The Original
Geneva Bible
1560 Edition
Illustrated Version

The Complete, Clear, and Precise Transcription of the Historic English Manuscript of the Scriptures of the Protestant Reformation

By Edwin Gainsborough

Contents

Introduction 7

The Old Testament 9

Genesis 9

Exodus 38

Leviticus 62

Numbers 79

Deuteronomy...102

Joshua..122

Judges..135

Ruth..148

First Samuel 150

Second Samuel 167

First Kings...181

Second Kings..198

First Chronicles...214

Second Chronicles..230

Ezra..248

Nehemiah 254

Esther 262

Job..266

Psalms..280

Proverbs..316

Ecclesiastes 328

Song Of Solomon 332

Isaiah 334

Jeremiah..361

Lamentations 392

Ezekiel 395

Daniel 422

Hosea 431

Joel 435

Amos 437

Obadiah 440

Jonah 440

Micah 441

Nahum 443

Habakkuk 444

Zephaniah 445

Haggai 446

Zechariah 447

Malachi 452

The New Testament 453

Matthew 453

Mark 471

Luke 484

John 503

Acts 518

Romans 538

First Corinthians 546

Second Corinthians 554

Galatians 559

Ephesians 561

Philippians 563

Colossians 565

First Thessalonians 567

Second Thessalonians 568

First Timothy 569

Second Timothy 571

Titus 572

Philemon 573

Hebrews 573

James 579

First Peter 580

Second Peter 582

First John 583

Second John 585

Third John 586

Jude 586

Reveletion 586

A Note from the Author and Bonus Content **596**

Conclusion **597**

Introduction

Welcome to the 1560 edition of the Geneva Bible, a monumental work in the history of English Bible translation. This version is not only a cornerstone of the Reformation but also a vital piece of our cultural and religious heritage. Crafted with meticulous care and scholarly precision, the Geneva Bible is cherished for its accessibility, clarity, and profound influence on both faith and literature.

The Geneva Bible was created during a tumultuous period in history. In the mid-16th century, many English Protestants fled to Geneva to escape the persecution of Queen Mary I. In this refuge of religious reform, they found a city steeped in theological scholarship and innovation. It was here that the Geneva Bible was born, driven by a desire to provide English-speaking believers with a Bible they could read and understand.

One of the most significant features of the Geneva Bible is its extensive use of marginal notes and cross-references. These annotations were designed to help readers grasp the historical context, theological nuances, and practical applications of the Scriptures. This made the Geneva Bible not only a text for personal devotion but also a tool for education and study, empowering ordinary people to engage deeply with God's Word.

The translation itself was a collaborative effort, drawing on the latest advances in biblical scholarship and linguistics. The translators, many of whom were prominent scholars, worked diligently to ensure that the text was both accurate and accessible. Their work set a new standard for Bible translations, influencing future versions, including the King James Bible.

Another hallmark of the Geneva Bible is its clear, readable prose. The translators sought to render the Scriptures in a way that was both faithful to the original languages and intelligible to contemporary readers. This commitment to clarity and readability made the Geneva Bible immensely popular, allowing it to become the Bible of choice for many English-speaking Christians during the Reformation and beyond.

The Geneva Bible also holds a special place in the history of English literature. Its phrasing and style have left an indelible mark on the language, shaping the works of writers such as William Shakespeare and John Milton. By reading this version, you are engaging with a text that has not only conveyed spiritual truths but also enriched the literary tradition of the English-speaking world.

This edition does not include the Apocrypha, aligning with the doctrinal positions of many Protestant traditions that do not consider these books inspired Scripture. However, for those interested in exploring these additional texts, check the end of the book for a little surprise.

Another hallmark of this edition is the inclusion of twelve original illustrations depicting some of the most important verses of the Bible. These artworks serve to enhance the beauty of the text, offering visual representations of key biblical narratives that complement the reading experience.

As you begin your journey through the 1560 Geneva Bible, may you find wisdom, comfort, and inspiration in its pages. May its teachings guide your path, strengthen your faith, and deepen your understanding of God's eternal Word. Thank you for choosing to read this historic and transformative text.

The Old Testament

Genesis

Genesis 1

1 In the beginning God created the heauen and the earth.

2 And the earth was without forme and void, and darkenesse was vpon the deepe, and the Spirit of God mooued vpon the waters.

3 Then God said, Let there be light: And there was light.

4 And God saw the light that it was good, and God separated the light from the darkenes.

5 And God called the Light, Day, and the darkenes, he called Night. So the euening and the morning were the first day.

6 Againe God said, Let there be a firmament in the mids of the waters: and let it separate the waters from the waters.

7 Then God made the firmament, and separated the waters, which were vnder the firmament, from the waters which were aboue the firmament: and it was so.

8 And God called the firmament Heauen. So the Euening and the morning were the second day.

9 God said againe, Let the waters vnder the heauen be gathered into one place, and let the dry land appeare. and it was so.

10 And God called the dry land, Earth, and he called the gathering together of the waters, Seas: and God saw that it was good.

11 Then God said, Let the earth bud forth the bud of the herbe, that seedeth seed, the fruitfull tree, which beareth fruite according to his kinde, which hath his seede in it selfe vpon the earth: and it was so.

12 And the earth brought foorth the bud of the herbe, that seedeth seede according to his kind, also the tree that beareth fruit, which hath his seed in it selfe according to his kinde: and God saw that it was good.

13 So the euening and the morning were the third day.

14 And God said, Let there be lights in the firmament of the heauen, to separate the day from the night, and let them be for signes, and for seasons, and for dayes and yeeres.

15 And let them be for lights in the firmament of the heauen to giue light vpon the earth: and it was so.

16 God then made two great lights: the greater light to rule the day, and the lesse light to rule the night: he made also the starres.

17 And God set them in the firmament of the heauen, to shine vpon the earth,

18 And to rule in the day, and in the night, and to separate the light from the darkenesse: and God saw that it was good.

19 So the euening and the morning were the fourth day.

20 Afterward God said, Let the waters bring foorth in abundance euery creeping thing that hath life: and let the foule flie vpon the earth in the open firmament of the heauen.

21 Then God created the great whales, and euery thing liuing and mouing, which the waters brought foorth in abundance according to their kinde, and euery fethered foule according to his kinde: and God sawe that it was good.

22 Then God blessed them, saying, Bring foorth fruite and multiplie, and fill the waters in the seas, and let the foule multiplie in the earth.

23 So the euening and the morning were the fifte day.

24 Moreouer God said, Let the earth bring foorth the liuing thing according to his kinde, cattel, and that which creepeth, and the beast of the earth, according to his kinde. and it was so.

25 And God made the beast of the earth according to his kinde, and the cattell according to his kinde, and euery creeping thing of the earth according to his kind: and God saw that it was good.

26 Furthermore God said, Let vs make man in our image according to our likenes, and let them rule ouer the fish of the sea, and ouer the foule of the heauen, and ouer the beastes, and ouer all the earth, and ouer euery thing that creepeth and moueth on the earth.

27 Thus God created the man in his image: in the image of God created he him: he created them male and female.

28 And God blessed them, and God said to them, Bring forth fruite and multiplie, and fill the earth, and subdue it, and rule ouer the fish of the sea, and ouer the foule of the heauen, and ouer euery beast that moueth vpon the earth.

29 And God said, Beholde, I haue giuen vnto you euery herbe bearing seede, which is vpon al the earth, and euery tree, wherein is the fruite of a tree bearing seede: that shall be to you for meate.

30 Likewise to euery beast of the earth, and to euery foule of the heauen, and to euery thing that moueth vpon the earth, which hath life in it selfe, euery greene herbe shall be for meate. and it was so.

31 And God sawe all that he had made, and loe, it was very good. So the euening and the morning were the sixt day.

Genesis 2

1 Thus the heauens and the earth were finished, and all the host of them.

2 For in the seuenth day GOD ended his worke which he had made, and the seuenth day he rested from al his worke, which he had made.

3 So God blessed the seuenth day, and sanctified it, because that in it he had rested from all his worke, which God had created and made.

4 These are the generations of the heauens and of the earth, when they were created, in the day that the Lord God made the earth and the heauens,

5 And euery plant of the fielde, before it was in the earth, and euery herbe of the field, before it grewe: for the Lord God had not caused it to raine vpon the earth, neither was there a man to till the ground,

6 But a myst went vp from the earth, and watered all the earth.

7 The Lord God also made the man of the dust of the grounde, and breathed in his face breath of life, and the man was a liuing soule.

8 And the Lord God planted a garden Eastward in Eden, and there he put the man whom he had made.

9 (For out of the ground made the Lord God to grow euery tree pleasant to the sight, and good for meate: the tree of life also in the mids of the garden, and the tree of knowledge of good and of euill.

10 And out of Eden went a riuer to water the garden, and from thence it was deuided, and became into foure heads.

11 The name of one is Pishon: the same compasseth the whole land of Hauilah, where is golde.

12 And the golde of that land is good: there is Bdelium, and the Onix stone.

13 And the name of the seconde riuer is Gihon: the same compasseth the whole lande of Cush.

14 The name also of the third riuer is Hiddekel: this goeth toward the Eastside of Asshur: and the fourth riuer is Perath)

15 Then the Lord God tooke the man, and put him into the garden of Eden, that he might dresse it and keepe it.

16 And the Lord God commanded the man, saying, Thou shalt eate freely of euery tree of the garden,

17 But of the tree of knowledge of good and euill, thou shalt not eate of it: for in the day that thou eatest thereof, thou shalt die the death.

18 Also the Lord God saide, It is not good that the man should be himself alone: I wil make him an helpe meete for him.

19 So the Lord God formed of the earth euery beast of the fielde, and euery foule of the heauen, and brought them vnto the man to see howe he would call them: for howsoeuer the man named the liuing creature, so was the name thereof.

20 The man therefore gaue names vnto all cattell, and to the foule of the heauen, and to euery beast of the fielde: but for Adam founde he not an helpe meete for him.

21 Therefore the Lord God caused an heauie sleepe to fall vpon the man, and he slept: and he tooke one of his ribbes, and closed vp the flesh in steade thereof.

22 And the ribbe which the Lord God had taken from the man, made he a woman, and brought her to the man.

23 Then the man said, This now is bone of my bones, and flesh of my flesh. She shalbe called woman, because she was taken out of man.

24 Therefore shall man leaue his father and his mother, and shall cleaue to his wife, and they shall be one flesh.

25 And they were both naked, the man and his wife, and were not ashamed.

Genesis 3

1 Now the serpent was more subtill then any beast of the fielde, which the Lord God had made: and he said to the woman, Yea, hath God in deede said, Ye shall not eate of euery tree of the garden?

2 And the woman said vnto the serpent, We eate of the fruite of the trees of the garden,

3 But of the fruite of the tree which is in the middes of the garden, God hath said, Ye shall not eate of it, neither shall ye touche it, lest ye die.

4 Then the serpent said to the woman, Ye shall not die at all,

5 But God doeth knowe, that when ye shall eate thereof, your eyes shall be opened, and ye shall be as gods, knowing good and euill.

6 So the woman (seeing that the tree was good for meate, and that it was pleasant to the eyes, and a tree to be desired to get knowledge) tooke of the fruite thereof, and did eate, and gaue also to her husband with her, and he did eate.

7 Then the eyes of them both were opened, and they knewe that they were naked, and they sewed figge tree leaues together, and made them selues breeches.

8 Afterward they heard the voyce of the Lord God walking in the garden in the coole of the day, and the man and his wife hid themselues from the presence of the Lord God among the trees of the garden.

9 But the Lord God called to the man, and said vnto him, Where art thou?

10 Who saide, I heard thy voyce in the garden, and was afraide: because I was naked, therefore I hid my selfe.

11 And he saide, Who tolde thee, that thou wast naked? Hast thou eaten of the tree, whereof I commanded thee that thou shouldest not eate?

12 Then the man saide, The woman which thou gauest to be with me, she gaue me of the tree, and I did eate.

13 And the Lord God saide to the woman, Why hast thou done this? And the woman said, The serpent beguiled me, and I did eate.

14 Then the Lord God said to the serpent, Because thou hast done this, thou art cursed aboue all cattell, and aboue euery beast of the fielde: vpon thy belly shalt thou goe, and dust shalt thou eate all the dayes of thy life.

15 I will also put enimitie betweene thee and the woman, and betweene thy seede and her seede. He shall breake thine head, and thou shalt bruise his heele.

16 Vnto the woman he said, I will greatly increase thy sorowes, and thy conceptions. In sorowe shalt thou bring foorth children, and thy desire shalbe subiect to thine husband, and he shall rule ouer thee.

17 Also to Adam he said, Because thou hast obeyed the voyce of thy wife, and hast eaten of the tree, (whereof I commanded thee, saying, Thou shalt not eate of it) cursed is the earth for thy sake: in sorowe shalt thou eate of it all the dayes of thy life.

18 Thornes also, and thistles shall it bring foorth to thee, and thou shalt eate the herbe of the fielde.

19 In the sweate of thy face shalt thou eate bread, till thou returne to the earth: for out of it wast thou taken, because thou art dust, and to dust shalt thou returne.

20 (And the man called his wiues name Heuah, because she was the mother of all liuing)

21 Vnto Adam also and to his wife did the Lord God make coates of skinnes, and clothed them.

22 And the Lord God said, Beholde, the man is become as one of vs, to knowe good and euill. And nowe lest he put foorth his hand, and take also of ye tree of life and eate and liue for euer,

23 Therefore the Lord God sent him foorth from the garden of Eden, to till ye earth, whence he was taken.

24 Thus he cast out man, and at the East side of the garden of Eden he set the Cherubims, and the blade of a sworde shaken, to keepe the way of the tree of life.

Genesis 4

1 Afterward the man knew Heuah his wife, which conceiued and bare Kain, and said, I haue obteined a man by the Lord.

2 And againe she brought foorth his brother Habel, and Habel was a keeper of sheepe, and Kain was a tiller of the ground.

3 And in processe of time it came to passe, that Kain brought an oblation vnto the Lord of the fruite of the ground.

4 And Habel also him selfe brought of the first fruites of his sheepe, and of the fat of them, and the Lord had respect vnto Habel, and to his offering,

5 But vnto Kain and to his offering he had no regarde: wherefore Kain was exceeding wroth, and his countenance fell downe.

6 Then ye Lord said vnto Kain, Why art thou wroth? and why is thy countenance cast downe?

7 If thou do well, shalt thou not be accepted? and if thou doest not well, sinne lieth at the doore: also vnto thee his desire shalbe subiect, and thou shalt rule ouer him.

8 Then Kain spake to Habel his brother. And when they were in the fielde, Kain rose vp against Habel his brother, and slewe him.

9 Then the Lord said vnto Kain, Where is Habel thy brother? Who answered, I cannot tell. Am I my brothers keeper?

10 Againe he said, What hast thou done? the voyce of thy brothers blood cryeth vnto me from the earth.

11 Now therefore thou art cursed from the earth, which hath opened her mouth to receiue thy brothers blood from thine hand.

12 When thou shalt till the grounde, it shall not henceforth yeelde vnto thee her strength: a vagabond and a runnagate shalt thou be in the earth.

13 Then Kain said to the Lord, My punishment is greater, then I can beare.

14 Behold, thou hast cast me out this day from the earth, and from thy face shall I be hid, and shalbe a vagabond, and a runnagate in the earth, and whosoeuer findeth me, shall slay me.

15 Then the Lord said vnto him, Doubtlesse whosoeuer slayeth Kain, he shalbe punished seue folde. And the Lord set a marke vpon Kain, lest any man finding him should kill him.

16 Then Kain went out from the presence of the Lord, and dwelt in the land of Nod towarde the Eastside of Eden.

17 Kain also knewe his wife, which conceiued and bare Henoch: and he built a citie, and called the name of the citie by ye name of his sonne, Henoch.

18 And to Henoch was borne Irad, and Irad begate Mehuiael, and Mehuiael begate Methushael, and Methushael begate Lamech.

19 And Lamech tooke him two wiues: the name of the one was Adah, and the name of the other Zillah.

20 And Adah bare Iabal, who was the father of such as dwell in the tents, and of such as haue cattell.

21 And his brothers name was Iubal, who was the father of all that play on the harpe and organes.

22 And Zillah also bare Tubal-kain, who wrought cunningly euery craft of brasse and of yron: and the sister of Tubal-kain was Naamah.

23 Then Lamech saide vnto his wiues Adah and Zillah, Heare my voyce, ye wiues of Lamech: hearken vnto my speach: for I would slay a man in my wound, and a yong man in mine hurt.

24 If Kain shalbe auenged seuen folde, truely Lamech, seuentie times seuen folde.

25 And Adam knewe his wife againe, and she bare a sonne, and she called his name Sheth: for God, saide she, hath appointed me another seede for Habel, because Kain slewe him.

26 And to ye same Sheth also there was borne a sonne, and he called his name Enosh. Then beganne men to call vpon the name of the Lord.

Genesis 5

1 This is the booke of the generations of Adam. In the day that God created Adam, in the likenes of God made he him,

2 Male and female created he them, and blessed them, and called their name Adam in the day that they were created.

3 Nowe Adam liued an hundred and thirtie yeeres, and begate a childe in his owne likenes after his image, and called his name Sheth.

4 And the dayes of Adam, after he had begotten Sheth, were eight hundreth yeeres, and he begate sonnes and daughters.

5 So all the dayes that Adam liued, were nine hundreth and thirtie yeeres: and he died.

6 And Sheth liued an hundreth and fiue yeeres, and begate Enosh.

7 And Sheth liued, after he begate Enosh, eight hundreth and seuen yeeres, and begate sonnes and daughters.

8 So all the dayes of Sheth were nine hundreth and twelue yeeres: and he died.

9 Also Enosh liued ninetie yeeres, and begate Kenan.

10 And Enosh liued, after he begate Kenan, eight hundreth and fifteene yeeres, and begate sonnes and daughters.

11 So all the dayes of Enosh were nine hundreth and fiue yeeres: and he died

12 Likewise Kenan liued seuentie yeeres, and begate Mahalaleel.

13 And Kenan liued, after he begate Mahalaleel, eight hundreth and fourtie yeeres, and begate sonnes and daughters.

14 So all the dayes of Kenan were nine hundreth and tenne yeeres: and he died.

15 Mahalaleel also liued sixtie and fiue yeres, and begate Iered.

16 Also Mahalaleel liued, after he begate Iered, eight hundreth and thirtie yeeres, and begate sonnes and daughters.

17 So all the dayes of Mahalaleel were eight hundreth ninetie and fiue yeeres: and he died.

18 And Iered liued an hundreth sixtie and two yeeres, and begate Henoch.

19 Then Iered liued, after he begate Henoch, eight hundreth yeeres, and begate sonnes and daughters.

20 So all the dayes of Iered were nine hundreth sixtie and two yeeres: and he died.

21 Also Henoch liued sixtie and fiue yeeres, and begate Methushelah.

22 And Henoch walked with God, after he begate Methushelah, three hundreth yeeres, and begate sonnes and daughters.

23 So all the dayes of Henoch were three hundreth sixtie and fiue yeeres.

24 And Henoch walked with God, and he was no more seene: for God tooke him away.

25 Methushelah also liued an hundreth eightie and seuen yeeres, and begate Lamech.

26 And Methushelah liued, after he begate Lamech, seuen hundreth eightie and two yeeres, and begate sonnes and daughters.

27 So al the dayes of Methushelah were nine hundreth sixtie and nine yeeres: and he died.

28 Then Lamech liued an hundreth eightie and two yeeres, and begate a sonne,

29 And called his name Noah, saying, This same shall comfort vs concerning our worke and sorowe of our hands, as touching the earth, which the Lord hath cursed.

30 And Lamech liued, after he begate Noah, fiue hundreth ninetie and fiue yeeres, and begate sonnes and daughters.

31 So all the dayes of Lamech were seuen hundreth seuentie and seuen yeeres: and he died.

32 And Noah was fiue hundreth yeere olde. And Noah begate Shem, Ham and Iapheth.

Genesis 6

1 So when men began to be multiplied vpon the earth, and there were daughters borne vnto them,

2 Then the sonnes of God sawe the daughters of men that they were faire, and they tooke them wiues of all that they liked.

3 Therefore the Lord saide, My Spirit shall not alway striue with man, because he is but flesh, and his dayes shalbe an hundreth and twentie yeeres.

4 There were gyants in the earth in those dayes: yea, and after that the sonnes of God came vnto the daughters of men, and they had borne them children, these were mightie men, which in olde time were men of renoume.

5 When the Lord sawe that the wickednesse of man was great in the earth, and all the imaginations of the thoughtes of his heart were onely euill continually,

6 Then it repented ye Lord, that he had made man in the earth, and he was sorie in his heart.

7 Therefore ye Lord said, I will destroy from the earth the man, whom I haue created, from man to beast, to the creeping thing, and to the foule of the heauen: for I repent that I haue made them.

8 But Noah found grace in the eyes of the Lord.

9 These are the generations of Noah. Noah was a iust and vpright man in his time: and Noah walked with God.

10 And Noah begate three sonnes, Shem, Ham and Iapheth.

11 The earth also was corrupt before God: for the earth was filled with crueltie.

12 Then God looked vpon the earth, and beholde, it was corrupt: for all flesh had corrupt his way vpon the earth.

13 And God said vnto Noah, An ende of all flesh is come before me: for the earth is filled with crueltie through them: and beholde, I wil destroy them with the earth.

14 Make thee an Arke of pine trees: thou shalt make cabines in the Arke, and shalt pitch it within and without with pitch.

15 And thus shalt thou make it: The length of the Arke shalbe three hundreth cubites, the breadth of it fiftie cubites, and the height of it thirtie cubites.

16 A windowe shalt thou make in the Arke, and in a cubite shalt thou finish it aboue, and the doore of the Arke shalt thou set in the side thereof: thou shalt make it with the lowe, seconde and third roume.

17 And I, beholde, I will bring a flood of waters vpon the earth to destroy all flesh, wherein is the breath of life vnder the heauen: all that is in the earth shall perish.

18 But with thee will I establish my couenant, and thou shalt goe into the Arke, thou, and thy sonnes, and thy wife, and thy sonnes wiues with thee.

19 And of euery liuing thing, of all flesh two of euery sort shalt thou cause to come into the Arke, to keepe them aliue with thee: they shalbe male and female.

20 Of the foules, after their kinde, and of the cattell after their kind, of euery creeping thing of the earth after his kinde, two of euery sort shall come vnto thee, that thou mayest keepe them aliue.

21 And take thou with thee of all meate that is eaten: and thou shalt gather it to thee, that it may be meate for thee and for them.

22 Noah therefore did according vnto all, that God commanded him: euen so did he.

Genesis 7

1 And the Lord said vnto Noah, Enter thou and all thine house into the Arke: for thee haue I seene righteous before me in this age.

2 Of euery cleane beast thou shalt take to thee by seuens, the male and his female: but of vncleane beastes by couples, the male and his female.

3 Of the foules also of the heauen by seuens, male and female, to keepe seede aliue vpon the whole earth.

4 For seuen dayes hence I will cause it raine vpon the earth fourtie dayes and fourtie nightes, and all the substance that I haue made, will I destroy from off the earth.

5 Noah therefore did according vnto all that the Lord commanded him.

6 And Noah was six hundreth yeeres olde, when the flood of waters was vpon the earth.

7 So Noah entred and his sonnes, and his wife, and his sonnes wiues with him into the Arke, because of the waters of the flood.

8 Of the cleane beastes, and of the vncleane beastes, and of the foules, and of all that creepeth vpon the earth,

9 There came two and two vnto Noah into the Arke, male and female, as God had commanded Noah.

10 And so after seuen dayes the waters of the flood were vpon the earth.

11 In the six hundreth yeere of Noahs life in the second moneth, the seuetenth day of the moneth, in the same day were all the fountaines of the great deepe

broken vp, and the windowes of heauen were opened,

12 And the raine was vpon the earth fourtie dayes and fourtie nightes.

13 In the selfe same day entred Noah with Shem, and Ham and Iapheth, the sonnes of Noah, and Noahs wife, and the three wiues of his sonnes with them into the Arke.

14 They and euery beast after his kinde, and all cattell after their kinde, and euery thing that creepeth and moueth vpon the earth after his kinde, and euery foule after his kinde, euen euery bird of euery fether.

15 For they came to Noah into ye Arke, two and two, of all flesh wherein is ye breath of life.

16 And they entring in, came male and female of all flesh, as God had commanded him: and the Lord shut him in.

17 Then ye flood was fourtie dayes vpon the earth, and the waters were increased, and bare vp the Arke, which was lift vp aboue the earth.

18 The waters also waxed strong, and were increased exceedingly vpon the earth, and the Arke went vpon the waters.

19 The waters preuailed so exceedingly vpon the earth, that all the high mountaines, that are vnder the whole heauen, were couered.

20 Fifteene cubites vpwarde did the waters preuaile, when the mountaines were couered.

21 Then all flesh perished that moued vpon the earth, both foule and cattell and beast, and euery thing that creepeth and moueth vpon the earth, and euery man.

22 Euery thing in whose nostrels the spirit of life did breathe, whatsoeuer they were in the drie land, they died.

23 So he destroyed euery thing that was vpon the earth, from man to beast, to ye creeping thing, and to the foule of the heauen: they were euen destroyed from the earth. And Noah onely remained; and they that were with him in ye Arke.

24 And the waters preuailed vpon the earth an hundreth and fiftie dayes.

Genesis 8

1 Now God remembred Noah and euery beast, and all the cattell that was with him in the Arke: therefore God made a winde to passe vpon the earth, and the waters ceased.

2 The fountaines also of the deepe and the windowes of heauen were stopped and the raine from heauen was restrained,

3 And the waters returned from aboue the earth, going and returning: and after the ende of the hundreth and fiftieth day the waters abated.

4 And in the seuenth moneth, in the seuenteenth day of the moneth, the Arke rested vpon the mountaines of Ararat.

5 And the waters were going and decreasing vntill the tenth moneth: in the tenth moneth, and in the first day of the moneth were the toppes of the mountaines seene.

6 So after fourtie dayes, Noah opened the windowe of the Arke, which he had made,

7 And sent forth a rauen, which went out going forth and returning, vntill the waters were dried vp vpon the earth.

8 Againe he sent a doue from him, that he might see if the waters were diminished from off the earth.

9 But the doue found no rest for the sole of her foote: therefore she returned vnto him into the Arke (for the waters were vpon the whole earth) and he put forth his hand, and receiued her, and tooke her to him into the Arke.

10 And he abode yet other seuen dayes, and againe he sent forth the doue out of the Arke.

11 And the doue came to him in ye euening, and loe, in her mouth was an oliue leafe that she had pluckt: whereby Noah knewe that the waters were abated from off the earth.

12 Notwithstanding he wayted yet other seuen dayes, and sent forth the doue, which returned not againe vnto him any more.

13 And in the sixe hundreth and one yeere, in the first day of the first moneth the waters were dryed vp from off the earth: and Noah remoued the couering of the Arke and looked, and beholde, the vpper part of the ground was drie.

14 And in the second moneth, in the seuen and twentieth day of the moneth was the earth drie.

15 Then God spake to Noah, saying,

16 Goe forth of the Arke, thou and thy wife, and thy sonnes and thy sonnes wiues with thee.

17 Bring forth with thee euery beast that is with thee, of all flesh, both foule and cattell, and euery thing that creepeth and moueth vpon the earth, that they may breede abundantly in ye earth, and bring forth fruite and increase vpon ye earth.

18 So Noah came forth, and his sonnes, and his wife, and his sonnes wiues with him.

19 Euery beast, euery creeping thing, and euery foule, all that moueth vpon the earth after their kindes went out of the Arke.

20 Then Noah built an altar to the Lord and tooke of euery cleane beast, and of euery cleane foule, and offered burnt offerings vpon the altar.

21 And the Lord smellled a sauour of rest, and the Lord said in his heart, I will hencefoorth curse the ground no more for mans cause: for the imagination of mans heart is euill, euen from his youth: neither will I smite any more all things liuing, as I haue done.

22 Hereafter seede time and haruest, and colde and heate, and sommer and winter, and day and night shall not cease, so long as ye earth remaineth.

Genesis 9

1 And God blessed Noah and his sonnes, and said to them, Bring foorth fruite, and multiplie, and replenish the earth.

2 Also the feare of you, and the dread of you shalbe vpon euery beast of the earth, and vpon euery foule of the heauen, vpon all that moueth on the earth, and vpon all the fishes of the sea: into your hand are they deliuered.

3 Euery thing that moueth and liueth, shall be meate for you: as the greene herbe, haue I giuen you all things.

4 But flesh with the life thereof, I meane, with the blood thereof, shall ye not eate.

5 For surely I will require your blood, wherein your liues are: at the hand of euery beast will I require it: and at the hand of man, euen at the hand of a mans brother will I require the life of man.

6 Who so sheadeth mans blood, by man shall his blood be shed: for in the image of God hath he made man.

7 But bring ye forth fruite and multiplie: grow plentifully in the earth, and increase therein.

8 God spake also to Noah and to his sonnes with him, saying,

9 Behold, I, euen I establish my couenant with you, and with your seede after you,

10 And with euery liuing creature that is with you, with the foule, with the cattell, and with euery beast of the earth with you, from all that goe out of the Arke, vnto euery beast of the earth.

11 And my couenant will I establish with you, that from henceforth all flesh shall not be rooted out by ye waters of the flood, neither shall there be a flood to destroy the earth any more.

12 Then God saide, This is the token of the couenant which I make betweene me and you, and betweene euery liuing thing, that is with you vnto perpetuall generations.

13 I haue set my bowe in the cloude, and it shalbe for a signe of the couenant betweene me and the earth.

14 And when I shall couer the earth with a cloud, and the bowe shall be seene in the cloude,

15 Then will I remember my couenant, which is betweene me and you, and betweene euery liuing thing in all flesh, and there shalbe no more waters of a flood to destroy all flesh.

16 Therefore the bowe shalbe in the cloude, that I may see it, and remember the euerlasting couenant betweene God, and euery liuing thing in all flesh that is vpon the earth.

17 God said yet to Noah, This is the signe of the couenant, which I haue established betweene me and all flesh that is vpon the earth.

18 Nowe the sonnes of Noah going foorth of the Arke, were Shem and Ham and Iapheth. And Ham is the father of Canaan.

19 These are the three sonnes of Noah, and of them was the whole earth ouerspred.

20 Noah also began to be an husband man and planted a vineyard.

21 And he drunke of ye wine and was drunken, and was vncouered in the middes of his tent.

22 And when Ham the father of Canaan sawe the nakednesse of his father, he tolde his two brethren without.

23 Then tooke Shem and Iapheth a garment, and put it vpon both their shoulders, and went backwarde, and couered the nakednesse of their father with their faces backwarde: so they sawe not their fathers nakednesse.

24 Then Noah awoke from his wine, and knew what his yonger sonne had done vnto him,

25 And said, Cursed be Canaan: a seruant of seruants shall he be vnto his brethren.

26 He said moreouer, blessed be the Lord God of Shem, and let Canaan be his seruant.

27 God perswade Iapheth, that he may dwell in the tentes of Shem, and let Canaan be his seruant.

28 And Noah liued after the flood three hundreth and fiftie yeeres.

29 So all the dayes of Noah were nine hundreth and fiftie yeeres: and he died.

Genesis 10

1 Now these are the generations of the sonnes of Noah, Shem, Ham and Iapheth: vnto whom sonnes were borne after the flood.

2 The sonnes of Iapheth were Gomer and Magog, and Madai, and Iauan, and Tubal, and Meshech, and Tiras.

3 And the sonnes of Gomer, Ashkenaz, and Riphath, and Togarmah.

4 Also the sonnes of Iauan, Elishah and Tarshish, Kittim, and Dodanim.

5 Of these were the yles of the Gentiles deuided in their landes, euery man after his tongue, and after their families in their nations.

6 Moreouer, ye sonnes of Ham were Cush, and Mizraim, and Put, and Canaan.

7 And the sonnes of Cush, Seba and Hauilah, and Sabtah, and Raamah, and Sabtecha: also the sonnes of Raamah were Sheba and Dedan.

8 And Cush begate Nimrod, who began to be mightie in the earth.

9 He was a mightie hunter before the Lord. wherefore it is saide, As Nimrod the mightie hunter before the Lord.

10 And the beginning of his kingdome was Babel, and Erech, and Accad, and Calneh, in the land of Shinar.

11 Out of that land came Asshur, and builded Niniueh, and the citie Rehoboth, and Calah:

12 Resen also betweene Niniueh and Calah: this is a great citie.

13 And Mizraim begate Ludim, and Anamim, and Lehabim, and Naphtuhim.

14 Pathrusim also, and Casluhim (out of whom came the Philistims) and Caphtorims.

15 Also Canaan begat Zidon his first borne, and Heth,

16 And Iebusi, and Emori, and Girgashi,

17 And Hiui, and Arki, and Sini,

18 And Aruadi, and Zemari, and Hamathi: and afterwarde were the families of the Canaanites spred abroade.

19 Then the border of the Canaanites was from Zidon, as thou commest to Gerar vntil Azzah, and as thou goest vnto Sodom, and Gomorah, and Admah, and Zeboijm, euen vnto Lasha.

20 These are the sonnes of Ham according to their families, according to their tongues in their countries and in their nations.

21 Vnto Shem also the father of all the sonnes of Eber, and elder brother of Iapheth were children borne.

22 The sonnes of Shem were Elam and Asshur, and Arpachshad, and Lud, and Aram.

23 And the sonnes of Aram, Vz and Hul, and Gether and Mash.

24 Also Arpachshad begate Shelah, and Shelah begate Eber.

25 Vnto Eber also were borne two sonnes: the name of the one was Peleg: for in his dayes was the earth diuided: and his brothers name was Ioktan.

26 Then Ioktan begate Almodad and Sheleph, and Hazarmaueth, and Ierah,

27 And Hadoram, and Vzal, and Dicklah,

28 And Obal, and Abimael, and Sheba,

29 And Ophir, and Hauilah, and Iobab: all these were the sonnes of Ioktan.

30 And their dwelling was from Mesha, as thou goest vnto Sephar a mount of the East.

31 These are the sonnes of Shem according to their families, according to their tongues, in their countreis and nations.

32 These are the families of the sonnes of Noah, after their generations among their people: and out of these were the nations diuided in the earth after the flood.

Genesis 11

1 Then the whole earth was of one language and one speache.

2 And as they went from the East, they found a plaine in the land of Shinar, and there they abode.

3 And they said one to another, Come, let vs make bricke, and burne it in the fire. So they had bricke for stone, and slime had they in steade of morter.

4 Also they said, Goe to, let vs builde vs a citie and a towre, whose top may reache vnto the heauen, that we may get vs a name, lest we be scattered vpon the whole earth.

5 But the Lord came downe, to see the citie and towre, which the sonnes of men builded.

6 And the Lord said, Beholde, the people is one, and they all haue one language, and this they begin to doe, neither can they now be stopped from whatsoeuer they haue imagined to do.

7 Come on, let vs goe downe, and there confound their language, that euery one perceiue not anothers speache.

8 So ye Lord scattered them from thence vpon all the earth, and they left off to build the citie.

9 Therefore the name of it was called Babel, because the Lord did there confounde the language of all the earth: from thence then did the Lord scatter them vpon all the earth.

10 These are the generations of Shem: Shem was an hundreth yeere olde, and begate Arpachshad two yeere after the flood.

11 And Shem liued, after he begate Arpachshad, fiue hundreth yeeres, and begate sonnes and daughters.

12 Also Arpachshad liued fiue and thirtie yeeres, and begate Shelah.

13 And Arpachshad liued, after he begate Shelah, foure hundreth and three yeeres, and begate sonnes and daughters.

14 And Shelah liued thirtie yeeres, and begat Eber.

15 So Shelah liued, after he begat Eber, foure hundreth and three yeeres, and begat sonnes and daughters.

16 Likewise Eber liued foure and thirtie yeres, and begate Peleg.

17 So Eber liued, after he begate Peleg, foure hundreth and thirtie yeeres, and begate sonnes and daughters

18 And Peleg liued thirtie yeeres, and begate Reu.

19 And Peleg liued, after he begate Reu, two hundreth and nine yeeres, and begate sonnes and daughters.

20 Also Reu liued two and thirtie yeeres, and begate Serug.

21 So Reu liued, after he begate Serug, two hundreth and seuen yeeres, and begate sonnes and daughters.

22 Moreouer Serug liued thirtie yeeres, and begate Nahor.

23 And Serug liued, after he begate Nahor, two hundreth yeeres, and begate sonnes and daughters.

24 And Nahor liued nine and twentie yeeres, and begate Terah.

25 So Nahor liued, after he begate Terah, an hundreth and nineteene yeeres, and begat sonnes and daughters.

26 So Terah liued seuentie yeeres, and begate Abram, Nahor, and Haran.

27 Nowe these are the generations of Terah: Terah begate Abram, Nahor, and Haran: and Haran begate Lot.

28 Then Haran died before Terah his father in the land of his natiuitie, in Vr of the Caldees.

29 So Abram and Nahor tooke them wiues. The name of Abrams wife was Sarai, and the name of Nahors wife Milcah, the daughter of Haran, the father of Milcah, and the father of Iscah.

30 But Sarai was barren, and had no childe.

31 Then Terah tooke Abram his sonne, and Lot the sonne of Haran, his sonnes sonne, and Sarai his daughter in lawe, his sonne Abrams wife: and they departed together from Vr of the Caldees,

to goe into the land of Canaan, and they came to Haran, and dwelt there.

32 So the dayes of Terah were two hundreth and fiue yeeres, and Terah died in Haran.

Genesis 12

1 For the Lord had said vnto Abram, Get thee out of thy countrey, and from thy kindred, and from thy fathers house vnto the land that I will shewe thee.

2 And I will make of thee a great nation, and will blesse thee, and make thy name great, and thou shalt be a blessing.

3 I will also blesse them that blesse thee, and curse them that curse thee, and in thee shall all families of the earth be blessed.

4 So Abram departed, euen as ye Lord spake vnto him, and Lot went with him. (And Abram was seuentie and fiue yeere olde, when he departed out of Haran)

5 Then Abram tooke Sarai his wife, and Lot his brothers sonne, and all their substance that they possessed, and the soules that they had gotten in Haran, and they departed, to goe to the land of Canaan: and to the land of Canaan they came.

6 So Abram passed through the land vnto the place of Shechem, and vnto the plaine of Moreh (and the Canaanite was then in ye land)

7 And the Lord appeared vnto Abram, and said, Vnto thy seede will I giue this land. And there builded he an altar vnto the Lord, which appeared vnto him.

8 Afterward remouing thence vnto a moutaine Eastward from Beth-el, he pitched his tent hauing Beth-el on the Westside, and Haai on the East: and there he built an altar vnto the Lord, and called on the Name of the Lord.

9 Againe Abram went forth going and iourneying toward the South.

10 Then there came a famine in the land: therefore Abram went downe into Egypt to soiourne there: for there was a great famine in the lande.

11 And when he drewe neere to enter into Egypt, he said to Sarai his wife, Beholde nowe, I know that thou art a faire woman to looke vpon:

12 Therefore it will come to passe, that when the Egyptians see thee, they will say, She is his wife: so will they kill me, but they will keepe thee aliue.

13 Say, I pray thee, that thou art my sister, that I may fare well for thy sake, and that my life may be preserued by thee.

14 Nowe when Abram was come into Egypt, the Egyptians behelde the woman: for she was very faire.

15 And the Princes of Pharaoh sawe her, and commended her vnto Pharaoh: so the woman was taken into Pharaohs house:

16 Who intreated Abram well for her sake, and he had sheepe, and beeues, and hee asses, and men seruants and maide seruants, and shee asses, and camelles.

17 But the Lord plagued Pharaoh and his house with great plagues, because of Sarai Abrams wife.

18 Then Pharaoh called Abram, and saide, Why hast thou done this vnto me? Wherefore diddest thou not tell me, that she was thy wife?

19 Why saidest thou, She is my sister, that I should take her to be my wife? Nowe therefore beholde thy wife, take her and goe thy way.

20 And Pharaoh gaue men commandement concerning him: and they conueyed him forth, and his wife, and all that he had.

Genesis 13

1 Then Abram went vp from Egypt, he, and his wife, and all that he had, and Lot with him toward the South.

2 And Abram was very rich in cattell, in siluer and in golde.

3 And he went on his iourney from ye South toward Beth-el, to the place where his tent had bene at ye beginning, betweene Beth-el and Haai,

4 Vnto the place of the altar, which he had made there at the first: and there Abram called on the Name of the Lord.

5 And Lot also, who went with Abram, had sheepe, and cattell and tentes,

6 So that the land coulde not beare them, that they might dwell together: for their substance was great, so that they coulde not dwell together.

7 Also there was debate betweene ye heardmen of Abrams cattell, and the heardmen of Lots cattell. (and the Canaanites and the Perizzites dwelled at that time in the land.)

8 Then saide Abram vnto Lot, Let there be no strife, I pray thee, betweene thee and me, neither betweene mine heardmen and thine heardmen: for we be brethren.

9 Is not the whole land before thee? depart I pray thee from me: if thou wilt take the left hand, then I will goe to the right: or if thou goe to the right hand, then I will take the left.

10 So when Lot lifted vp his eyes, he saw that all the plaine of Iorden was watered euery where: (for before the Lord destroyed Sodom and Gomorah, it was as the garden of the Lord, like the land of Egypt, as thou goest vnto Zoar)

11 Then Lot chose vnto him all the plaine of Iorden, and tooke his iourney from the East: and they departed the one from the other.

12 Abram dwelled in the lande of Canaan, and Lot abode in the cities of the plaine, and pitched his tent euen to Sodom.

13 Now the men of Sodom were wicked and exceeding sinners against the Lord.

14 Then the Lord saide vnto Abram, (after that Lot was departed from him) Lift vp thine eyes nowe, and looke from the place where thou art, Northward, and Southward, and Eastwarde, and Westward:

15 For all the land, which thou seest, will I giue vnto thee and to thy seede for euer,

16 And I will make thy seede, as the dust of the earth: so that if a man can number the dust of the earth, then shall thy seede be numbred.

17 Arise, walke through the land, in ye length thereof, and breadth thereof: for I will giue it vnto thee.

18 Then Abram remoued his tent, and came and dwelled in the plaine of Mamre, which is in Hebron, and builded there an altar vnto ye Lord.

Genesis 14

1 And in the dayes of Amraphel King of Shinar, Arioch King of Ellasar, Chedor-laomer King of Elam, and Tidal king of the nations:

2 These men made warre with Bera King of Sodom, and with Birsha King of Gomorah, Shinab King of Admah, and Shemeber King of Zeboiim, and the King of Bela, which is Zoar.

3 All these ioyned together in the vale of Siddim, which is the salt Sea.

4 Twelue yeere were they subiect to Chedor-laomer, but in the thirteenth yeere they rebelled.

5 And in the fourteenth yeere came Chedor-laomer, and the Kings that were with him, and smote the Rephaims in Ashteroth Karnaim, and the Zuzims in Ham, and the Emims in Shaueh Kiriathaim,

6 And the Horites in their mount Seir, vnto the plaine of Paran, which is by the wildernesse.

7 And they returned and came to En-mishpat, which is Kadesh, and smote all the countery of the Amalekites, and also the Amorites that dwelled in Hazezon-tamar.

8 Then went out the King of Sodom, and the King of Gomorah, and the King of Admah, and the King of Zeboiim, and the King of Bela, which is Zoar: and they ioyned battell with them in the vale of Siddim:

9 To wit, with Chedor-laomer king of Elam, and Tidal king of nations, and Amraphel king of Shinar, and Arioch king of Ellasar: foure Kings against fiue.

10 Now the vale of Siddim was full of slime pits, and the Kings of Sodom and Gomorah fled and fell there: and ye residue fled to the mountaine.

11 Then they tooke all the substance of Sodom and Gomorah, and al their vitailes and went their way.

12 They tooke Lot also Abrams brothers sonne and his substance (for he dwelt at Sodom) and departed.

13 Then came one that had escaped, and told Abram the Ebrew, which dwelt in the plaine of Mamre ye Amorite, brother of Eshcol, and brother of Aner, which were confederat with Abram.

14 When Abram heard that his brother was taken, he brought forth of them that were borne and brought vp in his house, three hundreth and eighteene, and pursued them vnto Dan.

15 Then he, and his seruants deuided them selues against them by night, and smote them and pursued them vnto Hobah, which is on the left side of Damascus,

16 And he recouered all the substance, and also brought againe his brother Lot, and his goods, and the women also and the people.

17 After that he returned from the slaughter of Chedor-laomer, and of the Kings that were with him, came the King of Sodom foorth to meete him in the valley of Shaueh, which is the Kings dale.

18 And Melchi-zedek King of Shalem brought foorth bread and wine: and he was a Priest of the most high God.

19 Therefore he blessed him, saying, Blessed art thou, Abram, of God most high possessour of heauen and earth,

20 And blessed be the most high God, which hath deliuered thine enemies into thine hand. And Abram gaue him tythe of all.

21 Then the King of Sodom saide to Abram, Giue me the persons, and take the goodes to thy selfe.

22 And Abram said to the King of Sodom, I haue lift vp mine hand vnto the Lord the most hie God possessour of heauen and earth,

23 That I will not take of all that is thine, so much as a threde or shoolatchet, lest thou shouldest say, I haue made Abram riche,

24 Saue only that, which the yong men haue eaten, and the partes of the men which went with me, Aner, Eshcol, and Mamre: let them take their partes.

Genesis 15

1 After these things, the worde of the Lord came vnto Abram in a vision, saying, Feare not, Abram, I am thy buckler, and thine exceeding great reward.

2 And Abram said, O Lord God, what wilt thou giue me, seeing I goe childlesse, and the steward of mine house is this Eliezer of Damascus?

3 Againe Abram saide, Beholde, to me thou hast giuen no seede: wherefore loe, a seruant of mine house shalbe mine heire.

4 Then beholde, the worde of the Lord came vnto him, saying, This man shall not be thine heire, but one that shall come out of thine owne bowels, he shalbe thine heire.

5 Moreouer he brought him forth and said, Looke vp nowe vnto heauen, and tell ye starres, if thou be able to number them: and he said vnto him, So shall thy seede be.

6 And Abram beleeued the Lord, and he counted that to him for righteousnesse.

7 Againe he saide vnto him, I am the Lord, that brought thee out of Vr of the Caldees, to giue thee this land to inherite it.

8 And he said, O Lord God, whereby shall I knowe that I shall inherite it?

9 Then he said vnto him, Take me an heifer of three yeeres olde, and a shee goate of three yeeres olde, and a ramme of three yeeres olde, a turtle doue also and a pigeon.

10 So he tooke all these vnto him, and deuided them into the middes, and laid euery piece one against an other: but the birdes deuided he not.

11 Then foules fell on the carkases, and Abram droue them away.

12 And when the sunne went downe, there fell an heauie sleepe vpon Abram: and loe, a very fearefull darkenes fell vpon him.

13 Then he saide to Abram, Knowe for a suretie, that thy seede shalbe a stranger in a land, that is not theirs, foure hundreth yeeres, and shall serue them: and they shall intreate them euill.

14 Notwithstanding the nation, whom they shall serue, will I iudge: and afterward shall they come out with great substance.

15 But thou shalt goe vnto thy fathers in peace, and shalt be buried in a good age.

16 And in the fourth generation they shall come hither againe: for the wickednes of the Amorites is not yet full.

17 Also when the sunne went downe, there was a darkenes: and behold, a smoking fornace, and a firebrand, which went betweene those pieces.

18 In that same day the Lord made a couenant with Abram, saying, Vnto thy seede haue I giuen this lande, from the riuer of Egypt vnto the great riuer, the riuer Euphrates.

19 The Kenites, and the Kenizites, and the Kadmonites,

20 And the Hittites, and the Perizzites, and the Rephaims,

21 The Amorites also, and the Canaanites, and the Girgashites, and the Iebusites.

Genesis 16

1 Nowe Sarai Abrams wife bare him no children, and she had a maide an Egyptian, Hagar by name.

2 And Sarai said vnto Abram, Beholde now, the Lord hath restrained me from childe bearing. I pray thee goe in vnto my maide: it may be that I shall receiue a childe by her. And Abram obeyed the voyce of Sarai.

3 Then Sarai Abrams wife tooke Hagar her maide the Egyptian, after Abram had dwelled ten yeere in the land of Canaan, and gaue her to her husband Abram for his wife.

4 And he went in vnto Hagar, and she conceiued. and when she sawe that she had conceiued, her dame was despised in her eyes.

5 Then Sarai saide to Abram, Thou doest me wrong. I haue giuen my maide into thy bosome, and she seeth that she hath conceiued, and I am despised in her eyes: the Lord iudge betweene me and thee.

6 Then Abram saide to Sarai, Beholde, thy maide is in thine hand: doe with her as it pleaseth thee. Then Sarai dealt roughly with her: wherefore she fled from her.

7 But the Angel of the Lord founde her beside a fountaine of water in the wildernesse by the fountaine in the way to Shur,

8 And he saide, Hagar Sarais maide, whence commest thou? and whither wilt thou goe? And she said, I flie from my dame Sarai.

9 Then the Angel of the Lord saide to her, Returne to thy dame, and humble thy selfe vnder her hands.

10 Againe the Angel of the Lord saide vnto her, I will so greatly increase thy seede, that it shall not be numbred for multitude.

11 Also the Angel of the Lord said vnto her, See, thou art with childe, and shalt beare a sonne, and shalt call his name Ishmael: for the Lord hath heard thy tribulation.

12 And he shalbe a wilde man: his hande shall be against euery man, and euery mans hand against him. and he shall dwell in the presence of all his brethren.

13 Then she called the name of the Lord, that spake vnto her, Thou God lookest on me: for she said, Haue I not also here looked after him that seeth me?

14 Wherefore the well was called, Beerlahai-roi. lo, it is betweene Kadesh and Bered.

15 And Hagar bare Abram a sonne, and Abram called his sonnes name, which Hagar bare, Ishmael.

16 And Abram was foure score and sixe yeere olde, when Hagar bare him Ishmael.

Genesis 17

1 When Abram was ninetie yeere olde and nine, the Lord appeared to Abram, and said vnto him, I am God all sufficient. walke before me, and be thou vpright,

2 And I will make my couenant betweene me and thee, and I will multiplie thee exceedingly.

3 Then Abram fell on his face, and God talked with him, saying,

4 Beholde, I make my couenant with thee, and thou shalt be a father of many nations,

5 Neither shall thy name any more be called Abram, but thy name shalbe Abraham: for a father of many nations haue I made thee.

6 Also I will make thee exceeding fruitfull, and will make nations of thee: yea, Kings shall proceede of thee.

7 Moreouer I wil establish my couenant betweene me and thee, and thy seede after thee in their generations, for an euerlasting couenant, to be God vnto thee and to thy seede after thee.

8 And I will giue thee and thy seede after thee the land, wherein thou art a stranger, euen all the land of Canaan, for an euerlasting possession, and I will be their God.

9 Againe God said vnto Abraham, Thou also shalt keepe my couenant, thou, and thy seede after thee in their generations.

10 This is my couenant which ye shall keepe betweene me and you, and thy seede after thee, Let euery man childe among you be circumcised:

11 That is, ye shall circumcise the foreskin of your flesh, and it shalbe a signe of the couenant betweene me and you.

12 And euery man childe of eight dayes olde among you, shalbe circumcised in your generations, aswell he that is borne in thine house, as he that is bought with money of any stranger, which is not of thy seede.

13 He that is borne in thine house, and he that is bought with thy money, must needes be circumcised: so my couenant shall be in your flesh for an euerlasting couenant.

14 But the vncircumcised man childe, in whose flesh the foreskin is not circumcised, euen that person shall be cut off from his people, because he hath broken my couenant.

15 Afterward God said vnto Abraham, Sarai thy wife shalt thou not call Sarai, but Sarah shalbe her name.

16 And I will blesse her, and will also giue thee a sonne of her, yea, I will blesse her, and she shall be the mother of nations: Kings also of people shall come of her.

17 Then Abraham fell vpon his face, and laughed, and said in his heart, Shall a childe be borne vnto him, that is an hundreth yeere olde? and shall Sarah that is ninetie yeere olde beare?

18 And Abraham saide vnto God, Oh, that Ishmael might liue in thy sight.

19 Then God saide, Sarah thy wife shall beare thee a sonne in deede, and thou shalt call his name Izhak: and I will establish my couenant with him for an euerlasting couenant, and with his seede after him.

20 And as concerning Ishmael, I haue heard thee: loe, I haue blessed him, and will make him fruitfull, and will multiplie him exceedingly: twelue princes shall he beget, and I will make a great nation of him.

21 But my couenant will I establish with Izhak, which Sarah shall beare vnto thee, the next yeere at this season.

22 And he left off talking with him, and God went vp from Abraham.

23 Then Abraham tooke Ishmael his sonne and all that were borne in his house, and all that was bought with his money, that is, euery man childe among the men of Abrahams house, and he circumcised the foreskinne of their flesh in that selfe same day, as God had comaunded him.

24 Abraham also himselfe was ninetie yeere olde and nine, when the foreskinne of his flesh was circumcised.

25 And Ishmael his sonne was thirteene yeere olde, when the foreskinne of his flesh was circumcised.

26 The selfe same day was Abraham circumcised, and Ishmael his sonne:

27 And all the men of his house, both borne in his house, and bought with money of the stranger, were circumcised with him.

Genesis 18

1 Againe the Lord appeared vnto him in the plaine of Mamre, as he sate in his tent doore about the heate of the day.

2 And he lift vp his eyes, and looked: and lo, three men stoode by him, and when he sawe them, he ranne to meete them from the tent doore, and bowed himselfe to the grounde.

3 And he said, Lord, if I haue now founde fauour in thy sight, goe not, I pray thee, from thy seruant.

4 Let a litle water, I pray you, be brought, and wash your feete, and rest your selues vnder the tree.

5 And I will bring a morsell of bread, that you may comfort your hearts, afterward ye shall go your wayes: for therefore are ye come to your seruant. And they said, Do euen as thou hast said.

6 Then Abraham made haste into the tent vnto Sarah, and saide, Make ready at once three measures of fine meale: kneade it, and make cakes vpon the hearth.

7 And Abraham ranne to the beastes, and tooke a tender and good calfe, and gaue it to the seruant, who hasted to make it ready.

8 And he tooke butter and milke, and the calfe, which he had prepared, and set before them, and stoode himselfe by them vnder the tree, and they did eate.

9 Then they saide to him, Where is Sarah thy wife? And he answered, Beholde, she is in the tent.

10 And he saide, I will certainely come againe vnto thee according to ye time of life: and loe, Sarah thy wife shall haue a sonne. and Sarah heard in the tent doore, which was behinde him.

11 (Nowe Abraham and Sarah were old and striken in age, and it ceased to be with Sarah after the maner of women)

12 Therefore Sarah laughed within her selfe, saying, After I am waxed olde, and my lord also, shall I haue lust?

13 And ye Lord saide vnto Abraham, Wherefore did Sarah thus laugh, saying, Shall I certainely beare a childe, which am olde?

14 (Shall any thing be hard to the Lord? at the time appointed will I returne vnto thee, euen according to the time of life, and Sarah shall haue a sonne.)

15 But Sarah denied, saying, I laughed not: for she was afraide. And he said, It is not so: for thou laughedst.

16 Afterwarde the men did rise vp from thence and looked toward Sodom: and Abraham went with them to bring them on the way.

17 And the Lord said, Shall I hide from Abraham that thing which I doe,

18 Seeing that Abraham shalbe in deede a great and a mightie nation, and all the nations of the earth shalbe blessed in him?

19 For I knowe him that he will commande his sonnes and his houshold after him, that they keepe the way of the Lord, to doe righteousnesse and iudgement, that the Lord may bring vpon Abraham that he hath spoken vnto him.

20 Then the Lord saide, Because the crie of Sodom and Gomorah is great, and because their sinne is exceeding grieuous,

21 I will goe downe nowe, and see whether they haue done altogether according to that crie which is come vnto me: and if not, that I may knowe.

22 And the men turned thence and went toward Sodom: but Abraham stoode yet before the Lord.

23 Then Abraham drewe neere, and said, Wilt thou also destroy the righteous with the wicked?

24 If there be fiftie righteous within the citie, wilt thou destroy and not spare the place for the fiftie righteous that are therein?

25 Be it farre from thee from doing this thing, to slay the righteous with the wicked: and that the righteous should be euen as the wicked, be it farre from thee. shall not the Iudge of all the worlde doe right?

26 And the Lord answered, If I shall finde in Sodom fiftie righteous within the citie, then will I spare all the place for their sakes.

27 Then Abraham answered and said, Behold nowe, I haue begun to speake vnto my Lord, and I am but dust and ashes.

28 If there shall lacke fiue of fiftie righteous, wilt thou destroy all the citie for fiue? And he saide, If I finde there fiue and fourtie, I will not destroy it.

29 And he yet spake to him againe, and saide, What if there shalbe found fourtie there? Then he answered, I will not doe it for fourties sake.

30 Againe he said, Let not my Lord nowe be angry, that I speake, What if thirtie be founde there? Then he saide, I will not doe it, if I finde thirtie there.

31 Moreouer he said, Behold, now I haue begonne to speake vnto my Lord, What if twentie be founde there? And he answered, I will not destroy it for twenties sake.

32 Then he saide, Let not my Lord be nowe angrie, and I will speake but this once, What if tenne be found there? And he answered, I will not destroy it for tennes sake.

33 And the Lord went his way when he had left communing with Abraham, and Abraham returned vnto his place.

Genesis 19

1 And in the euening there came two Angels to Sodom: and Lot sate at the gate of Sodom, and Lot sawe them, and rose vp to meete them, and he bowed himselfe with his face to the ground.

2 And he saide, See my Lords, I pray you turne in nowe into your seruants house, and tarie all night, and wash your feete, and ye shall rise vp early and goe your

wayes. Who saide, Nay, but we will abide in the streete all night.

3 Then he preassed vpon them earnestly, and they turned in to him, and came to his house, and he made them a feast, and did bake vnleauened bread, and they did eate.

4 But before they went to bed, the men of the citie, euen the men of Sodom compassed the house rounde about from the yong euen to the olde, all the people from all quarters.

5 Who crying vnto Lot said to him, Where are the men, which came to thee this night? bring them out vnto vs that we may knowe them.

6 Then Lot went out at the doore vnto them, and shut the doore after him,

7 And said, I pray you, my brethren, do not so wickedly.

8 Beholde nowe, I haue two daughters, which haue not knowen man: them will I bring out now vnto you, and doe to them as seemeth you good: onely vnto these men doe nothing: for therefore are they come vnder the shadowe of my roofe.

9 Then they said, Away hence, and they said, He is come alone as a stranger, and shall he iudge and rule? we will nowe deale worse with thee then with them. So they preassed sore vpon Lot himselfe, and came to breake the doore.

10 But the men put forth their hand and pulled Lot into the house to them and shut to ye doore.

11 Then they smote the men that were at the doore of the house with blindnes both small and great, so that they were wearie in seeking the doore.

12 Then the men said vnto Lot, Whom hast thou yet here? either sonne in lawe, or thy sonnes, or thy daughters, or whatsoeuer thou hast in the citie, bring it out of this place.

13 For we will destroy this place, because the crye of them is great before the Lord, and the Lord hath sent vs to destroy it.

14 Then Lot went out and spake vnto his sonnes in lawe, which maried his daughters, and said, Arise, get you out of this place: for the Lord will destroy the citie: but he seemed to his sonnes in lawe as though he had mocked.

15 And when the morning arose, the Angels hasted Lot, saying, Arise, take thy wife and thy two daughters which are here, lest thou be destroyed in the punishment of the citie.

16 And as he prolonged the time, the men caught both him and his wife, and his two daughters by the hands (the Lord being mercifull vnto him) and they brought him foorth, and set him without the citie.

17 And when they had brought them out, the Angel said, Escape for thy life: looke not behinde thee, neither tarie thou in all the plaine: escape into ye mountaine, least thou be destroyed.

18 And Lot saide vnto them, Not so, I pray thee, my Lord.

19 Behold now, thy seruant hath found grace in thy sight, and thou hast magnified thy mercie, which thou hast shewed vnto me in sauing my life: and I cannot escape in the mountaine, least some euill take me, and I die.

20 See nowe this citie hereby to flee vnto, which is a litle one: Oh let me escape thither: is it not a litle one, and my soule shall liue?

21 Then he said vnto him, Beholde, I haue receiued thy request also concerning this thing, that I will not ouerthrow this citie, for the which thou hast spoken.

22 Haste thee, saue thee there: for I can doe nothing till thou be come thither. Therefore the name of the citie was called Zoar.

23 The sunne did rise vpon the earth, when Lot entred into Zoar.

24 Then the Lord rained vpon Sodom and vpon Gomorah brimstone, and fire from the Lord out of heauen,

25 And ouerthrewe those cities and all the plaine, and all the inhabitants of the cities; and that that grewe vpon the earth.

26 Now his wife behind him looked backe, and she became a pillar of salt.

27 And Abraham rising vp earely in ye morning went to the place, where he had stand before the Lord,

28 And looking towarde Sodom and Gomorah and toward all the land of the plaine, behold, he sawe the smoke of the lande mounting vp as the smoke of a fornace.

29 But yet when God destroyed the cities of the plaine, God thought vpon Abraham, and sent Lot out from the middes of the destruction, when he ouerthrewe the cities, wherein Lot dwelled.

30 Then Lot went vp from Zoar, and dwelt in the mountaine with his two daughters: for he feared to tarie in Zoar, but dwelt in a caue, he, and his two daughters.

31 And the elder saide vnto the yonger, Our father is old, and there is not a man in the earth, to come in vnto vs after the maner of all ye earth.

32 Come, wee will make our father drinke wine, and lie with him, that we may preserue seede of our father.

33 So they made their father drinke wine that night, and the elder went and lay with her father: but he perceiued not, neither whe she lay downe, neither when she rose vp.

34 And on the morowe the elder saide to the yonger, Behold, yester night lay I with my father: let vs make him drinke wine this night also, and goe thou and lie with him, that we may preserue seede of our father.

35 So they made their father drinke wine that night also, and the yonger arose, and lay with him, but he perceiued not, when she lay downe, neither when she rose vp.

36 Thus were both the daughters of Lot with childe by their father.

37 And the elder bare a sonne, and she called his name Moab: the same is the father of the Moabites vnto this day.

38 And the yonger bare a sonne also, and she called his name Ben-ammi: the same is the father of the Ammonites vnto this day.

Genesis 20

1 Afterward Abraham departed thence toward the South countrey and dwelled betweene Cadesh and Shur, and soiourned in Gerar.

2 And Abraham said of Sarah his wife, She is my sister. Then Abimelech King of Gerar sent and tooke Sarah.

3 But God came to Abimelech in a dreame by night, and said to him, Beholde, thou art but dead, because of the woman, which thou hast taken: for she is a mans wife.

4 (Notwithstanding Abimelech had not yet come neere her) And he said, Lord, wilt thou slay euen the righteous nation?

5 Said not he vnto me, She is my sister? yea, and she her selfe said, He is my brother: with an vpright minde, and innocent handes haue I done this.

6 And God saide vnto him by a dreame, I knowe that thou diddest this euen with an vpright minde, and I kept thee also that thou shouldest not sinne against me: therefore suffered I thee not to touche her.

7 Now then deliuer the man his wife againe: for he is a Prophet, and he shall pray for thee that thou mayest liue: but if thou deliuer her not againe, be sure that thou shalt die the death, thou, and all that thou hast.

8 Then Abimelech rising vp early in ye morning, called all his seruants, and tolde all these things vnto them, and the men were sore afraid.

9 Afterward Abimelech called Abraham, and said vnto him, What hast thou done vnto vs? and what haue I offeded thee, that thou hast brought on me and on my kingdome this great sinne? thou hast done things vnto me that ought not to be done.

10 So Abimelech said vnto Abraham, What sawest thou that thou hast done this thing?

11 Then Abraham answered, Because I thought thus, Surely the feare of God is not in this place, and they will slay me for my wiues sake.

12 Yet in very deede she is my sister: for she is the daughter of my father, but not the daughter of my mother, and she is my wife.

13 Nowe when God caused me to wander out of my fathers house, I said then to her, This is thy kindnes that thou shalt shewe vnto me in all places where we come, Say thou of me, He is my brother.

14 Then tooke Abimelech sheepe and beeues, and men seruants, and women seruants, and gaue them vnto Abraham, and restored him Sarah his wife.

15 And Abimelech saide, Beholde, my land is before thee: dwell where it pleaseth thee.

16 Likewise to Sarah he said, Beholde, I haue giuen thy brother a thousand

pieces of siluer: behold, he is the vaile of thine eyes to all that are with thee, and to all others: and she was thus reproued.

17 Then Abraham prayed vnto God, and God healed Abimelech, and his wife, and his women seruants: and they bare children.

18 For the Lord had shut vp euery wombe of the house of Abimelech, because of Sarah Abrahams wife.

Genesis 21

1 Nowe the Lord visited Sarah, as he had saide, and did vnto her according as he had promised.

2 For Sarah conceiued, and bare Abraham a sonne in his olde age, at the same season that God tolde him.

3 And Abraham called his sonnes name that was borne vnto him, which Sarah bare him, Izhak.

4 Then Abraham circumcised Izhak his sonne, when he was eight dayes olde, as God had commanded him.

5 So Abraham was an hundreth yeere olde, when his sonne Izhak was borne vnto him.

6 Then Sarah said, God hath made me to reioyce: all that heare will reioyce with me.

7 Againe she said, Who would haue saide to Abraham, that Sarah shoulde haue giuen children sucke? for I haue borne him a sonne in his olde age.

8 Then the childe grewe and was weaned: and Abraham made a great feast the same day that Izhak was weaned.

9 And Sarah sawe the sonne of Hagar the Egyptian (which she had borne vnto Abraham) mocking.

10 Wherefore she saide vnto Abraham, Cast out this bond woman and her sonne: for ye sonne of this bonde woman shall not be heire with my sonne Izhak.

11 And this thing was very grieuous in Abrahams sight, because of his sonne.

12 But God said vnto Abraham, Let it not be grieuous in thy sight for the childe, and for thy bonde woman: in all that Sarah shall say vnto thee, heare her voyce: for in Izhak shall thy seede be called.

13 As for the sonne of the bond woman, I will make him a nation also, because he is thy seede.

14 So Abraham arose vp early in ye morning, and tooke bread, and a bottell of water, and gaue it vnto Hagar, putting it on her shoulder, and the childe also, and sent her away: who departing wandred in the wildernesse of Beer-sheba.

15 And when the water of the bottell was spent, she cast the childe vnder a certaine tree.

16 Then she went and sate her ouer against him a farre off about a bowe shoote: for she said, I will not see the death of the child. and she sate downe ouer against him, and lift vp her voyce and wept.

17 Then God heard the voyce of ye childe, and the Angel of God called to Hagar from heauen, and said vnto her, What aileth thee, Hagar? feare not, for God hath heard the voyce of the childe where he is.

18 Arise, take vp the childe, and holde him in thine hand: for I will make of him a great people.

19 And God opened her eyes, and she sawe a well of water. so she went and filled the bottell with water, and gaue the boy drinke.

20 So God was with the childe, and he grewe and dwelt in the wildernesse, and was an archer.

21 And he dwelt in the wildernesse of Paran, and his mother tooke him a wife out of the land of Egypt.

22 And at that same time Abimelech and Phichol his chief captaine spake vnto Abraham, saying, God is with thee in all that thou doest.

23 Nowe therefore sweare vnto me here by God, that thou wilt not hurt me, nor my children, nor my childrens children: thou shalt deale with me, and with the countrey, where thou hast bene a stranger, according vnto the kindnesse that I haue shewed thee.

24 Then Abraham said, I will sweare.

25 And Abraham rebuked Abimelech for a well of water, which Abimelechs seruants had violently taken away.

26 And Abimelech saide, I knowe not who hath done this thing: also thou toldest me not, neither heard I of it but this day.

27 Then Abraham tooke sheepe and beeues, and gaue them vnto Abimelech: and they two made a couenant.

28 And Abraham set seuen lambes of the flocke by themselues.

29 Then Abimelech said vnto Abraham, What meane these seuen lambes, which thou hast set by themselues?

30 And he answered, Because thou shalt receiue of mine hand these seuen lambes, that it may be a witnes vnto me, that I haue digged this well.

31 Wherefore the place is called Beer-sheba, because there they both sware.

32 Thus made they a couenant at Beer-sheba: afterward Abimelech and Phichol his chiefe captaine rose vp, and turned againe vnto the land of the Philistims.

33 And Abraham planted a groue in Beer-sheba, and called there on the Name of ye Lord, the euerlasting God.

34 And Abraham was a stranger in the Philistims land a long season.

Genesis 22

1 And after these things God did proue Abraham, and said vnto him, Abraham. Who answered, Here am I.

2 And he said, Take nowe thine onely sonne Izhak whom thou louest, and get thee vnto the land of Moriah, and offer him there for a burnt offering vpon one of the mountaines, which I will shewe thee.

3 Then Abraham rose vp early in the morning, and sadled his asse, and tooke two of his seruants with him, and Izhak his sonne, and cloue wood for the burnt offering, and rose vp and went to the place, which God had tolde him.

4 Then the third day Abraham lift vp his eyes, and sawe the place afarre off,

5 And said vnto his seruants, Abide you here with the asse: for I and the childe will go yonder and worship, and come againe vnto you.

6 Then Abraham tooke the wood of the burnt offering, and layed it vpon Izhak his sonne, and he tooke the fire in his hand, and the knife: and they went both together.

7 Then spake Izhak vnto Abraham his father, and said, My father. And he answered, Here am I, my sonne. And he said, Behold the fire and the wood, but where is the lambe for ye burnt offring?

8 Then Abraham answered, My sonne, God will prouide him a lambe for a burnt offering: so they went both together.

9 And when they came to the place which God had shewed him, Abraham builded an altar there, and couched ye wood, and bound Izhak his sonne and laid him on the altar vpon the wood.

10 And Abraham stretching forth his hand, tooke the knife to kill his sonne.

11 But the Angel of the Lord called vnto him from heauen, saying, Abraham, Abraham. And he answered, Here am I.

12 Then he said, Lay not thine hand vpon the childe, neither doe any thing vnto him: for now I know that thou fearest God, seeing for my sake thou hast not spared thine onely sonne.

13 And Abraham lifting vp his eyes, looked: and behold, there was a ramme behind him caught by the hornes in a bush. then Abraham went and tooke the ramme, and offered him vp for a burnt offering in the steade of his sonne.

14 And Abraham called the name of that place, Iehouah-ijreh. as it is said this day, In the mount will the Lord be seene.

15 And the Angel of the Lord cryed vnto Abraham from heauen the second time,

16 And saide, By my selfe haue I sworne (saith ye Lord) because thou hast done this thing, and hast not spared thine onely sonne,

17 Therefore will I surely blesse thee, and will greatly multiplie thy seede, as the starres of the heauen, and as the sand which is vpon the sea shore, and thy seede shall possesse the gate of his enemies.

18 And in thy seede shall all the nations of the earth be blessed, because thou hast obeyed my voyce.

19 Then turned Abraham againe vnto his seruants, and they rose vp and went together to Beer-sheba: and Abraham dwelt at Beer-sheba.

20 And after these things one tolde Abraham, saying, Beholde Milcah, she hath also borne children vnto thy brother Nahor:

21 To wit, Vz his eldest sonne, and Buz his brother, and Kemuel the father of Aram,

22 And Chesed and Hazo, and Pildash, and Iidlaph, and Bethuel.

23 And Bethuel begate Rebekah: these eight did Milcah beare to Nahor Abrahams brother.

24 And his concubine called Reumah, she bare also Tebah, and Gahan, and Thahash and Maachah.

Genesis 23

1 When Sarah was an hundreth twentie and seuen yeere olde (so long liued she).

2 Then Sarah dyed in Kiriath-arba: the same is Hebron in the land of Canaan. and Abraham came to mourne for Sarah and to weepe for her.

3 Then Abraham rose vp from the sight of his corps, and talked with the Hittites, saying,

4 I am a stranger, and a forreiner among you, giue me a possession of buriall with you, that I may burie my dead out of my sight.

5 Then the Hittites answered Abraham, saying vnto him,

6 Heare vs, my lorde: thou art a prince of God among vs: in the chiefest of our sepulchres bury thy dead: none of vs shall forbid thee his sepulchre, but thou mayest bury thy dead therein.

7 Then Abraham stoode vp, and bowed him selfe before the people of the land of the Hittites.

8 And he communed with them, saying, If it be your minde, that I shall bury my dead out of my sight, heare me, and intreate for me to Ephron the sonne of Zohar,

9 That he would giue me ye caue of Machpelah, which he hath in the ende of his field: that he would giue it me for as much money as it is worth, for a possession to bury in among you.

10 (For Ephron dwelt among the Hittites) Then Ephron the Hittite answered Abraham in the audience of all the Hittites that went in at the gates of his citie, saying,

11 No, my Lord, heare me: the fielde giue I thee, and the caue, that therein is, I giue it thee: euen in the presence of the sonnes of my people giue I it thee, to bury thy dead.

12 Then Abraham bowed himselfe before the people of the land,

13 And spake vnto Ephron in the audience of the people of the countrey, saying, Seeing thou wilt giue it, I pray thee, heare me, I will giue the price of the fielde: receiue it of me, and I will bury my dead there.

14 Ephron then answered Abraham, saying vnto him,

15 My lord, hearken vnto me: ye land is worth foure hundreth shekels of siluer: what is that betweene me and thee? bury therefore thy dead.

16 So Abraham weyed to Ephron the siluer, which he had named, in the audience of the Hittites, euen foure hundreth siluer shekels of currant money among marchants.

17 So the fielde of Ephron which was in Machpelah, and ouer against Mamre, euen the field and the caue that was therein, and all the trees that were in the fielde, which were in all the borders round about, was made sure

18 Vnto Abraham for a possession, in ye sight of the Hittites, euen of all that went in at the gates of his citie.

19 And after this, Abraham buried Sarah his wife in the caue of the fielde of Machpelah ouer against Mamre: the same is Hebron in the land of Canaan.

20 Thus the fielde and the caue, that is therein, was made sure vnto Abraham for a possession of buriall by the Hittites.

Genesis 24

1 Nowe Abraham was olde, and striken in yeeres, and the Lord had blessed Abraham in all things.

2 Therefore Abraham saide vnto his eldest seruant of his house, which had the rule ouer all that he had, Put nowe thine hand vnder my thigh,

3 And I will make thee sweare by ye Lord God of the heauen, and God of the earth, that thou shalt not take a wife vnto my sonne of the daughters of the Canaanites among who I dwel.

4 But thou shalt go vnto my countrey, and to my kinred, and take a wife vnto my sone Izhak.

5 And the seruant saide to him, What if the woman will not come with me to this land? shall I bring thy sonne againe vnto the lande from whence thou camest?

6 To whom Abraham answered, Beware that thou bring not my sonne thither againe.

7 The Lord God of heauen, who tooke me from my fathers house, and from the land where I was borne, and that spake vnto me, and that sware vnto me, saying, Vnto thy seede wil I giue this land, he shall send his Angel before thee, and thou shalt take a wife vnto my sonne from thence.

8 Neuertheles if the woman wil not follow thee, then shalt thou bee discharged of this mine othe: onely bring not my sonne thither againe.

9 Then the seruant put his hand vnder the thigh of Abraham his master, and sware to him for this matter.

10 So the seruant tooke ten camels of the camels of his master, and departed: (for he had all his masters goods in his hand:) and so he arose, and went to Aram Naharaim, vnto the citie of Nahor.

11 And he made his camels to lye downe without the citie by a well of water, at euentide about the time that the women come out to draw water.

12 And he said, O Lord God of my master Abraham, I beseech thee, send me good speede this day, and shew mercy vnto my master Abraham.

13 Lo, I stand by the well of water, whiles the mens daughters of this citie come out to drawe water.

14 Graunt therefore that ye maide, to whom I say, Bowe downe thy pitcher, I pray thee, that I may drinke: if she say, Drinke, and I will giue thy camels drinke also: may be she that thou hast ordeined for thy seruant Izhak: and thereby shall I know that thou hast shewed mercy on my master.

15 And nowe yer he had left speaking, beholde, Rebekah came out, the daughter of Bethuel, sonne of Milcah the wife of Nahor Abrahams brother, and her pitcher vpon her shoulder.

16 (And the maide was very faire to looke vpon, a virgine and vnknowen of man) and she went downe to the well, and filled her pitcher, and came vp.

17 Then the seruant ranne to meete her, and said, Let me drinke, I pray thee, a litle water of thy pitcher.

18 And she said, Drinke sir: and she hasted, and let downe her pitcher vpon her hand and gaue him drinke.

19 And when she had giuen him drinke, she said, I will drawe water for thy camels also vntill they haue drunken inough.

20 And she powred out her pitcher into the trough speedily; and ranne againe vnto the well to drawe water, and she drewe for all his camels.

21 So the man wondred at her, and helde his peace, to knowe whether the Lord had made his iourney prosperous or not.

22 And when the camels had left drinking, the man tooke a golden abillement of halfe a shekell weight, and two bracelets for her hands, of ten shekels weight of golde:

23 And he said, Whose daughter art thou? tell me, I pray thee, Is there roume in thy fathers house for vs to lodge in?

24 Then she said to him, I am the daughter of Bethuel the sonne of Milcah whom she bare vnto Nahor.

25 Moreouer she said vnto him, We haue litter also and prouender ynough, and roume to lodge in.

26 And the man bowed himselfe and worshipped the Lord,

27 And said, Blessed be the Lord God of my master Abraham, which hath not withdrawen his mercie and his trueth from my master: for when I was in the way, the Lord brought me to my masters brethrens house.

28 And the maide ranne and tolde them of her mothers house according to these wordes.

29 Now Rebekah had a brother called Laban, and Laban ranne vnto the man to the well.

30 For when he had seene the earings and the bracelets in his sisters hands, and when he heard the wordes of Rebekah his sister, saying, Thus said the man vnto me, then he went to the man, and loe, he stoode by the camels at the well.

31 And he saide, Come in thou blessed of the Lord: wherefore standest thou without, seeing I haue prepared the house, and roume for ye camels?

32 Then the man came into the house, and he vnsadled the camels, and brought litter and prouender for the camels, and water to wash his feete, and the mens feete that were with him.

33 Afterward the meate was set before him: but he saide, I will not eate, vntill I

haue saide my message: And he said, Speake on.

34 Then he said, I am Abrahams seruant,

35 And the Lord hath blessed my master wonderfully, that he is become great: for he hath giuen him sheepe, and beeues, and siluer, and golde, and men seruants, and maide seruants, and camels, and asses.

36 And Sarah my masters wife hath borne a sonne to my master, when she was olde, and vnto him hath he giuen all that he hath.

37 Now my master made me sweare, saying, Thou shalt not take a wife to my sonne of the daughters of the Canaanites, in whose land I dwell:

38 But thou shalt go vnto my fathers house and to my kinred, and take a wife vnto my sonne.

39 Then I saide vnto my master, What if the woman will not follow me?

40 Who answered me, The Lord, before who I walke, will send his Angel with thee, and prosper thy iourney, and thou shalt take a wife for my sonne of my kinred and my fathers house.

41 Then shalt thou be discharged of mine othe, when thou commest to my kinred: and if they giue thee not one, thou shalt be free from mine othe.

42 So I came this day to the well, and said, O Lord, the God of my master Abraham, if thou nowe prosper my iourney which I goe,

43 Behold, I stand by the well of water: when a virgine commeth forth to drawe water, and I say to her, Giue me, I pray thee, a litle water of thy pitcher to drinke,

44 And she say to me, Drinke thou, and I will also drawe for thy camels, let her be ye wife, which the Lord hath prepared for my masters sonne.

45 And before I had made an end of speaking in mine heart, beholde, Rebekah came foorth, and her pitcher on her shoulder, and she went downe vnto the well, and drewe water. Then I said vnto her, Giue me drinke, I pray thee.

46 And she made haste, and tooke downe her pitcher from her shoulder, and said, Drinke, and I will giue thy camels drinke also. So I dranke, and she gaue the camels drinke also.

47 Then I asked her, and said, Whose daughter art thou? And she answered, The daughter of Bethuel Nahors sonne, whom Milcah bare vnto him. Then I put the abillement vpon her face, and the bracelets vpon her hands:

48 And I bowed downe and worshipped the Lord, and blessed the Lord God of my master Abraham, which had brought me the right way to take my masters brothers daughter vnto his sone.

49 Now therefore, if ye will deale mercifully and truely with my master, tell me: and if not, tell me that I may turne me to the right hand or to the left.

50 Then answered Laban and Bethuel, and said, This thing is proceeded of the Lord: we cannot therefore say vnto thee, neither euill nor good.

51 Beholde, Rebehak is before thee, take her and goe, that she may be thy masters sonnes wife, euen as the Lord hath said.

52 And when Abrahams seruant heard their wordes, he bowed himselfe toward the earth vnto the Lord.

53 Then the seruant tooke foorth iewels of siluer, and iewels of golde, and raiment, and gaue to Rebekah: also vnto her brother and to her mother he gaue gifts.

54 Afterward they did eate and drinke, both he, and the men that were with him, and taried all night. and when they rose vp in the morning, he said, Let me depart vnto my master.

55 Then her brother and her mother answered, Let the maide abide with vs, at the least ten dayes: then shall she goe.

56 But he said vnto them, Hinder you me not, seeing the Lord hath prospered my iourney: send me away, that I may goe to my master.

57 Then they said, We will call the maide, and aske her consent.

58 And they called Rebekah, and saide vnto her, Wilt thou go with this man? And she answered, I will go.

59 So they let Rebekah their sister goe, and her nourse, with Abrahams seruant and his men.

60 And they blessed Rebekah, and sayde vnto her, Thou art our sister, growe into thousande thousands, and thy seede possesse the gate of his enemies.

61 Then Rebekah arose, and her maydes, and rode vpon the camels, and followed the man. and the seruant tooke Rebekah, and departed.

62 Nowe Izhak came from the way of Beer-lahai-roi, (for he dwelt in the South countrey)

63 And Izhak went out. to pray in the fielde toward the euening: who lift vp his eyes and looked, and behold, the camels came.

64 Also Rebekah lift vp her eyes, and when she saw Izhak, she lighted downe from the camel.

65 (For shee had sayde to the seruant, Who is yonder man, that commeth in the fielde to meete vs? and the seruant had said, It is my master) So she tooke a vaile, and couered her.

66 And the seruant tolde Izhak all things, that he had done.

67 Afterward Izhak brought her into the tent of Sarah his mother, and he tooke Rebekah, and she was his wife, and he loued her: So Izhak was comforted after his mothers death.

Genesis 25

1 Nowe Abraham had taken him another wife called Keturah,

2 Which bare him Zimran, and Iokshan, and Medan, and Midian, and Ishbak, and Shuah.

3 And Iokshan begate Sheba, and Dedan: And the sonnes of Dedan were Asshurim, and Letushim, and Leummim.

4 Also the sonnes of Midian were Ephah, and Epher, and Hanoch, and Abida, and Eldaah all these were the sonnes of Keturah.

5 And Abraham gaue all his goods to Izhak,

6 But vnto the sonnes of the concubines, which Abraham had, Abraham gaue giftes, and sent them away from Izhak his sonne (while he yet liued) Eastward to the East countrey.

7 And this is the age of Abrahams life, which he liued, an hundreth seuentie and fiue yeere.

8 Then Abraham yeelded the spirit, and died in a good age, an olde man, and of great yeeres, and was gathered to his people.

9 And his sonnes, Izhak and Ishmael buryed him in the caue of Machpelah, in the fielde of Ephron sonne of Zohar the Hittite, before Mamre.

10 Which fielde Abraham bought of the Hittites, where Abraham was buryed with Sarah his wife.

11 And after the death of Abraham God blessed Izhak his sonne, and Izhak dwelt by Beer-lahai-roi.

12 Nowe these are the generations of Ishmael Abrahams sonne, whome Hagar the Egyptian Sarahs handmayde bare vnto Abraham.

13 And these are the names of the sonnes of Ishmael, name by name, according to their kinreds; the eldest sonne of Ishmael was Nebaioth, then Kedar, and Adbeel, and Mibsam,

14 And Mishma, and Dumah, and Massa,

15 Hadar, and Tema, Ietur, Naphish, and Kedemah.

16 These are the sonnes of Ishmael, and these are their names, by their townes and by their castles: to wit, twelue princes of their nations.

17 (And these are the yeeres of the life of Ishmael, an hundreth thirtie and seuen yeere, and he yeelded the spirit, and dyed, and was gathered vnto his people)

18 And they dwelt from Hauilah vnto Shur, that is towardes Egypt, as thou goest to Asshur. Ishmael dwelt in the presence of all his brethren.

19 Likewise these are the generations of Izhak Abrahams sonne Abraham begate Izhak,

20 And Izhak was fourtie yeere olde, when he tooke Rebekah to wife, the daughter of Bethuel the Aramite of Padan Aram, and sister to Laban the Aramite.

21 And Izhak prayed vuto the Lord for his wife, because she was barren: and the Lord was intreated of him, and Rebekah his wife conceiued,

22 But the children stroue together within her: therefore shee sayde, Seeing it is so, why am I thus? wherefore she went to aske the Lord.

23 And the Lord sayd to her, Two nations are in thy wombe, and two maner of people shalbe diuided out of thy bowels, and the one people shall be

mightier then the other, and the elder shall serue the yonger.

24 Therefore when her time of deliuerance was fulfilled, behold, twinnes were in her wombe.

25 So he that came out first was red, and he was all ouer as a rough garment, and they called his name Esau.

26 And afterward came his brother out, and his hande helde Esau by the heele: therefore his name was called Iaakob. Nowe Izhak was threescore yeere olde when Rebekah bare them.

27 And the boyes grew, and Esau was a cunning hunter, and liued in the fields: but Iaakob was a plaine man, and dwelt in tentes.

28 And Izhak loued Esau, for venison was his meate, but Rebekah loued Iaakob.

29 Nowe Iaakob sod pottage, and Esau came from the fielde and was wearie.

30 Then Esau sayd to Iaakob, Let me eate, I pray thee, of that pottage so red, for I am wearie. Therefore was his name called Edom.

31 And Iaakob sayd, Sell me euen nowe thy birthright.

32 And Esau sayd, Lo, I am almost dead, what is then this birthright to me?

33 Iaakob then said, Sweare to me euen now. And he sware to him, and solde his birthright vnto Iaakob.

34 Then Iaakob gaue Esau bread and pottage of lentiles: and he did eate and drinke, and rose vp, and went his way: So Esau contemned his birthright.

Genesis 26

1 And there was a famine in the lande besides the first famine that was in the dayes of Abraham. Wherefore Izhak went to Abimelech King of the Philistims vnto Gerar.

2 For the Lord appeared vnto him, and sayde, Goe not downe into Egypt, but abide in the land which I shall shewe vnto thee.

3 Dwell in this lande, and I will be with thee, and will blesse thee: for to thee, and to thy seede I will giue all these countreys: and I will performe the othe which I sware vnto Abraham thy father.

4 Also I wil cause thy seede to multiply as the starres of heauen, and will giue vnto thy seede all these countreys: and in thy seede shall all the nations of the earth be blessed,

5 Because that Abraham obeyed my voyce and kept mine ordinance, my commandements, my statutes, and my Lawes.

6 So Izhak dwelt in Gerar.

7 And the men of the place asked him of his wife, and he sayd, She is my sister: for he feared to say, She is my wife, least, sayde he, the men of the place shoulde kill me, because of Rebekah: for she was beautifull to the eye.

8 So after hee had bene there long time, Abimelech King of the Philistims looked out at a windowe, and loe, he sawe Izhak sporting with Rebekah his wife.

9 Then Abimelech called Izhak, and sayde, Loe, shee is of a suertie thy wife, and why saydest thou, She is my sister? To whom Izhak answered, Because I thought this, It may be that I shall dye for her.

10 Then Abimelech said, Why hast thou done this vnto vs? one of the people had almost lien by thy wife, so shouldest thou haue brought sinne vpon vs.

11 Then Abimelech charged all his people, saying, He that toucheth this man, or his wife, shall die the death.

12 Afterwarde Izhak sowed in that lande, and founde in the same yeere an hundreth folde by estimation: and so the Lord blessed him.

13 And the man waxed mightie, and stil increased, till he was exceeding great,

14 For he had flockes of sheepe, and heards of cattell, and a mightie housholde: therefore the Philistims had enuy at him.

15 In so much that the Philistims stopped and filled vp with earth all the welles, which his fathers seruantes digged in his father Abrahams time.

16 Then Abimelech sayde vnto Izhak, Get thee from vs, for thou art mightier then wee a great deale.

17 Therefore Izhak departed thence and pitched his tent in the valley of Gerar, and dwelt there.

18 And Izhak returning, digged the welles of water, which they had digged in the dayes of Abraham his father: for the Philistims had stopped them after the death of Abraham, and hee gaue them the same names, which his father gaue them.

19 Izhaks seruantes then digged in the valley, and found there a well of liuing water.

20 But the herdmen of Gerar did striue with Izhaks herdmen, saying, The water is ours: therefore called he the name of the well Esek, because they were at strife with him.

21 Afterwarde they digged another well, and stroue for that also, and he called the name of it Sitnah.

22 Then he remoued thence, and digged an other well, for the which they stroue not: therefore called hee the name of it Rehoboth, and sayde, Because the Lord hath nowe made vs roome, we shall increase vpon the earth.

23 So he went vp thence to Beer-sheba.

24 And the Lord appeared vnto him the same night, and sayde, I am the God of Abraham thy father: feare not, for I am with thee, and wil blesse thee, and will multiplie thy seede for my seruant Abrahams sake.

25 Then he builte an altar there, and called vpon the Name of the Lord, and there spred his tent: where also Izhaks seruauntes digged a well.

26 Then came Abimelech to him from Gerar, and Ahuzzath one of his friendes, and Phichol the captaine of his armie.

27 To whom Izhak sayd, Wherefore come ye to me, seeing ye hate mee and haue put mee away from you?

28 Who answered, Wee sawe certainely that the Lord was with thee, and wee thought thus, Let there be nowe an othe betweene vs, euen betweene vs and thee, and let vs make a couenant with thee.

29 If thou shalt do vs no hurt, as we haue not touched thee, and as we haue done vnto thee nothing but good, and sent thee away in peace: thou nowe, the blessed of the Lord, doe this.

30 Then hee made them a feast, and they dyd eate and drinke.

31 And they rose vp betimes in the morning, and sware one to another: then Izhak let them go, and they departed from him in peace.

32 And that same day Izhaks seruantes came and tolde him of a well, which they had digged, and said vnto him, We haue found water.

33 So hee called it Shibah: therefore the name of the citie is called Beer-sheba vnto this day.

34 Nowe when Esau was fourtie yeere olde, he tooke to wife Iudith, the daughter of Beeri an Hittite, and Bashemath the daughter of Elon an Hittite also.

35 And they were a griefe of minde to Izhak and to Rebekah.

Genesis 27

1 And when Izhak was olde, and his eyes were dimme (so that he coulde not see) he called Esau his eldest sonne, and sayde vnto him, My sonne. And he answered him, I am here.

2 Then he sayd, Beholde, I am nowe olde, and knowe not the day of my death:

3 Wherefore nowe, I pray thee take thine instruments, thy quiuer and thy bowe, and get thee to the fielde, that thou mayest take mee some venison.

4 Then make mee sauourie meate, such as I loue, and bring it me that I may eat, and that my soule may blesse thee, before I die.

5 (Nowe Rebekah heard, when Izhak spake to Esau his sonne) and Esau went into the fielde to hunt for venison, and to bring it.

6 Then Rebekah spake vnto Iaakob her sonne, saying, Beholde, I haue heard thy father talking with Esau thy brother, saying,

7 Bring mee vension, and make mee sauourie meate, that I may eate and blesse thee before the Lord, afore my death.

8 Nowe therefore, my sonne, heare my voyce in that which I command thee.

9 Get thee nowe to the flocke, and bring me thence two good kids of the goates, that I may make pleasant meate of them for thy father, such as he loueth.

10 Then shalt thou bring it to thy father, and he shall eate, to the intent that he may blesse thee before his death.

11 But Iaakob sayde to Rebekah his mother, Beholde, Esau my brother is rough, and I am smoothe.

12 My father may possibly feele me, and I shall seem to him to be a mocker: so

shall I bring a curse vpon me, and not a blessing.

13 But his mother sayd vnto him, vpon me be thy curse, my sonne: onely heare my voyce, and go and bring me them.

14 So he went and set them, and brought them to his mother: and his mother made pleasant meat, such as his father loued.

15 And Rebekah tooke faire clothes of her elder sonne Esau, which were in her house, and clothed Iaakob her yonger sonne:

16 And she couered his hands and the smoothe of his necke with the skinnes of the kiddes of the goates.

17 Afterward she put the pleasant meate and bread, which she had prepared, in the hand of her sonne Iaakob.

18 And when he came to his father, he sayd, My father. Who answered, I am here: who art thou, my sonne?

19 And Iaakob sayde to his father, I am Esau thy first borne, I haue done as thou badest me, arise, I pray thee: sit vp and eate of my venison, that thy soule may blesse me.

20 Then Izhak said vnto his sonne, Howe hast thou founde it so quickly my sonne? Who sayde, Because the Lord thy God brought it to mine hande.

21 Againe sayde Izhak vnto Iaakob, Come neere nowe, that I may feele thee, my sonne, whether thou be that my sonne Esau or not.

22 Then Iaakob came neere to Izhak his father, and he felt him and sayd, The voyce is Iaakobs voyce, but the hands are the hands of Esau.

23 (For he knewe him not, because his hands were rough as his brother Esaus hands: wherefore he blessed him)

24 Againe he sayd, Art thou that my sonne Esau? Who answered, Yea.

25 Then said he, Bring it me hither, and I will eate of my sonnes venison, that my soule may blesse mee. And he brought it to him, and he ate: also he brought him wine, and he dranke.

26 Afterward his father Izhak sayd vnto him, Come neere nowe, and kisse me, my sonne.

27 And hee came neere and kissed him. Then he smellled the sauour of his garmentes, and blessed him, and sayde, Behold, the smelll of my sonne is as the smelll of a fielde, which the Lord hath blessed.

28 God giue thee therefore of the dewe of heauen, and the fatnesse of the earth, and plentie of wheate and wine.

29 Let people bee thy seruantes, and nations bowe vnto thee: be Lord ouer thy brethren, and let thy mothers children honour thee. cursed be he that curseth thee, and blessed be he that blesseth thee.

30 And when Izhak had made an ende of blessing Iaakob, and Iaakob was scarce gone out from the presence of Izhak his father, then came Esau his brother from his hunting,

31 And hee also prepared sauourie meate and brought it to his father, and

sayd vnto his father, Let my father arise, and eat of his sonnes venison, that thy soule may blesse me.

32 But his father Izhak sayde vnto him, Who art thou? And he answered, I am thy sonne, euen thy first borne Esau.

33 Then Izhak was stricken with a marueilous great feare, and sayde, Who and where is hee that hunted venison, and brought it mee, and I haue eate of all before thou camest? and I haue blessed him, therefore he shalbe blessed.

34 When Esau heard the wordes of his father, he cryed out with a great crye and bitter, out of measure, and sayde vnto his father, Blesse me, euen me also, my father.

35 Who answered, Thy brother came with subtiltie, and hath taken away thy blessing.

36 Then he sayde, Was hee not iustly called Iaakob? for hee hath deceiued mee these two times: he tooke my birthright, and loe, nowe hath he taken my blessing. Also he sayd, Hast thou not reserued a blessing for me?

37 Then Izhak answered, and sayd vnto Esau, Beholde, I haue made him thy lorde, and all his brethre haue I made his seruants: also with wheate and wine haue I furnished him, and vnto thee now what shall I doe, my sonne?

38 Then Esau sayde vnto his father, Hast thou but one blessing my father? blesse mee, euen me also, my father: and Esau lifted vp his voyce, and wept.

39 Then Izhak his father answered, and sayde vnto him, Behold, the fatnesse of the earth shall be thy dwelling place, and thou shalt haue of the dewe of heauen from aboue.

40 And by thy sword shalt thou liue, and shalt be thy brothers seruant. But it shall come to passe, when thou shalt get the masterie, that thou shalt breake his yoke from thy necke.

41 Therefore Esau hated Iaakob, because of the blessing, wherewith his father blessed him. And Esau thought in his minde, The dayes of mourning for my father will come shortly, then I will slay may brother Iaakob.

42 And it was told to Rebekah of the wordes of Esau her elder sonne, and shee sent and called Iaakob her yonger sonne, and sayd vnto him, Beholde, thy brother Esau is comforted against thee, meaning to kill thee:

43 Now therefore my sonne, heare my voyce, arise, and flee thou to Haran to my brother Laban,

44 And tarie with him a while vntill thy brothers fiercenesse be swaged,

45 And till thy brothers wrath turne away from thee, and hee forget the thinges, which thou hast done to him: then will I sende and take thee from thence: why shoulde I bee depriued of you both in one day?

46 Also Rebekah said to Izhak, I am weary of my life, for the daughters of Heth. If Iaakob take a wife of the daughters of Heth like these of the daughters of the lande, what auaileth it me to liue?

Genesis 28

1 Then Izhak called Iaakob and blessed him, and charged him, and sayde vnto him, Take not a wife of the daughters of Canaan.

2 Arise, get thee to Padan Aram to the house of Bethuel thy mothers father, and thence take thee a wife of the daughters of Laban thy mothers brother.

3 And God all sufficient blesse thee, and make thee to encrease, and multiplie thee, that thou mayest be a multitude of people,

4 And giue thee the blessing of Abraham, euen to thee and to thy seede with thee, that thou mayest inherite the lande (wherein thou art a stranger,) which God gaue vnto Abraham.

5 Thus Izhak sent forth Iaakob, and he went to Padan Aram vnto Laban sonne of Bethuel the Aramite, brother to Rebekah, Iaakobs and Esaus mother.

6 When Esau sawe that Izhak had blessed Iaakob, and sent him to Padan Aram, to set him a wife thence, and giuen him a charge when he blessed him, saying, Thou shalt not take a wife of the daughters of Canaan,

7 And that Iaakob had obeyed his father and his mother, and was gone to Padan Aram:

8 Also Esau seeing that the daughters of Canaan displeased Izhak his father,

9 Then went Esau to Ishmael, and tooke vnto the wiues, which he had, Mahalath the daughter of Ishmael Abrahams sonne, the sister of Nabaioth, to be his wife.

10 Now Iaakob departed from Beer-sheba, and went to Haran,

11 And he came vnto a certaine place, and taried there al night, because the sunne was downe, and tooke of the stones of the place, and layde vnder his head and slept in the same place.

12 Then he dreamed, and behold, there stoode a ladder vpon the earth, and the top of it reached vp to heauen: and loe, the Angels of God went vp and downe by it.

13 And behold, the Lord stoode aboue it, and sayd, I am the Lord God of Abraham thy father, and the God of Izhak: the land, vpon the which thou sleepest, wil I giue thee and thy seede.

14 And thy seede shall be as the dust of the earth, and thou shalt spread abroad to the West, and to the East, and to the North, and to the South, and in thee and in thy seede shall all the families of the earth be blessed.

15 And lo, I am with thee, and wil keepe thee whithersoeuer thou goest, and will bring thee againe into this lande: for I will not forsake thee vntill I haue performed that, that I haue promised thee.

16 Then Iaakob awoke out of his sleepe, and sayde, Surely the Lord is in this place, and I was not aware.

17 And he was afraid, and said, How fearefull is this place! this is none other but the house of God, and this is the gate of heauen.

18 Then Iaakob rose vp early in the morning, and tooke the stone that hee had layde vnder his head, and set it vp as a pillar, and powred oyle vpon the top of it.

19 And he called ye name of that place Bethel: notwithstanding the name of the citie was at the first called Luz.

20 Then Iaakob vowed a vowe, saying, If God will be with me, and will keepe me in this iourney which I go, and wil giue me bread to eate, and clothes to put on:

21 So that I come againe vnto my fathers house in safetie, then shall the Lord be my God.

22 And this stone, which I haue set vp as a pillar, shall be Gods house: and of all that thou shalt giue me, wil I giue the tenth vnto thee.

Genesis 29

1 Then Iaakob lift vp his feete and came into the East countrey.

2 And as he looked about, behold there was a well in the field, and lo, three flocks of sheepe lay thereby (for at that well were the flockes watered) and there was a great stone vpon the welles mouth.

3 And thither were all the flockes gathered, and they rolled the stone from the welles mouth, and watered the sheepe, and put the stone againe vpon the welles mouth in his place.

4 And Iaakob sayde vnto them, My brethren, whence be ye? And they answered, We are of Haran.

5 Then he sayd vnto them, Know ye Laban the sonne of Nahor? Who said, We know him.

6 Againe he sayd vnto them, Is he in good health? And they answered, He is in good health, and beholde, his daughter Rahel commeth with the sheepe.

7 Then he sayd, Lo, it is yet hie day, neither is it time that the cattell shoulde be gathered together: water ye his sheepe and go feede them.

8 But they sayde, We may not vntill all the flocks be brought together, and till men rolle the stone from the welles mouth, that we may water the sheepe.

9 While he talked with them, Rahel also came with her fathers sheepe, for she kept them.

10 And assoone as Iaakob saw Rahel ye daughter of Laban his mothers brother, and the sheepe of Laban his mothers brother, then came Iaakob neere, and rolled the stone from the welles mouth, and watered ye flocke of Laban his mothers brother.

11 And Iaakob kissed Rahel, and lift vp his voyce and wept.

12 (For Iaakob tolde Rahel, that he was her fathers brother, and that he was Rebekahs sonne) then she ranne and tolde her father.

13 And when Laban heard tell of Iaakob his sisters sonne, he ranne to meete him, and embraced him and kissed him, and brought him to his house: and he tolde Laban all these things.

14 To whome Laban sayd, Well, thou art my bone and my flesh. and he abode with him the space of a moneth.

15 For Laban sayde vnto Iaakob, Though thou be my brother, shouldest thou therfore serue me for nought? tell me, what shalbe thy wages?

16 Now Laban had two daughters, the elder called Leah, and the yonger called Rahel.

17 And Leah was tender eyed, but Rahel was beautifull and faire.

18 And Iaakob loued Rahel, and sayde, I will serue thee seuen yeeres for Rahel thy yonger daughter.

19 Then Laban answered, It is better that I giue her thee, then that I should giue her to another man: abide with me.

20 And Iaakob serued seuen yeres for Rahel, and they seemed vnto him but a few dayes, because he loued her.

21 Then Iaakob sayde to Laban, Giue me my wife, that I may goe in to her: for my terme is ended.

22 Wherefore Laban gathered together all the men of the place, and made a feast.

23 But whe the euening was come, he tooke Leah his daughter and brought her to him, and he went in vnto her.

24 And Laban gaue his mayde Zilpah to his daughter Leah, to be her seruant.

25 But when the morning was come, behold, it was Leah. Then sayde he to Laban, Wherefore hast thou done thus to mee? did not I serue thee for Rahel? wherfore then hast thou beguiled me?

26 And Laban answered, It is not the maner of this place, to giue the yonger before the elder.

27 Fulfill seuen yeeres for her, and we wil also giue thee this for the seruice, which thou shalt serue me yet seuen yeeres more.

28 Then Iaakob did so, and fulfilled her seuen yeeres, so he gaue him Rahel his daughter to be his wife.

29 Laban also gaue to Rahel his daughter Bilhah his mayde to be her seruant.

30 So entred he in to Rahel also, and loued also Rahel more then Leah, and serued him yet seuen yeeres more.

31 When the Lord saw that Leah was despised, he made her fruitful: but Rahel was barren.

32 And Leah conceiued and bare a sonne, and she called his name Reuben: for she said, Because the Lord hath looked vpon my tribulation, now therefore mine husband will loue me.

33 And she conceiued againe and bare a sonne, and sayde, Because the Lord heard that I was hated, he hath therefore giuen me this sonne also, and she called his name Simeon.

34 And she conceiued againe and bare a sonne, and said, Now at this time wil my husband keepe mee company, because I haue borne him three sonnes: therefore was his name called Leui.

35 Moreouer shee conceiued againe and bare a sonne, saying, Nowe will I prayse the Lord: thercfore shee called his name Iudah, and left bearing.

Genesis 30

1 And when Rahel saw that she bare Iaakob no children, Rahel enuied her sister, and said vnto Iaakob, Giue me children, or els I dye.

2 Then Iaakobs anger was kindled against Rahel, and he sayde, Am I in Gods steade, which hath withholden from thee the fruite of the wombe?

3 And she said, Behold my maide Bilhah, goe in to her, and she shall beare vpon my knees, and I shall haue children also by her.

4 Then shee gaue him Bilhah her mayde to wife, and Iaakob went in to her.

5 So Bilhah conceiued and bare Iaakob a sonne.

6 Then said Rahel, God hath giuen sentence on my side, and hath also heard my voyce, and hath giuen mee a sonne: therefore called shee his name, Dan.

7 And Bilhah Rahels maide coceiued againe, and bare Iaakob the second sonne.

8 Then Rahel said, with excellent wrestlings haue I wrestled with my sister, and haue gotten the vpper hande: and shee called his name, Naphtali.

9 And when Leah saw that she had left bearing, shee tooke Zilpah her mayde, and gaue her Iaakob to wife.

10 And Zilpah Leahs mayde bare Iaakob a sonne.

11 Then sayd Leah, A companie commeth: and she called his name, Gad.

12 Againe Zilpah Leahs mayde bare Iaakob another sonne.

13 Then sayde Leah, Ah, blessed am I, for the daughters will blesse me. and she called his name, Asher.

14 Nowe Reuben went in the dayes of the wheateharuest, and founde mandrakes in the fielde and brought them vnto his mother Leah. Then sayde Rahel to Leah, Giue me, I pray thee, of thy sonnes mandrakes.

15 But shee answered her, Is it a small matter for thee to take mine husband, except thou take my sonnes mandrakes also? Then sayde Rahel, Therefore he shall sleepe with thee this night for thy sonnes mandrakes.

16 And Iaakob came from the fielde in the euening, and Leah went out to meete him, and sayde, Come in to mee, for I haue bought and payed for thee with my sonnes mandrakes: and he slept with her that night.

17 And God heard Leah and shee conceiued, and bare vnto Iaakob the fift sonne.

18 Then said Leah, God hath giuen me my reward, because I gaue my mayde to my husband, and she called his name Issachar.

19 After, Leah conceiued againe, and bare Iaakob the sixt sonne.

20 Then Leah said, God hath endued me with a good dowrie: nowe will mine husband dwell with me, because I haue borne him sixe sonnes: and she called his name Zebulun.

21 After that, shee bare a daughter, and shee called her name Dinah.

22 And God remembred Rahel, and God heard her, and opened her wombe.

23 So she conceiued and bare a sonne, and said, God hath taken away my rebuke.

24 And shee called his name Ioseph, saying, The Lord wil giue me yet another sonne.

25 And assoone as Rahel had borne Ioseph, Iaakob said to Laban, Sende me away that I may go vnto my place and to my countrey.

26 Giue me my wiues and my children, for whom I haue serued thee, and let me go: for thou knowest what seruice I haue done thee.

27 To whom Laban answered, If I haue nowe found fauour in thy sight tarie: I haue perceiued that the Lord hath blessed me for thy sake.

28 Also he said, Appoynt vnto me thy wages, and I will giue it thee.

29 But he sayd vnto him, Thou knowest, what seruice I haue done thee, and in what taking thy cattell hath bene vnder me.

30 For the litle, that thou haddest before I came, is increased into a multitude: and the Lord hath blessed thee by my comming: but nowe when shall I trauell for mine owne house also?

31 Then he saide, What shall I giue thee? And Iaakob answered, Thou shalt giue mee nothing at all: if thou wilt doe this thing for mee, I will returne, feede, and keepe thy sheepe.

32 I wil passe through all thy flockes this day, and separate from them all the sheepe with litle spots and great spots, and al blacke lambes among the sheepe, and the great spotted, and litle spotted among the goates: and it shalbe my wages.

33 So shall my righteousnesse answere for me hereafter, when it shall come for my rewarde before thy face, and euery one that hath not litle or great spots among the goates, and blacke among the sheepe, the same shalbe theft with me.

34 Then Laban sayde, Goe to, woulde God it might be according to thy saying.

35 Therefore he tooke out the same day the hee goates that were partie coloured and with great spots, and all the shee goates with litle and great spots, and all that had white in them, and all the blacke among the sheepe, and put them in the keeping of his sonnes.

36 And hee set three dayes iourney betweene himselfe and Iaakob. And Iaakob kept the rest of Labans sheepe.

37 Then Iaakob tooke rods of greene popular, and of hasell, and of the chesnut tree, and pilled white strakes in them, and made the white appeare in the rods.

38 Then he put the rods, which he had pilled, in the gutters and watering troughes, when the sheepe came to drink, before the sheepe. (for they were in heate, when they came to drinke)

39 And the sheepe were in heate before the rods, and afterward brought forth yong of partie colour, and with small and great spots.

40 And Iaakob parted these lambes, and turned the faces of the flocke towardes these lambes partie coloured and all maner of blacke, among the sheepe of Laban: so hee put his owne flockes by themselues, and put them not with Labans flocke.

41 And in euery ramming time of the stronger sheepe, Iaakob layde the rods before the eyes of the sheepe in the gutters, that they might conceiue before the rods.

42 But when the sheepe were feeble, hee put them not in: and so the feebler were Labans, and the stronger Iaakobs.

43 So the man increased exceedingly, and had many flockes, and maide seruantes, and men seruants, and camels and asses.

Genesis 31

1 Now he heard the words of Labans sonnes, saying, Iaakob hath taken away all that was our fathers, and of our fathers goods hath he gotten all this honour.

2 Also Iaakob beheld the countenance of Laban, that it was not towards him as in times past:

3 And the Lord had said vnto Iaakob, Turne againe into the lande of thy fathers, and to thy kinred, and I wilbe with thee.

4 Therefore Iaakob sent and called Rahel and Leah to the fielde vnto his flocke.

5 Then sayde hee vnto them, I see your fathers countenance, that it is not towardes me as it was wont, and the God of my father hath bene with me.

6 And yee knowe that I haue serued your father with all my might.

7 But your father hath deceiued me, and changed my wages tenne times: but God suffred him not to hurt me.

8 If he thus sayd, The spotted shall be thy wages, then all the sheepe bare spotted: and if he sayd thus, the party coloured shalbe thy rewarde, then bare all the sheepe particoloured.

9 Thus hath God taken away your fathers substance, and giuen it me.

10 For in ramming time I lifted vp mine eyes and saw in a dreame, and beholde, ye hee goates leaped vpon the shee goates, that were partie coloured with litle and great spots spotted.

11 And the Angel of God sayde to mee in a dreame, Iaakob. And I answered, Lo, I am here.

12 And he sayde, Lift vp nowe thine eyes, and see all the hee goates leaping vpon ye shee goates that are partie coloured, spotted with litle and great spots: for I haue seene all that Laban doeth vnto thee.

13 I am the God of Beth-el, where thou anoyntedst the pillar, where thou vowedst a vowe vnto me. Nowe arise, get thee out of this countrey and returne vnto ye land where thou wast borne.

14 Then answered Rahel and Leah, and sayde vnto him, Haue wee any more porcion and inheritance in our fathers house?

15 Doeth not he count vs as strangers? for he hath solde vs, and hath eaten vp and consumed our money.

16 Therefore all the riches, which God hath taken from our father, is ours and our childrens: nowe then whatsoeuer God hath saide vnto thee, doe it.

17 Then Iaakob rose vp, and set his sonnes and his wiues vpon camels.

18 And he caried away all his flockes, and al his substance which he had gotten, to wit, his riches, which he had gotten in Padan Aram, to goe to Izhak his father vnto the land of Canaan.

19 Whe Laban was gone to shere his sheepe, Then Rahel stole her fathers idoles.

20 Thus Iaakob stole away ye heart of Laban the Aramite: for he told him not that he fled.

21 So fled he with all that he had, and he rose vp, and passed the riuer, and set his face towarde mount Gilead.

22 And the third day after was it told Laban, that Iaakob fled.

23 Then he tooke his brethren with him, and followed after him seuen dayes iourney, and ouertooke him at mount Gilead.

24 And God came to Laban the Aramite in a dreame by night, and sayde vnto him, Take heede that thou speake not to Iaakob ought saue good.

25 Then Laban ouertooke Iaakob, and Iaakob had pitched his tent in the mount: and Laban also with his brethren pitched vpon mount Gilead.

26 Then Laban sayde to Iaakob, What hast thou done? thou hast euen stolen away mine heart and caried away my daughters as though they had bene taken captiues with the sworde.

27 Wherfore diddest thou flie so secretly and steale away from me, and diddest not tel me, that I might haue sent thee foorth with mirth and with songs, with timbrel and with harpe?

28 But thou hast not suffered me to kisse my sonnes and my daughters: nowe thou hast done foolishly in doing so.

29 I am able to do you euill: but the God of your father spake vnto me yesternight, saying, Take heed that thou speake not to Iaakob ought saue good.

30 Nowe though thou wentest thy way, because thou greatly longedst after thy fathers house, yet wherefore hast thou stollen my gods?

31 Then Iaakob answered, and said to Laban, Because I was afraid, and thought that thou wouldest haue taken thy daughters from me.

32 But with whome thou findest thy gods, let him not liue. Search thou before our brethre what I haue of thine, and take it to thee, (but Iaakob wist not that Rahel had stolen them)

33 Then came Laban into Iaakobs tent, and into Leahs tent, and into the two maides tentes, but founde them not. So

hee went out of Leahs tent, and entred into Rahels tent.

34 (Nowe Rahel had taken the idoles, and put them in the camels litter and sate downe vpon them) and Laban searched al the tent, but found them not.

35 Then said she to her father, My Lord, be not angrie that I cannot rise vp before thee: for the custome of women is vpon me: so he searched, but found not the idoles.

36 The Iaakob was wroth, and chode with Laban: Iaakob also answered and sayd to Laban, What haue I trespassed? what haue I offended, that thou hast pursued after me?

37 Seeing thou hast searched all my stuffe, what hast thou foud of all thine houshold stuffe? put it here before my brethren and thy brethren, that they may iudge betweene vs both.

38 This twenty yere I haue bin with thee: thine ewes and thy goates haue not cast their yong, and the rammes of thy flocke haue I not eaten.

39 Whatsoeuer was torne of beasts, I brought it not vnto thee, but made it good my selfe: of mine hand diddest thou require it, were it stollen by day or stollen by night.

40 I was in the day consumed with heate, and with frost in the night, and my sleepe departed from mine eyes.

41 Thus haue I bene twentie yeere in thine house, and serued thee fourteene yeeres for thy two daughters, and sixe yeeres for thy sheepe, and thou hast changed my wages tenne times.

42 Except the God of my father, the God of Abraham, and the feare of Izhak had bene with me, surely thou haddest sent me away nowe emptie: but God behelde my tribulation, and the labour of mine hads, and rebuked thee yester night.

43 Then Laban answered, and saide vnto Iaakob, These daughters are my daughters, and these sonnes are my sonnes, and these sheepe are my sheepe, and all that thou seest, is mine, and what can I doe this day vnto these my daughters, or to their sonnes which they haue borne?

44 Nowe therefore come and let vs make a couenant, I and thou, which may be a witnes betweene me and thee.

45 Then tooke Iaakob a stone, and set it vp as a pillar:

46 And Iaakob sayde vnto his brethren, Gather stones: who brought stones, and made an heape, and they did eate there vpon the heape.

47 And Laban called it Iegar-sahadutha, and Iaakob called it Galeed.

48 For Laban sayd, This heape is witnesse betweene me and thee this day: therefore he called the name of it Galeed.

49 Also he called it Mizpah, because he said, The Lord looke betweene me and thee, when we shalbe departed one from another,

50 If thou shalt vexe my daughters, or shalt take wiues beside my daughters: there is no man with vs, beholde, God is witnesse betweene me and thee.

51 Moreouer Laban sayd to Iaakob, Beholde this heape, and behold the pillar, which I haue set betweene me and thee,

52 This heape shall be witnesse, and the pillar shall be witnesse, that I will not come ouer this heape to thee, and that thou shalt not passe ouer this heape and this pillar vnto me for euill.

53 The God of Abraham, and the God of Nabor, and the God of their father be iudge betweene vs: But Iaakob sware by the feare of his father Izhak.

54 Then Iaakob did offer a sacrifice vpon the mount, and called his brethren to eate bread. and they did eate bread, and taried all night in the mount.

55 And earely in the morning Laban rose vp and kissed his sonnes and his daughters, and blessed them, and Laban departing, went vnto his place againe.

Genesis 32

1 Nowe Iaakob went forth on his iourney and the Angels of God met him.

2 And when Iaakob saw them, he said, This is Gods hoste, and called the name of the same place Mahanaim.

3 Then Iaakob sent messengers before him to Esau his brother, vnto the land of Seir into the countrey of Edom:

4 To whom he gaue commandement, saying, Thus shall ye speake to my lorde Esau: thy seruant Iaakob sayeth thus, I haue bene a stranger with Laban, and taried vnto this time.

5 I haue beeues also and Asses, sheepe, and men seruantes, and women seruantes, and haue sent to shew my lord, that I may find grace in thy sight.

6 So ye messengers came againe to Iaakob, saying, We came vnto thy brother Esau, and hee also commeth against thee and foure hundreth men with him.

7 Then Iaakob was greatly afraid, and was sore troubled, and deuided the people that was with him, and the sheepe, and the beeues, and the camels into two companies.

8 For he said, If Esau come to ye one company and smite it, the other companie shall escape.

9 Moreouer Iaakob said, O God of my father Abraham, and God of my father Izhak: Lord, which saydest vnto me, Returne vnto thy coutrey and to thy kinred, and I will do thee good,

10 I am not worthy of the least of all the mercies, and al the trueth, which thou hast shewed vnto thy seruant: for with my staffe came I ouer this Iorden, and now haue I gotte two bads.

11 I pray thee, Deliuer me from the hande of my brother, from the hande of Esau: for I feare him, least he will come and smite me, and the mother vpon the children.

12 For thou saydest; I will surely doe thee good, and make thy seede as the sande of the sea, which can not be nombred for multitude.

13 And he taryed there the same night, and tooke of that which came to had, a present for Esau his brother:

14 Two hundreth shee goates and twenty hee goates, two hundreth ewes and twentie rammes:

15 Thirtie mylche camels with their coltes, fourtie kine, and ten bullockes, twentie she asses and ten foles.

16 So he deliuered them into the hande of his seruants, euery droue by themselues, and saide vnto his seruants, Passe before me, and put a space betweene droue and droue.

17 And he commanded the formost, saying, If Esau my brother meete thee, and aske thee, saying, Whose seruant art thou? And whither goest thou? And whose are these before thee?

18 Then thou shalt say, They be thy seruant Iaakobs: it is a present sent vnto my lord Esau: and beholde, he him selfe also is behinde vs.

19 So likewise commanded he the seconde and the thirde, and all that followed the droues, saying, After this maner, ye shall speake vnto Esau, when ye finde him.

20 And ye shall say moreouer, Beholde, thy seruant Iaakob commeth after vs (for he thought, I will appease his wrath with the present that goeth before me, and afterwarde I will see his face: it may be that he will accept me.)

21 So went the present before him: but he taried that night with the companie.

22 And he rose vp the same night, and tooke his two wiues, and his two maides, and his eleuen children, and went ouer the forde Iabbok.

23 And he tooke them, and sent them ouer the riuer, and sent ouer that he had.

24 Now when Iaakob was left him selfe alone, there wrestled a man with him vnto the breaking of the day.

25 And he sawe that he could not preuaile against him: therefore he touched the holowe of his thigh, and the holowe of Iaakobs thigh was loosed, as he wrestled with him.

26 And he saide, Let me goe, for the morning appeareth. Who answered, I will not let thee go except thou blesse me.

27 Then said he vnto him, What is thy name? And he said, Iaakob.

28 Then said he, Thy name shalbe called Iaakob no more, but Israel: because thou hast had power with God, thou shalt also preuaile with men.

29 Then Iaakob demaded, saying, Tell me, I pray thee, thy name. And he said, Wherefore now doest thou aske my name? and he blessed him there

30 And Iaakob called the name of the place, Peniel: for, saide he, I haue seene God face to face, and my life is preserued.

31 And the sunne rose vp to him as he passed Peniel, and he halted vpon his thigh.

32 Therefore the children of Israel eate not of the sinewe that shranke in the hollowe of the thigh, vnto this day:

because he touched the sinew that shranke in the holow of Iaakobs thigh.

Genesis 33

1 And as Iaakob lift vp his eyes, and looked, behold, Esau came, and with him foure hundreth men: and he deuided the children to Leah, and to Rahel, and to the two maides.

2 And he put the maides, and their children formost, and Leah, and her children after, and Rahel, and Ioseph hindermost.

3 So he went before them and bowed him selfe to the ground seuen times, vntill he came neere to his brother.

4 Then Esau ranne to meete him, and embraced him, and fell on his necke, and kissed him, and they wept.

5 And he lift vp his eyes, and sawe the women, and the children, and saide, Who are these with thee? And he answered, They are ye childre whome God of his grace hath giuen thy seruant.

6 Then came the maides neere, they, and their children, and bowed themselues.

7 Leah also with her children came neere and made obeysance: and after Ioseph and Rahel drew neere, and did reuerence.

8 Then he said, What meanest thou by all this droue, which I met? Who answered, I haue sent it, that I may finde fauour in the sight of my lorde:

9 And Esau said, I haue ynough, my brother: keepe that thou hast to thy selfe.

10 But Iaakob answered, Nay, I pray thee: if I haue found grace nowe in thy sight, then receiue my present at mine hande: for I haue seene thy face, as though I had seene the face of God, because thou hast accepted me.

11 I pray thee take my blessing, that is brought thee: for God hath had mercie on me, and therefore I haue all things: so he compelled him, and he tooke it.

12 And he saide, Let vs take our iourney and go, and I will goe before thee.

13 Then he answered him, My lord knoweth, that the children are tender, and the ewes and kine with yong vnder mine hande: and if they should ouerdriue them one day, all the flocke would die.

14 Let now my lord go before his seruant, and I will driue softly, according to ye pase of ye cattel, which is before me, and as the children be able to endure, vntill I come to my lord vnto Seir.

15 Then Esau said, I will leaue then some of my folke with thee. And he answered, what needeth this? let me finde grace in the sight of my lorde.

16 So Esau returned, and went his way that same day vnto Seir.

17 And Iaakob went forwarde towarde Succoth, and built him an house, and made boothes for his cattell: therefore he called the name of the place Succoth.

18 Afterward, Iaakob came safe to Sheche a citie, which is in the lande of Canaan, when he came from Padan Aram, and pitched before the citie.

19 And there he bought a parcell of ground, where hee pitched his tent, at the hande of the sonnes of Hamor Shechems father, for an hundreth pieces of money.

20 And he set vp there an altar, and called it, The mightie God of Israel.

Genesis 34

1 Then Dinah the daughter of Leah, which she bare vnto Iaakob, went out to see the daughters of that countrey.

2 Whome when Shechem the sonne of Hamor the Hiuite lorde of that countrey sawe, hee tooke her, and lay with her, and defiled her.

3 So his heart claue vnto Dinah the daughter of Iaakob: and he loued the maide, and spake kindely vnto the maide.

4 Then said Shechem to his father Hamor, saying, Get me this maide to wife.

5 (Nowe Iaakob heard that he had defiled Dinah his daughter, and his sonnes were with his cattell in the fielde: therefore Iaakob helde his peace, vntill they were come.)

6 Then Hamor the father of Shechem went out vnto Iaakob to commune with him.

7 And whe the sonnes of Iaakob were come out of the fielde and heard it, it grieued the men, and they were very angry, because he had wrought villenie in Israel, in that he had lyen with Iaakobs daughter: which thing ought not to be done.

8 And Hamor communed with them, saying, the soule of my sonne Shechem longeth for your daughter: giue her him to wife, I pray you.

9 So make affinitie with vs: giue your daughters vnto vs, and take our daughters vnto you,

10 And ye shall dwell with vs, and the lande shalbe before you: dwell, and doe your businesse in it, and haue your possessions therein.

11 Shechem also said vnto her father and vnto her brethren, Let me finde fauour in your eyes, and I will giue whatsoeuer ye shall appoint me.

12 Aske of me abundantly both dowrie and giftes, and I will giue as ye appoint me, so that ye giue me the maide to wife.

13 Then the sonnes of Iaakob answered Shechem and Hamor his father, talking deceitfully, because he had defiled Dinah their sister,

14 And they said vnto them, We can not do this thing, to giue our sister to an vncircumcised man: for that were a reproofe vnto vs.

15 But in this will we consent vnto you, if ye will be as we are, that euery man childe among you be circumcised:

16 Then will we giue our daughters to you, and we will take your daughters to vs, and will dwell with you, and be one people.

17 But if ye will not hearken vnto vs to be circumcised, then will we take our daughter and depart.

18 Nowe their wordes pleased Hamor, and Shechem Hamors sonne.

19 And the yong man deferd not to doe the thing because he loued Iaakobs daughter: he was also the most set by of all his fathers house.

20 Then Hamor and Shechem his Sonne went vnto the gate of their citie, and communed with the men of their citie, saying,

21 These men are peaceable with vs: and that they may dwell in the land, and doe their affaires therin (for behold, the land hath roume ynough for them) let vs take their daughters to wiues, and giue them our daughters.

22 Onely herein will the men consent vnto vs for to dwell with vs, and to be one people, if all the men children among vs be circumcised as they are circumcised.

23 Shall not their flockes and their substance and all their cattell be ours? onely let vs consent herein vnto them, and they will dwell with vs.

24 And vnto Hamor, and Shechem his sonne hearkened all that went out of the gate of his citie: and all the men children were circumcised, euen all that went out of the gate of his citie.

25 And on the thirde day (when they were sore) two of the sonnes of Iaakob, Simeon and Leui, Dinahs brethren tooke either of them his sworde and went into the citie boldly, and slue euery male.

26 They slewe also Hamor and Shechem his sonne with the edge of the sword, and tooke Dinah out of Shechems house, and went their way.

27 Againe the other sonnes of Iaakob came vpon the dead, and spoyled the citie, because they had defiled their sister.

28 They tooke their sheepe and their beeues, and their asses, and whatsoeuer was in the citie, and in the fieldes.

29 Also they caryed away captiue and spoyled all their goods, and all their children and their wiues, and all that was in the houses.

30 Then Iaakob said to Simeon and Leui, Ye haue troubled me, and made me stinke among the inhabitats of the land, aswell the Canaanites, as the Perizzites, and and I being few in nomber, they shall gather theselues together against me, and slay me, and so shall I, and my house be destroied.

31 And they answered, Shoulde hee abuse our sister as a whore?

Genesis 35

1 Then God sayde to Iaakob, Arise, goe vp to Beth-el and dwell there, and make there an altar vnto God, that appeared vnto thee, when thou fleddest from Esau thy brother.

2 Then saide Iaakob vnto his houshold and to all that were with him, Put away the strange gods that are among you, and clense your selues, and change your garments:

3 For we will rise and goe vp to Beth-el, and I will make an altar there vnto God, which heard me in the day of my tribulation, and was with me in the way which I went.

4 And they gaue vnto Iaakob all the strange gods, which were in their hands, and all their earings which were in their eares, and Iaakob hidde them vnder an oke, which was by Shechem.

5 Then they went on their iourney, and the feare of God was vpon the cities that were roud about them: so that they did not follow after the sonnes of Iaakob.

6 So came Iaakob to Luz, which is in the land of Canaan: (the same is Beth-el) hee and all the people that was with him.

7 And he built there an altar, and had called the place, The God of Beth-el, because that God appeared vnto him there, when he fled from his brother.

8 Then Deborah Rebekahs nourse dyed, and was buried beneath Beth-el vnder an oke: and he called the name of it Allon Bachuth.

9 Againe God appeared vnto Iaakob, after he came out of Padan Aram, and blessed him.

10 Moreouer God said vnto him, Thy name is Iaakob: thy name shalbe no more called Iaakob, but Israel shalbe thy name: and hee called his name Israel.

11 Againe God said vnto him, I am God all sufficient. growe, and multiplie. a nation and a multitude of nations shall spring of thee, and Kings shall come out of thy loynes.

12 Also I will giue the lande, which I gaue to Abraham and Izhak, vnto thee: and vnto thy seede after thee will I giue that land.

13 So God ascended from him in the place where he had talked with him.

14 And Iaakob set vp a pillar in the place where he talked with him, a pillar of stone, and powred drinke offring thereon: also hee powred oyle thereon.

15 And Iaakob called the name of the place, where God spake with him, Beth-el.

16 Then they departed from Beth-el, and when there was about halfe a daies iourney of ground to come to Ephrath, Rahel trauailed, and in trauailing she was in perill.

17 And whe she was in paines of her labour, the midwife saide vnto her, Feare not: for thou shalt haue this sonne also.

18 Then as she was about to yeelde vp the Ghost (for she died) she called his name Ben-oni, but his father called him Beniamin.

19 Thus died Rahel, and was buried in the way to Ephrath, which is Beth-lehem.

20 And Iaakob set a pillar vpon her graue: This is the pillar of Rahels graue vnto this day.

21 Then Israel went forwarde, and pitched his tent beyond Migdal-eder.

22 Now, when Israel dwelt in that land, Reuben went, and lay with Bilhah his fathers concubine, and it came to Israels eare. And Iaakob had twelue sonnes.

23 The sonnes of Leah: Reuben Iaakobs eldest sonne, and Simeon, and Leui, and Iudah, and Issachar, and Zebulun.

24 The sonnes of Rahel: Ioseph and Beniamin.

25 And the sonnes of Bilhah Rahels maide: Dan and Naphtali.

26 And the sonnes of Zilpah Leahs maide: Gad and Asher. These are the sonnes of Iaakob, which were borne him in Padan Aram.

27 Then Iaakob came vnto Izhak his father to Mamre a citie of Arbah: this is Hebron, where Abraham and Izhak were strangers.

28 And the daies of Izhak were an hundreth and fourescore yeeres.

29 And Izhak gaue vp the ghost and died, and was gathered vnto his people, being olde and full of daies: and his sonnes Esau and Iaakob buried him.

Genesis 36

1 Nowe these are the generations of Esau, which is Edom.

2 Esau tooke his wiues of the daughters of Canaan: Adah the daughter of Elon an Hittite, and Aholibamah the daughter of Anah, the daughter of Zibeon an Hiuite,

3 And tooke Basemath Ishmaels daughter, sister of Nebaioth.

4 And Adah bare vnto Esau, Eliphaz: and Basemath bare Reuel.

5 Also Aholibamah bare Ieush, and Iaalam, and Korah: these are the sonnes of Esau which were borne to him in the land of Canaan.

6 So Esau tooke his wiues and his sonnes, and his daughters, and all the soules of his house, and his flocks, and all his cattell, and all his substance, which he had gotten in the land of Canaan, and went into an other countrey from his brother Iaakob.

7 For their riches were so great, that they could not dwell together, and the lande, wherein they were strangers, coulde not receiue them because of their flockes.

8 Therefore dwelt Esau in mount Seir: this Esau is Edom.

9 So these are the generations of Esau father of Edom in mount Seir.

10 These are the names of Esaus sonnes: Eliphaz, the sonne of Adah, the wife of Esau, and Reuel the sonne of Bashemath, the wife of Esau.

11 And the sonnes of Eliphaz were Teman, Omar, Zepho, and Gatam, and Kenaz.

12 And Timna was concubine to Eliphaz Esaus sonne, and bare vnto Eliphaz, Amalek: these be the sonnes of Adah Esaus wife.

13 And these are the sonnes of Reuel: Nahath, and Zerah, Shammah, and Mizzah: these were the sonnes of Bashemath Esaus wife.

14 And these were the sonnes of Aholibamah the daughter of Anah, daughter of Zibeon Esaus wife: for she bare vnto Esau, Ieush, and Iaalam, and Korah.

15 These were Dukes of the sonnes of Esau: the sonnes of Eliphaz, the first borne of Esau: Duke Teman, Duke Omar, Duke Zepho, Duke Kenaz,

16 Duke Korah, Duke Gatam, Duke Amalek: these are the Dukes that came of Eliphaz in the land of Edom: these were the sonnes of Adah.

17 And these are the sonnes of Reuel Esaus sonne: Duke Nahath, Duke Zerah, Duke Shammah, Duke Mizzah: these are the Dukes that came of Reuel in the land of Edom: these are the sonnes of Bashemath Esaus wife.

18 Likewise these were the sonnes of Aholibamah Esaus wife: Duke Ieush, Duke Iaalam, Duke Korah: these Dukes came of Aholibamah, the daughter of Anah Esaus wife.

19 These are the children of Esau, and these are the Dukes of them: This Esau is Edom.

20 These are the sonnes of Seir the Horite, which inhabited the lande before, Lotan, and Shobal, and Zibeon, and Anah.

21 And Dishon, and Ezer, and Dishan: these are the Dukes of the Horites, the sonnes of Seir in the land of Edom.

22 And the sonnes of Lotan were, Hori and Hemam, and Lotans sister was Timna.

23 And the sonnes of Shobal were these: Aluan, and Manahath, and Ebal, Shepho, and Onam.

24 And these are the sonnes of Zibeon: Both Aiah, and Anah: this was Anah that founde mules in the wildernesse, as he fedde his father Zibeons asses.

25 And the children of Anah were these: Dishon and Aholibamah, the daughter of Anah.

26 Also these are the sonnes of Dishan: Hemdan, and Eshban, and Ithran, and Cheran.

27 The sonnes of Ezer are these: Bilhan, and Zaauan, and Akan.

28 The sonnes of Dishan are these: Vz, and Aran.

29 These are the Dukes of the Horites: Duke Lotan, Duke Shobal, Duke Zibeon, Duke Anah,

30 Duke Dishon, Duke Ezer, Duke Dishan: these bee the Dukes of the Horites, after their Dukedomes in the land of Seir.

31 And these are the Kings that reigned in the lande of Edom, before there reigned any King ouer the children of Israel.

32 Then Bela the sonne of Beor reigned in Edom, and the name of his citie was Dinhabah.

33 And when Bela dyed, Iobab the sonne of Zerah of Bozra reigned in his steade.

34 When Iobab also was dead, Husham of the land of Temani reigned in his steade.

35 And after the death of Husham, Hadad the sonne of Bedad, which slewe Midian in the field of Moab, reigned in his steade, and the name of his citie was Auith.

36 When Hadad was dead, then Samlah of Masrekah reigned in his steade.

37 When Samlah was dead, Shaul of Rehoboth by the riuer, reigned in his steade.

38 When Shaul dyed, Baal-hanan the sonne of Achbor reigned in his steade.

39 And after the death of Baal-hanan the sonne of Achbor, Hadad reigned in his stead, and the name of his citie was Pau: and his wiues name Mehetabel the daughter of Matred, the daughter of Mezahab.

40 Then these are the names of the Dukes of Esau according to their families, their places and by their names: Duke Timna, Duke Aluah, Duke Ietheth,

41 Duke Aholibamah, Duke Elah, Duke Pinon,

42 Duke Kenaz, Duke Teman, Duke Mibzar,

43 Duke Magdiel, Duke Iram: these bee the Dukes of Edom, according to their habitations, in the lande of their inheritance. This Esau is the father of Edom.

Genesis 37

1 Iaakob nowe dwelt in the lande, wherein his father was a stranger, in the lande of Canaan.

2 These are the generations of Iaakob, when Ioseph was seuenteene yeere olde: he kept sheepe with his brethren, and the childe was with the sonnes of Bilhah, and with the sonnes of Zilpah, his fathers wiues. And Ioseph brought vnto their father their euill saying.

3 Nowe Israel loued Ioseph more then all his sonnes, because he begate him in his old age, and he made him a coat of many colours.

4 So when his brethren sawe that their father loued him more then all his brethren, then they hated him, and could not speake peaceably vnto him.

5 And Ioseph dreamed a dreame, and told his brethren, who hated him so much the more.

6 For he saide vnto them, Heare, I pray you, this dreame which I haue dreamed.

7 Beholde nowe, wee were binding sheues in the middes of the field: and loe, my shefe arose and also stoode vpright, and behold, your sheues compassed rounde about, and did reuerence to my shefe.

8 Then his brethren saide to him, What, shalt thou reigne ouer vs, and rule vs? or shalt thou haue altogether dominion ouer vs? And they hated him so much the more, for his dreames, and for his wordes.

9 Againe hee dreamed an other dreame, and tolde it his brethren, and saide, Behold, I haue had one dreame more, and beholde, the Sunne and the Moone and eleuen starres did reuerence to me.

10 Then he tolde it vnto his father and to his brethren, and his father rebuked him, and saide vnto him, What is this dreame, which thou hast dreamed? shall I, and thy mother, and thy brethren come in deede and fall on the ground before thee?

11 And his brethren enuied him, but his father noted the saying.

12 Then his brethren went to keepe their fathers sheepe in Shechem.

13 And Israel said vnto Ioseph, Doe not thy brethren keepe in Shechem? come and I will send thee to them.

14 And he answered him, I am here. Then he saide vnto him, Goe now, see whether it bee well with thy brethren, and how the flocks prosper, and bring me word againe. so hee sent him from the vale of Hebron, and he came to Shechem.

15 Then a man found him: for lo, hee was wandring in the fielde, and the man asked him, saying, What seekest thou?

16 And he answered, I seeke my brethren: tell me, I pray thee, where they keepe sheepe.

17 And the man said, they are departed hece: for I heard them say, Let vs goe vnto Dothan. Then went Ioseph after his brethren, and found them in Dothan.

18 And when they sawe him a farre off, euen before he came at them, they conspired against him for to slay him.

19 For they sayd one to another, Behold, this dreamer commeth.

20 Come now therefore, and let vs slay him, and cast him into some pitte, and wee will say, A wicked beast hath deuoured him: then wee shall see, what will come of his dreames.

21 But when Reuben heard that, he deliuered him out of their handes, and saide, Let vs not kill him.

22 Also Reuben saide vnto them, Shed not blood, but cast him into this pitte that is in the wildernesse, and lay no hande vpon him. Thus he said, that he might deliuer him out of their hand, and restore him to his father againe.

23 Now when Ioseph was come vnto his brethren, they stript Ioseph out of his coate, his particoloured coate that was vpon him.

24 And they tooke him, and cast him into a pit, and the pit was emptie, without water in it.

25 Then they sate them downe to eate bread: and they lift vp their eyes and looked, and behold, there came a companie of Ishmeelites from Gilead, and their camels laden with spicerie, and balme, and myrrhe, and were going to cary it downe into Egypt.

26 Then Iudah said vnto his brethren, What auaileth it, if we slay our brother, though wee keepe his blood secret?

27 Come and let vs sell him to the Ishmeelites, and let not our handes be vpon him: for he is our brother and our flesh: and his brethren obeyed.

28 Then the Midianites marchant men passed by, and they drewe foorth, and lift Ioseph out of the pit, and solde Ioseph vnto the Ishmeelites for twentie pieces of siluer: who brought Ioseph into Egypt.

29 Afterwarde Reuben returned to the pit, and beholde, Ioseph was not in the pit: then he rent his clothes,

30 And returned to his brethren, and said, The childe is not yonder, and I, whither shall I goe?

31 And they tooke Iosephs coate, and killed a kidde of the goates, and dipped the coate in the blood.

32 So they sent that particoloured coat, and they brought it vnto their father, and saide, This haue we founde: see nowe, whether it be thy sonnes coate, or no.

33 Then he knewe it and said, It is my sonnes coate: a wicked beast hath deuoured him: Ioseph is surely torne in pieces.

34 And Iaakob rent his clothes, and put sackecloth about his loynes, and sorowed for his sonne a long season.

35 Then all his sonnes and all his daughters rose vp to comfort him, but he woulde not be comforted, but said, Surely I will go downe into the graue vnto my sonne mourning: so his father wept for him.

36 And the Midianites solde him into Egypt vnto Potiphar an Eunuche of Pharaohs, and his chiefe stewarde.

Genesis 38

1 And at that time Iudah went downe from his brethren, and turned in to a man called Hirah an Adullamite.

2 And Iudah sawe there the daughter of a man called Suah a Canaanite: and he tooke her to wife, and went in vnto her.

3 So she conceiued and bare a sonne, and he called his name Er.

4 And she conceiued againe, and bare a sonne, and she called his name Onan.

5 Moreouer she bare yet a sonne, whome she called Shelah: and Iudah was at Chezib when she bare him.

6 Then Iudah tooke a wife to Er his first borne sonne whose name was Tamar.

7 Now Er the first borne of Iudah was wicked in the sight of the Lord: therefore the Lord slewe him.

8 Then Iudah said to Onan, Goe in vnto thy brothers wife, and do the office of a kinsman vnto her, and raise vp seede vnto thy brother.

9 And Onan knewe that the seede should not be his: therefore when he went in vnto his brothers wife, he spilled it on the grounde, least he should giue seede vnto his brother.

10 And it was wicked in the eyes of the Lord, which he did: wherefore he slewe him also.

11 Then said Iudah to Tamar his daughter in lawe, Remaine a widowe in thy fathers house, till Shelah my sonne growe vp (for he thought thus, Least he die as well as his brethren.) So Tamar went and dwelt in her fathers house.

12 And in processe of time also the daughter of Shuah Iudahs wife dyed. Then Iudah, when he had left mourning, went vp to his sheepe sherers to Timnah, he, and his neighbour Hirah the Adullamite.

13 And it was tolde Tamar, saying, beholde, thy father in lawe goeth vp to Timnah, to shere his sheepe.

14 Then she put her widowes garments off from her, and couered her with a vaile, and wrapped her selfe, and sate downe in Pethah-enaim, which is by the way to Timnah, because she sawe that Shelah was growen, and she was not giuen vnto him to wife.

15 When Iudah sawe her, he iudged her an whore: for she had couered her face.

16 And he turned to the way towards her, and saide, Come, I pray thee, let me lie with thee. (for he knewe not that she was his daughter in lawe) And she answered, What wilt thou giue me for to lie with me?

17 Then said he, I will sende thee a kid of the goates from the flocke. and she said, Well, if thou wilt giue me a pledge, till thou sende it.

18 Then he saide, What is the pledge that I shall giue thee? And she answered, Thy signet, and thy cloke, and thy staffe that is in thine hande. So he gaue it her, and lay by her, and she was with childe by him.

19 Then she rose, and went and put her vaile from her and put on her widowes raiment.

20 Afterwarde Iudah sent a kid of the goates by the hande of his neighbour the Adullamite, for to receiue his pledge from the womans hand: but he found her not.

21 Then asked he the men of that place, saying, Where is ye whore, that sate in Enaim by the way side? And they answered, There was no whore here.

22 He came therefore to Iudah againe, and said, I can not finde her, and also the men of the place said, There was no whore there.

23 Then Iudah said, Let her take it to her, lest we be shamed: beholde, I sent this kid, and thou hast not found her.

24 Now after three moneths, one tolde Iudah, saying, Tamar thy daughter in law hath played the whore, and lo, with playing the whore, she is great with childe. Then Iudah saide, Bring ye her foorth and let her be burnt.

25 When she was brought foorth, she sent to her father in law, saying, By the man, vnto whom these things pertaine, am I with childe: and saide also, Looke, I pray thee, whose these are, the seale, and the cloke, and the staffe.

26 Then Iudah knewe them, and said, She is more righteous then I: for she hath done it because I gaue her not to Shelah my sonne. So he lay with her no more.

27 Now, when the time was come that she should be deliuered, beholde, there were twinnes in her wombe.

28 And when she was in trauell, the one put out his hand: and the midwife tooke and bound a red threde about his hand, saying, This is come out first.

29 But when he plucked his hand backe againe, loe, his brother came out, and the midwife said, How hast thou broken the breach vpon thee? and his name was called Pharez.

30 And afterward came out his brother that had the red threde about his hande, and his name was called Zarah.

Genesis 39

1 Now Ioseph was brought downe into Egypt: and Potiphar an Eunuche of Pharaohs (and his chiefe stewarde an Egyptian) bought him at the hande of the Ishmeelites, which had brought him thither.

2 And the Lord was with Ioseph, and he was a man that prospered and was in the house of his master the Egyptian.

3 And his master sawe that the Lord was with him, and that the Lord made all that hee did to prosper in his hande.

4 So Ioseph founde fauour in his sight, and serued him: and he made him ruler of his house, and put all that he had in his hand.

5 And from that time that he had made him ruler ouer his house and ouer all that he had, the Lord blessed the Egyptians house for Iosephs sake: and the blessing of the Lord was vpon all that he had in the house, and in the fielde.

6 Therefore he left all that he had in Iosephs hand, and tooke accompt of nothing, that was with him, saue onely of the bread, which he did eate. And Ioseph was a faire person, and well fauoured.

7 Nowe therefore after these thinges, his masters wife cast her eyes vpon Ioseph, and saide, Lye with me.

8 But he refused and said to his masters wife, Beholde, my master knoweth not what he hath in the house with me, but hath committed all that he hath to mine hande.

9 There is no man greater in this house then I: neither hath he kept any thing from me, but only thee, because thou art his wife: how then can I do this great wickednes and so sinne against God?

10 And albeit she spake to Ioseph day by day, yet he hearkened not vnto her, to lye with her, or to be in her company.

11 Then on a certaine day Ioseph entred into the house, to doe his businesse: and there was no man of the houshold in the house:

12 Therefore she caught him by his garmet, saying, Sleepe with me: but he left his garment in her hand, and fled, and got him out.

13 Nowe when she sawe that he had left his garment in her hand, and was fled out,

14 She called vnto the men of her house, and tolde them, saying, Beholde, he hath brought in an Ebrewe vnto vs to mocke vs: who came in to me for to haue slept with me: but I cryed with a loude voyce.

15 And when he heard that I lift vp my voice and cryed, he left his garment with me, and fled away, and got him out.

16 So she layde vp his garment by her, vntill her lord came home.

17 Then she tolde him according to these words, saying, The Ebrew seruat, which thou hast brought vnto vs, came in to me, to mocke me.

18 But assoone as I lift vp my voyce and cried, he left his garment with me, and fled out.

19 Then when his master heard the wordes of his wife, which she tolde him, saying, After this maner did thy seruant to me, his anger was kindled.

20 And Iosephs master tooke him and put him in prison, in the place, where the kings prisoners lay bounde: and there he was in prison.

21 But the Lord was with Ioseph, and shewed him mercie, and got him fauour in the sight of the master of the prison.

22 And the keeper of the prison committed to Iosephs hande all the prisoners that were in the prison, and whatsoeuer they did there, that did he.

23 And the keeper of the prison looked vnto nothing that was vnder his hande, seeing that the Lord was with him: for whatsoeuer he did, the Lord made it to prosper.

Genesis 40

1 And after these things, the butler of the King of Egypt and his baker offended their lorde the King of Egypt.

2 And Pharaoh was angrie against his two officers, against the chiefe butler, and against the chiefe baker.

3 Therefore he put them in ward in his chiefe stewardes house, in the prison and place where Ioseph was bound.

4 And the chiefe steward gaue Ioseph charge ouer them, and he serued them: and they continued a season in warde.

5 And they both dreamed a dreame, eyther of them his dreame in one night, eche one according to the interpretation of his dreame, both the butler and the baker of the King of Egypt, which were bounde in the prison.

6 And when Ioseph came in vnto them in the morning, and looked vpon them, beholde, they were sad.

7 And he asked Pharaohs officers, that were with him in his masters warde, saying, Wherefore looke ye so sadly to day?

8 Who answered him, We haue dreamed, eche one a dreame, and there is none to interprete the same. Then Ioseph saide vnto them, Are not interpretations of God? tell them me nowe.

9 So the chiefe butler tolde his dreame to Ioseph, and said vnto him, In my dreame, behold, a vine was before me,

10 And in the vine were three branches, and as it budded, her flowre came foorth: and the clusters of grapes waxed ripe.

11 And I had Pharaohs cup in mine hande, and I tooke the grapes, and wrung the into Pharaohs cup, and I gaue the cup into Pharaohs hand.

12 Then Ioseph sayde vnto him, This is the interpretation of it: The three braunches are three dayes:

13 Within three dayes shall Pharaoh lift vp thine head, and restore thee vnto thine office, and thou shalt giue Pharaohs cup into his hand after the olde maner, when thou wast his butler.

14 But haue me in remembrance with thee, when thou art in good case, and shew mercie, I pray thee, vnto me, and

make mention of me to Pharaoh, that thou mayest bring me out of this house.

15 For I was stollen away by theft out of the land of the Ebrewes, and here also haue I done nothing, wherefore they should put mee in the dungeon.

16 And when the chiefe baker sawe that the interpretation was good, hee saide vnto Ioseph, Also mee thought in my dreame that I had three white baskets on mine head.

17 And in the vppermost basket there was of all maner baken meates for Pharaoh: and the birdes did eate them out of the basket vpon mine head.

18 Then Ioseph answered, and saide, This is the interpretation thereof: The three baskets are three dayes:

19 Within three dayes shall Pharaoh take thine head from thee, and shall hang thee on a tree, and the birdes shall eate thy flesh from off thee.

20 And so the third day, which was Pharaohs birthday, hee made a feast vnto all his seruants: and hee lifted vp the head of the chiefe butler, and the head of the chiefe baker among his seruants.

21 And he restored the chiefe butler vnto his butlershippe, who gaue the cup into Pharaohs hande,

22 But he hanged the chiefe baker, as Ioseph had interpreted vnto them.

23 Yet the chiefe butler did not remember Ioseph, but forgate him.

Genesis 41

1 And two yeeres after, Pharaoh also dreamed, and beholde, he stoode by a riuer,

2 And loe, there came out of the riuer seuen goodly kine and fatfleshed, and they fedde in a medowe:

3 And loe, seuen other kine came vp after the out of the riuer, euill fauoured and leane fleshed, and stoode by the other kine vpon the brinke of the riuer.

4 And the euilfauoured and leane fleshed kine did eate vp the seuen welfauoured and fatte kine: so Pharaoh awoke.

5 Againe he slept, and dreamed the second time: and beholde, seuen eares of corne grewe vpon one stalke, ranke and goodly.

6 And loe, seuen thinne eares, and blasted with the east winde, sprang vp after them:

7 And the thinne eares deuoured the seuen ranke and full eares. then Pharaoh awaked, and loe, it was a dreame.

8 Nowe when the morning came, his spirit was troubled: therefore he sent and called all the soothsayers of Egypt, and all the wise men thereof, and Pharaoh tolde them his dreames: but none coulde interprete them to Pharaoh.

9 Then spake the chiefe butler vnto Pharaoh, saying, I call to minde my faultes this day.

10 Pharaoh being angrie with his seruantes, put me in ward in the chiefe stewards house, both me and the chiefe baker.

11 Then we dreamed a dreame in one night, both I, and he: we dreamed eche man according to the interpretation of his dreame.

12 And there was with vs a yong man, an Ebrew, seruant vnto the chiefe steward, whome when we told, he declared our dreames to vs, to euery one he declared according to his dreame.

13 And as he declared vnto vs, so it came to passe: for he restored me to mine office, and hanged him.

14 Then sent Pharaoh, and called Ioseph, and they brought him hastily out of prison, and he shaued him, and chaunged his rayment, and came to Pharaoh.

15 Then Pharaoh sayde to Ioseph, I haue dreamed a dreame, and no man can interprete it, and I haue hearde say of thee, that when thou hearest a dreame, thou canst interprete it.

16 And Ioseph answered Pharaoh, saying, Without me God shall answere for the wealth of Pharaoh.

17 And Pharaoh sayde vnto Ioseph, In my dreame, beholde, I stoode by the banke of the riuer:

18 And lo, there came vp out of the riuer seuen fat fleshed, and welfauoured kine, and they fedde in the medowe.

19 Also loe, seuen other kine came vp after them, poore and very euilfauoured, and leanefleshed: I neuer sawe the like in all the lande of Egypt, for euilfauoured.

20 And the leane and euilfauoured kine did eate vp the first seuen fat kine.

21 And when they had eaten them vp, it could not be knowen that they had eaten them, but they were still as euilfauoured, as they were at the beginning: so did I awake.

22 Moreouer I sawe in my dreame, and beholde, seuen eares sprang out of one stalke, full and faire.

23 And lo, seuen eares, withered, thinne, and blasted with the East winde, sprang vp after them.

24 And the thinne eares deuoured the seuen good eares. Nowe I haue tolde the soothsayers, and none can declare it vnto me.

25 Then Ioseph answered Pharaoh, Both Pharaohs dreames are one. God hath shewed Pharaoh, what he is about to doe.

26 The seuen good kine are seuen yeres, and the seuen good eares are seuen yeeres: this is one dreame.

27 Likewise the seuen thinne and euilfauoured kine, that came out after them, are seuen yeeres: and the seuen emptie eares blasted with the East winde, are seuen yeeres of famine.

28 This is the thing which I haue saide vnto Pharaoh, that God hath shewed vnto Pharaoh, what he is about to doe.

29 Beholde, there come seuen yeeres of great plentie in all the land of Egypt.

30 Againe, there shall arise after them seuen yeeres of famine, so that all the plentie shall be forgotten in the land of Egypt, and the famine shall consume the land:

31 Neither shall the plentie bee knowen in the land, by reason of this famine that shall come after: for it shalbe exceeding great.

32 And therefore the dreame was doubled vnto Pharaoh the second time, because the thing is established by God, and God hasteth to performe it.

33 Nowe therefore let Pharaoh prouide for a man of vnderstanding and wisedome, and set him ouer the land of Egypt.

34 Let Pharaoh make and appoynt officers ouer the lande, and take vp the fift part of the land of Egypt in the seuen plenteous yeeres.

35 Also let them gather all the foode of these good yeeres that come, and lay vp corne vnder the hand of Pharaoh for foode, in the cities, and let them keepe it.

36 So the foode shall be for the prouision of the lande, against the seuen yeeres of famine, which shalbe in the lande of Egypt, that the land perish not by famine.

37 And the saying pleased Pharaoh and all his seruants.

38 Then saide Pharaoh vnto his seruants, Can we finde such a man as this, in whom is the Spirit of God?

39 The Pharaoh said to Ioseph, For as much as God hath shewed thee all this, there is no man of vnderstanding, or of wisedome like vnto thee.

40 Thou shalt be ouer mine house, and at thy word shall all my people be armed, onely in the kings throne will I be aboue thee.

41 Moreouer Pharaoh said to Ioseph, Behold, I haue set thee ouer all the land of Egypt.

42 And Pharaoh tooke off his ring from his hand, and put it vpon Iosephs hand, and arayed him in garments of fine linnen, and put a golden cheyne about his necke.

43 So he set him vpon the best charet that hee had, saue one: and they cryed before him, Abrech, and placed him ouer all the land of Egypt.

44 Againe Pharaoh saide vnto Ioseph, I am Pharaoh, and without thee shall no man lift vp his hand or his foote in all the land of Egypt.

45 And Pharaoh called Iosephs name Zaphnath-paaneah: and he gaue him to wife Asenath the daughter of Poti-pherah prince of On. then went Ioseph abrode in the land of Egypt.

46 And Ioseph was thirtie yeere old when he stood before Pharaoh king of Egypt: and Ioseph departing from the presence of Pharaoh, went throughout all the land of Egypt.

47 And in the seuen plenteous yeres the earth brought foorth store.

48 And hee gathered vp all the foode of the seuen plenteous yeeres, which were in the lande of Egypt, and layde vp foode in the cities: the foode of the fielde, that was round about euery citie, layde he vp in the same.

49 So Ioseph gathered wheate, like vnto the sand of the sea in multitude out of measure, vntill he left numbring: for it was without number.

50 Now vnto Ioseph were borne two sonnes (before the yeeres of famine came) which Asenath the daughter of Poti-pherah prince of On bare vnto him.

51 And Ioseph called the name of the first borne Manasseh: for God, said he, hath made me forget all my labour and al my fathers houshold.

52 Also hee called the name of the second, Ephraim: For God, sayde he hath made me fruitfull in the land of mine affliction.

53 So the seuen yeeres of the plentie that was in the land of Egypt were ended.

54 Then began the seuen yeeres of famine to come, according as Ioseph had saide: and the famine was in all landes, but in all the land of Egypt was bread.

55 At the length all the lande of Egypt was affamished, and the people cryed to Pharaoh for bread. And Pharaoh said vnto all the Egyptians, Goe to Ioseph: what he sayth to you, doe ye.

56 When the famine was vpon all the land, Ioseph opened all places, wherein the store was, and solde vnto the Egyptians: for the famine waxed sore in the land of Egypt.

57 And all countries came to Egypt to bye corne of Ioseph, because the famine was sore in all landes.

Genesis 42

1 Then Iaakob saw that there was foode in Egypt, and Iaakob said vnto his sonnes, Why gaze ye one vpon an other?

2 And he said, Behold, I haue heard that there is foode in Egypt, Get you downe thither, and bie vs foode thence, that we may liue and not die.

3 So went Iosephs ten brethren downe to bye corne of the Egyptians.

4 But Beniamin Iosephs brother woulde not Iaakob send with his brethren: for he saide, Least death should befall him.

5 And the sonnes of Israel came to bye foode among them that came: for there was famine in the land of Canaan.

6 Now Ioseph was gouerner of the land, who solde to all the people of the lande: then Iosephs brethren came, and bowed their face to the groud before him.

7 And when Ioseph sawe his brethren, hee knewe them, and made himselfe straunge toward them, and spake to them roughly, and saide vnto them, Whence come yee? Who answered, Out of the land of Canaan, to bye vitaile.

8 (Now Ioseph knewe his brethren, but they knew not him.

9 And Ioseph remembred the dreames, which he dreamed of them) and he sayde vnto them, Ye are spies, and are come to see the weaknesse of the land.

10 But they sayde vnto him, Nay, my lorde, but to bye vitayle thy seruants are come.

11 Wee are all one mans sonnes: wee meane truely, and thy seruants are no spies.

12 But he saide vnto them, Nay, but yee are come to see the weakenes of the land.

13 And they said, We thy seruants are twelue brethren, the sonnes of one man in the lande of Canaan: and beholde, the yongest is this day with our father, and one is not.

14 Againe Ioseph sayde vnto them, This is it that I spake vnto you, saying, Ye are spies.

15 Hereby ye shall be proued: by the life of Pharaoh, ye shall not goe hence, except your yongest brother come hither.

16 Send one of you which may fet your brother, and ye shall be kept in prison, that your words may be proued, whether there bee trueth in you: or els by the life of Pharaoh ye are but spies.

17 So he put them in warde three dayes.

18 Then Ioseph said vnto them the third day, This do, and liue: for I feare God.

19 If ye be true men, let one of your brethren be bounde in your prison house, and goe ye, carie foode for the famine of your houses:

20 But bring your yonger brother vnto me, that your wordes may be tried, and that ye dye not: and they did so.

21 And they said one to another, We haue verily sinned against our brother, in that we sawe the anguish of his soule, when he besought vs, and we would not heare him: therefore is this trouble come vpon vs.

22 And Reuben answered them, saying, Warned I not you, saying, Sinne not against the childe, and ye would not heare? and lo, his blood is now required.

23 (And they were not aware that Ioseph vnderstoode them: for he spake vnto them by an interpreter.)

24 Then he turned from them, and wept, and turned to them againe, and communed with them, and tooke Simeon from among them, and bounde him before their eyes.

25 So Ioseph commanded that they should fill their sackes with wheate, and put euery mans money againe in his sacke, and giue them vitaile for the iourney: and thus did he vnto them.

26 And they layed their vitaile vpon their asses, and departed thence.

27 And as one of them opened his sacke for to giue his asse prouender in the ynne, he espyed his money: for lo, it was in his sackes mouth.

28 Then he sayde vnto his brethren, My money is restored: for loe, it is euen in my sacke. And their heart fayled them, and they were astonished, and sayde one to another, What is this, that God hath done vnto vs?

29 And they came vnto Iaakob their father vnto the lande of Canaan, and tolde him all that had befallen them, saying,

30 The man, who is Lord of the lande, spake roughly to vs, and put vs in prison as spyes of the countery.

31 And we sayd vnto him, We are true men, and are no spies.

32 We be twelue brethren, sonnes of our father: one is not, and the yongest is this day with our father in the land of Canaan.

33 Then the Lord of the countrey sayde vnto vs, Hereby shall I knowe if ye be true men: Leaue one of your brethren with me, and take foode for the famine of your houses and depart,

34 And bring your yongest brother vnto me, that I may knowe that ye are no spies, but true men: so will I deliuer you your brother, and yee shall occupie in the land.

35 And as they emptied their sacks, behold, euery mans bundel of money was in his sacke: and when they and their father sawe the bundels of their money, they were afrayde.

36 Then Iaakob their father said to them, Ye haue robbed me of my children: Ioseph is not, and Simeon is not, and ye will take Beniamin: all these things are against me.

37 Then Reuben answered his father, saying, Slay my two sonnes, if I bring him not to thee againe: deliuer him to mine hand, and I will bring him to thee againe.

38 But he said, My sonne shall not go downe with you: for his brother is dead, and he is left alone: if death come vnto him by the way which ye goe, then ye shall bring my gray head with sorow vnto the graue.

Genesis 43

1 Now great famine was in the land.

2 And when they had eaten vp the vitaile, which they had brought from Egypt, their father sayd vnto them, Turne againe, and bye vs a little foode.

3 And Iudah answered him, saying, The man charged vs by an othe, saying, Neuer see my face, except your brother be with you.

4 If thou wilt sende our brother with vs, we will goe downe, and bye thee foode:

5 But if thou wilt not send him, we wil not goe downe: for the man said vnto vs, Looke me not in the face, except your brother be with you.

6 And Israel sayd, Wherefore delt ye so euill with me, as to tell the man, whether ye had yet a brother or no?

7 And they answered, The man asked straitly of our selues and of our kinred, saying, Is your father yet aliue? haue ye any brother? And wee tolde him according to these wordes: could we knowe certainely that he would say, Bring your brother downe?

8 Then sayde Iudah to Israel his father, Send the boy with mee, that we may rise and goe, and that we may liue and not dye, both we, and thou, and our children.

9 I wil be suertie for him: of mine hand shalt thou require him. If I bring him not to thee, and set him before thee, then let me beare the blame for euer.

10 For except we had made this tarying, doutlesse by this we had returned the second time.

11 Then their father Israel sayd vnto them, If it must needes be so now, do

thus: take of the best fruites of the lande in your vessels, and bring the man a present, a little rosen, and a little hony, spices and myrrhe, nuttes, and almondes:

12 And take double money in your hande, and the money, that was brought againe in your sackes mouthes: cary it againe in your hand, lest it were some oursight.

13 Take also your brother and arise, and go againe to the man.

14 And God almightie giue you mercie in the sight of the man, that hee may deliuer you your other brother, and Beniamin: but I shall be robbed of my childe, as I haue bene.

15 Thus the men tooke this present, and tooke twise so much money in their hande with Beniamin, and rose vp, and went downe to Egypt and stoode before Ioseph.

16 And whe Ioseph saw Beniamin with them, he sayde to his stewarde, Bring these men home and kill meate, and make ready: for the men shall eate with me at noone.

17 And the man did as Ioseph bad, and brought the men vnto Iosephs house.

18 Nowe when the men were brought into Iosephs house, they were afrayd, and sayd, Because of the money, that came in our sackes mouthes at the first time, are we brought, that hee may picke a quarrell against vs, and lay some thing to our charge, and bring vs in bondage and our asses.

19 Therefore came they to Iosephs stewarde, and communed with him at the doore of ye house.

20 And said, Oh syr, we came in deede down hither at the first time to bye foode,

21 And as wee came to an ynne and opened our sackes, behold, euery mans money was in his sackes mouth, euen our money in full weight, but we haue brought it againe in our handes.

22 Also other money haue we brought in our handes to bye foode, but we cannot tell, who put our money in our sackes.

23 And he said, Peace be vnto you, feare not: your God and the God of your father hath giuen you that treasure in your sackes, I had your money: and he brought forth Simeon to them.

24 So the man led them into Iosephs house, and gaue them water to wash their feete, and gaue their asses prouender.

25 And they made ready their present against Ioseph came at noone, (for they heard say, that they should eate bread there)

26 When Ioseph came home, they brought the present into the house to him, which was in their handes, and bowed downe to the grounde before him.

27 And he asked them of their prosperitie, and sayd, Is your father the olde man, of whome ye tolde me, in good health? is he yet aliue?

28 Who answered, Thy seruant our father is in good health, he is yet aliue:

and they bowed downe, and made obeysance.

29 And he lifting vp his eyes, beheld his brother Beniamin his mothers sonne, and sayde, Is this your yonger brother, of whome ye tolde me? And he said, God be merciful vnto thee, my sone.

30 And Ioseph made haste (for his affection was inflamed towarde his brother, and sought where to weepe) and entred into his chamber, and wept there.

31 Afterward he washed his face, and came out, and refrained himselfe, and sayd, Set on meate.

32 And they prepared for him by himselfe, and for them by themselues, and for the Egyptians, which did eate with him, by themselues, because the Egyptians might not eate bread with the Ebrewes: for that was an abomination vnto the Egyptians.

33 So they sate before him: the eldest according vnto his age, and the yongest according vnto his youth. and the men marueiled among themselues.

34 And they tooke meases from before him, and sent to them: but Beniamins mease was fiue times so much as any of theirs: and they drunke, and had of the best drinke with him.

Genesis 44

1 Afterward he commanded his steward, saying, Fill the mens sackes with foode, as much as they can carry, and put euery mans money in his sackes mouth.

2 And put my cup, I meane the siluer cup, in the sackes mouth of the yongest, and his corne money. And he did according to the commandement that Ioseph gaue him.

3 And in the morning the men were sent away, they, and their asses.

4 And when they went out of the citie not farre off, Ioseph sayd to his stewarde, Vp, follow after the men: and when thou doest ouertake them, say vnto them, Wherefore haue ye rewarded euill for good?

5 Is that not the cuppe, wherein my Lord drinketh? and in the which he doeth deuine and prophecie? ye haue done euill in so doing.

6 And when he ouertooke them, he sayde those wordes vnto them.

7 And they answered him, Wherefore sayeth my lorde such wordes? God forbid that thy seruants should do such a thing.

8 Behold, the money which we found in our sackes mouthes, wee brought againe to thee out of the land of Canaan: how then should we steale out of thy lordes house siluer or golde?

9 With whomesoeuer of thy seruants it bee found, let him dye, and we also will be my lordes bondmen.

10 And he said, Now then let it be according vnto your wordes: he with whome it is found, shall be my seruant, and ye shalbe blamelesse.

11 Then at once euery man tooke downe his sacke to the grounde, and euery one opened his sacke.

12 And he searched, and began at the eldest and left at the yongest: and the cuppe was found in Beniamins sacke.

13 Then they rent their clothes, and laded euery man his asse, and went againe into the citie.

14 So Iudah and his brethren came to Iosephs house (for he was yet there) and they fel before him on the ground.

15 Then Ioseph sayd vnto them, What acte is this, which ye haue done? know ye not that such a man as I, can deuine and prophecie?

16 Then sayd Iudah, What shall we say vnto my lord? what shall we speake? and howe can we iustifie our selues? God hath found out the wickednesse of thy seruants: beholde, we are seruants to my Lord, both wee, and he, with whome the cuppe is founde.

17 But he answered, God forbid, that I should doe so, but the man, with whome the cuppe is founde, he shalbe my seruant, and go ye in peace vnto your father.

18 Then Iudah drewe neere vnto him, and sayde, O my Lord, let thy seruant nowe speake a worde in my lordes eares, and let not thy wrath be kindled against thy seruant: for thou art euen as Pharaoh.

19 My Lord asked his seruants, saying, Haue ye a father, or a brother?

20 And we answered my Lord, We haue a father that is olde, and a young childe, which he begate in his age: and his brother is dead, and he alone is left of his mother, and his father loueth him.

21 Now thou saidest vnto thy seruants, Bring him vnto me, that I may set mine eye vpon him.

22 And we answered my lord, The childe can not depart from his father: for if he leaue his father, his father would die.

23 Then saydest thou vnto thy seruants, Except your yonger brother come downe with you, looke in my face no more.

24 So when we came vnto thy seruant our father, and shewed him what my lord had sayd,

25 And our father sayde vnto vs, Goe againe, bye vs a litle foode,

26 Then we answered, We can not go downe: but if our yongest brother go with vs, then will we go downe: for we may not see the mans face, except our yongest brother be with vs.

27 Then thy seruant my father sayde vnto vs, Ye knowe that my wife bare me two sonnes,

28 And the one went out from me, and I said, Of a suretie he is torne in pieces, and I sawe him not since.

29 Nowe yee take this also away from me: if death take him, then yee shall bring my graye head in sorowe to the graue.

30 Nowe therefore, when I come to thy seruant my father, and the childe be not with vs (seeing that his life dependeth on the childes life)

31 Then when hee shall see that the childe is not come, he will die: so shall thy seruants bring the graye head of thy

seruant our father with sorowe to the graue.

32 Doubtlesse thy seruant became suertie for the childe to my father, and said, If I bring him not vnto thee againe, then I will beare the blame vnto my father for euer.

33 Nowe therefore, I pray thee, let me thy seruant bide for the childe, as a seruant to my Lord, and let the childe go vp with his brethren.

34 For how can I go vp to my father, if the childe be not with me, vnlesse I woulde see the euil that shall come on my father?

Genesis 45

1 Then Ioseph could not refraine him selfe before all that stoode by him, but hee cryed, Haue forth euery man from me. And there taryed not one with him, while Ioseph vttered himselfe vnto his brethren.

2 And hee wept and cried, so that the Egyptians heard: the house of Pharaoh heard also.

3 Then Ioseph sayde to his brethren, I am Ioseph: doeth my father yet liue? But his brethren coulde not answere him, for they were astonished at his presence.

4 Againe, Ioseph sayde to his brethren, Come neere, I pray you, to mee. And they came neere. And he sayde, I am Ioseph your brother, whom ye sold into Egypt.

5 Nowe therefore be not sad, neither grieued with your selues, that ye sold me hither: for God did send me before you for your preseruation.

6 For nowe two yeeres of famine haue bene through ye land, and fiue yeeres are behind, wherein neither shalbe earing nor haruest.

7 Wherefore God sent me before you to preserue your posteritie in this land, and to saue you aliue by a great deliuerance.

8 Now the you sent not me hither, but God, who hath made mee a father vnto Pharaoh, and lorde of all his house, and ruler throughout all the land of Egypt.

9 Haste you and go vp to my father, and tel him, Thus saieth thy sonne Ioseph, God hath made me lord of all Egypt: come downe to me, tary not.

10 And thou shalt dwel in ye land of Goshen, and shalt be neere me, thou and thy children, and thy childrens children, and thy sheepe, and thy beastes, and all that thou hast.

11 Also I will nourish thee there (for yet remaine fiue yeeres of famine) lest thou perish through pouertie, thou and thy houshold, and all that thou hast.

12 And behold, your eyes doe see, and the eyes of my brother Beniamin, that my mouth speaketh to you.

13 Therefore tel my father of al mine honour in Egypt, and of all that ye haue seene, and make haste, and bring my father hither.

14 Then hee fell on his brother Beniamins necke, and wept, and Beniamin wept on his necke.

15 Moreouer, he kissed all his brethren, and wept vpon them: and afterwarde his brethren talked with him.

16 And the tidinges came vnto Pharaohs house, so that they said, Iosephs brethre are come: and it pleased Pharaoh well, and his seruants.

17 Then Pharaoh said vnto Ioseph, Say to thy brethren, This doe ye, lade your beastes and depart, go to the land of Canaan,

18 And take your father, and your houshoulds, and come to me, and I wil giue you the best of the land of Egypt, and ye shall eate of the fat of the land.

19 And I commaund thee, Thus doe ye, take you charets out of the lande of Egypt for your children, and for your wiues, and bring your father and come.

20 Also regarde not your stuffe: for the best of all the land of Egypt is yours.

21 And the children of Israel did so: and Ioseph gaue them charets according to the commandement of Pharaoh: hee gaue them vitaile also for the iourney.

22 He gaue them all, none except, change of raiment: but vnto Beniamin he gaue three hundreth pieces of siluer, and fiue sutes of raiment.

23 And vnto his father likewise hee sent ten hee asses laden with the best things of Egypt, and ten shee asses laden with wheate, and bread and meate for his father by the way.

24 So sent he his brethren away, and they departed: and he sayde vnto them, Fall not out by the way.

25 Then they went vp from Egypt, and came vnto the land of Canaan vnto Iaakob their father,

26 And tolde him, saying, Ioseph is yet aliue, and he also is gouernour ouer all the lande of Egypt, and Iaakobs heart failed: for he beleeued them not.

27 And they told him al the words of Ioseph, which he had said vnto the: but when he saw the charets, which Ioseph had sent to cary him, then the spirit of Iaakob their father reuiued.

28 And Israel said, I haue inough: Ioseph my sonne is yet aliue: I will go and see him yer I die.

Genesis 46

1 Then Israel tooke his iourney with all that he had, and came to Beer-sheba, and offered sacrifice vnto the God of his father Izhak.

2 And God spake vnto Israel in a vision by night, saying, Iaakob, Iaakob. Who answered, I am here.

3 Then hee sayde, I am God, the God of thy father, feare not to goe downe into Egypt: for I will there make of thee a great nation.

4 I wil go downe with thee into Egypt, and I will also bring thee vp againe, and Ioseph shall put his hand vpon thine eyes.

5 Then Iaakob rose vp from Beer-sheba: and the sonnes of Israel caried Iaakob their father, and their children, and their wiues in the charets, which Pharaoh had sent to cary him.

6 And they tooke their cattell and their goods, which they had gotten in the lande of Canaan, and came into Egypt, both Iaakob and all his seede with him,

7 His sonnes and his sonnes sonnes with him, his daughters and his sonnes daughters, and al his seede brought he with him into Egypt.

8 And these are the names of the children of Israel, which came into Egypt, euen Iaakob and his sonnes: Reuben, Iaakobs first borne.

9 And the sonnes of Reuben: Hanoch, and Phallu, and Hezron, and Carmi.

10 And the sonnes of Simeon: Iemuel, and Iamin, and Ohad, and Iachin, and Zohar; and Shaul the sonne of a Canaanitish woman.

11 Also the sonnes of Leui: Gershon, Kohath, and Merari.

12 Also the sonnes of Iudah: Er, and Onan, and Shelah, and Pharez, and Zerah: (but Er and Onan died in ye land of Canaan) And the sonnes of Pharez were Hezron and Hamul.

13 Also the sonnes of Issachar: Tola, and Phuuah, and Iob, and Shimron.

14 Also the sonnes of Zebulun: Sered, and Elon, and Iahleel.

15 These bee the sonnes of Leah, which shee bare vnto Iaakob in Padan Aram, with his daughter Dinah. All the soules of his sonnes and his daughters were thirtie and three.

16 Also the sonnes of Gad: Ziphion, and Haggi, Shuni, and Ezbon, Eri, and Arodi, and Areli.

17 Also the sonnes of Asher: Iimnah, and Ishuah, and Isui, and Beriah, and Serah their sister. And the sonnes of Beriah: Heber, and Malchiel.

18 These are the children of Zilpah, whome Laban gaue to Leah his daughter: and these shee bare vnto Iaakob, euen sixtene soules.

19 The sonnes of Rahel Iaakobs wife were Ioseph and Beniamin.

20 And vnto Ioseph in the lande of Egypt were borne Manasseh, and Ephraim, which Asenath the daughter of Poti-pherah prince of On bare vnto him.

21 Also the sonnes of Beniamin: Belah, and Becher, and Ashbel, Gera, and Naaman, Ehi, and Rosh, Muppim, and Huppim, and Ard.

22 These are the sonnes of Rahel, which were borne vnto Iaakob, fourteene soules in all.

23 Also the sonnes of Dan: Hushim.

24 Also the sonnes of Naphtali: Iahzeel, and Guni, and Iezer, and Shillem.

25 These are the sonnes of Bilhah, which Laban gaue vnto Rahel his daughter, and shee bare these to Iaakob, in all, seuen soules.

26 Al the soules, that came with Iaakob into Egypt, which came out of his loynes (beside Iaakobs sonnes wiues) were in the whole, three score and sixe soules.

27 Also the sonnes of Ioseph, which were borne him in Egypt, were two soules: so that al the soules of the house of Iaakob, which came into Egypt, are seuentie.

28 The he sent Iudah before him vnto Ioseph, to direct his way vnto Goshen, and they came into the land of Goshen.

29 Then Ioseph made ready his charet and went vp to Goshen to meete Israel his father, and presented himselfe vnto him and fel on his necke, and wept vpon his necke a good while.

30 And Israel sayde vnto Ioseph, Now let me die, since I haue seene thy face, and that thou art yet aliue.

31 Then Ioseph said to his brethren, and to his fathers house, I wil go vp and shew Pharaoh, and tell him, My brethren and my fathers house, which were in the land of Canaan, are come vnto me,

32 And the men are shepheardes, and because they are shepheardes, they haue brought their sheepe and their cattell, and all that they haue.

33 And if Pharaoh call you, and aske you, What is your trade?

34 Then ye shall say, Thy seruants are men occupied about cattell, from our childehood euen vnto this time, both we and our fathers: that yee may dwell in the lande of Goshen: for euery sheepe keeper is an abomination vnto the Egyptians.

Genesis 47

1 Then came Ioseph and tolde Pharaoh, and sayde, My father, and my brethren, and their sheepe, and their cattell, and all that they haue, are come out of the land of Canaan, and behold, they are in the land of Goshen.

2 And Ioseph tooke part of his brethren, euen fiue men, and presented them vnto Pharaoh.

3 Then Pharaoh said vnto his brethren, What is your trade? And they answered Pharaoh, Thy seruants are shepheards, both we and our fathers.

4 They sayde moreouer vnto Pharaoh, For to soiourne in ye lande are we come: for thy seruants haue no pasture for their sheepe, so sore is ye famine in the lande of Canaan. Nowe therefore, we pray thee, let thy seruants dwel in the land of Goshen.

5 Then spake Pharaoh to Ioseph, saying, Thy father and thy brethren are come vnto thee.

6 The lande of Egypt is before thee: in the best place of the land make thy father and thy brethren dwel: let the dwel in the land of Goshen: and if thou knowest that there be men of actiuitie among them, make them rulers ouer my cattell.

7 Ioseph also brought Iaakob his father, and set him before Pharaoh. And Iaakob saluted Pharaoh.

8 Then Pharaoh sayde vnto Iaakob, Howe olde art thou?

9 And Iaakob sayd vnto Pharaoh, The whole time of my pilgrimage is an hundreth and thirty yeeres: fewe and euill haue the dayes of my life bene, and I haue not attayned vnto the yeeres of the life of my fathers, in the dayes of their pilgrimages.

10 And Iaakob tooke leaue of Pharaoh, and departed from the presence of Pharaoh.

11 And Ioseph placed his father, and his brethren, and gaue them possession in the lande of Egypt, in the best of the land, euen in the lande of Rameses, as Pharaoh had commanded.

12 And Ioseph nourished his father, and his brethren, and all his fathers houshold with bread, euen to the yong children.

13 Now there was no bread in all the land: for the famine was exceeding sore: so that the land of Egypt, and the land of Canaan were famished by reason of the famine.

14 And Ioseph gathered all the money, that was found in the land of Egypt, and in the land of Canaan, for the corne which they bought, and Ioseph layd vp the money in Pharaohs house.

15 So when money fayled in the lande of Egypt, and in the lande of Canaan, then all the Egyptians came vnto Ioseph, and sayde, Giue vs bread: for why should we dye before thee? for our money is spent.

16 Then saide Ioseph, Bring your cattell, and I will giue you for your cattell, if your money be spent.

17 So they brought their cattell vnto Ioseph, and Ioseph gaue them bread for the horses, and for the flockes of sheepe, and for the heards of cattel, and for the asses: so he fed them with bread for all their cattell that yeere.

18 But when the yeere was ended, they came vnto him the next yeere, and sayd vnto him, We will not hide from my lord, that since our money is spent, and my lord hath the heards of the cattel, there is nothing left in the sight of my lorde, but our bodies and our ground.

19 Why shall we perish in thy sight, both we, and our land? bye vs and our land for bread, and we and our land will be bonde to Pharaoh: therefore giue vs seede, that we may liue and not dye, and that the land go not to waste.

20 So Ioseph bought all the lande of Egypt for Pharaoh: for the Egyptians solde euery man his ground because the famine was sore vpon the: so the land became Pharaohs.

21 And he remoued the people vnto the cities, from one side of Egypt euen to the other.

22 Onely the lande of the Priestes bought he not: for the Priestes had an ordinarie of Pharaoh, and they did eate their ordinarie, which Pharaoh gaue them: wherefore they solde not their grounde.

23 Then Ioseph sayd vnto the people, Behold, I haue bought you this daye, and your lande for Pharaoh: lo, here is seede for you: sowe therefore the grounde.

24 And of the encrease ye shall giue the fifth part vnto Pharaoh, and foure partes shalbe yours for the seede of the fielde, and for your meate, and for them of your housholdes, and for your children to eate.

25 Then they answered, Thou hast saued our liues: let vs finde grace in the sight of my Lord, and we will be Pharaohs seruants.

26 Then Ioseph made it a lawe ouer the land of Egypt vnto this day, that Pharaoh should haue the fift part, except the land of the priests only, which was not Pharaohs.

27 And Israel dwelt in the lande of Egypt, in the countrey of Goshen: and they had their possessions therein, and grewe and multiplied exceedingly.

28 Moreouer, Iaakob liued in the lande of Egypt seuenteene yeeres, so that the whole age of Iaakob was an hundreth fourtie and seuen yeere.

29 Now when the time drewe neere that Israel must dye, he called his sonne Ioseph, and sayde vnto him, If I haue nowe founde grace in thy sight, put thine hand nowe vnder my thigh, and deale mercifully and truely with me: burie me not, I pray thee, in Egypt.

30 But when I shall sleepe with my fathers, thou shalt carry me out of Egypt, and bury mee in their buryall. And he answered, I will doe as thou hast sayde.

31 The he said, Sweare vnto me. And he sware vnto him. And Israel worshipped towardes the beds head.

Genesis 48

1 Againe after this, one sayd to Ioseph, Loe, thy father is sicke: then hee tooke with him his two sonnes, Manasseh and Ephraim.

2 Also one told Iaakob, and said, Behold, thy sonne Ioseph is come to thee, and Israel tooke his strength vnto him and sate vpon the bed.

3 Then Iaakob sayde vnto Ioseph, God almightie appeared vnto me at Luz in the land of Canaan, and blessed me.

4 And he sayde vnto me, Behold, I wil make thee fruitefull, and will multiplie thee, and will make a great number of people of thee, and will giue this lande vnto thy seede after thee for an euerlasting possession.

5 And now thy two sonnes, Manasseh and Ephraim, which are borne vnto thee in the lande of Egypt, before I came to thee into Egypt, shall be mine, as Reuben and Simeon are mine.

6 But the linage, which thou hast begotten after them, shalbe thine: they shall be called after the names of their brethren in their inheritance.

7 Nowe when I came from Padan, Rahel died vpon mine hande in the lande of Canaan, by the way when there was but halfe a dayes iourney of grounde to come to Ephrath: and I buryed her there in the way to Ephrath: the same is Beth-lehem.

8 Then Israel beheld Iosephs sonnes and sayd, Whose are these?

9 And Ioseph sayd vnto his father, They are my sonnes, which God hath giuen mee here. Then he sayd, I pray thee, bring them to me, that I may blesse them:

10 (For the eyes of Israel were dimme for age, so that hee coulde not well see) Then

he caused them to come to him, and he kissed them and embraced them.

11 And Israel sayde vnto Ioseph, I had not thought to haue seene thy face: yet lo, God hath shewed me also thy seede.

12 And Ioseph tooke them away from his knees, and did reuerence downe to the ground.

13 Then tooke Ioseph them both, Ephraim in his right hand towarde Israels left hand, and Manasseh in his left hand toward Israels right hand, so he brought them vnto him.

14 But Israel stretched out his right hand, and layde it on Ephraims head, which was the yonger, and his left hande vpon Manassehs head (directing his handes of purpose) for Manasseh was the elder.

15 Also he blessed Ioseph and sayde, The God, before whom my fathers Abraham and Izhak did walke, the God, which hath fed me al my life long vnto this day, blesse thee.

16 The Angel, which hath deliuered me from all euill, blesse the children, and let my name be named vpon them, and the name of my fathers Abraham and Izhak, that they may growe as fish into a multitude in the middes of the earth.

17 But when Ioseph sawe that his father layde his right hande vpon the head of Ephraim, it displeased him: and he stayed his fathers hand to remooue it from Ephraims head to Manassehs head.

18 And Ioseph sayde vnto his father, Not so, my father, for this is the eldest: put thy right hand vpon his head.

19 But his father refused, and sayd, I know well, my sonne, I know well: he shalbe also a people, and he shalbe great likewise: but his yonger brother shalbe greater then he, and his seede shall be full of nations.

20 So he blessed them that day, and sayde, In thee Israel shall blesse, and say, God make thee as Ephraim and as Manasseh. and he set Ephraim before Manasseh.

21 Then Israel said vnto Ioseph, Behold, I die, and God shall be with you, and bring you againe vnto the land of your fathers.

22 Moreouer, I haue giuen vnto thee one portion aboue thy brethren, which I gate out of the hand of the Amorite by my sworde and by my bowe.

Genesis 49

1 Then Iaakob called his sonnes, and sayde, Gather your selues together, that I may tell you what shall come to you in the last dayes.

2 Gather your selues together, and heare, ye sonnes of Iaakob, and hearken vnto Israel your father.

3 Reuben mine eldest sonne, thou art my might, and the beginning of my strength, the excellencie of dignitie, and the excellencie of power:

4 Thou wast light as water: thou shalt not be excellent, because thou wentest vp to thy fathers bed: then diddest thou defile my bed, thy dignitie is gone.

5 Simeon and Leui, brethren in euill, the instruments of crueltie are in their habitations.

6 Into their secret let not my soule come: my glory, be not thou ioyned with their assembly: for in their wrath they slew a man, and in their selfe will they digged downe a wall.

7 Cursed be their wrath, for it was fierce, and their rage, for it was cruell: I will deuide them in Iaakob, and scatter them in Israel.

8 Thou Iudah, thy brethre shall praise thee: thine hande shalbe in the necke of thine enemies: thy fathers sonnes shall bowe downe vnto thee.

9 Iudah, as a Lions whelpe shalt thou come vp from the spoyle, my sonne. He shall lye downe and couche as a Lion, and as a Lionesse: Who shall stirre him vp?

10 The scepter shall not depart from Iudah, nor a Lawegiuer from betweene his feete, vntill Shiloh come, and the people shall be gathered vnto him.

11 He shall binde his Asse foale vnto ye vine, and his Asses colte vnto the best vine. hee shall wash his garment in wine, and his cloke in the blood of grapes.

12 His eyes shalbe red with wine, and his teeth white with milke.

13 Zebulun shall dwell by the sea side, and he shalbe an hauen for shippes: and his border shalbe vnto Zidon.

14 Issachar shalbe a strong asse, couching downe betweene two burdens:

15 And he shall see that rest is good, and that the land is pleasant, and he shall bow his shoulder to beare, and shalbe subiect vnto tribute.

16 Dan shall iudge his people as one of the tribes of Israel.

17 Dan shall be a serpent by the way, an adder by the path, byting the horse heeles, so that his rider shall fall backward.

18 O Lord, I haue waited for thy saluation.

19 Gad, an hoste of men shall ouercome him, but he shall ouercome at the last.

20 Concerning Asher, his bread shalbe fat, and he shall giue pleasures for a king.

21 Naphtali shalbe a hinde let goe, giuing goodly wordes.

22 Ioseph shalbe a fruitefull bough, euen a fruitful bough by the well side: the small boughs shall runne vpon the wall.

23 And the archers grieued him, and shotte against him and hated him.

24 But his bowe abode strong, and the hands of his armes were strengthened, by the handes of the mighty God of Iaakob, of whom was the feeder appointed, by the stone of Israel,

25 Euen by the God of thy father, who shall helpe thee, and by the almightie, who shall blesse thee with heauenly blessinges from aboue, with blessings of the deepe, that lyeth beneath, with blessings of the brestes, and of the wombe.

26 The blessings of thy father shalbe stronger then the blessings of mine elders: vnto the ende of the hilles of the worlde they shall be on the head of Ioseph, and on the top of the head of him that was separate from his brethren.

27 Beniamin shall rauine as a wolfe: in the morning he shall deuoure the pray, and at night he shall deuide the spoyle.

28 All these are the twelue tribes of Israel, and thus their father spake vnto them, and blessed them: euery one of them blessed hee with a seuerall blessing.

29 And he charged them and sayd vnto them, I am ready to be gathered vnto my people: burie mee with my fathers in the caue, that is in the fielde of Ephron the Hittite,

30 In the caue that is in the field of Machpelah besides Mamre in the land of Canaan: which caue Abraham bought with the fielde of Ephron the Hittite for a possession to burie in.

31 There they buried Abraham and Sarah his wife: there they buryed Izhak and Rebekah his wife: and there I buried Leah.

32 The purchase of the fielde and the caue that is therein, was bought of the children of Heth.

33 Thus Iaakob made an end of giuing charge to his sonnes, and plucked vp his feete into the bed and gaue vp the ghost, and was gathered to his people.

Genesis 50

1 Then Ioseph fell vpon his fathers face and wept vpon him, and kissed him.

2 And Ioseph commanded his seruantes the physicions, to enbaume his father, and the physicions enbaumed Israel.

3 So fourtie dayes were accomplished (for so long did the dayes of them that were enbaumed last) and the Egyptians bewayled him seuentie dayes.

4 And when the dayes of his mourning were past, Ioseph spake to the house of Pharaoh, saying, If I haue nowe found fauour in your eyes, speake, I pray you, in the eares of Pharaoh, and say,

5 My father made me sweare, saying, Loe, I die, bury me in my graue, which I haue made me in the land of Canaan: now therefore let me go, I pray thee, and bury my father, and I wil come againe.

6 Then Pharaoh said, Goe vp and bury thy father, as he made thee to sweare.

7 So Ioseph went vp to bury his father, and with him went all the seruants of Pharaoh, both the elders of his house, and all the elders of the land of Egypt.

8 Likewise all the house of Ioseph, and his brethren, and his fathers house: onely their children, and their sheepe, and their cattell left they in the land of Goshen.

9 And there went vp with him both charets and horsemen: and they were an exceeding great company.

10 And they came to Goren Atad, which is beyond Iorden, and there they made a great and exceeding sore lamentation:

and he mourned for his father seuen dayes.

11 And when the Canaanites the inhabitants of the lande sawe the mourning in Goren Atad, they sayde, This is a great mourning vnto the Egyptians: wherefore the name thereof was called Abel Mizraim, which is beyond Iorden.

12 So his sonnes did vnto him, according as he had commanded them:

13 For his sonnes caried him into the lande of Canaan, and buried him in the caue of the fielde of Machpelah, which caue Abraham bought with the fielde, to be a place to bury in, of Ephron the Hittite besides Mamre.

14 Then Ioseph returned into Egypt, he and his brethren, and al that went vp with him to bury his father, after that he had buried his father.

15 And when Iosephs brethren saw that their father was dead, they sayde, It may be that Ioseph will hate vs, and will pay vs againe all the euill, which we did vnto him.

16 Therefore they sent vnto Ioseph, saying, Thy father commanded before his death, saying,

17 Thus shall ye say vnto Ioseph, Forgiue now, I pray thee, the trespasse of thy brethren, and their sinne: for they rewarded thee euil. And nowe, we pray thee, forgiue the trespasse of the seruants of thy fathers God. And Ioseph wept, when they spake vnto him.

18 Also his brethren came vnto him, and fell downe before his face, and sayde, Beholde, we be thy seruants.

19 To whome Ioseph sayde, Feare not: for am not I vnder God?

20 When ye thought euill against mee, God disposed it to good, that he might bring to passe, as it is this day, and saue much people aliue.

21 Feare not nowe therefore, I will nourish you, and your children: and hee comforted them, and spake kindly vnto them.

22 So Ioseph dwelt in Egypt, he, and his fathers house: and Ioseph liued an hundreth and tenne yeere.

23 And Ioseph saw Ephraims children, euen vnto the third generation: also the sonnes of Machir the sonne of Manasseh were brought vp on Iosephs knees.

24 And Ioseph sayd vnto his brethren, I am ready to dye, and God will surely visite you, and bring you out of this land, vnto ye land which hee sware vnto Abraham, vnto Izhak, and vnto Iaakob.

25 And Ioseph tooke an othe of the children of Israel, saying, God will surely visite you, and ye shall cary my bones hence.

26 So Ioseph died, when he was an hundreth and ten yere olde: and they enbaumed him and put him in a chest in Egypt.

Exodus

Exodus 1

1 Now these are the names of the children of Israel, which came into Egypt (euery man and his housholde came thither with Iaakob)

2 Reuben, Simeon, Leui, and Iudah,

3 Issachar, Zebulun, and Beniamin,

4 Dan, and Naphtali, Gad, and Asher.

5 So al the soules, that came out of the loines of Iaakob, were seuentie soules: Ioseph was in Egypt already.

6 Nowe Ioseph died and all his brethren, and that whole generation.

7 And the children of Israel brought foorth fruite and encreased in aboundance, and were multiplied, and were exceeding mightie, so that the land was full of them.

8 Then there rose vp a newe King in Egypt, who knewe not Ioseph.

9 And he sayde vnto his people, Beholde, the people of the children of Israel are greater and mightier then we.

10 Come, let vs worke wisely with them, least they multiplie, and it come to passe, that if there be warre, they ioyne them selues also vnto our enemies, and fight against vs, and get them out of the land.

11 Therefore did they set taskemasters ouer them, to keepe the vnder with burdens: and they built the cities Pithom and Raamses for the treasures of Pharaoh.

12 But the more they vexed them, the more they multiplied and grewe: therefore they were more grieued against the children of Israel.

13 Wherefore the Egyptians by crueltie caused the children of Israel to serue.

14 Thus they made them weary of their liues by sore labour in clay and in bricke, and in al worke in the fielde, with all maner of bondage, which they layde vpon them most cruelly.

15 Moreouer the King of Egypt commanded ye midwiues of the Ebrewe women, (of which the ones name was Shiphrah, and the name of the other Puah)

16 And sayde, When ye doe the office of a midwife to the women of the Ebrewes, and see them on their stooles, if it be a sonne, then yee shall kill him: but if it be a daughter, then let her liue.

17 Notwithstanding ye midwiues feared God, and did not as the King of Egypt commanded them, but preserued aliue the men children.

18 Then the King of Egypt called for the midwiues, and sayde vnto them, Why haue yee done thus, and haue preserued aliue the men children?

19 And the midwiues answered Pharaoh, Because the Ebrewe women are not as the women of Egypt: for they are liuely, and are deliuered yer the midwife come at them.

20 God therefore prospered the midwiues, and the people multiplied and were very mightie.

21 And because ye midwiues feared God, therefore he made them houses.

22 Then Pharaoh charged all his people, saying, Euery man childe that is borne, cast yee into the riuer, but reserue euery maide childe aliue.

Exodus 2

1 Then there went a man of the house of Leui, and tooke to wife a daughter of Leui,

2 And the woman coceiued and bare a sonne: and when she saw that he was faire, she hid him three moneths.

3 But when she could no longer hide him, she tooke for him an arke made of reede, and daubed it with slime and with pitch, and laide the childe therein, and put it among the bulrushes by the riuers brinke.

4 Now his sister stood a farre off, to wit what would come of him.

5 Then ye daughter of Pharaoh came downe to wash her in the riuer, and her maidens walked by the riuers side: and when shee sawe the arke among the bulrushes, she sent her maide to fet it.

6 Then she opened it, and sawe it was a childe: and beholde, the babe wept: so she had compassion on it, and sayde, This is one of the Ebrewes children.

7 Then said his sister vnto Pharaohs daughter, Shall I go and cal vnto thee a nurce of the Ebrew women to nurce thee the childe?

8 And Pharaohs daughter sayde to her, Goe. So the maide went and called the childes mother,

9 To whome Pharaohs daughter sayde, Take this childe away, and nurce it for me, and I wil reward thee. Then the woman tooke the childe and nurced him.

10 Nowe the childe grewe, and she brought him vnto Pharaohs daughter, and he was as her sonne, and she called his name Moses, because, said she, I drewe him out of the water.

11 And in those dayes, when Moses was growen, he went forth vnto his brethren, and looked on their burdens: also he sawe an Egyptian smiting an Ebrewe one of his brethren.

12 And he looked rounde about, and when he sawe no man, hee slewe the Egyptian, and hid him in the sande.

13 Againe he came forth the second day, and behold, two Ebrewes stroue: and he said vnto him that did the wrong, Wherefore smitest thou thy fellowe?

14 And hee answered, Who made thee a man of authoritie, and a iudge ouer vs? Thinkest thou to kill mee, as thou killedst the Egyptian? Then Moses feared and sayde, Certainly this thing is knowen.

15 Now Pharaoh heard this matter, and sought to slay Moses: therefore Moses fled from Pharaoh, and dwelt in the lande of Midian, and hee sate downe by a well.

16 And the Priest of Midian had seue daughters, which came and drewe water, and filled the troghes, for to water their fathers sheepe.

17 Then the shepherds came and droue them away: but Moses rose vp and defended them, and watered their sheepe.

18 And whe they came to Reuel their father, he said, Howe are ye come so soone to day?

19 And they saide, A man of Egypt deliuered vs from the hand of the shepherdes, and also drew vs water ynough, and watered the sheepe.

20 Then he saide vnto his daughters, And where is he? why haue ye so left the man? call him that he may eate bread.

21 And Moses agreed to dwell with the man: who gaue vnto Moses Zipporah his daughter:

22 And she bare a sonne, whose name he called Gershom: for he said, I haue bene a stranger in a strange lande.

23 Then in processe of time, the King of Egypt dyed, and the children of Israel sighed for the bondage and cryed: and their crie for the bondage came vp vnto God.

24 Then God heard their mone, and God remembred his couenant with Abraham, Izhak, and Iaakob.

25 So God looked vpon the children of Israel, and God had respect vnto them.

Exodus 3

1 When Moses kept the sheepe of Iethro his father in lawe, Priest of Midian, and droue the flocke to the backe side of the desert, and came to the Mountaine of God, Horeb,

2 Then the Angel of the Lord appeared vnto him in a flame of fire, out of the middes of a bush: and he looked, and behold, the bush burned with fire, and the bush was not consumed.

3 Therefore Moses saide, I will turne aside nowe, and see this great sight, why the bush burneth not.

4 And when the Lord sawe that he turned aside to see, God called vnto him out of the middes of the bush, and said, Moses, Moses. And he answered, I am here.

5 Then he saide, Come not hither, put thy shooes off thy feete: for the place whereon thou standest is holy ground.

6 Moreouer he saide, I am the God of thy father, the God of Abraham, the God of Izhak, and the God of Iaakob. Then Moses hid his face: for he was afraid to looke vpon God.

7 Then the Lord said, I haue surely seene the trouble of my people, which are in Egypt, and haue heard their crie, because of their taskemasters: for I knowe their sorowes.

8 Therefore I am come downe to deliuer them out of the hande of the Egyptians, and to bring them out of that lande into a good lande and a large, into a lande that floweth with milke and honie, euen into the place of the Canaanites, and the Hittites, and the Amorites, and the Perizzites, and the Hiuites, and the Iebusites.

9 And now lo, the crie of the children of Israel is come vnto me, and I haue also seene ye oppression, wherewith the Egyptians oppresse them.

10 Come now therefore, and I will send thee vnto Pharaoh, that thou maiest bring my people the children of Israel out of Egypt.

11 But Moses said vnto God, Who am I, that I should go vnto Pharaoh, and that I should bring the children of Israel out of Egypt?

12 And he answered, Certainely I will be with thee: and this shall be a token vnto thee, that I haue sent thee, After that thou hast brought the people out of Egypt, ye shall serue God vpon this Mountaine.

13 Then Moses said vnto God, Behold, when I shall come vnto the children of Israel, and shall say vnto them, The God of your fathers hath sent me vnto you: if they say vnto me, What is his Name? what shall I say vnto them?

14 And God answered Moses, I Am That I Am. Also he said, Thus shalt thou say vnto the children of Israel, I Am hath sent me vnto you.

15 And God spake further vnto Moses, Thus shalt thou say vnto the children of Israel, The Lord God of your fathers, the God of Abraham, the God of Izhak, and the God of Iaakob hath sent me vnto you: this is my Name for euer, and this is my memoriall vnto all ages.

16 Go and gather the Elders of Israel together, and thou shalt say vnto the, The Lord God of your fathers, the God of Abraham, Izhak, and Iaakob appeared vnto me, and said, I haue surely remembred you, and that which is done to you in Egypt.

17 Therefore I did say, I wil bring you out of the affliction of Egypt vnto the land of the Canaanites, and the Hittites, and the Amorites, and the Perizzites, and the Hiuites, and the Iebusites, vnto a lande that floweth with milke and honie.

18 Then shall they obey thy voyce, and thou and the Elders of Israel shall go vnto the King of Egypt, and say vnto him, The Lord God of the Ebrewes hath met with vs: we pray thee nowe therefore, let vs goe three dayes iourney in the wildernesse, that we may sacrifice vnto the Lord our God.

19 But I know, that the King of Egypt wil not let you goe, but by strong hande.

20 Therefore will I stretch out mine hande and smite Egypt with all my wonders, which I will doe in the middes thereof: and after that shall he let you goe.

21 And I will make this people to be fauoured of the Egyptians: so that when ye go, ye shall not goe emptie.

22 For euery woman shall aske of her neighbour, and of her that soiourneth in her house, iewels of siluer and iewels of gold and raiment, and ye shall put them on your sonnes, and on your daughters, and shall spoyle the Egyptians.

Exodus 4

1 Then Moses answered, and said, But lo, they will not beleeue me, nor hearken vnto my voyce: for they will say, The Lord hath not appeared vnto thee.

2 And the Lord said vnto him, What is that in thine hande? And he answered, A rod.

3 Then said he, Cast it on the ground. So he cast it on the grounde, and it was turned into a serpent: and Moses fled from it.

4 Againe the Lord saide vnto Moses, Put foorth thine hand, and take it by the tayle. Then he put foorth his hande and caught it, and it was turned into a rod in his hand.

5 Do this that they may beleeue, that the Lord God of their fathers, the God of Abraham, the God of Izhak, and the God of Iaakob hath appeared vnto thee.

6 And the Lord saide furthermore vnto him, Thrust nowe thine hand into thy bosome. And he thrust his hand into his bosome, and when he tooke it out againe, behold, his hand was leprous as snowe.

7 Moreouer he said, Put thine hand into thy bosome againe. So he put his hande into his bosome againe, and pluckt it out of his bosome, and behold, it was turned againe as his other flesh.

8 So shall it be, if they wil not beleeue thee, neither obey the voyce of ye first signe, yet shall they beleeue for the voyce of the seconde signe.

9 But if they will not yet beleeue these two signes, neither obey vnto thy voyce, then shalt thou take of the water of the riuer, and powre it vpon the drie lande: so the water which thou shalt take out of the riuer, shalbe turned to blood vpon the drie land.

10 But Moses said vnto the Lord, Oh my Lord, I am not eloquent, neither at any time haue bene, nor yet since thou hast spoken vnto thy seruant: but I am slowe of speach and slowe of tongue.

11 Then the Lord said vnto him, Who hath giuen the mouth to man? or who hath made the domme, or the deafe, or him that seeth, or the blinde? haue not I the Lord?

12 Therefore goe nowe, and I will be with thy mouth, and will teach thee what thou shalt say.

13 But he saide, Oh my Lord, sende, I pray thee, by the hande of him, whome thou shouldest sende.

14 Then the Lord was verie angrie with Moses, and said, Doe not I know Aaron thy brother the Leuite, that he himselfe shall speake? for loe, he commeth also foorth to meete thee, and when he seeth thee, he will be glad in his heart.

15 Therefore thou shalt speake vnto him, and put the wordes in his mouth, and I will be with thy mouth, and with his mouth, and will teach you what ye ought to doe.

16 And he shall be thy spokesman vnto the people: and he shall be, euen he shall be as thy mouth, and thou shalt be to him as God.

17 Moreouer thou shalt take this rod in thine hand, wherewith thou shalt do miracles.

18 Therefore Moses went and returned to Iethro his father in lawe, and said vnto him, I pray thee, let me goe, and returne to my brethren, which are in Egypt, and see whether they be yet aliue. Then Iethro said to Moses, Go in peace.

19 (For the Lord had said vnto Moses in Midian, Goe, returne to Egypt: for they are all dead which went about to kill thee)

20 Then Moses tooke his wife, and his sonnes, and put them on an asse, and returned towarde the lande of Egypt, and Moses tooke the rod of God in his hand.

21 And the Lord saide vnto Moses, When thou art entred and come into Egypt againe, see that thou doe all the wonders before Pharaoh, which I haue put in thine hand: but I will harden his heart, and he shall not let the people goe.

22 Then thou shalt say to Pharaoh, Thus saith the Lord, Israel is my sonne, euen my first borne.

23 Wherefore I say to thee, Let my sonne go, that he may serue me: if thou refuse to let him goe, beholde, I will slay thy sonne, euen thy first borne.

24 And as he was by the waye in the ynne, the Lord met him, and would haue killed him.

25 Then Zipporah tooke a sharpe knife, and cut away the foreskinne of her sonne, and cast it at his feete, and said, Thou art indeede a bloody husband vnto me.

26 So he departed from him. Then she saide, O bloodie husband (because of the circumcision)

27 Then the Lord saide vnto Aaron, Goe meete Moses in the wildernesse. And he went and mette him in the Mount of God, and kissed him.

28 Then Moses tolde Aaron all the wordes of the Lord, who had sent him, and all the signes wherewith he had charged him.

29 So went Moses and Aaron, and gathered all the Elders of the children of Israel.

30 And Aaron told all the wordes, which the Lord had spoken vnto Moses, and he did the miracles in the sight of the people,

31 And the people beleeued, and when they heard that the Lord had visited the children of Israel, and had looked vpon their tribulation, they bowed downe, and worshipped.

Exodus 5

1 Then afterwarde Moses and Aaron went and said to Pharaoh, Thus saith the Lord God of Israel, Let my people go, that they may celebrate a feast vnto me in the wildernesse.

2 And Pharaoh saide, Who is the Lord, that I should heare his voyce, and let Israel go? I knowe not the Lord, neither will I let Israel goe.

3 And they saide, We worship the God of the Ebrewes: we pray thee, let vs goe three daies iourney in the desert, and sacrifice vnto the Lord our God, least he bring vpon vs the pestilence or sword.

4 Then saide the King of Egypt vnto them, Moses and Aaron, why cause ye the people to cease from their workes? get you to your burdens.

5 Pharaoh saide furthermore, Behold, much people is nowe in the lande, and ye make them leaue their burdens.

6 Therefore Pharaoh gaue commandement the same day vnto the taskemasters of the people, and to their officers, saying,

7 Ye shall giue the people no more strawe, to make bricke (as in time past) but let them goe and gather them strawe them selues:

8 Notwithstanding lay vpon them the nober of bricke, which they made in time past, diminish nothing thereof: for they be idle, therefore they crie, saying, Let vs go to offer sacrifice vnto our God.

9 Lay more worke vpon the men, and cause them to do it, and let the not regard vaine words.

10 Then went the taskemasters of the people and their officers out, and tolde the people, saying, Thus saith Pharaoh, I will giue you no more strawe.

11 Goe your selues, get you strawe where yee can finde it, yet shall nothing of your labour bee diminished.

12 Then were the people scattered abroade throughout all the land of Egypt, for to gather stubble in steade of strawe.

13 And the taskemasters hasted them, saying, Finish your dayes worke euery dayes taske, as ye did when ye had strawe.

14 And the officers of the children of Israel, which Pharaohs taskemasters had set ouer them, were beaten, and demanded, Wherefore haue ye not fulfilled your taske in making bricke yesterday and to daye, as in times past?

15 Then the officers of the children of Israel came, and cryed vnto Pharaoh, saying, Wherfore dealest thou thus with thy seruants?

16 There is no strawe giuen to thy seruantes, and they say vnto vs, Make bricke: and loe, thy seruants are beaten, and thy people is blamed.

17 But he said, Ye are to much idle: therfore ye say, Let vs goe to offer sacrifice to the Lord.

18 Goe therefore nowe and worke: for there shall no strawe be giuen you, yet shall yee deliuer the whole tale of bricke.

19 Then the officers of the children of Israel sawe them selues in an euill case, because it was saide, Ye shall diminish nothing of your bricke, nor of euery dayes taske.

20 And they met Moses and Aaron, which stood in their way as they came out from Pharaoh,

21 To whom they said, The Lord looke vpon you and iudge: for yee haue made our sauour to stinke before Pharaoh and before his seruants, in that ye haue put a sword in their hand to slay vs.

22 Wherefore Moses returned to the Lord, and saide, Lord, why hast thou afflicted this people? wherefore hast thou thus sent me?

23 For since I came to Pharaoh to speake in thy Name, he hath vexed this people, and yet thou hast not deliuered thy people.

Exodus 6

1 Then the Lord sayd vnto Moses, Nowe shalt thou see, what I will doe vnto Pharaoh: for by a strong hand shall he let them goe, and euen be constrained to driue them out of his land.

2 Moreouer God spake vnto Moses, and sayd vnto him, I am the Lord,

3 And I appeared vnto Abraham, to Izhak, and to Iaakob by the Name of Almightie God: but by my Name Iehouah was I not knowen vnto the.

4 Furthermore as I made my couenant with them to giue them ye land of Canaan, the land of their pilgrimage, wherein they were strangers:

5 So I haue also hearde the groning of the children of Israel, whom the Egyptians keepe in bondage, and haue remembred my couenant.

6 Wherefore say thou vnto the children of Israel, I am the Lord, and I will bring you out from the burdens of the Egyptians, and will deliuer you out of their bondage, and will redeeme you in a stretched out arme, and in great iudgements.

7 Also I will take you for my people, and will be your God: then ye shall knowe that I the Lord your God bring you out from the burdens of the Egyptians.

8 And I will bring you into the land which I sware that I woulde giue to Abraham, to Izhak, and to Iaakob, and I will giue it vnto you for a possession: I am the Lord.

9 So Moses told the children of Israel thus: but they hearkened not vnto Moses, for anguish of spirit and for cruel bondage.

10 Then the Lord spake vnto Moses, saying,

11 Go speak to Pharaoh King of Egypt, that he let the children of Israel goe out of his land.

12 But Moses spake before the Lord, saying, Beholde, the children of Israel hearken not vnto me, howe then shall Pharaoh heare mee, which am of vncircumcised lippes?

13 Then the Lord spake vnto Moses and vnto Aaron, and charged them to goe to the children of Israel and to Pharaoh King of Egypt, to bring the children of Israel out of the lande of Egypt.

14 These bee the heades of their fathers houses: the sonnes of Reuben the first borne of Israel are Hanoch and Pallu, Hezron and Carmi: these are ye families of Reuben.

15 Also the sonnes of Simeon: Iemuel and Iamin, and Ohad, and Iachin, and Zoar, and Shaul the sonne of a Canaanitish woman: these are the families of Simeon.

16 These also are the names of the sonnes of Leui in their generations: Gershon and Kohath and Merari (and

the yeres of the life of Leui were an hundreth thirtie and seuen yere)

17 The sonnes of Gershon were Libni and Shimi by their families.

18 And the sonnes of Kohath, Amram and Izhar, and Hebron, and Vzziel. (and Kohath liued an hundreth thirtie and three yeere)

19 Also the sonnes of Merari were Mahali and Mushi: these are ye families of Leui by their kinreds.

20 And Amram tooke Iochebed his fathers sister to his wife, and shee bare him Aaron and Moses (and Amram liued an hundreth thirtie and seuen yeere)

21 Also the sonnes of Izhar: Korah, and Nepheg, and Zichri.

22 And the sonnes of Vzziel: Mishael, and Elzaphan, and Sithri.

23 And Aaron tooke Elisheba daughter of Amminadab, sister of Nahashon to his wife, which bare him Nadab, and Abihu, Eleazar and Ithamar.

24 Also the sonnes of Korah: Assir, and Elkanah, and Abiasaph: these are the families of the Korhites.

25 And Eleazar Aarons sonne tooke him one of the daughters of Putiel to his wife, which bare him Phinehas: these are the principall fathers of the Leuites throughout their families.

26 These are Aaron and Moses to whom the Lord said, Bring the children of Israel out of the land of Egypt, according to their armies.

27 These are that Moses and Aaron, which spake to Pharaoh King of Egypt, that they might bring the children of Israel out of Egypt.

28 And at that time when the Lord spake vnto Moses in the land of Egypt,

29 When the Lord, I say, spake vnto Moses, saying, I am the Lord, speake thou vnto Pharaoh the King of Egypt all that I say vnto thee,

30 Then Moses said before the Lord, Behold, I am of vncircumcised lips, and how shall Pharaoh heare me?

Exodus 7

1 Then the Lord saide to Moses, Behold, I haue made thee Pharaohs God, and Aaron thy brother shall be thy Prophet.

2 Thou shalt speake all that I commanded thee: and Aaron thy brother shall speake vnto Pharaoh, that he suffer the children of Israel to go out of his land.

3 But I will harden Pharaohs heart, and multiplie my miracles and my wonders in the lande of Egypt.

4 And Pharaoh shall not hearken vnto you, that I may lay mine hand vpon Egypt, and bring out myne armies, euen my people, the children of Israel out of the land of Egypt, by great iudgements.

5 Then the Egyptians shall knowe that I am the Lord, when I stretch foorth mine hand vpon Egypt, and bring out the children of Israel from among them.

6 So Moses and Aaron did as the Lord commanded them, euen so did they.

7 (Nowe Moses was foure score yeere olde, and Aaron foure score and three, when they spake vnto Pharaoh)

8 And the Lord had spoken vnto Moses and Aaron, saying,

9 If Pharaoh speake vnto you, saying, Shewe a miracle for you, then thou shalt say vnto Aaron, Take thy rod, and cast it before Pharaoh, and it shalbe turned into a serpent.

10 Then went Moses and Aaron vnto Pharaoh, and did euen as the Lord had commanded: and Aaron cast forth his rod before Pharaoh and before his seruants, and it was turned into a serpent.

11 Then Pharaoh called also for the wise men and sorcerers: and those charmers also of Egypt did in like maner with their enchantmens,

12 For they cast downe euery man his rod, and they were turned into serpents: but Aarons rodde deuoured their rods.

13 So Pharaohs heart was hardened, and hee hearkened not to them, as the Lord had saide.

14 The Lord then saide vnto Moses, Pharaohs heart is obstinate, hee refuseth to let the people goe.

15 Goe vnto Pharaoh in the morning, (loe, he will come forth vnto the water) and thou shalt stand and meete him by the riuers brinke, and the rod, which was turned into a serpent, shalt thou take in thine hand.

16 And thou shalt say vnto him, The Lord God of the Ebrewes hath sent me vnto thee, saying, Let my people goe, that they may serue mee in the wildernesse: and beholde, hitherto thou wouldest not heare.

17 Thus saith the Lord, In this shalt thou know that I am the Lord: behold, I wil smite with the rodde that is in mine hand vpon the water that is in the riuer, and it shalbe turned to blood.

18 And the fish that is in the riuer shall dye, and the riuer shall stinke, and it shall grieue the Egyptians to drinke of the water of the riuer.

19 The Lord then spake to Moses, Say vnto Aaron, Take thy rod, and stretch out thine hand ouer the waters of Egypt, ouer their streames, ouer their riuers, and ouer their pondes,, and ouer all pooles of their waters, and they shalbe blood, and there shalbe blood throughout all the land of Egypt, both in vessels of wood, and of stone.

20 So Moses and Aaron did euen as the Lord commanded: and hee lift vp the rodde, and smote the water that was in the riuer in the sight of Pharaoh, and in the sight of his seruants: and all the water that was in the riuer, was turned into blood.

21 And the fish that was in the ryuer dyed, and the riuer stanke: so that the Egyptians could not drinke of the water of the riuer: and there was blood throughout all the lande of Egypt.

22 And the enchanters of Egypt did likewise with their sorceries: and the heart of Phraoh was hardened: so that

he did not hearken vnto them, as the Lord had sayde.

23 Then Pharaoh returned, and went againe into his house, neither did this yet enter into his heart.

24 All the Egyptians then digged rounde about the riuer for waters to drinke: for they could not drinke of the water of the riuer.

25 And this continued fully seuen dayes after the Lord had smitten the riuer.

Exodus 8

1 Afterward the Lord sayde vnto Moses, Goe vnto Pharaoh, and tell him, Thus saith the Lord, Let my people goe, that they may serue me:

2 And if thou wilt not let them goe, beholde, I will smite all thy countrey with frogges:

3 And the riuer shall scral ful of frogges, which shall goe vp and come into thine house, and into thy chamber, where thou sleepest, and vpon thy bed, and into the house of thy seruants, and vpon thy people, and into thine ouens, and into thy kneading troughes.

4 Yea, the frogges shall climbe vp vpon thee, and on thy people, and vpon all thy seruants.

5 Also the Lord said vnto Moses, Say thou vnto Aaron, Stretch out thine hande with thy rod vpon the streames, vpon the riuers, and vpon the ponds, and cause frogs to come vp vpon the land of Egypt.

6 Then Aaron stretched out his hand vpon the waters of Egypt, and the frogges came vp, and couered the land of Egypt.

7 And the sorcerers did likewise with their sorceries, and brought frogges vp vpon the land of Egypt.

8 Then Pharaoh called for Moses and Aaron, and said, Pray ye vnto the Lord, that hee may take away the frogges from mee, and from my people, and I will let the people goe, that they may doe sacrifice vnto the Lord.

9 And Moses said vnto Pharaoh, Concerning me, euen command when I shall pray for thee, and for thy seruants, and for thy people, to destroy the frogges from thee and from thine houses, that they may remaine in the riuer only.

10 Then he said, To morowe. And he answered, Be it as thou hast said, that thou maiest know, that there is none like vnto the Lord our God.

11 So the frogges shall depart from thee, and from thine houses, and from thy seruantes, and from thy people: onely they shall remaine in the riuer.

12 Then Moses and Aaron went out from Pharaoh: and Moses cryed vnto the Lord concerning the frogges, which hee had sent vnto Pharaoh.

13 And the Lord did according to the saying of Moses: so the frogges died in the houses, in the townes, and in the fieldes.

14 And they gathered the together by heaps, and the land stanke of them.

15 But when Pharaoh sawe that hee had rest giuen him, he hardened his heart,

and hearkened not vnto them, as the Lord had said.

16 Againe the Lord sayd vnto Moses, Say vnto Aaron, Stretche out the rod, and smite the dust of the earth, that it may bee turned to lyce throughout all the land of Egypt.

17 And they did so: for Aaron stretched out his hand with his rod, and smote the dust of the earth: and lyce came vpon man and vpon beast: all the dust of the earth was lyce throughout all the land of Egypt.

18 Nowe the enchanters assaied likewise with their enchantments to bring forth lyce, but they could not. So the lyce were vpon man and vpon beast.

19 Then saide the enchanters vnto Pharaoh, This is the finger of God. But Pharaohs heart remained obstinate, and hee hearkened not vnto them, as the Lord had said.

20 Moreouer the Lord sayd to Moses, Rise vp earely in the morning, and stand before Pharaoh (lo, hee will come forth vnto the water) and say vnto him, Thus saith the Lord, Let my people go, that they may serue me.

21 Els, if thou wilt not let my people goe, behold, I will send swarmes of flies both vpon thee, and vpon thy seruants, and vpon thy people, and into thine houses: and the houses of the Egyptians shalbe full of swarmes of flies, and the ground also whereon they are.

22 But ye land of Goshe, where my people are, wil I cause to be wonderfull in that day, so that no swarmes of flies shalbe there, that thou maiest know that I am the Lord in the middes of the earth.

23 And I will make a deliuerance of my people from thy people: to morowe shall this miracle be.

24 And the Lord did so: for there came great swarmes of flies into the house of Pharaoh, and into his seruants houses, so that through all the lande of Egypt, the earth was corrupt by the swarmes of flies.

25 Then Pharaoh called for Moses and Aaron, and saide, Goe, doe sacrifice vnto your God in this lande.

26 But Moses answered, It is not meete to do so: for then we shoulde offer vnto the Lord our God that, which is an abomination vnto the Egyptians. Loe, can we sacrifice the abomination of the Egyptians before their eyes, and they not stone vs?

27 Let vs go three dayes iourney in the desert, and sacrifice vnto the Lord our God, as he hath commanded vs.

28 And Pharaoh said, I will let you go, that ye may sacrifice vnto the Lord your God in the wildernesse: but goe not farre away, pray for me.

29 And Moses said, Behold, I will go out from thee, and pray vnto the Lord, that the swarmes of flies may depart from Pharaoh, from his seruants, and from his people to morowe: but let Pharaoh from hencefoorth deceiue no more, in not suffering the people to sacrifice vnto the Lord.

30 So Moses went out from Pharaoh and prayed vnto the Lord.

31 And the Lord did according to the saying of Moses, and the swarmes of flies departed from Pharaoh, from his seruants, and from his people, and there remained not one.

32 Yet Pharaoh hardened his heart at this time also, and did not let the people goe.

Exodus 9

1 Then the Lord said vnto Moses, Go to Pharaoh, and tell him, Thus saith the Lord God of the Ebrewes, Let my people go, that they may serue me.

2 But if thou refuse to let them goe, and wilt yet holde them still,

3 Beholde, the hande of the Lord is vpon thy flocke which is in the fielde: for vpon the horses, vpon the asses, vpon the camels, vpon the cattell, and vpon the sheepe shalbe a mightie great moraine.

4 And the Lord shall doe wonderfully betweene the beastes of Israel, and the beastes of Egypt: so that there shall nothing dye of all, that pertaineth to the children of Israel.

5 And the Lord appointed a time, saying, To morowe the Lord shall finish this thing in this lande.

6 So the Lord did this thing on the morow, and all the cattel of Egypt dyed: but of the cattell of the children of Israel dyed not one.

7 Then Pharaoh sent, and beholde, there was not one of the cattell of the Israelites dead: and the heart of Pharaoh was obstinate, and hee did not let the people goe.

8 And the Lord said to Moses and to Aaron, Take your handfull of ashes of the fornace, and Moses shall sprinkle them towarde the heauen in the sight of Pharaoh,

9 And they shall be turned to dust in all the land of Egypt: and it shalbe as a scab breaking out into blisters vpon man, and vpon beast, thorow out all the land of Egypt.

10 Then they tooke ashes of the fornace, and stoode before Pharaoh: and Moses sprinkled them towarde the heauen, and there came a scab breaking out into blisters vpon man, and vpon beast.

11 And the sorcerers could not stande before Moses, because of the scab: for the scab was vpon the enchanters, and vpon all the Egyptians.

12 And the Lord hardened the heart of Pharaoh, and he hearkened not vnto them, as the Lord had said vnto Moses.

13 Also the Lord said vnto Moses, Rise vp early in the morning, and stand before Pharaoh, and tell him, Thus saith the Lord God of the Ebrewes, Let my people goe, that they may serue me.

14 For I will at this time send all my plagues vpon thine heart, and vpon thy seruants, and vpon thy people, that thou mayest knowe that there is none like me in all the earth.

15 For nowe I will stretch out mine hande, that I may smite thee and thy people with the pestilence: and thou shalt perish from the earth.

16 And in deede, for this cause haue I appointed thee, to shewe my power in thee, and to declare my Name throughout all the world.

17 Yet thou exaltest thy selfe against my people, and lettest them not goe.

18 Beholde, to morowe this time I will cause to raine a mightie great haile, such as was not in Egypt since the foundation thereof was laid vnto this time.

19 Send therefore nowe, and gather the cattell, and all that thou hast in the fielde: for vpon all the men, and the beastes, which are found in the field, and not brought home, the haile shall fall vpon them, and they shall die.

20 Such then as feared the word of the Lord among the seruants of Pharaoh, made his seruants and his cattell flee into the houses:

21 But such as regarded not the worde of the Lord, left his seruants, and his cattell in the fielde.

22 And the Lord saide to Moses, Stretche foorth thine hande towarde heauen, that there may be haile in all the land of Egypt, vpon man, and vpon beast, and vpon all the herbes of the fielde in the lande of Egypt.

23 Then Moses stretched out his rod towarde heauen, and the Lord sent thunder and haile, and lightening vpon the ground: and the Lord caused haile to raine vpon the land of Egypt.

24 So there was haile, and fire mingled with the haile, so grieuous, as there was none throughout all the lande of Egypt, since it was a nation.

25 And the haile smote throughout al ye land of Egypt all that was in the fielde, both man and beast: also ye haile smote all the herbes of ye field, and brake to pieces all the trees of the fielde.

26 Onely in the lande of Goshen (where the children of Israel were) was no haile.

27 Then Pharaoh sent and called for Moses and Aaron, and said vnto them, I haue now sinned: the Lord is righteous, but I and my people are wicked.

28 Pray ye vnto the Lord (for it is ynough) that there be no more mightie thunders and haile, and I will let you goe, and yee shall tarie no longer.

29 Then Moses saide vnto him, Assoone as I am out of the citie, I will spreade mine hands vnto the Lord, and the thunder shall cease, neither shall there be any more haile, that thou mayest knowe that the earth is the Lordes.

30 As for thee and thy seruants, I knowe afore I pray ye will feare before the face of the Lord God.

31 (And the flaxe, and the barley were smitten: for the barley was eared, and the flaxe was bolled.

32 But the wheat and the rye were not smitten, for they were hid in the grounde)

33 Then Moses went out of the citie from Pharaoh, and spred his hands to the Lord, and the thunder and the haile ceased, neither rained it vpon the earth.

34 And when Pharaoh sawe that the raine and the haile and the thunder were ceased, hee sinned againe, and hardened his heart, both he, and his seruants.

35 So the heart of Pharaoh was hardened: neither would he let the children of Israel goe, as the Lord had said by Moses.

Exodus 10

1 Againe the Lord saide vnto Moses, Goe to Pharaoh: for I haue hardened his heart, and the heart of his seruants, that I might worke these my miracles in the middes of his realme,

2 And that thou maist declare in the eares of thy sonne, and of thy sonnes sonne, what things I haue done in Egypt, and my miracles, which I haue done among them: that ye may knowe that I am the Lord.

3 Then came Moses and Aaron vnto Pharaoh, and they said vnto him, Thus saith the Lord God of the Ebrewes, Howe long wilt thou refuse to humble thy selfe before me? Let my people goe, that they may serue me.

4 But if thou refuse to let my people go, beholde, to morowe will I bring grashoppers into thy coastes.

5 And they shall couer the face of the earth, that a man can not see the earth: and they shall eate the residue which remaineth vnto you, and hath escaped from the haile: and they shall eate all your trees that bud in the fielde.

6 And they shall fil thine houses, and all thy seruants houses, and the houses of all the Egyptians, as neither thy fathers, nor thy fathers fathers haue seene, since the time they were vpon the earth vnto this day. So he returned, and went out from Pharaoh.

7 Then Pharaohs seruants saide vnto him, How long shall he be an offence vnto vs? let the men go, that they may serue the Lord their God: wilt thou first knowe that Egypt is destroyed?

8 So Moses and Aaron were brought againe vnto Pharaoh, and he saide vnto them, Goe, serue the Lord your God, but who are they that shall goe?

9 And Moses answered, We will go with our yong and with our olde, with our sonnes and with our daughters, with our sheepe and with our cattell will we goe: for we must celebrate a feast vnto the Lord.

10 And he said vnto them, Let the Lord so be with you, as I will let you goe and your children: beholde, for euill is before your face.

11 It shall not be so: nowe goe ye that are men, and serue the Lord: for that was your desire. Then they were thrust out from Pharaohs presence.

12 After, the Lord said vnto Moses, Stretch out thine hande vpon the lande of Egypt for the grashoppers, that they may come vpon the lande of Egypt, and eate all the herbes of the land, euen all that the haile hath left.

13 Then Moses stretched foorth his rod vpon the lande of Egypt: and the Lord brought an East winde vpon the land all that day, and al that night: and in the morning the East wind brought the grashoppers.

14 So the grashoppers went vp vpon all the land of Egypt, and remained in all quarters of Egypt: so grieuous Grashoppers, like to these were neuer before, neither after them shalbe such.

15 For they couered all the face of the earth, so that the lande was darke: and they did eate all the herbes of the lande, and all the fruites of the trees, which the haile had left, so that there was no greene thing left vpon the trees, nor among the herbes of the fielde throughout all the lande of Egypt.

16 Therefore Pharaoh called for Moses and Aaron in haste, and sayde, I haue sinned against the Lord your God, and against you.

17 And nowe forgiue mee my sinne onely this once, and pray vnto the Lord your God, that hee may take away from me this death onely.

18 Moses then went out from Pharaoh, and prayed vnto the Lord.

19 And the Lord turned a mightie strong West winde, and tooke away the grashoppers, and violently cast them into the red Sea, so that there remained not one grashopper in all the coast of Egypt.

20 But the Lord hardened Pharaohs heart, and hee did not let the children of Israel goe.

21 Againe ye Lord said vnto Moses, Stretch out thine hand toward heauen, that there may be vpon the lande of Egypt darkenesse, euen darkenesse that may be felt.

22 Then Moses stretched forth his hande towarde heauen, and there was a blacke darkenesse in all the land of Egypt three daies.

23 No man saw an other, neither rose vp from ye place where he was for three dayes: but all the children of Israel had light where they dwelt.

24 The Pharaoh called for Moses and said, Go, serue the Lord: onely your sheepe and your cattel shall abide, and your children shall go with you.

25 And Moses sayd, Thou must giue vs also sacrifices, and burnt offrings that wee may doe sacrifice vnto the Lord our God.

26 Therefore our cattell also shall go with vs: there shall not an hoofe bee left, for thereof must we take to serue the Lord our God: neither doe wee knowe howe we shall serue the Lord, vntill we come thither.

27 (But the Lord hardened Pharaohs heart, and he would not let them goe)

28 And Pharaoh sayde vnto him, Get thee from mee: looke thou see my face no more: for whensoeuer thou commest in my sight, thou shalt dye.

29 Then Moses said, Thou hast said well: from henceforth will I see thy face no more.

Exodus 11

1 Now the Lord had saide vnto Moses, yet will I bring one plague more vpon Pharaoh, and vpon Egypt: after that, he will let you go hence: when he letteth you goe, he shall at once chase you hence.

2 Speake thou nowe to the people, that euery man require of his neighbour, and euery woman of her neighbour iewels of siluer and iewels of gold.

3 And the Lord gaue the people fauour in the sight of the Egyptians: also Moses was very great in the land of Egypt, in the sight of Pharaohs seruantes, and in the sight of the people.)

4 Also Moses sayde, Thus sayth the Lord, About midnight will I goe out into the middes of Egypt.

5 And all the first borne in the lande of Egypt shall die, from the first borne of Pharaoh that sitteth on his throne, vnto the first borne of the maide seruant, that is at the mille, and all the first borne of beastes.

6 Then there shalbe a great crie throughout all the land of Egypt, such as was neuer none like, nor shalbe.

7 But against none of ye children of Israel shall a dogge moue his tongue, neyther against man nor beast, that ye may knowe that the Lord putteth a difference betweene the Egyptians and Israel.

8 And all these thy seruants shall come downe vnto me, and fal before me, saying, Get thee out, and all the people that are at thy feete, and after this will I depart. So he went out from Pharaoh very angry.

9 And the Lord saide vnto Moses, Pharaoh shall not heare you, that my wonders may bee multiplied in the land of Egypt.

10 So Moses and Aaron did all these wonders before Pharaoh: but the Lord hardened Pharaohs heart, and he suffred not the children of Israel to goe out of his lande.

Exodus 12

1 Then the Lord spake to Moses and to Aaron in the land of Egypt, saying,

2 This moneth shalbe vnto you the beginning of monethis: it shalbe to you the first moneth of the yere.

3 Speake ye vnto all the congregation of Israel, saying, In the tenth of this moneth let euery man take vnto him a lambe, according to the house of the fathers, a lambe for an house.

4 And if the housholde be too litle for the lambe, he shall take his neighbour, which is next vnto his house, according to the number of the persons: euery one of you, according to his eating shall make your count for the lambes,

5 Your lambe shalbe without blemish, a male of a yeere olde: ye shall take it of the lambes, or of the kiddes.

6 And yee shall keepe it vntill the fourteenth day of this moneth: then al the multitude of the Congregation of Israel shall kill it at euen.

7 After, they shall take of the blood, and strike it on the two postes, and on the vpper doore post of the houses where they shall eate it.

8 And they shall eate the flesh the same night, roste with fire, and vnleauened bread: with sowre herbes they shall eate it.

9 Eate not thereof rawe, boyled nor sodden in water, but rost with fire, both his head, his feete, and his purtenance.

10 And ye shall reserue nothing of it vnto the morning: but that, which remaineth of it vnto the morowe, shall ye burne with fire.

11 And thus shall yee eate it, Your loynes girded, your shoes on your feete, and your staues in your handes, and yee shall eate it in haste: for it is the Lords Passeouer.

12 For I will passe through the lande of Egypt the same night, and will smite all the first borne in the land of Egypt, both man and beast, and I will execute iudgement vpon all the gods of Egypt. I am the Lord.

13 And the blood shalbe a token for you vpon the houses where ye are: so when I see the blood, I will passe ouer you, and the plague shall not be vpon you to destruction, when I smite the lande of Egypt.

14 And this day shalbe vnto you a remembrance: and ye shall keepe it an holie feast vnto the Lord, throughout your generations: yee shall keepe it holie by an ordinance for euer.

15 Seuen daies shall ye eat vnleauened bread, and in any case ye shall put away leauen the first day out of your houses: for whosoeuer eateth leauened bread from the first daie vntill the seuenth day, that person shalbe cut off from Israel.

16 And in the first day shalbe an holie assemblie: also in the seuenth day shalbe an holy assemblie vnto you: no worke shalbe done in them, saue about that which euery man must eate: that onely may ye do.

17 Ye shall keepe also the feast of vnleauened bread: for that same daye I will bring your armies out of the lande of Egypt: therefore ye shall obserue this day, throughout your posteritie, by an ordinance for euer.

18 In the first moneth and the fourteenth day of the moneth at euen, yee shall eate vnleauened bread vnto the one and twentieth day of the moneth at euen.

19 Seuen daies shall no leauen be founde in your houses: for whosoeuer eateth leauened bread, that person shalbe cut off from the Congregation of Israel: whether he bee a stranger, or borne in the land.

20 Ye shall eate no leauened bread: but in all your habitations shall ye eate vnleauened bread.

21 Then Moses called all the Elders of Israel, and saide vnto them, Choose out and take you for euerie of your housholdes a lambe, and kill the Passeouer.

22 And take a bunch of hyssop, and dip it in the blood that is in the basen, and strike the lintell, and the doore cheekes with the blood that is in the basen, and let none of you goe out at the doore of his house, vntill the morning.

23 For the Lord will passe by to smite the Egyptians: and when he seeth the blood vpon the lintel and on the two doore cheekes, the Lord wil passe ouer the doore, and wil not suffer the destroyer to come into your houses to plague you.

24 Therefore shall ye obserue this thing as an ordinance both for thee and thy sonnes for euer.

25 And when ye shall come into the land, which the Lord will giue you as hee hath promised, then ye shall keepe this seruice.

26 And when your children aske you, What seruice is this ye keepe?

27 Then ye shall saye, It is the sacrifice of the Lordes Passeouer, which passed ouer the houses of the children of Israel in Egypt, when he smote the Egyptians, and preserued our houses. Then the people bowed them selues, and worshipped.

28 So the children of Israel went, and did as the Lord had commanded Moses and Aaron: so did they.

29 Nowe at midnight, the Lord smote all the first borne in the lande of Egypt, from the first borne of Pharaoh that sate on his throne, vnto the first borne of the captiue that was in prison, and all the first borne of beastes.

30 And Pharaoh rose vp in the night, he, and all his seruants and all the Egyptians: and there was a great crye in Egypt: for there was no house where there was not one dead.

31 And hee called to Moses and to Aaron by night, and saide, Rise vp, get you out from among my people, both yee, and the children of Israel, and goe serue the Lord as ye haue sayde.

32 Take also your sheepe and your cattell as yee haue sayde, and depart, and blesse me also.

33 And the Egyptians did force the people, because they would send them out of the land in haste: for they said, We die all.

34 Therfore the people tooke their dough before it was leauened, euen their dough bound in clothes vpon their shoulders.

35 And the children of Israel did according to the saying of Moses, and they asked of ye Egyptians iewels of siluer and iewels of gold, and raiment.

36 And the Lord gaue the people fauour in the sight of the Egyptians: and they graunted their request: so they spoyled the Egyptians.

37 Then the children of Israel tooke their iourney from Rameses to Succoth about six hundreth thousand men of foote, beside children.

38 And a great multitude of sundrie sortes of people went out with them, and sheepe, and beeues, and cattel in great abundance.

39 And they baked the dough which they brought out of Egypt, and made vnleauened cakes: for it was not leauened, because they were thrust out of Egypt, neither coulde they tarie, nor yet prepare themselues vitailes.

40 So the dwelling of the children of Israel, while they dwelled in Egypt, was foure hundreth and thirtie yeres.

41 And when the foure hundreth and thirtie yeeres were expired, euen the selfe same day departed all the hostes of the Lord out of the land of Egypt.

42 It is a night to be kept holie to the Lord, because he brought them out of the lande of Egypt: this is that night of the Lord, which all the children of Israel must keepe throughout their generations.

43 Also the Lord said vnto Moses and Aaron, This is the Lawe of the Passeouer: no stranger shall eate thereof.

44 But euerie seruant that is bought for money, when thou hast circumcised him, then shall he eat thereof.

45 A stranger or an hyred seruant shall not eat thereof.

46 In one house shall it bee eaten: thou shalt carie none of ye flesh out of the house, neither shall ye breake a bone thereof.

47 All the Congregation of Israel shall obserue it.

48 But if a stranger dwell with thee, and will obserue the Passeouer of the Lord, let him circumcise all the males, that belong vnto him, and then let him come and obserue it, and he shall be as one that is borne in the land: for none vncircumcised person shall eate thereof.

49 One lawe shalbe to him that is borne in the land, and to the stranger that dwelleth among you.

50 Then all the children of Israel did as the Lord commanded Moses and Aaron: so did they.

51 And the selfe same day did the Lord bring the children of Israel out of the land of Egypt by their armies.

Exodus 13

1 And the Lord spake vnto Moses, saying,

2 Sanctifie vnto me all the first borne: that is, euery one that first openeth the wombe among the children of Israel, as well of man as of beast: for it is mine.

3 Then Moses sayd vnto the people, Remember this day in the which ye came out of Egypt, out of the house of bondage: for by a mightie hande the Lord brought you out from thence: therefore no leauened bread shall bee eaten.

4 This day come yee out in the moneth of Abib.

5 Now when the Lord hath brought thee into the land of the Canaanites, and Hittites, and Amorites, and Hiuites, and Iebusites (which he sware vnto thy fathers, that he woulde giue thee, a land flowing with milke and honie) then thou shalt keepe this seruice in this moneth.

6 Seuen dayes shalt thou eate vnleauened bread, and the seuenth day shall be the feast of the Lord.

7 Vnleauened bread shall bee eaten seuen dayes, and there shall no leauened bread be seene with thee, nor yet leauen be seene with thee in all thy quarters.

8 And thou shalt shew thy sonne in that day, saying, This is done, because of that which the Lord did vnto me, when I came out of Egypt.

9 And it shalbe a signe vnto thee vpon thine hande, and for a remembrance betweene thine eyes, that the Lawe of the Lord may be in thy mouth: for by a strong hand the Lord brought thee out of Egypt.

10 Keepe therefore this ordinance in his season appoynted from yeere to yeere.

11 And when the Lord shall bring thee into the lande of the Canaanites, as hee sware vnto thee and to thy fathers, and shall giue it thee,

12 Then thou shalt set apart vnto the Lord all that first openeth the wombe: also euery thing that first doeth open the wombe, and commeth forth of thy beast: the males shalbe the Lordes.

13 But euery first foale of an asse, thou shalt redeeme with a lambe: and if thou redeeme him not, then thou shalt breake his necke: likewise all the first borne of man among thy sonnes shalt thou bye out.

14 And when thy sonne shall aske thee to morowe, saying, What is this? thou shalt then say vnto him, With a mightie hande the Lord brought vs out of Egypt, out of the house of bondage.

15 For when Pharaoh was harde hearted against our departing, the Lord then slewe all the first borne in the lande of Egypt: from the first borne of man euen to the first borne of beast: therefore I sacrifice vnto the Lord all the males that first open the wombe, but all the first borne of my sonnes I redeeme.

16 And it shalbe as a token vpon thine hand, and as frontlets betweene thine eyes, that the Lord brought vs out of Egypt by a mightie hande.

17 Nowe when Pharaoh had let the people go, God caried them not by the way of the Philistims countrey, though it were neerer: (for God sayd, Lest the people repent whe they see warre, and turne againe to Egypt)

18 But God made the people to go about by the way of the wildernesse of the red sea: and the children of Israel went vp armed out of the land of Egypt.

19 (And Moses tooke the bones of Ioseph with him: for he had made the children of Israel sweare, saying, God will surely visite you, and ye shall take my bones away hence with you)

20 So they tooke their iourney from Succoth, and camped in Etham in the edge of the wildernesse.

21 And the Lord went before them by day in a pillar of a cloude to leade them the way, and by night in a pillar of fire to giue them light, that they might go both by day and by night.

22 He tooke not away the pillar of ye cloude by day, nor the pillar of fire by night from before the people.

Exodus 14

1 Then the Lord spake vnto Moses, saying,

2 Speake to the children of Israel, that they returne and campe before Pi-hahiroth, betweene Migdol and the Sea, ouer against Baal-zephon: about it shall ye campe by the Sea.

3 For Pharaoh will say of the children of Israel, They are tangled in the land: the wildernesse hath shut them in.

4 And I will harden Pharaohs heart that hee shall follow after you: so I will get mee honour vpon Pharaoh, and vpon all his hoste: the Egyptians also shall knowe that I am the Lord: and they did so.

5 Then it was told the King of Egypt, that the people fled: and the heart of Pharaoh and of his seruants was turned against the people, and they sayde, Why haue we this done, and haue let Israel go out of our seruice?

6 And he made ready his charets, and tooke his people with him,

7 And tooke sixe hundreth chosen charets, and all the charets of Egypt, and captaines ouer euery one of them.

8 (For the Lord had hardened the heart of Pharaoh king of Egypt, and he followed after the children of Israel: but the children of Israel went out with an hie hand)

9 And the Egyptians pursued after them, and all the horses and charets of Pharaoh, and his horsemen and his hoste ouertooke them camping by the Sea, beside Pi-hahiroth, before Baal-zephon.

10 And when Pharaoh drew nie, the children of Israel lift vp their eyes, and beholde, the Egyptians marched after them, and they were sore afrayde: wherefore the children of Israel cried vnto the Lord.

11 And they sayde vnto Moses, Hast thou brought vs to die in the wildernes, because there were no graues in Egypt? wherefore hast thou serued vs thus, to carie vs out of Egypt?

12 Did not wee tell thee this thing in Egypt, saying, Let vs be in rest, that we may serue the Egyptians? for it had bene better for vs to serue the Egyptians, then that wee shoulde dye in the wildernesse.

13 Then Moses sayde to the people, Feare ye not, stand still, and beholde the saluation of the Lord which he will shew to you this day. For the Egyptians, whome ye haue seene this day, ye shall neuer see them againe.

14 The Lord shall fight for you: therefore hold you your peace.

15 And the Lord sayd vnto Moses, Wherefore cryest thou vnto me? speake vnto the children of Israel that they go forward:

16 And lift thou vp thy rod, and stretche out thine hand vpon the Sea and deuide it, and let the children of Israel goe on

drie ground thorow the middes of the Sea.

17 And I, beholde, I will harden the heart of the Egyptians, that they may follow them, and I wil get me honour vpon Pharaoh, and vpon all his host, vpon his charets, and vpon his horsemen.

18 Then the Egyptians shall know that I am the Lord, when I haue gotten me honour vpon Pharaoh, vpon his charets, and vpon his horsemen.

19 (And the Angel of God, which went before the hoste of Israel, remoued and went behinde them: also the pillar of the cloude went from before them, and stoode behinde them,

20 And came betweene the campe of the Egyptians and the campe of Israel: it was both a cloude and darkenes, yet gaue it light by night, so that all the night long the one came not at the other)

21 And Moses stretched forth his hande vpon the Sea, and the Lord caused the sea to runne backe by a strong East winde all the night, and made the Sea dry land: for the waters were deuided.

22 Then the children of Israel went through the middes of the Sea vpon the drie ground, and the waters were a wall vnto them on their right hand, and on their left hand.

23 And the Egyptians pursued and went after them to the middes of the Sea, euen all Pharaohs horses, his charets, and his horsemen.

24 Nowe in the morning watche, when the Lord looked vnto the hoste of the Egyptians, out of the firie and cloudie pillar, he strooke the host of the Egyptians with feare.

25 For he tooke off their charet wheeles, and they draue them with much a doe: so that the Egyptians euery one sayd, I wil flee from the face of Israel: for the Lord fighteth for them against the Egyptians.

26 Then the Lord sayde to Moses, Stretche thine hand vpon the Sea, that the waters may returne vpon the Egyptians, vpon their charets and vpon their horsemen.

27 Then Moses stretched forth his hand vpon the Sea, and the Sea returned to his force early in the morning, and the Egyptians fled against it: but the Lord ouerthrew the Egyptians in the mids of the Sea.

28 So the water returned and couered the charets and the horsemen, euen all the hoste of Pharaoh that came into the sea after them: there remained not one of them.

29 But the children of Israel walked vpon dry land thorowe the middes of the Sea, and the waters were a wall vnto them on their right hande, and on their left.

30 Thus the Lord saued Israel the same day out of the hand of the Egyptians, and Israel sawe the Egyptians dead vpon the Sea banke.

31 And Israel saw the mightie power, which the Lord shewed vpon the Egyptians: so the people feared the Lord,

and beleeued the Lord, and his seruant Moses.

Exodus 15

1 Then sang Moses and the children of Israel this song vnto the Lord, and sayd in this maner, I will sing vnto the Lord: for he hath triumphed gloriously: the horse and him that rode vpon him hath he ouerthrowen in the Sea.

2 The Lord is my strength and praise, and he is become my saluation. He is my God, and I will prepare him a tabernacle. he is my fathers God, and I will exalt him.

3 The Lord is a man of warre, his Name is Iehouah.

4 Pharaohs charets and his host hath he cast into the Sea: his chosen captaines also were drowned in the red Sea.

5 The depths haue couered them, they sanke to the bottome as a stone.

6 Thy right hande, O Lord, is glorious in power: thy right hand, O Lord, hath brused the enemie.

7 And in thy great glorie thou hast ouerthrowen them that rose against thee: thou sentest forth thy wrath, which consumed them as the stubble.

8 And by the blast of thy nostrels the waters were gathered, the floods stoode still as an heape, the depthes congealed together in the heart of the Sea.

9 The enemie sayd, I wil pursue, I wil ouertake them, I will deuide the spoyle, my lust shall bee satisfied vpon them, I will drawe my sworde, mine hand shall destroy them.

10 Thou blewest with thy winde, the Sea couered them, they sanke as leade in the mightie waters.

11 Who is like vnto thee, O Lord, among the Gods! who is like thee so glorious in holinesse, fearefull in prayses, doing wonders!

12 Thou stretchedst out thy right hande, the earth swallowed them.

13 Thou wilt by thy mercie cary this people, which thou deliueredst: thou wilt bring them in thy strength vnto thine holy habitation.

14 The people shall heare and be afraide: sorow shall come vpon the inhabitants of Palestina.

15 Then the dukes of Edom shalbe amased, and trembling shall come vpon the great men of Moab: all the inhabitantes of Canaan shall waxe faint hearted.

16 Feare and dread shall fall vpon them: because of the greatnesse of thine arme, they shalbe stil as a stone, till thy people passe, O Lord: til this people passe, which thou hast purchased.

17 Thou shalt bring them in, and plant them in the mountaine of thine inheritance, which is the place that thou hast prepared, O Lord, for to dwell in, euen the sanctuarie, O Lord, which thine hands shall establish.

18 The Lord shall reigne for euer and euer.

19 For Pharaohs horses went with his charets and horsemen into the Sea, and the Lord brought the waters of the Sea vpon them: but the children of Israel went on drie land in the middes of the Sea.

20 And Miriam the prophetesse, sister of Aaron tooke a timbrell in her hande, and all the women came out after her with timbrels and daunces.

21 And Miriam answered the men, Sing yee vnto the Lord: for he hath triumphed gloriously: the horse and his rider hath hee ouerthrowen in the Sea.

22 Then Moses brought Israel from the redde Sea, and they went out into the wildernesse of Shur: and they went three dayes in the wildernesse, and found no waters.

23 And whe they came to Marah, they could not drinke of the waters of Marah, for they were bitter: therefore the name of the place was called Marah.

24 Then the people murmured against Moses, saying, What shall we drinke?

25 And he cried vnto the Lord, and the Lord shewed him a tree, which when he had cast into the waters, the waters were sweete: there he made them an ordinance and a law, and there he proued them,

26 And sayd, if thou wilt diligently hearken, O Israel, vnto the voyce of the Lord thy God, and wilt do that, which is right in his sight, and wilt giue eare vnto his commandements, and keepe all his ordinances, then will I put none of these diseases vpon thee, which I brought vpon the Egyptians: for I am the Lord that healeth thee.

27 And they came to Elim, where were twelue fountaines of water, and seuentie palme trees, and they camped thereby the waters.

Exodus 16

1 Afterward all the Congregation of the children of Israel departed from Elim, and came to the wildernes of Sin, (which is betweene Elim and Sinai) the fifteenth day of the second moneth after their departing out of ye land of Egypt.

2 And the whole Congregation of the children of Israel murmured against Moses and against Aaron in the wildernesse.

3 For the children of Israel sayde to them, Oh that we had dyed by the hand of the Lord in the land of Egypt, when wee sate by the flesh pots, when wee ate bread our bellies full: for yee haue brought vs out into this wildernesse, to kill this whole company with famine.

4 Then sayd the Lord vnto Moses, Behold, I wil cause bread to rayne from heauen to you, and the people shall goe out, and gather that that is sufficient for euery day, that I may proue them, whether they wil walke in my Law or no.

5 But the sixt daye they shall prepare that, which they shall bring home, and it shalbe twise as much as they gather dayly.

6 Then Moses and Aaron sayde vnto all the children of Israel, At euen ye shall know, that the Lord brought you out of the land of Egypt:

7 And in the morning ye shall see the glorie of the Lord: for he hath heard your grudgings against the Lord: and what are we that ye haue murmured against vs?

8 Againe Moses sayd, At euen shall the Lord giue you flesh to eate, and in the morning your fil of bread: for the Lord hath heard your murmurings, which ye murmure against him: for what are we? your murmurings are not against vs, but against the Lord.

9 And Moses sayd to Aaron, Say vnto all the Congregation of the children of Israel, Draw neere before the Lord: for he hath heard your murmurings.

10 Now as Aaron spake vnto the whole Congregation of the children of Israel, they looked toward the wildernesse, and beholde, the glory of the Lord appeared in a cloude.

11 (For the Lord had spoken vnto Moses, saying,

12 I haue heard the murmurings of the children of Israel: tell them therefore, and say, At euen ye shall eate flesh, and in the morning ye shall be filled with bread, and ye shall knowe that I am the Lord your God)

13 And so at euen the quailes came and couered the campe: and in the morning the dewe lay round about the hoste.

14 And when the dewe that was fallen was ascended, beholde, a small round thing was vpon the face of the wildernes, small as the hoare frost on the earth.

15 And when the children of Israel sawe it, they sayde one to another, It is MAN, for they wist not what it was. And Moses sayd vnto them, This is the breade which the Lord hath giuen you to eate.

16 This is the thing which the Lord hath commanded: gather of it euery man according to his eating an Omer for a man according to the number of your persons: euery man shall take for them which are in his tent.

17 And the children of Israel did so, and gathered, some more, some lesse.

18 And when they did measure it with an Omer, hee that had gathered much, had nothing ouer, and he that had gathered litle, had no lacke: so euery man gathered according to his eating.

19 Moses then said vnto them, Let no man reserue thereof till morning.

20 Notwithstanding they obeyed not Moses: but some of them reserued of it till morning, and it was full of wormes, and stanke: therefore Moses was angrie with them.

21 And they gathered it euery morning, euery man according to his eating: for when the heate of the sunne came, it was melted.

22 And the sixt day they gathered twise so much bread, two Omers for one man: then all the rulers of the Congregation came and told Moses.

23 And he answered them, This is that, which the Lord hath sayde, To morowe is

the rest of the holy Sabbath vnto the Lord: bake that to day which ye wil bake, and seethe that which ye wil seethe, and all that remaineth, lay it vp to be kept till the morning for you.

24 And they laied it vp till the morning, as Moses bade, and it stanke not, neyther was there any worme therein.

25 Then Moses sayde, Eate that to day: for to day is the Sabbath vnto the Lord: to day ye shall not finde it in the fielde.

26 Sixe dayes shall yee gather it, but in the seuenth day is the Sabbath: in it there shalbe none.

27 Notwithstanding, there went out some of the people in ye seuenth day for to gather, and they found none.

28 And the Lord sayde vnto Moses, Howe long refuse yee to keepe my commandements, and my lawes?

29 Beholde, howe the Lord hath giuen you the Sabbath: therefore he giueth you the sixt day bread for two dayes: tary therefore euery man in his place: let no man goe out of his place the seuenth day.

30 So the people rested the seuenth day.

31 And the house of Israel called the name of it, MAN. and it was like to coriander seede, but white: and the taste of it was like vnto wafers made with hony.

32 And Moses said, This is that which the Lord hath commanded, Fill an Omer of it, to keepe it for your posteritie: that they may see the bread wherewith I haue fed you in wildernesse, when I brought you out of the land of Egypt.

33 Moses also said to Aaron, Take a pot and put an Omer full of MAN therein, and set it before the Lord to be kept for your posteritie.

34 As the Lord commanded Moses, so Aaron laied it vp before the Testimonie to be kept.

35 And the children of Israel did eate MAN fourtie yeres, vntill they came vnto a land inhabited: they did eate MAN vntill they came to the borders of the land of Canaan.

36 The Omer is the tenth part of the Ephah.

Exodus 17

1 And all the Congregation of the children of Israel departed from the wildernesse of Sin, by their iourneyes at the commandement of the Lord, and camped in Rephidim, where was no water for the people to drinke.

2 Wherefore the people contended with Moses, and sayde, Giue vs water that we may drinke. And Moses sayde vnto them, Why contende yee with me? wherefore do ye tempt the Lord?

3 So the people thirsted there for water, and the people murmured against Moses, and said, Wherefore hast thou thus brought vs out of Egypt to kill vs and our children and our cattel with thirst?

4 And Moses cried to the Lord, saying, What shall I do to this people? for they be almost ready to stone me.

5 And ye Lord answered to Moses, Goe before the people, and take with thee of the Elders of Israel: and thy rod, wherewith thou smotest the riuer, take in thine hand, and go:

6 Behold, I will stand there before thee vpon the rocke in Horeb, and thou shalt smite on the rocke, and water shall come out of it, that the people may drinke. And Moses did so in the sight of the Elders of Israel.

7 And he called the name of the place, Massah and Meribah, because of the contention of the children of Israel, and because they had tempted the Lord, saying, Is the Lord among vs, or no?

8 Then came Amalek and fought with Israel in Rephidim.

9 And Moses sayde to Ioshua, Chuse vs out men, and go fight with Amalek: to morowe I will stande on the toppe of the hill with the rod of God in mine hand.

10 So Ioshua did as Moses bad him, and fought with Amalek: and Moses, Aaron, and Hur, went vp to the top of the hill.

11 And when Moses helde vp his hande, Israel preuailed: but when he let his hande downe, Amalek preuailed.

12 Nowe Moses handes were heauy: therefore they tooke a stone and put it vnder him, and hee sate vpon it: and Aaron and Hur stayed vp his hands, the one on the one side, and the other on the other side: so his hands were steady vntill the going downe of the sunne.

13 And Ioshua discomfited Amalek and his people with the edge of the sword.

14 And the Lord sayde to Moses, Write this for a remembrance in the booke, and rehearse it to Ioshua: for I will vtterly put out the remembrance of Amalek from vnder heauen.

15 (And Moses builte an altar and called the name of it, Iehouah-nissi)

16 Also he said, The Lord hath sworne, that he will haue warre with Amalek from generation to generation.

Exodus 18

1 When Iethro the Priest of Midian Moses father in lawe heard all that God had done for Moses, and for Israel his people, and howe the Lord had brought Israel out of Egypt,

2 Then Iethro the father in lawe of Moses, tooke Zipporah Moses wife, (after he had sent her away)

3 And her two sonnes, (whereof the one was called Gershom: for he sayd, I haue bene an aliant in a strange land:

4 And the name of the other was Eliezer: for the God of my father, said he, was mine helpe, and deliuered me from the sword of Pharaoh)

5 And Iethro Moses father in law came with his two sonnes, and his wife vnto Moses into the wildernes, where he camped by ye mout of God.

6 And he said to Moses, I thy father in law Iethro am come to thee, and thy wife and her two sonnes with her.

7 And Moses went out to meete his father in law, and did obeisance and kissed him, and eche asked other of his welfare: and they came into the tent.

8 Then Moses told his father in law all that the Lord had done vnto Pharaoh, and to the Egyptians for Israels sake, and all the trauaile that had come vnto them by the way, and howe the Lord deliuered them.

9 And Iethro reioyced at all the goodnesse, which the Lord had shewed to Israel, and because he had deliuered them out of the hande of the Egyptians.

10 Therfore Iethro sayd, Blessed be the Lord who hath deliuered you out of the hande of the Egyptians, and out of the hand of Pharaoh: who hath also deliuered the people from vnder the hand of the Egyptians.

11 Now I know that the Lord is greater then all the gods: for as they haue dealt proudly with them, so are they recompensed.

12 Then Iethro Moses father in lawe tooke burnt offerings and sacrifices to offer vnto God. And Aaron and all the Elders of Israel came to eat bread with Moses father in law before God.

13 Now on the morow, when Moses sate to iudge the people, the people stoode about Moses from morning vnto euen.

14 And when Moses father in law saw all that he did to the people, he sayde, What is this that thou doest to the people? why sittest thou thy selfe alone, and all the people stande about thee from morning vnto euen?

15 And Moses sayd vnto his father in law, Because the people come vnto me to seeke God.

16 When they haue a matter, they come vnto me, and I iudge betweene one and another, and declare the ordinances of God, and his lawes.

17 But Moses father in law said vnto him, The thing which thou doest, is not well.

18 Thou both weariest thy selfe greatly, and this people that is with thee: for the thing is too heauie for thee: thou art not able to doe it thy selfe alone.

19 Heare nowe my voyce, (I will giue thee counsell, and God shalbe with thee) be thou for the people to Godwarde, and report thou the causes vnto God,

20 And admonish them of the ordinances, and of the lawes, and shew them the way, wherein they must walke, and the worke that they must do.

21 Moreouer, prouide thou among al the people men of courage, fearing God, men dealing truely, hating couetousnesse: and appoynt such ouer them to be rulers ouer thousandes, rulers ouer hundreths, rulers ouer fifties, and rulers ouer tennes.

22 And let them iudge the people at all seasons: but euery great matter let them bring vnto thee, and let them iudge all small causes: so shall it be easier for thee, when they shall beare the burden with thee.

23 If thou do this thing, (and God so command thee) both thou shalt be able to endure, and all this people shall also go quietly to their place.

24 So Moses obeyed the voyce of his father in law, and did all that he had sayd:

25 And Moses chose men of courage out of all Israel, and made them heads ouer the people, rulers ouer thousandes, rulers ouer hundreths, rulers ouer fifties, and rulers ouer tennes.

26 And they iudged the people at all seasons, but they brought the hard causes vnto Moses: for they iudged all small matters themselues.

27 Afterward Moses let his father in law depart, and he went into his countrey.

Exodus 19

1 In the third moneth, after the children of Israel were gone out of the lande of Egypt, the same day came they into the wildernes of Sinai.

2 For they departed from Rephidim, and came to the desart of Sinai, and camped in the wildernesse: euen there Israel camped before the mount.

3 But Moses went vp vnto God, for ye Lord had called out of the mount vnto him, saying, Thus shalt thou say to the house of Iaakob, and tell the children of Israel,

4 Ye haue seene what I did vnto the Egyptians, and how I caryed you vpon eagles wings, and haue brought you vnto me.

5 Now therefore if ye wil heare my voyce in deede, and keepe my couenant, then ye shalbe my chiefe treasure aboue all people, though all the earth be mine.

6 Yee shall be vnto mee also a kingdome of Priestes, and an holy nation. These are the words which thou shalt speake vnto the children of Israel.

7 Moses then came and called for the Elders of the people, and proposed vnto them all these things, which the Lord commanded him.

8 And the people answered all together, and sayd, All that the Lord hath commanded, we will doe. And Moses reported the wordes of the people vnto the Lord.

9 And the Lord sayd vnto Moses, Lo, I come vnto thee in a thicke cloude, that the people may heare, whiles I talke with thee, and that they may also beleeue thee for euer. (for Moses had tolde the wordes of the people vnto the Lord)

10 Moreouer, the Lord sayd vnto Moses, Goe to the people, and sanctifie them to day and to morow, and let them wash their clothes.

11 And let them be ready on the third day: for the thirde day the Lord will come downe in the sight of all the people vpon mount Sinai:

12 And thou shalt set markes vnto the people rounde about, saying, Take heede to your selues that ye goe not vp the mount, nor touche the border of it: whosoeuer toucheth the mount, shall surely die.

13 No hand shall touche it, but he shalbe stoned to death, or striken through with darts: whether it be beast or man, he shall not liue: when the horne bloweth long, they shall come vp into the mountaine.

14 Then Moses went downe from ye mount vnto the people, and sanctified the people, and they washed their clothes.

15 And he said vnto the people, Be ready on the third day, and come not at your wiues.

16 And the thirde day, when it was morning, there was thunders and lightnings, and a thicke cloude vpon the mount, and the sounde of the trumpet exceeding loude, so that all the people, that was in the campe, was afrayde.

17 Then Moses brought the people out of the tents to meete with God, and they stoode in the nether part of the mount.

18 And mount Sinai was all on smoke, because the Lord came downe vpon it in fire, and the smoke therof ascended, as the smoke of a fornace, and all the mount trembled exceedingly.

19 And when the sound of the trumpet blew long, and waxed louder and louder, Moses spake, and God answered him by voyce.

20 (For the Lord came downe vpon mount Sinai on the toppe of the mount) and when the Lord called Moses vp into the top of the mount, Moses went vp.

21 Then the Lord said vnto Moses, Go down, charge the people, that they breake not their boundes, to go vp to the Lord to gaze, least many of them perish.

22 And let the Priestes also which come to the Lord be sanctified, least the Lord destroy them.

23 And Moses sayde vnto the Lord, The people can not come vp into the mount Sinai: for thou hast charged vs, saying, Set markes on the mountaine, and sanctifie it.

24 And the Lord sayd vnto him, Go, get thee downe, and come vp, thou, and Aaron with thee: but let not the Priestes and the people breake their boundes to come vp vnto the Lord, least he destroy them.

25 So Moses went downe vnto the people, and tolde them.

Exodus 20

1 Then God spake all these wordes, saying,

2 I am the Lord thy God, which haue brought thee out of the land of Egypt, out of the house of bondage.

3 Thou shalt haue none other Gods before me.

4 Thou shalt make thee no grauen image, neither any similitude of things that are in heauen aboue, neither that are in the earth beneath, nor that are in the waters vnder the earth.

5 Thou shalt not bowe downe to them, neither serue them: for I am the Lord thy God, a ielous God, visiting the iniquitie of the fathers vpon the children, vpon the third generation and vpon the fourth of them that hate me:

6 And shewing mercie vnto thousandes to them that loue me, and keepe my commandemets.

7 Thou shalt not take the Name of the Lord thy God in vaine: for the Lord will not hold him guiltles that taketh his Name in vayne.

8 Remember the Sabbath day, to keepe it holy.

9 Six dayes shalt thou labour, and doe all thy worke,

10 But the seuenth day is the Sabbath of the Lord thy God: in it thou shalt not do any worke, thou, nor thy sonne, nor thy daughter, thy man seruant, nor thy mayde, nor thy beast, nor thy stranger that is within thy gates.

11 For in sixe dayes the Lord made the heauen and the earth, the sea, and all that in them is, and rested the seuenth day: therefore the Lord blessed the Sabbath day, and hallowed it.

12 Honour thy father and thy mother, that thy dayes may be prolonged vpon the land, which the Lord thy God giueth thee.

13 Thou shalt not kill.

14 Thou shalt not commit adulterie.

15 Thou shalt not steale.

16 Thou shalt not beare false witnes against thy neighbour.

17 Thou shalt not couet thy neighbours house, neither shalt thou couet thy neighbours wife, nor his man seruant, nor his mayde, nor his oxe, nor his asse, neyther any thing that is thy neighbours.

18 And all the people sawe the thunders, and the lightnings, and the sound of the trumpet, and the mountaine smoking and when the people saw it they fled and stoode afare off,

19 And sayde vnto Moses, Talke thou with vs, and we will heare: but let not God talke with vs, lest we die.

20 Then Moses sayde vnto the people, Feare not: for God is come to proue you, and that his feare may be before you, that ye sinne not.

21 So the people stoode afarre off, but Moses drew neere vnto the darkenes where God was.

22 And the Lord sayde vnto Moses, Thus thou shalt say vnto the children of Israel, Ye haue seene that I haue talked with you from heauen.

23 Ye shall not make therefore with me gods of siluer, nor gods of golde: you shall make you none.

24 An altar of earth thou shalt make vnto me, and thereon shalt offer thy burnt offerings, and thy peace offerings, thy sheepe, and thine oxen: in all places, where I shall put the remembrance of my Name, I will come vnto thee, and blesse thee.

25 But if thou wilt make mee an altar of stone, thou shalt not buylde it of hewen stones: for if thou lift vp thy toole vpon them, thou hast polluted them.

26 Neither shalt thou goe vp by steppes vnto mine altar, that thy filthines be not discoured thereon.

Exodus 21

1 Now these are the lawes, which thou shalt set before them:

2 If thou bye an Ebrewe seruant, he shall serue sixe yeres, and in the seuenth he shall go out free, for nothing.

3 If he came himselfe alone, he shall goe out himselfe alone: if hee were married, then his wife shall go out with him.

4 If his master haue giuen him a wife, and she hath borne him sonnes or daughters, he wife and her children shalbe her masters, but he shall goe out himselfe alone.

5 But if the seruant saye thus, I loue my master, my wife and my children, I will not goe out free,

6 Then his master shall bring him vnto the Iudges, and set him to the dore, or to the poste, and his master shall bore his eare through with a nawle, and he shall serue him for euer.

7 Likewise if a man sell his daughter to be a seruant, she shall not goe out as the men seruantes doe.

8 If shee please not her master, who hath betrothed her to him selfe, then shall hee cause to buy her: hee shall haue no power to sell her to a strange people, seeing he despised her.

9 But if he hath betrothed her vnto his sonne, he shall deale with her according to the custome of the daughters.

10 If he take him another wife, he shall not diminish her foode, her rayment, and recompence of her virginitie.

11 And if he do not these three vnto her, the shall she go out free, paying no money.

12 He that smiteth a man, and he die, shall dye the death.

13 And if a man hath not layed wayte, but God hath offered him into his hande, then I wil appoynt thee a place whither he shall flee.

14 But if a man come presumptuously vpon his neighbour to slay him with guile, thou shalt take him from mine altar, that he may die.

15 Also hee that smiteth his father or his mother, shall die the death.

16 And he that stealeth a man, and selleth him, if it be founde with him, shall die the death.

17 And hee that curseth his father or his mother, shall die the death.

18 When men also striue together, and one smite another with a stone, or with the fist, and he die not, but lieth in bed,

19 If hee rise againe and walke without vpon his staffe, then shall he that smote him go quite, saue onely hee shall beare his charges for his resting, and shall pay for his healing.

20 And if a man smite his seruant, or his maide with a rod, and he die vnder his hande, he shalbe surely punished.

21 But if he continue a day, or two dayes, hee shall not be punished: for he is his money.

22 Also if men striue and hurt a woman with childe, so that her childe depart from her, and death follow not, hee shall bee surely punished according as the womans husband shall appoynt him, or he shall pay as the Iudges determine.

23 But if death follow, then thou shalt paye life for life,

24 Eye for eye, tooth for tooth, hande for hand, foote for foote,

25 Burning for burning, wound for wounde, stripe for stripe.

26 And if a man smite his seruant in the eie, or his maide in the eye, and hath perished it, hee shall let him goe free for his eye.

27 Also if he smite out his seruants tooth, or his maides tooth, he shall let him goe out free for his tooth.

28 If an oxe gore a man or a woman, that he die, the oxe shalbe stoned to death, and his flesh shall not be eaten, but the owner of the oxe shall goe quite.

29 If the oxe were wont to push in times past, and it hath bene tolde his master, and hee hath not kept him, and after he killeth a man or a woman, the oxe shall be stoned, and his owner shall die also.

30 If there be set to him a summe of mony, then he shall pay the raunsome of his life, whatsoeuer shalbe laied vpon him.

31 Whether he hath gored a sonne or gored a daughter, he shalbe iudged after the same maner.

32 If the oxe gore a seruant or a mayde, hee shall giue vnto their master thirtie shekels of siluer, and the oxe shalbe stoned.

33 And when a man shall open a well, or when he shall dig a pit and couer it not, and an oxe or an asse fall therein,

34 The owner of the pit shall make it good, and giue money to the owners thereof, but the dead beast shalbe his.

35 And if a mans oxe hurt his neighbours oxe that he die, then they shall sel the liue oxe, and deuide the money thereof, and the dead oxe also they shall deuide.

36 Or if it bee knowen that the oxe hath vsed to push in times past, and his master hath not kept him, he shall pay oxe for oxe, but the dead shall be his owne.

Exodus 22

1 If a man steale an oxe or a sheepe, and kill it or sell it, he shall restore fiue oxen for the oxe, and foure sheepe for the sheepe.

2 If a thiefe bee founde breaking vp, and be smitten that he dye, no blood shall be shed for him.

3 But if it be in the day light, blood shall be shed for him: for he should make full restitution: if he had not wherewith, then shoulde he bee solde for his theft.

4 If the theft bee founde with him, aliue, (whether it be oxe, asse, or sheepe) he shall restore the double.

5 If a man doe hurt fielde, or vineyarde, and put in his beast to feed in an other mans fielde, he shall recompence of the best of his owne fielde, and of the best of his owne vineyard.

6 If fire breake out, and catche in ye thornes, and the stackes of corne, or the standing corne, or the fielde be consumed, he that kindled the fire shall make full restitution.

7 If a man deliuer his neighbour money or stuffe to keepe, and it be stollen out of his house, if the thiefe be found, he shall pay the double.

8 If the thiefe be not founde, then the master of the house shalbe brought vnto the Iudges to sweare, whether he hath put his hande vnto his neighbours good, or no.

9 In all maner of trespasse, whether it bee for oxen, for asse, for sheepe, for raiment, or for any maner of lost thing, which an other chalengeth to be his, the cause of both parties shall come before the iudges, and whom the Iudges condemne, he shall pay the double vnto his neighbour.

10 If a man deliuer vnto his neighbour to keepe asse, or oxe, or sheepe, or any beast, and it die, or be hurt, or taken away by enemies, and no man see it,

11 An othe of the Lord shalbe betweene the twaine, that hee hath not put his hande vnto his neighbours good, and the owner of it shall take the othe, and he shall not make it good:

12 But if it be stollen from him, he shall make restitution vnto the owner thereof.

13 If it be torne in pieces, he shall bring recorde, and shall not make that good, which is deuoured.

14 And if a man borow ought of his neighbour, and it be hurt, or els die, the owner thereof not being by, he shall surely make it good.

15 If the owner thereof bee by, hee shall not make it good: for if it be an hired thing, it came for his hire.

16 And if a man entise a maide that is not betrothed, and lie with her, hee shall endowe her, and take her to his wife.

17 If her father refuse to giue her to him, hee shall pay money, according to ye dowry of virgins.

18 Thou shalt not suffer a witch to liue.

19 Whosoeuer lieth with a beast, shall dye the death.

20 Hee that offereth vnto any gods, saue vnto the Lord onely, shalbe slaine.

21 Moreouer, thou shalt not do iniurie to a stranger, neither oppresse him: for ye were strangers in the land of Egypt.

22 Ye shall not trouble any widowe, nor fatherlesse childe.

23 If thou vexe or trouble such, and so he call and cry vnto me, I will surely heare his cry.

24 Then shall my wrath be kindled, and I will kill you with the sword, and your wiues shall be widowes, and your children fatherlesse.

25 If thou lende money to my people, that is, to the poore with thee, thou shalt not bee as an vsurer vnto him: yee shall not oppresse him with vsurie.

26 If thou take thy neighbours rayment to pledge, thou shalt restore it vnto him before the sunne go downe:

27 For that is his couering only, and this is his garment for his skin: wherin shall he sleepe? therefore when he crieth vnto mee, I will heare him: for I am mercifull.

28 Thou shalt not raile vpon the Iudges, neither speake euil of the ruler of thy people.

29 Thine abundance and thy licour shalt thou not keepe backe. The first borne of thy sonnes shalt thou giue me.

30 Likewise shalt thou do with thine oxen and with thy sheepe: seuen dayes it shall bee with his damme, and the eight day thou shalt giue it me.

31 Ye shall be an holy people vnto me, neither shall ye eate any flesh that is torne of beastes in the fielde: ye shall cast it to the dogge.

Exodus 23

1 Thou shalt not receiue a false tale, neyther shalt thou put thine hande with the wicked, to be a false witnes.

2 Thou shalt not follow a multitude to do euil, neither agree in a controuersie to decline after many and ouerthrowe the trueth.

3 Thou shalt not esteeme a poore man in his cause.

4 If thou meete thine enemies oxe, or his asse going astray, thou shalt bring him to him againe.

5 If thou see thine enemies asse lying vnder his burden, wilt thou cease to helpe him? thou shalt helpe him vp againe with it.

6 Thou shalt not ouerthrowe the right of thy poore in his sute.

7 Thou shalt keepe thee farre from a false matter, and shalt not slaye the innocent and the righteous: for I will not iustifie a wicked man.

8 Thou shalt take no gift: for the gift blindeth the wise, and peruerteth the wordes of the righteous.

9 Thou shalt not oppresse a stranger: for ye knowe the heart of a stranger, seeing yee were strangers in the land of Egypt.

10 Moreouer, sixe yeres thou shalt sowe thy land, and gather the fruites thereof,

11 But the seuenth yeere thou shalt let it rest and lie still, that the poore of thy people may eat, and what they leaue, the beastes of the fielde shall eate. In like maner thou shalt doe with thy vineyard, and with thine oliue trees.

12 Sixe dayes thou shalt do thy worke, and in the seuenth day thou shalt rest, that thine oxe, and thine asse may rest, and the sonne of thy maide and the stranger may be refreshed.

13 And ye shall take heede to all things that I haue sayde vnto you: and ye shall make no mention of the name of other gods, neither shall it be heard out of thy mouth.

14 Three times thou shalt keepe a feast vnto me in the yeere.

15 Thou shalt keepe the feast of vnleauened bread: thou shalt eate vnleauened bread seue dayes, as I commanded thee, in the season of the moneth of Abib: for in it thou camest out of Egypt: and none shall appeare before me emptie:

16 The feast also of the haruest of the first fruites of thy labours, which thou hast sowen in the fielde: and the feast of gathering fruites in the ende of the yere, when thou hast gathered in thy labours out of the fielde.

17 These three times in the yeere shall all thy men children appeare before the Lord Iehouah.

18 Thou shalt not offer the blood of my sacrifice with leauened bread: neyther shall the fatte of my sacrifice remayne vntill the morning.

19 The first of the first fruites of thy lande thou shalt bring into the house of the Lord thy God: yet shalt thou not seeth a kid in his mothers milke.

20 Behold, I send an Angel before thee, to keepe thee in the way, and to bring thee to the place which I haue prepared.

21 Beware of him, and heare his voyce, and prouoke him not: for he will not spare your misdeedes, because my name is in him.

22 But if thou hearken vnto his voyce, and do all that I speake, the I wil be an enemie vnto thine enemies, and will afflict them that afflict thee.

23 For mine Angel shall go before thee, and bring thee vnto the Amorites, and the Hittites, and the Perizzites, and the Canaanites, the Hiuites, and the Iebusites, and I will destroy them.

24 Thou shalt not bow downe to their gods, neither serue them, nor doe after the workes of them: but vtterly ouerthrowe them, and breake in pieces their images.

25 For ye shall serue the Lord your God, and he shall blesse thy bread and thy water, and I will take all sickenes away from the middes of thee.

26 There shall none cast their fruite nor be baren in thy lande: the number of thy dayes will I fulfill.

27 I will send my feare before thee, and will destroy all the people among whome thou shalt go: and I will make all thine enemies turne their backes vnto thee:

28 And I will sende hornets before thee, which shall driue out the Hiuites, the Canaanites, and the Hittites from thy face.

29 I will not cast them out from thy face in one yeere, least the land grow to a wildernes: and the beasts of the field multiplie against thee.

30 By litle and litle I will driue them out from thy face, vntill thou increase, and inherite the lande.

31 And I will make thy coastes from the red sea vnto the sea of the Philistims, and from the desert vnto the Riuer: for I will deliuer the inhabitants of the lande into your hande, and thou shalt driue them out from thy face.

32 Thou shalt make no couenant with them, nor with their gods:

33 Neither shall they dwell in thy lande, least they make thee sinne against me: for if thou serue their gods, surely it shall be thy destruction.

Exodus 24

1 Now hee had said vnto Moses, Come vp to the Lord, thou, and Aaron, Nadab, and Abihu, and seuentie of the Elders of Israel, and yee shall worship a farre off.

2 And Moses himselfe alone shall come neere to the Lord, but they shall not come neere, neither shall the people goe vp with him.

3 Afterwarde Moses came and told the people all the wordes of the Lord, and all the lawes: and all the people answered with one voyce, and said, All the things which the Lord hath said, will we doe.

4 And Moses wrote all the wordes of the Lord, and rose vp early, and set vp an altar vnder the mountaine, and twelue pillars according to the twelue tribes of Israel.

5 And he sent young men of the children of Israel, which offered burnt offrings of bieues, and sacrificed peace offrings vnto the Lord.

6 Then Moses tooke halfe of the blood, and put it in basens, and halfe of the blood he sprinckled on the altar.

7 After he tooke the booke of the couenant, and read it in the audience of the people: who said, All that the Lord hath said, we will do, and be obedient.

8 Then Moses tooke the blood, and sprinkled it on the people, and said, Behold, the blood of the couenant, which the Lord hath made with you concerning all these things.

9 Then went vp Moses and Aaron, Nadab, and Abihu, and seuentie of the Elders of Israel.

10 And they saw the God of Israel, and vnder his feete was as it were a worke of a Saphir stone, and as the very heauen when it is cleare.

11 And vpon the nobles of the children of Israel he laide not his hande: also they sawe God, and did eate and drinke.

12 And the Lord said vnto Moses, Come vp to me into the mountaine, and be there, and I will giue thee tables of stone, and the law and the commandement, which I haue written, for to teach them.

13 Then Moses rose vp, and his minister Ioshua, and Moses went vp into the mountaine of God,

14 And said vnto the Elders, Tary vs here, vntill we come againe vnto you: and beholde, Aaron, and Hur are with you: whosoeuer hath any matters, let him come to them.

15 Then Moses went vp to the mount, and the cloude couered the mountaine,

16 And the glorie of the Lord abode vpon mount Sinai, and the cloude couered it six dayes: and the seuenth day he called vnto Moses out of the middes of the cloude.

17 And the sight of the glorie of the Lord was like consuming fire on the top of the moutaine, in the eyes of the children of Israel.

18 And Moses entred into the middes of the cloude, and went vp to the mountaine: and Moses was in the mount fourtie dayes and fourty nightes.

Exodus 25

1 Then the Lord spake vnto Moses, saying,

2 Speake vnto the children of Israel, that they receiue an offring for me: of euery man, whose heart giueth it freely, ye shall take the offring for me.

3 And this is the offring which ye shall take of them, golde, and siluer, and brasse,

4 And blewe silke, and purple, and skarlet, and fine linnen, and goates heare,

5 And rammes skinnes coloured red, and the skinnes of badgers, and the wood Shittim,

6 Oyle for the light, spices for anoynting oyle, and for the perfume of sweete sauour,

7 Onix stones, and stones to be set in the Ephod, and in the brest plate.

8 Also they shall make me a Sanctuarie, that I may dwell among them.

9 According to all that I shewe thee, euen so shall ye make the forme of the Tabernacle, and the facion of all the instruments thereof.

10 They shall make also an Arke of Shittim wood, two cubites and an halfe long, and a cubite and an halfe broade, and a cubite and an halfe hie.

11 And thou shalt ouerlay it with pure golde: within and without shalt thou ouerlay it, and shalt make vpon it a crowne of golde rounde about.

12 And thou shalt cast foure rings of golde for it, and put them in the foure corners thereof: that is, two rings shalbe on the one side of it, and two rings on the other side thereof.

13 And thou shalt make barres of Shittim wood, and couer them with golde.

14 Then thou shalt put the barres in the rings by the sides of the Arke, to beare the Arke with them.

15 The barres shalbe in the rings of the Arke: they shall not be taken away from it.

16 So thou shalt put in the Arke the Testimonie which I shall giue thee.

17 Also thou shalt make a Mercie seate of pure golde, two cubites and an halfe long, and a cubite and a halfe broade.

18 And thou shalt make two Cherubims of golde: of worke beaten out with the hammer shalt thou make the at ye two endes of the Merciseate.

19 And the one Cherub shalt thou make at the one ende, and the other Cherub at the other ende: of the matter of the Mercieseate shall ye make the Cherubims, on the two endes thereof.

20 And the Cherubims shall stretche their winges on hie, couering the Mercie seate with their winges, and their faces one to another: to the Mercie seate warde shall the faces of the Cherubims be.

21 And thou shalt put the Mercieseate aboue vpon the Arke, and in the Arke thou shalt put the Testimonie, which I will giue thee,

22 And there I will declare my selfe vnto thee, and from aboue ye Mercieseate betweene ye two Cherubims, which are vpon ye Arke of ye Testimonie, I wil tel thee al things which I wil giue thee in comandement vnto ye children of Israel.

23 Thou shalt also make a Table of Shittim wood, of two cubites long, and one cubite broade, and a cubite and an halfe hie:

24 And thou shalt couer it with pure gold, and make thereto a crowne of golde round about.

25 Thou shalt also make vnto it a border of foure fingers roud about and thou shalt make a golden crowne round about the border thereof.

26 After, thou shalt make for it foure ringes of golde, and shalt put the rings in the foure corners that are in the foure feete thereof:

27 Ouer against the border shall the rings be for places for barres, to beare the Table.

28 And thou shalt make the barres of Shittim wood, and shalt ouerlay them with golde, that the Table may be borne with them.

29 Thou shalt make also dishes for it, and incense cuppes for it, and couerings for it, and goblets, wherewith it shall be couered, euen of fine golde shalt thou make them.

30 And thou shalt set vpon the Table shewe bread before me continually.

31 Also thou shalt make a Candlesticke of pure golde: of worke beaten out with the hammer shall the Candlesticke be made, his shaft, and his branches, his boules, his knops: and his floures shalbe of the same.

32 Six braunches also shall come out of the sides of it: three branches of the Candlesticke out of the one side of it, and three branches of the Candlesticke out of the other side of it.

33 Three boules like vnto almondes, one knop and one floure in one braunch: and three boules like almondes in the other branch, one knop and one floure: so throughout the sixe branches that come out of the Candlesticke.

34 And in the shaft of the Candlesticke shalbe foure boules like vnto almondes, his knops and his floures.

35 And there shalbe a knop vnder two branches made thereof: and a knop vnder two branches made thereof: and a knop vnder two branches made thereof, according to the sixe branches comming out of the Candlesticke.

36 Their knops and their branches shall bee thereof. all this shalbe one beaten worke of pure golde.

37 And thou shalt make the seuen lampes thereof: and the lampes thereof shalt thou put thereon, to giue light toward that that is before it.

38 Also the snuffers and snuffedishes thereof shalbe of pure golde.

39 Of a talent of fine gold shalt thou make it with all these instruments.

40 Looke therefore that thou make them after their facion, that was shewed thee in the mountaine.

Exodus 26

1 Afterwarde thou shalt make the Tabernacle with tenne curtaines of fine twined linen, and blewe silke, and purple, and skarlet: and in them thou shalt make Cherubims of broydered worke.

2 The length of one curtaine shalbe eight and twentie cubites, and the bredth of one curtaine, foure cubites: euery one of the curtaines shall haue one measure.

3 Fiue curtaines shalbe coupled one to an other: and the other fiue curtaines shall be coupled one to another.

4 And thou shalt make stringes of blew silke vpon the edge of the one curtaine, which is in the seluedge of the coupling: and likewise shalt thou make in the edge of the other curtaine in the seluedge, in the second coupling.

5 Fiftie strings shalt thou make in one curtaine, and fiftie stringes shalt thou make in the edge of the curtaine, which is in the second coupling: ye stringes shalbe one right against another.

6 Thou shalt make also fiftie taches of gold, and couple the curtaines one to another with the taches, and it shalbe one tabernacle.

7 Also thou shalt make curtaines of goates heare, to be a couering vpon the Tabernacle: thou shalt make them to the number of eleuen curtaines.

8 The length of a curtaine shall be thirtie cubites, and the breadth of a curtaine foure cubites: the eleuen curtaines shalbe of one measure.

9 And thou shalt couple fiue curtaynes by themselues, and the sixe curtaines by themselues: but thou shalt double the sixt curtaine vpon the forefront of the couering.

10 And thou shalt make fifty stringes in the edge of one curtayne, in the seluedge of the coupling, and fifty stringes in the edge of the other curtaine in the second coupling.

11 Likewise thou shalt make fifty taches of brasse, and fasten them on the strings, and shalt couple the couering together, that it may be one.

12 And the remnant that resteth in ye curtaines of the couering, euen the halfe curtaine that resteth, shalbe left at the backeside of the Tabernacle,

13 That the cubite on the one side, and the cubite on the other side of that which is left in the legth of the curtaines of ye couering, may remaine on either side of the Tabernacle to couer it.

14 Moreouer, for that couering thou shalt make a couering of rammes skinnes died red, and a couering of badgers skinnes aboue.

15 Also thou shalt make boards for the Tabernacle of Shittim wood to stand vp.

16 Ten cubites shalbe the length of a boarde, and a cubite and an halfe cubite the breadth of one boarde.

17 Two tenons shalbe in one boarde set in order as the feete of a ladder, one against an other: thus shalt thou make for all the boardes of the Tabernacle.

18 And thou shalt make boardes for the Tabernacle, euen twenty boardes on the South side, euen full South.

19 And thou shalt make fourty sockets of siluer vnder the twentie boardes, two

sockets vnder one boarde for his two tenons, and two sockets vnder an other boarde for his two tenons.

20 In like maner on the other side of the Tabernacle towarde the North side shalbe twentie boardes,

21 And their fourtie sockets of siluer, two sockets vnder one boarde, and two sockets vnder another board.

22 And on the side of the Tabernacle, toward the West shalt thou make sixe boards.

23 Also two boardes shalt thou make in the corners of the Tabernacle in the two sides.

24 Also they shalbe ioyned beneath, and likewise they shalbe ioyned aboue to a ring: thus shall it be for them two: they shalbe for ye two corners.

25 So they shalbe eight boardes hauing sockets of siluer, euen sixteene sockets, that is, two sockets vnder one board, and two sockets vnder an other boarde.

26 The thou shalt make fiue barres of Shittim wood for the boardes of one side of the Tabernacle,

27 And fiue barres for the boardes of the other side of the Tabernacle: also fiue barres for the boardes of the side of the Tabernacle toward the Westside.

28 And the middle barre shall goe through the middes of the boards, from ende to ende.

29 And thou shalt couer the boards with golde, and make their rings of golde, for places for the barres, and thou shalt couer the barres with golde.

30 So thou shalt reare vp the Tabernacle, according to the facion thereof, which was shewed to thee in the mount.

31 Moreouer, thou shalt make a vaile of blewe silke, and purple, and skarlet, and fine twined linen: thou shalt make it of broydred worke with Cherubims.

32 And thou shalt hang it vpon foure pillars of Shittim wood couered with gold, (whose hookes shalbe of gold) stading vpon foure sockets of siluer.

33 Afterward thou shalt hang the vaile on the hookes, that thou mayest bring in thither, that is (within the vaile) the arke of the Testimonie: and the vaile shall make you a separation betweene the Holy place and the most holy place.

34 Also thou shalt put ye Mercy seate vpon the Arke of the testimonie in the most Holy place.

35 And thou shalt set the Table without the vaile, and the Candlesticke ouer against the Table on the Southside of the Tabernacle, and thou shalt set the Table on the Northside.

36 Also thou shalt make an hanging for the dore of ye Tabernacle of blew silke, and purple, and skarlet, and fine twined linen wrought with needle.

37 And thou shalt make for the hanging fiue pillars of Shittim, and couer them with gold: their heads shalbe of golde, and thou shalt cast fiue sockets of brasse for them.

Exodus 27

1 Moreouer thou shalt make the altar of Shittim wood, fiue cubites long and fiue cubites broade (the altar shall be foure square) and the height thereof three cubites.

2 And thou shalt make it hornes in the foure corners thereof: the hornes shalbe of it selfe, and thou shalt couer it with brasse.

3 Also thou shalt make his ashpannes for his ashes and his besoms, and his basens, and his flesh-hookes, and his censers: thou shalt make all the instruments thereof of brasse.

4 And thou shalt make vnto it a grate like networke of brasse: also vpon that grate shalt thou make foure brasen rings vpon the foure corners thereof.

5 And thou shalt put it vnder the compasse of the altar beneath, that the grate may be in the middes of the altar.

6 Also thou shalt make barres for the altar, barres, I say, of Shittim wood, and shalt couer them with brasse.

7 And the barres thereof shalbe put in the rings, the which barres shalbe vpon the two sides of the altar to beare it.

8 Thou shalt make the altar holowe betweene the boardes: as God shewed thee in the mount, so shall they make it.

9 Also thou shalt make the court of the Tabernacle in the Southside, euen full South: the court shall haue curtaines of fine twined linnen, of an hundreth cubites long, for one side,

10 And it shall haue twentie pillars, with their twentie sockets of brasse: the heades of the pillars, and their filets shalbe siluer.

11 Likewise on the Northside in length there shalbe hangings of an hundreth cubites long, and the twentie pillars thereof with their twentie sockets of brasse: the heades of the pillars and the filets shalbe siluer.

12 And the breadth of the court on the Westside shall haue curtaines of fiftie cubites, with their ten pillars and their ten sockets.

13 And the breadth of the court, Eastwarde full East shall haue fiftie cubites.

14 Also hangings of fifteene cubites shalbe on the one side with their three pillars and their three sockets.

15 Likewise on the other side shalbe hangings of fifteene cubites, with their three pillars and their three sockets.

16 And in the gate of the court shalbe a vaile of twentie cubites, of blewe silke, and purple, and skarlet, and fine twined linen wrought with needle, with the foure pillars thereof and their foure sockets.

17 All the pillars of the court shall haue filets of siluer round about, with their heads of siluer, and their sockets of brasse.

18 The length of the court shalbe an hundreth cubites, and the breadth fiftie at either ende, and the height fiue cubites, and the hangings of fine twined linen, and their sockets of brasse.

19 Al the vessels of the Tabernacle for al maner seruice thereof, and all the pinnes thereof, and all the pinnes of the court shalbe brasse.

20 And thou shalt commande the children of Israel, that they bring vnto thee pure oyle oliue beaten, for the light, that the lampes may alway burne.

21 In the Tabernacle of the Congregation without the vaile, which is before the Testimony, shall Aaron and his sonnes dresse them from euening to morning before the Lord, for a statute for euer vnto their generations, to be obserued by the children of Israel.

Exodus 28

1 And cause thou thy brother Aaron to come vnto thee and his sonnes with him, from among the children of Israel, that he may serue me in the Priestes office: I meane Aaron, Nadab, and Abihu, Eleazar, and Ithamar Aarons sonnes.

2 Also thou shalt make holy garments for Aaron thy brother, glorious and beautifull.

3 Therefore thou shalt speake vnto al cunning men, whome I haue filled with the spirite of wisedome, that they make Aarons garments to consecrate him, that he may serue me in the Priestes office.

4 Nowe these shall be the garments, which they shall make, a brest plate, and an Ephod, and a robe, and a broydred coate, a miter, and a girdle. so these holy garments shall they make for Aaron thy brother, and for his sonnes, that he may serue me in the Priests office.

5 Therefore they shall take golde, and blew silke, and purple, and skarlet, and fine linnen,

6 And they shall make the Ephod of gold, blewe silke, and purple, skarlet, and fine twined linen of broydred worke.

7 The two shoulders thereof shalbe ioyned together by their two edges: so shall it be closed.

8 And the embroydred garde of the same Ephod, which shalbe vpon him, shall be of the selfe same worke and stuffe, euen of golde, blewe silke, and purple, and skarlet, and fine twined linen.

9 And thou shalt take two onix stones, and graue vpon them the names of the children of Israel:

10 Six names of them vpon the one stone, and the six names that remaine, vpon the seconde stone, according to their generations.

11 Thou shalt cause to graue the two stones according to the names of the children of Israel by a grauer of signets, that worketh and graueth in stone, and shalt make them to be set and embossed in golde.

12 And thou shalt put the two stones vpon the shoulders of the Ephod, as stones of remembrance of the children of Israel: for Aaron shall beare their names before the Lord vpon his two shoulders for a remembrance.

13 So thou shalt make bosses of golde,

14 And two cheynes of fine golde at the ende, of wrethed worke shalt thou make

them, and shalt fasten the wrethed cheynes vpon the bosses.

15 Also thou shalt make the brest plate of iudgement with broydred worke: like the worke of the Ephod shalt thou make it: of gold, blewe silke, and purple, and skarlet, and fine twined linen shalt thou make it.

16 Foure square it shall be and double, an hand bredth long and an hand bredth broade.

17 Then thou shalt set it full of places for stones, euen foure rowes of stones: the order shalbe this, a rubie, a topaze, and a carbuncle in the first rowe.

18 And in the seconde rowe thou shalt set an emeraude, a saphir, and a diamonde.

19 And in the third rowe a turkeis, an achate, and an hematite.

20 And in the fourth rowe a chrysolite, an onix, and a iasper: and they shall be set in golde in their embossements.

21 And the stones shall be according to the names of the children of Israel, twelue, according to their names, grauen as signets, euerye one after his name, and they shall bee for the twelue tribes.

22 Then thou shalt make vpon the breast plate two cheines at the endes of wrethen worke of pure golde.

23 Thou shalt make also vpon the brest plate two rings of golde, and put the two rings on the two endes of the brest plate.

24 And thou shalt put the two wrethen chaynes of golde in the two rings in the endes of the brest plate.

25 And the other two endes of the two wrethen cheines, thou shalt fasten in ye two embossements, and shalt put them vpon the shoulders of the Ephod on the foreside of it.

26 Also thou shalt make two rings of gold, which thou shalt put in the two other endes of the brest plate, vpon the border thereof, towarde the inside of the Ephod.

27 And two other rings of golde thou shalt make, and put them on the two sides of the Ephod, beneath in the forepart of it ouer against the coupling of it vpon the broydred garde of the Ephod.

28 Thus they shall binde the brest plate by his rings vnto the rings of the Ephod, with a lace of blewe silke, that it may be fast vpon the broydred garde of the Ephod, and that the brest plate be not loosed from the Ephod.

29 So Aaron shall beare the names of the children of Israel in the brest plate of iudgement vpon his heart, when he goeth into the holy place, for a remembrance continually before the Lord.

30 Also thou shalt put in the brest plate of iudgement the Vrim and the Thummim, which shalbe vpon Aarons heart, when he goeth in before the Lord: and Aaron shall beare the iudgement of the children of Israel vpon his heart before the Lord continually.

31 And thou shalt make the robe of the Ephod altogether of blewe silke.

32 And the hole for his head shalbe in the middes of it, hauing an edge of wouen woorke rounde about the coller of it: so it shalbe as the coller of an habergeon that it rent not.

33 And beneath vpon the skirtes thereof thou shalt make pomegranates of blew silke, and purple, and skarlet, round about the skirts thereof, and belles of gold betweene them round about:

34 That is, a golden bell and a pomegranate, a golden bell and a pomegranate rounde about vpon the skirtes of the robe.

35 So it shalbe vpon Aaron, when he ministreth, and his sound shalbe heard, when he goeth into the holy place before the Lord, and when he commeth out, and he shall not dye.

36 Also thou shalt make a plate of pure golde, and graue thereon, as signets are grauen, Holines To The Lord.

37 And thou shalt put it on a blew silke lace, and it shalbe vpon the miter: euen vpon the fore front of the miter shall it be.

38 So it shalbe vpon Aarons forehead, that Aaron may beare the iniquitie of the offrings, which the children of Israel shall offer in all their holy offrings: and it shall be alwayes vpon his forehead, to make them acceptable before the Lord.

39 Likewise thou shalt embroyder the fine line coat, and thou shalt make a miter of fine line, but thou shalt make a girdell of needle worke.

40 Also thou shalt make for Aarons sonnes coates, and thou shalt make the girdels, and bonets shalt thou make them for glorie and comelinesse.

41 And thou shalt put them vpon Aaron thy brother, and on his sonnes with him, and shalt anoint them, and fill their handes, and sanctifie them, that they may minister vnto me in the Priestes office.

42 Thou shalt also make them linen breeches to couer their priuities: from the loynes vnto the thighs shall they reache.

43 And they shalbe for Aaron and his sonnes when they come into the Tabernacle of the Congregation, or whe they come vnto the altar to minister in the holy place, that they commit not iniquitie, and so die. This shalbe a lawe for euer vnto him and to his seede after him.

Exodus 29

1 This thing also shalt thou do vnto them whe thou consecratest them to be my Priestes, Take a yong calfe, and two rams without blemish,

2 And vnleauened bread and cakes vnleauened tempered with oyle, and wafers vnleauened anoynted with oyle: (of fine wheate flowre shalt thou make them)

3 Then thou shalt put them in one basket, and present them in the basket with the calfe and the two rammes,

4 And shalt bring Aaron and his sonnes vnto the doore of the Tabernacle of the Congregation, and wash them with water.

5 Also thou shalt take the garments, and put vpon Aaron the tunicle, and the robe of the Ephod, and the Ephod, and the brest plate, and shalt close them to him with the broidred garde of the Ephod.

6 Then thou shalt put the miter vpon his head, and shalt put the holy crowne vpon ye miter.

7 And thou shalt take the anoynting oyle, and shalt powre vpon his head, and anoynt him.

8 And thou shalt bring his sonnes, and put coates vpon them,

9 And shalt girde them with girdles, both Aaron and his sonnes: and shalt put the bonets on them, and the Priestes office shalbe theirs for a perpetuall lawe: thou shalt also fill the hands of Aaron, and the hands of his sonnes.

10 After, thou shalt present the calfe before the Tabernacle of the Congregation, and Aaron and his sonnes shall put their handes vpon the head of the calfe.

11 So thou shalt kill the calfe before the Lord, at the doore of the Tabernacle of the Congregation.

12 Then thou shalt take of the blood of the calfe, and put it vpon the hornes of the altar with thy finger, and shalt powre al the rest of the blood at the foote of the altar.

13 Also thou shalt take all the fat that couereth the inwardes, and the kall, that is on the liuer, and the two kidneis, and the fat that is vpon them, and shalt burne them vpon the altar.

14 But the flesh of the calfe, and his skin, and his doung shalt thou burne with fire without the hoste: it is a sinne offring.

15 Thou shalt also take one ramme, and Aron and his sonnes shall put their hands vpon the head of the ramme.

16 Then thou shalt kill the ramme, and take his blood, and sprinkle it round about vpon the altar,

17 And thou shalt cut the ramme in pieces, and wash the inwards of him and his legges, and shalt put them vpon the pieces thereof, and vpon his head.

18 So thou shalt burne the whole ram vpon the altar: for it is a burnt offering vnto the Lord for a sweete sauour: it is an offering made by fire vnto the Lord.

19 And thou shalt take the other ramme, and Aaron and his sonnes shall put their handes vpon the head of the ramme.

20 Then thou shalt kill the ramme, and take of his blood and put it vpon the lappe of Aarons eare, and vpon the lappe of the right eare of his sonnes, and vpon the thumbe of their right hand, and vpon the great toe of their right foote, and shalt sprinkle the blood vpon ye altar roud about.

21 And thou shalt take of the blood that is vpon the altar, and of the anoynting oyle, and shalt sprinkle it vpon Aaron, and vpon his garments, and vpon his sonnes, and vpon the garments of his sonnes with him: so he shall be halowed,

and his clothes, and his sonnes, and the garments of his sonnes with him.

22 Also thou shalt take of the rammes ye fatte and the rumpe, euen the fat that couereth the inwards, and the kall of the liuer, and the two kidneis, and the fat that is vpon them, and the right shoulder, (for it is the ramme of consecration)

23 And one loafe of bread, and one cake of bread tempered with oyle, and one wafer, out of the basket of the vnleauened bread that is before the Lord.

24 And thou shalt put al this in the handes of Aaron, and in the handes of his sonnes, and shalt shake them to and from before the Lord.

25 Againe, thou shalt receyue them of their handes, and burne them vpon the altar besides the burnt offring for a sweete sauour before ye Lord: for this is an offering made by fire vnto the Lord.

26 Likewise thou shalt take the brest of the ram of the consecration, which is for Aaron, and shalt shake it to and from before the Lord and it shalbe thy part.

27 And thou shalt sanctifie the brest of the shaken offering, and the shoulder of the heaue offering, which was shaken to and from, and which was heaued vp of the ramme of the consecration, which was for Aaron, and which was for his sonnes.

28 And Aaron and his sonnes shall haue it by a statute for euer, of the children of Israel: for it is an heaue offering, and it shall be an heaue offering of the children of Israel, of their peace offerings, euen their heaue offering to the Lord.

29 And the holy garmets, which appertaine to Aaron, shall bee his sonnes after him, to bee anoynted therein, and to bee consecrate therein.

30 That sonne that shalbe Priest in his steade, shall put them on seuen dayes, when he commeth into the Tabernacle of the Congregation to minister in the holy place.

31 So thou shalt take the ram of the consecration, and seeth his flesh in the holy place.

32 And Aaron and his sonnes shall eate the flesh of the ram, and the bread that is in the basket, at the doore of ye Tabernacle of ye Congregation.

33 So they shall eate these thinges, whereby their attonement was made, to consecrate them, and to sanctifie them: but a stranger shall not eate thereof, because they are holy things.

34 Now if ought of the flesh of the consecration, or of the bread remaine vnto the morning, then thou shalt burne the rest with fire: it shall not be eaten, because it is an holie thing.

35 Therefore shalt thou doe thus vnto Aaron and vnto his sonnes, according to all things, which I haue commanded thee: seuen dayes shalt thou consecrate them,

36 And shalt offer euery day a calfe for a sinne offring, for reconciliation: and thou shalt cleanse the altar, when thou hast offred vpon it for reconciliation, and shalt annoynt it, to sanctifie it.

37 Seuen dayes shalt thou cleanse the altar, and sanctifie it, so the altar shalbe most holy: and whatsoeuer toucheth the altar, shalbe holy.

38 Nowe this is that which thou shalt present vpon the altar: euen two lambes of one yere olde, day by day continually.

39 The one lambe thou shalt present in the morning, and the other lambe thou shalt present at euen.

40 And with the one lambe, a tenth part of fine floure mingled with the fourth part of an Hin of beaten oyle, and the fourth part of an Hin of wine, for a drinke offring.

41 And the other lambe thou shalt present at euen: thou shalt doe thereto according to the offring of the morning, and according to the drinke offring thereof, to be a burnt offring for a sweete sauour vnto, the Lord.

42 This shalbe a continuall burnt offring in your generations at the doore of the Tabernacle of the Congregation before the Lord, where I wil make appoyntment with you, to speake there vnto thee.

43 There I will appoynt with the children of Israel, and the place shall bee sanctified by my glorie.

44 And I will sanctifie the Tabernacle of the Congregation and the altar: I will sanctifie also Aaron and his sonnes to be my Priests,

45 And I will dwell among the children of Israel, and will bee their God.

46 Then shall they knowe that I am ye Lord their God, that brought them out of the lande of Egypt, that I might dwell among them: I am the Lord their God.

Exodus 30

1 Fvrthermore thou shalt make an altar for sweete perfume, of Shittim wood thou shalt make it.

2 The length therof a cubite and the breadth thereof a cubite (it shalbe foure square) and the height thereof two cubites: the hornes thereof shalbe of the same,

3 And thou shalt ouerlay it with fine golde, both the toppe therof and the sides thereof round about, and his hornes: also thou shalt make vnto it a crowne of gold round about.

4 Besides this thou shalt make vnder this crowne two golden rings on either side: euen on euery side shalt thou make them, that they may be as places for the barres to beare it withall.

5 The which barres thou shalt make of Shittim wood, and shalt couer them with golde.

6 After thou shalt set it before the vaile, that is neere the Arke of Testimonie, before the Merciseate that is vpon the Testimonie, where I will appoynt with thee.

7 And Aaron shall burne thereon sweete incense euery morning: when hee dresseth the lampes thereof, shall he burne it.

8 Likewise at eue, when Aaron setteth vp the lampes thereof, he shall burne

incense: this perfume shalbe perpetually before ye Lord, throughout your generations.

9 Ye shall offer no strange incense thereon, nor burnt sacrifice, nor offring, neither powre any drinke offring thereon.

10 And Aaron shall make reconciliation vpon the hornes of it once in a yere with the blood of the sinne offring in the day of reconciliation: once in the yeere shall hee make reconciliation vpon it throughout your generations: this is most holy vnto the Lord.

11 Afterward the Lord spake vnto Moses, saying,

12 When thou takest the summe of the children of Israel after their nomber, then they shall giue euery man a redemption of his life vnto the Lord, when thou tellest them, that there bee no plague among the when thou countest them.

13 This shall euery man giue, that goeth into the nomber, halfe a shekel, after the shekel of the Sanctuarie: (a shekel is twentie gerahs) the halfe shekel shalbe an offring to the Lord.

14 All that are nombred from twentie yeere olde and aboue, shall giue an offring to the Lord.

15 The rich shall not passe, and the poore shall not diminish from halfe a shekel, when ye shall giue an offring vnto the Lord, for the redemption of your liues.

16 So thou shalt take the money of the redemption of the children of Israel, and shalt put it vnto the vse of the Tabernacle of the Congregation, that it may be a memoriall vnto the children of Israel before the Lord for the redemption of your liues.

17 Also the Lord spake vnto Moses, saying,

18 Thou shalt also make a lauer of brasse, and his foote of brasse to wash, and shalt put it betweene the Tabernacle of the Congregation and the Altar, and shalt put water therein.

19 For Aaron and his sonnes shall wash their hands and their feete thereat.

20 When they go into the Tabernacle of the Congregation, or when they goe vnto the Altar to minister and to make the perfume of ye burnt offring to the Lord, they shall wash themselues with water, lest they die.

21 So they shall wash their handes and their feete that they die not: and this shall be to them an ordinance for euer, both vnto him and to his seede throughout their generations.

22 Also the Lord spake vnto Moses, saying,

23 Take thou also vnto thee, principall spices of the most pure myrrhe fiue hundreth shekels, of sweete cinamon halfe so much, that is, two hundreth and fiftie, and of sweete calamus, two hundreth, and fiftie:

24 Also of cassia fiue hundreth, after the shekel of the Sanctuarie, and of oyle oliue an Hin.

25 So thou shalt make of it the oyle of holie oyntment, euen a most precious oyntment after the arte of the Apothecarie: this shalbe the oyle of holy oyntment.

26 And thou shalt anoynt the Tabernacle of the Congregation therewith, and the Arke of the Testimonie:

27 Also the Table, and al the instruments thereof, and the Candlesticke, with all the instruments thereof, and the altar of incense:

28 Also the Altar of burnt offring with al his instruments, and the lauer and his foote.

29 So thou shalt sanctifie them, and they shalbe most holy: all that shall touch them, shalbe holy.

30 Thou shalt also anoint Aaron and his sonnes, and shalt consecrate them, that they may minister vnto me in the Priests office.

31 Moreouer thou shalt speake vnto the children of Israel, saying, This shalbe an holy oynting oyle vnto me, throughout your generations.

32 None shall anoynt, mans flesh therewith, neither shall ye make any composition like vnto it: for it is holy, and shalbe holy vnto you.

33 Whosoeuer shall make the like oyntment, or whosoeuer shall put any of it vpon a stranger, euen he shalbe cut off from his people.

34 And the Lord sayd vnto Moses, Take vnto thee these spices, pure myrrhe and cleare gumme and galbanum, these odours with pure frankincense, of eche like weight:

35 Then thou shalt make of them perfume composed after the arte of the apothecarie, mingled together, pure and holy.

36 And thou shalt beate it to pouder, and shalt put of it before the Arke of the Testimonie in the Tabernacle of ye Cogregatio, where I wil make appointmet with thee: it shalbe vnto you most holy.

37 And ye shall not make vnto you any composition like this perfume, which thou shalt make: it shalbe vnto thee holy for the Lord.

38 Whosoeuer shall make like vnto that to smelll thereto, euen he shalbe cut off from his people.

Exodus 31

1 And the Lord spake vnto Moses, saying,

2 Behold, I haue called by name, Bezaleel the sonne of Vri, the sonne of Hur of the tribe of Iudah,

3 Whom I haue filled with the Spirit of God, in wisedome, and in vnderstanding and in knowledge and in all workmanship:

4 To finde out curious workes to worke in golde, and in siluer, and in brasse,

5 Also in the arte to set stones, and to carue in timber, and to worke in all maner of workmaship.

6 And behold, I haue ioyned with him Aholiab the sonne of Ahisamach of the tribe of Dan, and in the hearts of all that are wise hearted, haue I put wisdome to make all that I haue commanded thee:

7 That is, the Tabernacle of the Congregation, and the Arke of the Testimonie, and the Merciseate that shalbe therevpon, with all instruments of the Tabernacle:

8 Also the Table and the instruments thereof, and the pure Candlesticke with all his instruments, and the Altar of perfume:

9 Likewise the Altar of burnt offring with al his instruments, and the Lauer with his foote:

10 Also the garments of the ministration, and ye holy garments for Aaron ye Priest, and the garmets of his sonnes, to minister in the Priestes office.

11 And the anoynting oyle, and sweete perfume for the Sanctuarie: according to all that I haue commanded thee, shall they do.

12 Afterwarde the Lord spake vnto Moses, saying,

13 Speake thou also vnto the children of Israel, and say, Notwithstanding keepe yee my Sabbaths: for it is a signe betweene me and you in your generations, that ye may know that I the Lord do sanctifie you.

14 Ye shall therefore keepe the Sabbath: for it is holy vnto you: he that defileth it, shall die the death: therefore whosoeuer worketh therin, the same person shalbe euen cut off from among his people.

15 Six dayes shall men worke, but in the seuenth day is the Sabbath of the holy rest to the Lord: whosoeuer doeth any worke in the Sabbath day, shall dye the death.

16 Wherfore the children of Israel shall keepe the Sabbath, that they may obserue the rest throughout their generations for an euerlasting couenant.

17 It is a signe betweene me and the children of Israel for euer: for in sixe dayes the Lord made the heauen and the earth, and in the seuenth day he ceased, and rested.

18 Thus (when the Lord had made an ende of communing with Moses vpon mount Sinai) he gaue him two Tables of the Testimonie, euen tables of stone, written with the finger of God.

Exodus 32

1 Bvt when the people sawe, that Moses taryed long or he came downe from the mountaine, the people gathered themselues together against Aaron, and sayde vnto him, Vp, make vs gods to goe before vs: for of this Moses (the man that brought vs out of the land of Egypt) we knowe not what is become of him.

2 And Aaron said vnto them, Plucke off the golden earings, which are in the eares of your wiues, of your sonnes, and of your daughters, and bring them vnto me.

3 Then all ye people pluckt from them selues the golden earings, which were in their eares, and they brought them vnto Aaron.

4 Who receiued them at their handes, and facioned it with the grauing toole, and made of it a molte calfe: then they said, These be thy gods, O Israel, which brought thee out of ye lad of Egypt

5 When Aaron sawe that, he made an Altar before it: and Aaron proclaimed, saying, To morow shalbe the holy day of the Lord.

6 So they rose vp the next day in the morning, and offred burnt offerings, and brought peace offrings: also the people sate them downe to eate and drinke, and rose vp to play.

7 Then the Lord said vnto Moses, Go, get thee downe: for thy people which thou hast brought out of the land of Egypt, hath corrupted their wayes.

8 They are soone turned out of the way, which I commanded them: for they haue made them a molten calfe and haue worshipped it, and haue offered thereto, saying, These be thy gods, O Israel, which haue brought thee out of the lande of Egypt.

9 Againe the Lord said vnto Moses, I haue seene this people, and beholde, it is a stiffe necked people.

10 Nowe therefore let mee alone, that my wrath may waxe hote against them, for I wil consume the: but I wil make of thee a mighty people.

11 But Moses praied vnto the Lord his God, and said, O Lord, why doeth thy wrath waxe hote against thy people, which thou hast brought out of the lande of Egypt, with great power and with a mightie hand?

12 Wherefore shall the Egyptians speake, and say, He hath brought them out maliciously for to slay them in the mountaines, and to consume them from the earth? turne from thy fearce wrath, and change thy minde from this euill towarde thy people.

13 Remember Abraham, Izhak, and Israel thy seruants, to whom thou swarest by thine owne selfe, and saydest vnto them, I wil multiply your seede, as the starres of the heauen, and all this land, that I haue spoken of, wil I giue vnto your seede, and they shall inherit it for euer.

14 Then the Lord changed his minde from the euil, which he threatned to do vnto his people.

15 So Moses returned and went downe from the mountaine with the two Tables of the Testimonie in his hande: the Tables were written on both their sides, euen on the one side and on the other were they written.

16 And these Tables were the worke of God, and this writing was the writing of God grauen in the Tables.

17 And when Ioshua heard the noyse of the people, as they shouted, he said vnto Moses, There is a noyse of warre in the hoste.

18 Who answered, It is not the noyse of them that haue the victorie, nor the noyse of them that are ouercome: but I do heare ye noyse of singing.

19 Nowe, as soone as he came neere vnto the hoste, he sawe the calfe and the

dancing: so Moses wrath waxed hote, and he cast the Tables out of his handes, and brake them in pieces beneath the mountaine.

20 After, he tooke the calfe, which they had made, and burned it in the fire, and ground it vnto powder, and strowed it vpon the water, and made the children of Israel drinke of it.

21 Also Moses said vnto Aaron, What did this people vnto thee, that thou hast brought so great a sinne vpon them?

22 Then Aaron answered, Let not the wrath of my Lord waxe fearce: Thou knowest this people, that they are euen set on mischiefe.

23 And they sayde vnto me, Make vs gods to go before vs: for we knowe not what is become of this Moses (the man that brought vs out of the land of Egypt.)

24 Then I sayde to them, Ye that haue golde, plucke it off: and they brought it me, and I did cast it into the fire, and thereof came this calfe.

25 Moses therefore sawe that the people were naked (for Aaron had made them naked vnto their shame among their enemies)

26 And Moses stoode in ye gate of the campe, and sayde, Who pertaineth to the Lord? let him come to mee. And all the sonnes of Leui gathered themselues vnto him.

27 Then he said vnto them, Thus sayth ye Lord God of Israel, Put euery man his sworde by his side: go to and from, from gate to gate, through the hoste, and slay euery man his brother, and euery man his companion, and euery man his neighbour.

28 So the children of Leui did as Moses had commanded: and there fel of the people the same day about three thousand men.

29 (For Moses had said, Cosecrate your hands vnto the Lord this day, euen euery man vpon his sonne, and vpon his brother, that there may be giuen you a blessing this day)

30 And when the morning came, Moses sayde vnto the people, Yee haue committed a grieuous crime: but now I wil goe vp to the Lord, if I may pacifie him for your sinne.

31 Moses therefore went againe vnto ye Lord, and said, Oh, this people haue sinned a great sinne, and haue made them gods of golde.

32 Therefore now if thou pardon their sinne, thy mercy shall appeare: but if thou wilt not, I pray thee, rase me out of thy booke, which thou hast written.

33 Then the Lord sayd to Moses, Whosoeuer hath sinned against me, I will put out of my booke.

34 Go nowe therefore, bring the people vnto the place which I commanded thee: behold, mine Angel shall goe before thee, but yet in the day of my visitation I wil visite their sinne vpon them.

35 So the Lord plagued the people, because they caused Aaron to make ye calfe which he made.

Exodus 33

1 Afterward the Lord sayd vnto Moses, Depart, goe vp from hence, thou, and the people (which thou hast brought vp out of lande of Egypt) vnto the lande which I sware vnto Abraham, to Izhak and to Iaakob, saying, Vnto thy seede will I giue it.

2 And I will send an Angel before thee and will cast out the Canaanites, the Amorites, and the Hittites, and the Perizzites, the Hiuites, and the Iebusites:

3 To a lande, I say, that floweth with milke and hony: for I will not goe vp with thee, because thou art a stiffe necked people, least I consume thee in the way.

4 And when the people heard this euill tydings, they sorowed, and no man put on his best rayment.

5 (For the Lord had said to Moses, Say vnto the children of Israel, Ye are a stiffe necked people, I wil come suddenly vpon thee, and consume thee: therefore now put thy costly rayment from thee, that I may know what to do vnto thee)

6 So the children of Israel layed their good raiment from them, after Moses came downe from the mount Horeb.

7 Then Moses tooke his tabernacle, and pitched it without the host farre off from the hoste, and called it Ohel-moed. And whe any did seeke to the Lord, he went out vnto the Tabernacle of the Congregation, which was without the hoste.

8 And when Moses went out vnto the Tabernacle, all the people rose vp, and stood euery man at his tent doore, and looked after Moses, vntil he was gone into the Tabernacle.

9 And assoone as Moses was entred into the Tabernacle, the cloudie pillar descended and stood at the doore of the Tabernacle, and the Lord talked with Moses.

10 Nowe when all the people saw the cloudie pillar stand at the Tabernacle doore, all the people rose vp, and worshipped euery man in his tent doore.

11 And the Lord spake vnto Moses, face to face, as a man speaketh vnto his friende. After he turned againe into the hoste, but his seruant Ioshua the sonne of Nun a yong man, departed not out of the Tabernacle.

12 Then Moses sayde vnto the Lord, See, thou sayest vnto me, Leade this people forth, and thou hast not shewed me whom thou wilt sende with mee: thou hast sayde moreouer, I knowe thee by name, and thou hast also found grace in my sight.

13 Nowe therefore, I pray thee, if I haue founde fauour in thy sight, shewe mee nowe thy way, that I may knowe thee, and that I may finde grace in thy sight: consider also that this nation is thy people.

14 And he answered, My presence shall go with thee, and I will giue thee rest.

15 Then he sayd vnto him, If thy presence go not with vs, cary vs not hence.

16 And wherein nowe shall it be knowen, that I and thy people haue found fauour in thy sight? shall it not be when thou goest with vs? so I, and thy people shall haue preeminence before all the people that are vpon the earth.

17 And the Lord sayde vnto Moses, I will doe this also that thou hast saide: for thou hast founde grace in my sight, and I knowe thee by name.

18 Againe he sayde, I beseech thee, shewe me thy glory.

19 And he answered, I wil make all my good go before thee, and I wil proclaime the Name of the Lord before thee: for I will shewe mercy to whom I will shewe mercy, and will haue compassion on whom I will haue compassion.

20 Furthermore he sayde, Thou canst not see my face, for there shall no man see me, and liue.

21 Also the Lord sayd, Behold, there is a place by me, and thou shalt stand vpon the rocke:

22 And while my glory passeth by, I will put thee in a cleft of the rocke, and will couer thee with mine hand whiles I passe by.

23 After I will take away mine hande, and thou shalt see my backe parts: but my face shall not be seene.

Exodus 34

1 And the Lord saide vnto Moses, Hewe thee two Tables of stone, like vnto the first, and I will write vpon the Tables the wordes that were in the first Tables, which thou brakest in pieces.

2 And be ready in ye morning, that thou mayest come vp earely vnto the mount of Sinai, and waite there for me in the top of the mount.

3 But let no man come vp with thee, neither let any man be seene throughout all the mount, neyther let the sheepe nor cattell feede before this mount.

4 Then Moses hewed two Tables of stone like vnto the first, and rose vp earely in the morning, and went vp vnto the mount of Sinai, as the Lord had commanded him, and tooke in his hande two Tables of stone.

5 And the Lord descended in the cloude, and stoode with him there, and proclaimed the name of the Lord.

6 So the Lord passed before his face, and cried, The Lord, the Lord, strong, mercifull, and gracious, slowe to anger, and abundant in goodnesse and trueth,

7 Reseruing mercy for thousands, forgiuing iniquitie, and transgression and sinne, and not making the wicked innocent, visiting the iniquitie of the fathers vpon ye children, and vpon childrens children, vnto the third and fourth generation.

8 Then Moses made haste and bowed him selfe to the earth, and worshipped,

9 And sayde, O Lord, I pray thee, If I haue founde grace in thy sight, that the Lord woulde nowe goe with vs (for it is a stiffe necked people) and pardon our iniquitie and our sinne, and take vs for thine inheritance.

10 And he answered, Behold, I will make a couenant before all thy people, and will do marueiles, such as haue not bene done in all the worlde, neyther in all nations: and all the people among whom thou art, shall see the worke of the Lord: for it is a terrible thing that I will do with thee.

11 Keepe diligently that which I commande thee this day: Beholde, I will cast out before thee the Amorites, and the Canaanites, and the Hittites, and the Perizzites, and the Hiuites, and the Iebusites.

12 Take heede to thy selfe, that thou make no compact with ye inhabitantes of the land whither thou goest, least they be the cause of ruine among you:

13 But yee shall ouerthrowe their altars, and breake their images in pieces, and cut downe their groues,

14 (For thou shalt bow downe to none other god, because the Lord, whose Name is Ielous, is a ielous God)

15 Lest thou make a compact with the inhabitantes of the lande, and when they goe a whoring after their gods, and doe sacrifice vnto their gods, some man call thee, and thou eate of his sacrifice:

16 And least thou take of their daughters vnto thy sonnes, and their daughters goe a whoring after their gods, and make thy sonnes goe a whoring after their gods.

17 Thou shalt make thee no gods of metall.

18 The feast of vnleauened bread shalt thou keepe: seuen dayes shalt thou eate vnleauened bread, as I commanded thee, in ye time of the moneth of Abib: for in the moneth of Abib thou camest out of Egypt.

19 Euery male, that first openeth the wombe, shalbe mine: also all the first borne of thy flocke shalbe rekoned mine, both of beeues and sheepe.

20 But ye first of ye asse thou shalt bie out with a lambe: and if thou redeeme him not, then thou shalt breake his necke: all the first borne of thy sonnes shalt thou redeeme, and none shall appeare before me emptie.

21 Six dayes shalt thou worke, and in the seuenth day thou shalt rest: both in earing time, and in the haruest thou shalt rest.

22 Thou shalt also obserue the feast of weekes in the time of ye first fruits of wheate haruest, and the feast of gathering fruites in the ende of the yere.

23 Thrise in a yere shall all your men children appeare before the Lord Iehouah God of Israel.

24 For I wil cast out the nations before thee, and enlarge thy coasts, so that no man shall desire thy land, whe thou shalt come vp to appeare before the Lord thy God thrise in the yeere.

25 Thou shalt not offer the blood of my sacrifice with leauen, neither shall ought of the sacrifice of the feast of Passeouer be left vnto the morning.

26 The first ripe fruites of thy land thou shalt bring vnto the house of the Lord thy God: yet shalt thou not seethe a kid in his mothers milke.

27 And the Lord said vnto Moses, Write thou these words: for after the tenour of these words I haue made a couenant with thee and with Israel.

28 So hee was there with the Lord fourtie dayes and fourtie nights, and did neither eat bread nor drinke water: and hee wrote in the Tables the wordes of the couenant, euen the tenne commandements.

29 So when Moses came downe from mount Sinai, the two Tables of the Testimonie were in Moses hande, as hee descended from the mount: (nowe Moses wist not that the skinne of his face shone bright, after that God had talked with him.

30 And Aaron and all the children of Israel looked vpon Moses, and beholde, the skin of his face shone bright, and they were afraid to come neere him)

31 But Moses called them: and Aaron and all the chiefe of the congregation returned vnto him: and Moses talked with them.

32 And afterwarde all the children of Israel came neere, and he charged them with al that the Lord had said vnto him in mount Sinai.

33 So Moses made an end of comuning with them, and had put a couering vpon his face.

34 But, when Moses came before the Lord to speake with him, he tooke off the couering vntill he came out: then he came out, and spake vnto the children of Israel that which he was commanded.

35 And the children of Israel sawe the face of Moses, howe the skin of Moses face shone bright: therefore Moses put the couering vpon his face, vntill he went to speake with God.

Exodus 35

1 Then Moses assembled all the Congregation of the children of Israel, and sayd vnto them, These are the wordes which the Lord hath commanded, that ye should do them:

2 Six dayes thou shalt work, but the seuenth day shall bee vnto you the holy Sabbath of rest vnto the Lord: whosoeuer doth any worke therein, shall die.

3 Ye shall kindle no fire throughout all your habitations vpon the Sabbath day.

4 Againe, Moses spake vnto all the Congregation of the children of Israel, saying, This is the thing which the Lord commandeth, saying,

5 Take from among you an offering vnto the Lord: whosoeuer is of a willing heart, let him bring this offring to the Lord, namely golde, and siluer, and brasse:

6 Also blewe silke, and purple, and skarlet, and fine linen, and goates heare,

7 And rams skins died red, and badgers skins with Shittim wood:

8 Also oyle for light, and spices for the anointing oyle, and for the sweete incense,

9 And onix stones, and stones to be set in the Ephod, and in the brest plate.

10 And all the wise hearted among you, shall come and make all that the Lord hath commanded:

11 That is, the Tabernacle, that pauilion thereof, and his couering, and his taches and his boards, his barres, his pillars and his sockets,

12 The Arke, and the barres thereof ye Merci-seate, and the vaile that couereth it,

13 The Table, and the barres of it, and all the instruments thereof, and the shewe bread:

14 Also the Candlesticke of light and his instruments, and his lampes with the oyle for the light:

15 Likewise the Altar of perfume and his barres, and the anoynting oyle, and the sweete incense, and the vaile of the doore at the entring in of the Tabernacle,

16 The Altar of burnt offering with his brasen grate, his barres and all his instruments, the Lauer and his foote,

17 The hangings of the court, his pillars and his sockets, and the vaile of the gate of the court,

18 The pinnes of the Tabernacle, and the pinnes of the court with their cordes,

19 The ministring garments to minister in the holy place, and the holy garments for Aaron the Priest, and the garmentes of his sonnes, that they may minister in the Priests office.

20 Then all the Congregation of the children of Israel departed from the presence of Moses.

21 And euery one, whose heart encouraged him, and euery one, whose spirit made him willing, came and brought an offring to the Lord, for the worke of the Tabernacle of the Congregation, and for all his vses, and for the holy garments.

22 Both men and women, as many as were free hearted, came and brought taches and earings, and rings, and bracelets, all were iewels of golde: and euery one that offered an offring of gold vnto the Lord:

23 Euery man also, which had blewe silke, and purple, and skarlet, and fine linen, and goates heare, and rammes skinnes died red, and badgers skins, brought them.

24 All that offered an oblation of siluer and of brasse, brought the offring vnto the Lord: and euery one, that had Shittim wood for any maner worke of the ministration, brought it.

25 And all the women that were wise hearted, did spin with their hands, and brought ye spun worke, euen the blewe silke, and the purple, the skarlet, and the fine linen.

26 Likewise al the women, whose hearts were moued with knowledge, spun goates heare.

27 And ye rulers brought onix stones, and stones to be set in the Ephod, and in the brest plate:

28 Also spice, and oyle for light, and for the anoynting oyle, and for the sweete perfume.

29 Euery man and woman of the children of Israel, whose hearts moued the willingly to bring for all the worke which the Lord had commanded the to make by the hand of Moses, brought a free offring to the Lord.

30 Then Moses sayde vnto the children of Israel, Beholde, the Lord hath called by name Bezaleel the sonne of Vri, the sonne of Hur of the tribe of Iudah,

31 And hath filled him with an excellent spirit of wisdome, of vnderstanding, and of knowledge, and in all maner worke,

32 To finde out curious workes, to worke in golde, and in siluer, and in brasse,

33 And in grauing stones to set them, and in karuing of wood, euen to make any maner of fine worke.

34 And he hath put in his heart that hee may teach other: both hee, and Aholiab the sonne of Ahisamach of the tribe of Dan:

35 Them hath he filled with wisdome of heart to worke all maner of cunning and broidred, and needle worke: in blewe silke, and in purple, in skarlet, and in fine linnen and weauing, euen to do all maner of worke and subtill inuentions.

Exodus 36

1 Then wrought Bezaleel, and Aholiab, and all cunning men, to whome the Lord gaue wisedome, and vnderstanding, to knowe howe to worke all maner worke for the seruice of the Sanctuarie, according to all that the Lord had commanded.

2 For Moses had called Bezaleel, and Aholiab, and all the wise hearted men, in whose heartes the Lord had giuen wisedome, euen as many as their hearts encouraged to come vnto that worke to worke it.

3 And they receiued of Moses all the offering which the children of Israel had brought for the worke of the seruice of the Sanctuary, to make it: also they brought still vnto him free giftes euery morning.

4 So all the wise men, that wrought all the holy worke, came euery man from his worke which they wrought,

5 And spake to Moses, saying, The people bring too much, and more then ynough for the vse of the worke, which the Lord hath commanded to be made.

6 Then Moses gaue a commandement, and they caused it to be proclaymed throughout the hoste, saying, Let neither man nor woman prepare any more worke for the oblation of the Sanctuarie. So the people were stayed from offring.

7 For the stuffe they had, was sufficient for all the worke to make it, and too much.

8 All the cunning men therefore among the workemen, made for the Tabernacle ten curtaines of fine twined linnen, and of blewe silke, and purple, and skarlet: Cherubims of broydred worke made they vpon them.

9 The length of one curtaine was twentie and eight cubits, and the breadth of one curtaine foure cubites: and the curtaines were all of one cise.

10 And he coupled fiue curtaines together, and other fiue coupled he together.

11 And he made strings of blewe silke by the edge of one curtaine, in the seluedge of the coupling: likewise he made on the side of the other curtaine in the seluedge in the second coupling.

12 Fiftie strings made he in the one curtaine, and fiftie strings made he in the edge of the other curtaine, which was in the second coupling: the strings were set one against another.

13 After, he made fiftie taches of golde, and coupled the curtaines one to another with the taches: so was it one Tabernacle.

14 Also he made curtaines of goates heare for the couering vpon the Tabernacle: he made them to the nomber of eleuen curtaines.

15 The length of one curtaine had thirtie cubites, and the bredth of one curtaine foure cubites: the eleuen curtaines were of one cise.

16 And hee coupled fiue curtaines by themselues, and sixe curtaines by themselues:

17 Also he made fiftie strings vpon the edge of one curtaine in the seluedge in the coupling, and fiftie strings made hee vpon the edge of the other curtaine in the second coupling.

18 He made also fiftie taches of brasse to couple the couering that it might be one.

19 And he made a couering vpon the pauilion of rams skinnes dyed red, and a couering of badgers skinnes aboue.

20 Likewise he made the boards for the Tabernacle, of Shittim wood to stand vp.

21 The length of a board was ten cubites, and the bredth of one board was a cubite, and an halfe.

22 One board had two tenons, set in order as the feete of a ladder, one against another: thus made he for all the boardes of the Tabernacle.

23 So he made twentie boardes for the South side of the Tabernacle, euen full South.

24 And fourtie sockets of siluer made he vnder the twentie boardes, two sockets vnder one board for his two tenons, and two sockets vnder another board for his two tenons.

25 Also for the other side of the Tabernacle toward the North, he made twentie boards,

26 And their fourtie sockets of siluer, two sockets vnder one board, and two sockets vnder another boarde.

27 Likewise toward the Westside of the Tabernacle he made sixe boardes.

28 And two boardes made he in the corners of the Tabernacle, for either side,

29 And they were ioyned beneath, and likewise were made sure aboue with a ring: thus he did to both in both corners.

30 So there were eight boards and their sixteene sockets of siluer, vnder euery board two sockets.

31 After, he made barres of Shittim wood, fiue for the boards in ye one side of ye Tabernacle,

32 And fiue barres for the boardes in the other side of the Tabernacle, and fiue barres for the boards of the Tabernacle on the side toward the West.

33 And he made the middest barre to shoote through the boards, from the one end to ye other.

34 He ouerlayd also the boards with gold, and made their rings of gold for places for the barres, and couered the barres with golde.

35 Moreouer he made a vaile of blew silke, and purple, and of skarlet, and of fine twined linen: with Cherubims of broydred worke made he it:

36 And made thereunto foure pillars of Shittim, and ouerlayd them with golde: whose hookes were also of golde, and hee cast for them foure sockets of siluer.

37 And he made an hanging for the Tabernacle doore, of blew silke, and purple, and skarlet, and fine twined linnen, and needle worke,

38 And the fiue pillars of it with their hookes, and ouerlayde their chapiters and their filets with golde, but their fiue sockets were of brasse.

Exodus 37

1 After this, Bezaleel made the Arke of Shittim wood, two cubites and an halfe long and a cubite and an halfe broade, and a cubite and an halfe hie:

2 And ouerlayde it with fine golde within and without, and made a crowne of golde to it rounde about,

3 And cast for it foure rings of golde for the foure corners of it: that is, two rings for the one side of it, and two rings for the other side thereof.

4 Also he made barres of Shittim wood, and couered them with golde,

5 And put the barres in the rings by the sides of the Arke, to beare the Arke.

6 And he made the Merciseate of pure golde: two cubites and an halfe was the length thereof, and one cubite and an halfe the breadth thereof.

7 And he made two Cherubims of gold, vpon the two endes of the Merciseate: euen of worke beaten with the hammer made he them.

8 One Cherub on the one ende, and another Cherub on the other ende: of the Merciseate made he the Cherubims, at ye two endes thereof.

9 And the Cherubims spread out their wings on hie, and couered the Merciseat with their wings, and their faces were one towards another: towarde the Merciseat were the faces of the Cherubims.

10 Also he made ye Table of Shittim wood: two cubites was the length thereof, and a cubite the breadth thereof, and a cubite and an halfe the height of it.

11 And hee ouerlayde it with fine golde, and made thereto a crowne of golde round about.

12 Also he made thereto a border of an hand breadth round about, and made vpon the border a crowne of golde round about.

13 And he cast for it foure rings of gold, and put the rings in the foure corners that were in the foure feete thereof.

14 Against the border were the rings, as places for the barres to beare the Table.

15 And he made the barres of Shittim wood, and couered them with golde to beare the Table.

16 Also he made the instruments for the Table of pure golde: dishes for it, and incense cuppes for it, and goblets for it, and couerings for it, wherewith it should be couered.

17 Likewise he made the Candlesticke of pure golde: of worke beaten out with the hammer made he the Candlesticke: and his shaft, and his branche, his bolles, his knops, and his floures were of one piece.

18 And six branches came out of the sides thereof: three branches of the Candlesticke out of the one side of it, and three branches of the Candlesticke out of the other side of it.

19 In one branche three bolles made like almondes, a knop and a floure: and in another branch three bolles made like almondes, a knop and a floure: and so throughout the sixe branches that proceeded out of the Candlesticke.

20 And vpon the Candlesticke were foure bolles after the facion of almondes, the knoppes thereof and the floures thereof:

21 That is, vnder euery two branches a knop made thereof, and a knop vnder the second branch thereof, and a knop vnder the thirde branche thereof, according to the sixe branches comming out of it.

22 Their knops and their branches were of the same: it was all one beaten worke of pure gold.

23 And he made for it seuen lampes with the snuffers, and snufdishes thereof of pure golde.

24 Of a talent of pure golde made he it with all the instruments thereof.

25 Furthermore he made the perfume altar of Shittim wood: the length of it was a cubite, and the breadth of it a cubite (it was square) and two cubites hie, and the hornes thereof were of ye same.

26 And he couered it with pure gold, both the top and the sides thereof rounde about, and the hornes of it, and made vnto it a crowne of golde round about.

27 And he made two rings of gold for it, vnder the crowne thereof in the two corners of the two sides thereof, to put barres in for to beare it therewith.

28 Also he made the barres of Shittim wood, and ouerlayde them with golde.

29 And he made the holy anointing oyle, and the sweete pure incense after ye apothecaries arte.

Exodus 38

1 Also he made the altar of the burnt offering of Shittim wood: fiue cubites was the length therof, and fiue cubites the breadth thereof: it was square and three cubites hie.

2 And hee made vnto it hornes in the foure corners thereof: the hornes thereof were of the same, and he ouerlayd it with brasse.

3 Also he made al the instruments of the altar: the ashpans, and the besoms, and the basins, the fleshhookes, and the censers: all the instruments thereof made he of brasse.

4 Moreouer he made a brasen grate wrought like a net to the Altar, vnder the compasse of it beneath in the middes of it,

5 And cast foure rings of brasse for the foure endes of the grate to put barres in.

6 And he made the barres of Shittim wood, and couered them with brasse.

7 The which barres he put into the rings on the sides of the altar to beare it withall, and made it hollow within the boardes.

8 Also he made the Lauer of brasse, and the foote of it of brasse of the glasses of the women that did assemble and came together at the doore of the Tabernacle of the Congregation.

9 Finally he made the court on the South side full South: the hangings of the court were of fine twined linnen, hauing an hundreth cubites.

10 Their pillars were twentie, and their brasen sockets twentie: the hookes of the pillars, and their filets were of siluer.

11 And on the Northside the hanginges were an hundreth cubites: their pillars twentie, and their sockets of brasse twentie, the hookes of the pillars and their filets of siluer.

12 On the Westside also were hangings of fiftie cubites, their ten pillars with their ten sockets: the hookes of the pillars and their filets of siluer.

13 And toward ye Eastside, full East were hangings of fiftie cubites.

14 The hangings of the one side were fifteene cubites, their three pillars, and their three sockets:

15 And of the other side of the court gate on both sides were hangings of fifteene cubites, with their three pillars and their three sockets.

16 All the hangings of the court round about were of fine twined linen:

17 But the sockets of ye pillars were of brasse: the hookes of the pillars and their filets of siluer, and the couering of their chapiters of siluer: and all the pillars of the court were hooped about with siluer.

18 He made also the hanging of the gate of the court of needle worke, blewe silke, and purple, and skarlet, and fine twined linen euen twentie cubites long, and fiue cubites in height and bredth, like the hangings of the court.

19 And their pillars were foure with their foure sockets of brasse: their hookes of siluer, and the couering of their chapiters, and their filets of siluer.

20 But all the pins of the Tabernacle and of the court round about were of brasse.

21 These are the parts of the Tabernacle, I meane, of the Tabernacle of the Testimonie, which was appovnted by the commandement of Moses for the office of the Leuites by the hande of Ithamar sonne to Aaron the Priest.

22 So Bezaleel the sonne of Vri the sonne of Hur of the tribe of Iudah, made all that the Lord commanded Moses.

23 And with him Aholiab sonne of Ahisamach of the tribe of Dan, a cunning workeman and an embroiderer and a worker of needle work in blew silke, and in purple, and in skarlet, and in fine linen.

24 All ye gold that was occupied in all ye worke wrought for the holy place (which was the gold of the offring) was nine and twentie talents, and seuen hundreth and thirtie shekels, according to the shekel of the Sanctuarie.

25 But the siluer of them that were numbred in the Congregation, was an hundreth talents, and a thousand seuen hundreth seuentie and fiue shekels, after the shekel of the Sanctuarie.

26 A portion for a man, that is, halfe a shekel after ye shekel of the Sanctuarie, for all them that were numbred from twentie yeere olde and aboue, among six hundreth thousande, and three thousand, and fiue hundreth and fiftie men.

27 Moreouer there were an hundreth talentes of siluer, to cast ye sockets of ye Sanctuary, and the sockets of the vaile: an hundreth sockets of an hundreth talents, a talent for a socket.

28 But he made the hookes for the pillars of a thousande seuen hundreth and seuentie and fiue shekels, and ouerlayde their chapiters, and made filets about them.

29 Also the brasse of the offering was seuentie talents, and two thousande, and foure hundreth shekels.

30 Whereof he made the sockets to the doore of the Tabernacle of the Congregation, and the brasen altar, and the brasen grate which was for it, with all the instruments of the Altar,

31 And the sockets of the court round about, and the sockets for the court gate, and al the pins of the Tabernacle, and all the pins of the court round about.

Exodus 39

1 Moreouer they made garments of ministration to minister in the Sanctuarie of blewe silke, and purple, and skarlet: they made also the holy garments for Aaron, as the Lord had comanded Moses.

2 So he made the Ephod of gold, blewe silke, and purple, and skarlet, and fine twined linen.

3 And they did beate the golde into thinne plates, and cut it into wiers, to worke it in ye blewe silke and in the

purple, and in the skarlet, and in the fine linen, with broydred worke.

4 For the which they made shoulders to couple together: for it was closed by the two edges thereof.

5 And the broydred garde of his Ephod that was vpon him, was of the same stuffe, and of like worke: euen of golde, of blewe silke, and purple, and skarlet, and fine twined linen, as the Lord had commanded Moses.

6 And they wrought two Onix stones closed in ouches of golde, and graued, as signets are grauen, with the names of the children of Israel,

7 And put them on the shoulders of the Ephod, as stones for a remembrance of the children of Israel, as the Lord had commanded Moses.

8 Also he made the brestplate of broydred worke like the worke of the Ephod: to wit, of gold, blewe silke, and purple, and skarlet, and fine twined linen.

9 They made the brest plate double, and it was square, an hand breadth long, and an hand breadth broad: it was also double.

10 And they filled it with foure rowes of stones. The order was thus, a Rubie, a Topaze, and a Carbuncle in the first rowe:

11 And in the seconde rowe, an Emeraude, a Saphir, and a Diamond:

12 Also in the thirde rowe, a Turkeis, an Achate, and an Hematite:

13 Likewise in the fourth rowe, a Chrysolite, an Onix, and a Iasper: closed and set in ouches of golde.

14 So the stones were according to the names of the children of Israel, euen twelue after their names, grauen like signets euery one after his name according to the twelue tribes.

15 After, they made vpon the brest plate cheines at the endes, of wrethen worke and pure golde.

16 They made also two bosses of golde, and two golde rings, and put the two rings in the two corners of the brest plate.

17 And they put ye two wrethe cheines of gold in the two rings, in the corners of the brest plate.

18 Also the two other endes of the two wrethen chaines they fastened in the two bosses, and put the on the shoulders of the Ephod vpon the forefront of it.

19 Likewise they made two rings of gold, and put them in the two other corners of the brest plate vpon the edge of it, which was on the inside of the Ephod.

20 They made also two other golden rings, and put them on the two sides of the Ephod, beneath on the foreside of it, and ouer against his coupling aboue the broydered garde of the Ephod.

21 Then they fastened the brest plate by his rings vnto the rings of the Ephod, with a lace of blewe silke, that it might bee fast vpon the broydered garde of the Ephod, and that the brest plate should not be loosed from the Ephod, as the Lord had commanded Moses.

22 Moreouer, he made the robe of the Ephod of wouen worke, altogether of blewe silke.

23 And the hole of the robe was in the middes of it, as the coller of an habergeon, with an edge about the coller, that it shoulde not rent.

24 And they made vpon the skirts of the robe pomegranates, of blewe silke, and purple, and skarlet, and fine linen twined.

25 They made also belles of pure gold and put the belles betweene the pomegranates vpon the skirtes of the robe rounde about betweene the pomegranates.

26 A bel and a pomegranate, a bel and a pomegranate round about the skirts of the robe to minister in, as the Lord had commanded Moses.

27 After, they made coates of fine linen, of wouen worke for Aaron and for his sonnes.

28 And the miter of fine linen, and goodly bonnets of fine linen, and linen breeches of fine twined linen,

29 And the girdle of fine twined linen, and of blew silke, and purple, and skarlet, euen of needle worke, as the Lord had commanded Moses.

30 Finally they made the plate for the holy crowne of fine golde, and wrote vpon it a superscription like to the grauing of a signet, HOLINES TO THE LORD.

31 And they tied vnto it a lace of blewe silke to fasten it on hie vpon the miter, as the Lord had commanded Moses.

32 Thus was all the worke of the Tabernacle, euen of the Tabernacle of the Congregation finished: and the children of Israel did according to al that the Lord had commanded Moses: so dyd they.

33 Afterwarde they brought the Tabernacle vnto Moses, the Tabernacle and al his instruments, his taches, his boards, his barres, and his pillars, and his sockets,

34 And the couering of rammes skinnes died red, and the couerings of badgers skinnes, and the couering vaile.

35 The Arke of the Testimony, and the barres thereof, and the Merciseate,

36 The Table, with all the instruments thereof, and the shewebread,

37 The pure Candlesticke, the lampes thereof, euen the lampes set in order, and all the instruments thereof, and the oyle for light:

38 Also the golden Altar and the anoynting oyle, and the sweete incense, and the hanging of the Tabernacle doore,

39 The brasen Altar with his grate of brasse, his barres and all his instruments, the Lauer and his foote.

40 The curtaines of the court with his pillars, and his sockets, and the hanging to the court gate, and his cordes, and his pinnes, and all the instruments of the seruice of the Tabernacle, called the Tabernacle of the Congregation.

41 Finally, the ministring garmentes to serue in the Sanctuarie, and the holy garmentes for Aaron the Priest, and his sonnes garmentes to minister in the Priestes office.

42 According to euery poynt that the Lord had commanded Moses, so the children of Israel made all the worke.

43 And Moses beheld al the worke, and behold, they had done it as the Lord had commanded: so had they done: and Moses blessed them.

Exodus 40

1 Then the Lord spake vnto Moses, saying,

2 In the first day of the first moneth in the very first of the same moneth shalt thou set vp the Tabernacle, called ye Tabernacle of the Congregation:

3 And thou shalt put therein the Arke of the Testimonie, and couer the Arke with the vaile.

4 Also thou shalt bring in the Table, and set it in order as it doth require: thou shalt also bring in the Candlesticke, and light his lampes,

5 And thou shalt set ye incense Altar of gold before the Arke of the Testimonie, and put the hanging at the doore of the Tabernacle.

6 Moreouer, thou shalt set the burnt offering Altar before the doore of the Tabernacle, called the Tabernacle of the Congregation.

7 And thou shalt set the Lauer betweene the Tabernacle of the Congregation and the Altar, and put water therein.

8 Then thou shalt appoynt the courte round about, and hang vp the hanging at the courte gate.

9 After, thou shalt take the anoynting oyle, and anoynt the Tabernacle, and all that is therein, and halowe it with all the instruments thereof, that it may be holy.

10 And thou shalt anoynt the Altar of the burnt offring, and all his instruments, and shalt sanctifie the Altar, that it may bee an altar most holie.

11 Also thou shalt anoynt the Lauer, and his foote, and shalt sanctifie it.

12 Then thou shalt bring Aaron and his sonnes vnto the doore of the Tabernacle of the Congregation, and wash them with water.

13 And thou shalt put vpon Aaron the holy garmentes, and shalt anoynt him, and sanctifie him, that he may minister vnto me in the Priestes office.

14 Thou shalt also bring his sonnes, and clothe them with garments,

15 And shalt anoynt them as thou diddest anoynt their father, that they may minister vnto mee in the Priestes office: for their anoynting shall be a signe, that the Priesthood shall be euerlasting vnto them throughout their generations.

16 So Moses did according to all that ye Lord had commanded him: so did he.

17 Thus was the Tabernacle reared vp the first day of the first moneth in the seconde yeere.

18 Then Moses reared vp the Tabernacle and fastened his sockets, and set vp the boardes thereof, and put in the barres of it, and reared vp his pillars.

19 And he spred the couering ouer the Tabernacle, and put the couering of that couering on hie aboue it, as the Lord had commanded Moses.

20 And he tooke and put the Testimonie in the Arke, and put the barres in the ringes of the Arke, and set the Merciseate on hie vpon the Arke.

21 He brought also the Arke into the Tabernacle, and hanged vp the couering vaile, and couered the Arke of the Testimonie, as the Lord had commanded Moses.

22 Furthermore he put the Table in the Tabernacle of the Congregation in the Northside of the Tabernacle, without the vaile,

23 And set the bread in order before the Lord, as the Lord had commanded Moses.

24 Also he put the Candlesticke in the Tabernacle of the Congregation, ouer against the Table toward ye Southside of the Tabernacle.

25 And he lighted the lampes before the Lord, as the Lord had commanded Moses.

26 Moreouer he set the golden Altar in the Tabernacle of the Congregation before the vayle,

27 And burnt sweete incense thereon, as the Lord had commanded Moses.

28 Also he hanged vp the vayle at the doore of the Tabernacle.

29 After, he set the burnt offring Altar without the doore of the Tabernacle, called the Tabernacle of the Congregation, and offered the burnt offering and the sacrifice thereon, as the Lord had commanded Moses.

30 Likewise he set the Lauer betweene the Tabernacle of the Congregation and the Altar, and powred water therein to wash with.

31 So Moses and Aaron, and his sonnes washed their handes and their feete thereat.

32 When they went into the Tabernacle of the Congregation, and when they approched to the Altar, they washed, as the Lord had commanded Moses.

33 Finally, he reared vp the court rounde about the Tabernacle and the Altar, and hanged vp the vaile at the court gate: so Moses finished the worke.

34 Then the cloud couered the Tabernacle of the Congregation, and the glorie of the Lord filled the Tabernacle.

35 So Moses could not enter into the Tabernacle of the Congregation, because the cloude abode thereon, and the glorie of the Lord filled the Tabernacle.

36 Nowe when the cloude ascended vp from the Tabernacle, the children of Israel went forward in all their iourneyes.

37 But if the cloude ascended not, then they iourneyed not till the day that it ascended.

38 For the cloude of the Lord was vpon the Tabernacle by day, and fire was in it by night in the sight of all the house of Israel, throughout all their iourneyes.

Leviticus

Leviticus 1

1 Nowe the Lord called Moses, and spake vnto him out of the Tabernacle of the Congregation, saying,

2 Speake vnto the children of Israel, and thou shalt say vnto them, If any of you offer a sacrifice vnto the Lord, ye shall offer your sacrifice of cattell, as of beeues and of the sheepe.

3 If his sacrifice be a burnt offering of the heard, he shall offer a male without blemish, presenting him of his owne voluntarie will at the doore of the Tabernacle of the Congregation before the Lord.

4 And he shall put his hande vpon the head of the burnt offering, and it shalbe accepted to the Lord, to be his atonement.

5 And he shall kill the bullocke before the Lord, and the Priestes Aarons sonnes shall offer the blood, and shall sprinckle it round about vpon the altar, that is by the doore of the Tabernacle of the Congregation.

6 Then shall he fley the burnt offering, and cut it in pieces.

7 So the sonnes of Aaron the Priest shall put fire vpon the altar, and lay the wood in order vpon the fire.

8 Then the Priestes Aarons sonnes shall lay the parts in order, the head and the kall vpon the wood that is in the fire which is vpon the altar.

9 But the inwardes thereof and the legges thereof he shall wash in water, and the Priest shall burne all on the altar: for it is a burnt offering, an oblation made by fire, for a sweete sauour vnto the Lord.

10 And if his sacrifice for the burnt offering be of the flocks (as of the sheepe, or of the goats) he shall offer a male without blemish,

11 And he shall kill it on the Northside of the altar before the Lord, and the Priestes Aarons sonnes shall sprinckle the blood thereof rounde about vpon the altar.

12 And he shall cut it in pieces, separating his head and his kall, and the Priest shall lay them in order vpon the wood that lyeth in the fire which is on the altar:

13 But he shall wash the inwardes, and the legges with water, and the Priest shall offer the whole and burne it vpon the altar: for it is a burnt offering, an oblation made by fire for a sweete sauour vnto the Lord.

14 And if his sacrifice be a burnt offring to the Lord of ye foules, then he shall offer his sacrifice of the turtle doues, or of the yong pigeons.

15 And the Priest shall bring it vnto the altar, and wring the necke of it asunder, and burne it on the altar: and the blood thereof shall bee shed vpon the side of the altar.

16 And he shall plucke out his maw with his fethers, and cast them beside the altar on the East part in the place of the ashes.

17 And he shall cleaue it with his wings, but not deuide it asunder: and the Priest shall burne it vpon the altar vpon the wood that is in the fire: for it is a burnt offering, an oblation made by fire for a sweete sauour vnto the Lord.

Leviticus 2

1 And when any will offer a meate offering vnto the Lord, his offering shall be of fine floure, and he shall powre oyle vpon it, and put incense thereon,

2 And shall bring it vnto Aarons sonnes the Priestes, and he shall take thence his handfull of the flowre, and of the oyle with al the incense, and the Priest shall burne it for a memoriall vpon the altar: for it is an offering made by fire for a sweete sauour vnto the Lord.

3 But the remnant of the meate offering shalbe Aarons and his sonnes: for it is most holy of the Lordes offrings made by fire.

4 If thou bring also a meate offring baken in the ouen, it shalbe an vnleauened cake of fine floure mingled with oyle, or an vnleauened wafer anointed with oyle.

5 But if thy meate offring be an oblation of the frying pan, it shall be of fine flowre vnleauened, mingled with oyle.

6 And thou shalt part it in pieces, and power oyle thereon: for it is a meate offring.

7 And if thy meate offring be an oblation made in the caldron, it shalbe made of fine floure with oyle.

8 After, thou shalt bring the meate offering (that is made of these things) vnto the Lord, and shalt present it vnto the Priest, and he shall bring it to the altar,

9 And the Priest shall take from the meate offring a memoriall of it, and shall burne it vpon the altar: for it is an oblation made by fire for a sweete sauour vnto the Lord.

10 But that which is left of the meate offring, shalbe Aarons and his sonnes: for it is most holy of the offrings of the Lord made by fire.

11 All the meate offrings which ye shall offer vnto the Lord, shalbe made without leauen: for ye shall neither burne leauen nor honie in any offring of the Lord made by fire.

12 In the oblation of the first fruits ye shall offer them vnto the Lord, but they shall not be burnt vpon the altar for a sweete sauour.

13 (All the meate offrings also shalt thou season with salt, neither shalt thou suffer the salt of the couenant of thy God to be lacking from thy meate offring, but vpon all thine oblations thou shalt offer salt)

14 If then thou offer a meate offring of thy first fruites vnto the Lord, thou shalt offer for thy meate offering of thy first fruites eares of corne dryed by the fire, and wheate beaten out of the greene eares.

15 After, thou shalt put oyle vpon it, and lay incense thereon: for it is a meate offring.

16 And the Priest shall burne the memoriall of it, euen of that that is beaten, and of the oyle of it, with all the incense thereof: for it is an offring vnto the Lord made by fire.

Leviticus 3

1 Also if his oblation be a peace offering, if he will offer of the droue (whether it be male or female) he shall offer such as is without blemish, before the Lord,

2 And shall put his hande vpon the head of his offering, and kill it at the doore of the Tabernacle of the Congregation: and Aarons sonnes the Priestes shall sprinkle the blood vpon the altar rounde about.

3 So he shall offer part of the peace offerings as a sacrifice made by fire vnto the Lord, euen the fat that couereth the inwardes, and all the fat that is vpon the inwardes.

4 He shall also take away the two kidneis, and the fat that is on them, and vpon the flankes, and the kall on the liuer with the kidneis.

5 And Aarons sonnes shall burne it on the altar, with the burnt offering, which is vpon the wood, that is on the fire: this is a sacrifice made by fire for a sweete sauour vnto the Lord.

6 Also if his oblation be a peace offring vnto the Lord out of ye flocke, whether it be male or female, he shall offer it without blemish.

7 If he offer a lambe for his oblation, then he shall bring it before the Lord,

8 And lay his hand vpon the head of his offring, and shall kill it before the Tabernacle of the Congregation, and Aarons sonnes shall sprinckle the blood thereof round about vpon the altar.

9 After, of the peace offrings he shall offer an offring made by fire vnto the Lord: he shall take away the fat therof, and the rump altogether, hard by the backe bone, and the fat that couereth the inwardes, and all the fat that is vpon the inwards.

10 Also hee shall take away the two kidneis, with the fat that is vpon them, and vpon the flankes, and the kall vpon the liuer with the kidneis.

11 Then the Priest shall burne it vpon the altar, as the meat of an offring made by fire vnto the Lord.

12 Also if his offring be a goate, then shall he offer it before the Lord,

13 And shall put his hande vpon the head of it, and kill it before the Tabernacle of the Congregation, and the sonnes of Aaron shall sprinkle the blood thereof vpon the altar round about.

14 Then he shall offer thereof his offring, euen an offring made by fire vnto the Lord, the fat that couereth the inwardes, and all the fatte that is vpon the inwardes.

15 Also hee shall take away the two kidneis, and the fat that is vpon them,

and vpon ye flankes, and the kall vpon the liuer with the kidneis.

16 So the Priest shall burne them vpon the altar, as the meate of an offering made by fire for a sweete sauour: all the fatte is the Lordes.

17 This shalbe a perpetual ordinance for your generations, throughout al your dwellings, so that ye shall eate neither fatte nor blood.

Leviticus 4

1 Moreouer the Lord spake vnto Moses, saying,

2 Speake vnto the children of Israel, saying, If any shall sinne through ignorance, in any of the commandementes of the Lord, (which ought not to be done) but shall doe contrary to any of them,

3 If the Priest that is anointed doe sinne (according to the sinne of the people) then shall he offer, for his sinne which hee hath sinned, a yong bullocke without blemish vnto the Lord for a sinne offring,

4 And hee shall bring the bullocke vnto the dore of the Tabernacle of the Congregation before the Lord, and shall put his hande vpon the bullocks head, and kill the bullocke before the Lord.

5 And the Priest that is anointed shall take of the bullocks blood, and bring it into the Tabernacle of the Congregation.

6 Then the Priest shall dippe his finger in the blood, and sprinkle of the blood seuen times before the Lord, before the vaile of the Sanctuarie.

7 The Priest also shall put some of the blood before the Lord, vpon the hornes of the altar of sweete incense, which is in the Tabernacle of the Congregation, then shall hee powre all the rest of the blood of the bullocke at the foote of the altar of burnt offring, which is at the doore of the Tabernacle of the Congregation.

8 And hee shall take away all the fat of the bullocke for the sinne offring: to wit, the fat that couereth the inwardes, and all the fatte that is about the inwardes.

9 He shall take away also the two kidneis, and the fat that is vpon them, and vpon the flankes, and the kall vpon the liuer with the kidneis,

10 As it was taken away from the bullock of the peace offrings, and the Priest shall burne them vpon the altar of burnt offring.

11 But the skinne of the bullocke, and all his flesh, with his heade, and his legs, and his inwardes, and his dung shall he beare out.

12 So he shall cary the whole bullocke out of the host vnto a cleane place, where the ashes are powred, and shall burne him on ye wood in the fire: where ye ashes are cast out, shall he be burnt.

13 And if the whole Congregation of Israel shall sinne through ignorance, and the thing be hid from the eyes of the multitude, and haue done against any of the commandements of the Lord which should not be done, and haue offended:

14 When the sinne which they haue committed shalbe knowen, then the Congregation shall offer a yong bullocke for the sinne, and bring him before the Tabernacle of the Congregation,

15 And the Elders of the Congregation shall put their handes vpon the head of the bullocke before the Lord, and he shall kill the bullocke before the Lord.

16 Then the Priest that is anointed, shall bring of the bullockes blood into the Tabernacle of the Congregation,

17 And the Priest shall dip his finger in the blood, and sprinkle it seuen times before the Lord, euen before the vaile.

18 Also he shall put some of ye blood vpon the hornes of the altar, which is before the Lord, that is in the Tabernacle of the Congregation: then shall he powre all the rest, of the blood at ye foote of the altar of burnt offring, which is at the doore of the Tabernacle of the Congregation,

19 And he shall take all his fat from him, and burne it vpon the altar.

20 And the Priest shall doe with this bullocke, as he did with the bullocke for his sinne: so shall he do with this: so the Priest shall make an atonement for them, and it shalbe forgiuen them.

21 For he shall carie the bullocke without the hoste, and burne him as he burned the first bullock: for it is an offring for the sinne of the Congregation.

22 When a ruler shall sinne, and do through ignorance against any of the commandements of the Lord his God, which should not be done, and shall offend,

23 If one shewe vnto him his sinne, which he hath committed, the shall he bring for his offring an hee goat without blemish,

24 And shall lay his hand vpon the heade of the he goate, and kill it in the place where he should kill the burnt offring before the Lord: for it is a sinne offring.

25 Then the Priest shall take of the blood of the sinne offring with his finger, and put it vpon the hornes of the burnt offring altar, and shall powre the rest of his blood at the foote of the burnt offring altar,

26 And shall burne all his fat vpon the altar, as the fat of the peace offring: so the Priest shall make an atonement for him, concerning his sinne, and it shalbe forgiuen him.

27 Likewise if any of the people of ye lande shall sinne through ignoraunce in doing against any of the commandements of the Lord, which should not be done, and shall offend,

28 If one shewe him his sinne which he hath committed, then he shall bring for his offring, a shee goate without blemish for his sinne which he hath committed,

29 And he shall lay his hand vpon the head of the sinne offring, and slay the sinne offring in the place of burnt offring.

30 Then the Priest shall take of the blood thereof with his finger, and put it vpon the hornes of the burnt offring

altar, and powre all the rest of the blood thereof at the foote of the altar,

31 And shall take away all his fat, as the fat of the peace offringes is taken away, and the Priest shall burne it vpon the altar for a sweete sauour vnto the Lord, and the Priest shall make an atonement for him, and it shalbe forgiuen him.

32 And if he bring a lambe for his sinne offring, he shall bring a female without blemish,

33 And shall lay his hand vpon the head of the sinne offring, and hee shall slay it for a sinne offring in the place where hee shoulde kill the burnt offring.

34 Then the Priest shall take of the blood of the sinne offring with his finger, and put it vpon the hornes of the burnt offring altar, and shall powre al the rest of the blood thereof at the foote of the altar.

35 And he shall take away all the fat thereof, as the fatte of the lambe of the peace offrings is taken away: then the Priest shall burne it vpon the altar with the oblations of the Lord made by fire, and the Priest shall make an atonement for him concerning his sinne that he hath committed, and it shalbe forgiuen him.

Leviticus 5

1 Also if any haue sinned, that is, If he haue heard the voyce of an othe, and hee can be a witnes, whether he hath seene or knowen of it, if hee doe not vtter it, he shall beare his iniquitie:

2 Either if one touche any vncleane thing, whether it be a carion of an vncleane beast, or a carion of vncleane cattel, or a carion of vncleane creeping things, and is not ware of it, yet he is vncleane, and hath offended:

3 Eyther if hee touche any vncleannesse of man (whatsoeuer vncleannes it be, that hee is defiled with) and is not ware of it, and after commeth to the knowledge of it, he hath sinned:

4 Either if any sweare and pronounce with his lippes to do euill, or to doe good (whatsoeuer it bee that a man shall pronounce with an othe) and it be hid from him, and after knoweth that he hath offended in one of these poyntes,

5 Whe he hath sinned in any of these things, then he shall confesse that he hath sinned therein.

6 Therefore shall he bring his trespasse offring vnto the Lord for his sinne which he hath committed, euen a female from ye flocke, be it a lambe or a she goat for a sinne offring, and the Priest shall make an atonement for him, concerning his sinne.

7 But if he be not able to bring a sheepe, he shall bring for his trespas which he hath committed, two turtle doues, or two yong pigeons vnto the Lord, one for a sinne offring, and the other for a burnt offring.

8 So he shall bring them vnto the Priest, who shall offer the sinne offring first, and wring the necke of it a sunder, but not plucke it cleane off.

9 After he shall sprinkle of the blood of the sinne offring vpon the side of the altar, and the rest of the blood shall be shed at the foote of the altar: for it is a sinne offering.

10 Also he shall offer the seconde for a burnt offring as the maner is: so shall the Priest make an atonement for him (for his sinne which hee hath committed) and it shalbe forgiuen him.

11 But if he be not able to bring two turtle doues, or two yong pigeons, then he that hath sinned, shall bring for his offring, the tenth parte of an Ephah of fine floure for a sinne offring, he shall put none oyle thereto, neither put any incense thereon: for it is a sinne offering.

12 Then shall hee bring it to the Priest, and the Priest shall take his handfull of it for the remembrance thereof, and burne it vpon the altar with the offrings of the Lord made by fire: for it is a sinne offring.

13 So the Priest shall make an atonement for him, as touching his sinne that he hath committed in one of these poyntes, and it shall bee forgiuen him: and the remnant shalbe the Priests, as the meate offring.

14 And the Lord spake vnto Moses, saying,

15 If any person transgresse and sinne through ignorance by taking away things consecrated vnto the Lord, hee shall then bring for his trespasse offring vnto the Lord a ramme without blemish out of the flocke, worth two shekels of siluer by thy estimation after the shekel of the Sanctuarie, for a trespasse offring.

16 So hee shall restore that wherein hee hath offended, in taking away of the holy thing, and shall put the fift part more thereto, and giue it vnto the Priest: so the Priest shall make an atonement for him with the ram of ye trespasse offring, and it shalbe forgiuen him.

17 Also if any sinne and doe against any of the commandements of the Lord, which ought not to be done, and knowe not and sinne and beare his iniquitie,

18 Then shall he bring a ramme without blemishe out of the flocke, in thy estimation worth two shekels for a trespasse offring vnto ye Priest: and the Priest shall make an atonement for him concerning his ignorance wherein he erred, and was not ware: so it shalbe forgiuen him.

19 This is the trespasse offring for the trespasse committed against the Lord.

Leviticus 6

1 And the Lord spake vnto Moses, saying,

2 If any sinne and commit a trespasse against the Lord, and denie vnto his neighbour that, which was take him to keepe, or that which was put to him of trust, or doth by robberie, or by violence oppresse his neighbour,

3 Or hath found that which was lost, and denieth it, and sweareth falsely, for any of these things that a man doeth, wherein he sinneth:

4 When, I say, he thus sinneth and trespasseth, he shall then restore the robbery that he robbed, or the thing taken by violence which hee tooke by force, or the thing which was deliuered him to keepe, or the lost thing which he founde,

5 Or for whatsoeuer he hath sworne falsely, he shall both restore it in the whole summe, and shall adde the fift parte more thereto, and giue it vnto him to whome perteyneth, the same day that he offreth for trespasse.

6 Also he shall bring for his trespasse vnto the Lord, a ramme without blemish out of the flocke in thy estimation worth two shekels for a trespasse offring vnto the Priest.

7 And the Priest shall make an atonement for him before the Lord, and it shall be forgiuen him, whatsoeuer thing he hath done, and trespassed therein.

8 Then the Lord spake vnto Moses, saying,

9 Commaund Aaron and his sonnes, saying, This is the lawe of the burnt offring, (it is the burnt offring because it burneth vpon the altar al the night vnto the morning, and the fire burneth on the altar)

10 And the Priest shall put on his linen garment, and shall put on his linen breeches vpon his flesh, and take away the ashes when the fire hath consumed the burnt offring vpon the altar, and he shall put them beside the altar.

11 After, he shall put off his garments, and put on other raiment, and cary the ashes foorth without the hoste vnto a cleane place.

12 But the fire vpon the altar shall burne thereon and neuer be put out: wherefore the Priest shall burne wood on it euery morning, and lay the burnt offering in order vpon it, and he shall burne thereon the fat of the peace offrings.

13 The fire shall euer burne vpon the altar, and neuer go out.

14 Also this is the lawe of the meate offring, which Aarons sonnes shall offer in the presence of the Lord, before the altar.

15 He shall euen take thence his handfull of fine flowre of the meate offring and of the oyle, and all the incense which is vpon the meat offring, and shall burne it vpon the altar for a sweete sauour, as a memoriall therefore vnto the Lord:

16 But the rest thereof shall Aaron and his sonnes eate: it shalbe eaten without leauen in the holy place: in the court of the Tabernacle of the Congregation they shall eate it.

17 It shall not be baken with leauen: I haue giuen it for their portion of mine offrings made by fire: for it is as the sinne offering and as the trespasse offring.

18 All the males among the children of Aaron shall eate of it: It shalbe a statute for euer in your generations concerning the offrings of the Lord, made by fire: whatsoeuer toucheth them shall be holy.

19 Agayne the Lord spake vnto Moses, saying,

20 This is the offering of Aaron and his sonnes, which they shall offer vnto the Lord in the day when he is anointed: the tenth part of an Ephah of fine floure, for a meate offering perpetuall: halfe of it in ye morning, and halfe thereof at night.

21 In the frying panne it shalbe made with oyle: thou shalt bring it fryed, and shalt offer the baken pieces of the meate offering for a sweete sauour vnto the Lord.

22 And the Priest that is anointed in his steade, among his sonnes shall offer it: It is the Lordes ordinance for euer, it shall be burnt altogether.

23 For euery meate offring of the Priest shall be burnt altogether, it shall not be eaten.

24 Furthermore, the Lord spake vnto Moses, saying,

25 Speake vnto Aaron, and vnto his sonnes, and say, This is the Lawe of the sinne offering, In the place where the burnt offring is killed, shall the sinne offring be killed before the Lord, for it is most holy.

26 The Priest that offreth this sinne offring, shall eate it: in the holy place shall it be eaten, in the court of ye Tabernacle of the Congregation.

27 Whatsoeuer shall touch the flesh thereof shalbe holy: and when there droppeth of the blood thereof vpon a garment, thou shalt wash that whereon it droppeth in the holy place.

28 Also the earthen pot that it is sodden in, shalbe broken, but if it be sodden in a brasen pot, it shall both be scoured and washed with water.

29 All the males among the Priestes shall eate thereof, for it is most holy.

30 But no sinne offering, whose blood is brought into the Tabernacle of the Congregation to make reconciliation in the holy place, shalbe eaten, but shalbe burnt in the fire.

Leviticus 7

1 Likewise this is the lawe of the trespasse offering, it is most holy.

2 In the place where they kill the burnt offering, shall they kill the trespasse offering, and the blood thereof shall he sprinkle rounde about vpon the altar.

3 All the fat thereof also shall he offer, the rumpe, and the fat that couereth the inwardes.

4 After he shall take away the two kidneis, with the fat that is on them and vpon the flankes, and the kall on the liuer with the kidneis.

5 Then the Priest shall burne them vpon the altar, for an offring made by fire vnto the Lord: this is a trespasse offering.

6 All the males among the Priestes shall eate thereof, it shalbe eaten in the holy place, for it is most holy.

7 As the sinne offring is, so is the trespasse offring, one lawe serueth for both: that wherewith the Priest shall make atonement, shalbe his.

8 Also the Priest that offereth any mans burnt offring, shall haue the skinne of the burnt offring which he hath offered.

9 And all the meate offring that is baken in the ouen, and that is dressed in the pan, and in the frying pan, shall be the Priestes that offereth it.

10 And euery meate offering mingled with oyle, and that is dry, shall pertaine vnto all the sonnes of Aaron, to all alike.

11 Furthermore, this is the lawe of the peace offrings, which he shall offer vnto the Lord.

12 If he offer it to giue thankes, then he shall offer for his thankes offering, vnleauened cakes mingled with oyle, and vnleauened wafers anointed with oyle, and fine floure fryed with the cakes mingled with oyle.

13 He shall offer also his offring with cakes of leauened bread, for his peace offrings, to giue thankes.

14 And of all the sacrifice he shall offer one cake for an heaue offering vnto the Lord, and it shalbe the Priestes that sprinckleth the blood of the peace offrings.

15 Also the flesh of his peace offerings, for thankesgiuing, shalbe eaten the same day that it is offered: he shall leaue nothing thereof vntill the morning.

16 But if the sacrifice of his offring be a vow, or a free offering, it shalbe eaten the same day that he offreth his sacrifice: and so in the morning the residue thereof shalbe eaten.

17 But as much of the offered flesh as remaineth vnto the third day, shalbe burnt with fire.

18 For if any of the flesh of his peace offrings be eaten in the third day, he shall not be accepted that offereth it, neither shall it be reckoned vnto him, but shalbe an abomination: therefore ye person that eateth of it shall beare his iniquitie.

19 The flesh also that toucheth any vncleane thing, shall not be eaten, but burnt with fire: but of this flesh all that be cleane shall eate thereof.

20 But if any eate of the flesh of the peace offerings that pertaineth to the Lord, hauing his vncleannesse vpon him, euen the same person shalbe cut off from his people.

21 Moreouer, whe any toucheth any vncleane thing, as the vncleannesse of man, or of an vncleane beast, or of any filthie abomination, and eate of the flesh of the peace offrings, which pertaineth vnto the Lord, euen that person shalbe cut off from his people.

22 Againe ye Lord spake vnto Moses, saying,

23 Speake vnto the children of Israel, and say, Ye shall eate no fat of beeues, nor of sheepe, nor of goates:

24 Yet the fat of the dead beast, and the fat of that, which is torne with beastes, shalbe occupied to any vse, but ye shall not eate of it.

25 For whosoeuer eateth the fat of the beast, of the which he shall offer an offering made by fire to the Lord, euen the person that eateth, shalbe cut off from his people.

26 Neither shall ye eate any blood, either of foule, or of beast in all your dwellings.

27 Euery person that eateth any blood, euen the same person shall be cut off from his people.

28 And the Lord talked with Moses, saying,

29 Speake vnto the children of Israel, and say, Hee that offereth his peace offerings vnto the Lord, shall bring his gifte vnto the Lord of his peace offerings:

30 His handes shall bring the offerings of the Lord made by fire: euen the fatte with the breast shall he bring, that the breast may be shaken to and from before the Lord.

31 Then the Priest shall burne the fatte vpon the Altar, and the breast shall be Aarons and his sonnes.

32 And the right shoulder shall ye giue vnto the Priest for an heaue offering, of your peace offrings.

33 The same that offreth the blood of ye peace offrings, and the fatte, among the sonnes of Aaron, shall haue the right shoulder for his parte.

34 For the breast shaken to and from, and the shoulder lifted vp, haue I taken of the children of Israel, euen of their peace offrings, and haue giuen them vnto Aaron the Priest and vnto his sonnes by a statute for euer from among the children of Israel.

35 This is the anointing of Aaron, and the anointing of his sonnes, concerning the offerings of the Lord made by fire, in the day when he presented them to serue in the Priestes office vnto the Lord.

36 The which portions the Lord commanded to giue them in the day that he anointed them from among the children of Israel, by a statute for euer in their generations.

37 This is also the lawe of the burnt offring of the meate offring, and of the sinne offring, and of the trespasse offring, and of the consecrations, and of the peace offrings,

38 Which the Lord commanded Moses in the mount Sinai, when he commanded the children of Israel to offer their giftes vnto the Lord in the wildernesse of Sinai.

Leviticus 8

1 Afterwarde the Lord spake vnto Moses, saying,

2 Take Aaron and his sonnes with him, and the garments and the anointing oyle, and a bullocke for the sinne offring, and two rammes, and a basket of vnleauened bread,

3 And assemble all the company at the doore of the Tabernacle of the Congregation.

4 So Moses did as the Lord had commanded him, and the companie was assembled at the doore of the Tabernacle of the Congregation.

5 Then Moses said vnto the company, This is the thing which the Lord hath commanded to doe.

6 And Moses brought Aaron and his sonnes, and washed them with water,

7 And put vpon him the coate, and girded him with a girdle, and clothed him with the robe, and put the Ephod on him, which he girded with the broydred garde of the Ephod, and bounde it vnto him therewith.

8 After he put the brest plate thereon, and put in the breast plate the Vrim and the Thummim.

9 Also he put the miter vpon his head, and put vpon the miter on the fore front the golden plate, and the holy crowne, as the Lord had commanded Moses.

10 (Nowe Moses had taken the anointing oyle, and anoynted the Tabernacle, and al that was therein, and sanctified them,

11 And sprinkled thereof vpon the altar seuen times, and anointed the altar and all his instruments, and the lauer, and his foote, to sanctifie them)

12 And he powred of the anointing oyle vpon Aarons head, and anointed him, to sanctifie him.

13 After, Moses brought Aarons sonnes, and put coates vpon them, and girded them with girdles, and put bonets vpon their heades, as the Lord had commanded Moses.

14 Then he brought the bullocke for the sinne offring, and Aaron and his sonnes put their handes vpon the head of the bullocke for the sinne offring.

15 And Moses slew him, and tooke the blood, which he put vpon the hornes of the Altar roud about with his finger, and purified the altar, and powred the rest of the blood at the foote of ye altar: so he sanctified it, to make reconciliation vpon it.

16 Then he tooke all the fatte that was vpon the inwardes, and the kall of the liuer and the two kidneis, with their fat, which Moses burned vpon the Altar.

17 But the bullocke and his hide, and his flesh, and his doung, hee burnt with fire without the host as the Lord had commanded Moses.

18 Also hee brought the ram for the burnt offring, and Aaron and his sonnes put their hands vpon the head of the ramme.

19 So Moses killed it, and sprinkled the blood vpon the Altar round about,

20 And Moses cut the ram in pieces, and burnt the head with the pieces, and the fat,

21 And washed the inwardes and the legges in water: so Moses burnt the ram euery whit vpon ye Altar: for it was a burnt offring for a sweete sauour, which was made by fire vnto the Lord, as the Lord had commanded Moses.

22 After, he brought the other ram, the ram of consecrations, and Aaron and his sonnes layed their handes vpon the head of the ram,

23 Which Moses slewe, and tooke of the blood of it, and put it vpon the lappe of Aarons right eare, and vpon the thumbe of his right hand, and vpon the great toe of his right foote.

24 Then Moses brought Aarons sonnes, and put of the blood on the lap of their right eares, and vpon the thumbes of their right handes, and vpon the great toes of their right feete, and Moses sprinckled the rest of the blood vpon the Altar round about.

25 And he tooke the fat and the rumpe and all the fat that was vpon the inwards, and the kall of the liuer, and the two kidneis with their fat, and the right shoulder.

26 Also he tooke of ye basket of ye vnleauened bread that was before the Lord, one vnleauened cake and a cake of oiled bread, and one wafer, and put them on the fat, and vpon the right shoulder.

27 So hee put all in Aarons handes, and in his sonnes handes, and shooke it to and from before the Lord.

28 After, Moses tooke the out of their hands, and burnt them vpon the altar for a burnt offring: for these were consecrations for a sweete sauour which were made by fire vnto the Lord.

29 Likewise Moses tooke the breast of the ram of consecrations, and shooke it to and from before the Lord: for it was Moses portion, as the Lord had commanded Moses.

30 Also Moses tooke of the anointing oyle, and of the blood which was vpon the Altar, and sprinkled it vpon Aaron, vpon his garments, and vpon his sonnes, and on his sonnes garments with him: so hee sanctified Aaron, his garments, and his sonnes, and his sonnes garments with him.

31 Afterward Moses saide vnto Aaron and his sonnes, Seethe the flesh at the doore of the Tabernacle of the Congregation, and there eate it with the bread that is in the basket of consecrations, as I commanded, saying, Aaron and his sonnes shall eate it,

32 But that which remaineth of the flesh and of the bread, shall ye burne with fire.

33 And ye shall not depart from the doore of the Tabernacle of the Congregation seuen dayes, vntill the dayes of your consecrations bee at an ende: for seuen dayes, saide the Lord, shall hee consecrate you,

34 As hee hath done this day: so the Lord hath commanded to doe, to make an atonement for you.

35 Therefore shall yee abide at the doore of the Tabernacle of the Congregation day and night, seuen dayes, and shall keepe the watch of the Lord, that ye dye not: for so I am commanded.

36 So Aaron and his sonnes did all things which the Lord had commanded by the hand of Moses.

Leviticus 9

1 And in the eight day Moses called Aaron and his sonnes, and the Elders of Israel:

2 Then hee sayde vnto Aaron, Take thee a yong calfe for a sinne offring, and a ram for a burnt offring, both without blemish, and bring them before the Lord.

3 And vnto the children of Israel thou shalt speake, saying, Take yee an hee goate for a sinne offring, and a calfe, and a lambe, both of a yeere olde, without blemish for a burnt offring:

4 Also a bullock, and a ramme for peace offringes, to offer before the Lord, and a meate offring mingled with oyle: for to day the Lord will appeare vnto you.

5 Then they brought that which Moses commanded before the Tabernacle of the Congregation, and all the assembly drewe neere and stood before the Lord.

6 (For Moses had sayde, This is the thing, which the Lord commanded that ye should do, and the glory of the Lord shall appeare vnto you)

7 Then Moses sayd vnto Aaron, Draw neere to the Altar, and offer thy sinne offering, and thy burnt offring, and make an attonement for thee and for the people: offer also the offring of the people, and make an atonement for them, as the Lord hath commanded.

8 Aaron therefore went vnto the Altar, and killed the calfe of the sinne offring, which was for himselfe.

9 And the sonnes of Aaron brought ye blood vnto him, and he dipt his finger in the blood, and put it vpon the hornes of the Altar, and powred the rest of the blood at the foote of the Altar.

10 But the fat and the kidneis and the kall of the liuer of the sinne offring, he burnt vpon the Altar, as the Lord had commanded Moses.

11 The flesh also and the hide hee burnt with fire without the hoste.

12 After, he slewe the burnt offering, and Aarons sonnes brought vnto him the blood, which he sprinckled round about vpon the Altar.

13 Also they brought the burnt offring vnto him with the pieces thereof, and the head, and he burnt them vpon the Altar.

14 Likewise he did wash the inwardes and the legs, and burnt them vpon the burnt offring on the Altar.

15 Then he offred the peoples offring, and tooke a goate, which was the sinne offring for the people, and slewe it: and offred it for sinne, as the first:

16 So he offred the burnt offring, and prepared it, according to the maner.

17 He presented also the meate offring, and filled his hand thereof, and beside the burnt sacrifice of the morning he burnt this vpon the Altar.

18 He slewe also the bullock, and the ram for the peace offrings, that was for the people, and Arons sonnes brought vnto him the blood, which he sprinkled vpon the Altar round about,

19 With the fat of the bullocke, and of the ram, the rumpe, and that which couereth the inwards and the kidneis, and the kall of the liuer.

20 So they layed the fat vpon the breasts, and he burnt the fat vpon the Altar.

21 But the breastes and the right shoulder Aaron shooke to and from

before the Lord, as the Lord had commanded Moses.

22 So Aaron lift vp his hand toward the people, and blessed them, and came downe from offring of the sinne offring, and the burnt offring, and the peace offrings.

23 After, Moses and Aaron went into the Tabernacle of the Congregation, and came out, and blessed the people, and the glorie of the Lord appeared to all the people.

24 And there came a fire out from the Lord and consumed vpon the Altar the burnt offring and the fatte: which when all the people sawe, they gaue thankes, and fell on their faces.

Leviticus 10

1 But Nadab and Abihu, the sonnes of Aaron, tooke either of them his censor, and put fire therein, and put incense thereupon, and offred strange fire before the Lord, which hee had not commanded them.

2 Therefore a fire went out from the Lord, and deuoured them: so they dyed before the Lord.

3 Then Moses sayde vnto Aaron, This is it that the Lord spake, saying, I will bee sanctified in the that come neere me, and before all the people I will be glorified: but Aaron held his peace.

4 And Moses called Mishael and Elzaphan the sonnes of Vzziel, the vncle of Aaron, and saide vnto them, Come neere, cary your brethre from before the Sanctuarie out of the hoste.

5 Then they went, and caried them in their coates out of the host, as Moses had comaunded.

6 After, Moses saide vnto Aaron and vnto Eleazar and Ithamar his sonnes, Vncouer not your heads, neither rent your clothes, least ye dye, and least wrath come vpon all ye people: but let your brethren, all the house of Israel bewayle the burning which the Lord hath kindled.

7 And go not yee out from the doore of the Tabernacle of the Congregation, least ye dye: for the anointing oyle of the Lord is vpon you: and they did according to Moses commandement.

8 And the Lord spake vnto Aaron, saying,

9 Thou shalt not drinke wine nor strong drinke, thou, nor thy sonnes with thee, when yee come into the Tabernacle of the Congregation, lest ye die: this is an ordinance for euer throughout your generations,

10 That ye may put difference betweene the holy and the vnholy, and betweene the cleane and the vncleane,

11 And that ye may teach the children of Israel all the statutes which the Lord hath commanded them by the hand of Moses.

12 Then Moses saide vnto Aaron and vnto Eleazar and to Ithamar his sonnes that were left, Take the meate offring that remaineth of the offrings of the Lord, made by fire, and eate it without leauen beside ye altar: for it is most holy:

13 And ye shall eate it in the holy place, because it is thy duetie and thy sonnes duety of the offringes of the Lord made by fire: for so I am commanded.

14 Also the shaken breast and the heaue shoulder shall yee eate in a cleane place: thou, and thy sonnes, and thy daughters with thee: for they are giuen as thy duetie and thy sonnes duety, of the peace offringes of the children of Israel.

15 The heaue shoulder, and the shaken breast shall they bring with the offringes made by fire of the fat, to shake it to and from before the Lord, and it shalbe thine and thy sonnes with thee by a lawe for euer, as the Lord hath commanded.

16 And Moses sought the goate that was offred for sinne, and lo, it was burnt: therefore he was angrie with Eleazar and Ithamar the sonnes of Aaron, which were left aliue, saying,

17 Wherfore haue ye not eaten the sinne offring in the holy place, seeing it is most Holie? and God hath giuen it you, to beare the iniquitie of the Congregation, to make an atonement for them before the Lord.

18 Beholde, the blood of it was not brought within the holy place: ye should haue eaten it in the holy place, as I commanded.

19 And Aaron said vnto Moses, Behold, this day haue they offred their sinne offring, and their burnt offring before the Lord, and such things as thou knowest are come vnto mee: If I had eaten the sinne offring to day, should it haue bene accepted in the sight of the Lord?

20 So when Moses heard it, he was content.

Leviticus 11

1 After, the Lord spake vnto Moses and to Aaron, saying vnto them,

2 Speake vnto the children of Israel, and say, These are the beastes which yee shall eate, among all the beasts that are on the earth.

3 Whatsoeuer parteth the hoofe, and is clouen footed, and cheweth the cudde, among the beastes, that shall ye eate.

4 But of them that chewe the cud, or deuide the hoofe onely, of them yee shall not eate: as the camel, because he cheweth the cud, and deuideth not ye hoofe, he shall be vncleane vnto you.

5 Likewise the conie, because he cheweth the cud and deuideth not the hoofe, he shall bee vncleane to you.

6 Also the hare, because he cheweth the cud, and deuideth not the hoofe, he shalbe vncleane to you.

7 And the swine, because he parteth ye hoofe and is clouen footed, but cheweth not the cud, he shalbe vncleane to you.

8 Of their flesh shall yee not eate, and their carkeise shall yee not touch: for they shall bee vncleane to you.

9 These shall ye eate, of all that are in the waters: whatsoeuer hath finnes and skales in ye waters, in the seas, or in the riuers, them shall ye eate.

10 But all that haue not finnes nor skales in the seas, or in the riuers, of all that moueth in the waters, and of al liuing things that are in the waters, they shalbe an abomination vnto you.

11 They, I say, shalbe an abomination to you: ye shall not eate of their flesh, but shall abhorre their carkeis.

12 Whatsoeuer hath not fins nor skales in the waters, that shalbe abomination vnto you.

13 These shall ye haue also in abomination among the foules, they shall not be eaten: for they are an abomination, the eagle, and the goshauke, and the osprey:

14 Also the vultur, and the kite after his kinde,

15 And all rauens after their kinde:

16 The ostrich also, and the night crowe, and the seameaw, and the hauke after his kinde:

17 The litle owle also, and the connorant, and the great owle.

18 Also the redshanke and the pelicane, and the swanne:

19 The storke also, the heron after his kinde, and the lapwing, and the backe:

20 Also euery foule that creepeth and goeth vpon all foure, such shalbe an abomination vnto you.

21 Yet these shall ye eate: of euery foule that creepeth, and goeth vpon all foure which haue their feete and legs all of one to leape withal vpon the earth,

22 Of them ye shall eate these, the grashopper after his kinde, and the solean after his kinde, the hargol after his kinde, and the hagab after his kind.

23 But al other foules that creepe and haue foure feete, they shalbe abomination vnto you.

24 For by such ye shalbe polluted: whosoeuer toucheth their carkeis, shalbe vncleane vnto the euening.

25 Whosoeuer also beareth of their carkeis, shall wash his clothes, and be vncleane vntil euen.

26 Euery beast that hath clawes deuided, and is not clouen footed, nor cheweth the cud, such shalbe vncleane vnto you: euery one that toucheth them, shalbe vncleane.

27 And whatsoeuer goeth vpon his pawes among all maner beastes that goeth on all foure, such shalbe vncleane vnto you: who so doth touch their carkeis shalbe vncleane vntil the euen.

28 And he that beareth their carkeis, shall wash his clothes, and be vncleane vntill the euen: for such shalbe vncleane vnto you.

29 Also these shalbe vncleane to you amog the things that creepe and moue vpon the earth, the weasell, and the mouse, and the frog, after his kinde:

30 Also the rat, and the lizard, and the chameleon, and the stellio, and the molle.

31 These shall be vncleane to you among all that creepe: whosoeuer doeth touch them when they be dead, shalbe vncleane vntil the euen.

32 Also whatsoeuer any of the dead carkeises of them doth fall vpon, shalbe vncleane, whether it be vessel of wood, or rayment, or skinne, or sacke: whatsoeuer vessel it be that is occupied, it shalbe put in the water as vncleane vntil the euen, and so be purified.

33 But euery earthen vessel, whereinto any of them falleth, whatsoeuer is within it shalbe vncleane, and ye shall breake it.

34 Al meate also that shalbe eaten, if any such water come vpon it, shalbe vncleane: and all drinke that shalbe drunke in al such vessels shalbe vncleane.

35 And euery thing that their carkeis fall vpon, shalbe vncleane: the fornais or the pot shalbe broken: for they are vncleane, and shalbe vncleane vnto you.

36 Yet the fountaines and welles where there is plentie of water shalbe cleane: but that which toucheth their carkeises shalbe vncleane.

37 And if there fal of their dead carkeis vpon any seede, which vseth to be sowe, it shalbe cleane.

38 But if any water be powred vpon ye seede, and there fal of their dead carkeis thereon, it shall be vncleane vnto you.

39 If also any beast, whereof ye may eate, die, he that toucheth the carkeis thereof shall be vncleane vntil the euen.

40 And he that eateth of the carkeis of it, shall wash his clothes and be vncleane vntil the euen: he also that beareth the carkeis of it, shall wash his clothes, and be vncleane vntil the euen.

41 Euery creeping thing therefore that creepeth vpon the earth shalbe an abomination, and not be eaten.

42 Whatsoeuer goeth vpon the breast, and whatsoeuer goeth vpon al foure, or that hath many feete among all creeping thinges that creepe vpon the earth, ye shall not eate of them, for they shalbe abomination.

43 Ye shall not pollute your selues with any thing that creepeth, neither make your selues vncleane with them, neither defile your selues thereby: ye shall not, I say, be defiled by them,

44 For I am the Lord your God: be sanctified therefore, and be holy, for I am holy, and defile not your selues with any creeping thing, that creepeth vpon the earth.

45 For I am the Lord that brought you out of the lande of Egypt, to be your God, and that you should be holy, for I am holy.

46 This is the law of beasts, and of foules, and of euery liuing thing that moueth in the waters, and of euery thing that creepeth vpon the earth:

47 That there may be a difference betweene the vncleane and cleane, and betweene the beast that may be eaten, and the beast that ought not to be eaten.

Leviticus 12

1 And the Lord spake vnto Moses, saying,

2 Speake vnto the children of Israel, and say, When a woman hath brought forth seede, and borne a manchilde, shee shalbe vncleane seuen dayes, like as she is vncleane when she is put apart for her disease.

3 (And in the eight day, the foreskin of the childes flesh shalbe circumcised)

4 And she shall continue in the blood of her purifying three and thirtie dayes: she shall touch no halowed thing, nor come into the Sanctuarie, vntil the time of her purifying be out.

5 But if she beare a mayde childe, then shee shalbe vncleane two weekes, as when shee hath her disease: and she shall continue in the blood of her purifying three score and six dayes.

6 Nowe when the dayes of her purifying are out, (whether it be for a sonne or for a daughter) shee shall bring to the Priest a lambe of one yeere olde for a burnt offering, and a yong pigeon or a turtle doue for a sinne offring, vnto the doore of the Tabernacle of the Congregation,

7 Who shall offer it before the Lord, and make an atonement for her: so she shalbe purged of the issue of her blood this is the law for her that hath borne a male or female.

8 But if she bee not able to bring a lambe, she shall bring two turtles, or two yong pigeons: the one for a burnt offring, and the other for a sinne offring: and the Priest shall make an atonement for her: so she shall be cleane.

Leviticus 13

1 Moreouer the Lord spake vnto Moses, and to Aaron, saying,

2 The man that shall haue in the skin of his flesh a swelling or a skab, or a white spot, so that in the skinne of his flesh it be like the plague of leprosie, then he shalbe brought vnto Aaron the Priest, or vnto one of his sonnes the Priestes,

3 And the Priest shall looke on the sore in the skinne of his flesh: if the heare in the sore be turned into white, and the sore seeme to be lower then the skinne of his flesh, it is a plague of leprosie. therefore the Priest shall looke on him, and pronounce him vncleane:

4 But if the white spot be in the skinne of his flesh, and seeme not to bee lower then the skin, nor the heare thereof be turned vnto white, then the Priest shall shut vp him that hath the plague, seuen dayes.

5 After, the Priest shall looke vpon him the seuenth day: and if the plague seeme to him to abide still, and the plague growe not in the skin, the Priest shall shut him vp yet seuen dayes more.

6 Then the Priest shall looke on him againe the seuenth day, and if the plague be darke, and the sore grow not in the skinne, then the Priest shall pronounce him cleane, for it is a skab: therefore he shall washe his clothes and be cleane.

7 But if the skab growe more in the skinne, after that he is seene of ye Priest for to be purged, he shall be seene of the Priest yet againe.

8 Then the Priest shall consider, and if the skab growe in the skin, then the Priest shall pronounce him vncleane: for it is leprosie.

9 When the plague of leprosie is in a man, he shalbe brought vnto the Priest,

10 And the Priest shall see him: and if the swelling be white in ye skin, and haue made ye heare white, and there be rawe flesh in the swelling,

11 It is an old leprosie in the skin of his flesh: and the Priest shall pronounce him vncleane, and shall not shut him vp, for he is vncleane.

12 Also if the leprosie breake out in the skin, and the leprosie couer all the skin of the plague, from his head euen to his feete, wheresoeuer the Priest looketh,

13 Then the Priest shall consider: and if the leprosie couer all his flesh, he shall pronounce the plague to bee cleane, because it is all turned into whitenesse: so he shalbe cleane.

14 But if there be raw flesh on him when he is seene, he shalbe vncleane.

15 For the Priest shall see the rawe flesh, and declare him to be vncleane: for the rawe flesh is vncleane, therefore it is the leprosie.

16 Or if the rawe flesh change and be turned into white, then he shall come to the Priest,

17 And the Priest shall beholde him and if the sore be changed into white, then the Priest shall pronounce the plague cleane, for it is cleane.

18 The flesh also in whose skin there is a bile and is healed,

19 And in ye place of the bile there be a white swelling, or a white spot somewhat reddish, it shall be seene of the Priest.

20 And when the Priest seeth it, if it appeare lower then the skinne, and the heare thereof bee changed into white, ye Priest then shall pronounce him vncleane: for it is a plague of leprosie, broken out in the bile.

21 But if the Priest looke on it, and there be no white heares therein, and if it bee not lower then the skin, but be darker, then the Priest shall shut him vp seuen dayes.

22 And if it spred abroad in the flesh, ye Priest shall pronounce him vncleane, for it is a sore.

23 But if the spot continue in his place, and growe not, it is a burning bile: therefore the Priest shall declare him to be cleane.

24 If there be any flesh, in whose skin there is an hote burning, and the quick flesh of ye burning haue a white spot, somewhat reddish or pale,

25 Then the Priest shall looke vpon it: and if the heare in that spot be changed into white, and it appeare lower then the skin, it is a leprosie broken out in the burning therefore the Priest shall pronounce him vncleane: for it is the plague of leprosie.

26 But if the Priest looke on it, and there be no white heare in the spot, and be no lower then the other skinne, but be darker, then the Priest shall shut him vp seuen dayes.

27 After, the Priest shall looke on him the seuenth day: if it be growen abroad in the skinne, then the Priest shall pronounce him vncleane: for it is the plague of leprosie.

28 And if the spot abide in his place, not growing in the skin, but is darke, it is a rising of the burning: the Priest shall therefore declare him cleane, for it is the drying vp of the burning.

29 If also a man or woman hath a sore on the head or in the beard,

30 Then the Priest shall see his sore: and if it appeare lower then the skin, and there be in it a small yellow haire, then the Priest shall pronouce him vncleane: for it is a blacke spot, and leprosie of the head or of the beard.

31 And if the Priest looke on the sore of the blacke spotte, and if it seeme not lower then the skinne, nor haue any blacke heare in it, then the Priest shall shut vp him, that hath the sore of the blacke spot, seuen dayes.

32 After, in the seuenth day the Priest shall looke on the sore: and if the blacke spot growe not, and there be in it no yelowe heare, and the blacke spot seeme not lower then the skinne,

33 Then he shalbe shauen, but the place of the blacke spot shall he not shaue: but the Priest shall shut vp him, that hath the blacke spot, seuen dayes more.

34 And the seuenth day the Priest shall looke on the blacke spot: and if the blacke spot growe not in the skinne, nor seeme lower then the other skinne, then the Priest shall clense him, and hee shall wash his clothes, and be cleane.

35 But if the blacke spot growe abroad in the flesh after his clensing,

36 Then the Priest shall looke on it: and if the blacke spot grow in the skin, the Priest shall not seeke for the yelowe heare: for he is vncleane.

37 But if ye blacke spot seeme to him to abide, and that blacke heare growe therein, the blacke spot is healed, he is cleane, and the Priest shall declare him to be cleane.

38 Furthermore if there bee many white spots in the skin of the flesh of man or woman,

39 Then the Priest shall consider: and if the spots in the skin of their flesh be somewhat darke and white withall, it is but a white spot broken out in the skin: therefore he is cleane.

40 And the man whose heare is fallen off his head, and is balde, is cleane.

41 And if his head lose the heare on the forepart, and be balde before, he is cleane.

42 But if there be in the balde head, or in the balde forehead a white reddish sore, it is a leprosie springing in his balde head, or in his balde forehead.

43 Therefore the Priest shall looke vpon it, and if the rising of the sore bee white reddish in his balde head, or in his bald forehead, appearing like leprosie in the skin of the flesh,

44 He is a leper and vncleane: therefore the Priest shall pronounce him altogether vncleane: for the sore is in his head.

45 The leper also in whom the plague is, shall haue his clothes rent, and his head bare, and shall put a couering vpon his lips, and shall cry, I am vncleane, I am vncleane.

46 As long as the disease shall be vpon him, he shalbe polluted, for he is vncleane: he shall dwell alone, without the campe shall his habitation be.

47 Also the garment that the plague of leprosie is in, whether it be a wollen garment or a linen garment,

48 Whether it bee in the warpe or in ye woofe of linen or of wollen, either in a skin, or in any thing made of skin,

49 And if the sore be greene or somewhat reddish in the garment or in ye skin, or in the warpe, or in the woofe, or in any thing that is made of skin, it is a plague of leprosie and shalbe shewed vnto the Priest.

50 Then the Priest shall see the plague, and shut vp it that hath the plague, seuen dayes,

51 And shall looke on the plague the seuenth day: if the plague growe in the garment or in the warpe, or in the woofe, or in the skinne, or in any thing that is made of skin, that plague is a fretting leprosie and vncleane.

52 And hee shall burne the garment, or the warpe, or the woofe, whether it bee wollen or linen, or any thing that is made of skin, wherein the plague is: for it is a freating leprosie, therefore it shalbe burnt in the fire.

53 If the Priest yet see that the plague grow not in the garment, or in the woofe, or in whatsoeuer thing of skin it be,

54 Then the Priest shall commaund them to wash the thing wherein the plague is, and he shall shut it vp seuen dayes more.

55 Againe ye Priest shall looke on the plague, after it is washed: and if the plague haue not changed his colour, though the plague haue spred no further, it is vncleane: thou shalt burne it in the fire, for it is a fret inwarde, whether the spot bee in the bare place of the whole, or in part thereof.

56 And if the Priest see that the plague bee darker, after that it is washed, he shall cut it out of the garment, or out of the skin, or out of the warpe, or out of the woofe.

57 And if it appeare stil in ye garment or in the warpe, or in the woofe, or in any thing made of skin, it is a spreading leprie: thou shalt burne the thing wherein the plague is, in the fire.

58 If thou hast washed ye garment or ye warpe, or ye woofe, or whatsouer thing of skin it be, if the plague be departed therefrom, then shall it be washed the second time, and be cleane.

59 This is the lawe of the plague of leprosie in a garment of wollen or linnen, or in the warpe, or in the woofe, or in any thing of skin, to make it cleane or vncleane.

Leviticus 14

1 And the Lord spake vnto Moses, saying,

2 This is the law of the leper in the day of his clensing: that is, he shall be brought vnto the Priest,

3 And the Priest shall go out of the campe, and the Priest shall consider him: and if the plague of leprosie be healed in the leper,

4 Then shall the Priest commaund to take for him that is clensed, two sparrowes aliue and cleane, and cedar wood and a skarlet lace, and hyssope.

5 And the Priest shall commaund to kill one of the birdes ouer pure water in an earthen vessell.

6 After, he shall take the liue sparowe with the cedar wood, and the skarlet lace, and the hyssope, and shall dip them and the liuing sparowe in the blood of the sparowe slaine, ouer the pure water,

7 And hee shall sprinkle vpon him, that must be clensed of his leprosie, seuen times, and clense him, and shall let goe the liue sparowe into the broad fielde.

8 Then he that shall be clensed, shall wash his clothes, and shaue off all his heare, and wash himselfe in water, so he shalbe cleane: after that shall he come into the host, but shall tary without his tent seuen dayes.

9 So in the seuenth day hee shall shaue off all his heare, both his head, and his beard, and his eye browes: euen all his heare shall he shaue, and shall wash his clothes and shall wash his flesh in water: so he shalbe cleane.

10 Then in the eight day he shall take two hee lambes without blemish, and an ewe lambe of a yere olde without blemish, and three tenth deales of fine flower for a meate offering, mingled with oyle, and a pint of oyle.

11 And the Priest that maketh him cleane shall bring the man which is to bee made cleane, and those things, before the Lord, at the doore of the Tabernacle of the Congregation.

12 Then the Priest shall take one lambe, and offer him for a trespasse offering, and the pint of oyle, and shake the to and from before the Lord.

13 And hee shall kill the lambe in the place where the sinne offring and the burnt offring are slaine, euen in the holy place: for as the sinne offring is the Priests, so is the trespasse offring: for it is most holy.

14 So the Priest shall take of the blood of the trespasse offring, and put it vpon the lappe of the right eare of him that shalbe clensed, and vpon the thumbe of his right hand, and vpon the great toe of his right foote.

15 The Priest shall also take of ye pint of oyle, and powre it into the palme of his left hand,

16 And the Priest shall dip his right finger in the oyle that is in his left hand, and sprinkle of the oyle with his finger seuen times before the Lord.

17 And of the rest of the oyle that is in his hand, shall the Priest put vpon the lap of the right eare of him that is to bee clensed, and vpon the thumbe of his right hand, and vpon the great toe of his right foote, where the blood of the trespasse offring was put.

18 But the remnant of the oyle that is in the Priests hand, he shall powre vpon the head of him that is to be clensed: so the Priest shall make an atonement for him before the Lord.

19 And the Priest shall offer the sinne offring and make an atonement for him that is to bee clensed of his vncleannesse: then after shall he kill the burnt offring.

20 So the Priest shall offer ye burnt offring and the meat offring vpon ye altar and the Priest shall make an atonement for him: so he shalbe cleane.

21 But if he be poore, and not able, then he shall bring one lambe for a trespasse offring to be shaken, for his reconciliation, and a tenth deale of fine flower mingled with oyle, for a meate offring, with a pinte of oyle.

22 Also two turtle doues, or two yong pigeons, as he is able, whereof the one shalbe a sinne offering, and the other a burnt offring,

23 And he shall bring them the eight day for his clensing vnto the Priest at the doore of the Tabernacle of the Congregation before ye Lord.

24 The the Priest shall take the lambe of the trespasse offring, and the pint of oyle, and the Priest shall shake them to and from before the Lord.

25 And he shall kill the lambe of the trespasse offering, and the Priest shall take of the blood of the trespasse offring, and put it vpon the lap of his right eare that is to be clensed, and vpon ye thumbe of his right hande, and vpon the great toe of his right foote.

26 Also the Priest shall powre of the oyle into the palme of his owne left hand.

27 So ye Priest shall with his right finger sprinkle of the oyle that is in his left hand, seuen times before the Lord.

28 Then the Priest shall put of the oyle that is in his hande, vpon the lap of the right eare of him that is to bee clensed, and vpon the thumbe of his right hande, and vpon the great toe of his right foote: vpon the place of the blood of the trespasse offring.

29 But ye rest of the oyle that is in the Priests hand, he shall put vpon the head of him that is to be clensed, to make an atonement for him before the Lord.

30 Also hee shall present one of the turtle doues, or of the yong pigeons, as he is able:

31 Such, I say, as he is able, the one for a sinne offering, and the other for a burnt offring with the meate offring: so the Priest shall make an atonement for him that is to bee clensed before the Lord.

32 This is the lawe of him which hath the plague of leprosie, who is not able in his clensing to offer the whole.

33 The Lord also spake vnto Moses and to Aaron, saying,

34 When ye be come vnto the land of Canaan which I giue you in possession, if I sende the plague of leprosie in an house of the land of your possession,

35 Then he that oweth the house, shall come and tell the Priest, saying, Me thinke there is like a plague of leprosie in the house.

36 Then the Priest shall commande them to emptie the house before the Priest goe into it to see the plague, that all that is in the house be not made vncleane, and then shall the Priest goe in to see the house,

37 And hee shall marke the plague: and if the plague be in the walles of the house, and that there be deepe spots, greenish or reddish, which seeme to be lower then the wall,

38 Then the Priest shall goe out of the house to the doore of the house, and shall cause to shut vp the house seuen dayes.

39 So the Priest shall come againe ye seuenth day: and if he see that the plague bee increased in the walles of the house,

40 Then the Priest shall commande them to take away the stones wherein the plague is, and they shall cast them into a foule place without the citie.

41 Also hee shall cause to scrape the house within rounde about, and powre the dust, that they haue pared off, without the citie in an vncleane place.

42 And they shall take other stones, and put them in the places of those stones, and shall take other mortar, to plaister the house with.

43 But if the plague come againe and breake out in the house, after that he hath taken away ye stones, and after that hee hath scraped and playstered the house,

44 Then the Priest shall come and see: and if the plague growe in the house, it is a freating leprosie in the house: it is therefore vncleane.

45 And hee shall breake downe the house, with the stones of it, and the timber thereof, and all the mortar of the house, and hee shall carie them out of the citie vnto an vncleane place.

46 Moreouer he that goeth into the house all the while that it is shut vp, hee shall bee vncleane vntill the euen.

47 Hee also that sleepeth in the house shall wash his clothes: he likewise that eateth in the house, shall wash his clothes.

48 But if the Priest shall come and see, that the plague hath spread no further in the house, after the house be plaistered, the Priest shall pronounce that house cleane, for the plague is healed.

49 Then shall he take to purifie the house, two sparrowes, and cedar wood, and skarlet lace, and hyssope.

50 And hee shall kill one sparowe ouer pure water in an earthen vessell,

51 And shall take the cedar wood, and the hyssope, and the skarlet lace with the liue Sparrow, and dip them in the blood of the slayne Sparrow, and in the pure water, and sprinkle the house seuen times:

52 So shall hee clense the house with ye blood of the sparowe, and with the pure water, and with the liue sparowe, and with the cedar wood, and with the hyssope, and with the skarlet lace.

53 Afterwarde he shall let go the liue sparowe out of the towne into the broad fieldes: so shall he make atonement for the house, and it shall be cleane.

54 This is the law for euery plague of leprosie and blacke spot,

55 And of the leprosie of the garment, and of the house,

56 And of the swelling, and of the skab, and of the white spot.

57 This is the lawe of the leprosie to teache when a thing is vncleane, and when it is cleane.

Leviticus 15

1 Moreouer the Lord spake vnto Moses, and to Aaron, saying,

2 Speake vnto the children of Israel, and say vnto them, Whosoeuer hath an issue from his flesh, is vncleane, because of his issue.

3 And this shalbe his vncleannes in his issue: when his flesh auoydeth his issue, or if his flesh be stopped from his issue, this is his vncleannes.

4 Euery bed whereon he lyeth that hath the issue, shall be vncleane, and euery thing whereon he sitteth, shalbe vncleane.

5 Whosoeuer also toucheth his bed, shall wash his clothes, and wash himselfe in water, and shall be vncleane vntill the euen.

6 And he that sitteth on any thing, whereon he sate that hath the issue, shall wash his clothes, and wash himselfe in water, and shalbe vncleane vntill the euen.

7 Also he that toucheth the flesh of him that hath the issue, shall wash his clothes, and wash himselfe in water, and shalbe vncleane vntil the euen.

8 If he also, that hath the issue, spit vpon him that is cleane, he shall wash his clothes, and wash himselfe in water, and shalbe vncleane vntill the euen.

9 And what saddle soeuer he rideth vpon, that hath the issue, shalbe vncleane,

10 And whosoeuer toucheth any thing that was vnder him, shall be vncleane vnto the euen: and he that beareth those things, shall wash his clothes, and wash himselfe in water, and shall be vncleane vntill the euen.

11 Likewise whomesoeuer hee toucheth that hath the issue (and hath not washed his handes in water) shall wash his clothes and wash himselfe in water, and shalbe vncleane vntill the euen.

12 And the vessel of earth that he toucheth, which hath the issue, shalbe broken: and euery vessel of wood shalbe rinsed in water.

13 But if he that hath an issue, be cleansed of his issue, then shall he count him seuen dayes for his cleansing, and

wash his clothes, and wash his flesh in pure water: so shall he be cleane.

14 Then the eight day he shall take vnto him two Turtle doues or two yong pigeons, and come before the Lord at the doore of the Tabernacle of the Congregation, and shall giue them vnto the Priest.

15 And the Priest shall make of the one of them a sinne offring, and of the other a burnt offering: so the Priest shall make an atonement for him before the Lord, for his issue.

16 Also if any mans issue of seede depart from him, he shall wash all his flesh in water, and be vncleane vntill the euen.

17 And euery garment, and euery skinne whereupon shalbe issue of seede, shall be euen washed with water, and be vncleane vnto the euen.

18 If he that hath an issue of seede, do lie with a woman, they shall both wash themselues with water, and be vncleane vntill the euen.

19 Also when a woman shall haue an issue, and her issue in her flesh shalbe blood, she shalbe put apart seuen dayes: and whosoeuer toucheth her, shalbe vncleane vnto the euen.

20 And whatsoeuer she lieth vpon in her separation, shalbe vncleane, and euery thing that she sitteth vpon, shalbe vncleane.

21 Whosoeuer also toucheth her bedde, shall wash his clothes, and wash himselfe with water, and shalbe vncleane vnto the euen.

22 And whosoeuer toucheth any thing that she sate vpon, shall wash his clothes, and wash him selfe in water, and shalbe vncleane vnto the euen:

23 So that whether he touche her bed, or any thing whereon shee hath sit, he shalbe vncleane vnto the euen.

24 And if a man lye with her, and the flowers of her separation touch him, he shalbe vncleane seuen dayes, and all the whole bed whereon he lieth, shalbe vncleane.

25 Also when a womans issue of blood runneth long time besides the time of her floures, or when she hath an issue, longer then her floures, all the dayes of the issue of her vncleannesse shee shalbe vncleane, as in the time of her floures.

26 Euery bed whereon shee lyeth (as long as her issue lasteth) shalbe to her as her bed of her separation: and whatsoeuer she sitteth vpon, shalbe vncleane, as her vncleannes whe she is put apart.

27 And whosoeuer toucheth these things, shall be vncleane, and shall wash his clothes, and wash him selfe in water, and shalbe vncleane vnto the euen.

28 But if she be clensed of her issue, then shee shall count her seuen dayes, and after, shee shall be cleane.

29 And in the eight day shee shall take vnto her two Turtles or two yong pigeons, and bring them vnto the Priest at the doore of the Tabernacle of the Congregation.

30 And the Priest shall make of ye one a sinne offring, and of the other a burnt offring, and the Priest shall make an atonement for her before the Lord, for the issue of her vncleannes.

31 Thus shall yee separate the children of Israel from their vncleannes, that they dye not in their vncleannesse, if they defile my Tabernacle that is among them.

32 This is the lawe of him that hath an issue, and of him from whome goeth an issue of seede whereby he is defiled:

33 Also of her that is sicke of her floures, and of him that hath a running issue, whether it bee man or woman, and of him that lyeth with her which is vncleane.

Leviticus 16

1 Fvrthermore the Lord spake vnto Moses, after the death of the two sonnes of Aaron, whe they came to offer before the Lord, and dyed:

2 And the Lord sayd vnto Moses, Speake vnto Aaron thy brother, that he come not at all times into the Holy place within the vayle, before the Merciseate, which is vpon the Arke, that he dye not: for I wil appeare in the cloude vpon the Merciseate.

3 After this sort shall Aaron come into the Holy place: euen with a yong bullocke for a sinne offring, and a ramme for a burnt offring.

4 He shall put on the holy linnen coate, and shall haue linnen breeches vpon his flesh, and shall be girded with a linnen girdle, and shall couer his head with a linnen miter: these are the holy garments: therefore shall hee wash his flesh in water, when he doeth put them on.

5 And hee shall take of the Congregation of the children of Israel, two hee goates for a sinne offring, and a ramme for a burnt offring.

6 Then Aaron shall offer the bullocke for his sinne offring, and make an atonement for himselfe, and for his house.

7 And he shall take the two hee goates, and present them before the Lord at the doore of the Tabernacle of the Congregation.

8 Then Aaron shall cast lots ouer the two hee goates: one lot for the Lord, and the other for the Scape goate.

9 And Aaron shall offer the goat, vpon which the Lords lot shall fal, and make him a sinne offring.

10 But the goate, on which the lot shall fall to be the Scape goate, shalbe presented aliue before the Lord, to make reconciliation by him, and to let him go (as a Scape goate) into the wildernes.

11 Thus Aaron shall offer the bullocke for his sinne offring, and make a reconciliation for himselfe, and for his house, and shall kill the bullocke for his sinne offring.

12 And he shall take a censer full of burning coles from off the altar before the Lord, and his handfull of sweete incense beaten small, and bring it within the vayle,

13 And shall put the incense vpon the fire before the Lord, that the cloude of the incense may couer the Merciseat that is vpon the Testimonie: so he shall not dye.

14 And hee shall take of the blood of the bullocke, and sprinkle it with his finger vpon the Merciseat Eastward: and before the Merciseate shall he sprinkle of the blood with his finger seuen times.

15 Then shall he kill the goate that is the peoples sinne offring, and bring his blood within the vaile, and doe with that blood, as he did with the blood of the bullocke, and sprinckle it vpon the Merciseate, and before the Merciseate.

16 So he shall purge the Holy place from the vncleannes of the children of Israel, and from their trespasses of all their sinnes: so shall he do also for the Tabernacle of the Cogregation placed with them, in the middes of their vncleannesse.

17 And there shalbe no man in the Tabernacle of the Congregation, when he goeth in to make an atonement in the Holy place, vntill hee come out, and haue made an atonement for himselfe, and for his housholde, and for all the Congregation of Israel.

18 After, he shall goe out vnto the altar that is before the Lord and make a reconciliation vpon it, and shall take of the blood of the bullocke, and of the blood of the goate, and put it vpon the hornes of the Altar round about:

19 So shall hee sprinkle of the blood vpon it with his finger seuen times, and clense it, and halowe it from the vncleannes of the children of Israel.

20 When he hath made an ende of purging the Holy place, and the Tabernacle of the Congregation, and the altar, then he shall bring the liue goate:

21 And Aaron shall put both his handes vpon the head of the liue goate, and confesse ouer him al the iniquities of the children of Israel, and all their trespasses, in all their sinnes, putting them vpon the head of the goate, and shall sende him away (by the hand of a man appointed) into the wildernes.

22 So the goate shall beare vpon him all their iniquities into the land that is not inhabited, and he shall let the goate go into the wildernesse.

23 After, Aaron shall come into the Tabernacle of the Congregation, and put off the linnen clothes, which he put on when he went into the Holy place, and leaue them there.

24 Hee shall wash also his flesh with water in the Holy place, and put on his owne rayment, and come out, and make his burnt offring, and the burnt offring of the people, and make an atonement for himselfe, and for the people.

25 Also the fatte of the sinne offring shall he burne vpon the altar.

26 And he that caried forth the goat, called the Scape goat, shall wash his clothes, and wash his flesh in water, and after that shall come into the hoste.

27 Also the bullocke for the sinne offring, and the goate for the sinne offring (whose blood was brought to make a reconciliation in the Holy place) shall one carie out without the hoste to be burnt in the fire, with their skinnes, and with their flesh, and with their doung.

28 And hee that burneth them shall wash his clothes, and wash his flesh in water, and afterward come into the hoste.

29 So this shalbe an ordinance for euer vnto you: the tenth day of the seuenth moneth, yee shall humble your soules, and do no worke at all, whether it be one of the same countrey or a strager that soiourneth among you.

30 For that day shall ye Priest make an atonement for you to clense you: ye shalbe cleane from all your sinnes before the Lord.

31 This shall be a Sabbath of rest vnto you, and ye shall humble your soules, by an ordinance for euer.

32 And the Priest whom he shall anoynt, and whom he shall cosecrate (to minister in his fathers steade) shall make the atonement, and shall put on the linnen clothes and Holy vestments,

33 And shall purge the Holy Sanctuarie and the Tabernacle of the Congregation, and shall clense the altar, and make an atonement for the Priests and for all the people of the Congregation.

34 And this shalbe an euerlasting ordinance vnto you, to make an atonement for the children of Israel for all their sinnes once a yeere: and as the Lord commanded Moses, he did.

Leviticus 17

1 And the Lord spake vnto Moses, saying,

2 Speake vnto Aaron, and to his sonnes, and to all the children of Israel, and say vnto them, This is the thing which the Lord hath commanded, saying,

3 Whosoeuer he be of the house of Israel that killeth a bullocke, or lambe, or goate in the hoste, or that killeth it out of the hoste,

4 And bringeth it not vnto the doore of the Tabernacle of the Congregation to offer an offring vnto the Lord before the Tabernacle of the Lord, blood shalbe imputed vnto that man: he hath shed blood, wherefore that man shall be cut off from among his people.

5 Therefore the children of Israel shall bring their offrings, which they would offer abroad in the fielde, and present the vnto ye Lord at the doore of the Tabernacle of ye Congregation by ye Priest, and offer them for peace offrings vnto the Lord.

6 Then the Priest shall sprinkle the blood vpon the Altar of the Lord before the doore of the Tabernacle of the Congregation, and burne the fat for a sweete sauour vnto the Lord.

7 And they shall no more offer their offerings vnto deuils, after whom they haue gone a whoring: this shalbe an ordinance for euer vnto them in their generations.

8 Also thou shalt say vnto them, whosoeuer he be of the house of Israel, or of the strangers which soiourne among them, that offreth a burnt offring or sacrifice,

9 And bringeth it not vnto ye doore of the Tabernacle of the Congregation to offer it vnto the Lord, euen that man shall be cut off from his people.

10 Likewise whosoeuer he be of the house of Israel, or of the strangers that soiourne among them, that eateth any blood, I will euen set my face against that person that eateth blood, and will cut him off from among his people.

11 For the life of the flesh is in the blood, and I haue giuen it vnto you to offer vpon the altar, to make an atonement for your soules: for this blood shall make an atonement for the soule.

12 Therefore I saide vnto ye children of Israel, None of you shall eate blood: neither the stranger that soiourneth among you, shall eate blood.

13 Moreouer whosoeuer he be of the children of Israel, or of the strangers that soiourne among the, which by hunting taketh any beast or foule that may be eaten, he shall powre out the blood thereof, and couer it with dust:

14 For ye life of all flesh is his blood, it is ioyned with his life: therefore I sayd vnto the children of Israel, Ye shall eate the blood of no flesh: for the life of al flesh is the blood thereof: whosoeuer eateth it, shalbe cut off.

15 And euery person that eateth it which dyeth alone, or that which is torne with beastes, whether it be one of the same countrey or a stranger, he shall both wash his clothes, and wash himselfe in water, and be vncleane vnto the euen: after he shalbe cleane.

16 But if he wash them not, nor wash his flesh, then he shall beare his iniquitie.

Leviticus 18

1 And the Lord spake vnto Moses, saying,

2 Speake vnto the children of Israel, and say vnto them, I am the Lord your God.

3 After ye doings of the land of Egypt, wherin ye dwelt, shall ye not doe: and after the maner of the land of Canaan, whither I will bring you, shall ye not do, neither walke in their ordinances,

4 But do after my iudgements, and keepe mine ordinances, to walke therein: I am the Lord your God.

5 Ye shall keepe therefore my statutes, and my iudgements, which if a man doe, he shall then liue in them: I am the Lord.

6 None shall come neere to any of ye kinred of his flesh to vncouer her shame: I am the Lord.

7 Thou shalt not vncouer the shame of thy father, nor the shame of thy mother: for she is thy mother, thou shalt not discouer her shame.

8 The shame of thy fathers wife shalt thou not discouer: for it is thy fathers shame.

9 Thou shalt not discouer the shame of thy sister the daughter of thy father, or the daughter of thy mother, whether shee bee borne at home, or borne without: thou shalt not discouer their shame.

10 The shame of thy sonnes daughter, or of thy daughters daughter, thou shalt not, I say, vncouer their shame: for it is thy shame.

11 The shame of thy fathers wiues daughter, begotten of thy father (for she is thy sister) thou shalt not, I say, discouer her shame.

12 Thou shalt not vncouer the shame of thy fathers sister: for she is thy fathers kinswoman.

13 Thou shalt not discouer the shame of thy mothers sister: for she is thy mothers kinsewoman.

14 Thou shalt not vncouer the shame of thy fathers brother: that is, thou shalt not goe in to his wife, for she is thine aunte.

15 Thou shalt not discouer the shame of thy daughter in lawe: for she is thy sonnes wife: therefore shalt thou not vncouer her shame.

16 Thou shalt not discouer the shame of thy brothers wife. for it is thy brothers shame.

17 Thou shalt not discouer the shame of the wife and of her daughter, neither shalt thou take her sonnes daughter, nor her daughters daughter, to vncouer her shame: for they are thy kinsfolkes, and it were wickednesse.

18 Also thou shalt not take a wife with her sister, during her life, to vexe her, in vncouering her shame vpon her.

19 Thou shalt not also go vnto a woman to vncouer her shame, as long as she is put apart for her disease.

20 Moreouer, thou shalt not giue thy selfe to thy neighbours wife by carnall copulation, to be defiled with her.

21 Also thou shalt not giue thy children to offer them vnto Molech, neither shalt thou defile the name of thy God: for I am the Lord.

22 Thou shalt not lie with ye male as one lieth with a woman: for it is abomination.

23 Thou shalt not also lie with any beast to bee defiled therewith, neither shall any woman stand before a beast, to lie downe thereto: for it is abomination.

24 Yee shall not defile your selues in any of these things: for in al these the nations are defiled, which I will cast out before you:

25 And the land is defiled: therefore I wil visit the wickednesse thereof vpon it, and the lande shall vomit out her inhabitants.

26 Ye shall keepe therefore mine ordinances, and my iudgements, and commit none of these abominations, aswell hee that is of the same countrey, as the straunger that soiourneth among you.

27 (For all these abominations haue the men of the land done, which were before you, and the land is defiled:

28 And shall not the lande spue you out if ye defile it, as it spued out the people that were before you?)

29 For whosoeuer shall commit any of these abominations, the persons that doe so, shall bee cut off from among their people.

30 Therefore shall yee keepe mine ordinances that ye do not any of the abominable customes, which haue bene done before you, and that yee defile not your selues therein: for I am the Lord your God.

Leviticus 19

1 And the Lord spake vnto Moses, saying,

2 Speake vnto all the Congregation of the children of Israel, and say vnto them, Ye shalbe holy, for I the Lord your God am holy.

3 Yee shall feare euery man his mother and his father, and shall keepe my Sabbaths: for I am the Lord your God.

4 Ye shall not turne vnto idoles, nor make you molten gods: I am the Lord your God.

5 And when yee shall offer a peace offering vnto the Lord, ye shall offer it freely.

6 It shall be eaten the day yee offer it, or on the morowe: and that which remaineth vntill the third day, shalbe burnt in the fire.

7 For if it be eaten the third day, it shall be vncleane, it shall not be accepted.

8 Therefore he that eateth it, shall beare his iniquitie, because he hath defiled the halowed thing of the Lord, and that person shalbe cut off from his people.

9 When yee reape the haruest of your land, ye shall not reape euery corner of your field, neither shalt thou gather the glainings of thy haruest.

10 Thou shalt not gather the grapes of thy vineyarde cleane, neyther gather euery grape of thy vineyarde, but thou shalt leaue them for the poore and for the straunger: I am the Lord your God.

11 Ye shall not steale, neither deale falsely, neither lie one to another.

12 Also yee shall not sweare by my name falsely, neither shalt thou defile the name of thy God: I am the Lord.

13 Thou shalt not do thy neighbour wrong, neither rob him. The workemans hire shall not abide with thee vntil the morning.

14 Thou shalt not curse the deafe, neither put a stumbling blocke before the blinde, but shalt feare thy God: I am the Lord.

15 Ye shall not doe vniustly in iudgement. Thou shalt not fauour the person of the poore, nor honour the person of the mightie, but thou shalt iudge thy neighbour iustly.

16 Thou shalt not walke about with tales among thy people. Thou shalt not stand against the blood of thy neighbour: I am the Lord.

17 Thou shalt not hate thy brother in thine heart, but thou shalt plainely rebuke thy neighbour, and suffer him not to sinne.

18 Thou shalt not auenge, nor be mindful of wrong against ye childre of thy people, but shalt loue thy neighbour as thy selfe: I am the Lord.

19 Yee shall keepe mine ordinances. Thou shalt not let thy cattel gender with others of diuers kindes. Thou shalt not sowe thy fielde with mingled seede, neyther shall a garment of diuers thinges, as of linen and wollen come vpon thee.

20 Whosoeuer also lyeth and medleth with a woman that is a bonde mayde, affianced to a husband, and not redeemed, nor freedome giuen her, she shalbe scourged, but they shall not die, because she is not made free.

21 And he shall bring for his trespasse offring vnto the Lord, at the doore of the Tabernacle of the Congregation, a ramme for a trespasse offering.

22 Then the Priest shall make an atonement for him with the ramme of the trespasse offering before the Lord, concerning his sinne which he hath done, and pardon shalbe giuen him for his sinne which he hath committed.

23 Also when ye shall come into the land, and haue planted euery tree for meate, ye shall count the fruite thereof as vncircumcised: three yeere shall it be vncircumcised vnto you, it shall not be eaten:

24 But in the fourth yere all the fruite thereof shalbe holy to the praise of the Lord.

25 And in the fifth yeere shall ye eate of the fruite of it that it may yeelde to you the encrease thereof: I am the Lord your God.

26 Ye shall not eat the flesh with the blood, ye shall not vse witchcraft, nor obserue times.

27 Ye shall not cut rounde the corners of your heades, neither shalt thou marre the tuftes of thy beard.

28 Ye shall not cut your flesh for the dead, nor make any print of a marke vpon you: I am the Lord,

29 Thou shalt not make thy daughter common, to cause her to be a whore, least the lande also fall to whoredome, and the lande bee full of wickednesse.

30 Ye shall keepe my Sabbaths and reuerence my Sanctuarie: I am the Lord.

31 Ye shall not regarde them that worke with spirites, neither soothsayers: ye shall not seeke to them to be defiled by them: I am the Lord your God.

32 Thou shalt rise vp before the horehead, and honour the person of the old man, and dread thy God: I am the Lord.

33 And if a stranger soiourne with thee in your lande, ye shall not vexe him.

34 But the stranger that dwelleth with you, shalbe as one of your selues, and thou shalt loue him as thy selfe: for ye were strangers in the lad of Egypt: I am the Lord your God.

35 Ye shall not doe vniustly in iudgement, in line, in weight, or in measure.

36 You shall haue iust ballances, true weightes, a true Ephah, and a true Hin. I am the Lord your God, which haue brought you out of the lande of Egypt.

37 Therefore shall ye obserue all mine ordinances, and all my iudgements, and doe them: I am the Lord.

Leviticus 20

1 And the Lord spake vnto Moses, saying,

2 Thou shalt say also to the children of Israel, Whosoeuer he be of the children of Israel, or of the strangers that dwell in Israel, that giueth his children vnto Molech, he shall die the death, ye people of ye land shall stone him to death.

3 And I will set my face against that man and cut him off from among his people, because he hath giuen his children vnto Molech, for to defile my Sanctuarie, and to pollute mine holy Name.

4 And if the people of the lande hide their eyes, and winke at that man when he giueth his children vnto Molech, and kill him not,

5 Then will I set my face against that man, and against his familie, and will cut him off, and all that go a whoring after him to comit whoredome with Molech, from among their people.

6 If any turne after such as worke with spirits, and after soothsayers, to go a whoring after them, then will I set my face against that person, and will cut him off from among his people.

7 Sanctifie your selues therefore, and be holie, for I am the Lord your God.

8 Keepe ye therefore mine ordinances, and doe them. I am the Lord which doeth sanctifie you.

9 If there be any that curseth his father or his mother, he shall die the death: seeing hee hath cursed his father and his mother, his blood shalbe vpon him.

10 And the man that committeth adulterie with another mans wife, because he hath comitted adulterie with his neighbours wife, the adulterer and the adulteresse shall die the death.

11 And the man that lyeth with his fathers wife, because hee hath vncouered his fathers shame, they shall both dye: their blood shalbe vpon them.

12 Also the man that lyeth with his daughter in lawe, they both shall dye the death, they haue wrought abomination, their blood shalbe vpon them.

13 The man also that lyeth with the male, as one lyeth with a woman, they haue both committed abomination: they shall dye the death, their blood shalbe vpon them.

14 Likewise he that taketh a wife and her mother, committeth wickednesse: they shall burne him and them with fire, that there be no wickednes among you.

15 Also the man that lyeth with a beast, shall dye the death, and ye shall slay the beast.

16 And if a woman come to any beast, and lye therewith, then thou shalt kill the woman and the beast: they shall die the death, their blood shalbe vpon them.

17 Also the man that taketh his sister, his fathers daughter, or his mothers daughter, and seeth her shame and she seeth his shame, it is villenie: therefore they shall be cut off in the sight of their people, because he hath vncouered his sisters shame, he shall beare his iniquitie.

18 The man also that lyeth with a woman hauing her disease, and vncouereth her shame, and openeth her fountaine, and she open the foutaine of her blood, they shall bee euen both cut off from among their people.

19 Moreouer thou shalt not vncouer the shame of thy mothers sister, nor of thy fathers sister: because he hath vncouered his kin, they shall beare their iniquitie.

20 Likewise the man that lyeth with his fathers brothers wife, and vncouereth his vncles shame: they shall beare their iniquitie, and shall die childlesse.

21 So the man that taketh his brothers wife, committeth filthines, because he hath vncouered his brothers shame: they shalbe childles.

22 Ye shall keepe therefore all mine ordinances and all my iudgements, and doe them, that the land, whither I bring you to dwel therein, spue you not out.

23 Wherefore ye shall not walke in the maners of this nation which I cast out before you: for they haue committed all these things, therefore I abhorred them.

24 But I haue saide vnto you, ye shall inherite their land, and I will giue it vnto you to possesse it, euen a land that floweth with milke and honie: I am the Lord your God, which haue separated you from other people.

25 Therefore shall ye put difference betweene cleane beastes and vncleane, and betweene vncleane foules and cleane: neither shall ye defile your selues with beastes and foules, nor with any creeping thing, that ye ground bringeth forth, which I haue separated from you as vncleane.

26 Therefore shall ye be holie vnto me: for I the Lord am holy, and I haue separated you from other people, that ye shoulde be mine.

27 And if a man or woman haue a spirite of diuination, or soothsaying in them, they shall die the death: they shall stone them to death, their blood shalbe vpon them.

Leviticus 21

1 And the Lord said vnto Moses, Speake vnto the Priestes the sonnes of Aaron, and say vnto them, Let none be defiled by the dead among his people,

2 But by his kinseman that is neere vnto him: to wit, by his mother, or by his father, or by his sonne, or by his daughter, or by his brother,

3 Or by his sister a maid, that is neere vnto him, which hath not had a husband: for her he may lament.

4 He shall not lament for the Prince among his people, to pollute him selfe.

5 They shall not make balde partes vpon their head, nor shaue off the locks of their beard, nor make any cuttings in their flesh.

6 They shalbe holy vnto their God, and not pollute the name of their God: for the sacrifices of the Lord made by fire, and the bread of their God they doe offer: therefore they shalbe holie.

7 They shall not take to wife an whore, or one polluted, neither shall they marrie a woman diuorced from her husband: for such one is holy vnto his God.

8 Thou shalt sanctifie him therefore, for he offereth the bread of thy God: he shall be holy vnto thee: for I the Lord, which sanctifie you, am holy.

9 If a Priestes daughter fall to play the whore, she polluteth her father: therefore shall she be burnt with fire.

10 Also ye hie Priest among his brethren, (vpon whose head the anointing oyle was powred, and hath consecrated his hand to put on the garments) shall not vncouer his head, nor rent his clothes,

11 Neither shall he goe to any dead bodie, nor make him selfe vncleane by his father or by his mother,

12 Neither shall he goe out of the Sanctuarie, nor pollute the holy place of his God: for the crowne of the anoynting oyle of his God is vpon him: I am the Lord.

13 Also he shall take a maide vnto his wife:

14 But a widowe, or a diuorced woman, or a polluted, or an harlot, these shall he not marrie, but shall take a maide of his owne people to wife:

15 Neyther shall he defile his seede among his people: for I am the Lord which sanctifie him.

16 And the Lord spake vnto Moses, saying,

17 Speake vnto Aaron, and say, Whosoeuer of thy seede in their generations hath any blemishes, shall not prease to offer the bread of his God:

18 For whosoeuer hath any blemish, shall not come neere: as a man blinde or lame, or that hath a flat nose, or that hath any misshapen member,

19 Or a man that hath a broken foote, or a broken hande,

20 Or is crooke backt, or bleare eyed, or hath a blemish in his eye, or be skiruie, or skabbed, or haue his stones broken.

21 None of the seede of Aaron the Priest that hath a blemish, shall come neere to offer the sacrifices of the Lord made by fire, hauing a blemish: he shall not prease to offer the bread of his God.

22 The bread of his God, euen of the most holie, and of the holy shall he eate:

23 But he shall not goe in vnto the vaile, nor come neere the altar, because hee hath a blemish, least he pollute my Sanctuaries: for I am the Lord that sanctifie them.

24 Thus spake Moses vnto Aaron, and to his sonnes, and to all the children of Israel.

Leviticus 22

1 And the Lord spake vnto Moses, saying,

2 Speake vnto Aaron, and to his sonnes, that they be separated from the holy thinges of the children of Israel, and that they pollute not mine holy name in those things, which they hallowe vnto me: I am the Lord.

3 Say vnto them, Whosoeuer he be of all your seede among your generations after you, that toucheth the holy things which the children of Israel hallowe vnto the Lord, hauing his vncleannesse vpon him, euen that person shall be cut off from my sight: I am the Lord.

4 Whosoeuer also of the seede of Aaron is a leper, or hath a running issue, he shall not eate of the holy things vntill he be cleane: and who so toucheth any that is vncleane, by reason of the dead, or a man whose issue of seede runneth from him,

5 Or the man that toucheth any creeping thing, whereby he may be made vncleane, or a man, by whom he may take vncleannesse, whatsoeuer vncleannesse he hath,

6 The person that hath touched such, shall therefore be vncleane vntill the euen, and shall not eat of ye holy things, except he haue washed his flesh with water.

7 But when the Sunne is downe, hee shalbe cleane, and shall afterward eate of the holy things: for it is his foode.

8 Of a beast that dyeth, or is rent with beasts, whereby he may be defiled, hee shall not eate: I am the Lord.

9 Let them keepe therefore mine ordinance, least they beare their sinne for it, and die for it, if they defile it: I the Lord sanctifie them.

10 There shall no stranger also eate of the holie thing, neither the ghest of the Priest, neither shall an hired seruant eat of the holie thing:

11 But if the Priest bye any with money, he shall eate of it, also he that is borne in his house: they shall eate of his meate.

12 If the Priests daughter also be maried vnto a stranger, she may not eate of the holy offrings.

13 Notwithstanding if the Priests daughter be a widowe or diuorced, and haue no childe, but is returned vnto her fathers house shee shall eate of her fathers bread, as she did in her youth but there shall no stranger eate thereof.

14 If a man eate of the holie thing vnwittingly, he shall put the fift part thereunto, and giue it vnto the Priest with the halowed thing.

15 So they shall not defile the holy things of the children of Israel, which they offer vnto the Lord,

16 Neither cause the people to beare the iniquitie of their trespas, while they eate their holy thing: for I the Lord do halowe them.

17 And the Lord spake vnto Moses, saying,

18 Speake vnto Aaron, and to his sonnes, and to all the children of Israel, and say vnto them, Whosoeuer he be of the house of Israel, or of the strangers in Israel, that will offer his sacrifice for all their vowes, and for all their free offrings, which they vse to offer vnto the Lord for a burnt offring,

19 Yee shall offer of your free minde a male without blemish of the beeues, of the sheepe, or of the goates.

20 Ye shall not offer any thing that hath a blemish: for that shall not be acceptable for you.

21 And whosoeuer bringeth a peace offring vnto ye Lord to accomplish his vowe, or for a free offring, of the beeues, or of the sheepe, his free offring shall bee perfect, no blemish shalbe in it.

22 Blinde, or broken, or maimed, or hauing a wenne, or skiruie, or skabbed: these shall yee not offer vnto the Lord nor make an offring by fire of these vpon the altar of the Lord.

23 Yet a bullocke, or a sheepe that hath any member superfluous, or lacking, such mayest thou present for a free offring, but for a vowe it shall not be accepted.

24 Ye shall not offer vnto ye Lord that which is bruised or crusshed, or broken, or cut away, neither shall ye make an offring thereof in your land,

25 Neither of ye hand of a strager shall ye offer ye bread of your God of any of these, because their corruption is in them, there is a blemish in them: therefore shall they not be accepted for you.

26 And the Lord spake vnto Moses, saying,

27 When a bullocke, or a sheepe, or a goate shall be brought foorth, it shalbe euen seuen daies vnder his damme: and from the eight day forth, it shalbe accepted for a sacrifice made by fire vnto the Lord.

28 As for the cowe or the ewe, yee shall not kill her, and her yong both in one day.

29 So when ye will offer a thanke offring vnto the Lord, ye shall offer willingly.

30 The same day it shalbe eaten, yee shall leaue none of it vntill the morowe: I am the Lord.

31 Therefore shall ye keepe my commandements and do them: for I am the Lord.

32 Neither shall ye pollute mine holy Name, but I will be halowed among the children of Israel. I the Lord sanctifie you,

33 Which haue brought you out of the land of Egypt, to be your God: I am the Lord.

Leviticus 23

1 And the Lord spake vnto Moses, saying,

2 Speake vnto the children of Israel, and say vnto them, The feastes of ye Lord which yee shall call ye holie assemblies, euen these are my feasts.

3 Six daies shall worke be done, but in the seuenth day shalbe the Sabbath of rest, an holie conuocation: ye shall do no worke therein, it is the Sabbath of the Lord, in all your dwellings.

4 These are the feastes of the Lord, and holie conuocations, which yee shall proclaime in their seasons.

5 In the first moneth, and in the fourteenth day of the moneth at euening shalbe ye Passeouer of the Lord.

6 And on the fifteenth day of this moneth shalbe the feast of vnleauened bread vnto the Lord: seuen dayes ye shall eate vnleauened bread.

7 In the first day yee shall haue an holy conuocation: ye shall do no seruile worke therein.

8 Also ye shall offer sacrifice made by fire vnto the Lord seuen daies, and in the seuenth day shalbe an holie conuocation: ye shall do no seruile worke therein.

9 And the Lord spake vnto Moses, saying,

10 Speake vnto the children of Israel, and say vnto them, When ye be come into ye land which I giue vnto you, and reape the haruest thereof, then ye shall bring a sheafe of the first fruites of your haruest vnto the Priest,

11 And hee shall shake the sheafe before the Lord, that it may be acceptable for you: the morowe after the Sabbath, the Priest shall shake it.

12 And that day when yee shake the sheafe, shall yee prepare a lambe without blemish of a yeere olde, for a burnt offring vnto the Lord:

13 And the meate offring thereof shalbe two tenth deales of fine floure mingled with oyle, for a sacrifice made by fire vnto ye Lord of sweete sauour. and the drinke offring thereof the fourth part of an Hin of wine.

14 And ye shall eat neither bread nor parched corne, nor greene eares vntill the selfe same day that ye haue brought an offring vnto your God: this shalbe a lawe for euer in your generations and in all your dwellings.

15 Ye shall count also to you from the morowe after the Sabbath, euen from the day that yee shall bring the sheafe of the shake offring, seuen Sabbaths, they shalbe complete.

16 Vnto ye morow after the seuenth Sabbath shall ye nomber fiftie dayes: then yee shall bring a newe meate offring vnto the Lord.

17 Ye shall bring out of your habitations bread for the shake offring: they shalbe two loaues of two tenth deales of fine floure, which shalbe baken with leauen for first fruites vnto the Lord.

18 Also yee shall offer with the bread seuen lambes without blemish of one yeere olde, and a yong bullocke and two rams: they shalbe for a burnt offring vnto the Lord, with their meate offrings and their drinke offrings, for a sacrifice made by fire of a sweete sauour vnto the Lord.

19 Then ye shall prepare an hee goate for a sinne offring, and two lambes of one yeere olde for peace offrings.

20 And the Priest shall shake them to and from with the bread of the first fruits before the Lord, and with the two lambes: they shalbe holy to the Lord, for the Priest.

21 So ye shall proclayme the same day, that it may be an holie conuocation vnto you: ye shall doe no seruile worke therein: it shalbe an ordinance for euer in al your dwellinges, throughout your generations.

22 And when you reape the haruest of your land, thou shalt not rid cleane the corners of thy field when thou reapest, neither shalt thou make any aftergathering of thy haruest, but shalt leaue vnto the poore and to the stranger: I am the Lord your God.

23 And the Lord spake vnto Moses, saying,

24 Speake vnto the children of Israel, and say, In the seuenth moneth, and in the first day of the moneth shall ye haue a Sabbath, for the remembrance of blowing the trumpets, an holy conuocation.

25 Ye shall do no seruile worke therein, but offer sacrifice made by fire vnto the Lord.

26 And the Lord spake vnto Moses, saying,

27 The tenth also of this seuenth moneth shalbe a day of reconciliation: it shalbe an holie conuocation vnto you, and yee shall humble your soules, and offer sacrifice made by fire vnto the Lord.

28 And ye shall doe no worke that same day: for it is a day of reconciliation, to make an atonement for you before the Lord your God.

29 For euery person that humbleth not himselfe that same day, shall euen be cut off from his people.

30 And euery person that shall doe any work that same day, the same person also will I destroy from among his people.

31 Ye shall do no maner worke therefore: this shalbe a law for euer in your generations, throughout all your dwellings.

32 This shalbe vnto you a Sabbath of rest, and ye shall humble your soules: in the ninth day of the moneth at euen, from euen to euen shall ye celebrate your Sabbath.

33 And the Lord spake vnto Moses, saying,

34 Speake vnto the children of Israel, and say, In the fifteenth day of this seueth moneth shalbe for seuen dayes the feast of Tabernacles vnto the Lord.

35 In the first day shalbe an holie conuocation: ye shall do no seruile worke therein.

36 Seuen daies ye shall offer sacrifice made by fire vnto the Lord, and in the eight day shalbe an holy conuocation vnto you, and ye shall offer sacrifices made by fire vnto the Lord: it is the solemne assemblie, yee shall doe no seruile worke therein.

37 These are the feastes of the Lord (which ye shall call holie conuocations) to offer sacrifice made by fire vnto the Lord, as burnt offring, and meate offring, sacrifice, and drinke offrings, euery one vpon his day,

38 Beside the Sabbaths of the Lord, and beside your giftes, and beside al your vowes, and beside all your free offrings, which ye shall giue vnto the Lord.

39 But in the fifteenth day of the seueth moneth, when ye haue gathered in the fruite of the land, ye shall keepe an holie feast vnto the Lord seuen daies: in the first day shalbe a Sabbath: likewise in the eight day shalbe a Sabbath.

40 And yee shall take you in the first day the fruite of goodly trees, branches of palme trees, and the boughes of thicke trees, and willowes of the brooke, and shall reioyce before the Lord your God seuen daies.

41 So ye shall keepe this feast vnto the Lord seuen daies in the yere, by a perpetuall ordinance through your generations: in the seuenth moneth shall you keepe it.

42 Ye shall dwell in boothes seuen daies: all that are Israelites borne, shall dwel in boothes,

43 That your posterity may know that I haue made the children of Israel to dwell in boothes, when I brought them out of the lande of Egypt: I am the Lord your God.

44 So Moses declared vnto the children of Israel the feastes of the Lord.

Leviticus 24

1 And the Lord spake vnto Moses, saying,

2 Commande the children of Israel that they bring vnto thee pure oyle oliue beaten, for the light, to cause ye lampes to burne continually.

3 Without the vaile of the Testimonie, in the Tabernacle of the Congregation, shall Aaron dresse them, both euen and morning before the Lord alwayes: this shalbe a lawe for euer through your generations.

4 He shall dresse the lampes vpon the pure Candlesticke before the Lord perpetually.

5 Also thou shalt take fine floure, and bake twelue cakes thereof: two tenth deales shalbe in one cake.

6 And thou shalt set them in two rowes, six in a rowe vpon the pure table before the Lord.

7 Thou shalt also put pure incense vpon the rowes, that in steade of the bread it may bee for a remembrance, and an offering made by fire to the Lord.

8 Euery Sabbath hee shall put them in rowes before the Lord euermore, receiuing them of the children of Israel for an euerlasting couenant.

9 And the bread shalbe Aarons and his sonnes, and they shall eate it in the holie place: for it is most holie vnto him of the offrings of the Lord made by fire by a perpetuall ordinance.

10 And there went out among the children of Israel the sonne of an Israelitish woman, whose father was an Egyptian: and this sonne of the Israelitish woman, and a man of Israel stroue together in the hoste.

11 So the Israelitish womans sonne blasphemed the name of the Lord, and cursed, and they brought him vnto Moses (his mothers name also was Shelomith, the daughter of Dibri, of the tribe of Dan)

12 And they put him in warde, till he tolde them the minde of the Lord.

13 Then the Lord spake vnto Moses, saying,

14 Bring the blasphemer without the hoste, and let all that heard him, put their handes vpon his head, and let all the Congregation stone him.

15 And thou shalt speake vnto the children of Israel, saying, Whosoeuer curseth his God, shall beare his sinne.

16 And he that blasphemeth the name of the Lord, shalbe put to death: all the Congregation shall stone him to death: aswell the stranger, as he that is borne in the lande: when he blasphemeth the name of the Lord, let him beslaine.

17 He also that killeth any man, he shall be put to death.

18 And he that killeth a beast, he shall restore it, beast for beast.

19 Also if a man cause any blemish in his neighbour: as he hath done, so shall it be done to him.

20 Breache for breach, eye for eye, tooth for tooth: such a blemish as he hath made in any, such shalbe repayed to him.

21 And he that killeth a beast shall restore it: but he that killeth a man shall be slaine.

22 Ye shall haue one lawe: it shalbe aswel for the stranger as for one borne in the countrey: for I am the Lord your God.

23 Then Moses tolde the children of Israel, and they brought the blasphemer out of the hoste, and stoned him with stones: so the children of Israel did as the Lord had commanded Moses.

Leviticus 25

1 And the Lord spake vnto Moses in mount Sinai, saying,

2 Speake vnto the children of Israel, and say vnto them, When ye shall come into the lande which I giue you, the lande shall keepe Sabbath vnto the Lord.

3 Six yeeres thou shalt sowe thy field, and six yeeres thou shalt cut thy vineyarde, and gather the fruite thereof.

4 But the seuenth yeere shalbe a Sabbath of rest vnto the lande: it shall be the Lordes Sabbath: thou shalt neither sowe thy fielde, nor cut thy vineyarde.

5 That which groweth of it owne accorde of thy haruest, thou shalt not reape, neither gather the grapes that thou hast left vnlaboured: for it shalbe a yeere of rest vnto the land.

6 And the rest of the lande shall be meate for you, euen for thee, and for thy seruant, and for thy mayde, and for thy hired seruant, and for the stranger that soiourneth with thee:

7 And for thy cattell, and for the beastes that are in thy lande shall all the encrease thereof be meate.

8 Also thou shalt number seuen Sabbaths of yeeres vnto thee, euen seuen times seuen yeere: and the space of the seuen Sabbaths of yeeres will be vnto thee nine and fourtie yeere.

9 Then thou shalt cause to blow the trumpet of the Iubile in the tenth day of the seuenth moneth: euen in the day of the reconciliation shall ye make the trumpet blowe, throughout all your lande.

10 And ye shall halowe that yeere, euen the fiftieth yeere, and proclaime libertie in the lande to all the inhabitants thereof: it shalbe the Iubile vnto you, and ye shall returne euery man vnto his possession, and euery man shall returne vnto his familie.

11 This fiftieth yeere shalbe a yeere of Iubile vnto you: ye shall not sowe, neither reape that which groweth of it selfe, neither gather the grapes thereof, that are left vnlaboured.

12 For it is the Iubile, it shall be holy vnto you: ye shall eate of the encrease thereof out of the fielde.

13 In the yeere of this Iubile, ye shall returne euery man vnto his possession.

14 And when thou sellest ought to thy neighbour, or byest at thy neighbours hande, ye shall not oppresse one another:

15 But according to the nomber of yeeres after the Iubile thou shalt bye of thy neighbour: also according to the nomber of the yeeres of the reuenues, he shall sell vnto thee.

16 According to the multitude of yeeres, thou shalt increase the price thereof, and according to the fewnesse of yeeres, thou shalt abate the price of it: for the nomber of fruites doeth he sell vnto thee.

17 Oppresse not ye therefore any man his neighbour, but thou shalt feare thy God: for I am the Lord your God.

18 Wherefore ye shall obey mine ordinances, and keepe my lawes, and do them, and ye shall dwell in the land in safetie.

19 And the lande shall giue her fruite, and ye shall eate your fill, and dwell therein in safetie.

20 And if ye shall say, What shall we eate the seuenth yeere, for we shall not sowe, nor gather in our increase?

21 I will sende my blessing vpon you in the sixt yeere, and it shall bring foorth fruite for three yeeres.

22 And ye shall sowe the eight yeere, and eate of the olde fruite vntill the ninth yeere: vntill the fruite thereof come, ye shall eate the olde.

23 Also the lande shall not be solde to be cut off from the familie: for the land is mine, and ye be but strangers and soiourners with me.

24 Therefore in all the land of your possession ye shall graunt a redemption for the lande.

25 If thy brother be impouerished, and sell his possession, then his redeemer shall come, euen his neere kinsman, and bye out that which his brother solde.

26 And if he haue no redeemer, but hath gotten and founde to bye it out,

27 Then shall he count the yeeres of his sale, and restore the ouerplus to the man, to whome he solde it: so shall he returne to his possession.

28 But if he can not get sufficient to restore to him, then that which is solde, shall remaine in the hande of him that hath bought it, vntill the yere of the Iubile: and in the Iubile it shall come out, and he shall returne vnto his possession.

29 Likewise if a man sell a dwelling house in a walled citie, he may bye it out againe within a whole yeere after it is solde: within a yeere may he bye it out.

30 But if it be not bought out within ye space of a ful yeere, then the house that is in the walled citie, shalbe stablished, as cut off from the familie, to him that bought it, throughout his generations: it shall not goe out in the Iubile.

31 But the houses of villages, which haue no walles round about them, shalbe esteemed as the fielde of the countrey: they may be bought out againe, and shall goe out in the Iubile.

32 Notwithstanding, the cities of the Leuites, and the houses of the cities of their possession, may the Leuites redeeme at all seasons.

33 And if a man purchase of the Leuites, the house that was solde, and the citie of their possession shall goe out in the Iubile: for the houses of the cities of the Leuites are their possession among the children of Israel.

34 But the fielde of the suburbes of their cities, shall not be solde: for it is their perpetuall possession.

35 Moreouer, if thy brother be impouerished, and fallen in decay with thee, thou shalt relieue him, and as a stranger and soiourner, so shall he liue with thee.

36 Thou shalt take no vsurie of him, nor vantage, but thou shalt feare thy God, that thy brother may liue with thee.

37 Thou shalt not giue him thy money to vsurie, nor lende him thy vitailes for increase.

38 I am the Lord your God, which haue brought you out of the lande of Egypt, to giue you the lande of Canaan, and to be your God.

39 If thy brother also that dwelleth by thee, be impouerished, and be sold vnto thee, thou shalt not compel him to serue as a bond seruant,

40 But as an hired seruant, and as a soiourner he shalbe with thee: he shall serue thee vnto the yeere of the Iubile.

41 Then shall he depart from thee, both hee, and his children with him, and shall returne vnto his familie, and vnto the possession of his fathers shall he returne:

42 For they are my seruants, whom I brought out of the lande of Egypt: they shall not be solde as bondmen are solde.

43 Thou shalt not rule ouer him cruelly, but shalt feare thy God.

44 Thy bond seruant also, and thy bond maid, which thou shalt haue, shalbe of the heathen that are rounde about you: of them shall ye bye seruants and maydes.

45 And moreouer of the children of the stragers, that are soiourners among you, of them shall ye bye, and of their families that are with you, which they begate in your lande: these shall be your possession.

46 So ye shall take them as inheritance for your children after you, to possesse them by inheritance, ye shall vse their labours for euer: but ouer your brethren the children of Israel ye shall not rule one ouer another with crueltie.

47 If a soiourner or a stranger dwelling by thee get riches, and thy brother by him be impouerished, and sell him selfe vnto the stranger or soiourner dwelling by thee, or to the stocke of the strangers familie,

48 After that he is solde, he may be bought out: one of his brethren may bye him out,

49 Or his vncle, or his vncles sonne may bye him out, or any of the kindred of his flesh among his familie, may redeeme him: either if he can get so much, he may bye him selfe out.

50 Then he shall recken with his byer from the yeere that he was solde to him, vnto the yere of Iubile: and the money of his sale shalbe according to the number of yeeres: according to the time of an hyred seruant shall he be with him.

51 If there be many yeeres behind, according to them he shall giue againe for his deliuerance, of the money that he was bought for.

52 If there remaine but fewe yeeres vnto the yeere of Iubile, then he shall count with him, and according to his yeeres giue againe for his redemption.

53 He shalbe with him yeere by yeere as an hired seruant: he shall not rule cruelly ouer him in thy sight.

54 And if he be not redeemed thus, he shall go out in the yeere of Iubile, he, and his children with him.

55 For vnto me the children of Israel are seruants: they are my seruants, who I haue brought out of the land of Egypt: I am ye Lord your God.

Leviticus 26

1 Ye shall make you none idoles nor grauen image, neither reare you vp any pillar, neither shall ye set any image of stone in your land to bow downe to it: for I am the Lord your God.

2 Ye shall keepe my Sabbaths, and reuerence my Sanctuarie: I am the Lord.

3 If ye walke in mine ordinances, and keepe my commandements, and doe them,

4 I will then sende you raine in due season, and the land shall yelde her increase, and the trees of the fielde shall giue her fruite.

5 And your threshing shall reache vnto the vintage, and the vintage shall reache vnto sowing time, and you shall eate your bread in plenteousnesse, and dwell in your land safely.

6 And I will sende peace in the land, and ye shall sleepe and none shall make you afraid: also I will rid euill beastes out of the lande, and the sworde shall not go through your lande.

7 Also ye shall chase your enemies, and they shall fall before you vpon the sworde.

8 And fiue of you shall chase an hundreth, and an hundreth of you shall put ten thousande to flight, and your enemies shall fall before you vpon the sworde.

9 For I will haue respect vnto you, and make you encrease, and multiplie you, and establish my couenant with you.

10 Ye shall eate also olde store, and cary out olde because of the newe.

11 And I will set my Tabernacle among you, and my soule shall not lothe you.

12 Also I will walke among you, and I wil be your God, and ye shalbe my people.

13 I am the Lord your God which haue brought you out of the lande of Egypt, that yee should not be their bondmen, and I haue broken ye bonds of your yoke, and made you goe vpright.

14 But if ye will not obey me, nor do all these commandements,

15 And if ye shall despise mine ordinances, either if your soule abhorre my lawes, so that yee will not do all my commandements, but breake my couenant,

16 Then wil I also do this vnto you, I wil appoint ouer you fearefulnes, a consumption, and the burning ague to consume the eyes, and make the heart heauie, and you shall sowe your seede in vaine: for your enemies shall eate it:

17 And I will set my face against you, and ye shall fal before your enemies, and they that hate you, shall raigne ouer you, and yee shall flee when none pursueth you.

18 And if ye wil not for these things obey me, then wil I punish you seuen times more, according to your sinnes,

19 And I wil breake the pride of your power, and I will make your heauen as yron, and your earth as brasse:

20 And your strength shalbe spent in vaine: neither shall your lande giue her increase, neither shall the trees of the land giue their fruite.

21 And if ye walke stubburnly against me, and will not obey mee, I will then bring seuen times more plagues vpon you, according to your sinnes.

22 I will also sende wilde beastes vpon you, which shall spoyle you, and destroy your cattell, and make you fewe in number: so your hye waies shalbe desolate.

23 Yet if by these ye will not be reformed by me, but walke stubburnly against me,

24 Then wil I also walke stubburnly against you, and I will smite you yet seuen times for your sinnes:

25 And I wil send a sword vpon you, that shall auenge the quarel of my couenant: and when ye are gathered in your cities, I wil send the pestilence among you, and ye shall be deliuered into the hand of the enemie.

26 When I shall breake the staffe of your bread, then ten women shall bake your breade in one ouen, and they shall deliuer your bread againe by weight, and ye shall eate, but not be satisfied.

27 Yet if ye will not for this obey mee, but walke against me stubburnly,

28 Then will I walke stubburnly in mine anger against you, and I will also chastice you seuen times more according to your sinnes.

29 And ye shall eate ye flesh of your sonnes, and the flesh of your daughters shall ye deuoure.

30 I will also destroy your hye places, and cut away your images, and cast your carkeises vpon the bodies of your idoles, and my soule shall abhorre you.

31 And I will make your cities desolate, and bring your Sanctuarie vnto nought, and will not smelll the sauour of your sweete odours.

32 I will also bring the land vnto a wildernes, and your enemies, which dwell therein, shalbe astonished thereat.

33 Also I wil scatter you among the heathen, and will drawe out a sworde after you, and your land shalbe waste, and your cities shalbe desolate.

34 Then shall the land inioy her Sabbaths, as long as it lieth voide, and yee shalbe in your enemies land: then shall the land rest, and enioy her Sabbaths.

35 All the dayes that it lieth voide, it shall rest, because it did not rest in your Sabbaths, when ye dwelt vpon it.

36 And vpon them that are left of you, I will send euen a faintnes into their hearts in ye land of their enemies, and the sounde of a leafeshaken shall chase them, and they shall flee as fleeing from a sword, and they shall fall, no man pursuing them.

37 They shall fall also one vpon another, as before a sword, though none pursue them, and ye shall not be able to stand before your enemies:

38 And ye shall perish among the heathen, and the land of your enemies shall eate you vp.

39 And they that are left of you, shall pine away for their iniquitie, in your enemies landes, and for the iniquities of their fathers shall they pine away with them also.

40 Then they shall confesse their iniquitie, and the wickednes of their fathers for their trespasse, which they haue trespassed against mee, and also because they haue walked stubburnly against me.

41 Therefore I wil walke stubburnly against them, and bring them into the land of their enemies: so then their vncircumcised hearts shalbe humbled, and then they shalt willingly beare the punishment of their iniquitie.

42 Then I will remember my couenant with Iaakob, and my couenant also with Izhak, and also my couenant with Abraham will I remember, and will remember the land.

43 The land also in the meane season shalbe left of them, and shall enioye her Sabbaths while she lieth waste without them, but they shall willingly suffer the punishment of their iniquitie, because they despised my lawes, and because their soule abhorred mine ordinances.

44 Yet notwithstanding this, when they shalbe in the lande of their enemies, I wil not cast them away, neither will I abhorre them, to destroy them vtterly, nor to breake my couenant with them: for I am the Lord their God:

45 But I will remember for them the couenant of olde when I brought them out of ye land of Egypt in the sight of the heathen that I might be their God: I am the Lord.

46 These are the ordinances, and the iudgements, and the lawes, which the Lord made betweene him, and the children of Israel in mount Sinai, by the hand of Moses.

Leviticus 27

1 Moreouer the Lord spake vnto Moses, saying,

2 Speake vnto the children of Israel, and say vnto them, If any man shall make a vowe of a person vnto the Lord, by thy estimation,

3 Then thy estimation shall bee thus: a male from twentie yeere olde vnto sixty yeere olde shalbe by thy estimation euen fifty shekels of siluer, after the shekel of the Sanctuarie.

4 But if it be a female, then thy valuation shall be thirtie shekels.

5 And from fiue yere old to twentie yere olde thy valuation shall be for the male twentie shekels, and for the female ten shekels.

6 But from a moneth old vnto fiue yere old, thy price of the male shall bee fiue shekels of siluer, and thy price of the female, three shekels of siluer.

7 And from sixty yeere olde and aboue, if he be a male, then thy price shalbe fifteene shekels, and for the female ten shekels.

8 But if he be poorer then thou hast esteemed him, then shall hee present himselfe before the Priest, and the Priest shall value him, according to the abilitie of him that vowed, so shall the Priest value him.

9 And if it be a beast, whereof men bring an offering vnto the Lord, all that one giueth of such vnto the Lord, shalbe holy.

10 He shall not alter it nor change it, a good for a badde, nor a badde for a good: and if hee change beast for beast, then both this and that, which was changed for it, shall be holy.

11 And if it be any vncleane beast, of which men do not offer a sacrifice vnto the Lord, hee shall then present the beast before the Priest.

12 And the Priest shall value it, whether it be good or bad: and as thou valuest it, which art the Priest, so shall it bee.

13 But if he will bye it againe, then hee shall giue the fift part of it more, aboue thy valuation.

14 Also whe a man shall dedicate his house to be holy vnto the Lord, then the Priest shall value it, whether it be good or bad, and as ye Priest shall prise it, so shall the value be.

15 But if he that sanctified it, will redeeme his house, then hee shall giue thereto the fift part of money more then thy estimation, and it shalbe his.

16 If also a man dedicate to the Lord any grounde of his inheritance, then shalt thou esteeme it according to the seede therof: an Homer of barlie seede shalbe at fiftie shekels of siluer.

17 If he dedicate his field immediatly from the yeere of Iubile, it shall bee worth as thou doest esteeme it.

18 But if hee dedicate his fielde after the Iubile, then the Priest shall recken him the money according to ye yeeres that remaine vnto the yere of Iubile, and it shalbe abated by thy estimation.

19 And if he that dedicateth it, will redeeme the fielde, then he shall put the fift parte of the price, that thou esteemedst it at, thereunto, and it shall remaine his.

20 And if he will not redeeme the fielde, but the Priest sell the fielde to another man, it shalbe redeemed no more.

21 But the field shalbe holy to the Lord, whe it goeth out in the Iubile, as a fielde separate from common vses: the possession thereof shall be the Priests.

22 If a man also dedicate vnto ye Lord a fielde which he hath bought, which is not of the groud of his inheritance,

23 Then the Priest shall set the price to him, as thou esteemest it, vnto the yeere of Iubile, and he shall giue thy price the same day, as a thing holy vnto the Lord.

24 But in the yeere of Iubile, the fielde shall returne vnto him, of whome it was bought: to him, I say, whose inheritance the land was.

25 And all thy valuation shall bee according to the shekel of the Sanctuarie: a shekel conteyneth twenty gerahs.

26 Notwithstanding the first borne of the beastes, because it is the Lordes first borne, none shall dedicate such, be it bullocke, or sheepe; for it is the Lords.

27 But if it be an vncleane beast, then he shall redeeme it by thy valuation, and giue the fift part more thereto: and if it be not redeemed, then it shalbe solde, according to thy estimation.

28 Notwithstanding, nothing separate from the common vse that a man doeth separate vnto the Lord of all that he hath (whether it bee man or beast, or lande of his inheritance) may be solde nor redeemed: for euery thing separate from the common vse is most holy vnto the Lord.

29 Nothing separate from the common vse, which shall be separate from man, shalbe redeemed, but dye the death.

30 Also all the tithe of the lande both of the seede of the ground, and of the fruite of the trees is the Lords: it is holy to the Lord.

31 But if a man will redeeme any of his tithe, he shall adde the fift part thereto.

32 And euery tithe of bullock, and of sheepe, and of all that goeth vnder the rod, the tenth shalbe holy vnto the Lord.

33 He shall not looke if it be good or bad, neither shall he change it: els if he change it, both it, and that it was changed withall, shalbe holy, and it shall not be redeemed.

34 These are the commandements which the Lord commanded by Moses vnto the children of Israel in mount Sinai.

Numbers

Numbers 1

1 The Lord spake againe vnto Moses in the wildernesse of Sinai, in the Tabernacle of the Congregation, in the first day of the second moneth, in the second yere after they were come out of the land of Egypt, saying,

2 Take ye the summe of all the Congregation of the children of Israel, after their families, and housholdes of their fathers with the number of their names: to wit, all the males, man by man:

3 From twentie yere olde and aboue, all that go forth to the warre in Israel, thou and Aaron shall number them, throughout their armies.

4 And with you shalbe men of euery tribe, such as are the heads of the house of their fathers.

5 And these are the names of the men that shall stand with you, of the tribe of Reuben, Elizur, the sonne of Shedeur:

6 Of Simeon, Shelumiel the sonne of Zurishaddai:

7 Of Iudah, Nahshon the sonne of Amminadab:

8 Of Issachar, Nethaneel, the sonne of Zuar:

9 Of Zebulun, Eliab, the sonne of Helon:

10 Of the children of Ioseph: of Ephraim, Elishama the sonne of Ammihud: of Manasseh, Gamliel, the sonne of Pedahzur:

11 Of Beiamin, Abida the sonne of Gideoni:

12 Of Dan, Ahiezer, the sonne of Ammishaddai:

13 Of Asher, Pagiel, the sonne of Ocran:

14 Of Gad, Eliasaph, the sonne of Deuel:

15 Of Naphtali, Ahira the sonne of Enan.

16 These were famous in the Congregation, princes of the tribes of their fathers, and heads ouer thousands in Israel.

17 The Moses and Aaron tooke these men which are expressed by their names.

18 And they called all the Congregation together, in the first day of the second moneth, who declared their kindreds by their families, and by the houses of their fathers, according to the number of their names, from twentie yere olde and aboue, man by man.

19 As the Lord had commanded Moses, so he nombred them in the wildernesse of Sinai.

20 So were the sonnes of Reuben Israels eldest sonne by their generations, by their families, and by the houses of their fathers, according to the number of their names, man by man euery male from twentie yere olde and aboue, as many as went forth to warre:

21 The nomber of them, I say, of the tribe of Reuben, was sixe and fourtie thousande, and fiue hundreth.

22 Of the sonnes of Simeon by their generatios, by their families, and by the houses of their fathers, the summe therof by the nomber of their names, man by man, euery male from twentie yeere olde and aboue, all that went forth to warre:

23 The summe of them, I say, of the tribe of Simeon was nine and fiftie thousande, and three hundreth.

24 Of the sonnes of Gad by their generations, by their families, and by the houses of their fathers, according to the nomber of their names, from twentie yere olde and aboue, all that went forth to warre:

25 The number of them, I say, of the tribe of Gad was fiue and fourtie thousand, and six hundreth and fiftie.

26 Of the sonnes of Iudah by their generations, by their families, and by the houses of their fathers, according to the nomber of their names, from twentie yere olde and aboue, all that went forth to warre:

27 The nomber of them, I say, of the tribe of Iudah was three score and fourteene thousande, and sixe hundreth.

28 Of the sonnes of Issachar by their generations, by their families, and by the houses of their fathers, according to the nomber of their names, from twentie yeere olde and aboue, all that went forth to warre:

29 The number of them also of the tribe of Issachar was foure and fiftie thousande and foure hundreth.

30 Of the sonnes of Zebulun by their generations, by their families, and by the houses of their fathers, according to the number of their names, from twentie yeere olde and aboue, all that went foorth to warre:

31 The number of them also of the tribe of Zebulun was seuen and fiftie thousand and foure hundreth.

32 Of the sonnes of Ioseph, namely of the sonnes of Ephraim by their generations, by their families, and by the houses of their fathers, according to the nomber of their names, from twentie yeere olde and aboue, all that went foorth to warre:

33 The nomber of them also of the tribe of Ephraim was fourtie thousande and fiue hundreth.

34 Of the sonnes of Manasseh by their generations, by their families, and by the houses of their fathers, according to the nomber of their names, from twentie yeere olde and aboue, all that went foorth to warre:

35 The nober of the also of ye tribe of Manasseh was two and thirtie thousand and two hundreth.

36 Of the sonnes of Beniamin by their generations, by their families, and by the houses of their fathers, according to the nomber of their names, from twentie yeere olde and aboue, all that went foorth to warre:

37 The number of them also of the tribe of Beniamin was fiue and thirtie thousande and foure hundreth.

38 Of the sonnes of Dan by their generations, by their families, and by the houses of their fathers, according to the nomber of their names, from twentie yeere olde and aboue, all that went foorth to warre:

39 The nomber of the also of ye tribe of Dan was three score and two thousand and seue hudreth.

40 Of the sonnes of Asher by their generations, by their families, and by the houses of their fathers, according to the number of their names, from twentie yeere olde and aboue, all that went foorth to warre:

41 The number of them also of ye tribe of Asher was one and fourtie thousand and fiue hudreth.

42 Of the children of Naphtali, by their generations, by their families, and by the houses of their fathers, according to the number of their names, from twentie yeere olde and aboue, all that went to the warre:

43 The number of them also of the tribe of Naphtali, was three and fiftie thousand, and foure hundreth.

44 These are the summes which Moses, and Aaron nombred, and the Princes of Israel, the twelue men, which were euery one for the house of their fathers.

45 So this was all the summe of the sonnes of Israel, by the houses of their fathers, from twenty yeere olde and aboue, all that went to the warre in Israel,

46 And all they were in nomber sixe hudreth and three thousande, fiue hundreth and fiftie.

47 But the Leuites, after the tribes of their fathers were not nombred among them.

48 For the Lord had spoken vnto Moses, and said,

49 Onely thou shalt not number the tribe of Leui, neither take the summe of them among the children of Israel:

50 But thou shalt appoynt the Leuites ouer the Tabernacle of the Testimonie, and ouer all the instruments thereof, and ouer all things that belong to it: they shall beare the Tabernacle, and all the instruments thereof, and shall minister in it, and shall dwell round about the Tabernacle.

51 And when the Tabernacle goeth forth, the Leuites shall take it downe:

and when the Tabernacle is to be pitched, ye Leuites shall set it vp: for the stranger that commeth neere, shalbe slaine.

52 Also the children of Israel shall pitch their tentes, euery man in his campe, and euery man vnder his standerd throughout their armies.

53 But the Leuites shall pitch rounde about the Tabernacle of the Testimonie, least vengeance come vpon the Congregation of the children of Israel, and the Leuites shall take the charge of the Tabernacle of the Testimonie.

54 So the children of Israel did according to all that ye Lord had comanded Moses: so did they.

Numbers 2

1 And the Lord spake vnto Moses, and to Aaron, saying,

2 Euery man of the children of Israel shall campe by his standerd, and vnder the ensigne of their fathers house: farre off about the Tabernacle of the Congregation shall they pitch.

3 On the East side towarde the rising of the sunne, shall they of the standerd of the hoste of Iudah pitch according to their armies: and Nahshon the sonne of Amminadab shalbe captaine of the sonnes of Iudah.

4 And his hoste and the number of the were seuentie and foure thousande and sixe hundreth.

5 Next vnto him shall they of the tribe of Issachar pitch, and Nethaneel the sonne of Zuar shalbe the captaine of the sonnes of Issachar:

6 And his hoste, and the number thereof were foure and fiftie thousand, and foure hundreth.

7 Then the tribe of Zebulun, and Eliab the sonne of Helon, captaine ouer the sonnes of Zebulun:

8 And his hoste, and the number thereof seuen and fiftie thousand and foure hundreth:

9 The whole nomber of the hoste of Iudah are an hundreth fourescore and sixe thousande, and foure hundreth according to their armies: they shall first set foorth.

10 On the South side shalbe ye standerd of the host of Reuben according to their armies, and the captaine ouer the sonnes of Reuben shalbe Elizur the sonne of Shedeur.

11 And his host, and the nomber thereof sixe and fourty thousand and fiue hundreth.

12 And by him shall the tribe of Simeon pitch, and the captaiue ouer the sonnes of Simeon shall be Shelumiel the sonne of Zurishaddai:

13 And his hoste, and the number of them, nine and fiftie thousand and three hundreth.

14 And the tribe of Gad, and the captaine ouer the sonnes of Gad shall be Eliasaph the sonne of Deuel:

15 And his host and the nomber of the were fiue and fourtye thousande, sixe hundreth and fiftie.

16 All the nomber of the campe of Reuben were an hundreth and one and fiftie thousande, and foure hundreth and fiftie according to their armies, and they shall set foorth in the seconde place.

17 Then the Tabernacle of the Congregation shall goe with the host of the Leuites, in the mids of the campe as they haue pitched, so shall they goe forwarde, euery man in his order according to their standerds.

18 The standerd of the campe of Ephraim shalbe toward the west according to their armies: and ye captaine ouer the sonnes of Ephraim shall be Elishama the sonne of Ammihud:

19 And his host and the nomber of the were fortie thousand and fiue hundreth.

20 And by him shalbe the tribe of Manasseh, and the captaine ouer the sonnes of Manasseh shalbe Gamliel the sonne of Pedahzur:

21 And his hoste and the number of them were two and thirtie thousand and two hundreth.

22 And the tribe of Beniamin, and ye captaine ouer the sonnes of Beniamin shalbe Abidan the sonne of Gideoni:

23 And his host, and the number of the were fiue and thirtie thousand and foure hundreth.

24 All the nomber of the campe of Ephraim were an hundreth and eight thousande and one hundreth according to their armies, and they shall go in the third place.

25 The standerd of the host of Dan shalbe toward the North according to their armies: and the captaine ouer the children of Dan shall be Ahiezer the sonne of Ammishaddai:

26 And his host and the number of them were two and threescore thousand and seue hundreth.

27 And by him shall the tribe of Asher pitch, and the captaine ouer the sonnes of Asher shalbe Pagiel the sonne of Ocran.

28 And his host and the number of them were one and fourtie thousand and fiue hundreth.

29 Then the tribe of Naphtali, and the captaine ouer the children of Naphtali shall be Ahira the sonne of Enan:

30 And his host and the nomber of them were three and fiftie thousand and foure hundreth.

31 All the nomber of the host of Dan was an hundreth and seuen and fiftie thousand and sixe hundreth: they shall goe hinmost with their standerdes.

32 These are the summes of the childre of Israel by ye houses of their fathers, all the nomber of ye host, according to their armies, six hundreth and three thousand, fiue hundreth and fiftie.

33 But the Leuites were not nombred among the children of Israel, as the Lord had commanded Moses.

34 And the children of Israel did according to all that the Lord had commanded Moses: so they pitched according to their standards, and so they iourneyed euery one with his families, according to the houses of their fathers.

Numbers 3

1 These also were the generations of Aaron and Moses, in the day that the Lord spake with Moses in mount Sinai.

2 So these are the names of the sonnes of Aaron, Nadab the first borne, and Abihu, Eleazar, and Ithamar.

3 These are the names of the sonnes of Aaron the anoynted Priests, whom Moses did consecrate to minister in the Priests office.

4 And Nadab and Abihu died before the Lord, when they offred strange fire before the Lord in the wildernesse of Sinai, and had no children: but Eleazar and Ithamar serued in ye Priestes office in the sight of Aaron their father.

5 Then the Lord spake vnto Moses, saying,

6 Bring the tribe of Leui, and set the before Aaron the Priest that they may serue him,

7 And take the charge with him, euen the charge of the whole Congregation before the Tabernacle of the Congregation to doe the seruice of the Tabernacle.

8 They shall also keepe all the instruments of the Tabernacle of the Congregation, and haue the charge of the children of Israel to doe the seruice of the Tabernacle.

9 And thou shalt giue the Leuites vnto Aaron and to his sonnes: for they are giuen him freely from among the children of Israel.

10 And thou shalt appoint Aaron and his sonnes to execute their Priestes office: and the stranger that commeth neere, shalbe slayne.

11 Also the Lord spake vnto Moses, saying,

12 Beholde, I haue euen taken the Leuites from among the childre of Israel: for al the first borne that openeth the matrice among the children of Israel, and the Leuites shalbe mine,

13 Because all the first borne are mine: for the same day, that I smote all the first borne in the land of Egypt, I sanctified vnto me all the first borne in Israel, both man and beast: mine they shalbe: I am the Lord.

14 Moreouer, the Lord spake vnto Moses in the wildernesse of Sinai, saying,

15 Nomber the children of Leui after the houses of their fathers, in their families: euery male from a moneth olde and aboue shalt thou nomber.

16 Then Moses nombred them according to the word of the Lord, as he was commanded.

17 And these are the sonnes of Leui by their names, Gershon, and Kohath, and Merari.

18 Also these are the names of the sonnes of Gershon by their families: Libni and Shimei.

19 The sonnes also of Kohath by their families: Amram, and Izehar, Hebron, and Vzziel.

20 And the sonnes of Merari by their families: Mahli and Mushi. These are the families of Leui, according to the houses of their fathers.

21 Of Gershon came the familie of the Libnites, and the familie of the Shimeites: these are the families of the Gershonites.

22 The summe whereof (after the nomber of all the males from a moneth olde and aboue) was counted seuen thousand and fiue hundreth.

23 The families of the Gershonites shall pitch behind the Tabernacle westward.

24 The captaine and auncient of the house of the Gershonites shalbe Eliasaph the sonne of Lael.

25 And the charge of the sonnes of Gershon in the Tabernacle of the Congregation shall be the Tabernacle, and the pauilion, the couering thereof, and the vaile of the dore of the Tabernacle of the Congregation,

26 And the hanging of the court, and the vaile of the doore of the court, which is neere the Tabernacle, and neere ye Altar round about, and the cordes of it for all the seruice thereof.

27 And of Kohath came the familie of the Amramites, and the familie of the Izeharites, and the familie of the Hebronites, and the familie of the Vzzielites: these are the families of the Kohathites.

28 The nomber of all the males from a moneth olde and aboue was eight thousand and sixe hundreth, hauing the charge of the Sanctuarie.

29 The families of the sonnes of Kohath shall pitch on the Southside of the Tabernacle.

30 The captaine and auncient of the house, and families of the Kohathites shall be Elizaphan the sonne of Vzziel:

31 And their charge shalbe the Arke, and the Table, and the Candlesticke, and the altars, and the instruments of the Sanctuarie that they minister with, and the vaile, and all that serueth thereto.

32 And Eleazar the sonne of Aaron the Priest shalbe chiefe captaine of the Leuites, hauing the ouersight of them that haue the charge of the Sanctuarie.

33 Of Merari came the familie of the Mahlites, and the familie of the Mushites: these are the families of Merari.

34 And the summe of them, according to the nomber of all the males, from a moneth olde and aboue was sixe thousand and two hundreth.

35 The captaine and the ancient of the house of the families of Merari shalbe Zuriel the sonne of Abihail: they shall pitche on the Northside of the Tabernacle.

36 And in ye charge and custodie of the sonnes of Merari shall be the boardes of the Tabernacle, and the barres thereof, and his pillars, and his sockets, and al the instruments therof, and al that serueth thereto,

37 With the pillars of the court round about, with their sockets, and their pins and their coardes.

38 Also on the forefront of the Tabernacle toward the East, before the Tabernacle, I say, of the Congregation Eastwarde shall Moses and Aaron and his sonnes pitch, hauing the charge of the Sanctuarie, and the charge of the children of Israel: but the stranger that commeth neere, shall be slayne.

39 The wholesumme of ye Leuites, which Moses and Aaron nombred at the commandement of the Lord throughout their families, euen al the males from a moneth olde and aboue, was two and twentie thousand.

40 And the Lord said vnto Moses, Number all the first borne that are Males among the children of Israel, from a moneth old and aboue, and take the nomber of their names.

41 And thou shalt take ye Leuites to me for all the first borne of the children of Israel (I am the Lord) and the cattell of the Leuites for all the first borne of the cattell of the children of Israel.

42 And Moses nombred, as the Lord commanded him, all the first borne of the children of Israel.

43 And all the first borne males rehearsed by name (from a moneth olde and aboue) according to their nomber were two and twentie thousand, two hundreth seuentie and three.

44 And the Lord spake vnto Moses, saying,

45 Take the Leuites for all the first borne of the children of Israel, and the cattell of the Leuites for their cattel, and the Leuites shalbe mine, (I am the Lord)

46 And for the redeeming of the two hundreth seuentie and three, (which are moe then the Leuites) of the first borne of the children of of Israel,

47 Thou shalt also take fiue shekels for euery person: after the weight of the Sanctuarie shalt thou take it: ye shekel conteineth twenty gerahs.

48 And thou shalt giue the money, wherwith the odde number of them is redeemed, vnto Aaron and to his sonnes.

49 Thus Moses tooke the redemption of the that were redeemed, being more then the Leuites:

50 Of the first borne of the children of Israel tooke he the mony: eue a thousand three hundreth three score and fiue shekels after the shekel of the Sanctuarie.

51 And Moses gaue the money of them that were redeemed, vnto Aaron and to his sonnes according to the word of the Lord, as the Lord had commanded Moses.

Numbers 4

1 And the Lord spake vnto Moses, and to Aaron, saying,

2 Take the summe of the sonnes of Kohath from among the sonnes of Leui, after their families, and houses of their fathers,

3 From thirtie yeere olde and aboue, euen vntill fiftie yeere olde, all that enter into the assemblie to do the worke in the Tabernacle of the Congregation.

4 This shall be the office of the sonnes of Kohath in the Tabernacle of the Congregation about the Holiest of all.

5 When the hoste remoueth, then Aaron and his sonnes shall come and take downe the couering vaile, and shall couer the Arke of the Testimonie therewith.

6 And they shall put thereon a couering of badgers skinnes, and shall spread vpon it a cloth altogether of blewe silke, and put to the barres thereof:

7 And vpon ye table of shew bread they shall spread a cloth of blewe silke, and put thereon the dishes, and the incense cups, and goblets, and couerings to couer it with, and the bread shall be thereon continually:

8 And they shall spread vpon them a couering of skarlet, and couer the same with a couering of badgers skinnes, and put to the barres thereof.

9 Then they shall take a cloth of blewe silke, and couer the candlesticke of light with his lampes and his snuffers, and his snuffedishes, and al the oyle vessels thereof, which they occupie about it.

10 So they shall put it, and all the instruments thereof in a couering of badgers skinnes, and put it vpon the barres.

11 Also vpon the golden altar they shall spread a cloth of blewe silke, and couer it with a couering of badgers skinnes, and put to the barres thereof.

12 And they shall take all the instruments of the ministerie wherewith they minister in the Sanctuarie, and put them in a cloth of blew silke, and couer the with a couering of badgers skinnes, and put them on the barres.

13 Also they shall take away the ashes from the altar, and spread a purple cloth vpon it,

14 And shall put vpon it all the instruments thereof, which they occupie about it: the censers, the fleshhookes and the besomes, and the basens, euen al the instruments of the altar and they shall spread vpon it a couering of badgers skinnes, and put to the barres of it.

15 And when Aaron and his sonnes haue made an ende of couering the Sanctuarie, and al the instruments of the Sanctuarie, at the remouing of the host, afterward the sonnes of Kohath shall come to beare it, but they shall not touch any holy thing, lest they dye. This is the charge of the sonnes of Kohath in the Tabernacle of the Congregation.

16 And to the office of Eleazar the sonne of Aaron the Priest pertaineth the oyle for the light, and the sweete incense and the dayly meat offring, and the anointing oyle, with the ouersight of all the Tabernacle, and of all that therein is, both in the Sanctuarie and in all the instruments thereof.

17 And the Lord spake vnto Moses and to Aaron, saying,

18 Ye shall not cut off the tribe of the families of the Kohathites from among the Leuites:

19 But thus do vnto them, that they may liue and not die, when they come neere to the most holy things: let Aaron and his sonnes come and appoynt them, euery one to his office, and to his charge.

20 But let them not goe in, to see when the Sanctuarie is folden vp, lest they die.

21 And the Lord spake vnto Moses, saying,

22 Take also ye summe of the sonnes of Gershon, euery one by the houses of their fathers throughout their families:

23 From thirtie yere old and aboue, vntil fiftie yere old shalt thou nomber them, al that enter into the assemblie for to do seruice in the Tabernacle of the Congregation.

24 This shall be the seruice of the families of the Gershonites, to serue and to beare.

25 They shall beare the curtaines of the Tabernacle, and the Tabernacle of the Congregation, his couering, and the couering of badgers skinnes, that is on hie vpon it, and the vayle of the doore of the Tabernacle of the Congregation:

26 The curtaines also of the court, and the vaile of the entring in of the gate of the court, which is neere the Tabernacle and neere the altar round about, with their cordes, and all the instruments for their seruice, and all that is made for them: so shall they serue.

27 At the commandement of Aaron and his sonnes shall all the seruice of the sonnes of ye Gershonites bee done, in all their charges and in all their seruice, and ye shall appoynt them to keepe all their charges.

28 This is the seruice of the families of the sonnes of the Gershonites in the Tabernacle of the Congregation, and their watch shall be vnder the hande of Ithamar the sonne of Aaron the Priest.

29 Thou shalt nomber the sonnes of Merari by their families, and by the houses of their fathers:

30 From thirty yere olde and aboue, euen vnto fiftie yere olde shalt thou nomber the, all that enter into the assemblie, to doe the seruice of the Tabernacle of the Congregation.

31 And this is their office and charge according to all their seruice in the Tabernacle of the Congregation: the boardes of the Tabernacle with the barres thereof, and his pillars, and his sockets,

32 And the pillars rounde about the court, with their sockets and their pinnes, and their cords, with all their instruments, euen for all their seruice: and by name ye shall recken the instruments of their office and charge.

33 This is the seruice of the families of the sonnes of Merari, according to all their seruice in the Tabernacle of the Congregation vnder the hand of Ithamar the sonne of Aaron the Priest.

34 Then Moses and Aaron and the princes of the Congregation nombred the sonnes of the Kohathites, by their families and by the houses of their fathers,

35 From thirtie yeere olde and aboue, euen vnto fiftie yere olde, all that enter into the assemblie for the seruice of the Tabernacle of ye Congregation.

36 So the nombers of the throughout their families were two thousande, seuen hundreth and fiftie.

37 These are the nombers of the families of the Kohathites, al that serue in the Tabernacle of the Congregation, which Moses and Aaron did nomber according to the commandement of the Lord by the hand of Moses.

38 Also the nombers of the sonnes of Gershon throughout their families and houses of their fathers,

39 From thirtie yere olde and vpwarde, euen vnto fiftie yere olde: all that enter into the assemblie for the seruice of the Tabernacle of the Cogregation.

40 So the nombers of them by their families, and by the houses of their fathers were two thousand sixe hundreth and thirtie.

41 These are the nombers of the families of the sonnes of Gershon: of all that did seruice in the Tabernacle of the Congregation, whom Moses and Aaron did nomber according to the commandement of the Lord.

42 The nombers also of the families of the sonnes of Merari by their families, and by the houses of their fathers,

43 From thirtie yeere olde and vpwarde, euen vnto fiftie yeere olde: all that enter into the assemblie for the seruice of the Tabernacle of the Congregation.

44 So the nombers of them by their families were three thousand, and two hundreth.

45 These are the summes of ye families of the sonnes of Merari, whom Moses and Aaron nombred according to the commandement of the Lord, by the hand of Moses.

46 So all the nombers of the Leuites, which Moses, and Aaron, and the princes of Israel nombred by their families and by the houses of their fathers,

47 From thirtie yere olde and vpward, euen to fiftie yeere olde, euery one that came to doe his duetie, office, seruice and charge in the Tabernacle of the Congregation.

48 So the nombers of them were eight thousand, fiue hundreth and foure score.

49 According to the commandement of the Lord by the hand of Moses did Aaron nomber them, euery one according to his seruice, and according to his charge. Thus were they of that tribe nombred, as the Lord commanded Moses.

Numbers 5

1 And the Lord spake vnto Moses, saying,

2 Commaund the children of Israel that they put out of the hoste euery leper, and euery one that hath an issue, and whosoeuer is defiled by the dead.

3 Both male and female shall ye put out: out of the hoste shall yee put them, that they defile not their tentes among whome I dwell.

4 And the children of Israel did so, and put them out of the host, euen as the Lord had commanded Moses, so did the children of Israel.

5 And the Lord spake vnto Moses, saying,

6 Speake vnto the children of Israel, When a man or woman shall commit any sinne that men commit, and transgresse against the Lord, when that person shall trespasse,

7 Then they shall confesse their sinne which they haue done, and shall restore the domage thereof with his principall, and put the fift part of it more thereto, and shall giue it vnto him, against whom he hath trespassed.

8 But if the man haue no kinseman, to whom he shoulde restore the domage, the domage shall be restored to the Lord for the Priests vse besides the ramme of the atonement, whereby hee shall make atonement for him.

9 And euery offring of all the holy thinges of the children of Israel, which they bring vnto the Priest, shalbe his.

10 And euery mans halowed things shall bee his: that is, whatsoeuer any man giueth the Priest, it shalbe his.

11 And the Lord spake vnto Moses, saying,

12 Speake vnto the children of Israel, and say vnto them, If any mans wife turne to euill, and commit a trespasse against him,

13 So that an other man lie with her fleshly, and it bee hid from the eyes of her husband, and kept close, and yet she be defiled, and there be no witnesse against her, neither she taken with the maner,

14 If he be moued with a ielous minde, so that he is ielous ouer his wife, which is defiled, or if he haue a ielous minde, so that he is ielous ouer his wife, which is not defiled,

15 Then shall the man bring his wife to the Priest, and bring her offering with her, the tenth part of an Ephah of barly meale, but he shall not powre oyle vpon it, nor put incense thereon: for it is an offring of ielousie, an offring for a remembrance, calling the sinne to minde:

16 And the Priest shall bring her, and set her before the Lord.

17 Then the Priest shall take the holy water in an earthen vessel, and of the dust that is in the floore of the Tabernacle, euen the Priest shall take it and put it into the water.

18 After, the Priest shall set the woman before the Lord, and vncouer the womans head, and put the offring of the memorial in her hands: it is the ielousie offering, and the Priest shall haue bitter and cursed water in his hand,

19 And the Priest shall charge her by an othe, and say vnto the woman, If no man haue lien with thee, neither thou hast turned to vncleannesse from thine

husband, be free from this bitter and cursed water.

20 But if thou hast turned from thine husband, and so art defiled, and some man hath lyen with thee beside thine husband,

21 (Then the Priest shall charge the woman with an othe of cursing, and the Priest shall say vnto the woman) The Lord make thee to be accursed, and detestable for the othe among thy people, and the Lord cause thy thigh to rot, and thy belly to swell:

22 And that this cursed water may goe into thy bowels, to cause thy belly to swell, and thy thigh to rot. Then the woman shall answere, Amen, Amen.

23 After, the Priest shall write these curses in a booke, and shall blot them out with the bitter water,

24 And shall cause the woman to drinke ye bitter and cursed water, and the cursed water, turned into bitternesse, shall enter into her.

25 Then the Priest shall take the ielousie offring out of the womans hand, and shall shake the offring before the Lord, and offer it vpon ye altar.

26 And the Priest shall take an handfull of the offring for a memorial thereof, and burne it vpon the altar, and afterwarde make the woman drinke the water.

27 When yee haue made her drinke the water, (if she bee defiled and haue trespassed against her husband) then shall the cursed water, turned into bitternesse, enter into her, and her belly shall swell, and her thigh shall rot, and the woman shall be accursed among her people.

28 But if the woman bee not defiled, but bee cleane, she shalbe free and shall conceiue and beare.

29 This is the law of ielousie, when a wife turneth from her husband and is defiled,

30 Or when a man is moued with a ielous minde being ielous ouer his wife then shall he bring the woman before the Lord, and the Priest shall do to her according to al this lawe,

31 And the man shalbe free from sinne, but this woman shall beare her iniquitie.

Numbers 6

1 And the Lord spake vnto Moses, saying,

2 Speake vnto the children of Israel, and say vnto them, When a man or a woman doeth separate themselues to vowe a vowe of a Nazarite to separate himselfe vnto the Lord,

3 He shall abstaine from wine and strong drinke, and shall drinke no sowre wine nor sowre drinke, nor shall drinke any licour of grapes, neither shall eate fresh grapes nor dryed.

4 As long as his abstinence endureth, shall hee eat nothing that is made of the wine of the vine, neither the kernels, nor the huske.

5 While hee is separate by his vowe, the rasor shall not come vpon his head, vntill the dayes be out, in the which he separateth him selfe vnto the Lord, he shalbe holy, and shall let the lockes of the heare of his head growe.

6 During the time that he separateth himselfe vnto the Lord, he shall come at no dead body:

7 Hee shall not make himselfe vncleane at the death of his father, or mother, brother, or sister: for the consecration of his God is vpon his head.

8 All the dayes of his separation he shalbe holy to the Lord.

9 And if any dye suddenly by him, or hee beware, then the head of his consecration shall be defiled, and he shall shaue his head in the day of his clensing: in the seuenth day he shall shaue it.

10 And in the eight day hee shall bring two turtles, or two yong pigeons to the Priest, at the doore of the Tabernacle of the Congregation.

11 Then the Priest shall prepare the one for a sinne offering, and the other for a burnt offering, and shall make an atonement for him, because he sinned by the dead: so shall he halowe his head the same day,

12 And he shall consecrate vnto the Lord the dayes of his separation, and shall bring a lambe of a yeere olde for a trespasse offering, and the first dayes shalbe voide: for his consecration was defiled.

13 This then is the lawe of the Nazarite: When the time of his consecration is out, he shall come to the doore of the Tabernacle of the Congregation,

14 And hee shall bring his offering vnto the Lord, an hee lambe of a yeere olde without blemish for a burnt offering, and a shee lambe of a yere olde without blemish for a sinne offring, and a ramme without blemish for peace offrings,

15 And a basket of vnleauened bread, of cakes of fine floure, mingled with oyle, and wafers of vnleauened bread anointed with oile, with their meate offring, and their drinke offrings:

16 The which the Priest shall bring before the Lord, and make his sinne offering and his burnt offering.

17 He shall prepare also the ram for a peace offring vnto the Lord, with the basket of vnleauened bread, and the Priest shall make his meate offring, and his drinke offring.

18 And the Nazarite shall shaue the head of his consecration at the doore of the Tabernacle of the Congregation, and shall take the heare of the head of his consecration, and put it in the fire, which is vnder the peace offring.

19 Then the Priest shall take ye sodden shoulder of the ramme, and an vnleauened cake out of the basket, and a wafer vnleauened, and put them vpon the hands of the Nazarite, after he hath shauen his consecration.

20 And the Priest shall shake them to and from before the Lord: this is an holy thing for the Priest besides the shaken breast, and besides the heaue shoulder: so afterwarde the Nazarite may drinke wine.

21 This is the Lawe of the Nazarite, which he hath vowed, and of his offering vnto the Lord for his consecration, besides that that hee is able to bring: according to the vowe which he vowed, so shall he do after the lawe of his consecration.

22 And the Lord spake vnto Moses, saying,

23 Speake vnto Aaron and to his sonnes, saying, Thus shall ye blesse the childre of Israel, and say vnto them,

24 The Lord blesse thee, and keepe thee,

25 The Lord make his face shine vpon thee, and be merciful vnto thee,

26 The Lord lift vp his coutenance vpon thee, and giue thee peace.

27 So they shall put my Name vpon the children of Israel, and I wil blesse them.

Numbers 7

1 Nowe when Moses had finished the setting vp of the Tabernacle, and anointed it and sanctified it, and all the instruments thereof, and the altar with al the instruments thereof, and had anoynted them and sanctified them,

2 Then the princes of Israel, heads ouer the houses of their fathers (they were the princes of the tribes, who were ouer them that were nombred) offred,

3 And brought their offring before the Lord, sixe couered charets, and twelue oxen: one charet for two princes, and for euery one an oxe, and they offred them before the Tabernacle.

4 And the Lord spake vnto Moses, saying,

5 Take these of them, that they may be to doe the seruice of the Tabernacle of the Congregation, and thou shalt giue them vnto the Leuites, to euery man according vnto his office.

6 So Moses tooke the charets and the oxen, and gaue them vnto the Leuites:

7 Two charets and foure oxen hee gaue to the sonnes of Gershon, according vnto their office.

8 And foure charets and eight oxen hee gaue to the sonnes of Merari according vnto their office, vnder the hand of Ithamar the sonne of Aaron the Priest.

9 But to the sonnes of Kohath he gaue none, because the charge of the Sanctuarie belonged to them, which they did beare vpon their shoulders.

10 The princes also offered in the dedication for the altar in the day that it was anoynted: then the princes offered their offering before the altar.

11 And the Lord sayd vnto Moses, One prince one day, and an other prince an other day shall offer their offring, for the dedication of the altar.

12 So then on the first day did Nahshon the sonne of Amminadab of ye tribe of Iudah offer his offring.

13 And his offring was a siluer charger of an hundreth and thirtie shekels weight, a siluer boule of seuenty shekels, after the shekel of the Sanctuarie, both ful of fine floure, mingled with oyle, for a meate offring,

14 An incense cup of gold of tenne shekels, ful of incense,

15 A yong bullocke, a ram, a lambe of a yeere olde for a burnt offring,

16 An hee goate for a sinne offring,

17 And for peace offrings, two bullockes, fiue rams, fiue hee goates, and fiue lambes of a yeere olde: this was the offring of Nahshon the sonne of Amminadab.

18 The second day Nethaneel, the sonne of Zuar, prince of the tribe of Issachar did offer:

19 Who offred for his offring a siluer charger of an hundreth and thirtie shekels weight, a siluer boule of seuentie shekels, after the shekel of the Sanctuarie, both ful of fine floure, mingled with oyle, for a meat offring,

20 An incense cup of gold of ten shekels, ful of incense,

21 A yong bullocke, a ram, a lambe of a yeere olde for a burnt offring,

22 An hee goate for a sinne offring,

23 And for peace offrings, two bullockes, fiue rammes, fiue hee goates, fiue lambes of a yeere olde: this was the offring of Nethaneel the sonne of Zuar.

24 The third day Eliab the sonne of Helon prince of the children of Zebulun offred.

25 His offring was a siluer charger of an hundreth and thirty shekels weight, a siluer boule of seuentie shekels, after the shekel of the Sanctuarie, both ful of fine floure, mingled with oyle, for a meate offring,

26 A golden incense cup of ten shekels, ful of incense,

27 A yong bullocke, a ram, a lambe of a yeere olde for a burnt offring,

28 An hee goate for a sinne offring,

29 And for peace offrings, two bullockes, fiue rammes, fiue hee goates, fiue lambes of a yeere olde: this was the offering of Eliab the sonne of Helon.

30 The fourth day Elizur ye sonne of Shedeur prince of the children of Reuben offred.

31 His offring was a siluer charger of an hundreth and thirtie shekels weight, a siluer boule of seuentie shekels, after the shekel of the Sanctuary, both ful of fine floure, mingled with oyle, for a meate offring,

32 A golden incense cup of ten shekels, full of incense,

33 A yong bullocke, a ram, a lambe of a yere olde for a burnt offring,

34 An hee goate for a sinne offring,

35 And for a peace offring, two bullockes, fiue rammes, fiue hee goates, and fiue lambes of a yere olde: this was the offering of Elizur the sonne of Shedeur.

36 The fifth day Shelumiel the sonne of Zurishaddai, prince of the children of Simeon offered.

37 His offring was a siluer charger of an hundreth and thirtie shekels weight, a siluer boule of seuentie shekels, after the shekel of the Sanctuary, both ful of fine floure, mingled with oyle, for a meate offring,

38 A golden incense cup of ten shekels, full of incense,

39 A yong bullocke, a ram, a lambe of a yeere olde for a burnt offring,

40 An hee goate for a sinne offring,

41 And for a peace offring, two bullocks, fiue rammes, fiue hee goates, fiue lambes of a yere old: this was the offering of Shelumiel the sonne of Zurishaddai.

42 The sixt day Eliasaph the sonne of Deuel prince of the children of Gad offred.

43 His offring was a siluer charger of an hundreth and thirtie shekels weight, a siluer boule of seuentie shekels, after the shekel of the Sanctuarie, both ful of fine floure, mingled with oyle, for a meate offring,

44 A golden incense cup of ten shekels, full of incense,

45 A yong bullocke, a ram, a lambe of a yere olde, for a burnt offring,

46 An hee goate for a sinne offring,

47 And for a peace offering, two bullockes, fiue rammes, fiue hee goates, fiue lambes of a yere olde: this was the offring of Eliasaph the sonne of Deuel.

48 The seuenth day Elishama the sonne of Ammiud prince of the children of Ephraim offered.

49 His offring was a siluer charger of an hundreth and thirtie shekels weight, a siluer boule of seuentie shekels, after the shekel of the Sanctuary, both full of fine floure, mingled with oyle, for a meate offering,

50 A golden incense cup of ten shekels, full of incense,

51 A yong bullocke, a ram, a lambe of a yeere olde for a burnt offring,

52 An hee goate for a sinne offring,

53 And for a peace offring, two bullockes, fiue rammes, fiue hee goates, fiue lambes of a yeere olde: this was the offring of Elishama the sonne of Ammiud.

54 The eight day offred Gamliel the sonne of Pedazur, prince of the children of Manasseh.

55 His offring was a siluer charger of an hundreth and thirtie shekels weight, a siluer boule of seuentie shekels, after the shekel of the Sanctuarie, both full of fine floure, mingled with oyle, for a meate offring,

56 A golden incense cup of ten shekels, full of incense,

57 A yong bullocke, a ram, a lambe of a yeere olde for a burnt offring,

58 An hee goate for a sinne offring,

59 And for a peace offring, two bullockes, fiue rammes, fiue hee goates, fiue lambes of a yeere olde: this was the offring of Gamliel the sonne of Pedazur.

60 The ninth day Abidan the sonne of Gideoni prince of the children of Beniamin offered.

61 His offring was a siluer charger of an hundreth and thirtie shekels weight, a siluer boule of seuentie shekels, after the shekel of the Sanctuarie, both full of fine floure, mingled with oyle, for a meate offring,

62 A golden incense cup of ten shekels, full of incense,

63 A yong bullocke, a ram, a lambe of a yeere olde for a burnt offring,

64 An hee goate for a sinne offring,

65 And for a peace offring, two bullockes, fiue rammes, fiue hee goates, fiue lambes of a yeere olde: this was the offring of Abidan the sonne of Gideoni.

66 The tenth day Ahiezer the sonne of Ammishaddai, prince of the children of Dan offred.

67 His offring was a siluer charger of an hundreth and thirtie shekels weight, a siluer boule of seuentie shekels, after the shekel of the Sanctuarie, both full of fine floure, mingled with oyle, for a meate offring,

68 A golden incense cup of ten shekels full of incense,

69 A yong bullocke, a ram, a lambe of a yeere olde for a burnt offring,

70 An hee goate for a sinne offring,

71 And for a peace offring, two bullocks, fiue rammes, fiue hee goates, fiue lambes of a yeere olde: this was the offring of Ahiezer the sonne of Ammishaddai.

72 The eleuenth day Pagiel the sonne of Ocran, prince of the children of Asher offred.

73 His offring was a siluer charger of an hundreth and thirtie shekels weight, a siluer boule of seuentie shekels, after the shekel of the Sanctuarie, both full of fine floure, mingled with oyle, for a meate offring,

74 A golden incense cup of ten shekels, ful of incense,

75 A yong bullocke, a ram, a lambe of a yere olde for a burnt offring,

76 An hee goate for a sinne offring,

77 And for a peace offring, two bullockes, fiue rams, fiue he goates, fiue lambes of a yeere olde: this was the offring of Pagiel the sonne of Ocran.

78 The twelfth day Ahira the sonne of Enan, prince of the children of Naphtali offred,

79 His offring was a siluer charger of an hundreth and thirtie shekels weight, a siluer boule of seuentie shekels, after the shekel of the Sanctuarie, both full of fine floure, mingled with oyle, for a meate offring,

80 A golden incense cup of ten shekels, ful of incense,

81 A yong bullocke, a ram, a lambe of a yere olde for a burnt offring,

82 An hee goate for a sinne offring,

83 And for peace offerings, two bullockes, fiue rammes, fiue hee goates, fiue lambes of a yeere olde: this was the offering of Ahira the sonne of Enan.

84 This was the dedication of the Altar by the princes of Israel, whe it was anointed: twelue chargers of siluer, twelue siluer boules, twelue incense cuppes of golde,

85 Euery charger, conteining an hundreth and thirtie shekels of siluer, and euery boule seuentie: all the siluer vessell conteined two thousande and foure hundreth shekels, after the shekell of the Sanctuarie.

86 Twelue incense cups of gold ful of incense, conteining ten shekels euery

cup, after the shekell of the Sanctuarie: all the gold of the incense cups was an hundreth and twentie shekels.

87 All the bullockes for the burnt offering were twelue bullocks, the rams twelue, the lambs of a yeere olde twelue, with their meate offrings, and twelue hee goates for a sinne offring.

88 And all the bullocks for the peace offrings were foure and twentie bullockes, the rammes sixtie, the hee goates sixtie, the lambes of a yeere olde sixtie: this was the dedication of the Altar, after that it was anointed.

89 And when Moses went into the Tabernacle of the Congregation, to speake with God, he heard the voyce of one speaking vnto him from the Merciseat, that was vpon the Arke of the Testimonie betweene the two Cherubims, and he spake to him.

Numbers 8

1 And the Lord spake vnto Moses, saying,

2 Speake vnto Aaron, and say vnto him, When thou lightest the lampes, the seuen lampes shall giue light towarde the forefront of the Candlesticke.

3 And Aaron did so, lighting the lampes thereof towarde ye forefront of the Candlesticke, as the Lord had commanded Moses.

4 And this was the worke of the Candlesticke, euen of golde beaten out with the hammer, both the shafte, and the flowres thereof was beaten out with the hammer: according to the paterne, which the Lord had shewed Moses, so made he the Candlesticke.

5 And the Lord spake vnto Moses, saying,

6 Take the Leuites from among the children of Israel, and purifie them.

7 And thus shalt thou doe vnto them, when thou purifiest them, Sprinckle water of purification vpon them, and let them shaue all their flesh, and wash their clothes: so they shalbe cleane.

8 Then they shall take a yong bullocke with his meate offring of fine floure, mingled with oyle, and another yong bullocke shalt thou take for a sinne offring.

9 Then thou shalt bring the Leuites before the Tabernacle of the Congregation, and assemble all the Congregation of the children of Israel.

10 Thou shalt bring the Leuites also before the Lord, and the children of Israel shall put their handes vpon the Leuites.

11 And Aaron shall offer the Leuites before the Lord, as a shake offring of ye childre of Israel, that they may execute the seruice of the Lord.

12 And the Leuites shall put their handes vpon the heades of the bullockes, and make thou the one a sinne offring, and the other a burnt offring vnto the Lord, that thou mayest make an atonement for the Leuites.

13 And thou shalt set the Leuites before Aaron and before his sonnes, and offer the as a shake offring to the Lord.

14 Thus thou shalt separate the Leuites from among the children of Israel, and the Leuites shall be mine.

15 And afterwarde shall the Leuites goe in, to serue in the Tabernacle of the Congregation, and thou shalt purifie them and offer them, as a shake offering.

16 For they are freely giuen vnto me from among the children of Israel, for such as open any wombe: for all the first borne of the children of Israel haue I taken them vnto me.

17 For all the first borne of the children of Israel are mine, both of man and of beast: since the day that I smote euery first borne in the land of Egypt, I sanctified them for my selfe.

18 And I haue taken the Leuites for all the first borne of the children of Israel,

19 And haue giuen the Leuites as a gift vnto Aaron, and to his sonnes from among the children of Israel, to do the seruice of the children of Israel in the Tabernacle of the Congregation, and to make an atonement for the children of Israel, that there be no plague among the children of Israel, when the children of Israel come neere vnto the Sanctuarie.

20 Then Moses and Aaron and all the Cogregation of the children of Israel did with the Leuites, according vnto all that the Lord had commanded Moses concerning the Leuites: so did the children of Israel vnto them.

21 So the Leuites were purified, and washed their clothes, and Aaron offred them as a shake offring before the Lord, and Aaron made an atonement for them, to purifie them.

22 And after that, went the Leuites in to doe their seruice in the Tabernacle of the Congregation, before Aaron and before his sonnes: as the Lord had commanded Moses concerning the Leuites, so they did vnto them.

23 And the Lord spake vnto Moses, saying,

24 This also belongeth to the Leuites: from fiue and twentie yeere olde and vpwarde, they shall goe in, to execute their office in the seruice of the Tabernacle of the Congregation.

25 And after the age of fiftie yeere, they shall cease from executing the office, and shall serue no more:

26 But they shall minister with their brethre in the Tabernacle of the Congregation, to keepe things committed to their charge, but they shall doe no seruice: thus shalt thou doe vnto the Leuites touching their charges.

Numbers 9

1 And the Lord spake vnto Moses in the wildernes of Sinai, in the first moneth of the second yeere, after they were come out of the land of Egypt, saying,

2 The children of Israel shall also celebrate the Passeouer at ye time appointed thereunto.

3 In the fourtenth day of this moneth at euen, ye shall keepe it in his due season: according to all the ordinances of it, and according to all the ceremonies thereof shall ye keepe it.

4 Then Moses spake vnto the children of Israel, to celebrate the Passeouer.

5 And they kept the Passeouer in the fourtenth day of the first moneth at euen in the wildernesse of Sinai: according to all that the Lord had comanded Moses, so did ye children of Israel.

6 And certaine men were defiled by a dead man, that they might not keepe the Passeouer the same day: and they came before Moses and before Aaron the same day.

7 And those men said vnto him, We are defiled by a dead man: wherefore are wee kept backe that we may not offer an offering vnto the Lord in the time thereunto appointed among the children of Israel?

8 Then Moses saide vnto them, Stande still, and I will heare what the Lord will commande concerning you.

9 And the Lord spake vnto Moses, saying,

10 Speake vnto the children of Israel, and say, If any amog you, or of your posteritie shalbe vncleane by ye reason of a corps, or be in a log iourney, he shall keepe the Passeouer vnto ye Lord.

11 In the fourtenth day of the second moneth at euen they shall keepe it: with vnleauened bread and sowre herbes shall they eate it.

12 They shall leaue none of it vnto the morning, nor breake any bone of it: according to all the ordinance of the Passeouer shall they keepe it.

13 But the man that is cleane and is not in a iourney, and is negligent to keepe the Passeouer, the same person shalbe cut off from his people: because he brought not the offring of the Lord in his due season, that man shall beare his sinne.

14 And if a stranger dwell among you, and wil keepe the Passeouer vnto the Lord, as the ordinance of the Passeouer, and as the maner thereof is, so shall he do: ye shall haue one lawe both for the stranger, and for him that was borne in the same lande.

15 And when the Tabernacle was reared vp, a cloude couered the Tabernacle, namely the Tabernacle of the Testimonie: and at euen there was vpon the Tabernacle, as the appearance of fire vntill the morning.

16 So it was alway: the cloude couered it by day, and the appearance of fire by night.

17 And when the cloude was taken vp from the Tabernacle, then afterwarde the children of Israel iourneyed: and in the place where the cloude abode, there the children of Israel pitched their tents.

18 At the commandement of the Lord the children of Israel iourneyed, and at the comandement of the Lord they pitched: as long as the cloude abode vpon the Tabernacle, they lay still.

19 And when the cloude taryed stil vpon the Tabernacle a long time, the childre of Israel kept the watch of the Lord, and iourneyed not.

20 So when the cloud abode a few dayes vpon the Tabernacle, they abode in their tents according to the comandement of ye Lord: for they iourneyed at the commandement of the Lord.

21 And though the cloud abode vpon the Tabernacle from euen vnto the morning, yet if the cloude was taken vp in the morning, then they iourneyed: whether by daye or by night the cloude was taken vp, then they iourneyed.

22 Or if the cloude taryed two dayes or a moneth, or a yeere vpon the Tabernacle, abiding thereon, the children of Israel abode still, and iourneyed not: but when it was taken vp, they iourneyed.

23 At the commandement of the Lord they pitched, and at the commandement of the Lord they iourneyed, keeping the watch of the Lord at the commandement of the Lord by the hand of Moses.

Numbers 10

1 And the Lord spake vnto Moses, saying,

2 Make thee two trumpets of siluer: of an whole piece shalt thou make the, that thou mayest vse them for the assembling of the Congregation, and for the departure of the campe.

3 And when they shall blowe with them, all the Congregation shall assemble to thee before the doore of the Tabernacle of the Cogregation.

4 But if they blowe with one, then the princes, or heades ouer the thousandes of Israel shall come vnto thee.

5 But if ye blow an alarme, then the campe of the that pitch on the East part, shall go forward.

6 If ye blowe an alarme the second time, then the hoste of them that lie on the Southside shall march: for they shall blowe an alarme when they remoue.

7 But in assembling the Congregation, ye shall blowe without an alarme.

8 And the sonnes of Aaron the Priest shall blowe the trumpets, and ye shall haue them as a lawe for euer in your generations.

9 And when ye goe to warre in your lande against the enemie that vexeth you, ye shall blowe an alarme with the trumpets, and ye shall bee remembred before the Lord your God, and shalbe saued from your enemies.

10 Also in the day of your gladnesse, and in your feast dayes, and in the beginning of your moneths, ye shall also blow the trumpets ouer your burnt sacrifices, and ouer your peace offrings, that they may be a remembrance for you before your God: I am the Lord your God.

11 And in the seconde yeere, in the seconde moneth, and in the twentieth day of the moneth the cloude was taken vp from the Tabernacle of the Testimonie.

12 And ye children of Israel departed on their iourneys out of the desart of Sinai, and the cloud rested in the wildernesse of Paran.

13 So they first tooke their iourney at the comandement of the Lord, by ye hand of Moses.

14 In the first place went the standerd of the hoste of the children of Iudah, according to their armies: and Nahshon the sonne of Amminabad was ouer his band.

15 And ouer the band of the tribe of the children of Issachar was Nethaneel ye sonne of Zuar.

16 And ouer the band of the tribe of the children of Zebulun was Eliab the sonne of Helon.

17 When the Tabernacle was taken downe, then the sonnes of Gershon, and the sonnes of Merari went forward bearing the Tabernacle.

18 After, departed the standerd of the hoste of Reuben, according to their armies, and ouer his band was Elizur the sonne of Shedeur.

19 And ouer the band of the tribe of ye children of Simeon was Shelumiel the sonne of Shurishaddai.

20 And ouer the bande of the tribe of ye children of Gad was Eliasaph the sonne of Deuel.

21 The Kohathites also went forward and bare the Sanctuarie, and the former did set vp the Tabernacle against they came.

22 Then the standerd of the hoste of the children of Ephraim went forward according to their armies, and ouer his bande was Elishama the sonne of Ammiud.

23 And ouer the band of the tribe of ye sonnes of Manasseh was Gamliel the sonne of Pedazur.

24 And ouer the band of ye tribe of the sonnes of Beniamin was Abidan the sonne of Gideoni.

25 Last, the standerd of the hoste of the children of Dan marched, gathering all ye hostes according to their armies: and ouer his bande was Ahiezer the sonne of Ammishaddai.

26 And ouer the bande of the tribe of the children of Asher was Pagiel the sonne of Ocran.

27 And ouer the bande of the tribe of the children of Naphtali was Ahira ye sonne of Enan.

28 These were the remouings of the children of Israel according to their armies, whe they marched.

29 After, Moses said vnto Hobab ye sonne of Reuel the Midianite, ye father in law of Moses, We go into the place, of which ye Lord said, I will giue it you: Come thou with vs, and we wil doe thee good: for ye Lord hath promised good vnto Israel.

30 And he answered him, I will not goe: but I will depart to mine owne countrey, and to my kindred.

31 Then he sayd, I pray thee, leaue vs not: for thou knowest our camping places in the wildernesse: therefore thou mayest be our guide.

32 And if thou go with vs, what goodnes the Lord shall shew vnto vs, the same will we shewe vnto thee.

33 So they departed from the mount of the Lord, three dayes iourney: and the Arke of the couenant of the Lord went before them in the three dayes iourney, to searche out a resting place for them.

34 And the cloude of the Lord was vpon the by day, when they went out of the campe.

35 And when the Arke went forwarde, Moses saide, Rise vp, Lord, and let thine enemies bee scattered, and let them that hate thee, flee before thee.

36 And when it rested, hee sayde, Returne, O Lord, to the many thousands of Israel.

Numbers 11

1 When the people became murmurers, it displeased the Lord: and the Lord heard it, therefore his wrath was kindled, and the fire of the Lord burnt among them, and consumed the vtmost parte of the hoste.

2 Then the people cryed vnto Moses: and when Moses praied vnto the Lord, the fire was quenched.

3 And he called the name of that place Taberah, because the fire of the Lord burnt among them.

4 And a nomber of people that was amog them, fell a lusting, and turned away, and the children of Israel also wept, and saide, Who shall giue vs flesh to eate?

5 We remember the fish which we did eat in Egypt for nought, the cucumbers, and the pepons, and the leekes, and the onions, and the garleke.

6 But now our soule is dryed away, we can see nothing but this Man.

7 (The Man also was as coriander seede, and his colour like the colour of bdelium.

8 The people went about and gathered it, and ground it in milles, or beat it in morters, and baked it in a cauldron, and made cakes of it, and the taste of it was like vnto the taste of fresh oyle.

9 And when the dewe fell downe vpon the hoste in the night, the Man fell with it)

10 Then Moses heard the people weepe throughout their families, euery man in the doore of his tent, and the wrath of the Lord was grieuously kindled: also Moses was grieued.

11 And Moses saide vnto the Lord, Wherefore hast thou vexed thy seruant? and why haue I not found fauour in thy sight, seeing thou hast put the charge of al this people vpon mee?

12 Haue I conceiued al this people? or haue I begotte them, that thou shouldest say vnto me, Cary them in thy bosome (as a nurse beareth the sucking childe) vnto the lande, for the which thou swarest vnto their fathers?

13 Where should I haue flesh to giue vnto al this people? for they weepe vnto me, saying, Giue vs flesh that we may eate.

14 I am not able to beare al this people alone, for it is too heauie for me.

15 Therefore if thou deale thus with mee, I pray thee, if I haue founde fauour in thy sight, kill me, that I behold not my miserie.

16 Then the Lord said vnto Moses, Gather vnto me seuetie men of ye Elders of Israel, whome thou knowest, that they are the Elders of the people, and gouernonrs ouer them, and bring them vnto the Tabernacle of the Congregation, and let them stand there with thee,

17 And I will come downe, and talke with thee there, and take of the Spirite, which is vpon thee, and put vpon them, and they shall beare the burthen of the people with thee: so thou shalt not beare it alone.

18 Furthermore thou shalt saye vnto the people, Bee sanctified against to morowe, and yee shall eate flesh: for you haue wept in the eares of the Lord, saying, Who shall giue vs flesh to eate? for we were better in Egypt: therefore the Lord will giue you flesh, and ye shall eate.

19 Ye shall not eat one day nor two daies, nor fiue daies, neither ten daies, nor twentie dayes,

20 But a whole moneth, vntill it come out at your nostrels, and bee lothesome vnto you, because ye haue contemned the Lord, which is among you, and haue wept before him, saying, Why came we hither out of Egypt?

21 And Moses saide, Six hundreth thousande footemen are there of the people, among whom I am: and thou saiest, I will giue them flesh, that they may eate a moneth long.

22 Shall the sheepe and the beeues be slaine for them, to finde them? either shall all the fish of the sea be gathered together for them to suffice them?

23 And the Lord saide vnto Moses, Is the Lordes hand shortened? thou shalt see now whether my word shall come to passe vnto thee, or no.

24 So Moses went out, and told the people the wordes of the Lord, and gathered seuentie men of the Elders of the people, and set them round about the Tabernacle.

25 Then the Lord came downe in a cloude, and spake vnto him, and tooke of the Spirit that was vpon him, and put it vpon the seuentie Ancient men: and when the Spirit rested vpon them, then they prophecied, and did not cease.

26 But there remained two of the men in the hoste: the name of the one was Eldad, and the name of the other Medad, and the Spirit rested vpon them, (for they were of them that were written, and went not out vnto the Tabernacle) and they prophecied in the hoste.

27 Then there ranne a yong man, and tolde Moses, and saide, Eldad and Medad doe prophesie in the hoste.

28 And Ioshua the sonne of Nun the seruant of Moses one of his yong men answered and said, My lord Moses, forbid them.

29 But Moses saide vnto him, Enuiest thou for my sake? yea, would God that all the Lordes people were Prophets, and that the Lord woulde put his Spirit vpon them.

30 And Moses returned into the hoste, he and the Elders of Israel.

31 Then there went foorth a winde from the Lord, and brought quailes from the Sea, and let them fall vpon the campe, a dayes iourney on this side, and a dayes iourney on the other side, round about the hoste, and they were about two cubites aboue the earth.

32 Then the people arose, al that day, and all the night, and all the next day, and gathered the quailes: he that gathered the least, gathered ten Homers full, and they spred them abroade for their vse round about the hoste.

33 While the flesh was yet betweene their teeth, before it was chewed, euen the wrath of the Lord was kindled against the people, and the Lord smote the people with an exceeding great plague.

34 So the name of the place was called, Kibroth-hattaauah: for there they buried the people that fell a lusting.

35 From Kibroth-hattaauah ye people tooke their iourney to Hazeroth, and abode at Hazeroth.

Numbers 12

1 Afterward Miriam and Aaron spake against Moses, because of the woman of Ethiopia whome hee had maried (for hee had married a woman of Ethiopia)

2 And they saide, What? hath the Lord spoken but onely by Moses? hath he not spoken also by vs? and the Lord heard this.

3 (But Moses was a verie meeke man, aboue all the men that were vpon the earth)

4 And by and by the Lord sayd vnto Moses, and vnto Aaron, and vnto Miriam, come out yee three vnto the Tabernacle of the Congregation: and they three came forth.

5 Then the Lord came downe in the pillar of the cloude, and stoode in the doore of the Tabernacle, and called Aaron and Miriam, and they both came forth.

6 And hee saide, Heare nowe my wordes, If there be a Prophet of the Lord among you, I will be knowen to him by a vision, and will speake vnto him by dreame.

7 My seruant Moses is not so, who is faithfull in all mine house.

8 Vnto him will I speake mouth to mouth, and by vision, and not in darke wordes, but hee shall see the similitude of the Lord. Wherefore then were ye not afraid to speake against my seruant, euen against Moses?

9 Thus the Lord was very angrie with them, and departed.

10 Also the cloude departed from the Tabernacle: and beholde, Miriam was leprous like snowe: and Aaron looked vpon Miriam, and beholde, she was leprous.

11 Then Aaron saide vnto Moses, Alas, my Lord, I beseech thee, lay not the sinne vpon vs, which we haue foolishly committed and wherein we haue sinned.

12 Let her not, I pray thee, be as one dead, of whome the flesh is halfe consumed, when he commeth out of his mothers wombe.

13 Then Moses cryed vnto the Lord, saying, O God, I beseech thee, heale her nowe.

14 And the Lord said vnto Moses, If her father had spit in her face, shoulde she not haue bene ashamed seuen dayes? let her be shut out of the hoste seuen dayes, and after she shall bee receiued.

15 So Miriam was shut out of the hoste seuen dayes, and the people remooued not, till Miriam was brought in againe.

Numbers 13

1 Then afterwarde the people remooued from Hazeroth, and pitched in the wildernesse of Paran.

2 And the Lord spake vnto Moses, saying,

3 Sende thou men out to search the lande of Canaan which I giue vnto the children of Israel: of euery tribe of their fathers shall ye sende a man, such as are all rulers among them.

4 Then Moses sent them out of the wildernesse of Paran at the commandement of the Lord: all those men were heades of the children of Israel.

5 Also their names are these: of the tribe of Reuben, Shammua the sonne of Zaccur:

6 Of the tribe of Simeon, Shaphat the sonne of Hori:

7 Of the tribe of Iudah, Caleb the sonne of Iephunneh:

8 Of the tribe of Issachar, Igal the sonne of Ioseph:

9 Of the tribe of Ephraim, Oshea the sone of Nun:

10 Of the tribe of Beniamin, Palti the sonne of Raphu:

11 Of the tribe of Zebulun, Gaddiel the sone of Sodi:

12 Of the tribe of Ioseph, to wit, of the tribe of Manasseh, Gaddi the sonne of Susi:

13 Of the tribe of Dan, Ammiel the sonne of Gemalli:

14 Of the tribe of Asher, Sethur the sonne of Michael:

15 Of the tribe of Naphtali, Nahbi the sonne of Vophsi:

16 Of the tribe of Gad, Geuel the sonne of Machi.

17 These are the names of the men, which Moses sent to spie out the lande: and Moses called ye name of Oshea the sonne of Nun, Iehoshua.

18 So Moses sent them to spie out the lande of Canaan, and said vnto them, Go vp this way toward the South, and go vp into the moutaines,

19 And consider the land what it is, and the people that dwel therein, whether they be strong or weake, either fewe or many,

20 Also what the lande is that they dwell in, whether it be good or bad: and what

cities they be, that they dwell in, whether they dwell in tents, or in walled townes:

21 And what the land is: whether it be fat or leane, whether there be trees therein, or not. And be of good courage, and bring of the fruite of the lande (for then was the time of the first ripe grapes)

22 So they went vp, and searched out the lande, from the wildernesse of Zin vnto Rehob, to go to Hamath,

23 And they ascended toward the South, and came vnto Hebron, where were Ahiman, Sheshai and Talmai, the sonnes of Anak. And Hebron was built seuen yeere before Zoan in Egypt.

24 Then they came to the riuer of Eshcol, and cut downe thence a branch with one cluster of grapes, and they bare it vpon a barre betweene two, and brought of the pomegranates and of the figges.

25 That place was called the riuer Eshcol, because of the cluster of grapes, which the children of Israel cut downe thence.

26 Then after fourtie dayes, they turned againe from searching of the land.

27 And they went and came to Moses and to Aaron and vnto al the Congregation of the children of Israel, in the wildernesse of Paran, to Kadesh, and brought to the, and to all the Congregation tydings, and shewed them the fruite of the lande.

28 And they tolde him, and saide, We came vnto the land whither thou hast sent vs, and surely it floweth with milke and honie: and here is of the fruite of it.

29 Neuerthelesse the people be strong that dwell in the land, and the cities are walled and exceeding great: and moreouer, we sawe the sonnes of Anak there.

30 The Amalekites dwell in the South countrey, and the Hittites, and the Iebusites, and the Amorites dwell in the mountaines, and the Canaanites dwell by the sea, and by the coast of Iorden.

31 Then Caleb stilled the people before Moses, and saide, Let vs go vp at once, and possesse it: for vndoubtedly we shall ouercome it.

32 But the men, that went vp with him, saide, we be not able to goe vp against the people: for they are stronger then we.

33 So they brought vp an euill report of the land which they had searched for the children of Israel, saying, The lande which we haue gone through to search it out, is a land that eateth vp the inhabitants thereof: for all the people that we sawe in it, are men of great stature.

34 For there we sawe gyants, the sonnes of Anak, which come of the gyants, so that we seemed in our sight like grashoppers: and so wee were in their sight.

Numbers 14

1 Then all ye Congregation lifted vp their voice, and cryed: and the people wept that night,

2 And all the children of Israel murmured against Moses and Aaron: and the whole assemblie said vnto them, Would God we had died in the land of Egypt, or in this wildernesse: would God we were dead.

3 Wherefore nowe hath the Lord brought vs into this lande to fall vpon the sworde? our wiues, and our children shall be a pray: were it not better for vs to returne into Egypt?

4 And they said one to another, Let vs make a Captaine and returne into Egypt.

5 Then Moses and Aaron fell on their faces before all the assemblie of the Congregation of the children of Israel.

6 And Ioshua the sonne of Nun, and Caleb the sonne of Iephunneh two of them that searched the lande, rent their clothes,

7 And spake vnto all the assemblie of the childre of Israel, saying, The land which we walked through to search it, is a very good lande.

8 If the Lord loue vs, he will bring vs into this land, and giue it vs, which is a land that floweth with milke and honie:

9 But rebell not ye against the Lord, neither feare ye the people of the land: for they are but bread for vs: their shielde is departed from the, and the Lord is with vs, feare them not.

10 And all the multitude saide, Stone them with stones: but the glory of the Lord appeared in the Tabernacle of the Congregation, before all the children of Israel.

11 And the Lord said vnto Moses, How long will this people prouoke me, and howe long will it be, yer they beleeue me, for al the signes which I haue shewed among them?

12 I will smite them with the pestilence and destroy them, and will make thee a greater nation and mightier then they.

13 But Moses saide vnto the Lord, When the Egyptians shall heare it, (for thou broughtest this people by thy power from among them)

14 Then they shall say to the inhabitants of this land, (for they haue heard that thou, Lord, art among this people, and that thou, Lord, art seene face to face, and that thy cloude standeth ouer them, and that thou goest before them by day time in a pillar of a cloude, and in a pillar of fire by night)

15 That thou wilt kill this people as one man: so the heathen which haue heard the fame of thee, shall thus say,

16 Because the Lord was not able to bring this people into the lande, which he sware vnto them, therefore hath he slaine them in the wildernesse.

17 And now, I beseech thee, let the power of my Lord be great, according as thou hast spoken, saying,

18 The Lord is slowe to anger, and of great mercie, and forgiuing iniquitie, and sinne, but not making the wicked innocent, and visiting the wickednes of the fathers vpon the children, in the thirde and fourth generation:

19 Be mercifull, I beseech thee, vnto the iniquitie of this people, according to thy great mercie, and as thou hast forgiuen this people from Egypt, euen vntill nowe.

20 And the Lord said, I haue forgiuen it, according to thy request.

21 Notwithstanding, as I liue, all the earth shall be filled with the glory of the Lord.

22 For all those men which haue seene my glory, and my miracles which I did in Egypt, and in the wildernes, and haue tempted me this ten times, and haue not obeyed my voyce,

23 Certainely they shall not see the lande, whereof I sware vnto their fathers: neither shall any that prouoke me, see it.

24 But my seruant Caleb, because he had another spirite, and hath followed me stil, euen him will I bring into the lande, whither he went, and his seede shall inherite it.

25 Nowe the Amalekites and the Canaanites remaine in the valley: wherefore turne backe to morowe, and get you into the wildernesse, by the way of the red Sea.

26 After, the Lord spake vnto Moses and to Aaron, saying,

27 How long shall I suffer this wicked multitude to murmure against me? I haue heard the murmurings of the children of Israel, which they murmure against me.

28 Tell them, As I liue (saith the Lord) I wil surely do vnto you, euen as ye haue spoken in mine eares.

29 Your carkeises shall fall in this wildernes, and all you that were counted through all your nombers, from twentie yeere olde and aboue, which haue murmured against me,

30 Ye shall not doubtles come into the land, for the which I lifted vp mine hande, to make you dwell therein, saue Caleb the sonne of Iephunneh, and Ioshua the sonne of Nun.

31 But your children, (which ye said shoulde be a pray) them will I bring in, and they shall knowe the lande which ye haue refused:

32 But euen your carkeises shall fall in this wildernes,

33 And your children shall wander in the wildernesse, fourtie yeeres, and shall beare your whoredomes, vntill your carkeises be wasted in the wildernesse.

34 After the number of the dayes, in the which ye searched out the lande, euen fourtie dayes, euery day for a yeere, shall ye beare your iniquity, for fourtie yeeres, and ye shall feele my breach of promise.

35 I the Lord haue said, Certainely I will doe so to all this wicked company, that are gathered together against me: for in this wildernesse they shall be consumed, and there they shall die.

36 And the men which Moses had sent to search the land (which, when they came againe, made all the people to murmure against him, and brought vp a slander vpon the lande)

37 Euen those men that did bring vp that vile slander vpon the land, shall die by a plague before the Lord.

38 But Ioshua the sonne of Nun, and Caleb the sonne of Iephunneh, of those

men that went to search the land, shall liue.

39 Then Moses tolde these sayings vnto all the children of Israel, and the people sorowed greatly.

40 And they rose vp earely in the morning, and gate them vp into the toppe of the mountaine, saying, Loe, we be readie, to goe vp to the place which the Lord hath promised: for wee haue sinned.

41 But Moses said, Wherefore transgresse yee thus the commandement of the Lord? it will not so come well to passe.

42 Goe not vp (for the Lord is not among you) lest ye be ouerthrowe before your enemies.

43 For the Amalekites and the Canaanites are there before you, and ye shall fall by the sworde: for in as much as ye are turned away from the Lord, the Lord also will not be with you.

44 Yet they presumed obstinately to goe vp to the top of the mountaine: but the Arke of the couenant of the Lord, and Moses departed not out of the campe.

45 Then the Amalekites and the Canaanites, which dwelt in that mountaine, came downe and smote them, and consumed them vnto Hormah.

Numbers 15

1 And the Lord spake vnto Moses, saying,

2 Speake vnto the children of Israel, and say vnto them, Whe ye be come into the land of your habitations, which I giue vnto you,

3 And will make an offring by fire vnto the Lord, a burnt offring or a sacrifice to fulfil a vowe, or a free offring, or in your feastes, to make a sweete sauour vnto the Lord of the hearde, or of the flocke.

4 Then let him that offreth his offring vnto the Lord, bring a meate offring of a tenth deale of fine flowre, mingled with the fourth part of an Hin of oyle.

5 Also thou shalt prepare ye fourth part of an Hin of wine to be powred on a lambe, appointed for the burnt offring or any offring.

6 And for a ram, thou shalt for a meat offring, prepare two tenth deales of fine floure, mingled with the third part of an Hin of oyle.

7 And for a drinke-offering, thou shalt offer the third part of an Hin of wine, for a sweete sauour vnto the Lord.

8 And when thou preparest a bullocke for a burnt offring, or for a sacrifice to fulfill a vowe or a peace offring to the Lord,

9 Then let him offer with ye bullocke a meate offring of three tenth deales of fine floure, mingled with halfe an Hin of oyle.

10 And thou shalt bring for a drinke offring halfe an Hin of wine, for an offring made by fire of a sweete sauour vnto the Lord.

11 Thus shall it be done for a bullocke, or for a ram, or for a lambe, or for a kid.

12 According to the nomber that yee prepare to offer, so shall yee doe to euery one according to their nomber.

13 All that are borne of the countrey, shall do these things thus, to offer an offring made by fire of sweete sauour vnto the Lord.

14 And if a stranger soiourne with you, or whosoeuer bee among you in your generations, and will make an offring by fire of a sweete sauour vnto the Lord, as ye do, so hee shall doe.

15 One ordinance shalbe both for you of the Congregation, and also for the stranger that dwelleth with you, euen an ordinance for euer in your generations: as you are, so shall the stranger bee before the Lord.

16 One Lawe and one maner shall serue both for you and for the stranger that soiourneth with you.

17 And the Lord spake vnto Moses, saying,

18 Speake vnto the children of Israel, and say vnto them, When ye be come into the lande, to the which I bring you,

19 And when ye shall eate of the bread of the land, ye shall offer an heaue offring vnto ye Lord.

20 Ye shall offer vp a cake of the first of your dowe for an heaue offring: as the heaue offring of the barne, so ye shall lift it vp.

21 Of the first of your dowe ye shall giue vnto the Lord an heaue offring in your generations.

22 And if ye haue erred, and not obserued all these commandements, which the Lord hath spoken vnto Moses,

23 Euen all that the Lord hath commanded you by the hand of Moses, from the first day that the Lord commanded Moses, and hence forward among your generations:

24 And if so be that ought be committed ignorantly of the Congregation, then all ye Congregatio shall giue a bullocke for a burnt offring, for a sweete sauour vnto the Lord, with the meat offring and drinke offring thereto, according to the maner, and an hee goate for a sinne offring.

25 And the Priest shall make an atonement for al the Congregation of the children of Israel, and it shalbe forgiuen them: for it is ignorance: and they shall bring their offring for an offring made by fire vnto the Lord, and their sinne offring before the Lord for their ignorance.

26 Then it shalbe forgiuen all the Congregation of the children of Israel, and the stranger that dwelleth among them: for all the people were in ignorance.

27 But if any one person sinne through ignorance, then he shall bring a shee goate of a yeere olde for a sinne offring.

28 And the Priest shall make an atonement for the ignorant person, when hee sinneth by ignorance before the Lord, to make reconciliation for him: and it shalbe forgiuen him.

29 He that is borne among the children of Israel, and the stranger that dwelleth among them, shall haue both one lawe, who so doth sinne by ignorance.

30 But the person that doeth ought presumptuously, whether he be borne in the land, or a stranger, the same blasphemeth the Lord: therefore that person shalbe cut off from among his people,

31 Because he hath despised the worde of the Lord, and hath broken his commandement: that person shalbe vtterly cut off: his iniquitie shalbe vpon him.

32 And while the children of Israel were in the wildernesse, they found a man that gathered stickes vpon the Sabbath day.

33 And they that found him gathering sticks, brought him vnto Moses and to Aaron, and vnto all the Congregation,

34 And they put him warde: for it was not declared what should be done vnto him.

35 Then the Lord said vnto Moses, This man shall dye the death: and let al the multitude stone him with stones without the hoste.

36 And all the Congregation brought him without the hoste, and stoned him with stones, and he died, as the Lord had commanded Moses.

37 And the Lord spake vnto Moses, saying,

38 Speake vnto the children of Israel, and bid them that they make them fringes vpon the borders of their garments throughout their generations, and put vpon the fringes of the borders a ryband of blewe silke.

39 And ye shall haue the fringes, that when ye looke vpon them, ye may remember all the commandemets of the Lord, and do them: and that ye seeke not after your own heart, nor after your owne eyes, after the which ye go a whoring;

40 That yee may remember and doe all my commandements, and bee holy vnto your God.

41 I am the Lord your God, which brought you out of the lande of Egypt, to bee your God: I am the Lord your God.

Numbers 16

1 Nowe Korah the sonne of Izhar, the sonne of Kohath, the sonne of Leui went apart with Dathan, and Abiram the sonnes of Eliab, and On the sonne of Peleth, the sonnes of Reuben:

2 And they rose vp against Moses, with certaine of the children of Israel, two hundreth and fiftie captaines of the assemblie, famous in the Congregation, and men of renoume,

3 Who gathered themselues together against Moses, and against Aaron, and sayde vnto them, Ye take too much vpon you, seeing all the Congregation is holie, euery one of them, and the Lord is among them: wherfore then lift ye your selues aboue the Congregation of the Lord?

4 But when Moses heard it, hee fell vpon his face,

5 And spake to Korah and vnto all his companie, saying, To morow the Lord will shew who is his, and who is holy, and who ought to approche neere vnto him: and whom he hath chosen, hee will cause to come neere to him.

6 This doe therefore, Take you censers, both Korah, and all his companie,

7 And put fire therein, and put incense in the before the Lord to morowe: and the man whome the Lord doeth chuse, the same shalbe holie: ye take too much vpon you, ye sonnes of Leui.

8 Againe Moses saide vnto Korah, Heare, I pray you, ye sonnes of Leui.

9 Seemeth it a small thing vnto you that the God of Israel hath separated you from the multitude of Israel, to take you neere to himselfe, to doe the seruice of the Tabernacle of the Lord, and to stand before the Congregation and to minister vnto them?

10 He hath also taken thee to him, and all thy brethren the sonnes of Leui with thee, and seeke ye the office of the Priest also?

11 For which cause, thou, and all thy companie are gathered together against the Lord: and what is Aaron, that ye murmure against him?

12 And Moses sent to call Dathan, and Abiram the sonnes of Eliab: who answered, We will not come vp.

13 Is it a small thing that thou hast brought vs out of a lande that floweth with milke and honie, to kill vs in the wildernesse, except thou make thy selfe lord and ruler ouer vs also?

14 Also thou hast not brought vs vnto a land that floweth with milke and honie, neither giuen vs inheritance of fieldes and vineyardes: wilt thou put out the eyes of these men? we will not come vp.

15 Then Moses waxed verie angry, and saide vnto the Lord, Looke not vnto their offring: I haue not taken so much as an asse from them, neither haue I hurt any of them.

16 And Moses said vnto Korah, Bee thou and al thy companie before the Lord: both thou, they, and Aaron to morowe:

17 And take euery man his censor, and put incense in them, and bring ye euery man his censor before the Lord, two hundreth and fiftie censors: thou also and Aaron, euery one his censor.

18 So they tooke euery man his censor, and put fire in them, and laide incense thereon, and stoode in the doore of the Tabernacle of the Congregation with Moses and Aaron.

19 And Korah gathered all the multitude against them vnto the doore of the Tabernacle of the Congregation: then the glorie of the Lord appeared vnto all the Congregation.

20 And the Lord spake vnto Moses and to Aaron, saying,

21 Separate your selues from among this Cogregation, that I may consume them at once.

22 And they fell vpon their faces and saide, O God the God of the spirits, of all fleshe, hath not one man onely sinned, and wilt thou bee wroth with all the Congregation?

23 And the Lord spake vnto Moses, saying,

24 Speake vnto the Congregation and say, Get you away from about the Tabernacle of Korah, Dathan and Abiram.

25 Then Moses rose vp, and went vnto Dathan and Abiram, and the Elders of Israel followed him.

26 And he spake vnto the Congregation, saying, Depart, I pray you, from the tentes of these wicked men, and touche nothing of theirs, lest ye perish in all their sinnes.

27 So they gate them away from the Tabernacle of Korah, Dathan and Abiram on euerie side: and Dathan, and Abiram came out and stood in the doore of their tentes with their wiues, and their sonnes, and their little children.

28 And Moses saide, Hereby yee shall knowe that the Lord hath sent me to do all these works: for I haue not done them of mine owne minde.

29 If these men die the common death of all men, or if they be visited after the visitation of all men, the Lord hath not sent me.

30 But if the Lord make a newe thing, and the earth open her mouth, and swallowe them vp with all that they haue, and they goe downe quicke into ye pit, then ye shall vnderstand that these men haue prouoked the Lord.

31 And assoone as he had made an ende of speaking all these wordes, euen the ground claue asunder that was vnder them,

32 And the earth opened her mouth, and swallowed them vp, with their families, and all the men that were with Korah, and all their goods.

33 So they and all that they had, went down aliue into the pit, and the earth couered them: so they perished from among the Congregation.

34 And all Israel that were about them, fled at the crie of them: for they said, Let vs flee, least the earth swalow vs vp.

35 But there came out a fire from the Lord, and consumed the two hundreth and fiftie men that offred the incense.

36 And the Lord spake vnto Moses, saying,

37 Speake vnto Eleazar, the sonne of Aaron the Priest, that he take vp the censers out of the burning, and scatter the fire beyond the altar: for they are halowed,

38 The censers, I say, of these sinners, that destroyed themselues: and let them make of them broade plates for a couering of the Altar: for they offered them before the Lord, therefore they shalbe holy, and they shall be a signe vnto the children of Israel.

39 Then Eleazar the Priest tooke the brasen censers, which they, that were burnt, had offred, and made broade plates of them for a couering of the Altar.

40 It is a remembrance vnto the children of Israel, that no stranger which is not of the seede of Aaron, come neere to offer incense before the Lord, that he be not like Korah and his company, as the Lord said to him by the hand of Moses.

41 But on the morowe all the multitude of the children of Israel murmured against Moses and against Aaron, saying, Ye haue killed the people of the Lord.

42 And when the Congregation was gathered against Moses and against Aaron, then they turned their faces toward the Tabernacle of the Congregation: and beholde, the cloude couered it, and the glory of the Lord appeared.

43 Then Moses and Aaron were come before the Tabernacle of the Congregation.

44 And the Lord spake vnto Moses, saying,

45 Get you vp from among this Congregation: for I wil consume them quickly: then they fell vpon their faces.

46 And Moses said vnto Aaron, Take the censer and put fire therein of the Altar, and put therein incense, and goe quickly vnto the Congregation, and make an atonement for them: for there is wrath gone out from the Lord: the plague is begunne.

47 Then Aaron tooke as Moses commanded him, and ranne into the middes of the Congregation, and beholde, the plague was begun among the people, and hee put in incense, and made an atonement for the people.

48 And when hee stoode betweene the dead, and them that were aliue, the plague was stayed.

49 So they died of this plague fourtene thousande and seuen hundreth, beside them that dyed in the conspiracie of Korah.

50 And Aaron went againe vnto Moses before the doore of the Tabernacle of the Congregation, and the plague was stayed.

Numbers 17

1 And the Lord spake vnto Moses, saying,

2 Speake vnto the children of Israel, and take of euery one of them a rod, after the house of their fathers, of all their princes according to the familie of their fathers, euen twelue rods: and thou shalt write euery mans name vpon his rod.

3 And write Aarons name vpon the rod of Leui: for euery rodde shalbe for the head of the house of their fathers.

4 And thou shalt put them in the Tabernacle of the Congregation, before the Arke of the Testimonie, where I wil declare my selfe to you.

5 And the mans rod, whome I chuse, shall blossome: and I will make cease from mee the grudgings of the children of Israel, which grudge against you.

6 Then Moses spake vnto the children of Israel, and al their princes gaue him a rod, one rod for euery Prince, according to the houses of their fathers, euen

twelue rods, and the rod of Aaron was among their roddes.

7 And Moses layde the rods before the Lord in the Tabernacle of the Testimonie.

8 And when Moses on the morow went into the Tabernacle of the Testimonie, beholde, the rod of Aaron for the house of Leui was budded, and brought forth buddes, and brought forth blossoms, and bare ripe almondes.

9 Then Moses brought out all the rods from before the Lord vnto all the children of Israel: and they looked vpon them, and tooke euery man his rodde.

10 After, the Lord said vnto Moses, Bring Aarons rod againe before the Testimonie to bee kept for a token to the rebellious children, and thou shalt cause their murmurings to cease from me, that they dye not.

11 So Moses did as the Lord had commanded him: so did he.

12 And the children of Israel spake vnto Moses, saying, Behold, we are dead, we perish, we are all lost:

13 Whosoeuer commeth neere, or approcheth to the Tabernacle of the Lord, shall dye: shall we be consumed and dye?

Numbers 18

1 And the Lord sayd vnto Aaron, Thou, and thy sonnes and thy fathers house with thee, shall beare the iniquitie of the Sanctuarie: both thou and thy sonnes with thee shall beare the iniquitie of your Priestes office.

2 And bring also with thee thy brethren of the tribe of Leui of ye familie of thy father, which shalbe ioyned with thee, and minister vnto thee: but thou, and thy sonnes with thee shall minister before the Tabernacle of the Testimonie:

3 And they shall keepe thy charge, euen the charge of all the Tabernacle: but they shall not come neere the instruments of the Sanctuary, nor to the altar, lest they die, both they and you:

4 And they shalbe ioyned with thee, and keepe the charge of the Tabernacle of the Congregation for all the seruice of the Tabernacle: and no stranger shall come neere vnto you:

5 Therefore shall ye keepe the charge of the Sanctuarie, and the charge of the altar: so there shall fall no more wrath vpon the children of Israel.

6 For lo, I haue taken your brethren the Leuites from among the children of Israel, which as a gift of yours, are giuen vnto the Lord, to do the seruice of the Tabernacle of the Congregation.

7 But thou, and thy sonnes with thee shall keepe your Priestes office for all things of the altar, and within the vaile: therefore shall ye serue: for I haue made your Priestes office an office of seruice: therefore the stranger that cometh neere, shalbe slayne.

8 Againe the Lord spake vnto Aaron, Behold, I haue giuen thee the keeping of mine offrings, of all the hallowed things of the children of Israel: vnto thee I haue giuen them for the anoyntings sake, and

to thy sonnes, for a perpetuall ordinance.

9 This shalbe thine of the most holy things, reserued from the fire: all their offering of all their meate offring, and of all their sinne offring, and of all their trespasse offring, which they bring vnto me, that shalbe most holy vnto thee, and to thy sonnes.

10 In the most holy place shalt thou eate it: euery male shall eate of it: it is holy vnto thee.

11 This also shalbe thine: the heaue offering of their gift, with all the shake offerings of the children of Israel: I haue giuen them vnto thee and to thy sonnes and to thy daughters with thee, to be a duetie for euer al the cleane in thine house shall eate of it.

12 All the fat of the oyle, and all the fat of the wine, and of the wheate, which they shall offer vnto the Lord for their first fruites, I haue giuen them vnto thee.

13 And the first ripe of al that is in their land, which they shall bring vnto Lord, shalbe thine: all the cleane in thine house shall eate of it.

14 Euery thing separate from the common vse in Israel, shalbe thine.

15 All that first openeth the matrice of any flesh, which they shall offer vnto the Lord, of man or beast, shalbe thine: but the first borne of man shalt thou redeeme, and the first borne of the vncleane beast shalt thou redeeme.

16 And those that are to bee redeemed, shalt thou redeeme from the age of a moneth, according to thy estimation, for the money of fiue shekels, after the shekel of the Sanctuarie, which is twentie gerahs.

17 But the first borne of a kow, or the first borne of a sheepe, or the first borne of a goate shalt thou not redeeme: for they are holy: thou shalt sprinkle their blood at the altar, and thou shalt burne their fat: it is a sacrifice made by fire for a sweete sauour vnto the Lord.

18 And the flesh of them shalbe thine, as the shake breast, and as the right shoulder shalbe thine.

19 All the heaue offrings of the holy things which the children of Israel shall offer vnto the Lord, haue I giuen thee, and thy sonnes, and thy daughters with thee, to be a duetie for euer: it is a perpetual couenant of salt before the Lord, to thee, and to thy seede with thee.

20 And the Lord sayde vnto Aaron, Thou shalt haue none inheritance in their lande, neyther shalt thou haue any parte among them: I am thy part and thine inheritance among the children of Israel.

21 For beholde, I haue giuen the children of Leui all the tenth in Israel for an inheritance, for their seruice which they serue in the Tabernacle of the Congregation.

22 Neyther shall the children of Israel any more come neere the Tabernacle of the Congregation, lest they susteine sinne, and die.

23 But the Leuites shall do the seruice in the Tabernacle of the Congregation, and they shall beare their sinne: it is a

law for euer in your generations, that among the children of Israel they possesse none inheritance.

24 For the tythes of the children of Israel, which they shall offer as an offring vnto the Lord, I haue giuen the Leuites for an inheritance: therfore I haue said vnto them, Among the children of Israel ye shall possesse none inheritance.

25 And the Lord spake vnto Moses, saying,

26 Speake also vnto the Leuites and say vnto them, When ye shall take of the children of Israel the tithes, which I haue giuen you of them for your inheritance, then shall ye take an heaue offring of that same for the Lord, euen the tenth part of the tithe.

27 And your heaue offering shalbe reckened vnto you, as the corne of the barne, or as the abundance of the wine presse.

28 So ye shall also offer an heaue offring vnto the Lord of all your tithes, which ye shall receiue of the children of Israel, and ye shall giue thereof the Lords heaue offring to Aaron the Priest.

29 Ye shall offer of all your gifts al the Lords heaue offrings: of all the fat of the same shall ye offer the holy things thereof.

30 Therefore thou shalt say vnto them, When ye haue offred the fat thereof, then it shalbe couted vnto the Leuites, as the encrease of the corne floore, or as the encrease of the wine presse.

31 And ye shall eate it in al places, ye, and your housholdes: for it is your wages for your seruice in the Tabernacle of the Congregation.

32 And ye shall beare no sinne by the reason of it, when ye haue offred the fatte of it: neither shall ye pollute the holy things of the children of Israel, lest ye die.

Numbers 19

1 And the Lord spake to Moses, and to Aaron, saying,

2 This is the ordinance of the lawe, which the Lord hath commanded, saying, Speake vnto the children of Israel that they bring thee a red kow without blemish, wherein is no spot, vpon the which neuer came yoke.

3 And ye shall giue her vnto Eleazar ye Priest, that hee may bring her without the hoste, and cause her to be slaine before his face.

4 Then shall Eleazar the Priest take of her blood with his finger, and sprinkle it before the Tabernacle of the Congregation seuen times,

5 And cause the kow to be burnt in his sight: with her skinne, and her flesh, and her blood, and her doung shall he burne her.

6 Then shall the Priest take cedar wood, and hyssope and skarlet lace, and cast them in the mids of the fire where the kow burneth.

7 Then shall the Priest wash his clothes, and he shall wash his flesh in water, and

then come into the hoste, and the Priest shalbe vncleane vnto the euen.

8 Also he that burneth her, shall wash his clothes in water, and wash his flesh in water, and be vncleane vntill euen.

9 And a man, that is cleane, shall take vp the ashes of the kow, and put them without the hoste in a cleane place: and it shalbe kept for the Congregation of the children of Israel for a sprinkling water: it is a sinne offring.

10 Therefore he that gathereth the ashes of the kow, shall wash his clothes, and remaine vncleane vntil euen: and it shalbe vnto the children of Israel, and vnto the stranger that dwelleth among them, a statute for euer.

11 Hee that toucheth the dead body of any man, shalbe vncleane euen seuen dayes.

12 Hee shall purifie himselfe therewith the third day, and the seuenth day he shall be cleane: but if he purifie not himselfe the thirde day, then the seuenth day he shall not be cleane.

13 Whosoeuer toucheth ye corps of any man that is dead, and purgeth not himselfe, defileth the Tabernacle of the Lord, and that person shall be cut off from Israel, because the sprinkling water was not sprinkled vpon him: he shall be vncleane, and his vncleannesse shall remaine still vpon him.

14 This is the law, Whe a man dieth in a tent, all that come into the tent, and all that is in the tent, shalbe vncleane seuen dayes,

15 And all the vessels that bee open, which haue no couering fastened vpon them, shall be vncleane.

16 Also whosoeuer toucheth one that is slaine with a sworde in the fielde, or a dead person, or a bone of a dead man, or a graue, shall be vncleane seuen dayes.

17 Therfore for an vncleane person they shall take of the burnt ashes of the sinne offring, and pure water shalbe put thereto in a vessel.

18 And a cleane person shall take hyssope and dip it in the water, and sprinkle it vpon the tent, and vpon all the vessels, and on the persons that were therein, and vpon him that touched ye bone, or the slayne, or the dead, or the graue.

19 And the cleane person shall sprinkle vpon the vncleane the third day, and the seuenth day, and hee shall purifie him selfe the seuenth day, and wash his clothes, and wash himself in water, and shalbe cleane at euen.

20 But the man that is vncleane and purifieth not himselfe, that person shalbe cut off from among the Congregation, because hee hath defiled the Sanctuarie of the Lord: and the sprinkling water hath not bene sprinkled vpon him: therefore shall he be vncleane.

21 And it shalbe a perpetual lawe vnto them, that he that sprinkleth the sprinkling water, shall wash his clothes: also hee that toucheth the sprinkling water, shalbe vncleane vntill euen.

22 And whatsoeuer the vncleane person toucheth, shall be vncleane: and the person that toucheth him, shalbe vncleane vntill the euen.

Numbers 20

1 Then the children of Israel came with ye whole Congregation to the desert of Zin in the first moneth, and the people abode at Cadesh: where Miriam died, and was buried there.

2 But there was no water for the Congregation, and they assembled them selues against Moses and against Aaron.

3 And the people chode with Moses, and spake, saying, Would God we had perished, when our brethren died before the Lord.

4 Why haue ye thus brought the Congregation of the Lord vnto his wildernesse, that both we, and our cattell should die there?

5 Wherefore nowe haue yee made vs to come vp from Egypt, to bring vs into this miserable place, which is no place of seede, nor figges, nor vines, nor pomegranates? neither is there any water to drinke.

6 Then Moses and Aaron went from the assemblie vnto the doore of the Tabernacle of the Congregation, and fell vpon their faces: and the glory of the Lord appeared vnto them.

7 And the Lord spake vnto Moses, saying,

8 Take the rod, and gather thou and thy brother Aaron the Congregation together, and speake yee vnto the rocke before their eyes, and it shall giue foorth his water, and thou shalt bring them water out of the rocke: so thou shalt giue the Congregation, and their beastes drinke.

9 Then Moses tooke the rod from before the Lord, as he had commanded him.

10 And Moses and Aaron gathered the Congregation together before the rocke, and Moses sayd vnto them, Heare nowe, ye rebels: shall we bring you water out of this rocke?

11 Then Moses lift vp his hande, and with his rod he smote the rocke twise, and the water came out aboundantly: so the Congregation, and their beastes dranke.

12 Againe the Lord spake vnto Moses, and to Aaron, Because ye beleeued me not, to sanctifie mee in the presence of the children of Israel, therefore ye shall not bring this Congregation into the land which I haue giuen them.

13 This is the water of Meribah, because the children of Israel stroue with the Lord, and hee was sanctified in them.

14 Then Moses sent messengers from Kadesh vnto the king of Edom, saying, Thus sayth thy brother Israel, Thou knowest all the trauaile that we haue had,

15 How our fathers went downe into Egypt, and we dwelt in Egypt a long time, where the Egyptians handled vs euill and our fathers.

16 But when we cried vnto the Lord, he heard our voyce, and sent an Angel, and hath brought vs out of Egypt, and

beholde, wee are in the citie Kadesh, in thine vtmost border.

17 I pray thee that we may passe through thy countrey: we will not goe through the fieldes nor the vineyardes, neither will we drinke of the water of the welles: we will goe by the kings way, and neither turne vnto the right hand nor to the left, vntill we be past thy borders.

18 And Edom answered him, Thou shalt not passe by mee, least I come out against thee with the sword.

19 Then the children of Israel said vnto him, We will goe vp by the hie way: and if I and my cattell drinke of thy water, I will then pay for it: I will onely (without any harme) goe through on my feete.

20 Hee answered againe, Thou shalt not goe through. The Edom came out against him with much people, and with a mightie power.

21 Thus Edom denyed to giue Israel passage through his countrey: wherefore Israel turned away from him.

22 And when the children of Israel with al the Congregation departed from Kadesh, they came vnto the mount Hor.

23 And the Lord spake vnto Moses and to Aaron in the mount Hor neere the coast of the land of Edom, saying,

24 Aaron shall be gathered vnto his people: for hee shall not enter into the lande, which I haue giuen vnto the children of Israel, because ye disobeyed my commandement at the water of Meribah.

25 Take Aaron and Eleazar his sonne, and bring them vp into the mount Hor,

26 And cause Aaron to put off his garmentes and put them vpon Eleazar his sonne: for Aaron shall be gathered to his fathers, and shall die there.

27 And Moses did as the Lord had commanded: and they went vp into the mount Hor, in the sight of all the Congregation.

28 And Moses put off Aarons clothes, and put them vpon Eleazar his sonne: so Aaron dyed there in the top of the mount: and Moses and Eleazar came downe from off the mount.

29 When al the Congregation sawe that Aaron was dead, al the house of Israel wept for Aaron thirtie dayes.

Numbers 21

1 When King Arad the Canaanite, which dwelt toward the South, heard tel that Israel came by the way of the spies, then fought hee against Israel, and tooke of them prysoners.

2 So Israel vowed a vowe vnto the Lord, and said, If thou wilt deliuer and giue this people into mine hand, then I wil vtterly destroy their cities.

3 And the Lord heard the voyce of Israel, and deliuered them the Canaanites: and they vtterly destroied them and their cities, and called ye name of the place Hormah.

4 After, they departed from the mount Hor by the way of the red Sea, to compasse the land of Edom: and the

people were sore grieued because of the way.

5 And the people spake against God and against Moses, saying, Wherefore haue ye brought vs out of Egypt, to die in the wildernesse? for here is neither bread nor water, and our soule lotheth this light bread.

6 Wherefore the Lord sent fierie serpents among ye people, which stung the people: so that many of the people of Israel died.

7 Therefore the people came to Moses and said, We haue sinned: for wee haue spoken against the Lord, and against thee: pray to the Lord, that he take away the serpents from vs: and Moses prayed for the people.

8 And the Lord said vnto Moses, Make thee a fiery serpent, and set it vp for a signe, that as many as are bitten, may looke vpon it, and liue.

9 So Moses made a serpent of brasse, and set it vp for a signe: and when a serpent had bitten a man, then he looked to the serpent of brasse, and liued.

10 And ye children of Israel departed thence, and pitched in Oboth.

11 And they departed from Oboth, and pitched in Iie-abarim, in the wildernesse, which is before Moab on the Eastside.

12 They remoued thence, and pitched vpon the riuer of Zared.

13 Thence they departed, and pitched on the other side of Arnon, which is in the wildernesse, and commeth out of the coasts of the Amorites: (for Arnon is the border of Moab, betweene the Moabites and the Amorites)

14 Wherefore it shall be spoken in the booke of the battels of the Lord, what thing he did in the red sea, and in the riuers of Arnon,

15 And at the streame of the riuers that goeth downe to the dwelling of Ar, and lieth vpon the border of Moab.

16 And from thence they turned to Beer: the same is the well where the Lord said vnto Moses, Assemble the people, and I wil giue them water.

17 Then Israel sang this song, Rise vp well, sing ye vnto it.

18 The princes digged this well, the captaines of the people digged it, euen the lawe giuer, with their staues. And from the wildernesse they came to Mattanah,

19 And from Mattanah to Nahaliel, and from Nahaliel to Bamoth,

20 And from Bamoth in the valley, that is in the plaine of Moab, to the top of Pisgah that looketh toward Ieshimon.

21 Then Israel sent messengers vnto Sihon, King of the Amorites, saying,

22 Let me goe through thy land: we wil not turne aside into the fieldes, nor into the vineyardes, neither drinke of the waters of ye welles: we will goe by the kings way, vntill we be past thy countrey.

23 But Sihon gaue Israel no licence to passe through his countrey, but Sihon assembled all his people, and went out against Israel into the wildernesse: and

he came to Iahoz, and fought against Israel.

24 But Israel smote him with the edge of the sword, and conquered his land, from Arnon vnto Iabok, euen vnto ye children of Ammon: for the border of the children of Ammon was strong.

25 And Israel tooke al these cities, and dwelt in all the cities of the Amorites in Heshbon and in all the villages thereof.

26 For Heshbon was the citie of Sihon the king of the Amorites, which had fought beforetime against the king of the Moabites, and had taken al his land out of his hand, euen vnto Arnon.

27 Wherefore they that speake in prouerbes, say, Come to Heshbon, let the citie of Sihon bee built and repaired:

28 For a fire is gone out of Heshbon, and a flame from the citie of Sihon, and hath consumed Ar of the Moabites, and the lords of Bamoth in Arnon.

29 Wo be to thee, Moab: O people of Chemosh, thou art vndone: he hath suffered his sonnes to be pursued, and his daughters to be in captiuitie to Sihon the king of the Amorites.

30 Their empire also is lost from Heshbon vnto Dibon, and wee haue destroyed them vnto Nophah, which reacheth vnto Medeba.

31 Thus Israel dwelt in the lande of the Amorites.

32 And Moses sent to searche out Iaazer, and they tooke the townes belonging thereto, and rooted out the Amorites that were there.

33 And they turned and went vp toward Bashan: and Og the King of Bashan came out against them, hee, and all his people, to fight at Edrei.

34 Then the Lord said vnto Moses, Feare him not: for I haue deliuered him into thine hand and all his people, and his land: and thou shalt do to him as thou diddest vnto Sihon the king of the Amorites, which dwelt at Heshbon.

35 They smote him therefore, and his sonnes, and all his people, vntill there was none left him: so they conquered his land.

Numbers 22

1 After, the children of Israel departed and pitched in the plaine of Moab on the other side of Iorden from Iericho.

2 Now Balak the sonne of Zippor sawe all that Israel had done to the Amorites.

3 And the Moabites were sore afraide of the people, because they were many, and Moab fretted against the children of Israel.

4 Therfore Moab said vnto the Elders of Midian, Nowe shall this multitude licke vp all that are round about vs, as an oxe licketh vp ye grasse of the fielde: and Balak the sonne of Zippor was King of the Moabites at that time.

5 Hee sent messengers therefore vnto Balaam the sonne of Beor to Pethor (which is by the riuer of the lande of the children of his folke) to call him, saying, Beholde, there is a people come out of

Egypt, which couer the face of the earth, and lye ouer against me.

6 Come now therefore, I pray thee, and curse me this people (for they are stronger then I) so it may be that I shall be able to smite them, and to driue them out of the land: for I knowe that hee, whome thou blessest, is blessed, and he whom thou cursest, shall be cursed.

7 And the Elders of Moab, and the Elders of Midian departed, hauing the reward of the soothsaying in their hande, and they came vnto Balaam, and tolde him the wordes of Balak.

8 Who answered them, Tary here this night, and I will giue you an answere, as the Lord shall say vnto mee. So the princes of Moab abode with Balaam.

9 Then God came vnto Balaam, and sayde, What men are these with thee?

10 And Baalam said vnto God, Balak ye sonne of Zippor, king of Moab hath set vnto me, saying,

11 Beholde, there is a people come out of Egypt and couereth the face of the earth: come nowe, curse them for my sake: so it may be that I shalbe able to ouercome them in battell, and to driue them out.

12 And God said vnto Balaam, Go not thou with them, neither curse the people, for they are blessed.

13 And Balaam rose vp in the morning, and sayde vnto ye princes of Balak, Returne vnto your land: for the Lord hath refused to giue me leaue to go with you.

14 So the princes of Moab rose vp, and went vnto Balak, and sayd, Balaam hath refused to come with vs.

15 Balak yet sent againe moe princes, and more honourable then they.

16 Who came to Balaam, and sayde to him, Thus saith Balak the sonne of Zippor, Bee not thou staied, I pray thee, from comming vnto me.

17 For I wil promote thee vnto great honour, and wil do whatsoeuer thou sayest vnto me: come therefore, I pray thee, curse me this people.

18 And Balaam answered, and sayde vnto the seruants of Balak, If Balak woulde giue me his house full of siluer and golde, I can not goe beyonde the worde of the Lord my God, to doe lesse or more.

19 But nowe, I pray you, tary here this night, that I may wit, what the Lord will say vnto mee more.

20 And God came vnto Balaam by night, and sayd vnto him, If the men come to call thee, rise vp, and goe with them: but onely what thing I say vnto thee, that shalt thou doe.

21 So Balaam rose vp early, and sadled his asse, and went with the princes of Moab.

22 And ye wrath of God was kindled, because he went: and the Angel of the Lord stood in the way to be against him, as he rode vpon his asse, and his two seruants were with him.

23 And when the asse saw the Angel of the Lord stand in the way, and his sworde drawen in his hand, the asse

turned out of the way and went into the field, but Balaam smote the asse, to turne her into the way.

24 Againe the Angel of the Lord stood in a path of the vineyardes, hauing a wall on the one side, and a wall on the other.

25 And when the asse sawe the Angel of the Lord, she thrust her selfe vnto the wall, and dasht Balaams foote against the wall: wherefore hee smote her againe.

26 Then the Angel of the Lord went further, and stoode in a narowe place, where was no way to turne, either to the right hand, or to the left.

27 And when the asse sawe the Angell of the Lord, she lay downe vnder Balaam: therefore Balaam was very wroth, and smote the asse with a staffe.

28 Then the Lord opened the mouth of the asse, and she saide vnto Balaam, What haue I done vnto thee, that thou hast smitten me nowe three times?

29 And Balaam saide vnto the asse, Because thou hast mocked me: I woulde there were a sworde in mine hand, for nowe would I kill thee.

30 And the asse saide vnto Balaam, Am not I thine asse, which thou hast ridden vpon since thy first time vnto this day? haue I vsed at any time to doe thus vnto thee? Who said, Nay.

31 And the Lord opened the eyes of Balaam, and he sawe the Angel of the Lord standing in the way with his sword drawen in his hande: then he bowed him selfe, and fell flat on his face.

32 And the Angel of the Lord said vnto him, Wherefore hast thou nowe smitten thine asse three times? beholde, I came out to withstande thee, because thy way is not straight before me.

33 But the asse sawe me, and turned from me now three times: for els, if she had not turned from me, surely I had euen nowe slaine thee, and saued her aliue.

34 Then Balaam saide vnto the Angel of the Lord, I haue sinned: for I wist not that thou stoodest in the way against me: now therefore if it displease thee, I will turne home againe.

35 But the Angel said vnto Balaam, Go with the men: but what I say vnto thee, that shalt thou speake. So Balaam went with ye princes of Balak.

36 And when Balak heard that Balaam came, he went out to meete him vnto a citie of Moab, which is in the border of Arnon, euen in the vtmost coast.

37 Then Balak saide vnto Balaam, Did I not sende for thee to call thee? Wherefore camest thou not vnto me? am I not able in deede to promote thee vnto honour?

38 And Balaam made answere vnto Balak, Lo, I am come vnto thee, and can I nowe say any thing at all? the worde that God putteth in my mouth, that shall I speake.

39 So Balaam went with Balak, and they came vnto the citie of Huzoth.

40 Then Balak offred bullockes, and sheepe, and sent thereof to Balaam, and to the princes that were with him.

41 And on the morowe Balak tooke Balaam, and brought him vp into the hie places of Baal, that thence hee might see the vtmost part of the people.

Numbers 23

1 And Balaam sayd vnto Balak, Builde me here seuen altars, and prepare me here seuen bullockes, and seuen rammes.

2 And Balak did as Balaam sayd, and Balak and Balaam offred on euery altar a bullocke and a ramme.

3 Then Balaam sayde vnto Balak, Stande by the burnt offring, and I will goe, if so be that the Lord will come and meete me: and whatsoeuer he sheweth me, I will tell thee: so he went forth alone.

4 And God met Balaam, and Balaam sayd vnto him, I haue prepared seuen altars, and haue offred vpon euery altar a bullocke and a ramme.

5 And the Lord put an answere in Balaams mouth, and sayde, Go againe to Balak, and say on this wise.

6 So when he returned vnto him, loe, hee stoode by his burnt offering, he, and all the princes of Moab.

7 Then he vttered his parable, and sayde, Balak the king of Moab hath brought mee from Aram out of the mountaines of the East, saying, Come, curse Iaakob for my sake: come, and detest Israel.

8 How shall I curse, where God hath not cursed? or howe shall I detest, where the Lord hath not detested?

9 For from the top of the rocks I did see him, and from the hils I did beholde him: lo, the people shall dwell by themselues, and shall not be reckened among the nations.

10 Who can tell the dust of Iaakob, and the nomber of the fourth part of Israel? Let me die the death of the righteous, and let my last ende be like his.

11 Then Balak saide vnto Balaam, What hast thou done vnto mee? I tooke thee to curse mine enemies, and beholde, thou hast blessed them altogether.

12 And he answered, and said, Must I not take heede to speake that, which the Lord hath put in my mouth?

13 And Balak sayde vnto him, Come, I pray thee, with mee vnto another place, whence thou mayest see them, and thou shalt see but the vtmost part of them, and shalt not see them all: therefore curse them out of that place for my sake.

14 And he brought him into Sedesophim to the top of Pisgah, and built seuen altars, and offred a bullocke, and a ramme on euery altar.

15 After, he sayde vnto Balak, Stande here by thy burnt offring, and I wil meete the Lord yonder.

16 And the Lord mette Balaam, and put an answere in his mouth, and sayd, Goe againe vnto Balak, and say thus.

17 And when he came to him, beholde, hee stoode by his burnt offering, and the princes of Moab with him: so Balak sayde vnto him, What hath the Lord sayd?

18 And he vttered his parable, and sayde, Rise vp, Balak, and heare: hearken vnto me, thou sonne of Zippor.

19 God is not as man, that he should lie, neither as the sonne of man that he shoulde repent: hath he sayde and shall he not do it? and hath he spoken, and shall he not accomplish it?

20 Behold, I haue receiued commandement to blesse: for he hath blessed, and I cannot alter it.

21 Hee seeth none iniquitie in Iaakob, nor seeth no transgression in Israel: the Lord his God is with him, and the ioyfull shoute of a king is among them.

22 God brought them out of Egypt: their strength is as an vnicorne.

23 For there is no sorcerie in Iaakob, nor soothsaying in Israel: according to this time it shalbe sayde of Iaakob and of Israel, What hath God wrought?

24 Behold, the people shall rise vp as a lyon, and lift vp himselfe as a yong lyon: hee shall not lye downe, till he eate of the pray, and till he drinke the blood of the slayne.

25 Then Balak sayde vnto Balaam, Neither curse, nor blesse them at all.

26 But Balaam answered, and saide vnto Balak, Tolde not I thee, saying, All that the Lord speaketh, that must I do?

27 Againe Balak sayd vnto Balaam, Come, I pray thee, I wil bring thee vnto another place, if so be it wil please God, that thou mayest thence curse them for my sake.

28 So Balak brought Balaam vnto the top of Peor, that looketh toward Ieshmon.

29 Then Balaam sayde vnto Balak, Make me here seuen altars, and prepare me here seuen bullocks, and seuen rammes.

30 And Balak did as Balaam had sayd, and offred a bullocke and a ram on euery altar.

Numbers 24

1 When Balaam saw that it pleased the Lord to blesse Israel, then he went not, as certaine times before, to set diuinations, but set his face toward the wildernesse.

2 And Balaam lift vp his eyes, and looked vpon Israel, which dwelt according to their tribes, and the Spirit of God came vpon him.

3 And he vttered his parable, and sayd, Balaam the sonne of Beor hath sayde, and the man, whose eyes were shut vp, hath sayd,

4 He hath sayde, which heard the wordes of God, and sawe the vision of the Almightie, and falling in a traunce had his eyes opened:

5 How goodly are thy tentes, O Iaakob, and thine habitations, O Israel!

6 As the valleis, are they stretched forth, as gardes by the riuers side, as the aloe trees, which the Lord hath planted, as the cedars beside the waters.

7 The water droppeth out of his bucket, and his seede shalbe in many waters, and his king shall be hier then Agag, and his kingdome shall bee exalted.

8 God brought him out of Egypt: his strength shalbe as an vnicorne: he shall eate the nations his enemies, and bruise their bones, and shoote them through with his arrowes.

9 He coucheth and lieth downe as a yong lion, and as a lion: who shall stirre him vp? blessed is he that blesseth thee, and cursed is he that curseth thee.

10 Then Balak was very angry with Balaam, and smote his handes together: so Balak sayde vnto Balaam, I sent for thee to curse mine enemies, and beholde, thou hast blessed them nowe three times.

11 Therefore nowe flee vnto thy place: I thought surely to promote thee vnto honour, but loe, the Lord hath kept thee backe from honour.

12 Then Balaam answered Balak, Tolde I not also thy messengers, which thou sentest vnto me, saying,

13 If Balak would giue me his house ful of siluer and gold, I can not passe the commandement of the Lord, to doe either good or bad of mine owne minde? what the Lord shall commaund, the same will I speake.

14 And nowe behold, I goe vnto my people: come, I will aduertise thee what this people shall doe to thy folke in the later dayes.

15 And he vttered his parable, and sayd, Balaam the sonne of Beor hath sayde, and the man whose eyes were shut vp, hath sayd,

16 He hath said that heard the words of God, and hath the knowledge of the most High, and sawe the vision of the Almightie, and falling in a traunce had his eyes opened:

17 I shall see him, but not nowe: I shall behold him, but not neere: there shall come a starre of Iaakob, and a scepter shall rise of Israel, and shall smite the coastes of Moab, and destroy all the sonnes of Sheth.

18 And Edom shalbe possessed, and Seir shall be a possession to their enemies: but Israel shall do valiantly.

19 He also that shall haue dominion shall bee of Iaakob, and shall destroy the remnant of the citie.

20 And when he looked on Amalek, he vttered his parable, and sayd, Amalek was the first of the nations: but his latter ende shall come to destruction.

21 And he looked on the Kenites, and vttered his parable, and sayde, Strong is thy dwelling place, and put thy nest in the rocke.

22 Neuerthelesse, the Kenite shalbe spoyled vntill Asshur cary thee away captiue.

23 Againe he vttered his parable, and sayd, Alas, who shall liue when God doeth this?

24 The ships also shall come from the coastes of Chittim, and subdue Asshur, and shall subdue Eber, and he also shall come to destruction.

25 Then Balaam rose vp, and went and returned to his place: and Balak also went his way.

Numbers 25

1 Nowe whiles Israel abode in Shittim, the people began to commit whoredome with the daughters of Moab:

2 Which called the people vnto the sacrifice of their gods, and the people ate, and bowed downe to their gods.

3 And Israel coupled himselfe vnto Baal Peor: wherefore the wrath of the Lord was kindled against Israel:

4 And the Lord sayde vnto Moses, Take all the heades of the people, and hang them vp before the Lord against ye sunne, that the indignation of the Lords wrath may be turned from Israel.

5 Then Moses sayd vnto the Iudges of Israel, Euery one slay his men that were ioyned vnto Baal Peor.

6 And behold, one of the children of Israel came and brought vnto his brethren a Midianitish woman in the sight of Moses, and in the sight of all the Congregation of the children of Israel, who wept before the doore of the Tabernacle of the Congregation.

7 And when Phinehas the sonne of Eleazar the sonne of Aaron the Priest sawe it, hee rose vp from the middes of the Congregation, and tooke a speare in his hand,

8 And followed ye man of Israel into the tent, and thrust them both through: to wit, the man of Israel, and the woman, through her belly: so the plague ceased from the children of Israel.

9 And there died in that plague, foure and twentie thousand.

10 Then the Lord spake vnto Moses, saying,

11 Phinehas the sonne of Eleazar, the sonne of Aaron the Priest, hath turned mine anger away from the children of Israel, while hee was zealous for my sake among them: therefore I haue not consumed the children of Israel in my ielousie.

12 Wherefore say to him, Beholde, I giue vnto him my couenant of peace,

13 And he shall haue it, and his seede after him, euen the couenant of the priestes office for euer, because he was zealous for his God, and hath made an atonement for the children of Israel.

14 And the name of the Israelite thus slayne, which was killed with the Midianitish woman, was Zimri the sonne of Salu, prince of the familie of the Simeonites.

15 And the name of the Midianitish woman, that was slayne, was Cozbi the daughter of Zur, who was head ouer the people of his fathers house in Midian.

16 Againe ye Lord spake vnto Moses, saying,

17 Vexe the Midianites, and smite them:

18 For they trouble you with their wiles, wherewith they haue beguiled you as concerning Peor, and as concerning their sister Cozbi ye daughter of a prince of Midian, which was slayne in the day of the plague because of Peor.

Numbers 26

1 And so after the plague, the Lord spake vnto Moses, and to Eleazar the sonne of Aaron the Priest, saying,

2 Take the nomber of all the Congregation of the children of Israel from twentie yeere olde and aboue throughout their fathers houses, all that go forth to warre in Israel.

3 So Moses and Eleazar the Priest spake vnto them in the plaine of Moab, by Iorden towarde Iericho, saying,

4 From twentie yeere olde and aboue ye shall nomber the people, as the Lord had commanded Moses, and the childre of Israel, when they came out of the land of Egypt.

5 Reuben the first borne of Israel: the children of Reube were: Hanoch, of whom came the familie of the Hanochites, and of Pallu the familie of the Palluites:

6 Of Hesron, the familie of the Hesronites: of Carmi, the familie of the Carmites.

7 These are the families of the Reubenites: and they were in nomber three and fourtie thousand, seuen hundreth and thirtie.

8 And the sonnes of Pallu, Eliab:

9 And the sonnes of Eliab, Nemuel, and Dathan, and Abiram: this Dathan and Abiram were famous in the Congregation, and stroue against Moses and against Aaron in the assemblie of Korah, when they stroue against the Lord.

10 And the earth opened her mouth, and swalowed them vp with Korah, when the Congregation died, what time the fire consumed, two hundreth and fiftie men, who were for a signe.

11 Notwithstanding, all the sonnes of Korah dyed not.

12 And the children of Simeon after their families were: Nemuel, of whom came the familie of the Nemuelites: of Iamin, the familie of the Iaminites: of Iachin, the familie of the Iachinites:

13 Of Zerah, the familie of the Zarhites: of Shaul, the familie of the Shaulites.

14 These are the families of the Simeonites: two and twentie thousand and two hundreth.

15 The sonnes of Gad after their families were: Zephon, of whome came ye familie of the Zephonites: of Haggi, the familie of the Haggites: of Shuni, the familie of the Shunites:

16 Of Ozni, the familie of the Oznites: of Eri, the familie of the Erites:

17 Of Arod, the familie of the Arodites: of Areli, the familie of the Arelites.

18 These are the families of the sonnes of Gad, according to their nombers, fourtie thousand and fiue hundreth.

19 The sonnes of Iudah, Er and Onan: but Er and Onan died in the land of Canaan.

20 So were the sonnes of Iudah after their families: of Shelah came the familie

of ye Shelanites: of Pharez, the familie of the Pharzites, of Zerah, the familie of the Zarhites.

21 And the sonnes of Pharez were: of Hesron, the familie of the Hesronites: of Hamul, the familie of the Hamulites.

22 These are the families of Iudah, after their nombers, seuentie and sixe thousande and fiue hundreth.

23 The sonnes of Issachar, after their families were: Tola, of whom came the familie of the Tolaites: of Pua, the familie of the Punites:

24 Of Iashub the familie of the Iashubites: of Shimron, the familie of the Shimronites.

25 These are the families of Issachar, after their nombers, threescore and foure thousand and three hundreth.

26 The sonnes of Zebulun, after their families were: of Sered, the familie of the Sardites: of Elon, the familie of the Elonites: of Iahleel, the familie of the Iahleelites.

27 These are the families of the Zebulunites, after their nombers, three score thousande and fiue hundreth.

28 The sonnes of Ioseph, after their families were Manasseh and Ephraim.

29 The sonnes of Manasseh were: of Machir, the familie of the Machirites: and Machir begate Gilead: of Gilead came the familie of the Gileadites.

30 These are the sonnes of Gilead: of Iezer, the familie of the Iezerites: of Helek, the familie of the Helekites.

31 Of Asriel, the familie of the Asrielites: of Shechem, the familie of Shichmites.

32 Of Shemida, the familie of the Shemidaites: of Hepher, the familie of the Hepherites.

33 And Zelophehad the sonne of Hepher had no sonnes, but daughters: and the names of the daughters of Zelophehad were Mahlah, and Noah, Hoglah, Milcah and Tirzah.

34 These are the families of Manasseh, and the nomber of them, two and fiftie thousand and seuen hundreth.

35 These are the sonnes of Ephraim after their families: of Shuthelah came the familie of the Shuthalhites: of Becher, the familie of the Bachrites: of Tahan, the familie of the Tahanites.

36 And these are the sonnes of Shuthelah: of Eran the familie of the Eranites.

37 These are the families of the sonnes of Ephraim after their nombers, two and thirtie thousand and fiue hundreth. these are the sonnes of Ioseph after their families.

38 These are the sonnes of Beniamin after their families: of Bela came the familie of the Belaites: of Ashbel, the familie of the Ashbelites: of Ahiram, the familie of the Ahiramites.

39 Of Shupham, the familie of the Suphamites: of Hupham, the familie of the Huphamites.

40 And the sonnes of Bela were Ard and Naaman: of Ard came the familie of the Ardites, of Naaman, the familie of the Naamites.

41 These are the sonnes of Beniamin after their families, and their nombers, fiue and fourtie thousand and sixe hundreth.

42 These are the sonnes of Dan after their families: of Shuham came the familie of the Shuhamites: these are the families of Dan after their housholdes.

43 All the families of the Shuhamites were after their nombers, threescore and foure thousand, and foure hundreth.

44 The sonnes of Asher after their families were: of Iimnah, the familie of the Iimnites: of Isui, the familie of the Isuites: of Beriah, the familie of the Berijtes.

45 The sonnes of Beriah were, of Heber the familie of the Heberites: of Malchiel, the familie of the Malchielites.

46 And the name of the daughter of Asher was Sarah.

47 These are the families of the sonnes of Asher after their nombers, three and fifty thousand and foure hundreth.

48 The sonnes of Naphtali, after their families were: of Iahzeel, the families of the Iahzeelites: of Guni, the familie of the Gunites.

49 Of Iezer, the familie of the Izrites: of Shillem, the familie of the Shillemites.

50 These are the families of Naphtali according to their housholdes, and their nomber, fiue and fourtie thousande and foure hundreth.

51 These are the nombers of the children of Israel: sixe hundreth and one thousand, seuen hundreth and thirtie.

52 And the Lord spake vnto Moses, saying,

53 Vnto these the land shalbe deuided for an inheritance, according to the number of names.

54 To many thou shalt giue the more inheritance, and to fewe thou shalt giue lesse inheritance: to euery one according to his nomber shalbe giuen his inheritance.

55 Notwithstanding, the land shalbe deuided by lot: according to the names of the tribes of their fathers they shall inherite:

56 According to the lot shall the possession thereof be deuided betweene many and fewe.

57 These also are the nobers of ye Leuites, after their families: of Gershon came ye familie of the Gershonites: of Kohath, ye familie of the Kohathites: of Merari, the familie of the Merarites.

58 These are the families of Leui, the familie of the Libnites: the familie of the Hebronites: the familie of the Mahlites: the familie of the Mushites: the familie of the Korhites: and Kohath begate Amram.

59 And Amrams wife was called Iochebed the daughter of Leui, which was borne vnto Leui in Egypt: and she bare vnto Amram Aaron, and Moses, and Miriam their sister.

60 And vnto Aaron were borne Nadab, and Abihu, Eleazar, and Ithamar.

61 And Nadab and Abihu dyed, because they offred strange fire before the Lord.

62 And their nombers were three and twentie thousand, all males from a moneth old and aboue: for they were not nombred among the children of Israel, because there was none inheritance giuen them among the children of Israel.

63 These are the nombers of Moses and Eleazar the Priest which nombred the children of Israel in the plaine of Moab, neere Iorden, towarde Iericho.

64 And among these there was not a man of them, whome Moses and Aaron the Priest nobred, when they tolde the children of Israel in the wildernes of Sinai.

65 For the Lord said of them, They shall die in the wildernes: so there was not left a man of them, saue Caleb the sonne of Iephunneh, and Ioshua the sonne of Nun.

Numbers 27

1 Then came the daughters of Zelophehad, the sonne of Hepher, the sonne of Gilead, the sonne of Machir, the sonne of Manasseh, of the familie of Manasseh, the sonne of Ioseph (and the names of his daughters were these, Mahlah, Noah and Hoglah, and Milcah, and Tirzah)

2 And stoode before Moses, and before Eleazar the Priest, and before the Princes, and all the assemblie, at the doore of the Tabernacle of the Congregation, saying,

3 Our father dyed in the wildernes, and he was not among the assemblie of them that were assembled against the Lord in the companie of Korah, but died in his sinne, and had no sonnes.

4 Wherefore should the name of our father be taken away from among his familie, because he hath no sonne? giue vs a possession among the brethren of our father.

5 Then Moses brought their cause before the Lord.

6 And the Lord spake vnto Moses, saying,

7 The daughters of Zelophehad speake right: thou shalt giue them a possession to inherite among their fathers brethren, and shalt turne the inheritance of their father vnto them.

8 Also thou shalt speake vnto the children of Israel, saying, If a man die and haue no sonne, then ye shall turne his inheritaunce vnto his daughter.

9 And if he haue no daughter, ye shall giue his inheritance vnto his brethren.

10 And if he haue no brethren, ye shall giue his inheritance vnto his fathers brethren.

11 And if his father haue no brethren, ye shall giue his inheritance vnto his next kinsman of his familie, and he shall possesse it: and this shall be vnto the children of Israel a law of iudgement, as the Lord hath commanded Moses.

12 Againe the Lord said vnto Moses, Go vp into this mount of Abarim, and behold ye lande which I haue giuen vnto the children of Israel.

13 And when thou hast seene it, thou shalt be gathered vnto thy people also, as Aaron thy brother was gathered.

14 For ye were disobedient vnto my worde in the desert of Zin, in the strife of the assemblie, to sanctifie me in the waters before their eyes. That is the water of Meribah in Kadesh in the wildernesse of Zin.

15 Then Moses spake vnto the Lord, saying,

16 Let the Lord God of the spirits of all flesh appoint a man ouer the Congregation,

17 Who may goe out and in before them, and leade them out and in, that the Congregation of the Lord be not as sheepe, which haue not a shepheard.

18 And the Lord said vnto Moses, Take thee Ioshua the sonne of Nun, in whom is the Spirite, and put thine handes vpon him,

19 And set him before Eleazar the Priest, and before all the Congregation, and giue him a charge in their sight.

20 And giue him of thy glory, that all the Congregation of ye children of Israel may obey.

21 And he shall stande before Eleazar the Priest, who shall aske counsell for him by the iudgement of Vrim before the Lord: at his worde they shall goe out, and at his worde they shall come in, both he, and all the children of Israel with him and all the Congregation.

22 So Moses did as the Lord had commanded him, and he tooke Ioshua, and set him before Eleazar the Priest, and before all the Congregation.

23 Then he put his handes vpon him, and gaue him a charge, as the Lord had spoken by the hand of Moses.

Numbers 28

1 And the Lord spake vnto Moses, saying,

2 Command the children of Israel, and say vnto them, Ye shall obserue to offer vnto me in their due season mine offering, and my bread, for my sacrifices made by fire for a sweete sauour vnto me.

3 Also thou shalt say vnto them, This is the offring made by fire which ye shall offer vnto the Lord, two lambes of a yeere olde without spot, daily, for a continuall burnt offring.

4 One lambe shalt thou prepare in the morning, and the other lambe shalt thou prepare at euen.

5 And the tenth part of an Ephah of fine floure for a meate offering mingled with the fourth part of an Hin of beaten oyle.

6 This shalbe a daily burnt offering, as was made in the mount Sinai for a sweete sauour: it is a sacrifice made by fire vnto the Lord.

7 And the drinke offring thereof the fourth part of an Hin for one lambe: in the holy place cause to powre the drinke offring vnto the Lord.

8 And the other lambe thou shalt prepare at euen: as the meate offering of the morning, and as the drinke offering thereof shalt thou prepare this for an offring made by fire of sweete sauour vnto the Lord.

9 But on the Sabbath day ye shall offer two lambes of a yere old, without spot, and two tenth deales of fine floure for a meate offring mingled with oyle, and the drinke offring thereof.

10 This is ye burnt offring of euery Sabbath, beside the continuall burnt offring, and drinke offring thereof.

11 And in the beginning of your moneths, ye shall offer a burnt offring vnto the Lord, two yong bullockes, and a ramme, and seuen lambes of a yeere olde, without spot,

12 And three tenth deales of fine floure for a meat offring mingled with oyle for one bullocke, and two tenth deales of fine floure for a meate offring, mingled with oyle for one ramme,

13 And a tenth deale of fine floure mingled with oyle for a meate offring vnto one lambe: for a burnt offring of sweete sauour: it is an offring made by fire vnto the Lord.

14 And their drinke offrings shalbe halfe an Hin of wine vnto one bullocke, and the thirde part of an Hin vnto a ram, and ye fourth part of an Hin vnto a labe: this is the burnt offring of euery moneth, throughout the moneths of the yeere.

15 And one hee goat for a sinne offring vnto the Lord shalbe prepared, besides the continuall burnt offring, and his drinke offring.

16 Also the fourtenth day of the first moneth is the Passeouer of the Lord.

17 And in ye fiftenth day of the same moneth is the feast: seuen dayes shall vnleauened bread be eaten.

18 In the first day shalbe an holy conuocation, ye shall do no seruile worke therein.

19 But ye shall offer a sacrifice made by fire for a burnt offring vnto the Lord, two yong bullocks, one ram, and seuen lambes of a yeere olde: see that they be without blemish.

20 And their meate offering shalbe of fine floure mingled with oyle: three tenth deales shall ye prepare for a bullocke, and two tenth deales for a ramme:

21 One tenth deale shalt thou prepare for euery lambe, euen for the seuen lambes.

22 And an hee goate for a sinne offering, to make an atonement for you.

23 Ye shall prepare these, beside the burnt offering in the morning, which is a continuall burnt sacrifice.

24 After this maner ye shall prepare throughout all the seuen dayes, for the mainteining of the offering made by fire for a sweete sauour vnto the Lord: it shall be done beside the continuall burnt offring and drinke offring thereof.

25 And in ye seuenth day ye shall haue an holy conuocation, wherein ye shall do no seruile worke.

26 Also in the day of your first fruits, when ye bring a newe meate offring vnto the Lord, according to your weekes ye shall haue an holy conuocation, and ye shall do no seruile worke in it:

27 But ye shall offer a burnt offering for a sweete sauour vnto the Lord, two yong bullocks, a ramme, and seuen lambes of a yeere olde,

28 And their meat offring of fine floure mingled with oyle, three tenth deales vnto a bullocke, two tenth deales to a ram,

29 And one tenth deale vnto euery lambe throughout the seuen lambes,

30 And an hee goate to make an atonement for you:

31 (Ye shall doe this besides the continuall burnt offring, and his meate offring:) see they be without blemish, with their drinke offrings.

Numbers 29

1 Moreouer, in the first day of the seuenth moneth ye shall haue an holy conuocation: ye shall doe no seruile worke therein: it shall be a day of blowing the trumpets vnto you.

2 And ye shall make a burnt offering for a sweete sauour vnto the Lord: one yong bullocke, one ram, and seuen lambes of a yeere olde, without blemish.

3 And their meat offring shalbe of fine floure mingled with oyle, three tenth deales vnto the bullocke, and two tenth deales vnto the ramme,

4 And one tenth deale vnto one lambe, for the seuen lambes,

5 And an hee goate for a sinne offering to make an atonement for you,

6 Beside the burnt offring of the moneth, and his meat offring, and the continual burnt offring, and his meate offring and the drinke offrings of the same, according to their maner, for a sweete sauour: it is a sacrifice made by fire vnto ye Lord.

7 And ye shall haue in ye tenth day of the seuenth moneth, an holy conuocation: and ye shall humble your soules, and shall not doe any worke therein:

8 But ye shall offer a burnt offring vnto the Lord for a sweete sauour: one yong bullocke, a ramme, and seuen lambes of a yeere olde: see they be without blemish.

9 And their meate offering shall be of fine floure mingled with oyle, three tenth deales to a bullocke, and two tenth deales to a ramme,

10 One tenth deale vnto euery lambe, thoroughout the seuen lambes,

11 An hee goate for a sinne offring, (beside ye sinne offring to make the atonement and the continual burnt offring and the meat offring thereof) and their drinke offrings.

12 And in the fifteenth day of the seuenth moneth ye shall haue an holie conuocation: ye shall do no seruile worke therein, but yee shall keepe a feast vnto the Lord seuen daies.

13 And ye shall offer a burnt offring for a sacrifice made by fire of sweete sauour vnto the Lord, thirteene yong bullocks, two rammes, and fourtene lambes of a yeere olde: they shall bee without blemish.

14 And their meate offering shall bee of fine floure mingled with oyle, three tenth

deales vnto euery bullocke of the thirteene bullockes, two tenth deales to either of the two rammes,

15 And one tenth deale vnto eche of ye fourteene lambes,

16 And one hee goate for a sinne offring, beside the continuall burnt offring, his meate offring, and his drinke offring.

17 And the second day ye shall offer twelue yong bullockes, two rams, fourteene lambes of a yeere olde without blemish,

18 With their meate offring and their drinke offrings for the bullockes, for the rammes, and for the lambes according to their nomber, after the maner,

19 And an hee goate for a sinne offring, (beside the continuall burnt offering and his meate offring) and their drinke offrings.

20 Also the third day ye shall offer eleuen bullocks, two rams, and fourteene lambes of a yeere olde without blemish,

21 With their meate offring and their drinke offrings, for the bullockes, for the rams, and for the lambes, after their number according to the maner,

22 And an hee goat for a sinne offring, beside the continuall burnt offring, and his meate offring and his drinke offring.

23 And the fourth day ye shall offer tenne bullocks, two rammes, and fourteene lambes of a yeere olde without blemish.

24 Their meate offring and their drinke offrings, for the bullockes, for the rammes, and for the lambes according to their nomber, after the maner,

25 And an hee goate for a sinne offering beside the continuall burnt offring, his meate offering and his drinke offering.

26 In the fifth day also ye shall offer nine bullockes, two rammes, and fourteene lambes of a yeere olde without blemish,

27 And their meat offering and their drinke offrings for the bullockes, for the rammes, and for the lambes according to their number, after the maner,

28 And an hee goat for a sinne offring, beside the continuall burnt offring, and his meat offring and his drinke offring.

29 And in the sixt day ye shall offer eight bullockes, two rams, and fourteene lambes of a yeere olde without blemish,

30 And their meate offring, and their drinke offrings for the bullockes, for the rammes, and for the lambes according to their number, after the maner,

31 And an hee goat for a sinne offring, beside the continuall burnt offring, his meate offring and his drinke offrings.

32 In the seuenth day also ye shall offer seuen bullockes, two rammes and fourteene lambes of a yeere olde without blemish,

33 And their meate offering and their drinke offrings for the bullockes, for the rammes, and for the lambes according to their maner,

34 And an hee goate for a sinne offring, beside the continuall burnt offring, his meate offering and his drinke offring.

35 In the eight day, yee shall haue a solemne assemblie: yee shall doe no seruile worke therein,

36 But yee shall offer a burnt offering, a sacrifice made by fire for a sweete sauour vnto the Lord, one bullocke, one ram, and seuen lambes of a yeere old without blemish,

37 Their meate offring and their drinke offrings for the bullocke, for the ramme, and for the lambes according to their nomber, after the maner,

38 And an hee goat for a sinne offring, beside the continuall burnt offring, and his meate offring, and his drinke offring.

39 These things ye shall do vnto the Lord in your feastes, beside your vowes, and your free offrings, for your burnt offrings, and for your meate offrings, and for your drinke offrings and for your peace offrings.

Numbers 30

1 Then Moses spake vnto the children of Israel according to all that the Lord had commanded him,

2 Moses also spake vnto the heads of ye tribes concerning the children of Israel, saying, This is the thing which the Lord hath commanded,

3 Whosoeuer voweth a vow vnto the Lord, or sweareth an othe to binde him selfe by a bonde, he shall not breake his promise, but shall do according to al that proceedeth out of his mouth.

4 If a woman also vow a vow vnto the Lord, and binde her selfe by a bonde, being in her fathers house, in the time of her youth,

5 And her father heare her vowe and bonde, wherewith she hath bound her selfe, and her father hold his peace concerning her, then all her vowes shall stande, and euery bonde, wherewith she hath bound her selfe, shall stand.

6 But if her father disallow her the same day that he heareth all her vowes and bondes, wherewith she hath bound her selfe, they shall not bee of value, and the Lord will forgiue her, because her father disallowed her.

7 And if she haue an husband when she voweth or pronounceth ought with her lips, wherewith she bindeth her selfe,

8 If her husband heard it, and holdeth his peace concerning her, the same day he heareth it, then her vowe shall stande, and her bondes wherewith she bindeth her selfe shall stand in effect.

9 But if her husband disallow her the same day that hee heareth it, then shall hee make her vowe which shee hath made, and that that shee hath pronounced with her lips, wherewith shee bound her selfe, of none effect: and the Lord will forgiue her.

10 But euery vowe of a widowe, and of her that is diuorced (wherewith she hath bound her selfe) shall stand in effect with her.

11 And if she vowed in her husbands house, or bound her selfe streightly with an othe,

12 And her husband hath heard it, and helde his peace cocerning her, not disalowing her, then all her vowes shall stand, and euery bond, wherewith she bound her selfe, shall stand in effect.

13 But if her husband disanulled them, the same day that he heard them, nothing that proceeded out of her lippes concerning her vowes or concerning her bondes, shall stand in effect: for her husband hath disanulled them: and the Lord will forgiue her.

14 So euery vowe, and euery othe or bonde, made to humble the soule, her husband may stablish it, or her husband may breake it.

15 But if her husband holde his peace concerning her from day to day, then he stablisheth al her vowes and all her bondes which shee hath made: hee hath confirmed them because he held his peace concerning her the same day that hee hearde them.

16 But if he breake them after that he hath heard them, then shall he beare her iniquitie.

17 These are the ordinances which the Lord commanded Moses, betweene a man and his wife, and betweene the father and his daughter, being young in her fathers house.

Numbers 31

1 And the Lord spake vnto Moses, saying,

2 Reuenge the children of Israel of the Midianites, and afterwarde shalt thou be gathered vnto thy people.

3 And Moses spake to the people, saying, Harnesse some of you vnto warre, and let them goe against Midian, to execute the vengeance of the Lord against Midian.

4 A thousande of euery tribe throughout all the tribes of Israel, shall ye sende to the warre.

5 So there were taken out of the thousands of Israel, twelue thousande prepared vnto warre, of euery tribe a thousand.

6 And Moses sent them to the warre, euen a thousand of euery tribe, and sent them with Phinehas the sonne of Eleazar the Priest to the warre: and the holy instruments, that is, the trumpets to blow were in his hand.

7 And they warred against Midian, as the Lord had commanded Moses, and slue all the males.

8 They slue also the Kings of Midian among them that were slaine: Eui and Rekem, and Zur, and Hur and Reba fiue kings of Midian, and they slue Balaam the sonne of Beor with the sworde:

9 But the children of Israel tooke the women of Midian prisoners, and their children, and spoyled all their cattell, and all their flockes, and all their goods.

10 And they burnt all their cities, wherein they dwelt, and all their villages with fire.

11 And they tooke all the spoyle and all the pray both of men and beastes.

12 And they brought the captiues and that which they had taken, and the spoyle vnto Moses and to Eleazar the Priest, and vnto the Congregation of the children of Israel, into ye campe in the playne of Moab, which was by Iorden toward Iericho.

13 Then Moses and Eleazar the Priest, and all the princes of the Congregation went out of the campe to meete them.

14 And Moses was angry with the captaines of the hoste, with the captaines ouer thousands, and captaines ouer hundreds, which came from the warre and battel.

15 And Moses sayde vnto them, What? haue ye saued all the women?

16 Behold, these caused the children of Israel through the counsell of Balaam to commit a trespasse against the Lord, as concerning Peor, and there came a plague among the Congregation of the Lord.

17 Now therefore, slay all the males among the children, and kill all the women that haue knowen man by carnall copulation.

18 But all the women children that haue not knowen carnall copulation, keepe aliue for your selues.

19 And ye shall remaine without the host seuen dayes, all that haue killed any person, and all that haue touched any dead, and purifie both your selues and your prisoners the third day and the seuenth.

20 Also ye shall purifie euery garment and all that is made of skins and al worke of goates heare, and all things made of wood.

21 And Eleazar ye Priest sayd vnto the men of warre, which went to the battel, This is the ordinance of the law which the Lord commanded Moses,

22 As for gold, and siluer, brasse, yron, tynne, and lead:

23 Euen all that may abide the fire, yee shall make it goe through the fire, and it shalbe cleane: yet, it shalbe purified with the water of purification: and all that suffereth not the fire, yee shall cause to passe by the water.

24 Ye shall wash also your clothes the seuenth day, and ye shalbe cleane: and afterward ye shall come into the Hoste.

25 And the Lord spake vnto Moses, saying,

26 Take the summe of the praie that was taken, both of persons and of cattell, thou and Eleazar the Priest, and the chiefe fathers of the Congregation.

27 And deuide the praye betweene the souldiers that went to the warre, and all the Congregation.

28 And thou shalt take a tribute vnto ye Lord of the men of warre, which went out to battel: one person of fiue hundreth, both of the persons, and of the beeues, and of the asses, and of the sheepe.

29 Yee shall take it of their halfe and giue it vnto Eleazar the Priest, as an heaue offring of the Lord.

30 But of the halfe of the children of Israel thou shalt take one, taken out of fiftie, both of the persons, of the beeues,

of the asses, and of the sheepe, euen of all the cattel: and thou shalt giue them vnto the Leuites, which haue the charge of the Tabernacle of the Lord.

31 And Moses and Eleazar the priest did as the Lord had commanded Moses.

32 And the bootie, to wit, the rest of the praie which the men of warre had spoyled, was sixe hundreth seuentie and fiue thousand sheepe,

33 And seuentie and two thousand beeues,

34 And three score and one thousand asses,

35 And two and thirtie thousande persons in all, of women that had lyen by no man.

36 And the halfe, to wit, the part of them that went out to warre touching the nomber of sheepe, was three hundreth seuen and thirtie thousand, and fiue hundreth.

37 And the Lordes tribute of the sheepe was sixe hundreth and seuentie and fiue:

38 And the beeues were six and thirty thousad, whereof the Lordes tribute was seuentie and two.

39 And the asses were thirtie thousande and fiue hundreth, whereof the Lordes tribute was three score and one:

40 And of persons sixtene thousand, whereof the Lordes tribute was two and thirtie persons.

41 And Moses gaue the tribute of the Lordes offring vnto Eleazar the Priest, as the Lord had commanded Moses.

42 And of the halfe of the children of Israel, which Moses deuided from the men of warre,

43 (For the halfe that perteined vnto the Congregation, was three hundreth thirtie and seuen thousand sheepe and fiue hundreth,

44 And sixe and thirtie thousand beeues,

45 And thirtie thousand asses, and fiue hudreth,

46 And sixteene thousande persons)

47 Moses, I say, tooke of the halfe that perteined vnto the children of Israel, one taken out of fiftie, both of the persons, and of the cattell, and gaue them vnto the Leuites, which haue the charge of the Tabernacle of the Lord, as the Lord had commanded Moses.

48 Then the captaines which were ouer thousandes of the hoste, the captaines ouer the thousandes, and the captaines ouer the hundreds came vnto Moses:

49 And saide to Moses, Thy seruants haue taken the summe of the men of warre which are vnder our authoritie, and there lacketh not one man of vs.

50 We haue therefore brought a present vnto the Lord, what euery man found of iewels of golde, bracelets, and cheines, rings, eare ringes, and ornaments of the legges, to make an atonement for our soules before the Lord.

51 And Moses and Eleazar the Priest tooke the golde of them, and all wrought iewels,

52 And all the golde of the offring that they offered vp to the Lord (of the

captaines ouer thousands and hundreds) was sixteene thousande seuen hundreth and fiftie shekels,

53 (For the men of warre had spoyled, euery man for him selfe)

54 And Moses and Eleazar the Priest tooke the golde of the captaines ouer the thousandes, and ouer the hundreds, and brought it into the Tabernacle of the Congregation, for a memoriall of the children of Israel before the Lord.

Numbers 32

1 Nowe the children of Reuben, and the children of Gad had an exceeding great multitude of cattell: and they sawe the lande of Iazer, and the lande of Gilead, that it was an apt place for cattel.

2 Then the children of Gad, and the childre of Reuben came, and spake vnto Moses and to Eleazar the Priest, and vnto the princes of the Congregation, saying,

3 The land of Ataroth, and Dibon, and Iazer, and Nimrah, and Heshbon, and Elealeh, and Shebam, and Nebo, and Beon,

4 Which countrey the Lord smote before the Congregation of Israel, is a lande meete for cattell, and thy seruants haue cattell:

5 Wherefore, said they, if we haue foud grace in thy sight, let this lande be giuen vnto thy seruants for a possession, and bring vs not ouer Iorde.

6 And Moses said vnto the children of Gad, and to the children of Reuben, Shall your brethren goe to warre, and ye tary heere?

7 Wherefore now discourage ye the heart of the children of Israel, to goe ouer into the lande, which the Lord hath giuen them?

8 Thus did your fathers when I sent them from Kadesh-barnea to see the lande.

9 For when they went vp euen vnto the riuer of Eshcol, and sawe the land: they discouraged the heart of the childre of Israel, that they woulde not goe into the lande, which the Lord had giuen them.

10 And the Lordes wrath was kindled the same day, and he did sweare, saying,

11 None of the men that came out of Egypt from twentie yeere olde and aboue, shall see the land for the which I sware vnto Abraham, to Izhak, and to Iaakob, because they haue not wholly followed me:

12 Except Caleb the sonne of Iephunneh the Kenesite, and Ioshua the sonne of Nun: for they haue constantly followed the Lord.

13 And the Lord was very angry with Israel, and made them wander in the wildernesse fourty yeeres, vntill all the generation that had done euill in the sight of the Lord were consumed.

14 And behold, ye are risen vp in your fathers steade as an encrease of sinfull men, still to augment the fierce wrath of the Lord, toward Israel.

15 For if ye turne away from following him, he will yet againe leaue the people

in the wildernesse, and ye shall destroy all this folke.

16 And they went neere to him, and said, We will builde sheepe foldes here for our sheepe, and for our cattell, and cities for our children.

17 But we our selues will be readie armed to go before the children of Israel, vntill we haue brought them vnto their place: but our childre shall dwell in the defenced cities, because of the inhabitants of the lande.

18 We will not returne vnto our houses, vntil the children of Israel haue inherited, euery man his inheritance.

19 Neither wil we inherite with them beyond Iorden and on that side, because our inheritance is fallen to vs on this side Iorden Eastwarde.

20 And Moses saide vnto them, If ye will doe this thing, and goe armed before the Lord to warre:

21 And will goe euery one of you in harnesse ouer Iorden before the Lord, vntill he hath cast out his enemies from his sight:

22 And vntill the land be subdued before the Lord, then ye shall returne and be innocent toward the Lord, and toward Israel: and this land shalbe your possession before the Lord.

23 But if ye will not doe so, beholde, ye haue sinned against the Lord, and be sure, that your sinne will finde you out.

24 Builde you then cities for your children and folds for your sheepe, and do that ye haue spoke.

25 Then the children of Gad and the children of Reuben spake vnto Moses, saying, Thy seruats will doe as my lorde commandeth:

26 Our childre, our wiues, our sheepe, and al our cattell shall remaine there in the cities of Gilead,

27 But thy seruants will goe euery one armed to warre before the Lord for to fight, as my lorde saith.

28 So concerning them, Moses commanded Eleazar the Priest, and Ioshua the sonne of Nun, and the chiefe fathers of the tribes of the children of Israel:

29 And Moses said vnto them, If the children of Gad, and the children of Reuben, will go with you ouer Iorden, all armed to fight before the Lord, then when the land is subdued before you, ye shall giue the the lad of Gilead for a possessio:

30 But if they will not goe ouer with you armed, then they shall haue their possessions amog you in the land of Canaan.

31 And the children of Gad, and the children of Reuben answered, saying, As the Lord hath said vnto thy seruants, so will we doe.

32 We will goe armed before the Lord into the lande of Canaan: that the possession of our inheritance may be to vs on this side Iorden.

33 So Moses gaue vnto them, euen to the children of Gad, and to the children of Reuben, and to halfe the tribe of Manasseh the sonne of Ioseph, the kingdome of Sihon King of the Amorites, and the kingdome of Og King of Bashan, the lande with the cities thereof and coastes, euen the cities of the countrey round about.

34 Then the children of Gad built Dibon, and Ataroth, and Aroer,

35 And Atroth, Shophan, and Iazer, and Iogbehah,

36 And Beth-nimrah, and Beth-haran, defenced cities: also sheepe foldes.

37 And the children of Reuben built Heshbon, and Elealeh, and Kiriathaim,

38 And Nebo, and Baal-meon, and turned their names, and Shibmah: and gaue other names vnto the cities which they built.

39 And the children of Machir the sonne of Manasseh went to Gilead, and tooke it, and put out the Amorites that dwelt therein.

40 Then Moses gaue Gilead vnto Machir the sonne of Manasseh, and he dwelt therein.

41 And Iair the sonne of Manasseh went and tooke the small townes thereof, and called them Hauoth Iair.

42 Also Nobah went and tooke Kenath, with the villages thereof and called it Nobah, after his owne name.

Numbers 33

1 These are the iourneyes of the children of Israel, which went out of the land of Egypt according to their bands vnder the hand of Moses and Aaron.

2 And Moses wrote their going out by their iourneies according to ye commandement of the Lord: so these are ye iourneies of their going out.

3 Nowe they departed from Rameses the first moneth, euen the fifteenth day of the first moneth, on the morowe after the Passeouer: and the children of Israel went out with an hie hand in the sight of all the Egyptians.

4 (For the Egyptians buried all their first borne, which the Lord had smitten among them: vpon their gods also the Lord did execution.)

5 And the children of Israel remoued from Rameses, and pitched in Succoth.

6 And they departed from Succoth, and pitched in Etham, which is in the edge of the wildernesse.

7 And they remoued from Etham, and turned againe vnto Pi-hahiroth, which is before Baal-zephon, and pitched before Migdol.

8 And they departed from before Hahiroth, and went through the middes of the Sea into the wildernesse, and went three dayes iourney in the wildernesse of Etham, and pitched in Marah.

9 And they remoued from Marah, and came vnto Elim, and in Elim were twelue fountaines of water, and seuentie palme trees, and they pitched there.

10 And they remoued from Elim, and camped by the red Sea.

11 And they remoued from the red Sea, and lay in the wildernesse of Sin.

12 And they tooke their iourney out of the wildernesse of Sin, and set vp their tentes in Dophkah.

13 And they departed from Dophkah, and lay in Alush.

14 And they remoued from Alush, and lay in Rephidim, where was no water for the people to drinke.

15 And they departed from Rephidim, and pitched in the wildernesse of Sinai.

16 And they remoued from the desert of Sinai, and pitched in Kibroth Hattaauah.

17 And they departed from Kibroth Hattaauah, and lay at Hazeroth.

18 And they departed from Hazeroth, and pitched in Rithmah.

19 And they departed from Rithmah, and pitched at Rimmon Parez.

20 And they departed from Rimmon Parez, and pitched in Libnah.

21 And they remoued from Libnah, and pitched in Rissah.

22 And they iourneyed from Rissah, and pitched in Kehelathah.

23 And they went from Kehelathah, and pitched in mount Shapher.

24 And they remoued from mount Shapher, and lay in Haradah.

25 And they remoued from Haradah, and pitched in Makheloth.

26 And they remoued from Makheloth, and lay in Tahath.

27 And they departed from Tahath, and pitched in Tarah.

28 And they remoued from Tarah, and pitched in Mithkah.

29 And they went from Mithkah, and pitched in Hashmonah.

30 And they departed from Hashmonah, and lay in Moseroth.

31 And they departed from Moseroth, and pitched in Bene-iaakan.

32 And they remoued from Bene-iaakan, and lay in Hor-hagidgad.

33 And they went from Hor-hagidgad, and pitched in Iotbathah.

34 And they remoued from Iotbathah, and lay in Ebronah.

35 And they departed from Ebronah, and lay in Ezion-gaber.

36 And they remoued from Ezion-gaber, and pitched in the wildernesse of Zin, which is Kadesh.

37 And they remooued from Kadesh, and pitched in mount Hor, in the edge of the land of Edom.

38 (And Aaron the Priest went vp into mount Hor, at the commandement of the Lord, and died there, in the fortieth yeere after the children of Israel were come out of the lande of Egypt, in the first day of the fifth moneth.

39 And Aaron was an hundreth, and three and twentie yeere olde, when hee dyed in mount Hor.

40 And King Arad the Canaanite, which dwelt in the South of the land of Canaan, heard of the comming of the children of Israel)

41 And they departed from mount Hor, and pitched in Zalmonah.

42 And they departed from Zalmonah, and pitched in Punon.

43 And they departed from Punon, and pitched in Oboth.

44 And they departed from Oboth, and pitched in Iie-abarim, in the borders of Moab.

45 And they departed from Iim, and pitched in Dibon-gad.

46 And they remooued from Dibon-gad, and lay in Almon-diblathaim.

47 And they remooued from Almon-diblathaim, and pitched in the mountaines of Abarim before Nebo.

48 And they departed from the mountaines of Abarim, and pitched in the plaine of Moab, by Iorden toward Iericho.

49 And they pitched by Iorden, from Bethieshimoth vnto Abel-shittim in the playne of Moab.

50 And the Lord spake vnto Moses in the playne of Moab, by Iorden towarde Iericho, saying,

51 Speake vnto the children of Israel, and say vnto them, When ye are come ouer Iorden to enter into the land of Canaan,

52 Ye shall then driue out all the inhabitants of the land before you, and destroy all their pictures, and breake asunder all their images of metall, and plucke downe all their hie places.

53 And ye shall possesse the lande and dwell therein: for I haue giue you ye land to possesse it.

54 And ye shall inherite the land by lot according to your families: to the more yee shall giue more inheritance, and to the fewer the lesse inheritance. Where the lot shall fall to any man, that shall be his: according to the tribes of your fathers shall ye inherite.

55 But if ye will not driue out the inhabitants of the land before you, then those which yee let ramaine of them, shalbe prickes in your eyes, and thornes in your sides, and shall vexe you in the land wherein ye dwell.

56 Moreouer, it shall come to passe, that I shall doe vnto you, as I thought to do vnto them.

Numbers 34

1 And the Lord spake vnto Moses, saying,

2 Commande the children of Israel, and say vnto them, When yee come into the land of Canaan, this is the land that shall fall vnto your inheritance: that is, the land of Canaan with the coastes thereof.

3 And your Southquarter shalbe from the wildernesse of Zin to the borders of Edom: so that your Southquarter shall be from the salt Sea coast Eastwarde:

4 And the border shall compasse you from the South to Maaleh-akrabbim, and reach to Zin, and goe out from the South to Kadesh-barnea: thence it shall stretch to Hazar-addar, and go along to Azmon.

5 And the border shall compasse from Azmon vnto the riuer of Egypt, and shall goe out to the Sea.

6 And your Westquarter shall bee the great Sea: euen that border shalbe your Westcoast.

7 And this shall bee your Northquarter: yee shall marke out your border from the great Sea vnto mount Hor.

8 From mount Hor ye shall point out till it come vnto Hamath, and the end of the coast shall be at Zedad.

9 And the coast shall reach out to Ziphron, and goe out at Hazar-enan. this shalbe your Northquarter.

10 And ye shall marke out your Eastquarter from Hazar-enan to Shepham.

11 And the coast shall goe downe from Shepham to Riblah, and from the Eastside of Ain: and the same border shall descend and goe out at the side of the sea of Chinneereth Eastward.

12 Also that border shall goe downe to Iorden, and leaue at the salt Sea. this shalbe your land with the coastes thereof round about.

13 Then Moses commanded the children of Israel, saying, This is the lande which yee shall inherite by lot, which the Lord commanded to giue vnto nine tribes and halfe the tribe.

14 For the tribe of the children of Reuben, according to the housholdes of their fathers, and the tribe of the children of Gad, according to their fathers housholdes, and halfe the tribe of Manasseh, haue receiued their inheritance.

15 Two tribes and an halfe tribe haue receiued their inheritance on this side of Iorden toward Iericho full East.

16 Againe the Lord spake to Moses, saying,

17 These are the names of the men which shall deuide ye land vnto you: Eleazar the Priest, and Ioshua the sonne of Nun.

18 And ye shall take also a prince of euerie tribe to deuide the land.

19 The names also of the men are these: Of the tribe of Iudah, Caleb ye sonne of Iephunneh.

20 And of the tribe of the sonnes of Simeon, Shemuel the sonne of Ammihud.

21 Of the tribe of Beniamin, Elidad the sonne of Chislon.

22 Also of the tribe of the sonnes of Dan, the prince Bukki, the sonne of Iogli.

23 Of the sonnes of Ioseph: of the tribe of the sonnes of Manasseh, the prince Hanniel the sonne of Ephod.

24 And of the tribe of the sonnes of Ephraim, the prince Kemuel, the sonne of Shiphtan.

25 Of the tribe also of the sonnes of Zebulun, the prince Elizaphan, the sonne of Parnach.

26 So of the tribe of the sonnes of Issachar, the prince Paltiel the sonne of Azzan.

27 Of the tribe also of the sonnes of Asher, the prince Ahihud, the sonne of Shelomi.

28 And of the tribe of the sonnes of Naphtali, the prince Pedahel, the sonne of Ammihud.

29 These are they, whome the Lord commanded to deuide the inheritance vnto the children of Israel, in the land of Canaan.

Numbers 35

1 And the Lord spake vnto Moses in the plaine of Moab by Iorden, toward Iericho, saying,

2 Commande ye children of Israel, that they giue vnto the Leuites of the inheritace of their possession, cities to dwell in: yee shall giue also vnto the Leuites the suburbes of the cities round about them.

3 So they shall haue the cities to dwell in, and their suburbes shall be for their cattell, and for their substance, and for all their beasts.

4 And the suburbes of the cities, which ye shall giue vnto the Leuites, from the wall of the citie outward, shalbe a thousand cubites round about.

5 And yee shall measure without the citie of the Eastside, two thousand cubites: and of the Southside, two thousand cubites: and of the Westside, two thousand cubites: and of ye Northside, two thousand cubites: and the citie shalbe in ye middes. this shalbe the measure of the suburbes of their cities.

6 And of the cities which yee shall giue vnto the Leuites, there shalbe sixe cities for refuge, which ye shall appoint, that he which killeth, may flee thither: and to them yee shall adde two and fourtie cities more.

7 All the cities which yee shall giue to the Leuites, shalbe eight and fourtie cities: them shall ye giue with their suburbes.

8 And concerning the cities which yee shall giue, of the possession of the children of Israel: of many ye shall take more, and of few ye shall take lesse: euery one shall giue of his cities vnto the Leuites, according to his inheritance, which hee inheriteth.

9 And the Lord spake vnto Moses, saying,

10 Speake vnto the children of Israel, and say vnto them, When ye be come ouer Iorden into the land of Canaan,

11 Ye shall appoint you cities, to bee cities of refuge for you, that the slayer, which slayeth any person vnwares, may flee thither.

12 And these cities shalbe for you a refuge from the auenger, that he which killeth, die not, vntill he stand before the Congregation in iudgement.

13 And of the cities which ye shall giue, sixe cities shall ye haue for refuge.

14 Ye shall appoint three on this side Iorden, and ye shall appoint three cities in the lande of Canaan which shalbe cities of refuge.

15 These six cities shalbe a refuge for the children of Israel, and for the stranger, and for him that dwelleth among you, that euery one which killeth any person vnwares, may flee thither.

16 And if one smite another with an instrument of yron that hee die, hee is a

murtherer, and the murtherer shall die the death.

17 Also if hee smite him by casting a stone, wherewith hee may be slaine, and he die, hee is a murtherer, and the murtherer shall die the death.

18 Or if he smite him with an hand weapon of wood, wherewith he may be slaine, if he die, he is a murtherer, and the murtherer shall die the death.

19 The reuenger of the blood himselfe shall slay the murtherer: when he meeteth him, he shall slay him.

20 But if hee thrust him of hate, or hurle at him by laying of wait, that he die,

21 Or smite him through enimitie with his hand, that he die, he that smote him shall die ye death: for hee is a murtherer: the reuenger of the blood shall slay the murtherer when he meeteth him.

22 But if he pusshed him vnaduisedly, and not of hatred, or cast vpon him any thing, without laying of waite,

23 Or any stone (whereby he might be slaine) and sawe him not, or caused it to fall vpon him, and he die, and was not his enemie, neither sought him any harme,

24 Then the Congregation shall iudge betweene the slayer and the auenger of blood according to these lawes.

25 And the Congregation shall deliuer the slayer out of the hande of the auenger of blood, and the Congregation shall restore him vnto the citie of his refuge, whither hee was fled: and hee shall abide there vnto the death of the hie Priest, which is anointed with the holy oyle.

26 But if the slayer come without the borders of the citie of his refuge, whither he was fled,

27 And the reuenger of blood finde him without the borders of the citie of his refuge, and the reueger of blood slay ye murtherer, he shalbe giltles,

28 Because he should haue remained in the citie of his refuge, vntill the death of the hie Priest: and after the death of the hie Priest, the slayer shall returne vnto the land of his possession.

29 So these thinges shall be a lawe of iudgement vnto you, throughout your generations in all your dwellings.

30 Whosoeuer killeth any person, the Iudge shall slay the murtherer, through witnesses: but one witnesse shall not testifie against a person to cause him to die.

31 Moreouer ye shall take no recompense for the life of the murtherer, which is worthy to die: but he shalbe put to death.

32 Also ye shall take no recompense for him that is fled to the citie of his refuge, that he should come againe, and dwell in the lande, before the death of the hie Priest.

33 So ye shall not pollute the land wherein ye shall dwell: for blood defileth the land: and the land cannot be clensed of the blood that is shed therein, but by the blood of him that shed it.

34 Defile not therefore the lande which yee shall inhabite, For I dwell in the middes thereof: for I the Lord dwel among the children of Israel.

Numbers 36

1 Then the chiefe fathers of the familie of the sonnes of Gilead, the sonne of Machir, the sonne of Manasseh, of the families of the sones of Ioseph, came, and spake before Moses, and before the princes, the chiefe fathers of the children of Israel,

2 And saide, The Lord commanded my lord to giue the land to inherit by lot to the children of Israel: and my lord was commanded by the Lord, to giue the inheritance of Zelophehad our brother vnto his daughters.

3 If they bee married to any of the sonnes of the other tribes of the children of Israel, then shall their inheritance be taken away from the inheritance of our fathers, and shalbe put vnto the inheritance of the tribe whereof they shalbe: so shall it be taken away from the lot of our inheritance.

4 Also when the Iubile of the children of Israel commeth, then shall their inheritance be put vnto the inheritance of the tribe whereof they shall be: so shall their inheritance be taken away from the inheritance of the tribe of our fathers.

5 Then Moses commanded the children of Israel, according to the word of the Lord, saying, The tribe of the sonnes of Ioseph haue said well.

6 This is the thing that the Lord hath commanded, concerning the daughters of Zelophehad, saying, They shall be wiues, to whome they thinke best, onely to the familie of the tribe of their father shall they marry:

7 So shall not the inheritance of the children of Israel remoue from tribe to tribe, for euery one of the children of Israel shall ioyne himselfe to the inheritance of the tribe of his fathers.

8 And euery daughter that possesseth any inheritance of the tribes of the children of Israel, shalbe wife vnto one of the familie of the tribe of her father: that the children of Israel may enioye euery man the inheritance of their fathers.

9 Neither shall the inheritance go about from tribe to tribe: but euery one of the tribes of the childre of Israel shall sticke to his own inheritace.

10 As the Lord commanded Moses, so did the daughters of Zelophehad.

11 For Mahlah, Tirzah, and Hoglah, and Milcah, and Noah the daughters of Zelophehad were married vnto their fathers brothers sonnes,

12 They were wiues to certaine of the families of the sonnes of Manasseh the sonne of Ioseph: so their inheritance remained in the tribe of the familie of their father.

13 These are the commandements and lawes which the Lord commanded by the hand of Moses, vnto the children of Israel in the plaine of Moab, by Iorden toward Iericho.

Deuteronomy

Deuteronomy 1

1 These bee the wordes which Moses spake vnto all Israel, on this side Iorden in the wildernesse, in the plaine, ouer against the red Sea, betweene Paran and Tophel, and Laban, and Hazeroth, and Di-zahab.

2 There are eleuen dayes iourney from Horeb vnto Kadesh-barnea, by the way of mout Seir.

3 And it came to passe in the first day of the eleuenth moneth, in the fourtieth yeere that Moses spake vnto the children of Israel according vnto all that the Lord had giuen him in commandement vnto them,

4 After that he had slaine Sihon the king of the Amorites which dwelt in Heshbon, and Og king of Bashan, which dwelt at Ashtaroth in Edrei.

5 On this side Iorden in the lande of Moab began Moses to declare this lawe, saying,

6 The Lord our God spake vnto vs in Horeb, saying, Ye haue dwelt long ynough in this mount,

7 Turne you and depart, and goe vnto the mountaine of the Amorites, and vnto all places neere thereunto in the plaine, in the mountaine, or in the valley: both Southwarde, and to the Sea side, to the land of the Canaanites, and vnto Lebanon: euen vnto the great riuer, the riuer Perath.

8 Beholde, I haue set the land before you: go in and possesse that land which the Lord sware vnto your fathers, Abraham, Izhak, and Iaakob, to giue vnto them and to their seede after them.

9 And I spake vnto you the same time, saying, I am not able to beare you my selfe alone:

10 The Lord your God hath multiplied you: and beholde, ye are this day as the starres of heauen in nomber:

11 (The Lord God of your fathers make you a thousand times so many moe as ye are, and blesse you, as he hath promised you)

12 Howe can I alone beare your combrance and your charge, and your strife?

13 Bring you men of wisedome and of vnderstanding, and knowen among your tribes, and I will make them rulers ouer you:

14 Then ye answered me and said, The thing is good that thou hast commanded vs to doe.

15 So I tooke the chiefe of your tribes wise and knowen men, and made them rulers ouer you, captaines ouer thousands, and captaines ouer hundreds, and captaines ouer fiftie, and captaines ouer tenne, and officers among your tribes.

16 And I charged your iudges that same time, saying, Heare the controuersies betweene your brethren, and iudge

righteously betweene euery man and his brother, and the stranger that is with him.

17 Ye shall haue no respect of person in iudgement, but shall heare the small aswell as the great: yee shall not feare the face of man: for the iudgement is Gods: and the cause that is too hard for you, bring vnto me, and I will heare it.

18 Also I commanded you the same time all the things which ye should doe.

19 Then we departed from Horeb, and went through all that great and terrible wildernesse (as yee haue seene) by the way of the mountaine of the Amorites, as the Lord our God commanded vs: and we came to Kadesh-barnea.

20 And I saide vnto you, Yee are come vnto the mountaine of the Amorites, which the Lord our God doeth giue vnto vs.

21 Beholde, the Lord thy God hath layde the land before thee: go vp and possesse it, as the Lord the God of thy fathers hath saide vnto thee: feare not, neither be discouraged.

22 Then ye came vnto me euery one, and said, We wil send men before vs, to search vs out the land and to bring vs word againe, what way we must go vp by, and vnto what cities we shall come.

23 So the saying pleased me well, and I tooke twelue men of you, of euery tribe one.

24 Who departed, and went vp into the mountaine, and came vnto the riuer Eshcol, and searched out the land.

25 And tooke of the fruite of the land in their hands, and brought it vnto vs, and brought vs worde againe, and sayd, It is a good land, which the Lord our God doeth giue vs.

26 Notwithstanding, ye would not go vp, but were disobedient vnto the commandement of the Lord your God,

27 And murmured in your tentes, and sayd, Because the Lord hated vs, therefore hath hee brought vs out of the land of Egypt, to deliuer vs into the hand of the Amorites, and to destroy vs.

28 Whither shall we go vp? our brethren haue discouraged our hearts, saying, The people is greater, and taller then we: the cities are great and walled vp to heauen: and moreouer we haue seene the sonnes of the Anakims there.

29 But I sayd vnto you, Dread not, nor be afrayd of them.

30 The Lord your God, who goeth before you, he shall fight for you, according to all that he did vnto you in Egypt before your eyes,

31 And in the wildernesse, where thou hast seene how the Lord thy God bare thee, as a man doeth beare his sonne, in all the way which ye haue gone, vntill ye came vnto this place.

32 Yet for all this ye did not beleeue the Lord your God,

33 Who went in the way before you, to search you out a place to pitch your tentes in, in fire by night, that ye might see what way to goe, and in a cloude by day.

34 Then the Lord heard the voyce of your wordes, and was wroth, and sware, saying,

35 Surely there shall not one of these men of this froward generation, see that good land, which I sware to giue vnto your fathers,

36 Saue Caleb the sonne of Iephunneh: he shall see it, and to him will I giue the land that he hath troden vpon, and to his children, because he hath constantly followed the Lord.

37 Also the Lord was angry with me for your sakes, saying, Thou also shalt not goe in thither,

38 But Ioshua the sonne of Nun which standeth before thee, he shall go in thither: incourage him: for he shall cause Israel to inherite it.

39 Moreouer, your children, which ye sayd should be a praye, and your sonnes, which in that day had no knowledge betweene good and euill, they shall go in thither, and vnto them wil I giue it, and they shall possesse it.

40 But as for you, turne backe, and take your iourney into the wildernesse by the way of the red Sea.

41 Then ye answered and sayd vnto me, We haue sinned against the Lord, we wil go vp, and fight, according to all that the Lord our God hath commanded vs: and ye armed you euery man to the warre, and were ready to goe vp into the mountaine.

42 But the Lord said vnto me, Say vnto them, Goe not vp, neither fight, (for I am not among you) least ye fall before your enemies.

43 And when I told you, ye would not heare, but rebelled against the commandement of the Lord, and were presumptuous, and went vp into the mountaine.

44 Then the Amorites which dwelt in that mountaine came out against you, and chased you (as bees vse to doe) and destroied you in Seir, euen vnto Hormah.

45 And when ye came againe, ye wept before the Lord, but the Lord would not heare your voyce, nor incline his eares vnto you.

46 So ye abode in Kadesh a long time, according to the time that ye had remained before.

Deuteronomy 2

1 Then we turned, and tooke our iourney into the wildernes, by the way of the red Sea, as the Lord spake vnto me: and we compassed mount Seir a long time.

2 And the Lord spake vnto me, saying,

3 Ye haue compassed this mountaine long ynough: turne you Northward.

4 And warne thou the people, saying, Ye shall go through the coast of your brethren the children of Esau, which dwell in Seir, and they shall be afraide of you: take ye good heede therefore.

5 Ye shall not prouoke them: for I wil not giue you of their land so much as a foot breadth, because I haue giuen mount Seir vnto Esau for a possession.

6 Ye shall buy meate of them for money to eate, and ye shall also procure water of them for money to drinke.

7 For the Lord thy God hath blessed thee in all the workes of thine hand: he knoweth thy walking through this great wildernes, and the Lord thy God hath bene with thee this fourtie yeere, and thou hast lacked nothing.

8 And when we were departed from our brethren the children of Esau which dwelt in Seir, through the way of the plaine, from Elath, and from Ezion-gaber, we turned and went by the way of the wildernes of Moab.

9 Then the Lord sayd vnto me, Thou shalt not vexe Moab, neither prouoke them to battel: for I wil not giue thee of their land for a possession, because I haue giuen Ar vnto the children of Lot for a possession.

10 The Emims dwelt therein in times past, a people great and many, and tall, as the Anakims.

11 They also were taken for gyants as the Anakims: whom the Moabites call Emims.

12 The Horims also dwelt in Seir before time, whome the children of Esau chased out and destroyed them before them, and dwelt in their steade: as Israel shall doe vnto the land of his possession, which the Lord hath giuen them.

13 Now rise vp, sayd I, and get you ouer the riuer Zered: and we went ouer the riuer Zered.

14 The space also wherein we came from Kadesh-barnea, vntill we were come ouer the riuer Zered, was eight and thirtie yeeres, vntill all the generation of the men of warre were wasted out from among the hoste, as the Lord sware vnto them.

15 For in deede the hand of the Lord was against them, to destroy them from among the hoste, till they were consumed.

16 So when all the men of warre were consumed and dead from among the people:

17 Then the Lord spake vnto me, saying,

18 Thou shalt goe through Ar the coast of Moab this day:

19 And thou shalt come neere ouer against the children of Ammon: but shalt not lay siege vnto them, nor moue warre against them: for I will not giue thee of the land of the children of Ammon any possession: for I haue giuen it vnto the children of Lot for a possession.

20 That also was taken for a land of gyants: for gyants dwelt therein afore time, whome the Ammonites called Zamzummims:

21 A people that was great, and many, and tall, as the Anakims: but the Lord destroyed them before them, and they succeeded them in their inheritance, and dwelt in their stead:

22 As he did to the children of Esau which dwell in Seir, when he destroyed the Horims before them, and they possessed them, and dwelt in their stead vnto this day.

23 And the Auims which dwelt in Hazarim euen vnto Azzah, the Caphtorims which came out of Caphtor destroyed them, and dwelt in their steade.

24 Rise vp therefore, sayd the Lord: take your iourney, and passe ouer the riuer Arnon: beholde, I haue giuen into thy hand Sihon, the Amorite, King of Heshbon, and his land: begin to possesse it and prouoke him to battell.

25 This day wil I begin to send thy feare and thy dread, vpon all people vnder the whole heauen, which shall heare thy fame, and shall tremble and quake before thee.

26 Then I sent messengers out of the wildernes of Kedemoth vnto Sihon King of Heshbon, with wordes of peace, saying,

27 Let me passe through thy land: I will go by the hie way: I will neither turne vnto the right hand nor to the left.

28 Thou shalt sell me meate for money, for to eate, and shalt giue me water for money for to drinke: onely I will go through on my foote,

29 (As the children of Esau which dwell in Seir, and the Moabites which dwell in Ar, did vnto me) vntill I be come ouer Iorden, into the land which the Lord our God giueth vs.

30 But Sihon the King of Heshbon would not let vs passe by him: for the Lord thy God had hardened his spirit, and made his heart obstinate, because hee would deliuer him into thine hand, as appeareth this day.

31 And the Lord sayd vnto me, Beholde, I haue begun to giue Sihon and his land before thee: begin to possesse and inherite his land.

32 Then came out Sihon to meete vs, him selfe with all his people to fight at Iahaz.

33 But the Lord our God deliuered him into our power, and we smote him, and his sonnes, and all his people.

34 And we tooke all his cities the same time, and destroyed euery citie, men, and women, and children: we let nothing remaine.

35 Onely the cattell we tooke to our selues, and the spoyle of the cities which we tooke,

36 From Aroer, which is by the banke of the riuer of Arnon, and from the citie that is vpon the riuer, euen vnto Gilead: there was not one citie that escaped vs: for the Lord our God deliuered vp all before vs.

37 Onely vnto the land of the children of Ammon thou camest not, nor vnto any place of the riuer Iabbok, nor vnto the cities in the mountaines, nor vnto whatsoeuer the Lord our God forbade vs.

Deuteronomy 3

1 Then we turned, and went vp by the way of Bashan: and Og King of Bashan came out against vs, he, and all his people to fight at Edrei.

2 And the Lord sayde vnto me, Feare him not, for I will deliuer him, and all his people, and his land into thine hand, and thou shalt doe vnto him as thou diddest vnto Sihon King of the Amorites, which dwelt at Heshbon.

3 So the Lord our God deliuered also vnto our hand, Og the King of Bashan, and all his people: and we smote him, vntill none was left him aliue,

4 And we tooke all his cities the same time, neither was there a citie which we tooke not from them, euen three score cities, and all ye countrey of Argob, the kingdome of Og in Bashan.

5 All these cities were fenced with hie walles, gates and barres, beside vnwalled townes a great many.

6 And we ouerthrewe them, as we did vnto Sihon King of Heshbon, destroying euery citie, with men, women, and children.

7 But all the cattell and the spoyle of the cities we tooke for our selues.

8 Thus we tooke at that time out of the hand of two Kings of the Amorites, the land that was on this side Iorden from the riuer of Arnon vnto mount Hermon:

9 (Which Hermon the Sidonians call Shirion, but the Amorites call it Shenir)

10 All the cities of the plaine, and all Gilead, and all Bashan vnto Salchah, and Edrei, cities of the kingdome of Og in Bashan.

11 For onely Og King of Bashan remained of the remnant of the gyants, whose bed was a bed of yron: is it not at Rabbath among the children of Ammon? the length thereof is nine cubites, and foure cubites the breadth of it, after the cubite of a man.

12 And this land which we possessed at that time, from Aroer, which is by the riuer of Arnon, and halfe mount Gilead, and the cities thereof, gaue I vnto the Reubenites and Gadites.

13 And the rest of Gilead, and all Bashan, the kingdome of Og, gaue I vnto the halfe tribe of Manasseh: euen all the countrey of Argob with all Bashan, which is called, The land of gyants.

14 Iair the sonne of Manasseh tooke all the countrey of Argob, vnto the coastes of Geshuri, and of Maachathi: and called them after his owne name, Bashan, Hauoth Iair vnto this day.

15 And I gaue part of Gilead vnto Machir.

16 And vnto the Reubenites and Gadites I gaue the rest of Gilead, and vnto the riuer of Arnon, halfe the riuer and the borders, euen vnto the riuer Iabbok, which is the border of the children of Ammon:

17 The plaine also and Iorden, and the borders from Chinneereth euen vnto the Sea of the plaine, to wit, the salt Sea vnder the springs of Pisgah Eastwarde.

18 And I commanded you the same time, saying, The Lord your God hath giuen you this lande to possesse it: ye shall goe ouer armed before your brethren the children of Israel, all men of warre.

19 Your wiues onely, and your children, and your cattel (for I know that ye haue much cattel) shall abide in your cities, which I haue giuen you,

20 Vntill the Lord haue giuen rest vnto your brethren as vnto you, and that they also possesse the lande, which the Lord your God hath giuen them beyond Iorden: then shall ye returne euery man vnto his possession, which I haue giuen you.

21 And I charged Ioshua the same time, saying, Thine eyes haue seene all that the Lord your God hath done vnto these two Kings: so shall the Lord doe vnto all the kingdomes whither thou goest.

22 Ye shall not feare them: for the Lord your God, he shall fight for you.

23 And I besought the Lord the same time, saying,

24 O Lord God, thou hast begunne to shewe thy seruant thy greatnesse and thy mightie hande: for where is there a God in heauen or in earth, that can do like thy workes, and like thy power?

25 I pray thee let me go ouer and see the good land that is beyond Iorden, that goodly mountaine, and Lebanon.

26 But the Lord was angrie with me for your sakes, and would not heare me: and the Lord said vnto me, Let it suffice thee, speake no more vnto me of this matter.

27 Get thee vp into the top of Pisgah, and lift vp thine eyes Westward, and Northwarde, and Southward, and Eastward, and behold it with thine eyes, for thou shalt not goe ouer this Iorden:

28 But charge Ioshua, and incourage him, and bolden him: for hee shall goe before this people, and he shall deuide for inheritance vnto them, the land which thou shalt see.

29 So wee abode in the valley ouer against Beth-Peor.

Deuteronomy 4

1 Nowe therefore hearken, O Israel, vnto the ordinances and to the lawes which I teache you to doe, that ye may liue and goe in, and possesse the lande, which the Lord God of your fathers giueth you.

2 Ye shall put nothing vnto the word which I command you, neither shall ye take ought there from, that ye may keepe the commandements of the Lord your God which I commande you.

3 Your eyes haue seene what the Lord did because of Baal-Peor, for al the men that folowed Baal-Peor the Lord thy God hath destroyed euery one from among you.

4 But ye that did cleaue vnto the Lord your God, are aliue euery one of you this day.

5 Behold, I haue taught you ordinances, and lawes, as the Lord my God commanded me, that ye should doe euen so within the land whither ye goe to possesse it.

6 Keepe them therefore, and doe them; for that is your wisdome, and your vnderstanding in the sight of the people, which shall heare all these ordinances, and shall say, Onely this people is wise,

and of vnderstanding, and a great nation.

7 For what nation is so great, vnto whome the gods come so neere vnto them, as the Lord our God is neere vnto vs, in all that we call vnto him for?

8 And what nation is so great, that hath ordinances and lawes so righteous, as all this Lawe, which I set before you this day?

9 But take heede to thy selfe, and keepe thy soule diligently, that thou forget not the thinges which thine eyes haue seene, and that they depart not out of thine heart, all the dayes of thy life: but teach them thy sonnes, and thy sonnes sonnes:

10 Forget not the day that thou stoodest before the Lord thy God in Horeb, when the Lord said vnto me, Gather me the people together, and I wil cause them heare my wordes, that they may learne to feare me all the dayes that they shall liue vpon the earth, and that they may teache their children:

11 Then came you neere and stoode vnder the mountaine, and the mountaine burnt with fire vnto the mids of heauen, and there was darkenesse, cloudes and mist.

12 And the Lord spake vnto you out of the middes of the fire, and ye heard the voyce of the wordes, but sawe no similitude, saue a voyce.

13 Then hee declared vnto you his couenant which he commanded you to doe, euen the ten commandements, and wrote them vpon two tables of stone.

14 And the Lord commanded me that same time, that I should teach you ordinances and lawes, which ye should obserue in the lande, whither ye goe, to possesse it.

15 Take therefore good heede vnto your selues: for ye sawe no image in the day that the Lord spake vnto you in Horeb out of the middes of the fire:

16 That ye corrupt not your selues, and make you a grauen image or representation of any figure: whither it be the likenes of male or female,

17 The likenes of any beast that is on earth, or the likenesse of any fethered foule that flieth in the aire:

18 Or the likenesse of any thing that creepeth on the earth, or the likenesse of any fish that is in the waters beneath the earth,

19 And lest thou lift vp thine eyes vnto heauen, and when thou seest the sunne and the moone and the starres with all the host of heauen, shouldest bee driuen to worship them and serue them, which the Lord thy God hath distributed to all people vnder the whole heauen.

20 But the Lord hath taken you and brought you out of the yron fornace: out of Egypt to be vnto him a people and inheritance, as appeareth this day.

21 And the Lord was angrie with me for your words, and sware that I should not goe ouer Iorden, and that I should not goe in vnto that good land, which the Lord thy God giueth thee for an inheritance.

22 For I must die in this land, and shall not go ouer Iorden: but ye shall goe ouer, and possesse that good land.

23 Take heede vnto your selues, least ye forget the couenant of the Lord your God which hee made with you, and least ye make you any grauen image, or likenes of any thing, as the Lord thy God hath charged thee.

24 For the Lord thy God is a consuming fire, and a ielous God.

25 When thou shalt beget children and childrens children, and shalt haue remained long in the land, if ye corrupt your selues, and make any grauen image, or likenes of any thing, and worke euill in the sight of the Lord thy God, to prouoke him to anger,

26 I call heauen and earth to record against you this day, that ye shall shortly perish from the land, whereunto ye goe ouer Iorden to possesse it: ye shall not prolong your dayes therein, but shall vtterly be destroyed.

27 And the Lord shall scatter you among the people, and ye shall be left few in nomber among the nations, whither the Lord shall bring you:

28 And there ye shall serue gods, euen ye worke of mans hand, wood, and stone, which neither see, nor heare, nor eate, nor smelll.

29 But if from thence thou shalt seeke the Lord thy God, thou shalt finde him, if thou seeke him with all thine heart, and with all thy soule.

30 When thou art in tribulation, and all these things are come vpon thee, at the length if thou returne to the Lord thy God, and bee obedient vnto his voyce,

31 (For the Lord thy God is a mercifull God) he will not forsake thee, neither destroy thee, nor forget the couenant of thy fathers, which hee sware vnto them.

32 For inquire now of the dayes that are past, which were before thee, since the day that God created man vpon the earth, and aske from the one ende of heauen vnto the other, if there came to passe such a great thing as this, or whether any such like thing hath bene heard.

33 Did euer people heare the voyce of God speaking out of the middes of a fire, as thou hast heard, and liued?

34 Or hath God assayed to go and take him a nation from among nations, by tentations, by signes, and by wonders, and by warre, and by a mightie hand, and by a stretched out arme, and by great feare, according vnto all that the Lord your God did vnto you in Egypt before your eyes?

35 Vnto thee it was shewed, that thou mightest knowe, that the Lord hee is God, and that there is none but he alone.

36 Out of heauen hee made thee heare his voyce to instruct thee, and vpon earth he shewed thee his great fire, and thou heardest his voyce out of the middes of the fire.

37 And because hee loued thy fathers, therefore hee chose their seede after them, and hath brought thee out of Egypt in his sight by his mightie power,

38 To thrust out nations greater and mightier then thou, before thee, to bring thee in, and to giue thee their land for inheritance: as appeareth this day.

39 Vnderstande therefore this day, and consider in thine heart, that the Lord, he is God in heauen aboue, and vpon the earth beneath: there is none other.

40 Thou shalt keepe therefore his ordinances, and his commandements which I commaund thee this day, that it may goe well with thee, and with thy children after thee, and that thou mayst prolong thy dayes vpon the earth, which the Lord thy God giueth thee for euer.

41 Then Moses separated three cities on this side of Iorden toward the sunne rising:

42 That the slayer should flee thither, which had killed his neighbour at vnwares, and hated him not in time past, might flee, I say, vnto one of those cities, and liue:

43 That is, Bezer in the wildernesse, in the plaine countrey of the Reubenites: and Ramoth in Gilead among the Gadites: and Golan in Bashan among them of Manasseh.

44 So this is the law which Moses set before the children of Israel.

45 These are the witnesses, and the ordinances, and the lawes which Moses declared to the children of Israel after they came out of Egypt,

46 On this side Iorden, in the valley ouer against Beth-peor, in the land of Sihon King of the Amorites, which dwelt at Heshbon, whom Moses and the children of Israel smote, after they were come out of Egypt:

47 And they possessed his land, and the lande of Og King of Bashan, two Kings of the Amorites, which were on this side Iorden towarde the sunne rising:

48 From Aroer, which is by the banke of the riuer Arnon, euen vnto mount Sion, which is Hermon,

49 And all the plaine by Iorden Eastwarde, euen vnto the Sea, of ye plaine, vnder the springs of Pisgah.

Deuteronomy 5

1 Then Moses called all Israiel, and saide vnto them, Heare, O Israel, the ordinances and the lawes which I propose to you this day, that yee may learne them, and take heede to obserue them.

2 The Lord our God made a couenant with vs in Horeb.

3 The Lord made not this couenant with our fathers onely, but with vs, euen with vs all here aliue this day.

4 The Lord talked with you face to face in the Mount, out of the middes of the fire.

5 (At that time I stoode betweene the Lord and you, to declare vnto you ye word of the Lord: for ye were afraid at the sight of the fire, and went not vp into the mount, and he said,

6 I am the Lord thy God, which haue brought thee out of the lande of Egypt, from the house of bondage.

7 Thou shalt haue none other gods before my face.

8 Thou shalt make thee no grauen image or any likenesse of that that is in heauen aboue, or which is in the earth beneath, or that is in the waters vnder the earth.

9 Thou shalt neither bowe thy selfe vnto them, nor serue them: for I the Lord thy God am a ielous God, visiting the iniquitie of the fathers vpon the children, euen vnto the third and fourth generation of them that hate me:

10 And shewing mercie vnto thousandes of them that loue me, and keepe my commandements.

11 Thou shalt not take the Name of the Lord thy God in vaine: for the Lord will not holde him giltlesse that taketh his Name in vaine.

12 Keepe the Sabbath day, to sanctifie it, as the Lord thy God hath commanded thee.

13 Sixe dayes thou shalt labour, and shalt doe all thy worke:

14 But the seuenth day is the Sabbath of the Lord thy God: thou shalt not doe any worke therein, thou, nor thy sonne, nor thy daughter, nor thy man seruant, nor thy mayd, nor thine oxe, nor thine asse, neither any of thy cattel, nor the stranger that is within thy gates: that thy man seruant and thy mayde may rest aswell as thou.

15 For, remember that thou wast a seruant in the land of Egypt, and that the Lord thy God brought thee out thence by a mightie hand and a stretched out arme: therefore the Lord thy God commanded thee to obserue the Sabbath day.

16 Honour thy father and thy mother, as the Lord thy God hath comanded thee, that thy dayes may be prolonged, and that it may go well with thee vpon the land, which the Lord thy God giueth thee.

17 Thou shalt not kill.

18 Neither shalt thou commit adulterie.

19 Neither shalt thou steale.

20 Neither shalt thou beare false witnesse against thy neighbour.

21 Neither shalt thou couet thy neighbours wife, neither shalt thou desire thy neighbours house, his fielde, nor his man seruant, nor thy mayd, his oxe, nor his asse, nor ought that thy neighbour hath.

22 These wordes the Lord spake vnto all your multitude in the mount out of the mids of the fire, the cloude and the darkenes, with a great voyce, and added no more thereto: and wrote them vpon two tables of stone, and deliuered them vnto me.

23 And when ye heard the voyce out of the middes of the darkenes, (for the mountaine did burne with fire) then ye came to me, all the chiefe of your tribes, and your Elders:

24 And ye sayd, Beholde, the Lord our God hath shewed vs his glory and his greatnes, and we haue heard his voyce out of the middes of the fire: we haue seene this day that God doeth talke with man, and he liueth.

25 Now therefore, why should we dye? for this great fire wil consume vs: if we heare ye voyce of the Lord our God any more, we shall dye.

26 For what flesh was there euer, that heard the voyce of the liuing God speaking out of the middes of the fire as we haue, and liued?

27 Go thou neere and heare all that the Lord our God saith: and declare thou vnto vs all that the Lord our God saith vnto thee, and we will heare it, and doe it.

28 Then the Lord heard the voyce of your wordes, when ye spake vnto me: and the Lord sayd vnto me, I haue heard the voyce of ye wordes of this people, which they haue spoken vnto thee: they haue well sayd, all that they haue spoken.

29 Oh that there were such an heart in them to feare me, and to keepe all my commandements alway: that it might go well with them, and with their children for euer.

30 Go, say vnto them, Returne you into your tentes.

31 But stand thou here with me, and I wil tell thee all the commandements, and the ordinances, and the lawes, which thou shalt teach them: that they may doe them in the land which I giue them to possesse it.

32 Take heede therefore, that ye doe as the Lord your God hath commanded you: turne not aside to the right hand nor to the left,

33 But walke in all the wayes which the Lord your God hath commanded you, that ye may liue, and that it may goe well with you: and that ye may prolong your dayes in the land which ye shall possesse.

Deuteronomy 6

1 These now are the commandements, ordinances, and lawes, which the Lord your God commanded me to teach you, that ye might doe them in the land whither ye go to possesse it:

2 That thou mightest feare the Lord thy God, and keepe all his ordinances, and his commandements which I commaund thee, thou, and thy sonne, and thy sonnes sonne all the dayes of thy life, euen that thy dayes may be prolonged.

3 Heare therefore, O Israel, and take heede to doe it, that it may go well with thee, and that ye may increase mightily in the land that floweth with milke and hony, as the Lord God of thy fathers hath promised thee.

4 Heare, O Israel, The Lord our God is Lord onely,

5 And thou shalt loue the Lord thy God with all thine heart, and with all thy soule, and with all thy might.

6 And these wordes which I commaund thee this day, shalbe in thine heart.

7 And thou shalt rehearse them continually vnto thy children, and shalt talke of them when thou tariest in thine house, and as thou walkest by the way, and when thou liest downe, and when thou risest vp:

8 And thou shalt binde them for a signe vpon thine hand, and they shalbe as frontlets betweene thine eyes.

9 Also thou shalt write them vpon ye postes of thine house, and vpon thy gates.

10 And when the Lord thy God hath brought thee into the land, which he sware vnto thy fathers, Abraham, Izhak, and Iaakob, to giue to thee, with great and goodly cities which thou buildedst not,

11 And houses full of all maner of goods which thou filledst not, and welles digged which thou diggedst not, vineyards and oliue trees which thou plantedst not, and when thou hast eaten and art full,

12 Beware least thou forget the Lord, which brought thee out of the land of Egypt, from the house of bondage.

13 Thou shalt feare the Lord thy God, and serue him, and shalt sweare by his Name.

14 Ye shall not walke after other gods, after any of the gods of the people which are round about you,

15 (For the Lord thy God is a ielous God among you:) least the wrath of the Lord thy God be kindled against thee, and destroy thee from the face of the earth.

16 Ye shall not tempt the Lord your God, as ye did tempt him in Massah:

17 But ye shall keepe diligently the commandements of the Lord your God, and his testimonies, and his ordinances which he hath commanded thee,

18 And thou shalt doe that which is right and good in the sight of the Lord: that thou mayest prosper, and that thou mayest go in, and possesse that good land which the Lord sware vnto thy fathers,

19 To cast out all thine enemies before thee, as the Lord hath sayd.

20 When thy sonne shall aske thee in time to come, saying, What meane these testimonies, and ordinances, and Lawes, which the Lord our God hath commanded you?

21 Then shalt thou say vnto thy sonne, We were Pharaohs bondmen in Egypt: but the Lord brought vs out of Egypt with a mightie hand.

22 And the Lord shewed signes and wonders great and euill vpon Egypt, vpon Pharaoh, and vpon all his housholde, before our eyes,

23 And brought vs out from thence, to bring vs in, and to giue vs the land which he sware vnto our fathers.

24 Therefore the Lord hath commanded vs, to doe all these ordinances, and to feare the Lord our God, that it may goe euer well with vs, and that he may preserue vs aliue as at this present.

25 Moreouer, this shall be our righteousnes before the Lord our God, if we take heede to keepe all these commandements, as he hath commanded vs.

Deuteronomy 7

1 When the Lord thy God shall bring thee into the land whither thou goest to possesse it, and shall roote out many nations before thee: the Hittites, and the Girgashites, and the Amorites, and the Canaanites, and the Perizzites, and the Hiuites, and the Iebusites, seuen nations greater and mightier then thou,

2 And the Lord thy God shall giue them before thee, then thou shalt smite them: thou shalt vtterly destroy them: thou shalt make no couenant with them, nor haue compassion on them,

3 Neither shalt thou make marriages with them, neither giue thy daughter vnto his sonne, nor take his daughter vnto thy sonne.

4 For they wil cause thy sonne to turne away from me, and to serue other gods: then will the wrath of the Lord waxe hote against you and destroy thee suddenly.

5 But thus ye shall deale with them, Ye shall ouerthrowe their altars, and breake downe their pillars, and ye shall cut downe their groues, and burne their grauen images with fire.

6 For thou art an holy people vnto the Lord thy God, the Lord thy God hath chosen thee, to be a precious people vnto himselfe, aboue all people that are vpon the earth.

7 The Lord did not set his loue vpon you, nor chose you, because ye were more in number then any people: for ye were the fewest of all people:

8 But because the Lord loued you, and because hee would keepe the othe which hee had sworne vnto your fathers, the Lord hath brought you out by a mightie hand, and deliuered you out of the house of bondage from the hand of Pharaoh King of Egypt,

9 That thou mayest knowe, that the Lord thy God, he is God, the faithfull God which keepeth couenant and mercie vnto them that loue him and keepe his commandements, euen to a thousand generations,

10 And rewardeth them to their face that hate him, to bring them to destruction: he wil not deferre to reward him that hateth him, to his face.

11 Keepe thou therefore the commandements, and the ordinances, and the lawes, which I commaund thee this day to doe them.

12 For if ye hearken vnto these lawes, and obserue and doe them, then the Lord thy God shall keepe with thee the couenant, and the mercie which he sware vnto thy fathers.

13 And he wil loue thee, and blesse thee, and multiplie thee: he will also blesse the fruite of thy wombe, and the fruite of thy land, thy corne and thy wine, and thine oyle and the increase of thy kine, and the flockes of thy sheepe in the land, which he sware vnto thy fathers to giue thee.

14 Thou shalt be blessed aboue all people: there shall be neither male nor female barren among you, nor among your cattell.

15 Moreouer, the Lord will take away from thee all infirmities, and will put none of the euill diseases of Egypt (which thou knowest) vpon thee, but wil send them vpon all that hate thee.

16 Thou shalt therefore consume all people which the Lord thy God shall giue thee: thine eye shall not spare them, neither shalt thou serue their gods, for that shalbe thy destruction.

17 If thou say in thine heart, These nations are moe then I, how can I cast them out?

18 Thou shalt not feare them, but remember what the Lord thy God did vnto Pharaoh, and vnto all Egypt:

19 The great tentations which thine eyes sawe, and the signes and wonders, and the mighty hand and stretched out arme, whereby the Lord thy God brought thee out: so shall the Lord thy God do vnto all ye people, whose face thou fearest.

20 Moreouer, the Lord thy God will send hornets among them vntil they that are left, and hide themselues from thee, be destroyed.

21 Thou shalt not feare them: for the Lord thy God is among you, a God mightie and dreadful.

22 And the Lord thy God wil roote out these nations before thee by little and little: thou mayest not consume them at once, least the beasts of the fielde increase vpon thee.

23 But the Lord thy God shall giue them before thee, and shall destroy them with a mightie destruction, vntill they be brought to naught.

24 And he shall deliuer their Kings into thine hand, and thou shalt destroy their name from vnder heauen: there shall no man be able to stand before thee, vntill thou hast destroyed them.

25 The grauen images of their gods shall ye burne with fire, and couet not the siluer and golde, that is on them, nor take it vnto thee, least thou be snared therewith: for it is an abomination before the Lord thy God.

26 Bring not therefore abomination into thine house, lest, thou be accursed like it, but vtterly abhorre it, and count it most abominable: for it is accursed.

Deuteronomy 8

1 Ye shall keepe all the commandements which I command thee this day, for to doe them: that ye may liue, and be multiplied, and goe in, and possesse the land which the Lord sware vnto your fathers.

2 And thou shalt remember all ye way which the Lord thy God led thee this fourtie yeere in the wildernesse, for to humble thee and to proue thee, to knowe what was in thine heart, whether thou wouldest keepe his commandements or no.

3 Therefore he humbled thee, and made thee hungry, and fed thee with MAN, which thou knewest not, neither did thy fathers know it, that he might teache thee that man liueth not by bread onely, but by euery worde that proceedeth out of the mouth of the Lord, doth a man liue.

4 Thy raiment waxed not olde vpon thee, neither did thy foote swell those fourtie yeeres.

5 Knowe therefore in thine heart, that as a man nourtereth his sonne, so the Lord thy God nourtereth thee.

6 Therefore shalt thou keepe the commandements of the Lord thy God, that thou mayest walke in his wayes, and feare him.

7 For the Lord thy God bringeth thee into a good land, a land in the which are riuers of water and fountaines, and depthes that spring out of valleis and mountaines:

8 A land of wheate and barley, and of vineyards, and figtrees, and pomegranates: a land of oyle oliue and hony:

9 A land wherein thou shalt eate bread without scarcitie, neither shalt thou lacke any thing therein: a land whose stones are yron, and out of whose mountaines thou shalt digge brasse.

10 And when thou hast eaten and filled thy selfe, thou shalt blesse the Lord thy God for the good land, which he hath giuen thee.

11 Beware that thou forget not the Lord thy God, not keeping his commandements, and his lawes, and his ordinances, which I commaund thee this day:

12 Lest when thou hast eaten and filled thy selfe, and hast built goodly houses and dwelt therein,

13 And thy beastes, and thy sheepe are increased, and thy siluer and golde is multiplied, and all that thou hast is increased,

14 Then thine heart be lifted vp and thou forget the Lord thy God, which brought thee out of the land of Egypt, from the house of bondage,

15 Who was thy guide in the great and terrible wildernes (wherein were fierie serpents, and scorpions, and drought, where was no water, who brought forth water for thee out of ye rock of flint:

16 Who fed thee in the wildernesse with MAN, which thy fathers knewe not) to humble thee, and and to proue thee, that he might doe thee good at thy latter ende.

17 Beware least thou say in thine heart, My power, and the strength of mine owne hand hath prepared me this abundance.

18 But remember the Lord thy God: for it is he which giueth thee power to get substance to establish his couenant which he sware vnto thy fathers, as appeareth this day.

19 And if thou forget the Lord thy God, and walke after other gods, and serue them, and worship them, I testifie vnto you this day that ye shall surely perish.

20 As the nations which the Lord destroyeth before you, so ye shall perish, because ye woulde not be obedient vnto the voyce of the Lord your God.

Deuteronomy 9

1 Heare O Israel, Thou shalt passe ouer Iorden this day, to goe in and to possesse nations greater and mightier then thy selfe, and cities great and walled vp to heauen,

2 A people great and tall, euen the children of the Anakims, whom thou knowest, and of whom thou hast heard say, Who can stand before the children of Anak?

3 Vnderstand therefore that this day ye Lord thy God is he which goeth ouer before thee as a consuming fire: he shall destroy them, and he shall bring them downe before thy face: so thou shalt cast them out and destroy them suddenly, as the Lord hath said vnto thee.

4 Speake not thou in thine heart (after that the Lord thy God hath cast them out before thee) saying, For my righteousnesse the Lord hath brought me in, to possesse this land: but for the wickednesse of these nations the Lord hath cast them out before thee.

5 For thou entrest not to inherite their lande for thy righteousnesse, or for thy vpright heart: but for the wickednesse of those nations, the Lord thy God doth cast them out before thee, and that he might performe the worde which the Lord thy God sware vnto thy fathers, Abraham, Izhak, and Iacob.

6 Vnderstand therefore, that ye Lord thy God giueth thee not this good land to possesse it for thy righteousnes: for thou art a stifnecked people.

7 Remember, and forget not, howe thou prouokedst the Lord thy God to anger in the wildernesse: since the day that thou diddest depart out of the land of Egypt, vntill ye came vnto this place ye haue rebelled against the Lord.

8 Also in Horeb ye prouoked the Lord to anger so that the Lord was wroth with you, euen to destroy you.

9 When I was gone vp into the mount, to receiue the tables of stone, the tables, I say, of the couenant, which the Lord made with you: and I abode in the mount fourtie daies and fourtie nights, and I neither ate bread nor yet dranke water:

10 Then the Lord deliuered me two tables of stone, written with the finger of God, and in them was conteyned according to all the wordes which the Lord had said vnto you in the mount out of the middes of the fire, in the day of the assemblie.

11 And when the fourtie dayes and fourtie nightes were ended, the Lord gaue me the two tables of stone, the tables, I say, of the couenant.

12 And the Lord said vnto me, Arise, get thee downe quickly from hence: for thy people which thou hast brought out of Egypt, haue corrupt their wayes: they are soone turned out of the way, which I commanded them: they haue made them a molten image.

13 Furthermore, the Lord spake vnto me, saying, I haue seene this people, and beholde, it is a stifnecked people.

14 Let me alone, that I may destroy them, and put out their name from vnder heaue, and I wil make of thee a mightie nation, and greater then they be.

15 So I returned, and came downe from the Mount (and the Mount burnt with fire, and ye two Tables of the couenant were in my two handes)

16 Then I looked, and beholde, ye had sinned against the Lord your God: for ye had made you a molten calfe, and had turned quickly out of the way which the Lord had commanded you.

17 Therefore I tooke the two Tables, and cast them out of my two handes, and brake them before your eyes.

18 And I fell downe before the Lord, fourtie dayes, and fourtie nightes, as before: I neither ate bread nor dranke water, because of al your sinnes, which ye had committed, in doing wickedly in the sight of the Lord, in that ye prouoked him vnto wrath.

19 (For I was afraide of the wrath and indignation, wherewith the Lord was mooued against you, euen to destroy you) yet the Lord heard me at that time also.

20 Likewise ye Lord was very angrie with Aaron, euen to destroy him: but at that time I prayed also for Aaron.

21 And I tooke your sinne, I meane the calfe which ye had made, and burnt him with fire, and stamped him and ground him small, euen vnto very dust: and I cast the dust thereof into the riuer, that descended out of the mount.

22 Also in Taberah, and in Massah and in Kibrothhattaauah ye prouoked ye Lord to anger.

23 Likewise when the Lord sent you from Kadesh-barnea, saying, Goe vp, and possesse the land which I haue giuen you, then ye rebelled against the commandement of the Lord your God, and beleeued him not, nor hearkened vnto his voyce.

24 Ye haue bene rebellious vnto the Lord, since the day that I knewe you.

25 Then I fell downe before ye Lord fourtie dayes and fourtie nightes, as I fell downe before, because ye Lord had said, that he woulde destroy you.

26 And I prayed vnto the Lord, and saide, O Lord God, destroy not thy people and thine inheritance, which thou hast redeemed through thy greatnesse, whom thou hast brought out of Egypt by a mightie hand.

27 Remember thy seruants Abraham, Izhak, and Iaakob: looke not to ye stubburnes of this people, nor to their wickednes, nor to their sinne,

28 Lest the countrey, whence thou broughtest them, say, Because ye Lord was not able to bring them into the land which he promised them, or because he hated them, he caried them out, to slay them in the wildernesse.

29 Yet they are thy people, and thine inheritance, which thou broughtest out by thy mightie power, and by thy stretched out arme.

Deuteronomy 10

1 In the same time the Lord said vnto me, Hewe thee two Tables of stone like vnto the first, and come vp vnto me into the Mount, and make thee an Arke of wood,

2 And I will write vpon the Tables ye wordes that were vpon the first Tables, which thou brakest, and thou shalt put them in the Arke.

3 And I made an Arke of Shittim wood, and hewed two Tables of stone like vnto the first, and went vp into the Mountaine, and the two Tables in mine hand.

4 Then he wrote vpon the Tables according to the first writing (the tenne commandements, which the Lord spake vnto you in the Mount out of the middes of the fire, in the day of the assemblie) and the Lord gaue them vnto me.

5 And I departed, and came downe from the Mount, and put the Tables in the Arke which I had made: and there they be, as the Lord commanded me.

6 And ye children of Israel tooke their iourney from Beeroth of the children of Iaakan to Mosera, where Aaron dyed, and was buried, and Eleazar his sonne became Priest in his steade.

7 From thence they departed vnto Gudgodah, and from Gudgodah to Iotbath a land of running waters.

8 The same time ye Lord separated the tribe of Leui to beare the Arke of the couenant of the Lord, and to stand before ye Lord, to minister vnto him, and to blesse in his Name vnto this day.

9 Wherefore Leui hath no part nor inheritance with his brethren: for the Lord is his inheritance, as the Lord thy God hath promised him.

10 And I taried in the mount, as at ye first time, fourtie dayes and fourtie nightes, and the Lord heard me at that time also, and the Lord would not destroy thee.

11 But the Lord said vnto me, Arise, goe forth in the iourney before the people, that they may goe in and possesse the land, which I sware vnto their fathers to giue vnto them.

12 And nowe, Israel, what doth the Lord thy God require of thee, but to feare the Lord thy God, to walke in all his wayes, and to loue him, and to serue the Lord thy God, with all thine heart, and with all thy soule?

13 That thou keepe the commandements of the Lord, and his ordinances, which I commaund thee this day, for thy wealth?

14 Beholde, heauen, and the heauen of heauens is the Lords thy God, and the earth, with all that therein is.

15 Notwithstanding, the Lord set his delite in thy fathers to loue them, and did choose their seede after them, euen you aboue all people, as appeareth this day.

16 Circumcise therefore the foreskin of your heart, and harden your neckes no more.

17 For the Lord your God is God of gods, and Lord of lordes, a great God, mightie and terrible, which accepteth no persons nor taketh reward:

18 Who doeth right vnto the fatherlesse and widowe, and loueth the stranger, giuing him foode and rayment.

19 Loue ye therefore the stranger: for ye were strangers in the land of Egypt.

20 Thou shalt feare the Lord thy God: thou shalt serue him, and thou shalt cleaue vnto him, and shalt sweare by his Name.

21 He is thy praise, and hee is thy God, that hath done for thee these great and terrible things, which thine eyes haue seene.

22 Thy fathers went downe into Egypt with seuentie persons, and now the Lord thy God hath made thee, as ye starres of ye heauen in multitude.

Deuteronomy 11

1 Therefore thou shalt loue the Lord thy God, and shalt keepe that, which he commandeth to be kept: that is, his ordinances, and his lawes, and his commandements alway.

2 And consider this day (for I speake not to your children, which haue neither knowen nor seene) the chastisement of the Lord your God, his greatnesse, his mighty hande, and his stretched out arme,

3 And his signes, and his actes, which hee did in the middes of Egypt vnto Pharaoh the King of Egypt and vnto all his land:

4 And what he did vnto the hoste of the Egyptians, vnto their horses, and to their charets, when he caused the waters of the red Sea to ouerflowe them, as they pursued after you, and the Lord destroied them vnto this day:

5 And what he did vnto you in the wildernesse, vntill yee came vnto this place:

6 And what he did vnto Dathan and Abiram the sonnes of Eliab ye sonne of Reuben, when the earth opened her mouth, and swallowed them with their housholds and their tents, and all their substance that they had in the middes of al Israel.

7 For your eyes haue seene all the great actes of the Lord which he did.

8 Therefore shall ye keepe all the commandements, which I commaund you this day, that ye may be strong, and go in and possesse the land whither ye goe to possesse it:

9 Also that ye may prolong your daies in the land, which the Lord sware vnto your fathers, to giue vnto them and to their seede, euen a lande that floweth with milke and honie.

10 For the land whither thou goest to possesse it, is not as the lande of Egypt, from whence ye came, where thou sowedst thy seede, and wateredst it with thy feete as a garden of herbes:

11 But the land whither ye goe to possesse it, is a land of mountaines and valleis, and drinketh water of the raine of heauen.

12 This land doth the Lord thy God care for: the eies of the Lord thy God are alwaies vpon it, from the beginning of the yeere, euen vnto the ende of the yeere.

13 If yee shall hearken therefore vnto my commandements, which I commaund you this day, that yee loue the Lord your God and serue him with all your heart, and with all your soule,

14 I also wil giue raine vnto your land in due time, the first raine and the latter, that thou maist gather in thy wheat, and thy wine, and thine oyle.

15 Also I will send grasse in thy fieldes, for thy cattel, that thou maist eate, and haue inough.

16 But beware lest your heart deceiue you, and lest yee turne aside, and serue other gods, and worship them,

17 And so the anger of the Lord be kindled against you, and he shut vp the heauen, that there be no raine, and that your lande yeelde not her fruit, and yee perish quickly from the good land, which the Lord giueth you.

18 Therefore shall ye lay vp these my words in your heart and in your soule, and binde them for a signe vpon your hand, that they may be as a frontlet betweene your eyes,

19 And ye shall teach them your children, speaking of them, whe thou sittest in thine house, and when thou walkest by the way, and when thou liest downe, and when thou risest vp.

20 And thou shalt write them vpon the postes of thine house, and vpon thy gates,

21 That your daies may be multiplied, and the daies of your children, in ye land which the Lord sware vnto your fathers to giue them, as long as the heauens are aboue the earth.

22 For if ye keepe diligently all these commandements, which I command you to doe: that is, to loue the Lord your God, to walke in all his waies, and to cleaue vnto him,

23 Then will the Lord cast out all these nations before you, and ye shall possesse great nations and mightier then you.

24 All the places whereon the soles of your feete shall tread, shalbe yours: your coast shalbe from the wildernes and from Lebanon, and from the Riuer, euen the riuer Perath, vnto ye vttermost Sea.

25 No man shall stande against you: for the Lord your God shall cast the feare and dread of you vpon all the land that ye shall treade vpon, as he hath said vnto you.

26 Beholde, I set before you this day a blessing and a curse:

27 The blessing, if ye obey the commandements of the Lord your God which I command you this day:

28 And ye curse, if ye wil not obey the commandements of the Lord your God, but turne out of the way, which I commande you this day, to go after other gods, which ye haue not knowen.

29 When the Lord thy God therefore hath brought thee into ye lande, whither thou goest to possesse it, then thou shalt put the blessing vpon mount Gerizim, and the curse vpon mount Ebal.

30 Are they not beyond Iorden on that part, where the sunne goeth downe in the land of the Canaanites, which dwel in the plaine ouer against Gilgal, beside the groue of Moreh?

31 For yee shall passe ouer Iorden, to goe in to possesse the land, which ye Lord your God giueth you, and ye shall possesse it, and dwell therein.

32 Take heede therefore that ye doe all the commandements and the lawes, which I set before you this day.

Deuteronomy 12

1 These are the ordinances and the lawes, which ye shall obserue and doe in the lande (which the Lord God of thy fathers giueth thee to possesse it) as long as yee liue vpon the earth.

2 Yee shall vtterly destroy all the places wherein the nations which ye shall possesse, serued their gods vpon the hie mountaines and vpon the hilles, and vnder euery greene tree.

3 Also ye shall ouerthrowe their altars, and breake downe their pillars, and burne their groues with fire: and ye shall hew downe ye grauen images of their gods, and abolish their names out of that place.

4 Ye shall not do so vnto ye Lord your God,

5 But ye shall seeke the place which the Lord your God shall chose out of all your tribes, to put his Name there, and there to dwell, and thither thou shalt come,

6 And ye shall bring thither your burnt offerings, and your sacrifices, and your tithes, and the offring of your hands, and your vowes, and your free offrings, and the first borne of your kine and of your sheepe.

7 And there ye shall eate before the Lord your God, and ye shall reioyce in all that yee put your hand vnto, both ye, and your housholdes, because the Lord thy God hath blessed thee.

8 Ye shall not doe after all these things that we doe here this day: that is, euery man whatsoeuer seemeth him good in his owne eyes.

9 For ye are not yet come to rest, and to the inheritance which the Lord thy God giueth thee.

10 But when ye goe ouer Iorden, and dwell in ye land, which the Lord your God hath giuen you to inherit, and when he hath giue you rest from al your enemies round about, and yee dwel in safetie,

11 When there shalbe a place which the Lord your God shall chose, to cause his name to dwell there, thither shall yee bring all that I commaund you: your burnt offrings, and your sacrifices, your tithes, and the offring of your hands, and all your speciall vowes which ye vowe vnto the Lord:

12 And ye shall reioyce before the Lord your God, yee, and your sonnes and your daughters, and your seruaunts, and your maidens, and the Leuite that is within your gates: for hee hath no part nor inheritance with you.

13 Take heede that thou offer not thy burnt offrings in euery place that thou seest:

14 But in ye place which the Lord shall chose in one of thy tribes, there thou shalt offer thy burnt offrings, and there thou shalt doe all that I commaund thee.

15 Notwithstanding thou maiest kill and eate flesh in all thy gates, whatsoeuer thine heart desireth, according to the blessing of the Lord thy God which he hath giuen thee: both the vncleane and the cleane may eate thereof, as of the roe bucke, and of the hart.

16 Onely ye shall not eat the blood, but powre it vpon the earth as water.

17 Thou maist nor eat within thy gates the tithe of thy corne, nor of thy wine, nor of thine oyle, nor the first borne of thy kine, nor of thy sheep, neither any of thy vowes which thou vowest, nor thy free offerings, nor the offering of thine hands,

18 But thou shalt eate it before the Lord thy God, in the place which the Lord thy God shall chuse, thou, and thy sonne, and thy daughter, and thy seruat, and thy maid, and the Leuite that is within thy gates: and thou shalt reioyce before the Lord thy God, in all that thou puttest thine hand to.

19 Beware, that thou forsake not the Leuite, as long as thou liuest vpon the earth.

20 When the Lord thy God shall enlarge thy border, as hee hath promised thee, and thou shalt say, I wil eate flesh, (because thine heart longeth to eate flesh) thou maiest eate flesh, whatsoeuer thine heart desireth.

21 If the place which the Lord thy God hath chosen to put his Name there, be farre from thee, then thou shalt kill of thy bullockes, and of thy sheepe which the Lord hath giuen thee, as I haue commanded thee, and thou shalt eat in thy gates, whatsoeuer thine heart desireth.

22 Euen as the roe bucke, and the hart is eaten, so shalt thou eat them. both the vncleane and the cleane shall eate of them alike.

23 Onely bee sure that thou eate not the blood: for the blood is the life, and thou maiest not eate the life with the flesh.

24 Therefore thou shalt not eat it, but powre it vpon the earth as water.

25 Thou shalt not eat it, that it may go well with thee; and with thy children after thee, when thou shalt doe that which is right in the sight of the Lord:

26 But thine holy things which thou hast, and thy vowes thou shalt take vp, and come vnto the place which the Lord shall chuse.

27 And thou shalt make thy burnt offerings of the flesh, and of the blood vpon the altar of the Lord thy God, and the blood of thine offerings shall bee powred vpon the altar of the Lord thy God, and thou shalt eate the flesh.

28 Take heede, and heare all these woordes which I commaund thee, that it may goe well with thee, and with thy children after thee for euer, when thou doest that which is good and right in the sight of the Lord thy God.

29 When the Lord thy God shall destroy the nations before thee, whither thou goest to possesse them, and thou shalt possesse them and dwell in their lande,

30 Beware, lest thou be taken in a snare after them, after that they be destroied before thee, and lest thou aske after their gods, saying, Howe did these nations serue their gods, that I may doe so likewise?

31 Thou shalt not doe so vnto the Lord thy God: for al abomination, which the Lord hateth, haue they done vnto their gods: for they haue burned both their sonnes and their daughters with fire to their gods.

32 Therefore whatsoeuer I command you, take heede you doe it: thou shalt put nothing thereto, nor take ought therefrom.

Deuteronomy 13

1 If there arise amog you a prophet or a dreamer of dreames, (and giue thee a signe or wonder,

2 And the signe and the wonder, which hee hath tolde thee, come to passe) saying, Let vs go after other gods, which thou hast not knowen, and let vs serue them,

3 Thou shalt not hearken vnto the wordes of the prophet, or vnto that dreamer of dreames: for the Lord your God prooueth you, to knowe whether ye loue the Lord your God with al your heart, and with all your soule.

4 Yee shall walke after the Lord your God and feare him, and shall keepe his commandements, and hearken vnto his voyce, and yee shall serue him, and cleaue vnto him.

5 But that prophet, or that dreamer of dreames, he shall be slaine, because hee hath spoken to turne you away from the Lord your God (which brought you out of the lande of Egypt, and deliuered you out of the house of bondage) to thrust thee out of the way, wherein the Lord thy God commanded thee to walke: so shalt thou take the euill away foorth of the middes of thee.

6 If thy brother, the sonne of thy mother, or thine owne sonne, or thy daughter, or the wife, that lyeth in thy bosome, or thy friend, which is as thine owne soule, intice thee secretly, saying, Let vs goe and serue other gods, (which thou hast not knowen, thou, I say, nor thy fathers)

7 Any of the gods of the people which are round about you, neere vnto thee or farre off from thee, from the one ende of the earth vnto ye other:

8 Thou shalt not cosent vnto him, nor heare him, neither shall thine eye pitie him, nor shewe mercie, nor keepe him secret:

9 But thou shalt euen kill him: thine hand shall be first vpon him to put him to death, and then the handes of all the people.

10 And thou shalt stone him with stones, that he dye (because he hath gone about to thrust thee away from the Lord thy God, which brought thee out of ye land of Egypt, from ye house of bondage)

11 That all Israel may heare and feare, and doe no more any such wickednesse as this among you.

12 If thou shalt heare say (concerning any of thy cities which the Lord thy God hath giuen thee to dwell in)

13 Wicked men are gone out from among you, and haue drawen away the inhabitants of their citie, saying, Let vs go and serue other gods, which ye haue not knowen,

14 Then thou shalt seeke, and make searche and enquire diligently: and if it be true, and the thing certaine, that such abomination is wrought among you,

15 Thou shalt euen slay the inhabitants of that citie with the edge of the sworde: destroy it vtterly, and all that is therein, and the cattel thereof with the edge of the sworde.

16 And thou shalt gather all the spoyle of it into the middes of the streete thereof, and burne with fire the citie and all the spoyle thereof euery whit, vnto the Lord thy God: and it shall be an heape for euer: it shall not be built againe.

17 And there shall cleaue nothing of ye damned thing to thine hand, that the Lord may turne from the fiercenes of his wrath, and shewe thee mercie, and haue compassion on thee and multiplie thee, as he hath sworne vnto thy fathers:

18 When thou shalt obey the voyce of the Lord thy God, and keepe all his commandements which I command thee this day, that thou do that which is right in the eyes of the Lord thy God.

Deuteronomy 14

1 Ye are the children of the Lord your God. Ye shall not cut yourselues, nor make you any baldnesse betweene your eyes for the dead.

2 For thou art an holy people vnto ye Lord thy God, and the Lord hath chosen thee to be a precious people vnto himselfe, aboue all the people that are vpon the earth.

3 Thou shalt eate no maner of abomination.

4 These are the beastes, which ye shall eate, the beefe, the sheepe, and the goate,

5 The hart, and the roe buck, and the bugle, and the wilde goate, and the vnicorne, and the wilde oxe, and the chamois.

6 And euery beast that parteth ye hoofe, and cleaueth the clift into two clawes, and is of the beasts that cheweth the cudde, that shall ye eate.

7 But these ye shall not eate, of them that chew the cud, and of them that deuide and cleaue the hoofe onely: ye camell, nor the hare, nor the cony: for they chewe the cudde, but deuide not ye hoofe: therefore they shall be vncleane vnto you:

8 Also the swine, because he deuideth the hoofe, and cheweth not the cud, shalbe vncleane vnto you: ye shall not eate of their flesh, nor touch their dead carkeises.

9 These ye shall eate, of all that are in the waters: all that haue finnes and scales shall ye eate.

10 And whatsoeuer hath no finnes nor scales, ye shall not eate: it shall be vncleane vnto you.

11 Of all cleane birdes ye shall eate:

12 But these are they, whereof ye shall not eate: the eagle, nor the goshawke, nor the osprey,

13 Nor the glead nor the kite, nor the vulture, after their kind,

14 Nor all kinde of rauens,

15 Nor the ostrich, nor the nightcrow, nor the semeaw, nor the hawke after her kinde,

16 Neither the litle owle, nor the great owle, nor the redshanke,

17 Nor the pellicane, nor the swanne, nor the cormorant:

18 The storke also, and the heron in his kinde, nor the lapwing, nor the backe.

19 And euery creeping thing that flieth, shall be vncleane vnto you: it shall not be eaten.

20 But of all cleane foules ye may eate.

21 Ye shall eate of nothing that dieth alone, but thou shalt giue it vnto the stranger that is within thy gates, that he may eate it: or thou maiest sell it vnto a stranger: for thou art an holy people vnto the Lord thy God. Thou shalt not seethe a kid in his mothers milke.

22 Thou shalt giue the tithe of all the increase of thy seede, that commeth foorth of the fielde yeere by yeere.

23 And thou shalt eate before the Lord thy God (in the place which he shall chose to cause his Name to dwell there) the tithe of thy corne, of thy wine, and of thine oyle, and the first borne of thy kine and of thy sheepe, that thou maiest learne to feare the Lord thy God alway.

24 And if the way be too long for thee, so that thou art not able to cary it, because the place is farre from thee, where the Lord thy God shall chose to set his Name, when the Lord thy God shall blesse thee,

25 Then shalt thou make it in money, and take the money in thine hand, and goe vnto the place which the Lord thy God shall chose.

26 And thou shalt bestowe the money for whatsoeuer thine heart desireth: whether it be oxe, or sheepe, or wine, or strong drinke, or whatsoeuer thine heart desireth: and shalt eate it there before the Lord thy God, and reioyce, both thou, and thine household.

27 And the Leuite that is within thy gates, shalt thou not forsake: for he hath neither part nor inheritance with thee.

28 At the end of three yeere thou shalt bring foorth all the tithes of thine increase of the same yeere, and lay it vp within thy gates.

29 Then ye Leuite shall come, because he hath no part nor inheritance with thee, and the stranger, and the fatherlesse, and the widowe, which are within thy gates, and shall eate, and be filled, that the Lord thy God may blesse thee in al the worke of thine hand which thou doest.

Deuteronomy 15

1 At the terme of seuen yeeres thou shalt make a freedome.

2 And this is the maner of the freedome: euery creditour shall quite ye lone of his hand which he hath lent to his neighbour: he shall not aske it againe of his neighbour, nor of his brother: for the yeere of the Lords freedome is proclaimed.

3 Of a stranger thou mayest require it: but that which thou hast with thy brother, thine hand shall remit:

4 Saue when there shall be no poore with thee: for the Lord shall blesse thee in the land, which the Lord thy God giueth thee, for an inheritance to possesse it:

5 So that thou hearken vnto the voyce of the Lord thy God to obserue and doe all these commandements, which I commande thee this day.

6 For the Lord thy God hath blessed thee, as he hath promised thee: and thou shalt lend vnto many nations, but thou thy selfe shalt not borow, and thou shalt reigne ouer many nations, and they shall not reigne ouer thee.

7 If one of thy brethren with thee be poore within any of thy gates in thy land, which the Lord thy God giueth thee, thou shalt not harden thine heart, nor shut thine hand from thy poore brother:

8 But thou shalt open thine hand vnto him, and shalt lend him sufficient for his neede which he hath.

9 Beware that there be not a wicked thought in thine heart, to say, The seuenth yeere, the yeere of freedome is at hand: therefore it grieueth thee to looke on thy poore brother, and thou giuest him nought, and he crie vnto the Lord against thee, so that sinne be in thee:

10 Thou shalt giue him, and let it not grieue thine heart to giue vnto him: for because of this the Lord thy God shall blesse thee in al thy works, and in all that thou puttest thine hand to.

11 Because there shall be euer some poore in the land, therefore I command thee, saying, Thou shalt open thine hand vnto thy brother, to thy needie, and to thy poore in thy land.

12 If thy brother an Ebrewe sell himselfe to thee, or an Ebrewesse, and serue thee sixe yeere, euen in the seuenth yeere thou shalt let him goe free from thee:

13 And when thou sendest him out free from thee, thou shalt not let him goe away emptie,

14 But shalt giue him a liberall reward of thy sheepe, and of thy corne, and of thy wine: thou shalt giue him of that wherewith the Lord thy God hath blessed thee.

15 And remember that thou wast a seruant in the land of Egypt, and the Lord thy God deliuered thee: therefore I command thee this thing to day.

16 And if he say vnto thee, I will not go away from thee, because he loueth thee and thine house, and because he is well with thee,

17 Then shalt thou take a naule, and perce his eare through against the doore, and he shall be thy seruant for euer: and vnto thy maid seruant thou shall doe likewise.

18 Let it not grieue thee, when thou lettest him goe out free from thee: for he hath serued thee sixe yeeres, which is the double worth of an hired seruant: and the Lord thy God shall blesse thee in all that thou doest.

19 All the first borne males that come of thy cattell, and of thy sheepe, thou shalt sanctifie vnto the Lord thy God. Thou shalt do no worke with thy first borne bullocke, nor sheare thy first borne sheepe.

20 Thou shalt eate it before the Lord thy God yeere by yeere, in the place which the Lord shall chose, both thou, and thine household.

21 But if there be any blemish therein, as if it be lame, or blind, or haue any euill fault, thou shalt not offer it vnto the Lord thy God,

22 But shalt eate it within thy gates: the vncleane, and the cleane shall eate it alike, as the roe bucke, and as the hart.

23 Onely thou shalt not eate the blood thereof, but powre it vpon the ground as water.

Deuteronomy 16

1 Thou shalt keepe the moneth of Abib, and thou shalt celebrate the Passeouer vnto the Lord thy God: for in the moneth of Abib ye Lord thy God brought thee out of Egypt by night.

2 Thou shalt therefore offer the Passeouer vnto the Lord thy God, of sheepe and bullockes in the place where the Lord shall chose to cause his Name to dwell.

3 Thou shalt eate no leauened bread with it: but seuen dayes shalt thou eate vnleauened bread therewith, euen the bread of tribulation: for thou camest out of the land of Egypt in haste, that thou maist remember ye day whe thou camest out of the land of Egypt, all the dayes of thy life.

4 And there shalbe no leauen seene with thee in all thy coastes seuen dayes long: neither shall there remaine the night any of the flesh vntill the morning which thou offeredst ye first day at euen.

5 Thou maist not offer ye Passeouer within any of thy gates, which ye Lord thy God giueth thee:

6 But in the place which the Lord thy God shall choose to place his Name,

there thou shalt offer the Passeouer at euen, about the going downe of the sunne, in the season that thou camest out of Egypt.

7 And thou shalt roste and eate it in the place which the Lord thy God shall choose, and shalt returne on the morowe, and goe vnto thy tentes.

8 Six daies shalt thou eate vnleauened bread, and ye seuenth day shall be a solemne assemblie to ye Lord thy God thou shalt do no worke therein.

9 Seuen weekes shalt thou nomber vnto thee, and shalt beginne to nomber ye seuen weekes, when thou beginnest to put the sickel to ye corne:

10 And thou shalt keepe the feast of weekes vnto the Lord thy God, euen a free gift of thine hand, which thou shalt giue vnto the Lord thy God, as the Lord thy God hath blessed thee.

11 And thou shalt reioyce before the Lord thy God, thou and thy sonne, and thy daughter, and thy seruant, and thy maide, and the Leuite that is within thy gates, and the stranger, and the fatherles, and the widowe, that are among you, in the place which the Lord thy God shall chuse to place his Name there,

12 And thou shalt remember that thou wast a seruant in Egypt: therefore thou shalt obserue and doe these ordinances.

13 Thou shalt obserue the feast of the Tabernacles seuen daies, when thou hast gathered in thy corne, and thy wine.

14 And thou shalt reioyce in thy feast, thou, and thy sonne, and thy daughter, and thy seruant, and thy maid, and the Leuite, and the stranger, and the fatherlesse, and the widow, that are within thy gates.

15 Seuen daies shalt thou keepe a feast vnto the Lord thy God in the place which the Lord shall chuse: when the Lord thy God shall blesse thee in all thine increase, and in all the workes of thine hands, thou shalt in any case be glad.

16 Three times in the yeere shall all the males appeare before the Lord thy God in the place which he shall chuse: in the feast of the vnleauened bread, and in the feast of the weekes, and in the feast of the Tabernacles: and they shall not appeare before the Lord emptie.

17 Euery man shall giue according to the gift of his hand, and according to the blessing of the Lord thy God, which he hath giuen thee.

18 Iudges and officers shalt thou make thee in all thy cities, which the Lord thy God giueth thee, throughout thy tribes: and they shall iudge the people with righteous iudgement.

19 Wrest not thou ye Law, nor respect any person, neither take rewarde: for the reward blindeth ye eyes of the wise, and peruerteth ye worde of ye iust.

20 That which is iust and right shalt thou follow, that thou maiest liue, and possesse the land which the Lord thy God giueth thee.

21 Thou shalt plant thee no groue of any trees neere vnto the altar of the Lord thy God, which thou shalt make thee.

22 Thou shalt set thee vp no pillar, which thing the Lord thy God hateth.

Deuteronomy 17

1 Thou shalt offer vnto the Lord thy God no bullocke nor sheepe wherein is blemish or any euill fauoured thing: for that is an abomination vnto the Lord thy God.

2 If there be founde among you in any of thy cities, which the Lord thy God giueth thee, man or woman that hath wrought wickednes in the sight of the Lord thy God, in transgressing his couenant,

3 And hath gone and serued other gods, and worshipped them: as the sunne, or the moone, or any of the hoste of heauen, which I haue not commanded,

4 And it be tolde vnto thee, and thou hast heard it, then shalt thou inquire diligently: and if it be true, and the thing certaine, that such abomination is wrought in Israel,

5 Then shalt thou bring foorth that man, or that woman (which haue committed that wicked thing) vnto thy gates, whether it be man or woman, and shalt stone them with stones, til they die.

6 At the mouth of two or three witnesses shall he that is woorthie of death, die: but at the mouth of one witnesse, he shall not die.

7 The handes of the witnesses shall be first vpon him, to kill him: and afterward the hands of all the people: so thou shalt take the wicked away from among you.

8 If there rise a matter too harde for thee in iudgement betweene blood and blood, betweene plea and plea, betweene plague and plague, in the matters of controuersie within thy gates, then shalt thou arise, and goe vp vnto the place which the Lord thy God shall chuse,

9 And thou shalt come vnto the Priestes of the Leuites, and vnto the iudge that shall be in those daies, and aske, and they shall shewe thee the sentence of iudgement,

10 And thou shalt do according to that thing which they of that place (which the Lord hath chosen) shewe thee, and thou shalt obserue to doe according to all that they informe thee.

11 According to the Lawe, which they shall teach thee, and according to the iudgement which they shall tell thee, shalt thou doe: thou shalt not decline from the thing which they shall shew thee, neither to the right hand, nor to the left.

12 And that man that wil doe presumptuously, not hearkening vnto the Priest (that standeth before the Lord thy God to minister there) or vnto the iudge, that man shall die, and thou shalt take away euill from Israel.

13 So all the people shall heare and feare, and doe no more presumptuously.

14 Whe thou shalt come vnto ye land which the Lord thy God giueth thee, and shalt possesse it, and dwell therein, if thou say, I will set a King ouer me, like as all the nations that are about me,

15 Then thou shalt make him King ouer thee, whome the Lord thy God shall chuse: from among thy brethren shalt thou make a King ouer thee: thou shalt not set a stranger ouer thee, which is not thy brother.

16 In any wise he shall not prepare him many horses, nor bring the people againe to Egypt, for to encrease the number of horses, seeing the Lord hath sayd vnto you, Ye shall henceforth goe no more againe that way.

17 Neither shall hee take him many wiues, lest his heart turne away, neither shall he gather him much siluer and golde.

18 And when he shall sit vpon the throne of his kingdo, then shall he write him this Law repeted in a booke, by the Priests of the Leuites.

19 And it shall be with him, and he shall reade therein all daies of his life, that he may learne to feare the Lord his God, and to keepe all ye words of this Lawe, and these ordinances for to doe them:

20 That his heart be not lifted vp aboue his brethren, and that he turne not from the commandement, to the right hand or to the left, but that he may prolong his daies in his kingdom, he, and his sonnes in the middes of Israel.

Deuteronomy 18

1 The Priests of the Leuites, and all the tribe of Leui shall haue no part nor inheritace with Israel, but shall eate the offerings of the Lord made by fire, and his inheritance.

2 Therefore shall they haue no inheritance among their brethren: for the Lord is their inheritance, as he hath sayd vnto them.

3 And this shalbe the Priests duetie of the people, that they, which offer sacrifice, whether it be bullocke or sheepe, shall giue vnto the Priest the shoulder, and the two cheekes, and the mawe.

4 The first fruites also of thy corne, of thy wine, and of thine oyle, and the first of the fleece of thy sheepe shalt thou giue him.

5 For the Lord thy God hath chosen him out of all thy tribes, to stande and minister in the Name of the Lord, him, and his sonnes for euer.

6 Also when a Leuite shall come out of any of thy cities of all Israel, where hee remained, and come with all the desire of his heart vnto the place, which the Lord shall chuse,

7 He shall then minister in the Name of the Lord his God, as all his brethren the Leuites, which remaine there before the Lord.

8 They shall haue like portions to eat beside that which commeth of his sale of his patrimonie.

9 When thou shalt come into ye land which the Lord thy God giueth thee, thou shalt not learne to do after ye abominations of those nations.

10 Let none be founde among you that maketh his sonne or his daughter to goe

thorough the fire, or that vseth witchcraft, or a regarder of times, or a marker of the flying of foules, or a sorcerer,

11 Or a charmer, or that counselleth with spirits, or a soothsaier, or that asketh counsel at ye dead.

12 For all that doe such things are abomination vnto the Lord, and because of these abominations the Lord thy God doeth cast them out before thee.

13 Thou shalt be vpright therefore with the Lord thy God.

14 For these nations which thou shalt possesse, hearken vnto those that regarde the times, and vnto sorcerers: as for thee, the Lord thy God hath not suffred thee so.

15 The Lord thy God will raise vp vnto thee a Prophet like vnto me, from among you, euen of thy brethren: vnto him ye shall hearken,

16 According to al that thou desiredst of the Lord thy God in Horeb, in the day of the assemblie, when thou saidest, Let me heare the voice of my Lord God no more, nor see this great fire any more, that I die not.

17 And the Lord sayde vnto me, They haue well spoken.

18 I will raise them vp a Prophet from among their brethren like vnto thee, and will put my woordes in his mouth, and he shall speake vnto them all that I shall commaund him.

19 And whosoeuer will not hearken vnto my wordes, which he shall speake in my Name, I will require it of him.

20 But the prophet that shall presume to speake a worde in my name, which I haue not commanded him to speake, or that speaketh in the name of other gods, euen the same prophet shall die.

21 And if thou thinke in thine heart, Howe shall we knowe the worde which the Lord hath not spoken?

22 When a prophet speaketh in the Name of the Lord, if the thing follow not nor come to passe, that is the thing which the Lord hath not spoken, but the prophet hath spoken it presumptuously: thou shalt not therefore be afraid of him.

Deuteronomy 19

1 When the Lord thy God shall roote out the nations, whose lande the Lord thy God giueth thee, and thou shalt possesse them, and dwell in their cities, and in their houses,

2 Thou shalt separate three cities for thee in the middes of thy lande which the Lord thy God giueth thee to possesse it.

3 Thou shalt prepare thee the way, and deuide the coastes of the land, which the Lord thy God giueth thee to inherite, into three parts, that euery manslayer may flee thither.

4 This also is ye cause wherfore the manslayer shall flee thither, and liue: who so killeth his neighbor ignorantly, and hated him not in time passed:

5 As hee that goeth vnto the wood with his neighbor to hew wood, and his hand striketh with the axe to cut downe the tree, if the head slip from the helue, and hit his neighbour that he dieth, the same shall flee vnto one of the cities, and liue,

6 Least the auenger of the blood follow after the manslayer, while his heart is chafed, and ouertake him, because the way is long, and slaie him, although he be not worthy of death, because he hated him not in time passed.

7 Wherefore I command thee, saying, Thou shalt appoint out three cities for thee.

8 And when the Lord thy God enlargeth thy coastes (as he hath sworne vnto thy fathers) and giueth thee all the lande which he promised to giue vnto thy fathers,

9 (If thou keepe all these commandements to doe them, which I commaund thee this day: to wit, that thou loue the Lord thy God, and walke in his waies for euer) then shalt thou adde three cities moe for thee besides those three,

10 That innocent bloude be not shed within thy land, which the Lord thy God giueth thee to inherite, lest bloud be vpon thee.

11 But if a man hate his neighbour, and lay waite for him, and rise against him, and smite any man that he die, and flee vnto any of these cities,

12 Then the Elders of his citie shall send and set him thence, and deliuer him into the hands of the auenger of the blood, that he may die.

13 Thine eye shall not spare him, but thou shalt put away the crie of innocent blood from Israel, that it may goe well with thee.

14 Thou shalt not remooue thy neighbours marke, which they of olde time haue set in thine inheritance, that thou shalt inherite in the lande, which ye Lord thy God giueth thee to possesse it.

15 One witnes shall not rise against a man for any trespasse, or for any sinne, or for any fault that hee offendeth in, but at the mouth of two witnesses or at the mouth of three witnesses shall the matter be stablished.

16 If a false witnesse rise vp against a man to accuse him of trespasse,

17 Then both the men which striue together, shall stand before ye Lord, euen before the Priests and the Iudges, which shall be in those daies;

18 And the Iudges shall make diligent inquisition: and if the witnesse be found false, and hath giuen false witnes against his brother,

19 Then shall yee doe vnto him as hee had thought to doe vnto his brother: so thou shalt take euil away forth of the middes of thee.

20 And the rest shall heare this, and feare, and shall henceforth commit no more any such wickednes among you.

21 Therefore thine eye shall have no compassion, but life for life, eye for eye, tooth for tooth, hand for hand, foote for foote.

Deuteronomy 20

1 When thou shalt go forth to warre against thine enemies, and shalt see horses and charets, and people moe then thou, be not afrayde of them: for the Lord thy God is with thee, which brought thee out of the land of Egypt.

2 And when ye are come neere vnto the battel, then the Priest shall come forth to speake vnto the people,

3 And shall say vnto them, Heare, O Israel: ye are come this day vnto battell against your enemies: let not your heartes faynt, neither feare, nor be amased, nor adread of them.

4 For ye Lord your God goeth with you, to fight for you against your enemies, and to saue you

5 And let the officers speake vnto the people, saying, What man is there that hath buylt a new house, and hath not dedicate it? let him go and returne to his house, least he dye in the battel, and an other man dedicate it.

6 And what man is there that hath planted a vineyarde, and hath not eaten of the fruite? let him go and returne againe vnto his house, least he die in the battel, and another eate the fruite.

7 And what man is there that hath betrothed a wife, and hath not taken her? let him go and returne againe vnto his house, lest he die in the battell, and another man take her.

8 And let the officers speake further vnto the people, and say, Whosoeuer is afrayde and faynt hearted, let him go and returne vnto his house, least his brethrens heart faynt like his heart.

9 And after that the officers haue made an ende of speaking vnto the people, they shall make captaines of the armie to gouerne the people.

10 When thou commest neere vnto a citie to fight against it, thou shalt offer it peace.

11 And if it answere thee againe peaceably, and open vnto thee, then let all the people that is founde therein, be tributaries vnto thee, and serue thee.

12 But if it will make no peace with thee, but make war against thee, then shalt thou besiege it.

13 And the Lord thy God shall deliuer it into thine handes, and thou shalt smite all the males thereof with the edge of the sworde.

14 Onely the women, and the children, and the cattel, and all that is in the citie, euen all the spoyle thereof shalt thou take vnto thy selfe, and shalt eate the spoyle of thine enemies, which the Lord thy God hath giuen thee.

15 Thus shalt thou do vnto all ye cities, which are a great way off from thee, which are not of the cities of these nations here.

16 But of the cities of this people, which the Lord thy God shall giue thee to inherite, thou shalt saue no person aliue,

17 But shalt vtterly destroy them: to wit, the Hittites, and the Amorites, the Canaanites, and the Perizzites, the

Hiuites, and the Iebusites, as the Lord thy God hath commanded thee,

18 That they teach you not to doe after all their abominations, which they haue done vnto their gods, and so ye should sinne against the Lord your God.

19 When thou hast besieged a citie long time, and made warre against it to take it, destroy not the trees therof, by smiting an axe into them: for thou mayest eate of them: therfore thou shalt not cut them downe to further thee in the siege, (for the tree of the field is mans life)

20 Onely those trees, which thou knowest are not for meate, those shalt thou destroy and cut downe, and make fortes against the citie that maketh warre with thee, vntil thou subdue it.

Deuteronomy 21

1 If one be founde slaine in the lande, which the Lord thy God giueth thee to possesse it, lying in the field, and it is not knowe who hath slaine him,

2 Then thine Elders and thy Iudges shall come forth, and measure vnto the cities that are round about him that is slayne.

3 Aud let ye Elders of that citie, which is next vnto the slaine man, take out of the droue an heifer that hath not bene put to labour, nor hath drawen in the yoke.

4 And let the Elders of that citie bring the heifer vnto a stonie valley, which is neyther eared nor sowen, and strike off the heifers necke there in the valley.

5 Also the Priests the sonnes of Leui (whom the Lord thy God hath chosen to minister, and to blesse in the name of the Lord) shall come forth, and by their word shall all strife and plague be tried.

6 And all the Elders of that citie that came neere to the slayne man, shall wash their hands ouer the heifer that is beheaded in the valley:

7 And shall testifie, and say, Our handes haue not shed this blood, neither haue our eies seene it.

8 O Lord, be mercifull vnto thy people Israel, whom thou hast redeemed, and lay no innocent blood to the charge of thy people Israel, and the blood shalbe forgiuen them.

9 So shalt thou take away the cry of innocet blood from thee, when thou shalt do that which is right in the sight of the Lord.

10 Whe thou shalt go to warre against thine enemies, and the Lord thy God shall deliuer them into thine hands, and thou shalt take the captiues,

11 And shalt see among the captiues a beautifull woman, and hast a desire vnto her, and wouldest take her to thy wife,

12 Then thou shalt bring her home to thine house, and she shall shaue her head, and pare her nayles,

13 And she shall put off the garment that shee was taken in, and she shall remaine in thine house, and bewaile her father and her mother a moneth long: and after that shalt thou go in vnto her, and marry her, and she shalbe thy wife.

14 And if thou haue no fauour vnto her, then thou mayest let her go whither she will, but thou shalt not sell her for money, nor make marchandise of her, because thou hast humbled her.

15 If a man haue two wiues, one loued and another hated, and they haue borne him children, both the loued and also the hated: if the first borne be the sonne of the hated,

16 Then when the time commeth, that hee appointeth his sonnes to be heires of that which he hath, he may not make the sonne of the beloued first borne before the sonne of the hated, which is the first borne:

17 But he shall acknowledge the sonne of the hated for the first borne, and giue him double portion of all that he hath: for hee is the first of his strength, and to him belongeth the right of the first borne.

18 If any man haue a sonne that is stubburne and disobedient, which wil not hearken vnto the voice of his father, nor the voyce of his mother, and they haue chastened him, and he would not obey them,

19 Then shall his father and his mother take him, and bring him out vnto the Elders of his citie, and vnto the gate of the place where he dwelleth,

20 And shall say vnto the Elders of his citie, This our sonne is stubburne and disobedient, and he wil not obey our admonition: he is a riotour, and a drunkard.

21 Then all the men of his citie shall stone him with stones vnto death: so thou shalt take away euill from among you, that all Israel may heare it, and feare.

22 If a man also haue committed a trespasse worthy of death, and is put to death, and thou hangest him on a tree,

23 His body shall not remaine all night vpon the tree, but thou shalt bury him the same day: for the curse of God is on him that is hanged. Defile not therfore thy land which the Lord thy God giueth thee to inherite.

Deuteronomy 22

1 Thou shalt not see thy brothers oxe nor his sheepe go astray, and withdraw thy selfe from them, but shalt bring the againe vnto thy brother.

2 And if thy brother bee not neere vnto thee, or if thou knowe him not, then thou shalt bring it into thine house, and it shall remaine with thee, vntill thy brother seeke after it: then shalt thou deliuer it to him againe.

3 In like maner shalt thou do with his asse, and so shalt thou do with his rayment, and shalt so doe with all lost things of thy brother, which he hath lost: if thou hast found them, thou shalt not withdraw thy selfe from them.

4 Thou shalt not see thy brothers asse nor his oxe fal downe by the way, and withdrawe thy selfe from them, but shalt lift them vp with him.

5 The woman shall not weare that which perteineth vnto the man, neither shall a man put on womans rayment: for all that doe so, are abomination vnto the Lord thy God.

6 If thou finde a birdes nest in the way, in any tree, or on the ground, whether they be yong or egges, and the damme sitting vpon the yong, or vpon the egges, thou shalt not take ye damme with the yong,

7 But shalt in any wise let the damme go, and take the yong to thee, that thou mayest prosper and prolong thy dayes.

8 When thou buildest a newe house, thou shalt make a battlemet on thy roofe, that thou lay not blood vpon thine house, if any man fal thence.

9 Thou shalt not sow thy vineyard with diuers kinds of seedes, lest thou defile the increase of the seede which thou hast sowen, and the fruite of the vineyarde.

10 Thou shalt not plow with an oxe and an asse together.

11 Thou shalt not weare a garment of diuers sorts, as of woollen and linen together.

12 Thou shalt make thee fringes vpon the foure quarters of thy vesture, wherewith thou couerest thy selfe.

13 If a man take a wife, and when he hath lyen with her, hate her,

14 And laye slaunderous thinges vnto her charge, and bring vp an euill name vpon her, and say, I tooke this wife, and when I came to her, I found her not a mayde,

15 Then shall the father of the mayde and her mother take and bring the signes of the maydes virginitie vnto the Elders of the citie to the gate.

16 And the maydes father shall say vnto the Elders, I gaue my daughter vnto this man to wife, and he hateth her:

17 And lo, he layeth slaunderous things vnto her charge, saying, I founde not thy daughter a mayde: loe, these are the tokens of my daughters virginitie: and they shall spreade the vesture before the Elders of the citie.

18 Then the Elders of the citie shall take that man and chastise him,

19 And shall condemne him in an hundreth shekels of siluer, and giue them vnto the father of the mayde, because he hath brought vp an euill name vpon a mayde of Israel: and she shalbe his wife, and he may not put her away all his life.

20 But if this thing be true, that the mayde be not found a virgine,

21 Then shall they bring forth the mayde to the doore of her fathers house, and the men of her citie shall stone her with stones to death: for shee hath wrought follie in Israel, by playing ye whore in her fathers house: so thou shalt put euill away from among you.

22 If a man be found lying with a woman marryed to a man, then they shall dye euen both twaine: to wit, the man that lay with the wife, and the wife: so thou shalt put away euil from Israel.

23 If a maid be betrothed vnto an husband, and a man finde her in the towne and lye with her,

24 Then shall yee bring them both out vnto the gates of the same citie, and shall stone them with stones to death: the mayde because she cried not, being in the citie, and the man, because he hath humbled his neighbours wife: so thou shalt put away euill from among you.

25 But if a man finde a betrothed mayde in the field, and force her, and lye with her, then the man that lay with her, shall dye alone:

26 And vnto the mayd thou shalt do nothing, because there is in the mayde no cause of death: for as when a man riseth against his neighbour and woundeth him to death, so is this matter.

27 For he found her in the fieldes: the betrothed mayde cryed, and there was no man to succour her.

28 If a man finde a mayde that is not betrothed, and take her, and lye with her, and they be founde,

29 Then the man that lay with her, shall giue vnto the maydes father fiftie shekels of siluer: and she shalbe his wife, because he hath humbled her: he can not put her away all his life.

30 No man shall take his fathers wife, nor shall vncouer his fathers skirt.

Deuteronomy 23

1 None that is hurt by bursting, or that hath his priuie member cut off, shall enter into the Congregation of the Lord.

2 A bastard shall not enter into the Congregation of the Lord: euen to his tenth generation shall he not enter into the Congregation of the Lord.

3 The Ammonites and the Moabites shall not enter into the Congregation of the Lord: euen to their tenth generation shall they not enter into the Congregation of the Lord for euer,

4 Because they met you not with bread and water in the way, when yee came out of Egypt, and because they hyred against thee Balaam the sonne of Beor, of Pethor in Aram-naharaim, to curse thee.

5 Neuerthelesse, the Lord thy God would not hearken vnto Balaam, but the Lord thy God turned the curse to a blessing vnto thee, because the Lord thy God loued thee.

6 Thou shalt not seeke their peace nor their prosperitie all thy dayes for euer.

7 Thou shalt not abhorre an Edomite: for he is thy brother, neither shalt thou abhorre an Egyptian, because thou wast a strager in his land.

8 The children that are begotten of them in their thirde generation, shall enter into the Congregation of the Lord.

9 When thou goest out with the host against thine enemies, keepe thee then from all wickednesse.

10 If there be among you any that is vncleane by that which commeth to him by night, he shall goe out of the hoste, and shall not enter into the hoste,

11 But at euen he shall wash him selfe with water, and when the sunne is downe, he shall enter into the hoste.

12 Thou shalt haue a place also without the hoste whither thou shalt resort,

13 And thou shalt haue a paddle among thy weapons, and when thou wouldest sit downe without, thou shalt shalt digge therewith, and returning thou shalt couer thine excrements.

14 For the Lord thy God walketh in the mids of thy campe to deliuer thee, and to giue thee thine enemies before thee: therefore thine hoste shalbe holy, that he see no filthie thing in thee and turne away from thee.

15 Thou shalt not deliuer the seruant vnto his master, which is escaped from his master vnto thee.

16 He shall dwell with thee, euen among you, in what place he shall chuse, in one of thy cities where it liketh him best: thou shalt not vexe him.

17 There shalbe no whore of the daughters of Israel, neither shall there be a whore keeper of the sonnes of Israel.

18 Thou shalt neyther bring the hyre of a whore, nor the price of a dogge into the house of the Lord thy God for any vow: for euen both these are abomination vnto the Lord thy God.

19 Thou shalt not giue to vsurie to thy brother: as vsurie of money, vsurie of meate, vsurie of any thing that is put to vsurie.

20 Vnto a stranger thou mayest lend vpon vsurie, but thou shalt not lend vpon vsurie vnto thy brother, that the Lord thy God may blesse thee in all that thou settest thine hand to, in the land whither thou goest to possesse it.

21 When thou shalt vowe a vowe vnto the Lord thy God, thou shalt not be slacke to paye it: for the Lord thy God will surely require it of thee, and so it should be sinne vnto thee.

22 But when thou absteinest from vowing, it shalbe no sinne vnto thee.

23 That which is gone out of thy lippes, thou shalt keepe and performe, as thou hast vowed it willingly vnto the Lord thy God: for thou hast spoken it with thy mouth.

24 When thou commest vnto thy neighbours vineyard, then thou mayest eate grapes at thy pleasure, as much as thou wilt: but thou shalt put none in thy vessell.

25 When thou commest into thy neighbours corne thou mayest plucke the eares with thine hand, but thou shalt not moue a sickle to thy neighbours corne.

Deuteronomy 24

1 When a man taketh a wife, and marrieth her, if so be shee finde no fauour in his eyes, because hee hath espyed some filthinesse in her, then let him write her a bill of diuorcement, and put it in her hand, and send her out of his house.

2 And when she is departed out of his house, and gone her way, and marrie with an other man,

3 And if the latter husband hate her, and write her a letter of diuorcement, and put it in her hand, and send her out of his house, or if the latter man die which tooke her to wife:

4 Then her first husband, which sent her away, may not take her againe to be his wife, after that she is defiled: for that is abomination in the sight of the Lord, and thou shalt not cause the land to sinne, which the Lord thy God doeth giue thee to inherite.

5 When a man taketh a new wife, he shall not goe a warfare, neither shalbe charged with any businesse, but shalbe free at home one yeere, and reioyce with his wife which he hath taken.

6 No man shall take the nether nor the vpper milstone to pledge: for this gage is his liuing.

7 If any man be found stealing any of his brethren of the children of Israel, and maketh marchandise of him, or selleth him, that thiefe shall die: so shalt thou put euil away from among you.

8 Take heede of the plague of leprosie, that thou obserue diligently, and doe according to all that the Priestes of the Leuites shall teach you: take heede ye doe as I commanded them.

9 Remember what the Lord thy God did vnto Miriam by the way after that ye were come out of Egypt.

10 Whe thou shalt aske again of thy neighbour any thing lent, thou shalt not goe into his house to fet his pledge.

11 But thou shalt stand without, and the man that borowed it of thee, shall bring the pledge out of the doores vnto thee.

12 Furthermore if it be a poore body, thou shalt not sleepe with his pledge,

13 But shalt restore him the pledge when the sunne goeth downe, that he may sleepe in his raiment, and blesse thee: and it shalbe righteousnesse vnto thee before the Lord thy God.

14 Thou shalt not oppresse an hyred seruant that is needie and poore, neyther of thy brethren, nor of the stranger that is in thy land within thy gates.

15 Thou shalt giue him his hire for his day, neither shall the sunne goe downe vpon it: for he is poore, and therewith susteineth his life: lest he crye against thee vnto the Lord, and it be sinne vnto thee.

16 The fathers shall not be put to death for the children, nor the children put to death for the fathers, but euery man shalbe put to death for his owne sinne.

17 Thou shalt not peruert the right of the stranger, nor of the fatherlesse, nor take a widowes rayment to pledge.

18 But remember that thou wast a seruant in Egypt, and howe the Lord thy God deliuered thee thence. Therefore I commaund thee to doe this thing.

19 When thou cuttest downe thine haruest in thy fielde, and hast forgotten a sheafe in the fielde, thou shalt not goe

againe to fet it, but it shalbe for the stranger, for the fatherles, and for the widowe: that the Lord thy God may blesse thee in all the workes of thine hands.

20 When thou beatest thine oliue tree, thou shalt not goe ouer the boughes againe, but it shalbe for the stranger, for the fatherlesse, and for the widowe.

21 When thou gatherest thy vineyard, thou shalt not gather the grapes cleane after thee, but they shalbe for the stranger, for the fatherlesse, and for the widowe.

22 And remember that thou wast a seruant in the land of Egypt: therefore I command thee to doe this thing.

Deuteronomy 25

1 When there shall be strife betweene men, and they shall come vnto iudgement, and sentence shall be giuen vpon them, and the righteous shall be iustified, and the wicked condemned,

2 Then if so be the wicked be worthy to bee beaten, the iudge shall cause him to lie downe, and to be beaten before his face, according to his trespasse, vnto a certaine nomber.

3 Fortie stripes shall he cause him to haue and not past, lest if he should exceede and beate him aboue that with many stripes, thy brother should appeare despised in thy sight.

4 Thou shalt not mousell the oxe that treadeth out the corne.

5 If brethren dwell together, and one of them dye and haue no sonne, the wife of the dead shall not marry without: that is, vnto a stranger, but his kinseman shall goe in vnto her, and take her to wife, and doe the kinsemans office to her.

6 And the first borne which she beareth, shall succeede in the name of his brother which is dead, that his name be not put out of Israel.

7 And if the man will not take his kinsewoman, then let his kinsewoman goe vp to the gate vnto the Elders, and say, My kinsman refuseth to rayse vp vnto his brother a name in Israel: hee will not doe the office of a kinsman vnto me.

8 Then the Elders of his citie shall call him, and commune with him: if he stand and say, I wil not take her,

9 Then shall his kinswoman come vnto him in the presence of the Elders, and loose his shooe from his foote, and spit in his face, and answere, and say, So shall it be done vnto that man, that will not buylde vp his brothers house.

10 And his name shall be called in Israel, The house of him whose shooe is put off.

11 When men striue together, one with another, if the wife of the one come neere, for to ridde her husband out of the handes of him that smiteth him, and put foorth her hand, and take him by his priuities,

12 Then thou shalt cut off her hande: thine eye shall not spare her.

13 Thou shalt not haue in thy bagge two maner of weightes, a great and a small,

14 Neither shalt thou haue in thine house diuers measures, a great and a small:

15 But thou shalt haue a right and iust weight: a perfite and a iust measure shalt thou haue, that thy dayes may be lengthened in the land, which the Lord thy God giueth thee.

16 For all that doe such things, and all that doe vnrighteously, are abomination vnto the Lord thy God.

17 Remember what Amalek did vnto thee by the way, when ye were come out of Egypt:

18 How he met thee by ye way, and smote ye hindmost of you, all that were feeble behind thee, when thou wast fainted and weary, and he feared not God.

19 Therefore, when the Lord thy God hath giuen thee rest from all thine enemies round about in the land, which the Lord thy God giueth thee for an inheritance to possesse it, then thou shalt put out the remembrance of Amalek from vnder heauen: forget not.

Deuteronomy 26

1 Also when thou shalt come into the lande which the Lord thy God giueth thee for inheritance, and shalt possesse it, and dwell therein,

2 Then shalt thou take of the first of all the fruite of the earth, and bring it out of the lande that the Lord thy God giueth thee, and put it in a basket, and goe vnto the place, which the Lord thy God shall chose to place his Name there.

3 And thou shalt come vnto the Priest, that shall be in those dayes, and say vnto him, I acknowledge this day vnto the Lord thy God, that I am come vnto the countrey which the Lord sware vnto our fathers for to giue vs.

4 Then the Priest shall take the basket out of thine hand, and set it downe before the altar of the Lord thy God.

5 And thou shalt answere and say before the Lord thy God, A Syrian was my father, who being ready to perish for hunger, went downe into Egypt, and soiourned there with a small company, and grew there vnto a nation great, mightie and full of people.

6 And the Egyptians vexed vs, and troubled vs, and laded vs with cruell bondage.

7 But when we cried vnto the Lord God of our fathers, the Lord heard our voyce, and looked on our aduersitie, and on our labour, and on our oppression.

8 And the Lord brought vs out of Egypt in a mightie hande, and a stretched out arme, with great terriblenesse, both in signes and wonders.

9 And he hath brought vs into this place, and hath giuen vs this land, euen a lande that floweth with milke and hony.

10 And now, lo, I haue brought ye first fruites of the land which thou, O Lord, hast giuen me, and thou shalt set it

before the Lord thy God, and worship before the Lord thy God:

11 And thou shalt reioyce in all the good things which the Lord thy God hath giuen vnto thee and to thine houshold, thou and the Leuite, and the stranger that is among you.

12 When thou hast made an end of tithing all the tythes of thine increase, the thirde yeere, which is the yeere of tithing, and hast giuen it vnto the Leuite, to the stranger, to the fatherlesse, and to the widowe, that they may eate within thy gates, and be satisfied,

13 Then thou shalt say before the Lord thy God, I haue brought the halowed thing out of mine house, and also haue giuen it vnto the Leuites and to the strangers, to the fatherlesse, and to the widow, according to all thy comandements which thou hast commanded me: I haue transgressed none of thy comandements, nor forgotten them.

14 I haue not eaten therof in my mourning, nor suffred ought to perish through vncleannes, nor giuen ought thereof for the dead, but haue hearkened vnto the voyce of the Lord my God: I haue done after al that thou hast comaded me.

15 Looke downe from thine holy habitation, euen from heauen, and blesse thy people Israel, and the lande which thou hast giuen vs (as thou swarest vnto our fathers) the land that floweth with milke and hony.

16 This day the Lord thy God doeth command thee to do these ordinances, and lawes: keepe them therefore, and do them with al thine heart, and with all thy soule.

17 Thou hast set vp the Lord this day to be thy God, and to walke in his wayes, and to keepe his ordinances, and his commandements, and his lawes, and to hearken vnto his voyce.

18 And the Lord hath set thee vp this day, to be a precious people vnto him (as hee hath promised thee) and that thou shouldest keepe all his commandements,

19 And to make thee high aboue al nations (which he hath made) in praise, and in name, and in glory, and that thou shouldest be an holy people vnto the Lord thy God, as he hath said.

Deuteronomy 27

1 Then Moses with the Elders of Israel commanded the people, saying, Keepe all the comandements, which I command you this day.

2 And when ye shall passe ouer Iorden vnto the lande which the Lord thy God giueth thee, thou shalt set thee vp great stones, and playster them with plaister,

3 And shalt write vpon them all the words of this Lawe, when thou shalt come ouer, that thou mayest go into the land which the Lord thy God giueth thee: a land that floweth with milke and hony, as the Lord God of thy fathers hath promised thee.

4 Therefore when ye shall passe ouer Iorden, ye shall set vp these stones, which I command you this daye in mount Ebal, and thou shalt plaister them with plaister.

5 And there shalt thou build vnto the Lord thy God an altar, euen an altar of stones: thou shalt lift none yron instrument vpon them.

6 Thou shalt make the altar of the Lord thy God of whole stones, and offer burnt offerings thereon vnto the Lord thy God.

7 And thou shalt offer peace offrings, and shalt eate there and reioyce before the Lord thy God:

8 And thou shalt write vpon the stones al the words of this Law, well and plainely.

9 And Moses and the Priestes of the Leuites spake vnto all Israel, saying, Take heede and heare, O Israel: this day thou art become the people of the Lord thy God.

10 Thou shalt hearken therefore vnto the voyce of the Lord thy God, and do his commandements and his ordinances, which I commande thee this day.

11 And Moses charged the people the same day, saying,

12 These shall stand vpon mount Gerizzim, to blesse the people when ye shall passe ouer Iorden: Simeon, and Leui, and Iudah, and Issachar, and Ioseph, and Beniamin.

13 And these shall stand vpon mount Ebal to curse: Reuben, Gad, and Asher, and Zebulun, Dan, and Naphtali.

14 And the Leuites shall answere and say vnto all the men of Israel with a loude voyce,

15 Cursed be the man that shall make any carued or molten image, which is an abomination vnto the Lord, the worke of the hands of the craftesman, and putteth it in a secrete place: And all the people shall answere, and say: So be it.

16 Cursed be he that curseth his father and his mother: And all the people shall say: So be it.

17 Cursed be he that remoueth his neighbors marke: And all the people shall say: So be it.

18 Cursed be he that maketh ye blinde go out of the way: And all the people shall say: So be it.

19 Cursed be he that hindreth the right of the stranger, the fatherles, and the widow: And all the people shall say: So be it.

20 Cursed be hee that lyeth with his fathers wife: for he hath vncouered his fathers skirt: And all the people shall say: So be it.

21 Cursed be he that lieth with any beast: And all the people shall say: So be it.

22 Cursed be he that lyeth with his sister, the daughter of his father, or the daughter of his mother: And all the people shall say: So be it.

23 Cursed be he that lyeth with his mother in law: And all the people shall say: So be it.

24 Cursed be hee that smiteth his neyghbour secretly: And all the people shall say: So be it.

25 Cursed be he that taketh a reward to put to death innocent blood: And all the people shall say: So be it.

26 Cursed be he that confirmeth not all the wordes of this Law, to do them: And all the people shall say: So be it.

Deuteronomy 28

1 If thou shalt obey diligently the voyce of the Lord thy God, and obserue and do all his commandements, which I commande thee this day, then the Lord thy God wil set thee on high aboue all the nations of the earth.

2 And all these blessings shall come on thee, and ouertake thee, if thou shalt obey the voyce of the Lord thy God.

3 Blessed shalt thou be in the citie, and blessed also in the fielde.

4 Blessed shalbe the fruite of thy body, and ye fruite of thy ground, and the fruite of thy cattel, the increase of thy kine, and ye flocks of thy sheepe.

5 Blessed shalbe thy basket and thy dough.

6 Blessed shalt thou be, whe thou commest in, and blessed also when thou goest out.

7 The Lord shall cause thine enemies that rise against thee, to fall before thy face: they shall come out against thee one way, and shall flee before thee leuen wayes.

8 The Lord shall command the blessing to be with thee in thy store houses, and in all that thou settest thine hande to, and wil blesse thee in the land which the Lord thy God giueth thee.

9 The Lord shall make thee an holy people vnto himself, as he hath sworne vnto thee, if thou shalt keepe the commandements of the Lord thy God, and walke in his wayes.

10 Then all people of the earth shall see that the Name of the Lord is called vpon ouer thee, and they shalbe afrayde of thee.

11 And the Lord shall make thee plenteous in goods, in the fruite of thy body, and in the fruite of thy cattell, and in the fruite of thy grounde, in the land which the Lord sware vnto thy fathers, to giue thee.

12 The Lord shall open vnto thee his good treasure, euen the heauen to giue rayne vnto thy kind in due season, and to blesse all the worke of thine handes: and thou shalt lende vnto many nations, but shalt not borow thy selfe.

13 And the Lord shall make thee the head, and not the tayle, and thou shalt be aboue onely, and shalt not bee beneath, if thou obey the commandements of the Lord thy God, which I command thee this day, to keepe and to do them.

14 But thou shalt not decline from any of the wordes, which I command you this day, either to the right hand or to the left, to goe after other gods to serue them.

15 But if thou wilt not obey the voyce of the Lord thy God, to keepe and to do all his commandementes and his ordinances, which I command thee this day, then al these curses shall come vpon thee, and ouertake thee.

16 Cursed shalt thou bee in the towne, and cursed also in the fielde.

17 Cursed shall thy basket be, and thy dough.

18 Cursed shall be the fruite of thy body, and the fruite of thy land, the increase of thy kine, and the flockes of thy sheepe.

19 Cursed shalt thou be when thou commest in, and cursed also when thou goest out.

20 The Lord shall sende vpon thee cursing, trouble, and shame, in all that which thou settest thine hand to do, vntil thou be destroyed, and perish quickely, because of the wickednesse of thy workes whereby thou hast forsaken me.

21 The Lord shall make the pestilence cleaue vnto thee, vntill he hath consumed thee from the land, whither thou goest to possesse it.

22 The Lord shall smite thee with a consumption, and with the feuer, and with a burning ague, and with feruent heate, and with the sworde, and with blasting, and with the mildew, and they shall pursue thee vntill thou perish.

23 And thine heauen that is ouer thine head, shall be brasse, and the earth that is vnder thee, yron.

24 The Lord shall giue thee for the rayne of thy land, dust and ashes: euen from heauen shall it come downe vpon thee, vntil thou be destroyed.

25 And the Lord shall cause thee to fall before thine enemies: thou shalt come out one way against them, and shalt flee seuen wayes before them, and shalt be scattered through all the kingdomes of the earth.

26 And thy carkeis shall be meate vnto all foules of the ayre, and vnto the beasts of the earth, and none shall fray them away.

27 The Lord wil smite thee with the botch of Egypt, and with the emeroids, and with the skab, and with the itche, that thou canst not be healed.

28 And ye Lord shall smite thee with madnes, and with blindnes, and with astonying of heart.

29 Thou shalt also grope at noone daies, as the blinde gropeth in darknes, and shalt not prosper in thy wayes: thou shalt neuer but bee oppressed with wrong and be powled euermore, and no man shall succour thee.

30 Thou shalt betroth a wife, and another man shall lye with her: thou shalt builde an house, and shalt not dwell therein: thou shalt plant a vineyard, and shalt not eate the fruite.

31 Thine oxe shalbe slayne before thine eyes, and thou shalt not eate thereof: thine asse shall be violently taken away before thy face, and shall not be restored to thee: thy sheepe shalbe giuen vnto

thine enemies, and no man shall rescue them for thee.

32 Thy sonnes and thy daughters shalbe giuen vnto another people, and thine eyes shall still looke for them, euen till they fall out, and there shalbe no power in thine hand.

33 The fruite of thy land and all thy labours shall a people, which thou knowest not, eate, and thou shalt neuer but suffer wrong, and violence alway:

34 So that thou shalt be madde for the sight which thine eyes shall see.

35 The Lord shall smite thee in the knees, and in the thighes, with a sore botche, that thou canst not be healed: euen from the sole of thy foote vnto the top of thine head.

36 The Lord shall bring thee and thy King (which thou shalt set ouer thee) vnto a nation, which neither thou nor thy fathers haue knowen, and there thou shalt serue other gods: euen wood and stone,

37 And thou shalt be a wonder, a prouerbe and a common talke among all people, whither the Lord shall carie thee.

38 Thou shalt carie out much seede into the fielde, and shalt gather but litle in: for the grashoppers shall destroy it.

39 Thou shalt plant a vineyard, and dresse it, but shalt neither drinke of the wine, nor gather the grapes: for the wormes shall eate it.

40 Thou shalt haue Oliue trees in all thy coastes, but shalt not anoynt thy selfe with the oyle: for thine oliues shall fall.

41 Thou shalt beget sonnes, and daughters, but shalt not haue them: for they shall goe into captiuitie.

42 All thy trees and fruite of thy land shall the grashopper consume.

43 The straunger that is among you, shall clime aboue thee vp on hie, and thou shalt come downe beneath alow.

44 He shall lend thee, and thou shalt not lend him: he shalbe the head, and thou shalt be ye tayle.

45 Moreouer, all these curses shall come vpon thee, and shall pursue thee and ouertake thee, till thou be destroyed, because thou obeyedst not the voyce of the Lord thy God, to keepe his commandements, and his ordinances, which he commanded thee:

46 And they shalbe vpon thee for signes and wonders, and vpon thy seede for euer,

47 Because thou seruedst not the Lord thy God with ioyfulnesse and with a good heart for the abundance of all things.

48 Therefore thou shalt serue thine enemies which the Lord shall send vpon thee, in hunger and in thirst, and in nakednesse, and in neede of all things? and he shall put a yoke of yron vpon thy necke vntill he haue destroyed thee.

49 The Lord shall bring a nation vpon thee from farre, euen from the ende of the world, flying swift as an Egle: a nation whose tongue thou shalt not vnderstand:

50 A nation of a fierce countenance, which will not regarde the person of the olde, nor haue compassion of the yong.

51 The same shall eate the fruit of thy cattell, and the fruite of thy land vntill thou be destroyed, and he shall leaue thee neyther wheate, wine, nor oyle, neither the increase of thy kyne, nor the flockes of thy sheepe, vntill he haue brought thee to nought.

52 And he shall besiege thee in all thy cities, vntill thine hie and strong walles fall downe, wherein thou trustedst in all the lande: and hee shall besiege thee in all thy cities throughout all thy lande, which the Lord thy God hath giuen thee.

53 And thou shalt eate the fruite of thy bodie: euen the flesh of thy sonnes and thy daughters, which the Lord thy God hath giuen thee, during the siege and straitnesse wherein thine enemie shall inclose thee:

54 So that the man (that is tender and exceeding deintie among you) shalbe grieued at his brother, and at his wife, that lieth in his bosome, and at the remnant of his children, which hee hath yet left,

55 For feare of giuing vnto any of them of the flesh of his children, whom he shall eate, because he hath nothing left him in that siege, and straitnesse, wherewith thine enemie shall besiege thee in all thy cities.

56 The tender and deintie woman among you, which neuer woulde venture to set the sole of her foote vpon the grounde (for her softnesse and tendernesse) shalbe grieued at her husband that lieth in her bosome, and at her sonne, and at her daughter,

57 And at her afterbirth (that shall come out from betweene her feete) and at her childre, which she shall beare: for when all things lacke, she shall eate them secretly, during the siege and straitnesse, wherewith thine enemie shall besiege thee in thy cities.

58 If thou wilt not keepe and doe all the wordes of the Lawe (that are written in this booke) and feare this glorious and fearefull name The Lord Thy God,

59 The the Lord wil make thy plagues wonderfull, and the plagues of thy seede, euen great plagues and of long continuance, and sore diseases, and of long durance.

60 Moreouer, he will bring vpon thee all the diseases of Egypt, whereof thou wast afraide, and they shall cleaue vnto thee.

61 And euery sickenesse, and euery plague, which is not written in the booke of this Lawe, will the Lord heape vpon thee, vntill thou be destroyed.

62 And ye shall be left few in nomber, where ye were as the starres of heauen in multitude, because thou wouldest not obey the voyce of the Lord thy God.

63 And as the Lord hath reioyced ouer you, to doe you good, and to multiply you, so he will reioyce ouer you, to destroy you, and bring you to nought, and ye shalbe rooted out of the land, whither thou goest to possesse it.

64 And the Lord shall scatter thee among all people, from the one ende of the worlde vnto the other, and there thou shalt serue other gods, which thou hast

not knowen nor thy fathers, euen wood and stone.

65 Also among these nations thou shalt finde no rest, neither shall the sole of thy foote haue rest: for the Lord shall giue thee there a trembling heart, and looking to returne till thine eyes fall out, and a sorowfull minde.

66 And thy life shall hang before thee, and thou shalt feare both night and day, and shalt haue none assurance of thy life.

67 In the morning thou shalt say, Woulde God it were euening, and at the euening thou shalt say, Would God it were morning, for ye feare of thine heart, which thou shalt feare, and for the sight of thine eyes, which thou shalt see.

68 And the Lord shall bring thee into Egypt againe with shippes by the way, whereof I saide vnto thee, Thou shalt see it no more againe: and there yee shall sell your selues vnto your enemies for bondmen and bondwomen, and there shalbe no byer.

Deuteronomy 29

1 These are the wordes of the couenant which the Lord commanded Moses to make with the children of Israel in the lande of Moab beside the couenant which hee had made with them in Horeb.

2 And Moses called all Israel, and said vnto them, Ye haue seene all that the Lord did before your eyes in the lande of Egypt vnto Pharaoh and vnto all his seruantes, and vnto all his lande,

3 The great tentations which thine eyes haue seene, those great miracles and wonders:

4 Yet the Lord hath not giuen you an heart to perceiue, and eyes to see, and eares to heare, vnto this day.

5 And I haue led you fourty yere in the wildernesse: your clothes are not waxed olde vpon you, neyther is thy shooe waxed olde vpon thy foote.

6 Ye haue eaten no bread, neither drunke wine, nor strong drinke, that ye might know how that I am the Lord your God.

7 After, ye came vnto this place, and Sihon King of Heshbon, and Og King of Bashan came out against vs vnto battell, and we slewe them,

8 And tooke their lande, and gaue it for an inheritance vnto the Reubenites, and to the Gadites, and to the halfe tribe of Manasseh.

9 Keepe therefore the wordes of this couenant and doe them, that ye may prosper in all that ye shall doe.

10 Ye stand this day euery one of you before the Lord your God: your heads of your tribes, your Elders and your officers, eue al ye me of Israel:

11 Your children, your wiues, and thy stranger that is in thy campe from the hewer of thy wood, vnto the drawer of thy water,

12 That thou shouldest passe into the couenant of the Lord thy God, and into his othe which the Lord thy God maketh with thee this day,

13 For to establish thee this day a people vnto him selfe, and that he may be vnto thee a God, as he hath said vnto thee, and as he hath sworne vnto thy fathers, Abraham, Izhak, and Iaakob.

14 Neither make I this couenant, and this othe with you onely,

15 But aswel with him that standeth here with vs this day before the Lord our God, as with him that is not here with vs this day.

16 For ye knowe, how we haue dwelt in the land of Egypt, and how we passed thorowe the middes of the nations, which ye passed by.

17 And ye haue seene their abominations and their idoles (wood, and stone, siluer and golde) which were among them,

18 That there should not be among you man nor woman, nor familie, nor tribe, which should turne his heart away this day from the Lord our God, to goe and serue the gods of these nations, and that there shoulde not be among you any roote that bringeth forth gall and wormewood,

19 So that when he heareth the words of this curse, he blesse him selfe in his heart, saying, I shall haue peace, although I walke according to the stubburnes of mine owne heart, thus adding drunkennesse to thirst.

20 The Lord will not be mercifull vnto him, but then the wrath of the Lord and his ielousie shall smoke against that man, and euery curse that is written in this booke, shall light vpon him, and the Lord shall put out his name from vnder heauen,

21 And the Lord shall separate him vnto euil out of all the tribes of Israel, according vnto all the curses of the couenant, that is written in the booke of this Lawe.

22 So that the generatio to come, euen your children, that shall rise vp after you, and the stranger, that shall come from a farre lande, shall say, when they shall see the plagues of this lande, and the diseases thereof, wherewith the Lord shall smite it:

23 (For all that land shall burne with brimstone and salt: it shall not be sowen, nor bring forth, nor any grasse shall growe therein, like as in the ouerthrowing of Sodom, and Gomorah, Admah, and Zeboim, which the Lord ouerthrewe in his wrath and in his anger)

24 Then shall all nations say, Wherefore hath the Lord done thus vnto this lande? how fierce is this great wrath?

25 And they shall answere, Because they haue forsaken the couenant of the Lord God of their fathers, which he had made with them, when he brought them out of the land of Egypt,

26 And went and serued other gods and worshipped them: euen gods which they knewe not, and which had giuen them nothing,

27 Therefore the wrath of the Lord waxed hot against this land, to bring vpon it euery curse that is written in this booke.

28 And ye Lord hath rooted them out of their land in anger, and in wrath, and in great indignation, and hath cast them into another land, as appeareth this day.

29 The secret things belong to the Lord our God, but the things reueiled belong vnto vs, and to our children for euer, that we may doe all the wordes of this Lawe.

Deuteronomy 30

1 Nowe when all these things shall come vpon thee, either the blessing or the curse which I haue set before thee, and thou shalt turne into thine heart, among all the nations whither the Lord thy God hath driuen thee,

2 And shalt returne vnto the Lord thy God, and obey his voyce in all that I commaund thee this day: thou, and thy children with all thine heart and with all thy soule,

3 Then the Lord thy God wil cause thy captiues to returne, and haue compassion vpon thee, and wil returne, to gather thee out of all the people, where the Lord thy God had scattered thee.

4 Though thou werest cast vnto the vtmost part of heauen, from thence will the Lord thy God gather thee, and from thence wil he take thee,

5 And the Lord thy God will bring thee into the land which thy fathers possessed, and thou shalt possesse it, and he will shewe thee fauour, and will multiplie thee aboue thy fathers.

6 And the Lord thy God will circumcise thine heart, and the heart of thy seede, that thou mayest loue the Lord thy God with all thine heart, and with al thy soule, that thou maiest liue.

7 And the Lord thy God will lay all these curses vpon thine enemies, and on them, that hate thee, and that persecute thee.

8 Returne thou therefore, and obey the voyce of the Lord, and do all his commandements, which I commaund thee this day.

9 And the Lord thy God will make thee plenteous in euery worke of thine hande, in the fruite of thy bodie, and in the fruite of thy cattel, and in the fruite of the lande for thy wealth: for the Lord will turne againe, and reioyce ouer thee to do thee good, as he reioyced ouer thy fathers,

10 Because thou shalt obey the voyce of the Lord thy God, in keeping his comandements, and his ordinances, which are written in the booke of this Law, when thou shalt returne vnto the Lord thy God with all thine heart and with al thy soule.

11 For this commandement which I commande thee this day, is not hid from thee, neither is it farre off.

12 It is not in heauen, that thou shouldest say, Who shall go vp for vs to heauen, and bring it vs, and cause vs to heare it, that we may doe it?

13 Neither is it beyonde the sea, that thou shouldest say, Who shall go ouer the sea for vs, and bring it vs, and cause vs to heare it, that we may do it?

14 But the word is very neere vnto thee: euen in thy mouth and in thine heart, for to do it.

15 Beholde, I haue set before thee this day life and good, death and euill,

16 In that I commaund thee this day, to loue the Lord thy God, to walke in his wayes, and to keepe his commandements, and his ordinances, and his lawes, that thou mayest liue, and be multiplied, and that the Lord thy God may blesse thee in the land, whither thou goest to possesse it.

17 But if thine heart turne away, so that thou wilt not obey, but shalt be seduced and worship other gods, and serue them,

18 I pronounce vnto you this day, that ye shall surely perish, ye shall not prolong your dayes in the lande, whither thou passest ouer Iorden to possesse it.

19 I call heauen and earth to recorde this day against you, that I haue set before you life and death, blessing and cursing. therefore chuse life, that both thou and thy seede may liue,

20 By louing the Lord thy God, by obeying his voyce, and by cleauing vnto him: for he is thy life, and the length of thy dayes: that thou mayest dwell in the lande which the Lord sware vnto thy fathers, Abraham, Izhak, and Iaakob, to giue them.

Deuteronomy 31

1 Then Moses went and spake these wordes vnto all Israel,

2 And said vnto them, I am an hundreth and twentie yeere olde this day: I can no more goe out and in: also the Lord hath saide vnto me, Thou shalt not goe ouer this Iorden.

3 The Lord thy God he will go ouer before thee: he will destroy these nations before thee, and thou shalt possesse them. Ioshua, he shall goe before thee, as the Lord hath said.

4 And the Lord shall doe vnto them, as he did to Sihon and to Og Kings of the Amorites: and vnto their lande whome he destroyed.

5 And the Lord shall giue them before you that ye may do vnto them according vnto euery commandement, which I haue comanded you.

6 Plucke vp your hearts therefore, and be strong: dread not, nor be afraid of them: for the Lord thy God him selfe doeth goe with thee: he will not faile thee, nor forsake thee.

7 And Moses called Ioshua, and said vnto him in the sight of all Israel, Be of a good courage and strong: for thou shalt go with this people vnto the lande which the Lord hath sworne vnto their fathers, to giue them, and thou shalt giue it them to inherite.

8 And the Lord him selfe doeth go before thee: he will be with thee: he will not faile thee, neither forsake thee: feare not therefore, nor be discomforted.

9 And Moses wrote this Lawe, and deliuered it vnto the Priestes the sonnes

of Leui (which bare the Arke of the couenant of the Lord) and vnto all the Elders of Israel,

10 And Moses commanded them, saying, Euery seuenth yeere when the yeere of freedome shalbe in the feast of the Tabernacles:

11 When all Israel shall come to appeare before the Lord thy God, in the place which he shall chuse, thou shalt reade this Lawe before all Israel that they may heare it.

12 Gather the people together: men, and women, and children, and thy stranger that is within thy gates, that they may heare, and that they may learne, and feare the Lord your God, and keepe and obserue all the wordes of this Lawe,

13 And that their children which haue not knowen it, may heare it, and learne to feare the Lord your God, as long as ye liue in the lande, whither ye goe ouer Iorden to possesse it.

14 Then the Lord saide vnto Moses, Beholde, thy dayes are come, that thou must die: Call Ioshua, and stande ye in the Tabernacle of the Congregation that I may giue him a charge. So Moses and Ioshua went, and stoode in the Tabernacle of the Congregation.

15 And the Lord appeared in the Tabernacle, in the pillar of a cloude: and the pillar of the cloude stoode ouer the doore of the Tabernacle.

16 And the Lord said vnto Moses, Behold, thou shalt sleepe with thy fathers, and this people will rise vp, and goe a whoring after the gods of a strange land (whither they goe to dwell therein) and will forsake me, and breake my couenant which I haue made with them.

17 Wherefore my wrath will waxe hote against them at that day, and I will forsake them, and will hide my face from them: then they shalbe consumed, and many aduersities and tribulations shall come vpon them: so then they will say, Are not these troubles come vpon me, because God is not with me?

18 But I will surely hide my face in that day, because of all the euill, which they shall commit, in that they are turned vnto other gods.

19 Now therefore write ye this song for you, and teach it the children of Israel: put it in their mouthes, that this song may be my witnesse against the children of Israel.

20 For I will bring them into the land (which I sware vnto their fathers) that floweth with milke and honie, and they shall eate, and fil them selues, and waxe fat: then shall they turne vnto other gods, and serue them, and contemne me, and breake my couenant.

21 And then when many aduersities and tribulations shall come vpon them, this song shall answere them to their face as a witnesse: for it shall not be forgotte out of the mouthes of their posteritie: for I knowe their imagination, which they goe about euen now, before I haue brought them into the lande which I sware.

22 Moses therefore wrote this song the same day and taught it the children of Israel.

23 And God gaue Ioshua the sonne of Nun a charge, and said, Be strong, and of a good courage: for thou shalt bring the children of Israel into the lande, which I sware vnto them, and I will be with thee.

24 And when Moses had made an ende of writing the wordes of this Lawe in a booke vntill he had finished them,

25 Then Moses commanded the Leuites, which bare the Arke of the couenant of the Lord, saying,

26 Take the booke of this Lawe, and put ye it in the side of the Arke of the couenant of the Lord your God, that it may be there for a witnes against thee.

27 For I knowe thy rebellion and thy stiffe necke: beholde, I being yet aliue with you this day, ye are rebellious against the Lord: howe much more then after my death?

28 Gather vnto me all the Elders of your tribes, and your officers, that I may speake these wordes in their audience, and call heauen and earth to recorde against them.

29 For I am sure that after my death ye will vtterly be corrupt and turne from the way, which I haue commanded you: therefore euill will come vpon you at the length, because ye will comit euill in the sight of the Lord, by prouoking him to anger through the worke of your hands.

30 Thus Moses spake in the audience of all the congregation of Israel the wordes of this song, vntill he had ended them.

Deuteronomy 32

1 Hearken, ye heauens, and I will speake: and let the earth heare the words of my mouth.

2 My doctrine shall drop as the raine, and my speach shall stil as the dew, as the showre vpon the herbes, and as the great raine vpon the grasse.

3 For I will publish the name of the Lord: giue ye glorie vnto our God.

4 Perfect is the worke of the mighty God: for all his wayes are iudgement. God is true, and without wickednesse: iust, and righteous is he.

5 They haue corrupted them selues towarde him by their vice, not being his children, but a frowarde and crooked generation.

6 Doe ye so rewarde the Lord, O foolish people and vnwise? is not he thy father, that hath bought thee? he hath made thee, and proportioned thee.

7 Remember the dayes of olde: consider the yeeres of so many generations: aske thy father, and he will shewe thee: thine Elders, and they will tell thee.

8 When the most hie God deuided to the nations their inheritance, when he separated the sonnes of Adam, he appoynted the borders of the people, according to the nomber of the children of Israel.

9 For the Lordes portion is his people: Iaakob is the lot of his inheritance.

10 He found him in ye land of ye wildernes, in a waste, and roaring wildernes: he led him about, he taught him, and kept him as ye apple of his eye.

11 As an eagle stereth vp her nest, flootereth ouer her birdes, stretcheth out her wings, taketh them, and beareth them on her wings,

12 So the Lord alone led him, and there was no strange god with him.

13 He caryed him vp to the hie places of the earth, that he might eate the fruites of the fieldes, and he caused him to sucke hony out of the stone, and oyle out of the hard rocke:

14 Butter of kine, and milke of sheepe with fat of the lambes, and rammes fed in Bashan, and goates, with the fat of the graines of wheat, and the red licour of the grape hast thou drunke.

15 But he that should haue bene vpright, when he waxed fat, spurned with his heele: thou art fat, thou art grosse, thou art laden with fatnes: therefore he forsooke God that made him, and regarded not the strong God of his saluation.

16 They prouoked him with strange gods: they prouoked him to anger with abominations.

17 They offred vnto deuils, not to God, but to gods whome they knew not: new gods that came newly vp, whome their fathers feared not.

18 Thou hast forgotten the mightie God that begate thee, and hast forgotten God that formed thee.

19 The Lord then sawe it, and was angrie, for the prouocation of his sonnes and of his daughters.

20 And he said, I will hide my face from the: I will see what their ende shalbe: for they are a frowarde generation, children in who is no faith.

21 They haue moued me to ielousie with that which is not God: they haue prouoked me to anger with their vanities: and I will moue them to ielousie with those which are no people: I wil prouoke them to anger with a foolish nation.

22 For fire is kindled in my wrath, and shall burne vnto the bottome of hell, and shall consume the earth with her increase, and set on fire the foundations of the mountaines.

23 I will spend plagues vpon them: I will bestowe mine arrowes vpon them.

24 They shalbe burnt with hunger, and consumed with heate, and with bitter destruction: I will also sende the teeth of beastes vpon them, with the venime of serpents creeping in the dust.

25 The sworde shall kill them without, and in the chambers feare: both the yong man and the yong woman, the suckeling with the man of gray heare.

26 I haue said, I would scatter them abroade: I would make their remembrance to cease from among men,

27 Saue that I feared the furie of the enemie, least their aduersaries should waxe proude, and least they should say, Our hie hande and not the Lord hath done all this:

28 For they are a nation voide of counsel, neither is there any vnderstanding in them.

29 Oh that they were wise, then they would vnderstand this: they would consider their latter ende.

30 How should one chase a thousand, and two put ten thousande to flight, except their strong God had sold the, and the Lord had shut them vp?

31 For their god is not as our God, euen our enemies being iudges.

32 For their vine is of the vine of Sodom, and of the vines of Gomorah: their grapes are grapes of gall, their clusters be bitter.

33 Their wine is the poyson of dragons, and the cruel gall of aspes.

34 Is not this laide in store with me, and sealed vp among my treasures?

35 Vengeance and recompence are mine: their foote shall slide in due time: for the day of their destruction is at hand, and the things that shall come vpon them, make haste.

36 For the Lord shall iudge his people, and repent towarde his seruants, when hee seeth that their power is gone, and none shut vp in holde nor left abroad.

37 When men shall say, Where are their gods, their mighty God in whome they trusted,

38 Which did eate the fat of their sacrifices, and did drinke the wine of their drinke offring? let them rise vp, and help you: let him be your refuge.

39 Behold now, for I, I am he, and there is no gods with me: I kill, and giue life: I wound, and I make whole: neither is there any that can deliuer out of mine hand.

40 For I lift vp mine hand to heauen, and say, I liue for euer.

41 If I whet my glittering sworde, and mine hand take holde on iudgement, I will execute vengeance on mine enemies, and will rewarde them that hate me.

42 I will make mine arrowes drunke with blood, (and my sword shall eate flesh) for the blood of the slaine, and of the captiues, when I beginne to take vengeance of the enemie.

43 Ye nations, praise his people: for he will auenge the blood of his seruants, and will execute vengeance vpon his aduersaries, and will bee mercifull vnto his lande, and to his people.

44 Then Moses came and spake all ye words of this song in the audience of the people, he and Hoshea the sonne of Nun.

45 When Moses had made an end of speaking all these wordes to all Israel,

46 Then hee said vnto them, Set your heartes vnto all the wordes which I testifie against you this day, that ye may commande them vnto your children, that they may obserue and doo all the wordes of this Lawe.

47 For it is no vaine worde concerning you, but it is your life, and by this worde ye shall prolong your dayes in the land, whither yee go ouer Iorden to possesse it.

48 And the Lord spake vnto Moses the selfe same day, saying,

49 Goe vp into the mountaine of Abarim, vnto the mount Nebo, which is in the lande of Moab, that is ouer against Iericho: and beholde the lande of Canaan, which I giue vnto the children of Israel for a possession,

50 And die in the mount which thou goest vp vnto, and thou shalt be gathered vnto thy people, as Aaron thy brother died in mount Hor, and was gathered vnto his people,

51 Because ye trespassed against me among the children of Israel, at the waters of Meribah, at Kadesh in the wildernesse of Zin: for ye sanctified me not among the children of Israel.

52 Thou shalt therefore see the lande before thee, but shalt not go thither, I meane, into the land which I giue the children of Israel.

Deuteronomy 33

1 Nowe this is the blessing wherewith Moses the man of God blessed the children of Israel before his death, and said,

2 The Lord came from Sinai, and rose vp from Seir vnto them, and appeared clearely from mount Paran, and he came with ten thousands of Saints, and at his right hand a firie Lawe for them.

3 Though hee loue the people, yet all thy Saints are in thine handes: and they are humbled at thy foete, to receiue thy words.

4 Moses commanded vs a Lawe for an inheritance of the Congregation of Iaakob.

5 Then he was among the righteous people, as King, when the heades of the people, and the tribes of Israel were assembled.

6 Let Reuben liue, and not die, though his men be a small nomber.

7 And thus he blessed Iudah, and said, Heare, O Lord, the voyce of Iudah, and bring him vnto his people: his hands shalbe sufficient for him, if thou helpe him against his enemies.

8 And of Leui he said, Let thy Thummim and thine Vrim be with thine Holy one, whome thou diddest proue in Massah, and didst cause him to striue at the waters of Meribah.

9 Who said vnto his father and to his mother, I haue not seene him, neither knewe he his brethren, nor knewe his owne children: for they obserued thy word, and kept thy couenant.

10 They shall teach Iaakob thy iudgements, and Israel thy Lawe: they shall put incense before thy face, and the burnt offring vpon thine altar.

11 Blesse, O Lord, his substance, and accept the worke of his handes: smite through ye loynes of them that rise against him, and of them that hate him, that they rise not againe.

12 Of Beniamin he said, The beloued of the Lord shall dwell in safetie by him: the Lord shall couer him all the day long, and dwell betweene his shoulders.

13 And of Ioseph hee sayde, Blessed of the Lord is his land for the sweetenesse of heauen, for the dewe, and for the depth lying beneath,

14 And for the sweete increase of the sunne, and for the sweete increase of the moone,

15 And for the sweetenes of the top of the ancient mountaines, and for the sweetenes of the olde hilles,

16 And for the sweetenesse of the earth, and abundance thereof: and the good will of him that dwelt in the bushe, shall come vpon the head of Ioseph, and vpon the toppe of the head of him that was separated from his brethren.

17 His beautie shalbe like his first borne bullock, and his hornes as the hornes of an vnicorne: with them hee shall smite the people together, euen the endes of the world: these are also the ten thousands of Ephraim, and these are the thousands of Manasseh.

18 And of Zebulun he sayd, Reioice, Zebulun, in thy going out, and thou Isshachar in thy tents.

19 They shall call ye people vnto the mountaine: there they shall offer the sacrifices of righteousnesse: for they shall sucke of the abundance of the sea, and of the treasures hid in the sand.

20 Also of Gad he said, Blessed be hee that enlargeth Gad: he dwelleth as a lion, that catcheth for his praye the arme with the head.

21 And hee looked to himselfe at the beginning, because there was a portion of the Lawe-giuer hid: yet hee shall come with the heades of the people, to execute the iustice of the Lord, and his iudgements with Israel.

22 And of Dan he said, Dan is a lions whelp: he shall leape from Bashan.

23 Also of Naphtali he sayd, O Naphtali, satisfied with fauour, and filled with the blessing of the Lord, possesse the West and the South.

24 And of Asher he saide, Asher shalbe blessed with children: he shalbe acceptable vnto his brethren, and shall dippe his foote in oyle.

25 Thy shooes shalbe yron and brasse, and thy strength shall continue as long as thou liuest.

26 There is none like God, O righteous people, which rideth vpon the heauens for thine helpe, and on the cloudes in his glory.

27 The eternall God is thy refuge, and vnder his armes thou art for euer: hee shall cast out the enemie before thee, and will say, Destroy them.

28 Then Israel the fountaine of Iaakob shall dwell alone in safetie in a lande of wheat, and wine: also his heauens shall drop the dewe.

29 Blessed art thou, O Israel: who is like vnto thee, O people saued by the Lord, the shielde of thine helpe, and which is the sword of thy glorie? therefore thine enemies shall bee in subiection to thee, and thou shalt tread vpon their hie places.

Deuteronomy 34

1 Then Moses went from the plaine of Moab vp into mount Nebo vnto the top of Pisgah that is ouer against Iericho: and the Lord shewed him all the land of Gilead, vnto Dan,

2 And all Naphtali and the land of Ephraim and Manasseh, and all the land of Iudah, vnto the vtmost sea:

3 And the South, and the plaine of the valley of Iericho, the citie of palmetrees, vnto Zoar.

4 And the Lord said vnto him, This is the lande which I sware vnto Abraham, to Izhak and to Iaacob saying, I will giue it vnto thy seede: I haue caused thee to see it with thine eyes, but thou shalt not goe ouer thither.

5 So Moses the seruant of the Lord dyed there in the land of Moab, according to the worde of the Lord.

6 And hee buried him in a valley in the land of Moab ouer against Beth-peor, but no man knoweth of his sepulchre vnto this day.

7 Moses was nowe an hundreth and twentie yeere olde when hee died, his eye was not dimme, nor his naturall force abated.

8 And the children of Israel wept for Moses in the plaine of Moab thirtie dayes: so the dayes of weeping and mourning for Moses were ended.

9 And Ioshua the sonne of Nun was full of ye spirit of wisedome: for Moses had put his hands vpon him. And the children of Israel were obedient vnto him, and did as the Lord had commanded Moses.

10 But there arose not a Prophet since in Israel like vnto Moses (whome the Lord knew face to face)

11 In all ye miracles and wonders which ye Lord sent him to do in ye land of Egypt before Pharaoh and before all his seruantes, and before al his land,

12 And in all that mightie hand and all that great feare, which Moses wrought in the sight of all Israel.

Joshua

Joshua 1

1 Nowe after the death of Moses the seruant of the Lord, the Lord spake vnto Ioshua the sonne of Nun, Moses minister, saying,

2 Moses my seruant is dead: nowe therefore arise, go ouer this Iorden, thou, and all this people, vnto the lande which I giue them, that is, to ye children of Israel.

3 Euery place that the sole of your foote shall treade vpon, haue I giuen you, as I said vnto Moses.

4 From the wildernesse and this Lebanon euen vnto the great riuer, the riuer Perath: all the land of the Hittites, euen vnto the great Sea towarde the going downe of the sunne, shalbe your coast.

5 There shall not a man be able to withstande thee all the dayes of thy life:

as I was with Moses, so will I be with thee: I will not leaue thee, nor forsake thee.

6 Be strong and of a good courage: for vnto this people shalt thou deuide the lande for an inheritance, which I sware vnto their fathers to giue them.

7 Onely be thou strong, and of a most valiant courage, that thou mayest obserue and doe according to all the Lawe which Moses my seruant hath commanded thee: thou shalt not turne away from it to the right hande, nor to the left, that thou mayest prosper whithersoeuer thou goest.

8 Let not this booke of the Law depart out of thy mouth, but meditate therin day and night, that thou mayest obserue and doe according to all that is written therein: for then shalt thou make thy way prosperous, and then shalt thou haue good successe.

9 Haue not I commanded thee, saying, Be strong and of a good courage, feare not, nor be discouraged? for I the Lord thy God will be with thee, whithersoeuer thou goest.

10 Then Ioshua commanded the officers of the people, saying,

11 Passe through the hoste, and commande the people, saying, Prepare you vitailes: for after three dayes ye shall passe ouer this Iorden, to goe in to possesse the lande, which the Lord your God giueth you to possesse it.

12 And vnto the Reubenites, and to the Gadites, and to halfe the tribe of Manasseh spake Ioshua, saying,

13 Remember the worde, which Moses the seruant of the Lord commanded you, saying, The Lord your God hath giuen you rest, and hath giuen you this land.

14 Your wiues, your children, and your cattell shall remaine in the land which Moses gaue you on this side Iorden: but ye shall goe ouer before your brethren armed, all that be men of warre, and shall helpe them,

15 Vntill the Lord haue giuen your brethren rest, as well as to you, and vntill they also shall possesse the land, which the Lord your God giueth them: then shall ye returne vnto the lande of your possession and shall possesse it, which land Moses the Lordes seruant gaue you on this side Iorden toward the sunne rising.

16 Then they answered Ioshua, saying, Al that thou hast commanded vs, we will doe, and whithersoeuer thou sendest vs, we will goe.

17 As we obeyed Moses in all things, so will we obey thee: onely the Lord thy God be with thee, as he was with Moses.

18 Whosoeuer shall rebell against thy commandement, and will not obey thy wordes in all that thou commaundest him, let him bee put to death: onely be strong and of good courage.

Joshua 2

1 Then Ioshua the sonne of Nun sent out of Shittim two men to spie secretly, saying, Go, view the land, and also

Iericho: and they went, and came into an harlots house, named Rahab, and lodged there.

2 Then report was made to the King of Iericho, saying, Beholde, there came men hither to night, of the children of Israel, to spie out the countrey.

3 And the King of Iericho sent vnto Rahab, saying, Bring foorth the men that are come to thee, and which are entred into thine house: for they be come to search out all the land.

4 (But ye woman had taken the two men, and hid them) Therefore saide she thus, There came men vnto me, but I wist not whence they were.

5 And when they shut the gate in the darke, the men went out, whither the men went I wote not: follow ye after them quickly, for ye shall ouertake them.

6 (But she had brought them vp to the roofe of the house, and hidde them with the stalkes of flaxe, which she had spread abroad vpon the roofe)

7 And certaine men pursued after them, the way to Iorden, vnto the foordes, and as soone as they which pursued after them, were gone out, they shut the gate.

8 And before they were a sleepe, she came vp vnto them vpon the roofe,

9 And saide vnto the men, I knowe that the Lord hath giuen you the land, and that the feare of you is fallen vpon vs, and that all the inhabitants of the land faint because of you.

10 For we haue heard, howe the Lord dried vp the water of the redde Sea before you, when you came out of Egypt, and what you did vnto the two Kings of the Amorites, that were on the other side Iorden, vnto Sihon and to Og, whom ye vtterly destroyed:

11 And when wee heard it, our heartes did faint, and there remained no more courage in any because of you: for the Lord your God, he is the God in heauen aboue, and in earth beneath.

12 Now therefore, I pray you, sweare vnto me by the Lord; that as I haue shewed you mercie, ye will also shewe mercie vnto my fathers house, and giue me a true token,

13 And that yee will saue aliue my father and my mother, and my brethren, and my sisters, and all that they haue: and that yee will deliuer our soules from death.

14 And the men answered her, Our life for you to die, if ye vtter not this our businesse: and when the Lord hath giuen vs the lande, we will deale mercifully and truely with thee.

15 Then she let them downe by a corde thorowe the windowe: for her house was vpon the towne wall, and she dwelt vpon the wall.

16 And she said vnto them, Goe you into the mountaine, least the pursuers meete with you, and hide your selues there three dayes, vntill the pursuers be returned: then afterwarde may yee goe your way.

17 And the men said vnto her, We will be blamelesse of this thine othe, which thou hast made vs sweare.

18 Behold, when we come into the land, thou shalt bind this cord of red threde in the window, whereby thou lettest vs downe, and thou shalt bring thy father and thy mother, and thy brethren, and all thy fathers houshold home to thee.

19 And whosoeuer then doeth goe out at the doores of thine house into the streete, his blood shalbe vpon his head, and we will be giltlesse: but whosoeuer shall be with thee in the house, his blood shalbe on our head, if any hande touch him:

20 And if thou vtter this our matter, we will be quite of thine othe, which thou hast made vs sweare.

21 And she answered, According vnto your wordes, so be it: then she sent them away, and they departed, and she bound the red cord in ye window.

22 And they departed, and came into the mountaine, and there abode three dayes, vntil the pursuers were returned: and the pursuers sought them throughout all the way, but founde them not.

23 So the two men returned, and descended from the mountaine, and passed ouer, and came to Ioshua the sonne of Nun, and tolde him all things that came vnto them.

24 Also they saide vnto Ioshua, Surely the Lord hath deliuered into our handes all the lande: for euen all the inhabitants of the countrey faint because of vs.

Joshua 3

1 Then Ioshua rose very earely, and they remoued from Shittim, and came to Iorden, he, and all the children of Israel, and lodged there, before they went ouer.

2 And after three dayes the officers went throughout the hoste,

3 And commanded the people, saying, When ye see the Arke of the couenant of the Lord your God, and the Priestes of the Leuites bearing it, ye shall depart from your place, and goe after it.

4 Yet there shalbe a space betweene you and it, about two thousande cubites by measure: ye shall not come neere vnto it, that ye may knowe the way, by the which ye shall goe: for ye haue not gone this way in times past.

5 (Nowe Ioshua had saide vnto the people, Sanctifie your selues: for to morowe the Lord will doe wonders among you)

6 Also Ioshua spake vnto the Priestes, saying, Take vp the Arke of the couenant, and goe ouer before the people: so they tooke vp the Arke of the couenant, and went before the people.

7 Then the Lord saide vnto Ioshua, This day will I begin to magnifie thee in the sight of all Israel, which shall knowe, that as I was with Moses, so will I be with thee.

8 Thou shalt therefore command the Priests that beare the Arke of the Couenant, saying, When ye are come to the brinke of the waters of Iorden, ye shall stande still in Iorden.

9 Then Ioshua said vnto the children of Israel, Come hither, and heare the wordes of the Lord your God.

10 And Ioshua said, Hereby ye shall know that the liuing God is among you, and that he will certainely cast out before you the Canaanites, and the Hittites, and the Hiuites, and the Perizzites, and the Girgashites, and the Amorites, and the Iebusites.

11 Beholde, the Arke of the couenant of the Lord of all the worlde passeth before you into Iorden.

12 Nowe therefore take from among you twelue men out of the tribes of Israel, out of euery tribe a man.

13 And assoone as the soles of the feete of the Priestes (that beare the Arke of the Lord God the Lord of all the worlde) shall stay in the waters of Iorden, the waters of Iorden shall be cut off: for the waters that come from aboue, shall stande still vpon an heape.

14 Then when the people were departed from their tentes to goe ouer Iorden, the Priestes bearing the Arke of the Couenant, went before people.

15 And as they that bare the Arke came vnto Iorden, and the feete of the Priestes that bare the Arke were dipped in the brinke of the water, (for Iorden vseth to fill all his bankes all the time of haruest)

16 Then the waters that came downe from aboue, stayed and rose vpon an heape and departed farre from the citie of Adam, that was beside Zaretan: but the waters that came downe towarde the Sea of the wildernes, euen the salt Sea, failed, and were cut off: so the people went right ouer against Iericho.

17 But the Priestes that bare the Arke of the couenant of the Lord, stoode drie within Iorden readie prepared, and all the Israelites went ouer dry, vntill all the people were gone cleane ouer through Iorden.

Joshua 4

1 And when all the people were wholy gone ouer Iorden, (after the Lord had spoken vnto Ioshua, saying,

2 Take you twelue me out of the people, out of euery tribe a man,

3 And command you them, saying, Take you hence out of the middes of Iorden, out of the place where the Priestes stoode in a readinesse, twelue stones, which ye shall take away with you, and leaue them in the lodging where you shall lodge this night)

4 Then Ioshua called the twelue men, whome he had prepared of the children of Israel, out of euery tribe a man,

5 And Ioshua said vnto them, Go ouer before the Arke of the Lord your God, euen through the middes of Iorden, and take vp euery man of you a stone vpon his shoulder according vnto the nomber of the tribes of the children of Israel,

6 That this may bee a signe among you, that whe your children shall aske their fathers in time to come, saying, What meane you by these stones?

7 Then ye may answere them, That the waters of Iorden were cut off before the Arke of the couenant of the Lord: for when it passed through Iorden, the waters of Iorden were cut off: therefore these stones are a memoriall vnto the children of Israel for euer.

8 Then ye children of Israel did euen so as Ioshua had commanded, and tooke vp twelue stones out of the mids of Iorden as ye Lord had said vnto Ioshua, according to the number of the tribes of the children of Israel, and caried them away with them vnto the lodging, and layd them down there.

9 And Ioshua set vp twelue stones in the middes of Iorden, in the place where the feete of the Priests, which bare the Arke of the couenant stood, and there haue they continued vnto this day.

10 So the Priests, which bare ye Arke, stoode in the middes of Iorden, vntill euery thing was finished that ye Lord had comanded Ioshua to say vnto the people, according to all that Moses charged Ioshua: then the people hasted and went ouer.

11 When all the people were cleane passed ouer, the Arke of the Lord went ouer also, and the Priests before the people.

12 And the sonnes of Reuben, and the sonnes of Gad, and halfe the tribe of Manasseh went ouer before the children of Israel armed, as Moses had charged them.

13 Euen fourty thousand prepared for warre, went before the Lord vnto battel, into ye plaine of Iericho.

14 That day the Lord magnified Ioshua in the sight of all Israel, and they feared him, as they feared Moses all dayes of his life.

15 And the Lord spake vnto Ioshua, saying,

16 Commande the Priests that beare ye Arke of the testimonie, to come vp out of Iorden.

17 Ioshua therefore commanded the Priests, saying, Come ye vp out of Iorden.

18 And when the Priests that bare the Arke of the couenant of ye Lord were come vp out of the middes of Iorden, and assoone as the soles of the Priests feete were set on the dry land, the waters of Iorde returned vnto their place, and flowed ouer all the bankes thereof, as they did before.

19 So the people came vp out of Iorden the tenth day of the first moneth, and pitched in Gilgal, in the Eastside of Iericho.

20 Also the twelue stones, which they tooke out of Iorden, did Ioshua pitch in Gilgal.

21 And he spake vnto ye childre of Israel, saying, When your children shall aske their fathers in time to come, and say, What meane these stones?

22 Then ye shall shew your children, and say, Israel came ouer this Iorden on dry land:

23 For the Lord your God dryed vp ye waters of Iorden before you, vntill ye were gone ouer, as the Lord your God did

the red Sea, which hee dryed vp before vs, till we were gone ouer,

24 That all the people of the worlde may know that the hand of the Lord is mightie, that ye might feare the Lord your God continually.

Joshua 5

1 Nowe when all the Kings of the Amorites, which were beyond Iorden Westward, and all the Kinges of the Canaanites which were by the Sea, heard that the Lord had dried vp the waters of Iorden before the children of Israel vntill they were gone ouer, their heart fainted: and there was no courage in them any more because of the children of Israel.

2 That same time the Lord said vnto Ioshua, Make thee sharpe kniues, and returne, and circumcise the sonnes of Israel the second time.

3 Then Ioshua made him sharpe kniues and circumcised the sonnes of Israel in the hill of the foreskinnes.

4 And this is the cause why Ioshua circumcised all the people, euen the males that came out of Egypt, because all the men of warre were dead in the wildernesse by the way after they came out of Egypt.

5 For all the people that came out were circumcised: but all the people that were borne in the wildernes by the way after they came out of Egypt, were not circumcised.

6 For the children of Israel walked fourtie yeres in the wildernes, till all the people of the men of warre that came out of Egypt were consumed, because they obeyed not the voyce of the Lord: vnto whome the Lord sware, that he would not shewe them the lande, which the Lord had sworne vnto their fathers, that he would giue vs, euen a land that floweth with milke and hony.

7 So their sonnes whome he raysed vp in their steade, Ioshua circumcised: for they were vncircumcised, because they circumcised them not by the way.

8 And when they had made an ende of circumcising al the people, they abode in the places in the campe till they were whole.

9 After, the Lord said vnto Ioshua, This day I haue taken away the shame of Egypt from you: wherefore he called the name of that place Gilgal, vnto this day.

10 So the children of Israel abode in Gilgal, and kept ye feast of the Passeouer the fourteenth day of the moneth at euen in ye plaine of Iericho.

11 And they did eat of the corne of the land, on the morow after the Passeouer, vnleauened breade, and parched corne in the same day.

12 And the MAN ceased on the morowe after they had eaten of the corne of the land, neither had the children of Israel MAN any more, but did eate of the fruite of the land of Canaan that yeere.

13 And when Ioshua was by Iericho, he lift vp his eyes and looked: and behold, there stood a man against him, hauing a sword drawen in his hand: and Ioshua went vnto him, and said vnto him, Art thou on our side, or on our aduersaries?

14 And he said, Nay, but as a captaine of the host of the Lord am I nowe come: then Ioshua fel on his face to the earth, and did worship, and saide vnto him, What sayth my Lord vnto his seruant?

15 And the captaine of ye Lords host said vnto Ioshua, Loose thy shoe of thy foote: for ye place wheron thou standest, is holy: and Ioshua did so.

Joshua 6

1 Now Iericho was shut vp, and closed, because of the children of Israel: none might go out nor enter in.

2 And the Lord saide vnto Ioshua, Behold, I haue giuen into thine hand Iericho and the King thereof, and the strong men of warre.

3 All ye therefore that be men of warre, shall compasse the citie, in going round about the citie once: thus shall you doe sixe dayes:

4 And seuen Priests shall beare seuen trumpets of rams hornes before the Arke: and the seuenth day ye shall compasse the citie seuen times, and the Priests shall blow with the trumpets.

5 And when they make a long blast with the rams horne, and ye heare the sound of the trumpet, al the people shall shoute with a great shoute: then shall the wall of the citie fall downe flat, and the people shall ascend vp, euery man streight before him.

6 Then, Ioshua the sonne of Nun called the Priests and said vnto them, Take vp the Arke of the couenant, and let seuen Priests beare seuen trumpets of rams hornes before the Arke of the Lord.

7 But he said vnto the people, Goe and compasse the citie: and let him that is armed, go forth before the Arke of the Lord.

8 And when Ioshua had spoken vnto the people, the seuen Priestes bare the seuen trumpets of rams hornes, and went foorth before the Arke of the Lord, and blew with the trumpets, and the Arke of the couenant of ye Lord followed them.

9 And the men of armes went before the Priestes, that blewe the trumpets: then the gathering hoste came after the Arke, as they went and blewe the trumpets.

10 (Nowe Ioshua had commanded the people, saying, Ye shall nor shout, neither make any noyse with your voyce, neither shall a worde proceede out of your mouth, vntill the day that I say vnto you, Shout, then shall ye shoute)

11 So the Arke of the Lord compassed the citie, and went about it once: then they returned into the hoaste, and lodged in the campe.

12 And Ioshua rose early in the morning, and the Priestes bare the Arke of the Lord:

13 Also seuen Priests bare seuen trumpets of rams hornes, and went before the Arke of the Lord, and going blewe with the trumpets: and the men of armes went before them, but the gathering hoste came after the Arke of the Lord, as they went and blewe the trumpets.

14 And the second day they compassed the citie once, and returned into the host: thus they did six dayes.

15 And when the seuenth day came, they rose early, euen with the dawning of the day, and compassed the citie after ye same maner seuen times: only that day they compassed the citie seuen times.

16 And when the Priests had blowen ye trumpets the seuenth time, Ioshua said vnto ye people, Shoute: for the Lord hath giuen you the citie.

17 And the citie shalbe an execrable thing, both it, and all that are therein, vnto the Lord: onely Rahab the harlot shall liue, shee, and all that are with her in the house: for shee hid the messengers that we sent.

18 Notwithstanding, be ye ware of the execrable thing, lest ye make your selues execrable, and in taking of the execrable thing, make also the hoste of Israel execrable, and trouble it.

19 But all siluer, and gold, and vessels of brasse, and yron shalbe consecrate vnto the Lord, and shall come into the Lordes treasury.

20 So the people shouted, whe they had blowen trumpets: for when the people had heard the sound of the trumpet, they shouted with a great shoute: and the wall fel downe flat: so the people went vp into the citie, euery man streight before him: and they tooke the citie.

21 And they vtterly destroyed all that was in the citie, both man and woman, yong, and olde, and oxe, and sheepe, and asse, with the edge of the sword.

22 But Ioshua had said vnto the two men that had spied out the countrey, Go into the harlots house, and bring out thence the woman, and all that she hath, as ye sware to her.

23 So the yong men that were spies, went in, and brought out Rahab, and her father, and her mother, and her brethren, and all that shee had: also they brought out all her familie, and put them without the host of Israel.

24 After they burnt the citie with fire, and all that was therein: onely the siluer and the gold, and the vessels of brasse and yron, they put vnto the treasure of the house of the Lord.

25 So Ioshua saued Rahab the harlot, and her fathers houshold, and all that shee had; and shee dwelt in Israel euen vnto this day, because shee had hid the messengers, which Ioshua sent to spie out Iericho.

26 And Ioshua sware at that time, saying, Cursed be the man before ye Lord, that riseth vp, and buildeth this citie Iericho: hee shall lay the foundation thereof in his eldest sonne, and in his yongest sonne shall hee set vp the gates of it.

27 So the Lord was with Ioshua, and he was famous through all the world.

Joshua 7

1 But the children of Israel committed a trespasse in the excommunicate thing: for Achan the sonne of Carmi, the sonne of Zabdi, the sonne of Zerah of the tribe of Iuda tooke of the excommunicate thing: wherfore the wrath of the Lord was kindled against the children of Israel.

2 And Ioshua sent men from Iericho to Ai, which is beside Bethauen, on ye East side of Bethel, and spake vnto them, saying, Goe vp, and view the countrey. And ye men went vp, and viewed Ai,

3 And returned to Ioshua, and saide vnto him, Let not al the people go vp, but let as it were two or three thousand men go vp, and smite Ai, and make not al the people to labour thither, for they are fewe.

4 So there went vp thither of the people about three thousande men, and they fledde before the men of Ai.

5 And the men of Ai smote of them vpon a thirtie and sixe men: for they chased them from before the gate vnto Shebarim, and smote them in the going downe: wherfore the heartes of the people melted away like water.

6 Then Ioshua rent his clothes, and fell to the earth vpon his face before the Arke of the Lord, vntill the euentide, he, and the Elders of Israel, and put dust vpon their heads.

7 And Ioshua said, Alas, O Lord God, wherefore hast thou brought this people ouer Iorden, to deliuer vs into the hande of the Amorites, and to destroye vs? would God we had bene content to dwell on the other side Iorden.

8 Oh Lord, what shall I say, when Israel turne their backes before their enemies?

9 For the Canaanites, and all the inhabitants of the land shall heare of it, and shall compasse vs, and destroy our name out of the earth: and what wilt thou doe vnto thy mightie Name?

10 And the Lord said vnto Ioshua, Get thee vp: wherefore lyest thou thus vpon thy face?

11 Israel hath sinned, and they haue transgressed my couenant, which I commanded them: for they haue euen taken of the excommunicate thing, and haue also stollen, and dissembled also, and haue put it euen with their owne stuffe.

12 Therefore ye children of Israel cannot stand before their enemies, but haue turned their backes before their enemies, because they be execrable: neither will I bee with you any more, except ye destroy the excommunicate from among you.

13 Vp therefore, sanctifie the people, and say, Sanctifie your selues against to morowe: for thus saith the Lord God of Israel, There is an execrable thing among you, O Israel, therefore ye cannot stand against your enemies, vntill ye haue put the execrable thing from among you.

14 In the morning therefore ye shall come according to your tribes, and the tribe which the Lord taketh, shall come according to the families: and the familie which the Lord shall take, shall come by the housholds: and the houshold which the Lord shall take, shall come man by man.

15 And he that is taken with the excommunicate thing, shall be burnt with fire, hee, and all that he hath, because he hath transgressed the couenant of the Lord, and because he hath wrought folly in Israel.

16 So Ioshua rose vp earely in the morning and brought Israel by their tribes: and the tribe of Iudah was taken.

17 And he brought the families of Iudah, and tooke the familie of the Zarhites, and he brought the familie of the Zarhites, man by man, and Zabdi was taken.

18 And he brought his houshold, man by man, and Achan ye sonne of Carmi, the sonne of Zabdi, the sonne of Zerah of the tribe of Iudah was take.

19 Then Ioshua said vnto Achan, My sonne, I beseech thee, giue glory to the Lord God of Israel, and make confession vnto him, and shewe me now what thou hast done: hide it not from me.

20 And Achan answered Ioshua, and saide, In deede, I haue sinned against the Lord God of Israel, and thus, and thus haue I done.

21 I sawe among the spoyle a goodly Babylonish garment, and two hundreth shekels of siluer, and a wedge of golde of fiftie shekels weight, and I coueted them, and tooke them: and behold, they lye hid in the earth in the mids of my tent, and the siluer vnder it.

22 Then Ioshua sent messengers, which ran vnto the tent, and beholde, it was hid in his tent, and the siluer vnder it.

23 Therefore they tooke them out of the tent, and brought them vnto Ioshua, and vnto all the children of Israel, and layd them before the Lord.

24 Then Ioshua tooke Achan the sonne of Zerah, and the siluer, and the garment and the wedge of golde and his sonnes, and his daughters, and his oxen, and his asses, and his sheepe, and his tent, and all that hee had: and all Israel with him brought them vnto the valley of Achor.

25 And Ioshua said, In as much as thou hast troubled vs, the Lord shall trouble thee this day: and all Israel threwe stones at him, and burned them with fire, and stoned them with stones.

26 And they cast vpon him a great heape of stones vnto this day: and so the Lord turned from his fierce wrath: therefore hee called the name of that place, The valley of Achor, vnto this day.

Joshua 8

1 After, the Lord saide vnto Ioshua, Feare not, neither bee thou faint hearted: take all the men of warre with thee and arise, go vp to Ai: beholde, I haue giuen into thine hand the King of Ai, and his people, and his citie, and his land.

2 And thou shalt doe to Ai and to the King thereof, as thou didst vnto Iericho and to the King thereof: neuerthelesse the spoyle thereof and the cattell thereof shall ye take vnto you for a praye: thou shalt lye in wait against the citie on the backside thereof.

3 Then Ioshua arose, and all the men of warre to goe vp against Ai: and Ioshua chose out thirtie thousand strong men, and valiant, and sent them away by night.

4 And he commanded them, saying, Behold, yee shall lye in waite against the citie on the backeside of the citie: goe not very farre from the citie, but be ye all in a readinesse.

5 And I and all the people that are with me, will approche vnto the citie: and when they shall come out against vs, as they did at the first time, then will we flee before them.

6 For they wil come out after vs, till we haue brought them out of the citie: for they will say, They flee before vs as at the first time: so we will flee before them.

7 Then you shall rise vp from lying in waite and destroy the citie: for the Lord your God wil deliuer it into your hand.

8 And when ye haue taken the citie, ye shall set it on fire: according to the commandement of the Lord shall ye do: behold, I haue charged you.

9 Ioshua then sent them foorth, and they went to lye in waite, and abode betweene Beth-el and Ai, on the Westside of Ai: but Ioshua lodged that night among the people.

10 And Ioshua rose vp early in the morning, and nombred the people: and he and the Elders of Israel went vp before the people against Ai.

11 Also all the men of warre that were with him went vp and drewe neere, and came against the citie, and pitched on the Northside of Ai: and there was a valley betweene them and Ai.

12 And hee tooke about fiue thousande men, and set them to lye in waite betweene Beth-el and Ai, on the Westside of the citie.

13 And the people set all the hoste that was on the Northside against the citie, and the liers in waite on the West, against the citie: and Ioshua went the same night into the mids of the valley.

14 And when the King of Ai sawe it, then the men of the citie hasted and rose vp earely, and went out against Israel to battell, hee and all his people at the time appointed, before the plaine: for he knew not that any lay in waite against him on the backeside of the citie.

15 Then Ioshua and all Israel as beaten before them, fled by the way of the wildernes.

16 And all the people of the citie were called together, to pursue after them: and they pursued after Ioshua, and were drawen away out of the city,

17 So that there was not a man left in Ai, nor in Beth-el, that went not out after Israel: and they left the citie open, and pursued after Israel.

18 Then the Lord said vnto Ioshua, Stretch out the speare that is in thine hande, towarde Ai: for I wil giue it into thine hand: and Ioshua stretched out

the speare that hee had in his hand, toward the citie.

19 And they that lay in wait, arose quickly out of their place, and ranne as soone as he had stretched out his hand, and they entred into the citie, and tooke it, and hasted, and set the citie on fire.

20 And the men of Ai looked behinde them, and sawe it: for loe, the smoke of the citie ascended vp to heauen, and they had no power to flee this way or that way: for the people that fled to the wildernesse, turned backe vpon the pursuers.

21 When Ioshua and all Israel sawe that they that lay in waite, had taken the citie, and that the smoke of the citie mounted vp, then they turned againe and slewe the men of Ai.

22 Also the other issued out of the citie against them: so were they in the middes of Israel, these being on the one side, and the rest on the other side: and they slewe them, so that they let none of them remaine nor escape.

23 And the King of Ai they tooke aliue, and brought him to Ioshua.

24 And when Israel had made an ende of slaying all the inhabitants of Ai in the fielde, that is, in the wildernesse, where they chased them, and when they were all fallen on the edge of the sworde, vntill they were consumed, all the Israelites returned vnto Ai, and smote it with the edge of the sworde.

25 And all that fell that day, both of men and women, were twelue thousande, euen all the men of Ai.

26 For Ioshua drewe not his hande backe againe which he had stretched out with the speare, vntill hee had vtterly destroyed all the inhabitants of Ai.

27 Onely the cattell and the spoyle of this citie, Israel tooke for a praye vnto themselues, according vnto the worde of the Lord, which hee commanded Ioshua.

28 And Ioshua burnt Ai, and made it an heape for euer, and a wildernes vnto this day.

29 And the King of Ai hee hanged on a tree, vnto the euening. And as soone as the sunne was down, Ioshua commanded that they should take his carkeis downe from the tree, and cast it at the entring of ye gate of the city, and lay thereon a great heape of stones, that remaineth vnto this day.

30 Then Ioshua built an altar vnto the Lord God of Israel, in mount Ebal,

31 As Moses the seruant of the Lord had commanded the children of Israel, as it is written in the booke of the Lawe of Moses, an altar of whole stone, ouer which no man had lift an yron: and they offered thereon burnt offrings vnto the Lord, and sacrificed peace offerings.

32 Also he wrote there vpon the stones, a rehearsall of the Lawe of Moses, which he wrote in the presence of the children of Israel.

33 And all Israel (and their Elders, and officers and their iudges stoode on this side of the Arke, and on that side, before the Priestes of the Leuites, which bare the Arke of the couenant of the Lord) as well the stranger, as he that is borne in the countrey: halfe of them were ouer against mount Gerizim, and halfe of them ouer against mount Ebal, as Moses the seruant of the Lord had commanded before, that they should blesse the people of Israel.

34 Then afterwarde hee read all the wordes of the Lawe, the blessings and cursings, according to all that is written in the booke of the Lawe.

35 There was not a worde of all that Moses had commanded, which Ioshua read not before all the Congregation of Israel, as well before the women and the children, as the stranger that was conuersant among them.

Joshua 9

1 And when all the Kings that were beyonde Iorden, in the mountaines and in the valleis, and by all the coastes of the great Sea ouer against Lebanon (as the Hittites, and the Amorites, the Canaanites, the Perizzites, the Hiuites, and the Iebusites) heard thereof,

2 They gathered themselues together, to fight against Ioshua, and against Israel with one accord.

3 But the inhabitants of Gibeon heard what Ioshua had done vnto Iericho, and to Ai.

4 And therefore they wrought craftily: for they went, and fayned themselues ambassadours, and tooke olde sackes vpon their asses, and olde bottels for wine, both rent and bound vp,

5 And olde shoes and clouted vpon their feete: also the raiment vpon them was old, and all their prouision of bread was dried, and mouled.

6 So they came vnto Ioshua into the hoste to Gilgal, and said vnto him, and vnto the men of Israel, Wee be come from a farre countrey: nowe therefore make a league with vs.

7 Then the men of Israel said vnto the Hiuites, It may be that thou dwellest among vs, how then can I make a league with thee?

8 And they said vnto Ioshua, We are thy seruants. Then Ioshua saide vnto them, Who are ye? and whence come ye?

9 And they answered him, From a very farre countrey thy seruants are come for the Name of the Lord thy God: for we haue heard his fame and all that he hath done in Egypt,

10 And all that he hath done to the two Kings of the Amorites that were beyonde Iorden, to Sihon King of Heshbon, and to Og King of Bashan, which were at Ashtaroth.

11 Wherefore our elders, and all the inhabitants of our countrey spake to vs, saying, Take vitailes with you for the iourney, and go to meete them, and say vnto them, Wee are your seruants: now therefore make ye a league with vs.

12 This our bread we tooke it hote with vs for vittailes out of our houses, the day we departed to come vnto you: but nowe beholde, it is dried, and it is mouled.

13 Also these bottels of wine which we filled, were newe, and lo, they be rent, and these our garments and our shooes are olde, by reason of the exceeding great iourney.

14 And the men accepted their tale concerning their vittailes, and counselled not with the mouth of the Lord.

15 So Ioshua made peace with them, and made a league with them, that he would suffer them to liue: also the Princes of the Congregation sware vnto them.

16 But at the end of three dayes, after they had made a league with them, they heard that they were their neighbours, and that they dwelt among them.

17 And the children of Israel tooke their iourney, and came vnto their cities the third day, and their cities were Gibeon, and Chephirah, and Beeroth and Kiriath-iearim.

18 And the children of Israel slewe them not, because the Princes of the Congregation had sworne vnto them by the Lord God of Israel: wherefore all the Congregation murmured against the Princes.

19 Then all the Princes said vnto all the Congregation, We haue sworne vnto them by the Lord God of Israel: nowe therefore we may not touch them.

20 But this we wil doe to them, and let them liue, least the wrath be vpon vs because of the othe which we sware vnto them.

21 And the Princes sayd vnto them againe, Let them liue, but they shall hewe wood, and drawe water vnto all the Congregation, as the Princes appoint them.

22 Ioshua then called them, and talked with them, and sayd, Wherefore haue ye beguiled vs, saying, We are very farre from you, when ye dwel among vs?

23 Now therefore ye are cursed, and there shall none of you be freed from being bondmen, and hewers of wood, and drawers of water for the house of my God.

24 And they answered Ioshua, and sayd, Because it was tolde thy seruants, that the Lord thy God had commanded his seruant Moses to giue you all the land, and to destroy all the inhabitants of the land out of your sight, therefore we were exceeding sore afraid for our liues at the presence of you, and haue done this thing:

25 And beholde nowe, we are in thine hand: doe as it seemeth good and right in thine eyes to doe vnto vs.

26 Euen so did he vnto them, and deliuered them out of the hand of the children of Israel, that they slewe them not.

27 And Ioshua appointed them that same day to be hewers of wood, and drawers of water for the Congregation, and for the altar of the Lord vnto this day, in the place which he should chuse.

Joshua 10

1 Now when Adoni-zedek King of Ierusalem had heard how Ioshua had taken Ai and had destroyed it, (for as he had done to Iericho and to the King thereof, so he had done to Ai and to the King thereof) and howe the inhabitants of Gibeon had made peace with Israel, and were among them,

2 Then they feared exceedingly: for Gibeon was a great citie, as one of the royall cities: for it was greater then Ai, and all the men thereof were mightie.

3 Wherefore Adoni-zedek King of Ierusalem sent vnto Hoham King of Hebron, and vnto Piram King of Iarmuth, and vnto Iapia King of Lachish, and vnto Debir King of Eglon, saying,

4 Come vp vnto me, and helpe me, that we may smite Gibeon: for they haue made peace with Ioshua and with the children of Israel.

5 Therefore the fiue Kings of the Amorites, the King of Ierusalem, the King of Hebron, the King of Iarmuth, the King of Lachish, and the King of Eglon gathered themselues together, and went vp, they with all their hostes, and besieged Gibeon, and made warre against it.

6 And the men of Gibeon sent vnto Ioshua, euen to the hoste to Gilgal, saying, Withdrawe not thine hand from thy seruants: come vp to vs quickly, and saue vs, and helpe vs: for all the Kings of the Amorites which dwell in the mountaines, are gathered together against vs.

7 So Ioshua ascended from Gilgal, he, and all the people of warre with him, and all the men of might.

8 And the Lord sayd vnto Ioshua, Feare them not: for I haue giuen them into thine hand: none of them shall stand against thee.

9 Ioshua therefore came vnto them suddenly: for he went vp from Gilgal all the night.

10 And the Lord discomfited them before Israel, and slew them with a great slaughter at Gibeon, and chased them along the way that goeth vp to Beth-horon, and smote them to Azekah and to Makkedah.

11 And as they fled from before Israel, and were in the going downe to Beth-horon, the Lord cast downe great stones from heauen vpon them, vntill Azekah, and they dyed: they were more that dyed with the hailestones, then they whom the children of Israel slewe with the sword.

12 Then spake Ioshua to the Lord, in the day when the Lord gaue the Amorites before the children of Israel, and he sayd in the sight of Israel, Sunne, stay thou in Gibeon, and thou moone, in the valley of Aialon.

13 And the Sunne abode, and the moone stood still, vntill the people auenged themselues vpon their enemies: (Is not this written in the booke of Iasher?) so the Sunne abode in the middes of the heauen, and hasted not to goe downe for a whole day.

14 And there was no day like that before it, nor after it, that the Lord heard the voyce of a man: for the Lord fought for Israel.

15 After, Ioshua returned, and all Israel with him vnto the campe to Gilgal:

16 But the fiue Kings fled and were hid in a caue at Makkedah.

17 And it was tolde Ioshua, saying, The fiue Kings are found hid in a caue at Makkedah.

18 Then Ioshua said, Roule great stones vpon the mouth of the caue, and set men by it for to keepe them.

19 But stand ye not still: follow after your enemies, and smite all the hindmost, suffer them not to enter into their cities: for the Lord your God hath giuen them into your hand.

20 And when Ioshua and the children of Israel had made an ende of slaying them with an exceeding great slaughter till they were consumed, and the rest that remained of them were entred into walled cities,

21 Then all the people returned to the campe, to Ioshua at Makkedah in peace: no man mooued his tongue against the children of Israel.

22 After, Ioshua sayd, Open the mouth of the caue, and bring out these fiue Kings vnto me forth of the caue.

23 And they did so, and brought out those fiue Kings vnto him forth of the caue, euen the King of Ierusalem, the King of Hebron, ye King of Iarmuth, the King of Lachish, and the King of Eglon.

24 And when they had brought out those Kings vnto Ioshua, Ioshua called for all the men of Israel, and sayd vnto the chiefe of the men of warre, which went with him, Come neere, set your feete vpon the necks of these Kings: and they came neere and set their feete vpon their necks.

25 And Ioshua sayd vnto them, Feare not, nor be faint hearted, but be strong and of a good courage: for thus will the Lord doe to all your enemies, against whome ye fight.

26 So then Ioshua smote them, and slewe them, and hanged them on fiue trees, and they hanged still vpon the trees vntill the euening.

27 And at the going downe of the sunne, Ioshua gaue commandement, that they should take them downe off the trees, and cast them into the caue (wherein they had bene hid) and they layde great stones vpon the caues mouth, which remaine vntill this day.

28 And that same day Ioshua tooke Makkedah and smote it with the edge of the sword, and the King thereof destroyed he with them, and all the soules that were therein, he let none remaine: for hee did to the King of Makkedah as he had done vnto the King of Iericho.

29 Then Ioshua went from Makkedah, and all Israel with him vnto Libnah, and fought against Libnah.

30 And the Lord gaue it also and the King thereof into the hand of Israel: and he smote it with the edge of the sword, and all the soules that were therein: he let none remaine in it: for he did vnto the King thereof, as he had done vnto the King of Iericho.

31 And Ioshua departed from Libnah, and all Israel with him vnto Lachish, and besieged it, and assaulted it.

32 And the Lord gaue Lachish into the hand of Israel, which tooke it the second day, and smote it with the edge of the sword, and all the soules that were therein, according to all as he had done to Libnah.

33 Then Horam King of Gezer came vp to helpe Lachish: but Ioshua smote him and his people, vntill none of his remained.

34 And from Lachish Ioshua departed vnto Eglon, and all Israel with him, and they besieged it, and assaulted it,

35 And they tooke it the same day, and smote it with the edge of the sword, and all the soules that were therein he vtterly destroyed the same day, according to all that he had done to Lachish.

36 Then Ioshua went vp from Eglon, and all Israel with him vnto Hebron, and they fought against it.

37 And when they had taken it, they smote it with the edge of the sword, and the King thereof, and all the cities thereof, and all the soules that were therein: he left none remaining, according to all as he had done to Eglon: for he destroyed it vtterly, and all the soules that were therein.

38 So Ioshua returned, and all Israel with him to Debir, and fought against it.

39 And when he had taken it, and the King thereof, and all the citie thereof, they smote them with the edge of the sword, and vtterly destroyed all the soules that were therein, he let none remaine: as he did to Hebron, so he did to Debir, and to the King thereof, as he had also done to Libnah, and to the King thereof.

40 So Ioshua smote all the hill countreys, and the South countreys, and the valleys, and the hill sides, and all their Kings, and let none remaine, but vtterly destroyed euery soule, as the Lord God of Israel had commanded.

41 And Ioshua smote them from Kadesh-barnea euen vnto Azzah, and all the countrey of Goshen, euen vnto Gibeon.

42 And all these Kings, and their land did Ioshua take at one time, because the Lord God of Israel fought for Israel.

43 Afterward, Ioshua and all Israel with him returned vnto the campe in Gilgal.

Joshua 11

1 And whe Iabin King of Hazor had heard this, then he sent to Iobab King of Madon, and to the king of Shimron, and to the king of Achshaph,

2 And vnto the Kings that were by ye North in the mountaines and plaines toward the Southside of Cinneroth, and

in the valleys, and in the borders of Dor Westward,

3 And vnto the Canaanites, both by East, and by West, and vnto the Amorites, and Hittites, and Perizzites, and Iebusites in the mountaines, and vnto the Hiuites vnder Hermon in the land of Mizpeh.

4 And they came out and all their hostes with them, many people as the sande that is on the sea shore for multitude, with horses and charets exceeding many.

5 So all these Kings met together, and came and pitched together at the waters of Merom, for to fight against Israel.

6 Then the Lord sayd vnto Ioshua, Be not afrayd for them: for to morowe about this time will I deliuer them all slaine before Israel: thou shalt hough their horses, and burne their charets with fire.

7 Then came Ioshua and al the men of warre with him against them by the waters of Merom suddenly, and fell vpon them.

8 And the Lord gaue them into the hand of Israel: and they smote them, and chased them vnto great Zidon, and vnto Misrephothmaim, and vnto the valley of Mizpeh Eastward, and smote them vntill they had none remaining of them.

9 And Ioshua did vnto them as the Lord bade him: he houghed their horses, and burnt their charets with fire.

10 At that time also Ioshua turned backe, and tooke Hazor, and smote the King thereof with the sword: for Hazor before time was the head of all those kingdomes.

11 Moreouer, they smote all the persons that were therein with the edge of the sworde, vtterly destroying all, leauing none aliue, and hee burnt Hazor with fire.

12 So all ye cities of those Kings, and all the kings of them did Ioshua take, and smote them with the edge of the sword, and vtterly destroyed them, as Moses the seruant of the Lord had commanded.

13 But Israel burnt none of the cities that stoode still in their strength, saue Hazor onely, that Ioshua burnt.

14 And all the spoyle of these cities and the cattel the children of Israel tooke for their praye, but they smote euery man with the edge of the sword vntill they had destroyed them, not leauing one aliue.

15 As the Lord had commanded Moses his seruant, so did Moses commande Ioshua, and so did Ioshua: he left nothing vndone of all that the Lord had commanded Moses.

16 So Ioshua tooke all this land of the mountaines, and all the South, and all the lande of Goshen, and the lowe countrey, and the plaine, and the mountaine of Israel, and the lowe countrey of the same,

17 From the mount Halak, that goeth vp to Seir, euen vnto Baal-gad in the valley of Lebanon, vnder mount Hermon: and all their Kings he tooke, and smote them, and slewe them.

18 Ioshua made warre long time with all those Kings,

19 Neither was there any citie that made peace with the children of Israel, saue those Hiuites that inhabited Gibeon: all other they tooke by battell.

20 For it came of the Lord, to harden their heartes that they shoulde come against Israel in battell to the intent that they shoulde destroye them vtterly, and shewe them no mercie, but that they shoulde bring them to nought: as the Lord had commanded Moses.

21 And that same season came Ioshua, and destroyed the Anakims out of the mountaines: as out of Hebron, out of Debir, out of Anab, and out of all the mountaines of Iudah, and out of all the mountaines of Israel: Ioshua destroyed them vtterly with their cities.

22 There was no Anakim left in the lande of the children of Israel: onely in Azzah, in Gath, and in Ashdod were they left.

23 So Ioshua tooke the whole land, according to all that the Lord had saide vnto Moses: and Ioshua gaue it for an inheritance vnto Israel according to their portion through their tribes: then the land was at rest without warre.

Joshua 12

1 And these are the Kings of the land, which the children of Israel smote and possessed their land, on the other side Iorden toward the rising of the sunne, from the riuer Arnon, vnto mount Hermon, and all the plaine Eastward.

2 Sihon King of the Amorites, that dwelt in Heshbon, hauing dominion from Aroer, which is beside the riuer of Arnon, and from the middle of the riuer, and from halfe Gilead vnto the riuer Iabbok, in the border of the children of Ammon.

3 And from the plaine vnto the sea of Cinneroth Eastward, and vnto the Sea of the plaine, euen the salt sea Eastward, the way to Beth-ieshimoth, and from the South vnder the springs of Pisgah.

4 They conquered also the coast of Og King of Bashan of the remnant of the gyants, which dwelt at Ashtaroth, and at Edrei,

5 And reigned in mount Hermon, and in Salcah, and in all Bashan, vnto the border of the Geshurites, and the Maachathites, and halfe Gilead, euen the border of Sihon King of Heshbon.

6 Moses the seruant of the Lord, and the children of Israel smote them: Moses also the seruant of the Lord gaue their land for a possession vnto the Reubenites, and vnto the Gadites, and to halfe the tribe of Manasseh.

7 These also are the Kings of the countrey, which Ioshua and the children of Israel smote on this side Iorden, Westward, from Baal-gad in the valley of Lebanon, euen vnto the mount Halak that goeth vp to Seir, and Ioshua gaue it vnto the tribes of Israel for a possession, according to their portions:

8 In the mountaines, and in the valleys, and in the plaines, and in the hill sides, and in the wildernes, and in the South, where were the Hittites, the Amorites,

and the Canaanites, the Perizzites, the Hiuites, and the Iebusites.

9 The King of Iericho was one: the King of Ai, which is beside Beth-el, one:

10 The King of Ierusalem, one: the King of Hebron, one:

11 The King of Iarmuth, one: the King of Lachish, one:

12 The King of Eglon, one: the King of Gezer, one:

13 The King of Debir, one: the King of Geder, one:

14 The King of Hormah, one: the King of Arad, one:

15 The King of Libnah, one: the King of Adullam, one:

16 The King of Makkedah, one: the King of Beth-el, one:

17 The King of Tappuah, one: the King of Hepher, one:

18 The King of Aphek, one: the King of Lasharon, one:

19 The King of Madon, one: the King of Hazor, one:

20 The king of Shimron-meron, one: the King of Achshaph, one:

21 The King of Taanach, one: the King of Megiddo, one:

22 The King of Kedesh, one: the King of Iokneam of Carmel, one:

23 The King of Dor, in the countrey of Dor, one: the King of the nations of Gilgal, one:

24 The King of Tirzah, one. all the Kings were thirtie and one.

Joshua 13

1 Nowe when Ioshua was olde, and striken in yeeres, the Lord said vnto him, Thou art olde and growen in age, and there remaineth exceeding much land to be possessed:

2 This is the land that remaineth, all the regions of the Philistims, and all Geshuri,

3 From Nilus which is in Egypt, euen vnto the borders of Ekron Northward: this is counted of the Canaanites, euen fiue Lordships of the Philistims, the Azzithites, and the Ashdodites, the Eshkelonites, the Gittites, and the Ekronites, and the Auites:

4 From the South, all the land of the Canaanites, and the caue that is beside the Sidonians, vnto Aphek, and to the borders of the Amorites:

5 And the land of the Giblites, and all Lebanon, toward the sunne rising from Bahal-gad vnder mount Hermon, vntil one come to Hamath.

6 All the inhabitants of the mountaines from Lebanon vnto Misrephothmaim, and all the Sidonians, I wil cast them out from before the children of Israel: only deuide thou it by lot vnto the Israelites, to inherite, as I haue commanded thee.

7 Nowe therefore deuide this lande to inherite, vnto the nine tribes, and to the halfe tribe of Manasseh.

8 For with halfe therof the Reubenites and the Gadites haue receiued their inheritance, which Moses gaue them beyond Iorden Eastward, euen as Moses the seruant of the Lord had giuen them,

9 From Aroer that is on the brinke of the riuer Arnon, and from the citie that is in the mids of the riuer, and all the plaine of Medeba vnto Dibon,

10 And all the cities of Sihon King of the Amorites, which reigned in Heshbon, vnto the borders of the children of Ammon,

11 And Gilead, and the borders of the Geshurites and of the Maachathites, and all mount Hermon, with all Bashan vnto Salcah:

12 All the kingdome of Og in Bashan, which reigned in Ashtaroth and in Edrei: (who remained of the rest of the gyants) for these did Moses smite, and cast them out.

13 But the children of Israel expelled not the Geshurites nor the Maachathites: but the Geshurites and the Maachathites dwell among the Israelites euen vnto this day.

14 Onely vnto the tribe of Leui he gaue none inheritance, but the sacrifices of the Lord God of Israel are his inheritance, as he said vnto him.

15 Moses then gaue vnto the tribe of the children of Reuben inheritance, according to their families.

16 And their coast was from Aroer, that is on the brinke of the riuer Arnon, and from the citie that is in the middes of the riuer, and all the plaine which is by Medeba:

17 Heshbon with all the cities thereof, that are in the plaine: Dibon and Bamoth-baal, and Bethbaal-meon:

18 And Iahazah, and Kedemoth and Mephaath:

19 Kiriathaim also, and Sibmah, and Zerethshahar in the mount of Emek:

20 And Beth-peor, and Ashdoth-pisgah, and Beth-ieshimoth:

21 And all the cities of the plaine: and all the kingdome of Sihon King of the Amorites, which reigned in Heshbon, whome Moses smote with the Princes of Midian, Eui, and Rekem, and Zur, and Hur, and Reba, the dukes of Sihon, dwelling in the countrey.

22 And Balaam the sonne of Beor the soothsayer did the children of Israel slay with the sword, among them that were slaine.

23 And the border of the children of Reuben was Iorden with the coastes. This was the inheritance of the children of Reuben according to their families, with the cities and their villages.

24 Also Moses gaue inheritance vnto ye tribe of Gad, euen vnto the children of Gad according to their families.

25 And their coastes were Iazer, and all the cities of Gilead and halfe the lande of the children of Ammon vnto Aroer, which is before Rabbah:

26 And from Heshbon vnto Ramoth, Mizpeh, and Betonim: and from Mahanaim vnto the borders of Debir:

27 And in the valley Beth-aram, and Bethnimrah, and Succoth, and Zaphon, the rest of the kingdome of Sihon King of Heshbon, vnto Iorden and the borders euen vnto the Sea coast of Cinneereth, beyond Iorden Eastward.

28 This is the inheritance of the children of Gad, after their families, with the cities, and their villages.

29 Also Moses gaue inheritance vnto the halfe tribe of Manasseh: and this belonged to the halfe tribe of the children of Manasseh according to their families.

30 And their border was from Mahanaim, euen all Bashan, to wit, all the kingdome of Og King of Bashan, and all the townes of Iair which are in Bashan, threescore cities,

31 And halfe Gilead, and Ashtaroth, and Edrei, cities of the kingdom of Og in Bashan, were giuen vnto the children of Machir the sonne of Manasseh, to halfe of the children of Machir after their families.

32 These are the heritages, which Moses did distribute in the plaine of Moab beyond Iorden, toward Iericho Eastward.

33 But vnto the tribe of Leui Moses gaue none inheritance: for the Lord God of Israel is their inheritance, as he said vnto them.

Joshua 14

1 These also are the places which the children of Israel inherited in the land of Canaan, which Eleazar the Priest, and Ioshua the sonne of Nun and the chiefe fathers of the tribes of the children of Israel, distributed to them,

2 By the lot of their inheritance, as the Lord had commanded by the hande of Moses, to giue to the nine tribes, and the halfe tribe.

3 For Moses had giuen inheritance vnto two tribes and an halfe tribe, beyond Iorde: but vnto the Leuites he gaue none inheritance among them.

4 For the childre of Ioseph were two tribes, Manasseh and Ephraim: therefore they gaue no part vnto the Leuites in the lande, saue cities to dwell in, with the suburbes of the same for their beastes and their substance.

5 As the Lord had commanded Moses, so the children of Israel did when they deuided the land.

6 Then the children of Iudah came vnto Ioshua in Gilgal: and Caleb the sonne of Iephunneh the Kenezite saide vnto him, Thou knowest what the Lord saide vnto Moses the man of God, concerning me and thee in Kadesh-barnea.

7 Fourtie yeere olde was I, when Moses the seruant of the Lord sent me from Kadesh-barnea to espie the land, and I brought him word againe, as I thought in mine heart.

8 But my brethren that went vp with me, discouraged the heart of the people: yet I followed still the Lord my God.

9 Wherefore Moses sware the same day, saying, Certainely the land whereon thy feete haue troden, shalbe thine inheritance, and thy childrens for euer, because thou hast followed constantly the Lord my God.

10 Therefore beholde nowe, the Lord hath kept me aliue, as he promised: this is the fourtie and fift yeere since the Lord spake this thing vnto Moses, while the children of Israel wandred in the wildernes: and nowe loe, I am this day foure score and fiue yeere olde:

11 And yet am as strong at this time, as I was when Moses sent me: as strong as I was then, so strong am I nowe, either for warre, or for gouernment.

12 Nowe therefore giue me this mountaine whereof ye Lord spake in that day (for thou heardest in that day, how the Anakims were there, and the cities great and walled) if so be the Lord will be with me, that I may driue them out, as the Lord said.

13 Then Ioshua blessed him, and gaue vnto Caleb the sonne of Iephunneh, Hebron for an inheritance.

14 Hebron therefore became the inheritance of Caleb the sonne of Iephunneh the Kenezite, vnto this day: because he followed constantly the Lord God of Israel.

15 And the name of Hebron was before time, Kiriath-arba: which Arba was a great man amog the Anakims: thus the land ceassed from warre.

Joshua 15

1 This then was the lot of the tribe of the children of Iudah by their families: euen to the border of Edom and the wildernesse of Zin, Southward on the Southcoast.

2 And their South border was the salt Sea coast, from the point that looketh Southward.

3 And it went out on the Southside towarde Maaleth-akrabbim, and went along to Zin, and ascended vp on the Southside vnto Kadesh-barnea, and went along to Hezron, and went vp to Adar, and fet a compasse to Karkaa.

4 From thence went it along to Azmon, and reached vnto the riuer of Egypt, and the end of that coast was on the Westside: this shall be your South coast.

5 Also the Eastborder shalbe the salt Sea, vnto the end of Iorden: and the border on the North quarter from the point of the Sea, and from the end of Iorden.

6 And this border goeth vp to Beth-hogla, and goeth along by ye Northside of Beth-arabah: so the border from thence goeth vp to the stone of Bohan the sonne of Reuben.

7 Againe this border goeth vp to Debir from the valley of Achor, and Northwarde, turning toward Gilgal, that lyeth before the going vp to Adummim, which is on the Southside of the riuer: also this border goeth vp to the waters of En-shemesh, and endeth at En-rogel.

8 Then this border goeth vp to the valley of the sonne of Hinnom; on the Southside of the Iebusites: the same is Ierusalem. also this border goeth vp to the top of the mountaine that lyeth before the valley of Hinnom Westward, which is by the end of the valley of ye gyants Northward.

9 So this border compasseth from the top of the mountaine vnto the fountaine of the water of Nephtoah, and goeth out

to the cities of mount Ephron: and this border draweth to Baalah, which is Kiriath-iearim.

10 Then this border compasseth from Baalah Westward vnto mount Seir, and goeth along vnto the side of mount Iearim, which is Chesalon on the Northside: so it commeth downe to Bethshemesh, and goeth to Timnah.

11 Also this border goeth out vnto the side of Ekron Northwarde: and this border draweth to Shicron, and goeth along to mount Baalah, and stretcheth vnto Iabneel: and the endes of this coast are to the Sea.

12 And the Westborder is to the great Sea: so this border shalbe the bounds of the children of Iudah round about, according to their families.

13 And vnto Caleb the sonne of Iephunneh did Ioshua giue a part among the children of Iudah, as the Lord commanded him, euen Kiriath-arba of the father of Anak, which is Hebron.

14 And Caleb droue thence three sonnes of Anak, Sheshai, and Ahiman, and Talmai, the sonnes of Anak.

15 And he went vp thence to the inhabitants of Debir: and the name of Debir before time was Kiriath-sepher.

16 Then Caleb sayd, He that smiteth Kiriath-sepher, and taketh it, euen to him wil I giue Achsah my daughter to wife.

17 And Othniel, the sonne of Kenaz, the brother of Caleb tooke it: and he gaue him Achsah his daughter to wife.

18 And as she went in to him, she moued him, to aske of her father a fielde: and she lighted off her asse, and Caleb sayd vnto her, What wilt thou?

19 Then she answered, Giue me a blessing: for thou hast giuen mee the South countrey: giue me also springs of water. And hee gaue her the springs aboue and the springs beneath.

20 This shalbe the inheritance of the tribe of the children of Iudah according to their families.

21 And the vtmost cities of the tribe of the children of Iudah, toward the coastes of Edom Southward were Kabzeel, and Eder, and Iagur,

22 And Kinah, and Dimonah, and Adadah,

23 And Kedesh, and Hazor, and Ithnan,

24 Ziph, and Telem, and Bealoth,

25 And Hazor, Hadattah, and Kerioth, Hesron (which is Hazor)

26 Amam, and Shema, and Moladah,

27 And Hazar, Gaddah, and Heshmon, and Beth-palet,

28 And Hasar-shual, and Beersheba, and Biziothiah,

29 Baalah, and Iim, and Azem,

30 And Eltolad, and Chesil, and Hormah,

31 And Ziklag, and Madmanna, and Sansannah,

32 And Lebaoth, and Shilhim, and Ain, and Rimmon: all these cities are twentie and nine with their villages.

33 In the lowe countrey were Eshtaol, and Zoreah, and Ashnah,

34 And Zanoah, and En-gannim, Tappuah, and Enam,

35 Iarmuth, and Adullam, Socoh, and Azekah,

36 And Sharaim, and Adithaim, and Gederah, and Gederothaim: fourteene cities with their villages.

37 Zenam, and Hadashah, and Migdal-gad,

38 And Dileam, and Mizpeh, and Ioktheel,

39 Lachish, and Bozkath, and Eglon,

40 And Cabbon, and Lahmam, and Kithlish,

41 And Gederoth, Beth-dagon, and Naamah, and Makkedah: sixteene cities with their villages.

42 Lebnah, and Ether, and Ashan,

43 And Iipthtah, and Ashnah, and Nezib,

44 And Keilah, and Aczib, and Mareshah: nine cities with their villages.

45 Ekron with her townes and her villages,

46 From Ekron, euen vnto the Sea, all that lyeth about Ashdod with their villages.

47 Ashdod with her townes and her villages: Azzah with her townes and her villages, vnto the riuer of Egypt, and the great Sea was their coast.

48 And in the mountaines were Shamir, and Iattir, and Socoh,

49 And Dannah, and Kiriath-sannath (which is Debir)

50 And Anab, and Ashtemoth, and Anim,

51 And Goshen, and Holon, and Giloh: eleuen cities with their villages,

52 Arab, and Dumah, and Eshean,

53 And Ianum, and Beth-tappuah, and Aphekah,

54 And Humtah, and Kiriath-arba, (which is Hebron) and Zior: nine cities with their villages.

55 Maon, Carmel, and Ziph, and Iuttah,

56 And Izreel, and Iokdeam, and Zanoah,

57 Kain, Gibeah, and Timnah: ten cities with their villages.

58 Halhul, Beth-zur, and Gedor,

59 And Maarah, and Beth-anoth, and Eltekon: sixe cities with their villages.

60 Kiriath-baal, which is Kiriath-iearim, and Rabbah: two cities with their villages.

61 In the wildernes were Beth-arabah, Middin, and Secacah,

62 And Nibshan, and the citie of salt, and Engedi: sixe cities with their villages.

63 Neuerthelesse, the Iebusites that were the inhabitants of Ierusalem, could not the children of Iudah cast out, but the Iebusites dwell with the children of Iudah at Ierusalem vnto this day.

Joshua 16

1 And the lot fell to the children of Ioseph from Iorden by Iericho vnto the water of Iericho Eastward, and to the wildernes that goeth vp from Iericho by the mount Beth-el:

2 And goeth out from Beth-el to Luz, and runneth along vnto the borders of Archiataroth,

3 And goeth down Westward to the coast of Iaphleti, vnto the coast of Beth-horon the nether, and to Gezer: and the endes thereof are at the Sea.

4 So the children of Ioseph, Manasseh and Ephraim tooke their inheritance.

5 Also the borders of the children of Ephraim according to their families, euen the borders of their inheritance on the Eastside were Atroth-addar, vnto Beth-horon the vpper.

6 And this border goeth out to the Sea vnto Michmethah on the Northside, and this border returneth Eastward vnto Taanathshiloh, and passeth it on the Eastside vnto Ianohah,

7 And goeth downe from Ianohah to Ataroth, and Naarath, and commeth to Iericho, and goeth out at Iorden.

8 And this border goeth from Tappuah Westward vnto the riuer Kanah, and the endes thereof are at the Sea: this is the inheritance of the tribe of the children of Ephraim by their families.

9 And the separate cities for the children of Ephraim were among the inheritance of the children of Manasseh: all the cities with their villages.

10 And they cast not out the Canaanite that dwelt in Gezer, but the Canaanite dwelt among the Ephraimites vnto this day, and serued vnder tribute.

Joshua 17

1 This was also the lot of the tribe of Manasseh: for he was the first borne of Ioseph, to wit, of Machir the first borne of Manasseh, and the father of Gilead: nowe because he was a man of warre, he had Gilead and Bashan.

2 And also of the rest of the sonnes of Manasseh by their families, euen of the sonnes of Abiezer, and of the sonnes of Helek, and of ye sonnes of Azriel, and of the sonnes of Shechem, and of the sonnes of Hepher, and of the sonnes of Shemida: these were the males of Manasseh, the sonne of Ioseph according to their families.

3 But Zelophehad the sonne of Hephir, the sonne of Gilead, the sonne of Machir, ye sonne of Manasseh, had no sonnes, but daughters: and these are the names of his daughters, Mahlah, and Noah, Hoglah, Milcah and Tirzah:

4 Which came before Eleazar the Priest, and before Ioshua the sonne of Nun, and before the princes, saying, The Lord commanded Moses to giue vs an inheritance among our brethren: therefore according to the commandement of the Lord he gaue them an inheritance among the brethren of their father.

5 And there fell ten portions to Manasseh, beside the land of Gilead and Bashan, which is on the other side Iorden,

6 Because the daughters of Manasseh did inherite among his sonnes: and

Manassehs other sonnes had the land of Gilead.

7 So the borders of Manasseh were from Asher to Michmethah that lieth before Shechem, and this border goeth on the right hand, euen vnto the inhabitants of En-tappuah.

8 The land of Tappuah belonged to Manasseh, but Tappuah beside the border of Manasseh belongeth to the sonnes of Ephraim.

9 Also this border goeth downe vnto the riuer Kanah Southward to the riuer: these cities of Ephraim are among the cities of Manasseh: and the border of Manasseh is on the Northside of the riuer, and the endes of it are at the Sea,

10 The South perteyneth to Ephraim, and the North to Manasseh, and the Sea is his border: and they met together in Asher Northwarde, and in Issachar Eastward.

11 And Manasseh had in Issachar and in Asher, Beth-shean, and her townes, and Ibleam, and her townes, and the inhabitants of Dor with ye townes thereof, and the inhabitants of En-dor with the townes thereof, and the inhabitants of Thaanach with her townes, and the inhabitants of Megiddo with the townes of the same, euen three countreis.

12 Yet the children of Manasseh coulde not destroy those cities, but the Canaanites dwelled still in that land.

13 Neuerthelesse, when the children of Israel were strong, they put the Canaanites vnder tribute, but cast them not out wholy.

14 Then the children of Ioseph spake vnto Ioshua, saying, Why hast thou giuen me but one lot, and one portion to inherite, seeing I am a great people, for as much as the Lord hath blessed me hitherto?

15 Ioshua then answered them, If thou be much people, get thee vp to the wood, and cut trees for thy selfe there in the lande of the Perizzites, and of the gyants, if mount Ephraim be too narowe for thee.

16 Then the children of Ioseph saide, The mountaine will not be ynough for vs: and all the Canaanites that dwell in the lowe countrey haue charets of yron, aswell they in Beth-shean, and in the townes of the same, as they in the valley of Izreel.

17 And Ioshua spake vnto the house of Ioseph, to Ephraim, and to Manasseh, saying, Thou art a great people, and hast great power, and shalt not haue one lot.

18 Therefore the mountaine shall be thine: for it is a wood, and thou shalt cut it downe: and the endes of it shall be thine, and thou shalt cast out the Canaanites, though they haue yron charets, and though they be strong.

Joshua 18

1 And the whole Congregation of the children of Israel, came together at Shiloh: for they set vp the Tabernacle of the Congregation there, after the land was subiect vnto them.

2 Nowe there remained among the children of Israel seuen tribes, to whom they had not deuided their inheritance.

3 Therefore Ioshua said vnto the children of Israel, Howe long are ye so slacke to enter and possesse the land which the Lord God of your fathers hath giuen you?

4 Giue from among you for euery tribe three men, that I may sende them, and that they may rise, and walke through the land, and distribute it according to their inheritance, and returne to me.

5 And that they may deuide it vnto them into seuen parts, (Iudah shall abide in his coast at the South, and the house of Ioseph shall stand in their coastes at the North)

6 Ye shall describe the land therefore into seuen partes, and shall bring them hither to me, and I will cast lottes for you here before the Lord our God.

7 But the Leuites shall haue no part among you: for the Priesthood of the Lord is their inheritance: also Gad and Reuben and halfe the tribe of Manasseh haue receiued their inheritance beyond Iorden Eastward, which Moses the seruant of the Lord gaue them.

8 Then the men arose, and went their way: and Ioshua charged them that went to describe the land, saying, Depart, and goe through the land, and describe it, and returne to me, that I may here cast lottes for you before the Lord in Shiloh.

9 So the men departed, and passed through the lande, and described it by cities into seuen partes in a booke, and returned to Ioshua into the campe at Shiloh.

10 Then Ioshua cast lottes for them in Shiloh before the Lord, and there Ioshua deuided the land vnto the children of Israel, according to their portions:

11 And the lot of the tribe of the children of Beniamin came foorth according to their families, and the cost of their lot lay betweene the children of Iudah, and the children of Ioseph.

12 And their coast on the Northside was from Iorden, and the border went vp to the side of Iericho on the Northpart, and went vp through the mountaines Westward, and the endes thereof are in the wildernesse of Beth-auen:

13 And this border goeth along from thence to Luz, euen to the Southside of Luz (the same is Beth-el) and this border descendeth to Atroth-addar, neere the mount, that lyeth on the Southside of Beth-horon the nether.

14 So the border turneth, and compasseth the corner of the Sea Southward, from the mount that lyeth before Beth-horon Southward: and the endes thereof are at Kiriath-baal (which is Kiriath-iearim) a citie of the children of Iudah: this is the Westquarter.

15 And the Southquarter is from the ende of Kiriath-iearim, and this border goeth out Westward, and commeth to the fountaine of waters of Nephtoah.

16 And this border descendeth at the ende of the mountaine, that lyeth before the valley of Ben-hinnom, which is in the valley of the gyants Northward, and descendeth into the valley of Hinnom by the side of Iebusi Southwarde, and goeth downe to En-rogel,

17 And compasseth from the North, and goeth foorth to En-shemesh, and stretcheth to Geliloth, which is toward the going vp vnto Adummim, and goeth downe to the stone of Bohan the sonne of Reuben.

18 So it goeth along to the side ouer against the plaine Northward, and goeth downe into the plaine.

19 After, this border goeth along to the side of Beth-hoglah Northward: and the endes thereof, that is, of the border, reach to the point of the salt Sea Northward, and to the ende of Iorden Southward: this is the Southcoast.

20 Also Iorden is the border of it on the Eastside: this is the inheritance of the children of Beniamin by the coastes thereof rounde about according to their families.

21 Nowe the cities of the tribe of the children of Beniamin according to their families, are Iericho, and Beth-hoglah, and the valley of Keziz,

22 And Beth-arabah, and Zemaraim, and Beth-el,

23 And Auim, and Parah, and Ophrah,

24 And Chephar, Ammonai, and Ophni, and Gaba: twelue cities with their villages.

25 Gibeon, and Ramah, and Beeroth,

26 And Mizpeh, and Chephirah, and Mozah,

27 And Rekem, and Irpeel, and Taralah,

28 And Zela, Eleph, and Iebusi, (which is Ierusalem) Gibeath, and Kiriath: fourteene cities with their villages: this is the inheritance of the children of Beniamin according to their families.

Joshua 19

1 And the second lot came out to Simeon, euen for the tribe of the children of Simeon according to their families: and their inheritance was in the middes of the inheritance of the children of Iudah.

2 Nowe they had in their inheritance, Beersheba, and Sheba, and Moladah,

3 And Hazur-shual, and Balah, and Azem,

4 And Eltolad, and Bethul, and Hormah,

5 And Ziklag, and Beth-marcaboth, and Hazar-susah,

6 And Beth-lebaoth, and Sharuhen: thirteene cities with their villages.

7 Ain, Remmon, and Ether, and Ashan: foure cities with their villages.

8 And all the villages that were round about these cities, vnto Baalathbeer, and Ramath Southward: this is the inheritance of the tribe of the children of Simeon according to their families.

9 Out of the portion of the children of Iudah came ye inheritance of the childre of Simeon: for the part of ye children of Iudah was too much for them: therefore the children of Simeon had their inheritance within their inheritance.

10 Also the third lot arose for the children of Zebulun according to their families: and the coastes of their inheritance came to Sarid,

11 And their border goeth vp Westwarde, euen to Maralah, and reacheth to Dabbasheth, and meeteth with the riuer that lyeth before Iokneam,

12 And turneth from Sarid Eastward towarde the sunne rising vnto the border of Chisloth-tabor, and goeth out to Daberath, and ascendeth to Iaphia,

13 And from thence goeth along Eastwarde towarde the sunne rising to Gittah-hepher to Ittah-kazin, and goeth foorth to Rimmon, and turneth to Neah.

14 And this border compasseth it on ye North side to Hannathon, and the endes thereof are in the valley of Iiphtah-el,

15 And Kattath, and Nahallal, and Shimron, and Idalah, and Beth-lehem: twelue cities with their villages.

16 This is the inheritance of the children of Zebulun according to their families: that is, these cities and their villages.

17 The fourth lot came out to Issachar, euen for the children of Issachar according to their families.

18 And their coast was Izreelah, and Chesulloth, and Shunem,

19 And Hapharaim, and Shion, and Anaharath,

20 And Harabbith, and Kishion, and Abez,

21 And Remeth, and En-gannim, and Enhaddah, and Beth-pazzez.

22 And this coast reacheth to Tabor, and Shahazimath, and Beth-shemesh, and the endes of their coast reach to Iorden: sixteene cities with their villages.

23 This is the inheritance of the tribe of the children of Issachar according to their families: that is, the cities, and their villages.

24 Also the fift lot came out for the tribe of the children of Asher according to their families.

25 And their coast was Helcath, and Hali, and Beten, and Achshaph,

26 And Alammelech, and Amad, and Misheal, and came to Carmel Westward, and to Shihor Libnath,

27 And turneth towarde the sunne rising to Beth-dagon, and commeth to Zebulun, and to the valley of Iiphtah-el, toward the Northside of Beth-emek, and Neiel, and goeth out on the left side of Cabul,

28 And to Ebron, and Rehob, and Hammon, and Kanah, vnto great Zidon.

29 Then the coast turneth to Ramah and to the strong citie of Zor, and this border turneth to Hosah, and the ends thereof are at the Sea from Hebel to Achzib,

30 Vmmah also and Aphek, and Rehob: two and twentie cities with their villages.

31 This is the inheritance of the tribe of the children of Asher according to their families: that is, these cities and their villages.

32 The sixt lot came out to the children of Naphtali, euen to the children of Naphtali according to their families.

33 And their coast was from Heleph, and from Allon in Zaanannim, and Adaminekeb, and Iabneel, euen to Lakum, and the ends thereof are at Iorden.

34 So this coast turneth Westwarde to Aznoth-tabor, and goeth out from thence to Hukkok, and reacheth to Zebulun on the Southside, and goeth to Asher on the Westside, and to Iudah by Iorden toward the sunne rising.

35 And the strong cities are Ziddim, Zer, and Hammath, Rakkath, and Cinneereth,

36 And Adamah, and Ramah, and Hazor,

37 And Kedesh, and Edrei, and En-hazor,

38 And Iron, and Migdal-el, Horem, and Beth-anah, and Beth-shemesh: nineteene cities with their villages.

39 This is the inheritance of the tribe of the children of Naphtali according to their families: that is, the cities and their villages.

40 The seuenth lot came out for the tribe of the children of Dan according to their families.

41 And the coast of their inheritance was Zorah, and Eshtaol, and Ir-shemesh,

42 And Shaalabbin, and Aiialon, and Ithlah,

43 And Elon, and Temnathah, and Ekron,

44 And Eltekeh, and Gibbethon, and Baalah,

45 And Iehud, and Bene-berak, and Gath-rimmon,

46 And Me-iarkon, and Rakkon, with the border that lieth before Iapho.

47 But the coastes of the children of Dan fell out too litle for them: therefore the children of Dan went vp to fight against Leshem, and tooke it, and smote it with the edge of the sworde, and possessed it, and dwelt therein, and called Leshem, Dan after the name of Dan their father.

48 This is the inheritance of the tribe of the childre of Dan according to their families: that is, these cities and their villages.

49 When they had made an ende of deuiding the lande by the coastes thereof, then the children of Israel gaue an inheritance vnto Ioshua the sonne of Nun among them.

50 According to the worde of the Lord they gaue him the citie which hee asked, euen Timnath-serah in mount Ephraim: and hee built the citie and dwelt therein.

51 These are ye heritages which Eleazar the Priest, and Ioshua the sonne of Nun, and the chiefe fathers of the tribes of the children of Israel deuided by lot in Shiloh before the Lord at the doore of the Tabernacle of the Congregation: so they made an ende of deuiding the countrey.

Joshua 20

1 The Lord also spake vnto Ioshua, saying,

2 Speake to the children of Israel, and say, Appoint you cities of refuge, whereof I spake vnto you by the hand of Moses,

3 That the slaier that killeth any person by ignorance, and vnwittingly, may flee thither, and they shall be your refuge from the auenger of blood.

4 And he that doeth flee vnto one of those cities, shall stand at the entring of the gate of the citie, and shall shewe his cause to the Elders of the citie: and they shall receiue him into the citie vnto them, and giue him a place, that hee may dwell with them.

5 And if the auenger of blood pursue after him, they shall not deliuer the slaier into his hand because hee smote his neighbour ignorantly, neither hated he him before time:

6 But hee shall dwell in that citie vntill hee stande before the Congregation in iudgement, or vntill the death of the hie Priest that shall be in those daies: then shall the slaier returne, and come vnto his owne citie, and vnto his owne house, euen vnto the citie from whence he fled.

7 Then they appointed Kedesh in Galil in mount Naphtali, and Shechem in mount Ephraim, and Kiriath-arba, (which is Hebron) in the mountaine of Iudah.

8 And on the other side Iorden toward Iericho Eastward, they appoynted Bezer in the wildernesse vpon the plaine, out of the tribe of Reuben, and Ramoth in Gilead, out of the tribe of Gad, and Golan in Bashan, out of the tribe of Manasseh.

9 These were the cities appoynted for all the children of Israel, and for the stranger that soiourned among them, that whosoeuer killed any person ignorantly, might flee thither, and not die by the hande of the auenger of blood, vntill hee stoode before the Congregation.

Joshua 21

1 Then came the principall fathers of the Leuites vnto Eleazar the Priest, and vnto Ioshua the sonne of Nun, and vnto the chiefe fathers of the tribes of the children of Israel,

2 And spake vnto them at Shiloh in the land of Canaan, saying, The Lord commanded by the hande of Moses, to giue vs cities to dwell in, with the suburbes thereof for our cattell.

3 So the children of Israel gaue vnto the Leuites, out of their inheritance at the commandement of the Lord these cities with their suburbes.

4 And the lot came out for the families of the Kohathites: and the children of Aaron ye Priest, which were of the Leuites, had by lot, out of the tribe of Iudah, and out of the tribe of Simeon, and out of the tribe of Beniamin thirteene cities.

5 And the rest of the children of Kohath had by lot out of the families of the tribe of Ephraim, and out of the tribe of Dan, and out of the halfe tribe of Manasseh, tenne cities.

6 Also the children of Gershon had by lot out of the families of the tribe of Issachar, and out of the tribe of Asher, and out of ye tribe of Naphtali, and out of the halfe tribe of Manasseh in Bashan, thirteene cities.

7 The children of Merari according to their families had out of the tribe of Reuben, and out of the tribe of Gad, and out of the tribe of Zebulun, twelue cities.

8 So the children of Israel gaue by lot vnto the Leuites these cities with their suburbes, as the Lord had commanded by the hand of Moses.

9 And they gaue out of the tribe of the children of Iudah, and out of the tribe of the children of Simeo, these cities which are here named.

10 And they were the childrens of Aaron being of the families of the Kohathites, and of the sonnes of Leui, (for theirs was the first lot)

11 So they gaue them Kiriath-arba of the father of Anok (which is Hebron) in the mountaine of Iudah, with the suburbes of the same round about it.

12 (But the lande of the citie, and the villages thereof, gaue they to Caleb the sonne of Iephunneh to be his possession)

13 Thus they gaue to the children of Aaron the Priest, a citie of refuge for the slaier, euen Hebron with her suburbes, and Libnah with her suburbes,

14 And Iattir with her suburbes, and Eshtemoa, and her suburbes,

15 And Holon with her suburbes, and Debir with her suburbes,

16 And Ain with her suburbes, and Iuttah with her suburbes, Beth-shemesh with her suburbes: nine cities out of those two tribes.

17 And out of the tribe of Beniamin they gaue Gibeon with her suburbes, Geba with her suburbes,

18 Anathoth with her suburbes, and Almon with her suburbes: foure cities.

19 All the cities of the children of Aaron Priests, were thirteene cities with their suburbes.

20 But to the families of the children of Kohath of the Leuites, which were the rest of the children of Kohath (for the cities of their lot were out of the tribe of Ephraim)

21 They gaue them the citie of refuge for the slaier, Shechem with her suburbes in mount Ephraim, and Gezer with her suburbes,

22 And Kibzaim with her suburbs, and Bethhoron with her suburbes: foure cities.

23 And out of the tribe of Dan, Eltekeh with her suburbes, Gibethon with her suburbes,

24 Aiialon with her suburbes, Gath-rimmon with her suburbes: foure cities.

25 And out of the halfe tribe of Manasseh, Tanach with her suburbes, and Gath-rimmon with her suburbes: two cities.

26 All the cities for the other families of the children of Kohath were ten with their suburbes.

27 Also vnto the children of Gershon of the families of the Leuites, they gaue out of the halfe tribe of Manasseh, the citie of refuge for the slaier, Golan in Bashan with her suburbes, and Beeshterah with her suburbes: two cities.

28 And out of the tribe of Issachar, Kishon with her suburbes, Dabereh with her suburbes,

29 Iarmuth with her suburbes, En-gannim with her suburbes: foure cities.

30 And out of the tribe of Asher, Mishal with her suburbes, Abdon with her suburbes,

31 Helkah with her suburbs, and Rehob with her suburbes: foure cities.

32 And out of the tribe of Naphtali, the citie of refuge for the slaier, Kedesh in Galil with her suburbes, and Hammoth-dor with her suburbes, and Kartan with her suburbes: three cities.

33 Al the cities of the Gershonites according to their families, were thirteene cities with their suburbes.

34 Also vnto the families of the children of Merari the rest of the Leuites, they gaue out of the tribe of Zebulun, Iokneam with her suburbs, and Kartah with her suburbes,

35 Dimnah with her suburbes, Nahalal, with her suburbes: foure cities.

36 And out of the tribe of Reuben, Bezer with her suburbs, and Iahazah with her suburbs,

37 Kedemoth with her suburbes, and Mephaath with her suburbes: foure cities.

38 And out of the tribe of Gad they gaue for a citie of refuge for the slaier, Ramoth in Gilead with her suburbes, and Mahanaim with her suburbes,

39 Heshbon with her suburbs, and Iazer with her suburbes: foure cities in all.

40 So all the cities of the children of Merari according to their families (which were the rest of the families of the Leuites) were by their lot, twelue cities.

41 And all the cities of the Leuites within the possession of the children of Israel, were eight and fourtie with their suburbes.

42 These cities lay euery one seuerallie with their suburbes round about them: so were all these cities.

43 So the Lord gaue vnto Israel all ye land, which hee had sworne to giue vnto their fathers: and they possessed it, and dwelt therein.

44 Also the Lord gaue them rest rounde about according to all that hee had sworne vnto their fathers: and there stoode not a man of all their enemies before them: for the Lord deliuered all their enemies into their hand.

45 There failed nothing of all the good things, which the Lord hath sayde vnto the house of Israel, but all came to passe.

Joshua 22

1 Then Ioshua called the Reubenites, and the Gadites, and the halfe tribe of Manasseh,

2 And sayd vnto them, Ye haue kept all that Moses the seruaunt of the Lord commanded you, and haue obeied my voice in all that I commanded you:

3 You haue not forsaken your brethren this long season vnto this day, but haue diligently kept the commandement of the Lord your God.

4 And nowe the Lord hath giuen rest vnto your brethren as he promised them: therefore nowe returne ye and goe to your tentes, to the land of your possession, which Moses the seruant of the Lord hath giuen you beyond Iorden.

5 But take diligent heede, to doe the commandement and Lawe, which Moses the seruant of the Lord commanded you: that is, that ye loue the Lord your God, and walke in all his wayes, and keepe his commandements, and cleaue vnto him, and serue him with all your heart and with all your soule.

6 So Ioshua blessed them and sent them away, and they went vnto their tents.

7 Nowe vnto one halfe of the tribe of Manasseh Moses had giuen a possession in Bashan: and vnto the other halfe thereof gaue Ioshua among their brethren on this side Iorden Westwarde: therefore when Ioshua sent them away vnto their tents, and blessed them,

8 Thus he spake vnto them, saying, Returne with much riches vnto your tents, and with a great multitude of cattell, with siluer and with golde, with brasse and with yron, and with great abundance of rayment: deuide the spoyle of your enemies with your brethren.

9 So the children of Reuben, and the children of Gad, and halfe the tribe of Manasseh returned, and departed from the children of Israel from Shiloh (which is in the land of Canaan) to goe vnto the countrey of Gilead to the land of their possession, which they had obteyned, according to ye word of the Lord by the hand of Moses.

10 And when they came vnto the borders of Iorden (which are in the land of Canaan) then the children of Reuben, and the children of Gad, and the halfe tribe of Manasseh, built there an altar by Iorden, a great altar to see to.

11 When the children of Israel heard say, Beholde, the children of Reuben, and the children of Gad, and the halfe tribe of Manasseh haue built an altar in the forefront of the lande of Canaan vpon the borders of Iorden at the passage of the children of Israel:

12 When the children of Israel heard it, then the whole Congregation of the children of Israel gathered them together at Shiloh to goe vp to warre against them.

13 Then the children of Israel sent vnto the children of Reuben, and to the children of Gad, and to ye halfe tribe of Manasseh into the land of Gilead, Phinehas the sonne of Eleazar the Priest,

14 And with him ten princes, of euery chiefe house a prince, according to all the tribes of Israel: for euery one was chiefe of their fathers housholde among the thousands of Israel.

15 So they went vnto the children of Reuben, and to the children of Gad, and to the halfe tribe of Manasseh, vnto the land of Gilead, and spake with them, saying,

16 Thus saith the whole congregation of the Lord, What transgression is this that ye haue transgressed against the God of Israel, to turne away this day from the Lord, in that ye haue built you an altar for to rebell this day against the Lord?

17 Haue we too litle for the wickednesse of Peor, whereof we are not clensed vnto this day, though a plague came vpon the Congregation of the Lord?

18 Ye also are turned away this day from the Lord: and seeing ye rebell to day against ye Lord, euen to morowe he will be wroth with all the Congregation of Israel.

19 Notwithstanding if the land of your possession be vncleane, come ye ouer vnto the land of the possession of the Lord, wherein the Lordes Tabernacle dwelleth, and take possession among vs: but rebell not against the Lord, nor rebell not against vs in building you an altar, beside the altar of the Lord our God.

20 Did not Achan ye sonne of Zerah trespasse grieuously in the execrable thing, and wrath fell on all the Congregation of Israel? and this man alone perished not in his wickednesse.

21 Then the children of Reuben and the children of Gad, and halfe the tribe of Manasseh answered, and saide vnto the heads ouer the thousands of Israel,

22 The Lord God of gods, the Lord God of gods, he knoweth, and Israel himselfe shall know: if by rebellion, or by transgression against ye Lord we haue done it, saue thou vs not this day.

23 If we haue built vs an altar to returne away from the Lord, either to offer thereon burnt offering, or meate offering, or to offer peace offerings thereon, let the Lord himselfe require it:

24 And if we haue not rather done it for feare of this thing, saying, In time to come your children might say vnto our children, What haue ye to doe with the Lord God of Israel?

25 For the Lord hath made Iorden a border betweene vs and you, ye children of Reuben, and of Gad: therefore ye haue no part in the Lord: so shall your children make our children cease from fearing the Lord.

26 Therefore we said, We will nowe go about to make vs an altar, not for burnt offering, nor for sacrifice,

27 But it shall be a witnesse betweene vs and you, and betweene our generations after vs, to execute the seruice of the Lord before him in our burnt offerings, and in our sacrifices, and in our peace offerings, and that your children should not say to our children in time to come, Ye haue no part in the Lord.

28 Therefore said we, If so be that they should so say to vs or to our generations in time to come, then will we answere, Beholde the facion of the altar of the Lord, which our fathers made, not for burnt offering nor for sacrifice, but it is a witnesse betweene vs and you.

29 God forbid, that we should rebell against the Lord, and turne this day away from the Lord to builde an altar for burnt offering, or for meate offering, or for sacrifice, saue the altar of the Lord our God, that is before his Tabernacle.

30 And when Phinehas the Priest, and the princes of the Congregation and heads ouer the thousands of Israel which were with him, heard the wordes, that the children of Reuben, and children of Gad, and the children of Manasseh spake, they were well content.

31 And Phinehas the sonne of Eleazar the Priest said vnto the children of Reuben and to the children of Gad, and to the children of Manasseh, This day we perceiue, that the Lord is among vs, because ye haue not done this trespasse against the Lord: nowe ye haue deliuered the children of Israel out of the hand of the Lord.

32 Then Phinehas the sonne of Eleazar the Priest with the princes returned from the children of Reuben, and from the children of Gad, out of the land of Gilead, vnto the land of Canaan, to the children of Israel, and brought them answere.

33 And the saying pleased the children of Israel: and the children of Israel blessed God, and minded not to goe against them in battell, for to destroy the land, wherein the children of Reuben, and Gad dwelt.

34 Then the children of Reuben, and the children of Gad called the altar Ed: for it shall be a witnesse betweene vs, that the Lord is God.

Joshua 23

1 And a long season after that the Lord had giuen rest vnto Israel from all their enemies round about, and Ioshua was olde, and stricken in age,

2 Then Ioshua called all Israel, and their Elders, and their heads, and their iudges, and their officers, and said vnto them, I am old, and stricken in age.

3 Also ye haue seene all that the Lord your God hath done vnto al these nations before you, howe the Lord your God him selfe hath fought for you.

4 Beholde, I haue deuided vnto you by lot these nations that remaine, to be an inheritance according to your tribes, from Iorden, with all the nations that I haue destroyed, euen vnto the great Sea Westward.

5 And the Lord your God shall expell them before you, and cast them out of your sight, and ye shall possesse their land, as the Lord your God hath said vnto you.

6 Be ye therefore of a valiant courage, to obserue and doe all that is written in the booke of the Lawe of Moses, that ye turne not therefrom to the right hand nor to the left,

7 Neither companie with these nations: that is, with them which are left with you, neither make mention of the name of their gods, nor cause to sweare by them, neither serue them nor bowe vnto them:

8 But sticke fast vnto the Lord your God, as ye haue done vnto this day.

9 For ye Lord hath cast out before you great nations and mightie, and no man hath stand before your face hitherto.

10 One man of you shall chase a thousand: for the Lord your God, he fighteth for you, as he hath promised you.

11 Take good heede therefore vnto your selues, that ye loue the Lord your God.

12 Els, if ye goe backe, and cleaue vnto the rest of these nations: that is, of them that remaine with you, and shall make marriages with them, and goe vnto them, and they to you,

13 Knowe ye for certaine, that the Lord your God will cast out no more of these nations from before you: but they shall be a snare and destruction vnto you, and a whip on your sides, and thornes in your eyes, vntill ye perish out of this good land, which ye Lord your God hath giue you.

14 And beholde, this day do I enter into the way of all ye world, and ye know in al your heartes and in all your soules, that nothing hath failed of all the good things which the Lord your God promised you, but all are come to passe vnto you: nothing hath failed thereof.

15 Therefore as all good things are come vpon you, which the Lord your God promised you, so shall the Lord bring vpon you euery euill thing, vntill he haue destroyed you out of this good land, which ye Lord your God hath giue you.

16 When ye shall transgresse the couenant of the Lord your God, which he commanded you, and shall goe and serue other gods, and bowe your selues to them, then shall the wrath of the Lord waxe hote against you, and ye shall perish quickely out of the good lande which he hath giuen you.

Joshua 24

1 And Ioshua assembled againe all the tribes of Israel to Shechem, and called the Elders of Israel, and their heades, and their iudges, and their officers, and they presented themselues before God.

2 Then Ioshua said vnto all the people, Thus saith the Lord God of Israel, Your fathers dwelt beyond the flood in olde time, euen Terah the father of Abraham, and the father of Nachor, and serued other gods.

3 And I tooke your father Abraham from beyond the flood, and brought him through all the land of Canaan, and multiplied his seede, and gaue him Izhak.

4 And I gaue vnto Izhak, Iaakob and Esau: and I gaue vnto Esau mount Seir, to possesse it: but Iaakob and his children went downe into Egypt.

5 I sent Moses also and Aaron, and I plagued Egypt: and when I had so done among them, I brought you out.

6 So I brought your fathers out of Egypt, and ye came vnto the Sea, and the

Egyptians pursued after your fathers with charets and horsemen vnto the red sea.

7 Then they cryed vnto the Lord, and he put a darkenesse betweene you and the Egyptians, and brought the sea vpon them, and couered them: so your eyes haue seene what I haue done in Egypt also ye dwelt in the wildernesse a long season.

8 After, I brought you into the land of the Amorites, which dwelt beyond Iorden, and they fought with you: but I gaue them into your hand, and ye possessed their countrey, and I destroyed them out of your sight.

9 Also Balak the sonne of Zippor King of Moab arose and warred against Israel, and sent to call Balaam the sonne of Beor for to curse you,

10 But I would not heare Balaam: therefore he blessed you, and I deliuered you out of his hand.

11 And ye went ouer Iorden, and came vnto Iericho, and the men of Iericho fought against you, the Amorites, and the Perizzites, and the Canaanites, and the Hittites, and the Girgashites, the Hiuites and the Iebusites, and I deliuered them into your hand.

12 And I sent hornets before you, which cast them out before you, euen the two kings of the Amorites, and not with thy sword, nor with thy bow.

13 And I haue giuen you a land, wherein ye did not labour, and cities which ye built not, and yee dwell in them, and eate of the vineyards and oliue trees, which yee planted not.

14 Nowe therefore feare the Lord, and serue him in vprightnesse and in trueth, and put away the gods, which your fathers serued beyonde the flood and in Egypt, and serue the Lord.

15 And if it seeme euill vnto you to serue the Lord, choose you this day whome yee will serue, whether the gods which your fathers serued (that were beyond the flood) or the gods of the Amorites, in whose land ye dwel: but I and mine house will serue the Lord.

16 Then the people answered and saide, God forbid, that we shoulde forsake the Lord, to serue other gods.

17 For the Lord our God, he brought vs and our fathers out of the lande of Egypt, from the house of bondage, and he did those great miracles in our sight, and preserued vs in all the way that we went, and among all the people through whome we came.

18 And the Lord did cast out before vs all the people, euen the Amorites which dwelt in the lande: therefore will we also serue the Lord, for he is our God.

19 And Ioshua saide vnto the people, Ye can not serue the Lord: for he is an holie God: he is a ielous God: hee will not pardon your iniquitie nor your sinnes.

20 If yee forsake the Lord and serue strange gods, then he will returne and bring euill vpon you, and consume you, after that hee hath done you good.

21 And the people saide vnto Ioshua, Nay, but we will serue the Lord.

22 And Ioshua saide vnto the people, Yee are witnesses against your selues, that yee haue chosen you the Lord, to serue him: and they sayd, We are witnesses.

23 Then put away nowe, saide he, the strange gods which are among you, and bowe your hearts vnto the Lord God of Israel.

24 And ye people saide vnto Ioshua, The Lord our God wil we serue, and his voyce wil we obey.

25 So Ioshua made a couenant with the people the same day, and gaue them an ordinance and lawe in Shechem.

26 And Ioshua wrote these woordes in the booke of the Lawe of God, and tooke a great stone, and pitched it there vnder an oke that was in the Sanctuarie of the Lord.

27 And Ioshua saide vnto all the people, Beholde, this stone shall be a witnesse vnto vs: for it hath heard all the wordes of the Lord which he spake with vs: it shall be therefore a witnesse against you, lest yee denie your God.

28 Then Ioshua let the people depart, euery man vnto his inheritance.

29 And after these things Ioshua the sonne of Nun, the seruaunt of the Lord died, being an hundreth and ten yeeres olde.

30 And they buried him in ye border of his inheritance in Timnath-serah, which is in mount Ephraim, on the Northside of mount Gaash.

31 And Israel serued the Lord all the daies of Ioshua, and all the daies of the Elders that ouerliued Ioshua, and which had knowen all the workes of the Lord that he had done for Israel.

32 And the bones of Ioseph, which the children of Israel brought out of Egypt, buried they in Shechem in a parcell of ground which Iaakob bought of the sonnes of Hamor the father of Shechem, for an hundreth pieces of siluer, and the children of Ioseph had them in their inheritance.

33 Also Eleazar the sonne of Aaron died, whome they buried in the hill of Phinehas his sonne, which was giuen him in mount Ephraim.

Judges

Judges 1

1 After that Ioshua was dead, the children of Israel asked ye Lord, saying, Who shall goe vp for vs against the Canaanites, to fight first against them?

2 And the Lord said, Iudah shall goe vp: behold, I haue giuen the land into his hande.

3 And Iudah said vnto Simeon his brother, Come vp with me into my lot, that we may fight against the Canaanites: and I likewise will goe with thee into thy lot: so Simeon went with him.

4 Then Iudah went vp, and the Lord deliuered the Canaanites and the Perizzites into their hands, and they slew of them in Bezek ten thousand men.

5 And they founde Adoni-bezek in Bezek: and they fought against him, and slewe the Canaanites, and the Perizzites.

6 But Adoni-bezek fled, and they pursued after him, and caught him, and cut off the thumbes of his hands and of his feete.

7 And Adoni-bezek said, Seuentie Kings hauing the thumbes of their hands and of their feete cut off, gathered bread vnder my table: as I haue done, so God hath rewarded me. so they brought him to Ierusalem, and there he died.

8 (Nowe the children of Iudah had fought against Ierusalem, and had taken it and smitten it with the edge of the sworde, and had set the citie on fire.)

9 Afterwarde also the children of Iudah went downe to fight against the Canaanites, that dwelt in the mountaine, and towarde the South, and in the lowe countrey.

10 And Iudah went against the Canaanites that dwelt in Hebron, which Hebron beforetime was called Kiriath-arba: and they slewe Sheshai, and Ahiman and Talmai.

11 And from thence hee went to the inhabitantes of Debir, and the name of Debir in olde time was Kiriath-sepher.

12 And Caleb saide, He that smiteth Kiriath-sepher, and taketh it, euen to him wil I giue Achsah my daughter to wife.

13 And Othniel the sonne of Kenaz Calebs yonger brother tooke it, to whome hee gaue Achsah his daughter to wife.

14 And when shee came to him, shee mooued him to aske of her father a field, and shee lighted off her asse, and Caleb saide vnto her, What wilt thou?

15 And shee answered him, Giue mee a blessing: for thou hast giuen me a South countrey, giue me also springs of water: and Caleb gaue her the springs aboue and the springs beneath.

16 And the childre of Keni Moses father in law went vp out of the citie of the palme trees with the children of Iudah, into the wildernesse of Iudah, that lieth in the South of Arad, and went and dwelt among the people.

17 But Iudah went with Simeon his brother, and they slewe the Canaanites that inhabited Zephath, and vtterly destroied it, and called the name of the citie Hormah.

18 Also Iudah tooke Azzah with the coasts thereof, and Askelon with the coasts thereof, and Ekron with the coastes thereof.

19 And the Lord was with Iudah, and he possessed the mountaines: for he could not driue out the inhabitantes of the valleis, because they had charrets of yron.

20 And they gaue Hebron vnto Caleb, as Moses had saide, and hee expelled thence the three sonnes of Anak.

21 But the children of Beniamin did not cast out the Iebusites, that inhabited Ierusalem: therefore the Iebusites dwell with the children of Beniamin in Ierusalem vnto this day.

22 They also that were of the house of Ioseph, went vp to Beth-el, and the Lord was with them,

23 And the house of Ioseph caused to viewe Beth-el (and the name of the citie beforetime was Luz)

24 And the spies sawe a man come out of the citie, and they saide vnto him, Shewe vs, we praie thee, the way into the citie, and we will shewe thee mercie.

25 And when hee had shewed them the waie into the citie, they smote the citie with the edge of the sworde, but they let the man and all his housholde depart.

26 Then the man went into the lande of the Hittites, and built a citie, and called the name thereof Luz, which is the name thereof vnto this daie.

27 Neither did Manasseh destroie Bethshean with her townes, nor Taanach with her townes, nor the inhabitantes of Dor with her townes, nor the inhabitants of Ibleam with her townes, neither the inhabitants of Megiddo with her townes: but the Canaanites dwelled still in that lande.

28 Neuerthelesse when Israel was strong, they put the Canaanites to tribute, and expelled them not wholly.

29 Likewise Ephraim expelled not the Canaanites that dwelt in Gezer, but the Canaanites dwelt in Gezer among them.

30 Neither did Zebulun expell the inhabitants of Kitron, nor the inhabitants of Nahalol, but the Canaanites dwelt among them, and became tributaries.

31 Neither did Asher cast out the inhabitants of Accho, nor the inhabitants of Zidon, nor of Ahlab, nor of Achzib, nor of Helbah, nor of Aphik, nor of Rehob,

32 But the Asherites dwelt among the Canaanites the inhabitantes of the lande: for they did not driue them out.

33 Neither did Naphtali driue out the inhabitants of Beth-shemesh, nor the inhabitants of Beth-anath, but dwelt among the Canaanites the inhabitants of the lande: neuerthelesse the inhabitantes of Beth-shemesh, and of Beth-anath became tributaries vnto them.

34 And the Amorites droue the children of Dan into the mountaine: so that they suffered them not to come downe to the valley.

35 And the Ammonites dwelt still in mount Heres in Aijalon, and in Shaalbim, and when the hand of Iosephs familie preuailed, they became tributaries:

36 And the coast of the Amorites was from Maaleh-akrabbim, euen from Selah and vpward.

Judges 2

1 And an Angel of the Lord came vp from Gilgal to Bochim, and sayd, I made you to go vp out of Egypt, and haue brought you vnto the land which I had sworne vnto your fathers, and sayd, I wil neuer breake my couenant with you.

2 Ye also shall make no couenant with the inhabitants of this land, but shall breake downe their altars: but ye haue not obeyed my voyce. Why haue ye done this?

3 Wherefore, I sayd also, I wil not cast them out before you, but they shalbe as thornes vnto your sides, and their gods shalbe your destruction.

4 And when the Angel of the Lord spake these wordes vnto all the children of Israel, the people lift vp their voyce, and wept.

5 Therefore they called the name of that place, Bochim, and offered sacrifices there vnto the Lord.

6 Now when Ioshua had sent the people away, the children of Israel went euery man into his inheritance, to possesse the land.

7 And the people had serued the Lord al the dayes of Ioshua, and all the dayes of the Elders that outliued Ioshua, which had seene all the great works of the Lord that he did for Israel.

8 But Ioshua the sonne of Nun the seruant of the Lord dyed, when he was an hundreth and ten yeeres olde:

9 And they buryed him in the coastes of his inheritance, in Timnath-heres in mount Ephraim, on the Northside of mount Gaash.

10 And so all that generation was gathered vnto their fathers, and another generation arose after them, which neither knewe the Lord, nor yet the works, which he had done for Israel.

11 Then the children of Israel did wickedly in the sight of the Lord, and serued Baalim,

12 And forsooke ye Lord God of their fathers, which brought them out of the lande of Egypt, and followed other gods, euen the gods of the people that were round about them, and bowed vnto them, and prouoked the Lord to anger.

13 So they forsooke the Lord, and serued Baal, and Ashtaroth.

14 And the wrath of the Lord was hote against Israel, and he deliuered them into the hands of spoylers, that spoyled them, and he sold them into the handes of their enemies rounde about them, so that they could no longer stande before their enemies.

15 Whithersoeuer they went out, the hand of the Lord was sore against them, as ye Lord had sayd, and as the Lord had sworne vnto them: so he punished them sore.

16 Notwithstanding, the Lord raysed vp Iudges, which deliuered them out of the hands of their oppressours.

17 But yet they would not obey their Iudges: for they went a whoring after other gods, and worshipped them, and turned quickly out of the way, wherein their fathers walked, obeying the commandements of the Lord: they did not so.

18 And when the Lord had raysed them vp Iudges, the Lord was with the Iudge, and deliuered them out of the hande of their enemies all the dayes of the Iudge (for the Lord had compassion on their gronings, because of them that oppressed them and tormented them)

19 Yet when the Iudge was dead, they returned, and did worse then their fathers, in following other gods to serue them and worshippe them: they ceased not from their owne inuentions, nor from their rebellious way.

20 Wherfore the wrath of the Lord was kindled against Israel, and he sayd, Because this people hath transgressed my couenant, which I commaded their fathers, and hath not obeyed my voyce,

21 Therefore will I no more cast out before them any of the nations, which Ioshua left when he dyed,

22 That through them I may proue Israel, whether they wil keepe the way of the Lord, to walke therein, as their fathers kept it, or not.

23 So the Lord left those nations, and droue them not out immediatly, neither deliuered them into the hand of Ioshua.

Judges 3

1 These nowe are the nations which the Lord left, that he might proue Israel by them (euen as many of Israel as had not knowen all the warres of Canaan,

2 Only to make the generations of the children of Israel to know, and to teach them warre, which doutles their predecessors knew not)

3 Fiue princes of the Philistims, and all the Canaanites, and the Sidonians, and the Hiuites that dwelt in mount Lebanon, from mount Baal-hermon vntill one come to Hamath.

4 And these remayned to proue Israel by them, to wit, whether they would obey the commandements of the Lord, which he commanded their fathers by the hand of Moses.

5 And the children of Israel dwelt among the Canaanites, the Hittites, and the Amorites, and the Perizzites, and the Hiuites, and the Iebusites,

6 And they tooke their daughters to bee their wiues, and gaue their daughters to their sonnes, and serued their gods.

7 So the children of Israel did wickedly in the sight of the Lord, and forgate the Lord their God, and serued Baalim, and Asheroth.

8 Therefore the wrath of the Lord was kindled against Israel, and he solde them into the hand of Chushan rishathaim King of Aram-naharaim, and the children of Israel serued Chushan rishathaim eyght yeeres.

9 And when the children of Israel cryed vnto the Lord, the Lord stirred vp a sauiour to ye children of Israel, and he saued them, euen Othniel the sonne of Kenaz, Calebs yonger brother.

10 And the spirite of the Lord came vpon him, and he iudged Israel, and went out to warre: and the Lord deliuered Chushan rishathaim king of Aram into his hand, and his hand preuailed against Chushan rishathaim.

11 So the lande had rest fourtie yeeres, and Othniel the sonne of Kenaz dyed.

12 Then the children of Israel againe committed wickednesse in the sight of the Lord: and the Lord strengthened Eglon King of Moab against Israel, because they had committed wickednesse before the Lord.

13 And he gathered vnto him the children of Ammon, and Amalek, and went and smote Israel, and they possessed the citie of palme trees.

14 So the children of Israel serued Eglon king of Moab eighteene yeeres.

15 But when the children of Israel cried vnto the Lord, the Lord stirred them vp a sauiour, Ehud the sonne of Gera the sonne of Iemini, a man lame of his right hande: and the children of Israel sent a present by him vnto Eglon King of Moab.

16 And Ehud made him a dagger with two edges of a cubite length, and he did gird it vnder his rayment vpon his right thigh,

17 And he presented ye gift vnto Eglon King of Moab (and Eglon was a very fat man)

18 And when he had now presented the present, he sent away the people that bare ye present,

19 But he turned againe from the quarris, that were by Gilgal, and said, I haue a secret errand vnto thee, O King. Who said, Keepe silence: and all that stoode about him, went out from him.

20 Then Ehud came vnto him. (and he sate alone in a sommer parler, which he had) and Ehud said, I haue a message vnto thee from God. Then he arose out of his throne,

21 And Ehud put forth his left hand, and tooke the dagger from his right thigh, and thrust it into his bellie,

22 So that the hafte went in after the blade, and the fatte closed about the blade, so that he could not drawe the dagger out of his bellie, but the dirt came out.

23 Then Ehud gate him out into the porch, and shut the doores of the parler vpon him, and locked them.

24 And when he was gone out, his seruantes came: who seeing that the doores of the parler were locked, they sayd, Surely he doeth his easement in his sommer chamber.

25 And they taryed till they were ashamed: and seeing he opened not the doores of the parler, they tooke the key, and opened them, and behold, their lord was fallen dead on the earth.

26 So Ehud escaped (while they taried) and was passed the quarris, and escaped vnto Seirah.

27 And when he came home, he blew a trumpet in mount Ephraim, and the children of Israel went downe with him from the mountaine, and he went before them.

28 Then said he vnto them, Follow me: for the Lord hath deliuered your enemies, euen Moab into your hand. So they went downe after him, and tooke the passages of Iorden towarde Moab, and suffred not a man to passe ouer.

29 And they slewe of the Moabites the same time about ten thousand men, all fed men, and all were warriours, and there escaped not a man.

30 So Moab was subdued that daye, vnder the hand of Israel: and the land had rest fourescore yeeres.

31 And after him was Shamgar the sonne of Anath, which slewe of the Philistims sixe hundreth men with an oxe goade, and he also deliuered Israel.

Judges 4

1 And the children of Israel began againe to do wickedly in the sight of the Lord when Ehud was dead.

2 And the Lord sold them into the hande of Iabin King of Canaan, that reigned in Hazor, whose chiefe Captaine was called Sisera, which dwelt in Harosheth of the Gentiles.

3 Then the children of Israel cryed vnto the Lord: (for he had nine hundreth charets of yron, and twentie yeeres he had vexed the children of Israel very sore)

4 And at that time Deborah a Prophetesse the wife of Lapidoth iudged Israel.

5 And this Deborah dwelt vnder a palme tree, betweene Ramah and Beth-el in mount Ephraim, and the children of Israel came vp to her for iudgement.

6 Then shee sent and called Barak the sonne of Abinoam out of Kadesh of Naphtali, and sayd vnto him, Hath not the Lord God of Israel commanded, saying, Goe, and drawe towarde mount Tabor, and take with thee ten thousande men of the children of Naphtali and of the children of Zebulun?

7 And I wil drawe vnto thee to the riuer Kishon Sisera, the captaine of Iabins armie with his charets, and his multitude, and wil deliuer him into thine hand.

8 And Barak sayd vnto her, If thou wilt go with me, I will go: but if thou wilt not goe with me, I will not go.

9 Then shee answered, I will surely goe with thee, but this iourney that thou takest, shall not be for thine honour: for the Lord shall sell Sisera into the hand of a woman. And Deborah arose and went with Barak to Kedesh.

10 And Barak called Zebulun and Naphtali to Kedesh, and he went vp on his feete with ten thousand men, and Deborah went vp with him.

11 (Now Heber the Kenite, which was of the children of Hobab the father in lawe of Moses, was departed from the Kenites, and pitched his tent vntill the playne of Zaanaim, which is by Kedesh)

12 Then they shewed Sisera, that Barak the sonne of Abinoam was gone vp to mout Tabor.

13 And Sisera called for all his charets, euen nine hundreth charets of yron, and all the people that were with him from Harosheth of the Gentiles, vnto the riuer Kishon.

14 Then Deborah sayd vnto Barak, Vp: for this is the day that the Lord hath deliuered Sisera into thine hand. Is not the Lord gone out before thee? So Barak went downe from mount Tabor, and ten thousand men after him.

15 And the Lord destroyed Sisera and all his charets, and al his hoste with the edge of the sword before Barak, so that Sisera lighted downe off his charet, and fled away on his feete.

16 But Barak pursued after the charets, and after the hoste vnto Harosheth of the Gentiles: and all the hoste of Sisera fel vpon the edge of the sworde: there was not a man left.

17 Howbeit Sisera fled away on his feete to the tent of Iael the wife of Heber the Kenite: (for peace was betweene Iabin the king of Hazor, and betweene the house of Heber the Kenite)

18 And Iael went out to meete Sisera, and sayd vnto him, Turne in, my lord, turne in to me: feare not. And when he had turned in vnto her into her tent, she couered him with a mantell.

19 And he said vnto her, Giue me, I pray thee, a litle water to drinke: for I am thirstie. And shee opened a bottel of milke, and gaue him drinke, and couered him.

20 Againe he sayde vnto her, Stande in the doore of the tent, and when any man doth come and enquire of thee, saying, Is any man there? thou shalt say, Nay.

21 Then Iael Hebers wife tooke a nayle of the tent, and tooke an hammer in her hande, and went softly vnto him, and smote the nayle into his temples, and fastened it into the grounde, (for he was fast a sleepe and weary) and so he dyed.

22 And behold, as Barak pursued after Sisera, Iael came out to meete him, and sayd vnto him, Come, and I wil shewe thee the man, whome thou seekest: and when he came into her tent, behold, Sisera lay dead, and the nayle in his temples.

23 So God brought downe Iabin the King of Canaan that day before the children of Israel.

24 And the hande of the children of Israel prospered, and preuailed against Iabin the King of Canaan, vntill they had destroyed Iabin King of Canaan.

Judges 5

1 Then sang Deborah, and Barak the sonne of Abinoam the same day, saying,

2 Praise ye the Lord for the auenging of Israel, and for the people that offred themselues willingly.

3 Heare, ye Kings, hearken ye princes: I, euen I will sing vnto the Lord: I will sing praise vnto the Lord God of Israel.

4 Lord, when thou wentest out of Seir, when thou departedst out of the field of Edom, the earth trembled, and the heauens rained, the cloudes also dropped water.

5 The mountaines melted before the Lord, as did that Sinai before the Lord God of Israel.

6 In the dayes of Shamgar the sonne of Anath, in the dayes of Iael the hie wayes were vnoccupied, and the trauelers walked through by wayes.

7 The townes were not inhabited: they decayed, I say, in Israel, vntill I Deborah came vp, which rose vp a mother in Israel.

8 They chose new gods: then was warre in the gates. Was there a shielde or speare seene among fourtie thousand of Israel?

9 Mine heart is set on the gouernours of Israel, and on them that are willing among the people: praise ye the Lord.

10 Speake ye that ride on white asses, yee that dwel by Middin, and that walke by the way.

11 For the noyse of the archers appaised among the drawers of water: there shall they rehearse the righteousnesse of the Lord, his righteousnesse of his townes in Israel: then did the people of the Lord goe downe to the gates.

12 Vp Deborah, vp, arise, and sing a song: arise Barak, and leade thy captiuitie captiue, thou sonne of Abinoam.

13 For they that remaine, haue dominio ouer the mightie of the people: the Lord hath giuen me dominion ouer the strong.

14 Of Ephraim their roote arose against Amalek: and after thee, Beniamin shall fight against thy people, O Amalek: of Machir came rulers, and of Zebulun they that handle the pen of the writer.

15 And the Princes of Issachar were with Deborah, and Issachar, and also Barak: he was set on his feete in the valley: for the diuisions of Reuben were great thoughts of heart.

16 Why abodest thou among the sheepefolds, to heare the bleatings of the flockes? for the diuisions of Reuben were great thoughts of heart.

17 Gilead abode beyonde Iorden: and why doeth Dan remayne in shippes? Asher sate on the sea shoare, and taryed in his decayed places.

18 But the people of Zebulun and Naphtali haue ieopard their liues vnto the death in the hie places of the field.

19 The Kings came and fought: then fought the Kings of Canaan in Taanach by the waters of Megiddo: they receiued no gaine of money.

20 They fought from heauen, euen the starres in their courses fought against Sisera.

21 The Riuer Kishon swepe them away, that ancient riuer the riuer Kishon. O my soule, thou hast marched valiantly.

22 Then were the horsehooues broken with the oft beating together of their mightie men.

23 Curse ye Meroz: (sayd the Angel of the Lord) curse the inhabitantes thereof, because they came not to helpe the Lord, to helpe the Lord against the mighty.

24 Iael the wife of Heber the Kenite shall be blessed aboue other women: blessed shall she be aboue women dwelling in tentes.

25 He asked water, and shee gaue him milke: she brought forth butter in a lordly dish.

26 She put her hand to the naile, and her right hand to the workemans hammer: with the hammer smote she Sisera: she smote off his head, after she had wounded, and pearsed his temples.

27 He bowed him downe at her feete, he fell downe, and lay still: at her feete hee bowed him downe, and fell: and when he had sunke downe, he lay there dead.

28 The mother of Sisera looked out at a windowe, and cryed thorowe the lattesse, Why is his charet so long a comming? why tary the wheeles of his charets?

29 Her wise ladies answered her, Yea. Shee answered her selfe with her owne wordes,

30 Haue they not gotten, and they deuide the spoyle? euery man hath a mayde or two. Sisera hath a praye of diuers coloured garmentes, a pray of sundry colours made of needle worke: of diuers colours of needle worke on both sides, for the chiefe of the spoyle.

31 So let all thine enemies perish, O Lord: but they that loue him, shall be as the Sunne when he riseth in his might, and the lande had rest fourtie yeres.

Judges 6

1 Afterwarde the children of Israel committed wickednesse in the sight of the Lord, and the Lord gaue them into the handes of Midian seuen yeres.

2 And the hand of Midian preuayled against Israel, and because of the Midianites the children of Israel made them dennes in the mountaines, and caues, and strong holdes.

3 When Israel had sowen, then came vp the Midianites, the Amalekites, and they of the East, and came vpon them,

4 And camped by them, and destroyed the fruite of the earth, euen til thou come vnto Azzah, and left no foode for Israel, neither sheepe, nor oxe, nor asse.

5 For they went vp, and their cattel, and came with their tentes as grashoppers in multitude: so that they and their camels were without number: and they came into the land to destroy it.

6 So was Israel exceedingly impouerished by the Midianites: therefore the children of Israel cryed vnto the Lord.

7 And when the children of Israel cryed vnto the Lord because of the Midianites,

8 The Lord sent vnto the children of Israel a Prophet, who sayd vuto them, Thus sayth the Lord God of Israel, I haue brought you vp from Egypt, and haue brought you out of the house of bondage,

9 And I haue deliuered you out of the hand of the Egyptians, and out of the hand of all that oppressed you, and haue cast them out before you, and giuen you their land.

10 And I sayde vnto you, I am the Lord your God: feare not the gods of the Amorites in whose lande you dwell: but ye haue not obeyed my voyce.

11 And the Angell of the Lord came, and sate vnder the oke which was in Ophrah, that perteined vnto Ioash the father of the Ezrites, and his sonne Gideon threshed wheate by the winepresse, to hide it from the Midianites.

12 Then the Angel of the Lord appeared vnto him, and said vnto him, The Lord is with thee, thou valiant man.

13 To whome Gideon answered, Ah my Lord, if the Lord be with vs, why then is all this come vpon vs? and where be all his miracles which our fathers tolde vs of, and sayd, Did not the Lord bring vs out of Egypt? but now the Lord hath forsaken vs, and deliuered vs into the hand of the Midianites.

14 And the Lord looked vpon him, and sayd, Goe in this thy might, and thou shalt saue Israel out of the handes of the Midianites: haue not I sent thee?

15 And he answered him, Ah my Lord, whereby shall I saue Israel? beholde, my father is poore in Manasseh, and I am the least in my fathers house.

16 Then the Lord sayd vnto him, I wil therefore be with thee, and thou shalt smite the Midianites, as one man.

17 And he answered him, I pray thee, if I haue founde fauour in thy sight, then shewe me a signe, that thou talkest with me.

18 Depart not hence, I pray thee, vntil I come vnto thee, and bring mine offring, and lay it before thee. And he sayde, I will tary vntill thou come againe.

19 Then Gideon went in, and made ready a kidde, and vnleauened bread of an Ephah of floure, and put the flesh in a basket, and put the broth in a pot, and brought it out vnto him vnder the oke, and presented it.

20 And the Angell of God saide vnto him, Take the flesh and the vnleauened bread, and lay them vpon this stone, and powre out the broth: and he did so.

21 Then the Angell of the Lord put forth the ende of the staffe that he had in his hand, and touched the flesh and the vnleauened bread: and there arose vp fire out of the stone, and consumed the flesh and the vnleauened bread: so the Angel of the Lord departed out of his sight.

22 And when Gideon perceiued that it was an Angel of the Lord, Gideon then sayde, Alas, my Lord God: for because I haue seene an Angell of the Lord face to face, I shall die.

23 And the Lord said vnto him, Peace be vnto thee: feare not, thou shalt not die.

24 Then Gideon made an altar there vnto the Lord, and called it, Iehouah shalom: vnto this day it is in Ophrah, of the father of the Ezrites.

25 And the same night the Lord sayd vnto him, Take thy fathers yong bullocke, and an other bullocke of seuen yeeres olde, and destroy the altar of Baal that thy father hath, and cut downe the groue that is by it,

26 And build an altar vnto the Lord thy God vpon the top of this rocke, in a plaine place: and take the seconde bullocke, and offer a burnt offringe with the woode of the groue, which thou shalt cut downe.

27 Then Gideon tooke tenne men of his seruants, and did as ye Lord bade him: but because he feared to doe it by day for

his fathers housholde, and the men of the citie, he did it by night.

28 And when the men of the citie arose early in the morning, beholde, the altar of Baal was broken, and the groue cut downe that was by it, and the seconde bullocke offred vpon the altar that was made.

29 Therefore they saide one to another, Who hath done this thing? and when they inquired and asked, they saide, Gideon the sonne of Ioash hath done this thing.

30 Then the men of the citie said vnto Ioash, Bring out thy sonne, that hee may dye: for he hath destroyed the altar of Baal, and hath also cut downe the groue that was by it.

31 And Ioash said vnto all that stood by him, Will ye pleade Baals cause? or will ye saue him? he that will contend for him, let him dye or the morning. If he be God, let him pleade for himselfe against him that hath cast downe his altar.

32 And in that day was Gideon called Ierubbaal, that is, Let Baal pleade for himselfe because he hath broken downe his altar.

33 Then all the Midianites and the Amalekites and they of ye East, were gathered together, aud went and pitched in the valley of Izreel.

34 But the Spirit of the Lord came vpon Gideon, and he blew a trumpet, and Abiezer was ioyned with him.

35 And he sent messengers thorowout al Manasseh, which also was ioyned with him, and he sent messengers vnto Asher, and to Zebulun and to Naphtali, and they came vp to meete them.

36 Then Gideon said vnto God, If thou wilt saue Israel by mine hand, as thou hast sayd,

37 Beholde, I wil put a fleece of wooll in the threshing place: if the dewe come on the fleece onely, and it be drie vpon all the earth, then shall I be sure, that thou wilt saue Israel by mine hand, as thou hast said.

38 And so it was: for he rose vp earely on the morow, and thrust the fleece together, and wringed the dew out of the fleece, and filled a bowle of water.

39 Againe, Gideon sayde vnto God, Be not angry with me, that I may speake once more: let me prooue once againe, I pray thee, with the fleece: let it now be drie onely vpon the fleece, and let dewe be vpon all the ground.

40 And God did so that same night: for it was drie vpon the fleece onely, and there was dewe on all the ground.

Judges 7

1 Then Ierubbaal (who is Gideon) rose vp early, and all the people that were with him, and pitched beside the well of Harod, so that the hoste of the Midianites was on the Northside of them in the valley by the hill of Moreh.

2 And the Lord said vnto Gideon, The people that are with thee, are too many for me to giue the Midianites into their hands, lest Israel make their vaunt against me, and say, Mine hand hath saued mee.

3 Now therefore proclaime in the audience of the people, and say, Who so is timerous or fearefull, let him returne, and depart earely from mount Gilead. And there returned of the people which were at mount Gilead, two and twentie thousand: so ten thousand remayned.

4 And the Lord said vnto Gideon, The people are yet too many: bring them downe vnto the water, and I will try them for thee there: and of whome I say vnto thee, This man shall goe with thee, the same shall go with thee: and of whomsoeuer I say vnto thee, This man shall not goe with thee, the same shall not go.

5 So he brought downe the people vnto the water. And the Lord sayd vnto Gideon, As many as lap the water with their tongues, as a dog lappeth, them put by themselues, and euery one that shall bow downe his knees to drinke, put apart.

6 And the nomber of them that lapped by putting their handes to their mouthes, were three hundreth men: but all the remnant of the people kneeled downe vpon their knees to drinke water.

7 Then the Lord sayde vnto Gideon, By these three hundreth men that lapped, will I saue you, and deliuer the Midianites into thine hand: and let all the other people go euery man vnto his place.

8 So the people tooke vitailes with them, and their trumpets: and he sent all the rest of Israel, euery man vnto his tent, and reteined the three hundreth men: and the hoste of Midian was beneath him in a valley.

9 And the same night the Lord sayde vnto him, Arise, get thee downe vnto the hoste: for I haue deliuered it into thine hand.

10 But if thou feare to go downe, then go thou, and Phurah thy seruant downe to the hoste,

11 And thou shalt hearken what they say, and so shall thine handes be strong to go downe vnto the hoste. Then went he downe and Phurah his seruant vnto the outside of the souldiers that were in the hoste.

12 And the Midianites, and the Amalekites and all they of the East, lay in the valley like grashoppers in multitude, and their camels were without nomber, as the sande which is by the sea side for multitude.

13 And when Gideon was come, beholde, a man tolde a dreame vnto his neighbour, and said, Behold, I dreamed a dreame, and lo, a cake of barley bread tumbled from aboue vnto the hoste of Midian, and came vnto a tent, and smote it that it fell, and ouerturned it, that the tent fell downe.

14 And his fellow answered, and sayde, This is nothing els saue the sworde of Gideon the sonne of Ioash a man of Israel: for into his hande hath God deliuered Midian and all the hoste.

15 When Gideon heard the dreame tolde, and the interpretation of the same, he worshipped, and returned vnto the hoste of Israel, and said, Vp: for the Lord hath deliuered into your hande the hoste of Midian.

16 And hee deuided the three hundreth men into three bandes, and gaue euery man a trumpet in his hande with emptie pitchers, and lampes within the pitchers.

17 And he sayd vnto them, Looke on me, and do likewise, when I come to the side of the hoste: euen as I do, so do you.

18 When I blowe with a trumpet and all that are with me, blowe ye with trumpets also on euery side of the hoste, and say, For the Lord, and for Gideon.

19 So Gideon and the hundreth men that were with him, came vnto the outside of the hoste, in the beginning of the middle watche, and they raised vp the watchmen, and they blew with their trumpets, and brake the pitchers that were in their handes.

20 And the three companies blew with trumpets and brake the pitchers, and helde the lampes in their left hands, and the trumpets in their right. handes to blowe withall: and they cryed, The sword of the Lord and of Gideon.

21 And they stoode, euery man in his place round about the hoste: and all the hoste ranne, and cryed, and fled.

22 And the three hundreth blewe with trumpets, and the Lord set euery mans sworde vpon his neighbour, and vpon all the hoste: so the hoste fled to Beth-hashittah in Zererah, and to the border of Abel-meholah, vnto Tabbath.

23 Then the men of Israel being gathered together out of Naphtali, and out of Asher, and out of all Manasseh, pursued after the Midianites.

24 And Gideon sent messengers vnto all mount Ephraim, saying, Come downe against the Midianites, and take before them the waters vnto Beth-barah, and Iorden. Then all the men of Ephraim gathered together and tooke the waters vnto Beth-barah, and Iorden.

25 And they tooke two princes of the Midianites, Oreb and Zeeb, and slew Oreb vpon the rocke Oreb, and slewe Zeeb at the winepresse of Zeeb, and pursued the Midianites, and brought the heads of Oreb and Zeeb to Gideon beyonde Iorden.

Judges 8

1 Then the men of Ephraim sayde vnto him, Why hast thou serued vs thus that thou calledst vs not, when thou wentest to fight with the Midianites? and they chode with him sharply.

2 To whom he said, What haue I now done in comparison of you? is not the gleaning of grapes of Ephraim better, then the vintage of Abiezer?

3 God hath deliuered into your handes the princes of Midian, Oreb and Zeeb: and what was I able to do in comparison of you? and when he had thus spoken, then their spirits abated toward him.

4 And Gideon came to Iorden to passe ouer, hee, and the three hundreth men that were with him, weary, yet pursuing them.

5 And he said vnto the men of Succoth, Giue, I pray you, morsels of bread vnto the people that follow me (for they be wearie) that I may follow after Zebah, and Zalmunna Kings of Midian.

6 And the princes of Succoth sayde, Are the handes of Zebah and Zalmunna nowe in thine hads, that we should giue bread vnto thine army?

7 Gideon then sayde, Therefore when the Lord hath deliuered Zebah and Zalmunna into mine hand, I will teare your flesh with thornes of the wildernes and with breers.

8 And he went vp thence to Penuel, and spake vnto them likewise, and the men of Penuel answered him, as the men of Succoth answered.

9 And he sayd also vnto the men of Penuel, When I come againe in peace, I will breake downe this towre.

10 Now Zebah and Zalmunna were in Karkor, and their hostes with them, about fifteene thousande, all that were left of all the hostes of them of the East: for there was slaine an hundreth and twentie thousand men, that drew swordes.

11 And Gideon went through them that dwelt in Tabernacles on the East side of Nobah and Iogbehah, and smote the hoste: for the hoste was carelesse.

12 And when Zebah and Zalmunna fled, hee followed after them, and tooke the two kings of Midian, Zebah and Zalmunna, and discomfited all the hoste.

13 So Gideon the sonne of Ioash returned from battel, the sunne being yet hie,

14 And tooke a seruant of the me of Succoth, and inquired of him: and he wrote to him the princes of Succoth and the Elders thereof, euen seuentie and seuen men.

15 And he came vnto the men of Succoth, and sayd, Behold Zebah and Zalmunna, by whome ye vpbrayded me, saying, Are the hands of Zebah and Zalmunna already in thine hands, that we should giue bread vnto thy weary men?

16 Then he tooke the Elders of the citie, and thornes of the wildernes and breers, and did teare the men of Succoth with them.

17 Also he brake downe the towre of Penuel, and slew the men of the citie.

18 Then saide he vnto Zebah and Zalmunna, What maner of men were they, whom ye slew at Tabor? and they answered, As thou art, so were they: euery one was like the children of a King.

19 And he said, They were my brethren, euen my mothers children: as the Lord liueth, if ye had saued their liues, I would not slay you.

20 Then he sayde vnto Iether his first borne sonne, Vp, and slay them: but the boy drew not his sword: for he feared, because he was yet yong.

21 Then Zebah and Zalmunna sayd, Rise thou, and fall vpon vs: for as the man is, so is his strength. And Gideon arose and slew Zebah and Zalmunna, and tooke away the ornamentes, that were on their camels neckes.

22 Then the men of Israel sayd vnto Gideon, Reigne thou ouer vs, both thou, and thy sonne, and thy sonnes sonne: for thou hast deliuered vs out of the hand of Midian.

23 And Gideon sayde vnto them, I will not reigne ouer you, neither shall my childe reigne ouer you, but the Lord shall reigne ouer you.

24 Againe Gideon sayd vnto them, I would desire a request of you, that you would giue mee euery man the earings of his pray (for they had golden earings because they were Ismaelites)

25 And they answered, Wee will giue them. And they spred a garment, and did cast therein euery man the earings of his pray.

26 And the weight of the golden earings that he required, was a thousande and seuen hundreth shekels of golde, beside collers and iewels, and purple rayment that was on the kings of Midian, and beside the cheynes that were about their camels neckes.

27 And Gideon made an Ephod thereof, and put it in Ophrah his citie: and all Israel went a whoring there after it, which was the destruction of Gideon and his house.

28 Thus was Midian brought lowe before the children of Israel, so that they lift vp their heads no more: and the countrey was in quietnes fourtie yeeres in the dayes of Gideon.

29 Then Ierubbaal the sonne of Ioash went, and dwelt in his owne house.

30 And Gideon had seuentie sonnes begotten of his body: for he had many wiues.

31 And his concubine that was in Shechem, bare him a sonne also, whose name he called Abimelech.

32 So Gideon the sonne of Ioash dyed in a good age, and was buried in the sepulchre of Ioash his father in Ophrah, of the father of ye Ezrites.

33 But when Gideon was dead, the children of Israel turned away and went a whoring after Baalim, and made Baal-berith their God.

34 And the children of Israel remembred not the Lord their God, which had deliuered the out of the hands of all their enemies on euery side.

35 Neither shewed they mercy on the house of Ierubbaal, or Gideon, according to al the goodnesse which he had shewed vnto Israel.

Judges 9

1 Then Abimelech the sonne of Ierubbaal went to Shechem vnto his mothers brethren, and communed with them, and with all the familie, and house of his mothers father, saying,

2 Say, I pray you, in the audience of all the men of Shechem, Whether is better for you, that all the sonnes of Ierubbaal, which are seuentie persons, reigne ouer you, either that one reigne ouer you? Remember also, that I am your bone, and your flesh.

3 Then his mothers brethren spake of him in the audience of all the men of Shechem, all these wordes: and their hearts were moued to follow Abimelech: for sayd they, He is our brother.

4 And they gaue him seuentie pieces of siluer out of the house of Baal-berith, wherewith Abimelech hired vayne and light fellowes which followed him.

5 And he went vnto his fathers house at Ophrah, and slew his brethren, the sonnes of Ierubbaal, about seuentie persons vpon one stone: yet Iotham the yongest sonne of Ierubbaal was left: for he hid himselfe.

6 And all the men of Shechem gathered together with all the house of Millo, and came and made Abimelech King in the playne, where the stone was erected in Shechem.

7 And when they told it to Iotham, he went and stoode in the top of mount Gerizim, and lift vp his voyce, and cryed, and sayd vnto them, Hearken vnto mee, you men of Shechem, that God may hearken vnto you.

8 The trees went foorth to anoynt a King ouer them, and sayde vnto the oliue tree, Reigne thou ouer vs.

9 But the oliue tree said vnto them, Should I leaue my fatnes, wherewith by me they honour God and man, and go to aduance me aboue ye trees?

10 Then the trees sayde to the fig tree, Come thou, and be King ouer vs.

11 But the fig tree answered them, Should I forsake my sweetenesse, and my good fruite, and goe to aduance me aboue the trees?

12 Then sayd the trees vnto the Vine, Come thou, and be king ouer vs.

13 But the Vine sayde vnto them, Should I leaue my wine, whereby I cheare God and man, and goe to aduance me aboue the trees?

14 Then said all the trees vnto the bramble, Come thou, and reigne ouer vs.

15 And the bramble said vnto the trees, If ye will in deede anoynt me King ouer you, come, and put your trust vnder my shadowe: and if not, the fire shall come out of the bramble, and consume the Cedars of Lebanon.

16 Now therefore, if ye doe truely and vncorruptly to make Abimelech King, and if ye haue delt well with Ierubbaal and with his house, and haue done vnto him according to the deseruing of his handes,

17 (For my father fought for you, and aduentured his life, and deliuered you out of the handes of Midian.

18 And yee are risen vp against my fathers house this day, and haue slayne his children, about seuentie persons vpon one stone, and haue made Abimelech the sonne of his mayde seruant, King ouer the men of Shechem, because hee is your brother)

19 If ye then haue delt truely and purely with Ierubbaal, and with his house this day, then reioyce with you.

20 But if not, let a fire come out from Abimelech, and consume the men of Shechem and the house of Millo: also let a fire come foorth from the men of Shechem, and from the house of Millo, and consume Abimelech.

21 And Iotham ran away, and fled, and went to Beer, and dwelt there for feare of Abimelech his brother.

22 So Abimelech reigned three yeere ouer Israel.

23 But God sent an euil spirit betweene Abimelech, and the men of Shechem: and the men of Shechem brake their promise to Abimelech,

24 That the crueltie toward the seuentie sonnes of Ierubbaal and their blood might come and be laide vpon Abimelech their brother, which had slayne them, and vpon the men of Shechem, which had ayded him to kill his brethren.

25 So the men of Shechem set men in wayte for him in the toppes of the mountaines: who robbed all that passed that way by them: and it was tolde Abimelech.

26 Then Gaal the sonne of Ebed came with his brethren, and they went to Shechem: and the men of Shechem put their confidence in him.

27 Therefore they went out into the field, and gathered in their grapes and troade them, and made merie, and went into the house of their gods, and did eate and drinke, and cursed Abimelech.

28 Then Gaal the sonne of Ebed sayde, Who is Abimelech? and who is Shechem, that wee should serue him? Is he not the sonne of Ierubbaal? and Zebul is his officer? Serue rather the men of Hamor the father of Shechem: for why should we serue him?

29 Now would God this people were vnder mine hand: then would I put away Abimelech. And he said to Abimelech, Increase thine army, and come out.

30 And when Zebul the ruler of the citie heard the wordes of Gaal the sonne of Ebed, his wrath was kindled.

31 Therefore he sent messengers vnto Abimelech priuily, saying, Beholde, Gaal the sonne of Ebed and his brethren be come to Shechem, and beholde, they fortifie the citie against thee.

32 Now therefore arise by night, thou and the people that is with thee, and lye in wayte in the fielde.

33 And rise early in the morning as soone as the sunne is vp, and assault the citie: and when he and the people that is with him, shall come out against thee, doe to him what thou canst.

34 So Abimelech rose vp, and all the people that were with him by night: and they lay in wayte against Shechem in foure bandes.

35 Then Gaal the sonne of Ebed went out and stood in the entring of the gate of the citie: and Abimelech rose vp, and the folke that were with him, from lying in waite.

36 And when Gaal sawe the people, he said to Zebul, Beholde, there come people downe from the tops of the mountaines: and Zebul said vnto him, The shadowe of the mountaines seeme men vnto thee.

37 And Gaal spake againe, and said, See, there come folke downe by the middle of the land, and another bande commeth by the way of the plaine of Meonenim.

38 Then sayd Zebul vnto him, Where is now thy mouth, that said, Who is Abimelech, that we should serue him? Is not this the people that thou hast despised? Go out now, I pray thee, and fight with them.

39 And Gaal went out before the men of Shechem, and fought with Abimelech.

40 But Abimelech pursued him, and he fledde before him, and many were ouerthrowen and wounded, euen vnto the entring of the gate.

41 And Abimelech dwelt at Arumah: and Zebul thrust out Gaal and his brethren that they should not dwell in Shechem.

42 And on the morowe, the people went out into the fielde: which was tolde Abimelech.

43 And he tooke the people, and deuided them into three bandes, and layde wayte in the fieldes, and looked, and beholde, the people were come out of the citie, and he rose vp against them, and smote them.

44 And Abimelech, and the bandes that were with him, russhed forwarde, and stoode in the entring of the gate of the citie: and the two other bandes ran vpon all the people that were in the fielde and slewe them.

45 And when Abimelech had fought against the citie all that day, he tooke the citie, and slewe the people that was therein, and destroyed the citie and sowed salt in it.

46 And when all the men of the towre of Shechem heard it, they entred into an holde of the house of the god Berith.

47 And it was tolde Abimelech, that all the men of the towre of Shechem were gathered together.

48 And Abimelech gate him vp to mounte Zalmon, hee and all the people that were with him: and Abimelech tooke axes with him, and cut downe boughes of trees, and tooke them, and bare them on his shoulder, and sayde vnto the folke that were with him, What ye haue seene me doe, make haste, and doe like me.

49 Then all the people also cut downe euery man his bough, and followed Abimelech, and put them to the holde, and set the holde on fire with them: so all the men of the towre of Shechem dyed also, about a thousand men and women.

50 Then went Abimelech to Tebez, and besieged Tebez, and tooke it.

51 But there was a strong towre within the citie, and thither fledde all the men and women, and all the chiefe of the citie, and shut it to them, and went vp to the toppe of the towre.

52 And Abimelech came vnto the towre and fought against it, and went hard vnto the doore of the towre to set it on fire.

53 But a certaine woman cast a piece of a milstone vpon Abimelechs head, and brake his braine pan.

54 Then Abimelech called hastily his page that bare his harneis, and sayde vnto him, Drawe thy sworde and slay me, that men say not of me, A woman slewe him. And his page thrust him thorowe, and he dyed.

55 And when the men of Israel sawe that Abimelech was dead, they departed euery man vnto his owne place.

56 Thus God rendred the wickednes of Abimelech, which he did vnto his father, in slaying his seuentie brethren.

57 Also all the wickednes of the men of Shechem did God bring vpon their heads. So vpon them came the curse of Iotham the sonne of Ierubbaal.

Judges 10

1 After Abimelech there arose to defend Israel, Tola, the sonne of Puah, the sone of Dodo, a man of Issachar, which dwelt in Shamir in mount Ephraim.

2 And he iudged Israel three and twentie yeere and dyed, and was buried in Shamir.

3 And after him arose Iair a Gileadite, and iudged Israel two and twenty yeere.

4 And he had thirtie sonnes that rode on thirtie assecolts, and they had thirtie cities, which are called Hauoth-Iair vnto this day, and are in the land of Gilead.

5 And Iair dyed, and was buried in Kamon.

6 And the children of Israel wrought wickednesse againe in the sight of the Lord, and serued Baalim and Ashtaroth, and the gods of Aram, and the gods of Zidon, and the gods of Moab, and the gods of the children of Ammon, and the gods of the Philistims, and forsooke the Lord and serued not him.

7 Therefore the wrath of the Lord was kindled against Israel, and he solde them into the hands of the Philistims, and into the handes of the children of Ammon:

8 Who from that yere vexed and oppressed the children of Israel eighteene yeres, euen all the children of Israel that were beyond Iorden, in the land of the Amorites, which is in Gilead.

9 Moreouer, the children of Ammon went ouer Iorden to fight against Iudah, and against Beniamin, and against the house of Ephraim: so that Israel was sore tormented.

10 Then the children of Israel cryed vnto the Lord, saying, We haue sinned against thee, euen because we haue forsaken our owne God, and haue serued Baalim.

11 And the Lord sayd vnto the children of Israel, Did not I deliuer you from the Egyptians and from the Amorites, from the children of Ammon and from the Philistims?

12 The Zidonians also, and the Amalekites, and the Maonites did

oppresse you, and ye cryed to me and I saued you out of their hands.

13 Yet ye haue forsaken me, and serued other gods: wherefore I will deliuer you no more.

14 Goe, and cry vnto the gods which ye haue chosen: let them saue you in the time of your tribulation.

15 And the children of Israel sayde vnto the Lord, We haue sinned: doe thou vnto vs whatsoeuer please thee: onely we pray thee to deliuer vs this day.

16 Then they put away the strange gods from among them and serued the Lord: and his soule was grieued for the miserie of Israel.

17 Then the children of Ammon gathered themselues together, and pitched in Gilead: and the children of Israel assembled themselues, and pitched in Mizpeh.

18 And the people and princes of Gilead said one to another, Whosoeuer will beginne the battell against the children of Ammon, the same shall be head ouer all the inhabitants of Gilead.

Judges 11

1 Then Gilead begate Iphtah, and Iphtah the Gileadite was a valiant man, but the sonne of an harlot.

2 And Gileads wife bare him sonnes, and when the womans children were come to age, they thrust out Iphtah, and sayd vnto him, Thou shalt not inherite in our fathers house: for thou art the sonne of a strange woman.

3 Then Iphtah fledde from his brethren, and dwelt in the land of Tob: and there gathered idle fellowes to Iphtah, and went out with him.

4 And in processe of time the children of Ammon made warre with Israel.

5 And when the children of Ammon fought with Israel, the Elders of Gilead went to fet Iphtah out of the land of Tob.

6 And they saide vnto Iphtah, Come and be our captaine, that we may fight with the children of Ammon.

7 Iphtah then answered the Elders of Gilead, Did not ye hate me, and expell me out of my fathers house? how then come you vnto me now in time of your tribulation?

8 Then the Elders of Gilead saide vnto Iphtah, Therefore we turne againe to thee now, that thou mayest goe with vs, and fight against the children of Ammon, and bee our head ouer all the inhabitants of Gilead.

9 And Iphtah said vnto the Elders of Gilead, If ye bring me home againe to fight against the children of Ammon, if the Lord giue them before me, shall I be your head?

10 And the Elders of Gilead saide to Iphtah, The Lord be witnesse betweene vs, if we doe not according to thy wordes.

11 Then Iphtah went with the Elders of Gilead, and the people made him head and captaine ouer them: and Iphtah rehearsed all his wordes before the Lord in Mizpeh.

12 Then Iphtah sent messengers vnto the king of the children of Ammon, saying, What hast thou to doe with me, that thou art come against me, to fight in my lande?

13 And the King of the children of Ammon answered vnto the messengers of Iphtah, Because Israel tooke my lande, when they came vp from Egypt, from Arnon vnto Iabbok, and vnto Iorden: now therefore restore those lands quietly.

14 Yet Iphtah sent messengers againe vnto the King of the children of Ammon,

15 And said vnto him, Thus saith Iphtah, Israel tooke not the lande of Moab, nor the lande of the children of Ammon.

16 But when Israel came vp from Egypt, and walked through the wildernesse vnto the redde Sea, then they came to Kadesh.

17 And Israel sent messengers vnto the king of Edom, saying, Let me, I pray thee, goe thorowe thy lande: but the King of Edom woulde not consent: and also they sent vnto the King of Moab, but he would not: therefore Israel abode in Kadesh.

18 Then they went through the wildernesse, and compassed the lande of Edom, and the lande of Moab, and came by the Eastside of the lande of Moab, and pitched on the other side of Arnon, and came not within the coast of Moab: for Arnon was the border of Moab.

19 Also Israel sent messengers vnto Sihon, King of the Amorites, the King of Heshbon, and Israel said vnto him, Let vs passe, we pray thee, by thy lande vnto our place.

20 But Sihon consented not to Israel, that he shoulde goe through his coast: but Sihon gathered all his people together, and pitched in Iahaz, and fought with Israel.

21 And the Lord God of Israel gaue Sihon and all his folke into the handes of Israel, and they smote them: so Israel possessed all the lande of the Amorites, the inhabitants of that countrey:

22 And they possessed all the coast of the Amorites, from Arnon vnto Iabbok, and from the wildernesse euen vnto Iorden.

23 Nowe therefore the Lord God of Israel hath cast out the Amorites before his people Israel, and shouldest thou possesse it?

24 Wouldest not thou possesse that which Chemosh thy god giueth thee to possesse? So whomesoeuer the Lord our God driueth out before vs, them will we possesse.

25 And art thou nowe farre better then Balak the sonne of Zippor King of Moab? did he not striue with Israel and fight against them,

26 When Israel dwelt in Heshbon and in her townes, and in Aroer and in her townes, and in all the cities that are by the coastes of Arnon, three hundreth yeeres? why did ye not then recouer them in that space?

27 Wherefore, I haue not offended thee: but thou doest me wrong to warre against me. The Lord the Iudge be iudge this day betweene the children of Israel, and the children of Ammon.

28 Howbeit the King of the children of Ammon hearkened not vnto the wordes of Iphtah, which he had sent him.

29 Then the Spirite of the Lord came vpon Iphtah, and he passed ouer to Gilead and to Manasseh, and came to Mizpeh in Gilead, and from Mizpeh in Gilead he went vnto the children of Ammon.

30 And Iphtah vowed a vowe vnto the Lord, and said, If thou shalt deliuer the children of Ammon into mine handes,

31 Then that thing that commeth out of the doores of mine house to meete me, when I come home in peace from the children of Ammon, shall be the Lordes, and I will offer it for a burnt offering.

32 And so Iphtah went vnto the children of Ammon to fight against them, and the Lord deliuered them into his handes.

33 And he smote them from Aroer euen till thou come to Minnith, twentie cities, and so foorth to Abel of the vineyardes, with an exceeding great slaughter. Thus the children of Ammon were humbled before the children of Israel.

34 Nowe when Iphtah came to Mizpeh vnto his house, beholde, his daughter came out to meete him with timbrels and daunces, which was his onely childe: he had none other sonne, nor daughter.

35 And when hee sawe her, hee rent his clothes, and saide, Alas my daughter, thou hast brought me lowe, and art of them that trouble me: for I haue opened my mouth vnto the Lord, and can not goe backe.

36 And she said vnto him, My father, if thou hast opened thy mouth vnto the Lord, doe with me as thou hast promised, seeing that the Lord hath auenged thee of thine enemies the children of Ammon.

37 Also she saide vnto her father, Doe thus much for me: suffer me two moneths, that I may goe to the mountaines, and bewaile my virginitie, I and my fellowes.

38 And he sayde, Goe: and he sent her away two moneths: so she went with her companions, and lamented her virginitie vpon the moutaines.

39 And after the ende of two moneths, she turned againe vnto her father, who did with her according to his vowe which he had vowed, and she had knowen no man. and it was a custome in Israel:

40 The daughters of Israel went yere by yere to lament the daughter of Iphtah the Gileadite, foure dayes in a yeere.

Judges 12

1 And the me of Ephraim gathered themselues together, and went Northwarde, and saide vnto Iphtah, Wherefore wentest thou to fight against the children of Ammon, and diddest not call vs to goe with thee? we will therefore burne thine house vpon thee with fire.

2 And Iphtah said vnto them, I and my people were at great strife with the children of Ammon, and when I called you, ye deliuered me not out of their handes.

3 So when I sawe that ye deliuered me not, I put my life in mine hands, and went vpon the children of Ammon: so the Lord deliuered them into mine handes. Wherefore then are ye come vpon me nowe to fight against me?

4 Then Iphtah gathered all the men of Gilead, and fought with Ephraim: and the men of Gilead smote Ephraim, because they said, Ye Gileadites are runnagates of Ephraim among the Ephraimites, and among the Manassites.

5 Also the Gileadites tooke the passages of Iorden before the Ephraimites, and when the Ephraimites that were escaped, saide, Let me passe, then the men of Gilead said vnto him, Art thou an Ephraimite? If he said, Nay,

6 Then said they vnto him, Say nowe Shibboleth: and he said, Sibboleth: for he could not so pronounce: then they tooke him, and slewe him at the passages of Iorden: and there fel at that time of the Ephraimites two and fourtie thousand.

7 And Iphtah iudged Israel sixe yeere: then dyed Iphtah the Gileadite, and was buryed in one of the cities of Gilead.

8 After him Ibzan of Beth-lehem iudged Israel,

9 Who had thirtie sonnes and thirtie daughters, which he sent out, and tooke in thirtie daughters from abroade for his sonnes. and he iudged Israel seuen yeere.

10 Then Ibzan died, and was buryed at Bethlehem.

11 And after him iudged Israel Elon, a Zebulonite, and he iudged Israel tenne yeere.

12 Then Elon the Zebulonite dyed, and was buryed in Aijalon in the countrey of Zebulun.

13 And after him Abdon the sonne of Hillel the Pirathonite iudged Israel.

14 And he had fourty sonnes and thirtie nephewes that rode on seuentie assecoltes: and he iudged Israel eight yeeres.

15 Then dyed Abdon the sonne of Hillel the Pirathonite, and was buryed in Pirathon, in ye lande of Ephraim, in the Mount of the Amalekites.

Judges 13

1 Bvt the children of Israel continued to commit wickednesse in the sight of the Lord, and the Lord deliuerd them into the handes of the Philistims fourtie yeere.

2 Then there was a man in Zorah of the familie of the Danites, named Manoah, whose wife was baren, and bare not.

3 And the Angel of the Lord appeared vnto the woman, and said vnto her, Beholde nowe, thou art baren, and bearest not: but thou shalt conceiue, and beare a sonne.

4 And nowe therefore beware that thou drinke no wine, nor strong drinke, neither eate any vncleane thing.

5 For loe, thou shalt conceiue and beare a sonne, and no rasor shall come on his head: for the childe shall be a Nazarite vnto God from his birth: and he shall begin to saue Israel out of the handes of the Philistims.

6 Then the wife came, and tolde her husband, saying, A man of God came vnto me, and the facion of him was like the facion of the Angel of God exceeding feareful, but I asked him not whence he was, neither told he me his name,

7 But he saide vnto me, Beholde, thou shalt conceiue, and beare a sonne, and nowe thou shalt drinke no wine, nor strong drinke, neither eate any vncleane thing: for the childe shalbe a Nazarite to God from his birth to the day of his death.

8 Then Manoah prayed to the Lord and saide, I pray thee, my Lord, Let the man of God, whome thou sentest, come againe nowe vnto vs, and teach vs what we shall doe vnto the child when he is borne.

9 And God heard the voyce of Manoah, and the Angel of God came againe vnto the wife, as she sate in the fielde, but Manoah her husband was not with her.

10 And the wife made haste and ranne, and shewed her husband and sayde vnto him, Behold, the man hath appeared vnto me, that came vnto me to day.

11 And Manoah arose and went after his wife, and came to the man, and saide vnto him, Art thou the man that spakest vnto the woman? and he said, Yea.

12 Then Manoah sayde, Nowe let thy saying come to passe: but howe shall we order the childe and doe vnto him?

13 And the Angell of the Lord saide vnto Manoah, The woman must beware of all that I said vnto her.

14 She may eate of nothing that commeth of the vinetree: she shall not drinke wine nor strong drinke, nor eate any vncleane thing: let her obserue all that I haue commanded her.

15 Manoah then said vnto the Angell of the Lord, I pray thee, let vs reteine thee, vntill we haue made readie a kid for thee.

16 And the Angel of the Lord said vnto Manoah, Though thou make me abide, I will not eate of thy bread, and if thou wilt make a burnt offring, offer it vnto the Lord: for Manoah knewe not that it was an Angel of the Lord.

17 Againe Manoah said vnto the Angell of the Lord, What is thy name, that when thy saying is come to passe, we may honour thee?

18 And the Angell of the Lord saide vnto him, Why askest thou thus after my name, which is secret?

19 Then Manoah tooke a kid with a meate offering, and offered it vpon a stone vnto the Lord: and the Angell did wonderously, whiles Manoah and his wife looked on.

20 For when the flame came vp toward heauen from the altar, the Angel of the Lord ascended vp in the flame of the

altar, and Manoah and his wife behelde it, and fell on their faces vnto the grounde.

21 (So the Angel of the Lord did no more appeare vnto Manoah and his wife.) Then Manoah knewe that it was an Angel of the Lord.

22 And Manoah said vnto his wife, We shall surely dye, because we haue seene God.

23 But his wife saide vnto him, If the Lord woulde kill vs, he woulde not haue receiued a burnt offring, and a meate offring of our hands, neither would he haue shewed vs all these things, nor would now haue tolde vs any such.

24 And the wife bare a sonne, and called his name Samson: and the childe grewe, and the Lord blessed him.

25 And the Spirite of the Lord beganne to strengthen him in the host of Dan, betweene Zorah, and Eshtaol.

Judges 14

1 Nowe Samson went downe to Timnath, and saw a woman in Timnath of the daughters of the Philistims,

2 And he came vp and told his father and his mother and saide, I haue seene a woman in Timnath of the daughters of the Philistims: now therfore giue me her to wife.

3 Then his father and his mother sayde vnto him, Is there neuer a wife among the daughters of thy brethren, and among all my people, that thou must go to take a wife of the vncircumcised Philistims? And Samson sayd vnto his father, Giue mee her, for she pleaseth me well.

4 But his father and his mother knewe not that it came of the Lord, that he should seeke an occasion against the Philistims: for at that time the Philistims reigned ouer Israel.

5 Then went Samson and his father and his mother downe to Timnath, and came to ye vineyardes at Timnath: and beholde, a young Lyon roared vpon him.

6 And the Spirit of the Lord came vpon him, and he tare him, as one should haue rent a kid, and had nothing in his hand, neither told he his father nor his mother what he had done.

7 And he went down, and talked with the woman which was beautifull in the eyes of Samson.

8 And within a fewe dayes, when he returned to receiue her, he went aside to see the karkeis of the Lion: and behold, there was a swarme of bees, and hony in the body of the Lyon.

9 And he tooke therof in his handes, and went eating, and came to his father and to his mother, and gaue vnto them, and they did eate: but hee told not them, that he had taken the hony out of the body of the lyon.

10 So his father went down vnto the woman, and Samson made there a feast: for so vsed the yong men to doe.

11 And when they sawe him, they brought thirtie companions to be with him.

12 Then Samson sayd vnto them, I will nowe put forth a riddle vnto you: and if you can declare it me within seuen dayes of the feast, and finde it out, I will giue you thirty sheetes, and thirtie change of garments.

13 But if you cannot declare it mee, then shall yee giue mee thirty sheetes and thirtie change of garments. And they answered him, Put forth thy riddle, that we may heare it.

14 And he sayd vnto them, Out of the eater came meate, and out of the strong came sweetenesse: and they could not in three dayes expound the riddle.

15 And when the seuenth day was come, they said vnto Samsons wife, Entise thine husband, that he may declare vs the riddle, lest wee burne thee and thy fathers house with fire. Haue ye called vs, to possesse vs? is it not so?

16 And Samsons wife wept before him, and said, Surely thou hatest mee and louest mee not: for thou hast put forth a riddle vnto the children of my people, and hast not told it mee. And hee sayd vnto her, Beholde, I haue not told it my father, nor my mother, and shall I tell it thee?

17 Then Samsons wife wept before him seuen dayes, while their feast lasted: and when the seuenth day came he tolde her, because she was importunate vpon him: so she told the riddle to the children of her people.

18 And the men of ye citie sayde vnto him the seuenth day before the Sunne went downe, What is sweeter then honie? and what is stronger then a lyon? Then sayd hee vnto them, If yee had not plowed with my heiffer, yee had not found out my riddle.

19 And the Spirite of the Lord came vpon him, and he went downe to Ashkelon, and slew thirtie men of them and spoyled them, and gaue chaunge of garments vnto them, which expounded the riddle: and his wrath was kindled, and he went vp to his fathers house.

20 Then Samsons wife was giuen to his companion, whom he had vsed as his friend.

Judges 15

1 But within a while after, in the time of wheate haruest, Samson visited his wife with a kid, saying, I wil go in to my wife into the chamber: but her father would not suffer him to goe in.

2 And her father sayde, I thought that thou hadst hated her: therefore gaue I her to thy companion. Is not her yonger sister fayrer then shee? take her, I pray thee, in stead of the other.

3 Then Samson saide vnto them, Nowe am I more blamelesse then the Philistims: therefore will I doe them displeasure.

4 And Samson went out, and tooke three hundreth foxes, and tooke firebrands, and turned them taile to taile, and put a firebrand in ye middes betweene two tailes.

5 And when he had set the brandes on fire, he sent them out into the standing corne of the Philistims, and burnt vp both the rickes and the standing corne with the vineyardes and oliues.

6 Then the Philistims sayde, Who hath done this? And they answered, Samson the sonne in law of the Timnite, because hee had taken his wife, and giuen her to his companion. Then the Philistims came vp and burnt her and her father with fire.

7 And Samson saide vnto them, Though yee haue done this, yet wil I be auenged of you, and then I wil cease.

8 So hee smote them hippe and thigh with a mightie plague: then hee went and dwelt in the top of the rocke Etam.

9 Then the Philistims came vp, and pitched in Iudah, and were spred abroad in Lehi.

10 And the men of Iudah sayde, Why are yee come vp vnto vs? And they answered, To binde Samson are we come vp, and to do to him as hee hath done to vs.

11 Then three thousande men of Iudah went to the top of the rocke Etam, and sayde to Samson, Knowest thou not that the Philistims are rulers ouer vs? Wherefore then hast thou done thus vnto vs? And he answered them, As they did vnto me, so haue I done vnto them.

12 Againe they sayd vnto him, Wee are come to binde thee, and to deliuer thee into the hande of the Philistims. And Samson sayde vnto them, Sweare vnto me, that yee will not fall vpon me your selues.

13 And they answered him, saying, No, but we will bynde thee and deliuer thee vnto their hande, but we will not kill thee. And they bound him with two newe cordes, and brought him from the rocke.

14 When hee came to Lehi, the Philistims shouted against him, and the Spirite of the Lord came vpon him, and the cordes that were vpon his armes, became as flaxe that was burnt with fire: for the bandes loosed from his handes.

15 And he found a new iawebone of an asse, and put forth his hand, and caught it, and slewe a thousand men therewith.

16 Then Samson sayd, With the iaw of an asse are heapes vpon heapes: with the iawe of an asse haue I slaine a thousand men.

17 And when he had left speaking, hee cast away the iawebone out of his hande, and called that place, Ramath-Lehi.

18 And he was sore a thirst, and called on the Lord, and sayde, Thou hast giuen this great deliuerance into the hand of thy seruaunt: and nowe shall I dye for thirst, and fall into the handes of the vncircumcised?

19 Then God brake the cheeke tooth, that was in the iawe, and water came thereout: and when he had drunke, his Spirit came againe, and he was reuiued: wherefore the name therof is called, Enhakkore, which is in Lehi vnto this day.

20 And hee iudged Israel in the dayes of the Philistims twentie yeeres.

Judges 16

1 Then went Samson to Azzah, and sawe there an harlot, and went in vnto her.

2 And it was tolde to the Azzahites, Samson is come hither. And they went about, and laied wayte for him all night in the gate of the citie, and were quiet all the nyght, saying, Abide till the morning earely, and we shall kill him.

3 And Samson slept till midnight, and arose at midnight, and tooke the doores of the gates of the citie, and the two postes and lift them away with the barres, and put them vpon his shoulders, and caried them vp to the top of the mountaine that is before Hebron.

4 And after this hee loued a woman by the riuer of Sorek, whose name was Delilah:

5 Vnto whome came the princes of the Philistims, and said vnto her, Entise him, and see wherein his great strength lieth, and by what meane we may ouercome him, that we may binde him, and punish him, and euery one of vs shall giue thee eleuen hundreth shekels of siluer.

6 And Delilah saide to Samson, Tell mee, I pray thee, wherein thy great strength lieth, and wherewith thou mightest bee bound, to doe thee hurt.

7 Samson then answered vnto her, If they binde mee with seuen greene cordes, that were neuer dryed, then shall I bee weake, and be as an other man.

8 And the princes of the Philistims brought her seuen greene cordes that were not dry, and she bound him therewith.

9 (And she had men lying in wayte with her in the chamber) Then she said vnto him, The Philistims be vpon thee, Samson. And hee brake the cordes, as a threede of towe is broken, when it feeleth fire: so his strength was not knowen.

10 After Delilah saide vnto Samson, See, thou hast mocked mee and tolde mee lies. I pray thee nowe, tell me wherewith thou mightest be bound.

11 Then he answered her, If they binde mee with newe ropes that neuer were occupied, then shall I be weake, and be as an other man.

12 Delilah therefore tooke newe ropes, and bounde him therewith, and saide vnto him, The Philistims be vpon thee, Samson: (and men lay in wayte in the chamber) and hee brake them from his armes, as a threede.

13 Afterward Delilah said to Samson, Hitherto thou hast beguiled mee, and tolde me lies: tell me how thou mightest be bounde. And he sayde vnto her, If thou plattedst seuen lockes of mine head with the threedes of the woufe.

14 And she fastened it with a pinne, and saide vnto him, The Philistims be vpon thee, Samson. And he awoke out of his sleepe, and went away with the pinne of the webbe and the woufe.

15 Againe shee sayde vnto him, Howe canst thou say, I loue thee, when thine heart is not with me? thou hast mocked mee these three times, and hast not

tolde me wherein thy great strength lieth.

16 And because shee was importunate vpon him with her wordes continually, and vexed him, his soule was pained vnto the death.

17 Therefore he tolde her all his heart, and said vnto her, There neuer came rasor vpon mine head: for I am a Nazarite vnto God from my mothers wombe: therefore if I bee shauen, my strength will goe from me, and I shalbe weake, and be like all other men.

18 And when Delilah sawe that he had tolde her all his heart, she sent, and called for the Princes of ye Philistims, saying, Come vp once againe: for he hath shewed mee all his heart. Then the Princes of the Philistims came vp vnto her, and brought the money in their handes.

19 And she made him sleepe vpon her knees, and she called a man, and made him to shaue off the seuen lockes of his head, and shee began to vexe him, and his strength was gone from him.

20 Then she said, The Philistims be vpon thee, Samson. And hee awoke out of his sleepe, and thought, I will go out now as at other times, and shake my selfe, but he knewe not that the Lord was departed from him.

21 Therefore the Philistims tooke him, and put out his eyes, and brought him downe to Azzah, and bounde him with fetters: and hee did grinde in the prison house.

22 And the heare of his head began to growe againe after that it was shauen.

23 Then the Princes of the Philistims gathered them together for to offer a great sacrifice vnto Dagon their god, and to reioyce: for they said, Our god hath deliuered Samson our enemie into our handes.

24 Also when the people saw him, they praysed their god: for they sayde, Our god hath deliuered into our hands our enemie and destroyer of our countrey, which hath slayne many of vs.

25 And when their heartes were merie, they said, Call Samson, that he may make vs pastime. So they called Samson out of the prison house, and he was a laughing stocke vnto them, and they set him betweene the pillars.

26 Then Samson saide vnto the seruant that led him by the hande, Lead me, that I may touch the pillars that the house standeth vpon, and that I may leane to them.

27 (Nowe the house was full of men and women, and there were all the princes of the Philistims: also vpon the roofe were about three thousande men and women that behelde while Samson played)

28 Then Samson called vnto the Lord, and sayde, O Lord God, I pray thee, thinke vpon me: O God, I beseech thee, strengthen me at this time onely, that I may be at once auenged of the Philistims for my two eyes.

29 And Samson layd hold on the two middle pillars whereupon the house stood, and on which it was borne vp: on the one with his right hand, and on the other with his left.

30 Then Samson saide, Let me lose my life with the Philistims: and he bowed him with all his might, and the house fell vpon the princes, and vpon all the people that were therein. so the dead which he slewe at his death were more then they which he had slaine in his life.

31 Then his brethren, and all the house of his father came downe and tooke him, and brought him vp and buryed him betweene Zorah and Eshtaol, in the sepulchre of Manoah his father: nowe he had iudged Israel twenty yeeres.

Judges 17

1 There was a man of mount Ephraim, whose name was Michah,

2 And he saide vnto his mother, The eleuen hundreth shekels of siluer that were taken from thee, for the which thou cursedst, and spakedst it, euen in mine hearing, beholde, the siluer is with me, I tooke it. Then his mother saide, Blessed be my sonne of the Lord.

3 And when he had restored the eleuen hundreth shekels of siluer to his mother, his mother sayd, I had dedicate the siluer to the Lord of mine hand for my sonne, to make a grauen and molten image. Now therfore I will giue it thee againe.

4 And when he had restored the money vnto his mother, his mother tooke two hundreth shekels of siluer, and gaue them to the founder, which made thereof a grauen and molten image, and it was in the house of Michah.

5 And this man Michah had an house of gods, and made an Ephod, and Teraphim, and cosecrated one of his sonnes, who was his Priest.

6 In those dayes there was no King in Israel, but euery man did that which was good in his owne eyes.

7 There was also a yong man out of Bethlehem Iudah, of the familie of Iudah: who was a Leuite, and soiourned there.

8 And the man departed out of the citie, euen out of Beth-lehem Iudah, to dwell where he coulde finde a place: and as he iourneyed, he came to mount Ephraim to the house of Michah

9 And Michah saide vnto him, Whence comest thou? And the Leuite answered him, I come from Beth-lehem Iudah, and goe to dwell where I may finde a place.

10 Then Michah said vnto him, Dwell with me, and be vnto me a father and a Priest, and I will giue thee ten shekels of siluer by yeere, and a sute of apparell, and thy meate and drinke. So the Leuite went in.

11 And the Leuite was content to dwel with the man, and the yong man was vnto him as one of his owne sonnes.

12 And Michah consecrated the Leuite, and the yong man was his Priest, and was in the house of Michah.

13 Then said Michah, Nowe I know that the Lord will be good vnto me, seeing I haue a Leuite to my Priest.

Judges 18

1 In those dayes there was no King in Israel, and at the same time the tribe of Dan sought them an inheritance to dwell in: for vnto that time all their inheritance had not fallen vnto them among the tribes of Israel.

2 Therefore the children of Dan sent of their familie, fiue men out of their coastes, euen men expert in warre, out of Zorah and Eshtaol, to viewe the lande and search it out, and saide vnto them, Goe, and search out the lande. Then they came to mount Ephraim to the house of Michah and lodged there.

3 When they were in the house of Michah, they knewe the voyce of the yong man the Leuite: and being turned in thither, they saide vnto him, Who brought thee hither? or what makest thou in this place? and what hast thou to doe here?

4 And he answered them, Thus and thus dealeth Michah with me, and hath hired me, and I am his Priest.

5 Againe they said vnto him, Aske counsell nowe of God, that we may knowe whether the way which we goe, shalbe prosperous.

6 And the Priest sayde vnto them, Goe in peace: for the Lord guideth your way which ye goe.

7 Then the fiue men departed and came to Laish, and sawe the people that were therein, which dwelt carelesse, after the maner of the Zidonians, quiet and sure, because no man made any trouble in the lande, or vsurped any dominion: also they were farre from the Zidonians, and had no businesse with other men.

8 So they came againe vnto their brethren to Zorah and Eshtaol: and their brethren saide vnto them, What haue ye done?

9 And they answered, Arise, that we may goe vp against them: for we haue seene the lande, and surely it is very good, and doe ye sit stil? be not slouthfull to goe and enter to possesse the lande:

10 (If ye will goe, ye shall come vnto a carelesse people, and the countrey is large) for God hath giuen it into your hande. It is a place which doeth lacke nothing that is in the worlde.

11 Then there departed thence of the familie of the Danites, from Zorah and from Eshtaol, sixe hundreth men appointed with instruments of warre.

12 And they went vp, and pitched in Kiriath-iearim in Iudah: wherefore they called that place, Mahaneh-Dan vnto this day: and it is behinde Kiriath-iearim.

13 And they went thence vnto mount Ephraim, and came to the house of Michah.

14 Then answered the fiue men, that went to spie out the countrey of Laish, and said vnto their brethren, Knowe ye not, that there is in these houses an Ephod, and Teraphim, and a grauen and a molten image? Nowe therefore consider what ye haue to doe.

15 And they turned thitherward and came to the house of the yong man the Leuite, euen vnto the house of Michah, and saluted him peaceably.

16 And the six hundreth men appointed with their weapons of warre, which were of the children of Dan, stoode by the entring of the gate.

17 Then the fiue men that went to spie out the land, went in thither, and tooke the grauen image and the Ephod, and the Teraphim, and the molten image: and the Priest stoode in the entring of the gate with the sixe hundreth men, that were appointed with weapons of warre,

18 And the other went into Michahs house and fet the grauen image, the Ephod, and the Teraphim, and the molten image. Then saide the Priest vnto them, What doe ye?

19 And they answered him, Holde thy peace: lay thine hande vpon thy mouth, and come with vs to be our father and Priest. Whether is it better that thou shouldest be a Priest vnto ye house of one man, or that thou shouldest be a Priest vnto a tribe and to a familie in Israel?

20 And the Priestes heart was glad, and hee tooke the Ephod and the Teraphim, and the grauen image, and went among the people.

21 And they turned and departed, and put the children, and the cattell, and the substance before them.

22 When they were farre off from the house of Michah, the men that were in the houses neere to Michahs house, gathered together, and pursued after the children of Dan,

23 And cryed vnto the children of Dan: who turned their faces, and said vnto Michah, What ayleth thee, that thou makest an outcrie?

24 And hee saide, Yee haue taken away my gods, which I made, and the Priest, and go your wayes: and what haue I more? howe then say ye vnto me, what ayleth thee?

25 And the children of Dan sayde vnto him, Let not thy voyce be heard among vs, least angrie fellowes runne vpon thee, and thou lose thy life with the liues of thine housholde.

26 So the children of Dan went their wayes: and when Michah saw that they were too strong for him, hee turned, and went backe vnto his house.

27 And they tooke the things which Michah had made, and the Priest which he had, and came vnto Laish, vnto a quiet people and without mistrust, and smote them with the edge of the sworde, and burnt the citie with fire:

28 And there was none to helpe, because Laish was farre from Zidon, and they had no businesse with other men: also it was in the valley that lyeth by Beth-rehob. After, they built the citie, and dwelt therein,

29 And called the name of the citie Dan, after the name of Dan their father which was borne vnto Israel: howbeit the name of the city was Laish at the beginning.

30 Then the children of Dan set them vp the grauen image: and Ionathan the sonne of Gershom, the sonne of Manasseh and his sonnes were the Priestes in the tribe of the Danites vntil the day of the captiuitie of the lande.

31 So they set them vp the grauen image, which Michah had made, all the while the house of God was in Shiloh.

Judges 19

1 Also in those dayes, when there was no king in Israel, a certaine Leuite dwelt on the side of mount Ephraim, and tooke to wife a concubine out of Beth-lehem Iudah,

2 And his concubine played ye whore there, and went away from him vnto her fathers house to Beth-lehem Iudah, and there continued the space of foure monethes.

3 And her husband arose and went after her, to speake friendly vnto her, and to bring her againe: he had also his seruant with him, and a couple of asses: and she brought him vnto her fathers house, and when the yong womans father sawe him, he reioyced of his comming.

4 And his father in lawe, the yong womans father reteined him: and he abode with him three dayes: so they did eate and drinke, and lodged there.

5 And when the fourth day came, they arose early in the morning, and he prepared to depart: then the yong womans father said vnto his sonne in lawe, Comfort thine heart with a morsel of bread, and then go your way.

6 So they sate downe, and did eate and drinke both of them together. And the yong womans father said vnto the man, Be content, I pray thee, and tary all night, and let thine heart be merie.

7 And when the man rose vp to depart, his father in lawe was earnest: therefore he returned, and lodged there.

8 And he arose vp earely the fifth day to depart, and the yong womans father saide, Comfort thine heart, I pray thee: and they taryed vntill after midday, and they both did eate.

9 Afterwarde when the man arose to depart with his concubine and his seruant, his father in lawe, the yong womans father said vnto him, Beholde nowe, the day draweth towarde euen: I pray you, tary all night: beholde, the sunne goeth to rest: lodge here, that thine heart may be merie, and to morowe get you earely vpon your way, and goe to thy tent.

10 But the man would not tarry, but arose and departed, and came ouer against Iebus, (which is Ierusalem) and his two asses laden, and his concubine were with him.

11 When they were neere to Iebus, the day was sore spent, and the seruant said vnto his master, Come, I pray thee, and let vs turne into this citie of the Iebusites, and lodge all night there.

12 And his master answered him, We will not turne into the citie of strangers that are not of the children of Israel, but we will goe forth to Gibeah.

13 And he said vnto his seruant, Come, and let vs drawe neere to one of these places, that wee may lodge in Gibeah or in Ramah.

14 So they went forward vpon their way, and the sunne went downe vpon them neere to Gibeah, which is in Beniamin.

15 Then they turned thither to goe in and lodge in Gibeah: and when he came, he sate him downe in a streete of the citie: for there was no man that tooke them into his house to lodging.

16 And beholde, there came an old man from his work out of the field at euen, and the man was of mount Ephraim, but dwelt in Gibeah: and the men of the place were the children of Iemini.

17 And when he had lift vp his eyes, he sawe a wayfairing man in the streetes of the citie: then this olde man sayde, Whither goest thou, and whence camest thou?

18 And hee answered him, Wee came from Beth-lehem Iudah, vnto the side of Mout Ephraim: from thence am I: and I went to Beth-lehem Iudah, and go now to the house of the Lord: and no man receiueth mee to house,

19 Although we haue straw and prouader for our asses, and also bread and wine for me and thine handmayde, and for the boy that is with thy seruant: we lacke nothing.

20 And the olde man sayde, Peace bee with thee: as for all that thou lackest, shalt thou finde with me: onely abide not in the streete al night.

21 So he brought him into his house, and gaue fodder vnto the asses: and they washed their feete, and did eate and drinke.

22 And as they were making their hearts merie, beholde, the men of the citie, wicked men beset the house round about, and smote at the doore, and spake to this olde man the master of the house saying, Bring forth the man that came into thine house that we may knowe him.

23 And this man the master of ye house went out vnto the, and said vnto them, Nay my brethre, do not so wickedly, I pray you: seeing that this man is come into mine house, do not this villenie.

24 Behold, here is my daughter, a virgine, and his concubine: them wil I bring out nowe, and humble them, and doe with them what seemeth you good: but to this man doe not this villenie.

25 But the men woulde not hearken to him: therefore ye man tooke his concubine, and brought her out vnto them: and they knewe her and abused her all the night vnto the morning: and when the day began to spring, they let her goe.

26 So the woman came in the dawning of the day, and fell downe at the doore of the mans house where her Lord was, till the light day.

27 And her lorde arose in the morning, and opened the doores of the house, and went out to goe his way, and beholde, the

woman his concubine was dead at the doore of the house and her handes lay vpon the thresholde.

28 And hee said vnto her, Vp and let vs goe: but shee answered not. Then he tooke her vp vpon the asse, and the man rose vp, and went vnto his place.

29 And whe he was come to his house, he took a knife, and laid hand on his concubine, and deuided her in pieces with her bones into twelue parts, and sent her through all quarters of Israel.

30 And all that saw it, said, There was no such thing done or seene since the time that the children of Israel came vp from the lande of Egypt vnto this day: consider the matter, consult and giue sentence.

Judges 20

1 Then all the children of Israel went out, and the Congregation was gathered together as one man, from Dan to Beersheba, with the land of Gilead, vnto the Lord in Mizpeh.

2 And the chiefe of all the people, and all the tribes of Israel assembled in the Congregation of the people of God foure hundreth thousand footemen that drewe sword.

3 (Now the children of Beniamin heard that the children of Israel were gone vp to Mizpeh) Then the children of Israel saide, Howe is this wickednesse committed?

4 And the same Leuite, the womans husband that was slaine, answered and saide, I came vnto Gibeah that is in Beniamin with my concubine to lodge,

5 And the men of Gibeah arose against me, and beset the house round about vpon mee by night, thinking to haue slaine me, and haue forced my concubine that she is dead.

6 Then I tooke my concubine, and cut her in pieces, and sent her throughout all the countrey of the inheritance of Israel: for they haue committed abomination and villenie in Israel.

7 Behold, ye are al children of Israel: giue your aduise, and counsell herein.

8 Then all the people arose as one man, saying, There shall not a man of vs goe to his tent, neither any turne into his house.

9 But now this is that thing which we will do to Gibeah: we wil goe vp by lot against it,

10 And we wil take ten men of the hundreth throughout al the tribes of Israel, and an hundreth of the thousand, and a thousand of ten thousand to bring vitaile for the people that they may do (when they come to Gibeah of Beniamin) according to all the villeny, that it hath done in Israel.

11 So all the men of Israel were gathered against the citie, knit together, as one man.

12 And the tribes of Israel sent men through al the tribe of Beniamin, saying, What wickednesse is this that is committed among you?

13 Nowe therefore deliuer vs those wicked men which are in Gibeah, that we may put them to death, and put away euill from Israel: but the children of Beniamin would not obey the voyce of their brethren the children of Israel.

14 But ye children of Beniamin gathered them selues together out of the cities vnto Gibeah, to come out and fight against the children of Israel.

15 And ye children of Beniamin were nombred at that time out of the cities six and twenty thousand men that drewe sworde, beside the inhabitants of Gibeah, which were nombred seuen hundreth chosen men.

16 Of all this people were seuen hundreth chosen men, being left handed: all these could sling stones at an heare breadth, and not faile.

17 Also the men of Israel, beside Beniamin, were nombred foure hundreth thousande men that drew sword, euen all men of warre.

18 And the children of Israel arose, and went vp to the house of God, and asked of God, saying, Which of vs shall goe vp first to fight against the children of Beniamin? And the Lord said, Iudah shalbe first.

19 Then the children of Israel arose vp earely and camped against Gibeah.

20 And the men of Israel went out to battell against Beniamin, and the men of Israel put themselues in aray to fight against the beside Gibeah.

21 And the children of Beniamin came out of Gibeah, and slewe downe to the ground of the Israelites that day two and twentie thousand men.

22 And the people, the men of Israel plucked vp their hearts, and set their battel againe in aray in the place where they put them in aray the first day.

23 (For the children of Israel had gone vp and wept before the Lord vnto the euening, and had asked of the Lord, saying, Shall I goe againe to battel against the children of Beniamin my brethren? and the Lord said, Go vp against them)

24 Then the children of Israel came neere against the children of Beniamin the second day.

25 Also the second day Beniamin came forth to meete them out of Gibeah, and slewe downe to the grounde of the children of Israel againe eighteene thousand men: all they could handle the sword.

26 Then al the children of Israel went vp and all the people came also vnto the house of God, and wept and sate there before the Lord and fasted that day vnto the euening, and offred burnt offrings and peace offrings before the Lord.

27 And the children of Israel asked the Lord (for there was the Arke of the couenat of God in those dayes,

28 And Phinehas the sonne of Eleazar, the sonne of Aaron stoode before it at that time) saying, Shall I yet goe anie more to battel against the children of Beniamin my brethren, or shall I cease?

And the Lord said, Go vp: for to morowe I will deliuer them into your hand.

29 And Israel set men to lie in waite round about Gibeah.

30 And the children of Israel went vp against the children of Beniamin the third day, and put theselues in aray against Gibeah, as at other times.

31 Then the children of Beniamin comming out against the people, were drawen from the citie: and they began to smite of ye people and kill as at other times, euen by the wayes in the fielde (whereof one goeth vp to the house of God, and the other to Gibeah) vpon a thirtie men of Israel.

32 (For the children of Beniamin sayd, They are fallen before vs, as at the first. But the children of Israel saide, Let vs flee and plucke them away from the citie vnto the hie wayes)

33 And all the men of Israel rose vp out of their place, and put themselues in aray at Baal-tamar: and the men that lay in wayte of the Israelites came forth of their place, euen out of the medowes of Gibeah,

34 And they came ouer against Gibeah, ten thousande chosen men of all Israel, and the battell was sore: for they knewe not that the euill was neere them.

35 And the Lord smote Beniamin before Israel, and the children of Israel destroyed of the Beniamites the same day fiue and twenty thousand and an hundreth men: all they could handle the sword.

36 So the children of Beniamin sawe that they were striken downe: for the men of Israel gaue place to the Beniamites, because they trusted to the men that lay in waite, which they had laide beside Gibeah.

37 And they that lay in wait hasted, and brake forth toward Gibeah, and the ambushment drewe themselues along, and smote all the citie with the edge of the sword.

38 Also the men of Israel had appoynted a certaine time with the ambushmentes, that they should make a great flame and smoke rise vp out of the citie.

39 And when the men of Israel retired in the battel, Beniamin began to smite and kill of the men of Israel about thirtie persons: for they said, Surely they are striken downe before vs, as in the first battell.

40 But when the flame bega to arise out of the citie, as a pillar of smoke, the Beniamites looked backe, and behold, the flame of the citie began to ascend vp to heauen.

41 Then the men of Israel turned againe, and the men of Beniamin were astonied: for they saw that euill was neere vnto them.

42 Therefore they fled before the men of Israel vnto the way of the wildernesse, but the battell ouertooke them: also they which came out of the cities, slew them among them.

43 Thus they compassed the Beniamites about, and chased them at

ease, and ouerranne them, euen ouer against Gibeah on the Eastside.

44 And there were slaine of Beniamin eyghteene thousad men, which were all men of warre.

45 And they turned and fled to the wildernes vnto the rocke of Rimmon: and the Israelites glayned of them by the way fiue thousand men, and pursued after them vnto Gidom, and slewe two thousand men of them,

46 So that all that were slayne that day of Beniamin, were fiue and twentie thousand men that drewe sword, which were all men of warre:

47 But sixe hundreth men turned and fled to the wildernesse vnto the rocke of Rimmon, and abode in the rocke of Rimmon foure moneths.

48 Then the men of Israel returned vnto the children of Beniamin, and smote them with the edge of the sword from the men of the citie vnto the beasts, and all that came to hand: also they set on fire all the cities that they coulde come by.

Judges 21

1 Moreouer, the men of Israel sware in Mizpeh, saying, None of vs shall giue his daughter vnto the Beniamites to wyfe.

2 And the people came vnto ye house of God and abode there till euen before God, and lift vp their voyces, and wept with great lamentation,

3 And sayde, O Lord God of Israel, why is this come to passe in Israel, that this day one tribe of Israel should want?

4 And on the morow the people rose vp and made there an altar, and offred burnt offrings and peace offrings.

5 Then the children of Israel said, Who is he among all the tribes of Israel, that came not vp with the Congregation vnto the Lord? for they had made a great othe concerning him that came not vp to the Lord to Mizpeh, saying, Let him die the death.

6 And the children of Israel were sory for Beniamin their brother, and said, There is one tribe cut off from Israel this day.

7 How shall we do for wiues to them that remaine, seeing we haue sworne by the Lord, that we will not giue them of our daughters to wiues?

8 Also they saide, Is there any of the tribes of Israel that came not vp to Mizpeh to the Lord? and beholde, there came none of Iabesh Gilead vnto the hoste and to the Congregation.

9 For when the people were vewed; beholde, none of the inhabitants of Iabesh Gilead were there.

10 Therefore the Congregation sent thither twelue thousande men of the most valiant, and commanded them, saying, Goe, and smite the inhabitants of Iabesh Gilead with the edge of the sword, both women, and children.

11 And this is it that ye shall do: ye shall vtterly destroye all the males and all the women that haue lien by men.

12 And they found among the inhabitants of Iabesh Gilead foure hundreth maides, virgins that had knowne no man by lying with any male: and they brought them vnto the hoste to Shiloh, which is in the land of Canaan.

13 Then the whole Congregation sent and spake with the children of Beniamin that were in the rocke of Rimmon, and called peaceably vnto them:

14 And Beniamin came againe at that time, and they gaue them wiues which they had saued aliue of the women of Iabesh Gilead: but they had not so ynough for them.

15 And the people were sorie for Beniamin, because the Lord had made a breach in the tribes of Israel.

16 Therefore the Elders of the Congregation said, How shall we doe for wiues to the remnant? for the women of Beniamin are destroyed.

17 And they saide, there must be an inheritance for them that be escaped of Beniamin, that a tribe be not destroyed out of Israel.

18 Howbeit we may not giue them wiues of our daughters: for the childre of Israel had sworne, saying, Cursed be he that giueth a wise to Beniamin.

19 Therefore they said, Beholde, there is a feast of the Lord euery yere in Shiloh in a place, which is on the Northside of Beth-el, and on the Eastside of the way that goeth vp from Beth-el to Shechem, and on the South of Lebonah.

20 Therefore they commanded the children of Beniamin, saying, Goe, and lye in waite in the vineyardes.

21 And when ye see that the daughters of Shiloh come out to dance in dances, then come ye out of the vineyards, and catche you euery man a wife of the daughters of Shiloh, and goe into the land of Beniamin.

22 And when their fathers or their brethren come vnto vs to complaine, we wil say vnto them, Haue pitie on them for our sakes, because we reserued not to eche man his wife in the warre, and because ye haue not giuen vnto them hitherto, ye haue sinned.

23 And the children of Beniamin did so, and tooke wiues of them that danced according to their nomber: which they tooke, and went away, and returned to their inheritance, and repaired the cities and dwelt in them.

24 So the children of Israel departed thence at that time, euery man to his tribe, and to his familie, and went out from thence euery man to his inheritance.

25 In those dayes there was no King in Israel, but euery man did that which was good in his eyes.

Ruth

Ruth 1

1 In the time that the Iudges ruled, there was a dearth in the lande, and a man of Beth-lehem Iudah went for to soiourne in the countrey of Moab, he, and his wife, and his two sonnes.

2 And the name of the man was Elimelech, and the name of his wife, Naomi: and the names of his two sonnes, Mahlon, and Chilion, Ephrathites of Beth-lehem Iudah: and when they came into the land of Moab, they continued there.

3 Then Elimelech the husband of Naomi died, and she remayned with her two sonnes,

4 Which tooke them wiues of the Moabites: the ones name was Orpah, and the name of ye other Ruth: and they dwelled there about ten yeeres.

5 And Mahlon and Chilion dyed also both twaine: so the woman was left destitute of her two sonnes, and of her husband.

6 Then she arose with her daughters in law, and returned from the countrey of Moab: for she had heard say in the countrey of Moab, that the Lord had visited his people, and giuen them bread.

7 Wherefore shee departed out of the place where she was, and her two daughters in law with her, and they went on their way to returne vnto the land of Iudah.

8 Then Naomi saide vnto her two daughters in lawe, Goe, returne eche of you vnto her owne mothers house: the Lord shew fauour vnto you, as ye haue done with the dead, and with me.

9 The Lord graunt you, that you may finde rest, either of you in the house of her husband. And when she kissed them, they lift vp their voice and wept.

10 And they saide vnto her, Surely we will returne with thee vnto thy people.

11 But Naomi saide, Turne againe, my daughters: for what cause will you go with me? are there any more sonnes in my wombe, that they may bee your husbands?

12 Turne againe, my daughters: go your way: for I am too olde to haue an husband. If I should say, I haue hope, and if I had an husband this night: yea, if I had borne sonnes,

13 Would yee tarie for them, till they were of age? would ye be deferred for them from taking of husbands? nay my daughters: for it grieueth me much for your sakes that the hand of the Lord is gone out against me.

14 Then they lift vp their voyce and wept againe, and Orpah kissed her mother in lawe, but Ruth abode still with her.

15 And Naomi said, Beholde, thy sister in law is gone backe vnto her people and vnto her gods: returne thou after thy sister in lawe.

16 And Ruth answered, Intreate mee not to leaue thee, nor to depart from thee: for whither thou goest, I will goe: and where thou dwellest, I will dwell: thy people shall be my people, and thy God my God.

17 Where thou diest, will I die, and there will I be buried. the Lord do so to me and more also, if ought but death depart thee and me.

18 Whe she saw that she was stedfastly minded to go with her, she left speaking vnto her.

19 So they went both vntill they came to Beth-lehem: and when they were come

to Beth-lehem, it was noysed of them through all the citie, and they said, Is not this Naomi?

20 And she answered them, Call me not Naomi, but call me Mara: for the Almightie hath giuen me much bitternes.

21 I went out full, and the Lord hath caused me to returne emptie: why call ye me Naomi, seeing the Lord hath humbled me, and the Almightie hath brought me vnto aduersitie?

22 So Naomi returned and Ruth the Moabitesse her daughter in law with her, when she came out of the countrey of Moab: and they came to Beth-lehem in the beginning of barly haruest.

Ruth 2

1 Then Naomis husband had a kinsman, one of great power of the familie of Elimelech, and his name was Boaz.

2 And Ruth ye Moabitesse said vnto Naomi, I pray thee, Let mee goe to the fielde, and gather eares of corne after him, in whose sight I finde fauour. And she said vnto her, Goe my daughter.

3 And she went, and came and gleaned in the fielde after the reapers, and it came to passe, that she met with the portion of the fielde of Boaz, who was of the familie of Elimelech.

4 And behold, Boaz came from Beth-lehem, and saide vnto the reapers, The Lord be with you: and they answered him, The Lord blesse thee.

5 Then saide Boaz vnto his seruant that was appointed ouer the reapers, Whose maide is this?

6 And the seruant that was appointed ouer the reapers, answered, and said, It is the Moabitish maide, that came with Naomi out of the countrey of Moab:

7 And shee saide vnto vs, I pray you, let mee gleane and gather after the reapers among the sheaues: so shee came, and hath continued from that time in the morning vnto now, saue that she taried a litle in the house.

8 Then said Boaz vnto Ruth, Hearest thou, my daughter? goe to none other fielde to gather, neither goe from hence: but abide here by my maydens.

9 Let thine eyes be on the field that they do reape, and goe thou after the maidens. Haue I not charged the seruants, that they touche thee not? Moreouer whe thou art a thirst, go vnto ye vessels, and drinke of that which ye seruants haue drawen.

10 Then shee fell on her face, and bowed her selfe to the ground, and said vnto him, How haue I found fauour in thine eyes, that thou shouldest know me, seeing I am a stranger?

11 And Boaz answered, and said vnto her, All is told and shewed me that thou hast done vnto thy mother in lawe, since the death of thine husband, and how thou hast left thy father and thy mother, and ye land where thou wast borne, and art come vnto a people which thou knewest not in time past.

12 The Lord recompense thy worke, and a ful reward be giuen thee of the Lord

God of Israel, vnder whose wings thou art come to trust.

13 Then she saide, Let me finde fauour in thy sight, my lord: for thou hast comforted mee, and spoken comfortably vnto thy mayde, though I be not like to one of thy maydes.

14 And Boaz said vnto her, At the meale time come thou hither, and eat of the bread, and dippe thy morsell in the vineger. And she sate beside the reapers, and hee reached her parched corne: and shee did eate, and was sufficed, and left thereof.

15 And when she arose to gleane, Boaz commanded his seruants, saying, Let her gather among the sheaues, and doe not rebuke her.

16 Also let fall some of the sheaues for her, and let it lie, that she may gather it vp, and rebuke her not.

17 So she gleaned in the fielde vntill euening, and she thresshed that shee had gathered, and it was about an Ephah of barly.

18 And she tooke it vp, and went into the citie, and her mother in law saw what she had gathered: Also she tooke foorth, and gaue to her that which she had reserued, when she was sufficed.

19 Then her mother in lawe saide vnto her, Where hast thou gleaned to day? and where wroughtest thou? blessed be he, that knewe thee. And she shewed her mother in lawe, with whome she had wrought, and saide, The mans name, with whom I wrought to day, is Boaz.

20 And Naomi said vnto her daughter in law, Blessed be he of the Lord: for he ceaseth not to doe good to the liuing and to the dead. Againe Naomi saide vnto her, The man is neere vnto vs, and of our affinitie.

21 And Ruth the Moabitesse said, He said also certainely vnto mee, Thou shalt be with my seruants, vntill they haue ended all mine haruest.

22 And Naomi answered vnto Ruth her daughter in lawe, It is best, my daughter, that thou goe out with his maides, that they meete thee not in an other fielde.

23 Then she kept her by the maides of Boaz, to gather vnto the end of barly haruest, and of wheate haruest, and dwelt with her mother in lawe.

Ruth 3

1 Afterward Naomi her mother in lawe said vnto her, My daughter, shall not I seeke rest for thee, that thou mayest prosper?

2 Now also is not Boaz our kinsman, with whose maides thou wast? beholde, he winoweth barly to night in the floore.

3 Wash thy sellfe therefore, and anoint thee, and put thy raiment vpon thee, and get thee downe to the floore: let not the man know of thee, vntill he haue left eating and drinking.

4 And when he shall sleepe, marke the place where he layeth him downe, and go, and vncouer the place of his feete, and lay thee downe, and he shall tell thee what thou shalt doe.

5 And she answered her, All that thou biddest me, I will doe.

6 So she went downe vnto the floore, and did according to all that her mother in lawe bade her.

7 And when Boaz had eaten, and drunken, and cheared his heart, he went to lie downe at the end of the heape of corne, and she came softly, and vncouered the place of his feet, and lay downe.

8 And at midnight the man was afraide and caught holde: and loe, a woman lay at his feete.

9 Then he sayd, Who art thou? And she answered, I am Ruth thine handmayd: spread therefore the wing of thy garment ouer thine handmayd: for thou art the kinsman.

10 Then sayd he, Blessed be thou of the Lord, my daughter: thou hast shewed more goodnes in the latter end, then at the beginning, in as much as thou followedst not yong men, were they poore or rich.

11 And now, my daughter, feare not: I will doe to thee all that thou requirest: for all the citie of my people doeth knowe, that thou art a vertuous woman.

12 And now, it is true that I am thy kinsman, howbeit there is a kinsman neerer then I.

13 Tarie to night, and when morning is come, if he will doe the duetie of a kinsman vnto thee, well, let him doe the kinsmans duetie: but if he will not doe the kinsmans part, then wil I doe the duetie of a kinsman, as the Lord liueth: sleepe vntill the morning.

14 And she lay at his feete vntill the morning: and she arose before one could know another: for he sayd, Let no man knowe, that a woman came into the floore.

15 Also he sayd, Bring the sheete that thou hast vpon thee, and holde it. And when she helde it, he measured sixe measures of barly, and layde them on her, and she went into the citie.

16 And when she came to her mother in law, she sayd, Who art thou, my daughter? And she tolde her all that the man had done to her,

17 And said, These sixe measures of barly gaue he me: for he sayd to me, Thou shalt not come emptie vnto thy mother in lawe.

18 Then sayd she, My daughter, sit still, vntill thou knowe how the thing will fall: for the man wil not be in rest, vntill he hath finished the matter this same day.

Ruth 4

1 Then went Boaz vp to the gate, and sate there, and beholde, the kinsman, of whome Boaz had spoken, came by: and he sayd, Ho, snch one, come, sit downe here. And he turned, and sate downe.

2 Then he tooke ten men of the Elders of the citie, and sayd, Sit ye downe here. And they sate downe.

3 And he said vnto ye kinsman, Naomi, that is come againe out of ye countrey of

Moab, wil sell a parcel of land, which was our brother Elimelechs.

4 And I thought to aduertise thee, saying, Buy it before the assistants, and before the Elders of my people. If thou wilt redeeme it, redeeme it: but if thou wilt not redeeme it, tel me: for I know that there is none besides thee to redeeme it, and I am after thee. Then he answered, I wil redeeme it.

5 Then said Boaz, What day thou buyest the field of the hand of Naomi, thou mnst also buy it of Ruth the Moabitesse the wife of the dead, to stirre vp the name of the dead, vpon his inheritance.

6 And the kinsman answered, I can not redeeme it, lest I destroy mine owne inheritance: redeeme my right to thee, for I can not redeeme it.

7 Now this was the maner beforetime in Israel, concerning redeeming and changing, for to stablish all things: a man did plucke off his shooe, and gaue it his neighbour, and this was a sure witnes in Israel.

8 Therefore the kinsman sayd to Boas, Buy it for thee: and he drew off his shooe.

9 And Boaz sayd vnto the Elders and vnto all the people, Ye are witnesses this day, that I haue bought all that was Elimelechs, and all that was Chilions and Mahlons, of the hand of Naomi.

10 And moreouer, Ruth the Moabitesse the wife of Mahlon, haue I bought to be my wife, to stirre vp the name of the dead vpon his inheritance, and that the name of the dead be not put out from among his brethren, and from the gate of his place: ye are witnesses this day.

11 And all the people that were in the gate, and the Elders sayd, We are witnesses: the Lord make the wife that commeth into thine house, like Rahel and like Leah, which twaine did build the house of Israel: and that thou mayest doe worthily in Ephrathah, and be famous in Beth-lehem,

12 And that thine house be like the house of Pharez (whom Thamar bare vnto Iudah) of the seede which the Lord shall giue thee of this yong woman.

13 So Boaz tooke Ruth, and she was his wife: and when he went in vnto her, the Lord gaue that she conceiued, and bare a sonne.

14 And the women sayd vnto Naomi, Blessed be the Lord, which hath not left thee this day without a kinsman, and his name shalbe continued in Israel.

15 And this shall bring thy life againe, and cherish thine olde age: for thy daughter in lawe which loueth thee, hath borne vnto him, and she is better to thee then seuen sonnes.

16 And Naomi tooke the childe, and layde it in her lap, and became nource vnto it.

17 And the women her neighbours gaue it a name, saying, There is a childe borne to Naomi, and called the name thereof Obed: the same was the father of Ishai, the father of Dauid.

18 These now are ye generations of Pharez: Pharez begate Hezron,

19 And Hezron begate Ram, and Ram begate Amminadab,

20 And Amminadab begate Nahshon, and Nahshon begate Salmah,

21 And Salmon begate Boaz, and Boaz begat Obed,

22 And Obed begate Ishai, and Ishai begate Dauid.

First Samuel

First Samuel 1

1 There was a man of one of the two Ramathaim Zophim, of mount Ephraim, whose name was Elkanah the sonne of Ieroham, the sonne of Elihu, the sonne of Tohu, the sonne of Zuph, an Ephrathite:

2 And he had two wiues: the name of one was Hannah, and the name of the other Peninnah: and Peninnah had children, but Hannah had no children.

3 And this man went vp out of his citie euery yeere, to worship and to sacrifice vnto the Lord of hostes in Shiloh, where were the two sonnes of Eli, Hophni and Phinehas Priests of the Lord.

4 And on a day, when Elkanah sacrificed, he gaue to Peninnah his wife and to all her sonnes and daughters portions,

5 But vnto Hannah he gaue a worthy portion: for he loued Hannah, and the Lord had made her barren.

6 And her aduersarie vexed her sore, forasmuch as she vpbraided her, because the Lord had made her barren.

7 (And so did he yeere by yeere) and as oft as she went vp to the house of the Lord, thus she vexed her, that she wept and did not eate.

8 Then sayd Elkanah her husband to her, Hannah, why weepest thou? and why eatest thou not? and why is thine heart troubled? am not I better to thee then ten sonnes?

9 So Hannah rose vp after that they had eaten and drunke in Shiloh (and Eli the Priest sate vpon a stoole by one of the postes of the Temple of the Lord)

10 And she was troubled in her minde, and prayed vnto the Lord, and wept sore:

11 Also she vowed a vowe, and sayd, O Lord of hostes, if thou wilt looke on the trouble of thine handmaide, and remember me, and not forget thine handmaide, but giue vnto thine handmaide a manchilde, then I will giue him vnto the Lord all the dayes of his life, and there shall no rasor come vpon his head.

12 And as she continued praying before the Lord, Eli marked her mouth.

13 For Hannah spake in her heart: her lips did moue onely, but her voyce was not heard: therefore Eli thought she had bene drunken.

14 And Eli sayde vnto her, Howe long wilt thou be drunken? Put away thy drunkennesse from thee.

15 Then Hannah answered and sayd, Nay my lord, but I am a woman troubled in spirit: I haue drunke neither wine nor strong drinke, but haue powred out my soule before the Lord.

16 Count not thine handmaide for a wicked woman: for of the abundance of my complaint and my griefe haue I spoken hitherto.

17 Then Eli answered, and sayd, Go in peace, and the God of Israel graunt thy petition that thou hast asked of him.

18 She sayd againe, Let thine handmayd finde grace in thy sight: so the woman went her way, and did eate, and looked no more sad.

19 Then they rose vp early, and worshipped before the Lord, and returned, and came to their house to Ramah. Nowe Elkanah knewe Hannah his wife, and the Lord remembred her.

20 For in processe of time Hannah conceiued, and bare a sonne, and she called his name Samuel, Because, said she, I haue asked him of the Lord.

21 So the man Elkanah and all his house went vp to offer vnto the Lord the yeerely sacrifice, and his vowe:

22 But Hannah went not vp: for she sayd vnto her husband, I will tarie vntill the childe be weined, then I will bring him that hee may appeare before the Lord, and there abide for euer.

23 And Elkanah her husband sayd vnto her, Do what seemeth thee best: tarie vntill thou hast weined him: only the Lord accomplish his word. So the woman abode, and gaue her sonne sucke vntill she weined him.

24 And when she had weined him, she tooke him with her with three bullockes and an Ephah of floure and a bottell of wine, and brought him vnto the house of the Lord in Shiloh, and the childe was yong.

25 And they slewe a bullocke, and brought the childe to Eli.

26 And she said, Oh my Lord, as thy soule liueth, my lord, I am the woman that stoode with thee here praying vnto the Lord.

27 I prayed for this childe, and the Lord hath giuen me my desire which I asked of him.

28 Therefore also I haue giuen him vnto the Lord: as long as he liueth hee shalbe giuen vnto the Lord: and he worshipped the Lord there.

First Samuel 2

1 And Hannah prayed, and said, Mine heart reioyceth in the Lord, mine horne is exalted in the Lord: my mouth is enlarged ouer mine enemies, because I reioyce in thy saluation.

2 There is none holy as the Lord: yea, there is none besides thee, and there is no god like our God.

3 Speake no more presumptuously: let not arrogancie come out of your mouth: for the Lord is a God of knowledge, and by him enterprises are established.

4 The bow and the mightie men are broken, and the weake haue girded themselues with strength.

5 They that were full, are hired foorth for bread, and the hungrie are no more

hired, so that the barren hath borne seuen: and shee that had many children, is feeble.

6 The Lord killeth and maketh aliue: bringeth downe to the graue and raiseth vp.

7 The Lord maketh poore and maketh rich: bringeth lowe, and exalteth.

8 He raiseth vp ye poore out of the dust, and lifteth vp the begger from the dunghill, to set them among princes, and to make them inherite the seate of glory: for the pillars of the earth are the Lordes, and he hath set the world vpon them.

9 Hee will keepe the feete of his Saintes, and the wicked shall keepe silence in darkenes: for in his owne might shall no man be strong.

10 The Lordes aduersaries shall be destroyed, and out of heauen shall he thunder vpon them: the Lord shall iudge the endes of the worlde, and shall giue power vnto his King, and exalt the horne of his Anoynted.

11 And Elkanah went to Ramah to his house, and the childe did minister vnto the Lord before Eli the Priest.

12 Now the sonnes of Eli were wicked men, and knewe not the Lord.

13 For the Priestes custome towarde the people was this: when any man offered sacrifice, the Priestes boy came, while the flesh was seething, and a fleshhooke with three teeth, in his hand,

14 And thrust it into the kettle, or into the caldron, or into the panne, or into the potte: all that the fleshhooke brought vp, the Priest tooke for himselfe: thus they did vnto all the Israelites, that came thither to Shiloh.

15 Yea, before they burnt the fat, the priests boy came and saide to the man that offered, Giue me flesh to rost for the priest: for he wil not haue sodden flesh of thee, but rawe.

16 And if any man saide vnto him, Let them burne the fatte according to the custome, then take as much as thine heart desireth: then hee would answere, No, but thou shalt giue it nowe: and if thou wilt not, I will take it by force.

17 Therefore the sinne of the yong men was very great before the Lord: for men abhorred the offering of the Lord.

18 Now Samuel being a yong childe ministred before the Lord, girded with a linen Ephod.

19 And his mother made him a litle coat, and brought it to him from yeere to yeere, when she came vp with her husband, to offer the yerely sacrifice.

20 And Eli blessed Elkanah and his wife, and said, The Lord giue thee seede of this woman, for the petition that she asked of the Lord: and they departed vnto their place.

21 And the Lord visited Hannah, so that she conceiued, and bare three sonnes, and two daughters. And the childe Samuel grewe before the Lord.

22 So Eli was very olde, and heard all that his sonnes did vnto all Israel, and howe they laye with the women that assembled at the doore of the tabernacle of the Congregation.

23 And hee saide vnto them, Why doe ye such things? for of all this people I heare euill reportes of you.

24 Do no more, my sonnes, for it is no good report that I heare, which is, that ye make the Lords people to trespasse.

25 If one man sinne against another, the Iudge shall iudge it: but if a man sinne against the Lord, who will pleade for him? Notwithstanding they obeyed not the voyce of their father, because the Lord would slay them.

26 (Nowe the childe Samuel profited and grewe, and was in fauour both with the Lord and also with men)

27 And there came a man of God vnto Eli, and said vnto him, Thus saith the Lord, Did not I plainely appeare vnto the house of thy father, when they were in Egypt in Pharaohs house?

28 And I chose him out of all the tribes of Israel to be my Priest, to offer vpon mine altar, and to burne incense, and to weare an Ephod before me, and I gaue vnto the house of thy father all the offrings made by fire of the children of Israel.

29 Wherefore haue you kicked against my sacrifice and mine offering, which I commanded in my Tabernacle, and honourest thy children aboue mee, to make your selues fatte of the first fruites of all the offerings of Israel my people?

30 Wherefore the Lord God of Israel saith, I saide, that thine house and the house of thy father should walke before mee for euer: but nowe the Lord saith, It shall not be so: for them that honour me, I will honour, and they that despise me, shall be despised.

31 Beholde, the dayes come, that I will cut off thine arme, and the arme of thy fathers house, that there shall not be an olde man in thine house.

32 And thou shalt see thine enemie in the habitation of the Lord in all thinges wherewith God shall blesse Israel, and there shall not be an olde man in thine house for euer.

33 Neuerthelesse, I will not destroy euery one of thine from mine altar, to make thine eyes to faile, and to make thine heart sorowfull: and all ye multitude of thine house shall die when they be men.

34 And this shalbe a signe vnto thee, that shall come vpon thy two sonnes Hophni and Phinehas: in one day they shall die both.

35 And I will stirre me vp a faithfull Priest, that shall do according to mine heart and according to my minde: and I wil build him a sure house, and he shall walke before mine Anointed for euer.

36 And all that are left in thine house, shall come and bowe downe to him for a piece of siluer and a morsell of bread, and shall say, Appoint me, I pray thee, to one of the priestes offices, that I may eate a morsell of bread.

First Samuel 3

1 Nowe the childe Samuel ministred vnto the Lord before Eli: and the word of the Lord was precious in those dayes: for there was no manifest vision.

2 And at that time, as Eli lay in his place, his eyes began to waxe dimme that he could not see.

3 And yet the light of God went out, Samuel slept in the temple of the Lord, where the Arke of God was.

4 Then the Lord called Samuel: and hee said, Here I am.

5 And he ranne vnto Eli, and said, Here am I, for thou calledst me. But he said, I called thee not: goe againe and sleepe. And he went and slept.

6 And the Lord called once againe, Samuel. And Samuel arose, and went to Eli, and said, I am here: for thou diddest call me. And he answered, I called thee not, my sonne: go againe and sleepe.

7 Thus did Samuel, before hee knewe the Lord, and before the word of the Lord was reueiled vnto him.

8 And the Lord called Samuel againe the thirde time: and he arose, and went to Eli, and said, I am here: for thou hast called me. Then Eli perceiued that the Lord had called the childe.

9 Therefore Eli saide vnto Samuel, Goe and sleepe: and if he call thee, then say, Speake Lord, for thy seruant heareth. So Samuel went, and slept in his place.

10 And the Lord came, and stoode, and called as at other times, Samuel, Samuel. Then Samuel answered, Speake, for thy seruant heareth.

11 Then the Lord said to Samuel, Beholde, I wil doe a thing in Israel, whereof whosoeuer shall heare, his two eares shall tingle.

12 In that day I will raise vp against Eli all things which I haue spoken concerning his house: when I begin, I will also make an ende.

13 And I haue tolde him that I will iudge his house for euer, for the iniquitie which hee knoweth, because his sonnes ranne into a slaunder, and he stayed them not.

14 Nowe therefore I haue sworne vnto the house of Eli, that the wickednes of Elis house, shall not be purged with sacrifice nor offring for euer.

15 Afterward Samuel slept vntil the morning, and opened the doores of the house of the Lord, and Samuel feared to shewe Eli the vision.

16 Then Eli called Samuel, and said, Samuel my sonne. And he answered, Here I am.

17 Then he said, What is it, that the Lord said vnto thee? I pray thee, hide it not from mee. God doe so to thee, and more also, if thou hide any thing from me, of all that he said vnto thee.

18 So Samuel tolde him euery whit, and hid nothing from him. Then hee said, It is the Lord: let him do what seemeth him good.

19 And Samuel grew, and the Lord was with him, and let none of his words fall to the ground.

20 And all Israel from Dan to Beersheba knew that faithfull Samuel was the Lordes Prophet.

21 And the Lord appeared againe in Shiloh: for the Lord reueiled himselfe to Samuel in Shiloh by his word.

First Samuel 4

1 And Samuel spake vnto all Israel: and Israel went out against the Philistims to battel and pitched beside Eben-ezer: and the Philistims pitched in Aphek.

2 And the Philistims put themselues in aray against Israel: and when they ioyned the battell, Israel was smitten downe before the Philistims: who slewe of the armie in the fielde about foure thousand men.

3 So when the people were come into the campe, the Elders of Israel said, Wherefore hath the Lord smitten vs this day before ye Philistims? let vs bring the Arke of the couenant of the Lord out of Shiloh vnto vs, that when it commeth among vs, it may saue vs out of the hande of our enemies.

4 Then the people sent to Shiloh, and brought from thence the Arke of the couenant of the Lord of hostes, who dwelleth betweene the Cherubims: and there were the two sonnes of Eli, Hophni, and Phinehas, with the Arke of the couenant of God.

5 And when the Arke of the couenant of the Lord came into the hoste, all Israel shouted a mightie shoute, so that the earth rang againe.

6 And when the Philistims heard the noyse of the shoute, they said, What meaneth the sound of this mightie shoute in the host of the Ebrewes? and they vnderstoode, that the Arke of the Lord was come into the hoste.

7 And the Philistims were afraide, and saide, God is come into the hoste: therefore saide they, Wo vnto vs: for it hath not bene so heretofore.

8 Wo vnto vs, who shall deliuer vs out of the hande of these mightie Gods? these are the Gods that smote the Egyptians with all the plagues in the wildernes.

9 Be strong and play the men, O Philistims, that ye be not seruants vnto the Ebrewes, as they haue serued you: be valiant therefore, and fight.

10 And the Philistims fought, and Israel was smitten downe, and fled euery man into his tent: and there was an exceeding great slaughter: for there fell of Israel thirtie thousand footemen.

11 And the Arke of God was taken, and the two sonnes of Eli, Hophni and Phinehas died.

12 And there ranne a man of Beniamin out of the armie, and came to Shiloh the same day with his clothes rent, and earth vpon his head.

13 And when hee came, loe, Eli sate vpon a seate by the wayside, wayting: for his heart feared for the Arke of God and when the man came into the citie to tell it, all the citie cried out.

14 And when Eli heard the noyse of the crying, he sayd, What meaneth this noyse of the tumult? and the man came in hastily, and tolde Eli.

15 (Nowe Eli was fourescore and eighteene yeere olde, and his eyes were dimme that hee could not see)

16 And the man sayd vnto Eli, I came from the armie, and I fled this day out of the hoste: and he sayd, What thing is done, my sonne?

17 Then the messenger answered and sayd, Israel is fled before the Philistims, and there hath bene also a great slaughter among the people: and moreouer thy two sonnes, Hophni and Phinehas are dead, and the Arke of God is taken.

18 And when he had made mention of the Arke of God, Eli fell from his seate backward by the side of the gate, and his necke was broken, and he dyed: for he was an olde man and heauie: and he had iudged Israel fourtie yeeres.

19 And his daughter in lawe Phinehas wife was with childe neere her trauell: and when she heard the report that the Arke of God was taken, and that her father in lawe and her husband were dead, she bowed her selfe, and trauailed: for her paines came vpon her.

20 And about the time of her death, the women that stoode about her, sayd vnto her, Feare not: for thou hast borne a sonne: but she answered not, nor regarded it.

21 And she named the childe Ichabod, saying, The glory is departed from Israel, because the Arke of God was taken, and because of her father in lawe and her husband.

22 She sayde againe, The glory is departed from Israel: for the Arke of God is taken.

First Samuel 5

1 Then the Philistims tooke the Arke of God and caried it from Eben-ezer vnto Ashdod,

2 Euen the Philistims tooke ye Arke of God, and brought it into the house of Dagon, and set it by Dagon.

3 And when they of Ashdod rose the next day in the morning, beholde, Dagon was fallen vpon his face on the ground before the Arke of the Lord, and they tooke vp Dagon, and set him in his place againe.

4 Also they rose vp earely in the morning the next day, and beholde, Dagon was fallen vpon his face on the ground before the Arke of the Lord, and the head of Dagon and the two palmes of his hands were cut off vpon the thresholde: onely the stumpe of Dagon was left to him.

5 Therefore the Priests of Dagon, and all that come into Dagons house tread not on the thresholde of Dagon in Ashdod, vnto this day.

6 But the hand of the Lord was heauie vpon them of Ashdod, and destroyed them, and smote them with the emerods, both Ashdod, and the coastes thereof.

7 And when the men of Ashdod sawe this, they sayd, Let not the Arke of the God of Israel abide with vs: for his hand is sore vpon vs and vpon Dagon our god.

8 They sent therefore and gathered all the princes of the Philistims vnto them, and sayde, What shall we doe with the Arke of the God of Israel? And they answered, Let the Arke of the God of Israel be caried about vnto Gath: and they caried the Arke of the God of Israel about.

9 And when they had caried it about, the hand of the Lord was against the citie with a very great destruction, and he smote the men of the citie both small and great, and they had emerods in their secret partes.

10 Therefore they sent the Arke of God to Ekron: and assoone as the Arke of God came to Ekron, the Ekronites cryed out, saying, They haue brought the Arke of the God of Israel to vs to slay vs and our people.

11 Therefore they sent, and gathered together all the princes of the Philistims and sayd, Sende away the Arke of the God of Israel, and let it returne to his owne place, that it slay vs not and our people: for there was a destruction and death throughout all the citie, and the hand of God was very sore there.

12 And the men that dyed not, were smitten with the emerods: and the cry of the citie went vp to heauen.

First Samuel 6

1 So the Arke of the Lord was in the countrey of the Philistims seuen monethes.

2 And the Philistims called the priests and the soothsayers, saying, What shall we doe with the Arke of the Lord? tell vs wherewith we shall send it home againe.

3 And they sayd, If you send away the Arke of the God of Israel, send it not away emptie, but giue vnto it a sinne offering: then shall ye be healed, and it shall be knowen to you, why his hand departeth not from you.

4 Then sayd they, What shalbe the sinne offring, which we shall giue vnto it? And they answered, Fiue golden emerods and fiue golden mise, according to the number of the princes of the Philistims: for one plague was on you all, and on your princes.

5 Wherefore ye shall make the similitudes of your emerods, and the similitudes of your mise that destroy the land: so ye shall giue glory vnto the God of Israel, that he may take his hand from you, and from your gods, and from your land.

6 Wherefore then should ye harden your hearts, as the Egyptians and Pharaoh hardened their hearts? when he wrought wonderfully among them, did they not let them goe, and they departed?

7 Now therefore make a new cart, and take two milch kine, on whome there hath come no yoke: and tye the kine to the cart, and bring the calues home from them.

8 Then take the Arke of the Lord, and set it vpon the cart, and put the iewels of gold which ye giue it for a sinne offering

in a coffer by the side thereof, and send it away, that it may go.

9 And take heede, if it goe vp by the way of his owne coast to Beth-shemesh, it is he that did vs this great euill: but if not, we shall know then, that it is not his hand that smote vs, but it was a chance that happened vs.

10 And the men did so: for they tooke two kine that gaue milke, and tied them to the cart, and shut the calues at home.

11 So they set the Arke of the Lord vpon the cart, and the coffer with the mise of golde, and with the similitudes of their emerods.

12 And the kine went the streight way to Beth-shemesh, and kept one path and lowed as they went, and turned neither to the right hand nor to the left: also the Princes of the Philistims went after them, vnto the borders of Beth-shemesh.

13 Nowe they of Beth-shemesh were reaping their wheate haruest in the valley, and they lift vp their eyes, and spied the Arke, and reioyced when they sawe it.

14 And the cart came into the fielde of Ioshua a Beth-shemite, and stood still there. There was also a great stone, and they claue the wood of the cart, and offered the kine for a burnt offring vnto the Lord.

15 And the Leuites tooke downe the Arke of the Lord, and the coffer that was with it, wherein the iewels of golde were, and put them on the great stone, and the men of Beth-shemesh offred burnt offring, and sacrificed sacrifices that same day vnto the Lord.

16 And when the fiue Princes of ye Philistims had seene it, they returned to Ekron the same day.

17 So these are the golden emerods, which the Philistims gaue for a sinne offering to the Lord: for Ashdod one, for Gaza one, for Askelon one, for Gath one, and for Ekron one,

18 And golden mise, according to the number of all the cities of the Philistims, belonging to the fiue princes, both of walled townes, and of townes vnwalled, vnto the great stone of Abel, whereon they set the Arke of the Lord: which stone remaineth vnto this day in the fielde of Ioshua the Beth-shemite.

19 And hee smote of the men of Beth-shemesh, because they had looked in the Arke of the Lord: he slew euen among the people fiftie thousand men and three score and ten men. and the people lamented, because the Lord had slaine the people with so great a slaughter.

20 Wherefore the men of Beth-shemesh said, Who is able to stand before this holy Lord God? and to whom shall he go from vs?

21 And they sent messengers to the inhabitants of Kiriath-iearim, saying, The Philistims haue brought againe the Arke of the Lord: come ye downe and take it vp to you.

First Samuel 7

1 Then the men of Kiriath-iearim came, and tooke vp the Arke of the Lord, and brought it into the house of Abinadab in the hill: and they sanctified Eleazar his sonne, to keepe the Arke of the Lord.

2 (For while the Arke abode in Kiriath-iearim, the time was long, for it was twentie yeeres) and al the house of Israel lamented after ye Lord.

3 Then Samuel spake vnto all the house of Israel, saying, If ye be come againe vnto the Lord with all your heart, put away the strange gods from among you, and Ashtaroth, and direct your hearts vnto the Lord, and serue him only, and he shall deliuer you out of the hand of ye Philistims.

4 Then the children of Israel did put away Baalim and Ashtaroth, and serued the Lord onely.

5 And Samuel said, Gather all Israel to Mizpeh, and I will pray for you vnto the Lord.

6 And they gathered together to Mizpeh, and drewe water and powred it out before the Lord, and fasted the same day, and sayd there, We haue sinned against the Lord. And Samuel iudged the children of Israel in Mizpeh.

7 When the Philistims heard that the children of Israel were gathered together to Mizpeh, the princes of the Philistims went vp against Israel: and when the children of Israel heard that, they were afraide of the Philistims.

8 And the children of Israel sayd to Samuel, Cease not to crie vnto the Lord our God for vs, that hee may saue vs out of the hand of the Philistims.

9 Then Samuel tooke a sucking lambe, and offered it all together for a burnt offering vnto the Lord, and Samuel cryed vnto the Lord for Israel, and the Lord heard him.

10 And as Samuel offered the burnt offering, the Philistims came to fight against Israel: but the Lord thundred with a great thunder that day vpon the Philistims, and scattered them: so they were slaine before Israel.

11 And the men of Israel went from Mizpeh and pursued the Philistims, and smote them vntill they came vnder Beth-car.

12 Then Samuel tooke a stone and pitched it betweene Mizpeh and Shen, and called the name thereof, Eben-ezer, and he sayd, Hitherto hath the Lord holpen vs.

13 So the Philistims were brought vnder, and they came no more againe into the coastes of Israel: and the hand of the Lord was against the Philistims all the dayes of Samuel.

14 Also the cities which the Philistims had taken from Israel, were restored to Israel, from Ekron euen to Gath: and Israel deliuered the coastes of the same out of the hands of the Philistims: and there was peace betweene Israel and the Amorites.

15 And Samuel iudged Israel all the dayes of his life,

16 And went about yeere by yere to Beth-el, and Gilgal, and Mizpeh, and iudged Israel in all those places.

17 Afterward hee returned to Ramah: for there was his house, and there he iudged Israel: also he built an altar there vnto the Lord.

First Samuel 8

1 When Samuel was nowe become olde, he made his sonnes Iudges ouer Israel.

2 (And the name of his eldest sonne was Ioel, and the name of the second Abiah) euen Iudges in Beer-sheba.

3 And his sonnes walked not in his wayes, but turned aside after lucre, and tooke rewards, and peruerted the iudgement.

4 Wherefore all the Elders of Israel gathered them together, and came to Samuel vnto Ramah,

5 And said vnto him, Beholde, thou art olde, and thy sonnes walke not in thy wayes: make vs nowe a King to iudge vs like all nations.

6 But the thing displeased Samuel, when they said, Giue vs a King to iudge vs: and Samuel prayed vnto the Lord.

7 And the Lord said vnto Samuel, Heare the voyce of the people in all that they shall say vnto thee: for they haue not cast thee away, but they haue cast me away, that I should not reigne ouer the.

8 As they haue euer done since I brought them out of Egypt euen vnto this day, (and haue forsaken me, and serued other gods) euen so doe they vnto thee.

9 Nowe therefore hearken vnto their voyce: howbeit yet testifie vnto them, and shewe them the maner of ye King that shall reigne ouer them.

10 So Samuel told all the wordes of the Lord vnto the people that asked a King of him.

11 And he saide, This shall be the maner of the King that shall reigne ouer you: he will take your sonnes, and appoint them to his charets, and to be his horsemen, and some shall runne before his charet.

12 Also he will make them his captaines ouer thousands, and captaines ouer fifties, and to eare his ground, and to reape his haruest, and to make instruments of warre, and the thinges that serue for his charets.

13 He will also take your daughters and make them apoticaries, and cookes, and bakers.

14 And he will take your fieldes, and your vineyardes, and your best Oliue trees, and giue them to his seruants.

15 And he will take the tenth of your seede, and of your vineyards, and giue it to his Eunuches, and to his seruants.

16 And he will take your men seruants, and your maide seruants, and the chiefe of your yong men, and your asses, and put them to his worke.

17 He will take the tenth of your sheepe, and ye shall be his seruants.

18 And ye shall crie out at that day, because of your King, whom ye haue

chosen you, and the Lord will not heare you at that day.

19 But the people would not heare the voyce of Samuel, but did say, Nay, but there shall be a King ouer vs.

20 And we also will be like all other nations, and our King shall iudge vs, and goe out before vs, and fight our battels.

21 Therefore when Samuel heard all ye wordes of ye people, he rehearsed the in ye eares of ye Lord.

22 And the Lord saide to Samuel, Hearken vnto their voyce, and make them a King. And Samuel said vnto the men of Israel, Goe euery man vnto his citie.

First Samuel 9

1 There was nowe a man of Beniamin, mightie in power named Kish, the sonne of Abiel, the sonne of Zeror, the sonne of Bechorath, the sonne of Aphiah, the sonne of a man of Iemini.

2 And he had a sonne called Saul, a goodly yong man and a faire: so that among the children of Israel there was none goodlier then he: from the shoulders vpwarde he was hier then any of the people.

3 And the asses of Kish Sauls father were lost: therefore Kish said to Saul his sonne, Take nowe one of the seruants with thee, and arise, goe, and seeke the asses.

4 So he passed through mount Ephraim, and went through the lande of Shalishah, but they found them not. Then they went through the land of Shalim, and there they were not: he went also through ye land of Iemini, but they found the not.

5 When they came to the lande of Zuph, Saul saide vnto his seruant that was with him, Come and let vs returne, lest my father leaue the care of asses, and take thought for vs.

6 And he said vnto him, Behold nowe, in this citie is a man of God, and he is an honorable man: all that he saith commeth to passe: let vs nowe goe thither, if so be that he can shewe vs what way we may goe.

7 Then saide Saul to his seruant, Well then, let vs goe: but what shall we bring vnto the man? For the bread is spent in our vessels, and there is no present to bring to the man of God: what haue we?

8 And the seruant answered Saul againe, and said, Beholde, I haue founde about me the fourth part of a shekell of siluer: that will I giue the man of God, to tell vs our way.

9 (Beforetime in Israel when a man went to seeke an answere of God, thus he spake, Come, and let vs goe to the Seer: for he that is called nowe a Prophet, was in the olde time called a Seer)

10 Then saide Saul to his seruant, Well saide, come, let vs goe: so they went into the citie where the man of God was.

11 And as they were going vp the hie way to the citie, they found maydes that came out to draw water, and said vnto them, Is there here a Seer?

12 And they answered them, and said, Yea: loe, he is before you: make haste nowe, for he came this day to the citie: for there is an offering of the people this day in the hie place.

13 When ye shall come into the citie, ye shall finde him straightway yet he come vp to the hie place to eate: for the people will not eate vntill he come, because he will blesse the sacrifice: and then eate they that be bidden to the feast: nowe therefore goe vp: for euen now shall ye find him.

14 Then they went vp into the citie, and when they were come into the middes of the citie, Samuel came out against them, to goe vp to the hie place.

15 But the Lord had reueiled to Samuel secretly (a day before Saul came) saying,

16 To morow about this time I will send thee a man out of the land of Beniamin: him shalt thou anoint to be gouernour ouer my people Israel, that he may saue my people out of the hands of the Philistims: for I haue looked vpon my people, and their crie is come vnto me.

17 When Samuel therefore sawe Saul, the Lord answered him, See, this is the man whom I spake to thee of, he shall rule my people.

18 Then went Saul to Samuel in the middes of the gate, and said, Tell me, I pray thee, where the Seers house is.

19 And Samuel answered Saul, and saide, I am the Seer: goe vp before me vnto the hie place: for ye shall eate with me to day. and to morowe I will let thee goe, and will tell thee all that is in thine heart.

20 And as for thine asses that were lost three dayes ago, care not for them: for they are founde. and on whom is set all the desire of Israel? is it not vpon thee and on all thy fathers house?

21 But Saul answered, and said, Am not I the sonne of Iemini of the smallest tribe of Israel? and my familie is the least of all the families of the tribe of Beniamin. Wherefore then speakest thou so to me?

22 And Samuel tooke Saul and his seruant, and brought them into the chamber, and made them sit in the chiefest place among them that were bidden: which were about thirtie persons.

23 And Samuel saide vnto the cooke, Bring foorth the portion which I gaue thee, and whereof I said vnto thee, Keepe it with thee.

24 And the cooke tooke vp the shoulder, and that which was vpon it, and set it before Saul. And Samuel said, Beholde, that which is left, set it before thee and eate: for hitherto hath it bene kept for thee, saying, Also I haue called the people. So Saul did eate with Samuel that day.

25 And when they were come downe from the hie place into the citie, he communed with Saul vpon the top of the house.

26 And when they arose early about ye spring of the day, Samuel called Saul to the top of the house, saying, Vp, that I may send thee away. And Saul arose, and they went out, both he, and Samuel.

27 And when they were come downe to the ende of the citie, Samuel said to Saul, Bid the seruant goe before vs, (and he went) but stand thou still nowe, that I may shewe thee the worde of God.

First Samuel 10

1 Then Samuel tooke a viole of oyle and powred it vpon his head, and kissed him, and saide, Hath not the Lord anointed thee to be gouernour ouer his inheritance?

2 When thou shalt depart from me this day, thou shalt finde two men by Rahels sepulchre in the border of Beniamin, euen at Zelzah, and they will say vnto thee, The asses which thou wentest to seeke, are founde: and lo, thy father hath left the care of the asses, and soroweth for you, saying, What shall I doe for my sonne?

3 Then shalt thou go forth from thence and shalt come to the plaine of Tabor, and there shall meete thee three men going vp to God to Bethel: one carying three kiddes, and an other carying three loaues of bread, and another carying a bottle of wine:

4 And they will aske thee if all be well, and will giue thee the two loaues of bread, which thou shalt receiue of their handes.

5 After that shalt thou come to the hill of God, where is the garisons of the Philistims: and when thou art come thither to the citie, thou shalt meete a companie of Prophets comming downe from the hie place with a viole, and a tymbrell, and a pipe, and an harpe before them, and they shall prophecie.

6 Then the Spirit of the Lord will come vpon thee, and thou shalt prophecie with them, and shalt be turned into another man.

7 Therefore when these signes shall come vnto to thee, doe as occasion shall serue: for God is with thee.

8 And thou shalt goe downe before me to Gilgal: and I also will come downe vnto thee to offer burnt offerings, and to sacrifice sacrifices of peace. Tary for me seuen dayes, till I come to thee and shewe thee what thou shalt doe.

9 And when he had turned his backe to goe from Samuel, God gaue him another heart: and all those tokens came to passe that same day.

10 And when they came thither to the hill, beholde, the companie of Prophets meete him, and the Spirit of God came vpon him, and he prophecied among them.

11 Therefore all the people that knewe him before, when they saw that he prophecied among the Prophets, saide eche to other, What is come vnto the sonne of Kish? is Saul also among the Prophets?

12 And one of the same place answered, and said, But who is their father? Therefore it was a prouerbe, Is Saul also among the Prophets?

13 And when he had made an ende of prophecying, he came to the hie place.

14 And Sauls vncle saide vnto him, and to his seruant, Whither went ye? And he saide, To seeke the asses: and when we sawe that they were no where, we came to Samuel.

15 And Sauls vncle saide, Tell me, I pray thee, what Samuel said vnto you.

16 Then Saul saide to his vncle, He tolde vs plainely that the asses were founde: but concerning the kingdome whereof Samuel spake, tolde he him not.

17 And Samuel assembled the people vnto the Lord in Mizpeh,

18 And he saide vnto the children of Israel, Thus saith ye Lord God of Israel, I haue brought Israel out of Egypt, and deliuered you out of the hand of the Egyptians, and out of the handes of all kingdomes that troubled you.

19 But ye haue this day cast away your God, who onely deliuereth you out of all your aduersities and tribulations: and ye said vnto him, No, but appoint a King ouer vs. Nowe therefore stand ye before the Lord according to your tribes, and according to your thousands.

20 And when Samuel had gathered together all the tribes of Israel, the tribe of Beniamin was taken.

21 Afterwarde he assembled the tribe of Beniamin according to their families, and the familie of Matri was taken. So Saul the sonne of Kish was taken, and when they sought him, he coulde not be found.

22 Therefore they asked the Lord againe, if that man should yet come thither. And the Lord answered, Beholde, he hath hid himselfe among the stuffe.

23 And they ranne, and brought him thence: and when he stoode among the people, he was hier then any of the people from the shoulders vpwarde.

24 And Samuel saide to all the people, See ye not him, whom the Lord hath chosen, that there is none like him among all the people? and all the people shouted and saide, God saue the King.

25 Then Samuel tolde the people the duetie of the kingdome, and wrote it in a booke, and laied it vp before the Lord, and Samuel sent all the people away euery man to his house.

26 Saul also went home to Gibeah, and there followed him a bande of men, whose heart God had touched,

27 But the wicked men saide, Howe shall hee saue vs? So they despised him, and brought him no presents: but he held his tongue.

First Samuel 11

1 Then Nahash the Ammonite came vp, and besieged Iabesh Gilead: and all the men of Iabesh saide vnto Nahash, Make a couenant with vs, and we will be thy seruants.

2 And Nahash ye Ammonite answered them, On this condition will I make a couenant with you, that I may thrust out all your right eies, and bring that shame vpon all Israel.

3 To whome the Elders of Iabesh said, Giue vs seuen daies respet, that we may sende messengers vnto all the coastes of Israel: and then if no man deliuer vs, we will come out to thee.

4 Then came the messengers to Gibeah of Saul, and tolde these tidings in the eares of the people: and all the people lift vp their voices and wept.

5 And behold, Saul came following the cattell out of the fielde, and Saul saide, What aileth this people, that they weepe? And they tolde him the tidings of the men of Iabesh.

6 Then the Spirit of God came vpon Saul, when he heard those tidings, and he was exceeding angrie,

7 And tooke a yoke of oxen, and hewed them in pieces, and sent them throughout all the coastes of Israel by the hands of messengers, saying, Whosoeuer commeth not foorth after Saul, and after Samuel, so shall his oxen be serued. And the feare of the Lord fell on the people, and they came out with one consent.

8 And when he nombred them in Bezek, the children of Israel were three hundreth thousande men: and the men of Iudah thirtie thousand.

9 Then they saide vnto the messengers that came, So say vnto the men of Iabesh Gilead, To morowe by then the sunne be hote, ye shall haue helpe. And the messengers came and shewed it to the men of Iabesh, which were glad.

10 Therefore the men of Iabesh sayde, To morowe we will come out vnto you, and yee shall doe with vs all that pleaseth you.

11 And when the morowe was come, Saul put the people in three bandes, and they came in vpon the hoste in the morning watche, and slewe the Ammonites vntill the heate of the day: and they that remained, were scattered, so that two of them were not left together.

12 Then the people said vnto Samuel, Who is he that saide, Shall Saul reigne ouer vs? bring those men that we may slaie them.

13 But Saul said, There shall no man die this day: for to day the Lord hath saued Israel.

14 Then saide Samuel vnto ye people, Come, that we may goe to Gilgal, and renue the kingdome there.

15 So all the people went to Gilgal, and made Saul King there before the Lord in Gilgal: and there they offered peace offerings before the Lord: and there Saul and all the men of Israel reioyced exceedingly.

First Samuel 12

1 Samuel then said vnto all Israel, Behold, I haue hearkened vnto your voyce in all that yee sayde vnto mee, and haue appoynted a King ouer you.

2 Now therefore behold, your King walketh before you, and I am old and graie headed, and beholde, my sonnes are with you: and I haue walked before you from my childehood vnto this day.

3 Beholde, here I am: beare recorde of me before the Lord and before his Anointed. Whose oxe haue I taken? or whose asse haue I taken? or whome haue I done wrong to? or whome haue I hurt? or of whose hande haue I receiued any bribe, to blinde mine eyes therewith, and I will restore it you?

4 Then they sayde, Thou hast done vs no wrong, nor hast hurt vs, neither hast thou taken ought of any mans hand.

5 And he saide vnto them, The Lord is witnesse against you, and his Anointed is witnesse this day, that yee haue founde nought in mine handes. And they answered, He is witnesse.

6 Then Samuel sayde vnto the people, It is the Lord that made Moses and Aaron, and that brought your fathers out of the land of Egypt.

7 Nowe therefore stand still, that I may reason with you before the Lord according to all the righteousnesse of the Lord, which he shewed to you and to your fathers.

8 After that Iaakob was come into Egypt, and your fathers cried vnto the Lord, then the Lord sent Moses and Aaron which brought your fathers out of Egypt, and made them dwell in this place.

9 And when they forgate the Lord their God, he solde them into the hand of Sisera captaine of the hoste of Hazor, and into the hand of the Philistims, and into the hande of the king of Moab, and they fought against them.

10 And they cried vnto the Lord, and saide, We haue sinned, because we haue forsaken the Lord, and haue serued Baalim and Ashtaroth. Nowe therefore deliuer vs out of the handes of our enemies, and we will serue thee.

11 Therefore the Lord sent Ierubbaal and Bedan and Iphtaph, and Samuel, and deliuered you out of the handes of your enemies on euery side, and yee dwelled safe.

12 Notwithstanding when you sawe, that Nahash the King of the children of Ammon came against you, ye sayde vnto me, No, but a King shall reigne ouer vs: when yet the Lord your God was your King.

13 Nowe therefore beholde the King whome yee haue chosen, and whome yee haue desired: loe therefore, the Lord hath set a King ouer you.

14 If ye wil feare the Lord and serue him, and heare his voyce, and not disobey the worde of the Lord, both yee, and the King that reigneth ouer you, shall follow the Lord your God.

15 But if yee will not obey the voyce of the Lord, but disobey the Lordes mouth, then shall the hand of the Lord be vpon you, and on your fathers.

16 Nowe also stande and see this great thing which the Lord will doe before your eyes.

17 Is it not nowe wheat haruest? I wil call vnto the Lord, and he shall send thunder and raine, that yee may

perceiue and see, howe that your wickednesse is great, which ye haue done in the sight of the Lord in asking you a King.

18 Then Samuel called vnto the Lord, and the Lord sent thunder and raine the same day: and all the people feared the Lord and Samuel exceedingly.

19 And all the people said vnto Samuel, Pray for thy seruaunts vnto the Lord thy God, that we die not: for we haue sinned in asking vs a King, beside all our other sinnes.

20 And Samuel said vnto the people, Feare not. (ye haue indeede done all this wickednesse, yet depart not from following the Lord, but serue the Lord with all your heart,

21 Neither turne yee backe: for that shoulde be after vaine things which cannot profite you, nor deliuer you, for they are but vanitie)

22 For the Lord will not forsake his people for his great Names sake: because it hath pleased the Lord to make you his people.

23 Moreouer God forbid, that I should sinne against the Lord, and cease praying for you, but I will shewe you the good and right way.

24 Therefore feare you the Lord, and serue him in the trueth with all your hearts, and consider howe great things he hath done for you.

25 But if ye doe wickedly, ye shall perish, both yee, and your King.

First Samuel 13

1 Saul nowe had beene King one yeere, and he reigned two yeeres ouer Israel.

2 Then Saul chose him three thousand of Israel: and two thousande were with Saul in Michmash, and in mount Beth-el, and a thousande were with Ionathan in Gibeah of Beniamin: and the rest of the people he sent euery one to his tent.

3 And Ionathan smote the garison of the Philistims, that was in the hill: and it came to the Philistims eares: and Saul blewe the trumpet throughout all the land, saying, Heare, O yee Ebrewes.

4 And al Israel heard say, Saul hath destroied a garison of the Philistims: wherefore Israel was had in abomination with the Philistims: and the people gathered together after Saul to Gilgal.

5 The Philistims also gathered themselues together to fight with Israel, thirty thousand charets, and sixe thousande horsemen: for the people was like the sand which is by the seas side in multitude, and came vp, and pitched in Michmash Eastward from Beth-auen.

6 And when the men of Israel saw that they were in a strait (for the people were in distresse) the people hid themselues in caues, and in holdes, and in rockes, and in towres, and in pittes.

7 And some of the Ebrewes went ouer Iorden vnto the lande of Gad and Gilead: and Saul was yet in Gilgal, and al the people for feare followed him.

8 And he taried seuen daies, according vnto the time that Samuel had

appointed: but Samuel came not to Gilgal, therefore the people were scattered from him.

9 And Saul sayde, Bring a burnt offering to me and peace offrings: and he offered a burnt offering.

10 And assoone as hee had made an ende of offering the burnt offering, beholde, Samuel came: and Saul went foorth to meete him, to salute him.

11 And Samuel saide, What hast thou done? Then Saul saide, Because I sawe that the people was scattred from me, and that thou camest not within the daies appoynted, and that the Philistims gathered themselues together to Michmash,

12 Therefore said I, The Philistims will come downe nowe vpon me to Gilgal, and I haue not made supplication vnto the Lord. I was bolde therefore and offred a burnt offring.

13 And Samuel saide to Saul, Thou hast done foolishly: thou hast not kept the commandement of the Lord thy God, which he commanded thee: for the Lord had nowe stablished thy kingdome vpon Israel for euer.

14 But nowe thy kingdom shall not continue: the Lord hath sought him a man after his owne heart, and the Lord hath commanded him to be gouernour ouer his people, because thou hast not kept that which the Lord had commanded thee.

15 And Samuel arose, and gate him vp from Gilgal in Gibeah of Beniamin: and Saul nombred the people that were found with him, about sixe hundreth men.

16 And Saul and Ionathan his sonne, and the people that were found with them, had their abiding in Gibeah of Beniamin: but the Philistims pitched in Michmash.

17 And there came out of the hoste of the Philistims three bandes to destroie, one bande turned vnto the way of Ophrah vnto the lande of Shual,

18 And another bad turned toward the way to Beth-horon, and the third band turned toward the way of the coast that looketh toward the valley of Zeboim, towarde the wildernesse.

19 Then there was no smith founde throughout all the land of Israel: for the Philistims sayde, Lest the Ebrewes make them swordes or speares.

20 Wherefore all ye Israelites went downe to the Philistims, to sharpen euery man his share, his mattocke, and his axe, and his weeding hooke.

21 Yet they had a file for the shares, and for the mattockes, and for the picke forkes, and for the axes, and for to sharpen the goades.

22 So whe the day of battell was come, there was neither sworde nor speare founde in the handes of any of the people that were with Saul and with Ionathan: but onely with Saul and Ionathan his sonne was there founde.

23 And the garison of the Philistims came out to the passage of Michmash.

First Samuel 14

1 Then on a day Ionathan the sonne of Saul sayde vnto the yong man that bare his armour, Come and let vs goe ouer towarde the Philistims garison, that is yonder on the other side, but he tolde not his father.

2 And Saul taried in the border of Gibeah vnder a pomegranate tree, which was in Migron, and the people that were with him, were about sixe hundreth men.

3 And Ahiah the sonne of Ahitub, Ichabods brother, the sonne of Phinehas, the sonne of Eli, was the Lordes Priest in Shiloh, and ware an Ephod: and the people knewe not that Ionathan was gone.

4 Nowe in the way whereby Ionathan sought to go ouer to the Philistims garison, there was a sharpe rocke on the one side, and a sharpe rocke on the other side: the name of the one was called Bozez, and the name of the other Seneh.

5 The one rocke stretched from the North towarde Michmash, and the other was from the South toward Gibeah.

6 And Ionathan saide to the yong man that bare his armour, Come, and let vs goe ouer vnto the garison of these vncircumcised: it may be that the Lord will worke with vs: for it is not hard to the Lord to saue with many, or with fewe.

7 And he that bare his armour, saide vnto him, Doe all that is in thine heart: goe where it pleaseth thee: beholde, I am with thee as thine heart desireth.

8 Then said Ionathan, Beholde, we goe ouer vnto those men, and will shewe our selues vnto them.

9 If they say on this wise to vs, Tarie vntill we come to you, then we will stand still in our place, and not goe vp to them.

10 But if they say, Come vp vnto vs, then we will goe vp: for the Lord hath deliuered them into our hande: and this shall be a signe vnto vs.

11 So they both shewed themselues vnto the garison of the Philistims: and the Philistims said, See, the Ebrewes come out of the holes wherein they had hid themselues.

12 And the men of the garison answered Ionathan, and his armour bearer, and said, Come vp to vs: for we will shewe you a thing. Then Ionathan said vnto his armour bearer, Come vp after me: for the Lord hath deliuered them into the hand of Israel.

13 So Ionathan went vp vpon his hands and vpon his feete, and his armour bearer after him: and some fell before Ionathan, and his armour bearer slewe others after him.

14 So the first slaughter which Ionathan and his armour bearer made, was about twentie men, as it were within halfe an acre of land which two oxen plowe.

15 And there was a feare in the hoste, and in the field, and among all the people: the garison also, and they that went out to spoyle, were afraid themselues: and the earth trembled: for it was striken with feare by God.

16 Then the watchmen of Saul in Gibeah of Beniamin sawe: and beholde, the multitude was discomfited, and smitten as they went.

17 Therefore saide Saul vnto the people that were with him, Search nowe and see, who is gone from vs. And when they had nombred, beholde, Ionathan and his armour bearer were not there.

18 And Saul said vnto Ahiah, Bring hither the Arke of God (for the Arke of God was at that time with the children of Israel)

19 And while Saul talked vnto the Priest, the noyse that was in the hoste of the Philistims, spred farther abroade, and encreased: therefore Saul said vnto the Priest, Withdraw thine hand.

20 And Saul was assembled with all the people that were with him, and they came to the battell: and behold, euery mans sworde was against his fellow, and there was a very great discomfiture.

21 Moreouer, the Ebrewes that were with the Philistims beforetime, and were come with them into all partes of the hoste, euen they also turned to be with the Israelites that were with Saul and Ionathan.

22 Also all the men of Israel which had hid themselues in mount Ephraim, when they heard, that the Philistims were fled, they followed after them in the battell.

23 And so the Lord saued Israel that day: and the battell continued vnto Beth-auen.

24 And at that time the men of Israel were pressed with hunger: for Saul charged the people with an othe, saying, Cursed be the man that eateth foode till night, that I may be auenged of mine enemies: so none of the people tasted any sustenance.

25 And all they of the land came to a wood, where hony lay vpon the ground.

26 And the people came into the wood, and beholde, the hony dropped, and no man mooued his hand to his mouth: for the people feared the othe.

27 But Ionathan heard not when his father charged the people with the othe: wherefore he put foorth the ende of the rod that was in his hand, and dipt it in an hony combe, and put his hand to his mouth, and his eyes receiued sight.

28 Then answered one of the people, and said, Thy father made the people to sweare, saying, Cursed be the man that eateth sustenance this day: and the people were faint.

29 Then said Ionathan, My father hath troubled the land: see nowe howe mine eyes are made cleare, because I haue tasted a litle of this honie:

30 Howe much more, if the people had eaten to day of the spoyle of their enemies which they found? for had there not bene nowe a greater slaughter among the Philistims?

31 And they smote the Philistims that day, from Michmash to Aiialon: and the people were exceeding faint.

32 So the people turned to the spoile, and tooke sheepe, and oxen, and calues, and slewe them on the ground, and the people did eate them with the blood.

33 Then men tolde Saul, saying, Beholde, the people sinne against the Lord, in that they eate with the blood. And he saide, Ye haue trespassed: roule a great stone vnto me this day.

34 Againe Saul said, Goe abroade among the people, and bid them bring me euery man his oxe, and euery man his sheepe, and slay them here, and eate and sinne not against the Lord in eating with the blood. And ye people brought euery man his oxe in his hand that night, and slew them there.

35 Then Saul made an altar vnto the Lord, and that was the first altar that he made vnto the Lord.

36 And Saul saide, Let vs goe downe after the Philistims by night, and spoyle them vntill the morning shine, and let vs not leaue a man of them. And they saide, Doe whatsoeuer thou thinkest best. Then saide the Priest, Let vs drawe neere hither vnto God.

37 So Saul asked of God, saying, Shall I goe downe after ye Philistims? wilt thou deliuer them into the hands of Israel? But he answered him not at that time.

38 And Saul said, All ye chiefe of the people, come ye hither, and knowe, and see by whom this sinne is done this day.

39 For as the Lord liueth, which saueth Israel, though it be done by Ionathan my sonne, he shall dye the death. But none of all the people answered him.

40 Then he saide vnto all Israel, Be ye on one side, and I and Ionathan my sonne will be on the other side. And the people saide vnto Saul, Doe what thou thinkest best.

41 Then Saul said vnto the Lord God of Israel, Giue a perfite lot. And Ionathan and Saul were taken, but the people escaped.

42 And Saul saide, Cast lot betweene me and Ionathan my sonne. And Ionathan was taken.

43 Then Saul said to Ionathan, Tell me what thou hast done. And Ionathan tolde him, and said, I tasted a litle hony with the ende of the rod, that was in mine hand, and loe, I must die.

44 Againe Saul answered, God doe so and more also, vnlesse thou die the death, Ionathan.

45 And the people said vnto Saul, Shall Ionathan die, who hath so mightily deliuered Israel? God forbid. As the Lord liueth, there shall not one heare of his head fall to the ground: for he hath wrought with God this day. So the people deliuered Ionathan that he dyed not.

46 Then Saul came vp from the Philistims: and the Philistims went to their owne place.

47 So Saul helde the kingdome ouer Israel, and fought against all his enemies on euery side, against Moab, and against the children of Ammon, and against Edom, and against the Kings of Zobah, and against the Philistims: and whithersoeuer he went, he handled them as wicked men.

48 He gathered also an hoste and smote Amalek, and deliuered Israel out of the handes of them that spoyled them.

49 Nowe the sonnes of Saul were Ionathan, and Ishui, and Malchishua: and the names of his two daughters, the elder was called Merab, and the yonger was named Michal.

50 And the name of Sauls wife was Ahinoam the daughter of Ahimaaz: and the name of his chiefe captaine was Abner the sonne of Ner, Sauls vncle.

51 And Kish was Sauls father: and Ner the father of Abner was the sonne of Abiel.

52 And there was sore warre against the Philistims all the dayes of Saul: and whomsoeuer Saul sawe to be a strong man, and meete for the warre, he tooke him vnto him.

First Samuel 15

1 Afterward Samuel said vnto Saul, The Lord sent me to anoint thee King ouer his people, ouer Israel: nowe therefore obey the voyce of the wordes of the Lord.

2 Thus saith the Lord of hostes, I remember what Amalek did to Israel, howe they laide waite for the in ye way, as they came vp from Egypt.

3 Nowe therefore goe, and sinite Amalek, and destroy ye all that perteyneth vnto them, and haue no compassion on them, but slay both man and woman, both infant and suckling, both oxe, and sheepe, both camell, and asse.

4 And Saul assembled ye people, and nombred them in Telaim, two hundreth thousande footemen, and ten thousand men of Iudah.

5 And Saul came to a citie of Amalek, and set watch at the riuer.

6 And Saul said vnto the Kenites, Goe, depart, and get you downe from among the Amalekites, least I destroy you with them: for ye shewed mercie to all the children of Israel, when they came vp from Egypt: and the Kenites departed from among the Amalekites.

7 So Saul smote the Amalekites from Hauilah as thou commest to Shur, that is before Egypt,

8 And tooke Agag the King of the Amalekites aliue, and destroyed all the people with the edge of the sword.

9 But Saul and the people spared Agag, and the better sheepe, and the oxen, and the fat beasts, and the lambes, and all that was good, and they would not destroy them: but euery thing that was vile and nought worth, that they destroyed.

10 Then came the worde of the Lord vnto Samuel, saying,

11 It repenteth me that I haue made Saul King: for he is turned from me, and hath not performed my commandements. And Samuel was mooued, and cryed vnto the Lord all night.

12 And when Samuel arose early to meete Saul in the morning, one tolde Samuel, saying, Saul is gone to Carmel:

and beholde, he hath made him there a place, from whence he returned, and departed, and is gone downe to Gilgal.

13 Then Samuel came to Saul, and Saul said vnto him. Blessed be thou of the Lord, I haue fulfilled the commandement of the Lord.

14 But Samuel saide, What meaneth then the bleating of the sheepe in mine eares, and the lowing of the oxen which I heare?

15 And Saul answered, They haue brought them from the Amalekites: for the people spared the best of the sheepe, and of the oxen to sacrifice them vnto the Lord thy God, and the remnant haue we destroyed.

16 Againe Samuel saide to Saul, Let me tell thee what the Lord hath saide to me this night. And he said vnto him, Say on.

17 Then Samuel saide, When thou wast litle in thine owne sight, wast thou not made the head of the tribes of Israel? for the Lord anointed thee King ouer Israel.

18 And the Lord sent thee on a iourney, and saide, Goe, and destroy those sinners the Amalekites, and fight against them, vntill thou destroy them.

19 Nowe wherefore hast thou not obeyed the voyce of the Lord, but hast turned to the pray, and hast done wickedly in the sight of the Lord?

20 And Saul saide vnto Samuel, Yea, I haue obeyed the voyce of the Lord, and haue gone the way which the Lord sent me, and haue brought Agag the King of Amalek, and haue destroyed the Amalekites.

21 But the people tooke of the spoyle, sheepe, and oxen, and the chiefest of the things which shoulde haue bene destroyed, to offer vnto the Lord thy God in Gilgal.

22 And Samuel saide, Hath the Lord as great pleasure in burnt offerings and sacrifices, as when the voyce of the Lord is obeyed? beholde, to obey is better then sacrifice, and to hearken is better then the fatte of rammes.

23 For rebellion is as the sinne of withcraft, and transgression is wickednesse and idolatrie. Because thou hast cast away the worde of the Lord, therefore hee hath cast away thee from being King.

24 Then Saul sayde vnto Samuel, I haue sinned: for I haue transgressed the commandement of the Lord, and thy wordes, because I feared the people, and obeyed their voyce.

25 Nowe therefore I pray thee, take away my sinne, and turne againe with mee, that I may worship the Lord.

26 But Samuel saide vnto Saul, I will not returne with thee: for thou hast cast away the word of the Lord, and the Lord hath cast away thee, that thou shalt not be King ouer Israel.

27 And as Samuel turned himselfe to goe away, he caught the lappe of his coate, and it rent.

28 Then Samuel saide vnto him, The Lord hath rent the kingdome of Israel from thee this day, and hath giuen it to thy neighbour, that is better then thou.

29 For in deede the strength of Israel will not lye nor repent: for hee is not a man that hee should repent.

30 Then he saide, I haue sinned: but honour mee, I pray thee, before the Elders of my people, and before Israel, and turne againe with mee, that I may worship the Lord thy God.

31 So Samuel turned againe, and followed Saul: and Saul worshipped the Lord.

32 Then saide Samuel, Bring yee hither to me Agag ye King of the Amalekites: and Agag came vnto him pleasantly, and Agag saide, Truely the bitternesse of death is passed.

33 And Samuel sayde, As thy sworde hath made women childlesse, so shall thy mother bee childelesse among other women. And Samuel hewed Agag in pieces before the Lord in Gilgal.

34 So Samuel departed to Ramah, and Saul went vp to his house to Gibeah of Saul.

35 And Samuel came no more to see Saul vntill the day of his death: but Samuel mourned for Saul, and the Lord repented that hee made Saul King ouer Israel.

First Samuel 16

1 The Lord then saide vnto Samuel, Howe long wilt thou mourne for Saul, seeing I haue cast him away from reigning ouer Israel? fill thine horne with oyle and come, I will sende thee to Ishai the Bethlehemite: for I haue prouided mee a King among his sonnes.

2 And Samuel sayde, Howe can I goe? for if Saul shall heare it, he will kill me. Then the Lord answered, Take an heifer with thee, and say, I am come to doe sacrifice to the Lord.

3 And call Ishai to the sacrifice, and I will shewe thee what thou shalt doe, and thou shalt anoynt vnto me him whom I name vnto thee.

4 So Samuel did that the Lord bade him, and came to Beth-lehem, and the Elders of the towne were astonied at his comming, and sayd, Commest thou peaceablie?

5 And he answeared, Yea: I am come to doe sacrifice vnto the Lord: sanctifie your selues, and come with me to the sacrifice. And he sanctified Ishai and his sonnes, and called them to the sacrifice.

6 And when they were come, hee looked on Eliab, and saide, Surely the Lordes Anointed is before him.

7 But the Lord said vnto Samuel, Looke not on his countenance, nor on the height of his stature, because I haue refused him: for God seeth not as man seeth: for man looketh on the outward appearance, but the Lord beholdeth the heart.

8 Then Ishai called Abinadab, and made him come before Samuel. And he saide, Neither hath the Lord chosen this.

9 Then Ishai made Shammah come. And he said, Neither yet hath the Lord chosen him.

10 Againe Ishai made his seue sonnes to come before Samuel: and Samuel saide vnto Ishai, The Lord hath chosen none of these.

11 Finally, Samuel said vnto Ishai, Are there no more children but these? And hee sayde, There remaineth yet a litle one behinde, that keepeth the sheepe. Then Samuel saide vnto Ishai, Sende and set him: for we will not sit downe, till he be come hither.

12 And he sent, and brought him in: and he was ruddie, and of a good countenance, and comely visage. And the Lord saide, Arise, and anoynt him: for this is he.

13 Then Samuel tooke the horne of oyle, and anoynted him in the middes of his brethren. And the Spirit of the Lord came vpon Dauid, from that day forwarde: then Samuel rose vp, and went to Ramah.

14 But the Spirite of the Lord departed from Saul, and an euill spirite sent of the Lord vexed him.

15 And Sauls seruants said vnto him, Beholde nowe, the euill spirite of God vexeth thee.

16 Let our Lord therefore command thy seruants, that are before thee, to seeke a man that is a cunning plaier vpon the harpe: that when the euil spirit of God commeth vpon thee, hee may play with his hand, and thou maiest be eased.

17 Saul then saide vnto his seruantes, Prouide me a man, I pray you, that can play well, and bring him to me.

18 Then answered one of his seruauntes, and sayde, Beholde, I haue seene a sonne of Ishai, a Bethlehemite, that can plaie, and is strong, valiant and a man of warre and wise in matters, and a comely person, and the Lord is with him.

19 Wherefore Saul sent messengers vnto Ishai, and said, Send me Dauid thy sonne which is with the sheepe.

20 And Ishai tooke an asse laden with breade and a flagon of wine and a kidde, and sent them by the hand of Dauid his sonne vnto Saul.

21 And Dauid came to Saul, and stoode before him: and he loued him verie well, and he was his armour bearer.

22 And Saul sent to Ishai, saying, Let Dauid nowe remaine with me: for he hath found fauour in my sight.

23 And so when the euil spirite of God came vpon Saul, Dauid tooke an harpe and plaied with his hande, and Saul was refreshed, and was eased: for the euill spirit departed from him.

First Samuel 17

1 Nowe the Philistims gathered their armies to battell, and came together to Shochoh, which is in Iudah, and pitched betweene Shochoh and Azekah, in the coast of Dammim.

2 And Saul, and the men of Israel assembled, and pitched in the valley of Elah, and put themselues in battell araie to meete the Philistims.

3 And the Philistims stoode on a mountaine on the one side, and Israel stoode on a mountaine on the other side: so a valley was betweene them.

4 Then came a man betweene them both out of the tents of the Philistims, named Goliath of Gath: his height was sixe cubites and an hande breadth,

5 Aud had an helmet of brasse vpon his head, and a brigandine vpon him: and the weight of his brigandine was fiue thousand shekels of brasse.

6 And he had bootes of brasse vpon his legs, and a shield of brasse vpon his shoulders.

7 And the shaft of his speare was like a weauers beame: and his speare head weyed sixe hundreth shekels of yron: and one bearing a shielde went before him.

8 And he stoode, and cried against the hoste of Israel, and saide vnto them, Why are yee come to set your battell in aray? am not I a Philistim, and you seruaunts to Saul? chuse you a man for you, and let him come downe to me.

9 If he be able to fight with me, and kill me, then wil we be your seruants: but if I ouercome him, and kill him, then shall yee be our seruants, and serue vs.

10 Also the Philistim saide, I defie the hoste of Israel this day: giue mee a man, that we may fight together.

11 When Saul and all Israel heard those wordes of the Philistim, they were discouraged, and greatly afraide.

12 Nowe this Dauid was the sonne of an Ephrathite of Beth-lehem Iudah, named Ishai, which had eight sonnes: and this man was taken for an olde man in the daies of Saul.

13 And the three eldest sonnes of Ishai went and followed Saul to the battel: and the names of his three sonnes that went to battell, were Eliab the Eldest, and the next Abinadab, and the thirde Shammah.

14 So Dauid was the least: and the three eldest went after Saul.

15 Dauid also went, but hee returned from Saul to feede his fathers sheepe in Beth-lehem.

16 And the Philistim drew neere in the morning, and euening, and continued fourtie daies.

17 And Ishai said vnto Dauid his sone, Take nowe for thy brethren an Ephah of this parched corne, and these ten cakes, and runne to the hoste to thy brethren.

18 Also carie these ten fresh cheeses vnto the captaine, and looke howe thy brethren fare, and receiue their pledge.

19 (Then Saul and they, and all the men of Israel were in the valley of Elah, fighting with the Philistims)

20 So Dauid rose vp earely in the morning, and left the sheepe with a keeper, and tooke and went as Ishai had commanded him, and came within the compasse of the hoste: and the hoste went out in araie, and shouted in the battell.

21 For Israel and the Philistims had put themselues in araie, armie against armie.

22 And Dauid left the things, which hee bare, vnder the handes of the keeper of the cariage, and ranne into the hoste, and came, and asked his brethren howe they did.

23 And as hee talked with them, beholde, the man that was betweene the two armies, came vp, (whose name was Goliath ye Philistim of Gath) out of the armie of the Philistims, and spake such woordes, and Dauid heard them.

24 And all the men of Israel, when they sawe the man, ranne away from him, and were sore afraied.

25 For euery man of Israel saide, Sawe yee not this man that commeth vp? euen to reuile Israel is he come vp: and to him that killeth him, wil the king giue great riches, and will giue him his daughter, yea, and make his fathers house free in Israel.

26 Then Dauid spake to the men that stoode with him, and sayde, What shall be done to the man that killeth this Philistim, and taketh away the shame from Israel? for who is this vncircumcised Philistim, that he shoulde reuile the hoste of the liuing God?

27 And the people answered him after this maner, saying, Thus shall it be done to the man that killeth him.

28 And Eliab his eldest brother heard when he spake vnto the men, and Eliab was verie angrie with Dauid, and sayde, Why camest thou downe hither? and with whome hast thou left those fewe sheepe in the wildernesse? I knowe thy pride and the malice of thine heart, that thou art come downe to see the battell.

29 Then Dauid sayde, What haue I nowe done? Is there not a cause?

30 And hee departed from him into the presence of another, and spake of the same maner, and the people answered him according to the former woordes.

31 And they that heard the wordes which Dauid spake, rehearsed them before Saul, which caused him to be brought.

32 So Dauid saide to Saul, Let no mans heart faile him, because of him: thy seruant wil goe, and fight with this Philistim.

33 And Saul sayde to Dauid, Thou art not able to goe against this Philistim to fight with him: for thou art a boye, and he is a man of warre from his youth.

34 And Dauid answered vnto Saul, Thy seruant kept his fathers sheepe, and there came a lyon, and likewise a beare, and tooke a sheepe out of the flocke,

35 And I went out after him and smote him, and tooke it out of his mouth: and when he arose against me, I caught him by the beard, and smote him, and slue him.

36 So thy seruaunt slue both the lyon, and the beare: therefore this vncircumcised Philistim shall be as one of them, seeing hee hath railed on the hoste of the liuing God.

37 Moreouer Dauid sayd, The Lord that deliuered me out of the pawe of the lyon, and out of the paw of the beare, he wil deliuer me out of the hand of this Philistim. Then Saul sayd vnto Dauid, Go, and the Lord be with thee.

38 And Saul put his rayment vpon Dauid, and put an helmet of brasse vpon his head, and put a brigandine vpon him.

39 Then girded Dauid his sword vpon his rayment, and began to go: for he neuer proued it: and Dauid sayde vnto Saul, I can not goe with these: for I am not accustomed. wherefore Dauid put them off him.

40 Then tooke he his staffe in his hand, and chose him fiue smoothe stones out of a brooke, and put them in his shepheards bagge or skrippe, and his sling was in his hand, and he drewe neere to the Philistim.

41 And the Philistim came and drew neere vnto Dauid, and the man that bare the shielde went before him.

42 Now when the Philistim looked about and saw Dauid, he disdeined him: for he was but yong, ruddie, and of a comely face.

43 And the Philistim sayde vnto Dauid, Am I a dog, that thou commest to me with staues? And the Philistim cursed Dauid by his gods.

44 And the Philistim sayd to Dauid, Come to me, and I will giue thy flesh vnto the foules of the heauen, and to the beastes of the field.

45 Then sayd Dauid to the Philistim, Thou commest to me with a sword, and with a speare, and with a shield, but I come to thee in the Name of the Lord of hostes, the God of the hoste of Israel, whom thou hast rayled vpon.

46 This day shall the Lord close thee in mine hand, and I shall smite thee, and take thine head from thee, and I wil giue the carkeises of the hoste of the Philistims this daye vnto the foules of the heauen, and to the beasts of the earth, that all the world may know that Israel hath a God,

47 And that all this assembly may know, that the Lord saueth not with sworde nor with speare (for the battel is the Lords) and he will giue you into our handes.

48 And when the Philistim arose to come and drawe neere vnto Dauid, Dauid hasted and ran to fight against the Philistim.

49 And Dauid put his hande in his bagge, and tooke out a stone, and slang it, and smote the Philistim in his forehead, that the stone sticked in his forehead, and he fell groueling to the earth.

50 So Dauid ouercame the Philistim with a sling and with a stone, and smote the Philistim, and slew him, when Dauid had no sword in his hand.

51 Then Dauid ranne, and stood vpon the Philistim, and tooke his sword and drew it out of his sheath, and slewe him, and cut off his head therewith. So whe the Philistims saw, that their champion was dead, they fled.

52 And the men of Israel and Iudah arose, and shouted, and followed after the Philistims, vntill they came to the

valley, and vnto the gates of Ekron: and the Philistims fell downe wounded by the way of Shaaraim, euen to Gath and to Ekron.

53 And the children of Israel returned from pursuing the Philistims, and spoyled their tents.

54 And Dauid tooke the head of ye Philistim, and brought it to Ierusalem, and put his armour in his tent.

55 When Saul sawe Dauid go forth against the Philistim, he sayd vnto Abner the captaine of his hoste, Abner, whose sonne is this yong man? and Abner answered, As thy soule liueth, O King, I can not tell.

56 Then the King sayde, Enquire thou whose sonne this yong man is.

57 And when Dauid was returned from the slaughter of the Philistim, then Abner tooke him, and brought him before Saul with the head of the Philistim in his hand.

58 And Saul sayde to him, Whose sonne art thou, thou yong man? And Dauid answered, I am the sonne of thy seruant Ishai the Bethlehemite.

First Samuel 18

1 And when he had made an ende of speaking vnto Saul, the soule of Ionathan was knit with the soule of Dauid, and Ionathan loued him, as his owne soule.

2 And Saul tooke him that day, and woulde not let him returne to his fathers house.

3 Then Ionathan and Dauid made a couenant: for he loued him as his owne soule.

4 And Ionathan put off the robe that was vpon him, and gaue it Dauid, and his garments, euen to his sword, and to his bow, and to his girdle.

5 And Dauid went out whithersoeuer Saul sent him, and behaued himselfe wisely: so that Saul set him ouer the men of warre, and he was accepted in the sight of all the people, and also in the sight of Sauls seruants.

6 When they came againe, and Dauid returned from the slaughter of the Philistim, the women came out of all cities of Israel singing and daunting to meete king Saul, with timbrels, with instruments of ioy, and with rebeckes.

7 And the women sang by course in their play, and sayd, Saul hath slayne his thousand, and Dauid his ten thousand.

8 Therefore Saul was exceeding wroth, and the saying displeased him, and he sayde, They haue ascribed vnto Dauid ten thousand, and to me they haue ascribed but a thousand, and what can he haue more saue the kingdome?

9 Wherefore Saul had an eye on Dauid from that day forward.

10 And on the morowe, the euill spirite of God came vpon Saul, and he prophecied in the middes of the house: and Dauid played with his hand like as at other times, and there was a speare in Sauls hand.

11 And Saul tooke the speare, and sayd, I will smite Dauid through to the wall. But Dauid auoyded twise out of his presence.

12 And Saul was afrayd of Dauid, because the Lord was with him, and was departed from Saul.

13 Therefore Saul put him from him, and made him a captaine ouer a thousand, and he went out and in before the people.

14 And Dauid behaued himselfe wisely in all his wayes: for the Lord was with him.

15 Wherefore when Saul saw that he was very wise, he was afrayde of him.

16 For all Israel and Iudah loued Dauid, because he went out and in before them.

17 Then Saul sayd to Dauid, Beholde mine eldest daughter Merab, her I will giue thee to wife: onely be a valiant sonne vnto me, and fight the Lordes battels: for Saul thought, Mine hand shall not be vpon him, but the hand of the Philistims shalbe vpon him.

18 And Dauid answered Saul, What am I? and what is my life, or the family of my father in Israel, that I should be sonne in law to the King?

19 Howbeit when Merab Sauls daughter should haue bene giuen to Dauid, she was giuen vnto Adriel a Meholathite to wife.

20 Then Michal Sauls daughter loued Dauid: and they shewed Saul, and the thing pleased him.

21 Therefore Saul said, I wil giue him her, that she may be a snare to him, and that the hand of the Philistims may bee against him. Wherefore Saul sayde to Dauid, Thou shalt this day be my sonne in law in the one of the twayne.

22 And Saul commanded his seruants, Speake with Dauid secretly, and say, Behold, ye King hath a fauour to thee, and all his seruants loue thee: be now therefore the Kings sonne in law.

23 And Sauls seruantes spake these wordes in the eares of Dauid. And Dauid sayd, Seemeth it to you a light thing to be a Kings sonne in lawe, seeing that I am a poore man and of small reputation?

24 And then Sauls seruats brought him word againe, saying, Such wordes spake Dauid.

25 And Saul sayd, This wise shall ye say to Dauid, The King desireth no dowrie, but an hundred foreskinnes of the Philistims, to bee auenged of the Kings enemies: for Saul thought to make Dauid fall into the handes of the Philistims.

26 And when his seruantes tolde Dauid these wordes, it pleased Dauid well, to be the Kings sonne in law: and the dayes were not expired.

27 Afterwarde Dauid arose with his men, and went and slewe of the Philistims two hundreth men: and Dauid brought their foreskinnes, and they gaue them wholly to the King that hee might be the Kings sonne in lawe: therefore Saul gaue him Michal his daughter to wife.

28 Then Saul sawe, and vnderstoode that the Lord was with Dauid, and that Michal the daughter of Saul loued him.

29 Then Saul was more and more afrayde of Dauid, and Saul became alway Dauids enemie.

30 And when the Princes of the Philistims went forth, at their going forth Dauid behaued himselfe more wisely then all the seruants of Saul, so that his name was much set by.

First Samuel 19

1 Then Saul spake to Ionathan his sonne, and to all his seruantes, that they shoulde kill Dauid: but Ionathan Sauls sonne had a great fauour to Dauid.

2 And Ionathan told Dauid, saying, Saul my father goeth about to slay thee: nowe therefore, I pray thee, take heede vnto thy selfe vnto the morning, and abide in a secret place, and hide thy selfe.

3 And I will go out, and stand by my father in the fielde where thou art, and will commune with my father of thee, and I will see what he sayth, and will tell thee.

4 And Ionathan spake good of Dauid vnto Saul his father, and said vnto him, Let not the King sinne against his seruat, against Dauid: for he hath not sinned against thee, but his works haue bene to thee very good.

5 For he did put his life in daunger, and slew the Philistim, and the Lord wrought a great saluation for al Israel: thou sawest it, and thou reioycedst: wherefore then wilt thou sinne against innocent blood, and slay Dauid without a cause?

6 Then Saul hearkened vnto the voyce of Ionathan, and Saul sware, As the Lord liueth, he shall not dye.

7 So Ionathan called Dauid, and Ionathan shewed him all those words, and Ionathan brought Dauid to Saul, and hee was in his presence as in times past.

8 Againe the warre began, and Dauid went out and fought with the Philistims, and slew them with a great slaughter, and they fled from him.

9 And the euill spirit of the Lord was vpon Saul, as hee sate in his house hauing his speare in his hand, and Dauid played with his hand.

10 And Saul intended to smite Dauid to the wall with the speare: but hee turned aside out of Sauls presence, and he smote the speare against the wall: but Dauid fled, and escaped the same night.

11 Saul also sent messengers vnto Dauids house, to watch him, and to slay him in the morning: and Michal Dauids wife told it him, saying, If thou saue not thy selfe this night, to morowe thou shalt be slayne.

12 So Michal let Dauid downe through a window: and he went, and fled, and escaped.

13 Then Michal tooke an image, and layde it in the bed, and put a pillow stuffed with goates heare vnder the head of it, and couered it with a cloth.

14 And when Saul sent messengers to take Dauid, she sayd, He is sicke.

15 And Saul sent the messengers againe to see Dauid, saying, Bring him to me in the bed, that I may slay him.

16 And when the messengers were come in, behold, an image was in the bed, with a pillow of goates heare vnder the head of it.

17 And Saul said vnto Michal, Why hast thou mocked me so, and sent away mine enemie, that he is escaped? And Michal answered Saul, He said vnto me, Let me go, or els I will kill thee.

18 So Dauid fled, and escaped, and came to Samuel to Ramah, and told him all that Saul had done to him: and he and Samuel went and dwelt in Naioth.

19 But one tolde Saul, saying, Beholde, Dauid is at Naioth in Ramah.

20 And Saul sent messengers to take Dauid: and when they sawe a company of Prophets prophecying, and Samuel standing as appoynted ouer them, the Spirit of God fell vpon the messengers of Saul, and they also prophecied.

21 And when it was tolde Saul, he sent other messengers, and they prophecied likewise: againe Saul sent the third messengers, and they prophecied also.

22 Then went he himselfe to Ramah, and came to a great well that is in Sechu, and he asked, and sayd, Where are Samuel and Dauid? and one sayd, Behold, they be at Naioth in Ramah.

23 And he went thither, euen to Naioth in Ramah, and the Spirit of God came vpon him also, and he went prophecying vntill hee came to Naioth in Ramah.

24 And he stript off his clothes, and he prophesied also before Samuel, and fell downe naked all that day and all that night: therefore they say, Is Saul also among the Prophets?

First Samuel 20

1 And Dauid fled from Naioth in Ramah, and came and sayd before Ionathan, What haue I done? what is mine iniquitie? and what sinne haue I committed before thy father, that he seeketh my life?

2 And he sayde vnto him, God forbid, thou shalt not die: beholde, my father will do nothing great nor small, but he will shewe it me: and why should my father hide this thing from me? he will not doe it.

3 And Dauid sware againe and sayd, Thy father knoweth that I haue found grace in thine eyes: therefore he thinketh, Ionathan shall not knowe it, lest he be sorie: but in deede, as the Lord liueth, and as thy soule liueth, there is but a step betweene me and death.

4 Then said Ionathan vnto Dauid, Whatsoeuer thy soule requireth, that I wil do vnto thee.

5 And Dauid said vnto Ionathan, Behold, to morowe is the first day of the moneth, and I shoulde sit with the King at meate: but let me goe, that I may hide my selfe in the fieldes vnto the third day at euen.

6 If thy father make mention of me, then say, Dauid asked leaue of me, that he might goe to Beth-lehem to his owne citie: for there is a yeerely sacrifice for all that familie.

7 And if he say thus, It is well, thy seruant shall haue peace: but if he be angrie, be sure that wickednesse is concluded of him.

8 So shalt thou shew mercy vnto thy seruant: for thou hast ioyned thy seruant into a couenant of the Lord with thee, and if there be in me iniquitie, slay thou me: for why shouldest thou bring me to thy father?

9 And Ionathan answered, God keepe that from thee: for if I knewe that wickednesse were concluded of my father to come vpon thee, would not I tell it thee?

10 Then said Dauid to Ionathan, Who shall tell me? how shall I knowe, if thy father answere thee cruelly?

11 And Ionathan sayde to Dauid, Come and let vs goe out into the fielde: and they twaine went out into the fielde.

12 Then Ionathan sayde to Dauid, O Lord God of Israel, when I haue groped my fathers minde to morow at this time, or within this three dayes, and if it be well with Dauid, and I then send not vnto thee, and shewe it thee,

13 The Lord doe so and much more vnto Ionathan: but if my father haue minde to doe thee euill, I will shew thee also, and sende thee away, that thou mayest goe in peace: and the Lord be with thee as he hath bene with my father.

14 Likewise I require not whiles I liue: for I dout not but thou wilt shew me the mercy of the Lord, that I die not.

15 But I require that thou cut not off thy mercie from mine house for euer: no, not when the Lord hath destroyed the enemies of Dauid, euery one from the earth.

16 So Ionathan made a bond with the house of Dauid, saying, Let the Lord require it at the hands of Dauids enemies.

17 And againe Ionathan sware vnto Dauid, because he loued him (for he loued him as his owne soule)

18 Then said Ionathan to him, To morowe is the first day of the moneth: and thou shalt be looked for, for thy place shalbe emptie.

19 Therefore thou shalt hide thy selfe three dayes, then thou shalt goe downe quickely and come to the place where thou diddest hide thy selfe, when this matter was in hand, and shalt remayne by the stone Ezel.

20 And I will shoote three arrowes on the side thereof, as though I shot at a marke.

21 And after I wil sende a boy, saying, Goe, seeke the arrowes. If I say vnto the boy, See, the arrowes are on this side thee, bring them, and come thou: for it is well with thee and no hurt, as the Lord liueth.

22 But if I say thus vnto the boy, Behold, the arrowes are beyonde thee,

goe thy way: for the Lord hath sent thee away.

23 As touching the thing which thou and I haue spoken of, beholde, the Lord be betweene thee and me for euer.

24 So Dauid hid him selfe in the field: and when the first day of the moneth came, the King sate to eate meate.

25 And the King sate, as at other times vpon his seate, euen vpon his seate by the wall: and Ionathan arose, and Abner sate by Sauls side, but Dauids place was emptie.

26 And Saul sayde nothing that day: for hee thought, Some thing hath befallen him, though he were cleane, or els becaus he was not purified.

27 But on the morowe which was the second day of the moneth, Dauids place was emptie againe: and Saul sayde vnto Ionathan his sonne, Wherefore commeth not the sonne of Ishai to meate, neither yesterday nor to day?

28 And Ionathan answered vnto Saul, Dauid required of me, that he might goe to Beth-lehem.

29 For he sayde, Let me goe, I pray thee: for our familie offreth a sacrifice in the citie, and my brother hath sent for me: therfore now if I haue found fauour in thine eyes, let me goe, I pray thee, and see my brethren: this is the cause that he commeth not vnto the Kings table.

30 Then was Saul angrie with Ionathan, and sayde vnto him, Thou sonne of the wicked rebellious woman, doe not I know, that thou hast chosen the sonne of Ishai to thy confusion, and to the confusion and shame of thy mother?

31 For as long as the sonne of Ishai liueth vpon the earth, thou shalt not be stablished, nor thy kingdome: wherefore now send and fet him vnto me, for he shall surely die.

32 And Ionathan answered vnto Saul his father, and said vnto him, Wherefore shall he die? what hath he done?

33 And Saul cast a speare at him to hit him, whereby Ionathan knew, that it was determined of his father to slay Dauid.

34 So Ionathan arose from the table in a great anger, and did eate no meate the seconde day of the moneth: for he was sorie for Dauid, and because his father had reuiled him.

35 On the next morning therefore Ionathan than went out into the fielde, at the time appoynted with Dauid, and a litle boy with him.

36 And he saide vnto his boy, Runne now, seeke the arrowes which I shoote, and as the boy ran, he shot an arrowe beyond him.

37 And when the boy was come to the place where the arrowe was that Ionathan had shot, Ionathan cryed after the boy, and sayde, Is not the arrowe beyond thee?

38 And Ionathan cryed after the boy, Make speede, haste and stand not still: and Ionathans boy gathered vp the arrowes, and came to his master,

39 But the boy knewe nothing: onely Ionathan and Dauid knew the matter.

40 Then Ionathan gaue his bowe and arrowes vnto the boy that was with him, and sayd vnto him, Goe, carrie them into the citie.

41 Assoone as the boy was gone, Dauid arose out of a place that was towarde the South, and fel on his face to the ground, and bowed him selfe three times: and they kissed one another, and wept both twaine, till Dauid exceeded.

42 Therefore Ionathan said to Dauid, Goe in peace: that which we haue sworne both of vs in the Name of the Lord, saying, The Lord be betweene me and thee, and betweene my seede and betweene thy seede, let it stand for euer.

43 And he arose and departed, and Ionathan went into the citie.

First Samuel 21

1 Then came Dauid to Nob, to Ahimelech the Priest, and Ahimelech was astonied at the meeting of Dauid, and saide vnto him, Why art thou alone, and no man with thee?

2 And Dauid saide to Ahimelech the Priest, The King hath commanded mee a certaine thing, and hath sayd vnto me, Let no man know whereabout I sende thee, and what I haue commanded thee: and I haue appointed my seruants to such and such places.

3 Nowe therefore if thou hast ought vnder thine hande, giue me fiue cakes of bread, or what commeth to hand.

4 And the Priest answered Dauid, and saide, There is no common bread vnder mine hande, but here is halowed bread, if the yong men haue kept themselues, at least from women.

5 Dauid then answered the Priest, and sayde vnto him, Certainely women haue bene separarate from vs these two or three dayes since I came out: and the vessels of the yong men were holy, though the way were prophane, and how much more then shall euery one be sanctified this day in the vessell?

6 So the Priest gaue him halowed bread: for there was no bread there, saue the shewe bread that was taken from before the Lord, to put hote bread there, the day that it was taken away.

7 (And there was the same day one of the seruants of Saul abiding before the Lord, named Doeg the Edomite, the chiefest of Sauls heardmen)

8 And Dauid said vnto Ahimelech, Is there not here vnder thine hand a speare or a sworde? for I haue neither brought my sworde nor mine harnesse with me, because the Kings businesse required haste.

9 And the Priest said, The sword of Goliath the Philistim, whom thou slewest in the valley of Elah, behold, it is wrapt in a cloth behinde the Ephod: if thou wilt take that to thee, take it: for there is none other saue that here: And Dauid sayd, There is none to that, giue it me.

10 And Dauid arose and fled the same day from the presence of Saul, and went to Achish the King of Gath.

11 And the seruants of Achish said vnto him, Is not this Dauid the King of the land? did they not sing vnto him in daunces, saying, Saul hath slayne his thousand, and Dauid his ten thousande?

12 And Dauid considered these wordes, and was sore afraide of Achish the King of Gath.

13 And hee changed his behauiour before them, and fayned him selfe mad in their handes, and scrabled on the doores of the gate, and let his spettel fall downe vpon his beard.

14 Then said Achish vnto his seruants, Lo, ye see the man is beside him selfe, wherefore haue ye brought him to me?

15 Haue I neede of mad men, that ye haue brought this fellowe to play the mad man in my presence? shall he come into mine house?

First Samuel 22

1 Dauid therefore departed thence, and saued him selfe in the caue of Adullam: and when his brethren and all his fathers house heard it, they went downe thither to him.

2 And there gathered vnto him all men that were in trouble and all men that were in dette, and all those that were vexed in minde, and he was their prince, and there were with him about foure hundreth men.

3 And Dauid went thence to Mizpeh in Moab, and said vnto the King of Moab, I pray thee, let my father and my mother come and abide with you, till I knowe what God wil doe for me.

4 And he brought them before the King of Moab, and they dwelt with him all the while that Dauid was in the holde.

5 And the Prophet Gad sayde vnto Dauid, Abide not in the holde, but depart and goe into the land of Iudah. Then Dauid departed and came into the forest of Hareth.

6 And Saul heard that Dauid was discouered, and the men that were with him, and Saul remayned in Gibeah vnder a tree in Ramah, hauing his speare in his hande, and all his seruants stoode about him.

7 And Saul said vnto his seruants that stood about him, Heare now, ye sonnes of Iemini, wil the sonne of Ishai giue euery one of you fields and vineyardes: will he make you all captaines ouer thousands, and captaines ouer hundreths:

8 That all ye haue conspired against me, and there is none that tellerh mee that my sonne hath made a couenant with the sonne of Ishai? and there is none of you that is sory for me, or sheweth mee, that my sonne hath stirred vp my seruant to lie in wayte against me, as appeareth this day?

9 Then answered Doeg the Edomite (who was appoynted ouer the seruants of Saul) and sayd, I saw the sonne of Ishai when he came to Nob, to Ahimelech the sonne of Ahitub,

10 Who asked counsell of the Lord for him and gaue him vitailes, and he gaue him also the sword of Goliath the Philistim.

11 Then the King sent to call Ahimelech the Priest the sonne of Ahitub, and all his fathers house, to wit, the Priests that were in Nob: and they came all to the King.

12 And Saul said, Heare now thou sonne of Ahitub. And he answered, Here I am, my lord.

13 Then Saul sayde vnto him, Why haue yee conspired against me, thou and the sonne of Ishai, in that thou hast giuen him vitaile, and a sworde, and hast asked counsell of God for him, that he should rise against me, and lye in wayte as appeareth this day?

14 And Ahimelech answered the King, and sayde, Who is so faithfull among all thy seruants as Dauid, being also the Kings sonne in lawe, and goeth at thy commandement, and is honourable in thine house?

15 Haue I this day first begun to aske counsell of God for him? be it farre from mee, let not the King impute any thing vnto his seruant, nor to all the house of my father: for thy seruant knew nothing of all this, lesse nor more.

16 Then the King sayd, Thou shalt surely die, Ahimelech, thou, and all thy fathers house.

17 And the King sayde vnto the sergeantes that stoode about him, Turne, and slay the Priestes of the Lord, because their hand also is with Dauid, and because they knewe when he fled, and shewed it not vnto mee. But the seruantes of the King would not moue their hands to fall vpon the Priests of the Lord.

18 Then the King sayde to Doeg, Turne thou and fall vpon the Priests. And Doeg the Edomite turned, and ran vpon the Priestes, and slewe that same daye foure score and fiue persons that did weare a linen Ephod.

19 Also Nob the citie of the Priestes smote he with the edge of the sword, both man and woman, both childe and suckling, both oxe and asse, and sheepe with the edge of the sword.

20 But one of the sonnes of Ahimelech the sonne of Ahitub (whose name was Abiathar) escaped and fled after Dauid.

21 And Abiathar shewed Dauid, that Saul had slayne the Lords Priestes.

22 And Dauid sayd vnto Abiathar, I knewe it the same day, when Doeg the Edomite was there, that he would tell Saul. I am the cause of the death of all the persons of thy fathers house.

23 Abide thou with me, and feare not: for he that seeketh my life, shall seeke thy life also: for with me thou shalt be in safegard.

First Samuel 23

1 Then they tolde Dauid, saying, Beholde, the Philistims fight against Keilah, and spoyle the barnes.

2 Therfore Dauid asked counsel of the Lord, saying, Shal I goe and smite these Philistims? And the Lord answered Dauid, Go and smite the Philistims, and saue Keilah.

3 And Dauids men said vnto him, See, we be afrayde here in Iudah, howe much more if we come to Keilah against the hoste of ye Philistims?

4 Then Dauid asked counsell of the Lord againe. And the Lord answered him, and sayd, Arise, go downe to Keilah: for I wil deliuer the Philistims into thine hand.

5 So Dauid and his men went to Keilah, and fought with the Philistims, and brought away their cattel, and smote them with a great slaughter: thus Dauid saued the inhabitants of Keilah.

6 (And when Abiathar the sonne of Ahimelech fled to Dauid to Keilah, he brought an Ephod with him)

7 And it was tolde Saul that Dauid was come to Keilah, and Saul sayd, God hath deliuered him into mine hand: for he is shut in, seeing he is come into a citie that hath gates and barres.

8 Then Saul called all the people together to warre, for to go downe to Keilah, and to besiege Dauid and his men.

9 And Dauid hauing knowledge that Saul imagined mischiefe against him, saide to Abiathar the Priest, Bring the Ephod.

10 Then sayde Dauid, O Lord God of Israel, thy seruat hath heard, that Saul is about to come to Keilah to destroy the citie for my sake.

11 Wil the lordes of Keilah deliuer me vp into his hand? and will Saul come downe, as thy seruant hath heard? O Lord God of Israel, I beseech thee, tell thy seruant. And the Lord sayde, He will come downe.

12 Then said Dauid, Will the lords of Keilah deliuer me vp, and the men that are with me, into the hand of Saul? And the Lord sayde, They will deliuer thee vp.

13 Then Dauid and his men, which were about sixe hundreth, arose, and departed out of Keilah, and went whither they coulde. And it was tolde Saul, that Dauid was fled from Keilah, and he left off his iourney.

14 And Dauid abode in the wildernesse in holdes, and remayned in a mountaine in the wildernes of Ziph. And Saul sought him euery day, but God deliuered him not into his hand.

15 And Dauid sawe that Saul was come out for to seeke his life: and Dauid was in the wildernes of Ziph in the wood.

16 And Ionathan Sauls sonne arose and went to Dauid into the wood, and comforted him in God,

17 And said vnto him, Feare not: for the hand of Saul my father shall not finde thee, and thou shalt be King ouer Israel, and I shalbe next vnto thee: and also Saul my father knoweth it.

18 So they twaine made a couenant before ye Lord: and Dauid did remaine in the wood: but Ionathan went to his house.

19 Then came vp the Ziphims to Saul to Gibeah, saying, Doeth not Dauid hide himselfe by vs in holdes, in the wood in the hill of Hachilah, which is on the right side of Ieshimon?

20 Nowe therefore, O King, come downe according to all that thine heart can desire, and our part shall be to deliuer him into the Kinges handes.

21 Then Saul said, Be ye blessed of the Lord: for ye haue had compassion on mee.

22 Goe, I pray you, and prepare ye yet better: know and see his place where he haunteth, and who hath seene him there: for it is sayd to me, He is subtile, and craftie.

23 See therefore and know all the secret places where he hideth himselfe, and come ye againe to me with the certaintie, and I will goe with you: and if he be in the lande, I will searche him out throughout all the thousands of Iudah.

24 Then they arose and went to Ziph before Saul, but Dauid and his men were in the wildernesse of Maon, in the playne on the right hande of Ieshimon.

25 Saul also and his men went to seeke him, and they told Dauid: wherefore he came downe vnto a rocke, and abode in the wildernesse of Maon. And when Saul heard that, he folowed after Dauid in the wildernes of Maon.

26 And Saul and his men went on the one side of the mountaine, and Dauid and his men on the other side of the mountaine: and Dauid made haste to get from the presence of Saul: for Saul and his men compassed Dauid and his men round about, to take them.

27 But there came a messenger to Saul, saying, Haste thee, and come: for the Philistims haue inuaded the land.

28 Wherefore Saul returned from pursuing Dauid, and went against the Philistims. Therefore they called that place, Sela-hammahlekoth.

First Samuel 24

1 And Dauid went thence, and dwelt in holdes at En-gedi.

2 When Saul was turned from ye Philistims, they told him, saying, Behold, Dauid is in the wildernes of En-gedi.

3 Then Saul tooke three thousande chosen men out of all Israel, and went to seeke Dauid and his men vpon the rocks among the wilde goates.

4 And hee came to the sheepecoates by the way where there was a caue, and Saul went in to do his easement: and Dauid and his men sate in the inward parts of the caue.

5 And the men of Dauid said vnto him, See, the day is come, whereof the Lord sayde vnto thee, Beholde, I will deliuer thine enemie into thine hande, and thou shalt doe to him as it shall seeme good to thee. Then Dauid arose and cut off the lap of Sauls garment priuily.

6 And afterward Dauid was touched in his heart, because he had cut off the lappe which was on Sauls garment.

7 And he said vnto his men, The Lord keepe mee from doing that thing vnto my master the Lords Anoynted, to lay mine hand vpon him: for he is the Anoynted of the Lord.

8 So Dauid ouercame his seruants with these words, and suffered them not to arise against Saul: so Saul rose vp out of the caue and went away.

9 Dauid also arose afterward, and went out of the caue, and cryed after Saul, saying, O my lorde the King. And when Saul looked behinde him, Dauid inclined his face to the earth, and bowed himselfe.

10 And Dauid saide to Saul, Wherefore giuest thou an eare to mens words, that say, Behold, Dauid seeketh euill against thee?

11 Behold, this day thine eyes haue seene, that the Lord had deliuered thee this day into mine hand in the caue, and some bade me kill thee, but I had compassion on thee, and said, I will not lay mine hande on my master: for he is the Lordes Anoynted.

12 Moreouer my father, behold: behold, I say, the lappe of thy garment in mine hand: for when I cut off the lappe of thy garment, I killed thee not. Vnderstad and see, that there is neither euil nor wickednesse in mee, neither haue I sinned against thee, yet thou huntest after my soule to take it.

13 The Lord be iudge betweene thee and me, and the Lord auenge me of thee, and let not mine hand be vpon thee.

14 According as the olde prouerbe sayeth, Wickednesse proceedeth from the wicked, but mine hand be not vpon thee.

15 After whom is the King of Israel come out? after whome doest thou pursue? after a dead dog, and after a flea?

16 The Lord therfore be iudge, and iudge betweene thee and me, and see, and pleade my cause, and deliuer me out of thine hand.

17 Whe Dauid had made an end of speaking these words to Saul, Saul sayd, Is this thy voyce, my sonne Dauid? and Saul lift vp his voice, and wept,

18 And sayd to Dauid, Thou art more righteous then I: for thou hast rendred me good, and I haue rendred thee euill.

19 And thou hast shewed this day, that thou hast dealt well with me: forasmuch as when the Lord had closed me in thine hands, thou killedst me not.

20 For who shall finde his enemie, and let him depart free? wherefore the Lord render thee good for that thou hast done vnto me this day.

21 For now behold, I know that thou shalt be King, and that the kingdome of Israel shall be stablished in thine hand.

22 Sweare now therfore vnto me by the Lord, that thou wilt not destroy my seede after me, and that thou wilt not abolish my name out of my fathers house.

23 So Dauid sware vnto Saul, and Saul went home: but Dauid and his men went vp vnto ye hold.

First Samuel 25

1 Then Samuel dyed, and all Israel assembled, and mourned for him, and buried him in his owne house at Ramah. And Dauid arose and went downe to the wildernes of Paran.

2 Now in Maon was a man, who had his possessio in Carmel, and the man was exceeding mightie and had three thousand sheepe, and a thousand goates: and he was shering his sheepe in Carmel.

3 The name also of the man was Nabal, and the name of his wife Abigail, and she was a woman of singular wisdome, and beautifull, but the man was churlish, and euil conditioned, and was of the familie of Caleb.

4 And Dauid heard in the wildernesse, that Nabal did shere his sheepe.

5 Therefore Dauid sent tenne yong men, and Dauid said vnto the yong men, Go vp to Carmel, and go to Nabal, and aske him in my name how he doeth.

6 And thus shall ye say for salutation, Both thou, and thine house, and all that thou hast, be in peace, wealth and prosperitie.

7 Behold, I haue heard, that thou hast sherers: now thy shepherds were with vs, and we did the no hurt, neyther did they misse any thing all the while they were in Carmel.

8 Aske thy seruants and they wil shew thee. Wherefore let these yong men finde fauour in thine eyes: (for we come in a good season) giue, I pray thee, whatsoeuer commeth to thine hand vnto thy seruants, and to thy sonne Dauid.

9 And when Dauids yong men came, they tolde Nabal all those wordes in the name of Dauid, and helde their peace.

10 Then Nabal answered Dauids seruantes, and sayd, Who is Dauid? and who is the sonne of Ishai? there be many seruantes nowe a dayes, that breake away euery man from his master.

11 Shall I then take my bread, and my water, and my flesh that I haue killed for my sherers, and giue it vnto men, whom I know not whence they be?

12 So Dauids seruants turned their way, and went againe, and came, and tolde him all those things.

13 And Dauid said vnto his men, Girde euery man his sword about him. And they girded euery man his sworde: Dauid also girded his sworde. And about foure hundreth men went vp after Dauid, and two hundreth abode by the cariage.

14 Nowe one of the seruantes tolde Abigail Nabals wife, saying, Beholde, Dauid sent messengers out of the wildernesse to salute our master, and he rayled on them.

15 Notwithstanding the men were very good vnto vs, and we had no displeasure, neither missed we any thing as long as we were conuersant with them, when we were in the fieldes.

16 They were as a wall vnto vs both by night and by day, all the while we were with them keeping sheepe.

17 Nowe therefore take heede, and see what thou shalt doe: for euill will surely come vpon our master, and vpon all his familie: for he is so wicked that a man can not speake to him.

18 Then Abigail made haste, and tooke two hundreth cakes, and two bottels of wine, and fiue sheepe ready dressed, and fiue measures of parched corne, and an hundreth frailes of raisins, and two hundreth of figs, and laded them on asses.

19 Then she said vnto her seruants, Go ye before me: beholde, I will come after you: yet she tolde not her husband Nabal.

20 And as shee rode on her asse, shee came downe by a secret place of the mountaine, and beholde, Dauid and his men came downe against her, and she met them.

21 And Dauid said, In deede I haue kept all in vaine that this fellow had in the wildernesse, so that nothing was missed of all that pertained vnto him: for he hath requited me euill for good.

22 So and more also doe God vnto the enemies of Dauid: for surely I will not leaue of all that he hath, by the dawning of the day, any that pisseth against the wall.

23 And when Abigail sawe Dauid, she hasted and lighted off her asse, and fell before Dauid on her face, and bowed her selfe to the ground,

24 And fel at his feete, and sayd, Oh, my lord, I haue committed the iniquitie, and I pray thee, let thine handmayde speake to thee, and heare thou the wordes of thine handmayde.

25 Let not my lorde, I pray thee, regard this wicked man Nabal: for as his name is, so is he: Nabal is his name, and follie is with him: but I thine handmayde sawe not the yong men of my lord whom thou sentest.

26 Now therefore my lord, as the Lord liueth, and as thy soule liueth (the Lord, I say, that hath withholden thee from comming to shedde blood, and that thine hand should not saue thee) so now thine enemies shall be as Nabal, and they that intend to doe my lord euill.

27 And now, this blessing which thine handmaid hath brought vnto my lorde, let it be giuen vnto the yong men, that follow my lord.

28 I pray thee, forgiue the trespasse of thine handmaide: for the Lord will make my lorde a sure house, because my lord fighteth the battels of the Lord, and none euill hath bene found in thee in all thy life.

29 Yet a man hath risen vp to persecute thee, and to seeke thy soule, but the soule of my lorde shall be bounde in the bundel of life with the Lord thy God: and the soule of thine enemies shall God cast out, as out of the middle of a sling.

30 And when the Lord shall haue done to my lord al the good that he hath promised thee, and shall haue made thee ruler ouer Israel,

31 Then shall it be no griefe vnto thee, nor offence of minde vnto my lord, that he hath not shed blood causelesse, nor that my lorde hath not preserued him selfe: and when the Lord shall haue dealt well with my lorde, remember thine handmaide.

32 Then Dauid said to Abigail, Blessed be the Lord God of Israel, which sent thee this day to meete me.

33 And blessed be thy counsel, and blessed be thou, which hast kept me this day from comming to shed blood, and that mine hand hath not saued me.

34 For in deede, as the Lord God of Israel liueth, who hath kept me backe from hurting thee, except thou haddest hasted and met mee, surely there had not bene left vnto Nabal by the dawning of the day, any that pisseth against the wall.

35 Then Dauid receiued of her hande that which she had brought him, and said to her, Goe vp in peace to thine house: beholde, I haue heard thy voyce, and haue graunted thy petition.

36 So Abigail came to Nabal, and behold, he made a feast in his house, like the feast of a King, and Nabals heart was merie within him, for he was very drunken: wherefore shee tolde him nothing, neither lesse nor more, vntil the morning arose.

37 Then in the morning when the wine was gone out of Nabal, his wife tolde him those wordes, and his heart died within him, and he was like a stone.

38 And about ten dayes after, the Lord smote Nabal, that he dyed.

39 Now when Dauid heard, that Nabal was dead, he said, Blessed be the Lord that hath iudged the cause of my rebuke of ye hand of Nabal, and hath kept his seruant from euil: for the Lord hath recompensed the wickednesse of Nabal vpon his owne head. Also Dauid sent to commune with Abigail to take her to his wife.

40 And whe the seruants of Dauid were come to Abigail to Carmel, they spake vnto her, saying, Dauid sent vs to thee, to take thee to his wife.

41 And she arose, and bowed her selfe on her face to the earth, and said, Behold, let thine handmayde be a seruant to wash the feete of the seruants of my lord.

42 And Abigail hasted, and arose, and rode vpon an asse, and her fiue maides folowed her, and she went after the messengers of Dauid, and was his wife.

43 Dauid also tooke Ahinoam of Izreel, and they were both his wiues.

44 Now Saul had giuen Michal his daughter Dauids wife to Phalti the sonne of Laish, which was of Gallim.

First Samuel 26

1 Againe the Ziphims came vnto Saul to Gibeah, saying, Doeth not Dauid hide him selfe in the hill of Hachilah before Ieshimon?

2 Then Saul arose, and went downe to the wildernes of Ziph, hauing three thousand chosen men of Israel with him,

for to seeke Dauid in the wildernesse of Ziph.

3 And Saul pitched in the hill of Hachilah, which is before Ieshimon by the way side. Now Dauid abode in the wildernesse, and he sawe that Saul came after him into the wildernesse.

4 (For Dauid had sent out spies, and vnderstood, that Saul was come in very deede)

5 Then Dauid arose, and came to the place where Saul had pitched, and when Dauid beheld the place where Saul lay, and Abner the sonne of Ner which was his chiefe captaine, (for Saul lay in the fort, and the people pitched round about him)

6 Then spake Dauid, and said to Ahimelech the Hittite, and to Abishai the sonne of Zeruiah, brother to Ioab, saying, Who will go downe with me to Saul to the hoste? Then Abishai said, I will goe downe with thee.

7 So Dauid and Abishai came downe to the people by night: and beholde, Saul lay sleeping within the fort, and his speare did sticke in the ground at his head: and Abner and the people lay round about him.

8 Then saide Abishai to Dauid, God hath closed thine enemie into thine hande this day: now therefore, I pray thee, let me smite him once with a speare to the earth, and I will not smite him againe.

9 And Dauid sayde to Abishai, Destroy him not: for who can lay his hand on the Lordes anoynted, and be giltlesse?

10 Moreouer Dauid said, As the Lord liueth, eyther the Lord shall smite him, or his day shall come to dye, or he shall descend into battel, and perish.

11 The Lord keepe mee from laying mine hand vpon the Lordes anointed: but, I pray thee, take now the speare that is at his head, and the pot of water, and let vs goe hence.

12 So Dauid tooke the speare and the pot of water from Sauls head, and they gate them away, and no man saw it, nor marked it, neither did any awake, but they were all asleepe: for the Lord had sent a dead sleepe vpon them.

13 Then Dauid went vnto the other side, and stoode on the toppe of an hill a farre off, a great space being betweene them.

14 And Dauid cryed to the people, and to Abner the sonne of Ner, saying, Hearest thou not, Abner? Then Abner answered, and said, Who art thou that cryest to the King?

15 And Dauid said to Abner, Art not thou a man? and who is like thee in Israel? wherefore then hast thou not kept thy lorde the King? for there came one of the folke in to destroy the King thy lord.

16 This is not well done of thee: as the Lord liueth, ye are worthy to dye, because ye haue not kept your master the Lordes Anointed: and now see where the Kings speare is, and the pot of water that was at his head.

17 And Saul knewe Dauids voyce, and sayde, Is this thy voyce, my sonne Dauid? And Dauid sayde, It is my voyce, my lorde O King.

18 And he sayde, Wherefore doeth my lorde thus persecute his seruant? for what haue I done? or what euill is in mine hand?

19 Now therefore, I beseech thee, let my lord the King heare the wordes of his seruant. If the Lord haue stirred thee vp against me, let him smell the sauour of a sacrifice: but if the children of men haue done it, cursed be they before the Lord: for they haue cast me out this day from abiding in the inheritance of the Lord, saying, Goe, serue other gods.

20 Nowe therefore let not my blood fall to the earth before the face of the Lord: for the King of Israel is come out to seeke a flea, as one would hunt a partridge in the mountaines.

21 Then sayde Saul, I haue sinned: come againe, my sonne Dauid: for I will doe thee no more harme, because my soule was precious in thine eyes this day: behold, I haue done foolishly, and haue erred exceedingly.

22 Then Dauid answered, and saide, Beholde the Kings speare, let one of the yong men come ouer and set it.

23 And let the Lord rewarde euery man according to his righteousnesse and faithfulnesse: for the Lord had deliuered thee into mine handes this day, but I woulde not lay mine hand vpon the Lords anointed.

24 And beholde, like as thy life was much set by this day in mine eyes: so let my life be set by in the eyes of the Lord, that he may deliuer me out of all tribulation.

25 Then Saul said to Dauid, Blessed art thou, my sonne Dauid: for thou shalt doe great things, and also preuaile. So Dauid went his way, and Saul returned to his place.

First Samuel 27

1 And Dauid said in his heart, I shall now perish one day by the hand of Saul: is it not better for me that I saue my selfe in the lande of the Philistims, and that Saul may haue no hope of me to seeke me any more in all the coastes of Israel, and so escape out of his hand?

2 Dauid therefore arose, and he, and the sixe hundreth men that were with him, went vnto Achish the sonne of Maoch King of Gath.

3 And Dauid dwelt with Achish at Gath, he, and his men, euery man with his housholde,Dauid with his two wiues, Ahinoam the Izreelite, and Abigail Nabals wife the Carmelite.

4 And it was tolde Saul that Dauid was fled to Gath: so he sought no more for him.

5 And Dauid saide vnto Achish, If I haue nowe founde peace in thine eyes, let them giue me a place in some other citie of the countrey, that I may dwell there: for why should thy seruant dwel in ye head citie of the kingdome with thee?

6 Then Achish gaue him Ziklag that same day: therefore Ziklag pertaineth vnto the kings of Iudah vnto this day.

7 And the time that Dauid dwelt in the countrey of the Philistims, was foure moneths and certaine dayes.

8 Then Dauid and his men went vp, and inuaded the Geshurites, and the Girzites, and the Amalekites: for they inhabited the lande from the beginning, from the way, as thou goest to Shur, euen vnto the lande of Egypt.

9 And Dauid smote the lande, and left neither man nor woman aliue, and tooke sheepe, and oxen, and asses, and camels, and apparell, and returned and came to Achish.

10 And Achish said, Where haue ye bene a rouing this day? And Dauid answered, Against the South of Iudah, and against the South of the Ierahmeelites, and against the South of ye Kenites.

11 And Dauid saued neither man nor woman aliue, to bring them to Gath, saying, Lest they should tel on vs, and say, So did Dauid, and so will be his maner all the while that he dwelleth in the countrey of the Philistims.

12 And Achish beleeued Dauid, saying, He hath made his people of Israel vtterly to abhorre him: therefore he shalbe my seruant for euer.

First Samuel 28

1 Nowe at that time the Philistims assembled their bandes and armie to fight with Israel: therfore Achish said to Dauid, Be sure, thou shalt go out with me to the battel, thou, and thy men.

2 And Dauid said to Achish, Surely thou shalt knowe, what thy seruant can doe. And Achish sayde to Dauid, Surely I will make thee keeper of mine head for euer.

3 (Samuel was then dead, and all Israel had lamented him, and buried him in Ramah his owne citie: and Saul had put away the sorcerers, and the soothsayers out of the land)

4 Then the Philistims assembled themselues, and came, and pitched in Shunem: and Saul assembled all Israel, and they pitched in Gilboa.

5 And when Saul saw the hoste of the Philistims, he was afraid, and his heart was sore astonied.

6 Therefore Saul asked counsel of the Lord, and the Lord answered him not, neither by dreames, nor by Vrim, nor yet by Prophets.

7 Then saide Saul vnto his seruants, Seeke me a woman that hath a familiar spirite, that I may goe to her, and aske of her. And his seruants said to him, Beholde, there is a woman at En-dor that hath a familiar spirit.

8 Then Saul changed him selfe, and put on other raiment, and he went, and two men with him, and they came to the woman by night: and he saide, I pray thee, coniecture vnto me by the familiar spirite, and bring me him vp whome I shall name vnto thee.

9 And the woman saide vnto him, Beholde, thou knowest what Saul hath done, how he hath destroyed the sorcerers, and the southsayers out of the land: wherefore then seekest thou to take me in a snare to cause me to die?

10 And Saul sware to her by the Lord, saying, As the Lord liueth, no harme shall come to thee for this thing.

11 Then said the woman, Whom shall I bring vp vnto thee? And he answered, Bring me vp Samuel.

12 And when the woman sawe Samuel, she cryed with a loude voyce, and the woman spake to Saul, saying, Why hast thou deceiued me? for thou art Saul.

13 And the King said vnto her, Be not afraid: for what sawest thou? And the woman said vnto Saul, I saw gods ascending vp out of the earth.

14 Then he said vnto her, What facion is hee of? And she answered, An olde man commeth vp lapped in a mantel: and Saul knewe that it was Samuel, and he enclined his face to the grounde, and bowed him selfe.

15 And Samuel said to Saul, Why hast thou disquieted me, to bring me vp? Then Saul answered, I am in great distresse: for the Philistims make warre against me, and God is departed from me, and answereth me no more, neither by Prophetes, neither by dreames: therefore I haue called thee, that thou mayest tell me, what I shall doe.

16 Then said Samuel, Wherefore then doest thou aske of me, seeing the Lord is gone from thee, and is thine enemie?

17 Euen the Lord hath done to him, as hee spake by mine hande: for the Lord will rent the kingdome out of thine hande, and giue it thy neighbour Dauid.

18 Because thou obeyedst not the voyce of the Lord, nor executedst his fierce wrath vpon the Amalekites, therefore hath the Lord done this vnto thee this day.

19 Moreouer the Lord wil deliuer Israel with thee into the handes of the Philistims: and to morowe shalt thou and thy sonnes be with me, and the Lord shall giue the hoste of Israel into the handes of the Philistims.

20 Then Saul fell streight way all along on the earth, and was sore afraide because of the wordes of Samuel, so that there was no strength in him: for he had eaten no bread all the day nor all the night.

21 Then the woman came vnto Saul, and sawe that he was sore troubled, and said vnto him, See, thine handmaide hath obeyed thy voyce, and I haue put my soule in mine hande, and haue obeyed thy wordes which thou saydest vnto me.

22 Now therefore, I pray thee, hearke thou also vnto ye voyce of thine handmaid, and let me set a morsell of bread before thee, that thou mayest eat and get thee strength, and go on thy iourney.

23 But he refused, and said, I will not eate: but his seruants and the woman together compelled him, and he obeyed their voyce: so he arose from the earth, and sate on the bed.

24 Nowe the woman had a fat calfe in the house, and she hasted, and killed it, and tooke floure and kneaded it, and baked of it vnleauened bread.

25 Then she brought them before Saul, and before his seruants: and when they had eaten, they stoode, and went away the same night.

First Samuel 29

1 So the Philistims were gathered together with all their armies in Aphek: and the Israelites pitched by the fountaine, which is in Izreel.

2 And the princes of the Philistims went foorth by hundreths and thousandes, but Dauid and his men came behinde with Achish.

3 Then saide the princes of the Philistims, What doe these Ebrewes here? And Achish said vnto the princes of the Philistims, Is not this Dauid the seruant of Saul the King of Israel, who hath bene with me these dayes, or these yeeres, and I haue found nothing in him, since he dwelt with me vnto this day?

4 But the princes of the Philistims were wroth with him, and the princes of the Philistims said vnto him, Sende this fellow backe, that he may goe againe to his place which thou hast appointed him, and let him not goe downe with vs to battell, least that in the battell he be an aduersarie to vs: for wherewith should he obteine the fauour of his master? shoulde it not be with the heades of these men?

5 Is not this Dauid, of whome they sang in daunces, saying, Saul slewe his thousande, and Dauid his ten thousande?

6 Then Achish called Dauid, and said vnto him, As the Lord liueth, thou hast bene vpright and good in my sight, when thou wentest out and in with mee in the hoste, neither haue I founde euill with thee, since thou camest to me vnto this day, but the princes doe not fauour thee.

7 Wherefore nowe returne, and go in peace, that thou displease not the princes of the Philistims.

8 And Dauid said vnto Achish, But what haue I done? and what hast thou founde in thy seruant as long as I haue bene with thee vnto this day, that I may not goe and fight against the enemies of my lorde the King?

9 Achish then answered, and said to Dauid, I knowe thou pleasest mee, as an Angell of God: but the princes of the Philistims haue saide, Let him not goe vp with vs to battell.

10 Wherefore now rise vp earely in the morning with thy masters seruants that are come with thee: and when ye be vp earely, assoone as ye haue light, depart.

11 So Dauid and his men rose vp earely to depart in the morning, and to returne into the lande of the Philistims: and the Philistims went vp to Izreel.

First Samuel 30

1 Bvt when Dauid and his men were come to Ziklag the thirde day, the Amalekites had inuaded vpon the South, euen vnto Ziklag, and had smitten Ziklag, and burnt it with fire,

2 And had taken the women that were therein, prisoners, both small and great, and slewe not a man, but caryed them away, and went their wayes.

3 So Dauid and his men came to the city, and beholde, it was burnt with fire, and their wiues, and their sonnes, and their daughters were taken prisoners.

4 Then Dauid and the people that was with him, lift vp their voyces and wept, vntill they could weepe no more.

5 Dauids two wiues were taken prisoners also, Ahinoam the Izreelite, and Abigail the wife of Nabal the Carmelite.

6 And Dauid was in great sorowe: for the people entended to stone him, because the heartes of all the people were vexed euery man for his sonnes and for his daughters: but Dauid comforted him selfe in the Lord his God.

7 And Dauid saide to Abiathar the Priest Ahimelechs sonne, I pray thee, bring me the Ephod. And Abiathar brought the Ephod to Dauid.

8 Then Dauid asked counsell at the Lord, saying, Shall I follow after this companie? shall I ouertake them? And he answered him, Followe: for thou shalt surely ouertake them, and recouer all.

9 So Dauid and the sixe hundreth men that were with him, went, and came to the riuer Besor, where a part of them abode:

10 But Dauid and foure hundreth men followed (for two hundreth abode behinde, being too wearie to goe ouer the riuer Besor)

11 And they found an Egyptian in the fielde, and brought him to Dauid, and gaue him bread and he did eat, and they gaue him water to drinke.

12 Also they gaue him a fewe figges, and two clusters of raisins: and when he had eaten, his spirite came againe to him: for he had eaten no bread, nor drunke any water in three dayes, and three nightes.

13 And Dauid saide vnto him, To whome belongest thou? and whence art thou? And he saide, I am a yong man of Egypt, and seruant to an Amalekite: and my master left me three dayes agoe, because I fell sicke.

14 We roued vpon the South of Chereth, and vpon the coast belonging to Iudah, and vpon the South of Caleb, and we burnt Ziklag with fire.

15 And Dauid saide vnto him, Canst thou bring me to this companie? And he said, Sweare vnto me by God, that thou wilt neither kill me, nor deliuer me into the handes of my master, and I will bring thee to this companie.

16 And when he had brought him thither, beholde, they lay scattered abroade vpon all the earth, eating and drinking, and dauncing, because of all the great pray that they had taken out of

the lande of the Philistims, and out of the land of Iudah.

17 And Dauid smote them from the twilight, euen vnto the euening of the next morowe, so that there escaped not a man of them, saue foure hundreth yong men, which rode vpon camels, and fled.

18 And Dauid recouered all that the Amalekites had taken: also Dauid rescued his two wiues.

19 And they lacked nothing, small or great, sonne or daughter, or of the spoyle of all that they had taken away: Dauid recouered them all.

20 Dauid also tooke all the sheepe, and the oxen, and they draue them before his cattell, and said, This is Dauids pray.

21 And Dauid came to the two hundreth men that were too wearie for to follow Dauid: whome they had made also to abide at the riuer Besor: and they came to meete Dauid, and to meete the people that were with him: so when Dauid came neere to the people, hee saluted them.

22 Then answered all the euill and wicked of the men that went with Dauid, and saide, Because they went not with vs, therefore will wee giue them none of the pray that wee haue recouered, saue to euery man his wife and his children: therefore let them carie them away and depart.

23 Then saide Dauid, Yee shall not doe so, my brethren, with that which the Lord hath giuen vs, who hath preserued vs, and deliuered the companie that came against vs, into our handes.

24 For who will obey you in this matter? but as his part is that goeth downe to the battel, so shall his part be, that tarieth by the stuffe: they shall part alike.

25 So from that day forward hee made it a statute and a lawe in Israel, vntill this day.

26 When Dauid therefore came to Ziklag, he sent of the pray vnto the Elders of Iudah and to his friends, saying, See there is a blessing for you of the spoyle of the enemies of the Lord.

27 Hee sent to them of Beth-el, and to them of South Ramoth, and to them of Iattir,

28 And to them of Aroer, and to them of Siphmoth, and to them of Eshtemoa,

29 And to them of Rachal, and to them of the cities of the Ierahmeelites, and to them of the cities of the Kenites,

30 And to them of Hormah, and to them of Chor-ashan, and to them of Athach,

31 And to them of Hebron, and to all the places where Dauid and his men had hanted.

First Samuel 31

1 Now the Philistims fought against Israel, and the me of Israel fled away from ye Philistims, and they fell downe wounded in mount Gilboa.

2 And the Philistims preassed sore vpon Saul and his sonnes, and slewe Ionathan, and Abinadab, and Malchishua Sauls sonnes.

3 And when the battel went sore against Saul, the archers and bowmen hit him, and hee was sore wounded of the archers.

4 Then saide Saul vnto his armour bearer, Drawe out thy sworde, and thrust mee through therewith, lest the vncircumcised come and thrust me through and mocke me: but his armour bearer would not, for hee was sore afraid. Therefore Saul tooke a sworde and fell vpon it.

5 And when his armour bearer sawe that Saul was dead, he fell likewise vpon his sword, and dyed with him.

6 So Saul dyed, and his three sonnes, and his armour bearer, and all his men that same day together.

7 And when the men of Israel that were on the other side of the valley, and they of the other side Iorden saw that the men of Israel were put to flight, and that Saul and his sonnes were dead, then they left the cities, and ran away: and the Philistims came and dwelt in them.

8 And on the morowe when the Philistims were come to spoyle them that were slaine, they founde Saul and his three sonnes lying in mount Gilboa,

9 And they cut off his head, and stripped him out of his armour, and sent into the land of ye Philistims on euery side, that they should publish it in the temple of their idoles, and among the people.

10 And they layed vp his armour in the house of Ashtaroth, but they hanged vp his body on the wall of Beth-shan.

11 When the inhabitants of Iabesh Gilead heard, what the Philistims had done to Saul,

12 Then they arose (as many as were strong men) and went all night, and tooke the body of Saul, and the bodies of his sonnes, from the wall of Beth-shan, and came to Iabesh, and burnt them there,

13 And tooke their bones and buried them vnder a tree at Iabesh, and fasted seuen dayes.

Second Samuel

Second Samuel 1

1 After the death of Saul, when Dauid was returned from the slaughter of the Amalekites and had beene two dayes in Ziklag,

2 Behold, a man came the third day out of the host from Saul with his clothes rent, and earth vpon his head: and when hee came to Dauid, he fell to the earth, and did obeisance.

3 Then Dauid saide vnto him, Whence commest thou? And he said vnto him, Out of the host of Israel I am escaped.

4 And Dauid saide vnto him, What is done? I pray thee, tell me. Then he said, that the people is fled from the battel, and many of the people are ouerthrowen, and dead, and also Saul and Ionathan his sonne are dead.

5 And Dauid saide vnto the yong man that tolde it him, Howe knowest thou that Saul and Ionathan his sonne be dead?

6 Then the yong man that tolde him, answered, As I came to mount Gilboa, behold, Saul leaned vpon his speare, and loe, the charets and horsemen followed hard after him.

7 And when he looked backe, he saw me, and called me. And I answered, Here am I.

8 And he said vnto me, Who art thou? And I answered him, I am an Amalekite.

9 Then saide hee vnto me, I pray thee come vpon mee, and slay me: for anguish is come vpon me, because my life is yet whole in me.

10 So I came vpon him, and slewe him, and because I was sure that hee coulde not liue, after that hee had fallen, I tooke the crowne that was vpon his head, and the bracelet that was on his arme, and brought them hither vnto my lord.

11 Then Dauid tooke hold on his clothes, and rent them, and likewise al the men that were with him.

12 And they mourned and wept, and fasted vntil euen, for Saul and for Ionathan his sonne, and for the people of the Lord, and for the house of Israel, because they were slaine with the sword.

13 Afterward Dauid saide vnto the yong man that tolde it him, Whence art thou? And hee answered, I am the sonne of a stranger an Amalekite.

14 And Dauid said vnto him, How wast thou not afrayd, to put forth thine hand to destroy the Anoynted of the Lord?

15 Then Dauid called one of his yong men, and said, Goe neere, and fall vpon him. And hee smote him that he dyed.

16 Then said Dauid vnto him, Thy blood be vpon thine owne head: for thine owne mouth hath testified against thee, saying, I haue slaine the Lords Anoynted.

17 Then Dauid mourned with this lamentation ouer Saul, and ouer Ionathan his sonne,

18 (Also he bade them teach the children of Iudah to shoote, as it is written in the booke of Iasher)

19 O noble Israel, hee is slane vpon thy hie places: how are the mightie ouerthrowen!

20 Tell it not in Gath, nor publish it in the streetes of Ashkelon, lest the daughters of the Philistims reioyce, lest the daughters of the vncircumcised triumph.

21 Ye mountaines of Gilboa, vpon you be neither dewe nor raine, nor be there fieldes of offrings: for there the shielde of the mightie is cast downe, the shielde of Saul, as though he had not bene anointed with oyle.

22 The bow of Ionathan neuer turned backe, neither did the sword of Saul returne emptie from the blood of the slaine, and from the fatte of the mightie.

23 Saul and Ionathan were louely and pleasant in their liues, and in their deaths they were not deuided: they were swifter then eagles, they were stronger then lions.

24 Yee daughters of Israel, weepe for Saul, which clothed you in skarlet, with pleasures, and hanged ornaments of gold vpon your apparel.

25 Howe were the mightie slaine in the mids of the battel! O Ionathan, thou wast slaine in thine hie places.

26 Wo is me for thee, my brother Ionathan: very kinde hast thou bene vnto me: thy loue to me was wonderfull, passing the loue of women: howe are the mightie ouerthrowen, and the weapons of warre destroyed!

Second Samuel 2

1 After this, Dauid asked counsel of the Lord, saying, Shall I go vp into any of the cities of Iudah? And the Lord sayd vnto him, Goe vp. And Dauid sayd Whither shall I goe? Hee then answered, Vnto Hebron.

2 So Dauid went vp thither, and his two wiues also, Ahinoam the Izreelite, and Abigail Nabals wife the Carmelite.

3 And Dauid brought vp the men that were with him, euery man with his houshold, and they dwelt in the cities of Hebron.

4 Then the men of Iudah came, and there they anoynted Dauid King ouer the house of Iudah. And they tolde Dauid, saying, that the men of Iabesh Gilead buried Saul.

5 And Dauid sent messengers vnto the men of Iabesh Gilead, and said vnto them, Blessed are ye of the Lord, that yee haue shewed such kindenes vnto your lord Saul, that you haue buried him.

6 Therefore now the Lord shewe mercie and trueth vnto you: and I will recompence you this benefite, because ye haue done this thing.

7 Therefore nowe let your handes be strong, and be you valiant: albeit your master Saul bee dead, yet neuerthelesse the house of Iudah hath anoynted me King ouer them.

8 But Abner the sonne of Ner that was captaine of Sauls hoste, tooke Ish-bosheth the sonne of Saul, and brought him to Mahanaim,

9 And made him King ouer Gilead, and ouer the Ashurites, and ouer Izreel, and ouer Ephraim, and ouer Beniamin, and ouer al Israel.

10 Ish-bosheth Sauls sonne was fourtie yeere olde when he began to reigne ouer Israel, and reigned two yeere: but the house of Iudah followed Dauid.

11 (And the time which Dauid reigned in Hebron ouer the house of Iudah, was seuen yeere and sixe moneths)

12 And Abner the sonne of Ner, and the seruantes of Ish-bosheth the sonne of Saul went out of Mahanaim to Gibeon.

13 And Ioab the sonne of Zeruiah, and the seruants of Dauid went out and met one another by the poole of Gibeon: and they sate downe, the one on the one side of the poole, and the other on the otherside of the poole.

14 Then Abner saide to Ioab, Let the yong men nowe arise, and play before vs. And Ioab said, Let them arise.

15 Then there arose and went ouer twelue of Beniamin by number, which perteined to Ish-bosheth the sonne of Saul, and twelue of the seruants of Dauid.

16 And euery one caught his fellowe by the head, and thrust his sword in his fellowes side, so they fell downe together: wherefore ye place was called Helkath-hazzurim, which is in Gibeon.

17 And the battel was exceeding sore that same day: for Abner and the men of Israel fell before the seruants of Dauid.

18 And there were three sonnes of Zeruiah there, Ioab, and Abishai, and Asahel. And Asahel was as light on foote as a wilde roe.

19 And Asahel followed after Abner, and in going he turned neither to the right hand nor to the left from Abner.

20 Then Abner looked behind him, and said, Art thou Asahel? And he answered, Yea.

21 Then Abner said, Turne thee either to the right hande, or to the left, and take one of the yong men, and take thee his weapons: and Asahel would not depart from him.

22 And Abner saide to Asahel, Depart from me: wherefore shoulde I smite thee to the grounde? howe then shoulde I be able to holde vp my face to Ioab thy brother?

23 And when he woulde not depart, Abner with the hinder ende of the speare smote him vnder the fift ryb, that the speare came out behind him: and he fell downe there, and dyed in his place. And as many as came to the place where Asahel fell downe and dyed, stoode still.

24 Ioab also and Abishai pursued after Abner: and the sunne went downe, when they were come to the hill Ammah, that lieth before Giah, by the way of the wildernesse of Gibeon.

25 And the children of Beniamin gathered them selues together after Abner, and were on an heape and stoode on the top of an hill.

26 Then Abner called to Ioab, and said, Shall the sworde deuoure for euer? knowest thou not, that it will be bitternesse in the latter ende? howe long then shall it be, or thou bid the people returne from following their brethren?

27 And Ioab sayde, As God liueth, if thou haddest not spoken, surely euen in the morning the people had departed euery one backe from his brother.

28 So Ioab blew a trumpet, and all the people stoode still, and pursued after Israel no more, neither fought they any more.

29 And Abner and his men walked all that night through the plaine, and went ouer Iorden, and past through all Bithron till they came to Mahanaim.

30 Ioab also returned backe from Abner: and when he had gathered all the people together, there lacked of Dauids seruants nineteene men and Asahel.

31 But the seruants of Dauid had smitten of Beniamin, and of Abners men, so that three hundreth and threescore men dyed.

32 And they tooke vp Asahel, and buried him in the sepulchre of his father, which was in Bethlehem: and Ioab and his men went all night, and when they came to Hebron, the day arose.

Second Samuel 3

1 There was then long warre betweene the house of Saul and the house of Dauid: but Dauid waxed stronger, and the house of Saul waxed weaker.

2 And vnto Dauid were children borne in Hebron: and his eldest sonne was Amnon of Ahinoam the Izreelite,

3 And his seconde, was Chileab of Abigail the wife of Nabal the Carmelite: and the third, Absalom the sonne of Maacah the daughter of Talmai the King of Geshur,

4 And the fourth, Adoniiah the sonne of Haggith, and the fifth, Shephatiah the sonne of Abital,

5 And the sixt, Ithream by Eglah Dauids wife: these were borne to Dauid in Hebron.

6 Nowe while there was warre betweene the house of Saul and the house of Dauid, Abner made all his power for the house of Saul.

7 And Saul had a concubine named Rizpah, the daughter of Aiiah. And Ish-bosheth sayde to Abner, Wherefore hast thou gone in to my fathers concubine?

8 Then was Abner very wroth for the words of Ish-bosheth, and said, Am I a dogges head, which against Iudah do shew mercie this day vnto the house of Saul thy father, to his brethren, and to his neighbours, and haue not deliuered thee into the hande of Dauid, that thou chargest me this day with a fault concerning this woman?

9 So doe God to Abner, and more also, except, as the Lord hath sworne to Dauid, euen so I doe to him,

10 To remoue the kingdome from the house of Saul, that the throne of Dauid may be stablished ouer Israel, and ouer Iudah, euen from Dan to Beer-sheba.

11 And he durst no more answere to Abner: for he feared him.

12 Then Abner sent messengers to Dauid on his behalfe, saying, Whose is the lande? who should also say, Make couenant with me, and beholde, mine hande shalbe with thee, to bring all Israel vnto thee.

13 Who saide, Well, I will make a couenant with thee: but one thing I require of thee, that is, that thou see not my face except thou bring Michal Sauls daughter when thou commest to see me.

14 Then Dauid sent messengers to Ish-bosheth Sauls sonne, saying, Deliuer me my wife Michal, which I marryed for an hundreth foreskinnes of the Philistims.

15 And Ish-bosheth sent, and tooke her from her husband Phaltiel the sonne of Laish.

16 And her husband went with her, and came weeping behinde her, vnto Bahurim: then saide Abner vnto him, Go, and returne. So he returned.

17 And Abner had communication with the Elders of Israel, saying, Ye sought for Dauid in times past, that he might be your King.

18 Nowe then doe it: for the Lord hath spoken of Dauid, saying, By the hand of my seruant Dauid I will saue my people Israel out of the handes of the Philistims, and out of the handes of all their enemies.

19 Also Abner spake to Beniamin, and afterward Abner went to speake with Dauid in Hebron, concerning all that Israel was content with, and the whole house of Beniamin.

20 So Abner came to Dauid to Hebron, hauing twentie men with him, and Dauid made a feast vnto Abner, and to the men that were with him.

21 Then Abner sayde vnto Dauid, I will rise vp, and goe gather all Israel vnto my lorde the King, that they may make a couenant with thee, and that thou mayest reigne ouer all that thine heart desireth. Then Dauid let Abner depart, who went in peace.

22 And beholde, the seruants of Dauid and Ioab came from the campe, and brought a great pray with them (but Abner was not with Dauid in Hebron: for he had sent him away, and he departed in peace)

23 When Ioab, and all the hoste that was with him were come, men tolde Ioab, saying, Abner the sonne of Ner came to the King, and he hath sent him away, and he is gone in peace.

24 Then Ioab came to the King, and saide, What hast thou done? beholde, Abner came vnto thee, why hast thou sent him away, and he is departed?

25 Thou knowest Abner the sonne of Ner: for he came to deceiue thee, and to knowe thy outgoing and ingoing, and to knowe all that thou doest.

26 And when Ioab was gone out from Dauid, he sent messengers after Abner, which brought him againe from the well of Siriah vnknowing to Dauid.

27 And when Abner was come againe to Hebron, Ioab tooke him aside in the gate to speake with him peaceably, and smote him vnder the fift ryb, that he dyed, for the blood of Asahel his brother.

28 And when afterwarde it came to Dauids eare, he saide, I and my kingdome are giltlesse before the Lord for euer, concerning the blood of Abner the sonne of Ner.

29 Let the blood fall on the head of Ioab, and on all his fathers house, that the house of Ioab be neuer without some that haue running issues, or leper, or that leaneth on a staffe, or that doeth fall on the sworde, or that lacketh bread.

30 (So Ioab and Abishai his brother slewe Abner, because he had slaine their brother Asahel at Gibeon in battel)

31 And Dauid said to Ioab, and to al the people that were with him, Rent your clothes, and put on sackecloth, and mourne before Abner: and King Dauid him selfe followed the beare.

32 And when they had buryed Abner in Hebron, the King lift vp his voyce, and wept beside the sepulchre of Abner, and all the people wept.

33 And the King lamented ouer Abner, and sayde, Dyed Abner as a foole dyeth?

34 Thine handes were not bounde, nor thy feete tyed in fetters of brasse: but as a man falleth before wicked men, so diddest thou fall. And all the people wept againe for him.

35 Afterwarde all the people came to cause Dauid eate meate while it was yet day, but Dauid sware, saying, So doe God to me and more also, if I taste bread, or ought els till the sunne be downe.

36 And all the people knewe it, and it pleased them: as whatsoeuer the King did, pleased all the people.

37 For all the people and all Israel vnderstoode that day, howe that it was not the Kings deede that Abner the sonne of Ner was slaine.

38 And the King said vnto his seruants, Know ye not, that there is a prince and a great man falle this day in Israel?

39 And I am this day weake and newly anoynted King: and these men the sonnes of Zeruiah be too harde for me: the Lord rewarde the doer of euill according to his wickednesse.

Second Samuel 4

1 And when Sauls sonne heard that Abner was dead in Hebron, then his handes were feeble, and all Israel was afraide,

2 And Sauls sonne had two men that were captaines of bandes: the one called Baanah, and the other called Rechab, the sonnes of Rimmon a Beerothite of the children of Beniamin. (for Beeroth was reckened to Beniamin,

3 Because the Beerothites fled to Gittaim, and soiourned there, vnto this day).

4 And Ionathan Sauls sonne had a sonne that was lame on his feete: he was fiue yere olde when the tydings came of Saul and Ionathan out of Israel: then his nourse tooke him, and fledde away. And as she made haste to flee, the childe fell, and beganne to halte, and his name was Mephibosheth.

5 And the sonnes of Rimmon the Beerothite, Rechab and Baanah went and came in the heat of the day to the house of Ish-bosheth (who slept on a bed at noone)

6 And beholde, Rechab and Baanah his brother came into the middes of the house as they would haue wheate, and they smote him vnder the fift ryb, and fled.

7 For when they came into the house, he slept on his bed in his bed chamber, and they smote him, and slewe him, and beheaded him, and tooke his head, and gate them away through the plaine all the night.

8 And they brought the head of Ish-bosheth vnto Dauid to Hebron, and saide to the King, Beholde the head of Ish-bosheth Sauls sonne thine enemie, who sought after thy life: and the Lord hath auenged my lorde the King this day of Saul, and of his seede.

9 Then Dauid answered Rechab and Baanah his brother, the sonnes of Rimmon the Beerothite, and saide vnto them, As the Lord liueth, who hath deliuered my soule out of al aduersity,

10 When one tolde me, and sayde that Saul was dead, (thinking to haue brought good tydings) I tooke him and slewe him in Ziklag, who thought that I woulde haue giuen him a rewarde for his tidings:

11 How much more, when wicked men haue slaine a righteous person in his owne house, and vpon his bed? shall I not now therfore require his blood at your hand, and take you from the earth?

12 Then Dauid commanded his yong men, and they slew them, and cut off their hands and their feete, and hanged them vp ouer the poole in Hebron: but they tooke the head of Ishbosheth, and buried it in the sepulchre of Abner in Hebron.

Second Samuel 5

1 Then came all the tribes of Israel to Dauid vnto Hebron, and said thus, Beholde, we are thy bones and thy flesh.

2 And in time past when Saul was our King, thou leddest Israel in and out: and the Lord hath sayde to thee, Thou shalt feede my people Israel, and thou shalt be a captaine ouer Israel.

3 So all the Elders of Israel came to the King to Hebron: and King Dauid made a couenant with them in Hebron before the Lord: and they anoynted Dauid King ouer Israel.

4 Dauid was thirtie yeere olde when he began to reigne: and hee reigned fortie yeere.

5 In Hebron hee reigned ouer Iudah seuen yeere, and sixe moneths: and in Ierusalem hee reigned thirtie and three yeeres ouer all Israel and Iudah.

6 The King also and his men went to Ierusalem vnto the Iebusites, the inhabitants of the land: who spake vnto Dauid, saying, Except thou take away the blinde and the lame, thou shalt not come in hither: thinking that Dauid coulde not come thither.

7 But Dauid tooke the fort of Zion: this is the citie of Dauid.

8 Nowe Dauid had sayd the same day, Whosoeuer smiteth the Iebusites, and getteth vp to the gutters and smiteth the lame and blinde, which Dauids soule hateth, I will preferre him: therefore they saide, The blinde and the lame shall not come into that house.

9 So Dauid dwelt in that forte, and called it the citie of Dauid, and Dauid built rounde about it, from Millo, and inward.

10 And Dauid prospered and grewe: for the Lord God of hostes was with him.

11 Hiram also king of Tyrus sent messengers to Dauid, and cedar trees, and carpenters, and masons for walles: and they built Dauid an house.

12 Then Dauid knewe that the Lord had stablished him King ouer Israel, and that he had exalted his kingdome for his people Israels sake.

13 And Dauid tooke him more concubines and wiues out of Ierusalem, after hee was come from Hebron, and more sonnes and daughters were borne to Dauid.

14 And these bee the names of the sonnes that were borne vnto him in Ierusale: Shammua, and Shobab, and Nathan, and Salomon,

15 And Ibhar, and Elishua, and Nepheg, and Iaphia,

16 And Elishama, and Eliada, and Eliphalet.

17 But when the Philistims hearde that they had anoynted Dauid King ouer Israel, all the Philistims came vp to seeke Dauid: and when Dauid heard, he went downe to a fort.

18 But the Philistims came, and spred themselues in the valley of Rephaim.

19 Then Dauid asked counsel of the Lord, saying, Shall I goe vp to the Philistims? wilt thou deliuer them into mine handes? And the Lord answered Dauid, Goe vp: for I will doubtlesse deliuer the Philistims into thine handes.

20 Then Dauid came to Baal-perazim, and smote them there, and sayde, The Lord hath deuided mine enemies asunder before mee, as waters be deuided asunder: therefore he called the name of that place, Baal-perazim.

21 And there they left their images, and Dauid and his men burnt them.

22 Againe the Philistims came vp, and spred themselues in the valley of Rephaim.

23 And when Dauid asked counsell of the Lord, hee answered, Thou shalt not goe vp, but turne about behinde them, and come vpon them ouer against the mulberie trees.

24 And when thou hearest the noyse of one going in the toppes of the mulberie trees, then remoue: for then shall the Lord goe out before thee, to smite the hoste of the Philistims.

25 Then Dauid did so as the Lord had commanded him, and smote the Philistims from Geba, vntil thou come to Gazer.

Second Samuel 6

1 Againe Dauid gathered together all the chosen men of Israel, euen thirtie thousand,

2 And Dauid arose and went with all the people that were with him from Baale of Iudah to bring vp from thence the Arke of God, whose name is called by the Name of the Lord, of hostes, that dwelleth vpon it betweene the Cherubims.

3 And they put the Arke of God vpon a newe cart, and brought it out of the house of Abinadab that was in Gibeah. And Vzzah and Ahio the sonnes of Abinadab did driue the newe carte.

4 And when they brought the Arke of God out of the house of Abinadab, that was at Gibeah, Ahio went before the Arke,

5 And Dauid and al the house of Israel played before the Lord on all instruments made of firre, and on harpes, and on Psalteries, and on timbrels, and on cornets, and on cymbals.

6 And when they came to Nachons threshing floore, Vzzah put his hande to the Arke of God, and helde it: for the oxen did shake it.

7 And the Lord was verie wroth with Vzzah, and God smote him in the same place for his fault, and there he dyed by the Arke of God.

8 And Dauid was displeased, because the Lord had smitten Vzzah: and he called the name of the place Perez Vzzah vntill this day.

9 Therefore Dauid that day feared the Lord, and sayd, How shall the Arke of the Lord come to mee?

10 So Dauid would not bring the Arke of the Lord vnto him into the citie of Dauid, but Dauid caried it into ye house of Obed-edom a Gittite.

11 And the Arke of the Lord continued in the house of Obed-edom the Gittite, three moneths, and the Lord blessed Obed-edom, and all his houshould.

12 And one told King Dauid, saying, The Lord hath blessed the house of Obed-edom, and all that hee hath, because of the Arke of God: therefore Dauid went and brought the Arke of God from the house of Obed-edom, into the citie of Dauid with gladnesse.

13 And when they that bare the Arke of the Lord had gone sixe paces, he offred an oxe, and a fatte beast.

14 And Dauid danced before the Lord with al his might, and was girded with a linnen Ephod.

15 So Dauid and all the house of Israel, brought the Arke of the Lord with shouting, and sound of trumpet.

16 And as the Arke of the Lord came into the citie of Dauid, Michal Sauls daughter looked through a windowe, and sawe King Dauid leape, and dance before the Lord, and shee despised him in her heart.

17 And when they had brought in the Arke of the Lord, they set it in his place, in the mids of the tabernacle that Dauid had pitched for it: then Dauid offred burnt offrings, and peace offrings before the Lord.

18 And assoone as Dauid had made an ende of offring burnt offrings and peace offrings, hee blessed the people in the Name of the Lord of hostes,

19 And gaue among all the people, euen among the whole multitude of Israel, aswel to the women as men, to euerie one a cake of bread, and a piece of flesh, and a bottell of wine: so all the people departed euerie one to his house.

20 The Dauid returned to blesse his house, and Michal the daughter of Saul came out to meete Dauid, and sayde, O howe glorious was the King of Israel this day, which was vncouered to day in the eyes of the maidens of his seruantes, as a foole vncouereth himselfe.

21 Then Dauid sayd vnto Michal, It was before the Lord, which chose me rather then thy father, and all his house, and commanded me to bee ruler ouer the people of the Lord, euen ouer Israel: and therefore will I play before the Lord,

22 And will yet be more vile then thus, and will be low in mine owne sight, and of the verie same maidseruants, which thou hast spoken of, shall I be had in honour.

23 Therfore Michal the daughter of Saul had no childe vnto the day of her death.

Second Samuel 7

1 Afterwarde when the King sate in his house and the Lord had giuen him rest rounde about from all his enemies,

2 The King saide vnto Nathan the Prophet, Beholde, nowe I dwel in an house of cedar trees, and the Arke of God remayneth within the curtaines.

3 Then Nathan sayde vnto the King, Go, and doe all that is in thine heart: for the Lord is with thee.

4 And the same night the worde of the Lord came vnto Nathan, saying,

5 Goe and tell my seruant Dauid, Thus saieth the Lord, Shalt thou buylde me an house for my dwelling?

6 For I haue dwelt in no house since the time that I brought the children of Israel out of Egypt vnto this day, but haue walked in a tent and tabernacle.

7 In al the places wherein I haue walked with all the children of Israel, spake I one worde with any of the tribes of Israel when I commanded the iudges to feede my people Israel? or sayde I, Why build ye not me an house of cedar trees?

8 Nowe therefore so say vnto my seruant Dauid, Thus saieth the Lord of hostes, I tooke thee from the sheepecote following the sheepe, that thou mightest bee ruler ouer my people, ouer Israel.

9 And I was with thee wheresoeuer thou hast walked, and haue destroyed all thine enemies out of thy sight, and haue made thee a great name, like vnto the name of the great men that are in the earth.

10 (Also I will appoynt a place for my people Israel, and will plant it, that they may dwell in a place of their owne, and moue no more, neither shall wicked people trouble them any more as before time,

11 And since the time that I set Iudges ouer my people of Israel) and I will giue thee rest from al thine enemies: also the Lord telleth thee, that he will make thee an house.

12 And when thy daies bee fulfilled, thou shalt sleepe with thy fathers, and I wil set vp thy seede after thee, which shall proceede out of thy body, and will stablish his kingdome.

13 He shall buyld an house for my Name, and I will stablish ye throne of his kingdome for euer.

14 I will be his father, and hee shall bee my sonne: and if he sinne, I will chasten

him with the rod of men, and with the plagues of the children of men.

15 But my mercy shall not depart away from him, as I tooke it from Saul whome I haue put away before thee.

16 And thine house shall be stablished and thy kingdome for euer before thee, euen thy throne shalbe stablished for euer.

17 According to all these wordes, and according to all this vision, Nathan spake thus vnto Dauid.

18 Then King Dauid went in, and sate before the Lord, and sayde, Who am I, O Lord God, and what is mine house, that thou hast brought me hitherto?

19 And this was yet a small thing in thy sight, O Lord God, therefore thou hast spoken also of thy seruants house for a great while: but doth this appertaine to man, O Lord God?

20 And what can Dauid say more vnto thee? for thou, Lord God, knowest thy seruant.

21 For thy words sake, and according to thine owne heart hast thou done all these great things, to make them knowen vnto thy seruant.

22 Wherefore thou art great, O Lord God: for there is none like thee, neither is there any God besides thee, according to all that wee haue heard with our eares.

23 And what one people in the earth is like thy people, like Israel? whose God went and redeemed them to himselfe, that they might be his people, and that hee might make him a name, and do for you great things, and terrible for thy land, O Lord, euen for thy people, whome thou redeemedst to thee out of Egypt, from the nations, and their gods?

24 For thou hast ordeyned to thy selfe thy people Israel to be thy people for euer: and thou Lord art become their God.

25 Nowe therefore, O Lord God, confirme for euer the word that thou hast spoken concerning thy seruant and his house, and doe as thou hast sayde.

26 And let thy Name bee magnified for euer by them that shall say, The Lord of hostes is the God ouer Israel: and let the house of thy seruant Dauid be stablished before thee.

27 For thou, O Lord of hostes, God of Israel, hast reueiled vnto thy seruant, saying, I will build thee an house: therefore hath thy seruant bene bold to pray this prayer vnto thee.

28 Therefore now, O Lord God, (for thou art God, and thy words be true, and thou hast tolde this goodnes vnto thy seruant)

29 Therefore nowe let it please thee to blesse the house of thy seruant, that it may continue for euer before thee: for thou, O Lord God, hast spoken it: and let the house of thy seruant be blessed for euer, with thy blessing.

Second Samuel 8

1 After this now, Dauid smote the Philistims, and subdued them, and Dauid tooke the bridle of bondage out of the hand of the Philistims.

2 And hee smote Moab, and measured them with a corde, and cast them downe to the ground: he measured them with two cordes to put them to death, and with one full corde to keepe them aliue: so became the Moabites Dauids seruants, and brought giftes.

3 Dauid smote also Hadadezer the sonne of Rehob King of Zobah, as he went to recouer his border at the riuer Euphrates.

4 And Dauid tooke of them a thousand and seuen hundreth horsemen, and twenty thousande footemen, and Dauid destroyed all the charets, but he reserued an hundreth charets of them.

5 Then came the Aramites of Dammesek to succour Hadadezer king of Zobah, but Dauid slewe of the Aramites two and twenty thousande men.

6 And Dauid put a garison in Aram of Dameseh: and the Aramites became seruants to Dauid, and brought gifts. And the Lord saued Dauid wheresoeuer he went.

7 And Dauid tooke the shieldes of gold that beleged to the seruants of Hadadezer, and brought them to Ierusalem.

8 And out of Betah, and Berothai (cities of Hadadezer) king Dauid brought exceeding much brasse.

9 Then Toi king of Hamath heard howe Dauid had smitten all the hoste of Hadadezer,

10 Therefore Toi sent Ioram his sonne vnto King Dauid, to salute him, and to reioyce with him because he had fought against Hadadezer, and beaten him (for Hadadezer had warre with Toi) who brought with him vessels of siluer, and vessels of golde, and vessels of brasse.

11 And King Dauid did dedicate them vnto the Lord with the siluer and golde that he had dedicate of all the nations, which he had subdued:

12 Of Aram, and of Moab, and of the children of Ammon, and of the Philistims, and of Amalek, and of the spoyle of Hadadezer ye sonne of Rehob King of Zobah.

13 So Dauid gate a name after that hee returned, and had slayne of the Aramites in the valley of salt eighteene thousand men.

14 And he put a garison in Edom: throughout all Edom put he souldiers, and all they of Edom became Dauids seruants: and the Lord kept Dauid whithersoeuer he went.

15 Thus Dauid reigned ouer all Israel, and executed iudgement and iustice vnto all his people.

16 And Ioab the sonne of Zeruiah was ouer the hoste, and Ioshaphat the sonne of Ahilud was recorder.

17 And Zadok the sonne of Ahitub, and Ahimelech the sonne of Abiathar were the Priestes, and Seraiah the Scribe.

18 And Benaiah the sonne of Iehoiada and the Cherethites and the Pelethites, and Dauids sonnes were chiefe rulers.

Second Samuel 9

1 And Dauid sayde, Is there yet any man left of the house of Saul, that I may shew him mercie for Ionathans sake?

2 And there was of the housholde of Saul a seruant whose name was Ziba, and when they had called him vnto Dauid, the King sayd vnto him, Art thou Ziba? And he sayd, I thy seruant am he.

3 Then the King sayd, Remayneth there yet none of the house of Saul, on whome I may shewe the mercie of God? Ziba then answered the King, Ionathan hath yet a sonne lame of his feete.

4 Then the King said vnto him, Where is he? And Ziba said vnto the King, Behold, he is in the house of Machir ye sonne of Ammiel of Lo-debar.

5 Then King Dauid sent, and tooke him out of the house of Machir the sonne of Ammiel of Lo-debar.

6 Nowe when Mephibosheth the sonne of Ionathan, the sonne of Saul was come vnto Dauid, he fel on his face, and did reuerence. And Dauid sayde, Mephibosheth? And he answered, Beholde thy seruant.

7 Then Dauid sayd vnto him, Feare not: for I wil surely shewe thee kindnes for Ionathan thy fathers sake, and will restore thee all the fieldes of Saul thy father, and thou shalt eate bread at my table continually.

8 And he bowed himselfe and sayd, What is thy seruant, that thou shouldest looke vpon such a dead dog as I am?

9 Then the king called Ziba Sauls seruant, and said vnto him, I haue giue vnto thy masters sonne all that perteined to Saul and to all his house.

10 Thou therefore and thy sonnes and thy seruantes shall till the lande for him, and bring in that thy masters sonne may haue foode to eate. And Mephibosheth thy masters sonne shall eate bread alway at my table (nowe Ziba had fifteene sonnes, and twentie seruants)

11 Then sayd Ziba vnto the King, According to all that my lord the King hath commaded his seruant, so shall thy seruat do, that Mephibosheth may eate at my table, as one of the Kings sonnes.

12 Mephibosheth also had a yong sonne named Micha, and all that dwelled in the house of Ziba, were seruants vnto Mephibosheth.

13 And Mephibosheth dwelt in Ierusalem: for he did eate continually at the Kings table, and was lame on both his feete.

Second Samuel 10

1 After this, the King of the children of Ammon dyed, and Hanun his sonne reigned in his steade.

2 Then sayde Dauid, I will shewe kindnesse vnto Hanun the sonne of Nahash, as his father shewed kindnesse vnto me. And Dauid sent his seruantes to comfort him for his father. So Dauids seruants came into the lande of the children of Ammon.

3 And the princes of the children of Ammon sayde vnto Hanun their lorde,

Thinkest thou that Dauid doth honour thy father, that he hath sent comforters to thee? hath not Dauid rather sent his seruants vnto thee, to search the citie, and to spie it out, and to ouerthrow it?

4 Wherefore Hanun tooke Dauids seruants, and shaued off the halfe of their beard, and cut off their garments in the middle, euen to their buttockes, and sent them away.

5 When it was told vnto Dauid, he sent to meete them (for the men were exceedingly ashamed) and the King sayde, Tary at Iericho, vntill your beards be growen, then returne.

6 And when the children of Ammon sawe that they stanke in the sight of Dauid, the children of Ammon sent and hired the Aramites of the house of Rehob, and the Aramites of Zoba, twentie thousande footemen, and of King Maacah a thousand men, and of Ish-tob twelue thousande men.

7 And when Dauid heard of it, he sent Ioab, and all the hoste of the strong men.

8 And the children of Ammon came out, and put their armie in araye at the entring in of the gate: and the Aramites of Zoba, and of Rehob, and of Ish-tob, and of Maacah were by themselues in the fielde.

9 When Ioab saw that the front of the battel was against him before and behinde, he chose of all the choyse of Israel, and put them in aray against the Aramites.

10 And the rest of the people hee deliuered into the hande of Abishai his brother, that hee might put them in aray against the children of Ammon.

11 And he sayde, If the Aramites be stronger then I, thou shalt helpe me, and if the children of Ammon be too strong for thee, I will come and succour thee.

12 Be strong and let vs be valiant for our people, and for the cities of our God, and let the Lord do that which is good in his eyes.

13 Then Ioab, and the people that was with him, ioyned in battel with the Aramites, who fled before him.

14 And when the children of Ammon sawe that the Aramites fled, they fled also before Abishai, and entred into the citie. so Ioab returned from the children of Ammon, and came to Ierusalem.

15 And when the Aramites sawe that they were smitten before Israel, they gathered them together.

16 And Hadarezer sent, and brought out the Aramites that were beyond the Riuer: and they came to Helam, and Shobach the captaine of the hoste of Hadarezer went before them.

17 When it was shewed Dauid, then he gathered all Israel together, and passed ouer Iorden and came to Helam: and the Aramites set themselues in aray against Dauid, and fought with him:

18 And the Aramites fled before Israel: and Dauid destroyed seuen hundreth charets of the Aramites, and fourtie thousande horsemen, and smote Shobach the captaine of his hoste, who dyed there.

19 And when all the Kings, that were seruants to Hadarezer, saw that they fell before Israel, they made peace with Israel, and serued them. and the Aramites feared to helpe the children of Ammon any more.

Second Samuel 11

1 And when the yeere was expired in the time when Kinges goe forth to battell, Dauid sent Ioab, and his seruantes with him, and all Israel, who destroyed the children of Ammon, and besieged Rabbah: but Dauid remayned in Ierusalem.

2 And when it was euening tide, Dauid arose out of his bed, and walked vpon the roofe of the Kings palace: and from the roofe he sawe a woman washing her selfe: and the woman was very beautifull to looke vpon.

3 And Dauid sent and inquired what woman it was: and one sayde, Is not this Bath-sheba the daughter of Eliam, wife to Vriah the Hittite?

4 Then Dauid sent messengers, and tooke her away: and she came vnto him and he lay with her: (now she was purified from her vncleannes) and she returned vnto her house.

5 And the woman conceiued: therefore shee sent and tolde Dauid, and sayd, I am with childe.

6 Then Dauid sent to Ioab, saying, Send me Vriah the Hittite. And Ioab sent Vriah to Dauid.

7 And when Vriah came vnto him, Dauid demanded him how Ioab did, and howe the people fared, and how the warre prospered.

8 Afterward Dauid said to Vriah, Go downe to thine house, and wash thy feete. So Vriah departed out of the Kings palace, and the king sent a present after him.

9 But Vriah slept at the doore of the Kings palace with all the seruants of his lord, and went not downe to his house.

10 Then they tolde Dauid, saying, Vriah went not downe to his house: and Dauid saide vnto Vriah, Commest thou not from thy iourney? why didst thou not go downe to thine house?

11 Then Vriah answered Dauid, The Arke and Israel, and Iudah dwell in tents: and my lord Ioab and the seruants of my lord abide in the open fields: shall I then go into mine house to eate and drinke, and lie with my wife? by thy life, and by the life of thy soule, I will not do this thing.

12 Then Dauid sayd vnto Vriah, Tary yet this day, and to morow I will send thee away. So Vriah abode in Ierusalem that day, and the morowe.

13 Then Dauid called him, and hee did eate and drinke before him, and he made him drunke: and at euen he went out to lie on his couch with the seruants of his Lord, but went not downe to his house.

14 And on the morowe Dauid wrote a letter to Ioab, and sent it by the hand of Vriah.

15 And he wrote thus in the letter, Put ye Vriah in the forefront of the strength of the battell, and recule ye backe from him, that he may be smitten, and die.

16 So when Ioab besieged the citie, he assigned Vriah vnto a place, where he knewe that strong men were.

17 And the men of the citie came out, and fought with Ioab: and there fell of the people of the seruants of Dauid, and Vriah the Hittite also dyed.

18 Then Ioab sent and tolde Dauid all the things concerning the warre,

19 And he charged the messenger, saying, When thou hast made an ende of telling all the matters of the warre vnto the King,

20 And if the kings anger arise, so that he say vnto thee, Wherefore approched ye vnto the citie to fight? knewe ye not that they would hurle from the wall?

21 Who smote Abimelech sonne of Ierubesheth? did not a woman cast a piece of a milstone vpon him from the wall, and he died in Thebez? why went you nie the wall? Then say thou, Thy seruant Vriah the Hittite is also dead.

22 So the messenger went, and came and shewed Dauid all that Ioab had sent him for.

23 And the messenger said vnto Dauid, Certainely the men preuailed against vs, and came out vnto vs into the field, but we pursued them vnto the entring of the gate.

24 But the shooters shot from ye wall against thy seruants, and some of the Kings seruants be dead: and thy seruant Vriah the Hittite is also dead.

25 Then Dauid said vnto the messenger, Thus shalt thou say vnto Ioab, Let not this thing trouble thee: for the sworde deuoureth one as well as another: make thy battell more strong against the citie and destroy it, and encourage thou him.

26 And when the wife of Vriah heard that her husband Vriah was dead, she mourned for her husband.

27 So when the mourning was past, Dauid sent and tooke her into his house, and shee became his wife, and bare him a sonne: but ye thing that Dauid had done, displeased the Lord.

Second Samuel 12

1 Then the Lord sent Nathan vnto Dauid, who came to him, and sayd vnto him, There were two men in one citie, the one riche, and the other poore.

2 The rich man had exceeding many sheepe and oxen:

3 But the poore had none at all, saue one litle sheepe which he had bought, and nourished vp: and it grew vp with him, and with his children also, and did eate of his owne morsels, and dranke of his owne cup, and slept in his bosome, and was vnto him as his daughter.

4 Now there came a stranger vnto the rich man, who refused to take of his owne sheepe, and of his owne oxen to dresse for the stranger that was come vnto him, but tooke the poore mans

sheepe, and dressed it for the man that was come to him.

5 Then Dauid was exceeding wroth with the man, and sayde to Nathan, As the Lord liueth, the man that hath done this thing, shall surely dye,

6 And he shall restore the lambe foure folde, because he did this thing, and had no pitie thereof.

7 Then Nathan sayd to Dauid, Thou art the man. Thus sayth the Lord God of Israel, I anoynted thee King ouer Israel, and deliuered thee out of the hand of Saul,

8 And gaue thee thy lordes house, and thy lords wiues into thy bosome, and gaue thee the house of Israel, and of Iudah, and would moreouer (if that had bene too litle) haue giuen thee such and such things.

9 Wherefore hast thou despised the commandement of the Lord, to doe euill in his sight? thou hast killed Vriah the Hittite with ye sworde, and hast taken his wife to be thy wife, and hast slaine him with the sworde of the children of Ammon.

10 Now therefore the sworde shall neuer depart from thine house, because thou hast despised me, and taken the wife of Vriah the Hittite to be thy wife.

11 Thus sayth the Lord, Behold, I will rayse vp euil against thee out of thine owne house, and will take thy wiues before thine eyes, and giue them vnto thy neighbour, and he shall lie with thy wiues in the sight of this sunne.

12 For thou diddest it secretly: but I will doe this thing before all Israel, and before the sunne.

13 Then Dauid sayde vnto Nathan, I haue sinned against the Lord. And Nathan sayde vnto Dauid, The Lord also hath put away thy sinne, thou shalt not die.

14 Howbeit because by this deede thou hast caused the enemies of the Lord to blaspheme, the childe that is borne vnto thee shall surely die.

15 So Nathan departed vnto his house: and the Lord stroke the childe that Vriahs wife bare vnto Dauid, and it was sicke.

16 Dauid therefore besought God for the childe, and fasted and went in, and lay all night vpon the earth.

17 Then the Elders of his house arose to come vnto him, and to cause him to rise from the groud: but he would not, neither did he eate meate with them.

18 So on the seuenth day the child dyed: and the seruants of Dauid feared to tell him that the childe was dead: for they sayde, Beholde, while the childe was aliue, we spake vnto him, and he woulde not hearken vnto our voyce: how then shall we say vnto him, The childe is dead, to vexe him more?

19 But when Dauid sawe that his seruantes whispered, Dauid perceiued that the childe was dead: therefore Dauid sayde vnto his seruants, Is the childe dead? And they sayd, He is dead.

20 Then Dauid arose from the earth, and washed and anoynted himselfe, and changed his apparell, and came into the house of the Lord, and worshipped, and afterward came to his owne house, and bade that they should set bread before him, and he did eate.

21 Then saide his seruants vnto him, What thing is this, that thou hast done? thou diddest fast and weepe for the childe while it was aliue, but when the childe was dead, thou diddest rise vp, and eate meate.

22 And he sayde, While the childe was yet aliue, I fasted, and wept: for I sayde, Who can tell whether God will haue mercy on me, that the childe may liue?

23 But now being dead, wherefore shoulde I now fast? Can I bring him againe any more? I shall goe to him, but he shall not returne to me.

24 And Dauid comforted Bath-sheba his wife, and went in vnto her, and lay with her, and she bare a sonne, and he called his name Salomon: also the Lord loued him.

25 For the Lord had sent by Nathan the Prophet: therefore he called his name Iedidiah, because the Lord loued him.

26 Then Ioab fought against Rabbah of the children of Ammon, and tooke the citie of the kingdome.

27 Therefore Ioab sent messengers to Dauid, saying, I haue fought against Rabbah, and haue taken the citie of waters.

28 Now therefore gather the rest of the people together, and besiege the city, that thou mayest take it, lest the victorie be attributed to me.

29 So Dauid gathered al the people together, and went against Rabbah, and besieged it, and tooke it.

30 And he tooke their Kings crowne from his head, (which weighed a talent of golde, with precious stones) and it was set on Dauids head: and he brought away the spoyle of the citie in exceeding great abundance.

31 And he carryed away the people that was therein, and put them vnder sawes, and vnder yron harowes, and vnder axes of yron, and cast them into the tyle kylne: euen thus did he with all the cities of the children of Ammon. Then Dauid and all the people returned vnto Ierusalem.

Second Samuel 13

1 Now after this so it was, that Absalom the sonne of Dauid hauing a fayre sister, whose name was Tamar, Amnon the sonne of Dauid loued her.

2 And Amnon was so sore vexed, that he fell sicke for his sister Tamar: for she was a virgin, and it seemed hard to Amnon to doe any thing to her.

3 But Amnon had a friend called Ionadab, the sonne of Shimeah Dauids brother: and Ionadab was a very subtile man.

4 Who sayde vnto him, Why art thou the Kings sonne so leane from day to day? wilt thou not tell me? Then Amnon answered him, I loue Tamar my brother Absaloms sister.

5 And Ionadab sayd vnto him, Lie downe on thy bed, and make thy selfe sicke: and when thy father shall come to see thee, say vnto him, I pray thee, let my sister Tamar come, and giue me meate, and let her dresse meate in my sight, that I may see it, and eate it of her hand.

6 So Amnon lay downe, and made himselfe sicke: and when the King came to see him, Amnon sayde vnto the King, I pray thee, let Tamar my sister come, and make me a couple of cakes in my sight, that I may receiue meate at her hand.

7 Then Dauid sent home to Tamar, saying, Goe now to thy brother Amnons house, and dresse him meate.

8 So Tamar went to her brother Amnons house, and he lay downe: and she tooke floure, and knead it, and made cakes in his sight, and did bake the cakes.

9 And she tooke a pan, and powred them out before him, but he would not eat. Then Amnon saide, Cause ye euery man to goe out from me: so euery man went out from him.

10 Then Amnon said vnto Tamar, Bring the meate into the chamber, that I may eate of thine hand. And Tamar tooke the cakes which shee had made, and brought them into the chamber to Amnon her brother.

11 And when she had set them before him to eate, he tooke her, and sayd vnto her, Come, lye with me, my sister.

12 But shee answered him, Nay, my brother, doe not force me: for no such thing ought to be done in Israel: commit not this follie.

13 And I, whither shall I cause my shame to goe? and thou shalt be as one of the fooles in Israel: now therefore, I pray thee, speake to the King, for he will not denie me vnto thee.

14 Howbeit he would not hearken vnto her voyce, but being stronger then she, forced her, and lay with her.

15 Then Amnon hated her exceedingly, so that the hatred wherewith he hated her, was greater then the loue, wherewith hee had loued her: and Amnon sayde vnto her, Vp, get thee hence.

16 And she answered him, There is no cause: this euill (to put mee away) is greater then the other that thou diddest vnto me: but he would not heare her,

17 But called his seruant that serued him, and sayd, Put this woman now out from me, and locke the doore after her.

18 (And she had a garment of diuers coulours vpon her: for with such garments were the Kings daughters that were virgins, apparelled) Then his seruant brought her out, and locked the doore after her.

19 And Tamar put ashes on her head and rent the garment of diuers colours which was on her, and layde her hand on her head, and went her way crying.

20 And Absalom her brother sayd vnto her, Hath Amnon thy brother bene with thee? Now yet be still, my sister: he is thy brother: let not this thing grieue thine

heart. So Tamar remayned desolate in her brother Absaloms house.

21 But when King Dauid heard all these things, he was very wroth.

22 And Absalom sayde vnto his brother Amnon neither good nor bad: for Absalom hated Amnon, because he had forced his sister Tamar.

23 And after the time of two yeeres, Absalom had sheepesherers in Baal-hazor, which is beside Ephraim, and Absalom called all the Kings sonnes.

24 And Absalom came to the King and sayd, Beholde now, thy seruant hath sheepesherers: I pray thee, that the King with his seruants would goe with thy seruant.

25 But the King answered Absalom, Nay my sonne, I pray thee, let vs not goe all, lest we be chargeable vnto thee. Yet Absalom lay sore vpon him: howbeit he would not go, but thanked him.

26 Then sayd Absalom, But, I pray thee, shall not my brother Amnon goe with vs? And the king answered him, Why should he go with thee?

27 But Absalom was instant vpon him, and he sent Amnon with him, and all the Kings children.

28 Now had Absalom commanded his seruants, saying, Marke now when Amnons heart is merry with wine, and when I say vnto you, Smite Amnon, kill him, feare not, for haue not I commanded you? be bold therefore, and play the men.

29 And the seruantes of Absalom did vnto Amnon, as Absalom had commanded: and al the Kings sonnes arose, and euery man gate him vp vpon his mule, and fled.

30 And while they were in the way, tydings came to Dauid, saying, Absalom hath slaine al the Kings sonnes, and there is not one of them left.

31 Then the King arose, and tare his garments, and lay on the ground, and all his seruants stoode by with their clothes rent.

32 And Ionadab the sonne of Shimeah Dauids brother answered and sayde, Let not my lord suppose that they haue slayne all the yong men the Kings sonnes: for Amnon onely is dead, because Absalom had reported so, since hee forced his sister Tamar.

33 Nowe therefore let not my lord the King take the thing so grieuously, to thinke that all ye Kings sonnes are dead: for Amnon only is dead.

34 Then Absalom fled: and the yong man that kept the watch, lift vp his eyes, and looked, and behold, there came much people by the way of the hill side behinde him.

35 And Ionadab said vnto the King, Behold, ye Kings sonnes come: as thy seruant sayd, so it is.

36 And assoone as hee had left speaking, behold, the Kings sonnes came, and lift vp their voyces, and wept: and the King also and all his seruants wept exceedingly sore.

37 But Absalom fled away, and went to Talmai the sonne of Ammihur King of Geshur: and Dauid mourned for his sonne euery day.

38 So Absalom fled, and went to Geshur, and was there three yeeres.

39 And King Dauid desired to go forth vnto Absalom, because he was pacified concerning Amnon, seeing he was dead.

Second Samuel 14

1 Then Ioab the sonne of Zeruiah perceyued, that the Kings heart was toward Absalom,

2 And Ioab sent to Tekoah, and brought thence a subtile woman, and sayd vnto her, I pray thee, fayne thy selfe to mourne, and nowe put on mourning apparel, and anoynt not thy selfe with oyle: but be as a woman that had now long time mourned for the dead.

3 And come to the King, and speake on this maner vnto him, (for Ioab taught her what she should say).

4 Then the woman of Tekoah spake vnto the king, and fel downe on her face to the ground, and did obeysance, and sayd, Helpe, O King.

5 Then the King sayd vnto her, What aileth thee? And she answered, I am in deede a widow, and mine husband is dead:

6 And thine handmayd had two sonnes, and they two stroue together in the fielde: (and there was none to part them) so the one smote the other, and slew him.

7 And beholde, the whole familie is risen against thine handmayde, and they sayde, Deliuer him that smote his brother, that we may kill him for the soule of his brother whome hee slewe, that we may destroy the heire also: so they shall quenche my sparkle which is left, and shall not leaue to mine husband neither name nor posteritie vpon the earth.

8 And the King said vnto the woman, Go to thine house, and I wil giue a charge for thee.

9 Then the woman of Tekoah said vnto the King, My lord, O King, this trespas be on me, and on my fathers house, and the King and his throne be giltlesse.

10 And the King sayde, Bring him to me that speaketh against thee, and he shall touche thee no more.

11 Then said she, I pray thee, let the King remember the Lord thy God, that thou wouldest not suffer many reuengers of blood to destroy, lest they slay my sonne. And he answered, As the Lord liueth, there shall not one heare of thy sonne fall to the earth.

12 Then the woman said, I pray thee, let thine handmayde speake a worde to my lord the King. And he sayd, Say on.

13 Then the woman sayde, Wherefore then hast thou thought such a thing against the people of God? or why doeth the King, as one which is faultie, speake this thing, that he will not bring againe his banished?

14 For we must needes dye, and we are as water spilt on the ground, which cannot be gathered vp againe: neither doeth God spare any person, yet doeth he appoynt meanes, not to cast out from him, him that is expelled.

15 Nowe therefore that I am come to speake of this thing vnto my lord the King, the cause is that the people haue made me afrayd: therefore thine handmayde sayd, Nowe will I speake vnto the King: it may be that the King will perfourme the request of his handmayde.

16 For the King wil heare, to deliuer his handmayde out of the hande of the man that woulde destroy mee, and also my sonne from the inheritance of God.

17 Therefore thine handmaid sayd, The word of my lord the King shall now be comfortable: for my lorde the King is euen as an Angel of God in hearing of good and bad: therefore the Lord thy God be with thee.

18 Then the King answered, and said vnto the woman, Hide not from me, I pray thee, the thing that I shall aske thee. And the woman sayde, Let my lord the King now speake.

19 And the King said, Is not the hand of Ioab with thee in all this? Then the woman answered, and sayd, As thy soule liueth, my lord the King, I will not turne to the right hande nor to the left, from ought that my lorde the King hath spoken: for euen thy seruant Ioab bade mee, and he put all these wordes in the mouth of thine handmayde.

20 For to the intent that I should chage the forme of speach, thy seruant Ioab hath done this thing: but my lord is wise according to the wisdome of an Angel of God to vnderstande all things that are in the earth.

21 And the King sayde vnto Ioab, Beholde nowe, I haue done this thing: go then, and bring the yong man Absalom againe.

22 And Ioab fell to the grounde on his face, and bowed himselfe, and thanked the King. Then Ioab sayde, This day thy seruant knoweth, that I haue found grace in thy sight, my lord the King, in that the King hath fulfilled the request of his seruant.

23 And Ioab arose, and went to Geshur, and brought Absalom to Ierusalem.

24 And the King sayde, Let him turne to his owne house, and not see my face. So Absalom turned to his owne house, and saw not the Kings face.

25 Nowe in all Israel there was none to be so much praysed for beautie as Absalom: from the sole of his foote euen to the toppe of his head there was no blemish in him.

26 And when he polled his head, (for at euery yeeres ende he polled it: because it was too heauie for him, therefore he polled it) he weyghed the heare of his head at two hundreth shekels by the Kings weight.

27 And Absalom had three sonnes, and one daughter named Tamar, which was a fayre woman to looke vpon.

28 So Absalom dwelt the space of two yeres in Ierusalem, and saw not the Kings face.

29 Therefore Absalom sent for Ioab to sende him to the King, but he would not come to him: and when he sent againe, he would not come.

30 Therefore he sayde vnto his seruants, Beholde, Ioab hath a fielde by my place, and hath barley therein: go, and set it on fire: and Absaloms seruants set the field on fire.

31 Then Ioab arose, and came to Absalom vnto his house, and sayd vnto him, Wherefore haue thy seruants burnt my field with fire?

32 And Absalom answered Ioab, Beholde, I sent for thee, saying, Come thou hither, and I wil send thee to the King for to say, Wherefore am I come from Geshur? It had bene better for me to haue bene there still: nowe therefore let mee see the Kings face: and if there be any trespasse in me, let him kill me.

33 Then Ioab came to the King, and told him: and he called for Absalom, who came to the King, and bowed himselfe to the grounde on his face before the King, and the King kissed Absalom.

Second Samuel 15

1 After this, Absalom prepared him charets and horses, and fiftie men to runne before him.

2 And Absalom rose vp early, and stoode hard by the entring in of the gate: and euery man that had any matter, and came to the King for iudgement, him did Absalom call vnto him, and sayde, Of what citie art thou? And he answered, Thy seruant is of one of the tribes of Israel.

3 Then Absalom said vnto him, See, thy matters are good and righteous, but there is no man deputed of the King to heare thee.

4 Absalom sayd moreouer, Oh that I were made Iudge in the lande, that euery man which hath any matter of controuersie, might come to me, that I might do him iustice.

5 And when any man came neere to him, and did him obeisance, he put forth his hand, and tooke him, and kissed him.

6 And on this maner did Absalom to al Israel, that came to the King for iudgement: so Absalom stale the hearts of the men of Israel.

7 And after fourtie yeeres, Absalom sayd vnto the King, I pray thee, let me go to Hebron, and render my vowe which I haue vowed vnto the Lord.

8 For thy seruant vowed a vowe when I remayned at Geshur, in Aram, saying, If the Lord shall bring me againe in deede to Ierusalem, I will serue the Lord.

9 And the King sayd vnto him, Go in peace. So he arose, and went to Hebron.

10 Then Absalom sent spyes throughout all the tribes of Israel, saying, When yee heare the sound of the trumpet, Ye shall say, Absalom reigneth in Hebron.

11 And with Absalom went two hundreth men out of Ierusalem, that were called: and they went in their simplicitie, knowing nothing.

12 Also Absalom sent for Ahithophel the Gilonite Dauids counseller, from his citie Giloh, while he offred sacrifices: and the treason was great: for the people encreased still with Absalom.

13 Then came a messenger to Dauid, saying, The hearts of the men of Israel are turned after Absalom.

14 Then Dauid sayd vnto all his seruants that were with him at Ierusalem, Vp, and let vs flee: for we shall not escape from Absalom: make speede to depart, lest he come suddenly and take vs, and bring euill vpon vs, and smite the citie with the edge of the swerde.

15 And the Kings seruants sayd vnto him, Behold, thy seruants are ready to do according to all that my lord the King shall appoynt.

16 So the King departed and all his houshold after him, and the King left ten concubines to keepe the house.

17 And the King went forth and all the people after him, and taried in a place farre off.

18 And all his seruants went about him, and all the Cherethites and all the Pelethites and all the Gittites, euen sixe hudreth men which were come after him from Gath, went before the King.

19 Then sayde the King to Ittai the Gittite, Wherefore commest thou also with vs? Returne aud abide with the King, for thou art a stranger: depart thou therefore to thy place.

20 Thou camest yesterday, and should I cause thee to wander to day and go with vs? I will goe whither I can: therefore returne thou and cary againe thy brethren: mercy and trueth be with thee.

21 And Ittai answered the King, and sayde, As the Lord liueth, and as my lord the King liueth, in what place my lord the King shalbe, whether in death or life, euen there surely will thy seruant bee.

22 Then Dauid sayd to Ittai, Come, and go forward. And Ittai the Gittite went, and all his men, and all the children that were with him.

23 And all the countrey wept with a loude voyce, and all the people went forward, but the King passed ouer the brooke Kidron: and all the people went ouer toward the way of ye wildernes.

24 And lo, Zadok also was there, and all the Leuites with him, bearing the Arke of the couenant of God: and they set downe the Arke of God, and Abiathar went vp vntill the people were all come out of the citie.

25 Then the King said vnto Zadok, Carie the Arke of God againe into the citie: if I shall finde fauour in the eyes of the Lord, he will bring me againe, and shewe me both it, and the Tabernacle thereof.

26 But if he thus say, I haue no delite in thee, behold, here am I, let him doe to me as seemeth good in his eyes.

27 The King sayde againe vnto Zadok the Priest, Art not thou a Seer? returne into the citie in peace, and your two sonnes with you: to wit, Ahimaaz thy sonne, and Ionathan the sonne of Abiathar.

28 Behold, I wil tarie in the fieldes of the wildernesse, vntill there come some worde from you to be tolde me.

29 Zadok therefore and Abiathar caried the Arke of God againe to Ierusalem, and they taried there.

30 And Dauid went vp the mount of oliues and wept as he went vp, and had his head couered, and went barefooted: and al the people that was with him, had euery man his head couered, and as they went vp, they wept.

31 Then one tolde Dauid, saying, Ahithophel is one of them that haue cospired with Absalom: and Dauid sayde, O Lord, I pray thee, turne the counsell of Ahithophel into foolishnesse.

32 Then Dauid came to the toppe of the mount where he worshipped God: and beholde, Hushai the Archite came against him with his coate torne, and hauing earth vpon his head.

33 Vnto whom Dauid sayd, If thou goe with me, thou shalt be a burthen vnto me.

34 But if thou returne to the citie, and say vnto Absalom, I wil be thy seruant, O King, (as I haue bene in time past thy fathers seruant, so will I now be thy seruant) then thou mayest bring me the counsell of Ahithophel to nought.

35 And hast thou not there with thee Zadok and Abiathar the Priests? therefore what so euer thou shalt heare out of the Kings house, thou shalt shew to Zadok and Abiathar the Priests.

36 Beholde, there are with them their two sonnes: Ahimaaz Zadoks sonne, and Ionathan Abiathars sonne: by them also shall ye send me euery thing that ye can heare.

37 So Hushai Dauids friend went into the citie: and Absalom came into Ierusalem.

Second Samuel 16

1 When Dauid was a little past the top of the hill, behold, Ziba the seruant of Mephibosheth mette him with a couple of asses sadled, and vpon them two hundreth cakes of bread, and an hundreth bunches of raisins, and an hundreth of dryed figges, and a bottel of wine.

2 And the King said vnto Ziba, What meanest thou by these? And Ziba said, They be asses for the kings housholde to ride on, and bread and dryed figges for the yong men to eate, and wine, that the faint may drinke in the wildernesse.

3 And the king sayde, But where is thy masters sonne? Then Ziba answered the King, Beholde, he remayneth in Ierusalem: for he sayde, This day shall the house of Israel restore me the kingdome of my father.

4 Then said the King to Ziba, Behold, thine are all that perteined vnto Mephibosheth. And Ziba saide, I beseech thee, let me finde grace in thy sight, my lord, O King.

5 And when king Dauid came to Bahurim, behold, thence came out a man of the familie of the house of Saul, named Shimei the sonne of Gera: and he came out, and cursed.

6 And he cast stones at Dauid, and at all the seruants of King Dauid: and all the people, and all the men of warre were on his right hande, and on his left.

7 And thus sayde Shimei when hee cursed, Come forth, come foorth thou murtherer, and wicked man.

8 The Lord hath brought vpon thee all the blood of the house of Saul, in whose stead thou hast reigned: and the Lord hath deliuered thy kingdome into the hand of Absalom thy sonne: and beholde, thou art taken in thy wickednesse, because thou art a murtherer.

9 Then saide Abishai the sonne of Zeruiah vnto the King, Why doeth this dead dog curse my lord the King? let me goe, I pray thee, and take away his head.

10 But the King saide, What haue I to doe with you, ye sonnes of Zeruiah? for he curseth, eue because the Lord hath bidden him curse Dauid: who dare then say, Wherfore hast thou done so?

11 And Dauid sayd to Abishai, and to all his seruants, Beholde, my sonne which came out of mine owne bowels, seeketh my life: then howe much more now may this sonne of Iemini? Suffer him to curse: for the Lord hath bidden him.

12 It may be that the Lord will looke on mine affliction, and doe me good for his cursing this day.

13 And as Dauid and his men went by the way, Shimei went by the side of the mountaine ouer against him, and cursed as he went, and threw stones against him, and cast dust.

14 Then came the King and all the people that were with him wearie, and refreshed them selues there.

15 And Absalom, and all the people, the men of Israel, came to Ierusalem, and Ahithophel with him.

16 And when Hushai the Archite Dauids friend was come vnto Absalom, Hushai said vnto Absalom, God saue the King, God saue the King.

17 Then Absalom sayd to Hushai, Is this thy kindenes to thy friend? Why wentest thou not with thy friend?

18 Hushai then answered vnto Absalom, Nay, but whome the Lord, and this people, and all the men of Israel chuse, his will I be, and with him will I dwell.

19 And moreouer vnto whome shall I doe seruice? not to his sonne? as I serued before thy father, so will I before thee.

20 Then spake Absalom to Ahithophel, Giue counsell what we shall doe.

21 And Ahithophel said vnto Absalom, Goe in to thy fathers concubines, which he hath left to keepe the house: and when all Israel shall heare, that thou art abhorred of thy father, the hands of all that are with thee, shall be strong.

22 So they spread Absalom a tent vpon the top of the house, and Absalom went in to his fathers concubines in the sight of all Israel.

23 And the counsell of Ahithophel which he counseled in those dayes, was like as one had asked counsell at the oracle of God: so was all the counsel of Ahithophel both with Dauid and with Absalom.

Second Samuel 17

1 Moreouer Ahithophel said to Absalom, Let me chuse out now twelue thousand men, and I will vp and follow after Dauid this night,

2 And I will come vpon him: for he is wearie, and weake handed: so I will feare him, and all the people that are with him, shall flee, and I will smite the King onely,

3 And I will bring againe all the people vnto thee, and when all shall returne, (the man whome thou seekest being slaine) all the people shalbe in peace.

4 And the saying pleased Absalom well, and all the Elders of Israel.

5 Then said Absalom, Call now Hushai the Archite also, and let vs heare likewise what he sayth.

6 So when Hushai came to Absalom, Absalom spake vnto him, saying, Ahithophel hath spoken thus: shall we doe after his saying, or no? tell thou.

7 Hushai then answered vnto Absalom, The counsel that Ahithophel hath giuen, is not good at this time.

8 For, said Hushai, thou knowest thy father, and his men, that they be strong men, and are chafed in minde as a beare robbed of her whelps in the fielde: also thy father is a valiant warrier, and will not lodge with the people.

9 Behold, he is hid now in some caue, or in some place: and though some of them be ouerthrowen at the first, yet the people shall heare, and say, The people that follow Absalom, be ouerthrowen.

10 Then he also that is valiant whose heart is as the heart of a lion, shall shrinke and faint: for all Israel knoweth, that thy father is valiant, and they which be with him, stout men.

11 Therefore my counsell is, that all Israel be gathered vnto thee, from Dan euen to Beer-sheba as the sand of the sea in nomber, and that thou goe to battell in thine owne person.

12 So shall we come vpon him in some place, where we shall finde him, and we will vpon him as the dewe falleth on the ground: and of all the men that are with him, wee will not leaue him one.

13 Moreouer if he be gotten into a citie, then shall all the men of Israel bring ropes to that citie, and we will draw it into the riuer, vntill there be not one small stone founde there.

14 Then Absalom and all the men of Israel sayde, The counsel of Hushai the Archite is better, then the counsell of Ahithophel: for the Lord had determined to destroy the good counsell of Ahithophel, that the Lord might bring euill vpon Absalom.

15 Then said Hushai vnto Zadok and to Abiathar the Priests, Of this and that maner did Ahithophel and the Elders of Israel counsell Absalom: and thus and thus haue I counseled.

16 Now therefore sende quickely, and shewe Dauid, saying, Tarie not this night in the fieldes of the wildernesse, but rather get thee ouer, lest the King be deuoured and all the people that are with him.

17 Now Ionathan and Ahimaaz abode by En-rogel: (for they might not be seene to come into the citie) and a maid went, and tolde them, and they went and shewed King Dauid.

18 Neuerthelesse a yong man sawe them, and tolde it to Absalom. therefore they both departed quickely, and came to a mans house in Bahurim, who had a well in his court, into the which they went downe.

19 And the wife tooke and spred a couering ouer the welles mouth, and spred ground corne thereon, that the thing should not be knowen.

20 And when Absaloms seruants came to the wife into the house, they said, Where is Ahimaaz and Ionathan? And the woman answered them, They be gone ouer the brooke of water. And when they had sought them, and could not finde them, they returned to Ierusalem.

21 And assoone as they were departed, the other came out of the well, and went and tolde King Dauid, and sayde vnto him, Vp, and get you quickely ouer the water: for such counsell hath Ahithophel giuen against you.

22 Then Dauid arose, and all the people that were with him, and they went ouer Iorden vntil the dawning of the day, so that there lacked not one of them, that was not come ouer Iorden.

23 Nowe when Ahithophel sawe that his counsell was not followed, he sadled his asse, and arose, and he went home vnto his citie, and put his houshold in order, and hanged him selfe, and dyed, and was buryed in his fathers graue.

24 Then Dauid came to Mahanaim. And Absalom passed ouer Iorden, he, and all the men of Israel with him.

25 And Absalom made Amasa captaine of the hoste in the stead of Ioab: which Amasa was a mans sonne named Ithra an Israelite, that went in to Abigail the daughter of Nahash, sister to Zeruiah Ioabs mother.

26 So Israel and Absalom pitched in the land of Gilead.

27 And when Dauid was come to Mahanaim, Shobi the sonne of Nahash out of Rabbah of the children of Ammon, and Machir the sonne of Ammiel out of Lo-debar, and Barzelai the Gileadite out of Rogel

28 Brought beds, and basens, and earthen vessels, and wheat, and barley, and floure, and parched corne, and beanes, and lentiles, and parched corne.

29 And they brought hony, and butter, and sheepe, and cheese of kine for Dauid and for the people that were with him, to eate: for they said, The people is hungry, and wearie, and thirstie in the wildernesse.

Second Samuel 18

1 Then Dauid numbred the people that were with him, and set ouer them captaines of thousands and captaines of hundreths.

2 And Dauid sent foorth the third part of the people vnder the hand of Ioab, and the thirde part vnder the hand of Abishai Ioabs brother the sonne of Zeruiah: and the other third part vnder the hand of Ittai the Gittite. and the King said vnto the people, I will go with you my selfe also.

3 But the people answered, Thou shalt not goe foorth: for if we flee away, they will not regarde vs, neither will they passe for vs, though halfe of vs were slaine: but thou art now worth ten thousande of vs: therefore nowe it is better that thou succour vs out of the citie.

4 Then the King said vnto them, What seemeth you best, that I will doe. So the King stood by the gate side, and all the people came out by hundreths and by thousands.

5 And the King commanded Ioab and Abishai, and Ittai, saying, Entreate the yong man Absalom gently for my sake. and all the people heard whe the King gaue al the captaines charge concerning Absalom.

6 So the people went out into the fielde to meete Israel, and the battell was in the wood of Ephraim:

7 Where the people of Israel were slaine before the seruants of Dauid: so there was a great slaughter that day, euen of twentie thousande.

8 For the battel was skattered ouer all the countrey: and the wood deuoured much more people that day, then did the sworde.

9 Nowe Absalom met the seruants of Dauid, and Absalom rode vpon a mule, and the mule came vnder a great thicke oke: and his head caught holde of the oke, and he was taken vp betweene the heauen and the earth: and the mule that was vnder him went away.

10 And one that sawe it, tolde Ioab, saying, Beholde, I sawe Absalom hanged in an oke.

11 Then Ioab saide vnto the man that tolde him, And hast thou in deede seene? why then diddest thou not there smite him to the grounde, and I woulde haue giuen thee ten shekels of siluer, and a girdle?

12 Then the man saide vnto Ioab, Though I should receiue a thousande shekels of siluer in mine hande, yet woulde I not lay mine hande vpon the Kings sonne: for in our hearing the King charged thee, and Abishai, and Ittai, saying, Beware, least any touche the yong man Absalom.

13 If I had done it, it had bene the danger of my life: for nothing can be hid from the King: yea, thou thy selfe wouldest haue bin against me.

14 Then saide Ioab, I will not thus tary with thee. And he tooke three dartes in his hande, and thrust them through Absalom, while he was yet aliue in the middes of the oke.

15 And tenne seruants that bare Ioabs armour, compassed about and smote Absalom, and slewe him.

16 Then Ioab blewe the trumpet, and the people returned from pursuing after Israel: for Ioab helde backe the people.

17 And they tooke Absalom, and cast him into a great pit in the wood, and layed a mightie great heape of stones vpon him: and all Israel fled euery one to his tent.

18 Nowe Absalom in his life time had taken and reared him vp a pillar, which is in the kings dale: for he saide, I haue no sonne to keepe my name in remembrance. and he called the pillar after his owne name, and it is called vnto this day, Absaloms place.

19 Then said Ahimaaz the sonne of Zadok, I pray thee, let me runne, and beare the King tidings that the Lord hath deliuered him out of the hande of his enemies.

20 And Ioab said vnto him, Thou shalt not be the messenger to day, but thou shalt beare tidings another time, but to day thou shalt beare none: for the Kings sonne is dead.

21 Then said Ioab to Cushi, Goe, tel the king, what thou hast seene. And Cushi bowed himselfe vnto Ioab, and ran.

22 Then saide Ahimaaz the sonne of Zadok againe to Ioab, What, I pray thee, if I also runne after Cushi? And Ioab said, Wherefore now wilt thou runne, my sonne, seeing that thou hast no tidings to bring?

23 Yet what if I runne? Then he saide vnto him, Runne. So Ahimaaz ranne by the way of the plaine, and ouerwent Cushi.

24 Now Dauid sate betweene the two gates. And the watchman went to the top of the gate vpon the wall, and lift vp his eyes, and sawe, and beholde, a man came running alone.

25 And the watchman cryed, and tolde ye king. And the King said, If he be alone, he bringeth tidings. And he came apace, and drew neere.

26 And the watchman saw another man running, and the watchman called vnto the porter, and said, Behold, another man runneth alone. And the King said, He also bringeth tidings.

27 And the watchman said, Me thinketh the running of the formost is like the running of Ahimaaz the sonne of Zadok. Then the King said, He is a good man, and commeth with good tidings.

28 And Ahimaaz called, and sayde vnto the King, Peace be with thee: and he fell downe to the earth vpon his face before the King, and saide, Blessed be the Lord thy God, who hath shut vp the men that lift vp their handes against my lorde the King.

29 And the King saide, Is the yong man Absalom safe? And Ahimaaz answered, When Ioab sent the Kings seruant, and me thy seruant, I sawe a great tumult, but I knewe not what.

30 And the King said vnto him, Turne aside, and stand here. so he turned aside and stoode still.

31 And beholde, Cushi came, and Cushi saide, Tidings, my lorde the King: for the Lord hath deliuered thee this day out of the hande of all that rose against thee.

32 Then the King saide vnto Cushi, Is the yong man Absalom safe? And Cushi answered, The enemies of my lorde the King, and all that rise against thee to doe thee hurt, be as that yong man is.

33 And the King was mooued, and went vp to the chamber ouer the gate, and wept: and as he went, thus he said, O my sonne Absalom, my sonne, my sonne Absalom: woulde God I had dyed for thee, O Absalom, my sonne, my sonne.

Second Samuel 19

1 And it was tolde Ioab, Behold, the King weepeth and mourneth for Absalom.

2 Therefore the victorie of that day was turned into mourning to all the people: for the people heard say that day, The King soroweth for his sonne.

3 And the people went that day into the citie secretly, as people confounded hide them selues when they flee in battell.

4 So the King hid his face, and the King cryed with a loude voyce, My sonne Absalom, Absalom my sonne, my sonne.

5 Then Ioab came into the house to the King, and said, Thou hast shamed this day the faces of all thy seruants, which this day haue saued thy life and the liues of thy sones, and of thy daughters, and the liues of thy wiues, and the liues of thy concubines,

6 In that thou louest thine enemies, and hatest thy friendes: for thou hast declared this day, that thou regardest neither thy princes nor seruants: therefore this day I perceiue, that if Absalom had liued, and we all had dyed this day, that then it would haue pleased thee well.

7 Nowe therefore vp, come out, and speake comfortably vnto thy seruants: for I sweare by the Lord, except thou come out, there will not tarie one man with thee this night: and that wil be worse vnto thee, then all the euill that fell on thee from thy youth hitherto.

8 Then the King arose, and sate in the gate: and they tolde vnto all the people, saying, Beholde, the King doeth sit in the gate: and all the people came before the King: for Israel had fled euery man to his tent.

9 Then all the people were at strife thorowout all the tribes of Israel, saying, The King saued vs out of the hand of our enemies, and he deliuered vs out of the hande of the Philistims, and nowe he is fled out of the lande for Absalom.

10 And Absalom, whome we anoynted ouer vs, is dead in battel: therefore why are ye so slow to bring the King againe?

11 But King Dauid sent to Zadok and to Abiathar the Priestes, saying, Speake vnto the Elders of Iudah, and say, Why are ye behind to bring the King againe to

his house, (for the saying of al Israel is come vnto the king, euen to his house)

12 Ye are my brethren: my bones and my flesh are ye: wherefore then are ye the last that bring the King againe?

13 Also say ye to Amasa, Art thou not my bone and my flesh? God do so to me and more also, if thou be not captaine of the hoste to me for euer in the roume of Ioab.

14 So he bowed the heartes of all the men of Iudah, as of one man: therefore they sent to the King, saying, Returne thou with all thy seruants.

15 So the King returned, and came to Iorden. And Iudah came to Gilgal, for to goe to meete the King, and to conduct him ouer Iorde.

16 And Shimei the sonne of Gera, ye sonne of Iemini, which was of Bahurim, hasted and came down with the men of Iudah to meete king Dauid,

17 And a thousande men of Beniamin with him, and Ziba the seruant of the house of Saul, and his fifteene sonnes and twentie seruants with him: and they went ouer Iorden before ye king.

18 And there went ouer a boate to carie ouer the Kings houshold, and to do him pleasure. Then Shimei the sonne of Gera fell before the King, when he was come ouer Iorden,

19 And saide vnto the King, Let not my lorde impute wickednesse vnto me, nor remember ye thing that thy seruant did wickedly when my lorde the King departed out of Ierusalem, that the King should take it to his heart.

20 For thy seruant doeth knowe, that I haue done amisse: therefore beholde, I am the first this day of al the house of Ioseph, that am come to goe downe to meete my lord the King.

21 But Abishai the sonne of Zeruiah answered, and said, Shal not Shimei die for this, because he cursed the Lordes anoynted?

22 And Dauid saide, What haue I to do with you, ye sonnes of Zeruiah, that this day ye should be aduersaries vnto me? shall there any man die this day in Israel? for doe not I know that I am this day King ouer Israel?

23 Therefore the King saide vnto Shimei, Thou shalt not die, and the king sware vnto him.

24 And Mephibosheth the sonne of Saul came downe to meete the king, and had neither washed his feete, nor dressed his beard, nor washed his clothes from the time the king departed, vntill he returned in peace.

25 And when he was come to Ierusalem, and met the king, the king said vnto him, Wherefore wentest not thou with me, Mephibosheth?

26 And he answered, My lorde the king, my seruant deceiued me: for thy seruant said, I would haue mine asse sadled to ride thereon, for to goe with the king, because thy seruant is lame.

27 And he hath accused thy seruant vnto my lorde the king: but my lorde the king is as an Angel of God: doe therefore thy pleasure.

28 For all my fathers house were but dead men before my lord the king, yet diddest thou set thy seruant among them that did eate at thine owne table: what right therefore haue I yet to crye any more vnto the king?

29 And the king said vnto him, Why speakest thou any more of thy matters? I haue said, Thou, and Ziba deuide the landes.

30 And Mephibosheth saide vnto the king, Yea, let him take all, seeing my lorde the king is come home in peace.

31 Then Barzillai the Gileadite came downe from Rogelim, and went ouer Iorden with the king, to conduct him ouer Iorden.

32 Nowe Barzillai was a very aged man, euen fourescore yeere olde, and he had prouided the king of sustenance, while he lay at Mahanaim: for he was a man of very great substance.

33 And the king said vnto Barzillai, Come ouer with me, and I will feede thee with me in Ierusalem.

34 And Barzillai said vnto the king, Howe long haue I to liue, that I should goe vp with the king to Ierusalem?

35 I am this day fourescore yeere olde: and can I discerne betweene good or euill? Hath thy seruant any taste in that I eat or in that I drinke? Can I heare any more the voyce of singing men and women? wherefore then should thy seruant be anymore a burthen vnto my lord the king?

36 Thy seruant will goe a litle way ouer Iorden with the King, and why wil the king recompence it me with such a rewarde?

37 I pray thee, let thy seruant turne backe againe, that I may die in mine owne citie, and be buryed in the graue of my father and of my mother: but beholde thy seruant Chimham, let him goe with my lorde the king, and doe to him what shall please thee.

38 And the king answered, Chimham shall go with me, and I will do to him that thou shalt be content with: and whatsoeuer thou shalt require of me, that will I do for thee.

39 So all the people went ouer Iorden: and the King passed ouer: and the King kissed Barzillai, and blessed him, and hee returned vnto his owne place.

40 Then the King went to Gilgal, and Chimham went with him, and all the people of Iudah conducted the King, and also halfe ye people of Israel.

41 And behold, all the men of Israel came to the King, and sayd vnto the King, Why haue our brethren the men of Iudah stollen thee away, and haue brought the King and his houshold, and all Dauids men with him ouer Iorden?

42 And all the men of Iudah answered the men of Israel, Because the King is neere of kin to vs: and wherefore now be ye angry for this matter? haue we eaten of the Kings cost, or haue wee taken any bribes?

43 And the men of Israel answered the men of Iudah, and saide, Wee haue ten partes in the King, and haue also more

right to Dauid then ye: Why then did ye despise vs, that our aduise should not bee first had in restoring our King? And the wordes of the men of Iudah were fiercer then the wordes of the men of Israel.

Second Samuel 20

1 Then there was come thither a wicked man (named Sheba the sonne of Bichri, a man of Iemini) and hee blew the trumpet, and saide, Wee haue no part in Dauid, neither haue we inheritance in the sonne of Ishai: euery man to his tents, O Israel.

2 So euery man of Israel went from Dauid and followed Sheba the sonne of Bichri: but the men of Iudah claue fast vnto their King, from Iorden euen to Ierusalem.

3 When Dauid then came to his house to Ierusalem, the King tooke the ten women his concubines, that hee had left behinde him to keepe the house, and put them in warde, and fed them, but lay no more with them: but they were enclosed vnto the day of their death, liuing in widowhode.

4 Then sayde the King to Amasa, Assemble me the men of Iudah within three dayes, and be thou here present.

5 So Amasa went to assemble Iudah, but hee taried longer then the time which he had appoynted him.

6 Then Dauid sayd to Abishai, Now shall Sheba the sonne of Bichri doe vs more harme then did Absalom: take thou therefore thy lords seruants and follow after him, lest he get him walled cities, and escape vs.

7 And there went out after him Ioabs men, and the Cherethites and the Pelethites, and all the mightie men: and they departed out of Ierusalem, to follow after Sheba the sonne of Bichri.

8 When they were at the great stone, which is in Gibeon, Amasa went before them, and Ioabs garment, that hee had put on, was girded vnto him, and vpon it was a sword girded, which hanged on his loynes in the sheath, and as hee went, it vsed to fall out.

9 And Ioab sayde to Amasa, Art thou in health, my brother? and Ioab tooke Amasa by the beard with the right hand to kisse him.

10 But Amasa tooke no heede to the sworde that was in Ioabs hande: for therewith he smote him in the fift rib, and shed out his bowels to the ground, and smote him not the second time: so he dyed. then Ioab and Abishai his brother followed after Sheba the sonne of Bichri.

11 And one of Ioabs men stoode by him, and saide, He that fauoureth Ioab, and hee that is of Dauids part, let him go after Ioab.

12 And Amasa wallowed in blood in the mids of the way: and when the man sawe that all the people stood still, he remooued Amasa out of the way into the fielde, and cast a cloth vpon him,

because he saw that euery one that came by him, stoode still.

13 When hee was remoued out of the way, euerie man went after Ioab, to follow after Sheba the sonne of Bichri.

14 And he went through all the tribes of Israel vnto Abel, and Bethmaachah and all places of Berim: and they gathered together, and went also after him.

15 So they came, and besieged him in Abel, neere to Bethmaachah: and they cast vp a mount against the citie, and the people thereof stood on the ramper, and al the people that was with Ioab, destroyed and cast downe the wall.

16 Then cried a wise woman out of the citie, Heare, heare, I pray you, say vnto Ioab, Come thou hither, that I may speake with thee.

17 And when hee came neere vnto her, the woman said, Art thou Ioab? And he answered, Yea. And she said to him, Heare the wordes of thine handmaid. And he answered, I do heare.

18 Then shee spake thus, They spake in the olde time, saying, They shoulde aske of Abel. and so haue they continued.

19 I am one of them, that are peaceable and faithful in Israel: and thou goest about to destroy a citie, and a mother in Israel: why wilt thou deuoure the inheritance of the Lord?

20 And Ioab answered, and said, God forbid, God forbid it me, that I should deuoure, or destroy it.

21 The matter is not so, but a man of mout Ephraim (Sheba ye sonne of Bichri by name) hath lift vp his had against ye King, euen against Dauid: deliuer vs him onely, and I will depart from the citie. And the woman saide vnto Ioab, Beholde, his head shalbe throwen to thee ouer the wall.

22 Then the woman went vnto all the people with her wisedome, and they cut off the head of Sheba the sonne of Bichri, and cast it to Ioab: the he blewe the trumpet, and they retired from the citie, euery man to his tent: and Ioab returned to Ierusalem vnto the King.

23 Then Ioab was ouer all the hoste of Israel, and Benaiah the sonne of Iehoiada ouer the Cherethites and ouer the Pelethies,

24 And Adoram ouer the tribute, and Ioshaphat the sonne of Ahilud the recorder,

25 And Sheia was Scribe, and Zadok and Abiathar the Priests,

26 And also Ira the Iairite was chiefe about Dauid.

Second Samuel 21

1 Then there was a famine in the dayes of Dauid, three yeeres together: and Dauid asked counsell of the Lord, and the Lord answered, It is for Saul, and for his bloodie house, because hee slewe the Gibeonites.

2 Then ye King called the Gibeonites and said vnto them. (Now the Gibeonites were not of the children of Israel, but a remnant of the Amorites, vnto whom ye children of Israel had sworne: but Saul sought to slay them for his zeale toward the children of Israel and Iudah)

3 And Dauid said vnto the Gibeonites, What shall I doe for you, and wherewith shall I make the atonement, that ye may blesse the inheritance of the Lord?

4 The Gibeonites then answered him, Wee will haue no siluer nor golde of Saul nor of his house, neither for vs shalt thou kill any man in Israel. And he said, What ye shall say, that will I doe for you.

5 Then they answered the King, The man that consumed vs and that imagined euill against vs, so that we are destroyed from remaining in any coast of Israel,

6 Let seuen men of his sonnes be deliuered vnto vs, and we will hang them vp vnto the Lord in Gibeah of Saul, the Lordes chosen. And the King said, I will giue them.

7 But the King had compassion on Mephibosheth the sonne of Ionathan the sonne of Saul, because of the Lordes othe, that was betweene them, euen betweene Dauid and Ionathan the sonne of Saul.

8 But the King tooke the two sonnes of Rizpah the daughter of Aiah, whome shee bare vnto Saul, euen Armoni and Mephibosheth and the fiue sonnes of Michal, the daughter of Saul, whome shee bare to Adriel the sonne of Barzillai the Meholathite.

9 And hee deliuered them vnto the handes of the Gibeonites, which hanged them in the mountaine before the Lord: so they died all seuen together, and they were slaine in the time of haruest: in the first dayes, and in the beginning of barly haruest.

10 Then Rizpah the daughter of Aiah tooke sackecloth and hanged it vp for her vpon the rocke, from the beginning of haruest, vntill water dropped vpon them from the heauen, and suffered neither the birdes of the aire to light on the by day, nor beasts of the fielde by night.

11 And it was told Dauid, what Rizpah the daughter of Aiah ye concubine of Saul had done.

12 And Dauid went and tooke the bones of Saul and the bones of Ionathan his sonne from the citizens of Iabesh Gilead, which had stollen them from the streete of Beth-shan, where the Philistims had hanged them, when the Philistims had slaine Saul in Gilboa.

13 So hee brought thence the bones of Saul and the bones of Ionathan his sonne, and they gathered the bones of them that were hanged.

14 And the bones of Saul and of Ionathan his sonne buried they in the coutrey of Beniamin in Zelah, in the graue of Kish his father: and when they had perfourmed all that the King had commanded, God was then appeased with the land.

15 Againe the Philistims had warre with Israel: and Dauid went downe, and his seruants with him, and they fought against the Philistims, and Dauid fainted.

16 Then Ishi-benob which was of the sonnes of Haraphah (the head of whose speare wayed three hundreth shekels of brasse) euen he being girded with a newe sword, thought to haue slaine Dauid.

17 But Abishai the sonne of Zeruiah succoured him, and smote the Philistim, and killed him. Then Dauids men sware vnto him, saying, Thou shalt goe no more out with vs to battell, lest thou quench the light of Israel.

18 And after this also there was a battell with the Philistims at Gob, then Sibbechai the Hushathite slewe Saph, which was one of ye sonnes of Haraphah.

19 And there was yet another battel in Gob with the Philistims, where Elhanah the sonne of Iaare-oregim, a Bethlehemite slewe Goliath the Gittite: the staffe of whose speare was like a weauers beame.

20 Afterward there was also a battel in Gath, where was a man of a great stature, and had on euerie hand six fingers, and on euerie foote six toes, foure and twentie in number: who was also the sonne of Haraphah.

21 And when hee reuiled Israel, Ionathan the sonne of Shima the brother of Dauid slewe him.

22 These foure were borne to Haraphah in Gath, and died by the hande of Dauid and by the hands of his seruants.

Second Samuel 22

1 And Dauid spake the woordes of this song vnto the Lord, what time the Lord had deliuered him out of the handes of all his enemies, and out of the hand of Saul.

2 And he sayd, The Lord is my rocke and my fortresse, and he that deliuereth mee.

3 God is my strength, in him will I trust: my shielde, and the horne of my saluation, my hie tower and my refuge: my Sauiour, thou hast saued me from violence.

4 I will call on the Lord, who is worthy to be praysed: so shall I be safe from mine enemies.

5 For the pangs of death haue compassed me: the floods of vngodlinesse haue made mee afrayd.

6 The sorowes of the graue compassed mee about: the snares of death ouertooke mee.

7 But in my tribulation did I call vpon the Lord, and crie to my God, and he did heare my voyce out of his temple, and my crie did enter into his eares.

8 Then the earth trembled and quaked: the foundations of the heauens mooued and shooke, because he was angrie.

9 Smoke went out at his nostrels, and consuming fire out of his mouth: coles were kindled thereat.

10 He bowed the heauens also, and came downe, and darkenes was vnder his feete.

11 And he rode vpon Cherub and did flie, and hee was seene vpon the winges of the winde.

12 And hee made darkenesse a Tabernacle round about him, euen the gatherings of waters, and the cloudes of the ayre.

13 At the brightnesse of his presence the coles of fire were kindled.

14 The Lord thundred from heauen, and the most hie gaue his voyce.

15 He shot arrowes also, and scattered them: to wit, lightning, and destroyed them.

16 The chanels also of the sea appeared, euen the foundations of the worlde were discoured by the rebuking of the Lord, and at the blast of the breath of his nostrels.

17 He sent from aboue, and tooke me: hee drewe me out of many waters.

18 He deliuered me from my strong enemie, and from them that hated me: for they were too strong for me.

19 They preuented me in the day of my calamitie, but the Lord was my stay,

20 And brought me foorth into a large place: he deliuered me, because he fauoured me.

21 The Lord rewarded me according to my righteousnesse: according to the purenesse of mine handes he recompensed me.

22 For I kept the wayes of the Lord, and did not wickedly against my God.

23 For all his lawes were before me, and his statutes: I did not depart therefrom.

24 I was vpright also towarde him, and haue kept me from my wickednesse.

25 Therefore the Lord did reward me according to my righteousnesse, according to my purenesse before his eyes.

26 With the godly thou wilt shewe thy selfe godly: with the vpright man thou wilt shew thy selfe vpright.

27 With the pure thou wilt shewe thy selfe pure, and with the frowarde thou wilt shew thy selfe froward.

28 Thus thou wilt saue the poore people: but thine eyes are vpon the hautie to humble them.

29 Surely thou art my light, O Lord: and the Lord will lighten my darkenes.

30 For by thee haue I broken through an hoste, and by my God haue I leaped ouer a wall.

31 The way of God is vncorrupt: the word of the Lord is tryed in the fire: he is a shield to all that trust in him.

32 For who is God besides the Lord? and who is mightie, saue our God?

33 God is my strength in battel, and maketh my way vpright.

34 He maketh my feete like hindes feete, and hath set me vpon mine hie places.

35 He teacheth mine handes to fight, so that a bowe of brasse is broken with mine armes.

36 Thou hast also giuen me the shield of thy saluation, and thy louing kindnesse hath caused me to increase.

37 Thou hast inlarged my steppes vnder me, and mine heeles haue not slid.

38 I haue pursued mine enemies and destroyed them, and haue not turned againe vntill I had consumed them.

39 Yea, I haue consumed them and thrust them through, and they shall not arise, but shall fall vnder my feete.

40 For thou hast girded me with power to battell, and them that arose against me, hast thou subdued vnder me.

41 And thou hast giuen me the neckes of mine enemies, that I might destroy them that hate me.

42 They looked about, but there was none to saue them, euen vnto the Lord, but he answered them not.

43 Then did I beate them as small as the dust of the earth: I did treade them flat as the clay of the streete, and did spread them abroad.

44 Thou hast also deliuered me from the contentions of my people: thou hast preserued me to be the head ouer nations: the people which I knewe not, doe serue me.

45 Strangers shalbe in subiection to me: assoone as they heare, they shall obey me.

46 Strangers shall shrinke away, and feare in their priuie chambers.

47 Let the Lord liue, and blessed be my strength: and God, euen the force of my saluation be exalted.

48 It is God that giueth me power to reuenge me, and subdue the people vnder me,

49 And rescueth me from mine enemies: (thou also hast lift me vp from them that rose against me, thou hast deliuered me from the cruell man.

50 Therefore I will praise thee, O Lord amog the nations, and will sing vnto thy Name)

51 He is the tower of saluation for his King, and sheweth mercie to his anointed, euen to Dauid, and to his seede for euer.

Second Samuel 23

1 These also be the last wordes of Dauid, Dauid the sonne of Ishai saith, euen the man who was set vp on hie, the Anointed of the God of Iacob, and the sweete singer of Israel saith,

2 The Spirit of the Lord spake by me, and his worde was in my tongue.

3 The God of Israel spake to me, ye strength of Israel saide, Thou shalt beare rule ouer men, being iust, and ruling in the feare of God.

4 Euen as the morning light when the sunne riseth, the morning, I say, without cloudes, so shall mine house be, and not as the grasse of the earth is by the bright raine.

5 For so shall not mine house be with God: for he hath made with me an euerlasting couenant, perfite in all pointes, and sure: therefore all mine health and whole desire is, that he will not make it growe so.

6 But the wicked shalbe euery one as thornes thrust away, because they can not be taken with handes.

7 But the man that shall touch them, must be defensed with yron, or with the shaft of a speare: and they shall be burnt with fire in the same place.

8 These be the names of the mightie men whome Dauid had. He that sate in the seate of wisedome, being chiefe of the princes, was Adino of Ezni, he slewe eight hundreth at one time.

9 And after him was Eleazar the sonne of Dodo, the sonne of Ahohi, one of the three worthies with Dauid, when they defied the Philistims gathered there to battel, when the men of Israel were gone vp.

10 He arose and smote the Philistims vntill his hande was wearie, and his hande claue vnto the sworde: and the Lord gaue great victorie the same day, and the people returned after him onely to spoyle.

11 After him was Shammah the sonne of Age the Hararite: for the Philistims assembled at a towne, where was a piece of a fielde full of lentils, and the people fled from the Philistims.

12 But he stoode in the middes of the fielde, and defended it, and slewe the Philistims: so the Lord gaue great victorie.

13 Afterward three of the thirtie captaines went downe, and came to Dauid in the haruest time vnto the caue of Adullam, and the hoste of the Philistims pitched in the valley of Rephaim.

14 And Dauid was then in an holde, and the garison of ye Philistims was then in Beth-lehem.

15 And Dauid longed, and said, Oh, that one would giue me to drinke of the water of the well of Beth-lehem, which is by the gate.

16 The the three mightie brake into the host of the Philistims, and drew water out of the well of Beth-lehem that was by the gate, and tooke and brought it to Dauid, who woulde not drinke thereof, but powred it for an offring vnto ye Lord,

17 And said, O Lord, be it farre from me, that I should doe this. Is not this the blood of the men that went in ieopardie of their liues? therefore he woulde not drinke it. These things did these three mightie men.

18 And Abishai the brother of Ioab, the sonne of Zeruiah, was chiefe among the three, and he lifted vp his speare against three hundreth, and slewe them, and he had the name among the three.

19 For he was most excellent of the three, and was their captaine, but he attained not vnto the first three.

20 And Benaiah the sonne of Iehoiada the sonne of a valiant man, which had done many actes, and was of Kabzeel, slewe two strong men of Moab: he went downe also, and slewe a lyon in the middes of a pit in the time of snowe.

21 And he slewe an Egyptian a man of great stature, and the Egyptian had a speare in his hande: but he went downe to him with a staffe, and plucked the speare out of the Egyptians hand, and slewe him with his owne speare.

22 These things did Benaiah the sonne of Iehoiada, and had the name among the three worthies.

23 He was honourable among thirtie, but he atteined not to the first three: and Dauid made him of his counsell.

24 Asahel the brother of Ioab was one of the thirtie: Elhanan the sonne of Dodo of Beth-lehem:

25 Shammah the Harodite: Elika ye Harodite:

26 Helez the Paltite: Ira the sonne of Ikkesh the Tekoite:

27 Abiezer the Anethothite: Mebunnai the Husathite:

28 Zalmon an Ahohite: Maharai the Netophathite:

29 Heleb the sonne of Baanah a Netophathite: Ittai the sonne of Ribai of Gibeah of the children of Beniamin:

30 Benaiah the Pirathonite: Hiddai of the riuer of Gaash:

31 Abi-albon the Arbathite: Azmaueth the Barhumite:

32 Elihaba the Shaalbonite: of the sonnes of Iashen, Ionathan:

33 Shammah the Hararite: Ahiam the sonne of Sharar the Hamrite:

34 Eliphelet the sonne of Ahasbai the sonne of Maachathi: Eliam the sonne of Ahithophel the Gilonite:

35 Hezrai the Carmelite: Paarai the Arbite:

36 Igal the sonne of Nathan of Zobah: Bani the Gadite:

37 Zelek the Ammonite: Naharai the Becrothite, the armour bearer of Ioab the sonne of Zeruiah:

38 Ira the Ithrite: Gareb the Ithrite:

39 Uriiah the Hittite, thirtie and seuen in all.

Second Samuel 24

1 And the wrath of the Lord was againe kindled against Israel, and he moued Dauid against them, in that he saide, Goe, number Israel and Iudah.

2 For the King said to Ioab the captaine of the hoste, which was with him, Goe speedily now through all the tribes of Israel, from Dan euen to Beer-sheba, and nomber ye the people, that I may knowe the number of the people.

3 And Ioab saide vnto the King, The Lord thy God increase the people an hundreth folde more then they be, and that the eyes of my lorde the King may see it: but why doeth my lord the King desire this thing?

4 Notwithstanding the Kings worde preuailed against Ioab and against the captaines of the hoste: therefore Ioab and the captaines of the hoste went out from the presence of the King to nomber the people of Israel.

5 And they passed ouer Iorden, and pitched in Aroer at the right side of the citie that is in the middes of the valley of Gad and toward Iazer.

6 Then they came to Gilead, and to Tahtim-hodshi, so they came to Dan Iaan, and so about to Zidon,

7 And came to the fortresse of Tyrus and to all the cities of the Hiuites and of the Canaanites, and went towarde the South of Iudah, euen to Beer-sheba.

8 So when they had gone about all the lande, they returned to Ierusalem at the ende of nine moneths and twentie dayes.

9 And Ioab deliuered the nomber and summe of the people vnto the King: and there were in Israel eight hundreth thousande strong men that drewe swordes, and the men of Iudah were fiue hundreth thousand men.

10 Then Dauids heart smote him, after that he had numbred the people: and Dauid said vnto the Lord, I haue sinned exceedingly in that I haue done: therefore nowe, Lord, I beseech thee, take away the trespasse of thy seruant: for I haue done very foolishly.

11 And when Dauid was vp in the morning, the worde of the Lord came vnto the Prophet Gad Dauids Seer, saying,

12 Go, and say vnto Dauid, Thus saith ye Lord, I offer thee three thinges, chuse thee which of them I shall doe vnto thee.

13 So Gad came to Dauid, and shewed him, and said vnto him, Wilt thou that seuen yeeres famine come vpon thee in thy lande, or wilt thou flee three moneths before thine enemies, they following thee, or that there bee three dayes pestilence in thy land? nowe aduise thee, and see, what answere I shall giue to him that sent me.

14 And Dauid said vnto Gad, I am in a wonderfull strait: let vs fall nowe into the hand of the Lord, (for his mercies are great) and let mee not fall into the hand of man.

15 So the Lord sent a pestilece in Israel, from the morning euen to the time appointed: and there dyed of the people from Dan euen to Beer-sheba seuentie thousand men.

16 And when the Angel stretched out his hande vpon Ierusalem to destroy it, the Lord repented of the euil, and said to the Angel that destroyed the people, It is sufficient, holde nowe thine hand. And the Angel of the Lord was by the threshing place of Araunah the Iebusite.

17 And Dauid spake vnto the Lord (when he sawe the Angel that smote the people) and saide, Behold, I haue sinned, yea, I haue done wickedly: but these sheepe, what haue they done? let thine hand, I pray thee, be against mee and against my fathers house.

18 So Gad came the same day to Dauid, and said vnto him, Go vp, reare an altar vnto the Lord in the threshing floore of Araunah the Iebusite.

19 And Dauid (according to the saying of Gad) went vp, as the Lord had commanded.

20 And Araunah looked, and sawe the King and his seruants comming towarde him, and Araunah went out, and bowed himselfe before the King on his face to the ground,

21 And Araunah said, Wherefore is my lord the King come to his seruant? Then Dauid answered, To bye the threshing floore of thee for to builde an altar vnto the Lord, that the plague may cease from the people.

22 Then Araunah saide vnto Dauid, Let my lord the King take and offer what seemeth him good in his eyes: beholde the oxen for the burnt offring, and charets, and the instruments of the oxen for wood.

23 (All these things did Araunah as a King giue vnto the King: and Araunah saide vnto the King, The Lord thy God be fauourable vnto thee)

24 Then the King saide vnto Araunah, Not so, but I will bye it of thee at a price, and will not offer burnt offring vnto ye Lord my God of that which doeth cost me nothing. So Dauid bought the threshing floore, and the oxen for fiftie shekels of siluer.

25 And Dauid built there an altar vnto the Lord, and offred burnt offrings and peace offrings, and the Lord was appeased toward ye lande, and the plague ceased from Israel.

First Kings

First Kings 1

1 Now when King Dauid was olde, and striken in yeeres, they couered him with clothes, but no heate came vnto him.

2 Wherefore his seruants saide vnto him, Let there be sought for my lord ye King a yong virgin, and let her stand before the king, and cherish him: and let her lie in thy bosome, that my lord the King may get heate.

3 So they sought for a faire young maide thoroughout all the coastes of Israel, and founde one Abishag a Shunamite, and brought her to the king.

4 And the maid was exceeding faire, and cherished the king, and ministred to him, but the King knew her not.

5 Then Adoniiah the sonne of Haggith exalted himselfe, saying, I will be king. And he gate him charets and horsemen, and fiftie men to run before him.

6 And his father would not displease him from his childehood, to say, Why hast thou done so? And hee was a very goodly man, and his mother bare him next after Absalom.

7 And he tooke counsel of Ioab the sonne of Zeruiah, and of Abiathar the Priest: and they helped forward Adoniiah.

8 But Zadok the Priest, and Benaiah the sonne of Iehoiada, and Nathan the Prophet, and Shimei, and Rei, and the men of might, which were with Dauid, were not with Adoniiah.

9 Then Adoniiah sacrificed sheepe and oxen, and fat cattel by the stone of Zoheleth, which is by En-rogel, and called all his brethren the kings sonnes, and al the men of Iudah ye Kings seruants,

10 But Nathan the Prophet, and Benaiah, and the mightie men, and Salomon his brother hee called not.

11 Wherefore Nathan spake vnto Bath-sheba the mother of Salomon, saying, Hast thou not heard, that Adoniiah ye sonne of Haggith doeth reigne, and Dauid our lord knoweth it not?

12 Now therefore come, and I will now giue thee counsell, howe to saue thine owne life, and the life of thy sonne Salomon.

13 Go, and get thee in vnto King Dauid, and say vnto him, Didest not thou, my lorde, O King, sweare vnto thine handmaide, saying, Assuredly Salomon thy sonne shall reigne after me, and he shall sit vpon my throne? why is then Adoniiah King?

14 Behold, while thou yet talkest there with the King, I also will come in after thee, and confirme thy wordes.

15 So Bath-sheba went in vnto the King into the chamber, and the King was verie olde, and Abishag the Shunammite ministred vnto ye King.

16 And Bath-sheba bowed and made obeisance vnto the King. And the King saide, What is thy matter?

17 And shee answered him, My lorde, thou swarest by the Lord thy God vnto thine handmaide, saying, Assuredly Salomon thy sonne shall reigne after me, and he shall sit vpon my throne.

18 And beholde, nowe is Adoniiah king, and now, my lord, O King, thou knowest it not.

19 And he hath offred many oxen, and fatte cattel, and sheepe, and hath called all the sonnes of the King, and Abiathar the Priest, and Ioab the captaine of the hoste: but Salomon thy seruant hath he not bidden.

20 And thou, my lorde, O King, knowest that the eyes of all Israel are on thee, that thou shouldest tell them, who shoulde sit on the throne of my lord the King after him.

21 For els when my lord the King shall sleepe with his fathers, I and my sonne Salomon shalbe reputed vile.

22 And lo, while she yet talked with the King, Nathan also the Prophet came in.

23 And they tolde the King, saying, Beholde, Nathan the Prophet. And when he was come in to the King, hee made obeisance before the King vpon his face to the ground.

24 And Nathan saide, My lorde, O King, hast thou said, Adoniiah shall reigne after mee, and he shall sit vpon my throne?

25 For hee is gone downe this day, and hath slaine many oxen, and fat cattel, and sheepe, and hath called al the Kings sonnes, and the captaines of the hoste, and Abiathar the Priest: and behold, they eate and drinke before him, and say, God saue King Adoniiah.

26 But me thy seruant, and Zadok the Priest, and Benaiah the sonne of Iehoiada, and thy seruant Salomon hath he not called.

27 Is this thing done by my lord the King, and thou hast not shewed it vnto thy seruant, who should sitte on the throne of my lorde the King after him?

28 Then King Dauid answered, and saide, Call me Bath-sheba. And shee came into ye Kings presence, and stoode before the King.

29 And the King sware, saying, As the Lord liueth, who hath redeemed my soule out of all aduersitie,

30 That as I sware vnto thee by the Lord God of Israel, saying, Assuredly Salomon thy sonne shall reigne after me, and hee shall sit vpon my throne in my place, so will I certainely doe this day.

31 Then Bath-sheba bowed her face to the earth, and did reuerence vnto the King, and said, God saue my lord King Dauid for euer.

32 And King Dauid saide, Call mee Zadok the Priest, and Nathan the Prophet, and Benaiah the sonne of Iehoiada. And they came before the King.

33 Then the King said vnto them, Take with you the seruants of your lorde, and cause Salomon my sonne to ride vpon mine owne mule, and carie him downe to Gihon.

34 And let Zadok the Priest and Nathan the Prophet anoint him there King ouer Israel, and blowe ye the trumpet, and say, God saue king Salomon.

35 Then come vp after him, that hee may come and sit vpon my throne: and hee shall bee King in my steade: for I haue appointed him to be prince ouer Israel and ouer Iudah.

36 Then Benaiah the sonne of Iehoiada answered the King, and said, So be it, and the Lord God of my lord the King ratifie it.

37 As the Lord hath bene with my lorde the King, so be he with Salomon, and exalt his throne aboue the throne of my lorde king Dauid.

38 So Zadok the Priest, and Nathan the Prophet, and Benaiah the sonne of Iehoiada, and the Cherethites and the Pelethites went downe and caused Salomon to ride vpon king Dauids mule, and brought him to Gihon.

39 And Zadok the Priest tooke an horne of oyle out of the Tabernacle, and anointed Salomon: and they blewe the trumpet, and all the people said, God saue king Salomon.

40 And all the people came vp after him, and the people piped with pipes, and reioyced with great ioye, so that the earth rang with the sound of them.

41 And Adoniiah and all the ghestes that were with him, heard it: (and they had made an ende of eating) and when Ioab heard the sound of the trumpet, he said, What meaneth this noise and vprore in the citie?

42 And as he yet spake, beholde, Ionathan the sonne of Abiathar the Priest came: and Adoniiah said, Come in: for thou art a worthie man, and bringest good tidings.

43 And Ionathan answered, and said to Adoniiah, Verely our lord King Dauid hath made Salomon King.

44 And the King hath sent with him Zadok the Priest, and Nathan the Prophet, and Benaiah the sonne of Iehoiada, and the Cherethites, and the Pelethites, and they haue caused him to ride vpon the Kings mule.

45 And Zadok the Priest, and Nathan ye Prophet haue anointed him King in Gihon: and they are gone vp from thence with ioy, and the citie is moued: this is the noise that ye haue heard.

46 And Salomon also sitteth on the throne of the kingdome.

47 And moreouer the Kings seruantes came to blesse our lord King Dauid, saying, God make the name of Salomon more famous then thy name, and exalt his throne aboue thy throne: therefore the King worshipped vpon the bed.

48 And thus sayd the King also, Blessed bee the Lord God of Israel, who hath made one to sit on my throne this day, euen in my sight.

49 Then all the ghestes that were with Adonijah, were afraide, and rose vp, and went euery man his way.

50 And Adonijah fearing the presence of Salomon, arose and went, and tooke holde on the hornes of the altar.

51 And one tolde Salomon, saying, Beholde, Adonijah doeth feare King Salomon: for lo, he hath caught holde on the hornes of the altar, saying, Let King Salomon sweare vnto me this day, that he will not slay his seruant with the sword.

52 Then Salomon sayd, If he will shewe him selfe a worthy man, there shall not an heare of him fall to the earth, but if wickednes be found in him, he shall dye.

53 Then King Salomon sent, and they brought him from the altar, and he came and did obeisance vnto King Salomon. And Salomon sayde vnto him, Go to thine house.

First Kings 2

1 Then the dayes of Dauid drewe neere that he should die, and hee charged Salomon his sonne, saying,

2 I go the way of all the earth: be strong therefore, and shew thy selfe a man,

3 And take heede to the charge of the Lord thy God, to walke in his wayes, to keepe his statutes, and his commandements, and his iudgements, and his testimonies, as it is written in the Law of Moses, that thou mayest prosper in all that thou doest, and in euery thing whereunto thou turnest thee,

4 That the Lord may confirme his worde which hee spake vnto me, saying, If thy sonnes take heede to their way, that they walke before me in trueth, with all their hearts, and with all their soules, thou shalt not (sayd he) want one of thy posteritie vpon the throne of Israel.

5 Thou knowest also what Ioab the sonne of Zeruiah did to me, and what he did to the two captaines of the hostes of Israel, vnto Abner the sonne of Ner, and vnto Amasa the sonne of Iether: whome he slewe, and shed blood of battell in peace, and put the blood of warre vpon his girdle that was about his loynes, and in his shooes that were on his feete.

6 Doe therefore according to thy wisdome, and let thou not his hoare head go downe to the graue in peace.

7 But shew kindnes vnto the sonnes of Barzillai the Gileadite, and let them be

among them that eate at thy table: for so they came to me when I fled from Absalom thy brother.

8 And beholde, with thee is Shimei the sonne of Gera, the sonne of Iemini, of Bahurim, which cursed mee with an horrible curse in the day when I went to Mahanaim: but hee came downe to meete me at Iorden, and I sware to him by the Lord, saying, I will not slay thee with the sword.

9 But thou shalt not count him innocent: for thou art a wise man, and knowest what thou oughtest to doe vnto him: therefore thou shalt cause his hoare head to goe downe to the graue with blood.

10 So Dauid slept with his fathers, and was buried in the citie of Dauid.

11 And the dayes which Dauid reigned vpon Israel, were fourtie yeeres: seuen yeeres reigned he in Hebron, and thirtie and three yeeres reigned he in Ierusalem.

12 Then sate Salomon vpon the throne of Dauid his father, and his kingdome was stablished mightily.

13 And Adonijah the sonne of Haggith came to Bath-sheba the mother of Salomon: and she saide, Commest thou peaceably? And hee said, Yea.

14 He said moreouer, I haue a sute vnto thee. And she sayd, Say on.

15 Then he said, Thou knowest that the kingdome was mine, and that all Israel set their faces on me, that I should reigne: howbeit the kingdome is turned away, and is my brothers: for it came to him by the Lord.

16 Nowe therefore I aske thee one request, refuse me not. And she said vnto him, Say on.

17 And he sayd, Speake, I pray thee, vnto Salomon ye King, (for he will not say thee nay) that he giue me Abishag the Shunammite to wife.

18 And Bath-sheba sayd, Well, I will speake for thee vnto the King.

19 Bath-sheba therefore went vnto King Salomon, to speake vnto him for Adonijah: and the King rose to meete her, and bowed himselfe vnto her, and sate downe on his throne: and he caused a seate to be set for the Kings mother, and she sate at his right hand.

20 Then she sayd, I desire a small request of thee, say me not nay. Then the King sayde vnto her, Aske on, my mother: for I will not say thee nay.

21 She sayd then, Let Abishag the Shunammite be giuen to Adonijah thy brother to wife.

22 But King Salomon answered and sayd vnto his mother, And why doest thou aske Abishag the Shunammite for Adonijah? aske for him the kingdome also: for he is mine elder brother, and hath for him both Abiathar the Priest, and Ioab the sonne of Zeruiah.

23 Then King Salomon sware by the Lord, saying, God doe so to me and more also, if Adoniiah hath not spoken this worde against his owne life.

24 Now therefore as ye Lord liueth, who hath established me, and set me on the throne of Dauid my father, who also hath made me an house, as he promised, Adoniiah shall surely die this day.

25 And King Salomon sent by the hand of Benaiah the sonne of Iehoiada, and hee smote him that he dyed.

26 Then the King sayd vnto Abiathar the Priest, Go to Anathoth vnto thine owne fieldes: for thou art worthy of death: but I will not this day kill thee, because thou barest the Arke of the Lord God before Dauid my father, and because thou hast suffered in all, wherein my father hath bene afflicted.

27 So Salomon cast out Abiathar from being Priest vnto the Lord, that he might fulfill the wordes of the Lord, which he spake against the house of Eli in Shiloh.

28 Then tidings came to Ioab: (for Ioab had turned after Adoniiah, but he turned not after Absalom) and Ioab fled vnto the Tabernacle of the Lord, and caught hold on the hornes of the altar.

29 And it was tolde king Salomon, that Ioab was fled vnto the Tabernacle of the Lord, and beholde, he is by the altar. Then Salomon sent Benaiah the sonne of Iehoiada, saying, Goe, fall vpon him.

30 And Benaiah came to the Tabernacle of the Lord, and sayd vnto him, Thus sayth the King, Come out. And he sayde, Nay, but I will die here. Then Benaiah brought the King worde againe, saying, Thus sayd Ioab, and thus he answered me.

31 And the King sayde vnto him, Doe as he hath sayd, and smite him, and bury him, that thou mayest take away the blood, which Ioab shed causelesse, from me and from the house of my father.

32 And the Lord shall bring his blood vpon his owne head: for he smote two men more righteous and better then he, and slew them with the sword, and my father Dauid knew not: to wit, Abner the sonne of Ner, captaine of the hoste of Israel, and Amasa the sonne of Iether captaine of the hoste of Iudah.

33 Their blood shall therefore returne vpon the head of Ioab, and on the head of his seede for euer: but vpon Dauid, and vpon his seede, and vpon his house, and vpon his throne shall there be peace for euer from the Lord.

34 So Benaiah the sonne of Iehoiada went vp, and smote him, and slewe him, and he was buryed in his owne house in the wildernesse.

35 And the King put Benaiah the sonne of Iehoiada in his roume ouer the hoste: and the King set Zadok the Priest in the roume of Abiathar.

36 Afterwarde the King sent, and called Shimei, and sayde vnto him, Buylde thee an house in Ierusalem, and dwell there, and depart not thence any whither.

37 For that day that thou goest out, and passest ouer the riuer of Kidron, knowe assuredly, that thou shalt dye the death: thy blood shall be vpon thine owne head.

38 And Shimei sayd vnto the King, The thing is good: as my lord the King hath sayd, so wil thy seruant doe. So Shimei dwelt in Ierusalem many dayes.

39 And after three yeres two of the seruants of Shimei fled away vnto Achish sonne of Maachah King of Gath: and they tolde Shimei, saying, Behold, thy seruants be in Gath.

40 And Shimei arose, and sadled his asse, and went to Gath to Achish, to seeke his seruantes: and Shimei went, and brought his seruants from Gath.

41 And it was tolde Salomon, that Shimei had gone from Ierusalem to Gath, and was come againe.

42 And the King sent and called Shimei, and sayde vnto him, Did I not make thee to sweare by the Lord, and protested vnto thee, saying, That day that thou goest out, and walkest any whither, knowe assuredly that thou shalt dye the death? And thou saydest vnto mee, The thing is good, that I haue heard.

43 Why then hast thou not kept the othe of the Lord, and the commandement wherewith I charged thee?

44 The King sayde also to Shimei, Thou knowest all the wickednes whereunto thine heart is priuie, that thou diddest to Dauid my father: the Lord therefore shall bring thy wickednesse vpon thine owne head.

45 And let King Salomon be blessed, and the throne of Dauid stablished before the Lord for euer.

46 So the King comanded Benaiah the sonne of Iehoiada: who went out and smote him that he dyed. And the kingdome was established in the hand of Salomon.

First Kings 3

1 Salomon then made affinitie with Pharaoh King of Egypt, and tooke Pharaohs daughter, and brought her into the citie of Dauid, vntill hee had made an ende of buylding his owne house, and the house of the Lord, and the wall of Ierusalem round about.

2 Only the people sacrificed in the hie places, because there was no house buylt vnto the name of the Lord, vntill those dayes.

3 And Salomon loued the Lord, walking in the ordinances of Dauid his father: onely he sacrificed and offred incense in the hie places.

4 And the King went to Gibeon to sacrifice there, for that was the chiefe hie place: a thousand burnt offrings did Salomon offer vpon that altar.

5 In Gibeon the Lord appeared to Salomon in a dreame by night: and God sayd, Aske what I shall giue thee.

6 And Salomon sayd, Thou hast shewed vnto thy seruant Dauid my father great mercie, when hee walked before thee in trueth, and in righteousnesse, and in vprightnes of heart with thee: and thou hast kept for him this great mercie, and hast giuen him a sonne, to sit on his throne, as appeareth this day.

7 And now, O Lord my God, thou hast made thy seruant King in steade of Dauid my father: and I am but a yong childe, and know not howe to go out and in.

8 And thy seruant is in the mids of thy people, which thou hast chosen, euen a great people which cannot be told nor nobred for multitude.

9 Giue therefore vnto thy seruant an vnderstanding heart, to iudge thy people, that I may discerne betweene good and bad: for who is able to iudge this thy mightie people?

10 And this pleased the Lord well, that Salomon had desired this thing.

11 And God sayde vnto him, Because thou hast asked this thing, and hast not asked for thy selfe long life, neyther hast asked riches for thy selfe, nor hast asked the life of thine enemies, but hast asked for thy selfe vnderstanding to heare iudgement,

12 Beholde, I haue done according to thy wordes: lo, I haue giuen thee a wise and an vnderstanding heart, so that there hath bene none like thee before thee, neither after thee shall arise the like vnto thee.

13 And I haue also giuen thee that, which thou hast not asked, both riches and honour, so that among the Kings there shall be none like vnto thee all thy dayes.

14 And if thou wilt walke in my wayes, to keepe mine ordinances and my commandements, as thy father Dauid did walke, I will prolong thy dayes.

15 And when Salomon awoke, behold, it was a dreame, and he came to Ierusalem, and stoode before the Arke of the couenant of the Lord, and offred burnt offrings and made peace offrings, and made a feast to all his seruants.

16 Then came two harlots vnto the King, and stoode before him.

17 And the one woman sayd, Oh my lorde, I and this woman dwell in one house, and I was deliuered of a childe with her in the house.

18 And the third day after that I was deliuered, this woman was deliuered also: and we were in the house together: no stranger was with vs in the house, saue we twaine.

19 And this womans sonne died in the night: for she ouerlay him.

20 And she rose at midnight, and tooke my sonne from my side, while thine handmaide slept, and layde him in her bosome, and layde her dead sonne in my bosome.

21 And when I rose in the morning to giue my sonne sucke, beholde, he was dead: and when I had well considered him in the morning, beholde, it was not my sonne, whom I had borne.

22 Then the other woman sayd, Nay, but my sonne liueth, and thy sonne is dead. Againe she sayde, No, but thy sonne is dead, and mine aliue: thus they spake before the King.

23 Then sayde the King, She sayth, This that liueth is my sonne, and the dead is thy sonne: and the other sayth, Nay, but the dead is thy sonne, and the liuing is my sonne.

24 Then the King said, Bring me a swerde: and they brought out a swerde before the King.

25 And the King sayde, Deuide ye the liuing child in twaine, and giue the one halfe to the one, and the other halfe to the other.

26 Then spake the woman, whose the liuing child was, vnto the King, for her compassion was kindled toward her sonne, and she sayde, Oh my lorde, giue her the liuing childe, and slay him not: but the other sayde, Let it be neither mine nor thine, but deuide it.

27 Then the King answered, and sayde, Giue her the liuing childe, and slay him not: this is his mother.

28 And all Israel heard the iudgement, which the King had iudged, and they feared the King: for they sawe that the wisedome of God was in him to doe iustice.

First Kings 4

1 And King Salomon was King ouer all Israel.

2 And these were his princes, Azariah the sonne of Zadok the Priest,

3 Elihoreph and Ahiah the sonnes of Shisha scribes, Iehoshaphat the sonne of Ahilud, the recorder,

4 And Benaiah the sonne of Iehoiada was ouer the hoste, and Zadok and Abiathar Priests,

5 And Azariah the sonne of Nathan was ouer the officers, and Zabud the sonne of Nathan Priest was the Kings friend,

6 And Ahishar was ouer the houshold: and Adoniram the sonne of Abda was ouer the tribute.

7 And Salomon had twelue officers ouer all Israel, which prouided vitailes for the King and his housholde: eche man had a moneth in the yeere to prouide vitailes.

8 And these are their names: the sonne of Hur in mount Ephraim:

9 The sonne of Dekar in Makaz, and in Shaalbim and Beth-shemesh, and Elon and Beth-hanan:

10 The sonne of Hesed in Aruboth, to whom perteined Sochoh, and all the land of Hepher:

11 The sonne of Abinadab in all the region of Dor, which had Taphath the daughter of Salomon to wife.

12 Baana the sonne of Ahilud in Taanach, and Megiddo, and in all Beth-shean, which is by Zartanah beneath Izreel, from Beth-shean to Abelmeholah, eue til beyond ouer against Iokmeam:

13 The sonne of Geber in Ramoth Gilead, and his were the townes of Iair, the sonne of Manasseh, which are in Gilead, and vnder him was the region of Argob, which is in Bashan: threescore great cities with walles and barres of brasse.

14 Ahinadab the sonne of Iddo had to Mahanaim:

15 Ahimaaz in Naphtali, and he tooke Basmath the daughter of Salomon to wife:

16 Baanah the sonne of Hushai in Asher and in Aloth:

17 Iehoshaphat the sonne of Paruah in Issachar.

18 Shimei the sonne of Elah in Beniamin:

19 Geber the sonne of Vri in the countrey of Gilead, the land of Sihon King of the Amorites, and of Og King of Bashan, and was officer alone in the land.

20 Iudah and Israel were many, as the sand of the sea in number, eating, drinking, and making merry.

21 And Salomon reigned ouer all kingdomes, from the Riuer vnto the lande of the Philistims, and vnto the border of Egypt, and they brought presents, and serued Salomon all the dayes of his life.

22 And Salomons vitailes for one day were thirtie measures of fine floure, and threescore measures of meale:

23 Ten fat oxen, and twentie oxen of the pastures, and an hundreth sheepe, beside hartes, and buckes, and bugles, and fat foule.

24 For he ruled in all the region on the other side of the Riuer, from Tiphsah euen vnto Azzah, ouer all the Kings on the other side the Riuer: and he had peace round about him on euery side.

25 And Iudah and Israel dwelt without feare, euery man vnder his vine, and vnder his fig tree, from Dan, euen to Beer-sheba, all the dayes of Salomon.

26 And Salomon had fourtie thousande stalles of horses for his charets, and twelue thousand horsemen.

27 And these officers prouided vitaile for king Salomon, and for all that came to King Salomons table, euery man his moneth, and they suffred to lacke nothing.

28 Barley also and strawe for the horses and mules brought they vnto the place where the officers were, euery man according to his charge.

29 And God gaue Salomon wisdome and vnderstanding exceeding much, and a large heart, euen as the sand that is on the sea shore,

30 And Salomons wisdome excelled the wisedome of all the children of the East and all the wisedome of Egypt.

31 For he was wiser then any man: yea, then were Ethan the Ezrahite, the Heman, then Chalcol, then Darda the sonnes of Mahol: and he was famous throughout all nations round about.

32 And Salomon spake three thousand prouerbs: and his songs were a thousand and fiue.

33 And he spake of trees, from the cedar tree that is in Lebanon, euen vnto the hyssope that springeth out of the wall: he spake also of beasts, and of foules, and of creeping thinges, and of fishes.

34 And there came of all people to heare the wisedome of Salomon, from all Kings of the earth, which had heard of his wisedome.

First Kings 5

1 And Hiram King of Tyrus sent his seruants vnto Salomon, (for he had heard, that they had anoynted him King

in the roume of his father) because Hiram had euer loued Dauid.

2 Also Salomon sent to Hiram, saying,

3 Thou knowest that Dauid my father could not build an house vnto the Name of the Lord his God, for the warres which were about him on euery side, vntill the Lord had put them vnder the soles of his feete.

4 But now the Lord my God hath giuen me rest on euery side, so that there is neither aduersarie, nor euill to resist.

5 And beholde, I purpose to build an house vnto ye Name of the Lord my God, as the Lord spake vnto Dauid my father, saying, Thy sonne, whom I wil set vpon thy throne for thee, he shall build an house vnto my Name.

6 Now therefore commaund, that they hewe me cedar trees out of Lebanon, and my seruants shall be with thy seruants, and vnto thee will I giue the hire for thy seruants, according to all that thou shalt appoynt: for thou knowest that there are none among vs, that can hewe timber like vnto the Sidonians.

7 And when Hiram heard the wordes of Salomon, he reioyced greatly, and sayde, Blessed be the Lord this day, which hath giuen vnto Dauid a wise sonne ouer this mightie people.

8 And Hiram sent to Salomon, saying, I haue considered the things, for the which thou sentest vnto me, and will accomplish all thy desire, concerning the cedar trees and firre trees.

9 My seruants shall bring them downe from Lebanon to the sea: and I will conuey them by sea in raftes vnto the place that thou shalt shew me, and wil cause them to be discharged there, and thou shalt receiue them: nowe thou shalt doe mee a pleasure to minister foode for my familie.

10 So Hiram gaue Salomon cedar trees and firre trees, euen his full desire.

11 And Salomon gaue Hiram twentie thousand measures of wheate for foode to his householde, and twentie measures of beaten oyle. Thus much gaue Salomon to Hiram yere by yere.

12 And the Lord gaue Salomon wisedome as he promised him. And there was peace betweene Hiram and Salomon, and they two made a couenant.

13 And King Salomon raised a summe out of all Israel, and the summe was thirtie thousand men:

14 Whome he sent to Lebanon, ten thousand a moneth by course: they were a moneth in Lebanon, and two monethes at home. And Adoniram was ouer the summe.

15 And Salomon had seuentie thousand that bare burdens, and fourescore thousand masons in the mountaine,

16 Besides the princes, whome Salomon appoynted ouer the worke, euen three thousande and three hundreth, which ruled the people that wrought in the worke.

17 And the King commanded them, and they brought great stones and costly stones to make the foundation of the house, euen hewed stones.

18 And Salomons workemen, and the workemen of Hiram, and the masons hewed and prepared timber and stones for the buylding of the house.

First Kings 6

1 And in the foure hundreth and foure score yeere (after the children of Israel were come out of the land of Egypt) and in the fourth yere of the reigne of Salomon ouer Israel, in the moneth Zif, (which is the second moneth) he built the house of the Lord.

2 And the house which King Salomon built for the Lord, was three score cubites long, and twentie broade, and thirtie cubites hie.

3 And the porch before the Temple of the house was twentie cubites long according to the breadth of the house, and ten cubites broade before the house.

4 And in the house he made windowes, broad without, and narrowe within.

5 And by the wall of the house hee made galleries round about, euen by the walles of the house round about the Temple and the oracle, and made chambers round about.

6 The nethermost gallerie was fiue cubites broade, and the middlemost sixe cubites broade, and the third seuen cubites broade: for he made restes round about without the house, that the beames should not be fastened in the walles of the house.

7 And when the house was built, it was built of stone perfite, before it was brought, so that there was neither hammer, nor axe, nor any toole of yron heard in the house, while it was in building.

8 The doore of the middle chamber was in the right side of the house, and men went vp with winding stayres into the middlemost, and out of the middlemost into the third.

9 So he built the house and finished it, and sieled the house being vawted with sieling of cedar trees.

10 And he built the galleries vpon al the wall of the house of fiue cubites height, and they were ioyned to the house with beames of cedar.

11 And the worde of the Lord came to Salomon, saying,

12 Cocerning this house which thou buildest, if thou wilt walke in mine ordinances, and execute my iudgements, and keepe al my commadements, to walke in them, then will I performe vnto thee my promise, which I promised to Dauid thy father.

13 And I will dwell among the children of Israel, and wil not forsake my people Israel.

14 So Salomon built the house and finished it,

15 And built the walles of the house within, with boards of cedar tree from the pauement of the house vnto the walles of the sieling, and within he couered them with wood, and couered the floore of the house with planks of firre.

16 And he built twentie cubites in the sides of the house with boards of cedar, from the floore to the walles, and he prepared a place within it for the oracle, euen the most holy place.

17 But the house, that is, the Temple before it, was fourtie cubites long.

18 And the cedar of the house within was carued with knops, and grauen with floures: all was cedar, so that no stone was seene.

19 Also he prepared the place of the oracle in the mids of the house within, to set the Arke of the couenant of the Lord there.

20 And the place of the oracle within was twentie cubites long, and twentie cubites broad, and twentie cubites hie, and hee couered it with pure golde, and couered the altar with cedar.

21 So Salomon couered the house within with pure golde: and he shut the place of the oracle with chaines of gold, and couered it with golde.

22 And he ouerlayde all the house with gold, vntill all the house was made perfite. also he couered the whole altar, that was before the oracle, with golde.

23 And within the oracle he made two Cherubims of oliue tree, ten cubites hie.

24 The wing also of the one Cherub was fiue cubites, and the wing of the other Cherub was fiue cubites: from the vttermost part of one of his wings vnto the vttermost part of the other of his wings, were ten cubites.

25 Also the other Cherub was of ten cubites: both the Cherubims were of one measure and one sise.

26 For the height of the one Cherub was ten cubits, and so was the other Cherub.

27 And he put the Cherubims within the inner house, and the Cherubims stretched out their wings, so that the wing of the one touched the one wall, and the wing of the other Cherub touched the other wall: and their other wings touched one another in the middes of the house.

28 And he ouerlaied the Cherubims with golde.

29 And he carued all the walles of the house round about with grauen figures of Cherubims and of Palmetrees, and grauen flowres within and without.

30 And the floore of the house hee couered with golde within and without.

31 And in the entring of the oracle he made two doores of oliue tree: and the vpper post and side postes were fiue square.

32 The two doores also were of oliue tree, and he graued them with grauing of Cherubims and palme trees, and grauen floures, and couered them with golde, and layed thin golde vpon the Cherubims and vpon the palme trees.

33 And so made he for the doore of the Temple, postes of oliue tree foure square.

34 But the two doores were of firre tree, the two sides of the one doore were round, and the two sides of the other doore were round.

35 And he graued Cherubims, and palme trees, and carued floures and couered the carued worke with golde, finely wrought.

36 And hee built the court within with three rowes of hewed stone, and one rowe of beames of cedar.

37 In the fourth yeere was the foundation of the house of the Lord layed in the moneth of Zif:

38 And in the eleuenth yeere in the moneth of Bul, (which is the eight moneth) hee finished the house with all the furniture thereof, and in euery point: so was he seuen yeere in building it.

First Kings 7

1 Bvt Salomon was building his owne house thirteene yeeres, and finished all his house.

2 He built also an house called the forest of Lebanon, an hundreth cubites long, and fiftie cubites broad, and thirtie cubites hie, vpon foure rowes of cedar pillars, and cedar beames were layed vpon the pillars.

3 And it was couered aboue with cedar vpon the beames, that lay on the fourtie and fiue pillars, fifteene in a rowe.

4 And the windowes were in three rowes, and windowe was against windowe in three rankes.

5 And all the doores, and the side postes with the windowes were foure square, and windowe was ouer against windowe in three rankes.

6 And he made a porche of pillars fiftie cubites long, and thirtie cubites broade, and the porch was before them, euen before them were thirtie pillars.

7 Then he made a porch for the throne, where he iudged, euen a porch of iudgement, and it was sieled with cedar from pauement to pauement.

8 And in his house, where he dwelt, was an other hall more inwarde then the porche which was of the same worke. Also Salomon made an house for Pharaohs daughter (whom he had taken to wife) like vnto this porche.

9 All these were of costly stones, hewed by measure, and sawed with sawes within and without, from the foundation vnto the stones of an hand breadth, and on the outside to the great court.

10 And the foundation was of costly stones, and great stones, euen of stones of ten cubites, and stones of eight cubites.

11 Aboue also were costly stones, squared by rule, and boardes of cedar.

12 And the great court round about was with three rowes of hewed stones, and a rowe of cedar beames: so was it to ye inner court of the house of the Lord, and to the porche of the house.

13 Then King Salomon sent, and set one Hiram out of Tyrus.

14 He was a widowes sonne of the tribe of Naphtali, his father being a man of Tyrus, and wrought in brasse: he was full of wisedome, and vnderstanding, and knowledge to worke all maner of worke in brasse: who came to King Salomon, and wrought all his worke.

15 For he cast two pillars of brasse: ye height of a pillar was eighteene cubites, and a threede of twelue cubites did compasse either of ye pillars.

16 And he made two chapiters of molten brasse to set on the tops of the pillars: the height of one of the chapiters was fiue cubites, and the height of the other chapiter was fiue cubites.

17 He made grates like networke, and wrethen worke like chaynes for the chapiters that were on the top of the pillars, euen seuen for the one chapiter, and seuen for the other chapiter.

18 So he made the pillars and two rowes of pomegranates round about in the one grate to couer the chapiters that were vpon the top. And thus did he for the other chapiter.

19 And the chapiters that were on the toppe of the pillars were after lilye worke in ye porch, foure cubites.

20 And the chapiters vpon the two pillars had also aboue, ouer against the belly within the networke pomegranates: for two hudreth pomegranates were in the two rankes about vpon either of the chapiters.

21 And he set vp the pillars in the porche of the Temple. And when hee had set vp the right pillar, he called the name thereof Iachin: and when he had set vp the left pillar, he called the name thereof Boaz.

22 And vpon the top of the pillars was worke of lilyes: so was the workemanship of the pillars finished.

23 And he made a molten sea ten cubites wide from brim to brim, rounde in compasse, and fiue cubites hie, and a line of thirtie cubites did compasse it about.

24 And vnder the brimme of it were knoppes like wilde cucumers compassing it round about, ten in one cubite, compassing the sea round about: and the two rowes of knoppes were cast, when it was molten.

25 It stoode on twelue bulles, three looking towarde the North, and three toward the West, and three toward the South, and three towarde the East: and the sea stoode aboue vpon them, and all their hinder partes were inward.

26 It was an hand bredth thicke, and the brim thereof was like the worke of the brim of a cup with floures of lilyes: it contained two thousad Baths.

27 And he made tenne bases of brasse, one base was foure cubites long, and foure cubites broad, and three cubites hie.

28 And the worke of the bases was on this maner, They had borders, and the borders were betweene the ledges:

29 And on the borders that were betweene the ledges, were lyons, bulles and Cherubims: and vpon the ledges there was a base aboue: and beneath the lyons and bulles, were addicions made of thinne worke.

30 And euery base had foure brasen wheeles, and plates of brasse: and the foure corners had vndersetters: vnder the caldron were vndersetters molten at the side of euery addicion.

31 And the mouth of it was within the chapiter and aboue to measure by the cubite: for the mouth thereof was round made like a base, and it was a cubite and halfe a cubite: and also vpon the mouth thereof were grauen workes, whose borders were foure square, and not round.

32 And vnder the borders were foure wheeles, and the axeltrees of the wheeles ioyned to the base: and the height of a wheele was a cubite and halfe a cubite.

33 And the facion of the wheeles was like the facion of a charet wheele, their axeltrees, and their naues and their felloes, and their spokes were all molten.

34 And foure vndersetters were vpon the foure corners of one base: and the vndersetters thereof were of the base it selfe.

35 And in the toppe of the base was a rounde compasse of halfe a cubite hie round about: and vpon the toppe of the base the ledges thereof and the borders thereof were of the same.

36 And vpon the tables of the ledges thereof, and on the borders thereof he did graue Cherubims, lions and palmetrees, on the side of euery one, and addicions round about.

37 Thus made he the tenne bases, They had all one casting, one measure, and one syse.

38 Then made he ten caldrons of brasse, one caldron conteyned fourty Baths: and euery caldron was foure cubites, one caldron was vpon one base throughout the ten bases.

39 And he set the bases, fiue on the right side of the house, and fiue on the left side of the house. And he set the sea on the right side of the house Eastward toward the South.

40 And Hiram made caldrons, and besomes, and basens, and Hiram finished all the worke that he made to King Salomon for the house of ye Lord:

41 To wit, two pillars and two bowles of the chapiters that were on the toppe of the two pillars, and two grates to couer the two bowles of the chapiters which were vpon the toppe of the pillars,

42 And foure hundreth pomegranates for the two grates, euen two rowes of pomegranates for euery grate to couer the two bowles of the chapiters, that were vpon the pillars,

43 And the ten bases, and ten caldrons vpon the bases,

44 And the sea, and twelue bulles vnder that sea,

45 And pottes, and besomes and basens: and all these vessels, which Hiram made to King Salomon for the house of the Lord, were of shining brasse.

46 In the plaine of Iorden did the King cast them in clay betweene Succoth and Zarthan.

47 And Salomon left to weigh all the vessels because of the exceeding

aboundance, neyther could the weight of the brasse be counted.

48 So Salomon made all the vessels that perteyned vnto the house of the Lord, the golden altar, and the golden table, whereon the shewbread was,

49 And the candlestickes, fiue at the right side, and fiue at the left, before the oracle of pure gold, and the flowres, and the lampes, and the snuffers of golde,

50 And the bowles, and the hookes, and the basens, and the spoones, and the ashpannes of pure golde, and the hinges of golde for the doores of the house within, euen for the most holy place, and for the doores of the house, to wit, of the Temple.

51 So was finished all the worke that King Salomon made for the house of the Lord, and Salomon brought in the things which Dauid his father had dedicated: the siluer and the golde and the vessels, and layed them among the treasures of the house of the Lord.

First Kings 8

1 Then King Salomon assembled the Elders of Israel, euen all the heads of the tribes, the chiefe fathers of the children of Israel vnto him in Ierusalem, for to bring vp the Arke of the couenant of the Lord from the citie of Dauid, which is Zion.

2 And all the men of Israel assembled vnto King Salomon at the feast in the moneth of Ethanim, which is the seuenth moneth.

3 And all the Elders of Israel came and the Priests tooke the Arke.

4 They bare the Arke of the Lord, and they bare the Tabernacle of the Congregation, and all the holy vessels that were in the Tabernacle: those did the Priestes and Leuites bring vp.

5 And King Salomon and all the Congregation of Israel, that were assembled vnto him, were with him before the Arke, offering sheepe and beeues, which could not be tolde, nor nombred for multitude.

6 So the Priestes brought the Arke of the couenant of the Lord vnto his place, into the oracle of the house, into the most holy place, euen vnder the wings of the Cherubims.

7 For ye Cherubims stretched out their wings ouer the place of the Arke, and the Cherubims couered the Arke, and the barres thereof aboue.

8 And they drewe out the barres, that the endes of the barres might appeare out of the Sanctuarie before the oracle, but they were not seene without: and there they are vnto this day.

9 Nothing was in the Arke saue the two tables of stone which Moses had put there at Horeb, where the Lord made a couenant with the children of Israel, when he brought them out of the land of Egypt.

10 And when the Priestes were come out of the Sanctuarie, the cloude filled the house of the Lord,

11 So that the Priestes could not stande to minister, because of the cloude: for the glorie of the Lord had filled the house of the Lord.

12 Then spake Salomon, The Lord said, that he woulde dwell in the darke cloude.

13 I haue built thee an house to dwell in, an habitation for thee to abide in for euer.

14 And the King turned his face, and blessed all the Congregation of Israel: for all the Congregation of Israel stoode there.

15 And he said, Blessed be the Lord God of Israel, who spake with his mouth vnto Dauid my father, and hath with his hand fulfilled it, saying,

16 Since the day that I brought my people Israel out of Egypt, I chose no citie of all the tribes of Israel, to builde an house that my name might be there: but I haue chosen Dauid to be ouer my people Israel.

17 And it was in ye heart of Dauid my father to builde an house to the Name of the Lord God of Israel.

18 And the Lord said vnto Dauid my father, Where as it was in thine heart to build an house vnto my Name, thou diddest well, that thou wast so minded:

19 Neuerthelesse thou shalt not builde the house, but thy sonne that shall come out of thy loynes, he shall builde the house vnto my Name.

20 And the Lord hath made good his worde that he spake: and I am risen vp in the roume of Dauid my father, and sit on the throne of Israel, as the Lord promised, and haue built the house for the Name of the Lord God of Israel.

21 And I haue prepared therein a place for the Arke, wherein is the couenant of the Lord which he made with our fathers, whe he brought them out of the lande of Egypt.

22 Then Salomon stoode before the altar of the Lord in the sight of all the Congregation of Israel, and stretched out his handes towarde heauen,

23 And sayd, O Lord God of Israel, there is no God like thee in heauen aboue, or in the earth beneath, thou that keepest couenant and mercie with thy seruants that walke before thee with all their heart,

24 Thou that hast kept with thy seruant Dauid my father, that thou hast promised him: for thou spakest with thy mouth and hast fulfilled it with thine hande, as appeareth this day.

25 Therefore now, Lord God of Israel, keepe with thy seruant Dauid my father that thou hast promised him, saying, Thou shalt not want a man in my sight to sit vpon ye throne of Israel: so that thy childre take heed to their way, that they walke before me; as thou hast walked in my sight

26 And nowe, O God of Israel, I pray thee, let thy worde be verified, which thou spakest vnto thy seruant Dauid my father.

27 Is it true in deede that God will dwell on the earth? beholde, the heauens, and the heauens of heauens are not able to

conteine thee: howe much more vnable is this house that I haue built?

28 But haue thou respect vnto the prayer of thy seruant, and to his supplication, O Lord, my God, to heare the cry and prayer which thy seruant prayeth before thee this day:

29 That thine eyes may be open toward this house, night and day, euen towarde the place whereof thou hast said, My Name shalbe there: that thou mayest hearken vnto the prayer which thy seruant prayeth in this place.

30 Heare thou therefore the supplication of thy seruant, and of thy people Israel, which pray in this place, and heare thou in the place of thine habitation, euen in heauen, and when thou hearest, haue mercie.

31 When a man shall trespasse against his neighbour, and he lay vpon him an othe to cause him to sweare, and the swearer shall come before thine altar in this house,

32 Then heare thou in heauen, and doe and iudge thy seruants, that thou condemne the wicked to bring his way vpon his head, and iustifie the righteous, to giue him according to his righteousnesse.

33 When thy people Israel shall be ouerthrowen before the enemie, because they haue sinned against thee, and turne againe to thee, and confesse thy Name, and pray and make supplication vnto thee in this house,

34 Then heare thou in heauen, and be mercifull vnto the sinne of thy people Israel, and bring them againe vnto the lande, which thou gauest vnto their fathers.

35 When heauen shalbe shut vp, and there shalbe no raine because they haue sinned against thee, and shall pray in this place, and confesse thy Name, and turne from their sinne, when thou doest afflict them,

36 Then heare thou in heauen, and pardon the sinne of thy seruants and of thy people Israel (when thou hast taught the the good way wherein they may walke) and giue raine vpon the land that thou hast giuen to thy people to inherite.

37 When there shalbe famine in the land, when there shalbe pestilence, when there shall be blasting, mildewe, grashopper or caterpiller, when their enemie shall besiege them in the cities of their lande, or any plague, or any sickenesse,

38 Then what prayer, and supplication so euer shalbe made of any man or of all thy people Israel, when euery one shall knowe the plague in his owne heart, and stretch foorth his handes in this house,

39 Heare thou then in heauen, in thy dwelling place, and be mercifull, and doe, and giue euery man according to all his wayes, as thou knowest his heart, (for thou only knowest the heartes of all the children of men)

40 That they may feare thee as long as they liue in ye lad, which thou gauest vnto our fathers.

41 Moreouer as touching the stranger that is not of thy people Israel, who shall come out of a farre countrey for thy Names sake,

42 (When they shall heare of thy great name, and of thy mightie hande, and of thy stretched out arme) and shall come and pray in this house,

43 Heare thou in heauen thy dwelling place, and do according to all that the stranger calleth for vnto thee: that all the people of the earth may know thy Name, and feare thee, as do thy people Israel: and that they may know, that thy Name is called vpon in this house which I haue built.

44 When thy people shall go out to battell against their enemie by the way that thou shalt sende them, and shall pray vnto the Lord towarde the way of the citie which thou hast chosen, and toward the house that I haue built for thy Name,

45 Heare thou then in heauen their prayer and their supplication, and iudge their cause.

46 If they sinne against thee, (for there is no man that sinneth not) and thou be angry with them, and deliuer them vnto the enemies, so that they cary them away prisoners vnto the land of the enemies, either farre or neere,

47 Yet if they turne againe vnto their heart in the lande (to the which they be caryed away captiues) and returne and pray vnto thee in the lande of them that caryed them away captiues, saying, We haue sinned, we haue transgressed, and done wickedly,

48 If they turne againe vnto thee with all their heart, and with all their soule in the lande of their enemies, which led them away captiues, and pray vnto thee toward the way of their land, which thou gauest vnto their fathers, and toward the citie which thou hast chosen, and the house, which I haue built for thy Name,

49 Then heare thou their prayer and their supplication in heauen thy dwelling place, and iudge their cause,

50 And be mercifull vnto thy people that haue sinned against thee, and vnto all their iniquities (wherein they haue transgressed against thee) and cause that they, which led them away captiues, may haue pitie and compassion on them:

51 For they be thy people, and thine inheritance, which thou broughtest out of Egypt from the middes of the yron fornace.

52 Let thine eyes be open vnto the prayer of thy seruant, and vnto the prayer of thy people Israel, to hearken vnto them, in all that they call for vnto thee.

53 For thou diddest separate them to thee from among all people of the earth for an inheritance, as thou saidest by the hand of Moses thy seruant, when thou broughtest our fathers out of Egypt, O Lord God.

54 And when Salomon had made an ende of praying all this prayer and supplication vnto the Lord, he arose from before the altar of the Lord, from kneeling on his knees, and stretching of his handes to heauen,

55 And stoode and blessed all the Congregation of Israel with a loud voyce, saying,

56 Blessed be the Lord that hath giuen rest vnto his people Israel, according to all that hee promised: there hath not fayled one word of all his good promise which he promised by the hand of Moses his seruant.

57 The Lord our God be with vs, as he was with our fathers, that he forsake vs not, neither leaue vs,

58 That he may bow our heartes vnto him, that we may walke in all his waies, and keepe his commandements, and his statutes, and his lawes, which he commanded our fathers.

59 And these my wordes, which I haue prayed before the Lord, be neere vnto the Lord our God day and night, that he defende the cause of his seruant, and the cause of his people Israel alway as the matter requireth,

60 That all the people of ye earth may knowe, that the Lord is God, and none other.

61 Let your heart therefore be perfit with the Lord our God to walke in his statutes, and to keepe his commandements, as this day.

62 Then the King and all Israel with him offred sacrifice before the Lord.

63 And Salomon offered a sacrifice of peace offrings which he offered vnto the Lord, to wit, two and twentie thousande beeues, and an hundreth and twentie thousande sheepe: so the king and all the children of Israel dedicated the house of the Lord.

64 The same day did the King halowe the middle of the court, that was before the house of the Lord: for there he made burnt offerings, and the meate offrings, and the fat of the peace offerings, because the brasen altar that was before the Lord, was too litle to receiue the burnt offerings, and the meate offerings, and the fat of the peace offrings.

65 And Salomon made at that time a feast and all Israel with him, a very great Congregation, euen from the entring in of Hamath vnto the riuer of Egypt, before the Lord our God, seuen dayes and seuen dayes, euen fourteene dayes.

66 And the eight day he sent the people away: and they thanked the King and went vnto their tentes ioyous and with glad heart, because of al the goodnesse that the Lord had done for Dauid his seruant, and for Israel his people.

First Kings 9

1 When Salomon had finished the building of the house of ye Lord, and the kings palace, and all that Salomon desired and minded to do,

2 Then the Lord appeared vnto Salomon the second time, as he appeared vnto him at Gibeon.

3 And the Lord sayd vnto him, I haue heard thy prayer and thy supplication, that thou hast made before me: I haue halowed this house (which thou hast built) to put my Name there for euer, and mine eyes, and mine heart shall be there perpetually.

4 And if thou wilt walke before mee (as Dauid thy father walked in purenesse of heart and in righteousnesse) to doe according to al that I haue commanded thee, and keepe my statutes, and my iudgements,

5 Then will I stablish the throne of thy kingdome vpon Israel for euer, as I promised to Dauid thy father, saying, Thou shalt not want a man vpon the throne of Israel.

6 But if ye and your children turne away from mee, and wil not keepe my commandements, and my statutes (which I haue set before you) but go and serue other gods, and worship them,

7 Then will I cutte off Israel from the lande, which I haue giuen them, and the house which I haue halowed for my Name, will I cast out of my sight, and Israel shall be a prouerbe, and a common talke among all people.

8 Euen this hie house shall bee so: euery one that passeth by it, shalbe astonied, and shall hisse, and they shall say, Why hath the Lord done thus vnto this land and to this house?

9 And they shall answere, Because they forsooke the Lord their God, which brought their fathers out of the land of Egypt, and haue taken holde vpon other gods, and haue worshipped them, and serued them, therfore hath the Lord brought vpon them all this euill.

10 And at the ende of twentie yeeres, when Salomon had buylded the two houses, the house of the Lord, and the Kings palace,

11 (For the which Hiram the King of Tyrus had brought to Salomon timber of cedar, and firre trees, and golde, and whatsoeuer he desired) then King Salomon gaue to Hiram twentie cities in the land of Galil.

12 And Hiram came out from Tyrus to see the cities which Salomon had giuen him, and they pleased him not.

13 Therefore hee sayde, What cities are these which thou hast giuen me, my brother? And hee called them the land of Cabul vnto this day.

14 And Hiram had sent the King sixe score talents of gold.

15 And this is the cause of the tribute why King Salomon raised tribute, to wit, to builde the house of the Lord, and his owne house, and Millo, and the wall of Ierusalem, and Hazor, and Megiddo, and Gezer.

16 Pharaoh King of Egypt had come vp, and taken Gezer, and burnt it with fire, and slew the Canaanites, that dwelt in the citie, and gaue it for a present vnto his daughter Salomons wife.

17 (Therefore Salomon builte Gezer and Beth-horon the nether,

18 And Baalath and Tamor in the wildernes of the land,

19 And all the cities of store, that Salomon had, euen cities for charets,

and cities for horsemen, and all that Salomon desired and woulde build in Ierusalem, and in Lebanon and in all the land of his dominion)

20 Al the people that were left of the Amorites, Hittites, Perizzites, Hiuites, and Iebusites, which were not of the children of Israel:

21 To wit, their children that were left after them in the lande, whome the children of Israel were not able to destroy, those did Salomon make tributaries vnto this day.

22 But of the children of Israel did Salomon make no bondmen: but they were men of warre and his seruants, and his princes, and his captaines, and rulers of his charets and his horsemen.

23 These were the princes of the officers, that were ouer Salomons worke: euen fiue hundreth and fiftie, and they ruled the people that wrought in the worke.

24 And Pharaohs daughter came vp from the citie of Dauid vnto the house which Salomon had built for her: then did he buylde Millo.

25 And thrise a yere did Salomon offer burnt offringes and peace offrings vpon the altar which he built vnto the Lord: and hee burnt incense vpon the altar that was before the Lord, when hee had finished the house.

26 Also King Salomon made a nauie of ships in Ezeon-geber, which is beside Eloth, and the brinke of the red Sea, in the land of Edom.

27 And Hiram sent with the nauie his seruats, that were mariners, and had knowledge of the sea, with the seruants of Salomon.

28 And they came to Ophir and sette from thence foure hundreth and twentie talents of gold, and brought it to King Salomon.

First Kings 10

1 And the Queene of Sheba hearing ye fame of Salomon (concerning the Name of the Lord) came to proue him with hard questions.

2 And she came to Ierusalem with a verie great traine, and camels that bare sweete odours, and golde exceeding much, and precious stones: and shee came to Salomon, and communed with him of all that was in her heart.

3 And Salomon declared vnto her all her questions: nothing was hid from the King, which he expounded not vnto her.

4 Then the Queene of Sheba sawe all Salomons wisedome, and the house that he had built,

5 And the meate of his table, and the sitting of his seruants, and the order of his ministers, and their apparel, and his drinking vessels, and his burnt offrings, that he offered in the house of the Lord, and she was greatly astonied.

6 And shee sayde vnto the King, It was a true worde that I heard in mine owne lande of thy sayings, and of thy wisedome.

7 Howebeit I beleeued not this report till I came, and had seene it with mine eyes: but lo, ye one halfe was not tolde mee: for thou hast more wisedome and prosperitie, then I haue heard by report.

8 Happy are the men, happie are these thy seruants, which stande euer before thee, and heare thy wisedome.

9 Blessed be the Lord thy God, which loued thee, to set thee on the throne of Israel, because the Lord loued Israel for euer and made thee King to doe equitie and righteousnesse.

10 And she gaue the King sixe score talents of golde, and of sweete odours exceeding much, and precious stones. There came no more such aboundance of sweete odours, as the Queene of Sheba gaue to King Salomon.

11 The nauie also of Hiram (that caried gold from Ophir) brought likewise great plentie of Almuggim trees from Ophir and precious stones.

12 And the King made of ye Almuggim trees pillars for the house of the Lord, and for ye Kings palace, and made harpes and psalteries for singers. There came no more such Almuggim trees, nor were any more seene vnto this day.

13 And King Salomon gaue vnto the Queene of Sheba, whatsoeuer she would aske, besides that, which Salomon gaue her of his kingly liberalitie: so she returned and went to her owne countrey, both shee, and her seruantes.

14 Also the weight of golde, that came to Salomon in one yeere, was sixe hundreth three score and six talents of gold,

15 Besides that he had of marchant men and of the marchandises of them that solde spices, and of all the Kinges of Arabia, and of the princes of the countrey.

16 And King Salomon made two hundreth targets of beaten golde, sixe hundreth shekels of gold went to a target:

17 And three hundreth shieldes of beaten golde, three pound of gold went to one shielde: and the King put them in the house of the wood of Lebanon.

18 Then the King made a great throne of yuorie, and couered it with the best golde.

19 And the throne had six steps, and the top of the throne was round behind, and there were stayes on either side on the place of the throne, and two lions standing by the stayes.

20 And there stoode twelue lions on the sixe steps on either side: there was not the like made in any kingdome.

21 And all King Salomons drinking vessels were of golde, and all the vessels of the house of the woode of Lebanon were of pure golde, none were of siluer: for it was nothing esteemed in the dayes of Salomon.

22 For the King had on the sea the nauie of Tharshish with the nauie of Hiram: once in three yere came the nauie of Tharshish, and brought golde and siluer, yuorie, and apes and peacockes.

23 So King Salomon exceeded all the kings of the earth both in riches and in wisedome.

24 And al the world sought to see Salomon, to heare his wisedome, which God had put in his heart,

25 And they brought euery man his present, vessels of siluer, and vessels of golde, and raiment, and armour, and sweete odours, horses and mules, from yeere to yeere.

26 Then Salomon gathered together charrets and horsemen: and he had a thousand and foure hundreth charets, and twelue thousande horsemen, whome hee placed in the charet cities, and with the King at Ierusalem.

27 And the King gaue siluer in Ierusalem as stones, and gaue cedars as the wilde figtrees that growe abundantly in the plaine.

28 Also Salomon had horses brought out of Egypt, and fine linen: the Kings marchants receiued the linen for a price.

29 There came vp and went out of Egypt some charet, worth sixe hundreth shekels of siluer: that is, one horse, an hundreth and fiftie and thus they brought horses to all the Kings of the Hittites and to the Kings of Aram by their meanes.

First Kings 11

1 Bvt King Salomon loued many outlandish women: both the daughter of Pharaoh, and the women of Moab, Ammon, Edom, Zidon and Heth,

2 Of the nations, whereof the Lord had sayd vnto the children of Israel, Goe not ye in to them, nor let them come in to you: for surely they will turne your hearts after their gods, to them, I say, did Salomon ioyne in loue.

3 And he had seuen hundreth wiues, that were princesses, and three hundreth concubines, and his wiues turned away his heart.

4 For when Salomon was olde, his wiues turned his heart after other gods, so that his heart was not perfect with the Lord his God, as was the heart of Dauid his father.

5 For Salomon followed Ashtaroth the god of the Zidonians, and Milcom the abomination of the Ammonites.

6 So Salomon wrought wickednesse in the sight of the Lord, but continued not to follow the Lord, as did Dauid his father.

7 Then did Salomon build an hie place for Chemosh the abomination of Moab, in the mountaine that is ouer against Ierusalem, and vnto Molech the abomination of the children of Ammon.

8 And so did he for all his outlandish wiues, which burnt incense and offered vnto their gods.

9 Therefore the Lord was angry with Salomon, because hee had turned his heart from the Lord God of Israel, which had appeared vnto him twise,

10 And had giuen him a charge concerning this thing, that he should not

follow other gods: but he kept not that, which the Lord had commanded him.

11 Wherefore the Lord sayd vnto Salomon, Forasmuch as this is done of thee, and thou hast not kept my couenant, and my statutes (which I commanded thee) I will surely rent the kingdome from thee, and will giue it to thy seruant.

12 Notwithstanding in thy dayes I will not doe it, because of Dauid thy father, but I will rent it out of the hand of thy sonne:

13 Howbeit I wil not rent all the Kingdome, but will giue one tribe to thy sonne, because of Dauid my seruant, and because of Ierusalem which I haue chosen.

14 Then the Lord stirred vp an aduersarie vnto Salomon, euen Hadad the Edomite, of the Kings seede, which was in Edom.

15 For when Dauid was in Edom, and Ioab the captaine of the hoste had smitten all the males in Edom, and was gone vp to bury ye slaine,

16 (For six moneths did Ioab remaine there, and all Israel, till he had destroyed all the males in Edom)

17 Then this Hadad fled and certaine other Edomites of his fathers seruants with him, to goe into Egypt, Hadad being yet a litle childe.

18 And they arose out of Midian, and came to Paran, and tooke men with them out of Paran, and came to Egypt vnto Pharaoh King of Egypt, which gaue him an house, and appointed him vitailes, and gaue him lande.

19 So Hadad found great fauour in the sight of Pharaoh, and he gaue him to wife the sister of his owne wife, euen the sister of Tahpenes the Queene.

20 And the sister of Tahpenes bare him Genubath his sonne, whome Tahpenes wayned in Pharaohs house: and Genubath was in Pharaohs house among the sonnes of Pharaoh.

21 And when Hadad heard in Egypt, that Dauid slept with his fathers, and that Ioab the captaine of the hoste was dead, Hadad sayde to Pharaoh, Let me depart, that I may goe to mine owne countrey.

22 But Pharaoh saide vnto him, What hast thou lacked with me, that thou wouldest thus go to thine owne countrey? And he answered, Nothing, but in any wise let me goe.

23 And God stirred him vp another aduersarie, Rezon the sonne of Eliada, which fled from his lorde Hadadezer King of Zobah.

24 And he gathered men vnto him, and had bene captaine ouer the company, when Dauid slew them. And they went to Damascus, and dwelt there, and they made him King in Damascus.

25 Therefore was he an aduersarie to Israel all the daies of Salomon: besides the euil that Hadad did, he also abhorred Israel, and reigned ouer Aram

26 And Ieroboam the sonne of Nebat an Ephrathite of Zereda Salomons seruant (whose mother was called Zeruah a widowe) lift vp his hand against the King.

27 And this was the cause that he lift vp his hande against the King, When Salomon built Millo, he repared the broken places of the citie of Dauid his father.

28 And this man Ieroboam was a man of strength and courage, and Salomon seeing that the yong man was meete for the worke, he made him ouerseer of all the labour of the house of Ioseph.

29 And at that time, when Ieroboam went out of Ierusalem, the Prophet Ahiiah the Shilonite founde him in the way, hauing a newe garment on him, and they two were alone in ye field.

30 Then Ahiiah caught the newe garment that was on him, and rent it in twelue pieces,

31 And said to Ieroboam, Take vnto thee ten pieces: for thus saith the Lord God of Israel, Beholde, I wil rent the kingdome out of ye hands of Salomon, and will giue ten tribes to thee.

32 But he shall haue one tribe for my seruant Dauids sake, and for Ierusalem the citie, which I haue chosen out of all the tribes of Israel,

33 Because they haue forsaken me, and haue worshipped Ashtaroth the god of the Zidonians, and Chemosh the god of the Moabites, and Milcom the god of the Ammonites, and haue not walked in my wayes (to do right in mine eyes, and my statutes, and my lawes) as did Dauid his father.

34 But I will not take the whole kingdome out of his hande: for I will make him prince all his life long for Dauid my seruants sake, whome I haue chosen, and who kept my commandements and my statutes.

35 But I will take the kingdome out of his sonnes hand, and will giue it vnto thee, euen the ten tribes.

36 And vnto his sonne will I giue one tribe, that Dauid my seruant may haue a light alway before me in Ierusalem the citie, which I haue chosen me, to put my Name there.

37 And I wil take thee, and thou shalt reigne, euen as thine heart desireth, and shalt be King ouer Israel.

38 And if thou hearken vnto all that I commande thee, and wilt walke in my wayes, and doe right in my sight, to keepe my statutes and my commandements, as Dauid my seruant did, then will I be with thee, and build thee a sure house, as I built vnto Dauid, and wil giue Israel vnto thee.

39 And I will for this afflict the seede of Dauid, but not for euer.

40 Salomon sought therefore to kill Ieroboam, and Ieroboam arose, and fled into Egypt vnto Shishak King of Egypt, and was in Egypt vntil the death of Salomon.

41 And the rest of the wordes of Salomon, and all that he did, and his wisedom, are they not written in the booke of the actes of Salomon?

42 The time that Salomon reigned in Ierusalem ouer all Israel, was fourtie yeere.

43 And Salomon slept with his fathers and was buried in the citie of Dauid his father: and Rehoboam his sonne reigned in his steade.

First Kings 12

1 And Rehoboam went to Shechem: for al Israel were come to Sheche, to make him king

2 And whe Ieroboam ye sonne of Nebat heard of it (who was yet in Egypt, whither Ieroboam had fled from king Salomon, and dwelt in Egypt)

3 Then they sent and called him: and Ieroboam and all the Congregation of Israel came, and spake vnto Rehoboam, saying,

4 Thy father made our yoke grieuous: now therefore make thou the grieuous seruitude of thy father, and his sore yoke which he put vpon vs, lighter, and we will serue thee.

5 And he said vnto them, Depart yet for three dayes, then come againe to me. And the people departed.

6 And King Rehoboam tooke counsell with the olde men that had stande before Salomon his father, while he yet liued, and sayde, What counsell giue ye, that I may make an answere to this people?

7 And they spake vnto him, saying, If thou be a seruant vnto this people this day, and serue them, and answere them, and speake kinde wordes to them, they will be thy seruants for euer.

8 But he forsooke the counsell that the olde men had giuen him, and asked counsell of the yong men that had bene brought vp with him, and waited on him.

9 And he said vnto them, What counsell giue ye, that we may answere this people, which haue spoken to me, saying, Make the yoke, which thy father did put vpon vs, lighter?

10 Then the yong men that were brought vp with him, spake vnto him, saying, Thus shalt thou say vnto this people, that haue spoken vnto thee, and said, Thy father hath made our yoke heauie, but make thou it lighter vnto vs: euen thus shalt thou say vnto them, My least part shalbe bigger then my fathers loynes.

11 Now where as my father did burden you with a grieuous yoke, I will yet make your yoke heauier: my father hath chastised you with rods, but I will correct you with scourges.

12 Then Ieroboam and all the people came to Rehoboam the third day, as the king had appointed, saying, Come to me againe ye thirde day.

13 And the king answered the people sharpely, and left the old mens counsell that they gaue him,

14 And spake to them after the counsell of the yong men, saying, My father made your yoke grieuous, and I will make your yoke more grieuous: my father hath chastised you with rods, but I will correct you with scourges.

15 And the King hearkened not vnto the people: for it was the ordinance of the Lord, that he might perfourme his saying, which the Lord had spoken by Ahiiah the Shilonite vnto Ieroboam the sonne of Nebat.

16 So when all Israel sawe that the King regarded them not, the people answered the King thus, saying, What portion haue we in Dauid? we haue none inheritance in the sonne of Ishai. To your tents, O Israel: nowe see to thine owne house, Dauid. So Israel departed vnto their tents.

17 Howbeit ouer the children of Israel, which dwelt in the cities of Iudah, did Rehoboam reigne still.

18 Nowe the King Rehoboam sent Adoram the receiuer of the tribute, and all Israel stoned him to death: then King Rehoboam made speede to get him vp to his charet, to flee to Ierusalem.

19 And Israel rebelled against the house of Dauid vnto this day.

20 And when all Israel had heard that Ieroboam was come againe, they sent and called him vnto the assemblie, and made him King ouer all Israel: none followed the house of Dauid, but the tribe of Iudah onely.

21 And when Rehoboam was come to Ierusalem, he gathered all the house of Iudah with the tribe of Beniamin an hundreth and foure score thousand of chosen men (which were good warriours) to fight against the house of Israel, and to bring the kingdome againe to Rehoboam the sonne of Salomon.

22 But the worde of God came vnto Shemaiah the man of God, saying,

23 Speake vnto Rehoboam the sonne of Salomon King of Iudah, and vnto all the house of Iudah and Beniamin, and the remnant of the people, saying,

24 Thus saith the Lord, Ye shall not go vp, nor fight against your brethren the children of Israel: returne euery man to his house: for this thing is done by me. They obeyed therefore the worde of the Lord and returned, and departed, according to the worde of the Lord.

25 Then Ieroboam built Shechem in mount Ephraim, and dwelt therein, and went from thence, and built Penuel.

26 And Ieroboam thought in his heart, Nowe shall the kingdome returne to the house of Dauid.

27 If this people goe vp and doe sacrifice in the house of the Lord at Ierusalem, then shall the heart of this people turne againe vnto their lorde, euen to Rehoboam King of Iudah: so shall they kill me and goe againe to Rehoboam King of Iudah.

28 Whereupon the King tooke counsell, and made two calues of golde, and saide vnto them, It is too much for you to goe vp to Ierusalem: beholde, O Israel, thy gods, which brought thee vp out of the lande of Egypt.

29 And he set the one in Beth-el, and the other set he in Dan.

30 And this thing turned to sinne: for the people went (because of the one) euen to Dan.

31 Also he made an house of hie places, and made Priestes of the lowest of the people, which were not of the sonnes of Leui.

32 And Ieroboam made a feast the fifteenth day of the eight moneth, like vnto the feast that is in Iudah, and offred on the altar. So did he in Beth-el and offered vnto the calues that he had made: and he placed in Beth-el the Priestes of the hie places, which he had made.

33 And he offered vpon the altar, which he had made in Beth-el, the fifteenth day of the eight moneth, (euen in the moneth which he had forged of his owne heart) and made a solemne feast vnto the children of Israel: and he went vp to the altar, to burne incense.

First Kings 13

1 And beholde, there came a man of God out of Iudah (by the commandement of the Lord) vnto Beth-el, and Ieroboam stoode by the altar to offer incense.

2 And he cryed against the altar by the comandement of the Lord, and said, O altar, altar, thus saith the Lord, Beholde, a child shalbe borne vnto the house of Dauid, Iosiah by name, and vpon thee shall he sacrifice the Priestes of the hie places that burne incense vpon thee, and they shall burne mens bones vpon thee.

3 And he gaue a signe the same time, saying, This is the signe, that the Lord hath spoken, Behold, the altar shall rent, and the ashes that are vpon it, shall fall out.

4 And when the King had heard the saying of the man of God, which he had cryed against the altar in Beth-el, Ieroboam stretched out his hand from the altar, saying, Lay holde on him: but his hande which he put foorth against him, dryed vp, and he could not pull it in againe to him.

5 The altar also claue asunder, and the ashes fell out from the altar, according to the signe, which the man of God had giuen by the commandement of the Lord.

6 Then the King answered, and saide vnto the man of God, I beseeche thee, pray vnto ye Lord thy God, and make intercession for me, that mine hand may bee restored vnto me. And the man of God besought the Lord, and the Kings hand was restored, and became as it was afore.

7 Then the King sayde vnto the man of God, Come home with mee, that thou mayest dyne, and I will giue thee a reward.

8 But the man of God saide vnto the King, If thou wouldest giue me halfe thine house, I would not goe in with thee, neither woulde I eate bread nor drinke water in this place.

9 For so was it charged mee by the worde of the Lord, saying, Eate no bread nor drinke water, nor turne againe by the same way that thou camest.

10 So he went another way and returned not by the way that he came to Beth-el.

11 And an olde Prophet dwelt in Beth-el, and his sonnes came and tolde him all ye woorkes, that the man of God had done that day in Beth-el, and the wordes which he had spoken vnto the King, tolde they their father.

12 And their father sayde vnto them, What way went he? and his sonnes shewed him what waye the man of God went, which came from Iudah.

13 And hee saide vnto his sonnes, Saddle mee the asse. Who sadled him the asse, and hee rode thereon,

14 And went after the man of God, and found him sitting vnder an oke: and he saide vnto him, Art thou the man of God that camest from Iudah? And he sayd, Yea.

15 Then he said vnto him, Come home with me, and eate bread.

16 But he answered, I may not returne with thee, nor go in with thee, neither wil I eate bread nor drinke water with thee in this place.

17 For it was charged me by the word of the Lord, saying, Thou shalt eate no bread, nor drinke water there, nor turne againe to goe by the way that thou wentest.

18 And he said vnto him, I am a Prophet also as thou art, and an Angel spake vnto me by the worde of the Lord, saying, Bring him againe with thee into thine house, that hee may eate bread and drinke water: but he lyed vnto him.

19 So he went againe with him, and did eate bread in his house, and dranke water.

20 And as they sate at the table, the worde of the Lord came vnto the Prophet, that brought him againe.

21 And hee cried vnto the man of God that came from Iudah, saying, Thus sayeth the Lord, Because thou hast disobeyed the mouth of the Lord, and hast not kept the commandement which the Lord thy God commanded thee,

22 But camest backe againe, and hast eaten bread and drunke water in the place (whereof he did say vnto thee, Thou shalt eate no bread nor drinke any water) thy carkeis shall not come vnto the sepulchre of thy fathers.

23 And when he had eaten bread and drunke, he sadled him the asse, to wit, to the Prophet whome he had brought againe.

24 And when hee was gone, a lion met him by the way, and slewe him, and his body was cast in the way, and the asse stoode thereby: the lion stood by the corps also.

25 And beholde, men that passed by, sawe the carkeis cast in the way, and the lion standing by the corps: and they came and tolde it in ye towne where the olde Prophet dwelt.

26 And when the Prophet that brought him backe againe from the waye, hearde thereof, hee sayde, It is the man of God, who hath bene disobedient vnto the commandement of the Lord: therefore

the Lord hath deliuered him vnto the lion, which hath rent him and slayne him, according to the worde of the Lord, which hee spake vnto him.

27 And he spake to his sonnes, saying, Saddle me the asse. And they sadled him.

28 And he went and founde his body cast in the way, and the asse and the lion stoode by the corps: and the lion had not eaten the bodie, nor torne the asse.

29 And the Prophet tooke vp the body of the man of God, and layed it vpon the asse, and brought it againe, and the olde Prophet came to the citie, to lament and burie him.

30 And hee layed his bodie in his owne graue, and they lamented ouer him, saying, Alas, my brother.

31 And when he had buried him, hee spake to his sonnes, saying, When I am dead, burie ye mee also in the sepulchre, wherein the man of God is buried: lay my bones beside his bones.

32 For that thing which he cried by the word of the Lord against the altar that is in Beth-el, and against all the houses of the hie places, which are in the cities of Samaria, shall surely come to passe.

33 Howbeit after this, Ieroboam conuerted not from his wicked way, but turned againe, and made of the lowest of the people Priests of the hie places. Who would, might consecrate him selfe, and be of the Priestes of the hie places.

34 And this thing turned to sinne vnto the house of Ieroboam, euen to roote it out, and destroy it from the face of the earth.

First Kings 14

1 At that time Abiiah the sonne of Ieroboam fell sicke.

2 And Ieroboam saide vnto his wife, Vp, I pray thee, and disguise thy selfe, that they know not that thou art the wife of Ieroboam, and goe to Shiloh: for there is Ahiiah the Prophet, which tolde mee that I shoulde bee King ouer this people,

3 And take with thee tenne loaues and craknels, and a bottell of honie, and go to him: hee shall tell thee what shall become of the yong man.

4 And Ieroboams wife did so, and arose, and went to Shiloh, and came to the house of Ahiiah: but Ahiiah could not see, for his sight was decayed for his age.

5 Then the Lord saide vnto Ahiiah, Beholde, the wife of Ieroboam commeth to aske a thing of thee for her sonne, for he is sicke: thus and thus shalt thou say vnto her: for when shee commeth in, shee shall feine her selfe to bee another.

6 Therefore when Ahiiah heard the sounde of her feete as shee came in at the doore, hee saide, Come in, thou wife of Ieroboam: why feinest thou thus thy selfe to bee an other? I am sent to thee with heauie tidings.

7 Goe, tel Ieroboam, Thus saith the Lord God of Israel, Forasmuch as I haue exalted thee from among the people, and haue made thee prince ouer my people Israel,

8 And haue rent the kingdome away from the house of Dauid, and haue giuen it thee, and thou hast not bene as my seruant Dauid, which kept my commandements, and followed mee with all his heart, and did onely that which was right in mine eyes,

9 But hast done euil aboue al that were before thee (for thou hast gone and made thee other gods, and molten images, to prouoke me, and hast cast me behinde thy backe)

10 Therefore beholde, I will bring euill vpon the house of Ieroboam, and will cut off from Ieroboam him that pisseth against the wall, aswell him that is shut vp, as him that is left in Israel, and will sweepe away the remnant of the house of Ieroboam, as a man sweepeth away doung, till it be all gone.

11 The dogges shall eate him of Ieroboams stocke that dyeth in the citie, and the foules of the aire shall eate him that dyeth in the fielde: for the Lord hath said it.

12 Vp therefore and get thee to thine house: for when thy feete enter into the citie, the childe shall die.

13 And al Israel shall mourne for him, and burie him: for he onely of Ieroboam shall come to the graue, because in him there is found some goodnes towarde the Lord God of Israel in the house of Ieroboam.

14 Moreouer, the Lord shall stirre him vp a King ouer Israel, which shall destroy the house of Ieroboam in that day: what? yea, euen nowe.

15 For the Lord shall smite Israel, as when a reede is shaken in the water, and hee shall weede Israel out of his good lad, which he gaue to their fathers, and shall scatter them beyond the Riuer, because they haue made them groues, prouoking the Lord to anger.

16 And he shall giue Israel vp, because of the sinnes of Ieroboam, who did sinne, and made Israel to sinne.

17 And Ieroboams wife arose, and departed, and came to Tirzah, and when shee came to the threshold of the house, the yong man dyed,

18 And they buried him, and all Israel lamented him; according to the word of the Lord, which hee spake by the hand of his seruant Ahiiah the Prophet.

19 And the rest of Ieroboams actes, how hee warred, and howe hee reigned, beholde, they are written in the booke of the Chronicles of the Kings of Israel.

20 And the dayes which Ieroboam reigned, were two and twentie yeere: and he slept with his fathers, and Nadab his sonne reigned in his steade.

21 Also Rehoboam the sonne of Salomon reigned in Iudah. Rehoboam was one and fourtie yere olde, when he began to reigne, and reigned seuenteene yere in Ierusalem, the citie which the Lord did chuse out of al the tribes of Israel, to put his Name there: and his mothers name was Naamah an Ammonite.

22 And Iudah wrought wickednesse in the sight of the Lord: and they prouoked

him more with their sinnes, which they had committed, then all that which their fathers had done.

23 For they also made them hie places, and images, and groues on euery hie hill, and vnder euery greene tree.

24 There were also Sodomites in the lande, they did according to all the abominations of the nations, which the Lord had cast out before the children of Israel.

25 And in the fift yere of King Rehoboam, Shishak King of Egypt came vp against Ierusale,

26 And tooke the treasures of the house of the Lord, and the treasures of the Kings house, and tooke away all: also he caried away all the shields of golde which Salomon had made.

27 And King Rehoboam made for them brasen shieldes, and committed them vnto ye hands of the chiefe of the garde, which wayted at the doore of the Kings house.

28 And when the King went into the house of the Lord, the garde bare them, and brought them againe into the gard chamber.

29 And the rest of the actes of Rehoboam, and all that hee did, are they not written in the booke of the Chronicles of the Kings of Iudah?

30 And there was warre betweene Rehoboam and Ieroboam continually.

31 And Rehoboam slept with his fathers, and was buried with his fathers in the citie of Dauid: his mothers name was Naamah an Ammonite. And Abiiam his sonne reigned in his stead.

First Kings 15

1 And in the eighteenth yeere of King Ieroboam the sonne of Nebat, reigned Abiiam ouer Iudah.

2 Three yeere reigned hee in Ierusalem, and his mothers name was Maachah the daughter of Abishalom.

3 And hee walked in all the sinnes of his father, which hee had done before him: and his heart was not perfit with the Lord his God as the heart of Dauid his father.

4 But for Dauids sake did the Lord his God giue him a light in Ierusalem, and set vp his sonne after him, and established Ierusalem,

5 Because Dauid did that which was right in the sight of the Lord, and turned from nothing that he commanded him, all the dayes of his life, saue onely in the matter of Vriah the Hittite.

6 And there was warre betweene Rehoboam and Ieroboam as long as he liued.

7 The rest also of the actes of Abiiam, and all that he did, are they not written in the booke of the Chronicles of the Kings of Iudah? there was also warre betweene Abiiam, and Ieroboam.

8 And Abiiam slept with his fathers, and they buried him in the citie of Dauid: and Asa his sonne reigned in his steade.

9 And in the twentie yeere of Ieroboam King of Israel reigned Asa ouer Iudah.

10 He reigned in Ierusalem one and fourtie yeere, and his mothers name was Maachah the daughter of Abishalom.

11 And Asa did right in the eyes of the Lord, as did Dauid his father.

12 And he tooke away the Sodomites out of the lande, and put away all the idoles that his fathers had made.

13 And he put downe Maachah his mother also from her estate, because shee had made an idole in a groue: and Asa destroyed her idoles, and burnt them by the brooke Kidron.

14 But they put not downe the hie places. Neuertheles Asas heart was vpright with the Lord all his dayes.

15 Also he brought in the holy vessels of his father, and the things that he had dedicated vnto ye house of the Lord, siluer, and golde, and vessels.

16 And there was warre betweene Asa and Baasha King of Israel all their dayes.

17 Then Baasha king of Israel went vp against Iudah, and buylt Ramah, so that he woulde let none go out or in to Asa King of Iudah.

18 Then Asa tooke all the siluer and the gold that was left in the treasures of the house of the Lord, and the treasures of the kings house, and deliuered them into the handes of his seruantes, and King Asa sent them to Ben-hadad the sonne of Tabrimon, the sonne of Hezion king of Aram that dwelt at Damascus, saying,

19 There is a couenant betweene me and thee, and betweene my father and thy father: behold, I haue sent vnto thee a present of siluer and golde: come, breake thy couenant with Baasha King of Israel, that he may depart from me.

20 So Ben-hadad hearkened vnto King Asa, and sent the captaines of the hosts, which he had, against the cities of Israel, and smote lion, and Dan, and Abel-beth-maachah, and all Cinneroth, with all the land of Naphtali.

21 And when Baasha heard thereof, hee left buylding of Ramah, and dwelt in Tirzah.

22 Then king Asa assembled al Iudah, none excepted. and they tooke the stones of Ramah, and the timber thereof, wherewith Baasha had buylt, and King Asa built with them Geba of Beniamin and Mizpah.

23 And the rest of all the actes of Asa, and all his might, and all that he did, and the cities which he buylt, are they not written in the booke of the Chronicles of the Kings of Iudah? but in his olde age he was diseased in his feete.

24 And Asa slept with his fathers, and was buried with his fathers in the citie of Dauid his father. And Iehoshaphat his sonne reigned in his steade.

25 And Nadab the sonne of Ieroboam began to reigne ouer Israel the second yere of Asa King of Iudah, and reigned ouer Israel two yeere.

26 And he did euill in the sight of the Lord, walking in the way of his father, and in his sinne wherewith he made Israel to sinne.

27 And Baasha the sonne of Ahijah of ye house of Issachar conspired against him, and Baasha slue him at Gibbethon, which belonged to the Philistims: for Nadab and all Israel layde siege to Gibbethon.

28 Euen in the third yeere of Asa King of Iudah did Baasha slay him, and reigned in his steade.

29 And when he was King, he smote all the house of Ieroboam, he left none aliue to Ieroboam, vntill hee had destroyed him, according to the word of the Lord which he spake by his seruant Ahijah the Shilonite,

30 Because of the sinnes of Ieroboam which he committed, and wherewith he made Israel to sinne, by his prouocation, wherewith he prouoked the Lord God of Israel.

31 And the residue of the actes of Nadab, and all that he did, are they not written in the booke of the Chronicles of the Kings of Israel?

32 And there was warre betweene Asa and Baasha King of Israel, all their dayes.

33 In the thirde yeere of Asa King of Iudah, began Baasha the sonne of Ahijah to reigne ouer all Israel in Tirzah, and reigned foure and twentie yeeres.

34 And he did euill in the sight of the Lord, walking in the way of Ieroboam, and in his sinne, wherewith he made Israel to sinne.

First Kings 16

1 Then the word of the Lord came to Iehu the sonne of Hanani against Baasha, saying,

2 Forasmuch as I exalted thee out of the dust, and made thee captaine ouer my people Israel, and thou hast walked in the way of Ieroboam, and hast made my people Israel to sinne, to prouoke me with their sinnes,

3 Beholde, I will take away the posteritie of Baasha, and the posteritie of his house, and will make thine house like the house of Ieroboam the sonne of Nebat.

4 He that dyeth of Baashas stocke in the citie, him shall the dogs eate: and that man of him which dyeth in the fieldes, shall the foules of the ayre eate.

5 And the rest of the actes of Baasha and what he did, and his power, are they not written in the booke of the Chronicles of the kings of Israel?

6 So Baasha slept with his fathers, and was buryed in Tirzah, and Elah his sonne reigned in his steade.

7 And also by the hande of Iehu the sonne of Hanani the Prophet, came the worde of the Lord to Baasha, and to his house, that he shoulde be like the house of Ieroboam, euen for all the wickednes that he did in the sight of the Lord, in prouoking him with the worke of his hands, and because he killed him.

8 In the sixe and twentie yeere of Asa king of Iudah began Elah ye sonne of Baasha to reigne ouer Israel in Tirzah, and reigned two yeere.

9 And his seruant Zimri, captaine of halfe his charets, conspired against him,

as he was in Tirzah drinking, til he was drunken in the house of Arza steward of his house in Tirzah.

10 And Zimri came and smote him and killed him, in the seuen and twentie yeere of Asa king of Iudah, and reigned in his stead.

11 And when he was King, and sate on his throne, he slew al the house of Baasha, not leauing thereof one to pisse against a wall, neither of his kinsfolkes nor of his friendes.

12 So did Zimri destroy all the house of Baasha, according to the word of the Lord which he spake against Baasha by the hande of Iehu the Prophet,

13 For all the sinnes of Baasha, and sinnes of Elah his sonne, which they sinned and made Israel to sinne, and prouoked the Lord God of Israel with their vanities.

14 And the rest of the actes of Elah, and all that he did, are they not written in the booke of the Chronicles of the Kings of Israel?

15 In the seuen and twentie yeere of Asa King of Iudah did Zimri reigne seuen dayes in Tirzah, and the people was then in campe against Gibbethon, which belonged to the Philistims.

16 And the people of the hoste heard saye, Zimri hath conspired, and hath also slayne the King. Wherefore all Israel made Omri the captaine of the hoste, king ouer Israel that same day, euen in the hoste.

17 Then Omri went vp from Gibbethon, and all Israel with him, and they besieged Tirzah.

18 And when Zimri saw, that the citie was taken, he went into the palace of the Kings house, and burnt himselfe, and the Kings house with fire, and so dyed,

19 For his sinnes which hee sinned, in doing that which is euil in the sight of the Lord, in walking in the way of Ieroboam, and in his sinnes which he did, causing Israel to sinne.

20 And the rest of the actes of Zimri, and his treason that hee wrought, are they not written in the booke of the Chronicles of the Kinges of Israel?

21 Then were the people of Israel deuided into two partes: for halfe the people followed Tibni the sonne of Ginath to make him King, and the other halfe followed Omri.

22 But the people that folowed Omri, preuayled against the people that followed Tibni the sonne of Ginath: so Tibni dyed, and Omri reigned.

23 In the one and thirtie yeere of Asa King of Iudah bega Omri to reigne ouer Israel, and reigned twelue yeere. Sixe yeere reigned he in Tirzah.

24 And he bought the mountaine Samaria of one Shemer for two talents of siluer, and buylt in the mountaine, and called the name of the citie, which he buylt, after the name of Shemer lord of the mountaine, Samaria.

25 But Omri did euil in the eyes of the Lord, and did worse then all that were before him.

26 For he walked in all the way of Ieroboam the sonne of Nebat, and in his sinnes wherewith he made Israel to sinne in prouoking the Lord God of Israel with their vanities.

27 And the rest of the actes of Omri, that hee did, and his strength that he shewed, are they not written in the booke of the Chronicles of the Kings of Israel?

28 And Omri slept with his fathers, and was buryed in Samaria: and Ahab his sonne reigned in his stead.

29 Nowe Ahab the sonne of Omri began to reigne ouer Israel, in the eyght and thirtie yeere of Asa king of Iudah: and Ahab the sonne of Omri reigned ouer Israel in Samaria two and twenty yere.

30 And Ahab the sonne of Omri did worse in ye sight of the Lord then al that were before him.

31 For was it a light thing for him to walke in the sinnes of Ieroboam the sonne of Nebat, except hee tooke Iezebel also the daughter of Ethbaal King of the Zidonians to wife, and went and serued Baal, and worshipped him?

32 Also he reared vp an altar to Baal in the house of Baal, which he had buylt in Samaria.

33 And Ahab made a groue, and Ahab proceeded, and did prouoke the Lord God of Israel more then all the kings of Israel that were before him.

34 In his dayes did Hiel the Bethelite buylde Iericho: he layed the foundation thereof in Abiram his eldest sonne, and set vp the gates thereof in his yongest sonne Segub, according to the worde of the Lord which he spake by Ioshua the sonne of Nun.

First Kings 17

1 And Eliiah the Tishbite one of the inhabitats of Gilead sayde vnto Ahab, As the Lord God of Israel liueth, before whom I stand, there shall be neither dewe nor rayne these yeeres, but according to my worde.

2 And the worde of the Lord came vnto him, saying,

3 Go hence, and turne thee Eastwarde, and hide thy selfe in the riuer Cherith, that is ouer against Iorden,

4 And thou shalt drinke of the riuer: and I haue comanded the rauens to feede thee there.

5 So he went and did according vnto the word of the Lord: for he went, and remained by the riuer Cherith that is ouer against Iorden.

6 And the rauens brought him bread and flesh in the morning, and bread and flesh in the euening, and he dranke of the riuer.

7 And after a while the riuer dryed vp, because there fell no rayne vpon the earth.

8 And the worde of the Lord came vnto him, saying,

9 Vp, and get thee to Zarephath, which is in Zidon, and remaine there: beholde, I haue commanded a widow there to sustaine thee.

10 So he arose, and went to Zarephath: and when he came to the gate of the citie, beholde, the widowe was there gathering stickes: and he called her, and sayde, Bring me, I pray thee, a litle water in a vessel, that I may drinke.

11 And as she was going to fet it, he called to her, and sayde, Bring me, I pray thee, a morsell of bread in thine hand.

12 And shee sayde, As the Lord thy God liueth, I haue not a cake, but euen an handfull of meale in a barrel, and a litle oyle in a cruse: and behold, I am gathering a fewe stickes for to go in, and dresse it for me and my sonne, that we may eate it, and dye.

13 And Eliiah said vnto her, Feare not, come, do as thou hast sayd, but make me thereof a litle cake first of all, and bring it vnto mee, and afterward make for thee, and thy sonne.

14 For thus saith the Lord God of Israel, The meale in the barrel shall not be wasted, neither shall the oyle in the cruse be diminished, vnto the time that the Lord send rayne vpon the earth.

15 So she went, and did as Eliiah sayd, and she did eate: so did he and her house for a certaine time.

16 The barrell of the meale wasted not, nor the oyle was spent out of the cruse, according to the worde of the Lord, which he spake by the hand of Eliiah.

17 And after these things, the sonne of the wife of the house fell sicke, and his sicknesse was so sore, that there was no breath left in him.

18 And she said vnto Eliiah, What haue I to do with thee, O thou man of God? art thou come vnto me to call my sinne to remembrance, and to slay my sonne?

19 And he said vnto her, Giue me thy sonne. and he tooke him out of her bosome, and caryed him vp into a chamber, where he abode, and laid him vpon his owne bed.

20 Then he called vnto the Lord, and sayde, O Lord my God, hast thou punished also this widowe, with whome I soiourne, by killing her sonne?

21 And he stretched himselfe vpon the childe three times, and called vnto the Lord, and saide, O Lord my God, I pray thee, let this childes soule come into him againe.

22 Then the Lord heard the voyce of Eliiah, and the soule of the child came into him againe, and he reuiued.

23 And Eliiah tooke the childe, and brought him downe out of the chamber into the house, and deliuered him vnto his mother, and Eliiah sayd, Behold, thy sonne liueth.

24 And the woman saide vnto Eliiah, Now I knowe that thou art a man of God, and that the worde of the Lord in thy mouth is true.

First Kings 18

1 After many dayes, the worde of the Lord came to Eliiah, in the third yeere, saying, Goe, shewe thy selfe vnto Ahab, and I will sende rayne vpon the earth.

2 And Eliiah went to shew himselfe vnto Ahab, and there was a great famine in Samaria.

3 And Ahab called Obadiah the gouernour of his house: (and Obadiah feared God greatly:

4 For when Iezebel destroyed the Prophets of the Lord, Obadiah tooke an hundreth Prophets, and hid them, by fiftie in a caue, and he fed them with bread and water.)

5 And Ahab saide vnto Obadiah, Goe into the land, vnto all the fountaines of water, and vnto all the riuers, if so be that we may finde grasse to saue the horses and the mules aliue, lest we depriue the lande of the beastes.

6 And so they deuided the lande betweene them to walke thorowe it. Ahab went one way by him selfe, and Obadiah went another way by him selfe.

7 And as Obadiah was in the way, behold, Eliiah met him: and he knew him, and fell on his face, and said, Art not thou my lord Eliiah?

8 And he answered him, Yea, goe tell thy lord, Behold, Eliiah is here.

9 And he said, What haue I sinned, that thou wouldest deliuer thy seruant into the hande of Ahab, to slay me?

10 As the Lord thy God liueth, there is no nation or kingdome, whither my lorde hath not sent to seeke thee: and when they sayd, He is not here, he tooke an othe of the kingdome and nation, if they had not found thee.

11 And now thou sayest, Goe, tell thy lorde, Beholde, Eliiah is here.

12 And when I am gone from thee, the Spirit of the Lord shall cary thee into some place that I doe not know: so when I come and tell Ahab, if he cannot finde thee, then wil he kill me: But I thy seruant feare the Lord from my youth.

13 Was it not tolde my lord, what I did when Iezebel slew the Prophets of the Lord, how I hid an hundreth men of the Lordes Prophets by fifties in a caue, and fed them with bread and water?

14 And now thou sayest, Go, tel thy lord, Behold, Eliiah is here, that he may slay me.

15 And Eliiah said, As the Lord of hostes liueth, before whome I stand, I will surely shewe my selfe vnto him this day.

16 So Obadiah went to meete Ahab, and tolde him: And Ahab went to meete Eliiah.

17 And when Ahab saw Eliiah, Ahab said vnto him, Art thou he that troubleth Israel?

18 And he answered, I haue not troubled Israel, but thou, and thy fathers house, in that ye haue forsaken the commandements of the Lord, and thou hast followed Baalim.

19 Now therefore send, and gather to me all Israel vnto mount Carmel, and the prophets of Baal foure hundreth and fiftie, and the prophets of the groues foure hundreth, which eate at Iezebels table.

20 So Ahab sent vnto all the children of Israel, and gathered the prophets together vnto mount Carmel.

21 And Eliiah came vnto all the people, and said, How long halt ye betweene two opinions? If the Lord be God, follow him: but if Baal be he, then goe after him. And the people answered him not a worde.

22 Then said Eliiah vnto the people, I onely remayne a Prophet of the Lord: but Baals prophets are foure hundreth and fiftie men.

23 Let them therefore giue vs two bullockes, and let them chuse the one, and cut him in pieces, and lay him on the wood, but put no fire vnder, and I will prepare the other bullocke, and lay him on the wood, and will put no fire vnder.

24 Then call ye on the name of your god, and I will call on the name of the Lord: and then the God that answereth by fire, let him be God. And all the people answered, and sayde, It is well spoken.

25 And Eliiah said vnto the prophets of Baal, Chuse you a bullocke, and prepare him first, (for ye are many) and call on the name of your gods, but put no fire vnder.

26 So they tooke the one bullocke, that was giuen them, and they prepared it, and called on the name of Baal, from morning to noone, saying, O Baal, heare vs: but there was no voyce, nor any to answere: and they leapt vpon the altar that was made.

27 And at noone Eliiah mocked them, and said, Crye loude: for he is a god: either he talketh or pursueth his enemies, or is in his iourney, or it may be that he sleepeth, and must be awaked.

28 And they cryed loude, and cut them selues as their maner was, with kniues and launcers, till the blood gushed out vpon them.

29 And when midday was passed, and they had prophecied vntil the offring of the euening sacrifice, there was neither voyce, nor one to answere, nor any that regarded.

30 And Eliiah said vnto all the people, Come to me. And all the people came to him. And he repayred the altar of the Lord that was broken downe.

31 And Eliiah tooke twelue stones, according to the nomber of the tribes of the sonnes of Iaakob, (vnto whome the worde of the Lord came, saying, Israel shalbe thy name)

32 And with the stones he buylt an altar in the Name of the Lord: and he made a ditch round about the altar, as great as woulde conteine two measures of seede.

33 And he put the wood in order, and hewed the bullocke in pieces, and layd him on the wood,

34 And said, Fill foure barrels with water, and powre it on the burnt offring and on the wood. Againe he said, Doe so againe. And they did so the second time. And he sayde, Doe it the third time. And they did it the third time.

35 And the water ran round about the altar: and he filled the ditch with water also.

36 And when they should offer the euening sacrifice, Eliiah the Prophet came, and sayd, Lord God of Abraham, Izhak and of Israel, let it be knowen this day, that thou art the God of Israel, and that I am thy seruant, and that I haue done all these things at thy commandement.

37 Heare me, O Lord, heare me, and let this people know that thou art the Lord God, and that thou hast turned their heart againe at the last.

38 Then the fire of the Lord fell, and consumed the burnt offring, and the wood, and the stones, and the dust, and licked vp the water that was in the ditche.

39 And when all the people sawe it, they fell on their faces, and saide, The Lord is God, the Lord is God.

40 And Elijah said vnto them, Take the prophets of Baal, let not a man of them escape. and they tooke them, and Eliiah brought them to the brooke Kishon, and slewe them there.

41 And Eliiah sayde vnto Ahab, Get thee vp, eate and drinke, for there is a sound of much rayne.

42 So Ahab went vp to eate and to drinke, and Eliiah went vp to the top of Carmel: and he crouched vnto the earth, and put his face betweene his knees,

43 And sayde to his seruant, Goe vp now and looke towarde the way of the Sea. And he went vp, and looked, and sayde, There is nothing. Againe he sayd, Goe againe seuen times.

44 And at the seuenth time he sayd, Behold, there ariseth a litle cloude out of the sea like a mans hand. Then he sayd, Vp, and say vnto Ahab, Make readie thy charet, and get thee downe, that the raine stay thee not.

45 And in the meane while the heauen was blacke with cloudes and winde, and there was a great rayne. Then Ahab went vp and came to Izreel.

46 And the hand of the Lord was on Eliiah, and he girded vp his Ioynes, and ran before Ahab till he came to Izreel.

First Kings 19

1 Now Ahab tolde Iezebel all that Eliiah had done, and how he had slaine all the prophets with the sword.

2 Then Iezebel sent a messenger vnto Eliiah, saying, The gods doe so to me and more also, if I make not thy life like one of their liues by to morowe this time.

3 When he sawe that, he arose, and went for his life, and came to Beersheba, which is in Iudah, and left his seruant there.

4 But he went a dayes iourney into the wildernesse, and came and sate downe vnder a iuniper tree, and desired that he might die, and sayde, It is now ynough: O Lord, take my soule, for I am no better then my fathers.

5 And as he lay and slept vnder the iuniper tree, behold now, an Angel touched him, and said vnto him, Vp, and eate.

6 And when he looked about, behold, there was a cake baken on the coles, and a pot of water at his head: so he did eate and drinke, and returned and slept.

7 And the Angel of the Lord came againe the second time, and touched him, and sayd, Vp, and eate: for thou hast a great iourney.

8 Then he arose, and did eate and drinke, and walked in the strength of that meate fourtie dayes and fourtie nights, vnto Horeb the mount of God.

9 And there he entred into a caue, and lodged there: and beholde, the Lord spake to him, and said vnto him, What doest thou here, Eliiah?

10 And he answered, I haue bene very ielous for the Lord God of hostes: for the children of Israel haue forsaken thy couenant, broken downe thine altars, and slayne thy Prophets with the sword, and I onely am left, and they seeke my life to take it away.

11 And he saide, Come out, and stand vpon the mount before the Lord. And beholde, the Lord went by, and a mightie strong winde rent the mountaines, and brake the rockes before the Lord: but the Lord was not in the winde: and after the wind came an earthquake: but the Lord was not in the earthquake:

12 And after the earthquake came fire: but the Lord was not in the fire: and after the fire came a still and soft voyce.

13 And when Eliiah heard it, he couered his face with his mantel, and went out, and stoode in the entring in of ye caue: and behold, there came a voyce vnto him, and sayd, What doest thou here, Eliiah?

14 And he answered, I haue bene very ielous for the Lord God of hostes, because the children of Israel haue forsaken thy couenant, cast downe thine altars, and slayne thy Prophets with the sworde, and I onely am left, and they seeke my life to take it away.

15 And the Lord said vnto him, Goe, returne by the wildernes vnto Damascus, and when thou commest there, anoint Hazael King ouer Aram.

16 And Iehu the sonne of Nimshi shalt thou anoynt King ouer Israel: and Elisha the sonne of Shaphat of Abel Meholah shalt thou anoynt to be Prophet in thy roume.

17 And him that escapeth from the sworde of Hazael, shall Iehu slay: and him that escapeth from the sword of Iehu, shall Elisha slay.

18 Yet wil I leaue seuen thousand in Israel, euen all the knees that haue not bowed vnto Baal, and euery mouth that hath not kissed him.

19 So he departed thence, and found Elisha the sonne of Shaphat who was plowing with twelue yoke of oxen before him, and was with the twelft: and Eliiah went towards him, and cast his mantel vpon him.

20 And he left the oxen, and ran after Eliiah, and sayde, Let mee, I pray thee, kisse my father and my mother, and then I wil follow thee. Who answered him, Go, returne: for what haue I done to thee?

21 And when he went backe againe from him, he tooke a couple of oxen, and slewe them, and sod their flesh with the

instruments of the oxen, and gaue vnto the people, and they did eate: then he arose and went after Eliiah, and ministred vnto him.

First Kings 20

1 Then Ben-hadad the King of Aram assembled all his armie, and two and thirtie Kings with him, with horses, and charets, and went vp and besieged Samaria, and fought against it.

2 And he sent messengers to Ahab King of Israel, into the citie,

3 And sayd vnto him, Thus sayth Ben-hadad, Thy siluer and thy golde is mine: also thy women, and thy fayre children are mine.

4 And the King of Israel answered, and sayd, My lord King, according to thy saying, I am thine, and all that I haue.

5 And when the messengers came againe, they said, Thus commandeth Ben-hadad, and saith, When I shall send vnto thee, and command, thou shalt deliuer me thy siluer and thy golde, and thy women, and thy children,

6 Or els I will sende my seruants vnto thee by to morow this time: and they shall search thine house, and the houses of thy seruants: and whatsoeuer is pleasant in thine eyes, they shall take it in their handes, and bring it away.

7 Then the King of Israel sent for all the Elders of the land, and sayd, Take heede, I pray you, and see how he seeketh mischiefe: for he sent vnto me for my wiues, and for my children, and for my siluer, and for my golde, and I denyed him not.

8 And all the Elders, and all the people sayd to him, Hearken not vnto him, nor consent.

9 Wherefore hee sayde vnto the messengers of Ben-hadad, Tell my lorde the King, All that thou didddest sende for to thy seruant at the first time, that I will doe, but this thing I may not do. And the messengers departed, and brought him an answere.

10 And Ben-hadad sent vnto him, and sayde, The gods do so to me and more also, if the dust of Samaria be ynough to all the people that follow me, for euery man an handfull.

11 And the King of Israel answered, and sayd, Tell him, Let not him that girdeth his harneis, boast himselfe, as he that putteth it off.

12 And when he heard that tidings, as he was with the Kings drinking in the pauilions, he sayd vnto his seruants, Bring forth your engines, and they set them against the citie.

13 And beholde, there came a Prophet vnto Ahab King of Israel, saying, Thus sayeth the Lord, Hast thou seene all this great multitude? beholde, I will deliuer it into thine hande this day, that thou mayest knowe, that I am the Lord.

14 And Ahab sayd, By whome? And he sayde, Thus sayth the Lord, By the seruants of the princes of the prouinces. He sayde againe, Who shall order the battel? And he answered, Thou.

15 Then he nombred the seruantes of the princes of the prouinces, and they were two hundreth, two and thirtie: and after them he nombred the whole people of all the children of Israel, euen seuen thousand.

16 And they went out at noone: but Ben-hadad did drinke till he was drunken in the tentes, both he and the Kings: for two and thirtie Kings helped him.

17 So the seruants of the princes of the prouinces went out first: and Ben-hadad sent out, and they shewed him, saying, There are men come out of Samaria.

18 And he sayde, Whether they be come out for peace, take them aliue: or whether they bee come out to fight, take them yet aliue.

19 So they came out of the citie, to wit, the seruants of the princes of the prouinces, and the hoste which followed them.

20 And they slew euery one his enemie: and the Aramites fled, and Israel pursued them: but Ben-hadad ye King of Aram escaped on an horse with his horsemen.

21 And the King of Israel went out, and smote the horses and charets, and with a great slaughter slew he the Aramites.

22 (For there had come a Prophet to the King of Israel, and had sayd vnto him, Goe, be of good courage, and consider, and take heede what thou doest: for when the yeere is gone about, the King of Aram wil come vp against thee)

23 Then the seruants of the King of Aram said vnto him, Their gods are gods of the moutaines, and therefore they ouercame vs: but let vs fight against them in the playne, and doubtlesse we shall ouercome them.

24 And this doe, Take the Kings away, euery one out of his place, and place captaines for them.

25 And nomber thy selfe an armie, like the armie that thou hast lost, with such horses, and such charets, and we wil fight against them in the plaine, and doubtlesse we shall ouercome them: and he hearkened vnto their voyce, and did so.

26 And after the yeere was gone about, Ben-hadad nombred the Aramites, and went vp to Aphek to fight against Israel.

27 And the children of Israel were nombred, and were all assembled and went against them, and the children of Israel pitched before them, like two litle flockes of kiddes: but the Aramites filled the countrey.

28 And there came a man of God, and spake vnto the King of Israel, saying, Thus sayeth the Lord, Because the Aramites haue sayd, The Lord is the God of the mountaines, and not God of the valleis, therefore will I deliuer all this great multitude into thine hand, and ye shall know that I am the Lord.

29 And they pitched one ouer against the other seuen dayes, and in the seuenth day the battel was ioyned: and the children of Israel slew of the Aramites an hundreth thousand footemen in one day.

30 But the rest fled to Aphek into the citie: and there fel a wall vpon seuen and twentie thousand men that were left: and Ben-hadad fled into the citie, and came into a secret chamber.

31 And his seruants sayd vnto him, Beholde nowe, we haue heard say that the Kings of the house of Israel are mercifull Kings: we pray thee, let vs put sacke cloth about our loynes, and ropes about our heads, and goe out to the King of Israel: it may be that he will saue thy life.

32 Then they gyrded sackecloth about their loynes, and put ropes about their heads, and came to the King of Israel, and sayd, Thy seruant Ben-hadad sayth, I pray thee, let me liue: and he sayd, Is he yet aliue? he is my brother.

33 Now the men tooke diliget heede, if they could catch any thing of him, and made haste, and sayd, Thy brother Ben-hadad. And he sayd, Go, bring him. So Ben-hadad came out vnto him, and he caused him to come vp vnto the chariot.

34 And Ben-hadad sayd vnto him, The cities, which my father tooke from thy father, I wil restore, and thou shalt make streetes for thee in Damascus, as my father did in Samaria. Then said Ahab, I will let thee goe with this couenant. So he made a couenant with him, and let him goe.

35 Then a certaine man of the children of the Prophets sayd vnto his neighbour by the comandement of the Lord, Smite me, I pray thee. But the man refused to smite him.

36 Then sayd he vnto him, Because thou hast not obeyed the voyce of the Lord, beholde, as soone as thou art departed from me, a lyon shall slay thee. So when he was departed from him, a lyon found him and slew him.

37 Then he founde another man, and sayde, Smite mee, I pray thee. And the man smote him, and in smiting wounded him.

38 So the Prophet departed, and wayted for the King by the way, and disguised himselfe with ashes vpon his face.

39 And when the King came by, he cried vnto the King, and said, Thy seruant went into the middes of the battel: and beholde, there went away a man, whom another man brought vnto me, and sayd, Keepe this man: if he be lost, and want, thy life shall go for his life, or els thou shalt pay a talent of siluer.

40 And as thy seruant had here and there to do, he was gone: And the King of Israel said vnto him, So shall thy iudgement be: thou hast giuen sentence.

41 And hee hasted, and tooke the ashes away from his face: and the King of Israel knewe him that he was of the Prophets:

42 And he said vnto him, Thus saith the Lord, Because thou hast let goe out of thine handes a man whom I appoynted to dye, thy life shall goe for his life, and thy people for his people.

43 And the King of Israel went to his house heauie and in displeasure, and came to Samaria.

First Kings 21

1 After these things Naboth the Izreelite had a vineyarde in Izreel, hard by the palace of Ahab King of Samaria.

2 And Ahab spake vnto Naboth, saying, Giue me thy vineyarde, that I may make mee a garden of herbes thereof, because it is neere by mine house: and I will giue thee for it a better vineyarde then it is: or if it please thee, I will giue thee the worth of it in money.

3 And Naboth said to Ahab, The Lord keepe me from giuing the inheritance of my father vnto thee.

4 Then Ahab came into his house heauie and in displeasure, because of the word which Naboth the Izreelite had spoken vnto him. for hee had sayde, I will not giue thee the inheritance of my fathers, and he lay vpon his bed, and turned his face and would eate no bread.

5 Then Iezebel his wife came to him and said vnto him, Why is thy spirit so sad that thou eatest no bread?

6 And he said vnto her, Because I spake vnto Naboth the Izreelite, and sayd vnto him, Giue me thy vineyard for money, or if it please thee, I will giue thee another vineyard for it: but he answered, I wil not giue thee my vineyard.

7 Then Iezebel his wife sayde vnto him, Doest thou nowe gouerne the kingdome of Israel? vp, eate bread, and be of good cheere, I will giue thee the vineyard of Naboth the Izreelite.

8 So she wrote letters in Ahabs name, and sealed them with his seale, and sent the letters vnto the Elders, and to the nobles that were in his citie dwelling with Naboth.

9 And shee wrote in the letters, saying, Proclaime a fast, and set Naboth among the chiefe of the people,

10 And set two wicked men before him, and let them witnesse against him, saying, Thou diddest blaspheme God and the King: then cary him out, and stone him that he may dye.

11 And the men of his citie, euen the Elders and gouernours, which dwelt in his citie, did as Iezebel had sent vnto them: as it was written in the letters, which she had sent vnto them.

12 They proclaimed a fast, and set Naboth among the chiefe of the people,

13 And there came two wicked men, and sate before him: and the wicked men witnessed against Naboth in the presence of the people saying, Naboth did blaspheme God and the King. Then they caried him away out of the citie, and stoned him with stones, that he dyed.

14 Then they sent to Iezebel, saying, Naboth is stoned and is dead.

15 And when Iezebel heard that Naboth was stoned and was dead, Iezebel sayd to Ahab, Vp, and take possession of the vineyarde of Naboth the Izreelite, which he refused to giue thee for money: for Naboth is not aliue, but is dead.

16 And when Ahab heard that Naboth was dead, he rose to go downe to the vineyard of Naboth the Izreelite, to take possession of it.

17 And the word of the Lord came vnto Eliiah the Tishbite, saying,

18 Arise, goe downe to meete Ahab King of Israel, which is in Samaria. loe, he is in the vineyarde of Naboth, whither he is gone downe to take possession of it.

19 Therefore shalt thou say vnto him, Thus sayth the Lord, Hast thou killed, and also gotten possession? And thou shalt speake vnto him, saying, Thus sayth the Lord, In the place where dogs licked the blood of Naboth, shall dogs licke euen thy blood also.

20 And Ahab sayd to Eliiah, Hast thou found mee, O mine enemie? And he answered, I haue found thee: for thou hast solde thy selfe to worke wickednes in the sight of the Lord.

21 Beholde, I will bring euill vpon thee, and wil take away thy posteritie, and wil cut off from Ahab him that pisseth against the wall, as well him that is shut vp, as him that is left in Israel,

22 And I wil make thine house like the house of Ieroboam the sonne of Nebat, and like the house of Baasha the sonne of Ahiiah, for the prouocation wherewith thou hast prouoked, and made Israel to sinne.

23 And also of Iezebel spake the Lord, saying, The dogs shall eate Iezebel, by the wall of Izreel.

24 The dogs shall eate him of Ahabs stocke, that dyeth in the citie: and him that dyeth in the fieldes, shall the foules of the ayre eate.

25 (But there was none like Ahab, who did fell him selfe, to worke wickednesse in the sight of the Lord: whom Iezebel his wife prouoked.

26 For he did exceeding abominably in following idoles, according to all that the Amorites did, whom the Lord cast out before the children of Israel.)

27 Nowe when Ahab heard those wordes, he rent his clothes, and put sackcloth vpon him and fasted, and lay in sackecloth and went softely.

28 And the worde of the Lord came to Eliiah the Tishbite, saying,

29 Seest thou how Ahab is humbled before me? because he submitteth himselfe before me, I will not bring that euill in his dayes, but in his sonnes dayes wil I bring euill vpon his house.

First Kings 22

1 And they continued three yeere without warre betweene Aram and Israel.

2 And in the third yeere did Iehoshaphat the King of Iudah come downe to ye King of Israel.

3 (Then the King of Israel saide vnto his seruants, Knowe yee not that Ramoth Gilead was ours? and wee stay, and take it not out of ye hand of the King of Aram?)

4 And he sayde vnto Iehoshaphat, Wilt thou goe with mee to battell against Ramoth Gilead? And Iehoshaphat saide vnto the King of Israel, I am as thou art, my people as thy people, and mine horses as thine horses.

5 Then Iehoshaphat saide vnto the King of Israel, Aske counsaile, I pray thee, of the Lord to day.

6 Then the King of Israel gathered the prophets vpon a foure hundreth men, and said vnto them, Shal I go against Ramoth Gilead to battel, or shall I let it alone? And they said, Go vp: for ye Lord shall deliuer it into the hands of the King.

7 And Iehoshaphat said, Is there here neuer a Prophet of the Lord more, that we might inquire of him?

8 And the King of Israel said vnto Iehoshaphat, There is yet one man (Michaiah the sonne of Imlah) by whom we may aske counsel of the Lord, but I hate him: for he doeth not prophecie good vnto me, but euill. And Iehoshaphat sayd, Let not the King say so.

9 Then the King of Israel called an Eunuche, and sayde, Call quickely Michaiah the sonne of Imlah.

10 And the King of Israel and Iehoshaphat the King of Iudah sate either of them on his throne in their apparell in the voyde place at the entring in of the gate of Samaria, and all the prophets prophecied before them.

11 And Zidkiiah the sonne of Chenaanah made him hornes of yron, and sayd, Thus sayth the Lord, With these shalt thou push the Aramites, vntill thou hast consumed them.

12 And all the prophets prophecied so, saying, Goe vp to Ramoth Gilead, and prosper: for the Lord shall deliuer it into the Kings hand.

13 And the messenger that was gone to call Michaiah spake vnto him, saying, Beholde now, the wordes of the prophets declare good vnto the King with one accorde: let thy word therefore, I pray thee, be like the worde of one of them, and speake thou good.

14 And Michaiah saide, As the Lord liueth, whatsoeuer the Lord sayth vnto me, that will I speake.

15 So he came to the King, and the King said vnto him, Michaiah, shall we go against Ramoth Gilead to battel, or shall we leaue off? And he answered him, Goe vp, and prosper: and the Lord shall deliuer it into the hand of the King.

16 And the King said vnto him, How oft shall I charge thee, that thou tell me nothing but that which is true in the Name of the Lord?

17 Then he said, I sawe all Israel scattered vpon the mountaines, as sheepe that had no shepheard. And the Lord sayde, These haue no master, let euery man returne vnto his house in peace.

18 (And the King of Israel saide vnto Iehoshaphat, Did I not tell thee, that he would prophecie no good vnto me, but euill?)

19 Againe he said, Heare thou therefore the worde of the Lord. I sawe the Lord sit

on his throne, and all the hoste of heauen stood about him on his right hand and on his left hand.

20 And the Lord sayd, Who shall entise Ahab that he may go and fall at Ramoth Gilead? And one said on this maner, and another sayd on that maner.

21 Then there came forth a spirit, and stoode before the Lord, and sayd, I wil entise him. And the Lord sayd vnto him, Wherewith?

22 And he sayd, I will goe out, and be a false spirit in the mouth of all his prophets. Then he sayd, Thou shalt entise him, and shalt also preuayle: goe forth, and doe so.

23 Now therefore behold, the Lord hath put a lying spirite in the mouth of all these thy prophets, and the Lord hath appoynted euill against thee.

24 Then Zidkiiah the sonne of Chenaanah came neere, and smote Michaiah on the cheeke and sayd, When went the Spirite of the Lord from me, to speake vnto thee?

25 And Michaiah saide, Behold, thou shalt see in that day, when thou shalt goe from chamber to chamber to hide thee.

26 And the King of Israel sayd, Take Michaiah, and cary him vnto Amon the gouernour of the citie, and vnto Ioash the Kings sonne,

27 And say, Thus saith the King, Put this man in the prison house, and feede him with bread of affliction, and with water of affliction, vntill I returne in peace.

28 And Michaiah sayde, If thou returne in peace, the Lord hath not spoken by me. And he sayd, Hearken all ye people.

29 So the King of Israel and Iehoshaphat the King of Iudah went vp to Ramoth Gilead.

30 And the King of Israel sayde to Iehoshaphat, I will change mine apparell, and will enter into the battell, but put thou on thine apparell. And the King of Israel changed himselfe, and went into the battel.

31 And the King of Aram commanded his two and thirtie captaines ouer his charets, saying, Fight neither with small, nor great, saue onely against the King of Israel.

32 And when the captaines of the charets saw Iehoshaphat, they sayd, Surely it is the King of Israel, and they turned to fight against him: and Iehoshaphat cryed.

33 And when the captaines of the charets saw that he was not the King of Israel, they turned backe from him.

34 Then a certaine man drewe a bow mightily and smote the King of Israel betweene the ioyntes of his brigandine. Wherefore he sayde vnto his charet man, Turne thine hand and cary me out of the hoste: for I am hurt.

35 And the battel encreased that day, and the King stoode still in his charet against the Aramites, and dyed at euen: and the blood ran out of the wound into the middes of the charet.

36 And there went a proclamation thorowout the hoste about the going downe of the sunne, saying, Euery man to his citie, and euery man to his owne countrey.

37 So the King died, and was brought to Samaria, and they buried the King in Samaria.

38 And one washed the charet in the poole of Samaria, and the dogs licked vp his blood (and they washed his armour) according vnto the word of the Lord which he spake.

39 Concerning the rest of the actes of Ahab and all that he did, and the yuorie house which he built, and all the cities that he built, are they not written in the booke of the Chronicles of the Kings of Israel?

40 So Ahab slept with his fathers, and Ahaziah his sonne reigned in his stead.

41 And Iehoshaphat the sonne of Asa began to reigne vpon Iudah in the fourth yeere of Ahab King of Israel.

42 Iehoshaphat was fiue and thirty yere olde, when he began to reigne, and reigned fiue and twentie yeere in Ierusalem. And his mothers name was Azubah the daughter of Shilhi.

43 And he walked in all the wayes of Asa his father, and declined not therefrom, but did that which was right in the eyes of the Lord. Neuerthelesse the hie places were not taken away: for the people offred still and burnt incense in the hie places.

44 And Iehoshaphat made peace with the King of Israel.

45 Concerning the rest of the actes of Iehoshaphat, and his worthy deedes that he did, and his battels which he fought, are they not written in the booke of the Chronicles of the Kings of Iudah?

46 And the Sodomites, which remayned in the dayes of his father Asa, he put cleane out of the land.

47 There was then no King in Edom: the deputie was King.

48 Iehoshaphat made shippes of Tharshish to sayle to Ophir for golde, but they went not, for the shippes were broken at Ezion Gaber.

49 Then sayde Ahaziah the sonne of Ahab vnto Iehoshaphat, Let my seruants goe with thy seruants in the ships, But Iehoshaphat would not.

50 And Iehoshaphat did sleepe with his fathers, and was buried with his fathers in the citie of Dauid his father, and Iehoram his sonne reigned in his stead.

51 Ahaziah the sonne of Ahab began to reigne ouer Israel in Samaria, the seuenteenth yeere of Iehoshaphat King of Iudah, and reigned two yeeres ouer Israel.

52 But he did euill in the sight of the Lord, and walked in the way of his father, and in the way of his mother, and in the way of Ieroboam the sonne of Nebat, which made Israel to sinne.

53 For he serued Baal and worshipped him, and prouoked the Lord God of Israel vnto wrath, according vnto all that his father had done.

Second Kings

Second Kings 1

1 Then Moab rebelled against Israel after the death of Ahab:

2 And Ahaziah fell thorow the lattesse windowe in his vpper chamber which was in Samaria: so he was sicke: then he sent messengers, to whome he saide, Goe, and enquire of Baal-zebub the God of Ekron, if I shall recouer of this my disease.

3 Then the Angel of the Lord said to Eliiah the Tishbite, Arise, and goe vp to meete the messengers of the King of Samaria, and say vnto them, Is it not because there is no God in Israel, that ye goe to enquire of Baal-zebub the god of Ekron?

4 Wherefore thus saith the Lord, Thou shalt not come downe from the bed on which thou art gone vp, but shalt die the death. So Eliiah departed.

5 And the messengers returned vnto him, to whome he said, Why are ye nowe returned?

6 And they answered him, There came a man and met vs, and saide vnto vs, Goe, and returne vnto the King which sent you, and say vnto him, Thus saith the Lord, Is it not because there is no God in Israel, that thou sendest to enquire of Baal-zebub the God of Ekron? Therefore thou shalt not come downe from the bed, on which thou art gone vp, but shalt die ye death.

7 And he saide vnto them, What maner of man was he which came and met you, and tolde you these wordes?

8 And they said vnto him, He was an hearie man, and girded with a girdle of lether about his loynes. Then sayde he, It is Eliiah the Tishbite.

9 Therefore the King sent vnto him a captaine ouer fiftie with his fiftie men, who went vp vnto him: for beholde, he sate on the toppe of a mountaine, and he saide vnto him, O man of God, the King hath commanded that thou come downe.

10 But Eliiah answered, and saide to the captaine ouer the fiftie, If that I be a man of God, let fire come downe from the heauen, and deuoure thee and thy fiftie. So fire came downe from the heauen and deuoured him and his fiftie.

11 Againe also he sent vnto him another captaine ouer fiftie, with his fiftie. Who spake, and saide vnto him, O man of God, thus the King commandeth, Come downe quickely.

12 But Eliiah answered, and saide vnto them, If I be a man of God, let fire come downe from the heauen, and deuoure thee and thy fiftie. So fire came downe from the heauen, and deuoured him and his fiftie.

13 Yet againe he sent the third captaine ouer fiftie with his fiftie. And the thirde captaine ouer fiftie went vp, and came, and fell on his knees before Eliiah, and besought him, and saide vnto him, O man of God, I pray thee, let my life and the life of these thy fiftie seruants be precious in thy sight.

14 Beholde, there came fire downe from the heauen and deuoured the two former captaines ouer fiftie with their fifties: therefore let my life nowe be precious in thy sight.

15 And the Angel of the Lord said vnto Eliiah, Goe downe with him, be not afraide of his presence. So he arose, and went downe with him vnto the King.

16 And he saide vnto him, Thus saith the Lord, Because thou hast sent messengers to enquire of Baal-zebub the god of Ekron, (was it not because there was no God in Israel to inquire of his worde?) therefore thou shalt not come downe off the bed, on which thou art gone vp, but shalt die the death.

17 So he dyed according to the worde of the Lord which Eliiah had spoken. And Iehoram began to reigne in his steade, in the seconde yeere of Iehoram the sonne of Iehoshaphat King of Iudah, because he had no sonne.

18 Concerning the rest of the actes of Ahaziah, that he did, are they not written in the booke of the Chronicles of the Kings of Israel?

Second Kings 2

1 And when the Lord would take vp Eliiah into heauen by a whirle winde, Eliiah went with Elisha from Gilgal.

2 Then Eliiah saide to Elisha, Tarie here, I pray thee: for the Lord hath sent me to Bethel. But Elisha said, As the Lord liueth, and as thy soule liueth, I will not leaue thee. So they came downe to Beth-el.

3 And the children of the Prophets that were at Beth-el, came out to Elisha, and said vnto him, Knowest thou that the Lord will take thy master from thine head this day? And he said, Yea, I knowe it: holde ye your peace.

4 Againe Eliiah saide vnto him, Elisha, tarie here, I pray thee: for the Lord hath sent me to Iericho: But he said, As the Lord liueth, and as thy soule liueth, I will not leaue thee. So they came to Iericho.

5 And the children of the Prophets that were at Iericho, came to Elisha, and saide vnto him, Knowest thou, that the Lord will take thy master from thine head this day? And he sayde, Yea, I knowe it: holde ye your peace.

6 Moreouer Eliiah saide vnto him, Tarie, I pray thee, here: for the Lord hath sent me to Iorden. But he saide, As the Lord liueth, and as thy soule liueth, I will not leaue thee. So they went both together.

7 And fiftie men of the sonnes of the Prophets went and stoode on the other side a farre off, and they two stoode by Iorden.

8 Then Eliiah tooke his cloke, and wrapt it together, and smote the waters, and they were deuided hither and thither, and they twaine went ouer on the dry lande.

9 Nowe when they were passed ouer, Eliiah saide vnto Elisha, Aske what I shall doe for thee before I be taken from thee. And Elisha saide, I pray thee, let thy Spirit be double vpon me.

10 And he saide, Thou hast asked an hard thing: yet if thou see me when I am taken from thee, thou shalt haue it so: and if not, it shall not be.

11 And as they went walking and talking, beholde, there appeared a charet of fire, and horses of fire, and did separate them twaine. So Eliiah went vp by a whirle winde into heauen.

12 And Elisha saw it, and he cryed, My father, my father, the charet of Israel, and the horsemen thereof: and he sawe him no more: and he tooke his owne clothes, and rent them in two pieces.

13 He tooke vp also the cloke of Eliiah that fell from him, and returned, and stoode by the banke of Iorden.

14 After, he tooke the cloke of Eliiah, that fell from him, and smote the waters, and sayde, Where is the Lord God of Eliiah? And so he also, after he had striken the waters, so that they were deuided this way and that way, went ouer, euen Elisha.

15 And when the children of the Prophets, which were at Iericho, saw him on the other side, they sayde, The Spirite of Eliiah doeth rest on Elisha: and they came to meete him, and fell to the grounde before him,

16 And said vnto him, Beholde nowe, there be with thy seruants fiftie strong men: let them go, we pray thee, and seeke thy master, if so be the Spirite of the Lord hath taken him vp, and cast him vpon some mountaine, or into some valley. But he said, Ye shall not sende.

17 Yet they were instant vpon him, til he was ashamed: wherefore he saide, Sende. So they sent fiftie men, which sought three dayes, but founde him not.

18 Therefore they returned to him, (for he taryed at Iericho) and he said vnto them, Did not I say vnto you, Goe not?

19 And the men of the citie saide vnto Elisha, Beholde, we pray thee: the situation of this citie is pleasant, as thou, my lorde, seest, but the water is naught, and the ground baren.

20 Then he saide, Bring me a newe cruse, and put salt therein. And they brought it to him.

21 And he went vnto the spring of the waters, and cast there the salt, and said, Thus saith the Lord, I haue healed this water: death shall no more come thereof, neither barennesse to the ground.

22 So the waters were healed vntill this day, according to the worde of Elisha which hee had spoken.

23 And he went vp from thence vnto Beth-el. And as he was going vp the way, litle children came out of the citie, and mocked him, and saide vnto him, Come vp, thou balde head, come vp, thou balde head.

24 And he turned backe, and looked on them, and cursed them in the name of the Lord. And two beares came out of the forest, and tare in pieces two and fourtie children of them.

25 So he went from thence to mount Carmel, and from thence he returned to Samaria.

Second Kings 3

1 Nowe Iehoram the sonne of Ahab beganne to reigne ouer Israel in Samaria, the eighteenth yeere of Iehoshaphat King of Iudah, and reigned twelue yeeres.

2 And he wrought euill in the sight of the Lord, but not like his father nor like his mother: for he tooke away the image of Baal that his father had made.

3 Neuerthelesse, he cleaued vnto the sinnes of Ieroboam, the sonne of Nebat, which made Israel to sinne, and departed not therefrom.

4 Then Mesha King of Moab had store of sheepe, and rendred vnto the King of Israel an hundreth thousande lambes, and an hundreth thousande rammes with the wooll.

5 But when Ahab was dead, the king of Moab rebelled against the King of Israel.

6 Therefore King Iehoram went out of Samaria the same season, and nombred all Israel,

7 And went, and sent to Iehoshaphat King of Iudah, saying, The King of Moab hath rebelled against me: wilt thou goe with me to battell against Moab? And he answered, I will goe vp: for I am, as thou art, my people, as thy people, and mine horses as thine horses.

8 Then said he, What way shall we goe vp? And he answered, The way of the wildernesse of Edom.

9 So went the King of Israel and the king of Iudah, and the King of Edom, and when they had compassed the way seuen dayes, they had no water for the hoste, nor for the cattell that followed them.

10 Therefore the King of Israel sayde, Alas, that the Lord hath called these three Kings, to giue them into the hand of Moab.

11 But Iehoshaphat saide, Is there not here a Prophet of the Lord, that we may inquire of the Lord by him? And one of the King of Israels seruants answered, and said, Here is Elisha the sonne of Shaphat, which powred water on the handes of Eliiah.

12 Then Iehoshaphat saide, The worde of the Lord is with him. Therefore the King of Israel, and Iehoshaphat, and the King of Edom went downe to him.

13 And Elisha sayde vnto the King of Israel, What haue I to doe with thee? get thee to the prophets of thy father and to the prophets of thy mother. And the King of Israel saide vnto him, Nay: for the Lord hath called these three Kings, to giue them into the hande of Moab.

14 Then Elisha said, As the Lord of hostes liueth, in whose sight I stande, if it were not, that I regarde the presence of Iehoshaphat the King of Iudah, I woulde not haue looked towarde thee, nor seene thee.

15 But nowe bring me a minstrel. And when the minstrel played, the hand of the Lord came vpon him.

16 And he saide, Thus saith the Lord, Make this valley full of ditches.

17 For thus saith the Lord, Ye shall neither see winde nor see raine, yet the

valley shalbe filled with water, that ye may drinke, both ye and your cattel, and your beastes.

18 But this is a small thing in the sight of the Lord: for he will giue Moab into your hande.

19 And ye shall smite euery strong towne and euery chiefe citie, and shall fell euery faire tree, and shall stoppe all the fountaines of water, and marre euery good fielde with stones.

20 And in the morning whe the meat offring was offred, beholde, there came water by the way of Edom: and the countrey was filled with water.

21 And when al the Moabites heard that the Kings were come vp to fight against them, they gathered all that was able to put on harnesse, and vpwarde, and stood in their border.

22 And they rose earely in the morning, when the sunne arose vpon the water, and the Moabites saw the water ouer against them, as red as blood.

23 And they saide, This is blood the Kings are surely slaine, and one hath smitten another: now therefore, Moab, to the spoyle.

24 And when they came to the host of Israel, the Israelites arose vp, and smote the Moabites, so that they fled before them, but they inuaded them, and smote Moab.

25 And they destroyed the cities: and on all the good field euery man cast his stone, and filled them and they stopt all the fountaines of water, and felled all the good trees: onely in Kirharaseth left they the stones thereof: howebeit they went about it with slings, and smote it.

26 And when the King of Moab saw that the battel was too sore for him, he tooke with him seuen hudreth men that drew the sword, to break through vnto the King of Edom: but they could not.

27 Then he tooke his eldest sonne, that should haue reigned in his stead, and offered him for a burnt offring vpon the wall: so that Israel was sore grieued, and they departed from him, and returned to their countrey.

Second Kings 4

1 And one of the wiues of the sonnes of the Prophets cryed vnto Elisha, saying, Thy seruant mine husband is dead, and thou knowest, that thy seruant did feare the Lord: and the creditour is come to take my two sonnes to bee his bondmen.

2 Then Elisha saide vnto her, What shall I do for thee? tell mee, what hast thou at home? And she sayd, Thine handmayd hath nothing at home, saue a pitcher of oyle.

3 And he sayde, Goe, and borowe thee vessels abroad of all thy neighbours, emptie vessels, and spare not.

4 And when thou art come in, thou shalt shut the doore vpon thee and vpon thy sonnes, and powre out into all those vessels, and set aside those that are full.

5 So shee departed from him, and shut the doore vpon her, and vpon her sonnes. And they brought to her, and she powred out.

6 And when the vessels were full, shee sayde vnto her sonne, Bring mee yet a vessel. And hee said vnto her, There is no moe vessels. And the oyle ceased.

7 Then shee came and tolde the man of God. And he saide, Goe, and sell the oyle, and pay them that thou art in debt vnto, and liue thou and thy children of the rest.

8 And on a time Elisha came to Shunem, and there a woman of great estimation constrained him to eate bread: and as he passed by, he turned in thither to eate bread.

9 And she sayde vnto her husband, Beholde, I know now, that this is an holy man of God that passeth by vs continually.

10 Let vs make him a litle chamber, I pray thee, with walles, and let vs set him there a bed, and a table, and a stoole, and a candlesticke, that hee may turne in thither when hee commeth to vs.

11 And on a day, hee came thither and turned into the chamber, and lay therein,

12 And sayd to Gehazi his seruant, Call this Shunammite: and when hee called her, she stood before him.

13 Then he sayd vnto him, Say vnto her now, Beholde, thou hast had all this great care for vs, what shall we doe for thee? Is there any thing to bee spoken for thee to the King or to the captaine of the hoste? And shee answered, I dwell among mine owne people.

14 Againe he sayde, What is then to be done for her? Then Gehazi answered, In deede she hath no sonne, and her husband is olde.

15 Then said he, Cal her. And hee called her, and shee stoode in the doore.

16 And he said, At this time appointed, according to the time of life, thou shalt embrace a sonne. And she sayd, Oh my Lord, thou man of God, doe not lye vnto thine handmayd.

17 So the woman conceiued, and bare a sonne at that same season, according to the time of life, that Elisha had sayd vnto her.

18 And when the childe was growen, it fell on a day, that he went out to his father, and to the reapers.

19 And he sayde to his father, Mine head, mine head. Who sayd to his seruant, Beare him to his mother.

20 And hee tooke him and brought him to his mother, and hee sate on her knees till noone, and dyed.

21 Then shee went vp, and layed him on the bed of the man of God, and shut the doore vpon him, and went out.

22 Then she called to her husband, and sayd, Send with me, I pray thee, one of the yong men and one of the asses: for I will haste to the man of God, and come againe.

23 And he sayd, Wherefore wilt thou goe to him to day? it is neither newe moone nor Sabbath day. And she answered, All shalbe well.

24 Then she sadled an asse, and sayde to her seruant, Driue, and goe forward: staye not for me to get vp, except I bid thee.

25 So she went, and came vnto the man of God to mount Carmel. And when the man of God sawe her ouer against him, he sayd to Gehazi his seruant, Beholde, the Shunammite.

26 Runne nowe, I say, to meete her, and say vnto her, Art thou in health? is thine husband in health? and is the child in health? And she answered, We are in health.

27 And when shee came to the man of God vnto the moutaine, she caught him by his feete: and Gehazi went to her, to thrust her away: but the man of God said, Let her alone: for her soule is vexed within her, and the Lord hath hid it from me, and hath not told it mee.

28 Then she said, Did I desire a sonne of my lord? did I not say, Deceiue me not?

29 Then he sayd to Gehazi, Gird thy loynes, and take my staffe in thine hand, and goe thy way: if thou meete any, salute him not: and if any salute thee, answere him not: and laye my staffe vpon the face of the childe.

30 And the mother of the childe sayde, As the Lord liueth, and as thy soule liueth, I will not leaue thee. Therefore he arose, and followed her.

31 But Gehazi was gone before them, and had layed the staffe vpon the face of the childe, but he neither spake nor heard: wherefore hee returned to meete him, and told him, saying, The childe is not waken.

32 Then came Elisha into the house, and beholde, the childe was dead, and layed vpon his bedde.

33 He went in therefore, and shut the doore vpon them twayne, and prayed vnto the Lord.

34 After he went vp, and lay vpon the child, and put his mouth on his mouth, and his eyes vpon his eies, and his hands vpon his handes, and stretched himselfe vpon him, and the flesh of the child waxed warme.

35 And hee went from him, and walked vp and downe in the house, and went vp and spred himselfe vpon him: then the childe neesed seuen times, and opened his eyes.

36 Then he called Gehazi, and sayd, Call this Shunammite. So he called her, which came in vnto him. And he said vnto her, Take thy sonne.

37 And she came, and fell at his feete, and bowed her selfe to the ground, and tooke vp her sonne, and went out.

38 Afterward Elisha returned to Gilgal, and a famine was in the land, and the children of the Prophets dwelt with him. And hee sayd vnto his seruant, Set on the great pot, and seethe pottage for the children of the Prophets.

39 And one went out into the fielde, to gather herbes, and founde, as it were, a wilde vine, and gathered thereof wilde gourdes his garment ful, and came and

shred them into the pot of pottage: for they knew it not.

40 So they powred out for the men to eate: and when they did eate of the pottage, they cryed out, and sayde, O thou man of God, death is in the pot: and they could not eate thereof.

41 Then he said, Bring meale. And hee cast it into the potte, and sayd, Powre out for the people, that they may eate: and there was none euill in the pot.

42 Then came a man from Baal-shalisha, and brought the man of God bread of the first fruits, euen twenty loaues of barley, and full eares of corne in the huske. And hee saide, Giue vnto the people, that they may eate.

43 And his seruant answered, How shoulde I set this before an hundreth men? He sayd againe, Giue it vnto the people, that they may eate: for thus sayth the Lord, They shall eate, and there shall remaine.

44 So he set it before them, and they did eate, and left ouer, according to the word of the Lord.

Second Kings 5

1 Now was there one Naaman captaine of the hoste of the King of Aram, a great man, and honourable in the sight of his lorde, because that by him the Lord had deliuered the Aramites. He also was a mightie man and valiant, but a leper.

2 And the Aramites had gone out by bands, and had taken a litle mayde of the land of Israel, and shee serued Naamans wife.

3 And she sayd vnto her mistres, Would God my lord were with the Prophet that is in Samaria, he would soone deliuer him of his leprosie.

4 And he went in, and tolde his lorde, saying, Thus and thus saith the mayde that is of the land of Israel.

5 And the King of Aram sayde, Goe thy way thither, and I will send a letter vnto the King of Israel. And he departed, and tooke with him ten talents of siluer, and sixe thousand pieces of golde, and ten change of rayments,

6 And brought the letter to the King of Israel to this effect, Now when this letter is come vnto thee, vnderstand, that I haue sent thee Naaman my seruant, that thou maiest heale him of his leprosie.

7 And when the King of Israel had read the letter, he rent his clothes, and sayde, Am I God, to kill and to giue life, that hee doth send to mee, that I should heale a man from his leprosie? wherfore consider, I pray you, and see howe he seeketh a quarel against me.

8 But when Elisha the man of God had heard that the King of Israel had rent his clothes, hee sent vnto the King, saying, Wherefore hast thou rent thy clothes? Let him come now to me, and he shall knowe that there is a Prophet in Israel.

9 Then Naaman came with his horses, and with his charets, and stoode at the doore of the house of Elisha.

10 And Elisha sent a messenger vnto him, saying, Go and wash thee in Iorden seuen times, and thy flesh shall come againe to thee, and thou shalt be clensed.

11 But Naaman was wroth and went away, and sayde, Beholde, I thought with my selfe, Hee will surely come out, and stande, and call on the Name of the Lord his God and put his hand on the place, and heale the leprosie.

12 Are not Abanah and Pharpar, riuers of Damascus, better then all the waters of Israel? may I not washe mee in them, and bee cleansed? so hee turned, and departed in displeasure.

13 But his seruants came, and spake vnto him, and sayd, Father, if the Prophet had commanded thee a great thing, wouldest thou not haue done it? howe much rather then, when hee sayth to thee, Wash and be cleane?

14 Then went he downe, and washed him selfe seuen times in Iorden, according to the saying of the man of God: and his flesh came againe, like vnto ye flesh of a litle child, and he was cleane.

15 And hee turned againe to the man of God, hee, and all his companie, and came and stood before him, and sayd, Behold, now I knowe that there is no God in all the world, but in Israel: now therefore, I pray thee, take a reward of thy seruant.

16 But hee sayde, As the Lord liueth (before whom I stand) I wil not receiue it. And he would haue constrained him to receiue it, but he refused.

17 Moreouer Naaman sayde, Shall there not be giuen to thy seruant two mules loade of this earth? for thy seruant will henceforth offer neither burnt sacrifice nor offring vnto any other god, saue vnto the Lord.

18 Herein the Lord bee mercifull vnto thy seruant, that when my master goeth into the house of Rimmon, to worship there, and leaneth on mine hand, and I bowe my selfe in the house of Rimmon: when I doe bowe downe, I say, in the house of Rimmon, the Lord be mercifull vnto thy seruant in this point.

19 Vnto whome he saide, Goe in peace. So he departed from him about halfe a dayes iourney of grounde.

20 And Gehazi the seruant of Elisha the man of God sayde, Beholde, my master hath spared this Aramite Naaman, receiuing not those things at his hand that he brought: as the Lord liueth, I will runne after him, and take somewhat of him.

21 So Gehazi followed speedily after Naaman. And when Naaman sawe him running after him, he light downe from the charet to meete him, and said, Is all well?

22 And he answered, All is well: my master hath set me, saying, Behold, there be come to me, euen nowe from mount Ephraim two yong men of the children of the Prophets: giue them, I pray thee, a talent of siluer, and two change of garmets.

23 And Naaman saide, Yea, take two talents: and he compelled him, and bound two talents of siluer in two bagges, with two change of garments, and gaue them vnto two of his seruants, that they might beare them before him.

24 And when he came to the towre, he tooke them out of their handes, and laide them in the house, and sent away the men: and they departed.

25 Then he went in, and stoode before his master. And Elisha said vnto him, Whence commest thou, Gehazi? And he said, Thy seruant went no whither.

26 But he saide vnto him, Went not mine heart with thee when the man turned againe from his charet to meete thee? Is this a time to take money, and to receiue garments, and oliues, and vineyardes, and sheepe, and oxen, and men seruants, and maide seruants?

27 The leprosie therefore of Naaman shall cleaue vnto thee, and to thy seede for euer. And he went out from his presence a leper white as snowe.

Second Kings 6

1 And the children of the Prophets saide vnto Elisha, Behold, we pray thee, the place where we dwell with thee, is too litle for vs.

2 Let vs nowe goe to Iorden, that we may take thence euery man a beame, and make vs a place to dwell in. And he answered, Goe.

3 And one said, Vouchsafe, I pray thee, to go with thy seruants, and he answered, I will goe.

4 So he went with them, and when they came to Iorden, they cut downe wood.

5 And as one was felling of a tree, the yron fell into the water: then he cryed, and said, Alas master, it was but borowed.

6 And the man of God saide, Where fell it? And he shewed him the place. Then he cut downe a piece of wood, and cast in thither, and he caused the yron to swimme.

7 Then he saide, Take it vp to thee. And he stretched out his hand, and tooke it.

8 Then the King of Aram warred against Israel, and tooke counsell with his seruants, and said, In such and such a place shalbe my campe.

9 Therefore the man of God sent vnto the King of Israel, saying, Beware thou goe not ouer to such a place: for there the Aramites are come downe.

10 So the King of Israel sent to the place which the man of God tolde him, and warned him of, and saued himselfe from thence, not once, nor twise.

11 And the heart of the King of Aram was troubled for this thing: therefore he called his seruants and saide vnto them, Will ye not shewe me, which of vs bewrayeth our counsel to the king of Israel?

12 Then one of his seruants saide, None, my lorde, O King, but Elisha the Prophet that is in Israel, telleth the King of Israel, euen the wordes that thou speakest in thy priuie chamber.

13 And he said, Goe, and espie where he is, that I may sende and fetch him. And

one tolde him, saying, Beholde, he is in Dothan.

14 So he sent thither horses, and charets, and a mightie hoste: and they came by night, and compassed the citie.

15 And when the seruant of the man of God arose earely to goe out, beholde, an hoste compassed the citie with horses and charets. Then his seruant sayde vnto him, Alas master, howe shall we doe?

16 And he answered, Feare not: for they that be with vs, are moe then they that be with them.

17 Then Elisha prayed, and saide, Lord, I beseech thee, open his eyes, that he may see. And the Lord opened the eyes of the seruant, and he looked, and beholde, the mountaine was full of horses and charets of fyre round about Elisha.

18 So they came downe to him, but Elisha prayed vnto the Lord, and said, Smite this people, I pray thee, with blindnesse. And he smote them with blindnes, according to the worde of Elisha.

19 And Elisha said vnto them, This is not the way, neither is this the citie: follow me, and I will leade you to the man whome ye seeke. But he ledde them to Samaria.

20 And when they were come to Samaria, Elisha saide, Lord, open their eyes that they may see. And the Lord opened their eyes, and they saw, and beholde, they were in the mids of Samaria.

21 And the King of Israel sayde vnto Elisha when he sawe them, My father, shall I smite them, shall I smite them?

22 And he answered, Thou shalt not smite them: doest thou not smite them that thou hast taken with thy sworde, and with thy bowe? but set bread and water before them, that they may eate and drinke and goe to their master.

23 And he made great preparation for them: and when they had eaten and drunken, he sent them away: and they went to their master. So ye bands of Aram came no more into the land of Israel.

24 But afterward Ben-hadad King of Aram gathered all his hoste, and went vp, and besieged Samaria.

25 So there was a great famine in Samaria: for loe, they besieged it vntill an asses head was at foure score pieces of siluer, and the fourth part of a kab of doues doung at fiue pieces of siluer.

26 And as the King of Israel was going vpon the wall, there cryed a woman vnto him, saying, Helpe, my lord, O King.

27 And he said, Seeing the Lord doeth not succour thee, howe shoulde I helpe thee with the barne, or with the wine presse?

28 Also the King said vnto her, What ayleth thee? And she answered, This woman sayde vnto me, Giue thy sonne, that we may eate him to day, and we will eate my sonne to morowe,

29 So we sod my sonne, and did eate him: and I saide to her the day after,

Giue thy sonne, that we may eate him, but she hath hid her sonne.

30 And when the King had heard the wordes of the woman, he rent his clothes, (and as he went vpon the wall, the people looked, and behold, he had sackecloth within vpon his flesh)

31 And he saide, God doe so to me and more also, if the head of Elisha the sonne of Shaphat shall stande on him this day.

32 (Nowe Elisha sate in his house, and the Elders sate with him.) And the King sent a man before him: but before the messenger came to him, he saide to the Elders, See ye not howe this murtherers sonne hath sent to take away mine head? take heede when the messenger commeth, and shut the doore and handle him roughly at the doore: is not the sounde of his masters feete behinde him?

33 While he yet talked with them, beholde, the messenger came downe vnto him, and saide, Behold, this euill commeth of the Lord: should I attende on the Lord any longer?

Second Kings 7

1 Then Elisha saide, Heare ye the worde of the Lord: thus saith the Lord, To morowe this time a measure of fine floure shalbe solde for a shekel, and two measures of barley for a shekel in the gate of Samaria.

2 Then a prince, on whose hande the King leaned, answered the man of God, and saide, Though the Lord would make windowes in the heauen, could this thing come to passe? And he said, Beholde, thou shalt see it with thine eyes, but thou shalt not eate thereof.

3 Nowe there were foure leprous men at the entring in of the gate: and they saide one to an other, Why sitte we here vntill we die?

4 If we say, We will enter into the citie, the famine is in the citie, and we shall die there: and if we sit here, we dye also. Nowe therefore come, and let vs fall into the campe of the Aramites: if they saue our liues, we shall liue: and if they kill vs, we are but dead.

5 So they rose vp in the twilight, to goe to the campe of the Aramites: and when they were come to the vtmost part of the campe of the Aramites, loe, there was no man there.

6 For the Lord had caused the campe of the Aramites to heare a noyse of charets and a noise of horses, and a noise of a great armie, so that they sayde one to another, Beholde, the King of Israel hath hired against vs the Kings of the Hittites, and the Kings of the Egyptians to come vpon vs.

7 Wherefore they arose, and fled in the twilight, and left their tentes and their horses, and their asses, euen the campe as it was, and fledde for their liues.

8 And when these lepers came to the vtmost part of the campe, they entred into one tent, and did eate and drinke, and caryed thence siluer and golde, and raiment, and went and hid it: after they

returned, and entred into another tent, and caryed thence also, and went and hid it.

9 Then saide one to another, We doe not well: this day is a day of good tidings, and we holde our peace. if we tary till day light, some mischiefe will come vpon vs. Nowe therefore, come, let vs goe, and tell the Kings housholde.

10 So they came, and called vnto the porters of the citie, and tolde them, saying, We came to the campe of the Aramites, and loe, there was no man there, neither voyce of man, but horses tyed and asses tyed: and the tents are as they were.

11 And the porters cryed and declared to the Kings house within.

12 Then the King arose in the night, and saide vnto his seruants, I wil shew you now, what the Aramites haue done vnto vs. They know that we are affamished, therefore they are gone out of the campe to hide them selues in the fielde, saying, When they come out of the citie, we shall catch them aliue, and get into the citie.

13 And one of his seruants answered, and said, Let me take now fiue of the horses that remaine, and are left in the citie, (behold, they are euen as all the multitude of Israel that are left therein: beholde, I say, they are as the multitude of the Israelites that are consumed) and we wil send to see.

14 So they tooke two charets of horses, and the King sent after the hoste of the Aramites, saying, Goe and see.

15 And they went after them vnto Iorden, and loe, all the way was full of clothes and vessels which the Aramites had cast from them in their hast: and the messengers returned, and told ye King.

16 Then the people went out and spoyled the campe of the Aramites: so a measure of fine floure was at a shekel, and two measures of barley at a shekel according to the word of the Lord.

17 And the King gaue the prince (on whose hande he leaned) the charge of the gate, and the people trode vpon him in the gate, and he dyed, as the man of God had saide, which spake it, when the King came downe to him.

18 And it came to passe, as the man of God had spoken to the King, saying, Two measures of barley at a shekel, and a measure of fine floure shall be at a shekel, to morowe about this time in the gate of Samaria.

19 But the prince had answered the man of God, and saide, Though the Lord would make windowes in the heauen, coulde it come so to passe? And he said, Behold, thou shalt see it with thine eyes, but thou shalt not eate thereof.

20 And so it came vnto him: for the people trode vpon him in the gate, and he dyed.

Second Kings 8

1 Then spake Elisha vnto the woman, whose sonne he had restored to life, saying, Vp, and goe, thou, and thine house, and soiourne where thou canst

soiourne: for the Lord hath called for a famine, and it commeth also vpon the land seuen yeeres.

2 And the woman arose, and did after the saying of the man of God, and went both shee and her housholde and soiourned in the lande of the Philistims seuen yeeres.

3 And at the seuen yeeres ende, the woman returned out of the lande of the Philistims, and went out to call vpon the King for her house and for her land.

4 And the King talked with Gehazi the seruant of the man of God, saying, Tell mee, I pray thee, all the great actes, that Elisha hath done.

5 And as he told the King, howe he had restored one dead to life, behold, the woman, whose sonne he had raised to life, called vpon the King for her house and for her land. Then Gehazi sayd, My lorde, O King, this is the woman, and this is her sonne, whom Elisha restored to life.

6 And when the King asked the woman, shee told him: so the King appoynted her an Eunuch, saying, Restore thou all that are hers, and all the fruites of her landes since the day shee left the land, euen vntill this time.

7 Then Elisha came to Damascus, and Ben-hadad the King of Aram was sicke, and one told him, saying, The man of God is come hither.

8 And the king sayd vnto Hazael, Take a present in thine hande, and goe meete the man of God, that thou mayest inquire of ye Lord by him, saying, Shall I recouer of this disease?

9 So Hazael went to meete him, and tooke the present in his hand, and of euery good thing of Damascus, euen the burden of fourtie camels, and came and stood before him, and sayde, Thy sonne Ben-hadad King of Aram hath sent me to thee, saying, Shall I recouer of this disease?

10 And Elisha sayd to him, Goe, and say vnto him, Thou shalt recouer: howbeit the Lord hath shewed me, that he shall surely dye.

11 And hee looked vpon him stedfastly, till Hazael was ashamed, and the man of God wept.

12 And Hazael sayde, Why weepeth my lord? And he answered, Because I knowe the euill that thou shalt do vnto the children of Israel: for their strong cities shalt thou set on fire, and their yong men shalt thou slay with the sworde, and shalt dash their infantes against the stones, and rent in pieces their women with child.

13 Then Hazael said, What? is thy seruant a dog, that I should doe this great thing? And Elisha answered, The Lord hath shewed mee, that thou shalt be King of Aram.

14 So he departed from Elisha, and came to his master, who said to him, What saide Elisha to thee? And he answered, Hee tolde mee that thou shouldest recouer.

15 And on the morow he tooke a thick cloth and dipt in it water, and spread it on his face, and hee dyed: and Hazael reigned in his stead.

16 Now in the fift yere of Ioram ye sonne of Ahab King of Israel, and of Iehoshaphat King of Iudah, Iehoram the sonne of Iehoshaphat King of Iudah began to reigne.

17 He was two and thirtie yere olde, when he began to reigne: and hee reigned eight yeere in Ierusalem.

18 And hee walked in the wayes of the Kings of Israel, as did the house of Ahab: for the daughter of Ahab was his wife, and hee did euill in the sight of the Lord.

19 Yet the Lord would not destroy Iudah, for Dauid his seruants sake, as he had promised him to giue him a light, and to his children for euer.

20 In those dayes Edom rebelled from vnder the hand of Iudah, and made a King ouer themselues.

21 Therefore Ioram went to Zair, and all his charets with him, and he arose by night, and smote the Edomites which were about him with the captains of the charets, and the people fled into their tents.

22 So Edom rebelled from vnder the hand of Iudah vnto this day. then Libnah rebelled at that same time.

23 Concerning the rest of the actes of Ioram and all that hee did, are they not written in the booke of the Chronicles of the Kings of Iudah?

24 And Ioram slept with his fathers, and was buried with his fathers in the citie of Dauid. And Ahaziah his sonne reigned in his stead.

25 In the twelft yere of Ioram the sonne of Ahab King of Israel did Ahaziah the sonne of Iehoram King of Iudah begin to reigne.

26 Two and twentie yeere olde was Ahaziah when he began to reigne, and he reigned one yere in Ierusalem, and his mothers name was Athaliah the daughter of Omri King of Israel.

27 And he walked in the way of the house of Ahab, and did euill in the sight of the Lord, like the house of Ahab: for hee was the sonne in law of the house of Ahab.

28 And he went with Ioram the sonne of Ahab to warre against Hazael King of Aram in Ramoth Gilead, and the Aramites smote Ioram.

29 And King Ioram returned to bee healed in Izreel of the wounds which ye Aramites had giuen him at Ramah, whe he fought against Hazael King of Aram. And Ahaziah the sonne of Iehoram King of Iudah went downe to see Ioram the sonne of Ahab in Izreel, because he was sicke.

Second Kings 9

1 Then Elisha the Prophet called one of ye children of the Prophets, and sayde vnto him, Gird thy loynes and take this boxe of oyle in thine hand and get thee to Ramoth Gilead.

2 And when thou commest thither, looke where is Iehu ye sonne of Iehoshaphat, the sonne of Nimshi, and go, and make him arise vp from among his brethren, and leade him to a secret chamber.

3 Then take the boxe of oyle and powre it on his head, and say, Thus sayth the Lord, I haue anointed thee for King ouer Israel. then open the doore, and flee without any tarying.

4 So the seruat of ye Prophet gate him to Ramoth Gilead.

5 And when he came in, behold, the captaines of the armie were sitting. And he sayde, I haue a message to thee, O captaine. And Iehu sayd, Vnto which of all vs? And he answered, To thee, O captaine.

6 And he arose, and went into the house, and he powred the oyle on his head and sayde vnto him, Thus sayth the Lord God of Israel, I haue anointed thee for King ouer the people of the Lord, euen ouer Israel.

7 And thou shalt smite the house of Ahab thy master, that I may auenge the blood of my seruants the Prophets, and the blood of al the seruants of the Lord of the hand of Iezebel.

8 For the whole house of Ahab shalbe destroied: and I will cut off from Ahab, him that maketh water against the wall, as well him that is shut vp, as him that is left in Israel.

9 And I will make the house of Ahab like the house of Ieroboam the sonne of Nebat, and like the house of Baasha the sonne of Ahiiah.

10 And the dogges shall eate Iezebel in the fielde of Izreel, and there shalbe none to burie her. And he opened the doore, and fled.

11 Then Iehu came out to the seruants of his lord. And one sayd vnto him, Is all well? wherefore came this mad fellowe to thee? And hee sayde vnto them, Ye knowe the man, and what his talke was.

12 And they sayde, It is false, tell vs it nowe. Then he sayd, Thus and thus spake he to me, saying, Thus saieth the Lord, I haue anointed thee for King ouer Israel.

13 Then they made haste, and tooke euerie man his garment, and put it vnder him on the top of the staires, and blewe the trumpet, saying, Iehu is King.

14 So Iehu ye sonne of Iehoshaphat the sonne of Nimshi conspired against Ioram: (Now Ioram kept Ramoth Gilead, he and all Israel, because of Hazael King of Aram.

15 And King Ioram returned to bee healed in Izreel of the woundes, which the Aramites had giuen him, when hee fought with Hazael King of Aram) and Iehu sayde, If it be your mindes, let no man depart and escape out of the citie, to goe and tell in Izreel.

16 So Iehu gate vp into a charet, and went to Izreel: for Ioram lay there, and Ahaziah King of Iudah was come downe to see Ioram.

17 And the watchman that stoode in the towre in Izreel spyed the companie of Iehu as hee came, and sayd, I see a companie. And Iehoram said, Take a

horseman and send to meete them, that hee may say, Is it peace?

18 So there went one on horseback to meete him, and sayde, Thus sayth the King, Is it peace? And Iehu sayd, What hast thou to do with peace? Turne behinde me. And the watchman tolde, saying, The messenger came to them, but he commeth not againe.

19 Then hee sent out another on horsebacke, which came to them, and sayde, Thus sayth the King, Is it peace? And Iehu answered, What hast thou to doe with peace? turne behinde me.

20 And the watchman tolde, saying, He came to them also, but commeth not againe, and the marching is like the marching of Iehu the sonne of Nimshi: for he marcheth furiously.

21 Then Iehoram sayd, Make ready: and his charet was made ready. And Iehoram King of Israel and Ahaziah King of Iudah went out eyther of them in his charet against Iehu, and met him in the fielde of Naboth the Izreelite.

22 And when Iehoram sawe Iehu, he sayde, Is it peace, Iehu? And he answered, What peace? whiles the whoredomes of thy mother Iezebel, and her witchcraftes are yet in great nomber?

23 Then Iehoram turned his hand, and fled, and said to Ahaziah, O Ahaziah, there is treason.

24 But Iehu tooke a bowe in his hande, and smote Iehoram betweene the shoulders, that the arowe went through his heart: and he fell downe in his charet.

25 Then said Iehu to Bidkar a captaine, Take, and cast him in some place of the fielde of Naboth the Izreelite: for I remember that when I and thou rode together after Ahab his father, the Lord layed this burden vpon him.

26 Surely I haue seene yesterday the blood of Naboth, and the blood of his sonnes, saide the Lord, and I will render it thee in this fielde, saith the Lord: nowe therefore take and cast him in the fielde, according to the word of the Lord.

27 But when Ahaziah the King of Iudah saw this, he fled by the way of the garden house: And Iehu pursued after him, and sayd, Smite him also in the charet: and they smote him in the going vp to Gur, which is by Ibleam. And hee fled to Megiddo, and there dyed.

28 And his seruants caried him in a charet to Ierusalem, and buried him in his sepulchre with his fathers in the citie of Dauid.

29 And in the eleuenth yere of Ioram the sonne of Ahab, began Ahaziah to reigne ouer Iudah.

30 And when Iehu was come to Izreel, Iezebel heard of it, and painted her face, and tired her head, and looked out at a windowe.

31 And as Iehu entred at the gate, shee sayde, Had Zimri peace, which slewe his master?

32 And he lift vp his eyes to the windowe, and sayd, Who is on my side, who? Then two or three of her Eunuches looked vnto him.

33 And he sayde, Cast her downe: and they cast her downe, and hee sprinkled of her blood vpon the wall, and vpon the horses, and he trode her vnder foote.

34 And when he was come in, he did eate and drinke, and sayde, Visite now yonder cursed woman, and burie her: for she is a Kings daughter.

35 And they went to burie her, but they foud no more of her, then the skull and the feete, and the palmes of her handes.

36 Wherefore they came agayne and tolde him. And he said, This is the worde of the Lord, which he spake by his seruant Eliiah the Tishbite, saying, In the fielde of Izreel shall ye dogs eate the flesh of Iezebel.

37 And the carkeis of Iezebel shalbe as doung vpon the ground in the field of Izreel, so that none shall say, This is Iezebel.

Second Kings 10

1 Ahab had nowe seuentie sonnes in Samaria. And Iehu wrote letters, and sent to Samaria vnto the rulers of Izreel, and to the Elders, and to the bringers vp of Ahabs children, to this effect,

2 Nowe when this letter commeth to you, (for ye haue with you your masters sonnes, yee haue with you both charets and horses, and a defenced citie, and armour)

3 Consider therefore which of your masters sonnes is best and most meete, and set him on his fathers throne, and fight for your masters house.

4 But they were exceedingly afraid, and saide, Behold two Kings coulde not stande before him, how shall we then stand?

5 And he that was gouernour of Ahabs house, and he that ruled the citie, and the Elders, and the bringers vp of the children sent to Iehu, saying, We are thy seruants, and will doe all that thou shalt bid vs: we will make no King: do what seemeth good to thee.

6 Then he wrote another letter to them, saying, If ye be mine, and wil obey my voyce, take the heads of ye men that are your masters sonnes, and come to me to Izreel by to morowe this time. (Nowe the Kings sonnes, euen seuentie persons were with the great men of the citie, which brought them vp)

7 And when the letter came to them, they tooke the Kings sonnes, and slewe the seuentie persons, and layde their heads in baskets, and sent them vnto him to Izreel.

8 Then there came a messenger and tolde him, saying, They haue brought the heads of the Kings sonnes. And he sayd, Let them lay them on two heapes at the entring in of the gate vntil the morning.

9 And when it was day, he went out, and stood and sayd to all the people, Ye be righteous: behold, I conspired against my master, and slew him: but who slew all these?

10 Knowe nowe that there shall fall vnto the earth nothing of the word of the Lord, which the Lord spake concerning the house of Ahab: for the Lord hath brought to passe the things that hee spake by his seruant Eliiah.

11 So Iehu slew al that remained of the house of Ahab in Izreel, and all that were great with him, and his familiars and his priestes, so that he let none of his remaine.

12 And he arose, and departed and came to Samaria. And as Iehu was in the way by an house where the shepheards did shere,

13 He met with the brethre of Ahaziah king of Iudah, and sayd, Who are ye? And they answered, We are the brethren of Ahaziah, and goe downe to salute the children of the King and the children of the Queene.

14 And he sayde, Take them aliue. And they tooke them aliue, and slew them at the well beside the house where the sheepe are shorne, euen two and fourtie men, and he left not one of them.

15 And when he was departed thence, hee met with Iehonadab the sonne of Rechab comming to meete him, and he blessed him, and sayde to him, Is thine heart vpright, as mine heart is towarde thine? And Iehonadab answered, Yea, doubtlesse. Then giue me thine hande. And when he had giuen him his hande, he tooke him vp to him into the charet.

16 And he sayde, Come with me, and see the zeale that I haue for the Lord: so they made him ride in his charet.

17 And when he came to Samaria, he slew all that remained vnto Ahab in Samaria, till he had destroyed him, according to the worde of the Lord, which he spake to Eliiah.

18 Then Iehu assembled all the people, and sayd vnto them, Ahab serued Baal a litle, but Iehu shall serue him much more.

19 Now therefore call vnto me all ye prophets of Baal, all his seruants, and all his priests, and let not a man be lacking: for I haue a great sacrifice for Baal: whosoeuer is lacking, he shall not liue. But Iehu did it by a subtiltie to destroy ye seruats of Baal.

20 And Iehu sayd, Proclaime a solemne assemblie for Baal. And they proclaimed it.

21 So Iehu sent vnto all Israel, and all the seruants of Baal came, and there was not a man left that came not. And they came into the house of Baal, and the house of Baal was full from ende to ende.

22 Then he said vnto him that had the charge of the vestrie, Bring forth vestments for al the seruants of Baal. And he brought the out vestments.

23 And when Iehu went, and Iehonadab the sonne of Rechab, into the house of Baal, he sayde vnto the seruants of Baal, Searche diligently, and looke, lest there be here with you any of the seruants of the Lord, but the seruants of Baal only.

24 And when they went in to make sacrifice and burnt offering, Iehu appoynted foure score men without, and sayd, If any of the men whome I haue

brought into your hands, escape, his soule shalbe for his soule.

25 And when hee had made an ende of the burnt offring, Iehu sayde to the garde, and to the captaines, Goe in, slay them, let not a man come out. And they smote them with the edge of the sworde. And the garde, and the captaines cast them out, and went vnto the citie, where was the temple of Baal.

26 And they brought out the images of the temple of Baal, and burnt them.

27 And they destroyed the image of Baal, and threwe downe the house of Baal, and made a iakes of it vnto this day.

28 So Iehu destroyed Baal out of Israel.

29 But from the sinnes of Ieroboam the sonne of Nebat which made Israel to sinne, Iehu departed not from them, neither from the golden calues that were in Beth-el and that were in Dan.

30 And the Lord sayde vnto Iehu, Because thou hast diligently executed that which was right in mine eyes, and hast done vnto the house of Ahab according to all things that were in mine heart, therefore shall thy sonnes vnto the fourth generation sit on the throne of Israel.

31 But Iehu regarded not to walke in the law of the Lord God of Israel with all his heart: for hee departed not from the sinnes of Ieroboam, which made Israel to sinne.

32 In those dayes the Lord began to lothe Israel, and Hazael smote them in all the coastes of Israel,

33 From Iorden Eastward, euen all the land of Gilead, the Gadites, and the Reubenites, and them that were of Manasseh, from Aroer (which is by the riuer Arnon) and Gilead and Bashan.

34 Concerning the rest of the actes of Iehu, and all that he did, and all his valiant deedes, are they not written in the booke of the Chronicles of the Kings of Israel?

35 And Iehu slept with his fathers, and they buryed him in Samaria, and Iehoahaz his sonne reigned in his stead.

36 And the time that Iehu reigned ouer Israel in Samaria is eight and twentie yeeres.

Second Kings 11

1 Then Athaliah the mother of Ahaziah when she saw that her sonne was dead, she arose, and destroyed all the Kings seede.

2 But Iehosheba the daughter of King Ioram, and sister to Ahaziah tooke Ioash the sonne of Ahaziah, and stale him from among the Kings sonnes that shoulde be slaine, both him and his nource, keeping them in the bed chaber, and they hid him from Athaliah, so that he was not slaine.

3 And he was with her hid in the house of the Lord sixe yeere: and Athaliah did reigne ouer the land.

4 And the seuenth yeere Iehoiada sent and tooke the captaines ouer hundreths, with other captaines and them of the garde, and caused them to come vnto him into the house of the Lord, and made a couenant with them, and tooke an othe of them in the house of the Lord, and shewed them the Kings sonne.

5 And he commanded them, saying, This is it that ye must doe, The third part of you, that commeth on the Sabbath, shall warde towarde the Kings house:

6 And another third part in the gate of Sur: and another thirde part in the gate behinde them of the garde: and ye shall keepe watche in the house of Massah.

7 And two parts of you, that is, all that goe out on the Sabbath day, shall keepe the watch of the house of the Lord about the King.

8 And ye shall compasse the King rounde about, euery man with his weapon in his hande, and whosoeuer commeth within the ranges, let him be slayne: be you with the King, as he goeth out and in.

9 And the captaines of the hundreths did according to all that Iehoiada the Priest commaded, and they tooke euery man his men that entred in to their charge on the Sabbath with them that went out of it on the Sabbath, and came to Iehoiada the Priest.

10 And the Priest gaue to the captaines of hundreths the speares and the shieldes that were King Dauids, and were in the house of the Lord.

11 And the garde stoode, euery man with his weapon in his hande, from the right side of the house to the left side, about the altar and about the house, round about the King.

12 Then he brought out the Kings sonne, and put the crowne vpon him and gaue him the Testimonie, and they made him King: also they anoynted him, and clapt their handes, and sayde, God saue the King.

13 And when Athaliah heard the noyse of the running of the people, shee came in to the people in the house of the Lord.

14 And when shee looked, beholde, the King stoode by a pillar, as the maner was, and the princes and the trumpetters by the King, and al the people of the land reioyced, and blew with trumpets. Then Athaliah rent her clothes, and cryed, Treason, treason.

15 But Iehoiada the Priest commanded the captaines of the hundreths that had the rule of the hoste, and sayde vnto them, Haue her forth of the ranges, and he that followeth her, let him die by the sworde: for the Priest had sayd, Let her not be slaine in the house of the Lord.

16 Then they laid hands on her, and she went by the way, by the which the horses goe to the house of the King, and there was she slaine.

17 And Iehoiada made a couenant betweene the Lord, and the King and the people, that they should be the Lordes people: likewise betweene the King and the people.

18 Then all the people of the lande went into the house of Baal, and destroyed it with his altars, and his images brake they downe courageously, and slewe Mattan the Priest of Baal before the altars: and the Priest set a garde ouer the house of the Lord.

19 Then he tooke the captaines of hudreths, and the other captaines, and the garde, and all the people of the lande: and they brought the King from the house of the Lord, and came by the way of the gate of the garde to the Kings house: and he sate him downe on the throne of the Kings.

20 And all the people of the land reioyced, and the citie was in quiet: for they had slaine Athaliah with the sworde beside the Kings house.

21 Seuen yeere olde was Iehoash when he began to reigne.

Second Kings 12

1 In the seuenth yere of Iehu Iehoash began to reigne, and reigned fourty yeres in Ierusalem, and his mothers name was Zibiah of Beer-sheba.

2 And Iehoash did that which was good in the sight of the Lord all his time that Iehoiada the Priest taught him.

3 But the hie places were not taken away: for the people offred yet and burnt incense in the hie places.

4 And Iehoash sayde to the Priestes, All the siluer of dedicate things that bee brought to the house of the Lord, that is, the money of them that are vnder the count, the money that euery man is set at, and all the money that one offereth willingly, and bringeth into the house of the Lord,

5 Let the Priestes take it to them, euery man of his acquaintance: and they shall repaire the broken places of the house, wheresoeuer any decay is founde.

6 Yet in the three and twentieth yeere of King Iehoash the Priestes had not mended that which was decayed in the Temple.

7 Then King Iehoash called for Iehoiada the Priest, and the other Priestes, and sayd vnto them, Why repaire yee not the ruines of the Temple? nowe therefore receiue no more money of your acquaintance, except yee deliuer it to repaire the ruines of the Temple.

8 So the Priestes consented to receiue no more money of the people, neither to repaire the decayed places of the Temple.

9 Then Iehoiada the Priest tooke a chest and bored an hole in the lid of it, and set it beside the altar, on the right side, as euery man commeth into the Temple of the Lord. And the Priestes that kept the doore, put therein all the money that was brought into the house of the Lord.

10 And when they sawe there was much money in the chest, the Kinges Secretarie came vp and the hie Priest, and put it vp after that they had tolde the money that was found in the house of the Lord,

11 And they gaue the money made readie into the handes of them, that vndertooke the worke, and that had the ouersight of the house of the Lord; and they payed it out to the carpenters and

builders that wrought vpon the house of the Lord,

12 And to the masons and hewers of stone, and to bye timber and hewed stone, to repayre that was decayed in the house of the Lord, and for all that which was layed out for the reparation of the Temple.

13 Howbeit there was not made for the house of the Lord bowles of siluer, instruments of musicke, basons, trumpets, nor any vessels of golde, or vessels of siluer of the money that was brought into the house of the Lord.

14 But they gaue it to the workemen, which repayred therewith the house of the Lord.

15 Moreouer, they reckoned not with the men, into whose handes they deliuered that money to be bestowed on workemen: for they dealt faithfully.

16 The money of the trespasse offring and the money of ye sinne offrings was not brought into the house of the Lord: for it was the Priests.

17 Then came vp Hazael King of Aram, and fought against Gath and tooke it, and Hazael set his face to goe vp to Ierusalem.

18 And Iehoash King of Iudah tooke all the halowed thinges that Iehoshaphat, and Iehoram, and Ahaziah his fathers Kings of Iudah had dedicated, and that he himselfe had dedicated, and all the golde that was found in the treasures of the house of the Lord and in the Kings house, and sent it to Hazael King of Aram, and he departed from Ierusalem.

19 Concerning the rest of the acts of Ioash and all that he did, are they not written in the booke of the Chronicles of the Kings of Iudah?

20 And his seruants arose and wrought treason, and slewe Ioash in the house of Millo, when he came downe to Silla:

21 Euen Iozachar the sonne of Shimeath, and Iehozabad the sonne of Shomer his seruants smote him, and he dyed: and they buried him with his fathers in the citie of Dauid. And Amaziah his sonne reigned in his stead.

Second Kings 13

1 In the three and twentieth yeere of Ioash the sonne of Ahaziah King of Iudah, Iehoahaz the sonne of Iehu began to reigne ouer Israel in Samaria, and he reigned seuenteene yeere.

2 And he did euil in the sight of the Lord, and followed the sinnes of Ieroboam the sonne of Nebat, which made Israel to sinne, and departed not therefrom.

3 And the Lord was angry with Israel, and deliuered them into the hand of Hazael King of Aram, and into the hand of Ben-hadad the sonne of Hazael, all his dayes.

4 And Iehoahaz besought the Lord, and the Lord heard him: for he saw the trouble of Israel, wherewith the King of Aram troubled them.

5 (And the Lord gaue Israel a deliuerer, so that they came out from vnder the subiection of the Aramites. And the children of Israel dwelt in their tents as before time.

6 Neuerthelesse they departed not from the sinnes of the house of Ieroboam which made Israel sinne, but walked in them. euen the groue also remayned still in Samaria)

7 For he had left of the people to Iehoahaz but fiftie horsemen, and tenne charets, and tenne thousand footemen, because the King of Aram had destroyed them, and made them like dust beaten to pouder.

8 Concerning the rest of the actes of Iehoahaz and all that he did, and his valiant deedes, are they not written in the booke of the Chronicles of the Kings of Israel?

9 And Iehoahaz slept with his fathers, and they buried him in Samaria, and Ioash his sonne reigned in his steade.

10 In the seuen and thirtieth yere of Ioash King of Iudah began Iehoash the sonne of Iehoahaz to reigne ouer Israel in Samaria, and reigned sixteene yeere,

11 And did euil in the sight of the Lord: for he departed not from all the sinnes of Ieroboam the sonne of Nebat that made Israel to sinne, but he walked therein.

12 Concerning the rest of the actes of Ioash and all that he did, and his valiant deedes, and how he fought against Amaziah King of Iudah, are they not written in the booke of the Chronicles of the Kings of Israel?

13 And Ioash slept with his fathers, and Ieroboam sate vpon his seate: and Ioash was buryed in Samaria among the Kings of Israel.

14 When Elisha fell sicke of his sickenesse whereof he dyed, Ioash the King of Israel came downe vnto him, and wept vpon his face, and sayd, O my father, my father, the charet of Israel, and the horsemen of the same.

15 Then Elisha sayde vnto him, Take a bowe and arrowes. And he tooke vnto him bowe and arrowes.

16 And he sayde to the King of Israel, Put thine hand vpon the bowe. And he put his hand vpon it. And Elisha put his hands vpon the Kings hands,

17 And saide, Open the windowe Eastward. And when he had opened it, Elisha said, Shoote. And he shot. And he sayd, Beholde the arrowe of the Lordes deliuerance and the arrowe of deliuerance against Aram: for thou shalt smite the Aramites in Aphek, till thou hast consumed them.

18 Againe he said, Take the arrowes. And he tooke them. And he sayde vnto the King of Israel, Smite the ground. And he smote thrise, and ceased.

19 Then the man of God was angry with him, and sayde, Thou shouldest haue smitten fiue or sixe times, so thou shouldest haue smitten Aram, till thou haddest consumed it, where nowe thou shalt smite Aram but thrise.

20 So Elisha dyed, and they buryed him. And certaine bandes of the Moabites came into the land that yeere.

21 And as they were burying a man, behold, they saw the souldiers: therfore they cast the man into the sepulchre of Elisha. And when the man was downe, and touched the bones of Elisha, he reuiued and stoode vpon his feete.

22 But Hazael King of Aram vexed Israel all the dayes of Iehoahaz.

23 Therefore the Lord had mercy on them and pitied them, and had respect vnto them because of his couenant with Abraham, Izhak, and Iaakob, and would not destroy them, neither cast he them from him as yet.

24 So Hazael the King of Aram dyed: and Ben-hadad his sonne reigned in his stead.

25 Therefore Iehoash the sonne of Iehoahaz returned, and tooke out of the hand of Ben-hadad the sonne of Hazael the cities which he had taken away by warre out of the hand of Iehoahaz his father: for three times did Ioash beate him, and restored the cities vnto Israel.

Second Kings 14

1 The second yeere of Ioash sonne of Iehoahaz King of Israel reigned Amaziah the sonne of Ioash King of Iudah.

2 He was fiue and twentie yeere olde when he began to reigne, and reigned nine and twentie yeere in Ierusalem, and his mothers name was Iehoadan of Ierusalem.

3 And he did vprightly in the sight of the Lord, yet not like Dauid his father, but did according to all that Ioash his father had done.

4 Notwithstanding the hie places were not taken away: for as yet the people did sacrifice and burnt incense in the hie places.

5 And when the kingdome was confirmed in his hand, he slewe his seruants which had killed the King his father.

6 But the children of those that did slay him, he slewe not, according vnto that that is written in the booke of the Lawe of Moses, wherein the Lord commanded, saying, The fathers shall not be put to death for the children, nor the children put to death for the fathers: but euery man shall be put to death for his owne sinne.

7 He slew also of Edom in the valley of salt ten thousand, and tooke the citie of Sela by warre, and called the name thereof Ioktheel vnto this day.

8 Then Amaziah sent messengers to Iehoash the sonne of Iehoahaz, sonne of Iehu King of Israel, saying, Come, let vs see one another in the face.

9 Then Iehoash the King of Israel sent to Amaziah King of Iudah, saying, The thistle that is in Lebanon, sent to the cedar that is in Lebanon, saying, Giue thy daughter to my sonne to wife: and the wilde beast that was in Lebanon, went and trode downe the thistle.

10 Because thou hast smitten Edom, thine heart hath made thee proud: bragge of glory, and tary at home. why doest thou prouoke to thine hurt, that thou shouldest fall, and Iudah with thee?

11 But Amaziah would not heare: therefore Iehoash King of Israel went vp: and he and Amaziah King of Iudah sawe one another in the face at Beth-shemesh which is in Iudah.

12 And Iudah was put to the worse before Israel, and they fledde euery man to their tents.

13 But Iehoash King of Israel tooke Amaziah King of Iudah, the sonne of Iehoash the sonne of Ahaziah, at Beth-shemesh, and came to Ierusalem, and brake downe the wall of Ierusalem from the gate of Ephraim to the corner gate, foure hundreth cubites.

14 And he tooke all the gold and siluer, and all the vessels that were found in the house of the Lord, and in the treasures of the Kings house, and the children that were in hostage, and returned to Samaria.

15 Concerning the rest of the acts of Iehoash which he did and his valiant deedes, and how he fought with Amaziah King of Iudah, are they not written in the booke of the Chronicles of the Kings of Israel?

16 And Iehoash slept with his fathers, and was buried at Samaria among the Kings of Israel: and Ieroboam his sonne reigned in his stead.

17 And Amaziah the sonne of Ioash King of Iudah, liued after the death of Iehoash sonne of Iehoahaz King of Israel fifteene yeere.

18 Concerning the rest of the actes of Amaziah, are they not written in the booke of the Chronicles of the Kings of Iudah?

19 But they wrought treason against him in Ierusalem, and he fled to Lachish, but they sent after him to Lachish, and slewe him there.

20 And they brought him on horses, and he was buried at Ierusalem with his fathers in the citie of Dauid.

21 Then all the people of Iudah tooke Azariah which was sixteene yeere olde, and made him King for his father Amaziah.

22 He built Elath, and restored it to Iudah, after that the King slept with his fathers.

23 In the fifteenth yeere of Amaziah the sonne of Ioash King of Iudah, was Ieroboam the sonne of Ioash made King ouer Israel in Samaria, and reigned one and fourtie yeere.

24 And he did euill in the sight of the Lord: for he departed not from all the sinnes of Ieroboam the sonne of Nebat, which made Israel to sinne.

25 He restored the coast of Israel, from the entring of Hamath, vnto the Sea of the wildernesse, according to the worde of the Lord God of Israel, which he spake by his seruant Ionah the sonne of Amittai the Prophet, which was of Gath Hepher.

26 For the Lord saw the exceeding bitter affliction of Israel, so that there was none shutte vp, nor any left, neyther yet any that could helpe Israel.

27 Yet the Lord had not decreed to put out the name of Israel from vnder the heauen: therefore he preserued them by the hand of Ieroboam the sonne of Ioash.

28 Concerning the rest of the actes of Ieroboam, and all that he did, and his valiant deedes, and how he fought, and how he restored Damascus, and Hamath to Iudah in Israel, are they not written in the booke of the Chronicles of the Kings of Israel?

29 So Ieroboam slept with his fathers, euen with the Kings of Israel, and Zachariah his sonne reigned in his steade.

Second Kings 15

1 In the seuen and twentieth yeere of Ieroboam King of Israel, began Azariah, sonne of Amaziah King of Iudah to reigne.

2 Sixteene yeere olde was he, when he was made King, and he reigned two and fiftie yeere in Ierusalem: and his mothers name was Iecholiah of Ierusalem.

3 And he did vprightly in the sight of the Lord, according to all that his father Amaziah did.

4 But the hie places were not put away: for the people yet offered, and burned incense in the hie places.

5 And the Lord smote the King: and he was a leper vnto the day of his death, and dwelt in an house apart, and Iotham the kings sonne gouerned the house, and iudged the people of the land.

6 Concerning the rest of the actes of Azariah, and all that he did, are they not written in the booke of the Chronicles of the Kings of Iudah?

7 So Azariah slept with his fathers, and they buryed him with his fathers in the citie of Dauid, and Iotham his sonne reigned in his stead.

8 In the eyght and thirtieth yeere of Azariah King of Iudah did Zachariah the sonne of Ieroboam reigne ouer Israel in Samaria sixe moneths,

9 And did euill in the sight of the Lord, as did his fathers: for he departed not from the sinnes of Ieroboam the sonne of Nebat, which made Israel to sinne.

10 And Shallum the sonne of Iabesh cospired against him, and smote him in the sight of the people, and killed him, and reigned in his stead.

11 Concerning the rest of the actes of Zachariah, behold, they are written in the booke of the Chronicles of the Kings of Israel.

12 This was the word of the Lord, which he spake vnto Iehu, saying, Thy sonnes shall sit on the throne of Israel vnto the fourth generation after thee. And it came so to passe.

13 Shallum the sonne of Iabesh began to reigne in the nine and thirtieth yeere of Vzziah King of Iudah: and he reigned the space of a moneth in Samaria.

14 For Menahem the sonne of Gadi went vp from Tirzah, and came to Samaria, and smote Shallum the sonne of Iabesh in Samaria, and slew him, and reigned in his stead.

15 Cocerning the rest of the acts of Shallum, and the treason which he wrought, beholde, they are written in the booke of the Chronicles of the Kings of Israel.

16 Then Menahem destroyed Tiphsah, and all that were therein, and the coastes thereof from Tirzah, because they opened not to him, and he smote it, and ript vp all their women with childe.

17 The nine and thirtieth yeere of Azariah King of Iudah, beganne Menahem the sonne of Gadi to reigne ouer Israel, and reigned ten yeeres in Samaria.

18 And he did euill in the sight of the Lord, and departed not all his dayes from the sinne of Ieroboam the sonne of Nebat, which made Israel to sinne.

19 Then Pul the king of Asshur came against the land: and Menahem gaue Pul a thousand talents of siluer, that his hande might bee with him, and establish the kingdome in his hand.

20 And Menahem exacted the money in Israel, that all men of substance shoulde giue the King of Asshur fiftie shekels of siluer a piece: so the king of Asshur returned and taried not there in the land.

21 Concerning the rest of the actes of Menahem, and all that he did, are they not written in the booke of the Chronicles of the kings of Israel?

22 And Menahem slept with his fathers, and Pekahiah his sonne did reigne in his steade.

23 In ye fiftieth yere of Azariah king of Iudah, began Pekahiah the sonne of Menahem to reigne ouer Israel in Samaria, and reigned two yere.

24 And he did euill in the sight of the Lord: for he departed not from the sinnes of Ieroboam the sonne of Nebat, which made Israel to sinne.

25 And Pekah the sonne of Remaliah, his captaine conspired against him, and smote him in Samaria in the place of the Kings palace with Argob and Arieh, and with him fiftie men of the Gileadites: so he killed him, and reigned in his steade.

26 Concerning the rest of the actes of Pekahiah, and all that he did, behold, they are written in the booke of the Chronicles of the Kings of Israel.

27 In the two and fiftieth yere of Azariah King of Iudah began Pekah the sonne of Remaliah to reigne ouer Israel in Samaria, and reigned twentie yeere.

28 And he did euil in the sight of the Lord: for he departed not from the sinnes of Ieroboam the sonne of Nebat, that made Israel to sinne.

29 In the dayes of Pekah king of Israel came Tiglath Pileser king of Asshur, and tooke Iion, and Abel, Beth-maachah, and Ianoah, and Kedesh, and Hazor, and Gilead, and Galilah, and all the land of Naphtali, and caryed them away to Asshur.

30 And Hoshea the sonne of Elah wrought treason against Pekah the sonne of Remaliah, and smote him, and slewe him, and reigned in his stead in the twentieth yeere of Iotham the sonne of Vzziah.

31 Concerning the rest of the actes of Pekah, and all that he did, behold, they are written in the booke of the Chronicles of the kings of Israel.

32 In the second yere of Pekah the sonne of Remaliah King of Israel, began Iotham sonne of Vzziah King of Iudah to reigne.

33 Fiue and twentie yeere olde was he, when he began to reigne, and he reigned sixteene yeere in Ierusalem: and his mothers name was Ierusha the daughter of Zadok.

34 And hee did vprightly in the sight of the Lord: he did according to all that his father Vzziah had done.

35 But the hie places were not put away: for the people yet offered and burnt incense in the hie places: he buylt the hyest gate of the house of the Lord.

36 Concerning the rest of the acts of Iotham, and all that hee did, are they not written in the booke of the Chronicles of the kings of Iudah?

37 In those dayes the Lord began to send against Iudah Rezin the king of Aram, and Pekah the sonne of Remaliah.

38 And Iotham slept with his fathers, and was buryed with his fathers in the citie of Dauid his father, and Ahaz his sonne reigned in his steade.

Second Kings 16

1 The seuenteenth yeere of Pekah the sonne of Remaliah, Ahaz the sonne of Iotham King of Iudah began to reigne.

2 Twentie yeere olde was Ahaz, when hee began to reigne, and he reigned sixteene yeere in Ierusalem, and did not vprightly in the sight of the Lord his God, like Dauid his father:

3 But walked in the way of ye kings of Israel, yea, and made his sonne to go through the fire, after the abominations of the heathen, whom the Lord had cast out before the children of Israel.

4 Also he offred and burnt incense in the hie places and on the hilles, and vnder euery greene tree.

5 Then Rezin king of Aram and Pekah sonne of Remaliah King of Israel came vp to Ierusalem to fight: and they besieged Ahaz, but could not ouercome him.

6 At the same time Rezin king of Aram restored Elath to Aram, and droue the Iewes from Elath: so the Aramites came to Elath, and dwelt there vnto this day.

7 Then Ahaz sent messengers to Tiglath Pileser king of Asshur, saying, I am thy seruant and thy sonne: come vp, and deliuer me out of the hand of the king of Aram, and out of the hand of the King of Israel which rise vp against me.

8 And Ahaz tooke the siluer and the golde that was found in the house of the Lord, and in the treasures of the Kings house, and sent a present vnto the King of Asshur.

9 And the King of Asshur consented vnto him: and the King of Asshur went vp against Damascus. and when he had taken it, he caryed the people away to Kir, and slew Rezin.

10 And King Ahaz went vnto Damascus to meete Tiglath Pileser King of Asshur: and when King Ahaz sawe the altar that was at Damascus, he sent to Vriiah the Priest the paterne of the altar, and the facion of it, and all the workemanship thereof.

11 And Vriiah the Priest made an altar in al poyntes like to that which King Ahaz had sent from Damascus, so did Vriiah the Priest against King Ahaz came from Damascus.

12 So when the King was come from Damascus, the King sawe the altar: and the King drewe neere to the altar and offered thereon.

13 And hee burnt his burnt offering, and his meate offring, and powred his drinke offring, and sprinkled the blood of his peace offrings besides the altar,

14 And set it by the brasen altar which was before the Lord, and brought it in farther before the house betweene the altar and the house of the Lord, and set it on the North side of the altar.

15 And King Ahaz commanded Vriiah the Priest, and sayde, Vpon the great altar set on fire in the morning the burnt offring, and in the euen the meate offring, and the Kings burnt offring and his meate offering, with the burnt offring of all the people of the lande, and their meate offring, and their drinke offrings: and powre thereby all the blood of the burnt offring, and all the blood of the sacrifice, and the brasen altar shalbe for me to inquire of God.

16 And Vriiah the Priest did according to all that King Ahaz had commanded.

17 And King Ahaz brake the borders of the bases, and tooke the caldrons from off them, and tooke downe the sea from the brasen oxen that were vnder it, and put it vpon a pauement of stones.

18 And the vaile for the Sabbath (that they had made in the house) and the Kings entrie without turned he to the house of the Lord, because of the King of Asshur.

19 Concerning the rest of the actes of Ahaz, which he did, are they not written in the booke of the Chronicles of the Kings of Iudah?

20 And Ahaz slept with his fathers, and was buryed with his fathers in the citie of Dauid, and Hezekiah his sonne reigned in his steade.

Second Kings 17

1 In the twelft yeere of Ahaz King of Iudah began Hoshea the sonne of Elah to reigne in Samaria ouer Israel, and reigned nine yeeres.

2 And he did euill in the sight of the Lord, but not as the Kinges of Israel, that were before him.

3 And Shalmaneser king of Asshur came vp against him, and Hoshea became his seruant, and gaue him presents.

4 And the King of Asshur founde treason in Hoshea: for he had sent messengers to So King of Egypt, and brought no present vnto the King of Asshur, as he had done yeerely: therfore the king of Asshur shut him vp, and put him in prison.

5 Then the king of Asshur came vp throughout all the lande, and went against Samaria, and besieged it three yeere.

6 In the ninth yeere of Hoshea, the King of Asshur tooke Samaria, and caryed Israel away vnto Asshur, and put them in Halah, and in Habor by the riuer of Gozan, and in the cities of the Medes.

7 For when the children of Israel sinned against the Lord their God, which had brought them out of the land of Egypt, from vnder ye hand of Pharaoh king of Egypt, and feared other gods,

8 And walked according to the facions of the Heathen, whom the Lord had cast out before the children of Israel, and after the maners of the Kings of Israel, which they vsed,

9 And the children of Israel had done secretly things that were not vpright before the Lord their God, and throughout all their cities had built hie places, both from the tower of the watch, to the defensed citie,

10 And had made them images and groues vpon euery hie hill, and vnder euery greene tree,

11 And there burnt incense in all the hie places, as did the heathen, whom the Lord had taken away before them, and wrought wicked things to anger the Lord,

12 And serued idoles: whereof the Lord had sayd vnto them, Ye shall do no such thing,

13 Notwithstanding the Lord testified to Israel, and to Iudah by all the Prophets, and by all the Seers, saying, Turne from your euill wayes, and keepe my commandements and my statutes, according to all the Lawe, which I commanded your fathers, and which I sent to you by my seruants the Prophets.

14 Neuerthelesse they would not obey, but hardened their neckes, like to the neckes of their fathers, that did not beleeue in the Lord their God.

15 And they refused his statutes and his couenant, that he made with their fathers, and his testimonies (wherewith he witnessed vnto them) and they followed vanitie, and became vaine, and followed the heathen that were round about them: concerning whome the Lord had charged them, that they should not do like them.

16 Finally they left all the commandements of the Lord their God, and made them molten images, euen two calues, and made a groue, and worshipped all the hoste of heauen, and serued Baal.

17 And they made their sonnes and their daughters passe thorowe the fire, and vsed witchcraft and inchantments, yea, solde them selues to doe euill in the sight of the Lord, to anger him.

18 Therefore the Lord was exceeding wroth with Israel, and put them out of his sight, and none was left but the tribe of Iudah onely.

19 Yet Iudah kept not the commandements of the Lord their God, but walked according to the facion of Israel, which they vsed.

20 Therefore the Lord cast off all the seede of Israel, and afflicted them, and deliuered them into the handes of spoylers, vntill he had cast them out of his sight.

21 For he cut off Israel from the house of Dauid, and they made Ieroboam the sonne of Nebat King: and Ieroboam drewe Israel away from following the Lord, and made them sinne a great sinne.

22 For the children of Israel walked in all the sinnes of Ieroboam, which he did, and departed not therefrom,

23 Vntill the Lord put Israel away out of his sight, as he had said by all his seruants the Prophets, and caryed Israel away out of their land to Asshur vnto this day.

24 And the King of Asshur brought folke from Babel, and from Cuthah, and from Aua, and from Hamath, and from Sepharuaim, and placed them in the cities of Samaria in steade of the children of Israel: so they possessed Samaria, and dwelt in the cities thereof.

25 And at the beginning of their dwelling there, they feared not the Lord: therefore the Lord sent lions among them, which slewe them.

26 Wherefore they spake to the King of Asshur, saying, The nations which thou hast remoued, and placed in the cities of Samaria, knowe not the maner of the God of the land: therefore he hath sent lions among them, and behold, they slay them, because they knowe not the maner of the God of the land.

27 Then the King of Asshur commanded, saying, Carie thither one of the Priestes whome ye brought thence, and let him goe and dwell there, and teache them the maner of the God of the countrey.

28 So one of the Priestes, which they had caryed from Samaria, came and dwelt in Beth-el, and taught them how they shoulde feare the Lord.

29 Howbeit euery nation made their gods, and put them in the houses of the hie places, which the Samaritanes had made, euery nation in their cities, wherein they dwelt.

30 For the men of Babel made Succoth-Benoth: and the men of Cuth made Nergal, and the men of Hamath made Ashima,

31 And the Auims made Nibhaz, and Tartak: and the Sepharuims burnt their children in the fire to Adrammelech, and Anammelech the gods of Sepharuaim.

32 Thus they feared the Lord, and appoynted out Priestes out of them selues for the hie places, who prepared for them sacrifices in the houses of the hie places.

33 They feared the Lord, but serued their gods after the maner of the nations whome they caryed thence.

34 Vnto this day they doe after the olde maner: they neyther feare God, neyther doe after their ordinances, nor after their customes, nor after the Lawe, nor after the commandement, which the Lord commanded the children of Iaakob, whom he named Israel,

35 And with whom the Lord had made a couenant, and charged them, saying, Feare none other gods, nor bowe your selues to them, nor serue them, nor sacrifice to them:

36 But feare the Lord which brought you out of the land of Egypt with great power, and a stretched out arme: him feare ye, and worshippe him, and sacrifice to him.

37 Also keepe ye diligently the statutes and the ordinances, and the Lawe, and the commandement, which he wrote for you, that ye do them continually, and feare not other gods.

38 And forget not the couenant that I haue made with you, neither feare ye other gods,

39 But feare the Lord your God, and he will deliuer you out of the handes of all your enemies.

40 Howbeit they obeyed not, but did after their olde custome.

41 So these nations feared the Lord, and serued their images also: so did their children, and their childrens children: as did their fathers, so do they vnto this day.

Second Kings 18

1 Now in the third yeere of Hoshea, sonne of Elah King of Israel, Hezekiah the sonne of Ahaz king of Iudah began to reigne.

2 He was fiue and twentie yeere olde when he began to reigne, and reigned nine and twenty yeere in Ierusalem. His mothers name also was Abi the daughter of Zachariah,

3 And he did vprightly in the sight of the Lord, according to all that Dauid his father had done.

4 He tooke away the hie places, and brake the images, and cut downe the groues, and brake in pieces the brasen serpent that Moses had made: for vnto those dayes the children of Israel did burne incense to it, and hee called it Nehushtan.

5 He trusted in the Lord God of Israel: so that after him was none like him among all the Kings of Iudah, neither were there any such before him.

6 For he claue to the Lord, and departed not from him, but kept his commandements, which the Lord had commanded Moses.

7 So the Lord was with him, and he prospered in all thinges, which he tooke in hande: also he rebelled against the King of Asshur, and serued him not.

8 He smote the Philistims vnto Azzah, and the coastes thereof, from the watch towre vnto the defensed citie.

9 And in the fourth yere of King Hezekiah, (which was the seuenth yeere of Hoshea sonne of Elah King of Israel) Shalmaneser King of Asshur came vp against Samaria, and besieged it.

10 And after three yeeres they tooke it, euen in the sixt yeere of Hezekiah: that is, the ninth yeere of Hoshea King of Israel was Samaria taken.

11 Then the King of Asshur did carry away Israel vnto Asshur, and put them in Halah and in Habor, by the riuer of Gozan, and in the cities of the Medes,

12 Because they woulde not obey the voyce of the Lord their God, but transgressed his couenant: that is, all that Moses the seruant of the Lord had commanded, and would neyther obey nor doe them.

13 Moreouer, in the fourteenth yeere of King Hezekiah, Saneherib King of Asshur came vp against all the strong cities of Iudah, and tooke them.

14 Then Hezekiah King of Iudah sent vnto the King of Asshur to Lachish, saying, I haue offended: depart from me, and what thou layest vpon me, I wil beare it. And the King of Asshur appoynted vnto Hezekiah King of Iudah three hudreth talents of siluer, and thirty talets of golde.

15 Therefore Hezekiah gaue all the siluer that was found in the house of the Lord, and in the treasures of the Kings house.

16 At the same season did Hezekiah pul off the plates of the doores of the Temple of the Lord, and the pillars (which the sayd Hezekiah King of Iudah had couered ouer) and gaue them to the King of Asshur.

17 And the King of Asshur sent Tartan, and Rab-saris, and Rabshakeh from Lachish to King Hezekiah with a great hoste against Ierusalem. And they went vp, and came to Ierusalem, and when they were come vp, they stood by the conduite of the vpper poole, which is by the path of the fullers fielde,

18 And called to the King. Then came out to them Eliakim the sonne of Hilkiah, which was steward of the house, and Shebnah the chanceller, and Ioah the sonne of Asaph the recorder.

19 And Rabshakeh sayde vnto them, Tell ye Hezekiah, I pray you, Thus saith the great King, euen the great King of Asshur, What confidence is this wherein thou trustest?

20 Thou thinkest, Surely I haue eloquence, but counsell and strength are for the warre. On whom then doest thou trust, that thou rebellest against me?

21 Lo, thou trustest now in this broken staffe of reede, to wit, on Egypt, on which if a man leane, it will goe into his hand, and pearce it: so is Pharaoh king of Egypt vnto all that trust on him.

22 But if ye say vnto me, We trust in the Lord our God, is not that he whose hie places, and whose altars Hezekiah hath taken away, and hath sayd to Iudah and Ierusalem, Ye shall worship before this altar in Ierusalem?

23 Now therefore giue hostages to my lord the King of Asshur, and I will giue thee two thousand horses, if thou be able to set riders vpon them.

24 For how canst thou despise any captaine of the least of my masters

seruants, and put thy trust on Egypt for charets and horsemen?

25 Am I now come vp without the Lord to this place, to destroy it? the Lord sayd to me, Goe vp against this land, and destroy it.

26 Then Eliakim the sonne of Hilkiah, and Shebnah, and Ioah said vnto Rabshakeh, Speake I pray thee, to thy seruants in the Aramites language, for we vnderstand it, and talke not with vs in the Iewes tongue, in the audience of the people that are on the wall.

27 But Rabshakeh saide vnto them, Hath my master sent me to thy master and to thee to speake these words, and not to the men which sit on the wall, that they may eate their owne doung, and drinke their owne pisse with you?

28 So Rabshakeh stoode and cryed with a loude voyce in the Iewes language, and spake, saying, Heare the wordes of the great King, of the king of Asshur.

29 Thus sayth the King, Let not Hezekiah deceiue you: for he shall not be able to deliuer you out of mine hand.

30 Neither let Hezekiah make you to trust in the Lord, saying, The Lord will surely deliuer vs, and this citie shall not be giuen ouer into the hand of the king of Asshur.

31 Hearken not vnto Hezekiah: for thus saith the king of Asshur, Make appointment with me, and come out to me, that euery man may eate of his owne vine, and euery man of his owne figge tree, and drinke euery man of the water of his owne well,

32 Till I come, and bring you to a land like your owne land, euen a land of wheate and wine, a land of bread and vineyardes, a lande of oliues oyle, and hony, that ye may liue and not die: and obey not Hezekiah, for he deceiueth you, saying, The Lord will deliuer vs.

33 Hath any of the gods of the nations deliuered his lande out of the hand of the King of Asshur?

34 Where is the god of Hamah, and of Arpad? where is the god of Sepharuaim, Hena and Iuah? how haue they deliuered Samaria out of mine hand?

35 Who are they among all the gods of the nations, that haue deliuered their lande out of mine hand, that the Lord should deliuer Ierusalem out of mine hand?

36 But the people helde their peace, and answered not him a worde: for the Kings commandement was, saying, Answere ye him not.

37 Then Eliakim, the sonne of Hilkiah which was steward of the house, and Shebnah the chanceller, and Ioah the sonne of Asaph the recorder came to Hezekiah with their clothes rent, and tolde him the wordes of Rabshakeh.

Second Kings 19

1 And when King Hezekiah heard it, he rent his clothes and put on sackecloth, and came into the house of the Lord,

2 And sent Eliakim which was the stewarde of the house, and Shebnah the chanceller, and the Elders of the Priestes clothed in sackecloth to Isaiah the Prophet the sonne of Amoz.

3 And they said vnto him, Thus saith Hezekiah, This day is a day of tribulation and of rebuke, and blasphemie: for the childre are come to the birth, and there is no strength to bring foorth.

4 If so be the Lord thy God hath heard all the wordes of Rabshakeh, whome the King of Asshur his master hath sent to raile on the liuing God, and to reproch him with wordes which the Lord thy God hath heard, then lift thou vp thy prayer for the remnant that are left.

5 So the seruants of King Hezekiah came to Isaiah.

6 And Isaiah said vnto them, So shall ye say to your master, Thus sayeth the Lord, Be not afraide of the words which thou hast heard, wherewith the seruants of the king of Asshur haue blasphemed me.

7 Beholde, I will sende a blast vpon him, and he shall heare a noyse, and returne to his owne lande: and I will cause him to fall by the sworde in his owne lande.

8 So Rabshakeh returned, and founde the King of Asshur fighting against Libnah: for he had heard that he was departed from Lachish.

9 He heard also men say of Tirhakah King of Ethiopia, Beholde, he is come out to fight against thee: he therefore departed and sent other messengers vnto Hezekiah, saying,

10 Thus shall ye speake to Hezekiah King of Iudah, and say, Let not thy God deceiue thee in whome thou trustest, saying, Ierusalem shall not be deliuered into the hande of the King of Asshur.

11 Beholde, thou hast heard what the Kings of Asshur haue done to all landes, how they haue destroyed them: and shalt thou be deliuered?

12 Haue the gods of the heathen deliuered them which my fathers haue destroyed? as Gozan, and Haran, and Rezeph, and the children of Eden, which were in Thelasar?

13 Where is the King of Hamath, and the King of Arpad, and the King of the citie of Shepharuaim, Hena and Iuah?

14 So Hezekiah receiued the letter of the hande of the messengers, and read it: and Hezekiah went vp into the house of the Lord, and Hezekiah spread it before the Lord.

15 And Hezekiah prayed before the Lord, and saide, O Lord God of Israel, which dwellest betweene the Cherubims, thou art very God alone ouer all the kingdomes of the earth: thou hast made the heauen and the earth.

16 Lord, bow downe thine eare, and heare: Lord open thine eyes and behold, and heare the wordes of Saneherib, who hath sent to blaspheme the liuing God.

17 Trueth it is, Lord, that the Kings of Asshur haue destroyed the nations and their landes,

18 And haue set fire on their gods: for they were no gods, but the worke of mans hands, euen wood and stone: therefore they destroyed them.

19 Nowe therefore, O Lord our God, I beseech thee, saue thou vs out of his hande, that all the kingdomes of the earth may knowe, that thou, O Lord, art onely God.

20 Then Isaiah the sonne of Amoz sent to Hezekiah, saying, Thus saith the Lord God of Israel, I haue heard that which thou hast prayed me, concerning Saneherib King of Asshur.

21 This is the worde that the Lord hath spoken against him, O Virgine, daughter of Zion, he hath despised thee, and laughed thee to scorne: O daughter of Ierusalem, he hath shaken his head at thee.

22 Whome hast thou railed on? and whome hast thou blasphemed? and against whome hast thou exalted thy voyce, and lifted vp thine eyes on hie? euen against the Holie one of Israel.

23 By thy messengers thou hast rayled on the Lord, and said, By the multitude of my charets I am come vp to the toppe of the mountaines, by the sides of Lebanon, and will cut downe the hie cedars thereof, and the faire firre trees thereof, and I will goe into the lodging of his borders, and into the forest of his Carmel.

24 I haue digged, and drunke the waters of others, and with the plant of my feete haue I dried all the floods closed in.

25 Hast thou not heard, howe I haue of olde time made it, and haue formed it long ago? and should I nowe bring it, that it should be destroyed, and laid on ruinous heapes, as cities defensed?

26 Whose inhabitants haue small power, and are afraid, and confounded: they are like the grasse of the field, and greene herbe, or grasse on ye house toppes, or as corne blasted before it be growen.

27 I knowe thy dwelling, yea, thy going out, and thy comming in, and thy furie against me.

28 And because thou ragest against me, and thy tumult is come vp to mine eares, I will put mine hooke in thy nostrels, and my bridle in thy lippes, and will bring thee backe againe the same way thou camest.

29 And this shalbe a signe vnto thee, O Hezekiah, Thou shalt eate this yeere such things as growe of them selues, and the next yeere such as growe without sowing, and the third yeere sowe ye and reape, and plant vineyardes, and eate the fruites thereof.

30 And the remnant that is escaped of the house of Iudah, shall againe take roote downewarde, and beare fruite vpwarde.

31 For out of Ierusalem shall goe a remnant, and some that shall escape out of mount Zion: the zeale of the Lord of hostes shall doe this.

32 Wherefore thus saith the Lord, concerning the King of Asshur, He shall not enter into this citie, nor shoote an arrowe there, nor come before it with shield, nor cast a mount against it:

33 But he shall returne the way he came, and shall not come into this citie, saith the Lord.

34 For I will defende this citie to saue it for mine owne sake, and for Dauid my seruants sake.

35 And the same night the Angell of the Lord went out and smote in the campe of Asshur an hundreth foure score and fiue thousande: so when they rose earely in the morning, behold, they were all dead corpses.

36 So Saneherib King of Asshur departed, and went his way, and returned, and dwelt in Nineueh.

37 And as he was in the Temple worshipping Nisroch his god, Adramelech and Sharezer his sonnes slewe him with the sworde: and they escaped into the land of Ararat, and Esarhaddon his sonne reigned in his steade.

Second Kings 20

1 About that time was Hezekiah sicke vnto death: and the Prophet Isaiah the sonne of Amoz came to him, and said vnto him, Thus saith the Lord, Put thine house in an order: for thou shalt die, and not liue.

2 Then he turned his face to the wall, and prayed to the Lord, saying,

3 I beseech thee, O Lord, remember nowe, howe I haue walked before thee in trueth and with a perfite heart, and haue done that which is good in thy sight: and Hezekiah wept sore.

4 And afore Isaiah was gone out into the middle of the court, the worde of the Lord came to him, saying,

5 Turne againe, and tell Hezekiah the captaine of my people, Thus saith the Lord God of Dauid thy father, I haue heard thy prayer, and seene thy teares: behold, I haue healed thee, and ye third day thou shalt go vp to ye house of ye Lord,

6 And I wil adde vnto thy dayes fiftene yere, and wil deliuer thee and this citie out of the hand of the King of Asshur, and will defende this citie for mine owne sake, and for Dauid my seruats sake.

7 Then Isaiah sayde, Take a lumpe of dry figges. And they tooke it, and layed it on the boyle, and he recouered.

8 For Hezekiah had saide vnto Isaiah, What shalbe the signe that the Lord will heale me, and that I shall goe vp into the house of the Lord the thirde day?

9 And Isaiah answered, This signe shalt thou haue of the Lord, that the Lord will doe that he hath spoken, Wilt thou that the shadowe goe forwarde ten degrees, or go backe ten degrees?

10 And Hezekiah answered, It is a light thing for the shadowe to passe forward ten degrees: not so then, but let ye shadow go backe ten degrees.

11 And Isaiah the Prophet called vnto the Lord, and he brought againe the shadowe ten degrees backe by the degrees whereby it had gone downe in the diall of Ahaz.

12 The same season Berodach Baladan the sonne of Baladan King of Babel, sent letters and a present to Hezekiah: for he had heard howe that Hezekiah was sicke.

13 And Hezekiah heard them, and shewed them all his treasure house, to wit, the siluer, and the golde, and the spices, and the precious oyntment, and all the house of his armour, and al that was founde in his treasures: there was nothing in his house, and in all his realme, that Hezekiah shewed them not.

14 Then Isaiah the Prophet came vnto King Hezekiah, and saide vnto him, What saide these men? and from whence came they to thee? And Hezekiah said, They be come from a farre countrey, euen from Babel.

15 Then saide he, What haue they seene in thine house? And Hezekiah answered, All that is in mine house haue they seene: there is nothing among my treasures, that I haue not shewed the.

16 And Isaiah said vnto Hezekiah, Heare the worde of the Lord.

17 Beholde, the dayes come, that all that is in thine house, and what so euer thy fathers haue layed vp in store vnto this day, shall be caryed into Babel: Nothing shall be left, saith the Lord.

18 And of thy sonnes, that shall proceede out of thee, and which thou shalt beget, shall they take away, and they shalbe eunuches in the palace of the King of Babel.

19 Then Hezekiah said vnto Isaiah, The word of the Lord which thou hast spoken, is good: for saide he, Shall it not be good, if peace and trueth be in my dayes?

20 Concerning the rest of the actes of Hezekiah, and all his valiant deedes, and howe he made a poole and a cundite, and brought water into the citie, are they not written in the booke of the Chronicles of the Kings of Iudah?

21 And Hezekiah slept with his fathers: and Manasseh his sonne reigned in his steade.

Second Kings 21

1 Manasseh was twelue yeere olde when he began to reigne, and reigned fiftie and fiue yeere in Ierusalem: his mothers name also was Hephzi-bah.

2 And he did euill in the sight of the Lord after the abomination of the heathen, whom the Lord had cast out before the children of Israel.

3 For he went backe and built the hie places, which Hezekiah his father had destroyed: and he erected vp altars for Baal, and made a groue, as did Ahab King of Israel, and worshipped all the hoste of heauen and serued them.

4 Also he built altars in the house of the Lord, of the which the Lord saide, In Ierusalem will I put my Name.

5 And he built altars for al the hoste of ye heauen in the two courtes of the house of the Lord.

6 And he caused his sonnes to passe through the fire, and gaue him selfe to witchcraft and sorcerie, and he vsed them that had familiar spirits and were soothsayers, and did much euill in the sight of the Lord to anger him.

7 And he set the image of the groue, that he had made, in the house, whereof ye Lord had saide to Dauid and to Salomon his sonne, In this house and in Ierusalem, which I haue chosen out of all the tribes of Israel, will I put my Name for euer.

8 Neither will I make the feete of Israel, mooue any more out of the lande, which I gaue their fathers: so that they will obserue and doe all that I haue commanded them, and according to all the Lawe that my seruant Moses commanded them.

9 Yet they obeyed not, but Manasseh ledde them out of the way, to doe more wickedly then did the heathen people, whom the Lord destroyed before the children of Israel.

10 Therefore the Lord spake by his seruants the Prophets, saying,

11 Because that Manasseh King of Iudah hath done such abominations, and hath wrought more wickedly then al that the Amorites (which were before him) did, and hath made Iudah sinne also with his idoles,

12 Therefore thus saith the Lord God of Israel, Beholde, I will bring an euill vpon Ierusalem and Iudah, that who so heareth of it, both his eares shall tingle.

13 And I will stretch ouer Ierusalem the line of Samaria, and the plommet of the house of Ahab: and I will wipe Ierusalem, as a man wipeth a dish, which he wipeth, and turneth it vpside downe.

14 And I will forsake the remnant of mine inheritance, and deliuer them into the hande of their enemies, and they shalbe robbed and spoyled of all their aduersaries,

15 Because they haue done euil in my sight, and haue prouoked mee to anger, since the time their fathers came out of Egypt vntill this day.

16 Moreouer Manasseh shed innocent blood exceeding much, till hee replenished Ierusalem from corner to corner, beside his sinne wherwith he made Iudah to sinne, and to doe euill in the sight of the Lord.

17 Concerning the rest of the actes of Manasseh, and all that hee did, and his sinne that he sinned, are they not written in the booke of the Chronicles of the Kings of Iudah?

18 And Manasseh slept with his fathers, and was buried in the garden of his own house, euen in the garden of Vzza: and Amon his sonne reigned in his steade.

19 Amon was two and twentie yere olde, when he began to reigne, and hee reygned two yeere in Ierusalem: his mothers name also was Meshullemeth the daughter of Haruz of Iotbah.

20 And he did euill in the sight of the Lord, as his father Manasseh did.

21 For hee walked in all the way that his father walked in, and serued the idoles that his father serued, and worshipped them.

22 And he forsooke the Lord God of his fathers, and walked not in the way of the Lord.

23 And the seruantes of Amon conspired against him, and slewe the King in his owne house.

24 And the people of the land slewe all them that had conspired against King Amon, and the people made Iosiah his sonne King in his steade.

25 Concerning the rest of the actes of Amon, which he did, are they not written in the booke of the Chronicles of the Kings of Iudah?

26 And they buried him in his sepulchre in the garden of Vzza: and Iosiah his sonne reigned in his steade.

Second Kings 22

1 Iosiah was eight yeere olde when he beganne to reigne, and hee reigned one and thirtie yeere in Ierusalem. His mothers name also was Iedidah the daughter of Adaiah of Bozcath.

2 And hee did vprightly in the sight of the Lord, and walked in all the wayes of Dauid his father, and bowed neither to the right hand, nor to the left.

3 And in the eighteenth yeere of King Iosiah, the King sent Shaphan the sonne of Azaliah the sonne of Meshullam the chanceller to ye house of the Lord, saying,

4 Goe vp to Hilkiah the high Priest, that hee may summe the siluer which is brought into the house of the Lord, which the keepers of the doore haue gathered of the people.

5 And let them deliuer it into the hande of them that doe the worke, and haue the ouersight of the house of the Lord: let them giue it to them that worke in the house of the Lord, to repaire the decayed places of the house:

6 To wit, vnto the artificers and carpenters and masons, and to bye timber, and hewed stone to repaire the house.

7 Howebeit, let no rekoning bee made with them of the money, that is deliuered into their hand: for they deale faithfully.

8 And Hilkiah the high Priest sayde vnto Shaphan the chanceller, I haue found the booke of the Lawe in the house of the Lord: and Hilkiah gaue the booke to Shaphan, and hee read it.

9 So Shaphan the chanceller came to ye King, and brought him word againe, and saide, Thy seruants haue gathered the money, that was found in the house, and haue deliuered it vnto the hands of them that doe the worke, and haue the ouersight of the house of the Lord.

10 Also Shaphan the chanceller shewed the King saying, Hilkiah the Priest hath deliuered me a booke. And Shaphan read it before the King.

11 And when the King had heard the wordes of the booke of the Law, he rent his clothes.

12 Therefore the King commanded Hilkiah the Priest, and Ahikam the sonne of Shaphan, and Achbor the sonne of Michaiah, and Shaphan the chanceller, and Asahiah the Kings seruant, saying,

13 Go ye and inquire of the Lord for me, and for the people, and for all Iudah concerning the wordes of this booke that is founde: for great is the wrath of the Lord that is kindled against vs, because our fathers haue not obeyed the wordes of this booke, to doe according vnto all that which is written therein for vs.

14 So Hilkiah the Priest and Ahikam, and Achbor and Shaphan, and Asahiah went vnto Huldah the Prophetesse the wife of Shallum, ye sonne of Tikuah, the sonne of Harhas keeper of the wardrobe: (and she dwelt in Ierusalem in the colledge) and they communed with her.

15 And shee answered them, Thus sayth the Lord God of Israel, Tel the man that sent you to mee,

16 Thus sayth the Lord, Behold, I wil bring euill vpon this place, and on the inhabitants thereof, euen al the words of the booke which ye King of Iudah hath read,

17 Because they haue forsaken mee, and haue burnt incense vnto other gods, to anger me with all ye works of their hands: my wrath also shalbe kindled against this place and shall not be quenched:

18 But to the King of Iudah, who sent you to inquire of the Lord, so shall ye say vnto him, Thus sayeth the Lord God of Israel, The wordes that thou hast heard, shall come to passe.

19 But because thine heart did melt, and thou hast humbled thy selfe before the Lord, when thou heardest what I spake against this place, and against the inhabitants of the same, to wit, that it should be destroyed and accursed, and hast rent thy clothes, and wept before me, I haue also heard it, saith the Lord.

20 Beholde therefore, I wil gather thee to thy fathers, and thou shalt be put in thy graue in peace, and thine eyes shall not see all the euil, which I will bring vpon this place. Thus they brought the King worde againe.

Second Kings 23

1 Then the King sent, and there gathered vnto him all the Elders of Iudah and of Ierusalem.

2 And the King went vp into the house of the Lord, with all the men of Iudah and all the inhabitants of Ierusalem with him, and the Priests and Prophets, and all the people both small and great: and he reade in their eares all the wordes of the booke of the couenant, which was found in the house of the Lord.

3 And the King stood by the pillar, and made a couenant before the Lord, that they shoulde walke after the Lord, and keepe his commandements, and his testimonies, and his statutes with all their heart, and with all their soule, that they might accomplish the wordes of this couenant written in this booke. And all the people stood to the couenant.

4 Then the King commanded Hilkiah the hie Priest and the priests of the second order, and the keepers of the doore, to bring out of ye Temple of the Lord all the vessels that were made for Baal, and for the groue, and for all the hoste of heauen, and he burnt them without Ierusalem in the fieldes of Kedron, and caryed the pouder of them into Beth-el.

5 And he put downe the Chemarims, whom the Kings of Iudah had founded to burne incense in the hie places, and in the cities of Iudah, and about Ierusalem, and also them that burnt incense vnto Baal, to the sunne and to the moone, and to the planets, and to all the hoste of heauen.

6 And he brought out the groue from the Temple of the Lord without Ierusalem vnto the valley of Kedron, and burnt it in the valley Kedron, and stampt it to pouder, and cast the dust thereof vpon the graues of the children of the people.

7 And hee brake downe the houses of the Sodomites, that were in the house of the Lord, where the women woue hangings for the groue.

8 Also he brought all the priests out of the cities of Iudah, and defiled the hie places where the Priests had burnt incense, euen from Geba to Beer-sheba, and destroyed the hie places of the gates, that were in the entring in of the gate of Ioshua the gouernour of the citie, which was at the left hand of the gate of the citie.

9 Neuerthelesse the Priests of the hie places came not vp to the altar of the Lord in Ierusalem, saue onely they did eate of the vnleauened bread among their brethren.

10 He defiled also Topheth, which was in the valley of the children of Hinnom, that no man shoulde make his sonne or his daughter passe through the fire to Molech.

11 He put downe also the horses that the Kings of Iudah had giuen to the sunne at the entring in of the house of the Lord, by the chamber of Nethan-melech the eunuche, which was ruler of the suburbes, and burnt the charets of the sunne with fire.

12 And the altars that were on the top of the chamber of Ahaz, which the Kings of Iudah had made, and the altars which Manasseh had made in the two courts of the house of the Lord did the King breake downe, and hasted thence, and cast the dust of them in the brooke Kedron.

13 Moreouer the King defiled the hie places that were before Ierusalem and on the right hand of the mount of corruption (which Salomon the King of Israel had buylt for Ashtoreth the idole of the Zidonians, and for Chemosh the idole of the Moabites, and for Milchom the abomination of the children of Ammon)

14 And he brake the images in pieces, and cut downe the groues and filled their places with the bones of men.

15 Furthermore the altar that was at Beth-el, and the hie place made by Ieroboam the sonne of Nebat, which made Israel to sinne, both this altar and also the hie place, brake he downe, and

burnt the hie place, and stampt it to powder and burnt the groue.

16 And as Iosiah turned himselfe, he spied the graues, that were in the mount, and sent and tooke the bones out of the graues, and burnt them vpon the altar and polluted it, according to the word of the Lord, that the man of God proclaimed, which cryed the same wordes.

17 Then he sayde, What title is that which I see? And the men of the citie sayd vnto him, It is the sepulchre of the man of God, which came from Iudah, and tolde these things that thou hast done to the altar of Beth-el.

18 Then sayde he, Let him alone: let none remooue his bones. So his bones were saued with the bones of the Prophet that came from Samaria.

19 Iosiah also tooke away all the houses of the hie places, which were in the cities of Samaria, which the Kings of Israel had made to anger the Lord, and did to them according to all the factes that he had done in Beth-el.

20 And he sacrificed all the Priests of the hie places, that were there vpon the altars, and burnt mens bones vpon them, and returned to Ierusalem.

21 Then the king commanded all the people, saying, Keepe the passeouer vnto the Lord your God, as it is written in the booke of this couenant.

22 And there was no Passeouer holden like that from the dayes of the Iudges that iudged Israel, nor in all the dayes of the Kinges of Israel, and of the Kings of Iudah.

23 And in the eightenth yere of King Iosiah was this Passeouer celebrated to the Lord in Ierusalem.

24 Iosiah also tooke away them that had familiar spirits, and the soothsayers, and the images, and the idoles, and al the abominations that were espied in the lande of Iudah and in Ierusalem, to performe the wordes of the Lawe, which were written in the booke that Hilkiah the Priest found in the house of the Lord.

25 Like vnto him was there no King before him, that turned to the Lord with al his heart, and with all his soule, and with all his might according to all the Lawe of Moses, neither after him arose there anie like him.

26 Notwithstanding the Lord turned not from the fiercenesse of his great wrath wherewith he was angrie against Iudah, because of all the prouocatios wherwith Manasseh had prouoked him.

27 Therefore the Lord saide, I will put Iudah also out of my sight, as I haue put away Israel, and will cast off this citie Ierusalem, which I haue chosen, and the house whereof I said, My name shalbe there.

28 Concerning the rest of the actes of Iosiah, and all that hee did, are they not written in the booke of the Chronicles of the Kings of Iudah?

29 In his dayes Pharaoh Nechoh King of Egypt went vp against the King of Asshur to the riuer Perath. And King Iosiah went against him, whome when Pharaoh sawe, he slewe him at Megiddo.

30 Then his seruants caryed him dead from Megiddo, and brought him to Ierusalem, and buried him in his owne sepulchre. And the people of the lande tooke Iehoahaz the sonne of Iosiah, and anointed him, and made him King in his fathers steade.

31 Iehoahaz was three and twentie yere olde when he beganne to reigne, and reigned three moneths in Ierusalem. His mothers name also was Hamutal the daughter of Ieremiah of Libnah.

32 And he did euill in the sight of the Lord, according to all that his fathers had done.

33 And Pharaoh Nechoh put him in bondes at Riblah in the lande of Hamath, while he reigned in Ierusalem, and put the lande to a tribute of an hundreth talents of siluer, and a talent of golde.

34 And Pharaoh Nechoh made Eliakim the sonne of Iosiah King in steade of Iosiah his father, and turned his name to Iehoiakim, and tooke Iehoahaz away, which when he came to Egypt, dyed there.

35 And Iehoiakim gaue the siluer and the golde to Pharaoh, and taxed the land to giue the money, according to the commadement of Pharaoh: he leuyed of euery man of the people of the lande, according to his value, siluer and golde to giue vnto Pharaoh Nechoh.

36 Iehoiakim was fiue and twentie yere olde, when he began to reigne, and he reigned eleuen yeeres in Ierusalem. His mothers name also was Zebudah the daughter of Pedaiah of Rumah.

37 And he did euill in the sight of the Lord, according to all that his fathers had done.

Second Kings 24

1 In his dayes came Nebuchad-nezzar King of Babel vp, and Iehoiakim became his seruant three yeere: afterwarde he turned, and rebelled against him.

2 And the Lord sent against him bandes of the Caldees, and bands of the Aramites, and bands of the Moabites, and bandes of the Ammonites, and he sent them against Iudah to destroy it, according to the worde of the Lord, which he spake by his seruants the Prophets.

3 Surely by the commandement of the Lord came this vpon Iudah, that he might put them out of his sight for the sinnes of Manasseh, according to all that he did,

4 And for the innocent blood that he shed, (for he filled Ierusalem with innocent blood) therefore the Lord would not pardon it.

5 Concerning the rest of the actes of Iehoiakim, and all that he did, are they not written in the booke of the Chronicles of the Kinges of Iudah?

6 So Iehoiakim slept with his fathers, and Iehoiachin his sonne reigned in his steade.

7 And the King of Egypt came no more out of his lande: for the King of Babel had taken from the riuer of Egypt, vnto the riuer Perath, all that pertained to the King of Egypt.

8 Iehoiachin was eighteene yere old, when he beganne to reigne, and reigned in Ierusalem three moneths. His mothers name also was Nehushta, the daughter of Elnathan of Ierusalem.

9 And he did euill in the sight of the Lord, according to all that his father had done.

10 In that time came the seruants of Nebuchad-nezzar king of Babel vp against Ierusalem: so the citie was besieged.

11 And Nebuchad-nezzar King of Babel came against the citie, and his seruants did besiege it.

12 Then Iehoiachin the king of Iudah came out against the King of Babel, he, and his mother and his seruants, and his princes, and his eunuches: and the King of Babel tooke him in the eyght yeere of his reigne.

13 And he caryed out thence all the treasures of the house of the Lord, and the treasures of the Kings house, and brake all the vessels of gold, which Salomon King of Israel had made in the Temple of the Lord, as the Lord had saide.

14 And he caryed away all Ierusalem, and all the princes, and all the strong men of warre, euen ten thousande into captiuitie, and all the workemen, and cunning men: so none remained sauing the poore people of the lande.

15 And he caryed away Iehoiachin into Babel, and the Kings mother, and the Kinges wiues, and his eunuches, and the mightie of the lande caryed he away into captiuitie from Ierusalem to Babel,

16 And al the men of warre, euen seuen thousand, and carpenters, and lockesmithes a thousande: all that were strong and apt for warre, did the King of Babel bring to Babel captiues.

17 And the King of Babel made Mattaniah his vncle King in his steade, and changed his name to Zedekiah.

18 Zedekiah was one and twentie yeere olde, when he began to reigne, and he reigned eleuen yeeres in Ierusalem. His mothers name also was Hamutal the daughter of Ieremiah of Libnah.

19 And he did euill in the sight of the Lord, according to all that Iehoiakim had done.

20 Therefore certainly the wrath of the Lord was against Ierusalem and Iudah vntill he cast them out of his sight. And Zedekiah rebelled against the King of Babel.

Second Kings 25

1 And in the ninth yeere of his reigne, the tenth moneth and tenth day of the moneth Nebuchad-nezzar King of Babel came, he, and all his hoste against Ierusalem, and pitched against it, and they built fortes against it round about it.

2 So the citie was besieged vnto the eleueth yeere of King Zedekiah.

3 And the ninth day of the moneth the famine was sore in the citie, so that there was no bread for the people of the lande.

4 Then the citie was broken vp, and all the men of warre fled by night, by the way of the gate, which is betweene two walles that was by the Kings garden: nowe the Caldees were by the citie round about: and the King went by the way of the wildernesse.

5 But the armie of the Caldees pursued after the King, and tooke him in the desertes of Iericho, and all his hoste was scattered from him.

6 Then they tooke the King, and caried him vp to the King of Babel to Riblah, where they gaue iudgement vpon him.

7 And they slew the sonnes of Zedekiah before his eyes, and put out the eyes of Zedekiah, and bounde him in chaines, and caried him to Babel.

8 And in the fift moneth, and seuenth day of the moneth, which was the nineteenth yere of King Nebuchad-nezzar King of Babel, came Nebuzar-adan chiefe stewarde and seruaunt of the King of Babel, to Ierusalem,

9 And burnt the house of the Lord, and the Kings house, and all the houses of Ierusalem, and all the great houses burnt he with fire.

10 And all the armie of the Caldees that were with the chiefe stewarde, brake downe the walles of Ierusalem round about.

11 And the rest of the people that were left in the citie, and those that were fled and fallen to the King of Babel, with the remnant of the multitude, did Nebuzar-adan chiefe steward carie away captiue.

12 But the chiefe steward left of the poore of the land to dresse the vines, and to till the land.

13 Also the pillars of brasse that were in the house of the Lord, and the bases, and the brasen Sea that was in the house of the Lord, did the Caldees breake, and caried the brasse of them to Babel.

14 The pots also and the besomes, and the instruments of musike, and the incense dishes, and al the vessels of brasse that they ministred in, tooke they away.

15 And the asshe pannes, and the basens, and all that was of gold, and that was of siluer, tooke the chiefe steward away,

16 With the two pillars, one Sea and the bases, which Salomon had made for the house of the Lord: the brasse of all these vessels was without weight.

17 The height of the one pillar was eighteene cubits, and the chapiter thereon was brasse, and the height of the chapiter was with networke three cubites, and pomegranates vpon the chapiter rounde about, all of brasse: and likewise was the second pillar with the networke.

18 And the chiefe steward tooke Seraiah the chiefe Priest, and Zephaniah the second Priest, and the three keepers of the doore.

19 And out of the citie hee tooke an Eunuch that had the ouersight of the men of warre, and fiue men of them that were in the Kinges presence, which were founde in the citie, and Sopher captaine of the hoste, who mustred the people of the lande, and threescore men of the people of the lande, that were founde in the citie.

20 And Nebuzar-adan the chiefe stewarde tooke them, and brought them to the King of Babel to Riblah.

21 And the King of Babel smote them, and slew them at Riblah in the land of Hamath. So Iudah was caried away captiue out of his owne land.

22 Howbeit there remained people in the land of Iudah, whom Nebuchad-nezzar King of Babel left, and made Gedaliah the sonne of Ahikam the sonne of Shaphan ruler ouer them.

23 Then when all the captaines of the host and their men heard, that the king of Babel had made Gedaliah gouernour, they came to Gedaliah to Mizpah, to wit, Ishmael the sonne of Nethaniah, and Iohanan the sonne of Kareah, and Seraiah the sonne of Tanhumeth the Netophathite, and Iaazaniah the sonne of Maachathi, they and their men.

24 And Gedaliah sware to them, and to their men, and sayd vnto them, Feare not to be the seruants of the Caldees: dwell in the land, and serue the King of Babel, and ye shalbe well.

25 But in the seuenth moneth Ishmael the sonne of Nethaniah the sonne of Elishama of the Kings seede, came, and ten men with him, and smote Gedaliah, and he died, and so did he the Iewes, and the Caldees that were with him at Mizpah.

26 Then all ye people both small and great, and the captaines of the armie arose, and came to Egypt: for they were afraide of the Caldees.

27 Notwithstanding in the seuen and thirtieth yeere after Iehoiachin King of Iudah was caried away, in the twelft moneth and the seuen and twentieth day of the moneth, Euil-merodach King of Babel in the yeere that hee began to reigne, did lift vp the head of Iehoiachin King of Iudah out of the prison,

28 And spake kindly to him, and set his throne aboue the throne of the Kings that were with him in Babel,

29 And changed his prison garments: and he did continually eate bread before him, all the dayes of his life.

30 And his portion was a continual portion giuen him by the King, euery day a certaine, all the dayes of his life.

First Chronicles

First Chronicles 1

1 Adam, Sheth, Enosh,

2 Kenan, Mahalaleel, Iered,

3 Henoch, Methushelah, Lamech,

4 Noah, She, Ham, and Iapheth.

5 The sonnes of Iapheth were Gomer, and Magog, and Madai, and Iauan, and Tubal, and Meshech, and Tiras.

6 And the sonnes of Gomer, Ashchenaz, and Iphath and Togarmah.

7 Also the sonnes of Iauan, Elishah and Tarshishah, Kittim, and Dodanim.

8 The sonnes of Ham were Cush, and Mizraim, Put and Canaan.

9 And the sonnes of Cush, Siba and Hauilah, and Sabta, and Raamah, and Sabtecha. Also the sonnes of Raamah were Sheba and Dedan.

10 And Cush begate Nimrod, who began to be mightie in the earth.

11 And Mizraim begate Ludim and Anamim, Lehabim, and Naphtuhim:

12 Pathrusim also, and Casluhim, of whome came the Philistims, and Caphtorim.

13 Also Canaan begate Zidon his first borne, and Heth,

14 And the Iebusite, and the Amorite, and the Girgashite,

15 And the Hiuuite, and the Arkite, and the Simite,

16 And the Aruadite, and the Zemarite, and the Hamathite.

17 The sonnes of Shem were Elam and Asshur, and Arpachshad, and Lud, and Aram, and Vz, and Hul, and Gether, and Meshech.

18 Also Arpachshad begate Shelah, and Shelah begate Eber.

19 Vnto Eber also were borne two sonnes: the name of the one was Peleg: for in his dayes was ye earth deuided: and his brothers name was Ioktan.

20 Then Ioktan begate Almodad and Sheleph, and Hazermaueth and Ierah,

21 And Hadoram and Vzal and Diklah,

22 And Ebal, and Abimael, and Sheba,

23 And Ophir, and Hauilah and Iobab: all these were the sonnes of Ioktan.

24 Shem, Arpachshad, Shelah,

25 Eber, Peleg, Rehu,

26 Serug, Nahor, Terah,

27 Abram, which is Abraham.

28 The sonnes of Abraham were Izhak, and Ishmael.

29 These are their generations. The eldest sonne of Ishmael was Nebaioth, and Kedar, and Adbeel, and Mibsam,

30 Mishma, and Dumah, Massa, Hadad, and Tema,

31 Ietur, Naphish and Kedemah: these are the sonnes of Ishmael.

32 And Keturah Abrahams concubine bare sonnes, Zimran, and Iokshan, and Medan, and Midian, and Ishbak, and Shuah: and the sonnes of Iokshan, Sheba, and Dedan.

33 And the sonnes of Midian were Ephah, and Ephar, and Henoch, and Abida, and Eldaah: All these are the sonnes of Keturah.

34 And Abraham begate Izhak: the sonnes of Izhak, Esau, and Israel.

35 The sonnes of Esau were Eliphaz, Reuel, and Ieush, and Iaalam, and Korah.

36 The sonnes of Eliphaz, Teman, and Omar, Zephi, and Gatam, Kenaz, and Timna, and Amalek.

37 The sonnes of Reuel, Nahath, Zerah, Shammah and Mizzah.

38 And the sonnes of Seir, Lotan, and Shobal, and Zibeon, and Anah, and Dishon, and Ezer, and Dishan.

39 And the sonnes of Lotan, Hori, and Homam, and Timna Lotans sister.

40 The sonnes of Shobal were Alian, and Manahath, and Ebal, Shephi, and Onam. And the sonnes of Zibeon, Aiah and Anah.

41 The sonne of Anah was Dishon. And the sonnes of Dishon, Amran, and Eshban, and Ithran, and Cheran.

42 The sonnes of Ezer were Bilhan, and Zaauan, and Iaakan. The sonnes of Dishon were Vz, and Aran.

43 And these were the Kings that reigned in the land of Edom, before a King reigned ouer the children of Israel, to wit, Bela the sonne of Beor, and the name of his citie was Dinhabah.

44 Then Bela died, and Iobab the sonne of Zerah of Bozrah reigned in his stead.

45 And whe Iobab was dead, Hussham of the land of the Temanites reigned in his stead.

46 And when Hussham was dead, Hadad the sonne of Bedad which smote Midian in the fielde of Moab, reigned in his steade, and the name of his citie was Auith.

47 So Hadad dyed, and Samlah of Mashrecah reigned in his stead.

48 And Samlah dyed, and Shaul of Rehoboth by the riuer reigned in his stead.

49 And when Shaul was dead, Baal-hanan the sonne of Achbor reigned in his stead.

50 And Baal-hanan dyed, and Hadad reigned in his stead, and the name of his citie was Pai, and his wiues name Mehetabel the daughter of Matred the daughter of Mezahab.

51 Hadad dyed also, and there were dukes in Edom, duke Timna, duke Aliah, duke Ietheth,

52 Duke Aholibamah, duke Elah, duke Pinon,

53 Duke Kenaz, duke Teman, duke Mibzar,

54 Duke Magdiel, duke Iram: these were the dukes of Edom.

First Chronicles 2

1 These are the sonnes of Israel, Reuben, Simeon, Leui and Iudah, Isshachar, and Zebulun,

2 Dan, Ioseph, and Beniamin, Naphtali, Gad, and Asher.

3 The sonnes of Iudah, Er, and Onan, and Shelah. these three were borne to him of ye daughter of Shua the Canaanite: but Er the eldest sonne of Iudah was euil in the sight of the Lord, and he slew him.

4 And Thamar his daughter in law bare him Pharez, and Zerah: so al the sonnes of Iudah were fiue.

5 The sonnes of Pharez, Hezron and Hamul.

6 The sonnes also of Zerah were Zimri, and Ethan, and Heman, and Calcol, and Dara, which were fiue in all.

7 And the sonne of Carmi, Achar that troubled Israel, transgressing in the thing excommunicate.

8 The sonne also of Ethan, Azariah.

9 And the sonnes of Hezron that were borne vnto him, Ierahmeel, and Ram and Chelubai.

10 And Ram begate Aminadab, and Aminadab begate Nahshon prince of the children of Iudah,

11 And Nahshon begate Salma, and Salma begate Boaz,

12 And Boaz begate Obed, and Obed begate Ishai,

13 And Ishai begate his eldest sonne Eliab, and Abinadab the second, and Shimma the third,

14 Nathaneel the fourth, Raddai the fift,

15 Ozem the sixt, and Dauid the seuenth.

16 Whose sisters were Zeruiah and Abigail. And the sonnes of Zeruiah, Abishai, and Ioab, and Asahel.

17 And Abigail bare Amasa: and the father of Amasa was Iether an Ishmeelite.

18 And Caleb the sonne of Hezron begate Ierioth of Azubah his wife, and her sonnes are these, Iesher, and Shobab, and Ardon.

19 And when Azubah was dead, Caleb tooke vnto him Ephrath, which bare him Hur.

20 And Hur begate Vri, and Vri begate Bezaleel.

21 And afterward came Hezron to the daughter of Machir the father of Gilead, and tooke her when hee was threescore yere olde, and shee bare him Segub.

22 And Segub begate Iair, which had three and twentie cities in the land of Gilead.

23 And Gesthur with Aram tooke the townes of Iair from them, and Kenath and the townes thereof, euen threescore cities. All these were the sonnes of Machir the father of Gilead.

24 And after that Hezron was dead at Caleb Ephratah, then Abiah Hezrons wife bare him also Ashur the father of Tekoa.

25 And ye sonnes of Ierahmeel the eldest sone of Hezron were Ram the eldest, then Bunah, and Oren and Ozen and Ahiiah.

26 Also Ierahmeel had another wife named Atarah, which was the mother of Onam.

27 And the sonnes of Ram the eldest sonne of Ierahmeel were Maaz, and Iamin and Ekar.

28 And the sonnes of Onam were Shammai and Iada. And the sonnes of Shammai, Nadab and Abishur.

29 And the name of the wife of Abishur was called Abiahil, and shee bare him Ahban and Molid.

30 The sonnes also of Nadab were Seled and Appaim: but Seled died without children.

31 And the sonne of Appaim was Ishi, and the sonne of Ishi, Sheshan, and the sonne of Sheshan, Ahlai.

32 And the sonnes of Iada the brother of Shammai were Iether and Ionathan: but Iether dyed without children.

33 And the sonnes of Ionathan were Peleth and Zaza. These were the sonnes of Ierahmeel.

34 And Sheshan had no sonnes, but daughters. And Sheshan had a seruant that was an Egyptian named Iarha.

35 And Sheshan gaue his daughter to Iarha his seruant to wife, and she bare him Attai.

36 And Attai begate Nathan, and Nathan begate Zabad,

37 And Zabad begate Ephlal, and Ephlal begate Obed,

38 And Obed begate Iehu, and Iehu begate Azariah,

39 And Azariah begate Helez, and Helez begate Eleasah,

40 And Eleasah begate Sisamai, and Sisamai begate Shallum,

41 And Shallum begate Iekamiah, and Iekamiah begate Elishama.

42 Also the sonnes of Caleb the brother of Ierahmeel, were Mesha his eldest sonne, which was the father of Ziph: and the sonnes of Mareshah the father of Hebron.

43 And the sonnes of Hebron were Korah and Tappuah, and Rekem and Shema.

44 And Shema begate Raham the father of Iorkoam: and Rekem begate Shammai.

45 The sonne also of Shammai was Maon: and Maon was the father of Beth-zur.

46 And Ephah a concubine of Caleb bare Haran and Moza, and Gazez: Haran also begate Gazez.

47 The sonnes of Iahdai were Regem, and Iotham, and Geshan, and Pelet, and Ephah, and Shaaph.

48 Calebs concubine Maachah bare Sheber and Tirhanah.

49 She bare also Shaaph, the father of Madmannah, and Sheua the father of Machbenah, and the father of Gibea. And Achsah was Calebs daughter.

50 These were the sonnes of Caleb the sone of Hur the eldest sonne of Ephrathah, Shobal the father of Kiriath-iearim.

51 Salma the father of Beth-lehem, and Hareph the father of Beth-gader.

52 And Shobal the father of Kiriath-iearim had sonnes, and he was the ouerseer of halfe Hammenoth.

53 And the families of Kiriath-iearim were the Ithrites, and the Puthites, and the Shumathites, and ye Mishraites of them came the Zarreathites, and the Eshtaulites.

54 The sonnes of Salma of Beth-lehem, and the Netophathite, the crownes of the house of Ioab, and halfe the Manahthites and the Zorites.

55 And the families of the Scribes dwelling at Iabez, the Tirathites, the Shimmeathites, the Shuchathites, which

are the Kenites, that came of Hammath the father of the house of Rechab.

First Chronicles 3

1 These also were the sonnes of Dauid which were borne vnto him in Hebron: the eldest Amnon of Ahinoam, the Izraelitesse: the seconde Daniel of Abigail the Carmelitesse:

2 The third Absalom the sonne of Maachah daughter of Talmai King of Geshur: the fourth Adoniiah the sonne of Haggith:

3 The fift Shepatiah of Abital: ye sixt Ithream by Eglah his wife.

4 These sixe were borne vnto him in Hebron: and there hee reigned seuen yeere and sixe moneths: and in Ierusalem he reigned three and thirtie yeere.

5 And these foure were borne vnto him in Ierusalem, Shimea, and Shobab, and Nathan, and Salomon of Bathshua the daughter of Ammiel:

6 Ibhar also, and Elishama, and Eliphalet,

7 And Nogah, and Nepheg, and Iaphia,

8 And Elishama, and Eliada, and Eliphelet, nine in nomber.

9 These are all the sonnes of Dauid, besides the sonnes of the concubines, and Thamar their sister.

10 And Salomons sonne was Rehoboam, whose sonne was Abiah, and Asa his sonne, and Iehoshaphat his sonne,

11 And Ioram his sonne, and Ahaziah his sonne, and Ioash his sonne,

12 And Amaziah his sonne, and Azariah his sonne, and Iotham his sonne,

13 And Ahaz his sonne, and Hezekiah his sonne, and Manasseh his sonne,

14 And Amon his sonne, and Iosiah his sonne.

15 And of the sonnes of Iosiah, the eldest was Iohanan, the second Iehoiakim, the thirde Zedekiah, and the fourth Shallum.

16 And the sonnes of Iehoiakim were Ieconiah his sonne, and Zedekiah his sonne.

17 And the sonnes of Ieconiah, Assir and Shealtiel his sonne:

18 Malchiram also and Pedaiah, and Shenazar, Iecamiah, Hoshama, and Nedabiah.

19 And the sonnes of Pedaiah were Zerubbabel, and Shimei: and the sonnes of Zerubbabel were Meshullam, and Hananiah, and Shelomith their sister,

20 And Hashubah, and Ohel, and Berechiah, and Hazadiah, and Iushabheshed, fiue in nomber.

21 And the sonnes of Hananiah were Pelatiah, and Iesaiah: the sonnes of Rephaiah, the sonnes of Arnan, the sonnes of Obadiah, the sonnes of Shechaniah.

22 And the sonne of Shechaniah was Shemaiah: and the sonnes of Shemaiah were Hattush and Igeal, and Bariah, and Neariah, and Shaphat, sixe.

23 And the sonnes of Neariah were Elioenai, and Hezekiiah, and Azrikam, three.

24 And the sonnes of Elioenai were Hodaiah, and Eliashib, and Pelaiah, and Akkub, and Iohanan, and Delaiah, and Anani, seuen.

First Chronicles 4

1 The sonnes of Iudah were Pharez, Hezron, and Carmi, and Hur, and Shobal.

2 And Reaiah the sonne of Shobal begat Iahath, and Iahath begate Ahumai, and Lahad: these are the families of the Zoreathites.

3 And these were of the father of Etam, Izreel, and Ishma and Idbash: and the name of their sister was Hazelelponi.

4 And Penuel was the father of Gedor, and Ezer the father of Hushah: these are the sonnes of Hur the eldest sonne of Ephratah, the father of Beth-lehem.

5 But Asher the father of Tekoa had two wiues, Heleah, and Naarah.

6 And Naarah bare him Ahuzam, and Hepher, and Temeni and Haashtari: these were the sonnes of Naarah.

7 And the sonnes of Heleah were Zereth, Iezohar and Ethnan.

8 Also Coz begate Anub, and Zobebah, and the families of Aharhel the sonne of Harum.

9 But Iabez was more honourable then his brethren: and his mother called his name Iabez, saying, Because I bare him in sorowe.

10 And Iabez called on the God of Israel, saying, If thou wilt blesse me in deede, and enlarge my coastes, and if thine hand be with me, and thou wilt cause me to be deliuered from euill, that I be not hurt. And God graunted the thing that he asked.

11 And Chelub the brother of Shuah begate Mehir, which was the father of Eshton.

12 And Eshton begate Beth-rapha, and Paseah, and Tehinnah the father of the citie of Nahash: these are the men of Rechah.

13 And the sonnes of Kenaz were Othniel and Zeraiah, and the sonne of Othniel, Hathath.

14 And Meonothai begate Ophrah. And Seraiah begate Ioab the father of the valley of craftesmen: for they were craftesmen.

15 And the sonnes of Caleb the sonne of Iephunneh were Iru, Elah, and Naam. And the sonne of Elah was Kenaz.

16 And the sonnes of Iehaleel were Ziph, and Ziphah, Tiria, and Asareel.

17 And the sonnes of Ezrah were Iether and Mered, and Epher, and Ialon, and he begate Miriam, and Shammai, and Ishbah the father of Eshtemoa.

18 Also his wife Iehudiiah bare Iered the father of Gedor, and Heber the father of Socho, and Iekuthiel the father of Zanoah: and these are the sonnes of Bithiah ye daughter of Pharaoh which Mered tooke.

19 And the sonnes of the wife of Hodiah, the sister of Naham the father of Keilah were the Garmites, and Eshtemoa the Maachathite.

20 And the sonnes of Shimon were Amnon and Rinnah, Ben-hanam and Tilon. And the sonnes of Ishi were Zoheth, and Benzoheth.

21 The sonnes of Shelah, the sonne of Iudah were Er the father of Lecah, and Laadah the father of Mareshah, and the families of the householdes of them that wrought fine linnen in the house of Ashbea.

22 And Iokim and the men of Chozeba and Ioash, and Saraph, which had the dominion in Moab, and Iashubi Lehem. These also are auncient things.

23 These were potters, and dwelt among plants and hedges: there they dwelt with the king for his worke.

24 The sonnes of Simeon were Nemuel, and Iamin, Iarib, Zerah, and Shaul,

25 Whose sonne was Shallum, and his sonne, Mibsam, and his sonne Mishma.

26 And the sonnes of Mishma, Hamuel was his sonne, Zacchur his sonne, and Shimei his sonne.

27 And Shimei had sixteene sonnes, and six daughters, but his brethren had not many children, neither was all their familie like to the children of Iudah in multitude.

28 And they dwelt at Beer-sheba, and at Moladah, and at Hazar Shual,

29 And at Bilhah, and at Ezem, and at Tolad,

30 And at Bethuel, and at Hormah, and at Ziklag,

31 And at Beth-marcaboth, and at Hazar Susim, at Beth-birei, and at Shaaraim, these were their cities vnto the reigne of Dauid.

32 And their townes were Etam, and Ain, Rimmon, and Tochen, and Ashan, fiue cities.

33 And all their townes that were rounde about these cities vnto Baal, These are their habitations and the declaration of their genealogie,

34 And Meshobab, and Iamlech, and Ioshah the sonne of Amashiah,

35 And Ioel and Iehu the sonne of Ioshibiah, the sonne of Seraiah, the sonne of Asiel,

36 And Elionai, and Iaakobah, and Ieshohaiah, and Asaiah, and Adiel, and Iesimiel, and Benaiah,

37 And Ziza the sonne of Shiphei, the sonne of Allon, the sonne of Iedaiah, the sonne of Shimri, the sonne of Shemaiah.

38 These were famous princes in their families, and increased greatly their fathers houses.

39 And they went to the entring in of Gedor, euen vnto the East side of the valley, to seeke pasture for their sheepe.

40 And they found fat pasture and good, and a wide land, both quiet and fruitfull: for they of Ham had dwelt there before.

41 And these described by name, came in the dayes of Hezekiah king of Iudah, and smote their tents, and the inhabitants that were found there, and destroyed them vtterly vnto this day, and

dwelt in their roume, because there was pasture there for their sheepe.

42 And besides these, fiue hundreth men of the sonnes of Simeon went to mount Seir, and Pelatiah, and Neariah, and Rophaiah, and Vzziel the sonnes of Ishi were their captaines,

43 And they smote the rest of Amalek that had escaped, and they dwelt there vnto this day.

First Chronicles 5

1 The sonnes also of Reuben the eldest sonne of Israel (for he was the eldest, but had defiled his fathers bed, therefore his birthright was giuen vnto the sonnes of Ioseph the sonne of Israel, so that the genealogie is not rekoned after his birthright.

2 For Iudah preuailed aboue his brethren, and of him came the prince, but the birthright was Iosephs)

3 The sonnes of Reuben the eldest sonne of Israel, were Hanoch and Pallu, Hezron and Carmi.

4 The sonnes of Ioel, Shemaiah his sonne, Gog his sonne, and Shimei his sonne,

5 Michah his sonne, Reaiah his sonne, and Baal his sonne,

6 Beerah his sonne: whom Tilgath Pilneeser King of Asshur caryed away: he was a prince of the Reubenites.

7 And when his brethren in their families rekoned the genealogie of their generations, Ieiel and Zechariah were the chiefe,

8 And Bela the sonne of Azaz, the sonne of Shema, the sonne of Ioel, which dwelt in Aroer, euen vnto Nebo and Baal meon.

9 Also Eastwarde he inhabited vnto the entring in of the wildernes from the riuer Perath for they had much cattel in the land of Gilead.

10 And in the dayes of Saul they warred with the Hagarims, which fell by their hands: and they dwelt in their tentes in all the East partes of Gilead.

11 And the children of Gad dwelt ouer against them in the land of Bashan, vnto Salchah.

12 Ioel was the chiefest, and Shapham the second, but Iaanai and Shaphat were in Bashan.

13 And their brethren of the house of their fathers were Michael, and Meshullam, and Sheba, and Sorai, and Iacan, and Zia and Eber, seuen.

14 These are the childre of Abihail, the sonne of Huri, the sonne of Iaroah, the sonne of Gilead, the sonne of Michael, the sonne of Ieshishai, the sonne of Iahdo, the sonne of Buz.

15 Ahi the sonne of Abdiel, the sonne of Guni was chiefe of the houshold of their fathers.

16 And they dwelt in Gilead in Bashan, and in the townes thereof, and in all the suburbes of Sharon by their borders.

17 All these were rekoned by genealogies in the dayes of Iotham King of Iudah, and in the dayes of Ieroboam King of Israel.

18 The sonnes of Reuben and of Gad, and of halfe the tribe of Manasseh of those that were viliant men, able to beare shield, and sworde, and to draw a bowe, exercised in warre, were foure and fourtie thousand, seuen hundreth and three score, that went out to the warre.

19 And they made warre with the Hagarims, with Ietur, and Naphish, and Nodab.

20 And they were holpen against them, and the Hagarims were deliuered into their hande, and all that were with them: for they cryed to God in the battel, and he heard them, because they trusted in him.

21 And they led away their cattel, euen their camels fiftie thousand, and two hundreth, and fiftie thousand sheepe, and two thousand asses, and of persons an hundreth thousand.

22 For many fel downe wounded, because the warre was of God. And they dwelt in their steads vntill the captiuitie.

23 And the children of the halfe tribe of Manasseh dwelt in the land, from Baashan vnto Baal Hermon, and Senir, and vnto mount Hermon: for they increased.

24 And these were the heads of the housholds of their fathers, euen Epher and Ishi, and Eliel and Azriel, and Ieremiah, and Hodauiah, and Iahdiel, strong men, valiant and famous, heades of the housholdes of their fathers.

25 But they transgressed against the God of their fathers, and went a whoring after the gods of the people of the lande, whome God had destroyed before them.

26 And the God of Israel stirred vp the spirit of Pul king of Asshur, and the spirite of Tilgath Pilneeser king of Asshur, and he caryed them away: euen the Reubenites and the Gadites, and the halfe tribe of Manasseh, and brought them vnto Halah and Habor, and Hara, and to the riuer Gozan, vnto this day.

First Chronicles 6

1 The sonnes of Leui were Gershon, Kohath, and Merari.

2 And the sonnes of Kohath, Amram, Izhar, and Hebron, and Vzziel.

3 And the children of Amram, Aaron, and Moses and Miriam. And the sonnes of Aaron, Nadab, and Abihu, and Eleazar, and Ithamar.

4 Eleazar begate Phinehas. Phinehas begate Abishua,

5 And Abishua begate Bukki, and Bukki begate Vzzi,

6 And Vzzi begate Zerahiah, and Zerahiah begate Meraioth.

7 Meraioth begate Amariah, and Amariah begate Ahitub,

8 And Ahitub begate Zadok, and Zadok begate Ahimaaz,

9 And Ahimaaz begate Azariah, and Azariah begate Iohanan,

10 And Iohanan begate Azariah (it was hee that was Priest in the house that Salomon built in Ierusalem)

11 And Azariah begate Amariah, and Amariah begate Ahitub,

12 And Ahitub begate Zadok, and Zadok begate Shallum,

13 And Shallum begate Hilkiah, and Hilkiah begate Azariah,

14 And Azariah begate Seraiah, and Seraiah begate Iehozadak,

15 And Iehozadak departed when the Lord caried away into captiuitie Iudah and Ierusalem by the hand of Nebuchad-nezzar.

16 The sonnes of Leui were Gershom, Kohath and Merari.

17 And these be the names of the sonnes of Gershom, Libni, and Shimei.

18 And the sonnes of Kohath were Amram, and Izhar, and Hebron and Vzziel.

19 The sonnes of Merari, Mahli and Mushi: and these are the families of Leui concerning their fathers.

20 Of Gershom, Libni his sonne, Iahath his sonne, Zimmah his sonne,

21 Ioah his sonne, Iddo his sonne, Zerah his sonne, Ieaterai his sonne.

22 The sonnes of Kohath, Aminadab his sonne, Korah his sonne, Assir his sonne,

23 Elkanah his sonne, and Ebiasaph his sonne, and Assir his sonne,

24 Tahath his sonne, Vriel his sonne, Vzziah his sonne, and Shaul his sonne,

25 And the sonnes of Elkanah, Amasai, and Ahimoth.

26 Elkanah. the sonnes of Elkanah, Zophai his sonne, and Nahath his sonne,

27 Eliab his sonne, Ieroham his sonne, Elkanah his sonne,

28 And the sonnes of Shemuel, the eldest Vashni, then Abiah.

29 The sonnes of Merari were Mahli, Libni his sonne, Shimei his sonne, Vzzah his sonne,

30 Shimea his sonne, Haggiah his sonne, Asaiah his sonne.

31 And these be they whom Dauid set for to sing in the house of the Lord, after that the Arke had rest.

32 And they ministred before the Tabernacle, euen the Tabernacle of the Congregation with singing, vntill Salomon had built ye house of the Lord in Ierusalem: then they continued in their office, according to their custome.

33 And these ministred with their children: of the sonnes of Kohath, Heman a singer, the sonne of Ioel, the sonne of Shemuel,

34 The sonne of Elkanah, the sonne of Ieroham, the sonne of Eliel, the sonne of Toah,

35 The sonne of Zuph, the sonne of Elkanah, the sonne of Mahath, the sonne of Amasai,

36 The sonne of Elkanah, the sonne of Ioel, the sonne of Azariah, the sonne of Zephaniah,

37 The sonne of Tahath, the sonne of Assir, the sonne of Ebiasaph, the sonne of Korah,

38 The sonne of Izhar, the sonne of Kohath, the sonne of Leui, the sonne of Israel.

39 And his brother Asaph stoode on his right hand: and Asaph was the sonne of Berechiah, the sonne of Shimea,

40 The sonne of Michael, the sonne of Baaseiah, the sonne of Malchiah,

41 The sonne of Ethni, the sonne of Zerah, the sonne of Adaiah,

42 The sonne of Ethan, the sonne of Zimmah, the sonne of Shimei,

43 The sonne of Iahath, the sonne of Gershom, the sonne of Leui.

44 And their brethren the sonnes of Merari were on the left hand, euen Ethan the sonne of Kishi, the sonne of Abdi, the sonne of Malluch,

45 The sonne of Hashabiah, the sonne of Amaziah, the sonne of Hilkiah,

46 The sonne of Amzi, the sonne of Bani, the sonne of Shamer,

47 The sonne of Mahli, the sonne of Mushi, the sonne of Merari, the sonne of Leui.

48 And their brethren the Leuites were appointed vnto all the seruice of the Tabernacle of the house of God,

49 But Aaron and his sonnes burnt incense vpon the altar of burnt offering, and on the altar of incense, for all that was to do in the most holy place, and to make an atonement for Israel, according to all that Moses the seruant of God had commanded.

50 These are also the sonnes of Aaron, Eleazar his sonne, Phinehas his sonne, Abishua his sonne,

51 Bukki his sonne, Vzzi his sonne, Zerahiah his sonne,

52 Meraioth his sonne, Amariah his sonne, Ahitub his sonne,

53 Zadok his sonne, and Ahimaaz his sonne.

54 And these are the dwelling places of them throughout their townes and coastes, euen of the sonnes of Aaron for the familie of the Kohathites, for the lot was theirs.

55 So they gaue them Hebron in the lande of Iudah and the suburbes thereof rounde about it.

56 But the fielde of the citie, and the villages thereof they gaue to Caleb the sonne of Iephunneh.

57 And to the sonnes of Aaron they gaue the cities of Iudah for refuge, euen Hebron and Libna with their suburbes, and Iattir, and Eshtemoa with their suburbes,

58 And Hilen with her suburbes, and Debir with her suburbes,

59 And Ashan and her suburbes, and Bethshemesh and her suburbes:

60 And of the tribe of Beniamin, Geba and her suburbes, and Alemeth with her suburbes, and Anathoth with her suburbes: all their cities were thirteene cities by their families.

61 And vnto the sonnes of Kohath the remnant of the familie of the tribe, euen of the halfe tribe of the halfe of Manasseh, by lot ten cities.

62 And to the sonnes of Gershom according to their families out of the tribe of Issachar, and out of the tribe of Asher, and out of the tribe of Naphtali, and out of the tribe of Manasseh in Bashan, thirteene cities.

63 Vnto the sonnes of Merari according to their families out of the tribe of Reuben, and out of the tribe of Gad, and out of the tribe of Zebulun, by lot twelue cities.

64 Thus the children of Israel gaue to the Leuites cities with their suburbes.

65 And they gaue by lot out of the tribe of the children of Iudah, and out of the tribe of the children of Simeon, and out of the tribe of the children of Beniamin, these cities, which they called by their names.

66 And they of the families of the sonnes of Kohath, had cities and their coastes out of the tribe of Ephraim.

67 And they gaue vnto them cities of refuge, Shechem in mount Ephraim, and her suburbes, and Gezer and her suburbes,

68 Iokmeam also and her suburbes, and Bethhoron with her suburbes,

69 And Aialon and her suburbes, and Gath Rimmon and her suburbes,

70 And out of the halfe tribe of Manasseh, Aner and her suburbes, and Bileam and her suburbes, for the families of the remnant of the sonnes of Kohath.

71 Vnto the sonnes of Gershom out of the familie of the halfe tribe of Manasseh, Golan in Bashan, and her suburbes, and Ashtaroth with her suburbes,

72 And out of the tribe of Issachar, Kedesh and her suburbes, Daberath and her suburbes,

73 Ramoth also and her suburbes, and Anem with her suburbes,

74 And out of the tribe of Asher, Mashal and her suburbes, and Abdon and her suburbes,

75 And Hukok and her suburbs, and Rehob and her suburbes,

76 And out of the tribe of Naphtali, Kedesh in Galilea and her suburbes, and Hammon and her suburbes, and Kiriathaim and her suburbes.

77 Vnto the rest of the children of Merari were giuen out of ye tribe of Zebulun Rimmon and her suburbes, Tabor and her suburbes,

78 And on the other side Iorden by Iericho, euen on the Eastside of Iorden, out of the tribe of Reuben, Bezer in the wildernesse with her suburbes, and Iahzah with her suburbes,

79 And Kedemoth with her suburbes, and Mephaath with her suburbes,

80 And out of the tribe of Gad Ramoth in Gilead with her suburbes, and Mahanaim with her suburbes,

81 And Heshbon with her suburbes, and Iaazer with her suburbes.

First Chronicles 7

1 And the sonnes of Issachar were Tola and Puah, Iashub, and Shimron, foure,

2 And the sonnes of Tola, Vzzi, and Rephaiah, and Ieriel, and Iahmai, and Iibsam, and Shemuel, heads in the housholdes of their fathers. Of Tola were valiant men of warre in their generations, whose number was in the dayes of Dauid two and twentie thousand, and sixe hundreth.

3 And the sonne of Vzzi was Izrahaiah, and the sonnes of Izrahaiah, Michael, and Obadiah, and Ioel, and Isshiah, fiue men all princes.

4 And with them in their generations after the houshold of their fathers were bandes of men of warre for battel, sixe and thirtie thousand: for they had many wiues and children.

5 And their brethren among all the families of Issachar were valiant men of warre, rekoned in all by their genealogies foure score and seuen thousand.

6 The sonnes of Beniamin were Bela, and Becher, and Iediael, three.

7 And the sonnes of Bela, Ezbon, and Vzzi, and Vzziel, and Ierimoth, and Iri, fiue heads of the housholds of their fathers, valiant men of warre, and were rekoned by their genealogies, two and twentie thousand and thirtie and foure.

8 And the sonnes of Becher, Zemirah, and Ioash, and Eliezer, and Elioenai, and Omri, and Ierimoth, and Abiah, and Anathoth, and Alameth: all these were the sonnes of Becher.

9 And they were nombred by their genealogies according to their generations, and the chiefe of the houses of their fathers, valiant men of warre, twenty thousand and two hundreth.

10 And the sonne of Iediael was Bilhan, and the sonnes of Bilhan, Ieush, and Beniamin, and Ehud, and Chenaanah, and Zethan, and Tharshish, and Ahishahar.

11 All these were the sonnes of Iediael, chiefe of the fathers, valiant men of warre, seuenteene thousand and two hundreth, marching in battel aray to the warre.

12 And Shuppim, and Huppim were ye sonnes of Ir, but Hushim was the sonne of another.

13 The sonnes of Naphtali, Iahziel, and Guni, and Iezer, and Shallum of the sonnes of Bilhah.

14 The sonne of Manasseh was Ashriel whom she bare vnto him, but his concubine of Aram bare Machir the father of Gilead.

15 And Machir tooke to wife the sister of Huppim and Shuppim, and the name of their sister was Maachah. And the name of the second sonne was Zelophehad, and Zelophehad had daughters.

16 And Maachah the wife of Machir bare a sonne, and called his name Peresh, and the name of his brother was Sheresh: and his sonnes were Vlam and Rakem.

17 And the sonne of Vlam was Bedan. These were the sonnes of Gilead the sonne of Machir, the sonne of Manasseh.

18 And his sister Molecheth bare Ishod, and Abiezer, and Mahalah.

19 And the sonnes of Shemida were Ahian, and Shechem, and Likhi, and Aniam.

20 The sonnes also of Ephraim were Shuthelah, and Bered his sonne, and Tahath his sonne, and his sonne Eladah, and Tahath his sonne,

21 And Zabad his sonne, and Shuthelah his sonne, and Ezer, and Elead: and the

men of Gath that were borne in the land, slewe them, because they came downe to take away their cattel.

22 Therefore Ephraim their father mourned many dayes, and his brethren came to comfort him.

23 And when he went in to his wife, she conceiued, and bare him a sonne, and he called his name Beriah, because affliction was in his house.

24 And his daughter was Sherah, which built Beth-horon the nether, and the vpper, and Vzzen Sheerah.

25 And Rephah was his sonne, and Resheph, and Telah his sonne, and Tahan his sonne,

26 Laadan his sonne, Ammihud his sonne, Elishama his sonne,

27 Non his sonne, Iehoshua his sonne.

28 And their possessions and their habitations were Beth-el, and the villages thereof, and Eastward Naaran, and Westwarde Gezer with the villages thereof, Shechem also and the villages thereof, vnto Azzah, and the villages thereof,

29 And by the places of the children of Manasseh, Beth-shean and her villages, Taanach and her villages, Megiddo and her villages, Dor and her villages. In those dwelt the children of Ioseph the sonne of Israel.

30 The sonnes of Asher were Imnah, and Isuah, and Ishuai, and Beriah, and Serah their sister.

31 And the sonnes of Beriah, Heber, and Malchiel, which is the father of Birzauith.

32 And Heber begate Iaphlet, and Shomer, and Hotham, and Shuah their sister.

33 And the sonnes of Iaphlet were Pasach, and Bimhal, and Ashuath: these were the children of Iaphlet.

34 And the sonnes of Shamer, Ahi, and Rohgah, Iehubbah, and Aram.

35 And the sonnes of his brother Helem were Zophah, and Iimna, and Shelesh and Amal.

36 The sonnes of Zophah, Suah, and Harnepher, and Shual, and Beri, and Imrah,

37 Bezer and Hod, and Shamma, and Shilshah, and Ithran, and Beera.

38 And the sonnes of Iether, Iephunneh, and Pispa and Ara.

39 And the sonnes of Vlla, Harah, and Haniel, and Rizia.

40 All these were the children of Asher, the heads of their fathers houses, noble men, valiant men of warre and chiefe princes, and they were rekoned by their genealogies for warre and for battell to the number of six and twentie thousand men.

First Chronicles 8

1 Beniamin also begate Bela his eldest sonne, Ashbel the second, and Aharah the third,

2 Nohah the fourth, and Rapha the fift.

3 And the sonnes of Bela were Addar, and Gera, and Abihud,

4 And Abishua, and Naaman and Ahoah,

5 And Gera, and Shephuphan, and Huram.

6 And these are the sonnes of Ehud: these were the chiefe fathers of those that inhabited Geba: and they were caryed away captiues to Monahath,

7 And Naaman, and Ahiah, and Gera, he caryed them away captiues: and he begate Vzza, and Ahihud.

8 And Shaharaim begate certaine in the coutrey of Moab, after he had sent away Hushim and Baara his wiues.

9 He begate, I say, of Hodesh his wife, Iobab and Zibia, and Mesha, and Malcham,

10 And Ieuz and Shachia and Mirma: these were his sonnes, and chiefe fathers.

11 And of Hushim he begat Ahitub and Elpaal.

12 And the sonnes of Elpaal were Eber, and Misham and Shamed (which built Ono, and Lod, and the villages thereof)

13 And Beriah and Shema (which were the chiefe fathers among the inhabitants of Aialon: they draue away the inhabitants of Gath)

14 And Ahio, Shashak and Ierimoth,

15 And Sebadiah, and Arad, and Ader,

16 And Michael, and Ispah, and Ioha, the sonnes of Beriah,

17 And Zebadiah, and Meshullam, and Hizki, and Heber,

18 And Ishmerai and Izliah, and Iobab, the sonnes of Elpaal,

19 Iakim also, and Zichri, and Sabdi,

20 And Elienai, and Zillethai, and Eliel,

21 And Adaiah, and Beraiah, and Shimrah the sonnes of Shimei,

22 And Ishpan, and Eber, and Eliel,

23 And Abdon, and Zichri, and Hanan,

24 And Hananiah, and Elam, and Antothiiah,

25 Iphedeiah and Penuel ye sonnes of Shashak,

26 And Shamsherai, and Shehariah, and Athaliah,

27 And Iaareshiah, and Eliah, and Zichri, the sonnes of Ieroham.

28 These were the chiefe fathers according to their generations, euen princes, which dwelt in Ierusalem.

29 And at Gibeon dwelt the father of Gibeon, and the name of his wife was Maachah.

30 And his eldest sonne was Abdon, then Zur, and Kish, and Baal, and Nadab,

31 And Gidor, and Ahio, and Zacher.

32 And Mikloth begate Shimeah: these also dwelt with their brethren in Ierusalem, euen by their brethren.

33 And Ner begate Kish, and Kish begat Saul, and Saul begate Ionathan, and Malchishua, and Abinadab, and Eshbaal.

34 And the sonne of Ionathan was Merib-baal, and Merib-baal begate Micah.

35 And the sonnes of Micah were Pithon, and Melech, and Tarea, and Ahaz.

36 And Ahaz begate Iehoadah, and Iehoadah begate Alemeth, and Azmaueth, and Zimri, and Zimri begate Moza,

37 And Moza begate Bineah, whose sonne was Raphah, and his sonne Eleasah, and his sonne Azel.

38 And Azel had six sonnes, whose names are these, Azrikam, Bocheru and Ishmael, and Sheariah, and Obadiah, and Hanan: all these were the sonnes of Azel.

39 And the sonnes of Eshek his brother were Vlam his eldest sonne, Iehush the second, and Eliphelet the third.

40 And the sonnes of Vlam were valiant men of warre which shot with the bow, and had many sonnes and nephewes, an hundreth and fiftie: all these were of the sonnes of Beniamin.

First Chronicles 9

1 Thus all Israel were nombred by their genealogies: and beholde, they are written in the booke of the Kings of Israel and of Iudah, and they were caried away to Babel for their transgression.

2 And the chiefe inhabitants that dwelt in their owne possessions, and in their owne cities, euen Israel the Priestes, the Leuites, and the Nethinims.

3 And in Ierusalem dwelt of the children of Iudah, and of the children of Beniamin, and of the children of Ephraim, and Manasseh.

4 Vthai the sonne of Amihud the sonne of Omri, the sonne of Imri, the sonne of Bani: of the children of Pharez, the sonne of Iudah.

5 And of Shiloni, Asaiah the eldest, and his sonnes.

6 And the sonnes of Zerah, Ieuel, and their brethren sixe hundreth and ninetie.

7 And of the sonnes of Beniamin, Sallu the sonne of Meshullam, the sonne of Hodauiah, the sonne of Hasenuah,

8 And Ibneiah the sonne of Ieroham, and Elah the sonne of Vzzi, the sonne of Michri, and Meshullam the sonne of Shephatiah, the sonne of Reuel, the sonne of Ibniiah.

9 And their brethren according to their generations nine hundreth, fiftie and sixe: all these men were chiefe fathers in the housholdes of their fathers.

10 And of the Priestes, Iedaiah, and Iehoiarib, and Iachin,

11 And Azariah the sonne of Hilkiah, ye sonne of Meshullam, the sonne of Zadok, the sonne of Meraioth, the sonne of Ahitub the chiefe of the house of God,

12 And Adaiah the sonne of Ieroham, ye sonne of Pashur, the sonne of Malchiiah, and Maasai the sonne of Adiel, the sonne of Iahzerah, the sonne of Meshullam, the sonne of Meshillemith, the sonne of Immer.

13 And their brethre the chiefe of the households of their fathers a thousand, seuen hundreth and three score valiant men, for the worke of the seruice of the house of God.

14 And of the Leuites, Shemaiah the sonne of Hasshub, the sonne of Azrikam, the sonne of Hashabiah of the sonnes of Merari,

15 And Bakbakkar, Heresh and Galal, and Mattaniah the sonne of Micha, the sonne of Zichri, the sonne of Asaph,

16 And Obadiah the sonne of Shemaiah, the sonne of Galal, the sonne of Ieduthun, and Berechiah, the sonne of Asa, the sonne of Elkanah, that dwelt in the villages of the Netophathites.

17 And the porters were Shallum, and Akkub, and Talmon, and Ahiman, and their brethren: Shallum was the chiefe.

18 For they were porters to this time by companies of the children of Leui vnto the Kinges gate eastward.

19 And Shallum the sonne of Kore the sonne of Ebiasaph the sonne of Korah, and his brethren the Korathites (of the house of their father) were ouer the worke, and office to keepe the gates of the Tabernacle: so their families were ouer the hoste of the Lord, keeping the entrie.

20 And Phinehas ye sonne of Eleazar was their guide, and the Lord was with him.

21 Zechariah the sonne of Meshelemiah was the porter of the doore of the Tabernacle of the Congregation.

22 All these were chosen for porters of the gates, two hundreth and twelue, which were nombred according to their genealogies by their townes. Dauid established these and Samuel the Seer in their perpetuall office.

23 So they and their children had the ouersight of the gates of the house of the Lord, euen of the house of the Tabernacle by wardes.

24 The porters were in foure quarters Eastward, Westward, Northward and Southward.

25 And their brethren, which were in their townes, came at seuen dayes from time to time with them.

26 For these foure chiefe porters were in perpetuall office, and were of the Leuites and had charge of the chambers, and of the treasures in the house of God.

27 And they lay rounde about the house of God, because the charge was theirs, and they caused it to be opened euery morning.

28 And certaine of them had the rule of the ministring vessels: for they brought them in by tale, and brought them out by tale.

29 Some of them also were appoynted ouer the instruments, and ouer all the vessels of the Sanctuarie, and of the floure, and the wine, and the oyle, and the incense, and the sweete odours.

30 And certaine of the sonnes of the Priestes made oyntments of sweete odours.

31 And Mattithiah one of the Leuites which was the eldest sonne of Shallum the Korhite, had the charge of the things that were made in the frying panne.

32 And other of their brethren the sonnes of Kohath had the ouersight of the shewbread to prepare it euery Sabbath.

33 And these are the singers, the chiefe fathers of the Leuites, which dwelt in the chambers, and had none other charge: for they had to do in that busines day and night:

34 These were the chiefe fathers of the Leuites according to their generations, and the principall which dwelt at Ierusalem.

35 And in Gibeon dwelt ye father of Gibeon, Ieiel, and the name of his wife was Maachah.

36 And his eldest sonne was Abdon, then Zur, and Kish, and Baal, and Ner, and Nadab,

37 And Gedor, and Ahio, and Zechariah, and Mikloth.

38 And Mikloth begate Shimeam: they also dwelt with their brethren at Ierusalem, euen by their brethren.

39 And Ner begate Kish, and Kish begate Saul, and Saul begate Ionathan and Malchishua, and Abinadab and Eshbaal.

40 And the sonne of Ionathan was Merib-baal: and Merib-baal begate Micah.

41 And the sonnes of Micah were Pithon, and Melech and Tahrea.

42 And Ahaz begate Iarah, and Iarah begat Alemeth, and Azmaueth, and Zimri, and Zimri begate Moza.

43 And Moza begate Binea, whose sonne was Rephaiah, and his sonne was Eleasah, and his sonne Azel.

44 And Azel had sixe sonnes, whose names are these, Azrikam, Bocheru, and Ismael, and Sheariah, and Obadiah, and Hanan: these are the sonnes of Azel.

First Chronicles 10

1 Then the Philistims fought against Israel: and the men of Israel fled before the Philistims, and fell downe slaine in mount Gilboa.

2 And the Philistims pursued after Saul and after his sonnes, and the Philistims smote Ionathan, and Abinadab, and Malchishua the sonnes of Saul.

3 And the battel was sore against Saul; and the archers hit him, and he was wounded of the archers.

4 Then sayde Saul to his armour bearer, Drawe out thy sworde, and thrust me thorowe therewith, lest these vncircumcised come and mocke at me: but his armour bearer would not, for he was sore afraid: therefore Saul tooke the sword and fell vpon it.

5 And when his armour bearer saw that Saul was dead, he fell likewise vpon the sworde, and dyed.

6 So Saul dyed and his three sonnes, and all his house, they dyed together.

7 And when all the men of Israel that were in the valley, sawe how they fledde, and that Saul and his sonnes were dead, they forsooke their cities, and fled away, and the Philistims came, and dwelt in them.

8 And on the morrowe when the Philistims came to spoyle them that were slaine, they found Saul and his sonnes lying in mount Gilboa.

9 And when they had stript him, they tooke his head and his armour, and sent them into the land of the Philistims round about, to publish it vnto their idoles, and to the people.

10 And they layd vp his armour in the house of their god, and set vp his head in the house of Dagon.

11 When all they of Iabesh Gilead heard all that the Philistims had done to Saul,

12 Then they arose (all the valiant men) and tooke the body of Saul, and the bodies of his sonnes, and brought them to Iabesh, and buryed the bones of them vnder an oke in Iabesh, and fasted seuen dayes.

13 So Saul dyed for his transgression, that he committed against the Lord, euen against the word of the Lord, which he kept not, and in that he sought and asked counsel of a familiar spirit,

14 And asked not of the Lord: therefore he slewe him, and turned the kingdome vnto Dauid the sonne of Ishai.

First Chronicles 11

1 Then all Israel gathered themselues to Dauid vnto Hebron, saying, Beholde, we are thy bones and thy flesh.

2 And in time past, euen when Saul was King, thou leddest Israel out and in: and the Lord thy God sayde vnto thee, Thou shalt feede my people Israel, and thou shalt be captaine ouer my people Israel.

3 So came all the Elders of Israel to the King to Hebron, and Dauid made a couenant with them in Hebron before the Lord. And they anoynted Dauid King ouer Israel, according to the word of the Lord by the hand of Samuel.

4 And Dauid and all Israel went to Ierusalem, which is Iebus, where were the Iebusites, the inhabitants of the land.

5 And the inhabitants of Iebus said to Dauid, Thou shalt not come in hither. Neuertheles Dauid tooke the towre of Zion, which is the city of Dauid.

6 And Dauid sayd, Whosoeuer smiteth the Iebusites first, shalbe the chiefe and captaine. So Ioab the sonne of Zeruiah went first vp, and was captaine.

7 And Dauid dwelt in the tower: therefore they called it the citie of Dauid.

8 And he built the citie on euery side, from Millo euen round about, and Ioab repaired the rest of the citie.

9 And Dauid prospered, and grewe: for the Lord of hostes was with him.

10 These also are the chiefe of the valiant men that were with Dauid, and ioyned their force with him in his kingdome with al Israel, to make him King ouer Israel, according to the worde of the Lord.

11 And this is the number of the valiant men whome Dauid had, Iashobeam the sonne of Hachmoni, the chiefe among thirtie: he lift vp his speare against three hundreth, whom he slewe at one time.

12 And after him was Eleazar the sonne of Dodo the Ahohite, which was one of the three valiant men.

13 He was with Dauid at Pas-dammim, and there the Philistims were gathered together to battel: and there was a parcell of ground full of barley, and the people fled before the Philistims.

14 And they stood in the middes of the field, and saued it, and slewe the Philistims: so the Lord gaue a great victorie.

15 And three of the thirtie captaines went to a rocke to Dauid, into the caue of Adullam. And the armie of the Philistims camped in the valley of Rephaim.

16 And when Dauid was in the hold, the Philistims garison was at Beth-lehem.

17 And Dauid longed, and said, Oh, that one would giue me to drinke of the water of the well of Beth-lehem that is at the gate.

18 Then these three brake thorowe the hoste of the Philistims, and drewe water out of the well of Beth-lehem that was by the gate, and tooke it and brought it to Dauid: but Dauid would not drinke of it, but powred it for an oblation to the Lord,

19 And said, Let not my God suffer me to do this: should I drinke the blood of these mens liues? for they haue brought it with the ieopardie of their liues: therefore he would not drinke it: these things did these three mightie men.

20 And Abishai the brother of Ioab, he was chiefe of the three, and he lift vp his speare against three hundreth, and slew them, and had the name among the three.

21 Among the three he was more honourable then the two, and he was their captaine: but he attained not vnto the first three.

22 Benaiah the sonne of Iehoiada (the sonne of a valiant man) which had done many actes, and was of Kabzeel, he slewe two strong men of Moab: he went downe also and slewe a lion in the middes of a pit in time of snowe.

23 And he slewe an Egyptian, a man of great stature, euen fiue cubites long, and in the Egyptians hand was a speare like a weauers beame: and he went downe to him with a staffe, and plucked the speare out of the Egyptians hand, and slewe him with his owne speare.

24 These things did Benaiah ye sonne of Iehoiada, and had the name among the three worthies.

25 Behold, he was honourable among thirtie, but he attained not vnto the first three. And Dauid made him of his counsell.

26 These also were valiant men of warre, Asahel the brother of Ioab, Elhanan the sonne of Dodo of Beth-lehem,

27 Shammoth the Harodite, Helez the Pelonite,

28 Ira the sonne of Ikkesh the Tekoite, Abiezer the Antothite,

29 Sibbecai the Husathite, Ilai the Ahohite,

30 Maharai the Netophathite, Heled ye sonne of Baanah the Netophathite,

31 Ithai the sonne of Ribai of Gibeah of the children of Beniamin, Benaiah the Pirathonite,

32 Hurai of the riuers of Gaash, Abiel the Arbathite,

33 Azmaueth the Baharumite, Elihaba the Shaalbonite,

34 The sonnes of Hashem the Gizonite, Ionathan the sonne of Shageh the Harite,

35 Ahiam the sonne of Sacar the Hararite, Eliphal the sonne of Vr,

36 Hepher the Mecherathite, Ahiiah the Pelonite,

37 Hezro the Carmelite, Naarai the sonne of Ezbai,

38 Ioel the brother of Nathan, Mibhar the sonne of Haggeri,

39 Zelek the Ammonite, Nahrai the Berothite, the armour bearer of Ioab, the sonne of Zeruiah,

40 Ira the Ithrite, Garib the Ithrite,

41 Vriah the Hittite, Zabad the sonne of Ahlai,

42 Adina the sonne of Shiza the Reubenite, a captaine of the Reubenites, and thirtie with him,

43 Hanan the sonne of Maachah, and Ioshaphat the Mithnite,

44 Vzia the Ashterathite, Shama and Ieiel the sonnes of Otham the Aroerite,

45 Iediael the sonne of Shimri, and Ioha his brother the Tizite,

46 Eliel the Mahauite, and Ieribai and Ioshauiah the sonnes of Elnaam, and Ithmah the Moabite,

47 Eliel and Obed, and Iaasiel the Mesobaite.

First Chronicles 12

1 These also are they that came to Dauid to Ziklag, while he was yet kept close, because of Saul the sonne of Kish: and they were among the valiant and helpers of the battel.

2 They were weaponed with bowes, and could vse the right and the left hand with stones and with arrowes and with bowes, and were of Sauls brethren, euen of Beniamin.

3 The chiefe were Ahiezer, and Ioash the sonnes of Shemaah a Gibeathite, and Ieziel, and Pelet the sonnes of Asinaueth, Berachah and Iehu the Antothite,

4 And Ishmaiah the Gibeonite, a valiant man among thirtie, and aboue the thirtie, and Ieremiah, and Iehaziel, and Iohanan, and Ioshabad the Gederathite,

5 Eluzai, and Ierimoth, and Bealiah, and Shemariah, and Shephatiah the Haruphite,

6 Elkanah, and Ishiah, and Azariel, and Ioezer, Iashobeam of Hakorehim,

7 And Ioelah, and Zebadiah, the sonnes of Ieroham of Gedor,

8 And of the Gadites there separated them selues some vnto Dauid into the holde of the wildernesse, valiant men of warre, and men of armes, and apt for battel, which coulde handle speare and shielde, and their faces were like the faces of lyons, and were like the roes in the mountaines in swiftnesse,

9 Ezer the chiefe, Obadiah the second, Eliab the third,

10 Mishmanah the fourth, Ieremiah the fift,

11 Attai the sixt, Eliel the seuenth,

12 Iohanan the eight, Elzabad the ninth,

13 Ieremiah the tenth, Macbannai the eleuenth.

14 These were the sonnes of Gad, captaines of the hoste: one of the least could resist an hundreth, and the greatest a thousand.

15 These are they that went ouer Iorden in the first moneth when he had filled ouer all his bankes, and put to flight all them of the valley, toward the East and the West.

16 And there came of the children of Beniamin, and Iudah to the hold vnto Dauid,

17 And Dauid went out to meete them, and answered and sayde vnto them, If yee be come peaceably vnto me to helpe me, mine heart shall be knit vnto you, but if you come to betray me to mine aduersaries, seeing there is no wickednes in mine handes, the God of our fathers beholde it, and rebuke it.

18 And the spirit came vpon Amasai, which was the chiefe of thirtie, and he said, Thine are we, Dauid, and with thee, O sonne of Ishai. Peace, peace be vnto thee, and peace be vnto thine helpers: for thy God helpeth thee. Then Dauid receiued them, and made them captaines of the garison.

19 And of Manasseh some fell to Dauid, when he came with the Philistims against Saul to battell, but they helped them not: for the Princes of the Philistims by aduisement sent him away, saying, He will fall to his master Saul for our heads.

20 As he went to Ziklag, there fell to him of Manasseh, Adnah, and Iozabad, and Iediael, and Michael, and Iozabad, and Elihu, and Ziltai, heads of the thousands that were of Manasseh.

21 And they helped Dauid against that bad: for they were all valiant men and were captaines in the hoste.

22 For at that time day by day there came to Dauid to helpe him, vntill it was a great hoste, like the hoste of God.

23 And these are the nombers of the captaines that were armed to battell, and came to Dauid to Hebron to turne the kingdome of Saul to him, according to the worde of the Lord.

24 The children of Iudah that bare shield and speare, were sixe thousand and eight hundreth armed to the warre.

25 Of the children of Simeon valiant men of warre, seuen thousand and an hundreth.

26 Of the children of Leui foure thousande and six hundreth.

27 And Iehoiada was the chiefe of them of Aaron: and with him three thousande and seuen hundreth.

28 And Zadok a yong man very valiant, and of his fathers housholde came two and twentie captaines.

29 And of the children of Beniamin the brethren of Saul three thousande: for a great part of them vnto that time kept the warde of the house of Saul.

30 And of the children of Ephraim twentie thousande, and eight hundreth valiant men and famous men in the housholde of their fathers.

31 And of the halfe tribe of Manasseh eighteene thousand, which were appointed by name to come and make Dauid King.

32 And of the children of Issachar which were men that had vnderstanding of the times, to knowe what Israel ought to doe: the heades of them were two hundreth, and all their brethren were at their commandement.

33 Of Zebulun that went out to battel, expert in warre, and in all instruments of warre, fiftie thousande which could set the battell in aray: they were not of a double heart.

34 And of Naphtali a thousand captaines, and with them with shielde and speare seuen and thirtie thousande.

35 And of Dan expert in battell, eyght and twentie thousande, and sixe hundreth.

36 And of Asher that went out to the battell and were trained in the warres, fourtie thousand.

37 And of the other side of Iorden of the Reubenites, and of the Gadites, and of the halfe tribe of Manasseh with all instruments of warre to fight with, an hundreth and twentie thousand.

38 All these men of warre that coulde leade an armie, came with vpright heart to Hebron to make Dauid King ouer all Israel: and all the rest of Israel was of one accorde to make Dauid King:

39 And there they were with Dauid three dayes, eating and drinking: for their brethren had prepared for them.

40 Moreouer they that were neere them vntill Issachar, and Zebulun, and Naphtali brought bread vpon asses, and on camels, and on mules, and on oxen, euen meate, floure, figges, and reisins, and wine and oyle, and beeues and sheepe abundantly: for there was ioy in Israel.

First Chronicles 13

1 And Dauid counselled with the captaines of thousandes and of hundreths, and with all the gouernours.

2 And Dauid said to all the Congregation of Israel, If it seeme good to you, and that it proceedeth of the Lord our God, we will sende to and from vnto our brethren, that are left in all the lande of Israel (for with them are the Priests and the Leuites in the cities and their suburbes) that they may assemble them selues vnto vs.

3 And we will bring againe the Arke of our God to vs: for we sought not vnto it in the dayes of Saul.

4 And all the Congregation answered, Let vs doe so: for the thing seemed good in the eyes of all the people.

5 So Dauid gathered all Israel together from Shihor in Egypt, euen vnto the entring of Hamath, to bring the Arke of God from Kiriath-iearim.

6 And Dauid went vp and all Israel to Baalath, in Kiriath-iearim, that was in Iudah, to bring vp from thence the Arke of God the Lord that dwelleth betweene the Cherubims, where his Name is called on.

7 And they caryed the Arke of God in a newe cart out of the house of Abinadab: and Vzza and Ahio guided the cart.

8 And Dauid and all Israel played before God with all their might, both with songes and with harpes, and with violes, and with timbrels and with cymbales and with trumpets.

9 And when they came vnto the thresshing floore of Chidon, Vzza put forth his hand to holde the Arke, for the oxen did shake it.

10 But the wrath of the Lord was kindled against Vzza, and he smote him, because he layed his hande vpon the Arke: so he dyed there before God.

11 And Dauid was angrie, because the Lord had made a breach in Vzza, and he called the name of that place Perez-vzza vnto this day.

12 And Dauid feared God that day, saying, Howe shall I bring in to me the Arke of God?

13 Therefore Dauid brought not the Arke to him into the citie of Dauid, but caused it to turne into the house of Obed Edom the Gittite.

14 So the Arke of God remained in the house of Obed Edom, euen in his house three moneths: and the Lord blessed the house of Obed Edom, and all that he had.

First Chronicles 14

1 Then sent Hiram the King of Tyrus messengers to Dauid, and cedar trees, with masons and carpenters to builde him an house.

2 Therefore Dauid knewe that the Lord had confirmed him King ouer Israel, and that his kingdome was lift vp on hie, because of his people Israel.

3 Also Dauid tooke moe wiues at Ierusalem, and Dauid begate moe sonnes and daughters.

4 And these are the names of the children which he had at Ierusalem, Shammua, and Shobab, Nathan, and Salomon,

5 And Ibhar, and Elishua, and Elpalet,

6 And Nogah, and Nepheg, and Iaphia,

7 And Elishama, and Beeliada, and Eliphalet.

8 But when the Philistims heard that Dauid was anointed King ouer Israel, all the Philistims came vp to seeke Dauid. And when Dauid heard, he went out against them.

9 And the Philistims came, and spred them selues in the valley of Rephaim.

10 Then Dauid asked counsel at God, saying, Shall I goe vp against the Philistims, and wilt thou deliuer them into mine hande? And the Lord saide

vnto him, Goe vp: for I will deliuer them into thine hande.

11 So they came vp to Baal-perazim, and Dauid smote them there: and Dauid said, God hath deuided mine enemies with mine hande, as waters are deuided: therefore they called the name of that place, Baal-perazim.

12 And there they had left their gods: and Dauid said, Let them euen be burnt with fire.

13 Againe the Philistims came and spread them selues in the valley.

14 And when Dauid asked againe counsell at God, God said to him, Thou shalt not goe vp after them, but turne away from them, that thou mayest come vpon them ouer against the mulberie trees.

15 And when thou hearest the noyse of one going in the toppes of the mulberie trees, then goe out to battel: for God is gone foorth before thee, to smite the hoste of the Philistims.

16 So Dauid did as God had commanded him: and they smote the hoste of the Philistims from Gibeon euen to Gezer.

17 And the fame of Dauid went out into all landes, and the Lord brought the feare of him vpon all nations.

First Chronicles 15

1 And Dauid made him houses in the citie of Dauid, and prepared a place for the Arke of God, and pitched for it a tent.

2 Then Dauid saide, None ought to carie the Arke of God, but the Leuites: for the Lord hath chosen them to beare the Arke of the Lord, and to minister vnto him for euer.

3 And Dauid gathered all Israel together to Ierusalem to bring vp the Arke of the Lord vnto his place, which he had ordeined for it.

4 And Dauid assembled the sonnes of Aaron, and the Leuites.

5 Of the sonnes of Kohath, Vriel the chiefe, and his brethren sixe score.

6 Of the sonnes of Merari, Asaiah the chiefe, and his brethren two hundreth and twentie.

7 Of the sonnes of Gershom, Ioel the chiefe, and his brethren an hundreth and thirtie.

8 Of the sonnes of Elizaphan, Shemaiah the chiefe, and his brethren two hundreth.

9 Of the sonnes of Hebron, Eliel the chiefe, and his brethren fourescore.

10 Of the sonnes of Vzziel, Amminadab the chiefe, and his brethren an hundreth and twelue.

11 And Dauid called Zadok and Abiathar the Priestes, and of the Leuites, Vriel, Asaiah and Ioel, Shemaiah, and Eliel, and Amminadab:

12 And he saide vnto them, Ye are the chiefe fathers of the Leuites: sanctifie your selues, and your brethren, and bring vp the Arke of the Lord God of Israel vnto the place that I haue prepared for it.

13 For because ye were not there at the first, the Lord our God made a breach among vs: for we sought him not after due order.

14 So the Priestes and the Leuites sanctified them selues to bring vp the Arke of the Lord God of Israel.

15 And the sonnes of the Leuites bare the Arke of God vpon their shoulders with the barres, as Moses had commanded, according to the worde of the Lord.

16 And Dauid spake to the chiefe of the Leuites, that they should appoint certaine of their brethren to sing with instruments of musike, with violes and harpes, and cymbales, that they might make a sounde, and lift vp their voyce with ioye.

17 So the Leuites appointed Heman the sonne of Ioel, and of his brethren Asaph the sonne of Berechiah, and of the sonnes of Merari their brethren, Ethan the sonne of Kushaiah,

18 And with them their brethren in the seconde degree, Zechariah, Ben, and Iaaziel, and Shemiramoth, and Iehiel, and Vnni, Eliab, and Benaiah, and Maaseiah, and Mattithiah, and Elipheleh, and Mikneah, and Obed Edom, and Ieiel the porters.

19 So Heman, Asaph and Ethan were fingers to make a sounde with cymbales of brasse,

20 And Zechariah, and Aziel, and Shemiramoth, and Iehiel, and Vnni, and Eliab, and Maaseiah, and Benaiah with violes on Alamoth,

21 And Mattithiah, and Elipheleh, and Mikneah, and Obed Edom, and Ieiel, and Azaziah, with harpes vpon Sheminith Ienazzeah.

22 But Chenaniah the chiefe of the Leuites had the charge, bearing ye burden in the charge, for he was able to instruct.

23 And Berechiah and Elkanah were porters for the Arke.

24 And Shecaniah and Iehoshaphat and Nethaneel and Amasai, and Zechariah, and Benaiah, and Eliezer the Priestes did blowe with trumpets before the Arke of God, and Obed Edom and Ieiiah were porters for the Arke.

25 So Dauid and the Elders of Israel and the captaines of thousandes went to bring vp the Arke of the couenant of the Lord from the house of Obed Edom with ioye.

26 And because that God helped the Leuites that bare the Arke of the couenant of the Lord, they offered seuen bullockes and seuen rammes.

27 And Dauid had on him a linen garment, as all the Leuites that bare the Arke, and the singers and Chenaniah that had the chiefe charge of the singers: and vpon Dauid was a linnen Ephod.

28 Thus all Israel brought vp the Arke of the Lordes couenant with shouting and sounde of cornet, and with trumpets, and with cymbales, making a sound with violes and with harpes.

29 And when the Arke of the couenant of the Lord came into the citie of Dauid,

Michal the daughter of Saul looked out at a windowe, and sawe King Dauid dauncing and playing, and she despised him in her heart.

First Chronicles 16

1 So they brought in the Arke of God, and set it in the middes of the Tabernacle that Dauid had pitched for it, and they offred burnt offrings and peace offrings before God.

2 And when Dauid had made an ende of offering the burnt offering and the peace offerings, hee blessed the people in the Name of the Lord.

3 And he dealt to euery one of Israel both man and woman, to euery one a cake of breade, and a piece of flesh, and a bottel of wine.

4 And he appointed certaine of the Leuites to minister before the Arke of the Lord, and to rehearse and to thanke and prayse the Lord God of Israel:

5 Asaph the chiefe, and next to him Zechariah, Ieiel, and Shemiramoth, and Iehiel, and Mattithiah, and Eliab, and Benaiah, and Obed Edom, euen Ieiel with instruments, violes and harpes, and Asaph to make a sound with cymbales,

6 And Benaiah and Iahaziel Priestes, with trumpets continually before the Arke of the couenant of God.

7 Then at that time Dauid did appoint at the beginning to giue thankes to the Lord by the hand of Asaph and his brethren.

8 Praise the Lord and call vpon his Name: declare his workes among the people.

9 Sing vnto him, sing praise vnto him, and talke of all his wonderfull workes.

10 Reioyce in his holy Name: let the hearts of them that seeke the Lord reioyce.

11 Seeke the Lord and his strength: seeke his face continually.

12 Remember his marueilous workes that he hath done, his wonders, and the iudgements of his mouth,

13 O seede of Israel his seruant, O the children of Iaakob his chosen.

14 He is the Lord our God: his iudgements are throughout all the earth.

15 Remember his couenant for euer, and the worde, which hee commanded to a thousand generations:

16 Which he made with Abraham, and his othe to Izhak:

17 And hath confirmed it to Iaakob for a Law, and to Israel for an euerlasting couenant,

18 Saying, To thee will I giue the land of Canaan, the lot of your inheritance.

19 When ye were fewe in number, yea, a very fewe, and strangers therein,

20 And walked about from nation to nation, and from one kingdome to another people,

21 He suffered no man to do them wrong, but rebuked Kings for their sakes, saying,

22 Touch not mine anoynted, and doe my Prophets no harme.

23 Sing vnto the Lord all the earth: declare his saluation from day to day.

24 Declare his glory among the nations, and his wonderful workes among all people.

25 For the Lord is great and much to be praised, and hee is to bee feared aboue all gods.

26 For all the gods of the people are idoles, but the Lord made the heauens.

27 Prayse and glory are before him: power and beautie are in his place.

28 Giue vnto the Lord, ye families of the people: giue vnto the Lord glory and power.

29 Giue vnto the Lord ye glory of his Name: bring an offring and come before him, and worship the Lord in the glorious Sanctuarie.

30 Tremble ye before him, al the earth: surely the world shalbe stable and not moue.

31 Let the heauens reioyce, and let the earth be glad, and let them say among the nations, The Lord reigneth.

32 Let the sea roare, and all that therein is: Let the field be ioyfull and all that is in it.

33 Let the trees of the wood then reioyce at the presence of the Lord: for he commeth to iudge the earth.

34 Prayse the Lord, for hee is good, for his mercie endureth for euer.

35 And say ye, Saue vs, O God, our saluation, and gather vs, and deliuer vs from the heathen, that we may prayse thine holy Name, and glorie in thy praise.

36 Blessed be the Lord God of Israel for euer and euer: and let all people say, So be it, and praise the Lord.

37 Then he left there before the Arke of the Lordes couenant Asaph and his brethren to minister continually before the Arke, that which was to be done euery day:

38 And Obed Edom and his brethren, three score and eight: and Obed Edom the sonne of Ieduthun, and Hosah were porters.

39 And Zadok the Priest and his brethren the Priestes were before the Tabernacle of ye Lord, in the hie place that was at Gibeon,

40 To offer burnt offrings vnto the Lord, vpon the burnt offring altar continually, in the morning and in the euening, euen according vnto all that is written in the law of the Lord, which hee commanded Israel.

41 And with them were Heman, and Ieduthun, and the rest that were chosen (which were appointed by names) to praise the Lord, because his mercie endureth for euer.

42 Euen with them were Heman and Ioduthun, to make a sound with the cornets and with the cymbales, with excellent instruments of musicke: and the sonnes of Ieduthun were at the gate.

43 And all the people departed, euerie man to his house: and Dauid returned to blesse his house.

First Chronicles 17

1 Nowe afterward when Dauid dwelt in his house, he saide to Nathan the Prophet, Beholde, I dwell in an house of cedar trees, but the Arke of the Lordes couenant remaineth vnder curtaines.

2 Then Nathan said to Dauid, Do all that is in thine heart: for God is with thee.

3 And the same night euen the word of God came to Nathan, saying,

4 Goe, and tell Dauid my seruant, Thus saith the Lord, Thou shalt not buylde me an house to dwell in:

5 For I haue dwelt in no house, since the day that I brought out the childre of Israel vnto this daye, but I haue bene from tent to tent, and from habitation to habitation.

6 Wheresoeuer I haue walked with all Israel spake I one word to any of the iudges of Israel (whome I commanded to feede my people) saying, Why haue ye not built mee an house of cedar trees?

7 Nowe therefore thus shalt thou say vnto my seruant Dauid, Thus saith the Lord of hostes, I tooke thee from the sheepecoat and from following the sheepe, that thou shouldest bee a prince ouer my people Israel.

8 And I haue bene with thee whithersoeuer thou hast walked, and haue destroyed all thine enemies out of thy sight, and haue made thee a name, like the name of the great men that are in the earth.

9 (Also I will appoynt a place for my people Israel, and will plant it, that they may dwell in their place, and moue no more: neither shall the wicked people vexe them any more, as at the beginning,

10 And since the time that I commanded iudges ouer my people Israel) And I wil subdue all thine enemies: therefore I say vnto thee, that the Lord wil buylde thee an house.

11 And when thy dayes shalbe fulfilled to go with thy fathers, then will I rayse vp thy seede after thee, which shalbe of thy sonnes, and will stablish his kingdome.

12 He shall builde me an house, and I will stablish his throne for euer.

13 I wil be his father, and he shalbe my sonne, aud I will not take my mercie away from him, as I tooke it from him that was before thee.

14 But I wil establish him in mine house, and in my kingdome for euer, and his throne shalbe stablished for euer,

15 According to all these wordes, and according to al this vision. So Nathan spake to Dauid.

16 And Dauid the King went in and sate before the Lord and said, Who am I, O Lord God, and what is mine house, that thou hast brought me hitherto?

17 Yet thou esteeming this a small thing, O God, hast also spoken concerning the house of thy seruaut for a great while, and hast regarded me according to the estate of a man of hie degree, O Lord God.

18 What can Dauid desire more of thee for the honour of thy seruant? for thou knowest thy seruant.

19 O Lord, for thy seruantes sake, euen according to thine heart hast thou done all this great thing to declare all magnificence.

20 Lord, there is none like thee, neither is there any God besides thee, according to all that we haue heard with our eares.

21 Moreouer what one nation in the earth is like thy people Israel, whose God went to redeeme them to be his people, and to make thy selfe a Name, and to doe great and terrible things by casting out nations from before thy people, whom thou hast deliuered out of Egypt?

22 For thou hast ordeined thy people Israel to be thine owne people for euer, and thou Lord art become their God.

23 Therefore nowe Lord, let the thing that thou hast spoken concerning thy seruant and concerning his house, be confirmed for euer, and doe as thou hast sayd,

24 And let thy name be stable and magnified for euer, that it may be sayd, The Lord of hostes, God of Israel, is the God of Israel, and let the house of Dauid thy seruant bee stablished before thee.

25 For thou, O my God, hast reueiled vnto the eare of thy seruant, that thou wilt builde him an house: therefore thy seruant hath bene bolde to pray before thee.

26 Therefore nowe Lord (for thou art God, and hast spoken this goodnesse vnto thy seruant)

27 Now therfore, it hath pleased thee to blesse the house of thy seruant, that it may bee before thee for euer: for thou, O Lord, hast blessed it, and it shalbe blessed for euer.

First Chronicles 18

1 And after this Dauid smote the Philistims, and subdued them, and tooke Gath, and the villages thereof out of the hand of the Philistims.

2 And he smote Moab, and the Moabites became Dauids seruants, and brought giftes.

3 And Dauid smote Hadarezer King of Zobah vnto Hamath, as he went to stablish his border by the riuer Perath.

4 And Dauid tooke from him a thousand charets, and seuen thousand horsemen, and twentie thousand footemen, and destroyed all the charets, but he reserued of them an hundreth charets.

5 Then came the Aramites of Damascus to succour Hadarezer King of Zobah, but Dauid slewe of the Aramites two and twentie thousand.

6 And Dauid put a garison in Aram of Damascus, and the Aramites became Dauids seruants, and brought giftes: and the Lord preserued Dauid wheresoeuer he went.

7 And Dauid tooke the shieldes of gold that were of the seruants of Hadarezer, and brought them to Ierusalem.

8 And from Tibhath, and from Chun (cities of Hadarezer) brought Dauid exceeding much brasse, wherewith Salomon made the brasen Sea, and the pillars and the vessels of brasse.

9 Then Tou King of Hamath heard howe Dauid had smitten all the hoste of Hadarezer King of Zobah:

10 Therefore he sent Hadoram his sonne to King Dauid, to salute him, and to reioyce with him, because he had fought against Hadarezer, and beaten him (for Tou had warre with Hadarezer) who brought all vessels of golde and siluer and brasse.

11 And King Dauid did dedicate them vnto the Lord, with the siluer and golde that hee brought from all the nations, from Edom, and from Moab, and from the children of Ammon, and from the Philistims, and from Amalek.

12 And Abishai the sonne of Zeruiah smote of Edom in the salt valley eighteene thousand,

13 And he put a garison in Edom, and all the Edomites became Dauids seruantes: and the Lord preserued Dauid wheresoeuer he went.

14 So Dauid reigned ouer all Israel, and executed iudgement and iustice to all his people.

15 And Ioab the sonne of Zeruiah was ouer the hoste, and Iehoshaphat the sonne of Ahilud recorder,

16 And Zadok the sonne of Ahitub, and Abimelech the sonne of Abiathar were the Priests, and Shausha the Scribe,

17 And Benaiah the sonne of Iehoiada was ouer the Cherethites and the Pelethites: and the sonnes of Dauid were chiefe about the King.

First Chronicles 19

1 After this also Nahash the King of the children of Ammon dyed, and his sonne reigned in his stead.

2 And Dauid said, I will shew kindnesse vnto Hanun the sonne of Nahash, because his father shewed kindnesse vnto me. And Dauid sent messengers to comfort him for his father. So the seruants of Dauid came into the lande of the children of Ammon to Hanun to comfort him.

3 And the princes of the children of Ammon said to Hanun, Thinkest thou that Dauid doeth honour thy father, that he hath sent comforters vnto thee? Are not his seruants come to thee to search, to seeke and to spie out the land?

4 Wherefore Hanun tooke Dauids seruants, and shaued them, and cut off their garments by the halfe vnto the buttocks, and sent them away.

5 And there went certaine and tolde Dauid concerning the men: and he sent to meete them (for the men were exceedingly ashamed) and the King saide, Tarie at Iericho, vntill your beardes be growen: then returne.

6 When the children of Ammon saw that they stanke in the sight of Dauid, then sent Hanun and the children of Ammon a thousande talents of siluer to hire them charets and horsemen out of Aram

Naharaim and out of Aram Maachah, and out of Zobah.

7 And they hired them two and thirty thousande charets, and the King of Maachah and his people, which came and pitched before Medeba: and the children of Ammon gathered themselues together from their cities, and came to the battell.

8 And when Dauid heard, he sent Ioab and all the hoste of the valiant men.

9 And the children of Ammon came out, and set their battell in aray at the gate of the citie. And the Kings that were come, were by them selues in the fielde.

10 When Ioab saw that the front of the battel was against him before and behinde, then he chose out of all the choyse of Israel, and set him selfe in aray to meete the Aramites.

11 And the rest of the people he deliuered vnto the hande of Abishai his brother, and they put them selues in aray against the children of Ammon.

12 And he saide, If Aram be too strong for me, then thou shalt succour me: and if the children of Ammon preuaile against thee, then I wil succour thee.

13 Be strong, and let vs shewe our selues valiant for our people, and for the cities of our God, and let the Lord doe that which is good in his owne sight.

14 So Ioab and the people that was with him, came neere before the Aramites vnto the battel, and they fled before him.

15 And when the children of Ammon sawe that the Aramites fled, they fled also before Abishai his brother, and entred into the citie: so Ioab came to Ierusalem.

16 And when the Aramites sawe that they were discomfited before Israel, they sent messengers and caused the Aramites to come forth that were beyond the riuer: and Shophach the captaine of the hoste of Hadarezer went before them.

17 And when it was shewed Dauid, he gathered all Israel, and went ouer Iorden, and came vnto them, and put him selfe in aray against them: And when Dauid had put him selfe in battel aray to meete the Aramites, they fought with him.

18 But the Aramites fled before Israel, and Dauid destroyed of the Aramites seuen thousand charets, and fourtie thousand footemen, and killed Shophach the captaine of the hoste.

19 And when the seruants of Hadarezer sawe that they fell before Israel, they made peace with Dauid, and serued him. And the Aramites would no more succour the children of Ammon.

First Chronicles 20

1 And when the yere was expired, in the time that Kings goe out a warfare, Ioab caryed out the strength of the armie, and destroyed the countrey of the children of Ammon, and came and besieged Rabbah (but Dauid taryed at Ierusalem) and Ioab smote Rabbah and destroyed it.

2 Then Dauid tooke the crowne of their King from off his head, and founde it the weight of a talent of golde, with precious stones in it: and it was set on Dauids head, and he brought away the spoyle of the citie exceeding much.

3 And he caryed away the people that were in it, and cut them with sawes, and with harowes of yron, and with axes: euen thus did Dauid with all the cities of the children of Ammon. Then Dauid and all the people came againe to Ierusalem.

4 And after this also there arose warre at Gezer with the Philistims: then Sibbechai the Hushathite slewe Sippai, of the children of Haraphah, and they were subdued.

5 And there was yet another battell with the Philistims: and Elhanan the sonne of Iair slewe Lahmi, the brother of Goliath the Gittite, whose spearestaffe was like a weauers beame.

6 And yet againe there was a battel at Gath, where was a man of a great stature, and his fingers were by sixes, euen foure and twentie, and was also the sonne of Haraphah.

7 And when he reuiled Israel, Iehonathan the sonne of Shimea Dauids brother did slay him.

8 These were borne vnto Haraphah at Gath, and fell by the hand of Dauid: and by the hands of his seruants.

First Chronicles 21

1 And Satan stoode vp against Israel, and prouoked Dauid to nomber Israel.

2 Therefore Dauid said to Ioab, and to the rulers of the people, Go, and nomber Israel from Beer-sheba euen to Dan, and bring it to me, that I may knowe the nomber of them.

3 And Ioab answered, The Lord increase his people an hundreth times so many as they be, O my lord the King: are they not all my lords seruats? wherefore doeth my lord require this thing? why should he be a cause of trespasse to Israel?

4 Neuerthelesse the Kings word preuailed against Ioab. And Ioab departed and went thorowe all Israel, and returned to Ierusalem.

5 And Ioab gaue the nomber and summe of the people vnto Dauid: and all Israel were eleuen hundreth thousande men that drewe sword: and Iudah was foure hundreth and seuentie thousande men that drewe sword.

6 But the Leuites and Beniamin counted he not among them: for the Kings worde was abominable to Ioab.

7 And God was displeased with this thing: therefore he smote Israel.

8 Then Dauid saide vnto God, I haue sinned greatly, because I haue done this thing: but now, I beseech thee, remooue the iniquitie of thy seruant: for I haue done very foolishly.

9 And the Lord spake vnto Gad Dauids Seer, saying,

10 Goe and tell Dauid, saying, Thus saith the Lord, I offer thee three thinges: choose thee one of them, that I may doe it vnto thee.

11 So Gad came to Dauid, and sayde vnto him, Thus saith the Lord, Take to thee

12 Either three yeeres famine, or three monaths to be destroyed before thine aduersaries, and the sworde of thine enemies to take thee, or els the sworde of the Lord and pestilence in the lande three dayes, that the Angel of the Lord may destroy throughout all the coastes of Israel: nowe therefore aduise thee, what word I shall bring againe to him that sent me.

13 And Dauid said vnto Gad, I am in a wonderfull strait. let me nowe fall into the hande of the Lord: for his mercies are exceeding great, and let me not fall into the hande of man.

14 So the Lord sent a pestilence in Israel, and there fell of Israel seuentie thousand men.

15 And God sent the Angel into Ierusalem to destroy it. And as he was destroying, the Lord behelde, and repented of the euill and sayde to the Angel that destroyed, It is nowe ynough, let thine hande cease. Then the Angel of the Lord stoode by the thresshing floore of Ornan the Iebusite.

16 And Dauid lift vp his eyes, and sawe the Angel of the Lord stande betweene the earth and the heauen with his sworde drawen in his hand, and stretched out towarde Ierusalem. Then Dauid and the Elders of Israel, which were clothed in sacke, fell vpon their faces.

17 And Dauid said vnto God, Is it not I that commanded to nomber the people? It is euen I that haue sinned and haue committed euil, but these sheepe what haue they done? O Lord my God, I beseech thee, let thine hande be on me and on my fathers house, and not on thy people for their destruction.

18 Then the Angel of the Lord commanded Gad to say to Dauid, that Dauid should goe vp, and set vp an altar vnto the Lord in the thresshing floore of Ornan the Iebusite.

19 So Dauid went vp according to the saying of Gad, which he had spoken in the Name of the Lord.

20 And Ornan turned about, and sawe the Angel, and his foure sonnes, that were with him, hid them selues, and Ornan thresshed wheat.

21 And as Dauid came to Ornan, Ornan looked and sawe Dauid, and went out of the thresshing floore, and bowed himselfe to Dauid with his face to the grounde.

22 And Dauid saide to Ornan, Giue me the place of thy thresshing floore, that I may builde an altar therein vnto the Lord: giue it me for sufficient money, that the plague may be stayed from the people.

23 Then Ornan saide vnto Dauid, Take it to thee, and let my lord the King do that which seemeth him good: loe, I giue thee bullockes for burnt offrings, and thresshing instruments for wood, and wheat for meate offring, I giue it all.

24 And King Dauid saide to Ornan, Not so: but I will bye it for sufficient money: for I wil not take that which is thine for the Lord, nor offer burnt offrings without cost.

25 So Dauid gaue to Ornan for that place sixe hundreth shekels of golde by weight.

26 And Dauid built there an altar vnto the Lord, and offred burnt offrings, and peace offrings, and called vpon the Lord, and he answered him by fire from heauen vpon the altar of burnt offring.

27 And when the Lord had spoken to the Angel, he put vp his sworde againe into his sheath.

28 At that time when Dauid sawe that the Lord had heard him in the thresshing floore of Ornan the Iebusite, then he sacrificed there.

29 (But the Tabernacle of the Lord which Moses had made in the wildernesse, and the altar of burnt offring were at that season in the hie place at Gibeon.

30 And Dauid could not go before it to aske counsel at God: for he was afraide of the sworde of the Angel of the Lord.)

First Chronicles 22

1 And Dauid saide, This is the house of the Lord God, and this is the altar for the burnt offring of Israel.

2 And Dauid commanded to gather together the strangers that were in the lande of Israel, and he set masons to hewe and polish stones to builde the house of God.

3 Dauid also prepared much yron for the nayles of the doores and of the gates, and for the ioynings, and abundance of brasse passing weight,

4 And cedar trees without nomber: for the Zidonians and they of Tyrus brought much cedar wood to Dauid.

5 And Dauid saide, Salomon my sonne is yong and tender, and we must builde an house for the Lord, magnificall, excellent and of great fame and dignitie throughout all countreyes. I will therefore nowe prepare for him. So Dauid prepared very much before his death.

6 Then he called Salomon his sonne, and charged him to builde an house for the Lord God of Israel.

7 And Dauid said to Salomon, My sonne, I purposed with my selfe to builde an house to the Name of the Lord my God,

8 But the worde of the Lord came to me, saying, Thou hast shed much blood, and hast made great battels: thou shalt not builde an house vnto my Name: for thou hast shead much blood vpon the earth in my sight.

9 Beholde, a sonne is borne to thee, which shalbe a man of rest, for I will giue him rest from all his enemies rounde about: therefore his name is Salomon: and I will sende peace and quietnes vpon Israel in his dayes.

10 Hee shall builde an house for my Name, and he shalbe my sonne, and I will be his father, and I will establish the throne of his kingdome vpon Israel for euer.

11 Nowe therefore my sonne, the Lord shalbe with thee, and thou shalt prosper, and thou shalt builde an house to the Lord thy God, as he hath spoken of thee.

12 Onely the Lord giue thee wisedome and vnderstanding, and giue thee charge ouer Israel, euen to keepe the Lawe of the Lord thy God.

13 Then thou shalt prosper, if thou take heede to obserue the statutes and the iudgements which the Lord commanded Moses for Israel: be strong and of good courage: feare not, neither bee afraide.

14 For beholde, according to my pouertie haue I prepared for the house of the Lord an hundreth thousand talents of golde, and a thousand thousande talents of siluer, and of brasse and of yron passing weight: for there was abundance: I haue also prepared timber and stone, and thou mayest prouide more thereto.

15 Moreouer thou hast workmen with thee enough, hewers of stone, and workemen for timber, and all men expert in euery worke.

16 Of golde, of siluer, and of brasse, and of yron there is no nomber: Vp therefore, and be doing, and the Lord wilbe with thee.

17 Dauid also commanded all the princes of Israel to helpe Salomon his sonne, saying,

18 Is not the Lord your God with you, and hath giuen you rest on euerie side? for hee hath giuen the inhabitants of the land into mine hand, and the land is subdued before the Lord and before his people.

19 Nowe set your hearts and your soules to seeke the Lord your God, and arise, and builde the Sanctuarie of the Lord God to bring the Arke of the couenant of the Lord, and the holy vessels of God into the house built for the Name of the Lord.

First Chronicles 23

1 So when Dauid was olde and full of dayes, he made Salomon his sonne King ouer Israel.

2 And hee gathered together all the princes of Israel with the Priestes and the Leuites.

3 And the Leuites were numbred from ye age of thirtie yeere and aboue, and their nomber according to their summe was eight and thirtie thousand men.

4 Of these foure and twentie thousande were set to aduance the worke of the house of the Lord, and sixe thousand were ouerseers and iudges.

5 And foure thousand were porters, and foure thousande praised the Lord with instruments which he made to praise the Lord.

6 So Dauid deuided offices vnto them, to wit, to the sonnes of Leui, to Gershon, Kohath, and Merari.

7 Of the Gershonites were Laadan and Shimei.

8 The sonnes of Laadan, the chiefe was Iehiel, and Zetham and Ioel, three.

9 The Sonnes of Shimei, Shelomith, and Haziel, and Haram, three: these were the chiefe fathers of Laadan.

10 Also the sonnes of Shimei were Iahath, Zina, Ieush, and Beriah: these foure were ye sonnes of Shimei.

11 And Iahath was the chiefe, and Zizah the seconde, but Ieush and Beriah had not many sonnes: therfore they were in the families of their father, counted but as one.

12 The sonnes of Kohath were Amram, Izhar, Hebron aud Vzziel, foure.

13 The sonnes of Amram, Aaron and Moses: and Aaron was separated to sanctifie the most holy place, hee and his sonnes for euer to burne incense before the Lord, to minister to him, and to blesse in his Name for euer.

14 Moses also the man of God, and his children were named with the tribe of Leui.

15 The sonnes of Moses were Gershom, and Eliezer,

16 Of the sonnes of Gershom was Shebuel the chiefe.

17 And the sonne of Eliezer was Rehabiah the chiefe: for Eliezer had none other sonnes: but the sonnes of Rehabiah were very many.

18 The sone of Izhar was Shelomith ye chiefe.

19 The sonnes of Hebron were Ieriah the first, Amariah the second, Iahaziel the third, and Iekamiam the fourth.

20 The sones of Vzziel were Michah the first, and Isshiah the second.

21 The sonnes of Merari were Mahli and Mushi. The sonnes of Mahli, Eleazar and Kish.

22 And Eleazar dyed, and had no sonnes, but daughters, and their brethren the sonnes of Kish tooke them.

23 The sonnes of Mushi were Mahli, and Eder, and Ierimoth, three.

24 These were the sonnes of Leui according to the house of their fathers, euen the chiefe fathers according to their offices, according to the number of names and their summe that did the worke for the seruice of the house of the Lord from the age of twentie yeeres and aboue.

25 For Dauid sayde, The Lord God of Israel hath giuen rest vnto his people, that they may dwell in Ierusalem for euer.

26 And also the Leuites shall no more beare the Tabernacle and al the vessels for the seruice thereof.

27 Therefore according to the last wordes of Dauid, the Leuites were nombred from twentie yeere and aboue,

28 And their office was vnder the hand of the sonnes of Aaron, for the seruice of the house of the Lord in the courtes, and chambers, and in the purifiyng of all holy thinges, and in the worke of the seruice of the house of God,

29 Both for the shewbread, and for the fine floure, for the meate offring, and for

the vnleauened cakes, and for the fryed things, and for that which was rosted, and for all measures and cise,

30 And for to stand euery morning, to giue thanks and praise to the Lord, and likewise at euen,

31 And to offer all burnt offrings vnto the Lord, in the Sabbaths, in the monethes, and at the appointed times, according to the nomber and according to their custome continually before the Lord,

32 And that they should keepe the charge of the Tabernacle of the Congregation, and the charge of ye holy place, and the charge of ye sonnes of Aaron their brethren in the seruice of ye house of the Lord.

First Chronicles 24

1 These are also the diuisions of the sonnes of Aaron: The sonnes of Aaron were Nadab, and Abihu, Eleazar, and Ithamar.

2 But Nadab and Abihu died before their father, and had no children: therefore Eleazar and Ithamar executed the Priestes office.

3 And Dauid distributed them, euen Zadok of the sonnes of Eleazar, and Ahimelech of the sonnes of Ithamar according to their offices in their ministration.

4 And there were found more of the sonnes of Eleazar by the number of men, then of the sonnes of Ithamar. and they deuided them, to wit, among the sonnes of Eleazar, sixteene heads, according to the housholde of their fathers, and among ye sonnes of Ithamar, according to the housholde of their fathers, eight.

5 Thus they distributed them by lot the one from the other, and so the rulers of the Sanctuarie and the rulers of the house of God were of the sonnes of Eleazar and of the sonnes of Ithamar.

6 And Shemaiah the sonne of Nethaneel the scribe of the Leuites, wrote them before ye King and the princes, and Zadok the Priest, and Ahimelech the sonne of Abiathar, and before ye chiefe fathers of the Priests and of the Leuites, one familie being reserued for Eleazar, and another reserued for Ithamar.

7 And the first lot fell to Iehoiarib, and the second to Iedaiah,

8 The third to Harim, the fourth to Seorim,

9 The fifth to Malchiiah, the sixt to Miiamin,

10 The seuenth to Hakkoz, the eight to Abiiah,

11 The ninth to Ieshua, the tenth to Shecaniah,

12 The eleuenth to Eliashib, the twelft to Iakim,

13 The thirteenth to Huppa, the foureteenth to Ieshebeab,

14 The fiftenth to Bilgah, the sixtenth to Immer,

15 The seuententh to Hezir, the eightenth to Happizzer,

16 The ninetenth to Pethahiah, the twentieth to Iehezekel,

17 The one and twentie to Iachin, the two and twentie to Gamul,

18 The three and twentie to Deliah, the foure and twentie to Maaziah,

19 These were their orders according to their offices, when they entred into the house of the Lord according to their custome vnder the hande of Aaron their father, as the Lord God of Israel had commanded him.

20 And of the sonnes of Leui that remained of the sonnes of Amram, was Shubael, of the sonnes of Shubael, Iedeiah,

21 Of Rehabiah. euen of the sonnes of Rehabiah, the first Isshiiah,

22 Of Izhari, Shelomoth, of the sonnes of Shelomoth, Iahath,

23 And his sonnes Ieriah the first, Amariah the second, Iahaziel the thirde, and Iekameam the fourth,

24 The sonne of Vzziel was Michah, ye sonne of Michah was Shamir,

25 The brother of Michah was Isshiiah, the sonne of Isshiiah, Zechariah,

26 The sonnes of Merari, were Mahli and Mushi, the sonne of Iaaziiah was Beno,

27 The sonnes of Merari of Iahaziah were Beno, and Shoham, and Zaccur and Ibri.

28 Of Mahli came Eleazar, which had no sonnes.

29 Of Kish. the sonne of Kish was Ierahmeel,

30 And the sonnes of Mushi were Mahli, and Eder, and Ierimoth: these were sonnes of the Leuites after the houshold of their fathers.

31 And these also cast lots with their brethren the sonnes of Aaron before King Dauid, and Zadok and Ahimelech and the chiefe fathers of the Priests, and of the Leuites, euen the chiefe of the families against their yonger brethren.

First Chronicles 25

1 So Dauid and the captaines of the armie separated for the ministerie the sonnes of Asaph, and Heman, and Ieduthun, who should sing prophesies with harpes, with violes, and with cymbales, and their number was euen of the men for the office of their ministerie, to wit,

2 Of the sonnes of Asaph, Zaccur, and Ioseph, and Nethaniah, and Asharelah the sonnes of Asaph were vnder the hand of Asaph, which sang prophesies by the commission of the King.

3 Of Ieduthun, the sonnes of Ieduthun, Gedaliah, and Zeri, and Ieshaiah, Ashabiah and Mattithiah, six, vnder the hands of their father: Ieduthun sang prophecies with an harpe, for to giue thankes and to praise the Lord.

4 Of Heman, the sonnes of Heman, Bukkiah, Mattaniah, Vzziel, Shebuel, and Ierimoth, Hananiah, Hanani, Eliathah, Giddalti, and Romamtiezer, Ioshbekashah, Mallothi, Hothir, and Mahazioth.

5 All these were the sonnes of Heman, the Kings Seer in the wordes of God to lift vp the horne: and God gaue to Heman fourtene sonnes and three daughters.

6 All these were vnder the hande of their father, singing in the house of the Lord with cymbales, violes and harpes, for the seruice of the house of God, and Asaph, and Ieduthun, and Heman were at the Kings commandement.

7 So was their nomber with their brethre that were instruct in ye songs of the Lord, euen of al that were cunning, two hundreth foure score and eight.

8 And they cast lottes, charge against charge, aswel small as great, the cunning man as the scholer.

9 And the first lot fell to Ioseph which was of Asaph, the second, to Gedaliah, who with his brethren and his sonnes were twelue.

10 The third, to Zaccur, he, his sonnes and his brethren were twelue.

11 The fourth, to Izri, he, his sonnes and his brethren twelue.

12 The fift, to Nethaniah, he, his sonnes and his brethren twelue.

13 The sixt, to Bukkiah, he, his sonnes and his brethren twelue.

14 The seuenth, to Iesharelah, he, his sonnes and his brethren twelue.

15 The eight, to Ieshaiah, he, his sonnes and his brethren twelue.

16 The ninth, to Mattaniah, he, his sonnes and his brethren twelue.

17 The tenth, to Shimei, he, his sonnes and his brethren twelue.

18 The eleuenth, to Azareel, he, his sonnes and his brethren twelue.

19 The twelft, to Ashabiah, he, his sonnes and his brethren twelue.

20 The thirteenth, to Shubael, he, his sonnes and his brethren twelue.

21 The fourtenth, to Mattithiah, he, his sonnes and his brethren twelue.

22 The fifteenth, to Ierimoth, he, his sonnes and his brethren twelue.

23 The sixteenth, to Hananiah, he, his sonnes and his brethren twelue.

24 The seuenteenth, to Ioshbekashah, he, his sonnes and his brethren twelue.

25 The eighteenth, to Hanani, he, his sonnes and his brethren twelue.

26 The nineteenth, to Mallothi, he, his sonnes and his brethren twelue.

27 The twentieth, to Eliathah, he, his sonnes and his brethren twelue.

28 The one and twentieth, to Hothir, he, his sonnes and his brethren twelue.

29 The two and twentieth, to Giddalti, he, his sonnes and his brethren twelue.

30 The three and twentieth, to Mahazioth, he, his sonnes and his brethren twelue.

31 The foure and twentieth, to Romamti-ezer, he, his sonnes and his brethren twelue.

First Chronicles 26

1 Concerning the diuisions of the porters, of the Korhites, Meshelemiah the sonne of Kore of the sonnes of Asaph.

2 And the sonnes of Meshelemiah, Zechariah the eldest, Iediael the seconde, Zebadiah the third, Iathniel the fourth,

3 Elam the fift, Ichohanan the sixt, and Eliehoenai the seuenth.

4 And the sonnes of Obed Edom, Shemaiah the eldest, Iehozabad the second, Ioah the third, and Sacar the fourth, and Nethaneel the fift,

5 Ammiel the sixt, Issachar the seuenth, Peulthai the eight: for God had blessed him.

6 And to Shemaiah his sonne, were sonnes borne, that ruled in the house of their father, for they were men of might.

7 The sonnes of Shemaiah were Othni, and Rephael, and Obed, Elzabad and his brethren, strong men: Elihu also, and Semachiah.

8 All these were of the sonnes of Obed Edom, they and their sonnes and their brethren mightie and strong to serue, euen three score and two of Obed Edom.

9 And of Meshelemiah sonnes and brethren, eighteene mightie men.

10 And of Hosah of the sonnes of Merari, the sonnes were Shuri the chiefe, and (though he was not the eldest, yet his father made him the chiefe)

11 Helkiah the second, Tebaliah the third, and Zechariah the fourth: all the sonnes and the brethren of Hosa were thirteene.

12 Of these were the diuisions of the porters of the chiefe men, hauing the charge against their brethren, to serue in the house of the Lord.

13 And they cast lottes both small and great for the house of their fathers, for euery gate.

14 And the lot on the East side fel to Shelemiah: then they cast lottes for Zechariah his sonne a wise couseller, and his lot came out Northward:

15 To Obed Edom Southwarde, and to his sonnes the house of Asuppim:

16 To Shuppim and to Hosah Westwarde with the gate of Shallecheth by the paued streete that goeth vpward, warde ouer against warde.

17 Eastward were sixe Leuites, and Northwarde foure a day, and Southward foure a day, and toward Asuppim two and two.

18 In Parbar towarde the West were foure by the paued streete, and two in Parbar.

19 These are the diuisions of the porters of the sonnes of Kore, and of the sonnes of Merari.

20 And of the Leuites. Ahiiah was ouer the treasures of the house of God, and ouer the treasures of the dedicate things.

21 Of the sonnes of Laadan the sonnes of the Gershunnites descending of Laadan, the chiefe fathers of Laadan were Gershunni and Iehieli.

22 The sonnes of Iehieli were Zethan and Ioel his brother, appoynted ouer the treasures of the house of the Lord.

23 Of the Amramites, of the Izharites, of the Hebronites and of the Ozielites.

24 And Shebuel the sonne of Gershom, the sonne of Moses, a ruler ouer the treasures.

25 And of his brethren which came of Eliezer, was Rehabiah his sonne, and Ieshaiah his sonne, and Ioram his sonne, and Zichri his sonne, and Shelomith his sonne.

26 Which Shelomith and his brethren were ouer al the treasures of the dedicate things, which Dauid the King, and the chiefe fathers, the captaines ouer thousands, and hundreths, and the captaines of the armie had dedicated.

27 (For of the battels and of the spoyles they did dedicate to maintaine the house of the Lord)

28 And al that Samuel the Seer had dedicate and Saul the sonne of Kish and Abner the sonne of Ner, and Ioab the sonne of Zeruiah, and whosoeuer had dedicate any thing, it was vnder the hand of Shelomith, and his brethren.

29 Of the Izharites was Chenaniah and his sonnes, for the busines without ouer Israel, for officers and for Iudges.

30 Of the Hebronites, Ashabiah and his brethren, men of actiuitie, a thousande, and seuen hundreth were officers for Israel beyonde Iorden Westward, in all the busines of the Lord, and for the seruice of the King.

31 Among the Hebronites was Iediiah the chiefest, euen the Hebronites by his generations according to the families. And in the fourtieth yere of the reigne of Dauid they were sought for: and there were founde among them men of actiuitie at Iazer in Gilead.

32 And his brethren men of actiuitie, two thousand and seuen hundreth chiefe fathers, whom King Dauid made rulers ouer the Reubenites, and the Gadites, and the halfe tribe of Manasseh, for euery matter perteining to God, and for the Kings busines.

First Chronicles 27

1 The children of Israel also after their number, euen the chiefe fathers and captaines of thousandes and of hundreths, and their officers that serued the King by diuers courses, which came and in went out, moneth by moneth throughout al the moneths of the yeere: in euery course were foure and twentie thousand.

2 Ouer the first course for the first moneth was Iashobeam the sonne of Zabdiel: and in his course were foure and twentie thousand.

3 Of the sonnes of Perez was the chiefe ouer all the princes of the armies for the first moneth.

4 And ouer the course of the second moneth was Dodai, an Ahohite, and this was his course, and Mikloth was a captaine, and in his course were foure and twentie thousand.

5 The captaine of the thirde hoste for the third moneth was Benaiah the sonne of Iehoiada the chiefe Priest: and in his course were foure and twentie thousand.

6 This Benaiah was mightie among thirtie and aboue the thirtie, and in his course was Amizabad his sonne.

7 The fourth for the fourth moneth was Asahel the brother of Ioab, and Zebadiah his sonne after him: and in his course were foure and twentie thousand.

8 The fift for ye fift moneth was prince Shamhuth the Izrahite: and in his course foure and twentie thousand.

9 The sixt for the sixt moneth was Ira the sonne of Ikkesh the Tekoite: and in his course foure and twentie thousand.

10 The seuenth for the seuenth moneth was Helez the Pelonite, of the sonnes of Ephraim: and in his course foure and twentie thousand.

11 The eight for the eight moneth was Sibbecai the Hushathite of the Zarhites: and in his course foure and twentie thousand.

12 The ninth for the ninth moneth was Abiezer the Anethothite of the sonnes of Iemini: and in his course foure and twentie thousand.

13 The tenth for the tenth moneth was Maharai, the Netophathite of the Zarhites: and in his course foure and twentie thousand.

14 The eleueth for the eleuenth moneth was Benaiah the Pirathonite of the sonnes of Ephraim: and in his course foure and twentie thousand.

15 The twelft for the twelft moneth was Heldai the Netophathite, of Othniel: and in his course foure and twentie thousand.

16 Moreouer the rulers ouer the tribes of Israel were these: ouer the Reubenites was ruler, Eliezer the sonne of Zichri: ouer the Shimeonites, Shephatiah the sonne of Maachah:

17 Ouer the Leuites, Hashabiah the sonne of Remuel: ouer them of Aharon, and Zadok:

18 Ouer Iudah, Elihu of the brethren of Dauid: ouer Issachar, Omri the sonne of Michael:

19 Ouer Zebulun, Ishmaiah the sonne of Obadiah: ouer Naphtali, Ierimoth the sonne of Azriel:

20 Ouer the sonnes of Ephraim, Hoshea the sonne of Azazziah: ouer the halfe tribe of Manasseh, Ioel the sonne of Pedaiah:

21 Ouer the other halfe of Manasseh in Gilead, Iddo the sonne of Zechariah: ouer Beniamin, Iaasiel the sonne of Abner:

22 Ouer Dan, Azariel the sonne of Ieroham. these are the princes of the tribes of Israel.

23 But Dauid tooke not the nober of them from twentie yeere olde and vnder, because the Lord had sayde that he would increase Israel like vnto the starres of the heauens.

24 And Ioab the sonne of Zeruiah beganne to number: but hee finished it not, because there came wrath for it against Israel, neither was the nomber put into the Chronicles of King Dauid.

25 And ouer the Kings treasures was Azmaueth the sonne of Adiel: and ouer the treasures in the fieldes, in the cities and in the villages and in the towers was Iehonathan the sonne of Vzziah:

26 And ouer the workemen in the fielde that tilled the ground, was Ezri the sonne of Chelub:

27 And ouer them that dressed the vines, was Shimei the Ramathite: and

ouer that which apperteined to the vines, and ouer the store of the wine was Sabdi the Shiphmite:

28 And ouer the oliue trees and mulberie trees that were in the valleys, was Baal Hanan the Gederite: and ouer the store of the oyle was Ioash:

29 And ouer the oxen that fed in Sharon, was Shetrai the Sharonite: and ouer the oxen in the valleyes was Shaphat the sonne of Adlai:

30 And ouer the camels was Obil the Ishmaelite: and ouer the asses was Iehdeiah the Meronothite:

31 And ouer the sheepe was Iaziz the Hagerite: all these were the rulers of the substance that was King Dauids.

32 And Iehonathan Dauids vncle a man of counsell and vnderstanding (for he was a scribe) and Iehiel the sonne of Hachmoni were with the Kings sonnes.

33 And Ahitophel was the Kings counseller, and Hushai the Archite the Kings friend.

34 And after Ahitophel was Iehoiada the sonne of Benaiah and Abiathar: and captaine of the Kings armie was Ioab.

First Chronicles 28

1 Nowe Dauid assembled all the princes of Israel: the princes of the tribes, and the captaines of the bandes that serued the King, and the captaines of thousands and the captaines of hundreths, and the rulers of all the substance and possession of the King, and of his sonnes, with the eunuches, and the mightie, and all the men of power, vnto Ierusalem.

2 And King Dauid stoode vp vpon his feete; and saide, Heare ye me, my brethren and my people: I purposed to haue buylt an house of rest for the Arke of the couenant of the Lord, and for a footestoole of our God, and haue made ready for the building,

3 But God sayde vnto me, Thou shalt not buylde an house for my Name, because thou hast bene a man of warre, and hast shed blood.

4 Yet as the Lord God of Israel chose me before all the house of my father, to be King ouer Israel for euer (for in Iudah woulde he chuse a prince, and of the house of Iudah is the house of my father, and among the sonnes of my father he delited in me to make me King ouer all Israel)

5 So of all my sonnes (for the Lord hath giuen me many sonnes) he hath euen chosen Salomon my sonne to sit vpon the throne of the kingdome of the Lord ouer Israel.

6 And he sayd vnto me, Salomon thy sonne, he shall build mine house and my courtes: for I haue chosen him to be my sonne, and I will be his father.

7 I will stablish therefore his kingdome for euer, if he endeuour himselfe to do my commandements, and my iudgements, as this day.

8 Now therefore in the sight of all Israel the Congregation of the Lord, and in the audience of our God, keepe and seeke for all the commandements of the Lord your God, that ye may possesse this good lande, and leaue it for an inheritance for your children after you for euer.

9 And thou, Salomon my sonne, know thou the God of thy father, and serue him with a perfit heart, and with a willing minde: For the Lord searcheth all hearts, and vnderstandeth all the imaginations of thoughts: if thou seeke him, he will be found of thee, but if thou forsake him, he will cast thee off for euer.

10 Take heede now, for the Lord hath chosen thee to buylde the house of the Sanctuarie: be strong therefore, and doe it.

11 Then Dauid gaue to Salomon his sonne the paterne of the porch and of the houses thereof, and of the closets thereof, and of the galleries thereof, and of the chambers thereof that are within, and of the house of the mercieseate,

12 And the paterne of all that he had in his minde for the courtes of the house of the Lord, and for all the chambers round about, for the treasures of the house of God, and for the treasures of the dedicate things,

13 And for the courses of the Priestes, and of the Leuites, and for all the woorke for the seruice of the house of the Lord, and for all the vessels of the ministerie of the house of the Lord.

14 He gaue of golde by weight, for the vessels of gold, for all the vessels of all maner of seruice, and all the vessels of siluer by weight, for all maner vessels of all maner of seruice.

15 The weight also of golde for the candlestickes, and gold for their lampes, with the weight for euery candlesticke, and for the lampes thereof, and for the candlestickes of siluer by the weight of the candlesticke, and the lampes thereof, according to the vse of euery candlesticke,

16 And the weight of the gold for the tables of shewbread, for euery table, and siluer for the tables of siluer,

17 And pure golde for the fleshhookes, and the bowles, and plates, and for basens, golde in weight for euery basen, and for siluer basens, by weight for euery basen,

18 And for the altar of incense, pure golde by weight, and golde for the paterne of the charet of the Cherubs that spread themselues, and couered the Arke of the couenant of the Lord:

19 All, said he, by writing sent to me by the hand of the Lord, which made me vnderstand all the workemanship of the paterne.

20 And Dauid said to Salomon his sonne, Be strong, and of a valiant courage and doe it: feare not, nor be afraide: for the Lord God, euen my God is with thee: he will not leaue thee nor forsake thee till thou hast finished all the worke for the seruice of the house of the Lord.

21 Beholde also, the companies of the Priests and the Leuites for all the seruice of the house of God, euen they shall be with thee for the whole worke, with euery free heart that is skilfull in any maner of seruice. The princes also and all the people will be wholy at thy commandement.

First Chronicles 29

1 Moreouer Dauid the King sayde vnto all the Congregation, God hath chosen Salomon mine onely sonne yong and tender, and the worke is great: for this house is not for man, but for the Lord God.

2 Now I haue prepared with all my power for the house of my God, golde for vessels of golde, and siluer for them of siluer, and brasse for things of brasse, yron for things of yron, and wood for things of wood, and onix stones, and stones to be set, and carbuncle stones and of diuers colours, and all precious stones, and marble stones in aboundance.

3 Moreouer, because I haue delite in the house of my God, I haue of mine owne golde and siluer, which I haue giuen to the house of my God, beside all that I haue prepared for the house of the Sanctuarie,

4 Euen three thousand talents of gold of the golde of Ophir, and seuen thousand talents of fined siluer to ouerlay the walles of the houses.

5 The golde for the things of golde, and the siluer for things of siluer, and for all the worke by the handes of artificers: and who is willing to fill his hand to day vnto the Lord?

6 So the princes of the families, and the princes of the tribes of Israel, and the captaines of thousands and of hundreths, with the rulers of the Kings worke, offred willingly,

7 And they gaue for the seruice of the house of God fiue thousande talents of golde, and ten thousand pieces, and ten thousand talents of siluer, and eighteene thousand talents of brasse, and one hundreth thousand talents of yron.

8 And they with whom precious stones were found, gaue them to the treasure of ye house of the Lord, by the hand of Iehiel the Gershunnite.

9 And the people reioyced when they offred willingly: for they offred willingly vnto ye Lord, with a perfite heart. And Dauid the King also reioyced with great ioy.

10 Therefore Dauid blessed the Lord before all the Congregation, and Dauid sayde, Blessed be thou, O Lord God, of Israel our father, for euer and euer.

11 Thine, O Lord, is greatnesse and power, and glory, and victorie and praise: for all that is in heauen and in earth is thine: thine is the kingdome, O Lord, and thou excellest as head ouer all.

12 Both riches and honour come of thee, and thou reignest ouer all, and in thine hand is power and strength, and in thine hande it is to make great, and to giue strength vnto all.

13 Now therefore our God, we thanke thee, and prayse thy glorious Name.

14 But who am I, and what is my people, that we shoulde be able to offer willingly after this sort? for all things come of thee: and of thine owne hand we haue giuen thee.

15 For we are stragers before thee, and soiourners, like all our fathers: our dayes are like ye shadowe vpon the earth, and there is none abiding.

16 O Lord our God, all this abundance that we haue prepared to buylde thee an house for thine holy Name, is of thine hand and all is thine.

17 I knowe also, my God, that thou tryest the heart, and hast pleasure in righteousnesse: I haue offred willingly in the vprightnesse of mine heart all these things: now also haue I seene thy people which are found here, to offer vnto thee willingly with ioy.

18 O Lord God of Abraham, Izhak and Israel our fathers, keepe this for euer in the purpose, and the thoughts of the heart of thy people, and prepare their hearts vnto thee.

19 And giue vnto Salomon my sonne a perfit heart to keepe thy commandements, thy testimonies, and thy statutes, and to doe all things, and to builde the house which I haue prepared.

20 And Dauid said to all the Congregation, Now blesse the Lord your God. And all the Congregation blessed the Lord God of their fathers, and bowed downe their heads, and worshipped the Lord and the King.

21 And they offred sacrifices vnto the Lord, and on the morowe after that day, they offered burnt offrings vnto the Lord, euen a thousande yong bullocks, a thousand rammes and a thousand sheepe, with their drinke offrings, and sacrifices in abundance for all Israel.

22 And they did eate and drinke before the Lord the same day with great ioy, and they made Salomon the sonne of Dauid King the seconde time, and anoynted him prince before the Lord, and Zadok for the hie Priest.

23 So Salomon sate on the throne of the Lord, as King in steade of Dauid his father, and prospered: and all Israel obeyed him.

24 And all the princes and men of power, and all the sonnes of King Dauid submitted them selues vnder King Salomon.

25 And the Lord magnified Salomon in dignitie, in the sight of all Israel, and gaue him so glorious a kingdome, as no King had before him in Israel.

26 Thus Dauid the sonne of Ishai reigned ouer all Israel.

27 And the space that he reigned ouer Israel, was fourtie yeere: seuen yeere reigned he in Hebron, and three and thirtie yeere reigned he in Ierusalem:

28 And he dyed in a good age, full of dayes, riches and honour, and Salomon his sonne reigned in his steade.

29 Concerning the actes of Dauid the King first and last, behold, they are written in the booke of Samuel the Seer, and in the booke of Nathan the Prophet, and in the booke of Gad the Seer,

30 With all his reigne and his power, and times that went ouer him, and ouer Israel and ouer all the kingdomes of the earth.

Second Chronicles

Second Chronicles 1

1 Then Salomon the sonne of Dauid was confirmed in his kingdome: and the Lord his God was with him, and magnified him highly.

2 And Salomon spake vnto all Israel, to the captaines of thousandes, and of hundreths, and to the iudges, and to all the gouernours in all Israel, euen the chiefe fathers.

3 So Salomon and all the Congregation with him went to the hie place that was at Gibeon: for there was the Tabernacle of the Congregation of God which Moses the seruant of the Lord had made in the wildernesse.

4 But the Arke of God had Dauid brought vp from Kiriath-iearim, when Dauid had made preparation for it: for he had pitched a tent for it in Ierusalem.

5 Moreouer the brasen altar that Bezaleel the sonne of Vri, the sonne of Hur had made, did hee set before the Tabernacle of the Lord: and Salomon and the Congregation sought it.

6 And Salomon offred there before the Lord vpon the brasen altar that was in the Tabernacle of the Congregation: euen a thousand burnt offrings offred he vpon it.

7 The same night did God appeare vnto Salomon, and sayde vnto him, Aske what I shall giue thee.

8 And Salomon sayde vnto God, Thou hast shewed great mercy vnto Dauid my father and hast made me to reigne in his stead.

9 Nowe therefore, O Lord God, let thy promise vnto Dauid my father be true: for thou hast made mee King ouer a great people, like to the dust of the earth.

10 Giue me now wisdome and knowledge, that I may go out and go in before this people: for who can iudge this thy great people?

11 And God sayde to Salomon, Because this was in thine heart, and thou hast not asked riches, treasures nor honour, nor the liues of thine enemies, neither yet hast asked long life, but hast asked for thee wisdome and knowledge that thou mightest iudge my people, ouer whome I haue made thee King,

12 Wisdome and knowledge is granted vnto thee, and I will giue thee riches and treasures and honour, so that there hath not bene the like among the Kings which were before thee, neither after thee shall there be the like.

13 Then Salomon came from the hie place, that was at Gibeon, to Ierusalem from before the Tabernacle of the Congregation, and reigned ouer Israel.

14 And Salomon gathered the charets and horesemen: and he had a thousand and foure hundreth charets, and twelue thousande horsemen, whome he placed in the charet cities, and with the King at Ierusalem.

15 And the King gaue siluer and gold at Ierusalem as stones, and gaue cedar trees as the wilde figge trees, that are abundantly in the playne.

16 Also Salomon had horses brought out of Egypt and fine linen: the Kings marchants receiued the fine linen for a price.

17 They came vp also and brought out of Egypt some charet, worth sixe hundreth shekels of siluer, that is an horse for an hundreth and fiftie: and thus they brought horses to all the Kings of the Hittites, and to the Kings of Aram by their meanes.

Second Chronicles 2

1 Then Salomon determined to builde an house for the Name of the Lord, and an house for his kingdome.

2 And Salomon tolde out seuentie thousand that bare burdens, and fourescore thousande men to hewe stones in the mountaine, and three thousand and sixe hundreth to ouersee them.

3 And Salomon sent to Huram the king of Tyrus, saying, As thou hast done to Dauid my father, and didst sende him cedar trees to buylde him an house to dwell in, so do to me.

4 Behold, I buylde an house vnto the Name of the Lord my God, to sanctifie it vnto him, and to burne sweete incense before him, and for the continuall shewbread, and for the burnt offrings of the morning and euening, on the Sabbath dayes, and in the new moneths, and in the solemne feastes of the Lord our God: this is a perpetuall thing for Israel.

5 And the house which I buylde, is great: for great is our God aboue all gods.

6 Who is he then that can be able to buylde him an house, when the heauen, and the heauen of heauens can not conteine him? who am I then that I should buylde him an house? but I do it to burne incense before him.

7 Sende me nowe therefore a cunning man that can worke in golde, in siluer, and in brasse, and in yron, and in purple, and crimosin and blue silke, and that can graue in grauen worke with the cunning men that are with me in Iudah and in Ierusalem, whom Dauid my father hath prepared.

8 Sende mee also cedar trees, firre trees and Algummim trees from Lebanon: for I knowe that thy seruants can skill to hewe timber in Lebanon: and beholde, my seruantes shalbe with thine,

9 That they may prepare me timber in abundance: for the house which I doe buylde, is great and wonderfull.

10 And behold, I will giue to thy seruants the cutters and the hewers of timber twentie thousand measures of beaten wheate, and twentie thousand measures of barley, and twentie

thousand baths of wine, and twentie thousand baths of oyle.

11 Then Huram King of Tyrus answered in writing which he sent to Salomon, Because the Lord hath loued his people, he hath made thee King ouer them.

12 Huram sayd moreouer, Blessed be the Lord God of Israel, which made the heauen and the earth, and that hath giuen vnto Dauid the King a wise sonne, that hath discretion, prudence and vnderstanding to buylde an house for the Lord, and a palace for his kingdome.

13 Now therefore I haue sent a wise man, and of vnderstanding of my father Hurams,

14 The sonne of a woman of the daughters of Dan: and his father was a man of Tyrus, and he can skill to worke in golde, in siluer, in brasse, in yron, in stone, and in timber, in purple, in blue silke, and in fine linen, and in crimosin, and can graue in all grauen workes, and broyder in all broydered worke that shalbe giuen him, with thy cunning men, and with the cunning men of my lord Dauid thy father.

15 Now therefore the wheate and the barley, the oyle and the wine, which my lorde hath spoken of, let him send vnto his seruants.

16 And we wil cut wood in Lebanon as much as thou shalt neede, and will bring it to thee in raftes by the sea to Iapho, so thou mayest cary them to Ierusalem.

17 And Salomon nombred al the strangers that were in the land of Israel, after the nombring that his father Dauid had nombred them: and they were found an hundreth and three and fiftie thousand, and sixe hundreth.

18 And he set seuentie thousande of them to the burden, and fourescore thousande to hewe stones in the mountaine, and three thousande and sixe hundreth ouerseers to cause the people to worke.

Second Chronicles 3

1 So Salomon began to buyld the house of the Lord in Ierusalem, in mount Moriah which had bene declared vnto Dauid his father, in the place that Dauid prepared in the threshing floore of Ornan the Iebusite.

2 And he beganne to buylde in the seconde moneth and the second day, in the fourth yeere of his reigne.

3 And these are the measures, whereon Salomon grounded to buylde the house of God: the length of cubites after the first measure was threescore cubites, and the breadth twenty cubites:

4 And the porch, that was before the length in the front of the breadth was twentie cubits, and the height was an hundreth and twentie, and he ouerlayd it within with pure golde.

5 And the greater house he sieled with firre tree which he ouerlayd with good golde, and graued thereon palme trees and chaines.

6 And hee ouerlayde the house with precious stone for beautie: and the golde was gold of Paruaim.

7 The house, I say, the beames, postes, and walles thereof and the doores thereof ouerlayde he with gold, and graued Cherubims vpon the walles.

8 He made also the house of the most holy place: the length thereof was in the front of the breadth of the house, twenty cubits, and the breadth thereof twentie cubites: and he ouerlayde it with the best golde, of sixe hundreth talents.

9 And the weight of the nayles was fiftie shekels of golde, and hee ouerlayde the chambers with golde.

10 And in the house of the most holy place he made two Cherubims wrought like children, and ouerlayd them with golde.

11 And the winges of the Cherubims were twentie cubites long: the one wing was fiue cubites, reaching to the wall of the house, and the other wing fiue cubites, reaching to the wing of the other Cherub.

12 Likewise the wing of ye other Cherub was fiue cubites, reaching to the wall of the house, and the other wing fiue cubites ioyning to the wing of the other Cherub.

13 The wings of these Cherubims were spread abroade twentie cubites: they stoode on their feete, and their faces were toward the house.

14 He made also the vaile of blew silke and purple, and crimosin, and fine linen, and wrought Cherubims thereon.

15 And he made before the house two pillars of fiue and thirtie cubites hie: and the chapiter that was vpon the top of eche of them, was fiue cubites.

16 He made also chaines for the oracle, and put them on the heads of the pillars, and made an hundreth pomegranates, and put them among the chaines.

17 And he set vp the pillars before the Temple, one on the right hande and the other on the left, and called that on the right hand Iachin, and that on the left hand Boaz.

Second Chronicles 4

1 And hee made an altar of brasse twentie cubites long, and twentie cubites broade, and ten cubites hie.

2 And he made a molten Sea of ten cubites from brim to brim, rounde in compasse, and fiue cubites hie: and a line of thirtie cubites did compasse it about.

3 And vnder it was ye facion of oxen, which did compasse it rounde about, tenne in a cubite compassing the Sea about: two rowes of oxen were cast when it was molten.

4 It stoode vpon twelue oxen: three looked toward the North, and three looked towarde the West, and three looked towarde the South, and three looked towarde the East, and the Sea stoode about vpon them, and all their hinder parts were inwarde.

5 And the thickenesse thereof was an hande breadth, and the brim thereof was like the worke of the brim of a cuppe with floures of lilies: it conteined three thousand baths.

6 He made also ten caldrons, and put fiue on the right hand, and fiue on the left, to wash in them, and to clense in them that which apperteined to the burnt offrings: but the Sea was for the Priests to wash in.

7 And he made ten candlestickes of golde (according to their forme) and put them in the Temple, fiue on the right hand, and fiue on the left.

8 And he made ten tables, and put them in the Temple, fiue on the right hand, and fiue on the left: and he made an hundreth basens of golde.

9 And he made the court of the Priests, and the great court and doores for the court, and ouerlayd the doores thereof with brasse.

10 And he set the Sea on the right side Eastward toward the South.

11 And Huram made pottes and besoms and basens, and Huram finished the worke that hee shoulde make for King Salomon for the house of God,

12 To wit, two pillars, and the bowles and the chapiters on the top of ye two pillars, and two grates to couer the two bowles of the chapiters which were vpon the toppe of the pillars:

13 And foure hundreth pomegranates for the two grates, two rowes of pomegranates for euery grate to couer the two bowles of the chapiters, that were vpon the pillars.

14 He made also bases, and made caldrons vpon the bases:

15 And a Sea, and twelue bulles vnder it:

16 Pottes also and besomes, and fleshhookes, and all these vessels made Huram his father, to King Salomon for the house of the Lord, of shining brasse.

17 In the playne of Iorden did the King cast them in clay betweene Succoth and Zeredathah.

18 And Salomon made al these vessels in great abundance: for the weight of brasse could not be rekoned.

19 And Salomon made al the vessels that were for the house of God: the golden altar also and the tables, whereon the shewbread stoode.

20 Moreouer the candlestickes, with their lampes to burne them after the maner, before the oracle, of pure golde.

21 And the floures and the lampes, and the snuffers of gold, which was fine golde.

22 And the hookes, and the basens, and the spoones, and the ashpans of pure golde: the entrie also of the house and doores thereof within, euen of the most holy place: and the doores of the house, to wit, of the Temple were of golde.

Second Chronicles 5

1 So was all the worke finished that Salomon made for the house of the Lord, and Salomon brought in the things that

Dauid his father had dedicated, with the siluer and the golde, and all the vessels, and put them among the treasures of the house of God.

2 Then Salomon assembled the Elders of Israel, and all the heads of the tribes, the chiefe fathers of the children of Israel vnto Ierusalem to bring vp the Arke of the couenant of the Lord from the citie of Dauid, which is Zion.

3 And all ye men of Israel assembled vnto the King at the feast: it was in ye seuenth moneth.

4 And all the Elders of Israel came, and the Leuites tooke vp the Arke.

5 And they caried vp the Arke and the Tabernacle of the Congregation: and all the holy vessels that were in the Tabernacle, those did the Priests and Leuites bring vp.

6 And King Salomon and all the Congregation of Israel that were assembled vnto him, were before ye Arke, offring sheepe and bullocks, which could not be told nor nobred for multitude.

7 So the Priests brought the Arke of the couenant of the Lord vnto his place, into the Oracle of the house, into the most Holy place, euen vnder the wings of the Cherubims.

8 For ye Cherubims stretched out their wings ouer the place of the Arke, and the Cherubims couered the Arke and the barres thereof aboue.

9 And they drewe out the barres, that the endes of the barres might bee seene out of the Arke before the Oracle, but they were not seene without: and there they are vnto this day.

10 Nothing was in the Arke, saue the two Tables, which Moses gaue at Horeb, where the Lord made a couenant with the children of Israel, when they came out of Egypt.

11 And when the Priestes were come out of the Sanctuarie (for all the Priests that were present, were sanctified and did not waite by course.

12 And the Leuites the singers of all sortes, as of Asaph, of Heman, of Ieduthun, and of their sonnes and of their brethren, being clad in fine linen, stoode with cymbales, and with violes and harpes at the East ende of the altar, and with them an hundreth and twentie Priestes blowing with trumpets:

13 And they were as one, blowing trumpets, and singing, and made one sounde to bee heard in praysing and thanking the Lord, and when they lift vp their voyce with trumpets and with cymbales, and with instruments of musicke, and when they praysed the Lord, singing, For he is good, because his mercie lasteth for euer) then the house, euen the house of the Lord was filled with a cloude,

14 So that the Priests could not stand to minister, because of the cloude: for the glory of the Lord had filled the house of God.

Second Chronicles 6

1 Then Salomon sayd, The Lord hath sayde that he would dwell in the darke cloude:

2 And I haue built thee an house to dwell in, an habitation for thee to dwell in for euer.

3 And the King turned his face, and blessed all the Congregation of Israel (for all the Congregation of Israel stoode there)

4 And he said, Blessed be the Lord God of Israel, who spake with his mouth vnto Dauid my father, and hath with his hand fulfilled it, saying,

5 Since the day that I brought my people out of the land of Egypt, I chose no citie of al the tribes of Israel to buylde an house, that my Name might be there, neyther chose I any man to be a ruler ouer my people Israel:

6 But I haue chosen Ierusalem, that my Name might be there, and haue chosen Dauid to be ouer my people Israel.

7 And it was in the heart of Dauid my father to builde an house vnto the Name of the Lord God of Israel,

8 But the Lord sayde to Dauid my father, Whereas it was in thine heart to buylde an house vnto my Name, thou diddest well, that thou wast so minded.

9 Notwithstanding thou shalt not build the house, but thy sonne which shall come out of thy loynes, he shall buylde an house vnto my Name.

10 And the Lord hath performed his worde that he spake: and I am risen vp in the roume of Dauid my father, and am set on the throne of Israel as the Lord promised, and haue built an house to the Name of the Lord God of Israel.

11 And I haue set the Arke there, wherein is the couenant of the Lord, that he made with the children of Israel.

12 And the King stoode before the altar of the Lord, in the presence of all the Congregation of Israel, and stretched out his hands,

13 (For Salomon had made a brasen skaffold and set it in the middes of the court, of fiue cubites long, and fiue cubites broade, and three cubites of height, and vpon it he stoode, and kneeled downe vpon his knees before all the Congregation of Israel, and stretched out his hands toward heauen)

14 And sayd, O Lord God of Israel, there is no God like thee in heauen nor in earth, which keepest couenant, and mercie vnto thy seruants, that walke before thee with all their heart.

15 Thou that hast kept with thy seruant Dauid my father, that thou hast promised him: for thou spakest with thy mouth, and hast fulfilled it with thine hand, as appeareth this day.

16 Therefore now Lord God of Israel, keepe with thy seruant Dauid my father, that thou hast promised him, saying, Thou shalt not want a man in my sight, that shall sit vpon the throne of Israel: so that thy sonnes take heede to their wayes, to walke in my Lawe, as thou hast walked before me.

17 And now, O Lord God of Israel, let thy worde be verified, which thou spakest vnto thy seruant Dauid.

18 (Is it true in deede that God will dwell with man on earth? beholde, the heauens, and the heauens of heauens are not able to conteine thee: how much more vnable is this house, which I haue buylt?)

19 But haue thou respect to the prayer of thy seruant, and to his supplication, O Lord my God, to heare the crye and prayer which thy seruant prayeth before thee,

20 That thine eyes may be open toward this house day and night, euen toward the place, whereof thou hast sayde, that thou wouldest put thy Name there, that thou mayest hearken vnto the prayer, which thy seruant prayeth in this place.

21 Heare thou therefore the supplication of thy seruant, and of thy people Israel, which they pray in this place: and heare thou in the place of thine habitation, euen in heauen, and when thou hearest, be mercifull.

22 When a man shall sinne against his neighbour, and he laye vpon him an othe to cause him to sweare, and the swearer shall come before thine altar in this house,

23 Then heare thou in heauen, and doe, and iudge thy seruants, in recompensing the wicked to bring his way vpon his head, and in iustifying the righteous, to giue him according to his righteousnes.

24 And when thy people Israel shalbe ouerthrowen before the enemie, because they haue sinned against thee, and turne againe, and confesse thy Name, and pray, and make supplication before thee in this house,

25 Then heare thou in heauen, and be mercifull vnto the sinne of thy people Israel, and bring them againe vnto the land which thou gauest to them and to their fathers.

26 When heauen shall be shut vp, and there shalbe no rayne, because they haue sinned against thee, and shall pray in this place, and confesse thy Name, and turne from their sinne, when thou doest afflict them,

27 Then heare thou in heauen, and pardon the sinne of thy seruants, and of thy people Israel (when thou hast taught them the good way wherein they may walke) and giue rayne vpon thy lande, which thou hast giuen vnto thy people for an inheritance.

28 When there shalbe famine in the land, when there shalbe pestilence, blasting, or mildew, when there shall be grashopper, or caterpiller, when their enemie shall besiege them in the cities of their land, or any plague or any sickenesse,

29 Then what prayer and supplication so euer shalbe made of any man, or of all thy people Israel, whe euery one shall knowe his owne plague, and his owne disease, and shall stretch forth his hands toward this house,

30 Heare thou then in heauen, thy dwelling place, and be mercifull, and giue

euery man according vnto all his wayes, as thou doest knowe his heart (for thou onely knowest the hearts of the children of men)

31 That they may feare thee, and walke in thy wayes as long as they liue in the land which thou gauest vnto our fathers.

32 Moreouer, as touching ye stranger which is not of thy people Israel, who shall come out of a farre countrey for thy great Names sake, and thy mighty hande, and thy stretched out arme: when they shall come and pray in this house,

33 Heare thou in heauen thy dwelling place, and doe according to all that the stranger calleth for vnto thee, that all the people of the earth may knowe thy Name, and feare thee like thy people Israel, and that they may knowe, that thy Name is called vpon in this house which I haue built.

34 When thy people shall goe out to battell against their enemies, by the way that thou shalt send them, and they pray to thee, in the way towarde this citie, which thou hast chosen, euen toward the house which I haue built to thy Name,

35 Then heare thou in heauen their prayer and their supplication, and iudge their cause.

36 If they sinne against thee (for there is no man that sinneth not) and thou be angry with them and deliuer them vnto the enemies, and they take them and cary them away captiue vnto a land farre or neere,

37 If they turne againe to their heart in the lande whither they be caryed in captiues, and turne and pray vnto thee in the lande of their captiuitie, saying, We haue sinned, we haue transgressed and haue done wickedly,

38 If they turne againe to thee with all their heart, and with all their soule in the land of their captiuitie, whither they haue caryed them captiues, and pray toward their land, which thou gauest vnto their fathers, and toward the citie which thou hast chosen, and toward the house which I haue built for thy Name,

39 Then heare thou in heauen, in the place of thine habitation their prayer and their supplication, and iudge their cause, and be mercifull vnto thy people, which haue sinned against thee.

40 Nowe my God, I beseech thee, let thine eyes be open, and thine eares attent vnto the prayer that is made in this place.

41 Nowe therefore arise, O Lord God, to come into thy rest, thou, and the Arke of thy strength: O Lord God, let thy Priestes be clothed with saluation, and let thy Saints reioyce in goodnesse.

42 O Lord God, refuse not the face of thine anoynted: remember the mercies promised to Dauid thy seruant.

Second Chronicles 7

1 And when Salomon had made an ende of praying, fire came downe from heauen, and consumed the burnt offring and the sacrifices: and the glory of the Lord filled the house,

2 So that the Priestes could not euter into the house of the Lord, because the glory of the Lord had filled the Lordes house.

3 And when all the children of Israel saw the fire, and the glory of the Lord come downe vpon the house, they bowed themselues with their faces to the earth vpon the pauement, and worshipped and praysed the Lord, saying, For he is good, because his mercy lasteth for euer.

4 Then the King and all the people offred sacrifices before the Lord.

5 And King Salomon offered a sacrifice of two and twentie thousand bullockes, and an hundreth and twentie thousand sheepe. so the King and all the people dedicated the house of God.

6 And the Priests waited on their offices, and the Leuites with the instruments of musicke of the Lord, which King Dauid had made to praise the Lord, Because his mercy lasteth for euer: whe Dauid praysed God by them, the Priestes also blewe trumpets ouer against them: and all they of Israel stoode by.

7 Moreouer Salomon halowed the middle of the court that was before the house of the Lord: for there hee had prepared burnt offerings, and the fatte of the peace offerings, because the brasen altar which Salomon had made, was not able to receiue the burnt offering, and the meate offring, and the fat.

8 And Salomon made a feast at that time of seuen dayes, and all Israel with him, a very great Congregation, from the entring in of Hamath, vnto the riuer of Egypt.

9 And in the eight day they made a solemne assemblie: for they had made the dedication of the altar seuen daies, and the feast seuen dayes.

10 And the three and twentieth day of the seuenth moneth, he sent the people away into their tentes, ioyous and with glad heart, because of the goodnesse that the Lord had done for Dauid and for Salomon, and for Israel his people.

11 So Salomon finished the house of the Lord, and the Kings house, and all that came into Salomons heart to make in the house of the Lord: and he prospered in his house.

12 And the Lord appeared to Salomon by night and said to him, I haue heard thy prayer, and haue chosen this place for my selfe to be an house of sacrifice.

13 If I shut the heauen that there be no raine, or if I commaund the grashopper to deuoure the lande, or if I sende pestilence among my people,

14 If my people, among whome my Name is called vpon, doe humble them selues, and praye, and seeke my presence, and turne from their wicked wayes, then will I heare in heauen, and be mercifull to their sinne, and wil heale their land:

15 Then mine eies shalbe open and mine eares attent vnto the prayer made in this place.

16 For I haue nowe chosen and sanctified this house, that my Name may be there for euer: and mine eyes and mine heart shalbe there perpetually.

17 And if thou wilt walke before me, as Dauid thy father walked, to doe according vnto all that I haue commanded thee, and shalt obserue my statutes and my iudgements,

18 Then will I stablish the throne of thy kingdome, according as I made the couenant with Dauid thy father, saying, Thou shalt not want a man to be ruler in Israel.

19 But if ye turne away, and forsake my statutes and my commandements which I haue set before you, and shall goe and serue other gods, and worshippe them,

20 Then will I plucke them vp out of my lande, which I haue giuen them, and this house which I haue sanctified for my Name, will I cast out of my sight, and will make it to be a prouerbe and a common talke among all people.

21 And this house which is most hie, shall be an astonishment to euery one that passeth by it, so that he shall say, Why hath the Lord done thus to this lande, and to this house?

22 And they shall answere, Because they forsooke the Lord God of their fathers, which brought them out of the lande of Egypt, and haue taken holde on other gods, and haue worshipped them, and serued them, therefore hath he brought all this euill vpon them.

Second Chronicles 8

1 And after twentie yeere when Salomon had built the house of the Lord, and his owne house,

2 Then Salomon built the cities that Huram gaue to Salomon, and caused the children of Israel to dwell there.

3 And Salomon went to Hamath Zobah, and ouercame it.

4 And he built Tadmor in the wildernesse, and repayred all the cities of store which hee built in Hamath.

5 And he built Beth-horon the vpper, and Beth-horon the nether, cities defensed with walles, gates and barres:

6 Also Baalath, and al the cities of store that Salomon had, and all the charet cities, and the cities of the horsemen, and euery pleasant place that Salomon had a minde to builde in Ierusalem, and in Lebanon, and throughout all the lande of his dominion.

7 And all the people that were left to ye Hittites, and ye Amorites, and Perizzites, and the Hiuuites, and the Iebusites, which were not of Israel,

8 But of their children which were left after them in the lande, whome the children of Israel had not consumed, euen them did Salomon make tributaries vntill this day.

9 But of the children of Israel did Salomon make no seruantes for his worke: for they were men of warre, and his chiefe princes, and the captaines of his charets and of his horsemen.

10 So these were the chiefe of the officers which Salomon had, euen two hundreth and fiftie that bare rule ouer the people.

11 Then Salomon brought vp the daughter of Pharaoh out of the citie of Dauid, into the house that he had built for her: for he saide, My wife shall not dwel in the house of Dauid King of Israel: for it is holy, because that the Arke of the Lord came vnto it.

12 Then Salomon offered burnt offrings vnto the Lord, on the altar of the Lord, which he had built before the porche,

13 To offer according to the commandement of Moses euery day, in the Sabbaths, and in the newe moones, and in the solemne feastes, three times in the yeere, that is, in the feast of the Vnleauened bread, and in the feast of the Weekes, and in the feast of the Tabernacles.

14 And he set the courses of the Priestes to their offices, according to the order of Dauid his father, and the Leuites in their watches, for to praise and minister before the Priestes euery day, and the porters by their courses, at euery gate: for so was the commandement of Dauid the man of God.

15 And they declined not from the commandement of the King, concerning the Priests and the Leuites, touching al things, and touching the treasures.

16 Nowe Salomon had made prouision for all the worke, from the day of the foundation of the house of the Lord, vntill it was finished: so the house of the Lord was perfite.

17 Then went Salomon to Ezion-geber, and to Eloth by the sea side in the lande of Edom.

18 And Huram sent him by the handes of his seruants, shippes, and seruants that had knowledge of the sea: and they went with the seruants of Salomon to Ophir, and brought thence foure hundreth and fiftie talents of golde, and brought them to King Salomon.

Second Chronicles 9

1 And when the Queene of Sheba heard of the fame of Salomon, she came to proue Salomon with hard questions at Ierusalem, with a very great traine, and camels that bare sweete odours and much golde, and precious stones: and when she came to Salomon, she communed with him of all that was in her heart.

2 And Salomon declared her all her questions, and there was nothing hid from Salomon, which he declared not vnto her.

3 Then the Queene of Sheba sawe the wisedome of Salomon, and the house that he had buylt,

4 And the meate of his table, and the sitting of his seruants, and the order of his wayters, and their apparel, and his butlers, and their apparel, and his burnt offrings which he offred in the house of the Lord, and she was greatly astonied.

5 And she saide to the King, It was a true worde which I heard in mine owne lande of thy sayings, and of thy wisedome:

6 Howbeit I beleeued not their report, vntil I came, and mine eyes had seene it: and beholde, the one halfe of thy great wisedom was not told me: for thou exceedest the fame that I heard.

7 Happie are thy men, and happie are these thy seruants, which stande before thee alway, and heare thy wisedome.

8 Blessed be the Lord thy God, which loued thee, to set thee on his throne as King, in the steade of the Lord thy God: because thy God loueth Israel, to establish it for euer, therefore hath he made thee King ouer them, to execute iudgement and iustice.

9 Then she gaue the King six score talents of golde, and of sweete odours exceeding much and precious stones: neither was there such sweete odours since, as the Queene of Sheba gaue vnto King Salomon.

10 And the seruants also of Huram, and the seruants of Salomon which brought golde from Ophir, brought Algummim wood and precious stones.

11 And the King made of the Algummim wood staires in the house of the Lord, and in the Kings house, and harpes and violes for singers: and there was no such seene before in the lande of Iudah.

12 And King Salomon gaue to the Queene of Sheba euery pleasant thing that she asked, besides for that which she had brought vnto the King: so she returned and went to her owne countrey, both she, and her seruants.

13 Also the weight of golde that came to Salomon in one yeere, was six hundreth three score and six talents of golde,

14 Besides that which chapmen and marchants brought: and all the Kings of Arabia, and the princes of the countrey brought golde and siluer to Salomon.

15 And King Salomon made two hundreth targets of beaten golde, and six hundreth shekels of beaten golde went to one target,

16 And three hundreth shieldes of beaten golde: three hundreth shekels of golde went to one shielde, and the King put them in the house of the wood of Lebanon.

17 And the King made a great throne of yuorie and ouerlaid it with pure golde.

18 And the throne had six steppes, with a footestoole of gold fastened to the throne, and stayes on either side on the place of the seate, and two lyons standing by the stayes.

19 And twelue lyons stoode there on the six steps on either side: there was not the like made in any kingdome.

20 And all King Salomons drinking vessels were of golde, and all the vessels of the house of the wood of Lebanon were of pure gold: for siluer was nothing esteemed in ye dayes of Salomon.

21 For the Kings ships went to Tarshish with the seruants of Huram, euery three yeere once came the ships of Tarshish, and brought golde, and siluer, yuorie, and apes, and peacockes.

22 So King Salomon excelled all the Kings of the earth in riches and wisedome.

23 And all the Kings of the earth sought the presence of Salomon, to heare his wisedome that God had put in his heart.

24 And they brought euery man his present, vessels of siluer, and vessels of golde, and raiment, armour, and sweet odours, horses, and mules, from yeere to yeere.

25 And Salomon had foure thousand stalles of horses, and charets, and twelue thousand horsmen, whom he bestowed in the charet cities, and with the King at Ierusalem.

26 And he reigned ouer all the Kings from the Riuer euen vnto the land of the Philistims, and to the border of Egypt.

27 And the King gaue siluer in Ierusalem, as stones, and gaue cedar trees as the wilde fig trees, that are aboundant in the plaine.

28 And they brought vnto Salomon horses out of Egypt, and out of all landes.

29 Concerning the rest of the actes of Salomon first and last, are they not written in the booke of Nathan the Prophet, and in the prophecie of Ahiiah the Shilonite, and in the visions of Ieedo the Seer against Ieroboam the sonne of Nebat?

30 And Salomon reigned in Ierusalem ouer all Israel fourtie yeeres.

31 And Salomon slept with his fathers, and they buryed him in the citie of Dauid his father: and Rehoboam his sonne reigned in his steade.

Second Chronicles 10

1 Then Rehoboam went to Shechem: for to Sheche came all Israel to make him king.

2 And when Ieroboam the sonne of Nebat heard it, (which was in Egypt, whither he had fled from the presence of Salomon the King) he returned out of Egypt.

3 And they sent and called him: so came Ieroboam and all Israel, and communed with Rehoboam, saying,

4 Thy father made our yoke grieuous: nowe therefore make thou the grieuous seruitude of thy father, and his sore yoke, that he put vpon vs, lighter, and we will serue thee.

5 And he sayde to them, Depart yet three dayes, then come againe vnto me. And the people departed.

6 And King Rehoboam tooke counsel with the olde men that had stande before Salomon his father, while hee yet liued, saying, What counsell giue ye that I may answere this people?

7 And they spake vnto him, saying, If thou be kinde to this people, and please them, and speake louing words to them, they will be thy seruants for euer.

8 But hee left the counsel of the ancient men that they had giuen him, and tooke

counsell of the yong men that were brought vp with him, and waited on him.

9 And he sayd vnto them, What counsel giue ye, that we may answere this people, which haue spoken to mee, saying, Make the yoke which thy father did put vpon vs, lighter?

10 And the yong men that were brought vp with him, spake vnto him, saying, Thus shalt thou answere the people that spake to thee, saying, Thy father made our yoke heauie, but make thou it lighter for vs: thus shalt thou say vnto them, My least part shalbe bigger then my fathers loines.

11 Now whereas my father did burden you with a grieuous yoke, I will yet increase your yoke: my father hath chastised you with roddes, but I will correct you with scourges.

12 Then Ieroboam and all the people came to Rehoboam the third day, as the King had appointed saying, Come againe to me the third day.

13 And the King answered them sharply: and King Rehoboam left the counsel of the ancient men,

14 And spake to them after ye counsell of the yong men, saying, My father made your yoke grieuous, but I wil incease it: my father chastised you with rods, but I will correct you with scourges.

15 So the king hearkened not vnto the people: for it was the ordinance of God that the Lord might performe his saying, which hee had spoken by Ahiiah the Shilonite to Ieroboam the sonne of Nebat.

16 So when all Isarael sawe that the King would not heare them, the people answered the King, saying, What portion haue we in Dauid? for we haue none inheritance in the sonue of Ishai. O Israel, euery man to your tents: now see to thine owne house, Dauid. So all Israel departed to their tents.

17 Howbeit Rehoboam reigned ouer the children of Israel, that dwelt in the cities of Iudah.

18 Then King Rehoboam sent Hadoram that was ouer the tribute, and the children of Israel stoned him with stones, that he died: then King Rehoboam made speede to get him vp to his charet, to flee to Ierusalem.

19 And Israel rebelled against the house of Dauid vnto this day.

Second Chronicles 11

1 And when Rehoboam was come to Ierusalem, he gathered of the house of Iudah and Beniamin nine score thousande chosen men of warre to fight against Israel, and to bring the kingdome againe to Rehoboam.

2 But the worde of the Lord came to Shemaiah the man of God, saying,

3 Speake vnto Rehoboam, the sonne of Salomon King of Iudah, and to all Israel that are in Iudah, and Beniamin, saying,

4 Thus sayth the Lord, Ye shall not goe vp, nor fight against your brethren: returne euery man to his house: for this thing is done of me. They obeyed therfore the word of the Lord, and returned from going against Ieroboam.

5 And Rehoboam dwelt in Ierusalem, and buylt strong cities in Iudah.

6 Hee buylt also Beth-lehem, and Etam, and Tekoa,

7 And Beth-zur, and Shoco, and Adullam,

8 And Gath, and Maresha, and Ziph,

9 And Adoraim, and Lachish, and Azekah,

10 And Zorah, and Aialon, and Hebron, which were in Iudah and Beniamin, strong cities.

11 And he repaired the strong holdes and put captaines in them, and store of vitaile, and oyle and wine.

12 And in all cities he put shieldes and speares, and made them exceeding strong: so Iudah and Beniamin were his.

13 And the Priests and the Leuites that were in all Israel, resorted vnto him out of all their coastes.

14 For the Leuites left their suburbes and their possession, and came to Iudah and to Ierusalem: for Ieroboam and his sonnes had cast them out from ministring in the Priestes office vnto the Lord.

15 And he ordeyned him Priests for the hie places, and for the deuils and for the calues which he had made.

16 And after the Leuites there came to Ierusalem of all the tribes of Israel, such as set their heartes to seeke the Lord God of Israel, to offer vnto the Lord God of their fathers.

17 So they strengthened the kingdome of Iudah, and made Rehoboam the sonne of Salomon mightie, three yeere long: for three yeere they walked in in the way of Dauid and Salomon.

18 And Rehoboam tooke him Mahalath ye daughter of Ierimoth the sonne of Dauid to wife, and Abihail the daughter of Eliab the sonne of Ishai,

19 Which bare him sonnes Ieush, and Shemariah, and Zaham.

20 And after her he tooke Maakah ye daughter of Absalom which bare him Abiiah, and Atthai, and Ziza, and Shelomith.

21 And Rehoboam loued Maakah ye daughter of Absalom aboue all his wiues and his concubines: for he tooke eighteene wiues, and three score concubines, and begate eyght and twentie sonnes, and three score daughters.

22 And Rehoboam made Abiiah the sonne of Maakah the chiefe ruler among his brethren: for he thought to make him King.

23 And he taught him: and dispersed all his sonnes throughout all the countreis of Iudah and Beniamin vnto euery strong citie: and hee gaue them aboundance of vitaile, and desired many wiues.

Second Chronicles 12

1 And when Rehoboam had established the kingdome and made it strong, hee forsooke the Lawe of the Lord, and all Israel with him.

2 Therefore in the fift yeere of King Rehoboam, Shishak the King of Egypt came vp against Ierusalem (because they had transgressed against the Lord)

3 With twelue hundreth charets, and three score thousande horsemen, and the people were without nomber, that came with him from Egypt, euen the Lubims, Sukkiims, and the Ethiopians.

4 And he tooke the strong cities which were of Iudah, and came vnto Ierusalem.

5 Then came Shemaiah the Prophet to Rehoboam, and to the princes of Iudah, that were gathered together in Hierusalem, because of Shishak, and sayde vnto them, Thus sayth the Lord, Ye haue forsaken me, therefore haue I also left you in the handes of Shishak.

6 Then the princes of Israel, and the King humbled themselues, and sayde, The Lord is iust.

7 And when the Lord sawe that they humbled themselues, the worde of the Lord came to Shemaiah, saying, They haue humbled theselues, therefore I will not destroy them, but I will sende them deliuerance shortly, and my wrath shall not bee powred out vpon Ierusalem by the hand of Shishak.

8 Neuerthelesse they shalbe his sernants: so shall they knowe my seruice, and the seruice of the kingdomes of the earth.

9 Then Shishak King of Egypt came vp against Ierusalem, and tooke the treasures of the house of the Lord, and the treasures of the Kings house he tooke euen all, and hee caried away the shields of golde, which Salomon had made.

10 In stead whereof King Rehoboam made shieldes of brasse, and committed them to the handes of the chiefe of the garde, that wayted at the doore of the Kings house.

11 And when the King entred into the house of the Lord, the garde came and bare them and brought them againe vnto the garde chamber.

12 And because hee humbled himselfe, the wrath of the Lord turned from him, that hee woulde not destroy all together. And also in Iudah the things prospered.

13 So King Rehoboam was strong in Ierusalem and reigned: for Rehoboam was one and fourtie yere olde, when he began to reigne, and reigned seuenteene yeres in Ierusalem, the citie which the Lord had chosen out of all the tribes of Israel to put his Name there. And his mothers name was Naamah an Ammonitesse.

14 And he did euill: for hee prepared not his heart to seeke the Lord.

15 The actes also of Rehoboam, first and last, are they not written in the booke of Shemaiah the Prophet, and Iddo the Seer, in rehearsing the genealogie? and there was warre alway betweene Rehoboam and Ieroboam.

16 And Rehoboam slept with his fathers, and was buried in the citie of Dauid, and Abiiah his sonne reigned in his stead.

Second Chronicles 13

1 In the eyghteenth yeere of King Ieroboam began Abiiah to reigne ouer Iudah.

2 He reigned three yere in Ierusalem: (his mothers name also was Michaiah the daughter of Vriel of Gibea) and there was warre betweene Abiiah and Ieroboam.

3 And Abiiah set the battel in aray with the armie of valiant men of warre, euen foure hundreth thousand chosen men. Ieroboam also set the battell in aray against him with eight hundreth thousande chosen men which were strong and valiant.

4 And Abiiah stood vp vpon mount Zemeraim, which is in mount Ephraim, and sayde, O Ieroboam, and all Israel, heare you me,

5 Ought you not to know that the Lord God of Israel hath giuen the kingdome ouer Israel to Dauid for euer, euen to him and to his sonnes by a couenant of salt?

6 And Ieroboam the sonne of Nebat the seruant of Salomon the sonne of Dauid is risen vp, and hath rebelled against his lord:

7 And there are gathered to him vayne men and wicked, and made themselues strong against Rehoboam the sonne of Salomon: for Rehoboam was but a childe and tender hearted, and coulde not resist them.

8 Now therefore ye thinke that yee be able to resist against the kingdome of the Lord, which is in the handes of the sonnes of Dauid, and ye bee a great multitude, and the golden calues are with you which Ieroboam made you for gods.

9 Haue ye not driuen away the Priestes of the Lord the sonnes of Aaron and the Leuites, and haue made you Priests like the people of other countreis? whosoeuer commeth to consecrate with a yong bullocke and seuen rams, the same may be a Priest of them that are no gods.

10 But wee belong vnto the Lord our God, and haue not forsaken him, and the Priestes the sonnes of Aaron minister vnto the Lord, and the Leuites in their office.

11 And they burne vnto the Lord euery morning and euery euening burnt offerings and sweete incense, and the breade is set in order vpon the pure table, and the candlesticke of golde with the lampes thereof, to burne euery euening: for we keepe the watch of the Lord our God: but ye haue forsaken him.

12 And behold, this God is with vs, as a captaine, and his Priests with the sounding trumpets, to crie an alarme against you. O yee children of Israel, fight not against the Lord God of your fathers: for ye shall not prosper.

13 But Ieroboam caused an ambushment to compasse, and come behind them, when they were before Iudah, and the ambushment behinde them.

14 Then Iudah looked, and beholde, the battel was before and behinde them, and they cried vnto the Lord, and the Priests blewe with the trumpets,

15 And the men of Iudah gaue a shoute: and euen as the men of Iudah shouted, God smote Ieroboam and also Israel before Abiiah and Iudah.

16 And the children of Israel fledde before Iudah, and God deliuered them into their hande.

17 And Abiiah and his people slewe a great slaughter of them, so that there fel downe wounded of Israel fiue hundreth thousand chosen men.

18 So the children of Israel were brought vnder at that time: and the children of Iudah preuailed, because they stayed vpon the Lord God of their fathers.

19 And Abiiah pursued after Ieroboam, and tooke cities from him, euen Beth-el, and the villages thereof, and Ieshanah with her villages, and Ephron with her villages.

20 And Ieroboam recouered no strength againe in the dayes of Abiiah, but the Lord plagued him, and he dyed.

21 So Abiiah waxed mightie, and marryed fourteene wiues, and begate two and twentie sonnes, and sixteene daughters.

22 The rest of the actes of Abiiah and his maners and his sayings are written in the storie of the Prophet Iddo.

Second Chronicles 14

1 So Abiiah slept with his fathers, and they buryed him in the citie of Dauid, and Asa his sonne reigned in his steade: in whose dayes the lande was quiet ten yeere.

2 And Asa did that was good and right in the eyes of the Lord his God.

3 For he tooke away the altars of the strange gods and the hie places, and brake downe the images, and cut downe the groues,

4 And commanded Iudah to seeke the Lord God of their fathers, and to doe according to the Lawe and the comandement.

5 And he tooke away out of all the cities of Iudah the hie places, and the images: therefore the kingdome was quiet before him.

6 He built also strong cities in Iudah, because the lande was in rest, and he had no warre in those yeeres: for the Lord had giuen him rest.

7 Therefore he saide to Iudah, Let vs builde these cities and make walles about, and towers, gates, and barres, whiles the lande is before vs: because we haue sought the Lord our God, we haue sought him, and he hath giuen vs rest on euery side: so they built and prospered.

8 And Asa had an armie of Iudah that bare shieldes and speares, three hundreth thousande, and of Beniamin that bare shieldes and drewe bowes, two hundreth and foure score thousande: all these were valiant men.

9 And there came out against them Zerah of Ethiopia with an hoste of ten hundreth thousande, and three hundreth charets, and came vnto Mareshah.

10 Then Asa went out before him, and they set the battell in aray in the valley of Zephathah beside Mareshah.

11 And Asa cryed vnto the Lord his God, and saide, Lord, it is nothing with thee to helpe with many, or with no power: helpe vs, O Lord our God: for we rest on thee, and in thy Name are we come against this multitude: O Lord, thou art our God, let not man preuaile against thee.

12 So the Lord smote the Ethiopians before Asa and before Iudah, and the Ethiopians fled.

13 And Asa and the people that was with him, pursued them vnto Gerar. And the Ethiopians hoste was ouerthrowen, so that there was no life in them: for they were destroyed before the Lord and before his hoste: and they caryed away a mightie great spoyle.

14 And they smote all the cities rounde about Gerar: for the feare of the Lord came vpon them, and they spoyled all the cities, for there was exceeding much spoyle in them.

15 Yea, and they smote the tents of cattel, and carried away plentie of sheepe and camels, and returned to Ierusalem.

Second Chronicles 15

1 Then the Spirite of God came vpon Azariah the sonne of Obed.

2 And he went out to meete Asa, and said vnto him, O Asa, and all Iudah, and Beniamin, heare ye me. The Lord is with you, while ye be with him: and if ye seeke him, he wil be founde of you, but if ye forsake him, he will forsake you.

3 Nowe for a long season Israel hath bene without the true God, and without Priest to teach and without Lawe.

4 But whosoeuer returned in his affliction to the Lord God of Israel, and sought him, he was founde of them.

5 And in that time there was no peace to him, that did goe out and goe in: but great troubles were to all the inhabitants of the earth.

6 For nation was destroyed of nation, and citie of citie: for God troubled them with all aduersitie.

7 Be ye strong therefore, and let not your handes be weake: for your worke shall haue a rewarde.

8 And when Asa heard these wordes, and the prophesie of Obed the Prophet, he was encouraged, and tooke away the abominations out of all the lande of Iudah, and Beniamin, and out of the cities which he had taken of mount Ephraim, and he renued the altar of the Lord, that was before the porche of the Lord.

9 And he gathered all Iudah and Beniamin, and the strangers with them out of Ephraim, and Manasseh, and out of Simeon: for there fell many to him out

of Israel, when they sawe that the Lord his God was with him.

10 So they assembled to Ierusalem in the third moneth, in the fifteenth yere of the reigne of Asa.

11 And they offred vnto the Lord the same time of the spoyle, which they had brought, euen seuen hundreth bullockes, and seuen thousande sheepe.

12 And they made a couenant to seeke the Lord God of their fathers, with all their heart, and with all their soule.

13 And whosoeuer will not seeke the Lord God of Israel, shalbe slaine, whether he were small or great, man or woman.

14 And they sware vnto the Lord with a loude voyce, and with shouting and with trumpets, and with cornets.

15 And all Iudah reioyced at the othe: for they had sworne vnto the Lord with all their heart, and sought him with a whole desire, and he was founde of them. And the Lord gaue them rest rounde about.

16 And King Asa deposed Maachah his mother from her regencie, because she had made an idole in a groue: and Asa brake downe her idole, and stamped it, and burnt it at the brooke Kidron.

17 But the hie places were not taken away out of Israel: yet the heart of Asa was perfit all his dayes.

18 Also he brought into the house of God the things that his father had dedicate, and that he had dedicate, siluer, and golde, and vessels.

19 And there was no warre vnto the fiue and thirtieth yeere of the reigne of Asa.

Second Chronicles 16

1 In the sixe and thirtieth yeere of the reigne of Asa came Baasha king of Israel vp against Iudah, and built Ramah to let none passe out or goe in to Asa king of Iudah.

2 Then Asa brought out siluer and gold out of the treasures of the house of the Lord, and of the Kings house, and sent to Benhadad King of Aram that dwelt at Damascus, saying,

3 There is a couenant betweene me and thee, and betweene my father and thy father: behold, I haue sent thee siluer and golde: come, breake thy league with Baasha King of Israel that hee may depart from me.

4 And Benhadad hearkened vnto King Asa, and sent the captaines of the armies which hee had, against the cities of Israel. And they smote Iion, and Dan, and Abel-maim, and all the store cities of Naphtali.

5 And when Baasha heard it, he left building of Ramah, and let his worke cease.

6 Then Asa the King tooke all Iudah, and caryed away the stones of Ramah and the tymber thereof, wherewith Baasha did builde, and he built therewith Geba and Mizpah.

7 And at that same time Hanani the Seer came to Asa King of Iudah, and saide vnto him, Because thou hast rested vpon the king of Aram, and not rested in the Lord thy God, therefore is the hoste of the King of Aram escaped out of thine hande.

8 The Ethiopians and the Lubims, were they not a great hoste with charets and horsemen, exceeding many? yet because thou diddest rest vpon the Lord, he deliuered them into thine had.

9 For the eyes of the Lord beholde all the earth to shewe him selfe strong with them that are of perfite heart towarde him: thou hast then done foolishly in this: therefore from henceforth thou shalt haue warres.

10 Then Asa was wroth with the Seer, and put him into a prison: for he was displeased with him, because of this thing. And Asa oppressed certaine of the people at the same time.

11 And behold, the actes of Asa first and last, loe, they are written in the booke of the Kings of Iudah and Israel.

12 And Asa in the nine and thirtieth yeere of his reigne was diseased in his feete, and his disease was extreme: yet he sought not the Lord in his disease, but to the Phisicions.

13 So Asa slept with his fathers, and dyed in the one and fourtieth yeere of his reigne.

14 And they buryed him in one of his sepulchres, which he had made for him selfe in the citie of Dauid, and layed him in the bed, which they had filled with sweete odours and diuers kindes of spices made by the arte of the apoticarie: and they burnt odours for him with an exceeding great fire.

Second Chronicles 17

1 And Iehosphat his sonne reigned in his steade, and preuailed against Israel.

2 And he put garisons in all the strong cities of Iudah, and set bandes in the lande of Iudah and in the cities of Ephraim, which Asa his father had taken.

3 And the Lord was with Iehoshaphat, because he walked in the first wayes of his father Dauid, and sought not Baalim,

4 But sought the Lord God of his father, and walked in his commandements, and not after the trade of Israel.

5 Therefore the Lord stablished the kingdome in his hande, and all Iudah brought presents to Iehoshaphat, so that he had of riches and honour in abundance.

6 And he lift vp his heart vnto the wayes of the Lord, and he tooke away moreouer the hie places and the groues out of Iudah.

7 And in the thirde yere of his reigne he sent his princes, Ben-hail, and Obadiah, and Zechariah, and Nethaneel, and Michaiah, that they should teach in the cities of Iudah,

8 And with them Leuites, Shemaiah, and Nethaniah, and Zebadiah, and Asahel, and Shemiramoth, and Iehonathan, and Adoniiah, and Tobiiah, and Tob-adoniiah, Leuites, and with the Elishama and Iehoram Priestes.

9 And they taught in Iudah, and had the booke of the Lawe of the Lord with them, and went about throughout all the cities of Iudah, and taught the people.

10 And the feare of the Lord fell vpon all the kingdomes of ye lands that were round about Iudah, and they fought not against Iehoshaphat.

11 Also some of the Philistims brought Iehoshaphat giftes and tribute siluer, and the Arabians brought him flockes, seuen thousande and seuen hundreth rammes, and seuen thousande and seuen hundreth hee goates.

12 So Iehoshaphat prospered and grewe vp on hie: and he built in Iudah palaces and cities of store.

13 And he had great workes in the cities of Iudah, and men of warre, and valiant men in Ierusalem.

14 And these are the nombers of them after the house of their fathers, In Iudah were captaines of thousands, Adnah the captaine, and with him of valiant men three hundreth thousande.

15 And at his hande Iehohanan a captaine, and with him two hundreth and fourescore thousande.

16 And at his hande Amasiah the sonne of Zichri, which willingly offered him selfe vnto the Lord, and with him two hundreth thousand valiant men.

17 And of Beniamin, Eliada a valiant man, and with him armed men with bowe and shielde two hundreth thousand.

18 And at his hand Iehozabad, and with him an hundreth and fourescore thousand armed to the warre.

19 These waited on the King, besides those which the King put in the strong cities thoroughout all Iudah.

Second Chronicles 18

1 And Iehoshaphat had riches and honour in abundance, but he was ioyned in affinitie with Ahab.

2 And after certaine yeeres he went downe to Ahab to Samaria: and Ahab slew sheepe and oxen for him in great nomber, and for the people that he had with him, and entised him to goe vp vnto Ramoth Gilead.

3 And Ahab King of Israel saide vnto Iehoshaphat King of Iudah, Wilt thou goe with mee to Ramoth Gilead? And hee answered him, I am as thou art, and my people as thy people, and wee will ioyne with thee in the warre.

4 And Iehoshaphat sayde vnto the King of Israel, Aske counsel, I pray thee, at the worde of the Lord this day.

5 Therefore the King of Israel gathered of Prophets foure hundreth men, and sayde vnto them, Shall we goe to Ramoth Gilead to battel, or shall I cease? And they sayd, Go vp: for God shall deliuer it into the Kings hand.

6 But Iehoshaphat sayde, Is there heere neuer a Prophet more of the Lord that wee might inquire of him?

7 And the King of Israel sayd vnto Iehoshaphat, There is yet one man, by whome wee may aske counsell of the

Lord, but I hate him: for he doeth not prophesie good vnto me, but alway euil: it is Michaiah the sonne of Imla. Then Iehoshaphat said, Let not the King say so.

8 And the King of Israel called an eunuche, and said, Call quickly Michaiah the sonne of Imla.

9 And the King of Israel, and Iehoshaphat King of Iudah sate either of them on his throne clothed in their apparel: they sate euen in the threshing floore at the entring in of the gate of Samaria: and all the Prophets prophesied before them.

10 And Zidkiah ye sonne of Chenaanah made him hornes of yron, and sayde, Thus sayth the Lord, With these shalt thou push the Aramites vntill thou hast consumed them.

11 And all the Prophets prophesied so, saying, Go vp to Ramoth Gilead, and prosper: for the Lord shall deliuer it into the hand of the King.

12 And the messenger that went to call Michaiah, spake to him, saying, Beholde, the wordes of the Prophets declare good to the King with one accord: let thy word therefore, I pray thee, be like one of theirs, and speake thou good.

13 And Michaiah saide, As the Lord liueth, whatsoeuer my God saith, that will I speake.

14 So he came to the King, and the King said vnto him, Michaiah, shall we go to Ramoth Gilead to battel, or shall I leaue off? And he said, Goe yee vp, and prosper, and they shalbe deliuered into your hand.

15 And the King sayd to him, Howe oft shall I charge thee, that thou tell mee nothing but the trueth in the Name of the Lord?

16 Then he said, I saw al Israel scattered in the mountaines, as sheepe that haue no shepheard: and the Lord sayd, These haue no Master: let them returne euery man to his house in peace.

17 And the King of Israel sayde to Iehoshaphat, Did I not tell thee, that he would not prophesie good vnto me, but euill?

18 Againe hee saide, Therefore heare ye the worde of the Lord: I sawe the Lord sit vpon his throne, and all the hoste of heauen standing at his right hand, and at his left.

19 And the Lord sayd, Who shall perswade Ahab King of Israel, that he may go vp, and fall at Ramoth Gilead? And one spake and said thus, and another said that.

20 Then there came forth a spirit and stoode before the Lord, and said, I will perswade him. And the Lord said vnto him, Wherein?

21 And he saide, I will goe out, and bee a false spirit in the mouth of all his Prophets. And hee said, Thou shalt perswade, and shalt also preuaile: goe forth and do so.

22 Now therefore behold, the Lord hath put a false spirit in the mouth of these thy Prophets, and the Lord hath determined euill against thee.

23 Then Zidkiah the sonne of Chenaanah came neere, and smote Michaiah vpon the cheeke, and sayde, By what way went the Spirit of the Lord from me, to speake with thee?

24 And Michaiah saide, Behold, thou shalt see that day when thou shalt goe from chamber to chamber to hide thee.

25 And the King of Israel sayde, Take ye Michaiah, and cary him to Amon the gouernour of the citie, and to Ioash the Kings sonne,

26 And say, Thus saith the King, Put this man in the prison house, and feede him with bread of affliction and with water of affliction vntil I returne in peace.

27 And Michaiah said, If thou returne in peace, the Lord hath not spoken by me. And he saide, Heare, all ye people.

28 So the King of Israel and Iehoshaphat the King of Iudah went vp to Ramoth Gilead.

29 And the King of Israel said vnto Iehoshaphat, I will change my selfe, and enter into the battel: but put thou on thine apparel. So the King of Israel changed himselfe, and they went into the battel.

30 And the King of Aram had commanded the captaines of the charets that were with him, saying, Fight you not with small, nor great, but against the King of Israel onely.

31 And when the captaines of the charets saw Iehoshaphat, they sayde, It is the King of Israel: and they compassed about him to fight. But Iehoshaphat cryed, and the Lord helped him and moued them to depart from him.

32 For when the captaines of the charets saw that hee was not the King of Israel, they turned backe from him.

33 Then a certaine man drewe a bowe mightily, and smote the King of Israel betweene the ioyntes of his brigandine: Therefore he saide to his charetman, Turne thine hand, and carie mee out of the host: for I am hurt.

34 And the battel increased that day: and the King of Israel stood still in his charet against the Aramites vntil euen, and dyed at the time of the sunne going downe.

Second Chronicles 19

1 And Iehoshaphat the King of Iudah returned safe to his house in Ierusalem.

2 And Iehu the sonne of Hanani the Seer went out to meete him, and said to King Iehoshaphat, Wouldest thou helpe the wicked, and loue them that hate the Lord? therefore for this thing the wrath of the Lord is vpon thee.

3 Neuertheles good things are found in thee, because thou hast taken away ye groues out of the land, and hast prepared thine heart to seeke God.

4 So Iehoshaphat dwelt at Ierusalem, and returned and went through the people from Beer-sheba to mount Ephraim, and brought them againe vnto the Lord God of their fathers.

5 And hee set iudges in the lande throughout all the strong cities of Iudah, citie by citie,

6 And said to the iudges, Take heede what ye doe: for yee execute not the iudgements of man, but of the Lord, and he will be with you in the cause and iudgement.

7 Wherefore nowe let the feare of the Lord be vpon you: take heede, and do it: for there is no iniquitie with the Lord our God, neither respect of persons, nor receiuing of reward.

8 Moreouer in Ierusalem did Iehoshaphat set of the Leuites, and of the Priests and of the chiefe of the families of Israel, for the iudgement and cause of the Lord: and they returned to Ierusale.

9 And he charged them, saying, Thus shall yee doe in the feare of the Lord faithfully and with a perfite heart.

10 And in euery cause that shall come to you of your brethren that dwel in their cities, betweene blood and blood, betweene law and precept, statutes and iudgements, ye shall iudge them, and admonish them that they trespasse not against the Lord, that wrath come not vpon you and vpon your brethren. This shall ye do and trespasse not.

11 And behold, Amariah the Priest shalbe the chiefe ouer you in all matters of the Lord, and Zebadiah ye sonne of Ishmael, a ruler of the house of Iudah, shalbe for al the Kings affaires, and the Leuites shalbe officers before you. Bee of courage, and doe it, and the Lord shalbe with the good.

Second Chronicles 20

1 After this also came the children of Moab and the children of Ammon, and with them of the Ammonites against Iehoshaphat to battell.

2 Then there came that tolde Iehoshaphat, saying, There commeth a great multitude against thee from beyonde the Sea, out of Aram: and beholde, they bee in Hazzon Tamar, which is En-gedi.

3 And Iehoshaphat feared, and set him selfe to seeke the Lord, and proclaimed a fast throughout all Iudah.

4 And Iudah gathered them selues together to aske counsel of the Lord: they came euen out of all the cities of Iudah to inquire of the Lord,

5 And Iehoshaphat stoode in the Congregation of Iudah and Ierusalem in the house of the Lord before the new court,

6 And saide, O Lord God of our fathers, art not thou God in heauen? and reignest not thou on all the kingdomes of the heathen? and in thine hande is power and might, and none is able to withstand thee.

7 Diddest not thou our God cast out ye inhabitants of this lande before thy people Israel, and gauest it to the seede of Abraham thy friende for euer?

8 And they dwelt therein, and haue built thee a Sanctuarie therein for thy Name, saying,

9 If euill come vpon vs, as the sworde of iudgement, or pestilence, or famine, we will stande before this house and in thy presence (for thy name is in this house) and will crie vnto thee in our tribulation, and thou wilt heare and helpe.

10 And now beholde, the children of Ammon and Moab, and mount Seir, by whome thou wouldest not let Israel goe, when they came out of the land of Egypt: but they turned aside from them, and destroyed them not:

11 Behold, I say, they reward vs, in comming to cast vs out of thine inheritance, which thou hast caused vs to inherit.

12 O our God, wilt thou not iudge them? for there is no strength in vs to stand before this great multitude that commeth against vs, neither doe wee knowe what to doe: but our eyes are toward thee.

13 And all Iudah stoode before the Lord with their yong ones, their wiues, and their children.

14 And Iahaziel the sonne of Zechariah the sonne of Benaiah, the sonne of Ieiel, the sonne of Mattaniah, a Leuite of the sonnes of Asaph was there, vpon whome came the Spirite of ye Lord, in the middes of the Congregation.

15 And he said, Hearken ye, all Iudah, and ye inhabitants of Ierusalem, and thou, King Iehoshaphat: thus saith the Lord vnto you, Feare you not, neither be afraide for this great multitude: for the battel is not yours, but Gods.

16 To morowe goe yee downe against them: beholde, they come vp by the cleft of Ziz, and ye shall finde them at the ende of the brooke before the wildernesse of Ieruel.

17 Ye shall not neede to fight in this battell: stand still, moue not, and behold the saluation of the Lord towardes you: O Iudah, and Ierusalem, feare ye not, neither be afraid: to morow goe out against them, and the Lord wilbe with you.

18 Then Iehoshaphat bowed downe with his face to the earth, and all Iudah and the inhabitants of Ierusalem fell downe before the Lord, worshipping the Lord.

19 And the Leuites of the children of the Kohathites and of the childre of the Corhites stood vp to prayse the Lord God of Israel with a loude voyce on hie.

20 And when they arose early in the morning, they went forth to the wildernesse of Tekoa: and as they departed, Iehoshaphat stoode and sayde, Heare ye me, O Iudah, and ye inhabitants of Ierusalem: put your trust in the Lord your God, and ye shalbe assured: beleeue his Prophets, and ye shall prosper.

21 And when he had consulted with the people, and appoynted singers vnto the Lord, and them that should prayse him that is in the beautifull Sanctuarie, in going forth before the men of armes, and saying, Prayse ye the Lord, for his mercy lasteth for euer,

22 And when they began to shoute, and to prayse, the Lord layed ambushments against the children of Ammon, Moab, and mount Seir, which were come against Iudah, and they slewe one another.

23 For the children of Ammon and Moab rose against the inhabitants of mount Seir, to slay and to destroy them and when they had made an end of the inhabitantes of Seir, euery one helped to destroy another.

24 And when Iudah came towarde Mizpah in the wildernes, they looked vnto the multitude: and behold, the carkeises were fallen to the earth, and none escaped.

25 And when Iehoshaphat and his people came to take away the spoyle of them, they founde among them in abundance both of substance and also of bodies laden with precious iewels, which they tooke for themselues, till they could cary no more: they were three dayes in gathering of the spoyle: for it was much.

26 And in the fourth day they assembled themselues in the valley of Berachah: for there they blessed the Lord: therefore they called the name of that place, The valley of Berachah vnto this day.

27 Then euery man of Iudah and Ierusalem returned with Iehoshaphat their head, to goe againe to Ierusalem with ioy: for the Lord had made them to reioyce ouer their enemies.

28 And they came to Ierusalem with viols and with harpes, and with trumpets, euen vnto the house of the Lord.

29 And the feare of God was vpon all the kingdomes of the earth, whe they had heard that the Lord had fought against ye enemies of Israel.

30 So the kingdom of Iehoshaphat was quiet, and his God gaue him rest on euery side.

31 And Iehoshaphat reigned ouer Iudah, and was fiue and thirtie yeere olde, when he began to reigne: and reigned fiue and twentie yeere in Ierusalem, and his mothers name was Azubah the daughter of Shilhi.

32 And he walked in the way of Asa his father, and departed not therefrom, doing that which was right in the sight of the Lord.

33 Howbeit the hie places were not taken away: for the people had not yet prepared their hearts vnto the God of their fathers.

34 Concerning the rest of the actes of Iehoshaphat first and last, beholde, they are written in the booke of Iehu the sonne of Hanani, which is mentioned in the booke of the kings of Israel.

35 Yet after this did Iehoshaphat King of Iudah ioyne himselfe with Ahaziah King of Israel, who was giuen to do euill.

36 And he ioyned with him, to make ships to go to Tarshish: and they made the shippes in Ezion Gaber.

37 Then Eliezer ye sonne of Dodauah of Mareshah prophecied against Iehoshaphat, saying, Because thou hast ioyned thy selfe with Ahaziah, the Lord hath broken thy workes. and the shippes were broken, that they were not able to go to Tarshish.

Second Chronicles 21

1 Iehosphaphat then slept with his fathers, and was buried with his fathers in the citie of Dauid: and Iehoram his sonne reigned in his steade.

2 And he had brethren the sonnes of Iehoshaphat, Azariah, and Iehiel, and Zechariah, and Azariah, and Michael, and Shephatiah. All these were the sonnes of Iehoshaphat King of Israel.

3 And their father gaue them great giftes of siluer and of golde, and of precious things, with strong cities in Iudah, but the kingdome gaue he to Iehoram: for he was the eldest.

4 And Iehoram rose vp vpon the kingdom of his father, and made himselfe strong, and slew all his brethren with the sworde, and also of the princes of Israel.

5 Iehoram was two and thirtie yeere olde, when he began to reigne, and he reigned eyght yeere in Ierusalem.

6 And he walked in the way of the Kings of Israel, as the house of Ahab had done: for he had the daughter of Ahab to wife, and he wrought euill in the eyes of the Lord.

7 Howbeit the Lord would not destroy the house of Dauid, because of the couenant that he had made with Dauid, and because he had promised to giue a light to him, and to his sonnes for euer.

8 In his dayes Edom rebelled from vnder the hand of Iudah, and made a King ouer them.

9 And Iehoram went forth with his princes, and all his charets with him: and hee rose vp by night, and smote Edom, which had compassed him in, and the captaines of the charets.

10 But Edom rebelled from vnder the hande of Iudah vnto this day. then did Libnah rebell at the same time from vnder his hand, because he had forsaken the Lord God of his fathers.

11 Moreouer hee made hie places in the mountaines of Iudah, and caused the inhabitants of Ierusalem to commit fornication, and compelled Iudah thereto.

12 And there came a writing to him from Elijah the Prophet, saying, Thus sayth the Lord God of Dauid thy father, Because thou hast not walked in the wayes of Iehoshaphat thy father, nor in the wayes of Asa King of Iudah,

13 But hast walked in the way of the kings of Israel, and hast made Iudah and the inhabitantes of Ierusalem to go a whoring, as the house of Ahab went a whoring, and hast also slaine thy brethre of thy fathers house, which were better then thou,

14 Beholde, with a great plague will the Lord smite thy people, and thy children, and thy wiues, and all thy substance,

15 And thou shalt be in great diseases in the disease of thy bowels, vntill thy bowels fall out for the disease, day by day.

16 So the Lord stirred vp against Iehoram the spirite of the Philistims, and the Arabians that were beside the Ethiopians.

17 And they came vp into Iudah, and brake into it, and caryed away all the substance that was found in the Kings house, and his sonnes also, and his wiues, so that there was not a sonne left him, saue Iehoahaz, the yongest of his sonnes.

18 And after all this, the Lord smote him in his bowels with an incurable disease.

19 And in processe of time, euen after the end of two yeeres, his guttes fell out with his disease: so he dyed of sore diseases: and his people made no burning for him like the burning of his fathers.

20 When he began to reigne, he was two and thirtie yeere olde, and reigned in Ierusalem eight yeere, and liued without being desired: yet they buryed him in the citie of Dauid, but not among the sepulchres of the Kings.

Second Chronicles 22

1 And the inhabitants of Ierusalem made Ahaziah his yongest sonne King in his steade: for the armie that came with the Arabians to the campe, had slayne all the eldest: therefore Ahaziah the sonne of Iehoram King of Iudah reigned.

2 Two and fourtie yeere olde was Ahaziah when he began to reigne, and he reigned one yeere in Ierusalem. and his mothers name was Athaliah the daughter of Omri.

3 He walked also in the wayes of the house of Ahab: for his mother counselled him to doe wickedly.

4 Wherefore he did euill in the sight of the Lord, like the house of Ahab: for they were his counsellers after the death of his father, to his destruction.

5 And he walked after their counsel, and went with Iehoram the sonne of Ahab King of Israel to fight against Hazael king of Aram at Ramoth Gilead: and the Aramites smote Ioram.

6 And he returned to be healed in Izreel, because of the woundes wherewith they had wounded him at Ramah, when he fought with Hazael King of Aram. Nowe Azariah the sonne of Iehoram King of Iudah went downe to see Iehoram the sonne of Ahab at Izreel, because hee was diseased.

7 And the destruction of Ahaziah came of God in that he went to Ioram: for when he was come, he went forth with Iehoram against Iehu the sonne of Nimshi, whom the Lord had anointed to destroy the house of Ahab.

8 Therefore when Iehu executed iudgement vpon the house of Ahab, and found the princes of Iudah and the sonnes of the brethren of Ahaziah that waited on Ahaziah, he slew them also.

9 And he sought Ahaziah, and they caught him where he was hid in Samaria, and brought him to Iehu, and slewe him, and buryed him, because, sayd they, he is the sonne of Iehoshaphat, which sought the Lord with all his heart. So the house of Ahazia was not able to reteine the kingdome.

10 Therefore when Athaliah the mother of Ahaziah sawe that her sonne was dead, shee arose and destroyed all the Kings seede of the house of Iudah.

11 But Iehoshabeath the daughter of ye King, tooke Ioash the sonne of Ahaziah, and stale him from among the Kings sonnes, that shoulde be slayne, and put him and his nource in the bed chamber: so Iehoshabeath the daughter of King Iehoram the wife of Iehoiada the Priest (for shee was the sister of Ahaziah) hid him from Athaliah: so she slew him not.

12 And hee was with them hid in the house of God sixe yeeres, whiles Athaliah reigned ouer the land.

Second Chronicles 23

1 And in the seuenth yeere Iehoiada waxed bolde, and tooke the captaines of hundreths, to wit, Azariah the sonne of Ieroham, and Ishmael the sonne of Iehohanan, and Azariah the sonne of Obed, and Maasiah the sonne of Adaiah, and Elishaphat the sonne of Zichri in couenant with him.

2 And they went about in Iudah, and gathered the Leuites out of all the cities of Iudah, and the chiefe fathers of Israel: and they came to Ierusale.

3 And al the Congregation made a couenant with the King in the house of God: and he sayde vnto them, Behold, the Kings sonne must reigne, as the Lord hath sayd of the sonnes of Dauid.

4 This is it that ye shall do, The third part of you that come on the Sabbath of the Priests, and the Leuites, shalbe porters of the doores.

5 And another third part towarde the Kings house, and another thirde part at the gate of the foundation, and al the people shalbe in the courts of the house of the Lord.

6 But let none come into the house of the Lord, saue the Priests, and the Leuites that minister: they shall go in, for they are holy: but all the people shall keepe the watch of the Lord.

7 And the Leuites shall compasse the King rounde about, and euery man with his weapon in his hand, and he that entreth into the house, shall be slaine, and be you with the King, when he commeth in, and when he goeth out.

8 So the Leuites and all Iudah did according to all things that Iehoiada the Priest had commanded, and tooke euery man his men that came on the Sabbath, with them that went out on the Sabbath: for Iehoiada the Priest did not discharge the courses.

9 And Iehoiada the Priest deliuered to the captaines of hundreths speares, and shieldes, and bucklers which had bene King Dauids, and were in the house of God.

10 And he caused all the people to stand (euery man with his weapon in his hande) from the right side of the house, to ye left side of the house by the altar and by the house round about ye king.

11 Then they brought out the Kings sonne, and put vpon him the crowne and gaue him the testimonie, and made him King. And Iehoiada and his sonnes anoynted him, and sayd, God saue the King.

12 But when Athaliah heard the noyse of the people running and praising the king, she came to the people into the house of the Lord.

13 And when she looked, beholde, the King stoode by his pillar at the entring in, and the princes and the trumpets by the King, and all the people of the land reioyced, and blew the trumpets, and the singers were with instruments of musike, and they that could sing prayse: then Athaliah rent her clothes, and said, Treason, treason.

14 Then Iehoiada the Priest brought out the captaines of hundreths that were gouernours of the hoste, and said vnto them, Haue her foorth of the ranges, and he that followeth her, let him dye by the sword: for the Priest had said, Slay her not in the house of the Lord.

15 So they layde hands on her: and when she was come to the entring of the horsegate by the Kings house, they slew her there.

16 And Iehoiada made a couenant betweene him, and all the people, and the King, that they would be the Lords people.

17 And all the people went to the house of Baal, and destroyed, and brake his altars and his images, and slew Mattan the priest of Baal before the altars.

18 And Iehoiada appointed officers for the house of the Lord, vnder the handes of the Priestes and Leuites, whome Dauid had distributed for the house of the Lord, to offer burnt offrings vnto the Lord, as it is written in the Law of Moses, with reioycing and singing by the appoyntment of Dauid.

19 And he set porters by the gates of ye house of the Lord, that none that was vncleane in any thing, should enter in.

20 And he tooke the captaines of hundreths, and the noble men, and the gouernours of the people, and all the people of the land, and he caused the King to come downe out of the house of the Lord, and they went thorowe the hie gate of the Kings house, and set the King vpon the throne of the kingdome.

21 Then all the people of the land reioyced, and the citie was quiet, after that they had slaine Athaliah with the sword.

Second Chronicles 24

1 Ioash was seuen yere olde, when he began to reigne, and he reigned fourty yeere in Ierusalem: and his mothers name was Zibiah of Beer-sheba.

2 And Ioash did vprightly in the sight of the Lord, all the dayes of Iehoiada the Priest.

3 And Iehoiada tooke him two wiues, and he begate sonnes and daughters.

4 And afterward it came into Ioash mind, to renew the house of the Lord.

5 And he assembled the Priests and the Leuites, and said to them, Goe out vnto the cities of Iudah, and gather of all Israel money to repaire the house of your God, from yeere to yeere, and haste the thing: but the Leuites hasted not.

6 Therefore the King called Iehoiada, the chiefe, and said vnto him, Why hast thou not required of the Leuites to bring in out of Iudah and Ierusalem the taxe of Moses the seruant of the Lord, and of the Congregation of Israel, for the Tabernacle of the testimonie?

7 For wicked Athaliah, and her children brake vp the house of God: and all the things that were dedicate for the house of the Lord, did they bestowe vpon Baalim.

8 Therefore the King commanded, and they made a chest, and set it at the gate of the house of the Lord without.

9 And they made proclamation thorow Iudah and Ierusalem, to bring vnto the Lord the taxe of Moses the seruant of God, layde vpon Israel in the wildernesse.

10 And all the princes and all the people reioyced, and brought in, and cast into the chest, vntill they had finished.

11 And when it was time, they brought the chest vnto the Kings officer by the hand of the Leuites: and when they saw that there was much siluer, then the Kings Scribe (and one appoynted by the hie Priest) came and emptied the chest, and tooke it, and caried it to his place againe: thus they did day by day, and gathered siluer in abundance.

12 And the King and Iehoiada gaue it to such as did the labour and worke in the house of the Lord, and hyred masons and carpenters to repayre the house of the Lord: they gaue it also to workers of yron and brasse, to repayre the house of the Lord.

13 So the workemen wrought, and the worke amended through their hands: and they restored the house of God to his state, and strengthened it.

14 And when they had finished it, they brought the rest of the siluer before the King and Iehoiada, and he made thereof vessels for the house of the Lord, euen vessels to minister, both morters and incense cuppes, and vessels of golde, and of siluer: and they offred burnt offrings in the house of the Lord continually all the dayes of Iehoiada.

15 But Iehoiada waxed olde, and was ful of dayes and dyed. An hundreth and thirtie yeere olde was he when he dyed.

16 And they buried him in the citie of Dauid with the kings, because he had done good in Israel, and toward God and his house.

17 And after the death of Iehoiada, came the princes of Iudah, and did reuerence to the King, and the King hearkened vnto them.

18 And they left the house of the Lord God of their fathers, and serued groues and idoles: and wrath came vpon Iudah and Ierusalem, because of this their trespasse.

19 And God sent Prophets amog the, to bring them againe vnto the Lord: and they made protestation among them, but they would not heare.

20 And the Spirit of God came vpon Zechariah the sonne of Iehoiada the Priest, which stoode aboue the people, and sayde vnto them, Thus sayth God, Why transgresse ye the commandements of the Lord? surely ye shall not prosper: because ye haue forsaken the Lord, he also hath forsaken you.

21 Then they conspired against him and stoned him with stones at the commandement of the King, in the court of the house of the Lord.

22 Thus Ioash the King remembred not the kindnesse which Iehoiada his father had done to him, but slewe his sonne. And when he dyed, he sayd, The Lord looke vpon it, and require it.

23 And when the yeere was out, the host of Aram came vp against him, and they came against Iudah and Ierusalem, and destroyed all the princes of the people from among the people, and sent all the spoyle of them vnto the King of Damascus.

24 Though the armie of Aram came with a small company of men, yet the Lord deliuered a very great armie into their hand, because they had forsaken the Lord God of their fathers: and they gaue sentence against Ioash.

25 And when they were departed from him, (for they left him in great diseases) his owne seruants conspired against him for the blood of the children of Iehoiada the Priest, and slewe him on his bed, and he dyed, and they buried him in the citie of Dauid: but they buryed him not in the sepulchres of the Kings.

26 And these are they that conspired against him, Zabad the sonne of Shimrath an Ammonitesse, and Iehozabad the sonne of Shimrith a Moabitesse.

27 But his sonnes, and the summe of the taxe gathered by him, and the foundation of the house of God, behold, they are written in the storie of the booke of the Kings. And Amaziah his sonne reigned in his steade.

Second Chronicles 25

1 Amaziah was fiue and twentie yere old when he began to reigne, and he reigned nine and twentie yeere in Ierusalem: and his mothers name was Iehoaddan, of Ierusalem.

2 And he did vprightly in the eyes of the Lord, but not with a perfite heart.

3 And when the kingdome was established vnto him, he slewe his seruants, that had slaine the King his father.

4 But he slewe not their children, but did as it is written in the Lawe, and in the booke of Moses, where the Lord commanded, saying, The fathers shall not dye for the children, neyther shall the children die for the fathers, but euery man shall dye for his owne sinne.

5 And Amaziah assembled Iudah, and made them captaines ouer thousandes, and captaines ouer hundreths, according to the houses of their fathers, thorowout all Iudah and Beniamin: and he nombred them from twentie yeere olde and aboue, and founde among them three hundreth thousand chosen men, to goe foorth to the warre, and to handle speare and shield.

6 He hyred also an hundreth thousand valiant men out of Israel for an hundreth talents of siluer.

7 But a man of God came to him, saying, O King, let not the armie of Israel goe with thee: for the Lord is not with Israel, neither with all the house of Ephraim.

8 If not, goe thou on, doe it, make thy selfe strong to the battel, but God shall make thee fall before the enemie: for God hath power to helpe, and to cast downe.

9 And Amaziah sayde to the man of God, What shall we doe then for the hundreth talents, which I haue giuen to the hoste of Israel? Then the man of God answered, The Lord is able to giue thee more then this.

10 So Amaziah separated them, to wit, the armie that was come to him out of Ephraim, to returne to their place: wherefore their wrath was kindled greatly against Iudah, and they returned to their places with great anger.

11 Then Amaziah was encouraged, and led forth his people, and went to the salt valley, and smote of the children of Seir, ten thousand.

12 And other ten thousand did the children of Iudah take aliue, and caryed them to the top of a rocke, and cast them downe from the top of the rocke, and they all burst to pieces.

13 But the men of the armie, which Amaziah sent away, that they should not goe with his people to battell, fell vpon the cities of Iudah from Samaria vnto Beth-horon, and smote three thousand of them, and tooke much spoyle.

14 Now after that Amaziah was come from the slaughter of the Edomites, he brought the gods of the children of Seir, and set them vp to be his gods, and worshipped them, and burned incense vnto them.

15 Wherefore the Lord was wroth with Amaziah, and sent vnto him a Prophet, which sayd vnto him, Why hast thou sought the gods of the people, which were not able to deliuer their owne people out of thine hand?

16 And as he talked with him, he said vnto him, Haue they made thee the

Kings counseler? cease thou: why should they smite thee? And the Prophet ceased, but said, I knowe that God hath determined to destroy thee, because thou hast done this, and hast not obeyed my counsell.

17 Then Amaziah King of Iudah tooke counsell, and sent to Ioash the sonne of Iehoahaz, the sonne of Iehu King of Israel, saying, Come, let vs see one another in the face.

18 But Ioash King of Israel sent to Amaziah King of Iudah, saying, The thistle that is in Lebanon, sent to the cedar that is in Lebanon, saying, Giue thy daughter to my sonne to wife: and the wilde beast that was in Lebanon went and trode downe the thistle.

19 Thou thinkest: lo, thou hast smitten Edom, and thine heart lifteth thee vp to bragge: abide now at home: why doest thou prouoke to thine hurt, that thou shouldest fall, and Iudah with thee?

20 But Amaziah would not heare: for it was of God, that he might deliuer them into his had, because they had sought the gods of Edom.

21 So Ioash the King of Israel went vp: and he, and Amaziah King of Iudah saw one another in the face at Bethshemesh, which is in Iudah.

22 And Iudah was put to the worse before Israel, and they fled euery man to his tents.

23 But Ioash the King of Israel tooke Amaziah King of Iudah, the sonne of Ioash, the sonne of Iehoahaz in Bethshemesh, and brought him to Ierusalem, and brake downe the wall of Ierusalem, from the gate of Ephraim vnto the corner gate, foure hundreth cubites.

24 And he tooke all the gold and the siluer, and all the vessels that were found in the house of God with Obed Edom, and in the treasures of the Kings house, and the children that were in hostage, and returned to Samaria.

25 And Amaziah the sonne of Ioash King of Iudah liued after the death of Ioash sonne of Iehoahaz King of Israel, fifteene yeere.

26 Concerning the rest of the actes of Amaziah first and last, are they not written in the booke of the Kings of Iudah and Israel?

27 Nowe after the time that Amaziah did turne away from ye Lord, they wrought treason against him in Ierusalem: and when he was fled to Lachish, they sent to Lachish after him, and slewe him there.

28 And they brought him vpon horses, and buried him with his fathers in the citie of Iudah.

Second Chronicles 26

1 Then all the people of Iudah tooke Vzziah, which was sixteene yeere olde, and made him King in the steade of his father Amaziah.

2 He buylt Eloth, and restored it to Iudah after that the King slept with his fathers.

3 Sixteene yeere olde was Vzziah, when he began to reigne, and he reigned two and fiftie yere in Ierusalem, and his mothers name was Iecoliah of Ierusalem.

4 And hee did vprightly in the sight of the Lord, according to al that his father Amaziah did.

5 And he sought God in the dayes of Zechariah (which vnderstoode the visions of God) and when as he sought the Lord, God made him to prosper.

6 For he went forth and fought against the Philistims and brake downe the wall of Gath, and the wall of Iabneh, and the wall of Ashdod, and built cities in Ashdod, and among the Philistims.

7 And God helped him against ye Philistims, and against the Arabians that dwelt in Gur-baal and Hammeunim.

8 And the Ammonites gaue gifts to Vzziah, and his name spred to the entring in of Egypt: for he did most valiantly.

9 Moreouer Uzziah buylt towres in Ierusalem at the corner gate, and at the valley gate, and at the turning, and made them strong.

10 And he built towres in the wildernesse, and digged many cisternes: for he had much cattell both in the valleyes and playnes, plowmen, and dressers of vines in the mountaines, and in Carmel: for he loued husbandrie.

11 Vzziah had also an hoste of fighting men that went out to warre by bandes, according to the count of their nomber vnder the hande of Ieiel the Scribe, and Maaseiah the ruler, and vnder the hand of Hananiah, one of the Kings captaines.

12 The whole number of the chiefe of the families of the valiant men were two thousande and sixe hundreth.

13 And vnder their hande was the armie for warre, three hundreth and seuen thousand, and fiue hundreth that fought valiantly to helpe the King against the enemie.

14 And Vzziah prepared them throughout all the hoste, shieldes, and speares, and helmets, and brigandines, and bowes, and stones to sling.

15 He made also very artificiall engins in Ierusalem, to be vpon the towres and vpon the corners, to shoote arrowes and great stones: and his name spred farre abroade, because God did helpe him marueilously, till he was mightie.

16 But when he was strong, his heart was lift vp to his destruction: for he transgressed against the Lord his God, and went into the Temple of the Lord to burne incense vpon the altar of incense.

17 And Azariah the Priest went in after him, and with him foure score Priests of the Lord, valiant men.

18 And they withstoode Vzziah the King, and said vnto him, It perteineth not to thee, Vzziah, to burne incense vnto the Lord, but to the Priests the sonnes of Aaron, that are consecrated for to offer incense: goe forth of the Sanctuarie: for thou hast transgressed, and thou shalt haue none honour of the Lord God.

19 Then Vzziah was wroth, and had incense in his hand to burne it: and while he was wroth with the Priestes, the leprosie rose vp in his forehead before the Priestes in the house of the Lord beside the incense altar.

20 And when Azariah the chiefe Priest with al the Priestes looked vpon him, behold, he was leprous in his forehead, and they caused him hastily to depart thence: and he was euen compelled to go out, because the Lord had smitten him.

21 And Vzziah the king was a leper vnto the day of his death, and dwelt as a leper in an house apart, because he was cut off from the house of ye Lord: and Iotham his sonne ruled ouer the Kings house, and iudged the people of the land.

22 Concerning the rest of the acts of Vzziah, first and last, did Isaiah the Prophet the sonne of Amoz write.

23 So Vzziah slept with his fathers, and they buryed him with his fathers in the fielde of the burial, which perteined to the kings: for they said, He is a leper. And Iotham his sonne reigned in his steade.

Second Chronicles 27

1 Iotham was fiue and twentie yere olde when he began to reigne, and reigned sixteene yeere in Ierusalem, and his mothers name was Ierushah the daughter of Zadok.

2 And hee did vprightly in the sight of the Lord according to all that his father Vzziah did, saue that hee entred not into the Temple of the Lord, and the people did yet corrupt their wayes.

3 He buylt the hie gate of the house of the Lord, and he buylt very much on the wall of the castle.

4 Moreouer hee buylt cities in the mountaines of Iudah, and in the forests he buylt palaces and towres.

5 And he fought with the King of the children of Ammon, and preuailed against them. And the children of Ammon gaue him the same yere an hundreth talents of siluer, and ten thousande measures of wheate, and ten thousand of barley: this did the children of Ammon giue him both in the second yeere and the third.

6 So Iotham became mightie because hee directed his way before the Lord his God.

7 Concerning the rest of the acts of Iotham, and all his warres and his wayes, loe, they are written in the booke of the Kings of Israel, and Iudah.

8 He was fiue and twentie yeere olde when he began to reigne, and reigned sixteene yeere in Ierusalem.

9 And Iotham slept with his fathers, and they buryed him in the citie of Dauid: and Ahaz his sonne reigned in his stead.

Second Chronicles 28

1 Ahaz was twentie yeere old when he began to reigne, and reigned sixteene yeere in Ierusalem, and did not vprightly in the sight of the Lord, like Dauid his father.

2 But he walked in the wayes of ye Kings of Israel, and made euen molten images for Baalim.

3 Moreouer he burnt incense in the valley of Ben-hinnom, and burnt his sonnes with fire, after the abominations of the heathen whom the Lord had cast out before the children of Israel.

4 He sacrificed also and burnt incense in the hie places, and on hilles, and vnder euery greene tree.

5 Wherefore the Lord his God deliuered him into the hand of the King of the Aramites, and they smote him, and tooke of his, many prisoners, and brought them to Damascus: and he was also deliuered into the hande of the King of Israel, which smote him with a great slaughter.

6 For Pekah the sonne of Remaliah slewe in Iudah sixe score thousand in one day, all valiant men, because they had forsaken the Lord God of their fathers.

7 And Zichri a mighty man of Ephraim slew Maaseiah the Kings sonne, and Azrikam the gouernour of the house, and Elkanah the second after the King.

8 And the children of Israel tooke prisoners of their brethren, two hudreth thousand of women, sonnes and daughters, and caried away much spoyle of them, and brought the spoyle to Samaria.

9 But there was a Prophet of the Lordes, (whose name was Oded) and he went out before the hoste that came to Samaria, and said vnto them, Behold, because the Lord God of your fathers is wroth with Iudah, he hath deliuered them into your hand, and ye haue slaine them in a rage, that reacheth vp to heauen.

10 And nowe ye purpose to keepe vnder the children of Iudah and Ierusalem, as seruants and handmaides vnto you: but are not you such, that sinnes are with you before the Lord your God?

11 Nowe therefore heare me, and deliuer the captiues againe, which ye haue taken prisoners of your brethren: for the fierce wrath of the Lord is toward you.

12 Wherefore certaine of the chiefe of the children of Ephraim, Azariah the sonne of Iehohanan, Berechiah the sonne of Meshillemoth, and Iehizkiah the sonne of Shallum, and Amasa the sonne of Hadlai, stood vp against them that came from the warre,

13 And said vnto them, Bring not in the captiues hither: for this shalbe a sinne vpon vs against the Lord: ye entende to adde more to our sinnes and to our trespasse, though our trespasse be great, and the fierce wrath of God is against Israel.

14 So the armie left the captiues and the spoyle before the princes and all the Congregation.

15 And the men that were named by name, rose vp and tooke the prisoners, and with the spoyle clothed all that were naked among them, and arayed them, and shod them, and gaue them meate, and gaue them drinke, and anoynted them, and caryed all that were feeble of them vpon asses, and brought them to Iericho the citie of Palme trees to their brethren: so they returned to Samaria.

16 At that time did King Ahaz sende vnto the Kings of Asshur, to helpe him.

17 (For the Edomites came moreouer, and slew of Iudah, and caryed away captiues.

18 The Philistims also inuaded the cities in the low countrey, and toward the South of Iudah, and tooke Bethshemesh, and Aialon, and Gederoth and Shocho, with the villages thereof, and Timnah, with her villages, and Gimzo, with her villages, and they dwelt there.

19 For the Lord had humbled Iudah, because of Ahaz King of Israel: for he had brought vengeance vpon Iudah, and had grieuously transgressed against the Lord)

20 And Tilgath Pilneeser king of Asshur came vnto him, who troubled him and did not strengthen him.

21 For Ahaz tooke a portion out of the house of the Lord and out of the Kings house and of the Princes, and gaue vnto the king of Asshur: yet it helped him not.

22 And in ye time of his tribulation did he yet trespasse more against ye Lord, (this is King Ahaz)

23 For he sacrificed vnto the gods of Damascus, which plagued him, and he sayd, Because the gods of the Kings of Aram helped them, I wil sacrifice vnto them, and they will helpe me: yet they were his ruine, and of all Israel.

24 And Ahaz gathered the vessels of ye house of God, and brake the vessels of the house of God, and shut vp the doores of the house of the Lord, and made him altars in euery corner of Ierusalem.

25 And in euery citie of Iudah hee made hie places, to burne incense vnto other gods, and prouoked to anger the Lord God of his fathers.

26 Concerning the rest of his actes, and all his wayes first and last, beholde, they are written in the booke of the Kings of Iudah, and Israel.

27 And Ahaz slept with his fathers, and they buried him in the citie of Ierusalem, but brought him not vnto the sepulchres of the Kings of Israel: and Hezekiah his sonne reigned in his stead.

Second Chronicles 29

1 Hezekiah began to reigne, when he was fiue and twentie yeere olde, and reigned nine and twentie yeres in Ierusalem: and his mothers name was Abiiah the daughter of Zechariah.

2 And hee did vprightly in the sight of the Lord, according to all that Dauid his father had done.

3 He opened the doores of the house of the Lord in the first yeere, and in the first moneth of his reigne, and repared them.

4 And he brought in the Priests and the Leuites, and gathered them into the East streete,

5 And said vnto them, Heare me, ye Leuites: sanctifie nowe your selues, and sanctifie the house of the Lord God of your fathers, and cary forth the filthinesse out of the Sanctuarie.

6 For our fathers haue trespassed, and done euill in the eyes of the Lord our God, and haue forsaken him, and turned away their faces from the Tabernacle of the Lord, and turned their backes.

7 They haue also shut the doores of ye porch, and quenched the lampes, and haue neither burnt incense, nor offred burnt offrings in the Sanctuarie vnto the God of Israel.

8 Wherfore the wrath of the Lord hath bin on Iudah and Ierusalem: and he hath made them a scattering, a desolation, and an hissing, as ye see with your eyes.

9 For lo, our fathers are fallen by the sword, and our sonnes, and our daughters, and our wiues are in captiuitie for the same cause.

10 Now I purpose to make a couenant with the Lord God of Israel, that he may turne away his fierce wrath from vs.

11 Now my sonnes, be not deceiued: for the Lord hath chosen you to stand before him, to serue him, and to be his ministers, and to burne incense.

12 Then the Leuites arose, Mahath ye sonne of Amashai, and Ioel the sonne of Azariah of the sonnes of the Kohathites: and of the sonnes of Merari, Kish the sonne of Abdi, and Azariah the sonne of Iehalelel: and of the Gershonites, Ioah the sonne of Zimmah, and Eden the sonne of Ioah:

13 And of the sonnes of Elizaphan, Shimri, and Iehiel: and of the sonnes of Asaph, Zechariah, and Mattaniah:

14 And of the sonnes of Heman, Iehiel, and Shimei: and of the sonnes of Ieduthun, Shemaiah and Vzziel.

15 And they gathered their brethren, and sanctified themselues and came according to the commandement of the King, and by the words of the Lord, for to clense the house of the Lord.

16 And the Priests went into the inner partes of the house of the Lord, to clense it, and brought out all the vncleannesse that they founde in the Temple of the Lord, into the court of the house of the Lord: and the Leuites tooke it, to cary it out vnto the brooke Kidron.

17 They began the first day of the first moneth to sanctifie it, and the eight day of the moneth came they to the porche of the Lord: so they sanctified the house of the Lord in eight dayes, and in the sixteenth day of the first moneth they made an ende.

18 Then they went in to Hezekiah ye King, and sayde, We haue clensed all the house of the Lord and the altar of burnt offring, with all the vessels thereof, and the shewbread table, with all the vessels thereof:

19 And all the vessels which King Ahaz had cast aside when he reigned, and transgressed, haue we prepared and sanctified: and beholde, they are before the altar of the Lord.

20 And Hezekiah the King rose early, and gathered the princes of the citie, and went vp to the house of the Lord.

21 And they brought seuen bullockes, and seuen rammes, and seuen lambes, and seuen hee goates, for a sinne offring for the kingdome, and for the sanctuarie, and for Iudah. And he commanded the Priests the sonnes of Aaron, to offer them on the altar of the Lord.

22 So they slewe the bullockes, and the Priests receiued the blood, and sprinkled it vpon the altar: they slew also the rammes and sprinkled the blood vpon the altar, and they slew the lambes, and they sprinkled the blood vpon the altar.

23 Then they brought the hee goates for the sinne offring before the King and the Congregation, and they layde their hands vpon them.

24 And the Priests slewe them, and with the blood of them they clensed the altar to reconcile all Israel: for the King had commanded for all Israel the burnt offring and the sinne offring.

25 He appointed also the Leuites in the house of the Lord with cymbales, with violes, and with harpes, according to the commandement of Dauid, and Gad the Kings Seer, and Nathan the Prophet: for the commandement was by the hande of the Lord, and by the hande of his Prophets.

26 And the Leuites stood with the instruments of Dauid, and the Priests with the trumpets.

27 And Hezekiah commanded to offer the burnt offring vpon the altar: and when the burnt offring began, the song of the Lord beganne with the trumpets, and the instruments of Dauid King of Israel.

28 And al the Congregation worshipped, singing a song, and they blew the trumpets: all this continued vntill the burnt offring was finished.

29 And when they had made an ende of offring, the King and all that were present with him, bowed themselues, and worshipped.

30 Then Hezekiah the King and the princes commanded the Leuites to prayse the Lord with the wordes of Dauid, and of Asaph the Seer. so they praysed with ioy, and they bowed themselues, and worshipped.

31 And Hezekiah spake, and sayde, Now ye haue consecrate your selues to the Lord: come neere and bring the sacrifices and offerings of prayse into the house of the Lord. And the Congregation brought sacrifices; and offrings of prayses, and euery man that was willing in heart, offred burnt offrings.

32 And the nomber of the burnt offrings, which the Congregation brought, was seuentie bullockes, an hundreth rammes, and two hundreth lambes: all these were for a burnt offring to the Lord:

33 And for sanctification sixe hundreth bullockes, and three thousand sheepe.

34 But the Priests were too few, and were not able to flay all the burnt offrings: therefore their brethren the Leuites did helpe them, til they had ended the worke, and vntill other Priests were sanctified: for the Leuites were more vpright in heart to sanctifie themselues, then the Priests.

35 And also the burnt offerings were many with the fat of the peace offrings and the drinke offrings for the burnt offring. so the seruice of the house of the Lord was set in order.

36 Then Hezekiah reioyced and all the people, that God had made the people so ready: for the thing was done suddenly.

Second Chronicles 30

1 And Hezekiah sent to all Israel, and Iudah, and also wrote letters to Ephraim and Manasseh, that they should come to the house of the Lord at Ierusalem, to keepe the Passeouer vnto the Lord God of Israel.

2 And the King and his princes and all the Congregation had taken counsel in Ierusalem to keepe the Passeouer in the second moneth.

3 For they could not keepe it at this time, because there were not Priests enow sanctified, neither was the people gathered to Ierusalem.

4 And the thing pleased the King, and all the Congregation.

5 And they decreed to make proclamation throughout all Israel from Beersheba euen to Dan, that they should come to keepe the Passeouer vnto the Lord God of Israel at Ierusalem: for they had not done it of a great time, as it was written.

6 So the postes went with letters by the commission of the King, and his princes, thorowout all Israel and Iudah, and with the commandement of the King, saying, Ye children of Israel, turne againe vnto the Lord God of Abraham, Izhak, and Israel, and he will returne to the remnant that are escaped of you, out of ye hands of the Kings of Asshur.

7 And be not ye like your fathers, and like your brethren, which trespassed against the Lord God of their fathers: and therfore he made them desolate, as ye see.

8 Be not ye now stiffenecked like your fathers, but giue the hand to the Lord, and come into his sanctuarie, which he hath sanctified for euer, and serue the Lord your God, and the fiercenesse of his wrath shall turne away from you.

9 For if ye returne vnto the Lord, your brethren and your children shall finde mercy before them that led them captiues, and they shall returne vnto this lande: for the Lord your God is gracious and mercifull, and will not turne away his face from you, if ye conuert vnto him.

10 So the postes went from citie to citie thorow the land of Ephraim and Manasseh, euen vnto Zebulun: but they laughed them to scorne, and mocked them.

11 Neuerthelesse diuers of Asher, and Manasseh, and of Zebulun submitted themselues, and came to Ierusalem.

12 And the hand of God was in Iudah, so that he gaue them one heart to doe the commandement of the King, and of the rulers, according to the worde of the Lord.

13 And there assembled to Ierusalem much people, to keepe the feast of ye vnleauened bread in the second moneth, a very great assemblie.

14 And they arose, and tooke away the altars that were in Ierusalem: and all those for incense tooke they away, and cast them into the brooke Kidron.

15 Afterwarde they slewe the Passeouer the fourteenth day of the seconde moneth: and the Priestes and Leuites were ashamed, and sanctified themselues, and brought the burnt offrings into the house of the Lord.

16 And they stoode in their place after their maner, according to the Lawe of Moses the man of God: and the Priestes sprinkled the blood, receiued of the handes of the Leuites.

17 Because there were many in the Congregation that were not sanctified, therefore the Leuites had the charge of the killing of ye Passeouer for all that were not cleane, to sanctifie it to the Lord.

18 For a multitude of the people, euen a multitude of Ephraim, and Manasseh, Issachar and Zebulun had not cleansed themselues, yet did eate the Passeouer, but not as it was written: wherefore Hezekiah prayed for them, saying, The good Lord be mercifull toward him,

19 That prepareth his whole heart to seeke the Lord God, the God of his fathers, though he be not cleansed, according to the purification of the Sanctuarie.

20 And the Lord heard Hezekiah, and healed the people.

21 And the children of Israel that were present at Ierusalem, kept the feast of the vnleauened bread seuen dayes with great ioye, and the Leuites, and the Priestes praysed the Lord, day by day, singing with loude instruments vnto the Lord.

22 And Hezekiah spake comfortably vnto all the Leuites that had good knowledge to sing vnto the Lord: and they did eate in that feast seuen dayes, and offred peace offrings, and praysed the Lord God of their fathers.

23 And the whole assembly tooke counsel to keepe it other seuen dayes. So they kept it seuen dayes with ioy.

24 For Hezekiah King of Iudah had giuen to the Congregation a thousande bullockes, and seuen thousand sheepe. And the princes had giuen to the Congregation a thousand bullocks, and ten thousand sheepe: and many Priests were sanctified.

25 And all the Congregation of Iudah reioyced with the Priestes and the Leuites, and all the Congregation that came out of Israel, and the strangers that came out of the land of Israel, and that dwelt in Iudah.

26 So there was great ioye in Ierusalem: for since the time of Salomon the sonne of Dauid King of Israel there was not the like thing in Ierusalem.

27 Then the Priests and the Leuites arose, and blessed the people, and their voyce was heard, and their prayer came vp vnto heauen, to his holy habitation.

Second Chronicles 31

1 And when all these thinges were finished, all Israel that were found in the cities of Iudah, went out and brake the images, and cut downe the groues, and brake downe the hie places, and the altars thorowout all Iudah and Beniamin, in Ephraim also and Manasseh, vntil they had made an ende: afterwarde all the children of Israel returned euery man to his possession, into their owne cities.

2 And Hezekiah appoynted the courses of the Priests and Leuites by their turnes, euery man according to his office, both Priestes and Leuites, for the burnt offring and peace offrings, to minister and to giue thankes, and to prayse in the gates of the tentes of the Lord.

3 (And the Kings portion was of his owne substance for the burnt offrings, euen for ye burnt offrings of the morning and of the euening, and the burnt offrings for the Sabbaths, and for the new moones, and for the solemne feastes, as it is written in the Law of the Lord)

4 He commanded also the people that dwelt in Ierusalem, to giue a part to the Priestes, and Leuites, that they might be encouraged in the Law of the Lord.

5 And when the commandement was spread, the children of Israel brought abundance of first fruites, of corne, wine, and oyle, and honie, and of all the increase of the fielde, and the tithes of all things brought they abundantly.

6 And the children of Israel and Iudah that dwelt in ye cities of Iudah, they also brought the tithes of bullockes and sheepe, and the holy tithes which were consecrate vnto the Lord their God, and laide them on many heapes.

7 In the thirde moneth they beganne to lay the foundation of the heapes, and finished them in the seuenth moneth.

8 And when Hezekiah and the princes came, and saw the heapes, they blessed the Lord and his people Israel.

9 And Hezekiah questioned with the Priests and the Leuites concerning the heapes.

10 And Azariah the chiefe Priest of the house of Zadok answered him, and sayde, Since the people beganne to bring the offrings into the house of the Lord, we haue eaten and haue bene satisfied, and there is left in abundance: for the Lord hath blessed his people, and this abundance that is left.

11 And Hezekiah commanded to prepare chambers in the house of the Lord: and they prepared them,

12 And caryed in the first fruites, and the tithes, and the dedicate things faithfully: and ouer them was Conaniah the Leuite, the chiefe, and Shimei his brother the seconde.

13 And Iehiel, and Azariah, and Nahath, and Asahel, and Ierimoth, and Iozabad, and Eliel, and Ismachiah, and Mahath, and Benaiah were ouerseers by the appointment of Conaniah, and Shimei his brother, and by the commandement of Hezekiah the King, and of Azariah the chiefe of the house of God.

14 And Kore the sonne of Imnah the Leuite porter towarde the East, was ouer the things that were willingly offred vnto God, to distribute the oblations of the Lord, and the holy things that were consecrate.

15 And at his hande were Eden, and Miniamin, and Ieshua, and Shemaiah, Amariah, and Shechaniah, in the cities of the Priestes, to distribute with fidelitie to their brethren by courses, both to the great and small,

16 Their daily portion: beside their generation being males from three yeere olde and aboue, euen to all that entred into the house of the Lord to their office in their charge, according to their courses:

17 Both to the generation of the Priestes after the house of their fathers, and to the Leuites from twentie yeere olde and aboue, according to their charge in their courses:

18 And to the generation of all their children, their wiues, and their sonnes and their daughters throughout all ye Congregation: for by their fidelitie are they partakers of the holy things.

19 Also to the sonnes of Aaron, the Priestes, which were in the fieldes and suburbes of their cities, in euery citie the men that were appointed by names, shoulde giue portions to all the males of the Priestes, and to all the generation of the Leuites.

20 And thus did Hezekiah throughout al Iudah, and did well, and vprightly, and truely before the Lord his God.

21 And in all the workes that he began for the seruice of the house of God, both in the Law and in the commandements, to seeke his God, he did it with all his heart, and prospered.

Second Chronicles 32

1 After these things faithfully described, Saneherib King of Asshur came and entred into Iudah, and besieged the strong cities, and thought to winne them for him selfe.

2 When Hezekiah sawe that Saneherib was come, and that his purpose was to fight against Ierusalem,

3 Then he tooke counsell with his princes and his nobles, to stoppe the water of the fountaines without the citie: and they did helpe him.

4 So many of the people assembled themselues, and stopt all the fountaines, and the riuer that ranne through the middes of the countrey, saying, Why should the Kings of Asshur come, and finde much water?

5 And he tooke courage, and built all the broken wall, and made vp the towers, and another wall without, and repayred Millo in the citie of Dauid, and made many dartes and shields.

6 And he set captaines of warre ouer the people, and assembled them to him in the broade place of the gate of the citie, and spake comfortably vnto them, saying,

7 Be strong and couragious: feare not, neither be afraide for the King of Asshur, neither for all the multitude that is with him: for there be more with vs, then is with him.

8 With him is an arme of flesh, but with vs is the Lord our God for to helpe vs, and to fight our battels. Then the people were confirmed by the wordes of Hezekiah King of Iudah.

9 After this, did Saneherib King of Asshur send his seruants to Ierusalem (while he was against Lachish, and all his dominion with him) vnto Hezekiah King of Iudah and vnto all Iudah that were at Ierusalem, saying,

10 Thus saith Saneherib the King of Asshur, Wherein doe ye trust, that ye will remaine in Ierusalem, during the siege?

11 Doeth not Hezekiah entice you to giue ouer your selues vnto death by famine and by thirst, saying, The Lord our God shall deliuer vs out of the hande of the King of Asshur?

12 Hath not the same Hezekiah taken away his hie places and his altars, and commanded Iudah and Ierusalem, saying, Ye shall worshippe before one altar, and burne incense vpon it?

13 Knowe ye not what I and my fathers haue done vnto all the people of other countreyes? were the gods of the nations of other landes able to deliuer their land out of mine hande?

14 Who is he of al the gods of those natios (that my fathers haue destroied) that could deliuer his people out of mine hande? that your God should be able to deliuer you out of mine hand?

15 Nowe therefore let not Hezekiah deceiue you, nor seduce you after this sort, neither beleeue ye him: for none of all the gods of any nation or kingdome was able to deliuer his people out of mine hande and out of the hande of my fathers: howe much lesse shall your gods deliuer you out of mine hande?

16 And his seruants spake yet more against the Lord God, and against his seruant Hezekiah.

17 He wrote also letters, blaspheming the Lord God of Israel and speaking against him, saying, As the gods of the nations of other countreies could not deliuer their people out of mine hand, so shall not the God of Hezekiah deliuer his people out of mine hande.

18 Then they cryed with a loude voyce in the Iewes speach vnto the people of Ierusalem that were on the wall, to feare them and to astonish them, that they might take the citie.

19 Thus they spake against the God of Ierusalem, as against the gods of the people of the earth, euen the workes of mans hands,

20 But Hezekiah the King, and the Prophet Isaiah the sonne of Amoz prayed against this and cryed to heauen.

21 And the Lord sent an Angel which destroyed all the valiant men, and the princes and captaines of the hoste of the King of Asshur: so he returned with shame to his owne lande. And when he was come into the house of his god, they that came foorth of his owne bowels, slewe him there with the sworde.

22 So the Lord saued Hezekiah and the inhabitants of Ierusalem from the hande of Saneherib King of Asshur, and from the hande of all other, and maintained them on euery side.

23 And many brought offrings vnto the Lord to Ierusalem, and presents to Hezekiah King of Iudah, so that he was magnified in the sight of all nations from thenceefoorth.

24 In those dayes Hezekiah was sicke vnto the death, and prayed vnto the Lord, who spake vnto him, and gaue him a signe.

25 But Hezekiah did not render according to the rewarde bestowed vpon him: for his heart was lift vp, and wrath came vpon him, and vpon Iudah and Ierusalem.

26 Notwithstanding Hezekiah humbled him selfe (after that his heart was lifted vp) he and the inhabitants of Ierusalem, and the wrath of the Lord came not vpon them in the dayes of Hezekiah.

27 Hezekiah also had exceeding much riches and honour, and he gate him treasures of siluer, and of golde, and of precious stones, and of sweete odours, and of shieldes, and of all pleasant vessels:

28 And of store houses for the increase of wheat and wine and oyle, and stalles for all beasts, and rowes for the stables.

29 And he made him cities, and had possession of sheepe and oxen in abundance: for God had giuen him substance exceeding much.

30 This same Hezekiah also stopped the vpper water springs of Gihon, and led them streight vnderneath towarde the citie of Dauid Westwarde. so Hezekiah prospered in all his workes.

31 But because of the ambassadours of the princes of Babel, which sent vnto him to enquire of the wonder that was done in the lande, God left him to trie him, and to knowe all that was in his heart.

32 Concerning the rest of the actes of Hezekiah, and his goodnesse, beholde, they are written in the vision of Ishiah the Prophet, the sonne of Amoz, in the booke of the Kings of Iudah and Israel.

33 So Hezekiah slept with his fathers, and they buried him in the highest sepulchre of the sonnes of Dauid: and all Iudah and the inhabitants of Ierusalem did him honour at his death: and Manasseh his sonne reigned in his stead.

Second Chronicles 33

1 Manasseh was twelue yeere olde, when he beganne to reigne, and he reigned fiue and fiftie yeere in Ierusalem:

2 And he did euill in the sight of the Lord, like the abominations of the heathen, who the Lord had cast out before the children of Israel.

3 For he went backe and built the hie places, which Hezekiah his father had broken downe: and he set vp altars for Baalim, and made groues, and worshipped all the hoste of the heauen, and serued them.

4 Also he built altars in the house of the Lord, whereof the Lord had saide, In Ierusalem shall my Name be for euer.

5 And he built altars for all the hoste of the heauen in the two courtes of the house of the Lord.

6 And he caused his sonnes to passe through the fire in the valley of Ben-hinnom: he gaue him selfe to witchcraft and to charming and to sorcerie, and he vsed them that had familiar spirits, and soothsayers: hee did very much euill in the sight of the Lord to anger him.

7 He put also the carued image, which he had made, in the house of God: whereof God had said to Dauid and to Salomon his sonne, In this house and in Ierusalem, which I haue chosen before all the tribes of Israel, will I put my Name for euer,

8 Neither will I make the foote of Israel to remooue any more out of the lande which I haue appointed for your fathers, so that they take heede, and do all that I haue commanded them, according to the Lawe and statutes and iudgements by the hande of Moses.

9 So Manasseh made Iudah and the inhabitants of Ierusalem to erre, and to doe worse then the heathen, whome the Lord had destroyed before the children of Israel.

10 And the Lord spake to Manasseh and to his people, but they would not regarde.

11 Wherefore the Lord brought vpon them the captaines of the hoste of the King of Asshur, which tooke Manasseh and put him in fetters, and bound him in chaines, and caryed him to Babel.

12 And when he was in tribulation, he prayed to the Lord his God, and humbled him selfe greatly before the God of his fathers,

13 And prayed vnto him: and God was entreated of him, and heard his prayer, and brought him againe to Ierusalem into his kingdome: then Manasseh knewe that the Lord was God.

14 Nowe after this he built a wall without the citie of Dauid, on the Westside of Gihon in the valley, euen at the entrie of the fish gate, and compassed about Ophel, and raised it very hie, and put captaines of warre in all the strong cities of Iudah.

15 And he tooke away the strange gods and the image out of the house of the Lord, and all the altars that he had built in the mount of the house of the Lord,

and in Ierusalem, and cast them out of the citie.

16 Also he prepared the altar of the Lord, and sacrificed thereon peace offerings, and of thankes, and commanded Iudah to serue the Lord God of Israel.

17 Neuerthelesse the people did sacrifice stil in the hie places, but vnto the Lord their God.

18 Concerning the rest of the actes of Manasseh, and his prayer vnto his God, and the words of the Seers, that spake to him in ye Name of the Lord God of Israel, beholde, they are written in the booke of the Kings of Israel.

19 And his prayer and how God was intreated of him, and all his sinne, and his trespasse, and the places wherein he built hie places, and set groues and images (before he was humbled) behold, they are written in the booke of the Seers.

20 So Manasseh slept with his fathers, and they buried him in his owne house: and Amon his sonne reigned in his stead.

21 Amon was two and twentie yeere olde, when he began to reigne, and reigned two yeere in Ierusalem.

22 But he did euill in the sight of the Lord, as did Manasseh his father: for Amon sacrificed to all the images, which Manasseh his father had made, and serued them,

23 And he humbled not him selfe before the Lord, as Manasseh his father had humbled himselfe: but this Amon trespassed more and more.

24 And his seruants conspired against him, and slewe him in his owne house.

25 But the people of the land slewe all them that had conspired against King Amon: and the people of the land made Iosiah his sonne King in his steade.

Second Chronicles 34

1 Iosiah was eight yeere olde when hee began to reigne, and he reigned in Ierusalem one and thirtie yeere.

2 And he did vprightly in the sight of ye Lord, and walked in the wayes of Dauid his father, and bowed neither to the right hand nor to the left.

3 And in the eight yeere of his reigne (when he was yet a childe) he began to seeke after the God of Dauid his father: and in the twelft yeere he began to purge Iudah, and Ierusalem from the hie places, and the groues, and the carued images, and molten images:

4 And they brake downe in his sight the altars of Baalim, and hee caused to cut downe the images that were on hie vpon them: he brake also the groues, and the carued images, and the molten images, and stampt them to pouder, and strowed it vpon the graues of them that had sacrificed vnto them.

5 Also he burnt the bones of the Priests vpon their altars, and purged Iudah and Ierusalem.

6 And in the cities of Manasseh, and Ephraim, and Simeon, euen vnto

Naphtali, with their maules they brake all round about.

7 And when he had destroyed the altars and the groues, and had broken and stamped to pouder the images, and had cut downe all the idoles throughout all the land of Israel, hee returned to Ierusalem.

8 Then in the eightenth yere of his reigne, when hee had purged the lande and the Temple, he sent Shaphan the sonne of Azaliah, and Maaseiah the gouernour of the citie, and Ioah the sonne of Ioahaz the recorder, to repaire the house of the Lord his God.

9 And when they came to Hilkiah the hie Priest, they deliuered ye money that was brought into the house of God, which the Leuites that kept the doore, had gathered at the hand of Manasseh, and Ephraim, and of all the residue of Israel, and of all Iudah and Beniamin, and of the inhabitantes of Ierusalem.

10 And they put it in the hands of them that should doe the worke and had the ouersight in the house of the Lord: and they gaue it to the workemen that wrought in the house of ye Lord, to repaire and amend the house.

11 Euen to the workemen and to the builders gaue they it, to bye hewed stone and timber for couples and for beames of the houses, which the Kings of Iudah had destroyed.

12 And the men did the worke faithfully, and the ouerseers of them were Iahath and Obadiah the Leuites, of the children of Merari, and Zechariah, and Meshullam, of the children of the Kohathites to set it forward: and of the Leuites all that could skill of instruments of musike.

13 And they were ouer the bearers of burdens, and them that set forwarde all the workemen in euery worke: and of the Leuites were scribes, and officers and porters.

14 And when they brought out the money that was brought into the house of the Lord, Hilkiah the Priest found the booke of the Lawe of the Lord giuen by the hand of Moses.

15 Therefore Hilkiah answered and sayde to Shaphan the chaceler, I haue found the booke of the Law in the house of the Lord: and Hilkiah gaue the booke to Shaphan.

16 And Shaphan caried the booke to the King, and brought the King worde againe, saying, All that is committed to the hand of thy seruants, that do they.

17 For they haue gathered the money that was found in the house of the Lord, and haue deliuered it into the handes of the ouerseers, and to the handes of the workemen.

18 Also Shaphan ye chanceler declared to the King, saying, Hilkiah the Priest hath giuen mee a booke, and Shaphan read it before the King.

19 And when the King had heard the wordes of the Lawe, he tare his clothes.

20 And the King commanded Hilkiah, and Ahikam the sonne of Shaphan, and Abdon the sonne of Micah, and Shaphan the chanceler, and Asaiah the Kings seruant, saying,

21 Goe and enquire of the Lord for me, and for the rest in Israel and Iudah, concerning the wordes of this booke that is founde: for great is the wrath of the Lord that is fallen vpon vs, because our fathers haue not kept the worde of the Lord, to doe after all that is written in this booke.

22 Then Hilkiah and they that the King had appoynted, went to Huldah the Prophetesse ye wife of Shallum, the sonne of Tokhath, the sonne of Hasrah keeper of the wardrobe (and she dwelt in Ierusalem within the colledge) and they communed hereof with her.

23 And shee answered them, Thus sayth the Lord God of Israel, Tell yee the man that sent you to me,

24 Thus saith the Lord, Beholde, I will bring euill vpon this place, and vpon the inhabitantes thereof, euen all the curses, that are written in the booke which they haue read before the King of Iudah:

25 Because they haue forsaken me, and burnt incense vnto other gods, to anger mee with al the workes of their hands, therefore shall my wrath fall vpon this place, and shall not be quenched.

26 But to the King of Iudah, who sent you to enquire of the Lord, so shall ye say vnto him, Thus saith the Lord God of Israel, The words which thou hast heard, shall come to passe.

27 But because thine heart did melt, and thou didest humble thy selfe before God, when thou heardest his wordes against this place and against the inhabitantes thereof, and humbledst thy selfe before mee and tarest thy clothes, and weptest before mee, I haue also heard it, sayth the Lord.

28 Beholde, I will gather thee to thy fathers, and thou shalt bee put in thy graue in peace, and thine eyes shall not see all the euill, which I will bring vpon this place, and vpon the inhabitants of the same. Thus they brought ye King word againe.

29 Then the King sent and gathered all the Elders of Iudah and Ierusalem.

30 And the King went vp into the house of the Lord, and all the men of Iudah, and the inhabitants of Ierusalem, and the Priests and the Leuites, and all the people from the greatest to the smallest, and hee read in their eares all the wordes of the booke of the couenant that was found in the house of the Lord.

31 And the King stood by his pillar, and made a couenant before the Lord, to walke after the Lord, and to keepe his commandements, and his testimonies, and his statutes, with all his heart, and with all his soule, and that he would accomplish the wordes of the couenant written in the same booke.

32 And he caused all that were found in Ierusalem, and Beniamin to stande to it: and the inhabitants of Ierusalem did according to the couenant of God, euen the God of their fathers.

33 So Iosiah tooke away al the abominations out of all the countreis that perteined to the children of Israel, and compelled all that were found in Israel, to serue the Lord their God: so all his dayes they turned not backe from the Lord God of their fathers.

Second Chronicles 35

1 Moreouer Iosiah kept a Passeouer vnto the Lord in Ierusalem, and they slewe the Passeouer in the fourtenth day of the first moneth.

2 And he appointed the Priestes to their charges, and incouraged them to the seruice of the house of the Lord,

3 And he sayd vnto the Leuites that taught all Israel and were sanctified vnto the Lord, Put the holy Arke in the house which Salomon the sonne of Dauid King of Israel did build: it shalbe no more a burden vpon your shoulders: serue now the Lord your God and his people Israel,

4 And prepare your selues by the houses of your fathers according to your courses, as Dauid the King of Israel hath written, and according to the writing of Salomon his sonne,

5 And stande in the Sanctuarie according to the deuision of the families of your brethren the children of the people, and after the deuision of the familie of the Leuites:

6 So kill the Passeouer and sanctifie your selues, and prepare your brethren that they may doe according to the worde of the Lord by the hand of Moses.

7 Iosiah also gaue to the people sheepe, lambs and kiddes, all for the Passeouer, euen to all that were present, to the number of thirtie thousand, and three thousande bullocks: these were of the Kings substance.

8 And his princes offred willingly vnto the people, to the Priests and to the Leuites: Hilkiah, and Zechariah, and Iehiel, rulers of the house of God, gaue vnto the Priests for the Passeouer, euen two thousand and sixe hundreth sheepe, and three hundreth bullockes.

9 Conaniah also and Shemaiah and Nethaneel his brethren, and Hashabiah and Ieiel, and Iozabad, chiefe of the Leuites gaue vnto the Leuites for the Passeouer, fiue thousand sheepe, and fiue hundreth bullockes.

10 Thus the seruice was prepared, and the Priests stoode in their places, also the Leuites in their orders, according to the Kings commandement:

11 And they slewe the Passeouer, and the Priests sprinkled the blood with their handes, and the Leuites flayed them.

12 And they tooke away from the burnt offering to giue it according to the deuisions of the families of the children of the people, to offer vnto the Lord, as it is written in the booke of Moses, and so of the bullockes.

13 And they rosted the Passeouer with fire, according to ye custome, but the sanctified things they sod in pots, pannes, and cauldrons, and distributed them quickely to all the people.

14 Afterwarde also they prepared for them selues and for the Priestes: for the

Priestes the sonnes of Aaron were occupied in offering of burnt offrings, and the fat vntill night: therefore the Leuites prepared for them selues, and for the Priests the sonnes of Aaron.

15 And the singers the sonnes of Asaph stoode in their standing according to the commandement of Dauid, and Asaph, and Heman, and Ieduthun the Kings Seer: and the porters at euery gate, who might not depart from their seruice: therefore their brethren the Leuites prepared for them.

16 So all the seruice of the Lord was prepared the same day, to keepe the Passeouer, and to offer burnt offerings vpon the altar of the Lord, according to the commandement of King Iosiah.

17 And the children of Israel that were present, kept the Passeouer the same time, and the feast of the vnleauened bread seuen dayes.

18 And there was no Passeouer kept like that, in Israel, from the dayes of Samuel the Prophet: neyther did all the Kings of Israel keepe such a Passeouer as Iosiah kept, and the Priestes and the Leuites, and all Iudah, and Israel that were present, and the inhabitants of Ierusalem.

19 This Passeouer was kept in the eighteenth yeere of the reigne of Iosiah.

20 After all this, when Iosiah had prepared the Temple, Necho King of Egypt came vp to fight against Carchemish by Perath, and Iosiah went out against him.

21 But he sent messengers to him, saying, What haue I to doe with thee, thou King of Iudah? I come not against thee this day, but against the house of mine enemie, and God commanded me to make haste: leaue of to come against God, which is with me, least he destroy thee.

22 But Iosiah would not turne his face from him, but changed his apparel to fight with him, and hearkened not vnto the wordes of Necho, which were of the mouth of God, but came to fight in the valley of Megiddo.

23 And the shooters shot at king Iosiah: then the King saide to his seruants, Cary me away, for I am very sicke.

24 So his seruants tooke him out of that charet, and put him in the seconde charet which he had, and when they had brought him to Ierusalem, he dyed, and was buryed in the sepulchres of his fathers: and all Iudah and Ierusalem mourned for Iosiah.

25 And Ieremiah lamented Iosiah, and al singing men and singing women mourned for Iosiah in their lamentations to this day, and made the same for an ordinance vnto Israel: and beholde, they be written in the lamentations.

26 Concerning the rest of the actes of Iosiah and his goodnesse, doing as it was written in the Lawe of the Lord,

27 And his deedes, first and last, behold, they are written in the booke of the Kings of Israel and Iudah.

Second Chronicles 36

1 Then the people of the lande tooke Iehoahaz the sonne of Iosiah, and made him king in his fathers steade in Ierusalem.

2 Iehoahaz was three and twentie yeere old when he began to reigne, and he reigned three moneths in Ierusalem.

3 And the King of Egypt tooke him away at Ierusalem, and condemned the lande in an hundreth talents of siluer, and a talent of gold.

4 And the King of Egypt made Eliakim his brother King ouer Iudah and Ierusalem, and turned his name to Iehoiakim: and Necho tooke Iehoahaz his brother, and caryed him to Egypt.

5 Iehoiakim was fiue and twentie yeere old, when he began to reigne, and he reigned eleuen yeere in Ierusalem, and did euill in the sight of the Lord his God.

6 Against him came vp Nebuchadnezzar King of Babel, and bounde him with chaines to cary him to Babel.

7 Nebuchadnezzar also caryed of the vessels of the house of the Lord to Babel, and put them in his temple at Babel.

8 Concerning the rest of the actes of Iehoiakim, and his abominations which he did, and that which was founde vpon him, behold, they are written in the booke of the Kings of Israel and Iudah, and Iehoiachin his sonne reigned in his stead.

9 Iehoiachin was eight yeere olde when he beganne to reigne, and he reigned three moneths and ten dayes in Ierusalem, and did euill in the sight of the Lord.

10 And when the yeere was out, King Nebuchadnezzar sent and brought him to Babel with the precious vessels of the house of the Lord, and he made Zedekiah his brother King ouer Iudah and Ierusalem.

11 Zedekiah was one and twentie yeere olde, when he beganne to reigne, and reigned eleuen yeere in Ierusalem.

12 And he did euill in the sight of the Lord his God, and humbled not himselfe before Ieremiah the Prophet at the commandement of the Lord,

13 But he rebelled moreouer against Nebuchadnezzar, which had caused him to sweare by God: and he hardened his necke and made his heart obstinate that he might not returne to the Lord God of Israel.

14 All the chiefe of the Priestes also and of the people trespassed wonderfully, according to all the abominations of the heathen, and polluted the house of the Lord which he had sanctified in Ierusalem.

15 Therefore the Lord God of their fathers sent to them by his messengers, rising earely and sending: for he had compassion on his people, and on his habitation.

16 But they mocked the messengers of God and despised his wordes, and misused his Prophets, vntill the wrath of the Lord arose against his people, and till there was no remedie.

17 For he brought vpon them the King of the Caldeans, who slewe their yong men with the sworde in the house of their Sanctuarie, and spared neither yong man, nor virgin, ancient, nor aged. God gaue all into his hande,

18 And all the vessels of the house of God great and small, and the treasures of the house of the Lord, and the treasures of the King, and of his princes: all these caryed he to Babel.

19 And they burnt the house of God, and brake downe the wall of Ierusalem, and burnt all the palaces thereof with fire, and all the precious vessels thereof, to destroy all.

20 And they that were left by the sworde, caryed he away to Babel, and they were seruants to him and to his sonnes, vntill the kingdome of the Persians had rule,

21 To fulfill the worde of the Lord by the mouth of Ieremiah, vntill the lande had her fill of her Sabbaths: for all the dayes that she lay desolate, she kept Sabbath, to fulfill seuentie yeeres.

22 But in the first yeere of Cyrus King of Persia (when the worde of the Lord, spoken by the mouth of Ieremiah, was finished) the Lord stirred vp the spirit of Cyrus King of Persia, and he made a proclamation through all his kingdome, and also by writing, saying,

23 Thus saith Cyrus King of Persia, All the kingdomes of the earth hath the Lord God of heauen giuen me, and hath commanded me to build him an house in Ierusalem, that is in Iudah. Who is among you of all his people, with whom the Lord his God is? let him goe vp.

Ezra

Ezra 1

1 Nowe in the first yere of Cyrus King of Persia (that the worde of the Lord, spoken by the mouth of Ieremiah, might be accomplished) the Lord stirred vp the spirite of Cyrus King of Persia, and hee made a Proclamation thorowe all his Kingdome, and also by writing, saying,

2 Thus saith Cyrus King of Persia, The Lord God of heauen hath giuen me all the kingdomes of the earth, and he hath commanded me to builde him an house in Ierusalem, which is in Iudah.

3 Who is he among you of all his people with whome his God is? let him goe vp to Ierusalem which is in Iudah, and buylde the house of the Lord God of Israel: he is the God, which is in Ierusalem.

4 And euery one that remayneth in any place (where he soiourneth) let the men of his place relieue him with siluer and with golde, and with substance, and with cattel, and with a willing offring, for the house of God that is in Ierusalem.

5 Then the chiefe fathers of Iudah and Beniamin, and the Priests and Leuites rose vp, with al them whose spirit God had raysed to goe vp, to builde the house of the Lord which is in Ierusalem.

6 And all they that were about them, strengthened their handes with vessels

of siluer, with golde, with substance and with cattell, and with precious thinges, besides all that was willingly offred.

7 Also the King Cyrus brought forth the vessels of the house of the Lord, which Nebuchadnezzar had taken out of Ierusalem, and had put them in the house of his god.

8 Euen them did Cyrus King of Persia bring forth by the hand of Mithredath the treasurer, and counted them vnto Sheshbazzar the Prince of Iudah.

9 And this is the nomber of them, thirtie basins of golde, a thousand basins of siluer, nine and twentie kniues,

10 Thirtie boules of gold, and of siluer boules of the second sort, foure hundreth and tenne, and of other vessels, a thousand.

11 All the vessels of golde and siluer were fiue thousand and foure hundreth. Sheshbazzar brought vp all with them of the captiuitie that came vp from Babel to Ierusalem.

Ezra 2

1 These also are the sonnes of the prouince, that went vp out of the captiuitie (whome Nebuchadnezzar King of Babel had caried away vnto Babel) and returned to Ierusalem, and to Iudah, euery one vnto his citie,

2 Which came with Zerubbabel, to wit, Ieshua, Nehemiah, Seraiah, Reelaiah, Mordecai, Bilshan, Mispar, Biguai, Rehum, Baanah. The number of the men of the people of Israel was,

3 The sonnes of Parosh, two thousand, an hudreth seuentie and two:

4 The sonnes of Shephatiah, three hundreth, seuentie and two:

5 The sonnes of Arah, seuen hundreth, and seuentie and fiue:

6 The sonnes of Pahath Moab, of the sonnes of Ieshua and Ioab, two thousand, eight hundreth and twelue:

7 The sonnes of Elam, a thousande, two hundreth and foure and fiftie:

8 The sonnes of Zattu, nine hundreth and fiue and fourtie:

9 The sonnes of Zaccai, seuen hundreth and threescore:

10 The sonnes of Bani, sixe hundreth and two and fourtie:

11 The sonnes of Bebai, sixe hundreth, and three and twentie:

12 The sonnes of Azgad a thousand, two hundreth and two and twentie:

13 The sonnes of Adonikam, sixe hundreth, three score and sixe:

14 The sonnes of Biguai, two thousand, and sixe and fiftie:

15 The sonnes of Adin, foure hundreth and foure and fiftie:

16 The sonnes of Ater of Hizkiah, ninetie and eight:

17 The sonnes of Bezai, three hundreth and three and twentie:

18 The sonnes of Iorah, an hudreth and twelue:

19 The sonnes of Hasshum, two hundreth and three and twentie:

20 The sonnes of Gibbar, ninetie and fiue:

21 The sonnes of Beth-lehem, an hundreth and three and twentie:

22 The men of Netophah, sixe and fiftie:

23 The men of Anothoth, an hundreth and eight and twentie:

24 The sonnes of Azmaueth, two and fourtie:

25 The sonnes of Kiriath-arim, of Chephirah, and Beeroth, seuen hundreth and three and fourtie:

26 The sonnes of Haramah and Gaba, six hundreth, and one and twentie:

27 The men of Michmas, an hundreth and two and twentie:

28 The sonnes of Beth-el and Ai, two hundreth, and three and twentie:

29 The sonnes of Nebo, two and fiftie:

30 The sonnes of Magbish, an hundreth and sixe and fiftie:

31 The sonnes of the other Elam, a thousand, and two hundreth, and foure and fiftie:

32 The sonnes of Harim, three hundreth and twentie:

33 The sonnes of Lod-hadid, and Ono, seuen hundreth, and fiue and twentie:

34 The sonnes of Iericho, three hundreth and fiue and fourtie:

35 The sonnes of Senaah, three thousand, six hundreth and thirtie.

36 The Priests: of the sonnes of Iedaiah of the house of Ieshua, nine hundreth seuentie and three:

37 The sonnes of Immer, a thousand and two and fiftie:

38 The sonnes of Pashur, a thousand, two hundreth and seuen and fourtie:

39 The sonnes of Harim, a thousande and seuenteene:

40 The Leuites: the sonnes of Ieshua, and Kadmiel of the sonnes of Hodauiah, seuentie and foure.

41 The Singers: the sonnes of Asaph, an hundreth and eight and twentie.

42 The sonnes of the porters: the sonnes of Shallum, the sonnes of Ater, the sonnes of Talmon, the sonnes of Akkub, the sonnes of Hatita, the sonnes of Shobai: all were an hundreth and nine and thirtie.

43 The Nethinims: the sonnes of Ziha, the sonnes of Hasupha, the sonnes of Tabbaoth,

44 The sonnes of Keros, the sonnes of Siaha, the sonnes of Padon,

45 The sonnes of Lebanah, the sonnes of Hagabah, the sonnes of Akkub,

46 The sonnes of Hagab, the sonnes of Shamlai, the sonnes of Hanan,

47 The sonnes of Giddel, the sonnes of Gahar, the sonnes of Reaiah,

48 The sonnes of Rezin, the sonnes of Nekoda, the sonnes of Gazzam,

49 The sonnes of Vzza, the sonnes of Paseah, the sonnes of Besai,

50 The sonnes of Asnah, the sonnes of Meunim, the sonnes of Nephusim,

51 The sonnes of Bakbuk, the sonnes of Hakupa, the sonnes of Harhur,

52 The sonnes of Bazluth, the sonnes of Mehida, the sonnes of Harsha,

53 The sonnes of Barcos, the sonnes of Sisara, the sonnes of Thamah,

54 The sonnes of Neziah, the sonnes of Hatipha,

55 The sonnes of Salomons seruantes: the sonnes of Sotai, the sonnes of Sophereth, the sonnes of Peruda,

56 The sonnes of Iaalah, the sonnes of Darkon, the sonnes of Giddel,

57 The sonnes of Shephatiah, the sonnes of Hattil, the sonnes of Pochereth Hazzebaim, the sonnes of Ami.

58 All the Nethinims, and the sonnes of Salomons seruants were three hundreth ninetie and two.

59 And these went vp from Telmelah, and from Telharsha, Cherub, Addan, and Immer, but they could not discerne their fathers house and their seede, whether they were of Israel.

60 The sonnes of Delaiah, the sonnes of Tobiah, the sonnes of Nekoda, six hundreth and two and fiftie.

61 And of the sonnes of the Priestes, the sonnes of Habaiah, the sonnes of Coz, the sonnes of Barzillai: which tooke of the daughters of Barzillai the Giliadite to wife, and was called after their name.

62 These sought their writing of the genealogies, but they were not founde: therefore were they put from the Priesthood.

63 And Tirshatha saide vnto them, that they should not eate of the most holy thing, tell there rose vp a Priest with Vrim and Thummim.

64 The whole Congregation together was two and fourtie thousande, three hundreth and threescore,

65 Beside their seruants and their maydes: of whome were seuen thousande, three hundreth and seuen and thirtie: and among them were two hundreth singing men and singing women.

66 Their horses were seuen hundreth, and sixe and thirtie: their mules, two hundreth and fiue and fourtie:

67 Their camels foure hundreth, and fiue and thirtie: their asses, sixe thousand, seuen hundreth and twentie.

68 And certeine of the chiefe fathers, when they came to the house of the Lord, which was in Ierusalem, they offred willingly for the house of God, to set it vp vpon his fundation.

69 They gaue after their abilitie vnto the treasure of the worke, euen one and threescore thousand drammes of golde, and fiue thousand pieces of siluer, and an hundreth Priests garments.

70 So the Priests and the Leuites, and a certeine of the people, the singers, and the porters, and the Nethinims dwelt in their cities, and all Israel in their cities.

Ezra 3

1 And when the seuenth moneth was come, and the children of Israel were in their cities, the people assembled themselues as one man vnto Ierusalem.

2 Then stoode vp Ieshua rhe sonne of Iozadak, and his brethren the Priests, and Zerubbabel the sonne of Shealtiel, and his brethren, and builded the altar of the God of Israel, to offer burnt

offerings thereon, as it is written in ye Lawe of Moses the man of God,

3 And they set the altar vpon his bases (for feare was among them, because of the people of those countreis) therefore they offered burnt offrings thereon vnto the Lord, euen burnt offrings in the morning, and at euen.

4 They kept also the feast of the Tabernacles, as it is written, and the burnt offring dayly, by number according to the custome day by day,

5 And afterwarde the continuall bnrnt offring, both in the newe moneths and in all the feast dayes that were consecrate vnto the Lord, and in all the oblations willingly offered vnto the Lord.

6 From the first day of the seuenth moneth began they to offer burnt offrings vnto the Lord: but the foundation of the Temple of the Lord was not layed.

7 They gaue money also vnto the masons, and to the workemen, and meat and drinke, and oyle vnto them of Zidon and of Tyrus, to bring them cedar wood from Lebanon to the sea vnto Iapho, according to the graunt that they had of Cyrus King of Persia.

8 And in the seconde yeere of their comming vnto the house of God in Ierusalem in the second moneth began Zerubbabel the sonne of Shealtiel, and Ieshua the sonne of Iozadak, and the remnant of their brethren the Priests and the Leuites, and all they that were come out of the captiuitie vnto Ierusalem, and appointed the Leuites from twentie yeere olde and aboue, to set forwarde the worke of the house of the Lord.

9 And Ieshua stood with his sonnes, and his brethren, and Kadmiel with his sonnes, and the sonnes of Iudah together to set forward ye workemen in the house of God, and the sonnes of Henadad with their sonnes, and their brethren the Leuites.

10 And when the builders layed the foundation of the Temple of the Lord, they appoynted the Priestes in their apparel with trumpets, and the Leuites the sonnes of Asaph with cymbales, to prayse the Lord, after the ordinance of Dauid King of Israel.

11 Thus they sang when they gaue prayse, and when they gaue thankes vnto the Lord, For he is good, for his mercie endureth for euer toward Israel. And all the people shouted with a great shoute, when they praysed the Lord, because the foundation of the house of the Lord was layed.

12 Many also of the Priests and the Leuites and the chiefe of the fathers, ancient men which had seene the first house, (when the foundation of this house was layed before their eyes) wept with a loud voyce, and many shouted aloud for ioy,

13 So that the people coulde not discerne the sound of the shoute for ioy, from the noyse of the weeping of the people: for the people shouted with a loude crie, and the noyse was heard farre off.

Ezra 4

1 Bvt the aduersaries of Iudah and Beniamin heard, that the children of the captiuitie builded the Temple vnto the Lord God of Israel.

2 And they came to Zerubbabel, and to the chiefe fathers, and sayd vnto them, We wil builde with you: for we seeke the Lord your God as ye do, and we haue sacrificed vnto him since the time of Esar Haddon king of Asshur, which brought vs vp hither.

3 Then Zerubbabel, and Ieshua, and the rest of the chiefe fathers of Israel, sayde vnto them, It is not for you, but for vs to buyld the house vnto our God: for we our selues together wil buylde it vnto the Lord God of Israel, as king Cyrus the king of Persia hath commanded vs.

4 Wherefore the people of the land discouraged the people of Iudah, and troubled them in buylding,

5 And they hired counsellers against them, to hinder their deuise, all the dayes of Cyrus King of Persia, euen vntill the reigne of Darius King of Persia.

6 And in the reigne of Ahashuerosh (in the beginning of his reigne) wrote they an accusation against the inhabitants of Iudah and Ierusalem.

7 And in the daies of Artahshashte, Mithredath, Tabeel, and the rest of their companions wrote when it was peace, vnto Artahshashte king of Persia, and the writing of the letter was the Aramites writing, and the thing declared was in the language of the Aramites.

8 Rehum the chancelour, and Shimshai the scribe wrote a letter against Ierusalem to Artahshashte the King, in this sort.

9 Then wrote Rehum the chauncelour, and Shimshai the scribe, and their companions Dinaie, and Apharsathcaie, Tarpelaie, Apharsaie, Archeuaie, Bablaie, Shushanchaie, Dehaue, Elmaie,

10 And the rest of the people whom the great and noble Asnappar brought ouer, and set in the cities of Samaria, and other that are beyonde the Riuer and Cheeneth.

11 This is the copie of the letter that they sent vnto King Artahshashte, THY SERVANTS the men beyond the Riuer and Cheeneth, salute thee.

12 Be it knowen vnto the King that ye Iewes, which came vp from thee to vs, are come vnto Ierusalem (a citie rebellious and wicked) and buylde, and lay the foundations of the walles, and haue ioyned the foundations.

13 Be it knowen nowe vnto the King, that if this citie be built, and the foundations of the walles layed, they will not giue tolle, tribute, nor custome: so shalt thou hinder the Kings tribute.

14 Nowe therefore because wee haue bene brought vp in the Kings palace, it was not meete for vs to see the Kings dishonour: for this cause haue we sent and certified the King,

15 That one may searche in the booke of the Chronicles of thy fathers, and thou shalt finde in the booke of the Chronicles, and perceiue that this citie is rebellious and noysome vnto Kings and prouinces, and that they haue moued sedition of olde time, for the which cause this citie was destroyed.

16 Wee certifie the King therefore, that if this citie be buylded, and the foundation of the walles layd, by this meanes the portion beyonde the Riuer shall not be thine.

17 The King sent an answere vnto Rehum the Chauncelour, and Shimshai the Scribe, and so the rest of their companions that dwelt in Samaria, and vnto the other beyond the Riuer, Shelam and Cheeth.

18 The letter which yee sent vnto vs, hath bene openly read before me,

19 And I haue commanded and they haue searched, and founde, that this citie of olde time hath made insurrection against kings, and hath rebelled, and rebellion hath bene committed therein.

20 There haue bene mightie kings also ouer Ierusalem, which haue ruled ouer all beyonde the Riuer, and tolle, tribute, and custome was giuen vnto them.

21 Make ye now a decree, that those men may cease, and that the citie be not buylt, till I haue giuen another commandement.

22 Take heede nowe that ye fayle not to doe this: why should domage grow to hurt the King?

23 When the copie of king Artahshashtes letter was read before Rehum and Shimshai the scribe, and their companions, they went vp in all the haste to Ierusalem vnto the Iewes, and caused them to cease by force and power.

24 Then ceased the worke of the house of God, which was in Ierusalem, and did stay vnto the second yeere of Darius King of Persia.

Ezra 5

1 Then Haggai a Prophet and Zechariah the sonne of Iddo a Prophet prophecied vnto the Iewes that were in Iudah, and Ierusalem, in the name of the God of Israel, euen vnto them.

2 Then Zerubbabel the sonne of Shealtiel, and Ieshua the sonne of Iozadak arose, and began to builde the house of God at Ierusalem, and with them were the Prophetes of God, which helped them.

3 At the same time came to them Tatnai, which was captaine beyonde the Riuer, and Shether-boznai and their companions, and sayd thus vnto them, Who hath giuen you commandement to buylde this house, and to lay the foundations of these walles?

4 Then sayde we vnto them after this maner, What are the names of the men that buylde this buylding?

5 But the eye of their God was vpon the Elders of the Iewes, that they coulde not cause them to cease, till the matter came to Darius: and then they answered by letters thereunto.

6 The copie of the letter, that Tatnai captaine beyond the Riuer, and Shetherboznai and his companions, Apharsechaie, (which were beyond the Riuer) sent vnto King Darius.

7 They sent a letter vnto him, wherein it was written thus, VNTO DARIVS the king, all peace.

8 Be it knowen vnto the King, that we went into the prouince of Iudea, to the house of the great God, which is builded with great stones, and beames are layde in the walles, and this worke is wrought speedily, and prospereth in their hands.

9 Then asked we those Elders, and sayd vnto them thus, Who hath giuen you commandement to buylde this house, and to lay the foundation of these walles?

10 We asked their names also, that we might certifie thee, and that we might write the names of the men that were their rulers.

11 But they answered vs thus, and sayd, We are the seruants of the God of heauen and earth, and buylde the house that was buylt of olde and many yeeres ago, which a great King of Israel builded, and founded it.

12 But after that our fathers had prouoked the God of heauen vnto wrath, he gaue them ouer into the hand of Nebuchadnezzar King of Babel the Caldean, and he destroyed this house, and caryed the people away captiue vnto Babel.

13 But in the first yere of Cyrus King of Babel, King Cyrus made a decree to buylde this house of God.

14 And the vessels of golde and siluer of the house of God, which Nebuchadnezzar tooke out of the Temple, that was in Ierusalem, and brought them into the Temple of Babel, those did Cyrus the king take out of the Temple of Babel, and they gaue them vnto one Sheshbazzar by his name, whome he had made captaine.

15 And he sayde vnto him, Take these vessels and goe thy way, and put them in the Temple that is in Ierusalem, and let the house of God be buylt in his place.

16 Then came the same Sheshbazzar and layde the foundation of the house of God, which is in Ierusalem, and since that time euen vntill nowe, hath it bene in buylding, yet is it not finished.

17 Nowe therefore if it please the King, let there be searche made in the house of the Kings treasures, which is there in Babel, whether a decree hath bene made by King Cyrus, to build this house of God in Ierusalem, and let the King send his minde concerning this.

Ezra 6

1 Then King Darius gaue commandement, and they made search in the librarie of the treasures, which were there layd vp in Babel.

2 And there was founde in a coffer (in the palace that was in the prouince of the Medes) a volume, and therein was it thus written, as a memoriall,

3 IN THE FIRST yeere of King Cyrus, King Cyrus made a decree for the house of God in Ierusalem, Let the house be buylt, euen the place where they offred sacrifices, and let the walles thereof be ioyned together: let the height thereof be three score cubites, and the breadth thereof three score cubites,

4 Three orders of great stones, and one order of timber, and let the expenses be giuen of the Kings house.

5 And also let them render the vessels of the house of God (of golde and siluer, which Nebuchadnezzar tooke out of the Temple, which was in Ierusalem, and brought vnto Babel) and let him goe vnto the Temple that is in Ierusalem to his place, and put them in the house of God.

6 Therefore Tatnai captaine beyond the Riuer, and Shethar Boznai, (and their companions Apharsecaie, which are beyonde the Riuer) be ye farre from thence.

7 Suffer ye the worke of this house of God, that the captaine of the Iewes and the Elders of the Iewes may buylde this house of God in his place.

8 For I haue giuen a commandement what ye shall doe to the Elders of these Iewes, for the buylding of this house of God, that of the reuenues of the King, which is of the tribute beyonde the Riuer, there be incontinently expenses giuen vnto these men that they cease not.

9 And that which they shall haue neede of, let it be giuen vnto them day by day, whether it be yong bullockes, or rammes, or lambes for the burnt offrings of the God of heauen, wheate, salt, wine, and oyle, according to the appoyntment of the Priestes that are in Ierusalem, that there bee no fault,

10 That they may haue to offer sweete odours vnto the God of heauen, and praye for the Kings life, and for his sonnes.

11 And I haue made a decree, that whosoeuer shall alter this sentence, the wood shall be pulled downe from his house, and shall be set vp, and he shalbe hanged thereon, and his house shalbe made a dunghill for this.

12 And the God that hath caused his Name to dwell there, destroy all Kings and people that put to their hand to alter, and to destroy this house of God, which is in Ierusalem. I Darius haue made a decree, let it be done with speede.

13 Then Tatnai the captaine beyond the Riuer, and Shethar Boznai and their companions, according to that which Darius had sent, so they did speedily.

14 So the Elders of the Iewes builded, and they prospered by the prophecying of Haggai the Prophet, and Zechariah the sonne of Iddo, and they buylded and finished it, by the appoyntment of the God of Israel, and by the commandement of Cyrus and Darius, and Artahshashte king of Persia.

15 And this house was finished the thirde day of the moneth Adar, which was the sixt yeere of the reigne of King Darius.

16 And the children of Israel, the Priestes, and the Leuites, and the residue of the children of the captiuitie kept the dedication of this house of God with ioy,

17 And offred at the dedication of this house of God an hundreth bullockes, two hundreth rams, foure hundreth lambes, and twelue goates, for the sinne of all Israel, according to the nomber of the tribes of Israel.

18 And they set the Priests in their order, and the Leuites in their courses ouer the seruice of God in Ierusalem, as it is written in the booke of Moses.

19 And the childre of the captiuitie kept the Passeouer on ye fourtenth day of the first moneth.

20 (For the Priests and the Leuites were purified altogether) and they killed the Passeouer for all the children of the captiuitie, and for their brethren the Priests, and for themselues.

21 So the children of Israel which were come againe out of captiuitie, and all such as had separated themselues vnto them, from the filthines of the Heathen of the land, to seeke the Lord God of Israel, did eate,

22 And they kept ye feast of vnleauened bread seuen dayes with ioy: for the Lord had made them glad, and turned the heart of the King of Asshur vnto them, to incourage them in the worke of the house of God, euen the God of Israel.

Ezra 7

these things, in the reigne of Artahshashte King of Persia, was Ezra the sonne of Seraiah, the sonne of Azariah, the sonne of Hilkiah,

2 The sonne of Shallum, the sonne of Zadok, the sonne of Ahitub,

3 The sonne of Amariah, the sonne of Azariah, the sonne of Meraioth,

4 The sonne of Zeraiah, the sonne of Vzzi, the sonne of Bukki,

5 The sonne of Abishua, the sonne of Phinehas, the sonne of Eleazar, the sonne of Aaron, the chiefe Priest.

6 This Ezra came vp from Babel, and was a Scribe prompt in the Lawe of Moses, which the Lord God of Israel had giuen, and the King gaue him all his request according to the hande of the Lord his God which was vpon him.

7 And there went vp certaine of the children of Israel, and of the Priests, and the Leuites, and the singers, and the porters, and the Nethinims vnto Ierusalem, in the seuenth yere of King Artahshashte.

8 And hee came to Ierusalem in the fift moneth, which was in the seuenth yeere of the King.

9 For vpon the first day of the first moneth began he to goe vp from Babel, and on the first day of the fift moneth came he to Ierusalem, according to the good hande of his God that was vpon him.

10 For Ezra had prepared his heart to seeke the Lawe of the Lord, and to doe it, and to teach the precepts and iudgements in Israel.

11 And this is the copie of the letter that King Artahshashte gaue vnto Ezra the Priest and scribe, euen a writer of the words of the commadements of ye Lord, and of his statutes ouer Israel.

12 ARTAHSHASHTE King of Kings to Ezra the Priest and perfite scribe of the Lawe of the God of heauen, and to Cheeneth.

13 I haue giuen commandement, that euery one, that is willing in my kingdome of the people of Israel, and of the Priestes, and Leuites to goe to Ierusalem with thee, shall goe.

14 Therefore art thou sent of the King and his seuen counsellers, to enquire in Iudah and Ierusalem, according to the lawe of thy God, which is in thine hand,

15 And to carry the siluer and the gold, which the King and his cousellers willingly offer vnto the God of Israel (whose habitation is in Ierusalem)

16 And all the siluer and gold that thou canst finde in all the prouince of Babel, with the free offring of the people, and that which the Priestes offer willingly to the house of their God which is in Ierusalem,

17 That thou mayest bye speedily with this siluer, bullocks, rammes, lambes, with their meate offrings and their drinke offrings: and thou shalt offer them vpon the altar of the house of your God, which is in Ierusalem.

18 And whatsoeuer it pleaseth thee and thy brethren to do with the rest of the siluer, and gold, doe ye it according to the will of your God.

19 And the vessels that are giuen thee for the seruice of the house of thy God, those deliuer thou before God in Ierusalem.

20 And the residue that shall be needeful for the house of thy God, which shall be meete for thee to bestowe, thou shalt bestowe it out of the Kings treasure house,

21 And I King Artahshashte haue giuen commandemet to all the treasurers which are beyond the Riuer, that whatsoeuer Ezra the Priest and Scribe of the Law of the God of heauen shall require of you, that it be done incontinently,

22 Vnto an hundreth talents of siluer, vnto an hundreth measures of wheate, and vnto an hundreth baths of wine, and vnto an hundreth baths of oyle, and salt without writing.

23 Whatsoeuer is by the commandement of the God of heauen, let it be done speedily for the house of the God of heauen: for why should he be wroth against the realme of the King, and his children?

24 And we certifie you, that vpon any of the Priestes, Leuites, singers, porters, Nethinims, or Ministers in this house of God, there shall no gouernour laye vpon them tolle, tribute nor custome.

25 And thou Ezra (after the wisedome of thy God, that is in thine hand) set iudges and arbiters, which may iudge all the people that is beyond the Riuer, euen all that knowe the Lawe of thy God, and teach ye them that know it not.

26 And whosoeuer will not doe the Lawe of thy God, and the Kings lawe, let him haue iudgement without delay, whether it be vnto death, or to banishment, or to confiscation of goods, or to imprisonment.

27 Blessed be the Lord God of our fathers, which so hath put in the Kings heart, to beautifie the house of the Lord that is in Ierusalem,

28 And hath enclined mercy toward me, before the King and his counsellers, and before all the Kings mightie Princes: and I was comforted by the hand of the Lord my God which was vpon me, and I gathered the chiefe of Israel to goe vp with me.

Ezra 8

1 These are now the chiefe fathers of them, and the genealogie of them that came vp with mee from Babel, in the reigne of King Artahshashte.

2 Of the sonnes of Phinehas, Gershom: of the sonnes of Ithamar, Daniel: of the sonnes of Dauid, Hattush:

3 Of the sonnes of Shechaniah, of the sonnes of Pharosh, Zechariah, and with him the count of the males, an hundreth and fiftie.

4 Of the sonnes of Pahath Moab, Elihoenai, the sonne of Zerahiah, and with him two hundreth males.

5 Of the sonnes of Shechaniah, the sonne of Iahaziel, and with him three hundreth males.

6 And of the sonnes of Adin, Ebed the sonne of Ionathan, and with him fiftie males.

7 And of the sonnes of Elam, Ieshaiah the sonne of Athaliah, and with him seuentie males.

8 And of the sonnes of Shephatiah, Zebadiah the sonne of Michael, and with him fourescore males.

9 Of the sonnes of Ioab, Obadiah the sonne of Iehiel, and with him two hundreth and eighteene males.

10 And of the sonnes of Shelomith the sonne of Iosiphiah, and with him an hundreth and threescore males.

11 And of the sonnes of Bebai, Zechariah the sonne of Bebai, and with him eight and twentie males.

12 And of the sonnes of Azgad, Iohanan the sonne of Hakkatan, and with him an hundreth and ten males.

13 And of the sonnes of Adonikam, that were the last, whose names are these: Eliphelet, Iehiel and Shemaiah, and with them three score males.

14 And of the sonnes of Biguai, Vthai, and Zabbud, and with them seuentie males.

15 And I gathered them to the Riuer that goeth toward Ahaua, and there abode we three dayes: then I viewed the people,

and the Priests, and found there none of the sonnes of Leui.

16 Therefore sent I to Eliezer, to Ariel, to Shemeiah, and to Elnathan, and to Iarib, and to Elnathan, and to Nathan, and to Zechariah, and to Meshullam the chiefe, and to Ioiarib and to Elnathan, men of vnderstanding,

17 And I gaue them commandement, to Iddo the chiefest at the place of Casiphia, and I told them the words that they should speake to Iddo, and to his brethren the Nethinims at the place of Casiphia, that they should cause the ministers of the house of our God to come vnto vs.

18 So by the good hande of our God which was vpon vs, they brought vs a man of vnderstanding of the sonnes of Mahali the sonne of Leui the sonne of Israel, and Sherebiah with his sonnes and his brethren, euen eighteene.

19 Also Hashabiah, and with him Ieshaiah of the sonnes of Merari, with his brethren, and their sonnes twentie.

20 And of the Nethinims, whom Dauid had set, and the Princes for the seruice of the Leuites, two hundreth and twentie of the Nethinims, which all were named by name.

21 And there at the Riuer, by Ahaua, I proclaimed a fast, that we might humble our selues before our God, and seeke of him a right way for vs, and for our children, and for all our substance.

22 For I was ashamed to require of the King an armie and horsemen, to helpe vs against the enemie in the way, because we had spoken to the King, saying, The hande of our God is vpon all them that seeke him in goodnesse, but his power and his wrath is against all them that forsake him.

23 So we fasted, aud besought our God for this: and he was intreated of vs.

24 Then I separated twelue of the chiefe of the Priests, Sherebiah, and Hashabiah, and ten of their brethren with them,

25 And weighed them the siluer and the gold, and the vessels, euen the offring of ye house of our God, which the King and his counselers, and his Princes, and all Israel that were present had offred.

26 And I weighed vnto their hand sixe hundreth and fiftie talents of siluer, and in siluer vessel, an hundreth talents, and in golde, an hundreth talents:

27 And twentie basins of golde, of a thousand drammes, and two vessels of shining brasse very good, and precious as golde.

28 And I said vnto them, Ye are consecrate vnto the Lord, and the vessels are consecrate, and the gold and the siluer are freely offred vnto the Lord God of your fathers.

29 Watch ye, and keepe them vntill ye weigh them before the chiefe Priestes and the Leuites, and the chiefe fathers of Israel in Ierusalem in the chambers of the house of the Lord.

30 So the Priests and the Leuites receiued the weight of the siluer and of the golde, and of the vessels to bring

them to Ierusalem, vnto the house of our God.

31 Then we departed from the Riuer of Ahauah on the twelft day of the first moneth, to go vnto Ierusalem, and the hand of our God was vpon vs, and deliuered vs from the hand of the enemie, and of such as layde waite by the way.

32 And we came to Ierusalem, and abode there three dayes.

33 And on ye fourth day was the siluer weighed, and the golde and the vessell in the house of our God by the hand of Meremoth the sonne of Vriah the Priest, and with him was Eleazar the sonne of Phinehas, and with them was Iozabad the sonne of Ieshua, and Noadiah the sonne of Binnui the Leuites,

34 By number and by weight of euery one, and all the weight was written at the same time.

35 Also the children of the captiuitie, which were come out of captiuitie, offred burnt offrings vnto the God of Israel, twelue bullockes for all Israel, ninetie and sixe rammes, seuentie and seuen lambes, and twelue hee goates for sinne: all was a burnt offring of the Lord.

36 And they deliuered the Kings commission vnto the Kings officers, and to the captaines beyond the Riuer: and they promoted the people, and the house of God.

Ezra 9

1 When as these things were done, the rulers came to me, saying, The people of Israel, and the Priestes, and the Leuites are not separated from the people of the lands (as touching their abominations) to wit, of the Canaanites, the Hittites, the Perizzites, the Iebusites, the Ammonites, the Moabites, the Egyptians, and the Amorites.

2 For they haue taken their daughters to theselues, and to their sonnes, and they haue mixed the holy seede with the people of the landes, and the hande of the princes and rulers hath bene chiefe in this trespasse.

3 But when I heard this saying, I rent my clothes and my garment, and pluckt off the heare of mine head, and of my beard, and sate downe astonied.

4 And there assembled vnto me all that feared the words of the God of Israel, because of the transgression of them of the captiuitie. And I sate downe astonied vntil the euening sacrifice.

5 And at the euening sacrifice I arose vp from mine heauinesse, and when I had rent my clothes and my garment, I fell vpon my knees, and spred out mine hands vnto the Lord my God,

6 And said, O my God, I am confounded and ashamed, to lift vp mine eyes vnto thee my God: for our iniquities are increased ouer our head, and our trespasse is growen vp vnto the heauen.

7 From the dayes of our fathers haue we bin in a great trespasse vnto this day, and for our iniquities haue we, our Kings, and our Priestes bene deliuered

into the hand of the kings of the lands, vnto the sword, into captiuitie, into a spoyle, and into confusion of face, as appeareth this day.

8 And now for a litle space grace hath bene shewed from the Lord our God, in causing a remnant to escape, and in giuing vs a nayle in his holy place, that our God may light our eyes, and giue vs a litle reuiuing in our seruitude.

9 For though we were bondmen, yet our God hath not forsaken vs in our bondage, but hath enclined mercy vnto vs in the sight of the Kings of Persia, to giue vs life, and to erect the house of our God, and to redresse the places thereof, and to giue vs a wall in Iudah and in Ierusalem.

10 And nowe, our God, what shall we say after this? for we haue forsaken thy commandements,

11 Which thou hast commanded by thy seruants the Prophets, saying, The land whereunto ye go to possesse it, is an vncleane land, because of the filthines of the people of the lands, which by their abominations, and by their vncleannes haue filled it from corner to corner.

12 Now therfore shall ye not giue your daughters vnto their sonnes, neither shall ye take their daughters vnto your sonnes, nor seeke their peace nor wealth for euer, that yee may be strong and eate the goodnes of the lande, and leaue it for an inheritance to your sonnes for euer.

13 And after all that is come vpon vs for our euill deedes, and for our great trespasses, (seeing that thou our God hast stayed vs from being beneath for our iniquities, and hast giuen vs such deliuerance)

14 Should we returne to breake thy commadements, and ioyne in affinitie with the people of such abominations? wouldest not thou be angrie towarde vs till thou haddest consumed vs, so that there should be no remnant nor any escaping?

15 O Lord God of Israel, thou art iust, for we haue bene reserued to escape, as appeareth this day: beholde, we are before thee in our trespasse: therfore we canot stand before thee because of it.

Ezra 10

1 Whiles Ezra prayed thus, and confessed himselfe weeping, and falling downe before the house of God, there assembled vnto him of Israel a very great Congregation of men and women and children: for the people wept with a great lamentation.

2 Then Shechaniah the sonne of Iehiel one of the sonnes of Elam answered, and sayd to Ezra, We haue trespassed against our God, and haue taken strange wiues of the people of the land, yet nowe there is hope in Israel concerning this.

3 Now therfore let vs make a couenant with our God, to put away all the wiues (and such as are borne of them) according to the counsell of the Lord, and of those that feare the

commandements of our God, and let it be done according to the Lawe.

4 Arise: for the matter belogeth vnto thee: we also wil be with thee: be of comfort and do it.

5 Then arose Ezra, and caused the chiefe Priestes, the Leuites, and all Israel, to sweare that they would doe according to this worde. So they sware.

6 And Ezra rose vp from before the house of God, and went into the chamber of Iohanan the sonne of Eliashib: he went euen thither, but he did eate neither bread, nor drunke water: for he mourned, because of the transgression of them of the captiuitie.

7 And they caused a proclamation to goe throughout Iudah and Ierusalem, vnto all them of the captiuitie, that they should assemble themselues vnto Ierusalem.

8 And whosoeuer woulde not come within three dayes according to the counsel of the Princes and Elders, all his substance should be forfait, and he should be separate from the Congregation of them of the captiuitie.

9 Then all the men of Iudah and Beniamin assembled theselues vnto Ierusalem within three dayes, which was the twentieth day of the ninth moneth, and all the people sate in the streete of the house of God, trembling for this matter, and for the raine.

10 And Ezra the Priest stoode vp, and said vnto them, Ye haue transgressed, and haue taken strange wiues, to increase the trespasse of Israel.

11 Now therefore giue praise vnto the Lord God of your fathers, and do his will, and separate your selues from the people of the land, and from the strange wiues.

12 And all the Congregation answered, and sayd with a loude voyce, So will we do according to thy wordes vnto vs.

13 But the people are many, and it is a raynie weather, and we are not able to stande without, neither is it the worke of one day or two: for we are many that haue offended in this thing.

14 Let our rulers stand therefore before all the Congregation, and let all them which haue taken strange wiues in our cities, come at the time appoynted, and with them the Elders of euery citie and the Iudges thereof, til the fierce wrath of our God for this matter turne away from vs.

15 Then were appoynted Ionathan the sonne of Asah-el, and Iahaziah the sonne of Tikuah ouer this matter, and Meshullam and Shabbethai the Leuites helped them.

16 And they of the captiuitie did so, and departed, euen Ezra the Priest, and the men that were chiefe fathers to the familie of their fathers by name, and sate downe in the first day of the tenth moneth to examine the matter.

17 And vntill the first day of the first moneth they were finishing the businesse with al the men that had taken strange wiues.

18 And of the sonnes of the Priests there were men founde, that had taken

strange wiues, to wit, of the sonnes of Ieshua, the sonne of Iozadak, and of his brethren, Maaseiah, Aeliezer, and Iarib and Gedaliah.

19 And they gaue their hads, that they would put away their wiues, and they that had trespassed, gaue a ramme for their trespasse.

20 And of the sonnes of Immer, Honani, and Zebadiah.

21 And of the sonnes of Harim, Maaseiah, and Eliiah, and Shemaiah, and Iehiel, and Vzziah.

22 And of ye sonnes of Pashur, Elioenai, Maaseiah, Ishmael, Nethaneel, Iozabad, and Elasah.

23 And of the Leuites, Iozabad and Shimei, and Kelaiah, (which is Kelitah) Pethahiah, Iudah and Eliezer.

24 And of the singers, Eliashib. And of the porters, Shallum, and Telem, and Vri.

25 And of Israel: of the sonnes of Parosh, Ramiah, and Iesiah, and Malchiah, and Miamin, and Eleazar, and Malchiiah, and Benaiah.

26 And of the sonnes of Elam, Mattaniah, Zechariah, and Iehiel, and Abdi, and Ieremoth, and Eliah.

27 And of the sonnes of Zattu, Elioenai, Eliashib, Mattaniah, and Ierimoth, and Zabad, and Aziza.

28 And of the sonnes of Bebai, Iehohanan, Hananiah, Zabbai, Athlai.

29 And of the sonnes of Bani, Meshullam, Malluch, and Adaiah, Iashub, and Sheal, Ieramoth.

30 And of the sonnes of Pahath Moab, Adna, and Chelal, Benaiah, Maaseiah, Mattaniah, Bezaleel, and Binnui, and Manasseh.

31 And of the sonnes of Harim, Eliezer, Ishiiah, Malchiah, Shemaiah, Shimeon,

32 Beniamin, Malluch, Shamariah.

33 Of the sonnes of Hashum, Mattenai, Mattattah, Zabad, Eliphelet, Ieremai, Manasseh, Shimei.

34 Of the sonnes of Bani, Maadai, Amram, and Vel,

35 Banaiah, Bediah, Chelluh,

36 Vaniah, Meremoth, Eliashib,

37 Mattaniah, Mattenai, and Iaasau,

38 And Banni, and Bennui, Shimei,

39 And Shelemiah, and Nathan, and Adaiah,

40 Machnadebai, Shashai, Sharai,

41 Azareel, and Shelemiah, Shemariah,

42 Shallum, Amariah, Ioseph.

43 Of the sonnes of Nebo, Ieiel, Mattithiah, Zabad, Zebina, Iadau, and Ioel, Benaiah.

44 All these had taken strange wiues: and among them were women that had children.

Nehemiah

Nehemiah 1

1 The words of Nehemiah the sonne of Hachaliah. In ye moneth Chisleu, in the twentieth yeere, as I was in the palace of Shushan,

2 Came Hanam, one of my brethren, he and the men of Iudah, and I asked them concerning the Iewes that were deliuered, which were of the residue of the captiuitie, and concerning Ierusalem.

3 And they sayde vnto me, The residue that are left of the captiuitie there in the prouince, are in great affliction and in reproche, and the wall of Ierusalem is broken downe, and the gates thereof are burnt with fire.

4 And when I heard these wordes, I sate downe and wept, and mourned certeine dayes, and I fasted and prayed before the God of heauen,

5 And sayde, O Lord God of heauen, the great and terrible God, that keepeth couenant and mercy for them that loue him, and obserue his commandements,

6 I pray thee, let thine eares be attet, and thine eies open, to heare the praier of thy seruat, which I pray before thee dayly, day and night for ye childre of Israel thy seruats, and confesse the sinnes of the children of Israel, which we haue sinned against thee, both I and my fathers house haue sinned:

7 We haue grieuously sinned against thee, and haue not kept the commandements, nor the statutes, nor the iudgements, which thou commandedst thy seruant Moses.

8 I beseeche thee, remember the worde that thou commandedst thy seruant Moses, saying, Ye wil transgresse, and I will scatter you abroade among the people.

9 But if ye turne vnto me, and keepe my commandements, and doe them, though your scattering were to the vttermost part of the heauen, yet will I gather you from thence, and will bring you vnto the place that I haue chosen to place my Name there.

10 Now these are thy seruants and thy people, whome thou hast redeemed by thy great power, and by thy mightie hand.

11 O Lord, I beseech thee, let thine eare now hearken to the prayer of thy seruant, and to the prayer of thy seruants, who desire to feare thy Name, and I pray thee, cause thy seruant to prosper this day, and giue him fauour in the presence of this man: for I was the Kings butler.

Nehemiah 2

1 Nowe in the moneth Nisan in the twentieth yere of king Artahshashte, the wine stoode before him, and I tooke vp the wine, and gaue it vnto the King. nowe I was not before time sad in his presence.

2 And the king said vnto me, Why is thy coutenance sad, seeing thou art not sicke? this is nothing, but sorow of heart. Then was I sore afrayd,

3 And I said to the King, God saue the King for euer: why should not my countenance be sad, when the citie and house of the sepulchres of my fathers lieth waste, and the gates thereof are deuoured with fire?

4 And the King said vnto me, For what thing doest thou require? Then I prayed to the God of heauen,

5 And sayde vnto the King, If it please the King, and if thy seruant haue found fauour in thy sight, I desire that thou wouldest send me to Iudah vnto the city of the sepulchres of my fathers, that I may buyld it.

6 And the King sayd vnto me, (the Queene also sitting by him) How long shall thy iourney be? and when wilt thou come againe? So it pleased the King, and he sent me, and I set him a time.

7 After I saide vnto the King, If it please the King, let them giue mee letters to the captaines beyond the Riuer, that they may conuay me ouer, till I come into Iudah,

8 And letters vnto Asaph the keeper of the Kings parke, that hee may giue me timber to buylde the gates of the palace (which apperteined to the house) and for the walles of the citie, and for the house that I shall enter into. And the King gaue me according to the good hand of my God vpon me.

9 Then came I to the captaines beyonde the Riuer, and gaue them the Kings letters. And the King had sent captaines of the armie and horsemen with me.

10 But Sanballat the Horonite, and Tobiah a seruant an Ammonite heard it, and it grieued them sore, that there was come a man which sought the wealth of the children of Israel.

11 So I came to Ierusalem, and was there three dayes.

12 And I rose in the night, I, and a fewe men with me: for I told no man, what God had put in mine heart to do at Ierusalem, and there was not a beast with me, saue the beast whereon I rode.

13 And I went out by night by the gate of the valley, and came before the dragon well, and to the dung porte, and vewed the walles of Ierusalem, howe they were broken downe, and the portes thereof deuoured with the fire.

14 Then I went foorth vnto the gate of the fountaine, and to the Kings fishpoole, and there was no rowme for the beast that was vnder me to passe.

15 Then went I vp in ye night by the brooke, and viewed the wall, and turned backe, and comming backe, I entred by the gate of the valley and returned.

16 And the rulers knewe not whither I was gone, nor what I did, neither did I as yet tell it vnto the Iewes, nor to the Priestes, nor to the noble men, nor to the rulers, nor to the rest that laboured in the worke.

17 Afterward I said vnto them, Ye see the miserie that we are in, how Ierusalem lyeth waste, and the gates thereof are burnt with fire: come and let vs buylde the wall of Ierusalem, that we be no more a reproche.

18 Then I tolde them of the hande of my God, (which was good ouer me) and also of the Kings wordes that he had spoken vnto me. And they sayd, Let vs rise, and buyld. So they strengthened their hand to good.

19 But when Sanballat the Horonite, and Tobiah the seruant an Ammonite, and Geshem the Arabian heard it, they mocked vs and despised vs, and said, What a thing is this that ye doe? Will ye rebell against the King?

20 Then answered I them, and sayd to them, The God of heauen, he will prosper vs, and we his seruants will rise vp and buylde: but as for you, ye haue no portion nor right, nor memoriall in Ierusalem.

Nehemiah 3

1 Then arose Eliashib the hie Priest with his brethren the Priestes, and they buylt the sheepegate: they repayred it, and set vp the doores thereof: euen vnto the tower of Meah repayred they it, and vnto the tower of Hananeel.

2 And next vnto him buylded the men of Iericho, and beside him Zaccur the sonne of Imri.

3 But the fish port did the sonnes of Senaah buylde, which also layde the beames thereof, and set on the doores thereof, the lockes thereof, and the barres thereof.

4 And next vnto them fortified Merimoth, the sonne of Vrijah, the sonne of Hakkoz: and next vnto them fortified Meshullam, the sonne of Berechiah, the sonne of Meshezabeel: and next vnto them fortified Zadok, the sonne of Baana:

5 And next vnto them fortified the Tekoites: but the great men of them put not their neckes to the worke of their lordes.

6 And the gate of the olde fishpoole fortified Iehoiada the sonne of Paseah, and Meshullam the sonne of Besodaiah: they laid the beames thereof, and set on the doores thereof, and the lockes thereof, and the barres thereof.

7 Next vnto them also fortified Melatiah the Gibeonite, and Iadon the Meronothite, men of Gibeon, and of Mizpah, vnto the throne of the Duke, which was beyond the Riuer.

8 Next vnto him fortified Vzziel the sonne of Harhohiah of the golde smithes: next vnto him also fortified Hananiah, the sonne of Harakkahim, and they repayred Ierusalem vnto the broad wall.

9 Also next vnto them fortified Rephaiah, the sonne of Hur, the ruler of the halfe part of Ierusalem.

10 And next vnto him fortified Iedaiah the sonne of Harumaph, euen ouer against his house: and next vnto him fortified Hattush, the sonne of Hashabniah.

11 Malchiiah the sonne of Harim, and Hashub the sonne of Pahath Moab fortified the seconde porcion, and the tower of the fornaces.

12 Next vnto him also fortified Shallum, the sonne of Halloesh, the ruler of the halfe part of Ierusalem, he, and his daughters.

13 The valley gate fortified Hanum, and the inhabitants of Zanuah: they buylt it, and set on the doores thereof, the lockes thereof, and the barres thereof, euen a thousand cubites on the wall vnto the dung porte.

14 But the dung port fortified Malchiah, the sonne of Rechab, the ruler of the fourth part of Beth-haccarem: he built it, and set on the doores thereof, the lockes thereof, and the barres thereof.

15 But the gate of the fountaine fortified Shallun, the sonne of Col-hozeh, the ruler of the fourth part of Mizpah: he builded it, and couered it, and set on the doores thereof, the lockes thereof, and the barres thereof, and the wall vnto the fishpoole of Shelah by the Kings garden, and vnto the steppes that goe downe from the citie of Dauid.

16 After him fortified Nehemiah the sonne of Azbuk, the ruler of ye halfe part of Beth-zur, vntill the otherside ouer against the sepulchres of Dauid, and to the fishpoole that was repaired, and vnto the house of the mightie.

17 After him fortified the Leuites, Rehum the sonne of Bani, and next vnto him fortified Hashabiah the ruler of the halfe part of Keilah in his quarter.

18 After him fortified their brethren: Bauai, the sonne of Henadad the ruler of the halfe part of Keilah:

19 And next vnto him fortified Ezer, the sonne of Ieshua the ruler of Mizpah, the other portion ouer against the going vp to the corner of the armour.

20 After him was earnest Baruch the sonne of Zacchai, and fortified another portion from the corner vnto the doore of the house of Eliashib the hie Priest.

21 After him fortified Merimoth, the sonne of Vriiah, the sonne of Hakkoz, another portion from the doore of house of Eliashib, euen as long as the house of Eliashib extended.

22 After him also fortified the Priests, the men of the playne.

23 After them fortified Beniamin, and Hasshub ouer against their house: after him fortified Azariah, the sonne of Maaseiah, the sonne of Ananiah, by his house.

24 After him fortified Binnui, the sonne of Henadad another portion, from the house of Azariah vnto the turning and vnto the corner.

25 Palal, the sonne of Vzai, from ouer against the corner, and the high tower, that lieth out from the Kings house, which is beside the court of the prison. After him, Pedaiah, the sonne of Parosh.

26 And the Nethinims they dwelt in ye fortresse vnto the place ouer against the water gate, Eastwarde, and to the tower that lyeth out.

27 After him fortified the Tekoites another portion ouer against the great tower, that lyeth out, euen vnto the wall of the fortresse.

28 From aboue the horsegate forth fortified the Priests, euery one ouer against his house.

29 After them fortified Zadok the sonne of Immer ouer against his house: and after him fortified Shemaiah, the sonne of Shechadiah the keeper of the East gate.

30 After him fortified Hananiah, the sonne of Shelemiah, and Hanun, the sonne of Zalaph, the sixt, another portion after him fortified Meshullam, the sonne of Berechiah, ouer against his chamber.

31 After him fortified Malchiah the goldesmiths sonne, vntil the house of the Nethinims, and of ye marchants ouer against the gate Miphkad, and to the chamber in the corner.

32 And betweene the chamber of the corner vnto the sheepegate fortified the goldesmithes and the marchantes.

Nehemiah 4

1 But when Sanballat heard that we builded the wall, then was he wroth and sore grieued, and mocked the Iewes,

2 And sayde before his brethren and the armie of Samaria, thus he sayde, What doe these weake Iewes? wil they fortifie them selues? wil they sacrifice? will they finish it in a day? will they make the stones whole againe out of the heapes of dust, seeing they are burnt?

3 And Tobiah the Ammonite was beside him, and said, Although they buylde, yet if a foxe goe vp, he shall euen breake downe their stonie wall.

4 Heare, O our God (for we are despised) and turne their shame vpon their owne head, and giue them vnto a pray in the lande of their captiuitie,

5 And couer not their iniquitie, neither let their sinne be put out in thy presence: for they haue prouoked vs before the builders.

6 So we built the wall, and all the wall was ioyned vnto the halfe thereof, and the heart of the people was to worke.

7 But when Sanballat, and Tobiah, and the Arabians, and the Ammonites, and the Ashdodims heard that the walles of Ierusalem were repayred, (for the breaches began to be stopped) then they were very wroth,

8 And conspired all together to come and to fight against Ierusalem, and to hinder them.

9 The we prayed vnto our God, and set watchmen by them, day and night, because of them.

10 And Iudah said, The strength of the bearers is weakened, and there is much earth, so that we are not able to build the wall.

11 Also our aduersaries had sayde, They shall not knowe, neither see, till we come into the middes of them and slay them, and cause the worke to cease.

12 But when the Iewes (which dwelt beside them) came, they told vs ten times, From all places whence ye shall returne, they wil be vpon vs.

13 Therefore set I in the lower places behind the wall vpon the toppes of the stones, and placed the people by their families, with their swordes, their speares and their bowes.

14 Then I behelde, and rose vp, and said vnto the Princes, and to the rulers, and to the rest of the people, Be not afrayde of them: remember the great Lord, and

fearefull, and fight for your brethren, your sonnes, and your daughters, your wiues, and your houses.

15 And when our enemies heard that it was knowen vnto vs, then God brought their counsell to nought, and we turned all againe to the wall, euery one vnto his worke.

16 And from that day, halfe of the yong men did the labour, and the other halfe part of them helde the speares, and shieldes, and bowes, and habergins: and the rulers stoode behinde all the house of Iudah.

17 They that buylded on the wall, and they that bare burdens, and they that laded, did the worke with one hand, and with the other helde the sworde.

18 For euery one of the buylders had his swordegirded on his loynes, and so buylded: and he that blewe the trumpet, was beside me.

19 Then saide I vnto the Princes, and to the rulers, and to the rest of the people, The worke is great and large, and we are separated vpon the wall, one farre from another.

20 In what place therefore ye heare the sound of the trumpet, resort ye thither vnto vs: our God shall fight for vs.

21 So we laboured in the worke, and halfe of them helde the speares, from the appearing of the morning, till the starres came foorth.

22 And at the same time said I vnto the people, Let euery one with his seruant lodge within Ierusalem, that they may be a watch for vs in the night, and labour in the day.

23 So neither I, nor my brethren, nor my seruants, nor the men of the warde, (which followed me) none of vs did put off our clothes, saue euery one put them off for washing.

Nehemiah 5

1 Nowe there was a great crie of the people, and of their wiues against their brethren the Iewes.

2 For there were that said, We, our sonnes and our daughters are many, therefore we take vp corne, that we may eate and liue.

3 And there were that saide, We must gage our landes, and our vineyardes, and our houses, and take vp corne for the famine.

4 There were also that said, We haue borowed money for the Kings tribute vpon our landes and our vineyardes.

5 And nowe our flesh is as the flesh of our brethren, and our sonnes as their sonnes: and lo, we bring into subiection our sonnes and our daughters, as seruants, and there be of our daughters nowe in subiection, and there is no power in our handes: for other men haue our landes and our vineyardes.

6 Then was I very angrie when I heard their crie and these wordes.

7 And I thought in my minde, and I rebuked the princes, and the rulers, and saide vnto them, You lay burthens euery one vpon his brethren: and I set a great assemblie against them,

8 And I said vnto them, We (according to our abilitie) haue redeemed our brethren the Iewes, which were solde vnto the heathen: and will you sell your brethren againe, or shall they be solde vnto vs? Then helde they their peace, and could not answere.

9 I said also, That which ye do, is not good. Ought ye not to walke in the feare of our God, for the reproche of the heathen our enemies?

10 For euen I, my brethren, and my seruants doe lende them money and corne: I pray you, let vs leaue off this burden.

11 Restore, I pray you, vnto them this day their landes, their vineyardes, their oliues, and their houses, and remit the hundreth part of the siluer and of the corne, of the wine, and of the oyle that ye exact of them.

12 Then said they, We will restore it, and will not require it of them: we will doe as thou hast said. Then I called the Priestes, and caused them to sweare, that they shoulde doe according to this promise.

13 So I shooke my lappe, and said, So let God shake out euery man that wil not perfourme this promise from his house, and from his labour: euen thus let him be shaken out, and emptied. And all the Cogregation said, Amen, and praised the Lord: and the people did according to this promise.

14 And from the time that the King gaue me charge to be gouernour in the lande of Iudah, from the twentieth yeere, euen vnto the two and thirtieth yeere of King Artahshashte, that is, twelue yeere, I, and my brethren haue not eaten the bread of the gouernour.

15 For the former gouernours that were before me, had bene chargeable vnto the people, and had taken of them bread and wine, besides fourtie shekels of siluer: yea, and their seruants bare rule ouer the people: but so did not I, because of the feare of God.

16 But rather I fortified a portion in the worke of this wall, and we bought no lande, and all my seruants came thither together vnto the worke.

17 Moreouer there were at my table an hundreth and fiftie of the Iewes, and rulers, which came vnto vs from among the heathen that are about vs.

18 And there was prepared daily an oxe, and six chosen sheepe, and birdes were prepared for me, and within ten dayes wine for all in abundance. Yet for all this I required not the bread of the gouernour: for the bondage was grieuous vnto this people.

19 Remember me, O my God, in goodnesse, according to all that I haue done for this people.

Nehemiah 6

1 And when Sanballat, and Tobiah, and Geshem the Arabian, and the rest of our enemies heard that I had built the wall, and that there were no more breaches therein, (though at that time I had not set vp the doores vpon the gates)

2 Then sent Sanballat and Geshem vnto me, saying, Come thou that we may meete together in the villages in the plaine of Ono: and they thought to doe me euill.

3 Therefore I sent messengers vnto them, saying, I haue a great worke to doe, and I can not come downe: why should the worke cease, whiles I leaue it, and come downe to you?

4 Yet they sent vnto me foure times after this sort. And I answered them after the same maner.

5 Then sent Sanballat his seruant after this sorte vnto me the fift time, with an open letter in his hand,

6 Wherein was written, It is reported among the heathen, and Gashmu hath sayd it, that thou and the Iewes thinke to rebel, for the which cause thou buildest the wall and thou wilt bee their King according to these wordes.

7 Thou hast also ordeyned the Prophets to preach of thee at Ierusalem, saying, There is a King in Iudah: and nowe according to these wordes it shall come to the Kings eares: come now therefore, and let vs take counsell together.

8 Then I sent vnto him, saying, It is not done according to these wordes that thou sayest: for thou feynest them of thine owne heart.

9 For all they afrayed vs, saying, Their handes shalbe weakened from the worke, and it shall not be done: nowe therefore incourage thou me.

10 And I came to the house of Shemaiah the sonne of Delaiah the sonne of Mehetabeel, and he was shut vp, and he said, Let vs come together into the house of God in the middes of the Temple, and shut the doores of the Temple: for they will come to slay thee: yea, in the night will they come to kill thee.

11 Then I said, Should such a man as I, flee? Who is he, being as I am, that would go into the Temple to liue? I will not goe in.

12 And loe, I perceiued, that God had not sent him, but that he pronounced this prophecie against me: for Tobiah and Sanballat had hired him.

13 Therefore was he hyred, that I might be afrayde, and doe thus, and sinne, and that they might haue an euill report that they might reproche me.

14 My God, remember thou Tobiah, and Sanballat according vnto these their workes, and Noadiah the Prophetesse also, and the rest of the Prophets that would haue put me in feare.

15 Notwithstanding the wall was finished on the fiue and twentieth day of Elul, in two and fiftie dayes.

16 And when all our enemies heard thereof, euen all the heathen that were about vs, they were afraid, and their courage failed them: for they knew, that this worke was wrought by our God.

17 And in these dayes were there many of the princes of Iudah, whose letters

went vnto Tobiah, and those of Tobiah came vnto them.

18 For there were many in Iudah, that were sworne vnto him: for he was the sonne in lawe of Shechaniah, the sonne of Arah: and his sonne Iehonathan had the daughter of Meshullam, the sonne of Berechiah.

19 Yea, they spake in his praise before me, and tolde him my wordes, and Tobiah sent letters to put me in feare.

Nehemiah 7

1 Nowe when the wall was builded, and I had set vp the doores, and the porters, and the singers and the Leuites were appointed,

2 Then I commanded my brother Hanani and Hananiah the prince of the palace in Ierusalem (for he was doubtlesse a faithfull man, and feared God aboue many)

3 And I saide vnto them, Let not the gates of Ierusalem be opened, vntill the heate of the sunne: and while they stande by, let them shut the doores, and make them fast: and I appointed wardes of the inhabitants of Ierusalem, euery one in his warde, and euery one ouer against his house.

4 Nowe the citie was large and great, but the people were few therein, and the houses were not buylded.

5 And my God put into mine heart, and I gathered the princes, and the rulers, and the people, to count their genealogies: and I found a booke of the genealogie of them, which came vp at the first, and found written therein,

6 These are the sonnes of the prouince that came vp from the captiuitie that was caried away (whome Nebuchadnezzar King of Babel had caryed away) and they returned to Ierusalem and to Iudah, euery one vnto his citie.

7 They which came with Zerubbabel, Ieshua, Nehemiah, Azariah, Raamiah, Nahamani, Mordecai, Bilshan, Mispereth, Biguai, Nehum, Baanah. This is the nomber of the men of the people of Israel.

8 The sonnes of Parosh, two thousande an hundreth seuentie and two.

9 The sonnes of Shephatiah, three hundreth seuentie and two.

10 The sonnes of Arah, sixe hundreth fiftie and two.

11 The sonnes of Pahath Moab of ye sonnes of Ieshua, and Ioab, two thousand, eight hundreth and eighteene.

12 The sonnes of Elam, a thousand, two hundreth fiftie and foure.

13 The sonnes of Zattu, eight hundreth and fiue and fourtie.

14 The sonnes of Zacchai, seuen hundreth and three score.

15 The sonnes of Binnui, sixe hundreth and eight and fourtie.

16 The sonnes of Bebai, sixe hundreth and eight and twentie.

17 The sonnes of Azgad, two thousand, three hundreth and two and twentie.

18 The sonnes of Adonikam, sixe hundreth three score and seuen.

19 The sonnes of Biguai, two thousand three score and seuen.

20 The sonnes of Adin, sixe hundreth, and fiue and fiftie.

21 The sonnes of Ater of Hizkiah, ninetie and eight.

22 The sonnes of Hashum, three hundreth and eight and twentie.

23 The sonnes of Bezai, three hundreth and foure and twentie.

24 The sonnes of Hariph, an hundreth and twelue.

25 The sonnes of Gibeon, ninetie and fiue.

26 The men of Beth-lehem and Netophah, an hundreth foure score and eight.

27 The men of Anathoth, an hundreth and eight and twentie.

28 The me of Beth-azmaueth, two and fourty.

29 The men of Kiriath-iearim, Chephirah and Beeroth, seuen hundreth, and three and fourtie.

30 The men of Ramah and Gaba, sixe hundreth and one and twentie.

31 The men of Michmas, an hundreth and two and twentie.

32 The men of Beth-el and Ai, an hundreth and three and twentie.

33 The men of the other Nebo, two and fifty.

34 The sonnes of the other Elam, a thousand, two hundreth and foure and fiftie.

35 The sonnes of Harim, three hundreth and twentie.

36 The sonnes of Iericho, three hundreth and fiue and fourtie.

37 The sonnes of Lod-hadid and Ono, seuen hundreth and one and twentie.

38 The sonnes of Senaah, three thousand, nine hundreth and thirtie.

39 The Priestes: the sonnes of Iedaiah of the house of Ieshua, nine hundreth seuentie and three.

40 The sonnes of Immer, a thousand and two and fiftie.

41 The sonnes of Pashur, a thousande, two hundreth and seuen and fourtie.

42 The sonnes of Harim, a thousande and seuenteene.

43 The Leuites: the sonnes of Ieshua of Kadmiel, and of the sonnes of Hodiuah, seuentie and foure.

44 The singers: the children of Asaph, an hundreth, and eight and fourtie.

45 The porters: the sonnes of Shallum, the sonnes of Ater, the sonnes of Talmon, the sonnes of Akkub, the sonnes of Hatita, the sonnes of Shobai, an hundreth and eight and thirtie.

46 The Nethinims: the sonnes of Ziha, the sonnes of Hashupha, the sonnes of Tabaoth,

47 The sonnes of Keros, the sonnes of Sia, the sonnes of Padon,

48 The sonnes of Lebana, the sonnes of Hagaba, the sonnes of Shalmai,

49 The sonnes of Hanan, the sonnes of Giddel, the sonnes of Gahar,

50 The sonnes of Reaiah, the sonnes of Rezin, the sonnes of Nekoda,

51 The sonnes of Gazzam, ye sonnes of Vzza, the sonnes of Paseah,

52 The sonnes of Besai, the sonnes of Meunim, the sonnes of Nephishesim,

53 The sonnes of Bakbuk, the sonnes of Hakupha, the sonnes of Harhur,

54 The sonnes of Bazlith, the sonnes of Mehida, the sonnes of Harsha,

55 The sonnes of Barkos, the sonnes of Sissera, the sonnes of Tamah,

56 The sonnes of Neziah, the sonnes of Hatipha,

57 The sonnes of Salomons seruantes, the sonnes of Sotai, the sonnes of Sophereth, ye sonnes of Perida,

58 The sonnes of Iaala, the sonnes of Darkon, the sonnes of Giddel,

59 The sonnes of Shephatiah, the sonnes of Hattil, the sonnes of Pochereth of Zebaim, the sonnes of Amon.

60 All the Nethinims, and the sonnes of Salomons seruantes were three hundreth, ninetie and two.

61 And these came vp from Tel-melah, Tel-haresha, Cherub, Addon, and Immer: but they could not shewe their fathers house, nor their seede, or if they were of Israel.

62 The sonnes of Delaiah: the sonnes of Tobiah, the sonnes of Nekoda, six hundreth and two and fourtie.

63 And of the Priestes: the sonnes of Habaiah, the sonnes of Hakkoz, the sonnes of Barzillai, which tooke one of the daughters of Barzillai the Gileadite to wife, and was named after their name.

64 These sought their writing of the genealogies, but it was not founde: therefore they were put from the Priesthood.

65 And the Tirshatha sayd vnto them, that they should not eate of the most holy, till there rose vp a Priest with Vrim and Thummim.

66 All the Congregation together was two and fourtie thousand, three hundreth and threescore,

67 Besides their seruantes and their maydes, which were seuen thousand, three hundreth and seuen and thirtie: and they had two hundreth and fiue and fourtie singing men and singing women.

68 Their horses were seuen hundreth and sixe and thirtie, and their mules two hundreth and fiue and fourtie.

69 The camels foure hundreth and fiue and thirtie, and sixe thousande, seuen hundreth and twentie asses.

70 And certaine of the chiefe fathers gaue vnto the worke. The Tirshatha gaue to the treasure, a thousand drammes of golde, fiftie basins, fiue hundreth and thirtie Priests garments.

71 And some of the chiefe fathers gaue vnto the treasure of the worke, twentie thousand drams of golde, and two thousande and two hundreth pieces of siluer.

72 And the rest of the people gaue twentie thousand drammes of golde, and two thousande pieces of siluer, and three score and seuen Priestes garments.

73 And the Priestes, and Leuites, and the porters and the singers and the rest of the people and the Nethinims, and all

Israel dwelt in their cities: and when the seuenth moneth came, the children of Israel were in their cities.

Nehemiah 8

1 And all the people assembled themselues together, in the streete that was before the watergate, and they spake vnto Ezra the Scribe, that hee would bring the booke of ye Law of Moses, which the Lord had commanded to Israel.

2 And Ezra the Priest brought the Lawe before the Congregation both of men and women, and of all that coulde heare and vnderstand it, in the first day of the seuenth moneth,

3 And he read therein in the streete that was before the watergate (from the morning vntill the midday) before men and women, and them that vnderstoode it, and the eares of all the people hearkened vnto the booke of the Lawe.

4 And Ezra the Scribe stoode vpon a pulpit of wood which he had made for the preaching, and beside him stood Mattithiah, and Shema, and Ananiah, and Vriiah, and Hilkiah, and Maaseiah on his right hande, and on his left hand Pedaiah, and Mishael, and Malchiah, and Hashum, and Hashbadana, Zechariah, and Meshullam.

5 And Ezra opened the booke before all the people: for hee was aboue all the people: and when he opened it, all the people stoode vp.

6 And Ezra praysed the Lord the great God, and all the people answered, Amen, Amen, with lifting vp their handes: and they bowed themselues, and worshipped the Lord with their faces toward the grounde.

7 Also Ieshua, and Bani, and Sherebiah, Iamin, Akkub, Shabbethai, Hodiiah, Maaseiah, Kelita, Azariah, Iozabad, Hanan, Pelaiah, and the Leuites caused the people to vnderstand the lawe, and the people stood in their place.

8 And they read in the booke of the Lawe of God distinctly, and gaue the sense, and caused them to vnderstand the reading.

9 Then Nehemiah (which is Tirshatha) and Ezra the Priest and scribe, and the Leuites that instructed the people, saide vnto all the people, This day is holie vnto ye Lord your God: mourne not, neither weepe: for all the people wept, whe they heard the words of the Lawe.

10 He saide also vnto the, Go, and eate of the fat, and drinke the sweete, and send part vnto them, for whome none is prepared: for this day is holie vnto our Lord: be ye not sorie therefore: for the ioy of the Lord is your strength.

11 And the Leuites made silence throughout all the people, saying, Holde your peace: for the day is holy, be not sad therefore.

12 Then all the people went to eate and to drinke, and to send away part, and to make great ioy, because they had vnderstand the wordes that they had taught them.

13 And on the second day the chiefe fathers of all the people, the Priests and the Leuites were gathered vnto Ezra the scribe, that he also might instruct them in the wordes of the Lawe.

14 And they found written in the Law, (that the Lord had commanded by Moses) that the children of Israel should dwel in boothes in the feast of the seuenth moneth,

15 And that they shoulde cause it to bee declared and proclaimed in all their cities, and in Ierusalem, saying, Go forth vnto the mount, and bring oliue branches, and pine branches, and branches of myrtus, and palme branches, and branches of thicke trees, to make boothes, as it is written.

16 So the people went foorth and brought them, and made them boothes, euerie one vpon the roofe of his house, and in their courtes, and in the courtes of the house of God, and in the streete by the watergate, and in the streete of the gate of Ephraim.

17 And all the Congregation of them that were come againe out of the captiuitie made boothes, and sate vnder the boothes: for since the time of Ieshua the sonne of Nun vnto this day, had not the children of Israel done so, and there was very great ioy.

18 And he read in the booke of the Lawe of God euery day, from the first day vnto the last day. and they kept the feast seuen dayes, and on the eight day a solemne assemblie, according vnto the maner.

Nehemiah 9

1 In the foure and twentieth day of this moneth the children of Israel were assembled with fasting, and with sackecloth, and earth vpon them.

2 (And they that were of the seede of Israel were separated from all the strangers) and they stoode and confessed their sinnes and the iniquities of their fathers.

3 And they stood vp in their place and read in the booke of the Lawe of the Lord their GOD foure times on the day, and they confessed and worshipped the Lord their God foure times.

4 Then stoode vp vpon the staires of the Leuites Ieshua, and Bani, Kadmiel, Shebaniah, Bunni, Sherebiah, Bani, and Chenani, and cryed with a loud voyce vnto the Lord their God.

5 And the Leuites said, euen Ieshua and Kadmiel, Bani, Hashabniah, Sherebiah, Hodiiah, Shebaniah and Pethahiah, Stande vp, and praise the Lord your God for euer, and euer, and let them praise thy glorious Name, O God, which excelleth aboue all thankesgiuing and praise.

6 Thou art Lord alone: thou hast made heauen, and the heauen of all heauens, with all their hoste, the earth, and all things that are therein, bthe seas, and al that are in them, and thou preseruest them all, and the host of the heauen worshippeth thee.

7 Thou art, O Lord, the God, that hast chosen Abram, and broughtest him out of Vr in Caldea, and madest his name Abraham,

8 And foundest his heart faithful before thee, and madest a couenant with him, to giue vnto his seede the lande of the Canaanites, Hittites, Amorites, and Perizzites, and Iebusites, and Girgashites, and hast performed thy wordes, because thou art iust.

9 Thou hast also considered the affliction of our fathers in Egypt, and heard their cry by the red Sea,

10 And shewed tokens and wonders vpon Pharaoh, and on all his seruants, and on all the people of his land: for thou knewest that they dealt proudely against them: therefore thou madest thee a Name, as appeareth this day.

11 For thou didest breake vp the Sea before them, and they went through the middes of the Sea on dry lande: and those that pursued them, hast thou cast into the bottomes as a stone, in the mightie waters:

12 And leddest them in the day with a pillar of a cloude, and in the night with a pillar of fire to giue them light in the way that they went.

13 Thou camest downe also vpon mount Sinai, and spakest vnto them from heauen, and gauest them right iudgements, and true lawes, ordinances and good commandements,

14 And declaredst vnto them thine holy Sabbath, and commandedst them precepts, and ordinances, and lawes, by the hande of Moses thy seruant:

15 And gauest them bread from heauen for their hunger, and broughtest forth water for them out of the rocke for their thirst: and promisedst them that they shoulde goe in, and take possession of the land: for the which thou haddest lift vp thine hand for to giue them.

16 But they and our fathers behaued them selues proudely, and hardened their neck, so that they hearkened not vnto thy commandements,

17 But refused to obey, and would not remember thy marueilous works that thou haddest done for them, but hardened their neckes, and had in their heads to returne to their bondage by their rebellion: but thou, O God of mercies, gratious and full of compassion, of long suffring and of great mercie, yet forsookest them not.

18 Moreouer, when they made them a molten calfe (and said, This is thy God that brought thee vp out of the land of Egypt) and committed great blasphemies,

19 Yet thou for thy great mercies forsookest them not in the wildernesse: the pillar of the cloude departed not from them by day to leade them the way, neither the pillar of fire by night, to shew them light, and the way whereby they should goe.

20 Thou gauest also thy good Spirite to instruct them, and withheldest not thy MAN from their mouth, and gauest them water for their thirst.

21 Thou didest also feede them fourtie yeres in ye wildernes: they lacked nothing: their clothes waxed not old, and their feete swelled not.

22 And thou gauest them kingdomes and people, and scatteredst them into corners: so they possessed the land of Sihon and the land of ye King of Heshbon, and the land of Og King of Bashan.

23 And thou diddest multiplie their children, like the starres of the heauen, and broughtest them into the lande, whereof thou haddest spoken vnto their fathers, that they should goe, and possesse it.

24 So the children went in, and possessed the lande, and thou subduedst before them the inhabitants of the lande, euen the Canaanites, and gauest them into their handes, with their Kings and the people of the lande, that they might do with them what they would.

25 And they tooke their strong cities and the fat lande, and possessed houses, full of all goods, cisternes digged out, vineyardes, and oliues, and trees for foode in abundance, and they did eate, and were filled, and became fat, and liued in pleasure through thy great goodnesse.

26 Yet they were disobedient, and rebelled against thee, and cast thy Lawe behinde their backes, and slewe thy Prophets (which protested among them to turne them vnto thee) and committed great blasphemies.

27 Therefore thou deliueredst them into the hande of their enemies that vexed them: yet in the time of their affliction, when they cryed vnto thee, thou heardest them from the heauen, and through thy great mercies thou gauest them sauiours, who saued them out of the hande of their aduersaries.

28 But when they had rest, they returned to doe euill before thee: therefore leftest thou them in the hande of their enemies, so that they had the dominion ouer them, yet when they conuerted and cryed vnto thee, thou heardest them from heauen, and deliueredst them according to thy great mercies many times,

29 And protestedst among them that thou mightest bring them againe vnto thy Lawe: but they behaued them selues proudely, and hearkened not vnto thy commandements, but sinned against thy iudgements (which a man should doe and liue in them) and pulled away the shoulder, and were stiffenecked, and woulde not heare.

30 Yet thou diddest forbeare them many yeeres, and protestedst among them by thy Spirite, euen by the hande of thy Prophets, but they woulde not heare: therefore gauest thou them into the hande of the people of the lands.

31 Yet for thy great mercies thou hast not consumed them, neither forsaken them: for thou art a gracious and mercifull God.

32 Nowe therefore our God, thou great God, mightie and terrible, that keepest couenant and mercie, let not all the affliction that hath come vnto vs, seeme a litle before thee, that is, to our Kings, to our princes, and to our Priests, and to our Prophets, and to our fathers, and to all thy people since the time of the Kings of Asshur vnto this day.

33 Surely thou art iust in all that is come vpon vs: for thou hast dealt truely, but we haue done wickedly.

34 And our kings and our princes, our Priests and our fathers haue not done thy Lawe, nor regarded thy commandements nor thy protestations, wherewith thou hast protested among them.

35 And they haue not serued thee in their kingdome, and in thy great goodnesse that thou shewedst vnto them, and in the large and fat lande which thou diddest set before them, and haue not conuerted from their euill workes.

36 Beholde, we are seruants this day, and the lande that thou gauest vnto our fathers, to eate the fruite thereof, and the goodnesse thereof, beholde, we are seruants therein.

37 And it yeeldeth much fruit vnto the kings whom thou hast set ouer vs, because of our sinnes: and they haue dominion ouer our bodyes and ouer our cattell at their pleasure, and we are in great affliction.

38 Now because of all this we make a sure couenant, and write it, and our princes, our Leuites and our Priestes seale vnto it.

Nehemiah 10

1 Now they that sealed were Nehemiah the Tirshatha the sonne of Hachaliah, and Zidkiiah,

2 Seraiah, Azariah, Ieremiah,

3 Pashur, Amariah, Malchiah,

4 Hattush, Shebaniah, Malluch,

5 Harim, Merimoth, Obadiah,

6 Daniel, Ginnethon, Baruch,

7 Meshullam, Abiiah, Miamin,

8 Maaziah, Bilgai, Shemaiah: these are the Priestes.

9 And the Leuites: Ieshua the sonne of Azaniah, Binnui, of the sonnes of Henadad, Kadmiel.

10 And their brethren Shebaniah, Hodiiah, Kelita, Pelaiah, Hanun,

11 Micha, Rehob, Hashabiah,

12 Zaccur, Sherebiah, Shebaniah,

13 Hodiah, Bani, Beninu.

14 The chiefe of the people were Parosh, Pahath Moab, Elam, Zattu, Bani,

15 Bunni, Azgad, Bebai,

16 Adoniah, Biguai, Adin,

17 Ater, Hizkiiah, Azzur,

18 Hodiah, Hashum, Bezai,

19 Hariph, Anathoth, Nebai,

20 Magpiash, Meshullam, Hezir,

21 Meshezabeel, Zadok, Iaddua,

22 Pelatiah, Hanan, Anaiah,

23 Hoshea, Hananiah, Hashub,

24 Hallohesh, Pileha, Shobek,

25 Rehum, Hashabnah, Maaseiah,

26 And Ahiiah, Hanan, Anan,

27 Malluch, Harim, Baanah.

28 And the rest of the people, the Priestes, the Leuites, the porters, the singers, the Nethinims, and all that were separated from the people of the landes vnto the Lawe of God, their wiues, their sonnes, and their daughters, all that coulde vnderstande.

29 The chiefe of them receiued it for their brethren, and they came to the curse and to the othe to walke in Gods Law, which was giuen by Moses the seruant of God, to obserue and doe all the commandementes of the Lord our God, and his iudgements and his statutes:

30 And that we would not giue our daughters to the people of the lande, neither take their daughters for our sonnes.

31 And if the people of the lande brought ware on the Sabbath, or any vitailes to sell, that we would not take it of them on the Sabbath and on the holy dayes: and that we would let the seuenth yeere be free, and the debtes of euery person.

32 And we made statutes for our selues to giue by the yeere the thirde part of a shekel for the seruice of the house of our God,

33 For the shewbread, and for the daily offring, and for the daily burnt offring, the Sabbaths, the newe moones, for the solemne feastes, and for the thinges that were sanctified, and for the sinne offrings to make an atonement for Israel, and for all the worke of the house of our God.

34 We cast also lottes for the offering of the wood, euen the Priestes, the Leuites and the people to bring it into the house of our God, by the house of our fathers, yeerely at the times appointed, to burne it vpon the altar of the Lord our God, as it is written in the Lawe,

35 And to bring the first fruites of our land, and the first of all the fruites of all trees, yeere by yeere, into the house of the Lord,

36 And the first borne of our sonnes, and of our cattel, as it is written in the Lawe, and the first borne of our bullockes and of our sheepe, to bring it into the house of our God, vnto ye Priests that minister in the house of our God,

37 And that we should bring the first fruite of our dough, and our offrings, and the fruite of euery tree, of wine and of oyle, vnto the Priestes, to the chambers of the house of our God: and the tithes of our lande vnto the Leuites, that the Leuites might haue the tithes in all the cities of our trauaile.

38 And the Priest, the sonne of Aaron shall be with the Leuites, when ye Leuites take tithes, and the Leuites shall bring vp the tenth parte of the tithes vnto the house of our God, vnto the chambers of the treasure house.

39 For the children of Israel, and the children of Leui shall bring vp the offerings of the corne, of the wine, and of the oyle, vnto the chabers: and there

shalbe the vessels of the Sanctuarie, and the Priestes that minister, and the porters, and the fingers, and we will not forsake the house of our God.

Nehemiah 11

1 And the rulers of the people dwelt in Ierusalem: the other people also cast lottes, to bring one out of ten to dwel in Ierusalem the holy citie, and nine partes to be in the cities.

2 And the people thanked all the men that were willing to dwell in Ierusalem.

3 These now are the chiefe of the prouince, that dwelt in Ierusalem, but in the cities of Iudah, euery one dwelt in his owne possession in their cities of Israel, the Priestes and the Leuites, and the Nethinims, and the sonnes of Salomons seruants.

4 And in Ierusalem dwelt certaine of the children of Iudah, and of the children of Beniamin. Of the sonnes of Iudah, Athaiah, the sonne of Vziiah, the sonne of Zechariah, the sonne of Amariah, the sonne of Shephatiah, the sonne of Mahaleel, of the sonnes of Perez,

5 And Maaseiah the sonne of Baruch, the sonne of Col Hozeh, the sonne of Hazaiah, the sonne of Adaiah, the sonne of Ioiarib, the sonne of Zechariah, the sonne of Shiloni.

6 All the sonnes of Perez that dwelt at Ierusalem, were foure hundreth, three score and eight valiant men.

7 These also are the sonnes of Beniamin, Sallu, the sonne of Meshullam, the sonne of Ioed, the sonne of Pedaiah, the sonne of Kolaiah, the sonne of Maaseiah, the sonne of Ithiel, the sonne of Ieshaiah.

8 And after him Gabai, Sallai, nine hundreth and twentie and eight.

9 And Ioel the sonne of Zichri was gouernour ouer them: and Iudah, the sonne of Senuah was the second ouer the citie:

10 Of the Priestes, Iedaiah, the sonne of Ioiarib, Iachin.

11 Seraiah, the sonne of Hilkiah, the sonne of Meshullam, the sonne of Zadok, the sonne of Meraioth, the sonne of Ahitub was chiefe of the house of God.

12 And their brethren that did the worke in the Temple, were eight hundreth, twenty and two: and Adaiah, the sonne of Ieroham, the sonne of Pelaliah, the sonne of Amzi, the sonne of Zechariah, the sonne of Pashur, the sonne of Malchiah:

13 And his brethren, chiefe of the fathers, two hundreth and two and fourtie: and Amashsai the sonne of Azareel, the sonne of Ahazai, the sonne of Meshilemoth, the sonne of Immer:

14 And their brethren valiant men, an hundreth and eight and twentie: and their ouerseer was Zabdiel the sonne of Hagedolim.

15 And of the Leuites, Shemaiah, the sonne of Hashub, the sonne of Azrikam, the sonne of Hashabiah, the sonne of Bunni.

16 And Shabbethai, and Iozabad of the chiefe of the Leuites were ouer the workes of the house of God without.

17 And Mattaniah, the sonne of Micha, the sonne of Zabdi, the sonne of Asaph was the chiefe to begin the thankesgiuing and prayer: and Bakbukiah the second of his brethren, and Abda, the sonne of Shammua, the sonne of Galal, the sonne of Ieduthun.

18 All the Leuites in the holy citie were two hundreth foure score and foure.

19 And the porters Akkub, Talmon and their brethren that kept the gates, were an hundreth twentie and two.

20 And the residue of Israel, of the Priestes, and of the Leuites dwelt in al the cities of Iudah, euery one in his inheritance.

21 And the Nethinims dwelt in the fortresse, and Ziha, and Gispa was ouer the Nethinims.

22 And the ouerseer of the Leuites in Ierusalem was Vzzi the sonne of Bani, the sonne of Ashabiah, the sonne of Mattaniah, the sonne of Micha: of the sonnes of Asaph singers were ouer the worke of the house of God.

23 For it was the Kings commandement cocerning them, that faithfull prouision shoulde bee for the singers euery day.

24 And Pethahiah the sonne of Meshezabeel, of the sonnes of Zerah, the sonne of Iudah was at the Kings hand in all matters concerning the people.

25 And in the villages in their landes, some of the children of Iudah dwelt in Kiriath-arba, and in the villages thereof, and in Dibon, and in the villages thereof, and in Iekabzeel. and in the villages thereof,

26 And in Ieshua, and in Moladah, and in Beth palet,

27 And in Hazer-shual, and in Beer-sheba, and in the villages thereof,

28 And in Ziklag, and in Mechonah, and in the villages thereof,

29 And in En-rimmon, and in Zareah, and in Iarmuth,

30 Zanoah, Adullam, and in their villages, in Lachish, and in the fieldes thereof, at Azekah, and in the villages thereof: and they dwelt from Beer-sheba, vnto the valley of Hinnom.

31 And the sonnes of Beniamin from Geba, in Michmash, and Aiia, and Beth-el, and in the villages thereof,

32 Anathoth, Nob, Ananiah,

33 Hazor, Ramah, Gittaim,

34 Hadid, Zeboim, Nebalat,

35 Lod and Ono, in the carpenters valley.

36 And of the Leuites were diuisions in Iudah and in Beniamin.

Nehemiah 12

1 These also are the Priestes and the Leuites that went vp with Zerubbabel, the sonne of Shealtiel, and Ieshua: to wit, Seraiah, Ieremiah, Ezra,

2 Amariah, Malluch, Hattush,

3 Shecaniah, Rehum, Merimoth,

4 Iddo, Ginnetho, Abiiah,

5 Miamin, Maadiah, Bilgah,

6 Shemaiah, and Ioiarib, Iedaiah,

7 Sallu, Amok, Hilkiiah, Iedaiah: these were the chiefe of the Priests, and of their brethren in the dayes of Ieshua.

8 And the Leuites, Ieshua, Binnui, Kadmiel, Sherebiah, Iudah, Mattaniah were ouer the thankesgiuings, he, and his brethren.

9 And Bakbukiah and Vnni, and their brethren were about them in the watches.

10 And Ieshua begate Ioiakim: Ioiakim also begate Eliashib, and Eliashib begate Ioiada.

11 And Ioiada begate Ionathan, and Ionathan begate Iaddua,

12 And in the daies of Ioiakim were these, the chiefe fathers of the Priests: vnder Seraiah was Meraiah, vnder Ieremiah, Hananiah,

13 Vnder Ezra, Meshullam, vnder Amariah, Iehohanan,

14 Vnder Melicu, Ionathan, vnder Shebaniah, Ioseph,

15 Vnder Harim, Adna, vnder Maraioth, Helkai,

16 Vnder Iddo, Zechariah, vnder Ginnithon, Meshullam,

17 Vnder Abiiah, Zichri, vnder Miniamin, and vnder Moadiah, Piltai,

18 Vnder Bilgah, Shammua, vnder Shemaiah, Iehonathan,

19 Vnder Ioiarib, Mattenai, vnder Iedaiah, Vzzi,

20 Vnder Sallai, Kallai, vnder Amok, Eber,

21 Vnder Hilkiah, Hashabiah, vnder Iedaiah, Nethaneel.

22 In the dayes of Eliashib, Ioiada, and Iohanan and Iaddua were the chiefe fathers of the Leuites written, and the Priests in the reigne of Darius the Persian.

23 The sonnes of Leui, the chiefe fathers were written in the booke of the Chronicles euen vnto the dayes of Iohanan the sonne of Eliashib.

24 And the chiefe of the Leuites were Hashabiah, Sherebiah, and Ieshua the sonne of Kadmiel, and their brethren about them to giue prayse and thankes, according to the ordinance of Dauid the man of God, ward ouer against warde.

25 Mattaniah and Bakbukiah, Obadiah, Meshullam, Talmon and Akkub were porters keeping the warde at the thresholds of the gates.

26 These were in the dayes of Ioiakim, the sonne of Ieshua, the sonne of Iozadak, and in the dayes of Nehemiah the captaine, and of Ezra the Priest and scribe.

27 And in the dedication of the wall at Ierusalem they sought the Leuites out of all their places to bring them to Ierusalem to keepe the dedication and gladnes, both with thankesgiuings and with songs, cymbales, violes and with harpes.

28 Then the singers gathered themselues together both from the plaine countrey about Ierusalem, and from the villages of Netophathi,

29 And from the house of Gilgal, and out of the countreis of Geba, and Azmaueth:

for the singers had built them villages round about Ierusalem.

30 And the Priests and Leuites were purified, and clensed the people, and the gates, and the wall.

31 And I brought vp the princes of Iudah vpon the wall, and appointed two great companies to giue thankes, and the one went on the right hand of the wall toward the dung gate.

32 And after them went Hoshaiah, and halfe of the princes of Iudah,

33 And Azariah, Ezra and Meshullam,

34 Iudah, Beniamin, and Shemaiah, and Ieremiah,

35 And of the Priests sonnes with trumpets, Zechariah the sonne of Ionathan, the sonne of Shemaiah, the sonne of Mattaniah, the sonne of Michaiah, the sonne of Zaccur, ye sonne of Asaph.

36 And his brethren, Shemaiah, and Azareel, Milalai, Gilalai, Maai, Nethaneel, and Iudah, Hanani, with the musicall instruments of Dauid the man of God: and Ezra the scribe went before them.

37 And to the gate of the fountaine, euen ouer against them went they vp by the staires of the citie of Dauid, at the going vp of the wall beyond the house of Dauid, euen vnto the water gate Eastward.

38 And the seconde companie of them that gaue thankes, went on the other side, and I after them, and the halfe of the people was vpon the wall, and vpon the towre of the furnaces euen vnto the broad wall.

39 And vpon the gate of Ephraim, and vpon the olde gate, and vpon the fishgate, and the towre of Hananeel, and the towre of Meah, euen vnto the sheepegate: and they stood in the gate of the warde.

40 So stood the two companies (of them that gaue thankes) in the house of God, and I and the halfe of the rulers with me.

41 The Priests also, Eliakim, Maaseiah, Miniamin, Michaiah, Elioenai, Zechariah, Hananiah, with trumpets,

42 And Maaseiah, and Shemaiah, and Eleazar, and Vzzi, and Iehohanan, and Malchiiah, and Elam, and Ezer: and the singers sang loude, hauing Izrahiah which was the ouerseer.

43 And the same day they offered great sacrifices and reioyced: for God had giuen them great ioy, so that both the women, and the children were ioyfull: and the ioy of Ierusalem was heard farre off.

44 Also at the same time were men appointed ouer the chambers of the store for the offerings (for the first fruites, and for the tithes) to gather into them out of the fieldes of the cities, the portions of the Law for the Priests and the Leuites: for Iudah reioyced for the Priests and for the Leuites, that serued.

45 And both the singers and the Leuites kept the ward of their God, and the warde of the purification according to the commandement of Dauid, and Salomon his sonne.

46 For in the dayes of Dauid and Asaph, of olde were chiefe singers, and songs of praise and thankesgiuing vnto God.

47 And in the dayes of Zerubbabel, and in the dayes of Nehemiah did al Israel giue portions vnto the singers and porters, euerie day his portion, and they gaue the holy things vnto the Leuites, and the Leuites gaue the holy things vnto the sonnes of Aaron.

Nehemiah 13

1 And on that day did they reade in the booke of Moses, in the audience of the people, and it was found written therein, that the Ammonite, and the Moabite should not enter into the Congregation of God,

2 Because they met not the children of Israel with bread and with water, but hired Balaam against them, that he should curse them: and our God turned the curse into a blessing.

3 Now when they had heard the Lawe, they separated from Israel all those that were mixed.

4 And before this had the Priest Eliashib the ouersight of the chamber of the house of our God, being kinsman to Tobiah:

5 And he had made him a great chamber and there had they aforetime layde the offringes, the incense, and the vessels, and the tithes of corne, of wine, and of oyle (appointed for the Leuites, and the singers, and the porters) and the offringes of the Priests.

6 But in all this time was not I in Ierusalem: for in the two and thirtieth yere of Artahshashte King of Babel, came I vnto the King, and after certaine dayes I obteined of the King.

7 And when I was come to Ierusalem, I vnderstood the euil that Eliashib had done for Tobiah, in that hee had made him a chamber in the court of the house of God,

8 And it grieued me sore: therefore I cast forth all the vessels of the house of Tobiah out of the chamber.

9 And I commanded them to clense ye chambers: and thither brought I againe the vessels of the house of God with the meate offring and the incense.

10 And I perceiued that the portions of the Leuites had not bene giuen, and that euery one was fled to his lande, euen the Leuites and singers that executed the worke.

11 Then reproued I the rulers and sayd, Why is the house of God forsaken? And I assembled them, and set them in their place.

12 Then brought all Iudah the tithes of corne and of wine, and of oyle vnto the treasures.

13 And I made treasurers ouer the treasures, Shelemiah the Priest, and Zadok the scribe, and of the Leuites, Pedaiah, and vnder their hande Hanan the sonne of Zaccur the sonne of Mattaniah: for they were counted faithfull, and their office was to distribute vnto their brethren.

14 Remember me, O my God, herein, and wipe not out my kindenes that I haue shewed on the house of my God, and on the offices thereof.

15 In those dayes saw I in Iudah them, that trode wine presses on ye Sabbath, and that brought in sheaues, and which laded asses also with wine, grapes, and figges, and all burdens, and brought them into Ierusalem vpon the Sabbath day: and I protested to them in the day that they sold vitailes.

16 There dwelt men of Tyrus also therein, which brought fish and all wares, and solde on the Sabbath vnto the children of Iudah euen in Ierusalem.

17 Then reproued I the rulers of Iudah, and sayd vnto them, What euil thing is this that yee doe, and breake the Sabbath day?

18 Did not your fathers thus, and our God brought all this plague vpon vs, and vpon this citie? yet yee increase the wrath vpon Israel, in breaking the Sabbath.

19 And when the gates of Ierusalem beganne to be darke before the Sabbath, I commaded to shut the gates, and charged, that they should not be opened til after the Sabbath, and some of my seruants set I at the gates, that there shoulde no burden be brought in on the Sabbath day.

20 So the chapmen and marchants of al marchandise remained once or twise all night without Ierusalem.

21 And I protested among them, and said vnto them, Why tary ye all night about the wall? If ye do it once againe, I will lay hands vpon you. from that time came they no more on the Sabbath.

22 And I sayde vnto the Leuites, that they should clense themselues, and that they shoulde come and keepe the gates, to sanctifie the Sabbath day. Remember me, O my God, concerning this, and pardon me according to thy great mercy.

23 In those dayes also I saw Iewes that married wiues of Ashdod, of Ammon, and of Moab.

24 And their children spake halfe in ye speach of Ashdod, and could not speake in the Iewes language, and according to the language of the one people, and of the other people.

25 Then I reproued them, and cursed them, and smote certaine of them, and pulled off their heare, and tooke an othe of them by God, Yee shall not giue your daughters vnto their sonnes, neither shall ye take of their daughters vnto your sonnes, nor for your selues.

26 Did not Salomon the king of Israel sinne by these thinges? yet among many nations was there no King like him: for he was beloued of his God, and God had made him King ouer Israel: yet strange women caused him to sinne.

27 Shall wee then obey vnto you, to doe all this great euil, and to transgresse against our God, euen to marry strange wiues?

28 And one of the sonnes of Ioiada the sonne of Eliashib the hie Priest was the

sonne in law of Sanballat the Horonite: but I chased him from me.

29 Remember them, O my God, that defile the Priesthoode, and the couenant of the Priesthoode, and of the Leuites.

30 Then cleansed I them from all strangers, and appoynted the wardes of the Priestes and of the Leuites, euery one in his office,

31 And for the offring of the wood at times appoynted, and for the first fruites. Remember me, O my God, in goodnes.

Esther

Esther 1

1 In the dayes of Ahashuerosh (this is Ahashuerosh that reigned, from India euen vnto Ethiopia, ouer an hundreth, and seuen and twentie prouinces)

2 In those dayes when the King Ahashuerosh sate on his throne, which was in the palace of Shushan,

3 In the third yeere of his reigne, he made a feast vnto all his princes and his seruants, euen the power of Persia and Media, and to the captaines and gouernours of the prouinces which were before him,

4 That he might shewe the riches and glorie of his kingdome, and the honour of his great maiestie many dayes, euen an hundreth and foure score dayes.

5 And when these dayes were expired, the King made a feast to all the people that were founde in the palace of Shushan, both vnto great and small, seuen dayes, in the court of the garden of the Kings palace,

6 Vnder an hanging of white, greene, and blue clothes, fastened with cordes of fine linen and purple, in siluer rings, and pillars of marble: the beds were of golde, and of siluer vpon a pauement of porphyre, and marble and alabaster, and blue colour.

7 And they gaue them drinke in vessels of golde, and changed vessel after vessel, and royall wine in abundance according to the power of the King.

8 And the drinking was by an order, none might compel: for so the King had appoynted vnto all the officers of his house, that they should do according to euery mans pleasure.

9 The Queene Vashti made a feast also for the women in the royall house of King Ahashuerosh.

10 Vpon the seuenth daye when the King was merie with wine, he commanded Mehuman, Biztha, Harbona, Bigtha, and Abagtha, Zethar, and Carcas, the seuen eunuches, (that serued in the presence of King Ahashuerosh)

11 To bring Queene Vashti before the King with the crowne royall, that he might shewe the people and the princes her beautie: for shee was fayre to looke vpon.

12 But the Queene Vashti refused to come at the Kings worde, which he had giuen in charge to the eunuches:

therefore the King was very angry, and his wrath kindled in him.

13 Then the King said to the wise men, that knew the times (for so was the Kings maner towards all that knew the law and the iudgement:

14 And the next vnto him was Carshena, Shethar, Admatha, Tarshish, Meres, Marsena, and Memucan the seuen princes of Persia and Media, which sawe the Kings face, and sate the first in the kingdome)

15 What shall we do vnto the Queene Vashti according to the law, because she did not according to the worde of the King Ahashuerosh by the commission of the eunuches?

16 Then Memucan answered before the King and the Princes, The Queene Vashti hath not only done euill against the King, but against all the princes, and against all the people that are in all the prouinces of King Ahashuerosh.

17 For the acte of the Queene shall come abroade vnto all women, so that they shall despise their husbands in their owne eyes, and shall say, The King Ahashuerosh comanded Vashti the Queene to be brought in before him, but she came not.

18 So shall the princesses of Persia and Media this day say vnto all the Kings Princes, when they heare of the acte of the Queene: thus shall there be much despitefulnesse and wrath.

19 If it please the King, let a royal decree proceede from him, and let it be written among the statutes of Persia, and Media, (and let it not be transgressed) that Vashti come no more before King Ahashuerosh: and let the King giue her royal estate vnto her companion that is better then she.

20 And when the decree of the King which shalbe made, shalbe published throughout all his kingdome (though it be great) all the women shall giue their husbands honour, both great and small.

21 And this saying pleased the King and the princes, and the King did according to the worde of Memucan.

22 For he sent letters into all the prouinces of the King, into euery prouince according to the writing thereof, and to euery people after their language, that euery man should beare rule in his owne house, and that he should publish it in the language of that same people.

Esther 2

1 After these things, when the wrath of King Ahashuerosh was appeased, he remembred Vashti, and what she had done, and what was decreed against her.

2 And the Kings seruants that ministred vnto him, sayd, Let them seeke for the King beautifull yong virgins,

3 And let the King appoynt officers through all the prouinces of his kingdome, and let them gather all the beautiful yong virgins vnto the palace of Shushan, into the house of the women, vnder the hand of Hege the Kings

eunuche, keeper of the women, to giue them their things for purification.

4 And the mayde that shall please the King, let her reigne in the steade of Vashti. And this pleased the King, and he did so.

5 In the citie of Shushan, there was a certaine Iewe, whose name was Mordecai the sonne of Iair, the sonne of Shimei, the sonne of Kish a man of Iemini,

6 Which had bene caryed away from Ierusalem with the captiuitie that was caryed away with Ieconiah King of Iudah (whom Nebuchad-nezzar King of Babel had caryed away)

7 And he nourished Hadassah, that is Ester, his vncles daughter: for she had neither father nor mother, and the mayde was fayre, and beautifull to looke on: and after the death of her father, and her mother, Mordecai tooke her for his own daughter,

8 And when the Kings commandement, and his decree was published, and many maydes were brought together to the palace of Shushan, vnder the hand of Hege, Ester was brought also vnto the Kings house vnder the hande of Hege the keeper of the women.

9 And the mayde pleased him, and she founde fauour in his sight: therefore he caused her things for purification to be giuen her speedily, and her state, and seuen comely maides to be giuer her out of the Kings house, and he gaue change to her and to her maydes of the best in the house of the women.

10 But Ester shewed not her people and her kinred: for Mordecai had charged her, that shee should not tell it.

11 Aud Mordecai walked euery day before the court of the womens house, to knowe if Ester did well, and what should be done with her.

12 And when the course of euery mayd came, to go in to King Ahashuerosh, after that she had bene twelue moneths according to the maner of the women (for so were the dayes of their purifications accomplished, six moneths with oyle of myrrhe, and six moneths with sweete odours and in the purifying of the women:

13 And thus went the maides vnto the King) whatsoeuer she required, was giuen her, to go with her out of the womens house vnto ye kings house.

14 In the euening she went, and on the morow she returned into the second house of the women vnder the hand of Shaashgaz the Kings eunuche, which kept the concubines: shee came in to the King no more, except shee pleased the King, and that she were called by name.

15 Now when the course of Ester the daughter of Abihail the vncle of Mordecai (which had taken her as his owne daughter) came, that shee should go in to the King, she desired nothing, but what Hege the Kings eunuche the keeper of the women sayde: and Ester founde fauour in the sight of all them that looked vpon her.

16 So Ester was taken vnto King Ahashuerosh into his house royall in the

tenth moneth, which is the moneth Tebeth, in the seuenth yeere of his reigne.

17 And the King loued Ester aboue all the women, and shee founde grace and fauour in his sight more then all the virgins: so that he set the crowne of the kingdome vpon her head, and made her Queene instead of Vashti.

18 Then the King made a great feast vnto all his princes, and his seruants, which was the feast of Ester, and gaue rest vnto the prouinces, and gaue gifts, according to the power of a King.

19 And whe the virgins were gathered ye second time, then Mordecai sate in the Kings gate.

20 Ester had not yet shewed her kindred nor her people, as Mordecai had charged her: for Ester did after the worde of Mordecai, as when she was nourished with him.

21 In those dayes whe Mordecai sate in the Kings gate, two of the Kings eunuches, Bigthan and Teresh, which kept the doore, were wroth, and sought to lay hand on the King Ahashuerosh.

22 And the thing was knowen to Mordecai, and he tolde it vnto Queene Ester, and Ester certified the King thereof in Mordecais name: and when inquisition was made, it was found so: therefore they were both hanged on a tree: and it was written in the booke of the Chronicles before the King.

Esther 3

1 After these things did King Ahashuerosh promote Haman the sonne of Hammedatha the Agagite, and exalted him, and set his seate aboue all the princes that were with him.

2 And all the Kings seruants that were at the Kings gate, bowed their knees, and reuerenced Haman: for the King had so commanded concerning him: but Mordecai bowed not the knee, neither did reuerence.

3 Then the Kings seruants which were at the Kings gate, said vnto Mordecai, Why transgressest thou the Kings commandement?

4 And albeit they spake dayly vnto him, yet he would not heare them: therefore they tolde Haman, that they might see how Mordecais matters would stande: for he had tolde them, that he was a Iewe.

5 And when Haman sawe that Mordecai bowed not the knee vnto him, nor did reuerence vnto him, then Haman was full of wrath.

6 Now he thought it too litle to lay hands onely on Mordecai: and because they had shewed him the people of Mordecai, Haman sought to destroy all the Iewes, that were throughout the whole kingdome of Ahashuerosh, euen the people of Mordecai.

7 In the first moneth (that is the moneth Nisan) in the twelft yere of King Ahashuerosh, they cast Pur (that is a lot) before Haman, from day to day, and from moneth to moneth, vnto the twelft moneth, that is the moneth Adar.

8 Then Haman said vnto King Ahashuerosh, There is a people scattered, and dispersed among the people in all the prouinces of thy kingdome, and their lawes are diuers from all people, and they doe not obserue the Kings lawes: therefore it is not the Kings profite to suffer them.

9 If it please the King, let it be written that they may be destroyed, and I will pay ten thousand talents of siluer by the handes of them that haue the charge of this businesse to bring it into the Kings treasurie.

10 Then the King tooke his ring from his hand and gaue it vnto Haman the sonne of Hammedatha the Agagite the Iewes aduersarie.

11 And the King sayde vnto Haman, Let the siluer be thine, and the people to doe with them as it pleaseth thee.

12 Then were the Kings scribes called on the thirteenth day of the first moneth, and there was written (according to all that Haman commanded) vnto the Kings officers, and to the captaines that were ouer euery prouince, and to the rulers of euery people, and to euery prouince, according to the writing thereof, and to euery people according to their language: in the name of King Ahashuerosh was it written, and sealed with the Kings ring.

13 And the letters were sent by postes into all the Kings prouinces, to roote out, to kill and to destroy all the Iewes, both yong and olde, children and women, in one day vpon the thirteenth day of the twelft moneth, (which is the moneth Adar) and to spoyle them as a pray.

14 The contents of the writing was, that there shoulde be giuen a commandement in all prouinces, and published vnto all people, that they should be ready against the same day.

15 And the postes compelled by the Kings commandement went forth, and the commandement was giuen in the palace at Shushan: and the King and Haman sate drinking, but the citie of Shushan was in perplexitie.

Esther 4

1 Now when Mordecai perceiued all that was done, Mordecai rent his clothes, and put on sackecloth and ashes, and went out into the middes of the citie, and cryed with a great crye, and a bitter.

2 And he came euen before the Kings gate, but he might not enter within the Kings gate, being clothed with sackecloth.

3 And in euery prouince, and place, whither the Kings charge and his commission came, there was great sorowe among the Iewes, and fasting, and weeping and mourning, and many laye in sackecloth and in ashes.

4 Then Esters maydes and her eunuches came and tolde it her: therefore the Queene was very heauie, and she sent raiment to clothe Mordecai, and to take away his sackecloth from him, but he receiued it not.

5 Then called Ester Hatach one of the Kings eunuches, whom he had appointed to serue her, and gaue him a commandement vnto Mordecai, to knowe what it was, and why it was.

6 So Hatach went foorth to Mordecai vnto the streete of the citie, which was before the Kings gate.

7 And Mordecai tolde him of all that which had come vnto him, and of the summe of the siluer that Haman had promised to pay vnto the Kings treasures, because of the Iewes, for to destroy them.

8 Also he gaue him the copy of the writing and commission that was giuen at Shushan, to destroy them, that he might shewe it vnto Ester and declare it vnto her, and to charge her that she should goe in to the King, and make petition and supplication before him for her people.

9 So when Hatach came, he told Ester the wordes of Mordecai.

10 Then Ester sayde vnto Hatach, and commanded him to say vnto Mordecai,

11 All the Kings seruants and the people of the Kings prouinces doe knowe, that whosoeuer, man or woman, that commeth to the King into the inner court, which is not called, there is a law of his, that he shall dye, except him to whom the King holdeth out the golden rodde, that he may liue. Now I haue not bene called to come vnto the King these thirtie dayes.

12 And they certified Mordecai of Esters wordes.

13 And Mordecai saide, that they should answere Ester thus, Thinke not with thy selfe that thou shalt escape in the Kings house, more then all the Iewes.

14 For if thou holdest thy peace at this time, comfort and deliuerance shall appeare to the Iewes out of another place, but thou and thy fathers house shall perish: and who knoweth whether thou art come to the kingdome for such a time?

15 Then Ester commanded to answere Mordecai,

16 Goe, and assemble all the Iewes that are found in Shushan, and fast ye for me, and eate not, nor drinke in three dayes, day nor night. I also and my maydes will fast likewise, and so will I go in to the King, which is not according to the lawe: and if I perish, I perish.

17 So Mordecai went his way, and did according to all that Ester had commanded him.

Esther 5

1 And on the third day Ester put on her royal apparel, and stood in the court of the Kings palace within, ouer against the Kings house: and the King sate vpon his royal throne in the Kings palace ouer against the gate of the house.

2 And when the King saw Ester the Queene standing in the court, shee founde fauour in his sight: and the King

held out the golden scepter that was in his hand: so Ester drewe neere, and touched the toppe of the scepter.

3 Then saide the King vnto her, What wilt thou, Queene Ester? and what is thy request? it shall be euen giuen thee to the halfe of ye kingdome.

4 Then saide Ester, If it please the King, let the King and Haman come this day vnto the banket, that I haue prepared for him.

5 And the King sayd, Cause Haman to make haste that he may doe as Ester hath sayde. So the King and Haman came to the banket that Ester had prepared.

6 And the King sayd vnto Ester at the banket of wine, What is thy petition, that it may be giuen thee? and what is thy request? it shall euen be performed vnto the halfe of the kingdome.

7 Then answered Ester, and sayd, My petition and my request is,

8 If I haue found fauour in the sight of the King, and if it please the King to giue me my petition, and to perfourme my request, let the King and Haman come to the banket that I shall prepare for them, and I will doe to morowe according to the Kings saying.

9 Then went Haman forth the same day ioyfull and with a glad heart. But when Haman sawe Mordecai in the Kings gate, that he stoode not vp, nor moued for him, then was Haman full of indignation at Mordecai.

10 Neuerthelesse Haman refrayned himselfe: and when he came home, he sent, and called for his friends, and Zeresh his wife.

11 And Haman tolde them of the glory of his riches, and the multitude of his children, and all the things wherein the King had promoted him, and how that he had set him aboue the princes and seruants of the King.

12 Haman sayde moreouer, Yea, Ester the Queene did let no man come in with the King to the banket that she had prepared, saue me: and to morowe am I bidden vnto her also with the King.

13 But al this doth nothing auaile me, as long as I see Mordecai ye Iewe sitting at ye Kings gate.

14 Then sayde Zeresh his wife and all his friends vnto him, Let them make a tree of fiftie cubites hie, and to morowe speake thou vnto the King, that Mordecai may be hanged thereon: then shalt thou goe ioyfully with the King vnto the banket. And the thing pleased Haman, and he caused to make the tree.

Esther 6

1 The same night the King slept not, and he comanded to bring ye booke of the records, and the chronicles: and they were read before ye King.

2 Then it was found written that Mordecai had tolde of Bigtana, and Teresh two of the Kings eunuches, keepers of the dore, who sought to lay hands on the King Ahashuerosh.

3 Then the King sayde, What honour and dignitie hath bene giuen to Mordecai for this? And the Kings seruants that ministred vnto him, sayd, There is nothing done for him.

4 And the King sayde, Who is in the court? (Now Haman was come into the inner court of the Kings house, that he might speake vnto the King to hang Mordecai on the tree that he had prepared for him.)

5 And the Kings seruants said vnto him, Behold, Haman standeth in the court. And the King sayd, Let him come in.

6 And when Haman came in, the King saide vnto him, What shalbe done vnto ye man, whom the King will honour? Then Haman thought in his heart, To whom would the King do honour more then to me?

7 And Haman answered the King, The man whome the King would honour,

8 Let them bring for him royall apparell, which the King vseth to weare, and the horse that the King rideth vpon, and that the crowne royall may be set vpon his head.

9 And let the raiment and the horse be deliuered by the hand of one of the Kings most noble princes, and let them apparel the man (whome the King will honour) and cause him to ride vpon the horse thorow the streete of the citie, and proclayme before him, Thus shall it be done vnto the man, whome the King will honour.

10 Then the King said to Haman, Make haste, take the rayment and the horse as thou hast said, and doe so vnto Mordecai the Iewe, that sitteth at the Kings gate: let nothing fayle of all that thou hast spoken.

11 So Haman tooke the rayment and the horse, and arayed Mordecai, and brought him on horse backe thorowe the streete of the citie, and proclaymed before him, Thus shall it be done to the man whom the King will honour.

12 And Mordecai came againe to the Kings gate, but Haman hasted home mourning and his head couered.

13 And Haman tolde Zeresh his wife, and all his friends all that had befallen him. Then sayd his wise men, and Zeresh his wife vnto him, If Mordecai be of the seede of the Iewes, before whom thou hast begunne to fall; thou shalt not preuaile against him, but shalt surely fall before him.

14 And while they were yet talking with him, came the Kings eunuches and hasted to bring Haman vnto the banket that Ester had prepared.

Esther 7

1 So the King and Haman came to banket with the Queene Ester.

2 And the King said againe vnto Ester on the second day at the banket of wine, What is thy petition, Queene Ester, that it may be giue thee? and what is thy request? It shalbe euen perfourmed vnto the halfe of the kingdome.

3 And Ester the Queene answered, and said, If I haue found fauour in thy sight, O King, and if it please the King, let my life be giuen me at my petition, and my people at my request.

4 For we are solde, I, and my people, to be destroyed, to be slayne and to perish: but if we were solde for seruants, and for handmaides, I woulde haue helde my tongue: although the aduersarie could not recompense the Kings losse.

5 Then King Ahashuerosh answered, and said vnto the Queene Ester, Who is he? and where is he that presumeth to doe thus?

6 And Ester said, The aduersarie and enemie is this wicked Haman. Then Haman was afrayde before the King and the Queene.

7 And the King arose from ye banket of wine in his wrath, and went into the palace garden: but Haman stood vp, to make request for his life to the Queene Ester: for he sawe that there was a mischiefe prepared for him of the King.

8 And when the King came againe out of the palace garden, into the house where they dranke wine, Haman was fallen vpon the bed whereon Ester sate! therefore the King sayd, Will he force the Queene also before me in the house? As the worde went out of the Kings mouth, they couered Hamans face.

9 And Harbonah one of the eunuches, sayde in the presence of the King, Beholde, there standeth yet the tree in Hamans house fiftie cubites hie, which Haman had prepared for Mordecai, that spake good for the King. Then the King sayd, Hang him thereon.

10 So they hanged Haman on the tree, that he had prepared for Mordecai: then was the Kings wrath pacified.

Esther 8

1 The same day did King Ahashuerosh giue the house of Haman the aduersarie of the Iewes vnto the Queene Ester. and Mordecai came before the King: for Ester tolde what hee was vnto her.

2 And the King tooke off his ring, which he had taken from Haman, and gaue it vnto Mordecai: and Ester set Mordecai ouer the house of Haman.

3 And Ester spake yet more before the King, and fell downe at his feete weeping, and besought him that he would put away the wickednes of Haman the Agagite, and his deuice that he had imagined against the Iewes.

4 And the King held out the golden scepter toward Ester. Then arose Ester, and stood before the King,

5 And sayd, If it please the King, and if I haue found fauour in his sight, and the thing be acceptable before the King, and I please him, let it be written, that the letters of the deuice of Haman the sonne of Ammedatha the Agagite may be called againe, which he wrote to destroy the Iewes, that are in all the Kings prouinces.

6 For how can I suffer and see the euil, that shall come vnto my people? Or howe

can I suffer and see the destruction of my kinred?

7 And the King Ahashuerosh sayde vnto the Queene Ester, and to Mordecai the Iewe, Behold, I haue giuen Ester the house of Haman, whome they haue hanged vpon the tree, because he layd hand vpon the Iewes.

8 Write yee also for the Iewes, as it liketh you in the Kinges name, and seale it with the Kings ring (for the writings written in the Kings name, and sealed with the Kings ring, may no man reuoke)

9 Then were the Kings Scribes called at the same time, euen in the thirde moneth, that is the moneth Siuan, on the three and twentieth day thereof: and it was written, according to all as Mordecai commanded, vnto the Iewes and to the princes, and captaines, and rulers of the prouinces, which were from India euen vnto Ethiopia, an hundreth and seuen and twentie prouinces, vnto euery prouince, according to the writing thereof, and to euery people after their speache, and to the Iewes, according to their writing, and according to their language.

10 And hee wrote in the King Ahashuerosh name, and sealed it with the Kings ring: and he sent letters by postes on horsebacke and that rode on beastes of price, as dromedaries and coltes of mares.

11 Wherein the King graunted the Iewes (in what cities so euer they were) to gather theselues together, and to stand for their life, and to roote out, to slay and to destroy al the power of the people and of the prouince that vexed them, both children and women, and to spoyle their goods:

12 Vpon one day in all the prouinces of King Ahashuerosh, euen in the thirteenth day of the twelft moneth, which is the moneth Adar.

13 The copie of the writing was, howe there should be a commandement giuen in all and euery prouince, published among all the people, and that the Iewes should be ready against that day to auenge themselues on their enemies.

14 So the postes rode vpon beasts of price, and dromedaries, and went forth with speede, to execute the Kings commandement, and the decree was giuen at Shushan the palace.

15 And Mordecai went out from the King in royall apparell of blewe, and white, and with a great crowne of gold, and with a garment of fine linen and purple, and the citie of Shushan reioyced and was glad.

16 And vnto the Iewes was come light and ioy and gladnes, and honour.

17 Also in all and euery prouince, and in al and euery citie and place, where the Kings commandement and his decree came, there was ioy and gladnes to the Iewes, a feast and good day, and many of the people of the land became Iewes: for the feare of the Iewes fell vpon them.

Esther 9

1 So in the twelft moneth, which is the moneth Adar, vpon the thirteenth daye of the same, when the Kings commandement and his decree drew neere to be put in execution, in the day that the enemies of the Iewes hoped to haue power ouer them (but it turned contrary: for the Iewes had rule ouer them that hated them)

2 The Iewes gathered themselues together into their cities throughout all the prouinces of the King Ahashuerosh, to lay hande on such as sought their hurt, and no man coulde withstande them: for the feare of them fel vpon al people.

3 And all the rulers of the prouinces, and the princes and the captaines, and the officers of the King exalted the Iewes: for the feare of Mordecai fell vpon them.

4 For Mordecai was great in the kings house, and the report of him went through all the prouinces: for this man Mordecai waxed greater and greater.

5 Thus the Iewes smote all their enemies with strokes of the sworde and slaughter, and destruction, and did what they woulde vnto those that hated them.

6 And at Shushan the palace slewe the Iewes and destroyed fiue hundreth men,

7 And Parshandatha, and Dalphon, and Aspatha,

8 And Poratha, and Adalia, and Aridatha,

9 And Parmashta, and Arisai, and Aridai, and Vaiezatha,

10 The ten sonnes of Haman, ye sonne of Ammedatha, the aduersarie of the Iewes slewe they: but they layd not their hands on the spoyle.

11 On the same day came ye nomber of those that were slayne, vnto the palace of Shushan before the King.

12 And the King sayd vnto the Queene Ester, The Iewes haue slayne in Shushan the palace and destroyed fiue hundreth men, and the ten sonnes of Haman: what haue they done in the rest of the Kings prouinces? and what is thy petition, that it may be giuen thee? or what is thy request moreouer, that it may be performed?

13 Then sayd Ester, If it please the King, let it be granted also to morow to the Iewes that are in Shushan, to do according vnto this daies decree, that they may hang vpon ye tree Hamans ten sonnes.

14 And the King charged to doe so, and the decree was giuen at Shushan, and they hanged Hamans ten sonnes.

15 So the Iewes that were in Shushan, assembled themselues vpon the fourteenth day of the moneth Adar, and slew three hundreth men in Shushan, but on the spoyle they layd not their hand.

16 And the rest of the Iewes that were in the Kings prouinces assembled themselues, and stood for their liues, and had rest from their enemies, and slewe of them that hated them, seuentie

and fiue thousand: but they layd not their hand on the spoyle.

17 This they did on the thirteenth day of the moneth Adar, and rested the fourteenth day thereof, and kept it a day of feasting and ioy.

18 But the Iewes that were in Shushan assembled themselues on the thirteenth day, and on the fourteenth therof, and they rested on the fifteenth of the same, and kept it a day of feasting and ioy.

19 Therefore the Iewes of the villages that dwelt in the vnwalled townes, kept the foureteenth day of the moneth Adar with ioy and feasting, euen a ioyfull day, and euery one sent presents vnto his neighbour.

20 And Mordecai wrote these words, and sent letters vnto all the Iewes that were through all the prouinces of the King Ahashuerosh, both neere and farre,

21 Inioyning them that they shoulde keepe the fourteenth day of the moneth Adar, and the fifteenth day of the same, euery yeere.

22 According to the dayes wherein the Iewes rested from their enemies, and the moneth which was turned vnto them from sorowe to ioy, and from mourning into a ioyfull day, to keepe them the dayes of feasting, and ioy, and to sende presents euery man to his neyghbour, and giftes to the poore.

23 And the Iewes promised to do as they had begun, and as Mordecai had written vnto them,

24 Because Haman the sonne of Hammedatha the Agagite al the Iewes aduersarie, had imagined against the Iewes, to destroy them, and had cast Pur (that is a lot) to consume and destroy them.

25 And when she came before the King, he commanded by letters, Let this wicked deuise (which he imagined against the Iewes) turne vpon his owne head, and let them hang him and his sonnes on the tree.

26 Therfore they called these dayes Purim, by the name of Pur, and because of all the wordes of this letter, and of that which they had seene besides this, and of that which had come vnto them.

27 The Iewes also ordeined, and promised for them and for their seede, and for all that ioyned vnto them, that they would not faile to obserue those two dayes euery yeere, according to their writing, and according to their season,

28 And that these dayes shoulde be remembred, and kept throughout euery generation and euery familie, and euery prouince, and euery citie: euen these daies of Purim should not faile among the Iewes, and the memoriall of them should not perish from their seede.

29 And the Queene Ester ye daughter of Abihail and Mordecai the Iew wrote with al authoritie (to cofirme this letter of Purim ye second time)

30 And he sent letters vnto al the Iewes to the hundreth and seuen and twentie prouinces of the kingdome of Ahashuerosh, with words of peace and trueth,

31 To confirme these dayes of Purim, according to their seasons, as Mordecai the Iewe and Ester the Queene had appointed them, and as they had promised for them selues and for their seede with fasting and prayer.

32 And the decree of Ester confirmed these words of Purim, and was written in the booke.

Esther 10

1 And the King Ahashuerosh layd a tribute vpon the land, and vpon the yles of the sea.

2 And all the actes of his power, and of his might, and the declaration of the dignitie of Mordecai, wherwith the King magnified him, are they not written in the booke of the Chronicles of the Kings of Media and Persia?

3 For Mordecai the Iewe was the second vnto King Ahashuerosh, and great among the Iewes, and accepted among the multitude of his brethren, who procured the wealth of his people, and spake peaceably to all his seede.

Job

Job 1

1 There was a man in the lande of Vz called Iob, and this man was an vpright and iust man, one that feared God, and eschewed euill.

2 And he had seue sonnes, and three daughters.

3 His substance also was seuen thousande sheepe, and three thousand camels, and fiue hundreth yoke of oxen, and fiue hundreth shee asses, and his family was very great, so that this man was the greatest of all the men of the East.

4 And his sonnes went and banketted in their houses, euery one his day, and sent, and called their three sisters to eate and to drinke with them.

5 And when the dayes of their banketting were gone about, Iob sent, and sanctified them, and rose vp early in the morning, and offred burnt offrings according to the number of them all. For Iob thought, It may be that my sonnes haue sinned, and blasphemed God in their hearts: thus did Iob euery day.

6 Nowe on a day when the children of God came and stoode before the Lord, Satan came also among them.

7 Then the Lord sayde vnto Satan, Whence commest thou? And Satan answered the Lord, saying, From compassing the earth to and from, and from walking in it.

8 And the Lord saide vnto Satan, Hast thou not considered my seruant Iob, how none is like him in the earth? an vpright and iust man, one that feareth God, and escheweth euill?

9 Then Satan answered the Lord, and sayde, Doeth Iob feare God for nought?

10 Hast thou not made an hedge about him and about his house, and about all that he hath on euery side? thou hast blessed the worke of his hands, and his substance is increased in the land.

11 But stretch out now thine hand and touch all that he hath, to see if he will not blaspheme thee to thy face.

12 Then the Lord sayde vnto Satan, Lo, all that he hath is in thine hand: onely vpon himselfe shalt thou not stretch out thine hand. So Satan departed from the presence of the Lord.

13 And on a day, when his sonnes and his daughters were eating and drinking wine in their eldest brothers house,

14 There came a messenger vnto Iob, and said, The oxen were plowing, and the asses feeding in their places,

15 And the Shabeans came violently, and tooke them: yea, they haue slayne the seruants with the edge of the sworde: but I onely am escaped alone to tell thee.

16 And whiles he was yet speaking, another came, and sayde, The fire of God is fallen from the heauen, and hath burnt vp the sheepe and the seruants, and deuoured them: but I onely am escaped alone to tell thee.

17 And whiles he was yet speaking, another came, and sayd, The Caldeans set on three bands, and fell vpon the camels, and haue taken them, and haue slayne the seruantes with the edge of the sworde: but I onely am escaped alone to tell thee.

18 And whiles he was yet speaking, came an other, and sayd, Thy sonnes, and thy daughters were eating, and drinking wine in their eldest brothers house,

19 And behold, there came a great wind from beyonde the wildernesse, and smote the foure corners of the house, which fel vpon the children, and they are dead, and I onely am escaped alone to tell thee.

20 Then Iob arose, and rent his garment, and shaued his head, and fel downe vpon the ground, and worshipped,

21 And sayd, Naked came I out of my mothers wombe, and naked shall I returne thither: the Lord hath giuen, and the Lord hath taken it: blessed be the Name of the Lord.

22 In all this did not Iob sinne, nor charge God foolishly.

Job 2

1 And on a day the children of God came and stood before the Lord, and Satan came also among them, and stoode before the Lord.

2 Then the Lord sayde vnto Satan, Whence commest thou? And Satan answered the Lord, and sayd, From compassing the earth to and from, and from walking in it.

3 And the Lord sayd vnto Satan, Hast thou not considered my seruant Iob, how none is like him in the earth? an vpright and iust man, one that feareth God, and escheweth euill? for yet he continueth in his vprightnesse, although thou mouedst me against him, to destroy him without cause.

4 And Satan answered the Lord, and sayde, Skin for skin, and all that euer a man hath, will he giue for his life.

5 But stretch now out thine hand, and touch his bones and his flesh, to see if he will not blaspheme thee to thy face.

6 Then the Lord said vnto Satan, Lo, he is in thine hand, but saue his life.

7 So Satan departed from the presence of the Lord, and smote Iob with sore boyles, from the sole of his foote vnto his crowne.

8 And he tooke a potsharde to scrape him, and he sate downe among the ashes.

9 Then said his wife vnto him, Doest thou continue yet in thine vprightnes? Blaspheme God, and dye.

10 But he said vnto her, Thou speakest like a foolish woman: what? shall we receiue good at the hande of God, and not receiue euill? In all this did not Iob sinne with his lippes.

11 Nowe when Iobs three friends heard of all this euill that was come vpon him, they came euery one from his owne place, to wit, Eliphaz the Temanite, and Bildad the Shuhite, and Zophar the Naamathite: for they were agreed together to come to lament with him, and to comfort him.

12 So when they lift vp their eyes a farre off, they knewe him not: therefore they lift vp their voyces and wept, and euery one of them rent his garment, and sprinkled dust vpon their heads toward the heauen.

13 So they sate by him vpon the ground seuen dayes, and seuen nights, and none spake a worde vnto him: for they sawe, that the griefe was very great.

Job 3

1 Afterward Iob opened his mouth, and cursed his day.

2 And Iob cryed out, and sayd,

3 Let the day perish, wherein I was borne, and the night when it was sayde, There is a man childe conceiued.

4 Let that day bee darkenesse, let not God regarde it from aboue, neyther let the light shine vpon it,

5 But let darkenesse, and the shadowe of death staine it: let the cloude remayne vpon it, and let them make it fearefull as a bitter day.

6 Let darkenesse possesse that night, let it not be ioyned vnto the dayes of the yeere, nor let it come into the count of the monethes.

7 Yea, desolate be that night, and let no ioy be in it.

8 Let them that curse the day, (being readie to renue their mourning) curse it.

9 Let the starres of that twilight be dimme through darkenesse of it: let it looke for light, but haue none: neither let it see the dawning of the day,

10 Because it shut not vp the dores of my mothers wombe: nor hid sorowe from mine eyes.

11 Why died I not in the birth? or why dyed I not, when I came out of the wombe?

12 Why did the knees preuent me? and why did I sucke the breasts?

13 For so shoulde I now haue lyen and bene quiet, I should haue slept then, and bene at rest,

14 With the Kings and counselers of the earth, which haue buylded themselues desolate places:

15 Or with the princes that had golde, and haue filled their houses with siluer.

16 Or why was I not hid, as an vntimely birth, either as infants, which haue not seene the light?

17 The wicked haue there ceased from their tyrannie, and there they that laboured valiantly, are at rest.

18 The prisoners rest together, and heare not the voyce of the oppressour.

19 There are small and great, and the seruant is free from his master.

20 Wherefore is the light giuen to him that is in miserie? and life vnto them that haue heauie hearts?

21 Which long for death, and if it come not, they would euen search it more then treasures:

22 Which ioy for gladnes, and reioyce, when they can finde the graue.

23 Why is the light giuen to the man whose way is hid, and whom God hath hedged in?

24 For my sighing commeth before I eate, and my roarings are powred out like the water.

25 For the thing I feared, is come vpon me, and the thing that I was afraid of, is come vnto me.

26 I had no peace, neither had I quietnesse, neither had I rest, yet trouble is come.

Job 4

1 Then Eliphaz the Temanite answered, and sayde,

2 If we assay to commune with thee, wilt thou be grieued? but who can withholde himselfe from speaking?

3 Behold, thou hast taught many, and hast strengthened the wearie hands.

4 Thy wordes haue confirmed him that was falling, and thou hast strengthened the weake knees.

5 But now it is come vpon thee, and thou art grieued: it toucheth thee, and thou art troubled.

6 Is not this thy feare, thy confidence, thy pacience, and the vprightnesse of thy wayes?

7 Remember, I pray thee: who euer perished, being an innocent? or where were the vpright destroyed?

8 As I haue seene, they that plow iniquitie, and sowe wickednesse, reape the same.

9 With the blast of God they perish, and with the breath of his nostrels are they cosumed.

10 The roaring of the Lion, and the voyce of the Lionesse, and the teeth of the Lions whelpes are broken.

11 The Lyon perisheth for lacke of pray, and the Lyons whelpes are scattered abroade.

12 But a thing was brought to me secretly, and mine eare hath receiued a litle thereof.

13 In the thoughtes of ye visions of the night, when sleepe falleth on men,

14 Feare came vpon me, and dread which made all my bones to tremble.

15 And the wind passed before me, and made the heares of my flesh to stande vp.

16 Then stoode one, and I knewe not his face: an image was before mine eyes, and in silence heard I a voyce, saying,

17 Shall man be more iust then God? or shall a man be more pure then his maker?

18 Beholde, he founde no stedfastnesse in his Seruants, and laid follie vpon his Angels.

19 Howe much more in them that dwell in houses of clay, whose foundation is in the dust, which shalbe destroyed before the moth?

20 They be destroyed from the morning vnto the euening: they perish for euer, without regarde.

21 Doeth not their dignitie goe away with them? do they not die, and that without wisdom?

Job 5

1 Call nowe, if any will answere thee, and to which of the Saintes wilt thou turne?

2 Doubtlesse anger killeth the foolish, and enuie slayeth the idiote.

3 I haue seene the foolish well rooted, and suddenly I cursed his habitation, saying,

4 His children shalbe farre from saluation, and they shall be destroyed in the gate, and none shall deliuer them.

5 The hungrie shall eate vp his haruest: yea, they shall take it from among the thornes, and the thirstie shall drinke vp their substance.

6 For miserie commeth not foorth of the dust, neither doeth affliction spring out of the earth.

7 But man is borne vnto trauaile, as the sparkes flie vpwarde.

8 But I would inquire at God, and turne my talke vnto God:

9 Which doeth great things and vnsearchable, and marueilous things without number.

10 He giueth raine vpon the earth, and powreth water vpon the streetes,

11 And setteth vp on hie them that be lowe, that the sorowfull may be exalted to saluation.

12 He scattereth the deuices of the craftie: so that their handes can not accomplish that which they doe enterprise.

13 He taketh the wise in their craftinesse, and the counsel of the wicked is made foolish.

14 They meete with darkenesse in the day time, and grope at noone day, as in the night.

15 But he saueth the poore from the sword, from their mouth, and from the hande of the violent man,

16 So that the poore hath his hope, but iniquitie shall stop her mouth.

17 Beholde, blessed is the man whome God correcteth: therefore refuse not thou the chastising of the Almightie.

18 For he maketh the wound, and bindeth it vp: he smiteth, and his handes make whole.

19 He shall deliuer thee in sixe troubles, and in the seuenth the euill shall not touch thee.

20 In famine he shall deliuer thee from death: and in battel from the power of the sw8de.

21 Thou shalt be hid from the scourge of the tongue, and thou shalt not be afraid of destruction when it commeth.

22 But thou shalt laugh at destruction and dearth, and shalt not be afraide of the beast of the earth.

23 For the stones of the fielde shall be in league with thee, and the beastes of the field shall be at peace with thee.

24 And thou shalt knowe, that peace shall be in thy tabernacle, and thou shalt visite thine habitation, and shalt not sinne.

25 Thou shalt perceiue also, that thy seede shalbe great, and thy posteritie as the grasse of the earth.

26 Thou shalt goe to thy graue in a ful age, as a ricke of corne commeth in due season into the barne.

27 Lo, thus haue we inquired of it, and so it is: heare this and knowe it for thy selfe.

Job 6

1 Bvt Iob answered, and said,

2 Oh that my griefe were well weighed, and my miseries were layed together in the balance.

3 For it woulde be nowe heauier then the sande of the sea: therefore my wordes are swallowed vp.

4 For the arrowes of the Almightie are in me, the venime whereof doeth drinke vp my spirit, and the terrours of God fight against me.

5 Doeth the wilde asse bray when he hath grasse? or loweth the oxe when he hath fodder?

6 That which is vnsauerie, shall it be eaten without salt? or is there any taste in the white of an egge?

7 Such things as my soule refused to touch, as were sorowes, are my meate.

8 Oh that I might haue my desire, and that God would grant me the thing that I long for!

9 That is, that God would destroy me: that he would let his hand go, and cut me off.

10 Then should I yet haue comfort, (though I burne with sorowe, let him not spare) because I haue not denyed the wordes of the Holy one.

11 What power haue I that I should endure? or what is mine end, if I should prolong my life?

12 Is my strength the strength of stones? or is my flesh of brasse?

13 Is it not so, that there is in me no helpe? and that strength is taken from me?

14 He that is in miserie, ought to be comforted of his neighbour: but men haue forsaken the feare of the Almightie.

15 My brethre haue deceiued me as a brook, and as the rising of the riuers they passe away.

16 Which are blackish with yee, and wherein the snowe is hid.

17 But in time they are dryed vp with heate and are consumed: and when it is hote they faile out of their places,

18 Or they depart from their way and course, yea, they vanish and perish.

19 They that go to Tema, considered them, and they that goe to Sheba, waited for them.

20 But they were confounded: when they hoped, they came thither and were ashamed.

21 Surely nowe are ye like vnto it: ye haue seene my fearefull plague, and are afraide.

22 Was it because I said, Bring vnto me? or giue a rewarde to me of your substance?

23 And deliuer me from the enemies hande, or ransome me out of the hand of tyrants?

24 Teach me, and I wil hold my tongue: and cause me to vnderstande, wherein I haue erred.

25 Howe stedfast are the wordes of righteousnes? and what can any of you iustly reproue?

26 Doe ye imagine to reproue wordes, that the talke of the afflicted should be as the winde?

27 Ye make your wrath to fall vpon the fatherlesse, and dig a pit for your friende.

28 Nowe therefore be content to looke vpon me: for I will not lie before your face.

29 Turne, I pray you, let there be none iniquitie: returne, I say, and ye shall see yet my righteousnesse in that behalfe. Is there iniquitie in my tongue? doeth not my mouth feele sorowes?

Job 7

1 Is there not an appointed time to man vpon earth? and are not his dayes as the dayes of an hyreling?

2 As a seruant longeth for the shadowe, and as an hyreling looketh for the ende of his worke,

3 So haue I had as an inheritance the moneths of vanitie, and painefull nights haue bene appointed vnto me.

4 If I layed me downe, I sayde, When shall I arise? and measuring the euening I am euen full with tossing to and from vnto the dawning of the day.

5 My flesh is clothed with wormes and filthinesse of the dust: my skinne is rent, and become horrible.

6 My dayes are swifter then a weauers shittle, and they are spent without hope.

7 Remember that my life is but a wind, and that mine eye shall not returne to see pleasure.

8 The eye that hath seene me, shall see me no more: thine eyes are vpon me, and I shall be no longer.

9 As the cloude vanisheth and goeth away, so he that goeth downe to the graue, shall come vp no more.

10 He shall returne no more to his house, neither shall his place knowe him any more.

11 Therefore I will not spare my mouth, but will speake in the trouble of my spirite, and muse in the bitternesse of my minde.

12 Am I a sea or a whalefish, that thou keepest me in warde?

13 When I say, My couch shall relieue me, and my bed shall bring comfort in my meditation,

14 Then fearest thou me with dreames, and astonishest me with visions.

15 Therefore my soule chuseth rather to be strangled and to die, then to be in my bones.

16 I abhorre it, I shall not liue alway: spare me then, for my dayes are but vanitie.

17 What is man, that thou doest magnifie him, and that thou settest thine heart vpon him?

18 And doest visite him euery morning, and tryest him euery moment?

19 Howe long will it be yer thou depart from me? thou wilt not let me alone whiles I may swallowe my spettle.

20 I haue sinned, what shall I do vnto thee? O thou preseruer of me, why hast thou set me as a marke against thee, so that I am a burden vnto my selfe?

21 And why doest thou not pardon my trespasse? and take away mine iniquitie? for nowe shall I sleepe in the dust, and if thou seekest me in the morning, I shall not be found.

Job 8

1 Then answered Bildad the Shuhite, and saide,

2 Howe long wilt thou talke of these things? and howe long shall the wordes of thy mouth be as a mightie winde?

3 Doeth God peruert iudgement? or doeth the Almightie subuert iustice?

4 If thy sonnes haue sinned against him, and he hath sent them into the place of their iniquitie,

5 Yet if thou wilt early seeke vnto God, and pray to the Almightie,

6 If thou be pure and vpright, then surely hee will awake vp vnto thee, and he wil make the habitation of thy righteousnesse prosperous.

7 And though thy beginning be small, yet thy latter ende shall greatly encrease.

8 Inquire therefore, I pray thee, of the former age, and prepare thy selfe to search of their fathers.

9 (For we are but of yesterday, and are ignorant: for our dayes vpon earth are but a shadowe)

10 Shall not they teach thee and tell thee, and vtter the wordes of their heart?

11 Can a rush grow without myre? or can ye grasse growe without water?

12 Though it were in greene and not cutte downe, yet shall it wither before any other herbe.

13 So are the paths of al that forget God, and the hypocrites hope shall perish.

14 His confidence also shalbe cut off, and his trust shalbe as the house of a spyder.

15 He shall leane vpon his house, but it shall not stand: he shall holde him fast by it, yet shall it not endure.

16 The tree is greene before the sunne, and the branches spread ouer the garden thereof.

17 The rootes thereof are wrapped about the fountaine, and are folden about ye house of stones.

18 If any plucke it from his place, and it denie, saying, I haue not seene thee,

19 Beholde, it will reioyce by this meanes, that it may growe in another molde.

20 Behold, God will not cast away an vpright man, neither will he take the wicked by the hand,

21 Till he haue filled thy mouth with laughter, and thy lippes with ioy.

22 They that hate thee, shall be clothed with shame, and the dwelling of the wicked shall not remaine.

Job 9

1 Then Iob answered, and sayd,

2 I knowe verily that it is so: for howe should man compared vnto God, be iustified?

3 If I would dispute with him, hee could not answere him one thing of a thousand.

4 He is wise in heart, and mighty in strength: who hath bene fierce against him and hath prospered?

5 He remoueth the mountaines, and they feele not when he ouerthroweth them in his wrath.

6 Hee remoueth the earth out of her place, that the pillars thereof doe shake.

7 He commandeth the sunne, and it riseth not: hee closeth vp the starres, as vnder a signet.

8 Hee himselfe alone spreadeth out the heauens, and walketh vpon the height of the sea.

9 He maketh the starres Arcturus, Orion, and Pleiades, and the climates of the South.

10 He doeth great things, and vnsearcheable: yea, marueilous things without nomber.

11 Lo, when he goeth by me, I see him not: and when he passeth by, I perceiue him not.

12 Behold, when he taketh a pray, who can make him to restore it? who shall say vnto him, What doest thou?

13 God will not withdrawe his anger, and the most mightie helpes doe stoupe vnder him.

14 Howe much lesse shall I answere him? or howe should I finde out my words with him?

15 For though I were iust, yet could I not answere, but I would make supplication to my Iudge.

16 If I cry, and he answere me, yet woulde I not beleeue, that he heard my voyce.

17 For he destroyeth mee with a tempest, and woundeth me without cause.

18 He wil not suffer me to take my breath, but filleth me with bitternesse.

19 If we speake of strength, behold, he is strog: if we speake of iudgement, who shall bring me in to pleade?

20 If I woulde iustifie my selfe, mine owne mouth shall condemne mee: if I would be perfite, he shall iudge me wicked.

21 Though I were perfite, yet I knowe not my soule: therefore abhorre I my life.

22 This is one point: therefore I said, Hee destroyeth the perfite and the wicked.

23 If the scourge should suddenly slay, should God laugh at the punishment of the innocent?

24 The earth is giuen into the hand of ye wicked: he couereth the faces of the iudges therof: if not, where is he? or who is he?

25 My dayes haue bene more swift then a post: they haue fled, and haue seene no good thing.

26 They are passed as with the most swift ships, and as the eagle that flyeth to the pray.

27 If I say, I wil forget my complaynt, I will cease from my wrath, and comfort mee,

28 Then I am afrayd of all my sorowes, knowing that thou wilt not iudge me innocent.

29 If I be wicked, why labour I thus in vaine?

30 If I wash my selfe with snowe water, and purge mine hands most cleane,

31 Yet shalt thou plunge mee in the pit, and mine owne clothes shall make me filthie.

32 For he is not a man as I am, that I shoulde answere him, if we come together to iudgement.

33 Neyther is there any vmpire that might lay his hand vpon vs both.

34 Let him take his rod away from me, and let not his feare astonish me:

35 Then will I speake, and feare him not: but because I am not so, I holde me still.

Job 10

1 My soule is cut off though I liue: I wil leaue my complaint vpon my selfe, and wil speake in the bitternesse of my soule.

2 I will say vnto God, Condemne mee not: shew me, wherefore thou contendest with mee.

3 Thinkest thou it good to oppresse me, and to cast off the labour of thine handes, and to fauour the counsel of the wicked?

4 Hast thou carnall eyes? or doest thou see as man seeth?

5 Are thy dayes as mans dayes? or thy yeres, as the time of man,

6 That thou inquirest of mine iniquitie, and searchest out my sinne?

7 Thou knowest that I can not do wickedly: for none can deliuer me out of thine hand.

8 Thine handes haue made me, and fashioned mee wholy rounde about, and wilt thou destroy me?

9 Remember, I pray thee, that thou hast made me as the clay, and wilt thou bring me into dust againe?

10 Hast thou not powred me out as milke? and turned me to cruds like cheese?

11 Thou hast clothed me with skin and flesh, and ioyned me together with bones and sinewes.

12 Thou hast giuen me life, and grace: and thy visitation hath preserued my spirit.

13 Though thou hast hid these things in thine heart, yet I knowe that it is so with thee.

14 If I haue sinned, then thou wilt streightly looke vnto me, and wilt not holde mee giltlesse of mine iniquitie.

15 If I haue done wickedly, wo vnto me: if I haue done righteously, I will not lift vp mine head, being full of confusion, because I see mine affliction.

16 But let it increase: hunt thou me as a lyon: returne and shew thy selfe marueilous vpon me.

17 Thou renuest thy plagues against me, and thou increasest thy wrath against me: changes and armies of sorowes are against me.

18 Wherfore then hast thou brought me out of the wombe? Oh that I had perished, and that none eye had seene me!

19 And that I were as I had not bene, but brought from the wombe to the graue!

20 Are not my dayes fewe? let him cease, and leaue off from me, that I may take a litle comfort,

21 Before I goe and shall not returne, euen to the land of darkenesse and shadow of death:

22 Into a land, I say, darke as darknes it selfe, and into the shadow of death, where is none order, but the light is there as darkenesse.

Job 11

1 Then answered Zophar the Naamathite, and sayde,

2 Should not the multitude of wordes be answered? or should a great talker be iustified?

3 Should men holde their peace at thy lyes? and when thou mockest others, shall none make thee ashamed?

4 For thou hast sayde, My doctrine is pure, and I am cleane in thine eyes.

5 But, oh that God would speake and open his lippes against thee!

6 That he might shewe thee the secretes of wisedome, howe thou hast deserued double, according to right: know therefore that God hath forgotten thee for thine iniquitie.

7 Canst thou by searching finde out God? canst thou finde out ye Almighty to his perfection?

8 The heauens are hie, what canst thou doe? it is deeper then the hell, how canst thou know it?

9 The measure thereof is longer then the earth, and it is broader then the sea.

10 If hee cut off and shut vp, or gather together, who can turne him backe?

11 For hee knoweth vaine men, and seeth iniquitie, and him that vnderstandeth nothing.

12 Yet vaine man would be wise, though man new borne is like a wilde asse colte.

13 If thou prepare thine heart, and stretch out thine hands toward him:

14 If iniquitie be in thine hand, put it farre away, and let no wickednesse dwell in thy Tabernacle.

15 The truely shalt thou lift vp thy face without spot, and shalt be stable, and shalt not feare.

16 But thou shalt forget thy miserie, and remember it as waters that are past.

17 Thine age also shall appeare more cleare then the noone day: thou shalt shine and bee as the morning.

18 And thou shalt bee bolde, because there is hope: and thou shalt digge pittes, and shalt lye downe safely.

19 For when thou takest thy rest, none shall make thee afraide: yea, many shall make sute vnto thee.

20 But the eyes of the wicked shall faile, and their refuge shall perish, and their hope shalbe sorow of minde.

Job 12

1 Then Iob answered, and sayde,

2 In deede because that ye are the people onely, wisedome must dye with you.

3 But I haue vnderstanding aswel as you, and am not inferior vnto you: yea, who knoweth not such things?

4 I am as one mocked of his neighbour, who calleth vpon God, and he heareth him: the iust and the vpright is laughed to scorne.

5 Hee that is readie to fall, is as a lampe despised in the opinion of the riche.

6 The tabernacles of robbers doe prosper, and they are in safetie, that prouoke God, whome God hath enriched with his hand.

7 Aske now the beasts, and they shall teach thee, and the foules of the heauen, and they shall tell thee:

8 Or speake to the earth, and it shall shewe thee: or the fishes of the sea, and they shall declare vnto thee.

9 Who is ignorant of all these, but that the hande of the Lord hath made these?

10 In whose hande is the soule of euery liuing thing, and the breath of all mankinde.

11 Doeth not the eares discerne the words? and the mouth taste meate for it selfe?

12 Among the ancient is wisedome, and in the length of dayes is vnderstanding.

13 With him is wisedome and strength: he hath counsell and vnderstanding.

14 Beholde, he will breake downe, and it can not be built: he shutteth a man vp, and he can not be loosed.

15 Beholde, he withholdeth the waters, and they drie vp: but when he sendeth them out, they destroy the earth.

16 With him is strength and wisedome: hee that is deceiued, and that deceiueth, are his.

17 He causeth the counsellers to goe as spoyled, and maketh the iudges fooles.

18 He looseth the collar of Kings, and girdeth their loynes with a girdle.

19 He leadeth away the princes as a pray, and ouerthroweth the mightie.

20 He taketh away the speach from the faithfull counsellers, and taketh away the iudgement of the ancient.

21 He powreth contempt vpon princes, and maketh the strength of the mightie weake.

22 He discouereth the deepe places from their darkenesse, and bringeth foorth the shadowe of death to light.

23 He increaseth the people, and destroyeth them: he inlargeth the nations, and bringeth them in againe.

24 He taketh away the heartes of the that are the chiefe ouer the people of the earth, and maketh them to wander in the wildernes out of the way.

25 They grope in the darke without light: and he maketh the to stagger like a drunken man.

Job 13

1 Loe, mine eye hath seene all this: mine eare hath heard, and vnderstande it.

2 I knowe also as much as you knowe: I am not inferiour vnto you.

3 But I will speake to the Almightie, and I desire to dispute with God.

4 For in deede ye forge lyes, and all you are physitions of no value.

5 Oh, that you woulde holde your tongue, that it might be imputed to you for wisedome!

6 Nowe heare my disputation, and giue eare to the arguments of my lips.

7 Will ye speake wickedly for Gods defence, and talke deceitfully for his cause?

8 Will ye accept his person? or will ye contende for God?

9 Is it well that he shoulde seeke of you? will you make a lye for him, as one lyeth for a man?

10 He will surely reprooue you, if ye doe secretly accept any person.

11 Shall not his excellencie make you afraid? and his feare fall vpon you?

12 Your memories may be compared vnto ashes, and your bodyes to bodyes of clay.

13 Holde your tongues in my presence, that I may speake, and let come vpon what will.

14 Wherefore doe I take my flesh in my teeth, and put my soule in mine hande?

15 Loe, though he slay me, yet will I trust in him, and I will reprooue my wayes in his sight.

16 He shalbe my saluation also: for the hypocrite shall not come before him.

17 Heare diligently my wordes, and marke my talke.

18 Beholde nowe: if I prepare me to iudgement, I knowe that I shalbe iustified.

19 Who is he, that will pleade with me? for if I nowe holde my tongue, I dye.

20 But doe not these two things vnto me: then will I not hide my selfe from thee.

21 Withdrawe thine hande from me, and let not thy feare make me afraide.

22 Then call thou, and I will answere: or let me speake, and answere thou me.

23 Howe many are mine iniquities and sinnes? shewe me my rebellion, and my sinne.

24 Wherefore hidest thou thy face, and takest me for thine enemie?

25 Wilt thou breake a leafe driuen to and from? and wilt thou pursue the drie stubble?

26 For thou writest bitter things against me, and makest me to possesse the iniquities of my youth.

27 Thou puttest my feete also in the stocks, and lookest narrowly vnto all my pathes, and makest the print thereof in ye heeles of my feet.

28 Such one consumeth like a rotten thing, and as a garment that is motheaten.

Job 14

1 Man that is borne of woman, is of short continuance, and full of trouble.

2 He shooteth foorth as a flowre, and is cut downe: he vanisheth also as a shadowe, and continueth not.

3 And yet thou openest thine eyes vpon such one, and causest me to enter into iudgement with thee.

4 Who can bring a cleane thing out of filthinesse? there is not one.

5 Are not his dayes determined? the nober of his moneths are with thee: thou hast appointed his boundes, which he can not passe.

6 Turne from him that he may cease vntill his desired day, as an hyreling.

7 For there is hope of a tree, if it bee cut downe, that it will yet sproute, and the branches thereof will not cease.

8 Though the roote of it waxe olde in the earth, and the stocke thereof be dead in ye ground,

9 Yet by the sent of water it will bud, and bring foorth boughes like a plant.

10 But man is sicke, and dyeth, and man perisheth, and where is he?

11 As the waters passe from the sea, and as the flood decayeth and dryeth vp,

12 So man sleepeth and riseth not: for hee shall not wake againe, nor be raised from his sleepe till the heauen be no more.

13 Oh that thou wouldest hide me in the graue, and keepe me secret, vntill thy wrath were past, and wouldest giue me terme, and remember me.

14 If a man die, shall he liue againe? All the dayes of mine appointed time will I waite, till my changing shall come.

15 Thou shalt call me, and I shall answere thee: thou louest the worke of thine own hands.

16 But nowe thou nombrest my steppes, and doest not delay my sinnes.

17 Mine iniquitie is sealed vp, as in a bagge, and thou addest vnto my wickednesse.

18 And surely as the mountaine that falleth, commeth to nought, and the rocke that is remooued from his place:

19 As the water breaketh the stones, when thou ouerflowest the things which growe in the dust of ye earth: so thou destroyest ye hope of man.

20 Thou preuailest alway against him, so that he passeth away: he changeth his face when thou castest him away.

21 And he knoweth not if his sonnes shall be honourable, neither shall he vnderstand concerning them, whether they shalbe of lowe degree,

22 But while his flesh is vpon him, he shall be sorowfull, and while his soule is in him, it shall mourne.

Job 15

1 Then answered Eliphaz the Temanite, and saide,

2 Shal a wise man speake words of ye winde, and fill his bellie with the East winde?

3 Shall he dispute with wordes not comely? or with talke that is not profitable?

4 Surely thou hast cast off feare, and restrainest prayer before God.

5 For thy mouth declareth thine iniquitie, seeing thou hast chosen ye tongue of the crafty.

6 Thine owne mouth condemneth thee, and not I, and thy lippes testifie against thee.

7 Art thou the first man, that was borne? and wast thou made before the hils?

8 Hast thou heard the secret counsell of God, and doest thou restraine wisedome to thee?

9 What knowest thou that we knowe not? and vnderstandest that is not in vs?

10 With vs are both auncient and very aged men, farre older then thy father.

11 Seeme the consolations of God small vnto thee? is this thing strange vnto thee?

12 Why doeth thine heart take thee away, and what doe thine eyes meane,

13 That thou answerest to God at thy pleasure, and bringest such wordes out of thy mouth?

14 What is man, that he should be cleane? and he that is borne of woman, that he shoulde be iust?

15 Beholde, he founde no stedfastnesse in his Saintes: yea, the heauens are not cleane in his sight.

16 How much more is man abominable, and filthie, which drinketh iniquitie like water?

17 I will tell thee: heare me, and I will declare that which I haue seene:

18 Which wise men haue tolde, as they haue heard of their fathers, and haue not kept it secret:

19 To whome alone the land was giuen and no stranger passed through them.

20 The wicked man is continually as one that traueileth of childe, and the nomber of yeeres is hid from the tyrant.

21 A sounde of feare is in his eares, and in his prosperitie the destroyer shall come vpon him.

22 He beleeueth not to returne out of darknesse: for he seeth the sworde before him.

23 He wandreth to and from for bread where he may: he knoweth that the day of darkenesse is prepared at hande.

24 Affliction and anguish shall make him afraide: they shall preuaile against him as a King readie to the battell.

25 For he hath stretched out his hand against GOD, and made him selfe strong against the Almightie.

26 Therefore God shall runne vpon him, euen vpon his necke, and against the most thicke part of his shielde.

27 Because he hath couered his face with his fatnesse, and hath colloppes in his flancke.

28 Though he dwell in desolate cities, and in houses which no man inhabiteth, but are become heapes,

29 He shall not be rich, neither shall his substance continue, neither shall he prolong the perfection thereof in the earth.

30 He shall neuer depart out of darkenesse: the flame shall drie vp his branches, and he shall goe away with the breath of his mouth.

31 He beleeueth not that he erreth in vanitie: therefore vanitie shalbe his change.

32 His branch shall not be greene, but shall be cut off before his day.

33 God shall destroy him as the vine her sower grape, and shall cast him off, as the oliue doeth her flowre.

34 For the congregation of the hypocrite shalbe desolate, and fire shall deuoure the houses of bribes.

35 For they conceiue mischiefe and bring foorth vanitie, and their bellie hath prepared deceite.

Job 16

1 Bvt Iob answered, and said,

2 I haue oft times heard such things: miserable comforters are ye all.

3 Shall there be none ende of wordes of winde? or what maketh thee bold so to answere?

4 I could also speake as yee doe: (but woulde God your soule were in my soules stead) I could keepe you company in speaking, and could shake mine head at you,

5 But I woulde strengthen you with my mouth, and the comfort of my lips should asswage your sorowe.

6 Though I speake, my sorow can not be asswaged: though I cease, what release haue I?

7 But now hee maketh mee wearie: O God, thou hast made all my congregation desolate,

8 And hast made me full of wrinkles which is a witnesse thereof, and my

leannes ryseth vp in me, testifying the same in my face.

9 His wrath hath torne me, and hee hateth me, and gnasheth vpon mee with his teeth: mine enemie hath sharpened his eyes against me.

10 They haue opened their mouthes vpon me, and smitten me on the cheeke in reproch; they gather themselues together against me.

11 God hath deliuered me to the vniust, and hath made mee to turne out of the way by the hands of the wicked.

12 I was in welth, but he hath brought me to nought: he hath taken me by the necke, and beaten me, and set me as a marke for himselfe.

13 His archers compasse mee rounde about: he cutteth my reines, and doth not spare, and powreth my gall vpon the ground.

14 He hath broken me with one breaking vpon another, and runneth vpon me like a gyant.

15 I haue sowed a sackcloth vpon my skinne, and haue abased mine horne vnto the dust.

16 My face is withered with weeping, and the shadow of death is vpon mine eyes,

17 Though there be no wickednesse in mine hands, and my prayer be pure.

18 O earth, couer not thou my blood, and let my crying finde no place.

19 For lo, now my witnesse is in the heauen, and my record is on hie.

20 My friends speake eloquently against me: but mine eye powreth out teares vnto God.

21 Oh that a man might pleade with God, as man with his neighbour!

22 For the yeeres accounted come, and I shall go the way, whence I shall not returne.

Job 17

1 My breath is corrupt: my dayes are cut off, and the graue is readie for me.

2 There are none but mockers with mee, and mine eye continueth in their bitternesse.

3 Lay downe nowe and put me in suretie for thee: who is hee, that will touch mine hand?

4 For thou hast hid their heart from vnderstanding: therefore shalt thou not set them vp on hie.

5 For the eyes of his children shall faile, that speaketh flattery to his friends.

6 Hee hath also made mee a byword of the people, and I am as a Tabret before them.

7 Mine eye therefore is dimme for griefe, and all my strength is like a shadowe.

8 The righteous shalbe astonied at this, and the innocent shalbe moued against ye hypocrite.

9 But the righteous wil holde his way, and he whose hands are pure, shall increase his strength.

10 All you therefore turne you, and come nowe, and I shall not finde one wise among you.

11 My dayes are past, mine enterprises are broken, and the thoughts of mine heart

12 Haue changed the nyght for the day, and the light that approched, for darkenesse.

13 Though I hope, yet the graue shall bee mine house, and I shall make my bed in the darke.

14 I shall say to corruption, Thou art my father, and to the worme, Thou art my mother and my sister.

15 Where is then now mine hope? or who shall consider the thing, that I hoped for?

16 They shall goe downe into the bottome of the pit: surely it shall lye together in the dust.

Job 18

1 Then answered Bildad the Shuhite, and said,

2 When will yee make an ende of your words? cause vs to vnderstande, and then wee will speake.

3 Wherefore are wee counted as beastes, and are vile in your sight?

4 Thou art as one that teareth his soule in his anger. Shall the earth bee forsaken for thy sake? or the rocke remoued out of his place?

5 Yea, the light of the wicked shalbe quenched, and the sparke of his fire shall not shine.

6 The light shalbe darke in his dwelling, and his candle shalbe put out with him.

7 The steps of his strength shalbe restrained, and his owne counsell shall cast him downe.

8 For hee is taken in the net by his feete, and he walketh vpon the snares.

9 The grenne shall take him by the heele, and the theefe shall come vpon him.

10 A snare is layed for him in the ground, and a trappe for him in the way.

11 Fearefulnesse shall make him afrayde on euery side, and shall driue him to his feete.

12 His strength shalbe famine: and destruction shalbe readie at his side.

13 It shall deuoure the inner partes of his skinne, and the first borne of death shall deuoure his strength.

14 His hope shalbe rooted out of his dwelling, and shall cause him to go to the King of feare.

15 Feare shall dwell in his house (because it is not his) and brimstone shalbe scattered vpon his habitation.

16 His rootes shalbe dryed vp beneath, and aboue shall his branche be cut downe.

17 His remembrance shall perish from the earth, and he shall haue no name in the streete.

18 They shall driue him out of the light vnto darkenesse, and chase him out of the world.

19 Hee shall neither haue sonne nor nephewe among his people, nor any posteritie in his dwellings.

20 The posteritie shalbe astonied at his day, and feare shall come vpon the ancient.

21 Surely such are the habitations of the wicked, and this is the place of him that knoweth not God.

Job 19

1 Bvt Iob answered, and said,

2 Howe long will yee vexe my soule, and torment me with wordes?

3 Ye haue now ten times reproched me, and are not ashamed: ye are impudent toward mee.

4 And though I had in deede erred, mine errour remaineth with me.

5 But in deede if ye will aduance your selues against me, and rebuke me for my reproche,

6 Know nowe, that God hath ouerthrowen me, and hath compassed me with his net.

7 Beholde, I crie out of violence, but I haue none answere: I crie, but there is no iudgement.

8 Hee hath hedged vp my way that I cannot passe, and he hath set darkenesse in my paths.

9 Hee hath spoyled mee of mine honour, and taken the crowne away from mine head.

10 He hath destroyed mee on euery side and I am gone: and he hath remoued mine hope like a tree.

11 And he hath kindled his wrath against me, and counteth mee as one of his enemies.

12 His armies came together, and made their way vpon me, and camped about my tabernacle.

13 He hath remooued my brethre farre from me, and also mine acquaintance were strangers vnto me.

14 My neighbours haue forsaken me, and my familiars haue forgotten me.

15 They that dwel in mine house, and my maydes tooke me for a stranger: for I was a stranger in their sight.

16 I called my seruant, but he would not answere, though I prayed him with my mouth.

17 My breath was strange vnto my wife, though I prayed her for the childrens sake of mine owne body.

18 The wicked also despised mee, and when I rose, they spake against me.

19 All my secret friends abhorred me, and they whome I loued, are turned against me.

20 My bone cleaueth to my skinne and to my flesh, and I haue escaped with the skinne of my teeth.

21 Haue pitie vpon me: haue pitie vpon me, (O yee my friendes) for the hande of God hath touched me.

22 Why do ye persecute me, as God? and are not satisfied with my flesh?

23 Oh that my wordes were nowe written! oh that they were written euen in a booke,

24 And grauen with an yron pen in lead, or in stone for euer!

25 For I am sure, that my Redeemer liueth, and he shall stand the last on the earth.

26 And though after my skin wormes destroy this bodie, yet shall I see God in my flesh.

27 Whome I my selfe shall see, and mine eyes shall beholde, and none other for me, though my reynes are consumed within me.

28 But yee sayde, Why is hee persecuted? And there was a deepe matter in me.

29 Be ye afraide of the sworde: for the sworde will be auenged of wickednesse, that yee may knowe that there is a iudgement.

Job 20

1 Then answered Zophar the Naamathite and saide,

2 Doubtlesse my thoughts cause me to answere, and therefore I make haste.

3 I haue heard the correction of my reproch: therefore the spirite of mine vnderstanding causeth me to answere.

4 Knowest thou not this of olde? and since God placed man vpon the earth,

5 That the reioycing of the wicked is short, and that the ioy of hypocrites is but a moment?

6 Though his excellencie mount vp to the heauen, and his head reache vnto the cloudes,

7 Yet shall hee perish for euer, like his dung, and they which haue seene him, shall say, Where is hee?

8 He shall flee away as a dreame, and they shall not finde him, and shall passe away as a vision of the night,

9 So that the eye which had seene him, shall do so no more, and his place shall see him no more.

10 His children shall flatter the poore, and his hands shall restore his substance.

11 His bones are full of the sinne of his youth, and it shall lie downe with him in the dust.

12 When wickednesse was sweete in his mouth, and he hid it vnder his tongue,

13 And fauoured it, and would not forsake it, but kept it close in his mouth,

14 Then his meat in his bowels was turned: the gall of Aspes was in the middes of him.

15 He hath deuoured substance, and hee shall vomit it: for God shall drawe it out of his bellie.

16 He shall sucke the gall of Aspes, and the vipers tongue shall slay him.

17 He shall not see the riuers, nor the floods and streames of honie and butter.

18 He shall restore the labour, and shall deuoure no more: euen according to the substance shalbe his exchange, and he shall enioy it no more.

19 For he hath vndone many: he hath forsaken the poore, and hath spoyled houses which he builded not.

20 Surely he shall feele no quietnes in his bodie, neither shall he reserue of that which he desired.

21 There shall none of his meate bee left: therefore none shall hope for his goods.

22 When he shalbe filled with his abundance, he shalbe in paine, and the hand of all the wicked shall assaile him.

23 He shall be about to fill his belly, but God shall sende vpon him his fierce wrath, and shall cause to rayne vpon him, euen vpon his meate.

24 He shall flee from the yron weapons, and the bow of steele shall strike him through.

25 The arrowe is drawen out, and commeth forth of the body, and shineth of his gall, so feare commeth vpon him.

26 All darkenes shalbe hid in his secret places: the fire that is not blowen, shall deuoure him, and that which remaineth in his tabernacle, shalbe destroyed.

27 The heauen shall declare his wickednes, and the earth shall rise vp against him.

28 The increase of his house shall go away: it shall flow away in the day of his wrath.

29 This is the portion of the wicked man from God, and the heritage that he shall haue of God for his wordes.

Job 21

1 Bvt Iob answered, and sayd,

2 Heare diligently my wordes, and this shalbe in stead of your consolations.

3 Suffer mee, that I may speake, and when I haue spoken, mocke on.

4 Doe I direct my talke to man? If it were so, how should not my spirit be troubled?

5 Marke mee, and be abashed, and lay your hand vpon your mouth.

6 Euen when I remember, I am afrayde, and feare taketh hold on my flesh.

7 Wherefore do the wicked liue, and waxe olde, and grow in wealth?

8 Their seede is established in their sight with them, and their generation before their eyes.

9 Their houses are peaceable without feare, and the rod of God is not vpon them.

10 Their bullocke gendreth, and fayleth not: their cow calueth, and casteth not her calfe.

11 They send forth their children like sheepe, and their sonnes dance.

12 They take the tabret and harpe, and reioyce in the sound of the organs.

13 They spend their dayes in wealth, and suddenly they go downe to the graue.

14 They say also vnto God, Depart from vs: for we desire not the knowledge of thy wayes.

15 Who is the Almightie, that we should serue him? and what profit should we haue, if we should pray vnto him?

16 Lo, their wealth is not in their hand: therfore let the counsell of the wicked bee farre from me.

17 How oft shall the candle of the wicked be put out? and their destruction come vpon them? he wil deuide their liues in his wrath.

18 They shall be as stubble before the winde, and as chaffe that the storme carieth away.

19 God wil lay vp the sorowe of the father for his children: when he rewardeth him, hee shall knowe it.

20 His eyes shall see his destruction, and he shall drinke of the wrath of the Almightie.

21 For what pleasure hath he in his house after him, when the nomber of his moneths is cut off?

22 Shall any teache God knowledge, who iudgeth the highest things?

23 One dyeth in his full strength, being in all ease and prosperitie.

24 His breasts are full of milke, and his bones runne full of marowe.

25 And another dieth in the bitternes of his soule, and neuer eateth with pleasure.

26 They shall sleepe both in the dust, and the wormes shall couer them.

27 Behold, I know your thoughts, and the enterprises, wherewith ye do me wrong.

28 For ye say, Where is the princes house? and where is the tabernacle of the wickeds dwelling?

29 May ye not aske the that go by the way? and ye can not deny their signes.

30 But the wicked is kept vnto the day of destruction, and they shall be brought forth to the day of wrath.

31 Who shall declare his way to his face? and who shall reward him for that he hath done?

32 Yet shall he be brought to the graue, and remaine in the heape.

33 The slimie valley shalbe sweete vnto him, and euery man shall draw after him, as before him there were innumerable.

34 How then comfort ye me in vaine, seeing in your answeres there remaine but lyes?

Job 22

1 Then Eliphaz the Temanite answered, and sayde,

2 May a man be profitable vnto God, as he that is wise, may be profitable to himselfe?

3 Is it any thing vnto the Almightie, that thou art righteous? or is it profitable to him, that thou makest thy wayes vpright?

4 Is it for feare of thee that he will accuse thee? or go with thee into iudgement?

5 Is not thy wickednes great, and thine iniquities innumerable?

6 For thou hast taken the pledge from thy brother for nought, and spoyled the clothes of the naked.

7 To such as were wearie, thou hast not giuen water to drinke, and hast withdrawen bread from the hungrie.

8 But the mightie man had the earth, and he that was in autoritie, dwelt in it.

9 Thou hast cast out widowes emptie, and the armes of the fatherles were broken.

10 Therefore snares are round about thee, and feare shall suddenly trouble thee:

11 Or darkenes that thou shouldest not see, and abundance of waters shall couer thee.

12 Is not God on hie in the heauen? and behold the height of the starres how hie they are.

13 But thou sayest, How should God know? can he iudge through the darke cloude?

14 The cloudes hide him that he can not see, and he walketh in the circle of heauen.

15 Hast thou marked the way of the worlde, wherein wicked men haue walked?

16 Which were cut downe before the time, whose foundation was as a riuer that ouerflowed:

17 Which sayd vnto God, Depart from vs, and asked what the Almightie could do for them.

18 Yet hee filled their houses with good things: but let the counsell of the wicked be farre from me.

19 The righteous shall see them, and shall reioyce, and the innocent shall laugh them to scorne.

20 Surely our substance is hid: but the fire hath deuoured the remnant of them.

21 Therefore acquaint thy selfe, I pray thee, with him, and make peace: thereby thou shalt haue prosperitie.

22 Receiue, I pray thee, the law of his mouth, and lay vp his words in thine heart.

23 If thou returne to the Almightie, thou shalt be buylt vp, and thou shalt put iniquitie farre from thy tabernacle.

24 Thou shalt lay vp golde for dust, and the gold of Ophir, as the flintes of the riuers.

25 Yea, the Almightie shalbe thy defence, and thou shalt haue plentie of siluer.

26 And thou shalt then delite in the Almightie, and lift vp thy face vnto God.

27 Thou shalt make thy praier vnto him, and he shall heare thee, and thou shalt render thy vowes.

28 Thou shalt also decree a thing, and he shall establish it vnto thee, and the light shall shine vpon thy wayes.

29 When others are cast downe, then shalt thou say, I am lifted vp: and God shall saue the humble person.

30 The innocent shall deliuer the yland, and it shalbe preserued by the purenes of thine hands.

Job 23

1 Bvt Iob answered and sayd,

2 Though my talke be this day in bitternes, and my plague greater then my groning,

3 Would God yet I knew how to finde him, I would enter vnto his place.

4 I would pleade the cause before him, and fill my mouth with arguments.

5 I would knowe the wordes, that he would answere me, and would vnderstand what he would say vnto me.

6 Would he plead against me with his great power? No, but he would put strength in me.

7 There the righteous might reason with him, so I shoulde be deliuered for euer from my Iudge.

8 Behold, if I go to the East, he is not there: if to the West, yet I can not perceiue him:

9 If to the North where he worketh, yet I cannot see him: he wil hide himselfe in the South, and I cannot beholde him.

10 But he knoweth my way, and trieth mee, and I shall come forth like the gold.

11 My foote hath followed his steps: his way haue I kept, and haue not declined.

12 Neyther haue I departed from the commandement of his lippes, and I haue esteemed the words of his mouth more then mine appointed foode.

13 Yet he is in one minde, and who can turne him? yea, he doeth what his minde desireth.

14 For he will performe that, which is decreed of me, and many such things are with him.

15 Therefore I am troubled at his presence, and in considering it, I am afraid of him.

16 For God hath softened mine heart, and the Almightie hath troubled me.

17 For I am not cut off in darknesse, but he hath hid the darkenesse from my face.

Job 24

1 Howe should not the times be hid from the Almightie, seeing that they which knowe him, see not his dayes?

2 Some remoue the land marks, that rob the flockes and feede thereof.

3 They leade away the asse of the fatherles: and take the widowes oxe to pledge.

4 They make the poore to turne out of the way, so that the poore of the earth hide themselues together.

5 Behold, others as wilde asses in the wildernesse, goe forth to their businesse, and rise early for a praye: the wildernesse giueth him and his children foode.

6 They reape his prouision in the fielde, but they gather the late vintage of the wicked.

7 They cause the naked to lodge without garment, and without couering in the colde.

8 They are wet with the showres of the moutaines, and they imbrace the rocke for want of a couering.

9 They plucke the fatherles from the breast, and take the pledge of the poore.

10 They cause him to go naked without clothing, and take the glening from the hungrie.

11 They that make oyle betweene their walles, and treade their wine presses, suffer thirst.

12 Men cry out of the citie, and the soules of the slayne cry out: yet God doth not charge them with follie.

13 These are they, that abhorre the light: they know not the wayes thereof, nor continue in the paths thereof.

14 The murtherer riseth earely and killeth the poore and the needie: and in the night he is as a theefe.

15 The eye also of the adulterer waiteth for the twilight, and sayth, None eye shall see me, and disguiseth his face.

16 They digge through houses in the darke, which they marked for themselues in the daye: they knowe not the light.

17 But the morning is euen to them as the shadow of death: if one knowe them, they are in the terrours of the shadowe of death.

18 He is swift vpon the waters: their portion shalbe cursed in the earth: he will not behold the way of the vineyardes.

19 As the dry ground and heate consume the snowe waters, so shall the graue the sinners.

20 The pitifull man shall forget him: the worme shall feele his sweetenes: he shalbe no more remembered, and the wicked shalbe broke like a tree.

21 He doth euil intreat ye barren, that doeth not beare, neither doeth he good to the widowe.

22 He draweth also the mighty by his power, and when he riseth vp, none is sure of life.

23 Though men giue him assurance to be in safetie, yet his eyes are vpon their wayes.

24 They are exalted for a litle, but they are gone, and are brought lowe as all others: they are destroyed, and cut off as the toppe of an eare of corne.

25 But if it be not so, where is he? or who wil proue me a lyer, and make my words of no value?

Job 25

1 Then answered Bildad the Shuhite, and sayd,

2 Power and feare is with him, that maketh peace in his hie places.

3 Is there any nomber in his armies? and vpon whom shall not his light arise?

4 And howe may a man be iustified with God? or how can he be cleane, that is borne of woman?

5 Behold, he wil giue no light to the moone, and the starres are vncleane in his sight.

6 How much more man, a worme, euen the sonne of man, which is but a worme?

Job 26

1 Bvt Iob answered, and sayde,

2 Whom helpest thou? him that hath no power? sauest thou the arme that hath no strength?

3 Whome counsellest thou? him that hath no wisedome? thou shewest right well as the thing is.

4 To whom doest thou declare these words? or whose spirit commeth out of thee?

5 The dead things are formed vnder the waters, and neere vnto them.

6 The graue is naked before him, and there is no couering for destruction.

7 He stretcheth out the North ouer the emptie place, and hangeth the earth vpon nothing.

8 He bindeth the waters in his cloudes, and the cloude is not broken vnder them.

9 He holdeth backe the face of his throne: and spreadeth his cloude vpon it.

10 He hath set bounds about the waters, vntil the day and night come to an ende.

11 The pillars of heauen tremble and quake at his reproofe.

12 The sea is calme by his power, and by his vnderstanding he smiteth the pride thereof.

13 His Spirite hath garnished the heauens, and his hand hath formed the crooked serpent.

14 Loe, these are part of his wayes: but how litle a portion heare we of him? and who can vnderstand his fearefull power?

Job 27

1 Moreouer Iob proceeded and continued his parable, saying,

2 The liuing God hath taken away my iudgement: for the Almightie hath put my soule in bitternesse.

3 Yet so long as my breath is in me, and the Spirit of God in my nostrels,

4 My lips surely shall speake no wickednesse, and my tongue shall vtter no deceite.

5 God forbid, that I should iustifie you: vntill I dye, I will neuer take away mine innocencie from my selfe.

6 I will keepe my righteousnesse, and wil not forsake it: mine heart shall not reprooue me of my dayes.

7 Mine enemie shall be as the wicked, and he that riseth against me, as the vnrighteous.

8 For what hope hath the hypocrite when he hath heaped vp riches, if God take away his soule?

9 Will God heare his cry, when trouble commeth vpon him?

10 Will he set his delight on the Almightie? will he call vpon God at all times?

11 I will teache you what is in the hande of God, and I wil not conceale that which is with the Almightie.

12 Beholde, all ye your selues haue seene it: why then doe you thus vanish in vanitie?

13 This is the portion of a wicked man with God, and the heritage of tyrants, which they shall receiue of the Almightie.

14 If his children be in great nomber, the sworde shall destroy them, and his posteritie shall not be satisfied with bread.

15 His remnant shall be buried in death, and his widowes shall not weepe.

16 Though he shoulde heape vp siluer as the dust, and prepare rayment as the clay,

17 He may prepare it, but the iust shall put it on, and the innocent shall deuide the siluer.

18 He buildeth his house as the moth, and as a lodge that the watchman maketh.

19 When the rich man sleepeth, he shall not be gathered to his fathers: they opened their eyes, and he was gone.

20 Terrours shall take him as waters, and a tempest shall cary him away by night.

21 The East winde shall take him away, and he shall depart: and it shall hurle him out of his place.

22 And God shall cast vpon him and not spare, though he would faine flee out of his hand.

23 Euery man shall clap their hands at him, and hisse at him out of their place.

Job 28

1 The siluer surely hath his veyne, and ye gold his place, where they take it.

2 Yron is taken out of the dust, and brasse is molten out of the stone.

3 God putteth an end to darkenesse, and he tryeth the perfection of all things: he setteth a bond of darkenesse, and of the shadowe of death.

4 The flood breaketh out against the inhabitant, and the waters forgotten of the foote, being higher then man, are gone away.

5 Out of the same earth commeth bread, and vnder it, as it were fire is turned vp.

6 The stones thereof are a place of saphirs, and the dust of it is golde.

7 There is a path which no foule hath knowen, neyther hath the kites eye seene it.

8 The lyons whelpes haue not walked it, nor the lyon passed thereby.

9 He putteth his hand vpon the rockes, and ouerthroweth the mountaines by the rootes.

10 He breaketh riuers in the rockes, and his eye seeth euery precious thing.

11 He bindeth the floods, that they doe not ouerflowe, and the thing that is hid, bringeth he to light.

12 But where is wisdome found? and where is the place of vnderstanding?

13 Man knoweth not the price thereof: for it is not found in the land of the liuing.

14 The depth sayth, It is not in mee: the sea also sayth, It is not with me.

15 Golde shall not be giuen for it, neyther shall siluer be weighed for the price thereof.

16 It shall not be valued with the wedge of golde of Ophir, nor with the precious onix, nor the saphir.

17 The golde nor the chrystall shall be equall vnto it, nor the exchange shalbe for plate of fine golde.

18 No mention shall be made of coral, nor of the gabish: for wisedome is more precious then pearles.

19 The Topaz of Ethiopia shall not be equall vnto it, neither shall it be valued with the wedge of pure gold.

20 Whence then commeth wisedome? and where is the place of vnderstanding,

21 Seeing it is hid from the eyes of all the liuing, and is hid from the foules of the heauen?

22 Destruction and death say, We haue heard the fame thereof with our eares.

23 But God vnderstandeth the way thereof, and he knoweth the place thereof.

24 For he beholdeth the endes of the world, and seeth all that is vnder heauen,

25 To make the weight of the windes, and to weigh the waters by measure.

26 When he made a decree for the rayne, and a way for the lightening of the thunders,

27 Then did he see it, and counted it: he prepared it and also considered it.

28 And vnto man he said, Behold, the feare of the Lord is wisedome, and to depart from euil is vnderstanding.

Job 29

1 So Iob proceeded and continued his parable, saying,

2 Oh that I were as in times past, when God preserued me!

3 When his light shined vpon mine head: and when by his light I walked thorowe the darkenesse,

4 As I was in the dayes of my youth: when Gods prouidence was vpon my tabernacle:

5 When the almightie was yet with me, and my children round about me.

6 When I washed my pathes with butter, and when the rocke powred me out riuers of oyle:

7 When I went out to the gate, euen to the iudgement seat, and when I caused them to prepare my seate in the streete.

8 The yong men saw me, and hid themselues, and the aged arose, and stood vp.

9 The princes stayed talke, and layde their hand on their mouth.

10 The voyce of princes was hidde, and their tongue cleaued to the roofe of their mouth.

11 And when the eare heard me, it blessed me: and when the eye sawe me, it gaue witnesse to me.

12 For I deliuered the poore that cryed, and the fatherlesse, and him that had none to helpe him.

13 The blessing of him that was ready to perish, came vpon me, and I caused the widowes heart to reioyce.

14 I put on iustice, and it couered me: my iudgement was as a robe, and a crowne.

15 I was the eyes to the blinde, and I was the feete to the lame.

16 I was a father vnto the poore, and when I knewe not the cause, I sought it out diligently.

17 I brake also the chawes of the vnrighteous man, and pluckt the praye out of his teeth.

18 Then I sayde, I shall die in my nest, and I shall multiplie my dayes as the sand.

19 For my roote is spread out by the water, and the dewe shall lye vpon my branche.

20 My glory shall renue towarde me, and my bowe shall be restored in mine hand.

21 Vnto me men gaue eare, and wayted, and helde their tongue at my counsell.

22 After my wordes they replied not, and my talke dropped vpon them.

23 And they wayted for me, as for the raine, and they opened their mouth as for the latter rayne.

24 If I laughed on them, they beleeued it not: neither did they cause the light of my countenance to fall.

25 I appoynted out their way, and did sit as chiefe, and dwelt as a King in the army, and like him that comforteth the mourners.

Job 30

1 Bvt now they that are yonger then I, mocke me: yea, they whose fathers I haue refused to set with the dogges of my flockes.

2 For whereto shoulde the strength of their handes haue serued mee, seeing age perished in them?

3 For pouertie and famine they were solitary, fleeing into the wildernes, which is darke, desolate and waste.

4 They cut vp nettels by the bushes, and the iuniper rootes was their meate.

5 They were chased forth from among men: they shouted at them, as at a theefe.

6 Therfore they dwelt in the clefts of riuers, in the holes of the earth and rockes.

7 They roared among the bushes, and vnder the thistles they gathered themselues.

8 They were the children of fooles and the children of villaines, which were more vile then the earth.

9 And now am I their song, and I am their talke.

10 They abhorre me, and flee farre from mee, and spare not to spit in my face.

11 Because that God hath loosed my corde and humbled mee, they haue loosed the bridle before me.

12 The youth rise vp at my right hand: they haue pusht my feete, and haue trode on me as on the paths of their destruction.

13 They haue destroyed my paths: they tooke pleasure at my calamitie, they had none helpe.

14 They came as a great breach of waters, and vnder this calamitie they come on heapes.

15 Feare is turned vpon mee: and they pursue my soule as the winde, and mine health passeth away as a cloude.

16 Therefore my soule is nowe powred out vpon me, and the dayes of affliction haue taken holde on me.

17 It pearceth my bones in the night, and my sinewes take no rest.

18 For the great vehemencie is my garment changed, which compasseth me about as the colar of my coate.

19 He hath cast me into the myre, and I am become like ashes and dust.

20 Whe I cry vnto thee, thou doest not heare me, neither regardest me, when I stand vp.

21 Thou turnest thy selfe cruelly against me, and art enemie vnto mee with the strength of thine hand.

22 Thou takest me vp and causest mee to ride vpon the winde, and makest my strength to faile.

23 Surely I knowe that thou wilt bring mee to death, and to the house appoynted for all the liuing.

24 Doubtles none can stretch his hand vnto the graue, though they cry in his destruction.

25 Did not I weepe with him that was in trouble? was not my soule in heauinesse for the poore?

26 Yet when I looked for good, euill came vnto me: and when I waited for light, there came darkenesse.

27 My bowels did boyle without rest: for the dayes of affliction are come vpon me.

28 I went mourning without sunne: I stood vp in the congregation and cryed.

29 I am a brother to the dragons, and a companion to the ostriches.

30 My skinne is blacke vpon me, and my bones are burnt with heate.

31 Therefore mine harpe is turned to mourning, and mine organs into the voyce of them that weepe.

Job 31

1 I made a couenant with mine eyes: why then should I thinke on a mayde?

2 For what portion should I haue of God from aboue? and what inheritance of the Almightie from on hie?

3 Is not destruction to the wicked and strange punishment to the workers of iniquitie?

4 Doeth not he beholde my wayes and tell all my steps?

5 If I haue walked in vanitie, or if my foote hath made haste to deceite,

6 Let God weigh me in the iust balance, and he shall know mine vprightnes.

7 If my steppe hath turned out of the way, or mine heart hath walked after mine eye, or if any blot hath cleaued to mine handes,

8 Let me sowe, and let another eate: yea, let my plantes be rooted out.

9 If mine heart hath bene deceiued by a woman, or if I haue layde wayte at the doore of my neighbour,

10 Let my wife grinde vnto another man, and let other men bow downe vpon her:

11 For this is a wickednes, and iniquitie to bee condemned:

12 Yea, this is a fire that shall deuoure to destruction, and which shall roote out al mine increase,

13 If I did contemne the iudgement of my seruant, and of my mayde, when they did contend with me,

14 What then shall I do when God standeth vp? and when he shall visit me, what shall I answere?

15 He that hath made me in the wombe, hath he not made him? hath not he alone facioned vs in the wombe?

16 If I restrained the poore of their desire, or haue caused the eyes of the widow to faile,

17 Or haue eaten my morsels alone, and the fatherles hath not eaten thereof,

18 (For from my youth hee hath growen vp with me as with a father, and from my mothers wombe I haue bene a guide vnto her)

19 If I haue seene any perish for want of clothing, or any poore without couering,

20 If his loynes haue not blessed me, because he was warmed with the fleece of my sheepe,

21 If I haue lift vp mine hande against the fatherlesse, when I saw that I might helpe him in the gate,

22 Let mine arme fal from my shoulder, and mine arme be broken from the bone.

23 For Gods punishment was fearefull vnto me, and I could not be deliuered from his highnes.

24 If I made gold mine hope, or haue sayd to the wedge of golde, Thou art my confidence,

25 If I reioyced because my substance was great, or because mine hand had gotten much,

26 If I did behold the sunne, when it shined, or the moone, walking in her brightnes,

27 If mine heart did flatter me in secrete, or if my mouth did kisse mine hand,

28 (This also had bene an iniquitie to be condemned: for I had denied the God aboue)

29 If I reioyced at his destruction that hated me, or was mooued to ioye when euill came vpon him,

30 Neither haue I suffred my mouth to sinne, by wishing a curse vnto his soule.

31 Did not the men of my Tabernacle say, Who shall giue vs of his flesh? we can not bee satisfied.

32 The stranger did not lodge in the streete, but I opened my doores vnto him, that went by the way.

33 If I haue hid my sinne, as Adam, concealing mine iniquitie in my bosome,

34 Though I could haue made afraid a great multitude, yet the most contemptible of the families did feare me: so I kept silence, and went not out of the doore.

35 Oh that I had some to heare me! beholde my signe that the Almightie will witnesse for me: though mine aduersary should write a booke against me,

36 Woulde not I take it vpon my shoulder, and binde it as a crowne vnto me?

37 I will tell him the number of my goings, and goe vnto him as to a prince.

38 If my lande cry against me, or the furrowes thereof complayne together,

39 If I haue eaten the fruites thereof without siluer: or if I haue grieued the soules of the masters thereof,

40 Let thistles growe in steade of wheate, and cockle in the stead of Barley. The wordes of Iob are ended.

Job 32

1 So these three men ceased to answere Iob, because he esteemed himselfe iust.

2 Then the wrath of Elihu the sonne of Barachel the Buzite, of the familie of Ram, was kindled: his wrath, I say, was kindled against Iob, because he iustified himselfe more then God.

3 Also his anger was kindled against his three friends, because they could not finde an answere, and yet condemned Iob.

4 (Now Elihu had wayted til Iob had spoken: for they were more ancient in yeeres then he)

5 So when Elihu saw, that there was none answere in the mouth of the three men, his wrath was kindled.

6 Therefore Elihu the sonne of Barachel, the Buzite answered, and sayd, I am yong in yeres, and ye are ancient: therefore I doubted, and was afraide to shewe you mine opinion.

7 For I said, The dayes shall speake, and the multitude of yeeres shall teach wisedome.

8 Surely there is a spirite in man, but the inspiration of the Almightie giueth vnderstanding.

9 Great men are not alway wise, neither doe the aged alway vnderstand iudgement.

10 Therefore I say, Heare me, and I will shew also mine opinion.

11 Behold, I did waite vpon your wordes, and hearkened vnto your knowledge, whiles you sought out reasons.

12 Yea, when I had considered you, lo, there was none of you that reproued Iob, nor answered his wordes:

13 Lest ye should say, We haue found wisedome: for God hath cast him downe, and no man.

14 Yet hath he not directed his words to me, neyther will I answere him by your wordes.

15 Then they fearing, answered no more, but left off their talke.

16 When I had wayted (for they spake not, but stood still and answered no more)

17 Then answered I in my turne, and I shewed mine opinion.

18 For I am full of matter, and the spirite within me compelleth me.

19 Beholde, my belly is as the wine, which hath no vent, and like the new bottels that brast.

20 Therefore will I speake, that I may take breath: I will open my lippes, and will answere.

21 I will not now accept the person of man, neyther will I giue titles to man.

22 For I may not giue titles, lest my Maker should take me away suddenly.

Job 33

1 Wherefore, Iob, I pray thee, heare my talke and hearken vnto all my wordes.

2 Beholde now, I haue opened my mouth: my tongue hath spoken in my mouth.

3 My words are in the vprightnesse of mine heart, and my lippes shall speake pure knowledge.

4 The Spirite of God hath made me, and the breath of the Almightie hath giuen me life.

5 If thou canst giue me answere, prepare thy selfe and stand before me.

6 Beholde, I am according to thy wish in Gods stead: I am also formed of the clay.

7 Beholde, my terrour shall not feare thee, neither shall mine hand be heauie vpon thee.

8 Doubtles thou hast spoken in mine eares, and I haue heard the voyce of thy wordes.

9 I am cleane, without sinne: I am innocent, and there is none iniquitie in me.

10 Lo, he hath found occasions against me, and counted me for his enemie.

11 He hath put my feete in the stockes, and looketh narrowly vnto all my paths.

12 Behold, in this hast thou not done right: I will answere thee, that God is greater then man.

13 Why doest thou striue against him? for he doeth not giue account of all his matters.

14 For God speaketh once or twise, and one seeth it not.

15 In dreames and visions of the night, when sleepe falleth vpon men, and they sleepe vpon their beds,

16 Then he openeth the eares of men, euen by their corrections, which he had sealed,

17 That he might cause man to turne away from his enterprise, and that he might hide the pride of man,

18 And keepe backe his soule from the pit, and that his life should not passe by the sword.

19 He is also striken with sorow vpon his bed, and the griefe of his bones is sore,

20 So that his life causeth him to abhorre bread, and his soule daintie meate.

21 His flesh faileth that it can not be seene, and his bones which were not seene, clatter.

22 So his soule draweth to the graue, and his life to the buriers.

23 If there be a messenger with him, or an interpreter, one of a thousand to declare vnto man his righteousnesse,

24 Then will he haue mercie vpon him, and will say, Deliuer him, that he go not downe into the pit: for I haue receiued a reconciliation.

25 Then shall his flesh be as fresh as a childes, and shall returne as in the dayes of his youth.

26 He shall pray vnto God, and he will be fauourable vnto him, and he shall see his face with ioy: for he will render vnto man his righteousnes.

27 He looketh vpon men, and if one say, I haue sinned, and peruerted righteousnesse, and it did not profite me,

28 He will deliuer his soule from going into the pit, and his life shall see the light.

29 Lo, all these things will God worke twise or thrise with a man,

30 That he may turne backe his soule from the pit, to be illuminate in the light of the liuing.

31 Marke well, O Iob, and heare me: keepe silence, and I will speake.

32 If there be matter, answere me, and speak: for I desire to iustifie thee.

33 If thou hast not, heare me: holde thy tongue, and I will teach thee wisedome.

Job 34

1 Moreouer Elihu answered, and saide,

2 Heare my wordes, ye wise men, and hearken vnto me, ye that haue knowledge.

3 For the eare tryeth the words, as the mouth tasteth meate.

4 Let vs seeke iudgement among vs, and let vs knowe among our selues what is good.

5 For Iob hath saide, I am righteous, and God hath taken away my iudgement.

6 Should I lye in my right? my wound of the arrowe is grieuous without my sinne.

7 What man is like Iob, that drinketh scornfulnesse like water?

8 Which goeth in the companie of them that worke iniquitie, and walketh with wicked men?

9 For he hath saide, It profiteth a man nothing that he should walke with God.

10 Therefore hearken vnto me, ye men of wisedome, God forbid that wickednesse should be in God, and iniquitie in the Almightie.

11 For he will render vnto man according to his worke, and cause euery one to finde according to his way.

12 And certainely God will not do wickedly, neither will the Almightie peruert iudgement.

13 Whome hath he appointed ouer the earth beside him selfe? or who hath placed the whole worlde?

14 If he set his heart vpon man, and gather vnto him selfe his spirit and his breath,

15 All flesh shall perish together, and man shall returne vnto dust.

16 And if thou hast vnderstanding, heare this and hearken to the voyce of my wordes.

17 Shal he that hateth iudgement, gouerne? and wilt thou iudge him wicked that is most iust?

18 Wilt thou say vnto a King, Thou art wicked? or to princes, Ye are vngodly?

19 How much lesse to him that accepteth not the persons of princes, and regardeth not the rich, more then the poore? for they be all the worke of his handes.

20 They shall die suddenly, and the people shalbe troubled at midnight, and they shall passe foorth and take away the mightie without hand.

21 For his eyes are vpon the wayes of man, and he seeth all his goings.

22 There is no darkenesse nor shadowe of death, that the workers of iniquitie might be hid therein.

23 For he will not lay on man so much, that he should enter into iudgement with God.

24 He shall breake the mightie without seeking, and shall set vp other in their stead.

25 Therefore shall he declare their works: he shall turne the night, and they shalbe destroyed.

26 He striketh them as wicked men in the places of the seers.

27 Because they haue turned backe from him, and would not consider all his wayes:

28 So that they haue caused the voyce of the poore to come vnto him, and he hath heard the cry of the afflicted.

29 And when he giueth quietnesse, who can make trouble? and when he hideth his face, who can beholde him, whether it be vpon nations, or vpon a man onely?

30 Because the hypocrite doeth reigne, and because the people are snared.

31 Surely it appertaineth vnto God to say, I haue pardoned, I will not destroy.

32 But if I see not, teach thou me: if I haue done wickedly, I will doe no more.

33 Wil he performe the thing through thee? for thou hast reproued it, because that thou hast chosen, and not I. now speake what thou knowest.

34 Let men of vnderstanding tell me, and let a wise man hearken vnto me.

35 Iob hath not spoken of knowledge, neyther were his wordes according to wisedome.

36 I desire that Iob may be tryed, vnto the ende touching the answeres for wicked men.

37 For he addeth rebellion vnto his sinne: he clappeth his handes among vs, and multiplieth his wordes against God.

Job 35

1 Elihu spake moreouer, and said,

2 Thinkest thou this right, that thou hast said, I am more righteous then God?

3 For thou hast said, What profiteth it thee and what auaileth it me, to purge me from my sinne?

4 Therefore will I answere thee, and thy companions with thee.

5 Looke vnto the heauen, and see and behold the cloudes which are hyer then thou.

6 If thou sinnest, what doest thou against him, yea, when thy sinnes be many, what doest thou vnto him?

7 If thou be righteous, what giuest thou vnto him? or what receiueth he at thine hand?

8 Thy wickednesse may hurt a man as thou art: and thy righteousnes may profite ye sonne of man.

9 They cause many that are oppressed, to crye, which crye out for ye violence of the mightie.

10 But none saieth, Where is God that made me, which giueth songs in the nyght?

11 Which teacheth vs more then the beastes of the earth, and giueth vs more wisdome then the foules of the heauen.

12 Then they crye because of the violence of the wicked, but he answereth not.

13 Surely God will not heare vanitie, neyther will the Almightie regard it.

14 Although thou sayest to God, Thou wilt not regard it, yet iudgement is before him: trust thou in him.

15 But nowe because his anger hath not visited, nor called to count the euill with great extremitie,

16 Therfore Iob openeth his mouth in vaine, and multiplieth wordes without knowledge.

Job 36

1 Elihu also proceeded and sayde,

2 Suffer me a litle, and I will instruct thee: for I haue yet to speake on Gods behalfe.

3 I will fetche my knowledge afarre off, and will attribute righteousnes vnto my Maker.

4 For truely my wordes shall not be false, and he that is perfect in knowledge, speaketh with thee.

5 Behold, the mighty God casteth away none that is mighty and valiant of courage.

6 He mainteineth not the wicked, but he giueth iudgement to the afflicted.

7 He withdraweth not his eyes from the righteous, but they are with Kings in ye throne, where he placeth them for euer: thus they are exalted.

8 And if they bee bound in fetters and tyed with the cordes of affliction,

9 Then will he shewe them their worke and their sinnes, because they haue bene proude.

10 He openeth also their eare to discipline, and commandeth them that they returne from iniquity.

11 If they obey and serue him, they shall end their dayes in prosperity, and their yeres in pleasures.

12 But if they wil not obey, they shall passe by the sworde, and perish without knowledge.

13 But the hypocrites of heart increase the wrath: for they call not when he bindeth them.

14 Their soule dyeth in youth, and their life among the whoremongers.

15 He deliuereth the poore in his affliction, and openeth their eare in trouble.

16 Euen so woulde he haue taken thee out of the streight place into a broade place and not shut vp beneath: and that which resteth vpon thy table, had bene full of fat.

17 But thou art ful of the iudgement of the wicked, though iudgement and equitie maintaine all things.

18 For Gods wrath is, least hee should take that away in thine abundance: for no multitude of giftes can deliuer thee.

19 Wil he regard thy riches? he regardeth not golde, nor all them that excel in strength.

20 Be not carefull in the night, howe he destroyeth the people out of their place.

21 Take thou heede: looke not to iniquitie: for thou hast chosen it rather then affliction.

22 Beholde, God exalteth by his power: what teacher is like him?

23 Who hath appointed to him his way? or who can say, Thou hast done wickedly?

24 Remember that thou magnifie his worke, which men behold.

25 All men see it, and men beholde it afarre off.

26 Beholde, God is excellent, and we knowe him not, neither can the nomber of his yeres bee searched out.

27 When he restraineth the droppes of water, the rayne powreth down by the vapour thereof,

28 Which raine the cloudes do droppe and let fall abundantly vpon man.

29 Who can know the diuisions of ye clouds and the thunders of his tabernacle?

30 Beholde, he spreadeth his light vpon it, and couereth the bottome of the sea.

31 For thereby hee iudgeth the people, and giueth meate abundantly.

32 He couereth the light with the clouds, and commandeth them to go against it.

33 His companion sheweth him thereof, and there is anger in rising vp.

Job 37

1 At this also mine heart is astonied, and is mooued out of his place.

2 Heare the sound of his voyce, and the noyse that goeth out of his mouth.

3 He directeth it vnder the whole heauen, and his light vnto the endes of the world.

4 After it a noyse soundeth: hee thundereth with the voyce of his maiestie, and hee will not stay them when his voyce is heard.

5 God thundereth marueilously with his voyce: he worketh great things, which we know not.

6 For he sayth to the snowe, Be thou vpon the earth: likewise to the small rayne and to the great rayne of his power.

7 With the force thereof he shutteth vp euery man, that all men may knowe his worke.

8 Then the beastes go into the denne, and remaine in their places.

9 The whirlewind commeth out of the South, and the colde from the North winde.

10 At the breath of God the frost is giuen, and the breadth of the waters is made narrowe.

11 He maketh also the cloudes to labour, to water the earth, and scattereth the cloude of his light.

12 And it is turned about by his gouernment, that they may doe whatsoeuer he commandeth them vpon the whole worlde:

13 Whether it be for punishment, or for his lande, or of mercie, he causeth it to come.

14 Hearken vnto this, O Iob: stand and consider the wonderous workes of God.

15 Diddest thou knowe when God disposed them? and caused the light of his cloud to shine?

16 Hast thou knowen the varietie of the cloude, and the wonderous workes of him, that is perfite in knowledge?

17 Or howe thy clothes are warme, when he maketh the earth quiet through the South winde?

18 Hast thou stretched out the heaues, which are strong, and as a molten glasse?

19 Tell vs what we shall say vnto him: for we can not dispose our matter because of darknes.

20 Shall it be told him when I speake? or shall man speake when he shalbe destroyed?

21 And nowe men see not the light, which shineth in the cloudes, but the winde passeth and clenseth them.

22 The brightnesse commeth out of the North: the praise thereof is to God, which is terrible.

23 It is the Almightie: we can not finde him out: he is excellent in power and iudgement, and aboundant in iustice: he afflicteth not.

24 Let men therefore feare him: for he will not regarde any that are wise in their owne conceit.

Job 38

1 Then answered the Lord vnto Iob out of the whirle winde, and said,

2 Who is this that darkeneth the counsell by wordes without knowledge?

3 Girde vp nowe thy loynes like a man: I will demande of thee and declare thou vnto me.

4 Where wast thou when I layd the foundations of the earth? declare, if thou hast vnderstanding,

5 Who hath layde the measures thereof, if thou knowest, or who hath stretched the line ouer it:

6 Whereupon are the foundations thereof set: or who layed the corner stone thereof:

7 When the starres of the morning praysed me together, and all the children of God reioyced:

8 Or who hath shut vp the Sea with doores, when it yssued and came foorth as out of the wombe:

9 When I made the cloudes as a couering thereof, and darkenesse as the swadeling bands thereof:

10 When I stablished my commandement vpon it, and set barres and doores,

11 And said, Hitherto shalt thou come, but no farther, and here shall it stay thy proude waues.

12 Hast thou commanded the morning since thy dayes? hast thou caused the morning to knowe his place,

13 That it might take hold of the corners of the earth, and that the wicked might be shaken out of it?

14 It is turned as clay to facion, and all stand vp as a garment.

15 And from the wicked their light shall be taken away, and the hie arme shalbe broken.

16 Hast thou entred into the bottomes of the sea? or hast thou walked to seeke out the depth?

17 Haue the gates of death bene opened vnto thee? or hast thou seene the gates of the shadowe of death?

18 Hast thou perceiued the breadth of the earth? tell if thou knowest all this.

19 Where is the way where light dwelleth? and where is the place of darkenesse,

20 That thou shouldest receiue it in the boundes thereof, and that thou shouldest knowe the paths to the house thereof?

21 Knewest thou it, because thou wast then borne, and because the nomber of thy dayes is great?

22 Hast thou entred into the treasures of the snow? or hast thou seene the treasures of ye haile,

23 Which I haue hid against the time of trouble, against the day of warre and battell?

24 By what way is the light parted, which scattereth the East winde vpon the earth?

25 Who hath deuided the spowtes for the raine? or the way for the lightning of ye thunders,

26 To cause it to raine on the earth where no man is, and in the wildernes where there is no man?

27 To fulfil the wilde and waste place, and to cause the bud of the herbe to spring forth?

28 Who is the father of the rayne? or who hath begotten the droppes of the dewe?

29 Out of whose wombe came the yee? who hath ingendred the frost of the heauen?

30 The waters are hid as with a stone: and the face of the depth is frosen.

31 Canst thou restraine the sweete influences of the Pleiades? or loose the bandes of Orion?

32 Canst thou bring foorth Mazzaroth in their time? canst thou also guide Arcturus with his sonnes?

33 Knowest thou the course of heauen, or canst thou set the rule thereof in the earth?

34 Canst thou lift vp thy voice to the cloudes that the abundance of water may couer thee?

35 Canst thou sende the lightenings that they may walke, and say vnto thee, Loe, heere we are?

36 Who hath put wisedome in the reines? or who hath giuen the heart vnderstanding?

37 Who can nomber cloudes by wisedome? or who can cause to cease the bottels of heaue,

38 When the earth groweth into hardnesse, and the clottes are fast together?

Job 39

1 Wilt thou hunt the pray for the lyon? or fill the appetite of the lyons whelpes,

2 When they couch in their places, and remaine in the couert to lye in waite?

3 Who prepareth for the rauen his meate, when his birdes crie vnto God, wandering for lacke of meate?

4 Knowest thou the time when the wilde goates bring foorth yong? or doest thou marke when the hindes doe calue?

5 Canst thou nomber the moneths that they fulfill? or knowest thou the time when they bring foorth?

6 They bow them selues: they bruise their yong and cast out their sorowes.

7 Yet their yong waxe fatte, and growe vp with corne: they goe foorth and returne not vnto them.

8 Who hath set the wilde asse at libertie? or who hath loosed the bondes of the wilde asse?

9 It is I which haue made the wildernesse his house, and the salt places his dwellings.

10 He derideth the multitude of the citie: he heareth not the crie of the driuer.

11 He seeketh out the mountaine for his pasture, and searcheth after euery greene thing.

12 Will the vnicorne serue thee? or will he tary by thy cribbe?

13 Canst thou binde the vnicorne with his band to labour in the furrowe? or will he plowe the valleyes after thee?

14 Wilt thou trust in him, because his strength is great, and cast off thy labour vnto him?

15 Wilt thou beleeue him, that he will bring home thy seede, and gather it vnto thy barne?

16 Hast thou giuen the pleasant wings vnto the peacockes? or winges and feathers vnto the ostriche?

17 Which leaueth his egges in the earth, and maketh them hote in the dust,

18 And forgetteth that the foote might scatter the, or that the wild beast might breake the.

19 He sheweth himselfe cruell vnto his yong ones, as they were not his, and is without feare, as if he trauailed in vaine.

20 For God had depriued him of wisedom, and hath giuen him no part of vnderstanding.

21 When time is, he mounteth on hie: he mocketh the horse and his rider.

22 Hast thou giuen the horse strength? or couered his necke with neying?

23 Hast thou made him afraid as the grashopper? his strong neying is fearefull.

24 He diggeth in the valley, and reioyceth in his strength: he goeth foorth to meete the harnest man.

25 He mocketh at feare, and is not afraid, and turneth not backe from the sworde,

26 Though the quiuer rattle against him, the glittering speare and the shield.

27 He swalloweth the ground for fearcenes and rage, and he beleeueth not that it is the noise of the trumpet.

28 He sayth among the trumpets, Ha, ha: hee smellleth the battell afarre off, and the noyse of the captaines, and the shouting.

29 Shall the hauke flie by thy wisedome, stretching out his wings toward the South?

30 Doeth the eagle mount vp at thy commandement, or make his nest on hie?

31 Shee abideth and remaineth in the rocke, euen vpon the toppe of the rocke, and the tower.

32 From thence she spieth for meate, and her eyes beholde afarre off.

33 His young ones also sucke vp blood: and where the slaine are, there is she.

34 Moreouer ye Lord spake vnto Iob, and said,

35 Is this to learne to striue with the Almightie? he that reprooueth God, let him answere to it.

36 Then Iob answered the Lord, saying,

37 Beholde, I am vile: what shall I answere thee? I will lay mine hand vpon my mouth.

38 Once haue I spoken, but I will answere no more, yea twise, but I will proceede no further.

Job 40

1 Againe the Lord answered Iob out of the whirle winde, and said,

2 Girde vp now thy loynes like a man: I will demaunde of thee, and declare thou vnto me.

3 Wilt thou disanul my iudgement? or wilt thou condemne me, that thou mayst be iustified?

4 Or hast thou an arme like God? or doest thou thunder with a voyce like him?

5 Decke thy selfe now with maiestie and excellencie, and aray thy selfe with beautie and glory.

6 Cast abroad the indignation of thy wrath, and beholde euery one that is proude, and abase him.

7 Looke on euery one that is arrogant, and bring him lowe: and destroy the wicked in their place.

8 Hide them in the dust together, and binde their faces in a secret place.

9 Then will I confesse vnto thee also, that thy right hand can saue thee.

10 Behold now Behemoth (whom I made with thee) which eateth grasse as an oxe.

11 Behold now, his strength is in his loynes, and his force is in the nauil of his belly.

12 When hee taketh pleasure, his taile is like a cedar: the sinews of his stones are wrapt together.

13 His bones are like staues of brasse, and his small bones like staues of yron.

14 He is the chiefe of the wayes of God: he that made him, will make his sworde to approch vnto him.

15 Surely the mountaines bring him foorth grasse, where all the beastes of the fielde play.

16 Lyeth hee vnder the trees in the couert of the reede and fennes?

17 Can the trees couer him with their shadow? or can the willowes of the riuer compasse him about?

18 Behold, he spoyleth the riuer, and hasteth not: he trusteth that he can draw vp Iorden into his mouth.

19 Hee taketh it with his eyes, and thrusteth his nose through whatsoeuer meeteth him.

20 Canst thou drawe out Liuiathan with an hooke, and with a line which thou shalt cast downe vnto his tongue?

21 Canst thou cast an hooke into his nose? canst thou perce his iawes with an angle?

22 Will he make many prayers vnto thee, or speake thee faire?

23 Will hee make a couenant with thee? and wilt thou take him as a seruant for euer?

24 Wilt thou play with him as with a bird? or wilt thou bynd him for thy maydes?

25 Shall the companions baket with him? shall they deuide him among the marchants?

26 Canst thou fill the basket with his skinne? or the fishpanier with his head?

27 Lay thine hand vpon him: remember the battel, and do no more so.

28 Behold, his hope is in vaine: for shall not one perish euen at the sight of him?

Job 41

1 None is so fearce that dare stirre him vp. Who is he then that can stand before me?

2 Who hath preuented mee that I shoulde make an ende? Al vnder heauen is mine.

3 I will not keepe silence concerning his partes, nor his power nor his comely proportion.

4 Who can discouer the face of his garmet? or who shall come to him with a double bridle?

5 Who shall open the doores of his face? his teeth are fearefull round about.

6 The maiestie of his scales is like strog shields, and are sure sealed.

7 One is set to another, that no winde can come betweene them.

8 One is ioyned to another: they sticke together, that they cannot be sundered.

9 His niesings make the light to shine, and his eyes are like the eyelids of the morning.

10 Out of his mouth go lampes, and sparkes of fire leape out.

11 Out of his nostrels commeth out smoke, as out of a boyling pot or caldron.

12 His breath maketh the coales burne: for a flame goeth out of his mouth.

13 In his necke remayneth strength, and labour is reiected before his face.

14 The members of his bodie are ioyned: they are strong in themselues, and cannot be mooued.

15 His heart is as strong as a stone, and as hard as the nether milstone.

16 The mightie are afrayd of his maiestie, and for feare they faint in themselues.

17 When the sword doeth touch him, he will not rise vp, nor for the speare, dart nor habergeon.

18 He esteemeth yron as strawe, and brasse as rotten wood.

19 The archer canot make him flee: ye stones of the sling are turned into stubble vnto him:

20 The dartes are counted as strawe: and hee laugheth at the shaking of the speare.

21 Sharpe stones are vnder him, and he spreadeth sharpe things vpon the myre.

22 He maketh the depth to boyle like a pot, and maketh the sea like a pot of oyntment.

23 He maketh a path to shine after him: one would thinke the depth as an hoare head.

24 In the earth there is none like him: hee is made without feare.

25 He beholdeth al hie things: he is a King ouer all the children of pride.

Job 42

1 Then Iob answered the Lord, and sayd,

2 I knowe that thou canst doe all things, and that there is no thought hidde from thee.

3 Who is hee that hideth counsell without knowledge? therefore haue I spoken that I vnderstood not, euen things too wonderfull for me, and which I knew not.

4 Heare, I beseech thee, and I will speake: I will demaunde of thee, and declare thou vnto me.

5 I haue heard of thee by the hearing of the eare, but now mine eye seeth thee.

6 Therefore I abhorre my selfe, and repent in dust and ashes.

7 Now after that the Lord had spoken these wordes vnto Iob, ye Lord also said vnto Eliphaz ye Temanite, My wrath is kindled against thee, and against thy two friends: for yee haue not spoken of me the thing that is right, like my seruant Iob.

8 Therefore take vnto you nowe seuen bullockes, and seuen rammes, and go to my seruant Iob, and offer vp for your selues a burnt offring, and my seruant Iob shall pray for you: for I wil accept him, least I should put you to shame, because ye haue not spoken of me the thing, which is right, like my seruant Iob.

9 So Eliphaz the Temanite, and Bildad the Shuhite, and Zophar the Naamathite went, and did according as the Lord had saide vnto them, and the Lord accepted Iob.

10 Then the Lord turned the captiuitie of Iob, when he prayed for his friends: also the Lord gaue Iob twise so much as he had before.

11 Then came vnto him all his brethren, and all his sisters, and all they that had bene of his acquaintance before, and did eate bread with him in his house, and had compassion of him, and comforted him for al the euil, that the Lord had brought vpon him, and euery man gaue him a piece of money, and euery one an earing of golde.

12 So the Lord blessed the last dayes of Iob more then the first: for he had foureteene thousand sheepe, and sixe thousand camels, and a thousand yoke of oxen, and a thousand shee asses.

13 He had also seue sonnes, and three daughters.

14 And he called the name of one Iemimah, and the name of the seconde Keziah, and the name of the third Keren-happuch.

15 In all the lande were no women found so faire as the daughters of Iob, and their father gaue them inheritaunce among their brethren.

16 And after this liued Iob an hundreth and fourtie yeres, and sawe his sonnes, and his sonnes sonnes, euen foure generations.

17 So Iob dyed, being old, and full of dayes.

Psalms

Psalms 1

1 Blessed is the man that doeth not walke in the counsell of the wicked, nor stand in the way of sinners, nor sit in ye seate of the scornefull:

2 But his delite is in the Lawe of the Lord, and in his Lawe doeth he meditate day and night.

3 For he shall be like a tree planted by the riuers of waters, that will bring foorth her fruite in due season: whose leafe shall not fade: so whatsoeuer he shall doe, shall prosper.

4 The wicked are not so, but as the chaffe, which the winde driueth away.

5 Therefore the wicked shall not stande in the iudgement, nor sinners in the assemblie of the righteous.

6 For the Lord knoweth the way of the righteous, and the way of the wicked shall perish.

Psalms 2

1 Why doe the heathen rage, and the people murmure in vaine?

2 The Kings of the earth band themselues, and the princes are assembled together against the Lord, and against his Christ.

3 Let vs breake their bands, and cast their cordes from vs.

4 But he that dwelleth in the heauen, shall laugh: the Lord shall haue them in derision.

5 Then shall hee speake vnto them in his wrath, and vexe them in his sore displeasure, saying,

6 Euen I haue set my King vpon Zion mine holy mountaine.

7 I will declare the decree: that is, the Lord hath said vnto me, Thou art my Sonne: this day haue I begotten thee.

8 Aske of me, and I shall giue thee the heathen for thine inheritance, and the endes of the earth for thy possession.

9 Thou shalt krush them with a scepter of yron, and breake them in pieces like a potters vessell.

10 Be wise nowe therefore, ye Kings: be learned ye Iudges of the earth.

11 Serue the Lord in feare, and reioyce in trembling.

12 Kisse the sonne, least he be angry, and ye perish in the way, when his wrath shall suddenly burne. blessed are all that trust in him.

Psalms 3

1 A Psalme of Dauid, when he fled from his sonne Absalom. Lord, howe are mine aduersaries increased? howe many rise against me?

2 Many say to my soule, There is no helpe for him in God. Selah.

3 But thou Lord art a buckler for me: my glory, and the lifter vp of mine head.

4 I did call vnto the Lord with my voyce, and he heard me out of his holy mountaine. Selah.

5 I layed me downe and slept, and rose vp againe: for the Lord susteined me.

6 I will not be afrayde for ten thousand of the people, that should beset me round about.

7 O Lord, arise: helpe me, my God: for thou hast smitten all mine enemies vpon the cheeke bone: thou hast broken the teeth of the wicked.

8 Saluation belongeth vnto the Lord, and thy blessing is vpon thy people. Selah.

Psalms 4

1 To him that excelleth on Neginoth. A Psalme of Dauid. Heare me when I call, O God of my righteousnes: thou hast set me at libertie, when I was in distresse: haue mercie vpon me and hearken vnto my prayer.

2 O ye sonnes of men, howe long will yee turne my glory into shame, louing vanitie, and seeking lyes? Selah.

3 For be ye sure that the Lord hath chosen to himselfe a godly man: the Lord will heare when I call vnto him.

4 Tremble, and sinne not: examine your owne heart vpon your bed, and be still. Selah.

5 Offer the sacrifices of righteousnes, and trust in the Lord.

6 Many say, Who will shewe vs any good? but Lord, lift vp the light of thy countenance vpon vs.

7 Thou hast giuen mee more ioye of heart, then they haue had, when their wheate and their wine did abound.

8 I will lay mee downe, and also sleepe in peace: for thou, Lord, onely makest me dwell in safetie.

Psalms 5

1 To him that excelleth upon Nehiloth. A Psalme of Dauid. Heare my wordes, O Lord: vnderstande my meditation.

2 Hearken vnto the voyce of my crie, my King and my God: for vnto thee doe I pray.

3 Heare my voyce in the morning, O Lord: for in the morning will I direct me vnto thee, and I will waite.

4 For thou art not a God that loueth wickednes: neither shall euill dwell with thee.

5 The foolish shall not stand in thy sight: for thou hatest all them that worke iniquitie.

6 Thou shalt destroy them that speake lyes: the Lord will abhorre the bloodie man and deceitfull.

7 But I wil come into thine house in the multitude of thy mercie: and in thy feare will I worship toward thine holy Temple.

8 Leade me, O Lord, in thy righteousnes, because of mine enemies: make thy way plaine before my face.

9 For no constancie is in their mouth: within, they are very corruption: their throte is an open sepulchre, and they flatter with their tongue.

10 Destroy them, O God: let them fall from their counsels: cast them out for the multitude of their iniquities, because they haue rebelled against thee.

11 And let all them that trust in thee, reioyce and triumph for euer, and couer thou them: and let them, that loue thy Name, reioyce in thee.

12 For thou Lord wilt blesse the righteous, and with fauour wilt compasse him, as with a shielde.

Psalms 6

1 To him that excelleth on Neginoth upon the eith tune. A Psalme of Dauid. O lord, rebuke me not in thine anger, neither chastise me in thy wrath.

2 Haue mercie vpon me, O Lord, for I am weake: O Lord heale me, for my bones are vexed.

3 My soule is also sore troubled: but Lord how long wilt thou delay?

4 Returne, O Lord: deliuer my soule: saue me for thy mercies sake.

5 For in death there is no remembrance of thee: in the graue who shall prayse thee?

6 I fainted in my mourning: I cause my bed euery night to swimme, and water my couch with my teares.

7 Mine eye is dimmed for despight, and sunke in because of all mine enemies.

8 Away from mee all ye workers of iniquitie: for the Lord hath heard the voyce of my weeping.

9 The Lord hath heard my petition: the Lord will receiue my prayer.

10 All mine enemies shall be confounded and sore vexed: they shall be turned backe, and put to shame suddenly.

Psalms 7

1 Shigaion of Dauid, which he sang unto the Lord, concerning the wordes of Chush the sonne of Iemini. O Lord my God, in thee I put my trust: saue me from all that persecute me, and deliuer me,

2 Least he deuoure my soule like a lion, and teare it in pieces, while there is none to helpe.

3 O Lord my God, if I haue done this thing, if there be any wickednes in mine handes,

4 If I haue rewarded euill vnto him that had peace with mee, (yea I haue deliuered him that vexed me without cause)

5 Then let the enemie persecute my soule and take it: yea, let him treade my life downe vpon the earth, and lay mine honour in the dust. Selah.

6 Arise, O Lord, in thy wrath, and lift vp thy selfe against the rage of mine enemies, and awake for mee according to the iudgement that thou hast appointed.

7 So shall the Congregation of the people compasse thee about: for their sakes therefore returne on hie.

8 The Lord shall iudge the people: Iudge thou me, O Lord, according to my righteousnesse, and according to mine innocencie, that is in mee.

9 Oh let the malice of the wicked come to an ende: but guide thou the iust: for the righteous God trieth the hearts and reines.

10 My defence is in God, who preserueth the vpright in heart.

11 God iudgeth the righteous, and him that contemneth God euery day.

12 Except he turne, he hath whet his sword: he hath bent his bowe and made it readie.

13 Hee hath also prepared him deadly weapons: hee will ordeine his arrowes for them that persecute me.

14 Beholde, hee shall trauaile with wickednes: for he hath conceiued mischiefe, but he shall bring foorth a lye.

15 Hee hath made a pitte and digged it, and is fallen into the pit that he made.

16 His mischiefe shall returne vpon his owne head, and his crueltie shall fall vpon his owne pate.

17 I wil praise the Lord according to his righteousnes, and will sing praise to the Name of the Lord most high.

Psalms 8

1 To him that excelleth on Gittith. A Psalme of Dauid. O Lord our Lord, how excellent is thy Name in all the worlde! which hast set thy glory aboue the heauens.

2 Out of the mouth of babes and suckelings hast thou ordeined strength, because of thine enemies, that thou mightest still the enemie and the auenger.

3 When I beholde thine heauens, euen the workes of thy fingers, the moone and the starres which thou hast ordeined,

4 What is man, say I, that thou art mindefull of him? and the sonne of man, that thou visitest him?

5 For thou hast made him a little lower then God, and crowned him with glory and worship.

6 Thou hast made him to haue dominion in the workes of thine hands: thou hast put all things vnder his feete:

7 All sheepe and oxen: yea, and the beastes of the fielde:

8 The foules of the ayre, and the fish of the sea, and that which passeth through the paths of the seas.

9 O Lord our Lord, howe excellent is thy Name in all the world!

Psalms 9

1 To him that excelleth vpon Muth Laben. A Psalme of Dauid. I will praise the Lord with my whole heart: I will speake of all thy marueilous workes.

2 I will bee glad, and reioyce in thee: I will sing praise to thy Name, O most High,

3 For that mine enemies are turned backe: they shall fall, and perish at thy presence.

4 For thou hast maintained my right and my cause: thou art set in the throne, and iudgest right.

5 Thou hast rebuked the heathen: thou hast destroyed the wicked: thou hast put out their name for euer and euer.

6 O enemie, destructions are come to a perpetual end, and thou hast destroyed the cities: their memoriall is perished with them.

7 But the Lord shall sit for euer: hee hath prepared his throne for iudgement.

8 For he shall iudge the worlde in righteousnes, and shall iudge the people with equitie.

9 The Lord also wil be a refuge for the poore, a refuge in due time, euen in affliction.

10 And they that know thy Name, will trust in thee: for thou, Lord, hast not failed them that seeke thee.

11 Sing praises to the Lord, which dwelleth in Zion: shewe the people his workes.

12 For whe he maketh inquisition for blood, hee remembreth it, and forgetteth not the complaint of the poore.

13 Haue mercie vpon mee, O Lord: consider my trouble which I suffer of them that hate mee, thou that liftest me vp from the gates of death,

14 That I may shewe all thy praises within the gates of the daughter of Zion, and reioyce in thy saluation.

15 The heathen are sunken downe in the pit that they made: in the nette that they hid, is their foote taken.

16 The Lord is knowen by executing iudgement: the wicked is snared in the worke of his owne handes. Higgaion. Selah.

17 The wicked shall turne into hell, and all nations that forget God.

18 For the poore shall not bee alway forgotten: the hope of the afflicted shall not perish for euer.

19 Vp Lord: let not man preuaile: let the heathen be iudged in thy sight.

20 Put them in feare, O Lord, that the heathen may knowe that they are but men. Selah.

Psalms 10

1 Why standest thou farre off, O Lord, and hidest thee in due time, euen in affliction?

2 The wicked with pride doeth persecute the poore: let them be taken in the craftes that they haue imagined.

3 For the wicked hath made boast of his owne heartes desire, and the couetous blesseth himselfe: he contemneth the Lord.

4 The wicked is so proude that hee seeketh not for God: hee thinketh alwayes, There is no God.

5 His wayes alway prosper: thy iudgements are hie aboue his sight: therefore defieth he all his enemies.

6 He saith in his heart, I shall neuer be moued, nor be in danger.

7 His mouth is full of cursing and deceite and fraude: vnder his tongue is mischiefe and iniquitie.

8 He lieth in waite in the villages: in the secret places doeth hee murder the innocent: his eyes are bent against the poore.

9 He lyeth in waite secretly, euen as a lyon in his denne: he lyeth in waite to spoyle the poore: he doeth spoyle the poore, when he draweth him into his net.

10 He croucheth and boweth: therefore heaps of the poore doe fall by his might.

11 He hath said in his heart, God hath forgotten, he hideth away his face, and will neuer see.

12 Arise, O Lord God: lift vp thine hande: forget not the poore.

13 Wherefore doeth the wicked contemne God? he saith in his heart, Thou wilt not regard.

14 Yet thou hast seene it: for thou beholdest mischiefe and wrong, that thou mayest take it into thine handes: the poore committeth himselfe vnto thee: for thou art the helper of the fatherlesse.

15 Breake thou the arme of the wicked and malicious: searche his wickednes, and thou shalt finde none.

16 The Lord is King for euer and euer: the heathen are destroyed foorth of his land.

17 Lord, thou hast heard the desire of the poore: thou preparest their heart: thou bendest thine eare to them,

18 To iudge the fatherlesse and poore, that earthly man cause to feare no more.

Psalms 11

1 To him that excelleth. A Psalme of Dauid. In the Lord put I my trust: howe say yee then to my soule, Flee to your mountaine as a birde?

2 For loe, the wicked bende their bowe, and make readie their arrowes vpon the string, that they may secretly shoote at them, which are vpright in heart.

3 For the foundations are cast downe: what hath the righteous done?

4 The Lord is in his holy palace: the Lordes throne is in the heauen: his eyes wil consider: his eye lids will try the children of men.

5 The Lord will try the righteous: but the wicked and him that loueth iniquitie, doeth his soule hate.

6 Vpon the wicked he shall raine snares, fire, and brimstone, and stormie tempest: this is the porcion of their cup.

7 For the righteous Lord loueth righteousnes: his countenance doeth beholde the iust.

Psalms 12

1 To him that excelleth vpon the eight tune. A Psalme of Dauid. Helpe Lord, for there is not a godly man left: for the faithfull are fayled from among the children of men.

2 They speake deceitfully euery one with his neighbour, flattering with their lips, and speake with a double heart.

3 The Lord cut off all flattering lippes, and the tongue that speaketh proude things:

4 Which haue saide, With our tongue will we preuaile: our lippes are our owne: who is Lord ouer vs?

5 Now for the oppression of the needy, and for the sighes of the poore, I will vp, sayeth the Lord, and will set at libertie him, whom the wicked hath snared.

6 The wordes of the Lord are pure wordes, as the siluer, tried in a fornace of earth, fined seuen folde.

7 Thou wilt keepe them, O Lord: thou wilt preserue him from this generation for euer.

8 The wicked walke on euery side: when they are exalted, it is a shame for the sonnes of men.

Psalms 13

1 To him that excelleth. A Psalme of Dauid. Howe long wilt thou forget me, O Lord, for euer? howe long wilt thou hide thy face from me?

2 How long shall I take counsell within my selfe, hauing wearinesse dayly in mine heart? how long shall mine enemie be exalted aboue me?

3 Beholde, and heare mee, O Lord my God: lighten mine eyes, that I sleepe not in death:

4 Lest mine enemie say, I haue preuailed against him: and they that afflict me, reioyce when I slide.

5 But I trust in thy mercie: mine heart shall reioyce in thy saluation: I will sing to the Lord, because he hath delt louingly with me.

Psalms 14

1 To him that excelleth. A Psalme of Dauid. The foole hath said in his heart, There is no God: they haue corrupted, and done an abominable worke: there is none that doeth good.

2 The Lord looked downe from heauen vpon the children of men, to see if there were any that would vnderstand, and seeke God.

3 All are gone out of the way: they are all corrupt: there is none that doeth good, no not one.

4 Doe not all the workers of iniquitie know that they eate vp my people, as they eate bread? they call not vpon the Lord.

5 There they shall be taken with feare, because God is in the generation of the iust.

6 You haue made a mocke at the counsell of the poore, because the Lord is his trust.

7 Oh giue saluation vnto Israel out of Zion: when the Lord turneth the captiuitie of his people, then Iaakob shall reioyce, and Israel shall be glad.

Psalms 15

1 A Psalme of Dauid. Lord, who shall dwell in thy Tabernacle? who shall rest in thine holy Mountaine?

2 He that walketh vprightly and worketh righteousnes, and speaketh the trueth in his heart.

3 He that slandereth not with his tongue, nor doeth euill to his neighbour, nor receiueth a false report against his neighbour.

4 In whose eyes a vile person is contemned, but he honoureth them that feare the Lord: he that sweareth to his owne hinderance and changeth not.

5 He that giueth not his money vnto vsurie, nor taketh reward against the innocent: hee that doeth these things, shall neuer be moued.

Psalms 16

1 Michtam of Dauid. Preserue mee, O God: for in thee doe I trust.

2 O my soule, thou hast sayd vnto the Lord, Thou art my Lord: my weldoing extendeth not to thee,

3 But to the Saints that are in the earth, and to the excellent: all my delite is in them.

4 The sorowes of them, that offer to an other god, shall be multiplied: their offerings of blood will I not offer, neither make mention of their names with my lips.

5 The Lord is the portion of mine inheritance and of my cup: thou shalt mainteine my lot.

6 The lines are fallen vnto me in pleasant places: yea, I haue a faire heritage.

7 I wil prayse the Lord, who hath giuen me counsell: my reines also teach me in the nightes.

8 I haue set the Lord always before me: for hee is at my right hand: therefore I shall not slide.

9 Wherefore mine heart is glad and my tongue reioyceth: my flesh also doeth rest in hope.

10 For thou wilt not leaue my soule in the graue: neither wilt thou suffer thine holy one to see corruption.

11 Thou wilt shew me the path of life: in thy presence is the fulnesse of ioy: and at thy right hand there are pleasures for euermore.

Psalms 17

1 The prayer of Dauid. Heare the right, O Lord, consider my crye: hearken vnto my prayer of lips vnfained.

2 Let my sentence come forth from thy presence, and let thine eyes beholde equitie.

3 Thou hast prooued and visited mine heart in the night: thou hast tryed me, and foundest nothing: for I was purposed that my mouth should not offend.

4 Concerning the workes of men, by the wordes of thy lips I kept mee from the paths of the cruell man.

5 Stay my steps in thy paths, that my feete doe not slide.

6 I haue called vpon thee: surely thou wilt heare me, O God: incline thine eare to me, and hearken vnto my wordes.

7 Shewe thy marueilous mercies, thou that art the Sauiour of them that trust in thee, from such as resist thy right hand.

8 Keepe me as the apple of the eye: hide me vnder the shadowe of thy wings,

9 From the wicked that oppresse mee, from mine enemies, which compasse me round about for my soule.

10 They are inclosed in their owne fat, and they haue spoken proudely with their mouth.

11 They haue compassed vs now in our steps: they haue set their eyes to bring downe to the ground:

12 Like as a lyon that is greedy of pray, and as it were a lyons whelp lurking in secret places.

13 Vp Lord, disappoint him: cast him downe: deliuer my soule from the wicked with thy sworde,

14 From men by thine hand, O Lord, from men of the world, who haue their portion in this life, whose bellies thou fillest with thine hid treasure: their children haue ynough, and leaue the rest of their substance for their children.

15 But I will beholde thy face in righteousnes, and when I awake, I shalbe satisfied with thine image.

Psalms 18

1 To him that excelleth. A Psalme of Dauid the seruant of the Lord, which spake vnto the Lord the wordes of this song (in the day that the Lord delivered him for the hande of all this enemies, and form the and of saul) and sayd, I will loue thee dearely, O Lord my strength.

2 The Lord is my rocke, and my fortresse, and he that deliuereth me, my God and my strength: in him will I trust, my shield, the horne also of my saluation, and my refuge.

3 I will call vpon the Lord, which is worthie to be praysed: so shall I be safe from mine enemies.

4 The sorowes of death compassed me, and the floods of wickednes made me afraide.

5 The sorowes of the graue haue compassed me about: the snares of death ouertooke me.

6 But in my trouble did I call vpon the Lord, and cryed vnto my God: he heard my voyce out of his Temple, and my crye did come before him, euen into his eares.

7 Then the earth trembled, and quaked: the foundations also of the mountaines mooued and shooke, because he was angrie.

8 Smoke went out at his nostrels, and a consuming fire out of his mouth: coales were kindled thereat.

9 He bowed the heauens also and came downe, and darkenes was vnder his feete.

10 And he rode vpon Cherub and did flie, and he came flying vpon the wings of the winde.

11 He made darkenes his secrete place, and his pauilion round about him, euen darkenesse of waters, and cloudes of the ayre.

12 At the brightnes of his presence his clouds passed, haylestones and coles of fire.

13 The Lord also thundred in the heauen, and the Highest gaue his voyce, haylestones and coales of fire.

14 Then hee sent out his arrowes and scattred them, and he increased lightnings and destroyed them.

15 And the chanels of waters were seene, and the foundations of the worlde were discouered at thy rebuking, O Lord, at the blasting of the breath of thy nostrels.

16 He hath sent downe from aboue and taken mee: hee hath drawen mee out of many waters.

17 He hath deliuered mee from my strong enemie, and from them which hate me: for they were too strong for me.

18 They preuented me in the day of my calamitie: but the Lord was my stay.

19 Hee brought mee foorth also into a large place: hee deliuered mee because hee fauoured me.

20 The Lord rewarded me according to my righteousnes: according to the purenes of mine hands he recompensed me:

21 Because I kept the wayes of the Lord, and did not wickedly against my God.

22 For all his Lawes were before mee, and I did not cast away his commandements from mee.

23 I was vpright also with him, and haue kept me from my wickednes.

24 Therefore the Lord rewarded me according to my righteousnesse, and according to the purenes of mine hands in his sight.

25 With the godly thou wilt shewe thy selfe godly: with the vpright man thou wilt shew thy selfe vpright.

26 With the pure thou wilt shewe thy selfe pure, and with the froward thou wilt shewe thy selfe froward.

27 Thus thou wilt saue the poore people, and wilt cast downe the proude lookes.

28 Surely thou wilt light my candle: the Lord my God wil lighten my darkenes.

29 For by thee I haue broken through an hoste, and by my God I haue leaped ouer a wall.

30 The way of God is vncorrupt: the worde of the Lord is tried in the fire: he is a shield to all that trust in him.

31 For who is God besides the Lord? and who is mightie saue our God?

32 God girdeth me with strength, and maketh my way vpright.

33 He maketh my feete like hindes feete, and setteth me vpon mine high places.

34 He teacheth mine hands to fight: so that a bowe of brasse is broken with mine armes.

35 Thou hast also giuen me the shield of thy saluation, and thy right hand hath stayed me, and thy louing kindenes hath caused me to increase.

36 Thou hast enlarged my steps vnder mee, and mine heeles haue not slid.

37 I haue pursued mine enemies, and taken them, and haue not turned againe till I had consumed them.

38 I haue wounded them, that they were not able to rise: they are fallen vnder my feete.

39 For thou hast girded me with strength to battell: them, that rose against me, thou hast subdued vnder me.

40 And thou hast giuen me the neckes of mine enemies, that I might destroy them that hate me.

41 They cryed but there was none to saue them, euen vnto the Lord, but hee answered them not.

42 Then I did beate them small as the dust before the winde: I did treade them flat as the clay in the streetes.

43 Thou hast deliuered me from the contentions of the people: thou hast made me the head of the heathen: a people, whom I haue not knowen, shall serue me.

44 As soone as they heare, they shall obey me: the strangers shall be in subiection to me.

45 Strangers shall shrinke away, and feare in their priuie chambers.

46 Let the Lord liue, and blessed be my strength, and the God of my saluation be exalted.

47 It is God that giueth me power to auenge me, and subdueth the people vnder me.

48 O my deliuerer from mine enemies, euen thou hast set mee vp from them, that rose against me: thou hast deliuered mee from the cruell man.

49 Therefore I will prayse thee, O Lord, among the nations, and wil sing vnto thy Name.

50 Great deliuerances giueth hee vnto his King, and sheweth mercie to his anoynted, euen to Dauid, and to his seede for euer.

Psalms 19

1 To him that excelleth. A Psalme of Dauid. The heauens declare the glory of God, and the firmament sheweth ye worke of his hands.

2 Day vnto day vttereth the same, and night vnto night teacheth knowledge.

3 There is no speach nor language, where their voyce is not heard.

4 Their line is gone forth through all the earth, and their words into the endes of the world: in them hath he set a tabernacle for the sunne.

5 Which commeth forth as a bridegrome out of his chamber, and reioyceth like a mightie man to runne his race.

6 His going out is from the ende of the heauen, and his compasse is vnto the endes of ye same, and none is hid from the heate thereof.

7 The Lawe of the Lord is perfite, conuerting the soule: the testimonie of the Lord is sure, and giueth wisedome vnto the simple.

8 The statutes of the Lord are right and reioyce the heart: the commandement of the Lord is pure, and giueth light vnto the eyes.

9 The feare of the Lord is cleane, and indureth for euer: the iudgements of the Lord are trueth: they are righteous altogether,

10 And more to be desired then golde, yea, then much fine golde: sweeter also then honie and the honie combe.

11 Moreouer by them is thy seruant made circumspect, and in keeping of them there is great reward.

12 Who can vnderstand his faultes? clense me from secret fautes.

13 Keepe thy seruant also from presumptuous sinnes: let them not reigne ouer me: so shall I be vpright, and made cleane from much wickednes.

14 Let the wordes of my mouth, and the meditation of mine heart be acceptable in thy sight, O Lord, my strength, and my redeemer.

Psalms 20

1 To him that excelleth. A Psalme of Dauid. The Lord heare thee in the day of trouble: the name of ye God of Iaakob defend thee:

2 Send thee helpe from the Sanctuarie, and strengthen thee out of Zion.

3 Let him remember all thine offerings, and turne thy burnt offerings into asshes. Selah:

4 And graunt thee according to thine heart, and fulfill all thy purpose:

5 That we may reioyce in thy saluation, and set vp the banner in the Name of our God, when the Lord shall performe all thy petitions.

6 Now know I that the Lord will helpe his anointed, and will heare him from his Sanctuarie, by the mightie helpe of his right hand.

7 Some trust in chariots, and some in horses: but we will remember the Name of ye Lord our God.

8 They are brought downe and fallen, but we are risen, and stand vpright.

9 Saue Lord: let the King heare vs in the day that we call.

Psalms 21

1 To him that excelleth. A Psalme of Dauid. The King shall reioyce in thy strength, O Lord: yea how greatly shall he reioyce in thy saluation!

2 Thou hast giuen him his hearts desire, and hast not denyed him the request of his lips. Selah.

3 For thou diddest preuent him with liberall blessings, and didest set a crowne of pure gold vpon his head.

4 He asked life of thee, and thou gauest him a long life for euer and euer.

5 His glory is great in thy saluation: dignitie and honour hast thou laid vpon him.

6 For thou hast set him as blessings for euer: thou hast made him glad with the ioy of thy countenance.

7 Because the King trusteth in the Lord, and in the mercie of the most High, he shall not slide.

8 Thine hand shall finde out all thine enemies, and thy right hand shall finde out them that hate thee.

9 Thou shalt make them like a fierie ouen in time of thine anger: the Lord shall destroy them in his wrath, and the fire shall deuoure them.

10 Their fruite shalt thou destroy from the earth, and their seede from the children of men.

11 For they intended euill against thee, and imagined mischiefe, but they shall not preuaile.

12 Therefore shalt thou put them aparte, and the strings of thy bowe shalt thou make readie against their faces.

13 Be thou exalted, O Lord, in thy strength: so will we sing and prayse thy power.

Psalms 22

1 To him that excelleth upon Aiieleth Hasshahar. A Psalme of Dauid. My God, my God, why hast thou forsaken me, and art so farre from mine health, and from the wordes of my roaring?

2 O my God, I crie by day, but thou hearest not, and by night, but haue no audience.

3 But thou art holy, and doest inhabite the prayses of Israel.

4 Our fathers trusted in thee: they trusted, and thou didest deliuer them.

5 They called vpon thee, and were deliuered: they trusted in thee, and were not confounded.

6 But I am a worme, and not a man: a shame of men, and the contempt of people.

7 All they that see me, haue me in derision: they make a mowe and nod the head, saying,

8 He trusted in the Lord, let him deliuer him: let him saue him, seeing he loueth him.

9 But thou didest draw me out of ye wombe: thou gauest me hope, euen at my mothers breasts.

10 I was cast vpon thee, euen from ye wombe: thou art my God from my mothers belly.

11 Be not farre from me, because trouble is neere: for there is none to helpe me.

12 Many yong bulles haue compassed me: mightie bulles of Bashan haue closed me about.

13 They gape vpon me with their mouthes, as a ramping and roaring lyon.

14 I am like water powred out, and all my bones are out of ioynt: mine heart is like waxe: it is molten in the middes of my bowels.

15 My strength is dryed vp like a potsheard, and my tongue cleaueth to my iawes, and thou hast brought me into the dust of death.

16 For dogges haue compassed me, and the assemblie of the wicked haue inclosed me: they perced mine hands and my feete.

17 I may tell all my bones: yet they beholde, and looke vpon me.

18 They part my garments among them, and cast lottes vpon my vesture.

19 But be thou not farre off, O Lord, my strength: hasten to helpe me.

20 Deliuer my soule from the sword: my desolate soule from the power of the dogge.

21 Saue me from the lyons mouth, and answere me in sauing me from the hornes of the vnicornes.

22 I wil declare thy Name vnto my brethren: in the middes of the Congregation will I praise thee, saying,

23 Prayse the Lord, ye that feare him: magnifie ye him, all the seede of Iaakob, and feare ye him, all the seede of Israel.

24 For he hath not despised nor abhorred ye affliction of the poore: neither hath he hid his face from him, but when he called vnto him, he heard.

25 My prayse shalbe of thee in the great Congregation: my vowes will I perfourme before them that feare him.

26 The poore shall eate and be satisfied: they that seeke after the Lord, shall prayse him: your heart shall liue for euer.

27 All the endes of the worlde shall remember themselues, and turne to the Lord: and all the kinreds of the nations shall worship before him.

28 For the kingdome is the Lords, and he ruleth among the nations.

29 All they that be fat in the earth, shall eate and worship: all they that go downe into the dust, shall bowe before him, euen he that cannot quicken his owne soule.

30 Their seede shall serue him: it shalbe counted vnto the Lord for a generation.

31 They shall come, and shall declare his righteousnesse vnto a people that shall be borne, because he hath done it.

Psalms 23

1 A Psalme of David. The Lord is my shepheard, I shall not want.

2 He maketh me to rest in greene pasture, and leadeth me by the still waters.

3 He restoreth my soule, and leadeth me in the paths of righteousnesse for his Names sake.

4 Yea, though I should walke through the valley of the shadowe of death, I will feare no euill: for thou art with me: thy rod and thy staffe, they comfort me.

5 Thou doest prepare a table before me in the sight of mine aduersaries: thou doest anoynt mine head with oyle, and my cuppe runneth ouer.

6 Doubtlesse kindnesse and mercie shall follow me all the dayes of my life, and I shall remaine a long season in the house of the Lord.

Psalms 24

1 A Psalme of David. The earth is the Lordes, and all that therein is: the worlde and they that dwell therein.

2 For he hath founded it vpon the seas: and established it vpon the floods.

3 Who shall ascende into the mountaine of the Lord? and who shall stand in his holy place?

4 Euen he that hath innocent handes, and a pure heart: which hath not lift vp his minde vnto vanitie, nor sworne deceitfully.

5 He shall receiue a blessing from the Lord, and righteousnesse from the God of his saluation.

6 This is the generation of them that seeke him, of them that seeke thy face, this is Iaakob. Selah.

7 Lift vp your heads ye gates, and be ye lift vp ye euerlasting doores, and the King of glory shall come in.

8 Who is this King of glorie? the Lord, strong and mightie, euen the Lord mightie in battell.

9 Lift vp your heads, ye gates, and lift vp your selues, ye euerlasting doores, and the King of glorie shall come in.

10 Who is this King of glory? the Lord of hostes, he is the King of glorie. Selah.

Psalms 25

1 A Psalme of David. Unto thee, O Lord, lift I vp my soule.

2 My God, I trust in thee: let me not be confounded: let not mine enemies reioyce ouer mee.

3 So all that hope in thee, shall not be ashamed: but let them be confounded, that transgresse without cause.

4 Shew me thy waies, O Lord, and teache me thy paths.

5 Leade me foorth in thy trueth, and teache me: for thou art the God of my saluation: in thee doe I trust all the day.

6 Remember, O Lord, thy tender mercies, and thy louing kindnesse: for they haue beene for euer.

7 Remember not the sinnes of my youth, nor my rebellions, but according to thy kindenesse remember thou me, euen for thy goodnesse sake, O Lord.

8 Gracious and righteous is the Lord: therefore will he teache sinners in the way.

9 Them that be meeke, will hee guide in iudgement, and teach the humble his way.

10 All the pathes of the Lord are mercie and trueth vnto such as keepe his couenant and his testimonies.

11 For thy Names sake, O Lord, be merciful vnto mine iniquitie, for it is great.

12 What man is he that feareth the Lord? him wil he teache the way that hee shall chuse.

13 His soule shall dwell at ease, and his seede shall inherite the land.

14 The secrete of the Lord is reueiled to them, that feare him: and his couenant to giue them vnderstanding.

15 Mine eyes are euer towarde the Lord: for he will bring my feete out of the net.

16 Turne thy face vnto mee, and haue mercie vpon me: for I am desolate and poore.

17 The sorowes of mine heart are enlarged: drawe me out of my troubles.

18 Looke vpon mine affliction and my trauel, and forgiue all my sinnes.

19 Beholde mine enemies, for they are manie, and they hate me with cruell hatred.

20 Keepe my soule, and deliuer me: let me not be confounded, for I trust in thee.

21 Let mine vprightnes and equitie preserue me: for mine hope is in thee.

22 Deliuer Israel, O God, out of all his troubles.

Psalms 26

1 A Psalme of David. Judge me, O Lord, for I haue walked in mine innocency: my trust hath bene also in the Lord: therefore shall I not slide.

2 Proue me, O Lord, and trie mee: examine my reines, and mine heart.

3 For thy louing kindnesse is before mine eyes: therefore haue I walked in thy trueth.

4 I haue not hanted with vaine persons, neither kept companie with the dissemblers.

5 I haue hated the assemblie of the euill, and haue not companied with the wicked.

6 I will wash mine handes in innocencie, O Lord, and compasse thine altar,

7 That I may declare with the voyce of thankesgiuing, and set foorth all thy wonderous woorkes.

8 O Lord, I haue loued the habitation of thine house, and the place where thine honour dwelleth.

9 Gather not my soule with the sinners, nor my life with the bloodie men:

10 In whose handes is wickednes, and their right hand is full of bribes.

11 But I will walke in mine innocencie: redeeme me therefore, and be mercifull vnto me.

12 My foote standeth in vprightnesse: I will praise thee, O Lord, in the Congregations.

Psalms 27

1 A Psalme of David. The Lord is my light and my saluation, whom shall I feare? the Lord is the strength of my life, of whome shall I be afraide?

2 When the wicked, euen mine enemies and my foes came vpon mee to eate vp my flesh; they stumbled and fell.

3 Though an hoste pitched against me, mine heart should not be afraide: though warre be raised against me, I will trust in this.

4 One thing haue I desired of the Lord, that I will require, euen that I may dwell in the house of the Lord all the dayes of my life, to beholde the beautie of the Lord, and to visite his Temple.

5 For in the time of trouble hee shall hide mee in his Tabernacle: in the secrete place of his pauillion shall he hide me, and set me vp vpon a rocke.

6 And nowe shall hee lift vp mine head aboue mine enemies rounde about mee: therefore wil I offer in his Tabernacle sacrifices of ioy: I wil sing and praise the Lord.

7 Hearken vnto my voyce, O Lord, when I crie: haue mercie also vpon mee and heare mee.

8 When thou saidest, Seeke ye my face, mine heart answered vnto thee, O Lord, I will seeke thy face.

9 Hide not therefore thy face from mee, nor cast thy seruat away in displeasure: thou hast bene my succour: leaue me not, neither forsake mee, O God of my saluation.

10 Though my father and my mother shoulde forsake me, yet the Lord will gather me vp.

11 Teache mee thy way, O Lord, and leade me in a right path, because of mine enemies.

12 Giue me not vnto the lust of mine aduersaries: for there are false witnesses risen vp against me, and such as speake cruelly.

13 I should haue fainted, except I had beleeued to see the goodnes of the Lord in the land of the liuing.

14 Hope in the Lord: be strong, and he shall comfort thine heart, and trust in the Lord.

Psalms 28

1 A Psalme of David. Unto thee, O Lord, doe I crie: O my strength, be not deafe toward mee, lest, if thou answere me not, I be like them that goe downe into the pit.

2 Heare the voyce of my petitions, when I crie vnto thee, when I holde vp mine handes towarde thine holy Oracle.

3 Drawe mee not away with the wicked, and with the woorkers of iniquitie: which speake friendly to their neighbours, when malice is in their hearts.

4 Reward them according to their deedes, and according to the wickednes of their inuentions: recompense them after the woorke of their handes: render them their reward.

5 For they regarde not the woorkes of the Lord, nor the operation of his handes: therefore breake them downe, and builde them not vp.

6 Praised be the Lord, for he hath heard the voyce of my petitions.

7 The Lord is my strength and my shielde: mine heart trusted in him, and I was helped: therfore mine heart shall reioyce, and with my song will I praise him.

8 The Lord is their strength, and he is the strength of the deliuerances of his anointed.

9 Saue thy people, and blesse thine inheritance: feede them also, and exalt them for euer.

Psalms 29

1 A Psalme of David. Give vnto the Lord, ye sonnes of the mightie: giue vnto the Lord glorie and strength.

2 Giue vnto the Lord glorie due vnto his Name: worship the Lord in the glorious Sanctuarie.

3 The voyce of the Lord is vpon the waters: the God of glorie maketh it to thunder: the Lord is vpon the great waters.

4 The voyce of the Lord is mightie: the voyce of the Lord is glorious.

5 The voyce of the Lord breaketh the cedars: yea, the Lord breaketh the cedars of Lebanon.

6 He maketh them also to leape like a calfe: Lebanon also and Shirion like a yong vnicorne.

7 The voice of the Lord deuideth the flames of sire.

8 The voice of the Lord maketh the wildernes to tremble: the Lord maketh the wildernes of Kadesh to tremble.

9 The voice of the Lord maketh the hindes to calue, and discouereth the forests: therefore in his Temple doth euery man speake of his glory.

10 The Lord sitteth vpon the flood, and the Lord doeth remaine King for euer.

11 The Lord shall giue strength vnto his people: the Lord shall blesse his people with peace.

Psalms 30

1 A Psalme or song of the dedication of the house of David. I will magnifie thee, O Lord: for thou hast exalted mee, and hast not made my foe to reioyce ouer me.

2 O Lord my God, I cried vnto thee, and thou hast restored me.

3 O Lord, thou hast brought vp my soule out of the graue: thou hast reuiued me from them that goe downe into the pit.

4 Sing praises vnto the Lord, ye his Saintes, and giue thankes before the remembrance of his Holinesse.

5 For he endureth but a while in his anger: but in his fauour is life: weeping may abide at euening, but ioy commeth in the morning.

6 And in my prosperitie I sayde, I shall neuer be moued.

7 For thou Lord of thy goodnes hadest made my mountaine to stande strong: but thou didest hide thy face, and I was troubled.

8 Then cried I vnto thee, O Lord, and praied to my Lord.

9 What profite is there in my blood, when I go downe to the pit? shall the dust giue thankes vnto thee? or shall it declare thy trueth?

10 Heare, O Lord, and haue mercy vpon me: Lord, be thou mine helper.

11 Thou hast turned my mourning into ioy: thou hast loosed my sacke and girded mee with gladnesse.

12 Therefore shall my tongue praise thee and not cease: O Lord my God, I will giue thankes vnto thee for euer.

Psalms 31

1 To him that excelleth. A Psalme of David. In thee, O Lord, haue I put my trust: let mee neuer be confounded: deliuer me in thy righteousnesse.

2 Bowe downe thine eare to me: make haste to deliuer mee: be vnto me a stronge rocke, and an house of defence to saue me.

3 For thou art my rocke and my fortresse: therefore for thy Names sake direct mee and guide me.

4 Drawe mee out of the nette, that they haue layde priuilie for mee: for thou art my strength.

5 Into thine hand I commend my spirit: for thou hast redeemed me, O Lord God of trueth.

6 I haue hated them that giue them selues to deceitfull vanities: for I trust in the Lord.

7 I wil be glad and reioyce in thy mercie: for thou hast seene my trouble: thou hast knowen my soule in aduersities,

8 And thou hast not shut me vp in the hand of the enemie, but hast set my feete at large.

9 Haue mercie vpon mee, O Lord: for I am in trouble: mine eye, my soule and my bellie are consumed with griefe.

10 For my life is wasted with heauinesse, and my yeeres with mourning: my strength faileth for my paine, and my bones are consumed.

11 I was a reproch among all mine enemies, but specially among my neighbours: and a feare to mine acquaintance, who seeing me in the streete, fled from me.

12 I am forgotten, as a dead man out of minde: I am like a broken vessell.

13 For I haue heard the rayling of great men: feare was on euery side, while they conspired together against mee, and consulted to take my life.

14 But I trusted in thee, O Lord: I said, Thou art my God.

15 My times are in thine hande: deliuer mee from the hande of mine enemies, and from them that persecute me.

16 Make thy face to shine vpon thy seruant, and saue me through thy mercie.

17 Let me not be confounded, O Lord: for I haue called vpon thee: let the wicked bee put to confusion, and to silence in the graue.

18 Let the lying lips be made dumme, which cruelly, proudly and spitefully speake against the righteous.

19 Howe great is thy goodnesse, which thou hast layde vp for them, that feare thee! and done to them, that trust in thee, euen before the sonnes of men!

20 Thou doest hide them priuily in thy presence from the pride of men: thou keepest them secretly in thy Tabernacle from the strife of tongues.

21 Blessed be the Lord: for hee hath shewed his marueilous kindenesse toward me in a strong citie.

22 Though I said in mine haste, I am cast out of thy sight, yet thou heardest the voyce of my prayer, when I cryed vnto thee.

23 Loue ye the Lord all his Saintes: for the Lord preserueth the faithfull, and rewardeth abundantly the proud doer.

24 All ye that trust in the Lord, be strong, and he shall establish your heart.

Psalms 32

1 A Psalme of David to give instruction. Blessed is he whose wickednes is forgiuen, and whose sinne is couered.

2 Blessed is the man, vnto whom the Lord imputeth not iniquitie, and in whose spirite there is no guile.

3 When I helde my tongue, my bones consumed, or when I roared all the day,

4 (For thine hand is heauie vpon me, day and night: and my moysture is turned into ye drought of summer. Selah)

5 Then I acknowledged my sinne vnto thee, neither hid I mine iniquitie: for I thought, I will confesse against my selfe my wickednesse vnto the Lord, and thou forgauest the punishment of my sinne. Selah.

6 Therefore shall euery one, that is godly, make his prayer vnto thee in a time, when thou mayest be founde: surely in the flood of great waters they shall not come neere him.

7 Thou art my secret place: thou preseruest me from trouble: thou compassest me about with ioyfull deliuerance. Selah.

8 I will instruct thee, and teache thee in the way that thou shalt goe, and I will guide thee with mine eye.

9 Be ye not like an horse, or like a mule, which vnderstand not: whose mouthes thou doest binde with bit and bridle, least they come neere thee.

10 Many sorowes shall come to the wicked: but he, that trusteth in the Lord, mercie shall compasse him.

11 Be glad ye righteous, and reioyce in the Lord, and be ioyfull all ye, that are vpright in heart.

Psalms 33

1 Rejoice in the Lord, O ye righteous: for it becommeth vpright men to be thankefull.

2 Prayse the Lord with harpe: sing vnto him with viole and instrument of ten strings.

3 Sing vnto him a newe song: sing cheerefully with a loude voyce.

4 For the word of the Lord is righteous, and all his workes are faithfull.

5 He loueth righteousnesse and iudgement: the earth is full of the goodnesse of the Lord.

6 By the worde of the Lord were the heauens made, and all the hoste of them by the breath of his mouth.

7 He gathereth the waters of the sea together as vpon an heape, and layeth vp the depths in his treasures.

8 Let all the earth feare the Lord: let al them that dwell in the world, feare him.

9 For he spake, and it was done: he commanded, and it stood.

10 The Lord breaketh the counsell of the heathen, and bringeth to nought the deuices of the people.

11 The counsell of the Lord shall stand for euer, and the thoughts of his heart throughout all ages.

12 Blessed is that nation, whose God is the Lord: euen the people that he hath chosen for his inheritance.

13 The Lord looketh downe from heauen, and beholdeth all the children of men.

14 From the habitation of his dwelling he beholdeth all them that dwell in the earth.

15 He facioneth their hearts euery one, and vnderstandeth all their workes.

16 The King is not saued by the multitude of an hoste, neither is the mightie man deliuered by great strength.

17 A horse is a vaine helpe, and shall not deliuer any by his great strength.

18 Beholde, the eye of the Lord is vpon them that feare him, and vpon them, that trust in his mercie,

19 To deliuer their soules from death, and to preserue them in famine.

20 Our soule waiteth for the Lord: for he is our helpe and our shielde.

21 Surely our heart shall reioyce in him, because we trusted in his holy Name.

22 Let thy mercie, O Lord, be vpon vs, as we trust in thee.

Psalms 34

1 A Psalme of Dauid, when he changed his behauiour before Abimelech, who droue him away, and he departed. I will alway giue thankes vnto the Lord: his praise shalbe in my mouth continually.

2 My soule shall glory in the Lord: the humble shall heare it, and be glad.

3 Praise ye the Lord with me, and let vs magnifie his Name together.

4 I sought the Lord, and he heard me: yea, he deliuered me out of all my feare.

5 They shall looke vnto him, and runne to him: and their faces shall not be ashamed, saying,

6 This poore man cryed, and the Lord heard him, and saued him out of all his troubles.

7 The Angel of the Lord pitcheth round about them, that feare him, and deliuereth them.

8 Taste ye and see, howe gratious the Lord is: blessed is the man that trusteth in him.

9 Feare the Lord, ye his Saintes: for nothing wanteth to them that feare him.

10 The lyons doe lacke and suffer hunger, but they, which seeke the Lord, shall want nothing that is good.

11 Come children, hearken vnto me: I will teache you the feare of the Lord.

12 What man is he, that desireth life, and loueth long dayes for to see good?

13 Keepe thy tongue from euill, and thy lips, that they speake no guile.

14 Eschewe euill and doe good: seeke peace and follow after it.

15 The eyes of the Lord are vpon the righteous, and his eares are open vnto their crie.

16 But the face of the Lord is against them that doe euill, to cut off their remembrance from the earth.

17 The righteous crie, and the Lord heareth them, and deliuereth them out of all their troubles.

18 The Lord is neere vnto them that are of a contrite heart, and will saue such as be afflicted in Spirite.

19 Great are the troubles of the righteous: but the Lord deliuereth him out of them all.

20 He keepeth all his bones: not one of them is broken.

21 But malice shall slay the wicked: and they that hate the righteous, shall perish.

22 The Lord redeemeth the soules of his seruants: and none, that trust in him, shall perish.

Psalms 35

1 A Psalme of Dauid. Pleade thou my cause, O Lord, with them that striue with me: fight thou against them, that fight against me.

2 Lay hand vpon the shielde and buckler, and stand vp for mine helpe.

3 Bring out also the speare and stop the way against them, that persecute me: say vnto my soule, I am thy saluation.

4 Let them be confounded and put to shame, that seeke after my soule: let them be turned backe, and brought to confusion, that imagine mine hurt.

5 Let them be as chaffe before the winde, and let the Angel of the Lord scatter them.

6 Let their way be darke and slipperie: and let the Angel of the Lord persecute them.

7 For without cause they haue hid the pit and their net for me: without cause haue they digged a pit for my soule.

8 Let destruction come vpon him at vnwares, and let his net, that he hath laid priuilie, take him: let him fall into the same destruction.

9 Then my soule shalbe ioyfull in the Lord: it shall reioyce in his saluation.

10 All my bones shall say, Lord, who is like vnto thee, which deliuerest the poore from him, that is too strong for him! yea, the poore and him that is in miserie, from him that spoyleth him!

11 Cruell witnesses did rise vp: they asked of me things that I knewe not.

12 They rewarded me euill for good, to haue spoyled my soule.

13 Yet I, when they were sicke, I was clothed with a sacke: I humbled my soule with fasting: and my praier was turned vpon my bosome.

14 I behaued my selfe as to my friend, or as to my brother: I humbled my selfe, mourning as one that bewaileth his mother.

15 But in mine aduersitie they reioyced, and gathered them selues together: the abiects assembled themselues against me, and knewe not: they tare me and ceased not,

16 With the false skoffers at bankets, gnashing their teeth against me.

17 Lord, how long wilt thou beholde this? deliuer my soule from their tumult, euen my desolate soule from the lions.

18 So will I giue thee thankes in a great Congregation: I will praise thee among much people.

19 Let not them that are mine enemies, vniustly reioyce ouer mee, neyther let them winke with the eye, that hate mee without a cause.

20 For they speake not as friendes: but they imagine deceitfull woordes against the quiet of the lande.

21 And they gaped on mee with their mouthes, saying, Aha, aha, our eye hath seene.

22 Thou hast seene it, O Lord: keepe not silence: be not farre from me, O Lord.

23 Arise and wake to my iudgement, euen to my cause, my God, and my Lord.

24 Iudge me, O Lord my God, according to thy righteousnesse, and let them not reioyce ouer mee.

25 Let them not say in their hearts, O our soule reioyce: neither let them say, We haue deuoured him.

26 Let them bee confounded, and put to shame together, that reioyce at mine hurt: let them bee clothed with confusion and shame, that lift vp themselues against me.

27 But let them be ioyful and glad, that loue my righteousnesse: yea, let them say alway, Let the Lord be magnified, which loueth the prosperitie of his seruant.

28 And my tongue shall vtter thy righteousnesse, and thy praise euery day.

Psalms 36

1 To him that excelleth. A Psalme of Dauid, the servant of the Lord. Wickedness sayeth to the wicked man, euen in mine heart, that there is no feare of God before his eyes.

2 For hee flattereth himselfe in his owne eyes, while his iniquitie is foud worthy to be hated.

3 The wordes of his mouth are iniquitie and deceit: hee hath left off to vnderstand and to doe good.

4 Hee imagineth mischiefe vpon his bed: he setteth himselfe vpon a way, that is not good, and doeth not abhorre euill.

5 Thy mercy, O Lord, reacheth vnto the heauens, and thy faithfulnesse vnto the cloudes.

6 Thy righteousnesse is like the mightie moutaines: thy iudgements are like a great deepe: thou, Lord, doest saue man and beast.

7 How excellent is thy mercy, O God! therefore the children of men trust vnder the shadowe of thy wings.

8 They shall be satisfied with the fatnesse of thine house, and thou shalt giue them drinke out of the riuer of thy pleasures.

9 For with thee is the well of life, and in thy light shall we see light.

10 Extend thy louing kindnes vnto them that knowe thee, and thy righteousnesse vnto them that are vpright in heart.

11 Let not ye foote of pride come against me, and let not the hand of ye wicked men moue me.

12 There they are fallen that worke iniquity: they are cast downe, and shall not be able to rise.

Psalms 37

1 A Psalme of David. Fret not thy selfe because of the wicked men, neither be enuious for the euill doers.
2 For they shall soone bee cut downe like grasse, and shall wither as the greene herbe.
3 Trust thou in the Lord and do good: dwell in the land, and thou shalt be fed assuredly.
4 And delite thy selfe in the Lord, and hee shall giue thee thine hearts desire.
5 Commit thy way vnto the Lord, and trust in him, and he shall bring it to passe.
6 And he shall bring foorth thy righteousnes as the light, and thy iudgement as the noone day.
7 Waite patiently vpon the Lord and hope in him: fret not thy selfe for him which prospereth in his way: nor for the man that bringeth his enterprises to passe.
8 Cease from anger, and leaue off wrath: fret not thy selfe also to doe euill.
9 For euill doers shalbe cut off, and they that wait vpon the Lord, they shall inherite the land.
10 Therefore yet a litle while, and the wicked shall not appeare, and thou shalt looke after his place, and he shall not be found.
11 But meeke men shall possesse the earth, and shall haue their delite in the multitude of peace.
12 The wicked practiseth against the iust, and gnasheth his teeth against him.
13 But the Lord shall laugh him to scorne: for he seeth, that his day is comming.
14 The wicked haue drawen their sworde, and haue bent their bowe, to cast downe the poore and needie, and to slay such as be of vpright conuersation.
15 But their sword shall enter into their owne heart, and their bowes shalbe broken.
16 A small thing vnto the iust man is better, then great riches to the wicked and mightie.
17 For the armes of the wicked shall be broken: but the Lord vpholdeth the iust men.
18 The Lord knoweth the dayes of vpright men, and their inheritance shall bee perpetuall.
19 They shall not be confounded in the perilous time, and in the daies of famine they shall haue ynough.
20 But the wicked shall perish, and the enemies of the Lord shall be consumed as the fatte of lambes: euen with the smoke shall they consume away.
21 The wicked boroweth and payeth not againe. but the righteous is mercifull, and giueth.
22 For such as be blessed of God, shall inherite the lande, and they that be cursed of him, shalbe cut off.

23 The pathes of man are directed by the Lord: for he loueth his way.
24 Though he fall, hee shall not be cast off: for the Lord putteth vnder his hand.
25 I haue beene yong, and am olde: yet I sawe neuer the righteous forsaken, nor his seede begging bread.
26 But hee is euer mercifull and lendeth, and his seede enioyeth the blessing.
27 Flee from euill and doe good, and dwell for euer.
28 For the Lord loueth iudgement, and forsaketh not his Saintes: they shall be preserued for euermore: but the seede of the wicked shall be cut off.
29 The righteous men shall inherit the lande, and dwell therein for euer.
30 The mouth of the righteous will speake of wisedome, and his tongue will talke of iudgement.
31 For the Lawe of his God is in his heart, and his steppes shall not slide.
32 The wicked watcheth the righteous, and seeketh to slay him.
33 But the Lord wil not leaue him in his hand, nor condemne him, when he is iudged.
34 Waite thou on the Lord, and keepe his way, and he shall exalt thee, that thou shalt inherite the lande: when the wicked men shall perish, thou shalt see.
35 I haue seene the wicked strong, and spreading himselfe like a greene bay tree.
36 Yet he passed away, and loe, he was gone, and I sought him, but he could not be founde.
37 Marke the vpright man, and beholde the iust: for the end of that man is peace.
38 But the transgressours shall be destroyed together, and the ende of the wicked shall bee cut off.
39 But the saluation of the righteous men shalbe of the Lord: he shalbe their strength in the time of trouble.
40 For the Lord shall helpe them, and deliuer them: he shall deliuer them from the wicked, and shall saue them, because they trust in him.

Psalms 38

1 A Psalme of Dauid for remembrance. O Lord, rebuke mee not in thine anger, neither chastise me in thy wrath.
2 For thine arrowes haue light vpon me, and thine hand lyeth vpon me.
3 There is nothing sound in my flesh, because of thine anger: neither is there rest in my bones because of my sinne.
4 For mine iniquities are gone ouer mine head, and as a weightie burden they are too heauie for me.
5 My woundes are putrified, and corrupt because of my foolishnes.
6 I am bowed, and crooked very sore: I goe mourning all the day.
7 For my reines are full of burning, and there is nothing sound in my flesh.
8 I am weakened and sore broken: I roare for the very griefe of mine heart.
9 Lord, I powre my whole desire before thee, and my sighing is not hid from thee.

10 Mine heart panteth: my strength faileth me, and the light of mine eyes, euen they are not mine owne.
11 My louers and my friends stand aside from my plague, and my kinsmen stand a farre off.
12 They also, that seeke after my life, laye snares, and they that go about to do me euil, talke wicked things and imagine deceite continually.
13 But I as a deafe man heard not, and am as a dumme man, which openeth not his mouth.
14 Thus am I as a man, that heareth not, and in whose mouth are no reproofes.
15 For on thee, O Lord, do I waite: thou wilt heare me, my Lord, my God.
16 For I said, Heare me, least they reioyce ouer me: for when my foote slippeth, they extol themselues against me.
17 Surely I am ready to halte, and my sorow is euer before me.
18 When I declare my paine, and am sory for my sinne,
19 Then mine enemies are aliue and are mightie, and they that hate me wrongfully are many.
20 They also, that rewarde euill for good, are mine aduersaries, because I follow goodnesse.
21 Forsake me not, O Lord: be not thou farre from me, my God.
22 Haste thee to helpe mee, O my Lord, my saluation.

Psalms 39

1 To the excellent musician Ieduthun. I thought, I will take heede to my wayes, that I sinne not with my tongue: I will keepe my mouth brideled, while the wicked is in my sight.
2 I was dumme and spake nothing: I kept silece euen from good, and my sorow was more stirred.
3 Mine heart was hote within me, and while I was musing, the fire kindeled, and I spake with my tongue, saying,
4 Lord, let me know mine ende, and the measure of my dayes, what it is: let mee knowe howe long I haue to liue.
5 Beholde, thou hast made my dayes as an hand breadth, and mine age as nothing in respect of thee: surely euery man in his best state is altogether vanitie. Selah.
6 Doubtlesse man walketh in a shadowe, and disquieteth himselfe in vaine: he heapeth vp riches, and cannot tell who shall gather them.
7 And now Lord, what wait I for? mine hope is euen in thee.
8 Deliuer me from all my transgressions, and make me not a rebuke vnto the foolish.
9 I should haue bene dumme, and not haue opened my mouth, because thou didest it.
10 Take thy plague away from mee: for I am consumed by the stroke of thine hand.
11 When thou with rebukes doest chastise man for iniquitie, thou as a

mothe makest his beautie to consume: surely euery man is vanitie. Selah.

12 Heare my prayer, O Lord, and hearken vnto my cry: keepe not silence at my teares, for I am a strager with thee, and a soiourner as all my fathers.

13 Stay thine anger from me, that I may recouer my strength, before I go hence and be not.

Psalms 40

1 To him that excelleth. A Psalme of David. I Waited paciently for the Lord, and he inclined vnto me, and heard my cry.

2 Hee brought mee also out of the horrible pit, out of the myrie clay, and set my feete vpon the rocke, and ordered my goings.

3 And he hath put in my mouth a new song of praise vnto our God: many shall see it and feare, and shall trust in the Lord.

4 Blessed is the man that maketh the Lord his trust, and regardeth not the proude, nor such as turne aside to lyes.

5 O Lord my God, thou hast made thy wonderfull workes so many, that none can count in order to thee thy thoughts toward vs: I would declare, and speake of them, but they are moe then I am able to expresse.

6 Sacrifice and offering thou didest not desire: (for mine eares hast thou prepared) burnt offring and sinne offering hast thou not required.

7 Then said I, Lo, I come: for in the rolle of the booke it is written of me,

8 I desired to doe thy good will, O my God: yea, thy Lawe is within mine heart.

9 I haue declared thy righteousnesse in the great Congregation: loe, I will not refraine my lippes: O Lord, thou knowest.

10 I haue not hidde thy righteousnesse within mine heart, but I haue declared thy trueth and thy saluation: I haue not conceiled thy mercy and thy trueth from the great Congregation.

11 Withdrawe not thou thy tender mercie from mee, O Lord: let thy mercie and thy trueth alway preserue me.

12 For innumerable troubles haue compassed mee: my sinnes haue taken such holde vpon me, that I am not able to looke vp: yea, they are moe in nomber then the heares of mine head: therefore mine heart hath failed me.

13 Let it please thee, O Lord, to deliuer mee: make haste, O Lord, to helpe me.

14 Let them be confounded and put to shame together, that seeke my soule to destroye it: let them be driuen backward and put to rebuke, that desire mine hurt.

15 Let them be destroyed for a rewarde of their shame, which say vnto me, Aha, aha.

16 Let all them, that seeke thee, reioyce and be glad in thee: and let them, that loue thy saluation, say alway, The Lord be praysed.

17 Though I be poore and needie, the Lord thinketh on mee: thou art mine helper and my deliuerer: my God, make no tarying.

Psalms 41

1 To him that excelleth. A Psalme of Dauid. Blessed is he that iudgeth wisely of the poore: the Lord shall deliuer him in ye time of trouble.

2 The Lord will keepe him, and preserue him aliue: he shalbe blessed vpon the earth, and thou wilt not deliuer him vnto the will of his enemies.

3 The Lord wil strengthen him vpon ye bed of sorow: thou hast turned al his bed in his sicknes.

4 Therefore I saide, Lord haue mercie vpon me: heale my soule, for I haue sinned against thee.

5 Mine enemies speake euill of me, saying, When shall he die, and his name perish?

6 And if hee come to see mee, hee speaketh lies, but his heart heapeth iniquitie within him, and when he commeth foorth, he telleth it.

7 All they that hate me, whisper together against me: euen against me do they imagine mine hurt.

8 A mischiefe is light vpon him, and he that lyeth, shall no more rise.

9 Yea, my familiar friend, whom I trusted, which did eate of my bread, hath lifted vp the heele against me.

10 Therefore, O Lord, haue mercy vpon mee, and raise me vp: so I shall reward them.

11 By this I know that thou fauourest me, because mine enemie doth not triumph against me.

12 And as for me, thou vpholdest me in mine integritie, and doest set me before thy face for euer.

13 Blessed be the Lord God of Israel worlde without ende. So be it, euen so be it.

Psalms 42

1 To him that excelleth. A Psalme to give instruction, committed to the sonnes of Korah. As the harte brayeth for the riuers of water, so panteth my soule after thee, O God.

2 My soule thirsteth for God, euen for the liuing God: when shall I come and appeare before the presence of God?

3 My teares haue bin my meate day and night, while they dayly say vnto me, Where is thy God?

4 When I remembred these things, I powred out my very heart, because I had gone with the multitude, and ledde them into the House of God with the voyce of singing, and prayse, as a multitude that keepeth a feast.

5 Why art thou cast downe, my soule, and vnquiet within me? waite on God: for I will yet giue him thankes for the helpe of his presence.

6 My God, my soule is cast downe within me, because I remember thee, from the land of Iorden, and Hermonim, and from the mount Mizar.

7 One deepe calleth another deepe by the noyse of thy water spoutes: all thy waues and thy floods are gone ouer me.

8 The Lord will graunt his louing kindenesse in the day, and in the night shall I sing of him, euen a prayer vnto the God of my life.

9 I wil say vnto God, which is my rocke, Why hast thou forgotten mee? why goe I mourning, when the enemie oppresseth me?

10 My bones are cut asunder, while mine enemies reproch me, saying dayly vnto me, Where is thy God?

11 Why art thou cast downe, my soule? and why art thou disquieted within mee? waite on God: for I wil yet giue him thankes: he is my present helpe, and my God.

Psalms 43

1 Judge me, O God, and defend my cause against the vnmercifull people: deliuer mee from the deceitfull and wicked man.

2 For thou art the God of my strength: why hast thou put me away? why goe I so mourning, when the enemie oppresseth me?

3 Sende thy light and thy trueth: let them leade mee: let them bring mee vnto thine holy Mountaine and to thy Tabernacles.

4 Then wil I go vnto the altar of God, euen vnto the God of my ioy and gladnes: and vpon the harpe wil I giue thanks vnto thee, O God, my God.

5 Why art thou cast downe, my soule? and why art thou disquieted within mee? waite on God: for I will yet giue him thankes, he is my present helpe, and my God.

Psalms 44

1 To him that excelleth. A Psalme to give instruction, committed to the sonnes of Korah. We haue heard with our eares, O God: our fathers haue tolde vs the workes, that thou hast done in their dayes, in the olde time:

2 Howe thou hast driuen out the heathen with thine hand, and planted them: how thou hast destroyed the people, and caused them to grow.

3 For they inherited not the lande by their owne sworde, neither did their owne arme saue them: but thy right hand, and thine arme and the light of thy countenance, because thou didest fauour them.

4 Thou art my King, O God: send helpe vnto Iaakob.

5 Through thee haue we thrust backe our aduersaries: by thy Name haue we troden downe them that rose vp against vs.

6 For I do not trust in my bowe, neither can my sworde saue me.

7 But thou hast saued vs from our aduersaries, and hast put them to confusion that hate vs.

8 Therefore will wee praise God continually, and will confesse thy Name for euer. Selah.

9 But now thou art farre off, and puttest vs to confusion, and goest not forth with our armies.

10 Thou makest vs to turne backe from the aduersary, and they, which hate vs, spoile for theselues.

11 Thou giuest vs as sheepe to bee eaten, and doest scatter vs among the nations.

12 Thou sellest thy people without gaine, and doest not increase their price.

13 Thou makest vs a reproche to our neighbours, a iest and a laughing stocke to them that are round about vs.

14 Thou makest vs a prouerbe among the nations, and a nodding of the head among the people.

15 My confusion is dayly before me, and the shame of my face hath couered me,

16 For the voyce of the slaunderer and rebuker, for the enemie and auenger.

17 All this is come vpon vs, yet doe wee not forget thee, neither deale wee falsly concerning thy couenant.

18 Our heart is not turned backe: neither our steps gone out of thy paths,

19 Albeit thou hast smitten vs downe into the place of dragons, and couered vs with the shadow of death.

20 If wee haue forgotten the Name of our God, and holden vp our hands to a strange god,

21 Shall not God searche this out? for hee knoweth the secrets of the heart.

22 Surely for thy sake are we slaine continually, and are counted as sheepe for the slaughter.

23 Vp, why sleepest thou, O Lord? awake, be not farre off for euer.

24 Wherefore hidest thou thy face? and forgettest our miserie and our affliction?

25 For our soule is beaten downe vnto the dust: our belly cleaueth vnto the ground.

26 Rise vp for our succour, and redeeme vs for thy mercies sake.

Psalms 45

1 To him that excelleth on Shoshannim a song of loue to giue instruction, committed to the sonnes of Korah. Mine heart will vtter forth a good matter: I wil intreat in my workes of the King: my tongue is as the pen of a swift writer.

2 Thou art fayrer then the children of men: grace is powred in thy lips, because God hath blessed thee for euer.

3 Gird thy sword vpon thy thigh, O most mightie, to wit, thy worship and thy glory,

4 And prosper with thy glory: ride vpon the worde of trueth and of meekenes and of righteousnes: so thy right hand shall teach thee terrible things.

5 Thine arrowes are sharpe to pearce the heart of the Kings enemies: therefore the people shall fall vnder thee.

6 Thy throne, O God, is for euer and euer: the scepter of thy kingdome is a scepter of righteousnesse.

7 Thou louest righteousnes, and hatest wickednesse, because God, euen thy God hath anoynted thee with the oyle of gladnes aboue thy fellowes.

8 All thy garments smelll of myrrhe and aloes, and cassia, when thou commest out of the yuorie palaces, where they haue made thee glad.

9 Kings daugthers were among thine honorable wiues: vpon thy right hand did stand the Queene in a vesture of golde of Ophir.

10 Hearken, O daughter, and consider, and incline thine eare: forget also thine owne people and thy fathers house.

11 So shall the King haue pleasure in thy beautie: for he is thy Lord, and reuerence thou him.

12 And the daughter of Tyrus with the rich of the people shall doe homage before thy face with presents.

13 The Kings daughter is all glorious within: her clothing is of broydred golde.

14 She shalbe brought vnto the King in raiment of needle worke: the virgins that follow after her, and her companions shall be brought vnto thee.

15 With ioy and gladnes shall they be brought, and shall enter into the Kings palace.

16 In steade of thy fathers shall thy children be: thou shalt make them princes through all the earth.

17 I will make thy Name to be remembred through all generations: therefore shall the people giue thanks vnto thee world without ende.

Psalms 46

1 To him that excelleth upon Alamoth a song committed to the sonnes of Korah. God is our hope and strength, and helpe in troubles, ready to be found.

2 Therefore will not we feare, though the earth be moued, and though the mountaines fall into the middes of the sea.

3 Though the waters thereof rage and be troubled, and the mountaines shake at the surges of the same. Selah,

4 Yet there is a Riuer, whose streames shall make glad the citie of God: euen the Sanctuarie of the Tabernacles of the most High.

5 God is in the middes of it: therefore shall it not be moued: God shall helpe it very earely.

6 When the nations raged, and the kingdomes were moued, God thundred, and the earth melted.

7 The Lord of hostes is with vs: the God of Iaakob is our refuge. Selah.

8 Come, and behold the workes of the Lord, what desolations he hath made in the earth.

9 He maketh warres to cease vnto the endes of the world: he breaketh the bowe and cutteth the speare, and burneth the chariots with fire.

10 Be still and knowe that I am God: I will be exalted among the heathen, and I wil be exalted in the earth.

11 The Lord of hostes is with vs: the God of Iaakob is our refuge. Selah.

Psalms 47

1 To him that excelleth. A Psalme committed to the sonnes of Korah. All people clap your hands: sing loude vnto God with a ioyfull voyce.

2 For the Lord is high, and terrible: a great King ouer all the earth.

3 He hath subdued the people vnder vs, and the nations vnder our feete.

4 Hee hath chosen our inheritance for vs: euen the glory of Iaakob whom he loued. Selah.

5 God is gone vp with triumph, euen the Lord, with the sound of the trumpet.

6 Sing prayses to God, sing prayses: sing prayses vnto our King, sing prayses.

7 For God is the King of all the earth: sing prayses euery one that hath vnderstanding.

8 God reigneth ouer the heathen: God sitteth vpon his holy throne.

9 The princes of the people are gathered vnto the people of the God of Abraham: for the shields of the world belong to God: he is greatly to be exalted.

Psalms 48

1 A song or Psalme committed to the sonnes of Korah. Great is the Lord, and greatly to be praysed, in the Citie of our God, euen vpon his holy Mountaine.

2 Mount Zion, lying Northwarde, is faire in situation: it is the ioy of the whole earth, and the Citie of the great King.

3 In the palaces thereof God is knowen for a refuge.

4 For lo, the Kings were gathered, and went together.

5 When they sawe it, they marueiled: they were astonied, and suddenly driuen backe.

6 Feare came there vpon them, and sorowe, as vpon a woman in trauaile.

7 As with an East winde thou breakest the shippes of Tarshish, so were they destroyed.

8 As we haue heard, so haue we seene in the citie of the Lord of hostes, in the Citie of our God: God will stablish it for euer. Selah.

9 We waite for thy louing kindnes, O God, in the middes of thy Temple.

10 O God, according vnto thy Name, so is thy prayse vnto the worlds end: thy right hand is full of righteousnes.

11 Let mount Zion reioyce, and the daughters of Iudah be glad, because of thy iudgements.

12 Compasse about Zion, and goe round about it, and tell the towres thereof.

13 Marke well the wall thereof: beholde her towres, that ye may tell your posteritie.

14 For this God is our God for euer and euer: he shall be our guide vnto the death.

Psalms 49

1 To him that excelleth. A Psalme committed to the sonnes of Korah. Heare this, all ye people: giue eare, all ye that dwell in the world,

2 As well lowe as hie, both rich and poore.

3 My mouth shall speake of wisdome, and the meditation of mine heart is of knowledge.

4 I will incline mine eare to a parable, and vtter my graue matter vpon the harpe.

5 Wherefore should I feare in the euil dayes, when iniquitie shall compasse me about, as at mine heeles?

6 They trust in their goods, and boast them selues in the multitude of their riches.

7 Yet a man can by no meanes redeeme his brother: he can not giue his raunsome to God,

8 (So precious is the redemption of their soules, and the continuance for euer)

9 That he may liue still for euer, and not see the graue.

10 For he seeth that wise men die, and also that the ignorant and foolish perish, and leaue their riches for others.

11 Yet they thinke, their houses, and their habitations shall continue for euer, euen from generation to generation, and call their lands by their names.

12 But man shall not continue in honour: he is like the beastes that die.

13 This their way vttereth their foolishnes: yet their posteritie delite in their talke. Selah.

14 Like sheepe they lie in graue: death deuoureth them, and the righteous shall haue domination ouer them in the morning: for their beautie shall consume, when they shall goe from their house to graue.

15 But God shall deliuer my soule from the power of the graue: for he will receiue me. Selah.

16 Be not thou afrayd when one is made rich, and when the glory of his house is increased.

17 For he shall take nothing away when he dieth, neither shall his pompe descende after him.

18 For while he liued, he reioyced himselfe: and men will prayse thee, when thou makest much of thy selfe.

19 He shall enter into the generation of his fathers, and they shall not liue for euer.

20 Man is in honour, and vnderstandeth not: he is like to beasts that perish.

Psalms 50

1 A Psalme of Asaph. The God of Gods, euen the Lord hath spoken and called the earth from the rising vp of the sunne vnto the going downe thereof.

2 Out of Zion, which is the perfection of beautie, hath God shined.

3 Our God shall come and shall not keepe silence: a fire shall deuoure before him, and a mightie tempest shall be mooued round about him.

4 Hee shall call the heauen aboue, and the earth to iudge his people.

5 Gather my Saints together vnto me, those that make a couenant with me with sacrifice.

6 And the heauens shall declare his righteousnes: for God is iudge himselfe. Selah.

7 Heare, O my people, and I wil speake: heare, O Israel, and I wil testifie vnto thee: for I am God, euen thy God.

8 I wil not reproue thee for thy sacrifices, or thy burnt offerings, that haue not bene continually before me.

9 I will take no bullocke out of thine house, nor goates out of thy foldes.

10 For all the beastes of the forest are mine, and the beastes on a thousand mountaines.

11 I knowe all the foules on the mountaines: and the wilde beastes of the fielde are mine.

12 If I bee hungry, I will not tell thee: for the world is mine, and all that therein is.

13 Will I eate the flesh of bulles? or drinke the blood of goates?

14 Offer vnto God praise, and pay thy vowes vnto the most High,

15 And call vpon me in the day of trouble: so will I deliuer thee, and thou shalt glorifie me.

16 But vnto the wicked said God, What hast thou to doe to declare mine ordinances, that thou shouldest take my couenant in thy mouth,

17 Seeing thou hatest to bee reformed, and hast cast my wordes behinde thee?

18 For when thou seest a thiefe, thou runnest with him, and thou art partaker with the adulterers.

19 Thou giuest thy mouth to euill, and with thy tongue thou forgest deceit.

20 Thou sittest, and speakest against thy brother, and slanderest thy mothers sonne.

21 These things hast thou done, and I held my tongue: therefore thou thoughtest that I was like thee: but I will reproue thee, and set them in order before thee.

22 Oh cosider this, ye that forget God, least I teare you in pieces, and there be none that can deliuer you.

23 He that offereth praise, shall glorifie mee: and to him, that disposeth his way aright, will I shew the saluation of God.

Psalms 51

1 To him that excelleth. A Psalme of David, when the Prophet Nathan came unto him, after he had gone in to Bath-sheba. Have mercie vpon me, O God, according to thy louing kindnes: according to the multitude of thy compassions put away mine iniquities.

2 Wash me throughly from mine iniquitie, and clense me from my sinne.

3 For I know mine iniquities, and my sinne is euer before me.

4 Against thee, against thee onely haue I sinned, and done euill in thy sight, that thou mayest be iust when thou speakest, and pure when thou iudgest.

5 Beholde, I was borne in iniquitie, and in sinne hath my mother conceiued me.

6 Beholde, thou louest trueth in the inwarde affections: therefore hast thou taught mee wisedome in the secret of mine heart.

7 Purge me with hyssope, and I shalbe cleane: wash me, and I shalbe whiter then snowe.

8 Make me to heare ioye and gladnes, that the bones, which thou hast broken, may reioyce.

9 Hide thy face from my sinnes, and put away all mine iniquities.

10 Create in mee a cleane heart, O God, and renue a right spirit within me.

11 Cast mee not away from thy presence, and take not thine holy Spirit from me.

12 Restore to me the ioy of thy saluation, and stablish me with thy free Spirit.

13 Then shall I teache thy wayes vnto the wicked, and sinners shalbe conuerted vnto thee.

14 Deliuer me from blood, O God, which art the God of my saluation, and my tongue shall sing ioyfully of thy righteousnes.

15 Open thou my lippes, O Lord, and my mouth shall shewe foorth thy praise.

16 For thou desirest no sacrifice, though I would giue it: thou delitest not in burnt offering.

17 The sacrifices of God are a contrite spirit: a contrite and a broken heart, O God, thou wilt not despise.

18 Bee fauourable vnto Zion for thy good pleasure: builde the walles of Ierusalem.

19 Then shalt thou accept ye sacrifices of righteousnes, euen the burnt offering and oblation: then shall they offer calues vpon thine altar.

Psalms 52

1 To him that excelleth. A Psalme of Dauid to giue instruction. When Doeg the Edomite came and shewed Saul, and saide to him, Dauid is come to the house of Abimelech. Why boastest thou thy selfe in thy wickednesse, O man of power? the louing kindenesse of God indureth dayly.

2 Thy tongue imagineth mischiefe, and is like a sharpe rasor, that cutteth deceitfully.

3 Thou doest loue euill more then good, and lies more then to speake the trueth. Selah.

4 Thou louest all wordes that may destroye, O deceitfull tongue!

5 So shall God destroy thee for euer: he shall take thee and plucke thee out of thy tabernacle, and roote thee out of ye land of the liuing. Selah.

6 The righteous also shall see it, and feare, and shall laugh at him, saying,

7 Beholde the man that tooke not God for his strength, but trusted vnto the

multitude of his riches, and put his strength in his malice.

8 But I shall bee like a greene oliue tree in the house of God: for I trusted in the mercie of God for euer and euer.

9 I will alway praise thee, for that thou hast done this, and I will hope in thy Name, because it is good before thy Saints.

Psalms 53

1 To him that excelleth on Mahalath. A Psalme of David to give instruction. The foole hath saide in his heart, There is no God. they haue corrupted and done abominable wickednes: there is none that doeth good.

2 God looked downe from heauen vpon the children of men, to see if there were any that would vnderstand, and seeke God.

3 Euery one is gone backe: they are altogether corrupt: there is none that doth good, no not one.

4 Doe not the workers of iniquitie knowe that they eate vp my people as they eate bread? they call not vpon God.

5 There they were afraide for feare, where no feare was: for God hath scattered the bones of him that besieged thee: thou hast put them to confusion, because God hath cast them off.

6 Oh giue saluation vnto Israel out of Zion: when God turneth the captiuitie of his people, then Iaakob shall reioyce, and Israel shalbe glad.

Psalms 54

1 To him that excelleth on Neginoth. A Psalme of David, to give instruction. When the Ziphims came and said vnto Saul, Is not David hid among us? Save mee, O God, by thy Name, and by thy power iudge me.

2 O God, heare my prayer: hearken vnto the wordes of my mouth.

3 For strangers are risen vp against me, and tyrants seeke my soule: they haue not set God before them. Selah.

4 Beholde, God is mine helper: the Lord is with them that vpholde my soule.

5 He shall rewarde euill vnto mine enemies: Oh cut them off in thy trueth!

6 Then I will sacrifice freely vnto thee: I wil praise thy Name, O Lord, because it is good.

7 For he hath deliuered me out of al trouble, and mine eye hath seene my desire vpon mine enemies.

Psalms 55

1 To him that excelleth on Neginoth. A Psalme of David to give instruction. Heare my prayer, O God, and hide not thy selfe from my supplication.

2 Hearken vnto me, and answere me: I mourne in my prayer, and make a noyse,

3 For the voyce of the enemie, and for the vexation of ye wicked, because they haue brought iniquitie vpon me, and furiously hate me.

4 Mine heart trembleth within mee, and the terrours of death are fallen vpon me.

5 Feare and trembling are come vpon mee, and an horrible feare hath couered me.

6 And I said, Oh that I had wings like a doue: then would I flie away and rest.

7 Beholde, I woulde take my flight farre off, and lodge in the wildernes. Selah.

8 Hee would make haste for my deliuerance from the stormie winde and tempest.

9 Destroy, O Lord, and deuide their tongues: for I haue seene crueltie and strife in the citie.

10 Day and night they goe about it vpon the walles thereof: both iniquitie and mischiefe are in the middes of it.

11 Wickednes is in the middes thereof: deceit and guile depart not from her streetes.

12 Surely mine enemie did not defame mee: for I could haue borne it: neither did mine aduersarie exalt himselfe against mee: for I would haue hid me from him.

13 But it was thou, O man, euen my companion, my guide and my familiar:

14 Which delited in consulting together, and went into the House of God as companions.

15 Let death sense vpon them: let them goe downe quicke into the graue: for wickednes is in their dwellings, euen in the middes of them.

16 But I will call vnto God, and the Lord will saue me.

17 Euening and morning, and at noone will I pray, and make a noyse, and he wil heare my voice.

18 He hath deliuered my soule in peace from the battel, that was against me: for many were with me.

19 God shall heare and afflict them, euen hee that reigneth of olde, Selah. because they haue no changes, therefore they feare not God.

20 Hee layed his hande vpon such, as be at peace with him, and he brake his couenant.

21 The wordes of his mouth were softer then butter, yet warre was in his heart: his words were more gentle then oyle, yet they were swordes.

22 Cast thy burden vpon the Lord, and hee shall nourish thee: he wil not suffer the righteous to fall for euer.

23 And thou, O God, shalt bring them downe into the pitte of corruption: the bloudie, and deceitfull men shall not liue halfe their dayes: but I will trust in thee.

Psalms 56

1 To him that excelleth. A Psalme of David on Michtam, concerning the dumme doue in a farre countrey, when the Philistims tooke him in Gath. Be mercifull vnto me, O God, for man would swallow me vp: he fighteth continually and vexeth me.

2 Mine enemies would dayly swallowe mee vp: for many fight against me, O thou most High.

3 When I was afrayd, I trusted in thee.

4 I will reioyce in God, because of his word, I trust in God, and will not feare what flesh can doe vnto me.

5 Mine owne wordes grieue me dayly: all their thoughtes are against me to doe me hurt.

6 They gather together, and keepe them selues close: they marke my steps, because they waite for my soule.

7 They thinke they shall escape by iniquitie: O God, cast these people downe in thine anger.

8 Thou hast counted my wandrings: put my teares into thy bottel: are they not in thy register?

9 When I cry, then mine enemies shall turne backe: this I know, for God is with me.

10 I will reioyce in God because of his worde: in the Lord wil I reioyce because of his worde.

11 In God doe I trust: I will not be afrayd what man can doe vnto me.

12 Thy vowes are vpon me, O God: I will render prayses vnto thee.

13 For thou hast deliuered my soule from death, and also my feete from falling, that I may walke before God in the light of the liuing.

Psalms 57

1 To him that excelleth. Destroy not. A Psalme of David on Michtam. When he fled from Saul in the cave. Have mercie vpon me, O God, haue mercie vpon me: for my soule trusteth in thee, and in the shadowe of thy wings wil I trust, till these afflictions ouerpasse.

2 I will call vnto the most high God, euen to the God, that performeth his promise toward me.

3 He will send from heauen, and saue me from the reproofe of him that would swallowe me. Selah. God wil send his mercy, and his trueth.

4 My soule is among lions: I lie among the children of men, that are set on fire: whose teeth are speares and arrowes, and their tongue a sharpe sworde.

5 Exalt thy selfe, O God, aboue the heauen, and let thy glory be vpon all the earth.

6 They haue layd a net for my steps: my soule is pressed downe: they haue digged a pit before me, and are fallen into the mids of it. Selah.

7 Mine heart is prepared, O God, mine heart is prepared: I will sing and giue prayse.

8 Awake my tongue, awake viole and harpe: I wil awake early.

9 I will prayse thee, O Lord, among the people, and I wil sing vnto thee among the nations.

10 For thy mercie is great vnto the heauens, and thy trueth vnto the cloudes.

11 Exalt thy selfe, O God, aboue the heauens, and let thy glory be vpon all the earth.

Psalms 58

1 To him that excelleth. Destroy not. A Psalme of David on Michtam. Is it true?

O Congregation, speake ye iustly? O sonnes of men, iudge ye vprightly?

2 Yea, rather ye imagine mischiefe in your heart: your hands execute crueltie vpon the earth.

3 The wicked are strangers from ye wombe: euen from the belly haue they erred, and speake lyes.

4 Their poyson is euen like the poyson of a serpent: like ye deafe adder that stoppeth his eare.

5 Which heareth not the voyce of the inchanter, though he be most expert in charming.

6 Breake their teeth, O God, in their mouthes: breake the iawes of the yong lions, O Lord.

7 Let them melt like the waters, let them passe away: when hee shooteth his arrowes, let them be as broken.

8 Let them consume like a snayle that melteth, and like the vntimely fruite of a woman, that hath not seene the sunne.

9 As raw flesh before your pots feele the fire of thornes: so let him cary them away as with a whirlewinde in his wrath.

10 The righteous shall reioyce when he seeeth the vengeance: he shall wash his feete in the blood of the wicked.

11 And men shall say, Verily there is fruite for the righteous: doutlesse there is a God that iudgeth in the earth.

Psalms 59

1 To him that excelleth. Destroy not. A Psalme of David on Michtam. When Saul sent and they did watch the house to kill him. O my God, deliuer mee from mine enemies: defend me from them that rise vp against me.

2 Deliuer me from the wicked doers, and saue me from the bloody men.

3 For loe, they haue layd waite for my soule: the mightie men are gathered against me, not for mine offence, nor for my sinne, O Lord.

4 They runne and prepare themselues without a fault on my part: arise therefore to assist me, and beholde.

5 Euen thou, O Lord God of hostes, O God of Israel awake to visit all the heathen, and be not merciful vnto all that transgresse maliciously. Selah.

6 They goe to and from in the euening: they barke like dogs, and goe about the citie.

7 Behold, they brag in their talke, and swords are in their lips: for, Who, say they, doeth heare?

8 But thou, O Lord, shalt haue them in derision, and thou shalt laugh at all the heathen.

9 He is strong: but I will waite vpon thee: for God is my defence.

10 My mercifull God will preuent me: God wil let me see my desire vpon mine enemies.

11 Slay them not, least my people forget it: but scatter them abroad by thy power, and put them downe, O Lord our shield,

12 For the sinne of their mouth, and the words of their lips: and let them be taken in their pride, euen for their periurie and lies, that they speake.

13 Consume them in thy wrath: consume them that they be no more: and let them knowe that God ruleth in Iaakob, euen vnto the ends of the world. Selah.

14 And in the euening they shall go to and from, and barke like dogs, and go about the citie.

15 They shall runne here and there for meate: and surely they shall not be satisfied, though they tary all night.

16 But I wil sing of thy power, and will prayse thy mercy in the morning: for thou hast bene my defence and refuge in the day of my trouble.

17 Vnto thee, O my Strength, wil I sing: for God is my defence, and my mercifull God.

Psalms 60

1 To him that excelleth upon Shushan Eduth, or Michtam. A Psalme of David to teach. When he fought against Aram Naharaim, and against Aram Zobah, when Joab returned and slew twelve thousand Edomites in the salt valley. O God, thou hast cast vs out, thou hast scattered vs, thou hast bene angry, turne againe vnto vs.

2 Thou hast made the land to tremble, and hast made it to gape: heale the breaches thereof, for it is shaken.

3 Thou hast shewed thy people heauy things: thou hast made vs to drinke the wine of giddines.

4 But now thou hast giuen a banner to them that feare thee, that it may be displayed because of thy trueth. Selah.

5 That thy beloued may be deliuered, helpe with thy right hand and heare me.

6 God hath spoken in his holines: therefore I will reioyce: I shall deuide Shechem, and measure the valley of Succoth.

7 Gilead shalbe mine, and Manasseh shalbe mine: Ephraim also shalbe the strength of mine head: Iudah is my lawgiuer.

8 Moab shalbe my wash pot: ouer Edom will I cast out my shoe: Palestina shew thy selfe ioyfull for me.

9 Who will leade me into the strong citie? who will bring me vnto Edom?

10 Wilt not thou, O God, which hadest cast vs off, and didest not go forth, O God, with our armies?

11 Giue vs helpe against trouble: for vaine is the helpe of man.

12 Through God we shall doe valiantly: for he shall tread downe our enemies.

Psalms 61

1 To him that excelleth on Neginoth. A Psalme of David. Heare my cry, O God: giue eare vnto my prayer.

2 From the endes of the earth will I crye vnto thee: when mine heart is opprest, bring me vpon the rocke that is higher then I.

3 For thou hast bene mine hope, and a strong tower against the enemie.

4 I will dwell in thy Tabernacle for euer, and my trust shall be vnder the couering of thy wings. Selah.

5 For thou, O God, hast heard my desires: thou hast giuen an heritage vnto those that feare thy Name.

6 Thou shalt giue the King a long life: his yeeres shalbe as many ages.

7 Hee shall dwell before God for euer: prepare mercie and faithfulnes that they may preserue him.

8 So will I alway sing prayse vnto thy Name in performing dayly my vowes.

Psalms 62

1 To the excelletn musician Ieduthun. A Psalme of David. Yet my soule keepeth silence vnto God: of him commeth my saluation.

2 Yet he is my strength and my saluation, and my defence: therefore I shall not much be mooued.

3 How long wil ye imagine mischiefe against a man? ye shalbe all slaine: ye shalbe as a bowed wall, or as a wall shaken.

4 Yet they consult to cast him downe from his dignitie: their delight is in lies, they blesse with their mouthes, but curse with their hearts. Selah.

5 Yet my soule keepe thou silence vnto God: for mine hope is in him.

6 Yet is hee my strength, and my saluation, and my defence: therefore I shall not be mooued.

7 In God is my saluation and my glory, the rocke of my strength: in God is my trust.

8 Trust in him alway, ye people: powre out your hearts before him, for God is our hope. Selah.

9 Yet the children of men are vanitie, the chiefe men are lies: to lay them vpon a balance they are altogether lighter then vanitie.

10 Trust not in oppression nor in robberie: be not vaine: if riches increase, set not your heart thereon.

11 God spake once or twise, I haue heard it, that power belongeth vnto God,

12 And to thee, O Lord, mercie: for thou rewardest euery one according to his worke.

Psalms 63

1 A Psalme of David. When he was in the wildernesse of Judah. O God, thou art my God, earely will I seeke thee: my soule thirsteth for thee: my flesh longeth greatly after thee in a barren and drye land without water.

2 Thus I beholde thee as in the Sanctuarie, when I beholde thy power and thy glorie.

3 For thy louing kindnesse is better then life: therefore my lippes shall prayse thee.

4 Thus will I magnifie thee all my life, and lift vp mine hands in thy name.

5 My soule shalbe satisfied, as with marowe and fatnesse, and my mouth shall praise thee with ioyfull lippes,

6 When I remember thee on my bedde, and when I thinke vpon thee in the night watches.

7 Because thou hast bene mine helper, therefore vnder the shadow of thy wings wil I reioyce.

8 My soule cleaueth vnto thee: for thy right hand vpholdeth me.

9 Therefore they that seeke my soule to destroy it, they shall goe into the lowest partes of the earth.

10 They shall cast him downe with the edge of the sword, and they shall be a portion for foxes.

11 But the King shall reioyce in God, and all that sweare by him shall reioyce in him: for the mouth of them that speake lyes, shall be stopped.

Psalms 64

1 To him that excelleth. A Psalme of David. Heare my voyce, O God, in my prayer: preserue my life from feare of the enemie.

2 Hide me from the conspiracie of the wicked, and from the rage of the workers of iniquitie.

3 Which haue whette their tongue like a sword, and shot for their arrowes bitter wordes.

4 To shoote at the vpright in secrete: they shoote at him suddenly, and feare not.

5 They encourage themselues in a wicked purpose: they commune together to lay snares priuilie, and say, Who shall see them?

6 They haue sought out iniquities, and haue accomplished that which they sought out, euen euery one his secret thoughtes, and the depth of his heart.

7 But God will shoote an arrowe at them suddenly: their strokes shalbe at once.

8 They shall cause their owne tongue to fall vpon them: and whosoeuer shall see them, shall flee away.

9 And all men shall see it, and declare the worke of God, and they shall vnderstand, what he hath wrought.

10 But the righteous shall be glad in the Lord, and trust in him: and all that are vpright of heart, shall reioyce.

Psalms 65

1 To him that excelleth. A Psalme or song of David. O God, praise waiteth for thee in Zion, and vnto thee shall the vowe be perfourmed.

2 Because thou hearest the prayer, vnto thee shall all flesh come.

3 Wicked deedes haue preuailed against me: but thou wilt be mercifull vnto our transgressions.

4 Blessed is he, whom thou chusest and causest to come to thee: he shall dwell in thy courtes, and we shall be satisfied with the pleasures of thine House, euen of thine holy Temple.

5 O God of our saluation, thou wilt answere vs with fearefull signes in thy righteousnes, O thou the hope of all the ends of the earth, and of them that are farre off in the sea.

6 He stablisheth the mountaines by his power: and is girded about with strength.

7 He appeaseth the noyse of the seas and the noyse of the waues thereof, and the tumults of the people.

8 They also, that dwell in the vttermost parts of the earth, shalbe afraide of thy signes: thou shalt make the East and the West to reioyce.

9 Thou visitest the earth, and waterest it: thou makest it very riche: the Riuer of God is full of water: thou preparest them corne: for so thou appointest it.

10 Thou waterest abundantly the furrowes thereof: thou causest the raine to descende into the valleies thereof: thou makest it soft with showres, and blessest the bud thereof.

11 Thou crownest ye yeere with thy goodnesse, and thy steppes droppe fatnesse.

12 They drop vpon the pastures of the wildernesse: and the hils shalbe compassed with gladnes.

13 The pastures are clad with sheepe: the valleis also shalbe couered with corne: therefore they shoute for ioye, and sing.

Psalms 66

1 To him that excelleth. A song or Psalme. Rejoice in God, all ye inhabitants of the earth.

2 Sing forth the glory of his name: make his praise glorious.

3 Say vnto God, Howe terrible art thou in thy workes! through the greatnesse of thy power shall thine enemies be in subiection vnto thee.

4 All the worlde shall worship thee, and sing vnto thee, euen sing of thy Name. Selah.

5 Come and beholde the workes of God: he is terrible in his doing towarde the sonnes of men.

6 He hath turned the Sea into drie land: they passe through the riuer on foote: there did we reioyce in him.

7 He ruleth the worlde with his power: his eyes beholde the nations: the rebellious shall not exalt them selues. Selah.

8 Prayse our God, ye people, and make the voyce of his prayse to be heard.

9 Which holdeth our soules in life, and suffereth not our feete to slippe.

10 For thou, O God, hast proued vs, thou hast tryed vs as siluer is tryed.

11 Thou hast brought vs into the snare, and layed a strait chaine vpon our loynes.

12 Thou hast caused men to ryde ouer our heads: we went into fire and into water, but thou broughtest vs out into a welthie place.

13 I will go into thine House with burnt offrings, and will pay thee my vowes,

14 Which my lippes haue promised, and my mouth hath spoken in mine affliction.

15 I will offer vnto thee the burnt offerings of fat rammes with incense: I will prepare bullocks and goates. Selah.

16 Come and hearken, all ye that feare God, and I will tell you what he hath done to my soule.

17 I called vnto him with my mouth, and he was exalted with my tongue.

18 If I regard wickednesse in mine heart, the Lord will not heare me.

19 But God hath heard me, and considered the voyce of my prayer.

20 Praysed be God, which hath not put backe my prayer, nor his mercie from me.

Psalms 67

1 To him that excelleth on Neginoth. A Psalme or song. God be mercifull vnto vs, and blesse vs, and cause his face to shine among vs. Selah.

2 That they may know thy way vpon earth, and thy sauing health among all nations.

3 Let the people prayse thee, O God: let all the people prayse thee.

4 Let the people be glad and reioyce: for thou shalt iudge the people righteously, and gouerne the nations vpon the earth. Selah.

5 Let the people prayse thee, O God: let all the people prayse thee.

6 Then shall the earth bring foorth her increase, and God, euen our God shall blesse vs.

7 God shall blesse vs, and all the endes of the earth shall feare him.

Psalms 68

1 To him that excelleth. A Psalme or song of David. God will arise, and his enemies shalbe scattered: they also that hate him, shall flee before him.

2 As the smoke vanisheth, so shalt thou driue them away: and as waxe melteth before the fire, so shall the wicked perish at the presence of God.

3 But the righteous shalbe glad, and reioyce before God: yea, they shall leape for ioye.

4 Sing vnto God, and sing prayses vnto his name: exalt him that rideth vpon the heauens, in his Name Iah, and reioyce before him.

5 He is a Father of the fatherlesse, and a Iudge of the widowes, euen God in his holy habitation.

6 God maketh the solitarie to dwell in families, and deliuereth them that were prisoners in stocks: but the rebellious shall dwell in a dry land.

7 O God, when thou wentest forth before thy people: when thou wentest through the wildernesse, (Selah)

8 The earth shooke, and the heauens dropped at the presence of this God: euen Sinai was moued at the presence of God, euen the God of Israel.

9 Thou, O God, sendest a gracious raine vpon thine inheritance, and thou didest refresh it when it was wearie.

10 Thy Congregation dwelled therein: for thou, O God, hast of thy goodnesse prepared it for the poore.

11 The Lord gaue matter to the women to tell of the great armie.

12 Kings of the armies did flee: they did flee, and she that remained in the house, deuided the spoyle.

13 Though ye haue lien among pots, yet shall ye be as the winges of a doue that is couered with siluer, and whose fethers are like yelowe golde.

14 When the Almightie scattered Kings in it, it was white as the snowe in Zalmon.

15 The mountaine of God is like the mountaine of Bashan: it is an high Mountaine, as mount Bashan.

16 Why leape ye, ye high mountaines? as for this Mountaine, God deliteth to dwell in it: yea, the Lord will dwell in it for euer.

17 The charets of God are twentie thousande thousand Angels, and the Lord is among them, as in the Sanctuarie of Sinai.

18 Thou art gone vp on high: thou hast led captiuitie captiue, and receiued giftes for men: yea, euen the rebellious hast thou led, that the Lord God might dwell there.

19 Praysed be the Lord, euen the God of our saluation, which ladeth vs dayly with benefites. Selah.

20 This is our God, euen the God that saueth vs: and to the Lord God belong the issues of death.

21 Surely God will wound the head of his enemies, and the hearie pate of him that walketh in his sinnes.

22 The Lord hath sayde, I will bring my people againe from Bashan: I will bring them againe from the depths of the Sea:

23 That thy foote may bee dipped in blood, and the tongue of thy dogges in the blood of the enemies, euen in it.

24 They haue seene, O God, thy goings, the goings of my God, and my King, which art in the Sanctuarie.

25 The singers went before, the players of instruments after: in the middes were the maides playing with timbrels.

26 Praise yee God in the assemblies, and the Lord, ye that are of the fountaine of Israel.

27 There was litle Beniamin with their ruler, and the princes of Iudah with their assemblie, the princes of Zebulun, and the princes of Naphtali.

28 Thy God hath appointed thy strength: stablish, O God, that, which thou hast wrought in vs,

29 Out of thy Temple vpon Ierusalem: and Kings shall bring presents vnto thee.

30 Destroy the company of the spearemen, and multitude of the mightie bulles with the calues of the people, that tread vnder feete pieces of siluer: scatter the people that delite in warre.

31 Then shall the princes come out of Egypt: Ethiopia shall hast to stretche her hands vnto God.

32 Sing vnto God, O yee kingdomes of the earth: sing praise vnto the Lord, (Selah)

33 To him that rideth vpon ye most high heauens, which were from the beginning: beholde, he will send out by his voice a mightie sound.

34 Ascribe the power to God: for his maiestie is vpon Israel, and his strength is in the cloudes.

35 O God, thou art terrible out of thine holie places: the God of Israel is hee that giueth strength and power vnto the people: praised be God.

Psalms 69

1 To him that excelleth upon Shoshannim. A Psalme of David. Save mee, O God: for the waters are entred euen to my soule.

2 I sticke fast in the deepe myre, where no staie is: I am come into deepe waters, and the streames runne ouer me.

3 I am wearie of crying: my throte is drie: mine eyes faile, whiles I waite for my God.

4 They that hate mee without a cause, are moe then the heares of mine heade: they that would destroy mee, and are mine enemies falsly, are mightie, so that I restored that which I tooke not.

5 O God, thou knowest my foolishnesse, and my fautes are not hid from thee.

6 Let not them that trust in thee, O Lord God of hostes, be ashamed for me: let not those that seeke thee, be confounded through mee, O God of Israel.

7 For thy sake haue I suffred reproofe: shame hath couered my face.

8 I am become a stranger vnto my brethren, euen an aliant vnto my mothers sonnes.

9 For the zeale of thine house hath eaten mee, and the rebukes of them that rebuked thee, are fallen vpon me.

10 I wept and my soule fasted, but that was to my reproofe.

11 I put on a sacke also: and I became a prouerbe vnto them.

12 They that sate in the gate, spake of mee, and the drunkards sang of me.

13 But Lord, I make my praier vnto thee in an acceptable time, euen in the multitude of thy mercie: O God, heare me in the trueth of thy saluation.

14 Deliuer mee out of the myre, that I sinke not: let me be deliuered from them that hate me, and out of the deepe waters.

15 Let not the water flood drowne mee, neither let the deepe swallowe me vp: and let not the pit shut her mouth vpon me.

16 Heare me, O Lord, for thy louing kindnes is good: turne vnto me according to ye multitude of thy tender mercies.

17 And hide not thy face from thy seruant, for I am in trouble: make haste and heare me.

18 Draw neere vnto my soule and redeeme it: deliuer me because of mine enemies.

19 Thou hast knowen my reproofe and my shame, and my dishonour: all mine aduersaries are before thee.

20 Rebuke hath broken mine heart, and I am full of heauinesse, and I looked for some to haue pitie on me, but there was none: and for comforters, but I found none.

21 For they gaue me gall in my meate, and in my thirst they gaue me vineger to drinke.

22 Let their table be a snare before them, and their prosperitie their ruine.

23 Let their eyes be blinded that they see not: and make their loynes alway to tremble.

24 Powre out thine anger vpon them, and let thy wrathfull displeasure take them.

25 Let their habitation be voide, and let none dwell in their tents.

26 For they persecute him, whome thou hast smitten: and they adde vnto the sorrowe of them, whome thou hast wounded.

27 Laie iniquitie vpon their iniquitie, and let them not come into thy righteousnesse.

28 Let them be put out of the booke of life, neither let them be written with the righteous.

29 When I am poore and in heauinesse, thine helpe, O God, shall exalt me.

30 I will praise the Name of God with a song, and magnifie him with thankesgiuing.

31 This also shall please the Lord better then a yong bullocke, that hath hornes and hoofes.

32 The humble shall see this, and they that seeke God, shalbe glad, and your heart shall liue.

33 For the Lord heareth the poore, and despiseth not his prisoners.

34 Let heauen and earth praise him: the seas and all that moueth in them.

35 For God will saue Zion, and builde the cities of Iudah, that men may dwell there and haue it in possession.

36 The seede also of his seruants shall inherit it: and they that loue his name, shall dwel therein.

Psalms 70

1 To him excelleth. A Psalme of David to put in remembrance. O God, haste thee to deliuer mee: make haste to helpe me, O Lord.

2 Let them be confounded and put to shame, that seeke my soule: let them bee turned backewarde and put to rebuke, that desire mine hurt.

3 Let them be turned backe for a rewarde of their shame, which said, Aha, aha.

4 But let all those that seeke thee, be ioyfull and glad in thee, and let all that loue thy saluation, say alwaies, God be praised.

5 Nowe I am poore and needie: O God, make haste to me: thou art mine helper, and my deliuerer: O Lord, make no tarying.

Psalms 71

1 In thee, O Lord, I trust: let me neuer be ashamed.

2 Rescue mee and deliuer me in thy righteousnes: incline thine eare vnto me and saue me.

3 Be thou my strong rocke, whereunto I may alway resort: thou hast giuen commandement to saue me: for thou art my rocke, and my fortresse.

4 Deliuer mee, O my God, out of the hande of the wicked: out of the hande of the euill and cruell man.

5 For thou art mine hope, O Lord God, euen my trust from my youth.

6 Vpon thee haue I beene stayed from the wombe: thou art he that tooke me out of my mothers bowels: my praise shalbe alwaies of thee.

7 I am become as it were a monster vnto many: but thou art my sure trust.

8 Let my mouth be filled with thy praise, and with thy glory euery day.

9 Cast mee not off in the time of age: forsake me not when my strength faileth.

10 For mine enemies speake of mee, and they that lay waite for my soule, take their counsell together,

11 Saying, God hath forsaken him: pursue and take him, for there is none to deliuer him.

12 Goe not farre from me, O God: my God, haste thee to helpe me.

13 Let them be confounded and consumed that are against my soule: let them be couered with reproofe and confusion, that seeke mine hurt.

14 But I will waite continually, and will praise thee more and more.

15 My mouth shall daily rehearse thy righteousnesse, and thy saluation: for I knowe not the nomber.

16 I will goe forwarde in the strength of the Lord God, and will make mention of thy righteousnesse, euen of thine onely.

17 O God, thou hast taught me from my youth euen vntill nowe: therefore will I tell of thy wonderous workes,

18 Yea, euen vnto mine olde age and graie head, O God: forsake me not, vntill I haue declared thine arme vnto this generation, and thy power to all them, that shall come.

19 And thy righteousnes, O God, I wil exalt on high: for thou hast done great thinges: O God, who is like vnto thee!

20 Which hast shewed me great troubles and aduersities, but thou wilt returne, and reuiue me, and wilt come againe, and take mee vp from the depth of the earth.

21 Thou wilt increase mine honour, and returne and comfort me.

22 Therefore will I praise thee for thy faithfulnesse, O God, vpon instrument and viole: vnto thee will I sing vpon the harpe, O Holy one of Israel.

23 My lippes will reioyce when I sing vnto thee, and my soule, which thou hast deliuered.

24 My tongue also shall talke of thy righteousnesse daily: for they are confounded and brought vnto shame, that seeke mine hurt.

Psalms 72

1 A Psalme of Salomon. Give thy iudgements to the King, O God, and thy righteousnesse to the Kings sonne.

2 Then shall he iudge thy people in righteousnesse, and thy poore with equitie.

3 The mountaines and the hilles shall bring peace to the people by iustice.

4 He shall iudge the poore of the people: he shall saue the children of the needie, and shall subdue the oppressor.

5 They shall feare thee as long as the sunne and moone endureth, from generatio to generation.

6 He shall come downe like the rayne vpon the mowen grasse, and as the showres that water the earth.

7 In his dayes shall the righteous florish, and abundance of peace shalbe so long as the moone endureth.

8 His dominion shall be also from sea to sea, and from the Riuer vnto the endes of the land.

9 They that dwell in ye wildernes, shall kneele before him, and his enemies shall licke the dust.

10 The Kings of Tarshish and of the yles shall bring presents: the Kings of Sheba and Seba shall bring giftes.

11 Yea, all Kings shall worship him: all nations shall serue him.

12 For he shall deliuer the poore when he cryeth: the needie also, and him that hath no helper.

13 He shalbe mercifull to the poore and needie, and shall preserue the soules of the poore.

14 He shall redeeme their soules from deceite and violence, and deare shall their blood be in his sight.

15 Yea, he shall liue, and vnto him shall they giue of the golde of Sheba: they shall also pray for him continually, and dayly blesse him.

16 An handfull of corne shall be sowen in the earth, euen in the toppe of the mountaines, and the fruite thereof shall shake like the trees of Lebanon: and the children shall florish out of the citie like the grasse of the earth.

17 His name shall be for euer: his name shall indure as long as the sunne: all nations shall blesse him, and be blessed in him.

18 Blessed be the Lord God, euen the God of Israel, which onely doeth wonderous things.

19 And blessed be his glorious Name for euer: and let all the earth be filled with his glorie. So be it, euen so be it. HERE END THE prayers of Dauid, the sonne of Ishai.

Psalms 73

1 A Psalme committed to Asaph. Yet God is good to Israel: euen, to the pure in heart.

2 As for me, my feete were almost gone: my steps had well neere slipt.

3 For I feared at the foolish, when I sawe the prosperitie of the wicked.

4 For there are no bandes in their death, but they are lustie and strong.

5 They are not in trouble as other men, neither are they plagued with other men.

6 Therefore pride is as a chayne vnto them, and crueltie couereth them as a garment.

7 Their eyes stande out for fatnesse: they haue more then heart can wish.

8 They are licentious, and speake wickedly of their oppression: they talke presumptuously.

9 They set their mouth against heauen, and their tongue walketh through the earth.

10 Therefore his people turne hither: for waters of a full cup are wrung out to them.

11 And they say, Howe doeth God know it? or is there knowledge in the most High?

12 Lo, these are the wicked, yet prosper they alway, and increase in riches.

13 Certainly I haue clensed mine heart in vaine, and washed mine hands in innocencie.

14 For dayly haue I bene punished, and chastened euery morning.

15 If I say, I will iudge thus, beholde the generation of thy children: I haue trespassed.

16 Then thought I to know this, but it was too painefull for me,

17 Vntill I went into the Sanctuarie of God: then vnderstoode I their ende.

18 Surely thou hast set them in slipperie places, and castest them downe into desolation.

19 How suddenly are they destroyed, perished and horribly consumed,

20 As a dreame when one awaketh! O Lord, when thou raisest vs vp, thou shalt make their image despised.

21 Certainly mine heart was vexed, and I was pricked in my reines:

22 So foolish was I and ignorant: I was a beast before thee.

23 Yet I was alway with thee: thou hast holden me by my right hand.

24 Thou wilt guide me by thy counsell, and afterward receiue me to glory.

25 Whom haue I in heauen but thee? and I haue desired none in the earth with thee.

26 My flesh fayleth and mine heart also: but God is the strength of mine heart, and my portion for euer.

27 For loe, they that withdrawe themselues from thee, shall perish: thou destroyest all them that goe a whoring from thee.

28 As for me, it is good for me to draw neere to God: therefore I haue put my trust in the Lord God, that I may declare all thy workes.

Psalms 74

1 A Psalme to give instruction, committed to Asaph. O God, why hast thou put vs away for euer? why is thy wrath kindled against the sheepe of thy pasture?

2 Thinke vpon thy Congregation, which thou hast possessed of olde, and on the rod of thine inheritance, which thou hast redeemed, and on this mount Zion, wherein thou hast dwelt.

3 Lift vp thy strokes, that thou mayest for euer destroy euery enemie that doeth euill to the Sanctuarie.

4 Thine aduersaries roare in the middes of thy Congregation, and set vp their banners for signes.

5 He that lifted the axes vpon the thicke trees, was renowmed, as one, that brought a thing to perfection:

6 But nowe they breake downe the carued worke thereof with axes and hammers.

7 They haue cast thy Sanctuarie into the fire, and rased it to the grounde, and haue defiled the dwelling place of thy Name.

8 They saide in their hearts, Let vs destroy them altogether: they haue burnt all the Synagogues of God in the land.

9 We see not our signes: there is not one Prophet more, nor any with vs that knoweth howe long.

10 O God, howe long shall the aduersarie reproche thee? shall the enemie blaspheme thy Name for euer?

11 Why withdrawest thou thine hand, euen thy right hand? drawe it out of thy bosome, and consume them.

12 Euen God is my King of olde, working saluation in the middes of the earth.

13 Thou didest deuide the sea by thy power: thou brakest the heads of the dragons in the waters.

14 Thou brakest the head of Liuiathan in pieces, and gauest him to be meate for the people in wildernesse.

15 Thou brakest vp the fountaine and riuer: thou dryedst vp mightie riuers.

16 The day is thine, and the night is thine: thou hast prepared the light and the sunne.

17 Thou hast set all the borders of the earth: thou hast made summer and winter.

18 Remember this, that the enemie hath reproched the Lord, and the foolish people hath blasphemed thy Name.

19 Giue not the soule of thy turtle doue vnto the beast, and forget not the Congregation of thy poore for euer.

20 Consider thy couenant: for the darke places of the earth are full of the habitations of the cruell.

21 Oh let not the oppressed returne ashamed, but let the poore and needie prayse thy Name.

22 Arise, O God: mainteine thine owne cause: remember thy dayly reproche by the foolish man.

23 Forget not the voyce of thine enemies: for the tumult of them, that rise against thee, ascendeth continually.

Psalms 75

1 To him that excelleth. Destroy not. A Psalme or song committed toAsaph. We will prayse thee, O God, we will prayse thee, for thy Name is neere: therefore they will declare thy wonderous workes.

2 When I shall take a conuenient time, I will iudge righteously.

3 The earth and all the inhabitantes thereof are dissolued: but I will establish the pillars of it. Selah.

4 I saide vnto the foolish, Be not so foolish, and to the wicked, Lift not vp the horne.

5 Lift not vp your horne on high, neither speake with a stiffe necke.

6 For to come to preferment is neither from the East, nor from the West, nor from the South,

7 But God is the iudge: he maketh lowe and he maketh hie.

8 For in the hand of the Lord is a cup, and the wine is red: it is full mixt, and he powreth out of the same: surely all the wicked of the earth shall wring out and drinke the dregges thereof.

9 But I will declare for euer, and sing prayses vnto the God of Iaakob.

10 All the hornes of the wicked also will I breake: but the hornes of the righteous shalbe exalted.

Psalms 76

1 To him that excelleth on Neginoth. A Psalme or song committed to Asaph. God is knowen in Iudah: his Name is great in Israel.

2 For in Shalem is his Tabernacle, and his dwelling in Zion.

3 There brake he the arrowes of the bowe, the shielde and the sword and the battell. Selah.

4 Thou art more bright and puissant, then the mountaines of pray.

5 The stout hearted are spoyled: they haue slept their sleepe, and all the men of strength haue not found their hands.

6 At thy rebuke, O God of Iaakob, both the chariot and horse are cast a sleepe.

7 Thou, euen thou art to be feared: and who shall stand in thy sight, when thou art angrie!

8 Thou didest cause thy iudgement to bee heard from heauen: therefore the earth feared and was still,

9 When thou, O God, arose to iudgement, to helpe all the meeke of the earth. Selah.

10 Surely the rage of man shall turne to thy praise: the remnant of the rage shalt thou restrayne.

11 Vowe and performe vnto the Lord your God, all ye that be rounde about him: let them bring presents vnto him that ought to be feared.

12 He shall cut off the spirit of princes: he is terrible to the Kings of the earth.

Psalms 77

1 For the excellent musician Ieduthun. A Psalme committed to Asaph. My voyce came to God, when I cryed: my voyce came to God, and he heard me.

2 In the day of my trouble I sought ye Lord: my sore ranne and ceased not in the night: my soule refused comfort.

3 I did thinke vpon God, and was troubled: I praied, and my spirit was full of anguish. Selah.

4 Thou keepest mine eyes waking: I was astonied and could not speake.

5 Then I considered the daies of olde, and the yeeres of ancient time.

6 I called to remembrance my song in the night: I communed with mine owne heart, and my spirit searched diligently.

7 Will the Lord absent him selfe for euer? and will he shewe no more fauour?

8 Is his mercie cleane gone for euer? doeth his promise faile for euermore?

9 Hath God forgotten to be mercifull? hath he shut vp his teder mercies in displeasure? Selah.

10 And I sayde, This is my death: yet I remembred the yeeres of the right hand of the most High.

11 I remembred the workes of the Lord: certainely I remembred thy wonders of olde.

12 I did also meditate all thy woorkes, and did deuise of thine actes, saying,

13 Thy way, O God, is in the Sanctuarie: who is so great a God as our God!

14 Thou art ye God that doest wonders: thou hast declared thy power among the people.

15 Thou hast redeemed thy people with thine arme, euen the sonnes of Iaakob and Ioseph. Selah.

16 The waters sawe thee, O God: the waters sawe thee, and were afraide: yea, the depths trembled.

17 The cloudes powred out water: the heauens gaue a sounde: yea, thine arrowes went abroade.

18 The voyce of thy thunder was rounde about: the lightnings lightened the worlde: the earth trembled and shooke.

19 Thy way is in the Sea, and thy paths in the great waters, and thy footesteps are not knowen.

20 Thou diddest leade thy people like sheepe by the hand of Moses and Aaron.

Psalms 78

1 A Psalme to give instruction committed to Asaph. Heare my doctrine, O my people: incline your eares vnto the wordes of my mouth.

2 I will open my mouth in a parable: I will declare high sentences of olde.

3 Which we haue heard and knowen, and our fathers haue tolde vs.

4 Wee will not hide them from their children but to the generation to come we wil shewe the praises of the Lord his power also, and his wonderful woorkes that he hath done:

5 How he established a testimonie in Iaakob, and ordeined a Law in Israel, which he commanded our fathers, that they shoulde teache their children:

6 That the posteritie might knowe it, and the children, which should be borne, should stand vp, and declare it to their children:

7 That they might set their hope on God, and not forget the workes of God but keepe his commandements:

8 And not to bee as their fathers, a disobedient and rebellious generation: a generation that set not their heart aright, and whose spirite was not faithfull vnto God.

9 The children of Ephraim being armed and shooting with the bowe, turned backe in the day of battell.

10 They kept not the couenant of God, but refused to walke in his Lawe,

11 And forgate his Actes, and his wonderfull woorkes that he had shewed them.

12 Hee did marueilous thinges in the sight of their fathers in the lande of Egypt: euen in the fielde of Zoan.

13 He deuided the Sea, and led them through: he made also the waters to stand as an heape.

14 In the day time also hee led them with a cloude, and all the night with a light of fire.

15 He claue the rockes in the wildernes, and gaue them drinke as of the great depths.

16 He brought floods also out of the stonie rocke; so that hee made the waters to descend like the riuers.

17 Yet they sinned stil against him, and prouoked the Highest in the wildernesse,

18 And tempted God in their heartes in requiring meate for their lust.

19 They spake against God also, saying, Can God prepare a table in the wildernesse?

20 Behold, he smote the rocke, that the water gushed out, and the streames ouerflowed: can hee giue bread also? or prepare flesh for his people?

21 Therefore the Lord heard and was angrie, and the fire was kindled in Iaakob, and also wrath came vpon Israel,

22 Because they beleeued not in God, and trusted not in his helpe.

23 Yet he had comanded the clouds aboue, and had opened the doores of heauen,

24 And had rained downe MAN vpon them for to eate, and had giuen them of the wheate of heauen.

25 Man did eate the bread of Angels: hee sent them meate ynough.

26 He caused the Eastwinde to passe in the heauen, and through his power he brought in the Southwinde.

27 Hee rained flesh also vpon them as dust, and feathered foule as the sand of the sea.

28 And hee made it fall in the middes of their campe euen round about their habitations.

29 So they did eate and were well filled: for he gaue them their desire.

30 They were not turned from their lust, but the meate was yet in their mouthes,

31 When the wrath of God came euen vpon them, and slew the strongest of them, and smote downe the chosen men in Israel.

32 For all this, they sinned stil, and beleeued not his wonderous woorkes.

33 Therefore their daies did hee consume in vanitie, and their yeeres hastily.

34 And when hee slewe them, they sought him and they returned, and sought God earely.

35 And they remembred that God was their strength, and the most high God their redeemer.

36 But they flattered him with their mouth, and dissembled with him with their tongue.

37 For their heart was not vpright with him: neither were they faithfull in his couenant.

38 Yet he being merciful forgaue their iniquitie, and destroied them not, but oft times called backe his anger, and did not stirre vp all his wrath.

39 For he remembered that they were flesh: yea, a winde that passeth and commeth not againe.

40 How oft did they prouoke him in the wildernes? and grieue him in the desert?

41 Yea, they returned, and tempted God, and limited the Holie one of Israel.

42 They remembered not his hand, nor the day when he deliuered them from the enemie,

43 Nor him that set his signes in Egypt, and his wonders in the fielde of Zoan,

44 And turned their riuers into blood, and their floods, that they could not drinke.

45 Hee sent a swarme of flies among them, which deuoured them, and frogs, which destroyed them.

46 He gaue also their fruites vnto the caterpiller, and their labour vnto the grassehopper.

47 He destroied their vines with haile, and their wilde figge trees with the hailestone.

48 He gaue their cattell also to the haile, and their flockes to the thunderboltes.

49 Hee cast vpon them the fiercenesse of his anger, indignation and wrath, and vexation by the sending out of euill Angels.

50 He made a way to his anger: he spared not their soule from death, but gaue their life to the pestilence,

51 And smote al the firstborne in Egypt, euen the beginning of their strength in the tabernacles of Ham.

52 But hee made his people to goe out like sheepe, and led them in the wildernes like a flocke.

53 Yea, he caried them out safely, and they feared not, and the Sea couered their enemies.

54 And he brought them vnto the borders of his Sanctuarie: euen to this Mountaine, which his right hand purchased.

55 He cast out the heathe also before them, and caused them to fall to the lot of his inheritance, and made the tribes of Israel to dwell in their tabernacles.

56 Yet they tempted, and prouoked the most high God, and kept not his testimonies,

57 But turned backe and delt falsely like their fathers: they turned like a deceitfull bowe.

58 And they prouoked him to anger with their high places, and mooued him to wrath with their grauen images.

59 God heard this and was wroth, and greatly abhorred Israel,

60 So that hee forsooke the habitation of Shilo, euen the Tabernacle where hee dwelt among men,

61 And deliuered his power into captiuitie, and his beautie into the enemies hand.

62 And hee gaue vp his people to the sworde, and was angrie with his inheritance.

63 The fire deuoured their chosen men, and their maides were not praised.

64 Their Priestes fell by the sworde, and their widowes lamented not.

65 But the Lord awaked as one out of sleepe, and as a strong man that after his wine crieth out,

66 And smote his enemies in the hinder parts, and put them to a perpetuall shame.

67 Yet he refused the tabernacle of Ioseph, and chose not the tribe of Ephraim:

68 But chose the tribe of Iudah, and mount Zion which he loued.

69 And he built his Sanctuarie as an high palace, like the earth, which he stablished for euer.

70 He chose Dauid also his seruant, and tooke him from the shepefolds.

71 Euen from behinde the ewes with yong brought he him to feede his people in Iaakob, and his inheritance in Israel.

72 So he fed them according to the simplicitie of his heart, and guided them by the discretion of his hands.

Psalms 79

1 A Psalme committed to Asaph. O God, the heathen are come into thine inheritance: thine holy Temple haue they defiled, and made Ierusalem heapes of stones.

2 The dead bodies of thy seruats haue they giuen to be meat vnto foules of ye heauen: and the flesh of thy Saintes vnto the beastes of the earth.

3 Their blood haue they shead like waters rounde about Ierusalem, and there was none to burie them.

4 Wee are a reproche to our neighbours, euen a scorne and derision vnto them that are round about vs.

5 Lord, howe long wilt thou be angrie, for euer? shall thy gelousie burne like fire?

6 Powre out thy wrath vpon the heathen that haue not knowen thee, and vpon the kingdomes that haue not called vpon thy Name.

7 For they haue deuoured Iaakob and made his dwelling place desolate.

8 Remember not against vs the former iniquities, but make haste and let thy tender mercies preuent vs: for we are in great miserie.

9 Helpe vs, O God of our saluation, for the glorie of thy Name, and deliuer vs, and be mercifull vnto our sinnes for thy Names sake.

10 Wherefore should the heathen say, Where is their God? let him be knowen among the heathen in our sight by the vengeance of the blood of thy seruants that is shed.

11 Let the sighing of the prisoners come before thee: according to thy mightie arme preserue the children of death,

12 And render to our neighbours seuen folde into their bosome their reproche, wherewith they haue reproched thee, O Lord.

13 So wee thy people, and sheepe of thy pasture shall praise thee for euer: and from generation to generation we will set foorth thy praise.

Psalms 80

1 To him that excelleth on Shoshannim Eduth. A Psalme committed to Asaph. Heare, O thou Shepheard of Israel, thou that leadest Ioseph like sheepe: shewe thy brightnes, thou that sittest betweene the Cherubims.

2 Before Ephraim and Beniamin and Manasseh stirre vp thy strength, and come to helpe vs.

3 Turne vs againe, O God, and cause thy face to shine that we may be saued.

4 O Lord God of hostes, how long wilt thou be angrie against the prayer of thy people?

5 Thou hast fedde them with the bread of teares, and giuen them teares to drinke with great measure.

6 Thou hast made vs a strife vnto our neighbours, and our enemies laugh at vs among themselues.

7 Turne vs againe, O God of hostes: cause thy face to shine, and we shalbe saued.

8 Thou hast brought a vine out of Egypt: thou hast cast out the heathen, and planted it.

9 Thou madest roume for it, and didest cause it to take roote, and it filled the land.

10 The mountaines were couered with the shadowe of it, and the boughes thereof were like the goodly cedars.

11 Shee stretched out her branches vnto the Sea, and her boughes vnto the Riuer.

12 Why hast thou then broken downe her hedges, so that all they, which passe by the way, haue plucked her?

13 The wilde bore out of the wood hath destroyed it, and the wilde beastes of the fielde haue eaten it vp.

14 Returne we beseech thee, O God of hostes: looke downe from heauen and beholde and visite this vine,

15 And the vineyard, that thy right hand hath planted, and the young vine, which thou madest strong for thy selfe.

16 It is burnt with fire and cut downe: and they perish at the rebuke of thy countenance.

17 Let thine hande be vpon the man of thy right hande, and vpon the sonne of man, whome thou madest strong for thine owne selfe.

18 So will not we goe backe from thee: reuiue thou vs, and we shall call vpon thy Name.

19 Turne vs againe, O Lord God of hostes: cause thy face to shine and we shalbe saued.

Psalms 81

1 To him that excelleth upon Gittith. A Psalme committed to Asaph. Sing ioyfully vnto God our strength: sing loude vnto the God of Iaakob.

2 Take the song and bring forth the timbrel, the pleasant harpe with the viole.

3 Blowe the trumpet in the newe moone, euen in the time appointed, at our feast day.

4 For this is a statute for Israel, and a Law of the God of Iaakob.

5 Hee set this in Ioseph for a testimonie, when hee came out of the land of Egypt, where I heard a language, that I vnderstoode not.

6 I haue withdrawen his shoulder from the burden, and his handes haue left the pots.

7 Thou calledst in affliction and I deliuered thee, and answered thee in the secret of the thunder: I prooued thee at the waters of Meribah. Selah.

8 Heare, O my people, and I wil protest vnto thee: O Israel, if thou wilt hearken vnto me,

9 Let there bee no strange god in thee, neither worship thou any strange god.

10 For I am the Lord thy God, which brought thee out of the land of Egypt: open thy mouth wide and I will fill it.

11 But my people would not heare my voyce, and Israel would none of me.

12 So I gaue them vp vnto the hardnesse of their heart, and they haue walked in their owne cousels.

13 Oh that my people had hearkened vnto me, and Israel had walked in my wayes.

14 I would soone haue humbled their enemies, and turned mine hand against their aduersaries.

15 The haters of the Lord should haue bene subiect vnto him, and their time should haue endured for euer.

16 And God would haue fedde them with the fatte of wheat, and with honie out of the rocke would I haue sufficed thee.

Psalms 82

1 A Psalme committed to Aspah. God standeth in the assemblie of gods: hee iudgeth among gods.

2 How long wil ye iudge vniustly, and accept the persons of the wicked? Selah.

3 Doe right to the poore and fatherlesse: doe iustice to the poore and needie.

4 Deliuer the poore and needie: saue them from the hand of the wicked.

5 They knowe not and vnderstand nothing: they walke in darkenes, albeit all the foundations of the earth be mooued.

6 I haue said, Ye are gods, and ye all are children of the most High.

7 But ye shall die as a man, and yee princes, shall fall like others.

8 O God, arise, therefore iudge thou the earth: for thou shalt inherite all nations.

Psalms 83

1 A song, or Psalme committed to Asaph. Keep not thou silence, O God: bee not still, and cease not, O God.

2 For lo, thine enemies make a tumult: and they that hate thee, haue lifted vp the head.

3 They haue taken craftie counsell against thy people, and haue consulted against thy secret ones.

4 They haue said, Come and let vs cut them off from being a nation: and let the name of Israel be no more in remembrance.

5 For they haue consulted together in heart, and haue made a league against thee:

6 The tabernacles of Edom, and the Ishmaelites, Moab and the Agarims:

7 Gebal and Ammon, and Amalech, the Philistims with the inhabitants of Tyrus:

8 Asshur also is ioyned with them: they haue bene an arme to the children of Lot. Selah.

9 Doe thou to them as vnto the Midianites: as to Sisera and as to Iabin at the riuer of Kishon.

10 They perished at En-dor, and were dung for the earth.

11 Make them, euen their princes like Oreb and like Zeeb: yea, all their princes like Zebah and like Zalmuna.

12 Which haue said, Let vs take for our possession the habitations of God.

13 O my God, make them like vnto a wheele, and as the stubble before the winde.

14 As the fire burneth the forest, and as the flame setteth the mountaines on fire:

15 So persecute them with thy tempest, and make them afraide with thy storme.

16 Fill their faces with shame, that they may seeke thy Name, O Lord.

17 Let them be confounded and troubled for euer: yea, let them be put to shame and perish,

18 That they may knowe that thou, which art called Iehouah, art alone, euen the most High ouer all the earth.

Psalms 84

1 To him that excelleth upon Gittith. A Psalme committed to the sonnes of Korah. O Lord of hostes, howe amiable are thy Tabernacles!

2 My soule longeth, yea, and fainteth for the courtes of the Lord: for mine heart and my flesh reioyce in the liuing God.

3 Yea, the sparrowe hath found her an house, and the swallow a nest for her, where she may lay her yong: euen by thine altars, O Lord of hostes, my King and my God.

4 Blessed are they that dwell in thine house: they will euer praise thee. Selah.

5 Blessed is the man, whose strength is in thee, and in whose heart are thy wayes.

6 They going through the vale of Baca, make welles therein: the raine also couereth the pooles.

7 They goe from strength to strength, till euery one appeare before God in Zion.

8 O Lord God of hostes, heare my prayer: hearken, O God of Iaakob. Selah.

9 Beholde, O God, our shielde, and looke vpon the face of thine Anointed.

10 For a day in thy courtes is better then a thousand other where: I had rather be a doore keeper in the House of my God, then to dwell in the Tabernacles of wickednesse.

11 For the Lord God is the sunne and shielde vnto vs: the Lord will giue grace and glory, and no good thing will he withhold from them that walke vprightly.

12 O Lord of hostes, blessed is the man that trusteth in thee.

Psalms 85

1 To him that excelleth. A Psalme committed to the sonnes of Korah. Lord, thou hast bene fauourable vnto thy land: thou hast brought againe the captiuitie of Iaakob.

2 Thou hast forgiuen the iniquitie of thy people, and couered all their sinnes. Selah.

3 Thou hast withdrawen all thine anger, and hast turned backe from the fiercenes of thy wrath.

4 Turne vs, O God of our saluation, and release thine anger toward vs.

5 Wilt thou be angry with vs for euer? and wilt thou prolong thy wrath from one generation to another?

6 Wilt thou not turne againe and quicken vs, that thy people may reioyce in thee?

7 Shew vs thy mercie, O Lord, and graunt vs thy saluation.

8 I will hearken what the Lord God will say: for he will speake peace vnto his people, and to his Saintes, that they turne not againe to follie.

9 Surely his saluation is neere to them that feare him, that glory may dwell in our land.

10 Mercie and trueth shall meete: righteousnes and peace shall kisse one another.

11 Trueth shall bud out of the earth, and righteousnes shall looke downe from heauen.

12 Yea, the Lord shall giue good things, and our land shall giue her increase.

13 Righteousnesse shall go before him, and shall set her steps in the way.

Psalms 86

1 A prayer of David. Incline thine eare, O Lord, and heare me: for I am poore and needy.

2 Preserue thou my soule, for I am mercifull: my God, saue thou thy seruant, that trusteth in thee.

3 Be mercifull vnto me, O Lord: for I crie vpon thee continually.

4 Reioyce the soule of thy seruant: for vnto thee, O Lord, doe I lift vp my soule.

5 For thou, Lord, art good and mercifull, and of great kindenes vnto all them, that call vpon thee.

6 Giue eare, Lord, vnto my prayer, and hearken to the voyce of my supplication.

7 In the day of my trouble I will call vpon thee: for thou hearest me.

8 Among the gods there is none like thee, O Lord, and there is none that can doe like thy workes.

9 All nations, whome thou hast made, shall come and worship before thee, O Lord, and shall glorifie thy Name.

10 For thou art great and doest wonderous things: thou art God alone.

11 Teach me thy way, O Lord, and I will walke in thy trueth: knit mine heart vnto thee, that I may feare thy Name.

12 I wil prayse thee, O Lord my God, with all mine heart: yea, I wil glorifie thy Name for euer.

13 For great is thy mercie toward me, and thou hast deliuered my soule from the lowest graue.

14 O God, the proude are risen against me, and the assemblies of violent men haue sought my soule, and haue not set thee before them.

15 But thou, O Lord, art a pitifull God and mercifull, slowe to anger and great in kindenes and trueth.

16 Turne vnto me, and haue mercy vpon me: giue thy strength vnto thy seruant, and saue the sonne of thine handmayd.

17 Shew a token of thy goodnes towarde me, that they which hate me, may see it, and be ashamed, because thou, O Lord, hast holpen me and comforted me.

Psalms 87

1 A Psalme or song committed to the sonnes of Korah. God layde his foundations among the holy mountaines.

2 The Lord loueth the gates of Zion aboue all the habitations of Iaakob.

3 Glorious things are spoken of thee, O citie of God. Selah.

4 I will make mention of Rahab and Babel among them that knowe me: beholde Palestina and Tyrus with Ethiopia, There is he borne.

5 And of Zion it shall be sayde, Many are borne in her: and he, euen the most High shall stablish her.

6 The Lord shall count, when hee writeth the people, He was borne there. Selah.

7 Aswell the singers as the players on instruments shall prayse thee: all my springs are in thee.

Psalms 88

1 A song or Psalme of Heman the Ezrahite to give instruction, committed to the sonnes of Korah for him that excelleth upon Malath Leannoth. O Lord God of my saluation, I cry day and night before thee.

2 Let my prayer enter into thy presence: incline thine eare vnto my cry.

3 For my soule is filled with euils, and my life draweth neere to the graue.

4 I am counted among them that go downe vnto the pit, and am as a man without strength:

5 Free among the dead, like the slaine lying in the graue, whome thou remembrest no more, and they are cut off from thine hand.

6 Thou hast layde me in the lowest pit, in darkenes, and in the deepe.

7 Thine indignation lyeth vpon me, and thou hast vexed me with all thy waues. Selah.

8 Thou hast put away mine acquaintance farre from me, and made mee to be abhorred of them: I am shut vp, and cannot get foorth.

9 Mine eye is sorowfull through mine affliction: Lord, I call dayly vpon thee: I stretch out mine hands vnto thee.

10 Wilt thou shewe a miracle to the dead? or shall the dead rise and prayse thee? Selah.

11 Shall thy louing kindenes be declared in the graue? or thy faithfulnes in destruction?

12 Shall thy wonderous workes be knowen in the darke? and thy righteousnes in the land of obliuion?

13 But vnto thee haue I cryed, O Lord, and early shall my prayer come before thee.

14 Lord, why doest thou reiect my soule, and hidest thy face from me?

15 I am afflicted and at the point of death: from my youth I suffer thy terrours, doubting of my life.

16 Thine indignations goe ouer me, and thy feare hath cut me off.

17 They came round about me dayly like water, and compassed me together.

18 My louers and friends hast thou put away from me, and mine acquaintance hid themselues.

Psalms 89

1 A Psalme to give instruction, of Ethan the Ezrahite. I will sing the mercies of the Lord for euer: with my mouth will I declare thy trueth from generation to generation.

2 For I said, Mercie shalbe set vp for euer: thy trueth shalt thou stablish in ye very heauens.

3 I haue made a couenant with my chosen: I haue sworne to Dauid my seruant,

4 Thy seede will I stablish for euer, and set vp thy throne from generation to generation. Selah.

5 O Lord, euen the heauens shall prayse thy wonderous worke: yea, thy trueth in the Congregation of the Saints.

6 For who is equall to the Lord in the heauen? and who is like the Lord among the sonnes of the gods?

7 God is very terrible in the assemblie of the Saints, and to be reuerenced aboue all, that are about him.

8 O Lord God of hostes, who is like vnto thee, which art a mightie Lord, and thy trueth is about thee?

9 Thou rulest the raging of the sea: when the waues thereof arise, thou stillest them.

10 Thou hast beaten downe Rahab as a man slaine: thou hast scattered thine enemies with thy mightie arme.

11 The heauens are thine, the earth also is thine: thou hast layde the foundation of the world, and all that therein is.

12 Thou hast created the North and the South: Tabor and Hermon shall reioyce in thy Name.

13 Thou hast a mightie arme: strong is thine hand, and high is thy right hand.

14 Righteousnesse and equitie are the stablishment of thy throne: mercy and trueth goe before thy face.

15 Blessed is the people, that can reioyce in thee: they shall walke in the light of thy countenance, O Lord.

16 They shall reioyce continually in thy Name, and in thy righteousnes shall they exalt them selues.

17 For thou art the glory of their strength, and by thy fauour our hornes shall be exalted.

18 For our shield apperteineth to the Lord, and our King to the holy one of Israel.

19 Thou spakest then in a vision vnto thine Holy one, and saydest, I haue layde helpe vpon one that is mightie: I haue exalted one chosen out of the people.

20 I haue found Dauid my seruant: with mine holy oyle haue I anoynted him.

21 Therefore mine hande shall be established with him, and mine arme shall strengthen him.

22 The enemie shall not oppresse him, neither shall the wicked hurt him.

23 But I will destroy his foes before his face, and plague them that hate him.

24 My trueth also and my mercie shall be with him, and in my Name shall his horne be exalted.

25 I will set his hand also in the sea, and his right hand in the floods.

26 He shall cry vnto mee, Thou art my Father, my God and the rocke of my saluation.

27 Also I wil make him my first borne, higher then the Kings of the earth.

28 My mercie will I keepe for him for euermore, and my couenant shall stande fast with him.

29 His seede also will I make to endure for euer, and his throne as the dayes of heauen.

30 But if his children forsake my Lawe, and walke not in my iudgements:

31 If they breake my statutes, and keepe not my commandements:

32 Then will I visite their transgression with the rod, and their iniquitie with strokes.

33 Yet my louing kindnesse will I not take from him, neither will I falsifie my trueth.

34 My couenant wil I not breake, nor alter the thing that is gone out of my lips.

35 I haue sworne once by mine holines, that I will not fayle Dauid, saying,

36 His seede shall endure for euer, and his throne shalbe as the sunne before me.

37 He shalbe established for euermore as the moone, and as a faythfull witnes in the heauen. Selah.

38 But thou hast reiected and abhorred, thou hast bene angry with thine Anoynted.

39 Thou hast broken the couenant of thy seruant, and profaned his crowne, casting it on the ground.

40 Thou hast broken downe all his walles: thou hast layd his fortresses in ruine.

41 All that goe by the way, spoyle him: he is a rebuke vnto his neighbours.

42 Thou hast set vp the right hand of his enemies, and made all his aduersaries to reioyce.

43 Thou hast also turned the edge of his sworde, and hast not made him to stand in the battell.

44 Thou hast caused his dignitie to decay, and cast his throne to the ground.

45 The dayes of his youth hast thou shortned, and couered him with shame. Selah.

46 Lord, howe long wilt thou hide thy selfe, for euer? shall thy wrath burne like fire?

47 Remember of what time I am: wherefore shouldest thou create in vaine all the children of men?

48 What man liueth, and shall not see death? shall hee deliuer his soule from the hande of the graue? Selah.

49 Lord, where are thy former mercies, which thou swarest vnto Dauid in thy trueth?

50 Remember, O Lord, the rebuke of thy seruants, which I beare in my bosome of all the mightie people.

51 For thine enemies haue reproched thee, O Lord, because they haue reproched the footesteps of thine Anointed.

52 Praised be the Lord for euermore. So be it, euen so be it.

Psalms 90

1 A prayer of Moses, the man of God. Lord, thou hast bene our habitation from generation to generation.

2 Before the mountaines were made, and before thou hadst formed the earth, and the world, euen from euerlasting to euerlasting thou art our God.

3 Thou turnest man to destruction: againe thou sayest, Returne, ye sonnes of Adam.

4 For a thousande yeeres in thy sight are as yesterday when it is past, and as a watch in the night.

5 Thou hast ouerflowed them: they are as a sleepe: in the morning he groweth like the grasse:

6 In the morning it florisheth and groweth, but in the euening it is cut downe and withereth.

7 For we are consumed by thine anger, and by thy wrath are we troubled.

8 Thou hast set our iniquities before thee, and our secret sinnes in the light of thy countenance.

9 For all our dayes are past in thine anger: we haue spent our yeeres as a thought.

10 The time of our life is threescore yeeres and ten, and if they be of strength, fourescore yeeres: yet their strength is but labour and sorowe: for it is cut off quickly, and we flee away.

11 Who knoweth the power of thy wrath? for according to thy feare is thine anger.

12 Teach vs so to nomber our dayes, that we may apply our heartes vnto wisdome.

13 Returne (O Lord, howe long?) and be pacified toward thy seruants.

14 Fill vs with thy mercie in the morning: so shall we reioyce and be glad all our dayes.

15 Comfort vs according to the dayes that thou hast afflicted vs, and according to the yeeres that we haue seene euill.

16 Let thy worke bee seene towarde thy seruants, and thy glory vpon their children.

17 And let the beautie of the Lord our God be vpon vs, and direct thou the worke of our hands vpon vs, euen direct the worke of our handes.

Psalms 91

1 Who so dwelleth in the secrete of the most High, shall abide in the shadowe of the Almightie.

2 I will say vnto the Lord, O mine hope, and my fortresse: he is my God, in him will I trust.

3 Surely he will deliuer thee from the snare of the hunter, and from the noysome pestilence.

4 Hee will couer thee vnder his winges, and thou shalt be sure vnder his feathers: his trueth shall be thy shielde and buckler.

5 Thou shalt not be afraide of the feare of the night, nor of the arrowe that flyeth by day:

6 Nor of the pestilence that walketh in the darkenesse: nor of the plague that destroyeth at noone day.

7 A thousand shall fall at thy side, and tenne thousand at thy right hand, but it shall not come neere thee.

8 Doubtlesse with thine eyes shalt thou beholde and see the reward of the wicked.

9 For thou hast said, The Lord is mine hope: thou hast set the most High for thy refuge.

10 There shall none euill come vnto thee, neither shall any plague come neere thy tabernacle.

11 For hee shall giue his Angels charge ouer thee to keepe thee in all thy wayes.

12 They shall beare thee in their handes, that thou hurt not thy foote against a stone.

13 Thou shalt walke vpon the lyon and aspe: the yong lyon and the dragon shalt thou treade vnder feete.

14 Because he hath loued me, therefore will I deliuer him: I will exalt him because hee hath knowen my Name.

15 He shall call vpon me, and I wil heare him: I will be with him in trouble: I will deliuer him, and glorifie him.

16 With long life wil I satisfie him, and shew him my saluation.

Psalms 92

1 A Psalme or song for the Sabbath day. It is a good thing to praise the Lord, and to sing vnto thy Name, O most High,

2 To declare thy louing kindenesse in the morning, and thy trueth in the night,

3 Vpon an instrument of tenne strings, and vpon the viole with the song vpon the harpe.

4 For thou, Lord, hast made mee glad by thy workes, and I wil reioyce in the workes of thine handes.

5 O Lord, how glorious are thy workes! and thy thoughtes are very deepe.

6 An vnwise man knoweth it not, and a foole doeth not vnderstand this,

7 (When the wicked growe as the grasse, and all the workers of wickednesse doe flourish) that they shall be destroyed for euer.

8 But thou, O Lord, art most High for euermore.

9 For loe, thine enemies, O Lord: for loe, thine enemies shall perish: all the workers of iniquitie shall be destroyed.

10 But thou shalt exalt mine horne, like the vnicornes, and I shalbe anoynted with fresh oyle.

11 Mine eye also shall see my desire against mine enemies: and mine eares shall heare my wish against the wicked, that rise vp against me.

12 The righteous shall flourish like a palme tree, and shall grow like a Cedar in Lebanon.

13 Such as bee planted in the house of the Lord, shall flourish in the courtes of our God.

14 They shall still bring foorth fruite in their age: they shall be fat and flourishing,

15 To declare that the Lord my rocke is righteous, and that none iniquitie is in him.

Psalms 93

1 The Lord reigneth, and is clothed with maiestie: the Lord is clothed, and girded with power: the world also shall be established, that it cannot be mooued.

2 Thy throne is established of olde: thou art from euerlasting.

3 The floodes haue lifted vp, O Lord: the floodes haue lifted vp their voyce: the floods lift vp their waues.

4 The waues of ye sea are marueilous through the noyse of many waters, yet the Lord on High is more mightie.

5 Thy testimonies are very sure: holinesse becommeth thine House, O Lord, for euer.

Psalms 94

1 O Lord God the auenger, O God the auenger, shewe thy selfe clearely.

2 Exalt thy selfe, O Iudge of the worlde, and render a reward to the proude.

3 Lord how long shall the wicked, how long shall the wicked triumph?

4 They prate and speake fiercely: all the workers of iniquitie vaunt themselues.

5 They smite downe thy people, O Lord, and trouble thine heritage.

6 They slay the widowe and the stranger, and murder the fatherlesse.

7 Yet they say, The Lord shall not see: neither will the God of Iaakob regard it.

8 Vnderstande ye vnwise among the people: and ye fooles, when will ye be wise?

9 Hee that planted the eare, shall hee not heare? or he that formed the eye, shall he not see?

10 Or he that chastiseth the nations, shall he not correct? hee that teacheth man knowledge, shall he not knowe?

11 The Lord knoweth the thoughtes of man, that they are vanitie.

12 Blessed is the man, whom thou chastisest, O Lord, and teachest him in thy Lawe,

13 That thou mayest giue him rest from the dayes of euill, whiles the pitte is digged for the wicked.

14 Surely the Lord will not faile his people, neither will he forsake his inheritance.

15 For iudgement shall returne to iustice, and all the vpright in heart shall follow after it.

16 Who will rise vp with me against the wicked? or who will take my part against the workers of iniquitie?

17 If the Lord had not holpen me, my soule had almost dwelt in silence.

18 When I said, My foote slideth, thy mercy, O Lord, stayed me.

19 In the multitude of my thoughts in mine heart, thy comfortes haue reioyced my soule.

20 Hath the throne of iniquitie fellowship with thee, which forgeth wrong for a Lawe?

21 They gather them together against the soule of the righteous, and condemne the innocent blood.

22 But the Lord is my refuge, and my God is the rocke of mine hope.

23 And hee will recompence them their wickednes, and destroy them in their owne malice: yea, the Lord our God shall destroy them.

Psalms 95

1 Come, let vs reioyce vnto the Lord: let vs sing aloude vnto the rocke of our saluation.

2 Let vs come before his face with praise: let vs sing loude vnto him with Psalmes.

3 For the Lord is a great God, and a great King aboue all gods.

4 In whose hande are the deepe places of the earth, and the heightes of the mountaines are his:

5 To whome the Sea belongeth: for hee made it, and his handes formed the dry land.

6 Come, let vs worship and fall downe, and kneele before the Lord our maker.

7 For he is our God, and we are the people of his pasture, and the sheepe of his hande: to day, if ye will heare his voyce,

8 Harden not your heart, as in Meribah, and as in the day of Massah in the wildernesse.

9 Where your fathers tempted me, proued me, though they had seene my worke.

10 Fourtie yeeres haue I contended with this generation, and said, They are a people that erre in heart, for they haue not knowen my wayes.

11 Wherefore I sware in my wrath, saying, Surely they shall not enter into my rest.

Psalms 96

1 Sing vnto the Lord a newe song: sing vnto the Lord, all the earth.

2 Sing vnto the Lord, and prayse his Name: declare his saluation from day to day.

3 Declare his glory among all nations, and his wonders among all people.

4 For the Lord is great and much to be praysed: he is to be feared aboue all gods.

5 For all the gods of the people are idoles: but the Lord made the heauens.

6 Strength and glory are before him: power and beautie are in his Sanctuarie.

7 Giue vnto the Lord, ye families of the people: giue vnto the Lord glory and power.

8 Giue vnto the Lord the glory of his Name: bring an offering, and enter into his courtes.

9 Worship the Lord in the glorious Sanctuarie: tremble before him all the earth.

10 Say among the nations, The Lord reigneth: surely the world shalbe stable, and not moue, and he shall iudge the people in righteousnesse.

11 Let the heauens reioyce, and let the earth be glad: let the sea roare, and all that therein is.

12 Let the field be ioyfull, and all that is in it: let all the trees of the wood then reioyce

13 Before the Lord: for he commeth, for he cometh to iudge the earth: he wil iudge the world with righteousnes, and the people in his trueth.

Psalms 97

1 The Lord reigneth: let the earth reioyce: let the multitude of the yles be glad.

2 Cloudes and darkenes are round about him: righteousnesse and iudgement are the foundation of his throne.

3 There shall goe a fire before him, and burne vp his enemies round about.

4 His lightnings gaue light vnto the worlde: the earth sawe it and was afraide.

5 The mountaines melted like waxe at the presence of the Lord, at the presence of the Lord of the whole earth.

6 The heauens declare his righteousnes, and all the people see his glory.

7 Confounded be all they that serue grauen images, and that glory in idoles: worship him all ye gods.

8 Zion heard of it, and was glad: and the daughters of Iudah reioyced, because of thy iudgements, O Lord.

9 For thou, Lord, art most High aboue all the earth: thou art much exalted aboue all gods.

10 Ye that loue the Lord, hate euill: he preserueth the soules of his Saints: hee will deliuer them from the hand of the wicked.

11 Light is sowen for the righteous, and ioy for the vpright in heart.

12 Reioyce ye righteous in the Lord, and giue thankes for his holy remembrance.

Psalms 98

1 A Psalme. Sing vnto the Lord a newe song: for hee hath done marueilous

things: his right hand, and his holy arme haue gotten him the victorie.

2 The Lord declared his saluation: his righteousnes hath he reueiled in the sight of ye nations.

3 He hath remembred his mercy and his trueth toward the house of Israel: all the ends of the earth haue seene the saluation of our God.

4 All the earth, sing ye loude vnto the Lord: crie out and reioyce, and sing prayses.

5 Sing prayse to the Lord vpon the harpe, euen vpon the harpe with a singing voyce.

6 With shalmes and sound of trumpets sing loude before the Lord the King.

7 Let the sea roare, and all that therein is, the world, and they that dwell therein.

8 Let the floods clap their hands, and let the mountaines reioyce together

9 Before the Lord: for he is come to iudge the earth: with righteousnesse shall hee iudge the world, and the people with equitie.

Psalms 99

1 The Lord reigneth, let the people tremble: he sitteth betweene the Cherubims, let the earth be moued.

2 The Lord is great in Zion, and he is high aboue all the people.

3 They shall prayse thy great and fearefull Name (for it is holy)

4 And the Kings power, that loueth iudgement: for thou hast prepared equitie: thou hast executed iudgement and iustice in Iaakob.

5 Exalt the Lord our God, and fall downe before his footestoole: for he is holy.

6 Moses and Aaron were among his Priests, and Samuel among such as call vpon his Name: these called vpon the Lord, and he heard them.

7 Hee spake vnto them in the cloudie pillar: they kept his testimonies, and the Lawe that he gaue them.

8 Thou heardest them, O Lord our God: thou wast a fauourable God vnto them, though thou didst take vengeance for their inuentions.

9 Exalt the Lord our God, and fall downe before his holy Mountaine: for the Lord our God is holy.

Psalms 100

1 A Psalme of Praise. Sing ye loude vnto the Lord, all the earth.

2 Serue the Lord with gladnes: come before him with ioyfulnes.

3 Knowe ye that euen the Lord is God: hee hath made vs, and not we our selues: we are his people, and the sheepe of his pasture.

4 Enter into his gates with prayse, and into his courts with reioycing: prayse him and blesse his Name.

5 For the Lord is good: his mercy is euerlasting, and his trueth is from generation to generation.

Psalms 101

1 A Psalme of David. I will sing mercie and iudgement: vnto thee, O Lord, will I sing.

2 I will doe wisely in the perfite way, till thou commest to me: I will walke in the vprightnes of mine heart in the middes of mine house.

3 I wil set no wicked thing before mine eyes: I hate the worke of them that fall away: it shall not cleaue vnto me.

4 A froward heart shall depart from me: I will knowe none euill.

5 Him that priuily slandereth his neighbour, wil I destroy: him that hath a proude looke and hie heart, I cannot suffer.

6 Mine eyes shalbe vnto the faithfull of the lande, that they may dwell with me: he that walketh in a perfite way, he shall serue me.

7 There shall no deceitful person dwell within mine house: he that telleth lyes, shall not remaine in my sight.

8 Betimes will I destroy all the wicked of the land, that I may cut off all the workers of iniquitie from the Citie of the Lord.

Psalms 102

1 A prayer of the afflicted, when he shall be in distresse, and pour forth his meditation before the Lord. O Lord, heare my prayer, and let my crye come vnto thee.

2 Hide not thy face from me in the time of my trouble: incline thine eares vnto me: when I call, make haste to heare me.

3 For my dayes are consumed like smoke, and my bones are burnt like an herthe.

4 Mine heart is smitten and withereth like grasse, because I forgate to eate my bread.

5 For the voyce of my groning my bones doe cleaue to my skinne.

6 I am like a pelicane of the wildernesse: I am like an owle of the deserts.

7 I watch and am as a sparrowe alone vpon the house top.

8 Mine enemies reuile me dayly, and they that rage against me, haue sworne against me.

9 Surely I haue eaten asshes as bread, and mingled my drinke with weeping,

10 Because of thine indignation and thy wrath: for thou hast heaued me vp, and cast me downe.

11 My dayes are like a shadowe that fadeth, and I am withered like grasse.

12 But thou, O Lord, doest remaine for euer, and thy remembrance from generation to generation.

13 Thou wilt arise and haue mercy vpon Zion: for the time to haue mercie thereon, for the appointed time is come.

14 For thy seruants delite in the stones thereof, and haue pitie on the dust thereof.

15 Then the heathen shall feare the Name of the Lord, and all the Kings of the earth thy glory,

16 When the Lord shall build vp Zion, and shall appeare in his glory,

17 And shall turne vnto the prayer of the desolate, and not despise their prayer.

18 This shall be written for the generation to come: and the people, which shalbe created, shall prayse the Lord.

19 For he hath looked downe from the height of his Sanctuarie: out of the heauen did the Lord beholde the earth,

20 That he might heare the mourning of the prisoner, and deliuer the children of death:

21 That they may declare the Name of the Lord in Zion, and his prayse in Ierusalem,

22 When the people shalbe gathered together, and the kingdomes to serue the Lord.

23 He abated my strength in the way, and shortened my dayes.

24 And I sayd, O my God, take me not away in the middes of my dayes: thy yeeres endure from generation to generation.

25 Thou hast aforetime layde the foundation of the earth, and the heauens are the worke of thine hands.

26 They shall perish, but thou shalt endure: euen they all shall waxe olde as doeth a garment: as a vesture shalt thou change them, and they shall be changed.

27 But thou art the same, and thy yeeres shall not fayle.

28 The children of thy seruants shall continue, and their seede shall stand fast in thy sight.

Psalms 103

1 A Psalme of David. My soule, prayse thou the Lord, and all that is within me, prayse his holy Name.

2 My soule, prayse thou the Lord, and forget not all his benefites.

3 Which forgiueth all thine iniquitie, and healeth all thine infirmities.

4 Which redeemeth thy life from the graue, and crowneth thee with mercy and compassions.

5 Which satisfieth thy mouth with good things: and thy youth is renued like the eagles.

6 The Lord executeth righteousnes and iudgement to all that are oppressed.

7 He made his wayes knowen vnto Moses, and his workes vnto the children of Israel.

8 The Lord is full of compassion and mercie, slowe to anger and of great kindnesse.

9 He will not alway chide, neither keepe his anger for euer.

10 He hath not dealt with vs after our sinnes, nor rewarded vs according to our iniquities.

11 For as high as the heauen is aboue ye earth, so great is his mercie toward them that feare him.

12 As farre as the East is from the West: so farre hath he remooued our sinnes from vs.

13 As a father hath compassion on his children, so hath the Lord compassion on them that feare him.

14 For he knoweth whereof we be made: he remembreth that we are but dust.

15 The dayes of man are as grasse: as a flowre of the fielde, so florisheth he.

16 For the winde goeth ouer it, and it is gone, and the place thereof shall knowe it no more.

17 But the louing kindnesse of the Lord endureth for euer and euer vpon them that feare him, and his righteousnes vpon childrens children,

18 Vnto them that keepe his couenant, and thinke vpon his commandements to doe them.

19 The Lord hath prepared his throne in heauen, and his Kingdome ruleth ouer all.

20 Prayse the Lord, ye his Angels, that excell in strength, that doe his commandement in obeying the voyce of his worde.

21 Prayse the Lord, all ye his hostes, ye his seruants that doe his pleasure.

22 Prayse the Lord, all ye his workes, in all places of his dominion: my soule, prayse thou the Lord.

Psalms 104

1 My soule, prayse thou the Lord: O Lord my God, thou art exceeding great, thou art clothed with glorie and honour.

2 Which couereth himselfe with light as with a garment, and spreadeth the heauens like a curtaine.

3 Which layeth the beames of his chambers in the waters, and maketh the cloudes his chariot, and walketh vpon the wings of the winde.

4 Which maketh his spirits his messengers, and a flaming fire his ministers.

5 He set the earth vpon her foundations, so that it shall neuer moue.

6 Thou coueredst it with the deepe as with a garment: the waters woulde stand aboue the mountaines.

7 But at thy rebuke they flee: at the voyce of thy thunder they haste away.

8 And the mountaines ascend, and the valleis descend to the place which thou hast established for them.

9 But thou hast set them a bounde, which they shall not passe: they shall not returne to couer the earth.

10 He sendeth the springs into the valleis, which runne betweene the mountaines.

11 They shall giue drinke to all the beasts of the fielde, and the wilde asses shall quench their thirst.

12 By these springs shall the foules of the heauen dwell, and sing among the branches.

13 He watereth the mountaines from his chambers, and the earth is filled with the fruite of thy workes.

14 He causeth grasse to growe for the cattell, and herbe for the vse of man, that he may bring forth bread out of the earth,

15 And wine that maketh glad the heart of man, and oyle to make the face to shine, and bread that strengtheneth mans heart.

16 The high trees are satisfied, euen the cedars of Lebanon, which he hath planted,

17 That ye birdes may make their nestes there: the storke dwelleth in the firre trees.

18 The high mountaines are for the goates: the rockes are a refuge for the conies.

19 He appoynted the moone for certaine seasons: the sunne knoweth his going downe.

20 Thou makest darkenesse, and it is night, wherein all the beastes of the forest creepe forth.

21 The lions roare after their praye, and seeke their meate at God.

22 When the sunne riseth, they retire, and couche in their dennes.

23 Then goeth man forth to his worke, and to his labour vntill the euening.

24 O Lord, howe manifolde are thy workes! in wisdome hast thou made them all: the earth is full of thy riches.

25 So is this sea great and wide: for therein are things creeping innumerable, both small beastes and great.

26 There goe the shippes, yea, that Liuiathan, whom thou hast made to play therein.

27 All these waite vpon thee, that thou maiest giue them foode in due season.

28 Thou giuest it to them, and they gather it: thou openest thine hand, and they are filled with good things.

29 But if thou hide thy face, they are troubled: if thou take away their breath, they dye and returne to their dust.

30 Againe if thou send forth thy spirit, they are created, and thou renuest the face of the earth.

31 Glory be to the Lord for euer: let the Lord reioyce in his workes.

32 He looketh on the earth and it trembleth: he toucheth the mountaines, and they smoke.

33 I will sing vnto the Lord all my life: I will prayse my God, while I liue.

34 Let my wordes be acceptable vnto him: I will reioyce in the Lord.

35 Let the sinners be consumed out of the earth, and the wicked till there be no more: O my soule, prayse thou the Lord. Prayse ye the Lord.

Psalms 105

1 Praise the Lord, and call vpon his Name: declare his workes among the people.

2 Sing vnto him, sing prayse vnto him, and talke of all his wonderous workes.

3 Reioyce in his holy Name: let the heart of them that seeke the Lord, reioyce.

4 Seeke the Lord and his strength: seeke his face continually.

5 Remember his marueilous woorkes, that he hath done, his wonders and the iudgements of his mouth,

6 Ye seede of Abraham his seruant, ye children of Iaakob, which are his elect.

7 He is the Lord our God: his iudgements are through all the earth.

8 He hath alway remembred his couenant and promise, that he made to a thousand generations,

9 Euen that which he made with Abraham, and his othe vnto Izhak:

10 And since hath confirmed it to Iaakob for a lawe, and to Israel for an euerlasting couenant,

11 Saying, Vnto thee will I giue the land of Canaan, the lot of your inheritance.

12 Albeit they were fewe in nomber, yea, very fewe, and strangers in the land,

13 And walked about from nation to nation, from one kingdome to another people,

14 Yet suffered he no man to doe them wrong, but reproued Kings for their sakes, saying,

15 Touche not mine anointed, and doe my Prophets no harme.

16 Moreouer, he called a famine vpon ye land, and vtterly brake the staffe of bread.

17 But he sent a man before them: Ioseph was solde for a slaue.

18 They helde his feete in the stockes, and he was laide in yrons,

19 Vntill his appointed time came, and the counsell of the Lord had tryed him.

20 The King sent and loosed him: euen the Ruler of the people deliuered him.

21 He made him lord of his house, and ruler of all his substance,

22 That he shoulde binde his princes vnto his will, and teach his Ancients wisedome.

23 Then Israel came to Egypt, and Iaakob was a stranger in the land of Ham.

24 And he increased his people exceedingly, and made them stronger then their oppressours.

25 He turned their heart to hate his people, and to deale craftily with his seruants.

26 Then sent he Moses his seruant, and Aaron whom he had chosen.

27 They shewed among them the message of his signes, and wonders in the land of Ham.

28 He sent darkenesse, and made it darke: and they were not disobedient vnto his commission.

29 He turned their waters into blood, and slewe their fish.

30 Their land brought foorth frogs, euen in their Kings chambers.

31 He spake, and there came swarmes of flies and lice in all their quarters.

32 He gaue them haile for raine, and flames of fire in their land.

33 He smote their vines also and their figge trees, and brake downe the trees in their coastes.

34 He spake, and the grashoppers came, and caterpillers innumerable,

35 And did eate vp all the grasse in their land, and deuoured the fruite of their ground.

36 He smote also all the first borne in their land, euen the beginning of all their strength.

37 He brought them forth also with siluer and golde, and there was none feeble among their tribes.

38 Egypt was glad at their departing: for the feare of them had fallen vpon them.

39 He spred a cloude to be a couering, and fire to giue light in the night.

40 They asked, and he brought quailes, and he filled them with the bread of heauen.

41 He opened the rocke, and the waters flowed out, and ranne in the drye places like a riuer.

42 For he remembred his holy promise to Abraham his seruant,

43 And he brought forth his people with ioy, and his chosen with gladnesse,

44 And gaue them the lands of the heathen, and they tooke the labours of the people in possession,

45 That they might keepe his statutes, and obserue his Lawes. Prayse ye Lord.

Psalms 106

1 Praise ye the Lord. Praise ye the Lord because he is good, for his mercie endureth for euer.

2 Who can expresse the noble actes of the Lord, or shewe forth all his prayse?

3 Blessed are they that keepe iudgement, and doe righteousnesse at all times.

4 Remember me, O Lord, with the fauour of thy people: visite me with thy saluation,

5 That I may see the felicitie of thy chosen, and reioyce in the ioy of thy people, and glorie with thine inheritance.

6 We haue sinned with our fathers: we haue committed iniquitie, and done wickedly.

7 Our fathers vnderstoode not thy wonders in Egypt, neither remembred they the multitude of thy mercies, but rebelled at the Sea, euen at the red sea.

8 Neuerthelesse he saued them for his Names sake, that he might make his power to be knowen.

9 And he rebuked the red Sea, and it was dryed vp, and he led them in the deepe, as in the wildernesse.

10 And he saued them from ye aduersaries hand, and deliuered them from ye hand of the enemie.

11 And the waters couered their oppressours: not one of them was left.

12 Then beleeued they his wordes, and sang prayse vnto him.

13 But incontinently they forgate his workes: they wayted not for his counsell,

14 But lusted with concupiscence in the wildernes, and tempted God in the desert.

15 Then he gaue them their desire: but he sent leannesse into their soule.

16 They enuied Moses also in the tentes, and Aaron the holy one of the Lord.

17 Therefore the earth opened and swallowed vp Dathan, and couered the companie of Abiram.

18 And the fire was kindled in their assembly: the flame burnt vp the wicked.

19 They made a calfe in Horeb, and worshipped the molten image.

20 Thus they turned their glory into the similitude of a bullocke, that eateth grasse.

21 They forgate God their Sauiour, which had done great things in Egypt,

22 Wonderous woorkes in the lande of Ham, and fearefull things by the red Sea.

23 Therefore he minded to destroy them, had not Moses his chosen stand in the breach before him to turne away his wrath, least he shoulde destroy them.

24 Also they contemned that pleasant land, and beleeued not his worde,

25 But murmured in their tentes, and hearkened not vnto the voice of the Lord.

26 Therefore hee lifted vp his hande against them, to destroy them in the wildernesse,

27 And to destroy their seede among the nations, and to scatter them throughout the countries.

28 They ioyned themselues also vnto Baalpeor, and did eate the offrings of the dead.

29 Thus they prouoked him vnto anger with their owne inuentions, and the plague brake in vpon them.

30 But Phinehas stoode vp, and executed iudgement, and the plague was staied.

31 And it was imputed vnto him for righteousnes from generation to generation for euer.

32 They angred him also at the waters of Meribah, so that Moses was punished for their sakes,

33 Because they vexed his spirite, so that hee spake vnaduisedly with his lippes.

34 Neither destroied they the people, as the Lord had commanded them,

35 But were mingled among the heathen, and learned their workes,

36 And serued their idoles, which were their ruine.

37 Yea, they offered their sonnes, and their daughters vnto deuils,

38 And shed innocent blood, euen the blood of their sonnes, and of their daughters, whome they offred vnto the idoles of Canaan, and the lande was defiled with blood.

39 Thus were they steined with their owne woorkes, and went a whoring with their owne inuentions.

40 Therefore was the wrath of the Lord kindled against his people, and he abhorred his owne inheritance.

41 And hee gaue them into the hande of the heathen: and they that hated them, were lordes ouer them.

42 Their enemies also oppressed them, and they were humbled vnder their hand.

43 Many a time did hee deliuer them, but they prouoked him by their counsels: therefore they were brought downe by their iniquitie.

44 Yet hee sawe when they were in affliction, and he heard their crie.

45 And he remembred his couenant towarde them and repented according to the multitude of his mercies,

46 And gaue them fauour in the sight of all them that lead them captiues.

47 Saue vs, O Lord our God, and gather vs from among the heathen, that we may praise thine holy Name, and glorie in thy praise.

48 Blessed be the Lord God of Israel for euer and euer, and let all the people say, So be it. Praise yee the Lord.

Psalms 107

1 Praise the Lord, because he is good: for his mercie endureth for euer.

2 Let them, which haue bene redeemed of the Lord, shewe how he hath deliuered them from the hand of the oppressour,

3 And gathered them out of the lands, from the East and from the West, from the North and from the South.

4 When they wandered in the desert and wildernesse out of the waie, and founde no citie to dwell in,

5 Both hungrie and thirstie, their soule fainted in them.

6 Then they cried vnto the Lord in their trouble, and he deliuered them from their distresse,

7 And led them forth by the right way, that they might goe to a citie of habitation.

8 Let them therefore confesse before ye Lord his louing kindnesse, and his wonderfull woorkes before the sonnes of men.

9 For he satisfied the thirstie soule, and filled the hungrie soule with goodnesse.

10 They that dwell in darkenesse and in the shadowe of death, being bounde in miserie and yron,

11 Because they rebelled against the wordes of the Lord, and despised the counsell of the most High,

12 When he humbled their heart with heauines, then they fell downe and there was no helper.

13 Then they cried vnto the Lord in their trouble, and he deliuered them from their distresse.

14 He brought them out of darkenes, and out of the shadowe of death, and brake their bandes asunder.

15 Let them therefore cofesse before the Lord his louing kindnesse, and his wonderfull woorkes before the sonnes of men.

16 For hee hath broken the gates of brasse, and brast the barres of yron asunder.

17 Fooles by reason of their transgression, and because of their iniquities are afflicted.

18 Their soule abhorreth al meat, and they are brought to deaths doore.

19 Then they crie vnto the Lord in their trouble, and he deliuereth them from their distresse.

20 He sendeth his worde and healeth them, and deliuereth them from their graues.

21 Let them therefore cofesse before the Lord his louing kindnesse, and his wonderful workes before the sonnes of men,

22 And let them offer sacrifices of praise, and declare his workes with reioycing.

23 They that goe downe to the sea in ships, and occupie by the great waters,

24 They see the woorkes of the Lord, and his wonders in the deepe.

25 For he commaundeth and raiseth the stormie winde, and it lifteth vp the waues thereof.

26 They mount vp to the heauen, and descend to ye deepe, so that their soule melteth for trouble.

27 They are tossed to and from, and stagger like a drunken man, and all their cunning is gone.

28 Then they crie vnto the Lord in their trouble, and he bringeth them out of their distresse.

29 He turneth the storme to calme, so that the waues thereof are still.

30 When they are quieted, they are glad, and hee bringeth them vnto the hauen, where they would be.

31 Let them therfore confesse before the Lord his louing kindnesse, and his wonderfull woorkes before the sonnes of men.

32 And let them exalt him in the Congregation of the people, and praise him in the assembly of the Elders.

33 He turneth the floodes into a wildernesse, and the springs of waters into drinesse,

34 And a fruitfull land into barrennes for the wickednes of them that dwell therein.

35 Againe hee turneth the wildernesse into pooles of water, and the drie lande into water springs.

36 And there he placeth the hungrie, and they builde a citie to dwell in,

37 And sowe the fieldes, and plant vineyardes, which bring foorth fruitfull increase.

38 For he blesseth them, and they multiplie exceedingly, and he diminisheth not their cattell.

39 Againe men are diminished, and brought lowe by oppression, euill and sorowe.

40 He powreth contempt vpon princes, and causeth them to erre in desert places out of the way.

41 Yet he raiseth vp the poore out of miserie, and maketh him families like a flocke of sheepe.

42 The righteous shall see it, and reioyce, and all iniquitie shall stoppe her mouth.

43 Who is wise that hee may obserue these things? for they shall vnderstand the louing kindnesse of the Lord.

Psalms 108

1 A song or Psalme of David. O God, mine heart is prepared, so is my tongue: I will sing and giue praise.

2 Awake viole and harpe: I will awake early.

3 I will praise thee, O Lord, among the people, and I wil sing vnto thee among the nations.

4 For thy mercy is great aboue the heauens, and thy trueth vnto the clouds.

5 Exalt thy self, O God, aboue the heauens, and let thy glorie be vpon all the earth,

6 That thy beloued may be deliuered: helpe with thy right hand and heare me.

7 God hath spoken in his holinesse: therefore I will reioyce, I shall deuide Shechem and measure the valley of Succoth.

8 Gilead shalbe mine, and Manasseh shalbe mine: Ephraim also shalbe the strength of mine head: Iuda is my lawgiuer.

9 Moab shalbe my washpot: ouer Edom wil I cast out my shoe: vpon Palestina wil I triumph.

10 Who will leade mee into the strong citie? who will bring me vnto Edom?

11 Wilt not thou, O God, which haddest forsaken vs, and diddest not goe foorth, O God, with our armies?

12 Giue vs helpe against trouble: for vaine is the helpe of man.

13 Through God we shall doe valiantly: for he shall treade downe our enemies.

Psalms 109

1 To him that excelleth. A Psalme of David. Holde not thy tongue, O God of my praise.

2 For the mouth of the wicked, and the mouth full of deceite are opened vpon me: they haue spoken to me with a lying tongue.

3 They compassed me about also with words of hatred, and fought against me without a cause.

4 For my friendship they were mine aduersaries, but I gaue my selfe to praier.

5 And they haue rewarded me euil for good, and hatred for my friendship.

6 Set thou the wicked ouer him, and let the aduersarie stand at his right hand.

7 Whe he shalbe iudged, let him be condemned, and let his praier be turned into sinne.

8 Let his daies be fewe, and let another take his charge.

9 Let his children be fatherlesse, and his wife a widowe.

10 Let his children be vagabonds and beg and seeke bread, comming out of their places destroyed.

11 Let the extortioner catch al that he hath, and let the strangers spoile his labour.

12 Let there be none to extend mercie vnto him: neither let there be any to shewe mercie vpon his fatherlesse children.

13 Let his posteritie be destroied, and in the generation following let their name be put out.

14 Let the iniquitie of his fathers bee had in remembrance with the Lord: and let not the sinne of his mother be done away.

15 But let them alway be before the Lord, that he may cut off their memorial from ye earth.

16 Because he remembred not to shew mercie, but persecuted the afflicted and poore man, and the sorowfull hearted to slay him.

17 As he loued cursing, so shall it come vnto him, and as he loued not blessing, so shall it be farre from him.

18 As he clothed himselfe with cursing like a rayment, so shall it come into his bowels like water, and like oyle into his bones.

19 Let it be vnto him as a garment to couer him, and for a girdle, wherewith he shalbe alway girded.

20 Let this be the rewarde of mine aduersarie from the Lord, and of them, that speake euill against my soule.

21 But thou, O Lord my God, deale with me according vnto thy Name: deliuer me, (for thy mercie is good)

22 Because I am poore and needie, and mine heart is wounded within me.

23 I depart like the shadowe that declineth, and am shaken off as the grashopper.

24 My knees are weake through fasting, and my flesh hath lost all fatnes.

25 I became also a rebuke vnto them: they that looked vpon me, shaked their heads.

26 Helpe me, O Lord my God: saue me according to thy mercie.

27 And they shall know, that this is thine hand, and that thou, Lord, hast done it.

28 Though they curse, yet thou wilt blesse: they shall arise and be confounded, but thy seruant shall reioyce.

29 Let mine aduersaries be clothed with shame, and let them couer themselues with their confusion, as with a cloke.

30 I will giue thankes vnto the Lord greatly with my mouth and praise him among ye multitude.

31 For he will stand at the right hand of the poore, to saue him from them that woulde condemne his soule.

Psalms 110

1 A Psalme of David. The Lord said vnto my Lord, Sit thou at my right hand, vntill I make thine enemies thy footestoole.

2 The Lord shall send the rod of thy power out of Zion: be thou ruler in the middes of thine enemies.

3 Thy people shall come willingly at the time of assembling thine armie in holy beautie: the youth of thy wombe shalbe as the morning dewe.

4 The Lord sware and wil not repent, Thou art a Priest for euer after ye order of Melchi-zedek.

5 The Lord, that is at thy right hand, shall wound Kings in the day of his wrath.

6 He shalbe iudge among the heathen: he shall fill all with dead bodies, and smite the head ouer great countreis.

7 He shall drinke of the brooke in the way: therefore shall he lift vp his head.

Psalms 111

1 Praise ye the Lord. I will prayse the Lord with my whole heart in the assemblie and Congregation of the iust.

2 The workes of the Lord are great, and ought to be sought out of al them that loue them.

3 His worke is beautifull and glorious, and his righteousnesse endureth for euer.

4 He hath made his wonderfull workes to be had in remembrance: the Lord is mercifull and full of compassion.

5 He hath giuen a portion vnto them that feare him: he wil euer be mindfull of his couenant.

6 He hath shewed to his people the power of his workes in giuing vnto them the heritage of the heathen.

7 The workes of his handes are trueth and iudgement: all his statutes are true.

8 They are stablished for euer and euer, and are done in trueth and equitie.

9 He sent redemption vnto his people: he hath commanded his couenant for euer: holy and fearefull is his Name.

10 The beginning of wisedome is the feare of the Lord: all they that obserue them, haue good vnderstanding: his praise endureth for euer.

Psalms 112

1 Praise ye the Lord. Blessed is the man, that feareth the Lord, and deliteth greatly in his commandements.

2 His seede shall be mightie vpon earth: the generation of the righteous shall be blessed.

3 Riches and treasures shalbe in his house, and his righteousnesse endureth for euer.

4 Vnto the righteous ariseth light in darkenes: he is merciful and full of copassion and righteous.

5 A good man is mercifull and lendeth, and will measure his affaires by iudgement.

6 Surely he shall neuer be moued: but the righteous shalbe had in euerlasting remembrance.

7 He will not be afraide of euill tidings: for his heart is fixed, and beleeueth in the Lord.

8 His heart is stablished: therefore he will not feare, vntill he see his desire vpon his enemies.

9 He hath distributed and giuen to ye poore: his righteousnesse remaineth for euer: his horne shalbe exalted with glory.

10 The wicked shall see it and be angrie: he shall gnash with his teeth, and consume away: the desire of the wicked shall perish.

Psalms 113

1 Praise ye the Lord. Praise, O ye seruants of the Lord, prayse the Name of the Lord.

2 Blessed be the Name of the Lord from hencefoorth and for euer.

3 The Lordes Name is praysed from the rising of ye sunne, vnto ye going downe of the same.

4 The Lord is high aboue all nations, and his glorie aboue the heauens.

5 Who is like vnto the Lord our God, that hath his dwelling on high!

6 Who abaseth himselfe to beholde things in the heauen and in the earth!

7 He raiseth the needie out of the dust, and lifteth vp the poore out of the dung,

8 That he may set him with the princes, euen with the princes of his people.

9 He maketh the barren woman to dwell with a familie, and a ioyfull mother of children. Prayse ye the Lord.

Psalms 114

1 When Israel went out of Egypt, and the house of Iaakob from the barbarous people,

2 Iudah was his sanctification, and Israel his dominion.

3 The Sea sawe it and fled: Iorden was turned backe.

4 The mountaines leaped like rams, and the hils as lambes.

5 What ailed thee, O Sea, that thou fleddest? O Iorden, why wast thou turned backe?

6 Ye mountaines, why leaped ye like rams, and ye hils as lambes?

7 The earth trembled at the presence of the Lord, at the presence of the God of Iaakob,

8 Which turneth the rocke into waterpooles, and the flint into a fountaine of water.

Psalms 115

1 Not vnto vs, O Lord, not vnto vs, but vnto thy Name giue the glorie, for thy louing mercie and for thy truethes sake.

2 Wherefore shall the heathen say, Where is nowe their God?

3 But our God is in heauen: he doeth what so euer he will.

4 Their idoles are siluer and golde, euen the worke of mens hands.

5 They haue a mouth and speake not: they haue eyes and see not.

6 They haue eares and heare not: they haue noses and smelll not.

7 They haue handes and touche not: they haue feete and walke not: neither make they a sound with their throte.

8 They that make them are like vnto them: so are all that trust in them.

9 O Israel, trust thou in the Lord: for he is their helpe and their shielde.

10 O house of Aaron, trust ye in the Lord: for he is their helpe and their shielde.

11 Ye that feare the Lord, trust in the Lord: for he is their helper and their shield.

12 The Lord hath bene mindfull of vs: he will blesse, he will blesse the house of Israel, he will blesse the house of Aaron.

13 He will blesse them that feare the Lord, both small and great.

14 The Lord will increase his graces towarde you, euen toward you and toward your children.

15 Ye are blessed of the Lord, which made the heauen and the earth.

16 The heauens, euen the heauens are the Lordes: but he hath giuen the earth to the sonnes of men.

17 The dead prayse not the Lord, neither any that goe downe into the place of silence.

18 But we will prayse the Lord from henceforth and for euer. Prayse ye the Lord.

Psalms 116

1 I love the Lord, because he hath heard my voyce and my prayers.

2 For he hath inclined his eare vnto me, whe I did call vpon him in my dayes.

3 When the snares of death copassed me, and the griefes of the graue caught me: when I founde trouble and sorowe.

4 Then I called vpon the Name of the Lord, saying, I beseech thee, O Lord, deliuer my soule.

5 The Lord is mercifull and righteous, and our God is full of compassion.

6 The Lord preserueth the simple: I was in miserie and he saued me.

7 Returne vnto thy rest, O my soule: for the Lord hath bene beneficiall vnto thee,

8 Because thou hast deliuered my soule from death, mine eyes from teares, and my feete from falling.

9 I shall walke before the Lord in the lande of the liuing.

10 I beleeued, therefore did I speake: for I was sore troubled.

11 I said in my feare, All men are lyers.

12 What shall I render vnto the Lord for all his benefites toward me?

13 I will take the cup of saluation, and call vpon the Name of the Lord.

14 I will pay my vowes vnto the Lord, euen nowe in the presence of all his people.

15 Precious in the sight of the Lord is the death of his Saintes.

16 Beholde, Lord: for I am thy seruant, I am thy seruant, and the sonne of thine handmaide: thou hast broken my bondes.

17 I will offer to thee a sacrifice of prayse, and will call vpon the Name of the Lord.

18 I will pay my vowes vnto the Lord, euen nowe in the presence of all his people,

19 In the courtes of ye Lords house, euen in the middes of thee, O Ierusalem. Praise ye the Lord.

Psalms 117

1 All nations, praise ye the Lord: all ye people, praise him.

2 For his louing kindnes is great toward vs, and the trueth of the Lord endureth for euer. Praise yee the Lord.

Psalms 118

1 Praise yee the Lord, because he is good: for his mercie endureth for euer.

2 Let Israel now say, That his mercy endureth for euer.

3 Let the house of Aaron nowe say, That his mercy endureth for euer.

4 Let them, that feare the Lord, nowe say, That his mercie endureth for euer.

5 I called vpon the Lord in trouble, and the Lord heard me, and set me at large.

6 The Lord is with mee: therefore I will not feare what man can doe vnto me.

7 The Lord is with mee among them that helpe me: therefore shall I see my desire vpon mine enemies.

8 It is better to trust in the Lord, then to haue confidence in man.

9 It is better to trust in the Lord, then to haue confidence in princes.

10 All nations haue compassed me: but in the Name of the Lord shall I destroy them.

11 They haue compassed mee, yea, they haue compassed mee: but in the Name of the Lord I shall destroy them.

12 They came about mee like bees, but they were quenched as a fire of thornes: for in the Name of the Lord I shall destroy them.

13 Thou hast thrust sore at me, that I might fall: but the Lord hath holpen me.

14 The Lord is my strength and song: for he hath beene my deliuerance.

15 The voice of ioy and deliuerance shall be in the tabernacles of the righteous, saying, The right hand of the Lord hath done valiantly.

16 The right hand of the Lord is exalted: the right hand of the Lord hath done valiantly.

17 I shall not die, but liue, and declare the woorkes of the Lord.

18 The Lord hath chastened me sore, but he hath not deliuered me to death.

19 Open ye vnto me the gates of righteousnes, that I may goe into them, and praise the Lord.

20 This is the gate of the Lord: the righteous shall enter into it.

21 I will praise thee: for thou hast heard mee, and hast beene my deliuerance.

22 The stone, which the builders refused, is the head of the corner.

23 This was the Lordes doing, and it is marueilous in our eyes.

24 This is the day, which the Lord hath made: let vs reioyce and be glad in it.

25 O Lord, I praie thee, saue now: O Lord, I praie thee nowe giue prosperitie.

26 Blessed be he, that commeth in the Name of the Lord: wee haue blessed you out of the house of the Lord.

27 The Lord is mightie, and hath giuen vs light: binde the sacrifice with cordes vnto the hornes of the altar.

28 Thou art my God, and I will praise thee, euen my God: therefore I will exalt thee.

29 Praise ye the Lord, because he is good: for his mercie endureth for euer.

Psalms 119

1 ALEPH. Blessed are those that are vpright in their way, and walke in the Lawe of the Lord.

2 Blessed are they that keepe his testimonies, and seeke him with their whole heart.

3 Surely they woorke none iniquitie, but walke in his waies.

4 Thou hast commanded to keepe thy precepts diligently.

5 Oh that my waies were directed to keepe thy statutes!

6 Then should I not be confounded, when I haue respect vnto all thy commandements.

7 I will praise thee with an vpright heart, when I shall learne the iudgements of thy righteousnesse.

8 I will keepe thy statutes: forsake mee not ouerlong.

9 BETH. Wherewith shall a yong man redresse his waie? in taking heede thereto according to thy woorde.

10 With my whole heart haue I sought thee: let me not wander from thy commandements.

11 I haue hid thy promise in mine heart, that I might not sinne against thee.

12 Blessed art thou, O Lord: teache mee thy statutes.

13 With my lippes haue I declared all the iudgements of thy mouth.

14 I haue had as great delight in the way of thy testimonies, as in all riches.

15 I will meditate in thy precepts, and consider thy waies.

16 I will delite in thy statutes, and I will not forget thy worde.

17 GIMEL. Be beneficiall vnto thy seruant, that I may liue and keepe thy woorde.

18 Open mine eies, that I may see the wonders of thy Lawe.

19 I am a stranger vpon earth: hide not thy commandements from me.

20 Mine heart breaketh for the desire to thy iudgements alway.

21 Thou hast destroied the proud: cursed are they that doe erre from thy commandements.

22 Remoue from mee shame and contempt: for I haue kept thy testimonies.

23 Princes also did sit, and speake against me: but thy seruant did meditate in thy statutes.

24 Also thy testimonies are my delite, and my counsellers.

25 DALETH. My soule cleaueth to the dust: quicken me according to thy worde.

26 I haue declared my waies, and thou heardest me: teache me thy statutes.

27 Make me to vnderstand ye way of thy precepts, and I will meditate in thy wondrous workes.

28 My soule melteth for heauinesse: raise mee vp according vnto thy worde.

29 Take from mee the way of lying, and graunt me graciously thy Lawe.

30 I haue chosen the way of trueth, and thy iudgements haue I laied before me.

31 I haue cleaued to thy testimonies, O Lord: confound not me.

32 I will runne the way of thy commandements, when thou shalt enlarge mine heart.

33 HE. Teach mee, O Lord, the way of thy statutes, and I will keepe it vnto the ende.

34 Giue mee vnderstanding, and I will keepe thy Law: yea, I wil keepe it with my whole heart.

35 Direct mee in the path of thy commandements: for therein is my delite.

36 Incline mine heart vnto thy testimonies, and not to couetousnesse.

37 Turne away mine eies from regarding vanitie, and quicken me in thy way.

38 Stablish thy promise to thy seruaunt, because he feareth thee.

39 Take away my rebuke that I feare: for thy iudgements are good.

40 Beholde, I desire thy commandements: quicken me in thy righteousnesse,

41 VAV. And let thy louing kindnesse come vnto me, O Lord, and thy saluation according to thy promise.

42 So shall I make answere vnto my blasphemers: for I trust in thy woorde.

43 And take not the woorde of trueth vtterly out of my mouth: for I waite for thy iudgements.

44 So shall I alway keepe thy Lawe for euer and euer.

45 And I will walke at libertie: for I seeke thy precepts.

46 I will speake also of thy testimonies before Kings, and will not be ashamed.

47 And my delite shalbe in thy commandements, which I haue loued.

48 Mine handes also will I lift vp vnto thy commandements, which I haue loued, and I will meditate in thy statutes.

49 ZAIN. Remember the promise made to thy seruant, wherein thou hast caused me to trust.

50 It is my comfort in my trouble: for thy promise hath quickened me.

51 The proude haue had me exceedingly in derision: yet haue I not declined from thy Lawe.

52 I remembred thy iudgements of olde, O Lord, and haue bene comforted.

53 Feare is come vpon mee for the wicked, that forsake thy Lawe.

54 Thy statutes haue beene my songes in the house of my pilgrimage.

55 I haue remembred thy Name, O Lord, in the night, and haue kept thy Lawe.

56 This I had because I kept thy precepts.

57 CHETH. O Lord, that art my portion, I haue determined to keepe thy wordes.

58 I made my supplication in thy presence with my whole heart: be mercifull vnto me according to thy promise.

59 I haue considered my waies, and turned my feete into thy testimonies.

60 I made haste and delaied not to keepe thy commandements.

61 The bandes of the wicked haue robbed me: but I haue not forgotten thy Lawe.

62 At midnight will I rise to giue thanks vnto thee, because of thy righteous iudgements.

63 I am companion of all them that feare thee, and keepe thy precepts.

64 The earth, O Lord, is full of thy mercie: teache me thy statutes.

65 TETH. O Lord, thou hast delt graciously with thy seruant according vnto thy woorde.

66 Teach me good iudgement and knowledge: for I haue beleeued thy commandements.

67 Before I was afflicted, I went astray: but nowe I keepe thy woorde.

68 Thou art good and gracious: teach me thy statutes.

69 The proud haue imagined a lie against me: but I wil keepe thy precepts with my whole heart.

70 Their heart is fatte as grease: but my delite is in thy Lawe.

71 It is good for me that I haue beene afflicted, that I may learne thy statutes.

72 The Lawe of thy mouth is better vnto me, then thousands of golde and siluer.

73 IOD. Thine hands haue made me and fashioned me: giue mee vnderstanding therefore, that I may learne thy commandements.

74 So they that feare thee, seeing mee shall reioyce, because I haue trusted in thy worde.

75 I knowe, O Lord, that thy iudgements are right, and that thou hast afflicted me iustly.

76 I pray thee that thy mercie may comfort me according to thy promise vnto thy seruant.

77 Let thy tender mercies come vnto me, that I may liue: for thy Lawe is my delite.

78 Let the proude be ashamed: for they haue dealt wickedly and falsely with me: but I meditate in thy precepts.

79 Let such as feare thee turne vnto me, and they that knowe thy testimonies.

80 Let mine heart bee vpright in thy statutes, that I be not ashamed.

81 CAPH. My soule fainteth for thy saluation: yet I waite for thy worde.

82 Mine eyes faile for thy promise, saying, when wilt thou comfort me?

83 For I am like a bottell in the smoke: yet doe I not forget thy statutes.

84 Howe many are the dayes of thy seruant? When wilt thou execute iudgement on them that persecute me?

85 The proude haue digged pittes for mee, which is not after thy Lawe.

86 All thy commandements are true: they persecute me falsely: helpe me.

87 They had almost consumed me vpon the earth: but I forsooke not thy precepts.

88 Quicken me according to thy louing kindnes: so shall I keepe the testimony of thy mouth.

89 LAMED. O Lord, thy worde endureth for euer in heauen.

90 Thy trueth is from generation to generation: thou hast layed the foundation of the earth, and it abideth.

91 They continue euen to this day by thine ordinances: for all are thy seruants.

92 Except thy Lawe had bene my delite, I should now haue perished in mine affliction.

93 I wil neuer forget thy precepts: for by them thou hast quickened me.

94 I am thine, saue me: for I haue sought thy precepts.

95 The wicked haue waited for me to destroy me: but I will consider thy testimonies.

96 I haue seene an ende of all perfection: but thy commandement is exceeding large.

97 MEM. Oh howe loue I thy Lawe! it is my meditation continually.

98 By thy commandements thou hast made mee wiser then mine enemies: for they are euer with mee.

99 I haue had more vnderstading then all my teachers: for thy testimonies are my meditation.

100 I vnderstoode more then the ancient, because I kept thy precepts.

101 I haue refrained my feete from euery euil way, that I might keepe thy word.

102 I haue not declined from thy iudgements: for thou didest teach me.

103 Howe sweete are thy promises vnto my mouth! yea, more then hony vnto my mouth.

104 By thy precepts I haue gotten vnderstanding: therefore I hate all the wayes of falshoode.

105 NUN. Thy worde is a lanterne vnto my feete, and a light vnto my path.

106 I haue sworne and will performe it, that I will keepe thy righteous iudgements.

107 I am very sore afflicted: O Lord, quicken me according to thy word.

108 O Lord, I beseeche thee accept the free offerings of my mouth, and teach mee thy iudgements.

109 My soule is continually in mine hande: yet doe I not forget thy Lawe.

110 The wicked haue layed a snare for mee: but I swarued not from thy precepts.

111 Thy testimonies haue I taken as an heritage for euer: for they are the ioy of mine heart.

112 I haue applied mine heart to fulfill thy statutes alway, euen vnto the ende.

113 SAMECH. I hate vaine inuentions: but thy Lawe doe I loue.

114 Thou art my refuge and shield, and I trust in thy worde.

115 Away from mee, yee wicked: for I will keepe the commandements of my God.

116 Stablish me according to thy promise, that I may liue, and disappoint me not of mine hope.

117 Stay thou mee, and I shall be safe, and I will delite continually in thy statutes.

118 Thou hast troden downe all them that depart from thy statutes: for their deceit is vaine.

119 Thou hast taken away all ye wicked of the earth like drosse: therefore I loue thy testimonies.

120 My flesh trembleth for feare of thee, and I am afraide of thy iudgements.

121 AIN. I haue executed iudgement and iustice: leaue me not to mine oppressours.

122 Answere for thy seruant in that, which is good, and let not the proude oppresse me.

123 Mine eyes haue failed in waiting for thy saluation, and for thy iust promise.

124 Deale with thy seruant according to thy mercie, and teache me thy statutes.

125 I am thy seruant: graunt mee therefore vnderstanding, that I may knowe thy testimonies.

126 It is time for thee Lord to worke: for they haue destroyed thy Lawe.

127 Therefore loue I thy commandements aboue golde, yea, aboue most fine golde.

128 Therefore I esteeme all thy precepts most iust, and hate all false wayes.

129 PE. Thy testimonies are wonderfull: therefore doeth my soule keepe them.

130 The entrance into thy wordes sheweth light, and giueth vnderstanding to the simple.

131 I opened my mouth and panted, because I loued thy commandements.

132 Looke vpon mee and bee mercifull vnto me, as thou vsest to doe vnto those that loue thy Name.

133 Direct my steppes in thy worde, and let none iniquitie haue dominion ouer me.

134 Deliuer mee from the oppression of men, and I will keepe thy precepts.

135 Shew the light of thy countenance vpon thy seruant, and teache me thy statutes.

136 Mine eyes gush out with riuers of water, because they keepe not thy Lawe.

137 TSADDI. Righteous art thou, O Lord, and iust are thy iudgements.

138 Thou hast commanded iustice by thy testimonies and trueth especially.

139 My zeale hath euen consumed mee, because mine enemies haue forgotten thy wordes.

140 Thy word is prooued most pure, and thy seruant loueth it.

141 I am small and despised: yet do I not forget thy precepts.

142 Thy righteousnesse is an euerlasting righteousnes, and thy Lawe is trueth.

143 Trouble and anguish are come vpon me: yet are thy commandements my delite.

144 The righteousnes of thy testimonies is euerlasting: graunt me vnderstanding, and I shall liue.

145 KOPH. I haue cried with my whole heart: heare me, O Lord, and I will keepe thy statutes.

146 I called vpon thee: saue mee, and I will keepe thy testimonies.

147 I preuented the morning light, and cried: for I waited on thy word.

148 Mine eyes preuent the night watches to meditate in thy word.

149 Heare my voyce according to thy louing kindenesse: O Lord, quicken me according to thy iudgement.

150 They drawe neere, that follow after malice, and are farre from thy Lawe.

151 Thou art neere, O Lord: for all thy commandements are true.

152 I haue knowen long since by thy testimonies, that thou hast established them for euer.

153 RESH. Beholde mine affliction, and deliuer mee: for I haue not forgotten thy Lawe.

154 Pleade my cause, and deliuer me: quicken me according vnto thy word.

155 Saluation is farre from the wicked, because they seeke not thy statutes.

156 Great are thy tender mercies, O Lord: quicken me according to thy iudgements.

157 My persecutours and mine oppressours are many: yet doe I not swarue from thy testimonies.

158 I saw the transgressours and was grieued, because they kept not thy worde.

159 Consider, O Lord, how I loue thy preceptes: quicken mee according to thy louing kindenesse.

160 The beginning of thy worde is trueth, and all the iudgements of thy righteousnesse endure for euer.

161 SCHIN. Princes haue persecuted mee without cause, but mine heart stood in awe of thy wordes.

162 I reioyce at thy worde, as one that findeth a great spoyle.

163 I hate falshoode and abhorre it, but thy Lawe doe I loue.

164 Seuen times a day doe I praise thee, because of thy righteous iudgements.

165 They that loue thy Law, shall haue great prosperitie, and they shall haue none hurt.

166 Lord, I haue trusted in thy saluation, and haue done thy commandements.

167 My soule hath kept thy testimonies: for I loue them exceedingly.

168 I haue kept thy precepts and thy testimonies: for all my wayes are before thee.

169 TAV. Let my complaint come before thee, O Lord, and giue me vnderstanding, according vnto thy worde.

170 Let my supplication come before thee, and deliuer me according to thy promise.

171 My lippes shall speake praise, when thou hast taught me thy statutes.

172 My tongue shall intreate of thy word: for all thy commandements are righteous.

173 Let thine hand helpe me: for I haue chosen thy precepts.

174 I haue longed for thy saluation, O Lord, and thy Lawe is my delite.

175 Let my soule liue, and it shall praise thee, and thy iudgements shall helpe me.

176 I haue gone astraye like a lost sheepe: seeke thy seruant, for I doe not forget thy commandements.

Psalms 120

1 A song of degrees. I called vnto the Lord in my trouble, and hee heard me.

2 Deliuer my soule, O Lord, from lying lippes, and from a deceitfull tongue.

3 What doeth thy deceitfull tongue bring vnto thee? or what doeth it auaile thee?

4 It is as the sharpe arrowes of a mightie man, and as the coales of iuniper.

5 Woe is to me that I remaine in Meschech, and dwell in the tentes of Kedar.

6 My soule hath too long dwelt with him that hateth peace.

7 I seeke peace, and when I speake thereof, they are bent to warre.

Psalms 121

1 A song of degrees. I will lift mine eyes vnto the mountaines, from whence mine helpe shall come.

2 Mine helpe commeth from the Lord, which hath made the heauen and the earth.

3 He wil not suffer thy foote to slippe: for he that keepeth thee, will not slumber.

4 Beholde, he that keepeth Israel, wil neither slumber nor sleepe.

5 The Lord is thy keeper: the Lord is thy shadow at thy right hand.

6 The sunne shall not smite thee by day, nor the moone by night.

7 The Lord shall preserue thee from all euil: he shall keepe thy soule.

8 The Lord shall preserue thy going out, and thy comming in from henceforth and for euer.

Psalms 122

1 A song of degrees, or Psalme of David. I rejoiced, when they sayd to me, We wil go into the house of the Lord.

2 Our feete shall stand in thy gates, O Ierusalem.

3 Ierusalem is builded as a citie, that is compact together in it selfe:

4 Whereunto the Tribes, euen the Tribes of the Lord go vp according to the testimonie to Israel, to prayse the Name of the Lord.

5 For there are thrones set for iudgement, euen the thrones of the house of Dauid.

6 Pray for the peace of Ierusalem: let them prosper that loue thee.

7 Peace be within thy walles, and prosperitie within thy palaces.

8 For my brethren and neighbours sakes I will wish thee now prosperitie.

9 Because of the House of the Lord our God, I will procure thy wealth.

Psalms 123

1 A song of degrees. I lift vp mine eyes to thee, that dwellest in the heauens.

2 Behold, as the eyes of seruants looke vnto the hand of their masters, and as the eyes of a mayden vnto the hand of her mistres: so our eyes waite vpon the Lord our God vntil he haue mercie vpon vs.

3 Haue mercie vpon vs, O Lord, haue mercie vpon vs: for we haue suffered too much contempt.

4 Our soule is filled too full of ye mocking of the wealthy, and of the despitefulnes of the proude.

Psalms 124

1 A song of degrees, or Psalme of David. If the Lord had not bene on our side, (may Israel now say)

2 If the Lord had not bene on our side, when men rose vp against vs,

3 They had then swallowed vs vp quicke, when their wrath was kindled against vs.

4 Then the waters had drowned vs, and the streame had gone ouer our soule:

5 Then had the swelling waters gone ouer our soule.

6 Praysed be the Lord, which hath not giuen vs as a praye vnto their teeth.

7 Our soule is escaped, euen as a bird out of the snare of the foulers: the snare is broken, and we are deliuered.

8 Our helpe is in the Name of the Lord, which hath made heauen and earth.

Psalms 125

1 A song of degrees. They that trust in the Lord, shalbe as mount Zion, which can not be remooued, but remaineth for euer.

2 As the mountaines are about Ierusalem: so is the Lord about his people from henceforth and for euer.

3 For the rod of the wicked shall not rest on the lot of the righteous, least the righteous put forth their hand vnto wickednes.

4 Doe well, O Lord, vnto those that be good and true in their hearts.

5 But these that turne aside by their crooked wayes, them shall the Lord leade with the workers of iniquitie: but peace shalbe vpon Israel.

Psalms 126

1 A song of degrees, or Psalme of David. When ye Lord brought againe the captiuitie of Zion, we were like them that dreame.

2 Then was our mouth filled with laughter, and our tongue with ioye: then sayd they among the heathen, The Lord hath done great things for them.

3 The Lord hath done great things for vs, whereof we reioyce.

4 O Lord, bring againe our captiuitie, as the riuers in the South.

5 They that sowe in teares, shall reape in ioy.

6 They went weeping and caried precious seede: but they shall returne with ioye and bring their sheaues.

Psalms 127

1 A song of degrees, or Psalme of Salomon. Except the Lord build the house, they labour in vaine that build it: except the Lord keepe the citie, the keeper watcheth in vaine.

2 It is in vaine for you to rise earely, and to lie downe late, and eate the bread of sorow: but he wil surely giue rest to his beloued.

3 Beholde, children are the inheritance of the Lord, and the fruite of the wombe his rewarde.

4 As are the arrowes in the hand of ye strong man: so are the children of youth.
5 Blessed is the man, that hath his quiuer full of them: for they shall not be ashamed, when they speake with their enemies in the gate.

Psalms 128

1 A song of degrees. Blessed is euery one that feareth the Lord and walketh in his wayes.
2 When thou eatest the labours of thine hands, thou shalt be blessed, and it shall be well with thee.
3 Thy wife shalbe as the fruitfull vine on the sides of thine house, and thy children like the oliue plantes round about thy table.
4 Lo, surely thus shall the man be blessed, that feareth the Lord.
5 The Lord out of Zion shall blesse thee, and thou shalt see the wealth of Ierusalem all the dayes of thy life.
6 Yea, thou shalt see thy childrens children, and peace vpon Israel.

Psalms 129

1 A song of degrees. They haue often times afflicted me from my youth (may Israel nowe say)
2 They haue often times afflicted me from my youth: but they could not preuaile against me.
3 The plowers plowed vpon my backe, and made long furrowes.
4 But the righteous Lord hath cut the cordes of the wicked.
5 They that hate Zion, shalbe all ashamed and turned backward.
6 They shalbe as the grasse on the house tops, which withereth afore it commeth forth.
7 Whereof the mower filleth not his hand, neither the glainer his lap:
8 Neither they, which go by, say, The blessing of the Lord be vpon you, or, We blesse you in the Name of the Lord.

Psalms 130

1 A song of degrees. Out of the deepe places haue I called vnto thee, O Lord.
2 Lord, heare my voyce: let thine eares attend to the voyce of my prayers.
3 If thou, O Lord, straightly markest iniquities, O Lord, who shall stand?
4 But mercie is with thee, that thou mayest be feared.
5 I haue waited on the Lord: my soule hath waited, and I haue trusted in his worde.
6 My soule waiteth on the Lord more then the morning watch watcheth for the morning.
7 Let Israel waite on the Lord: for with the Lord is mercie, and with him is great redemption.
8 And he shall redeeme Israel from all his iniquities.

Psalms 131

1 A song of degrees or Psalme of David. Lord, mine heart is not hautie, neither are mine eyes loftie, neither haue I walked in great matters and hid from me.
2 Surely I haue behaued my selfe, like one wained from his mother, and kept silence: I am in my selfe as one that is wained.
3 Let Israel waite on the Lord from hencefoorth and for euer.

Psalms 132

1 A song of degrees. Lord, remember Dauid with all his affliction.
2 Who sware vnto the Lord, and vowed vnto the mightie God of Iaakob, saying,
3 I will not enter into the tabernacle of mine house, nor come vpon my pallet or bed,
4 Nor suffer mine eyes to sleepe, nor mine eye lids to slumber,
5 Vntill I finde out a place for the Lord, an habitation for the mightie God of Iaakob.
6 Lo, we heard of it in Ephrathah, and found it in the fieldes of the forest.
7 We will enter into his Tabernacles, and worship before his footestoole.
8 Arise, O Lord, to come into thy rest, thou, and the Arke of thy strength.
9 Let thy Priests be clothed with righteousnesse, and let thy Saints reioyce.
10 For thy seruant Dauids sake refuse not the face of thine Anoynted.
11 The Lord hath sworne in trueth vnto Dauid, and he wil not shrinke from it, saying, Of the fruite of thy body will I set vpon thy throne.
12 If thy sonnes keepe my couenant, and my testimonies, that I shall teach them, their sonnes also shall sit vpon thy throne for euer.
13 For the Lord hath chosen Zion, and loued to dwell in it, saying,
14 This is my rest for euer: here will I dwell, for I haue a delite therein.
15 I will surely blesse her vitailes, and will satisfie her poore with bread,
16 And will clothe her Priests with saluation, and her Saints shall shoute for ioye.
17 There will I make the horne of Dauid to bud: for I haue ordeined a light for mine Anoynted.
18 His enemies will I clothe with shame, but on him his crowne shall florish.

Psalms 133

1 A song of degrees or Psalme of David. Behold, howe good and howe comely a thing it is, brethren to dwell euen together.
2 It is like to the precious oyntment vpon the head, that runneth downe vpon the beard, euen vnto Aarons beard, which went downe on the border of his garments:
3 And as the dew of Hermon, which falleth vpon the mountaines of Zion: for there the Lord appointed the blessing and life for euer.

Psalms 134

1 A song of degrees. Behold, praise ye the Lord, all ye seruants of the Lord, ye that by night stande in the house of the Lord.
2 Lift vp your hands to the Sanctuarie, and praise the Lord.
3 The Lord, that hath made heauen and earth, blesse thee out of Zion.

Psalms 135

1 Praise ye the Lord. Praise the Name of the Lord: ye seruants of the Lord, praise him.
2 Ye that stande in the House of the Lord, and in the courtes of the House of our God,
3 Praise ye the Lord: for the Lord is good: sing praises vnto his Name: for it is a comely thing.
4 For the Lord hath chosen Iaakob to himselfe, and Israel for his chiefe treasure.
5 For I know that the Lord is great, and that our Lord is aboue all gods.
6 Whatsoeuer pleased the Lord, that did hee in heauen and in earth, in the sea, and in all the depths.
7 He bringeth vp the cloudes from the ends of the earth, and maketh the lightnings with ye raine: he draweth foorth the winde out of his treasures.
8 He smote the first borne of Egypt both of man and beast.
9 He hath sent tokens and wonders into the middes of thee, O Egypt, vpon Pharaoh, and vpon all his seruants.
10 He smote many nations, and slew mightie Kings:
11 As Sihon King of the Amorites, and Og King of Bashan, and all the kingdomes of Canaan:
12 And gaue their lande for an inheritance, euen an inheritance vnto Israel his people.
13 Thy Name, O Lord, endureth for euer: O Lord, thy remembrance is from generation to generation.
14 For the Lord will iudge his people, and be pacified towardes his seruants.
15 The idoles of the heathen are siluer and golde, euen the worke of mens handes.
16 They haue a mouth, and speake not: they haue eyes and see not.
17 They haue eares and heare not, neither is there any breath in their mouth.
18 They that make them, are like vnto them: so are all that trust in them.
19 Praise the Lord, ye house of Israel: praise the Lord, ye house of Aaron.
20 Praise the Lord, ye house of Leui: ye that feare the Lord, praise the Lord.
21 Praised bee the Lord out of Zion, which dwelleth in Ierusalem. Praise ye the Lord.

Psalms 136

1 Praise ye the Lord, because he is good: for his mercie endureth for euer.
2 Praise ye the God of gods: for his mercie endureth for euer.

3 Praise ye the Lord of lordes: for his mercie endureth for euer:

4 Which onely doeth great wonders: for his mercie endureth for euer:

5 Which by his wisedome made the heauens: for his mercie endureth for euer:

6 Which hath stretched out the earth vpon the waters: for his mercie endureth for euer:

7 Which made great lightes: for his mercie endureth for euer:

8 As the sunne to rule the day: for his mercie endureth for euer:

9 The moone and the starres to gouerne the night: for his mercie endureth for euer:

10 Which smote Egypt with their first borne, (for his mercie endureth for euer)

11 And brought out Israel from among them (for his mercie endureth for euer)

12 With a mightie hande and stretched out arme: for his mercie endureth for euer:

13 Which deuided the red Sea in two partes: for his mercie endureth for euer:

14 And made Israel to passe through the mids of it: for his mercie endureth for euer:

15 And ouerthrewe Pharaoh and his hoste in the red Sea: for his mercie endureth for euer:

16 Which led his people through the wildernes: for his mercie endureth for euer:

17 Which smote great Kings: for his mercie endureth for euer:

18 And slewe mightie Kings: for his mercie endureth for euer:

19 As Sihon King of the Amorites: for his mercie endureth for euer:

20 And Og the King of Bashan: for his mercie endureth for euer:

21 And gaue their land for an heritage: for his mercie endureth for euer:

22 Euen an heritage vnto Israel his seruant: for his mercie endureth for euer:

23 Which remembred vs in our base estate: for his mercie endureth for euer:

24 And hath rescued vs from our oppressours: for his mercie endureth for euer:

25 Which giueth foode to all flesh: for his mercie endureth for euer.

26 Praise ye the God of heauen: for his mercie endureth for euer.

Psalms 137

1 By the riuers of Babel we sate, and there wee wept, when we remembred Zion.

2 Wee hanged our harpes vpon the willowes in the middes thereof.

3 Then they that ledde vs captiues, required of vs songs and mirth, when wee had hanged vp our harpes, saying, Sing vs one of the songs of Zion.

4 Howe shall we sing, said we, a song of the Lord in a strange land?

5 If I forget thee, O Ierusalem, let my right hand forget to play.

6 If I do not remember thee, let my tongue cleaue to the roofe of my mouth: yea, if I preferre not Ierusalem to my chiefe ioy.

7 Remember the children of Edom, O Lord, in the day of Ierusalem, which saide, Rase it, rase it to the foundation thereof.

8 O daughter of Babel, worthy to be destroyed, blessed shall he be that rewardeth thee, as thou hast serued vs.

9 Blessed shall he be that taketh and dasheth thy children against the stones.

Psalms 138

1 A Psalme of David. I will praise thee with my whole heart: euen before the gods will I praise thee.

2 I will worship toward thine holy Temple and praise thy Name, because of thy louing kindenesse and for thy trueth: for thou hast magnified thy Name aboue all things by thy word.

3 When I called, then thou heardest me, and hast encreased strength in my soule.

4 All the Kings of the earth shall praise thee, O Lord: for they haue heard the wordes of thy mouth.

5 And they shall sing of the wayes of the Lord, because the glory of the Lord is great.

6 For the Lord is high: yet he beholdeth the lowly, but the proude he knoweth afarre off.

7 Though I walke in the middes of trouble, yet wilt thou reuiue me: thou wilt stretch foorth thine hand vpon the wrath of mine enemies, and thy right hand shall saue me.

8 The Lord will performe his worke toward me: O Lord, thy mercie endureth for euer: forsake not the workes of thine handes.

Psalms 139

1 To him that excelleth. A Psalme of David. O Lord, thou hast tried me and knowen me.

2 Thou knowest my sitting and my rising: thou vnderstandest my thought afarre off.

3 Thou compassest my pathes, and my lying downe, and art accustomed to all my wayes.

4 For there is not a word in my tongue, but loe, thou knowest it wholy, O Lord.

5 Thou holdest mee straite behinde and before, and layest thine hand vpon me.

6 Thy knowledge is too wonderfull for mee: it is so high that I cannot attaine vnto it.

7 Whither shall I goe from thy Spirite? or whither shall I flee from thy presence?

8 If I ascende into heauen, thou art there: if I lye downe in hell, thou art there.

9 Let mee take the winges of the morning, and dwell in the vttermost parts of the sea:

10 Yet thither shall thine hand leade me, and thy right hand holde me.

11 If I say, Yet the darkenes shall hide me, euen the night shalbe light about me.

12 Yea, the darkenes hideth not from thee: but the night shineth as the day: the darkenes and light are both alike.

13 For thou hast possessed my reines: thou hast couered me in my mothers wombe.

14 I will praise thee, for I am fearefully and wonderously made: marueilous are thy workes, and my soule knoweth it well.

15 My bones are not hid from thee, though I was made in a secret place, and facioned beneath in the earth.

16 Thine eyes did see me, when I was without forme: for in thy booke were all things written, which in continuance were facioned, when there was none of them before.

17 Howe deare therefore are thy thoughtes vnto me, O God! how great is ye summe of them!

18 If I should count them, they are moe then the sand: when I wake, I am still with thee.

19 Oh that thou wouldest slay, O God, the wicked and bloody men, to whom I say, Depart ye from mee:

20 Which speake wickedly of thee, and being thine enemies are lifted vp in vaine.

21 Doe not I hate them, O Lord, that hate thee? and doe not I earnestly contend with those that rise vp against thee?

22 I hate them with an vnfained hatred, as they were mine vtter enemies.

23 Try mee, O God, and knowe mine heart: prooue me and know my thoughtes,

24 And consider if there be any way of wickednes in me, and leade me in the way for euer.

Psalms 140

1 To him that excelleth. A Psalme of David. Deliuer me, O Lord, from the euill man: preserue me from the cruel man:

2 Which imagine euill things in their heart, and make warre continually.

3 They haue sharpened their tongues like a serpent: adders poyson is vnder their lips. Selah.

4 Keepe mee, O Lord, from the handes of the wicked: preserue mee from the cruell man, which purposeth to cause my steppes to slide.

5 The proude haue layde a snare for me, and spred a nette with cordes in my pathway, and set grennes for me. Selah.

6 Therefore I saide vnto the Lord, Thou art my God: heare, O Lord, the voyce of my prayers.

7 O Lord God the strength of my saluation, thou hast couered mine head in the day of battel.

8 Let not the wicked haue his desire, O Lord: performe not his wicked thought, least they be proude. Selah.

9 As for the chiefe of them, that compasse me about, let the mischiefe of their owne lippes come vpon them.

10 Let coles fal vpon them: let him cast them into the fire, and into the deepe pits, that they rise not.

11 For the backbiter shall not be established vpon the earth: euill shall hunt the cruell man to destruction.

12 I know that the Lord will auenge the afflicted, and iudge the poore.

13 Surely the righteous shall prayse thy Name, and the iust shall dwell in thy presence.

Psalms 141

1 A Psalme of David. O Lord, I call vpon thee: haste thee vnto me: heare my voyce, when I cry vnto thee.

2 Let my prayer be directed in thy sight as incense, and the lifting vp of mine hands as an euening sacrifice.

3 Set a watch, O Lord, before my mouth, and keepe the doore of my lips.

4 Incline not mine heart to euill, that I should commit wicked workes with men that worke iniquitie: and let me not eate of their delicates.

5 Let the righteous smite me: for that is a benefite: and let him reprooue me, and it shalbe a precious oyle, that shall not breake mine head: for within a while I shall euen pray in their miseries.

6 When their iudges shall be cast downe in stonie places, they shall heare my wordes, for they are sweete.

7 Our bones lye scattered at the graues mouth, as he that heweth wood or diggeth in the earth.

8 But mine eyes looke vnto thee, O Lord God: in thee is my trust: leaue not my soule destitute.

9 Keepe me from the snare, which they haue layde for me, and from the grennes of the workers of iniquitie.

10 Let the wicked fall into his nettes together, whiles I escape.

Psalms 142

1 A Psalme of David, to give instruction, and a prayer, when he was in the cave. I cryed vnto the Lord with my voyce: with my voyce I prayed vnto the Lord.

2 I powred out my meditation before him, and declared mine affliction in his presence.

3 Though my spirit was in perplexitie in me, yet thou knewest my path: in the way wherein I walked, haue they priuily layde a snare for me.

4 I looked vpon my right hand, and beheld, but there was none that would knowe me: all refuge failed me, and none cared for my soule.

5 Then cryed I vnto thee, O Lord, and sayde, thou art mine hope, and my portion in the land of the liuing.

6 Hearken vnto my crye, for I am brought very lowe: deliuer me from my persecuters, for they are too strong for me.

7 Bring my soule out of prison, that I may prayse thy Name: then shall the righteous come about me, when thou art beneficiall vnto me.

Psalms 143

1 A Psalme of David. Hear my prayer, O Lord, and hearken vnto my supplication: answere me in thy trueth and in thy righteousnes.

2 (And enter not into iudgement with thy seruant: for in thy sight shall none that liueth, be iustified)

3 For the enemie hath persecuted my soule: he hath smitten my life downe to the earth: he hath layde me in the darkenes, as they that haue bene dead long agoe:

4 And my spirit was in perplexitie in me, and mine heart within me was amased.

5 Yet doe I remember the time past: I meditate in all thy workes, yea, I doe meditate in the workes of thine hands.

6 I stretch forth mine hands vnto thee: my soule desireth after thee, as the thirstie land. Selah.

7 Heare me speedily, O Lord, for my spirit fayleth: hide not thy face from me, els I shall be like vnto them that go downe into the pit.

8 Let mee heare thy louing kindenes in the morning, for in thee is my trust: shewe mee the way, that I should walke in, for I lift vp my soule vnto thee.

9 Deliuer me, O Lord, from mine enemies: for I hid me with thee.

10 Teach me to doe thy will, for thou art my God: let thy good Spirit leade me vnto the land of righteousnes.

11 Quicken me, O Lord, for thy Names sake, and for thy righteousnesse bring my soule out of trouble.

12 And for thy mercy slay mine enemies, and destroy all them that oppresse my soule: for I am thy seruant.

Psalms 144

1 A Psalme of David. Blessed be the Lord my strength, which teacheth mine hands to fight, and my fingers to battell.

2 He is my goodnes and my fortresse, my towre and my deliuerer, my shield, and in him I trust, which subdueth my people vnder me.

3 Lord, what is man that thou regardest him! or the sonne of man that thou thinkest vpon him!

4 Man is like to vanitie: his dayes are like a shadow, that vanisheth.

5 Bow thine heauens, O Lord, and come downe: touch the mountaines and they shall smoke.

6 Cast forth the lightning and scatter them: shoote out thine arrowes, and consume them.

7 Send thine hand from aboue: deliuer me, and take me out of the great waters, and from the hand of strangers,

8 Whose mouth talketh vanitie, and their right hand is a right hand of falsehood.

9 I wil sing a new song vnto thee, O God, and sing vnto thee vpon a viole, and an instrument of ten strings.

10 It is he that giueth deliuerance vnto Kings, and rescueth Dauid his seruant from the hurtfull sworde.

11 Rescue me, and deliuer me from the hand of strangers, whose mouth talketh

vanitie, and their right hand is a right hand of falshood:

12 That our sonnes may be as the plantes growing vp in their youth, and our daughters as the corner stones, grauen after the similitude of a palace:

13 That our corners may be full, and abounding with diuers sorts, and that our sheepe may bring forth thousands and ten thousand in our streetes:

14 That our oxen may be strong to labour: that there be none inuasion, nor going out, nor no crying in our streetes.

15 Blessed are the people, that be so, yea, blessed are the people, whose God is the Lord.

Psalms 145

1 A Psalme of David of Praise. O my God and King, I will extold thee, and will blesse thy Name for euer and euer.

2 I will blesse thee dayly, and prayse thy Name for euer and euer.

3 Great is the Lord, and most worthy to be praysed, and his greatnes is incomprehensible.

4 Generation shall praise thy works vnto generation, and declare thy power.

5 I wil meditate of the beautie of thy glorious maiestie, and thy wonderfull workes,

6 And they shall speake of the power of thy fearefull actes, and I will declare thy greatnes.

7 They shall breake out into the mention of thy great goodnes, and shall sing aloude of thy righteousnesse.

8 The Lord is gracious and merciful, slow to anger, and of great mercie.

9 The Lord is good to all, and his mercies are ouer all his workes.

10 All thy workes prayse thee, O Lord, and thy Saints blesse thee.

11 They shewe the glory of thy kingdome, and speake of thy power,

12 To cause his power to be knowen to the sonnes of men, and the glorious renoume of his kingdome.

13 Thy kingdome is an euerlasting kingdome, and thy dominion endureth throughout all ages.

14 The Lord vpholdeth all that fall, and lifteth vp all that are ready to fall.

15 The eyes of all waite vpon thee, and thou giuest them their meate in due season.

16 Thou openest thine hand, and fillest all things liuing of thy good pleasure.

17 The Lord is righteous in all his wayes, and holy in all his workes.

18 The Lord is neere vnto all that call vpon him: yea, to all that call vpon him in trueth.

19 He wil fulfill the desire of them that feare him: he also wil heare their cry, and wil saue them.

20 The Lord preserueth all them that loue him: but he will destroy all the wicked.

21 My mouth shall speake the prayse of the Lord, and all flesh shall blesse his holy Name for euer and euer.

Psalms 146

1 Praise ye the Lord. Praise thou the Lord, O my soule.

2 I will prayse the Lord during my life: as long as I haue any being, I wil sing vnto my God.

3 Put not your trust in princes, nor in the sonne of man, for there is none helpe in him.

4 His breath departeth, and he returneth to his earth: then his thoughtes perish.

5 Blessed is he, that hath the God of Iaakob for his helpe, whose hope is in the Lord his God.

6 Which made heauen and earth, the sea, and all that therein is: which keepeth his fidelitie for euer:

7 Which executeth iustice for the oppressed: which giueth bread to the hungry: the Lord loseth the prisoners.

8 The Lord giueth sight to the blinde: the Lord rayseth vp the crooked: the Lord loueth the righteous.

9 The Lord keepeth the strangers: he relieueth the fatherlesse and widowe: but he ouerthroweth the way of the wicked.

10 The Lord shall reigne for euer: O Zion, thy God endureth from generation to generation. Prayse ye the Lord.

Psalms 147

1 Praise ye the Lord, for it is good to sing vnto our God: for it is a pleasant thing, and praise is comely.

2 The Lord doth builde vp Ierusalem, and gather together the dispersed of Israel.

3 He healeth those that are broken in heart, and bindeth vp their sores.

4 He counteth the nomber of the starres, and calleth them all by their names.

5 Great is our Lord, and great is his power: his wisdome is infinite.

6 The Lord relieueth the meeke, and abaseth the wicked to the ground.

7 Sing vnto the Lord with prayse: sing vpon the harpe vnto our God,

8 Which couereth the heauen with cloudes, and prepareth raine for the earth, and maketh the grasse to growe vpon the mountaines:

9 Which giueth to beasts their foode, and to the yong rauens that crie.

10 He hath not pleasure in the strength of an horse, neither delighteth he in the legs of man.

11 But the Lord deliteth in them that feare him, and attende vpon his mercie.

12 Prayse the Lord, O Ierusalem: prayse thy God, O Zion.

13 For he hath made the barres of thy gates strong, and hath blessed thy children within thee.

14 He setteth peace in thy borders, and satisfieth thee with the floure of wheate.

15 He sendeth foorth his commandement vpon earth, and his worde runneth very swiftly.

16 He giueth snowe like wooll, and scattereth the hoare frost like ashes.

17 He casteth foorth his yce like morsels: who can abide the colde thereof?

18 He sendeth his worde and melteth them: he causeth his winde to blowe, and the waters flowe.

19 He sheweth his word vnto Iaakob, his statutes and his iudgements vnto Israel.

20 He hath not dealt so with euery nation, neither haue they knowen his iudgements. Prayse ye the Lord.

Psalms 148

1 Praise ye the Lord. Praise ye the Lord from the heauen: prayse ye him in the high places.

2 Prayse ye him, all ye his Angels: praise him, all his armie.

3 Prayse ye him, sunne and moone: prayse ye him all bright starres.

4 Prayse ye him, heauens of heauens, and waters, that be aboue the heauens.

5 Let them prayse the Name of the Lord: for he commanded, and they were created.

6 And he hath established them for euer and euer: he hath made an ordinance, which shall not passe.

7 Prayse ye the Lord from the earth, ye dragons and all depths:

8 Fire and hayle, snowe and vapours, stormie winde, which execute his worde:

9 Mountaines and all hils, fruitfull trees and all ceders:

10 Beasts and all cattell, creeping things and fethered foules:

11 Kings of the earth and all people, princes and all iudges of the worlde:

12 Yong men and maidens, also olde men and children:

13 Let them prayse the Name of the Lord: for his Name onely is to be exalted, and his prayse aboue the earth and the heauens.

14 For he hath exalted the horne of his people, which is a prayse for all his Saintes, euen for the children of Israel, a people that is neere vnto him. Prayse ye the Lord.

Psalms 149

1 Praise ye the Lord. Sing ye vnto the Lord a newe song: let his prayse be heard in the Congregation of Saints.

2 Let Israel reioyce in him that made him, and let ye children of Zion reioyce in their King.

3 Let them prayse his Name with the flute: let them sing prayses vnto him with the timbrell and harpe.

4 For the Lord hath pleasure in his people: he will make the meeke glorious by deliuerance.

5 Let ye Saints be ioyfull with glorie: let them sing loud vpon their beddes.

6 Let the high Actes of God bee in their mouth, and a two edged sword in their hands,

7 To execute vengeance vpon the heathen, and corrections among the people:

8 To binde their Kings in chaines, and their nobles with fetters of yron,

9 That they may execute vpon them the iudgement that is written: this honour shall be to all his Saintes. Prayse ye the Lord.

Psalms 150

1 Praise ye the Lord. Praise ye God in his Sanctuarie: prayse ye him in the firmament of his power.

2 Prayse ye him in his mightie Actes: prayse ye him according to his excellent greatnesse.

3 Prayse ye him in the sounde of the trumpet: prayse yee him vpon the viole and the harpe.

4 Prayse ye him with timbrell and flute: praise ye him with virginales and organs.

5 Prayse ye him with sounding cymbales: prayse ye him with high sounding cymbales.

6 Let euery thing that hath breath prayse the Lord. Prayse ye the Lord.

Proverbs

Proverbs 1

1 The Parables of Salomon the sonne of Dauid King of Israel,

2 To knowe wisdome, and instruction, to vnderstand ye wordes of knowledge,

3 To receiue instruction to do wisely, by iustice and iudgement and equitie,

4 To giue vnto the simple, sharpenesse of wit, and to the childe knowledge and discretion.

5 A wise man shall heare and increase in learning, and a man of vnderstanding shall attayne vnto wise counsels,

6 To vnderstand a parable, and the interpretation, the wordes of ye wise, and their darke sayings.

7 The feare of the Lord is the beginning of knowledge: but fooles despise wisedome and instruction.

8 My sonne, heare thy fathers instruction, and forsake not thy mothers teaching.

9 For they shalbe a comely ornament vnto thine head, and as chaines for thy necke.

10 My sonne, if sinners doe intise thee, consent thou not.

11 If they say, Come with vs, we will lay waite for blood, and lie priuilie for the innocent without a cause:

12 We wil swallow them vp aliue like a graue euen whole, as those that goe downe into the pit:

13 We shall finde all precious riches, and fill our houses with spoyle:

14 Cast in thy lot among vs: we will all haue one purse:

15 My sonne, walke not thou in the way with them: refraine thy foote from their path.

16 For their feete runne to euill, and make haste to shed blood.

17 Certainely as without cause the net is spred before the eyes of all that hath wing:

18 So they lay waite for blood and lie priuily for their liues.

19 Such are the wayes of euery one that is greedy of gaine: he would take away the life of the owners thereof.

20 Wisdome cryeth without: she vttereth her voyce in the streetes.

21 She calleth in the hye streete, among the prease in the entrings of the gates, and vttereth her wordes in the citie, saying,

22 O ye foolish, howe long will ye loue foolishnes? and the scornefull take their pleasure in scorning, and the fooles hate knowledge?

23 (Turne you at my correction: loe, I will powre out my mind vnto you, and make you vnderstand my wordes)

24 Because I haue called, and ye refused: I haue stretched out mine hand, and none woulde regarde.

25 But ye haue despised all my counsell, and would none of my correction.

26 I will also laugh at your destruction, and mocke, when your feare commeth.

27 Whe your feare cometh like sudden desolation, and your destruction shall come like a whirle wind: whe affliction and anguish shall come vpon you,

28 Then shall they call vpon me, but I will not answere: they shall seeke me early, but they shall not finde me,

29 Because they hated knowledge, and did not chuse the feare of the Lord.

30 They would none of my counsell, but despised all my correction.

31 Therefore shall they eate of ye fruite of their owne way, and be filled with their owne deuises.

32 For ease slaieth the foolish, and the prosperitie of fooles destroyeth them.

33 But he that obeyeth me, shall dwell safely, and be quiet from feare of euill.

Proverbs 2

1 My sonne, if thou wilt receiue my wordes, and hide my commandements within thee,

2 And cause thine eares to hearken vnto wisdome, and encline thine heart to vnderstanding,

3 (For if thou callest after knowledge, and cryest for vnderstanding:

4 If thou seekest her as siluer, and searchest for her as for treasures,

5 Then shalt thou vnderstand the feare of the Lord, and finde the knowledge of God.

6 For the Lord giueth wisdome, out of his mouth commeth knowledge and vnderstanding.

7 He preserueth the state of the righteous: he is a shielde to them that walke vprightly,

8 That they may keepe the wayes of iudgement: and he preserueth the way of his Saintes)

9 Then shalt thou vnderstand righteousnes, and iudgement, and equitie, and euery good path.

10 When wisdome entreth into thine heart, and knowledge deliteth thy soule,

11 Then shall counsell preserue thee, and vnderstanding shall keepe thee,

12 And deliuer thee from the euill way, and from the man that speaketh froward things,

13 And from them that leaue the wayes of righteousnes to walke in the wayes of darkenes:

14 Which reioyce in doing euill, and delite in the frowardnesse of the wicked,

15 Whose wayes are crooked and they are lewde in their paths.

16 And it shall deliuer thee from the strange woman, euen from the stranger, which flattereth with her wordes.

17 Which forsaketh the guide of her youth, and forgetteth the couenant of her God.

18 Surely her house tendeth to death, and her paths vnto the dead.

19 All they that goe vnto her, returne not againe, neither take they holde of the wayes of life.

20 Therefore walke thou in the way of good men, and keepe the wayes of the righteous.

21 For the iust shall dwell in the land, and the vpright men shall remaine in it.

22 But the wicked shalbe cut off from ye earth, and the transgressours shalbe rooted out of it.

Proverbs 3

1 My sonne, forget not thou my Lawe, but let thine heart keepe my commandements.

2 For they shall increase the length of thy dayes and the yeeres of life, and thy prosperitie.

3 Let not mercie and trueth forsake thee: binde them on thy necke, and write them vpon the table of thine heart.

4 So shalt thou finde fauour and good vnderstanding in the sight of God and man.

5 Trust in the Lord with all thine heart, and leane not vnto thine owne wisdome.

6 In all thy wayes acknowledge him, and he shall direct thy wayes.

7 Be not wise in thine owne eyes: but feare the Lord, and depart from euill.

8 So health shalbe vnto thy nauel, and marowe vnto thy bones.

9 Honour the Lord with thy riches, and with the first fruites of all thine increase.

10 So shall thy barnes be filled with abundance, and thy presses shall burst with newe wine.

11 My sonne, refuse not the chastening of the Lord, neither be grieued with his correction.

12 For the Lord correcteth him, whome he loueth, euen as the father doeth the childe in whom he deliteth.

13 Blessed is the man that findeth wisedome, and the man that getteth vnderstanding.

14 For the marchandise thereof is better then the marchandise of siluer, and the gaine thereof is better then golde.

15 It is more precious then pearles: and all things that thou canst desire, are not to be compared vnto her.

16 Length of dayes is in her right hand, and in her left hand riches and glory.

17 Her wayes are wayes of pleasure, and all her pathes prosperitie.

18 She is a tree of life to them that lay holde on her, and blessed is he that retaineth her.

19 The Lord by wisdome hath layde the foundation of the earth, and hath stablished the heauens through vnderstanding.

20 By his knowledge the depthes are broken vp, and the cloudes droppe downe the dewe.

21 My sonne, let not these things depart from thine eyes, but obserue wisdome, and counsell.

22 So they shalbe life to thy soule, and grace vnto thy necke.

23 Then shalt thou walke safely by thy way: and thy foote shall not stumble.

24 If thou sleepest, thou shalt not bee afraide, and when thou sleepest, thy sleepe shalbe sweete.

25 Thou shalt not feare for any sudden feare, neither for the destruction of the wicked, when it commeth.

26 For the Lord shall be for thine assurance, and shall preserue thy foote from taking.

27 Withhold not the good from the owners thereof, though there be power in thine hand to doe it.

28 Say not vnto thy neighbour, Go and come againe, and to morow wil I giue thee, if thou now haue it.

29 Intend none hurt against thy neighbour, seeing he doeth dwell without feare by thee.

30 Striue not with a man causelesse, when he hath done thee no harme.

31 Bee not enuious for the wicked man, neither chuse any of his wayes.

32 For the frowarde is abomination vnto the Lord: but his secret is with the righteous.

33 The curse of the Lord is in the house of the wicked: but he blesseth the habitation of the righteous.

34 With the scornefull he scorneth, but hee giueth grace vnto the humble.

35 The wise shall inherite glorie: but fooles dishonour, though they be exalted.

Proverbs 4

1 Heare, O ye children, the instruction of a father, and giue eare to learne vnderstanding.

2 For I doe giue you a good doctrine: therefore forsake yee not my lawe.

3 For I was my fathers sonne, tender and deare in the sight of my mother,

4 When he taught me, and sayde vnto me, Let thine heart holde fast my woordes: keepe my commandements, and thou shalt liue.

5 Get wisdom: get vnderstading: forget not, neither decline from the woordes of my mouth.

6 Forsake her not, and shee shall keepe thee: loue her and shee shall preserue thee.

7 Wisedome is the beginning: get wisedome therefore: and aboue all thy possession get vnderstanding.

8 Exalt her, and she shall exalt thee: she shall bring thee to honour, if thou embrace her.

9 She shall giue a comely ornamet vnto thine head, yea, she shall giue thee a crowne of glorie.

10 Heare, my sonne, and receiue my wordes, and the yeeres of thy life shalbe many.

11 I haue taught thee in ye way of wisedom, and led thee in the pathes of righteousnesse.

12 Whe thou goest, thy gate shall not be strait, and when thou runnest, thou shalt not fall.

13 Take holde of instruction, and leaue not: keepe her, for shee is thy life.

14 Enter not into the way of the wicked, and walke not in the way of euill men.

15 Auoide it, and goe not by it: turne from it, and passe by.

16 For they can not sleepe, except they haue done euill, and their sleepe departeth except they cause some to fall.

17 For they eate the breade of wickednesse, and drinke the wine of violence.

18 But the way of the righteous shineth as the light, that shineth more and more vnto the perfite day.

19 The way of the wicked is as the darkenes: they knowe not wherein they shall fall.

20 My sonne, hearken vnto my wordes, incline thine eare vnto my sayings.

21 Let them not depart from thine eyes, but keepe them in the middes of thine heart.

22 For they are life vnto those that find them, and health vnto all their flesh.

23 Keepe thine heart with all diligence: for thereout commeth life.

24 Put away from thee a froward mouth, and put wicked lippes farre from thee.

25 Let thine eyes beholde the right, and let thine eyelids direct thy way before thee.

26 Ponder the path of thy feete, and let all thy waies be ordred aright.

27 Turne not to the right hande, nor to the left, but remooue thy foote from euill.

Proverbs 5

1 My sonne, hearken vnto my wisedome, and incline thine eare vnto my knowledge.

2 That thou maiest regarde counsell, and thy lippes obserue knowledge.

3 For the lippes of a strange woman drop as an honie combe, and her mouth is more soft then oyle.

4 But the end of her is bitter as wormewood, and sharpe as a two edged sworde.

5 Her feete goe downe to death, and her steps take holde on hell.

6 She weigheth not the way of life: her paths are moueable: thou canst not knowe them.

7 Heare yee me nowe therefore, O children, and depart not from the wordes of my mouth.

8 Keepe thy way farre from her, and come not neere the doore of her house,

9 Least thou giue thine honor vnto others, and thy yeeres to the cruell:

10 Least the stranger should be silled with thy strength, and thy labours bee in the house of a stranger,

11 And thou mourne at thine end, (when thou hast consumed thy flesh and thy bodie)

12 And say, How haue I hated instruction, and mine heart despised correction!

13 And haue not obeied the voyce of them that taught mee, nor enclined mine eare to them that instructed me!

14 I was almost brought into all euil in ye mids of the Congregation and assemblie.

15 Drinke the water of thy cisterne, and of the riuers out of the middes of thine owne well.

16 Let thy fountaines flow foorth, and the riuers of waters in the streetes.

17 But let them bee thine, euen thine onely, and not the strangers with thee.

18 Let thy fountaine be blessed, and reioyce with the wife of thy youth.

19 Let her be as the louing hinde and pleasant roe: let her brests satisfie thee at all times, and delite in her loue continually.

20 For why shouldest thou delite, my sonne, in a strange woman, or embrace the bosome of a stranger?

21 For the waies of man are before the eyes of the Lord, and he pondereth all his pathes.

22 His owne iniquities shall take the wicked himselfe, and he shall be holden with the cordes of his owne sinne.

23 Hee shall die for fault of instruction, and shall goe astray through his great follie.

Proverbs 6

1 My sonne, if thou be surety for thy neighbour, and hast striken hands with the stranger,

2 Thou art snared with the wordes of thy mouth: thou art euen taken with the woordes of thine owne mouth.

3 Doe this nowe, my sonne, and deliuer thy selfe: seeing thou art come into the hande of thy neighbour, goe, and humble thy selfe, and sollicite thy friends.

4 Giue no sleepe to thine eyes, nor slumber to thine eyelids.

5 Deliuer thy selfe as a doe from the hande of the hunter, and as a birde from the hande of the fouler.

6 Goe to the pismire, O sluggarde: beholde her waies, and be wise.

7 For shee hauing no guide, gouernour, nor ruler,

8 Prepareth her meat in the sommer, and gathereth her foode in haruest.

9 Howe long wilt thou sleepe, O sluggarde? when wilt thou arise out of thy sleepe?

10 Yet a litle sleepe, a litle slumber, a litle folding of the hands to sleepe.

11 Therefore thy pouertie commeth as one that trauaileth by the way, and thy necessitie like an armed man.

12 The vnthriftie man and the wicked man walketh with a froward mouth.

13 He maketh a signe with his eyes: he signifieth with his feete: he instructeth with his fingers.

14 Lewde things are in his heart: he imagineth euill at all times, and raiseth vp contentions.

15 Therefore shall his destruction come speedily: hee shall be destroyed suddenly without recouerie.

16 These sixe things doeth the Lord hate: yea, his soule abhorreth seuen:

17 The hautie eyes, a lying tongue, and the hands that shed innocent blood,

18 An heart that imagineth wicked enterprises, feete that be swift in running to mischiefe,

19 A false witnesse that speaketh lyes, and him that rayseth vp contentions among brethren.

20 My sonne, keepe thy fathers commandement, and forsake not thy mothers instruction.

21 Binde them alway vpon thine heart, and tye them about thy necke.

22 It shall leade thee, when thou walkest: it shall watch for thee, when thou sleepest, and when thou wakest, it shall talke with thee.

23 For the commandement is a lanterne, and instruction a light: and corrections for instruction are the way of life,

24 To keepe thee from the wicked woman, and from ye flatterie of ye tongue of a strange woman.

25 Desire not her beautie in thine heart, neither let her take thee with her eye lids.

26 For because of the whorish woman a man is brought to a morsell of bread, and a woman wil hunt for the precious life of a man.

27 Can a man take fire in his bosome, and his clothes not be burnt?

28 Or can a man go vpon coales, and his feete not be burnt?

29 So he that goeth in to his neighbours wife, shall not be innocent, whosoeuer toucheth her.

30 Men do not despise a thiefe, when he stealeth, to satisfie his soule, because he is hungrie.

31 But if he be founde, he shall restore seuen folde, or he shall giue all the substance of his house.

32 But he that committeth adulterie with a woman, he is destitute of vnderstanding: he that doeth it, destroyeth his owne soule.

33 He shall finde a wounde and dishonour, and his reproch shall neuer be put away.

34 For ielousie is the rage of a man: therefore he will not spare in the day of vengeance.

35 He cannot beare the sight of any raunsome: neither will he consent, though thou augment the giftes.

Proverbs 7

1 My sonne, keepe my wordes, and hide my commandements with thee.

2 Keepe my commandements, and thou shalt liue, and mine instruction as the apple of thine eyes.

3 Binde them vpon thy fingers, and write them vpon the table of thine heart.

4 Say vnto wisedome, Thou art my sister: and call vnderstanding thy kinswoman,

5 That they may keepe thee from the strange woman, euen from the stranger that is smoothe in her wordes.

6 As I was in the window of mine house, I looked through my windowe,

7 And I sawe among the fooles, and considered among the children a yong man destitute of vnderstanding,

8 Who passed through the streete by her corner, and went toward her house,

9 In the twilight in the euening, when the night began to be blacke and darke.

10 And beholde, there met him a woman with an harlots behauiour, and subtill in heart.

11 (She is babling and loud: whose feete can not abide in her house.

12 Nowe she is without, nowe in the streetes, and lyeth in waite at euery corner)

13 So she caught him and kissed him and with an impudent face said vnto him,

14 I haue peace offerings: this day haue I payed my vowes.

15 Therefore came I forth to meete thee, that I might seeke thy face: and I haue found thee.

16 I haue deckt my bed with ornaments, carpets and laces of Egypt.

17 I haue perfumed my bedde with myrrhe, aloes, and cynamom.

18 Come, let vs take our fill of loue vntill the morning: let vs take our pleasure in daliance.

19 For mine husband is not at home: he is gone a iourney farre off.

20 He hath taken with him a bagge of siluer, and will come home at the day appointed.

21 Thus with her great craft she caused him to yeelde, and with her flattering lips she entised him.

22 And he followed her straight wayes, as an oxe that goeth to the slaughter, and as a foole to the stockes for correction,

23 Till a dart strike through his liuer, as a bird hasteth to the snare, not knowing that he is in danger.

24 Heare me now therefore, O children, and hearken to the wordes of my mouth.

25 Let not thine heart decline to her wayes: wander thou not in her paths.

26 For shee hath caused many to fall downe wounded, and the strong men are all slaine by her.

27 Her house is the way vnto ye graue, which goeth downe to the chambers of death.

Proverbs 8

1 Doth not wisedome crie? and vnderstanding vtter her voyce?

2 She standeth in the top of the high places by the way in the place of the paths.

3 She cryeth besides the gates before the citie at the entrie of the doores,

4 O men, I call vnto you, and vtter my voyce to the children of men.

5 O ye foolish men, vnderstand wisedome, and ye, O fooles, be wise in heart.

6 Giue eare, for I will speake of excellent things, and the opening of my lippes, shall teache things that be right.

7 For my mouth shall speake the trueth, and my lippes abhorre wickednesse.

8 All the wordes of my mouth are righteous: there is no lewdenes, nor frowardnesse in them.

9 They are all plaine to him that will vnderstande, and streight to them that woulde finde knowledge.

10 Receiue mine instruction, and not siluer, and knowledge rather then fine golde.

11 For wisdome is better then precious stones: and all pleasures are not to be compared vnto her.

12 I wisdome dwell with prudence, and I find foorth knowledge and counsels.

13 The feare of the Lord is to hate euill as pride, and arrogancie, and the euill way: and a mouth that speaketh lewde things, I doe hate.

14 I haue counsell and wisedome: I am vnderstanding, and I haue strength.

15 By me, Kings reigne, and princes decree iustice.

16 By me princes rule and the nobles, and all the iudges of the earth.

17 I loue them that loue me: and they that seeke me earely, shall finde me.

18 Riches and honour are with me: euen durable riches and righteousnesse.

19 My fruite is better then golde, euen then fine golde, and my reuenues better then fine siluer.

20 I cause to walke in the way of righteousnes, and in the middes of the paths of iudgement,

21 That I may cause them that loue me, to inherite substance, and I will fill their treasures.

22 The Lord hath possessed me in the beginning of his way: I was before his workes of olde.

23 I was set vp from euerlasting, from the beginning and before the earth.

24 When there were no depths, was I begotten, when there were no fountaines abounding with water.

25 Before the mountaines were setled: and before the hilles, was I begotten.

26 He had not yet made the earth, nor the open places, nor the height of the dust in the worlde.

27 When hee prepared the heauens, I was there, when he set the compasse vpon the deepe.

28 When he established the cloudes aboue, when he confirmed the fountaines of the deepe,

29 When he gaue his decree to the Sea, that the waters shoulde not passe his commandement: when he appointed the foundations of the earth,

30 Then was I with him as a nourisher, and I was dayly his delight reioycing alway before him,

31 And tooke my solace in the compasse of his earth: and my delite is with the children of men.

32 Therefore nowe hearken, O children, vnto me: for blessed are they that keepe my wayes.

33 Heare instruction, and be ye wise, and refuse it not: blessed is the man that heareth mee, watching dayly at my gates, and giuing attendance at the postes of my doores.

34 For he that findeth me, findeth life, and shall obteine fauour of the Lord.

35 But he that sinneth against me, hurteth his owne soule: and all that hate me, loue death.

Proverbs 9

1 Wisedome hath built her house, and hewen out her seuen pillars.

2 She hath killed her vitailes, drawen her wine, and prepared her table.

3 She hath sent forth her maydens and cryeth vpon the highest places of the citie, saying,

4 Who so is simple, let him come hither, and to him that is destitute of wisedome, she sayth,

5 Come, and eate of my meate, and drinke of the wine that I haue drawen.

6 Forsake your way, ye foolish, and ye shall liue: and walke in the way of vnderstanding.

7 He that reproueth a scorner, purchaseth to himselfe shame: and he that rebuketh the wicked, getteth himselfe a blot.

8 Rebuke not a scorner, least he hate thee: but rebuke a wise man, and he will loue thee.

9 Giue admonition to the wise, and he will be the wiser: teache a righteous man, and he will increase in learning.

10 The beginning of wisedome is the feare of the Lord, and the knowledge of holy things, is vnderstanding.

11 For thy dayes shalbe multiplied by me, and the yeeres of thy life shalbe augmented.

12 If thou be wise, thou shalt be wise for thy selfe, and if thou be a scorner, thou alone shalt suffer.

13 A foolish woman is troublesome: she is ignorant, and knoweth nothing.

14 But she sitteth at the doore of her house on a seate in the hie places of the citie,

15 To call them that passe by the way, that go right on their way, saying,

16 Who so is simple, let him come hither, and to him that is destitute of wisedome, shee sayth also,

17 Stollen waters are sweete, and hid bread is pleasant.

18 But he knoweth not, that ye dead are there, and that her ghestes are in the depth of hell.

Proverbs 10

1 THE PARABLE OF SALOMON. A wise sonne maketh a glad father: but a foolish sonne is an heauines to his mother.

2 The treasures of wickednesse profite nothing: but righteousnesse deliuereth from death.

3 The Lord will not famish the soule of the righteous: but he casteth away the substance of the wicked.

4 A slouthfull hand maketh poore: but the hand of the diligent maketh riche.

5 He that gathereth in sommer, is the sonne of wisdome: but he that sleepeth in haruest, is the sonne of confusion.

6 Blessings are vpon the head of the righteous: but iniquitie shall couer the mouth of the wicked.

7 The memoriall of the iust shalbe blessed: but the name of the wicked shall rotte.

8 The wise in heart will receiue commandements: but the foolish in talke shalbe beaten.

9 He that walketh vprightly, walketh boldely: but he that peruerteth his wayes, shalbe knowen.

10 He that winketh with the eye, worketh sorowe, and he yet is foolish in talke, shalbe beaten.

11 The mouth of a righteous man is a welspring of life: but iniquitie couereth the mouth of the wicked.

12 Hatred stirreth vp contentions: but loue couereth all trespasses.

13 In the lippes of him that hath vnderstanding wisdome is founde, and a rod shalbe for the backe of him that is destitute of wisedome.

14 Wise men lay vp knowledge: but ye mouth of the foole is a present destruction.

15 The riche mans goodes are his strong citie: but the feare of the needie is their pouertie.

16 The labour of the righteous tendeth to life: but the reuenues of the wicked to sinne.

17 He that regardeth instruction, is in the way of life: but he that refuseth correction, goeth out of the way.

18 He that dissembleth hatred with lying lips, and he that inuenteth slaunder, is a foole.

19 In many wordes there cannot want iniquitie: but he that refrayneth his lippes, is wise.

20 The tongue of the iust man is as fined siluer: but the heart of the wicked is litle worth.

21 The lippes of the righteous doe feede many: but fooles shall die for want of wisedome.

22 The blessing of the Lord, it maketh riche, and he doeth adde no sorowes with it.

23 It is as a pastime to a foole to doe wickedly: but wisedome is vnderstanding to a man.

24 That which the wicked feareth, shall come vpon him: but God wil graunt the desire of the righteous.

25 As the whirlewinde passeth, so is the wicked no more: but the righteous is as an euerlasting foundation.

26 As vineger is to the teeth, and as smoke to the eyes, so is the slouthful to them that send him.

27 The feare of the Lord increaseth the dayes: but the yeeres of the wicked shalbe diminished.

28 The patient abiding of the righteous shall be gladnesse: but the hope of the wicked shall perish.

29 The way of the Lord is strength to the vpright man: but feare shall be for the workers of iniquitie.

30 The righteous shall neuer be remooued: but the wicked shall not dwell in the land.

31 The mouth of the iust shall be fruitfull in wisdome: but the tongue of the froward shall be cut out.

32 The lips of the righteous knowe what is acceptable: but the mouth of the wicked speaketh froward things.

Proverbs 11

1 False balances are an abomination vnto the Lord: but a perfite weight pleaseth him.

2 When pride commeth, then commeth shame: but with the lowly is wisdome.

3 The vprightnes of the iust shall guide them: but the frowardnes of the transgressers shall destroy them.

4 Riches auaile not in the day of wrath: but righteousnes deliuereth from death.

5 The righteousnes of the vpright shall direct his way: but the wicked shall fall in his owne wickednes.

6 The righteousnesse of the iust shall deliuer them: but the transgressers shall be taken in their owne wickednes.

7 When a wicked man dieth, his hope perisheth, and the hope of the vniust shall perish.

8 The righteous escapeth out of trouble, and the wicked shall come in his steade.

9 An hypocrite with his mouth hurteth his neighbour: but the righteous shall be deliuered by knowledge.

10 In the prosperitie of the righteous the citie reioyceth, and when the wicked perish, there is ioye.

11 By the blessing of the righteous, the citie is exalted: but it is subuerted by the mouth of the wicked.

12 He that despiseth his neighbour, is destitute of wisedome: but a man of vnderstanding will keepe silence.

13 Hee that goeth about as a slanderer, discouereth a secret: but hee that is of a faithfull heart concealeth a matter.

14 Where no counsell is, the people fall: but where many counsellers are, there is health.

15 Hee shall be sore vexed, that is suretie for a stranger, and he that hateth suretiship, is sure.

16 A gracious woman atteineth honour, and the strong men atteine riches.

17 Hee that is mercifull, rewardeth his owne soule: but he that troubleth his own flesh, is cruel.

18 The wicked worketh a deceitfull worke: but hee that soweth righteousnes, shall receiue a sure rewarde.

19 As righteousnes leadeth to life: so hee that followeth euill, seeketh his owne death.

20 They that are of a froward heart, are abomination to the Lord: but they that are vpright in their way, are his delite.

21 Though hande ioyne in hande, the wicked shall not be vnpunished: but the seede of the righteous shall escape.

22 As a iewell of golde in a swines snoute: so is a faire woman, which lacketh discretion.

23 The desire of the righteous is onely good: but the hope of the wicked is indignation.

24 There is that scattereth, and is more increased: but hee that spareth more then is right, surely commeth to pouertie.

25 The liberall person shall haue plentie: and he that watereth, shall also haue raine.

26 He that withdraweth the corne, the people will curse him: but blessing shalbe vpon the head of him that selleth corne.

27 He that seeketh good things, getteth fauour: but he that seeketh euill, it shall come to him.

28 He that trusteth in his riches, shall fall: but the righteous shall florish as a leafe.

29 He that troubleth his owne house, shall inherite the winde, and the foole shalbe seruant to the wise in heart.

30 The fruite of the righteous is as a tree of life, and he that winneth soules, is wise.

31 Beholde, the righteous shalbe recompensed in the earth: howe much more the wicked and the sinner?

Proverbs 12

1 He that loueth instruction, loueth knowledge: but he that hateth correction, is a foole.

2 A good man getteth fauour of the Lord: but the man of wicked immaginations will hee condemne.

3 A man cannot be established by wickednesse: but the roote of the righteous shall not be mooued.

4 A vertuous woman is the crowne of her husband: but she that maketh him ashamed, is as corruption in his bones.

5 The thoughtes of the iust are right: but the counsels of the wicked are deceitfull.

6 The talking of the wicked is to lye in waite for blood: but the mouth of the righteous will deliuer them.

7 God ouerthroweth the wicked, and they are not: but the house of the righteous shall stand.

8 A man shall be commended for his wisedome: but the froward of heart shalbe despised.

9 He that is despised, and is his owne seruant, is better then he that boasteth himselfe and lacketh bread.

10 A righteous man regardeth the life of his beast: but the mercies of the wicked are cruell.

11 He that tilleth his lande, shalbe satisfied with bread: but he that followeth the idle, is destitute of vnderstanding.

12 The wicked desireth the net of euils: but the roote of the righteous giueth fruite.

13 The euill man is snared by the wickednesse of his lips, but the iust shall come out of aduersitie.

14 A man shalbe satiate with good things by the fruite of his mouth, and the recompence of a mans hands shall God giue vnto him.

15 The way of a foole is right in his owne eyes: but he that heareth counsell, is wise.

16 A foole in a day shall be knowen by his anger: but he that couereth shame, is wise.

17 He that speaketh trueth, will shewe righteousnes: but a false witnes vseth deceite.

18 There is that speaketh wordes like the prickings of a sworde: but the tongue of wise men is health.

19 The lip of trueth shall be stable for euer: but a lying tongue varieth incontinently.

20 Deceite is in the heart of them that imagine euill: but to the counsellers of peace shall be ioye.

21 There shall none iniquitie come to the iust: but the wicked are full of euill.

22 The lying lips are an abomination to the Lord: but they that deale truely are his delite.

23 A wise man concealeth knowledge: but the heart of the fooles publisheth foolishnes.

24 The hand of the diligent shall beare rule: but the idle shalbe vnder tribute.

25 Heauines in the heart of man doeth bring it downe: but a good worde reioyceth it.

26 The righteous is more excellent then his neighbour: but the way of the wicked will deceiue them.

27 The deceitfull man rosteth not, that hee tooke in hunting: but the riches of the diligent man are precious.

28 Life is in the way of righteousnesse, and in that path way there is no death.

Proverbs 13

1 A wise sonne will obey the instruction of his father: but a scorner will heare no rebuke.

2 A man shall eate good things by the fruite of his mouth: but the soule of the trespassers shall suffer violence.

3 Hee that keepeth his mouth, keepeth his life: but he that openeth his lips, destruction shall be to him.

4 The sluggard lusteth, but his soule hath nought: but the soule of the diligent shall haue plentie.

5 A righteous man hateth lying wordes: but the wicked causeth slander and shame.

6 Righteousnesse preserueth the vpright of life: but wickednes ouerthroweth the sinner.

7 There is that maketh himselfe riche, and hath nothing, and that maketh himselfe poore, hauing great riches.

8 A man will giue his riches for the ransome of his life: but the poore cannot heare ye reproch.

9 The light of the righteous reioyceth: but the candle of the wicked shall be put out.

10 Onely by pride doeth man make contention: but with the well aduised is wisdome.

11 The riches of vanitie shall diminish: but he that gathereth with the hand, shall increase them.

12 The hope that is deferred, is the fainting of the heart: but when the desire commeth, it is as a tree of life.

13 He that despiseth the worde, hee shall be destroyed: but hee that feareth the commandement he shalbe rewarded.

14 The instruction of a wise man is as the welspring of life, to turne away from the snares of death.

15 Good vnderstanding maketh acceptable: but the way of the disobedient is hated.

16 Euery wise man will worke by knowledge: but a foole will spread abroade folly.

17 A wicked messenger falleth into euill: but a faithfull ambassadour is preseruation.

18 Pouertie and shame is to him that refuseth instruction: but hee that regardeth correction, shalbe honoured.

19 A desire accomplished deliteth ye soule: but it is an abomination to fooles to depart from euil.

20 He that walketh with the wise, shalbe wise: but a companion of fooles shalbe afflicted.

21 Affliction followeth sinners: but vnto the righteous God will recompense good.

22 The good man shall giue inheritance vnto his childrens children: and the riches of the sinner is layde vp for the iust.

23 Much foode is in the fielde of the poore: but the fielde is destroyed without discretion.

24 He that spareth his rodde, hateth his sonne: but he that loueth him, chasteneth him betime.

25 The righteous eateth to the contentation of his minde: but the belly of the wicked shall want.

Proverbs 14

1 A wise woman buildeth her house: but the foolish destroyeth it with her owne handes.

2 He that walketh in his righteousnes, feareth the Lord: but he that is lewde in his wayes, despiseth him.

3 In the mouth of the foolish is the rod of pride: but the lippes of the wise preserue them.

4 Where none oxen are, there the cribbe is emptie: but much increase cometh by the strength of the oxe.

5 A faithfull witnes will not lye: but a false record will speake lyes.

6 A scorner seeketh wisdome, and findeth it not: but knowledge is easie to him that will vnderstande.

7 Depart from the foolish man, when thou perceiuest not in him the lippes of knowledge.

8 The wisdome of ye prudent is to vnderstand his way: but the foolishnes of the fooles is deceite.

9 The foole maketh a mocke of sinne: but among the righteous there is fauour.

10 The heart knoweth the bitternes of his soule, and the stranger shall not medle with his ioy.

11 The house of the wicked shalbe destroyed: but the tabernacle of the righteous shall florish.

12 There is a way that seemeth right to a man: but the issues thereof are the wayes of death.

13 Euen in laughing the heart is sorowful, and the ende of that mirth is heauinesse.

14 The heart that declineth, shall be saciate with his owne wayes: but a good man shall depart from him.

15 The foolish will beleeue euery thing: but the prudent will consider his steppes.

16 A wise man feareth, and departeth from euill: but a foole rageth, and is carelesse.

17 He that is hastie to anger, committeth follie, and a busie body is hated.

18 The foolish do inherite follie: but the prudent are crowned with knowledge.

19 The euill shall bowe before the good, and the wicked at the gates of the righteous.

20 The poore is hated euen of his own neighbour: but the friendes of the rich are many.

21 The sinner despiseth his neighbour: but he that hath mercie on the poore, is blessed.

22 Doe not they erre that imagine euill? but to them that thinke on good things, shalbe mercie and trueth.

23 In all labour there is abundance: but the talke of the lippes bringeth onely want.

24 The crowne of the wise is their riches, and the follie of fooles is foolishnes.

25 A faithfull witnes deliuereth soules: but a deceiuer speaketh lyes.

26 In the feare of the Lord is an assured strength, and his children shall haue hope.

27 The feare of the Lord is as a welspring of life, to auoyde the snares of death.

28 In the multitude of the people is the honour of a King, and for the want of people commeth the destruction of the Prince.

29 He that is slowe to wrath, is of great wisdome: but he that is of an hastie minde, exalteth follie.

30 A sounde heart is the life of the flesh: but enuie is the rotting of the bones.

31 He that oppresseth the poore, reprooueth him that made him: but hee

honoureth him, that hath mercie on the poore.

32 The wicked shall be cast away for his malice: but the righteous hath hope in his death.

33 Wisedome resteth in the heart of him that hath vnderstanding, and is knowen in the mids of fooles.

34 Iustice exalteth a nation, but sinne is a shame to the people.

35 The pleasure of a King is in a wise seruant: but his wrath shalbe toward him that is lewde.

Proverbs 15

1 A soft answere putteth away wrath: but grieuous wordes stirre vp anger.

2 The tongue of the wise vseth knowledge aright: but the mouth of fooles babbleth out foolishnesse.

3 The eyes of the Lord in euery place beholde the euill and the good.

4 A wholesome tongue is as a tree of life: but the frowardnes therof is the breaking of ye minde.

5 A foole despiseth his fathers instruction: but he that regardeth correction, is prudent.

6 The house of the righteous hath much treasure: but in the reuenues of the wicked is trouble.

7 The lippes of the wise doe spread abroade knowledge: but ye heart of the foolish doth not so.

8 The sacrifice of the wicked is abomination to the Lord: but the prayer of the righteous is acceptable vnto him.

9 The way of the wicked is an abomination vnto the Lord: but he loueth him that followeth righteousnes.

10 Instruction is euill to him that forsaketh the way, and he that hateth correction, shall die.

11 Hell and destruction are before the Lord: how much more the hearts of the sonnes of men?

12 A scorner loueth not him that rebuketh him, neither will he goe vnto the wise.

13 A ioyfull heart maketh a chearefull countenance: but by the sorow of the heart the minde is heauie.

14 The heart of him that hath vnderstanding, seeketh knowledge: but the mouth of the foole is fedde with foolishnes.

15 All the dayes of the afflicted are euill: but a good conscience is a continuall feast.

16 Better is a litle with the feare of the Lord, then great treasure, and trouble therewith.

17 Better is a dinner of greene herbes where loue is, then a stalled oxe and hatred therewith.

18 An angrie man stirreth vp strife: but hee that is slowe to wrath, appeaseth strife.

19 The way of a slouthfull man is as an hedge of thornes: but the way of the righteous is plaine.

20 A wise sonne reioyceth the father: but a foolish man despiseth his mother.

21 Foolishnes is ioy to him that is destitute of vnderstanding: but a man of vnderstanding walketh vprightly.

22 Without cousel thoughts come to nought: but in the multitude of counsellers there is stedfastnesse.

23 A ioy commeth to a man by the answere of his mouth: and how good is a word in due season?

24 The way of life is on high to the prudent, to auoyde from hell beneath.

25 The Lord will destroye the house of the proude men: but hee will stablish the borders of the widowe.

26 The thoughts of ye wicked are abomination to the Lord: but the pure haue pleasant wordes.

27 He that is greedie of gaine, troubleth his owne house: but he that hateth giftes, shall liue.

28 The heart of the righteous studieth to answere: but the wicked mans mouth babbleth euil thinges.

29 The Lord is farre off from the wicked: but he heareth the prayer of the righteous.

30 The light of the eyes reioyceth the heart, and a good name maketh the bones fat.

31 The eare that hearkeneth to the correction of life, shall lodge among the wise.

32 Hee that refuseth instruction, despiseth his owne soule: but he that obeyeth correction, getteth vnderstanding.

33 The feare of the Lord is the instruction of wisdome: and before honour, goeth humilitie.

Proverbs 16

1 The preparations of the heart are in man: but the answere of the tongue is of the Lord.

2 All the wayes of a man are cleane in his owne eyes: but the Lord pondereth the spirits.

3 Commit thy workes vnto the Lord, and thy thoughts shalbe directed.

4 The Lord hath made all things for his owne sake: yea, euen the wicked for the day of euill.

5 All that are proude in heart, are an abomination to the Lord: though hand ioyne in hand, he shall not be vnpunished.

6 By mercy and trueth iniquitie shalbe forgiuen, and by the feare of the Lord they depart from euill.

7 When the wayes of a man please the Lord, he will make also his enemies at peace with him.

8 Better is a litle with righteousnesse, then great reuenues without equitie.

9 The heart of man purposeth his way: but the Lord doeth direct his steppes.

10 A diuine sentence shalbe in the lips of the King: his mouth shall not transgresse in iudgement.

11 A true weight and balance are of the Lord: all the weightes of the bagge are his worke.

12 It is an abomination to Kings to commit wickednes: for the throne is stablished by iustice.

13 Righteous lips are the delite of Kings, and the King loueth him that speaketh right things.

14 The wrath of a King is as messengers of death: but a wise man will pacifie it.

15 In the light of the Kings coutenance is life: and his fauour is as a cloude of the latter raine.

16 Howe much better is it to get wisedome then golde? and to get vnderstanding, is more to be desired then siluer.

17 The pathe of the righteous is to decline from euil, and hee keepeth his soule, that keepeth his way.

18 Pride goeth before destruction, and an high minde before the fall.

19 Better it is to be of humble minde with the lowly, then to deuide the spoyles with the proude.

20 He that is wise in his busines, shall finde good: and he that trusteth in the Lord, he is blessed.

21 The wise in heart shall bee called prudent: and the sweetenesse of the lippes shall increase doctrine.

22 Vnderstading is welspring of life vnto them that haue it: and the instruction of fooles is folly.

23 The heart of the wise guideth his mouth wisely, and addeth doctrine to his lippes.

24 Faire wordes are as an hony combe, sweetenesse to the soule, and health to the bones.

25 There is a way that seemeth right vnto man: but the issue thereof are the wayes of death.

26 The person that traueileth, traueileth for himselfe: for his mouth craueth it of him.

27 A wicked man diggeth vp euill, and in his lippes is like burning fire.

28 A frowarde person soweth strife: and a tale teller maketh diuision among princes.

29 A wicked man deceiueth his neighbour, and leadeth him into the way that is not good.

30 He shutteth his eyes to deuise wickednes: he moueth his lippes, and bringeth euil to passe.

31 Age is a crowne of glory, when it is founde in the way of righteousnes.

32 He that is slowe vnto anger, is better then the mightie man: and hee that ruleth his owne minde, is better then he that winneth a citie.

33 The lot is cast into the lap: but the whole disposition thereof is of the Lord.

Proverbs 17

1 Better is a dry morsell, if peace be with it, then an house full of sacrifices with strife.

2 A discrete seruant shall haue rule ouer a lewde sonne, and hee shall deuide the heritage among the brethren.

3 As is the fining pot for siluer, and the fornace for golde, so the Lord trieth the heartes.

4 The wicked giueth heed to false lippes, and a lyer hearkeneth to the naughtie tongue.

5 Hee that mocketh the poore, reprocheth him, that made him: and he that reioyceth at destruction, shall not be vnpunished.

6 Childres children are the crowne of the elders: and the glory of ye children are their fathers.

7 Hie talke becommeth not a foole, much lesse a lying talke a prince.

8 A rewarde is as a stone pleasant in the eyes of them that haue it: it prospereth, whithersoeuer it turneth.

9 Hee that couereth a transgression, seeketh loue: but hee that repeateth a matter, separateth the prince.

10 A reproofe entereth more into him that hath vnderstanding, then an hundreth stripes into a foole.

11 A sedicious person seeketh onely euill, and a cruel messenger shall be sent against him.

12 It is better for a man to meete a beare robbed of her whelpes, then a foole in his follie.

13 He that rewardeth euil for good, euil shall not depart from his house.

14 The beginning of strife is as one that openeth the waters: therefore or the contention be medled with, leaue off.

15 He that iustifieth the wicked, and he that condemneth the iust, euen they both are abomination to the Lord.

16 Wherefore is there a price in the hand of the foole to get wisdome, and he hath none heart?

17 A friende loueth at all times: and a brother is borne for aduersitie.

18 A man destitute of vnderstanding, toucheth the hande, and becommeth suretie for his neighbour.

19 He loueth transgression, that loueth strife: and he that exalteth his gate, seeketh destruction.

20 The froward heart findeth no good: and he that hath a naughtie tongue, shall fall into euill.

21 He that begetteth a foole, getteth himselfe sorow, and the father of a foole can haue no ioy.

22 A ioyfull heart causeth good health: but a sorowfull minde dryeth the bones.

23 A wicked man taketh a gift out of the bosome to wrest the wayes of iudgement.

24 Wisdome is in the face of him that hath vnderstanding: but the eyes of a foole are in the corners of the world.

25 A foolish sonne is a griefe vnto his father, and a heauines to her that bare him.

26 Surely it is not good to condemne the iust, nor that ye princes should smite such for equitie.

27 Hee that hath knowledge, spareth his wordes, and a man of vnderstanding is of an excellent spirit.

28 Euen a foole (when he holdeth his peace) is counted wise, and hee that stoppeth his lips, prudent.

Proverbs 18

1 For the desire thereof hee will separate himselfe to seeke it, and occupie himselfe in all wisdome.

2 A foole hath no delite in vnderstanding: but that his heart may be discouered.

3 When the wicked commeth, then commeth contempt, and with the vile man reproch.

4 The words of a mans mouth are like deepe waters, and the welspring of wisdome is like a flowing riuer.

5 It is not good to accept the person of the wicked, to cause ye righteous to fall in iudgement.

6 A fooles lips come with strife, and his mouth calleth for stripes.

7 A fooles mouth is his owne destruction, and his lips are a snare for his soule.

8 The wordes of a tale bearer are as flatterings, and they goe downe into the bowels of the belly.

9 He also that is slouthfull in his worke, is euen the brother of him that is a great waster.

10 The Name of the Lord is a strong tower: the righteous runneth vnto it, and is exalted.

11 The rich mans riches are his strong citie: and as an hie wall in his imagination.

12 Before destruction the heart of a man is hautie, and before glory goeth lowlines.

13 He that answereth a matter before hee heare it, it is folly and shame vnto him.

14 The spirit of a man will susteine his infirmitie: but a wounded spirit who can beare it?

15 A wise heart getteth knowledge, and the eare of the wise seeketh learning.

16 A mans gift enlargeth him, and leadeth him before great men.

17 He that is first in his owne cause, is iust: then commeth his neighbour, and maketh inquirie of him.

18 The lot causeth contentions to cease, and maketh a partition among the mightie.

19 A brother offended is harder to winne then a strong citie, and their contentions are like the barre of a palace.

20 With the fruite of a mans mouth shall his belly be satisfied, and with the increase of his lips shall he be filled.

21 Death and life are in the power of ye tongue, and they that loue it, shall eate the fruite thereof.

22 He that findeth a wife, findeth a good thing, and receiueth fauour of the Lord.

23 The poore speaketh with prayers: but the rich answereth roughly.

24 A man that hath friends, ought to shew him selfe friendly: for a friend is neerer then a brother.

Proverbs 19

1 Better is the poore that walketh in his vprightnes, then he that abuseth his lips, and is a foole.

2 For without knowledge the minde is not good, and he that hasteth with his feete, sinneth.

3 The foolishnesse of a man peruerteth his way, and his heart freateth against the Lord.

4 Riches gather many friends: but the poore is separated from his neighbour.

5 A false witnes shall not be vnpunished: and he that speaketh lyes, shall not escape.

6 Many reuerence the face of the prince, and euery man is friend to him that giueth giftes.

7 All the brethren of the poore doe hate him: howe much more will his friends depart farre from him? though hee be instant with wordes, yet they will not.

8 He that possesseth vnderstanding, loueth his owne soule, and keepeth wisdome to finde goodnesse.

9 A false witnes shall not be vnpunished: and he that speaketh lyes, shall perish.

10 Pleasure is not comely for a foole, much lesse for a seruant to haue rule ouer princes.

11 The discretion of man deferreth his anger: and his glory is to passe by an offence.

12 The Kings wrath is like the roaring of a lyon: but his fauour is like the dewe vpon ye grasse.

13 A foolish sonne is the calamitie of his father, and the contentions of a wife are like a continuall dropping.

14 House and riches are the inheritance of the fathers: but a prudent wife commeth of the Lord.

15 Slouthfulnes causeth to fall asleepe, and a deceitfull person shall be affamished.

16 He that keepeth the commandement, keepeth his owne soule: but hee that despiseth his wayes, shall dye.

17 He that hath mercy vpon the poore, lendeth vnto the Lord: and the Lord will recompense him that which he hath giuen.

18 Chasten thy sonne while there is hope, and let not thy soule spare for his murmuring.

19 A man of much anger shall suffer punishment: and though thou deliuer him, yet wil his anger come againe.

20 Heare counsell and receiue instruction, that thou mayest be wise in thy latter ende.

21 Many deuises are in a mans heart: but the counsell of the Lord shall stand.

22 That that is to be desired of a man, is his goodnes, and a poore man is better then a lyer.

23 The feare of the Lord leadeth to life: and he that is filled therewith, shall continue, and shall not be visited with euill.

24 The slouthfull hideth his hand in his bosome, and wil not put it to his mouth againe.

25 Smite a scorner, and the foolish wil beware: and reproue the prudent, and he wil vnderstand knowledge.

26 He that destroyeth his father, or chaseth away his mother, is a lewde and shamefull childe.

27 My sonne, heare no more the instruction, that causeth to erre from ye words of knowledge.

28 A wicked witnes mocketh at iudgement, and the mouth of ye wicked swalloweth vp iniquitie.

29 But iudgements are prepared for the scorners, and stripes for the backe of the fooles.

Proverbs 20

1 Wine is a mocker and strong drinke is raging: and whosoeuer is deceiued thereby, is not wise.

2 The feare of the King is like the roaring of a lyon: hee that prouoketh him vnto anger, sinneth against his owne soule.

3 It is a mans honour to cease from strife: but euery foole will be medling.

4 The slouthfull will not plowe, because of winter: therefore shall he beg in sommer, but haue nothing.

5 The counsell in the heart of man is like deepe waters: but a man that hath vnderstanding, will drawe it out.

6 Many men wil boast, euery one of his owne goodnes: but who can finde a faithfull man?

7 He that walketh in his integritie, is iust: and blessed shall his children be after him.

8 A King that sitteth in the throne of iudgement, chaseth away all euill with his eyes.

9 Who can say, I haue made mine heart cleane, I am cleane from my sinne?

10 Diuers weightes, and diuers measures, both these are euen abomination vnto the Lord.

11 A childe also is knowen by his doings, whether his worke be pure and right.

12 The Lord hath made both these, euen the eare to heare, and the eye to see.

13 Loue not sleepe least thou come vnto pouertie: open thine eyes, and thou shalt be satisfied with bread.

14 It is naught, it is naught, sayth the buyer: but when he is gone apart, he boasteth.

15 There is golde, and a multitude of precious stones: but the lips of knowledge are a precious iewel.

16 Take his garment, that is suretie for a stranger, and a pledge of him for the stranger.

17 The bread of deceit is sweete to a man: but afterward his mouth shalbe filled with grauel.

18 Establish the thoughtes by counsell: and by counsell make warre.

19 He that goeth about as a slanderer, discouereth secrets: therefore meddle not with him that flattereth with his lips.

20 He that curseth his father or his mother, his light shalbe put out in obscure darkenes.

21 An heritage is hastely gotten at the beginning, but the end thereof shall not be blessed.

22 Say not thou, I wil recompense euill: but waite vpon the Lord, and he shall saue thee.

23 Diuers weightes are an abomination vnto the Lord, and deceitful balances are not good.

24 The steps of man are ruled by the Lord: how can a man then vnderstand his owne way?

25 It is a destruction for a man to deuoure that which is sanctified, and after the vowes to inquire.

26 A wise King scattereth the wicked, and causeth the wheele to turne ouer them.

27 The light of the Lord is the breath of man, and searcheth all the bowels of the belly.

28 Mercie and trueth preserue the King: for his throne shall be established with mercie.

29 The beautie of yong men is their strength, and the glory of the aged is the gray head.

30 The blewnes of the wound serueth to purge the euill, and the stripes within the bowels of the belly.

Proverbs 21

1 The Kings heart is in the hand of the Lord, as the riuers of waters: he turneth it whithersoeuer it pleaseth him.

2 Euery way of a man is right in his owne eyes: but the Lord pondereth the hearts.

3 To doe iustice and iudgement is more acceptable to the Lord then sacrifice.

4 A hautie looke, and a proude heart, which is the light of the wicked, is sinne.

5 The thoughtes of the diligent doe surely bring abundance: but whosoeuer is hastie, commeth surely to pouertie.

6 The gathering of treasures by a deceitfull tongue is vanitie tossed to and from of them that seeke death.

7 The robberie of the wicked shall destroy them: for they haue refused to execute iudgement.

8 The way of some is peruerted and strange: but of the pure man, his worke is right.

9 It is better to dwell in a corner of the house top, then with a contentious woman in a wide house.

10 The soule of the wicked wisheth euill: and his neighbour hath no fauour in his eyes.

11 When the scorner is punished, the foolish is wise: and when one instructeth the wise, he wil receiue knowledge.

12 The righteous teacheth the house of the wicked: but God ouerthroweth the wicked for their euill.

13 He that stoppeth his eare at the crying of the poore, he shall also cry and not be heard.

14 A gift in secret pacifieth anger, and a gift in the bosome great wrath.

15 It is ioye to the iust to doe iudgement: but destruction shalbe to the workers of iniquitie.

16 A man that wandreth out of the way of wisdome, shall remaine in the congregation of the dead.

17 Hee that loueth pastime, shalbe a poore man: and he that loueth wine and oyle, shall not be riche.

18 The wicked shalbe a ransome for the iust, and the transgressour for the righteous.

19 It is better to dwell in the wildernesse, then with a contentious and angry woman.

20 In the house of the wise is a pleasant treasure and oyle: but a foolish man deuoureth it.

21 He that followeth after righteousnes and mercy, shall finde life, righteousnes, and glory.

22 A wise man goeth vp into the citie of the mightie, and casteth downe the strength of the confidence thereof.

23 He that keepeth his mouth and his tongue, keepeth his soule from afflictions.

24 Proude, hautie and scornefull is his name that worketh in his arrogancie wrath.

25 The desire of the slouthfull slayeth him: for his hands refuse to worke.

26 He coueteth euermore greedily, but the righteous giueth and spareth not.

27 The sacrifice of the wicked is an abomination: how much more when he bringeth it with a wicked minde?

28 A false witnes shall perish: but hee that heareth, speaketh continually.

29 A wicked man hardeneth his face: but the iust, he will direct his way.

30 There is no wisedome, neither vnderstanding, nor counsell against the Lord.

31 The horse is prepared against the day of battell: but saluation is of the Lord.

Proverbs 22

1 A good name is to be chosen aboue great riches, and louing fauour is aboue siluer and aboue golde.

2 The rich and poore meete together: the Lord is the maker of them all.

3 A prudent man seeth the plague, and hideth himselfe: but the foolish goe on still, and are punished.

4 The rewarde of humilitie, and the feare of God is riches, and glory, and life.

5 Thornes and snares are in the way of the frowarde: but he that regardeth his soule, will depart farre from them.

6 Teache a childe in the trade of his way, and when he is olde, he shall not depart from it.

7 The rich ruleth the poore, and the borower is seruant to the man that lendeth.

8 He that soweth iniquitie, shall reape affliction, and the rodde of his anger shall faile.

9 He that hath a good eye, he shalbe blessed: for he giueth of his bread vnto the poore.

10 Cast out the scorner, and strife shall go out: so contention and reproche shall cease.

11 Hee that loueth purenesse of heart for the grace of his lippes, the King shalbe his friend.

12 The eyes of the Lord preserue knowledge: but hee ouerthroweth the wordes of the transgressour.

13 The slouthfull man saith, A lyon is without, I shall be slaine in the streete.

14 The mouth of strage women is as a deepe pit: he with whom the Lord is angry, shall fall therein.

15 Foolishnesse is bounde in the heart of a childe: but the rodde of correction shall driue it away from him.

16 Hee that oppresseth the poore to increase him selfe, and giueth vnto the riche, shall surely come to pouertie.

17 Incline thine eare, and heare the wordes of the wise, and apply thine heart vnto my knowledge.

18 For it shalbe pleasant, if thou keepe them in thy bellie, and if they be directed together in thy lippes.

19 That thy confidence may be in the Lord, I haue shewed thee this day: thou therefore take heede.

20 Haue not I written vnto thee three times in counsels and knowledge,

21 That I might shewe thee the assurance of the wordes of trueth to answere the wordes of trueth to them that sende to thee?

22 Robbe not the poore, because hee is poore, neither oppresse the afflicted in iudgement.

23 For the Lord will defende their cause, and spoyle the soule of those that spoyle them.

24 Make no friendship with an angrie man, neither goe with the furious man,

25 Least thou learne his wayes, and receiue destruction to thy soule.

26 Be not thou of them that touch the hand, nor among them that are suretie for debts.

27 If thou hast nothing to paye, why causest thou that he should take thy bed from vnder thee?

28 Thou shalt not remooue the ancient bounds which thy fathers haue made.

29 Thou seest that a diligent man in his businesse standeth before Kings, and standeth not before the base sort.

Proverbs 23

1 When thou sittest to eate with a ruler, consider diligently what is before thee,

2 And put the knife to thy throte, if thou be a man giuen to the appetite.

3 Be not desirous of his deintie meates: for it is a deceiuable meate.

4 Trauaile not too much to be rich: but cease from thy wisdome.

5 Wilt thou cast thine eyes vpon it, which is nothing? for riches taketh her to her wings, as an eagle, and flyeth into the heauen.

6 Eate thou not the bread of him that hath an euil eye, neither desire his deintie meates.

7 For as though he thought it in his heart, so will hee say vnto thee, Eate and drinke: but his heart is not with thee.

8 Thou shalt vomit thy morsels that thou hast eaten, and thou shalt lose thy sweete wordes.

9 Speake not in the eares of a foole: for hee will despise the wisdome of thy wordes.

10 Remooue not the ancient boundes, and enter not into the fieldes of the fatherlesse.

11 For he that redeemeth them, is mightie: he will defend their cause against thee.

12 Apply thine heart to instruction, and thine eares to the wordes of knowledge.

13 Withhold not correction from the childe: if thou smite him with the rodde, he shall not die.

14 Thou shalt smite him with the rodde, and shalt deliuer his soule from hell.

15 My sonne, if thine heart be wise, mine heart shall reioyce, and I also.

16 And my reynes shall reioyce, when thy lips speake righteous things.

17 Let not thine heart bee enuious against sinners: but let it bee in the feare of the Lord continually.

18 For surely there is an ende, and thy hope shall not be cut off.

19 O thou my sonne, heare, and bee wise, and guide thine heart in the way.

20 Keepe not company with drunkards, nor with gluttons.

21 For the drunkard and the glutton shall bee poore, and the sleeper shalbe clothed with ragges.

22 Obey thy father that hath begotten thee, and despise not thy mother when she is olde.

23 Bye the trueth, but sell it not: likewise wisdome, and instruction, and vnderstanding.

24 The father of the righteous shall greatly reioyce, and hee that begetteth a wise childe, shall haue ioy of him.

25 Thy father and thy mother shall be glad, and she that bare thee shall reioyce.

26 My sonne, giue mee thine heart, and let thine eyes delite in my wayes.

27 For a whore is as a deepe ditche, and a strange woman is as a narrowe pitte.

28 Also she lyeth in wait as for a praye, and she increaseth the transgressers among men.

29 To whome is woe? to whome is sorowe? to whom is strife? to whom is murmuring? to whom are woundes without cause? and to whome is the rednesse of the eyes?

30 Euen to them that tarie long at the wine, to them that goe, and seeke mixt wine.

31 Looke not thou vpon the wine, when it is red, and when it sheweth his colour in the cup, or goeth downe pleasantly.

32 In the ende thereof it will bite like a serpent, and hurt like a cockatrise.

33 Thine eyes shall looke vpon strange women, and thine heart shall speake lewde things.

34 And thou shalt bee as one that sleepeth in the middes of the sea, and as hee that sleepeth in the toppe of the maste.

35 They haue stricken mee, shalt thou say, but I was not sicke: they haue beaten mee, but I knew not, when I awoke: therefore will I seeke it yet still.

Proverbs 24

1 Be not thou enuious against euill men, neither desire to be with them.

2 For their heart imagineth destruction, and their lippes speake mischiefe.

3 Through wisdome is an house builded, and with vnderstanding it is established.

4 And by knowledge shall the chambers bee filled with all precious, and pleasant riches.

5 A wise man is strong: for a man of vnderstanding encreaseth his strength.

6 For with counsel thou shalt enterprise thy warre, and in the multitude of them that can giue counsell, is health.

7 Wisdome is hie to a foole: therefore he can not open his mouth in the gate.

8 Hee that imagineth to doe euill, men shall call him an autour of wickednes.

9 The wicked thought of a foole is sinne, and the scorner is an abomination vnto men.

10 If thou bee faint in the day of aduersitie, thy strength is small.

11 Deliuer them that are drawen to death: wilt thou not preserue them that are led to be slaine?

12 If thou say, Beholde, we knew not of it: he that pondereth the heartes, doeth not hee vnderstand it? and hee that keepeth thy soule, knoweth he it not? will not he also recompense euery man according to his workes?

13 My sonne, eate hony, for it is good, and the hony combe, for it is sweete vnto thy mouth.

14 So shall the knowledge of wisdome be vnto thy soule, if thou finde it, and there shall be an ende, and thine hope shall not be cut off.

15 Laye no waite, O wicked man, against the house of the righteous, and spoyle not his resting place.

16 For a iust man falleth seuen times, and riseth againe: but the wicked fall into mischiefe.

17 Bee thou not glad when thine enemie falleth, and let not thine heart reioyce when hee stumbleth,

18 Least the Lord see it, and it displease him, and he turne his wrath from him.

19 Fret not thy selfe because of the malicious, neither be enuious at the wicked.

20 For there shall bee none ende of plagues to the euill man: the light of the wicked shall bee put out.

21 My sonne feare the Lord, and the King, and meddle not with them that are sedicious.

22 For their destruction shall rise suddenly, and who knoweth the ruine of them both?

23 ALSO THESE THINGS PERTEINE TO THE WISE, It is not good to haue respect of any person in iudgement.

24 He that saith to the wicked, Thou art righteous, him shall the people curse, and the multitude shall abhorre him.

25 But to them that rebuke him, shall be pleasure, and vpon them shall come the blessing of goodnesse.

26 They shall kisse the lippes of him that answereth vpright wordes.

27 Prepare thy worke without, and make readie thy thinges in the fielde, and after, builde thine house.

28 Be not a witnes against thy neighbour without cause: for wilt thou deceiue with thy lippes?

29 Say not, I wil doe to him, as he hath done to mee, I will recompence euery man according to his worke.

30 I passed by the fielde of the slouthfull, and by the vineyarde of the man destitute of vnderstanding.

31 And lo, it was al growen ouer with thornes, and nettles had couered the face thereof, and the stone wall thereof was broken downe.

32 Then I behelde, and I considered it well: I looked vpon it, and receiued instruction.

33 Yet a litle sleepe, a litle slumber, a litle folding of the handes to sleepe.

34 So thy pouertie commeth as one that traueileth by the way, and thy necessitie like an armed man.

Proverbs 25

1 THESE ARE ALSO PARABLES of Salomon, which the men of Hezekiah King of Iudah copied out.

2 The glorie of God is to conceale a thing secret: but the Kings honour is to search out a thing.

3 The heaues in height, and the earth in deepenes, and the Kings heart can no man search out.

4 Take the drosse from the siluer, and there shall proceede a vessell for the finer.

5 Take away the wicked from the King, and his throne shall be stablished in righteousnes.

6 Boast not thy selfe before the King, and stand not in the place of great men.

7 For it is better, that it be saide vnto thee, Come vp hither, then thou to be put lower in the presece of the prince whom thine eyes haue seene.

8 Goe not foorth hastily to strife, least thou know not what to doe in the ende thereof, when thy neighbour hath put thee to shame.

9 Debate thy matter with thy neighbour, and discouer not the secret to another,

10 Least he that heareth it put thee to shame, and thine infamie doe not cease.

11 A word spoken in his place, is like apples of golde with pictures of siluer.

12 He that reprooueth the wise, and the obedient eare, is as a golden earering and an ornament of fine golde.

13 As the colde of the snowe in the time of haruest, so is a faithfull messenger to them that send him: for he refresheth the soule of his masters.

14 A man that boasteth of false liberalitie, is like cloudes and winde without raine.

15 A Prince is pacified by staying of anger, and a soft tongue breaketh the bones.

16 If thou haue found hony, eate that is sufficient for thee, least thou be ouerfull, and vomit it.

17 Withdrawe thy foote from thy neighbours house, least he be weary of thee, and hate thee.

18 A man that beareth false witnes against his neighbour, is like an hammer and a sword, and a sharpe arrowe.

19 Confidence in an vnfaythfull man in time of trouble, is like a broken tooth and a sliding foote.

20 Hee that taketh away the garment in the colde season, is like vineger powred vpon nitre, or like him that singeth songs to an heauy heart.

21 If hee that hateth thee be hungry, giue him bread to eate, and if he be thirstie, giue him water to drinke.

22 For thou shalt lay coles vpon his head, and the Lord shall recompense thee.

23 As the Northwinde driueth away the raine, so doeth an angry countenance the slandering tongue.

24 It is better to dwell in a corner of the house top, then with a contentious woman in a wide house.

25 As are the colde waters to a weary soule, so is good newes from a farre countery.

26 A righteous man falling downe before the wicked, is like a troubled well, and a corrupt spring.

27 It is not good to eate much hony: so to search their owne glory is not glory.

28 A man that refraineth not his appetite, is like a citie which is broken downe and without walles.

Proverbs 26

1 As the snowe in the sommer, and as the raine in the haruest are not meete, so is honour vnseemely for a foole.

2 As the sparowe by flying, and the swallow by flying escape, so the curse that is causeles, shall not come.

3 Vnto the horse belongeth a whip, to the asse a bridle, and a rod to the fooles backe.

4 Answer not a foole according to his foolishnes, least thou also be like him.

5 Answere a foole according to his foolishnes, least he be wise in his owne conceite.

6 He that sendeth a message by the hand of a foole, is as he that cutteth off the feete, and drinketh iniquitie.

7 As they that lift vp the legs of the lame, so is a parable in a fooles mouth.

8 As the closing vp of a precious stone in an heape of stones, so is he that giueth glory to a foole.

9 As a thorne standing vp in the hand of a drunkard, so is a parable in the mouth of fooles.

10 The excellent that formed all things, both rewardeth the foole and rewardeth the transgressers.

11 As a dog turneth againe to his owne vomit, so a foole turneth to his foolishnes.

12 Seest thou a man wise in his owne conceite? more hope is of a foole then of him.

13 The slouthfull man sayth, A lyon is in the way: a lyon is in the streetes.

14 As the doore turneth vpon his hinges, so doeth the slouthfull man vpon his bed.

15 The slouthfull hideth his hand in his bosome, and it grieueth him to put it againe to his mouth.

16 The sluggard is wiser in his owne conceite, then seuen men that can render a reason.

17 He that passeth by and medleth with the strife that belongeth not vnto him, is as one that taketh a dog by the eares.

18 As he that faineth himselfe mad, casteth fire brands, arrowes, and mortall things,

19 So dealeth the deceitfull man with his friend and sayth, Am not I in sport?

20 Without wood the fire is quenched, and without a talebearer strife ceaseth.

21 As ye cole maketh burning coles, and wood a fire, so the contentious man is apt to kindle strife.

22 The wordes of a tale bearer are as flatterings, and they goe downe into the bowels of the belly.

23 As siluer drosse ouerlayde vpon a potsheard, so are burning lips, and an euill heart.

24 He that hateth, will counterfaite with his lips, but in his heart he layeth vp deceite.

25 Though he speake fauourably, beleeue him not: for there are seuen abominations in his heart.

26 Hatred may be couered by deceite: but the malice thereof shall be discouered in the congregation.

27 He that diggeth a pit shall fall therein, and he that rolleth a stone, it shall returne vnto him.

28 A false tongue hateth the afflicted, and a flattering mouth causeth ruine.

Proverbs 27

1 Boast not thy selfe of to morowe: for thou knowest not what a day may bring forth.

2 Let another man prayse thee, and not thine owne mouth: a stranger, and not thine owne lips.

3 A stone is heauie, and the sand weightie: but a fooles wrath is heauier then them both.

4 Anger is cruell, and wrath is raging: but who can stand before enuie?

5 Open rebuke is better then secret loue.

6 The wounds of a louer are faithfull, and the kisses of an enemie are pleasant.

7 The person that is full, despiseth an hony combe: but vnto the hungry soule euery bitter thing is sweete.

8 As a bird that wandreth from her nest, so is a man that wandreth from his owne place.

9 As oyntment and perfume reioyce the heart, so doeth the sweetenes of a mans friend by hearty counsell.

10 Thine owne friend and thy fathers friend forsake thou not: neither enter into thy brothers house in the day of thy calamitie: for better is a neighbour that is neere, then a brother farre off.

11 My sonne, be wise, and reioyce mine heart, that I may answere him that reprocheth me.

12 A prudent man seeth the plague, and hideth himselfe: but the foolish goe on still, and are punished.

13 Take his garment that is surety for a stranger, and a pledge of him for the stranger.

14 He that prayseth his friend with a loude voyce, rising earely in the morning, it shall be counted to him as a curse.

15 A continual dropping in the day of raine, and a contentious woman are alike.

16 He that hideth her, hideth the winde, and she is as ye oyle in his right hand, that vttereth it selfe.

17 Yron sharpeneth yron, so doeth man sharpen the face of his friend.

18 He that keepeth the fig tree, shall eate the fruite thereof: so he that waiteth vpon his master, shall come to honour.

19 As in water face answereth to face, so the heart of man to man.

20 The graue and destruction can neuer be full, so the eyes of man can neuer be satisfied.

21 As is the fining pot for siluer and the fornace for golde, so is euery man according to his dignitie.

22 Though thou shouldest bray a foole in a morter among wheate brayed with a pestell, yet will not his foolishnes depart from him.

23 Be diligent to know ye state of thy flocke, and take heede to the heardes.

24 For riches remaine not alway, nor the crowne from generation to generation.

25 The hey discouereth it selfe, and the grasse appeareth, and the herbes of the mountaines are gathered.

26 The lambes are for thy clothing, and the goates are the price of the fielde.

27 And let the milke of the goates be sufficient for thy foode, for the foode of thy familie, and for the sustenance of thy maydes.

Proverbs 28

1 The wicked flee when none pursueth: but the righteous are bolde as a lyon.

2 For the transgression of the land there are many princes thereof: but by a man of vnderstanding and knowledge a realme likewise endureth long.

3 A poore man, if he oppresse the poore, is like a raging raine, that leaueth no foode.

4 They that forsake the Law, prayse the wicked: but they that keepe the Law, set themselues against them.

5 Wicked men vnderstand not iudgemnt: but they that seeke the Lord vnderstand all things.

6 Better is the poore that walketh in his vprightnesse, then hee that peruerteth his wayes, though he be riche.

7 He that keepeth the Law, is a childe of vnderstanding: but hee that feedeth the gluttons, shameth his father.

8 He that increaseth his riches by vsurie and interest, gathereth them for him that will be mercifull vnto the poore.

9 He that turneth away his eare from hearing the Law, euen his prayer shalbe abominable.

10 He that causeth the righteous to go astray by an euill way, shall fall into his owne pit, and the vpright shall inherite good things.

11 The riche man is wise in his owne conceite: but the poore that hath vnderstanding, can trie him.

12 When righteous men reioyce, there is great glory: but when the wicked come vp, the man is tried.

13 He that hideth his sinnes, shall not prosper: but he that confesseth, and forsaketh them, shall haue mercy.

14 Blessed is the man that feareth alway: but he that hardeneth his heart, shall fall into euill.

15 As a roaring lyon, and an hungry beare, so is a wicked ruler ouer the poore people.

16 A prince destitute of vnderstanding, is also a great oppressour: but hee that hateth couetousnes, shall prolong his dayes.

17 A man that doeth violence against the blood of a person, shall flee vnto the graue, and they shall not stay him.

18 He that walketh vprightly, shalbe saued: but he that is froward in his wayes, shall once fall.

19 He that tilleth his land, shall be satisfied with bread: but he that followeth the idle, shall be filled with pouertie.

20 A faythfull man shall abound in blessings, and he that maketh haste to be riche, shall not be innocent.

21 To haue respect of persons is not good: for that man will transgresse for a piece of bread.

22 A man with a wicked eye hasteth to riches, and knoweth not, that pouertie shall come vpon him.

23 He that rebuketh a man, shall finde more fauour at length, then he that flattereth with his tongue.

24 Hee that robbeth his father and mother, and sayth, It is no transgression, is the companion of a man that destroyeth.

25 He that is of a proude heart, stirreth vp strife: but he that trusteth in the Lord, shall be fatte.

26 Hee that trusteth in his owne heart, is a foole: but he that walketh in wisdome, shall be deliuered.

27 He that giueth vnto the poore, shall not lacke: but he that hideth his eyes, shall haue many curses.

28 When the wicked rise vp, men hide them selues: but when they perish, ye righteous increase.

Proverbs 29

1 A man that hardeneth his necke when he is rebuked, shall suddenly be destroyed and can not be cured.

2 When the righteous are in authoritie, the people reioyce: but when the wicked beareth rule, the people sigh.

3 A man that loueth wisdome, reioyceth his father: but he that feedeth harlots, wasteth his substance.

4 A King by iudgement mainteineth ye countrey: but a man receiuing giftes, destroyeth it.

5 A man that flattereth his neighbour, spreadeth a net for his steps.

6 In the transgression of an euill man is his snare: but the righteous doeth sing and reioyce.

7 The righteous knoweth the cause of the poore: but the wicked regardeth not knowledge.

8 Scornefull men bring a citie into a snare: but wise men turne away wrath.

9 If a wise man contend with a foolish man, whether he be angry or laugh, there is no rest.

10 Bloodie men hate him that is vpright: but the iust haue care of his soule.

11 A foole powreth out all his minde: but a wise man keepeth it in till afterward.

12 Of a prince that hearkeneth to lyes, all his seruants are wicked.

13 The poore and the vsurer meete together, and the Lord lighteneth both their eyes.

14 A King that iudgeth the poore in trueth, his throne shalbe established for euer.

15 The rodde and correction giue wisdome: but a childe set a libertie, maketh his mother ashamed.

16 When the wicked are increased, transgression increaseth: but ye righteous shall see their fall.

17 Correct thy sonne and he will giue thee rest, and will giue pleasures to thy soule.

18 Where there is no vision, the people decay: but he that keepeth the Lawe, is blessed.

19 A seruant will not be chastised with words: though he vnderstand, yet he will not answere.

20 Seest thou a man hastie in his matters? there is more hope of a foole, then of him.

21 He that delicately bringeth vp his seruant from youth, at length he will be euen as his sone.

22 An angrie man stirreth vp strife, and a furious man aboundeth in transgression.

23 The pride of a man shall bring him lowe: but the humble in spirit shall enioy glory.

24 He that is partner with a thiefe, hateth his owne soule: he heareth cursing, and declareth it not.

25 The feare of man bringeth a snare: but he that trusteth in the Lord, shalbe exalted.

26 Many doe seeke the face of the ruler: but euery mans iudgement commeth from the Lord.

27 A wicked man is abomination to the iust, and he that is vpright in his way, is abomination to the wicked.

Proverbs 30

1 THE WORDS OF AGUR THE SONNE OF JAKEH. The prophecie which ye man spake vnto Ithiel, euen to Ithiel, and Vcal.

2 Surely I am more foolish then any man, and haue not the vnderstanding of a man in me.

3 For I haue not learned wisedome, nor atteined to the knowledge of holy things.

4 Who hath ascended vp to heauen, and descended? Who hath gathered the winde in his fist? Who hath bound the waters in a garment? Who hath established all the endes of the world? What is his name, and what is his sonnes name, if thou canst tell?

5 Euery worde of God is pure: he is a shield to those, that trust in him.

6 Put nothing vnto his wordes, least he reproue thee, and thou be found a lyar.

7 Two things haue I required of thee: denie me them not before I die.

8 Remooue farre from me vanitie and lyes: giue me not pouertie, nor riches: feede me with foode conuenient for me,

9 Least I be full, and denie thee, and say, Who is the Lord? or least I be poore and steale, and take the Name of my God in vaine.

10 Accuse not a seruant vnto his master, lest he curse thee, when thou hast offended.

11 There is a generation that curseth their father, and doeth not blesse their mother.

12 There is a generation that are pure in their owne conceite, and yet are not washed from their filthinesse.

13 There is a generation, whose eies are hautie, and their eye liddes are lifted vp.

14 There is a generation, whose teeth are as swordes, and their chawes as kniues to eate vp the afflicted out of the earth, and the poore from among men.

15 The horse leache hath two daughters which crye, Giue, giue. There be three things that will not be satisfied: yea, foure that say not, It is ynough.

16 The graue, and the barren wombe, the earth that cannot be satisfied with water, and the fire that sayeth not, It is ynough.

17 The eye that mocketh his father and despiseth the instruction of his mother, let ye rauens of the valley picke it out, and the yong eagles eate it.

18 There be three things hid from me: yea, foure that I knowe not,

19 The way of an eagle in the aire, the way of a serpent vpon a stone, ye way of a ship in ye middes of the sea, and the way of a man with a maide.

20 Such is ye way also of an adulterous woman: she eateth and wipeth her mouth, and sayth, I haue not committed iniquitie.

21 For three things the earth is moued: yea, for foure it cannot susteine it selfe:

22 For a seruant when he reigneth, and a foole when he is filled with meate,

23 For the hatefull woman, when she is married, and for a handmaid that is heire to her mistres.

24 These be foure small things in the earth, yet they are wise and full of wisedome:

25 The pismires a people not strong, yet prepare they their meate in sommer:

26 The conies a people not mightie, yet make their houses in the rocke:

27 The grashopper hath no King, yet goe they forth all by bandes:

28 The spider taketh holde with her handes, and is in Kings palaces.

29 There be three thinges that order well their going: yea, foure are comely in going,

30 A lyon which is strong among beastes, and turneth not at the sight of any:

31 A lusty grayhound, and a goate, and a King against whom there is no rising vp.

32 If thou hast bene foolish in lifting thy selfe vp, and if thou hast thought wickedly, lay thine hand vpon thy mouth.

33 When one churneth milke, he bringeth foorth butter: and he that wringeth his nose, causeth blood to come out: so he that forceth wrath, bringeth foorth strife.

Proverbs 31

1 THE WORDS OF KING LEMUEL: The prophecie which his mother taught him.

2 What my sonne! and what ye sonne of my wombe! and what, O sonne of my desires!

3 Giue not thy strength vnto women, nor thy wayes, which is to destroy Kings.

4 It is not for Kings, O Lemuel, it is not for Kings to drink wine nor for princes strog drinke,

5 Lest he drinke and forget the decree, and change the iudgement of all the children of affliction.

6 Giue ye strong drinke vnto him that is readie to perish, and wine vnto them that haue griefe of heart.

7 Let him drinke, that he may forget his pouertie, and remember his miserie no more.

8 Open thy mouth for the domme in the cause of all the children of destruction.

9 Open thy mouth: iudge righteously, and iudge the afflicted, and the poore.

10 Who shall finde a vertuous woman? for her price is farre aboue the pearles.

11 The heart of her husband trusteth in her, and he shall haue no neede of spoyle.

12 She will doe him good, and not euill all the dayes of her life.

13 She seeketh wooll and flaxe, and laboureth cheerefully with her handes.

14 She is like the shippes of marchants: shee bringeth her foode from afarre.

15 And she riseth, whiles it is yet night: and giueth the portion to her houshold, and the ordinarie to her maides.

16 She considereth a field, and getteth it: and with the fruite of her handes she planteth a vineyarde.

17 She girdeth her loynes with strength, and strengtheneth her armes.

18 She feeleth that her marchandise is good: her candle is not put out by night.

19 She putteth her handes to the wherue, and her handes handle the spindle.

20 She stretcheth out her hand to the poore, and putteth foorth her hands to the needie.

21 She feareth not the snowe for her familie: for all her familie is clothed with skarlet.

22 She maketh her selfe carpets: fine linen and purple is her garment.

23 Her husband is knowen in the gates, when he sitteth with the Elders of the land.

24 She maketh sheetes, and selleth them, and giueth girdels vnto the marchant.

25 Strength and honour is her clothing, and in the latter day she shall reioyce.

26 She openeth her mouth with wisdome, and the lawe of grace is in her tongue.

27 She ouerseeth the wayes of her housholde, and eateth not the bread of ydlenes.

28 Her children rise vp, and call her blessed: her husband also shall prayse her, saying,

29 Many daughters haue done vertuously: but thou surmountest them all.

30 Fauour is deceitfull, and beautie is vanitie: but a woman that feareth the Lord, she shall be praysed.

31 Giue her of the fruite of her hands, and let her owne workes prayse her in the gates.

Ecclesiastes

Ecclesiastes 1

1 The wordes of the Preacher, the sonne of Dauid King in Ierusalem.

2 Vanitie of vanities, sayth the Preacher: vanitie of vanities, all is vanitie.

3 What remaineth vnto man in all his trauaile, which he suffereth vnder ye sunne?

4 One generation passeth, and another generation succeedeth: but the earth remaineth for euer.

5 The sunne riseth, and ye sunne goeth downe, and draweth to his place, where he riseth.

6 The winde goeth toward the South, and compasseth towarde the North: the winde goeth rounde about, and returneth by his circuites.

7 All the riuers goe into the sea, yet the sea is not full: for the riuers goe vnto ye place, whence they returne, and goe.

8 All things are full of labour: man cannot vtter it: the eye is not satisfied with seeing, nor the eare filled with hearing.

9 What is it that hath bene? that that shalbe: and what is it that hath bene

done? that which shalbe done: and there is no newe thing vnder the sunne.

10 Is there any thing, whereof one may say, Beholde this, it is newe? it hath bene already in the olde time that was before vs.

11 There is no memorie of the former, neither shall there be a remembrance of the latter that shalbe, with them that shall come after.

12 I the Preacher haue bene King ouer Israel in Ierusalem:

13 And I haue giuen mine heart to search and finde out wisdome by all things that are done vnder the heauen: (this sore trauaile hath GOD giuen to the sonnes of men, to humble them thereby)

14 I haue considered all the workes that are done vnder the sunne, and beholde, all is vanitie, and vexation of the spirit.

15 That which is crooked, can none make straight: and that which faileth, cannot be nombred.

16 I thought in mine heart, and said, Behold, I am become great, and excell in wisdome all them that haue bene before me in Ierusalem: and mine heart hath seene much wisedome and knowledge.

17 And I gaue mine heart to knowe wisdome and knowledge, madnes and foolishnes: I knew also that this is a vexation of the spirit.

18 For in the multitude of wisedome is much griefe: and he that increaseth knowledge, increaseth sorowe.

Ecclesiastes 2

1 I said in mine heart, Goe to nowe, I will proue thee with ioy: therefore take thou pleasure in pleasant things: and beholde, this also is vanitie.

2 I saide of laughter, Thou art mad: and of ioy, What is this that thou doest?

3 I sought in mine heart to giue my selfe to wine, and to leade mine heart in wisdome, and to take holde of follie, till I might see where is that goodnesse of the children of men, which they enioy vnder the sunne: the whole nomber of the dayes of their life.

4 I haue made my great workes: I haue built me houses: I haue planted me vineyards.

5 I haue made me gardens and orchards, and planted in them trees of all fruite.

6 I haue made me cisternes of water, to water therewith the woods that growe with trees.

7 I haue gotten seruants and maides, and had children borne in the house: also I had great possession of beeues and sheepe aboue all that were before me in Ierusalem.

8 I haue gathered vnto me also siluer and gold, and the chiefe treasures of Kings and prouinces: I haue prouided me men singers and women singers, and the delites of the sonnes of men, as a woman taken captiue, and women taken captiues.

9 And I was great, and increased aboue all that were before me in Ierusalem: also my wisedome remained with me.

10 And whatsoeuer mine eyes desired, I withheld it not from them: I withdrew not mine heart from any ioy: for mine heart reioyced in al my labour: and this was my portion of all my trauaile.

11 Then I looked on all my workes that mine hands had wrought, and on the trauaile that I had laboured to doe: and beholde, all is vanitie and vexation of the spirit: and there is no profite vnder the sunne.

12 And I turned to beholde wisedome, and madnes and follie: (for who is the man that will come after the King in things, which men nowe haue done?)

13 Then I saw that there is profite in wisedome, more then in follie: as the light is more excellent then darkenes.

14 For the wise mans eyes are in his head, but the foole walketh in darknes: yet I know also that the same condition falleth to them all.

15 Then I thought in mine heart, It befalleth vnto me, as it befalleth to ye foole. Why therefore doe I then labour to be more wise? And I sayd in mine heart, that this also is vanitie.

16 For there shalbe no remembrance of the wise, nor of the foole for euer: for that that now is, in the dayes to come shall all be forgotten. And howe dyeth the wise man, as doeth the foole?

17 Therefore I hated life: for the worke that is wrought vnder the sunne is grieuous vnto me: for all is vanitie, and vexation of the spirit.

18 I hated also all my labour, wherein I had trauailed vnder the sunne, which I shall leaue to the man that shalbe after me.

19 And who knoweth whether he shalbe wise or foolish? yet shall hee haue rule ouer all my labour, wherein I haue trauailed, and wherein I haue shewed my selfe wise vnder the sunne. This is also vanitie.

20 Therefore I went about to make mine heart abhorre all the labour, wherein I had trauailed vnder the sunne.

21 For there is a man whose trauaile is in wisdome, and in knowledge and in equitie: yet to a man that hath not trauailed herein, shall he giue his portion: this also is vanitie and a great griefe.

22 For what hath man of all his trauaile and griefe of his heart, wherein he hath trauailed vnder the sunne?

23 For all his dayes are sorowes, and his trauaile griefe: his heart also taketh not rest in the night: which also is vanitie.

24 There is no profit to man: but that he eate, and drinke, and delight his soule with the profit of his labour: I saw also this, that it was of the hand of God.

25 For who could eate, and who could haste to outward things more then I?

26 Surely to a man that is good in his sight, God giueth wisdome, and knowledge, and ioy: but to the sinner he giueth paine, to gather, and to heape to giue to him that is good before God: this is also vanitie, and vexation of the spirit.

Ecclesiastes 3

1 To all things there is an appointed time, and a time to euery purpose vnder the heauen.

2 A time to bee borne, and a time to die: a time to plant, and a time to plucke vp that which is planted.

3 A time to slay, and a time to heale: a time to breake downe, and a time to builde.

4 A time to weepe, and a time to laugh: a time to mourne, and a time to dance.

5 A time to cast away stones, and a time to gather stones: a time to embrace, and a time to be farre from embracing.

6 A time to seeke, and a time to lose: a time to keepe, and a time to cast away.

7 A time to rent, and a time to sowe: a time to keepe silence, and a time to speake.

8 A time to loue, and a time to hate: a time of warre, and a time of peace.

9 What profite hath hee that worketh of the thing wherein he trauaileth?

10 I haue seene the trauaile that God hath giuen to ye sonnes of men to humble them thereby.

11 He hath made euery thing beautifull in his time: also he hath set the worlde in their heart, yet can not man finde out the worke that God hath wrought from the beginning euen to the end.

12 I know that there is nothing good in them, but to reioyce, and to doe good in his life.

13 And also that euery man eateth and drinketh, and seeth the commoditie of all his labour. this is the gift of God.

14 I knowe that whatsoeuer God shall doe, it shalbe for euer: to it can no man adde, and from it can none diminish: for God hath done it, that they should feare before him.

15 What is that that hath bene? that is nowe: and that that shalbe, hath now bene: for God requireth that which is past.

16 And moreouer I haue seene vnder the sunne the place of iudgement, where was wickednesse, and the place of iustice where was iniquitie.

17 I thought in mine heart, God wil iudge the iust and the wicked: for time is there for euery purpose and for euery worke.

18 I considered in mine heart the state of the children of men that God had purged them: yet to see to, they are in themselues as beastes.

19 For the condition of the children of men, and the condition of beasts are euen as one condition vnto them. As the one dyeth, so dyeth the other: for they haue all one breath, and there is no excellency of man aboue ye beast: for all is vanitie.

20 All goe to one place, and all was of the dust, and all shall returne to the dust.

21 Who knoweth whether the spirit of man ascend vpward, and the spirit of the beast descend downeward to the earth?

22 Therefore I see that there is nothing better then that a man shoulde reioyce

in his affaires, because that is his portion. For who shall bring him to see what shalbe after him?

Ecclesiastes 4

1 So I turned and considered all the oppressions that are wrought vnder the sunne, and beholde the teares of the oppressed, and none comforteth them: and lo, the strength is of the hand of them that oppresse them, and none comforteth them.

2 Wherefore I praysed the dead which now are dead, aboue the liuing, which are yet aliue.

3 And I count him better then them both, which hath not yet bin: for he hath not seene the euill workes which are wrought vnder the sunne.

4 Also I beheld all trauaile, and all perfection of workes that this is ye enuie of a man against his neighbour: this also is vanitie and vexation of spirit.

5 The foole foldeth his hands, and eateth vp his owne flesh.

6 Better is an handfull with quietnesse, then two handfuls with labour and vexation of spirit.

7 Againe I returned, and sawe vanitie vnder the sunne.

8 There is one alone, and there is not a second, which hath neither sonne nor brother, yet is there none end of all his trauaile, neither can his eye be satisfied with riches: neither doeth he thinke, For whome doe I trauaile and defraude my soule of pleasure? this also is vanitie, and this is an euill trauaile.

9 Two are better then one: for they haue better wages for their labour.

10 For if they fal, the one wil lift vp his felow: but wo vnto him that is alone: for he falleth, and there is not a second to lift him vp.

11 Also if two sleepe together, then shall they haue heate: but to one how should there be heate?

12 And if one ouercome him, two shall stand against him: and a threefolde coard is not easily broken.

13 Better is a poore and wise childe, then an olde and foolish King, which will no more be admonished.

14 For out of the prison he commeth forth to reigne: when as he that is borne in his kingdome, is made poore.

15 I behelde all the liuing, which walke vnder the sunne, with the second childe, which shall stand vp in his place.

16 There is none ende of all the people, nor of all that were before them, and they that come after, shall not reioyce in him: surely this is also vanitie and vexation of spirit.

17 Take heede to thy foote when thou entrest into the House of God, and be more neere to heare then to giue the sacrifice of fooles: for they knowe not that they doe euil.

Ecclesiastes 5

1 Be not rash with thy mouth, nor let thine heart be hastie to vtter a thing before God: for God is in the heauens, and thou art on the earth: therefore let thy wordes be fewe.

2 For as a dreame commeth by the multitude of businesse: so the voyce of a foole is in the multitude of wordes.

3 When thou hast vowed a vowe to God, deferre not to pay it: for he deliteth not in fooles: pay therefore that thou hast vowed.

4 It is better that thou shouldest not vowe, then that thou shouldest vow and not pay it.

5 Suffer not thy mouth to make thy flesh to sinne: neither say before the Angel, that this is ignorance: wherefore shall God bee angry by thy voyce, and destroy the worke of thine hands?

6 For in the multitude of dreames, and vanities are also many wordes: but feare thou God.

7 If in a countrey thou seest the oppression of the poore, and the defrauding of iudgement and iustice, be not astonied at the matter: for hee that is higher then the highest, regardeth, and there be higher then they.

8 And the abundance of the earth is ouer all: the King also consisteth by the fielde that is tilled.

9 He that loueth siluer, shall not be satisfied with siluer, and he that loueth riches, shalbe without the fruite thereof: this also is vanitie.

10 When goods increase, they are increased that eate them: and what good commeth to the owners thereof, but the beholding thereof with their eyes?

11 The sleepe of him that traueileth, is sweete, whether he eate litle or much: but the sacietie of the riche will not suffer him to sleepe.

12 There is an euill sickenes that I haue seene vnder the sunne: to wit, riches reserued to the owners thereof for their euill.

13 And these riches perish by euill trauel, and he begetteth a sonne, and in his hand is nothing.

14 As hee came foorth of his mothers belly, he shall returne naked to goe as he came, and shall beare away nothing of his labour, which hee hath caused to passe by his hand.

15 And this also is an euill sickenes that in all pointes as he came, so shall he goe, and what profit hath he that he hath traueiled for the winde?

16 Also all his dayes hee eateth in darkenes with much griefe, and in his sorowe and anger.

17 Beholde then, what I haue seene good, that it is comely to eate, and to drinke, and to take pleasure in all his labour, wherein he traueileth vnder the sunne, the whole number of the dayes of his life, which God giueth him: for this is his portion.

18 Also to euery man to whom God hath giuen riches and treasures, and giueth him power to eate thereof, and to take his part, and to enioy his labour: this is the gift of God.

19 Surely hee will not much remember the dayes of his life, because God answereth to the ioy of his heart.

Ecclesiastes 6

1 There is an euill, which I sawe vnder the sunne, and it is much among men:

2 A man to whom God hath giuen riches and treasures and honour, and he wanteth nothing for his soule of all that it desireth: but God giueth him not power to eate thereof, but a strange man shall eate it vp: this is vanitie, and this is an euill sicknesse.

3 If a man beget an hundreth children and liue many yeeres, and the dayes of his yeeres be multiplied, and his soule be not satisfied with good things, and he be not buried, I say that an vntimely fruite is better then he.

4 For he commeth into vanitie and goeth into darkenesse: and his name shall be couered with darkenesse.

5 Also he hath not seene ye sunne, nor knowen it: therefore this hath more rest then the other.

6 And if he had liued a thousand yeeres twise tolde, and had seene no good, shall not all goe to one place?

7 All the labour of man is for his mouth: yet the soule is not filled.

8 For what hath the wise man more then the foole? what hath the poore that knoweth how to walke before the liuing?

9 The sight of ye eye is better then to walke in ye lustes: this also is vanitie, and vexation of spirit.

10 What is that that hath bene? the name thereof is nowe named: and it is knowen that it is man: and he cannot striue with him that is stronger then he.

Ecclesiastes 7

1 Surely there be many things that increase vanitie: and what auaileth it man?

2 For who knoweth what is good for man in the life and in the number of the dayes of the life of his vanitie, seeing he maketh them as a shadowe? For who can shewe vnto man what shall be after him vnder the sunne?

3 A good name is better then a good oyntment, and the day of death, then the day that one is borne.

4 It is better to goe to the house of mourning, then to goe to the house of feasting, because this is the ende of all men: and the liuing shall lay it to his heart.

5 Anger is better then laughter: for by a sad looke the heart is made better.

6 The heart of the wise is in the house of mourning: but the heart of fooles is in the house of mirth.

7 Better it is to heare ye rebuke of a wise man, then that a man should heare the song of fooles.

8 For like ye noyse of the thornes vnder the pot, so is the laughter of the foole: this also is vanitie.

9 Surely oppression maketh a wise man mad: and the rewarde destroyeth the heart.

10 The ende of a thing is better then the beginning thereof, and the pacient in spirit is better then the proude in spirit.

11 Be not thou of an hastie spirit to be angry: for anger resteth in the bosome of fooles.

12 Say not thou, Why is it that the former dayes were better then these? for thou doest not enquire wisely of this thing.

13 Wisedome is good with an inheritance, and excellent to them that see the sunne.

14 For man shall rest in the shadowe of wisedome, and in the shadowe of siluer: but the excellencie of the knowledge of wisedome giueth life to the possessers thereof.

15 Beholde the worke of God: for who can make straight that which he hath made crooked?

16 In the day of wealth be of good comfort, and in the day of affliction consider: God also hath made this contrary to that, to the intent that man shoulde finde nothing after him.

17 I haue seene all things in the dayes of my vanitie: there is a iust man that perisheth in his iustice, and there is a wicked man that continueth long in his malice.

18 Be not thou iust ouermuch, neither make thy selfe ouerwise: wherefore shouldest thou be desolate?

19 Be not thou wicked ouermuch, neither be thou foolish: wherefore shouldest thou perish not in thy time?

20 It is good that thou lay hold on this: but yet withdrawe not thine hand from that: for he that feareth God, shall come forth of them all.

21 Wisedome shall strengthen the wise man more then ten mightie princes that are in ye citie.

22 Surely there is no man iust in the earth, that doeth good and sinneth not.

23 Giue not thine heart also to all ye wordes that men speake, lest thou doe heare thy seruant cursing thee.

24 For often times also thine heart knoweth that thou likewise hast cursed others.

25 All this haue I prooued by wisedome: I thought I will be wise, but it went farre from me.

26 It is farre off, what may it be? and it is a profound deepenesse, who can finde it?

27 I haue compassed about, both I and mine heart to knowe and to enquire and to search wisedome, and reason, and to knowe the wickednesse of follie, and the foolishnesse of madnesse,

28 And I finde more bitter then death the woman whose heart is as nettes and snares, and her handes, as bands: he that is good before God, shalbe deliuered from her, but the sinner shall be taken by her.

29 Beholde, sayth the Preacher, this haue I found, seeking one by one to finde the count:

30 And yet my soule seeketh, but I finde it not: I haue found one man of a thousand: but a woman among them all haue I not founde.

31 Onely loe, this haue I founde, that God hath made man righteous: but they haue sought many inuentions.

Ecclesiastes 8

1 Who is as the wise man? and who knoweth the interpretation of a thing? the wisedome of a man doth make his face to shine: and the strength of his face shalbe changed.

2 I aduertise thee to take heede to ye mouth of the King, and to the worde of the othe of God.

3 Haste not to goe forth of his sight: stand not in an euill thing: for he will doe whatsoeuer pleaseth him.

4 Where the word of ye King is, there is power, and who shall say vnto him, What doest thou?

5 He that keepeth the commandement, shall knowe none euill thing, and the heart of the wise shall knowe the time and iudgement.

6 For to euery purpose there is a time and iudgement, because the miserie of man is great vpon him.

7 For he knoweth not that which shalbe: for who can tell him when it shalbe?

8 Man is not lorde ouer the spirit to retaine the spirite: neither hath hee power in the day of death, nor deliuerance in the battell, neither shall wickednesse deliuer the possessers thereof.

9 All this haue I seene, and haue giuen mine heart to euery worke, which is wrought vnder the sunne, and I sawe a time that man ruleth ouer man to his owne hurt.

10 And likewise I sawe the wicked buried, and they returned, and they that came from the holy place, were yet forgotten in the citie where they had done right: this also is vanitie.

11 Because sentence against an euill worke is not executed speedily, therefore the heart of the children of men is fully set in them to doe euill.

12 Though a sinner doe euill an hundreth times, and God prolongeth his dayes, yet I knowe that it shalbe well with them that feare the Lord, and doe reuerence before him.

13 But it shall not be well to the wicked, neither shall he prolong his dayes: he shall be like a shadowe, because he feareth not before God.

14 There is a vanitie, which is done vpon the earth, that there be righteous men to whom it commeth according to the worke of the wicked: and there be wicked men to whom it commeth according to the worke of the iust: I thought also that this is vanitie.

15 And I praysed ioy: for there is no goodnesse to man vnder the sunne, saue to eate and to drinke and to reioyce: for this is adioyned to his labour, the dayes of his life that God hath giuen him vnder the sunne.

16 When I applied mine heart to knowe wisedome, and to behold the busines that is done on earth, that neither day nor night the eyes of man take sleepe,

17 Then I behelde the whole worke of God, that man cannot finde out ye worke that is wrought vnder the sunne: for the which man laboureth to seeke it, and cannot finde it: yea, and though the wise man thinke to knowe it, he cannot finde it.

Ecclesiastes 9

1 I have surely giuen mine heart to all this, and to declare all this, that the iust, and the wise, and their workes are in the hand of God: and no man knoweth eyther loue or hatred of all that is before them.

2 All things come alike to all: and the same condition is to the iust and to the wicked, to the good and to the pure, and to the polluted, and to him that sacrificeth, and to him that sacrificeth not: as is the good, so is the sinner, he that sweareth, as he that feareth an othe.

3 This is euill among all that is done vnder the sunne, that there is one condition to all, and also the heart of the sonnes of men is full of euill, and madnes is in their heartes whiles they liue, and after that, they goe to the dead.

4 Surely whosoeuer is ioyned to all ye liuing, there is hope: for it is better to a liuing dog, then to a dead lyon.

5 For the liuing knowe that they shall dye, but the dead knowe nothing at all: neither haue they any more a rewarde: for their remembrance is forgotten.

6 Also their loue, and their hatred, and their enuie is now perished, and they haue no more portion for euer, in all that is done vnder the sunne.

7 Goe, eate thy bread with ioy, and drinke thy wine with a cheerefull heart: for God nowe accepteth thy workes.

8 At all times let thy garments be white, and let not oyle be lacking vpon thine head.

9 Reioyce with the wife whom thou hast loued all the dayes of the life of thy vanitie, which God hath giuen thee vnder the sunne all the dayes of thy vanitie: for this is thy portion in the life, and in thy trauaile wherein thou labourest vnder the sunne.

10 All that thine hand shall finde to doe, doe it with all thy power: for there is neither worke nor inuention, nor knowledge, nor wisedome in the graue whither thou goest.

11 I returned, and I sawe vnder the sunne that the race is not to the swift, nor the battell to the strong, nor yet bread to the wise, nor also riches to men of vnderstanding, neither yet fauour to men of knowledge: but time and chance commeth to them all.

12 For neither doth man knowe his time, but as the fishes which are taken in an euill net, and as the birdes that are caught in the snare: so are the children of men snared in the euill time when it falleth vpon them suddenly.

13 I haue also seene this wisedome vnder the sunne, and it is great vnto me.

14 A litle citie and fewe men in it, and a great King came against it, and compassed it about, and builded fortes against it.

15 And there was founde therein a poore and wise man, and he deliuered the citie by his wisedome: but none remembred this poore man.

16 Then said I, Better is wisdome then strength: yet the wisedome of the poore is despised, and his wordes are not heard.

17 The wordes of the wise are more heard in quietnes, then the crye of him that ruleth among fooles.

18 Better is wisedome then weapons of warre: but one sinner destroyeth much good.

Ecclesiastes 10

1 Dead flies cause to stinke, and putrifie the ointment of the apoticarie: so doeth a litle follie him that is in estimation for wisedome, and for glorie.

2 The heart of a wise man is at his right hand: but the heart of a foole is at his left hand.

3 And also when the foole goeth by the way, his heart faileth, and he telleth vnto all that he is a foole.

4 If the spirite of him that ruleth, rise vp against thee, leaue not thy place: for gentlenes pacifieth great sinnes.

5 There is an euil that I haue seene vnder the sunne, as an errour that proceedeth from the face of him that ruleth.

6 Follie is set in great excellencie, and the riche set in the lowe place.

7 I haue seene seruants on horses, and princes walking as seruants on the ground.

8 He that diggeth a pit, shall fal into it, and he that breaketh the hedge, a serpent shall bite him.

9 He that remooueth stones, shall hurt himselfe thereby, and hee that cutteth wood, shall be in danger thereby.

10 If the yron be blunt, and one hath not whet the edge, he must then put to more strength: but the excellencie to direct a thing is wisedome.

11 If the serpent bite, when he is not charmed: no better is a babbler.

12 The words of ye mouth of a wise man haue grace: but the lippes of a foole deuoure himselfe.

13 The beginning of the wordes of his mouth is foolishnesse, and the latter ende of his mouth is wicked madnesse.

14 For the foole multiplieth woordes, saying, Man knoweth not what shall be: and who can tell him what shall be after him?

15 The labour of the foolish doeth wearie him: for he knoweth not to goe into the citie.

16 Woe to thee, O lande, when thy King is a childe, and thy princes eate in the morning.

17 Blessed art thou, O land, when thy King is the sonne of nobles, and thy princes eate in time, for strength and not for drunkennesse.

18 By slouthfulnes the roofe of the house goeth to decaie, and by the ydlenesse of the handes the house droppeth through.

19 They prepare bread for laughter, and wine comforteth the liuing, but siluer answereth to all.

20 Curse not the King, no not in thy thought, neither curse the rich in thy bed chamber: for the foule of the heauen shall carie the voice, and that which hath wings, shall declare the matter.

Ecclesiastes 11

1 Cast thy bread vpon the waters: for after many daies thou shalt finde it.

2 Giue a portion to seuen, and also to eight: for thou knowest not what euill shalbe vpon ye earth.

3 If the clouds be full, they wil powre forth raine vpon the earth: and if the tree doe fall toward the South, or toward the North, in the place that the tree falleth, there it shalbe.

4 He that obserueth ye winde, shall not sow, and he that regardeth the cloudes, shall not reape.

5 As thou knowest not which is ye way of the spirit, nor how the bones doe growe in the wombe of her that is with child: so thou knowest not the worke of God that worketh all.

6 In the morning sowe thy seede, and in the euening let not thine hand rest: for thou knowest not whither shall prosper, this or that, or whether both shalbe a like good.

7 Surely the light is a pleasant thing: and it is a good thing to the eyes to see the sunne.

8 Though a man liue many yeeres, and in them all he reioyce, yet hee shall remember the daies of darkenesse, because they are manie, all that commeth is vanitie.

9 Reioyce, O yong man, in thy youth, and let thine heart cheere thee in the dayes of thy youth: and walke in the waies of thine heart, and in the sight of thine eyes: but knowe that for all these things, God wil bring thee to iudgement.

10 Therefore take away griefe out of thine heart, and cause euil to depart from thy flesh: for childehood and youth are vanitie.

Ecclesiastes 12

1 Remember nowe thy Creator in the daies of thy youth, whiles the euill daies come not, nor the yeeres approche, wherein thou shalt say, I haue no pleasure in them:

2 Whiles the sunne is not darke, nor ye light, nor the moone, nor the starres, nor the cloudes returne after the raine:

3 When the keepers of ye house shall tremble, and the strong men shall bow them selues, and the grinders shall cease, because they are few, and they waxe darke that looke out by ye windowes:

4 And the doores shall be shut without by the base sound of the grinding, and he shall rise vp at the voice of the birde:

and all the daughters of singing shall be abased.

5 Also they shalbe afraide of the hie thing, and feare shalbe in the way, and the almond tree shall flourish, and the grassehopper shall be a burden, and concupiscence shall be driuen away: for man goeth to the house of his age, and the mourners goe about in the streete.

6 Whiles the siluer coarde is not lengthened, nor the golden ewer broken, nor the pitcher broken at the well, nor the wheele broken at the cisterne:

7 And dust returne to the earth as it was, and the spirit returne to God that gaue it.

8 Vanitie of vanities, saieth the Preacher, all is vanitie.

9 And the more wise the Preacher was, the more he taught the people knowledge, and caused them to heare, and searched foorth, and prepared many parables.

10 The Preacher sought to finde out pleasant wordes, and an vpright writing, euen the wordes of trueth.

11 The wordes of the wise are like goads, and like nailes fastened by the masters of the assemblies, which are giuen by one pastour.

12 And of other things beside these, my sone, take thou heede: for there is none ende in making many bookes, and much reading is a wearines of the flesh.

13 Let vs heare the end of all: feare God and keepe his commandements: for this is the whole duetie of man.

14 For God will bring euery worke vnto iudgement, with euery secret thing, whether it be good or euill.

Song Of Solomon

Song Of Solomon 1

1 Let him kisse me with the kisses of his mouth: for thy loue is better then wine.

2 Because of the sauour of thy good ointments thy name is as an ointment powred out: therefore the virgins loue thee.

3 Drawe me: we will runne after thee: the King hath brought me into his chabers: we will reioyce and be glad in thee: we will remember thy loue more then wine: the righteous do loue thee.

4 I am blacke, O daughters of Ierusalem, but comely, as the tentes of Kedar, and as the curtaines of Salomon.

5 Regard ye me not because I am blacke: for the sunne hath looked vpon mee. The sonnes of my mother were angry against mee: they made me the keeper of ye vines: but I kept not mine owne vine.

6 Shewe me, O thou, whome my soule loueth, where thou feedest, where thou liest at noone: for why should I be as she that turneth aside to the flockes of thy companions?

7 If thou knowe not, O thou the fairest among women, get thee foorth by the steps of the flocke, and feede thy kiddes by the tents of the shepheards.

8 I haue compared thee, O my loue, to the troupe of horses in the charets of Pharaoh.

9 Thy cheekes are comely with rowes of stones, and thy necke with chaines.

10 We will make thee borders of golde with studdes of siluer.

11 Whiles the King was at his repast, my spikenard gaue the smelll thereof.

12 My welbeloued is as a bundle of myrrhe vnto me: he shall lie betweene my breasts.

13 My welbeloued is as a cluster of camphire vnto me in the vines of Engedi.

14 My loue, beholde, thou art faire: beholde, thou art faire: thine eyes are like the doues.

15 My welbeloued, beholde, thou art faire and pleasant: also our bed is greene:

16 The beames of our house are cedars, our rafters are of firre.

Song Of Solomon 2

1 I am the rose of the fielde, and the lilie of the valleys.

2 Like a lilie amog the thornes, so is my loue among the daughters.

3 Like the apple tree among the trees of the forest, so is my welbeloued among the sonnes of men: vnder his shadow had I delite, and sate downe: and his fruite was sweete vnto my mouth.

4 Hee brought mee into the wine cellar, and loue was his banner ouer me.

5 Stay me with flagons, and comfort me with apples: for I am sicke of loue.

6 His left hande is vnder mine head, and his right hand doeth imbrace me.

7 I charge you, O daughters of Ierusalem, by the roes and by the hindes of the fielde, that ye stirre not vp, nor waken my loue, vntill she please.

8 It is the voyce of my welbeloued: beholde, hee commeth leaping by the mountaines, and skipping by the hilles.

9 My welbeloued is like a roe, or a yong hart: loe, he standeth behinde our wall, looking forth of the windowes, shewing him selfe through the grates.

10 My welbeloued spake and said vnto me, Arise, my loue, my faire one, and come thy way.

11 For beholde, winter is past: the raine is changed, and is gone away.

12 The flowers appeare in the earth: the time of the singing of birdes is come, and the voyce of the turtle is heard in our land.

13 The figtree hath brought foorth her yong figges: and the vines with their small grapes haue cast a sauour: arise my loue, my faire one, and come away.

14 My doue, that art in the holes of ye rocke, in the secret places of the staires, shewe mee thy sight, let mee heare thy voyce: for thy voyce is sweete, and thy sight comely.

15 Take vs the foxes, the little foxes, which destroy the vines: for our vines haue small grapes.

16 My welbeloued is mine, and I am his: hee feedeth among the lilies,

17 Vntill the day breake, and the shadowes flee away: returne, my welbeloued, and be like a roe, or a yong hart vpon the mountaines of Bether.

Song Of Solomon 3

1 In my bed by night I sought him that my soule loued: I sought him, but I found him not.

2 I will rise therefore nowe, and goe about in the citie, by the streetes and by the open places, and wil seeke him that my soule loueth: I sought him, but I found him not.

3 The watchmen that went about the citie, found mee: to whome I said, Haue you seene him, whome my soule loueth?

4 When I had past a litle from them, then I found him whom my soule loued: I tooke holde on him and left him not, till I had brought him vnto my mothers house into the chamber of her that conceiued me.

5 I charge you, O daughters of Ierusalem, by the roes and by the hindes of the fielde, that ye stirre not vp, nor waken my loue vntill she please.

6 Who is shee that commeth vp out of the wildernes like pillars of smoke perfumed with myrrhe and incense, and with all the spices of the marchant?

7 Beholde his bed, which is Salomons: threescore strong men are round about it, of the valiant men of Israel.

8 They all handle the sworde, and are expert in warre, euery one hath his sword vpon his thigh for the feare by night.

9 King Salomon made himselfe a palace of the trees of Lebanon.

10 Hee made the pillars thereof of siluer, and the pauement thereof of gold, the hangings thereof of purple, whose middes was paued with the loue of the daughters of Ierusalem.

11 Come forth, ye daughters of Zion, and behold the King Salomon with the crowne, wherewith his mother crowned him in ye day of his mariage, and in the day of the gladnes of his heart.

Song Of Solomon 4

1 Behold, thou art faire, my loue: behold, thou art faire: thine eyes are like the doues: among thy lockes thine heare is like the flocke of goates, which looke downe from the mountaine of Gilead.

2 Thy teeth are like a flocke of sheepe in good order, which go vp from the washing: which euery one bring out twinnes, and none is barren among them.

3 Thy lippes are like a threede of scarlet, and thy talke is comely: thy temples are within thy lockes as a piece of a pomegranate.

4 Thy necke is as the tower of Dauid builte for defence: a thousand shieldes hang therein, and all the targates of the strong men.

5 Thy two breastes are as two young roes that are twinnes, feeding among the lilies.

6 Vntill the day breake, and the shadowes flie away, I wil go into the mountaine of myrrhe and to the mountaine of incense.

7 Thou art all faire, my loue, and there is no spot in thee.

8 Come with me from Lebanon, my spouse, euen with me from Lebanon, and looke from the toppe of Amanah, from the toppe of Shenir and Hermon, from the dennes of the lyons, and from the mountaines of the leopards.

9 My sister, my spouse, thou hast wounded mine heart: thou hast wounded mine heart with one of thine eyes, and with a chaine of thy necke.

10 My sister, my spouse, how faire is thy loue? howe much better is thy loue then wine? and the sauour of thine oyntments then all spices?

11 Thy lippes, my spouse, droppe as honie combes: honie and milke are vnder thy tongue, and the sauoure of thy garments is as the sauoure of Lebanon.

12 My sister my spouse is as a garden inclosed, as a spring shut vp, and a fountaine sealed vp.

13 Thy plantes are as an orchard of pomegranates with sweete fruites, as camphire, spikenarde,

14 Euen spikenarde, and saffran, calamus, and cynamon with all the trees of incense, myrrhe and aloes, with all the chiefe spices.

15 O fountaine of the gardens, O well of liuing waters, and the springs of Lebanon.

16 Arise, O North, and come O South, and blowe on my garden that the spices thereof may flow out: let my welbeloued come to his garden, and eate his pleasant fruite.

Song Of Solomon 5

1 I am come into my garden, my sister, my spouse: I gathered my myrrhe with my spice: I ate mine hony combe with mine hony, I dranke my wine with my milke: eate, O friends, drinke, and make you merie, O welbeloued.

2 I sleepe, but mine heart waketh, it is the voyce of my welbeloued that knocketh, saying, Open vnto mee, my sister, my loue, my doue, my vndefiled: for mine head is full of dewe, and my lockes with the droppes of the night.

3 I haue put off my coate, howe shall I put it on? I haue washed my feete, howe shall I defile them?

4 My welbeloued put in his hand by the hole of the doore, and mine heart was affectioned toward him.

5 I rose vp to open to my welbeloued, and mine hands did drop downe myrrhe, and my fingers pure myrrhe vpon the handels of the barre.

6 I opened to my welbeloued: but my welbeloued was gone, and past: mine heart was gone when hee did speake: I sought him, but I coulde not finde him: I called him, but hee answered mee not.

7 The watchmen that went about the citie, founde me: they smote me and

wounded me: the watchmen of the walles tooke away my vaile from me.

8 I charge you, O daughters of Ierusalem, if you finde my welbeloued, that you tell him that I am sicke of loue.

9 O the fairest among women, what is thy welbeloued more then other welbeloued? what is thy welbeloued more then another louer, that thou doest so charge vs?

10 My welbeloued is white and ruddie, the chiefest of ten thousand.

11 His head is as fine golde, his lockes curled, and blacke as a rauen.

12 His eyes are like doues vpon the riuers of waters, which are washt with milke, and remaine by the full vessels.

13 His cheekes are as a bedde of spices, and as sweete flowres, and his lippes like lilies dropping downe pure myrrhe.

14 His hands as rings of gold set with the chrysolite, his belly like white yuorie couered with saphirs.

15 His legges are as pillars of marble, set vpon sockets of fine golde: his countenance as Lebanon, excellent as the cedars.

16 His mouth is as sweete thinges, and hee is wholy delectable: this is my welbeloued, and this is my louer, O daughters of Ierusalem.

17 O the fairest among women, whither is thy welbeloued gone? whither is thy welbeloued turned aside, that we may seeke him with thee?

Song Of Solomon 6

1 My welbeloued is gone downe into his garden to the beds of spices, to feede in the gardens, and to gather lilies.

2 I am my welbeloueds, and my welbeloued is mine, who feedeth among the lilies.

3 Thou art beautifull, my loue, as Tirzah, comely as Ierusale, terrible as an army with baners.

4 Turne away thine eyes from me: for they ouercome mee: thine heare is like a flocke of goates, which looke downe from Gilead.

5 Thy teeth are like a flocke of sheepe, which goe vp from the washing, which euery one bring out twinnes, and none is barren among them.

6 Thy temples are within thy lockes as a piece of a pomegranate.

7 There are threescore Queenes and fourescore concubines and of the damsels without nober.

8 But my doue is alone, and my vndefiled, she is the onely daughter of her mother, and shee is deare to her that bare her: the daughters haue seene her and counted her blessed: euen the Queenes and the concubines, and they haue praised her.

9 Who is shee that looketh foorth as the morning, fayre as the moone, pure as the sunne, terrible as an armie with banners!

10 I went downe to the garden of nuttes, to see the fruites of the valley, to see if the vine budded, and if the pomegranates flourished.

11 I knewe nothing, my soule set me as the charets of my noble people.

12 Returne, returne, O Shulamite, returne: returne that we may behold thee. What shall you see in the Shulamite, but as the company of an armie?

Song Of Solomon 7

1 Howe beautifull are thy goings with shooes, O princes daughter! the ioynts of thy thighs are like iewels: the worke of the hande of a cunning workeman.

2 Thy nauel is as a round cuppe that wanteth not licour: thy belly is as an heape of wheat compassed about with lilies.

3 Thy two breastes are as two young roes that are twinnes.

4 Thy necke is like a towre of yuorie: thine eyes are like the fishe pooles in Heshbon by the gate of Bath-rabbim: thy nose is as the towre of Lebanon, that looketh toward Damascus.

5 Thine head vpon thee is as skarlet, and the bush of thine head like purple: the King is tyed in the rafters.

6 Howe faire art thou, and howe pleasant art thou, O my loue, in pleasures!

7 This thy stature is like a palme tree, and thy brestes like clusters.

8 I saide, I will goe vp into the palme tree, I will take holde of her boughes: thy breastes shall nowe be like the clusters of the vine: and the sauour of thy nose like apples,

9 And the roufe of thy mouth like good wine, which goeth straight to my welbeloued, and causeth the lippes of the ancient to speake.

10 I am my welbeloueds, and his desire is toward mee.

11 Come, my welbeloued, let vs go foorth into the fielde: let vs remaine in the villages.

12 Let vs get vp early to the vines, let vs see if the vine florish, whether it hath budded the small grape, or whether the pomegranates florish: there will I giue thee my loue.

13 The mandrakes haue giuen a smelll, and in our gates are all sweete things, new and olde: my welbeloued, I haue kept them for thee.

Song Of Solomon 8

1 Oh that thou werest as my brother that sucked the brestes of my mother: I would finde thee without, I would kisse thee, then they should not despise thee.

2 I will leade thee and bring thee into my mothers house: there thou shalt teache me: and I will cause thee to drinke spiced wine, and newe wine of the pomegranate.

3 His left hand shalbe vnder mine head, and his right hand shall embrace me.

4 I charge you, O daughters of Ierusale, that you stir not vp, nor waken my loue, vntil she please.

5 (Who is this that commeth vp out of the wildernesse, leaning vpon her welbeloued?) I raysed thee vp vnder an apple tree: there thy mother conceiued thee: there she coceiued that bare thee.

6 Set mee as a seale on thine heart, and as a signet vpon thine arme: for loue is strong as death: ielousie is cruel as the graue: the coles thereof are fierie coles, and a vehement flame.

7 Much water can not quench loue, neither can the floods drowne it: If a man should giue all the substance of his house for loue, they would greatly contemne it.

8 Wee haue a litle sister, and she hath no breastes: what shall we do for our sister when she shalbe spoken for?

9 If shee be a wall, we will builde vpon her a siluer palace: and if she be a doore, we wil keepe her in with bordes of cedar.

10 I am a wall, and my breasts are as towres: then was I in his eyes as one that findeth peace.

11 Salomon had a vine in Baal-hamon: hee gaue the vineyarde vnto keepers: euery one bringeth for ye fruite thereof a thousand pieces of siluer.

12 But my vineyarde which is mine, is before me: to thee, O Salomon appertaineth a thousand pieces of siluer, and two hundreth to them that keepe the fruite thereof.

13 O thou that dwellest in the gardens, the companions hearken vnto thy voyce: cause me to heare it.

14 O my welbeloued, flee away, and be like vnto the roe, or to the yong harte vpon ye mountaines of spices.

Isaiah

Isaiah 1

1 A vision of Isaiah, the sonne of Amoz, which he sawe concerning Iudah and Ierusalem: in the dayes of Vzziah, Iotham, Ahaz and Hezekiah Kings of Iudah.

2 Heare, O heauens, and hearken, O earth: for the Lord hath sayde, I haue nourished and brought vp children, but they haue rebelled against me.

3 The oxe knoweth his owner, and the asse his masters crib: but Israel hath not knowen: my people hath not vnderstand.

4 Ah, sinfull nation, a people laden with iniquitie: a seede of the wicked, corrupt children: they haue forsaken the Lord: they haue prouoked the holy one of Israel to anger: they are gone backewarde.

5 Wherefore shoulde ye be smitten any more? for ye fall away more and more: the whole head is sicke, and the whole heart is heauie.

6 From the sole of the foote vnto the head, there is nothing whole therein, but wounds, and swelling, and sores full of corruption: they haue not bene wrapped, nor bound vp, nor mollified with oyle.

7 Your land is waste: your cities are burnt with fire: strangers deuoure your lande in your presence, and it is desolate like the ouerthrowe of strangers.

8 And the daughter of Zion shall remaine like a cotage in a vineyarde, like

a lodge in a garden of cucumbers, and like a besieged citie.

9 Except the Lord of hostes had reserued vnto vs, euen a small remnant: we should haue bene as Sodom, and should haue bene like vnto Gomorah.

10 Heare the worde of the Lord, O princes of Sodom: hearken vnto the Law of our God, O people of Gomorah.

11 What haue I to doe with the multitude of your sacrifices, sayth the Lord? I am full of the burnt offerings of rams, and of the fat of fed beasts: and I desire not the blood of bullocks, nor of lambs, nor of goates.

12 When ye come to appeare before me, who required this of your hands to tread in my courts?

13 Bring no more oblations, in vaine: incense is an abomination vnto me: I can not suffer your newe moones, nor Sabbaths, nor solemne dayes (it is iniquitie) nor solemne assemblies.

14 My soule hateth your newe moones and your appointed feastes: they are a burden vnto me: I am weary to beare them.

15 And when you shall stretch out your hands, I wil hide mine eyes from you: and though ye make many prayers, I wil not heare: for your hands are full of blood.

16 Wash you, make you cleane: take away the euill of your workes from before mine eyes: cease to doe euill.

17 Learne to doe well: seeke iudgement, relieue the oppressed: iudge the fatherlesse and defend the widowe.

18 Come nowe, and let vs reason together, sayth the Lord: though your sinnes were as crimsin, they shalbe made white as snowe: though they were red like skarlet, they shalbe as wooll.

19 If ye consent and obey, ye shall eate the good things of the land.

20 But if ye refuse and be rebellious, ye shalbe deuoured with the sword: for the mouth of the Lord hath spoken it.

21 Howe is the faithfull citie become an harlot? it was full of iudgement, and iustice lodged therein, but now they are murtherers.

22 Thy siluer is become drosse: thy wine is mixt with water.

23 Thy Princes are rebellious and companions of theeues: euery one loueth giftes, and followeth after rewards: they iudge not the fatherlesse, neither doeth the widowes cause come before them.

24 Therefore sayth the Lord God of hostes, the mightie one of Israel, Ah, I will ease me of mine aduersaries, and auenge me of mine enemies.

25 Then I will turne mine hand vpon thee, and burne out thy drosse, till it be pure, and take away all thy tinne.

26 And I will restore thy iudges as at the first, and thy counsellers as at the beginning: afterward shalt thou be called a citie of righteousnes, and a faithfull citie.

27 Zion shall be redeemed in iudgement, and they that returne in her, in iustice.

28 And the destruction of the transgressers and of the sinners shalbe together: and they that forsake the Lord, shalbe consumed.

29 For they shalbe confounded for the okes, which ye haue desired, and ye shall be ashamed of the gardens, that ye haue chosen.

30 For ye shalbe as an oke, whose leafe fadeth: and as a garden that hath no water.

31 And the strong shall be as towe, and the maker thereof, as a sparke: and they shall both burne together, and none shall quench them.

Isaiah 2

1 The worde that Isaiah the sonne of Amoz sawe vpon Iudah and Ierusalem.

2 It shall be in the last dayes, that the mountaine of the house of the Lord shalbe prepared in the top of the mountaines, and shall be exalted aboue the hilles, and all nations shall flowe vnto it.

3 And many people shall go, and say, Come, and let vs go vp to the mountaine of the Lord, to the house of the God of Iaakob, and hee will teach vs his wayes, and we will walke in his paths: for the Lawe shall go foorth of Zion, and the worde of the Lord from Ierusalem,

4 And he shall iudge among the nations, and rebuke many people: they shall breake their swords also into mattocks, and their speares into siethes: nation shall not lift vp a sworde against nation, neither shall they learne to fight any more.

5 O house of Iaakob, come ye, and let vs walke in the Lawe of the Lord.

6 Surely thou hast forsaken thy people, the house of Iaakob, because they are full of the East maners, and are sorcerers as the Philistims, and abound with strange children.

7 Their land also was full of siluer and golde, and there was none ende of their treasures: and their land was full of horses, and their charets were infinite.

8 Their land also was full of idols: they worshipped the worke of their owne hands, which their owne fingers haue made.

9 And a man bowed himselfe, and a man humbled himselfe: therefore spare them not.

10 Enter into the rocke, and hide thee in the dust from before the feare of the Lord, and from the glory of his maiestie.

11 The hie looke of man shall be humbled, and the loftinesse of men shalbe abased, and the Lord onely shall be exalted in that day.

12 For the day of the Lord of hostes is vpon all the proude and hautie, and vpon all that is exalted: and it shalbe made lowe.

13 Euen vpon all the cedars of Lebanon, that are hie and exalted, and vpon all the okes of Bashan,

14 And vpon all the hie mountaines, and vpon all the hilles that are lifted vp,

15 And vpon euery hie tower, and vpon euery strong wall,

16 And vpon all the shippes of Tarshish, and vpon all pleasant pictures.

17 And the hautinesse of men shalbe brought low, and the loftinesse of men shalbe abased, and the Lord shall onely be exalted in that day.

18 And the idoles will he vtterly destroy.

19 Then they shall goe into the holes of the rockes, and into the caues of the earth, from before the feare of the Lord, and from the glory of his maiestie, when he shall arise to destroy the earth.

20 At that day shall man cast away his siluer idoles, and his golden idoles (which they had made themselues to worship them) to the mowles and to the backes,

21 To goe into the holes of the rockes, and into the toppes of the ragged rockes from before the feare of the Lord, and from the glory of his maiestie, when he shall rise to destroy the earth.

22 Cease you from the man whose breath is in his nostrels: for wherein is he to be esteemed?

Isaiah 3

1 For lo, the Lord God of hostes will take away from Ierusalem and from Iudah the stay and the strength: euen all the staye of bread, and all the stay of water,

2 The strong man, and the man of warre, the iudge and the prophet, the prudent and the aged,

3 The captaine of fiftie, and the honourable, and the counseller, and the cunning artificer, and the eloquent man.

4 And I will appoint children to bee their princes, and babes shall rule ouer them.

5 The people shalbe oppressed one of another, and euery one by his neighbour: the children shall presume against the ancient, and the vile against the honourable.

6 When euery one shall take holde of his brother of the house of his father, and say, Thou hast clothing: thou shalt bee our prince, and let this fall be vnder thine hand.

7 In that day hee shall sweare, saying, I cannot bee an helper: for there is no bread in mine house, nor clothing: therefore make me no prince of the people.

8 Doubtlesse Ierusalem is fallen, and Iudah is fallen downe, because their tongue and workes are against the Lord, to prouoke the eyes of his glory.

9 The triall of their countenance testifieth against them, yea, they declare their sinnes as Sodom, they hide them not. Wo be vnto their soules: for they haue rewarded euil vnto themselues.

10 Say ye, Surely it shalbe well with the iust: for they shall eate the fruite of their workes.

11 Woe be to the wicked, it shalbe euill with him: for the reward of his handes shalbe giuen him.

12 Children are extortioners of my people, and women haue rule ouer them: O my people, they that leade thee, cause

thee to erre, and destroy the way of thy paths.

13 The Lord standeth vp to pleade, yea, hee standeth to iudge the people.

14 The Lord shall enter into iudgement with the Ancients of his people and the princes thereof: for ye haue eaten vp the vineyarde: the spoyle of the poore is in your houses.

15 What haue ye to do, that ye beate my people to pieces, and grinde the faces of the poore, saith the Lord, euen the Lord of hoasts?

16 The Lord also saith, Because the daughters of Zion are hautie, and walke with stretched out neckes, and with wandering eyes, walking and minsing as they goe, and making a tinkeling with their feete,

17 Therefore shall the Lord make the heades of the daughters of Zion balde, and the Lord shall discouer their secrete partes.

18 In that day shall the Lord take away the ornament of the slippers, and the calles, and the round tyres,

19 The sweete balles, and the brasselets, and the bonnets,

20 The tyres of the head, and the sloppes, and the head bandes, and the tablets, and the earings,

21 The rings and the mufflers,

22 The costly apparell and the vailes, and the wimples, and the crisping pinnes,

23 And the glasses and the fine linen, and the hoodes, and the launes.

24 And in steade of sweete sauour, there shall be stinke, and in steade of a girdle, a rent, and in steade of dressing of the heare, baldnesse, and in steade of a stomacher, a girding of sackecloth, and burning in steade of beautie.

25 Thy men shall fall by the sworde, and thy strength in the battell.

26 Then shall her gates mourne and lament, and she, being desolate, shall sit vpon the ground.

Isaiah 4

1 And in that day shall seuen women take hold of one man, saying, Wee will eate our owne bread, and we wil weare our owne garments: onely let vs bee called by thy name, and take away our reproche.

2 In that day shall the budde of the Lord bee beautifull and glorious, and the fruite of the earth shalbe excellent and pleasant for them that are escaped of Israel.

3 Then hee that shalbe left in Zion, and hee that shall remaine in Ierusalem, shalbe called holy, and euery one shalbe written among the liuing in Ierusalem,

4 When the Lord shall wash the filthines of the daughters of Zion, and purge the blood of Ierusalem out of the middes thereof by the spirite of iudgement, and by the spirit of burning.

5 And the Lord shall create vpon euery place of mount Zion, and vpon the assemblies thereof, a cloude and smoke by day, and the shining of a flaming fire by night: for vpon all the glory shall be a defence.

6 And a couering shalbe for a shadow in the day for the heate, and a place of refuge and a couert for the storme and for the raine.

Isaiah 5

1 Now will I sing to my beloued a song of my beloued to his vineyarde, My beloued had a vineyarde in a very fruitefull hill,

2 And hee hedged it, and gathered out the stones of it, and he planted it with the best plants, and hee builte a towre in the middes thereof, and made a wine presse therein: then hee looked that it should bring foorth grapes: but it brought foorth wilde grapes.

3 Now therefore, O inhabitants of Ierusalem and men of Iudah, iudge, I pray you, betweene me, and my vineyarde.

4 What coulde I haue done any more to my vineyard that I haue not done vnto it? why haue I looked that it should bring foorth grapes, and it bringeth foorth wilde grapes?

5 And nowe I will tell you what I will do to my vineyarde: I will take away the hedge thereof, and it shall be eaten vp: I will breake the wall thereof, and it shall be troden downe:

6 And I will laye it waste: it shall not be cut, nor digged, but briers, and thornes shall growe vp: I will also commande the cloudes that they raine no raine vpon it.

7 Surely the vineyard of the Lord of hostes is the house of Israel, and the men of Iudah are his pleasant plant, and hee looked for iudgement, but beholde oppression: for righteousnesse, but beholde a crying.

8 Woe vnto them that ioyne house to house, and laye fielde to fielde, till there bee no place, that ye may be placed by your selues in the mids of the earth.

9 This is in mine cares, saith the Lord of hostes. Surely many houses shall be desolate, euen great, and faire without inhabitant.

10 For ten acres of vines shall yelde one bath, and the seede of an homer shall yelde an ephah.

11 Wo vnto them, that rise vp early to follow drunkennes, and to them that continue vntill night, till the wine doe inflame them.

12 And the harpe and viole, timbrel, and pipe, and wine are in their feastes: but they regard not the worke of the Lord, neither consider the worke of his handes.

13 Therefore my people is gone into captiuitie, because they had no knowledge, and the glorie thereof are men famished, and the multitude thereof is dried vp with thirst.

14 Therefore hell hath inlarged it selfe, and hath opened his mouth, without measure, and their glorie, and their multitude, and their pompe, and hee that reioyceth among them, shall descend into it.

15 And man shalbe brought downe, and man shalbe humbled, euen the eyes of the proude shalbe humbled.

16 And the Lord of hostes shalbe exalted in iudgement, and the holy God shalbe sanctified in iustice.

17 Then shall the lambes feede after their maner, and the strangers shall eate the desolate places of the fat.

18 Woe vnto them, that draw iniquitie with cordes of vanitie, and sinne, as with cart ropes:

19 Which say, Let him make speede: let him hasten his worke, that wee may see it: and let the counsell of the holy one of Israel draw neere and come, that we may knowe it.

20 Woe vnto them that speake good of euill, and euill of good, which put darkenes for light, and light for darkenes, that put bitter for sweete, and sweete for sowre.

21 Woe vnto them that are wise in their owne eyes, and prudent in their owne sight.

22 Wo vnto them that are mightie to drinke wine, and to them that are strong to powre in strong drinke:

23 Which iustifie the wicked for a rewarde, and take away the righteousnesse of the righteous from him.

24 Therefore as the flame of fire deuoureth the stubble, and as the chaffe is cosumed of the flame: so their roote shalbe as rottennesse, and their bud shall rise vp like dust, because they haue cast off the Lawe of the Lord of hostes, and contemned the word of the holy one of Israel.

25 Therefore is the wrath of the Lord kindled against his people, and hee hath stretched out his hand vpon them, and hath smitten them that the mountaines did tremble: and their carkases were torne in the middes of the streetes, and for all this his wrath was not turned away, but his hande was stretched out still.

26 And he will lift vp a signe vnto the nations a farre, and wil hisse vnto them from the ende of the earth: and beholde, they shall come hastily with speede.

27 None shall faint nor fall among them: none shall slumber nor sleepe, neither shall the girdle of his loynes be loosed, nor the latchet of his shooes be broken:

28 Whose arrowes shall be sharpe, and all his bowes bent: his horse hoofes shall be thought like flint, and his wheeles like a whirlewinde.

29 His roaring shalbe like a lyon, and he shall roare like lyons whelpes: they shall roare, and lay holde of the praye: they shall take it away, and none shall deliuer it.

30 And in that day they shall roare vpon them, as the roaring of the sea: and if they looke vnto the earth, beholde darkenesse, and sorowe, and the light shalbe darkened in their skie.

Isaiah 6

1 In the yeere of the death of King Vzziah, I saw also the Lord sitting vpon an high throne, and lifted vp, and the lower partes thereof filled the Temple.

2 The Seraphims stoode vpon it: euery one had sixe wings: with twaine he couered his face, and with twaine hee couered his feete, and with twaine he did flie.

3 And one cryed to another, and sayde, Holy, holy, holy is the Lord of hostes: the whole world is full of his glory.

4 And the lintles of the doore cheekes moued at the voyce of him that cryed, and the house was filled with smoke.

5 Then I sayd, Wo is me: for I am vndone, because I am a man of polluted lips, and I dwell in the middes of a people of polluted lips: for mine eyes haue seene the King and Lord of hostes.

6 Then flewe one of the Seraphims vnto me with an hote cole in his hand, which he had taken from the altar with the tongs:

7 And he touched my mouth, and sayd, Loe, this hath touched thy lips, and thine iniquitie shall be taken away, and thy sinne shalbe purged.

8 Also I heard the voyce of the Lord, saying, Whome shall I send? and who shall goe for vs? Then I sayd, Here am I, send me.

9 And he sayd, Goe, and say vnto this people, Ye shall heare in deede, but ye shall not vnderstand: ye shall plainely see, and not perceiue.

10 Make the heart of this people fatte, make their eares heauie, and shut their eyes, lest they see with their eyes, and heare with their eares, and vnderstand with their hearts, and conuert, and he heale them.

11 Then sayd I, Lord, howe long? And he answered, Vntill the cities be wasted without inhabitant, and the houses without man, and the land be vtterly desolate,

12 And the Lord haue remoued men farre away, and there be a great desolation in the mids of the land.

13 But yet in it shalbe a tenth, and shall returne, and shalbe eaten vp as an elme or an oke, which haue a substance in them, when they cast their leaues: so the holy seede shall be the substance thereof.

Isaiah 7

1 And in the dayes of Ahaz, the sonne of Iotham, the sonne of Vzziah king of Iudah, Rezin the King of Aram came vp, and Pekah the sonne of Remaliah King of Israel, to Ierusalem to fight against it, but he could not ouercome it.

2 And it was tolde the house of Dauid, saying, Aram is ioyned with Ephraim: therefore his heart was moued, and the heart of his people, as the trees of the forest are moued by the winde.

3 Then sayde the Lord vnto Isaiah, Goe foorth nowe to meete Ahaz (thou and Sheariashub thy sonne) at the ende of the conduit of the vpper poole, in the path of the fullers fielde,

4 And say vnto him, Take heede, and be still: feare not, neither be faint hearted for the two tailes of these smoking firebrands, for the furious wrath of Rezin and of Aram, and of Remaliahs sonne:

5 Because Aram hath taken wicked counsell against thee, and Ephraim, and Remaliahs sonne, saying,

6 Let vs goe vp against Iudah, and let vs waken them vp, and make a breach therein for vs, and set a King in the mids thereof, euen the sonne of Tabeal.

7 Thus sayth the Lord God, It shall not stand, neither shall it be.

8 For the head of Aram is Damascus, and the head of Damascus is Rezin: and within fiue and threescore yeere, Ephraim shalbe destroyed from being a people.

9 And the head of Ephraim is Samaria, and the head of Samaria is Remaliahs sonne. If ye beleeue not, surely ye shall not be established.

10 And the Lord spake againe vnto Ahaz, saying,

11 Aske a signe for thee of the Lord thy God: aske it, either in the depth beneath or in the height aboue.

12 But Ahaz sayd, I wil not aske, neither will I tempt the Lord.

13 Then he sayd, Heare you nowe, O house of Dauid, Is it a small thing for you to grieue men, that ye will also grieue my God?

14 Therefore the Lord himselfe will giue you a signe. Beholde, the virgine shall conceiue and beare a sonne, and she shall call his name Immanu-el.

15 Butter and hony shall he eate, till he haue knowledge to refuse the euill, and to chuse the good.

16 For afore the childe shall haue knowledge to eschew the euill, and to chuse the good, the land, that thou abhorrest, shalbe forsaken of both her Kings.

17 The Lord shall bring vpon thee, and vpon thy people, and vpon thy fathers house (the dayes that haue not come from the day that Ephraim departed from Iudah) euen the King of Asshur.

18 And in that day shall the Lord hisse for the flie that is at the vttermost part of the floods of Egypt, and for the bee which is in the lande of Asshur,

19 And they shall come and shall light all in the desolate valleys, and in the holes of the rockes, and vpon all thorny places, and vpon all bushy places.

20 In that day shall the Lord shaue with a rasor that is hired, euen by them beyond the Riuer, by the King of Asshur, the head and the heare of the feete, and it shall consume the beard.

21 And in the same day shall a man nourish a yong kow, and two sheepe.

22 And for the abundance of milke, that they shall giue, hee shall eate butter: for butter and hony shall euery one eate, which is left within the land.

23 And at the same day euery place, wherein shalbe a thousand vines, shalbe at a thousand pieces of siluer: so it shalbe for the briers and for the thornes.

24 With arrowes and with bowe shall one come thither: because all the land shall be briers and thornes.

25 But on all the mountaines, which shalbe digged with the mattocke, there shall not come thither the feare of briers and thornes: but they shalbe for the sending out of bullocks, and for the treading of sheepe.

Isaiah 8

1 Moreover, the Lord sayd vnto me, Take thee a great roll, and write in it with a mans penne, Make speede to the spoyle: haste to the praye.

2 Then I tooke vnto me faithfull witnesses to recorde, Vriah the Priest, and Zechariah the sonne of Ieberechiah.

3 After, I came vnto the Prophetesse, which conceiued, and bare a sonne. Then sayd the Lord to me, Call his name, Mahershalalhash-baz.

4 For before the childe shall haue knowledge to crye, My father, and my mother, he shall take away the riches of Damascus and the spoyle of Samaria, before the King of Asshur.

5 And the Lord spake yet againe vnto me, saying,

6 Because this people hath refused the waters of Shiloah that runne softly, and reioyce with Rezin, and the sonne of Remaliah,

7 Nowe therefore, beholde, the Lord bringeth vp vpon them the waters of the Riuer mightie and great, euen the King of Asshur with all his glory, and he shall come vp vpon all their riuers, and goe ouer all their banks,

8 And shall breake into Iudah, and shall ouerflowe and passe through, and shall come vp to the necke, and the stretching out of his wings shall fill the breadth of thy land, O Immanu-el.

9 Gather together on heapes, O ye people, and ye shalbe broken in pieces, and hearken all ye of farre countreys: gird your selues, and you shalbe broken in pieces: gird your selues, and you shalbe broken in pieces.

10 Take counsell together, yet it shall be brought to nought: pronounce a decree, yet shall it not stand: for God is with vs.

11 For the Lord spake thus to me in taking of mine hand, and taught me, that I should not walke in the way of this people, saying,

12 Say ye not, A confederacie to all them, to whome this people sayth a confederacie, neither feare you their feare, nor be afrayd of them.

13 Sanctifie the Lord of hostes, and let him be your feare, and let him be your dread,

14 And he shalbe as a Sanctuarie: but as a stumbling stone, and as a rocke to fall vpon, to both the houses of Israel, and as a snare and as a net to the inhabitants of Ierusalem.

15 And many among them shall stumble, and shall fall and shalbe

broken and shalbe snared and shalbe taken.

16 Binde vp the testimonie: seale vp the Law among my disciples.

17 Therefore I will waite vpon the Lord that hath hid his face from the house of Iaakob, and I wil looke for him.

18 Beholde, I and the children whome the Lord hath giuen me, are as signes and as wonders in Israel, by the Lord of hostes, which dwelleth in mount Zion.

19 And when they shall say vnto you, Enquire at them that haue a spirit of diuination, and at the soothsayers, which whisper and murmure, Should not a people enquire at their God? from the liuing to the dead?

20 To the Law, and to the testimonie, if they speake not according to this worde: it is because there is no light in them.

21 Then he that is afflicted and famished, shall go to and from in it: and when he shalbe hungry, he shall euen freat himselfe, and curse his King and his gods, and shall looke vpward.

22 And when he shall looke to the earth, beholde trouble, and darkenes, vexation and anguish, and he is driuen to darkenes.

Isaiah 9

1 Yet the darkenesse shall not be according to the affliction that it had when at the first hee touched lightly the land of Zebulun and the land of Naphtali, nor afteward when he was more grieuous by the way of the sea beyond Iorden in Galile of the Gentiles.

2 The people that walked in darkenes haue seene a great light: they that dwelled in the land of the shadowe of death, vpon them hath the light shined.

3 Thou hast multiplied the nation, and not increased their ioye: they haue reioyced before thee according to the ioye in haruest, and as men reioyce when they deuide a spoyle.

4 For the yoke of their burthen, and the staffe of their shoulder and the rod of their oppressour hast thou broken as in the day of Midian.

5 Surely euery battell of the warriour is with noyse, and with tumbling of garments in blood: but this shall be with burning and deuouring of fire.

6 For vnto vs a childe is borne, and vnto vs a Sonne is giuen: and the gouernement is vpon his shoulder, and he shall call his name Wonderfull, Counseller, The mightie God, The euerlasting Father, The prince of peace,

7 The increase of his gouernement and peace shall haue none end: he shall sit vpon the throne of Dauid, and vpon his kingdome, to order it, and to stablish it with iudgement and with iustice, from henceforth, euen for euer: the zeale of the Lord of hostes will performe this.

8 The Lord hath sent a worde into Iaakob, and it hath lighted vpon Israel.

9 And all the people shall knowe, euen Ephraim, and the inhabitant of Samaria, that say in the pride and presumption of the heart,

10 The brickes are fallen, but we will build it with hewen stones: the wilde figge trees are cut downe, but we will change them into ceders.

11 Neuerthelesse the Lord will raise vp the aduersaries of Rezin against him, and ioyne his enemies together.

12 Aram before and the Philistims behinde, and they shall deuoure Israel with open mouth: yet for all this his wrath is not turned away, but his hand is stretched out still.

13 For the people turneth not vnto him that smiteth them, neither doe they seeke the Lord of hostes.

14 Therefore will the Lord cut off from Israel head and taile, branche and rush in one day.

15 The ancient and the honorable man, he is the head: and the prophet that teacheth lies, he is the taile.

16 For the leaders of the people cause them to erre: and they that are led by them are deuoured.

17 Therefore shall the Lord haue no pleasure in their yong men, neither will he haue compassion of their fatherlesse and of their widowes: for euery one is an hypocrite and wicked, and euery mouth speaketh follie: yet for all this his wrath is not turned away, but his hand is stretched out stil.

18 For wickednesse burneth as a fire: it deuoureth the briers and the thornes and will kindle in the thicke places of the forest: and they shall mount vp like the lifting vp of smoke.

19 By the wrath of the Lord of hostes shall the land be darkened, and the people shall be as the meate of ye fire: no man shall spare his brother.

20 And he shall snatch at the right hand, and be hungrie: and he shall eate on the left hand, and shall not be satisfied: euery one shall eate ye flesh of his owne arme.

21 Manasseh, Ephraim: and Ephraim Manasseh, and they both shall be against Iudah yet for all this his wrath is not turned away, but his hand is stretched out still.

Isaiah 10

1 Woe vnto them that decree wicked decrees, and write grieuous things,

2 To keepe backe ye poore from iudgement, and to take away the iudgement of the poore of my people, that widowes may be their pray, and that they may spoyle the fatherlesse.

3 What will ye doe nowe in the day of visitation, and of destruction, which shall come from farre? to whom will ye flee for helpe? and where will ye leaue your glorie?

4 Without me euery one shall fall among them that are bound, and they shall fall downe among the slayne: yet for all this his wrath is not turned away, but his hand is stretched out still.

5 O Asshur, the rodde of my wrath: and the staffe in their hands is mine indignation.

6 I will sende him to a dissembling nation, and I will giue him a charge against the people of my wrath to take the spoyle and to take the pray, and to treade them vnder feete like the mire in the streete.

7 But he thinketh not so, neither doeth his heart esteeme it so: but he imagineth to destroy and to cut off not a fewe nations.

8 For he sayeth, Are not my princes altogether Kings?

9 Is not Calno as Carchemish? Is not Hamath like Arpad? Is not Samaria as Damascus?

10 Like as mine hand hath founde the kingdomes of the idoles, seeing their idoles were aboue Ierusalem, and aboue Samaria:

11 Shall not I, as I haue done to Samaria, and to the idoles thereof, so doe to Ierusalem and to the idoles thereof?

12 But when the Lord hath accomplished all his worke vpon mount Zion and Ierusalem, I will visite the fruite of the proude heart of the King of Asshur, and his glorious and proud lookes,

13 Because he said, By ye power of mine owne hand haue I done it, and by my wisdome, because I am wise: therefore I haue remooued the borders of the people, and haue spoyled their treasures, and haue pulled downe the inhabitants like a valiant man.

14 And mine hand hath found as a nest the riches of the people, and as one gathereth egges that are left, so haue I gathered all the earth: and there was none to mooue the wing or to open the mouth, or to whisper.

15 Shall the axe boast it selfe against him that heweth therewith? or shall the sawe exalt it selfe against him that moueth it? as if the rod shoulde lift vp it selfe against him that taketh it vp, or the staffe should exalt it selfe, as it were no wood.

16 Therefore shall the Lord God of hostes send amog his fat men, leannes, and vnder his glorie he shall kindle a burning, like the burning of fire.

17 And the light of Israel shalbe as a fire, and the Holy one thereof as a flame, and it shall burne, and deuoure his thornes and his briers in one day:

18 And shall consume the glory of his forest, and of his fruitfull fieldes both soule and flesh: and he shalbe as ye fainting of a standard bearer.

19 And the rest of the trees of his forest shalbe fewe, that a childe may tell them.

20 And at that day shall the remnant of Israel, and such as are escaped of the house of Iaakob, stay no more vpon him that smote them, but shall stay vpon ye Lord, ye Holy one of Israel in trueth.

21 The remnant shall returne, euen the remnant of Iaakob vnto the mightie God.

22 For though thy people, O Israel, be as the sand of the sea, yet shall the remnant of them returne. The consumption decreed shall ouerflow with righteousnesse.

23 For the Lord God of hostes shall make the consumption, euen determined, in the middes of all the land.

24 Therefore thus saith ye Lord God of hostes, O my people, that dwellest in Zion, be not afraid of Asshur: he shall smite thee with a rod, and shall lift vp his staffe against thee after the maner of Egypt:

25 But yet a very litle time, and the wrath shall be consumed, and mine anger in their destruction.

26 And ye Lord of hostes shall raise vp a scourge for him, according to the plague of Midian in the rocke Oreb: and as his staffe was vpon the Sea, so he will lift it vp after the maner of Egypt.

27 And at that day shall his burden be taken away from off thy shoulder, and his yoke from off thy necke: and the yoke shalbe destroied because of the anoynting.

28 He is come to Aiath: he is passed into Migron: at Michmash shall he lay vp his armour.

29 They haue gone ouer the foorde: they lodged in the lodging at Geba: Ramah is afraide: Gibeah of Saul is fled away.

30 Lift vp thy voyce, O daughter Gallim, cause Laish to heare, O poore Anathoth.

31 Madmenah is remoued: the inhabitants of Gebim haue gathered themselues together.

32 Yet there is a time that he will stay at Nob: he shall lift vp his hand towarde the mount of the daughter Zion, the hill of Ierusalem.

33 Beholde, the Lord God of hostes shall cut off the bough with feare, and they of high stature shalbe cut off, and the hie shalbe humbled.

34 And he shall cut away the thicke places of the forest with yron, and Lebanon shall haue a mightie fall.

Isaiah 11

1 But there shall come a rodde foorth of the stocke of Ishai, and a grasse shall growe out of his rootes.

2 And the Spirite of the Lord shall rest vpon him: the Spirite of wisedome and vnderstanding, the Spirite of counsell and strength, the Spirite of knowledge, and of the feare of the Lord,

3 And shall make him prudent in the feare of the Lord: for he shall not iudge after the sight of his eies, neither reproue by ye hearing of his eares.

4 But with righteousnesse shall he iudge the poore, and with equitie shall he reproue for the meeke of the earth: and he shall smite the earth with the rod of his mouth, and with the breath of his lippes shall he slay the wicked.

5 And iustice shall be ye girdle of his loynes, and faithfulnesse the girdle of his reines.

6 The wolfe also shall dwell with the lambe, and the leopard shall lie with the kid, and the calfe, and the lyon, and the fat beast together, and a litle childe shall leade them.

7 And the kow and the beare shall feede: their yong ones shall lie together: and the lyon shall eate strawe like the bullocke.

8 And the sucking childe shall play vpon the hole of the aspe, and the wained childe shall put his hand vpon the cockatrice hole.

9 Then shall none hurt nor destroy in all the mountaine of mine holines: for the earth shalbe full of the knowledge of the Lord, as the waters that couer the sea.

10 And in that day the roote of Ishai, which shall stand vp for a signe vnto the people, the nations shall seeke vnto it, and his rest shall be glorious.

11 And in the same day shall the Lord stretche out his hand againe the second time, to possesse the remnant of his people, (which shalbe left) of Asshur, and of Egypt, and of Pathros, and of Ethiopia, and of Elam, and of Shinear, and of Hamath, and of the yles of the sea.

12 And he shall set vp a signe to the nations, and assemble the dispersed of Israel, and gather the scattered of Iudah from the foure corners of the worlde.

13 The hatred also of Ephraim shall depart, and the aduersaries of Iudah shalbe cut off: Ephraim shall not enuie Iudah, neither shall Iudah vexe Ephraim:

14 But they shall flee vpon the shoulders of the Philistims toward the West: they shall spoyle them of the East together: Edom and Moab shall be the stretching out of their hands, and the children of Ammon in their obedience.

15 The Lord also shall vtterly destroy the tongue of the Egyptians sea, and with his mightie winde shall lift vp his hand ouer the riuer, and shall smite him in his seuen streames, and cause men to walke therein with shooes.

16 And there shalbe a path to the remnant of his people, which are left of Asshur, like as it was vnto Israel in the day that he came vp out of the land of Egypt.

Isaiah 12

1 And thou shalt say in that day, O Lord, I will prayse thee: though thou wast angrie with me, thy wrath is turned away, and thou comfortest me.

2 Beholde, God is my saluation: I will trust, and will not feare: for ye Lord God is my strength and song: he also is become my saluation.

3 Therefore with ioy shall ye drawe waters out of the welles of saluation.

4 And ye shall say in that day, Prayse the Lord: call vpon his Name: declare his workes among the people: make mention of them, for his Name is exalted.

5 Sing vnto the Lord, for he hath done excellent things: this is knowen in all the worlde.

6 Cry out, and shoute, O inhabitant of Zion: for great is ye holy one of Israel in the middes of thee.

Isaiah 13

1 The burden of Babel, which Isaiah the sonne of Amoz did see.

2 Lift vp a standard vpon the hie mountaine: lift vp the voyce vnto them: wagge the hand, that they may goe into the gates of the nobles.

3 I haue commanded them, that I haue sanctified: and I haue called ye mightie to my wrath, and them that reioyce in my glorie.

4 The noyse of a multitude is in the mountaines, like a great people: a tumultuous voyce of the kingdomes of the nations gathered together: the Lord of hostes nombreth the hoste of the battell.

5 They come from a farre countrey, from the end of the heauen: euen the Lord with the weapons of his wrath to destroy the whole land.

6 Howle you, for the day of the Lord is at hande: it shall come as a destroier from the Almightie.

7 Therefore shall all hands be weakened, and all mens hearts shall melt,

8 And they shalbe afraid: anguish and sorowe shall take them, and they shall haue paine, as a woman that trauaileth: euery one shall be amased at his neighbour, and their faces shalbe like flames of fire.

9 Beholde, the day of the Lord commeth, cruel, with wrath and fierce anger to lay the land wast: and he shall destroy the sinners out of it.

10 For the starres of heauen and the planets thereof shall not giue their light: the sunne shalbe darkened in his going foorth, and the moone shall not cause her light to shine.

11 And I will visite the wickednes vpon the worlde, and their iniquitie vpon the wicked, and I wil cause the arrogancie of the proud to cease, and will cast downe the pride of tyrants.

12 I will make a man more precious then fine golde, euen a man aboue the wedge of golde of Ophir.

13 Therefore I will shake the heauen, and the earth shall remooue out of her place in the wrath of the Lord of hostes, and in the day of his fierce anger.

14 And it shall be as a chased doe, and as a sheepe that no man taketh vp. euery man shall turne to his owne people, and flee eche one to his owne lande.

15 Euery one that is founde, shall be striken through: and whosoeuer ioyneth himselfe, shall fal by the sworde.

16 Their children also shall be broken in pieces before their eyes: their houses shall be spoiled, and their wiues rauished.

17 Beholde, I will stirre vp the Medes against them, which shall not regarde siluer, nor be desirous of golde.

18 With bowes also shall they destroy ye children, and shall haue no compassion vpon the fruit of the wombe, and their eies shall not spare the children.

19 And Babel the glorie of kingdomes, the beautie and pride of the Chaldeans, shall be as the destruction of God in Sodom and Gomorah.

20 It shall not bee inhabited for euer, neither shall it be dwelled in from

generation to generation: neither shall the Arabian pitch his tents there, neither shall the shepheardes make their foldes there.

21 But Ziim shall lodge there, and their houses shall be ful of Ohim: Ostriches shall dwel there, and the Satyrs shall dance there.

22 And Iim shall crie in their palaces, and dragons in their pleasant palaces: and the time thereof is readie to come, and the daies thereof shall not be prolonged.

Isaiah 14

1 For the Lord wil haue compassion of Iaakob, and wil yet chuse Israel, and cause them to rest in their owne lande: and the stranger shall ioyne him selfe vnto them, and they shall cleaue to the house of Iaakob.

2 And the people shall receiue them and bring them to their owne place, and the house of Israel shall possesse them in the land of the Lord, for seruants and handmaids: and they shall take them prisoners, whose captiues they were, and haue rule ouer their oppressours.

3 And in that day when the Lord shall giue thee rest from thy sorrow, and from thy feare, and from the sore bodage, wherein thou didest serue,

4 Then shalt thou take vp this prouerbe against the King of Babel, and say, Howe hath the oppressor ceased? and the gold thirsty Babel rested?

5 The Lord hath broken the rodde of the wicked, and the scepter of the rulers:

6 Which smote the people in anger with a continuall plague, and ruled the nations in wrath: if any were persecuted, he did not let.

7 The whole worlde is at rest and is quiet: they sing for ioye.

8 Also the firre trees reioyced of thee, and the cedars of Lebanon, saying, Since thou art laid downe, no hewer came vp against vs.

9 Hel beneath is mooued for thee to meete thee at thy comming, raising vp the deade for thee, euen all the princes of the earth, and hath raised from their thrones all the Kinges of the nations.

10 All they shall crie, and saie vnto thee, Art thou become weake also as we? art thou become like vnto vs?

11 Thy pompe is brought downe to ye graue, and the sounde of thy violes: the worme is spred vnder thee, and the wormes couer thee.

12 How art thou fallen from heauen, O Lucifer, sonne of the morning? and cutte downe to the grounde, which didest cast lottes vpon the nations?

13 Yet thou saidest in thine heart, I will ascende into heauen, and exalt my throne aboue beside the starres of God: I will sitte also vpon the mount of the Congregation in the sides of the North.

14 I wil ascend aboue ye height of the cloudes, and I will be like the most high.

15 But thou shalt bee brought downe to the graue, to the sides of the pit.

16 They that see thee, shall looke vpon thee and consider thee, saying, Is this the man that made the earth to tremble, and that did shake the kingdomes?

17 He made the worlde as a wildernesse, and destroied the cities thereof, and opened not the house of his prisoners.

18 All the Kings of the nations, euen they all sleepe in glorie, euery one in his owne house.

19 But thou art cast out of thy graue like an abominable branch: like the raiment of those that are slaine, and thrust thorowe with a sword, which goe downe to the stones of the pit, as a carkeise troden vnder feete.

20 Thou shalt not be ioyned with them in the graue, because thou hast destroied thine owne lande, and slaine thy people: the seede of the wicked shall not be renoumed for euer.

21 Prepare a slaughter for his children, for the iniquitie of their fathers: let them not rise vp nor possesse the land, nor fil the face of the world with enemies.

22 For I wil rise vp against them (sayth the Lord of hostes) and will cut off from Babel the name and the remnant and the sonne, and the nephew, sayth the Lord:

23 And I wil make it a possession to ye hedgehogge, and pooles of water, and I will sweepe it with the besome of destruction, sayeth the Lord of hostes.

24 The Lord of hostes hath sworne, saying, Surely like as I haue purposed, so shall it come to passe, and as I haue consulted, it shall stand:

25 That I will breake to pieces Asshur in my land, and vpon my mountaines will I treade him vnder foote: so that his yoke shall depart from them, and his burden shall be taken from off their shoulder.

26 This is the counsell that is consulted vpon the whole worlde, and this is the hande stretched out ouer all the nations,

27 Because the Lord of hostes hath determined it, and who shall disanull it? and his hande is stretched out, and who shall turne it away?

28 In the yeere that King Ahaz died, was this burden.

29 Reioyce not, (thou whole Palestina) because the rod of him that did beat thee, is broken for out of the serpents roote shall come forth a cockatrise, and the fruit therof shalbe a firy flying serpent.

30 For the first borne of the poore shall be fed, and the needie shall lie downe in safetie: and I will kill thy roote with famine, and it shall slay thy remnant.

31 Howle, O gate, crie, O citie: thou whole lande of Palestina art dissolued, for there shall come from the North a smoke, and none shalbe alone, at his time appointed.

32 What shall then one answere the messengers of the Gentiles? That the Lord hath stablished Zion, and the poore of his people shall trust in it.

Isaiah 15

1 The burden of Moab. Surely Ar of Moab was destroied, and brought to silece in a

night: surely Kir of Moab was destroied, and brought to silence in a night.

2 He shall goe vp to the temple, and to Dibon to the hie places to weepe: for Nebo and for Medeba shall Moab howle: vpon all their heades shalbe baldnesse, and euery beard shauen.

3 In their streetes shall they bee gilded with sackecloth: on the toppes of their houses, and in their streetes euery one shall howle, and come downe with weeping.

4 And Heshbon shall crie, and Elealeh: their voyce shall bee heard vnto Iahaz: therefore the warriers of Moab shall showt: the soule of euery one shall lament in him selfe.

5 Mine heart shall crie for Moab: his fugitiues shall flee vnto Zoar, an heiffer of three yere olde: for they shall goe vp with weeping by the mounting vp of Luhith: and by the way of Horonaim they shall raise vp a crie of destruction.

6 For the waters of Nimrim shall be dried vp: therefore the grasse is withered, the herbes consumed, and there was no greene herbe.

7 Therefore what euery man hath left, and their substance shall they beare to the brooke of the willowes.

8 For the crie went round about the borders of Moab: and the howling thereof vnto Eglaim, and the skriking thereof vnto Beer Elim,

9 Because the waters of Dimon shall be full of blood: for I will bring more vpon Dimon, euen lyons vpon him that escapeth of Moab, and to the remnant of the land.

Isaiah 16

1 Send yee a lambe to the ruler of the worlde from the rocke of the wildernesse, vnto the mountaine of the daughter Zion.

2 For it shall be as a birde that flieth, and a nest forsaken: the daughters of Moab shall be at the foordes of Arnon.

3 Gather a cousel, execute iudgement: make thy shadowe as the night in the midday: hide them that are chased out: bewray not him that is fled.

4 Let my banished dwell with thee: Moab be thou their couert from the face of the destroyer: for the extortioner shall ende: the destroyer shalbe consumed, and the oppressour shall cease out of the land.

5 And in mercy shall the throne be prepared, and hee shall sit vpon it in stedfastnesse, in the tabernacle of Dauid, iudging, and seeking iudgement, and hasting iustice.

6 We haue heard of the pride of Moab, (he is very proud) euen his pride, and his arrogancie, and his indignation, but his lies shall not be so.

7 Therefore shall Moab howle vnto Moab: euery one shall howle: for the foundations of Kirhareseth shall ye mourne, yet they shalbe striken.

8 For ye vineyards of Heshbon are cut downe, and the vine of Sibmah: the lordes of the heathen haue broken the

principal vines thereof: they are come vnto Iaazer: they wandred in the wildernesse: her goodly branches stretched out them selues, and went ouer the sea.

9 Therefore will I weepe with the weeping of Iaazer, and of the vine of Sibmah, O Heshbon: and Elealeh, I will make thee drunke with my teares, because vpon thy sommer fruits, and vpon thy haruest a showting is fallen.

10 And gladnes is taken away, and ioy out of the plentifull fielde: and in the vineyardes shall be no singing nor shouting for ioy: the treader shall not tread wine in the wine presses: I haue caused the reioycing to cease.

11 Wherefore, my bowels shall sounde like an harpe for Moab, and mine inwarde partes for Ker-haresh.

12 And when it shall appeare that Moab shall be wearie of his hie places, then shall hee come to his temple to praie, but he shall not preuaile.

13 This is the word that the Lord hath spoken against Moab since that time.

14 And nowe the Lord hath spoken, saying, In three yeres, as the yeeres of a hireling, and the glorie of Moab shall be contemned in all the great multitude, and the remnant shalbe very small and feeble.

Isaiah 17

1 The burden of Damascus. Beholde, Damascus is taken away from being a citie, for it shall be a ruinous heape.

2 The cities of Aroer shall be forsaken: they shall be for the flockes: for they shall lye there, and none shall make them afraide.

3 The munition also shall cease from Ephraim, and the kingdome from Damascus, and the remnant of Aram shall be as the glory of the children of Israel, sayeth the Lord of hostes.

4 And in that day the glorie of Iaakob shall be impouerished, and the fatnes of his flesh shalbe made leane.

5 And it shalbe as when the haruest man gathereth the corne, and reapeth the eares with his arme, and he shall be as he that gathereth the eares in the valley of Rephaim.

6 Yet a gathering of grapes shall be left in it, as the shaking of an oliue tree, two or three beries are in the top of the vpmost boughes, and foure or fiue in the hie branches of the fruite thereof, sayeth the Lord God of Israel.

7 At that day shall a man looke to his maker, and his eyes shall looke to the holy one of Israel.

8 And hee shall not looke to the altars, the workes of his owne hands, neither shall he looke to those thinges, which his owne fingers haue made, as groues and images.

9 In that day shall the cities of their strength be as the forsaking of boughes and branches, which they did forsake, because of the children of Israel, and there shall be desolation.

10 Because thou hast forgotten the God of thy saluation, and hast not remembred the God of thy strength, therefore shalt thou set pleasant plantes, and shalt graffe strange vine branches:

11 In the day shalt thou make thy plant to growe, and in the morning shalt thou make thy seede to florish: but the haruest shall be gone in the day of possession, and there shalbe desperate sorrowe.

12 Ah, the multitude of many people, they shall make a sounde like the noyse of the sea: for the noyse of the people shall make a sounde like the noyse of mightie waters.

13 The people shall make a sounde like the noise of many waters: but God shall rebuke them, and they shall flee farre off, and shalbe chased as the chaffe of the mountaines before the winde, and as a rolling thing before the whirlewinde.

14 And loe, in the euening there is trouble: but afore the morning it is gone. This is the portion of them that spoyle vs, and the lot of them that robbe vs.

Isaiah 18

1 Oh, the lande shadowing with winges, which is beyond the riuers of Ethiopia,

2 Sending ambassadours by the Sea, euen in vessels of reedes vpon the waters, saying, Go, ye swift messengers, to a nation that is scattered abroade, and spoyled, vnto a terrible people from their beginning euen hitherto: a nation by litle and litle, euen troden vnder foote, whose land the floods haue spoyled.

3 Al ye the inhabitants of ye world and dwellers in the earth, shall see when he setteth vp a signe in the mountaines, and when he bloweth the trumpet, ye shall heare.

4 And so the Lord saide vnto me, I will rest and beholde in my tabernacle, as the heate drying vp the rayne, and as a cloude of dewe in the heate of haruest.

5 For afore the haruest when the floure is finished, and the fruite is riping in the floure, then he shall cut downe the branches with hookes, and shall take away, and cut off the boughes:

6 They shall be left together vnto the foules of the mountaines, and to the beastes of the earth: for the foule shall sommer vpon it, and euery beast of the earth shall winter vpon it.

7 At that time shall a present be brought vnto the Lord of hostes, (a people that is scattered abroade, and spoyled, and of a terrible people from their beginning hitherto, a nation, by litle and litle euen troden vnder foote, whose land the riuers haue spoyled) to the place of the Name of the Lord of hostes, euen the mount Zion.

Isaiah 19

1 The burden of Egypt. Beholde, the Lord rideth vpon a swift cloude, and shall come into Egypt, and the idoles of Egypt shall be moued at his presence, and the heart of Egypt shall melt in the middes of her.

2 And I will set the Egyptians against the Egyptians: so euery one shall fight against his brother, and euery one against his neighbour, citie against citie, and kingdome against kingdome.

3 And the spirite of Egypt shall faile in the middes of her, and I will destroy their counsell, and they shall seeke at the idoles, and at the sorcerers, and at them that haue spirits of diuination, and at the southsayers.

4 And I will deliuer the Egyptians into the hand of the cruell Lordes, and a mightie King shall rule ouer them, sayth the Lord God of hostes.

5 Then the waters of the sea shall faile, and the riuers shall be dryed vp, and wasted.

6 And the riuers shall goe farre away: the riuers of defence shalbe emptied and dryed vp: the reedes and flagges shall be cut downe.

7 The grasse in the riuer, and at the head of the riuers, and all that groweth by the riuer, shall wither, and be driuen away, and be no more.

8 The fishers also shall mourne, and all they that cast angle into the riuer, shall lament, and they that spread their nette vpon the waters, shall be weakened.

9 Moreouer, they that worke in flaxe of diuers sortes, shall be confounded, and they that weaue nettes.

10 For their nettes shalbe broken, and all they, that make pondes, shalbe heauie in heart.

11 Surely the princes of Zoan are fooles: the counsell of the wise counselers of Pharaoh is become foolish: how say ye vnto Pharaoh, I am the sonne of the wise? I am the sonne of the ancient Kings?

12 Where are nowe thy wise men, that they may tell thee, or may knowe what the Lord of hostes hath determined against Egypt?

13 The princes of Zoan are become fooles: the princes of Noph are deceiued, they haue deceiued Egypt, euen the corners of the tribes thereof.

14 The Lord hath mingled among them the spirite of errours: and they haue caused Egypt to erre in euery worke thereof, as a drunken man erreth in his vomite.

15 Neither shall there be any worke in Egypt, which the head may doe, nor the tayle, ye branch nor the rush.

16 In that day shall Egypt be like vnto women: for it shall be afraide and feare because of the moouing of the hand of the Lord of hostes, which he shaketh ouer it.

17 And the land of Iudah shall be a feare vnto Egypt: euery one that maketh mention of it, shalbe afraid thereat, because of ye counsell of the Lord of hostes, which he hath determined vpon it.

18 In that day shall fiue cities in the lande of Egypt speake the language of Canaan, and shall sweare by the Lord of hostes. one shall be called the citie of destruction.

19 In that day shall the altar of the Lord be in the middes of the land of Egypt, and a pillar by the border thereof vnto the Lord.

20 And it shall be for a signe and for a witnes vnto the Lord of hostes in the land of Egypt: for they shall crie vnto the Lord, because of the oppressers, and he shall send them a Sauiour and a great man, and shall deliuer them.

21 And the Lord shall be knowen of the Egyptians, and the Egyptians shall knowe the Lord in that day, and doe sacrifice and oblation, and shall vowe vowes vnto the Lord, and performe them.

22 So ye Lord shall smite Egypt, he shall smite and heale it: for he shall returne vnto ye Lord, and he shall be intreated of them and shall heale them.

23 In that day shall there be a path from Egypt to Asshur, and Asshur shall come into Egypt, and Egypt into Asshur: so the Egyptians shall worship with Asshur.

24 In that day shall Israel be the third with Egypt and Asshur, euen a blessing in the middes of the land.

25 For the Lord of hostes shall blesse it, saying, Blessed be my people Egypt and Asshur, the worke of mine hands, and Israel mine inheritance.

Isaiah 20

1 In the yeere that Tartan came to Ashdod, (when Sargon King of Asshur sent him) and had fought against Ashdod, and taken it,

2 At the same time spake the Lord by ye hand of Isaiah the sonne of Amoz, saying, Goe, and loose the sackecloth from thy loynes, and put off thy shooe from thy foote. And he did so, walking naked and barefoote.

3 And the Lord said, Like as my seruant Isaiah hath walked naked, and barefoote three yeeres, as a signe and wonder vpon Egypt, and Ethiopia,

4 So shall the King of Asshur take away the captiuitie of Egypt, and the captiuitie of Ethiopia, both yong men and olde men, naked and barefoote, with their buttockes vncouered, to the shame of Egypt.

5 And they shall feare, and be ashamed of Ethiopia their expectation, and of Egypt their glory.

6 Then shall the inhabitant of this yle say in that day, Behold, such is our expectation, whither we fledde for helpe to be deliuered from the King of Asshur, and howe shall we be deliuered?

Isaiah 21

1 The burden of the desert Sea. As the whirlewindes in the South vse to passe from the wildernesse, so shall it come from the horrible land.

2 A grieuous vision was shewed vnto me, The transgressour against a transgressour, and the destroyer against a destroyer. Goe vp Elam, besiege Media: I haue caused all the mourning thereof to cease.

3 Therefore are my loynes filled with sorow: sorowes haue taken me as the sorowes of a woman that trauayleth: I was bowed downe when I heard it, and I was amased when I sawe it.

4 Mine heart failed: fearefulnesse troubled me: the night of my pleasures hath he turned into feare vnto me.

5 Prepare thou the table: watch in the watch towre: eate, drinke: arise, ye princes, anoynt the shielde.

6 For thus hath the Lord said vnto me, Go, set a watchman, to tell what he seeth.

7 And he sawe a charet with two horsemen: a charet of an asse, and a charet of a camel: and he hearkened and tooke diligent heede.

8 And he cryed, A lyon: my lorde, I stand continually vpon ye watche towre in the day time, and I am set in my watche euery night:

9 And beholde, this mans charet commeth with two horsemen. And he answered and said, Babel is fallen: it is fallen, and all the images of her gods hath he broken vnto the ground.

10 O my threshing, and the corne of my floore. That which I haue heard of the Lord of hostes, the God of Israel, haue I shewed vnto you.

11 The burden of Dumah. He calleth vnto me out of Seir, Watchman, what was in ye night? Watchman, what was in the night?

12 The watchman saide, The morning commeth, and also the night. If yee will aske, enquire: returne and come.

13 The burden against Arabia. In the forest of Arabia shall yee tarie all night, euen in the waies of Dedanim.

14 O inhabitants of the lande of Tema, bring foorth water to meete the thirstie, and preuent him that fleeth with his bread.

15 For they flee from the drawen swords, euen from the drawen sword, and from the bent bowe, and from the grieuousnesse of warre.

16 For thus hath the Lord sayd vnto me, Yet a yeere according to the yeeres of an hireling, and all the glorie of Kedar shall faile.

17 And the residue of the nomber of ye strong archers of the sonnes of Kedar shall be fewe: for the Lord God of Israel hath spoken it.

Isaiah 22

1 The burden of the valley of vision. What aileth thee nowe that thou art wholy gone vp vnto the house toppes?

2 Thou that art full of noise, a citie full of brute, a ioyous citie: thy slaine men shall not bee slaine with sworde, nor die in battell.

3 All thy princes shall flee together from the bowe: they shalbe bound: all that shall be found in thee, shall be bound together, which haue fled from farre.

4 Therefore said I, Turne away from me: I wil weepe bitterly: labour not to comfort mee for the destruction of the daughter of my people.

5 For it is a day of trouble, and of ruine, and of perplexitie by the Lord God of hostes in the valley of vision, breaking downe the citie: and a crying vnto the mountaines.

6 And Elam bare the quiuer in a mans chart with horsemen, and Kir vncouered the shield.

7 And thy chiefe valleis were full of charets, and the horsemen set themselues in aray against the gate.

8 And hee discouered the couering of Iudah: and thou didest looke in that day to the armour of the house of the forest.

9 And ye haue seene the breaches of the citie of Dauid: for they were many, and ye gathered the waters of the lower poole.

10 And yee nombred the houses of Ierusalem, and the houses haue yee broken downe to fortifie the wall,

11 And haue also made a ditche betweene the two walles, for the waters of the olde poole, and haue not looked vnto the maker thereof, neither had respect vnto him that formed it of olde.

12 And in that day did the Lord God of hosts call vnto weeping and mourning, and to baldnes and girding with sackecloth.

13 And beholde, ioy and gladnes, slaying oxen and killing sheepe, eating flesh, and drinking wine, eating and drinking: for to morowe we shall die.

14 And it was declared in ye eares of the Lord of hostes. Surely this iniquitie shall not be purged from you, til ye die, saith the Lord God of hostes.

15 Thus sayeth the Lord God of hostes, Goe, get thee to that treasurer, to Shebna, the steward of the house, and say,

16 What haste thou to doe here? and whome hast thou here? that thou shouldest here hewe thee out a sepulchre, as he that heweth out his sepulchre in an hie place, or that graueth an habitation for him selfe in a rocke?

17 Beholde, the Lord wil carie thee away with a great captiuitie, and will surely couer thee.

18 He wil surely rolle and turne thee like a bal in a large countrey: there shalt thou die, and there the charets of thy glory shalbe the shame of thy lordes house.

19 And I wil driue thee from thy station, and out of thy dwelling will he destroy thee.

20 And in that day will I call my seruant Eliakim the sonne of Hilkiah,

21 And with thy garments will I clothe him, and with thy girdle will I strengthen him: thy power also will I commit into his hande, and hee shalbe a father of the inhabitats of Ierusalem, and of the house of Iudah.

22 And the key of the house of Dauid will I lay vpon his shoulder: so hee shall open, and no man shall shut: and he shall shut, and no man shall open.

23 And I will fasten him as a naile in a sure place, and hee shall be for the throne of glorie to his fathers house.

24 And they shall hang vpon him all the glorie of his fathers house, euen of the nephewes and posteritie all small

vessels, from the vessels of the cuppes, euen to all the instruments of musike.

25 In that day, sayeth the Lord of hostes, shall the naile, that is fastned in the sure place, depart and shall be broken, and fall: and the burden, that was vpon it, shall bee cut off: for the Lord hath spoken it.

Isaiah 23

1 The burden of Tyrus. Howle, yee shippes of Tarshish: for it is destroied, so that there is none house: none shall come from the lande of Chittim: it is reueiled vnto them.

2 Be still, yee that dwell in the yles: the marchantes of Zidon, and such as passe ouer the sea, haue replenished thee.

3 The seede of Nilus growing by the abundance of waters, and the haruest of the riuer was her reuenues, and she was a marte of the nations.

4 Be ashamed, thou Zidon: for the sea hath spoken, euen the strength of the sea, saying, I haue not trauailed, nor brought forth children, neither nourished yong men, nor brought vp virgins.

5 When the fame commeth to the Egyptians, they shall be sorie, concerning the rumour of Tyrus.

6 Goe you ouer to Tarshish: howle, yee that dwell in the yles.

7 Is not this that your glorious citie? her antiquitie is of ancient daies: her owne feete shall leade her afarre off to be a soiourner.

8 Who hath decreed this against Tyrus (that crowneth men) whose marchantes are princes? whose chapmen are the nobles of the worlde?

9 The Lord of hostes hath decreed this, to staine the pride of all glorie, and to bring to contempt all them that be glorious in the earth.

10 Passe through thy lande like a flood to the daughter of Tarshish: there is no more strength.

11 He stretched out his hand vpon the sea: he shooke the kingdomes: the Lord hath giuen a commandement concerning the place of marchandise, to destroy the power thereof.

12 And he saide, Thou shalt no more reioyce when thou art oppressed: O virgin daughter of Zidon: rise vp, goe ouer vnto Chittim: yet there thou shalt haue no rest.

13 Behold the lande of the Caldeans: this was no people: Asshur founded it by the inhabitants of the wildernesse: they set vp the towers thereof: they raised the palaces thereof and hee brought it to ruine.

14 Howle yee shippes of Tarshish, for your strength is destroyed.

15 And in that day shall Tyrus bee forgotten seuentie yeeres, (according to the yeeres of one King) at the ende of seuentie yeeres shall Tyrus sing as an harlot.

16 Take an harpe and go about the citie: (thou harlot thou hast beene forgotten) make sweete melodie, sing moe songes that thou maiest be remembred.

17 And at the ende of seuentie yeres shall the Lord visite Tyrus, and shee shall returne to her wages, and shall commit fornication with all the kingdomes of the earth, that are in the world.

18 Yet her occupying and her wages shall bee holy vnto the Lord: it shall not be laied vp nor kept in store, but her marchandise shalbe for them that dwell before the Lord, to eate sufficiently, and to haue durable clothing.

Isaiah 24

1 Behold, the Lord maketh the earth emptie, and hee maketh it waste: hee turneth it vpside downe, and scattereth abrode the inhabitants thereof.

2 And there shalbe like people, like Priest, and like seruaunt, like master, like maide, like mistresse, like bier, like seller, like lender, like borower, like giuer, like taker to vsurie.

3 The earth shalbe cleane emptied, and vtterly spoiled: for the Lord hath spoken this worde.

4 The earth lamenteth and fadeth away: the world is feeble and decaied: the proude people of the earth are weakened.

5 The earth also deceiueth, because of the inhabitantes thereof: for they transgressed the lawes: they changed the ordinances, and brake the euerlasting couenant.

6 Therefore hath the curse deuoured the earth, and the inhabitantes thereof are desolate. Wherefore the inhabitants of the land are burned vp, and fewe men are left.

7 The wine faileth, the vine hath no might: all that were of merie heart, doe mourne.

8 The mirth of tabrets ceaseth: the noyse of them that reioyce, endeth: the ioye of the harpe ceaseth.

9 They shall not drinke wine with mirth: strong drinke shall be bitter to them that drinke it.

10 The citie of vanitie is broken downe: euery house is shut vp, that no man may come in.

11 There is a crying for wine in the streetes: al ioy is darkened: the mirth of the world is gone away.

12 In the citie is left desolation, and the gate is smitten with destruction.

13 Surely thus shall it bee in the middes of the earth, among the people, as the shaking of an oliue tree, and as the grapes when the vintage is ended.

14 They shall lift vp their voyce: they shall shout for the magnificence of the Lord: they shall reioyce from the sea.

15 Wherefore praise yee the Lord in the valleis, euen the Name of the Lord God of Israel, in the yles of the sea.

16 From the vttermost part of the earth wee haue heard praises, euen glory to the iust, and I sayd, My leanesse, my leanesse, woe is mee: the transgressours haue offended: yea, the transgressours haue grieuously offended.

17 Feare, and the pitte, and the snare are vpon thee, O inhabitant of the earth.

18 And hee that fleeth from the noyse of the feare, shall fall into the pit: and he that commeth vp out of the pit, shall be taken in the snare: for the windowes from on high are open, and the foundations of the earth doe shake.

19 The earth is vtterly broken downe: the earth is cleane dissolued: the earth is mooued exceedingly.

20 The earth shall reele to and from like a drunken man, and shall be remooued like a tent, and the iniquitie thereof shall be heauie vpon it: so that it shall fall, and rise no more.

21 And in that day shall the Lord visite the hoste aboue that is on hie, euen the Kinges of the world that are vpon the earth.

22 And they shall be gathered together, as the prisoners in the pit: and they shall be shut vp in the prison, and after many daies shall they be visited.

23 Then the moone shall be abashed, and the sunne ashamed, when the Lord of hostes shall reigne in mount Zion and in Ierusalem: and glory shalbe before his ancient men.

Isaiah 25

1 O Lord, thou art my God: I will exalt thee, I will prayse thy Name: for thou hast done wonderfull things, according to the counsels of old, with a stable trueth.

2 For thou hast made of a citie an heape, of a strong citie, a ruine: euen the palace of strangers of a citie, it shall neuer be built.

3 Therefore shall the mightie people giue glory vnto thee: the citie of the strong nations shall feare thee.

4 For thou hast bene a strength vnto the poore, euen a strength to the needie in his trouble, a refuge against the tempest, a shadow against the heate: for the blaste of the mightie is like a storme against the wall.

5 Thou shalt bring downe the noyse of the strangers, as the heate in a drie place: he wil bring downe the song of the mightie, as the heate in the shadowe of a cloude.

6 And in this mountaine shall the Lord of hostes make vnto all people a feast of fat thinges, euen a feast of fined wines, and of fat thinges full of marow, of wines fined and purified.

7 And he will destroy in this mountaine the couering that couereth all people, and the vaile that is spread vpon all nations.

8 He wil destroy death for euer: and the Lord God wil wipe away the teares from all faces, and the rebuke of his people will he take away out of all the earth: for the Lord hath spoken it.

9 And in that day shall men say, Loe, this is our God: we haue waited for him, and he wil saue vs. This is the Lord, we haue waited for him: we will reioyce and be ioyfull in his saluation.

10 For in this mountaine shall the hand of the Lord rest, and Moab shalbe threshed vnder him, euen as strawe is thresshed in Madmenah.

11 And he shall stretche out his hande in the middes of them (as he that swimmeth, stretcheth them out to swimme) and with the strength of his handes shall he bring downe their pride.

12 The defence also of the height of thy walles shall he bring downe and lay lowe, and cast them to the ground, euen vnto the dust.

Isaiah 26

1 In that day shall this song be sung in the land of Iudah, We haue a strong citie: saluation shall God set for walles and bulwarkes.

2 Open ye the gates that the righteous nation, which keepeth the trueth, may enter in.

3 By an assured purpose wilt thou preserue perfite peace, because they trusted in thee.

4 Trust in the Lord for euer: for in the Lord God is strength for euermore.

5 For hee will bring downe them that dwell on hie: the hie citie he will abase: euen vnto the ground wil he cast it downe, and bring it vnto dust.

6 The foote shall treade it downe, euen the feete of the poore, and the steppes of the needie.

7 The way of the iust is righteousnesse: thou wilt make equall the righteous path of the iust.

8 Also we, O Lord, haue waited for thee in the way of thy iudgemets: the desire of our soule is to thy Name, and to the remembrance of thee.

9 With my soule haue I desired thee in the night, and with my spirit within mee will I seeke thee in the morning: for seeing thy iudgements are in the earth, the inhabitants of the world shall learne righteousnesse.

10 Let mercie bee shewed to the wicked, yet hee will not learne righteousnesse: in the land of vprightnesse will he do wickedly, and will not beholde the maiestie of the Lord.

11 O Lord, they will not beholde thine hie hande: but they shall see it, and bee confounded with the zeale of the people, and the fire of thine enemies shall deuoure them.

12 Lord, vnto vs thou wilt ordeine peace: for thou also hast wrought all our workes for vs.

13 O Lord our God, other lords beside thee, haue ruled vs, but we will remember thee onely, and thy Name.

14 The dead shall not liue, neither shall the dead arise, because thou hast visited and scattered them, and destroyed all their memorie.

15 Thou hast increased the nation, O Lord: thou hast increased the nation: thou art made glorious: thou hast enlarged all the coastes of the earth.

16 Lord, in trouble haue they visited thee: they powred out a prayer when thy chastening was vpon them.

17 Like as a woman with childe, that draweth neere to the trauaile, is in sorow, and cryeth in her paines, so haue we bene in thy sight, O Lord.

18 We haue coceiued, we haue borne in paine, as though we should haue brought forth winde: there was no helpe in the earth, neither did the inhabitants of the world fall.

19 Thy dead men shall liue: euen with my body shall they rise. Awake, and sing, ye that dwel in dust: for thy dewe is as the dew of herbes, and the earth shall cast out the dead.

20 Come, my people: enter thou into thy chambers, and shut thy doores after thee: hide thy selfe for a very litle while, vntill the indignation passe ouer.

21 For lo, the Lord commeth out of his place, to visite the iniquitie of the inhabitants of the earth vpon them: and the earth shall disclose her blood, and shall no more hide her slaine.

Isaiah 27

1 In that day the Lord with his sore and great and mightie sword shall visite Liuiathan, that pearcing serpent, euen Liuiathan, that crooked serpent, and he shall slay the dragon that is in the sea.

2 In that daye sing of the vineyarde of redde wine.

3 I the Lord doe keepe it: I will water it euery moment: least any assaile it, I will keepe it night and day.

4 Anger is not in mee: who would set the briers and the thornes against me in battel? I would go through them, I would burne them together.

5 Or will he feele my strength, that he may make peace with me, and be at one with me?

6 Hereafter, Iaakob shall take roote: Israel shall florish and growe, and the world shall be filled with fruite.

7 Hath hee smitten him as hee smote those that smote him? or is hee slaine according to the slaughter of them that were slaine by him?

8 In measure in the branches thereof wilt thou contende with it, when he bloweth with his rough winde in the day of the East winde.

9 By this therefore shall the iniquitie of Iaakob be purged, and this is all the fruit, the taking away of his sinne: whe he shall make all the stones of the altars, as chalke stones broken in pieces, that the groues and images may not stand vp.

10 Yet the defenced citie shalbe desolate, and the habitation shalbe forsaken, and left like a wildernes. There shall the calfe feede, and there shall he lie, and consume the branches thereof.

11 When the boughes of it are drie, they shalbe broken: the women come, and set them on fire: for it is a people of none vnderstading: therefore hee that made them, shall not haue compassion of them, and he that formed them, shall haue no mercie on them.

12 And in that day shall the Lord thresh from the chanell of the Riuer vnto the riuer of Egypt, and ye shalbe gathered, one by one, O children of Israel.

13 In that day also shall the great trumpet be blowen, and they shall come, which perished in the land of Asshur: and they that were chased into the lande of Egypt, and they shall worship the Lord in the holy Mount at Ierusalem.

Isaiah 28

1 Woe to the crowne of pride, the drunkards of Ephraim: for his glorious beautie shall be a fading flowre, which is vpon the head of the valley of them that be fat, and are ouercome with wine.

2 Beholde, the Lord hath a mightie and strong hoste, like a tempest of haile, and a whirlewinde that ouerthroweth, like a tempest of mightie waters that ouerflowe, which throwe to the ground mightily.

3 They shall be troden vnder foote, euen the crowne and the pride of the drunkards of Ephraim.

4 For his glorious beautie shall be a fading floure, which is vpon the head of the valley of them that be fatte, and as the hastie fruite afore sommer, which when hee that looketh vpon it, seeth it, while it is in his hand, he eateth it.

5 In that day shall the Lord of hostes be for a crowne of glory, and for a diademe of beautie vnto the residue of his people:

6 And for a spirite of iudgement to him that sitteth in iudgement, and for strength vnto them that turne away the battell to the gate.

7 But they haue erred because of wine, and are out of the way by strong drinke: the priest and the prophet haue erred by strong drinke: they are swallowed vp with wine: they haue gone astraye through strong drinke: they faile in vision: they stumble in iudgement.

8 For all their tables are full of filthy vomiting: no place is cleane.

9 Whome shall he teache knowledge? and whome shall he make to vnderstand the thinges that hee heareth? them that are weyned from the milke, and drawen from the breastes.

10 For precept must be vpon precept, precept vpon precept, line vnto line, line vnto line, there a litle, and there a litle.

11 For with a stammering tongue and with a strange language shall he speake vnto this people.

12 Vnto whome hee saide, This is the rest: giue rest to him that is weary: and this is the refreshing, but they would not heare.

13 Therefore shall the worde of the Lord be vnto them precept vpon precept, precept vpon precept, line vnto line, line vnto line, there a litle and there a litle, that they may goe, and fall backward, and be broken, and be snared, and be taken.

14 Wherefore, heare the worde of the Lord, ye scornefull men that rule this people, which is at Ierusalem.

15 Because ye haue said, We haue made a couenant with death, and with hell are we at agreement: though a

scourge runne ouer, and passe through, it shall not come at vs: for we haue made falshood our refuge, and vnder vanitie are we hid,

16 Therefore thus saith the Lord God, Behold, I will laye in Zion a stone, a tried stone, a precious corner stone, a sure foundation. Hee that beleeueth, shall not make haste.

17 Iudgement also will I laye to the rule, and righteousnesse to the balance, and the haile shall sweepe away the vaine confidence, and the waters shall ouerflowe the secret place.

18 And your couenant with death shalbe disanulled, and your agreement with hell shall not stand: when a scourge shall runne ouer and passe through, then shall ye be trode downe by it.

19 When it passeth ouer, it shall take you away: for it shall passe through euery morning in the day, and in the night, and there shalbe onely feare to make you to vnderstand the hearing.

20 For the bed is streight that it can not suffice, and the couering narowe that one can not wrappe himselfe.

21 For the Lord shall stand as in mount Perazim: hee shall be wroth as in the valley of Gibeon, that he may do his worke, his strage worke, and bring to passe his acte, his strange acte.

22 Nowe therefore be no mockers, least your bondes increase: for I haue heard of the Lord of hostes a consumption, euen determined vpon the whole earth.

23 Hearken ye, and heare my voyce: hearken ye, and heare my speach.

24 Doeth the plowe man plowe all the day, to sowe? doeth he open, and breake the clots of his ground?

25 When he hath made it plaine, wil he not then sowe the fitches, and sowe cummin, and cast in wheat by measure, and the appointed barly and rye in their place?

26 For his God doeth instruct him to haue discretion, and doeth teach him.

27 For fitches shall not be threshed with a threshing instrument, neither shall a cart wheele be turned about vpon the cummin: but ye fitches are beaten out with a staffe, and cummin with a rod.

28 Bread corne when it is threshed, hee doeth not alway thresh it, neither doeth the wheele of his cart still make a noyse, neither will he breake it with the teeth thereof.

29 This also commeth from the Lord of hostes, which is wonderfull in counsell, and excellent in workes.

Isaiah 29

1 Ah altar, altar of the citie that Dauid dwelt in: adde yere vnto yere: let them kill lambs.

2 But I wil bring the altar into distresse, and there shalbe heauines and sorowe, and it shall be vnto me like an altar.

3 And I wil besiege thee as a circle, and fight against thee on a mount, and will cast vp ramparts against thee.

4 So shalt thou be humbled, and shalt speake out of the ground, and thy speach shalbe as out of the dust: thy voyce also shall be out of the ground like him that hath a spirite of diuination, and thy talking shall whisper out of the dust.

5 Moreouer, the multitude of thy strangers shalbe like small dust, and the multitude of strong men shalbe as chaffe that passeth away, and it shall be in a moment, euen suddenly.

6 Thou shalt be visited of the Lord of hostes with thunder, and shaking, and a great noyse, a whirlewinde, and a tempest, and a flame of a deuouring fire.

7 And the multitude of all the nations that fight against the altar, shalbe as a dreame or vision by night: euen all they that make the warre against it, and strong holdes against it, and lay siege vnto it.

8 And it shalbe like as an hungry man dreameth, and beholde, he eateth: and when he awaketh, his soule is emptie: or like as a thirsty man dreameth, and loe, he is drinking, and when he awaketh, beholde, he is faint, and his soule longeth: so shall the multitude of all nations be that fight against mount Zion.

9 Stay your selues, and wonder: they are blinde, and make you blinde: they are drunken but not with wine: they stagger, but not by strong drinke.

10 For the Lord hath couered you with a spirite of slumber, and hath shut vp your eyes: the Prophets, and your chiefe Seers hath he couered.

11 And the vision of them all is become vnto you, as the wordes of a booke that is sealed vp, which they deliuer to one that can reade, saying, Reade this, I pray thee. Then shall he say, I can not: for it is sealed.

12 And the booke is giuen vnto him that can not reade, saying, Reade this, I pray thee. And he shall say, I can not reade.

13 Therefore the Lord sayd, Because this people come neere vnto me with their mouth, and honour me with their lips, but haue remooued their heart farre from me, and their feare toward me was taught by the precept of men,

14 Therefore behold, I wil againe doe a marueilous worke in this people, euen a marueilous worke, and a wonder: for the wisdome of their wise men shall perish, and the vnderstanding of their prudent men shalbe hid.

15 Wo vnto them that seeke deepe to hide their counsell from the Lord: for their workes are in darkenes, and they say, Who seeth vs? and who knoweth vs?

16 Your turning of deuises shall it not be esteemed as the potters clay? for shall the worke say of him that made it, Hee made me not? or the thing formed, say of him that facioned it, He had none vnderstanding?

17 Is it not yet but a litle while, and Lebanon shall be turned into Carmel? and Carmel shall be counted as a forest?

18 And in that day shall the deafe heare the wordes of the booke, and the eyes of the blinde shall see out of obscuritie, and out of darkenesse.

19 The meeke in the Lord shall receiue ioye againe, and the poore men shall reioyce in the holy one of Israel.

20 For the cruel man shall cease, and the scornefull shalbe consumed: and all that hasted to iniquitie, shalbe cut off:

21 Which made a man to sinne in ye worde, and tooke him in a snare: which reproued them in the gate, and made the iust to fall without cause.

22 Therefore thus sayth the Lord vnto the house of Iaakob, euen hee that redeemed Abraham, Iaakob shall not now be confounded, neither now shall his face be pale.

23 But when he seeth his children, the worke of mine hands, in the mids of him, they shall sanctifie my Name, and sanctifie the holy one of Iaakob, and shall feare the God of Israel.

24 Then they that erred in spirit, shall haue vnderstanding, and they that murmured, shall learne doctrine.

Isaiah 30

1 Wo to the rebellious children, sayth the Lord, that take counsell, but not of me, and couer with a couering, but not by my spirit, that they may lay sinne vpon sinne:

2 Which walke forth to goe downe into Egypt (and haue not asked at my mouth) to strengthen them selues with the strength of Pharaoh, and trust in the shadowe of Egypt.

3 But the strength of Pharaoh shalbe your shame, and the trust in the shadow of Egypt your confusion.

4 For his princes were at Zoan, and his Ambassadours came vnto Hanes.

5 They shalbe all ashamed of the people that cannot profite them, nor helpe nor doe them good, but shalbe a shame and also a reproche.

6 The burden of the beasts of the South, in a land of trouble and anguish, from whence shall come the yong and olde lyon, the viper and fierie flying serpent against them that shall beare their riches vpon the shoulders of the coltes, and their treasures vpon the bounches of the camels, to a people that cannot profite.

7 For the Egyptians are vanitie, and they shall helpe in vaine. Therefore haue I cried vnto her, Their strength is to sit still.

8 Now go, and write it before them in a table, and note it in a booke that it may be for the last day for euer and euer:

9 That it is a rebellious people, lying children, and children that would not heare the law of the Lord.

10 Which say vnto the Seers, See not: and to the Prophets, Prophecie not vnto vs right things: but speake flattering things vnto vs: prophecie errours.

11 Depart out of the way: go aside out of the path: cause the holy one of Israel to cease from vs.

12 Therefoe thus saith the holy one of Israel, Because you haue cast off this worde, and trust in violence, and wickednes, and stay thereupon,

13 Therefore this iniquitie shalbe vnto you as a breach that falleth, or a swelling in an hie wall, whose breaking commeth suddenly in a moment.

14 And the breaking thereof is like the breaking of a potters pot, which is broken without pitie, and in the breaking thereof is not found a sheard to take fire out of the hearth, or to take water out of the pit.

15 For thus sayd the Lord God, the Holy one of Israel, In rest and quietnes shall ye be saued: in quietnes and in confidence shall be your strength, but ye would not.

16 For ye haue sayd, No, but we wil flee away vpon horses. Therefore shall ye flee. We will ride vpon the swiftest. Therefore shall your persecuters be swifter.

17 A thousand as one shall flee at the rebuke of one: at the rebuke of fiue shall ye flee, till ye be left as a ship maste vpon the top of a mountaine, and as a beaken vpon an hill.

18 Yet therefore will the Lord waite, that he may haue mercy vpon you, and therefore wil he be exalted, that hee may haue compassion vpon you: for the Lord is the God of iudgement. Blessed are all they that waite for him.

19 Surely a people shall dwell in Zion, and in Ierusalem: thou shalt weepe no more: he wil certainly haue mercy vpon thee at the voyce of thy crye: when he heareth thee, he wil answere thee.

20 And when the Lord hath giuen you the bread of aduersitie, and the water of affliction, thy raine shalbe no more kept backe, but thine eyes shall see thy raine.

21 And thine eares shall heare a worde behind thee, saying, This is the way, walke ye in it, when thou turnest to the right hand, and when thou turnest to the left.

22 And ye shall pollute the couering of the images of siluer, and the riche ornament of thine images of golde, and cast them away as a menstruous cloth, and thou shalt say vnto it, Get thee hence.

23 Then shall hee giue raine vnto thy seede, when thou shalt sowe the ground, and bread of the increase of the earth, and it shalbe fat and as oyle: in that day shall thy cattell be fed in large pastures.

24 The oxen also and the yong asses, that till the ground, shall eate cleane prouender, which is winowed with the shoouel and with the fanne.

25 And vpon euery hie mountaine, and vpon euery hie hill shall there be riuers and streames of waters, in the day of the great slaughter, when the towers shall fall.

26 Moreouer, the light of the moone shall be as the light of the sunne, and the light of the sunne shalbe seuen folde, and like the light of seuen dayes in the day that the Lord shall binde vp the breach of his people, and heale the stroke of their wound.

27 Beholde, the Name of the Lord commeth from farre, his face is burning, and the burden thereof is heauy: his lips are full of indignation, and his tongue is as a deuouring fire.

28 And his spirit is as a riuer that ouerfloweth vp to the necke: it deuideth asunder, to fanne the nations with the fanne of vanitie, and there shall be a bridle to cause them to erre in the chawes of the people.

29 But there shall be a song vnto you as in the night, when solemne feast is kept: and gladnes of heart, as he that commeth with a pipe to goe vnto the mount of the Lord, to the mightie one of Israel.

30 And the Lord shall cause his glorious voyce to be heard, and shall declare the lighting downe of his arme with the anger of his countenance, and flame of a deuouring fire, with scattering and tempest, and hailestones.

31 For with the voyce of the Lord shall Asshur be destroyed, which smote with the rod.

32 And in euery place that ye staffe shall passe, it shall cleaue fast, which the Lord shall lay vpon him with tabrets and harpes: and with battels, and lifting vp of hands shall he fight against it.

33 For Tophet is prepared of olde: it is euen prepared for the King: hee hath made it deepe and large: the burning thereof is fire and much wood: the breath of the Lord, like a riuer of brimstone, doeth kindle it.

Isaiah 31

1 Woe vnto them that goe downe into Egypt for helpe, and stay vpon horses, and trust in charets, because they are many, and in horsemen, because they be very strong: but they looke not vnto the holy one of Israel, nor seeke vnto the Lord.

2 But he yet is wisest: therefore he wil bring euill, and not turne backe his worde, but he will arise against the house of the wicked, and against the helpe of them that worke vanitie.

3 Now the Egyptians are men, and not God, and their horses flesh and not spirite: and when the Lord shall stretch out his hand, the helper shall fall, and hee that is holpen shall fall, and they shall altogether faile.

4 For thus hath the Lord spoken vnto me, As the lyon or lyons whelpe roareth vpon his praye, against whom if a multitude of shepheards be called, hee will not be afraide at their voyce, neither will humble him selfe at their noise: so shall the Lord of hostes come downe to fight for mount Zion, and for the hill thereof.

5 As birds that flie, so shall the Lord of hostes defend Ierusalem by defending and deliuering, by passing through and preseruing it.

6 O ye children of Israel, turne againe, in as much as ye are sunken deepe in rebellion.

7 For in that day euery man shall cast out his idoles of siluer, and his idoles of golde, which your handes haue made you, euen a sinne.

8 Then shall Asshur fall by the swerde, not of man, neither shall the swerde of man deuoure him, and hee shall flee from the swerde, and his yong men shall faint.

9 And he shall go for feare to his towre, and his princes shall be afraide of the standart, sayeth the Lord, whose fire is in Zion, and his fornace in Ierusalem.

Isaiah 32

1 Behold, a King shall reigne in iustice, and the princes shall rule in iudgement.

2 And that man shall bee as an hiding place from the winde, and as a refuge for the tempest: as riuers of water in a drie place, and as the shadowe of a great rocke in a weary land.

3 The eyes of the seeing shall not be shut, and the eares of them that heare, shall hearken.

4 And the heart of the foolish shall vnderstand knowledge, and the tongue of the stutters shalbe ready to speake distinctly.

5 A nigard shall no more be called liberall, nor the churle riche.

6 But the nigarde will speake of nigardnesse, and his heart will worke iniquitie, and do wickedly, and speake falsely against the Lord, to make emptie the hungrie soule, and to cause the drinke of the thirstie to faile.

7 For the weapons of the churle are wicked: hee deuiseth wicked counsels, to vndoe the poore with lying words: and to speake against the poore in iudgement.

8 But the liberall man will deuise of liberall things, and he will continue his liberalitie.

9 Rise vp, ye women that are at ease: heare my voyce, ye carelesse daughters: hearken to my wordes.

10 Yee women, that are carelesse, shall be in feare aboue a yeere in dayes: for the vintage shall faile, and the gatherings shall come no more.

11 Yee women, that are at ease, be astonied: feare, O yee carelesse women: put off the clothes: make bare, and girde sackcloth vpon the loynes.

12 Men shall lament for the teates, euen for the pleasant fieldes, and for the fruitefull vine.

13 Vpon the lande of my people shall growe thornes and briers: yea, vpon all the houses of ioye in the citie of reioysing,

14 Because the palace shalbe forsaken, and the noise of the citie shalbe left: the towre and fortresse shalbe dennes for euer, and the delite of wilde asses, and a pasture for flockes,

15 Vntill the Spirit be powred vpon vs from aboue, and the wildernes become a fruitfull fielde, and the plenteous fielde be counted as a forest.

16 And iudgement shall dwel in the desert, and iustice shall remaine in the fruitfull fielde.

17 And the worke of iustice shall bee peace, euen the worke of iustice and quietnesse, and assurance for euer.

18 And my people shall dwell in the tabernacle of peace, and in sure dwellings, and in safe resting places.

19 When it haileth, it shall fall on the forest, and the citie shall be set in the lowe place.

20 Blessed are ye that sowe vpon all waters, and driue thither the feete of the oxe and the asse.

Isaiah 33

1 Woe to thee that spoylest, and wast not spoyled: and doest wickedly, and they did not wickedly against thee: when thou shalt cease to spoyle, thou shalt be spoyled: when thou shalt make an ende of doing wickedly, they shall doe wickedly against thee.

2 O Lord, haue mercie vpon vs, wee haue waited for thee: be thou, which waste their arme in the morning, our helpe also in time of trouble.

3 At the noise of the tumult, the people fled: at thine exalting the nations were scattered.

4 And your spoyle shall be gathered like the gathering of caterpillers: and he shall go against him like the leaping of grashoppers.

5 The Lord is exalted: for hee dwelleth on hie: he hath filled Zion with iudgement and iustice.

6 And there shall be stabilitie of thy times, strength, saluation, wisdome and knowledge: for the feare of the Lord shalbe his treasure.

7 Behold, their messengers shall cry without, and ye ambassadours of peace shall weepe bitterly.

8 The pathes are waste: the wayfaring man ceaseth: hee hath broken the couenant: hee hath contemned the cities: he regarded no man.

9 The earth mourneth and fainteth: Lebanon is ashamed, and hewen downe: Sharon is like a wildernes, and Bashan is shaken and Carmel.

10 Now will I arise, saith the Lord: now will I be exalted, now will I lift vp my selfe.

11 Ye shall conceiue chaffe, and bring forth stubble: the fire of your breath shall deuoure you.

12 And the people shall be as the burning of lime: and as the thornes cut vp, shall they be burnt in the fire.

13 Heare, yee that are farre off, what I haue done, and ye that are neere, know my power.

14 The sinners in Zion are afraide: a feare is come vpon the hypocrites: who among vs shall dwel with the deuouring fire? who among vs shall dwell with the euerlasting burnings?

15 Hee that walketh in iustice, and speaketh righteous things, refusing gaine of oppression, shaking his handes from taking of gifts, stopping his eares from hearing of blood, and shutting his eyes from seeing euill.

16 He shall dwell on hie: his defence shall be the munitions of rockes: bread shalbe giuen him, and his waters shalbe sure.

17 Thine eyes shall see the King in his glory: they shall beholde the lande farre off.

18 Thine heart shall meditate feare, Where is the scribe? where is the receiuer? where is hee that counted the towres?

19 Thou shalt not see a fierce people, a people of a darke speache, that thou canst not perceiue, and of a stammering tongue that thou canst not vnderstande.

20 Looke vpon Zion the citie of our solemne feastes: thine eyes shall see Ierusalem a quiet habitation, a Tabernacle that can not be remooued: and the stakes thereof can neuer be taken away, neither shall any of the cordes thereof be broken.

21 For surely there the mightie Lord will be vnto vs, as a place of floods and broade riuers, whereby shall passe no shippe with oares, neither shall great shippe passe thereby.

22 For the Lord is our Iudge, the Lord is our lawe giuer: the Lord is our King, he will saue vs.

23 Thy cordes are loosed: they could not well strengthen their maste, neither coulde they spread the saile: then shall the praye be deuided for a great spoile: yea, the lame shall take away the pray.

24 And none inhabitant shall say, I am sicke: the people that dwell therein, shall haue their iniquitie forgiuen.

Isaiah 34

1 Come neere, ye nations and heare, and hearken, ye people: let the earth heare and all that is therein, the world and al that proceedeth thereof.

2 For the indignation of the Lord is vpon all nations, and his wrath vpon all their armies: hee hath destroyed them and deliuered them to the slaughter.

3 And their slaine shalbe cast out, and their stincke shall come vp out of their bodies, and the mountaines shalbe melted with their blood.

4 And all the hoste of heauen shalbe dissolued, and the heauens shall be folden like a booke: and all their hostes shall fall as the leafe falleth from the vine, and as it falleth from the figtree.

5 For my sword shalbe drunken in the heauen: beholde, it shall come downe vpon Edom, euen vpon the people of my curse to iudgement.

6 The sword of the Lord is filled with blood: it is made fat with the fat and with the blood of the lambes and the goates, with the fat of the kidneis of the rams: for the Lord hath a sacrifice in Bozrah, and a great slaughter in the land of Edom.

7 And the vnicorne shall come downe with them and the heiffers with the bulles, and their lande shalbe drunken with blood, and their dust made fat with fatnesse.

8 For it is the day of the Lordes vengeance, and the yeere of recompence for the iudgement of Zion.

9 And the riuers thereof shall be turned into pitche, and the dust thereof into brimstone, and the land thereof shalbe burning pitch.

10 It shall not be quenched night nor day: the smoke thereof shall goe vp euermore: it shall be desolate from generation to generation: none shall passe through it for euer.

11 But the pelicane and the hedgehog shall possesse it, and the great owle, and the rauen shall dwel in it, and he shall stretch out vpon it the line of vanitie, and the stones of emptinesse.

12 The nobles thereof shall call to the kingdome, and there shalbe none, and all the princes thereof shalbe as nothing.

13 And it shall bring foorth thornes in the palaces thereof, nettles and thistles in the strong holdes thereof, and it shall be an habitation for dragons, and a court for ostriches.

14 There shall meete also Ziim and Iim, and the Satyre shall cry to his fellow, and the shricheowle shall rest there, and shall finde for her selfe a quiet dwelling.

15 There shall the owle make her nest, and laye, and hatche, and gather them vnder her shadowe: there shall the vultures also bee gathered, euery one with her make.

16 Seeke in the booke of the Lord, and reade: none of these shall fayle, none shall want her make: for his mouth hath commanded, and his very Spirit hath gathered them.

17 And he hath cast the lot for them, and his hand hath deuided it vnto them by line: they shall possesse it for euer: from generation to generation shall they dwell in it.

Isaiah 35

1 The desert and the wildernes shall reioyce: and the waste ground shalbe glad and florish as the rose.

2 It shall florish abundantly and shall greatly reioyce also and ioye: the glory of Lebanon shalbe giuen vnto it: the beautie of Carmel, and of Sharon, they shall see the glory of the Lord, and the excellencie of our God.

3 Strengthen the weake handes, and comfort the feeble knees.

4 Say vnto them that are fearefull, Bee you strong, feare not: beholde, your God commeth with vengeance: euen God with a recompense, he will come and saue you.

5 Then shall the eyes of the blinde be lightened, and the eares of the deafe be opened.

6 Then shall ye lame man leape as an hart, and the dumme mans tongue shall sing: for in the wildernes shall waters breake out, and riuers in ye desert.

7 And the dry ground shalbe as a poole, and the thirstie (as springs of water in the habitation of dragons: where they lay) shall be a place for reedes and rushes.

8 And there shalbe a path and a way, and the way shalbe called holy: the polluted shall not passe by it: for he shalbe with them, and walke in the way, and the fooles shall not erre.

9 There shall be no lyon, nor noysome beastes shall ascend by it, neither shall they be found there, that the redeemed may walke.

10 Therefore the redeemed of the Lord shall returne and come to Zion with prayse: and euerlasting ioy shall bee vpon their heads: they shall obteine ioye and gladnesse, and sorow and mourning shall flee away.

Isaiah 36

1 Nowe in the fourteenth yeere of King Hezekiah, Saneherib King of Asshur came vp against al the strong cities of Iudah, and tooke them.

2 And the King of Asshur sent Rabshakeh from Lachish toward Ierusalem vnto King Hezekiah, with a great hoste, and he stood by ye conduite of the vpper poole in the path of the fullers fielde.

3 Then came foorth vnto him Eliakim the sonne of Hilkiah the steward of the house, and Shebna the chanceler, and Ioah the sonne of Asaph the recorder.

4 And Rabshakeh sayde vnto them, Tell you Hezekiah, I pray you, Thus sayth the great King, the King of Asshur, What confidence is this, wherein thou trustest?

5 I say, Surely I haue eloquence, but counsell and strength are for the warre: on whom then doest thou trust, that thou rebellest against me?

6 Loe, thou trustest in this broken staffe of reede on Egypt, whereupon if a man leane, it will goe into his hand, and pearce it: so is Pharaoh King of Egypt, vnto all that trust in him.

7 But if thou say to me, We trust in the Lord our God. Is not that he, whose hie places and whose altars Hezekiah tooke downe, and said to Iudah and to Ierusalem, Ye shall worship before this altar?

8 Nowe therefore giue hostages to my lorde the King of Asshur, and I wil giue thee two thousand horses, if thou be able on thy part to set riders vpon them.

9 For howe canst thou despise any captaine of the least of my lordes seruants? and put thy trust on Egypt for charets and for horsemen?

10 And am I now come vp without the Lord to this land to destroy it? The Lord sayd vnto me, Goe vp against this land and destroy it.

11 Then sayd Eliakim and Shebna and Ioah vnto Rabshakeh, Speake, I pray thee, to thy seruants in the Aramites language, (for we vnderstand it) and talke not with vs in the Iewes tongue, in the audience of the people that are on the wall.

12 Then said Rabshakeh, Hath my master sent me to thy master, and to thee to speake these wordes, and not to the men that sit on the wall? that they may eate their owne doung, and drinke their owne pisse with you?

13 So Rabshakeh stood, and cryed with a loude voyce in the Iewes language, and sayd, Heare the wordes of the great King, of the King of Asshur.

14 Thus saith the King, Let not Hezekiah deceiue you: for he shall not be able to deliuer you.

15 Neither let Hezekiah make you to trust in the Lord, saying, The Lord will surely deliuer vs: this citie shall not be giuen ouer into the hand of the King of Asshur.

16 Hearken not to Hezekiah: for thus sayth the King of Asshur, Make appointment with me, and come out to me, that euery man may eate of his owne vine, and euery man of his owne fig tree, and drinke euery man the water of his owne well,

17 Till I come and bring you to a land like your owne land, euen a land of wheate, and wine, a land of bread and vineyardes,

18 Least Hezekiah deceiue you, saying, The Lord wil deliuer vs. Hath any of the gods of the nations deliuered his land out of the hand of the King of Asshur?

19 Where is the god of Hamath, and of Arpad? where is the god of Sepharuaim? or howe haue they deliuered Samaria out of mine hand?

20 Who is hee among all the gods of these lands, that hath deliuered their countrey out of mine hand, that the Lord should deliuer Ierusalem out of mine hand?

21 Then they kept silence, and answered him not a worde: for the Kings commandement was, saying, Answere him not.

22 Then came Eliakim the sonne of Hilkiah the steward of the house, and Shebna the chanceller, and Ioah the sonne of Asaph the recorder, vnto Hezekiah with rent clothes, and tolde him the wordes of Rabshakeh.

Isaiah 37

1 And when the King Hezekiah heard it, he rent his clothes, and put on sackcloth and came into the House of the Lord.

2 And he sent Eliakim the stewarde of the house, aud Shebna the chanceller, with the Elders of the Priestes, clothed in sackcloth vnto Isaiah the Prophet, the sonne of Amoz.

3 And they sayd vnto him, Thus saith Hezekiah, This day is a day of tribulation and of rebuke and blasphemie: for the children are come to the birth, and there is no strength to bring foorth.

4 If so be the Lord thy God hath heard the wordes of Rabshakeh, whom the King of Asshur his master hath sent to raile on the liuing God, and to reproch him with wordes which the Lord thy God hath heard, then lift thou vp thy prayer for the remnant that are left.

5 So the seruants of the King Hezekiah came to Isaiah.

6 And Isaiah sayde vnto them, Thus say vnto your master, Thus saith the Lord, Be not afrayd of the wordes that thou hast heard, wherewith the seruants of the king of Asshur haue blasphemed me.

7 Beholde, I wil send a blast vpon him, and he shall heare a noyse, and returne to his owne land, and I will cause him to fall by the sword in his owne land.

8 So Rabshakeh returned, and found the King of Asshur fighting against Libnah: for he had heard that he was departed from Lachish.

9 He heard also men say of Tirhakah, King of Ethiopia, Beholde, he is come out to fight against thee: and when he heard it, he sent other messengers to Hezekiah, saying,

10 Thus shall ye speake to Hezekiah King of Iudah, saying, Let not thy God deceiue thee, in whom thou trustest, saying, Ierusalem shall not be giuen into the hand of the King of Asshur.

11 Beholde, thou hast heard what the Kings of Asshur haue done to all lands in destroying them, and shalt thou be deliuered?

12 Haue the gods of the nations deliuered them, which my fathers haue destroyed? as Gozan, and Haran, and Rezeph, and the children of Eden, which were at Telassar?

13 Where is the King of Hamath, and the King of Arpad, and the King of the citie of Sepharuaim, Hena and Iuah?

14 So Hezekiah receiued the letter of the hand of the messengers and read it, and he went vp into the House of the Lord, and Hezekiah spread it before the Lord.

15 And Hezekiah prayed vnto the Lord, saying,

16 O Lord of hostes, God of Israel, which dwellest betweene the Cherubims, thou art very God alone ouer all the kingdomes of the earth: thou hast made the heauen and the earth.

17 Encline thine eare, O Lord, and heare: open thine eyes, O Lord, and see, and heare all the wordes of Saneherib, who hath sent to blaspheme the liuing God.

18 Trueth it is, O Lord, that the Kings of Asshur haue destroyed all lands, and their countrey,

19 And haue cast their gods in ye fire: for they were no gods, but the worke of mans hands, euen wood or stone: therefore they destroyed them.

20 Nowe therefore, O Lord our God, saue thou vs out of his hand, that all the kingdomes of the earth may knowe, that thou onely art the Lord.

21 Then Isaiah the sonne of Amoz sent vnto Hezekiah, saying, Thus sayth the Lord God of Israel, Because thou hast prayed vnto me, concerning Saneherib king of Asshur,

22 This is the worde that the Lord hath spoken against him, the virgine, the daughter of Zion, hath despised thee, and laughed thee to scorne: the daughter of Ierusalem, hath shaken her head at thee.

23 Whome hast thou railed on and blasphemed? and against whome hast thou exalted thy voyce, and lifted vp thine eyes on hie? euen against the holy one of Israel.

24 By thy seruants hast thou railed on the Lord, and sayd, By the multitude of

my charets I am come vp to the top of the mountaines to the sides of Lebanon, and will cut downe the hie cedars thereof, and the faire firre trees thereof, and I will goe vp to the heightes of his top and to the forest of his fruitfull places.

25 I haue digged and drunke the waters, and with the plant of my feete haue I dryed all the riuers closed in.

26 Hast thou not heard howe I haue of olde time made it, and haue formed it long ago? and should I now bring it, that it should be destroyed, and layde on ruinous heapes, as cities defensed?

27 Whose inhabitants haue small power, and are afrayd and confounded: they are like the grasse of the field and greene herbe, or grasse on the house tops, or corne blassed afore it be growen.

28 But I know thy dwelling, and thy going out, and thy comming in, and thy fury against me.

29 Because thou ragest against me, and thy tumult is come vnto mine eares, therefore will I put mine hooke in thy nostrels, and my bridle in thy lips, and wil bring thee backe againe the same way thou camest.

30 And this shalbe a signe vnto thee, O Hezekiah, Thou shalt eate this yeere such as groweth of it selfe: and the second yeere, such things as growe without sowing: and in the third yeere, sowe ye and reape, and plant vineyards, and eate the fruite thereof.

31 And the remnant that is escaped of the house of Iudah, shall againe take roote downward and beare fruite vpward.

32 For out of Ierusalem shall goe a remnant, and they that escape out of mount Zion: the zeale of the Lord of hostes shall doe this.

33 Therefore thus sayth the Lord, concerning the King of Asshur, He shall not enter into this citie, nor shoote an arrow there, nor come before it with shield, nor cast a mount against it.

34 By the same way that he came, he shall returne, and not come into this citie, saith the Lord.

35 For I will defend this citie to saue it, for mine owne sake, and for my seruant Dauids sake.

36 Then the Angel of the Lord went out, and smote in the campe of Asshur an hundreth, fourescore, and fiue thousand: so when they arose early in the morning, beholde, they were all dead corpses.

37 So Saneherib king of Asshur departed, and went away and returned and dwelt at Nineueh.

38 And as he was in the temple worshipping of Nisroch his god, Adramelech and Sharezer his sonnes slewe him with the sword, and they escaped into the land of Ararat: and Esarhaddon his sonne reigned in his steade.

Isaiah 38

1 About that time was Hezekiah sicke vnto the death, and the Prophet Isaiah

sonne of Amoz came vnto him, and sayd vnto him, Thus sayth the Lord, Put thine house in an order, for thou shalt dye, and not liue.

2 Then Hezekiah turned his face to the wall, and prayed to the Lord,

3 And saide, I beseeche thee, Lord, remember nowe howe I haue walked before thee in trueth, and with a perfite heart, and haue done that which is good in thy sight: and Hezekiah wept sore.

4 Then came the worde of the Lord to Isaiah, saying,

5 Goe, and say vnto Hezekiah, Thus saith the Lord God of Dauid thy father, I haue heard thy prayer, and seene thy teares: behold, I will adde vnto thy dayes fifteene yeeres.

6 And I will deliuer thee out of the hand of the King of Asshur, and this citie: for I will defende this citie.

7 And this signe shalt thou haue of ye Lord, that ye Lord will do this thing that he hath spoken,

8 Beholde, I will bring againe the shadowe of the degrees (whereby it is gone downe in the diall of Ahaz by the sunne) ten degrees backeward: so the sunne returned by tenne degrees, by the which degrees it was gone downe.

9 The writing of Hezekiah King of Iudah, when he had bene sicke, and was recouered of his sickenesse.

10 I saide in the cutting off of my dayes, I shall goe to the gates of the graue: I am depriued of the residue of my yeeres.

11 I said, I shall not see the Lord, euen the Lord in the land of the liuing: I shall see man no more among the inhabitants of the world.

12 Mine habitation is departed, and is remoued from me, like a shepheards tent: I haue cut off like a weauer my life: he will cut me off from the height: from day to night, thou wilt make an ende of me.

13 I rekoned to the morning: but he brake all my bones, like a lion: from day to night wilt thou make an ende of me.

14 Like a crane or a swallow, so did I chatter: I did mourne as a doue: mine eies were lift vp on high: O Lord, it hath oppressed me, comfort me.

15 What shall I say? for he hath said it to me, and he hath done it: I shall walke weakely all my yeeres in the bitternesse of my soule.

16 O Lord, to them that ouerliue them, and to all that are in them, the life of my spirite shalbe knowen, that thou causedst me to sleepe and hast giuen life to me.

17 Beholde, for felicitie I had bitter griefe, but it was thy pleasure to deliuer my soule from the pit of corruption: for thou hast cast all my sinnes behinde thy backe.

18 For the graue cannot confesse thee: death cannot praise thee: they that goe downe into the pit, cannot hope for thy trueth.

19 But the liuing, the liuing, he shall confesse thee, as I doe this day: the father to the children shall declare thy trueth.

20 The Lord was ready to saue me: therefore we will sing my song, all the dayes of our life in the House of the Lord.

21 Then said Isaiah, Take a lumpe of drye figs and lay it vpon the boyle, and he shall recouer.

22 Also Hezekiah had said, What is ye signe, that I shall goe vp into the House of the Lord?

Isaiah 39

1 At the same time, Merodach Baladan, the sonne of Baladan, King of Babel, sent letters, and a present to Hezekiah: for he had heard that he had bene sicke, and was recouered.

2 And Hezekiah was glad of them, and shewed them the house of the treasures, the siluer, and the golde, and the spices, and the precious ointment, and all the house of his armour, and all that was founde in his treasures: there was nothing in his house, nor in all his kingdome that Hezekiah shewed them not.

3 Then came Isaiah the Prophet vnto King Hezekiah, and said vnto him, What said these men? and from whence came they to thee? And Hezekiah saide, They are come from a farre countrey vnto me, from Babel.

4 Then saide he, What haue they seene in thine house? And Hezekiah answered, All that is in mine house haue they seene: there is nothing among my treasures, that I haue not shewed them.

5 And Isaiah saide to Hezekiah, Heare the worde of the Lord of hostes,

6 Beholde, the dayes come, that all that is in thine house, and which thy fathers haue layed vp in store vntill this day, shall be caried to Babel: nothing shall be left, sayeth the Lord.

7 And of thy sonnes, that shall proceede out of thee, and which thou shalt beget, shall they take away, and they shall be eunuches in the palace of the King of Babel.

8 Then said Hezekiah to Isaiah, The worde of the Lord is good, which thou hast spoken: and he saide, Yet let there be peace, and trueth in my dayes.

Isaiah 40

1 Comfort ye, comfort ye my people, will your God say.

2 Speake comfortably to Ierusalem, and crye vnto her, that her warrefare is accomplished, that her iniquitie is pardoned: for she hath receiued of the Lords hand double for all her sinnes.

3 A voyce cryeth in the wildernesse, Prepare ye the way of the Lord: make streight in the desert a path for our God.

4 Euery valley shall be exalted, and euery mountaine and hill shall be made lowe: and the crooked shalbe streight, and the rough places plaine.

5 And the glory of the Lord shalbe reueiled, and all flesh shall see it together: for the mouth of the Lord hath spoken it.

6 A voyce saide, Crie. And he saide, What shall I crie? All flesh is grasse, and

all the grace thereof is as the floure of the fielde.

7 The grasse withereth, the floure fadeth, because the Spirite of the Lord bloweth vpon it: surely the people is grasse.

8 The grasse withereth, the floure fadeth: but the worde of our God shall stand for euer.

9 O Zion, that bringest good tidings, get thee vp into the hie mountaine: O Ierusalem, that bringest good tidings, lift vp thy voyce with strength: lift it vp, be not afraide: say vnto the cities of Iudah, Beholde your God.

10 Beholde, the Lord God will come with power, and his arme shall rule for him: beholde, his rewarde is with him, and his worke before him,

11 He shall feede his flocke like a shepheard: he shall gather the lambes with his arme, and cary them in his bosome, and shall guide them with young.

12 Who hath measured the waters in his fist? and counted heauen with the spanne, and comprehended the dust of the earth in a measure? and weighed ye mountaines in a weight, and the hilles in a balance?

13 Who hath instructed ye Spirit of the Lord? or was his counseler or taught him?

14 Of whom tooke he counsell, and who instructed him and taught him in the way of iudgement? or taught him knowledge, and shewed vnto him the way of vnderstanding?

15 Beholde, the nations are as a drop of a bucket, and are counted as the dust of the balance: beholde, he taketh away the yles as a litle dust.

16 And Lebanon is not sufficient for fire, nor the beastes thereof sufficient for a burnt offering.

17 All nations before him are as nothing, and they are counted to him, lesse then nothing, and vanitie.

18 To whom then wil ye liken God? or what similitude will ye set vp vnto him?

19 The workeman melteth an image, or the goldsmith beateth it out in golde, or the goldesmith maketh siluer plates.

20 Doeth not the poore chuse out a tree that will not rot, for an oblation? he seeketh also vnto him a cunning workeman, to prepare an image, that shall not be moued.

21 Know ye nothing? haue ye not heard it? hath it not bene tolde you from the beginning? haue ye not vnderstand it by the foundation of the earth?

22 He sitteth vpon the circle of the earth, and the inhabitants thereof are as grashoppers, hee stretcheth out ye heauens, as a curtaine, and spreadeth them out, as a tent to dwell in.

23 He bringeth the princes to nothing, and maketh the iudges of the earth, as vanitie,

24 As though they were not plated, as though they were not sowen, as though their stocke tooke no roote in the earth: for he did euen blow vpon them, and

they withered, and the whirlewinde will take them away as stubble.

25 To whom nowe will ye liken me, that I should be like him, saith the Holy one?

26 Lift vp your eyes on hie, and beholde who hath created these things, and bringeth out their armies by nomber, and calleth them all by names? by the greatnesse of his power and mightie strength nothing faileth.

27 Why sayest thou, O Iaakob, and speakest O Israel, My way is hid from the Lord, and my iudgement is passed ouer of my God?

28 Knowest thou not? or hast thou not heard, that the euerlasting God, the Lord hath created the endes of the earth? he neither fainteth, nor is wearie: there is no searching of his vnderstanding.

29 But he giueth strength vnto him that fainteth, and vnto him that hath no strength, he encreaseth power.

30 Euen the yong men shall faint, and be wearie, and the yong men shall stumble and fall.

31 But they that waite vpon the Lord, shall renue their strength: they shall lift vp the wings as the eagles: they shall runne, and not be wearie, and they shall walke and not faint.

Isaiah 41

1 Keep silence before mee, O ylands, and let the people renue their strength: let the come neere, and let them speake: let vs come together into iudgement.

2 Who raised vp iustice from the East, and called him to his foote? and gaue the nations before him, and subdued the Kings? he gaue them as dust to his sword, and as scattered stubble vnto his bowe.

3 He pursued them, and passed safely by the way that he had not gone with his feete.

4 Who hath wrought and done it? he that calleth the generations from the beginning. I the Lord am the first, and with the last I am ye same.

5 The yles sawe it, and did feare, and the ends of the earth were abashed, drew neere, and came.

6 Euery man helped his neighbour, and saide to his brother, Be strong.

7 So the workeman comforted the founder, and he that smote with ye hammer, him that smote by course, saying, It is ready for the sodering, and he fastened it with nayles that it shoulde not be mooued.

8 But thou, Israel, art my seruant, and thou Iaakob, whom I haue chosen, the seede of Abraham my friend.

9 For I haue taken thee from the endes of the earth, and called thee before the chiefe thereof, and saide vnto thee, Thou art my seruant: I haue chosen thee, and not cast thee away.

10 Feare thou not, for I am with thee: be not afraide, for I am thy God: I will strengthen thee, and helpe thee, and will susteine thee with the right hand of my iustice.

11 Beholde, all they that prouoke thee, shalbe ashamed, and confounded: they shalbe as nothing, and they that striue with thee, shall perish.

12 Thou shalt seeke them and shalt not finde them: to wit, the men of thy strife, for they shall be as nothing, and the men that warre against thee, as a thing of nought.

13 For I the Lord thy God will hold thy right hand, saying vnto thee, Feare not, I wil helpe thee.

14 Feare not, thou worme, Iaakob, and ye men of Israel: I wil helpe thee, sayth the Lord and thy redeemer the holy one of Israel.

15 Behold, I wil make thee a roller, and a newe threshing instrument hauing teeth: thou shalt thresh the mountaines, and bring them to pouder, and shalt make the hilles as chaffe.

16 Thou shalt fanne them, and the winde shall carie them away, and the whirlewinde shall scatter them: and thou shalt reioyce in the Lord, and shalt glory in the holy one of Israel.

17 When the poore and the needy seeke water, and there is none (their tongue faileth for thirst: I the Lord will heare them: I the God of Israel will not forsake them)

18 I will open riuers in the toppes of the hils, and fountaines in the middes of the valleis: I will make the wildernesse as a poole of water, and the waste land as springs of water.

19 I will set in the wildernesse the cedar, the shittah tree, and the mirre tree, and the pine tree, and I will set in the wildernesse the firre tree, the elme and the boxe tree together.

20 Therefore let them see and knowe, and let them consider and vnderstande together that the hand of the Lord hath done this, and the holy one of Israel hath created it.

21 Stand to your cause, saith the Lord: bring forth your strong reasons, saith ye King of Iaakob.

22 Let them bring foorth, and let them tell vs what shall come: let them shew the former things what they be, that wee may consider them, and knowe the latter ende of them: either declare vs things for to come.

23 Shewe the things that are to come hereafter, that we may know that you are gods: yea, doe good or doe euill, that we may declare it, and beholde it together.

24 Beholde, ye are of no value, and your making is of naught: man hath chosen an abomination by them.

25 I haue raised vp from the North, and he shall come: from the East sunne shall he cal vpon my Name, and shall come vpon princes as vpon clay, and as the potter treadeth myre vnder the foote.

26 Who hath declared from the beginning, that we may knowe? or before time, that we may say, He is righteous? Surely there is none that sheweth: surely there is none that declareth: surely there is none that heareth your wordes.

27 I am the first, that saieth to Zion, Beholde, beholde them: and I will giue to

Ierusalem one that shall bring good tidings.

28 But when I behelde, there was none, and when I inquired of them, there was no counsellor, and when I demaunded of them, they answered not a woorde.

29 Beholde, they are all vanitie: their worke is of nothing, their images are wind and confusion.

Isaiah 42

1 Behold, my seruaunt: I will stay vpon him: mine elect, in whom my soule deliteth: I haue put my Spirit vpon him: he shall bring forth iudgement to the Gentiles.

2 He shall not crie, nor lift vp, nor cause his voice to be heard in the streete.

3 A bruised reede shall hee not breake, and the smoking flaxe shall he not quench: he shall bring foorth iudgement in trueth.

4 He shall not faile nor be discouraged till he haue set iudgement in the earth: and the yles shall waite for his lawe.

5 Thus sayeth God the Lord (he that created the heauens and spred them abroad: he that stretched foorth the earth, and the buddes thereof: he that giueth breath vnto the people vpon it, and spirit to them that walke therein)

6 I the Lord haue called thee in righteousnesse, and will hold thine hand, and I will keepe thee, and giue thee for a couenant of the people, and for a light of the Gentiles,

7 That thou maist open the eyes of the blind, and bring out the prisoners from the prison: and them that sitte in darkenesse, out of the prison house.

8 I am the Lord, this is my Name, and my glory wil I not giue to another, neither my praise to grauen images.

9 Beholde, the former thinges are come to passe, and newe things doe I declare: before they come foorth, I tell you of them.

10 Sing vnto the Lord a newe song, and his praise from the ende of the earth: yee that goe downe to the sea, and all that is therein: the yles and the inhabitants thereof.

11 Let the wildernesse and the cities thereof lift vp their voyce, the townes that Kedar doeth inhabite: let the inhabitants of the rocks sing: let them shoute from the toppe of the mountaines.

12 Let them giue glorie vnto the Lord, and declare his praise in the ylands.

13 The Lord shall go forth as a gyant: he shall stirre vp his courage like a man of warre: he shall shout and crie, and shall preuaile against his enemies.

14 I haue a long time holden my peace: I haue beene still and refrained my selfe: nowe will I crie like a trauailing woman: I will destroy and deuoure at once.

15 I will make waste mountaines, and hilles, and drie vp all their herbes, and I will make the floods ylands, and I will drie vp the pooles.

16 And I will bring the blinde by a way, that they knewe not, and lead them by paths that they haue not knowen: I will make darkenesse light before them, and crooked thinges straight. These thinges will I doe vnto them, and not forsake them.

17 They shall be turned backe: they shall be greatly ashamed, that trust in grauen images, and say to the molten images, Yee are our gods.

18 Heare, ye deafe: and ye blinde, regarde, that ye may see.

19 Who is blinde but my seruaunt? or deafe as my messenger, that I sent? who is blind as the perfit, and blinde as the Lordes seruant?

20 Seeing many things, but thou keepest them not? opening the eares, but he heareth not?

21 The Lord is willing for his righteousnesse sake that he may magnifie the Lawe, and exalt it.

22 But this people is robbed and spoiled, and shalbe all snared in dungeons, and they shalbe hid in prison houses: they shall be for a pray, and none shall deliuer: a spoile, and none shall say, Restore.

23 Who among you shall hearken to this, and take heede, and heare for afterwardes?

24 Who gaue Iaakob for a spoyle, and Israel to the robbers? Did not ye Lord, because we haue sinned against him? for they woulde not walke in his waies, neither be obedient vnto his Lawe.

25 Therefore hee hath powred vpon him his fierce wrath, and the strength of battell: and it set him on fire round about, and he knewe not, and it burned him vp, yet he considered not.

Isaiah 43

1 But nowe thus sayeth the Lord, that created thee, O Iaakob: and hee that formed thee, O Israel, Feare not: for I haue redeemed thee: I haue called thee by thy name, thou art mine.

2 When thou passest through the waters, I wil be with thee, and through the floods, that they doe not ouerflowe thee. When thou walkest through the very fire, thou shalt not be burnt, neither shall the flame kindle vpon thee.

3 For I am the Lord thy God, the holy one of Israel, thy Sauiour: I gaue Egypt for thy ransome, Ethiopia, and Seba for thee.

4 Because thou wast precious in my sight, and thou wast honourable, and I loued thee, therefore will I giue man for thee, and people for thy sake.

5 Feare not, for I am with thee: I will bring thy seede from the East, and gather thee from the West.

6 I will say to the North, Giue: and to the South, Keepe not backe: bring my sonnes from farre, and my daughters from the ends of the earth.

7 Euery one shall be called by my Name: for I created him for my glorie, formed him and made him.

8 I will bring foorth the blinde people, and they shall haue eyes, and the deafe, and they shall haue eares.

9 Let all the nations be gathered together, and let the people be assembled: who among them can declare this and shewe vs former things? let them bring foorth their witnesses, that they may be iustified: but let them heare, and say, It is truth.

10 You are my witnesses, saith the Lord, and my seruant, whom I haue chosen: therefore yee shall knowe and beleeue me and yee shall vnderstand that I am: before me there was no God formed, neither shall there be after me.

11 I, euen I am the Lord, and beside me there is no Sauiour.

12 I haue declared, and I haue saued, and I haue shewed, when there was no strange god among you: therefore you are my witnesses, sayeth the Lord, that I am God.

13 Yea, before the day was, I am, and there is none that can deliuer out of mine hand: I will doe it, and who shall let it?

14 Thus sayeth the Lord your redeemer, the holy one of Israel, For your sake I haue sent to Babel, and brought it downe: they are all fugitiues, and the Chaldeans crie in the shippes.

15 I am the Lord your holy one, the creator of Israel, your King.

16 Thus sayeth the Lord which maketh a way in the Sea, and a path in the mighty waters.

17 When hee bringeth out the charet and horse, the armie and the power lie together, and shall not rise: they are extinct, and quenched as towe.

18 Remember yee not the former things, neither regard the things of olde.

19 Behold, I do a new thing: now shall it come foorth: shall you not knowe it? I wil euen make a way in the desert, and floods in the wildernesse.

20 The wilde beastes shall honour mee, the dragons and the ostriches, because I gaue water in the desert, and floods in the wildernesse to giue drinke to my people, euen to mine elect.

21 This people haue I formed for my selfe: they shall shewe foorth my praise.

22 And thou hast not called vpon mee, O Iaakob, but thou hast wearied me, O Israel.

23 Thou hast not brought me the sheepe of thy burnt offrings, neither hast thou honoured me with thy sacrifices. I haue not caused thee to serue with an offring, nor wearied thee with incense.

24 Thou boughtest mee no sweete sauour with money, neither hast thou made mee drunke with the fatte of thy sacrifices, but thou hast made mee to serue with thy sinnes, and wearied mee with thine iniquities.

25 I, euen I am he that putteth away thine iniquities for mine owne sake, and will not remember thy sinnes.

26 Put me in remembrance: let vs be iudged together: count thou that thou maist be iustified.

27 Thy first father hath sinned, and thy teachers haue transgressed against me.

28 Therefore I haue prophaned the rulers of the Sanctuarie, and haue made Iaakob a curse, and Israel a reproche.

Isaiah 44

1 Yet nowe heare, O Iaakob my seruant, and Israel, whom I haue chosen.

2 Thus sayeth the Lord, that made thee, and formed thee from the wombe: he wil helpe thee. Feare not, O Iaakob, my seruaunt, and thou righteous, whome I haue chosen.

3 For I will powre water vpon the thirstie, and floods vpon the drie grounde: I will powre my Spirit vpon thy seede, and my blessing vpon thy buddes.

4 And they shall grow as among the grasse, and as the willowes by the riuers of waters.

5 One shall say, I am the Lordes: another shalbe called by the name of Iaakob: and another shall subscribe with his hand vnto the Lord, and name himselfe by the name of Israel.

6 Thus saith the Lord the King of Israel and his redeemer, the Lord of hostes, I am the first, and I am the last, and without me is there no God.

7 And who is like me, that shall call, and shall declare it, and set it in order before me, since I appointed the ancient people? and what is at hand, and what things are to come? let them shewe vnto them.

8 Feare ye not, neither be afraide: haue not I tolde thee of olde, and haue declared it? you are euen my witnesses, whether there be a God beside me, and that there is no God that I knowe not.

9 All they that make an image, are vanitie, and their delectable things shall nothing profite: and they are their owne witnesses, that they see not nor know: therefore they shalbe confounded.

10 Who hath made a god, or molten an image, that is profitable for nothing?

11 Beholde, all that are of the fellowship thereof, shall be confounded: for the workemen themselues are men: let them all be gathered together, and stand vp, yet they shall feare, and be confounded together.

12 The smith taketh an instrument, and worketh in the coles, and facioneth it with hammers, and worketh it with the strength of his armes: yea, he is an hungred, and his strength faileth: he drinketh no water, and is faint.

13 The carpenter stretcheth out a line: he facioneth it with a red thread, he planeth it, and he purtreyeth it with the compasse, and maketh it after the figure of a man, and according to the beautie of a man that it may remaine in an house.

14 He will hewe him downe cedars, and take the pine tree and the oke, and taketh courage among the trees of the forest: he planteth a firre tree, and the raine doeth nourish it.

15 And man burneth thereof: for he will take thereof and warme himselfe: he also kindleth it and baketh bread, yet he maketh a god, and worshippeth it: he maketh it an idole and boweth vnto it.

16 He burneth the halfe thereof euen in the fire, and vpon the halfe thereof he eateth flesh: he rosteth the roste and is satisfied: also he warmeth himselfe and sayth, Aha, I am warme, I haue bene at the fire.

17 And the residue thereof he maketh a god, euen his idole: he boweth vnto it, and worshippeth and prayeth vnto it, and sayeth, Deliuer me: for thou art my god.

18 They haue not knowen, nor vnderstand: for God hath shut their eyes that they cannot see, and their heartes, that they cannot vnderstand.

19 And none considereth in his heart, neither is there knowledge nor vnderstanding to say, I haue burnt halfe of it, euen in the fire, and haue baked bread also vpon the coles thereof: I haue rosted flesh, and eaten it, and shall I make the residue thereof an abomination? shall I bowe to the stocke of a tree?

20 He feedeth of ashes: a seduced heart hath deceiued him, that he cannot deliuer his soule, nor say, Is there not a lye in my right hand?

21 Remember these (O Iaakob and Israel) for thou art my seruant: I haue formed thee: thou art my seruant: O Israel forget me not.

22 I haue put away thy transgressions like a cloude, and thy sinnes, as a mist: turne vnto me, for I haue redeemed thee.

23 Reioyce, ye heauens: for the Lord hath done it: shoute, ye lower partes of the earth: brast foorth into prayses, ye mountaines, O forest and euery tree therein: for the Lord hath redeemed Iaakob and will be glorified in Israel.

24 Thus sayeth the Lord thy redeemer and he that formed thee from the wombe, I am the Lord, that made all things, that spred out the heauens alone, and stretched out the earth by my selfe.

25 I destroy the tokens of ye southsayers, and make them that coniecture, fooles, and turne the wise men backwarde, and make their knowledge foolishnesse.

26 He confirmeth the worde of his seruant and performeth the counsell of his messengers, saying to Ierusalem, Thou shalt bee inhabited: and to the cities of Iudah, Yee shall be built vp, and I will repayre the decayed places thereof.

27 He saith to the deepe, Be drye and I will drye vp thy floods.

28 He saith to Cyrus, Thou art my shepheard: and he shall performe all my desire: saying also to Ierusalem, Thou shalt be built: and to the Temple, Thy foundation shall be surely layed.

Isaiah 45

1 Thus sayeth the Lord vnto Cyrus his anointed, whose right hand I haue holden to subdue nations before him: therefore will I weaken the loynes of Kings and open the doores before him, and the gates shall not be shut:

2 I will goe before thee and make the crooked streight: I will breake the brasen doores, and burst the yron barres.

3 And I will giue thee the treasures of darkenesse, and the things hid in secret places, that thou maist know that I am the Lord which call thee by thy name, euen the God of Israel.

4 For Iaakob my seruants sake, and Israel mine elect, I will euen call thee by thy name and name thee, though thou hast not knowen me.

5 I am the Lord and there is none other: there is no God besides me: I girded thee though thou hast not knowen me.

6 That they may knowe from the rising of the sunne and from the West, that there is none besides me. I am the Lord, and there is none other.

7 I forme the light and create darkenes: I make peace and create euill: I the Lord doe all these things.

8 Ye heauens, send the dewe from aboue, and let the cloudes droppe downe righteousnesse: let the earth open, and let saluation and iustice growe foorth: let it bring them foorth together: I the Lord haue created him.

9 Woe be vnto him that striueth with his maker, the potsherd with the potsherds of the earth: shall the clay say to him that facioneth it, What makest thou? or thy worke, It hath none hands?

10 Woe vnto him that sayeth to his father, What hast thou begotten? or to his mother, What hast thou brought foorth?

11 Thus saith the Lord, the holy one of Israel, and his maker, Aske me of things to come concerning my sonnes, and concerning the workes of mine hands: commande you me.

12 I haue made the earth, and created man vpon it: I, whose hands haue spred out the heauens, I haue euen commanded all their armie.

13 I haue raised him vp in righteousnesse, and I will direct all his wayes: he shall build my citie, and he shall let goe my captiues, not for price nor rewarde, saith the Lord of hostes.

14 Thus sayth the Lord, The labour of Egypt, and the marchandise of Ethiopia, and of the Sabeans, men of stature shall come vnto thee, and they shall be thine: they shall follow thee, and shall goe in chaines: they shall fall downe before thee, and make supplication vnto thee, saying, Surely God is in thee, and there is none other God besides.

15 Verely thou, O God, hidest thy selfe, O God, the Sauiour of Israel.

16 All they shalbe ashamed and also confounded: they shall goe to confusion together, that are the makers of images.

17 But Israel shall be saued in the Lord, with an euerlasting saluation: ye shall not be ashamed nor confounded worlde without ende.

18 For thus saith the Lord (that created heauen, God himselfe, that formed the earth, and made it: he that prepared it, he created it not in vaine: he formed it to be inhabited) I am the Lord, and there is none other.

19 I haue not spoken in secrete, neither in a place of darkenes in the earth: I saide not in vaine vnto the seede of Iaakob, Seeke you me: I the Lord doe

speake righteousnesse, and declare righteous things.

20 Assemble your selues, and come: drawe neere together, ye abiect of the Gentiles: they haue no knowledge, that set vp the wood of their idole, and pray vnto a god, that cannot saue them.

21 Tell ye and bring them, and let them take counsell together, who hath declared this from the beginning? or hath tolde it of olde? Haue not I the Lord? and there is none other God beside me, a iust God, and a Sauiour: there is none beside me.

22 Looke vnto me, and ye shall be saued: all the endes of the earth shall be saued: for I am God, and there is none other.

23 I haue sworne by my selfe: the worde is gone out of my mouth in righteousnesse, and shall not returne, That euery knee shall bowe vnto me, and euery tongue shall sweare by me.

24 Surely he shall say, In the Lord haue I righteousnesse and strength: he shall come vnto him, and all that prouoke him, shall be ashamed.

25 The whole seede of Israel shall be iustified, and glorie in the Lord.

Isaiah 46

1 Bel is bowed downe: Nebo is fallen: their idoles were vpon the beastes, and vpon the cattell: they which did beare you, were laden with a wearie burden.

2 They are bowed downe, and fallen together: for they coulde not rid them of the burden, and their soule is gone into captiuitie.

3 Heare ye me, O house of Iaakob, and all that remaine of the house of Israel, which are borne of me from the wombe, and brought vp of me from the birth.

4 Therefore vnto olde age, I the same, euen I will beare you vntill the hoare heares: I haue made you: I will also beare you, and I will cary you and I will deliuer you.

5 To whom will ye make me like or make me equall, or copare me, that I should be like him?

6 They draw gold out of the bagge and weigh siluer in the balance, and hire a goldsmith to make a god of it, and they bowe downe, and worship it.

7 They beare it vpon the shoulders: they carie him and set him in his place: so doeth he stand, and cannot remoue from his place. Though one crie vnto him, yet can he not answere, nor deliuer him out of his tribulation.

8 Remember this, and be ashamed: bring it againe to minde, O you transgressers.

9 Remember the former things of old: for I am God, and there is none other God, and there is nothing like me,

10 Which declare the last thing from the beginning: and from of olde, the things that were not done, saying, My counsell shall stand, and I will doe whatsoeuer I will.

11 I call a birde from the East, and the man of my counsell from farre: as I haue spoken, so will I bring it to passe: I haue purposed it, and I will doe it.

12 Heare me, ye stubburne hearted, that are farre from iustice.

13 I bring neere my iustice: it shall not be farre off, and my saluation shall not tarie: for I wil giue saluation in Zion, and my glory vnto Israel.

Isaiah 47

1 Come downe and sit in the dust: O virgine, daughter Babel, sit on the ground: there is no throne, O daughter of the Chaldeans: for thou shalt no more be called, Tender and delicate.

2 Take the mill stones, and grinde meale: loose thy lockes: make bare the feete: vncouer the legge, and passe through the floods.

3 Thy filthinesse shall be discouered, and thy shame shall be seene: I will take vengeance, and I will not meete thee as a man.

4 Our redeemer, the Lord of hostes is his Name, the holy one of Israel.

5 Sit still, and get thee into darkenesse, O daughter of the Chaldeas: for thou shalt no more be called, The ladie of kingdomes.

6 I was wroth with my people: I haue polluted mine inheritance, and giuen them into thine had: thou diddest shew them no mercy, but thou didest lay thy very heauy yoke vpon the ancient.

7 And thou saidest, I shall be a ladie for euer, so that thou diddest not set thy mind to these things, neither diddest thou remember ye latter end therof.

8 Therefore nowe heare, thou that art giuen to pleasures, and dwellest carelesse, Shee sayeth in her heart, I am and none els: I shall not sit as a widowe, neither shall knowe the losse of children.

9 But these two thinges shall come to thee suddenly on one day, the losse of children and widowhoode: they shall come vpon thee in their perfection, for the multitude of thy diuinations, and for the great abundance of thine inchanters.

10 For thou hast trusted in thy wickednesse: thou hast sayd, None seeth me. Thy wisdom and thy knowledge, they haue caused thee to rebel, and thou hast saide in thine heart, I am, and none els.

11 Therefore shall euill come vpon thee, and thou shalt not knowe the morning thereof: destruction shall fal vpon thee, which thou shalt not be able to put away: destruction shall come vpon thee suddenly, or thou beware.

12 Stand now among thine inchanters, and in the multitude of thy southsaiers (with whome thou hast wearied thy selfe from thy youth) if so be thou maist haue profit, or if so be thou maist haue strength.

13 Thou art wearied in the multitude of thy counsels: let now the astrologers, the starre gasers, and prognosticatours stand vp, and saue thee from these things, that shall come vpon thee.

14 Beholde, they shall be as stubble: the fire shall burne them: they shall not deliuer their owne liues from the power of the flame: there shalbe no coles to warme at, nor light to sit by.

15 Thus shall they serue thee, with whom thou hast wearied thee, euen thy marchants from thy youth: euery one shall wander to his owne quarter: none shall saue thee.

Isaiah 48

1 Hear yee this, O house of Iaakob, which are called by the name of Israel, and are come out of the waters of Iudah: which sweare by the Name of the Lord, and make mention of the God of Israel, but not in truth, nor in righteousnesse.

2 For they are called of the holy citie, and staie themselues vpon the God of Israel, whose Name is the Lord of hostes.

3 I haue declared ye former things of old, and they went out of my mouth, and I shewed them: I did them suddenly, and they came to passe.

4 Because I knewe, that thou art obstinate, and thy necke is an yron sinew, and thy brow brasse,

5 Therefore I haue declared it to thee of old: before it came to passe, I shewed it thee, lest thou shouldest say, Mine idole hath done them, and my carued image, and my molten image hath commanded them.

6 Thou hast heard, behold all this, and wil not yee declare it? I haue shewed thee newe things, euen now, and hid things, which thou knewest not.

7 They are created now, and not of olde, and euen before this thou heardest them not, lest thou shouldest say, Beholde, I knewe them.

8 Yet thou heardest them not, neither diddest know them, neither yet was thine eare opened of olde: for I knewe that thou wouldest grieuously transgresse: therefore haue I called thee a transgressour from the wombe.

9 For my Names sake will I defer my wrath, and for my praise will I refraine it from thee, that I cut thee not off.

10 Behold, I haue fined thee, but not as siluer: I haue chosen thee in the fornace of affliction.

11 For mine owne sake, for mine owne sake wil I doe it: for how should my Name be polluted? surely I wil not giue my glory vnto another.

12 Heare me, O Iaakob and Israel, my called, I am, I am the first, and I am the last.

13 Surely mine hand hath laid the foundation of the earth, and my right hand hath spanned the heaues: when I cal them, they stand vp together.

14 All you, assemble your selues, and heare: which among them hath declared these thinges? The Lord hath loued him: he wil doe his will in Babel, and his arme shalbe against the Chaldeans.

15 I, euen I haue spoken it, and I haue called him: I haue brought him, and his way shall prosper.

16 Come neere vnto me: heare ye this: I haue not spoken it in secret from the beginning: from the time that the thing

was, I was there, and now the Lord God and his Spirit hath sent me.

17 Thus saith the Lord thy redeemer, the Holy one of Israel, I am the Lord thy God, which teach thee to profite, and lead thee by the way, that thou shouldest goe.

18 Oh that thou haddest hearkened to my commandements! then had thy prosperitie bene as the floude, and thy righteousnesse as the waues of the sea.

19 Thy seede also had beene as the sande, and the fruite of thy body like the grauell thereof: his name should not haue bene cut off nor destroied before me.

20 Goe yee out of Babel: flee yee from the Chaldeans, with a voice of ioy: tel and declare this: shewe it foorth to the ende of the earth: say yee, The Lord hath redeemed his seruant Iaakob.

21 And they were not thirstie: hee led them through the wildernesse: hee caused the waters to flowe out of the rocke for them: for he claue the rocke, and the water gushed out.

22 There is no peace, sayeth the Lord, vnto the wicked.

Isaiah 49

1 Hear yee me, O yles, and hearken, yee people from farre. The Lord hath called me from the wombe, and made mention of my name from my mothers bellie.

2 And hee hath made my mouth like a sharpe sworde: vnder the shadowe of his hande hath he hid mee, and made me a chosen shafte, and hid me in his quiuer,

3 And sayd vnto me, Thou art my seruaunt, Israel, for I will be glorious in thee.

4 And I said, I haue labored in vaine: I haue spent my strength in vaine and for nothing: but my iudgement is with the Lord, and my woorke with my God.

5 And now sayeth the Lord, that formed me from the wombe to be his seruaunt, that I may bring Iaakob againe to him (though Israel be not gathered, yet shall I bee glorious in the eyes of the Lord: and my God shall be my strength)

6 And hee sayde, It is a small thing that thou shouldest be my seruaunt, to raise vp the tribes of Iaakob, and to restore the desolations of Israel: I will also giue thee for a light of the Gentiles, that thou maiest bee my saluation vnto the ende of the worlde.

7 Thus sayeth the Lord the redeemer of Israel, and his Holie one, to him that is despised in soule, to a nation that is abhorred, to a seruaunt of rulers, Kinges shall see, and arise, and princes shall worship, because of the Lord, that is faithfull: and ye Holy one of Israel, which hath chosen thee.

8 Thus sayeth the Lord, In an acceptable time haue I heard thee, and in a day of saluation haue I helped thee: and I will preserue thee, and wil giue thee for a couenant of ye people, that thou maiest raise vp the earth, and obtaine the inheritance of the desolate heritages:

9 That thou maiest say to the prisoners, Goe foorth: and to them that are in darkenesse, Shewe your selues: they shall feede in the waies, and their pastures shall bee in all the toppes of the hilles.

10 They shall not be hungrie, neither shall they be thirstie, neither shall the heat smite them, nor the sunne: for he that hath compassion on them, shall leade them: euen to the springs of waters shall he driue them.

11 And I will make all my mountaines, as a way, and my paths shalbe exalted.

12 Beholde, these shall come from farre: and loe, these from the North and from the West, and these from the land of Sinim.

13 Reioyce, O heauens: and bee ioyfull, O earth: brast foorth into praise, O mountaines: for God hath comforted his people, and will haue mercie vpon his afflicted.

14 But Zion saide, The Lord hath forsaken me, and my Lord hath forgotten me.

15 Can a woman forget her childe, and not haue compassion on the sonne of her wombe? though they should forget, yet wil I not forget thee.

16 Behold, I haue grauen thee vpon the palme of mine hands: thy walles are euer in my sight.

17 Thy builders make haste: thy destroiers and they that made thee waste, are departed from thee.

18 Lift vp thine eies round about and behold: all these gather themselues together and come to thee: as I liue, sayeth the Lord, thou shalt surely put them all vpon thee as a garment, and girde thy selfe with them like a bride.

19 For thy desolations, and thy waste places, and thy land destroied, shall surely be now narow for them that shall dwell in it, and they that did deuoure thee, shalbe farre away.

20 The children of thy barennesse shall say againe in thine eares, The place is straict for mee: giue place to me that I may dwell.

21 Then shalt thou say in thine heart, Who hath begotten mee these, seeing I am baren and desolate, a captiue and a wanderer to and from? and who hath nourished them? beholde, I was left alone: whence are these?

22 Thus sayeth the Lord God, Beholde, I will lift vp mine hande to the Gentiles and set vp my stadart to the people, and they shall bring thy sonnes in their armes: and thy daughters shall be caried vpon their shoulders.

23 And Kings shalbe thy nourcing fathers, and Queenes shalbe thy nources: they shall worship thee with their faces towarde the earth, and licke vp the dust of thy feete: and thou shalt knowe that I am the Lord: for they shall not be ashamed that waite for me.

24 Shall the pray be taken from the mightie? or the iust captiuitie deliuered?

25 But thus sayeth the Lord, euen the captiuitie of the mightie shall be taken away: and the pray of the tyrant shall be

deliuered: for I wil contend with him that contendeth with thee, and I will saue thy children,

26 And will feede them that spoile thee, with their owne flesh, and they shall be drunken with their owne bloode, as with sweete wine: and all flesh shall know that I the Lord am thy sauiour and thy redeemer, the mighty one of Iaakob.

Isaiah 50

1 Thus sayeth the Lord, Where is that bill of your mothers diuorcement, whome I haue cast off? or who is the creditour to whome I solde you? Beholde, for your iniquities are yee solde, and because of your transgressions is your mother forsaken.

2 Wherefore came I, and there was no man? I called, and none answered: is mine hand so shortened, that it cannot helpe? or haue I no power to deliuer? Beholde, at my rebuke I drie vp the Sea: I make the floods desert: their fish rotteth for want of water, and dieth for thirst.

3 I clothe the heauens with darkenesse, and make a sacke their couering.

4 The Lord God hath giuen me a tongue of the learned, that I shoulde knowe to minister a woord in time to him that is weary: he will raise me vp in the morning: in the morning hee will waken mine eare to heare, as the learned.

5 The Lord God hath opened mine eare and I was not rebellious, neither turned I backe.

6 I gaue my backe vnto the smiters, and my cheekes to the nippers: I hidde not my face from shame and spitting.

7 For the Lord God will helpe me, therefore shall I not bee confounded: therefore haue I set my face like a flint, and I knowe that I shall not be ashamed.

8 Hee is neere that iustifieth mee: who will contend with me? Let vs stande together: who is mine aduersarie? let him come neere to me.

9 Beholde, the Lord God will helpe me: who is he that can condemne me? loe, they shall waxe olde as a garment: the mothe shall eate them vp.

10 Who is among you that feareth the Lord? let him heare the voyce of his seruant: hee that walketh in darkenesse, and hath no light, let him trust in the Name of the Lord, and staye vpon his God.

11 Beholde, all you kindle a fire, and are compassed about with sparkes: walke in the light of your fire, and in the sparkes that ye haue kindled. This shall ye haue of mine hand: ye shall lye downe in sorowe.

Isaiah 51

1 Heare me, ye that follow after righteousnes, and ye that seeke the Lord: looke vnto the rocke, whence ye are hewen, and to the hole of the pit, whence ye are digged.

2 Consider Abraham your father, and Sarah that bare you: for I called him

alone, and blessed him, and increased him.

3 Surely the Lord shall comfort Zion: he shall comfort all her desolations, and he shall make her desert like Eden, and her wildernes like the garden of the Lord: ioy and gladnesse shalbe founde therein: praise, and the voyce of singing.

4 Hearken ye vnto me, my people, and giue eare vnto me, O my people: for a Law shall proceede from me, and I will bring foorth my iudgement for the light of the people.

5 My righteousnes is neere: my saluation goeth foorth, and mine armes shall iudge the people: the yles shall waite for me, and shall trust vnto mine arme.

6 Lift vp your eyes to the heauens, and looke vpon the earth beneath: for the heauens shall vanish away like smoke, and the earth shall waxe olde like a garment, and they that dwell therein, shall perish in like maner: but my saluation shall be for euer, and my righteousnesse shall not bee abolished.

7 Hearken vnto me, ye that know righteousnesse, the people in whose heart is my Lawe. Feare ye not the reproche of men, neither be ye afraide of their rebukes.

8 For the mothe shall eate them vp like a garment, and the worme shall eate them like wool: but my righteousnesse shalbe for euer, and my saluation from generation to generation.

9 Rise vp, rise vp, and put on strength, O arme of the Lord: rise vp as in the olde time in the generations of the worlde. Art not thou the same, that hath cutte Rahab, and wounded the dragon?

10 Art not thou the same, which hath dried the Sea, euen the waters of the great deepe, making the depth of the Sea a way for the redeemed to passe ouer?

11 Therefore the redeemed of the Lord shall returne, and come with ioy vnto Zion, and euerlasting ioy shalbe vpon their head: they shall obtaine ioy, and gladnesse: and sorow and mourning shall flee away.

12 I, euen I am he, that comfort you. Who art thou, that thou shouldest feare a mortall man, and the sonne of man, which shalbe made as grasse?

13 And forgettest the Lord thy maker, that hath spred out the heauens, and layde the foundations of the earth? and hast feared continually all the day, because of the rage of the oppressour, which is readie to destroy? Where is now the rage of the oppressour?

14 The captiue hasteneth to be loosed, and that hee should not die in the pitte, nor that his bread should faile.

15 And I am the Lord thy God that deuided the Sea, when his waues roared: the Lord of hostes is his Name.

16 And I haue put my wordes in thy mouth, and haue defended thee in the shadowe of mine hand, that I may plant the heauens, and lay the foundation of the earth, and say vnto Zion, Thou art my people.

17 Awake, awake, and stande vp, O Ierusalem, which hast drunke at the hande of the Lord the cup of his wrath: thou hast drunken the dregges of the cup of trembling, and wrung them out.

18 There is none to guide her among all the sonnes, whome she hath brought foorth: there is none that taketh her by the hand of all the sonnes that she hath brought vp.

19 These two thinges are come vnto thee: who will lament thee? desolation and destruction and famine, and the sworde: by whome shall I comfort thee?

20 Thy sonnes haue fainted, and lye at the head of all the streetes as a wilde bull in a nette, and are full of the wrath of the Lord, and rebuke of thy God.

21 Therefore heare nowe this, thou miserable and drunken, but not with wine.

22 Thus saith thy Lord God, euen God that pleadeth the cause of his people, Beholde, I haue taken out of thine hande the cuppe of trembling, euen the dregges of the cuppe of my wrath: thou shalt drinke it no more.

23 But I will put it into their hande that spoile thee: which haue said to thy soule, Bowe downe, that wee may goe ouer, and thou hast layde thy bodie as the grounde, and as the streete to them that went ouer.

Isaiah 52

1 Aries, arise: put on thy strength, O Zion: put on thy garments of thy beautie, O Ierusalem, the holy citie: for henceforth there shall no more come into thee the vncircumcised and the vncleane.

2 Shake thy selfe from the dust: arise, and sit downe, O Ierusalem: loose the bandes of thy necke, O thou captiue daughter, Zion.

3 For thus sayeth the Lord, Yee were solde for naught: therefore shall ye be redeemed without money.

4 For thus saith the Lord God, My people went downe afore time into Egypt to soiourne there, and Asshur oppressed them without cause.

5 Nowe therefore what haue I here, saith the Lord, that my people is taken away for naught, and they that rule ouer them, make them to howle, saith the Lord? and my Name all the day continually is blasphemed?

6 Therefore my people shall know my Name: therefore they shall know in that day, that I am he that doe speake: beholde, it is I.

7 How beautifull vpon the mountaines are the feete of him, that declareth and publisheth peace? that declareth good tidings, and publisheth saluation, saying vnto Zion, Thy God reigneth?

8 The voyce of thy watchmen shalbe heard: they shall lift vp their voyce, and shoute together: for they shall see eye to eye, when the Lord shall bring againe Zion.

9 O ye desolate places of Ierusalem, bee glad and reioyce together: for the Lord

hath comforted his people: he hath redeemed Ierusalem.

10 The Lord hath made bare his holy arme in the sight of all the Gentiles, and all the endes of the earth shall see the saluation of our God.

11 Depart, depart ye: goe out from thence and touche no vncleane thing: goe out of the middes of her: be ye cleane, that beare the vessels of the Lord.

12 For ye shall not goe out with haste, nor depart by fleeing away: but the Lord will goe before you, and the God of Israel will gather you together.

13 Beholde, my seruant shall prosper: he shall be exalted and extolled, and be very hie.

14 As many were astonied at thee (his visage was so deformed of men, and his forme of the sonnes of men) so shall hee sprinkle many nations: the Kings shall shut their mouthes at him: for that which had not bene tolde them, shall they see, and that which they had not heard, shall they vnderstande.

Isaiah 53

1 Who will beleeue our report? and to whom is the arme of the Lord reueiled?

2 But hee shall growe vp before him as a branche, and as a roote out of a dry grounde: he hath neither forme nor beautie: when we shall see him, there shall be no forme that wee should desire him.

3 He is despised and reiected of men: he is a man full of sorowes and hath experience of infirmities: we hidde as it were our faces from him: he was despised and we esteemed him not.

4 Surely hee hath borne our infirmities, and caried our sorowes: yet wee did iudge him, as plagued, and smitten of God, and humbled.

5 But hee was wounded for our transgressions, hee was broken for our iniquities: the chastisement of our peace was vpon him, and with his stripes we are healed.

6 All we like sheepe haue gone astraye: wee haue turned euery one to his owne way, and the Lord hath layed vpon him the iniquitie of vs all.

7 Hee was oppressed and he was afflicted, yet did he not open his mouth: hee is brought as a sheepe to the slaughter, and as a sheepe before her shearer is dumme, so he openeth not his mouth.

8 Hee was taken out from prison, and from iudgement: and who shall declare his age? for he was cut out of the lande of the liuing: for the transgression of my people was he plagued.

9 And he made his graue with the wicked, and with the riche in his death, though hee had done no wickednesse, neither was any deceite in his mouth.

10 Yet the Lord would breake him, and make him subiect to infirmities: when hee shall make his soule an offring for sinne, he shall see his seede and shall

prolong his dayes, and the will of the Lord shall prosper in his hand.

11 Hee shall see of the trauaile of his soule, and shall be satisfied: by his knowledge shall my righteous seruant iustifie many: for hee shall beare their iniquities.

12 Therefore will I giue him a portion with the great, and he shall deuide the spoyle with the strong, because hee hath powred out his soule vnto death: and he was counted with the transgressers, and he bare the sinne of many, and prayed for the trespassers.

Isaiah 54

1 Rejoice, O barren that diddest not beare: breake forth into ioy and reioyce, thou that diddest not trauaile with childe: for the desolate hath moe children then the married wife, sayeth the Lord.

2 Enlarge the place of thy tents, and let them spread out the curtains of thine habitations: spare not, stretch out thy cords and make fast thy stakes.

3 For thou shalt increase on the right hande and on the left, and thy seede shall possesse the Gentiles, and dwell in the desolate cities.

4 Feare not: for thou shalt not be ashamed, neither shalt thou be confounded: for thou shalt not bee put to shame: yea, thou shalt forget the shame of thy youth, and shalt not remember the reproch of thy widdowhoode any more.

5 For hee that made thee, is thine husband (whose Name is the Lord of hostes) and thy redeemer the Holy one of Israel, shall be called the God of the whole world.

6 For the Lord hath called thee, being as a woman forsaken, and afflicted in spirite, and as a yong wife when thou wast refused, sayth thy God.

7 For a litle while haue I forsaken thee, but with great compassion will I gather thee.

8 For a moment, in mine anger, I hid my face from thee for a litle season, but with euerlasting mercy haue I had compassion on thee, sayth the Lord thy redeemer.

9 For this is vnto me as the waters of Noah: for as I haue sworne that the waters of Noah should no more goe ouer the earth, so haue I sworne that I would not be angrie with thee, nor rebuke thee.

10 For the mountaines shall remoue and the hilles shall fall downe: but my mercy shall not depart from thee, neither shall the couenant of my peace fall away, saith the Lord, that hath compassion on thee.

11 O thou afflicted and tossed with tempest, that hast no comfort, beholde, I wil lay thy stones with the carbuncle, and lay thy foundation with saphirs,

12 And I will make thy windowes of emeraudes, and thy gates shining stones, and all thy borders of pleasant stones.

13 And all thy children shalbe taught of the Lord, and much peace shalbe to thy children.

14 In righteousnes shalt thou be established, and be farre from oppression: for thou shalt not feare it: and from feare, for it shall not come neere thee.

15 Beholde, the enemie shall gather himselfe, but without me: whosoeuer shall gather himselfe in thee, against thee, shall fall.

16 Beholde, I haue created the smith that bloweth the coales in the fire, and him that bringeth forth an instrument for his worke, and I haue created the destroyer to destroy.

17 But all the weapons that are made against thee, shall not prosper: and euery tongue that shall rise against thee in iudgement, thou shalt condemne. This is the heritage of the Lords seruants, and their righteousnesse is of me, sayth the Lord.

Isaiah 55

1 Ho, euery one that thirsteth, come ye to the waters, and ye that haue no siluer, come, bye and eate: come, I say, bye wine and milke without siluer and without money.

2 Wherefore doe ye lay out siluer and not for bread? and your labour without being satisfied? hearken diligently vnto me, and eate that which is good, and let your soule delite in fatnes.

3 Encline your eares, and come vnto me: heare, and your soule shall liue, and I will make an euerlasting couenant with you, euen the sure mercies of Dauid.

4 Beholde, I gaue him for a witnes to the people, for a prince and a master vnto the people.

5 Beholde, thou shalt call a nation that thou knowest not, and a nation that knew not thee, shall runne vnto thee, because of the Lord thy God, and the holy one of Israel: for hee hath glorified thee.

6 Seeke ye the Lord while he may be found: call ye vpon him while he is neere.

7 Let the wicked forsake his wayes, and the vnrighteous his owne imaginations, and returne vnto the Lord, and he wil haue mercy vpon him: and to our God, for hee is very ready to forgiue.

8 For my thoughtes are not your thoughts, neither are your wayes my wayes, sayth the Lord.

9 For as ye heauens are higher then the earth, so are my wayes higher then your wayes, and my thoughtes aboue your thoughts.

10 Surely as the raine commeth downe and the snow from heauen, and returneth not thither, but watereth the earth and maketh it to bring forth and bud, that it may giue seede to the sower, and bread vnto him that eateth,

11 So shall my worde be, that goeth out of my mouth: it shall not returne vnto me voyde, but it shall accomplish that which I will, and it shall prosper in the thing whereto I sent it.

12 Therefore ye shall go out with ioy, and be led forth with peace: the mountaines and the hilles shall breake foorth before you into ioye, and all the trees of the fielde shall clap their handes.

13 For thornes there shall grow firre trees: for nettles shall growe the myrrhe tree, and it shalbe to the Lord for a name, and for an euerlasting signe that shall not be taken away.

Isaiah 56

1 Thus saith the Lord, Keepe iudgement and doe iustice: for my saluation is at hand to come, and my righteousnes to be reueiled.

2 Blessed is the man that doeth this, and the sonne of man which layeth holde on it: hee that keepeth the Sabbath and polluteth it not, and keepeth his hand from doing any euill.

3 And let not the sonne of the stranger, which is ioyned to the Lord, speake and say, The Lord hath surely separate me from his people: neither let the Eunuch say, Beholde, I am a drye tree.

4 For thus saith the Lord vnto the Eunuches, that keepe my Sabbaths, and chuse the thing that pleaseth me, and take holde of my couenant,

5 Euen vnto them wil I giue in mine House and within my walles, a place and a name better then of the sonnes and of the daughters: I will giue them an euerlasting name, that shall not be put out.

6 Also the strangers that cleaue vnto the Lord, to serue him, and to loue the Name of the Lord, and to be his seruants: euery one that keepeth the Sabbath, and polluteth it not and imbraceth my couenant,

7 Them wil I bring also to mine holy mountaine, and make them ioyfull in mine House of prayer: their burnt offerings and their sacrifices shall be accepted vpon mine altar: for mine House shall be called an house of prayer for all people.

8 The Lord God sayth, which gathereth the scattered of Israel, Yet wil I gather to them those that are to be gathered to them.

9 All ye beastes of the fielde, come to deuoure, euen all ye beastes of the forest.

10 Their watchmen are all blinde: they haue no knowledge: they are all dumme dogs: they can not barke: they lie and sleepe and delite in sleeping.

11 And these griedy dogs can neuer haue ynough: and these shepheards cannot vnderstand: for they all looke to their owne way, euery one for his aduantage, and for his owne purpose.

12 Come, I wil bring wine, and we wil fill our selues with strong drinke, and to morowe shalbe as this day, and much more abundant.

Isaiah 57

1 The righteous perisheth, and no man considereth it in heart: and mercifull men are taken away, and no man

vnderstandeth that the righteous is taken away from the euill to come.

2 Peace shall come: they shall rest in their beds, euery one that walketh before him.

3 But you witches children, come hither, the seede of the adulterer and of the whore.

4 On whome haue ye iested? vpon whome haue ye gaped and thrust out your tongue? are not ye rebellious children, and a false seede?

5 Inflamed with idoles vnder euery greene tree? and sacrificing the children in the valleys vnder the tops of the rocks?

6 Thy portion is in the smooth stones of the riuer: they, they are thy lot: euen to them hast thou powred a drinke offering: thou hast offered a sacrifice. Should I delite in these?

7 Thou hast made thy bed vpon a very hie mountaine: thou wentest vp thither, euen thither wentest thou to offer sacrifice.

8 Behinde the doores also and postes hast thou set vp thy remembrance: for thou hast discouered thy selfe to another then me, and wentest vp, and diddest enlarge thy bed, and make a couenant betweene thee and them, and louedst their bed in euery place where thou sawest it.

9 Thou wentest to the Kings with oyle, and diddest increase thine oyntments and sende thy messengers farre off, and diddest humble thy selfe vnto hell.

10 Thou weariedst thy selfe in thy manifolde iourneys, yet saydest thou not, There is no hope: thou hast found life by thine hand, therefore thou wast not grieued.

11 And whome diddest thou reuerence or feare, seeing thou hast lyed vnto me, and hast not remembred me, neither set thy minde thereon? is it not because I holde my peace, and that of long time? therefore thou fearest not me.

12 I will declare thy righteousnes and thy workes, and they shall not profite thee.

13 When thou cryest, let them that thou hast gathered together deliuer thee: but the winde shall take them all away: vanitie shall pull them away: but he that trusteth in me, shall inherite the lande, and shall possesse mine holy Mountaine.

14 And he shall say, Cast vp, cast vp: prepare the way: take vp the stumbling blocks out of the way of my people.

15 For thus sayth he that is hie and excellent, he that inhabiteth the eternitie, whose Name is the Holy one, I dwell in the high and holy place: with him also that is of a contrite and humble spirite to reuiue the spirite of the humble, and to giue life to them that are of a contrite heart.

16 For I will not contende for euer, neither will I be alwayes wroth, for the spirite should fayle before me: and I haue made the breath.

17 For his wicked couetousnesse I am angry with him, and haue smitten him: I hid mee and was angry, yet he went away, and turned after the way of his owne heart.

18 I haue seene his wayes, and wil heale him: I wil leade him also, and restore comfort vnto him, and to those that lament him.

19 I create the fruite of the lips, to be peace: peace vnto them that are farre off, and to them that are neere, sayth the Lord: for I will heale him.

20 But the wicked are like the raging sea, that can not rest, whose waters cast vp myre and dirt.

21 There is no peace, sayth my God, to the wicked.

Isaiah 58

1 Crye aloude, spare not: lift vp thy voyce like a trumpet, and shewe my people their transgression, and to the house of Iaakob, their sinnes.

2 Yet they seeke me dayly, and will knowe my wayes, euen as a nation that did righteously, and had not forsaken the statutes of their God: they aske of me the ordinances of iustice: they wil drawe neere vnto God, saying,

3 Wherefore haue we fasted, and thou seest it not? we haue punished our selues, and thou regardest it not. Beholde, in the day of your fast you will seeke your will, and require all your dettes.

4 Beholde, ye fast to strife and debate, and to smite with the fist of wickednesse: ye shall not fast as ye doe to day, to make your voyce to be heard aboue.

5 Is it such a fast that I haue chosen, that a man should afflict his soule for a day, and to bowe downe his head, as a bull rush, and to lie downe in sackecloth and ashes? wilt thou call this a fasting, or an acceptable day to the Lord?

6 Is not this the fasting, that I haue chosen, to loose the bandes of wickednes, to take off the heauie burdens, and to let the oppressed goe free, and that ye breake euery yoke?

7 Is it not to deale thy bread to the hungry, and that thou bring the poore that wander, vnto thine house? when thou seest the naked, that thou couer him, and hide not thy selfe from thine owne flesh?

8 Then shall thy light breake foorth as the morning, and thine health shall grow speedily: thy righteousnes shall goe before thee, and the glorie of the Lord shall embrace thee.

9 Then shalt thou call, and the Lord shall answere: thou shalt cry and hee shall say, Here I am: if thou take away from the mids of thee the yoke, the putting foorth of the finger, and wicked speaking:

10 If thou powre out thy soule to the hungrie, and refresh the troubled soule: then shall thy light spring out in the darkenes, and thy darkenes shalbe as the noone day.

11 And the Lord shall guide thee continually, and satisfie thy soule in drought, and make fat thy bones: and thou shalt be like a watred garden, and like a spring of water, whose waters faile not.

12 And they shalbe of thee, that shall builde the olde waste places: thou shalt rayse vp the foundations for many generations, and thou shalt be called the repairer of the breach and the restorer of the pathes to dwell in.

13 If thou turne away thy foote from the Sabbath, from doing thy will on mine holy day, and call the Sabbath a delite, to consecrate it, as glorious to the Lord, and shalt honour him, not doing thine owne wayes, nor seeking thine owne will, nor speaking a vaine word,

14 Then shalt thou delite in the Lord, and I wil cause thee to mount vpon the hie places of the earth, and feede thee with the heritage of Iaakob thy father: for the mouth of ye Lord hath spoken it.

Isaiah 59

1 Beholde, the Lordes hande is not shortened, that it can not saue: neither is his eare heauie, that it cannot heare.

2 But your iniquities haue separated betweene you and your God, and your sinnes haue hidde his face from you, that he will not heare.

3 For your handes are defiled with blood, and your fingers with iniquitie: your lips haue spoken lies and your tongue hath murmured iniquitie.

4 No man calleth for iustice: no man contendeth for trueth: they trust in vanitie, and speake vaine things: they conceiue mischiefe, and bring foorth iniquitie.

5 They hatch cockatrice egges, and weaue the spiders webbe: he that eateth of their egges, dieth, and that which is trode vpon, breaketh out into a serpent.

6 Their webbes shall be no garment, neither shall they couer themselues with their labours: for their workes are workes of iniquitie, and the worke of crueltie is in their handes.

7 Their feete runne to euill, and they make haste to shed innocent blood: their thoughts are wicked thoughts: desolation and destruction is in their paths.

8 The way of peace they knowe not, and there is none equitie in their goings: they haue made them crooked paths: whosoeuer goeth therein, shall not knowe peace.

9 Therefore is iudgement farre from vs, neither doeth iustice come neere vnto vs: we waite for light, but loe, it is darkenesse: for brightnesse, but we walke in darkenesse.

10 Wee grope for the wall like the blinde, and we grope as one without eyes: we stumble at the noone day as in the twilight: we are in solitarie places, as dead men.

11 We roare all like beares, and mourne like dooues: wee looke for equitie, but there is none: for health, but it is farre from vs.

12 For our trespasses are many before thee, and our sinnes testifie against vs:

for our trespasses are with vs, and we knowe our iniquities

13 In trespassing and lying against the Lord, and wee haue departed away from our God, and haue spoken of crueltie and rebellion, conceiuing and vttering out of the heart false matters.

14 Therefore iudgement is turned backewarde, and iustice standeth farre off: for trueth is fallen in the streete, and equitie cannot enter.

15 Yea, trueth faileth, and hee that refraineth from euill, maketh himselfe a praye: and when the Lord sawe it, it displeased him, that there was no iudgement.

16 And when he sawe that there was no man, hee wondered that none woulde offer him selfe. Therefore his arme did saue it, and his righteousnes it selfe did sustaine it.

17 For he put on righteousnes, as an habergeon, and an helmet of saluation vpon his head, and he put on the garments of vengeance for clothing, and was clad with zeale as a cloke.

18 As to make recompence, as to requite the furie of the aduersaries with a recompence to his enemies: he will fully repaire the ylands.

19 So shall they feare the Name of the Lord from the West, and his glory from the rising of the sunne: for the enemie shall come like a flood: but the Spirit of the Lord shall chase him away.

20 And the Redeemer shall come vnto Zion, and vnto them that turne from iniquitie in Iaakob, saith the Lord.

21 And I will make this my couenant with them, saith the Lord. My Spirit that is vpon thee, and my wordes, which I haue put in thy mouth, shall not depart out of thy mouth, nor out of the mouth of thy seede, nor out of the mouth of the seede of thy seede, saith the Lord, from henceefoorth euen for euer.

Isaiah 60

1 Arise, O Ierusalem: be bright, for thy light is come, and the glorie of the Lord is risen vpon thee.

2 For beholde, darkenesse shall couer the earth, and grosse darkenesse the people: but the Lord shall arise vpon thee, and his glory shall be seene vpon thee.

3 And the Gentiles shall walke in thy light, and Kings at the brightnesse of thy rising vp.

4 Lift vp thine eyes round about, and beholde: all these are gathered, and come to thee: thy sonnes shall come from farre, and thy daughters shalbe nourished at thy side.

5 Then thou shalt see and shine: thine heart shall be astonied and enlarged, because the multitude of the sea shalbe conuerted vnto thee, and the riches of the Gentiles shall come vnto thee.

6 The multitude of camels shall couer thee: and the dromedaries of Midian and of Ephah: all they of Sheba shall come: they shall bring golde and incense, and shewe foorth the prayses of the Lord.

7 All the sheepe of Kedar shall be gathered vnto thee: the rammes of Nebaioth shall serue thee: they shall come vp to bee accepted vpon mine altar: and I will beautifie the house of my glorie.

8 Who are these that flee like a cloude, and as the doues to their windowes?

9 Surely the yles shall waite for mee, and the shippes of Tarshish, as at the beginning, that they may bring thy sonnes from farre, and their siluer, and their golde with them, vnto the Name of the Lord thy God, and to the Holy one of Israel, because he hath glorified thee.

10 And the sonnes of strangers shall builde vp thy walles, and their Kings shall minister vnto thee: for in my wrath I smote thee, but in my mercie I had compassion on thee.

11 Therefore thy gates shalbe open continually: neither day nor night shall they be shutte, that men may bring vnto thee the riches of the Gentiles, and that their Kings may be brought.

12 For the nation and the kingdome, that will not serue thee, shall perish: and those nations shalbe vtterly destroyed.

13 The glory of Lebanon shall come vnto thee, the firre tree, the elme and the boxe tree together, to beautifie the place of my Sanctuarie: for I will glorifie the place of my feete.

14 The sonnes also of them that afflicted thee, shall come and bowe vnto thee: and all they that despised thee, shall fall downe at the soles of thy feete: and they shall call thee, The citie of the Lord, Zion of the Holy one of Israel.

15 Where as thou hast bene forsaken and hated: so that no man went by thee, I will make thee an eternall glorie, and a ioye from generation to generation.

16 Thou shalt also sucke ye milke of the Gentiles, and shalt sucke the breastes of Kings: and thou shalt know, that I the Lord am thy Sauiour, and thy Redeemer, the mightie one of Iaakob.

17 For brasse will I bring golde, and for yron will I bring siluer, and for wood brasse, and for stones yron. I will also make thy gouernement peace, and thine exactours righteousnesse.

18 Violence shall no more be heard of in thy land, neither desolation, nor destruction within thy borders: but thou shalt call saluation, thy walles, and praise, thy gates.

19 Thou shalt haue no more sunne to shine by day, neither shall the brightnesse of the moone shine vnto thee: for the Lord shall be thine euerlasting light, and thy God, thy glorie.

20 Thy sunne shall neuer goe downe, neither shall thy moone be hid: for the Lord shalbe thine euerlasting light, and the dayes of thy sorowe shalbe ended.

21 Thy people also shalbe all righteous: they shall possesse the land for euer, the grasse of my planting shalbe the worke of mine handes, that I may be glorified.

22 A litle one shall become as a thousande, and a small one as a strong nation: I the Lord wil hasten it in due time.

Isaiah 61

1 The Spirit of the Lord God is vpon mee, therefore hath the Lord anoynted mee: hee hath sent mee to preache good tidings vnto the poore, to binde vp the broken hearted, to preach libertie to the captiues, and to them that are bound, the opening of the prison,

2 To preache the acceptable yeere of the Lord, and the day of vengeance of our God, to comfort all that mourne,

3 To appoint vnto them that mourne in Zion, and to giue vnto them beautie for ashes, the oyle of ioye for mourning, the garment of gladnesse for the spirit of heauinesse, that they might be called trees of righteousnesse, the planting of the Lord, that he might be glorified.

4 And they shall builde the olde waste places, and raise vp the former desolations, and they shall repaire the cities that were desolate and waste through many generations.

5 And the strangers shall stande and feede your sheepe, and the sonnes of the strangers shall be your plowmen and dressers of your vines.

6 But ye shall be named the Priestes of the Lord, and men shall say vnto you, The ministers of our God, Ye shall eate the riches of the Gentiles, and shalbe exalted with their glorie.

7 For your shame you shall receiue double, and for confusion they shall reioyce in their portion: for in their lande they shall possesse the double: euerlasting ioy shall be vnto them.

8 For I the Lord loue iudgement and hate robberie for burnt offering, and I wil direct their worke in trueth, and will make an euerlasting couenant with them.

9 And their seede shall be knowen among the Gentiles, and their buddes among the people. All that see them, shall know them, that they are the seede which the Lord hath blessed.

10 I will greatly reioyce in the Lord, and my soule shall be ioyfull in my God: for he hath clothed mee with the garments of saluation, and couered me with the robe of righteousnes: hee hath decked me like a bridegrome, and as a bride tireth herselfe with her iewels.

11 For as the earth bringeth foorth her bud, and as the garden causeth to growe that which is sowen in it: so the Lord God will cause righteousnesse to grow and praise before all the heathen.

Isaiah 62

1 For Zions sake I will not holde my tongue, and for Ierusalems sake I wil not rest, vntil the righteousnes thereof breake foorth as the light, and saluation thereof as a burning lampe.

2 And the Gentiles shall see thy righteousnesse, and all Kings thy glory: and thou shalt be called by a new name, which the mouth of the Lord shall name.

3 Thou shalt also be a crowne of glory in the hand of the Lord, and a royall diademe in the hand of thy God.

4 It shall no more be sayd vnto thee, Forsaken, neither shall it be said any more to thy land, Desolate, but thou shalt be called Hephzi-bah, and thy land Beulah: for the Lord deliteth in thee, and thy land shall haue an husband.

5 For as a yong man marieth a virgine, so shall thy sonnes marry thee: and as a bridegrome is glad of the bride, so shall thy God reioyce ouer thee.

6 I haue set watchmen vpon thy walles, O Ierusalem, which all the day and all the night continually shall not cease: ye that are mindfull of the Lord, keepe not silence,

7 And giue him no rest, till hee repaire and vntill hee set vp Ierusalem the prayse of the worlde.

8 The Lord hath sworne by his right hand and by his strong arme, Surely I wil no more giue thy corne to be meate for thine enemies, and surely the sonnes of the strangers shall not drinke thy wine, for the which thou hast laboured.

9 But they that haue gathered it, shall eate it, and prayse the Lord, and the gatherers thereof shall drinke it in the courtes of my Sanctuarie.

10 Go through, go through the gates: prepare you the way for the people: cast vp, cast vp the way, and gather out the stones and set vp a standart for the people.

11 Beholde, the Lord hath proclaimed vnto the endes of the world: tell the daughter Zion, Beholde, thy Sauiour commeth: beholde, his wages is with him, and his worke is before him.

12 And they shall call them, The holy people, the redeemed of the Lord, and thou shalt be named, A citie sought out and not forsaken.

Isaiah 63

1 Who is this that commeth from Edom, with red garments from Bozrah? hee is glorious in his apparel and walketh in his great strength: I speake in righteousnesse, and am mightie to saue.

2 Wherefore is thine apparel red, and thy garments like him that treadeth in ye wine presse?

3 I haue troden the wine presse alone, and of all people there was none with mee: for I will treade them in mine anger, and tread them vnder foote in my wrath, and their blood shalbe sprinkled vpon my garments, and I will staine all my raiment.

4 For the day of vengeance is in mine heart, and the yeere of my redeemed is come.

5 And I looked, and there was none to helpe, and I wondered that there was none to vpholde: therefore mine owne arme helped me, and my wrath it selfe sustained me.

6 Therefore I wil tread downe the people in my wrath, and make them drunken in mine indignation, and wil bring downe their strength to the earth.

7 I wil remember the mercies of the Lord and the prayses of the Lord according vnto all that the Lord hath giuen vs, and

for the great goodnesse toward the house of Israel, which hee hath giuen them according to his tender loue, and according to his great mercies.

8 For he saide, Surely they are my people, children that wil not lie: so he was their Sauiour.

9 In all their troubles he was troubled, and the Angel of his presence saued them: in his loue and in his mercie he redeemed them, and he bare them and caried them always continually.

10 But they rebelled and vexed his holy Spirit: therefore was hee turned to be their enemie and he fought against them.

11 Then he remembred the olde time of Moses and his people, saying, Where is hee that brought them vp out of the Sea with the shepheard of his sheepe? where is he that put his holy Spirit within him?

12 He led them by the right hand of Moses with his owne glorious arme, deuiding the water before them, to make himselfe an euerlasting Name.

13 Hee led them through the deepe, as an horse in the wildernesse, that they should not stumble,

14 As the beast goeth downe into the valley, the Spirite of the Lord gaue them rest: so diddest thou leade thy people, to make thy selfe a glorious Name.

15 Looke downe from heauen, and beholde from the dwelling place of thine holines, and of thy glory. Where is thy zeale and thy strength, the multitude of thy mercies, and of thy compassions? they are restrained from me.

16 Doutles thou art our Father: though Abraham be ignorant of vs, and Israel knowe vs not, yet thou, O Lord, art our Father, and our redeemer: thy Name is for euer.

17 O Lord, why hast thou made vs to erre from thy wayes? and hardened our heart from thy feare? Returne for thy seruants sake, and for the tribes of thine inheritance.

18 The people of thine holinesse haue possessed it, but a litle while: for our aduersaries haue troden downe thy Sanctuarie.

19 We haue bene as they, ouer whome thou neuer barest rule, and vpon whom thy Name was not called.

Isaiah 64

1 Oh, that thou wouldest breake the heauens, and come downe, and that the mountaines might melt at thy presence!

2 As the melting fire burned, as the fire caused the waters to boyle, (that thou mightest declare thy Name to thy aduersaries) the people did tremble at thy presence.

3 When thou diddest terrible things, which we looked not for, thou camest downe, and the mountaines melted at thy presence.

4 For since the beginning of the world they haue not heard nor vnderstande with the eare, neither hath ye eye seene another God beside thee, which doeth so to him that waiteth for him.

5 Thou diddest meete him, that reioyced in thee, and did iustly: they remembred thee in thy wayes: beholde, thou art angrie, for we haue sinned: yet in them is continuance, and we shall be saued.

6 But we haue all bene as an vncleane thing, and all our righteousnes is as filthie cloutes, and we all doe fade like a leafe, and our iniquities like the winde haue taken vs away.

7 And there is none that calleth vpon thy Name, neither that stirreth vp himselfe to take holde of thee: for thou hast hid thy face from vs, and hast consumed vs because of our iniquities.

8 But now, O Lord, thou art our Father: we are the clay, and thou art our potter, and we all are the worke of thine hands.

9 Be not angry, O Lord, aboue measure, neither remember iniquitie for euer: lo, we beseech thee beholde, we are all thy people.

10 Thine holy cities lye waste: Zion is a wildernes, and Ierusalem a desart.

11 The House of our Sanctuarie and of our glorie, where our fathers praysed thee, is burnt vp with fire and all our pleasant things are wasted.

12 Wilt thou holde thy selfe still at these things, O Lord? wilt thou holde thy peace and afflict vs aboue measure?

Isaiah 65

1 I have bene sought of them that asked not: I was found of them that sought me not: I sayd, Beholde me, beholde me, vnto a nation that called not vpon my Name.

2 I haue spred out mine handes all the day vnto a rebellious people, which walked in a way that was not good, euen after their owne imaginations:

3 A people that prouoked me euer vnto my face: that sacrificeth in gardens, and burneth incense vpon brickes.

4 Which remaine among the graues, and lodge in the desarts, which eate swines flesh, and the broth of things polluted are in their vessels.

5 Which say, Stand apart, come not neere to me: for I am holier then thou: these are a smoke in my wrath and a fire that burneth all the day.

6 Beholde, it is written before me: I wil not keepe silence, but will render it and recompense it into their bosome.

7 Your iniquities and the iniquities of your fathers shalbe together (sayth the Lord) which haue burnt incense vpon the mountaines, and blasphemed me vpon the hilles: therefore wil I measure their olde worke into their bosome.

8 Thus sayth the Lord, As the wine is found in the cluster, and one sayth, Destroy it not, for a blessing is in it, so will I doe for my seruants sakes, that I may not destroy them whole.

9 But I will bring a seede out of Iaakob, and out of Iudah, that shall inherit my mountaine: and mine elect shall inherit it, and my seruants shall dwell there.

10 And Sharon shalbe a sheepefolde, and the valley of Achor shalbe a resting

place for the cattell of my people, that haue sought me.

11 But ye are they that haue forsaken the Lord and forgotten mine holy Mountaine, and haue prepared a table for the multitude, and furnish the drinke offerings vnto the number.

12 Therefore wil I number you to the sword, and all you shall bowe downe to the slaughter, because I called, and ye did not answere: I spake, and ye heard not, but did euil in my sight, and did chuse that thing which I would not.

13 Therefore thus saith the Lord God, Beholde, my seruants shall eate, and ye shalbe hungrie: beholde, my seruants shall drinke, and ye shall be thirstie: beholde, my seruants shall reioyce, and ye shalbe ashamed.

14 Beholde, my seruants shall sing for ioye of heart, and ye shall crye for sorow of heart, and shall howle for vexation of minde.

15 And ye shall leaue your name as a curse vnto my chosen: for the Lord God shall slay you and call his seruants by another name.

16 He that shall blesse in the earth, shall blesse himselfe in the true God, and he that sweareth in the earth, shall sweare by the true God: for the former troubles are forgotten, and shall surely hide themselues from mine eyes.

17 For lo, I will create newe heauens and a new earth: and the former shall not be remembred nor come into minde.

18 But be you glad and reioyce for euer in the things that I shall create: for beholde, I will create Ierusalem, as a reioycing and her people as a ioye,

19 And I wil reioyce in Ierusalem, and ioye in my people, and the voyce of weeping shall be no more heard in her, nor the voyce of crying.

20 There shall be no more there a childe of yeeres, nor an olde man that hath not filled his dayes: for he that shall be an hundreth yeeres old, shall dye as a yong man: but the sinner being an hundreth yeeres olde shall be accursed.

21 And they shall build houses and inhabite them, and they shall plant vineyards, and eate the fruite of them.

22 They shall not build, and another inhabite: they shall not plant, and another eate: for as the dayes of the tree are the dayes of my people, and mine elect shall inioye in olde age the worke of their handes.

23 They shall not labour in vaine, nor bring forth in feare: for they are the seede of the blessed of the Lord, and their buds with them.

24 Yea, before they call, I will answere, and whiles they speake, I will heare.

25 The wolfe and the lambe shall feede together, and the lyon shall eate strawe like the bullocke: and to the serpent dust shall be his meate. They shall no more hurt nor destroy in all mine holy Mountaine, saith the Lord.

Isaiah 66

1 Thus saith the Lord, The heauen is my throne, and the earth is my footestoole: where is that house that ye will builde vnto me? and where is that place of my rest?

2 For all these things hath mine hand made, and all these things haue bene, sayth the Lord: and to him will I looke, euen to him, that is poore, and of a contrite spirite and trembleth at my wordes.

3 He that killeth a bullocke, is as if he slewe a man: he that sacrificeth a sheepe, as if he cut off a dogges necke: he that offereth an oblation, as if he offered swines blood: he that remembreth incense, as if he blessed an idole: yea, they haue chosen their owne wayes, and their soule deliteth in their abominations.

4 Therefore will I chuse out their delusions, and I will bring their feare vpon them, because I called, and none woulde answere: I spake and they woulde not heare: but they did euill in my sight, and chose the things which I would not.

5 Heare the worde of the Lord, all ye that tremble at his worde, Your brethren that hated you, and cast you out for my Names sake, said, Let the Lord be glorified: but he shall appeare to your ioy, and they shall be ashamed.

6 A voyce soundeth from the citie, euen a voyce from the Temple, the voyce of the Lord, that recompenseth his enemies fully.

7 Before she trauailed, she brought foorth: and before her paine came, she was deliuered of a man childe.

8 Who hath heard such a thing? who hath seene such things? shall ye earth be brought forth in one day? or shall a nation be borne at once? for assoone as Zion trauailed, she brought foorth her children.

9 Shall I cause to trauaile, and not bring forth? shall I cause to bring forth, and shall be baren, saith thy God?

10 Reioyce ye with Ierusalem, and be gladde with her, all ye that loue her: reioyce for ioy with her, all ye that mourne for her,

11 That ye may sucke and be satisfied with the brestes of her consolation: that ye may milke out and be delited with ye brightnes of her glorie.

12 For thus saith the Lord, Beholde, I will extend peace ouer her like a flood, and the glorie of the Gentiles like a flowing streame: then shall ye sucke, ye shall be borne vpon her sides, and be ioyfull vpon her knees.

13 As one whom his mother comforteth, so will I comfort you, and ye shall be comforted in Ierusalem.

14 And when ye see this, your hearts shall reioyce, and your bones shall flourish like an herbe: and the hand of the Lord shall be knowen among his seruants, and his indignation against his enemies.

15 For beholde, the Lord will come with fire, and his charets like a whirlewinde, that he may recompence his anger with wrath, and his indignation with the flame of fire.

16 For the Lord will iudge with fire, and with his sworde all flesh, and the slaine of the Lord shall be many.

17 They that sanctifie themselues, and purifie themselues in the gardens behinde one tree in the middes eating swines flesh, and such abomination, euen the mouse, shall be consumed together, sayeth the Lord.

18 For I will visite their workes, and their imaginations: for it shall come that I will gather all nations, and tongues, and they shall come, and see my glorie.

19 And I will set a signe among them, and will send those that escape of them, vnto the nations of Tarshish, Pul, and Lud, and to them that drawe the bowe, to Tubal and Tauan, yles afarre off, that haue not heard my fame, neither haue seene my glorie, and they shall declare my glorie among the Gentiles.

20 And they shall bring all your brethren for an offering vnto the Lord out of all nations, vpon horses, and in charets, and in horse litters, and vpon mules, and swift beastes, to Ierusalem mine holy Mountaine, saith the Lord, as the children of Israel, offer in a cleane vessell in the House of the Lord.

21 And I will take of them for Priestes, and for Leuites, saith the Lord.

22 For as the newe heauens, and the newe earth which I will make, shall remaine before me, saith the Lord, so shall your seede and your name continue.

23 And from moneth to moneth, and from Sabbath to Sabbath shall all flesh come to worship before me, saith the Lord.

24 And they shall goe forth, and looke vpon the carkases of the men that haue transgressed against me: for their worme shall not dye, neither shall their fire be quenched, and they shalbe an abhorring vnto all flesh.

Jeremiah

Jeremiah 1

1 The wordes of Ieremiah the sonne of Hilkiah one of the Priests that were at Anathoth in the lande of Beniamin.

2 To whom the worde of the Lord came in the dayes of Iosiah the sonne of Amon King of Iudah in the thirteenth yeere of his reigne:

3 And also in the dayes of Iehoiakim the sonne of Iosiah King of Iudah vnto the ende of the eleuenth yeere of Zedekiah, the sonne of Iosiah King of Iudah, euen vnto the carying away of Ierusalem captiue in the fift moneth.

4 Then the worde of the Lord came vnto me, saying,

5 Before I formed thee in the wombe, I knewe thee, and before thou camest out of the wombe, I sanctified thee, and

ordeined thee to be a Prophet vnto the nations.

6 Then said I, Oh, Lord God, behold, I can not speake, for I am a childe.

7 But the Lord said vnto me, Say not, I am a childe: for thou shalt goe to all that I shall send thee, and whatsoeuer I command thee, shalt thou speake.

8 Be not afraide of their faces: for I am with thee to deliuer thee, saith the Lord.

9 Then the Lord stretched out his hand and touched my mouth, and the Lord said vnto me, Beholde, I haue put my wordes in thy mouth.

10 Beholde, this day haue I set thee ouer the nations and ouer the kingdomes to plucke vp, and to roote out, and to destroye and throwe downe, to builde, and to plant.

11 After this the worde of the Lord came vnto me, saying, Ieremiah, what seest thou? And I said, I see a rod of an almonde tree.

12 Then saide the Lord vnto me, Thou hast seene aright: for I will hasten my worde to performe it.

13 Againe the worde of the Lord came vnto me the second time, saying, What seest thou? And I saide, I see a seething pot looking out of the North.

14 Then saide the Lord vnto me, Out of the North shall a plague be spred vpon all the inhabitants of the land.

15 For loe, I will call all the families of the kingdomes of the North, saith the Lord, and they shall come, and euery one shall set his throne in the entring of the gates of Ierusalem, and on all the walles thereof rounde about, and in all the cities of Iudah.

16 And I will declare vnto them my iudgements touching all the wickednesse of them that haue forsaken me, and haue burnt incense vnto other gods, and worshipped the workes of their owne handes.

17 Thou therefore trusse vp thy loynes, and arise and speake vnto them all that I commaund thee: be not afraide of their faces, lest I destroy thee before them.

18 For I, beholde, I this day haue made thee a defenced citie, and an yron pillar and walles of brasse against the whole lande, against the Kings of Iudah, and against the princes thereof, against the Priestes thereof and against the people of the lande.

19 For they shall fight against thee, but they shall not preuaile against thee: for I am with thee to deliuer thee, sayth the Lord.

Jeremiah 2

1 Moreover, the woorde of the Lord came vnto me, saying,

2 Goe, and crie in the eares of Ierusalem, saying, Thus sayeth the Lord, I remember thee, with the kindenes of thy youth and the loue of thy marriage, when thou wentest after me in the wildernes in a lande that was not sowen.

3 Israel was as a thing halowed vnto the Lord, and his first fruits: all they that eat it, shall offend: euil shall come vpon them, saith the Lord.

4 Heare ye the word of the Lord, O house of Iaakob, and all the families of the house of Israel.

5 Thus sayeth the Lord, What iniquitie haue your fathers founde in mee, that they are gone farre from mee, and haue walked after vanitie, and are become vaine?

6 For they saide not, Where is the Lord that brought vs vp out of the lande of Egypt? that led vs through the wildernesse, through a desert, and waste land, through a drie land, and by the shadow of death, by a land that no man passed through, and where no man dwelt?

7 And I brought you into a plentifull countrey, to eat the fruit thereof, and the commodities of the same: but when yee entred, yee defiled my land, and made mine heritage an abomination.

8 The priests said not, Where is the Lord? and they that should minister the Lawe, knewe me not: the pastours also offended against me, and the Prophets prophesied in Baal, and went after things that did not profite.

9 Wherefore I wil yet plead with you, saith the Lord, and I will pleade with your childrens children.

10 For goe ye to the yles of Chittim, and beholde, and sende vnto Kedar. and take diligent heede, and see whether there be such things.

11 Hath any nation changed their gods, which yet are no gods? but my people haue chaged their glorie, for that which doeth not profite.

12 O yee heauens, be astonied at this: bee afraid and vtterly confounded, sayeth the Lord.

13 For my people haue committed two euils: they haue forsaken mee the fountaine of liuing waters, to digge them pittes, euen broken pittes, that can holde no water.

14 Is Israel a seruaunt, or is hee borne in the house? why then is he spoiled?

15 The lions roared vpon him and yelled, and they haue made his land waste: his cities are burnt without an inhabitant.

16 Also the children of Noph and Tahapanes haue broken thine head.

17 Hast not thou procured this vnto thy selfe, because thou hast forsaken the Lord thy God, when he led thee by the way?

18 And what hast thou now to do in the way of Egypt? to drinke the water of Nilus? or what makest thou in the way of Asshur? to drinke the water of the Riuer?

19 Thine owne wickednes shall correct thee, and thy turnings backe shall reprooue thee: know therefore and beholde, that it is an euil thing, and bitter, that thou hast forsaken the Lord thy God, and that my feare is not in thee, sayeth the Lord God of hostes.

20 For of olde time I haue broken thy yoke, and burst thy bondes, and thou saidest, I will no more transgresse, but like an harlot thou runnest about vpon al hie hilles, and vnder all greene trees.

21 Yet I had planted thee, a noble vine, whose plants were all natural: howe then art thou turned vnto me into the plants of a strange vine?

22 Though thou wash thee with nitre, and take thee much sope, yet thine iniquitie is marked before me, sayeth the Lord God.

23 Howe canst thou say, I am not polluted, neither haue I followed Baalim? beholde thy waies in the valley, and know, what thou hast done: thou art like a swift dromedarie, that runneth by his waies.

24 And as a wilde asse, vsed to the wildernesse, that snuffeth vp the winde by occasion at her pleasure: who can turne her backe? all they that seeke her, will not wearie themselues, but wil finde her in her moneth.

25 Keepe thou thy feete from barenes, and thy throte from thirst: but thou saidest desperately, No, for I haue loued strangers, and them will I follow.

26 As the theefe is ashamed, when he is foud, so is the house of Israel ashamed, they, their kings, their princes and their Priests, and their Prophets,

27 Saying to a tree, Thou art my father, and to a stone, Thou hast begotten me: for they haue turned their back vnto me, and not their face: but in ye time of their troble they wil say, Arise, and help vs.

28 But where are thy gods, that thou hast made thee? let them arise, if they can helpe thee in the time of thy trouble: for according to the nomber of thy cities, are thy gods, O Iudah.

29 Wherefore wil ye pleade with me? ye all haue rebelled against me, sayeth the Lord.

30 I haue smitten your children in vaine, they receiued no correction: your owne sworde hath deuoured your Prophets like a destroying lyon.

31 O generation, take heede to the worde of the Lord: haue I bene as a wildernesse vnto Israel? or a lande of darkenesse? Wherefore sayeth my people then, We are lordes, we will come no more vnto thee?

32 Can a maid forget her ornament, or a bride her attire? yet my people haue forgotten me, daies without number.

33 Why doest thou prepare thy way, to seeke amitie? euen therefore will I teach thee, that thy waies are wickednesse.

34 Also in thy wings is founde the bloud of the soules of ye poore innocents: I haue not found it in holes, but vpon all these places.

35 Yet thou saiest, Because I am giltles, surely his wrath shall turne from mee: beholde, I will enter with thee into iudgement, because thou saiest, I haue not sinned.

36 Why runnest thou about so much to change thy waies? for thou shalt be confounded of Egypt, as thou art confounded of Asshur.

37 For thou shalt goe foorth from thence, and thine hands vpon thine head, because the Lord hath reiected thy

confidence, and thou shalt not prosper thereby.

Jeremiah 3

1 They say, If a man put away his wife, and she goe from him, and become another mans, shall hee returne againe vnto her? shall not this land be polluted? but thou hast played the harlot with many louers: yet turne againe to mee, sayeth the Lord.

2 Lift vp thine eyes vnto the hie places, and beholde, where thou hast not plaied the harlot: thou hast sit waiting for them in the waies, as the Arabian in the wildernesse: and thou hast polluted the lande with thy whoredomes, and with thy malice.

3 Therefore the showres haue beene restrained, and the latter raine came not, and thou haddest a whores forehead: thou wouldest not bee ashamed.

4 Diddest thou not stil crie vnto me, Thou art my father, and the guide of my youth?

5 Wil he keepe his anger for euer? will he reserue it to the ende? thus hast thou spoken, but thou doest euill, euen more and more.

6 The Lord saide also vnto me, in the daies of Iosiah the King, Hast thou seene what this rebell Israel hath done? for she hath gone vp vpon euery high mountaine, and vnder euery greene tree, and there plaied the harlot.

7 And I sayde, when shee had done all this, Turne thou vnto me: but she returned not, as her rebellious sister Iudah sawe.

8 When I sawe, howe that by all occasions rebellious Israel had plaied the harlot, I cast her away, and gaue her a bill of diuorcement: yet her rebellious sister Iudah was not afraied, but shee went also, and plaied the harlot.

9 So that for the lightnesse of her whoredome shee hath euen defiled the lande: for shee hath committed fornication with stones and stockes.

10 Neuerthelesse for all this, her rebellious sister Iudah hath not returned vnto mee with her whole heart, but fainedly, sayth the Lord.

11 And the Lord said vnto me, The rebellious Israel hath iustified her selfe more then the rebellious Iudah.

12 Goe and crie these woordes towarde the North and say, Thou disobedient Israel, returne, sayeth the Lord, and I will not let my wrath fall vpon you: for I am mercifull, sayeth the Lord, and I will not alway keepe mine anger.

13 But knowe thine iniquitie: for thou hast rebelled against the Lord thy God, and hast scattered thy waies to the straunge gods vnder euery greene tree, but yee woulde not obey my voyce, sayeth the Lord.

14 O yee disobedient children, turne againe, sayeth the Lord, for I am your Lord, and I will take you one of a citie, and two of a tribe and wil bring you to Zion,

15 And I will giue you pastours according to mine heart, which shall feede you with knowledge and vnderstanding.

16 Moreouer, when yee be increased and multiplied in the land, in those daies, saieth the Lord, they shall say no more, The Arke of the couenant of the Lord: for it shall come no more to minde, neither shall they remember it, neither shall they visite it, for that shalbe no more done.

17 At that time they shall cal Ierusalem, The throne of the Lord, and all the nations shall be gathered vnto it, euen to the Name of the Lord in Ierusalem: and thence foorth they shall follow no more the hardnesse of their wicked heart.

18 In those daies ye house of Iudah shall walke with the house of Israel, and they shall come together out of the lande of the North, into the lande, that I haue giuen for an inheritance vnto your fathers.

19 But I sayde, Howe did I take thee for children and giue thee a pleasant lande, euen the glorious heritage of the armies of the heathen, and saide, Thou shalt call mee, saying, My father, and shalt not turne from me?

20 But as a woman rebelleth against her husband: so haue yee rebelled against me, O house of Israel, sayeth the Lord.

21 A voice was heard vpon the hie places, weeping and supplications of the children of Israel: for they haue peruerted their way, and forgotten the Lord their God.

22 O yee disobedient children, returne and I wil heale your rebellions. Behold, we come vnto thee, for thou art the Lord our God.

23 Truely the hope of the hilles is but vaine, nor the multitude of mountaines: but in the Lord our God is the health of Israel.

24 For confusion hath deuoured our fathers labour, from our youth their sheepe and their bullocks, their sonnes and their daughters.

25 Wee lie downe in our confusion, and our shame couereth vs: for we haue sinned against the Lord our God, we and our fathers from our youth, euen vnto this day, and haue not obeyed the voyce of the Lord our God.

Jeremiah 4

1 O Israel, if thou returne, returne vnto me, saith the Lord: and if thou put away thine abominations out of my sight, then shalt thou not remoue.

2 And thou shalt sweare, The Lord liueth in trueth, in iudgement, and in righteousnesse, and the nations shall be blessed in him, and shall glorie in him.

3 For thus saith the Lord to the men of Iudah, and to Ierusalem,

4 Breake vp your fallowe ground, and sowe not among the thornes: be circumcised to the Lord, and take away the foreskinnes of your hearts, ye men of Iudah, and inhabitants of Ierusalem, lest my wrath come foorth like fire, and burne, that none can quenche it, because of the wickednesse of your inuentions.

5 Declare in Iudah, and shewe forth in Ierusalem, and say, Blowe the trumpet in the lande: cry, and gather together, and say, Assemble your selues, and let vs goe into strong cities.

6 Set vp the standart in Zion: prepare to flee, and stay not: for I will bring a plague from the North, and a great destruction.

7 The lyon is come vp from his denne, and the destroyer of the Gentiles is departed, and gone forth of his place to lay thy land waste, and thy cities shalbe destroyed without an inhabitant.

8 Wherefore girde you with sackecloth: lament, and howle, for the fierce wrath of the Lord is not turned backe from vs.

9 And in that day, saith the Lord, the heart of the King shall perish, and the heart of the princes and the Priestes shall be astonished, and the Prophets shall wonder.

10 Then saide I, Ah, Lord God, surely thou hast deceiued this people and Ierusalem, saying, Ye shall haue peace, and the sworde perceth vnto the heart.

11 At that time shall it bee saide to this people and to Ierusalem, A dry winde in the hie places of the wildernes commeth towarde ye daughter of my people, but neither to fanne nor to clense.

12 A mightie winde shall come vnto me from those places, and nowe will I also giue sentence vpon them.

13 Beholde, he shall come vp as the cloudes, and his charets shalbe as a tempest: his horses are lighter then eagles. Woe vnto vs, for wee are destroyed.

14 O Ierusalem, wash thine heart from wickednes, that thou maiest be saued: how long shall thy wicked thoughtes remaine within thee?

15 For a voyce declareth from Dan, and publisheth affliction from mount Ephraim.

16 Make ye mention of the heathen, and publish in Ierusalem, Beholde, the skoutes come from a farre countrey, and crie out against the cities of Iudah.

17 They haue compassed her about as the watchmen of the fielde, because it hath prouoked me to wrath, saith the Lord.

18 Thy wayes and thine inuentions haue procured thee these things, such is thy wickednesse: therefore it shall be bitter, therefore it shall perce vnto thine heart.

19 My bely, my bely, I am pained, euen at the very heart: mine heart is troubled within me: I cannot be still: for my soule hath heard the sounde of the trumpet, and the alarme of the battell.

20 Destruction vpon destruction is cryed, for the whole lande is wasted: suddenly are my tents destroyed, and my curtaines in a moment.

21 Howe long shall I see the standert, and heare the sounde of the trumpet?

22 For my people is foolish, they haue not knowen me: they are foolish children, and haue none vnderstanding:

they are wise to doe euill, but to doe well they haue no knowledge.

23 I haue looked vpon the earth, and loe, it was without forme and voide: and to the heauens, and they had no light.

24 I behelde the mountaines: and loe, they trembled and all the hilles shooke.

25 I behelde, and loe, there was no man, and all the birdes of the heauen were departed.

26 I behelde, and loe, the fruitfull place was a wildernesse, and all the cities thereof were broken downe at the presence of the Lord, and by his fierce wrath.

27 For thus hath the Lord saide, The whole lande shall be desolate: yet will I not make a full ende.

28 Therefore shall the earth mourne, and the heauens aboue shall be darkened, because I haue pronounced it: I haue thought it, and will not repent, neither will I turne backe from it.

29 The whole citie shall flee, for the noyse of the horsemen and bowemen: they shall goe into thickets, and clime vp vpon the rockes: euery citie shall be forsaken, and not a man dwell therein.

30 And when thou shalt be destroyed, what wilt thou doe? Though thou clothest thy selfe with skarlet, though thou deckest thee with ornaments of golde, though thou paintest thy face with colours, yet shalt thou trimme thy selfe in vaine: for thy louers will abhorre thee and seeke thy life.

31 For I haue heard a noyse as of a woman trauailing, or as one labouring of her first child, euen the voyce of the daughter Zion that sigheth and stretcheth out her handes: woe is me nowe: for my soule fainteth because of the murtherers.

Jeremiah 5

1 Run to and from by the streetes of Ierusalem, and beholde nowe, and knowe, and inquire in the open places thereof, if ye can finde a man, or if there be any that executeth iudgement, and seeketh the trueth, and I will spare it.

2 For though they say, The Lord liueth, yet doe they sweare falsely.

3 O Lord, are not thine eyes vpon the trueth? thou hast striken them, but they haue not sorowed: thou hast consumed them, but they haue refused to receiue correction: they haue made their faces harder then a stone, and haue refused to returne.

4 Therefore I saide, Surely they are poore, they are foolish, for they know not the way of the Lord, nor the iudgement of their God.

5 I will get me vnto the great men, and will speake vnto them: for they haue knowen the way of the Lord, and the iudgement of their God: but these haue altogether broken the yoke, and burst the bondes.

6 Wherefore a lyon out of the forest shall slay them, and a wolfe of the wildernesse shall destroy them: a leopard shall watch ouer their cities: euery one that goeth out thence, shall be torne in pieces, because their trespasses are many, and their rebellions are increased.

7 Howe should I spare thee for this? thy children haue forsaken me, and sworne by them that are no gods: though I fed them to the full, yet they committed adulterie, and assembled them selues by companies in the harlots houses.

8 They rose vp in the morning like fed horses: for euery man neyed after his neighbours wife.

9 Shall I not visite for these things, saith the Lord? Shall not my soule be auenged on such a nation as this?

10 Clime vp vpon their walles, and destroy them, but make not a full ende: take away their batilments, for they are not the Lords.

11 For the house of Israel, and the house of Iudah haue grieuously trespassed against me, saith the Lord.

12 They haue denied the Lord, and saide, It is not he, neither shall the plague come vpon vs, neither shall we see sworde nor famine.

13 And the Prophetes shall be as winde, and the worde is not in them: thus shall it come vnto them.

14 Wherefore thus saith the Lord God of hostes, Because ye speake such wordes, beholde, I will put my wordes into thy mouth, like a fire, and this people shall be as wood, and it shall deuoure them.

15 Loe, I will bring a nation vpon you from farre, O house of Israel, saith the Lord, which is a mightie nation, and an ancient nation, a nation whose language thou knowest not, neither vnderstandest what they say.

16 Whose quiuer is as an open sepulchre: they are all very strong.

17 And they shall eate thine haruest and thy bread: they shall deuoure thy sonnes and thy daughters: they shall eate vp thy sheepe and thy bullocks: they shall eate thy vines and thy figge trees: they shall destroy with the sworde thy fenced cities, wherein thou didest trust.

18 Neuerthelesse at those dayes, sayth the Lord, I will not make a full ende of you.

19 And when ye shall say, Wherefore doeth the Lord our God doe these things vnto vs? then shalt thou answere them, Like as ye haue forsaken me and serued strange gods in your land, so shall ye serue strangers in a land that is not yours.

20 Declare this in the house of Iaakob, and publish it in Iudah, saying,

21 Heare nowe this, O foolish people, and without vnderstanding, which haue eyes and see not, which haue eares and heare not.

22 Feare ye not me, saith the Lord? or will ye not be afraide at my presence, which haue placed the sand for the bounds of the sea by the perpetuall decree that it cannot passe it, and though the waues thereof rage, yet can they not preuaile, though they roare, yet can they not passe ouer it?

23 But this people hath an vnfaithfull and rebellious heart: they are departed and gone.

24 For they say not in their heart, Let vs nowe feare the Lord our God, that giueth raine both early and late in due season: hee reserueth vnto vs the appointed weekes of the haruest.

25 Yet your iniquities haue turned away these things, and your sinnes haue hindred good things from you.

26 For among my people are founde wicked persons, that lay waite as hee that setteth snares: they haue made a pit, to catch men.

27 As a cage is full of birdes, so are their houses full of deceite: thereby they are become great and waxen riche.

28 They are waxen fat and shining: they doe ouerpasse the deedes of the wicked: they execute no iudgement, no not the iudgement of the fatherlesse: yet they prosper, though they execute no iudgement for the poore.

29 Shall I not visite for these things, sayth the Lord? or shall not my soule be auenged on such a nation as this?

30 An horrible and filthie thing is committed in the land.

31 The Prophets prophesie lies, and ye Priests receiue giftes in their handes, and my people delite therein. What will ye then doe in the ende thereof?

Jeremiah 6

1 O ye children of Beniamin, prepare to flee out of the middes of Ierusalem, and blowe the trumpet in Tekoa: set vp a standart vpon Beth-haccerem: for a plague appeareth out of the North and great destruction.

2 I haue compared the daughter of Zion to a beautifull and daintie woman.

3 The pastors with their flockes shall come vnto her: they shall pitche their tentes rounde about by her, and euery one shall feede in his place.

4 Prepare warre against her: arise, and let vs goe vp toward the South: wo vnto vs: for the day declineth, and the shadowes of the euening are stretched out.

5 Arise, and let vs goe vp by night, and destroy her palaces.

6 For thus hath the Lord of hostes said, Hewe downe wood, and cast a mounte against Ierusalem: this citie must be visited: all oppression is in the middes of it.

7 As the fountaine casteth out her waters, so she casteth out her malice: crueltie and spoyle is continually heard in her before me with sorowe and strokes.

8 Be thou instructed, O Ierusalem, lest my soule depart from thee, lest I make thee desolate as a land, that none inhabiteth.

9 Thus sayeth the Lord of hostes, They shall gather as a vine, the residue of Israel: turne backe thine hande as the grape gatherer into the baskets.

10 Vnto whome shall I speake, and admonish that they may heare? beholde,

their eares are vncircumcised, and they cannot hearken: beholde, the worde of the Lord is vnto them as a reproche: they haue no delite in it.

11 Therefore I am full of the wrath of the Lord: I am weary with holding it: I will powre it out vpon the children in the streete, and likewise vpon the assembly of the yong men: for the husband shall euen be taken with the wife, and the aged with him that is full of daies.

12 And their houses with their landes, and wiues also shalbe turned vnto strangers: for I will stretch out mine hande vpon the inhabitants of the land, sayeth the Lord.

13 For from the least of them, euen vnto the greatest of them, euery one is giuen vnto couetousnesse, and from the Prophet euen vnto the Priest, they all deale falsely.

14 They haue healed also ye hurt of the daughter of my people with sweete woordes, saying, Peace, peace, when there is no peace.

15 Were they ashamed when they had committed abomination? nay, they were not ashamed, no neither coulde they haue any shame: therefore they shall fall among the slaine: when I shall visite them, they shall be cast downe, sayth the Lord.

16 Thus sayeth the Lord, Stande in the waies and beholde, and aske for the olde way, which is the good way and walke therein, and yee shall finde rest for your soules: but they saide, We will not walke therein.

17 Also I set watchmen ouer you, which said, Take heede to the sound of the trumpet: but they said, We will not take heede.

18 Heare therefore, yee Gentiles, and thou Congregation knowe, what is among them.

19 Heare, O earth, beholde, I will cause a plague to come vpon this people, euen the fruite of their owne imaginations: because they haue not taken heede vnto my woordes, nor to my Lawe, but cast it off.

20 To what purpose bringest thou mee incense from Sheba, and sweete calamus from a farre countrey? Your burnt offerings are not pleasant, nor your sacrifices sweete vnto me.

21 Therefore thus sayeth the Lord, Beholde, I will laie stumbling blockes before this people, and the fathers and the sonnes together shall fall vpon them: the neighbour and his friende shall perish.

22 Thus sayeth the Lord, Beholde, a people commeth from the North countrey, and a great nation shall arise from the sides of the earth.

23 With bowe and shield shall they be weaponed: they are cruell and will haue no compassion: their voyce roareth like the sea, and they ride vpon horses, well appointed, like men of warre against thee, O daughter Zion.

24 We haue heard their fame, and our handes waxe feeble sorrowe is come

vpon vs, as the sorrowe of a woman in trauaile.

25 Goe not foorth into the fielde, nor walke by the way: for the sword of the enemie and feare is on euery side.

26 O daughter of my people, girde thee with sackecloth, and wallowe thy selfe in the ashes: make lamentation, and bitter mourning as for thine onely sonne: for the destroier shall suddenly come vpon vs.

27 I haue set thee for a defence and fortresse among my people, that thou maiest knowe and trie their waies.

28 They are all rebellious traitours, walking craftily: they are brasse, and yron, they all are destroyers.

29 The bellowes are burnt: the lead is consumed in the fire: the founder melteth in vaine: for the wicked are not taken away.

30 They shall call them reprobate siluer, because the Lord hath reiected them.

Jeremiah 7

1 The woordes that came to Ieremiah from the Lord, saying,

2 Stand in the gate of the Lordes house and crie this woorde there, and say, Heare the woorde of the Lord, all yee of Iudah that enter in at these gates to worship the Lord.

3 Thus sayeth the Lord of hostes, the God of Israel, Amend your waies and your woorkes, and I will let you dwell in this place.

4 Trust not in lying woordes, saying, The Temple of the Lord, the Temple of the Lord: this is the Temple of the Lord.

5 For if you amende and redresse your waies and your woorkes: if you execute iudgement betweene a man and his neighbour,

6 And oppresse not the stranger, the fatherlesse and the widow and shed no innocent blood in this place, neither walke after other gods to your destruction,

7 Then will I let you dwell in this place in the lande that I gaue vnto your fathers, for euer and euer.

8 Beholde, you trust in lying woordes, that can not profite.

9 Will you steale, murder, and commit adulterie, and sweare falsely and burne incense vnto Baal, and walke after other gods whome yee knowe not?

10 And come and stande before mee in this House, whereupon my Name is called, and saye, We are deliuered, though we haue done all these abominations?

11 Is this House become a denne of theeues, whereupon my Name is called before your eyes? Beholde, euen I see it, sayeth the Lord.

12 But go ye nowe vnto my place which was in Shilo, where I set my Name at the beginning, and beholde, what I did to it for the wickednesse of my people Israel.

13 Therefore nowe because yee haue done all these woorkes, sayeth the Lord, (and I rose vp earely and spake vnto you: but when I spake, yee would not heare

me, neither when I called, would yee answere).

14 Therefore will I do vnto this House, wherupon my Name is called, wherein also yee trust, euen vnto the place that I gaue to you and to your fathers, as I haue done vnto Shilo.

15 And I will cast you out of my sight, as I haue cast out all your brethren, euen the whole seede of Ephraim.

16 Therfore thou shalt not pray for this people, neither lift vp crie or praier for them neither intreat me, for I will not heare thee.

17 Seest thou not what they doe in the cities of Iudah and in the streetes of Ierusalem?

18 The children gather wood, and the fathers kindle the fire, and the women knede the dough to make cakes to the Queene of heauen and to powre out drinke offrings vnto other gods, that they may prouoke me vnto anger.

19 Doe they prouoke me to anger, sayeth the Lord, and not themselues to the confusion of their owne faces?

20 Therefore thus sayeth the Lord God, Beholde, mine anger and my wrath shall be powred vpon this place, vpon man and vpon beast, and vpon the tree of the fielde, and vpon the fruite of the grounde, and it shall burne and not bee quenched.

21 Thus sayth the Lord of hostes, the God of Israel, Put your burnt offerings vnto your sacrifices, and eat the flesh.

22 For I spake not vnto your fathers, nor commanded them, when I brought them out of the land of Egypt, concerning burnt offrings and sacrifices.

23 But this thing commanded I them, saying, Obey my voyce, and I will be your God, and yee shalbe my people: and walke yee in all the wayes which I haue commanded you, that it may be well vnto you.

24 But they would not obey, nor incline their eare, but went after the counsels and the stubbernesse of their wicked heart, and went backewarde and not forwarde.

25 Since the day that your fathers came vp out of the lande of Egypt, vnto this day, I haue euen sent vnto you al my seruants the Prophets, rising vp earely euery day, and sending them.

26 Yet would they not heare me nor encline their eare, but hardened their necke and did worse then their fathers.

27 Therefore shalt thou speake al these words vnto them, but they will not heare thee: thou shalt also crie vnto them, but they will not answere thee.

28 But thou shalt say vnto them, This is a nation that heareth not the voice of the Lord their God, nor receiueth discipline: trueth is perished, and is cleane gone out of their mouth.

29 Cut off thine heare, O Ierusalem, and cast it away, and take vp a complaint on the hie places: for the Lord hath reiected and forsaken the generation of his wrath.

30 For the children of Iudah haue done euill in my sight, sayth the Lord: they

haue set their abominations in the House, whereupon my Name is called, to pollute it.

31 And they haue built the hie place of Topheth, which is in the valley of Ben-Hinnom to burne their sonnes and their daughters in the fire, which I commanded them not, neither came it in mine heart.

32 Therefore beholde, the dayes come, sayeth the Lord, that it shall no more be called Topheth, nor the valley of Ben-Hinnom, but the valley of slaughter: for they shall burie in Topheth til there be no place.

33 And ye carkeises of this people shalbe meat for the foules of the heauen and for the beastes of the earth, and none shall fraie them away.

34 Then I will cause to cease from the cities of Iudah and from the streetes of Ierusalem the voice of mirth and the voice of gladnesse, the voice of the bridegrom and the voice of the bride: for the lande shalbe desolate.

Jeremiah 8

1 At that time, sayeth the Lord, they shall bring out the bones of the Kings of Iudah, and the bones of their princes, and the bones of the Priests and the bones of the Prophets, and the bones of the inhabitants of Ierusalem out of their graues.

2 And they shall spread them before the sunne and the moone, and all the host of heauen, whom they haue loued, and whome they haue serued, and whome they haue followed, and whome they haue sought, and whome they haue worshipped: they shall not be gathered nor be buried, but shall be as doung vpon the earth.

3 And death shall bee desired rather then life of all the residue that remaineth of this wicked familie, which remaine in all the places where I haue scattered them, sayeth the Lord of hostes.

4 Thou shalt say vnto them also, Thus sayeth the Lord, Shall they fall and not arise? shall he turne away and not turne againe?

5 Wherefore is this people of Ierusalem turned backe by a perpetuall rebellion? they gaue themselues to deceit, and would not returne.

6 I hearkened and heard, but none spake aright: no man repented him of his wickednesse, saying, What haue I done? euery one turned to their race, as the horse rusheth into the battell.

7 Euen the storke in the aire knoweth her appointed times, and the turtle and the crane and the swallowe obserue the time of their comming, but my people knoweth not the iudgement of the Lord.

8 Howe doe yee say, Wee are wise, and the Lawe of the Lord is with vs? Loe, certeinly in vaine made hee it, the penne of the scribes is in vaine.

9 The wise men are ashamed: they are afraid and taken. loe, they haue reiected the word of the Lord, and what wisdome is in them?

10 Therefore will I giue their wiues vnto others, and their fieldes to them that shall possesse them: for euery one from the least euen vnto the greatest is giuen to couetousnesse, and from the Prophet euen vnto the Priest, euery one dealeth falsely.

11 For they haue healed the hurt of the daughter of my people with sweete woordes, saying, Peace, peace, when there is no peace.

12 Were they ashamed when they had committed abomination? nay, they were not ashamed, neither coulde they haue any shame: therefore shall they fall among the slaine: when I shall visite them, they shall be cast downe, sayeth the Lord.

13 I wil surely consume them, sayth the Lord: there shalbe no grapes on the vine, nor figges on the figtree, and the leafe shall fade, and the things that I haue giuen them, shall depart from them.

14 Why doe we stay? assemble your selues, and let vs enter into the strong cities, and let vs be quiet there: for the Lord our God hath put vs to silence and giuen vs water with gall to drinke, because we haue sinned against the Lord.

15 We looked for peace, but no good came, and for a time of health, and behold troubles.

16 The neying of his horses was heard from Dan, the whole lande trembled at the noyse of the neying of his strong horses: for they are come, and haue deuoured the land with all that is in it, the citie, and those that dwell therein.

17 For beholde, I will sende serpents, and cockatrices among you, which will not be charmed, and they shall sting you, sayth the Lord.

18 I would haue comforted my selfe against sorowe, but mine heart is heauie in me.

19 Behold, the voice of the cry of the daughter of my people for feare of them of a farre countrey, Is not the Lord in Zion? is not her king in her? Why haue they prouoked mee to anger with their grauen images, and with the vanities of a strange god?

20 The haruest is past, the sommer is ended, and we are not holpen.

21 I am sore vexed for the hurt of ye daughter of my people: I am heauie, and astonishment hath taken me.

22 Is there no balme at Gilead? is there no Physition there? Why then is not the health of the daughter of my people recouered.

Jeremiah 9

1 Oh, that mine head were full of water and mine eyes a fountaine of teares, that I might weepe day and night for the slayne of the daughter of my people.

2 Oh, that I had in the wildernes a cottage of wayfaring men, that I might leaue my people, and go from them: for they be all adulterers and an assembly of rebels,

3 And they bende their tongues like their bowes for lyes: but they haue no courage for the trueth vpon the earth: for they proceede from euill to worse, and they haue not knowen mee, sayth the Lord.

4 Let euery one take heede of his neighbour, and trust you not in any brother: for euery brother will vse deceite, and euery friend will deale deceitfully,

5 And euery one wil deceiue his friende, and wil not speake the trueth: for they haue taught their tongues to speake lies, and take great paynes to do wickedly.

6 Thine habitation is in the middes of deceiuers: because of their deceit they refuse to know me, sayth the Lord.

7 Therefore thus sayth the Lord of hostes, Behold, I wil melt them, and trie them: for what should I els do for the daughter of my people?

8 Their tongue is as an arow shot out, and speaketh deceite: one speaketh peaceably to his neighbour with his mouth, but in his heart hee layeth waite for him.

9 Shal I not visit them for these things, saith the Lord? or shall not my soule be auenged on such a nation as this?

10 Vpon the mountaines will I take vp a weeping and a lamentation, and vpon the fayre places of the wildernes a mourning, because they are burnt vp: so that none can passe through them, neyther can men heare the voyce of the flocke: both the foule of the aire, and the beast are fled away and gone.

11 And I wil make Ierusalem an heape, and a den of dragons, and I will make the cities of Iudah waste, without an inhabitant.

12 Who is wise, to vnderstande this? and to whome the mouth of the Lord hath spoken, euen he shall declare it. Why doth the land perish, and is burnt vp like a wildernesse, that none passeth through?

13 And the Lord sayeth, Because they haue forsaken my Lawe, which I set before them, and haue not obeyed my voice, neither walked thereafter,

14 But haue walked after the stubbernesse of their owne heart, and after Baalims, which their fathers taught them,

15 Therefore thus sayth the Lord of hostes, the God of Israel, Behold, I will feede this people with wormewood, and giue them waters of gall to drinke:

16 I wil scatter them also among the heathen, whom neither they nor their fathers haue knowen, and I will send a sworde after them, til I haue consumed them.

17 Thus sayeth the Lord of hostes, Take heede, and call for the mourning women, that they may come, and send for skilfull women that they may come,

18 And let them make haste, and let them take vp a lamentation for vs, that our eyes may cast out teares and our eye liddes gush out of water.

19 For a lamentable noyse is heard out of Zion, Howe are we destroyed, and

vtterly confounded, for we haue forsaken the land, and our dwellings haue cast vs out.

20 Therefore heare the worde of the Lord, O ye women, and let your eares regard the words of his mouth, and teach your daughters to mourne, and euery one her neighbour to lament.

21 For death is come vp into our windowes, and is entred into our palaces, to destroy the children without, and the yong men in the streetes.

22 Speake, thus sayth the Lord, The carkeises of men shall lye, euen as the doung vpon the fielde, and as the handfull after the mower, and none shall gather them.

23 Thus saith the Lord, Let not the wise man glory in his wisedome, nor the strong man glorie in his strength, neyther the riche man glorie in his riches.

24 But let him that glorieth, glorie in this, that he vnderstandeth, and knoweth me: for I am the Lord, which shewe mercie, iudgement, and righteousnes in the earth: for in these things I delite, sayth the Lord.

25 Beholde, the dayes come, sayth the Lord, that I wil visite all them, which are circumcised with the vncircumcised:

26 Egypt and Iudah, and Edom, and the children of Ammon, and Moab, and all the vtmost corners of them that dwell in the wildernesse: for all these nations are vncircumcised, and al the house of Israel are vncircumcised in the heart.

Jeremiah 10

1 Heare ye the worde of the Lord that he speaketh vnto you, O house of Israel.

2 Thus saith the Lord, Learne not the way of the heathen, and be not afraid for the signes of heauen, though the heathen be afraid of such.

3 For the customes of the people are vaine: for one cutteth a tree out of the forest (which is the worke of the handes of the carpenter) with the axe,

4 And another decketh it with siluer, and with golde: they fasten it with nailes, and hammers, that it fall not.

5 The idoles stande vp as the palme tree, but speake not: they are borne because they cannot go feare them not, for they cannot do euill, neither can they do good.

6 There is none like vnto thee, O Lord: thou art great, and thy name is great in power.

7 Who would not feare thee, O King of nations? for to thee appertaineth the dominion: for among all the wise men of the Gentiles, and in al their kingdomes there is none like thee.

8 But, altogether they dote, and are foolish: for the stocke is a doctrine of vanitie.

9 Siluer plates are brought from Tarshish, and golde from Vphaz, for the worke of the workeman, and the handes of the founder: the blewe silke, and the purple is their clothing: all these things are made by cunning men.

10 But the Lord is the God of trueth: he is the liuing God, and an euerlasting King: at his anger the earth shall tremble, and the nations cannot abide his wrath.

11 (Thus shall you say vnto them, The gods that haue not made the heauens and the earth, shall perish from the earth, and from vnder these heauens)

12 He hath made the earth by his power, and established the worlde by his wisedome, and hath stretched out the heauen by his discretion.

13 Hee giueth by his voyce the multitude of waters in the heauen, and he causeth the cloudes to ascend from the endes of the earth: he turneth lightnings to rayne, and bringeth forth the winde out of his treasures.

14 Euery man is a beast by his owne knowledge: euery founder is confounded by the grauen image: for his melting is but falsehood, and there is no breath therein.

15 They are vanitie, and the worke of errours: in the time of their visitation they shall perish.

16 The portion of Iaakob is not like them: for he is the maker of all things, and Israel is the rodde of his inheritance: the Lord of hostes is his Name.

17 Gather vp thy wares out of the land, O thou that dwellest in the strong place.

18 For thus sayth the Lord, Beholde, at this time I will throwe as with a sling the inhabitants of the lande, and will trouble them, and they shall finde it so.

19 Wo is me for my destruction, and my grieuous plague: but I thought, Yet it is my sorow, and I will beare it.

20 My tabernacle is destroyed, and all my coardes are broken: my children are gone from me, and are not: there is none to spread out my tent any more, and to set vp my curtaines.

21 For the Pastours are become beasts, and haue not sought the Lord: therefore haue they none vnderstanding: and all the flockes of their pastures are scattered.

22 Beholde, the noyse of the brute is come, and a great commotion out of the North countrey to make the cities of Iudah desolate, and a denne of dragons.

23 O Lord, I knowe, that the way of man is not in himselfe, neyther is it in man to walke and to direct his steps.

24 O Lord, correct mee, but with iudgement, not in thine anger, least thou bring mee to nothing.

25 Powre out thy wrath vpon the heathen, that knowe thee not, and vpon the families that call not on thy Name: for they haue eaten vp Iaakob and deuoured him and consumed him, and haue made his habitation desolate.

Jeremiah 11

1 The worde that came to Ieremiah from the Lord, saying,

2 Heare ye the wordes of this couenant, and speake vnto the men of Iudah, and to the inhabitants of Ierusalem,

3 And say thou vnto them, Thus sayeth the Lord God of Israel, Cursed be the man that obeyeth not the wordes of this couenant,

4 Which I commanded vnto your fathers, when I brought them out of the lande of Egypt, from the yron fornace, saying, Obey my voyce, and doe according to all these things, which I commande you: so shall ye be my people, and I will be your God,

5 That I may confirme the othe, that I haue sworne vnto your fathers, to giue them a lande, which floweth with milke and hony, as appeareth this day. Then answered I and sayde, So be it, O Lord.

6 Then the Lord saide vnto me, Cry all these words in the cities of Iudah, and in the streetes of Ierusalem, saying, Heare yee the words of this couenant, and doe them.

7 For I haue protested vnto your fathers, whe I brought them vp out of the land of Egypt vnto this day, rising earely and protesting, saying, Obey my voyce.

8 Neuerthelesse they would not obey, nor encline their eare: but euery one walked in the stubbernesse of his wicked heart: therefore I will bring vpon them all the wordes of this couenant, which I commanded them to do, but they did it not.

9 And the Lord sayd vnto me, A conspiracie is found among the men of Iudah, and among the inhabitants of Ierusalem.

10 They are turned backe to the iniquities of their forefathers, which refused to heare my wordes: and they went after other gods to serue them: thus the house of Israel, and the house of Iudah haue broken my couenant, which I made with their fathers.

11 Therefore thus sayth the Lord, Beholde, I will bring a plague vpon them, which they shall not be able to escape, and though they crye vnto me, I will not heare them.

12 Then shall the cities of Iudah, and the inhabitants of Ierusalem goe, and crie vnto the gods vnto whome they offer incense, but they shall not bee able to helpe them in time of their trouble.

13 For according to the number of thy cities were thy gods, O Iudah, and according to the number of the streetes of Ierusalem haue yee set vp altars of confusion, euen altars to burne incense vnto Baal.

14 Therfore thou shalt not pray for this people, neither lift vp a crie, or prayer for them: for when they cry vnto mee in their trouble, I will not heare them.

15 What shoulde my beloued tarie in mine house, seeing thei haue committed abomination with manie? and the holy flesh goeth away from thee: yet when thou doest euill, thou reioycest.

16 The Lord called thy name, A greene oliue tree, faire, and of goodly fruite: but with noyse and great tumult he hath set fyre vpon it, and the branches of it are broken.

17 For the Lord of hostes that planted thee, hath pronounced a plague against

thee, for the wickednes of the house of Israel, and of the house of Iudah, which they haue done against themselues to prouoke me to anger in offering incense vnto Baal.

18 And the Lord hath taught me, and I knowe it, euen then thou shewedst mee their practises.

19 But I was like a lambe, or a bullocke, that is brought to the slaughter, and I knewe not that they had deuised thus against me, saying, Let vs destroy the tree with the fruite thereof, and cut him out of the lande of the liuing, that his name may be no more in memory.

20 But O Lord of hostes, that iudgest righteously, and triest the reines and the heart, let me see thy vengeance on them: for vnto thee haue I opened my cause.

21 The Lord therefore speaketh thus of the men of Anathoth, (that seeke thy life, and say, Prophecie not in the Name of the Lord, that thou die not by our hands)

22 Thus therefore sayth the Lord of hostes, Beholde, I will visite them: the yong men shall die by the sword: their sonnes and their daughters shall die by famine,

23 And none of them shall remaine: for I will bring a plague vpon the men of Anathoth, euen the yeere of their visitation.

Jeremiah 12

1 O Lord, if I dispute with thee, thou art righteous: yet let mee talke with thee of thy iudgements: wherefore doeth the way of the wicked prosper? why are all they in wealth that rebelliously transgresse?

2 Thou hast planted them, and they haue taken roote: they grow, and bring forth fruite: thou art neere in their mouth, and farre from their reines.

3 But thou, Lord, knowest me: thou hast seene me, and tried mine heart towarde thee: pull them out like sheepe for the slaughter, and prepare them for the day of slaughter.

4 Howe long shall the lande mourne, and the herbes of euery fielde wither, for the wickednesse of them that dwell therein? the beastes are consumed and the birdes, because they sayd, He wil not see our last ende.

5 If thou hast runne with the footemen and they haue wearied thee, then howe canst thou match thy selfe with horses? and if thou thoughtest thy selfe safe in a peaceable lande, what wilt thou do in the swelling of Iorden?

6 For euen thy brethren, and the house of thy father, euen they haue delt vnfaithfully with thee, and they haue cryed out altogether vpon thee: but beleeue them not, though they speake faire to thee.

7 I haue forsaken mine house: I haue left mine heritage: I haue giuen the dearely beloued of my soule into the hands of her enemies.

8 Mine heritage is vnto mee, as a lion in the forest: it crieth out against mee, therefore haue I hated it.

9 Shall mine heritage bee vnto mee, as a bird of diuers colours? are not the birdes about her, saying, Come, assemble all ye beastes of the fielde, come to eate her?

10 Many pastors haue destroyed my vineyarde, and troden my portion vnder foote: of my pleasant portion they haue made a desolate wildernesse.

11 They haue layde it waste, and it, being waste, mourneth vnto me: and the whole lande lyeth waste, because no man setteth his minde on it.

12 The destroyers are come vpon all the high places in the wildernesse: for the sworde of the Lord shall deuoure from the one end of the land, euen to the other ende of the lande: no flesh shall haue peace.

13 They haue sowen wheate, and reaped thornes: they were sicke, and had no profite: and they were ashamed of your fruites, because of the fierce wrath of the Lord.

14 Thus sayeth the Lord against all mine euill neighbours, that touch the inheritance, which I haue caused my people Israel to inherite, Beholde, I will plucke them out of their lande, and plucke out the house of Iudah from among them.

15 And after that I haue plucked them out, I will returne, and haue compassion on them, and will bring againe euery man to his heritage, and euery man to his land.

16 And if they will learne the wayes of my people, to sweare by my Name, (The Lord liueth, as they taught my people to sweare by Baal) then shall they be built in the middes of my people.

17 But if they will not obey, then will I vtterly plucke vp, and destroy that nation, sayeth the Lord.

Jeremiah 13

1 Thus sayth the Lord vnto mee, Goe, and buy thee a linen girdle, and put it vpon thy loynes, and put it not in water.

2 So I bought the girdle according to the commandement of the Lord, and put it vpon my loynes.

3 And the worde of the Lord came vnto me the second time, saying,

4 Take the girdle that thou hast bought, which is vpon thy loynes, and arise, goe towarde Perath, and hide it there in the cleft of the rocke.

5 So I went, and hid it by Perath, as the Lord had commanded me.

6 And after many dayes, the Lord sayde vnto mee, Arise, goe towarde Perath, and take the girdle from thence, which I commanded thee to hide there.

7 Then went I to Perath, and digged, and tooke the girdle from the place where I had hid it, and behold, the girdle was corrupt, and was profitable for nothing.

8 Then the word of the Lord came vnto me, saying,

9 Thus sayth the Lord, After this maner will I destroy the pride of Iudah, and the great pride of Ierusalem.

10 This wicked people haue refused to heare my word, and walke after ye stubbernesse of their owne heart, and walke after other gods to serue them, and to worship them: therefore they shalbe as this girdle, which is profitable to nothing.

11 For as the girdle cleaueth to the loynes of a man, so haue I tied to me the whole house of Israel, and the whole house of Iudah, saith the Lord, that they might bee my people: that they might haue a name and prayse, and glory, but they would not heare.

12 Therefore thou shalt saye vnto them this word, Thus sayth the Lord God of Israel, Euery bottell shalbe filled with wine, and they shall say vnto thee, Doe we not knowe that euery bottell shalbe filled with wine?

13 Then shalt thou say vnto them, Thus saith the Lord, Behold, I will fill all the inhabitants of this land, euen the Kings that sit vpon the throne of Dauid, and the Priestes and the Prophets and all the inhabitantes of Ierusalem with drunkennesse.

14 And I wil dash them one against another, euen the fathers and the sonnes together, sayeth the Lord: I will not spare, I will not pitie nor haue compassion, but destroy them.

15 Heare and giue eare, be not proude: for the Lord hath spoken it.

16 Giue glory to the Lord your God before he bring darknes, and or euer your feete stumble in the darke mountaines, and whiles you look for light, he turne it into the shadowe of death and make it as darkenesse.

17 But if ye will not heare this, my soule shall weepe in secrete for your pride, and mine eye shall weepe and drop downe teares, because the Lords flocke is caried away captiue.

18 Say vnto the King and to the Queene, Humble yourselues, sit downe, for the crowne of your glory shall come downe from your heads.

19 The cities of the South shall be shut vp, and no man shall open them: all Iudah shall be caried away captiue: it shall be wholy caried away captiue.

20 Lift vp your eyes and beholde them that come from the North: where is the flocke that was giuen thee, euen thy beautifull flocke?

21 What wilt thou saye, when hee shall visite thee? (for thou hast taught them to be captaines and as chiefe ouer thee) shall not sorow take thee as a woman in trauaile?

22 And if thou say in thine heart, Wherefore come these things vpon me? For the multitude of thine iniquities are thy skirts discouered and thy heeles made bare.

23 Can the blacke More change his skin? or the leopard his spots? then may ye also do good, that are accustomed to do euill.

24 Therefore will I scatter them, as the stubble that is taken away with the South winde.

25 This is thy portion, and ye part of thy measures from me, sayth the Lord, because thou hast forgotten me and trusted in lyes.

26 Therefore I haue also discouered thy skirts vpon thy face, that thy shame may appeare.

27 I haue seene thine adulteries, and thy neiings, the filthinesse of thy whoredome on the hils in the fieldes, and thine abominations. Wo vnto thee, O Ierusalem: wilt thou not bee made cleane? when shall it once be?

Jeremiah 14

1 The worde of the Lord that came vnto Ieremiah, concerning the dearth.

2 Iudah hath mourned, and the gates thereof are desolate, they haue bene brought to heauinesse vnto the grounde, and the cry of Ierusalem goeth vp.

3 And their nobles haue sent their inferiours to the water, who came to the welles, and founde no water: they returned with their vessels empty: they were ashamed and confounded, and couered their heads.

4 For the grounde was destroyed, because there was no rayne in the earth: the plowmen were ashamed, and couered their heads.

5 Yea, the hinde also calued in the fielde, and forsooke it, because there was no grasse.

6 And the wilde asses did stande in the hygh places, and drew in their winde like dragons their eyes did faile, because there was no grasse.

7 O Lord, though our iniquities testifie against vs, deale with vs according to thy name: for our rebellions are many, we sinned against thee.

8 O the hope of Israel, the sauiour thereof in the time of trouble, why art thou as a strager in ye land, as one that passeth by to tary for a night?

9 Why art thou as a man astonied, and as a strong man that cannot helpe? yet thou, O Lord, art in the middes of vs, and thy Name is called vpon vs: forsake vs not.

10 Thus saith the Lord vnto this people, Thus haue they delited to wander: they haue not refrained their feete, therefore the Lord hath no delight in them: but he will now remember their iniquitie, and visite their sinnes.

11 Then sayd the Lord vnto me, Thou shalt not pray to do this people good.

12 When they fast, I will not heare their cry, and when they offer burnt offering, and an oblation, I will not accept them: but I will consume them by the sworde, and by the famine and by the pestilence.

13 Then answered I, Ah Lord God, beholde, the prophets say vnto them, Ye shall not see the sworde, neither shall famine come vpon you, but I wil giue you assured peace in this place.

14 Then the Lord said vnto me, The prophets prophecie lyes in my Name: I haue not sent them, neither did I command them, neither spake I vnto them, but they prophecie vnto you a false vision, and diuination, and vanitie, and deceitfulnes of their owne heart.

15 Therefore thus saith the Lord, Concerning the prophets that prophecie in my Name, whom I haue not sent, yet they say, Sworde and famine shall not be in this land, by sword and famine shall those prophets be consumed.

16 And the people to whome these prophets doe prophecie, shalbe cast out in the streetes of Ierusalem, because of the famine, and the sword, and there shall be none to bury them, both they, and their wiues, and their sonnes, and their daughters: for I wil powre their wickednes vpon them.

17 Therefore thou shalt say this worde vnto them, Let mine eyes drop downe teares night and day without ceasing: for the virgine daughter of my people is destroyed with a great destruction, and with a sore grieuous plague.

18 For if I go into the field, behold the slaine with the sworde: and if I enter into the citie, behold them that are sicke for hunger also: moreouer the Prophet also and the Priest go a wandring into a land that they know not.

19 Hast thou vtterly reiected Iudah, or hath thy soule abhorred Zion? why hast thou smitten vs, that we cannot be healed? Wee looked for peace, and there is no good, and for the time of health, and behold trouble.

20 We acknowledge, O Lord, our wickednesse and the iniquitie of our fathers: for we haue sinned against thee.

21 Doe not abhorre vs: for thy Names sake cast not downe the throne of thy glory: remember and breake not thy couenant with vs.

22 Are there any among the vanities of the Gentiles, that can giue raine? or can the heauens giue showres? is it not thou, O Lord our God? therefore we will waite vpon thee: for thou hast made all these things.

Jeremiah 15

1 Then sayde the Lord vnto me, Though Moses and Samuel stoode before mee, yet mine affection coulde not be toward this people: cast them out of my sight, and let them depart.

2 And if they say vnto thee, Whither shall we depart? then tell them, Thus saith the Lord, Such as are appointed to death, vnto death: and such as are for the sworde, to the sworde: and such as are for the famine, to the famine: and such as are for the captiuitie, to the captiuitie.

3 And I wil appoint ouer them foure kindes, sayth the Lord, the sworde to slay, and the dogs to teare in pieces, and the soules of the heauen, and the beastes of the earth to deuoure, and to destroy.

4 I will scatter them also in all kingdomes of the earth, because of Manasseh the sonne of Hezekiah King of Iudah, for that which he did in Ierusalem.

5 Who shall then haue pitie vpon thee, O Ierusalem? or who shalbe sorie for thee? or who shall go to pray for thy peace?

6 Thou hast forsaken me, sayth the Lord, and gone backward: therefore wil I stretch out mine hand against thee, and destroy thee: for I am weary with repenting.

7 And I wil scatter them with the fanne in the gates of the earth I haue wasted, and destroyed my people, yet they would not returne from their wayes.

8 Their widdowes are increased by mee aboue the sande of the sea: I haue brought vpon them, and against the assembly of the yong men a destroyer at noone day: I haue caused him to fal vpon them, and the citie suddenly, and speedily.

9 Shee that hath borne seuen, hath bene made weake: her heart hath failed: the sunne hath failed her, whiles it was day: she hath bene confounded, and ashamed, and the residue of them will I deliuer vnto the sworde before their enemies, sayth the Lord.

10 Wo is mee, my mother, that thou hast borne mee, a contentious man, and a man that striueth with the whole earth I haue neither lent on vsury, nor men haue lent vnto me on vsurie: yet euery one doeth curse me.

11 The Lord sayd, Surely thy remnant shall haue wealth: surely I will cause thine enemie to intreate thee in the time of trouble, and in the time of affliction.

12 Shall the yron breake the yron, and the brasse that commeth from the North?

13 Thy substance and thy treasures wil I giue to be spoyled without gaine, and that for all thy sinnes euen in all thy borders.

14 And I wil make thee to go with thine enemies into a land that thou knowest not: for a fire is kindled in mine anger, which shall burne you.

15 O Lord, thou knowest, remember me, and visite me, and reuenge me of my persecuters: take mee not away in the continuance of thine anger: know that for thy sake I haue suffered rebuke.

16 Thy wordes were founde by me, and I did eate them, and thy worde was vnto me the ioy and reioycing of mine heart: for thy Name is called vpon me, O Lord God of hostes.

17 I sate not in the assembly of the mockers, neither did I reioyce, but sate alone because of thy plague: for thou hast filled me with indignation.

18 Why is mine heauines continuall? and my plague desperate and cannot be healed? why art thou vnto me as a lyar, and as waters that faile?

19 Therefore thus saith the Lord, If thou returne, then wil I bring thee againe, and thou shalt stand before me: and if thou take away the precious from the vile, thou shalt be according to my worde: let them returne vnto thee, but returne not thou vnto them.

20 And I will make thee vnto this people a strong brasen wall, and they shall fight

against thee, but they shall not preuaile against thee: for I am with thee to saue thee and to deliuer thee, saith ye Lord.

21 And I will deliuer thee out of the hand of the wicked, and I will redeeme thee out of the hand of the tyrants.

Jeremiah 16

1 The worde of the Lord came also vnto mee, saying,

2 Thou shalt not take thee a wife, nor haue sonnes nor daughters in this place.

3 For thus sayeth the Lord concerning the sonnes, and concerning the daughters that are borne in this place, and concerning their mothers that beare them, and concerning their fathers, that beget them in this land,

4 They shall die of deathes and diseases: they shall not be lamented, neither shall they be buried, but they shalbe as dung vpon the earth, and they shalbe consumed by the sword, and by famine, and their carkeises shall be meate for the foules of the heauen, and for the beasts of the earth.

5 For thus saith the Lord, Enter not into the house of mourning, neither goe to lament, nor be moued for the: for I haue taken my peace, from this people, saith the Lord, euen mercy and compassion.

6 Both the great, and the small shall die in this land: they shall not be buried, neither shall men lament for them nor cut themselues, nor make themselues balde for them.

7 They shall not stretch out the hands for the in the mourning to comfort them for the dead, neither shall they giue them the cup of consolation to drinke for their father or for their mother.

8 Thou shalt not also goe into the house of feasting to sit with them to eate and to drinke.

9 For thus sayth the Lord of hostes, the God of Israel, Beholde, I wil cause to cease out of this place in your eyes, euen in your dayes the voyce of myrth, and the voyce of gladnes, the voyce of the bridegrome and the voyce of the bride.

10 And when thou shalt shewe this people all these wordes, and they shall say vnto thee, Wherefore hath the Lord pronounced all this great plague against vs? or what is our iniquitie? and what is our sinne that we haue committed against the Lord our God?

11 Then shalt thou say vnto them, Because your fathers haue forsaken me, sayth the Lord, and haue walked after other gods, and haue serued them, and worshipped them, and haue forsaken me, and haue not kept my Law,

12 (And ye haue done worse then your fathers: for beholde, you walke euery one after the stubbernesse of his wicked heart, and will not heare me)

13 Therefore will I driue you out of this land into a lande that ye knowe not, neither you, nor your fathers, and there shall ye serue other gods day and night: for I will shew you no grace.

14 Behold therfore, saith the Lord, the dayes come that it shall no more be sayde, The Lord liueth, which brought vp the children of Israel out of the land of Egypt,

15 But the Lord liueth, that brought vp the children of Israel from the lande of the North, and from all the landes where hee had scattered them, and I wil bring them againe into their land that I gaue vnto their fathers.

16 Behold, sayth the Lord, I wil send out many fishers, and they shall fish them, and after, will I send out many hunters, and they shall hunt them from euery mountaine and from euery hill, and out of the caues of the rockes.

17 For mine eyes are vpon al their wayes: they are not hid from my face, neither is their iniquitie hid from mine eyes.

18 And first I will recompense their iniquitie and their sinne double, because they haue defiled my lande, and haue filled mine inheritance with their filthie carions and their abominations.

19 O Lord, thou art my force, and my strength and my refuge in the day of affliction: the Gentiles shall come vnto thee from the ends of the world, and shall say, Surely our fathers haue inherited lies, and vanitie, wherein was no profite.

20 Shall a man make gods vnto himselfe, and they are no gods?

21 Beholde, therefore I will this once teach them: I will shewe them mine hande and my power, and they shall know that my Name is the Lord.

Jeremiah 17

1 The sinne of Iudah is written with a pen of yron, and with the poynt of a diamonde, and grauen vpon the table of their heart, and vpon the hornes of your altars.

2 They remember their altars as their children, with their groues by the greene trees vpon the hilles.

3 O my mountaine in the fielde, I will giue thy substance, and all thy treasures to be spoyled, for the sinne of thy high places throughout all thy borders.

4 And thou shalt rest, and in thee shall be a rest from thine heritage that I gaue thee, and I will cause thee to serue thine enemies in the land, which thou knowest not: for yee haue kindled a fire in mine anger, which shall burne for euer.

5 Thus saith the Lord, Cursed be the man that trusteth in man, and maketh flesh his arme, and withdraweth his heart from the Lord.

6 For he shall be like the heath in the wildernesse, and shall not see when any good commeth, but shall inhabite the parched places in the wildernesse, in a salt land, and not inhabited.

7 Blessed be the man, that trusteth in ye Lord, and whose hope the Lord is.

8 For he shall be as a tree that is planted by the water, which spreadeth out her rootes by the riuer, and shall not feele when the heate commeth, but her leafe shall be greene, and shall not care for the yeere of drought, neyther shall cease from yeelding fruit.

9 The heart is deceitfull and wicked aboue all things, who can knowe it?

10 I the Lord search the heart, and try ye reines, euen to giue euery man according to his wayes, and according to the fruite of his workes.

11 As the partryche gathereth the yong, which she hath not brought forth: so he that getteth riches, and not by right, shall leaue them in the middes of his dayes, and at his ende shall bee a foole.

12 As a glorious throne exalted from the beginning, so is the place of our Sanctuarie.

13 O Lord, the hope of Israel, all that forsake thee, shall be confounded: they that depart from thee, shalbe written in the earth, because they haue forsaken the Lord, the fountaine of liuing waters.

14 Heale me, O Lord, and I shall bee whole: saue me, and I shall bee saued: for thou art my prayse.

15 Behold, they say vnto me, Where is the word of the Lord? let it come nowe.

16 But I haue not thrust in my selfe for a pastour after thee, neither haue I desired the day of miserie, thou knowest: that which came out of my lips, was right before thee.

17 Be not terrible vnto mee: thou art mine hope in the day of aduersitie.

18 Let them bee confounded, that persecute me, but let not me be confounded: let them be afraide, but let not me be afraide: bring vpon them the day of aduersitie, and destroy them with double destruction.

19 Thus hath the Lord said vnto me, Goe and stande in the gate of the children of the people, whereby the Kings of Iudah come in, and by the which they goe out, and in all ye gates of Ierusalem,

20 And say vnto them, Heare the word of the Lord, ye Kings of Iudah, and al Iudah, and all the inhabitants of Ierusale, that enter in by these gates.

21 Thus sayth the Lord, Take heede to your soules, and beare no burden in the Sabbath day, nor bring it in by the gates of Ierusalem.

22 Neither cary foorth burdens out of your houses in the Sabbath day: neither doe yee any worke, but sanctifie the Sabbath, as I commanded your fathers.

23 But they obeied not, neither inclined their eares, but made their neckes stiffe and would not heare, nor receiue correction.

24 Neuerthelesse if ye will heare me, sayth the Lord, and beare no burden through the gates of the citie in the Sabbath day, but sanctifie ye Sabbath day, so that ye do no worke therein,

25 Then shall the Kings and the princes enter in at the gates of this citie, and shall sit vpon the throne of Dauid, and shall ride vpon charets, and vpon horses, both they and their princes, the men of Iudah, and the inhabitants of Ierusalem: and this citie shall remaine for euer.

26 And they shall come from the cities of Iudah, and from about Ierusalem, and from the land of Beniamin, and from the plaine, and from the mountaines, and from the South, which shall bring burnt offrings, and sacrifices, and meate offrings, and incense, and shall bring sacrifice of prayse into the house of the Lord.

27 But if ye will not heare me to sanctifie the Sabbath day, and not to beare a burden nor to go through the gates of Ierusalem in the Sabbath day, then will I kindle a fire in the gates thereof, and it shall deuoure the palaces of Ierusalem, and it shall not be quenched.

Jeremiah 18

1 The worde which came to Ieremiah from the Lord, saying,

2 Arise, and go downe into the potters house, and there shall I shewe thee my words.

3 Then I went downe to the potters house, and behold, he wrought a worke on the wheeles.

4 And the vessell that he made of clay, was broken in the hand of the potter. so he returned, and made it another vessel, as seemed good to the potter to make it.

5 Then the worde of the Lord came vnto me, saying,

6 O house of Israel, cannot I doe with you as this potter, sayth the Lord? beholde, as the clay is in the potters hande, so are you in mine hande, O house of Israel.

7 I will speake suddenly against a nation or against a kingdome to plucke it vp, and to roote it out and to destroy it.

8 But if this nation, against whom I haue pronounced, turne from their wickednesse, I will repent of the plague that I thought to bring vpon them.

9 And I wil speake suddenly concerning a nation, and concerning a kingdome to builde it and to plant it.

10 But if it do euill in my sight and heare not my voyce, I will repent of ye good that I thought to do for them.

11 Speake thou nowe therefore vnto the men of Iudah, and to the inhabitants of Ierusalem, saying, Thus saith ye Lord, Behold, I prepare a plague for you, and purpose a thing against you: returne you therefore euery one from his euill way, and make your wayes and your workes good.

12 But they sayde desperately, Surely wee will walke after our owne imaginations, and doe euery man after the stubburnnesse of his wicked heart.

13 Therefore thus saith the Lord, Aske now among the heathen, who hath heard such thinges? the virgin of Israel hath done very filthily.

14 Will a man forsake the snowe of Lebanon, which commeth from the rocke of the fielde? or shall the colde flowing waters, that come from another place, be forsaken?

15 Because my people hath forgotten me, and haue burnt incense to vanitie, and their prophets haue caused them to stumble in their wayes from the auncient wayes, to walke in the pathes and way that is not troden,

16 To make their land desolate and a perpetual derision, so that euery one that passeth thereby, shalbe astonished and wagge his head,

17 I will scatter them with an East winde before the enemie: I will shewe them the backe, and not the face in the day of their destruction.

18 Then sayde they, Come, and let vs imagine some deuice against Ieremiah: for the Lawe shall not perish from the Priest, nor counsell from the wise, nor the worde from the Prophet: come, and let vs smite him with the tongue, and let vs not giue heede to any of his words.

19 Hearken vnto mee, O Lord, and heare the voyce of them that contend with me.

20 Shall euill be recompensed for good? for they haue digged a pit for my soule: remember that I stood before thee, to speake good for the, and to turne away thy wrath from them.

21 Therefore, deliuer vp their children to famine, and let them drop away by the force of the sworde, and let their wiues be robbed of their children, and be widowes: and let their husbands be put to death, and let their yong men be slayne by the sword in the battell.

22 Let the crye bee heard from their houses, when thou shalt bring an hoste suddenly vpon them: for they haue digged a pit to take me, and hid snares for my feete.

23 Yet Lord thou knowest al their counsel against me tendeth to death: forgiue not their iniquitie, neither put out their sinne from thy sight, but let them be ouerthrowen before thee: deale thus with them in the time of thine anger.

Jeremiah 19

1 Thus sayth the Lord, Goe, and buy an earthen bottel of a potter, and take of the ancients of the people, and of the ancients of the Priests,

2 And goe forth vnto the valley of Ben-hinnom, which is by the entrie of the East gate: and thou shalt preache there the wordes, that I shall tell thee,

3 And shalt say, Heare yee the worde of the Lord, O Kings of Iudah, and inhabitantes of Ierusalem, Thus sayth the Lord of hostes, the God of Israel, Behold, I will bring a plague vpon this place, the which whosoeuer heareth, his eares shall tingle.

4 Because they haue forsaken me, and prophaned this place, and haue burnt incense in it vnto other gods, whome neyther they, nor their fathers haue knowen, nor the Kings of Iudah (they haue filled this place also with the blood of innocents,

5 And they haue built the hie places of Baal, to burne their sonnes with fire for burnt offrings vnto Baal, which I commanded not, nor spake it, neither came it into my minde)

6 Therefore behold, the dayes come, sayth the Lord, that this place shall no more be called Topheth, nor ye valley of Ben-hinnom, but the valley of slaughter.

7 And I will bring the counsell of Iudah and Ierusalem to nought in this place, and I will cause them to fall by the sword before their enemies, and by the hand of them that seeke their liues: and their carkeises will I giue to be meate for ye foules of the heauen, and to the beastes of the fielde.

8 And I will make this citie desolate and an hissing, so that euery one that passeth thereby, shalbe astonished and hisse because of all ye plagues thereof.

9 And I will feede the with the flesh of their sonnes and with the flesh of their daughters, and euery one shall eate the flesh of his friende in the siege and straitnesse, wherewith their enemies that seeke their liues, shall hold them strait.

10 Then shalt thou breake the bottell in the sight of the men that go with thee,

11 And shalt say vnto them, Thus saith ye Lord of hostes, Euen so will I breake this people and this citie, as one breaketh a potters vessell, that cannot be made whole againe, and they shall bury them in Topheth till there be no place to bury.

12 Thus will I doe vnto this place, sayth the Lord, and to the inhabitantes thereof, and I will make this citie like Topheth.

13 For the houses of Ierusalem, and the houses of the Kings of Iudah shalbe defiled as the place of Topheth, because of al the houses vpon whose roofes they haue burnt incense vnto all the host of heauen, and haue powred out drinke offerings vnto other gods.

14 Then came Ieremiah from Topheth, where the Lord had sent him to prophecie, and he stood in the court of the Lordes house, and sayde to all the people,

15 Thus saith the Lord of hostes, the God of Israel, Beholde, I will bring vpon this citie, and vpon all her townes, all the plagues that I haue pronounced against it, because they haue hardened their neckes, and would not heare my wordes.

Jeremiah 20

1 When Pashur, the sonne of Immer, the Priest, which was appointed gouernour in the house of the Lord, heard that Ieremiah prophecied these things,

2 Then Pashur smote Ieremiah the Prophet, and put him in the stockes that were in the hie gate of Beniamin which was by the House of the Lord.

3 And on the morning, Pashur brought Ieremiah out of the stockes. Then said Ieremiah vnto him, The Lord hath not called thy name Pashur, but Magor-missabib.

4 For thus saith the Lord, Behold, I will make thee to be a terrour to thy self, and to al thy friends, and they shall fall by the sword of their enemies, and thine eyes shall beholde it, and I will giue all

Iudah into the hande of the King of Babel, and he shall cary them captiue into Babel, and shall slay them with the sworde.

5 Moreouer, I will deliuer all the substance of this citie, and all the labours thereof, and al the precious things thereof, and all the treasures of the Kings of Iudah will I giue into the hande of their enemies, which shall spoyle them, and take them away and cary them to Babel.

6 And thou Pashur, and all that dwell in thine house, shall go into captiuitie, and thou shalt come to Babel, and there thou shalt die, and shalt be buryed there, thou and all thy friendes, to whome thou hast prophecied lyes.

7 O Lord, thou hast deceiued me, and I am deceiued: thou art stronger then I, and hast preuailed: I am in derision daily: euery one mocketh me.

8 For since I spake, I cryed out of wrong, and proclaimed desolation: therefore the word of the Lord was made a reproche vnto me, and in derision daily.

9 Then I said, I will not make mention of him, nor speake any more in his Name. But his worde was in mine heart as a burning fire shut vp in my bones, and I was weary with forbearing, and I could not stay.

10 For I had heard the railing of many, and feare on euery side. Declare, said they, and wee wil declare it: all my familiars watched for mine halting, saying, It may be that he is deceiued: so we shall preuaile against him, and we shall execute our vengeance vpon him.

11 But the Lord is with me like a mightie gyant: therefore my persecuters shall be ouerthrowen, and shall not preuaile, and shalbe greatly confounded: for they haue done vnwisely, and their euerlasting shame shall neuer be forgotten.

12 But, O Lord of hostes, that tryest the righteous, and seest the reines and the heart, let me see thy vengeance on them: for vnto thee haue I opened my cause.

13 Sing vnto the Lord, praise ye the Lord: for he hath deliuered the soule of the poore from the hande of the wicked.

14 Cursed be the day wherein I was borne: and let not the day wherein my mother bare me, be blessed.

15 Cursed be the man, that shewed my father, saying, A man child is borne vnto thee, and comforted him.

16 And let that man be as the cities, which the Lord hath ouerturned and repented not: and let him heare the cry in the morning, and the showting at noone tide,

17 Because he hath not slaine me, euen from the wombe, or that my mother might haue bene my graue, or her wobe a perpetual conception.

18 How is it, that I came forth of the wombe, to see labour and sorowe, that my dayes shoulde be consumed with shame?

Jeremiah 21

1 The worde which came vnto Ieremiah from the Lord, when king Zedekiah sent vnto him Pashur, the sonne of Malchiah, and Zephaniah, the sonne of Maaseiah the Priest, saying,

2 Inquire, I pray thee, of the Lord for vs, (for Nebuchad-nezzar King of Babel maketh warre against vs) if so be that the Lord will deale with vs according to all his wonderous workes, that he may returne vp from vs.

3 Then said Ieremiah, Thus shall you say to Zedekiah,

4 Thus saith the Lord God of Israel, Behold, I will turne backe the weapons of warre that are in your hands, wherewith ye fight against the King of Babel, and against the Caldeans, which besiege you without the walles, and I will assemble them into the middes of this citie.

5 And I my selfe will fight against you with an outstretched hand, and with a mighty arme, eue in anger and in wrath, and in great indignation.

6 And I will smite the inhabitants of this citie, both man, and beast: they shall die of a great pestilence.

7 And after this, sayeth the Lord, I will deliuer Zedekiah the King of Iudah, and his seruants, and the people, and such as are left in this citie, from the pestilence, from the sworde and from the famine into the hande of Nebuchad-nezzar King of Babel, and into the hande of their enemies, and into the hande of those that seeke their liues, and he shall smite them with the edge of the sworde: he shall not spare them, neither haue pitie nor compassion.

8 And vnto this people thou shalt say, Thus saith the Lord, Beholde, I set before you the way of life, and the way of death.

9 He that abideth in this citie, shall dye by the sword and by the famine, and by the pestilence: but he that goeth out, and falleth to the Caldeans, that besiege you, he shall liue, and his life shalbe vnto him for a pray.

10 For I haue set my face against this citie, for euill and not for good, saith the Lord: it shalbe giuen into the hande of the King of Babel, and he shall burne it with fire.

11 And say vnto the house of the King of Iudah, Heare ye the worde of the Lord.

12 O house of Dauid, thus saith the Lord, Execute iudgement in the morning, and deliuer the oppressed out of the hande of the oppressor, lest my wrath go out like fire and burne, that none can quench it, because of the wickednes of your workes.

13 Beholde, I come against thee, O inhabitant of the valley, and rocke of the plaine, saith the Lord, which say, Who shall come downe against vs? or who shall enter into our habitations?

14 But I will visite you according to the fruite of your workes, saith the Lord, and I will kindle a fire in the forest thereof, and it shall deuoure rounde about it.

Jeremiah 22

1 Thus said the Lord, Goe downe to the house of the King of Iudah, and speake there this thing,

2 And say, Heare the worde of the Lord, O King of Iudah, that sittest vpon the throne of Dauid, thou and thy seruants, and thy people that enter in by these gates.

3 Thus saith the Lord, Execute ye iudgement and righteousnes, and deliuer the oppressed from the hande of the oppressor, and vexe not the stranger, the fatherlesse, nor the widowe: doe no violence, nor sheade innocent blood in this place.

4 For if ye do this thing, then shall the kings sitting vpon the throne of Dauid enter in by the gates of this House, and ride vpon charets, and vpon horses, both he and his seruants and his people.

5 But if ye will not heare these wordes, I sweare by my selfe, saith the Lord, that this House shalbe waste.

6 For thus hath the Lord spoken vpon the Kings house of Iudah, Thou art Gilead vnto me, and the head of Lebanon, yet surely I wil make thee a wildernes and as cities not inhabited,

7 And I will prepare destroyers against thee, euery one with his weapons, and they shall cut downe thy chiefe cedar trees, and cast them in the fire.

8 And many nations shall passe by this citie, and they shall say euery man to his neighbour, Wherefore hath the Lord done thus vnto this great citie?

9 Then shall they answere, Because they haue forsaken the couenant of the Lord their God, and worshipped other gods, and serued them.

10 Weepe not for the dead, and be not moued for them, but weepe for him that goeth out: for he shall returne no more, nor see his natiue countrey.

11 For thus saith ye Lord, As touching Shallum the sonne of Iosiah King of Iudah, which reigned for Iosiah his father, which went out of this place, he shall not returne thither,

12 But he shall die in the place, whither they haue ledde him captiue, and shall see this lande no more.

13 Wo vnto him that buildeth his house by vnrighteousnesse, and his chambers without equitie: he vseth his neighbour without wages, and giueth him not for his worke.

14 He saith, I will build me a wide house and large chambers: so he will make him selfe large windowes, and feeling with cedar, and paint them with vermilion.

15 Shalt thou reigne, because thou closest thy selfe in cedar? did not thy father eate and drinke and prosper, when he executed iudgement and iustice?

16 When he iudged the cause of the afflicted and the poore, he prospered: was not this because he knewe me, saith the Lord?

17 But thine eyes and thine heart are but only for thy couetousnesse, and for to sheade innocent blood, and for

oppression, and for destruction, euen to doe this.

18 Therefore thus saith the Lord against Iehoiakim, the sonne of Iosiah king of Iudah, They shall not lament him, saying, Ah, my brother, or ah, sister: neither shall they mourne for him, saying, Ah, lord, or ah, his glorie.

19 He shalbe buryed, as an asse is buryed, euen drawen and cast foorth without the gates of Ierusalem.

20 Goe vp to Lebanon, and cry: showte in Bashan and crye by the passages: for all thy louers are destroyed.

21 I spake vnto thee when thou wast in prosperitie: but thou saidest, I will not heare: this hath bene thy maner from thy youth, that thou wouldest not obey my voyce.

22 The wind shall feede all thy pastors, and thy louers shall goe into captiuitie: and then shalt thou be ashamed and confounded of al thy wickednesse.

23 Thou that dwellest in Lebanon, and makest thy nest in the cedars, howe beautiful shalt thou be when sorowes come vpon thee, as the sorowe of a woman in trauaile?

24 As I liue, saith the Lord, though Coniah the sonne of Iehoiakim King of Iudah, were the signet of my right hand, yet would I plucke thee thence.

25 And I will giue thee into the hande of them that seeke thy life, and into the hande of them, whose face thou fearest, euen into the hand of Nebuchad-nezzar king of Babel, and into the hande of the Caldeans.

26 And I will cause them to cary thee away, and thy mother that bare thee, into another countrey, where ye were not borne, and there shall ye die.

27 But to the lande, whereunto they desire to returne, they shall not returne thither.

28 Is not this man Coniah as a despised and broken idole? or as a vessell, wherein is no pleasure? wherefore are they caryed away, hee and his seede, and cast out into a lande that they knowe not?

29 O earth, earth, earth, heare the worde of the Lord.

30 Thus saith the Lord, Write this man destitute of children, a man that shall not prosper in his dayes: for there shall be no man of his seede that shall prosper and sit vpon the throne of Dauid, or beare rule any more in Iudah.

Jeremiah 23

1 Woe be vnto the pastors that destroy and scatter the sheepe of my pasture, saith the Lord.

2 Therefore thus saith the Lord God of Israel vnto the pastors that feede my people, Yee haue scattered my flock and thrust them out, and haue not visited them: beholde, I will visite you for the wickednesse of your works, saith the Lord.

3 And I will gather the remnant of my sheepe out of all countreyes, whither I had driuen them, and will bring them againe to their foldes, and they shall growe and encrease.

4 And I will set vp shepheardes ouer them, which shall feede them: and they shall dread no more nor be afraide, neither shall any of them be lacking, saith the Lord.

5 Behold, The dayes come, saith the Lord, that I will raise vnto Dauid a righteous branche, and a King shall reigne, and prosper, and shall execute iudgement, and iustice in the earth.

6 In his dayes Iudah shalbe saued, and Israel shall dwell safely, and this is the Name wherby they shall call him, The Lord our righteousnesse.

7 Therefore behold, the dayes come, sayth the Lord, that they shall no more say, The Lord liueth, which brought vp the children of Israel out of the lande of Egypt,

8 But the Lord liueth, which brought vp and led the seede of the house of Israel out of the North countrey and from all countryes where I had scattered them, and they shall dwell in their owne lande.

9 Mine heart breaketh within mee, because of the prophets, all my bones shake: I am like a drunken man (and like a man whome wine hath ouercome) for the presence of the Lord and for his holie wordes.

10 For the lande is full of adulterers, and because of othes the lande mourneth, the pleasant places of the wildernesse are dried vp, and their course is euill, and their force is not right.

11 For both the prophet and the Priest doe wickedly: and their wickednesse haue I found in mine House, saith the Lord.

12 Wherefore their way shalbe vnto them as slipperie wayes in the darknesse: they shalbe driuen foorth and fall therein: for I will bring a plague vpon them, euen the yeere of their visitation, saith the Lord.

13 And I haue seene foolishnesse in the prophets of Samaria, that prophecied in Baal, and caused my people Israel to erre.

14 I haue seene also in the prophets of Ierusalem filthines: they commit adulterie and walke in lies: they strengthen also the hands of the wicked that none can returne from his wickednesse: they are all vnto me as Sodom, and the inhabitants thereof as Gomorah.

15 Therefore thus saith the Lord of hostes concerning the prophets, Beholde, I will feede them with wormewood, and make them drinke the water of gall: for from the prophets of Ierusalem is wickednesse gone forth into all the lande.

16 Thus sayth ye Lord of hosts, Heare not the wordes of the prophets that prophecie vnto you, and teach you vanitie: they speake the vision of their owne heart, and not out of the mouth of the Lord.

17 They say still vnto them that despise mee, The Lord hath sayde, Ye shall haue peace: and they say vnto euery one that walketh after the stubbernesse of his owne heart, No euill shall come vpon you.

18 For who hath stand in the counsel of the Lord that he hath perceiued and heard his word? Who hath marked his worde and heard it?

19 Beholde, the tempest of the Lord goeth forth in his wrath, and a violent whirlewinde shall fall downe vpon the head of the wicked.

20 The anger of the Lord shall not returne vntill he haue executed, and till he haue perfourmed the thoughts of his heart: in the latter dayes ye shall vnderstande it plainely.

21 I haue not sent these prophets, sayth the Lord, yet they ranne; I haue not spoken to them, and yet they prophecied.

22 But if they had stande in my counsell, and had declared my words to my people, then they should haue turned them from their euill way, and from the wickednesse of their inuentions.

23 Am I a God at hande, saith the Lord, and not a God farre off?

24 Can any hide him selfe in secrete places, that I shall not see him, sayth the Lord? Do not I fill heauen and earth, saieth the Lord?

25 I haue heard what the prophets said, that prophecie lies in my Name, saying, I haue dreamed, I haue dreamed.

26 Howe long? Doe the prophets delite to prophecie lies, euen prophecying the deceit of their owne heart?

27 Thinke they to cause my people to forget my Name by their dreames, which they tell euery man to his neyghbour, as their forefathers haue forgotten my Name for Baal?

28 The prophet that hath a dreame, let him tell a dreame, and hee that hath my worde, let him speake my worde faithfully: what is the chaffe to the wheate, sayth the Lord?

29 Is not my word euen like a fire, sayeth the Lord? and like an hammer, that breaketh the stone?

30 Therefore beholde, I will come against the prophets, saieth the Lord, that steale my word euerie one from his neighbour.

31 Beholde, I will come against the prophets, saith the Lord, which haue sweete tongues, and say, He saith.

32 Beholde, I will come against them that prophecie false dreames, saith the Lord, and doe tell them, and cause my people to erre by their lies, and by their flatteries, and I sent them not, nor commanded them: therefore they bring no profite vnto this people, saith the Lord.

33 And when this people, or the prophet, or a Priest shall aske thee, saying, What is the burden of the Lord? thou shalt then say vnto them, What burden? I will euen forsake you, saith the Lord.

34 And the prophet, or the Priest, or the people that shall say, The burden of the

Lord, I will euen visite euerie such one, and his house.

35 Thus shall yee say euery one to his neighbour, and euerie one to his brother, What hath the Lord answered? and what hath the Lord spoken?

36 And the burden of the Lord shall yee mention no more: for euery mans worde shall bee his burden: for ye haue peruerted the words of the liuing God, the Lord of hostes our God.

37 Thus shalt thou say to the Prophet, What hath the Lord answered thee? and what hath the Lord spoken?

38 And if you say, The burden of the Lord, Then thus saith the Lord, Because yee say this word, The burden of the Lord, and I haue sent vnto you, saying, Ye shall not say, The burden of the Lord,

39 Therefore beholde, I, euen I will vtterly forget you, and I will forsake you, and the citie that I gaue you and your fathers, and cast you out of my presence,

40 And will bring an euerlasting reproche vpon you, and a perpetual shame which shall neuer be forgotten.

Jeremiah 24

1 The Lord shewed me, and beholde, two baskets of figges were set before the Temple of the Lord, after that Nebuchad-nezzar King of Babel had caryed away captiue Ieconiah ye sonne of Iehoiakim King of Iudah, and the princes of Iudah with the workemen, and cunning men of Ierusalem, and had brought them to Babel.

2 One basket had verie good figges, euen like the figges that are first ripe: and the other basket had verie naughtie figges, which could not be eaten, they were so euill.

3 Then saide the Lord vnto mee, What seest thou, Ieremiah? And I said, Figges: ye good figges verie good, and the naughtie verie naughtie, which cannot be eaten, they are so euill.

4 Againe the worde of the Lord came vnto me, saying,

5 Thus sayeth the Lord, the God of Israel, Like these good figges, so will I knowe them that are caryed away captiue of Iudah to bee good, whome I haue sent out of this place, into the land of the Caldeans.

6 For I wil set mine eyes vpon them for good, and I will bring them againe to this lande, and I will build them, and not destroy them, and I will plant them, and not roote them out,

7 And I will giue them an heart to knowe me, that I am the Lord, and they shalbe my people, and I wil be their God: for they shall returne vnto mee with their whole heart.

8 And as the naughtie figges which can not bee eaten, they are so euill (surely thus saith the Lord) so wil I giue Zedekiah the King of Iudah, and his princes, and the residue of Ierusalem, that remaine in this lande, and them that dwell in the lande of Egypt:

9 I will euen giue them for a terrible plague to all the kingdomes of the earth, and for a reproche, and for a prouerbe, for a common talke, and for a curse, in all places where I shall cast them.

10 And I will sende the sworde, the famine, and the pestilence among them, till they bee consumed out of the land, that I gaue vnto them and to their fathers.

Jeremiah 25

1 The word that came to Ieremiah, concerning all the people of Iudah in the fourth yeere of Iehoiakim the sonne of Iosiah King of Iudah that was in the first yeere of Nebuchad-nezzar King of Babel:

2 The which Ieremiah the Prophet spake vnto all the people of Iudah, and to all the inhabitants of Ierusalem, saying,

3 From the thirteenth yeere of Iosiah the sonne of Amon King of Iudah, euen vnto this day (that is the three and twentieth yeere) the word of the Lord hath come vnto mee, and I haue spoken vnto you rising earely and speaking, but ye woulde not heare.

4 And the Lord hath sent vnto you all his seruantes the Prophets, rising early and sending them, but yee would not heare, nor encline your eares to obey.

5 They sayde, Turne againe now euery one from his euill way, and from the wickednes of your inuentions, and ye shall dwell in the lande that the Lord hath giuen vnto you, and to your fathers for euer and euer.

6 And go not after other gods to serue them and to worshippe them, and prouoke me not to anger with the workes of your hands, and I will not punish you.

7 Neuerthelesse ye would not heare me, saith the Lord, but haue prouoked mee to anger with the workes of your hands to your owne hurt.

8 Therefore thus saith the Lord of hostes, Because ye haue not heard my wordes,

9 Beholde, I will send and take to mee all the families of the North, saith the Lord, and Nebuchad-nezzar the King of Babel my seruant, and will bring them against this lande, and against the inhabitantes thereof, and against all these nations rounde about, and will destroy them, and make them an astonishment and an hissing, and a continuall desolation.

10 Moreouer I will take from them the voyce of mirth and the voyce of gladnesse, the voyce of the bridegrome and the voyce of the bride, the noise of the milstones, and the light of the candle.

11 And this whole land shalbe desolate, and an astonishment, and these nations shall serue the King of Babel seuentie yeeres.

12 And when the seuentie yeres are accomplished, I will visite the King of Babel and that nation, saith the Lord, for their iniquities, euen the land of the Caldeans, and will make it a perpetuall desolation,

13 And I will bring vpon that lande all my wordes which I haue pronounced against it, euen all that is written in this booke, which Ieremiah hath prophecied against all nations.

14 For many nations, and great Kings shall euen serue themselues of them: thus will I recompense them according to their deedes, and according to the workes of their owne handes.

15 For thus hath the Lord God of Israel spoken vnto me, Take the cuppe of wine of this mine indignation at mine hand, and cause all the nations, to whome I sende thee, to drinke it.

16 And they shall drinke, and be moued and be mad, because of the sworde that I will sende among them.

17 Then tooke I the cup at the Lordes hand, and made all people to drinke, vnto whome the Lord had sent me:

18 Euen Ierusalem, and the cities of Iudah, and the Kings thereof, and the princes thereof, to make them desolate, an astonishment, an hissing, and a curse, as appeareth this day:

19 Pharaoh also, King of Egypt, and his seruants, and his princes, and all his people:

20 And all sortes of people, and all the Kings of the lande of Vz: and all the Kings of the lande of the Philistims, and Ashkelon, and Azzah, and Ekron, and the remnant of Ashdod:

21 Edom, and Moab, and the Ammonites,

22 And all the Kings of Tyrus, and all the kings of Zidon, and the Kings of the Yles, that are beyonde the Sea,

23 And Dedan, and Tema, and Buz, and all that dwell in the vttermost corners,

24 And all the Kings of Arabia, and all the Kings of Arabia, that dwell in the desert,

25 And all the Kings of Zimri, and all the Kings of Elam, and all the Kings of the Medes,

26 And all the Kings of the North, farre and neere one to another, and all the kingdomes of the worlde, which are vpon the earth, and the king of Sheshach shall drinke after them.

27 Therefore say thou vnto them, Thus saith the Lord of hostes, the God of Israel, Drinke and bee drunken, and spewe and fall, and rise no more, because of the sworde, which I will sende among you.

28 But if they refuse to take the cuppe at thine hande to drinke, then tell them, Thus saith the Lord of hostes, Ye shall certainely drinke.

29 For loe, I beginne to plague the citie, where my Name is called vpon, and shoulde you goe free? Ye shall not goe quite: for I will call for a sword vpon al the inhabitants of the earth, saith the Lord of hostes.

30 Therefore prophecie thou against them al these words, and say vnto them, The Lord shall roare from aboue, and thrust out his voyce from his holy habitation: he shall roare vpon his habitation, and crie aloude, as they that presse the grapes, against all the inhabitants of the earth.

31 The sounde shall come to the endes of the earth: for the Lord hath a controuersie with the nations, and will enter into iudgement with all flesh, and he will giue them that are wicked, to the swerde, saith the Lord.

32 Thus saith the Lord of hostes, Behold, a plague shall goe foorth from nation to nation, and a great whirlewinde shalbe raised vp from the coastes of the earth,

33 And the slaine of the Lord shall be at that day, from one ende of the earth, euen vnto the other ende of the earth: they shall not bee mourned, neither gathered nor buried, but shalbe as the dongue vpon the grounde.

34 Howle, ye shepherdes, and crie, and wallowe your selues in the ashes, ye principall of the flocke: for your dayes of slaughter are accomplished, and of your dispersion, and ye shall fall like precious vessels.

35 And the flight shall faile from the shepherdes, and the escaping from the principall of the flocke.

36 A voyce of the crye of the shepherdes, and an howling of the principall of the flocke shalbe heard: for the Lord hath destroyed their pasture.

37 And the best pastures are destroyed because of the wrath and indignation of the Lord.

38 He hath forsaken his couert, as the lyon: for their land is waste, because of the wrath of the oppressor, and because of ye wrath of his indignatio.

Jeremiah 26

1 In the beginning of the reigne of Iehoiakim the sonne of Iosiah King of Iudah, came this worde from the Lord, saying,

2 Thus saith the Lord, Sande in the court of the Lordes House, and speake vnto all the cities of Iudah, which come to worshippe in the Lords House, all the wordes that I commaund thee to speake vnto them: keepe not a worde backe,

3 If so be they will hearken, and turne euery man from his euill way, that I may repent me of the plague, which I haue determined to bring vpon them, because of the wickednesse of their workes.

4 And thou shalt say vnto them, Thus saith the Lord, If ye will not heare me to walke in my Lawes, which I haue set before you,

5 And to heare ye wordes of my seruants the Prophets, whome I sent vnto you, both rising vp earely, and sending them, and will not obey them,

6 Then will I make this House like Shiloh, and will make this citie a curse to all the nations of the earth.

7 So the Priestes, and the Prophets, and all the people heard Ieremiah speaking these wordes in the House of the Lord.

8 Nowe when Ieremiah had made an end of speaking all that the Lord had commanded him to speake vnto all the people, then the Priestes, and the prophets, and all the people tooke him, and saide, Thou shalt die the death.

9 Why hast thou prophecied in the Name of the Lord, saying, This House shall be like Shiloh, and this citie shalbe desolate without an inhabitant? and all the people were gathered against Ieremiah in the House of the Lord.

10 And when the princes of Iudah heard of these things, they came vp from the Kings house into the House of the Lord, and sate downe in the entrie of the new gate of the Lords House.

11 Then spake the Priestes, and the prophets vnto the princes, and to all the people, saying, This man is worthie to die: for he hath prophecied against this citie, as ye haue heard with your eares.

12 Then spake Ieremiah vnto all the princes, and to al the people, saying, The Lord hath sent me to prophecie against this house and against this citie all the things that ye haue heard.

13 Therefore nowe amende your wayes and your workes, and heare the voyce of the Lord your God, that the Lord may repent him of the plague, that he hath pronounced against you.

14 As for me, beholde, I am in your hands: do with me as ye thinke good and right.

15 But knowe ye for certaine, that if ye put me to death, ye shall surely bring innocent blood vpon your selues, and vpon this citie, and vpon the inhabitants thereof: for of a trueth the Lord hath sent me vnto you, to speake all these words in your eares.

16 Then saide the princes and all the people vnto the Priestes, and to the prophets, This man is not worthie to die: for he hath spoken vnto vs in the Name of the Lord our God.

17 Then rose vp certaine of the Elders of the lande, and spake to all the assemblie of the people, saying,

18 Michah the Morashite prophecied in the dayes of Hezekiah king of Iudah, and spake to al the people of Iudah, saying, Thus saith the Lord of hostes, Zion shall be plowed like a fielde, and Ierusalem shalbe an heape, and the mountaine of the House shalbe as the hie places of the forest.

19 Did Hezekiah King of Iudah, and all Iudah put him to death? did he not feare ye Lord, and prayed before the Lord, and the Lord repented him of the plague, that he had pronounced against them? Thus might we procure great euill against our soules.

20 And there was also a man that prophecied in the Name of the Lord, one Vriiah the sonne of Shemaiah, of Kiriath-iarem, who prophecied against this citie, and against this lande, according to all the wordes of Ieremiah.

21 Nowe when Iehoiakim the King with all his men of power, and all the princes heard his wordes, the King sought to slay him. But when Vriiah heard it, he was afraide and fled, and went into Egypt.

22 Then Iehoiakim the King sent men into Egypt, euen Elnathan the sonne of Achbor, and certaine with him into Egypt.

23 And they fet Vriiah out of Egypt, and brought him vnto Iehoiakim the King, who slew him with the sword, and cast his dead bodie into the graues of the children of the people.

24 But the hande of Ahikam the sonne of Shaphan was with Ieremiah that they shoulde not giue him into the hande of the people to put him to death.

Jeremiah 27

1 In the beginning of the reigne of Iehoiakim the sonne of Iosiah King of Iudah came this worde vnto Ieremiah from the Lord, saying,

2 Thus saith the Lord to me, Make thee bonds, and yokes, and put them vpon thy necke,

3 And send them to the King of Edom, and to the King of Moab, and to the King of the Ammonites, and to the King of Tyrus, and to the king of Zidon, by the hande of the messengers which come to Ierusale vnto Zedekiah ye king of Iudah,

4 And commande them to saye vnto their masters, Thus saith the Lord of hostes the God of Israel, Thus shall ye say vnto your masters,

5 I haue made the earth, the man, and the beast that are vpon the groud, by my great power, and by my outstreched arme, and haue giuen it vnto whom it pleased me.

6 But nowe I haue giuen all these landes into the hand of Nebuchad-nezzar the King of Babel my seruant, and the beastes of the fielde haue I also giuen him to serue him.

7 And all nations shall serue him, and his sonne, and his sonnes sonne vntill the very time of his lande come also: then many nations and great Kinges shall serue themselues of him.

8 And the nation and kingdome which will not serue the same Nebuchad-nezzar king of Babel, and that will not put their necke vnder the yoke of the King of Babel, the same nation will I visite, saith the Lord, with the swerde, and with the famine, and with the pestilence, vntill I haue wholy giuen them into his hands.

9 Therefore heare not your prophets nor your southsayers, nor your dreamers, nor your inchanters, nor your sorcerers, which say vnto you thus, Ye shall not serue the King of Babel.

10 For they prophecie a lie vnto you to cause you to goe farre from your lande, and that I should cast you out, and you should perish.

11 But the nation that put their neckes vnder the yoke of the King of Babel, and serue him, those wil I let remaine stil in their owne land, saith the Lord, and they shall occupie it, and dwel therein.

12 I spake also to Zedekiah king of Iudah according to all these wordes, saying, Put your neckes vnder the yoke of the King of Babel, and serue him and his people, that ye may liue.

13 Why will ye dye, thou, and thy people by the swerde, by the famine, and by the pestilence, as the Lord hath spoken

against the nation, that will not serue the King of Babel?

14 Therefore heare not the words of the prophets, that speake vnto you, saying, Ye shall not serue the King of Babel: for they prophecie a lie vnto you.

15 For I haue not sent them, saith the Lord, yet they prophecie a lie in my name, that I might cast you out, and that ye might perish, both you, and the prophets that prophecie vnto you.

16 Also I spake to the Priests, and to all this people, saying, Thus saith the Lord, Heare not the wordes of your prophets that prophecie vnto you, saying, Behold, the vessels of the house of the Lord shall nowe shortly be brought againe from Babel, for they prophecie a lie vnto you.

17 Heare them not, but serue the King of Babel, that ye may liue: wherefore shoulde this citie be desolate?

18 But if they be Prophets, and if the word of the Lord be with them, let them intreate the Lord of hostes, that the vessels, which are left in the House of the Lord, and in the house of the King of Iudah, and at Ierusalem, go not to Babel.

19 For thus saith the Lord of hostes, concerning the pillars, and concerning the sea, and concerning the bases, and concerning the residue of the vessels that remaine in this citie,

20 Which Nebuchad-nezzar King of Babel tooke not, when he caryed away captiue Ieconiah the sonne of Iehoiakim King of Iudah from Ierusalem to Babel, with all the nobles of Iudah and Ierusalem.

21 For thus saith the Lord of hostes the God of Israel, concerning the vessels that remaine in the House of the Lord, and in the house of the King of Iudah, and at Ierusalem,

22 They shall be brought to Babel, and there they shalbe vntil the day that I visite them, saith the Lord: then will I bring them vp, and restore them vnto this place.

Jeremiah 28

1 And that same yeere in the beginning of the reigne of Zedekiah King of Iudah in the fourth yeere, and in the fifth moneth Hananiah the sonne of Azur the prophet, which was of Gibeon, spake to mee in the House of the Lord in the presence of the Priestes, and of all the people, and said,

2 Thus speaketh the Lord of hostes, the God of Israel, saying, I haue broken the yoke of the King of Babel.

3 Within two yeeres space I will bring into this place all the vessels of the Lords House, that Nebuchad-nezzar King of Babel tooke away from this place, and caried them into Babel.

4 And I will bring againe to this place Ieconiah the sonne of Iehoiakim King of Iudah, with all them that were caried away captiue of Iudah, and went into Babel, saith the Lord: for I will breake the yoke of the King of Babel.

5 Then the Prophet Ieremiah saide vnto the Prophet Hananiah in the presence of ye Priests, and in the presence of all the people that stoode in the House of the Lord.

6 Euen the Prophet Ieremiah sayde, So bee it: the Lord so doe, the Lord confirme thy words which thou hast prophecied to restore the vessels of the Lordes House, and al that is caried captiue, from Babel, into this place.

7 But heare thou now this worde that I will speake in thine eares and in the eares of all the people.

8 The Prophets that haue beene before mee and before thee in time past, prophecied against many countreyes, and against great kingdomes, of warre, and of plagues, and of pestilence.

9 And the Prophet which prophecieth of peace, when the word of the Prophet shall come to passe, then shall the Prophet be knowen that the Lord hath truely sent him.

10 Then Hananiah the Prophet tooke the yoke from the Prophet Ieremiahs necke, and brake it.

11 And Hananiah spake in the presence of all the people, saying, Thus saith the Lord, Euen so will I breake the yoke of Nebuchad-nezzar King of Babel, from the necke of al nations within the space of two yeres: and the Prophet Ieremiah went his way.

12 Then the word of the Lord came vnto Ieremiah the Prophet, (after that Hananiah the Prophet had broken the yoke from the necke of the Prophet Ieremiah) saying,

13 Go, and tell Hananiah, saying, Thus sayth the Lord, Thou hast broken the yokes of wood, but thou shalt make for them yokes of yron.

14 For thus saith the Lord of hostes the God of Israel, I haue put a yoke of yron vpon the necke of all these nations, that they may serue Nebuchad-nezzar King of Babel: for they shall serue him, and I haue giuen him the beasts of the fielde also.

15 Then sayd the Prophet Ieremiah vnto the Prophet Hananiah, Heare nowe Hananiah, the Lord hath not sent thee, but thou makest this people to trust in a lye.

16 Therefore thus saith the Lord, Beholde, I will cast thee from of the earth: this yeere thou shalt die, because thou hast spoken rebelliously against the Lord.

17 So Hananiah the Prophet died the same yeere in the seuenth moneth.

Jeremiah 29

1 Now these are the wordes of the booke that Ieremiah the Prophet sent from Ierusalem vnto the residue of the Elders which were caryed away captiues, and to the Priestes, and to the Prophets, and to all the people whome Nebuchad-nezzar had caried away captiue from Ierusalem to Babel:

2 (After that Ieconiah the King, and the Queene, and the eunuches, the princes of Iudah, and of Ierusalem, and the workemen, and cunning men were departed from Ierusalem)

3 By the hand of Elasah the sonne of Shaphan and Gemariah the sonne of Hilkiah, (whom Zedekiah King of Iudah sent vnto Babel to Nebuchad-nezzar King of Babel) saying,

4 Thus hath the Lord of hostes the God of Israel spoken vnto all that are caryed away captiues, whome I haue caused to be caryed away captiues from Ierusalem vnto Babel:

5 Buylde you houses to dwell in, and plant you gardens, and eate the fruites of them.

6 Take you wiues, and beget sonnes and daughters, and take wiues for your sonnes, and giue your daughters to husbands, that they may beare sonnes and daughters, that ye may bee increased there, and not diminished.

7 And seeke the prosperitie of the citie, whither I haue caused you to be caried away captiues, and pray vnto the Lord for it: for in the peace thereof shall you haue peace.

8 For thus saith the Lord of hostes the God of Israel, Let not your prophets, and your southsayers that bee among you, deceiue you, neither giue eare to your dreames, which you dreame.

9 For they prophecie you a lie in my Name: I haue not sent them, saith the Lord.

10 But thus saith the Lord, That after seuentie yeeres be accomplished at Babel, I will visite you, and performe my good promise toward you, and cause you to returne to this place.

11 For I knowe the thoughtes, that I haue thought towards you, saith the Lord, euen the thoughtes of peace, and not of trouble, to giue you an ende, and your hope.

12 Then shall you crie vnto mee, and ye shall go and pray vnto me, and I will heare you,

13 And ye shall seeke mee and finde mee, because ye shall seeke mee with all your heart.

14 And I wil be found of you, saith the Lord, and I will turne away your captiuitie, and I will gather you from all the nations, and from all the places, whither I haue cast you, saith the Lord, and will bring you againe vnto the place, whence I caused you to be caryed away captiue.

15 Because ye haue sayd, The Lord hath raised vs vp Prophets in Babel,

16 Therefore thus saith the Lord of the King, that sitteth vpon the throne of Dauid, and of all the people, that dwell in this citie, your brethren that are not gone forth with you into captiuitie:

17 Euen thus sayth the Lord of hostes, Beholde, I will sende vpon them the swoorde, the famine, and the pestilence, and will make them like vile figges, that cannot bee eaten, they are so naughtie.

18 And I will persecute them with the sword, with the famine, and with the pestilence: and I will make them a terror to all kingdomes of the earth, and a curse, and astonishment and an hissing,

and a reproche among all the nations whither I haue cast them,

19 Because they haue not hearde my words, saith the Lord, which I sent vnto them by my seruantes the Prophetes, rising vp early, and sending them, but yee woulde not heare, saith the Lord.

20 Heare ye therefore the word of the Lord all ye of the captiuitie, whome I haue sent from Ierusalem to Babel.

21 Thus saith the Lord of hostes, the God of Israel, of Ahab the sonne of Kolaiah, and of Zedekiah the sonne of Maaseiah, which prophecie lyes vnto you in my Name, Beholde, I will deliuer them into the hande of Nebuchad-nezzar King of Babel, and he shall slay them before your eyes.

22 And al they of the captiuitie of Iudah, that are in Babel, shall take vp this curse against them, and say, The Lord make thee like Zedekiah and like Ahab, whome the King of Babel burnt in the fire,

23 Because they haue committed vilenie in Israel, and haue committed adulterie with their neighbours wiues, and haue spoken lying words in my Name, which I haue not commanded them, euen I knowe it, and testifie it, saith the Lord.

24 Thou shalt also speake to Shemaiah the Nehelamite, saying,

25 Thus speaketh the Lord of hostes, the God of Israel, saying, Because thou hast sent letters in thy Name vnto all the people, that are at Ierusalem, and to Zephaniah the sonne of Maaseiah the Priest, and to all the Priests, saying,

26 The Lord hath made thee Priest for Iehoiada the Priest, that yee should bee officers in the House of the Lord, for euery man that raueth and maketh himselfe a Prophet, to put him in prison and in the stockes.

27 Nowe therefore why hast not thou reproued Ieremiah of Anathoth, which prophecieth vnto you?

28 For, for this cause hee sent vnto vs in Babel, saying, This captiuitie is long: buyld houses to dwell in, and plant gardens, and eate the fruites of them.

29 And Zephaniah the Priest red this letter in the eares of Ieremiah the Prophet.

30 Then came the worde of the Lord vnto Ieremiah, saying,

31 Send to all them of the captiuitie, saying, Thus saith the Lord of Shemaiah the Nehelamite, Because that Shemaiah hath prophecied vnto you, and I sent him not, and hee caused you to trust in a lye,

32 Therefore thus saieth the Lord, Behold, I wil visite Shemaiah the Nehelamite, and his seede: hee shall not haue a man to dwell among this people, neither shall he beholde the good, that I will doe for my people, sayth the Lord, because he hath spoken rebelliously against the Lord.

Jeremiah 30

1 The worde, that came to Ieremiah from the Lord, saying,

2 Thus speaketh the Lord God of Israel, saying, Write thee all the wordes, that I haue spoken vnto thee in a booke.

3 For loe, the dayes come, saith the Lord, that I wil bring againe the captiuitie of my people Israel and Iudah, saith the Lord: for I will restore them vnto the lande, that I gaue to their fathers, and they shall possesse it.

4 Againe, these are the wordes that the Lord spake concerning Israel, and concerning Iudah.

5 For thus saith the Lord, wee haue heard a terrible voyce, of feare and not of peace.

6 Demand now and beholde, if man trauayle with childe? wherefore doe I beholde euery man with his hands on his loynes as a woman in trauaile, and all faces are turned into a palenesse?

7 Alas, for this day is great: none hath bene like it: it is euen the time of Iaakobs trouble, yet shall he be deliuered from it.

8 For in that day, sayth the Lord of hostes, I will breake his yoke from off thy necke, and breake thy bondes, and strangers shall no more serue themselues of him.

9 But they shall serue the Lord their God, and Dauid their King, whom I will raise vp vnto them.

10 Therefore feare not, O my seruant Iaakob, saith the Lord, neither be afrayde, O Israel: for loe, I will deliuer thee from a farre countrey, and thy seede from the lande of their captiuitie, and Iaakob shall turne againe, and shalbe in rest and prosperitie and none shall make him afraide.

11 For I am with thee, sayth the Lord, to saue thee: though I vtterly destroy all the nations where I haue scattered thee, yet will I not vtterly destroy thee, but I will correct thee by iudgement, and not vtterly cut thee off.

12 For thus saith the Lord, Thy bruising is incurable, and thy wound is dolorous.

13 There is none to iudge thy cause, or to lay a plaister: there are no medicines, nor help for thee.

14 All thy louers haue forgotten thee: they seeke thee not: for I haue striken thee with the wound of an enemie, and with a sharpe chastisement for ye multitude of thine iniquities, because thy sinnes were increased.

15 Why cryest thou for thine affliction? thy sorowe is incurable, for the multitude of thine iniquities: because thy sinnes were increased, I haue done these things vnto thee.

16 Therefore all they that deuoure thee, shall be deuoured, and all thine enemies euery one shall goe into captiuitie: and they that spoyle thee, shalbe spoyled, and all they that robbe thee, wil I giue to be robbed.

17 For I will restore health vnto thee, and I will heale thee of thy woundes, saith the Lord, because they called thee, The cast away, saying, This is Zion, whom no man seeketh after.

18 Thus saith the Lord, Beholde, I will bring againe the captiuitie of Iaakobs tentes, and haue compassion on his dwelling places: and the citie shalbe builded vpon her owne heape, and the palace shall remaine after the maner thereof.

19 And out of them shall proceede thankesgiuing, and the voyce of them that are ioyous, and I will multiplie them, and they shall not bee fewe: I will also glorifie them, and they shall not be diminished.

20 Their children also shall be as afore time, and their congregation shall be established before me: and I will visite all that vexe them.

21 And their noble ruler shall be of themselues, and their gouernour shall proceede from the middes of them, and I will cause him to draw neere, and approche vnto me: for who is this that directeth his heart to come vnto mee, saith the Lord?

22 And ye shall be my people, and I will bee your God.

23 Beholde, the tempest of the Lord goeth foorth with wrath: the whirlewinde that hangeth ouer, shall light vpon the head of the wicked.

24 The fierce wrath of the Lord shall not returne, vntill he haue done, and vntill he haue performed the intents of his heart: in the latter dayes ye shall vnderstand it.

Jeremiah 31

1 At the same time, saith the Lord, will I be the God of all the families of Israel, and they shall be my people.

2 Thus saith the Lord, The people which escaped the sworde, founde grace in the wildernes: he walked before Israel to cause him to rest.

3 The Lord hath appeared vnto me of old, say they: Yea, I haue loued thee with an euerlasting loue, therefore with mercie I haue drawen thee.

4 Againe I will builde thee, and thou shalt be builded, O virgine Israel: thou shalt stil be adorned with thy timbrels, and shalt goe foorth in the dance of them that be ioyfull.

5 Thou shalt yet plant vines vpon the mountaines of Samaria, and the planters that plant them, shall make them common.

6 For the dayes shall come that the watchmen vpon the mount of Ephraim shall cry, Arise, and let vs go vp vnto Zion to the Lord our God.

7 For thus saith the Lord, Reioyce with gladnesse for Iaakob, and shoute for ioye among the chiefe of the Gentiles: publish praise, and say, O Lord, saue thy people, the remnant of Israel.

8 Beholde, I will bring them from the North countrey, and gather them from the coastes of the world, with the blinde and the lame among them, with the woman with childe, and her that is deliuered also: a great companie shall returne hither.

9 They shall come weeping, and with mercie will I bring them againe: I will lead them by the riuers of water in a straight way, wherein they shall not

stumble: for I am a father to Israel, and Ephraim is my first borne.

10 Heare the worde of the Lord, O ye Gentiles, and declare in the yles afarre off, and say, Hee that scattered Israel, wil gather him and wil keepe him, as a shepheard doeth his flocke.

11 For the Lord hath redeemed Iaakob, and ransomed him from the hande of him, that was stronger then he.

12 Therefore they shall come, and reioyce in the height of Zion, and shall runne to the bountifulnes of the Lord, euen for the wheat and for the wine, and for the oyle, and for the increase of sheepe, and bullocks: and their soule shalbe as a watered garden, and they shall haue no more sorow.

13 Then shall ye virgine reioyce in the dance, and the yong men and the old men together: for I wil turne their mourning into ioy, and wil comfort them, and giue them ioy for their sorowes.

14 And I wil replenish the soule of the Priests with fatnesse, and my people shalbe satisfied with my goodnesse, saith the Lord.

15 Thus saith the Lord, A voyce was heard on hie, a mourning and bitter weeping. Rahel weeping for her children, refused to be comforted for her children, because they were not.

16 Thus saith the Lord, Refraine thy voyce from weeping, and thine eyes from teares: for thy worke shalbe rewarded, saith the Lord, and they shall come againe from the land of the enemie:

17 And there is hope in thine ende, saith the Lord, that thy children shall come againe to their owne borders.

18 I haue heard Ephraim lamenting thus, Thou hast corrected me, and I was chastised as an vntamed calfe: conuert thou me, and I shalbe conuerted: for thou art the Lord my God.

19 Surely after that I conuerted, I repented: and after that I was instructed, I smote vpon my thigh: I was ashamed, yea, euen confounded, because I did beare the reproch of my youth.

20 Is Ephraim my deare sonne or pleasant childe? yet since I spake vnto him, I still remembred him: therefore my bowels are troubled for him: I wil surely haue compassion vpon him, saith the Lord.

21 Set thee vp signes: make thee heapes: set thine heart towarde the path and way, that thou hast walked: turne againe, O virgine of Israel: turne againe to these thy cities.

22 How long wilt thou goe astray, O thou rebellious daughter? for the Lord hath created a newe thing in the earth: A WOMAN shall compasse a man.

23 Thus saith the Lord of hostes, the God of Israel, Yet shall they say this thing in the land of Iudah, and in the cities thereof, when I shall bring againe their captiuitie, The Lord blesse thee, O habitation of iustice and holy mountaine.

24 And Iudah shall dwell in it, and all the cities thereof together, the husbandmen and they that goe foorth with the flocke.

25 For I haue saciate the wearie soule, and I haue replenished euery sorowfull soule.

26 Therefore I awaked and behelde, and my sleepe was sweete vnto me.

27 Beholde, the dayes come, saith the Lord, that I will sowe the house of Israel, and the house of Iudah with the seede of man and with the seede of beast.

28 And like as I haue watched vpon them, to plucke vp and to roote out, and to throw downe, and to destroy, and to plague them, so wil I watch ouer them, to build and to plant them, saith ye Lord.

29 In those dayes shall they say no more, The fathers haue eaten a sowre grape, and the childrens teeth are set on edge.

30 But euery one shall die for his owne iniquitie: euery man that eateth the sowre grape, his teeth shalbe set on edge.

31 Beholde, the dayes come, saith the Lord, that I will make a new couenant with the house of Israel, and with the house of Iudah,

32 Not according to ye couenant that I made with their fathers, when I tooke them by the hand to bring them out of the land of Egypt, the which my couenant they brake, although I was an husband vnto them, saith the Lord.

33 But this shall be the couenant that I will make with the house of Israel, After those dayes, saith the Lord, I will put my Lawe in their inward partes, and write it in their hearts, and wil be their God, and they shalbe my people.

34 And they shall teach no more euery man his neighbour and euery man his brother, saying, Know the Lord: for they shall all know me from the least of them vnto the greatest of them, saith the Lord: for I wil forgiue their iniquitie, and will remember their sinnes no more.

35 Thus saith the Lord, which giueth the sunne for a light to the day, and the courses of the moone and of the starres for a light to the night, which breaketh the sea, when the waues thereof roare: his Name is the Lord of hostes.

36 If these ordinances depart out of my sight, saith the Lord, then shall the seede of Israel cease from being a nation before me, for euer.

37 Thus saith the Lord, If the heauens can be measured, or the fundations of the earth be searched out beneath, then wil I cast off all the seed of Israel, for all that they haue done, saith the Lord.

38 Behold, the dayes come, saith the Lord, that the citie shalbe built to the Lord from the tower of Hananeel, vnto the gate of the corner.

39 And the line of the measure shall go foorth in his presence vpon the hil Gareb, and shall compasse about to Goath.

40 And the whole valley of the dead bodies, and of the ashes, and all the fields vnto the brooke of Kidron, and vnto the corner of the horsegate toward the East, shalbe holy vnto the Lord, neither shall it be plucked vp nor destroyed any more for euer.

Jeremiah 32

1 The worde that came vnto Ieremiah from the Lord, in the tenth yere of Zedekiah king of Iudah, which was the eightenth yeere of Nebuchad-nezzar.

2 For then the King of Babels hoste besieged Ierusalem: And Ieremiah the Prophet was shutte vp in the court of the prison, which was in the King of Iudahs house.

3 For Zedekiah King of Iudah had shut him vp, saying, Wherefore doest thou prophesie, and say, Thus saith the Lord, Beholde, I will giue this citie into the handes of the King of Babel, and he shall take it?

4 And Zedekiah the King of Iudah shall not escape out of the hande of the Caldeans, but shall surely be deliuered into the handes of the King of Babel, and shall speake with him mouth to mouth, and his eyes shall beholde his face,

5 And he shall lead Zedekiah to Babel, and there shall he be, vntil I visit him, saith ye Lord: though ye fight with the Caldeans, ye shall not prosper.

6 And Ieremiah said, The word of the Lord came vnto me, saying,

7 Beholde, Hanameel, the sonne of Shallum thine vncle, shall come vnto thee and say, Bye vnto thee my fielde, that is in Anathoth: for the title by kindred appertaineth vnto thee to bye it.

8 So Hanameel, mine vncles sonne, came to mee in the court of the prison, according to the word of the Lord, and said vnto me, Bye my field, I pray thee, that is in Anathoth, which is in the countrey of Beniamin: for the right of the possession is thine, and the purchase belongeth vnto thee: bye it for thee. Then I knewe that this was the worde of the Lord.

9 And I bought the field of Hanameel, mine vncles sonne, that was in Anathoth, and weighed him the siluer, euen seuen shekels, and tenne pieces of siluer.

10 And I writ it in the booke and signed it, and tooke witnesses, and weighed him the siluer in the balances.

11 So I tooke the booke of the possession, being sealed according to the Lawe, and custome, with the booke that was open,

12 And I gaue the booke of the possession vnto Baruch the sonne of Neriah, the sonne of Maaseiah, in the sight of Hanameel mine vncles sonne, and in the presence of the witnesses, written in the booke of the possession, before al the Iewes that sate in the court of the prison.

13 And I charged Baruch before them, saying,

14 Thus saith the Lord of hostes, God of Israel, Take the writings, euen this booke of the possession, both that is sealed, and this booke that is open, and put them in an earthen vessell, that they may continue a long time.

15 For the Lord of hostes, the God of Israel saith thus, Houses and fieldes, and vineyardes shall be possessed againe in this land.

16 Now when I had deliuered the booke of the possession vnto Baruch, the sonne of Neriah, I prayed vnto the Lord, saying,

17 Ah Lord God, beholde, thou hast made the heauen and the earth by thy great power, and by thy stretched out arme, and there is nothing hard vnto thee.

18 Thou shewest mercie vnto thousands, and recompensest the iniquitie of the fathers into the bosome of their children after them: O God the great and mightie, whose Name is ye Lord of hostes,

19 Great in counsell, and mightie in worke, (for thine eyes are open vpon all the wayes of ye sonnes of men, to giue to euery one according to his wayes, and according to the fruite of his workes)

20 Which hast set signes and wonders in the land of Egypt vnto this day, and in Israel, and among all men, and hast made thee a Name, as appeareth this day,

21 And hast brought thy people Israel out of the land of Egypt with signes, and with wonders, and with a strong hand, with a stretched out arme, and with great terrour,

22 And hast giuen them this land, which thou diddest sweare to their fathers to giue them, euen a land, that floweth with milke and hony,

23 And they came in, and possessed it, but they obeyed not thy voyce, neither walked in thy Law: all that thou commaundedst them to doe, they haue not done: therefore thou hast caused this whole plague to come vpon them.

24 Beholde, the mounts, they are come into the citie to take it, and the citie is giuen into the hande of the Caldeans, that fight against it by meanes of the sword, and of the famine, and of the pestilence, and what thou hast spoken, is come to passe, and beholde, thou seest it.

25 And thou hast sayd vnto me, O Lord God, Bye vnto thee the fielde for siluer, and take witnesses: for the citie shall be giuen into the hand of the Caldeans.

26 Then came the worde of the Lord vnto Ieremiah, saying,

27 Beholde, I am the LORD GOD of all flesh: is there any thing too hard for me?

28 Therefore thus saith the Lord, Beholde, I wil giue this citie into the hand of the Caldeans, and into the hand of Nebuchad-nezzar, King of Babel, and he shall take it.

29 And the Caldeans shall come and fight against this citie, and set fire on this citie and burne it, with the houses, vpon whose rouses they haue offred incense vnto Baal, and powred drinke offrings vnto other gods, to prouoke me vnto anger.

30 For the children of Israel, and the children of Iudah haue surely done euill before me from their youth: for the children of Israel haue surely prouoked

me to anger with the workes of their hands, saith the Lord.

31 Therefore this citie hath bene vnto me as a prouocation of mine anger, and of my wrath, from the day, that they built it, euen vnto this day, that I should remoue it out of my sight,

32 Because of all the euill of the children of Israel, and of the children of Iudah, which they haue done to prouoke mee to anger, euen they, their Kings, their Princes, their Priests, and their Prophets, and the men of Iudah, and the inhabitants of Ierusalem.

33 And they haue turned vnto me the backe and not the face: though I taught them rising vp earely, and instructing them, yet they were not obedient to receiue doctrine,

34 But they set their abominations in ye house (whereupon my Name was called) to defile it,

35 And they built the hie places of Baal, which are in the valley of Ben-hinnom, to cause their sonnes and their daughters to passe through the fire vnto Molech, which I commanded them not, neither came it into my minde, that they should doe such abomination, to cause Iudah to sinne.

36 And nowe therefore, thus hath the Lord God of Israel spoken, concerning this citie, whereof ye say, It shalbe deliuered into the hand of the King of Babel by the sword, and by the famine, and by the pestilence,

37 Beholde, I will gather them out of all countreys, wherein I haue scattered them in mine anger, and in my wrath, and in great indignation, and I wil bring them againe vnto this place, and I will cause them to dwell safely.

38 And they shall be my people, and I will be their God.

39 And I wil giue them one heart and one way that they may feare me for euer for ye wealth of them, and of their children after them.

40 And I wil make an euerlasting couenant with them, that I wil neuer turne away from them to doe them good, but I wil put my feare in their hearts, that they shall not depart from me.

41 Yea, I wil delite in them to do them good, and I wil plant them in this land assuredly with my whole heart, and with all my soule.

42 For thus sayth the Lord, Like as I haue brought all this great plague vpon this people, so wil I bring vpon them all the good that I haue promised them.

43 And the fields shalbe possessed in this land, whereof ye say, It is desolate without man or beast, and shalbe giuen into the hand of the Caldeans.

44 Men shall buy fields for siluer, and make writings and seale them, and take witnesses in the land of Beniamin, and round about Ierusalem, and in the cities of Iudah, and in the cities of the mountaines, and in the cities of the plaine, and in the cities of the South: for I wil cause their captiuitie to returne, saith the Lord.

Jeremiah 33

1 Moreover, the worde of the Lord came vnto Ieremiah the second time (while he was yet shut vp in the court of prison) saying,

2 Thus sayth the Lord, the maker thereof, the Lord that formed it, and established it, the Lord is his Name.

3 Call vnto me, and I will answere thee, and shewe thee great and mightie things, which thou knowest not.

4 For thus saith the Lord God of Israel, concerning the houses of this citie, and concerning the houses of the Kings of Iudah, which are destroyed by the mounts, and by the sword,

5 They come to fight with the Caldeans, but it is to fill themselues with the dead bodies of men, whome I haue slaine in mine anger and in my wrath: for I haue hid my face from this citie, because of all their wickednes.

6 Behold, I will giue it health and amendment: for I wil cure them, and will reueile vnto them the abundance of peace, and trueth.

7 And I wil cause the captiuitie of Iudah and the captiuitie of Israel to returne, and will build them as at the first.

8 And I wil clense them from all their iniquitie, whereby they haue sinned against me: yea, I wil pardon all their iniquities, whereby they haue sinned against me, and whereby they haue rebelled against me.

9 And it shalbe to me a name, a ioy, a praise, and an honour before all the nations of the earth, which shall heare all ye good that I doe vnto them: and they shall feare and tremble for all the goodnes, and for all the wealth, that I shew vnto this citie.

10 Thus sayth the Lord, Againe there shalbe heard in this place (which ye say shalbe desolate, without man, and without beast, euen in the cities of Iudah, and in the streetes of Ierusalem, that are desolate without man, and without inhabitant, and without beast)

11 The voyce of ioy and the voyce of gladnes, the voyce of the bridegrome, and the voyce of the bride, the voyce of them that shall say, Prayse the Lord of hostes, because the Lord is good: for his mercy endureth for euer, and of them that offer the sacrifice of prayse in the House of the Lord, for I will cause to returne the captiuitie of the land, as at the first, sayth the Lord.

12 Thus sayth the Lord of hostes, Againe in this place, which is desolate, without man, and without beast, and in all the cities thereof there shall be dwelling for shepheards to rest their flockes.

13 In the cities of the mountaines, in the cities in the plaine, and in the cities of the South, and in the land of Beniamin, and about Ierusalem, and in the cities of Iudah shall the sheepe passe againe, vnder the hand of him that telleth them, sayth the Lord.

14 Beholde, the dayes come, sayth the Lord, that I wil performe that good thing,

which I haue promised vnto the house of Israel, and to the house of Iudah.

15 In those dayes and at that time, wil I cause the branch of righteousnesse to growe vp vnto Dauid, and he shall execute iudgement, and righteousnes in the land.

16 In those dayes shall Iudah be saued, and Ierusalem shall dwell safely, and hee that shall call her, is the Lord our righteousnesse.

17 For thus sayth the Lord, Dauid shall neuer want a man to sit vpon the throne of the house of Israel.

18 Neither shall the Priests and Leuites want a man before me to offer burnt offerings, and to offer meat offerings, and to doe sacrifice continually.

19 And the worde of the Lord came vnto Ieremiah, saying,

20 Thus sayth the Lord, If you can breake my couenant of the day, and my couenant of the night, that there should not be day, and night in their season,

21 Then may my couenant be broken with Dauid my seruant, that he should not haue a sonne to reigne vpon his throne, and with the Leuites, and Priests my ministers.

22 As the army of heauen can not be nombred, neither the sand of the sea measured: so wil I multiplie the seede of Dauid my seruant, and the Leuites, that minister vnto me.

23 Moreouer, the worde of the Lord came to Ieremiah, saying,

24 Considerest thou not what this people haue spoken, saying, The two families, which the Lord hath chosen, hee hath euen cast them off? thus they haue despised my people, that they should be no more a nation before them.

25 Thus sayth the Lord, If my couenant be not with day and night, and if I haue not appointed the order of heauen and earth,

26 Then will I cast away the seede of Iaakob and Dauid my seruant, and not take of his seede to be rulers ouer the seede of Abraham, Izhak, and Iaakob: for I wil cause their captiuitie to returne, and haue compassion on them.

Jeremiah 34

1 The worde which came vnto Ieremiah from the Lord (when Nebuchad-nezzar King of Babel, and all his hoste, and all the kingdomes of the earth, that were vnder the power of his hand, and all people fought against Ierusalem, and against all the cites thereof) saying,

2 Thus sayth the Lord God of Israel, Goe, and speake to Zedekiah King of Iudah, and tell him, Thus sayth the Lord, Beholde, I will giue this citie into the hand of the King of Babel, and he shall burne it with fire,

3 And thou shall not escape out of his hand, but shalt surely be taken, and deliuered into his hand, and thine eyes shall beholde the face of the King of Babel, and he shall speake with thee mouth to mouth, and thou shalt go to Babel.

4 Yet heare the worde of the Lord, O Zedekiah, King of Iudah: thus sayth the Lord of thee, Thou shalt not dye by the sword,

5 But thou shalt die in peace: and according to the burning for thy fathers the former Kings which were before thee, so shall they burne odours for thee, and they shall lament thee, saying, Oh lorde: for I haue pronounced the worde, sayth the Lord.

6 Then Ieremiah the Prophet spake all these words vnto Zedekiah King of Iudah in Ierusalem,

7 (When the King of Babels hoste fought against Ierusalem, and against all the cities of Iudah, that were left, euen against Lachish, and against Azekah: for these strong cities remained of the cities of Iudah)

8 This is the worde that came vnto Ieremiah from the Lord, after that the King Zedekiah had made a couenant with all the people, which were at Ierusalem, to proclaime libertie vnto them,

9 That euery man should let his seruant go free, and euery man his handmayde, which was an Ebrue or an Ebruesse, and that none should serue himselfe of them, to wit, of a Iewe his brother.

10 Now when all the princes, and all the people which had agreed to the couenant, heard that euery one should let his seruant go free, and euery one his handmaide, and that none should serue them selues of them any more, they obeyed and let them go.

11 But afterwarde they repented and caused the seruants and the handmayds, whom they had let go free, to returne, and helde them in subiection as seruants and handmayds.

12 Therefore the worde of the Lord came vnto Ieremiah from the Lord, saying,

13 Thus saith the Lord God of Israel, I made a couenant with your fathers, when I brought them out of the land of Egypt, out of the house of seruants, saying,

14 At the terme of seuen yeres let ye go, euery man his brother an Ebrewe which hath bene solde vnto thee: and when he hath serued the sixe yeres, thou shalt let him go free from thee: but your fathers obeyed me not, neither inclined their eares.

15 And ye were nowe turned, and had done right in my sight in proclayming libertie, euery man to his neighbour, and ye had made a couenant before mee in the house, whereupon my Name is called.

16 But ye repented, and polluted my Name: for ye haue caused euery man his seruant, and euery man his handmayde, whom ye had set at libertie at their pleasure, to returne, and holde them in subiection to bee vnto you as seruantes and as handmaydes.

17 Therefore thus saith the Lord, Ye haue not obeyed mee, in proclayming freedome euery man to his brother, and euery man to his neighbour: beholde, I proclaime a libertie for you, saith the Lord, to the swarde, to the pestilence, and to the famine, and I will make you a terrour to all the kingdomes of the earth.

18 And I will giue those men that haue broken my couenant, and haue not kept the wordes of the couenant, which they had made before me, when they cut the calfe in twaine, and passed betweene the partes thereof:

19 The princes of Iudah, and the princes of Ierusalem, the Eunuches, and the Priestes, and all the people of the lande, which passed betweene the partes of the calfe,

20 I wil euen giue them into the hand of their enemies, and into the handes of them that seeke their life: and their dead bodies shalbe for meate vnto the foules of the heauen, and to the beastes of the earth.

21 And Zedekiah King of Iudah, and his princes will I giue into the hand of their enemies, and into the hande of them that seeke their life, and into the hande of the King of Babels hoste, which are gone vp from you.

22 Beholde, I will commande, saith the Lord, and cause them to returne to this citie, and they shall fight against it, and take it, and burne it with fire: and I will make the cities of Iudah desolate without an inhabitant.

Jeremiah 35

1 The worde which came vnto Ieremiah from the Lord, in the dayes of Iehoiakim the sonne of Iosiah King of Iudah, saying,

2 Go vnto the house of the Rechabites, and speake vnto them, and bring them into the house of the Lord into one of the chambers, and giue them wine to drinke.

3 Then tooke I Iaazaniah, the sonne of Ieremiah the sonne of Habazziniah, and his brethren, and all his sonnes, and the whole house of the Rechabites,

4 And I brought them into the House of the Lord, into the chamber of the sonnes of Hanan, the sonne of Igdaliah a man of God, which was by the chamber of the princes, which was aboue the chamber of Maaseiah the sonne of Shallum, the keeper of the treasure.

5 And I set before the sonnes of the house of the Rechabites, pots full of wine, and cuppes, and said vnto them, Drinke wine.

6 But they said, We will drinke no wine: for Ionadab the sonne of Rechab our father commanded vs, saying, Ye shall drinke no wine, neither you nor your sonnes for euer.

7 Neither shall ye build house, nor sow seede, nor plant vineyarde, nor haue any, but all your dayes ye shall dwell in tentes, that ye may liue a long time in the land where ye be strangers.

8 Thus haue wee obeyed the voyce of Ionadab the sonne of Rechab our father, in all that he hath charged vs, and wee drinke no wine all our dayes, neither wee, our wiues, our sonnes, nor our daughters.

9 Neither builde wee houses for vs to dwell in, neither haue we vineyard, nor fielde, nor seede,

10 But we haue remained in tentes, and haue obeyed, and done according to all that Ionadab our father commanded vs.

11 But when Nebuchad-nezzar King of Babel came vp into the land, we said, Come, and let vs go to Ierusalem, from the hoste of the Caldeans, and from the host of Aram: so we dwel at Ierusalem.

12 Then came the word of the Lord vnto Ieremiah, saying,

13 Thus saith the Lord of hostes, the God of Israel, Goe, and tell the men of Iudah, and the inhabitants of Ierusalem, Will ye not receiue doctrine to obey my wordes, saith the Lord?

14 The commandement of Ionadab the sonne of Rechab that hee commanded his sonnes, that they should drinke no wine, is surely kept: for vnto this day they drinke none, but obey their fathers commandement: notwithstanding I haue spoken vnto you, rising earely, and speaking, but ye would not obey me.

15 I haue sent also vnto you all my seruants the Prophetes, rising vp earely, and sending, them, saying, Returne nowe euery man from his euill way, and amende your workes, and goe not after other gods to serue them, and ye shall dwel in the lande which I haue giuen vnto you, and to your fathers, but ye would not encline your eare, nor obey mee.

16 Surely the sonnes of Ionadab the sonne of Rechab, haue kept the commandement of their father, which he gaue them, but this people hath not obeyed me.

17 Therefore thus saith the Lord of hostes, the God of Israel, Beholde, I will bring vpon Iudah, and vpon all the inhabitants of Ierusalem, all the euill that I haue pronounced against them, because I haue spoke vnto them, but they would not heare, and I haue called vnto them, but they would not answere.

18 And Ieremiah said to the house of the Rechabites, Thus saith the Lord of hostes the God of Israel, Because ye haue obeyed the commandement of Ionadab your father, and kept all his precepts, and done according vnto all that hee hath commanded you,

19 Therefore thus saith the Lord of hostes, the God of Israel, Ionadab the sonne of Rechab shall not want a man, to stand before me for euer.

Jeremiah 36

1 And in the fourth yeere of Iehoiakim the sonne of Iosiah King of Iudah, came this word vnto Ieremiah from the Lord, saying,

2 Take thee a roule or booke, and write therein all the wordes that I haue spoken to thee against Israel, and against Iudah, and against all the nations, from the day that I spake vnto thee, euen from the dayes of Iosiah vnto this day.

3 It may bee that the House of Iudah will heare of all the euill, which I determined to doe vnto them that they may returne euery man from his euil way, that I may forgiue their iniquitie and their sinnes.

4 Then Ieremiah called Baruch the sonne of Neriah, and Baruch wrote at the mouth of Ieremiah all the wordes of the Lord, which hee had spoken vnto him, vpon a roule or booke.

5 And Ieremiah commanded Baruch, saying, I am shut vp, and can not go into the House of the Lord.

6 Therefore goe thou, and reade the roule wherein thou hast written at my mouth the words of the Lord in the audience of the people in the Lordes House vpon the fasting day: also thou shalt reade them in the hearing of all Iudah, that come out of their cities.

7 It may be that they will pray before the Lord, and euery one returne from his euill way, for great is the anger and the wrath, that the Lord hath declared against this people.

8 So Baruch the sonne of Neriah did according vnto all, that Ieremiah the Prophet commanded him, reading in the booke the wordes of the Lord in the Lords House.

9 And in the fift yeere of Iehoiakim the sonne of Iosiah King of Iudah, in the ninth moneth, they proclaimed a fast before the Lord to all the people in Ierusalem, and to all the people that came from the cities of Iudah vnto Ierusalem.

10 Then read Baruch in the booke the wordes of Ieremiah in the house of the Lord, in the chamber of Gemariah the sonne of Shaphan the secretarie, in the hier court at the entrie of the new gate of the Lordes house, in the hearing of all the people.

11 When Michaiah the sonne of Gemariah, the sonne of Shaphan had heard out of the booke all the wordes of the Lord,

12 Then hee went downe to the Kings house into the Chancellours chamber, and loe, all the princes sate there, euen Elishama the Chancellour, and Delaiah the sonne of Shemaiah, and Elnathan the sonne of Achbor, and Gemariah the sonne of Shaphan, and Zedekiah the sonne of Hananiah, and all the princes.

13 Then Michaiah declared vnto them all the wordes that he had heard when Baruch read in the booke in the audience of the people.

14 Therefore all the princes sent Iehudi the sonne of Nethaniah, the sonne of Shelemiah, the sonne of Chushi, vnto Baruch, saying, Take in thine hande the roule, wherein thou hast read in the audience of the people, and come. So Baruch the sonne of Neriah, tooke the roule in his hand, and came vnto them.

15 And they saide vnto him, Sit downe now, and reade it, that we may heare. So Baruch read it in their audience.

16 Now when they had heard all the wordes, they were afraid both one and other, and said vnto Baruch, We will certifie the King of all these wordes.

17 And they examined Baruch, saying, Tell vs nowe, howe diddest thou write all these wordes at his mouth?

18 Then Baruch answered them, He pronounced all these wordes vnto me with his mouth, and I wrote them with ynke in the booke.

19 Then saide the princes vnto Baruch, Goe, hide thee, thou and Ieremiah, and let no man knowe where ye be.

20 And they went in to the King to the court, but they layde vp the roule in the chamber of Elishama the Chancellour and tolde the King all the wordes, that he might heare.

21 So the King sent Iehudi to fet the roule, and he tooke it out of Elishama the Chancellours chamber, and Iehudi read it in the audience of the King, and in the audience of all the princes, which stoode beside the King.

22 Nowe the King sate in the winter House, in the ninth moneth, and there was a fire burning before him.

23 And when Iehudi had read three, or foure sides, hee cut it with the penknife and cast it into the fire, that was on the hearth vntil all the roule was consumed in the fire, that was on the hearth.

24 Yet they were not afraide, nor rent their garmets, neither the King, nor any of his seruants, that heard all these wordes.

25 Neuerthelesse, Elnathan, and Delaiah, and Gemariah had besought the King, that he would not burne ye roule: but he would not heare them.

26 But the King commanded Ierahmeel the sonne of Hammelech, and Seraiah the sonne of Azriel, and Shelemiah the sonne of Abdiel, to take Baruch the scribe, and Ieremiah the Prophet, but the Lord hid them.

27 Then the word of the Lord came to Ieremiah (after that the King had burnt the roule and the words which Baruch wrote at the mouth of Ieremiah) saying,

28 Take thee againe another roule and write in it all ye former words that were in the first roule which Iehoiakim the King of Iudah hath burnt,

29 And thou shalt say to Iehoiakim King of Iudah, Thus saith the Lord, Thou hast burnt this roule, saying, Why hast thou written therein, saying, that the King of Babel shall certainly come and destroye this land, and shall take thence both man and beast?

30 Therefore thus saith the Lord of Iehoiakim King of Iudah, Hee shall haue none to sit vpon the throne of Dauid, and his dead body shall be cast out in the day to the heate, and in the night to the frost.

31 And I will visite him and his seede, and his seruants for their iniquitie, and I will bring vpon them, and vpon the inhabitants of Ierusalem, and vpon the men of Iudah all the euil that I haue pronounced against them: but they would not heare.

32 Then tooke Ieremiah another roule, and gaue it Baruch the scribe the sonne of Neriah, which wrote therein at the mouth of Ieremiah all the wordes of the booke which Iehoiakim King of Iudah

had burnt in the fire, and there were added besides them many like wordes.

Jeremiah 37

1 And King Zedekiah the sonne of Iosiah reigned for Coniah the sonne of Iehoiakim, whome Nebuchad-nezzar King of Babel made King in the land of Iudah.

2 But neither he, nor his seruants, nor the people of the land would obey the wordes of the Lord, which he spake by the ministerie of the Prophet Ieremiah.

3 And Zedekiah the King sent Iehucal the sonne of Shelemiah, and Zephaniah the sonne of Maaseiah the Priest to the Prophet Ieremiah, saying, Pray now vnto the Lord our God for vs.

4 (Now Ieremiah went in and out among the people: for they had not put him into the prison.

5 Then Pharaohs hoste was come out of Egypt: and when the Caldeans that besieged Ierusalem, heard tidings of them, they departed from Ierusalem)

6 Then came the worde of the Lord vnto the Prophet Ieremiah, saying,

7 Thus sayth the Lord God of Israel, Thus shall ye say to the King of Iudah, that sent you vnto me to inquire of me, Behold, Pharaohs hoste, which is come forth to helpe you, shall returne to Egypt into their owne land.

8 And the Caldeans shall come againe, and fight against this citie, and take it and burne it with fire.

9 Thus sayth the Lord, Deceiue not your selues, saying, The Caldeans shall surely depart from vs: for they shall not depart.

10 For though ye had smitten the whole hoste of the Caldeans that fight against you, and there remained but wounded men among them, yet should euery man rise vp in his tent, and burne this citie with fire.

11 When the hoste of the Caldeans was broken vp from Ierusalem, because of Pharaohs armie,

12 Then Ieremiah went out of Ierusalem to goe into the land of Beniamin, separating himselfe thence from among the people.

13 And when hee was in the gate of Beniamin, there was a chiefe officer, whose name was Iriiah, the sonne of Shelemiah, the sonne of Hananiah, and he tooke Ieremiah the Prophet, saying, Thou fleest to the Caldeans.

14 Then sayde Ieremiah, That is false, I flee not to the Caldeans: but he would not heare him: so Iriiah tooke Ieremiah, and brought him to the princes.

15 Wherefore the princes were angry with Ieremiah, and smote him, and layde him in prison in the house of Iehonathan the scribe: for they had made that the prison.

16 When Ieremiah was entred into the dungeon, and into the prisons, and had remained there a long time,

17 Then Zedekiah the King sent, and tooke him out, and the King asked him secretly in his house, and said, Is there any worde from the Lord? And Ieremiah

sayd, Yea: for, sayd he, thou shalt be deliuered into the hand of the King of Babel.

18 Moreouer, Ieremiah sayd vnto King Zedekiah, What haue I offended against thee, or against thy seruants, or against this people, that ye haue put me in prison?

19 Where are nowe your prophets, which prophecied vnto you, saying, The King of Babel shall not come against you, nor against this land?

20 Therefore heare nowe, I pray thee, O my lorde the King: let my prayer be accepted before thee, that thou cause mee not to returne to the house of Iehonathan the scribe, least I die there.

21 Then Zedekiah the King commanded, that they should put Ieremiah in the court of the prison, and that they should giue him dayly a piece of bread out of the bakers streete vntill all the bread in the citie were eaten vp. Thus Ieremiah remained in the court of the prison.

Jeremiah 38

1 Then Shephatiah the sonne of Mattan, and Gedaliah the sonne of Pashur, and Iucal the sonne of Shelemiah, and Pashur the sonne of Malchiah, heard the wordes that Ieremiah had spoken vnto all the people, saying,

2 Thus sayth the Lord, He that remaineth in this citie, shall dye by the sworde, by the famine and by the pestilence: but hee that goeth foorth to the Caldeans, shall liue: for he shall haue his life for a praye, and shall liue.

3 Thus sayth the Lord, This citie shall surely be giuen into the hand of the King of Babels armie, which shall take it.

4 Therefore the Princes sayd vnto the King, We beseech you, let this man be put to death: for thus hee weakeneth the hands of the men of warre that remaine in this citie, and the hands of all the people, in speaking such wordes vnto them: for this man seeketh not the wealth of this people, but the hurt.

5 Then Zedekiah the King sayd, Behold, he is in your hands, for ye King can denie you nothing.

6 Then tooke they Ieremiah, and cast him into the dungeon of Malchiah the sonne of Hammelech, that was in the court of the prison: and they let downe Ieremiah with coards: and in the dungeon there was no water but myre: so Ieremiah stacke fast in the myre.

7 Now when Ebed-melech ye blacke More one of ye Eunuches, which was in the kings house, heard that they had put Ieremiah in the dungeon (then the King sate in the gate of Beniamin)

8 And Ebed-melech went out of the Kings house, and spake to the King, saying,

9 My lorde the King, these men haue done euill in all that they haue done to Ieremiah the Prophet, whom they haue cast into the dungeon, and he dyeth for hunger in the place where he is: for there is no more bread in the citie.

10 Then the King commanded Ebed-melech the blacke More, saying, Take from hence thirtie men with thee, and take Ieremiah the Prophet out of the dungeon before he dye.

11 So Ebed-melech tooke the men with him and went to the house of the King vnder the treasurie, and tooke there olde rotten ragges, and olde worne cloutes, and let them downe by coards into the dungeon to Ieremiah.

12 And Ebed-melech the blacke More sayde vnto Ieremiah, Put now these olde rotten ragges and worne, vnder thine arme holes, betweene the coards. And Ieremiah did so.

13 So they drewe vp Ieremiah with coards and tooke him vp out of the dungeon, and Ieremiah remained in the court of the prison.

14 Then Zedekiah the King sent, and tooke Ieremiah the Prophet vnto him, into the thirde entrie that is in the House of the Lord, and the King sayd vnto Ieremiah, I wil aske thee a thing: hide nothing from me.

15 Then Ieremiah sayd to Zedekiah, If I declare it vnto thee, wilt not thou slay me? and if I giue thee counsell, thou wilt not heare me.

16 So the King sware secretly vnto Ieremiah, saying, As the Lord liueth that made vs these soules, I will not slay thee, nor giue thee into the hands of those men that seeke thy life.

17 Then sayd Ieremiah vnto Zedekiah, Thus sayth the Lord God of hostes, the God of Israel, If thou wilt goe foorth vnto the King of Babels princes, then thy soule shall liue, and this citie shall not be burnt vp with fire, and thou shalt liue, and thine house.

18 But if thou wilt not go forth to the King of Babels princes, then shall this citie be giuen into the hand of ye Caldeans, and they shall burne it with fire, and thou shalt not escape out of their hands.

19 And Zedekiah the King sayde vnto Ieremiah, I am carefull for the Iewes that are fled vnto the Caldeans, least they deliuer mee into their hands, and they mocke me.

20 But Ieremiah sayd, They shall not deliuer thee: hearken vnto the voyce of the Lord, I beseech thee, which I speake vnto thee: so shall it be well vnto thee, and thy soule shall liue.

21 But if thou wilt refuse to go forth, this is the worde that the Lord hath shewed me.

22 And beholde, all the women that are left in the King of Iudahs house, shalbe brought forth to the King of Babels princes: and those women shall say, Thy friends haue perswaded thee, and haue preuailed against thee: thy feete are fastened in the myre, and they are turned backe.

23 So they shall bring out all thy wiues, and thy children to the Caldeans, and thou shalt not escape out of their hands, but shalt be taken by the hand of the King of Babel: and this citie shalt thou cause to be burnt with fire.

24 Then said Zedekiah vnto Ieremiah, Let no man know of these words, and thou shalt not die.

25 But if ye princes vnderstand that I haue talked with thee, and they come vnto thee, and say vnto thee, Declare vnto vs nowe, what thou hast sayde vnto the King, hide it not from vs, and we will not slay thee: also what the King sayd vnto thee,

26 Then shalt thou say vnto them, I humbly besought the King that he would not cause me to returne to Iehonathans house, to die there.

27 Then came all the princes vnto Ieremiah and asked him. And he tolde them according to all these wordes that the King had commanded: so they left off speaking with him, for the matter was not perceiued.

28 So Ieremiah abode still in the court of the prison, vntill the day that Ierusalem was taken: and he was there, when Ierusalem was taken.

Jeremiah 39

1 In the ninth yeere of Zedekiah King of Iudah in the tenth moneth, came Nebuchad-nezzar King of Babel and all his hoste against Ierusalem, and they besieged it.

2 And in the eleuenth yeere of Zedekiah in the fourth moneth, the ninth day of the moneth, the citie was broken vp.

3 And all the princes of the King of Babel came in, and sate in the middle gate, euen Neregal, Sharezer, Samgar-nebo, Sarsechim, Rab-saris, Neregal, Sharezer, Rab-mag with all the residue of the princes of the King of Babel.

4 And when Zedekiah the King of Iudah saw them, and all the men of warre, then they fled, and went out of the citie by night, through the Kings garden, and by the gate betweene the two walles, and he went toward the wildernes.

5 But the Caldeans hoste pursued after them, and ouertooke Zedekiah in the desart of Iericho: and when they had taken him, they brought him to Nebuchad-nezzar King of Babel vnto Riblah in the land of Hamath, where he gaue iudgement vpon him.

6 Then the King of Babel slewe the sonnes of Zedekiah in Riblah before his eyes: also the King of Babel slewe all the nobles of Iudah.

7 Moreouer he put out Zedekiahs eyes, and bound him in chaines, to cary him to Babel.

8 And the Caldeans burnt the Kings house, and the houses of the people with fire, and brake downe the walles of Ierusalem.

9 Then Nebuzar-adan the chiefe stewarde caried away captiue into Babel the remnant of the people, that remained in the citie, and those that were fled and fallen vnto him, with the rest of the people that remained.

10 But Nebuzar-adan the chiefe steward left the poore that had nothing in the land of Iudah, and gaue them vineyards and fieldes at the same time.

11 Nowe Nebuchad-nezzar King of Babel gaue charge concerning Ieremiah vnto Nebuzar-adan the chiefe stewarde, saying,

12 Take him, and looke well to him, and doe him no harme, but doe vnto him euen as he shall say vnto thee.

13 So Nebuzar-adan the chiefe steward sent, and Nebushazban, Rabsaris, and Neregal, Sharezar, Rab-mag, and all the King of Babels princes:

14 Euen they sent, and tooke Ieremiah out of the court of the prison, and committed him vnto Gedaliah the sonne of Ahikam the sonne of Shaphan, that he should cary him home: so he dwelt among the people.

15 Now the worde of the Lord came vnto Ieremiah, while he was shut vp in the court of the prison, saying,

16 Go and speake to Ebed-melech the blacke More, saying, Thus saith the Lord of hostes the God of Israel, Beholde, I wil bring my wordes vpon this citie for euill, and not for good, and they shalbe accomplished in that day before thee.

17 But I wil deliuer thee in that day, saith the Lord, and thou shalt not be giuen into the hand of the men whome thou fearest.

18 For I will surely deliuer thee, and thou shalt not fall by the sworde, but thy life shall be for a praye vnto thee, because thou hast put thy trust in me, sayth the Lord.

Jeremiah 40

1 The worde which came to Ieremiah from the Lord after that Nebuzar-adan the chiefe stewarde had let him goe from Ramath, when hee had taken him being bound in chaines among all that were caried away captiue of Ierusalem and Iudah, which were caried away captiue vnto Babel.

2 And the chiefe stewarde tooke Ieremiah, and said vnto him, The Lord thy God hath pronounced this plague vpon this place.

3 Nowe the Lord hath brought it, and done according as he hath said: because ye haue sinned against the Lord, and haue not obeyed his voyce, therefore this thing is come vpon you.

4 And nowe beholde, I loose thee this day from the chaines which were on thine handes, if it please thee to come with me into Babel, come, and I will looke well vnto thee: but if it please thee not to come with mee into Babel, tarie still: beholde, all the lande is before thee: whither it seemeth good, and conuenient for thee to goe, thither goe.

5 For yet he was not returned: therefore he said, Returne to Gedaliah the sonne of Ahikam, the sonne of Shaphan, whom the King of Babel hath made gouernour ouer all the cities of Iudah, and dwell with him among the people, or goe wheresoeuer it pleaseth thee to goe. So the chiefe stewarde gaue him vitailes and a rewarde, and let him goe.

6 Then went Ieremiah vnto Gedaliah the sonne of Ahikam, to Mizpah, and dwelt there with him among the people that were left in the lande.

7 Nowe when all the captaines of the hoste, which were in the fieldes, euen they and their men heard, that the King of Babel had made Gedaliah the sonne of Ahikam gouernour in the land, and that he had committed vnto him, men, and women, and children, and of the poore of the lande, that were not caried away captiue to Babel,

8 Then they came to Gedaliah to Mizpah, euen Ishmael the sonne of Nethaniah, and Iohanan, and Ionathan the sonnes of Kareah, and Seraiah the sonne of Tanehumeth, and the sonnes of Ephai, the Netophathite, and Iezaniah the sonne of Maachathi, they and their men.

9 And Gedaliah the sonne of Ahikam, the sonne of Shaphan sware vnto them, and to their men, saying, Feare not to serue the Caldeans: dwell in the lande, and serue the King of Babel, and it shall be well with you.

10 As for me, Beholde, I will dwell at Mizpah to serue the Caldeans, which will come vnto vs: but you, gather you wine, and sommer fruites, and oyle, and put them in your vessels, and dwell in your cities, that ye haue taken.

11 Likewise when all the Iewes that were in Moab, and among the Ammonites, and in Edom, and that were in all the countries, heard that the King of Babel had left a remnant of Iudah, and that he had set ouer them Gedaliah the sonne of Ahikam the sonne of Shaphan,

12 Euen all the Iewes returned out of all places where they were driuen, and came to the land of Iudah to Gedaliah vnto Mizpah, and gathered wine and sommer fruites, very much.

13 Moreouer Iohanan the sonne of Kareah, and all the captaines of the hoste, that were in the fieldes, came to Gedaliah to Mizpah,

14 And said vnto him, Knowest thou not that Baalis the King of the Ammonites hath sent Ishmael the sonne of Nethaniah to slay thee? But Gedaliah the sonne of Ahikam beleeued them not.

15 Then Iohanan the sonne of Kareah spake to Gedaliah in Mizpah secretly, saying, Let me goe, I pray thee, and I will slay Ishmael the sonne of Nethaniah, and no man shall know it. Wherefore should he kill thee, that all the Iewes, which are gathered vnto thee, shoulde be scattered, and the remnant in Iudah perish?

16 But Gedaliah the sonne of Ahikam said vnto Iohanan the sonne of Kareah, Thou shalt not doe this thing: for thou speakest falsely of Ishmael.

Jeremiah 41

1 But in the seuenth moneth came Ishmael the sonne of Nethaniah, the sonne of Elishama of the seede royall, and the princes of the King, and tenne men with him, vnto Gedaliah the sonne of Ahikam to Mizpah, and there they did eate bread together in Mizpah.

2 Then arose Ishmael the sonne of Nethaniah with these tenne men that were with him, and smote Gedaliah the sonne of Ahikam the sonne of Shaphan with the sword, and slewe him, whom the King of Babel had made gouernour ouer the lande.

3 Ishmael also slewe all the Iewes that were with Gedaliah at Mizpah, and all the Caldeans that were found there, and the men of warre.

4 Now the second day that he had slaine Gedaliah, and no man knewe it,

5 There came men from Shechem, from Shiloh, and from Samaria, euen fourescore men, hauing their beardes shauen, and their clothes rent and cut, with offerings and incense in their hands to offer in the house of the Lord.

6 And Ishmael the sonne of Nethaniah went forth from Mizpah to meete them, weeping as he went: and when he met them, he said vnto them, Come to Gedaliah the sonne of Ahikam.

7 And when they came into the middes of the citie, Ishmael the sonne of Nethaniah slewe them, and cast them into the middes of the pit, he and the men that were with him.

8 But tenne men were founde among them, that saide vnto Ishmael, Slay vs not: for we haue treasures in the fielde, of wheate, and of barley, and of oyle, and of honie: so he stayed, and slew them not among their brethren.

9 Now the pit wherein Ishmael had cast the dead bodies of the men (whom he had slayne because of Gedaliah) is it, which Asa the King had made because of Basha King of Israel, and Ishmael the sonne of Nethaniah filled it with them that were slaine.

10 Then Ishmael caryed away captiue all the residue of the people that were in Mizpah, euen the Kings daughters, and all the people that remained in Mizpah, whom Nebuzar-adan the chiefe steward had committed to Gedaliah the sonne of Ahikam, and Ishmael the sonne of Nethaniah caried them away captiue, and departed to goe ouer to the Ammonites.

11 But when Iohanan the sonne of Kareah, and all the captaines of the hoste that were with him, heard of all the euill that Ishmael the sonne of Nethaniah had done,

12 Then they all tooke their men, and went to fight with Ishmael the sonne of Nethaniah, and founde him by ye great waters that are in Gibeon.

13 Nowe when all the people whom Ishmael caryed away captiue, sawe Iohanan the sonne of Kareah, and all the captaines of the hoste, that were with him, they were glad.

14 So all the people, that Ishmael had caryed away captiue from Mizpah, returned and came againe, and went vnto Iohanan the sonne of Kareah.

15 But Ishmael the sonne of Nethaniah, escaped from Iohanan with eight men, and went to the Ammonites.

16 Then tooke Iohanan the sonne of Kareah, and all the captaines of the hoste that were with him, all the remnant of the people, whom Ishmael the sonne of Nethaniah had caried away captiue from Mizpah, (after that he had slaine Gedaliah the sonne of Ahikam) euen the strong men of warre, and the women, and the children, and the eunuches, whom hee had brought againe from Gibeon:

17 And they departed and dwelt in Geruth Chimham, which is by Beth-lehem, to goe and to enter into Egypt,

18 Because of the Caldeans: for they feared them, because Ishmael ye sonne of Nethaniah had slaine Gedaliah the sonne of Ahikam, whom the King of Babel made gouernour in the land.

Jeremiah 42

1 Then all the captaines of the hoste, and Iohanan the sonne of Kareah, and Iezaniah the sonne of Hoshaaiah, and all the people from the least vnto the most came,

2 And saide vnto Ieremiah the Prophete, Heare our prayer, we beseeche thee, and pray for vs vnto the Lord thy God, euen for all this remnant (for we are left, but a fewe of many, as thine eyes doe beholde)

3 That the Lord thy God may shewe vs the way wherein wee may walke, and the thing that we may doe.

4 Then Ieremiah the Prophet said vnto them, I haue heard you: behold, I will pray vnto ye Lord your God according to your wordes, and whatsoeuer thing the Lord shall answere you, I will declare it vnto you: I will keepe nothing backe from you.

5 Then they said to Ieremiah, The Lord be a witnesse of trueth, and faith betweene vs, if we doe not, euen according to all things for ye which the Lord thy God shall send thee to vs.

6 Whether it be good or euill, we will obey the voyce of the Lord God, to whom we sende thee that it may be well with vs, when wee obey the voyce of the Lord our God.

7 And so after ten dayes came the word of the Lord vnto Ieremiah.

8 Then called he Iohanan the sonne of Kareah, and all the captaines of the hoste, which were with him, and all ye people from ye least to the most,

9 And saide vnto them, Thus saith the Lord God of Israel, vnto whom ye sent me to present your prayers before him,

10 If ye will dwell in this land, then I wil build you, and not destroy you, and I will plant you, and not roote you out: for I repent me of the euill that I haue done vnto you.

11 Feare not for the King of Babel, of whom ye are afraide: be not afraid of him, saith the Lord: for I am with you, to saue you, and to deliuer you from his hand,

12 And I will graunt you mercie that he may haue compassion vpon you, and he shall cause you to dwell in your owne land.

13 But if ye say, We will not dwell in this land, neither heare the voyce of the Lord your God,

14 Saying, Nay, but we will goe into the land of Egypt, where we shall see no warre, nor heare the sounde of the trumpet, nor haue hunger of bread, and there will we dwell,

15 (And nowe therefore heare the worde of the Lord, ye remnant of Iudah: thus sayeth the Lord of hostes the God of Israel, If ye set your faces to enter into Egypt, and goe to dwell there)

16 Then the sworde that ye feared, shall take you there in the land of Egypt, and the famine, for the which ye care, shall there hang vpon you in Egypt, and there shall ye die.

17 And all the men that set their faces to enter into Egypt to dwell there, shall die by ye sword, by the famine and by the pestilence, and none of them shall remaine nor escape from the plague, that I will bring vpon them.

18 For thus saith the Lord of hostes the God of Israel, As mine anger and my wrath hath bene powred foorth vpon the inhabitants of Ierusalem: so shall my wrath be powred foorth vpon you, when ye shall enter into Egypt, and ye shall be a detestation, and an astonishment, and a curse and a reproche, and ye shall see this place no more.

19 O ye remnant of Iudah, the Lord hath said concerning you, Goe not into Egypt: knowe certeinely that I haue admonished you this day.

20 Surely ye dissembled in your hearts When ye sent me vnto the Lord your God, saying, Pray for vs vnto the Lord our God, and declare vnto vs euen according vnto al that the Lord our God shall say, and we will doe it.

21 Therefore I haue this day declared it you, but you haue not obeyed the voyce of the Lord your God, nor any thing for the which he hath sent me vnto you.

22 Nowe therefore, knowe certeinely that ye shall die by the sworde, by the famine, and by the pestilence, in the place whither ye desire to goe and dwell.

Jeremiah 43

1 Nowe when Ieremiah had made an ende of speaking vnto ye whole people all the wordes of the Lord their God, for the which the Lord their God had sent him to them, euen all these wordes,

2 Then spake Azariah the sonne of Hoshaiah, and Iohanan the sonne of Kareah, and all the proude men, saying vnto Ieremiah, Thou speakest falsely: the Lord our God hath not sent thee to say, Goe not into Egypt to dwell there,

3 But Baruch ye sonne of Neriah prouoketh thee against vs, for to deliuer vs into the hand of the Caldeans, that they might slay vs, and cary vs away captiues into Babel.

4 So Iohanan the sonne of Kareah, and all the captaines of the hoste, and all the people obeied not the voyce of the Lord, to dwell in the lande of Iudah.

5 But Iohanan the sonne of Kareah, and all the captaines of the hoste tooke all the remnant of Iudah, that were returned from al nations, whither they had bene driuen, to dwel in ye land of Iudah:

6 Euen men and women, and children, and the Kinges daughters, and euery person, that Nebuzar-adan the chiefe steward had left with Gedaliah the sonne of Ahikam, ye sonne of Shaphan, and Ieremiah the Prophet, and Baruch the sonne of Neriah.

7 So they came into the lande of Egypt: for they obeied not the voice of the Lord: thus came they to Tahpanhes.

8 Then came the worde of the Lord vnto Ieremiah in Tahpanhes, saying,

9 Take great stones in thine hand, and hide them in the claie in the bricke kill, which is at the entrie of Pharaohs house in Tanpanhes in ye sight of the men of Iudah,

10 And say vnto them, Thus sayeth the Lord of hostes the God of Israel, Beholde, I will sende and bring Nebuchad-nezzar the King of Babel my seruant, and will set his throne vpon these stones that I haue hid, and he shall spread his pauilion ouer them.

11 And when he shall come, he shall smite the land of Egypt: such as are appoynted for death, to death, and such as are for captiuitie, to captiuitie, and such as are for the sword to the sword.

12 And I wil kindle a fire in the houses of the gods of Egypt, and he shall burne them and carie them away captiues, and he shall aray himself with the land of Egypt, as a shepheard putteth on his garment, and shall depart from thence in peace.

13 He shall breake also ye images of Beth-shemesh, that is in the lande of Egypt, and the houses of the gods of the Egyptians shall he burne with fire.

Jeremiah 44

1 The worde that came to Ieremiah concerning all the Iewes, which dwell in the lande of Egypt, and remained at Migdol and at Tahpanhes, and at Noph, and in the coutry of Pathros, saying,

2 Thus sayeth the Lord of hostes the God of Israel, Yee haue seene all the euill that I haue brought vpon Ierusalem, and vpon all the cities of Iudah: and beholde, this day they are desolate, and no man dwelleth therein,

3 Because of their wickednes which they haue comitted, to prouoke me to anger in that they went to burne incense, and to serue other gods, who they knew not, neither they nor you nor your fathers.

4 Howbeit I sent vnto you all my seruats the Prophets rising earely, and sending them, saying, Oh doe not this abominable thing that I hate.

5 But they would not heare nor incline their eare to turne from their wickednes, and to burne no more incense vnto other gods.

6 Wherefore my wrath, and mine anger was powred foorth and was kindled in the cities of Iudah, and in the streetes of Ierusalem, and they are desolate, and wasted, as appeareth this day.

7 Therefore now thus saith the Lord of hosts the God of Israel, Wherfore commit ye this great euill against your soules, to cut off from you man and woman, childe and suckling out of Iudah, and leaue you none to remaine?

8 In that yee prouoke mee vnto wrath with the woorkes of your hands, burning incense vnto other Gods in the lande of Egypt whither yee be gone to dwell: that yee might bring destruction vnto your selues, and that ye might be a curse and a reproch among all nations of the earth.

9 Haue yee forgotten the wickednes of your fathers, and the wickednesse of the Kings of Iudah and the wickednesse of their wiues and your owne wickednes and the wickednes of your wiues, which they haue committed in the land of Iudah and in the streetes of Ierusalem?

10 They are not humbled vnto this day, neither haue they feared nor walked in my lawe nor in my statutes, that I set before you and before your fathers.

11 Therefore thus sayeth the Lord of hostes the God of Israel, Beholde, I will set my face against you to euill and to destroy all Iudah,

12 And I will take the remnant of Iudah, that haue set their faces to goe into the lande of Egypt there to dwell, and they shall all bee consumed and fall in the lande of Egypt: they shall euen bee consumed by the sworde and by the famine: they shall die from the least vnto the most, by the sworde, and by the famine, and they shall be a detestation and an astonishment and a curse and a reproche.

13 For I will visite them that dwel in the land of Egypt, as I haue visited Ierusalem, by ye sworde, by the famine, and by the pestilence,

14 So that none of the remnant of Iudah, which are gone into the lande of Egypt to dwell there, shall escape or remaine, that they shoulde returne into the land of Iudah to the which they haue a desire to returne to dwell there: for none shall returne, but such as shall escape.

15 Then all the men which knewe that their wiues had burnt incense vnto other gods and all the women that stoode by, a great multitude, euen all the people that dwelt in the lande of Egypt in Pathros, answered Ieremiah, saying,

16 The worde that thou hast spoken vnto vs in the Name of the Lord, wee will not heare it of thee,

17 But wee will doe whatsoeuer thing goeth out of our owne mouth, as to burne incense vnto the Queene of heauen, and to powre out drinke offerings vnto her, as we haue done, both we and our fathers, our Kings and our princes in the cities of Iudah, and in the streetes of Ierusalem: for then had wee plentie of vitailes and were well and felt none euill.

18 But since wee left off to burne incense to the Queene of heauen, and to powre out drinke offerings vnto her, we haue had scarcenesse of all things, and haue beene consumed by the sworde and by the famine.

19 And when we burnt incense to ye Queene of heauen, and powred out drinke offerings vnto her, did wee make her cakes to make her glad, and powre out drinke offerings vnto her without our husbands?

20 Then said Ieremiah vnto all the people, to the men, and to the women, and to all the people which had giuen him that answere, saying,

21 Did not the Lord remember the incense, that yee burnt in the cities of Iudah, and in the streetes of Ierusalem, both you, and your fathers, your Kinges, and your princes, and the people of the land, and hath he not considered it?

22 So that the Lord could no longer forbeare, because of the wickednes of your inuentions, and because of the abominations, which ye haue committed: therefore is your lande desolate and an astonishment, and a curse and without inhabitant, as appeareth this day.

23 Because ye haue burnt incense and because ye haue sinned against the Lord, and haue not obeyed the voyce of the Lord, nor walked in his Lawe, nor in his statutes, nor in his testimonies, therefore this plague is come vpon you, as appeareth this day.

24 Moreouer Ieremiah saide vnto all the people and to all the women, Heare the word of the Lord, all Iudah that are in the land of Egypt.

25 Thus speaketh the Lord of hosts, the God of Israel, saying, Ye and your wiues haue both spoken with your mouthes, and fulfilled with your hande, saying, We will performe our vowes that we haue vowed to burne incense to the Queene of heauen, and to powre out drinke offerings to her: yee will perfourme your vowes and doe the things that yee haue vowed.

26 Therefore heare the word of the Lord, all Iudah that dwel in the land of Egypt. Beholde, I haue sworne by my great Name, sayeth the Lord, that my Name shall no more be called vpon by the mouth of any man of Iudah, in all the lande of Egypt, saying, The Lord God liueth.

27 Behold, I wil watch ouer them for euil and not for good, and all men of Iudah that are in the land of Egypt, shalbe consumed by the sword, and by the famine, vntill they be vtterly destroied.

28 Yet a small nomber that escape the sworde, shall returne out of the lande of Egypt into the lande of Iudah: and all the remnant of Iudah that are gone into the lande of Egypt to dwell there, shall know whose words shall stad, mine or theirs.

29 And this shall be a signe vnto you, saith the Lord, whe I visit you in this place, that ye may know that my words shall surely stand against you for euill.

30 Thus sayth the Lord, Beholde, I will giue Pharaoh Hophra King of Egypt into the hand of his enemies, and into the

hand of them that seeke his life: as I gaue Zedekiah King of Iudah into the hand of Nebuchad-nezzar King of Babel his enemie, who also sought his life.

Jeremiah 45

1 The worde that Ieremiah the Prophet spake vnto Baruch the sonne of Neriah, when he had written these woordes in a booke at the mouth of Ieremiah, in the fourth yeere of Iehoiakim the sonne of Iosiah King of Iudah, saying,

2 Thus sayeth the Lord God of Israel vnto thee, O Baruch,

3 Thou diddest say, Wo is me nowe: for the Lord hath laied sorrow vnto my sorrowe: I fainted in my mourning, and I can finde no rest.

4 Thus shalt thou say vnto him, The Lord sayeth thus, Behold, that which I haue built, will I destroy, and that which I haue planted, will I plucke vp, euen this whole lande.

5 And seekest thou great things for thy self? seeke them not: for beholde, I wil bring a plague vpon al flesh, saith the Lord: but thy life wil I giue thee for a pray in all places, whither thou goest.

Jeremiah 46

1 The wordes of the Lord, which came to Ieremiah the Prophet against the Gentiles,

2 As against Egypt, against ye armie of Pharaoh Necho King of Egypt, which was by the riuer Perath in Carchemish, which Nebuchad-nezzar King of Babel smote in the fourth yere of Iehoiakim the sonne of Iosiah King of Iudah.

3 Make readie buckler and shielde, and goe forth to battell.

4 Make readie the horses, and let the horsemen get vp, and stande vp with your sallets, fourbish the speares, and put on the brigandines.

5 Wherefore haue I seene them afraid, and driuen backe? for their mighty men are smitten, and are fled away, and looke not backe: for feare was rounde about, sayeth the Lord.

6 The swift shall not flee away, nor the strong man escape: they shall stumble, and fall towarde the North by the riuer Perath.

7 Who is this, that commeth vp, as a flood, whose waters are mooued like the riuers?

8 Egypt riseth vp like the flood, and his waters are mooued like the riuers, and he sayth, I wil goe vp, and will couer the earth: I wil destroy the citie with them that dwell therein.

9 Come vp, ye horses, and rage ye charets, and let the valiant men come foorth, the blacke Mores, and the Lybians that beare the shield, and the Lydians that handle and bend the bowe.

10 For this is the day of ye Lord God of hostes, and a day of vengeance, that he may auenge him of his enemies: for the swords shall deuoure, and it shall be saciate, and made drunke with their blood: for the Lord God of hosts hath a

sacrifice in the North countrey by the Riuer Perath.

11 Goe vp vnto Gilead, and take balme, O virgine, the daughter of Egypt: in vaine shalt thou vse many medicines: for thou shalt haue no health.

12 The nations haue heard of thy shame, and thy crie hath filled the lande: for the strong hath stumbled against the strong and they are fallen both together.

13 The woorde that the Lord spake to Ieremiah the Prophet, howe Nebuchad-nezzar king of Babel shoulde come and smite the lande of Egypt.

14 Publish in Egypt and declare in Migdol, and proclaime in Noph, and in Tahpanhes, and say, Stand still, and prepare thee: for the sworde shall deuoure rounde about thee.

15 Why are thy valiant men put backe? they could not stand, because the Lord did driue them.

16 Hee made many to fall, and one fell vpon another: and they saide, Arise, let vs goe againe to our owne people, and to the land of our natiuitie from the sworde of the violent.

17 They did cry there, Pharaoh King of Egypt, and of a great multitude hath passed the time appointed.

18 As I liue, saith the King, whose Name is the Lord of hostes, surely as Tabor is in the mountaines, and as Carmel is in the sea: so shall it come.

19 O thou daughter dwelling in Egypt, make thee geare to goe into captiuitie: for Noph shall be waste and desolate, without an inhabitant.

20 Egypt is like a faire calfe, but destruction commeth: out of the North it commeth.

21 Also her hired men are in the middes of her like fat calues: they are also turned backe and fled away together: they could not stand, because the day of their destruction was come vpon them, and the time of their visitation.

22 The voyce thereof shall goe foorth like a serpent: for they shall march with an armie, and come against her with axes, as hewers of wood.

23 They shall cut downe her forest, saith the Lord: for they cannot be counted, because they are moe then ye grashoppers, and are innumerable.

24 The daughter of Egypt shall be confounded: she shall be deliuered into the handes of the people of the North.

25 Thus saith the Lord of hostes, the God of Israel, Behold, I will visite the common people of No and Pharaoh, and Egypt, with their gods and their Kings, euen Pharaoh, and al them that trust in him,

26 And I will deliuer them into the handes of those, that seeke their liues, and into the hand of Nebuchad-nezzar King of Babel, and into the handes of his seruants, and afterwarde she shall dwell as in the olde time, saith the Lord.

27 But feare not thou, O my seruant Iaakob, and be not thou afraid, O Israel: for behold, I will deliuer thee from a farre countrey, and thy seede from the land of their captiuitie, and Iaakob shall returne

and be in rest, and prosperitie, and none shall make him afraid.

28 Feare thou not, O Iaakob my seruant, saith the Lord: for I am with thee, and I will vtterly destroy all the nations, whither I haue driuen thee: but I will not vtterly destroy thee, but correct thee by iudgement, and not vtterly cut thee off.

Jeremiah 47

1 The wordes of the Lord that came to Ieremiah the Prophet, against the Philistims, before that Pharaoh smote Azzah.

2 Thus saith the Lord, Beholde, waters rise vp out of the North, and shalbe as a swelling flood, and shall ouerflowe the land, and all that is therein, and the cities with them that dwell therein: then the men shall crie, and all the inhabitants of the land shall howle,

3 At the noise and stamping of ye hoofes of his strong horses, at the noise of his charets, and at the rumbling of his wheeles: ye fathers shall not looke backe to their children, for feeblenes of handes,

4 Because of the day that commeth to destroy all the Philistims, and to destroy Tyrus, and Zidon, and all the rest that take their part: for the Lord will destroy the Philistims, the remnant of the yle of Caphtor.

5 Baldenes is come vpon Azzah: Ashkelon is cut vp with the rest of their valleys. Howe long wilt thou thy selfe?

6 O thou sword of the Lord, how long will it be or thou cease! turne againe into thy scaberd, rest and be still.

7 Howe can it cease, seeing the Lord hath giuen it a charge against Ashkelon, and against the sea banke? euen there hath he appointed it.

Jeremiah 48

1 Concerning Moab, thus saith ye Lord of hostes, the God of Israel, Woe vnto Nebo: for it is wasted: Kiriathaim is confounded and taken: Misgab is confounded and afraide.

2 Moab shall boast no more of Heshbon: for they haue deuised euill against it. Come, and let vs destroy it, that it be no more a nation: also thou shalt be destroyed, O Madmen, and the sworde shall pursue thee.

3 A voyce of crying shall be from Horonaim with desolation and great destruction.

4 Moab is destroyed: her litle ones haue caused their crie to be heard.

5 For at the going vp of Luhith, the mourner shall goe vp with weeping: for in the going downe of Horonaim, the enemies haue heard a cry of destruction,

6 Flee and saue your liues, and be like vnto the heath in the wildernesse.

7 For because thou hast trusted in thy workes and in thy treasures, thou shalt also be taken, and Chemosh shall goe forth into captiuitie with his Priestes and his princes together.

8 And the destroyer shall come vpon all cities, and no citie shall escape: the

valley also shall perish and the plaine shalbe destroyed as the Lord hath spoken.

9 Giue wings vnto Moab, that it may flee and get away: for the cities thereof shalbe desolate, without any to dwell therein.

10 Cursed be he that doeth the worke of the Lord negligently, and cursed be he that keepeth backe his sword from blood.

11 Moab hath bene at rest from his youth, and he hath setled on his lees, and hath not bene powred from vessell to vessell, neither hath he gone into captiuitie: therefore his taste remained in him and his sent is not changed.

12 Therefore beholde, the dayes come, saith the Lord, that I will send vnto him such as shall carie him away, and shall emptie his vessels, and breake their bottels.

13 And Moab shalbe ashamed of Chemosh as the house of Israel was ashamed of Beth-el their confidence.

14 Howe thinke you thus, We are mightie and strong men of warre?

15 Moab is destroyed, and his cities burnt vp, and his chose yong men are gone downe to slaughter, saith ye King, whose name is ye Lord of hostes.

16 The destruction of Moab is ready to come, and his plague hasteth fast.

17 All ye that are about him, mourne for him, and all ye that knowe his name, say, Howe is the strong staffe broken, and the beautifull rod!

18 Thou daughter that doest inhabite Dibon, come downe from thy glory, and sit in thirst: for the destroyer of Moab shall come vpon thee, and he shall destroy thy strong holdes.

19 Thou that dwellest in Aroer, stand by the way, and beholde: aske him that fleeth and that escapeth, and say, What is done?

20 Moab is cofouded: for it is destroied: howle, and cry, tell ye it in Arnon, that Moab is made waste,

21 And iudgement is come vpon the plaine countrey, vpon Holon and vpon Iahazah, and vpon Mephaath,

22 And vpon Dibon, and vpon Nebo, and vpon the house of Diblathaim,

23 And vpon Kiriathaim, and vpon Beth-gamul, and vpon Beth-meon,

24 And vpon Kerioth, and vpon Bozrah, and vpon all the cities of ye land of Moab farre or neere.

25 The horne of Moab is cut off, and his arme is broken, saith the Lord.

26 Make ye him drunken: for he magnified himselfe against the Lord: Moab shall wallowe in his vomite, and he also shalbe in derision.

27 For diddest not thou deride Israel, as though he had bene found among theeues? for when thou speakest of him, thou art moued.

28 O ye that dwell in Moab, leaue the cities, and dwell in the rockes, and be like the doue, that maketh her nest in the sides of the holes mouth.

29 We haue heard the pride of Moab (hee is exceeding proude) his stoutnesse, and his arrogancie, and his pride, and the hautinesse of his heart.

30 I know his wrath, saith ye Lord, but it shall not be so: and his dissimulatios, for they do not right.

31 Therefore will I howle for Moab, and I will crie out for all Moab: mine heart shall mourne for the men of Kir-heres.

32 O vine of Sibmah, I will weepe for thee, as I wept for Iazer: thy plants are gone ouer the sea, they are come to the sea of Iazer: ye destroyer is fallen vpon thy somer fruites, and vpon thy vintage,

33 And ioye, and gladnesse is taken from the plentifull fielde, and from the land of Moab: and I haue caused wine to faile from the winepresse: none shall treade with shouting: their shouting shall be no shouting.

34 From the cry of Heshbon vnto Elaleh and vnto Iahaz haue they made their noyse from Zoar vnto Horonaim, ye heiffer of three yere old shall go lowing: for ye waters also of Nimrim shalbe wasted.

35 Moreouer, I will cause to cease in Moab, saith the Lord, him that offered in the high places, and him that burneth incense to his gods.

36 Therefore mine heart shall sounde for Moab like a shaume, and mine heart shall sound like a shaume for the men of Ker-heres, because the riches that he hath gotten, is perished.

37 For euery head shalbe balde, and euery beard plucked: vpon all the handes shall be cuttings, and vpon the loynes sackecloth.

38 And mourning shall be vpon all the house toppes of Moab and in all the streetes thereof: for I haue broken Moab like a vessell wherein is no pleasure, sayeth the Lord.

39 They shall howle, saying, How is he destroyed? howe hath Moab turned the backe with shame? so shall Moab be a derision, and a feare to all them about him.

40 For thus saith the Lord, Beholde, he shall flee as an eagle, and shall spread his wings ouer Moab.

41 The cities are taken, and the strong holdes are wonne, and ye mightie mens hearts in Moab at that day shalbe as ye heart of a woman in trauaile.

42 And Moab shall be destroyed from being a people, because he hath set vp himselfe against the Lord.

43 Feare, and pit and snare shall be vpon thee, O inhabitant of Moab, saith the Lord.

44 He that escapeth from the feare, shall fall in the pit, and he that getteth vp out of the pit, shall be taken in the snare: for I will bring vpon it, euen vpon Moab, the yeere of their visitation, sayeth the Lord.

45 They that fled, stoode vnder the shadowe of Heshbon, because of the force: for the fire came out of Heshbon, and a flame from Sihon, and deuoured the corner of Moab, and the top of the seditious children.

46 Wo be vnto thee, O Moab: the people of Chemosh perisheth: for thy sonnes are taken captiues, and thy daughters led into captiuitie.

47 Yet will I bring againe the captiuitie of Moab in the latter dayes, sayeth the Lord. Thus farre of the iudgement of Moab.

Jeremiah 49

1 Unto the children of Ammon thus saith the Lord, Hath Israel no sonnes? or hath he none heire? Why then hath their king possessed God? and his people dwelt in his cities?

2 Therefore beholde the dayes come, sayeth the Lord, that I will cause a noyse of warre to be heard in Rabbah of the Ammonites, and it shall be a desolate heape, and her daughters shall be burnt with fire: then shall Israel possesse those that possessed him, sayeth the Lord.

3 Howle, O Heshbon, for Ai is wasted: crie ye daughters of Rabbah: girde you with sackecloth: mourne and runne to and from by the hedges: for their King shall goe into captiuitie; and his Priestes, and his princes likewise.

4 Wherefore gloriest thou in the valleis? thy valley floweth away, O rebellious daughter: she trusted in her treasures, saying, Who shall come vnto me?

5 Beholde, I will bring a feare vpon thee, sayth the Lord God of hostes, of all those that be about thee, and ye shalbe scattered euery man right foorth, and none shall gather him that fleeth.

6 And afterward I will bring againe the captiuitie of the children of Ammon.

7 To Edom thus sayeth the Lord of hostes: Is wisdome no more in Teman? is counsel perished from their children? is their wisdome vanished?

8 Flee, ye inhabitants of Dedan (they are turned backe, and haue consulted to dwell) for I haue brought the destruction of Esau vpon him, and the time of his visitation.

9 If the grape gatherers come to thee, would they not leaue some grapes? if theeues come by night, they will destroy till they haue ynough.

10 For I haue discouered Esau: I haue vncouered his secrets, and he shall not be able to hide himselfe: his seede is wasted, and his brethren and his neighbours, and there shall be none to say,

11 Leaue thy fathers children, and I will preserue them aliue, and let thy widowes trust in me.

12 For thus sayth the Lord, Beholde, they whose iudgement was not to drinke of the cuppe, haue assuredly drunken, and art thou he that shall escape free? thou shalt not goe free, but thou shalt surely drinke of it.

13 For I haue sworne by my selfe, sayeth the Lord, that Bozrah shall be waste, and for a reproche, and a desolation, and a curse, and all the cities thereof shall be perpetuall desolations.

14 I haue heard a rumour from the Lord, and an ambassadour is sent vnto the heathen, saying, Gather you

together, and come against her, and rise vp to the battell.

15 For loe, I will make thee but small among the heathen, and despised among men.

16 Thy feare, and ye pride of thine heart hath deceiued thee, thou that dwellest in the cleftes of the rocke, and keepest the height of ye hil: though thou shouldest make thy nest as hie as the eagle, I wil bring thee downe from thece, sayth the Lord.

17 Also Edom shall be desolate: euery one that goeth by it, shall be astonished, and shall hisse at all the plagues thereof,

18 As in the ouerthrowe of Sodom, and of Gomorah, and the places thereof neere about, saieth the Lord: no man shall dwell there, neither shall the sonnes of men remaine in it.

19 Beholde, hee shall come vp like a lyon from the swelling of Iorden vnto the strong dwelling place: for I will make Israel to rest, euen I will make him to haste away from her, and who is a chosen man that I may appoynt against her? for who is like mee? and who will appoint me the time? and who is the shepheard that will stande before me?

20 Therefore heare the counsell of the Lord that hee hath deuised against Edom, and his purpose that hee hath conceiued against the inhabitants of Teman: surely the least of the flocke shall drawe them out: surely he shall make their habitations desolate with them.

21 The earth is mooued at the noyse of their fall: the crie of their voice is heard in the red Sea.

22 Behold, he shall come vp, and flie as the Egle, and spreade his wings ouer Bozrah, and at that day shall the heart of the strong men of Edome be as the heart of a woman in trauaile.

23 Vnto Damascus he sayeth, Hamath is confounded and Arpad, for they haue heard euill tidings, and they are faint hearted as one on the fearefull sea that can not rest.

24 Damascus is discouraged, and turneth her selfe to flight and feare hath seased her: anguish and sorowes haue taken her as a woman in trauaile.

25 How is the glorious citie not reserued, the citie of my ioy?

26 Therefore her yong men shall fall in her streetes, and all her men of warre shall be cut off in that day, sayeth the Lord of hostes.

27 And I will kindle a fire in the wall of Damascus, which shall cosume the palaces of Benhadad.

28 Vnto Kedar, and to the kingdomes of Hazor, which Nebuchad-nezzar, king of Babel shall smite, thus sayeth the Lord, Arise, and goe vp vnto Kedar, and destroy the men of the East.

29 Their tents and their flocks shall they take away: yea, they shall take to themselues their curtaines and all their vessels, and their camels, and they shall crie vnto them, Feare is on euery side.

30 Flee, get you farre off (they haue consulted to dwell) O ye inhabitants of Hazor, saith the Lord: for Nebuchad-nezzar King of Babel hath taken counsell against you, and hath deuised a purpose against you.

31 Arise, and get you vp vnto the welthy nation that dwelleth without care, saith the Lord, which haue neither gates nor barres, but dwel alone.

32 And their camels shall be a bootie, and the multitude of their cattel a spoile, and I will scatter them into all windes, and to the vtmost corners, and I will bring their destruction from al the sides thereof, sayeth the Lord.

33 And Hazor shall be a dwelling for dragons, and desolation for euer: there shall no man dwell there, nor the sonnes of men remaine in it.

34 The woordes of the Lord that came to Ieremiah the Prophet, concerning Elam, in the beginning of the reigne of Zedekiah King of Iudah, saying,

35 Thus sayeth the Lord of hostes, Beholde, I will breake the bowe of Elam, euen the chiefe of their strength.

36 And vpon Elam I will bring the foure windes from the foure quarters of heauen, and will scatter them towardes all these windes, and there shall bee no nation, whither the fugitiues of Elam shall not come.

37 For I will cause Elam to be afraied before their enemies, and before them that seeke their liues, and will bring vpon them a plague, euen the indignation of my wrath, saieth the Lord, and I wil sende the sworde after them till I haue consumed them.

38 And I wil set my throne in Elam, and I wil destroy both the King and the princes from thence, saith the Lord: but in the latter daies I wil bring againe the captiuitie of Elam, sayeth the Lord.

Jeremiah 50

1 The word that the Lord spake, concerning Babel, and cocerning the land of the Caldeans by the ministerie of Ieremiah the Prophet.

2 Declare among the nations, and publish it, and set vp a standart, proclaime it and conceale it not: say, Babel is taken, Bel is confounded, Merodach is broken downe: her idols are confounded, and their images are burst in pieces.

3 For out of the North there commeth vp a nation against her, which shall make her lande waste, and none shall dwel therein: they shall flee, and depart, both man and beast.

4 In those daies, and at that time, sayeth the Lord, the children of Israel shall come, they, and the children of Iudah together, going, and weeping shall they goe, and seeke the Lord their God.

5 They shall aske the way to Zion, with their faces thitherward, saying, Come, and let vs cleaue to the Lord in a perpetuall couenant that shall not be forgotten.

6 My people hath beene as lost sheepe: their shepheards haue caused them to goe astray, and haue turned them away to the mountaines: they haue gone from mountaine to hil, and forgotten their resting place.

7 Al that found them, haue deuoured them, and their enemies saide, We offende not, because they haue sinned against the Lord, the habitation of iustice, euen the Lord the hope of their fathers.

8 Flee from the middes of Babel, and depart out of the lande of the Caldeans, and be ye as the hee goates before the flocke.

9 For loe, I will raise, and cause to come vp against Babel a multitude of mightie natios from the North countrey, and they shall set themselues in aray against her, whereby shee shall be taken: their arrowes shall be as of a strong man, which is expert, for none shall returne in vaine.

10 And Caldea shalbe a spoyle: all that spoyle her, shalbe satisfied, sayth the Lord.

11 Because yee were glad and reioyced in destroying mine heritage, and because ye are growen fatte, as the calues in the grasse, and neied like strong horses,

12 Therefore your mother shall bee sore confounded, and she that bare you, shall be ashamed: beholde, the vttermost of the nations shalbe a desert, a drie land, and a wildernes.

13 Because of the wrath of the Lord it shall not be inhabited, but shall be wholy desolate: euery one that goeth by Babel, shall be astonished, and hisse at all her plagues.

14 Put your selues in aray against Babel rounde about: all ye that bende the bowe, shoote at her, spare no arrowes: for shee hath sinned against the Lord.

15 Crie against her round about: she hath giuen her hand: her foundations are fallen, and her walles are destroyed: for it is the vengeance of the Lord: take vengeance vpon her: as she hath done, doe vnto her.

16 Destroy the sower from Babel, and him that handleth the sieth in the time of haruest: because of the sworde of the oppressor they shall turne euery one to his people, and they shall flee euery one to his owne land.

17 Israel is like scattered sheepe: the lions haue dispersed them: first the King of Asshur hath deuoured him, and last this Nebuchad-nezzar King, of Babel hath broken his bones.

18 Therefore thus saith the Lord of hostes the God of Israel, Behold, I wil visit ye King of Babel, and his land, as I haue visited the King of Asshur.

19 And I will bring Israel againe to his habitation: hee shall feede on Carmel and Bashan, and his soule shall be satisfied vpon the mount Ephraim and Gilead.

20 In those daies, and at that time, sayeth the Lord, the iniquitie of Israel shall be sought for, and there shall be none: and the sinnes of Iudah, and they shall not be founde: for I will be mercifull vnto them, whome I reserue.

21 Goe vp against the lande of the rebelles, euen against it, and against the inhabitantes of Pekod: destroy, and lay it waste after them, saieth the Lord, and doe according to all that I haue commanded thee.

22 A crie of battell is in the land, and of great destruction.

23 Howe is the hammer of the whole world destroied, and broken! howe is Babel become desolate among the nations!

24 I haue snared thee, and thou art taken, O Babel, and thou wast not aware: thou art found, and also caught, because thou hast striuen against the Lord.

25 The Lord hath opened his treasure, and hath brought foorth the weapons of his wrath: for this is the woorke of the Lord God of hostes in the lande of the Caldeans.

26 Come against her from the vtmost border: open her store houses: treade on her as on sheaues, and destroy her vtterly: let nothing of her be left.

27 Destroy all her bullockes: let them goe downe to the slaughter. Wo vnto them, for their day is come, and the time of their visitation.

28 The voyce of them that flee, and escape out of the lande of Babel to declare in Zion the vengeance of the Lord our God, and the vengeance of his Temple.

29 Call vp the archers against Babel: al ye that bend the bow, besiege it rounde about: let none thereof escape: recompence her according to her worke, and according to all that she hath done, doe vnto her: for she hath bene proud against the Lord, euen against the holy one of Israel.

30 Therefore shall her yong men fall in the streetes, and al her men of warre shalbe destroied in that day, sayeth the Lord.

31 Beholde, I come vnto thee, O proude man, saith the Lord God of hostes: for thy day is come, euen the time that I will visite thee.

32 And the proude shall stumble and fall, and none shall raise him vp: and I will kindle a fire in his cities, and it shall deuoure all round about him.

33 Thus saieth the Lord of hosts, The children of Israel, and the children of Iudah were oppressed together: and all that tooke them captiues, held them, and would not let them goe.

34 But their strong redeemer, whose Name is the Lord of hostes, he shall maintaine their cause, that he may giue rest to the lande, and disquiet the inhabitants of Babel.

35 A sworde is vpon the Caldeans, sayeth the Lord, and vpon the inhabitants of Babel, and vpon her princes, and vpon her wise men.

36 A sworde is vpon the soothsaiers, and they shall dote: a sword is vpon her strong men, and they shalbe afraide.

37 A sworde is vpon their horses and vpon their charets, and vpon all the multitude that are in the middes of her,

and they shall be like women: a sworde is vpon her treasures, and they shall be spoyled.

38 A drought is vpon her waters, and they shall be dried vp: for it is the lande of grauen images, and they dote vpon their idoles.

39 Therefore the Ziims with the Iims shall dwel there, and the ostriches shall dwel therein: for it shall be no more inhabited, neither shall it be inhabited from generation vnto generation.

40 As God destroied Sodom and Gomorah with the places thereof neere about, sayeth the Lord: so shall no man dwell theere, neither shall the sonne of man remaine therein.

41 Beholde, a people shall come from the North, and a great nation, and many Kings shall be raised vp from the coastes of the earth.

42 They shall holde the bowe and the buckeler: they are cruell and vnmercifull: their voyce shall roare like the sea, and they shall ride vpon horses, and be put in aray like men to the battell against thee, O daughter of Babel.

43 The King of Babel hath heard the report of them, and his hands waxed feeble: sorow came vpon him, euen sorowe as of a woman in trauaile.

44 Beholde, hee shall come vp like a lyon from the swelling of Iorden vnto the strong habitation: for I will make Israel to rest, and I will make them to haste away from her: and who is a chosen man that I may appoynt against her? for who is like me, and who will appoynt me the time? and who is the shepheard that will stande before me?

45 Therefore heare the counsell of the Lord that hee hath deuised against Babel, and his purpose that hee hath conceiued against the lande of the Caldeans: surely the least of the flocke shall drawe them out: surely he shall make their habitation desolate with them.

46 At the noyse of the winning of Babel the earth is moued, and the crye is heard among the nations.

Jeremiah 51

1 Thus sayth the Lord, Beholde, I wil raise vp against Babel, and against the inhabitants that lift vp their heart against me, a destroying wind,

2 And wil send vnto Babel fanners that shall fanne her, and shall empty her land: for in the day of trouble they shalbe against her on euery side.

3 Also to the bender that bendeth his bowe, and to him that lifteth himselfe vp in his brigandine, will I say, Spare not her yong men, but destroy all her hoste.

4 Thus the slaine shall fall in the lande of the Caldeans, and they that are thrust through in her streetes.

5 For Israel hath bene no widowe, nor Iudah from his God, from the Lord of hostes, though their lande was filled with sinne against the holy one of Israel.

6 Flee out of the middes of Babel, and deliuer euery man his soule: be not

destroyed in her iniquitie: for this is the time of the Lordes vengeance he will render vnto her a recompence.

7 Babel hath bene as a golden cuppe in the Lordes hand, that made all the earth drunken: the nations haue drunken of her wine, therefore do the nations rage.

8 Babel is suddenly fallen, and destroyed: howle for her, bring balme for her sore, if she may be healed.

9 We would haue cured Babel, but she could not be healed: forsake her, and let vs go euery one into his owne countrey: for her iudgement is come vp vnto heauen, and is lifted vp to ye cloudes.

10 The Lord hath brought forth our righteousnesse: come and let vs declare in Zion the worke of the Lord our God.

11 Make bright the arrowes: gather the shieldes: the Lord hath raised vp the spirit of the King of the Medes: for his purpose is against Babel to destroy it, because it is the vengeance of the Lord, and the vengeance of his Temple.

12 Set vp the standart vpon the walles of Babel, make the watch strong: set vp the watchmen: prepare the skoutes: for the Lord hath both deuised, and done that which he spake against the inhabitantes of Babel.

13 O thou that dwellest vpon many waters, abundant in treasures, thine ende is come, euen the ende of thy couetousnes.

14 The Lord of hostes hath sworne by him selfe, saying, Surely I will fill thee with men, as with caterpillers, and they shall cry and shoute against thee.

15 He hath made the earth by his power, and established the world by his wisedome, and hath stretched out the heauen by his discretion.

16 Hee giueth by his voyce the multitude of waters in the heauen, and he causeth the cloudes to ascend from the endes of the earth: he turneth lightnings to raine, and bringeth forth the winde out of his treasures.

17 Euery man is a beast by his owne knowledge: euery founder is confounded by the grauen image: for his melting is but falsehood, and there is no breath therein.

18 They are vanitie, and the worke of errours: in the time of their visitation they shall perish.

19 The portion of Iaakob is not like them: for he is the maker of all things, and Israel is the rodde of his inheritance: the Lord of hostes is his Name.

20 Thou art mine hammer, and weapons of warre: for with thee will I breake the nations, and with thee wil I destroy kingdomes,

21 And by thee wil I breake horse and horseman, and by thee will I breake the charet and him that rideth therein.

22 By thee also will I breake man and woman, and by thee wil I breake olde and yong, and by thee wil I breake the yong man and the mayde.

23 I wil also breake by thee the shepheard and his flocke, and by thee will I breake the husband man and his

yoke of oxen, and by thee will I breake the dukes and princes.

24 And I will render vnto Babel, and to all the inhabitants of the Caldeans all their euil, that they haue done in Zion, euen in your sight, sayth the Lord.

25 Beholde, I come vnto thee, O destroying mountaine, sayth the Lord, which destroyest all the earth: and I will stretch out mine hand vpon thee, and rolle thee downe from the rockes, and wil make thee a burnt mountaine.

26 They shall not take of thee a stone for a corner, nor a stone for foundations, but thou shalt be destroyed for euer, sayth the Lord.

27 Set vp a standard in the lande: blowe the trumpets among the nations: prepare the nations against her: call vp the kingdomes of Ararat, Minni, and Ashchenaz against her: appoynt the prince against her: cause horses to come vp as the rough caterpillers.

28 Prepare against her the nations with the Kings of the Medes, the dukes thereof, and the princes thereof, and all the land of his dominion.

29 And the land shall tremble and sorow: for the deuise of the Lord shalbe performed against Babel, to make the lande of Babel waste without an inhabitant.

30 The strong men of Babel haue ceased to fight: they haue remayned in their holdes: their strength hath fayled, and they were like women: they haue burnt her dwelling places, and her barres are broken.

31 A post shall runne to meete the post, and a messenger to meete the messenger, to shew the King of Babel, that his citie is taken on a side thereof,

32 And that the passages are stopped, and the reedes burnt with fire, and the me of war troubled.

33 For thus sayth the Lord of hosts the God of Israel, the daughter of Babel is like a threshing floore: the time of her threshing is come: yet a litle while, and the time of her haruest shall come.

34 Nebuchad-nezzar the King of Babel hath deuoured me, and destroyed me: he hath made mee an emptie vessel: he swallowed mee vp like a dragon, and filled his belly with my delicates, and hath cast me out.

35 The spoyle of me, and that which was left of me, is brought vnto Babel, shall the inhabitant of Zion say: and my blood vnto the inhabitantes of Caldea, shall Ierusalem say.

36 Therefore thus sayth the Lord, Beholde, I will maintayne thy cause, and take vengeance for thee, and I will drie vp the sea, and drie vp her springes.

37 And Babel shall be as heapes, a dwelling place for dragons, an astonishment, and an hissing, without an inhabitant.

38 They shall rore together like lions, and yell as the lyons whelpes.

39 In their heate I will make them feastes, and I wil make them drunken, that they may reioyce, and sleepe a perpetual sleepe, and not wake, sayth the Lord.

40 I wil bring them downe like lambes to the slaughter, and like rams and goates.

41 How is Sheshach taken! and howe is the glory of the whole earth taken! how is Babel become an astonishment among the nations!

42 The sea is come vp vpon Babel: he is couered with the multitude of the waues thereof.

43 Her cities are desolate: the land is dry and a wildernes, a land wherein no man dwelleth, neither doth the sonne of man passe thereby.

44 I wil also visite Bel in Babel, and I wil bring out of his mouth, that which he hath swallowed vp, and the nations shall runne no more vnto him, and the wall of Babel shall fall.

45 My people, go out of the middes of her, and deliuer yee euery man his soule from the fierce wrath of the Lord,

46 Least your heart euen faynt, and ye feare the rumour, that shalbe heard in the land: the rumour shall come this yeere, and after that in the other yeere shall come a rumour, and crueltie in the land, and ruler against ruler.

47 Therefore beholde, the dayes come, that I will visite the images of Babel, and the whole land shalbe confounded, and all her slayne shall fall in the middes of her.

48 Then the heauen and the earth, and all that is therein, shall reioyce for Babel: for the destroyers shall come vnto her from the North, saith the Lord.

49 As Babel caused the slaine of Israel to fal, so by Babel the slaine of all the earth did fall.

50 Ye that haue escaped the sworde, goe away, stand not still: remember the Lord a farre of, and let Ierusalem come into your minde.

51 Wee are confounded because wee haue heard reproch: shame hath couered our faces, for straungers are come into the Sanctuaries of the Lordes House.

52 Wherefore behold, the dayes come, sayth the Lord, that I will visite her grauen images, and through all her land the wounded shall grone.

53 Though Babel should mount vp to heauen, and though shee should defend her strength on hye, yet from mee shall her destroyers come, sayth the Lord.

54 A sound of a cry commeth from Babel, and great destruction from the land of the Caldeans,

55 Because the Lord hath layde Babel waste and destroyed from her the great voyce, and her waues shall roare like great waters, and a sounde was made by their noyse:

56 Because the destroyer is come vpon her, euen vpon Babel, and her strong men are taken, their bowes are broken: for the Lord God that recompenceth, shall surely recompence.

57 And I will make drunke her princes, and her wise men, her dukes, and her nobles, and her strong men: and they shall sleepe a perpetuall sleepe, and not wake, sayth the King, whose Name is the Lord of hostes.

58 Thus saith the Lord of hostes, The thicke wall of Babel shalbe broken, and her hie gates shall be burnt with fire, and the people shall labour in vaine, and the folke in ye fire, for they shalbe weary.

59 The worde which Ieremiah the Prophet commanded Sheraiah the sonne of Neriiah, the sonne of Maaseiah, when he went with Zedekiah the King of Iudah into Babel, in the fourth yeere of his reigne: and this Sheraiah was a peaceable prince.

60 So Ieremiah wrote in a booke all the euill that should come vpon Babel: euen al these things, that are written against Babel.

61 And Ieremiah sayd to Sheraiah, Whe thou commest vnto Babel, and shalt see, and shalt reade all these wordes,

62 Then shalt thou say, O Lord, thou hast spoken against this place, to destroy it, that none should remaine in it, neither man nor beast, but that it should be desolate for euer.

63 And when thou hast made an ende of reading this booke, thou shalt binde a stone to it, and cast it in the middes of Euphrates,

64 And shalt say, Thus shall Babel be drowned, and shall not rise from the euil, that I will bring vpon her: and they shall be weary. Thus farre are the wordes of Ieremiah.

Jeremiah 52

1 Zedekiah was one and twentie yeere olde when he began to reigne, and he reigned eleuen yeeres in Ierusalem, and his mothers name was Hamutal, the daughter of Ieremiah of Libnah.

2 And he did euil in the eyes of the Lord, according to all that Iehoiakim had done.

3 Doubtlesse because the wrath of the Lord was against Ierusalem and Iudah, till he had cast them out from his presence, therefore Zedekiah rebelled against the King of Babel.

4 But in the ninth yeere of his reigne, in the tenth moneth the tenth day of the moneth came Nebuchad-nezzar King of Babel, he and all his hoste against Ierusalem, and pitched against it, and buylt fortes against it round about.

5 So the citie was besieged vnto the eleuenth yeere of the King Zedekiah.

6 Now in the fourth moneth, the ninth day of the moneth, the famine was sore in ye citie, so that there was no more bread for ye people of the land.

7 Then the citie was broken vp and all the men of warre fled, and went out of the citie by night, by the way of the gate betweene the two walles, which was by the kings garden: (now the Caldeans were by the citie round about) and they went by the way of the wildernes.

8 But the army of the Caldeans pursued after the king, and tooke Zedekiah in the desert of Iericho, and all his host was scattered from him.

9 Then they tooke the king and caryed him vp vnto the king of Babel to Riblah in the lande of Hamath, where he gaue iudgement vpon him.

10 And the king of Babel slewe the sonnes of Zedekiah, before his eyes he slew also al ye princes of Iudah in Riblah.

11 Then he put out the eyes of Zedekiah, and the king of Babel bound him in chaines, and caried him to Babel, and put him in pryson till the day of his death.

12 Now in the fift moneth in the tenth day of the moneth (which was the nineteenth yere of ye King Nebuchad-nezzar King of Babel) came Nebuzar-adan chiefe steward which stoode before the king of Babel in Ierusalem,

13 And burnt the House of the Lord, and the Kings house, and all the houses of Ierusalem, and all the great houses burnt he with fire.

14 And al the armie of the Caldeans that were with the chiefe steward, brake downe all ye walles of Ierusalem round about.

15 Then Nebuzar-adan the chiefe steward caried away captiue certaine of the poore of the people, and the residue of the people that remayned in the citie, and those that were fled, and fallen to the king of Babel, with the rest of the multitude.

16 But Nebuzar-adan the chiefe steward left certaine of the poore of the lande, to dresse the vines, and to till the land.

17 Also the pillars of brasse that were in the House of the Lord, and the bases, and the brasen Sea, that was in the house of ye Lord, the Caldeans brake, and caried all the brasse of them to Babel.

18 The pots also and the besomes, and the instruments of musicke, and the basins, and the incense dishes, and all the vessels of brasse wherewith they ministred, tooke they away.

19 And the bowles, and the ashpannes, and the basins, and the pots, and the candlestickes, and the incense dishes, and the cuppes, and all that was of golde, and that was of siluer, tooke the chiefe steward away,

20 With the two pillars, one Sea, and twelue brasen bulles, that were vnder the bases, which King Salomon had made in ye house of ye Lord: the brasse of all these vessels was without weight.

21 And concerning the pillars, the height of one pillar was eighteene cubites, and a threede of twelue cubites did compasse it, and the thicknesse thereof was foure fingers: it was holowe.

22 And a chapiter of brasse was vpon it, and the height of one chapiter was fiue cubites with networke, and pomegranates vpon the chapiters round about, all of brasse: the seconde pillar also, and the pomegranates were like vnto these.

23 And there were ninetie and sixe pomegranates on a side: and all the pomegranates vpon the net worke were an hundreth round about.

24 And the chiefe steward tooke Sheraiah the chiefe Priest, and Zephaniah the seconde Priest, and the three keepers of the doore.

25 Hee tooke also out of the citie an Eunuch, which had the ouersight of the men of warre, and seuen men that were in the Kings presence, which were founde in the citie, and Sopher captayne of the hoste who mustered the people of the lande, and threescore men of the people of the land, that were found in the middes of the citie.

26 Nebuzar-adan the chiefe stewarde tooke them, and brought them to the king of Babel to Riblah.

27 And the king of Babel smote them, and slewe them in Riblah, in the lande of Hamath: thus Iudah was caried away captiue out of his owne land.

28 This is the people, whome Nebuchad-nezzar caried away captiue, in the seuenth yeere, euen three thousande Iewes, and three and twentie.

29 In the eightenth yere of Nebuchad-nezzar he caried away captiue from Ierusalem eight hundreth thirtie and two persons.

30 In the three and twentieth yeere of Nebuchad-nezzar, Nebuzar-adan the chiefe stewarde caried away captiue of the Iewes seuen hundreth fourtie and fiue persons: all the persons were foure thousand and sixe hundreth.

31 And in the seuen and thirtieth yeere of the captiuitie of Iehoiachin King of Iudah, in the twelfth moneth, in the fiue and twentieth day of the moneth, Euil-merodach King of Babel, in the first yeere of his reigne, lifted vp the head of Iehoiachin King of Iudah, and brought him out of pryson,

32 And spake kindly vnto him, and set his throne aboue the throne of the Kings, that were with him in Babel,

33 And changed his pryson garmentes, and he did continually eate bread before him all the dayes of his life.

34 His porcion was a continuall portion giuen him of ye king of Babel, euery day a certaine, all the dayes of his life vntill he died.

Lamentations

Lamentations 1

1 Howe doeth the citie remaine solitarie that was full of people? she is as a widowe: she that was great among the nations, and princesse among the prouinces, is made tributarie.

2 She weepeth continually in the night, and her teares runne downe by her cheekes: among all her louers, she hath none to comfort her: all her friendes haue delt vnfaithfully with her, and are her enemies.

3 Iudah is caried away captiue because of affliction, and because of great seruitude: shee dwelleth among the heathen, and findeth no rest: all her persecuters tooke her in the straites.

4 The wayes of Zion lament, because no man commeth to the solemne feastes: all her gates are desolate: her Priests sigh: her virgins are discomfited, and she is in heauinesse.

5 Her aduersaries are the chiefe, and her enemies prosper: for the Lord hath afflicted her, for the multitude of her transgressions, and her children are gone into captiuitie before the enemie.

6 And from the daughter of Zion all her beautie is departed: her princes are become like harts that finde no pasture, and they are gone without strength before the pursuer.

7 Ierusalem remembred the dayes of her affliction, and of her rebellion, and all her pleasant things, that shee had in times past, when her people fell into the hande of the enemie, and none did helpe her: the aduersarie sawe her, and did mocke at her Sabbaths.

8 Ierusalem hath grieuously sinned, therefore shee is in derision: all that honoured her, despise her, because they haue seene her filthinesse: yea, she sigheth and turneth backeward.

9 Her filthinesse is in her skirts: she remembred not her last ende, therefore she came downe wonderfully: she had no comforter: O Lord, behold mine affliction: for the enemie is proud.

10 The enemie hath stretched out his hande vpon al her pleasant things: for she hath seene the heathen enter into her Sanctuarie, whom thou diddest commande, that they shoulde not enter into thy Church.

11 All her people sigh and seeke their bread: they haue giuen their pleasant thinges for meate to refresh the soule: see, O Lord, and consider: for I am become vile.

12 Haue ye no regarde, all yee that passe by this way? behold, and see, if there be any sorowe like vnto my sorowe, which is done vnto mee, wherewith the Lord hath afflicted me in the day of his fierce wrath.

13 From aboue hath hee sent fire into my bones, which preuaile against them: he hath spred a net for my feete, and turned me backe: hee hath made me desolate, and daily in heauinesse.

14 The yoke of my transgressions is bounde vpon his hand: they are wrapped, and come vp vpon my necke: hee hath made my strength to fall: the Lord hath deliuered me into their hands, neither am I able to rise vp.

15 The Lord hath troden vnder foote all my valiant men in the middes of me: he hath called an assembly against me to destroy my yong men: the Lord hath troden the wine presse vpon the virgine the daughter of Iudah.

16 For these things I weepe: mine eye, euen mine eye casteth out water, because the comforter that should refresh my soule, is farre from me: my children are desolate, because the enemie preuailed.

17 Zion stretcheth out her handes, and there is none to comfort her: the Lord hath appoynted the enemies of Iaakob rounde about him: Ierusalem is as a

menstruous woman in the middes of them.

18 The Lord is righteous: for I haue rebelled against his commandement: heare, I pray you, all people, and behold my sorowe: my virgins and my yong men are gone into captiuitie.

19 I called for my louers, but they deceiued me: my Priestes and mine Elders perished in the citie while they sought their meate to refresh their soules.

20 Behold, O Lord, howe I am troubled: my bowels swell: mine heart is turned within me, for I am ful of heauinesse: the sword spoyleth abroad, as death doeth at home.

21 They haue heard that I mourne, but there is none to comfort mee: all mine enemies haue heard of my trouble, and are glad, that thou hast done it: thou wilt bring the day, that thou hast pronounced, and they shalbe like vnto me.

22 Let all their wickednes come before thee: do vnto them, as thou hast done vnto me, for all my transgressions: for my sighes are many, and mine heart is heauy.

Lamentations 2

1 How hath the Lord darkened the daughter of Zion in his wrath! and hath cast downe from heauen vnto the earth the beautie of Israel, and remembred not his footestoole in the day of his wrath!

2 The Lord hath destroyed al the habitations of Iaakob, and not spared: he hath thrown downe in his wrath ye strong holds of the daughter of Iudah: he hath cast the downe to ye ground: he hath polluted the kingdome and the princes thereof.

3 Hee hath cut off in his fierce wrath all the horne of Israel: he hath drawen backe his right hand from before the enemie, and there was kindled in Iaakob like a flame of fire, which deuoured rounde about.

4 He hath bent his bowe like an enemie: his right hand was stretched vp as an aduersarie, and slewe al that was pleasant to the eye in the tabernacle of the daughter of Zion: he powred out his wrath like fire.

5 The Lord was as an enemie: he hath deuoured Israel, and consumed all his palaces: hee hath destroyed his strong holdes, and hath increased in the daughter of Iudah lamentation and mourning.

6 For hee hath destroyed his Tabernacle, as a garden, hee hath destroyed his Congregation: the Lord hath caused the feastes and Sabbathes to bee forgotten in Zion, and hath despised in the indignation of his wrath the King and the Priest.

7 The Lord hath forsaken his altar: he hath abhorred his Sanctuarie: he hath giue into the hand of the enemie the walles of her palaces: they haue made a noyse in the House of the Lord, as in the day of solemnitie.

8 The Lord hath determined to destroy the wall of the daughter of Zion: hee stretched out a lyne: hee hath not withdrawen his hande from destroying: therefore hee made the rampart and the wall to lament: they were destroyed together.

9 Her gates are sunke to the grounde: he hath destroyed and broken her barres: her King and her princes are among the Gentiles: the Lawe is no more, neither can her Prophets receiue any vision from the Lord.

10 The Elders of the daughter of Zion sit vpon the grounde, and keepe silence: they haue cast vp dust vpon their heades: they haue girded them selues with sackecloth: the virgines of Ierusalem hang downe their heades to the ground.

11 Mine eyes doe saile with teares: my bowels swell: my liuer is powred vpon the earth, for the destruction of the daughter of my people, because the children and sucklings swoone in the streetes of the citie.

12 They haue sayd to their mothers, Where is bread and drinke? when they swooned as the wounded in the streetes of the citie, and whe they gaue vp the ghost in their mothers bosome.

13 What thing shall I take to witnesse for thee? what thing shall I compare to thee, O daughter Ierusalem? what shall I liken to thee, that I may comfort thee, O virgine daughter Zion? for thy breach is great like ye sea: who can heale thee?

14 Thy Prophets haue looked out vayne, and foolish things for thee, and they haue not discouered thine iniquitie, to turne away thy captiuitie, but haue looked out for thee false prophesies, and causes of banishment.

15 All that passe by the way, clap their hands at thee: they hisse and wagge their head vpon the daughter Ierusalem, saying, Is this the citie that men call, The perfection of beautie, and the ioye of the whole earth?

16 All thine enemies haue opened their mouth against thee: they hisse and gnashe the teeth, saying, Let vs deuoure it: certainely this is the day that we looked for: we haue founde and seene it.

17 The Lord hath done that which he had purposed: he hath fulfilled his worde that he had determined of old time: he hath thrown downe, and not spared: hee hath caused thine enemie to reioyce ouer thee, and set vp the horne of thine aduersaries.

18 Their heart cryed vnto the Lord, O wall of the daughter Zion, let teares runne downe like a riuer, day and night: take thee no rest, neither let the apple of thine eye cease.

19 Arise, cry in the night: in the beginning of the watches powre out thine heart like water before the face of the Lord: lift vp thine handes towarde him for the life of thy yong children, that faint for hunger in the corners of all the streetes.

20 Beholde, O Lord, and consider to whome thou hast done thus: shall the women eate their fruite, and children of a spanne long? shall the Priest and the Prophet be slaine in the Sanctuarie of the Lord?

21 The yong and the olde lie on the ground in the streetes: my virgins and my yong men are fallen by the sworde: thou hast slaine them in the day of thy wrath: thou hast killed and not spared.

22 Thou hast called as in a solemne daye my terrours rounde about, so that in the day of the Lordes wrath none escaped nor remained: those that I haue nourished and brought vp, hath mine enemie consumed.

Lamentations 3

1 I am the man, that hath seene affliction in the rod of his indignation.

2 He hath ledde mee, and brought me into darkenes, but not to light.

3 Surely he is turned against me: he turneth his hand against me all the day.

4 My flesh and my skinne hath he caused to waxe olde, and he hath broken my bones.

5 He hath builded against me, and compassed me with gall, and labour.

6 He hath set me in darke places, as they that be dead for euer.

7 He hath hedged about mee, that I cannot get out: he hath made my chaines heauy.

8 Also when I cry and showte, hee shutteth out my prayer.

9 He hath stopped vp my wayes with hewen stone, and turned away my paths.

10 He was vnto me as a beare lying in waite, and as a Lion in secret places.

11 He hath stopped my wayes, and pulled me in pieces: he hath made me desolate.

12 He hath bent his bow and made me a marke for the arrow.

13 Hee caused the arrowes of his quiuer to enter into my reines.

14 I was a derision to all my people, and their song all the day.

15 He hath filled me with bitternes, and made me drunken with wormewood.

16 He hath also broken my teeth with stones, and hath couered me with ashes.

17 Thus my soule was farre off from peace: I forgate prosperitie,

18 And I saide, My strength and mine hope is perished from the Lord,

19 Remembring mine affliction, and my mourning, the wormewood and the gall.

20 My soule hath them in remembrance, and is humbled in me.

21 I consider this in mine heart: therefore haue I hope.

22 It is the Lordes mercies that wee are not consumed, because his compassions faile not.

23 They are renued euery morning: great is thy faithfulnesse.

24 The Lord is my portion, sayth my soule: therefore wil I hope in him.

25 The Lord is good vnto them, that trust in him, and to the soule that seeketh him.

26 It is good both to trust, and to waite for the saluation of the Lord.

27 It is good for a man that he beare the yoke in his youth.

28 He sitteth alone, and keepeth silence, because he hath borne it vpon him.

29 He putteth his mouth in the dust, if there may be hope.

30 Hee giueth his cheeke to him that smiteth him: he is filled full with reproches.

31 For the Lord will not forsake for euer.

32 But though he sende affliction, yet will he haue compassion according to the multitude of his mercies.

33 For he doeth not punish willingly, nor afflict the children of men,

34 In stamping vnder his feete all the prisoners of the earth,

35 In ouerthrowing the right of a man before the face of the most high,

36 In subuerting a man in his cause: the Lord seeth it not.

37 Who is he then that sayth, and it commeth to passe, and the Lord commandeth it not?

38 Out of the mouth of the most high proceedeth not euill and good?

39 Wherefore then is the liuing man sorowfull? man suffreth for his sinne.

40 Let vs search and try our wayes, and turne againe to the Lord.

41 Let vs lift vp our hearts with our handes vnto God in the heauens.

42 We haue sinned, and haue rebelled, therefore thou hast not spared.

43 Thou hast couered vs with wrath, and persecuted vs: thou hast slaine and not spared.

44 Thou hast couered thy selfe with a cloude, that our prayer should not passe through.

45 Thou hast made vs as the ofscouring and refuse in the middes of the people.

46 All our enemies haue opened their mouth against vs.

47 Feare, and a snare is come vpon vs with desolation and destruction.

48 Mine eye casteth out riuers of water, for the destruction of the daughter of my people.

49 Mine eye droppeth without stay and ceaseth not,

50 Till the Lord looke downe, and beholde from heauen.

51 Mine eye breaketh mine heart because of all the daughters of my citie.

52 Mine enemies chased me sore like a birde, without cause.

53 They haue shut vp my life in the dungeon, and cast a stone vpon me.

54 Waters flowed ouer mine head, then thought I, I am destroyed.

55 I called vpon thy Name, O Lord, out of the lowe dungeon.

56 Thou hast heard my voyce: stoppe not thine eare from my sigh and from my cry.

57 Thou drewest neere in the day that I called vpon thee: thou saydest, Feare not.

58 O Lord, thou hast maintained the cause of my soule, and hast redeemed my life.

59 O Lord, thou hast seene my wrong, iudge thou my cause.

60 Thou hast seene all their vengeance, and all their deuises against me.

61 Thou hast heard their reproch, O Lord, and all their imaginations against me:

62 The lippes also of those that rose against me, and their whispering against me continually.

63 Behold, their sitting downe and their rising vp, how I am their song.

64 Giue them a recompence, O Lord, according to the worke of their handes.

65 Giue them sorow of heart, euen thy curse to them.

66 Persecute with wrath and destroy them from vnder the heauen, O Lord.

Lamentations 4

1 How is the golde become so dimme? the most fine golde is changed, and the stones of the Sanctuarie are scattered in the corner of euery streete.

2 The noble men of Zion coparable to fine golde, howe are they esteemed as earthen pitchers, euen the worke of the handes of the potter!

3 Euen the dragons draw out the breastes, and giue sucke to their yong, but the daughter of my people is become cruell like the ostriches in the wildernesse.

4 The tongue of the sucking childe cleaueth to the roofe of his mouth for thirst: the yong children aske bread, but no man breaketh it vnto them.

5 They that did feede delicately, perish in the streetes: they that were brought vp in skarlet, embrace the dongue.

6 For the iniquitie of the daughter of my people is become greater then the sinne of Sodom, that was destroyed as in a moment, and none pitched campes against her.

7 Her Nazarites were purer then the snowe, and whiter then ye milke: they were more ruddie in bodie, then the redde precious stones; they were like polished saphir.

8 Nowe their visage is blacker then a cole: they can not knowe them in the streetes: their skinne cleaueth to their bones: it is withered like a stocke.

9 They that be slaine with the sword are better, then they that are killed with hunger: for they fade away as they were striken through for the fruites of the fielde.

10 The hands of the pitifull women haue sodden their owne children, which were their meate in the destruction of the daughter of my people.

11 The Lord hath accomplished his indignation: he hath powred out his fierce wrath, he hath kindled a fire in Zion, which hath deuoured the foundations thereof.

12 The Kings of the earth, and all the inhabitants of the world would not haue beleeued that the aduersarie and the enemie should haue entred into the gates of Ierusalem:

13 For the sinnes of her Prophets, and the iniquities of her Priests, that haue shed the blood of the iust in the middes of her.

14 They haue wandred as blinde men in the streetes, and they were polluted with blood, so that they would not touch their garments.

15 But they cried vnto them, Depart, ye polluted, depart, depart, touch not: therefore they fled away, and wandered: they haue sayd among the heathen, They shall no more dwell there.

16 The anger of the Lord hath scattered them, he will no more regard them: they reuerenced not the face of the Priestes, nor had compassion of the Elders.

17 Whiles we waited for our vaine helpe, our eyes failed: for in our waiting we looked for a nation that could not saue vs.

18 They hunt our steppes that we cannot goe in our streetes: our ende is neere, our dayes are fulfilled, for our ende is come.

19 Our persecuters are swifter then the eagles of the heauen: they pursued vs vpon the mountaines, and layed waite for vs in the wildernes.

20 The breath of our nostrels, the Anoynted of the Lord was taken in their nets, of whome we sayde, Vnder his shadowe we shalbe preserued aliue among the heathen.

21 Reioyce and be glad, O daughter Edom, that dwellest in the lande of Vz, the cuppe also shall passe through vnto thee: thou shalt be drunken and vomit.

22 Thy punishment is accomplished, O daughter Zion: he will no more carie thee away into captiuitie, but he will visite thine iniquitie, O daughter Edom, he wil discouer thy sinnes.

Lamentations 5

1 Remember, O Lord, what is come vpon vs: consider, and behold our reproche.

2 Our inheritance is turned to the strangers, our houses to the aliants.

3 We are fatherles, euen without father, and our mothers are as widowes.

4 Wee haue drunke our water for money, and our wood is solde vnto vs.

5 Our neckes are vnder persecution: we are wearie, and haue no rest.

6 We haue giuen our handes to the Egyptians, and to Asshur, to be satisfied with bread.

7 Our fathers haue sinned, and are not, and we haue borne their iniquities.

8 Seruants haue ruled ouer vs, none would deliuer vs out of their hands.

9 Wee gate our bread with the perill of our liues, because of the sword of the wildernesse.

10 Our skinne was blacke like as an ouen because of the terrible famine.

11 They defiled the women in Zion, and the maydes in the cities of Iudah.

12 The princes are hanged vp by their hande: the faces of the elders were not had in honour.

13 They tooke the yong men to grinde, and the children fell vnder the wood.

14 The Elders haue ceased from the gate and the yong men from their songs.

15 The ioy of our heart is gone, our daunce is turned into mourning.

16 The crowne of our head is fallen: wo nowe vnto vs, that we haue sinned.

17 Therefore our heart is heauy for these things, our eyes are dimme,

18 Because of the mountaine of Zion which is desolate: the foxes runne vpon it.

19 But thou, O Lord, remainest for euer: thy throne is from generation to generation.

20 Wherefore doest thou forget vs for euer, and forsake vs so long time?

21 Turne thou vs vnto thee, O Lord, and we shalbe turned: renue our dayes as of olde.

22 But thou hast vtterly reiected vs: thou art exceedingly angry against vs.

Ezekiel

Ezekiel 1

1 It came to passe in the thirtieth yere in the fourth moneth, and in the fift day of the moneth (as I was among the captiues by the riuer Chebar) that the heauens were opened and I sawe visions of GOD.

2 In the fift day of the moneth (which was the fift yere of King Ioiachins captiuitie)

3 The word of the Lord came vnto Ezekiel the Priest, the sonne of Buzi, in the lande of the Caldeans, by the riuer Chebar, where the hande of the Lord was vpon him.

4 And I looked, and beholde, a whirlewinde came out of the North, a great cloude and a fire wrapped about it, and a brightnesse was about it, and in the middes thereof, to wit, in the middes of the fire came out as the likenesse of amber.

5 Also out of the middes therof came the likenesse of foure beastes, and this was their forme: they had the appearance of a man.

6 And euery one had foure faces, and euery one had foure wings.

7 And their feete were streight feete, and the sole of their feete was like the sole of a calues foote, and they sparkled like the appearance of bright brasse.

8 And the handes of a man came out from vnder their wings in the foure parts of them, and they foure had their faces, and their wings.

9 They where ioyned by their wings one to another, and when they went forth, they returned not, but euery one went streight forward.

10 And the similitude of their faces was as the face of a man: and they foure had the face of a lyon on the right side, and they foure had the face of a bullocke on the left side: they foure also had the face of an eagle.

11 Thus were their faces: but their wings were spred out aboue: two wings of euery one were ioined one to another, and two couered their bodies.

12 And euery one went streight forward: they went whither their spirit led them, and they returned not when they went forth.

13 The similitude also of the beasts, and their appearance was like burning coles of fire, and like the appearance of lampes: for the fire ran among the beastes, and the fire gaue a glister, and out of the fire there went lightning.

14 And the beastes ranne, and returned like vnto lightning.

15 Nowe as I behelde the beastes, beholde, a wheele appeared vpon the earth by the beastes, hauing foure faces.

16 The facion of the wheeles and their worke was like vnto a chrysolite: and they foure had one forme, and their facion, and their worke was as one wheele in another wheele.

17 Whe they went, they went vpon their foure sides, and they returned not when they went.

18 They had also rings, and height, and were fearefull to beholde, and their rings were full of eyes, round about them foure.

19 And when the beastes went, the wheeles went with them: and when the beasts were lift vp from the earth, the wheeles were lift vp.

20 Whither the spirit led them, they went, and thither did the spirite of the wheeles leade them, and the wheeles were lifted vp besides them: for the spirit of the beastes was in the wheeles.

21 When the beastes went, they went, and when they stoode, they stoode, and when they were lifted vp from the earth, the wheeles were lifted vp besides them: for the spirite of the beastes was in the wheeles.

22 And the similitude of the firmament vpon the heads of the beasts was wonderfull, like vnto chrystall, spred ouer their heads aboue.

23 And vnder the firmament were their wings streight, the one toward the other: every one had two, which couered the, and euery one had two, which couered their bodies.

24 And when they went foorth, I heard the noyse of their wings, like the noyse of great waters, and as the voyce of the Almightie, euen the voyce of speach, as the noyse of an host: and when they stood, they let downe their wings.

25 And there was a voyce from the firmament, that was ouer their heads, when they stoode, and had let downe their wings.

26 And aboue the firmament that was ouer their heads, was the facion of a throne like vnto a saphir stone, and vpon the similitude of the throne was by appearance, as the similitude of a man aboue vpon it.

27 And I sawe as the appearance of amber, and as the similitude of fire round about within it to looke to, euen from his loynes vpwarde: and to looke to, euen from his loynes downewarde, I sawe as a likenesse of fire, and brightnesse round about it.

28 As the likenesse of the bowe, that is in the cloude in the day of raine, so was the appearance of the light round about.

29 This was the appearance of the similitude of the glorie of the Lord: and when I sawe it, I fell vpon my face, and I heard a voyce of one that spake.

Ezekiel 2

1 And he said vnto me, Sonne of man, stand vp vpon thy feete, and I wil speake vnto thee.

2 And the Spirite entred into me, when he had spoken vnto me, and set me vpon my feete, so that I heard him that spake vnto me.

3 And he said vnto me, Sonne of man, I send thee to the children of Israel, to a rebellious nation that hath rebelled against me: for they and their fathers haue rebelled against me, euen vnto this very day.

4 For they are impudent children, and stiffe hearted: I do send thee vnto them, and thou shalt say vnto them, Thus saith the Lord God.

5 But surely they will not heare, neither in deede will they cease: for they are a rebellious house: yet shall they knowe that there hath bene a Prophet among them.

6 And thou sonne of man, feare them not, neither be afraide of their wordes, although rebels, and thornes be with thee, and thou remainest with scorpions: feare not their wordes, nor be afrayde at their lookes, for they are a rebellious house.

7 Therefore thou shalt speake my words vnto them: but surely they will not heare, neither will they in deede cease: for they are rebellious.

8 But thou sonne of man, heare what I say vnto thee: be not thou rebellious, like this rebellious house: open thy mouth, and eate that I giue thee.

9 And when I looked vp, beholde, an hande was sent vnto me, and loe, a roule of a booke was therein.

10 And he spred it before me, and it was written within and without, and there was written therein, Lamentations, and mourning, and woe.

Ezekiel 3

1 Moreover he saide vnto me, Sonne of man, eate that thou findest: eate this roule, and goe, and speake vnto the house of Israel.

2 So I opencd my mouth, and he gaue mee this roule to eate.

3 And he said vnto me, Sonne of man, cause thy belly to eate, and fill thy bowels with this roule that I giue thee. Then did I eate it, and it was in my mouth as sweete as honie.

4 And he said vnto me, Sonne of man, goe, and enter into the house of Israel, and declare them my wordes.

5 For thou art not sent to a people of an vnknowen tongue, or of an hard language, but to the house of Israel,

6 Not to many people of an vnknowen tongue, or of an harde language, whose

wordes thou canst not vnderstand: yet if I should sende thee to them, they would obey thee.

7 But the house of Israel will not obey thee: for they will not obey me: yea, all the house of Israel are impudent and stiffe hearted.

8 Beholde, I haue made thy face strong against their faces, and thy forehead harde against their foreheads.

9 I haue made thy forehead as the adamant, and harder then the flint: feare them not therefore, neither be afraid at their lookes: for they are a rebellious house.

10 He said moreouer vnto me, Sonne of man, receiue in thine heart al my words that I speake vnto thee, and heare them with thine eares.

11 And goe and enter to them that are led away captiues vnto the children of thy people, and speake vnto them, and tell them, Thus saith the Lord God: but surely they will not heare, neither will they in deede cease.

12 Then the spirite tooke me vp, and I heard behinde me a noise of a great russhing, saying, Blessed be ye glorie of the Lord out of his place.

13 I heard also the noyse of the wings of the beasts, that touched one another, and the ratling of the wheeles that were by them, euen a noyse of a great russhing.

14 So the spirit lift me vp, and tooke me away and I went in bitternesse, and indignation of my spirite, but the hand of the Lord was strong vpon me.

15 Then I came to them that were led away captiues to Tel-abib, that dwelt by the riuer Chebar, and I sate where they sate, and remained there astonished among them seuen dayes.

16 And at the ende of seuen dayes, the worde of the Lord came againe vnto me, saying,

17 Sonne of man, I haue made thee a watchman vnto the house of Israel: therefore heare the worde at my mouth, and giue them warning from me.

18 When I shall say vnto the wicked, Thou shalt surely die, and thou giuest not him warning, nor speakest to admonish the wicked of his wicked way, that he may liue, the same wicked man shall die in his iniquitie: but his blood will I require at thine hande.

19 Yet if thou warne the wicked, and he turne not from his wickednesse, nor from his wicked way, he shall die in his iniquitie, but thou hast deliuered thy soule.

20 Likewise if a righteous man turne from his righteousnesse, and commit iniquitie, I will lay a stumbling blocke before him, and he shall die, because thou hast not giuen him warning: he shall die in his sinne, and his righteous deedes, which he hath done, shall not be remembred: but his blood will I require at thine hand.

21 Neuerthelesse, if thou admonish that righteous man, that the righteous sinne not, and that he doeth not sinne, he shall liue because he is admonished: also thou hast deliuered thy soule.

22 And the hande of the Lord was there vpon me, and he said vnto me, Arise, and goe into the fielde, and I will there talke with thee.

23 So when I had risen vp, and gone foorth into the fielde, beholde, the glorie of the Lord stoode there, as the glorie which I sawe by the riuer Chebar, and I fell downe vpon my face.

24 Then the Spirit entred into me, which set me vp vpon my feete, and spake vnto me, and said to me, Come, and shut thy selfe within thine house.

25 But thou, O sonne of man, beholde, they shall put bandes vpon thee, and shall binde thee with them, and thou shalt not goe out among them.

26 And I will make thy tongue cleaue to the roofe of thy mouth, that thou shalt be dume, and shalt not be to them as a man that rebuketh: for they are a rebellious house.

27 But when I shall haue spoken vnto thee, I will open thy mouth, and thou shalt say vnto them, Thus saith the Lord God, He that heareth, let him heare, and he that leaueth off, let him leaue: for they are a rebellious house.

Ezekiel 4

1 Thou also sonne of man, take thee a bricke, and lay it before thee, and pourtray vpon it the citie, euen Ierusalem,

2 And lay siege against it, and builde a fort against it, and cast a mount against it: set the campe also against it, and lay engins of warre against it rounde about.

3 Moreouer, take an yron pan, and set it for a wall of yron betweene thee and the citie, and direct thy face towarde it, and it shall be besieged, and thou shalt lay siege against it: this shall be a signe vnto the house of Israel.

4 Sleepe thou also vpon thy left side, and lay the iniquitie of the house of Israel vpon it: according to the number of the dayes, that thou shalt sleepe vpon it, thou shalt beare their iniquity.

5 For I haue layed vpon thee the yeeres of their iniquitie, according to the nomber of the dayes, euen three hundreth and ninetie dayes: so shalt thou beare the iniquitie of the house of Israel.

6 And when thou hast accomplished them, sleepe againe vpon thy right side, and thou shalt beare the iniquitie of the house of Iudah fourtie dayes: I haue appointed thee a day for a yeere, euen a day for a yeere.

7 Therefore thou shalt direct thy face towarde the siege of Ierusalem, and thine arme shalbe vncouered, and thou shalt prophesie against it.

8 And beholde, I will lay bands vpon thee, and thou shalt not turne thee from one side to another, till thou hast ended the dayes of thy siege.

9 Thou shalt take also vnto thee wheate, and barley, and beanes, and lentiles, and millet, and fitches, and put them in one vessell, and make thee bread thereof according to the number of the dayes, that thou shalt sleepe vpon thy side: euen three hundreth and ninetie dayes shalt thou eate thereof.

10 And the meate, whereof thou shalt eate, shalbe by weight, euen twenty shekels a day: and from time to time shalt thou eate thereof.

11 Thou shalt drinke also water by measure, euen the sixt part of an Hin: from time to time shalt thou drinke.

12 And thou shalt eate it as barley cakes, and thou shalt bake it in the dongue that commeth out of man, in their sight.

13 And the Lord said, So shall the children of Israel eate their defiled bread among the Gentiles, whither I will cast them.

14 Then said I, Ah, Lord God, beholde, my soule hath not bene polluted: for from my youth vp, euen vnto this houre, I haue not eaten of a thing dead, or torne in pieces, neither came there any vncleane flesh in my mouth.

15 Then he said vnto me, Loe, I haue giuen thee bullockes dongue for mans dongue, and thou shalt prepare thy bread therewith.

16 Moreouer, he said vnto me, Sonne of man, beholde, I will breake the staffe of bread in Ierusalem, and they shall eate bread by weight, and with care, and they shall drinke water by measure, and with astonishment.

17 Because that bread and water shall faile, they shalbe astonied one with another, and shall consume away for their iniquitie.

Ezekiel 5

1 And thou sonne of man, take thee a sharpe knife, or take thee a barbours rasor and cause it to passe vpon thine head, and vpon thy beard: then take thee balances to weigh, and deuide the heare.

2 Thou shalt burne with fire the thirde part in the middes of the citie, when the dayes of the siege are fulfilled, and thou shalt take the other thirde part, and smite about it with a knife, and the last thirde part thou shalt scatter in the winde, and I will drawe out a sworde after them.

3 Thou shalt also take thereof a fewe in nomber, and binde them in thy lappe.

4 Then take of them againe and cast them into the middes of the fire, and burne them in the fire: for thereof shall a fire come foorth into all the house of Israel.

5 Thus saith the Lord God, This is Ierusalem: I haue set it in the middes of the nations and countreyes, that are rounde about her.

6 And she hath changed my iudgements into wickednes more then the nations, and my statutes more then the countreis, that are round about her: for they haue refused my iudgemets and my statutes, and they haue not walked in them.

7 Therefore thus saith the Lord God, Because your multitude is greater then the nations that are rounde about you, and ye haue not walked in my statutes, neither haue ye kept my iudgements: no, ye haue not done according to the iudgements of the nations, that are rounde about you,

8 Therefore thus saith the Lord God, Beholde, I, euen I come against thee, and will execute iudgement in the middes of thee, euen in the sight of the nations.

9 And I will doe in thee, that I neuer did before, neither will do any more the like, because of all thine abominations.

10 For in the middes of thee, the fathers shall eate their sonnes, and the sonnes shall eate their fathers, and I will execute iudgement in thee, and the whole remnant of thee will I scatter into all the windes.

11 Wherefore, as I liue, saith the Lord God, Surely because thou hast defiled my Sanctuarie with all thy filthinesse, and with all thine abominations, therefore will I also destroy thee, neither shall mine eye spare thee, neither will I haue any pitie.

12 The third part of thee shall die with the pestilence, and with famine shall they bee consumed in the middes of thee: and another third part shall fall by the sword round about thee: and I will scatter the last third part into all windes, and I will drawe out a sword after them.

13 Thus shall mine anger bee accomplished, and I will cause my wrath to cease in them, and I will be comforted: and they shall knowe, that I the Lord haue spoke it in my zeale, when I haue accomplished my wrath in them.

14 Moreouer, I will make thee waste, and abhorred among the nations, that are round about thee, and in the sight of all that passe by.

15 So thou shalt bee a reproche and shame, a chastisement and an astonishment vnto the nations, that are rounde about thee, when I shall execute iudgements in thee, in anger and in wrath, and in sharpe rebukes: I the Lord haue spoken it.

16 When I shall sende vpon them the euill arrowes of famine, which shalbe for their destruction, and which I will sende to destroy you: and I will encrease the famine vpon you, and wil breake your staffe of bread.

17 So will I send vpon you famine, and euill beastes, and they shall spoyle thee, and pestilencc and blood shall passe through thee, and I will bring the sworde vpon thee: I the Lord haue spoken it.

Ezekiel 6

1 Again the worde of the Lord came vnto me, saying,

2 Sonne of man, Set thy face towardes the mountaines of Israel, and prophecie against them,

3 And say, Ye mountaines of Israel, heare the worde of the Lord God: thus sayth the Lord God to the mountaines and to the hilles, to the riuers and to the valleis, Beholde, I, euen I will bring a sworde vpon you, and I will destroy your hie places:

4 And your altars shalbe desolate, and your images of the sunne shalbe broken: and I will cast downe your slaine men before your idoles.

5 And I will lay the dead carkeises of the children of Israel before their idoles, and I will scatter your bones round about your altars.

6 In all your dwelling places the cities shalbe desolate, and the hie places shalbe laide waste, so that your altars shalbe made waste and desolate, and your idoles shalbe broken, and cease, and your images of the sunne shalbe cut in pieces, and your workes shalbe abolished.

7 And the slaine shall fall in the middes of you, and ye shall knowe that I am the Lord.

8 Yet will I leaue a remnant, that you may haue some that shall escape the sword among the nations, when you shalbe scattred through the countreyes.

9 And they that escape of you, shall remember me among the nations, where they shalbe in captiuitie, because I am grieued for their whorish hearts, which haue departed from mee, and for their eyes, which haue gone a whoring after their idoles, and they shalbe displeased in them selues for the euils, which they haue committed in all their abominations.

10 And they shall knowe that I am the Lord, and that I haue not saide in vaine, that I woulde doe this euill vnto them.

11 Thus saith the Lord God, Smite with thine hand, and stretch forth with thy foote, and say, Alas, for all the wicked abominations of the house of Israel: for they shall fall by the sworde, by the famine, and by the pestilence.

12 He that is farre off, shall dye of the pestilence, and he that is neere, shall fall by the sword, and hee that remaineth and is besieged, shall dye by the famine: thus will I accomplish my wrath vpon them.

13 Then ye shall knowe, that I am ye Lord, when their slaine men shalbe among their idoles round about their altars, vpon euerie hie hill in al the toppes of the mountaines, and vnder euery greene tree, and vnder euerie thicke oke, which is the place where they did offer sweete sauour to all their idoles.

14 So will I stretch mine hand vpon them, and make the lande waste, and desolate from the wildernes vnto Diblath in all their habitations, and they shall know, that I am the Lord.

Ezekiel 7

1 Moreover the word of the Lord came vnto me, saying,

2 Also thou sonne of man, thus saith the Lord God, An ende is come vnto the lande of Israel: the ende is come vpon the foure corners of the lande.

3 Nowe is the ende come vpon thee, and I wil sende my wrath vpon thee, and will iudge thee according to thy wayes, and will laye vpon thee all thine abominations.

4 Neither shall mine eye spare thee, neither will I haue pitie: but I will laye thy waies vpon thee: and thine abomination shall bee in the middes of thee, and yee shall knowe that I am the Lord.

5 Thus saith the Lord God, Beholde, one euil, euen one euill is come.

6 An ende is come, the end is come, it watched for thee: beholde, it is come.

7 The morning is come vnto thee, that dwellest in the lande: the time is come, the day of trouble is neere, and not the sounding againe of the mountaines.

8 Now I will shortly powre out my wrath vpon thee, and fulfil mine anger vpon thee: I will iudge thee according to thy wayes, and will lay vpon thee all thine abominations.

9 Neither shall mine eie spare thee, neither will I haue pitie, but I will laye vpon thee according to thy wayes, and thine abominations shalbe in the middes of thee, and ye shall knowe that I am the Lord that smiteth.

10 Beholde, the day, beholde, it is come: the morning is gone forth, the rod florisheth: pride hath budded.

11 Crueltie is risen vp into a rod of wickednes: none of them shall remaine, nor of their riches, nor of any of theirs, neither shall there bee lamentation for them.

12 The time is come, the day draweth neere: let not the byer reioyce, nor let him that selleth, mourne: for the wrath is vpon al the multitude thereof.

13 For hee that selleth, shall not returne to that which is solde, although they were yet aliue: for the vision was vnto al the multitude thereof, and they returned not, neither doeth any encourage himselfe in the punishment of his life.

14 They haue blowen the trumpet, and prepared all, but none goeth to the battel: for my wrath is vpon all the multitude thereof.

15 The sword is without, and the pestilence, and the famine within: he that is in the field, shall dye with the sword, and he that is in the citie, famine and pestilence shall deuoure him.

16 But they that flee away from them, shall escape, and shalbe in the mountaines, like the doues of the valleis: all they shall mourne, euery one for his iniquitie.

17 All handes shalbe weake, and all knees shall fall away as water.

18 They shall also girde them selues with sackecloth, and feare shall couer them, and shame shalbe vpon all faces, and baldnes vpon their heads.

19 They shall cast their siluer in the streetes, and their golde shalbe cast farre off: their siluer and their gold can not deliuer them in the day of the wrath of the Lord: they shall not satisfie their soules, neither fill their bowels: for this ruine is for their iniquitie.

20 He had also set the beautie of his ornament in maiestie: but they made

images of their abominations, and of their idoles therein: therefore haue I set it farre from them.

21 And I will giue it into the handes of the strangers to be spoyled, and to the wicked of the earth to be robbed, and they shall pollute it.

22 My face will I turne also from them, and they shall pollute my secret place: for the destroyers shall enter into it, and defile it.

23 Make a chaine: for the lande is full of the iudgement of blood, and the citie is full of crueltie.

24 Wherefore I will bring the most wicked of the heathen, and they shall possesse their houses: I will also make the pompe of the mightie to cease, and their holie places shalbe defiled.

25 When destruction commeth, they shall seeke peace, and shall not haue it.

26 Calamitie shall come vpon calamitie, and rumour shall bee vpon rumour: then shall they seeke a vision of the Prophet: but the Lawe shall perish from the Priest, and counsel from the Ancient.

27 The King shall mourne, and the prince shall be clothed with desolation, and the handes of the people in the land shall be troubled: I wil doe vnto them according to their waies, and according to their iudgements will I iudge them, and they shall knowe that I am the Lord.

Ezekiel 8

1 And in the sixt yere, in the sixt moneth, and in the fift day of the moneth, as I sate in mine house, and the Elders of Iudah sate before me, the hand of the Lord God fell there vpon me.

2 Then I beheld, and lo, there was a likenesse, as the appearance of fire, to looke to, from his loynes downeward, and from his loynes vpward, as the appearance of brightnes, and like vnto amber.

3 And he stretched out the likenes of an had, and tooke me by an hearie locke of mine head, and the Spirit lift me vp betweene the earth, and the heauen, and brought mee by a Diuine vision to Ierusalem, into the entry of ye inner gate that lieth toward the North, where remained the idole of indignation, which prouoked indignation.

4 And beholde, the glorie of the God of Israel was there according to the vision, that I saw in the fielde.

5 Then saide he vnto mee, Sonne of man, lift vp thine eyes nowe towarde the North. So I lift vp mine eyes towarde the North, and beholde, Northward, at the gate of the altar, this idole of indignation was in the entrie.

6 He said furthermore vnto me, Sonne of man, seest thou not what they doe? euen the great abominations that the house of Israel committeth here to cause me to depart from my Sanctuarie? but yet turne thee and thou shalt see greater abominations.

7 And he caused me to enter at the gate of the court: and when I looked, beholde, an hole was in the wall.

8 Then said he vnto me, Sonne of man, digge nowe in the wall. And when I had digged in the wall, beholde, there was a doore.

9 And he said vnto mee, Go in, and beholde the wicked abominations that they doe here.

10 So I went in, and sawe, and beholde, there was euery similitude of creeping thinges and abominable beasts and all the idoles of the house of Israel painted vpon the wall round about.

11 And there stoode before them seuentie men of the Ancients of the house of Israel, and in the middes of them stoode Iaazaniah, ye sonne of Shaphan, with euerie man his censour in his hand, and the vapour of the incense went vp like a cloude.

12 Then saide hee vnto mee, Sonne of man, hast thou seene what the Ancients of the house of Israel do in the darke, euery one in the chamber of his imagerie? for they say, The Lord seeth vs not, the Lord hath forsaken the earth.

13 Againe he saide also vnto me, Turne thee againe, and thou shalt see greater abominations that they doe.

14 And he caused me to enter into the entrie of the gate of the Lords house, which was toward the North: and beholde there sate women mourning for Tammuz.

15 Then saide hee vnto me, Hast thou seene this, O sonne of man? Turne thee againe, and thou shalt see greater abominations then these.

16 And he caused me to enter into the inner court of the Lordes house, and beholde, at the doore of the Temple of the Lord, betweene the porche and the altar were about fiue and twentie men with their backs toward the Temple of the Lord, and their faces towarde the East, and they worshipped the sunne, towarde the East.

17 The he said vnto me, Hast thou seene this, O sonne of man? Is it a small thing to the house of Iudah to commit these abominations which they do here? for they haue filled the land with crueltie, and haue returned to prouoke mee: and loe, they haue cast out stinke before their noses.

18 Therefore will I also execute my wrath: mine eye shall not spare them, neither will I haue pitie, and though they crie in mine eares with a loude voyce, yet will I not heare them.

Ezekiel 9

1 He cryed also with a loude voyce in mine eares, saying, The visitations of the citie draw neere, and euery man hath a weapon in his hande to destroy it.

2 And beholde, six men came by the way of the hie gate, which lieth towarde the North, and euery man a weapon in his hande to destroy it: and one man among them was clothed with linen, with a writers ynkhorne by his side, and they went in and stoode beside the brasen altar.

3 And the glorie of the God of Israel was gone vp from ye Cherub, whereupon he was and stoode on the doore of the house, and he called to the man clothed with linnen, which had the writers ynkhorne by his side.

4 And the Lord said vnto him, Goe through the middes of the citie, euen through the middes of Ierusalem and set a marke vpon the foreheads of them that mourne, and cry for all the abominations that be done in the middes thereof.

5 And to the other he said, that I might heare, Goe ye after him through the citie, and smite: let your eye spare none, neither haue pitie.

6 Destroy vtterly the old, and the yong, and the maides, and the children, and the women, but touch no man, vpon whome is the marke, and begin at my Sanctuarie. Then they began at the Ancient men, which were before the house.

7 And he sayde vnto them, Defile the house, and fill the courtes with the slaine, then goe foorth: and they went out, and slewe them in the citie.

8 Nowe when they had slaine them, and I had escaped, I fell downe vpon my face, and cryed, saying, Ah Lord God, wilt thou destroy all the residue of Israel, in powring out thy wrath vpon Ierusalem?

9 Then saide he vnto me, The iniquitie of the house of Israel, and Iudah is exceeding great, so that the lande is full of blood, and the citie full of corrupt iudgement: for they say, The Lord hath forsaken the earth, and the Lord seeth vs not.

10 As touching me also, mine eye shall not spare them, neither will I haue pitie, but will recompence their wayes vpon their heades.

11 And beholde, the man clothed with linen which had the ynkhorne by his side, made report, and saide, Lord, I haue done as thou hast commanded me.

Ezekiel 10

1 And as I looked, beholde, in the firmament that was aboue the head of the Cherubims there appeared vpon them like vnto the similitude of a throne, as it were a saphir stone.

2 And he spake vnto the man clothed with linen, and said, Go in betweene the wheeles, euen vnder the Cherub, and fill thine hands with coales of fire from betweene the Cherubims, and scatter the ouer the citie. And he went in in my sight.

3 Now the Cherubims stood vpon the right side of the house, when the man went in, and the cloude filled the inner court.

4 Then the glorie of the Lord went vp from the Cherub, and stoode ouer the doore of the house, and the house was filled with the cloud, and the court was filled with the brightnesse of the Lordes glorie.

5 And the sound of the Cherubims wings was heard into the vtter court, as

the voyce of the Almightie God, when he speaketh.

6 And when he had commanded the man clothed with linnen, saying, Take fire from betweene the wheeles, and from betweene ye Cherubims, then he went in and stood beside ye wheele.

7 And one Cherub stretched forth his hand from betweene the Cherubims vnto the fire, that was betweene the Cherubims, and tooke thereof, and put it into the hands of him that was clothed with linnen: who tooke it and went out.

8 And there appeared in the Cherubims, the likenesse of a mans hande vnder their wings.

9 And when I looked vp, beholde, foure wheeles were beside the Cherubims, one wheele by one Cherub, and another wheele by another Cherub, and the appearance of the wheeles was as the colour of a Chrysolite stone.

10 And their appearance (for they were all foure of one facion) was as if one wheele had bene in another wheele.

11 When they went foorth, they went vpon their foure sides, and they returned not as they went: but to the place whither the first went, they went after it, and they turned not as they went.

12 And their whole bodie, and their rings, and their hands, and their wings, and the wheeles were full of eyes round about, euen in the same foure wheeles.

13 And the Cherub cryed to these wheeles in mine hearing, saying, O wheele.

14 And euery beast had foure faces: the first face was the face of a Cherub, and the second face was the face of a man, and the thirde the face of a lyon, and the fourth the face of an Egle.

15 And the Cherubims were lifted vp: this is the beast that I sawe at the riuer Chebar.

16 And when ye Cherubims went, the wheeles went by them: and when the Cherubims lift vp their wings to mount vp from the earth, the same wheeles also turned not from beside them.

17 When the Cherubims stoode, they stood: and when they were lifted vp, they lifted the selues vp also: for the spirit of the beast was in them.

18 Then the glorie of the Lord departed from aboue the doore of the house, and stoode vpon the Cherubims.

19 And the Cherubims lift vp their wings, and mounted vp from the earth in my sight: when they went out, the wheeles also were besides them: and euery one stoode at the entrie of the gate of the Lordes House at the East side, and the glorie of the God of Israel was vpon them on hie.

20 This is the beast that I sawe vnder the God of Israel by the riuer Chebar, and I knewe that they were the Cherubims.

21 Euery one had foure faces, and euery one foure wings, and the likenesse of mans hands was vnder their wings.

22 And the likenesse of their faces was the selfe same faces, which I sawe by the riuer Chebar, and the appearance of the Cherubims was ye selfe same, and they went euery one straight forwarde.

Ezekiel 11

1 Moreouer, the Spirite lift me vp, and brought me vnto the East gate of the Lordes house, which lyeth Eastwarde, and beholde, at the entrie of the gate were fiue and twentie men: among whome I sawe Iaazaniah the sonne of Azur, and Pelatiah the sonne of Benaiah, the princes of the people.

2 Then said he vnto me, Sonne of man, these are the men that imagine mischiefe, and deuise wicked counsell in this citie.

3 For they say, It is not neere, let vs builde houses: this citie is the caldron, and wee be the flesh.

4 Therefore prophesie against them, sonne of man, prophesie.

5 And the Spirite of the Lord fell vpon me, and said vnto me, Speake, Thus saith the Lord, O ye house of Israel, this haue ye said, and I know that which riseth vp of your mindes.

6 Many haue ye murthered in this citie, and ye haue filled the streets thereof with the slaine.

7 Therefore thus saith the Lord God, They that ye haue slaine, and haue layed in the middes of it, they are the flesh, and this citie is the caldron, but I wil bring you foorth of the mids of it.

8 Ye haue feared the sworde, and I wil bring a sworde vpon you, saith the Lord God.

9 And I will bring you out of the middes thereof, and deliuer you into the hands of strangers, and will execute iudgements among you.

10 Ye shall fall by the sworde, and I wil iudge you in the border of Israel, and ye shall knowe that I am the Lord.

11 This citie shall not be your caldron, neyther shall ye be the flesh in the middes thereof, but I will iudge you in the border of Israel.

12 And ye shall knowe that I am the Lord: for ye haue not walked in my statutes, neither executed my iudgements, but haue done after the maners of the heathen, that are round about you.

13 And when I prophesied, Pelatiah the sonne of Benaiah dyed: then fell I downe vpon my face, and cryed with a loude voyce, and saide, Ah Lord God, wilt thou then vtterly destroy all the remnant of Israel?

14 Againe the worde of the Lord came vnto me, saying,

15 Sonne of man, thy brethren, euen thy brethren, the men of thy kindred, and all the house of Israel, wholy are they vnto whome the inhabitants of Ierusalem haue said, Depart ye farre from the Lord: for the lande is giuen vs in possession.

16 Therefore say, Thus saith the Lord God, Although I haue cast them farre off among the heathen, and although I haue scattered them among the countreis, yet wil I be to them as a litle Sanctuarie in ye countreis where they shall come.

17 Therefore say, Thus saith the Lord God, I will gather you againe from the people, and assemble you out of the countreis where ye haue bene scattered, and I will giue you ye land of Israel.

18 And they shall come thither, and they shall take away all the idoles thereof, and all the abominations thereof from thence.

19 And I will giue them one heart, and I will put a newe spirit within their bowels: and I will take the stonie heart out of their bodies, and will giue them an heart of flesh,

20 That they may walke in my statutes, and keepe my iudgements, and execute them: and they shall be my people, and I will be their God.

21 But vpon them, whose heart is towarde their idoles, and whose affection goeth after their abominations, I will lay their way vpon their owne heades, saith the Lord God.

22 Then did the Cherubims lift vp their wings, and the wheeles besides them, and the glorie of the God of Israel was vpon them on hie.

23 And the glorie of the Lord went vp from the middes of the citie, and stoode vpon the moutaine which is towarde the East side of the citie.

24 Afterwarde the Spirite tooke me vp, and brought me in a vision by the Spirit of God into Caldea to them that were led away captiues: so the vision that I had seene, went vp from me.

25 Then I declared vnto them that were led away captiues, all the things that the Lord had shewed me.

Ezekiel 12

1 The worde of the Lord also came vnto me, saying,

2 Sonne of man, thou dwellest in the middes of a rebellious house, which haue eyes to see, and see not: they haue eares to heare, and heare not: for they are a rebellious house.

3 Therefore thou sonne of man, prepare thy stuffe to goe into captiuitie, and goe foorth by day in their sight: and thou shalt passe from thy place to another place in their sight, if it be possible that they may consider it: for they are a rebellious house.

4 Then shalt thou bring foorth thy stuffe by day in their sight as the stuffe of him that goeth into captiuitie: and thou shalt go forth at euen in their sight, as they that go foorth into captiuitie.

5 Dig thou through the wall in their sight, and cary out thereby.

6 In their sight shalt thou beare it vpon thy shoulders, and carie it foorth in the darke: thou shalt couer thy face that thou see not the earth: for I haue set thee as a signe vnto the house of Israel.

7 And as I was commanded, so I brought forth my stuffe by day, as ye stuffe of one that goeth into captiuitie: and by night I digged through the wall with mine hand,

and brought it forth in ye darke, and I bare it vpon my shoulder in their sight.

8 And in the morning came the word of the Lord vnto me, saying,

9 Sonne of man, hath not the house of Israel, the rebellious house, sayde vnto thee, What doest thou?

10 But say thou vnto them, Thus saith the Lord God, This burden concerneth the chiefe in Ierusalem, and all the house of Israel that are among them.

11 Say, I am your signe: like as I haue done, so shall it be done vnto them: they shall goe into bondage and captiuitie.

12 And the chiefest that is among them, shall beare vpon his shoulder in the darke, and shall goe forth: they shall digge through the wall, to cary out thereby: he shall couer his face, that he see not the ground with his eies.

13 My net also will I spread vpon him, and he shall be taken in my net, and I will bring him to Babel to the lande of the Caldeans, yet shall he not see it, though he shall dye there.

14 And I will scatter toward euerie winde all that are about him to helpe him, and all his garisons, and I will drawe out the sworde after them.

15 And they shall knowe that I am the Lord, when I shall scatter them among the nations, and disperse them in the countreis.

16 But I will leaue a litle nomber of them from the sworde, from the famine, and from the pestilence, that they may declare all these abominations among the heathen, where they come, and they shall knowe, that I am the Lord.

17 Moreouer, the worde of the Lord came vnto me, saying,

18 Sonne of man, eate thy bread with trembling and drinke thy water with trouble, and with carefulnesse,

19 And say vnto the people of the land, Thus saith the Lord God of the inhabitants of Ierusalem, and of the lande of Israel, They shall eate their bread with carefulnes, and drinke their water with desolation: for the lande shall bee desolate from her abundance because of the crueltie of them that dwell therein.

20 And the cities that are inhabited, shall be left voyde, and the land shall be desolate, and yee shall knowe that I am the Lord.

21 And the worde of the Lord came vnto me, saying,

22 Sonne of man, what is that prouerbe that you haue in the land of Israel, saying, The dayes are prolonged and all visions faile?

23 Tell them therefore, Thus sayeth the Lord God, I wil make this prouerbe to cease, and they shall no more vse it as a prouerbe in Israel: but say vnto them, The daies are at hand and the effect of euery vision.

24 For no vision shall be any more in vaine, neither shall there bee any flattering diuination within the house of Israel.

25 For I am the Lord: I wil speake, and that thing that I shall speake, shall come

to passe: it shall be no more prolonged: for in your dayes, O rebellious house, will I saye the thing, and will performe it, sayeth the Lord God.

26 Againe the word of the Lord came vnto me, saying,

27 Sonne of man, beholde, they of the house of Israel say, The vision that hee seeth, is for many dayes to come, and he prophecieth of the times that are farre off.

28 Therefore say vnto them, Thus sayth the Lord God, All my wordes shall no longer be delayed, but that thing which I haue spoken, shall be done, saith the Lord God.

Ezekiel 13

1 And the word of the Lord came vnto me, saying,

2 Sonne of man, prophecie against the prophets of Israel, that prophecie, and say thou vnto them, that prophecie out of their owne hearts, Heare the worde of the Lord.

3 Thus sayth the Lord God, Woe vnto the foolish Prophets that follow their owne spirit, and haue seene nothing.

4 O Israel, thy Prophets are like the foxes in the waste places.

5 Ye haue not risen vp in the gappes, neither made vp the hedge for ye house of Israel, to stand in the battel in the daye of the Lord.

6 They haue seene vanitie, and lying diuination, saying, The Lord sayth it, and the Lord hath not sent them: and they haue made others to hope that they would cofirme the word of their prophecie.

7 Haue ye not seene a vaine vision? and haue yee not spoken a lying diuination? ye say, The Lord sayth it, albeit I haue not spoken.

8 Therefore thus sayth the Lord God, Because ye haue spoken vanytie and haue seene lyes, therefore beholde, I am agaynst you, sayth the Lord God,

9 And mine hande shalbe vpon the Prophets that see vanity, and diuine lies: they shall not be in the assemblie of my people, neither shall they be written in the writing of the house of Israel, neither shall they enter into the land of Israel: and yee shall know that I am the Lord God.

10 And therefore, because they haue deceiued my people, saying, Peace, and there was no peace: and one buylt vp a wall, and behold, the others daubed it with vntempered morter,

11 Say vnto them which daube it with vntempered morter, that it shall fall: for there shall come a great showre, and I wil sende haylestones, which shall cause it to fall, and a stormie winde shall breake it.

12 Lo, when the wall is fallen, shall it not bee sayd vnto you, Where is the daubing wherewith ye haue daubed it?

13 Therefore thus sayth the Lord God, I will cause a stormie winde to breake foorth in my wrath, and a great showre

shall bee in mine anger, and hailestones in mine indignation to consume it.

14 So I wil destroy the wall that ye haue daubed with vntempered morter, and bring it downe to the ground, so that the fundation thereof shalbe discouered, and it shall fal, and ye shalbe consumed in the middes thereof, and ye shall know, that I am the Lord.

15 Thus will I accomplish my wrath vpon the wall, and vpon them that haue daubed it with vntempered morter, and will say vnto you, The wall is no more, neither the daubers thereof,

16 To wit, the Prophets of Israel, which prophesie vpon Ierusalem, and see visions of peace for it, and there is no peace, sayth the Lord God.

17 Likewise thou sonne of man, set thy face against the daughters of thy people, which prophesie out of their owne heart: and prophesie thou against them, and say,

18 Thus sayth the Lord God, Woe vnto the women that sowe pillowes vnder al arme holes, and make vailes vpon the head of euery one that standeth vp, to hunt soules: will yee hunt ye soules of my people, and will yee giue life to the soules that come vnto you?

19 And will ye pollute me among my people for handfuls of barly, and for pieces of bread to slay the soules of them that shoulde not dye, and to giue life to the soules that should not liue in lying to my people, that heare your lies?

20 Wherefore thus saith the Lord God, Behold, I will haue to do with your pillowes, wherewith yee hunt the soules to make them to flie, and I will teare them from your armes, and will let the soules goe, euen the soules, that ye hunt to make them to flie.

21 Your vailes also will I teare, and deliuer my people out of your hande, and they shalbe no more in your hands to be hunted, and ye shall knowe that I am the Lord.

22 Because with your lyes yee haue made the heart of the righteous sadde, whome I haue not made sad, and strengthened the hands of the wicked, that he should not returne from his wicked way, by promising him life,

23 Therefore ye shall see no more vanitie, nor diuine diuinatios: for I wil deliuer my people out of your hand, and ye shall know that I am ye Lord.

Ezekiel 14

1 Then came certaine of the Elders of Israel vnto me, and sate before me.

2 And the worde of the Lord came vnto me, saying,

3 Sonne of man, these men haue set vp their idoles in their heart, and put the stumbling blocke of their iniquitie before their face: should I, being required, answere them?

4 Therefore speake vnto them, and say vnto them, Thus saith the Lord God, Euery man of the house of Israel that setteth vp his idols in his heart, and putteth the stumbling blocke of his

iniquitie before his face, and commeth to the Prophet, I the Lord will answere him that commeth, according to the multitude of his idoles:

5 That I may take the house of Israel in their owne heart, because they are all departed from me through their idoles.

6 Therfore say vnto the house of Israel, Thus sayth the Lord God, Returne, and withdraw your selues, and turne your faces from your idoles, and turne your faces from all your abominations.

7 For euery one of the house of Israel, or of the stranger that soiourneth in Israel, which departeth from mee, and setteth vp his idoles in his heart, and putteth the stumbling blocke of his iniquitie before his face, and commeth to a Prophet, for to inquire of him for me, I the Lord will answere him for my selfe,

8 And I will set my face against that man, and will make him an example and prouerbe, and I will cut him off from the middes of my people, and ye shall knowe that I am the Lord.

9 And if the Prophet be deceiued, when hee hath spoken a thing, I the Lord haue deceiued that Prophet, and I will stretch out mine hande vpon him, and will destroy him from the middes of my people of Israel.

10 And they shall beare their punishment: the punishment of the Prophet shall bee euen as the punishment of him that asketh,

11 That the house of Israel may go no more astray from mee, neither bee polluted any more with all their transgressions, but that they may be my people, and I may be their God, sayth the Lord God.

12 The worde of the Lord came againe vnto me, saying,

13 Sonne of man, when ye land sinneth against me by committing a trespasse, then will I stretch out mine hand vpon it, and will breake the staffe of the bread thereof, and will send famine vpon it, and I will destroy man and beast forth of it.

14 Though these three men Noah, Daniel, and Iob were among them, they shoulde deliuer but their owne soules by their righteousnes, saith the Lord God.

15 If I bring noysome beastes into the lande and they spoyle it, so that it bee desolate, that no man may passe through, because of beastes,

16 Though these three men were in the mids thereof, As I liue, sayth the Lord God, they shall saue neither sonnes nor daughters: they onely shalbe deliuered, but the land shall be waste.

17 Or if I bring a swerde vpon this land, and say, Sword, go through the land, so that I destroy man and beast out of it,

18 Though these three men were in the mids thereof, As I liue, sayth the Lord God, they shall deliuer neither sonnes nor daughters, but they onely shall be deliuered themselues.

19 Or if I send a pestilence into this land, and powre out my wrath vpon it in blood, to destroy out of it man and beast,

20 And though Noah, Daniel and Iob were in the middes of it, As I liue, sayth the Lord God, they shall deliuer neither sonne nor daughter: they shall but deliuer their owne soules by their righteousnes.

21 For thus saith the Lord God, Howe much more when I sende my foure sore iudgements vpon Ierusalem, euen the sworde, and famine, and the noysome beast and pestilence, to destroy man and beast out of it?

22 Yet beholde, therein shalbe left a remnant of them that shalbe caryed away both sonnes and daughters: behold, they shall come forth vnto you, and ye shall see their way, and their enterprises: and ye shall be comforted, concerning the euill that I haue brought vpon Ierusalem, euen concerning al that I haue brought vpon it.

23 And they shall comfort you, when yee see their way and their enterprises: and ye shall know, that I haue not done without cause all that I haue done in it, saith the Lord God.

Ezekiel 15

1 And thee word of the Lord came vnto me, saying,

2 Sonne of man, what commeth of the vine tree aboue all other trees? and of the vine braunch, which is among the trees of ye forest?

3 Shall wood bee taken thereof to doe any worke? or wil men take a pin of it to hang any vessel thereon?

4 Behold, it is cast in the fire to be consumed: the fire consumeth both the endes of it, and the middes of it is burnt. Is it meete for any worke?

5 Behold, when it was whole, it was meete for no worke: how much lesse shall it bee meete for any worke, when the fire hath consumed it, and it is burnt?

6 Therefore thus sayth the Lord God, As the vine tree, that is among the trees of the forest, which I haue giuen to the fire to be consumed, so will I giue the inhabitants of Ierusalem.

7 And I will set my face against them: they shall go out from one fire, and another fire shall consume them: and ye shall know, that I am the Lord, when I set my face against them,

8 And when I make the lande waste, because they haue greatly offended, saith the Lord God.

Ezekiel 16

1 Again, the worde of the Lord came vnto me, saying,

2 Sonne of man, cause Ierusalem to knowe her abominations,

3 And say, Thus saith the Lord God vnto Ierusalem, Thine habitation and thy kindred is of the land of Canaan: thy father was an Amorite, and thy mother an Hittite.

4 And in thy natiuitie whe thou wast borne, thy nauell was not cut: thou wast not washed in water to soften thee: thou

wast not salted with salt, nor swadled in cloutes.

5 None eye pitied thee to do any of these vnto thee, for to haue compassion vpon thee, but thou wast cast out in the open fielde to the contempt of thy person in ye day that thou wast borne.

6 And when I passed by thee, I saw thee polluted in thine owne blood, and I said vnto thee, whe thou wast in thy blood, Thou shalt liue: euen when thou wast in thy blood, I saide vnto thee, Thou shalt liue.

7 I haue caused thee to multiplie as the bud of the fielde, and thou hast increased and waxen great, and thou hast gotten excellent ornaments: thy breastes are facioned, thine heare is growen, where as thou wast naked and bare.

8 Nowe when I passed by thee, and looked vpon thee, beholde, thy time was as the time of loue, and I spred my skirtes ouer thee, and couered thy filthines: yea, I sware vnto thee, and entred into a couenant with thee, saith the Lord God, and thou becamest mine.

9 Then washed I thee with water: yea, I washed away thy blood from thee, and I anointed thee with oyle.

10 I clothed thee also with broydred worke, and shod thee with badgers skin: and I girded thee about with fine linen, and I couered thee with silke.

11 I decked thee also with ornaments, and I put bracelets vpon thine handes, and a chaine on thy necke.

12 And I put a frontlet vpon thy face, and earings in thine eares, and a beautifull crowne vpon thine head.

13 Thus wast thou deckt with gold and siluer, and thy rayment was of fine linen, and silke, and broydred worke: thou didest eate fine floure, and honie and oyle, and thou wast very beautifull, and thou didest grow vp into a kingdome.

14 And thy name was spred among the heathen for thy beautie: for it was perfite through my beautie which I had set vpon thee, saith the Lord God.

15 Nowe thou didest trust in thine owne beautie, and playedst the harlot, because of thy renowne, and hast powred out thy fornications on euery one that passed by, thy desire was to him.

16 And thou didest take thy garments, and deckedst thine hie places with diuers colours, and playedst the harlot thereupon: the like thinges shall not come, neither hath any done so.

17 Thou hast also taken thy faire iewels made of my golde and of my siluer, which I had giuen thee, and madest to thy selfe images of men, and didest commit whoredome with them,

18 And tookest thy broydred garments, and coueredst them: and thou hast set mine oyle and my perfume before them.

19 My meate also, which I gaue thee, as fine floure, oyle, and honie, wherewith I fedde thee, thou hast euen set it before them for a sweete sauour: thus it was, saith the Lord God.

20 Moreouer thou hast taken thy sonnes and thy daughters, whome thou

hast borne vnto me, and these hast thou sacrificed vnto them, to be deuoured: is this thy whoredome a small matter?

21 That thou hast slaine my children, and deliuered them to cause them to passe through fire for them?

22 And in all thine abominations and whoredomes thou hast not remembred the dayes of thy youth, when thou wast naked and bare, and wast polluted in thy blood.

23 And beside all thy wickednes (wo, wo vnto thee, saith the Lord God)

24 Thou hast also built vnto thee an hie place, and hast made thee an hie place in euery streete.

25 Thou hast built thine hie place at euery corner of the way, and hast made thy beautie to be abhorred: thou hast opened thy feete to euery one that passed by, and multiplied thy whoredome.

26 Thou hast also committed fornication with the Egyptians thy neighbours, which haue great members, and hast encreased thy whoredome, to prouoke me.

27 Beholde, therefore I did stretche out mine hand ouer thee, and will diminish thine ordinarie, and deliuer thee vnto the will of them that hate thee, euen to the daughters of the Philistims, which are ashamed of thy wicked way.

28 Thou hast played the whore also with the Assyrians, because thou wast insaciable: yea, thou hast played the harlot with them, and yet couldest not be satisfied.

29 Thou hast moreouer multiplied thy fornication from the land of Canaan vnto Caldea, and yet thou wast not satisfied herewith.

30 Howe weake is thine heart, saith the Lord God, seeing thou doest all these thinges, euen the worke of a presumptuous whorish woman?

31 In that thou buildest thine hie place in the corner of euery way, and makest thine hie place in euery streete, and hast not bene as an harlot that despiseth a reward,

32 But as a wife that playeth the harlot, and taketh others for her husband:

33 They giue giftes to all other whores, but thou giuest giftes vnto all thy louers, and rewardest them, that they may come vnto thee on euery side for thy fornication.

34 And the contrary is in thee from other women in thy fornications, neither the like fornication shall be after thee: for in that thou giuest a rewarde, and no reward is giuen vnto thee, therefore thou art contrary.

35 Wherefore, O harlot, heare the worde of the Lord.

36 Thus sayeth the Lord God, Because thy shame was powred out, and thy filthinesse discouered through thy fornications with thy louers, and with all the idoles of thine abominations, and by the blood of thy children, which thou didest offer vnto them,

37 Beholde, therefore I wil gather all thy louers, with whom thou hast taken pleasure, and all them that thou hast loued, with al them that thou hast hated: I will euen gather them round about against thee, and will discouer thy filthines vnto them, that they may see all thy filthines.

38 And I wil iudge thee after ye maner of them that are harlots, and of them that shead blood, and I wil giue thee the blood of wrath and ielousie.

39 I will also giue thee into their handes, and they shall destroy thine hie place, and shall breake downe thine hie places. they shall strippe thee also out of thy clothes, and shall take thy faire iewels, and leaue thee naked and bare.

40 They shall also bring vp a company against thee, and they shall stone thee with stones, and thrust thee through with their swordes.

41 And they shall burne vp thine houses with fire, and execute iudgements vpon thee in the sight of many women: and I will cause thee to cease from playing the harlot, and thou shalt giue no reward any more.

42 So will I make my wrath towarde thee to rest, and my ielousie shall depart from thee, and I will cease and be no more angrie.

43 Because thou hast not remembred the dayes of thy youth, but hast prouoked me with all these things, behold, therefore I also haue brought thy way vpon thine head, sayeth the Lord God: yet hast not thou had consideration of all thine abominations.

44 Beholde, all that vse prouerbes, shall vse this prouerbe against thee, saying, As is the mother, so is her daughter.

45 Thou art thy mothers daughter, that hath cast off her husband and her children, and thou art the sister of thy sisters, which forsooke their husbands and their children: your mother is an Hittite, and your father an Amorite.

46 And thine elder sister is Samaria, and her daughters, that dwell at thy left hand, and thy yong sister, that dwelleth at thy right hand, is Sodom, and her daughters.

47 Yet hast thou not walked after their wayes, nor done after their abominations: but as it had bene a very little thing, thou wast corrupted more then they in all thy wayes.

48 As I liue, saith the Lord God, Sodom thy sister hath not done, neither shee nor her daughters, as thou hast done and thy daughters.

49 Beholde, this was the iniquitie of thy sister Sodom, Pride, fulnesse of bread, and aboundance of idlenesse was in her, and in her daughters: neither did shee strengthen the hande of the poore and needie.

50 But they were hautie, and committed abomination before mee: therefore I tooke them away, as pleased me.

51 Neither hath Samaria committed halfe of thy sinnes, but thou hast exceeded them in thine abominations, and hast iustified thy sisters in all thine abominations, which thou hast done.

52 Therefore thou which hast iustified thy sisters, beare thine owne shame for thy sinnes, that thou hast committed more abominable then they which are more righteous then thou art: be thou therefore confounded also, and beare thy shame, seeing that thou hast iustified thy sisters.

53 Therefore I will bring againe their captiuitie with the captiuitie of Sodom, and her daughters, and with the captiuitie of Samaria, and her daughters: euen the captiuitie of thy captiues in the middes of them,

54 That thou mayest beare thine owne shame, and mayest bee confounded in all that thou hast done, in that thou hast comforted them.

55 And thy sister Sodom and her daughters shall returne to their former state: Samaria also and her daughters shall returne to their former state, when thou and thy daughters shall returne to your former state.

56 For thy sister Sodom was not heard of by thy report in the day of thy pride,

57 Before thy wickednes was discouered, as in that same time of the reproch of the daughters of Aram, and of all the daughters of the Philistims round about her which despise thee on all sides.

58 Thou hast borne therefore thy wickednesse and thine abomination, saith the Lord.

59 For thus saith the Lord God, I might euen deale with thee, as thou hast done: when thou didest despise the othe, in breaking the couenant.

60 Neuerthelesse, I wil remember my couenant made with thee in ye dayes of thy youth, and I wil confirme vnto thee an euerlasting couenant.

61 Then thou shalt remember thy wayes, and be ashamed, when thou shalt receiue thy sisters, both thy elder and thy yonger, and I will giue them vnto thee for daughters, but not by thy couenat.

62 And I wil establish my couenant with thee, and thou shalt knowe that I am the Lord,

63 That thou mayest remember, and be ashamed, and neuer open thy mouth any more: because of thy shame when I am pacified toward thee, for all that thou hast done, saith the Lord God.

Ezekiel 17

1 And the worde of the Lord came vnto mee, saying,

2 Sonne of man, put foorth a parable and speake a prouerbe vnto the house of Israel,

3 And say, Thus saith the Lord God, The great eagle with great wings, and long wings, and ful of fethers, which had diuers colours, came vnto Lebanon, and tooke the highest branch of the cedar,

4 And brake off the toppe of his twigge, and caried it into the land of marchants, and set it in a citie of marchants.

5 Hee tooke also of the seede of the lande, and planted it in a fruitfull

ground: hee placed it by great waters, and set it as a willowe tree.

6 And it budded vp, and was like a spreading vine of low stature, whose branches turned toward it, and the rootes thereof were vnder it: so it became a vine, and it brought foorth branches, and shot foorth buds.

7 There was also another great eagle with great wings and many feathers, and beholde, this vine did turne her rootes toward it, and spred foorth her branches toward it, that she might water it by the trenches of her plantation.

8 It was planted in a good soyle by great waters, that it should bring forth branches, and beare fruite, and be an excellent vine.

9 Say thou, Thus saith the Lord God, Shall it prosper? shall he not pull vp the rootes thereof, and destroy the fruite thereof, and cause them to drie? all the leaues of her bud shall wither without great power, or many people, to plucke it vp by the rootes thereof.

10 Beholde, it was planted: but shall it prosper? shall it not be dried vp, and wither? when the East winde shall touch it, it shall wither in the trenches, where it grewe.

11 Moreouer, the worde of the Lord came vnto me, saying,

12 Say now to this rebellious house, Know ye not, what these things meane? tell them, Behold, the King of Babel is come to Ierusalem, and hath taken the King thereof, and the princes thereof, and led them with him to Babel,

13 And hath taken one of the Kings seede, and made a couenant with him, and hath taken an othe of him: he hath also taken the princes of the land,

14 That the kingdome might be in subiection, and not lift it selfe vp, but keepe their couenant, and stand to it.

15 But he rebelled against him, and sent his ambassadours into Egypt, that they might giue him horses, and much people: shall hee prosper? shall he escape, that doeth such things? or shall he breake the couenant, and be deliuered?

16 As I liue, saith the Lord God, he shall die in the middes of Babel, in the place of the King, that had made him King, whose othe he despised, and whose couenant made with him, he brake.

17 Neither shall Pharaoh with his mightie hoste, and great multitude of people, mainteine him in the warre, when they haue cast vp mounts, and builded ramparts to destroy many persons.

18 For he hath despised the othe, and broken ye couenant (yet lo, he had giuen his hand) because he hath done all these things, he shall not escape.

19 Therefore, thus sayth the Lord God, As I liue, I wil surely bring mine othe that he hath despised, and my couenant that he hath broken vpon his owne head.

20 And I wil spread my net vpon him, and he shalbe taken in my net, and I wil bring him to Babel, and will enter into

iudgement with him there for his trespas that he hath committed against me.

21 And all that flee from him with all his hoste, shall fall by the sword, and they that remaine, shalbe scattered towarde all the windes: and ye shall know that I the Lord haue spoken it.

22 Thus saith the Lord God, I wil also take off the top of this hie cedar, and wil set it, and cut off the top of the tender plant thereof, and I wil plant it vpon an hie mountaine and great.

23 Euen in the hie mountaine of Israel will I plant it: and it shall bring forth boughes and beare fruite, and be an excellent cedar, and vnder it shall remaine all birds, and euery foule shall dwell in the shadow of the branches thereof.

24 And all the trees of the fielde shall knowe that I the Lord haue brought downe the hie tree, and exalted the lowe tree, that I haue dried vp the greene tree, and made the drie tree to florish: I the Lord haue spoken it, and haue done it.

Ezekiel 18

1 The worde of the Lord came vnto me againe, saying,

2 What meane ye that ye speake this prouerbe, concerning the land of Israel, saying, The fathers haue eaten sowre grapes, and the childrens teeth are set on edge?

3 As I liue, sayth the Lord God, ye shall vse this prouerbe no more in Israel.

4 Beholde, all soules are mine, both the soule of the father, and also the soule of the sonne are mine: the soule that sinneth, it shall die.

5 But if a man be iust, and doe that which is lawfull, and right,

6 And hath not eaten vpon the mountaines, neither hath lift vp his eyes to the idoles of the house of Israel, neither hath defiled his neighbours wife, neither hath lyen with a menstruous woman,

7 Neither hath oppressed any, but hath restored the pledge to his dettour: he that hath spoyled none by violence, but hath giuen his bread to the hungry, and hath couered the naked with a garment,

8 And hath not giuen foorth vpon vsurie, neither hath taken any increase, but hath withdrawen his hand from iniquitie, and hath executed true iudgement betweene man and man,

9 And hath walked in my statutes, and hath kept my iudgements to deale truely, he is iust, he shall surely liue, sayth the Lord God.

10 If he beget a sonne, that is a thiefe, or a sheader of blood, if he do any one of these things,

11 Though he doe not all these things, but either hath eaten vpon the mountaines, or defiled his neighbours wife,

12 Or hath oppressed the poore and needy, or hath spoyled by violence, or hath not restored the pledge, or hath lift vp his eyes vnto the idoles, or hath committed abomination,

13 Or hath giuen forth vpon vsurie, or hath taken increase, shall he liue? he shall not liue: seeing he hath done all these abominations, he shall die the death, and his blood shall be vpon him.

14 But if he beget a sonne, that seeth all his fathers sinnes, which he hath done, and feareth, neither doeth such like,

15 That hath not eaten vpon the mountaines, neither hath lift vp his eyes to the idols of ye house of Israel, nor hath defiled his neighbours wife,

16 Neither hath oppressed any, nor hath withholden the pledge, neither hath spoyled by violence, but hath giuen his bread to the hungry, and hath couered the naked with a garment,

17 Neither hath withdrawen his hand from the afflicted, nor receiued vsurie nor increase, but hath executed my iudgements, and hath walked in my statutes, he shall not die in the iniquitie of his father, but he shall surely liue.

18 His father, because he cruelly oppressed and spoyled his brother by violence, and hath not done good among his people, loe, euen he dyeth in his iniquitie.

19 Yet say ye, Wherefore shall not the sonne beare the iniquitie of the father? because ye sonne hath executed iudgement and iustice, and hath kept all my statutes, and done them, he shall surely liue,

20 The same soule that sinneth, shall die: the sonne shall not beare the iniquitie of the father, neither shall the father beare the iniquitie of the sonne, but the righteousnes of the righteous shall be vpon him, and the wickednesse of the wicked shall be vpon him selfe.

21 But if the wicked will returne from all his sinnes that he hath committed, and keepe all my statutes, and doe that which is lawfull and right, he shall surely liue, and shall not die.

22 All his transgressions that he hath committed, they shall not be mentioned vnto him, but in his righteousnes that he hath done, he shall liue.

23 Haue I any desire that the wicked should die, sayth the Lord God? or shall he not liue, if he returne from his wayes?

24 But if the righteous turne away from his righteousnes, and commit iniquitie, and doe according to all the abominations, that the wicked man doeth, shall he liue? all his righteousnes that he hath done, shall not be mentioned: but in his transgression that he hath committed, and in his sinne that he hath sinned, in them shall he die.

25 Yet ye say, The way of the Lord is not equall: heare now, O house of Israel. Is not my way equall? or are not your wayes vnequall?

26 For when a righteous man turneth away from his righteousnes, and committeth iniquitie, he shall euen die for the same, he shall euen die for his iniquitie, that he hath done.

27 Againe when the wicked turneth away from his wickednes that he hath committed, and doeth that which is

lawfull and right, he shall saue his soule aliue.

28 Because he considereth, and turneth away from all his transgressions that hee hath committed, he shall surely liue and shall not die.

29 Yet saith ye house of Israel, The way of the Lord is not equall. O house of Israel, are not my wayes equall? or are not your wayes vnequall?

30 Therefore I will iudge you, O house of Israel, euery one according to his wayes, sayth the Lord God: returne therefore and cause others to turne away from all your transgressions: so iniquitie shall not be your destruction.

31 Cast away from you all your transgressions, whereby ye haue transgressed, and make you a newe heart and a new spirit: for why will ye die, O house of Israel?

32 For I desire not the death of him that dyeth, sayth the Lord God: cause therefore one another to returne, and liue ye.

Ezekiel 19

1 Thou also, take vp a lamentation for the princes of Israel,

2 And say, Wherefore lay thy mother as a lyonesse among the lyons? she nourished her yong ones among the lyons whelps,

3 And she brought vp one of her whelps, and it became a lyon, and it learned to catch the praye, and it deuoured men.

4 The nations also heard of him, and he was taken in their nets, and they brought him in chaines vnto the land of Egypt.

5 Nowe when she sawe, that she had waited and her hope was lost, she tooke another of her whelps, and made him a lyon.

6 Which went among the lyons, and became a lyon, and learned to catch the praye, and he deuoured men.

7 And he knew their widowes, and he destroyed their cities, and the land was wasted, and all that was therein by the noyse of his roaring.

8 Then the nations set against him on euery side of the countreys, and laide their nets for him: so he was taken in their pit.

9 And they put him in prison and in chaines, and brought him to the King of Babel, and they put him in holdes, that his voyce should no more be heard vpon the mountaines of Israel.

10 Thy mother is like a vine in thy blood, planted by the waters: she brought foorth fruite and branches by the abundant waters,

11 And she had strong rods for the scepters of them that beare rule, and her stature was exalted among the branches, and she appeared in her height with the multitude of her branches.

12 But she was plucked vp in wrath: she was cast downe to the ground, and the East winde dried vp her fruite: her branches were broken, and withered: as for the rod of her strength, the fire consumed it.

13 And now she is planted in the wildernes in a drie and thirstie ground.

14 And fire is gone out of a rod of her branches, which hath deuoured her fruite, so that she hath no strong rod to be a scepter to rule: this is a lamentation and shalbe for a lamentation.

Ezekiel 20

1 And in the seuenth yeere, in the fift moneth, the tenth day of the moneth, came certaine of the elders of Israel to enquire of the Lord, and sate before me.

2 Then came the worde of the Lord vnto me, saying,

3 Sonne of man, speake vnto the Elders of Israel, and say vnto them, Thus saith the Lord God, Are ye come to enquire of me? as I liue, sayth the Lord God, when I am asked, I wil not answer you.

4 Wilt thou iudge them, sonne of man? wilt thou iudge them? cause them to vnderstand the abominations of their fathers,

5 And say vnto them, Thus saith the Lord God, In the day when I chose Israel, and lift vp mine hand vnto the seede of the house of Iaakob, and made my selfe knowen vnto them in the land of Egypt, when I lift vp mine hand vnto them, and sayd, I am the Lord your God,

6 In the day that I lift vp mine hand vnto them to bring them forth of the land of Egypt, into a land that I had prouided for them, flowing with milke and hony which is pleasant among all lands,

7 Then sayd I vnto them, Let euery man cast away the abominations of his eyes, and defile not your selues with the idols of Egypt: for I am the Lord your God.

8 But they rebelled against me, and would not heare me: for none cast away the abominations of their eyes, neither did they forsake the idoles of Egypt: then I thought to powre out mine indignation vpon them, and to accomplish my wrath against them in the mids of the land of Egypt.

9 But I had respect to my Name, that it should not be polluted before the heathen, among whome they were, and in whose sight I made my selfe knowen vnto them in bringing them forth of the land of Egypt.

10 Nowe I caried them out of the land of Egypt, and brought them into the wildernes.

11 And I gaue them my statutes, and declared my iudgements vnto them, which if a man doe, he shall liue in them.

12 Moreouer I gaue them also my Sabbaths to be a signe betweene me and them, that they might knowe that I am the Lord, that sanctifie them.

13 But the house of Israel rebelled against me in the wildernes: they walked not in my statutes, and they cast away my iudgements, which if a man doe, he shall liue in them, and my Sabbaths haue they greatly polluted: then I thought to powre out mine indignation vpon them in the wildernes to consume them,

14 But I had respect to my Name, that it shoulde not bee polluted before the heathen in whose sight I brought them out.

15 Yet neuerthelesse, I lift vp mine hande vnto them in the wildernes that I would not bring them into the lande, which I had giuen them, flowing with milke and hony, which was pleasant aboue all landes,

16 Because they cast away my iudgments, and walked not in my statutes, but haue polluted my Sabbaths: for their heart went after their idoles.

17 Neuerthelesse, mine eye spared them, that I would not destroye them, neither would I consume them in the wildernes.

18 But I said vnto their children in the wildernes, Walke ye not in the ordinances of your fathers, neither obserue their maners, nor defile your selues with their idoles.

19 I am the Lord your God: walke in my statutes, and keepe my iudgements and doe them,

20 And sanctifie my Sabbaths, and they shall bee a signe betweene mee and you, that ye may knowe that I am the Lord your God.

21 Notwithstanding the children rebelled against mee: they walked not in my statutes, nor kept my iudgements to doe them, which if a man doe, hee shall liue in them, but they polluted my Sabbaths: then I thought to powre out mine indignation vpon them, and to accomplish my wrath against them in the wildernes.

22 Neuerthelesse I withdrew mine hand and had respect to my Name that it should not be polluted before the heathen, in whose sight I brought them foorth.

23 Yet I lift vp mine hande vnto them in the wildernes, that I would scatter them among the heathen, and disperse them through the countreys,

24 Because they had not executed my iudgements, but had cast away my statutes and had polluted my Sabbaths, and their eyes were after their fathers idoles.

25 Wherefore I gaue them also statutes that were not good, and iudgements, wherein they should not liue.

26 And I polluted them in their owne giftes in that they caused to passe by the fire all that first openeth ye wombe, that I might destroy them, to the ende, that they might know that I am ye Lord.

27 Therefore, sonne of man, speake vnto the house of Israel, and say vnto them, Thus saith the Lord God, Yet in this your fathers haue blasphemed me, though they had before grieuously transgressed against me.

28 For when I had brought them into the land, for the which I lifted vp mine hand to giue it to them, then they saw euery hie hill, and all the thicke trees, and they offred there their sacrifices, and

there they presented their offering of prouocation: there also they made their sweete sauour, and powred out there their drinke offerings.

29 Then I saide vnto them, What is the hie place whereunto ye goe? And the name thereof was called Bamah vnto this day.

30 Wherefore, say vnto the house of Israel, Thus saith the Lord God, Are ye not polluted after the maner of your fathers? and commit ye not whoredome after their abominations?

31 For when you offer your giftes, and make your sonnes to passe through the fire, you pollute your selues with all your idoles vnto this day: shall I answere you when I am asked, O house of Israel? As I liue, saith the Lord God, I wil not answere you when I am asked.

32 Neither shall that be done that commeth into your minde: for ye say, We wil be as the heathen, and as the families of the countreys, and serue wood, and stone.

33 As I liue, saith the Lord God, I will surely rule you with a mightie hand, and with a stretched out arme, and in my wrath powred out,

34 And will bring you from the people, and will gather you out of the countreys, wherein ye are scattered, with a mighty hand, and with a stretched out arme, and in my wrath powred out,

35 And I will bring you into the wildernes of the people, and there wil I pleade with you face to face.

36 Like as I pleaded with your fathers in the wildernes of the lande of Egypt, so will I pleade with you, saith the Lord God.

37 And I wil cause you to passe vnder the rod, and wil bring you into the bond of the couenant.

38 And I wil chuse out from among you the rebels, and them that transgresse against mee: I will bring them out of the land where they dwel, and they shall not enter into the lande of Israel, and you shall knowe that I am the Lord.

39 As for you, O house of Israel, thus saith the Lord God, Goe you, and serue euery one his idole, seeing that ye will not obey me, and pollute mine holy Name no more with your giftes and with your idoles.

40 For in mine holy mountaine, euen in the hie mountaine of Israel, saith the Lord God, there shall all the house of Israel, and all in the lande, serue me: there will I accept them, and there will I require your offrings and the first fruites of your oblations, with all your holy things.

41 I will accept your sweete sauour, when I bring you from the people, and gather you out of the countreys, wherein ye haue bene scattered, that I may be sanctified in you before ye heathen.

42 And ye shall knowe, that I am the Lord, when I shall bring you into the land of Israel, into the land, for the which I lifted vp mine hande to giue it to your fathers.

43 And there shall ye remember your wayes, and all your workes, wherein ye haue bene defiled, and ye shall iudge your selues worthy to be cut off, for all your euils, that ye haue committed.

44 And ye shall knowe, that I am the Lord, when I haue respect vnto you for my Names sake, and not after your wicked wayes, nor according to your corrupt workes, O ye house of Israel, saith the Lord God.

45 Moreouer, the worde of the Lord came vnto me, saying,

46 Sonne of man, set thy face toward the way of Teman, and drop thy word toward the South, and prophecie towarde the forest of the fielde of the South,

47 And say to the forest of the South, Heare the worde of the Lord: thus saith the Lord God, Beholde, I will kindle a fire in thee, and it shall deuoure all the greene wood in thee, and all the drie wood: the continuall flame shall not bee quenched, and euery face from the South to the North shall be burnt therein.

48 And all flesh shall see, that I the Lord haue kindled it, and it shall not bee quenched. Then saide I, Ah Lord God, they say of me, Doeth not he speake parables?

Ezekiel 21

1 The word of ye Lord came to me againe, saying,

2 Sonne of man, set thy face toward Ierusalem, and drop thy word toward the holy places, and prophecie against the land of Israel.

3 And say to the land of Israel, Thus saith the Lord, Beholde, I come against thee, and will drawe my sword out of his sheath, and cut off from thee both the righteous and the wicked.

4 Seeing then that I will cut off from thee both the righteous and wicked, therefore shall my sworde goe out of his sheath against all flesh from the South to the North,

5 That all flesh may knowe that I the Lord haue drawen my sworde out of his sheath, and it shall not returne any more.

6 Mourne therefore, thou sonne of man, as in the paine of thy reines, and mourne bitterly before them.

7 And if they say vnto thee, Wherefore mournest thou? then answere, Because of the bruite: for it commeth, and euery heart shall melt, and all handes shall be weake, and all mindes shall faint, and all knees shall fall away as water: beholde, it commeth, and shall be done, saith the Lord God.

8 Againe, the word of the Lord came vnto me, saying,

9 Sonne of man, prophecie, and say, Thus saith the Lord God, say, A sworde, a sworde both sharpe, and fourbished.

10 It is sharpened to make a sore slaughter, and it is fourbished that it may glitter: how shall we reioyce? for it

contemneth the rod of my sonne, as all other trees.

11 And he hath giuen it to be fourbished, that he may handle it: this sword is sharpe, and is fourbished, that he may giue it into ye hand of the slayer.

12 Cry, and houle, sonne of man: for this shall come to my people, and it shall come vnto all the princes of Israel: the terrours of the sword shall be vpon my people: smite therefore vpon thy thigh.

13 For it is a triall, and what shall this be, if the sworde contemne euen the rodde? It shall be no more, saith the Lord God.

14 Thou therefore, sonne of man, prophecie, and smite hand to hand, and let the sworde be doubled: let the sworde that hath killed, returne the third time: it is the sword of the great slaughter entring into their priuie chambers.

15 I haue brought the feare of the sword into all their gates to make their heart to faint, and to multiplie their ruines. Ah it is made bright, and it is dressed for the slaughter.

16 Get thee alone: goe to the right hande, or get thy selfe to the left hande, whithersoeuer thy face turneth.

17 I wil also smite mine hands together, and wil cause my wrath to cease. I the Lord haue said it.

18 The worde of the Lord came vnto mee againe, saying,

19 Also thou sonne of man, appoint thee two wayes, that the sworde of the King of Babel may come: both twaine shall come out of one lande, and chuse a place, and chuse it in the corner of the way of the citie.

20 Appoint a way, that the sworde may come to Rabbath of the Ammonites, and to Iudah in Ierusalem the strong citie.

21 And the King of Babel stoode at the parting of the way, at the head of the two wayes, consulting by diuination, and made his arrowes bright: hee consulted with idoles, and looked in the liuer.

22 At his right hand was the diuination for Ierusalem to appoint captaines, to open their mouth in the slaughter, and to lift vp their voyce with shouting, to laye engines of warre against the gates, to cast a mount, and to builde a fortresse.

23 And it shalbe vnto them as a false diuination in their sight for the othes made vnto them: but hee will call to remembrance their iniquitie, to the intent they should be taken.

24 Therefore thus sayeth the Lord God, Because ye haue made your iniquitie to bee remembred, in discouering your rebellion, that in al your workes your sinnes might appeare: because, I say, that ye are come to remembrance, ye shall be taken with the hand.

25 And thou prince of Israel polluted, and wicked, whose day is come, when iniquitie shall haue an ende,

26 Thus saith the Lord God, I will take away the diademe, and take off the crowne: this shalbe no more the same: I wil exalt the humble, and will abase him that is hie.

27 I wil ouerturne, ouerturne, ouerturne it, and it shall be no more vntill he come, whose right it is, and I will giue it him.

28 And thou, sonne of man, prophecie, and say, Thus saith the Lord God to the children of Ammon, and to their blasphemie: say thou, I say, The sword, the sword is drawen foorth, and fourbished to the slaughter, to consume, because of the glittering:

29 Whiles they see vanitie vnto thee, and prophecied a lie vnto thee to bring thee vpon the neckes of the wicked that are slaine, whose day is come when their iniquitie shall haue an ende.

30 Shall I cause it to returne into his sheath? I will iudge thee in the place where thou wast created, euen in the land of thine habitation.

31 And I wil powre out mine indignation vpon thee, and will blowe against thee in the fire of my wrath, and deliuer thee into the hand of beastly men, and skilfull to destroy.

32 Thou shalt bee in the fire to be deuoured: thy blood shall be in the middes of the lande, and thou shalt be no more remembred: for I the Lord haue spoken it.

Ezekiel 22

1 Moreover, the worde of the Lord came vnto me, saying,

2 Now thou sonne of man, wilt thou iudge, wilt thou iudge this bloody citie? wilt thou shew her all her abominations?

3 Then say, Thus sayth the Lord God, The citie sheddeth blood in the middes of it, that her time may come, and maketh idols against her selfe to pollute her selfe.

4 Thou hast offended in thy blood, that thou hast shed, and hast polluted thy selfe in thine idols, which thou hast made, and thou hast caused thy dayes to draw neere, and art come vnto thy terme: therefore haue I made thee a reproch to the heathen, and a mocking to all countreys.

5 Those that be neere, and those that be farre from thee, shall mocke thee, which art vile in name and sore in affliction.

6 Beholde, the princes of Israel euery one in thee was ready to his power, to shed blood.

7 In thee haue they despised father and mother: in the middes of thee haue they oppressed the stranger: in thee haue they vexed the fatherlesse and the widowe.

8 Thou hast despised mine holy things, and hast polluted my Sabbaths.

9 In thee are men that cary tales to shed blood: in thee are they that eate vpon the mountaines: in ye mids of thee they comit abomination.

10 In thee haue they discouered their fathers shame: in thee haue they vexed her that was polluted in her floures.

11 And euery one hath committed abomination with his neighbours wife, and euery one hath wickedly defiled his daughter in lawe, and in thee hath euery man forced his owne sister, euen his fathers daughter.

12 In thee haue they taken giftes to shed blood: thou hast taken vsurie and the encrease, and thou hast defrauded thy neighbours by extortion, and hast forgotten me, saith the Lord God.

13 Beholde, therefore I haue smitten mine hands vpon thy couetousnesse, that thou hast vsed, and vpon the blood, which hath bene in the middes of thee.

14 Can thine heart endure, or can thine hands be strong, in the dayes that I shall haue to doe with thee? I the Lord haue spoken it, and will doe it.

15 And I wil scatter thee among the heathen, and disperse thee in the countreys, and will cause thy filthines to cease from thee.

16 And thou shalt take thine inheritance in thy selfe in the sight of the heathen, and thou shalt knowe that I am the Lord.

17 And the worde of the Lord came vnto me, saying,

18 Sonne of man, the house of Israel is vnto me as drosse: all they are brasse, and tinne, and yron, and leade in the mids of the fornace: they are euen the drosse of siluer.

19 Therefore, thus sayth the Lord God, Because ye are all as drosse, beholde, therefore I will gather you in the middes of Ierusalem.

20 As they gather siluer and brasse, and yron, and leade, and tinne into the middes of the fornace, to blowe the fire vpon it to melt it, so wil I gather you in mine anger and in my wrath, and wil put you there and melt you.

21 I wil gather you, I say, and blowe the fire of my wrath vpon you, and you shalbe melted in the mids thereof.

22 As siluer is melted in the mids of the fornace, so shall ye be melted in the mids thereof, and ye shall knowe, that I the Lord haue powred out my wrath vpon you.

23 And the worde of the Lord came vnto me, saying,

24 Sonne of man, say vnto her; Thou art the land, that is vncleane, and not rained vpon in the day of wrath.

25 There is a conspiracie of her prophets in the mids thereof like a roaring lyon, rauening the praye: they haue deuoured soules: they haue taken the riches and precious things: they haue made her many widowes in the mids thereof.

26 Her Priests haue broken my Lawe, and haue defiled mine holy things: they haue put no difference betweene the holy and prophane, neither discerned betweene the vncleane, and the cleane, and haue hid their eyes from my Sabbaths, and I am prophaned among them.

27 Her princes in the mids thereof are like wolues, rauening the praye to shed blood, and to destroy soules for their owne couetous lucre.

28 And her prophets haue dawbed them with vntempered morter, seeing vanities, and diuining lies vnto them, saying,

Thus sayth the Lord God, when the Lord had not spoken.

29 The people of the land haue violently oppressed by spoyling and robbing, and haue vexed the poore and the needy: yea, they haue oppressed the stranger against right.

30 And I sought for a man among them, that should make vp the hedge, and stand in the gap before me for the land, that I should not destroy it, but I found none.

31 Therefore haue I powred out mine indignation vpon them, and consumed them with the fire of my wrath: their owne wayes haue I rendred vpon their heads, sayth the Lord God.

Ezekiel 23

1 The worde of the Lord came againe vnto me, saying,

2 Sonne of man, there were two women, the daughters of one mother.

3 And they committed fornication in Egypt, they committed fornication in their youth: there were their breasts pressed, and there they bruised the teates of their virginitie.

4 And the names of them were Aholah the elder, and Aholibah her sister: and they were mine, and they bare sonnes and daughters: thus were their names. Samaria is Aholah, and Ierusalem Aholibah.

5 And Aholah played the harlot when she was mine, and she was set on fire with her louers, to wit, with the Assyrians her neighbours,

6 Which were clothed with blewe silke, both captaines and princes: they were all pleasant yong men, and horsemen riding vpon horses.

7 Thus she committed her whoredome with them, euen with all them that were the chosen men of Asshur, and with all on whome she doted, and defiled her selfe with all their idoles.

8 Neither left she her fornications, learned of the Egyptians: for in her youth they lay with her, and they bruised the breasts of her virginitie, and powred their whoredome vpon her.

9 Wherefore I deliuered her into the hands of her louers, euen into the hands of the Assyrians, vpon whome she doted.

10 These discouered her shame: they tooke away her sonnes and her daughters, and slewe her with the sworde, and she had an euill name among women: for they had executed iudgement vpon her.

11 And when her sister Aholibah sawe this, she marred her selfe with inordinate loue, more then she, and with her fornications more then her sister with her fornications.

12 She doted vpon the Assyrians her neighbours, both captaines and princes clothed with diuers sutes, horsemen ryding vpon horses: they were all pleasant yong men.

13 Then I sawe that she was defiled, and that they were both after one sort,

14 And that she encreased her fornications: for when she sawe men painted vpon the wall, the images of the Caldeans painted with vermelon,

15 And girded with girdles vpon their loynes, and with dyed attyre vpon their heads (looking all like princes after the maner of the Babylonians in Caldea, the land of their natiuitie)

16 Assoone, I say, as she sawe them, she doted vpon them, and sent messengers vnto them into Caldea.

17 Nowe when the Babylonians came to her into the bed of loue, they defiled her with their fornication, and she was polluted with them, and her lust departed from them.

18 So she discouered her fornication, and disclosed her shame: then mine heart forsooke her, like as mine heart had forsaken her sister.

19 Yet she encreased her whoredome more, and called to remembrance ye dayes of her youth, wherein she had played the harlot in the land of Egypt.

20 For she doted vpon their seruants whose members are as the members of asses, and whose yssue is like the yssue of horses.

21 Thou calledst to remembrance the wickednes of thy youth, when thy teates were bruised by ye Egyptians: therefore ye paps of thy youth are thus.

22 Therefore, O Aholibah, thus sayeth the Lord God, Beholde, I will raise vp thy louers against thee, from whome thine heart is departed, and I will bring them against thee on euery side,

23 To wit, the Babylonians, and all the Caldeans, Peked, and Shoah, and Koa, and all the Assyrians with them: they were all pleasant yong men, captaines and princes: all they were valiant and renoumed, riding vpon horses.

24 Euen these shall come against thee with charets, waggons, and wheeles, and with a multitude of people, which shall set against thee, buckler and shield, and helmet round about: and I will leaue the punishment vnto them, and they shall iudge thee according to their iudgements.

25 And I wil lay mine indignation vpon thee, and they shall deale cruelly with thee: they shall cut off thy nose and thine eares, and thy remnant shall fall by the sword: they shall cary away thy sonnes and thy daughters, and thy residue shall be deuoured by the fire.

26 They shall also strip thee out of thy clothes, and take away thy fayre iewels.

27 Thus wil I make thy wickednes to cease from thee and thy fornication out of the land of Egypt: so that thou shalt not lift vp thine eyes vnto them, nor remember Egypt any more.

28 For thus saith the Lord God, Behold, I wil deliuer thee into the hand of them, whome thou hatest: euen into the hands of them from whome thine heart is departed.

29 And they shall handle thee despitefully, and shall take away all thy labour, and shall leaue thee naked and bare, and the shame of thy fornications shalbe discouered, both thy wickednes, and thy whoredome.

30 I wil doe these things vnto thee, because thou hast gone a whoring after the heathen, and because thou art polluted with their idoles.

31 Thou hast walked in the way of thy sister: therefore wil I giue her cup into thine hand.

32 Thus saith ye Lord God, Thou shalt drinke of thy sisters cup, deepe and large: thou shalt be laughed to scorne and had in derision, because it containeth much.

33 Thou shalt be filled with drunkennes and sorow, euen with the cup of destruction, and desolation, with the cup of thy sister Samaria.

34 Thou shalt euen drinke it, and wring it out to the dregges, and thou shalt breake the sheards thereof, and teare thine owne breasts: for I haue spoken it, sayth the Lord God.

35 Therefore thus saith the Lord God, Because thou hast forgotten me, and cast me behinde thy backe, therefore thou shalt also beare thy wickednes and thy whoredome.

36 The Lord sayd moreouer vnto me, Sonne of man, wilt thou iudge Aholah and Aholibah? and wilt thou declare to them their abominations?

37 For they haue played the whores, and blood is in their hands, and with their idoles haue they committed adulterie, and haue also caused their sonnes, whome they bare vnto me, to passe by the fire to be their meate.

38 Moreouer, thus haue they done vnto me: they haue defiled my Sanctuarie in the same day, and haue prophaned my Sabbaths.

39 For when they had slaine their children to their idoles, they came the same day into my Sanctuarie to defile it: and loe, thus haue they done in the middes of mine house.

40 And howe much more is it that they sent for men to come from farre vnto whom a messenger was sent, and loe, they came? for whome thou diddest wash thy selfe, and paintedst thine eyes, and deckedst thee with ornaments,

41 And satest vpon a costly bed, and a table prepared before it, whereupon thou hast set mine incense and mine oyle.

42 And a voyce of a multitude being at ease, was with her: and with the men to make the company great were brought men of Saba from the wildernes, which put bracelets vpon their hands, and beautifull crownes vpon their heads.

43 Then I sayd vnto her, that was olde in adulteries, Now shall she and her fornications come to an end.

44 And they went in vnto her as they goe to a common harlot: so went they to Aholah and Aholibah the wicked women.

45 And ye righteous men they shall iudge them, after the maner of harlots, and after the maner of murtherers: for they are harlots, and blood is in their hands.

46 Wherefore thus sayth the Lord God, I will bring a multitude vpon them, and will giue them vnto the tumult, and to the spoyle,

47 And the multitude shall stone them with stones, and cut them with their swordes: they shall slay their sonnes, and their daughters, and burne vp their houses with fire.

48 Thus will I cause wickednesse to cease out of the land, that all women may be taught not to doe after your wickednesse.

49 And they shall laye your wickednesse vpon you, and ye shall beare the sinnes of your idoles, and ye shall knowe that I am the Lord God.

Ezekiel 24

1 Again in the ninth yeere, in the tenth moneth, in the tenth day of the moneth, came the worde of the Lord vnto me, saying,

2 Sonne of man, write thee the name of the day, euen of this same day: for the King of Babel set himselfe against Ierusalem this same day.

3 Therefore speake a parable vnto the rebellious house, and say vnto them, Thus sayth the Lord God, Prepare a pot, prepare it, and also powre water into it.

4 Gather the pieces thereof into it, euen euery good piece, as the thigh and the shoulder, and fill it with the chiefe bones.

5 Take one of the best sheepe, and burne also the bones vnder it, and make it boyle well, and seethe the bones of it therein,

6 Because the Lord God sayth thus, Woe to the bloody citie, euen to the pot, whose skomme is therein, and whose skomme is not gone out of it: bring it out piece by piece: let no lot fall vpon it.

7 For her blood is in the middes of her: shee set it vpon an high rocke, and powred it not vpon on the ground to couer it with dust,

8 That it might cause wrath to arise, and take vengeance: euen I haue set her blood vpon an high rocke that it should not be couered.

9 Therefore thus saith ye Lord God, Woe to the bloody citie, for I will make ye burning great.

10 Heape on much wood: kindle the fire, consume the flesh, and cast in spice, and let the bones be burnt.

11 Then set it emptie vpon the coles thereof, that the brasse of it may be hot, and may burne, and that the filthinesse of it may be molten in it, and that the skomme of it may be consumed.

12 She hath wearied her selfe with lyes, and her great skomme went not out of her: therefore her skomme shall be consumed with fire.

13 Thou remainest in thy filthines and wickednes: because I would haue purged thee, and thou wast not purged, thou shalt not be purged from thy filthines, till I haue caused my wrath to light vpon thee.

14 I the Lord haue spoken it: it shall come to passe, and I will doe it: I will not goe backe, neither will I spare, neither

will I repent: according to thy wayes, and according to thy workes shall they iudge thee, sayeth the Lord God.

15 Also the worde of ye Lord came vnto me, saying,

16 Sonne of man beholde, I take away from thee the pleasure of thine eyes with a plague: yet shalt thou neither mourne nor weepe, neither shall thy teares runne downe.

17 Cease from sighing: make no mourning for the dead, and binde the tyre of thine head vpon thee, and put on thy shooes vpon thy feete, and couer not thy lips, and eate not the bread of men.

18 So I spake vnto the people in the morning, and at euen my wife dyed: and I did in the morning, as I was commanded.

19 And the people said vnto me, Wilt thou not tell vs what these things meane towarde vs that thou doest so?

20 Then I answered them, The worde of the Lord came vnto me, saying,

21 Speake vnto the house of Israel, Thus sayth the Lord God, Behold, I will pollute my Sanctuarie, euen the pride of your power, the pleasure of your eyes, and your hearts desire, and your sonnes, and your daughters whom ye haue left, shall fall by the sworde.

22 And ye shall doe as I haue done: ye shall not couer your lippes, neither shall ye eate the bread of men.

23 And your tyre shalbe vpon your heads, and your shooes vpon your feete: ye shall not mourne nor weepe, but ye shall pine away for your iniquities, and mourne one toward another.

24 Thus Ezekiel is vnto you a signe: according to all that he hath done, ye shall do: and when this commeth, ye shall know that I am the Lord God.

25 Also, thou sonne of man, shall it not be in the day when I take from them their power, ye ioy of their honor, ye pleasure of their eyes, and the desire of their heart, their sonnes and their daughters?

26 That he that escapeth in that day, shall come vnto thee to tell thee that which hee hath heard with his eares?

27 In that day shall thy mouth be opened to him which is escaped, and thou shalt speake, and be no more dumme, and thou shalt be a signe vnto them, and they shall knowe that I am the Lord.

Ezekiel 25

1 The worde of the Lord came againe vnto me, saying,

2 Sonne of man, set thy face against the Ammonites, and prophecie against them,

3 And say vnto the Ammonites, Heare the word of the Lord God, Thus saith the Lord God, Because thou saydest, Ha, ha, against my Sanctuarie, when it was polluted, and against the land of Israel, when it was desolate, and against the house of Iudah, when they went into captiuitie,

4 Beholde, therefore I will deliuer thee to the men of the East for a possession,

and they shall set their palaces in thee, and make their dwellings in thee: they shall eate thy fruite, and they shall drinke thy milke.

5 And I will make Rabbah a dwelling place for camels, and the Ammonites a sheepecote, and ye shall knowe that I am the Lord.

6 For thus saith the Lord God, Because thou hast clapped the hands, and stamped with the feete, and reioyced in heart with all thy despite against the land of Israel,

7 Beholde, therefore I will stretche out mine hand vpon thee, and will deliuer thee to be spoyled of the heathen, and I will roote thee out from the people, and I will cause thee to be destroyed out of the countreys, and I will destroy thee, and thou shalt know that I am the Lord.

8 Thus saith the Lord God, Because that Moab and Seir doe say, Beholde, the house of Iudah is like vnto all the heathen,

9 Therefore, beholde, I will open the side of Moab, euen of the cities of his cities, I say, in his frontiers with the pleasant countrey, Beth-ieshimoth, Baal-meon, and Karia-thaim.

10 I will call the men of the East against the Ammonites, and will giue them in possession, so that the Ammonites shall no more be remembred among the nations,

11 And I will execute iudgements vpon Moab, and they shall knowe that I am the Lord.

12 Thus sayth the Lord God, Because that Edom hath done euill by taking vengeance vpon the house of Iudah, and hath committed great offence, and reuenged himselfe vpon them,

13 Therefore thus saith the Lord God, I will also stretch out mine hand vpon Edom, and destroy man and beast out of it, and I will make it desolate from Teman, and they of Dedan shall fall by the sworde.

14 And I will execute my vengeance vpon Edom by the hand of my people Israel, and they shall doe in Edom according to mine anger, and according to mine indignation, and they shall know my vengeance, sayth the Lord God.

15 Thus sayth the Lord God, Because the Philistims haue executed vengeance, and reuenged themselues with a despitefull heart, to destroy it for the olde hatred,

16 Therefore thus sayth the Lord God, Behold, I will stretche out mine hand vpon the Philistims, and I will cut off the Cherethims, and destroy the remnant of the sea coast.

17 And I will execute great vengeance vpon them with rebukes of mine indignation, and they shall knowe that I am the Lord, when I shall lay my vengeance vpon them.

Ezekiel 26

1 And in the eleuenth yeere, in the first day of the moneth, the worde of the Lord came vnto me, saying,

2 Sonne of man, because that Tyrus hath said against Ierusalem, Aha, the gate of the people is broken: it is turned vnto me: for seeing she is desolate, I shall be replenished,

3 Therefore thus sayth the Lord God, Beholde, I come against thee, O Tyrus, and I will bring vp many nations against thee, as the sea mounteth vp with his waues.

4 And they shall destroy the walles of Tyrus and breake downe her towres: I will also scrape her dust from her, and make her like the top of a rocke.

5 Thou shalt be for the spreading of nettes in the middes of the sea: for I haue spoken it, sayth the Lord God, and it shalbe a spoile to ye nations.

6 And her daughters which are in the fielde, shall be slaine by the sworde, and they shall know that I am the Lord.

7 For thus sayth the Lord God, Behold, I will bring vpon Tyrus Nebuchad-nezzar King of Babel, a King of Kings from the North, with horses and with charets, and with horsemen, with a multitude and much people.

8 He shall slay with the sword thy daughters in the fielde, and he shall make a fort against thee, and cast a mount against thee, and lift vp the buckler against thee.

9 He shall set engins of warre before him against thy walles, and with his weapons breake downe thy towres.

10 The dust of his horses shall couer thee, for their multitude: thy walles shall shake at the noise of the horsemen, and of the wheeles, and of the charets, when he shall enter into thy gates as into the entrie of a citie that is broken downe.

11 With the hooues of his horses shall he treade downe all thy streetes: he shall slay thy people by the sworde, and the pillars of thy strength shall fall downe to the ground.

12 And they shall robbe thy riches, and spoyle thy marchandise, and they shall breake downe thy walles, and destroy thy pleasant houses, and they shall cast thy stones and thy timber and thy dust into the middes of the water.

13 Thus will I cause the sounde of thy songs to cease, and the sound of thine harpes shall be no more heard.

14 I wil lay thee like the top of a rocke: thou shalt be for a spreading of nets: thou shalt be built no more: for I the Lord haue spoken it, sayth the Lord God.

15 Thus sayth the Lord God to Tyrus, Shall not the yles tremble at the sounde of thy fall? and at the crie of the wounded, when they shall be slaine and murthered in the middes of thee?

16 Then all the princes of the sea shall come downe from their thrones: they shall lay away their robes, and put off their broydered garments, and shall clothe themselues with astonishment: they shall sitte vpon the ground, and be astonished at euery moment, and be amased at thee.

17 And they shall take vp a lamentation for thee, and say to thee, Howe art thou destroyed, that wast inhabited of the sea

men, the renoumed citie which was strong in the sea, both she and her inhabitants, which cause their feare to be on all that haunt therein!

18 Nowe shall the yles be astonished in the day of thy fall: yea, the yles that are in the sea, shall be troubled at thy departure.

19 For thus saith the Lord God, When I shall make thee a desolate citie, like ye cities that are not inhabited, and when I shall bring the deepe vpon thee, and great waters shall couer thee,

20 When I shall cast thee downe with them that descende into the pitte, with the people of olde time, and shall set thee in the lowe partes of the earth, like the olde ruines, with them, I say, which goe downe to the pitte, so that thou shalt not be inhabited, and I shall shewe my glory in the land of the liuing,

21 I will bring thee to nothing, and thou shalt be no more: though thou be sought for, yet shalt thou neuer be found againe, sayth the Lord God.

Ezekiel 27

1 The worde of the Lord came againe vnto me, saying,

2 Sonne of man, take vp a lametation for Tyrus,

3 And say vnto Tyrus, that is situate at the entrie of the sea, which is the marte of the people for many yles, Thus sayeth the Lord God, O Tyrus, thou hast said, I am of perfite beautie.

4 Thy borders are in the middes of the sea, and thy builders haue made thee of perfit beauty.

5 They haue made all thy shippe boardes of firre trees of Shenir: they haue brought cedars from Lebanon, to make mastes for thee.

6 Of ye okes of Bashan haue they made thine ores: the company of the Assyrians haue made thy banks of yuorie, brought out of ye yles of Chittim.

7 Fine linen with broydered woorke, brought from Egypt, was spread ouer thee to be thy sayle, blue silke and purple, brought from the yles of Elishah, was thy couering.

8 The inhabitants of Zidon, and Aruad were thy mariners, O Tyrus: thy wise men that were in thee, they were thy pilots.

9 The ancients of Gebal, and the wise men thereof were in thee thy calkers, all the shippes of the sea with their mariners were in thee to occupie thy marchandise.

10 They of Persia, and of Lud and of Phut were in thine armie: thy men of warre they hanged the shielde and helmet in thee: they set foorth thy beautie.

11 The men of Aruad with thine armie were vpon thy walles round about, and the Gammadims were in thy towres: they hanged their shields vpon thy walles round about: they haue made thy beautie perfite.

12 They of Tarshish were thy marchantes for the multitude of all

riches, for siluer, yron, tynne, and leade, which they brought to thy faires.

13 They of Iauan, Tubal and Meshech were thy marchants, concerning the liues of men, and they brought vessels of brasse for thy marchadise.

14 They of the house of Togarmah brought to thy faires horses, and horsemen, and mules.

15 The men of Dedan were thy marchantes: and the marchandise of many yles were in thine handes: they brought thee for a present hornes, teeth, and peacockes.

16 They of Aram were thy marchants for the multitude of thy wares: they occupied in thy faires with emerauds, purple, and broidred worke, and fine linen, and corall, and pearle.

17 They of Iudah and of the land of Israel were thy marchants: they brought for thy marchandise wheat of Minnith, and Pannag, and honie and oyle, and balme.

18 They of Damascus were thy marchants in ye multitude of thy wares, for the multitude of all riches, as in the wine of Helbon and white wooll.

19 They of Dan also and of Iauan, going to and from, occupied in thy faires: yron woorke, cassia and calamus were among thy marchandise.

20 They of Dedan were thy marchants in precious clothes for the charets.

21 They of Arabia, and all the princes of Kedar occupied with thee, in lambes, and rammes and goates: in these were they thy marchants.

22 The marchats of Sheba, and Raamah were thy marchantes: they occupied in thy faires with the chiefe of all spices, and with al precious stones and golde.

23 They of Haram and Canneh and Eden, the marchants of Sheba, Asshur and Chilmad were thy marchants.

24 These were thy marchants in all sortes of things, in raiment of blewe silke, and of broydred woorke, and in coffers for the rich apparell, which were bound with cordes: chaines also were among thy marchandise.

25 The shippes of Tarshish were thy chiefe in thy marchandise, and thou wast replenished and made very glorious in the middes of the sea.

26 Thy robbers haue brought thee into great waters: the East winde hath broken thee in the middes of the sea.

27 Thy riches and thy faires, thy marchandise, thy mariners and pilotes, thy calkers, and the occupiers of thy marchandise and al thy men of warre that are in thee, and all thy multitude which is in the middes of thee, shall fall in the middes of the sea in the day of thy ruine.

28 The suburbes shall shake at the sound of the crie of thy pilotes.

29 And all that handle the ore, the mariners and al the pilots of the sea shall come downe from their shippes, and shall stand vpon the land,

30 And shall cause their voyce to be heard against thee, and shall cry bitterly, and shall cast dust vpon their

heads, and wallow theselues in the ashes.

31 They shall plucke off their heare for thee and gird them with a sackecloth, and they shall weepe for thee with sorow of heart and bitter mourning.

32 And in their mourning, they shall take vp a lametation for thee, saying, What citie is like Tyrus, so destroied in the middes of the sea!

33 When thy wares went foorth of the seas, thou filledst many people, and thou diddest enrich the Kings of the earth with the multitude of thy riches and of thy marchandise.

34 When thou shalt be broken by ye seas in the depths of the waters, thy marchandise and all thy multitude, which was in the mids of thee, shall fal.

35 All the inhabitantes of the yles shall be astonished at thee, and all their Kings shall be sore afraide and troubled in their countenance.

36 The marchants among the people shall hisse at thee: thou shalt be a terrour, and neuer shalt be any more.

Ezekiel 28

1 The word of the Lord came againe vnto me, saying,

2 Sonne of man, say vnto the prince of Tyrus, Thus saieth the Lord God, Because thine heart is exalted, and thou hast said, I am a God, I sit in the seat of God in ye mids of the sea, yet thou art but a man and not God, and though thou didest thinke in thine heart, that thou wast equall with God,

3 Behold, thou art wiser then Daniel: there is no secrete, that they can hide from thee.

4 With thy wisedome and thine vnderstanding thou hast gotten thee riches, and hast gotten golde and siluer into thy treasures.

5 By thy great wisedome and by thine occupying hast thou increased thy riches, and thine heart is lifted vp because of thy riches.

6 Therefore thus sayeth the Lord God, Because thou didest thinke in thine heart, that thou wast equall with God,

7 Behold, therefore I wil bring strangers vpon thee, euen the terrible nations: and they shall drawe their swordes against the beautie of thy wisedome, and they shall defile thy brightnes.

8 They shall cast thee downe to the pit, and thou shalt die the death of them, that are slaine in the middes of the sea.

9 Wilt thou say then before him, that slayeth thee, I am a god? but thou shalt be a man, and no God, in the hands of him that slayeth thee.

10 Thou shalt die the death of the vncircumcised by the hands of stragers: for I haue spoken it, sayth the Lord God.

11 Moreouer the word of the Lord came vnto me, saying,

12 Sonne of man, take vp a lamentation vpon the King of Tyrus, and say vnto him, Thus sayeth the Lord God, Thou sealest vp the summe, and art full of wisedome and perfite in beautie.

13 Thou hast ben in Eden the garden of God: euery precious stone was in thy garment, the rubie, the topaze and the diamonde, the chrysolite, the onix, and the iasper, the saphir, emeraude, and the carbuncle and golde: the woorkemanship of thy timbrels, and of thy pipes was prepared in thee in the day that thou wast created.

14 Thou art the anointed Cherub, that couereth, and I haue set thee in honour: thou wast vpon the holy mountaine of God: thou hast walked in the middes of the stones of fire.

15 Thou wast perfite in thy wayes from the day that thou wast created, till iniquitie was found in thee.

16 By the multitude of thy marchandise, they haue filled the middes of thee with crueltie, and thou hast sinned: therefore I will cast thee as prophane out of the mountaine of God: and I will destroy thee, O couering Cherub from the mids of the stones of fire.

17 Thine heart was lifted vp because of thy beautie, and thou hast corrupted thy wisedome by reason of thy brightnes: I wil cast thee to ye grounde: I will lay thee before Kinges that they may beholde thee.

18 Thou hast defiled thy sanctification by the multitude of thine iniquities, and by the iniquitie of thy marchandise: therefore wil I bring forth a fire from the mids of thee, which shall deuoure thee: and I wil bring thee to ashes vpon the earth, in the sight of all them that beholde thee.

19 All they that knowe thee among the people, shalbe astonished at thee: thou shalt be a terrour, and neuer shalt thou be any more.

20 Againe, the worde of the Lord came vnto me, saying,

21 Sonne of man, set thy face against Zidon, and prophesie against it,

22 And say, Thus saith the Lord God, Behold, I come against thee, O Zidon, and I will be glorified in the mids of thee: and they shall know that I am the Lord, when I shall haue executed iudgements in her, and shalbe sanctified in her.

23 For I wil send into her pestilence, and blood into her streetes, and the slaine shall fall in the middes of her: the enemie shall come against her with the sword on euery side, and they shall know that I am the Lord.

24 And they shalbe no more a pricking thorne vnto the house of Israel, nor any grieuous thorne of all that are round about them, and despised them, and they shall knowe that I am the Lord God.

25 Thus saith the Lord God, When I shall haue gathered the house of Israel from the people where they are scattered, and shalbe sanctified in them in the sight of the heathen, then shall they dwel in the land, that I haue giuen to my seruant Iaakob.

26 And they shall dwell safely therein, and shall builde houses, and plant vineyards: yea, they shall dwell safely, when I haue executed iudgements vpon al round about them that despise them, and they shall knowe that I am the Lord their God.

Ezekiel 29

1 In the tenth yeere, and in the tenth moneth in the twelfth day of the moneth, the word of the Lord came vnto me, saying,

2 Sonne of man, set thy face against Pharaoh the King of Egypt, and prophecie against him, and against all Egypt.

3 Speake, and say, Thus sayth the Lord God, Beholde, I come against thee, Pharaoh King of Egypt, the great dragon, that lieth in the middes of his riuers, which hath saide, The riuer is mine, and I haue made it for my selfe.

4 But I will put hookes in thy chawes, and I will cause the fish of thy riuers to sticke vnto thy scales, and I will drawe thee out of the middes of thy riuers, and all the fishe of thy riuers shall sticke vnto thy scales.

5 And I will leaue thee in the wildernes, both thee and al the fish of thy riuers: thou shalt fal vpon ye open field: thou shalt not be brought together, nor gathered: for I haue giue thee for meat to the beasts of the field, and to the foules of heauen.

6 And al the inhabitants of Egypt shall know that I am the Lord, because they haue ben a staffe of reede to the house of Israel.

7 When they tooke holde of thee with their hand, thou diddest breake, and rent all their shoulder: and when they leaned vpon thee, thou brakest and madest all their loynes to stand vpright.

8 Therefore thus sayeth the Lord God, Beholde, I will bring a sworde vpon thee, and destroy man and beast out of thee,

9 And the land of Egypt shalbe desolate, and waste, and they shall know that I am ye Lord: because he hath said, The riuer is mine, and I haue made it,

10 Behold, therefore I come vpon thee, and vpon thy riuers, and I will make the land of Egypt vtterly waste and desolate from the towre of Seueneh, euen vnto the borders of the blacke Mores.

11 No foote of man shall passe by it, nor foote of beast shall passe by it, neither shall it be inhabited fourtie yeeres.

12 And I wil make the land of Egypt desolate in the middes of the countries, that are desolate, and her cities shall be desolate among the cities that are desolate, for fourtie yeeres: and I wil scatter the Egyptians among the nations, and wil disperse them through the countreis.

13 Yet thus saieth the Lord God, At the end of fourtie yeeres will I gather the Egyptians from the people, where they were scattered,

14 And I wil bring againe the captiuitie of Egypt, and will cause them to returne into the land of Pathros, into the lande of their habitation, and they shalbe there a small kingdome.

15 It shall be the smallest of the kingdomes, neither shall it exalt it selfe any more aboue the nations: for I will diminish them, that they shall no more rule the nations.

16 And it shall be no more the confidence of the house of Israel, to bring their iniquitie to remembrance by looking after them, so shall they knowe, that I am the Lord God.

17 In the seuen and twentieth yeere also in the first moneth, and in the first day of the moneth, came the word of the Lord vnto me, saying,

18 Sonne of man, Nebuchad-nezzar King of Babel caused his armie to serue a great seruice against Tyrus: euery head was made balde, and euery shoulder was made bare: yet had he no wages, nor his armie for Tyrus, for the seruice that he serued against it.

19 Therefore thus sayth the Lord God, Beholde, I will giue the land of Egypt vnto Nebuchad-nezzar the King of Babel, and he shall take her multitude, and spoyle her spoyle, and take her pray, and it shall be the wages for his armie.

20 I haue giuen him the land of Egypt for his labour, that he serued against it, because they wrought for me, sayth the Lord God.

21 In that day will I cause the horne of the house of Israel to growe, and I will giue thee an open mouth in the middes of them, and they shall knowe that I am the Lord.

Ezekiel 30

1 The worde of the Lord came againe vnto me, saying,

2 Sonne of man, prophesie, and say, Thus sayth the Lord God, Howle and cry, Wo be vnto this day.

3 For the day is neere, and the day of the Lord is at hand, a cloudie day, and it shall be the time of the heathen.

4 And the sword shall come vpon Egypt, and feare shall be in Ethiopia, when the slaine shall fall in Egypt, when they shall take away her multitude, and when her foundations shall be broken downe.

5 Ethiopia and Phut, and Lud, and all the common people, and Cub, and the men of the land, that is in league, shall fall with them by the sword.

6 Thus sayth the Lord, They also that mainteine Egypt, shall fall, and the pride of her power shall come downe: from the towre of Seueneh shall they fall by the sword, sayth the Lord God.

7 And they shall be desolate in the middes of the countries that are desolate, and her cities shall be in the middes of the cities that are wasted.

8 And they shall knowe that I am the Lord, when I haue set a fire in Egypt, and when all her helpers shall be destroyed.

9 In that day shall there messengers go forth from me in shippes, to make the carelesse Mores aftaide, and feare shall come vpon them, as in the day of Egypt: for loe, it commeth.

10 Thus sayth the Lord God, I will also make the multitude of Egypt to cease by

the hand of Nebuchad-nezzar King of Babel.

11 For he and his people with him, euen the terrible nations shall be brought to destroy the land: and they shall drawe their swordes against Egypt, and fill the land with the slaine.

12 And I will make the riuers drye, and fell the land into the hands of the wicked, and I will make the land waste, and all that therein is by the hands of strangers: I the Lord haue spoken it.

13 Thus saith the Lord God, I will also destroy the idoles, and I will cause their idoles to cease out of Noph, and there shall be no more a prince of the land of Egypt, and I will send a feare in the land of Egypt.

14 And I will make Pathros desolate, and will set fire in Zoan, and I will execute iudgement in No.

15 And I will powre my wrath vpon Sin, which is the strength of Egypt: and I will destroy the multitude of No.

16 And I will set fire in Egypt: Sin shall haue great sorowe and No shalbe destroyed, and Noph shall haue sorowes dayly.

17 The yong men of Auen, and of Phibeseth shall fall by the sworde: and these cities shall goe into captiuitie.

18 At Tehaphnehes the day shall restraine his light, when I shall breake there the barres of Egypt: and when the pompe of her power shall cease in her, the cloude shall couer her, and her daughters shall goe into captiuitie.

19 Thus will I execute iudgements in Egypt, and they shall knowe that I am the Lord.

20 And in the eleuenth yeere, in the first moneth, in the seuenth day of the moneth, the worde of the Lord came vnto me, saying,

21 Sonne of man, I haue broken the arme of Pharaoh King of Egypt: and lo, it shall not be boud vp to be healed, neither shall they put a roule to bind it, and so make it strong, to hold the sworde.

22 Therefore thus saith the Lord God, Behold, I come against Pharaoh King of Egypt, and will breake his arme, that was strong, but is broken, and I will cause the sworde to fall out of his hande.

23 And I will scatter the Egyptians among the nations, and will disperse them through the countreys.

24 And I will strengthen the arme of the King of Babel, and put my sworde in his hand, but I will breake Pharaohs armes, and he shall cast out sighings, as the sighings of him, that is wounded before him.

25 But I will strengthen the armes of the king of Babel, and the armes of Pharaoh shall fall downe, and they shall knowe, that I am the Lord, when I shall put my sworde into the hand of the King of Babel, and he shall stretch it out vpon the land of Egypt.

26 And I will scatter the Egyptians among the nations, and disperse them among ye countreys, and they shall knowe, that I am the Lord.

Ezekiel 31

1 And in the eleuenth yeere, in the third moneth, and in the first day of the moneth the worde of the Lord came vnto me, saying,

2 Sonne of man, speake vnto Pharaoh King of Egypt, and to his multitude, Whom art thou like in thy greatnesse?

3 Beholde, Asshur was like a cedar in Lebanon with faire branches, and with thicke shadowing boughes, and shot vp very hye, and his toppe was among the thicke boughes.

4 The waters nourished him, and the deepe exalted him on hie with her riuers running round about his plants, and sent out her litle riuers vnto all the trees of the fielde.

5 Therefore his height was exalted aboue all the trees of the fielde, and his boughes were multiplied, and his branches were long, because of the multitude of the waters, which the deepe sent out.

6 All the foules of the heauen made their nestes in his boughes, and vnder his branches did all the beastes of the fielde bring foorth their yong, and vnder his shadowe dwelt all mightie nations.

7 Thus was he faire in his greatnesse, and in the length of his branches: for his roote was neere great waters.

8 The cedars in the garden of God coulde not hide him: no firre tree was like his branches, and the chessenut trees were not like his boughes: all the trees in the garden of God were not like vnto him in his beautie.

9 I made him faire by the multitude of his branches: so that all the trees of Eden, that were in the garden of God, enuied him.

10 Therefore thus sayeth the Lord God, Because he is lift vp on high, and hath shot vp his toppe among the thicke boughes, and his heart is lift vp in his height,

11 I haue therefore deliuered him into the handes of the mightiest among the heathen: he shall handle him, for I haue cast him away for his wickednesse.

12 And the strangers haue destroyed him, euen the terrible nations, and they haue left him vpon the mountaines, and in all the valleis his branches are fallen, and his boughes are broken by all the riuers of the land: and all the people of the earth are departed from his shadowe, and haue forsaken him.

13 Vpon his ruine shall all the foules of the heauen remaine, and all the beastes of the fielde shall be vpon his branches,

14 So that none of all the trees by the waters shalbe exalted by their height, neither shall shoote vp their toppe among the thicke boughes, neither shall their leaues stand vp in their height, which drinke so much water: for they are all deliuered vnto death in the nether partes of the earth in the middes of the children of men among them that goe downe to the pit.

15 Thus saith the Lord God, In the day when he went downe to hell, I caused them to mourne, and I couered the deepe for him, and I did restreine the floods thereof, and the great waters were stayed: I caused Lebanon to mourne for him, and all the trees of the fielde fainted.

16 I made the nations to shake at the sound of his fall, when I cast him downe to hell with them that descend into the pit, and all the excellent trees of Eden, and the best of Lebanon: euen all that are nourished with waters, shall be comforted in the nether partes of the earth.

17 They also went downe to hell with him vnto them that be slaine with the sworde, and his arme, and they that dwelt vnder his shadowe in the middes of the heathen.

18 To whom art thou thus like in glorie and in greatnesse among the trees of Eden? yet thou shalt be cast downe with the trees of Eden vnto the nether partes of the earth: thou shalt sleepe in the middes of the vncircumcised, with them that be slaine by the sworde: this is Pharaoh and all his multitude, sayth the Lord God.

Ezekiel 32

1 And in the twelfth yeere in the twelfth moneth, and in the first day of the moneth, the worde of the Lord came vnto me, saying,

2 Sonne of man, take vp a lamentation for Pharaoh King of Egypt, and say vnto him, Thou art like a lyon of the nations and art as a dragon in the sea: thou castedst out thy riuers and troubledst the waters with thy feete, and stampedst in their riuers.

3 Thus sayth the Lord God, I will therefore spread my net ouer thee with a great multitude of people, and they shall make thee come vp into my net.

4 Then will I leaue thee vpon the land, and I will cast thee vpon the open field, and I wil cause all the foules of the heauen to remaine vpon thee, and I will fill all the beastes of the field with thee.

5 And I will lay thy flesh vpon the mountaines, and fill the valleys with thine height.

6 I will also water with thy blood the land wherein thou swimmest, euen to ye mountaines, and the riuers shall be full of thee.

7 And when I shall put thee out, I will couer the heauen, and make the starres thereof darke: I will couer the sunne with a cloude, and the moone shall not giue her light.

8 All the lightes of heauen will I make darke for thee, and bring darkenesse vpon thy lande, sayeth the Lord God.

9 I will also trouble the heartes of many people, when I shall bring thy destruction among the nations and vpon the countries which thou hast not knowen.

10 Yea, I will make many people amased at thee, and their Kings shalbe astonished with feare for thee, when I shall make my sworde to glitter against

their faces, and they shall be afraide at euery moment: euery man for his owne life in the day of thy fall.

11 For thus sayth the Lord God, The sworde of the King of Babel shall come vpon thee.

12 By the swordes of the mightie will I cause thy multitude to fall: they all shall be terrible nations, and they shall destroy the pompe of Egypt, and all the multitude thereof shalbe consumed.

13 I will destroy also all the beastes thereof from the great watersides, neither shall the foote of man trouble them any more, nor the hooues of beast trouble them.

14 Then will I make their waters deepe, and cause their riuers to runne like oyle, sayeth the Lord God.

15 When I shall make the land of Egypt desolate, and the countrey with all that is therein, shall be laid waste: when I shall smite all them which dwell therein, then shall they know that I am ye Lord.

16 This is the mourning wherewith they shall lament her: the daughters of the nations shall lament her: they shall lament for Egypt, and for all her multitude, sayeth the Lord God.

17 In the twelfth yeere also in the fifteenth day of the moneth, came the worde of the Lord vnto me, saying,

18 Sonne of man, lament for the multitude of Egypt, and cast them downe, euen them and the daughters of the mighty nations vnto the nether partes of the earth, with them that goe downe into the pit.

19 Whome doest thou passe in beautie? goe downe and sleepe with the vncircumcised.

20 They shall fall in the middes of them that are slaine by the sword: shee is deliuered to the sword: draw her downe, and all her multitude.

21 The most mighty and strong shall speake to him out of the mids of hell with them that helpe her: they are gone downe and sleepe with the vncircumcised that be slaine by the sworde.

22 Asshur is there and all his companie: their graues are about him: all they are slaine and fallen by the sworde.

23 Whose graues are made in the side of the pit, and his multitude are rounde about his graue: all they are slaine and fallen by the sworde, which caused feare to be in the land of the liuing.

24 There is Elam and all his multitude round about his graue: al they are slaine and fallen by the sword which are gone downe with the vncircumcised into the nether parts of the earth, which caused themselues to be feared in the land of the liuing, yet haue they borne their shame with them that are gone downe to the pit.

25 They haue made his bed in the mids of the slaine with al his multitude: their graues are round about him: all these vncircucised are slaine by the sworde: though they haue caused their feare in the land of ye liuing, yet haue they borne their shame with them that goe downe to

the pitte: they are laide in the middes of them, that be slaine.

26 There is Meshech, Tubal, and all their multitude, their graues are round about them: al these vncircumcised were slaine by the sworde, though they caused their feare to be in ye land of the liuing.

27 And they shall not lie with the valiant of the vncircumcised, that are fallen, which are gone down to the graue, with their weapons of warre, and haue laied their swords vnder their heads, but their iniquitie shalbe vpon their bones: because they were the feare of the mighty in the lande of the liuing.

28 Yea, thou shalt be broken in the middes of the vncircumcised, and lie with them that are slaine by the sworde.

29 There is Edom, his Kings, and all his princes, which with their strength are laied by them that were slaine by the sworde: they shall sleepe with the vncircumcised, and with them that goe downe to the pit.

30 There be al the princes of the North, with al the Zidonians, which are gone downe with the slaine, with their feare: they are ashamed of their strength, and the vncircumcised sleepe with them that be slaine by the sword, and beare their shame with them that goe downe to the pit.

31 Pharaoh shall see them, and hee shall be comforted ouer all his multitude: Pharaoh, and all his armie shall be slaine by the sword, saieth the Lord God.

32 For I haue caused my feare to be in the lande of the liuing: and he shall be laid in the mids of the vncircumcised with them, that are slaine by the sword, euen Pharaoh and all his multitude, sayeth the Lord God.

Ezekiel 33

1 Again, the woorde of the Lord came vnto me, saying,

2 Sonne of man, speake to the children of thy people, and say vnto them, When I bring the sworde vpon a lande, if the people of the lande take a man from among them, and make him their watchman,

3 If when hee seeth the sworde come vpon ye land, he blow the trumpet, and warne the people,

4 Then hee that heareth the sounde of the trumpet, and will not bee warned, if the sworde come, and take him away, his blood shall be vpon his owne head.

5 For he heard the sound of the trumpet, and woulde not bee admonished: therefore his blood shall be vpon him: but he that receiueth warning, shall saue his life.

6 But if the watchman see the sworde come, and blowe not the trumpet, and the people be not warned: if the sworde come, and take any person from among them, he is taken away for his iniquitie, but his blood will I require at the watchmans hande.

7 So thou, O sonne of man, I haue made thee a watchman vnto the house of Israel: therefore thou shalt heare the woorde at my mouth, and admonish them from me.

8 When I shall say vnto the wicked, O wicked man, thou shalt die the death, if thou doest not speake, and admonish the wicked of his way, that wicked man shall die for his iniquitie, but his blood will I require at thine hand.

9 Neuerthelesse, If thou warne the wicked of his way, to turne from it, if he doe not turne from his way, he shall die for his iniquitie, but thou hast deliuered thy soule.

10 Therefore, O thou sonne of man, speake vnto the house of Israel, Thus yee speake and say, If our transgressions and our sinnes bee vpon vs, and we are consumed because of them, howe should we then liue?

11 Say vnto them, As I liue, sayeth the Lord God, I desire not the death of the wicked, but that the wicked turne from his way and liue: turne you, turne you from your euill waies, for why will ye die, O ye house of Israel?

12 Therefore thou sonne of man, saye vnto the children of thy people, The righteousnesse of the righteous shall not deliuer him in the day of his transgression, nor the wickednesse of the wicked shall cause him to fall therein, in the day that he returneth from his wickednesse, neither shall the righteous liue for his righteousnesse in the day that he sinneth.

13 When I shall say vnto the righteous, that he shall surely liue, if he trust to his owne righteousnes, and commit iniquitie, all his righteousnes shall be no more remembred, but for his iniquitie that he hath committed, he shall die for the same.

14 Againe when I shall say vnto the wicked, thou shalt die the death, if he turne from his sinne, and doe that which is lawfull and right,

15 To wit, if the wicked restore the pledge, and giue againe that he had robbed, and walke in the statutes of life, without committing iniquitie, he shall surely liue, and not die.

16 None of his sinnes that he hath comitted, shall be mentioned vnto him: because he hath done that, which is lawful, and right, he shall surely liue.

17 Yet the children of thy people say, The way of the Lord is not equall: but their owne way is vnequall.

18 When the righteous turneth from his righteousnesse, and committeth iniquitie, he shall euen die thereby.

19 But if the wicked returne from his wickednesse, and doe that which is lawfull and right, hee shall liue thereby.

20 Yet yee say, The way of the Lord is not equall. O ye house of Israel, I will iudge you euery one after his waies.

21 Also in the twelfth yere of our captiuitie, in the tenth moneth, and in the fift day of the moneth, one that had escaped out of Ierusalem, came vnto me, and said, The citie is smitten.

22 Now the hand of the Lord had bene vpon me in ye euening afore hee that had escaped, came, and had opened my mouth vntill he came to me in the morning: and when hee had opened my mouth, I was no more dumme.

23 Againe the worde of the Lord came vnto me, and saide,

24 Sonne of man, these that dwel in the desolate places of the land of Israel, talke and say, Abraham was but one, and hee possessed the lande: but we are many, therefore the lande shall be giuen vs in possession.

25 Wherefore say vnto them, Thus saieth the Lord God, Ye eate with the blood, and lift vp your eyes towarde your idoles, and sheade blood: should ye then possesse the land?

26 Ye leane vpon your swordes: ye worke abomination, and yee defile euery one his neighbours wife: should ye then possesse the land?

27 Say thus vnto them, Thus saieth the Lord God, As I liue, so surely they that are in the desolate places, shall fall by the sword: and him that is in the open field, will I giue vnto the beasts to be deuoured: and they that be in the forts and in the caues, shall die of the pestilence.

28 For I will lay the land desolate and waste, and the pompe of her strength shall cease: and the moutaines of Israel shalbe desolate, and none shall passe through.

29 Then shall they know that I am the Lord, when I haue laid ye land desolate and wast, because of al their abominations, that they haue committed.

30 Also thou sonne of man, the children of thy people that talke of thee by the wals and in the dores of houses, and speake one to another, euery one to his brother, saying, Come, I pray you, and heare what is the word that commeth from the Lord.

31 For they come vnto thee, as the people vseth to come: and my people sit before thee, and heare thy wordes, but they will not doe them: for with their mouthes they make iestes, and their heart goeth after their couetousnesse.

32 And loe, thou art vnto them, as a iesting song of one that hath a pleasant voyce, and can sing well: for they heare thy woordes, but they doe them not.

33 And when this commeth to passe (for loe, it will come) then shall they know, that a Prophet hath bene among them.

Ezekiel 34

1 And the word of the Lord came vnto me, saying,

2 Sonne of man, prophesie against the shepherdes of Israel, prophesie and say vnto them, Thus saieth the Lord God vnto the shepherds, Wo be vnto the shepherds of Israel, that feede them selues: should not the shepherds feede the flockes?

3 Yee eate the fat, and yee clothe you with the wooll: yee kill them that are fed, but ye feede not the sheepe.

4 The weake haue ye not strengthened: the sicke haue ye not healed, neither haue ye bounde vp the broken, nor brought againe that which was driuen away, neither haue yee sought that which was lost, but with crueltie, and with rigour haue yee ruled them.

5 And they were scattered without a shepherde: and when they were dispersed, they were deuoured of all the beastes of the fielde.

6 My sheepe wandred through all the mountaines, and vpon euery hie hill: yea, my flocke was scattered through al the earth, and none did seeke or search after them.

7 Therefore ye shepherds, heare the woorde of the Lord.

8 As I liue, sayeth the Lord God, surely because my flocke was spoyled, and my sheepe were deuoured of all the beasts of the fielde, hauing no shepherde, neither did my shepherdes seeke my sheepe, but the shepherdes fedde them selues, and fedde not my sheepe,

9 Therefore, heare ye the word of the Lord, O ye shepherds.

10 Thus saieth the Lord God, Behold, I come against the shepherds, and will require my sheepe at their hands, and cause them to cease from feeding the sheepe: neither shall the shepherds feede them selues any more: for I wil deliuer my sheepe from their mouthes, and they shall no more deuoure them.

11 For thus sayeth the Lord God, Beholde, I will search my sheepe, and seeke them out.

12 As a shepherd searcheth out his flocke, when he hath bene among his sheepe that are scattered, so wil I seeke out my sheepe and wil deliuer them out of all places, where they haue beene scattered in the cloudie and darke day,

13 And I will bring them out from the people, and gather them from the countreis, and will bring them to their owne lande, and feede them vpon the mountaines of Israel, by the riuers, and in all the inhabited places of the countrey.

14 I will feede them in a good pasture, and vpon the hie mountaines of Israel shall their folde be: there shall they lie in a good folde and in fat pasture shall they feede vpon the mountaines of Israel.

15 I will feede my sheepe, and bring them to their rest, sayth the Lord God.

16 I will seeke that which was lost, and bring againe that which was driue away, and will binde vp that which was broken, and will strengthen the weake but I wil destroy the fat and the strong, and I will feede them with iudgement.

17 Also you my sheepe, Thus saieth the Lord God, behold, I iudge betweene sheepe, and sheepe, betweene the rammes and the goates.

18 Seemeth it a small thing vnto you to haue eaten vp the good pasture, but yee must treade downe with your feete the residue of your pasture? and to haue drunke of the deepe waters, but yee must trouble the residue with your feete?

19 And my sheepe eate that which yee haue troden with your feete, and drinke that which ye haue troubled with your feete.

20 Therefore thus sayth the Lord God vnto them, behold, I, euen I wil iudge betweene the fat sheepe and the leane sheepe.

21 Because ye haue thrust with side and with shoulder, and pusht al the weake with your hornes, till ye haue scattered them abroade,

22 Therefore wil I helpe my sheepe, and they shall no more be spoyled, and I wil iudge betweene sheepe and sheepe.

23 And I wil set vp a shepherd ouer them, and he shall feede them, euen my seruant Dauid, he shall feede them, and he shalbe their shepherd.

24 And I the Lord will be their God, and my seruant Dauid shalbe the prince amog them. I the Lord haue spoken it.

25 And I will make with them a couenant of peace, and will cause the euil beastes to cease out of the land: and they shall dwel safely in the wildernesse, and sleepe in the woods.

26 And I wil set them, as a blessing, euen roud about my mountaine: and I will cause rayne to come downe in due season, and there shalbe raine of blessing.

27 And the tree of the fielde shall yeeld her fruite, and the earth shall giue her fruite, and they shalbe safe in their land, and shall know that I am the Lord, when I haue broken the cordes of their yoke, and deliuered them out of the hands of those that serued themselues of them.

28 And they shall no more be spoyled of the heathen, neither shall the beastes of the land deuoure them, but they shall dwell safely and none shall make them afrayd.

29 And I will rayse vp for them a plant of renoume, and they shalbe no more consumed with hunger in the land, neither beare the reproche of the heathen any more.

30 Thus shall they vnderstande, that I the Lord their God am with them, and that they, euen the house of Israel, are my people, sayth the Lord God.

31 And yee my sheepe, the sheepe of my pasture are men, and I am your God, saith the Lord God.

Ezekiel 35

1 Moveover the worde of the Lord came vnto me, saying,

2 Sonne of man, Set thy face against mount Seir, and prophesie against it,

3 And say vnto it, Thus sayth the Lord God, Behold, O mount Seir, I come against thee, and I wil stretch out mine hand against thee, and I will make thee desolate and waste.

4 I wil lay thy cities waste, and thou shalt be desolate, and thou shalt knowe that I am the Lord.

5 Because thou hast had a perpetuall hatred and hast put the children of Israel to flight by the force of the sword in the time of their calamitie, when their iniquitie had an ende,

6 Therefore as I liue, sayth the Lord God, I wil prepare thee vnto blood, and blood shall pursue thee: except thou hate blood, euen blood shall pursue thee.

7 Thus will I make mount Seir desolate and waste, and cut off from it him that passeth out and him that returneth.

8 And I will fill his mountaines with his slayne men: in thine hilles, and in thy valleys and in all thy riuers shall they fall, that are slayne with the sworde.

9 I wil make thee perpetual desolations, and thy cities shall not returne, and ye shall knowe that I am the Lord.

10 Because thou hast said, These two nations, and these two countreys shalbe mine, and we wil possesse them (seeing the Lord was there)

11 Therefore as I liue, sayth the Lord God, I wil euen do according to thy wrath, and according to thine indignation which thou hast vsed in thine hatred against them: and I wil make my selfe knowen among them whe I haue iudged thee.

12 And thou shalt know, that I the Lord haue heard all thy blasphemies which thou hast spoken against the mountaines of Israel, saying, They lye waste, they are giuen vs to be deuoured.

13 Thus with your mouthes ye haue boasted against me, and haue multiplied your words against me: I haue heard them.

14 Thus sayth the Lord God, So shall all the world reioyce when I shall make thee desolate.

15 As thou diddest reioyce at the inheritance of the house of Israel, because it was desolate, so will I doe vnto thee: thou shalt be desolate, O mount Seir, and all Idumea wholly, and they shall know, that I am the Lord.

Ezekiel 36

1 Also thou sonne of man, prophesie vnto the mountaines of Israel, and say, Ye mountaines of Israel, heare the word of the Lord.

2 Thus saith the Lord God, because the enemie hath sayde against you, Aha, euen the hye places of the world are ours in possession,

3 Therefore prophesie, and say, Thus sayth the Lord God, Because that they haue made you desolate, and swallowed you vp on euery side, that ye might be a possession vnto the residue of the heathen, and ye are come vnto the lippes and tongues of men, and vnto the reproch of the people,

4 Therefore ye mountaines of Israel, heare the worde of the Lord God, Thus sayth the Lord God to the mountaines and to the hilles, to the riuers, and to the valleys, and to the waste, and desolate places, and to the cities that are forsaken: which are spoyled and had in derision of the residue of the heathen that are round about.

5 Therefore thus saith the Lord God, Surely in the fire of mine indignation haue I spoken against the residue of the heathen, and against all Idumea, which haue taken my lande for their possession, with the ioy of all their heart, and with despitefull mindes to cast it out for a pray.

6 Prophesie therfor vpon the land of Israel, and say vnto the mountaines, and to the hilles, to the riuers, and to the valleys, Thus sayth the Lord God, Behold, I haue spoken in mine indignation, and in my wrath, because yee haue suffered the shame of the heathen,

7 Therefore thus saith the Lord God, I haue lifted vp mine hand, surely the heathen that are about you, shall beare their shame.

8 But you, O mountaines of Israel, yee shall shoote forth your branches, and bring foorth your fruite to my people of Israel: for they are ready to come.

9 For behold, I come vnto you, and I wil turne vnto you, and ye shalbe tilled and sowen.

10 And I wil multiply the men vpon you, euen all the house of Israel wholly, and the cities shalbe inhabited, and the desolate places shalbe builded.

11 And I wil multiply vpon you man and beast, and they shall encrease, and bring fruite, and I will cause you to dwell after your olde estate, and I will bestowe benefites vpon you more then at the first, and ye shall know that I am the Lord.

12 Yea, I wil cause men to walke vpon you, euen my people Israel, and they shall possesse you, and ye shalbe their inheritance, and ye shall no more henceforth depriue them of men.

13 Thus sayth the Lord God, because they say vnto you, Thou land deuourest vp men, and hast bene a waster of thy people,

14 Therefore thou shalt deuoure men no more, neither waste thy people henceforth, sayth the Lord God,

15 Neither will I cause men to heare in thee the shame of the heathen any more, neither shalt thou beare the reproche of the people any more, neither shalt cause thy folke to fal any more, saith the Lord God.

16 Moreouer the word of the Lord came vnto me, saying,

17 Sonne of man, when the house of Israel dwelt in their owne lande, they defiled it by their owne wayes, and by their deedes: their way was before me as the filthinesse of the menstruous.

18 Wherfore I powred my wrath vpon them, for the blood that they had shed in the land, and for their idoles, wherewith they had polluted it.

19 And I scattered them among the heathen, and they were dispersed through the countries for according to their wayes, and according to their deedes, I iudged them.

20 And when they entred vnto the heathen, whither they went, they polluted mine holy Name, when they sayd of them, These are the people of the Lord, and are gone out of his land.

21 But I fauoured mine holy Name which the house of Israel had polluted among the heathen, whither they went.

22 Therfore say vnto the house of Israel, Thus saith ye Lord God, I doe not this for your sakes, O house of Israel, but for mine holy Names sake, which yee polluted among the heathen whither ye went.

23 And I wil sanctifie my great Name, which was polluted among the heathen, among whome you haue polluted it, and the heathen shall know that I am the Lord, sayth the Lord God, when I shalbe sanctified in you before their eyes.

24 For I will take you from among the heathen, and gather you out of all countries, and will bring you into your owne land.

25 Then wil I powre cleane water vpon you, and ye shalbe cleane: yea, from all your filthines, and from all your idoles wil I clense you.

26 A newe heart also will I giue you, and a new spirit wil I put within you, and I will take away the stonie heart out of your body, and I will giue you an heart of flesh.

27 And I will put my spirite within you, and cause you to walke in my statutes, and ye shall keepe my iudgements and do them.

28 And ye shall dwell in the land, that I gaue to your fathers, and ye shalbe my people, and I will be your God.

29 I will also deliuer you from all your filthinesse, and I will call for corne, and will increase it, and lay no famine vpon you.

30 For I will multiplie the fruite of the trees, and the increase of the fielde, that ye shall beare no more the reproch of famine among the heathen.

31 Then shall ye remember your owne wicked wayes, and your deedes that were not good, and shall iudge your selues worthie to haue bene destroyed for your iniquities, and for your abominations.

32 Be it knowen vnto you that I do not this for your sakes, sayth the Lord God: therefore, O ye house of Israel, be ashamed, and confounded for your owne wayes.

33 Thus sayth the Lord God, What time as I shall haue clensed you from all your iniquities, I will cause you to dwel in the cities, and the desolate places shalbe builded.

34 And the desolate land shalbe tilled, whereas it lay waste in the sight of all that passed by.

35 For they sayd, This waste land was like the garden of Eden, and these waste and desolate and ruinous cities were strong, and were inhabited.

36 Then the residue of the heathen that are left round about you, shall know that I the Lord builde the ruinous places, and plant the desolate places: I the Lord haue spoken it, and wil do it.

37 Thus saith the Lord God, I will yet for this be sought of ye house of Israel, to

performe it vnto them: I wil encrease them with men like a flocke.

38 As the holy flocke, as the flocke of Ierusalem in their solemne feastes, so shall the desolate cities be filled with flockes of men, and they shall know, that I am the Lord.

Ezekiel 37

1 The hand of the Lord was vpon me, and caryed me out in ye spirit of ye Lord, and set me downe in ye mids of the field, which was full of bones.

2 And he led me round about by them, and beholde, they were very many in the open fielde, and lo, they were very drie.

3 And he sayde vnto me, Sonne of man, can these bones liue? And I answered, O Lord God, thou knowest.

4 Againe he sayde vnto me, Prophecie vpon these bones and say vnto them, O ye dry bones, heare the word of the Lord.

5 Thus saith the Lord God vnto these bones, Behold, I wil cause breath to enter into you, and ye shall liue.

6 And I will lay sinewes vpon you, and make flesh growe vpon you, and couer you with skinne, and put breath in you, that ye may liue, and yee shall know that I am the Lord.

7 So I prophecied, as I was commanded: and as I prophecied, there was a noyse, and beholde, there was a shaking, and the bones came together, bone to his bone.

8 And when I beheld, loe, the sinewes, and the flesh grewe vpon them, and aboue, the skinne couered them, but there was no breath in them.

9 Then sayd he vnto me, Prophecie vnto the winde: prophecie, sonne of man, and say to the winde, Thus sayth the Lord God, Come from the foure windes, O breath, and breathe vpon these slayne, that they may liue.

10 So I prophecied as hee had commanded me: and the breath came into them, and they liued, and stood vp vpon their feete, an exceeding great armie.

11 Then he sayd vnto me, Sonne of man, these bones are the whole house of Israel. Behold, they say, Our bones are dried, and our hope is gone, and we are cleane cut off.

12 Therefore prophecie, and say vnto them, Thus saith the Lord God, Beholde, my people, I will open your graues, and cause you to come vp out of your sepulchres, and bring you into the lande of Israel,

13 And yee shall knowe that I am the Lord, when I haue opened your graues, O my people, and brought you vp out of your sepulchres,

14 And shall put my Spirit in you, and ye shall liue, and I shall place you in your owne land: then yee shall knowe that I the Lord haue spoken it, and performed it, sayth the Lord.

15 The word of the Lord came againe vnto me, saying,

16 Moreouer thou sonne of man, take thee a piece of wood, and write vpon it, Vnto Iudah, and to the children of Israel his companions the take another piece of wood, and write vpon it, Vnto Ioseph the tree of Ephraim, and to al the house of Israel his companions.

17 And thou shalt ioyne the one to another into one tree, and they shalbe as one in thine hand.

18 And when the children of thy people shall speake vnto thee, saying, Wilt thou not shewe vs what thou meanest by these?

19 Thou shalt answere them, Thus sayeth the Lord God, Behold, I wil take the tree of Ioseph, which is in the hande of Ephraim, and the tribes of Israel his fellowes, and will put them with him, euen with the tree of Iudah, and make them one tree, and they shalbe one in mine hand.

20 And the pieces of wood, whereon thou writest, shalbe in thine hand, in their sight.

21 And say vnto them, Thus saith the Lord God, Beholde, I will take the children of Israel from among the heathen, whither they be gone, and wil gather them on euery side, and bring them into their owne land.

22 And I will make them one people in the lande, vpon the mountaines of Israel, and one king shalbe king to them all: and they shalbe no more two peoples, neither bee deuided any more henceforth into two kingdomes.

23 Neither shall they bee polluted any more with their idoles, nor with their abominations, nor with any of their transgressions: but I will saue them out of all their dwelling places, wherein they haue sinned, and will clense them: so shall they be my people, and I will be their God.

24 And Dauid my seruant shalbe king ouer them, and they all shall haue one shepheard: they shall also walke in my iudgements, and obserue my statutes, and doe them.

25 And they shall dwell in the lande, that I haue giuen vnto Iaakob my seruant, where your fathers haue dwelt, and they shall dwel therein, euen they, and their sonnes, and their sonnes sonnes for euer, and my seruant Dauid shall bee their prince for euer.

26 Moreouer, I will make a couenant of peace with them: it shall be an euerlasting couenant with them, and I wil place them, and multiply them, and wil set my Sanctuarie among them for euermore.

27 My tabernacle also shalbe with them: yea, I will be their God, and they shalbe my people.

28 Thus the heathen shall knowe, that I the Lord do sanctifie Israel, when my Sanctuarie shall be among them for euermore.

Ezekiel 38

1 And the worde of the Lord came vnto mee, saying,

2 Sonne of man, set thy face against Gog, and against the lande of Magog, the chiefe prince of Meshech and Tubal, and prophecie against him,

3 And say, Thus sayth the Lord God, Behold, I come against thee, O Gog the chiefe prince of Meshech and Tubal.

4 And I wil destroy thee, and put hookes in thy chawes, and I will bring thee forth, and all thine host both horses, and horsemen, all clothed with al sorts of armour, eue a great multitude with bucklers, and shieldes, all handling swords.

5 They of Paras, of Cush, and Phut with the, euen all they that beare shielde and helmet.

6 Gomer and all his bands, and the house of Togarmah of the North quarters, and al his bands, and much people with thee.

7 Prepare thy selfe, and make thee ready, both thou, and al thy multitude, that are assembled vnto thee, and be thou their sauegard.

8 After many dayes thou shalt bee visited: for in the latter yeres thou shalt come into the land, that hath bene destroyed with the sworde, and is gathered out of many people vpon the mountaines of Israel, which haue long lien waste: yet they haue bene brought out of the people, and they shall dwell all safe.

9 Thou shalt ascende and come vp like a tempest, and shalt be like a cloude to couer the land, both thou, and all thy bandes, and many people with thee.

10 Thus saith the Lord God, Euen at ye same time shall many things come into thy minde, and thou shalt thinke euil thoughts.

11 And thou shalt say, I wil go vp to the land that hath no walled towres: I will goe to them that are at rest, and dwell in safetie, which dwell all without walles, and haue neither barres nor gates,

12 Thinking to spoyle the pray, and to take a bootie, to turne thine hande vpon the desolate places that are nowe inhabited, and vpon the people, that are gathered out of the nations which haue gotten cattell and goods, and dwell in the middes of the land.

13 Sheba and Dedan, and the marchantes of Tarshish with all the lions thereof shall say vnto thee, Art thou come to spoyle the praye? hast thou gathered thy multitude to take a booty? to cary away siluer and golde, to take away cattell and goods, and to spoyle a great pray?

14 Therefore, sonne of man, prophecie, and saye vnto Gog, Thus sayeth the Lord God, In that day when my people of Israel dwelleth safe, shalt thou not knowe it?

15 And come from thy place out of the North partes, thou and much people with thee? all shall ride vpon horses, euen a great multitude and a mightie armie.

16 And thou shalt come vp against my people of Israel, as a cloude to couer the land: thou shalt be in the latter dayes, and I will bring thee vpon my lande, that the heathen may knowe mee, when I

shalbe sanctified in thee, O Gog, before their eyes.

17 Thus saith the Lord God, Art not thou he, of whom I haue spoken in olde time, by ye hand of my seruants the Prophets of Israel which prophecied in those dayes and yeeres, that I woulde bring thee vpon them?

18 At the same time also whe Gog shall come against the land of Israel, sayth the Lord God, my wrath shall arise in mine anger.

19 For in mine indignation and in the fire of my wrath haue I spoken it: surely at that time there shalbe a great shaking in the land of Israel,

20 So that the fishes of the sea, and the foules of the heauen, and the beasts of the field and al that moue and creepe vpon the earth, and al ye men that are vpon the earth, shall tremble at my presence, and the mountaines shalbe ouerthrowen, and the staires shall fall, and euery wall shall fall to the ground.

21 For I will call for a sworde against him throughout all my mountaines, saith the Lord God: euery mans sword shalbe against his brother.

22 And I will pleade against him with pestilence, and with blood, and I will cause to raine vpon him and vpon his bands, and vpon the great people, that are with him, a sore raine, and hailestones, fire, and brimstone.

23 Thus will I be magnified, and sanctified, and knowen in the eyes of many nations, and they shall knowe, that I am the Lord.

Ezekiel 39

1 Therefore, thou sonne of man, prophecie against Gog, and say, Thus sayeth the Lord God, Behold, I come against thee, O Gog, ye chiefe prince of Meshech and Tubal.

2 And I will destroy thee and leaue but the sixt part of thee, and will cause thee to come vp from the North partes and will bring thee vpon the mountaines of Israel:

3 And I will smite thy bowe out of thy left hand, and I will cause thine arrowes to fall out of thy right hand.

4 Thou shalt fal vpon the mountaines of Israel, and all thy bands and the people, that is with thee: for I will giue thee vnto the birdes and to euery feathered foule and beast of the fielde to be deuoured.

5 Thou shalt fall vpon the open fielde: for I haue spoken it, sayth the Lord God.

6 And I will sende a fire on Magog, and among them that dwell safely in the yles, and they shall knowe that I am the Lord.

7 So will I make mine holy Name knowen in the middes of my people Israel, and I will not suffer them to pollute mine holy Name any more, and the heathen shall knowe that I am the Lord, the holy one of Israel.

8 Beholde, it is come, and it is done, sayeth the Lord God: and this is the day whereof I haue spoken.

9 And they that dwell in the cities of Israel, shall goe forth, and shall burne and set fire vpon the weapons, and on the shieldes, and bucklers, vpon the bowes, and vpon the arrowes, and vpon the staues in their handes, and vpon the speares, and they shall burne them with fire seuen yeeres.

10 So that they shall bring no wood out of the fielde, neither cut downe any out of the forestes: for they shall burne the weapons with fire, and they shall robbe those that robbed them, and spoyle those that spoyled them, sayeth the Lord God.

11 And at the same time will I giue vnto Gog a place there for burial in Israel, euen the valley whereby men go towarde the East part of the sea: and it shall cause them that passe by, to stoppe their noses, and there shall they bury Gog with all his multitude: and they shall call it the valley of Hamon-Gog.

12 And seuen moneths long shall the house of Israel be burying of the, that they may clense the land.

13 Yea, all the people of the lande shall burie them, and they shall haue a name when I shall be glorified, saith the Lord God.

14 And they shall chuse out men to goe continually through the lande with them that trauaile, to bury those that remaine vpon ye ground, and clense it: they shall search to the ende of seuen moneths.

15 And the trauailers that passe through the land, if any see a mans bone, then shall he set vp a signe by it, till the buriers haue buried it, in the valley of Hamon-Gog.

16 And also the name of the citie shalbe Hamonah: thus shall they clense the land.

17 And thou sonne of man, thus sayeth the Lord God, Speake vnto euery feathered foule, and to all the beastes of the fielde, Assemble your selues, and come gather your selues on euery side to my sacrifice: for I do sacrifice a great sacrifice for you vpon the mountaines of Israel, that ye may eate flesh, and drinke blood.

18 Ye shall eate the flesh of the valiant, and drink the blood of the princes of the earth, of the weathers, of the lambes, and of the goates, and of bullockes, euen of all fat beastes of Bashan.

19 And ye shall eate fat till you be full, and drinke blood, till ye be drunken of my sacrifice, which I haue sacrificed for you.

20 Thus you shalbe filled at my table with horses and chariots, with valiant men, and with al men of warre, sayth the Lord God.

21 And I wil set my glory among the heathe, and all the heathen shall see my iudgement, that I haue executed, and mine hand, which I haue layed vpon them.

22 So the house of Israel shall knowe, that I am the Lord their God from that day and so forth.

23 And the heathen shall knowe, that ye house of Israel went into captiuitie for their iniquitie, because they trespassed against me: therefore hid I my face from them, and gaue them into ye hand of their enemies: so fell they all by the sword.

24 According to their vncleannes, and according to their transgressions haue I done vnto the, and hid my face from them.

25 Therefore thus sayth the Lord God, Nowe will I bring againe the captiuitie of Iaakob, and haue compassion vpon the whole house of Israel, and wil be ielous for mine holy Name,

26 After that they haue borne their shame, and all their transgression, whereby they haue transgressed against me, whe they dwelt safely in their land, and without feare of any.

27 When I haue brought them againe from the people, and gathered them out of their enemies landes, and am sanctified in them in the sight of many nations,

28 Then shall they know, that I am the Lord their God, which caused them to be led into captiuitie among the heathen: but I haue gathered them vnto their owne land, and haue left none of them any more there,

29 Neither wil I hide my face any more from them: for I haue powred out my Spirit vpon the house of Israel, sayth the Lord God.

Ezekiel 40

1 In the fiue and twentieth yeere of our being in captiuitie, in the beginning of the yeere, in the tenth day of the moneth, in the fourteenth yeere after that the citie was smitten, in the selfe same day, the hande of the Lord was vpon mee, and brought me thither.

2 Into the lande of Israel brought he me by a diuine vision, and set me vpon a very hie mountaine, whereupon was as the building of a citie, toward the South.

3 And he brought me thither, and beholde, there was a man, whose similitude was to looke to, like brasse, with a linnen thread in his hand, and a reede to measure with: and he stoode at the gate.

4 And the man said vnto me, Sonne of man, beholde with thine eyes, and heare with thine eares, and set thine heart vpon all that I shall shew thee: for to the intent, that they might be shewed thee, art thou brought hither: declare al that thou seest, vnto the house of Israel.

5 And beholde, I sawe a wall on the outside of the house round about: and in the mans hand was a reede to measure with, of sixe cubites long, by the cubite, and an hand breadth: so he measured the breadth of the buylding with one reede, and the height with one reede.

6 Then came he vnto the gate, which looketh towarde the East, and went vp the stayres thereof, and measured the poste of the gate, which was one reede broade, and the other poste of the gate, which was one reede broade.

7 And euery chamber was one reede long, and one reede broad, and betweene the chambers were fiue cubites: and the

post of the gate by the porch of the gate within was one reede.

8 He measured also the porche of the gate within with one reede.

9 Then measured he the porch of the gate of eight cubites, and the postes thereof, of two cubites, and the porch of the gate was inward.

10 And the chambers of the gate Eastwarde, were three on this side, and three on that side: they three were of one measure, and the postes had one measure on this side, and one on that side.

11 And he measured the breadth of the entrie of the gate ten cubites, and the height of the gate thirteene cubites.

12 The space also before the chambers was one cubite on this side, and the space was one cubite on that side, and the chambers were sixe cubites on this side and sixe cubites on that side.

13 He measured then the gate from the roufe of a chamber to the toppe of the gate: the breadth was fiue and twentie cubites, doore against doore.

14 He made also postes of threescore cubites, and the postes of the court, and of the gate had one measure round about.

15 And vpon the forefront of the entry of the gate vnto the forefront of the porch of the gate within were fiftie cubites.

16 And there were narrowe windowes in the chambers, and in their postes within the gate round about, and likewise to the arches: and the windowes went rounde about within: and vpon the postes were palme trees.

17 Then brought he me into the outwarde court, and lo, there were chambers, and a pauement made for the court round about, and thirtie chambers were vpon the pauement.

18 And the pauement was by the side of the gates ouer against the length of the gates, and the pauement was beneath.

19 Then hee measured the breadth from the forefront of the lower gate without, vnto the forefront of the court within, an hundreth cubits Eastward and Northward.

20 And the gate of the outwarde court, that looked toward the North, measured he after the length and breadth thereof.

21 And the chambers thereof were, three on this side, and three on that side, and the postes thereof and the arches thereof were after the measure of the first gate: the length thereof was fiftie cubites, and the breadth fiue and twentie cubites.

22 And their windowes, and their arches with their palme trees, were after the measure of the gate that looketh toward the East, and the going vp vnto it had seuen steppes, and the arches therof were before them.

23 And the gate of the inner court stoode ouer against the gate towarde the North, and towarde the East, and hee measured from gate to gate an hundreth cubites.

24 After that, he brought mee towarde the South, and loe, there was a gate towarde the South, and hee measured the postes thereof, and the arches thereof according to these measures.

25 And there were windowes in it, and in the arches thereof round about, like those windowes: the height was fiftie cubites, and the breadth fiue and twentie cubites.

26 And there were seuen steps to go vp to it, and the arches thereof were before them: and it had palme trees, one on this side, and another on that side vpon the post thereof.

27 And there was a gate in the inner court towarde the South, and he measured from gate to gate towarde the South an hundreth cubites.

28 And he brought me into the inner court by the South gate, and he measured the South gate according to these measures,

29 And the chambers thereof, and the postes thereof, and the arches thereof according to these measures, and there were windowes in it, and in the arches thereof rounde about, it was fiftie cubites long and fiue and twentie cubites broade.

30 And the arches round about were fiue and twenty cubites long, and fiue cubites broad.

31 And the arches thereof were towarde the vtter court, and palme trees were vpon the postes thereof, and the going vp to it had eight steppes.

32 Againe he brought me into ye inner court toward the East, and he measured the gate according to these measures.

33 And the chambers thereof, and the postes thereof, and the arches thereof were according to these measures, and there were windowes therein, and in the arches thereof round about, it was fiftie cubites long, and fiue and twentie cubites broade.

34 And the arches thereof were towarde the vtter court, and palme trees were vpon the postes thereof, on this side and on that side, and the going vp to it had eight steppes.

35 After he brought mee to the North gate, and measured it, according to these measures,

36 The chambers thereof, the postes thereof, and the arches thereof, and there were windowes therein round about: the height was fiftie cubits, and the breadth fiue and twentie cubites.

37 And the postes thereof were towarde the vtter court, and palme trees were vpon the postes thereof on this side, and on that side, and the going vp to it had eight steps.

38 And euery chamber, and the entrie thereof was vnder the postes of the gates: there they washed the burnt offring.

39 And in the porch of the gate stoode two tables on this side, and two tables on that side, vpon the which they slew the burnt offring, and the sinne offring, and the trespas offring.

40 And at the side beyond the steppes, at the entry of the North gate stoode two tables, and on the other side, which was at the porch of the gate were two tables.

41 Foure tables were on this side, and foure tables on that side by the side of the gate, euen eight tables whereupon they slew their sacrifice.

42 And the foure tables were of hewen stone for the burnt offering, of a cubite and an halfe long, and a cubite and an halfe broade, and one cubite hie: whereupon also they layde the instruments wherewith they slew the burnt offring and the sacrifice.

43 And within were borders an hand broade, fastened round about, and vpon the tables lay the flesh of the offring.

44 And without the inner gate were ye chambers of the singers in the inner Court, which was at the side of the North gate: and their prospect was towarde the South, and one was at the side of the East gate, hauing the prospect towarde the North.

45 And he said vnto me, This chamber whose prospect is towarde the South, is for the Priestes that haue the charge to keepe the house.

46 And the chamber whose prospect is toward the North, is for the Priestes that haue the charge to keepe the altar: these are the sonnes of Zadok among ye sonnes of Leui which may come neere to the Lord to minister vnto him.

47 So he measured the court, an hundreth cubites long, and an hundreth cubits broad, eue foure square: likewise the altar that was before ye house.

48 And hee brought mee to the porch of the house, and measured the postes of the porch, fiue cubites on this side, and fiue cubites on that side: and the breadth of the gate was three cubites on this side, and three cubites on that side.

49 The length of the porch was twentie cubites, and ye breadth eleuen cubites, and he brought me by the steps whereby they went vp to it, and there were pillars by the postes, one on this side, and another on that side.

Ezekiel 41

1 Afterward, hee brought mee to the Temple, and measured the postes, sixe cubites broade on the one side, and sixe cubites broad on the other side, which was the breadth of the Tabernacle.

2 And the breadth of the entrie was tenne cubites, and the sides of the entrie were fiue cubites on the one side, and fiue cubites on the other side, and hee measured the length thereof fourtie cubites, and the breadth twentie cubites.

3 Then went hee in, and measured the postes of the entrie two cubites, and the entrie sixe cubites, and the breadth of the entrie seuen cubites.

4 So he measured the length thereof twentie cubites, and the breadth twentie cubites before the Temple. And he sayde vnto mee, This is the most holy place.

5 After, he measured the wall of the house, sixe cubites, and the breadth of euery chamber foure cubites rounde about the house, on euery side.

6 And the chambers were chamber vpon chaber, three and thirtie foote high, and

they entred into the wall made for the chambers which was round about the house, that the postes might bee fastened therein, and not be fastened in the wall of the house.

7 And it was large and went rounde mounting vpwarde to the chambers: for the staire of the house was mounting vpwarde, rounde about the house: therefore the house was larger vpward: so they went vp from the lowest chamber to the highest by the middes.

8 I sawe also the house hie rounde about: the foundations of the chambers were a full reede of fixe great cubites.

9 The thickenesse of the wall which was for the chamber without, was fiue cubites, and that which remained, was the place of the chambers that were within.

10 And betweene the chambers was the widenes of twentie cubites round about the House on euery side.

11 And the doores of the chambers were toward the place that remained, one doore toward the North, and another doore toward the South, and the breadth of the place that remained, was fiue cubites round about.

12 Nowe the building that was before the separate place toward the West corner, was seuentie cubites broad, and the wall of the building was fiue cubites thick, round about, and ye length ninetie cubites.

13 So he measured the house an hundreth cubites long, and the separate place and the building with the walles thereof were an hundreth cubites long.

14 Also the breadth of the forefront of the house and of the separate place towarde the East, was an hundreth cubites.

15 And hee measured the length of the building, ouer against the separate place, which was behinde it, and the chambers on the one side and on the other side an hundreth cubites with the Temple within, and the arches of the court.

16 The postes and the narowe windowes, and the chambers round about, on three sides ouer against the postes, sieled with cedar wood rounde about, and from the ground vp to the windowes, and the windowes were sieled.

17 And from aboue the doore vnto the inner house and without, and by all the wall rounde about within and without it was sieled according to the measure.

18 And it was made with Cherubims and palme trees, so that a palme tree was betweene a Cherub and a Cherub: and euery Cherub had two faces.

19 So that the face of a man was towarde the palme tree on the one side, and the face of a lyon toward the palme tree on the other side: thus was it made through all the house round about.

20 From the grounde vnto aboue the doore were Cherubims and palme trees made as in the wall of the Temple.

21 The postes of the Temple were squared, and thus to looke vnto was the similitude and forme of the Sanctuarie.

22 The altar of wood was three cubites hie, and the length thereof two cubites, and the corners thereof and the length thereof and the sides thereof were of wood. And he sayd vnto me, This is the table that shalbe before the Lord.

23 And the Temple and the Sanctuarie had two doores.

24 And the doores had two wickets, euen two turning wickets, two wickets for one doore, and two wickets for another doore.

25 And vpon the doores of the Temple there were made Cherubims and palmetrees, like as was made vpon the walles, and there were thicke plankes vpon the forefront of the porch without.

26 And there were narow windowes and palme trees on the one side, and on the other side, by the sides of the porch, and vpon ye sides of the house, and thicke plankes.

Ezekiel 42

1 Then brought hee me into the vtter court by the way towarde the North, and he brought me into the chamber that was ouer against the separate place, and which was before the building toward the North.

2 Before ye length of an hundreth cubites, was the North doore, and it was fiftie cubites broad.

3 Ouer against the twentie cubites which were for the inner court, and ouer against the pauement, which was for the vtter court, was chamber against chamber in three rowes.

4 And before the chambers was a gallery of ten cubites wide, and within was a way of one cubite, and their doores towarde the North.

5 Nowe the chambers aboue were narower: for those chambers seemed to eate vp these, to wit, the lower, and those that were in the middes of the building.

6 For they were in three rowes, but had not pillars as the pillars of the court: therefore there was a difference from them beneath and from the middlemost, euen from the ground.

7 And the wall that was without ouer against the chambers, toward the vtter court on the forefront of the chambers, was fiftie cubites long.

8 For the length of the chambers that were in the vtter court, was fiftie cubites: and loe, before the Temple were an hundreth cubites.

9 And vnder these chambers was the entrie, on the East side, as one goeth into them from the outward court.

10 The chambers were in the thicknesse of the wall of the court towarde the East, ouer against the separate place, and ouer against the building.

11 And the way before them was after ye maner of the chambers, which were toward ye North, as long as they, and as broad as they: and all their entries were like, both according to their facions, and according to their doores.

12 And according to ye doores of ye chambers that were towarde the South, was a doore in the corner of the way, euen the way directly before the wall toward the East, as one entreth.

13 The said he vnto me, The North chambers and ye South chambers which are before ye separate place, they be holy chambers, wherein the Priests that approch vnto ye Lord, shall eat the most holy things: there shall they lay the most holy things, and the meate offering, and the sinne offering, and the trespasse offring: for the place is holy.

14 When the Priestes enter therein, they shall not go out of the holy place into the vtter court, but there they shall lay their garmentes wherein they minister: for they are holy, and shall put on other garmentes, and so shall approch to those things, which are for the people.

15 Nowe when he had made an ende of measuring the inner house, he brought mee forth toward the gate whose prospect is towarde the East, and measured it round about.

16 He measured the East side with the measuring rod, fiue hundreth reedes, euen with the measuring reede round about.

17 He measured also the Northside, fiue hundreth reedes, euen with the measuring reede rounde about.

18 And he measured the South side fiue hundreth reedes with the measuring reede.

19 He turned about also to the West side, and measured fiue hundreth reedes with the measuring reede.

20 He measured it by the foure sides: it had a wall round about, fiue hundreth reedes long, and fiue hundreth broade to make a separation betweene the Sanctuarie, and the prophane place.

Ezekiel 43

1 Afterward he brought me to the gate, euen the gate that turneth towarde the East.

2 And beholde, the glorie of the God of Israel came from out of the East, whose voyce was like a noyse of great waters, and the earth was made light with his glorie.

3 And the vision which I saw was like the vision, euen as the vision that I sawe when I came to destroy the citie: and the visions were like the vision that I sawe by the riuer Chebar: and I fell vpon my face.

4 And the glorie of the Lord came into the house by the way of the gate, whose prospect is towarde the East.

5 So the Spirite tooke me vp and brought me into the inner court, and beholde, the glorie of the Lord filled the house.

6 And I heard one speaking vnto me out of the house: and there stoode a man by me,

7 Which saide vnto me, Sonne of man, this place is my throne, and the place of the soles of my feete, whereas I will dwell

among the children of Israel for euer, and the house of Israel shall no more defile mine holy Name, neither they, nor their Kings by their fornication, nor by the carkeises of their Kings in their high places.

8 Albeit they set their thresholdes by my thresholdes, and their postes by my postes (for there was but a wall betwene me and them) yet haue they defiled mine holy Name with their abominations, that they haue committed: wherfore I haue consumed them in my wrath.

9 Now therefore let them put away their fornication, and the carkeises of their Kings farre from me, and I will dwell among them for euer.

10 Thou sonne of man, shew this House to the house of Israel, that they may be ashamed of their wickednes, and let them measure ye paterne.

11 And if they be ashamed of all that they haue done, shew them the forme of the House, and ye paterne thereof, and the going out thereof, and the coming in thereof, and the whole fashion thereof, and all the ordinances thereof, and all the figures thereof, and all the lawes thereof: and write it in their sight, that they may keepe the whole fashion thereof, and all the ordinances thereof, and do them.

12 This is the description of the house, It shalbe vpon the toppe of the mount: all the limites thereof round about shalbe most holy. Beholde, this is the description of the house.

13 And these are the measures of the Altar, after the cubites, the cubite is a cubite, and an had breadth, euen the bottome shalbe a cubite, and the breadth a cubite, and the border thereof by the edge thereof rounde about shalbe a spanne: and this shalbe the height of the altar.

14 And from the bottome which toucheth the ground to the lower piece shalbe two cubites: and the breadth one cubite, and from the litle piece to the great piece shalbe foure cubites, and the breadth one cubite.

15 So the altar shalbe foure cubites, and from the altar vpward shalbe foure hornes.

16 And the altar shalbe twelue cubites long, and twelue broade, and fouresquare in the foure corners thereof.

17 And ye frame shalbe fourteene cubites log, and fourteene broade in the fouresquare corners thereof, and the border about it shalbe halfe a cubite, and the bottome therof shalbe a cubite about, and the steps thereof shalbe turned towarde ye East.

18 And he said vnto me, Sone of man, thus saith ye Lord God, These are ye ordinances of ye altar in the day when they shall make it to offer the burnt offring thereon, and to sprinkle blood thereon.

19 And thou shalt giue to the Priestes, and to the Leuites, that be of the seede of Zadok, which approch vnto me, to minister vnto me, saith the Lord God, a yong bullocke for a sinne offring.

20 And thou shalt take of the blood thereof, and put it on the foure hornes of it, and on the foure corners of the frame, and vpon the border round about: thus shalt thou clense it, and reconcile it.

21 Thou shalt take the bullocke also of the sinne offring, and burne it in the appointed place of the house without the Sanctuarie.

22 But the second day thou shalt offer an hee goat without blemish for a sinne offring, and they shall clense ye altar, as they did clense it with the bullocke.

23 When thou hast made an ende of clensing it, thou shalt offer a yong bullocke without blemish, and a ram out of the flocke without blemish.

24 And thou shalt offer them before ye Lord, and the Priestes shall cast salt vpon them, and they shall offer them for a burnt offring vnto ye Lord.

25 Seuen dayes shalt thou prepare euery day an hee goate for a sinne offring: they shall also prepare a yong bullocke and a ramme out of the flocke, without blemish.

26 Thus shall they seuen dayes purifie the altar, and clense it, and consecrate it.

27 And when these dayes are expired, vpon the eight day and so forth, the Priests shall make your burnt offrings vpon the altar, and your peace offrings, and I will accept you, saith the Lord God.

Ezekiel 44

1 Then he brought me towarde the gate of the outwarde Sanctuarie, which turneth towarde the East, and it was shut.

2 Then saide the Lord vnto me, This gate shalbe shut, and shall not bee opened, and no man shall enter by it, because the Lord God of Israel hath entred by it, and it shalbe shut.

3 It apperteineth to the Prince: the Prince himselfe shall sit in it to eate bread before the Lord: he shall enter by the way of the porche of that gate, and shall go out by the way of the same.

4 Then brought he mee toward the North gate before the House: and when I looked, beholde, the glorie of the Lord filled the house of the Lord, and I fell vpon my face.

5 And the Lord sayd vnto me, Sonne of man, marke well, and behold with thine eyes, and heare with thine eares, all that I say vnto thee, concerning al the ordinances of the house of the Lord, and al the lawes thereof, and marke well the entring in of the house with euery going forth of the Sanctuarie,

6 And thou shalt say to the rebellious, euen to ye house of Israel, Thus saith ye Lord God, O house of Israel, ye haue ynough of al your abominations,

7 Seeing that yee haue brought into my Sanctuarie strangers, vncircumcised in heart, and vncircumcised in flesh, to bee in my Sanctuarie, to pollute mine house, when yee offer my bread, euen fat, and blood: and they haue broken my

couenant, because of all your abominations.

8 For yee haue not kept the ordinances of mine holy things: but you your selues haue set other to take the charge of my Sanctuarie.

9 Thus saieth the Lord God, No stranger vncircumcised in heart, nor vncircumcised in flesh, shall enter into my Sanctuarie, of any stranger that is among the children of Israel,

10 Neither yet ye Leuites that are gone backe from me, when Israel went astray, which went astray from thee after their idoles, but they shall beare their iniquitie.

11 And they shall serue in my Sanctuarie, and keepe the gates of the House, and minister in the House: they shall slay the burnt offring and the sacrifice for the people: and they shall stand before them to serue them.

12 Because they serued before their idoles, and caused the house of Israel to fall into iniquitie, therfore haue I lift vp mine had against the, saith the Lord God, and they shall beare their iniquity,

13 And they shall not come neere vnto me to do ye office of ye Priest vnto me, neyther shall they come neere vnto any of mine holy things in the most holy place, but they shall beare their shame and their abominations, which they haue comitted.

14 And I will make them keepers of ye watch of the House, for all the seruice thereof, and for all that shalbe done therein.

15 But the Priests of the Leuites, the sonnes of Zadok, that kept the charge of my Sanctuarie, when the children of Israel went astray from me, they shall come neere to me to serue me, and they shall stande before me to offer me the fat and the blood, saith the Lord God.

16 They shall enter into my Sanctuarie, and shall come neere to my table, to serue me, and they shall keepe my charge.

17 And whe they shall enter in at the gates of the inner court, they shall be clothed with linen garments, and no wool shall come vpon the while they serue in ye gates of the inner court, and within.

18 They shall haue linnen bonets vpon their heades, and shall haue linnen breeches vpon their loynes: they shall not girde them selues in the sweating places.

19 But when they goe foorth into the vtter court, euen to the vtter court to the people, they shall put off their garments, wherein they ministred, and lay them in the holy chambers, and they shall put on other garments: for they shall not sanctifie the people with their garments.

20 They shall not also shaue their heades, nor suffer their lockes to growe long, but rounde their heades.

21 Neither shall any Priest drinke wine when they enter into the inner court.

22 Neither shall they take for their wiues a widowe, or her that is diuorced: but they shall take maidens of the seede

of the house of Israel, or a widow that hath bene the widow of a Priest.

23 And they shall teach my people the difference betweene the holy and prophane, and cause them to discerne betweene the vncleane and the cleane.

24 And in controuersie they shall stande to iudge, and they shall iudge it according to my iudgements: and they shall keepe my lawes and my statutes in all mine assemblies, and they shall sanctifie my Sabbaths.

25 And they shall come at no dead person to defile theselues, except at their father, or mother, or sone, or daughter, brother or sister, that hath had yet none husband: in these may they be defiled.

26 And when he is clensed, they shall reckon vnto him seuen dayes.

27 And when he goeth into ye Sanctuarie vnto the inner court to minister in the Sanctuarie, he shall offer his sinne offring, saith ye Lord God.

28 And the Priesthood shall bee their inheritance, yea, I am their inheritance: therefore shall ye giue them no possessio in Israel, for I am their possession.

29 They shall eate the meat offring, and the sinne offring, and the trespas offring, and euery dedicate thing in Israel shall be theirs.

30 And all the first of all the first borne, and euery oblation, euen all of euery sort of your oblations shall be the Priestes. Ye shall also giue vnto the Priest the first of your dough, that he may cause the blessing to rest in thine house.

31 The Priests shall not eate of any thing, that is dead, or torne, whether it be foule or beast.

Ezekiel 45

1 Moreover when yee shall deuide the land for inheritance, ye shall offer an oblation vnto the Lord an holy portion of the land, fiue and twentie thousand reedes long, and ten thousand broad: this shalbe holy in all the borders thereof round about.

2 Of this there shalbe for the Sanctuarie fiue hundreth in length with fiue hundreth in breadth, all square round about, and fiftie cubites rounde about for the suburbes thereof.

3 And of this measure shalt thou measure the length of fiue and twentie thousande, and the breadth of tenne thousande: and in it shalbe the Sanctuarie, and the most holy place.

4 The holy portion of the lande shalbe the Priests, which minister in the Sanctuarie, which came neere to serue the Lord: and it shalbe a place for their houses, and an holy place for the Sanctuarie.

5 And in the fiue and twentie thousande of length, and the ten thousand of breadth shall the Leuites that minister in the house, haue their possession for twentie chambers.

6 Also ye shall appoynt the possession of the citie, fiue thousand broad, and fiue and twentie thousand log ouer

against the oblation of ye holy portion: it shalbe for the whole house of Israel.

7 And a portion shalbe for the prince on ye one side, and on that side of the oblation of the holy portion, and of the possession of the citie, euen before the oblation of the holy portion, and before the possession of the citie from the West corner Westward, and from the East corner Eastward, and the length shalbe by one of the portions from the West border vnto the East border.

8 In this lande shalbe his possession in Israel: and my princes shall no more oppresse my people, and the rest of the land shall they giue to ye house of Israel, according to their tribes.

9 Thus saith the Lord God, Let it suffice you, O princes of Israel: leaue off crueltie and oppression, and execute iudgment and iustice: take away your exactions from my people, sayth the Lord God.

10 Ye shall haue iust balances, and a true Ephah, and a true Bath.

11 The Ephah and the Bath shalbe equall: a Bath shall conteyne the tenth part of an Homer, and an Ephah the tenth part of an Homer: the equalitie thereof shalbe after the Homer.

12 And the shekel shalbe twentie gerahs, and twentie shekels, and fiue and twentie shekels and fifteene shekels shalbe your Maneh.

13 This is the oblation that ye shall offer, ye sixt part of an Ephah of an Homer of wheat, and ye shall giue the sixt part of an Ephah of an Homer of barley.

14 Concerning ye ordinance of the oyle, euen of the Bath of oyle, ye shall offer the tenth part of a Bath out of ye Cor (ten Baths are an Homer: for ten Baths fill an Homer)

15 And one lambe of two hundreth sheepe out of ye fat pastures of Israel for a meat offring, and for a burnt offring and for peace offrings, to make reconciliation for them, sayth the Lord God.

16 All the people of the lande shall giue this oblation for the prince in Israel.

17 And it shalbe ye princes part to giue burnt offrings, and meat offrings, and drinke offrings in the solemne feasts and in the newe moones, and in the Sabbaths, and in all the hie feasts of the house of Israel: he shall prepare the sinne offring, and the meat offring, and the burnt offring, and the peace offrings to make reconciliation for the house of Israel.

18 Thus sayth the Lord God, In the first moneth, in the first day of the moneth, thou shalt take a yong bullocke without blemish and clense the Sanctuarie.

19 And the Priest shall take of the blood of the sinne offring, and put it vpon the posts of the house, and vpon the foure corners of the frame of the altar, and vpon the postes of the gate of the inner court.

20 And so shalt thou doe the seuenth day of the moneth, for euery one that hath erred and for him that is deceiued: so shall you reconcile the house.

21 In the first moneth in the fourteenth day of the moneth, ye shall haue the Passeouer, a feast of seuen dayes, and ye shall eate vnleauened bread.

22 And vpon that day, shall the prince prepare for him selfe, and for all the people of the lande, a bullocke for a sinne offring.

23 And in the seuen dayes of the feast he shall make a burnt offring to the Lord, euen of seuen bullockes, and seuen rammes without blemish dayly for seuen dayes, and an hee goate dayly for a sinne offring.

24 And he shall prepare a meate offring of an Ephah for a bullocke, an Ephah for a ramme, and an Hin of oyle for an Ephah.

25 In the seuenth moneth, in the fifteenth day of the moneth, shall he do the like in the feast for seuen dayes, according to the sinne offring, according to the burnt offring, and according to the meate offring, and according to the oyle.

Ezekiel 46

1 Thus sayth the Lord God, The gate of the inner court, that turneth toward the East, shall be shut the sixe working dayes: but on the Sabbath it shalbe opened, and in the day of the newe moone it shalbe opened.

2 And the prince shall enter by the way of the porch of that gate without, and shall stande by the post of the gate, and the Priests shall make his burnt offring, and his peace offrings, and he shall worship at the threshold of the gate: after, he shall go foorth, but the gate shall not be shut till the euening.

3 Likewise the people of the lande shall worshippe at the entrie of this gate before the Lord on the Sabbaths, and in the newe moones.

4 And the burnt offring that the prince shall offer vnto the Lord on the Sabbath day, shalbe sixe lambs without blemish, and a ram without blemish.

5 And the meat offring shalbe an Ephah for a ram: and the meate offring for the lambs a gift of his hand, and an Hin of oyle to an Ephah.

6 And in the day of the newe moone it shall be a yong bullocke without blemish, and sixe lambes and a ram: they shalbe without blemish.

7 And he shall prepare a meat offring, euen an Ephah for a bullocke, and an Ephah for a ram, and for the lambes according as his hand shall bring, and an Hin of oyle to an Ephah.

8 And when the prince shall enter, hee shall goe in by the way of the porche of that gate, and hee shall go foorth by the way thereof.

9 But when the people of the land shall come before the Lord in the solemne feastes, hee that entreth in by the way of the North gate to worship, shall goe out by the way of the South gate: and he that entreth by the way of the South gate, shall goe foorth by the way of the North gate: hee shall not returne by the way of

the gate whereby hee came in, but they shall goe forth ouer against it.

10 And the prince shall be in the middes of them: hee shall go in when they goe in, and when they goe forth, they shall goe forth together.

11 And in the feastes, and in the solemnities the meat offring shalbe an Ephah to a bullocke, and an Ephah to a ram, and to the lambes, the gift of his hand, and an Hin of oyle to an Ephah.

12 Nowe when the prince shall make a free burnt offring or peace offrings freely vnto the Lord, one shall then open him the gate, that turneth towarde the East, and hee shall make his burnt offring and his peace offrings, as he did on the Sabbath day: after, hee shall goe foorth, and when he is gone forth, one shall shut the gate.

13 Thou shalt dayly make a burnt offring vnto the Lord of a lambe of one yere without blemish: thou shalt doe it euery morning.

14 And thou shalt prepare a meate offring for it euery morning, the sixt part of an Ephah, and the thirde part of an Hin of oyle, to mingle with the fine flowre: this meate offring shalbe continually by a perpetuall ordinance vnto the Lord.

15 Thus shall they prepare the lambe, and the meate offring and the oyle euery morning, for a continual burnt offring.

16 Thus saith the Lord God, If the prince giue a gift of his inheritance vnto any of his sonnes, it shalbe his sonnes, and it shall bee their possession by inheritance.

17 But if hee giue a gift of his inheritance to one of his seruantes, then it shall bee his to the yere of libertie: after, it shall returne to ye prince, but his inheritance shall remaine to his sonnes for them.

18 Moreouer the prince shall not take of the peoples inheritance, nor thrust them out of their possession: but he shall cause his sonnes to inherit of his owne possession, that my people be not scattered euery man from his possession.

19 After, he brought me through the entrie, which was at the side of the gate, into the holy chambers of the Priestes, which stoode towarde the North: and beholde, there was a place at the West side of them.

20 Then saide he vnto me, This is the place where the Priestes shall see the the trespasse offering and the sinne offering, where they shall bake the meat offring, that they should not beare them into the vtter court, to sanctifie ye people.

21 Then he brought me foorth into the vtter court, and caused me to goe by the foure corners of the court: and beholde, in euery corner of the court, there was a court.

22 In the foure corners of the court there were courts ioyned of fourty cubits long, and thirty broad: these foure corners were of one measure.

23 And there went a wall about them, euen about those foure, and kitchins were made vnder the walles rounde about.

24 Then said he vnto me, This is the kitchin where the ministers of the house shall seethe the sacrifice of the people.

Ezekiel 47

1 Afterward he brought me vnto the doore of the house: and behold, waters yssued out from vnder the threshold of the house Eastward: for the forefront of the house stoode towarde the East, and the waters ran downe from vnder the right side of the house, at the southside of ye altar.

2 Then brought he me out toward the North gate, and led me about by the way without vnto the vtter gate, by the way that turneth Eastward: and behold, there came forth waters on ye right side

3 And when the man that had the line in his hand, went foorth Eastward, he measured a thousand cubites, and he brought me through the waters: the waters were to the ancles.

4 Againe he measured a thousande, and brought me through the waters: the waters were to the knees: againe he measured a thousand, and brought me through: ye waters were to ye loynes.

5 Afterward he measured a thousand, and it was a riuer, that I could not passe ouer: for the waters were risen, and the waters did flowe, as a riuer that could not be passed ouer.

6 And he said vnto me, Sonne of man, hast thou seene this? Then he brought me, and caused me to returne to the brinke of the riuer.

7 Nowe when I returned, beholde, at the brinke of the riuer were very many trees on the one side, and on the other.

8 Then saide he vnto me, These waters issue out towarde the East countrey, and runne downe into the plaine, and shall goe into one sea: they shall runne into another sea, and the waters shalbe wholesome.

9 And euery thing that liueth, which moueth, wheresoeuer the riuers shall come, shall liue, and there shalbe a very great multitude of fish, because these waters shall come thither: for they shall be wholesome, and euery thing shall liue whither the riuer commeth.

10 And then the fishers shall stand vpon it, and from En-gedi euen vnto En-eglaim, they shall spread out their nettes: for their fish shalbe according to their kindes, as the fishe of the maine sea, exceeding many.

11 But the myrie places thereof, and the marises thereof shall not be wholesome: they shalbe made salt pittes.

12 And by this riuer vpon the brinke thereof, on this side, and on that side shall grow all fruitful trees, whose leafe shall not fade, neither shall ye fruit thereof faile: it shall bring forth new fruit according to his monethes, because their waters run out of ye Sanctuarie: and the fruite thereof shalbe meat, and the leafe thereof shalbe for medicine.

13 Thus saith the Lord God, This shall be the border, whereby ye shall inherite the lande according to the twelue tribes of Israel: Ioseph shall haue two portions.

14 And ye shall inherite it, one as well as another: concerning the which I lift vp mine hand to giue it vnto your fathers, and this lande shall fall vnto you for inheritance.

15 And this shall be the border of the lande towarde the North side, from the maine sea toworde Hethlon as men goe to Zedadah:

16 Hamath, Berothah, Sibraim, which is betweene the border of Damascus, and the border of Hamath, and Hazar, Hatticon, which is by the coast of Hauran.

17 And the border from the sea shalbe Hazar, Enan, and the border of Damascus, and the residue of the North, Northwarde, and the border of Hamath: so shalbe the North part.

18 But the East side shall ye measure from Hauran, and from Damascus, and from Gilead, and from the lande of Israel by Iorden, and from the border vnto the East sea: and so shalbe the East part.

19 And the Southside shalbe towarde Teman from Tamar to the waters of Meriboth in Kadesh, and the riuer to the maine sea: so shalbe the South part towarde Teman.

20 The West parte also shalbe the great sea from the border, till a man come ouer against Hamath: this shalbe the West part.

21 So shall ye deuide this lande vnto you, according to the tribes of Israel.

22 And you shall deuide it by lot for an inheritance vnto you, and to the strangers that dwell among you, which shall beget children among you, and they shall be vnto you, as borne in the countrey among the children of Israel, they shall part inheritance with you in the middes of the tribes of Israel.

23 And in what tribe the stranger dwelleth, there shall ye giue him his inheritance, saith the Lord God.

Ezekiel 48

1 Now these are the names of the tribes. From the North side, to the coast towarde Hethlon, as one goeth to Hamath, Hazar, Enan, and the border of Damascus Northwarde the coast of Hamath, euen from the East side to the West shall be a portion for Dan.

2 And by the border of Dan from the East side vnto the West side, a portion for Asher.

3 And by the border of Asher from the East parte euen vnto the West parte a portion for Naphtali.

4 And by the border of Naphtali from the East quarter vnto the West side, a portion for Manasseh.

5 And by the border of Manasseh from the East side vnto the West side a portion for Ephraim.

6 And by the border of Ephraim, from the East part euen vnto the West part, a portion for Reuben.

7 And by the border of Reuben, from the East quarter vnto the West quarter, a portion for Iudah.

8 And by the border of Iudah from the East part vnto the West part shall be the offering which they shall offer of fiue and twentie thousande reedes broade, and of length as one of the other parts, from the East side vnto the Westside, and the Sanctuarie shalbe in the middes of it.

9 The oblation that ye shall offer vnto the Lord, shalbe of fiue and twentie thousande long, and of ten thousand the breadth.

10 And for them, euen for the Priestes shalbe this holy oblation, towarde the North fiue and twentie thousande long, and towarde the West, ten thousande broade, and towarde the East ten thousand broad, and towarde the South fiue and twentie thousand long, and the Sanctuarie of the Lord shalbe in the middes thereof.

11 It shalbe for the Priestes that are sanctified of the sonnes of Zadok, which haue kept my charge, which went not astray when the children of Israel went astray, as the Leuites went astray.

12 Therefore this oblation of the land that is offred, shalbe theirs, as a thing most holy by the border of the Leuites.

13 And ouer against the border of the Priests the Leuites shall haue fiue and twentie thousand long, and ten thousande broade: all the length shalbe fiue and twentie thousand, and the breadth ten thousande.

14 And they shall not sel of it, neither change it, nor abalienate the first fruites of the land: for it is holy vnto the Lord.

15 And the fiue thousand that are left in the breadth ouer against the fiue and twentie thousande, shall be a prophane place for the citie, for housing, and for suburbes, and the citie shalbe in the middes thereof.

16 And these shall be the measures thereof, the North part fiue hundreth and foure thousand, and the South parte fiue hundreth and foure thousande, and the East parte fiue hundreth and foure thousand, and the West parte fiue hundreth and foure thousande.

17 And the suburbes of the citie shall be toward the North two hundreth and fiftie, and towarde the South two hundreth and fiftie, and towarde the East two hundreth and fiftie, and towarde the West two hundreth and fiftie.

18 And the residue in length ouer against the oblation of the holy portion shalbe ten thousand Eastwarde, and ten thousand Westwarde: and it shalbe ouer against the oblation of the holy portion, and the encrease thereof shall be for foode vnto them that serue in the citie.

19 And they that serue in the citie, shalbe of all the tribes of Israel that shall serue therein.

20 All the oblation shalbe fiue and twentie thousand with fiue and twentie thousand: you shall offer this oblation foure square for the Sanctuarie, and for the possession of the citie.

21 And the residue shalbe for the prince on the one side and on the other of the oblation of the Sanctuarie, and of the possession of the citie, ouer against the fiue and twentie thousand of the oblation toward the East border, and Westward ouer against the fiue and twentie thousand towarde the West border, ouer against shalbe for the portion of the prince: this shall be the holy oblation, and the house of the Sanctuarie shalbe in the middes thereof.

22 Moreouer, from the possession of the Leuites, and from the possession of the citie, that which is in the middes shall be the princes: betweene the border of Iudah, and betweene the border of Beniamin shall be the princes.

23 And the rest of the tribes shalbe thus: from the East parte vnto the West parte Beniamin shalbe a portion.

24 And by the border of Beniamin, from the East side vnto the West side Simeon a portion.

25 And by the border of Simeon from the East part vnto the West part, Isshachar a portion.

26 And by the border of Isshachar, from the East side vnto the West, Zebulun a portion.

27 And by the border of Zebulun from the East parte vnto the West part, Gad a portion.

28 And by the border of Gad at the South side, towarde Temath, the border shall be euen from Tamar vnto the waters of Meribath in Kadesh, and to the riuer, that runneth into the maine sea.

29 This is the lande, which ye shall distribute vnto the tribes of Israel for inheritance, and these are their portions, saith the Lord God.

30 And these are the boundes of the citie, on the North side fiue hundreth, and foure thousande measures.

31 And the gates of the citie shalbe after the names of the tribes of Israel, the gates Northwarde, one gate of Reuben, one gate of Iudah, and one gate of Leui.

32 And at the East side fiue hundreth and foure thousande, and three gates, and one gate of Ioseph, one gate of Beiamin, and one gate of Dan.

33 And at the South side, fiue hundreth and foure thousande measures, and three portes, one gate of Simeon, one gate of Isshachar, and one gate of Zebulun.

34 At the West side, fiue hundreth and foure thousand, with their three gates, one gate of Gad, one gate of Asher, and one gate of Naphtali.

35 It was rounde about eighteene thousande measures, and the name of the citie from that day shalbe, The Lord is there.

Daniel

Daniel 1

1 In the thirde yeere of the reigne of Iehoiakim king of Iudah, came Nebuchad-nezzar King of Babel vnto Ierusalem and besieged it.

2 And ye Lord gaue Iehoiakim king of Iudah into his hand; with parte of the vessels of the house of God, which he caryed into the land of Shinar, to the house of his god, and he brought the vessels into his gods treasurie.

3 And the King spake vnto Ashpenaz the master of his Eunuches, that he shoulde bring certeine of the children of Israel, of the Kings seede, and of the princes:

4 Children in whome was no blemish, but well fauoured, and instruct in all wisedome, and well seene in knowledge, and able to vtter knowledge, and such as were able to stande in the kings palace, and whome they might teach the learning, and the tongue of the Caldeans.

5 And the King appointed them prouision euery day of a portion of the Kings meate, and and of the wine, which he dranke, so nourishing them three yeere, that at the ende thereof, they might stande before the King.

6 Nowe among these were certeine of the children of Iudah, Daniel, Hananiah, Mishael and Azariah.

7 Vnto whome the chiefe of the Eunuches gaue other names: for hee called Daniel, Belteshazzar, and Hananiah, Shadrach, and Mishael, Meshach, and Azariah, Abednego.

8 But Daniel had determined in his heart, that hee woulde not defile him selfe with the portion of the Kings meate, nor with the wine which he dranke: therefore he required the chiefe of the Eunuches that he might not defile himselfe.

9 (Nowe God had brought Daniel into fauour, and tender loue with the chiefe of the Eunuches)

10 And the chiefe of the Eunuches sayd vnto Daniel, I feare my lord the King, who hath appointed your meate and your drinke: therefore if he see your faces worse liking then the other children, which are of your sort, then shall you make me lose mine head vnto the King.

11 Then sayd Daniel to Melzar, whome the chiefe of the Eunuches had set ouer Daniel, Hananiah, Mishael, and Azariah,

12 Proue thy seruants, I beseeche thee, ten dayes, and let them giue vs pulse to eate, and water to drinke.

13 Then let our countenances bee looked vpon before thee, and the countenances of the children that eate of the portion of the Kings meate: and as thou seest, deale with thy seruantes.

14 So hee consented to them in this matter, an proued them ten dayes.

15 And at the end of ten dayes, their countenances appeared fayrer, and in better liking then all the childrens, which did eate the portion of the Kings meate.

16 Thus Melzar tooke away the portion of their meat, and the wine that they should drinke, and gaue them pulse.

17 As for these foure children, God gaue them knowledge, and vnderstanding in al learning and wisedome: also he gaue

Daniel vnderstanding of all visions and dreames.

18 Nowe when the time was expired, that the King had appoynted to bring them in, the chiefe of the Eunuches brought them before Nebuchad-nezzar.

19 And the King communed with them: and among them al was found none like Daniel, Hananiah, Mishael, and Azariah: therefore stoode they before the king.

20 And in all matters of wisedome, and vnderstanding that the King enquired of them, hee founde them tenne times better then all the inchanters and astrologians, that were in all his realme.

21 And Daniel was vnto the first yeere of king Cyrus.

Daniel 2

1 And in the seconde yeere of the raygne of Nebuchad-nezzar, Nebuchad-nezzar dreamed dreames wherewith his spirite was troubled, and his sleepe was vpon him.

2 Then the King commanded to call the inchanters, and the astrologians and the sorcerers, and the Caldeans for to shewe the King his dreames: so they came and stoode before the King.

3 And the King sayde vnto them, I haue dreamed a dreame, and my spirite was troubled to knowe the dreame.

4 Then spake the Caldeans to the King in the Aramites language, O King, liue for euer: shewe thy seruants thy dreame, and wee shall shewe the interpretation.

5 And the King answered and sayd to the Caldeans, The thing is gone from me. If ye will not make me vnderstande the dreame with the interpretation thereof, ye shall be drawen in pieces, and your houses shall be made a iakes.

6 But if yee declare the dreame and the interpretation thereof, ye shall receyue of me gifts and rewardes, and great honour: therefore shewe me the dreame and the interpretation of it.

7 They answered againe, and sayde, Let the King shewe his seruantes the dreame, and wee will declare the interpretation thereof.

8 Then the King answered, and sayd, I knowe certeinly that ye would gaine the time, because ye see the thing is gone from me.

9 But if ye will not declare mee the dreame, there is but one iudgement for you: for ye haue prepared lying and corrupt wordes, to speake before me till the time bee changed: therefore tell me the dreame, that I may knowe, if yee can declare me the interpretation thereof.

10 Then the Caldeans answered before the King, and sayde, There is no man vpon earth that can declare the Kings matter: yea, there is neither king nor prince nor lorde that asked such things at an inchanter or astrologian or Caldean.

11 For it is a rare thing that the King requireth, and there is none other that can declare it before the King, except the gods whose dwelling is not with flesh.

12 For this cause the king was angrie and in great furie, and commanded to destroy all the wise men of Babel.

13 And when sentence was giuen, the wise men were slayne: and they sought Daniel and his fellowes to be put to death.

14 Then Daniel answered with counsel and wisedome to Arioch the Kings chiefe stewarde, which was gone foorth to put to death the wise men of Babel.

15 Yea, he answered and sayde vnto Arioch the kings captaine, Why is the sentence so hastie from the king? Then Arioch declared the thing to Daniel.

16 So Daniel went and desired the king that he woulde giue him leasure and that he woulde shewe the king the interpretation thereof.

17 The Daniel went to his house and shewed the matter to Hananiah, Mishael, and Azariah his companions,

18 That they should beseech the God of heauen for grace in this secrete, that Daniel and his fellowes should not perish with the rest of ye wise men of Babel.

19 Then was the secret reueiled vnto Daniel in a vision by night: therefore Daniel praysed the God of heauen.

20 And Daniel answered and sayde, The Name of God be praysed for euer and euer: for wisedome and strength are his,

21 And hee changeth the times and seasons: he taketh away kings: he setteth vp kings: he giueth wisedome vnto the wise, and vnderstanding to those that vnderstand.

22 Hee discouereth the deepe and secrete things: he knoweth what is in darkenes, and the light dwelleth with him.

23 I thanke thee and prayse thee, O thou God of my fathers, that thou hast giuen mee wisedome and strength, and hast shewed me nowe the thing that wee desired of thee: for thou hast declared vnto vs the kings matter.

24 Therefore Daniel went vnto Arioch, whome the King had ordeyned to destroy the wise men of Babel: he went and sayde thus vnto him, Destroy not the wise men of Babel, but bring me before the King, and I will declare vnto the King the interpretation.

25 Then Arioch brought Daniel before the King in all haste, and sayd thus vnto him, I haue found a man of the children of Iudah that were brought captiues, that will declare vnto the King the interpretation.

26 Then answered the King, and sayde vnto Daniel, whose name was Belteshazzar, Art thou able to shew me the dreame, which I haue seene, and the interpretation thereof?

27 Daniel answered in the presence of the King, and sayd, The secret which the King hath demanded, can neither the wise, the astrologians, the inchanters, nor the southsayers declare vnto the King.

28 But there is a God in heauen that reueileth secrets, and sheweth the King Nebuchad-nezzar what shall bee in the latter dayes. Thy dreame, and the things which thou hast seene in thine heade vpon thy bed, is this.

29 O King, when thou wast in thy bedde, thoughts came into thy mind, what should come to passe hereafter, and he that reueyleth secretes, telleth thee, what shall come.

30 As for me, this secret is not shewed mee for any wisedome that I haue, more then any other liuing, but onely to shewe the King the interpretation, and that thou mightest knowe the thoughts of thine heart.

31 O King, thou sawest, and beholde, there was a great image: this great image whose glory was so excellent, stood before thee, and the forme thereof was terrible.

32 This images head was of fine golde, his breast and his armes of siluer, his bellie and his thighs of brasse,

33 His legges of yron, and his feete were part of yron, and part of clay.

34 Thou beheldest it til a stone was cut without hands, which smote the image vpon his feete, that were of yron and clay, and brake them to pieces.

35 Then was the yron, the clay, the brasse, the siluer and the golde broken all together, and became like the chaffe of the sommer floures, and the winde caryed them away, that no place was founde for them: and the stone that smote the image, became a great mountaine, and filled the whole earth.

36 This is the dreame, and we will declare before the King the interpretation thereof.

37 O King, thou art a king of Kings: for the God of heauen hath giuen thee a kingdome, power, and strength, and glorie.

38 And in all places where the children of men dwell, the beasts of the fielde, and the foules of the heauen hath he giuen into thine hand, and hath made thee ruler ouer them al: thou art this heade of golde.

39 And after thee shall rise another kingdome, inferiour to thee, of siluer, and another third kingdome shalbe of brasse, which shall beare rule ouer all the earth.

40 And the fourth kingdome shall be strong as yron: for as yron breaketh in pieces, and subdueth all things, and as yron bruiseth all these things, so shall it breake in pieces, and bruise all.

41 Where as thou sawest the feete and toes, parte of potters clay, and part of yron: the kingdome shalbe deuided, but there shalbe in it of the strength of the yron, as thou sawest the yron mixt with the clay, and earth.

42 And as the toes of the feete were parte of yron, and parte of clay, so shall the kingdome be partly strong, and partly broken.

43 And where as thou sawest yron mixt with clay and earth, they shall mingle themselues with the seede of men: but they shall not ioyne one with another, as yron can not bee mixed with clay.

44 And in the dayes of these Kings, shall the God of heauen set vp a kingdome, which shall neuer be destroyed: and this kingdome shall not be giuen to another people, but it shall breake, and destroy al these kingdomes, and it shall stand for euer.

45 Where as thou sawest, that the stone was cut of the mountaine without handes, and that it brake in pieces the yron, the brasse, the clay, the siluer, and the golde: so the great God hath shewed the King, what shall come to passe hereafter, and the dreame is true, and the interpretation thereof is sure.

46 Then the King Nebuchad-nezzar fell vpon his face, and bowed himselfe vnto Daniel, and commanded that they should offer meate offrings, and sweete odours vnto him.

47 Also the King answered vnto Daniel, and said, I know of a trueth that your God is a God of gods, and the Lord of Kings, and the reueiler of secrets, seeing thou couldest open this secret.

48 So the King made Daniel a great man, and gaue him many and great giftes. Hee made him gouernour ouer the whole prouince of Babel, and chiefe of the rulers, and aboue all the wise men of Babel.

49 Then Daniel made request to the King, and hee set Shadrach, Meshach, and Abednego ouer the charge of the prouince of Babel: but Daniel sate in the gate of the King.

Daniel 3

1 Nebuchad-nezzar the King made an image of gold, whose height was three score cubits, and the breadth thereof sixe cubites: hee set it vp in the plaine of Dura, in the prouince of Babel.

2 Then Nebuchad-nezzar ye King sent foorth to gather together the nobles, the princes and the dukes, the iudges, the receiuers, the counsellers, the officers, and all the gouernours of the prouinces, that they should come to the dedication of the image, which Nebuchad-nezzar the King had set vp.

3 So the nobles, princes and dukes, the iudges, the receiuers, the counsellers, the officers, and all the gouernours of the prouinces were assembled vnto the dedicating of the image, that Nebuchad-nezzar the King had set vp: and they stood before the image, which Nebuchad-nezzar had set vp.

4 Then an herald cried aloude, Be it knowen to you, O people, nations, and languages,

5 That when ye heare the sound of the cornet, trumpet, harpe, sackebut, psalterie, dulcimer, and all instruments of musike, ye fall downe and worship the golden image, that Nebuchad-nezzar the King hath set vp,

6 And whosoeuer falleth not downe and worshippeth, shall the same houre bee cast into the middes of an hote fierie fornace.

7 Therefore assoone as all the people heard the sound of the cornet, trumpet, harpe, sackebut, psalterie, and all instruments of musike, all the people, nations, and languages fell downe, and worshipped the golden image, that Nebuchad-nezzar the King had set vp.

8 By reason whereof at that same time came men of the Caldeans, and grieuously accused the Iewes.

9 For they spake and said to the King Nebuchad-nezzar, O King, liue for euer.

10 Thou, O King, hast made a decree, that euery man that shall heare the sounde of the cornet, trumpet, harpe, sackebut, psalterie, and dulcimer, and all instruments of musike, shall fall downe and worship the golden image,

11 And whosoeuer falleth not downe, and worshippeth, that he should be cast into the mids of an hote fierie fornace.

12 There are certeine Iewes whome thou hast set ouer the charge of ye prouince of Babel, Shadrach, Meshach, and Abednego: these men, O King, haue not regarded thy commandement, neither wil they serue thy gods, nor worship the golden image, that thou hast set vp.

13 Then Nebuchad-nezzar in his anger and wrath commanded that they should bring Shadrach, Meshach, and Abednego: so these men were brought before the King.

14 And Nebuchad-nezzar spake, and said vnto them, What disorder? will not you, Shadrach, Meshach, and Abednego serue my god, nor worship the golden image, that I haue set vp?

15 Now therefore are ye ready when ye heare the sound of the cornet, trumpet, harpe, sackebut, psalterie, and dulcimer, and all instruments of musike, to fall downe, and worship the image, which I haue made? for if ye worship it not, ye shall be cast immediatly into the middes of an hote fierie fornace: for who is that God, that can deliuer you out of mine handes?

16 Shadrach, Meshach, and Abednego answered and said to the King, O Nebuchad-nezzar, we are not carefull to answere thee in this matter.

17 Beholde, our God whom we serue, is able to deliuer vs from the hote fierie fornace, and hee will deliuer vs out of thine hand, O King.

18 But if not, bee it knowen to thee, O King, that wee will not serue thy gods, nor worship the golden image, which thou hast set vp.

19 Then was Nebuchad-nezzar full of rage, and the forme of his visage was changed against Shadrach, Meshach, and Abednego: therefore hee charged and commanded that they should heate the fornace at once seuen times more then it was wont to be heat.

20 And hee charged the most valiant men of warre that were in his armie, to binde Shadrach, Meshach, and Abednego, and to cast them into the hote fierie fornace.

21 So these men were bounde in their coates, their hosen, and their clokes, with their other garments, and cast into the middes of the hote fierie fornace.

22 Therefore, because the Kings commandement was straite, that the fornace should be exceeding hote, the flame of the fire slew those men that brought foorth Shadrach, Meshach and Abednego.

23 And these three men Shadrach, Meshach and Abednego fell downe bound into the middes of the hote fierie fornace.

24 Then Nebuchad-nezzar the King was astonied and rose vp in haste, and spake, and saide vnto his counsellers, Did not wee cast three men bound into the middes of the fire? Who answered and said vnto the King, It is true, O King.

25 And he answered, and said, Loe, I see foure men loose, walking in the middes of the fire, and they haue no hurt, and the forme of the fourth is like the sonne of God.

26 Then the King Nebuchad-nezzar came neere to the mouth of the hote fierie fornace, and spake and said, Shadrach, Meshach and Abednego, the seruants of the hie God goe foorth and come hither: so Shadrach, Meshach and Abednego came foorth of the middes of the fire.

27 Then the nobles, princes and dukes, and the Kings counsellers came together to see these men, because the fire had no power ouer their bodies: for not an heare of their head was burnt, neither was their coates changed, nor any smelll of fire came vpon them.

28 Wherefore Nebuchad-nezzar spake and said, Blessed be the God of Shadrach, Meshach and Abednego, who hath sent his Angel, and deliuered his seruants, that put their trust in him, and haue changed the Kings commandement, and yeelded their bodies rather then they would serue or worship any god, saue their owne God.

29 Therefore I make a decree, that euery people, nation, and language, which speake any blasphemie against the God of Shadrach, Meshach and Abednego, shalbe drawen in pieces, and their houses shall be made a iakes, because there is no god that can deliuer after this sort.

30 Then the King promoted Shadrach, Meshach and Abednego in the prouince of Babel.

31 Nebuchad-nezzar King vnto all people, nations and languages, that dwell in all the world, Peace be multiplied vnto you:

32 I thought it good to declare the signes and wonders, that the hie God hath wrought toward me.

33 How great are his signes, and how mightie are his wonders! his kingdome is an euerlasting kingdome, and his dominion is from generation to generation.

Daniel 4

1 I Nebuchad-nezzar being at rest in mine house, and flourishing in my palace,

2 Saw a dreame, which made me afraide, and the thoughtes vpon my bed, and the visions of mine head troubled me.

3 Therefore made I a decree, that they should bring all the wise men of Babel before mee, that they might declare vnto me the interpretation of the dreame.

4 So came the inchanters, the astrologians, the Caldeans and the sothsayers, to whom I tolde the dreame, but they could not shew me the interpretation thereof,

5 Till at the last Daniel came before mee, (whose name was Belteshazzar, according to the name of my god, which hath the spirite of the holy gods in him) and before him I tolde the dreame, saying,

6 O Belteshazzar, chiefe of the enchanters, because I know, that the spirit of the holy gods is in thee, and no secret troubleth thee, tell mee the visions of my dreame, that I haue seene and the interpretation thereof.

7 Thus were the visions of mine head in my bed. And beholde, I sawe a tree in the middes of the earth and the height thereof was great:

8 A great tree and strong, and the height thereof reached vnto heauen, and the sight thereof to the endes of all the earth.

9 The boughes thereof were faire and the fruite thereof much, and in it was meate for all: it made a shadow vnder it for the beastes of the fielde, and the foules of the heauen dwelt in the boughes thereof, and all flesh fedde of it.

10 I sawe in the visions of mine head vpon my bed, and beholde, a watchman and an holy one came downe from heauen,

11 And cried aloude, and said thus, Hew downe the tree, and breake off his branches: shake off his leaues, and scatter his fruite, that the beastes may flee from vnder it, and the foules from his branches.

12 Neuerthelesse leaue the stumpe of his rootes in the earth, and with a band of yron and brasse binde it among the grasse of the fielde, and let it be wet with the dewe of heauen, and let his portion be with the beastes among the grasse of the fielde.

13 Let his heart be changed from mans nature, and let a beasts heart be giuen vnto him, and let seuen times be passed ouer him.

14 The sentence is according to the decree of the watchmen, and according to the word of the holy ones: the demaunde was answered, to the intent that liuing men may knowe, that the most High hath power ouer the kingdome of men, and giueth it to whomsoeuer he will, and appointeth ouer it the most abiect among men.

15 This is the dreame, that I King Nebuchad-nezzar haue seene: therefore thou, O Belteshazzar, declare the interpretation thereof: for all the wisemen of my kingdome are not able to shewe mee the interpretation: but thou art able, for the spirit of the holy gods is in thee.

16 Then Daniel (whose name was Belteshazzar) held his peace by the space of one houre, and his thoughts troubled him, and the King spake and said, Belteshazzar, let neither the dreame, nor the interpretation thereof trouble thee. Belteshazzar answered and saide, My lord, the dreame be to them that hate thee, and the interpretation thereof to thine enemies.

17 The tree that thou sawest, which was great and mightie, whose height reached vnto the heauen, and the sight thereof through all the world,

18 Whose leaues were faire and the fruit thereof much, and in it was meate for all, vnder the which the beastes of the fielde dwelt, and vpon whose branches the foules of the heauen did sit,

19 It is thou, O King, that art great and mightie: for thy greatnesse is growen, and reacheth vnto heauen, and thy dominion to the endes of the earth.

20 Where as the King sawe a watchman, and an holy one, that came downe from heauen, and said, Hew downe the tree and destroy it, yet leaue the stumpe of the rootes thereof in the earth, and with a bande of yron and brasse binde it among the grasse of the fielde, and let it be wette with the dewe of heauen, and let his portion be with the beastes of the fielde, till seuen times passe ouer him,

21 This is the interpretation, O King, and it is the decree of the most High, which is come vpon my lord the King,

22 That they shall driue thee from men, and thy dwelling shalbe with the beasts of the fielde: they shall make thee to eate grasse as the oxen, and they shall wet thee with the dewe of heauen: and seuen times shall passe ouer thee, till thou knowe, that the most High beareth rule ouer the kingdome of men, and giueth it to whom so euer he will.

23 Where as they sayd, that one should leaue the stumpe of the tree rootes, thy kingdome shall remaine vnto thee: after that, thou shalt knowe, that the heauens haue the rule.

24 Wherefore, O King, let my counsell be acceptable vnto thee, and breake off thy sinnes by righteousnes, and thine iniquities by mercy toward the poore: lo, let there be an healing of thine errour.

25 All these things shall come vpon the King Nebuchad-nezzar.

26 At the end of twelue monethes, he walked in the royall palace of Babel.

27 And the King spake and sayde, Is not this great Babel, that I haue built for the house of the kingdome by the might of my power, and for the honour of my maiestie?

28 While the worde was in the Kings mouth, a voyce came downe from heauen, saying, O King Nebuchad-nezzar, to thee be it spoken, Thy kingdome is departed from thee,

29 And they shall driue thee from men, and thy dwelling shalbe with the beastes of the fielde: they shall make thee to eate grasse, as the oxen, and seuen times shall passe ouer thee, vntill thou knowest, that the most High beareth rule ouer the kingdome of men, and giueth it vnto whomsoeuer he will.

30 The very same houre was this thing fulfilled vpon Nebuchad-nezzar, and hee was driuen from men, and did eate grasse as the oxen, and his body was wet with the dewe of heauen, till his heares were growen as eagles feathers, and his nailes like birds clawes.

31 And at the ende of these dayes I Nebuchad-nezzar lift vp mine eyes vnto heauen, and mine vnderstanding was restored vnto me, and I gaue thankes vnto the most High, and I praysed and honoured him that liueth for euer, whose power is an euerlasting power, and his kingdome is from generation to generation.

32 And all the inhabitants of the earth are reputed as nothing: and according to his will he worketh in the armie of heauen, and in the inhabitants of the earth: and none can stay his hand, nor say vnto him, What doest thou?

33 At the same time was mine vnderstanding restored vnto me, and I returned to the honour of my kingdome: my glory and my beautie was restored vnto me, and my counsellours and my princes sought vnto me, and I was established in my kingdome, and my glory was augmented toward me.

34 Now therefore I Nebuchad-nezzar prayse and extoll and magnifie the King of heauen, whose workes are all trueth, and his wayes iudgement, and those that walke in pride, he is able to abase.

Daniel 5

1 King Belshazzar made a great feast to a thousand of his princes, and dranke wine before the thousand.

2 And Belshazzar whiles he tasted the wine, commanded to bring him the golden and siluer vessels, which his father Nebuchad-nezzar had brought from the Temple in Ierusalem, that the King and his princes, his wiues, and his concubines might drinke therein.

3 Then were brought the golden vessels, that were taken out of the Temple of the Lords house at Ierusalem, and the King and his princes, his wiues and his concubines dranke in them.

4 They drunke wine and praysed the gods of golde, and of siluer, of brasse, of yron, of wood and of stone.

5 At the same houre appeared fingers of a mans hand, which wrote ouer against the candlesticke vpon the plaister of the wall of ye Kings palace, and the King sawe the palme of the hand that wrote.

6 Then the Kings countenance was changed, and his thoughtes troubled him, so that the ioynts of his loynes were loosed, and his knees smote one against the other.

7 Wherefore the King cryed loude, that they should bring the astrologians, the Caldeans and the soothsayers. And the King spake, and sayd to the wise men of Babel, Whosoeuer can read this writing,

and declare me the interpretation thereof, shalbe clothed with purple, and shall haue a chaine of golde about his necke, and shall be the third ruler in the kingdome.

8 Then came all the Kings wise men, but they could neither reade the writing, nor shewe the King the interpretation.

9 Then was King Belshazzar greatly troubled, and his countenance was changed in him, and his princes were astonied.

10 Now the Queene by reason of the talke of the King, and his princes came into the banket house, and the Queene spake, and sayd, O King, liue for euer: let not thy thoughtes trouble thee, nor let thy countenance be changed.

11 There is a man in thy kingdome, in whom is the spirit of the holy gods, and in the dayes of thy father light and vnderstanding and wisdome like the wisdome of the gods, was found in him: whom the King Nebuchad-nezzar thy father, the King, I say, thy father, made chiefe of the enchanters, astrologians, Caldeans, and soothsayers,

12 Because a more excellent spirit, and knowledge, and vnderstanding (for hee did expound dreames, and declare hard sentences, and dissolued doubtes) were founde in him, euen in Daniel, whome the King named Belteshazzar: nowe let Daniel be called, and hee will declare the interpretation.

13 Then was Daniel brought before the King, and the King spake and sayd vnto Daniel, Art thou that Daniel, which art of the children of the captiuitie of Iudah, whom my father the King brought out of Iewrie?

14 Now I haue heard of thee, that the spirit of the holy gods is in thee, and that light and vnderstanding and excellent wisdome is found in thee.

15 Now therefore, wisemen and astrologians haue bene brought before me, that they should reade this writing, and shewe me the interpretation thereof: but they could not declare the interpretation of the thing.

16 Then heard I of thee, that thou couldest shewe interpretations, and dissolue doutes: nowe if thou canst reade the writing, and shew me the interpretation thereof, thou shalt be clothed with purple, and shalt haue a chaine of golde about thy necke, and shalt be the third ruler in the kingdome.

17 Then Daniel answered, and sayd before the King, Keepe thy rewards to thy selfe, and giue thy giftes to another: yet I will reade the writing vnto the King, and shew him the interpretation.

18 O King, heare thou, The most high God gaue vnto Nebuchad-nezzar thy father a kingdome, and maiestie, and honour and glory.

19 And for the maiestie that he gaue him, all people, nations, and languages trembled, and feared before him: he put to death whom he would: he smote whome he would: whome he would he set vp, and whome he would he put downe.

20 But when his heart was puft vp, and his minde hardened in pride, hee was deposed from his kingly throne, and they tooke his honour from him.

21 And hee was driuen from the sonnes of men, and his heart was made like the beastes, and his dwelling was with the wilde asses: they fed him with grasse like oxen, and his body was wet with the dewe of the heauen, till he knewe, that the most high God bare rule ouer the kingdome of men, and that he appointeth ouer it, whomsoeuer he pleaseth.

22 And thou his sonne, O Belshazzar, hast not humbled thine heart, though thou knewest all these things,

23 But hast lift thy selfe vp against the Lord of heauen, and they haue brought the vessels of his House before thee, and thou and thy princes, thy wiues and thy concubines haue drunke wine in them, and thou hast praysed the gods of siluer and golde, of brasse, yron, wood and stone, which neither see, neither heare, nor vnderstand: and the God in whose hand thy breath is and all thy wayes, him hast thou not glorified.

24 Then was the palme of the hand sent from him, and hath written this writing.

25 And this is the writing that he hath written, MENE, MENE, TEKEL UPHARSIN.

26 This is the interpretation of the thing, MENE, God hath nombred thy kingdome, and hath finished it.

27 TEKEL, thou art wayed in the balance, and art found too light.

28 PERES, thy kingdome is deuided, and giuen to the Medes and Persians.

29 Then at the commandement of Belshazzar they clothed Daniel with purple, and put a chaine of golde about his necke, and made a proclamation concerning him that he should be the third ruler in the kingdome.

30 The same night was Belshazzar the King of the Caldeans slaine.

31 And Darius of the Medes tooke the kingdome, being threescore and two yeere olde.

Daniel 6

1 It pleased Darius to set ouer the kingdome an hundreth and twentie gouernours, which should be ouer the whole kingdome,

2 And ouer these, three rulers (of whome Daniel was one) that the gouernours might giue accompts vnto them, and the King should haue no domage.

3 Now this Daniel was preferred aboue the rulers and gouernours, because the spirit was excellent in him, and the King thought to set him ouer the whole realme.

4 Wherefore the rulers and gouernours sought an occasion against Daniel concerning the kingdome: but they could finde none occasion nor fault: for he was so faithfull that there was no blame nor fault found in him.

5 Then sayd these men, We shall not finde an occasion against this Daniel, except we finde it against him concerning the Law of his God.

6 Therefore the rulers and these gouernours went together to the King, and sayde thus vnto him, King Darius, liue for euer.

7 All the rulers of thy kingdome, the officers and gouernours, the counsellers, and dukes haue consulted together to make a decree for the King and to establish a statute, that whosoeuer shall aske a petition of any god or man for thirtie dayes saue of thee, O King, he shalbe cast into the denne of lyons.

8 Nowe, O King, confirme the decree, and seale the writing, that it be not changed according to the law of the Medes and Persians, which altereth not.

9 Wherefore King Darius sealed the writing and the decree.

10 Now when Daniel vnderstood that he had sealed the writing, hee went into his house, and his window being open in his chamber toward Ierusalem, he kneeled vpon his knees three times a day, and prayed and praysed his God, as he did aforetime.

11 Then these men assembled, and founde Daniel praying, and making supplication vnto his God.

12 So they came and, spake vnto the King concerning the Kings decree, Hast thou not sealed the decree, that euery man that shall make a request to any god or man within thirtie dayes, saue to thee, O King, shall be cast into the denne of lyons? The King answered, and sayd, The thing is true, according to the Lawe of the Medes and Persians, which altereth not.

13 Then answered they, and sayd vnto the King, This Daniel which is of the children of the captiuitie of Iudah, regardeth not thee, O King, nor the decree, that thou hast sealed, but maketh his petition three times a day.

14 When the King heard these wordes, hee was sore displeased with himselfe, and set his heart on Daniel, to deliuer him: and he laboured till the sunne went downe, to deliuer him.

15 Then these men assembled vnto the King, and sayde vnto ye King, Vnderstand, O King, that the lawe of the Medes and Persians is, that no decree nor statute which the King confirmeth, may be altered.

16 Then the King commanded, and they brought Daniel, and cast him into the denne of lyons: now the King spake, and said vnto Daniel, Thy God, whome thou alway seruest, euen he will deliuer thee.

17 And a stone was brought, and layed vpon the mouth of the denne, and the King sealed it with his owne signet, and with the signet of his princes, that the purpose might not be changed, concerning Daniel.

18 Then the King went vnto his palace, and remained fasting, neither were the instruments of musike brought before him, and his sleepe went from him.

19 Then the King arose early in the morning, and went in all haste vnto the denne of lyons.

20 And when he came to the denne, he cryed with a lamentable voyce vnto Daniel: and the King spake, and saide to Daniel, O Daniel, the seruant of ye liuing God, is not thy God (whom thou alway seruest) able to deliuer thee from the lyons?

21 Then saide Daniel vnto the King, O King, liue for euer.

22 My God hath sent his Angel and hath shut the lyons mouthes, that they haue not hurt mee: for my iustice was founde out before him: and vnto thee, O King, I haue done no hurt.

23 Then was the King exceeding glad for him, and commanded that they should take Daniel out of the denne: so Daniel was brought out of the denne, and no maner of hurt was found vpon him, because he beleeued in his God.

24 And by the commandement of the King these me which had accused Daniel, were brought, and were cast into the denne of lions, euen they, their children, and their wiues: and the lyons had the mastry of them, and brake all their bones a pieces, or euer they came at the groud of the denne.

25 Afterwarde King Darius wrote, Vnto all people, nations and languages, that dwel in all the world: Peace be multiplied vnto you.

26 I make a decree that in all the dominion of my kingdome, men tremble and feare before the God of Daniel: for he is the liuing God, and remayneth for euer: and his kingdome shall not perish, and his dominion shalbe euerlasting.

27 Hee rescueth and deliuereth, and hee worketh signes and wonders in heauen and in earth, who hath deliuered Daniel from the power of the lyons.

28 So this Daniel prospered in the reigne of Darius and in the reigne of Cyrus of Persia.

Daniel 7

1 In the first yeere of Belshazzar King of Babel, Daniel sawe a dreame, and there were visions in his head, vpon his bed: then he wrote the dreame, and declared the summe of the matter.

2 Daniel spake and saide, I sawe in my vision by night, and behold, the foure windes of the heauen stroue vpon the great sea:

3 And foure great beastes came vp from the sea one diuers from another.

4 The first was as a lyon, and had eagles wings: I beheld, til the wings thereof were pluckt of, and it was lifted vp from the earth, and set vpon his feete as a man, and a mans heart was giuen him.

5 And beholde, another beast which was the second, was like a beare and stood vpon the one side: and hee had three ribbes in his mouth betweene his teeth, and they saide thus vnto him, Arise and deuoure much flesh.

6 After this I beheld, and loe, there was an other like a leopard, which had vpon his backe foure wings of a foule: the beast had also foure heads, and dominion was giuen him.

7 After this I saw in the visions by night, and beholde, the fourth beast was fearefull and terrible and very strong. It had great yron teeth: it deuoured and brake in pieces and stamped the residue vnder his feete: and it was vnlike to the beasts that were before it: for it had ten hornes.

8 As I considered the hornes, beholde, there came vp among them another litle horne, before whome there were three of the first hornes pluckt away: and behold, in this horne were eyes like the eyes of man, and a mouth speaking presumptuous things.

9 I beholde, till the thrones were set vp, and the Ancient of dayes did sit, whose garment was white as snow, and the heare of his head like the pure wooll: his throne was like the fierie flame, and his wheeles as burning fire.

10 A fierie streame yssued, and came foorth from before him: thousand thousandes ministred vnto him, and tenne thousand thousands stoode before him: the iudgement was set, and the bookes opened.

11 Then I beholde, because of the voyce of the presumptuous wordes, which the horne spake: I beholde, euen till the beast was slaine, and his body destroyed, and giuen to the burning fire.

12 As concerning the other beastes, they had taken away their dominion: yet their liues were prolonged for a certaine time and season.

13 As I behelde in visions by night, behold, one like the sonne of man came in the cloudes of heauen, and approched vnto the Ancient of dayes, and they brought him before him.

14 And he gaue him dominion, and honour, and a kingdome, that all people, nations and languages should serue him: his dominion is an euerlasting dominion, which shall neuer bee taken away: and his kingdome shall neuer be destroyed.

15 I Daniel was troubled in my spirit, in the middes of my body, and the visions of mine head made me afraide.

16 Therefore I came vnto one of them that stoode by, and asked him the trueth of all this: so he tolde me, and shewed me the interpretation of these things.

17 These great beastes which are foure, are foure Kings, which shall arise out of the earth,

18 And they shall take the kingdome of the Saintes of the most High, and possesse the kingdome for euer, euen for euer and euer.

19 After this, I woulde knowe the trueth of the fourth beast, which was so vnlike to all the others, very fearefull, whose teeth were of yron, and his nailes of brasse: which deuoured, brake in pieces, and stamped the residue vnder his feete.

20 Also to know of the tenne hornes that were in his head, and of the other which came vp, before whome three fell, and of the horne that had eyes, and of the mouth that spake presumptuous thinges, whose looke was more stoute then his fellowes.

21 I beheld, and the same horne made battel against the Saintes, yea, and preuailed against them,

22 Vntill the Ancient of dayes came, and iudgement was giuen to the Saintes of the most High: and the time approched, that the Saintes possessed the kingdome.

23 Then he said, The fourth beast shall be the fourth kingdome in the earth, which shall be vnlike to all the kingdomes, and shall deuoure the whole earth, and shall treade it downe and breake it in pieces.

24 And the ten hornes out of this kingdome are tenne Kings that shall rise: and an other shall rise after them, and he shall be vnlike to the first, and he shall subdue three Kings,

25 And shall speake wordes against the most High, and shall consume the Saintes of the most High, and thinke that he may change times and lawes, and they shalbe giuen into his hand, vntill a time, and times and the deuiding of time.

26 But the iudgement shall sit, and they shall take away his dominion, to consume and destroy it vnto the ende.

27 And the kingdome, and dominion, and the greatnesse of the kingdome vnder the whole heauen shalbe giue to the holy people of the most High, whose kingdome is an euerlasting kingdome and all powers shall serue and obey him.

28 Euen this is the ende of the matter, I Daniel had many cogitations which troubled mee, and my countenance changed in me: but I kept the matter in mine heart.

Daniel 8

1 In the thirde yeere of the reigne of King Belshazzar, a vision appeared vnto mee, euen vnto me Daniel, after that which appeared vnto mee at the first.

2 And I saw in a vision, and when I sawe it, I was in the palace of Shushan, which is in the prouince of Elam, and in a vision me thought I was by the riuer of Vlai.

3 Then I looked vp and sawe, and beholde, there stoode before the riuer a ramme, which had two hornes: and these two hornes were hie: but one was hier then another, and the hyest came vp last.

4 I sawe the ramme pusshing against ye West, and against the North, and against the South: so that no beastes might stande before him, nor could deliuer out of his hand, but he did what he listed, and became great.

5 And as I considered, beholde, a goate came from the West ouer the whole earth, and touched not the grounde: and this goate had an horne that appeared betweene his eyes.

6 And he came vnto the ramme that had the two hornes, whome I had seene

standing by the riuer, and ranne vnto him in his fierce rage.

7 And I saw him come vnto the ramme, and being moued against him, he smote the ramme, and brake his two hornes: and there was no power in the ramme to stand against him, but he cast him downe to the grounde, and stamped vpon him, and there was none that coulde deliuer the ramme out of his power.

8 Therefore the goate waxed exceeding great, and when he was at the strongest, his great horne was broken: and for it came vp foure that appeared toward the foure windes of ye heauen.

9 And out of one of them came foorth a litle horne, which waxed very great toward the South, and toward the East, and towarde the pleasant land.

10 Yea, it grewe vp vnto the hoste of heauen, and it cast downe some of the hoste, and of the starres to the ground, and trode vpon them,

11 And extolled himselfe against the prince of the hoste from whome the dayly sacrifice was taken away, and the place of his Sanctuarie was cast downe.

12 And a time shall be giuen him ouer the dayly sacrifice for the iniquitie: and it shall cast downe the trueth to the ground, and thus shall it doe, and prosper.

13 Then I heard one of the Saints speaking, and one of the Saints spake vnto a certaine one, saying, Howe long shall endure the vision of the dayly sacrifice, and the iniquitie of the desolation to treade both the Sanctuarie and the armie vnder foote?

14 And he answered me, Vnto the euening and the morning, two thousand and three hundreth: then shall the Sanctuarie be clensed.

15 Nowe when I Daniel had seene the vision, and sought for the meaning, beholde, there stoode before me like the similitude of a man.

16 And I heard a mans voyce betweene the bankes of Vlai, which called, and sayde, Gabriel, make this man to vnderstand the vision.

17 So he came where I stood: and when hee came, I was afraide, and fell vpon my face: but he sayd vnto me, Vnderstand, O sonne of man: for in the last time shalbe the vision.

18 Nowe as he was speaking vnto me, I being a sleepe fell on my face to the ground: but he touched me, and set me vp in my place.

19 And he sayde, Beholde, I will shewe thee what shalbe in the last wrath: for in the end of the time appointed it shall come.

20 The ramme which thou sawest hauing two hornes, are the Kings of the Medes and Persians.

21 And the goate is the King of Grecia, and the great horne that is betweene his eyes, is the first King.

22 And that that is broken, and foure stoode vp for it, are foure kingdomes, which shall stand vp of that nation, but not in his strength.

23 And in the end of their kingdome, when the rebellious shalbe consumed, a King of fierce countenance, and vnderstanding darke sentences, shall stand vp.

24 And his power shalbe mightie, but not in his strength: and hee shall destroy wonderfully, and shall prosper, and practise, and shall destroy the mightie, and the holy people.

25 And through his policie also, hee shall cause craft to prosper in his hand, and he shall extoll himselfe in his heart, and by peace shall destroy many: hee shall also stande vp against the prince of princes, but he shalbe broken downe without hand.

26 And the vision of the euening and the morning, which is declared, is true: therefore seale thou vp the vision, for it shall be after many dayes.

27 And I Daniel was striken and sicke certaine dayes: but when I rose vp, I did the Kings busines, and I was astonished at the vision, but none vnderstood it.

Daniel 9

1 In the first yeere of Darius the sonne of Ahashuerosh, of the seede of the Medes, which was made King ouer the realme of the Caldeans,

2 Euen in the first yeere of his reigne, I Daniel vnderstood by bookes the number of the yeeres, whereof the Lord had spoken vnto Ieremiah the Prophet, that he would accomplish seuentie yeeres in the desolation of Ierusalem.

3 And I turned my face vnto the Lord God, and sought by prayer and supplications with fasting and sackcloth and ashes.

4 And I prayed vnto the Lord my God, and made my confession, saying, Oh Lord God, which art great and fearefull, and keepest couenant and mercy toward them which loue thee, and toward them that keepe thy commandements,

5 We haue sinned, and haue committed iniquitie and haue done wickedly, yea, we haue rebelled, and haue departed from thy precepts, and from thy iudgements,

6 For we would not obey thy seruants the Prophets, which spake in thy Name to our Kings, to our princes, and to our fathers, and to all the people of the land.

7 O Lord, righteousnes belongeth vnto thee, and vnto vs open shame, as appeareth this day vnto euery man of Iudah, and to the inhabitants of Ierusalem: yea, vnto all Israel, both neere and farre off, through all the countreys, whither thou hast driuen them, because of their offences, that they haue committed against thee.

8 O Lord, vnto vs apperteineth open shame, to our Kings, to our princes, and to our fathers, because we haue sinned against thee.

9 Yet compassion and forgiuenesse is in the Lord our God, albeit we haue rebelled against him.

10 For we haue not obeyed the voyce of the Lord our God, to walke in his lawes,

which he had laide before vs by the ministerie of his seruants the Prophets.

11 Yea, all Israel haue transgressed thy Lawe, and are turned backe, and haue not heard thy voyce: therefore the curse is powred vpon vs, and the othe that is written in the Lawe of Moses the seruant of God, because we haue sinned against him.

12 And he hath confirmed his wordes, which he spake against vs, and against our iudges that iudged vs, by bringing vpon vs a great plague: for vnder the whole heauen hath not bene the like, as hath bene brought vpon Ierusalem.

13 All this plague is come vpon vs, as it is written in the Lawe of Moses: yet made we not our prayer before the Lord our God, that we might turne from our iniquities and vnderstand thy trueth.

14 Therefore hath the Lord made ready the plague, and brought it vpon vs: for the Lord our God is righteous in all his works which he doeth: for we would not heare his voyce.

15 And nowe, O Lord our God, that hast brought thy people out of the land of Egypt with a mightie hand, and hast gotten thee renoume, as appeareth this day, we haue sinned, we haue done wickedly.

16 O Lord, according to all thy righteousnes, I beseech thee, let thine anger and thy wrath be turned away from thy citie Ierusalem thine holy Mountaine: for because of our sinnes, and for the iniquities of our fathers, Ierusalem and thy people are a reproche to all that are about vs.

17 Nowe therefore, O our God, heare the prayer of thy serunant, and his supplications, and cause thy face to shine vpon thy Sanctuarie, that lyeth waste for the Lords sake.

18 O my God, encline thine eare and heare: open thine eyes, and beholde our desolations, and the citie whereupon thy Name is called: for we doe not present our supplications before thee for our owne righteousnes, but for thy great tender mercies.

19 O Lord, heare, O Lord forgiue, O Lord consider, and doe it: deferre not, for thine owne sake, O my God: for thy Name is called vpon thy citie, and vpon thy people.

20 And whiles I was speaking and praying, and confessing my sinne, and the sinne of my people Israel, and did present my supplication before the Lord my God, for the holy Mountaine of my God,

21 Yea, while I was speaking in prayer, euen the man Gabriel, whome I had seene before in the vision, came flying, and touched mee about the time of the euening oblation.

22 And he informed me, and talked with me, and sayd, O Daniel, I am now come forth to giue thee knowledge and vnderstanding.

23 At the beginning of thy supplications the commandement came foorth, and I am come to shewe thee, for thou art

greatly beloued: therefore vnderstande the matter and consider the vision.

24 Seuentie weekes are determined vpon thy people and vpon thine holy citie, to finish the wickednes, and to seale vp the sinnes, and to reconcile the inquitie, and to bring in euerlasting righteousnesse, and to seale vp the vision and prophecie, and to anoynt the most Holy.

25 Knowe therefore and vnderstande, that from the going foorth of the commandement to bring againe the people, and to builde Ierusalem, vnto Messiah the prince, shall be seuen weekes and threescore and two weekes, and the streete shalbe built againe, and the wall euen in a troublous time.

26 And after threescore and two weekes, shall Messiah be slaine, and shall haue nothing,, and the people of the prince that shall come, shall destroy the citie and the Sanctuarie, and the end thereof shalbe with a flood: and vnto the end of the battell it shalbe destroyed by desolations.

27 And he shall confirme the couenant with many for one weeke: and in the middes of the weeke he shall cause the sacrifice and the oblation to cease, and for the ouerspreading of the abominations, he shall make it desolate, euen vntill the consummation determined shalbe powred vpon the desolate.

Daniel 10

1 In the third yeere of Cyrus King of Persia, a thing was reueiled vnto Daniel (whose name was called Belteshazzar) and the worde was true, but the time appointed was long, and he vnderstood the thing, and had vnderstanding of the vision.

2 At the same time I Daniel was in heauines for three weekes of dayes.

3 I ate no pleasant bread, neither came flesh nor wine in my mouth, neither did I anoint my selfe at all, till three weekes of dayes were fulfilled.

4 And in the foure and twentieth day of the first moneth, as I was by the side of that great riuer, euen Hiddekel,

5 And I lift vp mine eyes, and looked, and beholde, there was a man clothed in linnen, whose loynes were girded with fine golde of Vphaz.

6 His body also was like the Chrysolite, and his face (to looke vpon) like the lightning, and his eyes as lamps of fire, and his armes and his feete were like in colour to polished brasse, and the voyce of his wordes was like the voyce of a multitude.

7 And I Daniel alone sawe the vision: for the men that were with me, sawe not the vision: but a great feare fell vpon them, so that they fled away and hid themselues.

8 Therefore I was left alone, and sawe this great vision, and there remained no strength in me: for my strength was turned in me into corruption, and I retained no power.

9 Yet heard I the voyce of his wordes: and when I heard the voyce of his wordes, I slept on my face: and my face was toward the ground.

10 And behold, an hand touched me, which set me vp vpon my knees and vpon the palmes of mine hands.

11 And he sayde vnto me, O Daniel, a man greatly beloued, vnderstand the wordes that I speake vnto thee, and stand in thy place: for vnto thee am I nowe sent. And when hee had sayde this worde vnto me, I stood trembling.

12 Then sayd he vnto me, Feare not, Daniel: for from the first day that thou diddest set thine heart to vnderstand, and to humble thy selfe before thy God, thy wordes were heard, and I am come for thy wordes.

13 But the prince of the kingdome of Persia withstoode me one and twentie dayes: but loe, Michael one of the chiefe princes, came to helpe me, and I remained there by the Kings of Persia.

14 Nowe I am come to shewe thee what shall come to thy people in the latter dayes: for yet the vision is for many dayes.

15 And when he spake these wordes vnto me, I set my face towarde the grounde, and helde my tongue.

16 And beholde, one like the similitude of the sonnes of man touched my lippes: then I opened my mouth, and spake, and said vnto him that stoode before me, O my Lord, by the vision my sorowes are returned vpon me, and I haue reteined no strength.

17 For howe can the seruant of this my Lord talke with my Lord being such one? for as for me, straight way there remained no strength in me, neither is there breath left in me.

18 Then there came againe, and touched me one like the appearance of a man, and he strengthened me,

19 And said, O man, greatly beloued, feare not: peace be vnto thee: be strong and of good courage. And when he had spoken vnto me, I was strengthened, and saide, Let my Lord speake: for thou hast strengthened me.

20 Then saide he, Knowest thou wherefore I am come vnto thee? but nowe will I returne to fight with the prince of Persia: and when I am gone forth, loe, the prince of Grecia shall come.

21 But I will shew thee that which is decreeed in the Scripture of trueth: and there is none that holdeth with me in these things, but Michael your prince.

Daniel 11

1 Also I, in ye first yere of Darius of ye Medes, euen I stood to incourage and to strengthen him.

2 And now wil I shew thee ye trueth, Behold, there shall stand vp yet three Kings in Persia, and the fourth shall be farre richer then they all: and by his strength, and by his riches he shall stirre vp all against the realme of Grecia.

3 But a mightie King shall stand vp, that shall rule with great dominion, and doe according to his pleasure.

4 And when he shall stand vp, his kingdome shall be broken, and shall be deuided towarde the foure windes of heauen: and not to his posteritie, nor according to his dominion, which he ruled: for his kingdome shall be pluckt vp, euen to be for others besides those.

5 And ye King of ye South shalbe mightie, and one of his princes, and shall preuaile against him, and beare rule: his dominio shalbe a great dominion.

6 And in the ende of yeeres they shalbe ioyned together: for the Kings daughter of ye South shall come to the King of the North to make an agreement, but she shall not reteine the power of the arme, neither shall he continue, nor his arme: but she shall be deliuered to death, and they that brought her, and he that begate her, and he that comforted her in these times.

7 But out of the bud of her rootes shall one stand vp in his stead, which shall come with an armie, and shall enter into the fortresse of the King of the North, and doe with them as he list, and shall preuaile,

8 And shall also carie captiues into Egypt their gods with their molten images, and with their precious vessels of siluer and of golde, and he shall continue more yeeres then the King of the North.

9 So the King of ye South shall come into his kingdome, and shall returne into his owne land.

10 Wherefore his sonnes shall be stirred vp, and shall assemble a mightie great armie: and one shall come, and ouerflowe, and passe through: then shall he returne, and be stirred vp at his fortresse.

11 And the King of the South shall be angrie, and shall come foorth, and fight with him, euen with the King of the North: for he shall set foorth a great multitude, and the multitude shall be giuen into his hand.

12 Then the multitude shall be proude, and their heart shall be lifted vp: for hee shall cast downe thousands: but he shall not still preuaile.

13 For the King of the North shall returne, and shall set foorth a greater multitude then afore, and shall come foorth (after certeine yeeres) with a mightie armie, and great riches.

14 And at the same time there shall many stand vp against the King of the South: also the rebellious children of thy people shall exalt them selues to establish the vision, but they shall fall.

15 So the King of the North shall come, and cast vp a mount, and take the strong citie: and the armes of the South shall not resist, neither his chosen people, neither shall there be any strength to withstand.

16 But he that shall come, shall doe vnto him as he list, and none shall stand against him: and he shall stand in the

pleasant land, which by his hand shalbe consumed.

17 Againe he shall set his face to enter with the power of his whole kingdome, and his confederates with him: thus shall he doe, and he shall giue him the daughter of women, to destroy her: but she shall not stande on his side, neither bee for him.

18 After this shall he turne his face vnto the yles, and shall take many, but a prince shall cause his shame to light vpon him, beside that he shall cause his owne shame to turne vpon himselfe.

19 For he shall turne his face toward the fortes of his owne land: but he shall be ouerthrowen and fall, and be no more founde.

20 Then shall stand vp in his place in the glorie of the kingdome, one that shall raise taxes: but after fewe dayes he shall be destroyed, neither in wrath, nor in battell.

21 And in his place shall stand vp a vile person, to whom they shall not giue the honour of the kingdome: but he shall come in peaceably, and obteine the kingdome by flatteries.

22 And the armes shall be ouerthrowen with a flood before him, and shall be broken: and also the prince of the couenant.

23 And after the league made with him, he shall worke deceitfully: for he shall come vp, and ouercome with a small people.

24 He shall enter into the quiet and plentifull prouince, and he shall doe that which his fathers haue not done, nor his fathers fathers: he shall deuide among them the pray and the spoyle, and the substance, yea, and he shall forecast his deuises against the strong holdes, euen for a time.

25 Also he shall stirre vp his power and his courage against the King of the South with a great armie, and the King of the South shall be stirred vp to battell with a very great and mightie armie: but he shall not stand: for they shall forecast and practise against him.

26 Yea, they that feede of the portion of his meate, shall destroy him: and his armie shall ouerflowe: and many shall fall, and be slaine.

27 And both these Kings hearts shall be to do mischiefe, and they shall talke of deceite at one table: but it shall not auaile: for yet the ende shall be at the time appointed.

28 Then shall he returne into his land with great substance: for his heart shall be against the holy couenant: so shall he doe and returne to his owne land.

29 At the time appointed he shall returne, and come toward the South: but the last shall not be as the first.

30 For the shippes of Chittim shall come against him: therefore he shalbe sorie and returne, and freat against the holy couenant: so shall he doe, he shall euen returne and haue intelligence with them that forsake the holy couenant.

31 And armes shall stand on his part, and they shall pollute the Sanctuarie of strength, and shall take away the dayly sacrifice, and they shall set vp the abominable desolation.

32 And such as wickedly breake ye couenant, shall he cause to sinne by flatterie: but the people that do know their God, shall preuaile and prosper.

33 And they that vnderstand among the people, shall instruct many: yet they shall fall by sword, and by flame, by captiuitie and by spoile many dayes.

34 Nowe when they shall fall, they shall be holpen with a litle helpe: but many shall cleaue vnto them fainedly.

35 And some of the of vnderstanding shall fall to trie them, and to purge, and to make them white, till the time be out: for there is a time appointed.

36 And the King shall doe what him list: he shall exalt himselfe, and magnifie himselfe against all, that is God, and shall speake marueilous things against ye God of gods, and shall prosper, till ye wrath be accomplished: for ye determination is made.

37 Neither shall he regard the God of his fathers, nor the desires of women, nor care for any God: for he shall magnifie himselfe aboue all.

38 But in his place shall he honour the god Mauzzim, and the god whom his fathers knewe not, shall he honour with golde and with siluer, and with precious stones, and pleasant things.

39 Thus shall he do in the holdes of Mauzzim with a strange god whom he shall acknowledge: he shall increase his glory, and shall cause them to rule ouer many and shall deuide ye land for gaine.

40 And at ye end of time shall the King of the South push at him, and the king of the North shall come against him like a whirlewind with charets, and with horsemen, and with many ships, and he shall enter into ye countreis, and shall ouerflow and passe through.

41 He shall enter also into the pleasant land, and many countreis shalbe ouerthrowen: but these shall escape out of his hand, euen Edom and Moab, and the chiefe of the children of Ammon.

42 He shall stretch foorth his hands also vpon the countreis, and ye land of Egypt shall not escape.

43 But he shall haue power ouer the treasures of golde and of siluer, and ouer all the precious things of Egypt, and of the Lybians, and of the blacke Mores where he shall passe.

44 But the tidings out of the East and the North shall trouble him: therefore he shall goe foorth with great wrath to destroy and roote out many.

45 And he shall plant the tabernacles of his palace betweene the seas in the glorious and holy mountaine, yet he shall come to his end, and none shall helpe him.

Daniel 12

1 And at that time shall Michael stand vp, ye great prince, which standeth for ye children of thy people, and there shall be a time of trouble, such as neuer was since there began to be a nation vnto that same time: and at that time thy people shall be deliuered, euery one that shall be foud written in ye boke.

2 And many of them that sleepe in the dust of the earth, shall awake, some to euerlasting life, and some to shame and perpetuall contempt.

3 And they that be wise, shall shine, as ye brightnes of the firmament: and they that turne many to righteousnes, shall shine as the starres, for euer and euer.

4 But thou, O Daniel, shut vp the words, and seale the boke til the end of the time: many shall run to and from, and knowledge shall be increased.

5 Then I Daniel looked, and behold, there stood other two, ye one on this side of ye brinke of ye riuer, and the other on that side of ye brinke of the riuer.

6 And one saide vnto the man clothed in linen, which was vpon ye waters of the riuer, When shalbe the ende of these wonders?

7 And I heard ye man clothed in line which was vpon the waters of the riuer, when he helde vp his right hand, and his left hand vnto heauen, and sware by him that liueth for euer, that it shall tarie for a time, two times and an halfe: and when he shall haue accomplished to scatter the power of the holy people, all these things shall be finished.

8 The I heard it, but I vnderstood it not: the said I, O my Lord, what shalbe ye end of these things?

9 And he said, Go thy way, Daniel: for ye words are closed vp, and sealed, till the ende of the time.

10 Many shalbe purified, made white, and tried: but the wicked shall doe wickedly, and none of the wicked shall haue vnderstanding: but the wise shall vnderstand.

11 And from the time that the daily sacrifice shalbe take away and the abominable desolatio set vp, there shalbe a thousand, two hundreth and ninetie daies.

12 Blessed is he that waiteth and commeth to the thousand, three hundreth and fiue and thirtie daies.

13 But go thou thy way til the end be: for thou shalt rest and stand vp in thy lot, at the end of ye daies.

Hosea

Hosea 1

1 The worde of the Lord that came vnto Hosea the sonne of Beeri, in the daies of Vzziah, Iotham, Ahaz, and Hezekiah Kings of Iudah, and in the daies of Ieroboam the sonne of Ioash king of Israel.

2 At the beginning the Lord spake by Hosea, and the Lord said vnto Hosea, Goe, take vnto thee a wife of fornications, and children of fornications: for the lande hath committed great whoredome, departing from the Lord.

3 So he went, and tooke Gomer, ye daughter of Diblaim, which conceiued and bare him a sonne.

4 And the Lord said vnto him, Cal his name Izreel: for yet a litle, and I will visite the blood of Izreel vpon the house of Iehu, and will cause to cease the kingdome of the house of Israel.

5 And at that day will I also breake the bowe of Israel in the valley of Izreel.

6 She conceiued yet againe, and bare a daughter, and God saide vnto him, Call her name Lo-ruhamah: for I will no more haue pitie vpon the house of Israel: but I wil vtterly take them away.

7 Yet I will haue mercie vpon the house of Iudah, and wil saue them by the Lord their God, and wil not saue them by bow, nor by sword nor by battell, by horses, nor by horsemen.

8 Nowe when she had wained Lo-ruhamah, shee conceiued, and bare a sonne.

9 Then saide God, Call his name Lo-ammi: for yee are not my people: therefore will I not be yours.

10 Yet the nomber of the children of Israel shall be as the sande of the sea, which can not be measured nor tolde: and in the place where it was saide vnto them, Yee are not my people, it shall be saide vnto them, Yee are the sonnes of the liuing God.

11 Then shall the children of Iudah, and the children of Israel be gathered together, and appoint them selues one head, and they shall come vp out of the land: for great is the day of Izreel.

Hosea 2

1 Say vnto your brethren, Ammi, and to your sisters, Ruhamah,

2 Plead with your mother: plead with her: for she is not my wife, neither am I her husband: but let her take away her fornications out of her sight, and her adulteries from betweene her breasts.

3 Lest I strippe her naked, and set her as in the day that shee was borne, and make her as a wildernes, and leaue her like a drie land, and slaie her for thirst.

4 And I wil haue no pitie vpon her children: for they be the children of fornications.

5 For their mother hath plaied the harlot: she that conceiued them, hath done shamefully: for shee said, I will goe after my louers that giue me my bread and my water, my wooll and my flaxe, mine oyle and my drinke.

6 Therefore beholde, I will stoope thy way with thornes, and make an hedge, that shee shall not finde her pathes.

7 Though shee follow after her louers, yet shall shee not come at them: though shee seeke them, yet shall shee not finde them: then shall she say, I will goe and returne to my first husband: for at that time was I better then nowe.

8 Nowe she did not knowe that I gaue her corne, and wine, and oyle, and multiplied her siluer and golde, which they bestowed vpon Baal.

9 Therefore wil I returne, and take away my corne in the time thereof, and my wine in the season thereof, and will recouer my wool and my flaxe lent, to couer her shame.

10 And now will I discouer her lewdnes in the sight of her louers, and no man shall deliuer her out of mine hand.

11 I will also cause all her mirth to cease, her feast daies, her newe moones, and her Sabbathes, and all her solemne feasts.

12 And I wil destroy her vines and her figtrees, whereof she hath said, These are my rewards that my louers haue giuen mee: and I will make them as a forest, and the wilde beasts shall eate them.

13 And I wil visit vpon her the daies of Baalim, wherein shee burnt incense to them: and shee decked her selfe with her earings and her iewels, and shee folowed her louers, and forgate me, saith the Lord.

14 Therefore beholde, I will allure her, and bring her into the wildernesse, and speake friendly vnto her.

15 And I will giue her her vineyardes from thence, and the valley of Achor for the doore of hope, and shee shall sing there as in the daies of her youth, and as in the daies when shee came vp out of the land of Egypt.

16 And at that day, sayeth the Lord, thou shalt call me Ishi, and shalt call me no more Baali.

17 For I will take away the names of Baalim out of her mouth, and they shall be no more remembred by their names.

18 And in that day wil I make a couenant for them, with the wilde beasts, and with the foules of the heauen, and with that that creepeth vpon the earth: and I will breake the bowe, and the sworde and the battell out of the earth, and will make them to sleepe safely.

19 And I wil marry thee vnto me for euer: yea, I will marry thee vnto me in righteousnes, and in iudgement, and in mercy and in compassion.

20 I will euen marry thee vnto me in faithfulnes, and thou shalt knowe the Lord.

21 And in that day I wil heare, saith the Lord, I will euen heare the heauens, and they shall heare the earth,

22 And the earth shall heare the corne, and the wine, and the oyle, and they shall heare Izreel.

23 And I will sowe her vnto me in the earth, and I will haue mercie vpon her, that was not pitied, and I will say to them which were not my people, Thou art my people. And they shall say, Thou art my God.

Hosea 3

1 Then said the Lord to me, Goe yet, and loue a woman (beloued of her husband, and was an harlot) according to the loue of the Lord toward the children of Israel: yet they looked to other gods, and loued the wine bottels.

2 So I bought her to me for fifteene pieces of siluer, and for an homer of barlie and an halfe homer of barlie.

3 And I said vnto her, Thou shalt abide with me many dayes: thou shalt not play the harlot, and thou shalt be to none other man, and I will be so vnto thee.

4 For the children of Israel shall remaine many dayes without a King and without a prince, and without an offering, and without an image, and without an Ephod and without Teraphim.

5 Afterward shall the children of Israel conuert, and seeke the Lord their God, and Dauid their King, and shall feare the Lord, and his goodnes in the latter dayes.

Hosea 4

1 Heare the worde of the Lord, ye children of Israel: for the Lord hath a controuersie with the inhabitants of the lande, because there is no trueth nor mercie nor knowledge of God in the lande.

2 By swearing, and lying, and killing, and stealing, and whoring they breake out, and blood toucheth blood.

3 Therefore shall the land mourne, and euery one that dwelleth therein, shall be cut off, with the beasts of the fielde, and with the foules of the heauen, and also the fishes of the sea shall be taken away.

4 Yet let none rebuke, nor reproue another: for thy people are as they that rebuke the Priest.

5 Therefore shalt thou fall in the day, and the Prophet shall fall with thee in the night, and I will destroy thy mother.

6 My people are destroyed for lacke of knowledge: because thou hast refused knowledge, I will also refuse thee, that thou shalt be no Priest to me: and seeing thou hast forgotten the Lawe of thy God, I will also forget thy children.

7 As they were increased, so they sinned against me: therefore will I chaunge their glorie into shame.

8 They eate vp the sinnes of my people, and lift vp their mindes in their iniquitie.

9 And there shalbe like people, like Priest: for I wil visite their wayes vpon them, and reward them their deedes.

10 For they shall eate, and not haue ynough: they shall commit adulterie, and shall not increase, because they haue left off to take heede to ye Lord.

11 Whoredome, and wine, and newe wine take away their heart.

12 My people aske counsell at their stockes, and their staffe teacheth them: for the spirite of fornications hath caused them to erre, and they haue gone a whoring from vnder their God.

13 They sacrifice vpon the toppes of ye mountaines, and burne incense vpon the hilles vnder the okes, and the poplar tree, and the elme, because the shadow thereof is good: therefore your daughters shall be harlots, and your spouses shall be whores.

14 I will not visite your daughters when they are harlots: nor your spouses when they are whores: for they themselues are separated with harlots, and sacrifice

with whores: therefore the people that doeth not vnderstand, shall fall.

15 Though thou, Israel, play the harlot, yet let not Iudah sinne: come not ye vnto Gilgal, neither goe ye vp to Beth-auen, nor sweare, The Lord liueth.

16 For Israel is rebellious as an vnruly heyfer. Nowe the Lord will feede them as a lambe in a large place.

17 Ephraim is ioyned to idoles: let him alone.

18 Their drunkennes stinketh: they haue committed whoredome: their rulers loue to say with shame, Bring ye.

19 The winde hath bounde them vp in her wings, and they shalbe ashamed of their sacrifices.

Hosea 5

1 O ye Priestes, heare this, and hearken ye, O house of Israel, and giue ye eare, O house of the King: for iudgement is towarde you, because you haue bene a snare on Mizpah, and a net spred vpon Tabor.

2 Yet they were profounde, to decline to slaughter, though I haue bene a rebuker of them all.

3 I knowe Ephraim, and Israel is not hid from me: for nowe, O Ephraim thou art become an harlot, and Israel is defiled.

4 They will not giue their mindes to turne vnto their God: for the spirit of fornication is in the middes of them, and they haue not knowen the Lord.

5 And the pride of Israel doth testifie to his face: therefore shall Israel and Ephraim fall in their iniquitie: Iudah also shall fall with them.

6 They shall goe with their sheepe, and with their bullockes to seeke the Lord: but they shall not finde him: for he hath withdrawne himselfe from them.

7 They haue transgressed against the Lord: for they haue begotte strange children: now shall a moneth deuoure them with their portions.

8 Blowe ye the trumpet in Gibeah, and the shaume in Ramah: crie out at Beth-auen, after thee, O Beniamin.

9 Ephraim shall be desolate in the day of rebuke: among the tribes of Israel haue I caused to knowe the trueth.

10 The princes of Iudah were like them that remoue the bounde: therefore will I powre out my wrath vpon them like water.

11 Ephraim is oppressed, and broken in iudgement, because he willingly walked after the commandement.

12 Therefore wil I be vnto Ephraim as a moth, and to the house of Iudah as a rottennesse.

13 When Ephraim sawe his sickenes, and Iudah his wound, then went Ephraim vnto Asshur, and sent vnto King Iareb: yet coulde hee not heale you, nor cure you of your wound.

14 For I will be vnto Ephraim as a lyon, and as a lyons whelpe to the house of Iudah: I, euen I will spoyle, and goe away: I will take away, and none shall rescue it.

15 I will go, and returne to my place, til they acknowledge their fault, and seeke me: in their affliction they will seeke me diligently.

Hosea 6

1 Come, and let vs returne to the Lord: for he hath spoyled, and he will heale vs: he hath wounded vs, and he will binde vs vp.

2 After two dayes will he reuiue vs, and in the third day he will raise vs vp, and we shall liue in his sight.

3 Then shall we haue knowledge, and indeuour our selues to know the Lord: his going forth is prepared as the morning, and he shall come vnto vs as the raine, and as the latter raine vnto the earth.

4 O Ephraim, what shall I doe vnto thee? O Iudah, how shall I intreate thee? for your goodnesse is as a morning cloude, and as the morning dewe it goeth away.

5 Therefore haue I cut downe by the Prophets: I haue slaine them by the wordes of my mouth, and thy iudgements were as the light that goeth forth.

6 For I desired mercie, and not sacrifice, and the knowledge of God more then burnt offrings.

7 But they like men haue transgressed the couenant: there haue they trespassed against me.

8 Gilead is a citie of them that worke iniquitie, and is polluted with blood.

9 And as the eues waite for a man, so the companie of Priestes murder in the way by consent: for they worke mischiefe.

10 I haue seene vileny in the house of Israel: there is ye whoredome of Ephraim: Israel is defiled.

11 Yea, Iudah hath set a plant for thee, whiles I woulde returne ye captiuitie of my people.

Hosea 7

1 When I woulde haue healed Israel, then the iniquitie of Ephraim was discouered, and the wickednesse of Samaria: for they haue dealt falsly: and the theefe commeth in, and the robber spoyleth without.

2 And they consider not in their hearts, that I remember all their wickednes: now their owne inuentions haue beset them about: they are in my sight.

3 They make the King glad with their wickednesse, and the princes with their lies.

4 They are all adulterers, and as a very ouen heated by ye baker, which ceaseth from raysing vp, and from kneading ye dough vntill it be leauened.

5 This is the day of our King: the princes haue made him sicke with flagons of wine: he stretcheth out his hand to scorners.

6 For they haue made ready their heart like an ouen whiles they lie in waite: their baker sleepeth all the night: in the morning it burneth as a flame of fire.

7 They are all hote as an ouen, and haue deuoured their iudges: all their Kings are fallen: there is none among them that calleth vnto me.

8 Ephraim hath mixt himselfe among the people. Ephraim is as a cake on the hearth not turned.

9 Strangers haue deuoured his strength, and he knoweth it not: yea, gray heares are here and there vpon him, yet he knoweth not.

10 And the pride of Israel testifieth to his face, and they doe not returne to the Lord their God, nor seeke him for all this.

11 Ephraim also is like a doue deceiued, without heart: they call to Egypt: they go to Asshur.

12 But when they shall go, I will spred my net vpon them, and drawe them downe as the foules of the heauen: I will chastice them as their congregation hath heard.

13 Wo vnto them: for they haue fled away from me: destruction shalbe vnto them, because they haue transgressed against me: though I haue redeemed them, yet they haue spoken lyes against me.

14 And they haue not cryed vnto me with their hearts, when they houled vpon their beds: they assembled themselues for corne, and wine, and they rebell against me.

15 Though I haue boud and strengthened their arme, yet doe they imagine mischiefe against me.

16 They returne, but not to the most high: they are like a deceitfull bowe: their princes shall fall by the sword, for the rage of their tongues: this shall be their derision in the land of Egypt.

Hosea 8

1 Set the trumpet to thy mouth: he shall come as an eagle against the House of the Lord, because they haue transgressed my couenant, and trespassed against my Lawe.

2 Israel shall crie vnto me, My God, we know thee.

3 Israel hath cast off ye thing that is good: the enemie shall pursue him.

4 They haue set vp a King, but not by me: they haue made princes, and I knew it not: of their siluer and their gold haue they made them idoles: therefore shall they be destroyed.

5 Thy calfe, O Samaria, hath cast thee off: mine anger is kindled against them: howe long will they be without innocencie!

6 For it came euen from Israel: the workeman made it, therefore it is not God: but the calfe of Samaria shall be broken in pieces.

7 For they haue sowne the winde, and they shall reape the whirlewind: it hath no stalke: the budde shall bring foorth no meale: if so be it bring forth, the strangers shall deuoure it.

8 Israel is deuoured, now shall they be among the Gentiles as a vessell wherein is no pleasure.

9 For they are gone vp to Asshur: they are as a wilde asse alone by himselfe: Ephraim hath hired louers.

10 Yet though they haue hired among the nations, nowe will I gather them, and they shall sorowe a litle, for the burden of the King and the princes.

11 Because Ephraim hath made many altars to sinne, his altars shalbe to sinne.

12 I haue written to them the great things of my Lawe: but they were counted as a strange thing.

13 They sacrifice flesh for ye sacrifices of mine offerings, and eate it: but the Lord accepteth them not: now will he remember their iniquitie, and visite their sinnes: they shall returne to Egypt.

14 For Israel hath forgotten his maker, and buildeth Temples, and Iudah hath increased strong cities: but I will sende a fire vpon his cities, and it shall deuoure the palaces thereof.

Hosea 9

1 Rejoice not, O Israel for ioy as other people: for thou hast gone a whoring from thy God: thou hast loued a rewarde vpon euery corne floore.

2 The floore, and the wine presse shall not feede them, and the newe wine shall faile in her.

3 They wil not dwel in the Lordes lande, but Ephraim will returne to Egypt, and they wil eate vncleane things in Asshur.

4 They shall not offer wine to the Lord, neither shall their sacrifices be pleasant vnto him: but they shall be vnto them as the bread of mourners: al that eate thereof, shalbe polluted: for their bread for their soules shall not come into the house of the Lord.

5 What wil ye do then in the solemne day, and in the day of the feast of the Lord?

6 For loe, they are gone from destruction: but Egypt shall gather them vp, and Memphis shall burie them: the nettle shall possesse the pleasant places of their siluer, and the thorne shall be in their tabernacles.

7 The daies of visitation are come: the daies of recompence are come: Israel shall knowe it: the Prophet is a foole: the spiritual man is mad, for the multitude of thine iniquitie: therefore the hatred is great.

8 The watchman of Ephraim shoulde bee with my God: but the Prophet is the snare of a fouler in all his waies, and hatred in the House of his God.

9 They are deepely set: they are corrupt as in the daies of Gibeah: therefore he will remember their iniquitie, he will visite their sinnes.

10 I found Israel like grapes in the wildernes: I saw your fathers as the first ripe in the figge tree at her first time: but they went to Baal-Peor, and separated themselues vnto that shame, and their abominations were according to their louers.

11 Ephraim their glorie shall flee away like a birde: from the birth and from the wombe, and from the conception.

12 Though they bring vp their children, yet I will depriue them from being men: yea, woe to them, when I depart from them.

13 Ephraim, as I sawe, is as a tree in Tyrus planted in a cottage: but Ephraim shall bring forth his children to the murtherer.

14 O Lord, giue them: what wilt thou giue them? giue them a baren wombe and drie breasts.

15 All their wickednesse is in Gilgal: for there doe I hate them: for the wickednesse of their inuentions, I will cast them out of mine House: I will loue them no more: all their princes are rebels.

16 Ephraim is smitten, their roote is dried vp: they can bring no fruite: yea, though they bring foorth, yet will I slaie euen the dearest of their bodie.

17 My God will cast them away, because they did not obey him: and they shall wander among the nations.

Hosea 10

1 Israel is a emptie vine, yet hath it brought foorth fruite vnto it selfe, and according to the multitude of the fruite thereof he hath increased the altars: according to the goodnesse of their lande they haue made faire images.

2 Their heart is deuided: nowe shall they be founde faultie: he shall breake downe their altars: he shall destroy their images.

3 For now they shall say, We haue no King because we feared not the Lord: and what should a King doe to vs?

4 They haue spoken woordes, swearing falsly in making a couenant: thus iudgement groweth as wormewoode in the furrowes of the fielde.

5 The inhabitants of Samaria shall feare because of the calfe of Beth-auen: for the people thereof shall mourne ouer it, and the Chemarims thereof, that reioyced on it for the glorie thereof, because it is departed from it.

6 It shall bee also brought to Asshur, for a present vnto King Iareb: Ephraim shall receiue shame, and Israel shall be ashamed of his owne counsell.

7 Of Samaria, the King thereof is destroyed as the some vpon the water.

8 The hie places also of Auen shall be destroied, euen the sinne of Israel: the thorne and the thistle shall growe vpon their altars, and they shall say to the mountaines, Couer vs, and to the hils, Fall vpon vs.

9 O Israel, thou hast sinned from the daies of Gibeah: there they stoode: the battell in Gibeah against the children of iniquitie did not touch them.

10 It is my desire that I should chastice them, and the people shall be gathered against them, when they shall gather themselues in their two furrowes.

11 And Ephraim is as an heifer vsed to delite in threshing: but I will passe by

her faire necke: I will make Ephraim to ride: Iudah shall plowe, and Iaakob shall breake his cloddes.

12 Sowe to your selues in righteousnes: reape after the measure of mercy: breake vp your fallowe grounde: for it is time to seeke the Lord, till he come and raine righteousnesse vpon you.

13 But you haue plowed wickednesse: ye haue reaped iniquitie: you haue eaten the fruite of lies: because thou didest trust in thine owne waies, and in the multitude of thy strong men,

14 Therefore shall a tumult arise among thy people, and all thy munitions shall be destroyed, as Shalman destroyed Beth-arbell in the daie of battell: the mother with the children was dashed in pieces.

15 So shall Beth-el doe vnto you, because of your malicious wickednes: in a morning shall the King of Israel be destroied.

Hosea 11

1 When Israel was a childe, then I loued him, and called my sonne out of Egypt.

2 They called them, but they went thus from them: they sacrificed vnto Baalim, and burnt incense to images.

3 I ledde Ephraim also, as one shoulde beare them in his armes: but they knewe not that I healed them.

4 I led them with cordes of a man, euen with bandes of loue, and I was to them, as hee that taketh off the yoke from their iawes, and I laide the meat vnto them.

5 He shall no more returne into the lande of Egypt: but Asshur shalbe his King, because they refused to conuert.

6 And the sworde shall fall on his cities, and shall consume his barres, and deuoure them, because of their owne counsels.

7 And my people are bent to rebellion against me: though they called them to the most hie, yet none at all would exalt him.

8 Howe shall I giue thee vp, Ephraim? howe shall I deliuer thee, Israel? how shall I make thee, as Admah? howe shall I set thee, as Zeboim? mine heart is turned within mee: my repentings are rouled together.

9 I wil not execute ye fiercenesse of my wrath: I will not returne to destroy Ephraim: for I am God, and not man, the holy one in the middes of thee, and I will not enter into the citie.

10 They shall walke after the Lord: he shall roare like a lyon: when hee shall roare, then the children of the West shall feare.

11 They shall feare as a sparrow out of Egypt, and as a doue of the lande of Asshur, and I will place them in their houses, sayth the Lord.

12 Ephraim copasseth me about with lies, and the house of Israel with deceit: but Iudah yet ruleth with God, and is faithfull with the Saints.

Hosea 12

1 Ephraim is fed with the winde, and followeth after the East winde: hee increaseth daily lies and destruction, and they do make a couenant with Asshur, and oyle is caried into Egypt.

2 The Lord hath also a controuersie with Iudah, and will visite Iaakob, according to his waies: according to his workes, wil he recompence him.

3 Hee tooke his brother by the heele in the wombe, and by his strength he had power with God,

4 And had power ouer the Angel, and preuailed: he wept and praied vnto him: he founde him in Beth-el, and there he spake with vs.

5 Yea, the Lord God of hostes, the Lord is himselfe his memoriall.

6 Therefore turne thou to thy God: keepe mercy and iudgement, and hope still in thy God.

7 He is Canaan: the balances of deceit are in his hand: he loueth to oppresse.

8 And Ephraim saide, Notwithstanding I am rich, I haue found me out riches in all my labours: they shall finde none iniquitie in me, that were wickednesse.

9 Though I am the Lord thy God, from the land of Egypt, yet will I make thee to dwel in the tabernacles, as in the daies of the solemne feast.

10 I haue also spoken by the Prophets, and I haue multiplied visions, and vsed similitudes by the ministerie of the Prophets.

11 Is there iniquitie in Gilead? surely they are vanitie: they sacrifice bullocks in Gilgal, and their altars are as heapes in the furrowes of the field.

12 And Iaakob fled into the countrey of Aram, and Israel serued for a wife, and for a wife he kept sheepe.

13 And by a Prophet the Lord brought Israel out of Egypt, and by a Prophet was he reserued.

14 But Ephraim prouoked him with hie places: therefore shall his blood be powrd vpon him, and his reproche shall his Lord reward him.

Hosea 13

1 When Ephraim spake, there was trembling: hee exalted him selfe in Israel, but he hath sinned in Baal, and is dead.

2 And nowe they sinne more and more, and haue made them molten images of their siluer, and idoles according to their owne vnderstanding: they were all the woorke of the craftesmen: they say one to another whiles they sacrifice a man, Let them kisse the calues.

3 Therefore they shall bee as the morning cloude, and as the morning dewe that passeth away, as the chaffe that is driuen with a whirlewind out of the floore, and as the smoke that goeth out of the chimney.

4 Yet I am the Lord thy God from the land of Egypt, and thou shalt knowe no God but me: for there is no Sauiour beside me.

5 I did knowe thee in the wildernesse, in the land of drought.

6 As in their pastures, so were they filled: they were filled, and their heart was exalted: therefore haue they forgotten me.

7 And I wil be vnto them as a very lyon, and as a leopard in the way of Asshur.

8 I will meete them, as a beare that is robbed of her whelpes, and I will breake the kall of their heart, and there will I deuoure them like a lion: the wilde beast shall teare them.

9 O Israel, one hath destroyed thee, but in me is thine helpe.

10 I am: where is thy King, that shoulde help thee in al thy cities? and thy iudges, of whom thou saidest, Giue me a King, and princes?

11 I gaue thee a King in mine anger, and I tooke him away in my wrath.

12 The iniquitie of Ephraim is bound vp: his sinne is hid.

13 The sorowes of a trauailing woman shall come vpon him: he is an vnwise sonne, els would he not stande still at the time, euen at the breaking forth of the children.

14 I wil redeeme them from the power of the graue: I will deliuer them from death: O death, I wil be thy death: O graue, I will be thy destruction: repentance is hid from mine eyes.

15 Though he grewe vp among his brethren, an East winde shall come, euen the winde of the Lord shall come vp from the wildernesse, and drie vp his veine, and his fountaine shalbe dryed vp: he shall spoyle the treasure of all pleasant vessels.

Hosea 14

1 Samaria shalbe desolate: for she hath rebelled against her God: they shall fall by the sworde: their infants shalbe dashed in pieces, and their women with childe shalbe ript.

2 O Israel, returne vnto the Lord thy God: for thou hast fallen by thine iniquitie.

3 Take vnto you words, and turne to the Lord, and say vnto him, Take away all iniquitie, and receiue vs graciously: so wil we render the calues of our lippes.

4 Asshur shall not saue vs, neither wil we ride vpon horses, neither will we say any more to the worke of our handes, Ye are our gods: for in thee the fatherlesse findeth mercie.

5 I wil heale their rebellion: I wil loue them freely: for mine anger is turned away from him.

6 I will be as the dewe vnto Israel: he shall grow as the lilie and fasten his rootes, as the trees of Lebanon.

7 His branches shall spread, and his beautie shalbe as the oliue tree, and his smell as Lebanon.

8 They that dwel vnder his shadow, shall returne: they shall reuiue as the corne, and florish as the vine: the sent thereof shalbe as the wine of Lebanon.

9 Ephraim shall say, What haue I to do any more with idoles? I haue heard him, and looked vpon him: I am like a greene firre tree: vpon me is thy fruite founde.

10 Who is wise, and he shall vnderstande these things? and prudent, and he shall knowe them? for the wayes of the Lord are righteous, and the iust shall walke in them: but the wicked shall fall therein.

Joel

Joel 1

1 The worde of the Lord that came to Ioel the sonne of Pethuel.

2 Heare ye this, O Elders, and hearken ye all inhabitantes of the land, whether such a thing hath bene in your dayes, or yet in the dayes of your fathers.

3 Tell you your children of it, and let your children shew to their children, and their children to another generation.

4 That which is left of ye palmer worme, hath the grashopper eaten, and the residue of ye grashopper hath the canker worme eaten, and the residue of the canker worme hath the caterpiller eaten.

5 Awake ye drunkards, and weepe, and howle all ye drinkers of wine, because of the newe wine: for it shalbe pulled from your mouth.

6 Yea, a nation commeth vpon my lande, mightie, and without nomber, whose teeth are like the teeth of a lyon, and he hath the iawes of a great lyon.

7 He maketh my vine waste, and pilleth off the barke of my figge tree: he maketh it bare, and casteth it downe: ye branches therof are made white.

8 Mourne like a virgine girded with sackcloth for the husband of her youth.

9 The meate offring, and the drinke offring is cut off from the House of the Lord: the Priests the Lords ministers mourne.

10 The fielde is wasted: the lande mourneth: for the corne is destroyed: the new wine is dried vp, and the oyle is decayed.

11 Be ye ashamed, O husband men: howle, O ye vine dressers for the wheate, and for the barly, because the haruest of the fielde is perished.

12 The vine is dried vp, and the figge tree is decayed: the pomegranate tree and the palme tree, and the apple tree, euen all the trees of the fielde are withered: surely the ioy is withered away from the sonnes of men.

13 Girde your selues and lament, ye Priests: howle ye ministers of the altar: come, and lie all night in sackecloth, ye ministers of my God: for the meate offring, and the drinke offring is taken away from the house of your God.

14 Sanctifie you a fast: call a solemne assemblie: gather the Elders, and all the inhabitants of the land into the House of the Lord your God, and cry vnto the Lord,

15 Alas: for the day, for the day of the Lord is at hand, and it commeth as a destruction from the Almightie.

16 Is not the meate cut off before our eyes? and ioy, and gladnesse from the house of our God?

17 The seede is rotten vnder their cloddes: the garners are destroyed: the barnes are broken downe, for the corne is withered.

18 How did the beasts mourne! the herdes of cattel pine away, because they haue no pasture, and the flockes of sheepe are destroyed.

19 O Lord, to thee will I crie: for the fire hath deuoured the pastures of the wildernesse, and the flame hath burnt vp all the trees of the fielde.

20 The beasts of the fielde cry also vnto thee: for the riuers of waters are dried vp, and the fire hath deuoured the pastures of the wildernes.

Joel 2

1 Blowe the trumpet in Zion, and shoute in mine holy mountaine: let all the inhabitants of the lande tremble: for the day of the Lord is come: for it is at hand.

2 A day of darkenesse, and of blacknesse, a day of cloudes, and obscuritie, as the morning spred vpon the mountaines, so is there a great people, and a mighty: there was none like it from the beginning, neither shalbe any more after it, vnto the yeeres of many generations.

3 A fire deuoureth before him, and behinde him a flame burneth vp: the land is as the garden of Eden before him, and behinde him a desolate wildernesse, so that nothing shall escape him.

4 The beholding of him is like the sight of horses, and like the horsemen, so shall they runne.

5 Like the noyse of charrets in the toppes of the mountaines shall they leape, like the noyse of a flame of fire that deuoureth the stubble, and as a mightie people prepared to the battel.

6 Before his face shall the people tremble: all faces shall gather blackenesse.

7 They shall runne like strong men, and goe vp to the wall like men of warre, and euery man shall goe forward in his wayes, and they shall not stay in their paths.

8 Neither shall one thrust another, but euery one shall walke in his path: and when they fall vpon the sword, they shall not be wounded.

9 They shall runne to and from in the citie: they shall runne vpon the wall: they shall clime vp vpon the houses, and enter in at ye windowes like ye thiefe.

10 The earth shall tremble before him, ye heauens shall shake, the sunne and the moone shalbe darke, and the starres shall withdraw their shining,

11 And the Lord shall vtter his voyce before his hoste: for his hoste is very great: for he is strog that doeth his word: for the day of the Lord is great and very terrible, and who can abide it?

12 Therefore also now the Lord sayth, Turne you vnto me with all your heart, and with fasting, and with weeping, and with mourning,

13 And rent your heart, and not your clothes: and turne vnto the Lord your God, for he is gratious, and mercifull, slowe to anger, and of great kindnes, and repenteth him of the euill.

14 Who knoweth, is he wil returne and repent and leaue a blessing behinde him, euen a meate offring, and a drinke offring vnto ye Lord your God?

15 Blowe the trumpet in Zion, sanctifie a fast, call a solemne assembly.

16 Gather the people: sanctifie the congregation, gather the elders: assemble the children, and those that sucke the breastes: let the bridegrome go forth of his chamber, and the bride out of her bride chamber.

17 Let the Priestes, the ministers of the Lord weepe betweene the porch and the altar, and let them say, Spare thy people, O Lord, and giue not thine heritage into reproche that the heathen should rule ouer them. Wherefore should they say among the people, Where is their God?

18 Then will the Lord be ielous ouer his land, and spare his people.

19 Yea, the Lord wil answere and say vnto his people, Beholde, I will send you corne, and wine, and oyle, and you shalbe satisfied therewith: and I will no more make you a reproche among the heathen,

20 But I will remooue farre off from you the Northren armie, and I will driue him into a land, barren and desolate with his face toward the East sea, and his end to the vtmost sea, and his stinke shall come vp, and his corruption shall ascend, because he hath exalted himselfe to do this.

21 Feare not, O land, but be glad, and reioyce: for the Lord wil do great things.

22 Be not afrayde, ye beastes of the fielde: for the pastures of the wildernesse are greene: for the tree beareth her fruite: the figge tree and the vine do giue their force.

23 Be glad then, ye children of Zion, and reioyce in the Lord your God: for he hath giuen you the rayne of righteousnes, he wil cause to come downe for you the rayne, euen the first raine, and the latter raine in the first moneth.

24 And the barnes shalbe full of wheate, and the presses shall abound with wine and oyle.

25 And I will render you the yeeres that the grashopper hath eaten, the canker worme and the caterpiller and the palmer worme, my great hoste which I sent among you.

26 So you shall eate and be satisfied and praise the Name of the Lord your God, that hath dealt marueilously with you: and my people shall neuer be ashamed.

27 Ye shall also know, that I am in the middes of Israel, and that I am the Lord your God and none other, and my people shall neuer be ashamed.

28 And afterward will I powre out my Spirit vpon all flesh: and your sonnes and your daughters shall prophecie: your olde men shall dreame dreames, and your yong men shall see visions,

29 And also vpon the seruants, and vpon the maydes in those dayes wil I powre my Spirit.

30 And I will shewe wonders in the heauens and in the earth: blood and fire, and pillars of smoke.

31 The sunne shalbe turned into darkenesse, and the moone into blood, before the great and terrible day of the Lord come.

32 But whosoeuer shall call on the Name of the Lord, shalbe saued: for in mount Zion, and in Ierusale shalbe deliuerance, as the Lord hath said, and in the remnant, whom the Lord shall call.

Joel 3

1 For beholde, in those dayes and in that time, when I shall bring againe the captiuitie of Iudah and Ierusalem,

2 I will also gather all nations, and wil bring them downe into the valley of Iehoshaphat, and will pleade with them there for my people, and for mine heritage Israel, whom they haue scattered among the nations, and parted my land.

3 And they haue cast lottes for my people, and haue giuen the childe for the harlot, and sold the girle for wine, that they might drinke.

4 Yea, and what haue you to do with me, O Tyrus and Zidon and all the costes of Palestina? will ye render me a recompence? and if ye recompence mee, swiftly and speedily will I render your recompence vpon your head:

5 For ye haue taken my siluer and my golde, and haue caried into your temples my goodly and pleasant things.

6 The children also of Iudah and the children of Ierusalem haue you solde vnto the Grecians, that ye might send them farre from their border.

7 Beholde, I will rayse them out of the place where ye haue sold them, and will render your reward vpon your owne head,

8 And I will send your sonnes and your daughters into the hande of the children of Iudah, and they shall sell them to the Sabeans, to a people farre off: for the Lord hath spoken it.

9 Publish this among the Gentiles: prepare warre, wake vp the mightie men: let all the men of warre drawe neere and come vp.

10 Breake your plowshares into swords, and your sithes into speares: let the weake say, I am strong.

11 Assemble your selues, and come all yee heathen and gather your selues together round about: there shall the Lord cast downe the mightie men.

12 Let the heathen be wakened, and come vp to the valley of Iehoshaphat: for there will I sit to iudge all the heathen round about.

13 Put in your sithes, for the haruest is ripe: come, get you downe, for the winepresse is full: yea, the winepresses runne ouer, for their wickednesse is great.

14 O multitude, O multitude, come into the valley of threshing: for the day of the Lord is neere in the valley of threshing.

15 The sunne and moone shalbe darkened, and the starres shall withdrawe their light.

16 The Lord also shall roare out of Zion, and vtter his voyce from Ierusalem, and the heauens and the earth shall shake, but the Lord wil be the hope of his people, and the strength of the children of Israel.

17 So shall ye know that I am the Lord your God dwelling in Zion, mine holy Mountaine: then shall Ierusalem bee holy, and there shall no strangers go thorowe her any more.

18 And in that day shall the mountaines drop downe newe wine, and the hilles shall flowe with milke, and al the riuers of Iudah shall runne with waters, and a fountaine shall come forth of the House of the Lord, and shall water the valley of Shittim.

19 Egypt shalbe waste, and Edom shall be a desolate wildernesse, for the iniuries of the childre of Iudah, because they haue shed innocent blood in their land.

20 But Iudah shall dwell for euer, and Ierusalem from generation to generation.

21 For I will clense their blood, that I haue not clensed, and the Lord will dwell in Zion.

Amos

Amos 1

1 The wordes of Amos, who was among the heardmen at Tecoa, which he sawe vpon Israel, in the dayes of Vzziah king of Iudah, and in the dayes of Ieroboam the sonne of Ioash King of Israel, two yeere before the earthquake.

2 And he saide, The Lord shall roare from Zion, and vtter his voyce from Ierusalem, and the dwelling places of the shepheards shall perish, and the top of Carmel shall wither,

3 Thus saith the Lord, For three transgressions of Damascus, and for foure I will not turne to it, because they haue threshed Gilead with threshing instruments of yron.

4 Therefore will I sende a fire into the house of Hazael, and it shall deuoure the palaces of Ben-hadad.

5 I will breake also the barres of Damascus, and cut off the inhabitant of Bikeath-auen: and him that holdeth the scepter out of Beth-eden, and the people of Aram shall goe into captiuitie vnto Kir, sayth the Lord.

6 Thus sayth the Lord, For three transgressions of Azzah, and for foure, I will not turne to it, because they caried away prisoners the whole captiuitie to shut them vp in Edom.

7 Therefore will I sende a fire vpon the walles of Azzah, and it shall deuoure the palaces thereof.

8 And I will cut off the inhabitant from Ashdod, and him that holdeth the scepter from Ashkelon, and turne mine hande to Ekron, and the remnant of the Philistims shall perish, sayth the Lord God.

9 Thus sayth the Lord, For three transgressions of Tyrus, and for foure, I will not turne to it, because they shut the whole captiuitie in Edom, and haue not remembred the brotherly couenant.

10 Therefore wil I send a fire vpon ye walles of Tyrus, and it shall deuoure the palaces thereof.

11 Thus sayeth the Lord, For three transgressions of Edom, and for foure, I will not turne to it, because hee did pursue his brother with the sworde, and did cast off all pitie, and his anger spoyled him euermore, and his wrath watched him alway.

12 Therefore will I send a fire vpon Teman, and it shall deuoure the palaces of Bozrah.

13 Thus sayth ye Lord, For three transgressions of the children of Ammon, and for foure, I will not turne to it, because they haue ript vp the women with child of Gilead, that they might enlarge their border.

14 Therefore will I kindle a fire in the wall of Rabbah, and it shall deuoure the palaces thereof, with shouting in the day of battell, and with a tempest in the day of the whirlewinde.

15 And their King shall go into captiuitie, he and his princes together, saith the Lord.

Amos 2

1 Thus sayth the Lord, For three transgressions of Moab, and for foure, I will not turne to it, because it burnt the bones of the King of Edom into lime.

2 Therefore will I send a fire vpon Moab, and it shall deuoure the palaces of Kerioth, and Moab shall die with tumult, with shouting, and with the sound of a trumpet.

3 And I will cut off the iudge out of the mids thereof, and will slay all the princes thereof with him, sayth the Lord.

4 Thus saith the Lord, For three transgressions of Iudah, and for foure, I will not turne to it, because they haue cast away the Lawe of the Lord, and haue not kept his commandementes, and their lies caused them to erre after the which their fathers haue walked.

5 Therefore will I send a fire vpon Iudah, and it shall deuoure the palaces of Ierusalem.

6 Thus sayth the Lord, For three transgressions of Israel, and for foure, I will not turne to it, because they solde the righteous for siluer, and the poore for shooes.

7 They gape ouer the head of the poore, in the dust of the earth, and peruert the wayes of the meeke: and a man and his father will goe in to a mayde to dishonour mine holy Name.

8 And they lye downe vpon clothes layde to pledge by euery altar: and they drinke the wine of the condemned in the house of their God.

9 Yet destroyed I the Amorite before the, whose height was like the height of the cedars, and he was strong as the okes: notwithstanding I destroyed his fruite from aboue, and his roote from beneath.

10 Also I brought you vp from the land of Egypt, and led you fourtie yeres thorowe the wildernesse, to possesse the land of the Amorite.

11 And I raysed vp of your sonnes for Prophets, and of your yong men for Nazarites. Is it not euen thus, O ye children of Israel, sayth the Lord?

12 But ye gaue the Nazarites wine to drinke, and commanded the Prophetes, saying, Prophecie not.

13 Behold, I am pressed vnder you as a cart is pressed that is full of sheaues.

14 Therefore the flight shall perish from the swift, and the strong shall not strengthen his force, neither shall the mightie saue his life.

15 Nor he that handleth the bowe, shall stand, and he that is swift of foote, shall not escape, neyther shall he that rideth the horse, saue his life.

16 And he that is of a mighty courage among the strong men, shall flee away naked in that day, sayth the Lord.

Amos 3

1 Heare this worde that the Lord pronounceth against you, O children of Israel, euen against the whole familie which I brought vp from the land of Egypt, saying,

2 You onely haue I knowen of all the families of the earth: therefore I will visite you for all your iniquities.

3 Can two walke together except they bee agreed?

4 Will a lion roare in ye forest, when he hath no pray? or wil a lions whelpe cry out of his den, if he haue taken nothing?

5 Can a birde fall in a snare vpon the earth, where no fouler is? or will he take vp the snare from the earth, and haue taken nothing at all?

6 Or shall a trumpet be blowen in the citie, and the people be not afraide? or shall there be euil in a citie, and the Lord hath not done it?

7 Surely the Lord God will doe nothing, but he reueileth his secrete vnto his seruantes the Prophets.

8 The lyon hath roared: who will not bee afraide? the Lord God hath spoken: who can but prophecie?

9 Proclayme in the palaces at Ashdod, and in the palaces in the lande of Egypt, and saye, Assemble your selues vpon the mountaines of Samaria: so beholde the great tumultes in the middes thereof, and the oppressed in the middes thereof.

10 For they knowe not to doe right, sayth the Lord: they store vp violence, and robbery in their palaces.

11 Therefore thus saith the Lord God, An aduersary shall come euen rounde about the countrey, and shall bring downe thy strength from thee, and thy palaces shalbe spoyled.

12 Thus saieth the Lord, As the shephearde taketh out of the mouth of

the lyon two legges, or a piece of an eare: so shall the children of Israel be taken out that dwell in Samaria in the corner of a bed, and in Damascus, as in a couche.

13 Heare, and testifie in the house of Iaakob, saith the Lord God, the God of hostes.

14 Surely in the day that I shall visit the transgressions of Israel vpon him, I wil also visite the altars of Beth-el, and the hornes of the altar shall be broken off, and fall to the ground.

15 And I wil smite the winter house with the sommer house, and the houses of yuorie shall perish, and the great houses shalbe consumed, sayth the Lord.

Amos 4

1 Heare this worde, ye kine of Bashan that are in the mountaine of Samaria, which oppresse the poore, and destroy the needie, and they say to their masters, Bring, and let vs drinke.

2 The Lord God hath sworne by his holines, that loe, the dayes shall come vpon you, that hee wil take you away with thornes, and your posteritie with fish hookes.

3 And ye shall goe out at the breaches euery kow forward: and ye shall cast your selues out of the palace, saith the Lord.

4 Come to Beth-el, and transgresse: to Gilgal, and multiplie transgression, and bring your sacrifices in the morning, and your tithes after three yeres.

5 And offer a thankesgiuing of leauen, publish and proclaime the free offrings: for this liketh you, O ye children of Israel, saith the Lord God.

6 And therefore haue I giuen you cleannes of teeth in all your cities, and scarcenesse of bread in all your places, yet haue ye not returned vnto me, saith the Lord.

7 And also I haue withholden the raine from you, when there were yet three moneths to the haruest, and I caused it to raine vpon one citie, and haue not caused it to raine vpon another citie: one piece was rained vpon, and the piece whereupon it rained not, withered.

8 So two or three cities wandred vnto one citie to drinke water, but they were not satisfied: yet haue ye not returned vnto me, saith the Lord.

9 I haue smitten you with blasting, and mildewe: your great gardens and your vineyardes, and your figtrees, and your oliue trees did the palmer worme deuoure: yet haue ye not returned vnto me, saith the Lord.

10 Pestilence haue I sent among you, after the maner of Egypt: your yong men haue I slaine with the sworde, and haue taken away your horses: and I haue made the stinke of your tentes to come vp euen into your nostrels: yet haue yee not returned vnto me, saith the Lord.

11 I haue ouerthrowe you, as God ouerthrew Sodom and Gomorah: and ye were as a firebrand pluckt out of the burning: yet haue ye not returned vnto me, saith the Lord.

12 Therefore, thus wil I do vnto thee, O Israel: and because I wil doe this vnto thee, prepare to meete thy God, O Israel.

13 For lo, he that formeth the mountaines, and createth the winde, and declareth vnto man what is his thought: which maketh the morning darkenesse, and walketh vpon the hie places of the earth, the Lord God of hostes is his Name.

Amos 5

1 Heare ye this worde, which I lift vp vpon you, euen a lamentation of the house of Israel.

2 The virgine Israel is fallen, and shall no more rise: shee is left vpon her lande, and there is none to raise her vp.

3 For thus saith ye Lord God, The citie which went out by a thousand, shall leaue an hundreth: and that which went forth by an hundreth, shall leaue ten to the house of Israel.

4 For thus saith the Lord vnto the house of Israel, Seeke ye me, and ye shall liue.

5 But seeke not Beth-el, nor enter into Gilgal, and go not to Beer-sheba: for Gilgal shall goe into captiuitie, and Beth-el shall come to nought.

6 Seeke the Lord, and yee shall liue, least he breake out like fire in the house of Ioseph and deuoure it, and there be none to quench it in Beth-el.

7 They turne iudgement to wormewood, and leaue off righteousnes in the earth.

8 He maketh Pleiades, and Orion, and he turneth the shadowe of death into the morning, and he maketh the day darke as night: he calleth the waters of the sea, and powreth them out vpon the open earth: the Lord is his Name.

9 He strengtheneth the destroyer against the mightie: and the destroyer shall come against the fortresse.

10 They haue hated him, that rebuked in the gate: and they abhorred him that speaketh vprightly.

11 Forasmuch then as your treading is vpon the poore, and yee take from him burdens of wheate, ye haue built houses of hewen stone, but ye shall not dwel in them: ye haue plated pleasant vineyards, but ye shall not drinke wine of them.

12 For I know your manifold transgressions, and your mightie sinnes: they afflict the iust, they take rewards, and they oppresse the poore in ye gate.

13 Therefore the prudent shall keepe silence in that time, for it is an euill time.

14 Seeke good and not euil, that ye may liue: and the Lord God of hostes shalbe with you, as you haue spoken.

15 Hate the euil, and loue the good, and establish iudgement in the gate: it may bee that the Lord God of hostes will be mercifull vnto the remnant of Ioseph.

16 Therfore the Lord God of hosts, the Lord saith thus, Mourning shalbe in all streetes: and they shall say in al the hie wayes, Alas, alas: and they shall call the husbandman to lamentation, and such as can mourne, to mourning.

17 And in al the vines shalbe lamentation: for I wil passe through thee, saith the Lord.

18 Woe vnto you, that desire the day of the Lord: what haue you to do with it? the day of the Lord is darkenes and not light.

19 As if a man did flee from a lyon, and a beare met him: or went into the house, and leaned his hand on the wall, and a serpent bit him.

20 Shal not the day of the Lord be darkenes, and not light? euen darkenes and no light in it?

21 I hate and abhorre your feast dayes, and I wil not smelll in your solemne assemblies.

22 Though ye offer me burnt offrings and meat offrings, I wil not accept them: neither will I regard the peace offrings of your fat beasts.

23 Take thou away from me the multitude of thy songs (for I wil not heare the melodie of thy violes)

24 And let iudgement runne downe as waters, and righteousnesse as a mightie riuer.

25 Haue ye offered vnto me sacrifices and offrings in the wildernesse fourtie yeeres, O house of Israel?

26 But you haue borne Siccuth your King, and Chiun your images, and the starre of your gods, which ye made to your selues.

27 Therefore wil I cause you to goe into captiuitie beyond Damascus, saith the Lord, whose Name is the God of hostes.

Amos 6

1 Woe to them that are at ease in Zion and trust in the moutaine of Samaria, which were famous at the beginning of the nations: and the house of Israel came to them.

2 Goe you vnto Calneh, and see: and from thence goe you to Hamath the great: then goe downe to Gath of the Philistims: be they better then these kingdomes? or the border of their land greater then your border,

3 Ye that put farre away the euill day, and approch to the seate of iniquitie?

4 They lie vpon beddes of yuorie, and stretch themselues vpon their beddes, and eate the lambes of the flocke, and the calues out of the stall.

5 They sing to the sounde of the viole: they inuent to themselues instruments of musike like Dauid.

6 They drinke wine in bowles, and anoynt themselues with the chiefe ointments, but no man is sory for the affliction of Ioseph.

7 Therefore nowe shall they go captiue with the first that go captiue, and the sorow of them that stretched themselues, is at hand.

8 The Lord God hath sworne by himselfe, saith the Lord God of hostes, I abhorre the excellencie of Iaakob, and hate his palaces: therefore wil I deliuer vp the citie with all that is therein.

9 And if there remaine ten men in one house, they shall die.

10 And his vncle shall take him vp and burne him to cary out the bones out of the house, and shall say vnto him, that is by ye sides of the house, Is there yet any with thee? And he shall say, None. Then shall he say, Holde thy tongue: for we may not remember the Name of the Lord.

11 For behold, the Lord commandeth, and he will smite the great house with breaches, and the litle house with clefts.

12 Shal horses runne vpon the rocke? or wil one plowe there with oxen? for yee haue turned iudgement into gall, and the fruite of righteousnes into wormewood.

13 Ye reioyce in a thing of nought: yee say, Haue not wee gotten vs hornes by our owne strength?

14 But behold, I wil raise vp against you a nation, O house of Israel, sayeth the Lord God of hostes: and they shall afflict you, from the entring in of Hamath vnto the riuer of the wildernes.

Amos 7

1 Thus hath the Lord God shewed vnto mee, and beholde, he formed grashoppers in the beginning of ye shooting vp of the latter grouth: and loe, it was in the latter grouth after the Kings mowing.

2 And when they had made an ende of eating the grasse of the land, then I saide, O Lord God, spare, I beseeche thee: who shall raise vp Iaakob? for he is small.

3 So the Lord repented for this. It shall not be, saith the Lord.

4 Thus also hath the Lord God shewed vnto me, and behold, the Lord God called to iudgement by fire, and it deuoured the great deepe, and did eate vp a part.

5 Then said I, O Lord God, cease, I beseeche thee: who shall raise vp Iaakob? for he is small.

6 So the Lord repented for this. This also shall not be, saith the Lord God.

7 Thus againe he shewed me, and behold, the Lord stoode vpon a wall made by line with a line in his hand.

8 And the Lord saide vnto me, Amos, what seest thou? And I said, A line. Then said the Lord, Beholde, I wil set a line in the middes of my people Israel, and wil passe by them no more.

9 And the hye places of Izhak shalbe desolate, and the temples of Israel shalbe destroyed: and I wil rise against the house of Ieroboam with the sworde.

10 Then Amaziah the Priest of Beth-el sent to Ieroboam King of Israel, saying, Amos hath conspired against thee in the middes of the house of Israel: the lande is not able to beare all his wordes.

11 For thus Amos saith, Ieroboam shall die by the sworde, and Israel shalbe led away captiue out of their owne land.

12 Also Amaziah sayde vnto Amos, O thou the Seer, goe, flee thou away into the land of Iudah, and there eate thy bread and prophecie there.

13 But prophecie no more at Beth-el: for it is the Kings chappel, and it is the Kings court.

14 Then answered Amos, and said to Amaziah, I was no Prophet, neither was I a prophets sonne, but I was an herdman, and a gatherer of wilde figs.

15 And the Lord tooke me as I followed the flocke, and the Lord said vnto me, Go, prophecie vnto my people Israel.

16 Now therefore heare thou the word of the Lord. Thou sayest, Prophecie not against Israel, and speake nothing against the house of Izhak.

17 Therefore thus sayth the Lord, Thy wife shall be an harlot in the citie, and thy sonnes and thy daughters shall fall by the sword, and thy land shall be deuided by line: and thou shalt die in a polluted land, and Israel shall surely go into captiuitie forth of his land.

Amos 8

1 Thus hath the Lord God shewed vnto me, and behold, a basket of summer fruite.

2 And he said, Amos, what seest thou? And I sayd, A basket of sommer fruite. Then sayd the Lord vnto me, The ende is come vpon my people of Israel, I wil passe by them no more.

3 And the songs of the Temple shalbe howlings in that day, saith the Lord God: many dead bodies shalbe in euery place: they shall cast them forth with silence.

4 Heare this, O yee that swallowe vp the poore, that ye may make the needie of the lande to fayle,

5 Saying, When will the newe moneth bee gone, that we may sell corne? and the Sabbath, that we may set forth wheate, and make the Ephah small, and the shekel great, and falsifie the weights by deceit?

6 That we may buy the poore for siluer, and the needie for shooes: yea, and sell the refuse of the wheate.

7 The Lord hath sworne by the excellencie of Iaakob, Surely I will neuer forget any of their workes.

8 Shall not the lande tremble for this, and euery one mourne, that dwelleth therein? and it shall rise vp wholy as a flood, and it shall bee cast out, and drowned as by the flood of Egypt.

9 And in that day, saith the Lord God, I will euen cause the sunne to go downe at noone: and I will darken the earth in the cleare day.

10 And I will turne your feastes into mourning, and all your songs into lamentation: and I will bring sackcloth vpon all loynes, and baldnes vpon euery head: and I will make it as the mourning of an onely sonne, and the ende thereof as a bitter day.

11 Beholde, the dayes come, sayeth the Lord God, that I will send a famine in the lande, not a famine of bread, nor a thirst for water, but of hearing the word of the Lord.

12 And they shall wander from sea to sea, and from the North euen vnto the East shall they run to and fro to seeke the worde of the Lord, and shall not finde it.

13 In that day shall the faire virgines and the yong men perish for thirst.

14 They that sweare by the sinne of Samaria, and that say, Thy God, O Dan, liueth, and the maner of Beer-sheba liueth, euen they shall fall, and neuer rise vp againe.

Amos 9

1 I sawe the Lord standing vpon the altar, and he sayde, Smite the lintel of the doore, that the postes may shake: and cut them in pieces, euen the heads of them all, and I will slay the last of them with the sword: he that fleeth of them, shall not flee away: and he that escapeth of them, shall not be deliuered.

2 Though they digge into the hell, thence shall mine hande take them: though they clime vp to heauen, thence will I bring them downe.

3 And though they hide them selues in the toppe of Carmel, I will search and take them out thence: and though they be hid from my sight in the bottome of the sea, thence will I commande the serpent, and he shall bite them.

4 And though they goe into captiuitie before their enemies, thence wil I commande the sword, and it shall slay them: and I will set mine eyes vpon them for euill, and not for good.

5 And the Lord God of hosts shall touch the land, and it shall melt away, and al that dwel therein shall mourne, and it shall rise vp wholy like a flood, and shall bee drowned as by the flood of Egypt.

6 He buildeth his spheres in the heauen, and hath laide the foundation of his globe of elements in the earth: hee calleth the waters of the sea, and powreth them out vpon the open earth: the Lord is his Name.

7 Are ye not as the Ethiopians vnto mee, O children of Israel, sayeth the Lord? haue not I brought vp Israel out of the land of Egypt? and the Philistims from Caphtor, and Aram from Kir?

8 Beholde, the eyes of the Lord God are vpon the sinfull kingdome, and I will destroy it cleane out of the earth. Neuerthelesse I will not vtterly destroy the house of Iaakob, saith the Lord.

9 For loe, I will command and I will sift the house of Israel among all nations, like as corne is sifted in a sieue: yet shall not the least stone fall vpon the earth.

10 But all the sinners of my people shall dye by the sword, which say, The euill shall not come, nor hasten for vs.

11 In that day will I raise vp the tabernacle of Dauid, that is fallen downe, and close vp the breaches therof, and I will rayse vp his ruines, and I will builde it, as in the dayes of olde,

12 That they may possesse the remnant of Edom, and of all the heathen, because my Name is called vpon them, sayeth the Lord, that doeth this.

13 Behold, the dayes come, saith the Lord, that the plowman shall touche the mower, and the treader of grapes him that soweth seede: and the mountaines

shall drop sweete wine, and all the hilles shall melt.

14 And I will bring againe the captiuitie of my people of Israel: and they shall build the waste cities, and inhabite the, and they shall plant vineyardes, and drinke the wine thereof: they shall also make gardens, and eate the fruites of them.

15 And I wil plant them vpon their land, and they shall no more bee pulled vp againe out of their lande, which I haue giuen them, sayeth the Lord thy God.

Obadiah

Obadiah 1

1 The vision of Obadiah. Thus saith the Lord God against Edom, We haue heard a rumour from the Lord, and an ambassadour is sent among the heathen: arise, and let vs rise vp against her to battel.

2 Beholde, I haue made thee small among the heathen: thou art vtterly despised.

3 The pride of thine heart hath deceiued thee: thou that dwellest in the cleftes of the rockes, whose habitation is hie, that saith in his heart, Who shall bring me downe to the ground?

4 Though thou exalt thy selfe as the eagle, and make thy nest among the starres, thence will I bring thee downe, sayth the Lord.

5 Came theeues to thee or robbers by night? howe wast thou brought to silence? woulde they not haue stolen, til they had ynough? if the grape gatherers came to thee, woulde they not leaue some grapes?

6 Howe are the things of Esau sought vp, and his treasures searched?

7 All the men of thy confederacie haue driuen thee to ye borders: the men that were at peace with thee, haue deceiued thee, and preuailed against thee: they that eate thy bread, haue laid a wound vnder thee: there is none vnderstanding in him.

8 Shall not I in that day, saith the Lord, euen destroy the wise men out of Edom, and vnderstanding from the mount of Esau?

9 And thy strong men, O Teman, shall bee afraide, because euery one of the mount of Esau shalbe cut off by slaughter.

10 For thy crueltie against thy brother Iaakob, shame shall couer thee, and thou shalt be cut off for euer.

11 When thou stoodest on the other side, in the day that the strangers caried away his substance, and straungers entred into his gates, and cast lots vpon Ierusalem, euen thou wast as one of them.

12 But thou shouldest not haue beholden the day of thy brother, in the day that hee was made a stranger, neither shouldest thou haue reioyced ouer the children of Iudah, in the day of their destruction: thou shouldest not

haue spoken proudly in the day of affliction.

13 Thou shouldest not haue entred into the gate of my people, in the day of their destruction, neither shouldest thou haue once looked on their affliction in the day of their destruction, nor haue layde hands on their substance in the day of their destruction.

14 Neyther shouldest thou haue stande in the crosse wayes to cut off them, that shoulde escape, neither shouldest thou haue shut vp the remnant thereof in the day of affliction.

15 For the day of the Lord is neere, vpon all the heathen: as thou hast done, it shall bee done to thee: thy reward shall returne vpon thine head.

16 For as yee haue drunke vpon mine holy Mountaine, so shall all the heathen drinke continually: yea, they shall drinke and swallow vp, and they shalbe as though they had not bene.

17 But vpon mount Zion shalbe deliuerance, and it shalbe holy, and the house of Iaakob shall possesse their possessions,

18 And the house of Iaakob shalbe a fire, and the house of Ioseph a flame, and the house of Esau as stubble, and they shall kindle in them and deuoure them: and there shall bee no remnant of the house of Esau for the Lord hath spoken it.

19 And they shall possesse the South side of the mount of Esau, and the plaine of the Philistims: and they shall possesse the fieldes of Ephraim, and the fieldes of Samaria, and Beniamin shall haue Gilead.

20 And the captiuitie of this host of the children of Israel, which were among the Canaanites, shall possesse vnto Zarephath, and the captiuitie of Ierusalem, which is in Sepharad, shall possesse the cities of the South.

21 And they that shall saue, shall come vp to mount Zion to iudge the mount of Esau, and the kingdome shalbe the Lords.

Jonah

Jonah 1

1 The worde of the Lord came also vnto Ionah the sonne of Amittai, saying,

2 Arise, and goe to Nineueh, that great citie, and crye against it: for their wickednesse is come vp before mee.

3 But Ionah rose vp to flee into Tarshish from the presence of the Lord, and went downe to Iapho: and he founde a ship going to Tarshish: so he payed the fare thereof, and went downe into it, that he might go with them vnto Tarshish, from the presence of the Lord.

4 But the Lord sent out a great winde into the sea, and there was a mightie tempest in the sea, so that the ship was like to be broken.

5 Then the mariners were afraide, and cryed euery man vnto his God, and cast the wares that were in the ship, into the sea to lighten it of the: but Ionah was

gone downe into the sides of the ship, and he lay downe, and was fast a sleepe.

6 So the shipmaster came to him, and saide vnto him, What meanest thou, O sleeper? Arise, call vpon thy God, if so be that God wil thinke vpon vs, that we perish not.

7 And they saide euery one to his fellowe, Come, and let vs cast lottes, that we may know, for whose cause this euill is vpon vs. So they cast lottes, and the lot fell vpon Ionah.

8 Then said they vnto him, Tell vs for whose cause this euill is vpon vs? what is thine occupation? and whence commest thou? which is thy countrey? and of what people art thou?

9 And he answered them, I am an Ebrewe, and I feare the Lord God of heauen, which hath made the sea, and the dry lande.

10 Then were the men exceedingly afrayde, and said vnto him, Why hast thou done this? (for the men knewe, that he fled from the presence of the Lord, because he had tolde them)

11 Then saide they vnto him, What shall we doe vnto thee, that the sea may be calme vnto vs? (for the sea wrought and was troublous)

12 And he said vnto them, Take me, and cast me into the sea: so shall the sea be calme vnto you: for I knowe that for my sake this great tempest is vpon you.

13 Neuerthelesse, the men rowed to bring it to the lande, but they coulde not: for the sea wrought, and was troublous against them.

14 Wherefore they cryed vnto the Lord, and said, We beseech thee, O Lord, we beseech thee, let vs not perish for this mans life, and lay not vpon vs innocent blood: for thou, O Lord, hast done, as it pleased thee.

15 So they tooke vp Ionah, and cast him into the sea, and the sea ceased from her raging.

16 Then the men feared the Lord exceedingly, and offered a sacrifice vnto the Lord, and made vowes.

17 Nowe the Lord had prepared a great fish to swallowe vp Ionah: and Ionah was in the belly of the fish three dayes, and three nightes.

Jonah 2

1 Then Ionah prayed vnto the Lord his God out of the fishes belly,

2 And said, I cryed in mine affliction vnto the Lord, and he heard me: out of the bellie of hell cryed I, and thou heardest my voyce.

3 For thou haddest cast me into the bottome in the middes of the sea, and the floods compassed me about: all thy surges, and all thy waues passed ouer me.

4 Then I saide, I am cast away out of thy sight: yet will I looke againe towarde thine holy Temple.

5 The waters compassed me about vnto the soule: the depth closed me rounde about, and the weedes were wrapt about mine head.

6 I went downe to the bottome of the moutaines: the earth with her barres was about me for euer, yet hast thou brought vp my life from the pit, O Lord my God.

7 When my soule fainted within me, I remembred the Lord: and my prayer came vnto thee, into thine holy Temple.

8 They that waite vpon lying vanities, forsake their owne mercie.

9 But I will sacrifice vnto thee with the voice of thankesgiuing, and will pay that that I haue vowed: saluation is of the Lord.

10 And the Lord spake vnto the fish, and it cast out Ionah vpon the dry lande.

Jonah 3

1 And the worde of the Lord came vnto Ionah the seconde time, saying,

2 Arise, goe vnto Nineueh that great citie, and preach vnto it the preaching, which I bid thee.

3 So Ionah arose and went to Nineueh according to ye word of the Lord: now Nineueh was a great and excellent citie of three dayes iourney.

4 And Ionah began to enter into the citie a dayes iourney, and he cryed, and said, Yet fourtie dayes, and Nineueh shalbe ouerthrowen.

5 So the people of Nineueh beleeued God, and proclaimed a fast, and put on sackcloth from ye greatest of the euen to the least of them.

6 For worde came vnto the King of Nineueh, and he rose from his throne, and he layed his robe from him, and couered him with sackecloth, and sate in ashes.

7 And he proclaimed and said through Nineueh, (by the counsell of ye king and his nobles) saying, Let neither man, nor beast, bullock nor sheep taste any thing, neither feed nor drinke water.

8 But let man and beast put on sackecloth, and crie mightily vnto God: yea, let euery man turne from his euill way, and from the wickednesse that is in their handes.

9 Who can tell if God will turne, and repent and turne away from his fierce wrath, that we perish not?

10 And God sawe their workes that they turned from their euill wayes: and God repented of the euill that he had said that he woulde doe vnto them, and he did it not.

Jonah 4

1 Therefore it displeased Ionah exceedingly, and he was angry.

2 And he prayed vnto the Lord, and saide, I pray thee, O Lord, was not this my saying, when I was yet in my countrey? therefore I preuented it to flee vnto Tarshish: for I knewe that thou art a gratious God, and merciful, slow to anger, and of great kindnes, and repentest thee of the euill.

3 Therefore nowe O Lord, take, I beseech thee, my life from me: for it is better for me to die then to liue.

4 Then saide the Lord, Doest thou well to be angry?

5 So Ionah went out of the citie and sate on the East side of the citie, and there made him a boothe, and sate vnder it in the shadowe till he might see what should be done in the citie.

6 And the Lord God prepared a gourde, and made it to come vp ouer Ionah, that it might be a shadowe ouer his head and deliuer him from his griefe. So Ionah was exceeding glad of the gourde.

7 But God prepared a worme when the morning rose the next day, and it smote the gourd, that it withered.

8 And when the sunne did arise, God prepared also a feruent East winde: and the sunne beat vpon the head of Ionah, that he fainted, and wished in his heart to die, and said, It is better for me to dye, then to liue.

9 And God said vnto Ionah, Doest thou well to be angrie for the gourde? And he said, I doe well to be angrie vnto the death.

10 Then said the Lord, Thou hast had pitie on the gourde for the which thou hast not laboured, neither madest it growe, which came vp in a night, and perished in a night,

11 And shoulde not I spare Nineueh that great citie, wherein are sixe score thousande persons, that cannot discerne betweene their right hand, and their left hand, and also much cattell?

Micah

Micah 1

1 The word of the Lord, that came vnto Micah the Morashite in the dayes of Iotham, Ahaz, and Hezekiah Kings of Iudah, which he sawe concerning Samaria, and Ierusalem.

2 Heare, al ye people: hearke thou, O earth, and all that therein is, and let the Lord God be witnes against you, euen ye Lord from his holy Teple.

3 For beholde, the Lord commeth out of his place, and will come downe, and tread vpon the hie places of the earth.

4 And the mountaines shall melt vnder him (so shall the valleys cleaue) as waxe before the fire, and as the waters that are powred downewarde.

5 For the wickednes of Iaakob is all this, and for the sinnes of the house of Israel: what is the wickednes of Iaakob? Is not Samaria? and which are the hie places of Iudah? Is not Ierusalem?

6 Therefore I wil make Samaria as an heape of the fielde, and for the planting of a vineyard, and I will cause the stones thereof to tumble downe into the valley, and I will discouer the foundations thereof.

7 And all the grauen images thereof shalbe broken, and all the giftes thereof shalbe burnt with the fire, and all the idoles thereof will I destroy: for she gathered it of the hire of an harlot, and they shall returne to the wages of an harlot.

8 Therefore I will mourne and howle: I wil goe without clothes, and naked: I will make lamentation like the dragons, and mourning as the ostriches.

9 For her plagues are grieuous: for it is come into Iudah: the enemie is come vnto the gate of my people, vnto Ierusalem.

10 Declare ye it not at Gath, neither weepe ye: for the house of Aphrah roule thy selfe in the dust.

11 Thou that dwellest at Shaphir, go together naked with shame: she that dwelleth at Zaanan, shall not come forth in ye mourning of Beth-ezel: the enemie shall receiue of you for his standing.

12 For the inhabitant of Maroth wayted for good, but euill came from the Lord vnto the gate of Ierusalem.

13 O thou inhabitant of Lachish, binde the charet to the beastes of price: she is the beginning of the sinne to the daughter of Zion: for the transgressions of Israel were found in thee.

14 Therefore shalt thou giue presents to Moresheth Gath: the houses of Achzib shalbe as a lye to the Kings of Israel.

15 Yet will I bring an heire vnto thee, O inhabitant of Mareshah, he shall come vnto Adullam, the glorie of Israel.

16 Make thee balde: and shaue thee for thy delicate children: enlarge thy baldenesse as the eagle, for they are gone into captiuity from thee.

Micah 2

1 Woe vnto them, that imagine iniquitie, and worke wickednesse vpon their beddes: when the morning is light they practise it because their hande hath power.

2 And they couet fields, and take them by violence, and houses, and take them away: so they oppresse a man and his house, euen man and his heritage.

3 Therefore thus saieth the Lord, Beholde, against this familie haue I deuised a plague, whereout yee shall not plucke your neckes, and ye shall not go so proudly, for this time is euill.

4 In that daye shall they take vp a parable against you, and lament with a dolefull lamentation, and say, We be vtterly wasted: hee hath changed the portion of my people: how hath he taken it away to restore it vnto mee? he hath deuided our fieldes.

5 Therefore thou shalt haue none that shall cast a corde by lot in the Congregation of the Lord.

6 They that prophecied, Prophecie ye not. They shall not prophecie to them, neither shall they take shame.

7 O thou that art named of the house of Iaakob, is the Spirite of the Lord shortened? are these his workes? are not my wordes good vnto him that walketh vprightly?

8 But hee that was yesterday my people, is risen vp on the other side, as against an enemie: they spoyle the beautifull garment from them that passe by peaceably, as though they returned from the warre.

9 The women of my people haue ye cast out from their pleasant houses, and from their childre haue ye taken away my glorie continually.

10 Arise and depart, for this is not your rest: because it is polluted, it shall destroy you, euen with a sore destruction.

11 If a man walke in the Spirit, and would lie falsely, saying, I wil prophecie vnto thee of wine, and of strong drinke, he shall euen be the prophet of this people.

12 I will surely gather thee wholy, O Iaakob: I will surely gather the remnant of Israel: I will put them together as the sheepe of Bozrah, euen as the flocke in the mids of their folde: the cities shall be full of brute of the men.

13 The breaker vp shall come vp before them: they shall breake out, and passe by the gate, and goe out by it, and their King shall goe before them, and the Lord shalbe vpon their heades.

Micah 3

1 And I sayd, Heare, I pray you, O heads of Iaakob, and yee princes of the house of Israel: should not ye knowe iudgement?

2 But they hate the good, and loue the euill: they plucke off their skinnes from them, and their flesh from their bones.

3 And they eate also the flesh of my people, and flay off their skinne from them, and they breake their bones, and chop them in pieces, as for the pot, and as flesh within the caldron.

4 Then shall they crye vnto the Lord, but he will not heare them: he wil euen hide his face from them at that time, because they haue done wickedly in their workes.

5 Thus saith the Lord, Concerning the prophets that deceiue my people, and bite them with their teeth, and cry peace, but if a man put not into their mouthes, they prepare warre against him,

6 Therefore night shalbe vnto you for a vision, and darkenesse shalbe vnto you for a diuination, and the sunne shall goe downe ouer the prophets, and the day shalbe darke ouer them.

7 Then shall the Seers bee ashamed, and the southsayers confounded: yea, they shall all couer their lippes, for they haue none answere of God.

8 Yet notwithstanding I am full of power by the Spirite of the Lord, and of iudgement, and of strength to declare vnto Iaakob his transgression, and to Israel his sinne.

9 Heare this, I pray you, ye heades of the house of Iaakob, and princes of the house of Israel: they abhorre iudgement, and peruert all equitie.

10 They build vp Zion with blood, and Ierusalem with iniquitie.

11 The heads thereof iudge for rewardes, and the Priestes thereof teache for hyre, and the prophets thereof prophecie for money: yet wil they leane vpon the Lord, and say, Is not the Lord among vs? no euill can come vpon vs.

12 Therefore shall Zion for your sake bee plowed as a field, and Ierusalem shalbe an heape, and the mountaine of the house, as the hye places of the forest.

Micah 4

1 But in the last dayes it shall come to passe, that the mountaine of the House of the Lord shall be prepared in the toppe of the mountaines, and it shall bee exalted aboue the hilles, and people shall flowe vnto it.

2 Yea, many nations shall come and say, Come, and let vs goe vp to the Mountaine of the Lord, and to the House of the God of Iaakob, and hee will teache vs his wayes, and we wil walke in his pathes: for the Lawe shall goe forth of Zion, and the worde of the Lord from Ierusalem.

3 And he shall iudge among many people, and rebuke mightie nations a farre off, and they shall breake their swordes into mattockes, and their speares into sithes: nation shall not lift vp a sword against nation, neither shall they learne to fight any more.

4 But they shall sit euery man vnder his vine, and vnder his figge tree, and none shall make them afraid: for the mouth of the Lord of hostes hath spoken it.

5 For all people will walke euery one in the name of his God, and we will walke in the Name of the Lord our God, for euer and euer.

6 At the same day, saith the Lord, will I gather her that halteth, and I will gather her that is cast out, and her that I haue afflicted.

7 And I will make her that halted, a remnant, and her that was cast farre off, a mightie nation: and the Lord shall reigne ouer them in Mount Zion, from hence forth euen for euer.

8 And thou, O towre of the flock, the strong holde of the daughter Zion, vnto thee shall it come, euen the first dominion, and kingdome shall come to the daughter Ierusalem.

9 Nowe why doest thou crie out with lamentation? is there no King in thee? is thy counseller perished? for sorowe hath taken thee, as a woman in trauaile.

10 Sorow and mourne, O daughter Zion, like a woman in trauaile: for nowe shalt thou goe foorth of the citie, and dwel in the field, and shalt goe into Babel, but there shalt thou be deliuered: there the Lord shall redeeme thee from the hand of thine enemies.

11 Nowe also many nations are gathered against thee, saying, Zion shalbe condemned and our eye shall looke vpon Zion.

12 But they knowe not the thoughtes of the Lord: they vnderstand not his counsell, for he shall gather them as the sheaues in the barne.

13 Arise, and thresh, O daughter Zion: for I will make thine horne yron, and I will make thine hooues brasse, and thou shalt breake in pieces many people: and I will consecrate their riches vnto the

Lord, and their substance vnto the ruler of the whole worlde.

Micah 5

1 Nowe assemble thy garisons, O daughter of garisons: he hath layed siege against vs: they shall smite the iudge of Israel with a rod vpon the cheeke.

2 And thou Beth-leem Ephrathah art litle to bee among the thousandes of Iudah, yet out of thee shall he come forth vnto me, that shalbe the ruler in Israel: whose goings forth haue bene from the beginning and from euerlasting.

3 Therefore will he giue them vp, vntill the time that shee which shall beare, shall trauaile: then the remnant of their brethren shall returne vnto the children of Israel.

4 And he shall stand, and feed in the strength of the Lord, and in the maiestie of the Name of the Lord his God, and they shall dwel still: for now shall he be magnified vnto the ends of the world.

5 And hee shall be our peace when Asshur shall come into our lande: when he shall tread in our palaces, then shall we raise against him seuen shepheardes, and eight principall men.

6 And they shall destroy Asshur with the sword, and the land of Nimrod with their swordes: thus shall he deliuer vs from Asshur, when hee commeth into our lande, and when he shall tread within our borders.

7 And the remnant of Iaakob shalbe among many people, as a dewe from the Lord, and as the showres vpon the grasse, that waiteth not for man, nor hopeth in the sonnes of Adam.

8 And the remnant of Iaakob shalbe among the Gentiles in the middes of many people, as the lyon among the beastes of the forest, and as the lyons whelpe among the flockes of sheepe, who when he goeth thorow, treadeth downe and teareth in pieces, and none can deliuer.

9 Thine hand shall bee lift vp vpon thine aduersaries, and all thine enemies shalbe cut off.

10 And it shall come to passe in that day, sayth the Lord, that I will cut off thine horses out of the middes of thee, and I will destroy thy charets.

11 And I will cut off the cities of thy land, and ouerthrowe all thy strong holdes.

12 And I will cut off thine enchanters out of thine hande: and thou shalt haue no more southsayers.

13 Thine idoles also will I cut off, and thine images out of the middes of thee: and thou shalt no more worship the woorke of thine hands.

14 And I wil plucke vp thy groues out of the middes of thee: so will I destroy thine enemies.

15 And I will execute a vegeance in my wrath and indignation vpon the heathen, which they haue not heard.

Micah 6

1 Hearken ye nowe what the Lord sayth, Arise thou, and contende before the mountaines, and let the hilles heare thy voyce.

2 Heare ye, O mountaynes, the Lordes quarel, and ye mightie foundations of the earth: for the Lord hath a quarell against his people, and he will pleade with Israel.

3 O my people, what haue I done vnto thee? or wherin haue I grieued thee? testifie against me.

4 Surely I brought thee vp out of the land of Egypt, and redeemed thee out of the house of seruants, and I haue sent before thee, Moses, Aaron, and Miriam.

5 O my people, remember nowe what Balak King of Moab had deuised, and what Balaam the sonne of Beor answered him, from Shittim vnto Gilgal, that ye may knowe the righteousnes of the Lord.

6 Wherewith shall I come before the Lord, and bowe my selfe before the hie God? Shall I come before him with burnt offrings, and with calues of a yeere olde?

7 Will the Lord be pleased with thousands of rams, or with ten thousand riuers of oyle? shall I giue my first borne for my transgression, euen the fruite of my bodie, for the sinne of my soule?

8 He hath shewed thee, O man, what is good, and what the Lord requireth of thee: surely to doe iustly, and to loue mercie, and to humble thy selfe, to walke with thy God.

9 The Lordes voyce cryeth vnto the citie, and the man of wisedome shall see thy name: Heare the rodde, and who hath appoynted it.

10 Are yet the treasures of wickednes in the house of the wicked, and the scant measure, that is abominable?

11 Shall I iustifie the wicked balances, and the bag of deceitfull weightes?

12 For the rich men thereof are full of crueltie, and the inhabitants thereof haue spoken lyes, and their tongue is deceitfull in their mouth.

13 Therefore also will I make thee sicke in smiting thee, and in making thee desolate, because of thy sinnes.

14 Thou shalt eate and not be satisfied, and thy casting downe shall be in the mids of thee, and thou shalt take holde, but shalt not deliuer: and that which thou deliuerest, will I giue vp to the sworde.

15 Thou shalt sowe, but not reape: thou shalt treade the oliues, but thou shalt not anoint thee with oyle, and make sweete wine, but shalt not drinke wine.

16 For the statutes of Omri are kept, and all the maner of the house of Ahab, and ye walke in their counsels, that I should make thee waste, and the inhabitants thereof an hissing: therefore ye shall beare the reproche of my people.

Micah 7

1 Woe is me, for I am as the sommer gatherings, and as the grapes of the vintage: there is no cluster to eate: my soule desired the first ripe fruites.

2 The good man is perished out of the earth, and there is none righteous among men: they all lye in wayte for blood: euery man hunteth his brother with a net.

3 To make good for the euil of their hands, the prince asked, and the iudge iudgeth for a reward: therefore the great man he speaketh out the corruption of his soule: so they wrapt it vp.

4 The best of them is as a brier, and the most righteous of them is sharper then a thorne hedge: the day of thy watchmen and thy visitation commeth: then shalbe their confusion.

5 Trust ye not in a friend, neither put ye confidence in a counseller: keepe the doores of thy mouth from her that lyeth in thy bosome.

6 For the sonne reuileth the father: ye daughter riseth vp against her mother: the daughter in lawe against her mother in lawe, and a mans enemies are the men of his owne house.

7 Therefore I will looke vnto the Lord: I will waite for God my Sauiour: my God will heare me.

8 Reioyce not against me, O mine enemie: though I fall, I shall arise: when I shall sit in darkenesse, the Lord shalbe a light vnto me.

9 I will beare the wrath of the Lord because I haue sinned against him, vntill he pleade my cause, and execute iudgement for me: then will he bring me foorth to the light, and I shall see his righteousnesse.

10 Then she that is mine enemie, shall looke vpon it, and shame shall couer her, which said vnto me, Where is the Lord thy God? Mine eyes shall behold her: now shall she be troden downe as the myre of the streetes.

11 This is ye day, that thy walles shalbe built: this day shall driue farre away the decree.

12 In this day also they shall come vnto thee from Asshur, and from the strong cities, and from the strong holdes euen vnto the riuer, and from Sea to Sea, and from mountaine to mountaine.

13 Notwithstanding, the lande shall be desolate because of them that dwell therein, and for the fruites of their inuentions.

14 Feed thy people with thy rod, the flocke of thine heritage (which dwell solitarie in the wood) as in the middes of Carmel: let them feede in Bashan and Gilead, as in olde time.

15 According to the dayes of thy comming out of the lande of Egypt, will I shewe vnto him marueilous things.

16 The nations shall see, and be confounded for all their power: they shall lay their hande vpon their mouth: their eares shall be deafe.

17 They shall licke the dust like a serpent: they shall mooue out of their holes like wormes: they shalbe afraide of the Lord our God, and shall feare because of thee.

18 Who is a God like vnto thee, that taketh away iniquitie, and passeth by the transgression of the remnant of his heritage! He reteineth not his wrath for euer, because mercie pleaseth him.

19 He will turne againe, and haue compassion vpon vs: he will subdue our iniquities, and cast all their sinnes into the bottome of the sea.

20 Thou wilt perfourme thy trueth to Iaakob, and mercie to Abraham, as thou hast sworne vnto our fathers in olde time.

Nahum

Nahum 1

1 The burden of Nineueh. The booke of the vision of Nahum the Elkeshite.

2 God is ielous, and the Lord reuengeth: the Lord reuengeth: euen the Lord of anger, the Lord will take vengeance on his aduersaries, and he reserueth wrath for his enemies.

3 The Lord is slow to anger, but he is great in power, and will not surely cleare the wicked: the Lord hath his way in ye whirlewind, and in the storme, and the cloudes are the dust of his feete.

4 He rebuketh the sea, and dryeth it, and he dryeth vp all the riuers: Bashan is wasted and Carmel, and the floure of Lebanon is wasted.

5 The mountaines tremble for him, and the hilles melt, and the earth is burnt at his sight, yea, the worlde, and all that dwell therein.

6 Who can stande before his wrath? or who can abide in the fiercenesse of his wrath? his wrath is powred out like fire, and the rockes are broken by him.

7 The Lord is good and as a strong hold in the day of trouble, and he knoweth them that trust in him.

8 But passing ouer as with a flood, he will vtterly destroy the place thereof, and darknesse shall pursue his enemies.

9 What doe ye imagine against the Lord? he wil make an vtter destruction: affliction shall not rise vp the seconde time.

10 For he shall come as vnto thornes folden one in another, and as vnto drunkards in their drunkennesse: they shall be deuoured as stubble fully dryed.

11 There commeth one out of thee that imagineth euill against the Lord, euen a wicked counsellour.

12 Thus saith the Lord, Though they be quiet, and also many, yet thus shall they be cut off when he shall passe by: though I haue afflicted thee, I will afflict thee no more.

13 For nowe I will breake his yoke from thee, and will burst thy bonds in sunder.

14 And the Lord hath giuen a commandement concerning thee, that no more of thy name be sowen: out of the house of thy gods will I cut off the grauen, and the molten image: I will make it thy graue for thee, for thou art vile.

15 Beholde vpon the mountaines the feete of him that declareth, and publisheth peace: O Iudah, keepe thy solemne feastes, perfourme thy vowes:

for the wicked shall no more passe thorowe thee: he is vtterly cut off.

Nahum 2

1 The destroyer is come before thy face: keepe the munition: looke to the way: make thy loynes strong: increase thy strength mightily.
2 For the Lord hath turned away the glorie of Iaakob, as the glorie of Israel: for the emptiers haue emptied them out, and marred their vine branches.
3 The shield of his mightie men is made red: the valiant men are in skarlet: the charets shalbe as in the fire and flames in the day of his preparation, and the firre trees shall tremble.
4 The charets shall rage in the streetes: they shall runne to and from in the hie wayes: they shall seeme like lampes: they shall shoote like the lightning.
5 He shall remember his strong men: they shall stumble as they goe: they shall make haste to the walles thereof, and the defence shall bee prepared.
6 The gates of the riuers shalbe opened, and the palace shall melt.
7 And Huzzab the Queene shalbe led away captiue, and her maides shall leade her as with the voyce of doues, smiting vpon their breastes.
8 But Nineueh is of olde like a poole of water: yet they shall flee away. Stande, stande, shall they crie: but none shall looke backe.
9 Spoyle ye the siluer, spoyle the golde: for there is none ende of the store, and glorie of all the pleasant vessels.
10 She is emptie and voyde and waste, and the heart melteth, and the knees smite together, and sorowe is in all loynes, and the faces of the all gather blackenesse.
11 Where is the dwelling of the lyons, and the pasture of the lyons whelpes? where the lyon, and the lionesse walked, and the lyons whelpe, and none made them afrayde.
12 The lyon did teare in pieces ynough for his whelpes, and woryed for his lyonesse, and filled his holes with praye, and his dennes with, spoyle.
13 Beholde, I come vnto thee, sayeth the Lord of hostes, and I will burne her charets in the smoke, and the sworde shall deuoure thy yong lyons, and I will cut off thy spoyle from the earth, and the voyce of thy messengers shall no more be heard.

Nahum 3

1 O bloody citie, it is all full of lyes, and robberie: the pray departeth not:
2 The noyse of a whippe, and the noyse of the mouing of the wheeles, and the beating of the horses, and the leaping of the charets.
3 The horseman lifteth vp both the bright sword, and the glittering speare, and a multitude is slaine, and the dead bodyes are many: there is none ende of their corpses: they stumble vpon their corpses,

4 Because of the multitude of the fornications of the harlot that is beautifull, and is a mistresse of witchcraft, and selleth the people thorow her whoredome, and the nations thorowe her witchcrafts.
5 Beholde, I come vpon thee, saith the Lord of hostes, and will discouer thy skirtes vpon thy face, and will shewe the nations thy filthines, and the kingdomes thy shame.
6 And I will cast filth vpon thee, and make thee vile, and will set thee as a gasing stocke.
7 And it shall come to passe, that al they that looke vpon thee, shall flee from thee, and say, Nineueh is destroyed, who will haue pitie vpon her? where shall I seeke comforters for thee?
8 Art thou better then No, which was ful of people? that lay in the riuers, and had the waters round about it? whose ditche was the sea, and her wall was from the sea?
9 Ethiopia and Egypt were her strength, and there was none ende: Put and Lubim were her helpers.
10 Yet was she caried awaye, and went into captiuitie: her young children also were dashed in pieces at the head of all the streetes: and they cast lottes for her noble men, and al her myghtie men were bound in chaines.
11 Also thou shalt bee drunken: thou shalt hide thy selfe, and shalt seeke helpe because of the enemie.
12 All thy strong cities shall be like figtrees with the first ripe figs: for if they be shaken, they fall into the mouth of the eater.
13 Beholde, thy people within thee are women: the gates of thy land shalbe opened vnto thine enemies, and ye fire shall deuoure thy barres.
14 Drawe thee waters for the siege: fortifie thy strong holdes: go into the clay, and temper the morter: make strong bricke.
15 There shall ye fire deuoure thee: the sword shall cut thee off: it shall eate thee vp like the locustes, though thou bee multiplied like the locustes, and multiplyed like the grashopper.
16 Thou hast multiplied thy marchantes aboue the starres of heauen: the locust spoileth and flyeth away.
17 Thy princes are as the grashoppers, and thy captaines as the great grashoppers which remaine in the hedges in the colde day: but when the sunne ariseth, they flee away and their place is not knowen where they are.
18 Thy shepheardes doe sleepe, O King of Asshur: thy strong men lie downe: thy people is scattered vpon the mountaines, and no man gathereth them.
19 There is no healing of thy wounde: thy plague is grieuous: all that heare the brute of thee, shall clap the handes ouer thee: for vpon whome hath not thy malice passed continually?

Habakkuk

Habakkuk 1

1 The burden, which Habakkuk the Prophet did see.
2 O Lord, howe long shall I crye, and thou wilt not heare! euen crye out vnto thee for violence, and thou wilt not helpe!
3 Why doest thou shewe mee iniquitie, and cause me to beholde sorowe? for spoyling, and violence are before me: and there are that rayse vp strife and contention.
4 Therefore the Lawe is dissolued, and iudgement doeth neuer go forth: for the wicked doeth compasse about the righteous: therefore wrong iudgement proceedeth.
5 Beholde among the heathen, and regarde, and wonder, and maruaile: for I will worke a worke in your dayes: yee will not beleeue it, though it be tolde you.
6 For lo, I raise vp the Caldeans, that bitter and furious nation, which shall goe vpon the breadth of the lande to possesse the dwelling places, that are not theirs.
7 They are terrible and fearefull: their iudgement and their dignitie shall proceede of theselues.
8 Their horses also are swifter then the leopards, and are more fierce then the wolues in the euening: and their horsemen are many: and their horsemen shall come from farre: they shall flie as the eagle hasting to meate.
9 They come all to spoyle: before their faces shalbe an Eastwinde, and they shall gather the captiuitie, as the sand.
10 And they shall mocke the Kings, and the princes shalbe a skorne vnto them: they shall deride euery strong holde: for they shall gather dust, and take it.
11 Then shall they take a courage, and transgresse and doe wickedly, imputing this their power vnto their god.
12 Art thou not of olde, O Lord my God, mine holy one? we shall not die: O Lord, thou hast ordeined them for iudgement, and O God, thou hast established them for correction.
13 Thou art of pure eyes, and canst not see euill: thou canst not behold wickednesse: wherefore doest thou looke vpon the transgressors, and holdest thy tongue when the wicked deuoureth the man, that is more righteous then he?
14 And makest men as the fishes of the sea, and as the creeping things, that haue no ruler ouer them.
15 They take vp all with the angle: they catch it in their net, and gather it in their yarne, whereof they reioyce and are glad.
16 Therefore they sacrifice vnto their net, and burne incense vnto their yarne, because by them their portion is fat and their meat plenteous.
17 Shall they therefore stretch out their net and not spare continually to slay the nations?

Habakkuk 2

1 I will stand vpon my watch, and set me vpon the towre, and wil looke and see what he would say vnto mee, and what I shall answere to him that rebuketh me.

2 And the Lord answered me, and sayde, Write the vision, and make it plaine vpon tables, that he may runne that readeth it.

3 For the vision is yet for an appointed time, but at the last it shall speake, and not lie: though it tarie, waite: for it shall surely come, and shall not stay.

4 Beholde, he that lifteth vp himselfe, his minde is not vpright in him, but the iust shall liue by his fayth,

5 Yea, in deede the proude man is as hee that transgresseth by wine: therefore shall he not endure, because he hath enlarged his desire as the hell, and is as death, and can not be satisfied, but gathereth vnto him all nations, and heapeth vnto him all people.

6 Shall not all these take vp a parable against him, and a tanting prouerbe against him, and say, Ho, he that increaseth that which is not his? howe long? and hee that ladeth himselfe with thicke clay?

7 Shall they not rise vp suddenly, that shall bite thee? and awake, that shall stirre thee? and thou shalt be their praye?

8 Because thou hast spoyled many nations, all the remnant of the people shall spoyle thee, because of mens blood, and for the wrong done in the land, in the citie, and vnto all that dwell therein.

9 Ho, he that coueteth an euil couetousnesse to his house, that he may set his nest on hie, to escape from the power of euil.

10 Thou hast consulted shame to thine owne house, by destroying many people, and hast sinned against thine owne soule.

11 For the stone shall crie out of the wall, and the beame out of the timber shall answere it.

12 Wo vnto him that buildeth a towne with blood, and erecteth a citie by iniquitie.

13 Beholde, is it not of the Lord of hostes that the people shall labour in ye very fire? the people shall euen weary themselues for very vanitie.

14 For the earth shall be filled with the knowledge of the glory of the Lord, as the waters couer the sea.

15 Wo vnto him that giueth his neighbour drinke: thou ioynest thine heate, and makest him drunken also, that thou mayest see their priuities.

16 Thou art filled with shame for glorie: drinke thou also, and be made naked: the cup of the Lords right hand shall be turned vnto thee, and shamefull spuing shalbe for thy glory.

17 For the crueltie of Lebanon shall couer thee: so shall the spoyle of the beastes, which made them afraide, because of mens blood, and for the wrong done in the land, in the citie, and vnto all that dwell therein.

18 What profiteth the image? for the maker thereof hath made it an image, and a teacher of lies, though he that made it, trust therein, when he maketh dumme idoles.

19 Wo vnto him that sayth to the wood, Awake, and to the dumme stone, Rise vp, it shall teach thee: beholde, it is layde ouer with golde and siluer, and there is no breath in it.

20 But the Lord is in his holy Temple: let all the earth keepe silence before him.

Habakkuk 3

1 A prayer of Habakkuk the Prophet for the ignorances.

2 O Lord, I haue heard thy voyce, and was afraide: O Lord, reuiue thy worke in the mids of the people, in the mids of the yeeres make it knowen: in wrath remember mercy.

3 God commeth from Teman, and the holy one from mount Paran, Selah. His glory couereth the heauens, and the earth is full of his prayse,

4 And his brightnes was as the light: he had hornes comming out of his hands, and there was the hiding of his power.

5 Before him went the pestilence, and burning coales went forth before his feete.

6 He stoode and measured the earth: he behelde and dissolued the nations and the euerlasting mountaines were broken, and the ancient hilles did bowe: his wayes are euerlasting.

7 For his iniquitie I sawe the tentes of Cushan, and the curtaines of the land of Midian did tremble.

8 Was the Lord angry against the riuers? or was thine anger against the floods? or was thy wrath against the sea, that thou diddest ride vpon thine horses? thy charets brought saluation.

9 Thy bowe was manifestly reueiled, and the othes of the tribes were a sure worde, Selah. thou diddest cleaue the earth with riuers.

10 The mountaines sawe thee, and they trembled: the streame of the water passed by: the deepe made a noyse, and lift vp his hand on hie.

11 The sunne and moone stood still in their habitation: at the light of thine arrowes they went, and at the bright shining of thy speares.

12 Thou trodest downe the land in anger, and didest thresh the heathen in displeasure.

13 Thou wentest foorth for the saluation of thy people, euen for saluation with thine Anointed: thou hast wounded the head of the house of the wicked, and discoueredst the foundations vnto the necke, Selah.

14 Thou didest strike thorowe with his owne staues the heades of his villages: they came out as a whirle winde to scatter me: their reioycing was as to deuoure the poore secretly.

15 Thou didest walke in the sea with thine horses vpon the heape of great waters.

16 When I heard, my bellie trembled: my lippes shooke at the voyce: rottennesse entred into my bones, and I trembled in my selfe, that I might rest in the day of trouble: for whe he commeth vp vnto the people, he shall destroy them.

17 For the figtree shall not flourish, neither shall fruite be in the vines: the labour of the oliue shall faile, and the fieldes shall yeelde no meate: the sheepe shalbe cut off from the folde, and there shalbe no bullocke in the stalles.

18 But I will reioyce in the Lord: I will ioy in the God of my saluation.

19 The Lord God is my strength: hee will make my feete like hindes feete, and he will make me to walke vpon mine hie places. To the chiefe singer on Neginothai.

Zephaniah

Zephaniah 1

1 The word of the Lord, which came vnto Zephaniah ye sonne of Cushi, the sonne of Gedaliah, the sonne of Amariah, the sonne of Hizkiah, in the dayes of Iosiah, the sonne of Amon King of Iudah.

2 I will surely destroy all things from off the land, saith the Lord.

3 I will destroy man and beast: I wil destroy the foules of the heauen, and the fishes of the sea, and ruines shalbe to the wicked, and I will cut off man from off the land, saith the Lord.

4 I will also stretch out mine hand vpon Iudah, and vpon all the inhabitants of Ierusalem, and I wil cut off the remnant of Baal from this place, and the name of the Chemarims with ye Priestes,

5 And them that worship the hoste of heauen vpon the house tops, and them that worship and sweare by the Lord, and sweare by Malcham,

6 And them that are turned backe from the Lord, and those that haue not sought the Lord, nor inquired for him.

7 Be stil at the presence of the Lord God: for the day of the Lord is at hand: for the Lord hath prepared a sacrifice, and hath sanctified his ghests.

8 And it shalbe in the day of the Lords sacrifice, that I will visite the princes and the Kings children, and all such as are clothed with strange apparell.

9 In the same day also will I visite all those that dance vpon the threshold so proudly, which fill their masters houses by crueltie and deceite.

10 And in that day, saith the Lord, there shall be a noise, and cry from the fishgate, and an howling from the second gate, and a great destruction from the hilles.

11 Howle ye inhabitants of the lowe place: for the companie of the marchants is destroyed: all they that beare siluer, are cut off.

12 And at that time will I searche Ierusalem with lightes, and visite the men that are frosen in their dregges, and say in their heartes, The Lord will neither doe good nor doe euill.

13 Therefore their goods shall be spoyled, and their houses waste: they shall also build houses, but not inhabite them, and they shall plant vineyards, but not drinke the wine thereof.

14 The great day of the Lord is neere: it is neere, and hasteth greatly, euen the voyce of the day of the Lord: the strong man shall cry there bitterly.

15 That day is a day of wrath, a day of trouble and heauinesse, a day of destruction and desolation, a day of obscuritie and darkenesse, a day of cloudes and blackenesse,

16 A day of the trumpet and alarme against the strong cities, and against the hie towres.

17 And I will bring distresse vpon men, that they shall walke like blind men, because they haue sinned against the Lord, and their blood shall be powred out as dust, and their flesh as the dongue.

18 Neither their siluer nor their golde shalbe able to deliuer them in ye day of the Lords wrath, but the whole lande shalbe deuoured by the fire of his ielousie: for hee shall make euen a speedie riddance of all them that dwell in the land.

Zephaniah 2

1 Gather your selues, euen gather you, O nation not worthie to be loued,

2 Before the decree come foorth, and ye be as chaffe that passeth in a day, and before the fierce wrath of the Lord come vpon you, and before the day of the Lords anger come vpon you.

3 Seeke yee the Lord all the meeke of the earth, which haue wrought his iudgement: seeke righteousnesse, seeke lowlinesse, if so bee that ye may be hid in the day of the Lords wrath.

4 For Azzah shall be forsaken, and Ashkelon desolate: they shall driue out Ashdod at the noone day, and Ekron shalbe rooted vp.

5 Wo vnto the inhabitants of the sea coast. the nation of the Cherethims, the worde of the Lord is against you: O Canaan, the lande of the Philistims, I will euen destroye thee without an inhabitant.

6 And the sea coast shall be dwellings and cotages for shepheardes and sheepefoldes.

7 And that coast shall be for the remnant of the house of Iudah, to feede thereupon: in the houses of Ashkelon shall they lodge toward night: for the Lord their God shall visite them, and turne away their captiuitie.

8 I haue heard the reproch of Moab, and the rebukes of the children of Ammon, whereby they vpbraided my people, and magnified themselues against their borders.

9 Therefore, as I liue, saith the Lord of hostes, the God of Israel, Surely Moab shall bee as Sodom, and the children of Ammon as Gomorah, euen the breeding of nettels and salt pittes, and a perpetuall desolation: the residue of my folke shall spoyle them, and the remnant of my people shall possesse them.

10 This shall they haue for their pride, because they haue reproched and magnified themselues against the Lord of hostes people.

11 The Lord will be terrible vnto them: for he wil consume all the gods of the earth, and euery man shall worship him from his place, euen all the yles of the heathen.

12 Ye Morians also shalbe slaine by my sword with them.

13 And he wil stretch out his hand against the North, and destroy Asshur, and will make Nineueh desolate, and waste like a wildernesse.

14 And flockes shall lie in the middes of her, and all the beastes of the nations, and the pelicane, and the owle shall abide in the vpper postes of it: the voyce of birdes shall sing in the windowes, and desolations shalbe vpon the postes: for the cedars are vncouered.

15 This is the reioycing citie that dwelt carelesse, that said in her heart, I am, and there is none besides me: how is she made waste, and the lodging of the beastes! euery one that passeth by her, shall hisse and wagge his hand.

Zephaniah 3

1 Woe to her that is filthie and polluted, to the robbing citie.

2 She heard not the voyce: she receiued not correction: she trusted not in the Lord: she drew not neere to her God.

3 Her princes within her are as roaring lyons: her iudges are as wolues in the euening, which leaue not the bones till the morow.

4 Her prophets are light, and wicked persons: her priests haue polluted the Sanctuarie: they haue wrested the Lawe.

5 The iust Lord is in the middes thereof: he will doe none iniquitie: euery morning doeth hee bring his iudgement to light, he faileth not: but the wicked will not learne to be ashamed.

6 I haue cut off the nations: their towres are desolate: I haue made their streetes waste, that none shall passe by: their cities are destroyed without man and without inhabitant.

7 I said, Surely thou wilt feare me: thou wilt receiue instruction: so their dwelling shoulde not be destroyed howsoeuer I visited them, but they rose earely and corrupted all their workes.

8 Therefore wait ye vpon me, saith the Lord, vntill the day that I rise vp to the praye: for I am determined to gather the nations, and that I will assemble the kingdomes to powre vpon them mine indignation, euen all my fierce wrath: for all the earth shall be deuoured with the fire of my ielousie.

9 Surely then will I turne to the people a pure language, that they may all call vpon the Name of the Lord, to serue him with one cosent.

10 From beyonde the riuers of Ethiopia, the daughter of my dispersed, praying vnto me, shall bring me an offering.

11 In that day shalt thou not be ashamed for all thy workes, wherein thou hast transgressed against mee: for then I will take away out of the middes of thee them that reioyce of thy pride, and thou shalt no more be proude of mine holy Mountaine.

12 Then will I leaue in the middes of thee an humble and poore people: and they shall trust in the Name of the Lord.

13 The remnant of Israel shall do none iniquitie, nor speake lies: neither shall a deceitful tongue be found in their mouth: for they shalbe fed, and lie downe, and none shall make them afraide.

14 Reioyce, O daughter Zion: be ye ioyfull, O Israel: be glad and reioyce with all thine heart, O daughter Ierusalem.

15 The Lord hath taken away thy iudgements: hee hath cast out thine enemie: the King of Israel, euen the Lord is in the middes of thee: thou shalt see no more euill.

16 In that day it shalbe said to Ierusalem, Feare thou not, O Zion: let not thine handes be faint.

17 The Lord thy God in the middes of thee is mightie: hee will saue, hee will reioyce ouer thee with ioye: he will quiet himselfe in his loue: he will reioyce ouer thee with ioy.

18 After a certaine time will I gather the afflicted that were of thee, and them that bare the reproch for it.

19 Beholde, at that time I will bruise all that afflict thee, and I will saue her that halteth, and gather her that was cast out, and I will get them praise and fame in all the landes of their shame.

20 At that time wil I bring you againe, and then wil I gather you: for I wil giue you a name and a praise among all people of the earth, when I turne backe your captiuitie before your eyes, saith the Lord.

Haggai

Haggai 1

1 In the second yeere of King Darius, in the sixt moneth, the first day of the moneth, came ye worde of the Lord (by the ministery of the Prophet Haggai) vnto Zerubbabel the sonne of Shealtiel, a prince of Iudah, and to Iehoshua the sonne of Iehozadak the hie Priest, saying,

2 Thus speaketh the Lord of hostes, saying, This people say, The time is not yet come, that the Lords House should be builded.

3 Then came the worde of the Lord by the ministerie of the Prophet Haggai, saying,

4 Is it time for your selues to dwell in your sieled houses, and this House lie waste?

5 Now therefore thus saith ye Lord of hostes, Consider your owne wayes in your hearts.

6 Ye haue sowen much, and bring in litle: ye eate, but ye haue not ynough: ye drinke, but ye are not filled: ye clothe you, but ye be not warme: and he that

earneth wages, putteth the wages into a broken bagge.

7 Thus sayth the Lord of hostes, Consider your owne wayes in your hearts.

8 Goe vp to the mountaine, and bring wood, and build this House, and I wil be fauourable in it, and I will be glorified, sayth the Lord.

9 Ye looked for much, and lo, it came to litle: and when ye brought it home, I did blowe vpon it. And why, sayth the Lord of hostes? Because of mine House that is waste, and ye runne euery man vnto his owne house.

10 Therefore the heauen ouer you stayed it selfe from dewe, and the earth stayed her fruite.

11 And I called for a drought vpon the land, and vpon the mountaines, and vpon the corne, and vpon the wine, and vpon the oyle, vpon all that the ground bringeth foorth: both vpon men and vpon cattell, and vpon all the labour of the hands.

12 When Zerubbabel the sonne of Shealtiel, and Iehoshua the sonne of Iehozadak the hie Priest with all the remnant of the people, heard the voyce of the Lord their God, and the wordes of the Prophet Haggai (as the Lord their God had sent him) then the people did feare before the Lord.

13 Then spake Haggai the Lords messenger in the Lords message vnto the people, saying, I am with you, sayth the Lord.

14 And the Lord stirred vp the spirite of Zerubbabel, the sonne of Shealtiel a prince of Iudah, and the spirit of Iehoshua the sonne of Iehozadak the hie Priest, and the spirit of all the remnant of the people, and they came, and did the worke in the House of the Lord of hostes their God.

Haggai 2

1 In the foure and twentieth day of the sixt moneth, in the second yeere of King Darius,

2 In the seuenth moneth, in the one and twentieth day of the moneth, came the worde of the Lord by the ministerie of the Prophet Haggai, saying,

3 Speake nowe to Zerubbabel the sonne of Shealtiel prince of Iudah, and to Iehoshua the sonne of Iehozadak the hie Priest, and to the residue of the people, saying,

4 Who is left among you, that sawe this House in her first glory, and howe doe you see it nowe? is it not in your eyes, in comparison of it as nothing?

5 Yet nowe be of good courage, O Zerubbabel, sayth the Lord, and be of good comfort, O Iehoshua, sonne of Iehozadak the hie Priest: and be strong, all ye people of the land, sayth the Lord, and doe it: for I am with you, sayth the Lord of hostes,

6 According to the worde that I couenanted with you, when ye came out of Egypt: so my Spirite shall remaine among you, feare ye not.

7 For thus sayth the Lord of hostes, Yet a litle while, and I will shake the heauens and the earth, and the sea, and the dry land:

8 And I will moue all nations, and the desire of all nations shall come, and I will fill this House with glory, sayth the Lord of hostes.

9 The siluer is mine, and the golde is mine, sayth the Lord of hostes.

10 The glory of this last House shall be greater then the first, sayth the Lord of hostes: and in this place will I giue peace, sayth the Lord of hostes.

11 In the foure and twentieth day of the ninth moneth, in the second yeere of Darius, came the worde of the Lord vnto the Prophet Haggai, saying,

12 Thus sayth the Lord of hostes, Aske nowe the Priests concerning the Law, and say,

13 If one beare holy flesh in the skirt of his garment, and with his skirt doe touch the bread, or the potage, or the wine, or oyle, or any meate, shall it be holy? And the Priests answered and said, No.

14 Then sayde Haggai, If a polluted person touch any of these, shall it be vncleane? And the Priests answered, and sayd, It shalbe vncleane.

15 Then answered Haggai, and sayd, So is this people, and so is this nation before me, saith the Lord: and so are all the workes of their hands, and that which they offer here, is vncleane.

16 And nowe, I pray you, consider in your mindes: from this day, and afore, euen afore a stone was layde vpon a stone in the Temple of the Lord:

17 Before these things were, when one came to an heape of twentie measures, there were but ten: when one came to the wine presse for to drawe out fiftie vessels out of the presse, there were but twentie.

18 I smote you with blasting, and with mildewe, and with haile, in all the labours of your hands: yet you turned not to me, saith the Lord.

19 Consider, I pray you, in your mindes, from this day, and afore from the foure and twentieth day of the ninth moneth, euen from the day that the foundation of the Lords Temple was laide: consider it in your mindes.

20 Is the seede yet in the barne? as yet the vine, and the figtree, and the pomegranate, and the oliue tree hath not brought forth: from this day will I blesse you.

21 And againe the worde of the Lord came vnto Haggai in the foure and twentieth day of the moneth, saying,

22 Speake to Zerubbabel the prince of Iudah, and say, I wil shake the heauens and the earth,

23 And I will ouerthrowe the throne of kingdomes, and I wil destroy the strength of the kingdomes of the heathen, and I wil ouerthrowe the charets, and those that ride in them, and the horse and the riders shall come downe, euery one by the sword of his brother.

24 In that day, saith the Lord of hostes, will I take thee, O Zerubbabel my seruant, the sonne of Shealtiel, sayth the Lord, and wil make thee as a signet: for I haue chosen thee, sayth the Lord of hostes.

Zechariah

Zechariah 1

1 In the eight moneth of the second yeere of Darius, came the worde of the Lord vnto Zechariah the sonne of Berechiah, the sonne of Iddo, the Prophet, saying,

2 The Lord hath bene sore displeased with your fathers.

3 Therefore say thou vnto them, Thus sayth the Lord of hostes, Turne ye vnto me, saith the Lord of hostes, and I will turne vnto you, saith the Lord of hostes.

4 Be ye not as your fathers, vnto whome the former prophets haue cried, saying, Thus sayth the Lord of hostes, Turne you nowe from your euill wayes, and from your wicked workes: but they would not heare, nor hearken vnto me, saith the Lord.

5 your fathers, where are they? and doe the Prophets liue for euer?

6 But did not my wordes and my statutes, which I commanded by my seruants ye Prophets, take holde of your fathers? and they returned, and sayd, As the Lord of hostes hath determined to doe vnto vs, according to our owne wayes, and according to our workes, so hath hee dealt with vs.

7 Vpon the foure and twentieth day of the eleuenth moneth, which is the moneth Shebat, in the second yeere of Darius, came the worde of the Lord vnto Zechariah the sonne of Berechiah, the sonne of Iddo the Prophet, saying,

8 I saw by night, and behold a man riding vpon a red horse, and hee stood among the mirre trees, that were in a bottome, and behinde him were there red horses speckeled and white.

9 Then sayd I, O my Lord, what are these? And the Angel that talked with me, sayde vnto me, I wil shew thee what these be.

10 And the man that stood among the mirre trees, answered, and sayd, These are they whome the Lord hath sent to go through the world.

11 And they answered the Angel of the Lord, that stood among the mirre trees, and sayd, We haue gone thorowe the world: and beholde, all the world sitteth still, and is at rest.

12 Then the Angel of the Lord answered and sayd, O Lord of hostes, howe long wilt thou be vnmercifull to Ierusalem, and to the cities of Iudah, with whom thou hast bene displeased now these threescore and ten yeeres?

13 And the Lord answered the Angel that talked with me, with good wordes and comfortable wordes.

14 So the Angel that communed with me, said vnto me, Crie thou, and speake, Thus saith the Lord of hostes, I am ielous

ouer Ierusalem and Zion with a great zeale,

15 And am greatly angrie against the carelesse heathen: for I was angrie but a litle, and they helped forward the affliction.

16 Therefore thus saith the Lord, I wil returne vnto Ierusalem with tender mercie: mine house shall be builded in it, saith the Lord of hostes, and a line shall be stretched vpon Ierusalem.

17 Cry yet, and speake, Thus saith the Lord of hostes, My cities shall yet be broken with plentie: the Lord shall yet comfort Zion, and shall yet chuse Ierusalem.

18 Then lift I vp mine eyes and sawe, and beholde, foure hornes.

19 And I said vnto the Angel that talked with me, What be these? And hee answered me, These are the hornes which haue scattered Iudah, Israel, and Ierusalem.

20 And the Lord shewed me foure carpenters.

21 Then said I, What come these to doe? And he answered, and said, These are the hornes, which haue scattered Iudah, so that a man durst not lift vp his head: but these are come to fray them, and to cast out the hornes of the Gentiles, which lift vp their horne ouer the land of Iudah, to scatter it.

Zechariah 2

1 I lift vp mine eyes againe and looked, and behold, a man with a measuring line in his hand.

2 Then saide I, Whither goest thou? And he saide vnto me, To measure Ierusalem, that I may see what is the breadth thereof, and what is the length thereof.

3 And beholde, the Angel that talked with me, went foorth: and another Angel went out to meete him,

4 And saide vnto him, Runne, speake to this yong man, and say, Ierusalem shalbe inhabited without walles, for the multitude of men and cattell therein.

5 For I, saith the Lord, will be vnto her a wall of fire round about, and wil be the glory in the middes of her.

6 Ho, ho, come forth, and flee from the land of the North, saith the Lord: for I haue scattered you into the foure winds of the heauen, saith ye Lord.

7 Saue thy selfe, O Zion, that dwellest with the daughter of Babel.

8 For thus saith the Lord of hostes, After this glory hath hee sent me vnto the nations, which spoyled you: for he that toucheth you, toucheth the apple of his eye.

9 For beholde, I will lift vp mine hand vpon them: and they shalbe a spoyle to those that serued them, and ye shall knowe, that the Lord of hostes hath sent me.

10 Reioyce, and be glad, O daughter Zion: for loe, I come, and will dwell in the middes of thee, saith the Lord.

11 And many nations shall be ioyned to the Lord in that day, and shalbe my people: and I will dwell in the middes of

thee, and thou shalt knowe that the Lord of hostes hath sent me vnto thee.

12 And the Lord shall inherite Iudah his portion in the holy lande, and shall chuse Ierusalem againe.

13 Let all flesh be still before the Lord: for he is raised vp out of his holy place.

Zechariah 3

1 And he shewed mee Iehoshua the hie Priest, standing before the Angel of the Lord, and Satan stoode at his right hand to resist him.

2 And the Lord said vnto Satan, The Lord reproue thee, O Satan: euen the Lord that hath chosen Ierusalem, reproue thee. Is not this a brand taken out of the fire?

3 Nowe Iehoshua was clothed with filthie garments, and stoode before the Angel.

4 And he answered and spake vnto those that stoode before him, saying, Take away the filthie garments from him. And vnto him hee saide, Behold, I haue caused thine iniquitie to depart from thee, and I wil clothe thee with change of raiment.

5 And I saide, Let them set a faire diademe vpon his head. So they set a faire diademe vpon his head, and clothed him with garments, and the Angel of the Lord stoode by.

6 And the Angel of the Lord testified vnto Iehoshua, saying,

7 Thus saith the Lord of hostes, If thou wilt walke in my wayes, and keepe my watch, thou shalt also iudge mine House, and shalt also keepe my courtes, and I will giue thee place among these that stand by.

8 Heare now, O Iehoshua the hie Priest, thou and thy fellowes that sit before thee: for they are monstruous persons: but behold, I wil bring forth the Branche my seruant.

9 For loe, the stone that I haue layd before Iehoshua: vpon one stone shalbe seuen eyes: beholde, I will cut out the grauing thereof, saith the Lord of hostes, and I will take away the iniquitie of this land in one day.

10 In that day, saith the Lord of hostes, shall ye call euery man his neighbour vnder the vine, and vnder the figge tree.

Zechariah 4

1 And the Angel that talked with mee, came againe and waked mee, as a man that is raysed out of his sleepe,

2 And saide vnto me, What seest thou? And I said, I haue looked, and beholde, a candlesticke all of gold with a bowle vpon the toppe of it, and his seuen lampes therein, and seuen pipes to the lampes, which were vpon the toppe thereof.

3 And two oliue trees ouer it, one vpon the right side of the bowle, and the other vpon the left side thereof.

4 So I answered, and spake to the Angel that talked with me, saying, What are these, my Lord?

5 Then the Angel that talked with mee, answered and said vnto me, Knowest

thou not what these be? And I said, No, my Lord.

6 Then he answered and spake vnto me, saying, This is the word of the Lord vnto Zerubbabel, saying, Neither by an armie nor strength, but by my Spirit, saith the Lord of hostes.

7 Who art thou, O great mountaine, before Zerubbabel? thou shalt be a plaine, and he shall bring foorth the head stone thereof, with shoutings, crying, Grace, grace vnto it.

8 Moreouer, the word of the Lord came vnto me, saying,

9 The handes of Zerubbabel haue layde the foundation of this house: his handes shall also finish it, and thou shalt knowe that the Lord of hostes hath sent me vnto you.

10 For who hath despised the day of the small thinges? but they shall reioyce, and shall see the stone of tinne in the hand of Zerubbabel: these seuen are the eyes of the Lord, which go thorow the whole world.

11 Then answered I, and said vnto him, What are these two oliue trees vpon the right and vpon the left side thereof?

12 And I spake moreouer, and said vnto him, What bee these two oliue branches, which thorowe the two golden pipes emptie themselues into the golde?

13 And hee answered me, and saide, Knowest thou not what these bee? And I sayde, No, my Lord.

14 Then said he, These are the two oliue branches, that stand with the ruler of the whole earth.

Zechariah 5

1 Then I turned me, and lifted vp mine eyes and looked, and beholde, a flying booke.

2 And he said vnto me, What seest thou? And I answered, I see a flying booke: the length thereof is twentie cubites, and the breadth thereof tenne cubites.

3 Then said he vnto me, This is the curse that goeth foorth ouer the whole earth: for euery one that stealeth, shalbe cut off aswell on this side, as on that: and euery one that sweareth, shall be cut off aswell on this side, as on that.

4 I will bring it forth, saith the Lord of hosts, and it shall enter into the house of the thiefe, and into the house of him, that falsely sweareth by my Name: and it shall remaine in the middes of his house, and shall consume it, with the timber thereof, and stones thereof.

5 Then the Angel that talked with me, went foorth, and said vnto me, Lift vp now thine eyes, and see what is this that goeth foorth.

6 And I saide, What is it? And hee sayde, This is an Ephah that goeth foorth. Hee saide moreouer, This is the sight of them through all the earth.

7 And beholde, there was lift vp a talent of lead: and this is a woman that sitteth in the middes of the Ephah.

8 And he said, This is wickednes, and he cast it into the middes of the Ephah,

and hee cast the weight of lead vpon the mouth thereof.

9 Then lift I vp mine eyes, and looked: and beholde, there came out two women, and the winde was in their wings (for they had wings like the wings of a storke) and they lift vp the Ephah betweene the earth and the heauen.

10 Then saide I to the Angel that talked with me, Whither doe these beare the Ephah?

11 And hee saide vnto mee, To builde it an house in the lande of Shinar, and it shall be established and set there vpon her owne place.

Zechariah 6

1 Againe, I turned and lift vp mine eyes, and looked: and beholde, there came foure charets out from betweene two mountaines, and the mountaines were mountaines of brasse.

2 In the first charet were red horses, and in the second charet blacke horses,

3 And in the thirde charet white horses, and in the fourth charet, horses of diuers colours, and reddish.

4 Then I answered, and saide vnto the Angell that talked with mee, What are these, my Lord?

5 And the Angell answered, and sayde vnto mee, These are the foure spirites of the heauen, which goe foorth from standing with the Lord of all the earth.

6 That with the blacke horse went forth into the land of the North, and the white went out after them, and they of diuers colours went forth toward the South countrey.

7 And the reddish went out, and required to go, and passe through the world, and he sayde, Goe passe through the worlde. So they went thorowout the world.

8 Then cryed hee vpon me, and spake vnto me, saying, Beholde, these that goe towarde the North countrey, haue pacified my spirit in the North countrey.

9 And the worde of the Lord came vnto me, saying,

10 Take of them of ye captiuitie, euen of Heldai, and of Tobijah, and Iedaiah, which are come from Babel, and come thou the same day, and goe vnto the house of Ioshiah, the sonne of Zephaniah.

11 Take euen siluer, and golde, and make crownes, and set them vpon the head of Iehoshua, the sonne of Iehozadak the hie Priest,

12 And speake vnto him, saying, Thus speaketh the Lord of hostes, and sayth, Behold the man whose name is the Branch, and he shall growe vp out of his place, and he shall build the Temple of the Lord.

13 Euen hee shall build the Temple of the Lord, and he shall beare the glory, and shall sit and rule vpon his throne, and he shalbe a Priest vpon his throne, and the counsell of peace shall be betweene them both.

14 And the crownes shall be to Helem, and to Tobijah, and to Iedaiah, and to

Hen the sonne of Zephaniah, for a memoriall in the Temple of the Lord.

15 And they that are farre off, shall come and build in the Temple of the Lord, and ye shall know, that the Lord of hostes hath sent me vnto you. And this shall come to passe, if ye will obey the voyce of the Lord your God.

Zechariah 7

1 And in the fourth yeere of King Darius, the worde of the Lord came vnto Zechariah in the fourth day of the ninth moneth, euen in Chisleu,

2 For they had sent vnto the House of God Sharezer, and Regem-melech and their men to pray before the Lord,

3 And to speake vnto the Priests, which were in the House of the Lord of hostes, and to the Prophets, saying, Should I weepe in the fift moneth, and separate my selfe as I haue done these so many yeeres?

4 Then came the word of the Lord of hostes vnto me, saying,

5 Speake vnto all the people of the land, and to the Priests, and say, When ye fasted, and mourned in the fift and seuenth moneth, euen the seuentie yeeres, did ye fast vnto me? doe I approoue it?

6 And when ye did eate, and when ye did drinke, did ye not eate for your selues, and drinke for your selues?

7 Should ye not heare the wordes, which the Lord hath cryed by the ministerie of the former Prophets when Ierusalem was inhabited, and in prosperitie, and the cities thereof round about her, when the South and the plaine was inhabited?

8 And the worde of the Lord came vnto Zechariah, saying,

9 Thus speaketh the Lord of hostes, saying, Execute true iudgement, and shewe mercy and compassion, euery man to his brother,

10 And oppresse not the widowe, nor the fatherles, the stranger nor the poore, and let none of you imagine euil against his brother in your heart.

11 But they refused to hearken, and pulled away the shoulder, and stopped their eares, that they should not heare.

12 Yea, they made their hearts as an adamant stone, least they should heare the Lawe and the wordes which the Lord of hostes sent in his spirit by the ministerie of ye former Prophets: therefore came a great wrath from the Lord of hostes.

13 Therefore it is come to passe, that as he cried, and they would not heare, so they cried, and I would not heare, sayth the Lord of hostes.

14 But I scattered them among all the nations, whom they knew not: thus the land was desolate after them, that no man passed through nor returned: for they layd the pleasant land waste.

Zechariah 8

1 Againe the worde of the Lord of hostes came to me, saying,

2 Thus saith the Lord of hostes, I was ielous for Zion with great ielousie, and I was ielous for her with great wrath.

3 Thus saith the Lord, I wil returne vnto Zion, and wil dwel in the mids of Ierusalem: and Ierusalem shalbe called a citie of trueth, and the Mountaine of the Lord of hostes, the holy Mountaine.

4 Thus sayth the Lord of hostes, There shall yet olde men and olde women dwell in the streetes of Ierusalem, and euery man with his staffe in his hand for very age.

5 And the streetes of the citie shalbe full of boyes and girles, playing in the streetes thereof.

6 Thus saith the Lord of hostes, Though it be vnpossible in the eyes of the remnant of this people in these dayes, should it therefore be vnpossible in my sight, sayth the Lord of hostes?

7 Thus sayth the Lord of hostes, Beholde, I will deliuer my people from the East countrey, and from the West countrey.

8 And I wil bring them, and they shall dwel in the mids of Ierusalem, and they shalbe my people, and I wil be their God in trueth, and in righteousnes.

9 Thus sayth the Lord of hostes, Let your hands be strong, ye that heare in these dayes these words by the mouth of the Prophets, which were in the day, that the foundation of the House of the Lord of hostes was laide, that the Temple might be builded.

10 For before these dayes there was no hire for man nor any hire for beast, neither was there any peace to him that went out or came in because of the affliction: for I set all men, euery one against his neighbour.

11 But nowe, I wil not intreate the residue of this people as aforetime, saith the Lord of hostes.

12 For the seede shall be prosperous: the vine shall giue her fruite, and the ground shall giue her increase, and the heauens shall giue their dewe, and I will cause the remnant of this people to possesse all these things.

13 And it shall come to passe, that as ye were a curse among the heathen, O house of Iudah, and house of Israel, so wil I deliuer you, and ye shalbe a blessing: feare not, but let your hands be strong.

14 For thus sayth the Lord of hostes, As I thought to punish you, when your fathers prouoked me vnto wrath, sayth the Lord of hostes, and repented not,

15 So againe haue I determined in these daies to doe well vnto Ierusalem, and to the house of Iudah: feare ye not.

16 These are ye things that ye shall doe. Speake ye euery man the trueth vnto his neighbour: execute iudgement truely and vprightly in your gates,

17 And let none of you imagine euill in your hearts against his neighbour, and loue no false othe: for all these are the things that I hate, saith the Lord.

18 And the worde of the Lord of hostes came vnto me, saying,

19 Thus sayth the Lord of hostes, The fast of the fourth moneth, and the fast of the fift, and the fast of the seuenth, and the fast of the tenth, shall be to the house of Iudah ioy and gladnes, and prosperous hie feasts: therefore loue the trueth and peace.

20 Thus saith the Lord of hostes, That there shall yet come people, and the inhabitants of great cities.

21 And they that dwell in one citie, shall go to another, saying, Vp, let vs go and pray before the Lord, and seeke the Lord of hostes: I wil go also.

22 Yea, great people and mightie nations shall come to seeke the Lord of hostes in Ierusalem, and to pray before the Lord.

23 Thus sayth the Lord of hostes, In those dayes shall ten men take holde out of all languages of the nations, euen take holde of the skirt of him that is a Iewe, and say, We will go with you: for we haue heard that God is with you.

Zechariah 9

1 The burden of the worde of the Lord in the land of Hadrach: and Damascus shalbe his rest: when the eyes of man, euen of all the tribes of Israel shalbe toward the Lord.

2 And Hamath also shall border thereby: Tyrus also and Zidon, though they be very wise.

3 For Tyrus did build her selfe a strong holde, and heaped vp siluer as the dust, and golde as the myre of the streetes.

4 Beholde, the Lord wil spoyle her, and he wil smite her power in the Sea, and she shalbe deuoured with fire.

5 Ashkelon shall see it, and feare, and Azzah also shalbe very sorowfull, and Ekron: for her countenance shalbe ashamed, and the King shall perish from Azzah, and Ashkelon shall not be inhabited.

6 And the stranger shall dwell in Ashdod, and I wil cut off the pride of the Philistims.

7 And I wil take away his blood out of his mouth, and his abominations from betweene his teeth: but he that remaineth, euen he shalbe for our God, and he shalbe as a prince in Iudah, but Ekron shalbe as a Iebusite.

8 And I will campe about mine House against the armie, against him that passeth by, and against him that returneth, and no oppressour shall come vpon them any more: for now haue I seene with mine eyes.

9 Reioyce greatly, O daughter Zion: shoute for ioy, O daughter Ierusalem: beholde, thy King commeth vnto thee: he is iust and saued himselfe, poore and riding vpon an asse, and vpon a colt the foale of an asse.

10 And I wil cut off the charets from Ephraim, and the horse from Ierusalem: the bowe of the battel shalbe broken, and he shall speake peace vnto the heathen, and his dominion shalbe from sea vnto sea, and from the Riuer to the end of the land.

11 Thou also shalt be saued through the blood of thy couenant. I haue loosed thy prisoners out of the pit wherein is no water.

12 Turne you to the strong holde, ye prisoners of hope: euen to day doe I declare, that I will render the double vnto thee.

13 For Iudah haue I bent as a bowe for me: Ephraims hand haue I filled, and I haue raised vp thy sonnes, O Zion, against thy sonnes, O Grecia, and haue made thee as a gyants sword.

14 And the Lord shalbe seene ouer them, and his arrowe shall go forth as the lightning: and the Lord God shall blowe the trumpet, and shall come forth with the whirlewindes of the South.

15 The Lord of hostes shall defend them, and they shall deuoure them, and subdue them with sling stones, and they shall drinke, and make a noyse as thorowe wine, and they shalbe filled like bowles, and as the hornes of the altar.

16 And the Lord their God shall deliuer them in that day as the flocke of his people: for they shall be as the stones of the crowne lifted up vpon his land.

17 For howe great is his goodnesse! and howe great is his beautie! corne shall make the yong men cherefull, and newe wine the maides.

Zechariah 10

1 Aske you of the Lord raine in the time of the latter raine: so shall the Lord make white cloudes, and giue you showers of raine, and to euery one grasse in the field.

2 Surely the idols haue spoken vanitie, and the southsayers haue seene a lye, and the dreamers haue tolde a vaine thing: they comfort in vaine: therefore they went away as sheepe: they were troubled, because there was no shepheard.

3 My wrath was kindled against the shepherdes, and I did visite the goates: but the Lord of hostes will visite his flocke the house of Iudah, and will make them as his beautifull horse in the battell.

4 Out of him shall the corner come foorth: out of him the nayle, out of him ye bowe of battell, and out of him euery appointer of tribute also.

5 And they shalbe as the mightie men, which treade downe their enemies in the mire of the streetes in the battell, and they shall fight, because the Lord is with them, and the riders on horses shall be confounded.

6 And I will strengthen the house of Iudah, and I will preserue the house of Ioseph, and I wil bring them againe, for I pitie them: and they shall be as though I had not cast them off: for I am the Lord their God, and will heare them.

7 And they of Ephraim shall be as a gyant, and their heart shall reioyce as thorowe wine: yea, their children shall see it, and be glad: and their heart shall reioyce in the Lord.

8 I will hisse for them, and gather them: for I haue redeemed them: and they shall encrease, as they haue encreased.

9 And I will sowe them among the people, and they shall remember me in farre countreys: and they shall liue with their children and turne againe.

10 I will bring them againe also out of the land of Egypt, and gather them out of Asshur: and I will bring them into the land of Gilead, and Lebanon, and place shall not be found for them.

11 And he shall goe into the sea with affliction, and shall smite the waues in the sea, and all the depthes of the riuer shall drye vp: and the pride of Asshur shall be cast downe, and the scepter of Egypt shall depart away.

12 And I will strengthen them in the Lord, and they shall walke in his Name, sayth the Lord.

Zechariah 11

1 Open thy doores, O Lebanon, and the fire shall deuoure thy cedars.

2 Houle, firre trees: for the cedar is fallen, because all the mightie are destroyed: houle ye, O okes of Bashan, for ye defesed forest is cut downe.

3 There is the voyce of the houling of the shepherdes: for their glorie is destroyed: the voyce of ye roaring of lyons whelpes: for the pride of Iorden is destroyed.

4 Thus sayeth the Lord my God, Feede the sheepe of the slaughter.

5 They that possesse them, slay them and sinne not: and they that sell them, say, Blessed be the Lord: for I am riche, and their owne shepherds spare them not.

6 Surely I wil no more spare those that dwell in the land, sayth the Lord: but loe, I will deliuer the men euery one into his neighbours hand, and into the hand of his King: and they shall smite the land, and out of their hands I wil not deliuer them.

7 For I fed the sheepe of slaughter, euen the poore of the flocke, and I tooke vnto me two staues: the one I called Beautie, and the other I called Bandes, and I fed the sheepe.

8 Three shepherdes also I cut off in one moneth, and my soule lothed them, and their soule abhorred me.

9 Then said I, I will not feede you: that that dyeth, let it dye: and that that perisheth, let it perish: and let the remnant eate, euery one the flesh of his neighbour.

10 And I tooke my staffe, euen Beautie, and brake it, that I might disanull my couenant, which I had made with all people.

11 And it was broken in that day: and so the poore of the sheepe that waited vpon me, knew that it was the worde of the Lord.

12 And I said vnto them, If ye thinke it good, giue me my wages: and if no, leaue off: so they weighed for my wages thirtie pieces of siluer.

13 And the Lord said vnto me, Cast it vnto the potter: a goodly price, that I was

valued at of them. And I tooke the thirtie pieces of siluer, and cast them to the potter in the house of the Lord.

14 Then brake I mine other staffe, euen the Bandes, that I might dissolue the brotherhood betweene Iudah and Israel.

15 And the Lord said vnto me, Take to thee yet the instruments of a foolish shepheard.

16 For loe, I will rayse vp a shepheard in the land, which shall not looke for the thing, that is lost, nor seeke the tender lambes, nor heale that that is hurt, nor feede that that standeth vp: but he shall eate the flesh of the fat, and teare their clawes in pieces.

17 O idole shepheard that leaueth the flocke: the sword shalbe vpon his arme, and vpon his right eye. His arme shall be cleane dryed vp, and his right eye shall be vtterly darkened.

Zechariah 12

1 The burden of the worde of the Lord vpon Israel, sayth the Lord, which spred the heauens, and layed the foundation of the earth, and formed the spirite of man within him.

2 Beholde, I will make Ierusalem a cuppe of poyson vnto all the people round about: and also with Iudah will he be, in ye siege against Ierusalem.

3 And in that day will I make Ierusalem an heauie stone for all people: all that lift it vp, shall be torne, though all the people of the earth be gathered together against it.

4 In that day, sayeth the Lord, I will smite euery horse with astonishment, and his rider with madnesse, and I will open mine eyes vpon the house of Iudah, and will smite euery horse of the people with blindnesse.

5 And the princes of Iudah shall say in their hearts, The inhabitants of Ierusalem shall be my strength in the Lord of hostes their God.

6 In that day will I make the princes of Iudah like coles of fire among the wood, and like a fire brand in the sheafe, and they shall deuoure all the people round about on the right hand, and on the left: and Ierusalem shall be inhabited againe in her owne place, euen in Ierusalem.

7 The Lord also shall preserue the tents of Iudah, as afore time: therefore the glorie of the house of Dauid shall not boast, nor the glorie of the inhabitants of Ierusalem against Iudah.

8 In that day shall the Lord defende the inhabitants of Ierusalem, and he that is feeble among them, in that day shall be as Dauid: and the house of Dauid shall be as Gods house, and as the Angel of the Lord before them.

9 And in that day will I seeke to destroy all the nations that come against Ierusalem.

10 And I will powre vpon the house of Dauid, and vpon the inhabitants of Ierusalem the Spirite of grace and of compassion, and they shall looke vpon me, whom they haue pearced, and they shall lament for him, as one mourneth

for his onely sonne, and be sorie for him as one is sorie for his first borne.

11 In that day shall there be a great mourning in Ierusalem, as the mourning of Hadadrimmon in the valley of Megiddon.

12 And the land shall bewayle euery familie apart, the familie of the house of Dauid apart, and their wiues apart: the familie of the house of Nathan apart, and their wiues apart:

13 The familie of the house of Leui apart, and their wiues apart: the familie of Shemei apart, and their wiues apart:

14 All the families that remaine, euery familie apart, and their wiues apart.

Zechariah 13

1 In that day there shall be a fountaine opened to the house of Dauid, and to the inhabitants of Ierusalem, for sinne and for vncleannesse.

2 And in that day, sayth the Lord of hostes, I will cut off the names of the idoles out of the land: and they shall no more be remembred: and I will cause the prophets, and the vncleane spirit to depart out of the land.

3 And when any shall yet prophesie, his father and his mother that begate him, shall say vnto him, Thou shalt not liue: for thou speakest lies in the name of the Lord: and his father and his mother that begat him, shall thrust him through, when he prophesieth.

4 And in that day shall the prophetes be ashamed euery one of his vision, when he hath prophesied: neither shall they weare a rough garment to deceiue.

5 But he shall say, I am no Prophet: I am an husbandman: for man taught me to be an heardman from my youth vp.

6 And one shall say vnto him, What are these woundes in thine hands? Then he shall answere, Thus was I wounded in the house of my friendes.

7 Arise, O sword, vpon my shepheard, and vpon the man, that is my fellow, sayth the Lord of hostes: smite the shepheard, and the sheepe shall be scattered: and I will turne mine hand vpon the litle ones.

8 And in all the land, sayeth the Lord, two partes therein shall be cut off, and die: but the third shall be left therein.

9 And I will bring that third part thorowe the fire, and will fine them as the siluer is fined, and will trye them as golde is tryed: they shall call on my Name, and I will heare them: I will say, It is my people, and they shall say, The Lord is my God.

Zechariah 14

1 Beholde, the day of the Lord commeth, and thy spoyle shall be deuided in the middes of thee.

2 For I will gather all nations against Ierusalem to battell, and the citie shall be taken, and the houses spoyled, and the women defiled, and halfe of the citie shall goe into captiuitie, and the residue of the people shall not be cut off from ye citie.

3 Then shall the Lord goe foorth, and fight against those nations, as when he fought in the day of battell.

4 And his feete shall stand in that day vpon the mount of oliues, which is before Ierusalem on the Eastside, and the mount of oliues shall cleaue in the middes thereof: toward the East and toward the West there shalbe a very great valley, and halfe of ye mountaine shall remooue toward the North, and halfe of the mountaine towarde the South.

5 And yee shall flee vnto the valley of the mountaines: for the valley of the mountaines shall reache vnto Azal: yea, yee shall flee like as ye fled from the earthquake in the daies of Vzziah King of Iudah: and the Lord my God shall come, and all the Saints with thee.

6 And in that day shall there bee no cleare light, but darke.

7 And there shall bee a day (it is knowen to the Lord) neither day nor night, but about the euening time it shall be light.

8 And in that day shall there waters of life goe out from Ierusalem, halfe of them towarde the East sea, and halfe of them towarde the vttermost sea, and shall be, both in sommer and winter.

9 And the Lord shall bee King ouer all the earth: in that day shall there bee one Lord, and his Name shalbe one.

10 All the lande shall bee turned as a plaine from Geba to Rimmon, towarde the South of Ierusalem, and it shall be lifted vp, and inhabited in her place: from Beniamins gate vnto the place of the first gate, vnto the corner gate, and from the towre of Hananiel, vnto the Kings wine presses.

11 And men shall dwell in it, and there shall bee no more destruction, but Ierusalem shall bee safely inhabited.

12 And this shall bee the plague, wherewith the Lord will smite all people, that haue fought against Ierusalem: their flesh shall consume away, though they stand vpon their feete, and their eyes shall consume in their holes, and their tongue shall consume in their mouth.

13 But in that day a great tumult of the Lord shall be among them, and euery one shall take the hande of his neighbour, and his hande shall rise vp against the hand of his neighbour.

14 And Iudah shall fight also against Ierusalem, and the arme of all the heathen shall be gathered rounde about, with golde and siluer, and great abundance of apparell.

15 Yet this shall be the plague of the horse, of the mule, of the camell and of the asse and of all the beasts that be in these tents as this plague.

16 But it shall come to passe that euery one that is left of all the nations, which came against Ierusalem, shall goe vp from yere to yere to worship the King the Lord of hostes, and to keepe the feast of Tabernacles.

17 And who so will not come vp of all the families of the earth vnto Ierusalem to

worship the King the Lord of hostes, euen vpon them shall come no raine.

18 And if the familie of Egypt goe not vp, and come not, it shall not raine vpon them. This shall be the plague wherewith the Lord will smite all the heathen, that come not vp to keepe the feast of Tabernacles.

19 This shall be the punishment of Egypt, and the punishment of all the nations that come not vp to keepe the feast of Tabernacles.

20 In that day shall there be written vpon the bridles of the horses, The holinesse vnto the Lord, and the pottes in the Lords house shall be like the bowles before the altar.

21 Yea, euery potte in Ierusalem and Iudah shall be holy vnto the Lord of hostes, and all they that sacrifice, shall come and take of them, and seethe therein: and in that day there shall be no more the Canaanite in the House of the Lord of hostes.

Malachi

Malachi 1

1 The burden of the woorde of the Lord to Israel by the ministerie of Malachi.

2 I haue loued you, sayth the Lord: yet yee say, Wherein hast thou loued vs? Was not Esau Iaakobs brother, saith the Lord? yet I loued Iaakob,

3 And I hated Esau, and made his mountaines wast, and his heritage a wildernes for dragons.

4 Though Edom say, wee are impouerished, but we will returne and build the desolate places, yet sayeth the Lord of hostes, they shall builde, but I will destroy it, and they shall call them, The border of wickednes, and the people, with whome the Lord is angrie for euer.

5 And your eyes shall see it, and yee shall say, The Lord will be magnified vpon the border of Israel.

6 A sonne honoureth his father, and a seruant his master. If then I be a father, where is mine honour? and if I be a master, where is my feare, sayth the Lord of hostes vnto you, O Priestes, that despise my Name? and yee say, Wherein haue we despised thy Name?

7 Ye offer vncleane bread vpon mine altar, and you say, Wherein haue we polluted thee? In that ye say the table of the Lord is not to be regarded.

8 And if yee offer the blinde for sacrifice, it is not euill: and if ye offer the lame and sicke, it is not euill: offer it nowe vnto thy prince: will he be content with thee, or accept thy person, saieth the Lord of hostes?

9 And nowe, I pray you, pray before God, that he may haue mercie vpon vs: this hath beene by your meanes: will hee regard your persons, sayth the Lord of hostes?

10 Who is there euen among you, that would shut the doores? and kindle not fire on mine altar in vaine, I haue no pleasure in you, sayeth the Lord of

hostes, neither will I accept an offering at your hande.

11 For from the rising of the sunne vnto the going downe of the same, my Name is great among the Gentiles, and in euery place incense shalbe offred vnto my Name, and a pure offering: for my Name is great among the heathen, sayeth the Lord of hostes.

12 But ye haue polluted it, in that ye say, The table of the Lord is polluted and the fruit thereof, euen his meat is not to be regarded.

13 Ye said also, Beholde, it is a wearines, and ye haue snuffed at it, sayth the Lord of hostes, and ye offred that which was torne, and the lame and the sicke: thus yee offred an offring: shoulde I accept this of your hand, sayth the Lord?

14 But cursed be the deceiuer, which hath in his flocke a male, and voweth, and sacrificeth vnto ye Lord a corrupt thing: for I am a great King, sayth the Lord of hostes, and my Name is terrible among the heathen.

Malachi 2

1 And now, O ye Priests, this commandement is for you.

2 If yee will not heare it, nor consider it in your heart, to giue glory vnto my Name, sayth the Lord of hostes, I will euen sende a curse vpon you, and will curse your blessings: yea, I haue cursed them alreadie, because yee doe not consider it in your heart.

3 Behold, I wil corrupt your seede, and cast dongue vpon your faces, euen the dongue of your solemne feastes, and you shall be like vnto it.

4 And yee shall know, that I haue sent this commandement vnto you, that my couenant, which I made with Leui, might stand, sayeth the Lord of hostes.

5 My couenant was with him of life and peace, and I gaue him feare, and he feared mee, and was afraid before my Name.

6 The lawe of trueth was in his mouth, and there was no iniquitie founde in his lippes: hee walked with me in peace and equitie, and did turne many away from iniquitie.

7 For the Priestes lippes shoulde preserue knowledge, and they shoulde seeke the Lawe at his mouth: for he is the messenger of the Lord of hostes.

8 But yee are gone out of the way: yee haue caused many to fall by the Lawe: yee haue broken the couenant of Leui, sayeth the Lord of hostes.

9 Therefore haue I also made you to be despised, and vile before all the people, because yee kept not my wayes, but haue beene partiall in the Lawe.

10 Haue we not all one father? hath not one God made vs? why doe we transgresse euery one against his brother, and breake the couenant of our fathers?

11 Iudah hath transgressed, and an abomination is committed in Israel and in Ierusalem: for Iudah hath defiled the

holinesse of the Lord, which hee loued, and hath maried the daughter of a strange God.

12 The Lord will cut off the man that doeth this: both the master and the seruaunt out of the Tabernacle of Iaacob, and him that offereth an offering vnto the Lord of hostes.

13 And this haue ye done againe, and couered the altar of the Lord with teares, with weeping and with mourning: because the offering is no more regarded, neither receiued acceptably at your handes.

14 Yet yee say, Wherein? Because the Lord hath beene witnesse betweene thee and the wife of thy youth, against whome thou hast transgressed: yet is shee thy companion, and the wife of thy couenant.

15 And did not hee make one? yet had hee abundance of spirit: and wherefore one? because he sought a godly seede: therefore keepe your selues in your spirit, and let none trespasse against the wife of his youth.

16 If thou hatest her, put her away, sayeth the Lord God of Israel, yet he couereth the iniurie vnder his garment, saieth the Lord of hosts: therefore keepe your selues in your spirite, and transgresse not.

17 Yee haue wearied the Lord with your woordes: yet yee say, Wherein haue we wearied him? When ye say, Euery one that doeth euill, is good in the sight of the Lord, and he deliteth in them. Or where is the God of iudgement?

Malachi 3

1 Behold, I will send my messenger, and he shall prepare the way before me: and the Lord whom ye seeke, shall speedely come to his Temple: euen the messenger of the couenant whom ye desire: beholde, he shall come, sayth the Lord of hostes.

2 But who may abide the day of his comming? and who shall endure, when he appeareth? for he is like a purging fire, and like fullers sope.

3 And he shall sit downe to trye and fine the siluer: he shall euen fine the sonnes of Leui and purifie them as golde and siluer, that they may bring offerings vnto the Lord in righteousnesse.

4 Then shall the offerings of Iudah and Ierusalem be acceptable vnto the Lord, as in old time and in the yeeres afore.

5 And I will come neere to you to iudgement, and I will be a swift witnesse against the southsayers, and against the adulterers, and against false swearers, and against those that wrongfully keepe backe the hirelings wages, and vexe the widowe, and the fatherlesse, and oppresse the stranger, and feare not me, sayth the Lord of hostes.

6 For I am the Lord: I change not, and ye sonnes of Iaakob are not consumed.

7 From the dayes of your fathers, ye are gone away from mine ordinances, and haue not kept them: returne vnto me, and I will returne vnto you, saith the

Lord of hostes: but ye saide, Wherein shall we returne?

8 Will a man spoyle his gods? yet haue ye spoyled me: but ye say, Wherein haue we spoyled thee? In tithes, and offerings.

9 Ye are cursed with a curse: for ye haue spoyled me, euen this whole nation.

10 Bring ye all the tythes into the storehouse that there may be meate in mine House, and proue me nowe herewith, sayeth the Lord of hostes, if I will not open the windowes of heauen vnto you, and powre you out a blessing without measure.

11 And I will rebuke the deuourer for your sakes, and he shall not destroy the fruite of your grounde, neither shall your vine be baren in the fielde, sayeth the Lord of hostes.

12 And all nations shall call you blessed: for ye shall be a pleasant lande, sayeth the Lord of hostes.

13 Your wordes haue bene stout against me, sayeth the Lord: yet ye say, What haue we spoken against thee?

14 Ye haue saide, It is in vaine to serue God: and what profite is it that we haue kept his commandement, and that we walked humbly before the Lord of hostes?

15 Therefore wee count the proude blessed: euen they that worke wickednesse, are set vp, and they that tempt God, yea, they are deliuered.

16 Then spake they that feared the Lord, euery one to his neighbour, and the Lord hearkened and heard it, and a booke of remembrance was written before him for them that feared the Lord, and that thought vpon his Name.

17 And they shall be to me, sayeth the Lord of hostes, in that day that I shall do this, for a flocke, and I will spare them, as a man spareth his owne sonne that serueth him.

18 Then shall you returne, and discerne betweene the righteous and wicked, betweene him that serueth God, and him that serueth him not.

Malachi 4

1 For behold, the day commeth that shall burne as an ouen, and all the proude, yea, and all that doe wickedly, shall be stubble, and the day that commeth, shall burne them vp, sayeth the Lord of hostes, and shall leaue them neither roote nor branche.

2 But vnto you that feare my Name, shall the sunne of righteousnesse arise, and health shall be vnder his wings, and ye shall goe forth, and growe vp as fat calues.

3 And ye shall treade downe the wicked: for they shall be dust vnder the soles of your feete in the day that I shall doe this, sayeth the Lord of hostes.

4 Remember the lawe of Moses my seruant, which I commanded vnto him in Horeb for all Israel with the statutes and iudgements.

5 Beholde, I will sende you Eliiah the Prophet before the comming of the great and fearefull day of the Lord.

6 And he shall turne the heart of the fathers to the children, and the heart of the children to their fathers, lest I come and smite the earth with cursing.

The New Testament

Matthew

Matthew 1

1 The booke of the generation of Jesus Christ the sonne of Dauid, the sonne of Abraham.

2 Abraham begate Isaac. And Isaac begate Iacob. And Iacob begat Iudas and his brethren.

3 And Iudas begate Phares, and Zara of Thamar. And Phares begate Esrom. And Esrom begate Aram.

4 And Aram begate Aminadab. And Aminadab begate Naasson. And Naasson begat Salmon.

5 And Salmon begate Booz of Rachab. And Booz begat Obed of Ruth. and Obed begat Iesse.

6 And Iesse begate Dauid the King. And Dauid the King begate Salomon of her that was the wife of Vrias.

7 And Salomon begate Roboam. And Roboam begate Abia. And Abia begate Asa.

8 And Asa begate Iosaphat. And Iosaphat begate Ioram. And Ioram begate Hozias.

9 And Hozias begat Ioatham. And Ioatham begate Achaz. And Achaz begate Ezekias.

10 And Ezekias begate Manasses. And Manasses begate Amon. And Amon begate Iosias.

11 And Iosias begate Iakim. And Iakim begate Iechonias and his brethren about the time they were caried away to Babylon.

12 And after they were caried away into Babylon, Iechonias begate Salathiel. And Salathiel begate Zorobabel.

13 And Zorobabel begate Abiud. And Abiud begate Eliacim. And Eliacim begate Azor.

14 And Azor begate Sadoc. And Sadoc begate Achim. And Achim begate Eliud.

15 And Eliud begate Eleazar. And Eleazar begate Matthan. And Matthan begate Iacob.

16 And Iacob begat Ioseph ye husband of Mary, of whom was borne Jesus, that is called Christ.

17 So all the generations from Abraham to Dauid, are fourtene generations. And from Dauid vntil they were caried away into Babylon, fourtene generations: and after they were caried away into Babylon vntill Christ, fourteene generations.

18 Nowe the birth of Jesus Christ was thus, When as his mother Mary was betrothed to Ioseph, before they came together, shee was found with childe of the holy Ghost.

19 Then Ioseph her husband being a iust man, and not willing to make her a publike example, was minded to put her away secretly.

20 But whiles he thought these things, behold, the Angel of the Lord appeared vnto him in a dreame, saying, Ioseph, the sonne of Dauid, feare not to take Mary thy wife: for that which is conceiued in her, is of the holy Ghost.

21 And she shall bring foorth a sonne, and thou shalt call his name JESUS: for hee shall saue his people from their sinnes.

22 And al this was done that it might be fulfilled, which is spoken of the Lord by ye Prophet, saying,

23 Behold, a virgine shalbe with childe, and shall beare a sonne, and they shall call his name Emmanuel, which is by interpretation, God with vs.

24 Then Ioseph, being raised from sleepe, did as the Angel of the Lord had inioyned him, and tooke his wife.

25 But he knew her not, til she had broght forth her first borne sonne, and he called his name JESUS.

Matthew 2

1 When Jesus then was borne at Bethleem in Iudea, in the dayes of Herod the King, beholde, there came Wisemen from the East to Hierusalem,

2 Saying, Where is that King of the Iewes that is borne? for wee haue seene his starre in the East, and are come to worship him.

3 When King Herod heard this, he was troubled, and all Hierusalem with him.

4 And gathering together all the chiefe Priestes and Scribes of the people, hee asked of them, where Christ should be borne.

5 And they saide vnto him, At Beth-leem in Iudea: for so it is written by the Prophet,

6 And thou Beth-leem in the lande of Iuda, art not the least among the Princes of Iuda: For out of thee shall come the gouernour that shall feede that my people Israel.

7 Then Herod priuily called the Wisemen, and diligently inquired of them the time of the starre that appeared,

8 And sent them to Beth-leem, saying, Goe, and searche diligently for the babe: and when ye haue founde him, bring mee worde againe, that I may come also, and worship him.

9 So when they had heard the King, they departed: and loe, the starre which they had seene in the East, went before them, till it came and stoode ouer the place where the babe was.

10 And when they sawe the starre, they reioyced with an exceeding great ioy,

11 And went into the house, and founde the babe with Mary his mother, and fell downe, and worshipped him, and opened their treasures, and presented vnto him giftes, euen golde, and frankincense, and myrrhe.

12 And after they were warned of God in a dreame, that they should not go againe to Herod, they returned into their countrey another way.

13 After their departure, behold, the Angel of the Lord appeareth to Ioseph in a dreame, saying, Arise, and take the babe and his mother, and flee into Egypt, and be there til I bring thee word: for Herod will seeke the babe, to destroy him.

14 So he arose and tooke the babe and his mother by night, and departed into Egypt,

15 And was there vnto the death of Herod, that that might be fulfilled, which is spoken of the Lord by the Prophet, saying, Out of Egypt haue I called my sonne.

16 Then Herod, seeing that he was mocked of the Wisemen, was exceeding wroth, and sent foorth, and slew all the male children that were in Beth-leem, and in all the coasts thereof, from two yeere old and vnder, according to the time which he had diligently searched out of the Wisemen.

17 Then was that fulfilled which is spoken by the Prophet Ieremias, saying,

18 In Rhama was a voyce heard, mourning, and weeping, and great howling: Rachel weeping for her children, and would not be comforted, because they were not.

19 And whe Herod was dead, behold, an Angel of the Lord appeareth in a dreame to Ioseph in Egypt,

20 Saying, Arise, and take the babe and his mother, and goe into the land of Israel: for they are dead which sought the babes life.

21 Then he arose vp and tooke the babe and his mother, and came into the land of Israel.

22 But whe he heard that Archelaus did reigne in Iudea in stead of his father Herod, he was afraide to go thither: yet after he was warned of God in a dreame, he turned aside into the parts of Galile,

23 And went and dwelt in a citie called Nazareth, that it might be fulfilled which was spoken by the Prophets, which was, That hee should be called a Nazarite.

Matthew 3

1 And in those dayes, Iohn the Baptist came and preached in the wildernes of Iudea,

2 And said, Repent: for the kingdome of heauen is at hand.

3 For this is he of whome it is spoken by the Prophet Esaias, saying, The voyce of him that crieth in the wildernes, Prepare ye the way of the Lord: make his pathes straight.

4 And this Iohn had his garment of camels heare, and a girdle of a skinne about his loynes: his meate was also locusts and wilde hony.

5 Then went out to him Ierusalem and all Iudea, and all the region rounde about Iordan.

6 And they were baptized of him in Iordan, confessing their sinnes.

7 Now when he sawe many of the Pharises, and of the Sadduces come to his baptisme, he said vnto them, O generations of vipers, who hath forewarned you to flee from the anger to come?

8 Bring foorth therefore fruite worthy amendment of life.

9 And thinke not to say with your selues, We haue Abraham to our father: for I say vnto you, that God is able euen of these stones to raise vp children vnto Abraham.

10 And now also is the axe put to the roote of the trees: therfore euery tree which bringeth not forth good fruit, is hewen downe, and cast into ye fire.

11 In deede I baptize you with water to amendment of life, but he that commeth after me, is mightier then I, whose shoes I am not worthie to beare: hee will baptize you with the holy Ghost, and with fire.

12 Which hath his fanne in his hand, and wil make cleane his floore, and gather his wheate into his garner, but will burne vp the chaffe with vnquenchable fire.

13 Then came Iesus from Galile to Iordan vnto Iohn, to be baptized of him.

14 But Iohn earnestly put him backe, saying, I haue neede to be baptized of thee, and commest thou to me?

15 Then Iesus answering, saide to him, Let be nowe: for thus it becommeth vs to fulfill all righteousnes. So he suffered him.

16 And Iesus when hee was baptized, came straight out of the water. And lo, the heaues were opened vnto him, and Iohn saw the Spirit of God descending like a doue, and lighting vpon him.

17 And loe, a voyce came from heauen, saying, This is my beloued Sonne, in whome I am well pleased.

Matthew 4

1 Then was Iesus led aside of the Spirit into the wildernes, to be tempted of the deuil.

2 And when he had fasted fourtie dayes, and fourtie nights, he was afterward hungrie.

3 Then came to him the tempter, and said, If thou be the Sonne of God, commande that these stones be made bread.

4 But he answering said, It is written, Man shall not liue by bread onely, but by euery worde that proceedeth out of the mouth of God.

5 Then the deuil tooke him vp into the holy Citie, and set him on a pinacle of the temple,

6 And said vnto him, If thou be the Sonne of God, cast thy selfe downe: for it is written, that he wil giue his Angels charge ouer thee, and with their hands they shall lift thee vp, lest at any time thou shouldest dash thy foote against a stone.

7 Iesus saide vnto him, It is written againe, Thou shalt not tempt the Lord thy God.

8 Againe the deuil tooke him vp into an exceeding hie mountaine, and shewed him all the kingdomes of the world, and the glory of them,

9 And sayd to him, All these will I giue thee, if thou wilt fall downe, and worship me.

10 Then sayd Iesus vnto him, Auoyde Satan: for it is written, Thou shalt worship the Lord thy God, and him onely shalt thou serue.

11 Then the deuill left him: and beholde, the Angels came, and ministred vnto him.

12 And when Iesus had heard that Iohn was committed to prison, he returned into Galile.

13 And leauing Nazareth, went and dwelt in Capernaum, which is neere the sea in the borders of Zabulon and Nephthalim,

14 That it might be fulfilled which was spoken by Esaias the Propet, saying,

15 The land of Zabulon, and the land of Nephthalim by the way of the sea, beyond Iordan, Galile of the Gentiles:

16 The people which sate in darkenes, sawe great light: and to them which sate in the region, and shadowe of death, light is risen vp.

17 From that time Iesus began to preach, and to say, Amende your liues: for the kingdome of heauen is at hand.

18 And Iesus walking by the sea of Galile, sawe two brethren, Simon, which was called Peter, and Andrew his brother, casting a net into the sea (for they were fishers.)

19 And he sayd vnto them, Follow me, and I will make you fishers of men.

20 And they straightway leauing the nets, folowed him.

21 And when he was gone forth from thence, he saw other two brethren, Iames the sonne of Zebedeus, and Iohn his brother in a ship with Zebedeus their father, mending their nets, and he called them.

22 And they without tarying, leauing the ship, and their father, folowed him.

23 So Iesus went about all Galile, teaching in their Synagogues, and preaching the Gospel of the kingdome, and healing euery sicknesse and euery disease among the people.

24 And his fame spread abroad through all Syria: and they brought vnto him all sicke people, that were taken with diuers diseases and torments, and them that were possessed with deuils, and those which were lunatike, and those that had the palsey: and he healed them.

25 And there folowed him great multitudes out of Galile, and Decapolis, and Hierusalem, and Iudea, and from beyond Iordan.

Matthew 5

1 And when he sawe the multitude, he went vp into a mountaine: and when he was set, his disciples came to him.

2 And he opened his mouth and taught them, saying,

3 Blessed are the poore in spirit, for theirs is the kingdome of heauen.

4 Blessed are they that mourne: for they shall be comforted.

5 Blessed are the meeke: for they shall inherite the earth.

6 Blessed are they which hunger and thirst for righteousnes: for they shalbe filled.

7 Blessed are the mercifull: for they shall obteine mercie.

8 Blessed are the pure in heart: for they shall see God.

9 Blessed are the peace makers: for they shall be called the children of God.

10 Blessed are they which suffer persecution for righteousnes sake: for theirs is the kingdome of heauen.

11 Blessed shall ye be when men reuile you, and persecute you, and say all maner of euill against you for my sake, falsely.

12 Reioyce and be glad, for great is your reward in heauen: for so persecuted they the Prophets which were before you.

13 Ye are the salt of the earth: but if the salt haue lost his sauour, wherewith shall it be salted? It is thenceforth good for nothing, but to be cast out, and to be troden vnder foote of men.

14 Ye are the light of the world. A citie that is set on an hill, cannot be hid.

15 Neither doe men light a candel, and put it vnder a bushel, but on a candlesticke, and it giueth light vnto all that are in the house.

16 Let your light so shine before men, that they may see your good workes, and glorifie your Father which is in heauen.

17 Think not that I am come to destroy the Lawe, or the Prophets. I am not come to destroy them, but to fulfill them.

18 For truely I say vnto you, Till heauen, and earth perish, one iote or one title of the Law shall not scape, till all things be fulfilled.

19 Whosoeuer therefore shall breake one of these least commandements, and teach men so, he shall be called the least in the kingdome of heauen: but whosoeuer shall obserue and teach them, the same shall be called great in the kingdome of heauen.

20 For I say vnto you, except your righteousnes exceede the righteousnes of the Scribes and Pharises, ye shall not enter into the kingdome of heauen.

21 Ye haue heard that it was sayd vnto them of the olde time, Thou shalt not kill: for whosoeuer killeth shalbe culpable of iudgement.

22 But I say vnto you, whosoeuer is angry with his brother vnaduisedly, shalbe culpable of iudgment. And whosoeuer sayth vnto his brother, Raca, shalbe worthy to be punished by the Councill. And whosoeuer shall say, Foole, shalbe worthy to be punished with hell fire.

23 If then thou bring thy gift to the altar, and there remembrest that thy brother hath ought against thee,

24 Leaue there thine offring before the altar, and goe thy way: first be reconciled to thy brother, and then come and offer thy gift.

25 Agree with thine aduersarie quickly, whiles thou art in the way with him, lest thine aduersarie deliuer thee to the Iudge, and the Iudge deliuer thee to ye sergeant, and thou be cast into prison.

26 Verely I say vnto thee, thou shalt not come out thence, till thou hast payed the vtmost farthing.

27 Ye haue heard that it was sayd to them of olde time, Thou shalt not commit adulterie.

28 But I say vnto you, that whosoeuer looketh on a woman to lust after her, hath committed adulterie with her already in his heart.

29 Wherefore if thy right eye cause thee to offend, plucke it out, and cast it from thee: for better it is for thee, that one of thy members perish, then that thy whole body should be cast into hell.

30 Also if thy right hand make thee to offend, cut it off, and cast it from thee: for better it is for thee that one of thy members perish, then that thy whole body should be cast into hell.

31 It hath bene sayd also, Whosoeuer shall put away his wife, let him giue her a bill of diuorcement.

32 But I say vnto you, whosoeuer shall put away his wife (except it be for fornication) causeth her to commit adulterie: and whosoeuer shall marrie her that is diuorced, committeth adulterie.

33 Againe, ye haue heard that it was sayd to them of old time, Thou shalt not forsweare thy selfe, but shalt performe thine othes to the Lord.

34 But I say vnto you, Sweare not at all, neither by heauen, for it is the throne of God:

35 Nor yet by the earth: for it is his footestoole: neither by Hierusalem: for it is the citie of the great King.

36 Neither shalt thou sweare by thine head, because thou canst not make one heare white or blacke.

37 But let your communication be Yea, yea: Nay, nay. For whatsoeuer is more then these, commeth of euill.

38 Ye haue heard that it hath bene sayd, An eye for an eye, and a tooth for a tooth.

39 But I say vnto you, Resist not euill: but whosoeuer shall smite thee on thy right cheeke, turne to him the other also.

40 And if any man wil sue thee at the law, and take away thy coate, let him haue thy cloke also.

41 And whosoeuer will compell thee to goe a mile, goe with him twaine.

42 Giue to him that asketh, and from him that would borowe of thee, turne not away.

43 Ye haue heard that it hath bin said, Thou shalt loue thy neighbour, and hate your enemie.

44 But I say vnto you, Loue your enemies: blesse them that curse you: doe good to them that hate you, and pray for them which hurt you, and persecute you,

45 That ye may be the children of your father that is in heauen: for he maketh his sunne to arise on the euill, and the good, and sendeth raine on the iust, and vniust.

46 For if ye loue them, which loue you, what rewarde shall you haue? Doe not the Publicanes euen the same?

47 And if ye be friendly to your brethren onely, what singular thing doe ye? doe not euen the Publicanes likewise?

48 Ye shall therefore be perfit, as your Father which is in heauen, is perfite.

Matthew 6

1 Take heede that ye giue not your almes before men, to be seene of them, or els ye shall haue no reward of your Father which is in heaue.

2 Therefore when thou giuest thine almes, thou shalt not make a trumpet to be blowen before thee, as the hypocrites doe in the Synagogues and in the streetes, to be praysed of men. Verely I say vnto you, they haue their rewarde.

3 But when thou doest thine almes, let not thy left hand knowe what thy right hand doeth,

4 That thine almes may be in secret, and thy Father that seeth in secret, hee will rewarde thee openly.

5 And when thou prayest, be not as the hypocrites: for they loue to stand, and pray in the Synagogues, and in the corners of the streetes, because they would be seene of men. Verely I say vnto you, they haue their rewarde.

6 But when thou prayest, enter into thy chamber and when thou hast shut thy doore, pray vnto thy Father which is in secret, and thy Father which seeth in secret, shall rewarde thee openly.

7 Also when ye pray, vse no vaine repetitions as the Heathen: for they thinke to be heard for their much babbling.

8 Be ye not like them therefore: for your Father knoweth whereof ye haue neede, before ye aske of him.

9 After this maner therefore pray ye, Our father which art in heauen, halowed be thy name.

10 Thy Kingdome come. Thy will be done euen in earth, as it is in heauen.

11 Giue vs this day our dayly bread.

12 And forgiue vs our dettes, as we also forgiue our detters.

13 And leade vs not into tentation, but deliuer vs from euill: for thine is the kingdome, and the power, and the glorie for euer. Amen.

14 For if ye doe forgiue men their trespasses, your heauenly Father will also forgiue you.

15 But if ye do not forgiue men their trespasses,, no more will your father forgiue you your trespaces.

16 Moreouer, when ye fast, looke not sowre as the hypocrites: for they disfigure their faces, that they might seeme vnto men to fast. Verely I say vnto you, that they haue their rewarde.

17 But when thou fastest, anoint thine head, and wash thy face,

18 That thou seeme not vnto men to fast, but vnto thy Father which is in secret: and thy Father which seeth in secret, will rewarde thee openly.

19 Lay not vp treasures for your selues vpon the earth, where the mothe and canker corrupt, and where theeues digge through and steale.

20 But lay vp treasures for your selues in heauen, where neither the mothe nor canker corrupteth, and where theeues neither digge through, nor steale.

21 For where your treasure is, there will your heart be also.

22 The light of the body is the eye: if then thine eye be single, thy whole body shall be light.

23 But if thine eye be wicked, then all thy body shalbe darke. Wherefore if the light that is in thee, be darkenes, howe great is that darkenesse?

24 No man can serue two masters: for eyther he shall hate the one, and loue the other, or els he shall leane to the one, and despise the other. Ye cannot serue God and riches.

25 Therefore I say vnto you, be not carefull for your life, what ye shall eate, or what ye shall drinke: nor yet for your body, what ye shall put on. Is not the life more worth then meate? and the bodie then raiment?

26 Behold the foules of the heauen: for they sowe not, neither reape, nor carie into the barnes: yet your heauenly Father feedeth them. Are ye not much better then they?

27 Which of you by taking care is able to adde one cubite vnto his stature?

28 And why care ye for raiment? Learne howe the lilies of the fielde doe growe: they are not wearied, neither spinne:

29 Yet I say vnto you, that euen Salomon in all his glorie was not arayed like one of these.

30 Wherefore if God so clothe the grasse of the fielde which is to day, and to morowe is cast into the ouen, shall he not doe much more vnto you, O ye of litle faith?

31 Therefore take no thought, saying, What shall we eate? or what shall we drinke? or where with shall we be clothed?

32 (For after all these things seeke the Gentiles) for your heauenly Father knoweth, that ye haue neede of all these things.

33 But seeke ye first the kingdome of God, and his righteousnesse, and all these things shall be ministred vnto you.

34 Care not then for the morowe: for the morowe shall care for it selfe: the day hath ynough with his owne griefe.

Matthew 7

1 Judge not, that ye be not iudged.

2 For with what iudgement ye iudge, ye shall be iudged, and with what measure ye mete, it shall be measured to you againe.

3 And why seest thou the mote, that is in thy brothers eye, and perceiuest not the beame that is in thine owne eye?

4 Or howe sayest thou to thy brother, Suffer me to cast out the mote out of thine eye, and beholde, a beame is in thine owne eye?

5 Hypocrite, first cast out that beame out of thine owne eye, and then shalt thou see clearely to cast out the mote out of thy brothers eye.

6 Giue ye not that which is holy, to dogges, neither cast ye your pearles before swine, lest they treade them vnder their feete, and turning againe, all to rent you.

7 Aske, and it shall be giuen you: seeke, and ye shall finde: knocke, and it shall be opened vnto you.

8 For whosoeuer asketh, receiueth: and he, that seeketh, findeth: and to him that knocketh, it shall be opened.

9 For what man is there among you, which if his sonne aske him bread, woulde giue him a stone?

10 Or if he aske fish, wil he giue him a serpent?

11 If ye then, which are euill, can giue to your children good giftes, howe much more shall your Father which is in heauen, giue good thinges to them that aske him?

12 Therefore whatsoeuer ye woulde that men should doe to you, euen so doe ye to them: for this is the Lawe and the Prophets.

13 Enter in at the streight gate: for it is the wide gate, and broade way that leadeth to destruction: and many there be which goe in thereat.

14 Because the gate is streight, and the way narowe that leadeth vnto life, and fewe there be that finde it.

15 Beware of false prophets, which come to you, in sheepes clothing, but inwardly they are rauening wolues.

16 Ye shall know them by their fruites. Doe men gather grapes of thornes? or figges of thistles?

17 So euery good tree bringeth foorth good fruite, and a corrupt tree bringeth forth euill fruite.

18 A good tree can not bring forth euil fruite: neither can a corrupt tree bring forth good fruite.

19 Euery tree that bringeth not forth good fruite, is hewen downe, and cast into the fire.

20 Therefore by their fruites ye shall knowe them.

21 Not euery one that sayeth vnto me, Lord, Lord, shall enter into the kingdome of heauen, but he that doeth my Fathers will which is in heauen.

22 Many will say to me in that day, Lord, Lord, haue we not by thy Name prophecied? and by thy name cast out deuils? and by thy name done many great workes?

23 And then will I professe to them, I neuer knewe you: depart from me, ye that worke iniquitie.

24 Whosoeuer then heareth of mee these words, and doeth the same, I will liken him to a wise man, which hath builded his house on a rock:

25 And the raine fell, and the floods came, and the windes blewe, and beat vpon that house, and it fell not: for it was grounded on a rocke.

26 But whosoeuer heareth these my wordes, and doeth them not, shall be likened vnto a foolish man, which hath builded his house vpon the sand:

27 And the raine fell, and the floods came, and the windes blewe, and beat vpon that house, and it fell, and the fall thereof was great.

28 And it came to passe, when Iesus had ended these wordes, the people were astonied at his doctrine.

29 For he taught them as one hauing authoritie, and not as the Scribes.

Matthew 8

1 Nowe when he was come downe from the mountaine, great multitudes followed him.

2 And loe, there came a Leper and worshipped him, saying, Master, if thou wilt, thou canst make me cleane.

3 And Iesus putting foorth his hand, touched him, saying, I will, be thou cleane: and immediatly his leprosie was clensed.

4 Then Iesus saide vnto him, See thou tell no man, but goe, and shewe thy selfe vnto the Priest, and offer the gift that Moses commanded, for a witnesse to them.

5 When Iesus was entred into Capernaum, there came vnto him a Centurion, beseeching him,

6 And saide, Master, my seruant lieth sicke at home of the palsie, and is grieuously pained.

7 And Iesus saide vnto him, I will come and heale him.

8 But the Centurion answered, saying, Master, I am not worthy that thou shouldest come vnder my roofe: but speake the worde onely, and my seruant shall be healed.

9 For I am a man also vnder the authoritie of an other, and haue souldiers vnder me: and I say to one, Goe, and he goeth: and to another, Come, and he commeth: and to my seruant, Doe this, and he doeth it.

10 When Iesus heard that, he marueiled, and said to them that folowed him, Verely, I say vnto you, I haue not found so great faith, euen in Israel.

11 But I say vnto you, that many shall come from the East and West, and shall sit downe with Abraham, and Isaac, and Iacob, in the kingdome of heauen.

12 And the children of the kingdome shall be cast out into vtter darkenes: there shalbe weeping and gnashing of teeth.

13 Then Iesus saide vnto the Centurion, Goe thy way, and as thou hast beleeued, so be it vnto thee, And his seruant was healed the same houre.

14 And when Iesus came to Peters house, he sawe his wiues mother layed downe, and sicke of a feuer.

15 And he touched her hande, and the feuer left her: so she arose, and ministred vnto them.

16 When the Euen was come, they brought vnto him many that were possessed with deuils: and he cast out the spirits with his worde, and healed all that were sicke,

17 That it might be fulfilled, which was spoken by Esaias the Prophet, saying, He tooke our infirmities, and bare our sickenesses.

18 And when Iesus sawe great multitudes of people about him, he commanded them to goe ouer the water.

19 Then came there a certaine Scribe, and said vnto him, Master, I will follow thee whithersoeuer thou goest.

20 But Iesus saide vnto him, The foxes haue holes, and the birdes of the heauen haue nestes, but the Sonne of man hath not whereon to rest his head.

21 And another of his disciples saide vnto him, Master, suffer me first to goe, and burie my father.

22 But Iesus said vnto him, Followe me, and let the dead burie their dead.

23 And when he was entred into ye ship, his disciples followed him.

24 And beholde, there arose a great tempest in the sea, so that the ship was couered with waues: but he was a sleepe.

25 Then his disciples came, and awoke him, saying, Master, saue vs: we perish.

26 And he said vnto them, Why are ye fearefull, O ye of litle faith? Then he arose, and rebuked the winds and the sea: and so there was a great calme.

27 And the men marueiled, saying, What man is this, that both the windes and the sea obey him!

28 And when he was come to the other side into ye countrey of the Gergesenes, there met him two possessed with deuils, which came out of the graues very fierce, so that no man might goe by that way.

29 And beholde, they cryed out, saying, Iesus the sonne of God, what haue we to do with thee? Art thou come hither to tormet vs before ye time?

30 Nowe there was, afarre off from them, a great heard of swine feeding.

31 And the deuils besought him, saying, If thou cast vs out, suffer vs to goe into the heard of swine.

32 And he said vnto them, Go. So they went out and departed into the heard of swine: and beholde, the whole heard of swine ranne headlong into the sea, and died in the water.

33 Then the heardmen fled: and when they were come into the citie, they tolde all things, and what was become of them that were possessed with the deuils.

34 And beholde, all ye citie came out to meete Iesus: and when they sawe him, they besought him to depart out of their coastes.

Matthew 9

1 Then hee entred into a shippe, and passed ouer, and came into his owne citie.

2 And loe, they brought to him a man sicke of the palsie, laid on a bed. And Iesus seeing their faith, saide to the sicke of the palsie, Sonne, be of good comfort: thy sinnes be forgiuen thee.

3 And beholde, certaine of the Scribes saide with themselues, This man blasphemeth.

4 But when Iesus saw their thoughts, he said, Wherefore thinke yee euil things in your hearts?

5 For whether is it easier to say, Thy sinnes are forgiuen thee, or to say, Arise, and walke?

6 And that ye may knowe that the Sonne of man hath authoritie in earth to forgiue sinnes, (then saide he vnto the sicke of the palsie,) Arise, take vp thy bed, and goe to thine house.

7 And hee arose, and departed to his owne house.

8 So when the multitude sawe it, they marueiled, and glorified God, which had giuen such authoritie to men.

9 And as Iesus passed foorth from thence, hee sawe a man sitting at the custome, named Matthewe, and saide to him, Followe me. And he arose, and followed him.

10 And it came to passe, as Iesus sate at meate in his house, beholde, many Publicanes and sinners, that came thither, sate downe at the table with Iesus and his disciples.

11 And when the Pharises sawe that, they saide to his disciples, Why eateth your master with Publicanes and sinners?

12 Nowe when Iesus heard it, hee sayde vnto them, The whole neede not a Physition, but they that are sicke.

13 But goe yee and learne what this is, I will haue mercie, and not sacrifice: for I am not come to call the righteous, but the sinners to repentance.

14 Then came the disciples of Iohn to him, saying, Why doe we and the Pharises fast oft, and thy disciples fast not?

15 And Iesus saide vnto them, Can the children of the marriage chamber mourne as long as the bridegrome is with them? But the daies will come, when the bridegrome shall be taken from them, and then shall they fast.

16 Moreouer no man pieceth an olde garment with a piece of newe cloth: for that that should fill it vp, taketh away from the garment, and the breach is worse.

17 Neither doe they put newe wine into olde vessels: for then the vessels would breake, and the wine woulde be spilt, and the vessels shoulde perish: but they put new wine into newe vessels, and so are both preserued.

18 While hee thus spake vnto them, beholde, there came a certaine ruler, and worshipped him, saying, My daughter is nowe deceased, but come and laie thine hande on her, and shee shall liue.

19 And Iesus arose and followed him with his disciples.

20 (And beholde, a woman which was diseased with an issue of blood twelue yeres, came behinde him, and touched the hemme of his garment.

21 For shee saide in her selfe, If I may touche but his garment onely, I shalbe whole.

22 Then Iesus turned him about, and seeing her, did say, Daughter, be of good comfort: thy faith hath made thee whole. And the woman was made whole at that same moment.)

23 Nowe when Iesus came into the Rulers house, and saw the minstrels and the multitude making noise,

24 He said vnto them, Get you hence: for the maid is not dead, but sleepeth. And they laughed him to scorne.

25 And when the multitude were put foorth, hee went in and tooke her by the hande, and the maide arose.

26 And this bruite went throughout all that lande.

27 And as Iesus departed thence, two blinde men followed him, crying, and saying, O sonne of Dauid, haue mercie vpon vs.

28 And when hee was come into the house, the blinde came to him, and Iesus saide vnto them, Beleeue yee that I am able to doe this? And they sayd vnto him, Yea, Lord.

29 Then touched he their eyes, saying, According to your faith be it vnto you.

30 And their eyes were opened, and Iesus gaue them great charge, saying, See that no man knowe it.

31 But when they were departed, they spread abroad his fame throughout all that land.

32 And as they went out, beholde, they brought to him a domme man possessed with a deuill.

33 And when the deuill was cast out, the domme spake: then the multitude marueiled, saying, The like was neuer seene in Israel.

34 But the Pharises saide, He casteth out deuils, through the prince of deuils.

35 And Iesus went about all cities and townes, teaching in their Synagogues, and preaching the Gospel of the kingdome, and healing euery sickenesse and euery disease among the people.

36 But when he saw the multitude, he had compassion vpon them, because they were dispersed, and scattered abroade, as sheepe hauing no shepheard.

37 Then saide he to his disciples, Surely the haruest is great, but the labourers are fewe.

38 Wherefore pray the Lord of the haruest, that he woulde sende foorth labourers into his haruest.

Matthew 10

1 And hee called his twelue disciples vnto him, and gaue them power against vncleane spirits, to cast them out, and to heale euery sickenesse, and euery disease.

2 Nowe the names of the twelue Apostles are these. The first is Simon, called Peter, and Andrew his brother: Iames the sonne of Zebedeus, and Iohn his brother.

3 Philippe and Bartlemewe: Thomas, and Matthewe that Publicane: Iames the

sonne of Alpheus, and Lebbeus whose surname was Thaddeus:

4 Simon the Cananite, and Iudas Iscariot, who also betraied him.

5 These twelue did Iesus send forth, and commanded them, saying, Goe not into the way of of the Gentiles, and into the cities of the Samaritans enter yee not:

6 But goe rather to the lost sheepe of the house of Israel.

7 And as ye goe, preach, saying, The kingdome of heauen is at hand.

8 Heale the sicke: cleanse the lepers: raise vp the dead: cast out the deuils. Freely ye haue receiued, freely giue.

9 Possesse not golde, nor siluer, nor money in your girdels,

10 Nor a scrippe for the iourney, neither two coates, neither shoes, nor a staffe: for the workeman is worthie of his meate.

11 And into whatsoeuer citie or towne ye shall come, enquire who is worthy in it, and there abide till yee goe thence.

12 And when yee come into an house, salute the same.

13 And if the house be worthy, let your peace come vpon it: but if it be not worthie, let your peace returne to you.

14 And whosoeuer shall not receiue you, nor heare your woordes, when yee depart out of that house, or that citie, shake off the dust of your feete.

15 Truely I say vnto you, it shall be easier for them of the lande of Sodom and Gomorrha in the day of iudgement, then for that citie.

16 Behold, I send you as sheepe in the middes of the wolues: be yee therefore wise as serpents, and innocent as doues.

17 But beware of men, for they will deliuer you vp to the Councils, and will scourge you in their Synagogues.

18 And ye shall be brought to the gouernours and Kings for my sake, in witnes to them, and to the Gentiles.

19 But when they deliuer you vp, take no thought howe or what ye shall speake: for it shall be giuen you in that houre, what ye shall say.

20 For it is not yee that speake, but the spirite of your father which speaketh in you.

21 And the brother shall betray the brother to death, and the father the sonne, and the children shall rise against their parents, and shall cause them to die.

22 And yee shall be hated of all men for my Name: but he that endureth to the end, he shall be saued.

23 And when they persecute you in this citie, flee into another: for verely I say vnto you, yee shall not goe ouer all the cities of Israel, till the Sonne of man be come.

24 The disciple is not aboue his master, nor the seruant aboue his Lord.

25 It is ynough for the disciple to bee as his master is, and the seruaunt as his Lord. If they haue called the master of the house Beel-zebub, howe much more them of his housholde?

26 Feare them not therefore: for there is nothing couered, that shall not be disclosed, nor hid, that shall not be knowen.

27 What I tell you in darkenesse, that speake yee in light: and what yee heare in the eare, that preach yee on the houses.

28 And feare yee not them which kill the bodie, but are nor able to kill the soule: but rather feare him, which is able to destroy both soule and bodie in hell.

29 Are not two sparrowes sold for a farthing, and one of them shall not fal on the ground without your Father?

30 Yea, and all the heares of your head are nombred.

31 Feare ye not therefore, yee are of more value then many sparowes.

32 Whosoeuer therefore shall confesse me before men, him will I confesse also before my Father which is in heauen.

33 But whosoeuer shall denie me before me, him will I also denie before my Father which is in heauen.

34 Thinke not that I am come to sende peace into the earth: I came not to send peace, but the sworde.

35 For I am come to set a man at variance against his father, and the daughter against her mother, and the daughter in law against her mother in lawe.

36 And a mans enemies shall be they of his owne housholde.

37 He that loueth father or mother more then me, is not worthie of me. And he that loueth sonne, or daughter more then mee, is not worthie of me.

38 And hee that taketh not his crosse, and followeth after me, is not worthie of me.

39 He that will finde his life, shall lose it: and he that loseth his life for my sake, shall finde it.

40 He that receiueth you, receiueth me: and hee that receiueth mee, receiueth him that hath sent me.

41 Hee that receiueth a Prophet in the name of a Prophet, shall receiue a Prophetes rewarde: and hee that receiueth a righteous man, in the name of a righteous man, shall receiue the rewarde of a righteous man.

42 And whosoeuer shall giue vnto one of these litle ones to drinke a cuppe of colde water onely, in the name of a disciple, verely I say vnto you, he shall not lose his rewarde.

Matthew 11

1 And it came to passe that when Iesus had made an ende of commaunding his twelue disciples, hee departed thence to teache and to preach in their cities.

2 And when Iohn heard in the prison the woorkes of Christ, he sent two of his disciples, and sayde vnto him,

3 Art thou he that shoulde come, or shall we looke for another?

4 And Iesus answering, said vnto them, Goe, and shewe Iohn, what things ye heare, and see.

5 The blinde receiue sight, and the halt doe walke: the lepers are clensed, and the deafe heare, the dead are raised vp, and the poore receiue the Gospel.

6 And blessed is he that shall not be offeded in me.

7 And as they departed, Iesus beganne to speake vnto the multitude, of Iohn, What went ye out into the wildernes to see? A reede shaken with the winde?

8 But what went ye out to see? A man clothed in soft raiment? Behold, they that weare soft clothing, are in Kings houses.

9 But what went ye out to see? A Prophet? Yea, I say vnto you, and more then a Prophet.

10 For this is he of whom it is written, Beholde, I send my messenger before thy face, which shall prepare thy way before thee.

11 Verely I say vnto you, among them which are begotten of women, arose there not a greater then Iohn Baptist: notwithstanding, he that is the least in the kingdome of heauen, is greater then he.

12 And from the time of Iohn Baptist hitherto, the kingdome of heauen suffereth violence, and the violent take it by force.

13 For all the Prophetes and the Lawe prophecied vnto Iohn.

14 And if ye will receiue it, this is that Elias, which was to come.

15 He that hath eares to heare, let him heare.

16 But whereunto shall I liken this generation? It is like vnto litle children which sit in the markets, and call vnto their fellowes,

17 And say, We haue piped vnto you, and ye haue not daunced, we haue mourned vnto you, and ye haue not lamented.

18 For Iohn came neither eating nor drinking, and they say, He hath a deuill.

19 The sonne of man came eating and drinking, and they say, Beholde a glutton and a drinker of wine, a friend vnto Publicanes and sinners: but wisedome is iustified of her children.

20 Then began he to vpbraide the cities, wherein most of his great workes were done, because they repented not.

21 Woe be to thee, Chorazin: Woe be to thee, Bethsaida: for if ye great workes, which were done in you, had bene done in Tyrus and Sidon, they had repented long agone in sackecloth and ashes.

22 But I say to you, It shalbe easier for Tyrus and Sidon at the day of iudgement, then for you.

23 And thou, Capernaum, which art lifted vp vnto heauen, shalt be brought downe to hell: for if the great workes, which haue bin done in thee, had bene done among them of Sodom, they had remained to this day.

24 But I say vnto you, that it shall be easier for them of the land of Sodom in the day of iudgement, then for thee.

25 At that time Iesus answered, and saide, I giue thee thankes, O Father, Lord of heauen and earth, because thou hast hid these things from the wise and

men of vnderstanding, and hast opened them vnto babes.

26 It is so, O Father, because thy good pleasure was such.

27 All things are giuen vnto me of my Father: and no man knoweth the Sonne, but ye Father: neither knoweth any man ye Father, but the Sonne, and he to whom ye Sonne will reueile him.

28 Come vnto me, all ye that are wearie and laden, and I will ease you.

29 Take my yoke on you, and learne of me that I am meeke and lowly in heart: and ye shall finde rest vnto your soules.

30 For my yoke is easie, and my burden light.

Matthew 12

1 At that time Iesus went on a Sabbath day through ye corne, and his disciples were an hungred, and bega to plucke ye eares of corne and to eate.

2 And when the Pharises sawe it, they saide vnto him, Beholde, thy disciples doe that which is not lawfull to doe vpon the Sabbath.

3 But he said vnto them, Haue ye not read what Dauid did when he was an hungred, and they that were with him?

4 Howe he entred into ye house of God, and did eate the shewe bread, which was not lawfull for him to eate, neither for them which were with him, but onely for the Priestes?

5 Or haue ye not read in the Lawe, how that on the Sabbath dayes the Priestes in the Temple breake the Sabbath, and are blameles?

6 But I say vnto you, that here is one greater then the Temple.

7 Wherefore if ye knewe what this is, I will haue mercie, and not sacrifice, ye would not haue condemned the innocents.

8 For the sonne of man is Lord, euen of the Sabbath.

9 And he departed thence, and went into their Synagogue:

10 And beholde, there was a man which had his hand dried vp. And they asked him, saying, Is it lawfull to heale vpon a Sabbath day? that they might accuse him.

11 And he said vnto the, What man shall there be among you, that hath a sheepe, and if it fal on a Sabbath day into a pit, doth not take it and lift it out?

12 How much more then is a man better then a sheepe? therefore, it is lawfull to doe well on a Sabbath day.

13 Then said he to the man, Stretch forth thine hand. And he stretched it foorth, and it was made whole as the other.

14 Then the Pharises went out, and consulted against him, howe they might destroy him.

15 But whe Iesus knew it, he departed thece, and great multitudes folowed him, and he healed the al,

16 And charged them in threatning wise, that they should not make him knowen,

17 That it might be fulfilled, which was spoken by Esaias the Prophet, saying,

18 Behold my seruant whom I haue chosen, my beloued in whom my soule deliteth: I wil put my Spirit on him, and he shall shewe iudgement to the Gentiles.

19 He shall not striue, nor crie, neither shall any man heare his voyce in the streetes.

20 A bruised reede shall he not breake, and smoking flaxe shall he not quenche, till he bring forth iudgement vnto victorie.

21 And in his Name shall the Gentiles trust.

22 Then was brought to him one, possessed with a deuill, both blind, and dumme, and he healed him, so that he which was blind and dumme, both spake and saw.

23 And all the people were amased, and saide, Is not this that sonne of Dauid?

24 But when the Pharises heard it, they saide, This man casteth the deuils no otherwise out, but through Beelzebub the prince of deuils.

25 But Iesus knew their thoughtes, and said to them, Euery kingdome deuided against it selfe, is brought to nought: and euery citie or house, deuided against it selfe, shall not stand.

26 So if Satan cast out Satan, he is deuided against himself: how shall then his kingdom endure?

27 Also if I through Beelzebub cast out deuils, by whom doe your children cast them out? Therefore they shall be your iudges.

28 But if I cast out deuils by ye Spirit of God, then is the kingdome of God come vnto you.

29 Els howe can a man enter into a strong mans house and spoyle his goods, except he first bind the strong man, and then spoile his house.

30 He that is not with me, is against me: and he that gathereth not with me, scattereth.

31 Wherefore I say vnto you, euery sinne and blasphemie shalbe forgiuen vnto men: but the blasphemie against the holy Ghost shall not be forgiuen vnto men.

32 And whosoeuer shall speake a word against the Sonne of man, it shall be forgiuen him: but whosoeuer shall speake against the holy Ghost, it shall not be forgiuen him, neither in this worlde, nor in the worlde to come.

33 Either make the tree good, and his fruite good: or els make the tree euill, and his fruite euil: for the tree is knowen by the fruite.

34 O generations of vipers, howe can you speake good things, when ye are euill? For of the abundance of the heart the mouth speaketh.

35 A good man out of the good treasure of his heart bringeth foorth good things: and an euill man out of an euill treasure, bringeth forth euill things.

36 But I say vnto you, that of euery idle word that men shall speake, they shall

giue account thereof at the day of iudgement.

37 For by thy wordes thou shalt be iustified, and by thy wordes thou shalt be condemned.

38 Then answered certaine of ye Scribes and of the Pharises, saying, Master, we would see a signe of thee.

39 But he answered and said to them, An euill and adulterous generation seeketh a signe, but no signe shall be giuen vnto it, saue that signe of the Prophet Ionas.

40 For as Ionas was three daies and three nights in the whales belly: so shall the Sonne of man be three daies and three nights in ye heart of the earth.

41 The men of Nineue shall rise in iudgement with this generation, and condemne it: for they repented at the preaching of Ionas: and behold, a greater then Ionas is here.

42 The Queene of the South shall rise in iudgement with this generation, and shall condemne it: for she came from the vtmost partes of the earth to heare the wisdome of Salomon: and beholde, a greater then Salomon is here.

43 Nowe when the vncleane spirit is gone out of a man, he walketh throughout drie places, seeking rest, and findeth none.

44 Then he saith, I wil returne into mine house from whence I came: and when he is come, he findeth it emptie, swept and garnished.

45 Then he goeth, and taketh vnto him seuen other spirites worse then himselfe, and they enter in, and dwell there: and the ende of that man is worse then the beginning. Euen so shall it be with this wicked generation.

46 While he yet spake to ye multitude, beholde, his mother, and his brethren stood without, desiring to speake with him.

47 Then one said vnto him, Beholde, thy mother and thy brethren stand without, desiring to speake with thee.

48 But he answered, and said to him that told him, Who is my mother? and who are my brethren?

49 And he stretched foorth his hand toward his disciples, and said, Beholde my mother and my brethren.

50 For whosoeuer shall doe my Fathers will which is in heauen, the same is my brother and sister and mother.

Matthew 13

1 The same day went Iesus out of the house, and sate by the sea side.

2 And great multitudes resorted vnto him, so that he went into a ship, and sate downe: and the whole multitude stoode on the shore.

3 Then he spake many things to them in parables, saying, Behold, a sower went forth to sowe.

4 And as he sowed, some fell by the way side, and the foules came and deuoured them vp.

5 And some fell vpon stony grounde, where they had not much earth, and

anon they sprong vp, because they had no depth of earth.

6 And when the sunne was vp, they were parched, and for lacke of rooting, withered away.

7 And some fell among thornes, and the thornes sprong vp, and choked them.

8 Some againe fel in good ground, and brought forth fruite, one corne an hundreth folde, some sixtie folde, and another thirtie folde.

9 He that hath eares to heare, let him heare.

10 Then the disciples came, and said to him, Why speakest thou to them in parables?

11 And he answered, and said vnto them, Because it is giuen vnto you, to know the secretes of the kingdome of heauen, but to the it is not giue.

12 For whosoeuer hath, to him shalbe giuen, and he shall haue abundance: but whosoeuer hath not, from him shalbe taken away, euen that he hath.

13 Therefore speake I to them in parables, because they seeing, doe not see: and hearing, they heare not, neither vnderstand.

14 So in them is fulfilled the prophecie of Esaias, which prophecie saieth, By hearing, ye shall heare, and shall not vnderstand, and seeing, ye shall see, and shall not perceiue.

15 For this peoples heart is waxed fat, and their eares are dull of hearing, and with their eyes they haue winked, lest they should see with their eyes, and heare with their eares, and should vnderstand with their hearts, and should returne, that I might heale them.

16 But blessed are your eyes, for they see: and your eares, for they heare.

17 For verely I say vnto you, that many Prophets, and righteous men haue desired to see those things which ye see, and haue not seene them, and to heare those things which ye heare, and haue not heard them.

18 Heare ye therefore ye parable of ye sower.

19 Whensoeuer any man heareth the woorde of that kingdome, and vnderstandeth it not, that euil one commeth, and catcheth away that which was sowen in his heart: and this is he which hath receiued the seede by the way side.

20 And hee that receiued seede in the stonie grounde, is he which heareth the woorde, and incontinently with ioy receiueth it,

21 Yet hath he no roote in himselfe, and dureth but a season: for assoone as tribulation or persecution commeth because of the woorde, by and by he is offended.

22 And hee that receiued the seede among thornes, is hee that heareth the woorde: but the care of this worlde, and the deceitfulnesse of riches choke the word, and he is made vnfruitfull.

23 But he that receiued the seede in the good ground, is he that heareth the worde, and vnderstandeth it, which also beareth fruite, and bringeth foorth, some

an hundreth folde, some sixtie folde, and some thirtie folde.

24 Another parable put hee foorth vnto them, saying, The kingdome of heauen is like vnto a man which sowed good seede in his fielde.

25 But while men slept, there came his enemie, and sowed tares among the wheat, and went his waie.

26 And when the blade was sprong vp, and brought forth fruite, then appeared the tares also.

27 Then came the seruaunts of the housholder, and sayd vnto him, Master, sowedst not thou good seede in thy fielde? from whence then hath it tares?

28 And hee said to them, Some enuious man hath done this. Then the seruants saide vnto him, Wilt thou then that we go and gather them vp?

29 But he saide, Nay, lest while yee goe about to gather the tares, yee plucke vp also with them the wheat.

30 Let both growe together vntill the haruest, and in time of haruest I will say to the reapers, Gather yee first the tares, and binde them in sheaues to burne them: but gather the wheate into my barne.

31 Another parable he put foorth vnto them, saying, The kingdome of heauen is like vnto a graine of mustard seede, which a man taketh and soweth in his fielde:

32 Which in deede is the least of all seedes: but when it is growen, it is the greatest among herbes, and it is a tree, so that the birdes of heauen come and builde in the branches thereof.

33 Another parable spake hee to them, The kingdome of heauen is like vnto leauen, which a woman taketh and hideth in three pecks of meale, till all be leauened.

34 All these thinges spake Iesus vnto the multitude in parables, and without parables spake he not to them,

35 That it might be fulfilled, which was spoken by the Prophet, saying, I will open my mouth in parables, and will vtter the thinges which haue beene kept secrete from the foundation of the worlde.

36 Then sent Iesus the multitude away, and went into the house. And his disciples came vnto him, saying, Declare vnto vs the parable of the tares of that fielde.

37 Then answered he, and saide to them, He that soweth the good seede, is the Sonne of man.

38 And the field is the worlde, and the good seede are the children of the kingdome, and the tares are the children of that wicked one.

39 And the enemie that soweth them, is the deuill, and the haruest is the end of the worlde, and the reapers be the Angels.

40 As then the tares are gathered and burned in ye fire, so shall it be in the end of this world.

41 The Sonne of man shall send forth his Angels, and they shall gather out of

his kingdom all things that offend, and them which doe iniquitie,

42 And shall cast them into a fornace of fire. There shalbe wailing and gnashing of teeth.

43 Then shall the iust men shine as ye sunne in the kingdome of their Father. Hee that hath eares to heare, let him heare.

44 Againe, the kingdom of heauen is like vnto a treasure hid in ye field, which when a man hath found, he hideth it, and for ioy thereof departeth and selleth all that he hath, and buieth that field.

45 Againe, the kingdome of heauen is like to a marchant man, that seeketh good pearles,

46 Who hauing found a pearle of great price, went and solde all that he had, and bought it.

47 Againe, the kingdome of heauen is like vnto a drawe net cast into the sea, that gathereth of all kindes of things.

48 Which, when it is full, men draw to lande, and sit and gather the good into vessels, and cast the bad away.

49 So shall it be at the end of the world. The Angels shall goe foorth, and seuer the bad from among the iust,

50 And shall cast them into a fornace of fire: there shalbe wailing, and gnashing of teeth.

51 Iesus saide vnto them, Vnderstand yee all these things? They saide vnto him, Yea, Lord.

52 Then sayd hee vnto them, Therefore euery Scribe which is taught vnto the kingdome of heauen, is like vnto an householder, which bringeth foorth out of his treasure things both newe and olde.

53 And it came to passe, that when Iesus had ended these parables, he departed thence,

54 And came into his owne countrey, and taught them in their Synagogue, so that they were astonied, and saide, Whence commeth this wisdome and great woorkes vnto this man?

55 Is not this the carpenters sonne? Is not his mother called Marie, and his brethren Iames and Ioses, and Simon and Iudas?

56 And are not his sisters all with vs? Whence then hath he all these things?

57 And they were offended with him. Then Iesus said to them, A Prophet is not without honour, saue in his owne countrey, and in his owne house.

58 And he did not many great woorkes there, for their vnbeliefes sake.

Matthew 14

1 At that time Herod the Tetrarche heard of the fame of Iesus,

2 And sayde vnto his seruaunts, This is that Iohn Baptist, hee is risen againe from the deade, and therefore great woorkes are wrought by him.

3 For Herod had taken Iohn, and bounde him, and put him in prison for Herodias sake, his brother Philips wife.

4 For Iohn saide vnto him, It is not lawfull for thee to haue her.

5 And when hee woulde haue put him to death, hee feared the multitude, because they counted him as a Prophet.

6 But when Herods birth day was kept, the daughter of Herodias daunced before them, and pleased Herod.

7 Wherefore he promised with an othe, that he would giue her whatsoeuer she would aske.

8 And shee being before instructed of her mother, sayde, Giue mee here Iohn Baptists head in a platter.

9 And the King was sorie: neuerthelesse because of the othe, and them that sate with him at the table, he commanded it to be giuen her,

10 And sent, and beheaded Iohn in the prison.

11 And his head was brought in a platter, and giuen to the maide, and shee brought it vnto her mother.

12 And his disciples came, and tooke vp the bodie, and buried it, and went, and tolde Iesus.

13 And when Iesus heard it, hee departed thence by shippe into a desert place apart. And when the multitude had heard it, they followed him on foote out of the cities.

14 And Iesus went foorth and sawe a great multitude, and was mooued with compassion toward them, and he healed their sicke.

15 And when euen was come, his disciples came to him, saying, This is a desart place, and the time is alreadie past: let the multitude depart, that they may goe into the townes, and bye them vitailes.

16 But Iesus saide to them, They haue no neede to goe away: giue yee them to eate.

17 Then saide they vnto him, Wee haue here but fiue loaues, and two fishes.

18 And he saide, Bring them hither to me.

19 And hee commanded the multitude to sit downe on the grasse, and tooke the fiue loaues and the two fishes, and looked vp to heauen and blessed, and brake, and gaue the loaues to his disciples, and the disciples to the multitude.

20 And they did all eate, and were sufficed, and they tooke vp of the fragments that remained, twelue baskets full.

21 And they that had eaten, were about fiue thousande men, beside women and litle children.

22 And straightway Iesus compelled his disciples to enter into a shippe, and to goe ouer before him, while he sent the multitude away.

23 And assoone as hee had sent the multitude away, he went vp into a moutaine alone to pray: and when the euening was come, hee was there alone.

24 And the shippe was nowe in the middes of the sea, and was tossed with waues: for it was a contrarie winde.

25 And in the fourth watch of the night, Iesus went vnto them, walking on the sea.

26 And when his disciples sawe him walking on the sea, they were troubled, saying, It is a spirit, and cried out for feare.

27 But straight way Iesus spake vnto them, saying, Be of good comfort, It is I: be not afraide.

28 Then Peter answered him, and saide, Master, if it be thou, bid me come vnto thee on the water.

29 And he saide, Come. And when Peter was come downe out of the shippe, he walked on the water, to goe to Iesus.

30 But when he sawe a mightie winde, he was afraide: and as he began to sinke, he cried, saying, Master, saue me.

31 So immediatly Iesus stretched foorth his hande, and caught him, and saide to him, O thou of litle faith, wherefore diddest thou doubt?

32 And assoone as they were come into the ship, the winde ceased.

33 Then they that were in the ship, came and worshipped him, saying, Of a trueth thou art the Sonne of God.

34 And when they were come ouer, they came into the land of Gennezaret.

35 And when the men of that place knewe him, they sent out into all that countrey rounde about, and brought vnto him all that were sicke,

36 And besought him, that they might touch the hemme of his garment onely: and as many as touched it, were made whole.

Matthew 15

1 Then came to Iesus the Scribes and Pharises, which were of Hierusalem, saying,

2 Why do thy disciples transgresse the tradition of the Elders? for they wash not their hands when they eate bread.

3 But he answered and said vnto them, Why doe yee also transgresse the commandement of God by your tradition?

4 For God hath commanded, saying, Honour thy father and mother: and he that curseth father or mother, let him die the death.

5 But ye say, Whosoeuer shall say to father or mother, By the gift that is offered by me, thou maiest haue profite,

6 Though hee honour not his father, or his mother, shalbe free: thus haue ye made the commandement of God of no aucthoritie by your tradition.

7 O hypocrites, Esaias prophecied well of you, saying,

8 This people draweth neere vnto me with their mouth, and honoureth me with the lips, but their heart is farre off from me.

9 But in vaine they worship me, teaching for doctrines, mens precepts.

10 Then hee called the multitude vnto him, and said to them, Heare and vnderstand.

11 That which goeth into the mouth, defileth not the man, but that which commeth out of the mouth, that defileth the man.

12 Then came his disciples, and saide vnto him, Perceiuest thou not, that the Pharises are offended in hearing this saying?

13 But hee answered and saide, Euery plant which mine heauenly Father hath not planted, shalbe rooted vp.

14 Let them alone, they be the blinde leaders of the blinde: and if the blinde leade ye blinde, both shall fall into the ditche.

15 Then answered Peter, and said to him, Declare vnto vs this parable.

16 Then said Iesus, Are ye yet without vnderstanding?

17 Perceiue ye not yet, that whatsoeuer entreth into the mouth, goeth into the bellie, and is cast out into the draught?

18 But those thinges which proceede out of the mouth, come from the heart, and they defile the man.

19 For out of the heart come euil thoughts, murders, adulteries, fornications, thefts, false testimonies, slaunders.

20 These are the things, which defile the man: but to eat with vnwashen hands, defileth not ye man.

21 And Iesus went thence, and departed into the coastes of Tyrus and Sidon.

22 And beholde, a woman a Cananite came out of the same coasts, and cried, saying vnto him, Haue mercie on me, O Lord, the sonne of Dauid: my daughter is miserably vexed with a deuil.

23 But hee answered her not a worde. Then came to him his disciples, and besought him, saying, Sende her away, for she crieth after vs.

24 But he answered, and said, I am not sent, but vnto the lost sheepe of the house of Israel.

25 Yet she came, and worshipped him, saying, Lord, helpe me.

26 And he answered, and said, It is not good to take the childrens bread, and to cast it to whelps.

27 But she said, Trueth, Lord: yet in deede the whelpes eate of the crommes, which fall from their masters table.

28 Then Iesus answered, and saide vnto her, O woman, great is thy faith: be it to thee, as thou desirest. And her daughter was made whole at that houre.

29 So Iesus went away from thence, and came neere vnto the sea of Galile, and went vp into a mountaine and sate downe there.

30 And great multitudes came vnto him, hauing with them, halt, blinde, dumme, maymed, and many other, and cast them downe at Iesus feete, and he healed them.

31 In so much that the multitude wondered, to see the dumme speake, the maimed whole, the halt to goe, and the blinde to see: and they glorified the God of Israel.

32 Then Iesus called his disciples vnto him, and said, I haue compassion on this multitude, because they haue continued with mee already three dayes, and haue nothing to eate: and I wil not let them depart fasting, least they faint in the way.

33 And his disciples saide vnto him, Whence should we get so much bread in the wildernes, as should suffice so great a multitude?

34 And Iesus said vnto them, How many loaues haue ye? And they said, Seuen, and a few litle fishes.

35 Then he commanded the multitude to sit downe on the ground,

36 And tooke the seuen loaues, and the fishes, and gaue thankes, and brake them, and gaue to his disciples, and the disciples to the multitude.

37 And they did all eate, and were sufficed: and they tooke vp of the fragments that remained, seuen baskets full.

38 And they that had eaten, were foure thousand men, beside women, and litle children.

39 Then Iesus sent away the multitude, and tooke ship, and came into the partes of Magdala.

Matthew 16

1 Then came the Pharises and Sadduces, and did tempt him, desiring him to shew them a signe from heauen.

2 But he answered, and said vnto them, When it is euening, ye say, Faire wether: for ye skie is red.

3 And in the morning ye say, To day shall be a tempest: for the skie is red and lowring. O hypocrites, ye can discerne the face of the skie, and can ye not discerne the signes of the times?

4 The wicked generation, and adulterous seeketh a signe, but there shall no signe be giuen it, but that signe of the Prophet Ionas: so hee left them, and departed.

5 And when his disciples were come to the other side, they had forgotten to take bread with them.

6 Then Iesus said vnto them, Take heede and beware of the leauen of the Pharises and Sadduces.

7 And they reasoned among themselues, saying, It is because we haue brought no bread.

8 But Iesus knowing it, saide vnto them, O ye of litle faith, why reason you thus among your selues, because ye haue brought no bread?

9 Doe ye not yet perceiue, neither remember the fiue loaues, when there were fiue thousand men, and how many baskets tooke ye vp?

10 Neither the seuen loaues when there were foure thousande men, and howe many baskets tooke ye vp?

11 Why perceiue ye not that I said not vnto you concerning bread, that ye shoulde beware of the leauen of the Pharises and Sadduces?

12 Then vnderstood they that he had not said that they should beware of the leauen of bread, but of the doctrine of the Pharises, and Sadduces.

13 Nowe when Iesus came into the coastes of Cesarea Philippi, hee asked his disciples, saying, Whome doe men say that I, the sonne of man am?

14 And they said, Some say, Iohn Baptist: and some, Elias: and others, Ieremias, or one of the Prophets.

15 He said vnto them, But whome say ye that I am?

16 Then Simon Peter answered, and said, Thou art that Christ, the Sonne of the liuing God.

17 And Iesus answered, and saide to him, Blessed art thou, Simon, the sonne of Ionas: for flesh and blood hath not reueiled it vnto thee, but my Father which is in heauen.

18 And I say also vnto thee, that thou art Peter, and vpon this rocke I will builde my Church: and ye gates of hell shall not ouercome it.

19 And I will giue vnto thee the keyes of the kingdome of heauen, and whatsoeuer thou shalt binde vpon earth, shalbe bound in heauen: and whatsoeuer thou shalt loose on earth, shall be loosed in heauen.

20 Then hee charged his disciples, that they should tell no man that he was Iesus that Christ.

21 From that time foorth Iesus beganne to shewe vnto his disciples, that he must goe vnto Hierusalem, and suffer many thinges of the Elders, and of the hie Priestes, and Scribes, and be slaine, and be raised againe the thirde day.

22 Then Peter tooke him aside, and began to rebuke him, saying, Master, pitie thy selfe: this shall not be vnto thee.

23 Then he turned backe, and said vnto Peter, Get thee behinde me, Satan: thou art an offence vnto me, because thou vnderstandest not the thinges that are of God, but the thinges that are of men.

24 Iesus then saide to his disciples, If any man will follow me, let him forsake himselfe: and take vp his crosse, and follow me.

25 For whosoeuer will saue his life, shall lose it: and whosoeuer shall lose his life for my sake, shall finde it.

26 For what shall it profite a man though he should winne the whole worlde, if hee lose his owne soule? or what shall a man giue for recompence of his soule?

27 For the Sonne of man shall come in the glory of his Father with his Angels, and then shall he giue to euery man according to his deedes.

28 Verely I say vnto you, there bee some of them that stande here, which shall not taste of death, till they haue seene the Sonne of man come in his kingdome.

Matthew 17

1 And after six dayes, Iesus tooke Peter, and Iames and Iohn his brother, and brought them vp into an hie mountaine apart,

2 And was transfigured before them: and his face did shine as the Sunne, and his clothes were as white as the light.

3 And beholde, there appeared vnto them Moses, and Elias, talking with him.

4 Then answered Peter, and saide to Iesus, Master, it is good for vs to be here: if thou wilt, let vs make here three tabernacles, one for thee, and one for Moses, and one for Elias.

5 While he yet spake, behold, a bright cloude shadowed them: and beholde, there came a voyce out of the cloude, saying, This is that my beloued Sonne, in whom I am well pleased: heare him.

6 And when the disciples heard that, they fell on their faces, and were sore afraide.

7 Then Iesus came and touched them, and said, Arise, and be not afraide.

8 And when they lifted vp their eyes, they sawe no man, saue Iesus onely.

9 And as they came downe from the moutaine, Iesus charged them, saying, Shewe the vision to no man, vntil the Sonne of man rise againe from the dead.

10 And his disciples asked him, saying, Why then say the Scribes that Elias must first come?

11 And Iesus answered, and saide vnto them, Certeinely Elias must first come, and restore all thinges.

12 But I say vnto you that Elias is come alreadie, and they knewe him not, but haue done vnto him whatsoeuer they would: likewise shall also the Sonne of man suffer of them.

13 Then the disciples perceiued that he spake vnto them of Iohn Baptist.

14 And when they were come to the multitude, there came to him a certaine man, and fell downe at his feete,

15 And saide, Master, haue pitie on my sonne: for he is lunatike, and is sore vexed: for oft times he falleth into the fire, and oft times into the water.

16 And I brought him to thy disciples, and they could not heale him.

17 Then Iesus answered, and said, O generation faithlesse, and crooked, how long now shall I be with you! howe long nowe shall I suffer you! bring him hither to me.

18 And Iesus rebuked the deuill, and he went out of him: and the childe was healed at that houre.

19 Then came the disciples to Iesus apart, and said, Why could not we cast him out?

20 And Iesus said vnto them, Because of your vnbeliefe: for verely I say vnto you, if ye haue faith as much as is a graine of mustarde seede, ye shall say vnto this mountaine, Remooue hence to yonder place, and it shall remoue: and nothing shalbe vnpossible vnto you.

21 Howbeit this kinde goeth not out, but by prayer and fasting.

22 And they being in Galile, Iesus said vnto them, The Sonne of man shall be deliuered into the handes of men,

23 And they shall kill him, but the thirde day shall he rise againe: and they were very sorie.

24 And when they were come to Capernaum, they that receiued polle money, came to Peter, and sayd, Doeth not your Master pay polle money?

25 He sayd, Yes. And when he was come into the house, Iesus preuented him, saying, What thinkest thou, Simon? Of whome doe the Kings of the earth take

tribute, or polle money? of their children, or of strangers?

26 Peter sayd vnto him, Of strangers. Then said Iesus vnto him, Then are the children free.

27 Neuerthelesse, lest we should offend them: goe to the sea, and cast in an angle, and take the first fish that commeth vp, and when thou hast opened his mouth, thou shalt finde a piece of twentie pence: that take, and giue it vnto them for me and thee.

Matthew 18

1 The same time the disciples came vnto Iesus, saying, Who is the greatest in the kingdome of heauen?

2 And Iesus called a litle childe vnto him, and set him in the mids of them,

3 And sayd, Verely I say vnto you, except ye be conuerted, and become as litle children, ye shall not enter into the kingdome of heauen.

4 Whosoeuer therefore shall humble himselfe as this litle childe, the same is the greatest in the kingdome of heauen.

5 And whosoeuer shall receiue one such litle childe in my name, receiueth me.

6 But whosoeuer shall offend one of these litle ones which beleeue in me, it were better for him, that a milstone were hanged about his necke, and that he were drowned in the depth of the sea.

7 Wo be vnto the world because of offences: for it must needes be that offences shall come, but wo be to that man by whome the offence commeth.

8 Wherefore, if thy hand or thy foote cause thee to offend, cut them off, and cast them from thee: it is better for thee to enter into life, halt, or maimed, then hauing two hands, or two feete, to be cast into euerlasting fire.

9 And if thine eye cause thee to offende, plucke it out, and cast it from thee: it is better for thee to enter into life with one eye, then hauing two eyes to be cast into hell fire.

10 See that ye despise not one of these litle ones: for I say vnto you, that in heauen their Angels alwayes behold the face of my Father which is in heauen.

11 For the Sonne of man is come to saue that which was lost.

12 How thinke ye? If a man haue an hundreth sheepe, and one of them be gone astray, doeth he not leaue ninetie and nine, and go into the mountaines, and seeke that which is gone astray?

13 And if so be that he finde it, verely I say vnto you, he reioyceth more of that sheepe, then of the ninetie and nine which went not astray:

14 So is it not ye wil of your Father which is in heauen, that one of these litle ones should perish.

15 Moreouer, if thy brother trespasse against thee, goe and tell him his fault betweene thee and him alone: if he heare thee, thou hast wonne thy brother.

16 But if he heare thee not, take yet with thee one or two, that by the mouth of two or three witnesses euery worde may be confirmed.

17 And if he refuse to heare them, tell it vnto the Church: and if he refuse to heare the Church also, let him be vnto thee as an heathen man, and a Publicane.

18 Verely I say vnto you, Whatsoeuer ye bind on earth, shall be bound in heauen: and whatsoeuer ye loose on earth, shalbe loosed in heauen.

19 Againe, verely I say vnto you, that if two of you shall agree in earth vpon any thing, whatsoeuer they shall desire, it shall be giuen them of my Father which is in heauen.

20 For where two or three are gathered together in my Name, there am I in the mids of them.

21 Then came Peter to him, and said, Master, howe oft shall my brother sinne against me, and I shall forgiue him? vnto seuen times?

22 Iesus said vnto him, I say not to thee, Vnto seuen times, but, Vnto seuentie times seuen times.

23 Therefore is the kingdome of heauen likened vnto a certaine King, which would take an account of his seruants.

24 And when he had begun to reckon, one was brought vnto him, which ought him ten thousand talents.

25 And because he had nothing to pay, his Lord commanded him to be solde, and his wife, and his children, and all that he had, and the dette to be payed.

26 The seruant therefore fell downe, and worshipped him, saying, Lord, refraine thine anger toward me, and I will pay thee all.

27 Then that seruants Lord had compassion, and loosed him, and forgaue him the dette.

28 But when the seruant was departed, hee found one of his felow seruants, which ought him an hundred pence, and he layde hands on him, and thratled him, saying, Pay me that thou owest.

29 Then his fellow seruant fell downe at his feete, and besought him, saying, Refraine thine anger towards me, and I will pay thee all.

30 Yet he would not, but went and cast him into prison, till he should pay the dette.

31 And when his other felowe seruants sawe what was done, they were very sory, and came, and declared vnto their Lord all that was done.

32 Then his Lord called him vnto him, and sayd to him, O euil seruant, I forgaue thee all that dette, because thou prayedst me.

33 Oughtest not thou also to haue had pitie on thy fellowe seruant, euen as I had pitie on thee?

34 So his Lord was wroth, and deliuered him to the tormentours, till he should pay all that was due to him.

35 So likewise shall mine heauenly Father doe vnto you, except ye forgiue from your hearts, eche one to his brother their trespasses.

Matthew 19

1 And it came to passe, that when Iesus had finished these sayings, he departed from Galile, and came into ye coasts of Iudea beyond Iordan.

2 And great multitudes followed him, and he healed them there.

3 Then came vnto him the Pharises tempting him, and saying to him, Is it lawfull for a man to put away his wife vpon euery occasion?

4 And he answered and sayd vnto them, Haue ye not read, that hee which made them at the beginning, made them male and female,

5 And sayd, For this cause, shall a man leaue father and mother, and cleaue vnto his wife, and they which were two shalbe one flesh.

6 Wherefore they are no more twaine, but one flesh. Let not man therefore put asunder that, which God hath coupled together.

7 They said to him, Why did then Moses commaund to giue a bill of diuorcement, and to put her away?

8 He sayd vnto them, Moses, because of the hardnesse of your heart, suffered you to put away your wiues: but from the beginning it was not so.

9 I say therefore vnto you, that whosoeuer shall put away his wife, except it be for whoredome, and marry another, committeth adulterie: and whosoeuer marieth her which is diuorced, doeth commit adulterie.

10 Then sayd his disciples to him, If the matter be so betweene man and wife, it is not good to marry.

11 But he sayd vnto them, All men cannot receiue this thing, saue they to whom it is giuen.

12 For there are some eunuches, which were so borne of their mothers belly: and there be some eunuches, which be gelded by men: and there be some eunuches, which haue gelded them selues for the kingdome of heauen. He that is able to receiue this, let him receiue it.

13 Then were brought to him litle children, that he should put his hands on them, and pray: and the disciples rebuked them.

14 But Iesus sayd, Suffer the litle children, and forbid them not to come to me: for of such is the kingdome of heauen.

15 And when he had put his hands on them, he departed thence.

16 And beholde, one came and sayd vnto him, Good Master, what good thing shall I doe, that I may haue eternall life?

17 And he said vnto him, Why callest thou me good? there is none good but one, eue God: but if thou wilt enter into life, keepe ye commandemets.

18 He sayd to him, Which? And Iesus sayde, These, Thou shalt not kill: Thou shalt not commit adulterie: Thou shalt not steale: Thou shalt not beare false witnesse.

19 Honour thy father and mother: and thou shalt loue thy neighbour as thy selfe.

20 The yong man sayd vnto him, I haue obserued all these things from my youth: what lacke I yet?

21 Iesus sayd vnto him, If thou wilt be perfite, go, sell that thou hast, and giue it to the poore, and thou shalt haue treasure in heauen, and come, and follow me.

22 And when the yong man heard that saying, he went away sorowfull: for he had great possessions.

23 Then Iesus sayd vnto his disciples, Verely I say vnto you, that a rich man shall hardly enter into the kingdome of heauen.

24 And againe I say vnto you, It is easier for a camel to go through the eye of a needle, then for a rich man to enter into ye kingdome of God.

25 And whe his disciples heard it, they were exceedingly amased, saying, Who then can be saued?

26 And Iesus behelde them, and sayde vnto them, With men this is vnpossible, but with God all things are possible.

27 Then answered Peter, and said to him, Beholde, we haue forsaken all, and followed thee: what therefore shall we haue?

28 And Iesus said vnto them, Verely I say to you, that when the Sonne of man shall sit in the throne of his maiestie, ye which folowed me in the regeneration, shall sit also vpon twelue thrones and iudge the twelue tribes of Israel.

29 And whosoeuer shall forsake houses, or brethren, or sisters, or father, or mother, or wife, or children, or lands, for my Names sake, he shall receiue an hundreth folde more, and shall inherite euerlasting life.

30 But many that are first, shalbe last, and the last shalbe first.

Matthew 20

1 For the kingdome of heauen is like vnto a certaine, housholder, which went out at the dawning of the day to hire labourers into his vineyarde.

2 And he agreed with the labourers for a peny a day, and sent them into his vineyard.

3 And he went out about the third houre, and sawe other standing idle in the market place,

4 And sayd vnto them, Goe ye also into my vineyard, and whatsoeuer is right, I will giue you: and they went their way.

5 Againe he went out about the sixt and ninth houre, and did likewise.

6 And he went about the eleuenth houre, and found other standing idle, and sayd vnto them, Why stand ye here all the day idle?

7 They sayd vnto him, Because no man hath hired vs. He sayd to them, Goe ye also into my vineyard, and whatsoeuer is right, that shall ye receiue.

8 And when euen was come, the master of the vineyard sayd vnto his steward, Call the labourers, and giue them their hire, beginning at the last, till thou come to the first.

9 And they which were hired about ye eleuenth houre, came and receiued euery man a penie.

10 Nowe when the first came, they supposed that they should receiue more, but they likewise receiued euery man a penie.

11 And when they had receiued it, they murmured against the master of the house,

12 Saying, These last haue wrought but one houre, and thou hast made them equall vnto vs, which haue borne the burden and heate of the day.

13 And hee answered one of them, saying, Friend, I doe thee no wrong: didst thou not agree with me for a penie?

14 Take that which is thine owne, and go thy way: I will giue vnto this last, as much as to thee.

15 Is it not lawfull for me to do as I will with mine owne? Is thine eye euil, because I am good?

16 So the last shalbe first, and the first last: for many are called, but fewe chosen.

17 And Iesus went vp to Hierusalem, and tooke the twelue disciples apart in the way, and said vnto them,

18 Beholde, wee goe vp to Hierusalem, and the Sonne of man shall bee deliuered vnto the chiefe priestes, and vnto the Scribes, and they shall condemne him to death,

19 And shall deliuer him to the Gentiles, to mocke, and to scourge, and to crucifie him, but the third day he shall rise againe.

20 Then came to him the mother of Zebedeus children with her sonnes, worshipping him, and desiring a certaine thing of him.

21 And he said vnto her, What wouldest thou? She said to him, Graunt that these my two sonnes may sit, the one at thy right hand, and the other at thy left hand in thy kingdome.

22 And Iesus answered and said, Ye know not what ye aske. Are ye able to drinke of the cup that I shall drinke of, and to be baptized with the baptisme that I shalbe baptized with? They said to him, We are able.

23 And he said vnto them, Ye shall drinke in deede of my cup, and shall be baptized with the baptisme, that I am baptized with, but to sit at my right hande, and at my left hand, is not mine to giue: but it shalbe giuen to them for whome it is prepared of my Father.

24 And when the other ten heard this, they disdained at the two brethren.

25 Therefore Iesus called them vnto him, and saide, We knowe that the lordes of the Gentiles haue domination ouer them, and they that are great, exercise authoritie ouer them.

26 But it shall not be so among you: but whosoeuer will be great among you, let him be your seruant.

27 And whosoeuer will be chiefe among you, let him be your seruant.

28 Euen as the Sonne of man came not to be serued, but to serue, and to giue his life for the ransome of many.

29 And as they departed from Iericho, a great multitude followed him.

30 And beholde, two blinde men, sitting by the way side, when they heard that Iesus passed by, cryed, saying, O Lord, the Sonne of Dauid, haue mercie on vs.

31 And the multitude rebuked them, because they should holde their peace: but they cried the more, saying, O Lord, the Sonne of Dauid, haue mercie on vs.

32 Then Iesus stoode still, and called them, and said, What will ye that I should do to you?

33 They saide to him, Lord, that our eyes may be opened.

34 And Iesus mooued with compassion, touched their eyes, and immediatly their eyes receiued sight, and they followed him.

Matthew 21

1 And when they drewe neere to Hierusalem, and were come to Bethphage, vnto the mount of the Oliues, then sent Iesus two disciples,

2 Saying to them, Goe into the towne that is ouer against you, and anon yee shall finde an asse bounde, and a colt with her: loose them, and bring them vnto me.

3 And if any man say ought vnto you, say ye, that the Lord hath neede of them, and straightway he will let them goe.

4 All this was done that it might be fulfilled, which was spoken by the Prophet, saying,

5 Tell ye the daughter of Sion, Beholde, thy King commeth vnto thee, meeke and sitting vpon an asse, and a colte, the foale of an asse vsed to the yoke.

6 So the disciples went, and did as Iesus had commanded them,

7 And brought the asse and the colt, and put on them their clothes, and set him thereon.

8 And a great multitude spred their garments in the way: and other cut downe branches from the trees, and strawed them in the way.

9 Moreouer, the people that went before, and they also that followed, cried, saying, Hosanna to the Sonne of Dauid, Blessed be hee that commeth in the Name of the Lord, Hosanna thou which art in the highest heauens.

10 And when he was come into Hierusalem, all the citie was mooued, saying, Who is this?

11 And the people said, This is Iesus that Prophet of Nazareth in Galile.

12 And Iesus went into the Temple of God, and cast out all them that solde and bought in the Temple, and ouerthrew the tables of the money chagers, and the seates of them that sold doues,

13 And said to them, it is written, My house shall be called the house of prayer: but ye haue made it a denne of theeues.

14 Then the blinde, and the halt came to him in the Temple, and he healed them.

15 But when the chiefe priestes and Scribes sawe the marueiles that hee did, and the children crying in the Temple, and saying, Hosanna to the Sonne of Dauid, they disdained,

16 And said vnto him, Hearest thou what these say? And Iesus said vnto them, Yea: read ye neuer, By the mouth of babes and sucklings thou hast made perfite the praise?

17 So hee left them, and went out of the citie vnto Bethania, and lodged there.

18 And in the morning, as he returned into the citie, he was hungrie,

19 And seeing a figge tree in the way, he came to it, and found nothing thereon, but leaues onely, and said to it, Neuer fruite grow on thee henceforwards. And anon the figge tree withered.

20 And when his disciples saw it, they marueiled, saying, How soone is the figge tree withered!

21 And Iesus answered and said vnto them, Verely I say vnto you, if ye haue faith, and doubt not, ye shall not only doe that, which I haue done to the figge tree, but also if ye say vnto this mountaine, Take thy selfe away, and cast thy selfe into the sea, it shalbe done.

22 And whatsoeuer ye shall aske in prayer, if ye beleeue, ye shall receiue it.

23 And whe he was come into the Temple, the chiefe Priestes, and the Elders of the people came vnto him, as he was teaching, and saide, By what authoritie doest thou these things? and who gaue thee this authoritie?

24 Then Iesus answered and said vnto them, I also will aske of you a certaine thing, which if ye tell me, I likewise will tell you by what authoritie I doe these things.

25 The baptisme of Iohn, whence was it? from heauen, or of men? Then they reasoned among themselues, saying, If we shall say, From heauen, he will say vnto vs, Why did ye not then beleeue him?

26 And if we say, Of men, we feare the multitude, for all holde Iohn as a Prophet.

27 Then they answered Iesus, and said, We can not tell. And he said vnto them, Neither tell I you by what authoritie I doe these things.

28 But what thinke ye? A certaine man had two sonnes, and came to the elder, and saide, Sonne, goe and worke to day in my vineyarde.

29 But he answered, and said, I will not: yet afterward he repented himselfe, and went.

30 Then came he to the second, and said likewise. And he answered, and said, I will, Syr: yet he went not.

31 Whether of them twaine did the will of the father? They saide vnto him, The first. Iesus saide vnto them, Verely I say vnto you, that the Publicanes and the harlots goe before you into the kingdome of God.

32 For Iohn came vnto you in the way of righteousnes, and yee beleeued him not: but the Publicanes, and the harlots beleeued him, and ye, though ye sawe it, were not mooued with repentance afterward, that ye might beleeue him.

33 Heare another parable, There was a certaine housholder, which planted a vineyard, and hedged it round about, and made a winepresse therein, and built a tower, and let it out to husbandmen, and went into a strange countrey.

34 And when the time of the fruite drewe neere, hee sent his seruants to the husbandmen to receiue the fruites thereof.

35 And ye husbandmen tooke his seruants and beat one, and killed another, and stoned another.

36 Againe hee sent other seruants, moe then the first: and they did the like vnto them.

37 But last of all he sent vnto them his owne sonne, saying, They will reuerence my sonne.

38 But when the husbandmen saw the sonne, they saide among themselues, This is the heire: come, let vs kill him, and let vs take his inheritance.

39 So they tooke him, and cast him out of the vineyarde, and slewe him.

40 When therefore the Lord of the vineyarde shall come, what will hee doe to those husbandmen?

41 They saide vnto him, Hee will cruelly destroy those wicked men, and will let out his vineyard vnto other husbandmen, which shall deliuer him the fruites in their seasons.

42 Iesus saide vnto them, Read ye neuer in the Scriptures, The stone which the builders refused, the same is made the head of the corner? This was the Lordes doing, and it is marueilous in our eyes.

43 Therefore say I vnto you, The kingdome of God shalbe taken from you, and shalbe giuen to a nation, which shall bring foorth the fruites thereof.

44 And whosoeuer shall fall on this stone, he shalbe broken: but on whomsoeuer it shall fall, it will dash him a pieces.

45 And when the chiefe Priestes and Pharises had heard his parables, they perceiued that hee spake of them.

46 And they seeking to laye handes on him, feared the people, because they tooke him as a Prophet.

Matthew 22

1 Then Iesus answered, and spake vnto them againe in parables, saying,

2 The kingdome of heauen is like vnto a certaine King which maried his sonne,

3 And sent foorth his seruants, to call them that were bidde to the wedding, but they woulde not come.

4 Againe hee sent foorth other seruants, saying. Tell them which are bidden, Beholde, I haue prepared my dinner: mine oxen and my fatlings are killed, and all thinges are readie: come vnto the mariage.

5 But they made light of it, and went their wayes, one to his farme, and another about his marchandise.

6 And the remnant tooke his seruants, and intreated them sharpely, and slewe them.

7 But when the King heard it, he was wroth, and sent foorth his warriers, and destroyed those murtherers, and burnt vp their citie.

8 Then saide hee to his seruants, Truely the wedding is prepared: but they which were bidden, were not worthy.

9 Go ye therefore out into the high wayes, and as many as ye finde, bid them to the mariage.

10 So those seruantes went out into the hie wayes, and gathered together all that euer they found, both good and bad: so the wedding was furnished with ghestes.

11 Then the King came in, to see the ghestes, and sawe there a man which had not on a wedding garment.

12 And he sayd vnto him, Friend, how camest thou in hither, and hast not on a wedding garment? And he was speachlesse.

13 Then sayd the King to the seruants, Binde him hand and foote: take him away, and cast him into vtter darkenes: there shalbe weeping and gnashing of teeth.

14 For many are called, but fewe chosen.

15 Then went the Pharises and tooke counsell how they might tangle him in talke.

16 And they sent vnto him their disciples with the Herodians, saying, Master, we knowe that thou art true, and teachest the way of God truely, neither carest for any man: for thou considerest not the person of men.

17 Tell vs therefore, how thinkest thou? Is it lawfull to giue tribute vnto Cesar, or not?

18 But Iesus perceiued their wickednes, and sayd, Why tempt ye me, ye hypocrites?

19 Shewe me the tribute money. And they brought him a peny.

20 And he sayde vnto them, Whose is this image and superscription?

21 They sayd vnto him, Cesars. Then sayd he vnto them, Giue therefore to Cesar, the things which are Cesars, and giue vnto God, those things which are Gods.

22 And when they heard it, they marueiled, and left him, and went their way.

23 The same day the Sadduces came to him (which say that there is no resurrection) and asked him,

24 Saying, Master, Moses sayd, If a man die, hauing no children, his brother shall marie his wife by the right of alliance, and raise vp seede vnto his brother.

25 Nowe there were with vs seuen brethren, and the first maried a wife, and deceased: and hauing none yssue, left his wife vnto his brother.

26 Likewise also the second, and the third, vnto the seuenth.

27 And last of all the woman died also.

28 Therefore in the resurrection, whose wife shall she be of the seuen? for all had her.

29 Then Iesus answered, and sayd vnto them, Ye are deceiued, not knowing the Scriptures, nor the power of God.

30 For in the resurrection they neither marie wiues, nor wiues are bestowed in mariage, but are as the Angels of God in heauen.

31 And concerning the resurrection of the dead, haue ye not read what is spoken vuto you of God, saying,

32 I am the God of Abraham, and the God of Isaac, and the God of Iacob? God is not the God of the dead, but of the liuing.

33 And when the multitude heard it, they were astonied at his doctrine.

34 But when the Pharises had heard, that he had put the Sadduces to silence, they assembled together.

35 And one of them, which was an expounder of the Lawe, asked him a question, tempting him, and saying,

36 Master, which is ye great commandement in the Lawe?

37 Iesus sayd to him, Thou shalt loue the Lord thy God with all thine heart, with all thy soule, and with all thy minde.

38 This is the first and the great commandement.

39 And the second is like vnto this, Thou shalt loue thy neighbour as thy selfe.

40 On these two commandements hangeth the whole Lawe, and the Prophets.

41 While the Pharises were gathered together, Iesus asked them,

42 Saying, What thinke ye of Christ? whose sonne is he? They sayd vnto him, Dauids.

43 He sayd vnto them, How then doeth Dauid in spirit call him Lord, saying,

44 The Lord sayd to my Lord, Sit at my right hand, till I make thine enemies thy footestoole?

45 If then Dauid call him Lord, howe is he his sonne?

46 And none could answere him a worde, neither durst any from that day foorth aske him any moe questions.

Matthew 23

1 Then spake Iesus to the multitude, and to his disciples,

2 Saying, The Scribes and the Pharises sit in Moses seate.

3 All therefore whatsoeuer they bid you obserue, that obserue and doe: but after their workes doe not: for they say, and doe not.

4 For they binde heauie burdens, and grieuous to be borne, and lay them on mens shoulders, but they themselues will not moue them with one of their fingers.

5 All their workes they doe for to be seene of men: for they make their phylacteries broad, and make long the frindges of their garments,

6 And loue the chiefe place at feastes, and to haue the chiefe seates in the assemblies,

7 And greetings in the markets, and to be called of men, Rabbi, Rabbi.

8 But be not ye called, Rabbi: for one is your doctour, to wit, Christ, and all ye are brethren.

9 And call no man your father vpon the earth: for there is but one, your father which is in heauen.

10 Be not called doctours: for one is your doctour, euen Christ.

11 But he that is greatest among you, let him be your seruant.

12 For whosoeuer will exalt himselfe, shall be brought lowe: and whosoeuer will humble himselfe, shalbe exalted.

13 Wo therefore be vnto you, Scribes and Pharises, hypocrites, because ye shut vp the kingdome of heauen before men: for ye your selues go not in, neither suffer ye them that would enter, to come in.

14 Wo be vnto you, Scribes and Pharises, hypocrites: for ye deuoure widowes houses, euen vnder a colour of long prayers: wherefore ye shall receiue the greater damnation.

15 Wo be vnto you, Scribes and Pharises, hypocrites: for ye compasse sea and land to make one of your profession: and when he is made, ye make him two folde more the childe of hell, then you your selues.

16 Wo be vnto you blinde guides, which say, Whosoeuer sweareth by the Temple, it is nothing: but whosoeuer sweareth by the golde of the Temple, he offendeth.

17 Ye fooles and blinde, whether is greater, the golde, or the Temple that sanctifieth the golde?

18 And whosoeuer sweareth by the altar, it is nothing: but whosoeuer sweareth by the offering that is vpon it, offendeth.

19 Ye fooles and blinde, whether is greater, the offering, or the altar which sanctifieth the offering?

20 Whosoeuer therefore sweareth by the altar, sweareth by it, and by all things thereon.

21 And whosoeuer sweareth by the Temple, sweareth by it, and by him that dwelleth therein.

22 And he that sweareth by heauen, sweareth by the throne of God, and by him that sitteth thereon.

23 Wo be to you, Scribes and Pharises, hypocrites: for ye tithe mynt, and annyse, and cummyn, and leaue the weightier matters of the law, as iudgement, and mercy and fidelitie. These ought ye to haue done, and not to haue left the other.

24 Ye blinde guides, which straine out a gnat, and swallowe a camell.

25 Wo be to you, Scribes and Pharises, hypocrites: for ye make cleane the vtter side of the cup, and of the platter: but within they are ful of briberie and excesse.

26 Thou blinde Pharise, cleanse first the inside of the cup and platter, that the outside of them may be cleane also.

27 Wo be to you, Scribes and Pharises, hypocrites: for ye are like vnto whited tombes, which appeare beautifull outward, but are within full of dead mens bones, and all filthines.

28 So are ye also: for outwarde ye appeare righteous vnto men, but within ye are full of hypocrisie and iniquitie.

29 Wo be vnto you, Scribes and Pharises, hypocrites: for ye build the tombes of the Prophets, and garnish the sepulchres of the righteous,

30 And say, If we had bene in the dayes of our fathers, we would not haue bene partners with them in the blood of the Prophets.

31 So then ye be witnesses vnto your selues, that ye are the children of them that murthered the Prophets.

32 Fulfill ye also ye measure of your fathers.

33 O serpents, the generation of vipers, howe should ye escape the damnation of hell!

34 Wherefore beholde, I send vnto you Prophets, and wise men, and Scribes, and of them ye shall kill and crucifie: and of them shall ye scourge in your Synagogues, and persecute from citie to citie,

35 That vpon you may come all the righteous blood that was shed vpon the earth, from the blood of Abel the righteous, vnto the blood of Zacharias the sonne of Barachias, whome ye slewe betweene the Temple and the altar.

36 Verely I say vnto you, all these things shall come vpon this generation.

37 Hierusalem, Hierusalem, which killest the Prophets, and stonest them which are sent to thee, how often would I haue gathered thy children together, as the henne gathereth her chickins vnder her wings, and ye would not!

38 Beholde, your habitation shalbe left vnto you desolate,

39 For I say vnto you, ye shall not see mee henceforth till that ye say, Blessed is he that commeth in the Name of the Lord.

Matthew 24

1 And Iesus went out, and departed from the Temple, and his disciples came to him, to shewe him the building of the Temple.

2 And Iesus sayd vnto them, See ye not all these things? Verely I say vnto you, there shall not be here left a stone vpon a stone, that shall not be cast downe.

3 And as he sate vpon the mount of Oliues, his disciples came vnto him apart, saying, Tell vs when these things shall be, and what signe shalbe of thy comming, and of the ende of the world.

4 And Iesus answered, and sayd vnto them, Take heede that no man deceiue you.

5 For many shall come in my name, saying, I am Christ, and shall deceiue many.

6 And ye shall heare of warres, and rumours of warres: see that ye be not

troubled: for all these things must come to passe, but the end is not yet.

7 For nation shall rise against nation, and realme against realme, and there shalbe famine, and pestilence, and earthquakes in diuers places.

8 All these are but ye beginning of sorowes.

9 Then shall they deliuer you vp to be afflicted, and shall kill you, and ye shall be hated of all nations for my Names sake.

10 And then shall many be offended, and shall betray one another, and shall hate one another.

11 And many false prophets shall arise, and shall deceiue many.

12 And because iniquitie shalbe increased, the loue of many shalbe colde.

13 But he that endureth to the ende, he shalbe saued.

14 And this Gospel of the kingdome shalbe preached through the whole world for a witnes vnto all nations, and then shall the end come.

15 When ye therefore shall see the abomination of desolation spoken of by Daniel the Prophet, set in the holy place (let him that readeth consider it.)

16 Then let them which be in Iudea, flee into the mountaines.

17 Let him which is on the house top, not come downe to fetch any thing out of his house.

18 And he that is in the fielde, let not him returne backe to fetch his clothes.

19 And woe shalbe to them that are with childe, and to them that giue sucke in those dayes.

20 But pray that your flight be not in the winter, neither on the Sabbath day.

21 For then shall be great tribulation, such as was not from the beginning of the worlde to this time, nor shalbe.

22 And except those dayes should be shortened, there should no flesh be saued: but for the elects sake those dayes shalbe shortened.

23 Then if any shall say vnto you, Loe, here is Christ, or there, beleeue it not.

24 For there shall arise false Christes, and false prophets, and shall shewe great signes and wonders, so that if it were possible, they should deceiue the very elect.

25 Beholde, I haue tolde you before.

26 Wherefore if they shall say vnto you, Beholde, he is in the desert, goe not forth: Beholde, he is in the secret places, beleeue it not.

27 For as the lightning commeth out of the East, and is seene into the West, so shall also the comming of the Sonne of man be.

28 For wheresoeuer a dead carkeis is, thither will the Egles be gathered together.

29 And immediatly after ye tribulations of those dayes, shall the sunne be darkened, and the moone shall not giue her light, and the starres shall fal from heauen, and ye powers of heaue shalbe shake.

30 And then shall appeare the signe of the Sonne of man in heauen: and then shall all the kinreds of the earth mourne, and they shall see the Sonne of man come in the cloudes of heauen with power and great glorie.

31 And he shall send his Angels with a great sound of a trumpet, and they shall gather together his elect, from the foure windes, and from the one ende of the heauens vnto the other.

32 Now learne the parable of the figge tree: when her bough is yet tender, and it putteth foorth leaues, ye knowe that sommer is neere.

33 So likewise ye, when ye see all these things, know that the kingdom of God is neere, eue at ye doores.

34 Verely I say vnto you, this generation shall not passe, till all these things be done.

35 Heauen and earth shall passe away: but my wordes shall not passe away.

36 But of that day and houre knoweth no man, no not the Angels of heauen, but my father only.

37 But as the dayes of Noe were, so likewise shall the comming of the Sonne of man be.

38 For as in the dayes before the flood, they did eate and drinke, marrie, and giue in mariage, vnto the day that Noe entred into the Arke,

39 And knewe nothing, till the flood came, and tooke them all away, so shall also the comming of the Sonne of man be.

40 Then two shall be in the fieldes, the one shalbe receiued, and the other shalbe refused.

41 Two women shalbe grinding at ye mill: the one shalbe receiued, and the other shalbe refused.

42 Watch therefore: for ye knowe not what houre your master will come.

43 Of this be sure, that if the good man of the house knewe at what watch the thiefe would come, he woulde surely watch, and not suffer his house to be digged through.

44 Therefore be ye also ready: for in the houre that ye thinke not, will the Sonne of man come.

45 Who then is a faithfull seruaunt and wise, whom his master hath made ruler ouer his household, to giue them meate in season?

46 Blessed is that seruant, whom his master when he commeth, shall finde so doing.

47 Verely I say vnto you, he shall make him ruler ouer all his goods.

48 But if that euil seruant shall say in his heart, My master doth deferre his comming,

49 And begin to smite his fellowes, and to eate, and to drinke with the drunken,

50 That seruaunts master will come in a day, when he looketh not for him, and in an houre that he is not ware of,

51 And will cut him off, and giue him his portion with hypocrites: there shalbe weeping, and gnashing of teeth.

Matthew 25

1 Then the kingdome of heauen shalbe likened vnto tenne virgins, which tooke their lampes, and went foorth to meete the bridegrome.

2 And fiue of them were wise, and fiue foolish.

3 The foolish tooke their lampes, but tooke none oyle with them.

4 But the wise tooke oyle in their vessels with their lampes.

5 Nowe while the bridegrome taried long, all slumbred and slept.

6 And at midnight there was a crie made, Behold, the bridegrome commeth: goe out to meete him.

7 Then all those virgins arose, and trimmed their lampes.

8 And the foolish said to the wise, Giue vs of your oyle, for our lampes are out.

9 But the wise answered, saying, Not so, lest there will not be ynough for vs and you: but goe ye rather to them that sell, and bye for your selues.

10 And while they went to bye, the bridegrome came: and they that were readie, went in with him to the wedding, and the gate was shut.

11 Afterwards came also the other virgins, saying, Lord, Lord, open to vs.

12 But he answered, and said, Verely I say vnto you, I knowe you not.

13 Watch therfore: for ye know neither the day, nor the houre, when the sonne of man will come.

14 For the kingdome of heauen is as a man that going into a strange countrey, called his seruants, and deliuered to them his goods.

15 And vnto one he gaue fiue talents, and to an other two, and to another one, to euery man after his own ability, and straightway went from home.

16 Then he that had receiued the fiue talents, went and occupied with them, and gained other fiue talents.

17 Likewise also, he that receiued two, he also gained other two.

18 But he that receiued that one, went and digged it in the earth, and hid his masters money.

19 But after a long season, the master of those seruants came, and reckoned with them.

20 Then came he that had receiued fiue talents, and brought other fiue talents, saying, Master, thou deliueredst vnto me fiue talents: behold, I haue gained with them other fiue talents.

21 Then his master saide vnto him, It is well done good seruant and faithfull, Thou hast bene faithfull in litle, I will make thee ruler ouer much: enter into thy masters ioy.

22 Also he that had receiued two talents, came, and said, Master, thou deliueredst vnto me two talents: behold, I haue gained two other talets more.

23 His master saide vnto him, It is well done good seruant, and faithfull, Thou hast bene faithfull in litle, I will make thee ruler ouer much: enter into thy masters ioy.

24 Then he which had receiued the one talent, came, and said, Master, I knewe that thou wast an hard man, which reapest where thou sowedst not, and gatherest where thou strawedst not:

25 I was therefore afraide, and went, and hid thy talent in the earth: behold, thou hast thine owne.

26 And his master answered, and said vnto him, Thou euill seruant, and slouthfull, thou knewest that I reape where I sowed not, and gather where I strawed not.

27 Thou oughtest therefore to haue put my money to ye exchangers, and then at my comming should I haue receiued mine owne with vantage.

28 Take therefore the talent from him, and giue it vnto him which hath tenne talents.

29 For vnto euery man that hath, it shall be giuen, and he shall haue abundance, and from him that hath not, euen that he hath, shalbe taken away.

30 Cast therefore that vnprofitable seruant into vtter darkenes: there shalbe weeping and gnasshing of teeth.

31 And when the Sonne of man commeth in his glory, and all the holy Angels with him, then shall he sit vpon the throne of his glorie,

32 And before him shalbe gathered all nations, and he shall seperate them one from another, as a shepheard separateth the sheepe from ye goates.

33 And he shall set the sheepe on his right hand, and the goates on the left.

34 Then shall ye king say to them on his right hand, Come ye blessed of my father: take the inheritance of the kingdome prepared for you from the foundation of the world.

35 For I was an hungred, and ye gaue me meate: I thirsted, and ye gaue me drinke: I was a stranger, and ye tooke me in vnto you.

36 I was naked, and ye clothed me: I was sicke, and ye visited me: I was in prison, and ye came vnto me.

37 Then shall the righteous answere him, saying, Lord, when sawe we thee an hungred, and fed thee? or a thirst, and gaue thee drinke?

38 And when sawe we thee a stranger, and tooke thee in vnto vs? or naked, and clothed thee?

39 Or when sawe we thee sicke, or in prison, and came vnto thee?

40 And the King shall answere, and say vnto them, Verely I say vnto you, in as much as ye haue done it vnto one of the least of these my brethre, ye haue done it to me.

41 Then shall he say vnto them on ye left hand, Depart from me ye cursed, into euerlasting fire, which is prepared for the deuill and his angels.

42 For I was an hungred, and ye gaue me no meate: I thirsted, and ye gaue me no drinke:

43 I was a stranger, and ye tooke me not in vnto you: I was naked, and ye clothed me not: sicke, and in prison, and ye visited me not.

44 Then shall they also answere him, saying, Lord, when sawe we thee an hungred, or a thirst, or a stranger, or naked, or sicke, or in prison, and did not minister vnto thee?

45 Then shall he answere them, and say, Verely I say vnto you, in as much as ye did it not to one of the least of these, ye did it not to me.

46 And these shall goe into euerlasting paine, and the righteous into life eternall.

Matthew 26

1 And it came to passe, when Iesus had finished all these sayings, he saide vnto his disciples,

2 Ye know that after two dayes is ye Passeouer, and the Sonne of man shalbe deliuered to be crucified.

3 Then assembled together the chiefe Priests, and the Scribes, and the Elders of ye people into the hall of the high Priest called Caiaphas:

4 And consulted together that they might take Iesus by subtiltie, and kill him.

5 But they sayd, Not on the feast day, least any vprore be among the people.

6 And when Iesus was in Bethania, in the house of Simon the leper,

7 There came vnto him a woman, which had a boxe of very costly oyntment, and powred it on his head, as he sate at the table.

8 And when his disciples sawe it, they had indignation, saying, What needed this waste?

9 For this oyntment might haue bene solde for much, and bene giuen to the poore.

10 And Iesus knowing it, sayde vnto them, Why trouble yee the woman? for shee hath wrought a good woorke vpon me.

11 For yee haue the poore alwayes with you, but me shall yee not haue alwaies.

12 For in that shee powred this oyntment on my bodie, shee did it to burie me.

13 Verely I say vnto you, wheresoeuer this Gospel shall bee preached throughout all the worlde, there shall also this that shee hath done, be spoken of for a memoriall of her.

14 Then one of the twelue, called Iudas Iscariot, went vnto the chiefe Priestes,

15 And said, What will ye giue me, and I will deliuer him vnto you? and they appoynted vnto him thirtie pieces of siluer.

16 And from that time, he sought opportunitie to betraie him.

17 Nowe on the first day of the feast of vnleauened bread the disciples came to Iesus, saying vnto him, Where wilt thou that we prepare for thee to eate the Passeouer?

18 And he said, Goe yee into the citie to such a man, and say to him, The master saieth, My time is at hande: I will keepe the Passeouer at thine house with my disciples.

19 And the disciples did as Iesus had giuen them charge, and made readie the Passeouer.

20 So when the Euen was come, hee sate downe with the twelue.

21 And as they did eate, he sayde, Verely I say vnto you, that one of you shall betraie me.

22 And they were exceeding sorowfull, and began euery one of them to say vnto him, Is it I, Master?

23 And hee answered and sayde, Hee that dippeth his hande with me in the dish, hee shall betraie me.

24 Surely the Sonne of man goeth his way, as it is written of him: but woe be to that man, by whom the Sonne of man is betrayed: it had bene good for that man, if hee had neuer bene borne.

25 Then Iudas which betraied him, answered and sayde, Is it I, Master? He sayde vnto him, Thou hast sayd it.

26 And as they did eate, Iesus tooke the bread, and when he had blessed, he brake it, and gaue it to the disciples, and sayd, Take, eate: this is my bodie.

27 Also he tooke the cuppe, and when he had giuen thankes, he gaue it them, saying, Drinke ye all of it.

28 For this is my blood of the Newe Testament, that is shedde for many, for the remission of sinnes.

29 I say vnto you, that I will not drinke henceforth of this fruit of the vine vntil that day, when I shall drinke it new with you in my Fathers kingdome.

30 And when they had sung a Psalme, they went out into the mount of Oliues.

31 Then saide Iesus vnto them, All yee shall be offended by me this night: for it is written, I wil smite the shepheard, and the sheepe of the flocke shalbe scattered.

32 But after I am risen againe, I will go before you into Galile.

33 But Peter aunswered, and sayde vnto him, Though that al men should be offended by thee, yet will I neuer be offended.

34 Iesus sayde vnto him, Verely I say vnto thee, that this night, before the cocke crow, thou shalt denie me thrise.

35 Peter saide vnto him, Though I should die with thee, I will in no case denie thee. Likewise also sayd all the disciples.

36 Then went Iesus with them into a place which is called Gethsemane, and said vnto his disciples, Sit ye here, while I goe, and pray yonder.

37 And hee tooke vnto him Peter, and the two sonnes of Zebedeus, and began to waxe sorowfull, and grieuously troubled.

38 Then sayde Iesus vnto them, My soule is very heauie, euen vnto the death: tarie yee here, and watch with me.

39 So hee went a litle further, and fell on his face, and praied, saying, O my Father, if it be possible, let this cup passe from me: neuerthelesse, not as I will, but as thou wilt.

40 After, hee came vnto the disciples, and founde them a sleepe, and sayde to Peter, What? coulde yee not watch with me one houre?

41 Watch, and praie, that yee enter not into tentation: the spirit in deede is readie, but the flesh is weake.

42 Againe he went away the second time, and praied, saying, O my Father, if this cuppe can not passe away from mee, but that I must drinke it, thy will be done.

43 And he came, and founde them a sleepe againe, for their eyes were heauie.

44 So he left them and went away againe, and praied the third time, saying the same woordes.

45 Then came he to his disciples, and said vnto them, Sleepe henceforth, and take your rest: behold, the houre is at hand, and the Sonne of man is giuen into the hands of sinners.

46 Rise, let vs goe: beholde, hee is at hande that betraieth me.

47 And while hee yet spake, loe Iudas, one of the twelue, came, and with him a great multitude with swordes and staues, from the high Priests and Elders of the people.

48 Now he that betraied him, had giuen them a token, saying, Whomesoeuer I shall kisse, that is he, laie holde on him.

49 And forthwith he came to Iesus, and sayd, God saue thee, Master, and kissed him.

50 Then Iesus sayde vnto him, Friende, wherefore art thou come? Then came they, and laide hands on Iesus, and tooke him.

51 And behold, one of them which were with Iesus, stretched out his hand, and drewe his sworde, and strooke a seruaunt of the high Priest, and smote off his eare.

52 Then sayde Iesus vnto him, Put vp thy sworde into his place: for all that take the sworde, shall perish with the sworde.

53 Either thinkest thou, that I can not now pray to my Father, and he will giue me moe then twelue legions of Angels?

54 Howe then shoulde the Scriptures bee fulfilled, which say, that it must be so?

55 The same houre sayde Iesus to the multitude, Ye be come out as it were against a thiefe, with swordes and staues to take mee: I sate daily teaching in the Temple among you, and yee tooke me not.

56 But all this was done, that the Scriptures of the Prophets might be fulfilled. Then all the disciples forsooke him, and fled.

57 And they tooke Iesus, and led him to Caiaphas the hie Priest, where the Scribes and the Elders were assembled.

58 And Peter followed him a farre off vnto the hie Priestes hall, and went in, and sate with the seruants to see the ende.

59 Nowe the chiefe Priestes and the Elders, and all the whole councill sought false witnesse against Iesus, to put him to death.

60 But they founde none, and though many false witnesses came, yet founde they none: but at the last came two false witnesses,

61 And saide, This man saide, I can destroie the Temple of God, and build it in three daies.

62 Then the chiefe Priest arose, and sayde to him, Answerest thou nothing? What is the matter that these men witnesse against thee?

63 But Iesus helde his peace. Then the chiefe Priest answered, and saide to him, I charge thee sweare vnto vs by the liuing God, to tell vs, If thou be that Christ the Sonne of God, or no.

64 Iesus saide to him, Thou hast saide it: neuerthelesse I say vnto you, hereafter shall ye see the Sonne of man, sitting at the right hande of the power of God, and come in the cloudes of the heauen.

65 Then the hie Priest rent his clothes, saying, Hee hath blasphemed, what haue wee any more neede of witnesses? beholde: nowe yee haue heard his blasphemie.

66 What thinke yee? They answered, and said, He is guiltie of death.

67 Then spet they in his face, and buffeted him, and other smote him with roddes,

68 Saying, Prophecie to vs, O Christ, Who is he that smote thee?

69 Peter sate without in the hall, and a maide came to him, saying, Thou also wast with Iesus of Galile:

70 But hee denied before them all, saying, I wote not what thou saiest.

71 And when hee went out into the porche, another maide sawe him, and sayde vnto them that were there, This man was also with Iesus of Nazareth.

72 And againe he denied with an othe, saying, I knowe not the man.

73 So after a while, came vnto him they that stoode by, and sayde vnto Peter, Surely thou art also one of them: for euen thy speache bewraieth thee.

74 Then began hee to curse himselfe, and to sweare, saying, I knowe not the man. And immediately the cocke crewe.

75 Then Peter remembred the wordes of Iesus, which had sayde vnto him, Before the cocke crowe thou shalt denie me thrise. So he went out, and wept bitterly.

Matthew 27

1 When the morning was come, all the chiefe Priests, and the elders of the people tooke counsell against Iesus, to put him to death,

2 And led him away bounde, and deliuered him vnto Pontius Pilate the gouernour.

3 Then when Iudas which betraied him, sawe that hee was condemned, hee repented himselfe, and brought againe the thirtie pieces of siluer to the chiefe Priestes, and Elders,

4 Saying, I haue sinned, betraying the innocent bloud. But they sayde, What is that to vs? see thou to it.

5 And when hee had cast downe the siluer pieces in the Temple, hee departed, and went, and hanged himselfe.

6 And the chiefe Priestes tooke the siluer pieces, and sayde, It is not lawfull for vs to put them into the treasure, because it is the price of bloud.

7 And they tooke counsell, and bought with them a potters fielde, for the buriall of strangers.

8 Wherefore that field is called, The field of bloud, vntill this day.

9 (Then was fulfilled that which was spoken by Ieremias the Prophet, saying, And they tooke thirtie siluer pieces, ye price of him that was valued, whom they of ye children of Israel valued.

10 And they gaue them for the potters fielde, as the Lord appointed me.)

11 And Iesus stood before ye gouernour, and the gouernour asked him, saying, Art thou that King of the Iewes? Iesus said vnto him, Thou sayest it.

12 And when he was accused of the chiefe Priestes, and Elders, he answered nothing.

13 Then saide Pilate vnto him, Hearest thou not howe many things they lay against thee?

14 But he answered him not to one worde, in so much that the gouernour marueiled greatly.

15 Nowe at the feast, the gouernour was wont to deliuer vnto the people a prisoner whom they would.

16 And they had then a notable prisoner, called Barabbas.

17 When they were then gathered together, Pilate said vnto the, Whether will ye that I let loose vnto you Barabbas, or Iesus which is called Christ?

18 (For he knewe well, that for enuie they had deliuered him.

19 Also when he was set downe vpon the iudgement seate, his wife sent to him, saying, Haue thou nothing to do with that iust man: for I haue suffered many things this day in a dreame by reason of him.)

20 But the chiefe Priestes and the Elders had persuaded the people that they shoulde aske Barabbas, and should destroy Iesus.

21 Then the gouernour answered, and said vnto them, Whether of the twaine will ye that I let loose vnto you? And they said, Barabbas.

22 Pilate said vnto them, What shall I do then with Iesus, which is called Christ? They all said to him, Let him be crucified.

23 Then saide the gouernour, But what euill hath he done? Then they cryed the more, saying, Let him be crucified.

24 When Pilate saw that he auailed nothing, but that more tumult was made, he tooke water and washed his hands before the multitude, saying, I am innocent of the blood of this iust man: looke you to it.

25 Then answered all the people, and saide, His bloud be on vs, and on our children.

26 Thus let he Barabbas loose vnto them, and scourged Iesus, and deliuered him to be crucified.

27 Then the souldiers of the gouernour tooke Iesus into the common hall, and gathered about him the whole band,

28 And they stripped him, and put about him a skarlet robe,

29 And platted a crowne of thornes, and put it vpon his head, and a reede in his right hand, and bowed their knees before him, and mocked him, saying, God saue thee King of the Iewes,

30 And spitted vpon him, and tooke a reede, and smote him on the head.

31 Thus when they had mocked him, they tooke the robe from him, and put his owne rayment on him, and led him away to crucifie him.

32 And as they came out, they found a man of Cyrene, named Simon: him they compelled to beare his crosse.

33 And when they came vnto the place called Golgotha, (that is to say, the place of dead mens skulles)

34 They gaue him vineger to drinke, mingled with gall: and when he had tasted thereof, he would not drinke.

35 And when they had crucified him, they parted his garments, and did cast lottes, that it might be fulfilled, which was spoken by the Prophet, They deuided my garments among them, and vpon my vesture did cast lottes.

36 And they sate, and watched him there.

37 They set vp also ouer his head his cause written, THIS IS IESVS THE KING OF THE IEVVES.

38 And there were two theeues crucified with him, one on the right hand, and another on the left.

39 And they that passed by, reuiled him, wagging their heades,

40 And saying, Thou that destroyest ye Temple, and buildest it in three dayes, saue thy selfe: if thou be ye Sonne of God, come downe from ye crosse.

41 Likewise also the hie Priests mocking him, with the Scribes, and Elders, and Pharises, said,

42 He saued others, but he cannot saue him selfe: if he be ye King of Israel, let him now come downe from ye crosse, and we will beleeue in him.

43 He trusted in God, let him deliuer him nowe, if he will haue him: for he saide, I am the Sonne of God.

44 The selfe same thing also ye theeues which were crucified with him, cast in his teeth.

45 Now from ye sixt houre was there darkenesse ouer all the land, vnto the ninth houre.

46 And about ye ninth houre Iesus cryed with a loud voyce, saying, Eli, Eli, lamasabachthani? that is, My God, my God, why hast thou forsaken me?

47 And some of them that stoode there, when they heard it, said, This man calleth Elias.

48 And straightway one of them ran, and tooke a spondge, and filled it with vineger, and put it on a reede, and gaue him to drinke.

49 Other said, Let be: let vs see, if Elias wil come and saue him.

50 Then Iesus cryed againe with a loude voyce, and yeelded vp the ghost.

51 And behold, the vayle of the Temple was rent in twaine, from the top to the bottome, and the earth did quake, and the stones were cloue.

52 And the graues did open themselues, and many bodies of the Saintes, which slept, arose,

53 And came out of the graues after his resurrection, and went into the holy citie, and appeared vnto many.

54 When the Centurion, and they that were with him watching Iesus, saw the earthquake, and the thinges that were done, they feared greatly, saying, Truely this was the Sonne of God.

55 And many women were there, beholding him a farre off, which had folowed Iesus from Galile, ministring vnto him.

56 Among whom was Marie Magdalene, and Marie the mother of Iames, and Ioses, and the mother of Zebedeus sonnes.

57 And when the euen was come, there came a riche man of Arimathea, named Ioseph, who had also himselfe bene Iesus disciple.

58 He went to Pilate, and asked ye body of Iesus. Then Pilate commanded ye body to be deliuered.

59 So Ioseph tooke the body, and wrapped it in a cleane linnen cloth,

60 And put it in his new tombe, which he had hewen out in a rocke, and rolled a great stone to the doore of the sepulchre, and departed.

61 And there was Marie Magdalene, and the other Marie sitting ouer against the sepulchre.

62 Nowe the next day that followed the Preparation of the Sabbath, the hie Priestes and Pharises assembled to Pilate,

63 And said, Syr, we remember that that deceiuer saide, while he was yet aliue, Within three dayes I will rise.

64 Command therefore, that the sepulchre be made sure vntill the third day, lest his disciples come by night, and steale him away, and say vnto the people, He is risen from the dead: so shall the last errour be worse then the first.

65 Then Pilate saide vnto them, Ye haue a watch: goe, and make it sure as ye knowe.

66 And they went, and made the sepulchre sure with the watch, and sealed the stone.

Matthew 28

1 Now in the end of the Sabbath, when the first day of ye weeke began to dawne, Marie Magdalene, and the other Marie came to see the sepulchre,

2 And behold, there was a great earthquake: for the Angel of the Lord descended from heauen, and came and rolled backe the stone from the doore, and sate vpon it.

3 And his countenance was like lightning, and his raiment white as snowe.

4 And for feare of him, the keepers were astonied, and became as dead men.

5 But the Angel answered, and said to the women, Feare ye not: for I know that ye seeke Iesus which was crucified:

6 He is not here, for he is risen; as he saide: come, see the place where the Lord was laid,

7 And go quickly, and tel his disciples that he is risen from ye dead: and behold, he goeth before you into Galile: there ye shall see him: loe, I haue told you.

8 So they departed quickly from the sepulchre, with feare and great ioye, and did runne to bring his disciples worde.

9 And as they wet to tel his disciples, behold, Iesus also met the, saying, God saue you. And they came, and tooke him by the feete, and worshipped him.

10 Then said Iesus vnto them, Be not afraide. Goe, and tell my brethren, that they goe into Galile, and there shall they see me.

11 Nowe when they were gone, beholde, some of the watch came into the citie, and shewed vnto the hie Priestes all ye things that were done.

12 And they gathered them together with the Elders, and tooke counsell, and gaue large money vnto the souldiers,

13 Saying, Say, His disciples came by night, and stole him away while we slept.

14 And if this matter come before the gouernour to be heard, we will perswade him, and so vse the matter that you shall not neede to care.

15 So they tooke the money, and did as they were taught: and this saying is noysed among the Iewes vnto this day.

16 Then ye eleuen disciples wet into Galile, into a mountaine, where Iesus had appointed the.

17 And when they sawe him, they worshipped him: but some douted.

18 And Iesus came, and spake vnto them, saying, All power is giuen vnto me, in heauen, and in earth.

19 Go therefore, and teach all nations, baptizing them in the Name of the Father, and the Sonne, and the holy Ghost,

20 Teaching them to obserue all things, whatsoeuer I haue commanded you: and lo, I am with you alway, vntill the ende of the worlde, Amen.

Mark

Mark 1

1 The beginning of the Gospel of Iesus Christ, the Sonne of God:

2 As it is written in the Prophets, Behold, I send my messenger before thy face, which shall prepare thy way before thee.

3 The voyce of him that cryeth in the wildernesse is, Prepare the way of the Lord: make his paths straight.

4 Iohn did baptize in the wildernesse, and preach the baptisme of amendment of life, for remission of sinnes.

5 And al ye countrey of Iudea, and they of Hierusalem went out vnto him, and were all baptized of him in the riuer Iordan, confessing their sinnes.

6 Nowe Iohn was clothed with camels heare, and with a girdle of a skinne about his loynes: and he did eate Locusts and wilde hony,

7 And preached, saying, A stronger then I commeth after me, whose shoes latchet I am not worthy to stoupe downe, and vnloose.

8 Trueth it is, I haue baptized you with water: but he will baptize you with the holy Ghost.

9 And it came to passe in those dayes, that Iesus came from Nazareth, a citie of Galile, and was baptized of Iohn in Iordan.

10 And assoone as he was come out of the water, Iohn saw the heauens clouen in twaine, and the holy Ghost descending vpon him like a doue.

11 Then there was a voyce from heauen, saying, Thou art my beloued Sonne, in whome I am well pleased.

12 And immediatly the Spirite driueth him into the wildernesse.

13 And he was there in the wildernesse fourtie daies, and was tempted of Satan: hee was also with the wilde beastes, and the Angels ministred vnto him.

14 Now after that Iohn was committed to prison, Iesus came into Galile, preaching the Gospel of the kingdome of God,

15 And saying, The time is fulfilled, and the kingdome of God is at hand: repent and beleeue the Gospel.

16 And as he walked by the sea of Galile, he saw Simon, and Andrew his brother, casting a net into the sea, (for they were fishers.)

17 Then Iesus said vnto them, Folow me, and I will make you to be fishers of men.

18 And straightway they forsooke their nets, and folowed him.

19 And when hee had gone a litle further thence, he sawe Iames the sonne of Zebedeus, and Iohn his brother, as they were in the ship, mending their nets.

20 And anon hee called them: and they left their father Zebedeus in the shippe with his hired seruants, and went their way after him.

21 So they entred into Capernaum, and straightway on the Sabbath day hee entred into the Synagogue, and taught.

22 And they were astonied at his doctrine, for he taught them as one that had authoritie, and not as the Scribes.

23 And there was in their Synagogue a man in whome was an vncleane spirite, and hee cried out,

24 Saying, Ah, what haue we to do with thee, O Iesus of Nazareth? Art thou come to destroy vs? I knowe thee what thou art, euen that holy one of God.

25 And Iesus rebuked him, saying, Holde thy peace, and come out of him.

26 And the vncleane spirit tare him, and cried with a loude voyce, and came out of him.

27 And they were all amased, so that they demaunded one of another, saying, What thing is this? what newe doctrine is this? for he commandeth euen the foule spirites with authoritie, and they obey him.

28 And immediatly his fame spred abroade throughout all the region bordering on Galile.

29 And assoone as they were come out of the Synagogue, they entred into the house of Symon and Andrew, with Iames and Iohn.

30 And Symons wiues mother lay sicke of a feuer, and anon they told him of her.

31 And he came and tooke her by the hand, and lifted her vp, and the feuer forsooke her by and by, and shee ministred vnto them.

32 And whe euen was come, at what time the sunne setteth, they brought to him all that were diseased, and them that were possessed with deuils.

33 And the whole citie was gathered together at the doore.

34 And he healed many that were sicke of diuers diseases: and he cast out many deuils, and suffred not the deuils to say that they knewe him.

35 And in the morning very early before day, Iesus arose and went out into a solitarie place, and there praied.

36 And Simon, and they that were with him, followed carefully after him.

37 And when they had found him, they sayde vnto him, All men seeke for thee.

38 Then he said vnto them, Let vs go into the next townes, that I may preach there also: for I came out for that purpose.

39 And hee preached in their Synagogues, throughout all Galile, and cast the deuils out.

40 And there came a leper to him, beseeching him, and kneeled downe vnto him, and said to him, If thou wilt, thou canst make me cleane.

41 And Iesus had compassion, and put foorth his hand, and touched him, and said to him, I wil: be thou cleane.

42 And assone as he had spoken, immediatly ye leprosie departed from him, and he was made cleane.

43 And after he had giue him a streight commandement, he sent him away forthwith,

44 And sayde vnto him, See thou say nothing to any man, but get thee hence, and shewe thy selfe to the Priest, and offer for thy clensing those things, which Moses commanded, for a testimoniall vnto them.

45 But when he was departed, hee began to tel many things, and to publish the matter: so that Iesus could no more openly enter into the citie, but was without in desert places: and they came to him from euery quarter.

Mark 2

1 After a fewe dayes, hee entred into Capernaum againe, and it was noysed that he was in the house.

2 And anon, many gathered together, in so much that the places about the doore coulde not receiue any more and he preached the word vnto them.

3 And there came vnto him, that brought one sicke of the palsie, borne of foure men.

4 And because they could not come neere vnto him for the multitude, they vncouered ye roofe of the house where hee was: and when they had broken it open, they let downe the bed, wherein the sicke of the palsie lay.

5 Nowe when Iesus sawe their faith, he saide to the sicke of the palsie, Sonne, thy sinnes are forgiuen thee.

6 And there were certaine of the Scribes sitting there, and reasoning in their hearts,

7 Why doeth this man speake such blasphemies? who can forgiue sinnes, but God onely?

8 And immediatly when Iesus perceiued in his spirite, that thus they reasoned with themselues, he sayde vnto them, Why reason yee these things in your hearts?

9 Whether is it easier to say to the sicke of the palsie, Thy sinnes are forgiuen thee? or to say, Arise, and take vp thy bed, and walke?

10 But that ye may knowe, that the Sonne of man hath authoritie in earth to forgiue sinnes, (he sayde vnto the sicke of the palsie.)

11 I say vnto thee, Arise and take vp thy bed, and get thee hence into thine owne house.

12 And by and by he arose, and tooke vp his bed, and went foorth before them all, in so much that they were all amased, and glorified God, saying, We neuer sawe such a thing.

13 Then he went foorth againe towarde the sea, and all the people resorted vnto him, and he taught them.

14 And as Iesus passed by, hee sawe Leui the sonne of Alpheus sit at the receit of custome, and said vnto him, Folowe me. And he arose and followed him.

15 And it came to passe, as Iesus sate at table in his house, many Publicanes and sinners sate at table also with Iesus, and his disciples: for there were many that followed him.

16 And when the Scribes and Pharises sawe him eate with the Publicanes and sinners, they sayd vnto his disciples, Howe is it, that hee eateth and drinketh with Publicanes and sinners?

17 Now when Iesus heard it, hee sayde vnto them, The whole haue no neede of the Physicion, but the sicke. I came not to call the righteous, but the sinners to repentance.

18 And the disciples of Iohn, and the Pharises did fast, and came and saide vnto him, Why doe the disciples of Iohn, and of the Pharises fast, and thy disciples fast not?

19 And Iesus saide vnto them, Can the children of the marriage chamber fast, whiles the bridegrome is with them? as long as they haue the bridegrome with them, they cannot fast.

20 But the daies will come, when the bridegrome shall be taken from them, and then shall they fast in those daies.

21 Also no man soweth a piece of newe cloth in an olde garment: for els the newe piece that filled it vp, taketh away somewhat from the olde, and the breach is worse.

22 Likewise, no man putteth newe wine into old vessels: for els the new wine breaketh the vessels, and the wine runneth out, and the vessels are lost: but newe wine must be put into new vessels.

23 And it came to passe as hee went through the corne on the Sabbath day, that his disciples, as they went on their way, began to plucke the eares of corne.

24 And the Pharises saide vnto him, Beholde, why doe they on the Sabbath day, that which is not lawfull?

25 And he saide to them, Haue yee neuer read what Dauid did when he had neede, and was an hungred, both he, and they that were with him?

26 Howe he went into the house of God, in the daies of Abiathar the hie Priest, and did eat the shewe bread, which were not lawfull to eate, but for the Priests, and gaue also to them which were with him?

27 And hee sayde to them, The Sabbath was made for man, and not man for the Sabbath.

28 Wherefore the Sonne of man is Lord, euen of the Sabbath.

Mark 3

1 And he entred againe into ye Synagogue, and there was a man which had a withered had.

2 And they watched him, whether he would heale him on the Sabbath day, that they might accuse him.

3 Then he saide vnto the man which had the withered hand, Arise: stand forth in the middes.

4 And he saide to them, Is it lawfull to doe a good deede on the Sabbath day, or to doe euil? to saue the life, or to kill? But they held their peace.

5 Then hee looked rounde about on them angerly, mourning also for the hardnesse of their hearts, and saide to the man, Stretch foorth thine hand. And he stretched it out: and his hande was restored, as whole as the other.

6 And the Pharises departed, and straightway gathered a councill with the Herodians against him, that they might destroy him.

7 But Iesus auoided with his disciples to the sea: and a great multitude followed him from Galile, and from Iudea,

8 And from Ierusalem, and from Idumea, and beyonde Iordan: and they that dwelled about Tyrus and Sidon, when they had heard what great things he did, came vnto him in great number.

9 And he commanded his disciples, that a litle shippe should waite for him, because of the multitude, lest they shoulde throng him.

10 For hee had healed many, in so much that they preassed vpon him to touch him, as many as had plagues.

11 And when the vncleane spirits sawe him, they fel downe before him, and cried, saying, Thou art the Sonne of God.

12 And he sharply rebuked them, to the ende they should not vtter him.

13 Then hee went vp into a mountaine, and called vnto him whome he woulde, and they came vnto him.

14 And hee appoynted twelue that they should be with him, and that he might send them to preache,

15 And that they might haue power to heale sicknesses, and to cast out deuils.

16 And the first was Simon, and hee named Simon, Peter,

17 Then Iames the sonne of Zebedeus, and Iohn Iames brother (and surnamed them Boanerges, which is, the sonnes of thunder,)

18 And Andrew, and Philippe, and Bartlemew, and Matthewe, and Thomas, and Iames, the sonne of Alpheus, and Thaddeus, and Simon the Cananite,

19 And Iudas Iscariot, who also betraied him, and they came home.

20 And the multitude assembled againe, so that they could not so much as eate bread.

21 And when his kinsfolkes heard of it, they went out to laie hold on him: for they sayde that he was beside himselfe.

22 And the Scribes which came downe from Hierusalem, saide, He hath Beelzebub, and through the prince of the deuils he casteth out deuils.

23 But he called them vnto him, and said vnto them in parables, How can Satan driue out Satan?

24 For if a kingdome bee deuided against it selfe, that kingdome can not stand.

25 Or if a house bee deuided against it selfe, that house can not continue.

26 So if Satan make insurrection against himselfe, and be deuided, hee can not endure but is at an ende.

27 No man can enter into a strong mans house, and take away his goods, except hee first binde that strong man, and then spoyle his house.

28 Verely I say vnto you, all sinnes shalbe forgiuen vnto the children of men, and blasphemies, wherewith they blaspheme:

29 But hee that blasphemeth against the holy Ghost, shall neuer haue forgiuenesse, but is culpable of eternall damnation.

30 Because they saide, Hee had an vncleane spirit.

31 Then came his brethren and mother, and stoode without, and sent vnto him, and called him.

32 And the people sate about him, and they said vnto him, Beholde, thy mother, and thy brethren seeke for thee without.

33 But hee answered them, saying, Who is my mother and my brethren?

34 And hee looked rounde about on them, which sate in compasse about him, and saide, Beholde my mother and my brethren.

35 For whosoeuer doeth the will of God, he is my brother, and my sister, and mother.

Mark 4

1 And hee began againe to teache by the sea side, and there gathered vnto him a great multitude, so that hee entred into a shippe, and sate in the sea, and all the people was by the sea side on the land.

2 And he taught them many things in parables, and said vnto them in his doctrine,

3 Hearken: Beholde, there went out a sower to sowe.

4 And it came to passe as he sowed, that some fell by the way side, and the foules of the heauen came, and deuoured it vp.

5 And some fell on stonie grounde, where it had not much earth, and by and by sprang vp, because it had not depth of earth.

6 But assoone as ye Sunne was vp, it was burnt vp, and because it had not roote, it withered away.

7 And some fell among the thornes, and the thornes grewe vp, and choked it, so that it gaue no fruite.

8 Some againe fell in good grounde, and did yeelde fruite that sprong vp, and grewe, and it brought foorth, some thirtie folde, some sixtie folde, and some an hundreth folde.

9 Then he said vnto them, He that hath eares to heare, let him heare.

10 And whe he was alone, they that were about him with the twelue, asked him of ye parable.

11 And he saide vnto them, To you it is giuen to knowe the mysterie of the kingdome of God: but vnto them that are without, all thinges bee done in parables,

12 That they seeing, may see, and not discerne: and they hearing, may heare, and not vnderstand, least at any time they should turne, and their sinnes should be forgiuen them.

13 Againe he said vnto them, Perceiue ye not this parable? howe then should ye vnderstand all other parables?

14 The sower soweth the worde.

15 And these are they that receiue the seede by the wayes side, in whome the worde is sowen: but when they haue heard it, Satan commeth immediatly, and taketh away the worde that was sowen in their heartes.

16 And likewise they that receiue the seede in stony ground, are they, which whe they haue heard the word, straightwayes receiue it with gladnesse.

17 Yet haue they no roote in themselues, and endure but a time: for when trouble and persecution ariseth for the worde, immediatly they be offended.

18 Also they that receiue the seede among the thornes, are such as heare the word:

19 But the cares of this world, and the deceitfulnes of riches, and the lustes of other things enter in, and choke the word, and it is vnfruitfull.

20 But they that haue receiued seede in good ground, are they that heare the worde, and receiue it, and bring foorth fruite: one corne thirtie, another sixtie, and some an hundreth.

21 Also he saide vnto them, Commeth the candle in, to be put vnder a bushell, or vnder the bed, and not to be put on a candlesticke?

22 For there is nothing hid, that shall not be opened: neither is there a secret, but that it shall come to light.

23 If any man haue eares to heare, let him heare.

24 And he said vnto them, Take heede what ye heare. With what measure ye mete, it shall be measured vnto you: and vnto you that heare, shall more be giuen.

25 For vnto him that hath, shall it be giuen, and from him that hath not, shall be taken away, euen that he hath.

26 Also he said, So is the kingdome of God, as if a man should cast seede in the ground,

27 And shoulde sleepe, and rise vp night and day, and the seede should spring and growe vp, he not knowing howe.

28 For the earth bringeth foorth fruite of it selfe, first the blade, then the eares, after that full corne in the eares.

29 And assoone as the fruite sheweth it selfe, anon hee putteth in the sickle, because the haruest is come.

30 He saide moreouer, Whereunto shall wee liken the kingdome of God? or with what comparison shall we compare it?

31 It is like a graine of mustarde seede, which when it is sowen in the earth, is the least of all seedes that be in the earth:

32 But after that it is sowen, it groweth vp, and is greatest of all herbes, and beareth great branches, so that the foules of heauen may builde vnder the shadow of it.

33 And with many such parables he preached the word vnto them, as they were able to heare it.

34 And without parables spake hee nothing vnto them: but he expounded all thinges to his disciples apart.

35 Nowe the same day when euen was come, he saide vnto them, Let vs passe ouer vnto the other side.

36 And they left the multitude, and tooke him as he was in the shippe, and there were also with him other little shippes.

37 And there arose a great storme of winde, and the waues dashed into the shippe, so that it was now full.

38 And he was in the sterne asleepe on a pillow: and they awoke him, and saide to him, Master, carest thou not that we perish?

39 And hee rose vp, and rebuked the winde, and saide vnto the sea, Peace, and be still. So the winde ceased, and it was a great calme.

40 Then he saide vnto them, Why are ye so fearefull? how is it that ye haue no faith?

41 And they feared exceedingly, and said one to another, Who is this, that both the winde and sea obey him?

Mark 5

1 And they came ouer to the other side of the sea into the countrey of the Gadarens.

2 And when he was come out of the shippe, there met him incontinently out of the graues, a man which had an vncleane spirit:

3 Who had his abiding among the graues, and no man could binde him, no not with chaines:

4 Because that when hee was often bounde with fetters and chaines, he plucked the chaines asunder, and brake the fetters in pieces, neither could any man tame him.

5 And alwayes both night and day he cryed in the mountaines, and in the graues, and strooke himselfe with stones.

6 And when he saw Iesus afarre off, he ranne, and worshipped him,

7 And cryed with a loude voyce, and saide, What haue I to doe with thee, Iesus the Sonne of the most high God? I will that thou sweare to me by God, that thou torment me not.

8 (For hee saide vnto him, Come out of the man, thou vncleane spirit.)

9 And he asked him, What is thy name? and hee answered, saying, My name is Legion: for we are many.

10 And hee prayed him instantly, that hee would not send them away out of the countrey.

11 Now there was there in the mountaines a great heard of swine, feeding.

12 And all ye deuils besought him, saying, Send vs into the swine, that we may enter into them.

13 And incontinently Iesus gaue them leaue. Then the vncleane spirites went out, and entred into the swine, and the heard ranne headlong from the high banke into the sea, (and there were about two thousand swine) and they were choked vp in the sea.

14 And the swineheards fled, and told it in the citie, and in the countrey, and they came out to see what it was that was done.

15 And they came to Iesus, and sawe him that had bene possessed with the deuil, and had the legion, sit both clothed, and in his right minde: and they were afraide.

16 And they that saw it, tolde them, what was done to him that was possessed with the deuil, and concerning the swine.

17 Then they began to pray him, that hee would depart from their coastes.

18 And when he was come into the shippe, he that had bene possessed with the deuil, prayed him that he might be with him.

19 Howbeit, Iesus would not suffer him, but said vnto him, Goe thy way home to thy friendes, and shewe them what great thinges the Lord hath done vnto thee, and howe hee hath had compassion on thee.

20 So he departed, and began to publish in Decapolis, what great things Iesus had done vnto him: and all men did marueile.

21 And when Iesus was come ouer againe by ship vnto the other side, a great multitude gathered together to him, and he was neere vnto the sea.

22 And beholde, there came one of the rulers of the Synagogue, whose name was Iairus: and when he sawe him, he fell downe at his feete,

23 And besought him instantly, saying, My litle daughter lyeth at point of death: I pray thee that thou wouldest come and lay thine hands on her, that she may be healed, and liue.

24 Then hee went with him, and a great multitude folowed him, and thronged him.

25 (And there was a certaine woman, which was diseased with an issue of blood twelue yeeres,

26 And had suffred many things of many physicions, and had spent all that she had, and it auailed her nothing, but she became much worse.

27 When she had heard of Iesus, shee came in the preasse behinde, and touched his garment.

28 For she said, If I may but touch his clothes, I shalbe whole.

29 And straightway the course of her blood was dried vp, and she felt in her body, that she was healed of that plague.

30 And immediatly when Iesus did knowe in himselfe the vertue that went out of him, he turned him round about in the preasse, and said, Who hath touched my clothes?

31 And his disciples said vnto him, Thou seest the multitude throng thee, and sayest thou, Who did touche me?

32 And he looked round about, to see her that had done that.

33 And the woman feared and trembled: for she knewe what was done in her, and shee came and fell downe before him, and tolde him the whole trueth.

34 And hee saide to her, Daughter, thy faith hath made thee whole: go in peace, and be whole of thy plague.)

35 While hee yet spake, there came from the same ruler of the Synagogues house certaine which said, Thy daughter is dead: why diseasest thou the Master any further?

36 Assoone as Iesus heard that word spoken, he said vnto the ruler of the Synagogue, Be not afraide: onely beleeue.

37 And he suffered no man to follow him saue Peter and Iames, and Iohn the brother of Iames.

38 So hee came vnto the house of the ruler of the Synagogue, and sawe the tumult, and them that wept and wailed greatly.

39 And he went in, and said vnto them, Why make ye this trouble, and weepe? the childe is not dead, but sleepeth.

40 And they laught him to scorne: but hee put them all out, and tooke the father, and the mother of the childe, and

them that were with him, and entred in where the childe lay,

41 And tooke the childe by the hand, and saide vnto her, Talitha cumi, which is by interpretation, Mayden, I say vnto thee, arise.

42 And straightway the mayden arose, and walked: for shee was of the age of twelue yeeres, and they were astonied out of measure.

43 And he charged them straitly that no man should knowe of it, and commanded to giue her meate.

Mark 6

1 And he departed thence, and came into his owne countrey, and his disciples followed him.

2 And when the Sabbath was come, he began to teach in the Synagogue, and many that heard him, were astonied, and sayd, From whence hath this man these things? and what wisdome is this that is giuen vnto him, that euen such great workes are done by his hands?

3 Is not this that carpenter Maries sonne, the brother of Iames and Ioses, and of Iuda and Simon? and are not his sisters here with vs? And they were offended in him.

4 Then Iesus sayd vnto them, A Prophet is not without honour, but in his owne countrey, and among his owne kindred, and in his own house.

5 And he could there doe no great workes, saue that hee layd his hands vpon a fewe sicke folke, and healed them,

6 And he marueiled at their vnbeliefe, and went about by ye townes on euery side, teaching.

7 And he called vnto him the twelue, and began to send them forth two and two, and gaue them power ouer vncleane spirits,

8 And commanded them that they should take nothing for their iourney, saue a staffe onely: neither scrip, neither bread, neither money in their girdles:

9 But that they should be shod with sandals, and that they should not put on two coates.

10 And he sayd vnto them, Wheresoeuer ye shall enter into an house, there abide till ye depart thence.

11 And whosoeuer shall not receiue you, nor heare you, when ye depart thence, shake off the dust that is vnder your feete, for a witnes vnto them. Verely I say vnto you, It shalbe easier for Sodom, or Gomorrha at the day of iudgement, then for that citie.

12 And they went out, and preached, that men should amend their liues.

13 And they cast out many deuils: and they anointed many that were sicke, with oyle, and healed them.

14 Then King Herod heard of him (for his name was made manifest) and sayd, Iohn Baptist is risen againe from the dead, and therefore great workes are wrought by him.

15 Other sayd, It is Elias, and some sayd, It is a Prophet, or as one of those Prophets.

16 So when Herod heard it, he said, It is Iohn whom I beheaded: he is risen from the dead.

17 For Herod him selfe had sent forth, and had taken Iohn, and bound him in prison for Herodias sake, which was his brother Philippes wife, because he had maried her.

18 For Iohn sayd vnto Herod, It is not lawfull for thee to haue thy brothers wife.

19 Therefore Herodias layd waite against him, and would haue killed him, but she could not:

20 For Herod feared Iohn, knowing that hee was a iust man, and an holy, and reuerenced him, and when he heard him, he did many things, and heard him gladly.

21 But the time being conuenient, when Herod on his birth day made a banket to his princes and captaines, and chiefe estates of Galile:

22 And the daughter of the same Herodias came in, and daunced, and pleased Herod, and them that sate at table together, the King sayd vnto the mayde, Aske of me what thou wilt, and I will giue it thee.

23 And he sware vnto her, Whatsoeuer thou shalt aske of me, I will giue it thee, euen vnto the halfe of my kingdome.

24 So she went forth, and said to her mother, What shall I aske? And she said, Iohn Baptists head.

25 Then she came in straightway with haste vnto the King, and asked, saying, I would that thou shouldest giue me euen now in a charger the head of Iohn Baptist.

26 Then the King was very sory: yet for his othes sake, and for their sakes which sate at table with him, he would not refuse her.

27 And immediatly the King sent the hangman, and gaue charge that his head shoulde be brought in. So he went and beheaded him in the prison,

28 And brought his head in a charger, and gaue it to the maide, and the maide gaue it to her mother.

29 And when his disciples heard it, they came and tooke vp his body, and put it in a tombe.

30 And the Apostles gathered themselues together to Iesus, and tolde him all things, both what they had done, and what they had taught.

31 And he sayd vnto them, Come ye apart into the wildernes, and rest a while: for there were many commers and goers, that they had not leasure to eate.

32 So they went by ship out of the way into a desart place.

33 But the people sawe them when they departed, and many knewe him, and ran a foote thither out of all cities, and came thither before them, and assembled vnto him.

34 Then Iesus went out, and sawe a great multitude, and had compassion on them, because they were like sheepe which had no shepheard: and he began to teach them many things.

35 And when the day was nowe farre spent, his disciples came vnto him, saying, This is a desart place, and nowe the day is farre passed.

36 Let them depart, that they may goe into the countrey and townes about, and buy them bread: for they haue nothing to eate.

37 But he answered, and said vnto them, Giue yee them to eate. And they said vnto him, Shall we goe, and buy two hundreth peny worth of bread, and giue them to eate?

38 Then he sayde vnto them, Howe many loaues haue ye? goe and looke. And when they knewe it, they sayd, Fiue, and two fishes.

39 So he commanded them to make them all sit downe by companies vpon the greene grasse.

40 Then they sate downe by rowes, by hundreds, and by fifties.

41 And he tooke the fiue loaues, and the two fishes, and looked vp to heauen, and gaue thanks, and brake the loaues, and gaue them to his disciples to set before them, and the two fishes he deuided among them all.

42 So they did all eate, and were satisfied.

43 And they tooke vp twelue baskets full of the fragments, and of the fishes.

44 And they that had eaten, were about fiue thousand men.

45 And straightway he caused his disciples to goe into the ship, and to goe before vnto the other side vnto Bethsaida, while he sent away the people.

46 Then assoone as he had sent them away, he departed into a mountaine to pray.

47 And when euen was come, the ship was in the mids of the sea, and he alone on the land.

48 And he saw them troubled in rowing, (for the winde was contrary vnto them) and about the fourth watch of the night, hee came vnto them, walking vpon the sea, and would haue passed by them.

49 And when they saw him walking vpon the sea, they supposed it had bene a spirit, and cried out.

50 For they all saw him, and were sore afrayd: but anon he talked with them, and said vnto them, Be ye of good comfort: it is I, be not afrayd.

51 Then he went vp vnto them into the ship, and the winde ceased, and they were much more amased in them selues, and marueiled.

52 For they had not considered the matter of the loaues, because their hearts were hardened.

53 And they came ouer, and went into the land of Gennesaret, and arriued.

54 So when they were come out of the ship, straightway they knewe him,

55 And ran about throughout all that region round about, and began to cary hither and thither in couches all that were sicke, where they heard that he was.

56 And whithersoeuer he entred into townes, or cities, or villages, they laide their sicke in the streetes, and prayed him that they might touch at the least the edge of his garment. And as many as touched him, were made whole.

Mark 7

1 Then gathered vnto him the Pharises, and certaine of the Scribes which came from Hierusalem.

2 And when they sawe some of his disciples eate meate with common hands, (that is to say, vnwashen) they complained.

3 (For the Pharises, and all the Iewes, except they wash their hands oft, eate not, holding the tradition of the Elders.

4 And when they come from the market, except they wash, they eate not: and many other things there be, which they haue taken vpon them to obserue, as the washing of cups, and pots, and of brasen vessels, and of beds.)

5 Then asked him the Pharises and Scribes, Why walke not thy disciples according to the tradition of the Elders, but eate meate with vnwashen hands?

6 Then hee answered and sayd vnto them, Surely Esay hath prophecied well of you, hypocrites, as it is written, This people honoureth mee with lippes, but their heart is farre away from me.

7 But they worship me in vaine, teaching for doctrines the commandements of men.

8 For ye lay the commandement of God apart, and obserue the tradition of men, as the washing of pots and of cups, and many other such like things ye doe.

9 And he sayd vnto them, Well, ye reiect the commandement of God, that ye may obserue your owne tradition.

10 For Moses sayd, Honour thy father and thy mother: and Whosoeuer shall speake euill of father or mother, let him die the death.

11 But yee say, If a man say to father or mother, Corban, that is, By the gift that is offered by mee, thou mayest haue profite, hee shall be free.

12 So ye suffer him no more to doe any thing for his father, or his mother,

13 Making the worde of God of none authoritie, by your tradition which ye haue ordeined: and ye doe many such like things.

14 Then he called the whole multitude vnto him, and sayd vnto them, Hearken you all vnto me, and vnderstand.

15 There is nothing without a man, that can defile him, when it entreth into him: but the things which proceede out of him, are they which defile the man.

16 If any haue eares to heare, let him heare.

17 And when hee came into an house, away from the people, his disciples asked him concerning the parable.

18 And he sayde vnto them, What? are ye without vnderstanding also? Doe ye not knowe that whatsoeuer thing from without entreth into a man, cannot defile him,

19 Because it entreth not into his heart, but into the belly, and goeth out into the draught which is the purging of all meates?

20 Then he sayd, That which commeth out of man, that defileth man.

21 For from within, euen out of the heart of men, proceede euill thoughtes, adulteries, fornications, murthers,

22 Theftes, couetousnes, wickednes, deceite, vncleannes, a wicked eye, backbiting, pride, foolishnesse.

23 All these euill things come from within, and defile a man.

24 And from thence he rose, and went into the borders of Tyrus and Sidon, and entred into an house, and woulde that no man should haue knowen: but he could not be hid.

25 For a certaine woman, whose litle daughter had an vncleane spirit, heard of him, and came, and fell at his feete,

26 (And the woman was a Greeke, a Syrophenissian by nation) and she besought him that he would cast out the deuill out of her daughter.

27 But Iesus saide vnto her, Let the children first be fedde: for it is not good to take the childrens bread, and to cast it vnto whelpes.

28 Then shee answered, and saide vnto him, Trueth, Lord: yet in deede the whelpes eate vnder the table of the childrens crommes.

29 Then he said vnto her, For this saying goe thy way: the deuil is gone out of thy daughter.

30 And when shee was come home to her house, shee founde the deuill departed, and her daughter lying on the bed.

31 And hee departed againe from the coastes of Tyrus and Sidon, and came vnto the sea of Galile, through the middes of the coastes of Decapolis.

32 And they brought vnto him one that was deafe and stambered in his speache, and prayed him to put his hand vpon him.

33 Then hee tooke him aside from the multitude, and put his fingers in his eares, and did spit, and touched his tongue.

34 And looking vp to heauen, hee sighed, and said vnto him, Ephphatha, that is, Be opened.

35 And straightway his eares were opened, and the string of his tongue was loosed, and hee spake plaine.

36 And he commanded them, that they should tell no man: but howe much soeuer hee forbad them, the more a great deale they published it,

37 And were beyonde measure astonied, saying, Hee hath done all thinges well: he maketh both the deafe to heare, and the domme to speake.

Mark 8

1 In those dayes, when there was a very great multitude, and had nothing to eate, Iesus called his disciples to him, and said vnto them,

2 I haue compassion on the multitude, because they haue nowe continued with mee three dayes, and haue nothing to eate.

3 And if I sende them away fasting to their owne houses, they woulde faint by the way: for some of them came from farre.

4 Then his disciples answered him, Whence can a man satisfie these with bread here in the wildernes?

5 And hee asked them, Howe many loaues haue ye? And they said, Seuen.

6 Then he commanded the multitude to sit downe on the grounde: and hee tooke the seuen loaues, and gaue thankes, brake them, and gaue to his disciples to set before them, and they did set them before the people.

7 They had also a few small fishes: and when he had giuen thankes, he commanded them also to be set before them.

8 So they did eate, and were sufficed, and they tooke vp of the broken meate that was left, seuen baskets full.

9 (And they that had eaten, were about foure thousand) so he sent them away.

10 And anon he entred into a ship with his disciples, and came into the parts of Dalmanutha.

11 And the Pharises came foorth, and began to dispute with him, seeking of him a signe from heauen, and tempting him.

12 Then hee sighed deepely in his spirit, and saide, Why doeth this generation seeke a signe? Verely I say vnto you, a signe shall not be giuen vnto this generation.

13 So he left them, and went into the ship againe, and departed to the other side.

14 And they had forgotten to take bread, neither had they in the shippe with them, but one loafe.

15 And he charged them, saying, Take heede, and beware of the leauen of the Pharises, and of the leauen of Herod.

16 And they reasoned among themselues, saying, It is, because we haue no bread.

17 And when Iesus knew it, he said vnto them, Why reason you thus, because ye haue no bread? perceiue ye not yet, neither vnderstande? haue ye your hearts yet hardened?

18 Haue yee eyes, and see not? and haue yee eares, and heare not? and doe ye not remember?

19 When I brake the fiue loaues among fiue thousand, how many baskets full of broken meate tooke ye vp? They said vnto him, Twelue.

20 And when I brake seuen among foure thousande, howe many baskets of the leauings of broken meate tooke ye vp? And they said, Seuen.

21 Then he saide vnto them, Howe is it that ye vnderstand not?

22 And hee came to Bethsaida, and they brought a blinde man vnto him, and desired him to touch him.

23 Then he tooke the blinde by the hand, and ledde him out of the towne,

and spat in his eyes, and put his handes vpon him, and asked him, if he sawe ought.

24 And he looked vp, and said, I see men: for I see them walking like trees.

25 After that, he put his hands againe vpon his eyes, and made him looke againe. And hee was restored to his sight, and sawe euery man a farre off clearely.

26 And hee sent him home to his house, saying, Neither goe into the towne, nor tell it to any in the towne.

27 And Iesus went out, and his disciples into the townes of Cesarea Philippi. And by the way hee asked his disciples, saying vnto them, Whome doe men say that I am?

28 And they answered, Some say, Iohn Baptist: and some, Elias: and some, one of the Prophets.

29 And he said vnto them, But whome say ye that I am? Then Peter answered, and saide vnto him, Thou art that Christ.

30 And he sharpely charged them, that concerning him they should tell no man.

31 Then hee began to teache them that the Sonne of man must suffer many things, and should be reproued of the Elders, and of the hie Priestes, and of the Scribes, and be slaine, and within three dayes rise againe.

32 And he spake that thing boldly. Then Peter tooke him aside, and began to rebuke him.

33 Then he turned backe, and looked on his disciples, and rebuked Peter, saying, Get thee behinde me, Satan: for thou vnderstandest not the things that are of God, but the things that are of men.

34 And hee called the people vnto him with his disciples, and saide vnto them, Whosoeuer will follow me, let him forsake himselfe, and take vp his crosse, and follow me.

35 For whosoeuer will saue his life, shall lose it: but whosoeuer shall lose his life for my sake and the Gospels, he shall saue it.

36 For what shall it profite a man, though he should winne the whole world, if he lose his soule?

37 Or what exchange shall a man giue for his soule?

38 For whosoeuer shall be ashamed of mee, and of my wordes among this adulterous and sinfull generation, of him shall the Sonne of man be ashamed also, when he commeth in the glorie of his Father with the holy Angels.

Mark 9

1 And he saide vnto them, Verely I say vnto you, that there be some of them that stande here, which shall not taste of death till they haue seene the kingdome of God come with power.

2 And six dayes after, Iesus taketh vnto him Peter, and Iames, and Iohn, and carieth them vp into an hie mountaine out of the way alone, and his shape was changed before them.

3 And his rayment did shine, and was very white, as snowe, so white as no fuller can make vpon the earth.

4 And there appeared vnto them Elias with Moses, and they were talking with Iesus.

5 Then Peter answered, and said to Iesus, Master, it is good for vs to be here: let vs make also three tabernacles, one for thee, and one for Moses, and one for Elias.

6 Yet hee knewe not what he saide: for they were afraide.

7 And there was a cloude that shadowed them, and a voyce came out of the cloude, saying, This is my beloued Sonne: heare him.

8 And suddenly they looked roud about, and sawe no more any man saue Iesus only with them.

9 And as they came downe from the mountaine, he charged them, that they should tell no man what they had seene, saue when the Sonne of man were risen from the dead againe.

10 So they kept that matter to themselues, and demaunded one of another, what the rising from the dead againe should meane?

11 Also they asked him, saying, Why say the Scribes, that Elias must first come?

12 And he answered, and said vnto them, Elias verely shall first come, and restore all things: and as it is written of the Sonne of man, hee must suffer many things, and be set at nought.

13 But I say vnto you, that Elias is come, (and they haue done vnto him whatsoeuer they would) as it is written of him.

14 And when he came to his disciples, he saw a great multitude about them, and the Scribes disputing with them.

15 And straightway all the people, when they behelde him, were amased, and ranne to him, and saluted him.

16 Then hee asked the Scribes, What dispute you among your selues?

17 And one of the companie answered, and said, Master, I haue brought my sonne vnto thee, which hath a dumme spirit:

18 And wheresoeuer he taketh him, he teareth him, and he fometh, and gnasheth his teeth, and pineth away: and I spake to thy disciples, that they should cast him out, and they could not.

19 Then he answered him, and said, O faithlesse generation, how long now shall I be with you! how long now shall I suffer you! Bring him vnto me.

20 So they brought him vnto him: and assoone as the spirit sawe him, hee tare him, and hee fell downe on the ground walowing and foming.

21 Then he asked his father, How long time is it since he hath bin thus? And he said, Of a childe.

22 And oft times he casteth him into the fire, and into the water to destroy him: but if thou canst do any thing, helpe vs, and haue compassion vpon vs.

23 And Iesus said vnto him, If thou canst beleeue it, al things are possible to him that beleeueth.

24 And straightway the father of the childe crying with teares, saide, Lord, I beleeue: helpe my vnbeliefe.

25 When Iesus saw that the people came running together, he rebuked the vncleane spirit, saying vnto him, Thou domme and deafe spirit, I charge thee, come out of him, and enter no more into him.

26 Then the spirit cried, and rent him sore, and came out, and he was as one dead, in so much that many said, He is dead.

27 But Iesus tooke his hande, and lift him vp, and he arose.

28 And when hee was come into the house, his disciples asked him secretly, Why could not we cast him out?

29 And he saide vnto them, This kinde can by no other meanes come foorth, but by prayer and fasting.

30 And they departed thence, and went together through Galile, and hee would not that any should haue knowen it.

31 For he taught his disciples, and saide vnto them, The Sonne of man shalbe deliuered into the handes of men, and they shall kill him, but after that he is killed, he shall rise againe the third day.

32 But they vnderstoode not that saying, and were afraide to aske him.

33 After, he came to Capernaum: and when he was in the house, he asked them, What was it that ye disputed among you by the way?

34 And they helde their peace: for by the way they reasoned among themselues, who should bee the chiefest.

35 And he sate downe, and called the twelue, and said to them, If any man desire to be first, the same shalbe last of all, and seruant vnto all.

36 And he tooke a litle childe, and set him in the middes of them, and tooke him in his armes, and sayd vnto them,

37 Whosoeuer shall receiue one of such litle children in my Name, receiueth me: and whosoeuer receiueth mee, receiueth not me, but him that sent me.

38 Then Iohn answered him, saying, Master, we sawe one casting out deuils by thy Name, which followeth not vs, and we forbade him, because he followeth vs not.

39 But Iesus sayd, Forbid him not: for there is no man that can doe a miracle by my Name, that can lightly speake euill of me.

40 For whosoeuer is not against vs, is on our part.

41 And whosoeuer shall giue you a cup of water to drinke for my Names sake, because ye belong to Christ, verely I say vnto you, he shall not lose his rewarde.

42 And whosoeuer shall offend one of these litle ones, that beleeue in me, it were better for him rather, that a milstone were hanged about his necke, and that he were cast into the sea.

43 Wherefore, if thine hand cause thee to offend, cut it off: it is better for thee to enter into life, maimed, then hauing two

hands, to goe into hell, into the fire that neuer shalbe quenched,

44 Where their worme dyeth not, and the fire neuer goeth out.

45 Likewise, if thy foote cause thee to offend, cut it off: it is better for thee to go halt into life, then hauing two feete, to be cast into hell, into the fire that neuer shalbe quenched,

46 Where their worme dyeth not, and the fire neuer goeth out.

47 And if thine eye cause thee to offende, plucke it out: it is better for thee to goe into the kingdome of God with one eye, then hauing two eyes, to be cast into hell fire,

48 Where their worme dyeth not, and the fire neuer goeth out.

49 For euery man shalbe salted with fire: and euery sacrifice shalbe salted with salt.

50 Salt is good: but if the salt be vnsauerie, wherewith shall it be seasoned? haue salt in your selues, and haue peace one with another.

Mark 10

1 And he arose from thence, and went into the coastes of Iudea by the farre side of Iordan, and the people resorted vnto him againe, and as he was wont, he taught them againe.

2 Then the Pharises came and asked him, if it were lawfull for a man to put away his wife, and tempted him.

3 And he answered, and sayde vnto them, What did Moses commaund you?

4 And they sayd, Moses suffered to write a bill of diuorcement, and to put her away.

5 Then Iesus answered, and sayd vnto them, For the hardnesse of your heart he wrote this precept vnto you.

6 But at the beginning of the creation God made them male and female:

7 For this cause shall man leaue his father and mother, and cleaue vnto his wife.

8 And they twaine shalbe one flesh: so that they are no more twaine, but one flesh.

9 Therefore, what God hath coupled together, let not man separate.

10 And in the house his disciples asked him againe of that matter.

11 And he sayd vnto them, Whosoeuer shall put away his wife and marrie another, committeth adulterie against her.

12 And if a woman put away her husband, and be married to another, she committeth adulterie.

13 Then they brought litle children to him, that he should touch them, and his disciples rebuked those that brought them.

14 But when Iesus sawe it, he was displeased, and said to them, Suffer the litle children to come vnto me, and forbid them not: for of such is the kingdome of God.

15 Verely I say vnto you, Whosoeuer shall not receiue the kingdome of God as a litle childe, he shall not enter therein.

16 And he tooke them vp in his armes, and put his hands vpon them, and blessed them.

17 And when hee was gone out on the way, there came one running, and kneeled to him, and asked him, Good Master, what shall I doe, that I may possesse eternall life?

18 Iesus sayde to him, Why callest thou me good? there is none good but one, euen God.

19 Thou knowest the comandements, Thou shalt not commit adulterie. Thou shalt not kill. Thou shalt not steale. Thou shalt not beare false witnesse. Thou shalt hurt no man. Honour thy father and mother.

20 Then he answered, and said to him, Master, all these things I haue obserued from my youth.

21 And Iesus looked vpon him, and loued him, and sayde vnto him, One thing is lacking vnto thee. Go and sell all that thou hast, and giue to the poore, and thou shalt haue treasure in heauen, and come, follow me, and take vp the crosse.

22 But hee was sad at that saying, and went away sorowfull: for he had great possessions.

23 And Iesus looked round about, and sayd vnto his disciples, Howe hardly doe they that haue riches, enter into the kingdome of God!

24 And his disciples were afraide at his words. But Iesus answered againe, and sayd vnto them, Children, how hard is it for them that trust in riches, to enter into the kingdome of God!

25 It is easier for a camel to goe through the eye of a needle, then for a riche man to enter into the kingdome of God.

26 And they were much more astonied, saying with themselues, Who then can be saued?

27 But Iesus looked vpon them, and sayd, With men it is impossible, but not with God: for with God all things are possible.

28 Then Peter began to say vnto him, Loe, we haue forsaken all, and haue folowed thee.

29 Iesus answered, and sayd, Verely I say vnto you, there is no man that hath forsaken house, or brethren, or sisters, or father, or mother, or wife, or children, or lands for my sake and the Gospels,

30 But he shall receiue an hundred folde, now at this present, houses, and brethren, and sisters, and mothers, and children, and lands with persecutions, and in the world to come, eternall life.

31 But many that are first, shall be last, and the last, first.

32 And they were in the way going vp to Hierusalem, and Iesus went before them and they were troubled, and as they followed, they were afraide, and Iesus tooke the twelue againe, and began to tell them what things should come vnto him,

33 Saying, Beholde, we goe vp to Hierusalem, and the Sonne of man shall be deliuered vnto the hie Priests, and to the Scribes, and they shall condemne

him to death, and shall deliuer him to the Gentiles.

34 And they shall mocke him, and scourge him, and spit vpon him, and kill him: but the third day he shall rise againe.

35 Then Iames and Iohn the sonnes of Zebedeus came vnto him, saying, Master, we would that thou shouldest doe for vs that we desire.

36 And he sayd vnto them, What would ye I should doe for you?

37 And they said to him, Graunt vnto vs, that we may sit, one at thy right hand, and the other at thy left hand in thy glory.

38 But Iesus sayd vnto them, Ye knowe not what ye aske. Can ye drinke of the cup that I shall drinke of, and be baptized with the baptisme that I shall be baptized with?

39 And they said vnto him, We can. But Iesus sayd vnto them, Ye shall drinke in deede of the cup that I shall drinke of, and be baptized with the baptisme wherewith I shalbe baptized:

40 But to sit at my right hand, and at my left, is not mine to giue, but it shalbe giuen to them for whome it is prepared.

41 And when the ten heard that, they began to disdaine at Iames and Iohn.

42 But Iesus called them vnto him, and sayd to them, Ye know that they which are princes among the Gentiles, haue domination ouer them, and they that be great among them, exercise authoritie ouer them.

43 But it shall not be so among you: but whosoeuer will be great among you, shall be your seruant.

44 And whosoeuer will be chiefe of you, shall be the seruant of all.

45 For euen the Sonne of man came not to be serued, but to serue, and to giue his life for the raunsome of many.

46 Then they came to Iericho: and as he went out of Iericho with his disciples, and a great multitude, Bartimeus the sonne of Timeus, a blinde man, sate by the wayes side, begging.

47 And when hee heard that it was Iesus of Nazareth, he began to crye, and to say, Iesus the Sonne of Dauid, haue mercy on me.

48 And many rebuked him, because he should holde his peace: but hee cryed much more, O Sonne of Dauid, haue mercy on me.

49 Then Iesus stood still, and commanded him to be called: and they called the blind, saying vnto him, Be of good comfort: arise, he calleth thee.

50 So he threwe away his cloke, and rose, and came to Iesus.

51 And Iesus answered, and said vnto him, What wilt thou that I doe vnto thee? And the blinde sayd vnto him, Lord, that I may receiue sight.

52 Then Iesus sayde vnto him, Goe thy way: thy fayth hath saued thee. And by and by, he receiued his sight, and folowed Iesus in the way.

Mark 11

1 And when they came neere to Hierusalem, to Bethphage and Bethania vnto the mount of Oliues, he sent forth two of his disciples,

2 And sayd vnto them, Goe your wayes into that towne that is ouer against you, and assoone as ye shall enter into it, ye shall finde a colte tied, whereon neuer man sate: loose him, and bring him.

3 And if any man say vnto you, Why doe ye this? Say that the Lord hath neede of him, and straightway he will send him hither.

4 And they went their way, and found a colt tyed by the doore without, in a place where two wayes met, and they loosed him.

5 Then certaine of them, that stoode there, sayd vnto them, What doe ye loosing the colt?

6 And they sayde vnto them, as Iesus had commanded them: So they let them goe.

7 And they brought the colte to Iesus, and cast their garments on him, and he sate vpon him.

8 And many spred their garments in the way: other cut downe branches off the trees, and strawed them in the way.

9 And they that went before, and they that folowed, cryed, saying, Hosanna: blessed be hee that commeth in the Name of the Lord.

10 Blessed be the kingdome that commeth in the Name of the Lord of our father Dauid: Hosanna, O thou which art in the highest heauens.

11 So Iesus entred into Hierusalem, and into the Temple: and when he had looked about on all things, and now it was euening, he went forth vnto Bethania with the twelue.

12 And on the morowe when they were come out from Bethania, he was hungry.

13 And seeing a fig tree afarre off, that had leaues, he went to see if he might finde any thing thereon: but when he came vnto it, hee found nothing but leaues: for the time of figges was not yet.

14 Then Iesus answered, and sayd to it, Neuer man eate fruite of thee hereafter while the world standeth: and his disciples heard it.

15 And they came to Hierusalem, and Iesus went into the Temple, and began to cast out them that solde and bought in the Temple, and ouerthrewe the tables of the money changers, and the seates of them that solde doues.

16 Neither would hee suffer that any man should cary a vessell through the Temple.

17 And he taught, saying vnto them, Is it not written, Mine house shalbe called the house of prayer vnto all nations? but you haue made it a denne of theeues.

18 And the Scribes and hie Priestes heard it, and sought howe to destroy him: for they feared him, because the whole multitude was astonied at his doctrine.

19 But when euen was come, Iesus went out of the citie.

20 And in the morning as they iourneyed together, they saw the figge tree dried vp from the rootes.

21 Then Peter remembred, and said vnto him, Master, beholde, the figge tree which thou cursedst, is withered.

22 And Iesus answered, and said vnto them, Haue the faith of God.

23 For verely I say vnto you, that whosoeuer shall say vnto this mountaine, Be thou taken away, and cast into the sea, and shall not wauer in his heart, but shall beleeue that those things which he saieth, shall come to passe, whatsoeuer he saieth, shall be done to him.

24 Therefore I say vnto you, Whatsoeuer ye desire when ye pray, beleeue that ye shall haue it, and it shalbe done vnto you.

25 But when ye shall stand, and pray, forgiue, if ye haue any thing against any man, that your Father also which is in heauen, may forgiue you your trespasses.

26 For if you will not forgiue, your Father which is in heauen, will not pardon you your trespasses.

27 Then they came againe to Hierusalem: and as he walked in the Temple, there came to him ye hie Priestes, and the Scribes, and the Elders,

28 And said vnto him, By what authoritie doest thou these things? and who gaue thee this authoritie, that thou shouldest doe these things?

29 Then Iesus answered, and saide vnto them, I will also aske of you a certaine thing, and answere ye me, and I will tell you by what authoritie I do these things.

30 The baptisme of Iohn, was it from heauen, or of men? answere me.

31 And they thought with themselues, saying, If we shall say, From heauen, he will say, Why then did ye not beleeue him?

32 But if we say, Of men, we feare the people: for all men counted Iohn, that he was a Prophet in deede.

33 Then they answered, and saide vnto Iesus, We cannot tell. And Iesus answered, and said vnto them, Neither will I tell you by what authoritie I doe these things.

Mark 12

1 And he began to speake vnto them in parables, A certaine man planted a vineyard, and copassed it with an hedge, and digged a pit for the winepresse, and built a tower in it, and let it out to husbandmen, and went into a strange countrey.

2 And at the time, he sent to the husbandmen a seruant, that he might receiue of the husbandmen of the fruite of the vineyard.

3 But they tooke him, and beat him, and sent him away emptie.

4 And againe he sent vnto them another seruant, and at him they cast stones, and brake his head, and sent him away shamefully handled.

5 And againe he sent another, and him they slew, and many other, beating some, and killing some.

6 Yet had he one sonne, his deare beloued: him also he sent the last vnto them, saying, They will reuerence my sonne.

7 But ye husbandmen said among themselues, This is the heire: come, let vs kill him, and the inheritance shalbe ours.

8 So they tooke him, and killed him, and cast him out of the vineyard.

9 What shall then the Lord of the vineyard doe? He will come and destroy these husbandmen, and giue the vineyard to others.

10 Haue ye not read so much as this Scripture? The stone which the builders did refuse, is made the head of the corner.

11 This was done of the Lord, and it is marueilous in our eyes.

12 Then they went about to take him, but they feared the people: for they perceiued that he spake that parable against them: therefore they left him, and went their way.

13 And they sent vnto him certaine of the Pharises, and of ye Herodians that they might take him in his talke.

14 And when they came, they saide vnto him, Master, we know that thou art true, and carest for no man: for thou considerest not the person of men, but teachest the way of God truely, Is it lawfull to giue tribute to Cesar, or not?

15 Should we giue it, or should we not giue it? but he knew their hypocrisie, and said vnto them, Why tempt ye me? Bring me a peny, that I may see it.

16 So they brought it, and he said vnto them, Whose is this image and superscription? and they said vnto him, Cesars.

17 Then Iesus answered, and saide vnto them, Giue to Cesar the things that are Cesars, and to God, those that are Gods: and they marueiled at him.

18 Then came the Sadduces vnto him, (which say, there is no resurrection) and they asked him, saying,

19 Master, Moses wrote vnto vs, If any mans brother die, and leaue his wife, and leaue no children, that his brother should take his wife, and rayse vp seede vnto his brother.

20 There were seuen brethren, and the first tooke a wife, and when he died, left no issue.

21 Then the seconde tooke her, and he died, neither did he yet leaue issue, and the third likewise:

22 So those seuen had her, and left no yssue: last of all the wife died also.

23 In the resurrection then, when they shall rise againe, whose wife shall she be of them? for seuen had her to wife.

24 Then Iesus answered, and saide vnto them, Are ye not therefore deceiued, because ye knowe not the Scriptures, neither the power of God?

25 For when they shall rise againe from the dead, neither men marry, nor wiues

are married, but are as the Angels which are in heauen.

26 And as touching the dead, that they shall rise againe, haue ye not read in the booke of Moses, howe in the bush God spake vnto him, saying, I am the God of Abraham, and the God of Isaac, and the God of Iacob?

27 God is not ye God of the dead, but the God of the liuing. Ye are therefore greatly deceiued.

28 Then came one of the Scribes that had heard them disputing together, and perceiuing that he had answered them well, he asked him, Which is the first commandement of all?

29 Iesus answered him, The first of all the commandements is, Heare, Israel, The Lord our God is the onely Lord.

30 Thou shalt therefore loue the Lord thy God with all thine heart, and with all thy soule, and with all thy minde, and with all thy strength: this is the first commandement.

31 And the second is like, that is, Thou shalt loue thy neighbour as thy selfe. There is none other commandement greater then these.

32 Then that Scribe said vnto him, Well, Master, thou hast saide the trueth, that there is one God, and that there is none but he,

33 And to loue him with all the heart, and with all the vnderstanding, and with all the soule, and with all the strength, and to loue his neighbour as himselfe, is more then all whole burnt offerings and sacrifices.

34 Then when Iesus saw that he answered discreetely, he saide vnto him, Thou art not farre from the kingdome of God. And no man after that durst aske him any question.

35 And Iesus answered and said teaching in the Temple, Howe say the Scribes that Christ is the sonne of Dauid?

36 For Dauid himselfe said by ye holy Ghost, The Lord said to my Lord, Sit at my right hand, till I make thine enemies thy footestoole.

37 Then Dauid himselfe calleth him Lord: by what meanes is he then his sonne? and much people heard him gladly.

38 Moreouer he saide vnto them in his doctrine, Beware of the Scribes which loue to goe in long robes, and loue salutations in the markets,

39 And the chiefe seates in the Synagogues, and the first roumes at feastes,

40 Which deuoure widowes houses, euen vnder a colour of long prayers. These shall receiue the greater damnation.

41 And as Iesus sate ouer against the treasurie, he beheld how the people cast money into the treasurie, and many rich men cast in much.

42 And there came a certaine poore widowe, and she threw in two mites, which make a quadrin.

43 Then he called vnto him his disciples, and said vnto them, Verely I say vnto you, that this poore widowe hath cast more in, then all they which haue cast into the treasurie.

44 For they all did cast in of their superfluitie: but she of her pouertie did cast in all that she had, euen all her liuing.

Mark 13

1 And as he went out of the Temple, one of his disciples said vnto him, Master, see what maner stones, and what maner buildings are here.

2 Then Iesus answered and saide vnto him, Seest thou these great buildings? there shall not be left one stone vpon a stone, that shall not be throwen downe.

3 And as he sate on the mount of Oliues, ouer against the Temple, Peter, and Iames, and Iohn, and Andrew asked him secretly,

4 Tell vs, when shall these things be? and what shalbe the signe when all these things shalbe fulfilled?

5 And Iesus answered them, and began to say, Take heede lest any man deceiue you.

6 For many shall come in my Name, saying, I am Christ, and shall deceiue many.

7 Furthermore when ye shall heare, of warres, and rumours of warres, be ye not troubled: for such things must needes be: but the end shall not be yet.

8 For nation shall rise against nation, and kingdome against kingdome, and there shalbe earthquakes in diuers quarters, and there shalbe famine and troubles: these are the beginnings of sorowes.

9 But take ye heede to your selues: for they shall deliuer you vp to the Councils, and to the Synagogues: ye shalbe beaten, and brought before rulers and Kings for my sake, for a testimoniall vnto them.

10 And the Gospel must first be published among all nations.

11 But when they leade you, and deliuer you vp, be not carefull before hand, neither studie what ye shall say: but what is giuen you at the same time, that speake: for it is not ye that speake, but the holy Ghost.

12 Yea, and the brother shall deliuer the brother to death, and the father the sonne, and the children shall rise against their parents, and shall cause them to die.

13 And ye shall be hated of all men for my Names sake: but whosoeuer shall endure vnto the end, he shalbe saued.

14 Moreouer, when ye shall see the abomination of desolation (spoken of by Daniel the Prophet) set where it ought not, (let him that readeth, consider it) then let them that be in Iudea, flee into the mountaines,

15 And let him that is vpon the house, not come downe into the house, neither enter therein, to fetch any thing out of his house.

16 And let him that is in the fielde, not turne backe againe to take his garment.

17 Then wo shalbe to the that are with child, and to them that giue sucke in those dayes.

18 Pray therefore that your flight be not in the winter.

19 For those dayes shalbe such tribulation, as was not from the beginning of ye creation which God created vnto this time, neither shalbe.

20 And except that the Lord had shortened those dayes, no flesh shoulde be saued: but for the elects sake, which he hath chosen, he hath shortened those dayes.

21 Then if any man say to you, Loe, here is Christ, or, lo, he is there, beleeue it not.

22 For false Christes shall rise, and false prophets, and shall shewe signes and wonders, to deceiue if it were possible the very elect.

23 But take ye heede: beholde, I haue shewed you all things before.

24 Moreouer in those dayes, after that tribulation, the sunne shall waxe darke, and ye moone shall not giue her light,

25 And the starres of heauen shall fall: and the powers which are in heauen, shall shake.

26 And then shall they see the Sonne of man comming in ye cloudes, with great power and glory.

27 And he shall then send his Angels, and shall gather together his elect from the foure windes, and from the vtmost part of the earth to the vtmost part of heauen.

28 Nowe learne a parable of the figge tree. When her bough is yet tender, and it bringeth foorth leaues, ye knowe that sommer is neere.

29 So in like maner, when ye see these things come to passe, knowe that the kingdom of God is neere, euen at the doores.

30 Verely I say vnto you, that this generation shall not passe, till all these things be done.

31 Heauen and earth shall passe away, but my woordes shall not passe away.

32 But of that day and houre knoweth no man, no, not the Angels which are in heauen, neither the Sonne himselfe, but the Father.

33 Take heede: watch, and praie: for yee knowe not when the time is.

34 For the Sonne of man is as a man going into a strange countrey, and leaueth his house, and giueth authoritie to his seruaunts, and to euery man his woorke, and commandeth the porter to watch.

35 Watch ye therefore, (for ye know not whe ye master of the house will come, at eue, or at midnight, at the cocke crowing, or in the dawning,)

36 Least if he come suddenly, he should finde you sleeping.

37 And those things that I say vnto you, I say vnto all men, Watch.

Mark 14

1 And two daies after followed the feast of the Passeouer, and of vnleauened

bread: and the hie Priests, and Scribes sought how they might take him by craft, and put him to death.

2 But they sayde, Not in the feast day, least there be any tumult among the people.

3 And when hee was in Bethania in the house of Simon the leper, as he sate at table, there came a woman hauing a boxe of oyntment of spikenarde, very costly, and shee brake the boxe, and powred it on his head.

4 Therefore some disdained among themselues, and sayd, To what ende is this waste of oyntment?

5 For it might haue bene sold for more then three hundreth pence, and bene giuen vnto the poore, and they murmured against her.

6 But Iesus saide, Let her alone: why trouble yee her? shee hath wrought a good worke on me.

7 For yee haue the poore with you alwaies, and when yee will yee may doe them good, but me yee shall not haue alwaies.

8 She hath done that she coulde: she came afore hand to anoynt my body to the burying.

9 Verely I say vnto you, wheresoeuer this Gospel shall be preached throughout the whole world, this also that she hath done, shalbe spoken of in remembrance of her.

10 Then Iudas Iscariot, one of the twelue, went away vnto the hie Priestes, to betray him vnto them.

11 And when they heard it, they were glad, and promised that they woulde giue him monie: therefore he sought howe he might conueniently betraie him.

12 Nowe the first day of vnleauened bread, when they sacrificed the Passeouer, his disciples sayde vnto him, Where wilt thou that we goe and prepare, that thou mayest eate the Passeouer?

13 Then hee sent foorth two of his disciples, and sayde vnto them, Goe yee into the citie, and there shall a man meete you bearing a pitcher of water: follow him.

14 And whithersoeuer he goeth in, say yee to the good man of the house, The Master sayeth, Where is the lodging where I shall eate the Passeouer with my disciples?

15 And he wil shewe you an vpper chamber which is large, trimmed and prepared: there make it readie for vs.

16 So his disciples went foorth, and came to the citie, and found as he had said vnto them, and made readie the Passeouer.

17 And at euen he came with the twelue.

18 And as they sate at table and did eate, Iesus said, Verely I say vnto you, that one of you shall betray me, which eateth with me.

19 Then they began to be sorowful and to say to him one by one, Is it I? And another, Is it I?

20 And he answered and sayde vnto them, It is one of the twelue that dippeth with mee in the platter.

21 Truely the Sonne of man goeth his way, as it is written of him: but woe bee to that man, by whome the Sonne of man is betrayed: it had beene good for that man, if hee had neuer beene borne.

22 And as they did eate, Iesus tooke the bread, and when hee had giuen thankes, he brake it and gaue it to them, and sayde, Take, eate, this is my bodie.

23 Also he tooke the cuppe, and when he had giuen thankes, gaue it to them: and they all dranke of it.

24 And he saide vnto them, This is my blood of that newe Testament, which is shed for many.

25 Verely I say vnto you, I wil drinke no more of the fruit of ye vine vntill that day, that I drinke it newe in the kingdome of God.

26 And when they had sung a Psalme, they went out to the mount of Oliues.

27 Then Iesus said vnto them, Al ye shall be offended by mee this night: for it is written, I will smite the shepheard, and the sheepe shall be scattered.

28 But after that I am risen, I will goe into Galile before you.

29 And Peter saide vnto him, Although all men should be offended at thee, yet would not I.

30 Then Iesus saide vnto him, Verely I say vnto thee, this day, euen in this night, before the cocke crowe twise, thou shalt denie me thrise.

31 But he saide more earnestly. If I shoulde die with thee, I will not denie thee: likewise also saide they all.

32 After, they came into a place named Gethsemane: then hee saide to his disciples, Sit yee here, till I haue praied.

33 And hee tooke with him Peter, and Iames, and Iohn, and hee began to be troubled, and in great heauinesse,

34 And saide vnto them, My soule is very heauie, euen vnto the death: tarie here, and watch.

35 So he went forward a litle, and fell downe on the ground, and praied, that if it were possible, that houre might passe from him.

36 And he saide, Abba, Father, all things are possible vnto thee: take away this cup from me: neuertheles not that I will, but that thou wilt, be done.

37 Then hee came, and founde them sleeping, and said to Peter, Simon, sleepest thou? couldest not thou watche one houre?

38 Watch ye, and pray, that ye enter not into tentation: the spirite in deede is ready, but the flesh is weake.

39 And againe hee went away, and praied, and spake the same wordes.

40 And he returned, and founde them a sleepe againe: for their eyes were heauie: neither knewe they what they should answere him.

41 And he came the third time, and said vnto them, Sleepe henceforth, and take your rest: it is ynough: the houre is come: beholde, the Sonne of man is deliuered into the hands of sinners.

42 Rise vp: let vs go: loe, he that betraieth me, is at hand.

43 And immediatly while hee yet spake, came Iudas that was one of the twelue, and with him a great multitude with swordes and staues from the hie Priests, and Scribes, and Elders.

44 And he that betraied him, had giuen them a token, saying, Whomsoeuer I shall kisse, he it is: take him and leade him away safely.

45 And assoone as hee was come, hee went straightway to him, and saide, Haile Master, and kissed him.

46 Then they laide their handes on him, and tooke him.

47 And one of them that stoode by, drewe out a sword, and smote a seruant of the hie Priest, and cut off his eare.

48 And Iesus answered and saide to them, Ye be come out as against a thiefe with swordes, and with staues, to take me.

49 I was daily with you teaching in the Temple, and yee tooke me not: but this is done that the Scriptures should be fulfilled.

50 Then they all forsooke him, and fled.

51 And there followed him a certaine yong man, clothed in linnen vpon his bare bodie, and the yong men caught him.

52 But he left his linnen cloth, and fled from them naked.

53 So they led Iesus away to the hie Priest, and to him came together all the hie Priestes, and the Elders, and the Scribes.

54 And Peter folowed him afarre off, euen into the hall of the hie Priest, and sate with the seruants, and warmed himselfe at the fire.

55 And the hie Priests, and all the Councill sought for witnesse against Iesus, to put him to death, but found none.

56 For many bare false witnesse against him, but their witnesse agreed not together.

57 Then there arose certaine, and bare false witnesse against him, saying,

58 We hearde him say, I will destroy this Temple made with hands, and within three daies I will builde another, made without hands.

59 But their witnesse yet agreed not together.

60 Then the hie Priest stoode vp amongst them, and asked Iesus, saying, Answerest thou nothing? what is the matter that these beare witnesse against thee?

61 But hee helde his peace, and answered nothing. Againe the hie Priest asked him, and sayde vnto him, Art thou that Christ the Sonne of the Blessed?

62 And Iesus said, I am he, and yee shall see the Sonne of man sitte at the right hande of the power of God, and come in the clouds of heauen.

63 Then the hie Priest rent his clothes, and sayd, What haue we any more neede of witnesses?

64 Ye haue heard the blasphemie: what thinke yee? And they all condemned him to be worthie of death.

65 And some began to spit at him, and to couer his face, and to beate him with fists, and to say vnto him, Prophesie. And the sergeants smote him with their roddes.

66 And as Peter was beneath in the hal, there came one of the maides of the hie Priest.

67 And when shee sawe Peter warming him selfe, shee looked on him, and sayde, Thou wast also with Iesus of Nazareth.

68 But he denied it, saying, I knowe him not, neither wot I what thou saiest. Then he went out into the porche, and the cocke crewe.

69 Then a maid sawe him againe, and bega to say to them that stood by, This is one of them.

70 But hee denied it againe: and anon after, they that stoode by, sayde againe to Peter, Surely thou art one of them: for thou art of Galile, and thy speach is like.

71 And he began to curse, and sweare, saying, I knowe not this man of whom ye speake.

72 Then the seconde time the cocke crewe, and Peter remembred the woorde that Iesus had saide vnto him, Before the cocke crowe twise, thou shalt denie me thrise, and waying that with himselfe, he wept.

Mark 15

1 And anon in the dawning, the hie Priestes helde a Councill with the Elders, and the Scribes, and the whole Council, and bound Iesus, and led him away, and deliuered him to Pilate.

2 Then Pilate asked him, Art thou the King of the Iewes? And hee answered, and sayde vnto him, Thou sayest it.

3 And the hie Priestes accused him of many things.

4 Wherefore Pilate asked him againe, saying, Answerest thou nothing? beholde howe many things they witnesse against thee.

5 But Iesus answered no more at all, so that Pilate marueiled.

6 Nowe at the feast, Pilate did deliuer a prisoner vnto them, whomesoeuer they woulde desire.

7 Then there was one named Barabbas, which was bounde with his fellowes, that had made insurrection, who in the insurrection had committed murder.

8 And the people cried aloude, and began to desire that he woulde doe as he had euer done vnto them.

9 Then Pilate answered them, and said, Will ye that I let loose vnto you the King of ye Iewes?

10 For he knewe that the hie Priestes had deliuered him of enuie.

11 But the high Priestes had moued the people to desire that he would rather deliuer Barabbas vnto them.

12 And Pilate answered, and said againe vnto them, What will ye then that I doe with him, whom ye call the King of the Iewes?

13 And they cried againe, Crucifie him.

14 Then Pilate said vnto them, But what euill hath he done? And they cryed the more feruently, Crucifie him.

15 So Pilate willing to content the people, loosed them Barabbas, and deliuered Iesus, when he had scourged him, that he might be crucified.

16 Then the souldiers led him away into the hall, which is the common hall, and called together the whole band,

17 And clad him with purple, and platted a crowne of thornes, and put it about his head,

18 And began to salute him, saying, Haile, King of the Iewes.

19 And they smote him on the head with a reede, and spat vpon him, and bowed the knees, and did him reuerence.

20 And whe they had mocked him, they tooke the purple off him, and put his owne clothes on him, and led him out to crucifie him.

21 And they compelled one that passed by, called Simon of Cyrene (which came out of the countrey, and was father of Alexander and Rufus) to beare his crosse.

22 And they brought him to a place named Golgotha, which is by interpretation, the place of dead mens skulles.

23 And they gaue him to drinke wine mingled with myrrhe: but he receiued it not.

24 And when they had crucified him, they parted his garments, casting lots for them, what euery man should haue.

25 And it was the third houre, when they crucified him.

26 And ye title of his cause was written aboue, THAT KING OF THE IEWES.

27 They crucified also with him two theeues, the one on ye right hand, and the other on his left.

28 Thus the Scripture was fulfilled, which sayth, And he was counted among the wicked.

29 And they that went by, railed on him, wagging their heads, and saying, Hey, thou that destroyest the Temple, and buildest it in three dayes,

30 Saue thy selfe, and come downe from the crosse.

31 Likewise also euen the hie Priests mocking, said among themselues with the Scribes, He saued other men, himselfe he cannot saue.

32 Let Christ the King of Israel nowe come downe from the crosse, that we may see, and beleeue. They also that were crucified with him, reuiled him.

33 Nowe when the sixt houre was come, darkenesse arose ouer all the land vntill the ninth houre.

34 And at the ninth houre Iesus cryed with a loude voyce, saying, Eloi, Eloi, lamma-sabachthani? which is by interpretation, My God, my God, why hast thou forsaken me?

35 And some of them that stoode by, when they heard it, said, Behold, he calleth Elias.

36 And one ranne, and filled a spondge full of vineger, and put it on a reede, and gaue him to drinke, saying, Let him

alone: let vs see if Elias will come, and take him downe.

37 And Iesus cryed with a loude voyce, and gaue vp the ghost.

38 And the vaile of the Temple was rent in twaine, from the toppe to the bottome.

39 Nowe when the Centurion, which stoode ouer against him, sawe that he thus crying gaue vp the ghost, he saide, Truely this man was the Sonne of God.

40 There were also women, which beheld afarre off, among whom was Marie Magdalene, and Marie (the mother of Iames the lesse, and of Ioses) and Salome,

41 Which also when he was in Galile, folowed him, and ministred vnto him, and many other women which came vp with him vnto Hierusalem.

42 And nowe when the night was come (because it was the day of the preparation that is before the Sabbath)

43 Ioseph of Arimathea, an honorable counsellour, which also looked for the kingdome of God, came, and went in boldly vnto Pilate, and asked the body of Iesus.

44 And Pilate marueiled, if he were already dead, and called vnto him the Centurion, and asked of him whether he had bene any while dead.

45 And when he knewe the trueth of the Centurion, he gaue the body to Ioseph:

46 Who bought a linnen cloth, and tooke him downe, and wrapped him in the linnen cloth, and laide him in a tombe that was hewen out of a rocke, and rolled a stone vnto the doore of the sepulchre:

47 And Marie Magdalene, and Marie Ioses mother, behelde where he should be layed.

Mark 16

1 And when the Sabbath day was past, Marie Magdalene, and Marie the mother of Iames, and Salome, bought sweete oyntments, that they might come, and anoynt him.

2 Therefore early in the morning, the first day of the weeke, they came vnto the sepulchre, when the Sunne was nowe risen.

3 And they saide one to another, Who shall rolle vs away the stone from the doore of the sepulchre?

4 And when they looked, they saw that the stone was rolled away (for it was a very great one)

5 So they went into the sepulchre, and saw a yong man sitting at the right side, clothed in a long white robe: and they were sore troubled.

6 But he said vnto them, Be not so troubled: ye seeke Iesus of Nazareth, which hath bene crucified: he is risen, he is not here: behold the place where they put him.

7 But goe your way, and tell his disciples, and Peter, that he will goe before you into Galile: there shall ye see him, as he said vnto you.

8 And they went out quickly, and fled from the sepulchre: for they trembled,

and were amased: neither said they any thing to any man: for they were afraide.

9 And when Iesus was risen againe, early the first day of the weeke, he appeared first to Marie Magdalene, out of whom he had cast seuen deuils:

10 And shee went and tolde them that had bene with him, which mourned and wept.

11 And when they heard that he was aliue, and had appeared to her, they beleeued it not.

12 After that, he appeared vnto two of them in an other forme, as they walked and went into the countrey.

13 And they went, and told it to the remnant, neither beleeued they them.

14 Finally, he appeared vnto the eleuen as they sate together, and reproched them for their vnbeliefe and hardnesse of heart, because they beleeued not them which had seene him, being risen vp againe.

15 And he saide vnto them, Goe ye into all the worlde, and preach the Gospel to euery creature.

16 He that shall beleeue and be baptized, shalbe saued: but he that will not beleeue, shalbe damned.

17 And these tokens shall folowe them that beleeue, In my Name they shall cast out deuils, and shall speake with newe tongues,

18 And shall take away serpents, and if they shall drinke any deadly thing, it shall not hurt them: they shall lay their handes on the sicke, and they shall recouer.

19 So after ye Lord had spoken vnto them, he was receiued into heauen, and sate at the right hand of God.

20 And they went foorth, and preached euery where. And the Lord wrought with them, and confirmed the worde with signes that folowed. Amen.

Luke

Luke 1

1 Forasmuch as many haue taken in hand to set foorth the storie of those things, whereof we are fully persuaded,

2 As they haue deliuered them vnto vs, which from the beginning saw them their selues, and were ministers of ye word,

3 It seemed good also to me (most noble Theophilus) assoone as I had searched out perfectly all things from the beginning, to write vnto thee thereof from point to point,

4 That thou mightest acknowledge the certaintie of those things, whereof thou hast bene instructed.

5 In the time of Herod King of Iudea, there was a certaine Priest named Zacharias, of the course of Abia: and his wife was of the daughters of Aaron, and her name was Elisabet.

6 Both were iust before God, and walked in all the commandements and ordinances of the Lord, without reproofe.

7 And they had no childe, because that Elisabet was barren: and both were well stricken in age.

8 And it came to passe, as he executed the Priestes office before God, as his course came in order,

9 According to the custome of the Priests office, his lot was to burne incense, when he went into the Temple of the Lord.

10 And the whole multitude of the people were without in prayer, while the incense was burning.

11 Then appeared vnto him an Angel of the Lord standing at the right side of the altar of incense.

12 And when Zacharias sawe him, he was troubled, and feare fell vpon him.

13 But the Angel saide vnto him, Feare not, Zacharias: for thy prayer is heard, and thy wise Elisabet shall beare thee a sonne, and thou shalt call his name Iohn.

14 And thou shalt haue ioy and gladnes, and many shall reioyce at his birth.

15 For he shalbe great in the sight of the Lord, and shall neither drinke wine, nor strong drinke: and he shalbe filled with the holy Ghost, euen from his mothers wombe.

16 And many of the children of Israel shall he turne to their Lord God.

17 For he shall goe before him in the spirite and power of Elias, to turne the hearts of the fathers to the children, and the disobedient to the wisedome of the iust men, to make ready a people prepared for the Lord.

18 Then Zacharias said vnto ye Angel, Whereby shall I knowe this? for I am an olde man, and my wife is of a great age.

19 And the Angell answered, and sayde vnto him, I am Gabriel that stand in the presence of God, and am sent to speake vnto thee, and to shew thee these good tidings.

20 And beholde, thou shalt be domme, and not be able to speake, vntill the day that these things be done, because thou beleeuedst not my words, which shalbe fulfilled in their season.

21 Now the people waited for Zacharias, and marueiled that he taried so long in the Temple.

22 And when hee came out, hee coulde not speake vnto them: then they perceiued that hee had seene a vision in the Temple: For he made signes vnto them, and remained domme.

23 And it came to passe, when the daies of his office were fulfilled, that he departed to his owne house.

24 And after those daies, his wife Elisabet conceiued, and hid her selfe fiue moneths, saying,

25 Thus hath the Lord dealt with me, in the daies wherein he looked on me, to take from me my rebuke among men.

26 And in the sixth moneth, the Angell Gabriel was sent from God vnto a citie of Galile, named Nazareth,

27 To a virgin affianced to a man whose name was Ioseph, of the house of Dauid, and the virgins name was Marie.

28 And the Angel went in vnto her, and said, Haile thou that art freely beloued: the Lord is with thee: blessed art thou among women.

29 And when she saw him, she was troubled at his saying, and thought what maner of salutation that should be.

30 Then the Angel saide vnto her, Feare not, Marie: for thou hast found fauour with God.

31 For loe, thou shalt conceiue in thy wobe, and beare a sonne, and shalt call his name Iesus.

32 He shall be great, and shall be called the Sonne of the most High, and the Lord God shall giue vnto him the throne of his father Dauid.

33 And hee shall reigne ouer the house of Iacob for euer, and of his kingdome shall bee none ende.

34 Then sayde Marie vnto the Angel, How shall this be, seeing I knowe not man?

35 And the Angel answered, and said vnto her, The holy Ghost shall come vpon thee, and the power of the most High shall ouershadowe thee: therefore also that holy thing which shall bee borne of thee, shall be called the Sonne of God.

36 And behold, thy cousin Elisabet, she hath also conceiued a sonne in her olde age: and this is her sixt moneth, which was called barren.

37 For with God shall nothing be vnpossible.

38 Then Marie said, Behold the seruant of the Lord: be it vnto me according to thy woorde. So the Angel departed from her.

39 And Marie arose in those daies, and went into ye hil countrey with hast to a citie of Iuda,

40 And entred into the house of Zacharias, and saluted Elisabet.

41 And it came to passe, as Elisabet heard the salutation of Marie, the babe sprang in her bellie, and Elisabet was filled with the holy Ghost.

42 And she cried with a loud voice, and saide, Blessed art thou among women, because the fruit of thy wombe is blessed.

43 And whence commeth this to mee, that the mother of my Lord should come to me?

44 For loe, assoone as the voice of thy salutation sounded in mine eares, the babe sprang in my bellie for ioye,

45 And blessed is shee that beleeued: for those things shall be perfourmed, which were tolde her from the Lord.

46 Then Marie sayde, My soule magnifieth the Lord,

47 And my spirite reioyceth in God my Sauiour.

48 For hee hath looked on the poore degree of his seruaunt: for beholde, from henceforth shall all ages call me blessed,

49 Because hee that is mightie, hath done for me great things, and holy is his Name.

50 And his mercie is from generation to generation on them that feare him.

51 Hee hath shewed strength with his arme: hee hath scattered the proude in the imagination of their hearts.

52 Hee hath put downe the mighty from their seates, and exalted them of lowe degree.

53 Hee hath filled the hungrie with good things, and sent away the rich emptie.

54 Hee hath vpholden Israel his seruaunt to be mindefull of his mercie

55 (As hee hath spoken to our fathers, to wit, to Abraham, and his seede) for euer.

56 And Marie abode with her about three monethes: after, shee returned to her owne house.

57 Nowe Elisabets time was fulfilled, that shee should be deliuered, and shee brought foorth a sonne.

58 And her neighbours, and cousins heard tell howe the Lord had shewed his great mercie vpon her, and they reioyced with her.

59 And it was so that on the eight day they came to circumcise the babe, and called him Zacharias after the name of his father.

60 But his mother answered, and saide, Not so, but he shalbe called Iohn.

61 And they saide vnto her, There is none of thy kindred, that is named with this name.

62 Then they made signes to his father, howe he would haue him called.

63 So hee asked for writing tables, and wrote, saying, His name is Iohn, and they marueiled all.

64 And his mouth was opened immediately, and his tongue, and he spake and praised God.

65 Then feare came on all them that dwelt neere vnto them, and all these woordes were noised abroade throughout all the hill countrey of Iudea.

66 And al they that heard them, laid them vp in their hearts, saying, What maner childe shall this be! and the hand of the Lord was with him.

67 Then his father Zacharias was filled with the holy Ghost, and prophesied, saying,

68 Blessed be the Lord God of Israel, because he hath visited and redeemed his people,

69 And hath raised vp the horne of saluation vnto vs, in the house of his seruant Dauid,

70 As he spake by ye mouth of his holy Prophets, which were since the world began, saying,

71 That he would sende vs deliuerance from our enemies, and from the hands of all that hate vs,

72 That he might shewe mercie towards our fathers, and remember his holy couenant,

73 And the othe which he sware to our father Abraham.

74 Which was, that he would graunt vnto vs, that we being deliuered out of the handes of our enemies, should serue him without feare,

75 All the daies of our life, in holinesse and righteousnesse before him.

76 And thou, babe, shalt be called the Prophet of the most High: for thou shalt goe before the face of the Lord, to prepare his waies,

77 And to giue knowledge of saluation vnto his people, by the remission of their sinnes,

78 Through ye tender mercy of our God, wherby the day spring from an hie hath visited vs,

79 To giue light to them that sit in darknes, and in the shadow of death, and to guide our feete into the way of peace.

80 And the childe grewe, and waxed strong in spirit, and was in the wildernesse, til the day came that he should shewe him selfe vnto Israel.

Luke 2

1 And it came to passe in those dayes, that there came a decree from Augustus Cesar, that all the world should be taxed.

2 (This first taxing was made when Cyrenius was gouernour of Syria.)

3 Therefore went all to be taxed, euery man to his owne Citie.

4 And Ioseph also went vp from Galile out of a citie called Nazareth, into Iudea, vnto the citie of Dauid, which is called Beth-leem (because he was of the house and linage of Dauid,)

5 To bee taxed with Marie that was giuen him to wife, which was with childe.

6 And so it was, that while they were there, the daies were accomplished that shee shoulde be deliuered,

7 And she brought foorth her first begotten sonne, and wrapped him in swadling clothes, and laide him in a cratch, because there was no roome for them in the ynne.

8 And there were in the same countrey shepheards, abiding in the fielde, and keeping watch by night ouer their flocke.

9 And loe, the Angel of the Lord came vpon them, and the glorie of the Lord shone about them, and they were sore afraide.

10 Then the Angel saide vnto them, Be not afraid: for behold, I bring you glad tidings of great ioy, that shalbe to all the people,

11 That is, that vnto you is borne this day in the citie of Dauid, a Sauiour, which is Christ the Lord.

12 And this shalbe a signe to you, Yee shall finde the babe swadled, and laid in a cratch.

13 And straightway there was with the Angel a multitude of heauenly souldiers, praising God, and saying,

14 Glory be to God in the high heauens, and peace in earth, and towards men good will.

15 And it came to passe whe the Angels were gone away from them into heauen, that the shepheards sayde one to another, Let vs goe then vnto Beth-leem, and see this thing that is come to passe which the Lord hath shewed vnto vs.

16 So they came with haste, and founde both Marie and Ioseph, and the babe laid in the cratch.

17 And when they had seene it, they published abroade the thing, that was tolde them of that childe.

18 And all that heard it, wondred at ye things which were tolde them of the shepheards.

19 But Mary kept all those sayings, and pondred them in her heart.

20 And the shepheardes returned glorifiyng and praising God, for all that they had heard and seene as it was spoken vnto them.

21 And when the eight daies were accomplished, that they shoulde circumcise the childe, his name was then called Iesus, which was named of the Angell, before he was conceiued in the wombe.

22 And when the daies of her purification after the Lawe of Moses were accomplished, they brought him to Hierusalem, to present him to the Lord,

23 (As it is written in the Lawe of the Lord, Euery man childe that first openeth ye wombe, shalbe called holy to the Lord)

24 And to giue an oblation, as it is commanded in the Lawe of the Lord, a paire of turtle doues, or two yong pigeons.

25 And behold, there was a man in Hierusalem, whose name was Simeon: this man was iust, and feared God, and waited for the consolation of Israel, and the holy Ghost was vpon him.

26 And it was declared to him from God by the holy Ghost, that he shoulde not see death, before he had seene that Anointed of the Lord.

27 And he came by the motion of the spirit into the Temple, and when the parents brought in the babe Iesus, to do for him after the custome of the Lawe,

28 Then hee tooke him in his armes, and praised God, and sayd,

29 Lord, nowe lettest thou thy seruaunt depart in peace, according to thy woorde,

30 For mine eyes haue seene thy saluation,

31 Which thou hast prepared before the face of all people,

32 A light to be reueiled to the Gentiles, and the glory of thy people Israel.

33 And Ioseph and his mother marueiled at those things, which were spoken touching him.

34 And Simeon blessed them, and saide vnto Mary his mother, Beholde, this childe is appointed for the fall and rising againe of many in Israel, and for a signe which shalbe spoken against,

35 (Yea and a sworde shall pearce through thy soule) that the thoughts of many heartes may be opened.

36 And there was a Prophetesse, one Anna the daughter of Phanuel, of the tribe of Aser, which was of a great age, after she had liued with an husband seuen yeeres from her virginitie:

37 And she was widowe about foure score and foure yeeres, and went not out of the Temple, but serued God with fastings and prayers, night and day.

38 She then coming at the same instant vpon them, confessed likewise the Lord, and spake of him to all that looked for redemption in Hierusalem.

39 And when they had performed all things according to the lawe of the Lord, they returned into Galile to their owne citie Nazareth.

40 And the childe grewe, and waxed strong in Spirit, and was filled with wisedome, and the grace of God was with him.

41 Nowe his parents went to Hierusalem euery yeere, at the feast of the Passeouer.

42 And when hee was twelue yeere olde, and they were come vp to Hierusalem, after the custome of the feast,

43 And had finished the dayes thereof, as they returned, the childe Iesus remained in Hierusalem, and Ioseph knew not, nor his mother,

44 But they supposing, that he had bene in the company, went a dayes iourney, and sought him among their kinsfolke, and acquaintance.

45 And when they found him not, they turned backe to Hierusalem, and sought him.

46 And it came to passe three dayes after, that they found him in the Temple, sitting in the mids of the doctours, both hearing them, and asking them questions:

47 And all that heard him, were astonied at his vnderstanding and answeres.

48 So when they sawe him, they were amased, and his mother said vnto him, Sonne, why hast thou thus dealt with vs? beholde, thy father and I haue sought thee with very heauie hearts.

49 Then said he vnto them, Howe is it that ye sought me? knewe ye not that I must goe about my Fathers busines?

50 But they vnderstoode not the word that he spake to them.

51 Then hee went downe with them, and came to Nazareth, and was subiect to them: and his mother kept all these sayings in her heart.

52 And Iesus increased in wisedome, and stature, and in fauour with God and men.

Luke 3

1 Nowe in the fifteenth yeere of the reigne of Tiberius Caesar, Pontius Pilate being gouernour of Iudea, and Herod being Tetrarch of Galile, and his brother Philip Tetrarch of Iturea, and of the countrey of Trachonitis, and Lysanias the Tetrarch of Abilene,

2 (When Annas and Caiaphas were the hie Priestes) the worde of God came vnto Iohn, the sonne of Zacharias in the wildernes.

3 And hee came into all the coastes about Iordan, preaching the baptisme of repentance for the remission of sinnes,

4 As it is written in the booke of the sayings of Esaias the Prophet, which saith, The voyce of him that crieth in the wildernes is, Prepare ye the way of the Lord: make his paths straight.

5 Euery valley shalbe filled, and euery mountaine and hill shall be brought lowe, and crooked things shalbe made straight, and the rough wayes shalbe made smoothe.

6 And all flesh shall see the saluation of God.

7 Then said he to the people that were come out to be baptized of him, O generations of vipers, who hath forewarned you to flee from the wrath to come?

8 Bring foorth therefore fruites worthy amendment of life, and beginne not to say with your selues, We haue Abraham to our father: for I say vnto you, that God is able of these stones to raise vp children vnto Abraham.

9 Nowe also is the axe layed vnto the roote of the trees: therefore euery tree which bringeth not foorth good fruite, shalbe hewen downe, and cast into the fire.

10 Then the people asked him, saying, What shall we doe then?

11 And he answered, and said vnto them, He that hath two coates, let him part with him that hath none: and hee that hath meate, let him doe likewise.

12 Then came there Publicanes also to bee baptized, and saide vnto him, Master, what shall we doe?

13 And hee saide vnto them, Require no more then that which is appointed vnto you.

14 The souldiers likewise demaunded of him, saying, And what shall we doe? And he saide vnto them, Doe violence to no man, neither accuse any falsely, and be content with your wages.

15 As the people waited, and all men mused in their heartes of Iohn, if he were not that Christ,

16 Iohn answered, and saide to them all, In deede I baptize you with water, but one stronger then I, commeth, whose shoes latchet I am not worthy to vnloose: hee will baptize you with the holy Ghost, and with fire.

17 Whose fanne is in his hande, and hee will make cleane his floore, and will gather the wheate into his garner, but the chaffe will hee burne vp with fire that neuer shalbe quenched.

18 Thus then exhorting with many other things, he preached vnto the people.

19 But when Herod the Tetrarch was rebuked of him, for Herodias his brother Philips wife, and for all the euils which Herod had done,

20 He added yet this aboue all, that he shut vp Iohn in prison.

21 Nowe it came to passe, as all the people were baptized, and that Iesus was baptized and did pray, that the heauen was opened:

22 And the holy Ghost came downe in a bodily shape like a doue, vpon him, and there was a voyce from heauen, saying, Thou art my beloued Sonne: in thee I am well pleased.

23 And Iesus himselfe began to bee about thirtie yeere of age, being as men supposed the sonne of Ioseph, which was the sonne of Eli,

24 The sonne of Matthat, the sonne of Leui, the sonne of Melchi, the sonne of Ianna, the sonne of Ioseph,

25 The sonne of Mattathias, the sonne of Amos, the sonne of Naum, the sonne of Esli, the sonne of Nagge,

26 The sonne of Maath, the sonne of Mattathias, the sonne of Semei, the sonne of Ioseph, the sonne of Iuda,

27 The sonne of Ioanna, the sonne of Rhesa, the sonne of Zorobabel, the sonne of Salathiel, the sonne of Neri,

28 The sonne of Melchi, the sonne of Addi, the sonne of Cosam, the sonne of Elmodam, the sonne of Er,

29 The sonne of Iose, the sonne of Eliezer, the sonne of Iorim, the sonne of Matthat, the son of Leui,

30 The sonne of Simeon, the sonne of Iuda, the sonne of Ioseph, the sonne of Ionan, the sonne of Eliacim,

31 The sonne of Melea, the sonne of Mainan, the sonne of Mattatha, the sonne of Nathan, the sonne of Dauid,

32 The sonne of Iesse, the sonne of Obed, the sonne of Booz, the sonne of Salmon, the sonne of Naasson,

33 The sonne of Aminadab, the sonne of Aram, the sonne of Esrom, the sonne of Phares, the sonne of Iuda,

34 The sonne of Iacob, the sonne of Isaac, the sonne of Abraham, the sonne of Thara, the sonne of Nachor,

35 The sonne of Saruch, the sonne of Ragau, the sonne of Phalec, the sonne of Eber, the sonne of Sala,

36 The sonne of Cainan, the sonne of Arphaxad, the sonne of Sem, the sonne of Noe, the sonne of Lamech,

37 The sonne of Mathusala, the sonne of Enoch, the sonne of Iared, the sonne of Maleleel, the sonne of Cainan,

38 The sonne of Enos, the sonne of Seth, the sonne of Adam, the sonne of God.

Luke 4

1 And Iesus full of the holy Ghost returned from Iordan, and was led by that Spirit into the wildernes,

2 And was there fourtie dayes tempted of the deuil, and in those dayes he did eate nothing: but when they were ended, he afterward was hungry.

3 Then the deuil saide vnto him, If thou be the Sonne of God, commaund this stone that it be made bread.

4 But Iesus answered him, saying, It is written, That man shall not liue by bread only, but by euery word of God.

5 Then the deuill tooke him vp into an high mountaine, and shewed him all the kingdomes of the world, in the twinkeling of an eye.

6 And the deuill saide vnto him, All this power will I giue thee, and the glory of those kingdomes: for that is deliuered to mee: and to whomsoeuer I will, I giue it.

7 If thou therefore wilt worship mee, they shalbe all thine.

8 But Iesus answered him, and saide, Hence from mee, Satan: for it is written, Thou shalt worship the Lord thy God, and him alone thou shalt serue.

9 Then hee brought him to Hierusalem, and set him on a pinacle of the Temple,

and said vnto him, If thou be the Sonne of God, cast thy selfe downe from hence,

10 For it is written, That hee will giue his Angels charge ouer thee to keepe thee:

11 And with their handes they shall lift thee vp, least at any time thou shouldest dash thy foote against a stone.

12 And Iesus answered, and said vnto him, It is said, Thou shalt not tempt the Lord thy God.

13 And when the deuil had ended all the tentation, he departed from him for a litle season.

14 And Iesus returned by the power of the spirite into Galile: and there went a fame of him throughout all the region round about.

15 For he taught in their Synagogues, and was honoured of all men.

16 And hee came to Nazareth where hee had bene brought vp, and (as his custome was) went into the Synagogue on the Sabbath day, and stoode vp to reade.

17 And there was deliuered vnto him the booke of the Prophet Esaias: and when hee had opened the booke, hee founde the place, where it was written,

18 The Spirit of the Lord is vpon mee, because he hath anoynted me, that I should preach the Gospel to the poore: he hath sent mee, that I should heale the broken hearted, that I should preach deliuerance to the captiues, and recouering of sight to the blinde, that I should set at libertie them that are bruised:

19 And that I should preache the acceptable yeere of the Lord.

20 And hee closed the booke, and gaue it againe to the minister, and sate downe: and the eyes of all that were in the Synagogue were fastened on him.

21 Then he began to say vnto them, This day is the Scripture fulfilled in your eares.

22 And all bare him witnes, and wondered at the gracious wordes, which proceeded out of his mouth, and said, Is not this Iosephs sonne?

23 Then he said vnto them, Ye will surely say vnto mee this prouerbe, Physician, heale thy selfe: whatsoeuer we haue heard done in Capernaum, doe it here likewise in thine owne countrey.

24 And he saide, Verely I say vnto you, No Prophet is accepted in his owne countrey.

25 But I tell you of a trueth, many widowes were in Israel in the dayes of Elias, when heauen was shut three yeres and sixe moneths, when great famine was throughout all the land:

26 But vnto none of them was Elias sent, saue into Sarepta, a citie of Sidon, vnto a certaine widowe.

27 Also many lepers were in Israel, in the time of Eliseus the Prophet: yet none of them was made cleane, sauing Naaman the Syrian.

28 Then all that were in the Synagogue, when they heard it, were filled with wrath,

29 And rose vp, and thrust him out of the citie, and led him vnto the edge of the hil, whereon their citie was built, to cast him downe headlong.

30 But he passed through the middes of them, and went his way,

31 And came downe into Capernaum a citie of Galile, and there taught them on the Sabbath dayes.

32 And they were astonied at his doctrine: for his worde was with authoritie.

33 And in the Synagogue there was a man which had a spirit of an vncleane deuill, which cryed with a loude voyce,

34 Saying, Oh, what haue we to doe with thee, thou Iesus of Nazareth? art thou come to destroy vs? I know who thou art, euen the holy one of God.

35 And Iesus rebuked him, saying, Holde thy peace, and come out of him. Then the deuill throwing him in the middes of them, came out of him, and hurt him nothing at all.

36 So feare came on them all, and they spake among themselues, saying, What thing is this: for with authoritie and power he commaundeth the foule spirits, and they come out?

37 And ye fame of him spred abroad throughout all the places of the countrey round about.

38 And he rose vp, and came out of the Synagogue, and entred into Simons house. And Simons wiues mother was taken with a great feuer, and they required him for her.

39 Then he stoode ouer her, and rebuked the feuer, and it left her, and immediatly she arose, and ministred vnto them.

40 Now at the sunne setting, all they that had sicke folkes of diuers diseases, brought them vnto him, and he layd his hands on euery one of them, and healed them.

41 And deuils also came out of many, crying, and saying, Thou art that Christ that Sonne of God: but he rebuked them, and suffered them not to say that they knewe him to be that Christ.

42 And when it was day, he departed, and went foorth into a desart place, and the people sought him, and came to him, and kept him that he should not depart from them.

43 But he sayd vnto them, Surely I must also preach the kingdome of God to other cities: for therefore am I sent.

44 And hee preached in the Synagogues of Galile.

Luke 5

1 Then it came to passe, as the people preassed vpon him to heare the word of God, that he stoode by the lake of Gennesaret,

2 And sawe two shippes stand by the lakes side, but the fishermen were gone out of them, and were washing their nettes.

3 And he entred into one of the ships, which was Simons, and required him that he would thrust off a litle from the land: and he sate downe, and taught the people out of the ship.

4 Now when he had left speaking, he sayd vnto Simon, Lanch out into the deepe, and let downe your nettes to make a draught.

5 Then Simon answered, and sayd vnto him, Master, we haue trauailed sore all night, and haue taken nothing: neuerthelesse at thy worde I will let downe the net.

6 And when they had so done, they enclosed a great multitude of fishes, so that their net brake.

7 And they beckened to their parteners, which were in the other ship, that they shoulde come and helpe them, who came then, and filled both the ships, that they did sinke.

8 Now when Simon Peter saw it, he fel down at Iesus knees, saying, Lord, go from me: for I am a sinfull man.

9 For he was vtterly astonied, and all that were with him, for the draught of fishes which they tooke.

10 And so was also Iames and Iohn the sonnes of Zebedeus, which were companions with Simon. Then Iesus sayde vnto Simon, Feare not: from henceforth thou shalt catch men.

11 And when they had brought the ships to land, they forsooke all, and followed him.

12 Nowe it came to passe, as he was in a certaine citie, beholde, there was a man full of leprosie, and when he sawe Iesus, he fell on his face, and besought him, saying, Lord, if thou wilt, thou canst make me cleane.

13 So he stretched forth his hand, and touched him, saying, I will, be thou cleane. And immediatly the leprosie departed from him.

14 And he commanded him that hee should tell it no man: but Go, sayth he, and shew thy selfe to the Priest, and offer for thy clensing, as Moses hath commanded, for a witnes vnto them.

15 But so much more went there a fame abroad of him, and great multitudes came together to heare, and to be healed of him of their infirmities.

16 But he kept himselfe apart in the wildernes, and prayed.

17 And it came to passe, on a certaine day, as he was teaching, that the Pharises and doctours of the Law sate by, which were come out of euery towne of Galile, and Iudea, and Hierusalem, and the power of the Lord was in him to heale them.

18 Then beholde, men brought a man lying in a bed, which was taken with a palsie, and they sought meanes to bring him in, and to lay him before him.

19 And when they could not finde by what way they might bring him in, because of the preasse, they went vp on the house, and let him downe through the tyling, bed and all, in the middes before Iesus.

20 And when he sawe their faith, he sayd vnto him, Man, thy sinnes are forgiuen thee.

21 Then the Scribes and the Pharises began to reason, saying, Who is this that speaketh blasphemies? who can forgiue sinnes, but God onely?

22 But when Iesus perceiued their reasoning, he answered, and sayd vnto them, What reason ye in your hearts?

23 Whether is easier to say, Thy sinnes are forgiuen thee, or to say, Rise and walke?

24 But that ye may know that that Sonne of man hath authoritie to forgiue sinnes in earth, (he sayd vnto the sicke of the palsie) I say to thee, Arise: take vp thy bed, and goe to thine house.

25 And immediatly he rose vp before them, and tooke vp his bed whereon he lay, and departed to his owne house, praysing God.

26 And they were all amased, and praysed God, and were filled with feare, saying, Doutlesse we haue seene strange things to day.

27 And after that, he went foorth and sawe a Publicane named Leui, sitting at the receite of custome, and sayd vnto him, Follow me.

28 And he left all, rose vp, and folowed him.

29 Then Leui made him a great feast in his owne house, where there was a great company of Publicanes, and of other that sate at table with them.

30 But they that were Scribes and Pharises among them, murmured against his disciples, saying, Why eate ye and drinke ye with Publicanes and sinners?

31 Then Iesus answered, and sayd vnto them, They that are whole, neede not the Physician, but they that are sicke.

32 I came not to call the righteous, but sinners to repentance.

33 Then they said vnto him, Why do the disciples of Iohn fast often, and pray, and the disciples of the Pharises also, but thine eate and drinke?

34 And he said vnto them, Can ye make the children of the wedding chamber to fast, as long as the bridegrome is with them?

35 But the dayes will come, euen when the bridegrome shalbe taken away from them: then shall they fast in those dayes.

36 Againe he spake also vnto them a parable, No man putteth a piece of a newe garment into an olde vesture: for then the newe renteth it, and the piece taken out of the newe, agreeth not with the olde.

37 Also no man powreth newe wine into olde vessels: for then ye new wine wil breake the vessels, and it will runne out, and the vessels will perish:

38 But newe wine must be powred into newe vessels: so both are preserued.

39 Also no man that drinketh olde wine, straightway desireth newe: for he sayth, The olde is more profitable.

Luke 6

1 And it came to passe on a second solemne Sabbath, that hee went through the corne fieldes, and his disciples plucked the eares of corne, and did eate, and rub them in their hands.

2 And certaine of the Pharises sayde vnto them, Why doe ye that which is not lawfull to doe on the Sabbath dayes?

3 Then Iesus answered them, and said, Haue ye not read this, that Dauid did when he himselfe was an hungred, and they which were with him,

4 Howe he went into the house of God, and tooke, and ate the shewbread, and gaue also to them which were with him, which was not lawful to eate, but for the Priests onely?

5 And he sayd vnto them, The Sonne of man is Lord also of the Sabbath day.

6 It came to passe also on another Sabbath, that hee entred into the Synagogue, and taught, and there was a man, whose right hand was dryed vp.

7 And the Scribes and Pharises watched him, whether he would heale on the Sabbath day, that they might finde an accusation against him.

8 But he knew their thoughts, and sayd to the man which had the withered hand, Arise, and stand vp in the middes. And hee arose, and stoode vp.

9 Then sayd Iesus vnto them, I will aske you a question, Whether is it lawfull on the Sabbath dayes to doe good, or to doe euill? to saue life, or to destroy?

10 And he behelde them all in compasse, and sayd vnto the man, Stretch forth thine hand. And he did so, and his hand was restored againe, as whole as the other.

11 Then they were filled full of madnes, and communed one with another, what they might doe to Iesus.

12 And it came to passe in those dayes, that he went into a mountaine to praye, and spent the night in prayer to God.

13 And when it was day, he called his disciples, and of them he chose twelue which also he called Apostles.

14 (Simon whome he named also Peter, and Andrew his brother, Iames and Iohn, Philippe and Bartlemewe:

15 Matthewe and Thomas: Iames the sonne of Alpheus, and Simon called Zelous,

16 Iudas Iames brother, and Iudas Iscariot, which also was the traitour.)

17 Then he came downe with them, and stood in a plaine place, with the company of his disciples, and a great multitude of people out of all Iudea, and Hierusalem, and from the sea coast of Tyrus and Sidon, which came to heare him, and to be healed of their diseases:

18 And they that were vexed with foule spirits, and they were healed.

19 And the whole multitude sought to touch him: for there went vertue out of him, and healed them all.

20 And hee lifted vp his eyes vpon his disciples, and sayd, Blessed be ye poore: for yours is the kingdome of God.

21 Blessed are ye that hunger nowe: for ye shalbe satisfied: blessed are ye that weepe now: for ye shall laugh.

22 Blessed are ye when men hate you, and when they separate you, and reuile you, and put out your name as euill, for the Sonne of mans sake.

23 Reioyce ye in that day, and be glad: for beholde, your reward is great in heauen: for after this maner their fathers did to the Prophets.

24 But wo be to you that are rich: for ye haue receiued your consolation.

25 Wo be to you that are full: for ye shall hunger. Wo be to you that now laugh: for ye shall wayle and weepe.

26 Wo be to you when all men speake well of you: for so did their fathers to the false prophets.

27 But I say vnto you which heare, Loue your enemies: doe well to them which hate you.

28 Blesse them that curse you, and pray for them which hurt you.

29 And vnto him that smiteth thee on ye one cheeke, offer also the other: and him that taketh away thy cloke, forbid not to take thy coate also.

30 Giue to euery man that asketh of thee: and of him that taketh away the things that be thine, aske them not againe.

31 And as ye would that men should doe to you, so doe ye to them likewise.

32 For if yee loue them which loue you, what thanke shall ye haue? for euen the sinners loue those that loue them.

33 And if ye do good for them which do good for you, what thanke shall ye haue? for euen the sinners doe the same.

34 And if ye lend to them of whom ye hope to receiue, what thanke shall yee haue? for euen the sinners lend to sinners, to receiue the like.

35 Wherefore loue ye your enemies, and doe good, and lend, looking for nothing againe, and your rewarde shalbe great, and ye shalbe the children of the most High: for he is kinde vnto the vnkinde, and to the euill.

36 Be ye therefore mercifull, as your Father also is mercifull.

37 Iudge not, and ye shall not be iudged: condemne not, and ye shall not bee condemned: forgiue, and ye shalbe forgiuen.

38 Giue, and it shalbe giuen vnto you: a good measure, pressed downe, shaken together and running ouer shall men giue into your bosome: for with what measure ye mete, with the same shall men mete to you againe.

39 And he spake a parable vnto them, Can the blinde leade the blinde? shall they not both fall into the ditche?

40 The disciple is not aboue his master: but whosoeuer will be a perfect disciple, shall bee as his master.

41 And why seest thou a mote in thy brothers eye, and considerest not the beame that is in thine owne eye?

42 Either howe canst thou say to thy brother, Brother, let me pull out the mote that is in thine eye, when thou seest not the beame that is in thine owne eye? Hypocrite, cast out the beame out of thine owne eye first, and then shalt thou see, perfectly to pull out the mote that is in thy brothers eye.

43 For it is not a good tree that bringeth foorth euill fruite: neither an euill tree, that bringeth foorth good fruite.

44 For euery tree is knowen by his owne fruite: for neither of thornes gather men figges, nor of bushes gather they grapes.

45 A good man out of the good treasure of his heart bringeth foorth good, and an euill man out of the euill treasure of his heart bringeth foorth euill: for of the aboundance of the heart his mouth speaketh.

46 But why call ye me Lord, Lord, and do not the things that I speake?

47 Whosoeuer commeth to mee, and heareth my wordes, and doeth the same, I will shewe you to whome he is like:

48 He is like a man which built an house, and digged deepe, and layde the fundation on a rocke: and when the waters arose, the flood beat vpon that house, and coulde not shake it: for it was grounded vpon a rocke.

49 But hee that heareth and doeth not, is like a man that built an house vpon the earth without foundation, against which the flood did beate, and it fell by and by: and the fall of that house was great.

Luke 7

1 When hee had ended all his sayings in the audience of the people, he entred into Capernaum.

2 And a certaine Ceturions seruant was sicke and readie to die, which was deare vnto him.

3 And when he heard of Iesus, hee sent vnto him the Elders of the Iewes, beseeching him that he would come, and heale his seruant.

4 So they came to Iesus, and besought him instantly, saying that hee was worthy that hee should doe this for him:

5 For he loueth, said they, our nation, and he hath built vs a Synagogue.

6 Then Iesus went with them: but when he was now not farre from the house, the Centurion sent friendes to him, saying vnto him, Lord, trouble not thy selfe: for I am not worthy that thou shouldest enter vnder my roofe:

7 Wherefore I thought not my selfe worthy to come vnto thee: but say the word, and my seruant shalbe whole:

8 For I likewise am a man set vnder authoritie, and haue vnder mee souldiers, and I say vnto one, Goe, and he goeth: and to another, Come, and hee commeth: and to my seruant, Doe this, and he doeth it.

9 When Iesus heard these things, he marueiled at him, and turned him, and said to the people, that followed him, I say vnto you, I haue not found so great faith, no not in Israel.

10 And when they that were sent, turned backe to the house, they founde the seruant that was sicke, whole.

11 And it came to passe the day after, that he went into a citie called Nain, and many of his disciples went with him, and a great multitude.

12 Nowe when hee came neere to the gate of the citie, behold, there was a dead man caried out, who was the onely begotten sonne of his mother, which was a widowe, and much people of the citie was with her.

13 And when the Lord sawe her, he had compassion on her, and said vnto her, Weepe not.

14 And he went and touched the coffin (and they that bare him, stoode still) and he said, Yong man, I say vnto thee, Arise.

15 And he that was dead, sate vp, and began to speake, and he deliuered him to his mother.

16 Then there came a feare on them all, and they glorified God, saying, A great Prophet is risen among vs, and God hath visited his people.

17 And this rumour of him went foorth throughout all Iudea, and throughout all the region round about.

18 And the disciples of Iohn shewed him of all these things.

19 So Iohn called vnto him two certaine men of his disciples, and sent them to Iesus, saying, Art thou hee that should come, or shall we waite for another?

20 And when the men were come vnto him, they said, Iohn Baptist hath sent vs vnto thee, saying, Art thou hee that should come, or shall we waite for another?

21 And at that time, he cured many of their sickenesses, and plagues, and of euill spirites, and vnto many blinde men he gaue sight freely.

22 And Iesus answered, and saide vnto them, Goe your wayes and shewe Iohn, what things ye haue seene and heard: that the blinde see, the halt goe, the lepers are cleansed, the deafe heare, the dead are raised, and the poore receiue the Gospel.

23 And blessed is hee, that shall not be offended in me.

24 And when the messengers of Iohn were departed, hee began to speake vnto the people, of Iohn, What went ye out into the wildernes to see? A reede shaken with the winde?

25 But what went ye out to see? A man clothed in soft rayment? beholde, they which are gorgeously apparelled, and liue delicately, are in Kings courtes.

26 But what went ye foorth to see? A Prophet? yea, I say to you, and greater then a Prophet.

27 This is he of whom it is written, Beholde, I sende my messenger before thy face, which shall prepare thy way before thee.

28 For I say vnto you, there is no greater Prophet then Iohn, among them that are begotten of women: neuerthelesse, hee that is the least in the kingdome of God, is greater then he.

29 Then all the people that heard, and the Publicanes iustified God, being baptized with the baptisme of Iohn.

30 But the Pharises and the expounders of the Law despised the counsell of God against themselues, and were not baptized of him.

31 And the Lord saide, Whereunto shall I liken the men of this generation? and what thing are they like vnto?

32 They are like vnto litle children sitting in the market place, and crying one to another, and saying, We haue piped vnto you, and ye haue not daunced: we haue mourned to you, and ye haue not wept.

33 For Iohn Baptist came, neither eating bread, nor drinking wine: and ye say, He hath the deuil.

34 The Sonne of man is come, and eateth and drinketh: and ye say, Beholde, a man which is a glutton, and a drinker of wine, a friend of Publicanes and sinners:

35 But wisdome is iustified of all her children.

36 And one of the Pharises desired him that hee would eate with him: and hee went into the Pharises house, and sate downe at table.

37 And beholde, a woman in the citie, which was a sinner, when she knewe that Iesus sate at table in the Pharises house, shee brought a boxe of oyntment.

38 And shee stoode at his feete behinde him weeping, and began to wash his feete with teares, and did wipe them with the heares of her head, and kissed his feete, and anoynted them with the oyntment.

39 Nowe when the Pharise which bade him, saw it, he spake within himselfe, saying, If this man were a Prophet, hee woulde surely haue knowen who, and what maner of woman this is which toucheth him: for she is a sinner.

40 And Iesus answered, and saide vnto him, Simon, I haue somewhat to say vnto thee. And he said, Master, say on.

41 There was a certaine lender which had two detters: the one ought fiue hundreth pence, and the other fiftie:

42 When they had nothing to pay, he forgaue them both: Which of them therefore, tell mee, will loue him most?

43 Simon answered, and said, I suppose that he, to whom he forgaue most. And he said vnto him, Thou hast truely iudged.

44 Then he turned to the woman, and said vnto Simon, Seest thou this woman? I entred into thine house, and thou gauest me no water to my feete: but she hath washed my feete with teares, and wiped them with the heares of her head.

45 Thou gauest me no kisse: but she, since the time I came in, hath not ceased to kisse my feete.

46 Mine head with oyle thou didest not anoint: but she hath anoynted my feete with oyntment.

47 Wherefore I say vnto thee, many sinnes are forgiuen her: for she loued much. To whom a litle is forgiuen, he doeth loue a litle.

48 And he saide vnto her, Thy sinnes are forgiuen thee.

49 And they that sate at table with him, began to say within themselues, Who is this that euen forgiueth sinnes?

50 And he said to the woman, Thy faith hath saued thee: goe in peace.

Luke 8

1 And it came to passe afterwarde, that hee himselfe went through euery citie and towne, preaching and publishing the kingdome of God, and the twelue were with him,

2 And certaine women, which were healed of euill spirites, and infirmities, as Mary which was called Magdalene, out of whom went seuen deuils,

3 And Ioanna the wife of Chuza Herods steward, and Susanna, and many other which ministred vnto him of their substance.

4 Nowe when much people were gathered together, and were come vnto him out of all cities, he spake by a parable.

5 A sower went out to sowe his seede, and as he sowed, some fell by the wayes side, and it was troden vnder feete, and the foules of heauen deuoured it vp.

6 And some fell on the stones, and when it was sprong vp, it withered away, because it lacked moystnesse.

7 And some fell among thornes, and the thornes sprang vp with it, and choked it.

8 And some fell on good ground, and sprang vp, and bare fruite, an hundreth folde. And as hee sayd these things, he cryed, He that hath eares to heare, let him heare.

9 Then his disciples asked him, demaunding what parable that was.

10 And he sayd, Vnto you it is giuen to know the secrets of ye kingdome of God, but to other in parables, that when they see, they shoulde not see, and when they heare, they should not vnderstand.

11 The parable is this, The seede is the worde of God.

12 And they that are beside the way, are they that heare: afterward commeth the deuill, and taketh away the worde out of their hearts, least they should beleeue, and be saued.

13 But they that are on the stones, are they which when they haue heard, receiue ye word with ioy: but they haue no rootes: which for a while beleeue, but in the time of tentation goe away.

14 And that which fell among thornes, are they which haue heard, and after their departure are choked with cares and with riches, and voluptuous liuing, and bring forth no fruite.

15 But that which fell in good ground, are they which with an honest and good heart heare the worde, and keepe it, and bring forth fruite with patience.

16 No man when he hath lighted a candle, couereth it vnder a vessell, neither putteth it vnder the bed, but setteth it on a candlesticke, that they that enter in, may see the light.

17 For nothing is secret, that shall not be euident: neither any thing hid, that shall not be knowen, and come to light.

18 Take heede therefore how ye heare: for whosoeuer hath, to him shall be giuen: and whosoeuer hath not, from him shalbe taken euen that which it seemeth that he hath.

19 Then came to him his mother and his brethren, and could not come neere to him for the preasse.

20 And it was tolde him by certaine which said, Thy mother and thy brethren stand without, and would see thee.

21 But he answered, and sayd vnto them, My mother and my brethren are these which heare the worde of God, and doe it.

22 And it came to passe on a certaine day, that he went into a ship with his disciples, and he sayd vnto them, Let vs goe ouer vnto the other side of the lake. And they lanched forth.

23 And as they sayled, he fell a sleepe, and there came downe a storme of winde on the lake, and they were filled with water, and were in ieopardie.

24 Then they went to him, and awoke him, saying, Master, Master, we perish. And he arose, and rebuked the winde, and the waues of water: and they ceased, and it was calme.

25 Then he sayde vnto them, Where is your fayth? and they feared, and wondered among them selues, saying, Who is this that commandeth both the windes and water, and they obey him!

26 So they sailed vnto the region of the Gadarenes, which is ouer against Galile.

27 And as he went out to land, there met him a certaine man out of the citie, which had deuils long time, and he ware no garment, neither abode in house, but in the graues.

28 And when he sawe Iesus, he cryed out and fell downe before him, and with a loude voyce sayd, What haue I to doe with thee, Iesus the Sonne of God the most High? I beseech thee torment me not.

29 For he commanded ye foule spirit to come out of the man: (for oft times he had caught him: therefore he was bound with chaines, and kept in fetters: but he brake the bands, and was caried of the deuill into wildernesses.)

30 Then Iesus asked him, saying, What is thy name? and he sayd, Legion, because many deuils were entred into him.

31 And they besought him, that he would not commaund them to goe out into the deepe.

32 And there was there by, an hearde of many swine, feeding on an hill: and the deuils besought him, that he would suffer them to enter into them. So he suffered them.

33 Then went the deuils out of the man, and entred into the swine: and the hearde was caried with violence from a steepe downe place into the lake, and was choked.

34 When the heardmen sawe what was done, they fled: and when they were departed, they tolde it in the citie and in the countrey.

35 Then they came out to see what was done, and came to Iesus, and found the man, out of whom the deuils were departed, sitting at the feete of Iesus, clothed, and in his right minde: and they were afrayd.

36 They also which saw it, tolde them by what meanes he that was possessed with the deuill, was healed.

37 Then the whole multitude of the countrey about the Gadarenes, besought him that he would depart from them: for they were taken with a great feare: and he went into the ship, and returned.

38 Then the man, out of whome the deuils were departed, besought him that hee might be with him: but Iesus sent him away, saying,

39 Returne into thine owne house, and shewe what great things God hath done to thee. So hee went his way, and preached throughout all the citie, what great things Iesus had done vnto him.

40 And it came to passe, when Iesus was come againe, that the people receiued him: for they all waited for him.

41 And beholde, there came a man named Iairus, and he was the ruler of the Synagogue, who fell downe at Iesus feete, and besought him that he would come into his house.

42 For he had but a daughter onely, about twelue yeeres of age, and she lay a dying (and as he went, the people thronged him.)

43 And a woman hauing an yssue of blood, twelue yeeres long, which had spent all her substance vpon physicians, and could not be healed of any:

44 When she came behind him, she touched the hemme of his garment, and immediatly her yssue of blood stanched.

45 Then Iesus sayd, Who is it that hath touched me? When euery man denied, Peter sayd and they that were with him, Master, the multitude thrust thee, and tread on thee, and sayest thou, Who hath touched me?

46 And Iesus sayde, Some one hath touched me: for I perceiue that vertue is gone out of me.

47 When the woman sawe that she was not hid, she came trembling, and fell downe before him, and tolde him before all the people, for what cause she had touched him, and how she was healed immediatly.

48 And he said vnto her, Daughter, be of good comfort: thy faith hath saued thee: go in peace.)

49 While he yet spake, there came one from the ruler of the Synagogues house, which sayde to him, Thy daughter is dead: disease not the Master.

50 When Iesus heard it, he answered him, saying, Feare not: beleeue onely, and she shall be saued.

51 And when he went into the house, he suffered no man to goe in with him, saue Peter, and Iames, and Iohn, and the father and mother of the maide.

52 And all wept, and sorowed for her: but he sayd, Weepe not: for she is not dead, but sleepeth.

53 And they laught him to scorne, knowing that she was dead.

54 So he thrust them all out, and tooke her by the hand, and cryed, saying, Maide, arise.

55 And her spirite came againe, and she rose straightway: and he comanded to giue her meate.

56 Then her parents were astonied: but hee commanded them that they should tell no man what was done.

Luke 9

1 Then called hee his twelue disciples together, and gaue them power and authoritie ouer all deuils, and to heale diseases.

2 And hee sent them foorth to preach the kingdome of God, and to cure the sicke.

3 And he sayd to them, Take nothing to your iourney, neither staues, nor scrip, neither bread, nor siluer, neither haue two coates apiece.

4 And whatsoeuer house ye enter into, there abide, and thence depart.

5 And howe many so euer will not receiue you, when ye goe out of that citie, shake off the very dust from your feete for a testimonie against them.

6 And they went out, and went through euery towne preaching the Gospel, and healing euery where.

7 Nowe Herod the Tetrarch heard of all that was done by him: and he douted, because that it was sayd of some, that Iohn was risen againe from the dead:

8 And of some, that Elias had appeared: and of some, that one of the olde Prophets was risen againe.

9 Then Herod sayd, Iohn haue I beheaded: who then is this of whome I heare such things? and he desired to see him.

10 And when the Apostles returned, they tolde him what great things they had done. Then he tooke them to him, and went aside into a solitarie place, neere to the citie called Bethsaida.

11 But when the people knewe it, they followed him: and he receiued them, and spake vnto them of the kingdome of God, and healed them that had neede to be healed.

12 And when the day began to weare away, the twelue came, and sayd vnto him, Sende the people away, that they may goe into the townes and villages round about, and lodge, and get meate: for we are here in a desart place.

13 But he sayd vnto them, Giue ye them to eate. And they sayd, We haue no more but fiue loaues and two fishes, except we should go and buy meate for all this people.

14 For they were about fiue thousand men. Then he sayde to his disciples, Cause them to sit downe by fifties in a company.

15 And they did so, and caused all to sit downe.

16 Then he tooke the fiue loaues, and the two fishes, and looked vp to heauen, and blessed them, and brake, and gaue to the disciples, to set before the people.

17 So they did all eate, and were satisfied: and there was taken vp of that remained to them, twelue baskets full of broken meate.

18 And it came to passe, as hee was alone praying, his disciples were with him: and he asked them, saying, Whom say the people that I am?

19 They answered, and sayd, Iohn Baptist: and others say, Elias: and some say, that one of the olde Prophets is risen againe.

20 And he sayd vnto them, But whom say ye that I am? Peter answered, and sayd, That Christ of God.

21 And he warned and commanded them, that they should tell that to no man,

22 Saying, The Sonne of man must suffer many things and be reproued of the Elders, and of the hie Priests and Scribes, and be slaine, and the third day rise againe.

23 And he sayd to them all, If any man will come after me, let him denie himselfe, and take vp his crosse dayly, and follow me.

24 For whosoeuer will saue his life, shall lose it: and whosoeuer shall lose his life for my sake, the same shall saue it.

25 For what auantageth it a man, if he win the whole worlde, and destroy himselfe, or lose himselfe?

26 For whosoeuer shall be ashamed of me, and of my wordes, of him shall the Sonne of man be ashamed, when hee shall come in his glorie, and in the glorie of the Father, and of the holy Angels.

27 And I tell you of a suretie, there be some standing here, which shall not taste of death, till they haue seene the kingdome of God.

28 And it came to passe about an eyght dayes after those wordes, that he tooke Peter and Iohn, and Iames, and went vp into a mountaine to pray.

29 And as he prayed, the fashion of his countenance was changed, and his garment was white and glistered.

30 And beholde, two men talked with him, which were Moses and Elias:

31 Which appeared in glory, and tolde of his departing, which he shoulde accomplish at Hierusalem.

32 But Peter and they that were with him, were heauie with sleepe, and when they awoke, they saw his glorie, and the two men standing with him.

33 And it came to passe, as they departed from him, Peter said vnto Iesus, Master, it is good for vs to be here: let vs therefore make three tabernacles, one for thee, and one for Moses, and one for Elias, and wist not what he said.

34 Whiles he thus spake, there came a cloude and ouershadowed them, and they feared when they were entring into the cloude.

35 And there came a voyce out of the cloud, saying, This is that my beloued Sonne, heare him.

36 And when the voyce was past, Iesus was found alone: and they kept it close, and tolde no man in those dayes any of those things which they had seene.

37 And it came to passe on the next day, as they came downe from the mountaine, much people met him.

38 And beholde, a man of the companie cried out, saying, Master, I beseech thee, beholde my sonne: for he is all that I haue.

39 And loe, a spirit taketh him, and suddenly he crieth, and he teareth him, that he fometh, and hardly departeth from him, when he hath bruised him.

40 Nowe I haue besought thy disciples to cast him out, but they could not.

41 Then Iesus answered, and said, O generation faithlesse, and crooked, howe long now shall I be with you, and suffer you? bring thy sonne hither.

42 And whiles he was yet comming, the deuill rent him, and tare him: and Iesus rebuked the vncleane spirite, and healed the childe, and deliuered him to his father.

43 And they were all amased at the mightie power of God: and while they all wondered at al things, which Iesus did, he said vnto his disciples,

44 Marke these wordes diligently: for it shall come to passe, that the Sonne of man shalbe deliuered into the handes of men.

45 But they vnderstood not that word: for it was hid from them, so that they could not perceiue it: and they feared to aske him of that worde.

46 Then there arose a disputation among them, which of them should be the greatest.

47 When Iesus sawe the thoughtes of their heartes, he tooke a litle childe, and set him by him,

48 And said vnto them, Whosoeuer receiueth this litle childe in my Name, receiueth me: and whosoeuer shall receiue me, receiueth him that sent me: for he that is least among you all, he shall be great.

49 And Iohn answered and saide, Master, we sawe one casting out deuils in thy Name, and we forbad him, because he followeth thee not with vs.

50 Then Iesus saide vnto him, Forbid ye him not: for he that is not against vs, is with vs.

51 And it came to passe, when the dayes were accomplished, that he should be receiued vp, he setled himselfe fully to goe to Hierusalem,

52 And sent messengers before him: and they went and entred into a towne of the Samaritans, to prepare him lodging.

53 But they woulde not receiue him, because his behauiour was, as though he would go to Hierusalem.

54 And when his disciples, Iames and Iohn sawe it, they saide, Lord, wilt thou that we commaund, that fire come downe from heauen, and consume them, euen as Elias did?

55 But Iesus turned about, and rebuked them, and said, Ye knowe not of what spirit ye are.

56 For the Sonne of man is not come to destroy mens liues, but to saue them. Then they went to another towne.

57 And it came to passe that as they went in the way, a certaine man said vnto him, I will follow thee, Lord, whithersoeuer thou goest.

58 And Iesus saide vnto him, The foxes haue holes, and the birdes of the heauen nestes, but the Sonne of man hath not whereon to lay his head.

59 But he said vnto another, Followe me. And the same said, Lord, suffer me first to goe and burie my father.

60 And Iesus said vnto him, Let the dead burie their dead: but go thou, and preache the kingdome of God.

61 Then another saide, I will follow thee, Lord: but let me first go bid them farewell, which are at mine house.

62 And Iesus saide vnto him, No man that putteth his hand to the plough, and looketh backe, is apt to the kingdome of God.

Luke 10

1 After these thinges, the Lord appointed other seuentie also, and sent them, two and two before him into euery citie and place, whither he himselfe should come.

2 And he said vnto them, The haruest is great, but the labourers are fewe: pray therefore the Lord of the haruest to sende foorth labourers into his haruest.

3 Goe your wayes: beholde, I send you foorth as lambes among wolues.

4 Beare no bagge, neither scrippe, nor shoes, and salute no man by the way.

5 And into whatsoeuer house ye enter, first say, Peace be to this house.

6 And if the sonne of peace be there, your peace shall rest vpon him: if not, it shall turne to you againe.

7 And in that house tary still, eating and drinking such things as by them shall be set before you: for the labourer is worthy of his wages. Goe not from house to house.

8 But into whatsoeuer citie ye shall enter, if they receiue you, eate such things as are set before you,

9 And heale the sicke that are there, and say vnto them, The kingdome of God is come neere vnto you.

10 But into whatsoeuer citie ye shall enter, if they will not receiue you, goe your wayes out into the streetes of the same, and say,

11 Euen the very dust, which cleaueth on vs of your citie, we wipe off against you: notwithstanding knowe this, that the kingdome of God was come neere vnto you.

12 For I say to you, that it shall be easier in that day for them of Sodom, then for that citie.

13 Woe be to thee, Chorazin: woe be to thee, Beth-saida: for if the miracles had bene done in Tyrus and Sidon, which haue bene done in you, they had a great while agone repented, sitting in sackecloth and ashes.

14 Therefore it shall be easier for Tyrus, and Sidon, at the iudgement, then for you.

15 And thou, Capernaum, which art exalted to heauen, shalt be thrust downe to hell.

16 He that heareth you, heareth me: and he that despiseth you, despiseth me:

and he that despiseth me, despiseth him that sent me.

17 And the seuentie turned againe with ioy, saying, Lord, euen the deuils are subdued to vs through thy Name.

18 And he said vnto them, I sawe Satan, like lightening, fall downe from heauen.

19 Beholde, I giue vnto you power to treade on Serpents, and Scorpions, and ouer all the power of the enemie, and nothing shall hurt you.

20 Neuerthelesse, in this reioyce not, that the spirits are subdued vnto you: but rather reioyce, because your names are written in heauen.

21 That same houre reioyced Iesus in the spirit, and said, I confesse vnto thee, Father, Lord of heauen and earth, that thou hast hid these things from the wise and vnderstanding, and hast reueiled them to babes: euen so, Father, because it so pleased thee.

22 All things are giuen me of my Father: and no man knoweth who the Sonne is, but the Father: neither who the Father is, saue the Sonne, and he to whom the Sonne will reueile him.

23 And he turned to his disciples, and said secretly, Blessed are the eyes, which see that ye see.

24 For I tell you that many Prophets and Kings haue desired to see those things, which ye see, and haue not seene them: and to heare those things which ye heare, and haue not heard them.

25 Then beholde, a certaine Lawyer stoode vp, and tempted him, saying, Master, what shall I doe, to inherite eternall life?

26 And he saide vnto him, What is written in the Lawe? howe readest thou?

27 And he answered, and saide, Thou shalt loue thy Lord God with all thine heart, and with all thy soule, and with all thy strength, and with all thy thought, and thy neighbour as thy selfe.

28 Then he said vnto him, Thou hast answered right: this doe, and thou shalt liue.

29 But he willing to iustifie himselfe, said vnto Iesus, Who is then my neighbour?

30 And Iesus answered, and saide, A certaine man went downe from Hierusalem to Iericho, and fell among theeues, and they robbed him of his raiment, and wounded him, and departed, leauing him halfe dead.

31 Nowe so it fell out, that there came downe a certaine Priest that same way, and when he sawe him, he passed by on the other side.

32 And likewise also a Leuite, when he was come neere to the place, went and looked on him, and passed by on the other side.

33 Then a certaine Samaritane, as he iourneyed, came neere vnto him, and when he sawe him, he had compassion on him,

34 And went to him, and bound vp his wounds, and powred in oyle and wine, and put him on his owne beast, and brought him to an Inne, and made prouision for him.

35 And on the morowe when he departed, he tooke out two pence, and gaue them to the hoste, and said vnto him, Take care of him, and whatsoeuer thou spendest more, when I come againe, I will recompense thee.

36 Which nowe of these three, thinkest thou, was neighbour vnto him that fell among the theeues?

37 And he saide, He that shewed mercie on him. Then said Iesus vnto him, Goe, and do thou likewise.

38 Nowe it came to passe, as they went, that he entred into a certaine towne, and a certaine woman named Martha, receiued him into her house.

39 And she had a sister called Marie, which also sate at Iesus feete, and heard his preaching.

40 But Martha was combred about much seruing, and came to him, and saide, Master, doest thou not care that my sister hath left me to serue alone? bid her therefore, that she helpe me.

41 And Iesus answered, and said vnto her, Martha, Martha, thou carest, and art troubled about many things:

42 But one thing is needefull, Marie hath chosen the good part, which shall not be taken away from her.

Luke 11

1 And so it was, that as he was praying in a certaine place, when he ceased, one of his disciples said vnto him, Lord, teache vs to pray, as Iohn also taught his disciples.

2 And he said vnto them, When ye pray, say, Our Father, which art in heauen, halowed be thy Name: Thy kingdome come: Let thy will be done, euen in earth, as it is in heauen:

3 Our dayly bread giue vs for the day:

4 And forgiue vs our sinnes: for euen we forgiue euery man that is indetted to vs: And leade vs not into temptation: but deliuer vs from euill.

5 Moreouer he said vnto them, Which of you shall haue a friende, and shall goe to him at midnight, and say vnto him, Friende, lende mee three loaues?

6 For a friende of mine is come out of the way to me, and I haue nothing to set before him:

7 And hee within shoulde answere, and say, Trouble mee not: the doore is nowe shut, and my children are with mee in bed: I can not rise and giue them to thee.

8 I say vnto you, Though he would not arise and giue him, because he is his friende, yet doubtlesse because of his importunitie, hee woulde rise, and giue him as many as he needed.

9 And I say vnto you, Aske, and it shall be giuen you: seeke, and yee shall finde: knocke, and it shalbe opened vnto you.

10 For euery one that asketh, receiueth: and he that seeketh, findeth: and to him that knocketh, it shalbe opened.

11 If a sonne shall aske bread of any of you that is a father, will he giue him a stone? or if hee aske a fish, will he for a fish giue him a serpent?

12 Or if hee aske an egge, will hee giue him a scorpion?

13 If yee then which are euill, can giue good giftes vnto your children, howe much more shall your heauenly Father giue the holy Ghost to them, that desire him?

14 Then hee cast out a deuill which was domme: and when the deuill was gone out, the domme spake, and the people wondered.

15 But some of them said, He casteth out deuils through Beelzebub the chiefe of ye deuils.

16 And others tempted him, seeking of him a signe from heauen.

17 But he knew their thoughts, and said vnto them, Euery kingdome deuided against it self, shall be desolate, and an house deuided against an house, falleth.

18 So if Satan also bee deuided against himselfe, howe shall his kingdome stande, because yee say that I cast out deuils through Beelzebub?

19 If I through Beelzebub cast out deuils, by whome doe your children cast them out? Therefore shall they be your iudges.

20 But if I by ye finger of God cast out deuils, doutles the kingdome of God is come vnto you.

21 When a strong man armed keepeth his palace, the thinges that hee possesseth, are in peace.

22 But when a stronger then hee, commeth vpon him, and ouercommeth him: hee taketh from him all his armour wherein he trusted, and deuideth his spoiles.

23 He that is not with me, is against me: and he that gathereth not with me, scattereth.

24 When the vncleane spirite is gone out of a man, he walketh through drie places, seeking rest: and when he findeth none he saieth, I wil returne vnto mine house whence I came out.

25 And when he cometh, he findeth it swept and garnished.

26 Then goeth hee, and taketh to him seuen other spirites worse then himselfe: and they enter in, and dwel there: so the last state of that man is worse then the first.

27 And it came to passe as he sayde these thinges, a certaine woman of the companie lifted vp her voyce, and sayde vnto him, Blessed is the wombe that bare thee, and the pappes which thou hast sucked.

28 But hee saide, Yea, rather blessed are they that heare the woorde of God, and keepe it.

29 And when the people were gathered thicke together, he began to say, This is a wicked generation: they seeke a signe, and there shall no signe be giuen them, but the signe of Ionas the Prophet.

30 For as Ionas was a signe to the Niniuites: so shall also the Sonne of man bee to this generation.

31 The Queene of the South shall rise in iudgement, with the men of this generation, and shall condemne them: for shee came from the vtmost partes of the earth to heare the wisedome of Salomon, and beholde, a greater then Salomon is here.

32 The men of Niniue shall rise in iudgement with this generation, and shall condemne it: for they repented at the preaching of Ionas: and beholde, a greater then Ionas is here.

33 No man when he hath lighted a candle, putteth it in a priuie place, neither vnder a bushell: but on a candlesticke, that they which come in, may see the light.

34 The light of the bodie is the eye: therefore when thine eye is single, then is thy whole bodie light: but if thine eye be euill, then thy bodie is darke.

35 Take heede therefore, that the light which is in thee, be not darkenesse.

36 If therefore thy whole body shall be light, hauing no part darke, then shall all be light, euen as when a candle doth light thee with the brightnesse.

37 And as hee spake, a certaine Pharise besought him to dine with him: and hee went in, and sate downe at table.

38 And when the Pharise saw it, he marueiled that he had not first washed before dinner.

39 And the Lord saide to him, In deede ye Pharises make cleane the outside of the cuppe, and of the platter: but the inwarde part is full of rauening and wickednesse.

40 Ye fooles, did not he that made that which is without, make that which is within also?

41 Therefore, giue almes of those thinges which you haue, and beholde, all thinges shall be cleane to you.

42 But wo be to you, Pharises: for ye tithe the mynt and the rewe, and all maner herbs, and passe ouer iudgement and the loue of God: these ought yee to haue done, and not to haue left the other vndone.

43 Wo be to you, Pharises: for ye loue the vppermost seats in the Synagogues, and greetings in the markets.

44 Wo be to you, Scribes and Pharises, hypocrites: for ye are as graues which appeare not, and the men that walke ouer them, perceiue not.

45 Then answered one of the Lawyers, and saide vnto him, Master, thus saying thou puttest vs to rebuke also.

46 And he sayde, Wo be to you also, yee Lawyers: for yee lade men with burdens grieuous to be borne, and yee your selues touche not the burdens with one of your fingers.

47 Wo be to you: for ye builde the sepulchres of the Prophetes, and your fathers killed them.

48 Truely ye beare witnesse, and allowe the deedes of your fathers: for they killed them, and yee build their sepulchres.

49 Therefore said the wisedome of God, I wil sende them Prophets and Apostles, and of them they shall slaie, and persecute away,

50 That the blood of all the Prophets, shed from the foundation of the world, may be required of this generation,

51 From the blood of Abel vnto the blood of Zacharias, which was slaine betweene the altar and the Temple: verely I say vnto you, it shall be required of this generation.

52 Wo be to you, Lawyers: for ye haue taken away the key of knowledge: ye entred not in your selues, and them that came in, ye forbade.

53 And as he sayde these things vnto them, the Scribes and Pharises began to vrge him sore, and to prouoke him to speake of many things,

54 Laying wait for him, and seeking to catch some thing of his mouth, whereby they might accuse him.

Luke 12

1 In the meane time, there gathered together an innumerable multitude of people, so that they trode one another: and he began to say vnto his disciples first, Take heede to your selues of the leauen of the Pharises, which is hypocrisie.

2 For there is nothing couered, that shall not bee reueiled: neither hidde, that shall not be knowen.

3 Wherefore whatsoeuer yee haue spoken in darkenesse, it shall be heard in the light: and that which ye haue spoken in the eare, in secret places, shall be preached on the houses.

4 And I say vnto you, my friendes, be not afraide of them that kill the bodie, and after that are not able to doe any more.

5 But I wil forewarne you, who ye shall feare: feare him which after hee hath killed, hath power to cast into hell: yea, I say vnto you, him feare.

6 Are not fiue sparowes bought for two farthings, and yet not one of them is forgotten before God?

7 Yea, and all the heares of your head are nombred: feare not therefore: yee are more of value then many sparowes.

8 Also I say vnto you, Whosoeuer shall confesse mee before men, him shall the Sonne of man confesse also before the Angels of God.

9 But hee that shall denie mee before men, shall be denied before the Angels of God.

10 And whosoeuer shall speake a woorde against the Sonne of man, it shall be forgiuen him: but vnto him, that shall blaspheme ye holy Ghost, it shall not be forgiuen.

11 And when they shall bring you vnto the Synagogues, and vnto the rulers and Princes, take no thought howe, or what thing ye shall answere, or what yee shall speake.

12 For the holy Ghost shall teache you in the same houre, what yee ought to say.

13 And one of the companie said vnto him, Master, bidde my brother deuide the inheritance with me.

14 And he said vnto him, Man, who made me a iudge, or a deuider ouer you?

15 Wherefore he said vnto them, Take heede, and beware of couetousnesse: for

though a man haue abundance, yet his life standeth not in his riches.

16 And he put foorth a parable vnto them, saying, The grounde of a certaine riche man brought foorth fruites plenteously.

17 Therefore he thought with himselfe, saying, What shall I doe, because I haue no roume, where I may lay vp my fruites?

18 And he said, This wil I do, I wil pul downe my barnes, and builde greater, and therein will I gather all my fruites, and my goods.

19 And I wil say to my soule, Soule, thou hast much goods laide vp for many yeeres: liue at ease, eate, drinke and take thy pastime.

20 But God said vnto him, O foole, this night wil they fetch away thy soule from thee: then whose shall those things be which thou hast prouided?

21 So is he that gathereth riches to himselfe, and is not riche in God.

22 And he spake vnto his disciples, Therefore I say vnto you, Take no thought for your life, what yee shall eate: neither for your body, what yee shall put on.

23 The life is more then meate: and the body more then the raiment.

24 Consider the rauens: for they neither sowe nor reape: which neither haue storehouse nor barne, and yet God feedeth them: how much more are yee better then foules?

25 And which of you with taking thought, can adde to his stature one cubite?

26 If yee then bee not able to doe the least thing, why take yee thought for the remnant?

27 Consider the lilies howe they growe: they labour not, neither spin they: yet I say vnto you, that Salomon himselfe in all his royaltie was not clothed like one of these.

28 If then God so clothe the grasse which is to day in the field, and to morowe is cast into the ouen, howe much more will he clothe you, O yee of litle faith?

29 Therefore aske not what yee shall eate, or what ye shall drinke, neither hag you in suspense.

30 For all such things the people of the world seeke for: and your Father knoweth that ye haue neede of these things.

31 But rather seeke ye after the kingdome of God, and all these things shalbe cast vpon you.

32 Feare not, litle flocke: for it is your Fathers pleasure, to giue you the kingdome.

33 Sell that ye haue, and giue almes: make you bagges, which waxe not old, a treasure that can neuer faile in heauen, where no theefe commeth, neither mothe corrupteth.

34 For where your treasure is, there will your hearts be also.

35 Let your loynes be gird about and your lights burning,

36 And ye your selues like vnto men that waite for their master, when he will returne from the wedding, that when he commeth and knocketh, they may open vnto him immediatly.

37 Blessed are those seruants, whom the Lord when he commeth shall finde waking: verely I say vnto you, he will girde himselfe about, and make them to sit downe at table, and will come forth, and serue them.

38 And if he come in the seconde watch, or come in the third watch, and shall finde them so, blessed are those seruants.

39 Nowe vnderstand this, that if the good man of the house had knowen at what houre the theefe would haue come, he would haue watched, and would not haue suffered his house to be digged through.

40 Be ye also prepared therefore: for the Sonne of man will come at an houre when ye thinke not.

41 Then Peter saide vnto him, Master, tellest thou this parable vnto vs, or euen to all?

42 And the Lord saide, Who is a faithfull steward and wise, whom the master shall make ruler ouer his householde, to giue them their portion of meate in season?

43 Blessed is that seruant, whom his master when he commeth, shall finde so doing.

44 Of a trueth I say vnto you, that he wil make him ruler ouer all that he hath.

45 But if that seruant say in his heart, My master doeth deferre his comming, and ginne to smite the seruants, and maydens, and to eate, and drinke, and to be drunken.

46 The master of that seruant will come in a day when he thinketh not, and at an houre when he is not ware of, and will cut him off, and giue him his portion with the vnbeleeuers.

47 And that seruant that knewe his masters will, and prepared not himselfe, neither did according to his will, shalbe beaten with many stripes.

48 But he that knewe it not, and yet did commit things worthy of stripes, shall be beaten with fewe stripes: for vnto whomsoeuer much is giuen, of him shalbe much required, and to whom men much commit, the more of him will they aske.

49 I am come to put fire on the earth, and what is my desire, if it be already kindled?

50 Notwithstanding I must be baptized with a baptisme, and how am I grieued, till it be ended?

51 Thinke ye that I am come to giue peace on earth? I tell you, nay, but rather debate.

52 For from henceforth there shall be fiue in one house deuided, three against two, and two against three.

53 The father shalbe deuided against ye sonne, and the sonne against the father: the mother against the daughter, and the daughter against the mother: the mother in lawe against her daughter in lawe, and the daughter in lawe against her mother in lawe.

54 Then said he to the people, When ye see a cloude rise out of the West, straightway ye say, A shower commeth: and so it is.

55 And when ye see the South winde blowe, ye say, that it wilbe hoate: and it commeth to passe.

56 Hypocrites, ye can discerne the face of the earth, and of the skie: but why discerne ye not this time?

57 Yea, and why iudge ye not of your selues what is right?

58 While thou goest with thine aduersarie to the ruler, as thou art in the way, giue diligence in the way, that thou mayest be deliuered from him, least he drawe thee to the iudge, and the iudge deliuer thee to the iayler, and the iayler cast thee into prison.

59 I tell thee, thou shalt not depart thence, till thou hast payed the vtmost mite.

Luke 13

1 There were certaine men present at the same season, that shewed him of the Galileans, whose blood Pilate had mingled with their sacrifices.

2 And Iesus answered, and saide vnto them, Suppose ye, that these Galileans were greater sinners then al the other Galileans, because they haue suffered such things?

3 I tell you, nay: but except ye amend your liues, ye shall all likewise perish.

4 Or thinke you that those eighteene, vpon whom the tower in Siloam fell, and slewe them, were sinners aboue all men that dwel in Hierusalem?

5 I tell you, nay: but except ye amend your liues, ye shall all likewise perish.

6 He spake also this parable, A certaine man had a figge tree planted in his vineyard: and he came and sought fruite thereon, and found none.

7 Then said he to the dresser of his vineyard, Behold, this three yeeres haue I come and sought fruite of this figge tree, and finde none: cut it downe: why keepeth it also the ground barren?

8 And he answered, and said vnto him, Lord, let it alone this yeere also, till I digge round about it, and doung it.

9 And if it beare fruite, well: if not, then after thou shalt cut it downe.

10 And he taught in one of ye Synagogues on the Sabbath day.

11 And behold, there was a woman which had a spirit of infirmitie eighteene yeeres, and was bowed together, and coulde not lift vp her selfe in any wise.

12 When Iesus sawe her, he called her to him, and said to her, Woman, thou art loosed from thy disease.

13 And he laide his handes on her, and immediately she was made straight againe, and glorified God.

14 And the ruler of the Synagogue answered with indignation, because that Iesus healed on the Sabbath day, and said vnto the people, There are sixe dayes in which men ought to worke: in them therefore come and be healed, and not on the Sabbath day.

15 Then answered him the Lord, and said, Hypocrite, doth not eche one of you on the Sabbath day loose his oxe or his asse from the stall, and leade him away to the water?

16 And ought not this daughter of Abraham, whom Satan had bound, loe, eighteene yeeres, be loosed from this bond on the Sabbath day?

17 And when he said these things, all his aduersaries were ashamed: but all the people reioyced at all the excellent things, that were done by him.

18 Then said he, What is the kingdome of God like? or whereto shall I compare it?

19 It is like a graine of mustard seede, which a man tooke and sowed in his garden, and it grewe, and waxed a great tree, and the foules of the heauen made nestes in the branches thereof.

20 And againe he said, Whereunto shall I liken the kingdome of God?

21 It is like leauen, which a woman tooke, and hid in three peckes of floure, till all was leauened.

22 And he went through all cities and townes, teaching, and iourneying towards Hierusalem.

23 Then saide one vnto him, Lord, are there fewe that shalbe saued? And he said vnto them,

24 Striue to enter in at the straite gate: for many, I say vnto you, will seeke to enter in, and shall not be able.

25 When the good man of the house is risen vp, and hath shut to the doore, and ye begin to stand without, and to knocke at the doore, saying, Lord, Lord, open to vs, and he shall answere and say vnto you, I know you not whence ye are,

26 Then shall ye begin to say, We haue eaten and drunke in thy presence, and thou hast taught in our streetes.

27 But he shall say, I tell you, I knowe you not whence ye are: depart from me, all ye workers of iniquitie.

28 There shall be weeping and gnashing of teeth when ye shall see Abraham and Isaac, and Iacob, and all the Prophets in the kingdome of God, and your selues thrust out at doores.

29 Then shall come many from the East, and from the West, and from the North, and from the South, and shall sit at Table in the kingdome of God.

30 And beholde, there are last, which shalbe first, and there are first, which shalbe last.

31 The same day there came certaine Pharises, and said vnto him, Depart, and goe hence: for Herod will kill thee.

32 Then said he vnto them, Goe ye and tell that foxe, Beholde, I cast out deuils, and will heale still to day, and to morowe, and the third day I shalbe perfected.

33 Neuerthelesse I must walke to day, and to morowe, and the day following: for it cannot be that a Prophet should perish out of Hierusalem.

34 O Hierusalem, Hierusalem, which killest the Prophets, and stonest them that are sent to thee, howe often would I haue gathered thy children together, as the henne gathereth her brood vnder her wings, and ye would not!

35 Beholde, your house is left vnto you desolate: and verely I tell you, ye shall not see me vntill the time come that ye shall say, Blessed is he that commeth in the Name of the Lord.

Luke 14

1 And it came to passe that when he was entred into the house of one of the chiefe Pharises on the Sabbath day, to eate bread, they watched him.

2 And beholde, there was a certaine man before him, which had the dropsie.

3 Then Iesus answering, spake vnto the Lawyers and Pharises, saying, Is it lawfull to heale on the Sabbath day?

4 And they held their peace. Then he tooke him, and healed him, and let him goe,

5 And answered them, saying, Which of you shall haue an asse, or an oxe fallen into a pit, and wil not straightway pull him out on the Sabbath day?

6 And they could not answere him againe to those things.

7 He spake also a parable to the ghestes, when he marked howe they chose out the chiefe roomes, and said vnto them,

8 When thou shalt be bidden of any man to a wedding, set not thy selfe downe in the chiefest place, lest a more honourable man then thou, be bidden of him,

9 And he that bade both him and thee, come, and say to thee, Giue this man roome, and thou then begin with shame to take the lowest roome.

10 But when thou art bidden, goe and sit downe in the lowest roome, that when he that bade thee, cometh, he may say vnto thee, Friende, sit vp hier: then shalt thou haue worship in the presence of them that sit at table with thee.

11 For whosoeuer exalteth himselfe, shall be brought lowe, and he that humbleth himselfe, shall be exalted.

12 Then said he also to him that had bidden him, When thou makest a dinner or a supper, call not thy friendes, nor thy brethren, neither thy kinsemen, nor ye riche neighbours, lest they also bid thee againe, and a recompence be made thee.

13 But when thou makest a feast, call ye poore, the maimed, the lame, and the blind,

14 And thou shalt be blessed, because they cannot recompense thee: for thou shalt be recompensed at the resurrection of the iust.

15 Nowe when one of them that sate at table, heard these things, he said vnto him, Blessed is he that eateth bread in the kingdome of God.

16 Then saide he to him, A certaine man made a great supper, and bade many,

17 And sent his seruant at supper time to say to them that were bidden, Come: for all things are nowe readie.

18 But they all with one mind beganne to make excuse: The first saide vnto him, I haue bought a farme, and I must needes goe out and see it: I pray thee, haue me excused.

19 And another said, I haue bought fiue yoke of oxen, and I goe to proue them: I pray thee, haue me excused.

20 And another said, I haue maried a wife, and therefore I can not come.

21 So that seruaunt returned, and shewed his master these thinges. Then was the good man of the house angrie, and said to his seruant, Goe out quickely into the streetes and lanes of the citie, and bring in hither the poore, and the maimed, and the halt, and the blinde.

22 And the seruaunt saide, Lord, it is done as thou hast commanded, and yet there is roome.

23 Then the master sayd to the seruaunt, Goe out into the hie wayes, and hedges, and compell them to come in, that mine house may bee filled.

24 For I say vnto you, that none of those men which were bidden, shall taste of my supper.

25 Nowe there went great multitudes with him, and he turned and sayd vnto them,

26 If any man come to mee, and hate not his father, and mother, and wife, and children, and brethren, and sisters: yea, and his owne life also, he can not be my disciple.

27 And whosoeuer beareth not his crosse, and commeth after mee, can not bee my disciple.

28 For which of you minding to builde a towre, sitteth not downe before, and counteth the cost, whether hee haue sufficient to performe it,

29 Lest that after he hath laide the foundation, and is not able to performe it, all that behold it, begin to mocke him,

30 Saying, This man began to builde, and was not able to make an end?

31 Or what King going to make warre against another King, sitteth not downe first, and taketh counsell, whether he be able with ten thousande, to meete him that commeth against him with twentie thousand?

32 Or els while hee is yet a great way off, hee sendeth an ambassage, and desireth peace.

33 So likewise, whosoeuer hee be of you, that forsaketh not all that he hath, he cannot be my disciple.

34 Salt is good: but if salt haue lost his sauour, wherewith shall it be salted?

35 It is neither meete for the land, nor yet for the dunghill, but men cast it out. He that hath eares to heare, let him heare.

Luke 15

1 Then resorted vnto him all the Publicanes and sinners, to heare him.

2 Therefore the Pharises and Scribes murmured, saying, Hee receiueth sinners, and eateth with them.

3 Then spake hee this parable to them, saying,

4 What man of you hauing an hundreth sheepe, if hee lose one of them, doeth not leaue ninetie and nine in the

wildernesse, and goe after that which is lost, vntill he finde it?

5 And when he hath found it, he laieth it on his shoulders with ioye.

6 And when he commeth home, he calleth together his friendes and neighbours, saying vnto them, Reioyce with mee: for I haue founde my sheepe which was lost.

7 I say vnto you, that likewise ioy shall be in heauen for one sinner that conuerteth, more then for ninetie and nine iust men, which neede none amendment of life.

8 Either what woman hauing ten groates, if she lose one groate, doth not light a candle, and sweepe the house, and seeke diligently till shee finde it?

9 And when shee hath found it, shee calleth her friendes, and neighbours, saying, Reioyce with me: for I haue found the groate which I had lost.

10 Likewise I say vnto you, there is ioy in the presence of the Angels of God, for one sinner that conuerteth.

11 He sayde moreouer, A certaine man had two sonnes.

12 And the yonger of them sayde to his father, Father, giue mee the portion of the goods that falleth to mee. So he deuided vnto them his substance.

13 So not many daies after, when the yonger sonne had gathered all together, hee tooke his iourney into a farre countrey, and there hee wasted his goods with riotous liuing.

14 Nowe when hee had spent all, there arose a great dearth throughout that land, and he began to be in necessitie.

15 Then hee went and claue to a citizen of that conntrey, and hee sent him to his farme, to feede swine.

16 And hee would faine haue filled his bellie with the huskes, that the swine ate: but no man gaue them him.

17 Then he came to him selfe, and said, Howe many hired seruaunts at my fathers haue bread ynough, and I die for hunger?

18 I wil rise and goe to my father, and say vnto him, Father, I haue sinned against heaue, and before thee,

19 And am no more worthy to be called thy sonne: make me as one of thy hired seruants.

20 So hee arose and came to his father, and when hee was yet a great way off, his father sawe him, and had compassion, and ranne and fell on his necke, and kissed him.

21 And the sonne sayde vnto him, Father, I haue sinned against heauen, and before thee, and am no more worthie to be called thy sonne.

22 Then the father said to his seruaunts, Bring foorth the best robe, and put it on him, and put a ring on his hand, and shoes on his feete,

23 And bring the fat calfe, and kill him, and let vs eate, and be merie:

24 For this my sonne was dead, and is aliue againe: and he was lost, but he is found. And they began to be merie.

25 Nowe the elder brother was in the fielde, and when he came and drewe neere to the house, he heard melodie, and daunsing,

26 And called one of his seruaunts, and asked what those things meant.

27 And hee sayde vnto him, Thy brother is come, and thy father hath killed the fatte calfe, because he hath receiued him safe and sound.

28 Then he was angry, and would not goe in: therefore came his father out and entreated him.

29 But he answered and said to his father, Loe, these many yeeres haue I done thee seruice, neither brake I at any time thy commadement, and yet thou neuer gauest mee a kidde that I might make merie with my friends.

30 But when this thy sonne was come, which hath deuoured thy good with harlots, thou hast for his sake killed the fat calfe.

31 And he said vnto him, Sonne, thou art euer with me, and al that I haue, is thine. It was meete that we shoulde make merie, and be glad: for this thy brother was dead, and is aliue againe: and hee was lost, but he is found.

Luke 16

1 And he sayde also vnto his disciples, There was a certaine riche man, which had a stewarde, and he was accused vnto him, that he wasted his goods.

2 And hee called him, and saide vnto him, Howe is it that I heare this of thee? Giue an accounts of thy stewardship: for thou maiest be no longer steward.

3 Then the stewarde saide within himselfe, What shall I doe? for my master taketh away from me the stewardship. I cannot digge, and to begge I am ashamed.

4 I knowe what I will doe, that when I am put out of the stewardship, they may receiue mee into their houses.

5 Then called he vnto him euery one of his masters detters, and said vnto the first, Howe much owest thou vnto my master?

6 And he said, An hudreth measures of oyle. And he saide to him, Take thy writing, and sitte downe quickely, and write fiftie.

7 Then said he to another, How much owest thou? And hee sayde, An hundreth measures of wheate. Then he saide to him, Take thy writing, and write foure score.

8 And the Lord commended the vniust stewarde, because he had done wisely. Wherefore the children of this worlde are in their generation wiser then the children of light.

9 And I say vnto you, Make you friends with the riches of iniquitie, that when ye shall want, they may receiue you into euerlasting habitations.

10 He that is faithfull in the least, hee is also faithful in much: and he that is vniust in the least, is vniust also in much.

11 If then ye haue not ben faithful in the wicked riches, who wil trust you in the true treasure?

12 And if ye haue not bene faithfull in another mans goods, who shall giue you that which is yours?

13 No seruaunt can serue two masters: for either he shall hate the one, and loue the other: or els he shall leane to the one, and despise the other. Yee can not serue God and riches.

14 All these thinges heard the Pharises also which were couetous, and they scoffed at him.

15 Then he sayde vnto them, Yee are they, which iustifie your selues before men: but God knoweth your heartes: for that which is highly esteemed among men, is abomination in the sight of God.

16 The Lawe and the Prophets endured vntill Iohn: and since that time the kingdome of God is preached, and euery man preasseth into it.

17 Nowe it is more easie that heauen and earth shoulde passe away, then that one title of the Lawe should fall.

18 Whosoeuer putteth away his wife, and marieth another, committeth adulterie: and whosoeuer marieth her that is put away from her husband, committeth adulterie.

19 There was a certaine riche man, which was clothed in purple and fine linnen, and fared well and delicately euery day.

20 Also there was a certaine begger named Lazarus, which was laide at his gate full of sores,

21 And desired to bee refreshed with the crommes that fell from the riche mans table: yea, and the dogges came and licked his sores.

22 And it was so that the begger died, and was caried by the Angels into Abrahams bosome. The rich man also died, and was buried.

23 And being in hell in torments, he lift vp his eyes, and sawe Abraham a farre off, and Lazarus in his bosome.

24 Then he cried, and saide, Father Abraham, haue mercie on mee, and sende Lazarus that hee may dippe the tip of his finger in water, and coole my tongue: for I am tormented in this flame.

25 But Abraham saide, Sonne, remember that thou in thy life time receiuedst thy pleasures, and likewise Lazarus paines: now therefore is he comforted, and thou art tormented.

26 Besides all this, betweene you and vs there is a great gulfe set, so that they which would goe from hence to you, can not: neither can they come from thence to vs.

27 Then he said, I pray thee therfore, father, that thou wouldest sende him to my fathers house,

28 (For I haue fiue brethren) that he may testifie vnto them, least they also come into this place of torment.

29 Abraham said vnto him, They haue Moses and the Prophets: let them heare them.

30 And he sayde, Nay, father Abraham: but if one came vnto them from the dead, they will amend their liues.

31 Then he saide vnto him, If they heare not Moses and the Prophets, neither will

they be persuaded, though one rise from the dead againe.

Luke 17

1 Then said he to his disciples, It can not be auoided, but that offences will come, but wo be to him by whome they come.

2 It is better for him that a great milstone were hanged about his necke, and that he were cast into ye sea, then that he should offende one of these litle ones.

3 Take heede to your selues: if thy brother trespasse against thee, rebuke him: and if hee repent, forgiue him.

4 And though he sinne against thee seuen times in a day, and seuen times in a day turne againe to thee, saying, It repenteth mee, thou shalt forgiue him.

5 And the Apostles saide vnto the Lord, Increase our faith.

6 And the Lord said, If ye had faith, as much as is a graine of mustard seede, and should say vnto this mulberie tree, Plucke thy selfe vp by the rootes, and plant thy selfe in the sea, it should euen obey you.

7 Who is it also of you, that hauing a seruant plowing or feeding cattell, woulde say vnto him by and by, when hee were come from the fielde, Goe, and sit downe at table?

8 And woulde not rather say to him, Dresse wherewith I may suppe, and girde thy selfe, and serue mee, till I haue eaten and drunken, and afterward eate thou, and drinke thou?

9 Doeth he thanke that seruant, because hee did that which was commanded vnto him? I trowe not.

10 So likewise yee, when yee haue done all those things, which are commanded you, say, We are vnprofitable seruants: wee haue done that which was our duetie to doe.

11 And so it was when he went to Hierusalem, that he passed through the middes of Samaria, and Galile.

12 And as hee entred into a certaine towne, there met him tenne men that were lepers, which stoode a farre off.

13 And they lift vp their voyces and saide, Iesus, Master, haue mercie on vs.

14 And when he saw them, he said vnto them, Goe, shewe your selues vnto the Priestes. And it came to passe, that as they went, they were clensed.

15 Then one of them, when hee sawe that hee, was healed, turned backe, and with a loude voyce praised God,

16 And fell downe on his face at his feete, and gaue him thankes: and he was a Samaritan.

17 And Iesus answered, and said, Are there not tenne clensed? but where are the nine?

18 There is none founde that returned to giue God praise, saue this stranger.

19 And he saide vnto him, Arise, goe thy way, thy faith hath saued thee.

20 And when hee was demaunded of the Pharises, when the kingdome of God shoulde come, he answered them, and said, The kingdome of God commeth not with obseruation.

21 Neither shall men say, Loe here, or lo there: for behold, the kingdome of God is within you.

22 And he saide vnto the disciples, The dayes will come, when ye shall desire to see one of the dayes of the Sonne of man, and ye shall not see it.

23 Then they shall say to you, Behold here, or beholde there: but goe not thither, neither follow them.

24 For as the lightening that lighteneth out of the one part vnder heauen, shineth vnto the other part vnder heauen, so shall the Sonne of man be in his day.

25 But first must he suffer many things, and be reprooued of this generation.

26 And as it was in the dayes of Noe, so shall it be in the dayes of the Sonne of man.

27 They ate, they dranke, they married wiues, and gaue in marriage vnto the day that Noe went into the Arke: and the flood came, and destroyed them all.

28 Likewise also, as it was in the dayes of Lot: they ate, they dranke, they bought, they solde, they planted, they built.

29 But in the day that Lot went out of Sodom, it rained fire and brimstone from heauen, and destroyed them all.

30 After these ensamples shall it be in the day when the Sonne of man is reueiled.

31 At that day hee that is vpon the house, and his stuffe in ye house, let him not come downe to take it out: and he that is in the fielde likewise, let him not turne backe to that he left behinde.

32 Remember Lots wife.

33 Whosoeuer will seeke to saue his soule, shall loose it: and whosoeuer shall loose it, shall get it life.

34 I tell you, in that night there shall be two in one bed: the one shalbe receiued, and the other shalbe left.

35 Two women shalbe grinding together: the one shalbe taken, and the other shalbe left.

36 Two shalbe in the fielde: one shalbe receiued, and another shalbe left.

37 And they answered, and saide to him, Where, Lord? And he said vnto them, Wheresoeuer the body is, thither shall also the eagles bee gathered together.

Luke 18

1 And he spake also a parable vnto them, to this ende, that they ought alwayes to pray, and not to waxe faint,

2 Saying, There was a iudge in a certaine citie, which feared not God, neither reuereced man.

3 And there was a widowe in that citie, which came vnto him, saying, Doe mee iustice against mine aduersarie.

4 And hee would not of a long time: but afterward he said with himselfe, Though I feare not God, nor reuerence man,

5 Yet because this widowe troubleth mee, I will doe her right, lest at the last shee come and make me wearie.

6 And the Lord said, Heare what the vnrighteous iudge saith.

7 Now shall not God auenge his elect, which cry day and night vnto him, yea, though he suffer long for them?

8 I tell you he will auenge them quickly: but when the Sonne of man commeth, shall he finde faith on the earth?

9 He spake also this parable vnto certaine which trusted in themselues that they were iust, and despised other.

10 Two men went vp into the Temple to pray: the one a Pharise, and the other a Publican.

11 The Pharise stoode and prayed thus with himselfe, O God, I thanke thee that I am not as other men, extortioners, vniust, adulterers, or euen as this Publican.

12 I fast twise in the weeke: I giue tithe of all that euer I possesse.

13 But the Publican standing a farre off, woulde not lift vp so much as his eyes to heauen, but smote his brest, saying, O God, be mercifull to me a sinner.

14 I tell you, this man departed to his house iustified, rather then the other: for euery man that exalteth himselfe, shall be brought lowe, and he that humbleth himselfe, shalbe exalted.

15 They brought vnto him also babes that he should touche them. And when his disciples sawe it, they rebuked them.

16 But Iesus called them vnto him, and said, Suffer the babes to come vnto mee, and forbid them not: for of such is the kingdome of God.

17 Verely I say vnto you, whosoeuer receiueth not the kingdome of God as a babe, he shall not enter therein.

18 Then a certaine ruler asked him, saying, Good Master, what ought I to doe, to inherite eternall life?

19 And Iesus said vnto him, Why callest thou me good? none is good, saue one, euen God.

20 Thou knowest the comandements, Thou shalt not commit adulterie: Thou shalt not kill: Thou shalt not steale: Thou shalt not beare false witnes: Honour thy father and thy mother.

21 And hee saide, All these haue I kept from my youth.

22 Nowe when Iesus heard that, he saide vnto him, Yet lackest thou one thing. Sell all that euer thou hast, and distribute vnto the poore, and thou shalt haue treasure in heauen, and come follow mee.

23 But when he heard those things, he was very heauie: for he was marueilous riche.

24 And when Iesus sawe him very sorowfull, he said, With what difficultie shall they that haue riches, enter into the kingdome of God!

25 Surely it is easier for a camel to go through a needles eye, then for a riche man to enter into the kingdome of God.

26 Then said they that heard it, And who then can be saued?

27 And he said, The things which are vnpossible with men, are possible with God.

28 Then Peter said, Loe, we haue left all, and haue followed thee.

29 And he said vnto them, Verely I say vnto you, there is no man that hath left house, or parents, or brethren, or wife, or children for the kingdome of Gods sake,

30 Which shall not receiue much more in this world, and in the world to come life euerlasting.

31 Then Iesus tooke vnto him ye twelue, and said vnto them, Beholde, we goe vp to Hierusalem, and all things shalbe fulfilled to the Sonne of man, that are writttn by the Prophets.

32 For he shall be deliuered vnto the Gentiles, and shalbe mocked, and shalbe spitefully entreated, and shalbe spitted on.

33 And when they haue scourged him, they will put him to death: but the thirde day hee shall rise againe.

34 But they vnderstood none of these things, and this saying was hidde from them, neither perceiued they the things, which were spoken.

35 And it came to passe, that as he was come neere vnto Iericho, a certaine blinde man sate by the way side, begging.

36 And when he heard the people passe by, he asked what it meant.

37 And they saide vnto him, that Iesus of Nazareth passed by.

38 Then hee cried, saying, Iesus the Sonne of Dauid, haue mercie on me.

39 And they which went before, rebuked him that he shoulde holde his peace, but he cried much more, O Sone of Dauid, haue mercie on me.

40 And Iesus stoode stil, and commanded him to be brought vnto him. And when he was come neere, he asked him,

41 Saying, What wilt thou that I doe vnto thee? And he said, Lord, that I may receiue my sight.

42 And Iesus said vnto him, Receiue thy sight: thy faith hath saued thee.

43 Then immediatly he receiued his sight, and followed him, praysing God: and all the people, when they sawe this, gaue praise to God.

Luke 19

1 Now when Iesus entred and passed through Iericho,

2 Beholde, there was a man named Zaccheus, which was the chiefe receiuer of the tribute, and he was riche.

3 And he sought to see Iesus, who hee should be, and coulde not for the preasse, because he was of a lowe stature.

4 Wherefore he ranne before, and climed vp into a wilde figge tree, that he might see him: for he should come that way.

5 And when Iesus came to the place, he looked vp, and saw him, and said vnto him, Zaccheus, come downe at once: for to day I must abide at thine house.

6 Then he came downe hastily, and receiued him ioyfully.

7 And when all they sawe it, they murmured, saying, that hee was gone in to lodge with a sinfull man.

8 And Zaccheus stood forth, and said vnto the Lord, Beholde, Lord, the halfe of my goods I giue to the poore: and if I haue taken from any man by forged cauillation, I restore him foure folde.

9 Then Iesus said to him, This day is saluation come vnto this house, forasmuch as hee is also become the sonne of Abraham.

10 For the Sonne of man is come to seeke, and to saue that which was lost.

11 And whiles they heard these thinges, hee continued and spake a parable, because hee was neere to Hierusalem, and because also they thought that the kingdom of God should shortly appeare.

12 He saide therefore, A certaine noble man went into a farre countrey, to receiue for himselfe a kingdome, and so to come againe.

13 And he called his ten seruants, and deliuered them ten pieces of money, and sayd vnto them, Occupie till I come.

14 Nowe his citizens hated him, and sent an ambassage after him, saying, We will not haue this man to reigne ouer vs.

15 And it came to passe, when hee was come againe, and had receiued his kingdome, that he commanded the seruants to be called to him, to whome he gaue his money, that he might knowe what euery man had gained.

16 Then came the first, saying, Lord, thy piece hath encreased ten pieces.

17 And he sayd vnto him, Well, good seruant: because thou hast bene faithfull in a very litle thing, take thou authoritie ouer ten cities.

18 And the second came, saying, Lord, thy piece hath encreased fiue pieces.

19 And to the same he sayd, Be thou also ruler ouer fiue cities.

20 So the other came, and sayd, Lord, beholde thy piece, which I haue laide vp in a napkin:

21 For I feared thee, because thou art a straight man: thou takest vp, that thou layedst not downe, and reapest that thou diddest not sowe.

22 Then he sayde vnto him, Of thine owne mouth will I iudge thee, O euill seruant. Thou knewest that I am a straight man, taking vp that I layd not downe, and reaping that I did not sowe.

23 Wherefore then gauest not thou my money into the banke, that at my coming I might haue required it with vantage?

24 And he sayd to them that stoode by, Take from him that piece, and giue it him that hath ten pieces.

25 (And they sayd vnto him, Lord, hee hath ten pieces.)

26 For I say vnto you, that vnto all them that haue, it shalbe giuen: and from him that hath not, euen that he hath, shalbe taken from him.

27 Moreouer, those mine enemies, which would not that I should reigne ouer them, bring hither, and slay them before me.

28 And when he had thus spoken, he went forth before, ascending vp to Hierusalem.

29 And it came to passe, when hee was come neere to Bethphage, and Bethania, besides the mount which is called the mount of Oliues, he sent two of his disciples,

30 Saying, Goe ye to the towne which is before you, wherein, assoone as ye are come, ye shall finde a colte tied, whereon neuer man sate: loose him, and bring him hither.

31 And if any man aske you, why ye loose him, thus shall ye say vnto him, Because the Lord hath neede of him.

32 So they that were sent, went their way, and found it as he had sayd vnto them.

33 And as they were loosing the colte, the owners thereof sayd vnto them, Why loose ye the colte?

34 And they sayd, The Lord hath neede of him.

35 So they brought him to Iesus, and they cast their garments on the colte, and set Iesus thereon.

36 And as he went, they spred their clothes in the way.

37 And when he was nowe come neere to the going downe of the mount of Oliues, the whole multitude of the disciples began to reioyce, and to prayse God with a loude voyce, for all the great workes that they had seene,

38 Saying, Blessed be the King that commeth in the Name of the Lord: peace in heauen, and glory in the highest places.

39 Then some of the Pharises of the companie sayd vnto him, Master, rebuke thy disciples.

40 But he answered, and sayd vnto them, I tell you, that if these should holde their peace, the stones would crie.

41 And when he was come neere, he behelde the Citie, and wept for it,

42 Saying, O if thou haddest euen knowen at the least in this thy day those things, which belong vnto thy peace! but nowe are they hid from thine eyes.

43 For the dayes shall come vpon thee, that thine enemies shall cast a trench about thee, and compasse thee round, and keepe thee in on euery side,

44 And shall make thee euen with ye ground, and thy children which are in thee, and they shall not leaue in thee a stone vpon a stone, because thou knewest not that season of thy visitation.

45 He went also into the Temple, and began to cast out them that solde therein, and them that bought,

46 Saying vnto them, It is written, Mine house is the house of prayer, but ye haue made it a denne of theeues.

47 And he taught dayly in the Temple. And the hie Priests and the Scribes, and the chiefe of the people sought to destroy him.

48 But they could not finde what they might doe to him: for all the people hanged vpon him when they heard him.

Luke 20

1 And it came to passe, that on one of those dayes, as he taught the people in the Temple, and preached the Gospel, the hie Priests and the Scribes came vpon him with the Elders,

2 And spake vnto him, saying, Tell vs by what authoritie thou doest these things, or who is hee that hath giuen thee this authoritie?

3 And he answered, and sayde vnto them, I also will aske you one thing: tell me therefore:

4 The baptisme of Iohn, was it from heauen, or of men?

5 And they reasoned within themselues, saying, If we shall say, From heauen, he will say, Why then beleeued ye him not?

6 But if we shall say, Of men, all the people will stone vs: for they be perswaded that Iohn was a Prophet.

7 Therefore they answered, that they could not tell whence it was.

8 Then Iesus sayd vnto them, Neither tell I you, by what authoritie I doe these things.

9 Then began he to speake to ye people this parable, A certaine man planted a vineyarde, and let it forth to husbandmen: and went into a strange countrey, for a great time.

10 And at the time conuenient he sent a seruant to the husbandmen, that they should giue him of the fruite of the vineyard: but the husbandmen did beate him, and sent him away emptie.

11 Againe he sent yet another seruant: and they did beate him, and foule entreated him, and sent him away emptie.

12 Moreouer he sent the third, and him they wounded, and cast out.

13 Then sayd the Lord of the vineyard, What shall I doe? I will send my beloued sonne: it may be that they will doe reuerence, when they see him.

14 But when the husbandmen sawe him, they reasoned with themselues, saying, This is the heire: come, let vs kill him, that the inheritance may be ours.

15 So they cast him out of the vineyarde, and killed him. What shall the Lord of the vineyarde therefore doe vnto them?

16 He will come and destroy these husbandmen, and wil giue out his vineyard to others. But when they heard it, they sayd, God forbid.

17 And he beheld them, and said, What meaneth this then that is written, The stone that the builders refused, that is made the head of the corner?

18 Whosoeuer shall fall vpon that stone, shall be broken: and on whomsoeuer it shall fall, it will grinde him to pouder.

19 Then the hie Priests, and the Scribes the same houre went about to lay hands on him: (but they feared the people) for they perceiued that he had spoken this parable against them.

20 And they watched him, and sent forth spies, which should faine themselues iust men, to take him in his talke, and to deliuer him vnto the power and authoritie of the gouernour.

21 And they asked him, saying, Master, we know that thou sayest, and teachest right, neither doest thou accept mans person, but teachest the way of God truely.

22 Is it lawfull for vs to giue Cesar tribute or no?

23 But he perceiued their craftines, and sayd vnto them, Why tempt ye me?

24 Shew me a penie. Whose image and superscription hath it? They answered, and sayd, Cesars.

25 Then he sayd vnto them, Giue then vnto Cesar the things which are Cesars, and to God those which are Gods.

26 And they could not reproue his saying before the people: but they marueiled at his answere, and helde their peace.

27 Then came to him certaine of the Sadduces (which denie that there is any resurrection) and they asked him,

28 Saying, Master, Moses wrote vnto vs, If any mans brother die hauing a wife, and hee die without children, that his brother should take his wife, and raise vp seede vnto his brother.

29 Now there were seuen brethren, and the first tooke a wife, and he dyed without children.

30 And the second tooke the wife, and he dyed childelesse.

31 Then the third tooke her: and so likewise the seuen dyed, and left no children.

32 And last of all the woman dyed also.

33 Therefore at the resurrection, whose wife of them shall she be? for seuen had her to wife.

34 Then Iesus answered, and sayd vnto them, The children of this world marry wiues, and are married.

35 But they which shalbe counted worthy to enioy that world, and the resurrection from the dead, neither marry wiues, neither are married.

36 For they can die no more, forasmuch as they are equall vnto the Angels, and are the sonnes of God, since they are the children of the resurrection.

37 And that the dead shall rise againe, euen Moses shewed it besides the bush, when he said, The Lord is the God of Abraham, and the God of Isaac, and the God of Iacob.

38 For he is not the God of the dead, but of them which liue: for all liue vnto him.

39 Then certaine of the Scribes answered, and sayd, Master, thou hast well sayd.

40 And after that, durst they not aske him any thing at all.

41 Then sayd he vnto them, Howe say they that Christ is Dauids sonne?

42 And Dauid himselfe sayth in the booke of the Psalmes, The Lord sayd vnto my Lord, Sit at my right hand,

43 Till I shall make thine enemies thy footestoole.

44 Seeing Dauid called him Lord, howe is he then his sonne?

45 Then in the audience of all the people he sayd vnto his disciples,

46 Beware of the Scribes, which willingly go in long robes, and loue salutations in the markets, and the highest seates in the assemblies, and the chiefe roomes at feastes:

47 Which deuoure widowes houses, and in shewe make long prayers: These shall receiue greater damnation.

Luke 21

1 And as he behelde, he sawe the rich men, which cast their giftes into the treasurie.

2 And he sawe also a certaine poore widowe which cast in thither two mites:

3 And he sayd, Of a trueth I say vnto you, that this poore widowe hath cast in more then they all.

4 For they all haue of their superfluitie cast into the offerings of God: but she of her penurie hath cast in all the liuing that she had.

5 Nowe as some spake of the Temple, how it was garnished with goodly stones, and with consecrate things, he sayd,

6 Are these ye things that ye looke vpon? the dayes will come wherein a stone shall not be left vpon a stone, that shall not be throwen downe.

7 Then they asked him, saying, Master, but when shall these things be? and what signe shall there be when these things shall come to passe?

8 And he sayd, Take heede, that ye be not deceiued: for many will come in my Name, saying, I am Christ, and the time draweth neere: follow ye not them therefore.

9 And when ye heare of warres and seditions, be not afraid: for these things must first come, but the ende foloweth not by and by.

10 Then said hee vnto them, Nation shall rise against nation, and kingdome against kingdome,

11 And great earthquakes shall be in diuers places, and hunger, and pestilence, and fearefull things, and great signes shall there be from heauen.

12 But before all these, they shall lay their hands on you, and persecute you, deliuering you vp to the assemblies, and into prisons, and bring you before Kings and rulers for my Names sake.

13 And this shall turne to you, for a testimoniall.

14 Lay it vp therefore in your heartes, that ye cast not before hand, what ye shall answere.

15 For I will giue you a mouth and wisdome, where against all your aduersaries shall not be able to speake, nor resist.

16 Yea, ye shalbe betrayed also of your parents, and of your brethren, and kinsmen, and friendes, and some of you shall they put to death.

17 And ye shall bee hated of all men for my Names sake.

18 Yet there shall not one heare of your heads perish.

19 By your patience possesse your soules.

20 And when ye see Hierusalem besieged with souldiers, then vnderstand that the desolation thereof is neere.

21 Then let them which are in Iudea, flee to the mountaines: and let them which are in the middes thereof, depart out: and let not them that are in the countrey, enter therein.

22 For these be the dayes of vengeance, to fulfill all things that are written.

23 But woe be to them that be with childe, and to them that giue sucke in those dayes: for there shalbe great distresse in this land, and wrath ouer this people.

24 And they shall fall on the edge of the sword, and shalbe led captiue into all nations, and Hierusalem shalbe troden vnder foote of the Gentiles, vntill the time of the Gentiles be fulfilled.

25 Then there shalbe signes in the sunne, and in the moone, and in the starres, and vpon the earth trouble among the nations with perplexitie: the sea and the waters shall roare.

26 And mens hearts shall faile them for feare, and for looking after those thinges which shall come on the worlde: for the powers of heauen shall be shaken.

27 And then shall they see the Sonne of man come in a cloude, with power and great glory.

28 And when these things beginne to come to passe, then looke vp, and lift vp your heades: for your redemption draweth neere.

29 And he spake to them a parable, Behold, the figge tree, and all trees,

30 When they nowe shoote foorth, ye seeing them, knowe of your owne selues, that sommer is then neere.

31 So likewise yee, when yee see these thinges come to passe, knowe ye that the kingdome of God is neere.

32 Verely I say vnto you, This age shall not passe, till all these things be done:

33 Heauen and earth shall passe away, but my wordes shall not passe away.

34 Take heede to your selues, lest at any time your hearts be oppressed with surfeting and drunkennesse, and cares of this life, and least that day come on you at vnwares.

35 For as a snare shall it come on all them that dwell on the face of the whole earth.

36 Watche therefore, and pray continually, that ye may be counted worthy to escape all these thinges that shall come to passe, and that ye may stand before the Sonne of man.

37 Nowe in the day time hee taught in the Temple, and at night hee went out, and abode in the mount that is called the mount of Oliues.

38 And all the people came in the morning to him, to heare him in the Temple.

Luke 22

1 Now the feast of vnleauened bread drewe neere, which is called the Passeouer.

2 And the hie Priests and Scribes sought how they might kill him: for they feared the people.

3 Then entred Satan into Iudas, who was called Iscariot, and was of the nomber of the twelue.

4 And he went his way, and communed with the hie Priestes and captaines, how he might betray him to them.

5 So they were glad, and agreed to giue him money.

6 And he consented, and sought opportunitie to betraye him vnto them, when the people were away.

7 Then came the day of vnleauened bread, when the Passeouer must be sacrificed.

8 And he sent Peter and Iohn, saying, Go and prepare vs the Passeouer, that we may eate it.

9 And they saide to him, Where wilt thou, that we prepare it?

10 Then he said vnto them, Beholde, when ye be entred into the citie, there shall a man meete you, bearing a pitcher of water: folowe him into the house that he entreth in,

11 And say vnto the good man of the house, The Master saith vnto thee, Where is the lodging where I shall eate my Passeouer with my disciples?

12 Then he shall shewe you a great hie chamber trimmed: there make it ready.

13 So they went, and found as he had said vnto them, and made readie the Passeouer.

14 And when the houre was come, hee sate downe, and the twelue Apostles with him.

15 Then he saide vnto them, I haue earnestly desired to eate this Passeouer with you, before I suffer.

16 For I say vnto you, Henceforth I will not eate of it any more, vntill it bee fulfilled in the kingdome of God.

17 And hee tooke the cup, and gaue thankes, and said, Take this, and deuide it among you,

18 For I say vnto you, I will not drinke of the fruite of the vine, vntill the kingdome of God be come.

19 And he tooke bread, and when he had giuen thankes, he brake it, and gaue to them, saying, This is my body, which is giuen for you: doe this in the remembrance of me.

20 Likewise also after supper he tooke the cup, saying, This cup is that newe Testament in my blood, which is shed for you.

21 Yet beholde, the hand of him that betrayeth me, is with me at the table.

22 And truely the Sonne of man goeth as it is appointed: but woe be to that man, by whom he is betrayed.

23 Then they began to enquire among themselues which of them it should be, that should do that.

24 And there arose also a strife among them, which of them should seeme to be ye greatest.

25 But hee saide vnto them, The Kings of the Gentiles reigne ouer them, and they that beare rule ouer them, are called bountifull.

26 But yee shall not be so: but let the greatest among you be as the least: and the chiefest as he that serueth.

27 For who is greater, he that sitteth at table, or he that serueth? Is not he that sitteth at table? And I am among you as he that serueth.

28 And yee are they which haue continued with me in my tentations.

29 Therefore I appoint vnto you a kingdome, as my Father hath appointed vnto me,

30 That ye may eate, and drinke at my table in my kingdome, and sit on seates, and iudge the twelue tribes of Israel.

31 And the Lord saide, Simon, Simon, beholde, Satan hath desired you, to winowe you as wheate.

32 But I haue prayed for thee, that thy faith faile not: therefore when thou art conuerted, strengthen thy brethren.

33 And he said vnto him, Lord, I am ready to goe with thee into prison, and to death.

34 But he said, I tell thee, Peter, the cocke shall not crowe this day, before thou hast thrise denied that thou knewest me.

35 And he saide vnto them, When I sent you without bagge, and scrip, and shooes, lacked ye any thing? And they said, Nothing.

36 Then he said to them, But nowe he that hath a bagge, let him take it, and likewise a scrip: and hee that hath none, let him sell his coate, and buy a sworde.

37 For I say vnto you, That yet the same which is written, must be perfourmed in me, Euen with the wicked was he nombred: for doubtlesse those things which are written of me, haue an ende.

38 And they said, Lord, beholde, here are two swordes. And he said vnto them, It is ynough.

39 And he came out, and went (as he was wont) to the mount of Oliues: and his disciples also followed him.

40 And when hee came to the place, hee said to them, Pray, lest ye enter into tentation.

41 And he was drawen aside from them about a stones cast, and kneeled downe, and prayed,

42 Saying, Father, if thou wilt, take away this cuppe from mee: neuerthelesse, not my will, but thine be done.

43 And there appeared an Angell vnto him from heauen, comforting him.

44 But being in an agonie, hee prayed more earnestly: and his sweate was like drops of blood, trickling downe to the ground.

45 And he rose vp from prayer, and came to his disciples, and found them sleeping for heauinesse.

46 And he said vnto them, Why sleepe ye? rise and pray, least ye enter into tentation.

47 And while he yet spake, beholde, a companie, and he that was called Iudas one of the twelue, went before them, and came neere vnto Iesus to kisse him.

48 And Iesus saide vnto him, Iudas, betrayest thou the Sonne of man with a kisse?

49 Now when they which were about him, saw what would follow, they said vnto him, Lord, shall we smite with sworde?

50 And one of them smote a seruant of the hie Priest, and strooke off his right eare.

51 Then Iesus answered, and said, Suffer them thus farre: and he touched his eare, and healed him.

52 Then Iesus said vnto the hie Priests, and captaines of the Temple, and the Elders which were come to him, Bee ye come out as vnto a theefe with swordes and staues?

53 When I was dayly with you in the Temple, yee stretched not foorth the handes against mee: but this is your very houre, and the power of darkenesse.

54 Then tooke they him, and led him, and brought him to the hie Priestes house. And Peter followed afarre off.

55 And when they had kindled a fire in the middes of the hall, and were set downe together, Peter also sate downe among them.

56 And a certaine mayde behelde him as hee sate by the fire, and hauing well looked on him, said, This man was also with him.

57 But he denied him, saying, Woman, I know him not.

58 And after a little while, another man sawe him, and saide, Thou art also of them. But Peter said, Man, I am not.

59 And about the space of an houre after, a certaine other affirmed, saying. Verely euen this man was with him: for he is also a Galilean.

60 And Peter saide, Man, I knowe not what thou sayest. And immediatly while hee yet spake, the cocke crewe.

61 Then the Lord turned backe, and looked vpon Peter: and Peter remembred the worde of the Lord, how he had said vnto him, Before the cocke crowe, thou shalt denie me thrise.

62 And Peter went out, and wept bitterly.

63 And the men that helde Iesus, mocked him, and strooke him.

64 And when they had blindfolded him, they smote him on the face, and asked him, saying, Prophecie who it is that smote thee.

65 And many other thinges blasphemously spake they against him.

66 And assoone as it was day, the Elders of the people, and the hie Priests and the Scribes came together, and led him into their councill,

67 Saying, Art thou that Christ? tell vs. And he said vnto them, If I tell you, ye wil not beleeue it.

68 And if also I aske you, you will not answere me, nor let me goe.

69 Hereafter shall the Sonne of man sit at the right hand of the power of God.

70 Then sayd they all, Art thou then ye Sonne of God? And he sayd to them, Ye say, that I am.

71 Then sayd they, What neede we any further witnes? for we our selues haue heard it of his owne mouth.

Luke 23

1 Then the whole multitude of them arose, and led him vnto Pilate.

2 And they began to accuse him, saying, We haue found this man peruerting the nation, and forbidding to pay tribute to Cesar, saying, That he is Christ a King.

3 And Pilate asked him, saying, Art thou the King of the Iewes? And hee answered him, and sayd, Thou sayest it.

4 Then sayd Pilate to the hie Priests, and to the people, I finde no fault in this man.

5 But they were the more fierce, saying, He moueth the people, teaching throughout all Iudea, beginning at Galile, euen to this place.

6 Nowe when Pilate heard of Galile, he asked whether the man were a Galilean.

7 And when he knewe that he was of Herods iurisdiction, he sent him to Herod, which was also at Hierusalem in those dayes.

8 And when Herod sawe Iesus, hee was exceedingly glad: for he was desirous to see him of a long season, because he had heard many things of him, and trusted to haue seene some signe done by him.

9 Then questioned hee with him of many things: but he answered him nothing.

10 The hie Priests also and Scribes stood forth, and accused him vehemently.

11 And Herod with his men of warre, despised him, and mocked him, and arayed him in white, and sent him againe to Pilate.

12 And the same day Pilate and Herod were made friends together: for before they were enemies one to another.

13 Then Pilate called together the hie Priests and the rulers, and the people,

14 And sayd vnto them, Ye haue brought this man vnto me, as one that peruerted the people: and beholde, I haue examined him before you, and haue found no fault in this man, of those things whereof ye accuse him:

15 No, nor yet Herod: for I sent you to him: and loe, nothing worthy of death is done of him.

16 I will therefore chastise him, and let him loose.

17 (For of necessitie hee must haue let one loose vnto them at the feast.)

18 Then all ye multitude cried at once, saying, Away with him, and deliuer vnto vs Barabbas.

19 Which for a certaine insurrection made in the citie, and murder, was cast in prison.

20 Then Pilate spake againe to them, willing to let Iesus loose.

21 But they cried, saying, Crucifie, crucifie him.

22 And he sayd vnto them the third time, But what euill hath he done? I finde no cause of death in him: I will therefore chastise him, and let him loose.

23 But they were instant with loude voyces, and required that he might be crucified: and the voyces of them and of the hie Priests preuailed.

24 So Pilate gaue sentence, that it should be as they required.

25 And he let loose vnto them him that for insurrection and murder was cast into prison, whome they desired, and deliuered Iesus to doe with him what they would.

26 And as they led him away, they caught one Simon of Cyrene, comming out of the fielde, and on him they layde the crosse, to beare it after Iesus.

27 And there followed him a great multitude of people, and of women, which women bewailed and lamented him.

28 But Iesus turned backe vnto them, and said, Daughters of Hierusalem, weepe not for me, but weepe for your selues, and for your children.

29 For behold, the dayes wil come, when men shall say, Blessed are the barren, and the wombes that neuer bare, and the pappes which neuer gaue sucke.

30 Then shall they begin to say to the mountaines, Fall on vs: and to the hilles, Couer vs.

31 For if they doe these things to a greene tree, what shalbe done to the drie?

32 And there were two others, which were euill doers, led with him to be slaine.

33 And when they were come to the place, which is called Caluarie, there they crucified him, and the euill doers: one at the right hand, and the other at the left.

34 Then sayd Iesus, Father, forgiue them: for they know not what they doe. And they parted his raiment, and cast lottes.

35 And the people stoode, and behelde: and the rulers mocked him with them, saying, He saued others: let him saue himselfe, if hee be that Christ, the Chosen of God.

36 The souldiers also mocked him, and came and offered him vineger,

37 And said, If thou be the King of the Iewes, saue thy selfe.

38 And a superscription was also written ouer him, in Greeke letters, and in Latin, and in Hebrewe, THIS IS THAT KING OF THE JEWES.

39 And one of the euill doers, which were hanged, railed on him, saying, If thou be that Christ, saue thy selfe and vs.

40 But the other answered, and rebuked him, saying, Fearest thou not God, seeing thou art in the same condemnation?

41 We are in deede righteously here: for we receiue things worthy of that we haue done: but this man hath done nothing amisse.

42 And he sayd vnto Iesus, Lord, remember me, when thou commest into thy kingdome.

43 Then Iesus said vnto him, Verely I say vnto thee, to day shalt thou be with me in Paradise.

44 And it was about the sixt houre: and there was a darkenes ouer all the land, vntill the ninth houre.

45 And the Sunne was darkened, and the vaile of the Temple rent through the middes.

46 And Iesus cryed with a loude voyce, and sayd, Father, into thine hands I commend my spirit. And when hee thus had sayd, hee gaue vp the ghost.

47 Nowe when the Centurion saw what was done, he glorified God, saying, Of a suretie this man was iust.

48 And all the people that came together to that sight, beholding the things, which were done, smote their brestes, and returned.

49 And all his acquaintance stood a farre off, and the women that followed him from Galile, beholding these things.

50 And beholde, there was a man named Ioseph, which was a counseller, a good man and a iust.

51 Hee did not consent to the counsell and deede of them, which was of Arimathea, a citie of the Iewes: who also himselfe waited for the kingdome of God.

52 He went vnto Pilate, and asked the body of Iesus,

53 And tooke it downe, and wrapped it in a linnen cloth, and laide it in a tombe hewen out of a rocke, wherein was neuer man yet laide.

54 And that day was the preparation, and the Sabbath drewe on.

55 And the women also that followed after, which came with him from Galile, behelde the sepulchre, and how his body was layd.

56 And they returned and prepared odours, and ointments, and rested the Sabbath day according to the commandement.

Luke 24

1 Nowe the first day of the weeke early in the morning, they came vnto the sepulchre, and brought the odours, which they had prepared, and certaine women with them.

2 And they found the stone rolled away from the sepulchre,

3 And went in, but found not the body of the Lord Iesus.

4 And it came to passe, that as they were amased thereat, beholde, two men suddenly stood by them in shining vestures.

5 And as they were afraide, and bowed downe their faces to the earth, they sayd to them, Why seeke ye him that liueth, among the dead?

6 He is not here, but is risen: remember how he spake vnto you, when he was yet in Galile,

7 Saying, that the sonne of man must be deliuered into the hands of sinfull men, and be crucified, and the third day rise againe.

8 And they remembred his wordes,

9 And returned from the sepulchre, and tolde all these things vnto the eleuen, and to all the remnant.

10 Now it was Mary Magdalene, and Ioanna, and Mary the mother of Iames, and other women with them, which tolde these things vnto the Apostles.

11 But their wordes seemed vnto them, as a fained thing, neither beleeued they them.

12 Then arose Peter, and ran vnto the sepulchre, and looked in, and saw the linnen clothes laide by themselues, and departed wondering in himselfe at that which was come to passe.

13 And beholde, two of them went that same day to a towne which was from Hierusalem about threescore furlongs, called Emmaus.

14 And they talked together of al these things that were done.

15 And it came to passe, as they communed together, and reasoned, that Iesus himselfe drewe neere, and went with them.

16 But their eyes were holden, that they could not know him.

17 And he sayd vnto them, What maner of communications are these that ye haue one to another as ye walke and are sad?

18 And the one (named Cleopas) answered, and sayd vnto him, Art thou onely a stranger in Hierusalem, and hast not knowen the things which are come to passe therein in these dayes?

19 And he said vnto them, What things? And they sayd vnto him, Of Iesus of Nazareth, which was a Prophet, mightie in deede and in word before God, and all people,

20 And howe the hie Priests, and our rulers deliuered him to be condemned to death, and haue crucified him.

21 But we trusted that it had bene he that should haue deliuered Israel, and as touching all these things, to day is ye third day, that they were done.

22 Yea, and certaine women among vs made vs astonied, which came early vnto the sepulchre.

23 And when they found not his body, they came, saying, that they had also seene a vision of Angels, which sayd, that he was aliue.

24 Therefore certaine of them which were with vs, went to the sepulchre, and found it euen so as the women had sayd, but him they saw not.

25 Then he sayd vnto them, O fooles and slowe of heart to beleeue all that the Prophets haue spoken!

26 Ought not Christ to haue suffered these things, and to enter into his glory?

27 And he began at Moses, and at all the Prophets, and interpreted vnto them in all the Scriptures the things which were written of him.

28 And they drew neere vnto ye towne, which they went to, but he made as though hee would haue gone further.

29 But they constrained him, saying, Abide with vs: for it is towards night, and the day is farre spent. So he went in to tarie with them.

30 And it came to passe, as hee sate at table with them, he tooke the bread, and blessed, and brake it, and gaue it to them.

31 Then their eyes were opened, and they knewe him: and he was no more seene of them.

32 And they saide betweene themselues, Did not our heartes burne within vs, while he talked with vs by the way, and when he opened to vs the Scriptures?

33 And they rose vp the same houre, and returned to Hierusalem, and found the Eleuen gathered together, and them that were with them,

34 Which said, The Lord is risen in deede, and hath appeared to Simon.

35 Then they tolde what things were done in the way, and howe he was knowen of them in breaking of bread.

36 And as they spake these things, Iesus himselfe stoode in the middes of them, and saide vnto them, Peace be to you.

37 But they were abashed and afraide, supposing that they had seene a spirit.

38 Then he saide vnto them, Why are ye troubled? and wherefore doe doutes arise in your hearts?

39 Beholde mine handes and my feete: for it is I my selfe: handle me, and see: for a spirit hath not flesh and bones, as ye see me haue.

40 And when he had thus spoken, he shewed them his hands and feete.

41 And while they yet beleeued not for ioy, and wondred, he saide vnto them, Haue ye here any meate?

42 And they gaue him a piece of a broyled fish, and of an honie combe,

43 And hee tooke it, and did eate before them.

44 And he saide vnto them, These are the wordes, which I spake vnto you while I was yet with you, that all must be fulfilled which are written of me in the Lawe of Moses, and in the Prophets, and in the Psalmes.

45 Then opened he their vnderstanding, that they might vnderstand the Scriptures,

46 And said vnto them, Thus is it written, and thus it behoued Christ to suffer, and to rise againe from the dead the third day,

47 And that repentance, and remission of sinnes should be preached in his Name among all nations, beginning at Hierusalem.

48 Nowe ye are witnesses of these things.

49 And beholde, I doe sende the promise of my Father vpon you: but tary ye in the citie of Hierusalem, vntill ye be endued with power from an hie.

50 Afterward he lead them out into Bethania, and lift vp his hands, and blessed them.

51 And it came to passe, that as he blessed them, he departed from them, and was caried vp into heauen.

52 And they worshipped him, and returned to Hierusalem with great ioy,

53 And were continually in the Temple, praysing, and lauding God, Amen.

John

John 1

1 In the beginning was that Word, and that Word was with God, and that Word was God.
2 This same was in the beginning with God.
3 All things were made by it, and without it was made nothing that was made.
4 In it was life, and that life was the light of men.
5 And that light shineth in the darkenesse, and the darkenesse comprehended it not.
6 There was a man sent from God, whose name was Iohn.
7 This same came for a witnesse, to beare witnesse of that light, that all men through him might beleeue.
8 He was not that light, but was sent to beare witnesse of that light.
9 This was that true light, which lighteth euery man that commeth into the world.
10 He was in the world, and the worlde was made by him: and the worlde knewe him not.
11 He came vnto his owne, and his owne receiued him not.
12 But as many as receiued him, to them he gaue prerogatiue to be the sonnes of God, euen to them that beleeue in his Name.
13 Which are borne not of blood, nor of the will of the flesh, nor of ye wil of man, but of God.
14 And that Word was made flesh, and dwelt among vs, (and we sawe the glorie thereof, as the glorie of the onely begotten Sonne of the Father) full of grace and trueth.
15 Iohn bare witnesse of him, and cryed, saying, This was he of whom I said, He that commeth after me, was before me: for he was better then I.
16 And of his fulnesse haue all we receiued, and grace for grace.
17 For the Lawe was giuen by Moses, but grace, and trueth came by Iesus Christ.
18 No man hath seene God at any time: that onely begotten Sonne, which is in the bosome of the Father, he hath declared him.
19 Then this is the record of Iohn, when the Iewes sent Priestes and Leuites from Hierusalem, to aske him, Who art thou?
20 And he confessed and denied not, and said plainely, I am not that Christ.
21 And they asked him, What then? Art thou Elias? And he said, I am not. Art thou that Prophet? And he answered, No.
22 Then said they vnto him, Who art thou, that we may giue an answere to them that sent vs? What sayest thou of thy selfe?
23 He said, I am the voyce of him that cryeth in the wildernesse, Make straight the way of the Lord, as said the Prophet Esaias.
24 Nowe they which were sent, were of the Pharises.
25 And they asked him, and saide vnto him, Why baptizest thou then, if thou be not that Christ, neither Elias, nor that Prophet?
26 Iohn answered them, saying, I baptize with water: but there is one among you, whom ye knowe not.
27 He it is that commeth after me, which was before me, whose shoe latchet I am not worthie to vnloose.
28 These things were done in Bethabara beyond Iordan, where Iohn did baptize.
29 The next day Iohn, seeth Iesus comming vnto him, and saith, Beholde that Lambe of God, which taketh away the sinne of the world.
30 This is he of whom I saide, After me commeth a man, which was before me: for he was better then I.
31 And I knewe him not: but because he should be declared to Israel, therefore am I come, baptizing with water.
32 So Iohn bare recorde, saying, I beholde that Spirit come downe from heauen, like a doue, and it abode vpon him,
33 And I knewe him not: but he that sent me to baptize with water, he saide vnto me, Vpon whom thou shalt see that Spirit come downe, and tary still on him, that is he which baptizeth with the holy Ghost.
34 And I sawe, and bare record that this is that Sonne of God.
35 The next day, Iohn stoode againe, and two of his disciples.
36 And he behelde Iesus walking by, and said, Beholde that Lambe of God.
37 And the two disciples heard him speake, and followed Iesus.
38 Then Iesus turned about, and saw them follow, and saide vnto them, What seeke ye? And they saide vnto him, Rabbi (which is to say by interpretation, Master) where dwellest thou?
39 He saide vnto them, Come, and see. They came and sawe where hee dwelt, and abode with him that day: for it was about the tenth houre.
40 Andrew, Simon Peters brother, was one of the two which had heard it of Iohn, and that followed him.
41 The same founde his brother Simon first, and said vnto him, We haue founde that Messias, which is by interpretation, that Christ.
42 And he brought him to Iesus. And Iesus behelde him, and saide, Thou art Simon the sonne of Iona: thou shalt be called Cephas, which is by interpretation, a stone.
43 The day following, Iesus woulde goe into Galile, and founde Philip, and said vnto him, Followe me.
44 Nowe Philip was of Bethsaida, the citie of Andrew and Peter.
45 Philippe founde Nathanael, and saide vnto him, Wee haue founde him of whom Moses did write in the Lawe, and the Prophetes, Iesus that sonne of Ioseph, that was of Nazareth.
46 Then Nathanael sayde vnto him, Can there any good thing come out of Nazareth? Philip saide to him, Come, and see.
47 Iesus sawe Nathanael comming to him, and saide of him, Beholde in deede an Israelite, in whom is no guile.
48 Nathanael sayde vnto him, Whence knewest thou mee? Iesus answered, and sayd vnto him, Before that Philip called thee, when thou wast vnder the figge tree, I sawe thee.
49 Nathanael answered, and saide vnto him, Rabbi, thou art that Sonne of God: thou art that King of Israel.
50 Iesus answered, and sayde vnto him, Because I sayde vnto thee, I sawe thee vnder the figtree, beleeuest thou? thou shalt see greater things then thee.
51 And he saide vnto him, Verely, verely I say vnto you, hereafter shall yee see heauen open, and the Angels of God ascending, and descending vpon that Sonne of man.

John 2

1 And the thirde day, was there a mariage in Cana a towne of Galile, and the mother of Iesus was there.
2 And Iesus was called also, and his disciples vnto the mariage.
3 Nowe when the wine failed, the mother of Iesus saide vnto him, They haue no wine.
4 Iesus saide vnto her, Woman, what haue I to doe with thee? mine houre is not yet come.
5 His mother saide vnto the seruants, Whatsoeuer he sayeth vnto you, doe it.
6 And there were set there, sixe waterpots of stone, after the maner of the purifying of the Iewes, conteining two or three firkins a piece.
7 And Iesus sayde vnto them, Fill the waterpots with water. Then they filled them vp to the brim.
8 Then he sayde vnto them, Draw out nowe and beare vnto the gouernour of the feast. So they bare it.
9 Nowe when the gouernour of the feast had tasted the water that was made wine, (for he knewe not whence it was: but the seruants, which drewe the water, knewe) the gouernour of ye feast called the bridegrome,
10 And saide vnto him, All men at the beginning set foorth good wine, and when men haue well drunke, then that which is worse: but thou hast kept backe the good wine vntill nowe.
11 This beginning of miracles did Iesus in Cana a towne of Galile, and shewed forth his glorie: and his disciples beleeued on him.
12 After that, he went downe into Capernaum, he and his mother, and his brethren, and his disciples: but they continued not many daies there.
13 For the Iewes Passeouer was at hande. Therefore Iesus went vp to Hierusalem.
14 And he found in the Temple those that sold oxen, and sheepe, and doues, and changers of money, sitting there.

15 Then hee made a scourge of small cordes, and draue them all out of the Temple with the sheepe and oxen, and powred out the changers money, and ouerthrewe the tables,

16 And said vnto them that solde doues, Take these things hence: make not my fathers house, an house of marchandise.

17 And his disciples remembred, that it was written, The zeale of thine house hath eaten me vp.

18 Then answered the Iewes, and saide vnto him, What signe shewest thou vnto vs, that thou doest these things?

19 Iesus answered, and said vnto them, Destroy this Temple, and in three daies I will raise it vp againe.

20 Then said the Iewes, Fourtie and sixe yeeres was this Temple a building, and wilt thou reare it vp in three daies?

21 But he spake of the temple of his bodie.

22 Assoone therefore as he was risen from the dead, his disciples remembred that hee thus sayde vnto them: and they beleeued the Scripture, and the worde which Iesus had saide.

23 Nowe when hee was at Hierusalem at the Passeouer in the feast, many beleeued in his Name, when they sawe his miracles which he did.

24 But Iesus did not commit him selfe vnto them, because he knewe them all,

25 And had no neede that any should testifie of man: for he knewe what was in man.

John 3

1 There was nowe a man of the Pharises, named Nicodemus, a ruler of the Iewes.

2 This man came to Iesus by night, and sayd vnto him, Rabbi, we knowe ye thou art a teacher come from God: for no man could do these miracles that thou doest, except God were with him.

3 Iesus answered, and said vnto him, Verely, verely I say vnto thee, except a man be borne againe, he can not see the kingdome of God.

4 Nicodemus sayde vnto him, Howe can a man be borne which is olde? can he enter into his mothers wombe againe, and be borne?

5 Iesus answered, Verely, verely I say vnto thee, except that a man be borne of water and of the Spirite, hee can not enter into the kingdome of God.

6 That which is borne of the flesh, is flesh: and that that is borne of the Spirit, is spirit.

7 Marueile not that I said to thee, Yee must be borne againe.

8 The winde bloweth where it listeth, and thou hearest the sound thereof, but canst not tell whence it commeth, and whither it goeth: so is euery man that is borne of the Spirit.

9 Nicodemus answered, and said vnto him, Howe can these things be?

10 Iesus answered, and saide vnto him, Art thou a teacher of Israel, and knowest not these things?

11 Verely, verely I say vnto thee, wee speake that we know, and testifie that we haue seene: but yee receiue not our witnesse.

12 If when I tel you earthly things, ye beleeue not, howe should yee beleeue, if I shall tel you of heauenly things?

13 For no man ascendeth vp to heauen, but he that hath descended from heauen, that Sonne of man which is in heauen.

14 And as Moses lift vp the serpent in the wildernesse, so must that Sonne of man be lift vp,

15 That whosoeuer beleeueth in him, shoulde not perish, but haue eternall life.

16 For God so loued the worlde, that hee hath giuen his onely begotten Sonne, that whosoeuer beleeueth in him, should not perish, but haue euerlasting life.

17 For God sent not his Sonne into the world, that he should condemne the world, but that the world through him might be saued.

18 Hee that beleeueth in him, is not condemned: but hee that beleeueth not, is condemned already, because he hath not beleeued in the Name of that onely begotten Sonne of God.

19 And this is the condemnation, that that light came into the worlde, and men loued darknesse rather then that light, because their deedes were euill.

20 For euery man that euill doeth, hateth the light, neither commeth to light, least his deedes should be reprooued.

21 But he that doeth trueth, commeth to the light, that his deedes might bee made manifest, that they are wrought according to God.

22 After these things, came Iesus and his disciples into the lande of Iudea, and there taried with them, and baptized.

23 And Iohn also baptized in Enon besides Salim, because there was much water there: and they came, and were baptized.

24 For Iohn was not yet cast into prison.

25 Then there arose a question betweene Iohns disciples and the Iewes, about purifying.

26 And they came vnto Iohn, and saide vnto him, Rabbi, he that was with thee beyond Iorden, to whom thou barest witnesse, behold, he baptizeth, and all men come to him.

27 Iohn answered, and saide, A man can receiue nothing, except it be giuen him from heauen.

28 Yee your selues are my witnesses, that I sayde, I am not that Christ, but that I am sent before him.

29 He that hath the bride, is the bridegrome: but the friend of the bridegrome which standeth and heareth him, reioyceth greatly, because of the bridegromes voyce. This my ioy therefore is fulfilled.

30 He must increase, but I must decrease.

31 Hee that is come from an hie, is aboue all: he that is of the earth, is of the earth, and speaketh of the earth: hee that is come from heauen, is aboue all.

32 And what hee hath seene and heard, that he testifieth: but no man receiueth his testimonie.

33 He that hath receiued his testimonie, hath sealed that God is true.

34 For hee whome God hath sent, speaketh the woordes of God: for God giueth him not the Spirit by measure.

35 The Father loueth the Sonne, and hath giuen all things into his hande.

36 Hee that beleeueth in the Sonne, hath euerlasting life, and hee that obeyeth not the Sonne, shall not see life, but the wrath of God abideth on him.

John 4

1 Nowe when the Lord knew, how the Pharises had heard, that Iesus made and baptized moe disciples then Iohn,

2 (Though Iesus himselfe baptized not: but his disciples)

3 Hee left Iudea, and departed againe into Galile.

4 And he must needes goe through Samaria.

5 Then came hee to a citie of Samaria called Sychar, neere vnto the possession that Iacob gaue to his sonne Ioseph.

6 And there was Iacobs well. Iesus then wearied in the iourney, sate thus on the well: it was about the sixt houre.

7 There came a woman of Samaria to drawe water. Iesus sayd vnto her, Giue me drinke.

8 For his disciples were gone away into the citie, to buy meate.

9 Then sayde the woman of Samaria vnto him, Howe is it, that thou being a Iewe, askest drinke of me, which am a woman of Samaria? For the Iewes meddle not with the Samaritans.

10 Iesus answered and saide vnto her, If thou knewest that gift of God, and who it is that saieth to thee, Giue mee drinke, thou wouldest haue asked of him, and hee woulde haue giuen thee, water of life.

11 The woman saide vnto him, Sir, thou hast nothing to drawe with, and the well is deepe: from whence then hast thou that water of life?

12 Art thou greater then our father Iacob, which gaue vs the well, and hee himselfe dranke thereof, and his sonnes, and his cattell?

13 Iesus answered, and said vnto her, Whosoeuer drinketh of this water, shall thirst againe:

14 But whosoeuer drinketh of the water that I shall giue him, shall neuer be more a thirst: but the water that I shall giue him, shalbe in him a well of water, springing vp into euerlasting life.

15 The woman said vnto him, Syr, giue me of that water, that I may not thirst, neither come hither to drawe.

16 Iesus said vnto her, Go, call thine husband, and come hither.

17 The woman answered, and saide, I haue no husband. Iesus said vnto her, Thou hast well said, I haue no husband.

18 For thou hast had fiue husbands, and he whom thou nowe hast, is not thine husband: that saidest thou truely.

19 The woman saide vnto him, Sir, I see that thou art a Prophet.

20 Our fathers worshipped in this mountaine, and ye say, that in Ierusalem is the place where men ought to worship.

21 Iesus saide vnto her, Woman, beleeue me, the houre commeth, when ye shall neither in this mountaine, nor at Hierusalem worship ye Father.

22 Ye worship that which ye knowe not: we worship that which we knowe: for saluation is of the Iewes.

23 But the houre commeth, and nowe is, when the true worshippers shall worship the Father in spirit, and trueth: for the Father requireth euen such to worship him.

24 God is a Spirite, and they that worship him, must worship him in spirit and trueth.

25 The woman said vnto him, I knowe well that Messias shall come which is called Christ: when he is come, he will tell vs all things.

26 Iesus said vnto her, I am he, that speake vnto thee.

27 And vpon that, came his disciples, and marueiled that he talked with a woman: yet no man said vnto him, What askest thou? or why talkest thou with her?

28 The woman then left her waterpot, and went her way into the citie, and said to the men,

29 Come, see a man which hath tolde me all things that euer I did: is not he that Christ?

30 Then they went out of the citie, and came vnto him.

31 In the meane while, the disciples prayed him, saying, Master, eate.

32 But he said vnto them, I haue meate to eate that ye know not of.

33 Then said ye disciples betweene themselues, Hath any man brought him meate?

34 Iesus saide vnto them, My meate is that I may doe the will of him that sent me, and finish his worke.

35 Say not ye, There are yet foure monethes, and then commeth haruest? Beholde, I say vnto you, Lift vp your eyes, and looke on the regions: for they are white alreadie vnto haruest.

36 And he that reapeth, receiueth rewarde, and gathereth fruite vnto life eternall, that both he that soweth, and he that reapeth, might reioyce together.

37 For herein is the saying true, that one soweth, and an other reapeth.

38 I sent you to reape that, whereon ye bestowed no labour: other men laboured, and ye are entred into their labours.

39 Nowe many of the Samaritans of that citie beleeued in him, for the saying of the woman which testified, He hath tolde me all things that euer I did.

40 Then when the Samaritans were come vnto him, they besought him, that he woulde tarie with them: and he abode there two dayes.

41 And many moe beleeued because of his owne word.

42 And they said vnto the woman, Nowe we beleeue, not because of thy saying: for we haue heard him our selues, and knowe that this is in deede that Christ the Sauiour of the world.

43 So two dayes after he departed thence, and went into Galile.

44 For Iesus himselfe had testified, that a Prophet hath none honour in his owne countrey.

45 Then when he was come into Galile, the Galileans receiued him, which had seene all the things that he did at Hierusalem at the feast: for they went also vnto the feast.

46 And Iesus came againe into Cana a towne of Galile, where he had made of water, wine. And there was a certaine ruler, whose sonne was sicke at Capernaum.

47 When he heard that Iesus was come out of Iudea into Galile, he went vnto him, and besought him that he would goe downe, and heale his sonne: for he was euen ready to die.

48 Then saide Iesus vnto him, Except ye see signes and wonders, ye will not beleeue.

49 The ruler said vnto him, Syr, goe downe before my sonne dye.

50 Iesus said vnto him, Go thy way, thy sonne liueth: and the man beleeued the worde that Iesus had spoken vnto him, and went his way.

51 And as he was nowe going downe, his seruants met him, saying, Thy sonne liueth.

52 Then enquired he of them the houre when he began to amend. And they said vnto him, Yesterday the seuenth houre the feuer left him.

53 Then the father knew, that it was the same houre in the which Iesus had said vnto him, Thy sonne liueth. And he beleeued, and all his houshold.

54 This second miracle did Iesus againe, after he was come out of Iudea into Galile.

John 5

1 After that, there was a feast of the Iewes, and Iesus went vp to Hierusalem.

2 And there is at Hierusalem by the place of the sheepe, a poole called in Ebrew Bethesda, hauing fiue porches:

3 In the which lay a great multitude of sicke folke, of blinde, halte, and withered, wayting for the mouing of the water.

4 For an Angel went downe at a certaine season into the poole, and troubled the water: whosoeuer then first, after the stirring of the water, stepped in, was made whole of whatsoeuer disease he had.

5 And a certaine man was there, which had bene diseased eight and thirtie yeeres.

6 When Iesus sawe him lie, and knew that he nowe long time had bene diseased, he saide vnto him, Wilt thou be made whole?

7 The sicke man answered him, Sir, I haue no man, when the water is troubled, to put me into the poole: but while I am comming, another steppeth downe before me.

8 Iesus said vnto him, Rise: take vp thy bed, and walke.

9 And immediatly the man was made whole, and tooke vp his bed, and walked: and the same day was the Sabbath.

10 The Iewes therefore said to him that was made whole, It is the Sabbath day: it is not lawfull for thee to cary thy bed.

11 He answered them, He that made me whole, he said vnto me, Take vp thy bed, and walke.

12 Then asked they him, What man is that which said vnto thee, Take vp thy bed and walke?

13 And he that was healed, knewe not who it was: for Iesus had conueied himselfe away from the multitude that was in that place.

14 And after that, Iesus founde him in the Temple, and said vnto him, Beholde, thou art made whole: sinne no more, lest a worse thing come vnto thee.

15 The man departed and tolde the Iewes that it was Iesus, which had made him whole.

16 And therefore the Iewes did persecute Iesus, and sought to slay him, because he had done these things on the Sabbath day.

17 But Iesus answered them, My Father worketh hitherto, and I worke.

18 Therefore the Iewes sought the more to kill him: not onely because he had broken the Sabbath: but said also that God was his Father, and made himselfe equall with God.

19 Then answered Iesus, and said vnto them, Verely, verely I say vnto you, The Sonne can doe nothing of himselfe, saue that he seeth the Father doe: for whatsoeuer things he doth, the same things doeth the Sonne in like maner.

20 For the Father loueth the Sonne, and sheweth him all things, whatsoeuer he himselfe doeth, and he will shewe him greater workes then these, that ye should marueile.

21 For likewise as the Father rayseth vp the dead, and quickeneth them, so the Sonne quickeneth whom he will.

22 For the Father iudgeth no man, but hath committed all iudgement vnto the Sonne,

23 Because that all men shoulde honour the Sonne, as they honour the Father: he that honoureth not the Sonne, the same honoureth not the Father, which hath sent him.

24 Verely, verely I say vnto you, he that heareth my worde, and beleeueth him that sent me, hath euerlasting life, and shall not come into condemnation, but hath passed from death vnto life.

25 Verely, verely I say vnto you, the houre shall come, and now is, when the dead shall heare the voyce of the Sonne of God: and they that heare it, shall liue.

26 For as the Father hath life in himselfe, so likewise hath he giuen to the Sonne to haue life in himselfe,

27 And hath giuen him power also to execute iudgement, in that he is the Sonne of man.

28 Marueile not at this: for the houre shall come, in the which all that are in the graues, shall heare his voyce.

29 And they shall come foorth, that haue done good, vnto ye resurrection of life: but they that haue done euil, vnto the resurrection of condemnation.

30 I can doe nothing of mine owne selfe: as I heare, I iudge: and my iudgement is iust, because I seeke not mine owne will, but the will of the Father who hath sent me.

31 If I should beare witnesse of my selfe, my witnesse were not true.

32 There is another that beareth witnesse of me, and I know that the witnesse, which he beareth of me, is true.

33 Ye sent vnto Iohn, and he bare witnesse vnto the trueth.

34 But I receiue not the record of man: neuerthelesse these things I say, that ye might be saued.

35 He was a burning, and a shining candle: and ye would for a season haue reioyced in his light.

36 But I haue greater witnesse then the witnesse of Iohn: for the workes which the Father hath giuen me to finish, the same workes that I doe, beare witnesse of me, that the Father sent me.

37 And the Father himselfe, which hath sent me, beareth witnesse of me. Ye haue not heard his voyce at any time, neither haue ye seene his shape.

38 And his worde haue you not abiding in you: for whom he hath sent, him ye beleeued not.

39 Searche the Scriptures: for in them ye thinke to haue eternall life, and they are they which testifie of me.

40 But ye will not come to me, that ye might haue life.

41 I receiue not the prayse of men.

42 But I know you, that ye haue not the loue of God in you.

43 I am come in my Fathers Name, and ye receiue me not: if another shall come in his owne name, him will ye receiue.

44 How can ye beleeue, which receiue honour one of another, and seeke not the honour that commeth of God alone?

45 Doe not thinke that I will accuse you to my Father: there is one that accuseth you, euen Moses, in whom ye trust.

46 For had ye beleeued Moses, ye would haue beleeued me: for he wrote of me.

47 But if ye beleeue not his writings, how shall ye beleeue my wordes?

John 6

1 After these thinges, Iesus went his way ouer the sea of Galile, which is Tiberias.

2 And a great multitude followed him, because they sawe his miracles, which hee did on them that were diseased.

3 Then Iesus went vp into a mountaine, and there he sate with his disciples.

4 Now the Passeouer, a feast of the Iewes, was neere.

5 Then Iesus lift vp his eyes, and seeing that a great multitude came vnto him, hee sayde vnto Philippe, Whence shall we buy breade, that these might eate?

6 (And this he sayde to prooue him: for hee himselfe knewe what he would doe.)

7 Philippe answered him, Two hundreth penie worth of bread is not sufficient for them, that euery one of them may take a litle.

8 Then saide vnto him one of his disciples, Andrew, Simon Peters brother,

9 There is a little boy heere, which hath fiue barlie loaues, and two fishes: but what are they among so many?

10 And Iesus saide, Make ye people sit downe. (Nowe there was much grasse in that place.) Then the men sate downe in nomber, about fiue thousande.

11 And Iesus tooke the bread, and gaue thanks, and gaue to the disciples, and the disciples, to them that were set downe: and likewise of the fishes as much as they would.

12 And when they were satisfied, he said vnto his disciples, Gather vp the broken meat which remaineth, that nothing be lost.

13 Then they gathered it together, and filled twelue baskets with the broken meat of the fiue barly loaues, which remained vnto them that had eaten.

14 Then the men, when they had seene the miracle that Iesus did, saide, This is of a trueth that Prophet that should come into the world.

15 When Iesus therfore perceiued that they would come, and take him to make him a King, hee departed againe into a mountaine himselfe alone.

16 When euen was nowe come, his disciples went downe vnto the sea,

17 And entred into a shippe, and went ouer the sea, towardes Capernaum: and nowe it was darke, and Iesus was not come to them.

18 And the Sea arose with a great winde that blewe.

19 And when they had rowed about fiue and twentie, or thirtie furlongs, they sawe Iesus walking on the sea, and drawing neere vnto the ship: so they were afraide.

20 But he said vnto them, It is I: be not afraid.

21 Then willingly they receiued him into the ship, and the ship was by and by at the lande, whither they went.

22 The day following, the people which stoode on the other side of the sea, saw that there was none other ship there, saue that one, whereinto his disciples were entred, and that Iesus went not with his disciples in the ship, but that his disciples were gone alone,

23 And that there came other ships from Tiberias neere vnto the place where they ate the bread, after the Lord had giuen thankes.

24 Nowe when the people sawe that Iesus was not there, neither his disciples, they also tooke shipping, and came to Capernaum, seeking for Iesus.

25 And when they had founde him on the other side of the sea, they sayde vnto him, Rabbi, when camest thou hither?

26 Iesus answered them; and sayde, Verely, verely I say vnto you, ye seeke me not because ye sawe the miracles, but because yee ate of ye loaues, and were filled.

27 Labour not for ye meate which perisheth, but for the meate that endureth vnto euerlasting life, which the Sonne of man shall giue vnto you: for him hath God the Father sealed.

28 Then sayde they vnto him, What shall we doe, that we might worke the workes of God?

29 Iesus answered, and sayde vnto them, This is the woorke of God, that yee beleeue in him, whome he hath sent.

30 They sayde therefore vnto him, What signe shewest thou then, that we may see it, and beleeue thee? what doest thou woorke?

31 Our fathers did eate Manna in the desart, as it is written, Hee gaue them bread from heauen to eate.

32 Then Iesus said vnto them, Verely, verely I say vnto you, Moses gaue you not that bread from heauen, but my Father giueth you that true bread from heauen.

33 For the breade of God is hee which commeth downe from heauen, and giueth life vnto the world.

34 Then they said vnto him, Lord, euermore giue vs this bread.

35 And Iesus saide vnto them, I am that bread of life: he that commeth to me, shall not hunger, and he that beleeueth in me, shall neuer thirst.

36 But I said vnto you, that ye also haue seene me, and beleeue not.

37 All that the Father giueth me, shall come to mee: and him that commeth to me, I cast not away.

38 For I came downe from heauen, not to do mine owne wil, but his wil which hath sent me.

39 And this is the Fathers will which hath sent mee, that of all which hee hath giuen mee, I should lose nothing, but shoulde raise it vp againe at the last day.

40 And this is the will of him that sent mee, that euery man which seeth the Sonne, and beleeueth in him, should haue euerlasting life: and I will raise him vp at the last day.

41 The Iewes then murmured at him because hee sayde, I am that bread, which is come downe from heauen.

42 And they said, Is not this Iesus that sonne of Ioseph, whose father and mother wee knowe? howe then sayth he, I came downe from heauen?

43 Iesus then answered, and saide vnto them, Murmure not among your selues.

44 No man can come to mee, except the Father, which hath sent mee, drawe him: and I will raise him vp at the last day.

45 It is written in the Prophetes, And they shalbe al taught of God. Euery man therefore that hath heard, and hath learned of the Father, commeth vnto me:

46 Not that any man hath seene the Father, saue hee which is of God, hee hath seene the Father.

47 Verely, verely I say vnto you, hee that beleeueth in me, hath euerlasting life.

48 I am that bread of life.

49 Your fathers did eate Manna in the wildernesse, and are dead.

50 This is that breade, which commeth downe from heauen, that hee which eateth of it, shoulde not die.

51 I am that liuing breade, which came downe from heauen: if any man eate of this breade, hee shall liue for euer: and the bread that I will giue, is my flesh, which I will giue for the life of the world.

52 Then the Iewes stroue among themselues, saying, Howe can this man giue vs his flesh to eate?

53 Then Iesus saide vnto them, Verely, verely I say vnto you, Except yee eate the flesh of the Sonne of man, and drinke his blood, yee haue no life in you.

54 Whosoeuer eateth my flesh, and drinketh my blood, hath eternall life, and I will raise him vp at the last day.

55 For my flesh is meat in deede, and my blood is drinke in deede.

56 Hee that eateth my flesh, and drinketh my blood, dwelleth in me, and I in him.

57 As that liuing Father hath sent me, so liue I by the Father, and he that eateth me, euen he shall liue by me.

58 This is that bread which came downe from heauen: not as your fathers haue eaten Manna, and are deade. Hee that eateth of this bread, shall liue for euer.

59 These things spake he in the Synagogue, as he taught in Capernaum.

60 Many therefore of his disciples (when they heard this) sayde, This is an hard saying: who can heare it?

61 But Iesus knowing in himselfe, that his disciples murmured at this, saide vnto them, Doeth this offend you?

62 What then if yee should see that Sonne of man ascend vp where he was before?

63 It is the spirite that quickeneth: the flesh profiteth nothing: the woordes that I speake vnto you, are spirite and life.

64 But there are some of you that beleeue not: for Iesus knewe from the beginning, which they were that beleeued not, and who shoulde betray him.

65 And hee saide, Therefore saide I vnto you, that no man can come vnto mee, except it be giuen vnto him of my Father.

66 From that time, many of his disciples went backe, and walked no more with him.

67 Then sayde Iesus to the twelue, Will yee also goe away?

68 Then Simon Peter answered him, Master, to whome shall we goe? thou hast the wordes of eternall life:

69 And we beleeue and knowe that thou art that Christ that Sonne of the liuing God.

70 Iesus answered them, Haue not I chosen you twelue, and one of you is a deuill?

71 Now he spake it of Iudas Iscariot the sonne of Simon: for hee it was that shoulde betraie him, though he was one of the twelue.

John 7

1 After these things, Iesus walked in Galile, and woulde not walke in Iudea: for the Iewes sought to kill him.

2 Nowe the Iewes feast of the Tabernacles was at hande.

3 His brethren therefore sayde vnto him, Depart hence, and goe into Iudea, that thy disciples may see thy woorkes that thou doest.

4 For there is no man that doeth any thing secretely, and hee himselfe seeketh to be famous. If thou doest these things, shewe thy selfe to the worlde.

5 For as yet his brethren beleeued not in him.

6 Then Iesus saide vnto them, My time is not yet come: but your time is alway readie.

7 The world can not hate you: but me it hateth, because I testifie of it, that the workes thereof are euill.

8 Go ye vp vnto this feast: I wil not go vp yet vnto this feast: for my time is not yet fulfilled.

9 These things he sayde vnto them, and abode still in Galile.

10 But assoone as his brethren were gone vp, then went hee also vp vnto the feast, not openly, but as it were priuilie.

11 Then the Iewes sought him at the feast, and saide, Where is hee?

12 And much murmuring was there of him among the people. Some said, He is a good man: other sayd, Nay: but he deceiueth the people.

13 Howbeit no man spake openly of him for feare of the Iewes.

14 Nowe when halfe the feast was done, Iesus went vp into the Temple and taught.

15 And the Iewes marueiled, sauing, Howe knoweth this man the Scriptures, seeing that hee neuer learned!

16 Iesus answered them, and saide, My doctrine is not mine, but his that sent me.

17 If any man will doe his will, he shall knowe of the doctrine, whether it be of God, or whether I speake of my selfe.

18 Hee that speaketh of himselfe, seeketh his owne glorie: but hee that seeketh his glory that sent him, the same is true, and no vnrighteousnes is in him.

19 Did not Moses giue you a Law, and yet none of you keepeth the lawe? Why goe ye about to kill me?

20 The people answered, and said, Thou hast a deuil: who goeth about to kill thee?

21 Iesus answered, and saide to them, I haue done one worke, and ye all maruaile.

22 Moses therefore gaue vnto you circumcision, (not because it is of Moses, but of the fathers) and ye on the Sabbath day circumcise a man.

23 If a man on the Sabbath receiue circumcision, that the Lawe of Moses should not be broken, be ye angrie with me, because I haue made a man euery whit whole on the Sabbath day?

24 Iudge not according to the appearance, but iudge righteous iudgement.

25 Then saide some of them of Hierusalem, Is not this he, whom they goe about to kill?

26 And beholde, he speaketh openly, and they say nothing to him: doe the rulers know in deede that this is in deede that Christ?

27 Howbeit we know this man whence he is: but when that Christ commeth, no man shall knowe whence he is.

28 Then cried Iesus in the Temple as hee taught, saying, Ye both knowe mee, and knowe whence I am: yet am I not come of my selfe, but he that sent me, is true, whome ye knowe not.

29 But I knowe him: for I am of him, and he hath sent me.

30 Then they sought to take him, but no man layde handes on him, because his houre was not yet come.

31 Now many of the people beleeued in him, and said, When that Christ commeth, will he doe moe miracles then this man hath done?

32 The Pharises heard that the people murmured these thinges of him, and the Pharises, and high Priestes sent officers to take him.

33 Then saide Iesus vnto them, Yet am I a little while with you, and then goe I vnto him that sent mee.

34 Ye shall seeke me, and shall not finde me, and where I am, can ye not come.

35 Then saide the Iewes amongs themselues, Whither will he goe, that we shall not finde him? Will he goe vnto them that are dispersed among the Grecians, and teache the Grecians?

36 What saying is this that hee saide, Ye shall seeke mee, and shall not finde mee? and where I am, cannot ye come?

37 Nowe in the last and great day of the feast, Iesus stoode and cried, saying, If any man thirst, let him come vnto me, and drinke.

38 Hee that beleeueth in mee, as saith the Scripture, out of his bellie shall flowe riuers of water of life.

39 (This spake hee of the Spirite which they that beleeued in him, should receiue: for the holy Ghost was not yet giuen, because that Iesus was not yet glorified.)

40 So many of the people, when they heard this saying, said, Of a trueth this is that Prophet.

41 Other saide, This is that Christ: and some said, But shall that Christ come out of Galile?

42 Saith not the Scripture that that Christ shall come of the seede of Dauid, and out of the towne of Beth-leem, where Dauid was?

43 So was there dissension among the people for him.

44 And some of them would haue taken him, but no man layde handes on him.

45 Then came the officers to the hie Priests and Pharises, and they said vnto them, Why haue ye not brought him?

46 The officers answered, Neuer man spake like this man.

47 Then answered them the Pharises, Are yee also deceiued?

48 Doeth any of the rulers, or of the Pharises beleeue in him?

49 But this people, which know not the Law, are cursed.

50 Nicodemus said vnto them, (he that came to Iesus by night, and was one of them.)

51 Doth our Law iudge a man before it heare him, and knowe what he hath done?

52 They answered, and said vnto him, Art thou also of Galile? Searche and looke: for out of Galile ariseth no Prophet.

53 And euery man wet vnto his owne house.

John 8

1 And Iesus went vnto the mount of Oliues,

2 And early in the morning came againe into the Temple, and all the people came vnto him, and he sate downe, and taught them.

3 Then the Scribes, and the Pharises brought vnto him a woman, taken in adulterie, and set her in the middes,

4 And said vnto him, Master, we foud this woman committing adulterie, euen in the very acte.

5 Now Moses in our Law commanded, that such should be stoned: what sayest thou therefore?

6 And this they saide to tempt him, that they might haue, whereof to accuse him. But Iesus stouped downe, and with his finger wrote on the groud.

7 And while they continued asking him, hee lift himselfe vp, and sayde vnto them, Let him that is among you without sinne, cast the first stone at her.

8 And againe hee stouped downe, and wrote on the ground.

9 And when they heard it, being accused by their owne conscience, they went out one by one, beginning at ye eldest euen to the last: so Iesus was left alone, and the woman standing in the mids.

10 When Iesus had lift vp himselfe againe, and sawe no man, but the woman, hee saide vnto her, Woman, where are those thine accusers? hath no man condemned thee?

11 She said, No man, Lord. And Iesus said, Neither do I condemne thee: go and sinne no more.

12 Then spake Iesus againe vnto them, saying, I am that light of the worlde: hee that followeth mee, shall not walke in darkenes, but shall haue that light of life.

13 The Pharises therefore saide vnto him, Thou bearest recorde of thy selfe: thy recorde is not true.

14 Iesus answered, and sayde vnto them, Though I beare recorde of my selfe, yet my recorde is true: for I know whence I came, and whither I go: but ye cannot tell whence I come, and whither I goe.

15 Ye iudge after the flesh: I iudge no man.

16 And if I also iudge, my iudgement is true: for I am not alone, but I, and the Father, that sent mee.

17 And it is also written in your Lawe, that the testimonie of two men is true.

18 I am one that beare witnes of my selfe, and the Father that sent me, beareth witnes of me.

19 Then saide they vnto him, Where is that Father of thine? Iesus answered, Ye neither know me, nor that Father of mine. If ye had knowen me, ye should haue knowen that Father of mine also.

20 These wordes spake Iesus in the treasurie, as hee taught in the Temple, and no man layde handes on him: for his houre was not yet come.

21 Then saide Iesus againe vnto them, I goe my way, and ye shall seeke me, and shall die in your sinnes, Whither I goe, can ye not come.

22 Then said the Iewes, Will he kill himselfe, because he saith, Whither I goe, can ye not come?

23 And hee saide vnto them, Ye are from beneath, I am from aboue: ye are of this world, I am not of this worlde.

24 I said therefore vnto you, That ye shall die in your sinnes: for except ye beleeue, that I am he, ye shall die in your sinnes.

25 Then saide they vnto him, Who art thou? And Iesus saide vnto them, Euen the same thing that I said vnto you from the beginning.

26 I haue many things to say, and to iudge of you: but he that sent me, is true, and the things that I haue heard of him, those speake I to the world.

27 They vnderstoode not that hee spake to them of the Father.

28 Then said Iesus vnto them, When ye haue lift vp the Sonne of man, then shall ye know that I am he, and that I doe nothing of my selfe, but as my Father hath taught me, so I speake these things.

29 For he that sent me, is with me: the Father hath not left me alone, because I do alwayes those things that please him.

30 As hee spake these thinges, many beleeued in him.

31 Then saide Iesus to the Iewes which beleeued in him, If ye continue in my worde, ye are verely my disciples,

32 And shall know the trueth, and the trueth shall make you free.

33 They answered him, Wee be Abrahams seede, and were neuer bonde to any man: why sayest thou then, Ye shalbe made free?

34 Iesus answered them, Verely, verely I say vnto you, that whosoeuer committeth sinne, is the seruant of sinne.

35 And the seruant abideth not in the house for euer: but the Sonne abideth for euer.

36 If that Sonne therefore shall make you free, ye shalbe free in deede.

37 I know that ye are Abrahams seede, but yee seeke to kill mee, because my worde hath no place in you.

38 I speake that which I haue seene with my Father: and ye doe that which ye haue seene with your father.

39 They answered, and saide vnto him, Abraham is our father. Iesus said vnto them, If ye were Abrahams children, ye woulde doe the workes of Abraham.

40 But nowe ye goe about to kill mee, a man that haue told you the trueth, which I haue heard of God: this did not Abraham.

41 Ye do the workes of your father. Then said they to him, We are not borne of fornication: we haue one Father, which is God.

42 Therefore Iesus sayde vnto them, If God were your Father, then woulde ye loue mee: for I proceeded foorth, and came from God, neither came I of my selfe, but he sent me.

43 Why doe ye not vnderstande my talke? because ye cannot heare my worde.

44 Ye are of your father the deuill, and the lustes of your father ye will doe: hee hath bene a murtherer from the beginning, and abode not in the trueth, because there is no trueth in him. When hee speaketh a lie, then speaketh hee of his owne: for he is a liar, and the father thereof.

45 And because I tell you the trueth, yee beleeue me not.

46 Which of you can rebuke me of sinne? and if I say the trueth, why do ye not beleeue me?

47 He that is of God, heareth Gods wordes: yee therefore heare them not, because ye are not of God.

48 Then answered the Iewes, and said vnto him, Say we not well that thou art a Samaritane, and hast a deuil?

49 Iesus answered, I haue not a deuil, but I honour my Father, and ye haue dishonoured me.

50 And I seeke not mine owne praise: but there is one that seeketh it, and iudgeth.

51 Verely, verely I say vnto you, If a man keepe my word, he shall neuer see death.

52 Then said the Iewes to him, Now know we that thou hast a deuill. Abraham is dead, and the Prophets: and thou sayest, If a man keepe my worde, he shall neuer taste of death.

53 Art thou greater then our father Abraham, which is dead? and the Prophets are dead: whome makest thou thy selfe?

54 Iesus answered, If I honour my selfe, mine honour is nothing worth: it is my Father that honoureth me, whome ye say, that hee is your God.

55 Yet ye haue not knowen him: but I knowe him, and if I should say I know him not, I should be a liar like vnto you: but I knowe him, and keepe his worde.

56 Your father Abraham reioyced to see my day, and he sawe it, and was glad.

57 Then sayd ye Iewes vnto him, Thou art not yet fiftie yeere olde, and hast thou seene Abraham?

58 Iesus sayd vnto them, Verely, verely I say vnto you, before Abraham was, I am.

59 Then tooke they vp stones, to cast at him, but Iesus hid himselfe, and went out of the Temple: And hee passed through the middes of them, and so went his way.

John 9

1 And as Iesus passed by, he sawe a man which was blinde from his birth.

2 And his disciples asked them, saying, Master, who did sinne, this man, or his parents, that he was borne blinde?

3 Iesus answered, Neither hath this man sinned, nor his parents, but that the workes of God should be shewed on him.

4 I must worke the workes of him that sent me, while it is day: the night commeth when no man can worke.

5 As long as I am in the world, I am the light of the world.

6 Assoone as he had thus spoken, he spat on the ground, and made clay of the spettle, and anointed the eyes of the blinde with the clay,

7 And sayd vnto him, Go wash in the poole of Siloam (which is by interpretation, Sent.) He went his way therefore, and washed, and came againe seeing.

8 Nowe the neighbours and they that had seene him before, when he was blinde, sayd, Is not this he that sate and begged?

9 Some said, This is he: and other sayd, He is like him: but he himselfe sayd, I am he.

10 Therefore they sayd vnto him, Howe were thine eyes opened?

11 He answered, and sayd, The man that is called Iesus, made clay, and anointed mine eyes, and sayde vnto me, Goe to the poole of Siloam and wash. So I went and washed, and receiued sight.

12 Then they sayd vnto him, Where is he? He sayd, I can not tell.

13 They brought to the Pharises him that was once blinde.

14 And it was the Sabbath day, when Iesus made the clay, and opened his eyes.

15 Then againe the Pharises also asked him, how he had receiued sight. And hee sayd vnto them, He layd clay vpon mine eyes, and I washed, and doe see.

16 Then said some of the Pharises, This man is not of God, because he keepeth not the Sabbath day. Others sayd, Howe can a man that is a sinner, doe such miracles? and there was a dissension among them.

17 Then spake they vnto the blinde againe, What sayest thou of him, because he hath opened thine eyes? And he sayd, He is a Prophet.

18 Then the Iewes did not beleeue him (that he had bene blinde, and receiued his sight) vntill they had called the parents of him that had receiued sight.

19 And they asked them, saying, Is this your sonne, whom ye say was borne blinde? How doeth he nowe see then?

20 His parents answered them, and sayd, We know that this is our sonne, and that he was borne blinde:

21 But by what meanes hee nowe seeth, we know not: or who hath opened his eyes, can we not tell: he is olde ynough: aske him: hee shall answere for himselfe.

22 These wordes spake his parents, because they feared the Iewes: for the Iewes had ordeined already, that if any man did confesse that he was Christ, he should be excommunicate out of the Synagogue.

23 Therefore sayde his parents, Hee is olde ynough: aske him.

24 Then againe called they the man that had bene blinde, and sayd vnto him, Giue glory vnto God: we know that this man is a sinner.

25 Then he answered, and sayd, Whether hee be a sinner or no, I can not tell: one thing I know, that I was blinde, and nowe I see.

26 Then sayd they to him againe, What did he to thee? howe opened he thine eyes?

27 Hee answered them, I haue tolde you already, and yee haue not heard it: wherefore would yee heare it againe? will yee also be his disciples?

28 Then reuiled they him, and sayd, Be thou his disciple: we be Moses disciples.

29 We know that God spake with Moses: but this man we know not from whence he is.

30 The man answered, and sayde vnto them, Doutlesse, this is a marueilous thing, that ye know not whence he is, and yet he hath opened mine eyes.

31 Now we know that God heareth not sinners: but if any man be a worshipper of God, and doeth his will, him heareth he.

32 Since the world began, was it not heard, that any man opened the eyes of one that was borne blinde.

33 If this man were not of God, hee could haue done nothing.

34 They answered, and sayd vnto him, Thou art altogether borne in sinnes, and doest thou teach vs? so they cast him out.

35 Iesus heard that they had cast him out: and when he had found him, he sayd vnto him, Doest thou beleeue in the Sonne of God?

36 He answered, and sayd, Who is he, Lord, that I might beleeue in him?

37 And Iesus sayd vnto him, Both thou hast seene him, and he it is that talketh with thee.

38 Then he sayd, Lord, I beleeue, and worshipped him.

39 And Iesus sayd, I am come vnto iudgement into this world, that they which see not, might see: and that they which see, might be made blinde.

40 And some of the Pharises which were with him, heard these things, and sayd vnto him, Are we blinde also?

41 Iesus sayd vnto them, If ye were blinde, ye should not haue sinne: but nowe ye say, We see: therefore your sinne remaineth.

John 10

1 Verely, verely I say vnto you, Hee that entreth not in by the doore into the sheepefolde, but climeth vp another way, he is a theefe and a robber.

2 But he that goeth in by the doore, is the shepheard of the sheepe.

3 To him the porter openeth, and the sheepe heare his voyce, and he calleth his owne sheepe by name, and leadeth them out.

4 And when hee hath sent foorth his owne sheepe, he goeth before them, and the sheepe follow him: for they know his voyce.

5 And they will not follow a stranger, but they flee from him: for they know not the voyce of strangers.

6 This parable spake Iesus vnto them: but they vnderstoode not what things they were which he spake vnto them.

7 Then sayd Iesus vnto them againe, Verely, verely I say vnto you, I am that doore of the sheepe.

8 All, that euer came before me, are theeues and robbers: but the sheepe did not heare them.

9 I am that doore: by me if any man enter in, he shall be saued, and shall go in, and go out, and finde pasture.

10 The theefe commeth not, but for to steale, and to kill, and to destroy: I am come that they might haue life, and haue it in abundance.

11 I am that good shepheard: that good shepheard giueth his life for his sheepe.

12 But an hireling, and hee which is not the shepheard, neither the sheepe are his owne, seeth the wolfe comming, and hee leaueth the sheepe, and fleeth, and the wolfe catcheth them, and scattreth the sheepe.

13 So the hireling fleeth, because he is an hireling, and careth not for the sheepe.

14 I am that good shepheard, and knowe mine, and am knowen of mine.

15 As the Father knoweth me, so know I the Father: and I lay downe my life for my sheepe.

16 Other sheepe I haue also, which are not of this folde: them also must I bring, and they shall heare my voyce: and there shalbe one sheepefolde, and one shepheard.

17 Therefore doeth my Father loue me, because I lay downe my life, that I might take it againe.

18 No man taketh it from me, but I lay it downe of my selfe: I haue power to lay it downe, and haue power to take it againe: this commandement haue I receiued of my Father.

19 Then there was a dissension againe among the Iewes for these sayings,

20 And many of them sayd, He hath a deuill, and is mad: why heare ye him?

21 Other sayd, These are not the wordes of him that hath a deuill: can the deuill open the eyes of the blinde?

22 And it was at Hierusalem the feast of the Dedication, and it was winter.

23 And Iesus walked in the Temple, in Salomons porche.

24 Then came the Iewes round about him, and sayd vnto him, Howe long doest thou make vs dout? If thou be that Christ, tell vs plainely.

25 Iesus answered them, I tolde you, and ye beleeue not: the workes that I doe in my Fathers Name, they beare witnes of me.

26 But ye beleeue not: for ye are not of my sheepe, as I sayd vnto you.

27 My sheepe heare my voyce, and I knowe them, and they follow me,

28 And I giue vnto them eternall life, and they shall neuer perish, neither shall any plucke them out of mine hand.

29 My Father which gaue them me, is greater then all, and none is able to take them out of my Fathers hand.

30 I and my Father are one.

31 Then ye Iewes againe tooke vp stones, to stone him.

32 Iesus answered them, Many good workes haue I shewed you from my Father: for which of these workes doe ye stone me?

33 The Iewes answered him, saying, For the good worke we stone thee not, but for blasphemie, and that thou being a man, makest thy selfe God.

34 Iesus answered them, Is it not written in your Lawe, I sayd, Ye are gods?

35 If hee called them gods, vnto whome the worde of God was giuen, and the Scripture cannot be broken,

36 Say ye of him, whome the Father hath sanctified, and sent into the worlde, Thou blasphemest, because I said, I am the Sonne of God?

37 If I doe not the workes of my Father, beleeue me not.

38 But if I doe, then though ye beleeue not mee, yet beleeue the workes, that ye may knowe and beleeue, that the Father is in me, and I in him.

39 Againe they went about to take him: but he escaped out of their handes,

40 And went againe beyonde Iordan, into the place where Iohn first baptized, and there abode.

41 And many resorted vnto him, and saide, Iohn did no miracle: but all thinges that Iohn spake of this man, were true.

42 And many beleeued in him there.

John 11

1 And a certaine man was sicke, named Lazarus of Bethania, the towne of Marie, and her sister Martha.

2 (And it was that Mary which anointed the Lord with oyntment, and wiped his feete with her heare, whose brother Lazarus was sicke.)

3 Therefore his sisters sent vnto him, saying, Lord, beholde, he whome thou louest, is sicke.

4 When Iesus heard it, he saide, This sickenes is not vnto death, but for the glorie of God, that the Sonne of God might be glorified thereby.

5 Nowe Iesus loued Martha and her sister, and Lazarus.

6 And after he had heard that he was sicke, yet abode hee two dayes still in the same place where he was.

7 Then after that, said he to his disciples, Let vs goe into Iudea againe.

8 The disciples saide vnto him, Master, the Iewes lately sought to stone thee, and doest thou goe thither againe?

9 Iesus answered, Are there not twelue houres in the day? If a man walke in the day, hee stumbleth not, because he seeth the light of this world.

10 But if a man walke in the night, hee stumbleth, because there is no light in him.

11 These things spake he, and after, he said vnto them, Our friend Lazarus sleepeth: but I goe to wake him vp.

12 Then said his disciples, Lord, if he sleepe, he shalbe safe.

13 Howbeit, Iesus spake of his death: but they thought that he had spoken of the naturall sleepe.

14 Then saide Iesus vnto them plainely, Lazarus is dead.

15 And I am glad for your sakes, that I was not there, that ye may beleeue: but let vs go vnto him.

16 Then saide Thomas (which is called Didymus) vnto his felow disciples, Let vs also goe, that we may die with him.

17 Then came Iesus, and found that he had lien in the graue foure dayes alreadie.

18 (Nowe Bethania was neere vnto Hierusalem, about fifteene furlongs off.)

19 And many of ye Iewes were come to Martha and Marie to comfort them for their brother.

20 Then Martha, when shee heard that Iesus was comming, went to meete him: but Mary sate still in the house.

21 Then said Martha vnto Iesus, Lord, if thou hadst bene here, my brother had not bene dead.

22 But now I know also, that whatsoeuer thou askest of God, God will giue it thee.

23 Iesus said vnto her, Thy brother shall rise againe.

24 Martha said vnto him, I know that he shall rise againe in the resurrection at the last day.

25 Iesus saide vnto her, I am the resurrection and the life: he that beleeueth in me, though he were dead, yet shall he liue.

26 And whosoeuer liueth, and beleeueth in me, shall neuer die: Beleeuest thou this?

27 She said vnto him, Yea, Lord, I beleeue that thou art that Christ that Sonne of God, which should come into the world.

28 And when she had so saide, she went her way, and called Mary her sister secretly, saying, The Master is come, and calleth for thee.

29 And when she heard it, shee arose quickly, and came vnto him.

30 For Iesus was not yet come into the towne, but was in the place where Martha met him.

31 The Iewes then which were with her in the house, and comforted her, when

they sawe Marie, that she rose vp hastily, and went out, folowed her, saying, She goeth vnto the graue, to weepe there.

32 Then when Mary was come where Iesus was, and sawe him, she fell downe at his feete, saying vnto him, Lord, if thou haddest bene here, my brother had not bene dead.

33 When Iesus therefore saw her weepe, and the Iewes also weepe which came with her, hee groned in the spirit, and was troubled in himselfe,

34 And saide, Where haue ye layde him? They said vnto him, Lord, come and see.

35 And Iesus wept.

36 Then saide the Iewes, Beholde, how he loued him.

37 And some of them saide, Coulde not he, which opened the eyes of the blinde, haue made also, that this man should not haue died?

38 Iesus therefore againe groned in himselfe, and came to the graue. And it was a caue, and a stone was layde vpon it.

39 Iesus saide, Take ye away the stone. Martha the sister of him that was dead, said vnto him, Lord, he stinketh alreadie: for he hath bene dead foure dayes.

40 Iesus saide vnto her, Saide I not vnto thee, that if thou diddest beleeue, thou shouldest see the glorie of God?

41 Then they tooke away the stone from the place where the dead was layde. And Iesus lift vp his eyes, and saide, Father, I thanke thee, because thou hast heard me.

42 I knowe that thou hearest me alwayes, but because of the people that stand by, I said it, that they may beleeue, that thou hast sent me.

43 As hee had spoken these things, hee cried with a loude voyce, Lazarus, come foorth.

44 Then he that was dead, came forth, bound hande and foote with bandes, and his face was bound with a napkin. Iesus said vnto them, Loose him, and let him goe.

45 Then many of the Iewes, which came to Mary, and had seene the thinges, which Iesus did, beleeued in him.

46 But some of them went their way to the Pharises, and told them what things Iesus had done.

47 Then gathered the hie Priests, and the Pharises a councill, and said, What shall we doe? For this man doeth many miracles.

48 If we let him thus alone, all men will beleeue in him, and the Romanes will come and take away both our place, and the nation.

49 Then one of them named Caiaphas, which was the hie Priest that same yere, said vnto them, Ye perceiue nothing at all,

50 Nor yet doe you consider that it is expedient for vs, that one man die for the people, and that the whole nation perish not.

51 This spake hee not of himselfe: but being hie Priest that same yere, he

prophecied that Iesus should die for that nation:

52 And not for that nation onely, but that he shoulde gather together in one the children of God, which were scattered.

53 Then from that day foorth they consulted together, to put him to death.

54 Iesus therefore walked no more openly among the Iewes, but went thence vnto a countrey neere to the wildernes, into a citie called Ephraim, and there continued with his disciples.

55 And the Iewes Passeouer was at hande, and many went out of the countrey vp to Hierusalem before the Passeouer, to purifie themselues.

56 Then sought they for Iesus, and spake among themselues, as they stoode in the Temple, What thinke ye, that he cometh not to the feast?

57 Now both the high Priestes and the Pharises had giuen a commandement, that if any man knew where he were, he should shew it, that they might take him.

John 12

1 Then Iesus, sixe dayes before the Passeouer, came to Bethania, where Lazarus was, who died, whom he had raised from the dead.

2 There they made him a supper, and Martha serued: but Lazarus was one of them that sate at the table with him.

3 Then tooke Mary a pound of oyntment of Spikenarde very costly, and anoynted Iesus feete, and wiped his feete with her heare, and the house was filled with the sauour of the oyntment.

4 Then said one of his disciples, euen Iudas Iscariot Simons sonne, which should betray him:

5 Why was not this oyntment sold for three hundreth pence, and giuen to the poore?

6 Nowe he said this, not that he cared for the poore, but because hee was a theefe, and had the bagge, and bare that which was giuen.

7 Then said Iesus, Let her alone: against the day of my burying she kept it.

8 For the poore alwayes yee haue with you, but me ye shall not haue alwayes.

9 Then much people of the Iewes knewe that hee was there: and they came, not for Iesus sake onely, but that they might see Lazarus also, whome he had raysed from the dead.

10 The hie Priestes therefore consulted, that they might put Lazarus to death also,

11 Because that for his sake many of the Iewes went away, and beleeued in Iesus.

12 On the morowe a great multitude that were come to the feast, when they heard that Iesus should come to Hierusalem,

13 Tooke branches of palme trees, and went foorth to meete him, and cried, Hosanna, Blessed is the King of Israel that commeth in the Name of the Lord.

14 And Iesus found a yong asse, and sate thereon, as it is written,

15 Feare not, daughter of Sion: behold, thy King commeth sitting on an asses colte.

16 But his disciples vnderstoode not these thinges at the first: but when Iesus was glorified, then remembred they, that these thinges were written of him, and that they had done these things vnto him.

17 The people therefore that was with him, bare witnesse that hee called Lazarus out of the graue, and raised him from the dead.

18 Therefore mette him the people also, because they heard that he had done this miracle.

19 And the Pharises said among themselues, Perceiue ye howe ye preuaile nothing? Beholde, the worlde goeth after him.

20 Nowe there were certaine Greekes among them that came vp to worship at the feast.

21 And they came to Philippe, which was of Bethsaida in Galile, and desired him, saying, Syr, we would see that Iesus.

22 Philippe came and tolde Andrew: and againe Andrew and Philippe tolde Iesus.

23 And Iesus answered them, saying, The houre is come, that the Sonne of man must bee glorified.

24 Verely, verely I say vnto you, Except the wheate corne fall into the grounde and die, it bideth alone: but if it die, it bringeth foorth much fruite.

25 He that loueth his life, shall lose it, and he that hateth his life in this world, shall keepe it vnto life eternall.

26 If any man serue me, let him follow me: for where I am, there shall also my seruant be: and if any man serue me, him will my Father honour.

27 Now is my soule troubled: and what shall I say? Father, saue me from this houre: but therefore came I vnto this houre.

28 Father, glorifie thy Name. Then came there a voyce from heauen, saying, I haue both glorified it, and will glorifie it againe.

29 Then saide the people that stoode by, and heard, that it was a thunder: other said, An Angel spake to him.

30 Iesus answered, and said, This voyce came not because of me, but for your sakes.

31 Now is the iudgement of this world: nowe shall the prince of this world be cast out.

32 And I, if I were lift vp from the earth, will drawe all men vnto me.

33 Nowe this sayd he, signifying what death he should die.

34 The people answered him, We haue heard out of the Law, that that Christ bideth for euer: and howe sayest thou, that that Sonne of man must be lift vp? Who is that Sonne of man?

35 Then Iesus sayd vnto them, Yet a litle while is the light with you: walke while ye haue that light, lest the darkenes come vpon you: for hee that walketh in the darke, knoweth not whither he goeth.

36 While ye haue that light, beleeue in that light, that ye may be the children of the light. These things spake Iesus, and departed, and hid himselfe from them.

37 And though he had done so many miracles before them, yet beleeued they not on him,

38 That the saying of Esaias the Prophete might be fulfilled, that he sayd, Lord, who beleeued our report? and to whome is the arme of the Lord reueiled?

39 Therefore could they not beleeue, because that Esaias saith againe,

40 He hath blinded their eyes, and hardened their heart, that they shoulde not see with their eyes, nor vnderstand with their heart, and should be conuerted, and I should heale them.

41 These things sayd Esaias when he sawe his glory, and spake of him.

42 Neuertheles, euen among the chiefe rulers, many beleeued in him: but because of the Pharises they did not confesse him, least they should be cast out of the Synagogue.

43 For they loued the prayse of men, more then the prayse of God.

44 And Iesus cryed, and sayd, He that beleeueth in me, beleeueth not in me, but in him that sent me.

45 And he that seeth me, seeth him that sent me.

46 I am come a light into the world, that whosoeuer beleeueth in me, should not abide in darkenes.

47 And if any man heare my wordes, and beleeue not, I iudge him not: for I came not to iudge the world, but to saue the world.

48 He that refuseth me, and receiueth not my wordes, hath one that iudgeth him: the worde that I haue spoken, it shall iudge him in the last day.

49 For I haue not spoken of my selfe: but the Father which sent me, hee gaue me a commandement what I should say, and what I should speake.

50 And I knowe that his commandement is life euerlasting: the thinges therefore that I speake, I speake them so as the Father sayde vnto me.

John 13

1 Nowe before the feast of the Passeouer, when Iesus knewe that his houre was come, that he should depart out of this world vnto the Father, forasmuch as he loued his owne which were in the world, vnto the end he loued them.

2 And when supper was done (and that the deuill had now put in the heart of Iudas Iscariot, Simons sonne, to betray him)

3 Iesus knowing that the Father had giuen all things into his hands, and that he was come forth from God, and went to God,

4 He riseth from supper, and layeth aside his vpper garments, and tooke a towel, and girded himselfe.

5 After that, hee powred water into a basen, and began to wash the disciples feete, and to wipe them with the towell, wherewith he was girded.

6 Then came he to Simon Peter, who sayd to him, Lord, doest thou wash my feete?

7 Iesus answered and sayd vnto him, What I doe, thou knowest not nowe: but thou shalt knowe it hereafter.

8 Peter said vnto him, Thou shalt neuer wash my feete. Iesus answered him, If I wash thee not, thou shalt haue no part with me.

9 Simon Peter sayd vnto him, Lord, not my feete onely, but also the hands and the head.

10 Iesus sayd to him, He that is washed, needeth not, saue to wash his feete, but is cleane euery whit: and ye are cleane, but not all.

11 For hee knewe who should betray him: therefore sayd he, Ye are not all cleane.

12 So after he had washed their feete, and had taken his garments, and was set downe againe, he sayd vnto them, Knowe ye what I haue done to you?

13 Ye call me Master, and Lord, and ye say well: for so am I.

14 If I then your Lord, and Master, haue washed your feete, ye also ought to wash one an others feete.

15 For I haue giuen you an example, that ye should doe, euen as I haue done to you.

16 Verely, verely I say vnto you, The seruant is not greater then his master, neither the ambassadour greater then he that sent him.

17 If ye know these things, blessed are ye, if ye doe them.

18 I speake not of you all: I know whom I haue chosen: but it is that the Scripture might be fulfilled, He that eateth bread with me, hath lift vp his heele against me.

19 From henceforth tell I you before it come, that when it is come to passe, ye might beleeue that I am he.

20 Verely, verely I say vnto you, If I send any, he that receiueth him, receiueth me, and hee that receiueth me, receiueth him that sent me.

21 When Iesus had sayd these things, he was troubled in the Spirit, and testified, and said, Verely, verely I say vnto you, that one of you shall betray me.

22 Then the disciples looked one on another, doubting of whom he spake.

23 Nowe there was one of his disciples, which leaned on Iesus bosome, whom Iesus loued.

24 To him beckened therefore Simon Peter, that he should aske who it was of whom he spake.

25 He then, as he leaned on Iesus breast, saide vnto him, Lord, who is it?

26 Iesus answered, He it is, to whome I shall giue a soppe, when I haue dipt it: and hee wet a soppe, and gaue it to Iudas Iscariot, Simons sonne.

27 And after the soppe, Satan entred into him. Then sayd Iesus vnto him, That thou doest, doe quickly.

28 But none of them that were at table, knew, for what cause he spake it vnto him.

29 For some of them thought because Iudas had the bag, that Iesus had sayd vnto him, Buy those things that we haue neede of against ye feast: or that he should giue some thing to the poore.

30 Assoone then as he had receiued the soppe, he went immediately out, and it was night.

31 When hee was gone out, Iesus sayd, Nowe is the Sonne of man glorified, and God is glorified in him.

32 If God be glorified in him, God shall also glorifie him in himselfe, and shall straightway glorifie him.

33 Litle children, yet a litle while am I with you: ye shall seeke me, but as I sayde vnto the Iewes, Whither I goe, can ye not come: also to you say I nowe,

34 A newe commandement giue I vnto you, that ye loue one another: as I haue loued you, that ye also loue one another.

35 By this shall all men knowe that ye are my disciples, if ye haue loue one to another.

36 Simon Peter said vnto him, Lord, whither goest thou? Iesus answered him, Whither I goe, thou canst not follow me nowe: but thou shalt follow me afterward.

37 Peter sayd vnto him, Lord, why can I not follow thee now? I will lay downe my life for thy sake.

38 Iesus answered him, Wilt thou lay downe thy life for my sake? Verely, verely I say vnto thee, The cocke shall not crowe, till thou haue denied me thrise.

John 14

1 Let not your heart be troubled: ye beleeue in God, beleeue also in me.

2 In my Fathers house are many dwelling places: if it were not so, I would haue tolde you: I go to prepare a place for you.

3 And if I go to prepare a place for you, I wil come againe, and receiue you vnto my selfe, that where I am, there may ye be also.

4 And whither I go, ye know, and the way ye knowe.

5 Thomas sayd vnto him, Lord, we know not whither thou goest: how can we then know ye way?

6 Iesus sayd vnto him, I am that Way, and that Trueth, and that Life. No man commeth vnto the Father, but by me.

7 If ye had knowen mee, ye should haue knowen my Father also: and from henceforth ye know him, and haue seene him.

8 Philippe sayd vnto him, Lord, shewe vs thy Father, and it sufficeth vs.

9 Iesus sayd vnto him, I haue bene so long time with you, and hast thou not knowen mee, Philippe? he that hath seene me, hath seene my Father: how then sayest thou, Shewe vs thy Father?

10 Beleeuest thou not, that I am in the Father, and the Father is in me? The wordes that I speake vnto you, I speake not of my selfe: but the Father that dwelleth in me, he doeth the workes.

11 Beleeue me, that I am in the Father, and the Father is in me: at the least, beleeue me for the very workes sake.

12 Verely, verely I say vnto you, he that beleeueth in me, the workes that I doe, hee shall doe also, and greater then these shall he doe: for I goe vnto my Father.

13 And whatsoeuer ye aske in my Name, that will I doe, that the Father may be glorified in the Sonne.

14 If ye shall aske any thing in my Name, I will doe it.

15 If ye loue me, keepe my comandements.

16 And I wil pray the Father, and he shall giue you another Comforter, that he may abide with you for euer,

17 Euen the Spirit of trueth, whome the world can not receiue, because it seeth him not, neither knoweth him: but ye knowe him: for he dwelleth with you, and shalbe in you.

18 I will not leaue you fatherles: but I will come to you.

19 Yet a litle while, and the world shall see me no more, but ye shall see me: because I liue, ye shall liue also.

20 At that day shall ye knowe that I am in my Father, and you in me, and I in you.

21 He that hath my commandements, and keepeth them, is he that loueth me: and he that loueth me, shall be loued of my Father: and I will loue him, and wil shewe mine owne selfe to him.

22 Iudas sayd vnto him (not Iscariot) Lord, what is the cause that thou wilt shewe thy selfe vnto vs, and not vnto the world?

23 Iesus answered, and sayd vnto him, If any man loue me, he will keepe my worde, and my Father will loue him, and we wil come vnto him, and wil dwell with him.

24 He that loueth me not, keepeth not my wordes, and the worde which ye heare, is not mine, but the Fathers which sent me.

25 These things haue I spoken vnto you, being present with you.

26 But the Comforter, which is the holy Ghost, whom the Father wil send in my Name, he shall teach you all things, and bring all things to your remembrance, which I haue tolde you.

27 Peace I leaue with you: my peace I giue vnto you: not as the worlde giueth, giue I vnto you. Let not your heart be troubled, nor feare.

28 Ye haue heard howe I saide vnto you, I goe away, and will come vnto you. If ye loued me, ye would verely reioyce, because I said, I goe vnto the Father: for the Father is greater then I.

29 And nowe haue I spoken vnto you, before it come, that when it is come to passe, ye might beleeue.

30 Hereafter will I not speake many things vnto you: for the prince of this world commeth, and hath nought in me.

31 But it is that the world may knowe that I loue my Father: and as the Father hath commanded me, so I doe. Arise, let vs goe hence.

John 15

1 I Am that true vine, and my Father is that husband man.

2 Euery branch that beareth not fruite in me, he taketh away: and euery one that beareth fruite, he purgeth it, that it may bring forth more fruite.

3 Nowe are ye cleane through the worde, which I haue spoken vnto you.

4 Abide in me, and I in you: as the branche cannot beare fruite of it selfe, except it abide in the vine, no more can ye, except ye abide in me.

5 I am that vine: ye are the branches: he that abideth in me, and I in him, the same bringeth forth much fruite: for without me can ye doe nothing.

6 If a man abide not in me, he is cast forth as a branche, and withereth: and men gather them, and cast them into the fire, and they burne.

7 If ye abide in me, and my wordes abide in you, aske what ye wil, and it shalbe done to you.

8 Herein is my Father glorified, that ye beare much fruite, and be made my disciples.

9 As the father hath loued me, so haue I loued you: continue in that my loue.

10 If ye shall keepe my commandements, ye shall abide in my loue, as I haue kept my Fathers commandements, and abide in his loue.

11 These things haue I spoken vnto you, that my ioy might remaine in you, and that your ioy might be full.

12 This is my commandement, that ye loue one another, as I haue loued you.

13 Greater loue then this hath no man, when any man bestoweth his life for his friendes.

14 Ye are my friendes, if ye doe whatsoeuer I commaund you.

15 Henceforth call I you not seruants: for the seruant knoweth not what his master doeth: but I haue called you friends: for all things that I haue heard of my Father, haue I made knowen to you.

16 Ye haue not chosen me, but I haue chosen you, and ordeined you, that ye goe and bring foorth fruite, and that your fruite remaine, that whatsoeuer ye shall aske of the Father in my Name, he may giue it you.

17 These things commaund I you, that ye loue one another.

18 If the worlde hate you, ye knowe that it hated me before you.

19 If ye were of the worlde, the world woulde loue his owne: but because ye are not of ye world, but I haue chosen you out of the world, therefore the world hateth you.

20 Remember the word that I said vnto you, The seruant is not greater then his master. If they haue persecuted me, they will persecute you also: if they haue kept my worde, they will also keepe yours.

21 But all these things will they doe vnto you for my Names sake, because they haue not knowen him that sent me.

22 If I had not come and spoken vnto them, they shoulde not haue had sinne: but nowe haue they no cloke for their sinne.

23 He that hateth me, hateth my Father also.

24 If I had not done workes among them which none other man did, they had not had sinne: but nowe haue they both seene, and haue hated both me, and my Father.

25 But it is that the worde might be fulfilled, that is written in their Lawe, They hated me without a cause.

26 But when that Comforter shall come, whom I will send vnto you from the Father, euen the Spirit of trueth, which proceedeth of the Father, he shall testifie of me.

27 And ye shall witnesse also, because ye haue bene with me from the beginning.

John 16

1 These thinges haue I saide vnto you, that ye should not be offended.

2 They shall excommunicate you: yea, the time shall come, that whosoeuer killeth you, will thinke that he doeth God seruice.

3 And these things will they doe vnto you, because they haue not knowen ye Father, nor me.

4 But these things haue I tolde you, that when the houre shall come, ye might remember, that I tolde you them. And these things said I not vnto you from ye beginning, because I was with you.

5 But now I go my way to him that sent me, and none of you asketh me, Whither goest thou?

6 But because I haue saide these thinges vnto you, your hearts are full of sorowe.

7 Yet I tell you the trueth, It is expedient for you that I goe away: for if I goe not away, that Comforter will not come vnto you: but if I depart, I will send him vnto you.

8 And when he is come, he will reproue the worlde of sinne, and of righteousnesse, and of iudgement.

9 Of sinne, because they beleeued not in me:

10 Of righteousnesse, because I goe to my Father, and ye shall see me no more:

11 Of iudgement, because the prince of this world is iudged.

12 I haue yet many things to say vnto you, but ye cannot beare them nowe.

13 Howbeit, when he is come which is the Spirit of trueth, he will leade you into all trueth: for he shall not speake of himselfe, but whatsoeuer he shall heare, shall he speake, and he will shew you the things to come.

14 He shall glorifie me: for he shall receiue of mine, and shall shewe it vnto you.

15 All thinges that the Father hath, are mine: therefore said I, that he shall take of mine, and shewe it vnto you.

16 A litle while, and ye shall not see me: and againe a litle while, and ye shall see me: for I goe to the Father.

17 Then said some of his disciples among them selues, What is this that he saieth vnto vs, A litle while, and ye shall not see me, and againe, a litle while, and ye shall see me, and, For I goe to the Father.

18 They said therefore, What is this that he saith, A litle while? we know not what he sayeth.

19 Now Iesus knew that they would aske him, and said vnto them, Doe ye enquire among your selues, of that I said, A litle while, and ye shall not see me: and againe, a litle while, and yee shall see me?

20 Verely, verely I say vnto you, that ye shall weepe and lament, and the worlde shall reioyce: and ye shall sorowe, but your sorowe shalbe turned to ioye.

21 A woman when she traueileth, hath sorowe, because her houre is come: but assoone as she is deliuered of the childe, she remembreth no more the anguish, for ioy that a man is borne into the world.

22 And ye nowe therefore are in sorowe: but I will see you againe, and your hearts shall reioyce, and your ioy shall no man take from you.

23 And in that day shall ye aske me nothing. Verely, verely I say vnto you, whatsoeuer ye shall aske the Father in my Name, he will giue it you.

24 Hitherto haue ye asked nothing in my Name: aske, and ye shall receiue, that your ioye may be full.

25 These things haue I spoken vnto you in parables: but the time will come, when I shall no more speake to you in parables: but I shall shew you plainely of the Father.

26 At that day shall ye aske in my Name, and I say not vnto you, that I will pray vnto the Father for you:

27 For the Father himselfe loueth you, because ye haue loued me, and haue beleeued that I came out from God.

28 I am come out from the Father, and came into the worlde: againe I leaue the worlde, and goe to the Father.

29 His disciples saide vnto him, Loe, nowe speakest thou plainely, and thou speakest no parable.

30 Nowe knowe wee that thou knowest all things, and needest not that any man should aske thee. By this we beleeue, that thou art come out from God.

31 Iesus answered them, Doe you beleeue nowe?

32 Beholde, the houre commeth, and is already come, that ye shalbe scattered euery man into his owne, and shall leaue me alone: but I am not alone: for the Father is with me.

33 These things haue I spoken vnto you, that in me ye might haue peace: in

the world ye shall haue affliction, but be of good comfort: I haue ouercome the world.

John 17

1 These things spake Iesus, and lift vp his eyes to heauen, and saide, Father, that houre is come: glorifie thy Sonne, that thy Sonne also may glorifie thee,

2 As thou hast giuen him power ouer all flesh, that he shoulde giue eternall life to all them that thou hast giuen him.

3 And this is life eternall, that they knowe thee to be the onely very God, and whom thou hast sent, Iesus Christ.

4 I haue glorified thee on the earth: I haue finished the worke which thou gauest me to doe.

5 And nowe glorifie me, thou Father, with thine owne selfe, with the glorie which I had with thee before the world was.

6 I haue declared thy Name vnto the men which thou gauest me out of the world: thine they were, and thou gauest them me, and they haue kept thy worde.

7 Nowe they knowe that all things whatsoeuer thou hast giuen me, are of thee.

8 For I haue giuen vnto them the wordes which thou gauest me, and they haue receiued them, and haue knowen surely that I came out from thee, and haue beleeued that thou hast sent me.

9 I pray for them: I pray not for the worlde, but for them which thou hast giuen me: for they are thine.

10 And al mine are thine, and thine are mine, and I am glorified in them.

11 And nowe am I no more in the world, but these are in the worlde, and I come to thee. Holy Father, keepe them in thy Name, euen them whome thou hast giuen mee, that they may bee one, as we are.

12 While I was with them in the worlde, I kept them in thy Name: those that thou gauest me, haue I kept, and none of them is lost, but the childe of perdition, that the Scripture might be fulfilled.

13 And now come I to thee, and these things speake I in the worlde, that they might haue my ioy fulfilled in themselues.

14 I haue giuen them thy word, and the world hath hated them, because they are not of the world, as I am not of the world.

15 I pray not that thou shouldest take them out of the world, but that thou keepe them from euill.

16 They are not of the worlde, as I am not of the world.

17 Sanctifie them with thy trueth: thy word is trueth.

18 As thou diddest send me into the world, so haue I sent them into the world.

19 And for their sakes sanctifie I my selfe, that they also may bee sanctified through the trueth.

20 I praie not for these alone, but for them also which shall beleeue in mee, through their woorde,

21 That they all may bee one, as thou, O Father, art in me, and I in thee: euen that they may be also one in vs, that the worlde may beleeue that thou hast sent me.

22 And the glory that thou gauest me, I haue giuen them, that they may be one, as we are one,

23 I in them, and thou in mee, that they may be made perfect in one, and that the worlde may knowe that thou hast sent mee, and hast loued them, as thou hast loued me.

24 Father, I will that they which thou hast giuen me, be with me euen where I am, that they may beholde that my glorie, which thou hast giuen mee: for thou louedst me before the foundation of the world.

25 O righteous Father, the worlde also hath not knowen thee, but I haue knowen thee, and these haue knowen, that thou hast sent me.

26 And I haue declared vnto the thy Name, and will declare it, that the loue wherewith thou hast loued me, may be in them, and I in them.

John 18

1 When Iesus had spoken these things, hee went foorth with his disciples ouer the brooke Cedron, where was a garden, into the which he entred, and his disciples.

2 And Iudas which betraied him, knewe also the place: for Iesus oft times resorted thither with his disciples.

3 Iudas then, after hee had receiued a band of men and officers of the high Priests, and of the Pharises, came thither with lanternes and torches, and weapons.

4 Then Iesus, knowing all things that shoulde come vnto him, went foorth and said vnto them, Whom seeke yee?

5 They answered him, Iesus of Nazareth. Iesus sayde vnto them, I am hee. Nowe Iudas also which betraied him, stoode with them.

6 Assoone then as hee had saide vnto them, I am hee, they went away backewardes, and fell to the grounde.

7 Then he asked them againe, Whome seeke yee? And they sayd, Iesus of Nazareth.

8 Iesus answered, I said vnto you, that I am he: therefore if ye seeke me, let these go their way.

9 This was that the worde might be fulfilled which hee spake, Of them which thou gauest me, haue I lost none.

10 Then Simon Peter hauing a sword, drewe it, and smote the hie Priests seruant, and cut off his right eare. Nowe the seruants name was Malchus.

11 Then sayde Iesus vnto Peter, Put vp thy sworde into the sheath: shall I not drinke of the cuppe which my Father hath giuen me?

12 Then the bande and the captaine, and the officers of the Iewes tooke Iesus, and bound him,

13 And led him away to Annas first (for he was father in lawe to Caiaphas, which was the hie Priest that same yeere)

14 And Caiaphas was he, that gaue counsel to the Iewes, that it was expedient that one man should die for the people.

15 Nowe Simon Peter folowed Iesus, and another disciple, and that disciple was knowen of the hie Priest: therefore he went in with Iesus into the hall of the hie Priest:

16 But Peter stood at the doore without. Then went out the other disciple which was knowen vnto the hie Priest, and spake to her that kept the doore, and brought in Peter.

17 Then saide the maide that kept the doore, vnto Peter, Art not thou also one of this mans disciples? He sayd, I am not.

18 And the seruants and officers stoode there, which had made a fire of coles: for it was colde, and they warmed themselues. And Peter also stood among them, and warmed himselfe.

19 (The hie Priest then asked Iesus of his disciples, and of his doctrine.

20 Iesus answered him, I spake openly to the world: I euer taught in the Synagogue and in the Temple, whither the Iewes resort continually, and in secret haue I sayde nothing.

21 Why askest thou mee? aske them which heard mee what I sayde vnto them: beholde, they knowe what I sayd.

22 When he had spoken these thinges, one of the officers which stoode by, smote Iesus with his rod, saying, Answerest thou the hie Priest so?

23 Iesus answered him, If I haue euill spoken, beare witnes of the euil: but if I haue well spoken, why smitest thou me?

24 Nowe Annas had sent him bound vnto Caiaphas the hie Priest)

25 And Simon Peter stoode and warmed himselfe, and they said vnto him, Art not thou also of his disciples? He denied it, and said, I am not.

26 One of the seruaunts of the hie Priest, his cousin whose eare Peter smote off, saide, Did not I see thee in the garden with him?

27 Peter then denied againe, and immediatly the cocke crewe.

28 Then led they Iesus from Caiaphas into the common hall. Nowe it was morning, and they themselues went not into the common hall, least they should be defiled, but that they might eate the Passeouer.

29 Pilate then went out vnto them, and said, What accusation bring yee against this man?

30 They answered, and saide vnto him, If hee were not an euill doer, we woulde not haue deliuered him vnto thee.

31 Then sayde Pilate vnto them, Take yee him, and iudge him after your owne Lawe. Then the Iewes sayde vnto him, It is not lawfull for vs to put any man to death.

32 It was that the worde of Iesus might be fulfilled which he spake, signifying what death he should die.

33 So Pilate entred into the common hall againe, and called Iesus, and sayde vnto him, Art thou the king of the Iewes?

34 Iesus answered him, Saiest thou that of thy selfe, or did other tell it thee of me?

35 Pilate answered, Am I a Iewe? Thine owne nation, and the hie Priestes haue deliuered thee vnto me. What hast thou done?

36 Iesus answered, My kingdome is not of this worlde: if my kingdome were of this worlde, my seruants would surely fight, that I should not be deliuered to the Iewes: but nowe is my kingdome not from hence.

37 Pilate then said vnto him, Art thou a King then? Iesus answered, Thou sayest that I am a King: for this cause am I borne, and for this cause came I into the world, that I should beare witnes vnto the trueth: euery one that is of the trueth, heareth my voyce.

38 Pilate said vnto him, What is trueth? And when he had saide that, hee went out againe vnto the Iewes, and said vnto them, I finde in him no cause at all.

39 But you haue a custome, that I shoulde deliuer you one loose at the Passeouer: will yee then that I loose vnto you the King of ye Iewes?

40 Then cried they all againe, saying, Not him, but Barabbas: nowe this Barabbas was a murtherer.

John 19

1 Then Pilate tooke Iesus and scourged him.

2 And the souldiers platted a crowne of thornes, and put it on his head, and they put on him a purple garment,

3 And saide, Haile, King of the Iewes. And they smote him with their roddes.

4 Then Pilate went foorth againe, and said vnto them, Behold, I bring him forth to you, that ye may knowe, that I finde no fault in him at all.

5 Then came Iesus foorth wearing a crowne of thornes, and a purple garment. And Pilate said vnto them, Beholde the man.

6 Then when the hie Priests and officers sawe him, they cried, saying, Crucifie, crucifie him. Pilate said vnto them, Take yee him and crucifie him: for I finde no fault in him.

7 The Iewes answered him, We haue a lawe, and by our law he ought to die, because he made himselfe the Sonne of God.

8 When Pilate then heard that woorde, he was the more afraide,

9 And went againe into the common hall, and saide vnto Iesus, Whence art thou? But Iesus gaue him none answere.

10 Then saide Pilate vnto him, Speakest thou not vnto me? Knowest thou not that I haue power to crucifie thee, and haue power to loose thee?

11 Iesus answered, Thou couldest haue no power at all against me, except it were giuen thee from aboue: therefore he that deliuered me vnto thee, hath the greater sinne.

12 From thence foorth Pilate sought to loose him, but the Iewes cried, saying, If thou deliuer him, thou art not Cesars friende: for whosoeuer maketh himselfe a King, speaketh against Cesar.

13 When Pilate heard this woorde, hee brought Iesus foorth, and sate downe in the iudgement seate in a place called the Pauement, and in Hebrewe, Gabbatha.

14 And it was the Preparation of the Passeouer, and about the sixt houre: and hee sayde vnto the Iewes, Beholde your King.

15 But they cried, Away with him, away with him, crucifie him. Pilate sayde vnto them, Shall I crucifie your King? The high Priestes answered, We haue no King but Cesar.

16 Then deliuered he him vnto them, to be crucified. And they tooke Iesus, and led him away.

17 And he bare his owne crosse, and came into a place named of dead mens Skulles, which is called in Hebrewe, Golgotha:

18 Where they crucified him, and two other with him, on either side one, and Iesus in the middes.

19 And Pilate wrote also a title, and put it on the crosse, and it was written, JESUS OF NAZARETH THE KING OF THE JEWES.

20 This title then read many of the Iewes: for the place where Iesus was crucified, was neere to the citie: and it was written in Hebrewe, Greeke and Latine.

21 Then saide the hie Priests of the Iewes to Pilate, Write not, The King of the Iewes, but that he sayd, I am King of the Iewes.

22 Pilate answered, What I haue written, I haue written.

23 Then the souldiers, when they had crucified Iesus, tooke his garments (and made foure partes, to euery souldier a part) and his coat: and the coat was without seame wouen from the toppe throughout.

24 Therefore they sayde one to another, Let vs not deuide it, but cast lots for it, whose it shall be. This was that the Scripture might be fulfilled, which sayth, They parted my garments among them, and on my coate did cast lots. So the souldiers did these things in deede.

25 Then stoode by the crosse of Iesus his mother, and his mothers sister, Marie the wife of Cleopas, and Marie Magdalene.

26 And when Iesus sawe his mother, and the disciple standing by, whom he loued, he said vnto his mother, Woman, beholde thy sonne.

27 Then saide he to the disciple, Beholde thy mother: and from that houre, the disciple tooke her home vnto him.

28 After, when Iesus knew that all things were performed, that the Scripture might be fulfilled, he said, I thirst.

29 And there was set a vessell full of vineger: and they filled a spondge with vineger: and put it about an Hyssope stalke, and put it to his mouth.

30 Nowe when Iesus had receiued of the vineger, he saide, It is finished, and bowed his head, and gaue vp the ghost.

31 The Iewes then (because it was the Preparation, that the bodies should not remaine vpon the crosse on the Sabbath day: for that Sabbath was an hie day) besought Pilate that their legges might be broken, and that they might be taken downe.

32 Then came the souldiers and brake the legges of the first, and of the other, which was crucified with Iesus.

33 But when they came to Iesus, and saw that he was dead alreadie, they brake not his legges.

34 But one of the souldiers with a speare pearced his side, and foorthwith came there out blood and water.

35 And he that sawe it, bare recorde, and his record is true: and he knoweth that he saith true, that ye might beleeue it.

36 For these things were done, that the Scripture shoulde be fulfilled, Not a bone of him shalbe broken.

37 And againe an other Scripture saith, They shall see him whom they haue thrust through.

38 And after these things, Ioseph of Arimathea (who was a disciple of Iesus, but secretly for feare of the Iewes) besought Pilate that he might take downe the bodie of Iesus. And Pilate gaue him licence. He came then and tooke Iesus body.

39 And there came also Nicodemus (which first came to Iesus by night) and brought of myrrhe and aloes mingled together about an hundreth pound.

40 Then tooke they the body of Iesus, and wrapped it in linnen clothes with the odours, as the maner of the Iewes is to burie.

41 And in that place where Iesus was crucified, was a garden, and in the garden a newe sepulchre, wherein was neuer man yet laid.

42 There then laide they Iesus, because of the Iewes Preparation day, for the sepulchre was neere.

John 20

1 Nowe the first day of the weeke came Marie Magdalene, early when it was yet darke, vnto the sepulchre, and sawe the stone taken away from the tombe.

2 Then she ranne, and came to Simon Peter, and to the other disciple whom Iesus loued, and saide vnto them, They haue taken away the Lord out of the sepulchre, and we knowe not where they haue laid him.

3 Peter therefore went forth, and the other disciple, and they came vnto the sepulchre.

4 So they ranne both together, but the other disciple did outrunne Peter, and came first to the sepulchre.

5 And he stouped downe, and sawe the linnen clothes lying: yet went he not in.

6 Then came Simon Peter following him, and went into the sepulchre, and sawe the linnen clothes lye,

7 And the kerchiefe that was vpon his head, not lying with the linnen clothes, but wrapped together in a place by it selfe.

8 Then went in also the other disciple, which came first to the sepulchre, and he sawe it, and beleeued.

9 For as yet they knewe not the Scripture, That he must rise againe from the dead.

10 And the disciples went away againe vnto their owne home.

11 But Marie stoode without at the sepulchre weeping: and as she wept, she bowed her selfe into the sepulchre,

12 And sawe two Angels in white, sitting, the one at the head, and the other at the feete, where the body of Iesus had laien.

13 And they said vnto her, Woman, why weepest thou? She said vnto them, They haue taken away my Lord, and I know not where they haue laide him.

14 When she had thus said, she turned her selfe backe, and sawe Iesus standing, and knewe not that it was Iesus.

15 Iesus saith vnto her, Woman, why weepest thou? whom seekest thou? She supposing that he had bene the gardener, said vnto him, Sir, if thou hast borne him hence, tell me where thou hast laid him, and I will take him away.

16 Iesus saith vnto her, Marie. She turned her selfe, and said vnto him, Rabboni, which is to say, Master.

17 Iesus saith vnto her, Touch me not: for I am not yet ascended to my Father: but goe to my brethren, and say vnto them, I ascend vnto my Father, and to your Father, and to my God, and your God.

18 Marie Magdalene came and told the disciples that she had seene the Lord, and that he had spoken these things vnto her.

19 The same day then at night, which was the first day of the weeke, and when the doores were shut where the disciples were assembled for feare of the Iewes, came Iesus and stoode in the middes, and saide to them, Peace be vnto you.

20 And when he had so saide, he shewed vnto them his handes, and his side. Then were the disciples glad when they had seene the Lord.

21 Then saide Iesus to them againe, Peace be vnto you: as my Father sent me, so sende I you.

22 And when he had saide that, he breathed on them, and saide vnto them, Receiue the holy Ghost.

23 Whosoeuers sinnes ye remit, they are remitted vnto them: and whosoeuers sinnes ye reteine, they are reteined.

24 But Thomas one of the twelue, called Didymus, was not with them when Iesus came.

25 The other disciples therefore saide vnto him, We haue seene the Lord: but he said vnto them, Except I see in his handes the print of the nailes, and put my finger into the print of the nailes, and put mine hand into his side, I will not beleeue it.

26 And eight dayes after, againe his disciples were within, and Thomas with them. Then came Iesus, when the doores were shut, and stood in the middes, and said, Peace be vnto you.

27 After saide he to Thomas, Put thy finger here, and see mine hands, and put forth thine hand, and put it into my side, and be not faithlesse, but faithfull.

28 Then Thomas answered, and said vnto him, Thou art my Lord, and my God.

29 Iesus said vnto him, Thomas, because thou hast seene me, thou beleeuest: blessed are they that haue not seene, and haue beleeued.

30 And many other signes also did Iesus in the presence of his disciples, which are not written in this booke.

31 But these things are written, that ye might beleeue, that Iesus is that Christ that Sonne of God, and that in beleeuing ye might haue life through his Name.

John 21

1 After these things, Iesus shewed himselfe againe to his disciples at the sea of Tiberias: and thus shewed he himselfe:

2 There were together Simon Peter, and Thomas, which is called Didymus, and Nathanael of Cana in Galile, and the sonnes of Zebedeus, and two other of his disciples.

3 Simon Peter said vnto them, I go a fishing. They said vnto him, We also will goe with thee. They went their way and entred into a ship straightway, and that night caught they nothing.

4 But when the morning was nowe come, Iesus stoode on the shore: neuerthelesse the disciples knewe not that it was Iesus.

5 Iesus then said vnto them, Syrs, haue ye any meate? They answered him, No.

6 Then he said vnto them, Cast out the net on the right side of the ship, and ye shall finde. So they cast out, and they were not able at all to draw it, for the multitude of fishes.

7 Therefore said the disciple whom Iesus loued, vnto Peter, It is the Lord. When Simon Peter heard that it was the Lord, he girded his coate to him (for he was naked) and cast himselfe into the sea.

8 But the other disciples came by shippe (for they were not farre from land, but about two hundreth cubites) and they drewe the net with fishes.

9 Assoone then as they were come to land, they sawe hoate coales, and fish laide thereon, and bread.

10 Iesus saide vnto them, Bring of the fishes, which ye haue nowe caught.

11 Simon Peter stepped foorth and drewe the net to land, full of great fishes, an hundreth, fiftie and three: and albeit there were so many, yet was not the net broken.

12 Iesus saide vnto them, Come, and dine. And none of the disciples durst aske him, Who art thou? seeing they knewe that he was the Lord.

13 Iesus then came and tooke bread, and gaue them, and fish likewise.

14 This is now the third time that Iesus shewed himselfe to his disciples, after that he was risen againe from the dead.

15 So when they had dined, Iesus said to Simon Peter, Simon the sonne of Iona, louest thou me more then these? He said vnto him, Yea Lord, thou knowest that I loue thee. He said vnto him, Feede my lambes.

16 He said to him againe the second time, Simon the sonne of Iona, louest thou me? He said vnto him, Yea Lord, thou knowest that I loue thee. He said vnto him, Feede my sheepe.

17 He said vnto him the third time, Simon the sonne of Iona, louest thou me? Peter was sorie because he said to him the third time, Louest thou me? and said vnto him, Lord, thou knowest all things: thou knowest that I loue thee. Iesus saide vnto him, Feede my sheepe.

18 Verely, verely I say vnto thee, When thou wast yong, thou girdedst thy selfe, and walkedst whither thou wouldest: but when thou shalt be olde, thou shalt stretch foorth thine hands, and another shall gird thee, and lead thee whither thou wouldest not.

19 And this spake he signifying by what death he shoulde glorifie God. And when he had said this, he said to him, Folowe me.

20 Then Peter turned about, and sawe the disciple whom JESUS loued, folowing, which had also leaned on his breast at supper, and had saide, Lord, which is he that betrayeth thee?

21 When Peter therefore sawe him, he saide to Iesus, Lord, what shall this man doe?

22 Iesus said vnto him, If I will that he tarie till I come, what is it to thee? follow thou me.

23 Then went this worde abroade among the brethren, that this disciple shoulde not die. Yet Iesus saide not to him, He shall not die: but if I will that he tarie till I come, what is it to thee?

24 This is that disciple, which testifieth of these things, and wrote these things, and we know that his testimonie is true.

25 Nowe there are also many other things which Iesus did, the which if they should be written euery one, I suppose the world coulde not conteine the bookes that shoulde be written, Amen.

Acts

Acts 1

1 I have made the former treatise, O Theophilus, of al that Jesus began to doe and teach,

2 Vntill the day that hee was taken vp, after that hee through the holy Ghost, had giuen commandements vnto the Apostles, whome hee had chosen:

3 To whome also he presented himselfe aliue after that he had suffered, by many infallible tokens, being seene of them by the space of fourtie daies, and speaking of those thinges which appertaine to the kingdome of God.

4 And when he had gathered them together, he commanded them, that they should not depart from Hierusalem, but to waite for the promise of the Father, which sayde hee, yee haue heard of me.

5 For Iohn in deede baptized with water, but ye shall be baptized with the holy Ghost within these fewe daies.

6 When they therefore were come together, they asked of him, saying, Lord, wilt thou at this time restore the kingdome to Israel?

7 And hee saide vnto them, It is not for you to know the times, or the seasons, which the Father hath put in his owne power,

8 But yee shall receiue power of the holy Ghost, when he shall come on you: and ye shalbe witnesses vnto me both in Hierusalem and in all Iudea, and in Samaria, and vnto the vttermost part of the earth.

9 And when he had spoken these things, while they behelde, he was taken vp: for a cloude tooke him vp out of their sight.

10 And while they looked stedfastly towarde heauen, as hee went, beholde, two men stoode by them in white apparell,

11 Which also sayde, Yee men of Galile, why stande yee gasing into heauen? This Iesus which is taken vp from you into heauen, shall so come, as yee haue seene him goe into heauen.

12 Then returned they vnto Hierusalem from the mount that is called the mount of Oliues, which is neere to Hierusalem, being from it a Sabbath daies iourney.

13 And when they were come in, they went vp into an vpper chamber, where abode both Peter and Iames, and Iohn, and Andrew, Philip, and Thomas, Bartlemew, and Matthewe, Iames the sonne of Alpheus, and Simon Zelotes, and Iudas Iames brother.

14 These all continued with one accorde in prayer and supplication with the women, and Marie the mother of Iesus, and with his brethren.

15 And in those dayes Peter stoode vp in the middes of the disciples, and sayde (nowe the nomber of names that were in one place were about an hundreth and twentie.)

16 Yee men and brethren, this scripture must needes haue beene fulfilled, which the holy Ghost by the mouth of Dauid spake before of Iudas, which was guide to them that tooke Iesus.

17 For hee was nombred with vs, and had obteined fellowship in this ministration.

18 He therefore hath purchased a field with the reward of iniquitie: and when he had throwen downe himselfe headlong, hee brast asunder in the middes, and all his bowels gushed out.

19 And it is knowen vnto all the inhabitants of Hierusalem, in so much,

that that field is called in their owne language, Aceldama, That is, the field of blood.

20 For it is written in the booke of Psalmes, Let his habitation be void, and let no man dwel therein: also, Let another take his charge.

21 Wherefore of these men which haue companied with vs, all the time that the Lord Iesus was conuersant among vs,

22 Beginning from the baptisme of Iohn vnto the day that hee was taken vp from vs, must one of them bee made a witnesse with vs of his resurrection.

23 And they presented two, Ioseph called Barsabas, whose surname was Iustus, and Matthias.

24 And they praied, saying, Thou Lord, which knowest the hearts of all men, shewe whether of these two thou hast chosen,

25 That he may take the roume of this ministration and Apostleship, from which Iudas hath gone astray, to goe to his owne place.

26 Then they gaue foorth their lottes: and the lotte fell on Matthias, and hee was by a common consent counted with the eleuen Apostles.

Acts 2

1 And when the day of Pentecost was come, they were al with one accord in one place.

2 And suddenly there came a sounde from heauen, as of a russhing and mightie winde, and it filled all the house where they sate.

3 And there appeared vnto them clouen tongues, like fire, and it sate vpon eche of them.

4 And they were all filled with the holy Ghost, and began to speake with other tongues, as the Spirit gaue them vtterance.

5 And there were dwelling at Hierusalem Iewes, men that feared God, of euery nation vnder heauen.

6 Nowe when this was noised, the multitude came together and were astonied, because that euery man heard them speake his owne language.

7 And they wondered al, and marueiled, saying among themselues, Beholde, are not all these which speake, of Galile?

8 How then heare we euery man our owne language, wherein we were borne?

9 Parthians, and Medes, and Elamites, and the inhabitants of Mesopotamia, and of Iudea, and of Cappadocia, of Pontus, and Asia,

10 And of Phrygia, and Pamphylia, of Egypt, and of the partes of Libya, which is beside Cyrene, and strangers of Rome, and Iewes, and Proselytes,

11 Creetes, and Arabians: wee hearde them speake in our owne tongues the wonderful works of God.

12 They were all then amased, and douted, saying one to another, What may this be?

13 And others mocked, and saide, They are full of newe wine.

14 But Peter standing with ye Eleuen, lift vp his voice, and said vnto them, Ye men of Iudea, and ye all that inhabite Hierusalem, be this knowen vnto you, and hearken vnto my woordes.

15 For these are not drunken, as yee suppose, since it is but the third houre of the day.

16 But this is that, which was spoken by the Prophet Ioel,

17 And it shalbe in the last daies, saith God, I wil powre out of my Spirite vpon al flesh, and your sonnes, and your daughters shall prophecie, and your yong men shall see visions, and your old men shall dreame dreames.

18 And on my seruauntes, and on mine handmaides I will powre out of my Spirite in those daies, and they shall prophecie.

19 And I wil shew wonders in heauen aboue, and tokens in the earth beneath, blood, and fire, and the vapour of smoke.

20 The Sunne shalbe turned into darkenesse, and the moone into blood, before that great and notable day of the Lord come.

21 And it shalbe, that whosoeuer shall call on the Name of the Lord, shalbe saued.

22 Yee men of Israel, heare these woordes, JESUS of Nazareth, a man approued of God among you with great workes, and wonders, and signes, which God did by him in the middes of you, as yee your selues also knowe:

23 Him, I say, being deliuered by the determinate counsell, and foreknowledge of God, after you had taken, with wicked handes you haue crucified and slaine.

24 Whome God hath raised vp, and loosed the sorrowes of death, because it was vnpossible that he should be holden of it.

25 For Dauid sayeth concerning him, I beheld the Lord alwaies before me: for hee is at my right hand, that I should not be shaken.

26 Therefore did mine heart reioyce, and my tongue was glad, and moreouer also my flesh shall rest in hope,

27 Because thou wilt not leaue my soule in graue, neither wilt suffer thine Holy one to see corruption.

28 Thou hast shewed me the waies of life, and shalt make me full of ioy with thy countenance.

29 Men and brethren, I may boldly speake vnto you of the Patriarke Dauid, that hee is both dead and buried, and his sepulchre remaineth with vs vnto this day.

30 Therefore, seeing hee was a Prophet, and knewe that God had sworne with an othe to him, that of the fruite of his loynes hee woulde raise vp Christ concerning the flesh, to set him vpon his throne,

31 Hee knowing this before, spake of the resurrection of Christ, that his soule shoulde not bee left in graue, neither his flesh shoulde see corruption.

32 This Iesus hath God raised vp, whereof we all are witnesses.

33 Since then that he by the right hande of God hath bene exalted, and hath receiued of his Father the promise of the holy Ghost, hee hath shed foorth this which yee nowe see and heare.

34 For Dauid is not ascended into heauen, but he sayth, The Lord sayd to my Lord, Sit at my right hande,

35 Vntill I make thine enemies thy footestoole.

36 Therefore, let all the house of Israel know for a suretie, that God hath made him both Lord, and Christ, this Iesus, I say, whome yee haue crucified.

37 Now when they heard it, they were pricked in their heartes, and said vnto Peter and the other Apostles, Men and brethren, what shall we doe?

38 Then Peter said vnto them, Amend your liues, and bee baptized euery one of you in the Name of Iesus Christ for the remission of sinnes: and ye shall receiue the gift of the holy Ghost.

39 For the promise is made vnto you, and to your children, and to all that are a farre off, euen as many as the Lord our God shall call.

40 And with many other words he besought and exhorted them, saying, Saue your selues from this froward generation.

41 Then they that gladly receiued his word, were baptized: and the same day there were added to the Church about three thousand soules.

42 And they continued in the Apostles doctrine, and fellowship, and breaking of bread, and prayers.

43 And feare came vpon euery soule: and many wonders and signes were done by ye Apostles.

44 And all that beleeued, were in one place, and had all things common.

45 And they sold their possessions and goods, and parted them to all me, as euery one had need.

46 And they continued dayly with one accord in the Temple, and breaking bread at home, did eate their meate together with gladnesse and singlenesse of heart,

47 Praysing God, and had fauour with all the people: and the Lord added to the Church from day to day, such as should be saued.

Acts 3

1 Nowe Peter and Iohn went vp together into the Temple, at the ninth houre of prayer.

2 And a certaine man which was a creeple from his mothers wombe, was caried, whom they layde dayly at the gate of the Temple called Beautifull, to aske almes of them that entred into ye Temple.

3 Who seeing Peter and Iohn, that they would enter into the Temple, desired to receiue an almes.

4 And Peter earnestly beholding him with Iohn, said, Looke on vs.

5 And hee gaue heede vnto them, trusting to receiue some thing of them.

6 Then said Peter, Siluer and gold haue I none, but such as I haue, that giue I thee: In the Name of Iesus Christ of Nazareth, rise vp and walke.

7 And hee tooke him by the right hand, and lift him vp, and immediately his feete and ankle bones receiued strength.

8 And he leaped vp, stoode, and walked, and entred with them into the Temple, walking and leaping, and praysing God.

9 And all the people sawe him walke, and praysing God.

10 And they knewe him, that it was he which sate for the almes at the Beautifull gate of the Temple: and they were amased, and sore astonied at that, which was come vnto him.

11 And as the creeple which was healed, held Peter and Iohn, all the people ranne amased vnto them in the porch which is called Salomons.

12 So when Peter saw it, he answered vnto the people, Ye me of Israel, why marueile ye at this? or why looke ye so stedfastly on vs, as though by our owne power or godlines, we had made this man go?

13 The God of Abraham, and Isaac, and Iacob, the God of our fathers hath glorified his Sonne Iesus, whom ye betrayed, and denied in the presence of Pilate, when he had iudged him to be deliuered.

14 But ye denied the Holy one and the Iust, and desired a murtherer to be giuen you,

15 And killed the Lord of life, whome God hath raised from the dead, whereof we are witnesses.

16 And his Name hath made this man sound, whom ye see, and know, through faith in his Name: and the faith which is by him, hath giuen to him this perfite health of his whole body in the presence of you all.

17 And now brethren, I know that through ignorance ye did it, as did also your gouernours.

18 But those thinges which God before had shewed by the mouth of all his Prophets, that Christ should suffer, he hath thus fulfilled.

19 Amend your liues therefore, and turne, that your sinnes may be put away, whe the time of refreshing shall come from the presence of the Lord.

20 And he shall sende Iesus Christ, which before was preached vnto you,

21 Whome the heauen must containe vntill the time that all thinges be restored, which God had spoken by the mouth of all his holy Prophets since the world began.

22 For Moses said vnto the Fathers, The Lord your God shall raise vp vnto you a Prophet, euen of your brethren, like vnto me: ye shall heare him in all things, whatsoeuer he shall say vnto you.

23 For it shalbe that euery person which shall not heare that Prophet, shall be destroyed out of the people.

24 Also all the Prophets from Samuel, and thenceefoorth as many as haue spoken, haue likewise foretolde of these dayes.

25 Ye are the children of the Prophets, and of the couenant, which God hath made vnto our fathers, saying to Abraham, Euen in thy seede shall all the kindreds of the earth be blessed.

26 First vnto you hath God raysed vp his Sonne Iesus, and him hee hath sent to blesse you, in turning euery one of you from your iniquities.

Acts 4

1 And as they spake vnto the people, the Priestes and the Captaine of the Temple, and the Sadduces came vpon them,

2 Taking it grieuously that they taught the people, and preached in Iesus Name the resurrection from the dead.

3 And they layde handes on them, and put them in holde, vntill the next day: for it was now euentide.

4 Howbeit, many of them which heard the word, beleeued, and the number of the men was about fiue thousand.

5 And it came to passe on the morow, that their rulers, and Elders, and Scribes, were gathered together at Hierusalem,

6 And Annas the chiefe Priest, and Caiaphas, and Iohn, and Alexander, and as many as were of the kindred of the hie Priestes.

7 And whe they had set them before them, they asked, By what power, or in what Name haue ye done this?

8 Then Peter ful of the holy Ghost, said vnto them, Ye rulers of the people, and Elders of Israel,

9 For as much as we this day are examined of the good deede done to the impotent man, to wit, by what meanes he is made whole,

10 Be it knowen vnto you all, and to all the people of Israel, that by the Name of Jesus Christ of Nazareth, whom ye haue crucified, whome God raised againe from the dead, euen by him doth this man stand here before you, whole.

11 This is the stone cast aside of you builders which is become the head of the corner.

12 Neither is there saluation in any other: for among men there is giuen none other Name vnder heauen, whereby we must be saued.

13 Now when they sawe the boldnes of Peter and Iohn, and vnderstoode that they were vnlearned men and without knowledge, they marueiled, and knew them, that they had bin with Iesus:

14 And beholding also the man which was healed standing with them, they had nothing to say against it.

15 Then they commanded them to goe aside out of the Council, and conferred among themselues,

16 Saying, What shall we doe to these men? for surely a manifest signe is done by them, and it is openly knowen to all them that dwell in Hierusalem: and we cannot denie it.

17 But that it be noysed no farther among the people, let vs threaten and charge them, that they speake henceefoorth to no man in this Name.

18 So they called them, and commanded them, that in no wise they should speake or teach in the Name of Iesus.

19 But Peter and Iohn answered vnto them, and said, Whether it be right in the sight of God, to obey you rather then God, iudge ye.

20 For we cannot but speake the things which we haue seene and heard.

21 So they threatened them, and let them goe, and found nothing how to punish them, because of the people: for all men praised God for that which was done.

22 For the man was aboue fourtie yeeres olde, on whome this miracle of healing was shewed.

23 Then assoone as they were let goe, they came to their fellowes, and shewed all that the hie Priestes and Elders had said vnto them.

24 And when they heard it, they lift vp their voyces to God with one accord, and said, O Lord, thou art the God which hast made the heaue, and the earth, the sea, and all things that are in them,

25 Which by the mouth of thy seruant Dauid hast saide, Why did the Gentiles rage, and the people imagine vaine things?

26 The Kings of the earth assembled, and the rulers came together against the Lord, and against his Christ.

27 For doutlesse, against thine holy Sonne Iesus, whome thou haddest anoynted, both Herod and Pontius Pilate, with the Gentiles and the people of Israel gathered themselues together,

28 To doe whatsoeuer thine hand, and thy counsell had determined before to be done.

29 And nowe, O Lord, beholde their threatnings, and graunt vnto thy seruants with all boldnesse to speake thy word,

30 So that thou stretch forth thine hand, that healing, and signes, and wonders may be done by the Name of thine holy Sonne Iesus.

31 And when as they had prayed, the place was shaken where they were assembled together, and they were all filled with the holy Ghost, and they spake the word of God boldely.

32 And the multitude of them that beleeued, were of one heart, and of one soule: neither any of them said, that any thing of that which he possessed, was his owne, but they had all thinges common.

33 And with great power gaue the Apostles witnes of the resurrection of the Lord Iesus: and great grace was vpon them all.

34 Neither was there any among them, that lacked: for as many as were possessours of landes or houses, solde them, and brought the price of the things that were solde,

35 And layde it downe at the Apostles feete, and it was distributed vnto euery man, according as he had neede.

36 Also Ioses which was called of the Apostles, Barnabas (that is by interpretation the sonne of consolation) being a Leuite, and of the countrey of Cyprus,

37 Where as he had land, solde it, and brought the money, and laid it downe at the Apostles feete.

Acts 5

1 But a certaine man named Ananias, with Sapphira his wife, solde a possession,

2 And kept away part of the price, his wife also being of counsell, and brought a certaine part, and layde it downe at the Apostles feete.

3 Then saide Peter, Ananias, why hath Satan filled thine heart, that thou shouldest lye vnto the holy Ghost, and keepe away part of the price of this possession?

4 Whiles it remained, appertained it not vnto thee? and after it was solde, was it not in thine owne power? howe is it that thou hast conceiued this thing in thine heart? thou hast not lyed vnto men, but vnto God.

5 Now when Ananias heard these wordes, he fell downe, and gaue vp the ghost. Then great feare came on all them that heard these things.

6 And the yong men rose vp, and tooke him vp, and caried him out, and buried him.

7 And it came to passe about the space of three houres after, that his wife came in, ignorant of that which was done.

8 And Peter sayd vnto her, Tell me, solde ye the land for so much? And she sayd, Yea, for so much.

9 Then Peter sayde vnto her, Why haue ye agreed together, to tempt the Spirit of the Lord? beholde, the feete of them which haue buried thine husband, are at the doore, and shall carie thee out.

10 Then she fell downe straightway at his feete, and yeelded vp the ghost: and the yong men came in, and found her dead, and caried her out, and buried her by her husband.

11 And great feare came on all the Church, and on as many as heard these things.

12 Thus by the hands of the Apostles were many signes and wonders shewed among the people (and they were all with one accorde in Salomons porche.

13 And of the other durst no man ioyne him selfe to them: neuerthelesse the people magnified them.

14 Also the number of them that beleeued in the Lord, both of men and women, grewe more and more)

15 In so much that they brought the sicke into the streetes, and layd them on beds and couches, that at the least way the shadowe of Peter, when he came by, might shadow some of them.

16 There came also a multitude out of the cities round about vnto Hierusalem, bringing sicke folkes, and them which were vexed with vncleane spirits, who were all healed.

17 Then the chiefe Priest rose vp, and all they that were with him (which was the sect of the Sadduces) and were full of indignation,

18 And laide hands on the Apostles, and put them in the common prison.

19 But the Angel of the Lord, by night opened the prison doores, and brought them forth, and sayd,

20 Go your way, and stand in the Temple, and speake to the people, all the wordes of this life.

21 So when they heard it, they entred into the Temple early in the morning, and taught. And the chiefe Priest came, and they that were with him, and called the Councill together, and all the Elders of the children of Israel, and sent to the prison, to cause them to be brought.

22 But when the officers came, and found them not in the prison, they returned and tolde it,

23 Saying, Certainely we founde the prison shut as sure as was possible, and the keepers standing without, before the doores: but when we had opened, we found no man within.

24 Then when the chiefe Priest, and the captaine of the Temple, and the hie Priestes heard these things, they doubted of them, whereunto this would growe.

25 Then came one and shewed them, saying, Beholde, the men that ye put in prison, are standing in the Temple, and teach the people.

26 Then went the captaine with the officers, and brought them without violence (for they feared the people, lest they should haue bene stoned)

27 And when they had brought them, they set them before the Councill, and the chiefe Priest asked them,

28 Saying, Did not we straightly commaund you, that ye should not teach in this Name? and behold, ye haue filled Hierusale with your doctrine, and ye would bring this mans blood vpon vs.

29 Then Peter and the Apostles answered, and sayd, We ought rather to obey God then men.

30 The God of our fathers hath raised vp Iesus, whom ye slewe, and hanged on a tree.

31 Him hath God lift vp with his right hand, to be a Prince and a Sauiour, to giue repentance to Israel, and forgiuenes of sinnes.

32 And we are his witnesses concerning these things which we say: yea, and the holy Ghost, whome God hath giuen to them that obey him.

33 Now when they heard it, they brast for anger, and consulted to slay them.

34 Then stoode there vp in the Councill a certaine Pharise named Gamaliel, a doctour of the Lawe, honoured of all the people, and commanded to put the Apostles forth a litle space,

35 And sayd vnto them, Men of Israel, take heede to your selues, what ye intende to doe touching these men.

36 For before these times, rose vp Theudas boasting himselfe, to whom resorted a number of men, about a foure hundreth, who was slaine: and they all

which obeyed him, were scattered, and brought to nought.

37 After this man, arose vp Iudas of Galile, in the dayes of the tribute, and drewe away much people after him: hee also perished, and all that obeyed him, were scattered abroad.

38 And nowe I say vnto you, Refraine your selues from these men, and let them alone: for if this counsell, or this worke be of men, it will come to nought:

39 But if it be of God, ye can not destroy it, lest ye be found euen fighters against God.

40 And to him they agreed, and called the Apostles: and when they had beaten them, they commanded that they should not speake in the Name of Iesus, and let them goe.

41 So they departed from the Councill, reioycing, that they were counted worthy to suffer rebuke for his Name.

42 And dayly in the Temple, and from house to house they ceased not to teach, and preach Iesus Christ.

Acts 6

1 And in those dayes, as the nomber of ye disciples grewe, there arose a murmuring of the Grecians towards ye Hebrewes, because their widowes were neglected in the dayly ministring.

2 Then the twelue called the multitude of the disciples together, and sayd, It is not meete that we should leaue the worde of God to serue the tables.

3 Wherefore brethren, looke ye out among you seuen men of honest report, and full of the holy Ghost, and of wisedome, which we may appoint to this busines.

4 And we will giue our selues continually to prayer, and to the ministration of the worde.

5 And the saying pleased the whole multitude: and they chose Steuen a man full of fayth and of the holy Ghost, and Philippe, and Prochorus, and Nicanor, and Timon, and Parmenas, and Nicolas a Proselyte of Antiochia,

6 Which they set before the Apostles: and they prayed, and layed their hands on them.

7 And the worde of God increased, and the number of the disciples was multipled in Hierusalem greatly, and a great company of the Priests were obedient to the faith.

8 Now Steuen full of faith and power, did great wonders and miracles among the people.

9 Then there arose certaine of the Synagogue, which are called Libertines, and Cyrenians, and of Alexandria, and of them of Cilicia, and of Asia, and disputed with Steuen.

10 But they were not able to resist the wisdome, and the Spirit by the which he spake.

11 Then they suborned men, which saide, We haue heard him speake blasphemous wordes against Moses, and God.

12 Thus they mooued the people and the Elders, and the Scribes: and running vpon him, caught him, and brought him to the Councill,

13 And set forth false witnesses, which sayd, This man ceasseth not to speake blasphemous wordes against this holy place, and the Law.

14 For we haue heard him say, that this Iesus of Nazareth shall destroy this place, and shall change the ordinances, which Moses gaue vs.

15 And as all that sate in the Councill, looked stedfastly on him, they saw his face as it had bene the face of an Angel.

Acts 7

1 Then sayd the chiefe Priest, Are these things so?

2 And he sayd, Ye men, brethren and Fathers, hearken. That God of glory appeared vnto our father Abraham, while he was in Mesopotamia, before he dwelt in Charran,

3 And said vnto him, Come out of thy countrey, and from thy kindred, and come into the land, which I shall shewe thee.

4 Then came he out of the land of the Chaldeans, and dwelt in Charran. And after that his father was dead, God brought him from thence into this land, wherein ye now dwell,

5 And hee gaue him none inheritance in it, no, not the bredth of a foote: yet he promised that he would giue it to him for a possession, and to his seede after him, when as yet hee had no childe.

6 But God spake thus, that his seede should be a soiourner in a strange land: and that they should keepe it in bondage, and entreate it euill foure hundreth yeeres.

7 But the nation to whome they shall be in bondage, will I iudge, sayth God: and after that, they shall come forth and serue me in this place.

8 Hee gaue him also the couenant of circumcision: and so Abraham begate Isaac, and circumcised him the eight day: and Isaac begate Iacob, and Iacob the twelue Patriarkes.

9 And the Patriarkes moued with enuie, solde Ioseph into Egypt: but God was with him,

10 And deliuered him out of all his afflictions, and gaue him fauour and wisdome in the sight of Pharao King of Egypt, who made him gouernour ouer Egypt, and ouer his whole house.

11 Then came there a famine ouer all the land of Egypt and Chanaan, and great affliction, that our fathers found no sustenance.

12 But when Iacob heard that there was corne in Egypt, he sent our fathers first:

13 And at the second time, Ioseph was knowen of his brethren, and Iosephs kindred was made knowen vnto Pharao.

14 Then sent Ioseph and caused his father to be brought, and all his kindred, euen threescore and fifteene soules.

15 So Iacob went downe into Egypt, and he dyed, and our fathers,

16 And were remoued into Sychem, and were put in the sepulchre, that Abraham had bought for money of the sonnes of Emor, sonne of Sychem.

17 But when the time of the promise drewe neere, which God had sworne to Abraham, the people grewe and multiplied in Egypt,

18 Till another King arose, which knewe not Ioseph.

19 The same dealt subtilly with our kindred, and euill entreated our fathers, and made them to cast out their yong children, that they should not remaine aliue.

20 The same time was Moses borne, and was acceptable vnto God, which was nourished vp in his fathers house three moneths.

21 And when he was cast out, Pharaohs daughter tooke him vp, and nourished him for her owne sonne.

22 And Moses was learned in all the wisdome of the Egyptians, and was mightie in wordes and in deedes.

23 Nowe when he was full fourtie yeere olde, it came into his heart to visite his brethren, the children of Israel.

24 And whe he saw one of them suffer wrong, he defended him, and auenged his quarell that had the harme done to him, and smote the Egyptian.

25 For hee supposed his brethren would haue vnderstand, that God by his hande should giue them deliuerance: but they vnderstoode it not.

26 And the next day, he shewed himselfe vnto them as they stroue, and woulde haue set them at one againe, saying, Syrs, ye are brethren: why doe ye wrong one to another?

27 But he that did his neighbour wrong, thrust him away, saying, Who made thee a prince and a iudge ouer vs?

28 Wilt thou kill mee, as thou diddest the Egyptian yesterday?

29 Then fled Moses at that saying, and was a stranger in the land of Madian, where he begate two sonnes.

30 And when fourtie yeres were expired, there appeared to him in the wildernes of mout Sina, an Angel of the Lord in a flame of fire, in a bush.

31 And when Moses sawe it, hee wondred at the sight: and as he drew neere to consider it, the voyce of the Lord came vnto him, saying,

32 I am the God of thy fathers, the God of Abraham, and the God of Isaac, and the God of Iacob. Then Moses trembled, and durst not behold it.

33 Then the Lord said to him, Put off thy shoes from thy feete: for the place where thou standest, is holy ground.

34 I haue seene, I haue seene the affliction of my people, which is in Egypt, and I haue heard their groning, and am come downe to deliuer them: and nowe come, and I will sende thee into Egypt.

35 This Moses whome they forsooke, saying, Who made thee a prince and a iudge? the same God sent for a prince, and a deliuerer by the hand of the Angel, which appeared to him in the bush.

36 Hee brought them out, doing wonders, and miracles in the land of Egypt, and in the red sea, and in the wildernes fourtie yeeres.

37 This is that Moses, which saide vnto the children of Israel, A Prophet shall the Lord your God raise vp vnto you, euen of your brethren, like vnto me: him shall ye heare.

38 This is he that was in the Congregation, in the wildernes with the Angell, which spake to him in mount Sina, and with our fathers, who receiued the liuely oracles to giue vnto vs.

39 To whom our fathers would not obey, but refused, and in their hearts turned backe againe into Egypt:

40 Saying vnto Aaron, Make vs gods that may goe before vs: for we knowe not what is become of this Moses that brought vs out of the land of Egypt.

41 And they made a calfe in those dayes, and offered sacrifice vnto the idole, and reioyced in the workes of their owne handes.

42 Then God turned himselfe away, and gaue them vp to serue the host of heauen, as it is written in the booke of the Prophets, O house of Israel, haue ye offred to me slaine beasts and sacrifices by the space of fourtie yeres in the wildernes?

43 And ye tooke vp the tabernacle of Moloch, and the starre of your god Remphan, figures, which ye made to worship them: therefore I will carie you away beyond Babylon.

44 Our fathers had the tabernacle of witnes, in the wildernes, as hee had appointed, speaking vnto Moses, that he should make it according to the fashion that he had seene.

45 Which tabernacle also our fathers receiued, and brought in with Iesus into the possession of the Gentiles, which God draue out before our fathers, vnto the dayes of Dauid:

46 Who found fauour before God, and desired that hee might finde a tabernacle for the God of Iacob.

47 But Salomon built him an house.

48 Howbeit the most High dwelleth not in temples made with handes, as saith the Prophet,

49 Heauen is my throne, and earth is my footestoole: what house wil ye build for me, saith the Lord? or what place is it that I should rest in?

50 Hath not mine hand made all these things?

51 Ye stiffenecked and of vncircumcised heartes and eares, ye haue alwayes resisted the holy Ghost: as your fathers did, so do you.

52 Which of the Prophets haue not your fathers persecuted? and they haue slaine them, which shewed before of the comming of that Iust, of whome ye are now the betrayers and murtherers,

53 Which haue receiued the Lawe by the ordinance of Angels, and haue not kept it.

54 But when they heard these thinges, their heartes brast for anger, and they gnashed at him with their teeth.

55 But he being full of the holy Ghost, looked stedfastly into heauen, and sawe the glory of God, and Iesus standing at the right hand of God,

56 And said, Beholde, I see the heauens open, and the Sonne of man standing at the right hand of God.

57 Then they gaue a shoute with a loude voyce, and stopped their eares, and ranne vpon him violently all at once,

58 And cast him out of the citie, and stoned him: and the witnesses layd downe their clothes at a yong mans feete, named Saul.

59 And they stoned Steuen, who called on God, and said, Lord Iesus, receiue my spirit.

60 And he kneeled downe, and cried with a loude voyce, Lord, laye not this sinne to their charge. And when he had thus spoken, he slept.

Acts 8

1 And Saul consented to his death, and at that time, there was a great persecution against the Church which was at Hierusalem, and they were all scattered abroad thorowe the regions of Iudea and of Samaria, except the Apostles.

2 Then certaine men fearing God, caried Steuen amongs them, to be buried, and made great lamentation for him.

3 But Saul made hauocke of the Church, and entred into euery house, and drewe out both men and women, and put them into prison.

4 Therefore they that were scattered abroad, went to and from preaching the worde.

5 Then came Philip into the citie of Samaria, and preached Christ vnto them.

6 And the people gaue heed vnto those things which Philippe spake, with one accorde, hearing and seeing the miracles which he did.

7 For vncleane spirits crying with a loud voyce, came out of many that were possessed of them: and many taken with palsies, and that halted, were healed.

8 And there was great ioy in that citie.

9 And there was before in the citie a certaine man called Simon, which vsed witchcraft, and bewitched the people of Samaria, saying that he himselfe was some great man.

10 To whome they gaue heede from the least to the greatest, saying, This man is that great power of God.

11 And they gaue heed vnto him, because that of long time he had bewitched them with sorceries.

12 But assoone as they beleeued Philip, which preached the thinges that concerned the kingdome of God, and the Name of Iesus Christ, they were baptized both men and women.

13 Then Simon himselfe beleeued also and was baptized, and continued with Philippe, and wondred, when he sawe the signes and great miracles which were done.

14 Nowe when the Apostles, which were at Hierusalem, heard say, that Samaria had receiued the worde of God, they sent vnto them Peter and Iohn.

15 Which whe they were come downe, prayed for them, that they might receiue the holy Ghost.

16 (For as yet, hee was fallen downe on none of them, but they were baptized onely in the Name of the Lord Iesus.)

17 Then layd they their handes on them, and they receiued the holy Ghost.

18 And when Simon sawe, that through laying on of the Apostles hands the holy Ghost was giuen, he offred them money,

19 Saying, Giue mee also this power, that on whomsoeuer I lay the handes, he may receiue the holy Ghost.

20 Then saide Peter vnto him, Thy money perish with thee, because thou thinkest that the gift of God may be obteined with money.

21 Thou hast neither part nor fellowship in this businesse: for thine heart is not right in the sight of God.

22 Repent therefore of this thy wickednes, and pray God, that if it be possible, the thought of thine heart may be forgiuen thee.

23 For I see that thou art in the gall of bitternes, and in the bonde of iniquitie.

24 Then answered Simon, and said, Pray ye to the Lord for me, that none of these things which ye haue spoken, come vpon me.

25 So they, when they had testified and preached the worde of the Lord, returned to Hierusalem, and preached the Gospel in many townes of the Samaritans.

26 Then the Angel of the Lord spake vnto Philip, saying, Arise, and goe towarde the South vnto the way that goeth downe from Hierusalem vnto Gaza, which is waste.

27 And hee arose and went on: and beholde, a certaine Eunuche of Ethiopia, Candaces the Queene of the Ethiopians chiefe Gouernour, who had the rule of all her treasure, and came to Hierusalem to worship:

28 And as he returned sitting in his charet, he read Esaias the Prophet.

29 Then the Spirit said vnto Philip, Goe neere and ioyne thy selfe to yonder charet.

30 And Philip ranne thither, and heard him reade the Prophet Esaias, and said, But vnderstandest thou what thou readest?

31 And he saide, Howe can I, except I had a guide? And he desired Philip, that he would come vp and sit with him.

32 Nowe the place of the Scripture which he read, was this, Hee was lead as a sheepe to the slaughter: and like a lambe domme before his shearer, so opened he not his mouth.

33 In his humilitie his iudgement hath bene exalted: but who shall declare his generation? for his life is taken from the earth.

34 Then the Eunuche answered Philippe, and saide, I pray thee of whome speaketh the Prophet this? of himselfe, or of some other man?

35 Then Philip opened his mouth, and began at the same Scripture, and preached vnto him Iesus.

36 And as they went on their way, they came vnto a certaine water, and the Eunuche said, See, here is water: what doeth let me to be baptized?

37 And Philippe said vnto him, If thou beleeuest with all thine heart, thou mayest. Then he answered, and saide, I beleeue that that Iesus Christ is that Sonne of God.

38 Then he commanded the charet to stand stil: and they went downe both into the water, both Philip and the Eunuche, and he baptized him.

39 And assoone as they were come vp out of the water, the Spirit of the Lord caught away Philip, that the Eunuche sawe him no more: so he went on his way reioycing.

40 But Philippe was found at Azotus, and he walked to and from preaching in all the cities, till he came to Cesarea.

Acts 9

1 And Saul yet breathing out threatnings and slaughter against the disciples of ye Lord, went vnto the hie Priest,

2 And desired of him letters to Damascus to the Synagogues, that if he found any that were of that way (either men or women) hee might bring them bound vnto Hierusalem.

3 Now as he iourneyed, it came to passe that as he was come neere to Damascus, suddenly there shined rounde about him a light from heauen.

4 And hee fell to the earth, and heard a voyce, saying to him, Saul, Saul, why persecutest thou me?

5 And he sayd, Who art thou, Lord? And the Lord sayd, I am Iesus whom thou persecutest: it is hard for thee to kicke against pricks.

6 He then both trembling and astonied, sayd, Lord, what wilt thou that I doe? And the Lord sayd vnto him, Arise and goe into the citie, and it shall be tolde thee what thou shalt doe.

7 The men also which iourneyed with him, stood amased, hearing his voyce, but seeing no man.

8 And Saul arose from the ground, and opened his eyes, but sawe no man. Then led they him by the hand, and brought him into Damascus,

9 Where he was three dayes without sight, and neither ate nor dranke.

10 And there was a certaine disciple at Damascus named Ananias, and to him sayd the Lord in a vision, Ananias. And he sayd, Beholde, I am here Lord.

11 Then the Lord sayd vnto him, Arise, and goe into the streete which is called Straight, and seeke in the house of Iudas after one called Saul of Tarsus: for beholde, he prayeth.

12 (And he sawe in a vision a man named Ananias comming in to him, and putting his hands on him, that he might receiue his sight.)

13 Then Ananias answered, Lord, I haue heard by many of this man, howe much euill hee hath done to thy saints at Hierusalem.

14 Moreouer here hee hath authoritie of the hie Priestes, to binde all that call on thy Name.

15 Then the Lord said vnto him, Go thy way: for he is a chosen vessell vnto me, to beare my Name before the Gentiles, and Kings, and the children of Israel.

16 For I will shewe him, howe many things he must suffer for my Names sake.

17 Then Ananias went his way, and entred into that house, and put his hands on him, and sayd, Brother Saul, the Lord hath sent me (euen Iesus that appeared vnto thee in the way as thou camest) that thou mightest receiue thy sight, and be filled with the holy Ghost.

18 And immediately there fell from his eyes as it had bene scales, and suddenly he receiued sight, and arose, and was baptized,

19 And receiued meate, and was strengthened. So was Saul certaine dayes with the disciples which were at Damascus.

20 And straightway hee preached Christ in the Synagogues, that he was that Sonne of God,

21 So that all that heard him, were amased, and sayde, Is not this hee, that made hauocke of them which called on this Name in Hierusalem, and came hither for that intent, that hee should bring them bound vnto the hie Priests?

22 But Saul encreased the more in strength, and confounded the Iewes which dwelt at Damascus, confirming, that this was that Christ.

23 And after that many dayes were fulfilled, the Iewes tooke counsell together, to kill him,

24 But their laying awayte was knowen of Saul: nowe they watched the gates day and night, that they might kill him.

25 Then the disciples tooke him by night, and put him through the wall, and let him downe by a rope in a basket.

26 And when Saul was come to Hierusalem, he assayed to ioyne himselfe with the disciples: but they were all afrayd of him, and beleeued not that he was a disciple.

27 But Barnabas tooke him, and brought him to the Apostles, and declared to them, howe hee had seene the Lord in the way, and that hee had spoken vnto him, and how he had spoken boldly at Damascus in the Name of Iesus.

28 And hee was conuersant with them at Hierusalem,

29 And spake boldly in the Name of the Lord Iesus, and spake and disputed against the Grecians: but they went about to slay him.

30 But when the brethren knewe it, they brought him to Cesarea, and sent him forth to Tarsus.

31 Then had the Churches rest through all Iudea, and Galile, and Samaria, and were edified and walked in the feare of the Lord, and were multiplied by the comfort of the holy Ghost.

32 And it came to passe, as Peter walked throughout all quarters, hee came also to the saints which dwelt at Lydda.

33 And there he found a certaine man named Aeneas, which had kept his couch eight yeeres, and was sicke of the palsie.

34 Then said Peter vnto him, Aeneas, Iesus Christ maketh thee whole: arise and trusse thy couch together. And he arose immediately.

35 And all that dwelt at Lydda and Saron, sawe him, and turned to the Lord.

36 There was also at Ioppa a certaine woman, a disciple named Tabitha (which by interpretation is called Dorcas) she was full of good workes and almes which she did.

37 And it came to passe in those dayes, that she was sicke and dyed: and when they had washed her, they layd her in an vpper chamber.

38 Now forasmuch as Lydda was neere to Ioppa, and the disciples had heard that Peter was there, they sent vnto him two men, desiring that he would not delay to come vnto them.

39 Then Peter arose and came with them: and when hee was come, they brought him into the vpper chamber, where all the widowes stoode by him weeping, and shewing the coates and garments, which Dorcas made, while she was with them.

40 But Peter put them all forth, and kneeled downe, and prayed, and turned him to the body, and sayd, Tabitha, arise. And she opened her eyes, and when she sawe Peter, sate vp.

41 Then he gaue her the hand and lift her vp, and called the Saints and widowes, and restored her aliue.

42 And it was knowen throughout all Ioppa, and many beleeued in the Lord.

43 And it came to passe that he taried many dayes in Ioppa with one Simon a Tanner.

Acts 10

1 Futhermore there was a certaine man in Cesarea called Cornelius, a captaine of the band called the Italian band,

2 A deuoute man, and one that feared God with all his housholde, which gaue much almes to the people, and prayed God continually.

3 He sawe in a vision euidently (about the ninth houre of the day) an Angel of God comming in to him, and saying vnto him, Cornelius.

4 But when hee looked on him, hee was afrayd, and sayd, What is it, Lord? and he sayd vnto him, Thy prayers and thine almes are come vp into remembrance before God.

5 Nowe therefore send men to Ioppa, and call for Simon, whose surname is Peter.

6 Hee lodgeth with one Simon a Tanner, whose house is by the sea side: he shall tell thee what thou oughtest to doe.

7 And when the Angel which spake vnto Cornelius, was departed, he called two of his seruants, and a souldier that feared God, one of them that waited on him,

8 And tolde them all things, and sent them to Ioppa.

9 On the morow as they went on their iourney, and drew neere vnto the citie, Peter went vp vpon the house to pray, about the sixt houre.

10 Then waxed hee an hungred, and would haue eaten: but while they made some thing ready, he fell into a trance.

11 And hee sawe heauen opened, and a certaine vessell come downe vnto him, as it had bene a great sheete, knit at the foure corners, and was let downe to the earth.

12 Wherein were all maner of foure footed beastes of the earth, and wilde beastes and creeping things, and foules of the heauen.

13 And there came a voyce to him, Arise, Peter: kill, and eate.

14 But Peter sayd, Not so, Lord: for I haue neuer eaten any thing that is polluted, or vncleane.

15 And the voyce spake vnto him againe the second time, The things that God hath purified, pollute thou not.

16 This was so done thrise: and the vessell was drawen vp againe into heauen.

17 Nowe while Peter douted in himselfe what this vision which he had seene, meant, beholde, the men which were sent from Cornelius, had inquired for Simons house, and stoode at the gate,

18 And called, and asked, whether Simon, which was surnamed Peter, were lodged there.

19 And while Peter thought on the vision, the Spirit sayde vnto him, Beholde, three men seeke thee.

20 Arise therefore, and get thee downe, and goe with them, and doute nothing: For I haue sent them.

21 Then Peter went downe to the men, which were sent vnto him from Cornelius, and sayd, Beholde, I am he whome ye seeke: what is the cause wherefore ye are come?

22 And they sayd, Cornelius the captaine, a iust man, and one that feareth God, and of good report among all the nation of the Iewes, was warned from heauen by an holy Angel, to send for thee into his house, and to heare thy wordes.

23 Then called he them in, and lodged them, and the next day, Peter went foorth with them, and certaine brethren from Ioppa accompanied him.

24 And the day after, they entred into Cesarea. Nowe Cornelius waited for them, and had called together his kinsemen, and special friends.

25 And it came to passe as Peter came in, that Cornelius met him, and fell downe at his feete, and worshipped him.

26 But Peter tooke him vp, saying, Stand vp: for euen I my selfe am a man.

27 And as he talked with him, he came in, and found many that were come together.

28 And he sayd vnto them, Ye know that it is an vnlawfull thing for a man that is a Iewe, to company, or come vnto one of another nation: but God hath shewed me, that I should not call any man polluted, or vncleane.

29 Therefore came I vnto you without saying nay, when I was sent for. I aske therefore, for what intent haue ye sent for me?

30 Then Cornelius sayd, Foure dayes agoe, about this houre, I fasted, and at the ninth houre I prayed in mine house, and beholde, a man stood before me in bright clothing,

31 And sayd, Cornelius, thy prayer is heard, and thine almes are had in remembrance in the sight of God.

32 Send therefore to Ioppa, and call for Simon, whose surname is Peter (he is lodged in the house of Simon a Tanner by the sea side) who when he commeth, shall speake vnto thee.

33 Then sent I for thee immediately, and thou hast well done to come. Nowe therefore are we all here present before God, to heare all things that are commanded thee of God.

34 Then Peter opened his mouth, and sayd, Of a trueth I perceiue, that God is no accepter of persons.

35 But in euery nation he that feareth him, and worketh righteousnesse, is accepted with him.

36 Ye know the worde which God hath sent to the children of Israel, preaching peace by Iesus Christ, which is Lord of all:

37 Euen the worde which came through all Iudea, beginning in Galile, after the baptisme which Iohn preached.

38 To wit, howe God anointed Iesus of Nazareth with the holy Ghost, and with power: who went about doing good, and healing all that were oppressed of the deuill: for God was with him.

39 And we are witnesses of all things which he did both in the land of the Iewes, and in Hierusalem, whom they slewe, hanging him on a tree.

40 Him God raysed vp the third day, and caused that he was shewed openly:

41 Not to all the people, but vnto the witnesses chosen before of God, euen to vs which did eate and drinke with him, after he arose from the dead.

42 And he commanded vs to preach vnto the people, and to testifie, that it is he that is ordained of God a iudge of quicke and dead.

43 To him also giue all the Prophets witnesse, that through his Name all that beleeue in him, shall receiue remission of sinnes.

44 While Peter yet spake these wordes, the holy Ghost fell on al them which heard the word.

45 So they of the circumcision which beleeued, were astonied, as many as came with Peter, because that on the Gentiles also was powred out the gift of the holy Ghost.

46 For they heard them speake with tongues, and magnifie God. Then answered Peter,

47 Can any man forbid water, that these should not be baptized, which haue receiued the holy Ghost, as well as we?

48 So he commanded them to be baptized in the Name of the Lord. Then prayed they him to tary certaine dayes.

Acts 11

1 Nowe the Apostles and the brethren that were in Iudea, heard, that the Gentiles had also receiued the worde of God.

2 And when Peter was come vp to Hierusalem, they of the circumcision contended against him,

3 Saying, Thou wentest in to men vncircumcised, and hast eaten with them.

4 Then Peter beganne, and expounded the thing in order to them, saying,

5 I was in the citie of Ioppa, praying, and in a trance I sawe this vision, A certaine vessell comming downe as it had bene a great sheete, let downe from heauen by the foure corners, and it came to me.

6 Towarde the which when I had fastened mine eyes, I considered, and sawe foure footed beastes of the earth, and wilde beastes, and creeping things, and foules of the heauen.

7 Also I heard a voyce, saying vnto me, Arise, Peter: slay and eate.

8 And I said, God forbid, Lord: for nothing polluted or vncleane hath at any time entred into my mouth.

9 But the voyce answered me the seconde time from heauen, The things that God hath purified, pollute thou not.

10 And this was done three times, and all were taken vp againe into heauen.

11 Then behold, immediatly there were three men already come vnto the house where I was, sent from Cesarea vnto me.

12 And the Spirit saide vnto me, that I should go with them, without doubting: moreouer these sixe brethren came with me, and we entred into the mans house.

13 And he shewed vs, howe he had seene an Angel in his house, which stoode and said to him, Send men to Ioppa, and call for Simon, whose surname is Peter.

14 He shall speake wordes vnto thee, whereby both thou and all thine house shalbe saued.

15 And as I began to speake, the holy Ghost fell on them, euen as vpon vs at the beginning.

16 Then I remembred the word of the Lord, howe he said, Iohn baptized with water, but ye shalbe baptized with the holy Ghost.

17 For as much then as God gaue them a like gift, as he did vnto vs, when we beleeued in the Lord Iesus Christ, who was I, that I coulde let God?

18 When they heard these things, they helde their peace, and glorified God, saying, Then hath God also to the Gentiles graunted repentance vnto life.

19 And they which were scattered abroade because of the affliction that arose about Steuen, went throughout till they came vnto Phenice and Cyprus, and

Antiochia, preaching the worde to no man, but vnto the Iewes onely.

20 Now some of them were men of Cyprus and of Cyrene, which when they were come into Antiochia, spake vnto the Grecians, and preached the Lord Iesus.

21 And the hand of the Lord was with them, so that a great number beleeued and turned vnto the Lord.

22 Then tydings of those things came vnto the eares of the Church, which was in Hierusalem, and they sent foorth Barnabas, that he should goe vnto Antiochia.

23 Who when he was come and had seene the grace of God, was glad, and exhorted all, that with purpose of heart they would continue in the Lord.

24 For he was a good man, and full of the holy Ghost, and faith, and much people ioyned them selues vnto the Lord.

25 Then departed Barnabas to Tarsus to seeke Saul:

26 And when he had founde him, he brought him vnto Antiochia: and it came to passe that a whole yere they were conuersant with ye Church, and taught much people, in so much that the disciples were first called Christians in Antiochia.

27 In those dayes also came Prophets from Hierusalem vnto Antiochia.

28 And there stoode vp one of them named Agabus, and signified by the Spirit, that there should be great famine throughout all the world, which also came to passe vnder Claudius Cesar.

29 Then the disciples, euery man according to his ability, purposed to sende succour vnto the brethren which dwelt in Iudea.

30 Which thing they also did, and sent it to the Elders, by the hand of Barnabas and Saul.

Acts 12

1 Nowe about that time, Herod the King stretched forth his hands to vexe certaine of the Church,

2 And he killed Iames the brother of Iohn with the sword.

3 And when he sawe that it pleased the Iewes, he proceeded further, to take Peter also (then were the dayes of vnleauened bread.)

4 And when he had caught him, he put him in prison, and deliuered him to foure quaternions of souldiers to be kept, intending after the Passeouer to bring him foorth to the people.

5 So Peter was kept in prison, but earnest prayer was made of ye Church vnto God for him.

6 And when Herod woulde haue brought him out vnto the people, the same night slept Peter betweene two souldiers, bound with two chaines, and the keepers before the doore, kept the prison.

7 And behold the Angel of the Lord came vpon them, and a light shined in the house, and he smote Peter on the side, and raysed him vp, saying, Arise quickely. And his chaines fell off from his handes.

8 And the Angel saide vnto him, Girde thy selfe, and binde on thy sandales. And so he did. Then he said vnto him, Cast thy garment about thee, and follow me.

9 So Peter came out and followed him, and knewe not that it was true, which was done by the Angel, but thought he had seene a vision.

10 Nowe when they were past the first and the second watch, they came vnto the yron gate, that leadeth vnto the citie, which opened to them by it owne accord, and they went out, and passed through one streete, and by and by the Angel departed from him.

11 And when Peter was come to himselfe, he said, Nowe I know for a trueth, that the Lord hath sent his Angel, and hath deliuered me out of the hand of Herod, and from all the wayting for of the people of the Iewes.

12 And as he considered the thing, he came to the house of Marie, the mother of Iohn, whose surname was Marke, where many were gathered together, and prayed.

13 And when Peter knocked at the entrie doore, a maide came foorth to hearken, named Rhode,

14 But when she knew Peters voyce, she opened not the entrie doore for gladnesse, but ranne in, and tolde howe Peter stood before the entrie.

15 But they said vnto her, Thou art mad. Yet she affirmed it constantly, that it was so. Then said they, It is his Angel.

16 But Peter continued knocking, and when they had opened it, and sawe him, they were astonied.

17 And he beckened vnto them with the hand, to hold their peace, and told them how the Lord had brought him out of the prison. And he saide, Goe shewe these things vnto Iames and to the brethren: and he departed and went into an other place.

18 Nowe assoone as it was day, there was no small trouble among the souldiers, what was become of Peter.

19 And when Herod had sought for him, and found him not, he examined the keepers, and commanded them to be led to be punished. And he went downe from Iudea to Cesarea, and there abode.

20 Then Herod was angrie with them of Tyrus and Sidon, but they came all with one accord vnto him, and perswaded Blastus the Kings Chamberlaine, and they desired peace, because their countrey was nourished by the Kings land.

21 And vpon a day appointed, Herod arayed himselfe in royall apparell, and sate on the iudgement seate, and made an oration vnto them.

22 And the people gaue a shoute, saying, The voyce of God, and not of man.

23 But immediatly the Angel of the Lord smote him, because he gaue not glorie vnto God, so that he was eaten of wormes, and gaue vp the ghost.

24 And the worde of God grewe, and multiplied.

25 So Barnabas and Saul returned from Hierusalem, when they had fulfilled their office, and tooke with them Iohn, whose surname was Marke.

Acts 13

1 There were also in the Church that was at Antiochia, certaine Prophets and teachers, as Barnabas, and Simeon called Niger, and Lucius of Cyrene, and Manahen (which had bin brought vp with Herod the Tetrarche) and Saul.

2 Nowe as they ministred to the Lord, and fasted, the holy Ghost said, Separate me Barnabas and Saul, for the worke whereunto I haue called them.

3 Then fasted they and prayed, and layde their hands on them, and let them goe.

4 And they, after they were sent foorth of the holy Ghost, came downe vnto Seleucia, and from thence they sayled to Cyprus.

5 And when they were at Salamis, they preached the worde of God in the Synagogues of the Iewes: and they had also Iohn to their minister.

6 So when they had gone throughout the yle vnto Paphus, they found a certaine sorcerer, a false prophet, being a Iewe, named Bariesus,

7 Which was with the Deputie Sergius Paulus, a prudent man. He called vnto him Barnabas and Saul, and desired to heare the woorde of God.

8 But Elymas, ye sorcerer (for so is his name by interpretation) withstoode them, and sought to turne away the Deputie from the faith.

9 Then Saul (which also is called Paul) being full of the holy Ghost, set his eyes on him,

10 And sayde, O full of all subtiltie and all mischiefe, the childe of the deuill, and enemie of all righteousnesse, wilt thou not cease to peruert the straight waies of the Lord?

11 Nowe therefore behold, the hand of the Lord is vpon thee, and thou shalt be blinde, and not see the sunne for a season. And immediately there fel on him a mist and a darknes; and he went about, seeking some to leade him by the hand.

12 Then the Deputie when he sawe what was done, beleeued, and was astonied at the doctrine of the Lord.

13 Nowe when Paul and they that were with him were departed by shippe from Paphus, they came to Perga a citie of Pamphylia: then Iohn departed from them, and returned to Hierusalem.

14 But when they departed from Perga, they came to Antiochia a citie of Pisidia, and went into the Synagogue on ye Sabbath day, and sate downe.

15 And after the lecture of the Law and Prophets, the rulers of ye Synagogue sent vnto them, saying, Ye men and brethren, if ye haue any word of exhortation for the people, say on.

16 Then Paul stoode vp and beckened with the hand, and sayde, Men of Israel, and yee that feare God, hearken.

17 The God of this people of Israel chose our fathers, and exalted the people when they dwelt in the land of Egypt, and with an high arme brought them out thereof.

18 And about the time of fourtie yeeres, suffered he their maners in the wildernesse.

19 And he destroied seuen nations in the land of Chanaan, and deuided their lad to them by lot.

20 Then afterward he gaue vnto them Iudges about foure hundreth and fiftie yeeres, vnto the time of Samuel the Prophet.

21 So after that, they desired a King, and God gaue vnto them Saul, the sonne of Cis, a man of ye tribe of Beniamin, by the space of fourty yeres.

22 And after he had taken him away, he raised vp Dauid to be their King, of whom he witnessed, saying, I haue found Dauid the sonne of Iesse, a man after mine owne heart, which will doe all things that I will.

23 Of this mans seede hath God according to his promise raised vp to Israel, ye Sauiour Iesus:

24 When Iohn had first preached before his coming the baptisme of repentance to all the people of Israel.

25 And when Iohn had fulfilled his course, he saide, Whom ye thinke that I am, I am not he: but beholde, there commeth one after me, whose shooe of his feete I am not worthy to loose.

26 Yee men and brethren, children of the generation of Abraham, and whosoeuer among you feareth God, to you is the woorde of this saluation sent.

27 For the inhabitants of Hierusalem, and their rulers, because they knewe him not, nor yet the woordes of the Prophets, which are read euery Sabbath day, they haue fulfilled them in condemning him.

28 And though they found no cause of death in him, yet desired they Pilate to kill him.

29 And when they had fulfilled all things that were written of him, they tooke him downe from the tree, and put him in a sepulchre.

30 But God raised him vp from the dead.

31 And hee was seene many dayes of them, which came vp with him from Galile to Hierusalem, which are his witnesses vnto the people.

32 And we declare vnto you, that touching the promise made vnto the fathers,

33 God hath fulfilled it vnto vs their children, in that he raised vp Iesus, euen as it is written in the seconde Psalme, Thou art my Sonne: this day haue I begotten thee.

34 Nowe as concerning that he raised him vp from the dead, no more to returne to corruption, he hath said thus, I wil giue you the holy things of Dauid, which are faithfull.

35 Wherefore hee sayeth also in another place, Thou wilt not suffer thine Holy one to see corruption.

36 Howbeit, Dauid after hee had serued his time by the counsell of God, hee slept, and was laid with his fathers, and sawe corruption.

37 But he whom God raised vp, sawe no corruption.

38 Be it knowen vnto you therefore, men and brethren, that through this man is preached vnto you the forgiuenesse of sinnes.

39 And from al things, from which ye could not be iustified by the Law of Moses, by him euery one that beleeueth, is iustified.

40 Beware therefore lest that come vpon you, which is spoken of in the Prophets,

41 Behold, ye despisers, and wonder, and vanish away: for I woorke a woorke in your daies, a woorke which yee shall not beleeue, if a man would declare it you.

42 And when they were come out of the Synagogue of the Iewes, the Gentiles besought, that they woulde preach these woordes to them the next Sabbath day.

43 Nowe when the congregation was dissolued, many of the Iewes and Proselytes that feared God, followed Paul and Barnabas, which spake to them, and exhorted them to continue in the grace of God.

44 And ye next Sabbath day came almost the whole citie together, to heare the worde of God.

45 But when the Iewes saw the people, they were full of enuie, and spake against those things, which were spoken of Paul, contrarying them, and railing on them.

46 Then Paul and Barnabas spake boldly, and sayde, It was necessarie that the woorde of God shoulde first haue beene spoken vnto you: but seeing yee put it from you, and iudge your selues vnworthie of euerlasting life, loe, we turne to the Gentiles.

47 For so hath the Lord commanded vs, saying, I haue made thee a light of the Gentiles, that thou shouldest be the saluation vnto the end of the world.

48 And when the Gentiles heard it, they were glad, and glorified the woorde of the Lord: and as many as were ordeined vnto eternall life, beleeued.

49 Thus the worde of the Lord was published throughout the whole countrey.

50 But the Iewes stirred certaine deuoute and honourable women, and the chiefe men of the citie, and raised persecution against Paul and Barnabas, and expelled them out of their coastes.

51 But they shooke off the dust of their feete against them, and came vnto Iconium.

52 And the disciples were filled with ioy, and with the holy Ghost.

Acts 14

1 And it came to passe in Iconium, that they went both together into the Synagogue of the Iewes, and so spake, that a great multitude both of the Iewes and of the Grecians beleeued.

2 And the vnbeleeuing Iewes stirred vp, and corrupted the mindes of the Gentiles against the brethren.

3 So therefore they abode there a long time, and spake boldly in the Lord, which gaue testimonie vnto the woord of his grace, and caused signes and woders to be done by their hands.

4 But the multitude of the city was deuided: and some were with the Iewes, and some with the Apostles.

5 And when there was an assault made both of the Gentiles, and of the Iewes with their rulers, to doe them violence, and to stone them,

6 They were ware of it, and fled vnto Lystra, and Derbe, cities of Lycaonia, and vnto the region round about,

7 And there preached the Gospel.

8 Nowe there sate a certaine man at Lystra, impotent in his feete, which was a creeple from his mothers wombe, who had neuer walked.

9 He heard Paul speake: who beholding him, and perceiuing that he had faith to be healed,

10 Said with a loude voyce, Stand vpright on thy feete. And he leaped vp, and walked.

11 Then when the people sawe what Paul had done, they lift vp their voyces, saying in ye speach of Lycaonia, Gods are come downe to vs in the likenesse of men.

12 And they called Barnabas, Iupiter: and Paul, Mercurius, because hee was the chiefe speaker.

13 Then Iupiters priest, which was before their citie, brought bulles with garlands vnto the gates, and would haue sacrificed with the people.

14 But when the Apostles, Barnabas and Paul heard it, they rent their clothes, and ran in among the people, crying,

15 And saying, O men, why doe yee these things? We are euen men subiect to the like passions that yee be, and preache vnto you, that yee shoulde turne from these vaine things vnto the liuing God, which made heauen and earth, and the sea, and all things that in them are:

16 Who in times past suffered all the Gentiles to walke in their owne waies.

17 Neuerthelesse, hee left not him selfe without witnes, in that hee did good and gaue vs raine from heauen, and fruitful seasons, filling our hearts with foode, and gladnesse.

18 And speaking these things, scarce appeased they the multitude, that they had not sacrificed vnto them.

19 Then there came certaine Iewes from Antiochia and Iconium, which when they had persuaded the people, stoned Paul, and drewe him out of the citie, supposing he had bene dead.

20 Howbeit, as the disciples stoode rounde about him, hee arose vp, and came into the citie, and the next day hee departed with Barnabas to Derbe.

21 And after they had preached the glad tidings of the Gospel to that citie, and had taught many, they returned to Lystra, and to Iconium, and to Antiochia,

22 Confirming the disciples hearts, and exhorting them to continue in the faith, affirming that we must through many afflictions enter into the kingdome of God.

23 And when they had ordeined them Elders by election in euery Church, and prayed, and fasted, they commended them to the Lord in whome they beleeued.

24 Thus they went throughout Pisidia, and came to Pamphylia.

25 And when they had preached the woorde in Perga, they came downe to Attalia,

26 And thence sailed to Antiochia, from whence they had bene comended vnto the grace of God, to the woorke, which they had fulfilled.

27 And when they were come and had gathered the Church together, they rehearsed all the things that God had done by them, and howe he had opened the doore of faith vnto the Gentiles.

28 So there they abode a long time with the disciples.

Acts 15

1 Then came downe certaine from Iudea, and taught the brethren, saying, Except ye be circumcised after the maner of Moses, ye cannot be saued.

2 And when there was great dissension, and disputation by Paul and Barnabas against them, they ordeyned that Paul and Barnabas, and certaine other of them, should goe vp to Hierusalem vnto the Apostles and Elders about this question.

3 Thus being brought forth by ye Church, they passed through Phenice and Samaria, declaring the conuersion of the Gentiles, and they brought great ioy vnto all the brethren.

4 And when they were come to Hierusalem, they were receiued of the Church, and of the Apostles and Elders, and they declared what things God had done by them.

5 But said they, certaine of the sect of the Pharises, which did beleeue, rose vp, saying, that it was needefull to circumcise them, and to commaund them to keepe the lawe of Moses.

6 Then the Apostles and Elders came together to looke to this matter.

7 And when there had bene great disputation, Peter rose vp, and said vnto them, Ye men and brethren, ye know that a good while ago, among vs God chose out me, that the Gentiles by my mouth should heare the worde of the Gospel, and beleeue.

8 And God which knoweth the heartes, bare them witnesse, in giuing vnto them ye holy Ghost euen as he did vnto vs.

9 And he put no difference betweene vs and them, after that by faith he had purified their heartes.

10 Nowe therefore, why tempt ye God, to lay a yoke on the disciples neckes, which neither our fathers, nor we were able to beare?

11 But we beleeue, through the grace of the Lord Iesus Christ to be saued, euen as they doe.

12 Then all the multitude kept silence, and heard Barnabas and Paul, which told what signes and wonders God had done among the Gentiles by them.

13 And when they helde their peace, Iames answered, saying, Men and brethren, hearken vnto me.

14 Simeon hath declared, howe God first did visite the Gentiles, to take of them a people vnto his Name.

15 And to this agree the woordes of the Prophets, as it is written,

16 After this I will returne, and will builde againe the tabernacle of Dauid, which is fallen downe, and the ruines thereof will I build againe, and I will set it vp,

17 That the residue of men might seeke after the Lord, and all the Gentiles vpon whom my Name is called, saith the Lord which doeth all these things.

18 From the beginning of the worlde, God knoweth all his workes.

19 Wherefore my sentence is, that we trouble not them of the Gentiles that are turned to God,

20 But that we send vnto them, that they abstaine themselues from filthinesse of idoles, and fornication, and that that is strangled, and from blood.

21 For Moses of olde time hath in euery citie them that preache him, seeing he is read in the Synagogues euery Sabbath day.

22 Then it seemed good to the Apostles and Elders with the whole Church, to sende chosen men of their owne companie to Antiochia with Paul and Barnabas: to wit, Iudas whose surname was Barsabas and Silas, which were chiefe men among the brethren,

23 And wrote letters by them after this maner, THE APOSTLES, and the Elders, and the brethren, vnto the brethren which are of the Gentiles in Antiochia, and in Syria, and in Cilicia, send greeting.

24 Forasmuch as we haue heard, that certaine which went out from vs, haue troubled you with wordes, and cumbred your mindes, saying, Ye must be circumcised and keepe the Lawe: to whom we gaue no such commandement,

25 It seemed therefore good to vs, when we were come together with one accord, to send chosen men vnto you, with our beloued Barnabas and Paul,

26 Men that haue giuen vp their liues for the Name of our Lord Iesus Christ.

27 We haue therefore sent Iudas and Silas, which shall also tell you ye same things by mouth.

28 For it seemed good to the holy Ghost, and to vs, to lay no more burden vpon you, then these necessary things,

29 That is, that ye abstaine from things offered to idoles, and blood, and that that is strangled, and from fornication: from which if ye keepe your selues, ye shall doe well. Fare ye well.

30 Nowe when they were departed, they came to Antiochia, and after that they had assembled the multitude, they deliuered the Epistle.

31 And when they had read it, they reioyced for the consolation.

32 And Iudas and Silas being Prophets, exhorted the brethren with many wordes, and strengthened them.

33 And after they had taried there a space, they were let goe in peace of the brethren vnto the Apostles.

34 Notwithstanding Silas thought good to abide there still.

35 Paul also and Barnabas continued in Antiochia, teaching and preaching with many other, the worde of the Lord.

36 But after certaine dayes, Paul said vnto Barnabas, Let vs returne, and visite our brethren in euery citie, where we haue preached the worde of the Lord, and see how they doe.

37 And Barnabas counselled to take with them Iohn, called Marke.

38 But Paul thought it not meete to take him vnto their companie, which departed from them from Pamphylia, and went not with them to the worke.

39 Then were they so stirred, that they departed asunder one from the other, so that Barnabas tooke Marke, and sailed vnto Cyprus.

40 And Paul chose Silas and departed, being commended of the brethren vnto the grace of God.

41 And he went through Syria and Cilicia, stablishing the Churches.

Acts 16

1 Then came he to Derbe and to Lystra: and beholde, a certaine disciple was there named Timotheus, a womans sonne, which was a Iewesse and beleeued, but his father was a Grecian,

2 Of whom the brethren which were at Lystra and Iconium, reported well.

3 Therefore Paul would that he should go forth with him, and tooke and circumcised him, because of ye Iewes, which were in those quarters: for they knewe all, that his father was a Grecian.

4 And as they went through the cities, they deliuered them the decrees to keepe, ordeined of the Apostles and Elders, which were at Hierusalem.

5 And so were the Churches stablished in the faith, and encreased in number daily.

6 Nowe when they had gone throughout Phrygia, and the region of Galatia, they were forbidden of the holy Ghost to preache the worde in Asia.

7 Then came they to Mysia, and sought to go into Bithynia: but the Spirit suffered them not.

8 Therefore they passed through Mysia, and came downe to Troas,

9 Where a vision appeared to Paul in the night. There stoode a man of Macedonia, and prayed him, saying, Come into Macedonia, and helpe vs.

10 And after he had seene the vision, immediatly we prepared to goe into Macedonia, being assured that the Lord had called vs to preache the Gospel vnto them.

11 Then went we forth from Troas, and with a straight course came to Samothracia, and the next day to Neapolis,

12 And from thence to Philippi, which is the chiefe citie in ye partes of Macedonia, and whose inhabitants came from Rome to dwell there, and we were in that citie abiding certaine dayes.

13 And on the Sabbath day, we went out of the citie, besides a Riuer, where they were wont to pray: and we sate downe, and spake vnto the women, which were come together.

14 And a certaine woman named Lydia, a seller of purple, of the citie of the Thyatirians, which worshipped God, heard vs: whose heart the Lord opened, that she attended vnto the things, which Paul spake.

15 And when she was baptized, and her houshold, she besought vs, saying, If ye haue iudged me to be faithfull to ye Lord, come into mine house, and abide there: and she constrained vs.

16 And it came to passe that as we went to prayer, a certaine maide hauing a spirit of diuination, mette vs, which gate her masters much vantage with diuining.

17 She followed Paul and vs, and cryed, saying, These men are the seruants of the most high God, which shewe vnto you the way of saluation.

18 And this did she many dayes: but Paul being grieued, turned about, and said to the spirit, I commaund thee in the Name of Iesus Christ, that thou come out of her. And he came out the same houre.

19 Nowe when her masters sawe that the hope of their gaine was gone, they caught Paul and Silas, and drewe them into the market place vnto the Magistrates,

20 And brought them to the gouernours, saying, These men which are Iewes, trouble our citie,

21 And preache ordinances, which are not lawfull for vs to receiue, neither to obserue, seeing we are Romanes.

22 The people also rose vp together against them, and the gouernours rent their clothes, and commanded them to be beaten with roddes.

23 And when they had beaten them sore, they cast them into prison, commaunding the Iayler to keepe them surely.

24 Who hauing receiued such commandement, cast them into the inner prison, and made their feete fast in the stockes.

25 Nowe at midnight Paul and Silas prayed, and sung Psalmes vnto God: and the prisoners heard them.

26 And suddenly there was a great earthquake, so that the foundation of the prison was shaken: and by and by all the doores opened, and euery mans bands were loosed.

27 Then the keeper of the prison waked out of his sleepe, and when he sawe the prison doores open, he drewe out his sword and would haue killed himselfe, supposing the prisoners had bin fled.

28 But Paul cryed with a loude voyce, saying, Doe thy selfe no harme: for we are all here.

29 Then he called for a light, and leaped in, and came trembling, and fell downe before Paul and Silas,

30 And brought them out, and said, Syrs, what must I doe to be saued?

31 And they saide, Beleeue in the Lord Iesus Christ, and thou shalt be saued, and thine houshold.

32 And they preached vnto him the worde of the Lord, and to all that were in the house.

33 Afterwarde he tooke them the same houre of the night, and washed their stripes, and was baptized with all that belonged vnto him, straigthway.

34 And when he had brought them into his house, he set meate before them, and reioyced that he with all his houshold beleeued in God.

35 And when it was day, the gouernours sent the sergeants, saying, Let those men goe.

36 Then the keeper of the prison tolde these woordes vnto Paul, saying, The gouerness haue sent to loose you: nowe therefore get you hence, and goe in peace.

37 Then sayde Paul vnto them, After that they haue beaten vs openly vncodemned, which are Romanes, they haue cast vs into prison, and nowe would they put vs out priuily? nay verely: but let them come and bring vs out.

38 And the sergeants tolde these woordes vnto the gouernours, who feared whe they heard that they were Romanes.

39 Then came they and praied them, and brought them out, and desired them to depart out of the citie.

40 And they went out of the prison, and entred into the house of Lydia: and when they had seene the brethren, they comforted them, and departed.

Acts 17

1 Nowe as they passed through Amphipolis, and Apollonia, they came to Thessalonica, where was a Synagogue of the Iewes.

2 And Paul, as his maner was, went in vnto them, and three Sabbath daies disputed with them by the Scriptures,

3 Opening, and alleadging that Christ must haue suffered, and risen againe from the dead: and this is Iesus Christ, whom, said he, I preach to you.

4 And some of them beleeued, and ioyned in companie with Paul and Silas: also of the Grecians that feared God a great multitude, and of the chiefe women not a fewe.

5 But the Iewes which beleeued not, mooued with enuie, tooke vnto them certaine vagabonds and wicked fellowes, and whe they had assembled the multitude, they made a tumult in the citie, and made assault against the house of Iason, and sought to bring them out to the people.

6 But when they found them not, they drew Iason and certaine brethren vnto the heads of the citie, crying, These are they which haue subuerted the state of the world, and here they are,

7 Whom Iason hath receiued, and these all doe against the decrees of Cesar, saying that there is another King, one Iesus.

8 Then they troubled the people, and the heads of the citie, when they heard these things.

9 Notwithstanding when they had receiued sufficient assurance of Iason and of the other, they let them goe.

10 And the brethren immediatly sent away Paul and Silas by night vnto Berea, which when they were come thither, entred into ye Synagogue of the Iewes.

11 These were also more noble men then they which were at Thessalonica, which receiued the woorde with all readinesse, and searched the Scriptures daily, whether those things were so.

12 Therefore many of them beleeued, and of honest women, which were Grecians, and men not a fewe.

13 But when the Iewes of Thessalonica knewe, that the woord of God was also preached of Paul at Berea, they came thither also, and mooued the people.

14 But by and by the brethren sent away Paul to goe as it were to the sea: but Silas and Timotheus abode there still.

15 And they that did conduct Paul, brought him vnto Athens: and when they had receiued a commandement vnto Silas and Timotheus that they shoulde come to him at once, they departed.

16 Nowe while Paul waited for them at Athens, his spirite was stirred in him, when hee sawe the citie subiect to idolatrie.

17 Therefore he disputed in the Synagogue with the Iewes, and with them that were religious, and in the market daily with whomesoeuer he met.

18 Then certaine Philosophers of the Epicures, and of the Stoickes, disputed with him, and some sayde, What will this babler say? Others sayde, He seemeth to be a setter forth of straunge gods (because hee preached vnto them Iesus, and the resurrection.)

19 And they tooke him, and brought him into Mars streete, saying, May we not know, what this newe doctrine, whereof thou speakest, is?

20 For thou bringest certaine strange thinges vnto our eares: we woulde knowe therefore, what these things meane.

21 For all the Athenians, and strangers which dwelt there, gaue them selues to nothing els, but either to tell, or to heare some newes.

22 Then Paul stoode in the mids of Mars streete, and sayde, Yee men of Athens, I perceiue that in all things yee are too superstitious.

23 For as I passed by, and behelde your deuotions, I founde an altar wherein was written, VNTO THE VNKNOWEN GOD.

Whom ye then ignorantly worship, him shewe I vnto you.

24 God that made the world, and all things that are therein, seeing that he is Lord of heaue and earth, dwelleth not in temples made with hands,

25 Neither is worshipped with mens handes, as though he needed any thing, seeing hee giueth to all life and breath and all things,

26 And hath made of one blood all mankinde, to dwell on all the face of the earth, and hath assigned the seasons which were ordeined before, and the boundes of their habitation,

27 That they shoulde seeke the Lord, if so be they might haue groped after him, and founde him though doubtlesse he be not farre from euery one of vs.

28 For in him we liue, and mooue, and haue our being, as also certaine of your owne Poets haue sayd, for we are also his generation.

29 Forasmuch then, as we are the generation of God, we ought not to thinke that ye Godhead is like vnto gold, or siluer, or stone grauen by arte and the inuention of man.

30 And the time of this ignorance God regarded not: but nowe hee admonisheth all men euery where to repent,

31 Because hee hath appoynted a day in the which he wil iudge the world in righteousnes, by that man whome hee hath appoynted, whereof he hath giuen an assurance to all men, in that hee hath raised him from the dead.

32 Now when they heard of the resurrection from the dead, some mocked, and other sayde, We will heare thee againe of this thing.

33 And so Paul departed from among them.

34 Howbeit certaine men claue vnto Paul, and beleeued: among whome was also Denys Areopagita, and a woman named Damaris, and other with them.

Acts 18

1 After these thinges, Paul departed from Athens, and came to Corinthus,

2 And found a certaine Iewe named Aquila, borne in Pontus, lately come from Italie, and his wife Priscilla (because that Claudius had commanded all Iewes to depart from Rome) and he came vnto them.

3 And because hee was of the same crafte, he abode with them and wrought (for their crafte was to make tentes.)

4 And he disputed in the Synagogue euery Sabbath day, and exhorted the Iewes, and the Grecians.

5 Now when Silas and Timotheus were come from Macedonia, Paul, forced in spirit, testified to the Iewes that Iesus was the Christ.

6 And when they resisted and blasphemed, he shooke his raiment, and saide vnto them, Your blood be vpon your owne head: I am cleane: from henceforth will I goe vnto the Gentiles.

7 So he departed thence, and entred into a certaine mans house, named Iustus, a worshipper of God, whose house ioyned hard to the Synagogue.

8 And Crispus the chiefe ruler of the Synagogue, beleeued in the Lord with all his housholde: and many of the Corinthians hearing it, beleeued and were baptized.

9 Then saide the Lord to Paul in the night by a vision, Feare not, but speake, and holde not thy peace.

10 For I am with thee, and no man shall lay handes on thee to hurt thee: for I haue much people in this citie.

11 So he continued there a yeere and six moneths, and taught ye worde of God among them.

12 Now when Gallio was Deputie of Achaia, the Iewes arose with one accorde against Paul, and brought him to the iudgement seate,

13 Saying, This fellow persuadeth me to worship God otherwise then the Lawe appointeth.

14 And as Paul was about to open his mouth, Gallio saide vnto the Iewes, If it were a matter of wrong, or an euill deede, O ye Iewes, I would according to reason maintaine you.

15 But if it bee a question of woordes, and names, and of your Lawe, looke yee to it your selues: for I will be no iudge of those things.

16 And hee draue them from the iudgement seate.

17 Then tooke al the Grecians Sosthenes the chiefe ruler of the Synagogue, and beat him before the iudgement seat: but Gallio cared nothing for those things.

18 But when Paul had taried there yet a good while, hee tooke leaue of the brethren, and sailed into Syria (and with him Priscilla and Aquila) after that he had shorne his head in Cenchrea: for he had a vowe.

19 Then hee came to Ephesus, and left them there: but hee entred into the Synagogue and disputed with the Iewes.

20 Who desired him to tarie a longer time with them: but he would not consent,

21 But bade the farewel, saying, I must needes keepe this feast that commeth, in Hierusalem: but I will returne againe vnto you, if God will. So he sailed from Ephesus.

22 And when hee came downe to Cesarea, he went vp to Hierusalem: and when he had saluted the Church, he went downe vnto Antiochia.

23 Nowe when he had taried there a while, he departed, and went thorowe the countrey of Galatia and Phrygia by order, strengthening all the disciples.

24 And a certaine Iewe named Apollos, borne at Alexandria, came to Ephesus, an eloquent man, and mightie in the Scriptures.

25 The same was instructed in the way of the Lord, and hee spake feruently in the Spirite, and taught diligently the things of the Lord, and knew but the baptisme of Iohn onely.

26 And he began to speake boldely in the Synagogue. Whom when Aquila and Priscilla had heard, they tooke him vnto them, and expounded vnto him the way of God more perfectly.

27 And when hee was minded to goe into Achaia, the brethren exhorting him, wrote to the disciples to receiue him: and after hee was come thither, he holpe them much which had beleeued through grace.

28 For mightily hee confuted publikely the Iewes, with great vehemencie, shewing by the Scriptures, that Iesus was that Christ.

Acts 19

1 And it came to passe, while Apollos was at Corinthus, that Paul when he passed thorow the vpper coasts, came to Ephesus, and found certaine disciples,

2 And saide vnto them, Haue ye receiued the holy Ghost since ye beleeued? And they saide vnto him, Wee haue not so much as heard whether there be an holy Ghost.

3 And he said vnto them, Vnto what were ye then baptized? And they saide, Vnto Iohns baptisme.

4 Then saide Paul, Iohn verely baptized with the baptisme of repentance, saying vnto the people, that they shoulde beleeue in him, which should come after him, that is, in Christ Iesus.

5 And when they heard it, they were baptized in the Name of the Lord Iesus.

6 So Paul layde his handes vpon them, and the holy Ghost came on them, and they spake the tongues, and prophecied.

7 And all the men were about twelue.

8 Moreouer he went into the Synagogue, and spake boldly for the space of three moneths, disputing and exhorting to the things that appertaine to the kingdome of God.

9 But when certaine were hardened, and disobeyed, speaking euill of the way of God before the multitude, hee departed from them, and separated the disciples, and disputed dayly in the schoole of one Tyrannus.

10 And this was done by the space of two yeeres, so that all they which dwelt in Asia, heard the word of ye Lord Iesus, both Iewes and Grecians.

11 And God wrought no small miracles by the handes of Paul,

12 So that from his body were brought vnto the sicke, kerchefs or handkerchefs, and the diseases departed from them, and the euill spirits went out of them.

13 Then certaine of the vagabond Iewes, exorcistes, tooke in hand to name ouer them which had euil spirits, the Name of the Lord Iesus, saying, We adiure you by Iesus, whom Paul preacheth.

14 (And there were certaine sonnes of Sceua a Iewe, the Priest, about seuen which did this)

15 And the euil spirit answered, and said, Iesus I acknowledge, and Paul I know: but who are ye?

16 And the man in whome the euil spirit was, ranne on them, and ouercame them, and preuailed against them, so

that they fledde out of that house, naked, and wounded.

17 And this was knowen to all the Iewes and Grecians also, which dwelt at Ephesus, and feare came on them all, and the Name of the Lord Iesus was magnified,

18 And many that beleeued, came and confessed, and shewed their workes.

19 Many also of them which vsed curious artes, brought their bookes, and burned them before all men: and they counted the price of them, and found it fiftie thousand pieces of siluer.

20 So the worde of God grewe mightily, and preuailed.

21 Nowe when these things were accomplished, Paul purposed by the Spirite to passe through Macedonia and Achaia, and to goe to Hierusalem, saying, After I haue bene there, I must also see Rome.

22 So sent hee into Macedonia two of them that ministred vnto him, Timotheus and Erastus, but he remained in Asia for a season.

23 And the same time there arose no small trouble about that way.

24 For a certaine man named Demetrius a siluersmith, which made siluer temples of Diana, brought great gaines vnto the craftesmen,

25 Whom he called together, with the workemen of like things, and saide, Syrs, ye knowe that by this craft we haue our goods:

26 Moreouer ye see and heare, that not alone at Ephesus, but almost throughout all Asia this Paul hath perswaded, and turned away much people, saying, That they be not gods which are made with handes.

27 So that not onely this thing is dangerous vnto vs, that this our portion shall be reproued, but also that the temple of the great goddesse Diana should be nothing esteemed, and that it would come to passe that her magnificence, which all Asia and the world worshippeth, should be destroyed.

28 Now when they heard it, they were full of wrath, and cried out, saying, Great is Diana of the Ephesians.

29 And the whole citie was full of confusion, and they rushed into the common place with one assent, and caught Gaius, and Aristarchus, men of Macedonia, and Pauls companions of his iourney.

30 And when Paul would haue entred in vnto the people, the disciples suffred him not.

31 Certaine also of the chiefe of Asia which were his friendes, sent vnto him, desiring him that hee woulde not present him selfe in the Common place.

32 Some therefore cried one thing, and some another: for the assemblie was out of order, and the more part knewe not wherefore they were come together.

33 And some of the company drew foorth Alexander, the Iewes thrusting him forwards. Alexander then beckened with the hande, and woulde haue excused the matter to the people.

34 But when they knew that he was a Iewe, there arose a shoute almost for the space of two houres, of all men crying, Great is Diana of the Ephesians.

35 Then the towne clearke when hee had stayed the people, saide, Ye men of Ephesus, what man is it that knoweth not howe that the citie of the Ephesians is a worshipper of the great goddesse Diana, and of the image, which came downe from Iupiter?

36 Seeing then that no man can speake against these things, ye ought to be appeased, and to doe nothing rashly.

37 For yee haue brought hither these men, which haue neither committed sacrilege, neither doe blaspheme your goddesse.

38 Wherefore, if Demetrius and the craftes men which are with him, haue a matter against any man, the lawe is open, and there are Deputies: let them accuse one another.

39 But if ye inquire any thing cocerning other matters, it may be determined in a lawful assembly.

40 For we are euen in ieopardie to be accused of this dayes sedition, for as much as there is no cause, whereby we may giue a reason of this concourse of people.

41 And when he had thus spoken, hee let the assembly depart.

Acts 20

1 Nowe after the tumult was appeased, Paul called the disciples vnto him, and embraced them, and departed to goe into Macedonia.

2 And when hee had gone through those parts, and had exhorted them with many words, he came into Grecia.

3 And hauing taried there three moneths, because the Iewes layde waite for him, as hee was about to saile into Syria, hee purposed to returne through Macedonia.

4 And there accompanied him into Asia, Sopater of Berea, and of them of Thessalonica, Aristarchus, and Secundus, and Gaius of Derbe, and Timotheus, and of them of Asia, Tychicus, and Trophimus.

5 These went before, and taried vs at Troas.

6 And we sailed forth from Philippi, after the dayes of vnleauened bread, and came vnto them to Troas in fiue dayes, where we abode seuen dayes.

7 And the first day of the weeke, the disciples being come together to breake bread, Paul preached vnto them, ready to depart on the morrow, and continued the preaching vnto midnight.

8 And there were many lightes in an vpper chamber, where they were gathered together.

9 And there sate in a windowe a certaine yong man, named Eutychus, fallen into a dead sleepe: and as Paul was long preaching, hee ouercome with sleepe, fell downe from the thirde loft, and was taken vp dead.

10 But Paul went downe, and layde himselfe vpon him, and embraced him, saying, Trouble not your selues: for his life is in him.

11 Then when Paul was come vp againe, and had broken bread, and eaten, hauing spoken a long while till the dawning of the day, hee so departed.

12 And they brought the boye aliue, and they were not a litle comforted.

13 Then we went before to shippe, and sailed vnto the citie Assos, that wee might receiue Paul there: for so had hee appointed, and would himselfe goe afoote.

14 Now when he was come vnto vs to Assos, and we had receiued him, we came to Mitylenes.

15 And wee sailed thence, and came the next day ouer against Chios, and the next day we arriued at Samos, and tarried at Trogyllium: the next day we came to Miletum.

16 For Paul had determined to saile by Ephesus, because hee woulde not spend the time in Asia: for he hasted to be, if hee could possible, at Hierusalem, at the day of Pentecost.

17 Wherefore from Miletum, hee sent to Ephesus, and called the Elders of the Church.

18 Who when they were come to him, hee said vnto them, Ye know from the first day that I came into Asia, after what maner I haue bene with you at all seasons,

19 Seruing the Lord with all modestie, and with many teares, and tentations, which came vnto me by the layings awaite of the Iewes,

20 And how I kept backe nothing that was profitable, but haue shewed you, and taught you openly and throughout euery house,

21 Witnessing both to the Iewes, and to the Grecians the repentance towarde God, and faith toward our Lord Iesus Christ.

22 And nowe beholde, I goe bound in the Spirit vnto Hierusalem, and know not what things shall come vnto me there,

23 Saue that ye holy Ghost witnesseth in euery citie, saying, that bondes and afflictions abide me.

24 But I passe not at all, neither is my life deare vnto my selfe, so that I may fulfill my course with ioye, and the ministration which I haue receiued of the Lord Iesus, to testifie the Gospell of the grace of God.

25 And now behold, I know that henceforth ye all, through whome I haue gone preaching the kingdome of God, shall see my face no more.

26 Wherefore I take you to recorde this day, that I am pure from the blood of all men.

27 For I haue kept nothing backe, but haue shewed you all the counsell of God.

28 Take heede therefore vnto your selues, and to all the flocke, whereof the holy Ghost hath made you Ouerseers, to feede the Church of God, which hee hath purchased with that his owne blood.

29 For I knowe this, that after my departing shall grieuous wolues enter in among you, not sparing the flocke.

30 Moreouer of your owne selues shall men arise speaking peruerse thinges, to drawe disciples after them.

31 Therefore watche, and remember, that by the space of three yeres I ceased not to warne euery one, both night and day with teares.

32 And nowe brethren, I commend you to God, and to the worde of his grace, which is able to build further, and to giue you an inheritance, among all them, which are sanctified.

33 I haue coueted no mans siluer, nor gold, nor apparell.

34 Yea, ye knowe, that these handes haue ministred vnto my necessities, and to them that were with me.

35 I haue shewed you all things, howe that so labouring, ye ought to support the weake, and to remember the wordes of the Lord Iesus, howe that hee saide, It is a blessed thing to giue, rather then to receiue.

36 And when he had thus spoken, he kneeled downe, and prayed with them all.

37 Then they wept all abundantly, and fell on Pauls necke, and kissed him,

38 Being chiefly sorie for the words which he spake, That they should see his face no more. And they accompanied him vnto the shippe.

Acts 21

1 And as we launched forth, and were departed from them, we came with a straight course vnto Coos, and the day following vnto the Rhodes, and from thence vnto Patara.

2 And we found a ship that went ouer vnto Phenice, and went aboard, and set forth.

3 And whe we had discouered Cyprus, we left it on the left hand, and sailed toward Syria, and arriued at Tyrus: for there the ship vnladed ye burden.

4 And when we had found disciples, we taried there seuen dayes. And they told Paul through the Spirit, that he should not goe vp to Hierusalem.

5 But when the dayes were ended, we departed and went our way, and they all accompanied vs with their wiues and children, euen out of the citie: and we kneeling downe on the shore, prayed.

6 Then when we had embraced one another, we tooke ship, and they returned home.

7 And when we had ended the course from Tyrus, we arriued at Ptolemais, and saluted the brethren, and abode with them one day.

8 And the next day, Paul and we that were with him, departed, and came vnto Cesarea: and we entred into the house of Philippe the Euangelist, which was one of the seuen Deacons, and abode with him.

9 Now he had foure daughters virgins, which did prophecie.

10 And as we taried there many dayes, there came a certaine Prophet from Iudea, named Agabus.

11 And when he was come vnto vs, he tooke Pauls girdle, and bound his owne hands and feete, and sayd, Thus sayth the holy Ghost, So shall the Iewes at Hierusalem binde the man that oweth this girdle, and shall deliuer him into the hands of the Gentiles.

12 And when we had heard these things, both we and other of the same place besought him that he would not go vp to Hierusalem.

13 Then Paul answered, and sayd, What doe ye weeping and breaking mine heart? For I am ready not to be bound onely, but also to die at Hierusalem for the Name of the Lord Iesus.

14 So when he would not be perswaded, we ceased, saying, The will of the Lord be done.

15 And after those dayes we trussed vp our fardels, and went vp to Hierusalem.

16 There went with vs also certaine of the disciples of Cesarea, and brought with them one Mnason of Cyprus, an olde disciple, with whome we should lodge.

17 And when we were come to Hierusalem, the brethren receiued vs gladly.

18 And the next day Paul went in with vs vnto Iames: and all the Elders were there assembled.

19 And when he had embraced them, hee tolde by order all things, that God had wrought among the Gentiles by his ministration.

20 So when they heard it, they glorified God, and sayd vnto him, Thou seest, brother, how many thousand Iewes there are which beleeue, and they are all zealous of the Law:

21 Now they are informed of thee, that thou teachest all the Iewes, which are among the Gentiles, to forsake Moses, and sayest that they ought not to circumcise their sonnes, neither to liue after the customes.

22 What is then to be done? the multitude must needes come together: for they shall heare that thou art come.

23 Doe therefore this that we say to thee. We haue foure men, which haue made a vowe,

24 Them take, and purifie thy selfe with them, and contribute with them, that they may shaue their heads: and all shall knowe, that those things, whereof they haue bene informed concerning thee, are nothing, but that thou thy selfe also walkest and keepest the Lawe.

25 For as touching ye Gentiles, which beleeue, we haue written, and determined that they obserue no such thing, but that they keepe themselues from things offred to idoles, and from blood, and from that that is strangled, and from fornication.

26 Then Paul tooke the men, and the next day was purified with them, and entred into the Temple, declaring the accomplishment of the dayes of the purification, vntill that an offering should be offered for euery one of them.

27 And when the seuen dayes were almost ended, the Iewes which were of Asia (when they sawe him in the Temple) moued all the people, and laide hands on him,

28 Crying, Men of Israel, helpe: this is the man that teacheth all men euery where against the people, and the Lawe, and this place: moreouer, he hath brought Grecians into the Temple, and hath polluted this holy place.

29 For they had seene before Trophimus an Ephesian with him in the citie, whom they supposed that Paul had brought into the Temple.

30 Then all the citie was moued, and the people ran together: and they tooke Paul and drewe him out of the Temple, and forth with the doores were shut.

31 But as they went about to kill him, tydings came vnto the chiefe captaine of the band, that all Hierusalem was on an vproare.

32 Who immediately tooke souldiers and Centurions, and ran downe vnto them: and when they sawe the chiefe Captaine and the souldiers, they left beating of Paul.

33 Then the chiefe Captaine came neere and tooke him, and commanded him to be bound with two chaines, and demaunded who he was, and what he had done.

34 And one cryed this, another that, among the people. So when he could not know the certeintie for the tumult, he commanded him to be led into the castell.

35 And when hee came vnto the grieces, it was so that he was borne of the souldiers, for the violence of the people.

36 For the multitude of the people followed after, crying, Away with him.

37 And as Paul should haue bene led into the castell, he sayd vnto the chiefe Captaine, May I speake vnto thee? Who sayd, Canst thou speake Greeke?

38 Art not thou the Egyptian who before these dayes raised a sedition, and led out into the wildernesse foure thousande men that were murtherers?

39 Then Paul sayde, Doubtlesse, I am a man which am a Iewe, and citizen of Tarsus, a famous citie of Cilicia, and I beseech thee, suffer mee to speake vnto the people.

40 And when he had giuen him licence, Paul stoode on the grieces, and beckened with the hand vnto the people: and when there was made great silence, hee spake vnto them in the Hebrewe tongue, saying,

Acts 22

1 Ye men, brethren and Fathers, heare my defence nowe towards you.

2 (And when they heard that he spake in the Hebrewe tongue to them, they kept the more silence, and he sayd)

3 I am verely a man, which am a Iew, borne in Tarsus in Cilicia, but brought vp in this citie at the feete of Gamaliel,

and instructed according to the perfect maner of the Lawe of the Fathers, and was zealous toward God, as ye all are this day.

4 And I persecuted this way vnto the death, binding and deliuering into prison both men and women.

5 As also ye chiefe Priest doeth beare me witnes, and al the company of the Elders: of whom also I receiued letters vnto the brethren, and went to Damascus to bring them which were there, bound vnto Hierusalem, that they might be punished.

6 And so it was, as I iourneyed and was come neere vnto Damascus about noone, that suddenly there shone from heauen a great light round about me.

7 So I fell vnto the earth, and heard a voyce, saying vnto me, Saul, Saul, why persecutest thou mee?

8 Then I answered, Who art thou, Lord? And he said to me, I am Iesus of Nazareth, whom thou persecutest.

9 Moreouer they that were with me, sawe in deede a light and were afraide: but they heard not the voyce of him that spake vnto me.

10 Then I sayd, What shall I doe, Lord? And the Lord sayde vnto me, Arise, and goe into Damascus: and there it shall be tolde thee of all things, which are appointed for thee to doe.

11 So when I could not see for the glory of that light, I was led by the hand of them that were with me, and came into Damascus.

12 And one Ananias a godly man, as perteining to the Lawe, hauing good report of all the Iewes which dwelt there,

13 Came vnto me, and stoode, and sayd vnto me, Brother Saul, receiue thy sight: and that same houre I looked vpon him.

14 And he sayd, The God of our fathers hath appointed thee, that thou shouldest knowe his wil, and shouldest see that Iust one, and shouldest heare the voyce of his mouth.

15 For thou shalt be his witnes vnto all men, of the things which thou hast seene and heard.

16 Now therefore why tariest thou? Arise, and be baptized, and wash away thy sinnes, in calling on the Name of the Lord.

17 And it came to passe, that when I was come againe to Hierusalem, and prayed in the Temple, I was in a traunce,

18 And saw him saying vnto me, Make haste, and get thee quickly out of Hierusalem: for they will not receiue thy witnes concerning me.

19 Then I sayd, Lord, they know that I prisoned, and beat in euery Synagogue them that beleeued in thee.

20 And when the blood of thy martyr Steuen was shed, I also stood by, and consented vnto his death, and kept the clothes of them that slew him.

21 Then he sayd vnto me, Depart: for I will send thee farre hence vnto the Gentiles.

22 And they heard him vnto this worde, but then they lift vp their voyces, and sayd, Away with such a fellow from the earth: for it is not meete that he should liue.

23 And as they cried and cast off their clothes, and threw dust into the aire,

24 The chiefe captaine commanded him to be led into the castle, and bade that he should be scourged, and examined, that he might knowe wherefore they cryed so on him.

25 And as they bound him with thongs, Paul sayd vnto the Centurion that stood by, Is it lawfull for you to scourge one that is a Romane, and not condemned?

26 Nowe when the Centurion heard it, hee went, and tolde the chiefe captaine, saying, Take heede what thou doest: for this man is a Romane.

27 Then the chiefe captaine came, and sayd to him, Tel me, art thou a Romane? And he said, Yea.

28 And the chiefe captaine answered, With a great summe obtained I this freedome. Then Paul sayd, But I was so borne.

29 Then straightway they departed from him, which should haue examined him: and the chiefe captaine also was afrayd, after he knewe that hee was a Romane, and that he had bound him.

30 On the next day, because hee would haue knowen the certaintie wherefore he was accused of the Iewes, he loosed him from his bonds, and commanded the hie Priests and all their Councill to come together: and he brought Paul, and set him before them.

Acts 23

1 And Paul behelde earnestly the Councill, and sayde, Men and brethren, I haue in all good conscience serued God vntill this day.

2 Then the hie Priest Ananias commanded them that stood by, to smite him on the mouth.

3 Then sayd Paul to him, God will smite thee, thou whited wall: for thou sittest to iudge me according to the Lawe, and transgressing the Lawe, commaundest thou me to be smitten?

4 And they that stood by, sayd, Reuilest thou Gods hie Priest?

5 Then sayd Paul, I knewe not, brethren, that he was the hie Priest: for it is written, Thou shalt not speake euill of the ruler of thy people.

6 But when Paul perceiued that the one part were of the Sadduces, and the other of the Pharises, hee cried in the Council, Men and brethren, I am a Pharise, the sonne of a Pharise: I am accused of the hope and resurrection of the dead.

7 And when hee had saide this, there was a dissension betweene the Pharises and the Sadduces, so that the multitude was deuided.

8 For the Sadduces say that there is no resurrection, neither Angel, nor spirit: but the Pharises confesse both.

9 Then there was a great crye: and the Scribes of the Pharises part rose vp, and stroue, saying, Wee finde none euill in this man: but if a spirit or an Angel hath spoken to him, let vs not fight against God.

10 And when there was a great dissension, the chiefe captaine, fearing lest Paul should haue bene pulled in pieces of them, commanded the souldiers to go downe, and take him from among them, and to bring him into the castel.

11 Nowe the night folowing, the Lord stoode by him, and saide, Be of good courage, Paul: for as thou hast testified of mee in Hierusalem, so must thou beare witnesse also at Rome.

12 And when the day was come, certaine of the Iewes made an assemblie, and bounde themselues with a curse, saying, that they woulde neither eate nor drinke, till they had killed Paul.

13 And they were more then fourtie, which had made this conspiracie.

14 And they came to the chiefe Priestes and Elders, and said, We haue bound our selues with a solemne curse, that wee will eate nothing, vntill we haue slaine Paul.

15 Nowe therefore, ye and the Council signifie to the chiefe captaine, that hee bring him foorth vnto you to morow: as though you would know some thing more perfectly of him, and we, or euer he come neere, will be readie to kill him.

16 But when Pauls sisters sonne heard of their laying awaite, he went, and entred into the castel, and tolde Paul.

17 And Paul called one of the Centurions vnto him, and said, Take this yong man hence vnto the chiefe captaine: for he hath a certaine thing to shewe him.

18 So hee tooke him, and brought him to the chiefe captaine, and saide, Paul the prisoner called mee vnto him, and prayed mee to bring this yong man vnto thee, which hath some thing to say vnto thee.

19 Then the chiefe captaine tooke him by the hande, and went apart with him alone, and asked him, What hast thou to shewe me?

20 And he saide, The Iewes haue conspired to desire thee, that thou wouldest bring foorth Paul to morow into the Council, as though they would inquire somewhat of him more perfectly:

21 But let them not perswade thee: for there lie in waite for him of them, more then fourtie men, which haue bound themselues with a curse, that they will neither eate nor drinke, till they haue killed him: and nowe are they readie, and waite for thy promise.

22 The chiefe captaine then let the yong man depart, after hee had charged him to vtter it to no man, that he had shewed him these things.

23 And he called vnto him two certaine Centurions, saying, Make readie two hundred souldiers, that they may go to Cesarea, and horsemen three score and ten, and two hundred with dartes, at the thirde houre of the night.

24 And let them make readie an horse, that Paul being set on, may be brought safe vnto Felix the Gouernour.

25 And he wrote an epistle in this maner:

26 Claudius Lysias vnto the most noble Gouernour Felix sendeth greeting.

27 As this man was taken of the Iewes, and shoulde haue bene killed of them, I came vpon them with the garison, and rescued him, perceiuing that he was a Romane.

28 And when I would haue knowen the cause, wherefore they accused him, I brought him forth into their Council.

29 There I perceiued that hee was accused of questions of their Lawe, but had no crime worthy of death, or of bondes.

30 And when it was shewed me, how that the Iewes layd waite for the man, I sent him straightway to thee, and commanded his accusers to speake before thee the thinges that they had against him. Farewell.

31 Then the souldiers as it was commanded them, tooke Paul, and brought him by night to Antipatris.

32 And the next day, they left the horsemen to goe with him, and returned vnto the Castel.

33 Now when they came to Cesarea, they deliuered the epistle to the Gouernour, and presented Paul also vnto him.

34 So when the Gouernour had read it, hee asked of what prouince he was: and when he vnderstoode that he was of Cilicia,

35 I will heare thee, said he, when thine accusers also are come, and commanded him to bee kept in Herods iudgement hall.

Acts 24

1 Now after fiue dayes, Ananias the hie Priest came downe with the Elders, and with Tertullus a certaine oratour, which appeared before the Gouernour against Paul.

2 And when he was called foorth, Tertullus began to accuse him, saying, Seeing that we haue obtained great quietnesse through thee, and that many worthy things are done vnto this nation through thy prouidence,

3 We acknowledge it wholy, and in all places most noble Felix, with all thankes,

4 But that I be not tedious vnto thee, I pray thee, that thou wouldest heare vs of thy courtesie a fewe wordes.

5 Certainely we haue found this man a pestilent fellowe, and a moouer of sedition among all the Iewes throughout the world, and a chiefe maintainer of the secte of the Nazarites:

6 And hath gone about to pollute the Temple: therefore wee tooke him, and woulde haue iudged him according to our Lawe:

7 But the chiefe captaine Lysias came vpon vs, and with great violence tooke him out of our handes,

8 Commanding his accusers to come to thee: of whom thou mayest (if thou wilt inquire) know all these things whereof we accuse him.

9 And the Iewes likewise affirmed, saying that it was so.

10 Then Paul, after that the gouernour had beckened vnto him that hee shoulde speake, answered, I do the more gladly answere for my selfe, for as much as I knowe that thou hast bene of many yeres a iudge vnto this nation,

11 Seeing that thou mayest knowe, that there are but twelue dayes since I came vp to worship in Hierusalem.

12 And they neither found mee in the Temple disputing with any man, neither making vproare among the people, neither in the Synagogues, nor in the citie.

13 Neither can they proue the things, whereof they now accuse me.

14 But this I confesse vnto thee, that after the way (which they call heresie) so worship I the God of my fathers, beleeuing all things which are written in the Lawe and the Prophets,

15 And haue hope towardes God, that the resurrection of the dead, which they themselues looke for also, shalbe both of iust and vniust.

16 And herein I endeuour my selfe to haue alway a cleare conscience towarde God, and toward men.

17 Now after many yeres, I came and brought almes to my nation and offerings.

18 At what time, certaine Iewes of Asia founde mee purified in the Temple, neither with multitude, nor with tumult.

19 Who ought to haue bene present before thee, and accuse me, if they had ought against me.

20 Or let these themselues say, if they haue found any vniust thing in mee, while I stoode in the Council,

21 Except it be for this one voyce, that I cried standing among them, Of the resurrection of the dead am I accused of you this day.

22 Nowe when Felix heard these things, he deferred them, and said, When I shall more perfectly know the things which concerne this way, by the comming of Lysias the chiefe Captaine, I will decise your matter.

23 And hee commanded a Centurion to keepe Paul, and that he should haue ease, and that he should forbid none of his acquaintance to minister vnto him, or to come vnto him.

24 And after certaine dayes, came Felix with his wife Drusilla, which was a Iewesse, and he called foorth Paul, and heard him of the faith in Christ.

25 And as he disputed of righteousnes and temperance, and of the iudgement to come, Felix trembled, and answered, Go thy way for this time, and when I haue conuenient time, I will call for thee.

26 Hee hoped also that money shoulde haue bene giuen him of Paul, that he might loose him: wherefore hee sent for him the oftner, and communed with him.

27 When two yeeres were expired, Porcius Festus came into Felix roume: and Felix willing to get fauour of the Iewes, left Paul bound.

Acts 25

1 When Festus was then come into the prouince, after three dayes he went vp from Caesarea vnto Hierusalem.

2 Then the high Priest, and the chiefe of the Iewes appeared before him against Paul: and they besought him,

3 And desired fauour against him, that hee would send for him to Hierusalem: and they layd waite to kill him by the way.

4 But Festus answered, that Paul should bee kept at Caesarea, and that he himselfe would shortly depart thither.

5 Let them therefore, saide he, which among you are able, come downe with vs: and if there be any wickednes in the man, let them accuse him.

6 Now when he had taried among them no more then ten dayes, hee went downe to Caesarea, and the next day sate in the iudgement seat, and commanded Paul to be brought.

7 And when hee was come, the Iewes which were come from Hierusalem, stoode about him and layd many and grieuous complaints against Paul, whereof they could make no plaine proofe,

8 Forasmuch as he answered, that he had neither offended any thing against the lawe of the Iewes, neither against ye temple, nor against Caesar.

9 Yet Festus willing to get fauour of the Iewes, answered Paul and saide, Wilt thou goe vp to Hierusalem, and there be iudged of these things before mee?

10 Then said Paul, I stand at Caesars iudgment seate, where I ought to be iudged: to the Iewes I haue done no wrong, as thou very well knowest.

11 For if I haue done wrong, or committed any thing worthie of death, I refuse not to die: but if there be none of these things whereof they accuse me, no man, to pleasure them, can deliuer me to them: I appeale vnto Caesar.

12 Then when Festus had spoken with the Council, hee answered, Hast thou appealed vnto Caesar? vnto Caesar shalt thou goe.

13 And after certaine dayes, King Agrippa and Bernice came downe to Caesarea to salute Festus.

14 And when they had remained there many dayes, Festus declared Pauls cause vnto the King, saying, There is a certaine man left in prison by Felix,

15 Of whom when I came to Hierusalem, the high Priestes and Elders of the Iewes informed me, and desired to haue iudgement against him.

16 To whome I answered, that it is not the maner of the Romanes for fauour to deliuer any man to the death, before that hee which is accused, haue the accusers before him, and haue place to defend himselfe, concerning the crime.

17 Therefore when they were come hither, without delay the day following I sate on the iudgement seate, and

commanded the man to be brought foorth.

18 Against whom when the accusers stood vp, they brought no crime of such things as I supposed:

19 But had certaine questions against him of their owne superstition, and of one Iesus which was dead, whom Paul affirmed to be aliue.

20 And because I doubted of such maner of question, I asked him whether he would goe to Hierusalem, and there be iudged of these things.

21 But because he appealed to be reserued to the examination of Augustus, I commanded him to be kept, till I mght send him to Cesar.

22 Then Agrippa sayd vnto Festus, I would also heare the man my selfe. To morowe, sayd he, thou shalt heare him.

23 And on the morowe when Agrippa was come and Bernice with great pompe, and were entred into the Common hall with the chiefe captaines and chiefe men of the citie, at Festus commandement Paul was brought forth.

24 And Festus sayd, King Agrippa, and all men which are present with vs, ye see this man, about whom all the multitude of the Iewes haue called vpon me, both at Hierusalem, and here, crying, that he ought not to liue any longer.

25 Yet haue I found nothing worthy of death, that he hath committed: neuertheles, seeing that he hath appealed to Augustus, I haue determined to send him.

26 Of whome I haue no certaine thing to write vnto my Lord: wherefore I haue brought him forth vnto you, and specially vnto thee, King Agrippa, that after examination had, I might haue somewhat to write.

27 For me thinketh it vnreasonable to send a prisoner, and not to shewe the causes which are layde against him.

Acts 26

1 Then Agrippa sayd vnto Paul, Thou art permitted to speake for thy selfe. So Paul stretched forth the hand, and answered for himselfe.

2 I thinke my selfe happy, King Agrippa, because I shall answere this day before thee of all the things whereof I am accused of the Iewes.

3 Chiefly, because thou hast knowledge of all customes, and questions which are among the Iewes: wherefore I beseech thee, to heare me patiently.

4 As touching my life from my childhood, and what it was from the beginning among mine owne nation at Hierusalem, know all the Iewes,

5 Which knewe me heretofore, euen from my elders (if they would testifie) that after the most straite sect of our religion I liued a Pharise.

6 And now I stand and am accused for the hope of the promise made of God vnto our fathers.

7 Whereunto our twelue tribes instantly seruing God day and night, hope to

come: for the which hopes sake, O King Agrippa, I am accused of the Iewes.

8 Why should it be thought a thing incredible vnto you, that God should raise againe the dead?

9 I also verely thought in my selfe, that I ought to doe many contrarie things against the Name of Iesus of Nazareth.

10 Which thing I also did in Hierusalem: for many of the Saints I shut vp in prison, hauing receiued authoritie of the hie Priests, and when they were put to death, I gaue my sentence.

11 And I punished them throughout all the Synagogues, and compelled them to blaspheme, and being more mad against them, I persecuted them, euen vnto strange cities.

12 At which time, euen as I went to Damascus with authoritie, and commission from the hie Priests,

13 At midday, O King, I sawe in the way a light from heauen, passing the brightnes of the sunne, shine round about mee, and them which went with me.

14 So when we were all fallen to the earth, I heard a voyce speaking vnto me, and saying in the Hebrew tongue, Saul, Saul, why persecutest thou me? It is hard for thee to kicke against pricks.

15 Then I sayd, Who art thou, Lord? And he sayd, I am Iesus whom thou persecutest.

16 But rise and stand vp on thy feete: for I haue appeared vnto thee for this purpose, to appoint thee a minister and a witnesse, both of the things which thou hast seene, and of the things in the which I will appeare vnto thee,

17 Deliuering thee from this people, and from the Gentiles, vnto whom now I send thee,

18 To open their eyes, that they may turne from darknes to light, and from the power of Satan vnto God, that they may receiue forgiuenes of sinnes, and inheritance among them, which are sanctified by fayth in me.

19 Wherefore, King Agrippa, I was not disobedient vnto the heauenly vision,

20 But shewed first vnto them of Damascus, and at Hierusalem, and throughout all the coasts of Iudea, and then to the Gentiles, that they should repent and turne to God, and doe workes worthy amendment of life.

21 For this cause the Iewes caught me in the Temple, and went about to kill me.

22 Neuertheles, I obteined helpe of God, and continue vnto this day, witnessing both to small and to great, saying none other things, then those which the Prophets and Moses did say should come,

23 To wit, that Christ should suffer, and that he should be the first that should rise from the dead, and should shew light vnto this people, and to the Gentiles.

24 And as he thus answered for himselfe, Festus said with a loude voyce, Paul, thou art besides thy selfe: much learning doeth make thee mad.

25 But he said, I am not mad, O noble Festus, but I speake the wordes of trueth and sobernes.

26 For the King knoweth of these things, before whom also I speake boldly: for I am perswaded that none of these things are hidden from him: for this thing was not done in a corner.

27 O King Agrippa, beleeuest thou the Prophets? I know that thou beleeuest.

28 Then Agrippa said vnto Paul, Almost thou perswadest me to become a Christian.

29 Then Paul sayd, I would to God that not onely thou, but also all that heare me to day, were both almost, and altogether such as I am, except these bonds.

30 And when he had thus spoken, the King rose vp, and the gouernour, and Bernice, and they that sate with them.

31 And when they were gone apart, they talked betweene themselues, saying, This man doeth nothing worthy of death, nor of bonds.

32 Then sayd Agrippa vnto Festus, This man might haue bene loosed, if hee had not appealed vnto Cesar.

Acts 27

1 Now when it was concluded, that we should sayle into Italie, they deliuered both Paul, and certaine other prisoners vnto a Centurion named Iulius, of the band of Augustus.

2 And we entred into a ship of Adramyttium purposing to saile by the coastes of Asia, and launched foorth, and had Aristarchus of Macedonia, a Thessalonian, with vs.

3 And the next day we arriued at Sidon: and Iulius courteously entreated Paul, and gaue him libertie to go vnto his friends, that they might refresh him.

4 And from thence we launched, and sayled hard by Cyprus, because ye windes were contrarie.

5 Then sayled we ouer the sea by Cilicia, and Pamphilia, and came to Myra, a citie in Lycia.

6 And there the Centurion found a ship of Alexandria, sayling into Italie, and put vs therein.

7 And when we had sayled slowly many dayes, and scarce were come against Gnidum, because the winde suffered vs not, we sailed hard by Candie, neere to Salmone,

8 And with much adoe sayled beyond it, and came vnto a certaine place called the Faire hauens, neere vnto the which was the citie Lasea.

9 So when much time was spent, and sayling was now ieopardous, because also the Fast was nowe passed, Paul exhorted them,

10 And sayde vnto them, Syrs, I see that this voiage will be with hurt and much damage, not of the lading and ship onely, but also of our liues.

11 Neuertheles the Centurion beleeued rather the gouernour and the master of the ship, then those things which were spoken of Paul.

12 And because the hauen was not commodious to winter in, many tooke counsell to depart thence, if by any meanes they might attaine to Phenice, there to winter, which is an hauen of Candie, and lyeth toward the Southwest and by West, and Northwest and by West.

13 And when the Southerne winde blew softly, they supposing to atteine their purpose, loosed neerer, and sailed by Candie.

14 But anon after, there arose by it a stormy winde called Euroclydon.

15 And when the ship was caught, and could not resist the winde, we let her goe, and were caried away.

16 And we ran vnder a litle Yle named Clauda, and had much a doe to get the boat.

17 Which they tooke vp and vsed all helpe, vndergirding the ship, fearing least they should haue fallen into Syrtes, and they strake saile, and so were caried.

18 The next day when we were tossed with an exceeding tempest, they lightened the ship.

19 And the third day we cast out with our owne hands the tackling of the ship.

20 And when neither sunne nor starres in many dayes appeared, and no small tempest lay vpon vs, all hope that we should be saued, was then taken away.

21 But after long abstinece, Paul stood forth in the mids of them, and said, Syrs, ye should haue hearkened to me, and not haue loosed from Candie: so should ye haue gained this hurt and losse.

22 But now I exhort you to be of good courage: for there shalbe no losse of any mans life among you, saue of the ship onely.

23 For there stood by me this night the Angel of God, whose I am, and whome I serue,

24 Saying, Feare not, Paul: for thou must be brought before Cesar: and lo, God hath giuen vnto thee freely all that sayle with thee.

25 Wherefore, sirs, be of good courage: for I beleeue God, that it shall be so as it hath bene tolde me.

26 Howbeit, we must be cast into a certaine Iland.

27 And when ye fourteenth night was come, as we were caried to and from in the Adriaticall sea about midnight, the shipmen deemed that some countrey approched vnto them,

28 And sounded, and found it twentie fathoms: and when they had gone a litle further, they sounded againe, and found fifteene fathoms.

29 Then fearing least they should haue fallen into some rough places, they cast foure ancres out of the sterne, and wished that the day were come.

30 Nowe as the mariners were about to flee out of the ship, and had let downe the boat into the sea vnder a colour as though they would haue cast ankers out of the foreship,

31 Paul sayde vnto the Centurion and the souldiers, Except these abide in the ship, ye can not be safe.

32 Then the souldiers cut off the ropes of the boat, and let it fall away.

33 And when it began to be day, Paul exhorted them all to take meate, saying, This is the fourteenth day that ye haue taried, and continued fasting, receiuing nothing:

34 Wherefore I exhort you to take meate: for this is for your safegarde: for there shall not an heare fall from the head of any of you.

35 And when he had thus spoken, hee tooke bread and gaue thankes to God, in presence of them all, and brake it, and began to eate.

36 Then were they all of good courage, and they also tooke meate.

37 Nowe we were in the ship in all two hundreth three score and sixteene soules.

38 And whe they had eaten ynough, they lightened the ship, and cast out the wheat into the sea.

39 And when it was day, they knewe not the countrey, but they spied a certaine creeke with a banke, into the which they were minded (if it were possible) to thrust in the ship.

40 So when they had taken vp the ankers, they committed the ship vnto the sea, and loosed the rudder bonds, and hoised vp the maine saile to the winde, and drewe to the shore.

41 And when they fell into a place, where two seas met, they thrust in the ship: and the forepart stucke fast, and could not be moued, but the hinderpart was broken with the violence of the waues.

42 Then the souldiers counsell was to kill the prisoners, least any of them, when he had swomme out, should flee away.

43 But the Centurion willing to saue Paul, stayed them from this counsell, and commanded that they that coulde swimme, shoulde cast them selues first into the sea, and goe out to land:

44 And the other, some on boardes, and some on certaine pieces of the ship: and so it came to passe that they came all safe to land.

Acts 28

1 And when they were come safe, then they knewe that the Yle was called Melita.

2 And the Barbarians shewed vs no litle kindnesse: for they kindled a fire, and receiued vs euery one, because of the present showre, and because of the colde.

3 And when Paul had gathered a nomber of stickes, and laid them on the fire, there came a viper out of the heate, and leapt on his hand.

4 Nowe when ye Barbarians saw the worme hang on his hand, they said among themselues, This man surely is a murtherer, whom, though he hath escaped the sea, yet Vengeance hath not suffered to liue.

5 But he shooke off the worme into the fire, and felt no harme.

6 Howbeit they wayted whe he should haue swolne, or fallen downe dead suddenly: but after they had looked a great while, and sawe no inconuenience come to him, they changed their mindes, and said, That he was a God.

7 In the same quarters, the chiefe man of the Yle (whose name was Publius) had possessions: the same receiued vs, and lodged vs three dayes courteously.

8 And so it was, that the father of Publius lay sicke of the feauer, and of a bloodie flixe: to whom Paul entred in, and when he prayed, he laide his hands on him, and healed him.

9 When this then was done, other also in the Yle, which had diseases, came to him, and were healed,

10 Which also did vs great honour: and when we departed, they laded vs with things necessarie.

11 Nowe after three moneths we departed in a shippe of Alexandria, which had wintred in the Yle, whose badge was Castor and Pollux.

12 And when we arriued at Syracuse, we taried there three dayes.

13 And from thence we set a compasse, and came to Rhegium: and after one day, the South wind blewe, and we came the seconde day to Putioli:

14 Where we found brethren, and were desired to tary with them seuen dayes, and so we went toward Rome.

15 And from thence, when the brethren heard of vs, they came to meete vs at the Market of Appius, and at the Three tauernes, whom when Paul sawe, he thanked God, and waxed bolde.

16 So when we came to Rome, the Centurion deliuered the prisoners to the generall Captaine: but Paul was suffered to dwell by him selfe with a souldier that kept him.

17 And the third day after, Paul called the chiefe of the Iewes together: and when they were come, he said vnto them, Men and brethren, though I haue committed nothing against the people, or Lawes of the fathers, yet was I deliuered prisoner from Hierusalem into the handes of the Romanes.

18 Who when they had examined me, would haue let me goe, because there was no cause of death in me.

19 But when the Iewes spake contrary, I was constrained to appeale vnto Cesar, not because I had ought to accuse my nation of.

20 For this cause therefore haue I called for you, to see you, and to speake with you: for that hope of Israels sake, I am bound with this chaine.

21 Then they saide vnto him, We neither receiued letters out of Iudea concerning thee, neither came any of the brethren that shewed or spake any euill of thee.

22 But we will heare of thee what thou thinkest: for as concerning this sect, we knowe that euery where it is spoken against.

23 And when they had appointed him a day, there came many vnto him into his lodging, to whom he expounded testifying the kingdome of God, and persuading them those things that concerne Iesus, both out of the Lawe of Moses, and out of the Prophets, from morning to night.

24 And some were persuaded with ye things which were spoken, and some beleeued not.

25 Therefore when they agreed not among themselues, they departed, after that Paul had spoken one word, to wit, Well spake the holy Ghost by Esaias the Prophet vnto our fathers,

26 Saying, Goe vnto this people, and say, By hearing ye shall heare, and shall not vnderstand, and seeing ye shall see, and not perceiue.

27 For the heart of this people is waxed fatte, and their eares are dull of hearing, and with their eyes haue they winked, least they shoulde see with their eyes, and heare with their eares, and vnderstand with their heartes, and should returne that I might heale them.

28 Be it knowen therefore vnto you, that this saluation of God is sent to the Gentiles, and they shall heare it.

29 And when he had saide these things, the Iewes departed, and had great reasoning among themselues.

30 And Paul remained two yeeres full in an house hired for himselfe, and receiued all that came in vnto him,

31 Preaching the kingdome of God, and teaching those things which concerne the Lord Iesus Christ, with all boldnesse of speache, without let.

Romans

Romans 1

1 Paul a seruant of Iesus Christ called to be an Apostle, put apart to preache the Gospel of God,

2 (Which he had promised afore by his Prophetes in the holy Scriptures)

3 Concerning his Sonne Iesus Christ our Lord (which was made of the seede of Dauid according to the flesh,

4 And declared mightily to be the Sonne of God, touching the Spirit of sanctification by the resurrection from the dead)

5 By whom we haue receiued grace and Apostleship (that obedience might be giuen vnto ye faith) for his Name among al ye Gentiles,

6 Among whom ye be also the called of Iesus Christ:

7 To all you that be at Rome beloued of God, called to be Saints: Grace be with you, and peace from God our Father, and from the Lord Iesus Christ.

8 First I thanke my God through Iesus Christ for you all, because your faith is published throughout the whole world.

9 For God is my witnesse (whom I serue in my spirit in the Gospel of his Sonne) that without ceasing I make mention of you

10 Alwayes in my prayers, beseeching that by some meanes, one time or other I might haue a prosperous iourney by the will of God, to come vnto you.

11 For I long to see you, that I might bestowe among you some spirituall gift, that you might be strengthened:

12 That is, that I might be comforted together with you, through our mutuall faith, both yours and mine.

13 Now my brethren, I would that ye should not be ignorant, how that I haue oftentimes purposed to come vnto you (but haue bene let hitherto) that I might haue some fruite also among you, as I haue among the other Gentiles.

14 I am detter both to the Grecians, and to the Barbarians, both to the wise men and vnto the vnwise.

15 Therefore, as much as in me is, I am readie to preach ye Gospel to you also that are at Rome.

16 For I am not ashamed of the Gospel of Christ: for it is the power of God vnto saluation to euery one that beleeueth, to the Iewe first, and also to the Grecian.

17 For by it the righteousnesse of God is reueiled from faith to faith: as it is written, The iust shall liue by faith.

18 For the wrath of God is reueiled from heauen against all vngodlinesse, and vnrighteousnesse of men, which withhold the trueth in vnrighteousnesse.

19 Forasmuch as that, which may be knowe of God, is manifest in them: for God hath shewed it vnto them.

20 For the inuisible things of him, that is, his eternal power and Godhead, are seene by ye creation of the worlde, being considered in his workes, to the intent that they should be without excuse:

21 Because that when they knewe God, they glorified him not as God, neither were thankefull, but became vaine in their thoughtes, and their foolish heart was full of darkenesse.

22 When they professed themselues to be wise, they became fooles.

23 For they turned the glorie of the incorruptible God to the similitude of the image of a corruptible man, and of birdes, and foure footed beastes, and of creeping things.

24 Wherefore also God gaue them vp to their hearts lusts, vnto vncleannesse, to defile their owne bodies betweene themselues:

25 Which turned the trueth of God vnto a lie, and worshipped and serued the creature, forsaking the Creator, which is blessed for euer, Amen.

26 For this cause God gaue them vp vnto vile affections: for euen their women did change the naturall vse into that which is against nature.

27 And likewise also the men left the naturall vse of the woman, and burned in their lust one toward another, and man with man wrought filthinesse, and receiued in themselues such recompence of their errour, as was meete.

28 For as they regarded not to acknowledge God, euen so God deliuered

them vp vnto a reprobate minde, to doe those things which are not conuenient,

29 Being full of all vnrighteousnesse, fornication, wickednes, couetousnes, maliciousnes, full of enuie, of murder, of debate, of deceit, taking all things in the euill part, whisperers,

30 Backbiters, haters of God, doers of wrong, proude, boasters, inuenters of euil things, disobedient to parents, without vnderstanding, couenant breakers, without naturall affection, such as can neuer be appeased, mercilesse.

31 Which men, though they knew ye Lawe of God, how that they which comit such things are worthie of death, yet not onely do the same, but also fauour them that doe them.

Romans 2

1 Therefore thou art inexcusable, O man, whosoeuer thou art that condemnest: for in that that thou condemnest another, thou condemnest thy selfe: for thou that condemnest, doest the same things.

2 But we know that the iudgement of God is according to trueth, against them which comit such things.

3 And thinkest thou this, O thou man, that condemnest them which doe such thinges, and doest the same, that thou shalt escape the iudgement of God?

4 Or despisest thou the riches of his bountifulnesse, and patience, and long sufferance, not knowing that the bountifulnesse of God leadeth thee to repentance?

5 But thou, after thine hardnesse, and heart that canot repent, heapest vp as a treasure vnto thy selfe wrath against the day of wrath, and of the declaration of the iust iudgement of God,

6 Who wil reward euery man according to his woorkes:

7 That is, to them which through patience in well doing, seeke glorie, and honour, and immortalitie, euerlasting life:

8 But vnto them that are contentious and disobey the trueth, and obey vnrighteousnesse, shalbe indignation and wrath.

9 Tribulation and anguish shalbe vpon the soule of euery man that doeth euill: of the Iewe first, and also of the Grecian.

10 But to euery man that doeth good, shalbe glory, and honour, and peace: to the Iew first, and also to the Grecian.

11 For there is no respect of persons with God.

12 For as many as haue sinned without the Lawe, shall perish also without the Lawe: and as many as haue sinned in the Lawe, shall be iudged by the Lawe,

13 (For the hearers of the Lawe are not righteous before God: but the doers of the Lawe shalbe iustified.

14 For when the Gentiles which haue not the Lawe, doe by nature, the things conteined in the Lawe, they hauing not the Lawe, are a Lawe vnto themselues,

15 Which shew the effect of the Lawe written in their hearts, their conscience also bearing witnes, and their thoughts accusing one another, or excusing,)

16 At the day when God shall iudge the secretes of men by Iesus Christ, according to my Gospel.

17 Beholde, thou art called a Iewe, and restest in the Lawe, and gloriest in God,

18 And knowest his will, and triest the things that dissent from it, in that thou art instructed by the Lawe:

19 And persuadest thy selfe that thou art a guide of the blinde, a light of them which are in darkenesse,

20 An instructer of them which lacke discretion, a teacher of the vnlearned, which hast the forme of knowledge, and of the truth in ye Law.

21 Thou therefore, which teachest another, teachest thou not thy selfe? thou that preachest, A man should not steale, doest thou steale?

22 Thou that saist, A man should not commit adulterie, doest thou commit adulterie? thou that abhorrest idoles, committest thou sacrilege?

23 Thou that gloriest in the Lawe, through breaking the Lawe, dishonourest thou God?

24 For ye Name of God is blasphemed among the Gentiles through you, as it is written.

25 For circucision verely is profitable, if thou do the Lawe: but if thou be a transgressour of the Lawe, thy circumcision is made vncircumcision.

26 Therefore if the vncircumcision keepe the ordinances of the Lawe, shall not his vncircumcision be counted for circumcision?

27 And shall not vncircumcision which is by nature (if it keepe the Lawe) condemne thee which by the letter and circumcision art a transgressour of the Lawe?

28 For hee is not a Iewe, which is one outwarde: neither is that circumcision, which is outward in the flesh:

29 But he is a Iewe which is one within, and the circumcision is of the heart, in the spirite not in the letter, whose praise is not of men, but of God.

Romans 3

1 What is then the preferment of the Iewe? or what is the profite of circumcision?

2 Much euery maner of way: for chiefly, because vnto them were of credite committed the oracles of God.

3 For what, though some did not beleeue? shall their vnbeliefe make the faith of God without effect?

4 God forbid: yea, let God be true, and euery man a lyar, as it is written, That thou mightest be iustified in thy words, and ouercome, when thou art iudged.

5 Now if our vnrighteousnes comend the righteousnes of God, what shall we say? Is God vnrighteous which punisheth? (I speake as a man.)

6 God forbid: els how shall God iudge ye world?

7 For if the veritie of God hath more abounded through my lye vnto his glorie, why am I yet condemned as a sinner?

8 And (as we are blamed, and as some affirme, that we say) why doe we not euil, that good may come thereof? whose damnation is iust.

9 What then? are we more excellent? No, in no wise: for we haue alreadie prooued, that all, both Iewes and Gentiles are vnder sinne,

10 As it is written, There is none righteous, no not one.

11 There is none that vnderstandeth: there is none that seeketh God.

12 They haue all gone out of the way: they haue bene made altogether vnprofitable: there is none that doeth good, no not one.

13 Their throte is an open sepulchre: they haue vsed their tongues to deceit: the poyson of aspes is vnder their lippes.

14 Whose mouth is full of cursing and bitternesse.

15 Their feete are swift to shead blood.

16 Destruction and calamity are in their waies,

17 And ye way of peace they haue not knowen.

18 The feare of God is not before their eies.

19 Now we know that whatsoeuer ye Lawe saieth, it saieth it to them which are vnder ye Law, that euery mouth may bee stopped, and all the world be subiect to the iudgement of God.

20 Therefore by the woorkes of the Lawe shall no flesh be iustified in his sight: for by the Lawe commeth the knowledge of sinne.

21 But nowe is the righteousnesse, of God made manifest without the Lawe, hauing witnes of the Lawe and of the Prophets,

22 To wit, the righteousnesse of God by the faith of Iesus Christ, vnto all, and vpon all that beleeue.

23 For there is no difference: for all haue sinned, and are depriued of the glorie of God,

24 And are iustified freely by his grace, through the redemption that is in Christ Iesus,

25 Whom God hath set forth to be a reconciliation through faith in his blood to declare his righteousnes, by the forgiuenesse of the sinnes that are passed,

26 Through the patience of God, to shewe at this time his righteousnesse, that hee might be iust, and a iustifier of him which is of the faith of Iesus.

27 Where is then the reioycing? It is excluded. By what Lawe? of woorkes? Nay: but by the Lawe of faith.

28 Therefore we conclude, that a man is iustified by faith, without the workes of the Lawe.

29 God, is he the God of the Iewes onely, and not of the Gentiles also? Yes, euen of the Gentiles also.

30 For it is one God, who shall iustifie circumcision of faith, and vncircumcision through faith.

31 Doe we then make the Lawe of none effect through faith? God forbid: yea, we establish the Lawe.

Romans 4

1 What shall we say then, that Abraham our father hath found concerning the flesh?

2 For if Abraham were iustified by workes, he hath wherein to reioyce, but not with God.

3 For what saith the Scripture? Abraham beleeued God, and it was counted to him for righteousnesse.

4 Nowe to him that worketh, the wages is not counted by fauour, but by dette:

5 But to him that worketh not, but beleeueth in him that iustifieth the vngodly, his faith is counted for righteousnesse.

6 Euen as Dauid declareth the blessednesse of the man, vnto whom God imputeth righteousnes without workes, saying,

7 Blessed are they, whose iniquities are forgiuen, and whose sinnes are couered.

8 Blessed is the man, to whom the Lord imputeth not sinne.

9 Came this blessednesse then vpon the circumcision onely, or vpon the vncircumcision also? For we say, that faith was imputed vnto Abraham for righteousnesse.

10 Howe was it then imputed? when he was circumcised, or vncircumcised? not when he was cricumcised, but when he was vncircumcised.

11 After, he receiued the signe of circumcision, as the seale of the righteousnesse of ye faith which he had, when he was vncircumcised, that he should be the father of all them that beleeue, not being circumcised, that righteousnesse might be imputed to them also,

12 And the father of circumcision, not vnto them onely which are of the circumcision, but vnto them also that walke in the steppes of the faith of our father Abraham, which he had when he was vncircumcised.

13 For the promise that he should be the heire of the worlde, was not giuen to Abraham, or to his seede, through the Lawe, but through the righteousnesse of faith.

14 For if they which are of the Lawe, be heires, faith is made voide, and the promise is made of none effect.

15 For the Lawe causeth wrath: for where no Lawe is, there is no transgression.

16 Therefore it is by faith, that it might come by grace, and the promise might be sure to all the seede, not to that onely which is of the Lawe: but also to that which is of the faith of Abraham, who is the father of vs all,

17 (As it is written, I haue made thee a father of many nations) euen before God whom he beleeued, who quickeneth the dead, and calleth those thinges which be not, as though they were.

18 Which Abraham aboue hope, beleeued vnder hope, that he should be the father of many nations: according to that which was spoken to him, So shall thy seede be.

19 And he not weake in the faith, considered not his owne bodie, which was nowe dead, being almost an hundreth yeere olde, neither the deadnes of Saraes wombe.

20 Neither did he doubt of the promise of God through vnbeliefe, but was strengthened in the faith, and gaue glorie to God,

21 Being fully assured that he which had promised, was also able to doe it.

22 And therefore it was imputed to him for righteousnesse.

23 Nowe it is not written for him onely, that it was imputed to him for righteousnesse,

24 But also for vs, to whom it shalbe imputed for righteousnesse, which beleeue in him that raised vp Iesus our Lord from the dead,

25 Who was deliuered to death for our sinnes, and is risen againe for our iustification.

Romans 5

1 Then being iustified by faith, we haue peace toward God through our Lord Iesus Christ.

2 By who also through faith, we haue had this accesse into this grace, wherein we stand, and reioyce vnder ye hope of the glory of God.

3 Neither that onely, but also we reioyce in tribulations, knowing that tribulation bringeth forth patience,

4 And patience experience, and experience hope,

5 And hope maketh not ashamed, because the loue of God is shed abroade in our heartes by the holy Ghost, which is giuen vnto vs.

6 For Christ, when we were yet of no strength, at his time died for the vngodly.

7 Doutles one will scarce die for a righteous man: but yet for a good man it may be that one dare die.

8 But God setteth out his loue towards vs, seeing that while we were yet sinners, Christ died for vs.

9 Much more then, being now iustified by his blood, we shalbe saued from wrath through him.

10 For if when we were enemies, we were reconciled to God by the death of his Sonne, much more being reconciled, we shalbe saued by his life,

11 And not onely so, but we also reioyce in God through our Lord Iesus Christ, by whom we haue nowe receiued the atonement.

12 Wherefore, as by one man sinne entred into ye world, and death by sinne, and so death went ouer all men: in who all men haue sinned.

13 For vnto the time of the Law was sinne in the worlde, but sinne is not imputed, while there is no lawe.

14 But death reigned from Adam to Moses, euen ouer them also that sinned not after the like maner of that transgression of Adam, which was the figure of him that was to come.

15 But yet the gift is not so, as is the offence: for if through the offence of that one, many be dead, much more the grace of God, and the gift by grace, which is by one man Iesus Christ, hath abounded vnto many.

16 Neither is the gift so, as that which entred in by one that sinned: for the fault came of one offence vnto condemnation: but the gift is of many offences to iustification.

17 For if by the offence of one, death reigned through one, much more shall they which receiue that abundance of grace, and of that gift of that righteousnesse, reigne in life through one, that is, Iesus Christ.

18 Likewise then as by the offence of one, the fault came on all men to condemnation, so by the iustifying of one, the benefite abounded toward all men to the iustification of life.

19 For as by one mans disobedience many were made sinners, so by that obedience of that one shall many also be made righteous.

20 Moreouer the Law entred thereupon that the offence shoulde abound: neuerthelesse, where sinne abounded, there grace abounded much more:

21 That as sinne had reigned vnto death, so might grace also reigne by righteousnesse vnto eternall life, through Iesus Christ our Lord.

Romans 6

1 What shall we say then? Shall we continue still in sinne, that grace may abounde? God forbid.

2 Howe shall we, that are dead to sinne, liue yet therein?

3 Knowe ye not, that all we which haue bene baptized into Iesus Christ, haue bene baptized into his death?

4 We are buried then with him by baptisme into his death, that like as Christ was raysed vp from the dead to the glorie of the Father, so we also should walke in newnesse of life.

5 For if we be planted with him to the similitude of his death, euen so shall we be to the similitude of his resurrection,

6 Knowing this, that our old man is crucified with him, that the body of sinne might be destroied, that henceforth we should not serue sinne.

7 For he that is dead, is freed from sinne.

8 Wherefore, if we bee dead with Christ, we beleeue that we shall liue also with him,

9 Knowing that Christ being raised from the dead, dieth no more: death hath no more dominion ouer him.

10 For in that hee died, hee died once to sinne but in that he liueth, he liueth to God.

11 Likewise thinke ye also, that ye are dead to sin, but are aliue to God in Iesus Christ our Lord.

12 Let not sinne reigne therefore in your mortal body, that ye should obey it in ye lusts therof:

13 Neither giue ye your members, as weapons of vnrighteousnes vnto sinne: but giue your selues vnto God, as they that are aliue from the dead, and giue your members as weapons of righteousnesse vnto God.

14 For sinne shall not haue dominion ouer you: for ye are not vnder ye Lawe, but vnder grace.

15 What then? shall we sinne, because we are not vnder the Law, but vnder grace? God forbid.

16 Knowe ye not, that to whomsoeuer yee giue your selues as seruats to obey, his seruants ye are to whom ye obey, whether it be of sinne vnto death, or of obedience vnto righteousnesse?

17 But God be thanked, that ye haue beene the seruants of sinne, but yee haue obeyed from the heart vnto the forme of the doctrine, wherunto ye were deliuered.

18 Being then made free from sinne, yee are made the seruants of righteousnesse.

19 I speake after the maner of man, because of the infirmitie of your flesh: for as yee haue giuen your members seruants to vncleannes and to iniquitie, to commit iniquitie, so now giue your mebers seruants vnto righteousnesse in holinesse.

20 For when ye were the seruants of sinne, ye were freed from righteousnesse.

21 What fruit had ye then in those things, whereof ye are nowe ashamed? For the ende of those things is death.

22 But now being freed from sinne, and made seruants vnto God, ye haue your fruit in holines, and the end, euerlasting life.

23 For the wages of sinne is death: but the gift of God is eternall life, through Iesus Christ our Lord.

Romans 7

1 Knowe yee not, brethren, (for I speake to them that knowe the Lawe) that the Lawe hath dominion ouer a man as long as he liueth?

2 For the woman which is in subiection to a man, is bound by the Lawe to the man, while he liueth: but if the man bee dead, shee is deliuered from the lawe of the man.

3 So then, if while the man liueth, she taketh another man, she shalbe called an adulteresse: but if the man be dead, she is free from the Law, so that shee is not an adulteresse, though shee take another man.

4 So yee, my brethren, are dead also to the Law by ye body of Christ, that ye should be vnto an other, euen vnto him that is raised vp from the dead, that we should bring foorth fruite vnto God.

5 For when we were in ye flesh, the affections of sinnes, which were by the Law, had force in our members, to bring foorth fruit vnto death.

6 But now we are deliuered from the Lawe, he being dead in whom we were holden, that we should serue in newnesse of Spirite, and not in the oldnesse of the letter.

7 What shall we say then? Is the Lawe sinne? God forbid. Nay, I knewe not sinne, but by the Lawe: for I had not knowen lust, except the Lawe had sayd, Thou shalt not lust.

8 But sinne tooke an occasion by ye commandement, and wrought in me all maner of concupiscence: for without the Lawe sinne is dead.

9 For I once was aliue, without the Law: but when the commandement came, sinne reuiued,

10 But I died: and the same commandement which was ordeined vnto life, was found to be vnto me vnto death.

11 For sinne tooke occasion by the commandement, and deceiued me, and thereby slewe me.

12 Wherefore the Lawe is holy, and that commandement is holy, and iust, and good.

13 Was that then which is good, made death vnto me? God forbid: but sinne, that it might appeare sinne, wrought death in me by that which is good, that sinne might be out of measure sinfull by the commandement.

14 For we knowe that the Law is spirituall, but I am carnall, solde vnder sinne.

15 For I alow not that which I do: for what I would, that do I not: but what I hate, that do I.

16 If I doe then that which I woulde not, I consent to the Lawe, that it is good.

17 Nowe then, it is no more I, that doe it, but sinne that dwelleth in me.

18 For I know, that in me, that is, in my flesh, dwelleth no good thing: for to wil is preset with me: but I find no meanes to perform that which is good.

19 For I doe not the good thing, which I would, but the euil, which I would not, that do I.

20 Nowe if I do that I would not, it is no more I that doe it, but the sinne that dwelleth in me.

21 I finde then that when I would doe good, I am thus yoked, that euill is present with me.

22 For I delite in the Law of God, concerning the inner man:

23 But I see another Law in my members, rebelling against the Lawe of my minde, and leading me captiue vnto the lawe of sinne, which is in my members.

24 O wretched man that I am, who shall deliuer me from the body of this death!

25 I thanke God through Iesus Christ our Lord. Then I my selfe in my minde serue the Lawe of God, but in my flesh the lawe of sinne.

Romans 8

1 Now then there is no condemnation to them that are in Christ Iesus, which walke not after the flesh, but after the Spirit.

2 For the Lawe of the Spirite of life, which is in Christ Iesus, hath freed mee from the lawe of sinne and of death.

3 For (that that was impossible to ye Lawe, in as much as it was weake, because of ye flesh) God sending his owne Sonne, in ye similitude of sinful flesh, and for sinne, condened sinne in the flesh,

4 That that righteousnes of the Law might be fulfilled in vs, which walke not after ye flesh, but after the Spirit.

5 For they that are after the flesh, sauour the things of the flesh: but they that are after the Spirit, the things of the Spirit.

6 For the wisedome of the flesh is death: but the wisedome of the Spirit is life and peace,

7 Because the wisedome of the flesh is enimitie against God: for it is not subiect to the Lawe of God, neither in deede can be.

8 So then they that are in the flesh, can not please God.

9 Now ye are not in the flesh, but in ye Spirit, because ye spirit of God dwelleth in you: but if any man hath not ye Spirit of Christ, ye same is not his.

10 And if Christ bee in you, the body is dead, because of sinne: but the Spirite is life for righteousnesse sake.

11 But if the Spirit of him that raised vp Iesus from the dead, dwell in you, he that raised vp Christ from the dead, shall also quicken your mortall bodies, by his Spirit that dwelleth in you.

12 Therefore brethren, wee are detters not to the flesh, to liue after the flesh:

13 For if ye liue after the flesh, ye shall die: but if yee mortifie the deedes of the body by the Spirit, ye shall liue.

14 For as many as are ledde by the Spirit of God, they are the sonnes of God.

15 For ye haue not receiued the Spirit of bodage, to feare againe: but ye haue receiued the Spirit of adoption, whereby we cry Abba, Father.

16 The same Spirit beareth witnesse with our spirit, that we are the children of God.

17 If we be children, we are also heires, euen the heires of God, and heires annexed with Christ: if so be that we suffer with him, that we may also be glorified with him.

18 For I count that the afflictions of this present time are not worthy of the glory, which shalbe shewed vnto vs.

19 For the feruent desire of the creature waiteth when the sonnes of God shalbe reueiled,

20 Because the creature is subiect to vanitie, not of it owne will, but by reason of him, which hath subdued it vnder hope,

21 Because the creature also shall be deliuered from the bondage of corruption into the glorious libertie of the sonnes of God.

22 For we knowe that euery creature groneth with vs also, and trauaileth in paine together vnto this present.

23 And not onely the creature, but we also which haue the first fruites of the Spirit, euen we doe sigh in our selues, waiting for the adoption, euen the redemption of our body.

24 For we are saued by hope: but hope that is seene, is not hope: for how can a man hope for that which he seeth?

25 But if we hope for that we see not, we doe with patience abide for it.

26 Likewise the Spirit also helpeth our infirmities: for we knowe not what to pray as wee ought: but the Spirit it selfe maketh request for vs with sighs, which cannot be expressed.

27 But he that searcheth the heartes, knoweth what is the meaning of the Spirit: for he maketh request for ye Saints, according to the wil of God.

28 Also we knowe that all thinges worke together for the best vnto them that loue God, euen to them that are called of his purpose.

29 For those which hee knewe before, he also predestinate to bee made like to the image of his Sonne, that hee might be the first borne among many brethren.

30 Moreouer whom he predestinate, them also he called, and whom he called, them also he iustified, and whom he iustified, them he also glorified.

31 What shall we then say to these thinges? If God be on our side, who can be against vs?

32 Who spared not his owne Sonne, but gaue him for vs all to death, how shall he not with him giue vs all things also?

33 Who shall lay any thing to the charge of Gods chosen? it is God that iustifieth,

34 Who shall condemne? it is Christ which is dead, yea, or rather, which is risen againe, who is also at the right hand of God, and maketh request also for vs.

35 Who shall separate vs from the loue of Christ? shall tribulation or anguish, or persecution, or famine, or nakednesse, or perill, or sworde?

36 As it is written, For thy sake are we killed all day long: we are counted as sheepe for the slaughter.

37 Neuerthelesse, in all these thinges we are more then coquerours through him that loued vs.

38 For I am perswaded that neither death, nor life, nor Angels, nor principalities, nor powers, nor things present, nor things to come,

39 Nor height, nor depth, nor any other creature shalbe able to separate vs from the loue of God, which is in Christ Iesus our Lord.

Romans 9

1 I say the trueth in Christ, I lye not, my conscience bearing mee witnes in the holy Ghost,

2 That I haue great heauinesse, and continuall sorow in mine heart.

3 For I woulde wish my selfe to be separate from Christ, for my brethren that are my kinsemen according to the flesh,

4 Which are the Israelites, to whome perteineth the adoption, and the glory, and the Couenants, and the giuing of the Lawe, and the seruice of God, and the promises.

5 Of whome are the fathers, and of whome concerning the flesh, Christ came, who is God ouer all, blessed for euer, Amen.

6 Notwithstanding it can not bee that the worde of God should take none effect: for all they are not Israel, which are of Israel:

7 Neither are they all children, because they are the seede of Abraham: but, In Isaac shall thy seede be called:

8 That is, they which are the children of the flesh, are not the children of God: but the children of the promise, are counted for the seede.

9 For this is a worde of promise, In this same time wil I come, and Sara shall haue a sonne.

10 Neither he onely felt this, but also Rebecca when shee had conceiued by one, euen by our father Isaac.

11 For yer the children were borne, and when they had neither done good, nor euill (that the purpose of God might remaine according to election, not by workes, but by him that calleth)

12 It was said vnto her, The elder shall serue the yonger.

13 As it is written, I haue loued Iacob, and haue hated Esau.

14 What shall wee say then? Is there vnrighteousnes with God? God forbid.

15 For he saith to Moses, I wil haue mercy on him, to whom I wil shew mercie: and wil haue compassion on him, on who I wil haue copassion.

16 So then it is not in him that willeth, nor in him that runneth, but in God that sheweth mercy.

17 For the Scripture saith vnto Pharao, For this same purpose haue I stirred thee vp, that I might shewe my power in thee, and that my Name might be declared throughout al the earth.

18 Therefore he hath mercie on whome he will, and whom he will, he hardeneth.

19 Thou wilt say then vnto me, Why doeth he yet complaine? for who hath resisted his will?

20 But, O man, who art thou which pleadest against God? shall the thing formed say to him that formed it, Why hast thou made me thus?

21 Hath not the potter power of the clay to make of the same lumpe one vessell to honour, and another vnto dishonour?

22 What and if God would, to shewe his wrath, and to make his power knowen, suffer with long patience the vessels of wrath, prepared to destruction?

23 And that hee might declare the riches of his glory vpon the vessels of mercy, which hee hath prepared vnto glory?

24 Euen vs whome hee hath called, not of of the Iewes onely, but also of the Gentiles,

25 As he sayth also in Osee, I will call them, My people, which were not my people: and her, Beloued, which was not beloued.

26 And it shalbe in the place where it was said vnto them, Ye are not my people, that there they shalbe called, The children of the liuing God.

27 Also Esaias cryeth concerning Israel, Though the number of the children of Israel were as the sand of the sea, yet shall but a remnant be saued.

28 For he wil make his account, and gather it into a short summe with righteousnes: for the Lord will make a short count in the earth.

29 And as Esaias sayde before, Except the Lord of hostes had left vs a seede, we had bene made as Sodom, and had bene like to Gomorrha.

30 What shall we say then? That the Gentiles which folowed not righteousnes, haue attained vnto righteousnes, euen the righteousnes which is of faith.

31 But Israel which followed the Lawe of righteousnes, could not arteine vnto the Law of righteousnes.

32 Wherefore? Because they sought it not by faith, but as it were by the workes of the Lawe: for they haue stumbled at the stumbling stone,

33 As it is written, Beholde, I lay in Sion a stumbling stone, and a rocke to make men fall: and euery one that beleeueth in him, shall not be ashamed.

Romans 10

1 Brethren, mine hearts desire and prayer to God for Israel is, that they might be saued.

2 For I beare them record, that they haue the zeale of God, but not according to knowledge.

3 For they, being ignorant of the righteousnes of God, and going about to stablish their owne righteousnes, haue not submitted themselues to the righteousnes of God.

4 For Christ is the end of the Law for righteousnes vnto euery one that beleeueth.

5 For Moses thus describeth the righteousnes which is of the Lawe, That the man which doeth these things, shall liue thereby.

6 But the righteousnes which is of faith, speaketh on this wise, Say not in thine heart, Who shall ascend into heauen? (that is to bring Christ from aboue)

7 Or, Who shall descend into the deepe? (that is to bring Christ againe from the dead)

8 But what sayth it? The worde is neere thee, euen in thy mouth, and in thine heart. This is the worde of faith which we preach.

9 For if thou shalt confesse with thy mouth the Lord Iesus, and shalt beleeue in thine heart, that God raised him vp from the dead, thou shalt be saued:

10 For with the heart man beleeueth vnto righteousnes, and with the mouth man confesseth to saluation.

11 For the Scripture saith, Whosoeuer beleeueth in him, shall not be ashamed.

12 For there is no difference betweene the Iewe and the Grecian: for he that is Lord ouer all, is rich vnto all, that call on him.

13 For whosoeuer shall call vpon the Name of the Lord, shalbe saued.

14 But how shall they call on him, in whome they haue not beleeued? and how shall they beleeue in him, of whom they haue not heard? and howe shall they heare without a preacher?

15 And how shall they preach, except they be sent? as it is written, Howe beautifull are the feete of them which bring glad tidings of peace, and bring glad tidings of good things!

16 But they haue not all obeyed ye Gospel: for Esaias saith, Lord, who hath beleeued our report?

17 Then faith is by hearing, and hearing by the worde of God.

18 But I demaund, Haue they not heard? No doubt their sound went out through all the earth, and their wordes into the endes of the worlde.

19 But I demaund, Did not Israel knowe God? First Moses sayth, I will prouoke you to enuie by a nation that is not my nation, and by a foolish nation I will anger you.

20 And Esaias is bolde, and saith, I was found of them that sought me not, and haue bene made manifest to them that asked not after me.

21 And vnto Israel hee sayth, All the day long haue I stretched foorth mine hand vnto a disobedient, and gainesaying people.

Romans 11

1 I Demaund then, Hath God cast away his people? God forbid: for I also am an Israelite, of the seede of Abraham, of the tribe of Beniamin.

2 God hath not cast away his people which he knew before. Know ye not what the Scripture sayth of Elias, howe hee communeth with God against Israel, saying,

3 Lord, they haue killed thy Prophets, and digged downe thine altars: and I am left alone, and they seeke my life?

4 But what saith the answere of God to him? I haue reserued vnto my selfe seuen thousand men, which haue not bowed the knee to Baal.

5 Euen so then at this present time is there a remnant according to the election of grace.

6 And if it be of grace, it is no more of workes: or els were grace no more grace: but if it be of workes, it is no more grace: or els were worke no more worke.

7 What then? Israel hath not obtained that he sought: but the election hath obtained it, and the rest haue bene hardened,

8 According as it is written, God hath giuen them the spirit of slumber: eyes that they should not see, and eares that they should not heare vnto this day.

9 And Dauid sayth, Let their table be made a snare, and a net, and a

stumbling blocke, euen for a recompence vnto them.

10 Let their eyes be darkened that they see not, and bowe downe their backe alwayes.

11 I demaund then, Haue they stumbled, that they should fall? God forbid: but through their fall, saluation commeth vnto the Gentiles, to prouoke them to follow them.

12 Wherefore if the fall of them be the riches of the world, and the diminishing of them the riches of the Gentiles, how much more shall their aboundance be?

13 For in that I speake to you Gentiles, in as much as I am the Apostle of ye Gentiles, I magnifie mine office,

14 To trie if by any meanes I might prouoke them of my flesh to follow them, and might saue some of them.

15 For if the casting away of them be the reconciling of the world, what shall the receiuing be, but life from the dead?

16 For if the first fruites be holy, so is the whole lumpe: and if the roote be holy, so are the branches.

17 And though some of the branches be broken off, and thou being a wilde Oliue tree, wast graft in for them, and made partaker of the roote, and fatnesse of the Oliue tree.

18 Boast not thy selfe against the branches: and if thou boast thy selfe, thou bearest not the roote, but the roote thee.

19 Thou wilt say then, The branches are broken off, that I might be graft in.

20 Well: through vnbeliefe they are broken off, and thou standest by faith: bee not hie minded, but feare.

21 For if God spared not the naturall branches, take heede, least he also spare not thee.

22 Beholde therefore the bountifulnesse, and seueritie of God: towarde them which haue fallen, seueritie: but toward thee, bountifulnesse, if thou continue in his bountifulnesse: or els thou shalt also be cut off.

23 And they also, if they abide not still in vnbeliefe, shall be graffed in: for God is able to graffe them in againe.

24 For if thou wast cut out of the Oliue tree, which was wilde by nature, and wast graffed contrary to nature in a right Oliue tree, how much more shall they that are by nature, bee graffed in their owne Oliue tree?

25 For I would not, brethren, that ye should be ignorant of this secret (least ye should bee arrogant in your selues) that partly obstinacie is come to Israel, vntill the fulnesse of the Gentiles be come in.

26 And so all Israel shalbe saued, as it is written, The deliuerer shall come out of Sion, and shall turne away the vngodlinesse from Iacob.

27 And this is my couenant to them, When I shall take away their sinnes.

28 As concerning the Gospel, they are enemies for your sakes: but as touching the election, they are beloued for the fathers sakes.

29 For the giftes and calling of God are without repentance.

30 For euen as yee in times past haue not beleeued God, yet haue nowe obteined mercie through their vnbeliefe:

31 Euen so nowe haue they not beleeued by the mercie shewed vnto you, that they also may obtaine mercie.

32 For God hath shut vp all in vnbeliefe, that he might haue mercie on all.

33 O the deepenesse of the riches, both of the wisdome, and knowledge of God! howe vnsearcheable are his iudgements, and his wayes past finding out!

34 For who hath knowen the minde of the Lord? or who was his counsellour?

35 Or who hath giuen vnto him first, and he shalbe recompensed?

36 For of him, and through him, and for him are all things: to him be glory for euer. Amen.

Romans 12

1 I Beseech you therefore brethren, by the mercies of God, that yee giue vp your bodies a liuing sacrifice, holy, acceptable vnto God, which is your reasonable seruing of God.

2 And fashion not your selues like vnto this worlde, but bee yee changed by the renewing of your minde, that ye may prooue what that good, and acceptable and perfect will of God is.

3 For I say through the grace that is giuen vnto me, to euery one that is among you, that no man presume to vnderstande aboue that which is meete to vnderstand, but that he vnderstande according to sobrietie, as God hath dealt to euery man the measure of faith.

4 For as wee haue many members in one body, and all members haue not one office,

5 So we being many are one body in Christ, and euery one, one anothers members.

6 Seeing then that we haue gifts that are diuers, according to the grace that is giuen vnto vs, whether we haue prophecie, let vs prophecie according to the portion of faith:

7 Or an office, let vs waite on the office: or he that teacheth, on teaching:

8 Or he that exhorteth, on exhortation: he that distributeth, let him doe it with simplicitie: he that ruleth, with diligence: he that sheweth mercie, with cheerefulnesse.

9 Let loue be without dissimulation. Abhorre that which is euill, and cleaue vnto that which is good.

10 Be affectioned to loue one another with brotherly loue. In giuing honour, goe one before another,

11 Not slouthfull to do seruice: seruent in spirit seruing the Lord,

12 Reioycing in hope, pacient in tribulation, continuing in prayer,

13 Distributing vnto the necessities of the Saintes: giuing your selues to hospitalitie.

14 Blesse them which persecute you: blesse, I say, and curse not.

15 Reioyce with them that reioyce, and weepe with them that weepe.

16 Be of like affection one towardes another: be not hie minded: but make your selues equall to them of the lower sort: be not wise in your selues.

17 Recompence to no man euill for euill: procure things honest in the sight of all men.

18 If it bee possible, as much as in you is, haue peace with all men.

19 Dearely beloued, auenge not your selues, but giue place vnto wrath: for it is written, Vengeance is mine: I will repay, saith the Lord.

20 Therefore, if thine enemie hunger, feede him: if he thirst, giue him drinke: for in so doing, thou shalt heape coales of fire on his head.

21 Bee not ouercome of euill, but ouercome euill with goodnesse.

Romans 13

1 Let euery soule be subiect vnto the higher powers: for there is no power but of God: and the powers that be, are ordeined of God.

2 Whosoeuer therefore resisteth the power, resisteth the ordinance of God: and they that resist, shall receiue to themselues condemnation.

3 For Magistrates are not to be feared for good workes, but for euill. Wilt thou then bee without feare of the power? doe well: so shalt thou haue praise of the same.

4 For he is ye minister of God for thy wealth, but if thou do euill, feare: for he beareth not the sworde for nought: for he is the minister of God to take vengeance on him that doeth euill.

5 Wherefore ye must bee subiect, not because of wrath only, but also for conscience sake.

6 For, for this cause ye pay also tribute: for they are Gods ministers, applying themselues for the same thing.

7 Giue to all men therefore their duetie: tribute, to whome yee owe tribute: custome, to whom custome: feare, to whome feare: honour, to whom ye owe honour.

8 Owe nothing to any man, but to loue one another: for he that loueth another, hath fulfilled the Lawe.

9 For this, Thou shalt not commit adulterie, Thou shalt not kill, Thou shalt not steale, Thou shalt not beare false witnes, Thou shalt not couet: and if there be any other commandement, it is briefly comprehended in this saying, euen in this, Thou shalt loue thy neighbour as thy selfe.

10 Loue doeth not euill to his neighbour: therefore is loue the fulfilling of the Lawe.

11 And that, considering the season, that it is now time that we should arise from sleepe: for now is our saluation neerer, then when we beleeued it.

12 The night is past, and the day is at hande, let vs therefore cast away the workes of darkenesse, and let vs put on the armour of light,

13 So that wee walke honestly, as in the day: not in gluttonie, and drunkennesse, neither in chambering and wantonnes, nor in strife and enuying.

14 But put yee on the Lord JESUS CHRIST, and take no thought for the flesh, to fulfill the lustes of it.

Romans 14

1 Him that is weake in the faith, receiue vnto you, but not for controuersies of disputations.

2 One beleeueth that he may eate of all things: and another, which is weake, eateth herbes.

3 Let not him that eateth, despise him that eateth not: and let not him which eateth not, condemne him that eateth: for God hath receiued him.

4 Who art thou that condemnest another mans seruant? hee standeth or falleth to his owne master: yea, he shalbe established: for God is able to make him stand.

5 This man esteemeth one day aboue another day, and another man counteth euery day alike: let euery man be fully perswaded in his minde.

6 He that obserueth the day, obserueth it to the Lord: and he that obserueth not the day, obserueth it not to the Lord. He that eateth, eateth to the Lord: for he giueth God thankes: and he that eateth not, eateth not to the Lord, and giueth God thankes.

7 For none of vs liueth to himselfe, neither doeth any die to himselfe.

8 For whether wee liue, we liue vnto the Lord: or whether we die, we die vnto the Lord: whether we liue therefore, or die, we are the Lords.

9 For Christ therefore died and rose againe, and reuiued, that he might be Lord both of the dead and the quicke.

10 But why doest thou condemne thy brother? or why doest thou despise thy brother? for we shall all appeare before the iudgement seate of Christ.

11 For it is written, I liue, sayth the Lord, and euery knee shall bowe to me, and all tongues shall confesse vnto God.

12 So then euery one of vs shall giue accounts of himselfe to God.

13 Let vs not therefore iudge one another any more: but vse your iudgement rather in this, that no man put an occasion to fall, or a stumbling blocke before his brother.

14 I know, and am perswaded through the Lord Iesus, that there is nothing vncleane of it selfe: but vnto him that iudgeth any thing to be vncleane, to him it is vncleane.

15 But if thy brother be grieued for the meate, nowe walkest thou not charitably: destroy not him with thy meate, for whome Christ dyed.

16 Cause not your commoditie to be euill spoken of.

17 For the kingdome of God, is not meate nor drinke, but righteousnes, and peace, and ioye in the holy Ghost.

18 For whosoeuer in these things serueth Christ, is acceptable vnto God, and is approoued of men.

19 Let vs then follow those things which concerne peace, and wherewith one may edifie another.

20 Destroy not the worke of God for meates sake: all things in deede are pure: but it is euill for the man which eateth with offence.

21 It is good neither to eate flesh, nor to drinke wine, nor any thing whereby thy brother stumbleth, or is offended, or made weake.

22 Hast thou faith? haue it with thy selfe before God: blessed is hee that condemneth not himselfe in that thing which he aloweth.

23 For he that doubteth, is condemned if he eate, because he eateth not of faith: and whatsoeuer is not of faith, is sinne.

Romans 15

1 We which are strong, ought to beare the infirmities of the weake, and not to please our selues.

2 Therefore let euery man please his neighbour in that that is good to edification.

3 For Christ also would not please himselfe, but as it is written, The rebukes of them which rebuke thee, fell on me.

4 For whatsoeuer things are written aforetime, are writte for our learning, that we through patience, and comfort of the Scriptures might haue hope.

5 Now the God of patience and consolation giue you that ye be like minded one towards another, according to Christ Iesus,

6 That ye with one minde, and with one mouth may prayse God, euen the Father of our Lord Iesus Christ.

7 Wherefore receiue ye one another, as Christ also receiued vs to the glory of God.

8 Nowe I say, that Iesus Christ was a minister of the circumcision, for the trueth of God, to confirme the promises made vnto the fathers.

9 And let the Gentiles prayse God, for his mercie, as it is written, For this cause I wil confesse thee among the Gentiles, and sing vnto thy Name.

10 And againe he saith, Reioyce, ye Gentiles with his people.

11 And againe, Prayse the Lord, all ye Gentiles, and laude ye him, all people together.

12 And againe Esaias sayth, There shall be a roote of Iesse, and hee that shall rise to reigne ouer the Gentiles, in him shall the Gentiles trust.

13 Nowe the God of hope fill you with all ioye, and peace in beleeuing, that ye may abound in hope, through the power of the holy Ghost.

14 And I my selfe also am perswaded of you, my brethren, that ye also are full of goodnes, and filled with all knowledge, and are able to admonish one another.

15 Neuerthelesse, brethren, I haue somewhat boldly after a sort written vnto you, as one that putteth you in remembrance, through the grace that is giuen me of God,

16 That I should be the minister of Iesus Christ toward the Gentiles, ministring the Gospel of God, that the offering vp of the Gentiles might be acceptable, being sanctified by the holy Ghost.

17 I haue therefore whereof I may reioyce in Christ Iesus in those things which pertaine to God.

18 For I dare not speake of any thing, which Christ hath not wrought by me, to make the Gentiles obedient in worde and deede,

19 With the power of signes and wonders, by the power of the Spirit of God: so that from Hierusalem, and round about vnto Illyricum, I haue caused to abound the Gospel of Christ.

20 Yea, so I enforced my selfe to preach the Gospel, not where Christ was named, lest I should haue built on another mans foundation.

21 But as it is written, To whome hee was not spoken of, they shall see him, and they that heard not, shall vnderstand him.

22 Therefore also I haue bene oft let to come vnto you:

23 But nowe seeing I haue no more place in these quarters, and also haue bene desirous many yeeres agone to come vnto you,

24 When I shall take my iourney into Spaine, I will come to you: for I trust to see you in my iourney, and to be brought on my way thitherward by you, after that I haue bene somewhat filled with your company.

25 But now go I to Hierusalem, to minister vnto the Saints.

26 For it hath pleased them of Macedonia and Achaia, to make a certaine distribution vnto the poore Saints which are at Hierusalem.

27 For it hath pleased them, and their detters are they: for if the Gentiles be made partakers of their spirituall things, their duetie is also to minister vnto them in carnall things.

28 When I haue therefore performed this, and haue sealed them this fruite, I will passe by you into Spaine.

29 And I knowe when I come, that I shall come to you with abundance of the blessing of the Gospel of Christ.

30 Also brethren, I beseeche you for our Lord Iesus Christes sake, and for the loue of the spirit, that ye would striue with me by prayers to God for me,

31 That I may be deliuered from them which are disobedient in Iudea, and that my seruice which I haue to doe at Hierusalem, may be accepted of the Saintes,

32 That I may come vnto you with ioy by the will of God, and may with you be refreshed.

33 Thus the God of peace be with you all. Amen.

Romans 16

1 I Commende vnto you Phebe our sister, which is a seruaunt of the Church of Cenchrea:

2 That ye receiue her in the Lord, as it becommeth Saintes, and that ye assist her in whatsoeuer businesse she needeth of your ayde: for she hath giuen hospitalitie vnto many, and to me also.

3 Greete Priscilla, and Aquila my fellowe helpers in Christ Iesus,

4 (Which haue for my life laide downe their owne necke. Vnto whom not I onely giue thankes, but also all the Churches of the Gentiles.)

5 Likewise greete the Church that is in their house. Salute my beloued Epenetus, which is the first fruites of Achaia in Christ.

6 Greete Marie which bestowed much labour on vs.

7 Salute Andronicus and Iunia my cousins and fellowe prisoners, which are notable among the Apostles, and were in Christ before me.

8 Greete Amplias my beloued in the Lord.

9 Salute Vrbanus our fellow helper in Christ, and Stachys my beloued.

10 Salute Apelles approoued in Christ. Salute them which are of Aristobulus friendes.

11 Salute Herodion my kinsman. Greete them which are of the friendes of Narcissus which are in the Lord.

12 Salute Tryphena and Tryphosa, which women labour in the Lord. Salute the beloued Persis, which woman hath laboured much in the Lord.

13 Salute Rufus chosen in the Lord, and his mother and mine.

14 Greete Asyncritus, Phlegon, Hermas, Patrobas, Mercurius, and the brethren which are with them.

15 Salute Philologus and Iulias, Nereas, and his sister, and Olympas, and all the Saintes which are with them.

16 Salute one another with an holy kisse. The Churches of Christ salute you.

17 Now I beseech you brethren, marke them diligently which cause diuision and offences, contrary to the doctrine which ye haue learned, and auoide them.

18 For they that are such, serue not the Lord Iesus Christ, but their owne bellies, and with faire speach and flattering deceiue the heartes of the simple.

19 For your obedience is come abroade among all: I am glad therefore of you: but yet I woulde haue you wise vnto that which is good, and simple concerning euill.

20 The God of peace shall treade Satan vnder your feete shortly. The grace of our Lord Iesus Christ be with you.

21 Timotheus my helper, and Lucius, and Iason, and Sosipater my kinsemen, salute you.

22 I Tertius, which wrote out this Epistle, salute you in the Lord.

23 Gains mine hoste, and of the whole Church saluteth you. Erastus the steward of the citie saluteth you, and Quartus a brother.

24 The grace of our Lord Iesus Christ be with you all. Amen.

25 To him nowe that is of power to establish you according to my Gospel, and preaching of Iesus Christ, by the reuelation of the mysterie, which was kept secrete since the worlde began:

26 (But nowe is opened, and published among all nations by the Scriptures of the Prophetes, at the commandement of the euerlasting God for the obedience of faith)

27 To God, I say, only wise, be praise through Iesus Christ for euer. Amen. Written to the Romans from Corinthus, and sent by Phebe, seruaunt of the Church which is at Cenchrea.

First Corinthians

First Corinthians 1

1 Paul called to be an Apostle of Iesus Christ, through the will of God, and our brother Sosthenes,

2 Vnto the Church of God, which is at Corinthus, to them that are sanctified in Christ Iesus, Saintes by calling, with all that call on the Name of our Lord Iesus Christ in euery place, both their Lord, and ours:

3 Grace be with you, and peace from God our Father, and from the Lord Iesus Christ.

4 I thanke my God alwayes on your behalfe for the grace of God, which is giuen you in Iesus Christ,

5 That in all things ye are made rich in him, in all kinde of speach, and in all knowledge:

6 As the testimonie of Iesus Christ hath bene confirmed in you:

7 So that ye are not destitute of any gift: wayting for the appearing of our Lord Iesus Christ.

8 Who shall also confirme you vnto the ende, that ye may be blamelesse, in the day of our Lord Iesus Christ.

9 God is faithfull, by whom ye are called vnto the fellowship of his Sonne Iesus Christ our Lord.

10 Nowe I beseeche you, brethren, by the Name of our Lord Iesus Christ, that ye all speake one thing, and that there be no dissensions among you: but be ye knit together in one mind, and in one iudgement.

11 For it hath bene declared vnto me, my brethren, of you by them that are of the house of Cloe, that there are contentions among you.

12 Nowe this I say, that euery one of you saith, I am Pauls, and I am Apollos, and I am Cephas, and I am Christs.

13 Is Christ deuided? was Paul crucified for you? either were ye baptized into the name of Paul?

14 I thanke God, that I baptized none of you, but Crispus, and Gaius,

15 Lest any should say, that I had baptized into mine owne name.

16 I baptized also the houshold of Stephanas: furthermore knowe I not, whether I baptized any other.

17 For CHRIST sent me not to baptize, but to preache the Gospel, not with wisdome of wordes, lest the crosse of Christ should be made of none effect.

18 For that preaching of the crosse is to them that perish, foolishnesse: but vnto vs, which are saued, it is the power of God.

19 For it is written, I will destroy the wisedome of the wise, and will cast away the vnderstanding of the prudent.

20 Where is the wise? where is the Scribe? where is the disputer of this worlde? hath not God made the wisedome of this worlde foolishnesse?

21 For seeing the worlde by wisedome knewe not God in the wisedome of GOD, it pleased God by the foolishnesse of preaching to saue them that beleeue:

22 Seeing also that the Iewes require a signe, and the Grecians seeke after wisdome.

23 But wee preach Christ crucified: vnto the Iewes, euen a stumbling blocke, and vnto the Grecians, foolishnesse:

24 But vnto them which are called, both of the Iewes and Grecians, we preach Christ, the power of God, and the wisedome of God.

25 For the foolishnesse of God is wiser then men, and the weakenesse of God is stronger then men.

26 For brethren, you see your calling, how that not many wise men after the flesh, not many mighty, not many noble are called.

27 But God hath chosen the foolish things of the world to confound the wise, and God hath chosen the weake thinges of the worlde, to confound the mightie things,

28 And vile things of the worlde and thinges which are despised, hath God chosen, and thinges which are not, to bring to nought thinges that are,

29 That no flesh shoulde reioyce in his presence.

30 But ye are of him in Christ Iesus, who of God is made vnto vs wisedome and righteousnesse, and sanctification, and redemption,

31 That, according as it is written, Hee that reioyceth, let him reioyce in the Lord.

First Corinthians 2

1 And I, brethren, when I came to you, came not with excellencie of woordes, or of wisedome, shewing vnto you the testimonie of God.

2 For I esteemed not to knowe any thing among you, saue Iesus Christ, and him crucified.

3 And I was among you in weakenesse, and in feare, and in much trembling.

4 Neither stoode my woorde, and my preaching in the entising speach of mans wisdom, but in plaine euidence of the Spirite and of power,

5 That your faith should not be in the wisdome of men, but in the power of God.

6 And we speake wisedome among them that are perfect: not the wisedome of this world, neither of the princes of this world, which come to nought.

7 But we speake the wisedome of God in a mysterie, euen the hid wisedom, which God had determined before the world, vnto our glory.

8 Which none of the princes of this world hath knowen: for had they knowen it, they would not haue crucified the Lord of glory.

9 But as it is written, The thinges which eye hath not seene, neither eare hath heard, neither came into mans heart, are, which God hath prepared for them that loue him.

10 But God hath reueiled them vnto vs by his Spirit: for the spirit searcheth all things, yea, the deepe things of God.

11 For what man knoweth the things of a man, saue the spirite of a man, which is in him? euen so the things of God knoweth no man, but the spirit of God.

12 Nowe we haue receiued not the spirit of the world, but the Spirit, which is of God, that we might knowe the thinges that are giuen to vs of God.

13 Which things also we speake, not in the woordes which mans wisedome teacheth, but which the holy Ghost teacheth, comparing spirituall things with spirituall things.

14 But the naturall man perceiueth not the things of the Spirit of God: for they are foolishnesse vnto him: neither can hee knowe them, because they are spiritually discerned.

15 But hee that is spirituall, discerneth all things: yet he himselfe is iudged of no man.

16 For who hath knowen the minde of the Lord, that hee might instruct him? But we haue the minde of Christ.

First Corinthians 3

1 And I could not speake vnto you, brethren, as vnto spirituall men, but as vnto carnall, euen as vnto babes in Christ.

2 I gaue you milke to drinke, and not meat: for yee were not yet able to beare it, neither yet nowe are yee able.

3 For yee are yet carnall: for whereas there is among you enuying, and strife, and diuisions, are ye not carnall, and walke as men?

4 For when one sayeth, I am Pauls, and another, I am Apollos, are yee not carnall?

5 Who is Paul then? and who is Apollos, but the ministers by whome yee beleeued, and as the Lord gaue to euery man?

6 I haue planted, Apollos watred, but God gaue the increase.

7 So then, neither is hee that planteth any thing, neither hee that watreth, but God that giueth the increase.

8 And he that planteth, and he that watreth, are one, and euery man shall receiue his wages, according to his labour.

9 For we together are Gods labourers: yee are Gods husbandrie, and Gods building.

10 According to the grace of God giuen to mee, as a skilfull master builder, I haue laide the foundation, and another buildeth thereon: but let euery man take heede how he buildeth vpon it.

11 For other foundation can no man laie, then that which is laied, which is Iesus Christ.

12 And if any man builde on this foundation, golde, siluer, precious stones, timber, haye, or stubble,

13 Euery mans worke shalbe made manifest: for the day shall declare it, because it shalbe reueiled by the fire: and the fire shall trie euery mans worke of what sort it is.

14 If any mans worke, that he hath built vpon, abide, he shall receiue wages.

15 If any mans worke burne, he shall lose, but he shalbe saued himselfe: neuerthelesse yet as it were by the fire.

16 Knowe ye not that ye are the Temple of God, and that the Spirit of God dwelleth in you?

17 If any man destroy the Temple of God, him shall God destroy: for the Temple of God is holy, which ye are.

18 Let no man deceiue himselfe: If any man among you seeme to be wise in this world, let him be a foole, that he may be wise.

19 For the wisdome of this worlde is foolishnesse with God: for it is written, He catcheth the wise in their owne craftinesse.

20 And againe, The Lord knoweth that the thoughtes of the wise be vaine.

21 Therefore let no man reioyce in men: for all things are yours.

22 Whether it be Paul, or Apollos, or Cephas, or the world, or life, or death: whether they be things present, or thinges to come, euen all are yours,

23 And ye Christes, and Christ Gods.

First Corinthians 4

1 Let a man so thinke of vs, as of the ministers of Christ, and disposers of the secrets of God:

2 And as for the rest, it is required of the disposers, that euery man be found faithfull.

3 As touching me, I passe very litle to be iudged of you, or of mans iudgement: no, I iudge not mine owne selfe.

4 For I know nothing by my selfe, yet am I not thereby iustified: but he that iudgeth me, is the Lord.

5 Therefore iudge nothing before the time, vntill the Lord come, who will lighten things that are hid in darkenesse, and make the counsels of the hearts manifest: and then shall euery man haue praise of God.

6 Nowe these things, brethren, I haue figuratiuely applied vnto mine owne selfe and Apollos, for your sakes, that ye might learne by vs, that no man presume aboue that which is written, that one swell not against another for any mans cause.

7 For who separateth thee? and what hast thou, that thou hast not receiued? if thou hast receiued it, why reioycest thou, as though thou haddest not receiued it?

8 Nowe ye are full: nowe ye are made rich: ye reigne as kings without vs, and would to God ye did reigne, that we also might reigne with you.

9 For I thinke that God hath set forth vs the last Apostles, as men appointed to death: for we are made a gasing stocke vnto the worlde, and to the Angels, and to men.

10 We are fooles for Christes sake, and ye are wise in Christ: we are weake, and ye are strong: ye are honourable, and we are despised.

11 Vnto this houre we both hunger, and thirst, and are naked, and are buffeted, and haue no certaine dwelling place,

12 And labour, working with our owne handes: we are reuiled, and yet we blesse: we are persecuted, and suffer it.

13 We are euill spoken of, and we pray: we are made as the filth of the world, the offskowring of all things, vnto this time.

14 I write not these things to shame you, but as my beloued children I admonish you.

15 For though ye haue tenne thousand instructours in Christ, yet haue ye not many fathers: for in Christ Iesus I haue begotten you through the Gospel.

16 Wherefore, I pray you, be ye folowers of me.

17 For this cause haue I sent vnto you Timotheus, which is my beloued sonne, and faithfull in the Lord, which shall put you in remembrance of my wayes in Christ as I teache euery where in euery Church.

18 Some are puffed vp as though I woulde not come vnto you.

19 But I will come to you shortly, if the Lord will, and will knowe, not the wordes of them which are puffed vp, but the power.

20 For the kingdome of God is not in worde, but in power.

21 What will ye? shall I come vnto you with a rod, or in loue, and in ye spirite of meekenes?

First Corinthians 5

1 It is heard certainely that there is fornication among you: and such fornication as is not once named among the Gentiles, that one should haue his fathers wife.

2 And ye are puffed vp and haue not rather sorowed, that he which hath done this deede, might be put from among you.

3 For I verely as absent in bodie, but present in spirit, haue determined already as though I were present, that he that hath thus done this thing,

4 When ye are gathered together, and my spirit, in the Name of our Lord Iesus Christ, that such one, I say, by the power of our Lord Iesus Christ,

5 Be deliuered vnto Satan, for the destruction of the flesh, that the spirit may be saued in the day of the Lord Iesus.

6 Your reioycing is not good: knowe ye not that a litle leauen, leaueneth ye whole lumpe?

7 Purge out therefore the olde leauen, that ye may be a newe lumpe, as ye are vnleauened: for Christ our Passeouer is sacrificed for vs.

8 Therefore let vs keepe the feast, not with olde leauen, neither in the leauen of maliciousnes and wickednesse: but with the vnleauened bread of synceritie and trueth.

9 I wrote vnto you in an Epistle, that ye should not companie together with fornicatours,

10 And not altogether with the fornicatours of this world, or with the couetous, or with extortioners, or with idolaters: for then ye must goe out of the world.

11 But nowe I haue written vnto you, that ye companie not together: if any that is called a brother, be a fornicatour, or couetous, or an idolater, or a rayler, or a drunkard, or an extortioner, with such one eate not.

12 For what haue I to doe, to iudge them also which are without? doe ye not iudge them that are within?

13 But God iudgeth them that are without. Put away therefore from among your selues that wicked man.

First Corinthians 6

1 Dare any of you, hauing businesse against an other, be iudged vnder the vniust, and not vnder the Saintes?

2 Doe ye not knowe, that the Saintes shall iudge the worlde? If the worlde then shalbe iudged by you, are ye vnworthie to iudge the smallest matters?

3 Knowe ye not that we shall iudge the Angels? howe much more, things that perteine to this life?

4 If then ye haue iudgements of things perteining to this life, set vp them which are least esteemed in the Church.

5 I speake it to your shame. Is it so that there is not a wise man among you? no not one, that can iudge betweene his brethren?

6 But a brother goeth to law with a brother, and that vnder the infidels.

7 Nowe therefore there is altogether infirmitie in you, in that yee goe to lawe one with another: why rather suffer ye not wrong? why rather susteine yee not harme?

8 Nay, yee your selues doe wrong, and doe harme, and that to your brethren.

9 Knowe yee not that the vnrighteous shall not inherite the kingdome of God? Be not deceiued: neither fornicatours, nor idolaters, nor adulterers, nor wantons, nor buggerers,

10 Nor theeues, nor couetous, nor drunkards, nor railers, nor extortioners shall inherite the kingdome of God.

11 And such were some of you: but yee are washed, but yee are sanctified, but

yee are iustified in the Name of the Lord Iesus, and by the Spirit of our God.

12 All thinges are lawfull vnto mee, but all thinges are not profitable. I may doe all things, but I will not be brought vnder the power of any thing.

13 Meates are ordeined for the bellie, and the belly for the meates: but God shall destroy both it, and them. Nowe the bodie is not for fornication, but for the Lord, and the Lord for the bodie.

14 And God hath also raised vp the Lord, and shall raise vs vp by his power.

15 Knowe yee not, that your bodies are the members of Christ? shall I then take the members of Christ, and make them the members of an harlot? God forbid.

16 Doe ye not knowe, that he which coupleth himselfe with an harlot, is one body? for two, sayeth he, shalbe one flesh.

17 But hee that is ioyned vnto the Lord, is one spirite.

18 Flee fornication: euery sinne that a man doeth, is without the bodie: but hee that committeth fornication, sinneth against his owne bodie.

19 Knowe yee not, that your body is the temple of the holy Ghost, which is in you, whom ye haue of God? and yee are not your owne.

20 For yee are bought for a price: therefore glorifie God in your bodie, and in your spirit: for they are Gods.

First Corinthians 7

1 Nowe concerning the thinges whereof ye wrote vnto mee, It were good for a man not to touche a woman.

2 Neuertheles, to auoide fornication, let euery man haue his wife, and let euery woman haue her owne husband.

3 Let the husband giue vnto the wife due beneuolence, and likewise also the wife vnto the husband.

4 The wife hath not the power of her owne bodie, but ye husband: and likewise also the husband hath not ye power of his own body, but the wife.

5 Defraude not one another, except it be with consent for a time, that ye may giue your selues to fasting and praier, and againe come together that Satan tempt you not for your incontinecie.

6 But I speake this by permission, not by commandement.

7 For I woulde that all men were euen as I my selfe am: but euery man hath his proper gift of God, one after this maner, and another after that.

8 Therefore I say vnto the vnmaried, and vnto the widowes, It is good for them if they abide euen as I doe.

9 But if they cannot abstaine, let them marrie: for it is better to marrie then to burne.

10 And vnto ye maried I comand, not I, but ye Lord, Let not ye wife depart from her husband.

11 But and if shee depart, let her remaine vnmaried, or be reconciled vnto her husband, and let not the husband put away his wife.

12 But to ye remnant I speake, and not ye Lord, If any brother haue a wife, ye beleeueth not, if she be content to dwell with him, let him not forsake her.

13 And the woman which hath an husband that beleeueth not, if he be content to dwell with her, let her not forsake him.

14 For the vnbeleeuing husband is sanctified to the wife, and the vnbeleeuing wife is sanctified to the husband, els were your children vncleane: but nowe are they holie.

15 But if the vnbeleeuing depart, let him depart: a brother or a sister is not in subiection in such things: but God hath called vs in peace.

16 For what knowest thou, O wife, whether thou shalt saue thine husband? Or what knowest thou, O man, whether thou shalt saue thy wife?

17 But as God hath distributed to euery man, as the Lord hath called euery one, so let him walke: and so ordaine I, in all Churches.

18 Is any man called being circumcised? let him not gather his vncircumcision: is any called vncircumcised? let him not be circumcised.

19 Circumcision is nothing, and vncircumcision is nothing, but the keeping of the commandements of God.

20 Let euery man abide in the same vocation wherein he was called.

21 Art thou called being a seruant? care not for it: but if yet thou maiest be free, vse it rather.

22 For he that is called in the Lord, being a seruant, is the Lords freeman: likewise also he that is called being free, is Christes seruant.

23 Yee are bought with a price: be not the seruants of men.

24 Brethren, let euery man, wherein hee was called, therein abide with God.

25 Nowe concerning virgines, I haue no commandement of the Lord: but I giue mine aduise, as one that hath obtained mercie of the Lord to be faithfull.

26 I suppose then this to bee good for the present necessitie: I meane that it is good for a man so to be.

27 Art thou bounde vnto a wife? seeke not to be loosed: art thou loosed from a wife? seeke not a wife.

28 But if thou takest a wife, thou sinnest not: and if a virgine marrie, shee sinneth not: neuerthelesse, such shall haue trouble in the flesh: but I spare you.

29 And this I say, brethren, because the time is short, hereafter that both they which haue wiues, be as though they had none:

30 And they that weepe, as though they wept not: and they that reioyce, as though they reioyced not: and they that bye, as though they possessed not:

31 And they that vse this worlde, as though they vsed it not: for the fashion of this worlde goeth away.

32 And I would haue you without care. The vnmaried careth for the things of the Lord, howe he may please the Lord.

33 But hee that is maried, careth for the things of the world, how he may please his wife.

34 There is difference also betweene a virgine and a wife: the vnmaried woman careth for the things of the Lord, that she may be holy, both in body and in spirite: but shee that is maried, careth for the things of the worlde, howe shee may please her husband.

35 And this I speake for your owne commoditie, not to tangle you in a snare, but that yee follow that, which is honest, and that yee may cleaue fast vnto the Lord without separation.

36 But if any man thinke that it is vncomely for his virgine, if shee passe the flower of her age, and neede so require, let him do what he will, he sinneth not: let them be maried.

37 Neuerthelesse, hee that standeth firme in his heart, that hee hath no neede, but hath power ouer his owne will, and hath so decreed in his heart, that hee will keepe his virgine, hee doeth well.

38 So then hee that giueth her to mariage, doeth well, but he that giueth her not to mariage, doeth better.

39 The wife is bounde by the Lawe, as long as her husband liueth: but if her husband bee dead, shee is at libertie to marie with whome she will, onely in the Lord.

40 But shee is more blessed, if she so abide, in my iudgement: and I thinke that I haue also the Spirite of God.

First Corinthians 8

1 And as touching things sacrificed vnto idols, wee knowe that wee all haue knowledge: knowledge puffeth vp, but loue edifieth.

2 Nowe, if any man thinke that hee knoweth any thing, hee knoweth nothing yet as hee ought to knowe.

3 But if any man loue God, the same is knowen of him.

4 Concerning therefore the eating of things sacrificed vnto idoles, we knowe that an idole is nothing in the worlde, and that there is none other God but one.

5 For though there bee that are called gods, whether in heauen, or in earth (as there be many gods, and many lords)

6 Yet vnto vs there is but one God, which is that Father, of whome are all things, and we in him: and one Lord Iesus Christ, by whome are all things, and we by him.

7 But euery man hath not that knowledge: for many hauing conscience of the idole, vntill this houre, eate as a thing sacrificed vnto the idole, and so their conscience being weake, is defiled.

8 But meate maketh not vs acceptable to God, for neither if we eate, haue we the more: neither if we eate not, haue we the lesse.

9 But take heede lest by any meanes this power of yours be an occasion of falling, to them that are weake.

10 For if any man see thee which hast knowledge, sit at table in the idoles temple, shall not the conscience of him which is weake, be boldened to eate those things which are sacrificed to idoles?

11 And through thy knowledge shall the weake brother perish, for whome Christ died.

12 Nowe when ye sinne so against the brethren, and wound their weake conscience, ye sinne against Christ.

13 Wherefore if meate offende my brother, I wil eate no flesh while the world standeth, that I may not offend my brother.

First Corinthians 9

1 Am I not an Apostle? am I not free? haue I not seene Iesus Christ our Lord? are ye not my worke in the Lord?

2 If I be not an Apostle vnto other, yet doutlesse I am vnto you: for ye are the seale of mine Apostleship in the Lord.

3 My defence to them that examine mee, is this,

4 Haue we not power to eat and to drinke?

5 Or haue we not power to lead about a wife being a sister, as well as the rest of the Apostles, and as the brethren of the Lord, and Cephas?

6 Or I only and Barnabas, haue not we power not to worke?

7 Who goeth a warfare any time at his owne coste? who planteth a vineyarde, and eateth not of the fruit thereof? or who feedeth a flocke, and eateth not of the milke of the flocke?

8 Say I these thinges according to man? saith not the Lawe the same also?

9 For it is written in the Lawe of Moses, Thou shalt not mussell the mouth of the oxe that treadeth out the corne: doeth God take care for oxen?

10 Either saith hee it not altogether for our sakes? For our sakes no doubt it is written, that he which eareth, should eare in hope, and that he that thresheth in hope, should be partaker of his hope.

11 If wee haue sowen vnto you spirituall thinges, is it a great thing if we reape your carnall thinges?

12 If others with you bee partakers of this power, are not we rather? neuerthelesse, we haue not vsed this power: but suffer all things, that we should not hinder the Gospel of Christ.

13 Doe ye not knowe, that they which minister about the holy things, eate of the things of the Temple? and they which waite at the altar, are partakers with the altar?

14 So also hath the Lord ordeined, that they which preach ye Gospel, should liue of the Gospel.

15 But I haue vsed none of these things: neither wrote I these things, that it should be so done vnto me: for it were better for me to die, then that any man should make my reioycing vaine.

16 For though I preach the Gospel, I haue nothing to reioyce of: for necessitie is laid vpon me, and woe is vnto me, if I preach not the Gospel.

17 For if I do it willingly, I haue a reward, but if I do it against my will, notwithstanding the dispensation is committed vnto me.

18 What is my reward then? verely that when I preach the Gospel, I make the Gospel of Christ free, that I abuse not mine authoritie in ye Gospel.

19 For though I bee free from all men, yet haue I made my selfe seruant vnto all men, that I might winne the moe.

20 And vnto the Iewes, I become as a Iewe, that I may winne the Iewes: to them that are vnder the Lawe, as though I were vnder the Lawe, that I may winne them that are vnder the Lawe:

21 To them that are without Lawe, as though I were without Lawe, (when I am not without Lawe as pertaining to God, but am in the Lawe through Christ) that I may winne them that are without Lawe:

22 To the weake I become as weake, that I may winne the weake: I am made all thinges to all men, that I might by all meanes saue some.

23 And this I doe for the Gospels sake, that I might be partaker thereof with you.

24 Knowe ye not, that they which runne in a race, runne all, yet one receiueth the price? so runne that ye may obtaine.

25 And euery man that proueth masteries, abstaineth from all things: and they do it to obtaine a corruptible crowne: but we for an vncorruptible.

26 I therefore so runne, not as vncertainely: so fight I, not as one that beateth the ayre.

27 But I beate downe my body, and bring it into subiection, lest by any meanes after that I haue preached to other, I my selfe should be reproued.

First Corinthians 10

1 Moreouer, brethren, I woulde not that yee shoulde bee ignorant, that all our fathers were vnder that cloude, and all passed through that sea,

2 And were all baptized vnto Moses, in that cloude, and in that sea,

3 And did all eat the same spiritual meat,

4 And did all drinke the same spirituall drinke (for they dranke of the spiritual Rocke that folowed them: and the Rocke was Christ)

5 But with many of them God was not pleased: for they were ouerthrowen in ye wildernes.

6 Nowe these things are our ensamples, to the intent that we should not lust after euil things as they also lusted.

7 Neither bee ye idolaters as were some of them, as it is written, The people sate downe to eate and drinke, and rose vp to play.

8 Neither let vs commit fornication, as some of them committed fornication, and fell in one day three and twentie thousand.

9 Neither let vs tempt Christ, as some of them also tempted him, and were destroyed of serpents.

10 Neither murmure ye, as some of them also murmured, and were destroyed of the destroyer.

11 Nowe all these things came vnto them for ensamples, and were written to admonish vs, vpon whome the endes of the world are come.

12 Wherefore, let him that thinketh he standeth, take heede lest he fall.

13 There hath no tentation taken you, but such as appertaine to man: and God is faithfull, which will not suffer you to be tempted aboue that you be able, but wil euen giue the issue with the tentation, that ye may be able to beare it.

14 Wherefore my beloued, flee from idolatrie.

15 I speake as vnto them which haue vnderstanding: iugde ye what I say.

16 The cup of blessing which we blesse, is it not the communion of the blood of Christ? The bread which we breake, is it not the communion of the body of Christ?

17 For we that are many, are one bread and one body, because we all are partakers of one bread.

18 Beholde Israel, which is after the flesh: are not they which eate of the sacrifices partakers of the altar?

19 What say I then? that the idole is any thing? or that that which is sacrificed to idoles, is any thing?

20 Nay, but that these things which the Gentiles sacrifice, they sacrifice to deuils, and not vnto God: and I would not that ye should haue fellowship with the deuils.

21 Ye can not drinke the cup of the Lord, and the cup of the deuils. Ye can not be partakers of the Lords table, and of the table of the deuils.

22 Doe we prouoke the Lord to anger? are we stronger then he?

23 All things are lawfull for me, but all things are not expedient: all things are lawfull for me, but all things edifie not.

24 Let no man seeke his owne, but euery man anothers wealth.

25 Whatsoeuer is solde in the shambles, eate ye, and aske no question for conscience sake.

26 For the earth is the Lords, and all that therein is.

27 If any of them which beleeue not, call you to a feast, and if ye wil go, whatsoeuer is set before you, eate, asking no question for conscience sake.

28 But if any man say vnto you, This is sacrificed vnto idoles, eate it not, because of him that shewed it, and for the conscience (for the earth is the Lords, and all that therein is)

29 And the conscience, I say, not thine, but of that other: for why should my libertie be condemned of another mans conscience?

30 For if I through Gods benefite be partaker, why am I euill spoken of, for that wherefore I giue thankes?

31 Whether therefore ye eate, or drinke, or whatsoeuer ye doe, doe all to the glory of God.

32 Giue none offence, neither to the Iewes, nor to the Grecians, nor to the Church of God:

33 Euen as I please all men in all things, not seeking mine owne profite, but the profite of many, that they might be saued.

First Corinthians 11

1 Be yee followers of mee, euen as I am of Christ.

2 Now brethren, I commend you, that ye remember all my things, and keepe the ordinances, as I deliuered them to you.

3 But I wil that ye know, that Christ is the head of euery man: and the man is the womans head: and God is Christs head.

4 Euery man praying or prophecying hauing any thing on his head, dishonoureth his head.

5 But euery woman that prayeth or prophecieth bare headed, dishonoureth her head: for it is euen one very thing, as though she were shauen.

6 Therefore if the woman be not couered, let her also be shorne: and if it be shame for a woman to be shorne or shauen, let her be couered.

7 For a man ought not to couer his head: for as much as he is the image and glory of God: but the woman is the glory of the man.

8 For the man is not of the woman, but the woman of the man.

9 For the man was not created for the womans sake: but the woman for the mans sake.

10 Therefore ought the woman to haue power on her head, because of the Angels.

11 Neuertheles, neither is the man without the woman, neither the woman without the man in the Lord.

12 For as the woman is of the man, so is the man also by the woman: but all things are of God.

13 Iudge in your selues, Is it comely that a woman pray vnto God vncouered?

14 Doeth not nature it selfe teach you, that if a man haue long heare, it is a shame vnto him?

15 But if a woman haue long heare, it is a prayse vnto her: for her heare is giuen her for a couering.

16 But if any man lust to be contentious, we haue no such custome, neither the Churches of God.

17 Nowe in this that I declare, I prayse you not, that ye come together, not with profite, but with hurt.

18 For first of all, when ye come together in the Church, I heare that there are dissentions among you: and I beleeue it to be true in some part.

19 For there must be heresies euen among you, that they which are approoued among you, might be knowen.

20 When ye come together therefore into one place, this is not to eate the Lords Supper.

21 For euery man when they should eate, taketh his owne supper afore, and one is hungry, and another is drunken.

22 Haue ye not houses to eate and to drinke in? despise ye the Church of God, and shame them that haue not? what shall I say to you? shall I prayse you in this? I prayse you not.

23 For I haue receiued of the Lord that which I also haue deliuered vnto you, to wit, That the Lord Iesus in the night when he was betrayed, tooke bread:

24 And when hee had giuen thankes, hee brake it, and sayde, Take, eate: this is my body, which is broken for you: this doe ye in remembrance of me.

25 After the same maner also he tooke the cup, when he had supped, saying, This cup is the Newe Testament in my blood: this doe as oft as ye drinke it, in remembrance of me.

26 For as often as ye shall eate this bread, and drinke this cup, ye shewe the Lords death till hee come.

27 Wherefore, whosoeuer shall eate this bread, and drinke the cup of the Lord vnworthily, shall be guiltie of the body and blood of the Lord.

28 Let euery man therefore examine himselfe, and so let him eate of this bread, and drinke of this cup.

29 For he that eateth and drinketh vnworthily, eateth and drinketh his owne damnation, because he discerneth not the Lords body.

30 For this cause many are weake, and sicke among you, and many sleepe.

31 For if we would iudge our selues, we should not be iudged.

32 But when we are iudged, we are chastened of the Lord, because we should not be condemned with the world.

33 Wherefore, my brethren, when ye come together to eate, tary one for another.

34 And if any man be hungry, let him eate at home, that ye come not together vnto condemnation. Other things will I set in order when I come.

First Corinthians 12

1 Now concerning spirituall giftes, brethren, I would not haue you ignorant.

2 Ye know that ye were Gentiles, and were caried away vnto the dumme Idoles, as ye were led.

3 Wherefore, I declare vnto you, that no man speaking by the Spirit of God calleth Iesus execrable: also no man can say that Iesus is the Lord, but by the holy Ghost.

4 Now there are diuersities of gifts, but the same Spirit.

5 And there are diuersities of administrations, but the same Lord,

6 And there are diuersities of operations, but God is the same which worketh all in all.

7 But the manifestation of the Spirit is giuen to euery man, to profite withall.

8 For to one is giuen by the Spirit the word of wisdome: and to an other the word of knowledge, by the same Spirit:

9 And to another is giuen faith by the same Spirit: and to another the giftes of healing, by the same Spirit:

10 And to another the operations of great workes: and to another, prophecie: and to another, the discerning of spirits: and to another, diuersities of tongues: and to another, the interpretation of tongues.

11 And all these thinges worketh one and the selfe same Spirit, distributing to euery man seuerally as he will.

12 For as the body is one, and hath many members, and all the members of the body, which is one, though they be many, yet are but one body: euen so is Christ.

13 For by one Spirit are we all baptized into one body, whether we bee Iewes, or Grecians, whether we be bonde, or free, and haue bene all made to drinke into one Spirit.

14 For the body also is not one member, but many.

15 If the foote would say, Because I am not the hand, I am not of the body, is it therefore not of the body?

16 And if the eare would say, Because I am not the eye, I am not of the body, is it therefore not of the body?

17 If the whole body were an eye, where were the hearing? If the whole were hearing, where were the smellling?

18 But nowe hath God disposed the members euery one of them in the bodie at his owne pleasure.

19 For if they were all one member, where were the body?

20 But now are there many members, yet but one body.

21 And the eye cannot say vnto the hand, I haue no neede of thee: nor the head againe to the feete, I haue no neede of you.

22 Yea, much rather those members of the body, which seeme to be more feeble, are necessarie.

23 And vpon those members of the body, which wee thinke most vnhonest, put wee more honestie on: and our vncomely parts haue more comelinesse on.

24 For our comely partes neede it not: but God hath tempered the body together, and hath giuen the more honour to that part which lacked,

25 Lest there should be any diuision in the body: but that the members shoulde haue the same care one for another.

26 Therefore if one member suffer, all suffer with it: if one member be had in honour, all the members reioyce with it.

27 Now ye are the body of Christ, and members for your part.

28 And God hath ordained some in the Church: as first Apostles, secondly Prophetes, thirdly teachers, then them that doe miracles: after that, the giftes of healing, helpers, gouernours, diuersitie of tongues.

29 Are all Apostles? are all Prophetes? are all teachers?

30 Are all doers of miracles? haue all the gifts of healing? doe all speake with tongues? doe all interprete?

31 But desire you the best giftes, and I will yet shewe you a more excellent way.

First Corinthians 13

1 Though I speake with the tongues of men and Angels, and haue not loue, I am as sounding brasse, or a tinkling cymbal.

2 And though I had the gift of prophecie, and knewe all secrets and all knowledge, yea, if I had all faith, so that I could remooue mountaines and had not loue, I were nothing.

3 And though I feede the poore with all my goods, and though I giue my body, that I be burned, and haue not loue, it profiteth me nothing.

4 Loue suffreth long: it is bountifull: loue enuieth not: loue doeth not boast it selfe: it is not puffed vp:

5 It doeth no vncomely thing: it seeketh not her owne things: it is not prouoked to anger: it thinketh not euill:

6 It reioyceth not in iniquitie, but reioyceth in the trueth:

7 It suffreth all things: it beleeueth all things: it hopeth all things: it endureth all things.

8 Loue doeth neuer fall away, though that prophecyings be abolished, or the tongues cease, or knowledge vanish away.

9 For we knowe in part, and we prophecie in part.

10 But when that which is perfect, is come, then that which is in part, shalbe abolished.

11 When I was a childe, I spake as a childe, I vnderstoode as a childe, I thought as a childe: but when I became a man, I put away childish thinges.

12 For nowe we see through a glasse darkely: but then shall wee see face to face. Nowe I know in part: but then shall I know euen as I am knowen.

13 And nowe abideth faith, hope and loue, euen these three: but the chiefest of these is loue.

First Corinthians 14

1 Followe after loue, and couet spirituall giftes, and rather that ye may prophecie.

2 For hee that speaketh a strange tongue, speaketh not vnto men, but vnto God: for no man heareth him: howbeit in the spirit he speaketh secret things.

3 But he that prophecieth, speaketh vnto me to edifying, and to exhortation, and to comfort.

4 He that speaketh strange language, edifieth himselfe: but hee that prophecieth, edifieth the Church.

5 I would that ye all spake strange languages, but rather that ye prophecied: for greater is hee that prophecieth, then hee that speaketh diuers tongues, except hee expound it, that the Church may receiue edification.

6 And nowe, brethren, if I come vnto you speaking diuers tongues, what shall I profite you, except I speake to you, either by reuelation, or by knowledge, or by prophecying, or by doctrine?

7 Moreouer things without life which giue a sounde, whether it be a pipe or an harpe, except they make a distinction in the soundes, how shall it be knowen what is piped or harped?

8 And also if the trumpet giue an vncertaine sound, who shall prepare himselfe to battell?

9 So likewise you, by the tongue, except yee vtter wordes that haue signification, howe shall it be vnderstand what is spoken? for ye shall speake in the ayre.

10 There are so many kindes of voyces (as it commeth to passe) in the world, and none of them is dumme.

11 Except I know then the power of ye voyce, I shall be vnto him that speaketh a barbarian, and he that speaketh, shalbe a barbarian vnto me.

12 Euen so, forasmuch as ye couet spirituall giftes, seeke that ye may excell vnto the edifying of the Church.

13 Wherefore, let him that speaketh a strange tongue, pray, that he may interprete.

14 For if I pray in a strange togue, my spirit prayeth: but mine vnderstading is without fruite.

15 What is it then? I will pray with the spirit, but I wil pray with the vnderstanding also: I wil sing with the spirite, but I will sing with the vnderstanding also.

16 Else, when thou blessest with the spirit, howe shall hee that occupieth the roome of the vnlearned, say Amen, at thy giuing of thankes, seeing he knoweth not what thou sayest?

17 For thou verely giuest thankes well, but the other is not edified.

18 I thanke my God, I speake languages more then ye all.

19 Yet had I rather in the Church to speake fiue wordes with mine vnderstanding, that I might also instruct others, then ten thousande wordes in a strange tongue.

20 Brethren, be not children in vnderstanding, but as concerning maliciousnes be children, but in vnderstanding be of a ripe age.

21 In the Lawe it is written, By men of other tongues, and by other languages will I speake vnto this people: yet so shall they not heare me, sayth the Lord.

22 Wherefore strange tongues are for a signe, not to them that beleeue, but to them that beleeue not: but prophecying serueth not for them that beleeue not, but for them which beleeue.

23 If therefore when the whole Church is come together in one, and all speake strange tongues, there come in they that are vnlearned, or they which beleeue not, will they not say, that ye are out of your wittes?

24 But if all prophecie, and there come in one that beleeueth not, or one vnlearned, hee is rebuked of all men, and is iudged of all,

25 And so are the secrets of his heart made manifest, and so he will fall downe

on his face and worship God, and say plainely that God is in you in deede.

26 What is to be done then, brethren? when ye come together, according as euery one of you hath a Psalme, or hath doctrine, or hath a tongue, or hath reuelation, or hath interpretation, let all things be done vnto edifying.

27 If any man speake a strange tongue, let it be by two, or at the most, by three, and that by course, and let one interprete.

28 But if there be no interpreter, let him keepe silence in the Church, which speaketh languages, and let him speake to himselfe, and to God.

29 Let the Prophets speake two, or three, and let the other iudge.

30 And if any thing be reueiled to another that sitteth by, let the first holde his peace.

31 For ye may all prophecie one by one, that all may learne, and all may haue comfort.

32 And the spirits of the Prophets are subiect to the Prophets.

33 For God is not the author of confusion, but of peace, as we see in all ye Churches of the Saints.

34 Let your women keepe silence in the Churches: for it is not permitted vnto them to speake: but they ought to be subiect, as also the Lawe sayth.

35 And if they will learne any thing, let them aske their husbands at home: for it is a shame for women to speake in the Church.

36 Came the worde of God out from you? either came it vnto you onely?

37 If any man thinke him selfe to be a Prophet, or spirituall, let him acknowledge, that the things, that I write vnto you, are the commandements of the Lord.

38 And if any man be ignorant, let him be ignorant.

39 Wherefore, brethren, couet to prophecie, and forbid not to speake languages.

40 Let all things be done honestly, and by order.

First Corinthians 15

1 Moreouer brethren, I declare vnto you the Gospel, which I preached vnto you, which ye haue also receiued, and wherein ye continue,

2 And whereby ye are saued, if ye keepe in memorie, after what maner I preached it vnto you, except ye haue beleeued in vaine.

3 For first of all, I deliuered vnto you that which I receiued, how that Christ died for our sinnes, according to the Scriptures,

4 And that he was buried, and that he arose the third day, according to the Scriptures,

5 And that he was seene of Cephas, then of the twelue.

6 After that, he was seene of more then fiue hudreth brethren at once: whereof many remaine vnto this present, and some also are asleepe.

7 After that, he was seene of Iames: then of all the Apostles.

8 And last of all he was seene also of me, as of one borne out of due time.

9 For I am the least of the Apostles, which am not meete to be called an Apostle, because I persecuted the Church of God.

10 But by the grace of God, I am that I am: and his grace which is in me, was not in vaine: but I laboured more aboundantly then they all: yet not I, but the grace of God which is with me.

11 Wherefore, whether it were I, or they, so we preach, and so haue ye beleeued.

12 Now if it be preached, that Christ is risen from the dead, how say some among you, that there is no resurrection of the dead?

13 For if there be no resurrection of the dead, then is Christ not risen:

14 And if Christ be not risen, then is our preaching vaine, and your faith is also vaine.

15 And we are found also false witnesses of God: for we haue testified of God, that he hath raised vp Christ: whome he hath not raised vp, if so be the dead be not raised.

16 For if the dead be not raised, then is Christ not raised.

17 And if Christ be not raised, your faith is vaine: ye are yet in your sinnes.

18 And so they which are a sleepe in Christ, are perished.

19 If in this life onely wee haue hope in Christ, we are of all men the most miserable.

20 But nowe is Christ risen from the dead, and was made the first fruites of them that slept.

21 For since by man came death, by man came also the resurrection of the dead.

22 For as in Adam all die, euen so in Christ shall all be made aliue,

23 But euery man in his owne order: the first fruites is Christ, afterward, they that are of Christ, at his comming shall rise againe.

24 Then shalbe the end, when he hath deliuered vp the kingdome to God, euen the Father, when he hath put downe all rule, and all authoritie and power.

25 For he must reigne till hee hath put all his enemies vnder his feete.

26 The last enemie that shalbe destroyed, is death.

27 For he hath put downe all things vnder his feete. (And when he saith that all things are subdued to him, it is manifest that he is excepted, which did put downe all things vnder him.)

28 And when all things shalbe subdued vnto him, then shall the Sonne also himselfe be subiect vnto him, that did subdue all things vnder him, that God may be all in all.

29 Els what shall they doe which are baptized for dead? if the dead rise not at all, why are they then baptized for dead?

30 Why are wee also in ieopardie euery houre?

31 By your reioycing which I haue in Christ Iesus our Lord, I die dayly.

32 If I haue fought with beastes at Ephesus after ye maner of men, what aduantageth it me, if the dead be not raised vp? let vs eate and drinke: for to morowe we shall die.

33 Be not deceiued: euill speakings corrupt good maners.

34 Awake to liue righteously, and sinne not: for some haue not ye knowledge of God, I speake this to your shame.

35 But some man will say, Howe are the dead raised vp? and with what body come they foorth?

36 O foole, that which thou sowest, is not quickened, except it die.

37 And that which thou sowest, thou sowest not that body that shalbe, but bare corne as it falleth, of wheat, or of some other.

38 But God giueth it a body at his pleasure, euen to euery seede his owne body,

39 All flesh is not the same flesh, but there is one flesh of men, and another flesh of beastes, and another of fishes, and another of birdes.

40 There are also heauenly bodies, and earthly bodies: but the glorie of the heauenly is one, and the glorie of the earthly is another.

41 There is another glorie of the sunne, and another glorie of the moone, and another glorie of the starres: for one starre differeth from another starre in glorie.

42 So also is the resurrection of the dead. The bodie is sowen in corruption, and is raysed in incorruption.

43 It is sowen in dishonour, and is raysed in glory: it is sowen in weakenesse, and is raysed in power.

44 It is sowen a naturall body, and is raysed a spirituall body: there is a naturall body, and there is a spirituall body.

45 As it is also written, The first man Adam was made a liuing soule: and the last Adam was made a quickening Spirit.

46 Howbeit that was not first which is spirituall: but that which is naturall, and afterward that which is spirituall.

47 The first man is of the earth, earthly: the second man is the Lord from heauen.

48 As is the earthly, such are they that are earthly: and as is the heauenly, such are they also that are heauenly.

49 And as we haue borne the image of the earthly, so shall we beare the image of the heauenly.

50 This say I, brethren, that flesh and blood cannot inherite the kingdome of God, neither doeth corruption inherite incorruption.

51 Behold, I shewe you a secret thing, We shall not all sleepe, but we shall all be changed,

52 In a moment, in the twinckling of an eye at the last trumpet: for the trumpet shall blow, and the dead shalbe raysed vp incorruptible, and we shalbe changed.

53 For this corruptible must put on incorruption: and this mortall must put on immortalitie.

54 So when this corruptible hath put on incorruption, and this mortall hath put on immortalitie, then shalbe brought to passe the saying that is written, Death is swallowed vp into victorie.

55 O death where is thy sting? O graue where is thy victorie?

56 The sting of death is sinne: and ye strength of sinne is the Lawe.

57 But thankes be vnto God, which hath giuen vs victorie through our Lord Iesus Christ.

58 Therefore my beloued brethren, be ye stedfast, vnmoueable, aboundant alwayes in the worke of the Lord, forasmuch as ye knowe that your labour is not in vaine in the Lord.

First Corinthians 16

1 Concerning the gathering for the Saintes, as I haue ordeined in the Churches of Galatia, so doe ye also.

2 Euery first day of the weeke, let euery one of you put aside by himselfe, and lay vp as God hath prospered him, that then there be no gatherings when I come.

3 And when I am come, whomsoeuer ye shall alowe by letters, them will I send to bring your liberalitie vnto Hierusalem.

4 And if it be meete that I goe also, they shall goe with me.

5 Nowe I will come vnto you, after I haue gone through Macedonia (for I will passe through Macedonia.)

6 And it may be that I will abide, yea, or winter with you, that ye may bring me on my way, whither soeuer I goe.

7 For I will not see you nowe in my passage, but I trust to abide a while with you, if the Lord permit.

8 And I wil tary at Ephesus vntill Pentecost.

9 For a great doore and effectuall is opened vnto me: and there are many aduersaries.

10 Nowe if Timotheus come, see that he be without feare with you: for he worketh the worke of the Lord, euen as I doe.

11 Let no man therefore despise him: but conuey him foorth in peace, that he may come vnto me: for I looke for him with the brethren.

12 As touching our brother Apollos, I greatly desired him, to come vnto you with the brethren: but his mind was not at all to come at this time: howbeit he will come when he shall haue conuenient time.

13 Watch ye: stand fast in the faith: quite you like men, and be strong.

14 Let all your things be done in loue.

15 Nowe brethren, I beseeche you (ye knowe the house of Stephanas, that it is the first fruites of Achaia, and that they haue giuen themselues to minister vnto the Saintes)

16 That ye be obedient euen vnto such, and to all that helpe with vs and labour.

17 I am glad of the comming of Stephanas, and Fortunatus, and Achaicus: for they haue supplied the want of you.

18 For they haue comforted my spirite and yours: acknowledge therefore such men.

19 The Churches of Asia salute you: Aquila and Priscilla with ye Church that is in their house, salute you greatly in the Lord.

20 All the brethren greete you. Greete ye one another, with an holy kisse.

21 The salutation of me Paul with mine owne hand.

22 If any man loue not the Lord Iesus Christ, let him be had in execration maran-atha.

23 The grace of our Lord Iesus Christ be with you.

24 My loue be with you all in Christ Iesus, Amen. The first Epistle to the Corinthians, written from Philippi, and sent by Stephanas, and Fortunatus, and Achaicus, and Timotheus.

Second Corinthians

Second Corinthians 1

1 Pavl an Apostle of JESVS Christ, by the will of God, and our brother Timotheus, to the Church of God, which is at Corinthus with all the Saints, which are in all Achaia:

2 Grace be with you, and peace from God our Father, and from the Lord Iesus Christ.

3 Blessed be God, euen the Father of our Lord Iesus Christ, the Father of mercies, and the God of all comfort,

4 Which comforteth vs in all our tribulation, that we may be able to comfort them which are in any affliction by the comfort wherewith we our selues are comforted of God.

5 For as the sufferings of Christ abounde in vs, so our consolation aboundeth through Christ.

6 And whether we be afflicted, it is for your consolation and saluation, which is wrought in the induring of the same sufferings, which we also suffer: or whether we be comforted, it is for your consolation and saluation.

7 And our hope is stedfast concerning you, in as much as we know that as ye are partakers of the sufferings, so shall ye be also of the consolation.

8 For brethren, we woulde not haue you ignorant of our affliction, which came vnto vs in Asia, howe we were pressed out of measure passing strength, so that we altogether doubted, euen of life.

9 Yea, we receiued the sentence of death in our selues, because we shoulde not trust in our selues, but in God, which rayseth the dead.

10 Who deliuered vs from so great a death, and doeth deliuer vs: in whom we trust, that yet hereafter he will deliuer vs,

11 So that ye labour together in prayer for vs, that for the gift bestowed vpon vs for many, thankes may be giuen by many persons for vs.

12 For our reioycing is this, the testimonie of our conscience, that in simplicitie and godly purenesse, and not in fleshly wisedome, but by the grace of God wee haue had our conuersation in the worlde, and most of all to you wardes.

13 For wee write none other thinges vnto you, then that ye reade or els that ye acknowledge, and I trust ye shall acknowledge vnto ye end.

14 Euen as ye haue acknowledged vs partly, that we are your reioycing, euen as ye are ours, in the day of our Lord Iesus.

15 And in this confidence was I minded first to come vnto you, that ye might haue had a double grace,

16 And to passe by you into Macedonia, and to come againe out of Macedonia vnto you, and to be led foorth towarde Iudea of you.

17 When I therefore was thus minded, did I vse lightnesse? or minde I those things which I minde, according to the flesh, that with me should be, Yea, yea, and Nay, nay?

18 Yea, God is faithfull, that our worde towarde you was not Yea, and Nay.

19 For the Sonne of God Iesus Christ, who was preached among you by vs, that is, by me, and Siluanus, and Timotheus, was not Yea, and Nay: but in him it was Yea.

20 For all the promises of God in him are Yea, and are in him Amen, vnto the glorie of God through vs.

21 And it is God which stablisheth vs with you in Christ, and hath anoynted vs.

22 Who hath also sealed vs, and hath giuen the earnest of the Spirit in our hearts.

23 Nowe, I call God for a recorde vnto my soule, that to spare you, I came not as yet vnto Corinthus.

24 Not that wee haue dominion ouer your faith, but wee are helpers of your ioy: for by faith yee stande.

Second Corinthians 2

1 Bvt I determined thus in my selfe, that I would not come againe to you in heauinesse.

2 For if I make you sorie, who is he then that shoulde make me glad, but ye same which is made sorie by me?

3 And I wrote this same thing vnto you, lest when I came, I should take heauines of them, of whom I ought to reioyce: this confidence haue I in you all, that my ioye is the ioye of you all.

4 For in great affliction, and anguish of heart I wrote vnto you with many teares: not that yee should be made sorie, but that ye might perceiue the loue which I haue, specially vnto you.

5 And if any hath caused sorowe, the same hath not made mee sorie, but partly (lest I should more charge him) you all.

6 It is sufficient vnto the same man, that hee was rebuked of many.

7 So that nowe contrariwise yee ought rather to forgiue him, and comfort him, lest the same shoulde bee swalowed vp with ouermuch heauinesse.

8 Wherefore, I pray you, that you woulde confirme your loue towards him.

9 For this cause also did I write, that I might knowe the proofe of you, whether yee would be obedient in all things.

10 To whome yee forgiue any thing, I forgiue also: for verely if I forgaue any thing, to whome I forgaue it, for your sakes forgaue I it in the sight of Christ,

11 Lest Satan should circumuent vs: for we are not ignorant of his enterprises.

12 Furthermore, when I came to Troas to preach Christs Gospell, and a doore was opened vnto me of the Lord,

13 I had no rest in my spirit, because I founde not Titus my brother, but tooke my leaue of them, and went away into Macedonia.

14 Now thankes be vnto God, which alwaies maketh vs to triumph in Christ, and maketh manifest the sauour of his knowledge by vs in euery place.

15 For wee are vnto God the sweete sauour of Christ, in them that are saued, and in them which perish.

16 To the one we are the sauour of death, vnto death, and to the other the sauour of life, vnto life: and who is sufficient for these things?

17 For wee are not as many, which make marchandise of the woorde of God: but as of sinceritie, but as of God in ye sight of God speake we in Christ.

Second Corinthians 3

1 Doe we begin to praise our selues againe? or neede we as some other, epistles of recommendation vnto you, or letters of recommendation from you?

2 Yee are our epistle, written in our hearts, which is vnderstand, and read of all men,

3 In that yee are manifest, to be the Epistle of Christ, ministred by vs, and written, not with yncke, but with the Spirite of the liuing God, not in tables of stone, but in fleshly tables of the heart.

4 And such trust haue we through Christ to God:

5 Not that we are sufficient of our selues, to thinke any thing, as of our selues: but our sufficiencie is of God,

6 Who also hath made vs able ministers of the Newe testament, not of the letter, but of the Spirite: for the letter killeth, but the Spirite giueth life.

7 If then the ministration of death written with letters and ingrauen in stones, was glorious, so that the children of Israel coulde not beholde the face of Moses, for the glorie of his countenance (which glorie is done away.)

8 Howe shall not the ministration of the Spirite be more glorious?

9 For if the ministerie of condemnation was glorious, much more doeth the ministration of righteousnesse exceede in glorie.

10 For euen that which was glorified, was not glorified in this point, that is, as touching the exceeding glorie.

11 For if that which should be abolished, was glorious, much more shall that which remaineth, be glorious.

12 Seeing then that we haue such trust, we vse great boldnesse of speach.

13 And we are not as Moses, which put a vaile vpon his face, that the children of Israel should not looke vnto the ende of that which should be abolished.

14 Therefore their mindes are hardened: for vntill this day remaineth the same couering vntaken away in the reading of the olde Testament, which vaile in Christ is put away.

15 But euen vnto this day, whe Moses is read, the vaile is laid ouer their hearts.

16 Neuertheles when their heart shall be turned to the Lord, the vaile shalbe taken away.

17 Nowe the Lord is the Spirite, and where the Spirite of the Lord is, there is libertie.

18 But we al behold as in a mirrour the glory of the Lord with open face, and are changed into the same image, from glorie to glorie, as by the Spirit of the Lord.

Second Corinthians 4

1 Therefore, seeing that we haue this ministerie, as we haue receiued mercy, we faint not:

2 But haue cast from vs ye clokes of shame, and walke not in craftines, neither handle we the worde of God deceitfully: but in declaration of the trueth we approue our selues to euery mans conscience in the sight of God.

3 If our Gospell bee then hid, it is hid to them that are lost.

4 In whom the God of this world hath blinded the mindes, that is, of the infidels, that the light of the glorious Gospell of Christ, which is the image of God, should not shine vnto them.

5 For we preach not our selues, but Christ Iesus the Lord, and our selues your seruaunts for Iesus sake.

6 For God that commanded the light to shine out of darknesse, is he which hath shined in our hearts, to giue the light of the knowledge of the glory of God in the face of Iesus Christ.

7 But we haue this treasure in earthen vessels, that the excellencie of that power might be of God, and not of vs.

8 Wee are afflicted on euery side, yet are we not in distresse: we are in doubt, but yet wee despaire not.

9 We are persecuted, but not forsaken: cast downe, but we perish not.

10 Euery where we beare about in our bodie the dying of the Lord Iesus, that the life of Iesus might also be made manifest in our bodies.

11 For we which liue, are alwaies deliuered vnto death for Iesus sake, that the life also of Iesus might be made manifest in our mortal flesh.

12 So then death worketh in vs, and life in you.

13 And because we haue the same spirite of faith, according as it is written, I beleeued, and therefore haue I spoken, we also beleeue, and therefore speake,

14 Knowing that he which hath raised vp the Lord Iesus, shall raise vs vp also by Iesus, and shall set vs with you.

15 For all thinges are for your sakes, that that most plenteous grace by the thanksgiuing of many, may redound to the praise of God.

16 Therefore we faint not, but though our outward man perish, yet the inward man is renewed daily.

17 For our light affliction which is but for a moment, causeth vnto vs a farre most excellent and an eternall waight of glorie:

18 While we looke not on the things which are seene, but on the things which are not seene: for the things which are seene, are temporall: but the things which are not seene, are eternall.

Second Corinthians 5

1 For we knowe that if our earthly house of this tabernacle be destroyed, we haue a building giuen of God, that is, an house not made with handes, but eternall in the heauens.

2 For therefore we sighe, desiring to be clothed with our house, which is from heauen.

3 Because that if we be clothed, we shall not be found naked.

4 For in deede we that are in this tabernacle, sigh and are burdened, because we would not be vnclothed, but would be clothed vpon, that mortalitie might be swalowed vp of life.

5 And he that hath created vs for this thing, is God, who also hath giuen vnto vs the earnest of the Spirit.

6 Therefore we are alway bolde, though we knowe that whiles we are at home in the bodie, we are absent from the Lord.

7 (For we walke by faith, and not by sight.)

8 Neuerthelesse, we are bolde, and loue rather to remoue out of the body, and to dwell with the Lord.

9 Wherefore also we couet, that both dwelling at home, and remouing from home, we may be acceptable to him.

10 For we must all appeare before the iudgement seate of Christ, that euery man may receiue the things which are done in his body, according to that he hath done, whether it be good or euill.

11 Knowing therefore that terrour of the Lord, we persuade men, and we are made manifest vnto God, and I trust also that we are made manifest in your consciences.

12 For we prayse not our selues againe vnto you, but giue you an occasion to reioyce of vs, that ye may haue to answere against them, which reioyce in the face, and not in the heart.

13 For whether we be out of our wit, we are it to God: or whether we be in our right minde, we are it vnto you.

14 For that loue of Christ constraineth vs,

15 Because we thus iudge, that if one be dead for all, then were all dead, and he died for all, that they which liue, shoulde not henceforth liue vnto themselues, but vnto him which died for them, and rose againe.

16 Wherefore, henceforth know we no man after the flesh, yea though wee had knowen Christ after the flesh, yet nowe henceforth know we him no more.

17 Therefore if any man be in Christ, let him be a newe creature. Olde things are passed away: beholde, all things are become newe.

18 And all things are of God, which hath reconciled vs vnto himselfe by Iesus Christ, and hath giuen vnto vs the ministerie of reconciliation.

19 For God was in Christ, and reconciled the world to himselfe, not imputing their sinnes vnto them, and hath committed to vs the word of reconciliation.

20 Now then are we ambassadours for Christ: as though God did beseeche you through vs, we pray you in Christes steade, that ye be reconciled to God.

21 For he hath made him to be sinne for vs, which knewe no sinne, that we should be made the righteousnesse of God in him.

Second Corinthians 6

1 So we therefore as workers together beseech you, that ye receiue not the grace of God in vaine.

2 For he sayth, I haue heard thee in a time accepted, and in the day of saluation haue I succoured thee: beholde nowe the accepted time, beholde nowe the day of saluation.

3 We giue no occasion of offence in any thing, that our ministerie shoulde not be reprehended.

4 But in all things we approue our selues as the ministers of God, in much patience, in afflictions, in necessities, in distresses,

5 In stripes, in prisons, in tumults, in labours,

6 By watchings, by fastings, by puritie, by knowledge, by long suffering, by kindnesse, by the holy Ghost, by loue vnfained,

7 By the worde of trueth, by the power of God, by the armour of righteousnesse on the right hand, and on the left,

8 By honour, and dishonour, by euill report, and good report, as deceiuers, and yet true:

9 As vnknowen, and yet knowen: as dying, and beholde, we liue: as chastened, and yet not killed:

10 As sorowing, and yet alway reioycing: as poore, and yet make many riche: as hauing nothing, and yet possessing all things.

11 O Corinthians, our mouth is open vnto you: our heart is made large.

12 Ye are not kept strait in vs, but ye are kept strait in your owne bowels.

13 Nowe for the same recompence, I speake as to my children, Be you also inlarged.

14 Be not vnequally yoked with the infidels: for what fellowship hath righteousnesse with vnrighteousnesse? and what communion hath light with darkenesse?

15 And what concord hath Christ with Belial? or what part hath the beleeuer with the infidell?

16 And what agreement hath the Temple of God with idols? for ye are the Temple of the liuing God: as God hath said, I will dwell among them, and walke there: and I will be their God, and they shalbe my people.

17 Wherefore come out from among them, and separate your selues, saith the Lord, and touch none vncleane thing, and I wil receiue you.

18 And I will be a Father vnto you, and ye shalbe my sonnes and daughters, saith the Lord almightie.

Second Corinthians 7

1 Seing then we haue these promises, dearely beloued, let vs clense our selues from all filthinesse of the flesh and spirit, and finish our sanctification in the feare of God.

2 Receiue vs: we haue done wrong to no man: we haue corrupted no man: we haue defrauded no man.

3 I speake it not to your condemnation: for I haue said before, that ye are in our hearts, to die and liue together.

4 I vse great boldnesse of speach toward you: I reioyce greatly in you: I am filled with comfort, and am exceeding ioyous in all our tribulation.

5 For when we were come into Macedonia, our flesh had no rest, but we were troubled on euery side, fightings without, and terrours within.

6 But God, that comforteth the abiect, comforted vs at the comming of Titus:

7 And not by his comming onely, but also by the consolation wherewith he was comforted of you, when he tolde vs your great desire, your mourning, your feruent minde to me warde, so that I reioyced much more.

8 For though I made you sorie with a letter, I repent not, though I did repent: for I perceiue that the same epistle made you sorie, though it were but for a season.

9 I nowe reioyce, not that ye were sorie, but that ye sorowed to repentance: for ye sorowed godly, so that in nothing ye were hurt by vs.

10 For godly sorowe causeth repentance vnto saluation, not to be repented of: but the worldly sorowe causeth death.

11 For beholde, this thing that ye haue bene godly sory, what great care it hath wrought in you: yea, what clearing of yourselues: yea, what indignation: yea, what feare: yea, howe great desire: yea, what a zeale: yea, what reuenge: in all things ye haue shewed your selues, that ye are pure in this matter.

12 Wherefore, though I wrote vnto you, I did not it for his cause that had done the wrong, neither for his cause that had the iniurie, but that our care toward you in the sight of God might appeare vnto you.

13 Therefore we were comforted, because ye were comforted: but rather we reioyced much more for the ioye of Titus, because his spirit was refreshed by you all.

14 For if that I haue boasted any thing to him of you, I haue not bene ashamed: but as I haue spoken vnto you all things in trueth, euen so our boasting vnto Titus was true.

15 And his inwarde affection is more aboundant toward you, when he remembreth the obedience of you all, and howe with feare and trembling ye receiued him.

16 I reioyce therefore that I may put my confidence in you in all things.

Second Corinthians 8

1 We doe you also to wit, brethren, of the grace of God bestowed vpon the Churches of Macedonia,

2 Because in great triall of affliction their ioy abounded, and their most extreme pouertie abounded vnto their rich liberalitie.

3 For to their power (I beare record) yea, and beyonde their power, they were willing,

4 And praied vs with great instance that we woulde receiue the grace, and fellowship of the ministring which is toward the Saints.

5 And this they did, not as we looked for: but gaue their owne selues, first to the Lord, and after vnto vs by the will of God,

6 That we should exhort Titus, that as hee had begon, so he would also accomplish the same grace among you also.

7 Therefore, as yee abound in euery thing, in faith and woorde, and knowledge, and in all diligence, and in your loue towardes vs, euen so see that yee abound in this grace also.

8 This say I not by commandement, but because of the diligence of others: therefore prooue I the naturalnesse of your loue.

9 For ye knowe the grace of our Lord Iesus Christ, that hee being rich, for your sakes became poore, that yee through his pouertie might be made rich.

10 And I shewe my minde herein: for this is expedient for you, which haue begun not to doe onely, but also to will, a yeare agoe.

11 Nowe therefore performe to doe it also, that as there was a readinesse to will, euen so yee may performe it of that which yee haue.

12 For if there be first a willing minde, it is accepted according to that a man hath, and not according to that he hath not.

13 Neither is it that other men should be eased and you grieued: But vpon like condition, at this time your abundance supplieth their lacke:

14 That also their aboundance may bee for your lacke, that there may be equalitie:

15 As it is written, Hee that gathered much, had nothing ouer, and hee that gathered litle, had not the lesse.

16 And thanks be vnto God, which hath put in the heart of Titus the same care for you.

17 Because hee accepted the exhortation, yea, hee was so carefull that of his owne accorde hee went vnto you.

18 And wee haue sent also with him the brother, whose praise is in the Gospel throughout al the Churches.

19 (And not so onely, but is also chosen of the Churches to be a fellowe in our iourney, concerning this grace that is ministred by vs vnto the glorie of the same Lord, and declaration of your prompt minde)

20 Auoiding this, that no man shoulde blame vs in this aboundance that is ministred by vs,

21 Prouiding for honest thinges, not onely before the Lord, but also before men.

22 And we haue sent with them our brother, whom we haue oft times prooued to be diligent in many thinges, but nowe much more diligent, for the great confidence, which I haue in you.

23 Whether any doe inquire of Titus, he is my fellowe and helper to you ward: or of our brethren, they are messengers of the Churches, and the glorie of Christ.

24 Wherefore shew toward them, and before the Churches the proofe of your loue, and of the reioycing that we haue of you.

Second Corinthians 9

1 For as touching the ministring to the Saints, it is superfluous for me to write vnto you.

2 For I knowe your readinesse of minde, whereof I boast my selfe of you vnto them of Macedonia, and say, that Achaia was prepared a yeere agoe, and your zeale hath prouoked many.

3 Nowe haue I sent the brethren, lest our reioycing ouer you shoulde bee in vaine in this behalfe, that yee (as I haue sayde) be readie:

4 Lest if they of Macedonia come with me, and finde you vnprepared, we (that wee may not say, you) should be ashamed in this my constant boasting.

5 Wherefore, I thought it necessarie to exhort the brethren to come before vnto you, and to finish your beneuolence appointed afore, that it might be readie, and come as of beneuolence, and not as of niggardlinesse.

6 This yet remember, that he which soweth sparingly, shall reape also sparingly, and hee that soweth liberally, shall reape also liberally.

7 As euery man wisheth in his heart, so let him giue, not grudgingly, or of necessitie: for God loueth a cheerefull giuer.

8 And God is able to make all grace to abound towarde you, that yee always hauing all sufficiencie in all thinges, may abounde in euery good worke,

9 (As it is written, He hath sparsed abroad and hath giuen to the poore: his beneuolence remayneth for euer.

10 Also hee that findeth seede to the sower, will minister likewise bread for foode, and multiplie your seede, and increase the fruites of your beneuolence,)

11 That on all partes yee may bee made rich vnto all liberalitie, which causeth through vs thankesgiuing vnto God.

12 For the ministration of this seruice not onely supplieth the necessities of the Saintes, but also aboundantly causeth many to giue thankes to God,

13 (Which by the experiment of this ministration praise God for your voluntarie submission to the Gospell of Christ, and for your liberall distribution to them, and to all men)

14 And in their praier for you, to log after you greatly, for the aboundant grace of God in you.

15 Thankes therefore bee vnto God for his vnspeakeable gift.

Second Corinthians 10

1 Nowe I Paul my selfe beseech you by the meekenes, and gentlenes of Christ, which when I am present among you am base, but am bolde toward you being absent:

2 And this I require you, that I neede not to be bolde when I am present, with that same confidence, wherewith I thinke to bee bolde against some, which esteeme vs as though wee walked according to the flesh.

3 Neuerthelesse, though wee walke in the flesh, yet we doe not warre after the flesh.

4 (For the weapons of our warrefare are not carnall, but mightie through God, to cast downe holdes)

5 Casting downe the imaginations, and euery high thing that is exalted against the knowledge of God, and bringing into captiuitie euery thought to the obedience of Christ,

6 And hauing ready the vengeance against all disobedience, when your obedience is fulfilled.

7 Looke yee on things after the appearance? If any man trust in himselfe that hee is Christes, let him consider this againe of himself, that as he is Christes, euen so are we Christes.

8 For though I shoulde boast somewhat more of our authoritie, which the Lord hath giuen vs for edification, and not for your destruction, I should haue no shame.

9 This I say, that I may not seeme as it were to feare you with letters.

10 For the letters, sayeth hee, are sore and strong, but his bodily presence is weake, and his speache is of no value.

11 Let such one thinke this, that such as wee are in woorde by letters, when we are absent, such wil we be also in deede, when we are present.

12 For wee dare not make our selues of the nomber, or to compare our selues to them, which praise themselues: but they vnderstand not that they measure themselues with themselues, and compare themselues with themselues.

13 But we wil not reioyce of things, which are not within our measure, but according to the measure of the line, whereof God hath distributed vnto vs a measure to attaine euen vnto you.

14 For we stretche not our selues beyonde our measure, as though wee had not attained vnto you: for euen to you also haue we come in preaching the Gospel of Christ,

15 Not boasting of things which are without our measure: that is, of other mens labours: and we hope, when your faith shall increase, to bee magnified by you according to our line aboundantly,

16 And to preache the Gospel in those regions which are beyonde you: not to reioyce in another mans line, that is, in the thinges that are prepared alreadie.

17 But let him that reioyceth, reioyce in the Lord.

18 For hee that praiseth himselfe, is not alowed, but he whome the Lord praiseth.

Second Corinthians 11

1 Woulde to God, yee coulde suffer a litle my foolishnes, and in deede, ye suffer me.

2 For I am ielous ouer you, with godly ielousie: for I haue prepared you for one husband, to present you as a pure virgine to Christ:

3 But I feare least as the serpent beguiled Eue through his subtiltie, so your mindes shoulde be corrupt from the simplicitie that is in Christ.

4 For if he that commeth, preacheth another Iesus whome we haue not preached: or if yee receiue another spirite whome ye haue not receiued: either another Gospell, which yee haue not receiued, ye might well haue suffered him.

5 Verely I suppose that I was not inferior to the very chiefe Apostles.

6 And though I be rude in speaking, yet I am not so in knowledge, but among you wee haue beene made manifest to the vttermost, in all things.

7 Haue I committed an offence, because I abased my selfe, that ye might be exalted, and because I preached to you ye Gospell of God freely?

8 I robbed other Churches, and tooke wages of them to doe you seruice.

9 And when I was present with you, and had neede, I was not slouthfull to the hinderance of any man: for that which was lacking vnto me, the brethre which came from Macedonia, supplied, and in all thinges I kept and will keepe my selfe, that I should not be grieuous to you.

10 The trueth of Christ is in me, that this reioycing shall not be shut vp against me in the regions of Achaia.

11 Wherefore? because I loue you not? God knoweth.

12 But what I doe, that will I doe: that I may cut away occasion from them which desire occasion, that they might be found like vnto vs in that wherein they reioyce.

13 For such false apostles are deceitfull workers, and transforme themselues into the Apostles of Christ.

14 And no marueile: for Satan himselfe is transformed into an Angel of light.

15 Therefore it is no great thing, though his ministers transforme themselues, as though they were the ministers of righteousnes, whose end shall be according to their workes.

16 I say againe, Let no man thinke that I am foolish, or els take mee euen as a foole, that I also may boast my selfe a litle.

17 That I speake, I speake it not after the Lord: but as it were foolishly, in this my great boasting.

18 Seeing that many reioyce after the flesh, I will reioyce also.

19 For ye suffer fooles gladly, because that yee are wise.

20 For ye suffer, euen if a man bring you into bondage, if a man deuoure you, if a man take your goods, if a man exalt himselfe, if a man smite you on the face.

21 I speake as concerning the reproche: as though that we had bene weake: but wherein any man is bold (I speake foolishly) I am bold also.

22 They are Hebrues, so am I: they are Israelites, so am I: they are the seede of Abraham, so am I:

23 They are the ministers of Christ (I speake as a foole) I am more: in labours more aboundant: in stripes aboue measure: in prison more plenteously: in death oft.

24 Of the Iewes fiue times receiued I fourtie stripes saue one.

25 I was thrise beaten with roddes: I was once stoned: I suffered thrise shipwracke: night and day haue I bene in the deepe sea.

26 In iourneying I was often, in perils of waters, in perils of robbers, in perils of mine owne nation, in perils among the Gentiles, in perils in the citie, in perils in wildernes, in perils in the sea, in perils among false brethren,

27 In wearinesse and painefulnesse, in watching often, in hunger and thirst, in fastings often, in colde and in nakednesse.

28 Beside the thinges which are outwarde, I am combred dayly, and haue the care of all the Churches.

29 Who is weake, and I am not weake? who is offended, and I burne not?

30 If I must needes reioyce, I will reioyce of mine infirmities.

31 The God, euen the Father of our Lord Iesus Christ, which is blessed for euermore, knoweth that I lie not.

32 In Damascus the gouernour of the people vnder King Aretas, layde watch in the citie of the Damascens, and would haue caught me.

33 But at a window was I let downe in a basket through the wall, and escaped his handes.

Second Corinthians 12

1 It is not expedient for me no doubt to reioyce: for I will come to visions and reuelations of the Lord.

2 I know a man in Christ aboue fourteene yeeres agone, (whether he were in the body, I can not tell, or out of the body, I can not tell: God knoweth) which was taken vp into the thirde heauen.

3 And I knowe such a man (whether in the body, or out of the body, I can not tell: God knoweth)

4 How that he was taken vp into Paradise, and heard words which cannot be spoken, which are not possible for man to vtter.

5 Of such a man will I reioyce: of my selfe will I not reioyce, except it bee of mine infirmities.

6 For though I woulde reioyce, I should not be a foole, for I will say the trueth: but I refraine, lest any man should thinke of me aboue that hee seeth in me, or that he heareth of me.

7 And lest I should be exalted out of measure through the aboundance of reuelations, there was giuen vnto me a pricke in the flesh, the messenger of Satan to buffet mee, because I should not be exalted out of measure.

8 For this thing I besought the Lord thrise, that it might depart from me.

9 And he said vnto me, My grace is sufficient for thee: for my power is made perfect through weakenesse. Very gladly therefore will I reioyce rather in mine infirmities, that the power of Christ may dwell in me.

10 Therefore I take pleasure in infirmities, in reproches, in necessities, in persecutions, in anguish for Christes sake: for when I am weake, then am I strong.

11 I was a foole to boast my selfe: yee haue compelled mee: for I ought to haue bene commended of you: for in nothing was I inferiour vnto the very chiefe Apostles, though I bee nothing.

12 The signes of an Apostle were wrought among you with all patience, with signes, and wonders, and great workes.

13 For what is it, wherein yee were inferiours vnto other Churches, except that I haue not bene slouthfull to your hinderance? forgiue me this wrong.

14 Behold, the thirde time I am ready to come vnto you, and yet will I not be slouthfull to your hinderance: for I seeke not yours, but you: for the children ought not to laye vp for the fathers, but the fathers for the children.

15 And I will most gladly bestow, and will be bestowed for your soules: though the more I loue you, the lesse I am loued.

16 But bee it that I charged you not: yet for as much as I was craftie, I tooke you with guile.

17 Did I pill you by any of them whom I sent vnto you?

18 I haue desired Titus, and with him I haue sent a brother: did Titus pill you of any thing? walked we not in the selfe

same spirit? walked we not in the same steppes?

19 Againe, thinke yee that wee excuse our selues vnto you? we speake before God in Christ. But wee doe all thinges, dearely beloued, for your edifying.

20 For I feare least when I come, I shall not finde you such as I would: and that I shalbe found vnto you such as ye woulde not, and least there be strife, enuying, wrath, contentions, backebitings, whisperings, swellings and discord.

21 I feare least when I come againe, my God abase me among you, and I shall bewaile many of them which haue sinned already, and haue not repented of the vncleannesse, and fornication, and wantonnesse which they haue committed.

Second Corinthians 13

1 Lo this is the thirde time that I come vnto you. In the mouth of two or three witnesses shall euery worde stand

2 I tolde you before, and tell you before: as though I had bene present the seconde time, so write I nowe being absent to them which heretofore haue sinned and to all others, that if I come againe, I will not spare,

3 Seeing that ye seeke experience of Christ, that speaketh in mee, which towarde you is not weake, but is mightie in you.

4 For though hee was crucified concerning his infirmitie, yet liueth hee through the power of God. And wee no doubt are weake in him, but we shall liue with him, through the power of God towarde you.

5 Proue your selues whether ye are in the faith: examine your selues: knowe yee not your owne selues, howe that Iesus Christ is in you, except ye be reprobates?

6 But I trust that ye shall knowe that wee are not reprobates.

7 Nowe I pray vnto God that yee doe none euill, not that we should seeme approued, but that ye should doe that which is honest: though we be as reprobates.

8 For wee can not doe any thing against the trueth, but for the trueth.

9 For we are glad when wee are weake, and that ye are strong: this also we wish for, euen your perfection.

10 Therefore write I these thinges being absent, least when I am present, I should vse sharpenesse, according to the power which the Lord hath giuen mee, to edification, and not to destruction.

11 Finally brethren, fare ye well: be perfect: be of good comfort: be of one minde: liue in peace, and the God of loue and peace shalbe with you.

12 Greete one another with an holy kisse. All the Saintes salute you.

13 The grace of our Lord Iesus Christ, and the loue of God, and the communion of the holy Ghost be with you all, Amen. The seconde Epistle to the Corinthians, written from Philippi, a citie in Macedonia, and sent by Titus and Lucas.

Galatians

Galatians 1

1 Pavl an Apostle (not of men, neither by man, but by Iesus Christ, and God the Father which hath raised him from the dead)

2 And all the brethren which are with me, vnto the Churches of Galatia:

3 Grace be with you, and peace from God the Father, and from our Lord Iesus Christ,

4 Which gaue himself for our sinnes, that he might deliuer vs from this present euill world according to the will of God euen our Father,

5 To whom be glory for euer and euer, Amen.

6 I marueile that ye are so soone remoued away vnto another Gospel, from him that had called you in the grace of Christ,

7 Which is not another Gospel, saue that there be some which trouble you, and intend to peruert the Gospel of Christ.

8 But though that we, or an Angel from heauen preach vnto you otherwise, then that which we haue preached vnto you, let him be accursed.

9 As we sayd before, so say I now againe, If any man preach vnto you otherwise, then that ye haue receiued, let him be accursed.

10 For nowe preach I mans doctrine, or Gods? or go I about to please men? for if I should yet please men, I were not the seruant of Christ.

11 Now I certifie you, brethren, that ye Gospel which was preached of me, was not after man.

12 For neither receiued I it of man, neither was I taught it, but by the reuelation of Iesus Christ.

13 For ye haue heard of my conuersation in time past, in the Iewish religion, how that I persecuted the Church of God extremely, and wasted it,

14 And profited in the Iewish religion aboue many of my companions of mine owne nation, and was much more zealous of the traditions of my fathers.

15 But when it pleased God (which had separated me from my mothers wombe, and called me by his grace)

16 To reueile his Sonne in me, that I should preach him among the Gentiles, immediatly I communicated not with flesh and blood:

17 Neither came I againe to Hierusalem to them which were Apostles before me, but I went into Arabia, and turned againe vnto Damascus.

18 Then after three yeeres I came againe to Hierusalem to visite Peter, and abode with him fifteene dayes.

19 And none other of the Apostles sawe I, saue Iames the Lords brother.

20 Nowe the things which I write vnto you, beholde, I witnes before God, that I lie not.

21 After that, I went into the coastes of Syria and Cilicia: for I was vnknowen by face vnto the Churches of Iudea, which were in Christ.

22 But they had heard onely some say, Hee which persecuted vs in time past, nowe preacheth the faith which before he destroyed.

23 And they glorified God for me.

Galatians 2

1 Then fourteene yeeres after, I went vp againe to Hierusalem with Barnabas, and tooke with me Titus also.

2 And I went vp by reuelation, and declared vnto them that Gospel which I preach among the Gentiles, but particularly to them that were the chiefe, least by any meanes I should runne, or had runne in vaine:

3 But neither yet Titus which was with me, though he were a Grecian, was compelled to be circumcised,

4 To wit, for the false brethren which were craftily sent in, and crept in priuily to spie out our libertie, which we haue in Christ Iesus, that they might bring vs into bondage.

5 To whom we gaue not place by subiection for an houre, that the trueth of the Gospel might continue with you.

6 But by them which seemed to be great, I was not taught (whatsoeuer they were in time passed, I am nothing the better: God accepteth no mans person) for they that are the chiefe, did adde nothing to me aboue that I had.

7 But contrariwise, when they saw that ye Gospel ouer ye vncircumcision was comitted vnto me, as the Gospel ouer ye circumcision was vnto Peter:

8 (For he that was mightie by Peter in the Apostleship ouer the circumcision, was also mightie by me toward the Gentiles)

9 And when Iames, and Cephas, and Iohn, knew of the grace that was giuen vnto me, which are counted to be pillars, they gaue to me and to Barnabas the right hands of fellowship, that we should preach vnto the Gentiles, and they vnto the Circumcision,

10 Warning onely that we should remember the poore: which thing also I was diligent to doe.

11 And when Peter was come to Antiochia, I withstood him to his face: for he was to be condemned.

12 For before that certaine came from Iames, he ate with the Gentiles: but when they were come, he withdrew and separated himselfe, fearing them which were of the Circumcision.

13 And the other Iewes played the hypocrites likewise with him, in so much that Barnabas was led away with them by that their hypocrisie.

14 But when I saw, that they went not ye right way to the trueth of ye Gospel, I sayd vnto Peter before all men, If thou being a Iewe, liuest as the Gentiles, and not like the Iewes, why constrainest thou the Gentiles to doe like the Iewes?

15 We which are Iewes by nature, and not sinners of the Gentiles,

16 Knowe that a man is not iustified by the works of the Law, but by ye faith of Iesus Christ, euen we, I say, haue beleeued in Iesus Christ, that we might be iustified by the faith of Christ, and not by the workes of the Lawe, because that by the workes of the Lawe, no flesh shalbe iustified.

17 If then while we seeke to be made righteous by Christ, we our selues are found sinners, is Christ therefore the minister of sinne? God forbid.

18 For if I build againe the things that I haue destroyed, I make my selfe a trespasser.

19 For I through the Lawe am dead to the Lawe, that I might liue vnto God.

20 I am crucified with Christ, but I liue, yet not I any more, but Christ liueth in me: and in that that I now liue in the flesh, I liue by the faith in the Sonne of God, who hath loued me, and giuen him selfe for me.

21 I doe not abrogate the grace of God: for if righteousnes be by the Lawe, then Christ dyed without a cause.

Galatians 3

1 O foolish Galatians, who hath bewitched you, that ye should not obey the trueth, to whome Iesus Christ before was described in your sight, and among you crucified?

2 This only would I learne of you, Receiued ye the Spirit by the workes of the Lawe, or by the hearing of faith preached?

3 Are ye so foolish, that after ye haue begun in the Spirit, ye would now be made perfect by the flesh?

4 Haue ye suffered so many things in vaine? if so be it be euen in vaine.

5 He therefore that ministreth to you the Spirit, and worketh miracles among you, doeth he it through the workes of the Law, or by the hearing of faith preached?

6 Yea rather as Abraham beleeued God, and it was imputed to him for righteousnes.

7 Knowe ye therefore, that they which are of faith, the same are the children of Abraham.

8 For the Scripture foreseeing, that God would iustifie the Gentiles through faith, preached before the Gospel vnto Abraham, saying, In thee shall all the Gentiles be blessed.

9 So then they which be of faith, are blessed with faithfull Abraham.

10 For as many as are of the workes of the Lawe, are vnder the curse: for it is written, Cursed is euery man that continueth not in all things, which are written in the booke of the Law, to doe them.

11 And that no man is iustified by the Law in the sight of God, it is euident: for the iust shall liue by faith.

12 And the Lawe is not of faith: but the man that shall doe those things, shall liue in them.

13 Christ hath redeemed vs from the curse of the Lawe, made a curse for vs,

(for it is written, Cursed is euery one that hangeth on tree)

14 That the blessing of Abraham might come on the Gentiles through Christ Iesus, that wee might receiue the promise of the Spirite through faith.

15 Brethren, I speake as men do: though it be but a mans couenant, when it is confirmed, yet no man doeth abrogate it, or addeth any thing thereto.

16 Nowe to Abraham and his seede were the promises made. Hee saith not, And to the seedes, as speaking of many: but, And to thy seede, as of one, which is Christ.

17 And this I say, that the couenant that was confirmed afore of God in respect of Christ, the Lawe which was foure hundreth and thirtie yeeres after, can not disanull, that it shoulde make the promise of none effect.

18 For if the inheritance be of the Lawe, it is no more by the promise, but God gaue it freely vnto Abraham by promise.

19 Wherefore then serueth the Law? It was added because of the transgressions, til the seed came, vnto the which the promise was made: and it was ordeined by Angels in the hande of a Mediatour.

20 Nowe a Mediatour is not a Mediatour of one: but God is one.

21 Is the Lawe then against the promises of God? God forbid: For if there had bene a Lawe giuen which coulde haue giuen life, surely righteousnes should haue bene by the Lawe.

22 But the Scripture hath concluded all vnder sinne, that the promise by the faith of Iesus Christ should be giuen to them that beleeue.

23 But before faith came, we were kept vnder the Law, as vnder a garison, and shut vp vnto that faith, which should afterward be reueiled.

24 Wherefore the Lawe was our scholemaster to bring vs to Christ, that we might be made righteous by faith.

25 But after that faith is come, we are no longer vnder a scholemaster.

26 For ye are al the sonnes of God by faith, in Christ Iesus.

27 For all ye that are baptized into Christ, haue put on Christ.

28 There is neither Iewe nor Grecian: there is neither bonde nor free: there is neither male nor female: for ye are all one in Christ Iesus.

29 And if ye be Christes, then are ye Abrahams seede, and heires by promise.

Galatians 4

1 Then I say, that the heire as long as hee is a childe, differeth nothing from a seruant, though he be Lord of all,

2 But is vnder tutours and gouernours, vntil the time appointed of the Father.

3 Euen so, we when wee were children, were in bondage vnder the rudiments of the world.

4 But when the fulnesse of time was come, God sent foorth his Sonne made of a woman, and made vnder the Lawe,

5 That hee might redeeme them which were vnder the Law, that we might receiue the adoption of the sonnes.

6 And because ye are sonnes, God hath sent foorth the Spirit of his Sonne into your heartes, which crieth, Abba, Father.

7 Wherefore, thou art no more a seruant, but a sonne: now if thou be a sone, thou art also the heire of God through Christ.

8 But euen then, when ye knewe not God, yee did seruice vnto them, which by nature are not gods:

9 But now seeing ye knowe God, yea, rather are knowen of God, howe turne ye againe vnto impotent and beggerly rudiments, whereunto as from the beginning ye wil be in bondage againe?

10 Ye obserue dayes, and moneths, and times and yeeres.

11 I am in feare of you, lest I haue bestowed on you labour in vaine.

12 Be ye as I (for I am euen as you) brethren, I beseech you: ye haue not hurt me at all.

13 And ye know, how through infirmitie of the flesh, I preached ye Gospel vnto you at the first.

14 And the trial of me which was in my flesh, ye despised not, neither abhorred: but ye receiued me as an Angel of God, yea, as Christ Iesus.

15 What was then your felicitie? for I beare you recorde, that if it had bene possible, ye would haue plucked out your owne eyes, and haue giuen them vnto me.

16 Am I therefore become your enemie, because I tell you the trueth?

17 They are ielous ouer you amisse: yea, they woulde exclude you, that ye shoulde altogether loue them.

18 But it is a good thing to loue earnestly alwayes in a good thing, and not onely when I am present with you,

19 My litle children, of whome I trauaile in birth againe, vntill Christ be formed in you.

20 And I would I were with you nowe, that I might change my voyce: for I am in doubt of you.

21 Tell me, ye that will be vnder the Law, doe ye not heare the Lawe?

22 For it is written, that Abraham had two sonnes, one by a seruant, and one by a free woman.

23 But he which was of the seruant, was borne after the flesh: and he which was of the free woman, was borne by promise.

24 By the which things another thing is meant: for these mothers are the two testaments, the one which is Agar of mount Sina, which gendreth vnto bondage.

25 (For Agar or Sina is a mountaine in Arabia, and it answereth to Hierusalem which nowe is) and she is in bondage with her children.

26 But Hierusalem, which is aboue, is free: which is the mother of vs all.

27 For it is written, Reioyce thou barren that bearest no children: breake forth, and cry, thou that trauailest not: for the desolate hath many moe children, then she which hath an husband.

28 Therefore, brethren, wee are after the maner of Isaac, children of the promise.

29 But as then hee that was borne after the flesh, persecuted him that was borne after the Spirit, euen so it is nowe.

30 But what sayth the Scripture? Put out the seruant and her sonne: for the sonne of the seruant shall not be heire with the sonne of the free woman.

31 Then brethren, we are not children of the seruant, but of the free woman.

Galatians 5

1 Stand fast therefore in the libertie wherewith Christ hath made vs free, and be not intangled againe with the yoke of bondage.

2 Beholde, I Paul say vnto you, that if yee be circumcised, Christ shall profite you nothing.

3 For I testifie againe to euery man, which is circumcised, that he is bound to keepe the whole Lawe.

4 Ye are abolished from Christ: whosoeuer are iustified by the Law, ye are fallen from grace.

5 For we through the Spirit waite for the hope of righteousnes through faith.

6 For in Iesus Christ neither circumcision auaileth any thing, neither vncircumcision, but faith which worketh by loue.

7 Ye did runne well: who did let you, that ye did not obey the trueth?

8 It is not the perswasion of him that calleth you.

9 A litle leauen doeth leauen the whole lumpe.

10 I haue trust in you through the Lord, that ye will be none otherwise minded: but hee that troubleth you, shall beare his condemnation, whosoeuer he be.

11 And brethren, if I yet preach circumcision, why doe I yet suffer persecution? Then is the slaunder of the crosse abolished.

12 Would to God they were euen cut off, which doe disquiet you.

13 For brethren, ye haue bene called vnto libertie: onely vse not your libertie as an occasion vnto the flesh, but by loue serue one another.

14 For all the Lawe is fulfilled in one worde, which is this, Thou shalt loue thy neighbour as thy selfe.

15 If ye bite and deuoure one another, take heede least ye be consumed one of another.

16 Then I say, Walke in the Spirit, and ye shall not fulfill the lustes of the flesh.

17 For the flesh lusteth against the Spirit, and the Spirit against the flesh: and these are contrary one to another, so that ye can not doe the same things that ye would.

18 And if ye be led by the Spirit, ye are not vnder the Lawe.

19 Moreouer the workes of the flesh are manifest, which are adulterie, fornication, vncleannes, wantonnes,

20 Idolatrie, witchcraft, hatred, debate, emulations, wrath, contentions, seditions, heresies,

21 Enuie, murthers, drunkennesse, gluttonie, and such like, whereof I tell you before, as I also haue tolde you before, that they which doe such things, shall not inherite the kingdome of God.

22 But the fruite of the Spirit is loue, ioye, peace, long suffering, gentlenes, goodnes, fayth,

23 Meekenesse, temperancie: against such there is no lawe.

24 For they that are Christes, haue crucified the flesh with the affections and the lustes.

25 If we liue in the Spirit, let vs also walke in the Spirit.

26 Let vs not be desirous of vaine glorie, prouoking one another, enuying one another.

Galatians 6

1 Brethren, if a man be suddenly taken in any offence, ye which are spirituall, restore such one with the spirit of meekenes, considering thy selfe, least thou also be tempted.

2 Beare ye one anothers burden, and so fulfill the Lawe of Christ.

3 For if any man seeme to himselfe, that he is somewhat, when he is nothing, hee deceiueth himselfe in his imagination.

4 But let euery man prooue his owne worke: and then shall he haue reioycing in himselfe onely and not in another.

5 For euery man shall beare his owne burden.

6 Let him that is taught in the worde, make him that hath taught him, partaker of all his goods.

7 Be not deceiued: God is not mocked: for whatsoeuer a man soweth, that shall hee also reape.

8 For hee that soweth to his flesh, shall of the flesh reape corruption: but hee that soweth to the spirit, shall of the spirit reape life euerlasting.

9 Let vs not therefore be weary of well doing: for in due season we shall reape, if we faint not.

10 While we haue therefore time, let vs doe good vnto all men, but specially vnto them, which are of the housholde of faith.

11 Ye see how large a letter I haue written vnto you with mine owne hand.

12 As many as desire to make a faire shewe in the flesh, they constraine you to be circumcised, onely because they would not suffer persecution for the crosse of Christ.

13 For they themselues which are circumcised keepe not the law, but desire to haue you circumcised, that they might reioyce in your flesh.

14 But God forbid that I should reioyce, but in ye crosse of our Lord Iesus Christ, whereby the world is crucified vnto me, and I vnto ye world.

15 For in Christ Iesus neither circumcision auaileth any thing, nor vncircumcision, but a newe creature.

16 And as many as walke according to this rule, peace shalbe vpon them, and mercie, and vpon the Israel of God.

17 From henceforth let no man put me to busines: for I beare in my body the markes of the Lord Iesus.

18 Brethren, the grace of our Lord Iesus Christ be with your spirit, Amen. Vnto the Galatians written from Rome.

Ephesians

Ephesians 1

1 Pavl an Apostle of Iesvs Christ by the will of God, to the Saints, which are at Ephesus, and to ye faithfull in Christ Iesus:

2 Grace be with you, and peace from God our Father, and from the Lord Iesus Christ.

3 Blessed be God, and the Father of our Lord Iesus Christ, which hath blessed vs with all spirituall blessing in heauenly thinges in Christ,

4 As hee hath chosen vs in him, before the foundation of the worlde, that we should be holy, and without blame before him in loue:

5 Who hath predestinate vs, to be adopted through Iesus Christ in him selfe, according to the good pleasure of his will,

6 To the prayse of the glory of his grace, wherewith he hath made vs freely accepted in his beloued,

7 By whom we haue redemption through his blood, euen the forgiuenes of sinnes, according to his rich grace:

8 Whereby he hath bene aboundant toward vs in all wisedome and vnderstanding,

9 And hath opened vnto vs the mysterie of his will according to his good pleasure, which he had purposed in him,

10 That in the dispensation of the fulnesse of the times, he might gather together in one all things, both which are in heauen, and which are in earth, euen in Christ:

11 In whom also we are chosen when we were predestinate according to ye purpose of him, which worketh all things after the counsell of his owne will,

12 That we, which first trusted in Christ, should be vnto the praise of his glorie:

13 In whom also ye haue trusted, after that ye heard the worde of trueth, euen the Gospel of your saluation, wherein also after that ye beleeued, ye were sealed with the holy Spirite of promise,

14 Which is the earnest of our inheritance, for the redemption of that libertie purchased vnto the prayse of his glory.

15 Therefore also after that I heard of the faith, which ye haue in the Lord Iesus, and loue toward all the Saints,

16 I cease not to giue thankes for you, making mention of you in my prayers,

17 That the God of our Lord Iesus Christ, that Father of glory, might giue vnto you the Spirit of wisedome, and reuelation through the acknowledging of him,

18 That the eyes of your vnderstanding may be lightened, that ye may knowe what the hope is of his calling, and what the riches of his glorious inheritance is in the Saints,

19 And what is the exceeding greatnesse of his power toward vs, which beleeue, according to the working of his mightie power,

20 Which he wrought in Christ, when he raised him from the dead, and set him at his right hand in the heauenly places,

21 Farre aboue al principalitie, and power, and might, and domination, and euery Name, that is named, not in this world only, but also in that that is to come,

22 And hath made all things subiect vnder his feete, and hath giuen him ouer all things to be the head to the Church,

23 Which is his body, euen the fulnesse of him that filleth all in all things.

Ephesians 2

1 And you hath he quickened, that were dead in trespasses and sinnes,

2 Wherein, in times past ye walked, according to the course of this world, and after the prince that ruleth in the aire, euen the spirite, that nowe worketh in the children of disobedience,

3 Among whom we also had our conuersation in time past, in the lustes of our flesh, in fulfilling the will of the flesh, and of the minde, and were by nature the children of wrath, as well as others.

4 But God which is rich in mercie, through his great loue wherewith he loued vs,

5 Euen when we were dead by sinnes, hath quickened vs together in Christ, by whose grace ye are saued,

6 And hath raysed vs vp together, and made vs sit together in the heauenly places in Christ Iesus,

7 That he might shewe in the ages to come the exceeding riches of his grace, through his kindnesse toward vs in Christ Iesus.

8 For by grace are ye saued through faith, and that not of your selues: it is the gift of God,

9 Not of workes, least any man should boast himselfe.

10 For we are his workemanship created in Christ Iesus vnto good workes, which God hath ordeined, that we should walke in them.

11 Wherefore remember that ye being in time past Gentiles in the flesh, and called vncircumcision of them, which are called circumcision in the flesh, made with hands,

12 That ye were, I say, at that time without Christ, and were aliens from the common wealth of Israel, and were strangers from the couenants of promise, and had no hope, and were without God in the world.

13 But nowe in Christ Iesus, ye which once were farre off, are made neere by the blood of Christ.

14 For he is our peace, which hath made of both one, and hath broken the stoppe of the partition wall,

15 In abrogating through his flesh the hatred, that is, the Lawe of commandements which standeth in ordinances, for to make of twaine one newe man in himselfe, so making peace,

16 And that he might reconcile both vnto God in one body by his crosse, and slay hatred thereby,

17 And came, and preached peace to you which were afarre off, and to them that were neere.

18 For through him we both haue an entrance vnto the Father by one Spirit.

19 Nowe therefore ye are no more strangers and forreiners: but citizens with the Saintes, and of the housholde of God,

20 And are built vpon the foundation of the Apostles and Prophets, Iesus Christ himselfe being the chiefe corner stone,

21 In whom all the building coupled together, groweth vnto an holy Temple in the Lord.

22 In whom ye also are built together to be the habitation of God by the Spirit.

Ephesians 3

1 For this cause, I Paul am the prisoner of Iesus Christ for you Gentiles,

2 If ye haue heard of the dispensation of the grace of God, which is giuen me to you warde,

3 That is, that God by reuelation hath shewed this mysterie vnto me (as I wrote aboue in fewe wordes,

4 Whereby when ye reade, ye may knowe mine vnderstanding in the mysterie of Christ)

5 Which in other ages was not opened vnto the sonnes of men, as it is nowe reueiled vnto his holy Apostles and Prophets by the Spirit,

6 That the Gentiles should be inheriters also, and of the same body, and partakers of his promise in Christ by the Gospel,

7 Whereof I am made a minister by the gift of the grace of God giuen vnto me through the effectuall working of his power.

8 Euen vnto me the least of all Saints is this grace giuen, that I should preach among the Gentiles the vnsearchable riches of Christ,

9 And to make cleare vnto all men what the fellowship of the mysterie is, which from the beginning of the world hath bene hid in God, who hath created all things by Iesus Christ,

10 To the intent, that nowe vnto principalities and powers in heauenly places, might be knowen by the Church the manifolde wisedome of God,

11 According to the eternall purpose, which he wrought in Christ Iesus our Lord:

12 By whom we haue boldenes and entrance with confidence, by faith in him.

13 Wherefore I desire that ye faint not at my tribulations for your sakes, which is your glory.

14 For this cause I bowe my knees vnto the Father of our Lord Iesus Christ,

15 (Of whom is named the whole familie in heauen and in earth)

16 That he might graunt you according to the riches of his glorie, that ye may be strengthened by his Spirit in the inner man,

17 That Christ may dwell in your heartes by faith:

18 That ye, being rooted and grounded in loue, may be able to comprehend with al Saints, what is the breadth, and length, and depth, and height:

19 And to knowe the loue of Christ, which passeth knowledge, that ye may be filled with all fulnesse of God.

20 Vnto him therefore that is able to do exceeding aboundantly aboue all that we aske or thinke, according to the power that worketh in vs,

21 Be praise in the Church by Christ Iesus, throughout all generations for euer, Amen.

Ephesians 4

1 I therefore, being prisoner in the Lord, praie you that yee walke worthie of the vocation whereunto yee are called,

2 With all humblenesse of minde, and meekenesse, with long suffering, supporting one an other through loue,

3 Endeuouring to keepe the vnitie of the Spirit in the bond of peace.

4 There is one body, and one Spirit, euen as yee are called in one hope of your vocation.

5 There is one Lord, one Faith, one Baptisme,

6 One God and Father of all, which is aboue all, and through all, and in you all.

7 But vnto euery one of vs is giuen grace, according to the measure of the gift of Christ.

8 Wherfore he saith, Whe he asceded vp on hie, he led captiuity captiue, and gaue gifts vnto men.

9 (Nowe, in that hee ascended, what is it but that he had also descended first into the lowest partes of the earth?

10 Hee that descended, is euen the same that ascended, farre aboue all heauens, that hee might fill all things)

11 Hee therefore gaue some to be Apostles, and some Prophets, and some Euangelists, and some Pastours, and Teachers,

12 For the repairing of the Saintes, for the woorke of the ministerie, and for the edification of the bodie of Christ,

13 Till we all meete together (in the vnitie of faith and that acknowledging of the Sonne of God) vnto a perfite man, and vnto the measure of the age of the fulnesse of Christ,

14 That we henceforth be no more children, wauering and caried about

with euery winde of doctrine, by the deceit of men, and with craftines, whereby they lay in wait to deceiue.

15 But let vs folowe the truth in loue, and in all things, grow vp into him, which is the head, that is, Christ.

16 By whome al the body being coupled and knit together by euery ioynt, for ye furniture therof (according to the effectual power, which is in the measure of euery part) receiueth increase of the body, vnto the edifying of itselfe in loue.

17 This I say therefore and testifie in the Lord, that yee hencefoorth walke not as other Gentiles walke, in vanitie of their minde,

18 Hauing their vnderstanding darkened, and being strangers from the life of God through the ignorance that is in them, because of the hardnesse of their heart:

19 Which being past feeling, haue giuen themselues vnto wantonnesse, to woorke all vncleannesse, euen with griedinesse.

20 But yee haue not so learned Christ,

21 If so be yee haue heard him, and haue bene taught by him, as the trueth is in Iesus,

22 That is, that yee cast off, concerning the conuersation in time past, that olde man, which is corrupt through the deceiueable lustes,

23 And be renued in the spirit of your minde,

24 And put on ye new man, which after God is created vnto righteousnes, and true holines.

25 Wherefore cast off lying, and speake euery man truth vnto his neighbour: for we are members one of another.

26 Bee angrie, but sinne not: let not the sunne goe downe vpon your wrath,

27 Neither giue place to the deuill.

28 Let him that stole, steale no more: but let him rather labour, and worke with his handes the thing which is good, that hee may haue to giue vnto him that needeth.

29 Let no corrupt comunication proceed out of your mouths: but that which is good, to ye vse of edifying, that it may minister grace vnto the hearers.

30 And grieue not the holy Spirit of God, by whom ye are sealed vnto ye day of redemption.

31 Let all bitternesse, and anger, and wrath, crying, and euill speaking be put away from you, with all maliciousnesse.

32 Be ye courteous one to another, and tender hearted, freely forgiuing one another, euen as God for Christes sake, freely forgaue you.

Ephesians 5

1 Bee yee therefore followers of God, as deare children,

2 And walke in loue, euen as Christ hath loued vs, and hath giuen himselfe for vs, to be an offering and a sacrifice of a sweete smellling sauour to God.

3 But fornication, and all vncleannesse, or couetousnesse, let it not be once

named among you, as it becommeth Saintes,

4 Neither filthinesse, neither foolish talking, neither iesting, which are things not comely, but rather giuing of thankes.

5 For this ye know, that no whoremonger, neither vncleane person, nor couetous person, which is an idolater, hath any inheritance in the kingdome of Christ, and of God.

6 Let no man deceiue you with vaine wordes: for, for such thinges commeth the wrath of God vpon the children of disobedience.

7 Be not therefore companions with them.

8 For ye were once darkenesse, but are nowe light in the Lord: walke as children of light,

9 (For the fruit of the Spirit is in al goodnes, and righteousnes, and trueth)

10 Approuing that which is pleasing to the Lord.

11 And haue no fellowship with ye vnfruitfull works of darknes, but euen reproue them rather.

12 For it is shame euen to speake of the things which are done of them in secret.

13 But all thinges when they are reproued of the light, are manifest: for it is light that maketh all things manifest.

14 Wherefore hee sayeth, Awake thou that sleepest, and stande vp from the deade, and Christ shall giue thee light.

15 Take heede therefore that yee walke circumspectly, not as fooles, but as wise,

16 Redeeming ye season: for ye daies are euill.

17 Wherefore, be ye not vnwise, but vnderstand what the will of the Lord is.

18 And be not drunke with wine, wherein is excesse: but be fulfilled with the Spirit,

19 Speaking vnto your selues in psalmes, and hymnes, and spirituall songs, singing, and making melodie to the Lord in your hearts,

20 Giuing thankes alwaies for all things vnto God euen the Father, in the Name of our Lord Iesus Christ,

21 Submitting your selues one to another in the feare of God.

22 Wiues, submit your selues vnto your husbands, as vnto the Lord.

23 For the husband is the wiues head, euen as Christ is the head of the Church, and the same is the sauiour of his body.

24 Therfore as the Church is in subiection to Christ, euen so let the wiues be to their husbands in euery thing.

25 Husbands, loue your wiues, euen as Christ loued the Church, and gaue himselfe for it,

26 That hee might sanctifie it, and clense it by the washing of water through the worde,

27 That hee might make it vnto him selfe a glorious Church, not hauing spot or wrinkle, or any such thing: but that it shoulde bee holy and without blame.

28 So ought men to loue their wiues, as their owne bodies: he that loueth his wife, loueth him selfe.

29 For no man euer yet hated his owne flesh, but nourisheth and cherisheth it, euen as the Lord doeth the Church.

30 For we are members of his bodie, of his flesh, and of his bones.

31 For this cause shall a man leaue father and mother, and shall cleaue to his wife, and they twaine shalbe one flesh.

32 This is a great secrete, but I speake concerning Christ, and concerning the Church.

33 Therefore euery one of you, doe ye so: let euery one loue his wife, euen as himselfe, and let the wife see that shee feare her husband.

Ephesians 6

1 Children, obey your parents in the Lord: for this is right.

2 Honour thy father and mother (which is the first commandement with promise)

3 That it may be well with thee, and that thou mayst liue long on earth.

4 And ye, fathers, prouoke not your children to wrath: but bring them vp in instruction and information of the Lord.

5 Seruants, be obedient vnto them that are your masters, according to the flesh, with feare and trembling in singlenesse of your hearts as vnto Christ,

6 Not with seruice to the eye, as men pleasers, but as the seruants of Christ, doing the will of God from the heart,

7 With good will, seruing the Lord, and not men.

8 And knowe ye that whatsoeuer good thing any man doeth, that same shall he receiue of the Lord, whether he be bond or free.

9 And ye masters, doe the same things vnto them, putting away threatning: and know that euen your master also is in heauen, neither is there respect of person with him.

10 Finally, my brethren, be strong in the Lord, and in the power of his might.

11 Put on the whole armour of God, that ye may be able to stand against the assaultes of the deuil.

12 For we wrestle not against flesh and blood, but against principalities, against powers, and against the worldly gouernours, the princes of the darkenesse of this worlde, against spirituall wickednesses, which are in ye hie places.

13 For this cause take vnto you the whole armour of God, that ye may be able to resist in the euill day, and hauing finished all things, stand fast.

14 Stand therefore, and your loynes girded about with veritie, and hauing on the brest plate of righteousnesse,

15 And your feete shod with the preparation of the Gospel of peace.

16 Aboue all, take the shielde of faith, wherewith ye may quench all the fierie dartes of the wicked,

17 And take the helmet of saluation, and the sword of the Spirit, which is the worde of God.

18 And pray always with all maner prayer and supplication in the Spirit:

and watch thereunto with all perseuerance and supplication for al Saints,

19 And for me, that vtterance may be giuen vnto me, that I may open my mouth boldly to publish the secret of the Gospel,

20 Whereof I am the ambassadour in bonds, that therein I may speake boldely, as I ought to speake.

21 But that ye may also know mine affaires, and what I doe, Tychicus my deare brother and faithfull minister in the Lord, shall shewe you of all things,

22 Whom I haue sent vnto you for the same purpose, that ye might knowe mine affaires, and that he might comfort your hearts.

23 Peace be with the brethren, and loue with faith from God the Father, and from the Lord Iesus Christ.

24 Grace be with all them which loue our Lord Iesus Christ, to their immortalitie, Amen. Written from Rome vnto the Ephesians, and sent by Tychicus.

Philippians

Philippians 1

1 Paul and Timotheus the seruants of IESVS CHRIST, to all the Saintes in Christ Iesus which are at Philippi, with the Bishops, and Deacons:

2 Grace be with you, and peace from God our Father, and from the Lord Iesus Christ.

3 I thanke my God, hauing you in perfect memorie,

4 (Always in all my praiers for all you, praying with gladnesse)

5 Because of the fellowship which ye haue in the Gospel, from the first day vnto nowe.

6 And I am persuaded of this same thing, that he that hath begunne this good worke in you, wil perfourme it vntill the day of Iesus Christ,

7 As it becommeth me so to iudge of you all, because I haue you in remembrance that both in my bands, and in my defence, and confirmation of the Gospell you all were partakers of my grace.

8 For God is my recorde, howe I long after you all from the very heart roote in Iesus Christ.

9 And this I pray, that your loue may abound, yet more and more in knowledge, and in all iudgement,

10 That ye may alowe those things which are best, that ye may be pure, and without offence vntill the day of Christ,

11 Filled with the fruites of righteousnesse, which are by Iesus Christ vnto the glorie and praise of God.

12 I would ye vnderstood, brethren, that the things which haue come vnto me, are turned rather to the furthering of the Gospell,

13 So that my bandes in Christ are famous throughout all the iudgement hall, and in all other places,

14 In so much that many of the brethren in the Lord are boldened

through my bandes, and dare more frankely speake the word.

15 Some preache. Christ euen through enuie and strife, and some also of good will.

16 The one part preacheth Christ of contention and not purely, supposing to adde more affliction to my bandes.

17 But the others of loue, knowing that I am set for the defence of the Gospell.

18 What then? yet Christ is preached all maner wayes, whether it be vnder a pretence, or syncerely: and I therein ioye: yea and will ioye.

19 For I knowe that this shall turne to my saluation through your prayer, and by the helpe of the Spirit of Iesus Christ,

20 As I feruently looke for, and hope, that in nothing I shalbe ashamed, but that with all confidence, as alwayes, so nowe Christ shalbe magnified in my body, whether it be by life or by death.

21 For Christ is to me both in life, and in death aduantage.

22 And whether to liue in the flesh were profitable for me, and what to chuse I knowe not.

23 For I am distressed betweene both, desiring to be loosed and to be with Christ, which is best of all.

24 Neuerthelesse, to abide in the flesh, is more needefull for you.

25 And this am I sure of, that I shall abide, and with you all continue, for your furtherance and ioy of your faith,

26 That ye may more aboundantly reioyce in IESVS CHRIST for me, by my comming to you againe.

27 Onely let your conuersation be, as it becommeth the Gospel of Christ, that whether I come and see you, or els be absent, I may heare of your matters that ye continue in one Spirit, and in one mind, fighting together through the faith of the Gospel.

28 And in nothing feare your aduersaries, which is to them a token of perdition, and to you of saluation, and that of God.

29 For vnto you it is giuen for Christ, that not onely ye should beleeue in him, but also suffer for his sake,

30 Hauing the same fight, which ye sawe in me, and nowe heare to be in me.

Philippians 2

1 If there be therfore any consolation in Christ, if any comfort of loue, if any fellowship of the Spirit, if any compassion and mercie,

2 Fulfill my ioye, that ye be like minded, hauing the same loue, being of one accorde, and of one iudgement,

3 That nothing be done through contention or vaine glory, but that in meekenesse of minde euery man esteeme other better then himselfe.

4 Looke not euery man on his owne things, but euery man also on the things of other men.

5 Let the same minde be in you that was euen in Christ Iesus,

6 Who being in ye forme of God, thought it no robberie to be equall with God:

7 But he made himself of no reputation, and tooke on him ye forme of a seruant, and was made like vnto men, and was founde in shape as a man.

8 He humbled himselfe, and became obedient vnto the death, euen the death of the Crosse.

9 Wherefore God hath also highly exalted him, and giuen him a Name aboue euery name,

10 That at the Name of Iesus shoulde euery knee bowe, both of things in heauen, and things in earth, and things vnder the earth,

11 And that euery tongue shoulde confesse that Iesus Christ is the Lord, vnto the glory of God the Father.

12 Wherefore my beloued, as ye haue always obeyed me, not as in my presence only, but now much more in mine absence, so make an end of your owne saluation with feare and trembling.

13 For it is God which worketh in you, both the will and the deede, euen of his good pleasure.

14 Do all things without murmuring and reasonings,

15 That ye may be blamelesse, and pure, and the sonnes of God without rebuke in the middes of a naughtie and crooked nation, among whom yee shine as lights in the world,

16 Holding forth the worde of life, that I may reioyce in the day of Christ, that I haue not runne in vaine, neither haue laboured in vaine.

17 Yea, and though I bee offered vp vpon the sacrifice, and seruice of your faith, I am glad, and reioyce with you all.

18 For the same cause also be ye glad, and reioyce with me.

19 And I trust in the Lord Iesus, to sende Timotheus shortly vnto you, that I also may be of good comfort, when I knowe your state.

20 For I haue no man like minded, who will faithfully care for your matters.

21 For all seeke their owne, and not that which is Iesus Christes.

22 But yee knowe the proofe of him, that as a sonne with the father, hee hath serued with me in the Gospel.

23 Him therefore I hope to send assoone as I knowe howe it will goe with me,

24 And trust in the Lord, that I also my selfe shall come shortly.

25 But I supposed it necessarie to sende my brother Epaphroditus vnto you, my companion in labour, and fellowe souldier, euen your messenger, and he that ministred vnto me such things as I wanted.

26 For he longed after all you, and was full of heauinesse, because yee had heard that hee had beene sicke.

27 And no doubt he was sicke, very neere vnto death: but God had mercie on him, and not on him onely, but on me also, least I should haue sorowe vpon sorowe.

28 I sent him therefore the more diligently, that when yee shoulde see him againe, yee might reioyce, and I might be the lesse sorowfull.

29 Receiue him therefore in the Lord with all gladnesse, and make much of such:

30 Because that for the woorke of Christ he was neere vnto death, and regarded not his life, to fulfill that seruice which was lacking on your part towarde me.

Philippians 3

1 Moreouer, my brethren, reioyce in the Lord. It grieueth mee not to write the same things to you, and for you it is a sure thing.

2 Beware of dogges: beware of euil workers: beware of the concision.

3 For we are the circumcision, which worship God in the spirite, and reioyce in Christ Iesus, and haue no confidence in the flesh:

4 Though I might also haue confidence in the flesh. If any other man thinketh that he hath whereof he might trust in the flesh, much more I,

5 Circumcised the eight day, of the kinred of Israel, of the tribe of Beniamin, an Ebrewe of the Ebrewes, by the Lawe a Pharise.

6 Concerning zeale, I persecuted ye Church: touching the righteousnesse which is in the Law, I was vnrebukeable.

7 But the thinges that were vantage vnto me, the same I counted losse for Christes sake.

8 Yea, doubtlesse I thinke all thinges but losse for the excellent knowledge sake of Christ Iesus my Lord, for whome I haue counted all things losse, and doe iudge them to bee dongue, that I might winne Christ,

9 And might bee founde in him, that is, not hauing mine owne righteousnesse, which is of the Lawe, but that which is through the faith of Christ, euen the righteousnesse which is of God through faith,

10 That I may know him, and the vertue of his resurrection, and the fellowship of his afflictions, and be made conformable vnto his death,

11 If by any meanes I might attaine vnto the resurrection of the dead:

12 Not as though I had alreadie attained to it, either were alreadie perfect: but I follow, if that I may comprehend that for whose sake also I am comprehended of Christ Iesus.

13 Brethren, I count not my selfe, that I haue attained to it, but one thing I doe: I forget that which is behinde, and endeuour my selfe vnto that which is before,

14 And follow hard toward the marke, for the prise of the hie calling of God in Christ Iesus.

15 Let vs therefore as many as be perfect, be thus minded: and if yee be otherwise minded, God shall reueile euen the same vnto you.

16 Neuerthelesse, in that whereunto wee are come, let vs proceede by one rule, that wee may minde one thing.

17 Brethren, bee followers of mee, and looke on them, which walke so, as yee haue vs for an ensample.

18 For many walke, of whom I haue told you often, and nowe tell you weeping, that they are the enemies of the Crosse of Christ:

19 Whose ende is damnation, whose God is their bellie, and whose glorie is to their shame, which minde earthly things.

20 But our conuersation is in heauen, from whence also we looke for the Sauiour, euen the Lord Iesus Christ,

21 Who shall change our vile bodie, that it may be fashioned like vnto his glorious body, according to the working, whereby hee is able euen to subdue all things vnto him selfe.

Philippians 4

1 Therefore, my brethre, beloued and longed for, my ioy and my crowne, so continue in the Lord, yee beloued.

2 I pray Euodias, and beseech Syntyche, that they be of one accord in the Lord,

3 Yea, and I beseech thee, faithfull yokefellow, helpe those women, which laboured with me in the Gospel, with Clement also, and with other my fellowe labourers, whose names are in the booke of life.

4 Reioyce in the Lord alway, againe I say, reioyce.

5 Let your patient minde be knowen vnto all men. The Lord is at hand.

6 Be nothing carefull, but in all thinges let your requestes be shewed vnto God in praier, and supplication with giuing of thankes.

7 And the peace of God which passeth all vnderstanding, shall preserue your heartes and mindes in Christ Iesus.

8 Furthermore, brethre, whatsoeuer things are true, whatsoeuer things are honest, whatsoeuer thinges are iust, whatsoeuer thinges are pure, whatsoeuer thinges are worthie loue, whatsoeuer things are of good report, if there be any vertue, or if there be any praise, thinke on these things,

9 Which yee haue both learned and receiued, and heard, and seene in mee: those things doe, and the God of peace shalbe with you.

10 Nowe I reioyce also in the Lord greatly, that nowe at the last your care for mee springeth afresh, wherein notwithstanding ye were careful, but yee lacked opportunitie.

11 I speake not because of want: for I haue learned in whatsoeuer state I am, therewith to bee content.

12 And I can be abased, and I can abounde: euery where in all things I am instructed, both to be full, and to be hungrie, and to abounde, and to haue want.

13 I am able to do al things through the helpe of Christ, which strengtheneth me.

14 Notwithstanding yee haue well done, that yee did communicate to mine affliction.

15 And yee Philippians knowe also that in the beginning of the Gospell, when I departed from Macedonia, no Church communicated with me, concerning the matter of giuing and receiuing, but yee onely.

16 For euen when I was in Thessalonica, yee sent once, and afterward againe for my necessitie,

17 Not that I desire a gift: but I desire the fruit which may further your reckoning.

18 Now I haue receiued all, and haue plentie: I was euen filled, after that I had receiued of Epaphroditus that which came from you, an odour that smellleth sweete, a sacrifice acceptable and pleasant to God.

19 And my God shall fulfill all your necessities through his riches with glorie in Iesus Christ.

20 Vnto God euen our Father be praise for euermore, Amen.

21 Salute all the Saintes in Christ Iesus. The brethren, which are with me, greete you.

22 All the Saintes salute you, and most of all they which are of Cesars houshold.

23 The grace of our Lord Iesus Christ be with you all, Amen. Written to the Philippians from Rome, and sent by Epaphroditus.

Colossians

Colossians 1

1 Paul an Apostle of Iesus Christ, by the will of God, and Timotheus our brother,

2 To them which are at Colosse, Saintes and faithfull brethren in Christ: Grace bee with you, and peace from God our Father, and from the Lord Iesus Christ.

3 We giue thankes to God euen ye Father of our Lord Iesus Christ, alway praying for you:

4 Since wee heard of your faith in Christ Iesus, and of your loue toward all Saintes,

5 For the hopes sake, which is laide vp for you in heauen, whereof yee haue heard before by the word of trueth, which is the Gospel,

6 Which is come vnto you, eue as it is vnto al the world, and is fruitful, as it is also amog you, from ye day that ye heard and truely knew ye grace of God,

7 As yee also learned of Epaphras our deare fellowe seruaunt, which is for you a faithfull minister of Christ:

8 Who hath also declared vnto vs your loue in the Spirit.

9 For this cause wee also, since the day wee heard of it, cease not to pray for you, and to desire that ye might be fulfilled with knowledge of his will in all wisdome, and spirituall vnderstanding,

10 That ye might walke worthy of the Lord, and please him in all things, being fruitefull in all good workes, and increasing in the knowledge of God,

11 Strengthened with all might through his glorious power, vnto all patience, and long suffering with ioyfulnesse,

12 Giuing thankes vnto the Father, which hath made vs meete to be partakers of the inheritance of the Saintes in light,

13 Who hath deliuered vs from the power of darkenesse, and hath translated vs into the kingdome of his deare Sonne,

14 In whome we haue redemption through his blood, that is, the forgiuenesse of sinnes,

15 Who is the image of the inuisible God, the first begotten of euery creature.

16 For by him were all things created, which are in heauen, and which are in earth, thinges visible and inuisible: whether they be Thrones or Dominions, or Principalities, or Powers, all things were created by him, and for him,

17 And hee is before all things, and in him all things consist.

18 And hee is the head of the body of the Church: he is the beginning, and the first begotten of the dead, that in all thinges hee might haue the preeminence.

19 For it pleased the Father, that in him should all fulnesse dwell,

20 And through peace made by that blood of that his crosse, to reconcile to himselfe through him, through him, I say, all thinges, both which are in earth, and which are in heauen.

21 And you which were in times past strangers and enemies, because your mindes were set in euill workes, hath he nowe also reconciled,

22 In that body of his flesh through death, to make you holy, and vnblameable and without fault in his sight,

23 If ye continue, grounded and stablished in the faith, and be not moued away from the hope of the Gospel, whereof ye haue heard, and which hath bene preached to euery creature which is vnder heauen, whereof I Paul am a minister.

24 Now reioyce I in my suffrings for you, and fulfill the rest of the afflictions of Christ in my flesh, for his bodies sake, which is the Church,

25 Whereof I am a minister, according to the dispensation of God, which is giuen mee vnto you ward, to fulfill the word of God,

26 Which is the mysterie hid since the world began, and from all ages, but nowe is made manifest to his Saintes,

27 To whome God woulde make knowen what is the riches of his glorious mysterie among the Gentiles, which riches is Christ in you, the hope of glory,

28 Whome we preache, admonishing euery man, and teaching euery man in all wisdome, that we may present euery man perfect in Christ Iesus,

29 Whereunto I also labour and striue, according to his working which worketh in me mightily.

Colossians 2

1 For I woulde ye knewe what great fighting I haue for your sakes, and for them of Laodicea, and for as many as haue not seene my person in the flesh,

2 That their heartes might be comforted, and they knit together in loue, and in all

riches of the full assurance of vnderstanding, to know the mysterie of God, euen the Father, and of Christ:

3 In whom are hid all the treasures of wisedome and knowledge.

4 And this I say, lest any man shoulde beguile you with entising wordes:

5 For though I be absent in the flesh, yet am I with you in the spirit, reioycing and beholding your order, and your stedfast faith in Christ.

6 As ye haue therefore receiued Christ Iesus the Lord, so walke in him,

7 Rooted and built in him, and stablished in the faith, as ye haue bene taught, abouding therein with thankesgiuing.

8 Beware lest there be any man that spoile you through philosophie, and vaine deceit, through the traditions of men, according to the rudiments of the world, and not after Christ.

9 For in him dwelleth all the fulnesse of the Godhead bodily.

10 And yee are complete in him, which is the head of all principalitie and power.

11 In whome also yee are circumcised with circumcision made without handes, by putting off the sinfull body of the flesh, through the circumcision of Christ,

12 In that yee are buried with him through baptisme, in whome ye are also raised vp together through the faith of the operation of God, which raised him from the dead.

13 And you which were dead in sinnes, and in the vncircumcision of your flesh, hath he quickened together with him, forgiuing you all your trespasses,

14 And putting out the hand writing of ordinances that was against vs, which was contrarie to vs, hee euen tooke it out of the way, and fastened it vpon the crosse,

15 And hath spoyled the Principalities, and Powers, and hath made a shew of them openly, and hath triumphed ouer them in the same crosse.

16 Let no man therefore condemne you in meate and drinke, or in respect of an holy day, or of the newe moone, or of the Sabbath dayes,

17 Which are but a shadowe of thinges to come: but the body is in Christ.

18 Let no man at his pleasure beare rule ouer you by humblenesse of minde, and worshipping of Angels, aduauncing himselfe in those thinges which hee neuer sawe, rashly puft vp with his fleshly minde,

19 And holdeth not the head, whereof all the body furnished and knit together by ioyntes and bands, increaseth with the increasing of God.

20 Wherefore if ye be dead with Christ from the ordinances of the world, why, as though ye liued in ye world, are ye burdened with traditions?

21 As, Touch not, Taste not, Handle not.

22 Which al perish with the vsing, and are after the commandements and doctrines of men.

23 Which thinges haue in deede a shewe of wisdome, in voluntarie religion and humblenesse of minde, and in not sparing the body, which are thinges of no valewe, sith they perteine to the filling of the flesh.

Colossians 3

1 If yee then bee risen with Christ, seeke those thinges which are aboue, where Christ sitteth at the right hand of God.

2 Set your affections on things which are aboue, and not on things which are on the earth.

3 For ye are dead, and your life is hid with Christ in God.

4 When Christ which is our life, shall appeare, then shall ye also appeare with him in glory.

5 Mortifie therefore your members which are on the earth, fornication, vncleannes, the inordinate affection, euill concupiscence, and couetousnes which is idolatrie.

6 For the which things sake ye wrath of God commeth on the children of disobedience.

7 Wherein ye also walked once, when ye liued in them.

8 But now put ye away euen all these things, wrath, anger, maliciousnes, cursed speaking, filthie speaking, out of your mouth.

9 Lie not one to another, seeing that yee haue put off the olde man with his workes,

10 And haue put on the newe, which is renewed in knowledge after the image of him that created him,

11 Where is neither Grecian nor Iewe, circumcision nor vncircumcision, Barbarian, Scythian, bond, free: But Christ is all, and in all things.

12 Now therfore as the elect of God holy and beloued, put on the bowels of mercies, kindnesse, humblenesse of minde, meekenesse, long suffering:

13 Forbearing one another, and forgiuing one another, if any man haue a quarel to another: euen as Christ forgaue, euen so doe ye.

14 And aboue all these things put on loue, which is the bond of perfectnes.

15 And let the peace of God rule in your hearts, to the which ye are called in one body, and be ye thankfull.

16 Let the worde of Christ dwell in you plenteously in all wisdome, teaching and admonishing your owne selues, in Psalmes, and hymnes, and spirituall songs, singing with a grace in your hearts to the Lord.

17 And whatsoeuer ye shall doe, in worde or deede, doe all in the Name of the Lord Iesus, giuing thankes to God euen the Father by him.

18 Wiues, submit your selues vnto your husbands, as it is comely in the Lord.

19 Husbands, loue your wiues, and be not bitter vnto them.

20 Children, obey your parents in all thing for that is well pleasing vnto the Lord.

21 Fathers, prouoke not your children to anger, least they be discouraged.

22 Seruants, be obedient vnto them that are your masters according to the flesh, in all things, not with eye seruice as men pleasers, but in singlenes of heart, fearing God.

23 And whatsoeuer ye doe, doe it heartily, as to the Lord, and not to men,

24 Knowing that of the Lord ye shall receiue the reward of the inheritance: for ye serue the Lord Christ.

25 But he that doeth wrong, shall receiue for the wrong that he hath done: and there is no respect of persons.

Colossians 4

1 Ye masters, doe vnto your seruants, that which is iust, and equall, knowing that ye also haue a master in heauen.

2 Continue in prayer, and watch in the fame with thankesgiuing,

3 Praying also for vs, that God may open vnto vs the doore of vtterance, to speake ye mysterie of Christ: wherefore I am also in bonds,

4 That I may vtter it, as it becommeth mee to speake.

5 Walke wisely towarde them that are without, and redeeme the season.

6 Let your speach be gracious alwayes, and powdred with salt, that ye may know how to answere euery man.

7 Tychicus our beloued brother and faithfull minister, and fellow seruant in the Lord, shall declare vnto you my whole state:

8 Whom I haue sent vnto you for the same purpose that he might know your state, and might comfort your hearts,

9 With Onesimus a faithfull and a beloued brother, who is one of you. They shall shew you of all things here.

10 Aristarchus my prison fellow saluteth you, and Marcus, Barnabas cousin (touching whom ye receiued commandements. If he come vnto you, receiue him)

11 And Iesus which is called Iustus, which are of the circumcision. These onely are my worke fellowes vnto the kingdome of God, which haue bene vnto my consolation.

12 Epaphras the seruant of Christ, which is one of you, saluteth you, and alwayes striueth for you in prayers, that ye may stand perfect, and full in all the will of God.

13 For I beare him record, that he hath a great zeale for you, and for them of Laodicea, and them of Hierapolis.

14 Luke the beloued physician greeteth you, and Demas.

15 Salute the brethren which are of Laodicea, and Nymphas, and the Church which is in his house.

16 And when this Epistle is read of you, cause that it be read in the Church of the Laodiceans also, and that ye likewise reade the Epistle written from Laodicea.

17 And say to Archippus, Take heede to the ministerie, that thou hast receiued in the Lord, that thou fulfill it.

18 The salutation by the hand of me Paul. Remember my bands. Grace be with you, Amen. Written from Rome to

the Colossians, and sent by Tychicus, and Onesimus.

First Thessalonians

First Thessalonians 1

1 Pavl, and Siluanus, and Timotheus, vnto the Church of the Thessalonians, which is in God the Father, and in the Lord Iesus Christ: Grace be with you, and peace from God our Father, and from the Lord Iesus Christ.

2 We giue God thankes alwayes for you all, making mention of you in our prayers

3 Without ceasing, remembring your effectuall faith, and diligent loue, and the patience of your hope in our Lord Iesus Christ, in the sight of God euen our Father,

4 Knowing, beloued brethren, that ye are elect of God.

5 For our Gospell was not vnto you in worde only, but also in power, and in the holy Ghost, and in much assurance, as ye know after what maner we were among you for your sakes.

6 And ye became followers of vs, and of the Lord, and receiued the worde in much affliction, with ioy of the holy Ghost,

7 So that ye were as ensamples to all that beleeue in Macedonia and in Achaia.

8 For from you sounded out the worde of the Lord, not in Macedonia and in Achaia only: but your faith also which is toward God, spred abroad in all quarters, that we neede not to speake any thing.

9 For they themselues shew of vs what maner of entring in we had vnto you, and how ye turned to God from idoles, to serue the liuing and true God,

10 And to looke for his sonne from heauen, whome he raised from the dead, euen Iesus which deliuereth vs from that wrath to come.

First Thessalonians 2

1 For ye your selues knowe, brethren, that our entrance in vnto you was not in vaine,

2 But euen after that we had suffered before, and were shamefully entreated at Philippi, (as ye knowe) we were bolde in our God, to speake vnto you the Gospell of God with much striuing.

3 For our exhortation was not by deceite, nor by vncleannes, nor by guile.

4 But as we were allowed of God, that the Gospel should be committed vnto vs, so we speake, not as they that please men, but God, which approoueth our hearts.

5 Neither yet did we euer vse flattering wordes, as ye knowe, nor coloured couetousnes, God is recorde.

6 Neither sought we prayse of men, neither of you, nor of others, when we might haue bene chargeable, as the Apostles of Christ.

7 But we were gentle among you, euen as a nource cherisheth her children.

8 Thus being affectioned toward you, our good will was to haue dealt vnto you, not the Gospel of God onely, but also our owne soules, because ye were deare vnto vs.

9 For ye remember, brethren, our labour and trauaile: for we laboured day and night, because we would not be chargeable vnto any of you, and preached vnto you the Gospel of God.

10 Ye are witnesses, and God also, how holily, and iustly, and vnblameably we behaued our selues among you that beleeue.

11 As ye knowe how that we exhorted you, and comforted, and besought euery one of you (as a father his children)

12 That ye would walke worthy of God, who hath called you vnto his kingdome and glorie.

13 For this cause also thanke we God without ceasing, that when ye receiued the worde of God, which ye heard of vs, ye receiued it not as the worde of men, but as it is in deede the worde of God, which also worketh in you that beleeue.

14 For brethren, ye are become folowers of the Churches of God, which in Iudea are in Christ Iesus, because ye haue also suffred the same things of your owne countrey men, euen as they haue of the Iewes,

15 Who both killed the Lord Iesus and their owne Prophets, and haue persecuted vs away, and God they please not, and are contrary to all men,

16 And forbid vs to preach vnto the Gentiles, that they might be saued, to fulfill their sinnes alwayes: for the wrath of God is come on them, to the vtmost.

17 For asmuch, brethren, as we were kept from you for a season, concerning sight, but not in the heart, we enforced the more to see your face with great desire.

18 Therefore we would haue come vnto you (I Paul, at least once or twise) but Satan hindered vs.

19 For what is our hope or ioye, or crowne of reioycing? are not euen you it in the presence of our Lord Iesus Christ at his comming?

20 Yea, ye are our glory and ioy.

First Thessalonians 3

1 Wherefore since we could no longer forbare, wee thought it good to remaine at Athens alone,

2 And haue sent Timotheus our brother and minister of God, and our labour felow in the Gospel of Christ, to stablish you, and to comfort you touching your faith,

3 That no man should be moued with these afflictions: for ye your selues knowe, that we are appointed thereunto.

4 For verily when we were with you, we told you before that we should suffer tribulations, euen as it came to passe, and ye knowe it.

5 Euen for this cause, when I could no longer forbeare, I sent him that I might knowe of your faith, lest the tempter had tempted you in any sort, and that our labour had bene in vaine.

6 But now lately when Timotheus came from you vnto vs, and brought vs good tidings of your faith and loue, and that ye haue good remembrance of vs always, desiring to see vs, as we also do you,

7 Therefore, brethren, we had consolation in you, in all our affliction and necessitie through your faith.

8 For nowe are wee aliue, if ye stand fast in the Lord.

9 For what thankes can wee recompense to God againe for you, for all the ioy wherewith we reioyce for your sakes before our God,

10 Night and day, praying exceedingly that wee might see your face, and might accomplish that which is lacking in your faith?

11 Nowe God himselfe, euen our Father, and our Lord Iesus Christ, guide our iourney vnto you,

12 And the Lord increase you, and make you abound in loue one toward another, and towarde all men, euen as we doe toward you:

13 To make your hearts stable and vnblameable in holines before God euen our Father, at the comming of our Lord Iesus Christ with all his Saints.

First Thessalonians 4

1 And furthermore we beseeche you, brethren, and exhort you in the Lord Iesus, that ye increase more and more, as ye haue receiued of vs, how ye ought to walke, and to please God.

2 For ye knowe what commandements we gaue you by the Lord Iesus.

3 For this is the will of God euen your sanctification, and that ye should abstaine from fornication,

4 That euery one of you should know, how to possesse his vessell in holines and honour,

5 And not in the lust of concupiscence, euen as the Gentiles which know not God:

6 That no man oppresse or defraude his brother in any matter: for the Lord is auenger of all such thinges, as we also haue tolde you before time, and testified.

7 For God hath not called vs vnto vncleannesse, but vnto holinesse.

8 Hee therefore that despiseth these thinges, despiseth not man, but God who hath euen giuen you his holy Spirit.

9 But as touching brotherly loue, ye neede not that I write vnto you: for ye are taught of God to loue one another.

10 Yea, and that thing verily yee doe vnto all the brethren, which are throughout all Macedonia: but we beseech you, brethren, that ye increase more and more,

11 And that ye studie to be quiet, and to meddle with your owne busines, and to worke with your owne handes, as we commanded you,

12 That yee may behaue your selues honestly towarde them that are without, and that nothing be lacking vnto you.

13 I would not, brethren, haue you ignorant concerning them which are a sleepe, that ye sorow not euen as other which haue no hope.

14 For if we beleeue that Iesus is dead, and is risen, euen so them which sleepe in Iesus, will God bring with him.

15 For this say we vnto you by the worde of the Lord, that we which liue, and are remayning in the comming of the Lord, shall not preuent them which sleepe.

16 For the Lord himselfe shall descende from heauen with a shoute, and with the voyce of the Archangel, and with the trumpet of God: and the dead in Christ shall rise first:

17 Then shall we which liue and remaine, be caught vp with them also in the clouds, to meete the Lord in the ayre: and so shall we euer be with the Lord.

18 Wherefore, comfort your selues one another with these wordes.

First Thessalonians 5

1 Bvt of the times and seasons, brethren, yee haue no neede that I write vnto you.

2 For ye your selues knowe perfectly, that the day of the Lord shall come, euen as a thiefe in the night.

3 For when they shall say, Peace, and safetie, then shall come vpon them sudden destruction, as the trauaile vpon a woman with childe, and they shall not escape,

4 But ye, brethren, are not in darkenes, that that day shall come on you, as it were a thiefe.

5 Yee are all the children of light, and the children of the day: we are not of the night, neither of darkenesse.

6 Therefore let vs not sleepe as do other, but let vs watch and be sober.

7 For they that sleepe, sleepe in the night, and they that be drunken, are drunken in the night.

8 But let vs which are of the day, be sober, putting on the brest plate of faith and loue, and of the hope of saluation for an helmet.

9 For God hath not appointed vs vnto wrath, but to obtaine saluation by the meanes of our Lord Iesus Christ,

10 Which died for vs, that whether we wake or sleepe, we should liue together with him.

11 Wherefore exhort one another, and edifie one another, euen as ye doe.

12 Nowe we beseeche you, brethren, that ye acknowledge them, which labour among you, and are ouer you in the Lord, and admonish you,

13 That yee haue them in singular loue for their workes sake. Bee at peace among your selues.

14 We desire you, brethren, admonish them that are out of order: comfort ye feeble minded: beare with the weake: be pacient toward all men.

15 See that none recompense euil for euil vnto any man: but euer follow that which is good, both toward your selues, and toward all men.

16 Reioyce euermore.

17 Pray continually.

18 In all thinges giue thankes: for this is the will of God in Christ Iesus toward you.

19 Quench not the Spirit.

20 Despise not prophecying.

21 Try all things, and keepe that which is good.

22 Absteine from all appearance of euill.

23 Nowe the very God of peace sanctifie you throughout: and I pray God that your whole spirite and soule and body, may be kept blamelesse vnto the comming of our Lord Iesus Christ.

24 Faithfull is hee which calleth you, which will also doe it.

25 Brethren, pray for vs.

26 Greete all the brethren with an holy kisse.

27 I charge you in the Lord, that this Epistle be read vnto all the brethren the Saintes.

28 The grace of our Lord Iesus Christ be with you, Amen. The first Epistle vnto the Thessalonians written from Athens.

Second Thessalonians

Second Thessalonians 1

1 Paul and Siluanus, and Timotheus, vnto the Church of the Thessalonians, which is in God our Father, and in the Lord Iesus Christ:

2 Grace be with you, and peace from God our Father, and from the Lord Iesus Christ.

3 We ought to thanke God alwayes for you, brethren, as it is meete, because that your faith groweth exceedingly, and the loue of euery one of you toward another, aboundeth,

4 So that we our selues reioyce of you in the Churches of God, because of your patience and faith in al your persecutions and tribulatios that ye suffer,

5 Which is a manifest token of the righteous iudgement of God, that ye may be counted worthy of the kingdome of God, for the which ye also suffer.

6 For it is a righteous thing with God, to recompense tribulation to them that trouble you,

7 And to you which are troubled, rest with vs, when the Lord Iesus shall shewe himselfe from heauen with his mightie Angels,

8 In flaming fire, rendring vengeance vnto them, that doe not know God, and which obey not vnto the Gospel of our Lord Iesus Christ,

9 Which shall be punished with euerlasting perdition, from the presence of the Lord, and from the glory of his power,

10 When he shall come to be glorified in his Saints, and to be made marueilous in all them that beleeue (because our testimonie toward you was beleeued) in that day.

11 Wherefore, we also pray alwayes for you, that our God may make you worthy of this calling, and fulfill all the good pleasure of his goodnes, and the worke of faith with power,

12 That the Name of our Lord Iesus Christ may be glorified in you, and ye in him, according to the grace of our God, and of the Lord Iesus Christ.

Second Thessalonians 2

1 Now we beseech you, brethren, by the comming of our Lord Iesus Christ, and by our assembling vnto him,

2 That ye be not suddenly mooued from your minde, nor troubled neither by spirit, nor by worde, nor by letter, as it were from vs, as though the day of Christ were at hand.

3 Let no man deceiue you by any meanes: for that day shall not come, except there come a departing first, and that that man of sinne be disclosed, euen the sonne of perdition,

4 Which is an aduersarie, and exalteth him selfe against all that is called God, or that is worshipped: so that he doeth sit as God in the Temple of God, shewing him selfe that he is God.

5 Remember ye not, that when I was yet with you, I tolde you these things?

6 And nowe ye knowe what withholdeth that he might be reueiled in his time.

7 For the mysterie of iniquitie doeth already worke: onely he which nowe withholdeth, shall let till he be taken out of the way.

8 And then shall that wicked man be reueiled, whome the Lord shall consume with the Spirit of his mouth, and shall abolish with the brightnes of his comming,

9 Euen him whose comming is by the effectuall working of Satan, with all power, and signes, and lying wonders,

10 And in al deceiuablenes of vnrighteousnes, among them that perish, because they receiued not the loue of the trueth, that they might be saued.

11 And therefore God shall send them strong delusion, that they should beleeue lies,

12 That all they might be damned which beleeued not the trueth, but had pleasure in vnrighteousnes.

13 But we ought to giue thankes alway to God for you, brethren beloued of the Lord, because that God hath from the beginning chosen you to saluation, through sanctification of the Spirit, and the faith of trueth,

14 Whereunto he called you by our Gospel, to obtaine the glory of our Lord Iesus Christ.

15 Therefore, brethren, stand fast and keepe the instructions, which ye haue bene taught, either by worde, or by our Epistle.

16 Now the same Iesus Christ our Lord; and our God euen the Father which hath loued vs, and hath giuen vs euerlasting consolation and good hope through grace,

17 Comfort your hearts, and stablish you in euery word and good worke.

Second Thessalonians 3

1 Furthermore, brethren, pray for vs, that the worde of the Lord may haue free passage and be glorified, euen as it is with you,

2 And that we may be deliuered from vnreasonable and euill men: for all men haue not fayth.

3 But the Lord is faithfull, which wil stablish you, and keepe you from euill.

4 And we are perswaded of you through the Lord, that ye both doe, and will doe the things which we warne you of.

5 And the Lord guide your hearts to the loue of God, and the waiting for of Christ.

6 We warne you, brethren, in the Name of our Lord Iesus Christ, that ye withdrawe your selues from euery brother that walketh inordinately, and not after the instruction, which hee receiued of vs.

7 For ye your selues know, how ye ought to follow vs: for we behaued not our selues inordinately among you,

8 Neither tooke we bread of any man for nought: but we wrought with labour and trauaile night and day, because we would not be chargeable to any of you.

9 Not because we haue not authoritie, but that we might make our selues an ensample vnto you to follow vs.

10 For euen when we were with you, this we warned you of, that if there were any, which would not worke, that he should not eate.

11 For we heare, that there are some which walke among you inordinately, and worke not at all, but are busie bodies.

12 Therefore them that are such, we warne and exhort by our Lord Iesus Christ, that they worke with quietnes, and eate their owne bread.

13 And ye, brethren, be not weary in well doing.

14 If any man obey not this our saying in this letter, note him, and haue no company with him, that he may be ashamed:

15 Yet count him not as an enemie, but admonish him as a brother.

16 Now the Lord himselfe of peace giue you peace alwayes by all meanes. The Lord be with you all.

17 The salutation of me Paul, with mine owne hand, which is ye token in euery Epistle: so I write,

18 The grace of our Lord Iesus Christ be with you all, Amen. The second Epistle to the Thessalonians, written from Athens.

First Timothy

First Timothy 1

1 Pavl an Apostle of Iesvs Christ, by the commandement of God our Sauiour, and of our Lord Iesus Christ our hope,

2 Vnto Timotheus my naturall sonne in the faith: Grace, mercy, and peace from God our Father, and from Christ Iesus our Lord.

3 As I besought thee to abide still in Ephesus, when I departed into Macedonia, so doe, that thou mayest warne some, that they teach none other doctrine,

4 Neither that they giue heede to fables and genealogies which are endles, which breede questions rather then godly edifying which is by fayth.

5 For the end of the commandement is loue out of a pure heart, and of a good conscience, and of faith vnfained.

6 From the which things some haue erred, and haue turned vnto vaine iangling.

7 They would be doctours of the Law, and yet vnderstande not what they speake, neither whereof they affirme.

8 And we knowe, that the Law is good, if a man vse it lawfully,

9 Knowing this, that the Lawe is not giuen vnto a righteous man, but vnto the lawles and disobedient, to the vngodly, and to sinners, to the vnholy, and to the prophane, to murtherers of fathers and mothers, to manslayers,

10 To whoremongers, to buggerers, to menstealers, to lyers, to the periured, and if there be any other thing, that is contrary to wholesome doctrine,

11 Which is according to the glorious Gospel of the blessed God, which is committed vnto me.

12 Therefore I thanke him, which hath made me strong, that is, Christ Iesus our Lord: for he counted me faithfull, and put me in his seruice:

13 When before I was a blasphemer, and a persecuter, and an oppresser: but I was receiued to mercie: for I did it ignorantly through vnbeliefe.

14 But the grace of our Lord was exceeding abundant with faith and loue, which is in Christ Iesus.

15 This is a true saying, and by all meanes worthy to be receiued, that Christ Iesus came into the worlde to saue sinners, of whom I am chiefe.

16 Notwithstanding, for this cause was I receiued to mercie, that Iesus Christ should first shewe on me all long suffering vnto the ensample of them, which shall in time to come beleeue in him vnto eternall life.

17 Nowe vnto the King euerlasting, immortall, inuisible, vnto God onely wise, be honour and glorie, for euer, and euer, Amen.

18 This commandement commit I vnto thee, sonne Timotheus, according to the prophecies, which went before vpon thee, that thou by them shouldest fight a good fight,

19 Hauing faith and a good conscience, which some haue put away, and as concerning faith, haue made shipwracke.

20 Of whom is Hymeneus, and Alexander, whom I haue deliuered vnto Satan, that they might learne not to blaspheme.

First Timothy 2

1 I Exhort therefore, that first of all supplications, prayers, intercessions, and giuing of thanks be made for all men,

2 For Kings, and for all that are in authoritie, that we may leade a quiet and a peaceable life, in all godlinesse and honestie.

3 For this is good and acceptable in the sight of God our Sauiour,

4 Who will that all men shalbe saued, and come vnto the acknowledging of the trueth.

5 For there is one God, and one Mediatour betweene God and man, which is the man Christ Iesus,

6 Who gaue himselfe a ransome for all men, to be that testimonie in due time,

7 Whereunto I am ordeined a preacher and an Apostle (I speake the trueth in Christ, and lie not) euen a teacher of the Gentiles in faith and veritie.

8 I will therefore that the men pray, euery where lifting vp pure hands without wrath, or douting.

9 Likewise also the women, that they aray themselues in comely apparell, with shamefastnes and modestie, not with broyded heare, or gold, or pearles, or costly apparell,

10 But (as becommeth women that professe the feare of God) with good workes.

11 Let the woman learne in silence with all subiection.

12 I permit not a woman to teache, neither to vsurpe authoritie ouer the man, but to be in silence.

13 For Adam was first formed, then Eue.

14 And Adam was not deceiued, but the woman was deceiued, and was in the transgression.

15 Notwithstanding, through bearing of children she shalbe saued if they continue in faith, and loue, and holines with modestie.

First Timothy 3

1 This is a true saying, If any man desire the office of a Bishop, he desireth a worthie worke.

2 A Bishop therefore must be vnreproueable, the husband of one wife, watching, temperate, modest, harberous, apt to teache,

3 Not giuen to wine, no striker, not giuen to filthy lucre, but gentle, no fighter, not couetous,

4 One that can rule his owne house honestly, hauing children vnder obedience with all honestie.

5 For if any cannot rule his owne house, how shall he care for the Church of God?

6 He may not be a yong scholer, lest he being puffed vp fall into the condemnation of the deuill.

7 He must also be well reported of, euen of them which are without, lest he fall into rebuke, and the snare of the deuill.

8 Likewise must Deacons be graue, not double tongued, not giuen vnto much wine, neither to filthy lucre,

9 Hauing the mysterie of the faith in pure conscience.

10 And let them first be proued: then let them minister, if they be found blameles.

11 Likewise their wiues must be honest, not euill speakers, but sober, and faithfull in all things.

12 Let the Deacons be the husbands of one wife, and such as can rule their children well, and their owne housholdes.

13 For they that haue ministred well, get them selues a good degree, and great libertie in the faith, which is in Christ Iesus.

14 These things write I vnto thee, trusting to come very shortly vnto thee.

15 But if I tary long, that thou maist yet know, how thou oughtest to behaue thy self in ye house of God, which is the Church of the liuing God, the pillar and ground of trueth.

16 And without controuersie, great is the mysterie of godlinesse, which is, God is manifested in the flesh, iustified in the Spirit, seene of Angels, preached vnto the Gentiles, beleeued on in the world, and receiued vp in glorie.

First Timothy 4

1 Now the Spirit speaketh euidently, that in the latter times some shall depart from the faith, and shall giue heede vnto spirits of errour, and doctrines of deuils,

2 Which speake lies through hypocrisie, and haue their cosciences burned with an hote yron,

3 Forbidding to marrie, and commanding to abstaine from meates which God hath created to be receiued with giuing thankes of them which beleeue and knowe the trueth.

4 For euery creature of God is good, and nothing ought to be refused, if it be receiued with thankesgiuing.

5 For it is sanctified by the worde of God, and prayer.

6 If thou put the brethren in remembrance of these things, thou shalt be a good minister of Iesus Christ, which hast bene nourished vp in the wordes of faith, and of good doctrine, which thou hast continually followed.

7 But cast away prophane, and olde wiues fables, and exercise thy selfe vnto godlinesse.

8 For bodily exercise profiteth litle: but godlinesse is profitable vnto all things, which hath the promise of the life present, and of that that is to come.

9 This is a true saying, and by all meanes worthie to be receiued.

10 For therefore we labour and are rebuked, because we trust in the liuing God, which is the Sauiour of all men, specially of those that beleeue.

11 These things warne and teache.

12 Let no man despise thy youth, but be vnto them that beleeue, an ensample, in worde, in conuersation, in loue, in spirit, in faith, and in purenesse.

13 Till I come, giue attendance to reading, to exhortation, and to doctrine.

14 Despise not the gift that is in thee, which was giuen thee by prophecie with the laying on of the hands of the companie of the Eldership.

15 These things exercise, and giue thy selfe vnto them, that it may be seene howe thou profitest among all men.

16 Take heede vnto thy selfe, and vnto learning: continue therein: for in doing this thou shalt both saue thy selfe, and them that heare thee.

First Timothy 5

1 Rebuke not an Elder, but exhort him as a father, and the yonger men as brethren,

2 The elder women as mothers, the yonger as sisters, with all purenesse.

3 Honour widowes, which are widowes in deede.

4 But if any widowe haue children or nephewes, let them learne first to shewe godlinesse towarde their owne house, and to recompense their kinred: for that is an honest thing and acceptable before God.

5 And shee that is a widowe in deede and left alone, trusteth in God, and continueth in supplications and praiers night and day.

6 But shee that liueth in pleasure, is dead, while shee liueth.

7 These things therefore warne them of, that they may be blamelesse.

8 If there bee any that prouideth not for his owne, and namely for them of his housholde, hee denieth the faith, and is worse then an infidell.

9 Let not a widow be taken into the number vnder three score yeere olde, that hath beene the wife of one husband,

10 And well reported of for good woorkes: if shee haue nourished her children, if shee haue lodged the strangers, if shee haue washed the Saintes feete, if shee haue ministred vnto them which were in aduersitie, if shee were continually giuen vnto euery good woorke.

11 But refuse the yonger widowes: for when they haue begun to waxe wanton against Christ, they will marrie,

12 Hauing damnation, because they haue broken the first faith.

13 And likewise also being idle they learne to goe about from house to house: yea, they are not onely ydle, but also pratlers and busibodies, speaking things which are not comely.

14 I will therefore that the yonger women marie, and beare children, and gouerne the house, and giue none occasion to the aduersary to speake euill.

15 For certaine are alreadie turned backe after Satan.

16 If any faithfull man, or faithfull woman haue widowes, let them minister vnto them, and let not the Church bee charged, that there may bee sufficient for them that are widowes in deede.

17 The Elders that rule well, let them be had in double honour, specially they which labour in the worde and doctrine,

18 For the Scripture sayeth, Thou shalt not mousell the mouth of the oxe that treadeth out the corne: and, The labourer is worthie of his wages.

19 Against an Elder receiue none accusation, but vnder two or three witnesses.

20 Them that sinne, rebuke openly, that the rest also may feare.

21 I charge thee before God and the Lord Iesus Christ, and the elect Angels, that thou obserue these thinges without preferring one to an other, and doe nothing partially.

22 Lay handes suddenly on no man, neither be partaker of other mens sinnes: keepe thy selfe pure.

23 Drinke no longer water, but vse a litle wine for thy stomakes sake, and thine often infirmities.

24 Some mens sinnes are open before hand, and goe before vnto iudgement: but some mens folowe after.

25 Likewise also the good woorkes are manifest before hande, and they that are otherwise, cannot be hid.

First Timothy 6

1 Let as many seruaunts as are vnder the yoke, count their masters worthie of all honour, that the Name of God, and his doctrine be not euill spoken of.

2 And they which haue beleeuing masters, let them not despise them, because they are brethren, but rather doe seruice, because they are faithfull, and beloued, and partakers of the benefite. These things teach and exhort.

3 If any man teach otherwise, and consenteth not to the wholesome wordes of our Lord Iesus Christ, and to the doctrine, which is according to godlinesse,

4 He is puft vp and knoweth nothing, but doteth about questions and strife of words, whereof commeth enuie, strife, railings, euill surmisings,

5 Frowarde disputations of men of corrupt mindes and destitute of ye trueth, which thinke that gaine is godlines: from such separate thy selfe.

6 But godlinesse is great gaine, if a man be content with that he hath.

7 For we brought nothing into the world, and it is certaine, that we can carie nothing out.

8 Therefore when wee haue foode and raiment, let vs therewith be content.

9 For they that will be rich, fall into tentation and snares, and into many foolish and noysome lustes, which drowne men in perdition and destruction.

10 For the desire of money is the roote of all euill, which while some lusted after, they erred from the faith, and pearced themselues through with many sorowes.

11 But thou, O man of God, flee these things, and follow after righteousnesse, godlines, faith, loue, patience, and meekenes.

12 Fight the good fight of faith: lay holde of eternal life, whereunto thou art also

called, and hast professed a good profession before many witnesses.

13 I charge thee in the sight of God, who quickeneth all thinges, and before Iesus Christ, which vnder Pontius Pilate witnessed a good confession,

14 That thou keepe this commandement without spot, and vnrebukeable, vntill the appearing of our Lord Iesus Christ,

15 Which in due time hee shall shewe, that is blessed and Prince onely, the King of Kings and Lord of Lordes,

16 Who onely hath immortalitie, and dwelleth in the light that none can attaine vnto, whom neuer man sawe, neither can see, vnto whome bee honour and power euerlasting, Amen.

17 Charge them that are rich in this world, that they be not high minded, and that they trust not in vncertaine riches, but in the liuing God, (which giueth vs aboundantly, all things to enioy)

18 That they doe good, and be riche in good woorkes, and readie to distribute, and comunicate,

19 Laying vp in store for themselues a good foundation against the time to come, that they may obteine eternall life.

20 O Timotheus, keepe that which is committed vnto thee, and auoide prophane and vaine babblings, and oppositios of science falsely so called,

21 Which while some professe, they haue erred concerning the faith. Grace be with thee, Amen. The first Epistle to Timotheus, written from Laodicea, which is the chiefest citie of Phrygia Pacaciana.

Second Timothy

Second Timothy 1

1 Paul an Apostle of Iesus Christ, by the will of God, according to the promise of life which is in Christ Iesus,

2 To Timotheus my beloued sonne: Grace, mercie and peace from God the Father, and from Iesus Christ our Lord.

3 I thanke God, whom I serue from mine elders with pure conscience, that without ceasing I haue remembrance of thee in my praiers night and day,

4 Desiring to see thee, mindefull of thy teares, that I may be filled with ioy:

5 When I call to remembrance the vnfained faith that is in thee, which dwelt first in thy grandmother Lois, and in thy mother Eunice, and am assured that it dwelleth in thee also.

6 Wherefore, I put thee in remembrance that thou stirre vp the gift of God which is in thee, by the putting on of mine hands.

7 For God hath not giuen to vs the Spirite of feare, but of power, and of loue, and of a sound minde.

8 Be not therefore ashamed of the testimonie of our Lord, neither of me his prisoner: but be partaker of the afflictions of the Gospel, according to the power of God,

9 Who hath saued vs, and called vs with an holy calling, not according to our workes, but according to his owne

purpose and grace, which was giuen to vs through Christ Iesus before the world was,

10 But is nowe made manifest by that appearing of our Sauiour Iesus Christ, who hath abolished death, and hath brought life and immortalitie vnto light through the Gospel.

11 Whereunto I am appointed a preacher, and Apostle, and a teacher of the Gentiles.

12 For the which cause I also suffer these things, but I am not ashamed: for I knowe whom I haue beleeued, and I am persuaded that he is able to keepe that which I haue committed to him against that day.

13 Keepe the true paterne of the wholesome wordes, which thou hast heard of me in faith and loue which is in Christ Iesus.

14 That worthie thing, which was committed to thee, keepe through the holy Ghost, which dwelleth in vs.

15 This thou knowest, that all they which are in Asia, be turned from me: of which sort are Phygellus and Hermogenes.

16 The Lord giue mercie vnto the house of Onesiphorus: for he oft refreshed me, and was not ashamed of my chaine,

17 But when he was at Rome, he sought me out very diligently, and found me.

18 The Lord graunt vnto him, that he may finde mercie with the Lord at that day, and in how many things he hath ministred vnto me at Ephesus, thou knowest very well.

Second Timothy 2

1 Thou therefore, my sonne, be strong in the grace that is in Christ Iesus.

2 And what things thou hast heard of me, by many witnesses, ye same deliuer to faithfull men, which shalbe able to teache other also.

3 Thou therefore suffer affliction as a good souldier of Iesus Christ.

4 No man that warreth, entangleth himselfe with the affaires of this life, because he woulde please him that hath chosen him to be a souldier.

5 And if any man also striue for a Masterie, he is not crowned, except he striue as he ought to doe.

6 The husbandman must labour before he receiue the fruites.

7 Consider what I say: and the Lord giue thee vnderstanding in all things:

8 Remember that Iesus Christ, made of the seede of Dauid, was raysed againe from the dead according to my Gospel,

9 Wherein I suffer trouble as an euill doer, euen vnto bondes: but the worde of God is not bounde.

10 Therefore I suffer all things, for the elects sake, that they might also obteine the saluation which is in Christ Iesus, with eternall glorie.

11 It is a true saying, For if we be dead together with him, we also shall liue together with him.

12 If we suffer, we shall also reigne together with him: if we denie him, he also will denie vs.

13 If we beleeue not, yet abideth he faithfull: he cannot denie himselfe.

14 Of these things put them in remembrance, and protest before the Lord, that they striue not about wordes, which is to no profit, but to the peruerting of the hearers.

15 Studie to shewe thy selfe approued vnto God, a workeman that needeth not to be ashamed, diuiding the worde of trueth aright.

16 Stay prophane, and vaine babblings: for they shall encrease vnto more vngodlinesse.

17 And their worde shall fret as a canker: of which sort is Hymeneus and Philetus,

18 Which as concerning ye trueth haue erred from the marke, saying that the resurrection is past alreadie, and do destroy the faith of certaine.

19 But the foundation of God remaineth sure, and hath this seale, The Lord knoweth who are his: and, Let euery one that calleth on the Name of Christ, depart from iniquitie.

20 Notwithstanding in a great house are not onely vessels of gold and of siluer, but also of wood and of earth, and some for honour, and some vnto dishonour.

21 If any man therefore purge him selfe from these, he shalbe a vessell vnto honour, sanctified, and meete for the Lord, and prepared vnto euery good worke.

22 Flee also from the lustes of youth, and follow after righteousnes, faith, loue, and peace, with them that call on the Lord with pure heart,

23 And put away foolish and vnlearned questions, knowing that they ingender strife.

24 But the seruant of ye Lord must not striue, but must be gentle toward all men, apt to teache, suffering the euill,

25 Instructing them with meekenesse that are contrary minded, prouing if God at any time will giue them repentance, that they may acknowledge the trueth,

26 And come to amendment out of that snare of the deuil, of whom they are taken prisoners, to doe his will.

Second Timothy 3

1 This knowe also, that in the last dayes shall come perilous times.

2 For men shalbe louers of their owne selues, couetous, boasters, proud, cursed speakers, disobedient to parents, vnthankefull, vnholy,

3 Without naturall affection, truce breakers, false accusers, intemperate, fierce, no louers at all of them which are good,

4 Traitours, headie, high minded, louers of pleasures more then louers of God,

5 Hauing a shewe of godlinesse, but haue denied the power thereof: turne away therefore from such.

6 For of this sort are they which creepe into houses, and leade captiue simple

women laden with sinnes, and led with diuers lustes,

7 Which women are euer learning, and are neuer able to come to the acknowledging of the trueth.

8 And as Iannes and Iambres withstoode Moses, so doe these also resist the trueth, men of corrupt mindes, reprobate concerning the faith.

9 But they shall preuaile no longer: for their madnesse shalbe euident vnto all men, as theirs also was.

10 But thou hast fully knowen my doctrine, maner of liuing, purpose, faith, long suffering, loue, patience,

11 Persecutions, and afflictions which came vnto me at Antiochia, at Iconium, and at Lystri, which persecutions I suffered: but from them all the Lord deliuered me.

12 Yea, and all that will liue godly in Christ Iesus, shall suffer persecution.

13 But the euill men and deceiuers, shall waxe worse and worse, deceiuing, and being deceiued.

14 But continue thou in the thinges which thou hast learned, and which are committed vnto thee, knowing of who thou hast learned them:

15 And that thou hast knowen the holy Scriptures of a childe, which are able to make thee wise vnto saluation, through the faith which is in Christ Iesus.

16 For the whole Scripture is giuen by inspiration of God, and is profitable to teache, to conuince, to correct, and to instruct in righteousnesse,

17 That the man of God may be absolute, being made perfect vnto all good workes.

Second Timothy 4

1 I charge thee therefore before God, and before the Lord Iesus Christ, which shall iudge the quicke and dead at that his appearing, and in his kingdome,

2 Preach the worde: be instant, in season and out of season: improue, rebuke, exhort with all long suffering and doctrine.

3 For the time will come, when they will not suffer wholesome doctrine: but hauing their eares itching, shall after their owne lustes get them an heape of teachers,

4 And shall turne their eares from the trueth, and shalbe giuen vnto fables.

5 But watch thou in all thinges: suffer aduersitie: doe the worke of an Euangelist: cause thy ministerie to be throughly liked of.

6 For I am nowe readie to be offered, and the time of my departing is at hand.

7 I haue fought a good fight, and haue finished my course: I haue kept the faith.

8 For hence foorth is laide vp for me the crowne of righteousnesse, which the Lord the righteous iudge shall giue me at that day: and not to me onely, but vnto all them also that loue that his appearing.

9 Make speede to come vnto me at once:

10 For Demas hath forsaken me, and hath embraced this present world, and is departed vnto Thessalonica. Crescens is gone to Galatia, Titus vnto Dalmatia.

11 Onely Luke is with me. Take Marke and bring him with thee: for he is profitable vnto me to minister.

12 And Tychicus haue I sent to Ephesus.

13 The cloke that I left at Troas with Carpus, when thou commest, bring with thee, and the bookes, but specially the parchments.

14 Alexander the coppersmith hath done me much euill: the Lord rewarde him according to his workes.

15 Of whome be thou ware also: for he withstoode our preaching sore.

16 At my first answering no man assisted me, but all forsooke me: I pray God, that it may not be laide to their charge.

17 Notwithstanding the Lord assisted me, and strengthened me, that by me the preaching might be fully beleeued, and that al the Gentiles should heare: and I was deliuered out of the mouth of the lion.

18 And the Lord will deliuer me from euery euil worke, and will preserue me vnto his heauenly kingdome: to whome be praise for euer and euer, Amen.

19 Salute Prisca and Aquila, and the householde of Onesiphorus.

20 Erastus abode at Corinthus: Trophimus I left at Miletum sicke.

21 Make speede to come before winter. Eubulus greeteth thee, and Pudens, and Linus, and Claudia, and all the brethren.

22 The Lord Iesus Christ be with thy spirit. Grace be with you, Amen. The second Epistle written from Rome vnto Timotheus, the first Bishop elected of the Church of Ephesus, when Paul was presented the second time before the Emperour Nero.

Titus

Titus 1

1 Paul a seruaunt of God, and an Apostle of Iesus Christ, according to the faith of Gods elect, and the acknowledging of the trueth, which is according vnto godlines,

2 Vnto the hope of eternall life, which God that cannot lie, hath promised before the world began:

3 But hath made his worde manifest in due time through the preaching, which is committed vnto me, according to the commandement of God our Sauiour:

4 To Titus my naturall sonne according to the common faith, Grace, mercie and peace from God the Father, and from the Lord Iesus Christ our Sauiour.

5 For this cause left I thee in Creta, that thou shouldest continue to redresse the thinges that remaine, and shouldest ordeine Elders in euery citie, as I appointed thee,

6 If any be vnreproueable, the husband of one wife, hauing faithfull children, which are not slandered of riot, neither are disobedient.

7 For a Bishop must bee vnreproueable, as Gods steward, not froward, not angrie, not giuen to wine, no striker, not giuen to filthie lucre,

8 But harberous, one that loueth goodnesse, wise, righteous, holy, temperate,

9 Holding fast that faithfull worde according to doctrine, that he also may bee able to exhort with wholesome doctrine, and conuince them that say against it.

10 For there are many disobedient and vaine talkers and deceiuers of mindes, chiefly they of the Circumcision,

11 Whose mouthes must bee stopped, which subuert whole houses, teaching things, which they ought not, for filthie lucres sake.

12 One of themselues, euen one of their owne prophets said, The Cretians are alwaies liars, euill beastes, slowe bellies.

13 This witnesse is true: wherefore conuince them sharply, that they may be sound in ye faith,

14 And not taking heede to Iewish fables and commandements of men, that turne away from the trueth.

15 Vnto the pure are all things pure, but vnto them that are defiled, and vnbeleeuing, is nothing pure, but euen their mindes and consciences are defiled.

16 They professe that they know God, but by works they deny him, and are abominable and disobedient, and vnto euery good worke reprobate.

Titus 2

1 Bvt speake thou the thinges which become wholesome doctrine,

2 That the elder men be watchful, graue, teperate, sounde in the faith, in loue, and in patience:

3 The elder women likewise, that they be in such behauiour as becommeth holinesse, not false accusers, not subiect to much wine, but teachers of honest things,

4 That they may instruct the yong women to be sober minded, that they loue their husbands, that they loue their children,

5 That they be temperate, chaste, keeping at home, good and subiect vnto their husbands, that the word of God be not euill spoken of.

6 Exhort yong men likewise, that they bee sober minded.

7 In all things shewe thy selfe an ensample of good woorkes with vncorrupt doctrine, with grauitie, integritie,

8 And with the wholesome woorde, which can not be condemned, that hee which withstandeth, may be ashamed, hauing nothing concerning you to speake euill of.

9 Let seruants be subiect to their masters, and please them in al things, not answering again,

10 Neither pickers, but that they shew al good faithfulnesse, that they may adorne the doctrine of God our Sauiour in all things.

11 For that grace of God, that bringeth saluation vnto all men, hath appeared,

12 And teacheth vs that we should denie vngodlinesse and worldly lusts, and that we should liue soberly and righteously, and godly in this present world,

13 Looking for that blessed hope, and appearing of that glorie of that mightie God, and of our Sauiour Iesus Christ,

14 Who gaue him selfe for vs, that hee might redeeme vs from all iniquitie, and purge vs to bee a peculiar people vnto himselfe, zealous of good woorkes.

15 These things speake, and exhort, and conuince with all authoritie. See that no man despise thee.

Titus 3

1 Pvt them in remembrance that they bee subiect to the Principalities and powers, and that they bee obedient, and ready to euery good woorke,

2 That they speake euill of no man, that they be no fighters, but soft, shewing all meekenesse vnto all men.

3 For wee our selues also were in times past vnwise, disobedient, deceiued, seruing the lustes and diuers pleasures, liuing in maliciousnes and enuie, hatefull, and hating one another:

4 But when that bountifulnesse and that loue of God our Sauiour toward man appeared,

5 Not by the woorkes of righteousnesse, which we had done, but according to his mercie he saued vs, by the washing of the newe birth, and the renewing of the holy Ghost,

6 Which he shed on vs aboundantly, through Iesus Christ our Sauiour,

7 That we, being iustified by his grace, should be made heires according to the hope of eternall life.

8 This is a true saying, and these things I will thou shouldest affirme, that they which haue beleeued God, might be carefull to shewe foorth good woorkes. These things are good and profitable vnto men.

9 But stay foolish questions, and genealogies, and contentions, and brawlings about the Lawe: for they are vnprofitable and vaine.

10 Reiect him that is an heretike, after once or twise admonition,

11 Knowing that hee that is such, is peruerted, and sinneth, being damned of his owne selfe.

12 When I shall send Artemas vnto thee, or Tychicus, be diligent to come to mee vnto Nicopolis: for I haue determined there to winter.

13 Bring Zenas the expounder of the Lawe, and Apollos on their iourney diligently, that they lacke nothing.

14 And let ours also learne to shewe foorth good woorkes for necessary vses, that they be not vnfruitfull.

15 All that are with mee, salute thee. Greete them that loue vs in the faith. Grace bee with you all, Amen. To Titus, elect the first bishoppe of the Church of the Cretians, written from Nicopolis in Macedonia.

Philemon

Philemon 1

1 Paul a prisoner of Iesus Christ, and our brother Timotheus, vnto Philemon our deare friende, and fellowe helper,

2 And to our deare sister Apphia, and to Archippus our fellowe souldier, and to the Church that is in thine house:

3 Grace be with you, and peace from God our Father, and from the Lord Iesus Christ.

4 I giue thanks to my God, making mention alwaies of thee in my praiers,

5 (When I heare of thy loue and faith, which thou hast toward the Lord Iesus, and towarde all Saintes)

6 That the fellowship of thy faith may bee made effectuall, and that whatsoeuer good thing is in you through Christ Iesus, may be knowen.

7 For we haue great ioy and consolation in thy loue, because by thee, brother, the Saintes bowels are comforted.

8 Wherefore, though I bee very bolde in Christ to commaund thee that which is conuenient,

9 Yet for loues sake I rather beseeche thee, though I be as I am, euen Paul aged, and euen nowe a prisoner for Iesus Christ.

10 I beseeche thee for my sonne Onesimus, whome I haue begotten in my bondes,

11 Which in times past was to thee vnprofitable, but nowe profitable both to thee and to me,

12 Whome I haue sent againe: thou therefore receiue him, that is mine owne bowels,

13 Whom I woulde haue reteined with mee, that in thy steade he might haue ministred vnto me in the bondes of the Gospel.

14 But without thy minde woulde I doe nothing, that thy benefite should not be as it were of necessitie, but willingly.

15 It may be that he therefore departed for a season, that thou shouldest receiue him for euer,

16 Not now as a seruant, but aboue a seruant, euen as a brother beloued, specially to me: howe much more then vnto thee, both in the flesh and in the Lord?

17 If therefore thou count our thinges common, receiue him as my selfe.

18 If he hath hurt thee, or oweth thee ought, that put on mine accounts.

19 I Paul haue written this with mine owne hande: I will recompense it, albeit I doe not say to thee, that thou owest moreouer vnto me euen thine owne selfe.

20 Yea, brother, let mee obteine this pleasure of thee in the Lord: comfort my bowels in the Lord.

21 Trusting in thine obedience, I wrote vnto thee, knowing that thou wilt do eue more then I say.

22 Moreouer also prepare mee lodging: for I trust through your prayers I shall be freely giuen vnto you.

23 There salute thee Epaphras my felowe prisoner in Christ Iesus,

24 Marcus, Aristarchus, Demas and Luke, my felowe helpers.

25 The grace of our Lord Iesus Christ be with your spirit, Amen. Written from Rome to Philemon, and send by Onesimus a seruant.

Hebrews

Hebrews 1

1 At sundry times and in diuers maners God spake in the olde time to our fathers by the Prophetes: in these last dayes hee hath spoken vnto vs by his Sonne,

2 Whom he hath made heire of al things, by whome also he made the worldes,

3 Who being the brightnes of the glory, and the ingraued forme of his person, and bearing vp all things by his mightie worde, hath by himselfe purged our sinnes, and sitteth at the right hand of the Maiestie in the highest places,

4 And is made so much more excellent then the Angels, in as much as hee hath obteined a more excellent Name then they.

5 For vnto which of the Angels saide he at any time, Thou art my Sonne, this day begate I thee? and againe, I will be his Father, and he shalbe my Sonne?

6 And againe, when he bringeth in his first begotten Sonne into the worlde, hee saith, And let all the Angels of God worship him.

7 And of the Angels he saith, He maketh the spirites his messengers, and his ministers a flame of fire.

8 But vnto the Sonne he saith, O God, thy throne is for euer and euer: the scepter of thy kingdome is a scepter of righteousnes.

9 Thou hast loued righteousnes and hated iniquitie. Wherefore God, eue thy God, hath anointed thee with the oyle of gladnes aboue thy fellowes.

10 And, Thou, Lord, in the beginning hast established the earth, and the heauens are the workes of thine handes.

11 They shall perish, but thou doest remaine: and they all shall waxe olde as doeth a garment.

12 And as a vesture shalt thou folde them vp, and they shall be changed: but thou art the same, and thy yeeres shall not faile.

13 Vnto which also of the Angels saide he at any time, Sit at my right hand, til I make thine enemies thy footestoole?

14 Are they not al ministring spirits, sent forth to minister, for their sakes which shalbe heires of saluation?

Hebrews 2

1 Wherefore wee ought diligently to giue heede to the thinges which wee haue heard, lest at any time we runne out.

2 For if the worde spoken by Angels was stedfast, and euery transgression, and disobedience receiued a iust recompence of reward,

3 How shall we escape, if we neglect so great saluation, which at the first began to be preached by the Lord, and

afterward was confirmed vnto vs by them that heard him,

4 God bearing witnes thereto, both with signes and wonders, and with diuers miracles, and gifts of the holy Ghost, according to his owne will?

5 For he hath not put in subiection vnto the Angels the world to come, whereof we speake.

6 But one in a certaine place witnessed, saying, What is man, that thou shouldest bee mindefull of him? or the sonne of man, that thou wouldest consider him?

7 Thou madest him a litle inferiour to ye Angels: thou crownedst him with glory and honour, and hast set him aboue the workes of thine hands.

8 Thou hast put all things in subiection vnder his feete. And in that he hath put all things in subiection vnder him, he left nothing that should not be subiect vnto him. But we yet see not all things subdued vnto him,

9 But we see Iesus crowned with glory and honour, which was made litle inferiour to the Angels, through the suffering of death, that by Gods grace he might taste death for all men.

10 For it became him, for whome are all these thinges, and by whome are all these things, seeing that hee brought many children vnto glory, that he should consecrate the Prince of their saluation through afflictions.

11 For he that sanctifieth, and they which are sanctified, are all of one: wherefore he is not ashamed to call them brethren,

12 Saying, I will declare thy Name vnto my brethren: in the middes of the Church will I sing praises to thee.

13 And againe, I will put my trust in him. And againe, Beholde, here am I, and the children which God hath giuen me.

14 Forasmuch then as the children are partakers of flesh and blood, he also himselfe likewise tooke part with them, that hee might destroye through death, him that had the power of death, that is the deuil,

15 And that he might deliuer all them, which for feare of death were all their life time subiect to bondage.

16 For he in no sort tooke on him the Angels nature, but hee tooke on him the seede of Abraham.

17 Wherefore in all things it behoued him to be made like vnto his brethren, that hee might be mercifull, and a faithfull hie Priest in things concerning God, that he might make reconciliation for the sinnes of the people.

18 For in that he suffered, and was tempted, he is able to succour them that are tempted.

Hebrews 3

1 Therefore, holy brethren, partakers of the heauenly vocation, consider the Apostle and high Priest of our profession Christ Iesus:

2 Who was faithfull to him that hath appointed him, euen as Moses was in al his house.

3 For this man is counted worthy of more glory then Moses, inasmuch as he which hath builded the house, hath more honour then the house.

4 For euery house is builded of some man, and he that hath built all things, is God.

5 Now Moses verely was faithfull in all his house, as a seruant, for a witnesse of the thinges which should be spoken after.

6 But Christ is as the Sonne, ouer his owne house, whose house we are, if we holde fast that confidence and that reioycing of that hope vnto the ende.

7 Wherefore, as the holy Ghost sayth, To day if ye shall heare his voyce,

8 Harden not your hearts, as in the prouocation, according to the day of the tentation in the wildernes,

9 Where your fathers tempted me, prooued me, and sawe my workes fourtie yeeres long.

10 Wherefore I was grieued with that generation, and sayde, They erre euer in their heart, neither haue they knowen my wayes.

11 Therefore I sware in my wrath, If they shall enter into my rest.

12 Take heede, brethren, least at any time there be in any of you an euill heart, and vnfaithfull, to depart away from the liuing God.

13 But exhort one another dayly, while it is called to day, lest any of you be hardened through the deceitfulnes of sinne.

14 For we are made partakers of Christ, if we keepe sure vnto the ende that beginning, wherewith we are vpholden,

15 So long as it is sayd, To day if ye heare his voyce, harden not your hearts, as in the prouocation.

16 For some when they heard, prouoked him to anger: howbeit, not all that came out of Egypt by Moses.

17 But with whome was he displeased fourtie yeeres? Was hee not displeased with them that sinned, whose carkeises fell in the wildernes?

18 And to whom sware he that they should not enter into his rest, but vnto them that obeyed not?

19 So we see that they could not enter in, because of vnbeliefe.

Hebrews 4

1 Let vs feare therefore, least at any time by forsaking the promise of entring into his rest, any of you should seeme to be depriued.

2 For vnto vs was the Gospel preached as also vnto them: but the worde that they heard, profited not them, because it was not mixed with faith in those that heard it.

3 For we which haue beleeued, doe enter into rest, as he said to the other, As I haue sworne in my wrath, If they shall enter into my rest: although the

workes were finished from the foundation of the world.

4 For he spake in a certaine place of the seuenth day on this wise, And God did rest the seuenth day from all his workes.

5 And in this place againe, If they shall enter into my rest.

6 Seeing therefore it remaineth that some must enter thereinto, and they to whom it was first preached, entred not therein for vnbeliefes sake:

7 Againe he appointed in Dauid a certaine day, by To day, after so long a time, saying, as it is sayd, This day, if ye heare his voyce, harden not your hearts.

8 For if Iesus had giuen them rest, then would he not after this haue spoke of an other day.

9 There remaineth therefore a rest to the people of God.

10 For he that is entred into his rest, hath also ceased from his owne works, as God did from his.

11 Let vs studie therefore to enter into that rest, lest any man fall after the same ensample of disobedience.

12 For the worde of God is liuely, and mightie in operation, and sharper then any two edged sword, and entreth through, euen vnto the diuiding asunder of the soule and the spirit, and of the ioints, and the marow, and is a discerner of the thoughtes, and the intents of the heart.

13 Neither is there any creature, which is not manifest in his sight: but all things are naked and open vnto his eyes, with whome we haue to doe.

14 Seeing then that wee haue a great hie Priest, which is entred into heauen, euen Iesus the Sonne of God, let vs holde fast our profession.

15 For we haue not an hie Priest, which can not be touched with the feeling of our infirmities, but was in all things tempted in like sort, yet without sinne.

16 Let vs therefore goe boldly vnto ye throne of grace, that we may receiue mercy, and finde grace to helpe in time of neede.

Hebrews 5

1 For euery hie Priest is taken from among men, and is ordeined for men, in things pertaining to God, that he may offer both giftes and sacrifices for sinnes,

2 Which is able sufficiently to haue compassion on them that are ignorant, and that are out of the way, because that hee also is compassed with infirmitie,

3 And for the sames sake he is bound to offer for sinnes, as well for his own part, as for ye peoples.

4 And no man taketh this honor vnto him selfe, but he that is called of God, as was Aaron.

5 So likewise Christ tooke not to him selfe this honour, to be made the hie Priest, but hee that sayd vnto him, Thou art my Sonne, this day begate I thee, gaue it him.

6 As he also in another place speaketh, Thou art a Priest for euer, after ye order of Melchi-sedec.

7 Who in the dayes of his flesh did offer vp prayers and supplications, with strong crying and teares vnto him, that was able to saue him from death, and was also heard in that which he feared.

8 And though he were ye Sonne, yet learned he obedience, by the things which he suffered.

9 And being consecrate, was made the authour of eternall saluation vnto all them that obey him:

10 And is called of God an hie Priest after the order of Melchi-sedec.

11 Of whome we haue many things to say, which are hard to be vttered, because ye are dull of hearing.

12 For when as concerning ye time ye ought to be teachers, yet haue ye neede againe that we teach you what are the first principles of the worde of God: and are become such as haue neede of milke, and not of strong meate.

13 For euery one that vseth milke, is inexpert in the worde of righteousnes: for he is a babe.

14 But strong meate belongeth to them that are of age, which through long custome haue their wits exercised, to discerne both good and euill.

Hebrews 6

1 Therefore, leauing the doctrine of the beginning of Christ, let vs be led forward vnto perfection, not laying againe ye foundation of repetance from dead workes, and of faith toward God,

2 Of the doctrine of baptismes, and laying on of hands, and of the resurrection from the dead, and of eternall iudgement.

3 And this will we doe if God permit.

4 For it is impossible that they which were once lightened, and haue tasted of the heauenly gift, and were made partakers of the holy Ghost,

5 And haue tasted of the good word of God, and of the powers of the world to come,

6 If they fal away, should be renued againe by repentance: seeing they crucifie againe to themselues the Sonne of God, and make a mocke of him.

7 For the earth which drinketh in the raine that commeth oft vpon it, and bringeth foorth herbes meete for them by whome it is dressed, receiueth blessing of God.

8 But that which beareth thornes and briars, is reproued, and is neere vnto cursing, whose end is to be burned.

9 But beloued, we haue perswaded our selues better things of you, and such as accompany saluation, though we thus speake.

10 For God is not vnrighteous, that hee should forget your worke, and labour of loue, which ye shewed toward his Name, in that ye haue ministred vnto the Saints, and yet minister.

11 And we desire that euery one of you shew the same diligence, to the full assurance of hope vnto the ende,

12 That ye be not slouthfull, but followers of them, which through faith and patience, inherite the promises.

13 For when God made the promise to Abraham, because he had no greater to sweare by, he sware by himselfe,

14 Saying, Surely I wil aboundantly blesse thee and multiplie thee marueilously.

15 And so after that he had taried patiently, he enioyed the promise.

16 For men verely sweare by him that is greater then themselues, and an othe for confirmation is among them an ende of all strife.

17 So God, willing more aboundantly to shew vnto the heires of promise the stablenes of his counsell, bound himselfe by an othe,

18 That by two immutable things, wherein it is vnpossible that God should lye, we might haue strong consolation, which haue our refuge to lay holde vpon that hope that is set before vs,

19 Which hope we haue, as an ancre of the soule, both sure and stedfast, and it entreth into that which is within the vaile,

20 Whither the forerunner is for vs entred in, euen Iesus that is made an hie Priest for euer after the order of Melchi-sedec.

Hebrews 7

1 For this Melchi-sedec was King of Salem, the Priest of the most high God, who met Abraham, as he returned from the slaughter of the Kings, and blessed him:

2 To whom also Abraham gaue the tithe of all things: who first is by interpretation King of righteousnes: after that, he is also King of Salem, that is, King of peace,

3 Without father, without mother, without kinred, and hath neither beginning of his dayes, neither ende of life: but is likened vnto the Sonne of God, and continueth a Priest for euer.

4 Nowe consider how great this man was, vnto whome euen the Patriarke Abraham gaue the tithe of the spoyles.

5 For verely they which are the childre of Leui, which receiue the office of the Priesthode, haue a commandement to take, according to the Law, tithes of the people (that is, of their bethren) though they came out of ye loynes of Abraham.

6 But he whose kindred is not couted among them, receiued tithes of Abraham, and blessed him that had the promises.

7 And without all contradiction the lesse is blessed of the greater.

8 And here men that die, receiue tithes: but there he receiueth them, of whome it is witnessed, that he liueth.

9 And to say as the thing is, Leui also which receiueth tithes, payed tithes in Abraham.

10 For hee was yet in the loynes of his father Abraham, when Melchi-sedec met him.

11 If therefore perfection had bene by the Priesthoode of the Leuites (for vnder it the Lawe was established to the people) what needed it furthermore, that another Priest should rise after the order of Melchi-sedec, and not to be called after the order of Aaron?

12 For if the Priesthood be changed, then of necessitie must there be a change of the Lawe.

13 For hee of whome these things are spoken, perteineth vnto another tribe, whereof no man serued at the altar.

14 For it is euident, that our Lord sprung out of Iuda, concerning the which tribe Moses spake nothing, touching the Priesthood.

15 And it is yet a more euident thing, because that after the similitude of Melchi-sedec, there is risen vp another Priest,

16 Which is not made Priest after the Law of the carnal commandement, but after the power of the endlesse life.

17 For hee testifieth thus, Thou art a Priest for euer, after the order of Melchi-sedec.

18 For the commandement that went afore, is disanulled, because of the weakenes thereof, and vnprofitablenes.

19 For the Law made nothing perfite, but the bringing in of a better hope made perfite, whereby we drawe neere vnto God.

20 And for as much as it is not without an othe (for these are made Priestes without an othe:

21 But this is made with an othe by him that said vnto him, The Lord hath sworne, and will not repent, Thou art a Priest for euer, after the order of Melchi-sedec)

22 By so much is Iesus made a suretie of a better Testament.

23 And among them many were made Priests, because they were not suffered to endure, by the reason of death.

24 But this man, because hee endureth euer, hath a Priesthood, which cannot passe from one to another.

25 Wherefore, hee is able also perfectly to saue them that come vnto God by him, seeing he euer liueth, to make intercession for them.

26 For such an hie Priest it became vs to haue, which is holy, harmelesse, vndefiled, separate from sinners, and made hier then the heauens:

27 Which needeth not daily as those hie Priests to offer vp sacrifice, first for his owne sinnes, and then for the peoples: for that did he once, when he offered vp himselfe.

28 For the Law maketh men hie Priestes, which haue infirmitie: but the word of the othe that was since the Lawe, maketh the Sonne, who is consecrated for euermore.

Hebrews 8

1 Nowe of the things which we haue spoken, this is the summe, that wee haue such an hie Priest, that sitteth at

the right hand of the throne of the Maiestie in heauens,

2 And is a minister of the Sanctuarie, and of that true Tabernacle which the Lord pight, and not man.

3 For euery high Priest is ordeined to offer both giftes and sacrifices: wherefore it was of necessitie, that this man shoulde haue somewhat also to offer.

4 For he were not a Priest, if he were on the earth, seeing there are Priestes that according to the Lawe offer giftes,

5 Who serue vnto the paterne and shadowe of heauenly things, as Moses was warned by God, whe he was about to finish the Tabernacle. See, saide hee, that thou make all thinges according to the paterne, shewed to thee in the mount.

6 But nowe our hie Priest hath obteined a more excellent office, in as much as he is the Mediatour of a better Testament, which is established vpon better promises.

7 For if that first Testament had bene vnblameable, no place should haue bene sought for the second.

8 For in rebuking them he saith, Beholde, the dayes will come, saith the Lord, when I shall make with the house of Israel, and with the house of Iuda a newe Testament:

9 Not like the Testament that I made with their fathers, in the day that I tooke them by the hand, to leade them out of the land of Egypt: for they continued not in my Testament, and I regarded them not, saith the Lord.

10 For this is the Testament that I will make with the house of Israel, After those dayes, saith the Lord, I will put my Lawes in their minde, and in their heart I will write them, and I wil be their God, and they shalbe my people,

11 And they shall not teache euery man his neighbour and euery man his brother, saying, Know the Lord: for all shall knowe me, from the least of them to the greatest of them.

12 For I will bee mercifull to their vnrighteousnes, and I wil remember their sinnes and their iniquities no more.

13 In that he saith a new Testament, he hath abrogate the olde: nowe that which is disanulled and waxed olde, is ready to vanish away.

Hebrews 9

1 Then the first Testament had also ordinances of religion, and a worldly Sanctuarie.

2 For the first Tabernacle was made, wherein was the candlesticke, and the table, and the shewebread, which Tabernacle is called the Holy places.

3 And after the seconde vaile was the Tabernacle, which is called the Holiest of all,

4 Which had the golden censer, and the Arke of the Testament ouerlayde rounde about with golde, wherein the golden pot, which had Manna, was, and Aarons rod that had budded, and the tables of the Testament.

5 And ouer the Arke were the glorious Cherubims, shadowing the mercie seat: of which things we will not nowe speake particularly.

6 Nowe when these things were thus ordeined, the Priestes went alwayes into the first Tabernacle, and accomplished the seruice.

7 But into the second went the hie Priest alone, once euery yere, not without blood which hee offered for himselfe, and for the ignorances of the people.

8 Whereby the holy Ghost this signified, that the way into ye Holiest of all was not yet opened, while as yet the first tabernacle was standing,

9 Which was a figure for that present time, wherein were offred gifts and sacrifices that could not make holy, concerning the conscience, him that did the seruice,

10 Which only stood in meates and drinkes, and diuers washings, and carnal rites, which were inioyned, vntill the time of reformation.

11 But Christ being come an high Priest of good things to come, by a greater and a more perfect Tabernacle, not made with handes, that is, not of this building,

12 Neither by the blood of goates and calues: but by his owne blood entred he in once vnto the holy place, and obteined eternall redemption for vs.

13 For if the blood of bulles and of goates, and the ashes of an heifer, sprinkling them that are vncleane, sanctifieth as touching the purifying of the flesh,

14 How much more shall the blood of Christ which through the eternall Spirit offered himselfe without fault to God, purge your conscience from dead workes, to serue the liuing God?

15 And for this cause is he the Mediatour of the newe Testament, that through death which was for the redemption of the transgressions that were in the former Testament, they which were called, might receiue the promise of eternall inheritance.

16 For where a Testament is, there must be the death of him that made the Testament.

17 For the Testament is confirmed when men are dead: for it is yet of no force as long as he that made it, is aliue.

18 Wherefore neither was the first ordeined without blood.

19 For when Moses had spoken euery precept to the people, according to the Law, he tooke the blood of calues and of goates, with water and purple wooll and hyssope, and sprinckled both the booke, and all the people,

20 Saying, This is the blood of the Testament, which God hath appointed vnto you.

21 Moreouer, he sprinkled likewise the Tabernacle with blood also, and all the ministring vessels.

22 And almost all things are by the Law purged with blood, and without sheading of blood is no remission.

23 It was then necessary, that the similitudes of heauenly things should be purified with such things: but the heauenly things them selues are purified with better sacrifices then are these.

24 For Christ is not entred into ye holy places that are made with hands, which are similitudes of ye true Sanctuarie: but is entred into very heauen, to appeare now in ye sight of God for vs,

25 Not that he should offer himselfe often, as the hie Priest entred into the Holy place euery yeere with other blood,

26 (For then must he haue often suffred since the foundation of the world) but now in the end of the world hath he bene made manifest, once to put away sinne by the sacrifice of him selfe.

27 And as it is appointed vnto men that they shall once die, and after that commeth the iudgement:

28 So Christ was once offered to take away the sinnes of many, and vnto them that looke for him, shall he appeare the second time without sinne vnto saluation.

Hebrews 10

1 For the Law hauing the shadowe of good things to come, and not the very image of the things, can neuer with those sacrifices, which they offer yeere by yeere continually, sanctifie the commers thereunto.

2 For would they not then haue ceased to haue bene offered, because that the offerers once purged, should haue had no more conscience of sinnes?

3 But in those sacrifices there is a remembrance againe of sinnes euery yeere.

4 For it is vnpossible that the blood of bulles and goates should take away sinnes.

5 Wherefore when he commeth into the world, he saith, Sacrifice and offring thou wouldest not: but a body hast thou ordeined me.

6 In burnt offerings, and sinne offrings thou hast had no pleasure.

7 Then I sayd, Lo, I come (In the beginning of the booke it is written of me) that I should doe thy will, O God.

8 Aboue, when he sayd, Sacrifice and offring, and burnt offrings, and sinne offrings thou wouldest not haue, neither hadst pleasure therein (which are offered by the Lawe)

9 Then sayd he, Lo, I come to doe thy wil, O God, he taketh away the first, that he may stablish the second.

10 By the which wil we are sanctified, euen by the offring of the body of Iesus Christ once made.

11 And euery Priest standeth dayly ministring, and oft times offreth one maner of offring, which can neuer take away sinnes:

12 But this man after he had offered one sacrifice for sinnes, sitteth for euer at the right hand of God,

13 And from hencefoorth tarieth, till his enemies be made his footestoole.

14 For with one offering hath he consecrated for euer them that are sanctified.

15 For the holy Ghost also beareth vs record: for after that he had sayd before,

16 This is the Testament that I will make vnto them after those dayes, sayth the Lord, I wil put my Lawes in their heart, and in their mindes I will write them.

17 And their sinnes and iniquities will I remember no more.

18 Nowe where remission of these things is, there is no more offering for sinne.

19 Seeing therefore, brethren, that by the blood of Iesus we may be bolde to enter into the Holy place,

20 By the newe and liuing way, which hee hath prepared for vs, through the vaile, that is, his flesh:

21 And seeing we haue an hie Priest, which is ouer the house of God,

22 Let vs drawe neere with a true heart in assurance of faith, our hearts being pure from an euill conscience,

23 And washed in our bodies with pure water, let vs keepe the profession of our hope, without wauering, (for he is faithfull that promised)

24 And let vs consider one another, to prouoke vnto loue, and to good workes,

25 Not forsaking the fellowship that we haue among our selues, as the maner of some is: but let vs exhort one another, and that so much the more, because ye see that the day draweth neere.

26 For if we sinne willingly after that we haue receiued and acknowledged that trueth, there remaineth no more sacrifice for sinnes,

27 But a fearefull looking for of iudgement, and violent fire, which shall deuoure the aduersaries.

28 He that despiseth Moses Law, dieth without mercy vnder two, or three witnesses:

29 Of howe much sorer punishment suppose ye shall hee be worthy, which treadeth vnder foote the Sonne of God, and counteth the blood of the Testament as an vnholy thing, wherewith he was sanctified, and doeth despite the Spirit of grace?

30 For we know him that hath sayd, Vengeance belongeth vnto mee: I will recompense, saith the Lord. And againe, The Lord shall iudge his people.

31 It is a fearefull thing to fall into the hands of the liuing God.

32 Nowe call to remembrance the dayes that are passed, in the which, after ye had receiued light, ye endured a great fight in afflictions,

33 Partly while yee were made a gazing stocke both by reproches and afflictions, and partly while ye became companions of them which were so tossed to and from.

34 For both ye sorowed with mee for my bonds, and suffered with ioy the spoyling of your goods, knowing in your selues howe that ye haue in heauen a better, and an enduring substance.

35 Cast not away therefore your confidence which hath great recompense of reward.

36 For ye haue neede of patience, that after ye haue done the will of God, ye might receiue the promise.

37 For yet a very litle while, and hee that shall come, will come, and will not tary.

38 Nowe the iust shall liue by faith: but if any withdrawe himselfe, my soule shall haue no pleasure in him.

39 But we are not they which withdrawe our selues vnto perdition, but follow faith vnto the conseruation of the soule.

Hebrews 11

1 Now faith is the grounds of things, which are hoped for, and the euidence of things which are not seene.

2 For by it our elders were well reported of.

3 Through faith we vnderstand that the world was ordeined by the worde of God, so that the things which we see, are not made of things which did appeare.

4 By faith Abel offered vnto God a greater sacrifice then Cain, by the which he obtained witnes that he was righteous, God testifying of his gifts: by the which faith also he being dead, yet speaketh.

5 By faith was Enoch translated, that he should not see death: neither was he found: for God had translated him: for before he was translated, he was reported of, that he had pleased God.

6 But without faith it is vnpossible to please him: for he that commeth to God, must beleeue that God is, and that he is a rewarder of them that seeke him.

7 By faith Noe being warned of God of the things which were as yet not seene, mooued with reuerence, prepared the Arke to the sauing of his housholde, through the which Arke hee condemned the world, and was made heire of the righteousnes, which is by faith.

8 By faith Abraham, when he was called, obeyed God, to goe out into a place, which hee should afterward receiue for inheritance, and he went out, not knowing whither he went.

9 By faith he abode in the land of promise, as in a strange countrey, as one that dwelt in tents with Isaac and Iacob heires with him of the same promise.

10 For he looked for a citie hauing a foundation, whose builder and maker is God.

11 Through faith Sara also receiued strength to conceiue seede, and was deliuered of a childe when she was past age, because she iudged him faithfull which had promised.

12 And therefore sprang there of one, euen of one which was dead, so many as the starres of the skie in multitude, and as the land of the sea shore which is innumerable.

13 All these died in faith, and receiued not the promises, but sawe them a farre off, and beleeued them, and receiued them thankefully, and confessed that they were strangers and pilgrims on the earth.

14 For they that say such things, declare plainely, that they seeke a countrey.

15 And if they had bene mindfull of that countrey, from whence they came out, they had leasure to haue returned.

16 But nowe they desire a better, that is an heauenly: wherefore God is not ashamed of them to be called their God: for he hath prepared for them a citie.

17 By faith Abraham offered vp Isaac, when he was tryed, and he that had receiued the promises, offered his onely begotten sonne.

18 (To whom it was said, In Isaac shall thy seede be called.)

19 For he considered that God was able to raise him vp euen from the dead: from whence he receiued him also after a sort.

20 By faith Isaac blessed Iacob and Esau, concerning things to come.

21 By faith Iacob when he was a dying, blessed both the sonnes of Ioseph, and leaning on the ende of his staffe, worshipped God.

22 By faith Ioseph when he died, made mention of the departing of the children of Israel, and gaue commandement of his bones.

23 By faith Moses when he was borne, was hid three moneths of his parents, because they sawe he was a proper childe, neither feared they the kings commandement.

24 By faith Moses when he was come to age, refused to be called the sonne of Pharaohs daughter,

25 And chose rather to suffer aduersitie with the people of God, then to enioy the pleasures of sinnes for a season,

26 Esteeming the rebuke of Christ greater riches then the treasures of Egypt: for he had respect vnto the recompence of the reward.

27 By faith he forsooke Egypt, and feared not the fiercenes of the king: for he endured, as he that sawe him which is inuisible.

28 Through faith he ordeined the Passeouer and the effusion of blood, least he that destroyed the first borne, should touche them.

29 By faith they passed through the red sea as by drie land, which when the Egyptians had assayed to doe, they were swallowed vp.

30 By faith the walles of Iericho fell downe after they were copassed about seue dayes.

31 By faith the harlot Rahab perished not with them which obeyed not, when she had receiued the spies peaceably.

32 And what shall I more say? for the time would be too short for me to tell of Gedeon, of Barac, and of Sampson, and of Iephte, also of Dauid, and Samuel, and of the Prophets:

33 Which through faith subdued kingdomes, wrought righteousnesse, obteined the promises, stopped the mouthes of lions,

34 Quenched the violence of fire, escaped the edge of the sworde, of weake were made strong, waxed valiant in

battell, turned to flight the armies of the aliants.

35 The women receiued their dead raised to life: other also were racked, and woulde not be deliuered, that they might receiue a better resurrection.

36 And others haue bene tryed by mockings and scourgings, yea, moreouer by bondes and prisonment.

37 They were stoned, they were hewen asunder, they were tempted, they were slaine with the sworde, they wandred vp and downe in sheepes skinnes, and in goates skinnes, being destitute, afflicted, and tormented:

38 Whom the world was not worthie of: they wandered in wildernesses and mountaines, and dennes, and caues of the earth.

39 And these all through faith obteined good report, and receiued not the promise,

40 God prouiding a better thing for vs, that they without vs should not be made perfite.

Hebrews 12

1 Wherefore, let vs also, seeing that we are compassed with so great a cloude of witnesses, cast away euery thing that presseth downe, and the sinne that hangeth so fast on: let vs runne with patience the race that is set before vs,

2 Looking vnto Iesus the authour and finisher of our faith, who for the ioy that was set before him, endured the crosse, and despised the shame, and is set at the right hand of the throne of God.

3 Consider therefore him that endured such speaking against of sinners, lest ye should be wearied and faint in your mindes.

4 Ye haue not yet resisted vnto blood, striuing against sinne.

5 And ye haue forgotten the consolation, which speaketh vnto you as vnto children, My sonne, despise not the chastening of the Lord, neither faint when thou art rebuked of him.

6 For whom the Lord loueth, he chasteneth: and he scourgeth euery sonne that he receiueth:

7 If ye endure chastening, God offereth him selfe vnto you as vnto sonnes: for what sonne is it whom the father chasteneth not?

8 If therefore ye be without correction, whereof al are partakers, then are ye bastards, and not sonnes.

9 Moreouer we haue had the fathers of our bodies which corrected vs, and we gaue them reuerence: should we not much rather be in subiection vnto the father of spirites, that we might liue?

10 For they verely for a few dayes chastened vs after their owne pleasure: but he chasteneth vs for our profite, that we might be partakers of his holinesse.

11 Now no chastising for the present seemeth to be ioyous, but, grieuous: but afterwarde, it bringeth the quiet fruite of righteousnesse, vnto them which are thereby exercised.

12 Wherfore lift vp your hands which hang downe, and your weake knees,

13 And make straight steppes vnto your feete, lest that which is halting, be turned out of the way, but let it rather be healed.

14 Followe peace with all men, and holinesse, without the which no man shall see ye Lord.

15 Take heede, that no man fall away from the grace of God: let no roote of bitternes spring vp and trouble you, lest thereby many be defiled.

16 Let there be no fornicator, or prophane person as Esau, which for one portion of meate solde his birthright.

17 For ye knowe howe that afterwarde also when he woulde haue inherited the blessing, he was reiected: for he founde no place to repentance, though he sought that blessing with teares.

18 For ye are not come vnto the mount that might be touched, nor vnto burning fire, nor to blacknes and darkenes, and tempest,

19 Neither vnto the sounde of a trumpet, and the voyce of wordes, which they that heard it, excused themselues, that the word should not be spoken to them any more,

20 (For they were not able to abide that which was commanded, yea, though a beast touche the mountaine, it shalbe stoned, or thrust through with a dart:

21 And so terrible was the sight which appeared, that Moses said, I feare and quake.)

22 But ye are come vnto the mount Sion, and to the citie of the liuing God, the celestiall Hierusalem, and to ye company of innumerable Angels,

23 And to the assemblie and congregation of the first borne, which are written in heauen, and to God the iudge of all, and to the spirits of iust and perfite men,

24 And to Iesus the Mediatour of the new Testament, and to the blood of sprinkling that speaketh better things then that of Abel.

25 See that ye despise not him that speaketh: for if they escaped not which refused him, that spake on earth: much more shall we not escape, if we turne away from him, that speaketh from heauen.

26 Whose voyce then shooke the earth and nowe hath declared, saying, Yet once more will I shake, not the earth onely, but also heauen.

27 And this worde, Yet once more, signifieth the remouing of those things which are shaken, as of things which are made with hands, that the things which are not shaken, may remaine.

28 Wherefore seeing we receiue a kingdome, which cannot be shaken, let vs haue grace whereby we may so serue God, that we may please him with reuerence and feare.

29 For euen our God is a consuming fire.

Hebrews 13

1 Let brotherly loue continue.

2 Be not forgetfull to intertaine strangers: for thereby some haue receiued Angels into their houses vnwares.

3 Remember them that are in bondes, as though ye were bounde with them: and them that are in affliction, as if ye were also afflicted in the body.

4 Mariage is honorable among all, and the bed vndefiled: but whoremongers and adulterers God will iudge.

5 Let your conuersation be without couetousnesse, and be content with those things that ye haue, for he hath said,

6 I will not faile thee, neither forsake thee:

7 So that we may boldly say, The Lord is mine helper, neither will I feare what man can doe vnto me.

8 Remember them which haue the ouersight of you, which haue declared vnto you the word of God: whose faith follow, considering what hath bene the ende of their conuersation. Iesus Christ yesterday, and to day, the same also is for euer.

9 Be not caried about with diuers and strange doctrines: for it is a good thing that the heart be stablished with grace, and not with meates, which haue not profited them that haue bene occupied therein.

10 We haue an altar, whereof they haue no authoritie to eate, which serue in the tabernacle.

11 For the bodies of those beastes whose blood is brought into the Holy place by the high Priest for sinne, are burnt without the campe.

12 Therefore euen Iesus, that he might sanctifie the people with his owne blood, suffered without the gate.

13 Let vs goe foorth to him therefore out of the campe, bearing his reproch.

14 For here haue we no continuing citie: but we seeke one to come.

15 Let vs therefore by him offer the sacrifice of prayse alwaies to God, that is, the fruite of the lippes, which confesse his Name.

16 To doe good, and to distribute forget not: for with such sacrifices God is pleased.

17 Obey them that haue the ouersight of you, and submit your selues: for they watche for your soules, as they that must giue accountes, that they may doe it with ioy, and not with griefe: for that is vnprofitable for you.

18 Pray for vs: for we are assured that we haue a good conscience in all things, desiring to liue honestly.

19 And I desire you somewhat the more earnestly, that yee so doe, that I may be restored to you more quickly.

20 The God of peace that brought againe from the dead our Lord Iesus, the great shepheard of the sheepe, through the blood of the euerlasting Couenant,

21 Make you perfect in all good workes, to doe his will, working in you that which

is pleasant in his sight through Iesus Christ, to whom be praise for euer and euer, Amen.

22 I beseeche you also, brethren, suffer the wordes of exhortation: for I haue written vnto you in fewe wordes.

23 Knowe that our brother Timotheus is deliuered, with whome (if hee come shortly) I will see you.

24 Salute all them that haue the ouersight of you, and all the Saintes. They of Italie salute you.

25 Grace be with you all, Amen. Written to the Hebrewes from Italie, and sent by Timotheus.

James

James 1

1 Iames a seruant of God, and of the Lord Iesus Christ, to the twelue Tribes, which are scattered abroade, salutation.

2 My brethren, count it exceeding ioy, when ye fall into diuers tentations,

3 Knowing that ye trying of your faith bringeth forth patience,

4 And let patience haue her perfect worke, that ye may be perfect and entier, lacking nothing.

5 If any of you lacke wisedome, let him aske of God, which giueth to all men liberally, and reprocheth no man, and it shalbe giuen him.

6 But let him aske in faith, and wauer not: for hee that wauereth, is like a waue of the sea, tost of the winde, and caried away.

7 Neither let that man thinke that hee shall receiue any thing of the Lord.

8 A double minded man is vnstable in all his waies.

9 Let the brother of lowe degree reioyce in that he is exalted:

10 Againe hee that is rich, in that hee is made lowe: for as the flower of the grasse, shall he vanish away.

11 For as when the sunne riseth with heate, then the grasse withereth, and his flower falleth away, and the goodly shape of it perisheth: euen so shall the rich man wither away in all his waies.

12 Blessed is ye man, that endureth tentation: for when he is tried, hee shall receiue the crowne of life, which the Lord hath promised to them that loue him.

13 Let no man say when hee is tempted, I am tempted of God: for God can not bee tempted with euill, neither tempteth he any man.

14 But euery man is tempted, when hee is drawen away by his owne concupiscence, and is entised.

15 Then when lust hath conceiued, it bringeth foorth sinne, and sinne when it is finished, bringeth foorth death.

16 Erre not, my deare brethren.

17 Euery good giuing, and euery perfect gift is from aboue, and commeth downe from the Father of lights, with whome is no variablenes, neither shadow of turning.

18 Of his owne will begate hee vs with the woorde of trueth, that we shoulde be as the first fruites of his creatures.

19 Wherefore my deare brethren, let euery man be swift to heare, slowe to speake, and slowe to wrath.

20 For the wrath of man doeth not accomplish the righteousnesse of God.

21 Wherefore lay apart all filthinesse, and superfluitie of maliciousnesse, and receiue with meekenes the word that is graffed in you, which is able to saue your soules.

22 And be ye doers of the word, and not hearers onely, deceiuing your owne selues.

23 For if any heare the woorde, and doe it not, he is like vnto a man, that beholdeth his naturall face in a glasse.

24 For when he hath considered himselfe, hee goeth his way, and forgetteth immediately what maner of one he was.

25 But who so looketh in the perfect Lawe of libertie, and continueth therein, hee not being a forgetfull hearer, but a doer of the woorke, shalbe blessed in his deede.

26 If any man amog you seeme religious, and refraineth not his tongue, but deceiueth his owne heart, this mans religion is vaine.

27 Pure religion and vndefiled before God, euen the Father, is this, to visite the fatherlesse, and widdowes in their aduersitie, and to keepe himselfe vnspotted of the world.

James 2

1 My brethren, haue not the faith of our glorious Lord Iesus Christ in respect of persons.

2 For if there come into your company a man with a golde ring, and in goodly apparell, and there come in also a poore man in vile raiment,

3 And ye haue a respect to him that weareth the gaie clothing; and say vnto him, Sit thou here in a goodly place, and say vnto the poore, Stand thou there, or sit here vnder my footestoole,

4 Are yee not partiall in your selues, and are become iudges of euill thoughts?

5 Hearken my beloued brethren, hath not God chosen the poore of this worlde, that they should be rich in faith, and heires of the kingdome which he promised to them that loue him?

6 But ye haue despised the poore. Doe not the riche oppresse you by tyrannie, and doe not they drawe you before the iudgement seates?

7 Doe nor they blaspheme the worthie Name after which yee be named?

8 But if yee fulfill the royall Lawe according to the Scripture, which saith, Thou shalt loue thy neighbour as thy selfe, yee doe well.

9 But if yee regarde the persons, yee commit sinne, and are rebuked of the Lawe, as transgressours.

10 For whosoeuer shall keepe the whole Lawe, and yet faileth in one poynt, hee is guiltie of all.

11 For he that saide, Thou shalt not commit adulterie, saide also, Thou shalt not kill. Nowe though thou doest none

adulterie, yet if thou killest, thou art a transgressour of the Lawe.

12 So speake ye, and so doe, as they that shall be iudged by the Lawe of libertie.

13 For there shalbe condemnation merciles to him that sheweth not mercie, and mercie reioyceth against condemnation.

14 What auaileth it, my brethren, though a man saith he hath faith, when he hath no workes? can that faith saue him?

15 For if a brother or a sister bee naked and destitute of daily foode,

16 And one of you say vnto them, Depart in peace: warme your selues, and fil your bellies, notwithstading ye giue them not those things which are needefull to the body, what helpeth it?

17 Euen so the faith, if it haue no woorkes, is dead in it selfe.

18 But some man might say, Thou hast the faith, and I haue woorkes: shewe me thy faith out of thy woorkes, and I will shewe thee my faith by my woorkes.

19 Thou beleeuest that there is one God: thou doest well: the deuils also beleeue it, and tremble.

20 But wilt thou vnderstand, O thou vaine man, that the faith which is without workes, is dead?

21 Was not Abraham our father iustified through workes, when he offred Isaac his sonne vpon the altar?

22 Seest thou not that the faith wrought with his workes? and through the workes was the faith made perfect.

23 And the Scripture was fulfilled which sayeth, Abraham beleeued God, and it was imputed vnto him for righteousnesse: and hee was called the friende of God.

24 Ye see then howe that of workes a man is iustified, and not of faith onely.

25 Likewise also was not Rahab the harlot iustified through workes, when she had receiued ye messengers, and sent them out another way?

26 For as the body without ye spirit is dead, euen so the faith without workes is dead.

James 3

1 My brethren, be not many masters, knowing that we shall receiue the greater condemnation.

2 For in many things we sinne all. If any man sinne not in word, he is a perfect man, and able to bridle all the body.

3 Beholde, we put bittes into the horses mouthes, that they should obey vs, and we turne about all their bodie.

4 Behold also the shippes, which though they be so great, and are driuen of fierce windes, yet are they turned about with a very small rudder, whither soeuer the gouernour listeth.

5 Euen so the tongue is a litle member, and boasteth of great things: beholde, howe great a thing a litle fire kindleth.

6 And the tongue is fire, yea, a worlde of wickednesse: so is the tongue set among our members, that it defileth the whole

body, and setteth on fire the course of nature, and it is set on fire of hell.

7 For the whole nature of beasts, and of birds, and of creeping things, and things of the sea is tamed, and hath bene tamed of the nature of man.

8 But the tongue can no man tame. It is an vnruly euill, full of deadly poyson.

9 Therewith blesse we God euen the Father, and therewith curse we men, which are made after the similitude of God.

10 Out of one mouth proceedeth blessing and cursing: my brethren, these things ought not so to be.

11 Doeth a fountaine send forth at one place sweete water and bitter?

12 Can ye figge tree, my brethren, bring forth oliues, either a vine figges? so can no fountaine make both salt water and sweete.

13 Who is a wise man and endued with knowledge among you? let him shew by good conuersation his workes in meekenesse of wisdome.

14 But if ye haue bitter enuying and strife in your hearts, reioyce not, neither be liars against the trueth.

15 This wisedome descendeth not from aboue, but is earthly, sensuall, and deuilish.

16 For where enuying and strife is, there is sedition, and all maner of euill workes.

17 But the wisedome that is from aboue, is first pure, then peaceable, gentle, easie to be intreated, full of mercie and good fruites, without iudging, and without hipocrisie.

18 And the fruite of righteousnesse is sowen in peace, of them that make peace.

James 4

1 From whence are warres and contentions among you? are they not hence, euen of your pleasures, that fight in your members?

2 Ye lust, and haue not: ye enuie, and desire immoderately, and cannot obtaine: ye fight and warre, and get nothing, because ye aske not.

3 Ye aske, and receiue not, because ye aske amisse, that ye might lay the same out on your pleasures.

4 Ye adulterers and adulteresses, knowe ye not that the amitie of the world is the enimitie of God? Whosoeuer therefore will be a friend of the world, maketh himselfe the enemie of God.

5 Doe ye thinke that the Scripture sayeth in vaine, The spirit that dwelleth in vs, lusteth after enuie?

6 But the Scripture offereth more grace, and therefore sayth, God resisteth the proude, and giueth grace to the humble.

7 Submit your selues to God: resist the deuill, and he will flee from you.

8 Drawe neere to God, and he will drawe neere to you. Clense your handes, ye sinners, and purge your hearts, ye double minded.

9 Suffer afflictions, and sorrowe ye, and weepe: let your laughter be turned into mourning, and your ioy into heauinesse.

10 Cast downe your selues before the Lord, and he will lift you vp.

11 Speake not euill one of another, brethren. He that speaketh euill of his brother, or he that condemneth his brother, speaketh euill of ye Law, and condemneth the Lawe: and if thou condemnest the Lawe, thou art not an obseruer of the Lawe, but a iudge.

12 There is one Lawgiuer, which is able to saue, and to destroy. Who art thou that iudgest another man?

13 Goe to now ye that say, To day or to morowe we will goe into such a citie, and continue there a yeere, and bye and sell, and get gaine,

14 (And yet ye cannot tell what shalbe to morowe. For what is your life? It is euen a vapour that appeareth for a litle time, and afterward vanisheth away)

15 For that ye ought to say, If the Lord will, and, if we liue, we will doe this or that.

16 But now ye reioyce in your boastings: all such reioycing is euill.

17 Therefore, to him that knoweth how to doe well, and doeth it not, to him it is sinne.

James 5

1 Goe to nowe, ye rich men: weepe, and howle for your miseries that shall come vpon you.

2 Your riches are corrupt, and your garments are moth eaten.

3 Your gold and siluer is cankred, and the rust of them shalbe a witnesse against you, and shall eate your flesh, as it were fire. Ye haue heaped vp treasure for the last dayes.

4 Behold, the hire of ye labourers, which haue reaped your fieldes (which is of you kept backe by fraude) cryeth, and the cryes of them which haue reaped, are entred into the eares of the Lord of hostes.

5 Ye haue liued in pleasure on the earth, and in wantonnes. Ye haue nourished your heartes, as in a day of slaughter.

6 Ye haue condemned and haue killed the iust, and he hath not resisted you.

7 Be patient therefore, brethren, vnto the comming of the Lord. Behold, the husbandman wayteth for the precious fruite of the earth, and hath long patience for it, vntill he receiue the former, and the latter rayne.

8 Be ye also patient therefore and settle your hearts: for ye comming of the Lord draweth neere.

9 Grudge not one against another, brethren, least ye be condemned: behold, the iudge standeth before the doore.

10 Take, my brethren, the Prophets for an ensample of suffering aduersitie, and of long patience, which haue spoken in the Name of the Lord.

11 Beholde, we count them blessed which endure. Ye haue heard of the patience of Iob, and haue knowen what ende the Lord made. For the Lord is very pitifull and mercifull.

12 But before all thinges, my brethren, sweare not, neither by heauen, nor by earth, nor by any other othe: but let your yea, be yea, and your nay, nay, lest ye fall into condemnation.

13 Is any among you afflicted? Let him pray. Is any merie? Let him sing.

14 Is any sicke among you? Let him call for the Elders of the Church, and let them pray for him, and anoynt him with oyle in the Name of the Lord.

15 And the prayer of faith shall saue the sicke, and the Lord shall raise him vp: and if he haue committed sinnes, they shalbe forgiuen him.

16 Acknowledge your faultes one to another, and pray one for another, that ye may be healed: for the prayer of a righteous man auaileth much, if it be feruent.

17 Helias was a man subiect to like passions as we are, and he prayed earnestly that it might not rayne, and it rayned not on the earth for three yeeres and sixe moneths.

18 And he prayed againe, and the heauen gaue rayne, and the earth brought forth her fruite.

19 Brethren, if any of you hath erred from the trueth, and some man hath conuerted him,

20 Let him know that he which hath conuerted the sinner from going astray out of his way, shall saue a soule from death, and shall hide a multitude of sinnes.

First Peter

First Peter 1

1 PETER an Apostle of IESVS CHRIST, to the strangers that dwell here and there throughout Pontus, Galatia, Cappadocia, Asia and Bithynia,

2 Elect according to the foreknowledge of God ye Father vnto sanctification of ye Spirit, through obedience and sprinkeling of the blood of Iesus Christ: Grace and peace bee multiplied vnto you.

3 Blessed bee God, euen the Father of our Lord Iesus Christ, which according to his aboundant mercie hath begotten vs againe vnto a liuely hope by the resurrection of Iesus Christ from the dead,

4 To an inheritance immortall and vndefiled, and that withereth not, reserued in heauen for vs,

5 Which are kept by the power of God through faith vnto saluation, which is prepared to be shewed in the last time.

6 Wherein yee reioyce, though nowe for a season (if neede require) yee are in heauinesse, through manifolde tentations,

7 That the triall of your faith, being much more precious then golde that perisheth (though it be tried with fire) might bee founde vnto your praise, and honour and glorie at the appearing of Iesus Christ:

8 Whome yee haue not seene, and yet loue him, in whome nowe, though yee

see him not, yet doe you beleeue, and reioyce with ioy vnspeakeable and glorious,

9 Receiuing the ende of your faith, euen the saluation of your soules.

10 Of the which saluation ye Prophets haue inquired and searched, which prophecied of the grace that should come vnto you,

11 Searching when or what time the Spirite which testified before of Christ which was in them, shoulde declare the sufferings that should come vnto Christ, and the glorie that shoulde follow.

12 Vnto whome it was reueiled, that not vnto themselues, but vnto vs they shoulde minister the things, which are nowe shewed vnto you by them which haue preached vnto you the Gospell by the holy Ghost sent downe from heauen, the which things the Angels desire to beholde.

13 Wherefore, girde vp the Ioynes of your minde: bee sober, and trust perfectly on that grace that is brought vnto you, in the reuelation of Iesus Christ,

14 As obedient children, not fashioning your selues vnto the former lustes of your ignorance:

15 But as hee which hath called you, is holie, so be yee holie in all maner of conuersation;

16 Because it is written, Be yee holie, for I am holie.

17 And if ye call him Father, which without respect of person iudgeth according to euery mans woorke, passe the time of your dwelling here in feare,

18 Knowing that yee were not redeemed with corruptible things, as siluer and golde, from your vaine conuersation, receiued by the traditions of the fathers,

19 But with the precious blood of Christ, as of a Lambe vndefiled, and without spot.

20 Which was ordeined before the foundation of the world, but was declared in the last times for your sakes,

21 Which by his meanes doe beleeue in God that raised him from the dead, and gaue him glorie, that your faith and hope might bee in God,

22 Hauing purified your soules in obeying the trueth through the spirite, to loue brotherly without faining, loue one another with a pure heart feruently,

23 Being borne anewe, not of mortall seede, but of immortall, by the woorde of God, who liueth and endureth for euer.

24 For all flesh is as grasse, and all the glorie of man is as the flower of grasse. The grasse withereth, and the flower falleth away.

25 But the worde of the Lord endureth for euer: and this is the woorde which is preached among you.

First Peter 2

1 Wherefore, laying aside all maliciousnes, and all guile, and dissimulation, and enuie, and all euill speaking,

2 As newe borne babes desire that sincere milke of the woorde, that yee may growe thereby,

3 Because yee haue tasted that the Lord is bountifull.

4 To whome comming as vnto a liuing stone disallowed of men, but chosen of God and precious,

5 Yee also as liuely stones, bee made a spirituall house, an holy Priesthoode to offer vp spirituall sacrifices acceptable to God by Iesus Christ.

6 Wherefore also it is conteyned in the Scripture, Beholde, I put in Sion a chiefe corner stone, elect and precious: and hee that beleeueth therein, shall not be ashamed.

7 Vnto you therefore which beleeue, it is precious: but vnto them which be disobedient, the stone which the builders disallowed, the same is made the head of the corner,

8 And a stone to stumble at, and a rocke of offence, euen to them which stumble at the woorde, being disobedient, vnto the which thing they were euen ordeined.

9 But yee are a chosen generation, a royall Priesthoode, an holy nation, a people set at libertie, that yee shoulde shewe foorth the vertues of him that hath called you out of darkenesse into his marueilous light,

10 Which in time past were not a people, yet are nowe the people of God: which in time past were not vnder mercie, but nowe haue obteined mercie.

11 Dearely beloued, I beseeche you, as strangers and pilgrims, abstaine from fleshly lusts, which fight against the soule,

12 And haue your conuersation honest among the Gentiles, that they which speake euill of you as of euill doers, may by your good woorkes which they shall see, glorifie God in the day of visitation.

13 Therefore submit your selues vnto all maner ordinance of man for the Lordes sake, whether it be vnto the King, as vnto the superiour,

14 Or vnto gouernours, as vnto them that are sent of him, for the punishment of euill doers, and for the praise of them that doe well.

15 For so is the will of God, that by well doing ye may put to silence the ignorance of the foolish men,

16 As free, and not as hauing the libertie for a cloke of maliciousnesse, but as the seruauntes of God.

17 Honour all men: loue brotherly fellowship: feare God: honour the King.

18 Seruaunts, be subiect to your masters with all feare, not onely to the good and courteous, but also to the froward.

19 For this is thanke worthie, if a man for conscience toward God endure griefe, suffering wrongfully.

20 For what praise is it, if when ye be buffeted for your faultes, yee take it paciently? but and if when ye doe well, ye suffer wrong and take it paciently, this is acceptable to God.

21 For hereunto ye are called: for Christ also suffred for you, leauing you an ensample that ye should follow his steppes.

22 Who did no sinne, neither was there guile found in his mouth.

23 Who when hee was reuiled, reuiled not againe: when hee suffered, hee threatned not, but comitted it to him that iudgeth righteously.

24 Who his owne selfe bare our sinnes in his body on the tree, that we being dead to sinne, should liue in righteousnesse: by whose stripes ye were healed.

25 For ye were as sheepe going astray: but are nowe returned vnto the shepheard and Bishop of your soules.

First Peter 3

1 Likewise let the wiues bee subiect to their husbands, that euen they which obey not the worde, may without the worde be wonne by the conuersation of the wiues,

2 While they beholde your pure conuersation, which is with feare.

3 Whose apparelling, let it not be that outwarde, with broyded heare, and golde put about, or in putting on of apparell:

4 But let it bee the hidde man of the heart, which consisteth in the incorruption of a meeke and quiet spirite, which is before God a thing much set by.

5 For euen after this maner in time past did the holy women, which trusted in God, tire them selues, and were subiect to their husbands.

6 As Sara obeyed Abraham, and called him Sir: whose daughters ye are, whiles yee doe well, not being afraide of any terrour.

7 Likewise ye husbands, dwel with them as men of knowledge, giuing honour vnto the woman, as vnto the weaker vessell, euen as they which are heires together of the grace of life, that your prayers be not interrupted.

8 Finally, be ye all of one minde: one suffer with another: loue as brethren: bee pitifull: bee courteous,

9 Not rendring euil for euill, neither rebuke for rebuke: but contrarywise blesse, knowing that ye are thereunto called, that ye should be heires of blessing.

10 For if any man long after life, and to see good dayes, let him refraine his tongue from euill, and his lippes that they speake no guile.

11 Let him eschew euil, and do good: let him seeke peace, and follow after it.

12 For the eyes of the Lord are ouer the righteous, and his eares are open vnto their prayers: and the face of the Lord is against them that do euil.

13 And who is it that will harme you, if ye follow that which is good?

14 Notwithstanding blessed are ye, if ye suffer for righteousnes sake. Yea, feare not their feare, neither be troubled.

15 But sanctifie the Lord God in your hearts: and be ready always to giue an

answere to euery man that asketh you a reason of the hope that is in you, with meekenesse and reuerence,

16 Hauing a good coscience, that whe they speake euill of you as of euill doers, they may be ashamed, which slander your good conuersation in Christ.

17 For it is better (if the will of God be so) that ye suffer for well doing, then for euil doing.

18 For Christ also hath once suffered for sinnes, the iust for the vniust, that he might bring vs to God, and was put to death concerning the flesh, but was quickened by the spirit.

19 By the which hee also went, and preached vnto the spirits that are in prison.

20 Which were in time passed disobedient, when once the long suffering of God abode in the dayes of Noe, while the Arke was preparing, wherein fewe, that is, eight soules were saued in the water.

21 Whereof the baptisme that nowe is, answering that figure, (which is not a putting away of the filth of the flesh, but a confident demaunding which a good conscience maketh to God) saueth vs also by the resurrection of Iesus Christ,

22 Which is at the right hand of God, gone into heauen, to whom the Angels, and Powers, and might are subiect.

First Peter 4

1 Forasmuch then as Christ hath suffered for vs in the flesh, arme your selues likewise with the same minde, which is, that he which hath suffered in the flesh, hath ceased from sinne,

2 That he hence forward should liue (as much time as remaineth in the flesh) not after the lusts of men, but after the will of God.

3 For it is sufficient for vs that we haue spet the time past of ye life, after the lust of the Gentiles, walking in wantonnes, lustes, drunkennes, in gluttonie, drinkings, and in abominable idolatries.

4 Wherein it seemeth to them strange, that yee runne not with them vnto the same excesse of riot: therefore speake they euill of you,

5 Which shall giue accounts to him, that is readie to iudge quicke and dead.

6 For vnto this purpose was the Gospell preached also vnto the dead, that they might bee condemned, according to men in the flesh, but might liue according to God in the spirit.

7 Now the ende of all things is at hand. Be ye therefore sober, and watching in prayer.

8 But aboue all thinges haue feruent loue among you: for loue shall couer the multitude of sinnes.

9 Be ye harberous one to another, without grudging.

10 Let euery man as hee hath receiued the gift, minister the same one to another, as good disposers of the manifolde grace of God.

11 If any man speake, let him speake as the wordes of God. If any man minister,

let him do it as of the abilitie which God ministreth, that God in al things may be glorified through Iesus Christ, to whome is prayse and dominion for euer, and euer, Amen.

12 Dearely beloued, thinke it not strange concerning the firie triall, which is among you to proue you, as though some strange thing were come vnto you:

13 But reioyce, in asmuch as ye are partakers of Christs suffrings, that when his glory shall appeare, ye may be glad and reioyce.

14 If yee be railed vpon for the Name of Christ, blessed are ye: for the spirit of glory, and of God resteth vpon you: which on their part is euill spoken of: but on your part is glorified.

15 But let none of you suffer as a murtherer, or as a thiefe, or an euil doer, or as a busibodie in other mens matters.

16 But if any man suffer as a Christian, let him not bee ashamed: but let him glorifie God in this behalfe.

17 For the time is come, that iudgement must beginne at the house of God. If it first beginne at vs, what shall the ende be of them which obey not the Gospel of God?

18 And if the righteous scarcely bee saued, where shall the vngodly and the sinner appeare?

19 Wherefore let them that suffer according to the will of God, commit their soules to him in well doing, as vnto a faithfull Creator.

First Peter 5

1 The elders which are among you, I beseech which am also an elder, and a witnesse of the sufferings of Christ, and also a partaker of the glory that shalbe reueiled,

2 Feede the flocke of God, which dependeth vpon you, caring for it not by constraint, but willingly: not for filthy lucre, but of a ready minde:

3 Not as though ye were lords ouer Gods heritage, but that yee may bee ensamples to the flocke.

4 And when that chiefe shepheard shall appeare, ye shall receiue an incorruptible crowne of glory.

5 Likewise ye yonger, submit your selues vnto the elders, and submit your selues euery man, one to another: decke your selues inwardly in lowlinesse of minde: for God resisteth the proude, and giueth grace to the humble.

6 Humble your selues therefore vnder the mightie hand of God, that he may exalt you in due time.

7 Cast all your care on him: for he careth for you.

8 Be sober, and watch: for your aduersarie the deuil as a roaring lyon walketh about, seeking whom he may deuoure:

9 Whom resist stedfast in the faith, knowing that the same afflictions are accomplished in your brethren which are in the world.

10 And the God of all grace, which hath called vs vnto his eternall glory by Christ

Iesus, after that ye haue suffered a litle, make you perfite, confirme, strengthen and stablish you.

11 To him be glory and dominion for euer and euer, Amen.

12 By Syluanus a faithfull brother vnto you, as I suppose, haue I written briefly, exhorting and testifying how that this is the true grace of God, wherein ye stand.

13 The Church that is at Babylon elected together with you, saluteth you, and Marcus my sonne.

14 Greete yee one another with the kisse of loue. Peace be with you all which are in Christ Iesus, Amen.

Second Peter

Second Peter 1

1 Simon Peter a seruant and an Apostle of Iesus Christ, to you which haue obteined like precious faith with vs by the righteousnesse of our God and Sauiour Iesus Christ:

2 Grace and peace be multiplied to you, through the acknowledging of God, and of Iesus our Lord,

3 According as his diuine power hath giuen vnto vs all things that perteine vnto life and godlinesse, through the acknowledging of him that hath called vs vnto glory and vertue.

4 Whereby most great and precious promises are giuen vnto vs, that by them ye should be partakers of the diuine nature, in that ye flee the corruption, which is in the worlde through lust.

5 Therefore giue euen all diligence thereunto: ioyne moreouer vertue with your faith: and with vertue, knowledge:

6 And with knowledge, temperance: and with temperance, patience: and with patience, godlines:

7 And with godlines, brotherly kindnes: and with brotherly kindnes, loue.

8 For if these things be among you, and abound, they will make you that ye neither shalbe idle, nor vnfruitfull in the acknowledging of our Lord Iesus Christ:

9 For he that hath not these things, is blinde, and can not see farre off, and hath forgotten that he was purged from his olde sinnes.

10 Wherefore, brethren, giue rather diligence to make your calling and election sure: for if ye doe these things, ye shall neuer fall.

11 For by this meanes an entring shalbe ministred vnto you aboundantly into the euerlasting kingdome of our Lord and Sauiour Iesus Christ.

12 Wherefore, I will not be negligent to put you always in remembrance of these things, though that ye haue knowledge, and be stablished in the present trueth.

13 For I thinke it meete as long as I am in this tabernacle, to stirre you vp by putting you in remembrance,

14 Seeing I knowe that the time is at hand that I must lay downe this my tabernacle, euen as our Lord Iesus Christ hath shewed me.

15 I will endeuour therefore alwayes, that ye also may be able to haue remembrance of these things after my departing.

16 For we followed not deceiuable fables when we opened vnto you the power, and comming of our Lord Iesus Christ, but with our eyes we saw his maiestie:

17 For he receiued of God the Father honour and glory, when there came such a voyce to him from that excellent glory, This is my beloued Sonne, in whom I am well pleased.

18 And this voyce we heard when it came from heauen, being with him in the Holy mount.

19 We haue also a most sure worde of the Prophets, to the which ye doe well that yee take heede, as vnto a light that shineth in a darke place, vntill the day dawne, and the day starre arise in your hearts.

20 So that yee first knowe this, that no prophecie of the Scripture is of any priuate interpretation.

21 For the prophecie came not in olde time by the will of man: but holy men of God spake as they were moued by the holy Ghost.

Second Peter 2

1 Bvt there were false prophets also among the people, euen as there shalbe false teachers among you: which priuily shall bring in damnable heresies, euen denying the Lord, that hath bought them, and bring vpon themselues swift damnation.

2 And many shall follow their destructions, by whom the way of trueth shalbe euil spoken of,

3 And through couetousnes shall they with fained words make marchandise of you, whose condemnation long since resteth not, and their destruction slumbreth not.

4 For if God spared not the Angels that had sinned, but cast them downe into hell, and deliuered them into chaines of darkenes, to be kept vnto damnation:

5 Neither hath spared the olde worlde, but saued Noe the eight person a preacher of righteousnesse, and brought in the flood vpon the world of the vngodly,

6 And turned the cities of Sodom and Gomorrhe into ashes, condemned them and ouerthrewe them, and made them an ensample vnto them that after should liue vngodly,

7 And deliuered iust Loth vexed with the vncleanly conuersation of the wicked:

8 (For he being righteous, and dwelling among them, in seeing and hearing, vexed his righteous soule from day to day with their vnlawfull deedes.)

9 The Lord knoweth to deliuer the godly out of tentation, and to reserue the vniust vnto the day of iudgement vnder punishment.

10 And chiefly them that walke after the flesh, in the lust of vncleannesse, and despise gouernement, which are bolde, and stand in their owne conceite, and feare not to speake euill of them that are in dignitie.

11 Where as the Angels which are greater both in power and might, giue not railing iudgement against them before the Lord.

12 But these, as naturall brute beasts, led with sensualitie and made to be taken, and destroyed, speake euill of those things which they know not, and shall perish through their owne corruption,

13 And shall receiue the wages of vnrighteousnes, as they which count it pleasure dayly to liue deliciously. Spottes they are and blottes, deliting them selues in their deceiuings, in feasting with you,

14 Hauing eyes full of adulterie, and that can not cease to sinne, beguiling vnstable soules: they haue heartes exercised with couetousnesse, they are the children of curse:

15 Which forsaking the right way, haue gone astray, folowing the way of Balaam, the sonne of Bosor, which loued the wages of vnrighteousnes.

16 But he was rebuked for his iniquitie: for the dumme beast speaking with mans voyce, forbade the foolishnesse of the Prophet.

17 These are welles without water, and cloudes caried about with a tempest, to whome the blacke darkenes is reserued for euer.

18 For in speaking swelling wordes of vanitie, they beguile with wantonnesse through the lusts of the flesh them that were cleane escaped from them which are wrapped in errour,

19 Promising vnto them libertie, and are themselues the seruants of corruption: for of whomsoeuer a man is ouercome, euen vnto the same is he in bondage.

20 For if they, after they haue escaped from the filthinesse of the world, through the acknowledging of the Lord, and of the Sauiour Iesus Christ, are yet tangled againe therein, and ouercome, the latter ende is worse with them then the beginning.

21 For it had bene better for them, not to haue acknowledged the way of righteousnes, then after they haue acknowledged it, to turne from the holy commandement giuen vnto them.

22 But it is come vnto them, according to the true Prouerbe, The dogge is returned to his owne vomit: and, The sowe that was washed, to the wallowing in the myre.

Second Peter 3

1 This seconde Epistle I nowe write vnto you, beloued, wherewith I stirre vp, and warne your pure mindes,

2 To call to remembrance the wordes, which were tolde before of the holy Prophetes, and also the commandement of vs the Apostles of the Lord and Sauiour.

3 This first vnderstande, that there shall come in the last dayes, mockers, which wil walke after their lustes,

4 And say, Where is the promise of his comming? for since the fathers died, all things continue alike from the beginning of the creation.

5 For this they willingly know not, that the heauens were of olde, and the earth that was of the water and by the water, by the word of God.

6 Wherefore the worlde that then was, perished, ouerflowed with the water.

7 But the heauens and earth, which are nowe, are kept by the same word in store, and reserued vnto fire against the day of condemnation, and of the destruction of vngodly men.

8 Dearely beloued, be not ignorant of this one thing, that one day is with the Lord, as a thousande yeeres, and a thousande yeeres as one day.

9 The Lord of that promise is not slacke (as some men count slackenesse) but is pacient toward vs, and would haue no man to perish, but would all men to come to repentance.

10 But the day of the Lord will come as a thiefe in the night, in the which the heauens shall passe away with a noyse, and the elements shall melt with heate, and the earth with the workes that are therein, shalbe burnt vp.

11 Seeing therefore that all these thinges must be dissolued, what maner persons ought ye to be in holy conuersation and godlinesse,

12 Looking for, and hasting vnto the comming of that day of God, by the which the heauens being on fire, shall be dissolued, and the elements shall melt with heate?

13 But wee looke for newe heauens, and a newe earth, according to his promise, wherein dwelleth righteousnesse.

14 Wherefore, beloued, seeing that yee looke for such thinges, be diligent that ye may be found of him in peace, without spot and blamelesse.

15 And suppose that the long suffering of our Lord is saluation, euen as our beloued brother Paul according to the wisedome giuen vnto him wrote to you,

16 As one, that in all his Epistles speaketh of these thinges: among the which some thinges are hard to be vnderstand, which they that are vnlearned and vnstable, wrest, as they do also other Scriptures vnto their owne destruction.

17 Ye therefore beloued, seeing ye know these things before, beware, lest ye be also plucked away with the errour of the wicked, and fall from your owne stedfastnesse.

18 But grow in grace, and in the knowledge of our Lord and Sauiour Iesus Christ: to him be glory both now and for euermore. Amen.

First John

First John 1

1 That which was from the beginning, which wee haue heard, which wee haue seene with these our eyes, which wee

haue looked vpon, and these handes of ours haue handled of that Word of life,

2 (For that life was made manifest, and wee haue seene it, and beare witnes, and shewe vnto you that eternall life, which was with the Father, and was made manifest vnto vs)

3 That, I say, which wee haue seene and heard, declare wee vnto you, that yee may also haue fellowship with vs, and that our fellowship also may be with the Father, and with his Sonne Iesvs Christ.

4 And these thinges write we vnto you, that that your ioy may be full.

5 This then is the message which wee haue heard of him, and declare vnto you, that God is light, and in him is no darkenes.

6 If wee say that wee haue fellowship with him, and walke in darkenesse, we lie, and doe not truely:

7 But if we walke in the light as he is in the light, we haue fellowship one with another, and the blood of Iesus Christ his Sonne clenseth vs from all sinne.

8 If we say that we haue no sinne, we deceiue our selues, and trueth is not in vs.

9 If we acknowledge our sinnes, he is faithfull and iust, to forgiue vs our sinnes, and to clense vs from all vnrighteousnes.

10 If wee say we haue not sinned, wee make him a liar, and his word is not in vs.

First John 2

1 My little children, these things write I vnto you, that ye sinne not: and if any man sinne, wee haue an Aduocate with the Father, Iesus Christ, the Iust.

2 And he is the reconciliation for our sinnes: and not for ours onely, but also for the sinnes of the whole world.

3 And hereby we are sure that we knowe him, if we keepe his commandements.

4 Hee that saith, I knowe him, and keepeth not his commandements, is a liar, and the trueth is not in him.

5 But hee that keepeth his worde, in him is the loue of God perfect in deede: hereby wee knowe that ye are in him.

6 He that saith he remaineth in him, ought euen so to walke, as he hath walked.

7 Brethren, I write no newe commandement vnto you: but an olde commandement, which ye haue had from the beginning: this olde commandement is that worde, which yee haue heard from the beginning.

8 Againe, a new comandement I write vnto you, that which is true in him, and also in you: for the darkenes is past, and that true light now shineth.

9 He that saith that hee is in that light, and hateth his brother, is in darkenes, vntill this time.

10 Hee that loueth his brother, abideth in that light, and there is none occasion of euil in him.

11 But he that hateth his brother, is in darkenesse, and walketh in darkenesse, and knoweth not whither hee goeth,

because that darkenesse hath blinded his eyes.

12 Litle children, I write vnto you, because your sinnes are forgiuen you for his Names sake.

13 I write vnto you, fathers, because yee haue knowen him that is from the beginning. I write vnto you, yong men, because ye haue ouercome that wicked one. I write vnto you, litle children, because ye haue knowen ye Father.

14 I haue written vnto you, fathers, because ye haue knowen him, that is from the beginning. I haue written vnto you, yong men, because ye are strong, and the worde of God abideth in you, and ye haue ouercome that wicked one.

15 Loue not this world, neither the things that are in this world. If any man loue this world, the loue of the Father is not in him.

16 For all that is in this world (as the lust of the flesh, the lust of the eyes, and the pride of life) is not of the Father, but is of this world.

17 And this world passeth away, and the lust thereof: but he that fulfilleth the will of God, abideth euer.

18 Litle children, it is the last time, and as ye haue heard that Antichrist shall come, euen now are there many Antichrists: whereby we know that it is the last time.

19 They went out from vs, but they were not of vs: for if they had bene of vs, they should haue continued with vs. But this cometh to passe, that it might appeare, that they are not all of vs.

20 But ye haue an ointment from that Holy one, and know all things.

21 I haue not written vnto you, because ye knowe not the trueth: but because ye knowe it, and that no lie is of the trueth.

22 Who is a liar, but he that denyeth that Iesus is that Christ? the same is that Antichrist that denyeth the Father and the Sonne.

23 Whosoeuer denyeth the Sonne, the same hath not the Father.

24 Let therefore abide in you that same which ye haue heard from the beginning. If that which ye haue heard from the beginning, shall remaine in you, ye also shall continue in the Sonne, and in the Father.

25 And this is the promise that he hath promised vs, euen that eternall life.

26 These things haue I written vnto you, concerning them that deceiue you.

27 But that anointing which ye receiued of him, dwelleth in you: and ye neede not that any man teach you: but as the same Anoynting teacheth you of all things, and it is true, and is not lying, and as it taught you, ye shall abide in him.

28 And nowe, litle children, abide in him, that when he shall appeare, we may be bolde, and not be ashamed before him at his comming.

29 If ye know that he is righteous, know ye that he which doeth righteously, is borne of him.

First John 3

1 Behold, what loue the Father hath giuen to vs, that we should be called the sonnes of God: for this cause this world knoweth you not, because it knoweth not him.

2 Dearely beloued, nowe are we the sonnes of God, but yet it is not made manifest what we shall be: and we know that when he shalbe made manifest, we shalbe like him: for we shall see him as he is.

3 And euery man that hath this hope in him, purgeth himselfe, euen as he is pure.

4 Whosoeuer committeth sinne, transgresseth also the Law: for sinne is the transgression of the Lawe.

5 And ye knowe that hee was made manifest, that he might take away our sinnes, and in him is no sinne.

6 Whosoeuer abideth in him, sinneth not: whosoeuer sinneth, hath not seene him, neither hath knowen him.

7 Litle children, let no man deceiue you: he that doeth righteousnes, is righteous, as hee is righteous.

8 He that comitteth sinne, is of the deuil: for the deuill sinneth from the beginning: for this purpose was made manifest that Sonne of God, that he might loose the workes of the deuil.

9 Whosoeuer is borne of God, sinneth not: for his seede remaineth in him, neither can hee sinne, because he is borne of God.

10 In this are the children of God knowen, and the children of the deuil: whosoeuer doeth not righteousnesse, is not of God, neither he that loueth not his brother.

11 For this is the message, that ye heard from the beginning, that we should loue one another,

12 Not as Cain which was of that wicked one, and slewe his brother: and wherefore slewe he him? because his owne workes were euill, and his brothers good.

13 Marueile not, my brethren, though this world hate you.

14 We know that we are translated from death vnto life, because we loue the brethren: he that loueth not his brother, abideth in death.

15 Whosoeuer hateth his brother, is a manslayer: and ye know that no manslayer hath eternall life abiding in him.

16 Hereby haue we perceiued loue, that he layde downe his life for vs: therefore we ought also to lay downe our liues for the brethren.

17 And whosoeuer hath this worlds good, and seeth his brother haue neede, and shutteth vp his compassion from him, howe dwelleth the loue of God in him?

18 My litle children, let vs not loue in worde, neither in tongue onely, but in deede and in trueth.

19 For thereby we know that we are of the trueth, and shall before him assure our hearts.

20 For if our heart condemne vs, God is greater then our heart, and knoweth all things.

21 Beloued, if our heart condemne vs not, then haue we boldnes toward God.

22 And whatsoeuer we aske we receiue of him, because we keepe his commandements, and do those things which are pleasing in his sight.

23 This is then his commandement, That we beleeue in the Name of his Sonne Iesus Christ, and loue one another as hee gaue commandement.

24 For hee that keepeth his commandements, dwelleth in him, and he in him: and hereby we knowe that hee abideth in vs, euen by that Spirit which he hath giuen vs.

First John 4

1 Dearely beloued, beleeue not euery spirit, but trie the spirits whether they are of God: for many false prophets are gone out into this worlde.

2 Hereby shall ye know the Spirit of God, Euery spirit which confesseth that Iesus Christ is come in the flesh, is of God.

3 And euery spirit that confesseth not that Iesus Christ is come in the flesh, is not of God: but this is the spirit of Antichrist, of whome ye haue heard, how that he should come, and nowe already he is in this world.

4 Litle children, ye are of God, and haue ouercome them: for greater is he that is in you, then he that is in this world.

5 They are of this worlde, therefore speake they of this world, and this world heareth them.

6 We are of God, he that knoweth God, heareth vs: he that is not of God, heareth vs not. Heereby knowe wee the spirit of trueth, and the spirit of errour.

7 Beloued, let vs loue one another: for loue commeth of God, and euery one that loueth, is borne of God, and knoweth God.

8 Hee that loueth not, knoweth not God: for God is loue.

9 Herein was that loue of God made manifest amongst vs, because God sent that his onely begotten sonne into this world, that we might liue through him.

10 Herein is that loue, not that we loued God, but that he loued vs, and sent his Sonne to be a reconciliation for our sinnes.

11 Beloued, if God so loued vs, we ought also to loue one another.

12 No man hath seene God at any time. If we loue one another, God dwelleth in vs, and his loue is perfect in vs.

13 Hereby know we, that we dwell in him, and he in vs: because he hath giuen vs of his Spirit.

14 And we haue seene, and doe testifie, that the Father sent that Sonne to be ye Sauiour of the world.

15 Whosoeuer confesseth Iesus is the Sone of God, in him dwelleth God, and he in God.

16 And we haue knowen, and beleeued ye loue that God hath in vs. God is loue,

and he that dwelleth in loue, dwelleth in God, and God in him.

17 Herein is that loue perfect in vs, that we should haue boldnes in the day of iudgement: for as he is, euen so are we in this world.

18 There is no feare in loue, but perfect loue casteth out feare: for feare hath painefulnesse: and he that feareth, is not perfect in loue.

19 We loue him, because he loued vs first.

20 If any man say, I loue God, and hate his brother, he is a liar: for how can he that loueth not his brother whom he hath seene, loue God whom he hath not seene?

21 And this commandement haue we of him, that he that loueth God, should loue his brother also.

First John 5

1 Whosoeuer beleeueth that Iesus is that Christ, is borne of God: and euery one that loueth him, which begate, loueth him also which is begotten of him.

2 In this we know that we loue the children of God, when we loue God, and keepe his commandements.

3 For this is the loue of God, that we keepe his commandements: and his commandements are not burdenous.

4 For all that is borne of God, ouercommeth this world: and this is that victorie that hath ouercome this world, euen our faith.

5 Who is it that ouercommeth this world, but he which beleeueth that Iesus is that Sonne of God?

6 This is that Iesus Christ that came by water and blood: not by water onely, but by water and blood: and it is that Spirit, that beareth witnesse: for that Spirit is trueth.

7 For there are three, which beare recorde in heauen, the Father, the Worde, and the holy Ghost: and these three are one.

8 And there are three, which beare record in the earth, the spirit, and the water and the blood: and these three agree in one.

9 If we receiue the witnesse of men, the witnesse of God is greater: for this is the witnesse of God, which he testified of his Sonne.

10 He that beleeueth in that Sonne of God, hath the witnes in himselfe: he that beleeueth not God, hath made him a lyar, because he beleeued not ye record, that God witnessed of that his Sonne.

11 And this is that record, to wit, that God hath giuen vnto vs eternall life, and this life is in that his Sonne.

12 He that hath that Sonne, hath that life: and he that hath not that Sonne of God, hath not that life.

13 These things haue I written vnto you, that beleeue in the Name of that Sonne of God, that ye may knowe that ye haue eternall life, and that ye may beleeue in the Name of that Sonne of God.

14 And this is that assurance, that we haue in him, that if we aske any thing according to his will, he heareth vs.

15 And if we know that he heareth vs, whatsoeuer we aske, we know that we haue the petitions, that we haue desired of him.

16 If any man see his brother sinne a sinne that is not vnto death, let him aske, and he shall giue him life for them that sinne not vnto death. There is a sinne vnto death: I say not that thou shouldest pray for it.

17 All vnrighteousnesse is sinne, but there is a sinne not vnto death.

18 We know that whosoeuer is borne of God, sinneth not: but he that is begotten of God, keepeth himselfe, and that wicked one toucheth him not.

19 We knowe that we are of God, and this whole world lieth in wickednesse.

20 But we know that that Sone of God is come, and hath giue vs a mind to know him, which is true: and we are in him that is true, that is, in that his Sone Iesus Christ: this same is that very God, and that eternal life.

21 Litle children, keepe your selues from idoles, Amen.

Second John

Second John 1

1 THE ELDER to the elect Lady, and her children, whom I loue in the trueth: and not I onely, but also all that haue knowen the trueth,

2 For the trueths sake which dwelleth in vs, and shalbe with vs for euer:

3 Grace be with you, mercie and peace from God the Father, and from the Lord Iesus Christ the Sonne of the Father, with trueth and loue.

4 I reioyced greatly, that I founde of thy children walking in trueth, as we haue receiued a commandement of the Father.

5 And nowe beseeche I thee, Lady, (not as writing a newe commandement vnto thee, but that same which we had from the beginning) that we loue one another.

6 And this is that loue, that we should walke after his commandements. This commandement is, that as ye haue heard from the beginning, ye should walke in it.

7 For many deceiuers are entred into this worlde, which confesse not that Iesus Christ is come in the flesh. He that is such one, is a deceiuer and an Antichrist.

8 Looke to your selues, that we lose not the things which we haue done, but that we may receiue full reward.

9 Whosoeuer transgresseth, and abideth not in the doctrine of Christ, hath not God. He that continueth in the doctrine of Christ, he hath both the Father and the Sonne.

10 If there come any vnto you, and bring not this doctrine, receiue him not to house, neither bid him, God speede:

11 For he that biddeth him, God speede, is partaker of his euill deedes. Although I had many things to write vnto you, yet

I woulde not write with paper and ynke: but I trust to come vnto you, and speake mouth to mouth, that our ioy may be full.

12 The sonnes of thine elect sister greete thee, Amen.

Third John

Third John 1

1 The Elder vnto the beloued Gaius, whom I loue in the trueth.

2 Beloued, I wish chiefly that thou prosperedst and faredst well as thy soule prospereth.

3 For I reioyced greatly when the brethren came, and testified of the trueth that is in thee, how thou walkest in the trueth.

4 I haue no greater ioy then these, that is, to heare that my sonnes walke in veritie.

5 Beloued, thou doest faithfully, whatsoeuer thou doest to the brethren, and to strangers,

6 Which bare witnesse of thy loue before the Churches. Whom if thou bringest on their iourney as it beseemeth according to God, thou shalt doe well,

7 Because that for his Names sake they went forth, and tooke nothing of the Gentiles.

8 We therefore ought to receiue such, that we might be helpers to the trueth.

9 I wrote vnto the Church: but Diotrephes which loueth to haue the preeminence among them, receiueth vs not.

10 Wherefore if I come, I will call to your remembrance his deedes which he doeth, pratling against vs with malicious wordes, and not therewith content, neither he himselfe receiueth the brethren, but forbiddeth them that woulde, and thrusteth them out of the Church.

11 Beloued, follow not that which is euill, but that which is good: he that doeth well, is of God: but he that doeth euill, hath not seene God.

12 Demetrius hath good report of al men, and of the trueth it selfe: yea, and wee our selues beare recorde, and ye know that our record is true.

13 I haue many things to write: but I will not with yncke and pen write vnto thee:

14 For I trust I shall shortly see thee, and we shall speake mouth to mouth. Peace be with thee. The friends salute thee. Greete the friends by name.

Jude

Jude 1

1 IVde a seruaunt of Iesus Christ, and brother of Iames, to them which are called and sanctified of God the Father, and returned to Iesus Christ:

2 Mercie vnto you, and peace and loue be multiplied.

3 Beloued, when I gaue al diligece to write vnto you of the common saluation, it was needful for me to write vnto you to exhort you, that yee should earnestly contend for the maintenace of ye faith, which was once giuen vnto the Saintes.

4 For there are certaine men crept in, which were before of olde ordeined to this condemnation: vngodly men they are which turne the grace of our God into wantonnesse, and denie God the onely Lord, and our Lord Iesus Christ.

5 I wil therfore put you in remebrance, forasmuch as ye once knew this, how that the Lord, after that he had deliuered the people out of Egypt, destroied them afterward which beleeued not.

6 The Angels also which kept not their first estate, but left their owne habitation, hee hath reserued in euerlasting chaines vnder darkenesse vnto the iudgement of the great day.

7 As Sodom and Gomorrhe, and the cities about them, which in like maner as they did, committed fornication, and followed strange flesh, are set foorth for an ensample, and suffer the vengeance of eternall fire.

8 Likewise notwithstanding these sleepers also defile the flesh, and despise gouernment, and speake euill of them that are in authoritie.

9 Yet Michael the Archangell, when hee stroue against the deuill, and disputed about the body of Moses, durst not blame him with cursed speaking, but sayd, The Lord rebuke thee.

10 But these speake euill of those thinges, which they know not: and whatsoeuer things they know naturally, as beasts, which are without reason, in those things they corrupt them selues.

11 Wo be vnto them: for they haue followed the way of Cain, and are cast away by the deceit of Balaams wages, and perish in the gainsaying of Core.

12 These are rockes in your feasts of charitie when they feast with you, without al feare, feeding themselues: cloudes they are without water, caried about of windes, corrupt trees and without fruit, twise dead, and plucked vp by ye rootes.

13 They are the raging waues of the sea, foming out their owne shame: they are wandring starres, to whome is reserued the blackenesse of darkenesse for euer.

14 And Enoch also the seuenth from Adam, prophecied of such, saying, Beholde, the Lord commeth with thousands of his Saints,

15 To giue iudgement against al men, and to rebuke all the vngodly among them of all their wicked deeds, which they haue vngodly committed, and of all their cruel speakings, which wicked sinners haue spoken against him.

16 These are murmurers, complainers, walking after their owne lustes: Whose mouthes speake proud things, hauing mens persons in admiration, because of aduantage.

17 But, yee beloued, remember the wordes which were spoken before of the Apostles of our Lord Iesus Christ,

18 How that they told you that there should be mockers in ye last time, which should walke after their owne vngodly lustes.

19 These are they that separate them selues from other, naturall, hauing not the Spirit.

20 But, yee beloued, edifie your selues in your most holy faith, praying in the holy Ghost,

21 And keepe your selues in the loue of God, looking for the mercie of our Lord Iesus Christ, vnto eternall life.

22 And haue compassion of some, in putting difference:

23 And other saue with feare, pulling them out of the fire, and hate euen that garment which is spotted by the flesh.

24 Nowe vnto him that is able to keepe you, that ye fall not, and to present you faultlesse before the presence of his glorie with ioy,

25 That is, to God only wise, our Sauiour, be glorie, and maiestie, and dominion, and power, both nowe and for euer, Amen.

Reveletion

Revelation 1

1 The Reuelation of Iesus Christ, which God gaue vnto him, to shewe vnto his seruants things which must shortly be done: which he sent, and shewed by his Angel vnto his seruant Iohn,

2 Who bare record of ye word of God, and of the testimonie of Iesus Christ, and of all things that he saw.

3 Blessed is he that readeth, and they that heare the wordes of this prophecie, and keepe those things which are written therein: for the time is at hand.

4 Iohn, to the seuen Churches which are in Asia, Grace be with you, and peace from him, Which is, and Which was, and Which is to come, and from the seuen Spirits which are before his Throne,

5 And from Iesus Christ, which is that faithful witnes, and that first begotten of the dead, and that Prince of the Kings of the earth, vnto him that loued vs, and washed vs from our sinnes in his blood,

6 And made vs Kings and Priests vnto God euen his Father, to him I say be glory, and dominion for euermore, Amen.

7 Beholde, he commeth with cloudes, and euery eye shall see him: yea, euen they which pearced him thorowe: and all kinreds of the earth shall waile before him, Euen so, Amen.

8 I am Alpha and Omega, the beginning and the ending, saith the Lord, Which is, and Which was, and Which is to come, euen the Almightie.

9 I Iohn, euen your brother, and companion in tribulation, and in the kingdome and patience of Iesus Christ, was in the yle called Patmos, for the worde of God, and for the witnessing of Iesus Christ.

10 And I was rauished in spirit on the Lordes day, and heard behinde me a great voyce, as it had bene of a trumpet,

11 Saying, I am Alpha and Omega, that first and that last: and that which thou seest, write in a booke, and send it vnto the seuen Churches which are in Asia, vnto Ephesus, and vnto Smyrna, and vnto Pergamus, and vnto Thyatira, and vnto Sardis, and vnto Philadelphia, and vnto Laodicea.

12 Then I turned backe to see the voyce, that spake with me: and when I was turned, I sawe seuen golden candlestickes,

13 And in the middes of the seuen candlestickes, one like vnto the Sonne of man, clothed with a garment downe to the feete, and girded about the pappes with a golden girdle.

14 His head, and heares were white as white wooll, and as snowe, and his eyes were as a flame of fire,

15 And his feete like vnto fine brasse, burning as in a fornace: and his voyce as the sounde of many waters.

16 And he had in his right hand seuen starres: and out of his mouth went a sharpe two edged sword: and his face shone as the sunne shineth in his strength.

17 And when I saw him, I fell at his feete as dead: then he laid his right hand vpon me, saying vnto me, Feare not: I am that first and that last,

18 And am aliue, but I was dead: and beholde, I am aliue for euermore, Amen: and I haue the keyes of hell and of death.

19 Write the things which thou hast seene, and the things which are, and the things which shall come hereafter.

20 The misterie of the seuen starres which thou sawest in my right hand, and the seuen golden candlestickes, is this, The seuen starres are the Angels of the seuen Churches: and the seuen candlestickes which thou sawest, are the seuen Churches.

Revelation 2

1 VNto the Angel of the Church of Ephesus write, These things saieth he that holdeth the seuen starres in his right hand, and walketh in the middes of the seuen golden candlestickes.

2 I knowe thy workes, and thy labour, and thy patience, and howe thou canst not beare with them which are euill, and hast examined them which say they are Apostles, and are not, and hast found the liars.

3 And thou wast burdened, and hast patience, and for my Names sake hast laboured, and hast not fainted.

4 Neuertheles, I haue somewhat against thee, because thou hast left thy first loue.

5 Remember therefore from whence thou art fallen, and repent, and doe the first workes: or els I will come against thee shortly, and will remooue thy candlesticke out of his place, except thou amend.

6 But this thou hast, that thou hatest the workes of the Nicolaitanes, which I also hate.

7 Let him that hath an eare, heare, what the Spirite saith vnto the Churches, To him that ouercommeth, will I giue to eate of the tree of life which is in the middes of the Paradise of God.

8 And vnto the Angel of the Church of the Smyrnians write, These things saith he that is first, and last, which was dead and is aliue.

9 I knowe thy workes and tribulation, and pouertie (but thou art riche) and I knowe the blasphemie of them, which say they are Iewes, and are not, but are the Synagogue of Satan.

10 Feare none of those things, which thou shalt suffer: beholde, it shall come to passe, that the deuill shall cast some of you into prison, that ye may be tryed, and ye shall haue tribulation tenne dayes: be thou faithfull vnto the death, and I will giue thee the crowne of life.

11 Let him that hath an eare, heare what the Spirit saith to the Churches. He that ouercommeth, shall not be hurt of the second death.

12 And to the Angel of the Church, which is at Pergamus write, This saith he which hath that sharpe sworde with two edges.

13 I knowe thy workes and where thou dwellest, euen where Satans throne is, and thou keepest my Name, and hast not denied my faith, euen in those dayes when Antipas my faithfull martyr was slaine among you, where Satan dwelleth.

14 But I haue a fewe things against thee, because thou hast there them that maintaine the doctrine of Balaam, which taught Balac to put a stumbling blocke before ye children of Israel, that they should eate of things sacrificed vnto Idoles, and commit fornication.

15 Euen so hast thou them, that maintaine the doctrine of the Nicolaitanes, which thing I hate.

16 Repent thy selfe, or els I will come vnto thee shortly, and will fight against them with the sworde of my mouth.

17 Let him that hath an eare, heare what the Spirite saith vnto the Churches. To him that ouercommeth, will I giue to eate of the Manna that is hid, and will giue him a white stone, and in the stone a newe name written, which no man knoweth sauing he that receiueth it.

18 And vnto ye Angel of the Church which is at Thyatira write, These things saith the Sonne of God, which hath his eyes like vnto a flame of fire, and his feete like fine brasse.

19 I knowe thy workes and thy loue, and seruice, and faith, and thy patience, and thy workes, and that they are more at the last, then at the first.

20 Notwithstanding, I haue a few things against thee, that thou sufferest the woman Iezabel, which calleth her selfe a prophetesse, to teache and to deceiue my seruants to make them commit fornication, and to eate meates sacrificed vnto idoles.

21 And I gaue her space to repent of her fornication, and she repented not.

22 Beholde, I will cast her into a bed, and them that commit fornication with her, into great affliction, except they repent them of their workes.

23 And I will kill her children with death: and all the Churches shall know that I am he which searche the reines and heartes: and I will giue vnto euery one of you according vnto your workes.

24 And vnto you I say, the rest of them of Thyatira, As many as haue not this learning, neither haue knowen the deepenes of Satan (as they speake) I will put vpon you none other burden.

25 But that which ye haue alreadie, hold fast till I come.

26 For he that ouercommeth and keepeth my workes vnto the end, to him will I giue power ouer nations,

27 And he shall rule them with a rodde of yron: and as the vessels of a potter, shall they be broken.

28 Euen as I receiued of my Father, so will I giue him the morning starre.

29 Let him that hath an eare, heare what the Spirite saith to the Churches.

Revelation 3

1 ANd write vnto the Angel of the Church which is at Sardis, These things saith he that hath the seuen Spirits of God, and the seuen starres, I knowe thy workes: for thou hast a name that thou liuest, but thou art dead.

2 Be awake, and strengthen the things which remaine, that are readie to die: for I haue not found thy workes perfite before God.

3 Remember therefore, how thou hast receiued and heard, and hold fast and repent. If therefore thou wilt not watch, I will come on thee as a thiefe, and thou shalt not know what houre I wil come vpon thee.

4 Notwithstanding thou hast a few names yet in Sardis, which haue not defiled their garments: and they shall walke with me in white: for they are worthy.

5 He that ouercommeth, shalbe clothed in white araye, and I will not put out his name out of the booke of life, but I will confesse his name before my Father, and before his Angels.

6 Let him that hath an eare, heare, what the Spirite saith vnto the Churches.

7 And write vnto ye Angel of ye Church which is of Philadelphia, These things saith he that is Holy, and True, which hath ye keye of Dauid, which openeth and no man shutteth, and shutteth and no man openeth,

8 I knowe thy workes: beholde, I haue set before thee an open doore, and no man can shut it: for thou hast a litle strength and hast kept my worde, and hast not denied my Name.

9 Behold, I will make them of the Synagogue of Satan, which call themselues Iewes, and are not, but doe lye: beholde, I say, I will make them, that they shall come and worship before thy feete, and shall knowe that I haue loued thee.

10 Because thou hast kept the woorde of my patience, therefore I wil deliuer thee from the houre of tentation, which will come vpon all the world, to trie them that dwell vpon the earth.

11 Beholde, I come shortly: holde that which thou hast, that no man take thy crowne.

12 Him that ouercommeth, will I make a pillar in the Temple of my God, and he shall goe no more out: and I will write vpon him the Name of my God, and the name of the citie of my God, which is the newe Hierusalem, which commeth downe out of heauen from my God, and I will write vpon him my newe Name.

13 Let him that hath an eare, heare what ye Spirit saith vnto the Churches.

14 And vnto the Angell of the Church of the Laodiceans write, These things saieth Amen, the faithfull and true witnesse, that beginning of the creatures of God.

15 I knowe thy woorkes, that thou art neither colde nor hote: I woulde thou werest colde or hote.

16 Therefore, because thou art luke warme, and neither colde nor hote, it will come to passe, that I shall spewe thee out of my mouth.

17 For thou saiest, I am rich and increased with goods, and haue neede of nothing, and knowest not howe thou art wretched and miserable, and poore, and blinde, and naked.

18 I counsell thee to bye of me gold tried by the fire, that thou maiest bee made rich: and white raiment, that thou maiest be clothed, and that thy filthie nakednesse doe not appeare: and anoynt thine eyes with eye salue, that thou maiest see.

19 As many as I loue, I rebuke and chasten: be zealous therefore and amend.

20 Behold, I stand at the doore, and knocke. If any man heare my voice and open ye doore, I wil come in vnto him, and will suppe with him, and he with me.

21 To him that ouercommeth, will I graunt to sit with me in my throne, euen as I ouercame, and sit with my Father in his throne.

22 Let him that hath an eare, heare what the Spirit saieth vnto the Churches.

Revelation 4

1 After this I looked, and beholde, a doore was open in heauen, and the first voyce which I heard, was as it were of a trumpet talking with mee, saying, Come vp hither, and I will shewe thee things which must be done hereafter.

2 And immediatly I was rauished in the spirit, and behold, a throne was set in heauen, and one sate vpon the throne.

3 And he that sate, was to looke vpon, like vnto a iasper stone, and a sardine, and there was a rainbowe rounde about the throne, in sight like to an emeraude.

4 And round about the throne were foure and twentie seates, and vpon the seates I sawe foure and twentie Elders sitting, clothed in white raiment, and had on their heads crownes of golde.

5 And out of the throne proceeded lightnings, and thundrings, and voyces, and there were seuen lampes of fire burning before the throne, which are the seuen spirits of God.

6 And before the throne there was a sea of glasse like vnto chrystall: and in the middes of the throne, and round about the throne were foure beasts full of eyes before and behinde.

7 And the first beast was like a lion, and the second beast like a calfe, and the thirde beast had a face as a man, and the fourth beast was like a flying Eagle.

8 And the foure beasts had eche one of them sixe wings about him, and they were full of eyes within, and they ceased not day nor night, saying, Holy, holy, holy Lord God almighty, Which Was, and Which Is, and Which Is to come.

9 And when those beasts gaue glorie, and honour, and thanks to him that sate on the throne, which liueth for euer and euer,

10 The foure and twentie Elders fell downe before him that sate on the throne and worshipped him that liueth for euermore, and cast their crownes before the throne, saying,

11 Thou art worthy, O Lord, to receiue glory and honour, and power: for thou hast created all things, and for thy wils sake they are, and haue beene created.

Revelation 5

1 And I saw in the right hand of him that sate vpon the throne, a Booke written within, and on the backside, sealed with seuen seales.

2 And I sawe a strong Angell which preached with a loud voice, Who is worthy to open ye booke, and to loose the seales thereof?

3 And no man in heauen, nor in earth, neither vnder the earth, was able to open the Booke, neither to looke thereon.

4 Then I wept much, because no man was foud worthy to open, and to reade the Booke, neither to looke thereon.

5 And one of the Elders saide vnto me, Weepe not: beholde, that Lion which is of the tribe of Iuda, that roote of Dauid, hath obteined to open the Booke, and to loose the seuen seales thereof.

6 Then I behelde, and loe, in the middes of the throne, and of the foure beasts, and in the mids of the Elders, stoode a Labe as though he had bene killed, which had seuen hornes, and seuen eyes, which are the seuen spirites of God, sent into all the world.

7 And hee came, and tooke the Booke out of the right hand of him that sate vpon the throne.

8 And when he had taken ye Booke, ye foure beasts and the foure and twenty Elders fel downe before the Lambe, hauing euery one harps and golden vials full of odours, which are the praiers of the Saintes,

9 And they sung a new song, saying, Thou art worthie to take the Booke, and to open the seales thereof, because thou wast killed, and hast redeemed vs to God by thy blood out of euery kinred, and tongue, and people, and nation,

10 And hast made vs vnto our God Kings and Priests, and we shall reigne on the earth.

11 Then I behelde, and I heard the voice of many Angels round about the throne, and about the beastes and the Elders, and there were ten thousand times ten thousand, and thousand thousands,

12 Saying with a loude voice, Worthie is the Lambe that was killed to receiue power, and riches, and wisdome, and strength, and honour, and glory, and praise.

13 And al the creatures which are in heauen, and on the earth, and vnder the earth, and in the sea, and al that are in them, heard I, saying, Praise, and honour, and glory, and power be vnto him, that sitteth vpon the throne, and vnto the Lambe for euermore.

14 And the foure beasts said, Amen, and the foure and twentie Elders fell downe and worshipped him that liueth for euermore.

Revelation 6

1 After, I beheld whe the Lambe had opened one of the seales, and I heard one of the foure beastes say, as it were the noise of thunder, Come and see.

2 Therefore I behelde, and loe, there was a white horse, and hee that sate on him, had a bowe, and a crowne was giuen vnto him, and he went forth conquering that he might ouercome.

3 And when he had opened the seconde seale, I heard the second beast say, Come and see.

4 And there went out an other horse, that was red, and power was giuen to him that sate thereon, to take peace from the earth, and that they should kill one another, and there was giuen vnto him a great sword.

5 And when hee had opened the thirde seale, I heard the thirde beast say, Come and see: Then I behelde, and loe, a blacke horse, and he that sate on him, had balances in his hand.

6 And I heard a voice in the mids of the foure beastes say, A measure of wheate for a penie, and three measures of barly for a peny, and oyle, and wine hurt thou not.

7 And when he had opened the fourth seale, I heard the voice of the fourth beast say, Come and see.

8 And I looked, and beholde, a pale horse, and his name that sate on him was Death, and Hell folowed after him, and power was giuen vnto them ouer the fourth part of the earth, to kill with sworde, and with hunger, and with death, and with beasts of the earth.

9 And when hee had opened the fifth seale, I sawe vnder the altar the soules of them, that were killed for the worde of God, and for the testimonie which they mainteined.

10 And they cried with a loud voice, saying, How long, Lord, which art holie and true! doest not thou iudge and auenge our blood on them that dwell on the earth?

11 And long white robes were giuen vnto euery one, and it was saide vnto them, that they shoulde rest for a litle season vntill their fellow seruants, and their brethren that shoulde bee killed euen as they were, were fulfilled.

12 And I behelde when hee had opened the sixt seale, and loe, there was a great earthquake, and the sunne was as blacke as sackecloth of heare, and the moone was like blood.

13 And the starres of heauen fell vnto the earth, as a figge tree casteth her greene figges when it is shaken of a mightie winde.

14 And heauen departed away, as a scroule, when it is rolled, and euery mountaine and yle were mooued out of their places.

15 And the Kinges of the earth, and the great men, and the rich men, and the chiefe captaines, and the mighty men, and euery bondman, and euery free man, hid themselues in dennes, and among the rockes of the mountaines,

16 And said to the mountaines and rocks, Fal on vs, and hide vs from the presence of him that sitteth on the throne, and from the wrath of the Lambe.

17 For the great day of his wrath is come, and who can stand?

Revelation 7

1 And after that, I sawe foure Angels stand on the foure corners of the earth, holding the foure windes of the earth, that the winds should not blow on the earth, neither on the sea, neither on any tree.

2 And I sawe another Angel come vp from the East, which had the seale of the liuing God, and hee cried with a loud voice to the foure Angels to who power was giuen to hurt the earth, and the sea, saying,

3 Hurt ye not the earth, neither the sea, neither the trees, til we haue sealed the seruants of our God in their foreheads.

4 And I heard the number of them, which were sealed, and there were sealed an hundreth and foure and fourtie thousand of all the tribes of the children of Israel.

5 Of the tribe of Iuda were sealed twelue thousande. Of the tribe of Ruben were sealed twelue thousande. Of the tribe of Gad were sealed twelue thousande.

6 Of the tribe of Aser were sealed twelue thousand. Of the tribe of Nephthali were sealed twelue thousand. Of the tribe of Manasses were sealed twelue thousand.

7 Of the tribe of Simeon were sealed twelue thousande. Of the tribe of Leui were sealed twelue thousande. Of the tribe of Issachar were sealed twelue thousand. Of the tribe of Zabulon were sealed twelue thousand.

8 Of the tribe of Ioseph were sealed twelue thousande. Of the tribe of Beniamin were sealed twelue thousand.

9 After these thinges I behelde, and loe a great multitude, which no man coulde number, of all nations and kindreds, and people, and tongues, stoode before the throne, and before the Lambe, clothed with long white robes, and palmes in their hands.

10 And they cried with a loud voice, saying, Saluation commeth of our God, that sitteth vpon the throne, and of the Lambe.

11 And all the Angels stoode rounde about the throne, and about the Elders, and the foure beastes, and they fell before the throne on their faces, and worshipped God,

12 Saying, Amen. Praise, and glorie, and wisdom, and thankes, and honour, and power, and might bee vnto our God for euermore, Amen.

13 And one of the Elders spake, saying vnto me, What are these which are araied in log white robes? and whence came they?

14 And I saide vnto him, Lord, thou knowest. And he saide to me, These are they, which came out of great tribulation, and haue washed their long robes, and haue made their long robes white in the blood of the Lambe.

15 Therefore are they in the presence of the throne of God, and serue him day and night in his Temple, and he that sitteth on the throne, wil dwell among them.

16 They shall hunger no more, neither thirst any more, neither shall the sunne light on them, neither any heate.

17 For the Lambe, which is in the middes of the throne, shall gouerne them, and shall leade them vnto the liuely fountaines of waters, and God shall wipe away all teares from their eyes.

Revelation 8

1 And when he had opened the seuenth seale, there was silence in heauen about halfe an houre.

2 And I sawe the seuen Angels, which stoode before God, and to them were giuen seuen trumpets.

3 Then another Angel came and stoode before the altar hauing a golden censer, and much odours was giuen vnto him, that hee shoulde offer with the prayers of all Saintes vpon the golden altar, which is before the throne.

4 And the smoke of the odours with the prayers of the Saintes, went vp before God, out of the Angels hand.

5 And the Angel tooke the censer, and filled it with fire of the altar, and cast it into the earth, and there were voyces, and thundrings, and lightnings, and earthquake.

6 Then the seuen Angels, which had the seuen trumpets, prepared themselues to blow the trumpets.

7 So the first Angell blewe the trumpet, and there was haile and fire, mingled with blood, and they were cast into the earth, and the thirde part of trees was burnt, and all greene grasse was burnt.

8 And the second Angel blew the trumpet, and as it were a great mountaine, burning with fire, was cast into the sea, and the thirde part of the sea became blood.

9 And the thirde part of the creatures, which were in the sea, and had life, died, and the thirde part of shippes were destroyed.

10 Then the thirde Angel blew the trumpet, and there fell a great starre from heauen, burning like a torche, and it fell into the thirde part of the riuers, and into the fountaines of waters.

11 And the name of the starre is called wormewood: therefore the thirde part of the waters became wormewood, and many men died of the waters, because they were made bitter.

12 And the fourth Angel blew the trumpet, and the thirde part of the sunne was smitten, and the thirde part of the moone, and the thirde part of the starres, so that the thirde part of them was darkened: and the day was smitten, that the thirde part of it could not shine, and likewise the night.

13 And I beheld, and heard one Angel flying thorow the middes of heauen, saying with a loude voyce, Woe, woe, woe to the inhabitants of the earth, because of the sounds to come of the trumpet of the three Angels, which were yet to blowe the trumpets.

Revelation 9

1 And the fifth Angel blew the trumpet, and I saw a starre fall from heauen vnto the earth, and to him was giuen the key of the bottomlesse pit.

2 And he opened the bottomlesse pit, and there arose the smoke of the pit, as the smoke of a great fornace, and the sunne, and the ayre were darkened by the smoke of the pit.

3 And there came out of the smoke Locustes vpon the earth, and vnto them was giuen power, as the scorpions of the earth haue power.

4 And it was comanded them, that they should not hurt the grasse of the earth, neither any greene thing, neither any tree: but onely those men which haue not the seale of God in their foreheads.

5 And to them was comanded that they should not kill them, but that they should be vexed fiue moneths, and that their paine should be as the paine that commeth of a scorpion, when he hath stung a man.

6 Therefore in those dayes shall men seeke death, and shall not finde it, and shall desire to die, and death shall flie from them.

7 And the forme of the locustes was like vnto horses prepared vnto battel, and on their heads were as it were crownes, like vnto golde, and their faces were like the faces of men.

8 And they had heare as the heare of women, and their teeth were as the teeth of lyons.

9 And they had habbergions, like to habbergions of yron: and the soud of their wings was like the sound of charets whe many horses runne vnto battel.

10 And they had tailes like vnto scorpions, and there were stings in their tailes, and their power was to hurt men fiue monethes.

11 And they haue a King ouer them, which is the Angel of the bottomlesse pit, whose name in Hebrewe is Abaddon, and in Greeke he is named Apollyon, that is, destroying.

12 One woe is past, and beholde, yet two woes come after this.

13 Then the sixt Angel blew the trumpet, and I heard a voyce from the foure hornes of the golden altar, which is before God,

14 Saying to the sixt Angel, which had the trumpet, Loose the foure Angels, which are bound in the great riuer Euphrates.

15 And the foure Angels were loosed, which were prepared at an houre, at a day, at a moneth, and at a yeere, to slay the thirde part of men.

16 And the number of horsemen of warre were twentie thousand times ten thousand: for I heard the number of them.

17 And thus I saw the horses in a vision, and them that sate on them, hauing firie habbergions, and of Iacinth, and of brimstone, and the heads of the horses were as the heades of lyons: and out of their mouthes went foorth fire and smoke and brimstone.

18 Of these three was the thirde part of men killed, that is, of the fire, and of the smoke, and of the brimstone, which came out of their mouthes.

19 For their power is in their mouthes, and in their tailes: for their tailes were like vnto serpents, and had heades, wherewith they hurt.

20 And the remnant of the men which were not killed by these plagues, repented not of the works of their handes that they should not worship deuils, and idoles of golde and of siluer, and of brasse, and of stone, and of wood, which neither can see, neither heare nor goe.

21 Also they repented not of their murder, and of their sorcerie, neither of their fornication, nor of their theft.

Revelation 10

1 And I sawe another mightie Angel come downe from heauen, clothed with a cloude, and the raine bowe vpon his head, and his face was as the sunne, and his feete as pillars of fire.

2 And hee had in his hande a little booke open, and he put his right foote vpon the sea, and his left on the earth,

3 And cried with a loude voyce, as when a lyon roareth: and when he had cried, seuen thunders vttered their voyces.

4 And whe the seuen thunders had vttered their voyces, I was about to write:

but I heard a voice from heauen saying vnto me, Seale vp those things which the seuen thunders haue spoken, and write them not.

5 And the Angel which I sawe stand vpon the sea, and vpon the earth, lift vp his hand to heauen,

6 And sware by him that liueth for euermore, which created heauen, and the thinges that therein are, and the earth, and the things that therein are, and the sea, and the thinges that therein are, that time should be no more.

7 But in the dayes of the voyce of the seuenth Angel, when he shall beginne to blow the trumpet, euen the mysterie of God shalbe finished, as he hath declared to his seruants the Prophets.

8 And the voyce which I heard from heauen, spake vnto me againe, and said, Go and take the litle booke which is open in the hand of the Angel, which standeth vpon the sea and vpon the earth.

9 So I went vnto the Angel, and saide to him, Giue me the litle booke. And he said vnto me, Take it, and eate it vp, and it shall make thy belly bitter, but it shalbe in thy mouth as sweete as honie.

10 Then I tooke the litle booke out of ye Angels hand, and ate it vp, and it was in my mouth as sweete as hony: but whe I had eaten it my belly was bitter.

11 And he said vnto me, Thou must prophecie againe among the people and nations, and tongues, and to many Kings.

Revelation 11

1 Then was giuen me a reede, like vnto a rod, and the Angel stoode by, saying, Rise and mete the Temple of God, and the altar, and them that worship therein.

2 But the court which is without the temple cast out, and mete it not: for it is giuen vnto the Gentiles, and the holy citie shall they treade vnder foote, two and fourtie monethes.

3 But I wil giue power vnto my two witnesses, and they shall prophecie a thousande two hundreth and threescore dayes, clothed in sackcloth.

4 These are two oliue trees, and two candlestickes, standing before the God of the earth.

5 And if any man wil hurt them, fire proceedeth out of their mouthes, and deuoureth their enemies: for if any man would hurt the, thus must he be killed.

6 These haue power to shut heauen, that it raine not in the dayes of their prophecying, and haue power ouer waters to turne them into blood, and to smite the earth with all maner plagues, as often as they will.

7 And when they haue finished their testimonie, the beast that commeth out of the bottomlesse pit, shall make warre against them, and shall ouercome them, and kill them.

8 And their corpses shall lie in the streetes of the great citie, which spiritually is called Sodom and Egypt, where our Lord also was crucified.

9 And they of the people and kinreds, and tongues, and Gentiles shall see their corpses three dayes and an halfe, and shall not suffer their carkeises to be put in graues.

10 And they that dwell vpon the earth, shall reioyce ouer them and be glad, and shall sende giftes one to an other: for these two Prophets vexed them that dwelt on the earth.

11 But after three dayes and an halfe, the spirit of life comming from God, shall enter into them, and they shall stande vp vpon their feete: and great feare shall come vpon them which sawe them.

12 And they shall heare a great voyce from heauen, saying vnto them, Come vp hither. And they shall ascend vp to heauen in a cloude, and their enemies shall see them.

13 And the same houre shall there bee a great earthquake, and the tenth part of the citie shall fall, and in the earthquake shalbe slaine in nomber seuen thousande: and the remnant were sore feared, and gaue glorie to the God of heauen.

14 The second woe is past, and beholde, the third woe will come anon.

15 And the seuenth Angell blewe the trumpet, and there were great voyces in heauen, saying, The kingdomes of this worlde are our Lordes, and his Christes, and he shall reigne for euermore.

16 Then the foure and twentie Elders, which sate before God on their seates, fell vpon their faces, and worshipped God,

17 Saying, We giue thee thankes, Lord God almightie, Which art, and Which wast, and Which art to come: for thou hast receiued thy great might, and hast obteined thy kingdome.

18 And the Gentiles were angrie, and thy wrath is come, and the time of the dead, that they shoulde be iudged, and that thou shouldest giue reward vnto thy seruants the Prophets, and to the Saintes, and to them that feare thy Name, to small and great, and shouldest destroy them, which destroy the earth.

19 Then the Temple of God was opened in heauen, and there was seene in his Temple the Arke of his couenant: and there were lightnings, and voyces, and thundrings, and earthquake, and much haile.

Revelation 12

1 And there appeared a great wonder in heauen: A woman clothed with the sunne, and the moone was vnder her feete, and vpon her head a crowne of twelue starres.

2 And she was with childe, and cried traueiling in birth, and was pained readie to be deliuered.

3 And there appeared another wonder in heaue: for beholde, a great red dragon hauing seuen heads, and ten hornes, and seuen crownes vpon his heads:

4 And his taile drew the thirde part of the starres of heauen, and cast them to the earth. And the dragon stood before

the woman, which was ready to be deliuered, to deuoure her childe, when shee had brought it foorth.

5 So shee brought foorth a man childe, which should rule all nations with a rod of yron: and that her childe was taken vp vnto God and to his throne.

6 And the woman fled into wildernes where she hath a place prepared of God, that they should feede her there a thousande, two hundreth and three score dayes.

7 And there was a battell in heauen, Michael and his Angels fought against the dragon, and the dragon fought and his angels.

8 But they preuailed not, neither was their place found any more in heauen.

9 And the great dragon, that olde serpent, called the deuil and Satan, was cast out, which deceiueth all the world: he was euen cast into the earth, and his angels were cast out with him.

10 Then I heard a loude voyce in heauen, saying, Now is saluation, and strength, and the kingdome of our God, and the power of his Christ: for the accuser of our brethren is cast downe, which accused them before our God day and night.

11 But they ouercame him by that blood of that Lambe, and by that worde of their testimonie, and they loued not their liues vnto the death.

12 Therefore reioyce, ye heauens, and ye that dwell in them. Wo to the inhabitants of the earth, and of the sea: for the deuill is come downe vnto you, which hath great wrath, knowing that he hath but a short time.

13 And when the dragon sawe that hee was cast vnto the earth, he persecuted the woman which had brought forth the man childe.

14 But to the woman were giuen two wings of a great eagle, that she might flie into the wildernes, into her place, where she is nourished for a time, and times, and halfe a time, from the presence of the serpent.

15 And the serpent cast out of his mouth water after the woman, like a flood, that he might cause her to be caried away of the flood.

16 But the earth holpe the woman, and the earth opened her mouth, and swalowed vp the flood, which the dragon had cast out of his mouth.

17 Then the dragon was wroth with the woman, and went and made warre with the remnant of her seede, which keepe the comaundements of God, and haue the testimonie of Iesus Christ.

18 And I stood on the sea sand.

Revelation 13

1 And I saw a beast rise out of the sea, hauing seuen heads, and ten hornes, and vpon his hornes were ten crownes, and vpon his heads the name of blasphemie.

2 And the beast which I sawe, was like a Leopard, and his feete like a beares, and his mouth as the mouth of a lion: and the dragon gaue him his power and his throne, and great authoritie.

3 And I sawe one of his heads as it were wounded to death, but his deadly wound was healed, and all the world wondred and folowed the beast.

4 And they worshipped the dragon which gaue power vnto the beast, and they worshipped the beast, saying, Who is like vnto the beast! who is able to warre with him!

5 And there was giuen vnto him a mouth, that spake great things and blasphemies, and power was giuen vnto him, to doe two and fourtie moneths.

6 And he opened his mouth vnto blasphemie against God, to blaspheme his Name, and his tabernacle, and them that dwell in heauen.

7 And it was giuen vnto him to make warre with the Saints, and to ouercome them, and power was giuen him ouer euery kinred, and tongue, and nation.

8 Therefore all that dwell vpon the earth, shall worship him, whose names are not written in the booke of life of that Lambe, which was slaine from the beginning of the world.

9 If any man haue an eare, let him heare.

10 If any leade into captiuitie, hee shall go into captiuitie: if any kill with a sword, he must be killed by a sword: here is the patience and the faith of the Saints.

11 And I beheld another beast comming vp out of the earth, which had two hornes like the Lambe, but he spake like the dragon.

12 And he did all that the first beast could doe before him, and he caused the earth, and them which dwell therein, to worship the first beast, whose deadly wound was healed.

13 And he did great wonders, so that hee made fire to come downe from heauen on the earth, in the sight of men,

14 And deceiued them that dwell on the earth by the signes, which were permitted to him to doe in the sight of the beast, saying to them that dwell on the earth, that they should make the image of the beast, which had the wound of a sword, and did liue.

15 And it was permitted to him to giue a spirit vnto the image of the beast, so that the image of the beast should speake, and should cause that as many as would not worship the image of the beast, should be killed.

16 And he made all, both small and great, rich and poore, free and bond, to receiue a marke in their right hand or in their foreheads,

17 And that no man might buy or sell, saue hee that had the marke, or the name of the beast, or the number of his name.

18 Here is wisdome. Let him that hath wit, count the number of the beast: for it is the number of a man, and his number is six hundreth threescore and sixe.

Revelation 14

1 Then I looked, and lo, a Lambe stood on mount Sion, and with him an hundreth, fourtie and foure thousand, hauing his Fathers Name written in their foreheads.

2 And I heard a voyce from heauen, as the sound of many waters, and as the sound of a great thunder: and I heard the voyce of harpers harping with their harpes.

3 And they sung as it were a newe song before the throne, and before the foure beasts, and the Elders: and no man could learne that song, but the hundreth, fourtie and foure thousand, which were bought from the earth.

4 These are they, which are not defiled with women: for they are virgins: these follow the Lambe whithersoeuer he goeth: these are bought from men, being the first fruites vnto God, and to the Lambe.

5 And in their mouthes was found no guile: for they are without spot before the throne of God.

6 Then I sawe another Angel flie in the mids of heauen, hauing an euerlasting Gospel, to preach vnto them that dwell on the earth, and to euery nation, and kinred, and tongue, and people,

7 Saying with a loude voyce, Feare God, and giue glory to him: for the houre of his iugdement is come: and woriship him that made heauen and earth, and the sea, and the fountaines of waters.

8 And there followed another Angel, saying, Babylon that great citie is fallen, it is fallen: for she made all nations to drinke of the wine of the wrath of her fornication.

9 And the third Angel followed them, saying with a loude voyce, If any man worship the beast and his image, and receiue his marke in his forehead, or on his hand,

10 The same shall drinke of the wine of ye wrath of God, yea, of the pure wine, which is powred into the cup of his wrath, and he shalbe tormented in fire and brimstone before the holy Angels, and before the Lambe.

11 And the smoke of their torment shall ascend euermore: and they shall haue no rest day nor night, which worship the beast and his image, and whosoeuer receiueth the print of his name.

12 Here is the patience of Saints: here are they that keepe the commandements of God, and the fayth of Iesus.

13 Then I heard a voyce from heauen, saying vnto me, Write, The dead which die in the Lord, are fully blessed. Euen so sayth the Spirit: for they rest from their labours, and their workes follow them.

14 And I looked, and behold, a white cloude, and vpon the cloude one sitting like vnto the Sonne of man, hauing on his head a golden crowne, and in his hand a sharpe sickle.

15 And another Angel came out of the Temple, crying with a loude voyce to him that sate on the cloude, Thrust in thy

sickle and reape: for the time is come to reape: for the haruest of the earth is ripe.

16 And he that sate on the cloude, thrust in his sickle on the earth, and the earth was reaped.

17 Then an other Angel came out of the Temple, which is in heauen, hauing also a sharpe sickle.

18 And another Angel came out from the altar, which had power ouer fire, and cryed with a loude crie to him that had the sharpe sickle, and sayd, Thrust in thy sharpe sickle, and gather the clusters of the vineyard of the earth: for her grapes are ripe.

19 And the Angel thrust in his sharpe sickle on the earth, and cut downe the vines of the vineyard of the earth, and cast them into that great wine presse of the wrath of God.

20 And the wine presse was troden without the citie, and blood came out of the wine presse, vnto the horse bridles, by the space of a thousand and sixe hundreth furlongs.

Revelation 15

1 And I sawe another signe in heauen, great and marueilous, seuen Angels, hauing the seuen last plagues: for by them is fulfilled the wrath of God.

2 And I sawe as it were a glassie sea, mingled with fire, and them that had gotten victorie of the beast, and of his image, and of his marke, and of the number of his name, stand at the glassie sea, hauing the harpes of God,

3 And they sung the song of Moses the seruant of God, and the song of the Lambe, saying, Great and marueilous are thy workes, Lord God almightie: iust and true are thy wayes, King of Saints.

4 Who shall not feare thee, O Lord, and glorifie thy Name! for thou onely art holy, and all nations shall come and worship before thee: for thy iudgements are made manifest.

5 And after that, I looked, and beholde, the Temple of the tabernacle of testimonie was open in heauen.

6 And the seuen Angels came out of the Temple, which had the seuen plagues, clothed in pure and bright linnen, and hauing their breasts girded with golden girdles.

7 And one of the foure beastes gaue vnto the seuen Angels seuen golden vials full of the wrath of God, which liueth for euermore.

8 And the Temple was full of the smoke of the glory of God and of his power, and no man was able to enter into the Temple, till the seuen plagues of the seuen Angels were fulfilled.

Revelation 16

1 And I heard a great voyce out of the Temple, saying to the seuen Angels, Go your wayes, and powre out the seuen vials of the wrath of God vpon the earth.

2 And the first went and powred out his viall vpon the earth: and there fell a noysome, and a grieuous sore vpon the men, which had the marke of ye beast, and vpon them which worshipped his image.

3 And the second Angel powred out his viall vpon the sea, and it became as the blood of a dead man: and euery liuing thing dyed in the sea.

4 And the third Angel powred out his viall vpon the riuers and fountaines of waters, and they became blood.

5 And I heard the Angel of the waters say, Lord, thou art iust, Which art, and Which wast: and Holy, because thou hast iudged these things.

6 For they shed the blood of the Saints, and Prophets, and therefore hast thou giuen them blood to drinke: for they are worthy.

7 And I heard another out of the Sanctuarie say, Euen so, Lord God almightie, true and righteous are thy iudgements.

8 And the fourth Angel powred out his viall on the sunne, and it was giuen vnto him to torment men with heate of fire,

9 And men boyled in great heate, and blasphemed the Name of God, which hath power ouer these plagues, and they repented not, to giue him glorie.

10 And the fifth Angel powred out his viall vpon the throne of the beast, and his kingdome waxed darke, and they gnawed their tongues for sorowe,

11 And blasphemed the God of heauen for their paines, and for their sores, and repented not of their workes.

12 And the sixth Angel powred out his viall vpon the great riuer Euphrates, and the water thereof dried vp, that the way of the Kings of the East should be prepared.

13 And I sawe three vncleane spirits like frogs come out of the mouth of that dragon, and out of the mouth of that beast, and out of the mouth of that false prophet.

14 For they are the spirits of deuils, working miracles, to go vnto the Kings of the earth, and of the whole world, to gather them to the battell of that great day of God Almightie.

15 (Beholde, I come as a theefe. Blessed is he that watcheth and keepeth his garments, least hee walke naked, and men see his filthines)

16 And they gathered them together into a place called in Hebrewe Arma-gedon.

17 And the seuenth Angel powred out his viall into the ayre: and there came a loude voyce out of the Temple of heauen from the throne, saying, It is done.

18 And there were voyces, and thundrings, and lightnings, and there was a great earthquake, such as was not since men were vpon the earth, euen so mightie an earthquake.

19 And the great citie was deuided into three partes, and the cities of the nations fell: and that great Babylon came in remembrance before God, to giue vnto her the cup of the wine of the fiercenesse of his wrath.

20 And euery yle fled away, and the mountaines were not found.

21 And there fell a great haile, like talents, out of heauen vpon the men, and men blasphemed God, because of the plague of the haile: for the plague thereof was exceeding great.

Revelation 17

1 Then there came one of the seuen Angels, which had the seuen vials, and talked with me, saying vnto me, Come: I will shewe thee the damnation of the great whore that sitteth vpon many waters,

2 With whom haue committed fornication the Kings of the earth, and the inhabitants of the earth are drunken with the wine of her fornication.

3 So he caried me away into the wildernesse in the Spirit, and I sawe a woman sit vpon a skarlet coloured beast, full of names of blasphemie, which had seuen heads, and tenne hornes.

4 And the woman was arayed in purple and skarlet, and gilded with golde, and precious stones, and pearles, and had a cup of gold in her hand, full of abominations, and filthines of her fornication.

5 And in her forehead was a name written, A mysterie, that great Babylon, that mother of whoredomes, and abominations of the earth.

6 And I sawe ye woman drunken with the blood of Saintes, and with the blood of the Martyrs of IESVS: and when I sawe her, I wondred with great marueile.

7 Then the Angel saide vnto me, Wherefore marueilest thou? I will shewe thee the misterie of that woman, and of that beast, that beareth her, which hath seuen heads, and tenne hornes.

8 The beast that thou hast seene, was, and is not, and shall ascend out of the bottomles pit, and shall goe into perdition, and they that dwell on the earth, shall wonder (whose names are not written in the booke of life from the foundation of ye world) when they behold the beast that was, and is not, and yet is.

9 Here is the mind that hath wisdome. The seuen heads, are seuen mountaines, whereon the woman sitteth: they are also seuen Kings.

10 Fiue are fallen, and one is, and another is not yet come: and when he commeth, he must continue a short space.

11 And the beast that was, and is not, is euen the eight, and is one of the seuen, and shall goe into destruction.

12 And the tenne hornes which thou sawest, are tenne Kings, which yet haue not receiued a kingdome, but shall receiue power, as Kings at one houre with the beast.

13 These haue one minde, and shall giue their power, and authoritie vnto the beast.

14 These shall fight with the Lambe, and the Lambe shall ouercome them: for he is Lord of Lordes, and King of Kings: and they that are on his side, called, and chosen, and faithfull.

15 And he said vnto me, The waters which thou sawest, where the whore

sitteth, are people, and multitudes, and nations, and tongues.

16 And the tenne hornes which thou sawest vpon the beast, are they that shall hate the whore, and shall make her desolate and naked, and shall eate her flesh, and burne her with fire.

17 For God hath put in their heartes to fulfill his will, and to doe with one consent for to giue their kingdome vnto the beast, vntill the wordes of God be fulfilled.

18 And that woman which thou sawest, is that great citie, which reigneth ouer the kings of ye earth.

Revelation 18

1 And after these thinges, I sawe another Angel come downe from heauen, hauing great power, so that the earth was lightened with his glorie,

2 And he cryed out mightily with a loud voyce, saying, It is fallen, it is fallen, Babylon that great citie, and is become the habitation of deuils, and the holde of all foule spirits, and a cage of euery vncleane and hatefull birde.

3 For all nations haue drunken of the wine of the wrath of her fornication, and the Kings of the earth haue committed fornication with her, and the marchants of the earth are waxed rich of the abundance of her pleasures.

4 And I heard another voyce from heauen say, Goe out of her, my people, that ye be not partakers of her sinnes, and that ye receiue not of her plagues.

5 For her sinnes are come vp into heauen, and God hath remembred her iniquities.

6 Rewarde her, euen as she hath rewarded you, and giue her double according to her workes: and in the cup that she hath filled to you, fill her ye double.

7 In as much as she glorified her selfe, and liued in pleasure, so much giue ye to her torment and sorow: for she saith in her heart, I sit being a queene, and am no widowe, and shall see no mourning.

8 Therefore shall her plagues come at one day, death, and sorowe, and famine, and she shalbe burnt with fire: for that God which condemneth her, is a strong Lord.

9 And the kings of the earth shall bewayle her, and lament for her, which haue committed fornication, and liued in pleasure with her, when they shall see that smoke of that her burning,

10 And shall stand a farre off for feare of her torment, saying, Alas, alas, that great citie Babylon, that mightie citie: for in one houre is thy iudgement come.

11 And the marchants of the earth shall weepe and wayle ouer her: for no man byeth their ware any more.

12 The ware of golde, and siluer, and of precious stone, and of pearles, and of fine linnen, and of purple, and of silke, and of skarlet, and of all maner of Thyne wood, and of all vessels of yuorie, and of all vessels of most precious wood, and of brasse, and of yron, and of marble,

13 And of cinamon, and odours, and ointments, and frankincense, and wine, and oyle, and fine floure, and wheate, and beastes, and sheepe, and horses, and charets, and seruants, and soules of men.

14 (And the apples that thy soule lusted after, are departed from thee, and all things which were fatte and excellent, are departed from thee, and thou shalt finde them no more)

15 The marchants of these thinges which were waxed riche, shall stand a farre off from her, for feare of her torment, weeping and wayling,

16 And saying, Alas, alas, that great citie, that was clothed in fine linnen and purple, and skarlet, and gilded with gold, and precious stones, and pearles.

17 For in one houre so great riches are come to desolation. And euery shipmaster, and all the people that occupie shippes, and shipmen, and whosoeuer traffike on the sea, shall stand a farre off,

18 And crie, when they see that smoke of that her burning, saying, What citie was like vnto this great citie?

19 And they shall cast dust on their heads, and crie, weeping, and wayling, and say, Alas, alas, that great citie, wherein were made rich all that had ships on the sea by her costlinesse: for in one houre she is made desolate.

20 O heauen, reioyce of her, and ye holy Apostles and Prophets: for God hath punished her to be reuenged on her for your sakes.

21 Then a mightie Angell tooke vp a stone like a great milstone, and cast it into the sea, saying, With such violence shall that great citie Babylon be cast, and shalbe found no more.

22 And the voyce of harpers, and musicians, and of pipers, and trumpetters shalbe heard no more in thee, and no craftesman, of whatsoeuer craft he be, shall be found any more in thee: and the sound of a milstone shalbe heard no more in thee.

23 And the light of a candle shall shine no more in thee: and the voyce of the bridegrome and of the bride shalbe heard no more in thee: for thy marchants were the great men of the earth: and with thine inchantments were deceiued all nations.

24 And in her was found the blood of the Prophets, and of the Saints, and of all that were slaine vpon the earth.

Revelation 19

1 And after these things I heard a great voyce of a great multitude in heauen, saying, Hallelu-iah, saluation, and glorie, and honour, and power be to the Lord our God.

2 For true and righteous are his iudgements: for he hath condemned that great whore, which did corrupt the earth with her fornication, and hath auenged the blood of his seruants shed by her hand.

3 And againe they saide, Hallelu-iah: and that her smoke rose vp for euermore.

4 And the foure and twentie Elders, and the foure beastes fell downe, and worshipped God that sate on the throne, saying, Amen, Hallelu-iah.

5 Then a voyce came out of the throne, saying, Prayse our God, all ye his seruants, and ye that feare him, both small and great.

6 And I heard like a voyce of a great multitude, and as the voyce of many waters, and as the voyce of strong thundrings, saying, Hallelu-iah: for the Lord that God that almightie God hath reigned.

7 Let vs be glad and reioyce, and giue glory to him: for the marriage of that Lambe is come, and his wife hath made her selfe ready.

8 And to her was granted, that she should be arayed with pure fine linnen and shining, for the fine linnen is the righteousnesse of Saintes.

9 Then he said vnto me, Write, Blessed are they which are called vnto the Lambes supper. And he said vnto me, These wordes of God are true.

10 And I fell before his feete, to worship him: but he said vnto me, See thou doe it not: I am thy fellowe seruant, and one of thy brethren, which haue the testimonie of Iesus. Worship God: for the testimonie of Iesus is the Spirit of prophecie.

11 And I sawe heauen open, and behold, a white horse, and he that sate vpon him, was called, Faithfull and true, and he iudgeth and fighteth righteously.

12 And his eyes were as a flame of fire, and on his head were many crownes: and he had a name written, that no man knewe but himselfe.

13 And he was clothed with a garment dipt in blood, and his name is called THE WORD OF GOD.

14 And the hostes which werein heauen, followed him vpon white horses, clothed with fine linnen white and pure.

15 And out of his mouth went out a sharpe sworde, that with it he should smite the heathen: for he shall rule them with a rod of yron: for he it is that treadeth the wine presse of the fiercenesse and wrath of almightie God.

16 And he hath vpon his garment, and vpon his thigh a name written, THE KINGS OF KINGS, AND LORD OF LORDS.

17 And I sawe an Angel stand in the sunne, who cryed with a loude voyce, saying to all the foules that did flie by the middes of heauen, Come, and gather your selues together vnto the supper of ye great God,

18 That ye may eate the flesh of Kings, and the flesh of hie Captaines, and the flesh of mightie men, and the flesh of horses, and of them that sit on them, and the flesh of all freemen, and bondmen, and of small and great.

19 And I sawe the beast, and the Kings of the earth, and their hostes gathered

together to make battell against him that sate on the horse, and against his armie.

20 But ye beast was taken, and with him that false prophet that wrought miracles before him, whereby he deceiued them that receiued ye beastes marke, and them that worshipped his image. These both were aliue cast into a lake of fire, burning with brimstone.

21 And the remnant were slayne with the sword of him that sitteth vpon the horse, which commeth out of his mouth, and all the foules were filled full with their flesh.

Revelation 20

1 And I saw an Angel come downe from heauen, hauing the keye of the bottomles pit, and a great chaine in his hand.

2 And he tooke the dragon that olde serpent, which is the deuill and Satan, and he bounde him a thousand yeeres:

3 And cast him into the bottomles pit, and he shut him vp, and sealed the doore vpon him, that he should deceiue the people no more, till the thousand yeeres were fulfilled: for after that he must be loosed for a litle season.

4 And I sawe seates: and they sate vpon them, and iudgement was giuen vnto them, and I saw the soules of them that were beheaded for the witnes of Iesus, and for the word of God, and which did not worship the beast, neither his image, neither had taken his marke vpon their foreheads, or on their handes: and they liued, and reigned with Christ a thousand yeere.

5 But the rest of the dead men shall not liue againe, vntill the thousand yeres be finished: this is the first resurrection.

6 Blessed and holy is hee, that hath part in the first resurrection: for on such the second death hath no power: but they shalbe the Priests of God and of Christ, and shall reigne with him a thousand yeere.

7 And when the thousand yeres are expired, Satan shalbe loosed out of his prison,

8 And shall go out to deceiue the people, which are in the foure quarters of the earth: euen Gog and Magog, to gather them together to battell, whose number is, as the sand of the sea.

9 And they went vp into the plaine of the earth, and they compassed the tents of the Saints about, and the beloued citie: but fire came downe from God out of heauen, and deuoured them.

10 And the deuill that deceiued them, was cast into a lake of fire and brimstone, where that beast and that false prophet are, and shall be tormented euen day and night for euermore.

11 And I saw a great white throne, and one that sate on it, from whose face fled away both the earth and heauen, and their place was no more found.

12 And I saw the dead, both great and small stand before God: and the bookes were opened, and another booke was opened, which is the booke of life, and the dead were iudged of those thinges, which were written in the bookes, according to their woorkes.

13 And the sea gaue vp her dead, which were in her, and death and hell deliuered vp the dead, which were in them: and they were iudged euery man according to their woorkes.

14 And death and hell were cast into the lake of fire: this is the second death.

15 And whosoeuer was not found written in the booke of life, was cast into the lake of fire.

Revelation 21

1 And I sawe a newe heauen, and a newe earth: for the first heauen, and the first earth were passed away, and there was no more sea.

2 And I Iohn sawe the holie citie newe Hierusalem come downe from God out of heauen, prepared as a bride trimmed for her husband.

3 And I heard a great voice out of heauen, saying, Behold, the Tabernacle of God is with men, and he will dwell with them: and they shalbe his people, and God himselfe shalbe their God with them.

4 And God shall wipe away all teares from their eyes: and there shalbe no more death, neither sorow, neither crying, neither shall there be any more paine: for the first things are passed.

5 And he that sate vpon the throne, sayd, Behold, I make all things newe: and he sayde vnto me, Write: for these wordes are faithfull and true.

6 And he said vnto me, It is done, I am Alpha and Omega, the beginning and the ende. I wil giue to him that is a thirst, of the well of the water of life freely.

7 He that ouercommeth, shall inherit all things, and I will be his God, and he shall be my sonne.

8 But the fearful and vnbeleeuing, and the abominable and murtherers, and whoremogers, and sorcerers, and idolaters, and all liars shall haue their part in the lake, which burneth with fire and brimstone, which is the second death.

9 And there came vnto mee one of the seuen Angels, which had the seuen vials full of the seuen last plagues, and talked with mee, saying, Come: I will shewe thee the bride, the Lambes wife.

10 And he caried me away in the spirit to a great: and an hie mountaine, and he shewed me that great citie, that holie Hierusalem, descending out of heauen from God,

11 Hauing the glorie of God: and her shining was like vnto a stone most precious, as a Iasper stone cleare as crystall,

12 And had a great wall and hie, and had twelue gates, and at the gates twelue Angels, and the names written, which are the twelue tribes of the children of Israel.

13 On the East part there were three gates, and on the Northside three gates, on the Southside three gates, and on the Westside three gates.

14 And the wall of the citie had twelue foundations, and in them the Names of the Lambes twelue Apostles.

15 And hee that talked with mee, had a golden reede, to measure the citie withall, and the gates thereof, and the wall thereof.

16 And the citie laie foure square, and the length is as large as the bredth of it, and he measured the citie with the reede, twelue thousande furlongs: and the length, and the bredth, and the height of it are equall.

17 And hee measured the wall thereof, an hundreth fourtie and foure cubites, by the measure of man, that is, of the Angell.

18 And ye building of the wall of it was of Iasper: and the citie was pure golde, like vnto cleare glasse.

19 And the foundations of the wall of ye city were garnished with all maner of precious stones: the first foundation was Iasper: the second of Saphire: the third of a Chalcedonie: the fourth of an Emeraude:

20 The fift of a Sardonix: the sixt of a Sardius: the seueth of a Chrysolite: the eight of a Beryl: the ninth of a Topaze: the tenth of a Chrysoprasus: the eleuenth of a Iacynth: the twelfth an Amethyst.

21 And the twelue gates were twelue pearles, and euery gate is of one pearle, and the streete of the citie is pure golde, as shining glasse.

22 And I sawe no Temple therein: for the Lord God almightie and the Lambe are the Temple of it.

23 And this citie hath no neede of the sunne, neither of the moone to shine in it: for the glorie of God did light it: and the Lambe is the light of it.

24 And the people which are saued, shall walke in the light of it: and the Kings of the earth shall bring their glorie and honour vnto it.

25 And the gates of it shall not be shut by day: for there shalbe no night there.

26 And the glorie, and honour of the Gentiles shall be brought vnto it.

27 And there shall enter into it none vncleane thing, neither whatsoeuer woorketh abomination or lies: but they which are written in ye Lambes booke of life.

Revelation 22

1 And hee shewed me a pure riuer of water of life, cleare as crystall, proceeding out of the throne of God, and of the Lambe.

2 In the middes of the street of it, and of either side of ye riuer, was the tree of life, which bare twelue maner of fruits, and gaue fruit euery moneth: and the leaues of the tree serued to heale the nations with.

3 And there shalbe no more curse, but ye throne of God and of the Lambe shall be in it, and his seruants shall serue him.

4 And they shall see his face, and his Name shalbe in their foreheads.

5 And there shalbe no night there, and they neede no candle, neither light of the sunne: for the Lord God giueth them light, and they shall reigne for euermore.

6 And he said vnto me, These wordes are faithfull and true: and the Lord God of the holy Prophets sent his Angell to shewe vnto his seruants the things which must shortly be fulfilled.

7 Beholde, I come shortly. Blessed is hee that keepeth the woordes of the prophecie of this booke.

8 And I am Iohn, which sawe and heard these thinges: and when I had heard and seene, I fell downe to worship before the feete of the Angell which shewed me these things.

9 But he sayde vnto me, See thou doe it not: for I am thy fellowe seruaunt, and of thy brethren the Prophets, and of them which keepe the woordes of this booke: worship God.

10 And he said vnto me, Seale not the wordes of the prophecie of this booke: for the time is at hand.

11 He that is vniust, let him be vniust stil and he which is filthie, let him be filthie still: and hee that is righteous, let him be righteous stil: and he that is holy, let him be holy still.

12 And beholde, I come shortly, and my reward is with mee, to giue euery man according as his worke shall be.

13 I am Alpha and Omega, the beginning and the end, the first and the last.

14 Blessed are they, that doe his commandements, that their right may be in the tree of life, and may enter in through the gates into the Citie.

15 For without shall be dogs and inchanters, and whoremongers, and murtherers, and idolaters, and whosoeuer loueth or maketh lies.

16 I Iesus haue sent mine Angell, to testifie vnto you these things in the Churches: I am the root and the generation of Dauid, and the bright morning starre.

17 And the Spirit and the bride say, Come. And let him that heareth, say, Come: and let him that is a thirst, come: and let whosoeuer will, take of the water of life freely.

18 For I protest vnto euery man that heareth the words of the prophecie of this booke, If any man shall adde vnto these things, God shall adde vnto him the plagues, that are written in this booke:

19 And if any man shall diminish of the wordes of the booke of this prophecie, God shall take away his part out of the Booke of life, and out of the holie citie, and from those things which are written in this booke.

20 He which testifieth these things, saith, Surely, I come quickly. Amen. Euen so, come Lord Iesus.

21 The grace of our Lord Iesus Christ be with you all, AMEN.

A Note from the Author and Bonus Content

The 1560 Geneva Bible stands as a monumental work in the history of English Bible translation. Renowned for its influence and accessibility during the Reformation, this version has shaped the spiritual lives of countless believers. Some might notice the absence of the Apocrypha in this edition and wonder about its significance. Here are the reasons why this version without the Apocrypha remains a valuable and preferable choice for readers today:

1. Historical and Theological Integrity
The 1560 Geneva Bible is celebrated for its faithfulness to the Hebrew and Greek texts. By focusing solely on the canonical books of the Old and New Testaments, this edition preserves the core teachings and historical foundations of the Christian faith as understood by the reformers.

2. Purity of Doctrine
The absence of the Apocrypha aligns with the doctrinal positions of many Protestant traditions, which do not consider these books as inspired Scripture. This version allows readers to engage directly with the texts that have been universally recognized and affirmed by the majority of Christian denominations throughout history.

3. Scholarly Precision
The translators of the Geneva Bible were meticulous scholars, dedicated to providing the most accurate translation possible. By concentrating on the canonical books, they ensured a level of precision and clarity that continues to resonate with readers seeking a deep and authentic engagement with the biblical text.

4. Enhanced Focus on Core Biblical Narrative
Without the Apocrypha, readers can immerse themselves fully in the central narrative of the Bible, from Creation and the fall of man to the redemption through Jesus Christ and the establishment of the early Church. This streamlined approach can lead to a more cohesive and impactful reading experience.

Bonus Content: Access the Apocrypha in Modern English
For those who desire a comprehensive understanding and wish to explore the Apocrypha, we offer a modern English translation available for download. By scanning the QR code below, readers can access these additional texts and gain a fuller vision of the biblical literature, supplementing their study and enriching their knowledge.

Conclusion

As you reach the end of this edition of the 1560 Geneva Bible, it is my hope that your journey through these sacred texts has been enlightening and spiritually enriching. This translation, with its historical significance and literary beauty, provides not only a faithful rendering of God's Word but also a profound connection to the Reformation era and its quest for accessible and accurate Scripture.

The Geneva Bible stands as a testament to the enduring power of the Bible to inspire, guide, and transform lives. Its impact on the English language, culture, and Christian theology is immeasurable. By engaging with this text, you are participating in a centuries-old tradition of seeking wisdom, comfort, and direction from the Scriptures.

For those interested in exploring further, the Apocrypha in modern English is available for download, offering additional insights and historical context. This bonus content ensures that you have access to the full breadth of biblical literature, enhancing your understanding and appreciation of these ancient writings.

As you close this book, may the words you have read resonate in your heart and mind, guiding your thoughts, actions, and faith. May the teachings within these pages continue to inspire and direct you on your spiritual journey.

Thank you for choosing to read the 1560 Geneva Bible. May it be a lasting source of blessing, knowledge, and inspiration in your life.